DISCOPAEDIA OF THE VIOLIN 1889-1971

DISCOPAEDIA OF THE VIOLIN
1889-1971

James Creighton

UNIVERSITY OF TORONTO PRESS

© James Creighton 1974
Published by University of Toronto Press
Toronto and Buffalo
Printed in USA
ISBN 0-8020-1810-6
LC 79-185708

To the many violinists
whose recorded performances are listed
on the following pages

CONTENTS

FOREWORD

In a little over half a century, a complete historical process can be seen to have transpired. It is indicative of our era that this should have taken place within the ordinary course of our particular type of progress-by-multiplication with its implied order of experimentation, selection, and cross-fertilization in the fields of the intellect and applied science on a scale never before equalled except perhaps biologically by the fruit-fly.

This mechanical proliferation and the improvement of reproducing and of recording devices have occurred in fields subservient to men and women and even children, and at least in the world of music we can study this evolution as quietly and dispassionately as we might trace in archaeology the layers evidencing the travails of birth and the throes of death of civilizations long since departed.

Such a "record of records" as is this violin discopaedia provides one not only with a fascinating story of the progress of recording techniques, but, for me as a musician, with an exciting and revealing guide to the actual performance in terms of the differing styles of interpretation, the evolution of fashion in tone production, in vibrato, tempi, rubato, and fingerings, all of which prove strangely indicative of the national, personal, and social background of my eminent predecessors.

Again, such a discopaedia furthers the important study of the interaction between the aesthetics of musical performance and all the other branches of culture and behaviour – psychological, social, and economic – as well as covering the interesting transition between the last of the romantics and the first of the robots.

Finding myself somewhere in between these two factors and still copiously contributing to the volume of this and, I hope, future editions of this book, I am pleased and grateful to have been allowed to comment in what one might call the complementary capacities both of embalmed relic and ever constant contributor.

YEHUDI MENUHIN

PREFACE

The recorded works of almost seventeen hundred violinists are listed in this discopaedia, from the cylinders of 1889 to the quadra-sonic discs of our own time. All records, published and unpublished, made by interpreters of serious violin music for commercial organizations come within its purview. It is intended to serve as a source of reference for teachers and students of the violin; a guide for future discographic researchers and collectors; an aid to musicological researchers in comparing trends in popularity and repertoire over the years and from one country to another; a research tool for archival institutions, recorded-sound repositories, libraries, critics, broadcasting companies, and violinists generally; an aid to enlightened record manufacturers who want to record hitherto unrecorded materials; and a guide to concert goers who are interested in performances of the past as well as those of the present. The discopaedia will help provide its users with an insight into the repertoire of individual violinists and therefore into various playing styles. Some violinists place emphasis on a broad tone and tend to choose repertoire that will display that particular side of their art to the best advantage. Some may exhibit the more virtuosic aspect of violin playing, with the emphasis upon technique and its exploitation, while others may favour music of the baroque and classical periods. Still others, and particularly the contemporary performers, are at home with a wide range of compositions.

One of the primary services of the discopaedia will be to separate fact from fiction. The discographer works at the edge of a land of fantasy, full of dark mysteries that confuse an already fragmented situation. Most myths do have some foundation in fact, and important discographic discoveries of every nature have stemmed from delightful rumours. This process of discovery shows no sign of ending.

It has been rumoured that there exist private recordings by Kubelík, Kreisler, and Maud Powell. Coincidence might be the source of this rumour, for all three artists were contracted to the same record company (Victor) at the same time and could have made records which were never issued commercially. However, one would assume that such discs would appear in the company's register, and that is not the case. If, on the other hand, the rumour does refer to private rather than commercially unissued discs, there is a decided possibility that they still exist, for we know that artists such as Joseph Szigeti made recordings in their own homes or in hotel rooms even though the whereabouts of the cylinders are a mystery.

There was a rumour that Johannes Brahms had recorded all three of his violin and piano sonatas with violinist Joseph Joachim on a group of cylinders. Unfortunately there has never been any clear evidence of the existence of that wondrous combination. Such performances could have existed at one time, although complete sonata performances in the 1890s seem highly unlikely. One could speculate that Thibaud and Cortot might have recorded the ten Beethoven violin and piano sonatas half a century ago for the Pathé company, for both artists were then under contract to Pathé. Were this true, the recording would have predated by nearly fifteen years the first known complete set of the sonatas, performed by Kreisler and Franz Rupp. But there are no such grounds for speculation about Ole Bull and Henri Vieuxtemps who were still performing in 1877 when the phonograph was invented but who probably never heard of it, for it lay dormant for a decade while its inventor gave us light. The information contained in this book is the result of years of checking and rechecking the contents of countless record catalogues, supplements, advertisements, musical trade journals, periodicals, books, trade lists, and musical miscellanies of many countries. For information not given in the printed sources, examinations of rare recordings had to be made at the major national sound collections and radio centres of Europe and North America. Individual collectors and antiquarian dealers also played a large role in providing information. Ultimately the painstakingly assembled details upon thousands of pages of notes graduated into a manuscript.

This kind of documentation should have begun over three decades ago, before the European nations began the destruction of much of our phonographic history in the course of creating a history of another kind. What remains is still largely unorganized except where individual specialists have created the few essential guides which do exist. We owe an immense debt of gratitude to men like Harold M. Barnes, Roberto Bauer, John R. Bennett, George Cherrington, Francis F. Clough, G.J. Cuming, Charles Delaunay, Fred Gaisberg, Victor Girard, David Hall, P.G. Hurst, Brian Knight, Horst Lange, Bernard Lebow, Philip L. Miller, Jerrold N. Moore, Julian Morton Moses, Kurtz Myers, Herbert Rosenberg, Brian Rust, William Seltsam, Michael Smith, and Wilhelm Wimmer who have been foremost in trying to piece together what little phonographic history is at present available.

The present decade is crucial for discographical research. Much of the ground has been surveyed in part, yet the gargantuan task of collating, sifting, and verifying what has come our way is still to be done. It will be too late when turn-of-the-century catalogues and supplements are crumbled to dust and when discs or cylinders become hopelessly unplayable or broken. There appears to be no solution to the problems of organization, yet in this age of electronics, when tape recorders, videotape, microfilm, and computers serve as basic tools, there is no reason, other than financial (and that is not insurmountable), why the governments of the world could not be interested in building an international repository where all sound recording of whatever nature can be preserved for posterity. Only then will we have access to our recorded heritage.

I can only express my gratitude for services rendered by inadequately thanking the following people for their kind help and co-operation in lending assistance to me when it was most needed: Miss Valentine Britten, retired BBC Gramophone Librarian, London; Mr Roland Teutchler, Vienna; Mr Carl L. Bruun, Stockholm; Dr Boyd Neel, Toronto; Dr Herbert Rosenberg, director Nationaldiskoteket, Lyngby/Copenhagen; Dr André Ross, Handleman Institute of Recorded Sound, Miami; Dr Jerrold N. Moore, Sound Recordings, Yale University, New Haven; Mr Allan J. Crane, Vancouver; Mr David Hall, Rodgers & Hammerstein Collection, Lincoln Center, New York; Mr Joseph Szigeti, Clarens, Switzerland; Mr Steven Staryk, Toronto; Francine Bloch, Phonothèque national, Paris; Mrs Irmgaard von Broich-Oppen, Hessischer Rundfunk, Frankfurt; Mr Colin Shreve, London; Miss Janet Luck, BBC Reference Library, London; Mr Lorenzo Germani, director RAI Discoregistroteca, Rome; Mr Christer Östland, National Fonoteket, Stockholm; Miss Rita Soguel, Radio Suisse Romande, Geneva.

Sincere thanks also go to the personnel of many institutions, national archives, and radio centres throughout Europe and North America. Special thanks are due to the Humanities and Social Sciences Division of the Canada Council for a generous grant for my sound research project.

Lastly, a debt is owing to the person who made the suggestion for this work some thirteen years ago and who helped it grow from a mass of notations to its present encyclopaedic proportion with the encouragement and helpful suggestions that only an understanding wife could give to the mono-rail mind of a discographer.

INTRODUCTION

The discopaedia is concerned with the recording careers of violinists who have devoted themselves to serious (as opposed to "popular") works, but because of its emphasis on interpreters rather than on the music itself it includes occasional popular recordings such as Heifetz' performance of "White Christmas," many bits of memorable trash played by Kreisler, and some folksong arrangements, anonymous works, and concert arrangements of what purports to be gypsy music. It omits artists who recorded only popular music such as William Craig, Eugene A. Jaudas, Leopold Moeslein, and the more popular J. Scott Skinner whose discs and cylinders in the jig and reel category were widely circulated. A few more notable exclusions are the jazz greats Joe Venuti, Stuff Smith, Eddie South and Stéphane Grappelly who were among the few artists to use the violin in a fashion accepted by jazz purists. Also omitted is that popular master of the "catch" tune, Paul Nero, whose speciality was novelty pieces combined with phonographic tricks. Florian Zabach and Helmut Zacharias, both classically trained, are extraordinary examples of what great popular violinists sound like. Only Zacharias has recorded "straight" performances and so is included in this work. Another example of a violinist who combined serious solos with "bread and butter" selections was Charles D'Almaine. He successfully bridged the cultural gap to offer short concert works as well as traditional fiddle tunes. The discopaedia includes only his concert pieces and occasional arrangements of popular melodies.

The basic material of the discopaedia is sonatas, concerti, and shorter recital fare. Symphonies are included only when there is an extended solo passage and when the violinist is an acknowledged soloist in his own right. In chamber works for various instrumental combinations such as trios, quartets, quintets, and sextets, the same rule applies: a violinist is not listed if he recorded only as a member of an established chamber group.

In a work of this magnitude and complexity, there are undoubtedly errors and omissions. Because of the great numbers of minor and fly-by-night labels early in the century completeness is almost impossible to achieve. Some recordings have doubtless been overlooked altogether. Some kinds of information were not always available, even in company registers. An accompaniment may only be identified as "with piano." The opus numbers of some obscure compositions could not be found. The birth and death dates for some violinists were unavailable. And information about the dates of recordings was so scanty that no useful purpose would have been served by including what there was at this printing.

Another great problem in discographical research is the matrix number. There is such a large number of collectors of vocal recordings that their cumulative knowledge has produced near-complete matrix information for these records. This is not the case for the violin. Some information is found in manufacturers' catalogues and supplements, but most of it must come from the files of the manufacturers themselves and from the records. Unfortunately the great majority of turn-of-the-century companies are long since extinct and their files and registers have disappeared with them. I was able to examine at most perhaps one-quarter of the early 78 rpm discs, so matrix information from this source is patchy. However, I have included as many matrices as could be added up to the time of going to press, and the search for completion continues as does the quest for recording dates.

Matrices are of inestimable importance as an aid in the identification of different performances resulting from one or more recording sessions but released on the same label and possibly even bearing the same disc number. Most recording companies assign matrix numbers sequentially, and if one is in the possession of an assigned block of matrix numbers beginning and ending with those connected with a known recording date, it follows that one knows at least the approximate recording date of a given release with a matrix taken from that block. The "take" number of any matrix furthermore provides us with the knowledge of which of several versions of the same piece might have been chosen for commercial release. However, only a company's complete register of recording sessions can tell the full story.

The discopaedia includes many instances where an entirely different version coexists with what was hitherto considered a one-and-the-same performance. A case in point is the discovery of several "takes" of a record by Jan Kubelík. It appears that at least three versions of Drdla's serenade played by Kubelík have found their way into Fonotipia 39193, a disc released in Italy. The group of copies viewed of this disc included the following matrices: XPh 284^2, XPh 284^4, and XPh 4307 – take IV; the first two are shown by the raised digits or superscripts to be "takes" 2 and 4 of one session, while the "take" given for XPh 4307 indicates that a further session produced at least another four "takes" or versions. In all, Fonotipia 39193 could conceivably have been issued in up to eight different versions, taken from two distinct recording sessions, if all available (or known) "takes" had been used in subsequent pressings.

Because it is the artist and his repertoire that is to be highlighted in this work, the violinists form the main entries of the discopaedia. They are listed alphabetically, and within each entry are listed, also alphabetically, the composers and their compositions.

A typical listing is Paganini's Sonata a preghièra recorded by Barylli:

Walter BARYLLI   (1921-)

PAGANINI
[1]**Sonata a preghièra** [2]"Moses Fantasia" [3](on the aria "Dal tuo stellato soglio" from Rossini's opera "Mosè in Egitto") Op. 24 (1818 or 1819) [4]vln & orch.
  [5]with O.A. Graef pf [6]3515/6 GN 8 [7]Decca PO5127 Polydor 10810

The parts of the listing are:
1. title of composition (in bold face)
2. popular title (in quotation marks)
3. source, if applicable (in parentheses), followed by opus number, and date(s) of publication (in parentheses)
4. original scoring, plus arrangement if known
5. accompaniment
6. matrix number if known
7. catalogue number(s)

Key signatures are indicated by a capital letter for a major key and a lower case letter for a minor key.

The Index of Composers (p.843) will be the first point of contact for readers whose main interest is the composer and his work rather than the performer and his art.

The composers' surnames are listed alphabetically, followed by given names and the year of birth and death. The Paganini sonata listed in the example above appears in the Index of Composers thus:

Paganini, Niccolo (1782-1840)

[1]**Sonata a preghièra** [2]"Moses Fantasia" [3]*(on the aria "Dal tuo stellato soglio" from Rossini's opera "Mosè in Egitto")* Op. 24 (1818 or 1819) [4]*(vln & orch.*
  [5]*Accardo – Barylli – Garnier – Haendel* [6]*(2) – Kawaciuk – Lorant – Menuhin – D. Oistrakh – F. Reuter – R. Ricci (3) – Shkolníková – Sitkovetsky – Sobolevsky – Szentgyörgi – Zhuk*

The entry consists of:

1   title of composition
2   popular title (in quotation marks)
3   source, if applicable (in parentheses and italics) followed by opus number, and date(s) of publication (in parentheses)
4   scoring (in parentheses and italics)
5   alphabetical listing of artists' surnames (in italics) including
6   the number of versions recorded by the artists.

The List of Manufacturers (p.929) may be read in conjunction with the listings under artists to find country of origin, series, and size of record. The list includes only 33 1/3 rpm long playing (LP), 78 rpm, and 45 rpm (standard and extended play) records, and occasional 16 2/3 rpm items and cylinders.[1] All labels are listed alphabetically with their countries of origin in parentheses. The indicators of the varying series follows. This, in turn, is followed by the speed indicator columns, under which the size of the record is indicated.

The Index of Popular Titles lists the popular name, or subtitle, by which many works are best known. This title is given in bold face, followed by the composer's name and the formal title and instrumentation.

Finally, I have provided a summary alphabetical listing of the artists, with their birth and death dates where known.

---

[1]   In the older 78 rpm discs, speeds were anything but constant and were at variance with what we call "78s" by tracking at between 74 and 82 rpm; some early Pathé discs tracked at 90 rpm. Cylinders were more consistant, with 120 rpm as the norm.

ABBREVIATIONS

a	alto (contralto)
acc	accompaniment
arr	arranged
att	attributed
b	baritone
bar	baryton
bs	bass
bs-cl	bass clarinet
bsn	bassoon
BWV	Bach Werke-Verzeichnis, Wolfang Schmieder (b. 1901): *Thematischsystematisches Verzeichnis der Musikalischen Werke von Johann Sebastian Bach,* Breitkopf & Härtel, Leipzig 1950
C	Capri, A.: thematic index numbers assigned to Tartini's works in Padua, Milan 1945
c	continuo
cbns	combinations
cbs	contra bass
cel	celeste
cha	chamber
chit	chitarrone
cho	choir or chorus
cl	clarinet
clav	clavier
cond	conductor or conducted by
D	Deutsch, Otto Erich (1883-): biographer of Schubert
D	Dounias, Minos (1900-): catalog of Tartini concerti with assigned numbers
dir	directed
drms	drums
dul	dulcimer
ed	edited
E.hrn	English horn
EIAR	Ente Italiano Audizioni Radiofoniche (or Radio Turin orchestra)
ens	ensemble
F.	Falck, Martin (1888-): Wilhelm Friedemann Bach thematic index, *Thematisches Verzeichnis,* C.F. Kahnt, Leipzig 1913 (2nd ed. 1919)
F.	Fanna, Antonio (1926-): instrumental classification, *Indice Tematico di 200 opere strumentali di A. Vivaldi,* I Serie, Venezia 1955)
FAE	Frei aber einsam (reference to vln sonata composed jointly by Brahms, Dietrich & Schumann)
fl	flute
F.O.K.	Prague Film & Concert Orchestra
G	Grove, Sir George (1820-1900): reference to Beethoven
gamba	viola da gamba
gtr	guitar
H.	Hoboken, Anthony van (1887-): Dutch bibliographer; Haydn thematic catalog, 1st volume, 1957
hp	harp
hpsi	harpsichord

hpsi-c	harpsichord-continuo
hrn	French horn
I.C.B.S.	In Cimbalis Bene Sonantibus
inst	instrument
J	Jähns, Freidrich Wilhelm (1809-1888): *Carl Maria Friedrich Ernst von Weber Chronologisch-Thematisches Verzeichnis,* Schlesinger 1871
K	Köchel, Ludwig (1800-1877): Mozart bibliographer; *Chronolgisch-Thematisches Verzeichnis,* Leipzig 1862
L	Longo, Alessandro (1864-1945): edited & published the near-complete harpsichord works of Domenico Scarlatti
mand	mandolin
m-s	mezzo-soprano
ob	oboe
obb	obbligato
op	opus
orch	orchestra or orchestrated
org	organ
orig	originally
P	Pincherle, Marc (1888-): musicologist; *Antonio Vivaldi et la musique instrumentale,* Paris 1948
pcn	percussion
pf	piano
pic	piccolo
posth	posthumous
qnt	quintet
qt	quartet
R	Raabe, Peter: assigned numbers, 2nd volume of *Franz Liszt,* Stuttgart 1931
real	realized or realization
rec	recorder
res	restored or restoration
rev	revised
RIAS	Berlin Radio Orchestra (Rundfunk im amerikanischen Sektor)
s	soprano
sax	saxophone
spin	spinnet
s-s	single-sided
str(s)	string(s)
t	tenor
T	Tafelmusik: 3 groups of chamber works composed in 1733 by George Philipp Telemann
T	Terry, Charles Sanford: Bach scholar & J.C. Bach bibliographer; *Johann Christian Bach,* Oxford University Press 1929
tbn	trombone
timp	timpani or kettle drum
tpt	trumpet
transcr.	transcribed or transcription
t-viol	tenor-viol
unid	unidentified
unsp	unspecified
v	vocal
var	various
vir	virginals
vla	viola
vlc	violoncello
vln	violin
vol	volume
W	Wotquenne, Alfred (1867-1939): C.P.E. Bach bibliographer
WoO	Werke ohne Opus (work without opus) – Beethoven reference
w-wnds	woodwinds or wind instruments
Z	Zimmerman, Franklin B: *Purcell Thematic Catalog,* Macmillan 1963

DISCOPAEDIA OF THE VIOLIN 1889-1971

Vasco ABADIEV

BACH

(3) Sonatas & 3 Partitas BWV1001/6 solo vln
Sonata No. 2, in a: Grave (1st mvt) BWV1003
(unaccompanied)   Radioprom & Orfei 1336

MASSENET

Thaïs (1894) – opera
Méditation
with Norddeutscher Symphony Orch.   Europa E133

PAGANINI

(24) Caprices, Op. 1 (1801/7) solo vln
Caprice No. 9, in E
(unaccompanied)   Europa E133

Concerto No. 1, in D Op. 6 vln & orch.
with Sofia Philharmonic Orch.   Radioprom & Orfei 1355/9

SARASATE

Introduction & Tarantelle, Op. 43 vln & pf
with P. Vladigerov pf   Radioprom & Orfei 1359

TCHAIKOVSKY

Sérénade mélancolique in b flat, Op. 26 vln & orch. – arr. vln & pf
Wilhelmj
with P. Vladigerov pf   Radioprom & Orfei 1337

Michelangelo ABBADO (1900–)

ALBINONI

(12) Concerti, Op. 9 (1722) var. cbns & strs
Concerto No. 4, in A vln, strs & c
with Milan String Orch. – Abbado   Columbia FCX370

CASTELNUOVO–TEDESCO

Capitan Fracassa (1921) vln & pf
with L. Garezzeni pf   HMV GW1062

FALLA

(7) Canciones populares españolas (1914) v & pf
No. 6. Canción arr. vln & pf Kochański
L. Garezzeni pf   HMV GW1062

MORTARI

Largo in d (1928) vln & pf
with L. Garezzeni pf   HMV GW1062

PERGOLESI

Concerto in B flat vln & strs – ed. Lualdi
with Milan String Orch. – Abbado   Columbia FCX370

TARTINI

Concerto in D, D15 (C79) vln & orch. – ed. Abbado
with Milan String Orch. Abbado   Columbia FCX368

(12) Sonatas, Op. 1 (1734) vln & c
Sonata No. 3, in A: Pastorale arr. orch. Abbado
with Milan String Orch. – Abbado   Columbia FCS369

VIVALDI

Concerto in A, P.238 vln, vlc, strs & c
with R. Caruana (vlc)   Columbia FCX368
& Milan String Orch. – Abbado

Concerto in F, P.278 (F.I, No. 34) 3 vlns, strs & c
with M. Borgo vln, L. d'Annibale vln   Columbia FCX370
& Milan String Orch. – Abbado

Concerto in B flat, P.367 (F.I, No. 59) 4 vlns, strs & c
with M. Borgo vln, L. d'Annibale vln,   Columbia FCX369
T. Pasquale vln & Milan String
Orch. – Abbado

Jenny ABEL

BRAHMS

Sonata No. 1, in G, Op. 78 vln & pf
with L. Hokanson pf   Harmonia Mundi HM30952

WAGNER, S.

Concerto (1915) vln & orch.
with Nürnberg Symphony   Colosseum SM532
Orch. – Graf

Andrei ABRAMENKOV

BACH

Cantata No. 47 (Wer sich sebst erhöhet, der soll erniedriget werden)
BWV47
with G. Pisarenko s, A. Vedernikov bs,   Mezhdunarodnaya Kniga
Republican Russian Chorus (dir. A.   D017685/6, S01259/60
Yurlov) & Moscow Chamber
Orch. – Barshai with N. Gureyeva org

Concerto in c, BWV1060 vln & ob or 2 vlns, strs & c
with Y. Nepalo ob & Moscow   Mezhdunarodnaya Kniga
Chamber Orch. – Barshai   D11675, S549

JANÁČEK

Concertino (1925) pf, 2 vlns, vla, cl, hrn & bsn
with J. Páleniček pf, L. Poleess vln,   Mezhdunarodnaya Kniga
G. Talalyan vla, V. Tupikin cl, B.   D06267
Afanasyev hrn & Y. Kurpekov bsn

TELEMANN

Concerto in B flat 3 obs, 3 vlns, hpsi & strs
with P. Pierlot ob, E. Nepalov ob,   Angel 36264
P. Dubrov ob, R. Barshai vln &   Le Chant du Monde LDX–
L. Poleess vln & Moscow Chamber   A8340, LDX–A48348
Orch. – Barshai   Electrola SME91415
          Mezhdunarodnaya Kniga
          D022145/6

VIVALDI

Concerto in G, P.132 (F.I, No. 6) 2 vlns, strs & c
with E. Smirnov vln & Moscow   Le Chant du Monde LDX8326,
Chamber Orch. – Barshai   LDX48326
          Philips 835172 AY, A02296 L

Antonio ABUSSI (1909–)

CHAMINADE
Sérénade espagnole pf – arr. vln & pf Kreisler
  with E. Calace pf   Columbia CQ564

CHOPIN
(3) Nocturnes, Op. 9 pf
  No. 2. Nocturne No. 2, in E flat arr. vln & pf Sarasate
  with E. Calace pf   Columbia CQ565

DEBUSSY
(12) Préludes – Book I (1910) pf
  No. 8. La Fille aux cheveux de lin arr. vln & pf Hartmann
  with E. Calace pf   Columbia CQ564

SAMMARTINI, G.B.
Concerto No. 2, in C vln & orch.
  with Italian Chamber Orch. – Jenkins   Haydn Society HSL74
  (set HSL C)

SARASATE
Zigeunerweisen, Op. 20 vln & pf or orch.
  with E. Calace pf   Columbia CQ565

VIOTTI
Concerto in E flat "Double" pf, vln & str orch.
  with C. Bussotti pf & Italian Chamber   Haydn Society HSL78,
  Orch. – Jenkins   (set HSL C)
  Erato LDE3029

Concerto No. 4, in D vln & orch.
  with Italian Chamber Orch. – Jenkins   Haydn Society HSL137
  (set HSL N)

Salvatore ACCARDO (1941–)

BACH
(3) Sonatas & 3 Partitas, BWV1001/6 solo vln
  Partita No. 2, in d, BWV1004
  (unaccompanied)   Victor SL20245
(4) Suites, BWV1066/9 strs & c
  Suite No. 3, in D: Air (2nd mvt) BWV1068 2 obs, 3 tpts, drms & strs
  arr. vln & pf as "Air on the G-string" by Wilhelmj
  with A. Beltrami pf   Victor KVIS199, ML20221

BAZZINI
(La) Ronde des lutins, Op. 25 vln & pf
  with A. Beltrami pf   Victor KVIS199, ML20221
  (in set ML40003)

BEETHOVEN
Quartet No. 4, in E flat, Op. 16 pf, vln, vla & vlc
  with L. Lessona pf, L. Moffa vla, & U.   Cetra LPS21
  Egaddi vlc
(Die) Ruinen von Athen, Op. 113 – Incidental music orch.
  No. 4. Marcia alla turca arr. vln & pf Auer
  with A. Beltrami pf   Victor KVIS199
(3) Sonatas, Op. 12 vln & pf
  No. 1. Sonata No. 1, in D
  with L. Lessona pf   Cetra LPS20
Sonata no. 9, in A, Op. 47 "Kreutzer" vln & pf
  with L. Lessona pf   Cetra LPS20

BEETHOVEN – Continued
Trio in B flat, Op. 11 cl, vlc & pf
  with L. Lessona pf & U. Egaddi vlc   Cetra LPS21

BLOCH
Baal Shem (3 Pictures of Chassidic life) (1923) vln & pf
  No. 2. Nigun (Improvisation)
  with A. Beltrami pf   Victor ML20221

BOTTESINI
Grand duo concertante in a vln, cbs & orch.
  with L. Buccarella cbs & M.T. Garatti   Victor (in set ML40003)
  pf

BRAHMS
(21) Hungarian Dances pf duet
  Hungarian dance No. 4, in f arr. vln & pf "in b" Joachim
  with A. Beltrami pf   Victor KVIS199

CORELLI
(12) Sonatas, Op. 5 vln & c
  Sonata No. 12, in d "La Follia" arr. vln & pf Kreisler
  with A. Beltrami pf   Camden ML80
  Victor ML20180

DEBUSSY
(12) Préludes – Book I (1910) pf
  No. 8. La Fille aux cheveux de lin arr. vln & pf Hartmann
  with A. Collard pf   Vega MT10144

FALLA
(7) Canciones populares españolas (1914) v & pf
  No. 4. Jota arr. vln & pf Kochański
  with A. Collard pf   Saga XID5108
  Vega MT10144

KREISLER
Recitative & Scherzo–caprice, Op. 6 solo vln
  (unaccompanied)   Victor SL20245

LALO
Symphonie espagnole, Op. 21 vln orch.*
  with Pasdeloup Concerts   Classics Club X531
  Orch. – Albert   Prétoria CL8014
  Saga XID5108

MENDELSSOHN
Concerto in e, Op. 64 vln & orch.
  with Pasdeloup Concerts   Prétoria CL8013
  Orch. – Albert   Vega C30A328
(6) Gesänge, Op. 34 v & pf
  No. 2. Auf Flügeln des Gesanges arr. vln & pf Achron
  with A. Beltrami pf   Victor KVIS199

MILSTEIN
Paganiniana solo vln
  (unaccompanied)   Victor SL20245

* Including Intermezzo.

NOVAČEK

(8) Concert Caprices, Op. 5 vln & pf
No. 4. Perpetuum mobile
  with A. Beltrami pf   Victor ML20221

PAGANINI

Cantabile in D, Op. 17 vln & gtr
  with A. Beltrami pf   Victor ML20221

(24) Caprices, Op. 1 (1801/7) solo vln
Caprice No. 1, in E
  (unaccompanied)   Victor ML20213
Caprice No. 2, in b
  (unaccompanied)   Victor ML20213
Caprice No. 3, in e
  (unaccompanied)   Victor ML20213
Caprice No. 4, in c
  (unaccompanied)   Victor ML20213
Caprice No. 5, in a
  (unaccompanied)   Victor ML20213
                        (in set ML40003)
Caprice No. 6, in g
  (unaccompanied)   Victor ML20213
Caprice No 7, in a
  (unaccompanied)   Victor ML20213
Caprice No. 8, in E flat
  (unaccompanied)   Victor ML20213
Caprice No. 9, in E
  (unaccompanied)   Victor ML20213
                        (in set ML40003)
Caprice No. 10, in g
  (unaccompanied)   Victor ML20213
Caprice No. 11, in C
  (unaccompanied)   Victor ML20213
                        (in set ML40003)
Caprice No. 12, in A flat
  (unaccompanied)   Victor ML20213
Caprice No. 13, in B flat
  (unaccompanied)   Victor ML20214
Caprice No. 14, in E flat
  (unaccompanied)   Victor ML20214
Caprice No. 15, in e
  (unaccompanied)   Victor ML20214
Caprice no. 16, in g
  (unaccompanied)   Victor ML20214
Caprice No. 17, in E flat
  (unaccompanied)   Victor ML20214
                        (in set ML20214
Caprice No. 18, in C
  (unaccompanied)   Victor ML20214
Caprice No. 19, in E flat
  (unaccompanied)   Victor ML20214
Caprice No. 20, in D
  (unaccompanied)   Victor ML20214
Caprice No. 21, in A
  (unaccompanied)   Victor ML20214
Caprice No. 22, in F
  (unaccompanied)   Victor ML20214
Caprice No. 23, E flat
  (unaccompanied)   Victor ML20214

PAGANINI – *Continued*

Caprice No. 24, in a
  (unaccompanied)   Victor ML20214
Concerto No. 2, in b, Op. 7 (cadenza by Baller) vln & orch.
  with Rome Philharmonic   Victor ML20216
  Orch. – Boncompagni   (in set ML40003)
God save the King – variations, Op. 9 (1829) vln & orch.
  with A. Beltrami pf   Victor ML20216
Moto perpetuo (Allegro di concert) Op. 11 (1830) vln & orch.
  with A. Beltrami   Victor KVIS199, ML20216
Nel cor più non mi sento "Sonata appassionata con variazioni" (on the aria
  from Paisiello's opera "La bella molinara") Op. 38 (1820 or 1821)
  solo vln
  (unaccompanied)   Camden ML79
                        Victor ML20179
                        Prétoria CL8011
(I) Palpiti (variations on the aria "Di tanti palpiti" from Rossini's opera
  "Tancredi") Op. 13 (1819) vln & orch. – arr. vln & pf Kreisler
  with A. Beltrami pf   Camden ML79
                        Victor ML20179
                        Prétoria CL8011
(6) Sonatas, Op. 3 (1801/6) vln & gtr
No. 6. Sonata No. 12, in e
  with A. Beltrami pf   Camden ML79
                        Victor ML20179
                        Prétoria CL8011
Sonata a preghièra "Moses Fantasia" (on the aria "Dal tuo stellato soglio"
  from Rossini's opera "Mosè in Egitto") Op. 24 (1818 or 1819)
  vln & orch.
  with A. Beltrami pf   Camden ML79
                        Victor ML20179
                        Prétoria CL8011
(Le) Streghe (variations on a theme from Süssmeyer's opera "Il Noce di
  Benevento") Op. 8 (1813) vln & orch. – arr. vln & pf Kreisler
  with A. Beltrami pf   Camden ML79
                        Victor ML20179
                        Prétoria CL8011
(60) Variations (on the Genoese air "Barucaba") Op. 14 (1835) vln &
  gtr or pf*
  with piano

POLDINI

(7) Marionnettes pf
No. 2. Poupée valsante arr. vln & pf Kreisler
  with A. Beltrami pf   Victor KVIS199, ML20221

PORPORA

(12) Sonatas (1754) vln & c
Sonata No. 2, in G (ed. David)
  with A. Beltrami pf   Camden ML80
                        Victor ML20180

SARASATE

(8) Danzas españolas vln & pf
No. 3. Romanza andaluza, Op. 22, No. 1
  with A. Collard pf   Saga XID5108
                        Vega MT10144

* Unpublished Italian disc. This performance is played upon the Guarneri
violin once owned by Paganini and now kept in Genoa's town hall.

SARASATE – *Continued*

No. 6. Zapateado, Op. 23, No. 2
  with A. Beltrami pf   Victor KVIS199, ML20221

SCHUBERT

Fantasia in C, Op. 159 (D934) vln & pf
  with L. Lessona pf   Victor (in set MLDS61006)

**Introduction & Variations on "Trockne Blumen" from "Die Schöne
  Müllerin"** Op. 160 (D802) fl & pf – arr. vln & pf
  with L. Lessona pf   Victor (in set MLDS61006)

Rondo brillante in b, Op. 70 (D895) vln & pf
  with L. Lessona pf   Victor (in set MLDS61006)

Sonata in A, Op. 162 (D574) "Duo" vln & pf
  with L. Lessona pf   Victor (in set MLDS61006)

(3) Sonatinas, Op. 137 (D384, D385 & D408) vln & pf
  No. 1. Sonatina No. 1, in D, D384
    with L. Lessona pf   Victor (in set MLDS61006)
  No. 2. Sonatina No. 2, in a, D385
    with L. Lessona pf   Victor (in set MLDS61006)
  No. 3. Sonatina No. 3, in g, D408
    with L. Lessona pf   Victor (in set MLDS61006)

STRAVINSKY

Mavra (1922) – opera
  Russian maiden's song (Parasha's aria) arr. vln & pf Dushkin
  with A. Beltrami pf   Victor KVIS199, ML20221

SZYMANOWSKI

Notturno & Tarantella, Op. 28 vln & pf
  with A. Beltrami pf   Victor ML20221

TARTINI

Sonata in g, "Il Trillo del Diavolo" vln & c – arr. vln & pf Kreisler
  with A. Beltrami pf   Camden ML80
                               Victor ML20180

TCHAIKOVSKY

Concerto in D, Op. 35 vln & orch.
  with Pasdeloup Concerts   Prétoria CL8013
  Orch. – Albert   Vega C30 A328

Souvenir d'un lieu cher, Op. 42 vln & pf
  No. 3. Mélodie
    with A. Beltrami pf   Victor KVIS199, ML20221

VIOTTI

Concerto No. 22, in a (cadenza by Ysaÿe) vln & orch.
  with Rome Philharmonic   Victor ML20217
  Orch. – Boncompagni

VITALI

Chaconne in g vln & c – arr. vln & pf Charlier
  with A. Beltrami pf   Victor ML20217

VIVALDI

(12) Concerti, Op. 8 (1725) "Il Cimento dell Armonia dell Invenzione"
  (Nos. 1/4: Le quattro Stagioni) vln & strs
  Concerto no. 1, in E, F.I, No. 22 "La Primavera"
    with Orch. da Camera Italiana   Victor VICS1469
  Concerto No. 2, in B flat, F.I, No. 23 "L'Estate"
    with Orch. da Camera Italiana   Victor VICS1469

VIVALDI – *Continued*

  Concerto No. 3, in F, F.I, No. 24 "L'Autunno"
    with Orch. da Camera Italiana   Victor VICS1469
  Concerto No. 4, in f, F.I, No. 25 "L'Inverno"
    with Orch. da Camera Italiana   Victor VICS1469
Sonata in D, F.XII, No. 6 vln & c – arr. vln & pf Respighi
  with A. Beltrami pf   Camden ML80
                               Victor ML20180

WIENIAWSKI

Légende, Op. 17 vln & pf or orch.
  with A. Collard pf   Vega MT10144

Polonaise brillante No. 1, in D, Op. 4 vln & pf
  with A. Collard pf   Vega MT10144

Scherzo–Tarantelle, Op. 16 vln & pf
  with A. Beltrami pf   Victor KVIS199, ML20221

YSAŸE

(6) Sonatas, Op. 27 solo vln
  Sonata No. 3, in d
  (unaccompanied)   Victor SL20245

Murray ADASKIN (1906–)

ADASKIN

Sonata (1946) vln & pf
  with M. Bernardi pf   CBC Transcription Program 73
Sonatina baroque solo vln
  (unaccompanied)   CBC Transcription Program 73

M. ADDASH

BRAHMS

(16) Waltzes, Op. 39 pf duet
  No. 15. Waltz No. 15, in A flat arr. vln & pf "in A" Hochstein
  with piano   Imperial 1428

GLUCK

Orphée et Eurydice (1762) – opera
  Dance of the blessed spirits: Lento "Mélodie" (No. 2) arr. vln & pf
  Kreisler
  with piano   A 62X–2 Imperial 1400

MOZART

Divertimento No. 17, in D, K334 2 hrns & strs
  Minuet (3rd mvt) arr. vln & pf Burmester
  with piano   A 67X–3 Imperial 1400

RIMSKY–KORSAKOV

Sadko (1892) – opera
  Chant hindou arr. vln & pf Kreisler
  with piano   Imperial 1428

Ruben AGARONYAN (1948–)

KHACHATURIAN

Gayaneh (Suite No. 1) (1942) – ballet orch.
No. 2. Dance of Ayshe arr. vln & pf Fichtenholz
with N. Danielyan–Bek pf   Mezhdunarodnaya Kniga
D021809/10

KOMITAS

Keler Tsoler pf – arr. vln & pf K. Dombayev
with N. Danielyan–Bek pf   Mezhdunarodnaya Kniga
D021809/10

Krunk (Crane) pf - arr. vln & pf S. Aslamazyan
with S. Navasardyan pf   Mezhdunarodnaya Kniga
SM02093/4

Vagarshapat dance pf – arr. vln & pf K. Dombayev
with S. Navasardyan pf   Mezhdunarodnaya Kniga
SM02093/4

MANSURYAN

Sonata No. 1 (1962) vln & pf
with N. Danielyan–Bek pf   Mezhdunarodnaya Kniga
D021809/10

PAGANINI

(24) Caprices, Op. 1 (1801/7) solo vln
Caprice No. 17, in E flat
(unaccompanied)   Mezhdunarodnaya Kniga
SM02093/4

Nel cor più non mi sento "Sonata appassionata con variazioni" (on the aria from Paisiello's opera "La bella molinara") Op. 38 (1820 or 1821) solo vln
(unaccompanied)   Mezhdunarodnaya Kniga
D021809/10

(Le) Streghe (variations on a theme from Süssmeyer's opera "Il Noce di Benevento") Op. 8 (1813) vln & orch. – arr. vln & pf Kreisler
with S. Navasardyan pf   Mezhdunarodnaya Kniga
SM02093/4

STRAUSS, R.

Sonata in E flat, Op. 18 vln & pf
with S. Navasardyan pf   Mezhdunarodnaya Kniga
SM02093/4

TARTINI

Sonata in g "Il Trillo del Diavolo" vln & c – arr. vln & pf Kreisler
with N. Danielyan–Bek pf   Mezhdunarodnaya Kniga
D021809/10

Andrei AGOSTON (1947–)

PAGANINI

(24) Caprices, Op. 1 (1801/7) solo vln
Caprice No. 17, in E flat
(unaccompanied)   Mezhdunarodnaya Kniga
D028103/4

José de AGUIAR

BEETHOVEN

(6) Minuets, G167 pf
No. 2. Minuet No. 2, in G arr. vln & pf Burmester
with piano   Ultraphon AP315

LUCCHESI

Sérénade à une belle vln & pf
with piano   Ultraphon AP314

MARTINI (Il Tedesco)

Plaisir d'amour v & pf – arr. vln & pf
with piano   Ultraphon AP314

MASSENET

Élégie v & pf – arr. vln & pf
with piano   Ultraphon AP316

MOZART

(Le) Nozze di Figaro, K492 (1786) – opera
Vedro mentr'io sospiro arr. vln & pf
with piano   Ultraphon AP315

Fritz AHBERG

NACHÈZ

(4) Danses Tziganes, Op. 14 vln & pf
No. 1. Danse Tzigane No. 1, in a
with piano   Ekophon 320
Favorite 84017

SIMONETTI

Madrigale pf – arr. vln & pf
with piano   Ekophon 320
Favorite 84016

Helen AIROFF

BEETHOVEN

(3) Sonatas, Op. 30 vln & pf
No. 3. Sonata No. 8, in G
with C. Chailley–Richez pf   Concerteum CR225
Remington R199–95

MOZART

Concerto No. 7, in D, K271a (cadenzas by Enescu) vln & orch.
with Austrian Symphony   Remington R199–46
Orch. – Wöss

Victor AITAY

BARTÓK

(44) Duos (1931) 2 vlns
with M. Kuttner vln   Bartók BRS907

RIMSKY-KORSAKOV

Scheherazade, Op. 35 (1888) orch.
with Chicago Symphony   Angel 36034
Orch. – Ozawa

SCHOENBERG

Suite, Op. 29 (1927) cl, bs–cl, vln, vla, vlc & pf
  with Kreiselman cl, Neidich cl,   Period SPL705
  Keil cl, Layefsky vla, Sophos vlc,
  Sherman pf – cond. Schuller

Anahid AJEMIAN (1926–   )

BEETHOVEN

(3) Sonatas, Op. 12 vln & pf
  No. 3. Sonata No. 3, in E flat
  with M. Ajemian pf   MGM E3416
Sonata No. 9, in A, Op. 47 "Kreutzer" vln & pf
  with M. Ajemian pf   MGM E3416

CHAVEZ

Sonatina (1924) vln & pf
  with M. Ajemian pf   MGM E3180

COWELL

Set of five (1952) vln, pf & pcn
  with M. Ajemian pf & E. Bailey pcn   MGM E3454

HARRISON

Suite (1951) vln, pf & small orch.
  with M. Ajemian pf &   Composers Recordings CRI114
  orch. – Stokowski   Victor LM1785

HOVHANESS

Concerto No. 2 (1957) vln & orch.
  with MGM String Orch. – Surinach   Heliodor H25040, HS25040
                            MGM E3674
Kirgiz Suite, Op. 93 (1951) vln & pf
  with M. Ajemian pf   MGM E3454
Shatakh vln & pf
  with M. Ajemian pf   Dial LP6
                            Metronome CLP505

Suite, Op. 99 (1952) vln, pf & pcn
  with M. Ajemian pf & E. Bailey pcn   Columbia ML5179
Tzaikerk vln, fl & orch.
  with P. Kaplan fl &   Dial LP6
  Orch. – Hovhaness   Disc (in Set 876)
                            Metronome CLP505

IVES

Sonata No. 4 "Childrens' day at the camp meeting" (1916) vln & pf
  with M. Ajemian pf   MGM E3454

KHACHATURIAN

Chanson poème in e (1929) vln & pf
  with M. Ajemian pf   Victor 12–0343

KRENEK

Concerto, Op. 29 (1924) vln, pf & orch.
  with M. Ajemian pf & MGM   MGM E3218
  Orch. – Solomon

REVUELTAS

(3) Pieces (1932) vln & pf
  with M. Ajemian pf   MGM E3180

RIEGGER

Sonatina (1947) vln & pf
  with M. Ajemian pf   MGM E3218

SCHUBERT

Fantasia in C, Op. 159 (D934) vln & pf
  with M. Ajemian pf   MGM E3383

SCHUMANN

Sonata No. 1, in a, Op. 105 vln & pf
  with M. Ajemian pf   MGM E3383

SURINACH

Doppio Concertino (1954) vln, pf & cha orch.
  with M. Ajemian pf & MGM   MGM E3180
  Chamber Orch. – Surinach

WEBERN

(4) Pieces, Op. 7 (1910) vln & pf
  with M. Ajemian pf   MGM E3179

WEILL

Concerto, Op. 12 (1926) vln & w–wnds
  with MGM Wind Orch. – Solomon   MGM E3179

M. AKHMETOV

VALIULLIN

Lyric dance vln & pf
  with L. Akhmetova pf   Mezhdunarodnaya Kniga
                            D027091/2

Khalida AKHTYAMOVA

BRAHMS

(21) Hungarian Dances pf duet
  Hungarian dance No. 9, in e arr. vln & pf Joachim
  with F. Bauer pf   Mezhdunarodnaya Kniga
                            D11939

  Hungarian dance No. 16, in d arr. vln & pf Joachim
  with F. Bauer pf   Mezhdunarodnaya Kniga
                            D11939

SCHUMANN

(3) Fantasiestücke, Op. 73 cl & pf
  with F. Bauer pf   Mezhdunarodnaya Kniga
                            D11939

STRAVINSKY

Divertissement vln & pf
  with F. Bauer pf   Mezhdunarodnaya Kniga
                            D11940

Francis AKOS (1922–   )

BACH

(4) Suites, BWV1066/9 strs & c
Suite No. 3, in D: Air (2nd mvt) BWV1068 2 obs, 3 tpts, drms & strs – arr. vln & pf as "Air on the G–string" by Wilhelmj
with Berlin Municipal Opera Ensemble   Telefunken A11159, TEL585, UV228

DVOŘÁK

(8) Humoresques, Op. 101 pf
No. 7. Humoresque No. 7, in G flat arr. vln & pf "in G" Kreisler
with H. Altmann pf   HMV EG7934

(8) Slavonic Dances, Op. 46 pf duet; orch.
No. 2. Slavonic dance No. 2, in e arr vln & pf "in g" Kreisler
with H. Altmann pf   HMV EG8177

ELGAR

(La) Capricieuse, Op. 17 vln & pf
with H. Altmann pf   HMV EG8177

FOSTER

(The) Old folks at home "Swanee River" (1851) v & pf – arr. vln & pf Kreisler
with H. Altmann pf   HMV EG7938

GRIEG

Peer Gynt (Suite No. 2) Op. 55 orch.
No. 4. Solveig's song arr. vln & pf Sitt
with Berlin Municipal Opera Ensemble   Telefunken A11187, U45187, UV228

HANDEL

Serse (1738) – opera
Ombra mai fu "Largo" arr. vln & orch.
with Berlin Municipal Opera Ensemble   Telefunken A11159, TEL585, U45515

KREISLER

Liebesfreud vln & pf
with H. Altmann pf   HMV EG7937

Liebesleid vln & pf
with H. Altmann pf   HMV EG7937

LILIUCKALANI, Queen

Aloha Oe (1892) v & pf – arr. vln & pf Kreisler
with H. Altmann pf   HMV EG7938

SCHUMANN

(13) Kinderscenen, Op. 15 pf
No. 7. Träumerei arr. vln & orch.
with Berlin Municipal Opera Ensemble   Telefunken A11187, U45187, UV228

VIVALDI

(12) Sonatas, Op. 2 (1712) vln & c
Sonata No. 1, in g, F.XIII, No. 29
with E. Müller hpsi & J. Dawson gamba   Columbia C80550, QCX10423, SCXW7534, STC80550, WSX617, CXN1

VIVALDI – *Continued*

Sonata No. 2, in A, F.XIII, No. 30
with E. Müller hpsi & J. Dawson gamba   Columbia C80550, QCX10423, SCXW7534, STC80550, WSX617, CXH1

Sonata No. 3, in d, F.XIII, No. 31
with E. Müller hpsi & J. Dawson gamba   Columbia C80550, QCX10423, SCXW7534, STC80550, WSX617

Sonata No. 4, in F F.XIII, No. 32
with E. Müller hpsi & J. Dawson gamba   Columbia C80550, QCX10423, SCXW7534, STC80550, WSX617

Sonata No. 5, in b, F.XIII, No. 33
with E. Müller hpsi & J. Dawson gamba   Columbia C80550, QCX10423, SCXW7534, STC80550, WSX617

Sonata No. 6, in C, F.XIII, No. 34
with E. Müller hpsi & J. Dawson gamba   Columbia C80550, QCX10423, SCXW7534, STC80550, WSX617

François D'ALBERT (1918–   )

HUBAY

Impression de la Puszta (3 Morceaux caractéristiques hongrois) Op. 44 vln & pf
No. 2. Les fileuses
with Symphonic Strings – Lawner   B & F Budapest SG1001

(Le) Luthier de Crémone, Op. 40 (1894) – opera
Intermezzo orch. – arr. vln & pf Hubay
with Symphonic Strings – Lawner   B & F Budapest SG1001

(3) Morceaux, Op. 10 vln & pf
No. 1. Arioso
with Symphonic Strings – Lawner   B & F Budapest SG1001

(6) Nouveaux Poèmes (on popular themes) Op. 76 vln & pf
No. 4. Magyar Költemény
with Symphonic Strings – Lawner   B & F Budapest SG1001

(2) Pieces, Op. 38 vln & pf
No. 1. A Képe elött
with Symphonic Strings – Lawner   B & F Budapest SG1001

(6) Pieces (Pusztai hangok Hat zenedarab eredeti magyar dalokután) Op. 57 vln & pf
No. 6. Magyar Cigány dal
with Symphonic Strings – Lawner   B & F Budapest SG1001

(14) Scènes de la Csárda vln & pf
No. 3. Maros vize, Op. 18
with Symphonic Strings – Lawner   B & F Budapest SG1001

No. 4. Hejre Kati, Op. 32
with Symphonic Strings – Lawner   B & F Budapest SG1001

No. 5. Hullámzó balaton, Op. 33
with Symphonic Strings – Lawner   B & F Budapest SG1001

LEHÁR

Giuditta (1934) – operetta
Selection arr. vln & orch.
with orch.   B & F Budapest B7001

Selection arr. vln & orch.
with orch.   B & F Budapest SG1000

(Der) Graf von Luxemburg (1909) – operetta
Selection arr. vln & orch.
with orch.   B & F Budapest B7000

LEHÁR – *Continued*

(Das) Land des Lächelns (1923) – operetta
  Selection arr. vln & orch.
  with orch.   B & F Budapest B7001

Paganini (1925) – operetta
  Selection arr. vln & orch.
  with orch.   B & F Budapest B7000
  Selection arr. vln & orch.
  with orch.   B & F Budapest SG1000

LYSENKO

Capriccio élégiaque, Op. 32 vln & pf
  with C.S. Smith pf   Ikar IK3812M, IK3812S
Élégie in a (1912) vln & pf
  with C.S. Smith pf   Ikar IK3812M, IK3812S
Fantasia, Op. 21 vln & pf
  with C.S. Smith pf   Ikar IK3812M, IK3812S
Low sinks the sun vln & pf
  with C.S. Smith pf   Ikar IK3812M, IK3812S
Moment of disappointment (1901) vln & pf
  with C.S. Smith pf   Ikar IK3812M, IK3812S
Rhapsody No. 2 (Dumka–Shoomka on Ukrainian themes) Op. 18 vln & pf
  with C.S. Smith pf   Ikar IK3812M, IK3812S
Romance in A flat, Op. 27 vln & pf
  with C.S. Smith pf   Ikar IK3812M, IK3812S

MARKAITIS

Sonata in D (1960) vln & pf
  with G. Lawner pf   B & F Budapest SG2001, ST1001

György ALBERT

SZELÉNYI

(8) Duo Sonatinas "Little Duos" 2 vlns
  No. 1. Chase
  with T. Zalay vln   Qualiton LPX1188
  No. 2. Cuckoo chattering
  with T. Zalay vln   Qualiton LPX1188
  No. 3. Rondino
  with T. Zalay vln   Qualiton LPX1188

István ALBERT

ANONYMOUS

Esztergomi verbunkos (Esztergom recruiting dance) solo vln*
  (unaccompanied)   Qualiton LPX1216

CSERMÁK

Lassú magyar (Slow Hungarian dance) dul,† vlc & vln
  with L. Rálogh dul & T. Rácz vlc   Qualiton LPX1216

*Pre 1761 manuscript.

† Dulcimer – known as cimbalom in Hungary.

Giulio ALBERTI

GRIEG

Peer Gynt (Suite No. 2) Op. 55 orch.
  No. 4. Solveig's song arr. vln & pf Sitt
  with piano   9527   Gennett 3105

HERBERT

(The) Fortune Teller (1898) – operetta
  Gypsy love song arr. vln & pf
  with piano   9528   Gennett 3105

Lilia d'ALBORE (1914–)

BRAHMS

Sonata No. 3, in d, Op. 108 vln & pf
  with G. Frid pf   02330/2 LWH   Polydor 72053/4

DVOŘÁK

Sonatina in G, Op. 100 vln & pf
  Larghetto (2nd mvt)
  with H. Giesen pf 1178^2GE   Polydor 67681

FRANCK

Sonata in A (1886) vln & pf
  with H. Giesen pf   Polydor 68002/5

GLUCK

Orphée et Eurydice (1762) opera
  Dance of the blessed spirits: Lento "Mélodie" (No. 2) arr. vln & pf
  Kreisler
  with H. Giesen pf   Polydor 62838

MOZART

Sonata No. 31, in C, K404 vln & pf
  with H. Giesen pf   Polydor 67848

PIZZETTI

(3) Canti ad una giovane fidanzata (1924) vln & pf
  No. 3. Appassionato
  with G. Frid pf   Polydor 72054

SCHUBERT

(3) Sonatinas, Op. 137 (D384, D385 & D408) vln & pf
  No. 1. Sonatina No. 1, in D, D384
  with H. Giesen pf   Polydor 67847/8

SIMONETTI

Madrigale pf – arr. vln & pf
  with H. Giesen pf   Polydor 62838

VERACINI

(12) Sonatas, Op. 2 (1744) "Sonate accademiche" vln & c
  Sonata No. 6, in A: Largo (2nd mvt) ed. Corti
  with H. Giesen pf   1748½GE   Polydor 67681

Georges ALÈS (1903–)

BACH, J.C.

Sinfonia concertante in A, T. P284 (1770) vln, vlc & orch.
  with P. Coddée vlc & L'Oiseau-Lyre   L'Oiseau-Lyre OL50074
  Ensemble – Froment

BACH, J.S.

Concerto in D, BWV1045 vln, tpts, strs & c
  with R. Delmotte tpt & Collegium   Editions phonographiques
Musicum, Paris – Douatte   parisiennes APG124
Concerto in c, BWV1060 vln & ob or 2 vlns, strs & c
  with P. Pierlot ob & L'Oiseau–Lyre   L'Oiseau–Lyre OL50074
Ensemble – Froment

BRAHMS

Trio in E flat, Op. 40 hrn, vln & pf
  with J. Devémy hrn   M6 121553/60   Classic C2103/6, CL6005
  & A. d'Arco pf   Esquire TN22–001
                              Mercury MG15015

BRANDL

(Der) Liebe Augustin – operetta
Du alter Stefansturm arr. vln & pf as "The old refrain" by Kreisler
  with Orch. des Concerts,   Capitol CTL7076, (in set
Paris – Dupré   KCF273), L273, LC6537

COUPERIN, F.

(L') Apothéose de Lully (1725) 2 vlns & c
  with H. Merckel vln, M. Frécheville   L'Oiseau–Lyre LD1
vlc, M. Morel ob & R. Gerlin hpsi
(Les) Nations – 4 suites (1726) 2 vlns & c
Suite No. 4, in g "La Piémontoise"
  with G. Tessier vln, D. Gouarne hpsi   Club français du Disque 11
& G. Schwartz vlc
(Le) Parnesse, ou l'Apothéose de Corelli (1725) 2 vlns & c
       PART 1280–1, 1281–2, 1282/3   L'Oiseau–Lyre OL57/8
  with H. Merckel vln, M. Frécheville
vlc & R. Gerlin hpsi

EGK

(La) Tentation de Saint–Antoine (1945) b, 2 vlns, vla & vlc
  with B. Lefort b, P. Doukan vln,   L'Oiseau–Lyre OL50134
P. Ladhuite vla & R. Albin vlc

FALLA

Concerto in D (1926) hpsi, fl, ob, cl, vln, vlc & orch.
  with J–C. Richard hpsi, C. Lardé fl,   Nonesuch H1135, H71135
C. Maisonneuve ob, G. Deplus cl,   Valois MB440, MB940
J. Lamy vlc & Valois Instrumental
Ensemble – Ravier

FAURÉ

Berceuse, Op. 16 vln & pf
  with orch. – Cebron
                    Lumen 30104, 208003

HANDEL

Apollo e Dafne (Cantata No. 16) s, bs, fl, obs, bsn, strs & c
  with M. Ritchie s, B. Boyce b,   L'Oiseau–Lyre LD14, OL50038
P. Pierlot ob, A. Geoffroy-Dechaume
hpsi & L'Oiseau–Lyre
Ensemble – Lewis

HAYDN

Sinfonia concertante in B flat, Op. 84 (H.I, No. 105) vln, vlc, ob, bsn &
orch.
  with A. Rémond vlc, E. Mayousse ob,   Deutsche Grammophon
R. Droulez bsn & Lamoureux   LPEM19169
Orchestra – Markevitch   Heliodor 89509, H25015,
                            HS25015

KREISLER

Caprice viennois, Op. 2 vln & pf
  with L'Orch. des Concerts,   Capitol CTL7076, (in set
Paris – Dupré   KCF273), L273, LC6537
Liebesfreud vln & pf
  with L'Orch. des Concerts,   Capitol CTL7076, (in set
Paris – Dupré   KCF273), L273, LC6537
Liebesleid vln & pf
  with L'Orch. des Concerts,   Capitol CTL7076, (in set
Paris – Dupré   KCF273), L273, LC6537
Schön Rosmarin vln & pf
  with L'Orch. des Concerts,   Capitol CTL7076, (in set
Paris – Dupré   KCF273), L273, LC6537
Tambourin chinois, Op. 3 vln & pf
  with L'Orch. des Concerts,   Capitol CTL7076, (in set
Paris – Dupré   KCF273), L273, LC6537

LECLAIR

(12) Sonatas, Op. 1 – Book I (1723) vln & c
Sonata No. 8, in G
  with I. Nef hpsi   L'Oiseau–Lyre LD47, OL50087
(12) Sonatas, , Op. 2 – Book II (1728) vln & c
Sonata No. 1, in e
  with I. Nef hpsi   L'Oiseau–Lyre LD47, OL50087
                         Philips 839314EGY
Sonata No. 12, in g
  with I. Nef hpsi   L'Oiseau–Lyre LD47, OL50087
                         Philips 839314EGY
(12) Sonatas, Op. 5 – Book III (1734) vln & c
Sonata No. 1, in A
  with I. Nef hpsi   L'Oiseau–Lyre LD48, OL50088
                         Philips 839314EGY
Sonata No. 4, in B flat
  with I. Nef hpsi   L'Oiseau–Lyre LD48, OL50088
                         Philips 839314EGY
(12) Sonatas, Op. 9 – Book IV (1738) vln & c
Sonata No. 4, in A
  with I. Nef hpsi   L'Oiseau–Lyre LD48, OL50088

LOEILLET

(12) Sonatas, Op. 2 Nos. 1/6: 2 vlns & c – 7/9: 2 fls & c – 10/12: ob, fl
& c*
Sonata No. 1, in B flat arr. vln & hpsi as "No. 10, in B flat"
  with R. Gerlin hpsi   L'Oiseau–Lyre LD49, OL50018
Sonata No. 2, in F arr. vln & c as "No. 13, in G"
  with R. Gerlin hpsi & P. Coddée vlc   L'Oiseau–Lyre LD49, OL50018
Sonata No. 6, in c arr. vln & c as "No. 2, in b"
  with R. Gerlin hpsi & P. Coddée vlc   L'Oiseau–Lyre LD49, OL50018

MANCINI

Concerto a quattro in e (1729) fl, 2 vlns & hpsi
  with J–P. Rampal fl, P. Doukan vln   L'Oiseau–Lyre LD66, OL50009
& R. Gerlin hpsi

*Also published as op. 5

PURCELL

(The) Fairy Queen, Z629 (1692) – opera
 O let me sleep "The plaint"
  with M. Ritchie s, P. Coddée vlc,   L'Oiseau–Lyre LD16, OL50029
  A. Geoffroy–Dechaume hpsi
  & L'Oiseau–Lyre Ensemble – Lewis

(12) Sonatas, Z790/801 (1683) 3 part – 2 vlns & c
 Sonata No. 1, in g, Z190
                0111³GCP, 0112²GCP   L'Oiseau–Lyre 207/8, (in set
  with H. Merckel vln, I. Nef hpsi &   OLP1)
  A. Navarra vlc
 Sonata No. 2, in B flat, Z791
  with H. Merckel vln,   0113/4²GCP   L'Oiseau–Lyre 209/10, (in set
  I. Nef hpsi & A. Navarra vlc   OLP1)
 Sonata No. 3, in d, Z792
                0115/6²GCP   L'Oiseau–Lyre 211/2, (in set
  I. Nef hpsi & A. Navarra vlc   OLP1)
 Sonata No. 4, in F, Z793
                0117³GCP, 0118²GCP   L'Oiseau–Lyre 211/2, (in set
  with H. Merckel vln, I. Nef hpsi &   OLP1)
  A. Navarra vlc
 Sonata No. 5, in a, Z794
                0119²GCP, 0120³GCP   L'Oiseau–Lyre 209/10, (in set
  with H. Merckel vln, I. Nef hpsi &   OLP1)
  A. Navarra vlc
 Sonata No. 6, in C, Z795
                0121²GCP, 0122⁴GCP   L'Oiseau–Lyre 207/8, (in set
  with H. Merckel vln, I. Nef hpsi &   OLP1)
  A. Navarra vlc
 Sonata No. 7, in e, Z796
                0123³GCP, 0124²GCP   L'Oiseau–Lyre 213/4, (in set
  with H. Merckel vln, I. Nef hpsi &   OLP1)
  A. Navarra vlc
 Sonata No. 8, in G, Z797
  with H. Merckel vln,   0125/6²GCP   L'Oiseau–Lyre 215/6, (in set
  I. Nef hpsi & A. Navarra vlc   OLP1)
 Sonata No. 9, in c, Z798
  with H. Merckel   0129/30³GCP   L'Oiseau–Lyre 217/8, (in set
  vln, I. Nef hpsi & A. Navarra vlc   OLP1)
 Sonata No. 10, in A, Z799
                0131²GCP, 0132¹GCP   L'Oiseau–Lyre 217/8, (in set
  with H. Merckel vln, I. Nef hpsi &   OLP1)
  A. Navarra vlc
 Sonata No. 11, in f, Z800
                0133²GCP, 0134³GCP   L'Oiseau–Lyre 215/6, (in set
  with H. Merckel vln, I. Nef hpsi &   OLP1)
  A. Navarra vlc
 Sonata No. 12, in D, Z801
                0127²GCP, 0128¹GCP   L'Oiseau–Lyre 213/4, (in set
  with H. Merckel vln, I. Nef hpsi &   OLP1)
  A. Navarra vlc

Timon of Athens, Z632 (1694) – opera
 excerpts
  with M. Ritchie s, A. Geoffroy–   L'Oiseau–Lyre LD16, OL50029
  Dechaume hpsi & L'Oiseau–Lyre
  Ensemble – Lewis

SCHUBERT

(6) Moments musicaux, Op. 94 (D780) (1823/7) pf
 No. 3. Moment musicale No. 3, in f "Air russe" arr. vln & pf Kreisler
  with orch. – Cebron   Lumen 30104, 208003

STRAVINSKY

(L') Histoire du Soldat (1918) 3 narrators, cl, bsn, tpt, tbn, vln & cbs
  with M. Auclair, M. Herrand &   Pathé DTX124, DTX30008
  J. Marchat, narrators – P. Lefebvre cl,   Vox PL7960
  P. Hongne bsn, R. Delmotte tpt,
  M. Galiegue tbn, H. Moreau cbs,
  cond – Oubradous

TORELLI

(12) Concerti, Op. 8 (1709) Nos. 1/6: 2 vlns, strs & c – 7/2: vln, strs & c
 Concerto No. 1, in C
  with L. Kaufman vln, R. Albin vlc,   L'Oiseau–Lyre LD115, OL50089
  R. Gerlin hpsi & L'Oiseau–Lyre
  Ensemble – Kaufman
 Concerto No. 2, in a
  with L. Kaufman vln, R. Albin vlc,   L'Oiseau–Lyre LD115, OL50089
  R. Gerlin hpsi & L'Oiseau–Lyre
  Ensemble – Kaufman
 Concerto No. 3, in E
  with L. Kaufman vln, R. Albin vlc,   L'Oiseau–Lyre LD115, OL50089
  R. Gerlin hpsi & L'Oiseau–Lyre
  Ensemble – Kaufman
 Concerto No. 4, in B flat
  with L. Kaufman vln, R. Albin vlc,   L'Oiseau–Lyre LD116, OL50090
  R. Gerlin hpsi & L'Oiseau–Lyre
  Ensemble – Kaufman
 Concerto No. 5, in G
  with L. Kaufman vln, R. Albin vlc,   L'Oiseau–Lyre LD116, OL50090
  R. Gerlin hpsi & L'Oiseau–Lyre
  Ensemble – Kaufman
 Concerto No. 6, in g
  with L. Kaufman vln, R. Albin vlc,   L'Oiseau–Lyre LD116, OL50090
  R. Gerlin hpsi & L'Oiseau–Lyre
  Ensemble – Kaufman

VIVALDI

(12) Concerti, Op. 4 "La Stravaganza" vln & strs
 Concerto No. 5, in A, F.I, No. 184
  with M–L. Girod org, J. Wiederker vlc Les Quatre Saisons LQS103
  & Collegium Musicum,
  Paris – Douatte
 Concerto No. 6, in g, F.I, No. 185
  with M–L. Girod org, J. Wiederker vlc Les Quatre Saisons LQS103
  & Collegium Musicum,
  Paris – Douatte
 Concerto No. 7, in C, F.I, No. 186
  with M–L. Girod org, J. Wiederker vlc Les Quatre Saisons LQS104
  & Collegium Musicum,
  Paris – Douatte
 Concerto No. 8, in d, F.I, No. 187
  with M–L. Girod org, J. Wiederker vlc Les Quatre Saisons LQS104
  & Collegium Musicum,
  Paris – Douatte
 Concerto No. 9, in F, F.I, No. 188
  with M–L. Girod org, J. Wiederker vlc Les Quatre Saisons LQS104
  & Collegium Musicum,
  Paris – Douatte
 Concerto No. 10, in c, F.I, No. 189
  with M–L. Girod org, J. Wiederker vlc Les Quatre Saisons LQS104
  & Collegium Musicum,
  Paris – Douatte

VIVALDI – *Continued*

Concerto No. 11, in D, F.I, No. 190
with M–L. Girod org, J. Wiederker vlc Les Quatre Saisons LQS103
& Collegium Musicum,
Paris – Douatte

Concerto No. 12, in G, F.I, No. 191
with M–L. Girod org, J. Wiederker vlc Les Quatre Saisons LQS103
& Collegium Musicum,
Paris – Douatte

(12) Concerti, Op. 8 (1725) "Il Cimento dell' Armonia e dell Invenzione"
(Nos. 1/4: Le Quattro Stagioni) vln & strs
Concerto No. 1, in E, F.I, No. 22 "La Primavera"
with Collegium Musicum,   Concerteum CCX227
Paris – Douatte   Guilde Européenne du
                                       Microsillon GEM8
                                       Period SHO309
                                       Les Quatre Saisons LQS102

Concerto No. 2, in B flat, F.I, No. 23 "L'Estate"
with Collegium Musicum,   Concerteum CCX227
Paris – Douatte   Guilde Européenne du
                                       Microsillon GEM8
                                       Period SHO309
                                       Les Quatre Saisons LQS102

Concerto No. 3, in F, F.I, No. 24 "L'Autunno"
with Collegium Musicum,   Concerteum CCX227
Paris – Douatte   Guilde Européenne du
                                       Microsillon GEM8
                                       Period SHO309
                                       Les Quatre Saisons LQS102

Concerto No. 4, in f, F.I, No. 25 "L'Inverno"
with Collegium Musicum,   Concerteum CCX227
Paris – Douatte   Guilde Européenne du
                                       Microsillon GEM8
                                       Period SHO309
                                       Les Quatre Saisons LQS102

Concerto in G, P.135 (F.IV, No. 1) 2 vlns, 2 vlcs, strs & c
with R. Gendre vln, R. Albin vlc,   La Boîte à Musique LD84
A. Rémond vlc & L'Oiseau–Lyre   Fontana 695300KL
Ensemble – Froment   L'Oiseau–Lyre LD84 OL50124

Concerto in F, P.325 vln, strs & c
with Collegium Musicum,   Les Quatre Saisons LQS1,
Paris – Douatte   LQS101

Concerto in B flat, P.373 vln, strs & c
with Collegium Musicum,   Les Quatre Saisons LQS1,
Paris – Douatte   LQS101

Concerto in B flat, P.388 (F.IV, No. 2) (Op. 22. No. 2) vln, vlc, strs & c
with R. Albin vlc & L'Oiseau–Lyre   Fontana 695300KL
Ensemble – Froment   L'Oiseau–Lyre LD84, OL50124

Concerto in B flat, P.406 (F.XII, No. 16) vln, ob, strs & c
with C. Maisonneuve ob & L'Oiseau   L'Oiseau–Lyre LD73, OL50073
–Lyre Ensemble – Froment

Concerto in g, P.407 vln, strs & c
with L'Oiseau–Lyre   Fontana 695300KL
Ensemble – Froment   L'Oiseau–Lyre LD84, OL50124

Giannini ALESSANDRO

de ANGELIS
Rêve d'amour vln & pf
with piano   Odeon 51837

HERRMANN
Canzonetta, Op. 57 vln & pf
with piano   Odeon 51836

Azad ALIEV

GAJIEV
Concerto vln & orch.
with Azerbaijanian State Symphony   Mezhdunarodnaya Kniga
Orch. – Niyazi   D02392

MAMEDOV
Symphonic Variations vln & orch.
with Azerbaijanian State Symphony   Mezhdunarodnaya Kniga
Orch. – Niyazi   D02393, D015710

Phyllis ALLAN

FRANCK
Sonata in A (1886) vln & pf
Allegretto ben moderato (1st mvt)
with E. Hobday pf   Vocalion D02093

KREISLER
Andantino (Padre Martini) vln & pf
with E. Hobday pf   Vocalion R6064

MARTIN
From the Rialto vln & pf
with E. Hobday pf   Vocalion K05209
Morning song vln & pf
with E. Hobday pf   Vocalion K05209

STEWART
Capriccietto vln & pf
with E. Hobday pf   Vocalion R6064
Ecstasy vln & pf
with E. Hobday pf   Vocalion D02028

WAGNER
(Die) Meistersinger von Nürnberg (1868) – opera
Morgenlich leuchtend "Prize song" arr. vln & pf Wilhelmj
with E. Hobday pf   Vocalion D02028

Charles D'ALMAINE (1871–1943)

ADAMS
(The) Holy city (1892) v & pf – arr. vln & orch.
with orch.   Edison cylinder 7590
(The) Holy city (1892) v & pf – arr. vln & orch.
with orch.   Victor 433

ALARD

(10) Morceaux de Salon, Op. 49 vln & pf
No. 10. Brindisi
with orch.   Victor 31542

ANONYMOUS

(La) Carnevale di Venizia – variations arr. vln & orch. D'Almaine
with orch.   Edison cylinder 7824

(La) Carnevale di Venizia – variations arr. vln & orch. D'Almaine
with orch.   Columbia 31495

Polish national dance unid – arr. vln & orch.
with orch.   Edison cylinder B332

BALFE

(The) Bohemian Girl (1843) – opera
Then you'll remember me
with orch.   Edison cylinder B369

Then you'll remember me arr. vln & orch. D'Almaine
with orch.   Victor 1985

Then you'll remember me arr. vln & orch. D'Almaine
with orch.   Columbia 216

BÉRIOT

(6) Airs varié, Op. 12 vln & pf
No. 6 Air varié No. 6, in a arr. Schradieck
with piano   Edison cylinder 7930

No. 6. Air varié No. 6, in a arr. Schradieck
with piano   Edison cylinder 8431

No. 6 Air varié No. 6, in a arr. Schradieck
with piano   Columbia 214

Concerto No. 2, in b, Op. 32 vln & orch.
Andante (2nd mvt)
with orch.   Victor 2920, 16050

BERLIN

When I lost you (1912) v & pf – arr. vln & orch.
with orch.   Edison cylinder 2131

BRAHMS

(21) Hungarian Dances pf duet
Hungarian dance unid – arr. vln & orch.
with orch.   Columbia 66

(5) Lieder, Op. 49 v & pf
No. 4. Wiegenlied "Cradle song" arr. vln & pf
with piano   Gramophone & Typewriter 7994

FISHER

Peg o' my heart v & pf – arr. vln & orch.
with orch.   Edison cylinder 2263

GARBIEL–MARIE

(La) Cinquantaine (1894) pf duet – arr. vln & orch.
with orch.   Victor 2924, 31271

GANZ

Sing, sweet bird v & pf – arr. vln, fl & orch.
with D. Lyons fl & orch.   Victor 5007, 16242

GERMAN

Henry VIII (1892) – Incidental music orch.
Morris dance arr. vln & orch.
with orch.   Victor 2973

GERMAN – *Continued*

Shepherd's dance arr. vln & orch.
with orch.   Edison cylinder 8070

Shepherd's dance arr. vln & orch.
with orch.   United States Everlasting
                                          Indestructible cylinder 1115

Shepherd's dance arr. vln & orch.
with orch.   Victor 2872

GOUNOD

Faust (1859) – opera
selection arr. vln & orch. D'Almaine
with orch.   Columbia 1533, 31493, A229

selection arr. vln & orch. D'Almaine
with orch.   B 1361   Victor 2922, 31312

HALÉVY

(L') Éclair (1835) – opera
Call me thine own (Romance) arr. vln & orch.
with orch.   Victor 31491

Call me thine own (Romance) arr. vln, fl & orch.
with D. Lyons fl & orch.   Victor 35140

HANDEL

Serse (1738) – opera
Ombra mai fu "Largo" arr. vln & org
with organ   Victor 2925

d'HARDELOT

Because (1902) v & pf – arr. vln & pf
with piano   Edison cylinder B335

KNEASS

Ben Bolt (Oh! don't you remember sweet Alice?) (1848) v & pf – arr. vln & pf D'Almaine*
with orch.   Edison cylinder 7326, B333

Ben Bolt (Oh! don't you remember sweet Alice?) (1848) v & pf – arr. vln & pf D'Almaine*
with orch.   Columbia A202

LABITZKY

(Der) Traum der Sennerin (Dream of the mountains – Idyll) Op. 45 orch.
with D. Lyons fl & orch.   73892   Victor 31598

LÉONARD

Fantaisie militaire, Op. 15 vln & pf
with piano   Gramophone & Typewriter 7985
                                          Victor 2828, 16242

(5) Scènes humoristiques, Op. 61 vln & pf
No. 4. L'Ane et l'Anier
with piano   Victor 2770, 16169

MASCAGNI

Cavalleria Rusticana (1890) – opera
Intermezzo orch. – arr. vln & orch.
with orch.   Columbia 62, 27001

*Based on a German air.

MENDELSSOHN

(6) Songs without words, Op. 62 pf
No. 6. Song without words No. 30, in A "Spring song" arr. vln & pf
with piano   Victor 2923
No. 6. Song without words No. 30, in A "Spring song" arr. vln & orch.
with orch.   Victor 4358

MENZEL

Romanze, Op. 40 "Sweet longing" fl & var. inst – arr. vln, fl & orch.
with D. Lyons fl & orch.   C 2780   Victor 31455

OLCOTT

Mother Machree v & pf – arr. vln & orch.
with orch.   Edison cylinder 2119

PIERNÉ

Sérénade in A, Op. 7 (1875) pf – arr. vln & pf
with piano   Victor 4024, 16051

PRINCE

(The) White cockade vln & orch.
with orch. – Prince   Columbia 1023, 3749

RAFF

(6) Pieces, Op. 85 vln & pf
No. 3. Cavatina in D arr. vln & orch.
with orch.   Edison cylinder 7633, B449
No. 3. Cavatina in D
with piano   Leeds 4044
No. 3. Cavatina in D arr. vln & orch.
with orch.   Victor 4191

READING

O come all ye faithful (Adeste Fideles) hymn – arr. vln & orch.
with orch.   Edison cylinder B450

RIES

Suite No. 1, Op. 26 vln & pf
No. 5. Gavotte
with piano   Victor 2972

SARASATE

Faust Fantasia (on themes from the opera by Gounod) vln & pf or orch.
Valse
with orch.   Edison cylinder 7659
Valse
with orch.   Columbia 217

SCHUBERT

(14) Schwanengesang, D957 (1828) v & pf
No. 4. Ständchen "Serenade" arr. vln & orch.
with orch.   Edison cylinder 7192
No. 4. Ständchen "Serenade" arr. vln & orch.
with orch.   Columbia 212
No. 4. Ständchen "Serenade" arr. vln & orch.
with orch.   Victor 31493, 35140
No. 4. Ständchen "Serenade" arr. vln, fl & orch.
with D. Lyons fl & orch.   Victor 35493

SCHUMANN

(13) Kinderscenen, Op. 15 pf
No. 7. Träumerei arr. vln & orch
with orch.   Columbia 63
No. 7. Träumerei arr. vln & pf
with piano   Victor 246

THOMAS

Mignon (1866) – opera
Entr'acte (Gavotte) (Act II) orch – arr. vln & pf Sarasate
with piano   Gramophone & Typewriter 7987
                           Victor 2802

VERDI

(Il) Trovatore (1853) – opera
Miserere arr. vln & orch. D'Almaine
with orch.   Edison cylinder 7324, B331
Miserere arr. vln & pf D'Almaine
with piano   218–5–X   Columbia 218, 27013
Miserere arr. vln & orch. D'Almaine
with orch.   Victor 245

WALLACE

Lurline (1860) – opera
Sweet spirit, hear my prayer arr. vln & orch. D'Almaine
with orch.   Victor 16522
Maritana (1845) – opera
Scenes that are brightest arr. vln & orch. D'Almaine
with orch.   Edison cylinder 7455, B336
Scenes that are brightest arr. vln & orch. D'Almaine
with orch.   Columbia 27005
Scenes that are brightest arr. vln & orch. D'Almaine
with orch.   Victor 1211, 16093

WIENIAWSKI

Fantaisie brillante (on themes from Gounod's "Faust") Op. 20 vln & orch.
Garden scene
with orch.   Victor 1208, 16093

WINNER

(The) Mocking bird vln & orch.
with orch.   Edison cylinder 5352, 8099
(The) Mocking bird vln & orch.
with orch.   Victor 249, 16538

Has also recorded numerous jigs, reels, hornpipes, etc.

Juan ALÓS (1914–)

BACH

(3) Sonatas & 3 Partitas, BWV1001/6 solo vln
Partita No. 2, in d: Gigue (4th mvt) BWV1004 arr. vln & pf
with A.P. Santasusana pf   Odeon 184539

BRAHMS

(21) Hungarian Dances pf duet
Hungarian dance No. 5, in f sharp. arr. vln & pf "in g" Joachim
with A.P. Santasusana pf   Odeon 121175

PAGANINI

(24) Caprices, Op. 1 (1801/7) solo vln
Caprice No. 13, in B flat arr. vln & pf Kreisler
with A.P. Santasusana pf   Odeon 184539

(6) Sonatas, Op. 3 (1801/6) vln & gtr
No. 6. Sonata No. 12, in e
with A.P. Santasusana pf   Odeon 121177

SARASATE

Zigeunerweisen, Op. 20 vln & pf or orch.
with C. Lozaud pf   Odeon 184426

TCHAIKOVSKY

Souvenir d'un lieu cher, Op. 42 vln & pf
No. 3. Mélodie arr. Wilhelmj
with A.P. Santasusana pf   Odeon 121175

Vladimir ALOUME

BARTÓK

Sonata in g (1944) solo vln
(unaccompanied)   Mezhdunarodnaya Kniga
D024403/4

ELLER

Pines vln & pf
with piano   Mezhdunarodnaya Kniga
D024403/4

Sonata vln & pf
with C. Sepp pf   Mezhdunarodnaya Kniga
D3900/1

SARASATE

(8) Danzas españolas vln & pf
No. 3. Romanza andaluza, op. 22, No. 1
with piano   Mezhdunarodnaya Kniga
D024403/4

SUK

(4) Pieces Op. 17 vln & pf
No. 1. Quasi ballata
with piano   Mezhdunarodnaya Kniga
D024403/4

No. 2. Appassionato
with piano   Mezhdunarodnaya Kniga
D024403/4

E. ALTERMANN

ALTERMANN

Petite annonce vln & pf
with pf   Odeon 33587

THOMÉ

Simple aveu, Op. 25 pf – arr. vln & pf
with pf   Odeon 33670

Gaby ALTMANN

BACH

Sonata in d, BWV1036 2 vlns & c
with J–L. Lardinois vln & J. Louel pf   Decca FAT173454

Sonata in C, BWV1037 2 vlns & c
with J–L. Lardinois vln & J. Louel pf   Decca FAT173454

Sonata in G, BWV1038 fl, vln & c
with J–L. Lardinois vln & J. Louel pf   Decca FAT173454

Sonata in G, BWV1039 2 fls or vlns & c
with J–L. Lardinois vln & J. Louel pf   Decca FAT173454

BARTÓK

Contrasts (1938) vln, cl & pf
with P. Bulte cl & J. Louel pf   Decca FAT173400
London–Globe GLB1022

(44) Duos (1931) 2 vlns
with J–L. Lardinois vln   Decca FAT173400
London–Globe GLB1022

Licco AMAR (1891–1959)

BACH

(6) Sonatas, BWV1014/9 vln & clav
Sonata No. 4, in C: Largo (1st mvt); **Adagio ma non tanto** (2nd mvt)
BWV1017
with G. Ramin hpsi   87/8 bs   Brunswick 90258
Decca LY6013
Polydor 19869

BARTÓK

Quartet No. 2, in a, Op. 17 (1917) 2 vlns, vla & vlc
with W. Casper vln, P.   415/22 bg   Gramophone shop (in set GS52)
Hindemith vla & R. Hindemith vlc   Polydor 66425/8

BEETHOVEN

Quartet No. 11, in f, Op. 95 2 vlns, vla & vlc
with W. Casper vln, P. Hindemith vla   Polydor 66571/3
& R. Hindemith vlc

DVOŘÁK

Quartet No. 6, in f, Op. 96 "American" 2 vlns, vla & vlc
Vivace ma non troppo (4th mvt)
with W. Casper vln,   428 bg   Polydor 66421
P. Hindemith vla & R. Hindemith vlc

HINDEMITH

Quartet No. 3, in c, Op. 22 (1922) 2 vlns, vla & vlc
     905az, 906½az, 907/10az   Polydor 66198/200
with W. Casper vln, P. Hindemith vla
& R. Hindemith vlc

Quartet No. 3, in C, Op. 22 (1922) 2 vlns, vla & vlc
with W. Casper vln, P.   429/34 bg   Polydor 66422/4
Hindemith vla & R. Hindemith vlc

Trio No. 1, Op. 34 (1924) vln, vla & vlc
Toccata (1st mvt); **Mässig schnelle Viertel** (3rd mvt)
with P. Hindemith vla &   76/9 bo   Polydor 66573/4
R. Hindemith vlc

KRENEK

Quartet No. 3, Op. 20 2 vlns, vla & vlc
Waltz
with W. Casper vln, P. Hindemith vla   Polydor 66201
& R. Hindemith vlc

LECLAIR

(12) Sonatas, Op. 9 – Book IV (1738) vln & c
Sonata No. 3, in D
with G. Ramin   91 bs & 91½ bs Polydor 19871
hpsi

MOZART

Quartet No. 15, in d, K421 2 vlns, vla & vlc
Andante (2nd mvt): Minuetto ma non troppo (4th mvt)
with W. Casper vln, P. Hindemith vla   Parlophone P9351
& R. Hindemith vlc

Quartet No. 16, in E flat, K428 2 vlns, vla & vlc
with W. Casper vln,   138/43 bi Polydor 66568/70
P. Hindemith vla & R. Hindemith vlc

Quartet No. 16, in E flat, K428 2 vlns, vla & vlc
Allegro vivace (4th mvt)
with W. Casper vln,   414 bg Polydor 95005
P. Hindemith vla & R. Hindemith vlc

Quartet No. 23, in F, K590 2 vlns, vla & vlc
with W. Casper vln,   409/413 bg Polydor 95003/5
P. Hindemith vla & R. Hindemith vlc

REGER

Trio in a, Op. 77b vln, vla & vlc
with P. Hindemith vla &   71/6 bo Gramophone Shop (in set GS53)
R. Hindemith vlc   Polydor 66575/7

STRAVINSKY

Concertino (1920) 2 vlns, vla & vlc
with W. Casper vln, P. Hindemith vla   Polydor 12049, 66201
& R. Hindemith vlc

VERACINI

(12) Sonatas, Op. 2 (1744) "Sonate accademiche" vln & c
Sonata No. 8, in e: Largo & Allegro con fuoco
with G. Ramin hpsi   89/90 bs Polydor 19870

VERDI

Quartet in e (1873) 2 vlns, vla & vlc
with W. Casper vln,   423/7 bg Polydor 66419/21
P. Hindemith vla & R. Hindemith vlc

Richard AMBODEN

GOLDBERG

Sonata in g 2 vlns & c
with A. Trippner vln, M.G. Schneider   Da Camera SM92206
hpsi & H. Schäfer vlc

Priscilla Ann (Penny) AMBROSE (1946–1963)

KROLL

Banjo & fiddle vln & pf
with L.L. Smith pf   Golden Crest GC8000

PAGANINI

(24) Caprices, Op. 1 (1801/7) solo vln
Caprice No. 13, in B flat arr. vln & pf Kreisler
with L.L. Smith pf   Golden Crest GC8000

SCHUBERT

(7) Gesänge (set to Scott's "Lady of the Lake") Op. 52 v & pf
No. 6. Ave Maria, D839 arr. vln & pf Wilhelmj
with L.L. Smith pf   Golden Crest GC8000

TARTINI

Sonata in g "Il Trillo del Diavolo" vln & c – arr. vln & pf Kreisler
with L.L. Smith pf   Golden Crest GC8000

WIENIAWSKI

Concerto No. 2, in d, Op. 22 vln & orch.
Romance (2nd mvt)
with L.L. Smith pf   Golden Crest GC8000
Scherzo–Tarantelle, Op. 16 vln & pf
with L.L. Smith pf   Golden Crest GC8000

Alfredo d'AMBROSIO (1871–1914)

d'AMBROSIO

Aria, Op. 22 vln & pf
with piano   Association phonique de Grande
Artiste 150207

(2) Morceaux, Op. 17 vln & pf
No. 1. Aubade rêverie
with piano   Association phonique de Grande
Artiste 150204

Petit chanson, Op. 28 vln & pf
with piano   Asssociation phonique de Grande
Artiste 150195

Petite Suite, Op. 37 vln & pf
No. 1. Chanson napolitaine
with piano   Association phonique de Grande
Artiste 150191

Romance in D, Op. 9 vln & pf
with piano   Association phonique de Grande
Artiste 150196

FAURÉ

Berceuse, Op. 16 vln & pf
with piano   (untraced)

LECLAIR

(12) Sonatas, Op. 9 – Book IV (1738) vln & c
Sonata No. 3, in D: Sarabande (1st mvt); Tambourin (3rd mvt)
with piano   (untraced)

SAINT–SAËNS

(Le) Carnaval des animaux (1886) small orch.
Le cygne arr. vln & pf
with piano   Association phonique de Grande
Artiste 150203

SARASATE

Zigeunerweisen, Op. 20 vln & pf or orch.*
   with piano   Association phonique de Grande
                             Artiste 150211

SCHUMANN

(13) Kinderscenen, Op. 15 pf
   No. 7. Träumerei arr. vln & pf
   with piano   Association phonique de Grande
                             Artiste 150194

Alfred AMRHEIN

AUBER

Fra Diavolo (1830) – opera
   Overture arr. vln & pf
   with piano   Edison cylinder 9

GILLET

Entr'acte Gavotte, Op. 13 pf – arr. vln & pf
   with piano   Edison cylinder 14

SPIES

Polonaise, Op. 34 vln & pf
   with piano   Edison cylinder 3

WANGEMANN

Oberlandler (Tyrolean airs) pf – arr. vln & pf
   with piano   Edison cylinder 6

Carlo ANDERSEN (1904–   )

LUMBYE

Concert Polka (1863) 2 vlns & orch. – arr. P.T. Wallin
              OPF 179ᴵᴵ△, 182ᴵᴵ△   HMV X4224
   with K.P. Andersen vln & Tivoli Orch.

Concert Polka (1863) 2 vlns & orch.
   with P. Lynged vln & Royal Opera   London T5039
   House Orch. – Høeberg   Polyphon Z60130

SVENDSEN

Romance in G, Op. 26 vln & orch.
   with Copenhagen   2CS 1508/9ᴵ☐   HMV DB5232
   Philharmonic Orch. – Jensen

Kai Polycarp ANDERSEN

LUMBYE

Concert Polka (1863) 2 vlns & orch. – arr. P.T. Wallin
              OPF 179ᴵᴵ△, 182ᴵᴵ△   HMV X4224
   with C. Andersen vln & Tivoli Orch.

*Middle section only.

Walfred ANDERSEN

ANONYMOUS

Ack Varmeland du sköna Swedish folksong – arr. vln & pf
   with piano   1263–S   Sonata 22
                             Sonora 1074

Fjorton ar tror jag visst att jag var Swedish folksong – arr. vln & pf
   with piano   1263–S   Sonata 20
                             Sonora 1066

Om dagen vid mitt arbete Swedish folksong – arr. vln & pf
   with piano   1262–S   Sonata 20
                             Sonora 1066

BACKER–GRØNDAHL

Barntes Vaardag (cycle of 8 songs) Op. 42 v & pf
   No. 7. Mot Kvaeld (At eventide) arr. vln & pf
   with piano   1264–S   Sonata 31
                             Sonora 1067

Sommarsäng v & pf – arr. vln & pf
   with piano   1265–S   Sonata 31
                             Sonora 1067

BRAHMS

(16) Waltzes, Op. 39 pf duet
   No. 15. Waltz No. 15, in A flat arr. vln & pf "in A" Hochstein
   with G. Enders pf   6313–S–S   Sonora 1123

BULL

Säterjäntens søndag v & pf – arr. vln & pf Svendsen
   with piano   1647–S–B   Sonata 52
                             Sonora 1069

DRDLA

Souvenir vln & pf
   with piano   1664–S–C   Sonora 1072

DRIGO

(Les) Millions d'Arlequin (1900) – ballet orch.
   Sérénade arr. vln & pf Auer
   with ensemble   1651–S–B   Sonora 1071

DVOŘÁK

(8) Humoresques, Op. 101 pf
   No. 7. Humoresque No. 7, in G flat arr. vln & pf "in G" Kreisler
   with G. Enders pf   6312–S–S   Sonora 1123

GRIEG

Peer Gynt (Suite No. 2) Op. 55 orch.
   No. 4. Solveig's song arr. vln & pf Sitt
   with piano   1662–S–B   Sonata 52
                             Sonora 1069

(6) Songs, Op. 33 v & pf
   No. 3. Rundarne (Vol. II) arr. 2 vlns, vla & vlc
   with vln, vla & cl   1261–S   Sonora 1068

HALVORSEN

(4) Mosaïques (Suite des morceaux caractéristiques) vln & pf
   No. 4. Chant de Veslemøy arr. 2 vlns, vla & vlc
                  1266–S   Sonora 1068

HEYKENS

Serenade, Op. 21 orch. – arr. vln, vla & vlc
   with vln, vla & vlc   1401   Sonora 1057

JÄRNEFELT

Berceuse in g orch. – arr. vln & pf
with piano   1268–S   Sonata 220
                                    Sonora 1074

KREISLER

Liebesleid vln & pf
with G. Enders pf   6314–S–S   Sonora 1124
Schön Rosmarin vln & pf
with piano   1402   Sonora 1056

MASSENET

Élégie v & pf – arr. vln & pf
with piano   1403–S   Sonata 34
                                    Sonora 1065

MERIKANTO

Mustalainen pf – arr. vln & pf
with piano   1649–S–B   Sonora 1070

MONTI

Csárdas (1904) vln & pf
with piano   1670 SC   Sonora 1057, 1073

OFFENBACH

(Les) Contes d'Hoffmann (1881) – opera
    Belle Nuit, O nuit d'amour "Barcarolle" arr. vln & ens
with ensemble   1648–S–B   Sonora 1071

PROVOST

Intermezzo (1940) vln & pf
with G. Enders pf   6311–S–S–B   Sonora 1122

RAFF

(6) Pieces, Op. 85 vln & pf
    No. 3. Cavatina in D
with piano   1663–S–B   Sonora 1073

RENÖ

Sorgens söndag vln & pf
with piano   1878–S–B   Sonora 1082

SAINT–SAËNS

(Le) Carnaval des animaux (1886) small orch.
    Le cygne arr. vln & pf
with piano   1395–S   Sonata 34
                                    Sonora 1065

SCHEBECK

Violinens sång vln & pf
with G. Enders pf   6315–S–S   Sonora 1124

SCHUBERT

(7) Gesänge (set to Scott's "Lady of the Lake") Op. 52 v & pf
    No. 6 Ave Maria, D839 arr. vln & pf Wilhelmj
with piano   1398–S   Sonata 28
(14) Schwanengesang, D957 (1828) v & pf
    No. 4. Ständchen "Serenade" arr. vln & pf
with piano   1400–S   Sonora 1056

SJÖBERG

Tonerna vln & pf
with piano   1650–S–B   Sonora 1070

SVENDSEN

Romance in G, Op. 26 vln & orch. – arr. vln & pf Wilhelmj
with piano   1871–S   Sonora 1082

THIELEMANN

Canzonetta vln & pf
with G. Enders pf   6310–S–S–B   Sonora 1122

TOSELLI

Serenade, Op. 6 vln & pf
with piano   1669–S–B   Sonora 1072

Folke ANDERSSON

KREISLER

Liebesleid vln & pf
with N. Lind pf   W44817   Columbia 18445

Eileen ANDJELKOVITCH

ADAMS

(The) Bells of St. Mary's (1917) v & pf – arr. v, vln & pf
with vocal interlude & piano   Broadcast 174

ANONYMOUS

Beautiful evening – unid – arr. v, vln & pf
with B. Desmond v & piano   Aco G16206

BEETHOVEN

(6) Minuets, G167 pf
    No. 2 Minuet No. 2, in G arr. vln & pf Burmester
with piano   Aco G15721

BERLIN

Because I love you (1926) v & pf – arr. vln & pf
with piano   Aco G16145

COWARD

Nina v & pf – arr. v, vln & pf
with B. Desmond v & piano   Aco G16206

DVOŘÁK

(8) Humoresques, Op. 101 pf
    No. 7. Humoresque No. 7, in G flat (arr. vln & pf "in G" Kreisler)
with piano   Z2   Broadcast 122

GOUNOD

Ave Maria (Méditation on Bach's "Prelude No. 1, in C" from Book I of
    "Das Wohltemperirte Clavier") v & pf – arr. vln & pf
with piano   Z4   Broadcast 121

HERBERT

Naughty Marietta (1910) – operetta
    Ah! sweet mystery of life arr. vln & pf
with piano   Broadcast B1048

LOHR

Little grey home in the west (1911) v & pf – arr. vln & orch.
with salon orch.   Broadcast 322

MASSENET

Thaïs (1894) – opera
Méditation arr. vln & pf Marsick
with piano   Z1X   Broadcast 121

MOSZKOWSKI

(6) Klavierstücke, Op. 15 pf – 4 hands
No. 1. Serenata arr. vln & pf
with piano   Aco G15802

MOZART

Divertimento No. 17, in D, K334, strs & 2 hrns
Minuet (3rd mvt) arr. vln & pf Burmester
with piano   Aco G15802

RIMSKY–KORSAKOV

Sadko (1898) – opera
Chant hindou arr. vln & pf Kreisler
with piano   Aco G15721

SCHUMANN

(13) Kinderscenen, Op. 15 pf
No. 7. Träumerei arr. vln & pf
with piano   Aco G15820

SILÉSU

(A) Little love, a little kiss (1912) v & pf – arr. v, vln & pf
with vocal interlude & piano   Broadcast 174

TATE

Somewhere a voice is calling (1911) v & pf – arr. vln & orch.
with salon orch.   Broadcast 322

THOMÉ

Simple aveu, Op. 25 pf – arr. vln & pf
with piano   Z3   Broadcast 122

WALLER

Princess Charming – musical
I want you so arr. vln & pf
with piano   Aco G16145

WOLSTENHOLME

(The) Answer arr. vln & pf Moffat
with piano   Aco G15820

WOOD

Bird of love divine v & pf arr. v, vln & pf
with T. Phillips s & piano   Broadcast 220
Roses of Picardy (1916) v & pf – arr. v, vln & pf
with vocal interlude & piano   Broadcast 220, B1048

Janine ANDRADE (1918–   )

ALBÉNIZ

Malagueña, Op. 71, No. 6 pf – arr. vln & pf Kreisler
with A. Holeček pf   Supraphon SUA10690,
SUAST50690, SV8293

BRAHMS

Concerto in D, Op. 77 (Cadenza by Kreisler) vln & orch.
with Hamburg State Philharmonic   Vega C30, MT10121
Orch. – Jurgen–Walther

DELVINCOURT

Danceries vln & pf
with C. Delvincourt pf   Columbia LFX643/4

FALLA

(La) Vida Breve (1913) – opera
Danza española orch. – arr. vln & pf Kreisler
with A. Holeček pf   Supraphon SUA10690,
SUAST50690, SV8293

GLUCK

Orphée et Eurydice (1762) – opera
Dance of the blessed spirits: Lento "Mélodie" (No. 2) arr. vln & pf
Kreisler
with A. Holeček pf   Supraphon SUA10690,
SUAST50690, SV8293

KREISLER

Rondino on a theme by Beethoven vln & pf
with A. Holeček pf   Supraphon SUA10690,
SUAST50690, SV8293

Grave (W.F. Bach) vln & pf
with A. Holeček pf   Supraphon SUA10690,
SUAST50690, SV8293

Minuet (Porpora) vln & pf
with A. Holeček pf   Supraphon SUA10690,
SUAST50690, SV8293

Sicilienne & Rigaudon (Francoeur) vln & pf
with A. Holeček pf   Supraphon SUA10690,
SUAST50690, SV8293

MATTHESON

(12) Suites (1714) hpsi
Suite No. 5, in c: Air arr. vln & pf Burmester
with A. Holeček pf   Supraphon LPM390, SUEC853,
SUK30321

de MONDONVILLE

(6) Sonatas, Op. 3 vln & c
Sonata No. 4, in C
with A. Holeček pf   Supraphon LPM390

MOZART

Serenade No. 7, in D, K250 "Haffner" orch.
Rondo (4th mvt) arr. vln & pf Kreisler
with A. Holeček pf   Supraphon SUA10690,
SUAST50690, SV8293

PAGANINI

Concerto No. 2, in b, Op. 7 vln & orch.
Ronde à la clochette (3rd mvt) "La Campanella" arr. vln & pf Kreisler
with J. Panenka pf   Supraphon LPM390, SUEC853,
SUK30321

Ronde à la clochette (3rd mvt) "La Campanella" arr. vln & pf Kreisler
with A. Holeček pf   Supraphon SUA10690,
SUAST50690, SV8293

PERGOLESI

(14) Sonatas (1770) 2 vlns & c
 Sonata No. 1, in G arr. vln & pf Longo
 with J. Panenka pf　　　　　　Supraphon LPM390

RAMEAU

(Le) Temple de la Gloire (1745) – opera
 Gavotte in D arr. vln & pf Burmester
 with J. Panenka pf　　　　　　Supraphon LPM390

RAVEL

Pièce en forme d'Habanera v & pf – arr. vln & pf Kreisler
 with A. Holeček pf　　　　　　Supraphon SUA10690,
 　　　　　　　　　　　　　　　　SUAST50690, SV8293

RIES

Suite No. 3, in G, Op. 34 vln & pf
 No. 5. Perpetuum mobile
 with A. Holeček pf　　　　　　Supraphon LPM390, SUEC853,
 　　　　　　　　　　　　　　　　SUK30321

SIBELIUS

Concerto in d, Op. 47 vln & orch.
 with Finnish Radio Symphony Orch. – Decca DLP9001
 Fougstedt

TCHAIKOVSKY

Concerto in D, Op. 35 vln & orch.
 with Hamburg State Philharmonic　Classics Club X3002
 Orch. – Jurgen–Walther
(3) Souvenirs de Hapsal, pf
 No. 3. Chant sans paroles in f arr. vln & pf Kreisler
 with A. Holeček pf　　　　　　Supraphon SUA10690,
 　　　　　　　　　　　　　　　　SUAST50690, SV8293

Lucien ANDRÉ

ACCORETI

(Die) Verführung vln & pf
 with piano　　　　　　　　　　Favorite D4102

ANONYMOUS

Wörthersee – waltz unid – arr. vln & pf
 with piano　　　　　　　　　　Favorite D5041

BECUCCI

Tesoro mio – waltz, Op. 228 orch. – arr. vln & pf
 with piano　　　　　　　　　　Favorite D4102

MASCAGNI

Cavalleria Rusticana (1890) – opera
 Intermezzo orch. – arr. vln & pf
 with piano　　　　　　　　　　Favorite 1–4105D

THOMÉ

Simple aveu, Op. 25 pf – arr. vln & pf
 with piano　　　　　　　　　　Favorite 1–4100D

TICHÝ

Walzer–Zauber (Intermezzo) Op. 66 vln & pf
 with piano　　　　　　　　　　Favorite D5041

Roger ANDRÉ

MASSENET

Thaïs (1894) – opera
 Méditation arr. vln & pf Marsick
 with B. Galais hp　　　　　　Pathé ASTX336, DTX336

Lottie ANDREASSON (1903–)

BERWALD

(3) Trios, Op. 1 (1845) pf, vln & vlc
 No. 3. Trio No. 3, in d
 with A. Berwald pf* &　　SD 504/9A　Radiojanst RD5213
 C. de Frumerie-Lutharder vlc

FIBICH

Images, Impressions & Souvenirs, Op. 41 pf
 No. 14. Poem (from "Souvenirs", Part IV) arr. vln & pf Kubelík
 with piano　　　　　　Sto 2429　Odeon A162205, D4707
 No. 14. Poem (from "Souvenirs", Part IV) arr. vln & pf Kubelík
 with piano　　　　　　Sto 2723　Odeon (unissued)

JÄRNEFELT

Berceuse in g orch. – arr. vln & pf
 with piano　　　　　　Sto 2428　Odeon A162205, D4707

LECLAIR

(12) Sonatas, Op. 9 – Book IV (1738) vln & c
 Sonata No. 3, in D: Tambourin (3rd mvt) arr. vln & pf Kreisler
 with piano　　　　　　Sto 2678　Odeon A162336, D4835

MERIKANTO

Valse lente pf – arr. vln & pf Burmester
 with piano　　　　　　Sto 2676　Odeon (unissued)

RANZATO

Serenata galante vln & pf
 with piano　　　　　　Sto 2677　Odeon (unissued)

SCHILDKNECHT

Berceuse élégiaque vln & pf
 with Nils Grevillius Orch.　Sto 4290　Odeon A162753, D1045
Venetian serenade vln & pf
 with Nils Grevillius Orch.　Sto 4291　Odeon A162753, D1045

SJÖGREN

Sonata No. 2, in e, Op. 24 vln & pf
 Andante sostenuto (2nd movement)
 with piano　　　　　　Sto 2675　Odeon D4835, A162336

Pedro D'ANDURAIN

BARTÓK

(6) Rumanian folk dances (1915) pf – arr. vln & pf Székely
 with C. Oxley pf　　　　　　Capitol P18010

*Astrid Maria Beatrice Berwald, grand-daughter of Franz Adolf Berwarld
 1796–1868.

FALLA

(La) Vida Breve (1913) – opera
Danza española orch. – arr. vln & pf Kreisler
   with C. Oxley pf   Capitol P18010

FRASER

Cueca (1926) vln & pf
   with C. Oxley pf   Capitol P18010

GARRIDO

Divertimento (1951) vln & pf
Movimento perpetuo
   with C. Oxley pf   Capitol P18010

KROLL

Banjo & fiddle vln & pf
   with C. Oxley pf   Capitol P18010

LAVÍN

Cadencias Tehuelehes vln & pf
Nos. 1, 2 & 4
   with A. Coisne pf   Dirección General de
                                     Informaciones y Culture V–S2

NIN

(20) Cantos de España (1923) v & pf
No.7. Granadina arr. vln & pf Kochański
   with C. Oxley pf   Capitol P18010

PONCE

Sonata (1933) vln & pf
   with C. Oxley pf   Capitol P18010

PROKOFIEV

(The) Love for Three Oranges, Op. 33 (1919) – opera
No. 3. March arr. vln & pf. Heifetz
   with C. Oxley pf   Capitol P18010

SAS

Cantos del Perú (1927) vln & pf
Kchachampa (Incan war dance)
   with C. Oxley pf   Capitol P18010

SORO

Serenatella vln & pf
   with C. Oxley pf   Capitol P18010

ANEMOYANNI

HUBAY

(6) Poèmes hongroise, Op. 27 vln & pf
Poème hongrois No. 6, in B flat
   with piano   Odeon 36477

SCHUMANN

(13) Kinderscenen, Op. 15 pf
No. 7. Träumerei arr. vln & pf
   with piano   Odeon 36477

Loredana d'ANNIBALE

VIVALDI

Concerto in F, P.278 (F.I, No. 34) 3 vlns, strs & c
   with M. Abbado vln, M. Borgo vln   Columbia FCX370
   & Milan String Orch. – Abbado
Concerto in B flat, P.367 (F.I, No. 59) 4 vlns, strs & c
   with M. Abbado vln, M. Borgo vln,   Columbia FCX369
   T. Pasquali vln & Milan String
   Orch. – Abbado

ANONYMOUS VIOLINISTS

ALETTER

Fantasy vln & pf
   with piano   HMV B528177

d'AMBROSIO

Canzonetta, Op. 6 vln & pf
   with piano   HMV AL496

ANONYMOUS

Min Skat – waltz arr. vln & pf
   with piano   Pathé cylinder 5106

BECUCCI

Tesoro mio – waltz, Op. 228 orch. – arr. vln & pf
   with piano   HMV X287984

BRAGA

(7) Melodies (1867) v & pf
No. 5. La serenata "Angel's serenade" arr. v, vln & pf
   with H. Haydn a & piano   Gramophone & Typewriter 3555

BRAHMS

(21) Hungarian Dances pf duet
Hungarian dance No. 5, in f sharp arr. vln & pf "in g" Joachim
   with piano   Musicraft 8501
Hungarian dance No. 8, in a arr. vln & pf Joachim
   with piano   HMV AL639
Hungarian dance No. 17, in f sharp arr. vln & pf Joachim
   with piano   Stinson 5359

BULL

Säterjëntens søndag v & pf – arr. vln & pf
   with piano   HMV B587912

di CAPUA

O sole mio v & pf – arr. vln & pf
   with piano   01671   HMV Z0287900
O sole mio v & pf – arr. vln & orch.
   with orch.   Odeon 0170, 36411

CAROSIO

Ritorna mia rondinella (Mazurka) mand & pf – arr. vln & pf
   with piano   Artiphon D2187

DRDLA

Serenade No. 1, in A vln & pf
   with piano   Artiphon D1267
Souvenir vln & pf
   with piano   Little Wonder 1362

DRDLA – *Continued*

Souvenir vln & pf
with piano   0416   Odeon 5136

Souvenir vln & pf
with piano   Gennett 4286

DVOŘÁK

(8) Humoresques, Op. 101 pf
   No. 7. Humoresque No. 7, in G flat arr. vln & pf "in G" Kreisler
   with piano   HMV AL496
   No. 7. Humoresque No. 7, in G flat arr. vln & pf "in G" Kreisler
   with piano   Artiphon D1266

ELGAR

Salut d'amour, Op. 12 orch. – arr. vln & pf Elgar
with piano   Columbia 30168

FLIES

Wiegenlied (Schlafe, mein Prinzchen) v & pf – arr. vln & pf
with piano   HMV AL571, X287983

GIORDANI

Caro mio ben v & pf – arr. vln & pf
with piano   Artiphon D392

GODARD

Jocelyn (1888) – opera
   Cachés dans cet asile "Berceuse" arr. vln & pf
   with piano   Pathé cylinder 5069
   Cachés dans cet asile "Berceuse" arr. vln & pf
   with piano   01686n HMV Z0287901
   Cachés dans cet asile "Berceuse" arr. vln & pf
   with piano   Odeon 0171, 36404
   Cachés dans cet asile "Berceuse" arr. vln & pf
   with piano   0418 Odeon 5071

GOUBLIER

Love's serenade vln & pf
with orch.   Odeon 0605, X66902

GOUNOD

Ave Maria (Méditation on Bach's "Prelude No. 1, in C" from Book I of "Das Wohltemperirte Clavier") v & pf – arr. vln & pf
with piano   HMV X287982

Ave Maria (Méditation on Bach's "Prelude No. 1, in C" from Book I of "Das Wohltemperirte Clavier") v & pf – arr. v, vln & pf
with A. Patti s & L. Ronald pf   International Record Collector's Club 33

Ave Maria (Méditation on Bach's "Prelude No. 1, in C" from Book I of "Das Wohltemperirte Clavier") v & pf – arr. vln & pf
with piano   Artiphon D300

GRIEG

Peer Gynt (Suite No. 2) Op. 55 orch.
   No. 4. Solveig's song arr. vln & pf Sitt
   with piano   HMV B587913
   No. 4. Solveig's song arr. vln & pf Sitt
   with piano   1565 Masterpiece 8507

HANDEL

Serse (1738) – opera
   Ombra mai fu "Largo" arr. vln & pf
   with piano   Artiphon D302

HAYDN

(31) Trios, H.XV, Nos. 1/31 pf, vln & vlc
   Trio No. 27, in C: Presto (Rondo) (3rd mvt) H.XV, No. 27
   (Op. 75, No. 1) arr. vln & pf
   with H.G. Kincella pf   Victor 22018

KETLAR

Monte Cristo – valse–tzigane orch. – arr. vln & orch.
with orch.   Gennett 4286

LALO

Symphonie espagnole, Op. 21 vln & orch.*
with Berlin Symphony Orch. – Balzer   Royale 1287

LANGER

Grandfather, Op. 22 salon orch. – arr. vln & orch.
with orch.   Odeon UA40850

Grandmother, Op. 20 pf – arr. vln & orch.
with orch.   Odeon UA40851

LINCKE

Amina (Egyptian serenade) pf – arr. vln & pf
with piano   HMV B528178

MASCAGNI

Cavalleria Rusticana (1890) – opera
   Intermezzo orch. – arr. vln & pf
   with piano   Pathé cylinder 5128
   Intermezzo orch. – arr. vln & orch.
   with orch.   62 Columbia A209

MASSENET

Thaïs (1894) – opera
   Méditation arr. vln & pf Marsick
   with piano   Odeon 0171, 36410
   Méditation arr. vln & pf Marsick
   with piano   HMV AL639
   Méditation arr. vln & pf Marsick
   with D. Steele pf   Cameo NL2

MENDELSSOHN

Concerto in e, Op. 64 vln & orch.†
with symphony orch. – List   Pacific LDAD45

Concerto in e, Op. 64 vln & orch.
with Viennese Symphony Orch.   Plymouth P12–78

Concerto in e, Op. 64 vln & orch.
with National Opera Orch.   Gramophone (RCA) 2071

Concerto in e, Op. 64 vln & orch.
with orch.   Philharmonic Family Library of Great Music 9

*Including Intermezzo.
†Allegro appassionato or 1st mvt is also on Elite 3068.

MOZART

Sonata No. 22, in A, K305 vln & pf
Allegro di molto (1st mvt)
with H.G. Kincella pf   Victor 22018

PADEREWSKI

(6) Humoresques de concert, Op. 14 pf
No. 1. Minuet in G arr. vln & pf Kreisler
with orch.   0421   Odeon 5064

PAPINI

(4) Morceaux, Op. 28 vln & pf
No. 1. Souvenir du Tage (Larghetto)
with piano   0415   Odeon 5136

(2) Morceaux de salon, Op. 55 "Souvenir di Sorrento" vln & pf
No. 2. Saltarella
with piano   0417   Odeon 5071

POLIAKIN

(Le) Canari (Concert–polka) vln & pf
with piano   26264   Polyphon 30355
                                Zonophone X507905

RAFF

(6) Pieces, Op. 85 vln & pf
No. 3. Cavatina in D
with orch.   Odeon 0170, 36408

RAVEL

Tzigane (Rapsodie de concert) (1924) vln & pf or orch.
with Berlin Symphony Orch. – Rubahn Royale 1458

RUBINSTEIN

(2) Melodies, Op. 3 pf
No. 1. Melody in F arr. vln & pf
with piano   E 141   Marspen 271

No. 1. Melody in F arr. vln & orch.
with orch.   0422   Odeon 5064

SARASATE

Faust Fantasia (on themes from the opera by Gounod) vln & pf or orch.
Valse
with piano   Pathé cylinder 5126

SCHUBERT

(14) Schwanengesang, D957 (1828) v & pf
No. 4. Ständchen "Serenade" arr. vln & pf
with piano   212–10–3 Columbia 212

SCHUMANN

Concerto in d (1853) vln & orch.
with orch.   Music Appreciation Records
                                CM23/6, (set S126)

(13) Kinderscenen, Op. 15 pf
No. 7. Träumerei arr. vln & pf
with piano   Pathé cylinder 5069

No. 7. Träumerei arr. vln & pf
with piano   Odeon 0172, 36409

(9) Waldscenen, Op. 82 pf
No. 7. Vogel als Prophet arr. vln & pf Auer
with piano   1566   Masterpiece 8507

TCHAIKOVSKY

Concerto in D, Op. 35 vln & orch.
Allegro moderato (1st mvt)
with National Opera Orch.   Royale 6954
                                Webster Vol. 1 (side 1)

Allegro vivacissimo (3rd mvt)
with National Opera Orch.   Royale 6954

(The) Months, Op. 37a pf
No. 2. Carnival time (February) arr. vln & pf as "Neapolitan" by
Burmester
with piano   Mezhdunarodnaya Kniga D5359

Sérénade mélancolique in b flat, Op. 26 vln & orch.
with Columbia Symphony   Columbia ML4671
Orch. – Kurtz

THOMÉ

Simple aveu, Op. 25 pf – arr. vln & pf
with piano   Odeon 0172, 36407

TICHÝ

Triton – valse pf – arr. vln & pf
with piano   HMV X287985

VERDI

(Il) Trovatore (1853) – opera
selection arr. vln & orch. as "Fantasia"
with orch.   Columbia A215

VIVALDI

Concerto in d, P.311 (Op. 22, No. 4) vln, strs & c
with Scarlatti Orch. of   Angel 35254
Naples – Caracciolo   Columbia CX1276, QCX10138

Concerto in g, P.383 (F.XII, No. 3) "Per l'orch. di Dresda" vln, 2 fls, 2 obs,
2 bsns & c
with Paris Chamber Orch. – Jouve   Ducretet-Thomson LP8702
                                Telefunken NLB6081
                                Westminster WL5341

WIENIAWSKI

(2) Mazurkas, Op. 19 vln & pf
No. 1. Mazurka No. 1, in G "Obertass"
with D. Steele pf   Cameo NL2

Arnaldo APOSTOLI

CORELLI

(12) Concerti grossi, Op. 6 orch.
Concerto grosso No. 1, in D (rev. Negri)
with F. Ayo vln, E. Altobelli vlc &   Philips 802761LY, (in set SC71
I Musici   AX304)

Concerto grosso No. 2, in F (rev. Negri)
with F. Ayo vln, E. Altobelli vlc &   Philips 802761 LY, (in set SC71
I Musici   AX304)

Concerto grosso No. 3, in c (rev. Negri)
with F. Ayo vln, E. Altobelli vlc &   Philips 802761 LY, (in set SC71
I Musici   AX304)

Concerto grosso No. 4, in D (rev. Negri)
with F. Ayo vln, E. Altobelli vlc &   Philips. 802761 LY, (in set SC71
I Musici   AX304)

CORELLI – *Continued*

Concerto grosso No. 5, in B flat (rev. Negri)
with F. Ayo vln, E. Altobelli vlc &
I Musici   Philips 802762 LY, (in set SC71 AX304)

Concerto grosso No. 6, in F (rev. Negri)
with F. Ayo vln, E. Altobelli vlc &
I Musici   Philips 802762 LY, (in set SC71 AX304)

Concerto grosso No. 7, in D (rev. Negri)
with F. Ayo vln, E. Altobelli vlc &
I Musici   Philips 802762 LY, (in set SC71 AX304)

Concerto grosso Nó. 8, in g "Christmas Concerto" (rev. Negri)
with F. Ayo vln, E. Altobelli vlc &
I Musici   Philips 802762 LY, (in set SC71 AX304)

Concerto grosso No. 9, in F (rev. Negri)
with F. Ayo vln, F. Altobelli vlc &
I Musici   Philips 802763 LY, (in set SC71 AX304)

Concerto grosso No. 10, in C (rev. Negri)
with F. Ayo vln, E. Altobelli vlc &
I Musici   Philips. 802763 LY, (in set SC71 AX304)

Concerto grosso No. 11, in B flat (rev. Negri)
with F. Ayo vln, F. Altobelli vlc &
I Musici   Philips 802763 LY, (in set SC71 AX304)

Concerto grosso No. 12, in F (rev. Negri)
with F. Ayo vln, E. Altobelli vlc &
I Musici   Philips 802763 LY, (in set SC71 AX304)

TELEMANN

Concerto in F, T.II, No. 3, 3 vlns, strs & c
with F. Ayo vln, I. Colandrea vln &
I Musici   Philips 802864 DXY, PHS900188, SAL3737

Nobuko ARAKI

PERGOLESI

(14) Sonatas (1770) 2 vlns & c
  Sonata No. 1, in G
  with J–W. Jahn vln, M.G. Schneider   Da Camera SM92207
  hpsi & G. Reith vlc

  Sonata No. 2, in B
  with J–W. Jahn vln, M.G. Schneider   Da Camera SM92207
  hpsi & G. Reith vlc

  Sonata No. 3, in c
  with J–W. Jahn vln, M.G. Schneider   Da Camera SM92207
  hpsi & G. Reith vlc

  Sonata No. 4, in G
  with J–W. Jahn vln, M.G. Schneider   Da Camera SM92207
  hpsi & G. Reith vlc

  Sonata No. 5, in C
  with J–W. Jahn vln, M.G. Schneider   Da Camera SM92207
  hpsi & G. Reith vlc

  Sonata No. 6, in D
  with J–W. Jahn vln, M.G. Schneider   Da Camera SM92207
  hpsi & G. Reith vlc

  Sonata No. 7, in g
  with J–W. Jahn vln, M.G. Schneider   Da Camera SM92208
  hpsi & G. Reith vlc

  Sonata No. 8, in E flat
  with J–W. Jahn vln, M.G. Schneider   Da Camera SM92208
  hpsi & G. Reith vlc

PERGOLESI – *Continued*

  Sonata No. 9, in A
  with J–W. Jahn vln, M.G. Schneider   Da Camera SM92208
  hpsi & G. Reith vlc

  Sonata No. 10, in F
  with J–W. Jahn vln, M.G. Schneider   Da Camera SM92208
  hpsi & G. Reith vlc

  Sonata No. 11, in d
  with J–W. Jahn vln, M.G. Schneider   Da Camera SM92208
  hpsi & G. Reith vlc

  Sonata No. 12, in E
  with J–W. Jahn vln, M.G. Schneider   Da Camera SM92208
  hpsi & G. Reith vlc

  Sonata No. 13, in g
  with J–W. Jahn vln, M.G. Schneider   Da Camera SM92208
  hpsi & G. Reith vlc

  Sonata No. 14, in C
  with J–W. Jahn vln, M.G. Schneider   Da Camera SM92208
  hpsi & G. Reith vlc

Gèza ARANY

DONIZETTI

(L') Elisir d'Amore (1832) – opera
  Una furtiva lagrima arr. vln & pf
  with F. Kark pf   Artiphon D1845

GRIEG

Peer Gynt (Suite No. 2) Op. 55 (orch.)
  No. 4. Solveig's song arr. vln & pf Sitt
  with F. Kark pf   Artiphon D1846

LAMA

Cara piccina vln & pf
  with F. Kark pf   Artiphon D1849

SAINT-SAËNS

(Le) Carnaval des animaux (1886) small orch.
  Le cygne arr. vln & pf
  with F. Kark pf   Artiphon 420 D1847,

SCHUMANN

(12) Duets, Op. 85 pf, 4 hands
  No. 12. Abendlied arr. vln & pf Wilhelmj
  with F. Kark pf   Artiphon 420 D1848,

TOSTI

Invanno mand & pf – arr. vln & pf
  with F. Kark pf   Artiphon D1850

Yelli D'ARANYI (1893–1966)

ALBÉNIZ

Espana (6 Feuilles d'album) Op. 165 pf
  No. 2. Tango in D arr. vln & pf Dushkin
  with A. Bergh pf   147932   Columbia 2126D, 2144M, DB108, DO150

BACH

Concerto in d, BWV1043 2 vlns, strs & c
   with A. Fachiri vln & Aeolian   Vocalion A0252/3
   Orch. – Chapple

Concerto in d, BWV1043 2 vlns, strs & c
   Largo (2nd mvt)
                03294 X & 03295   Vocalion D02107
   with A. Fachiri vln
   & E. Hobday pf

Concerto in c, BWV1060 vln & ob or 2 vlns, strs & c
   Allegro (3rd mvt)
   with A. Fachiri vln   03559   Vocalion K05110
   & E. Hobday pf

Sonata in C, BWV1037 2 vlns & c
   Gigue: Presto (4th mvt)
   with A. Fachiri vln   03489   Vocalion D02146
   & E. Hobday pf

Toccata, Adagio & Fugue in C, BWV564 org
   Adagio (2nd mvt) arr. vln & pf Siloti
   with A. Bergh pf   151412   Columbia 2443D

BOCCHERINI

Sonata in c vla & pf
   Andante expressivo (2nd mvt) arr. 2 vlns & pf Moffat
   with A. Fachiri vln   03709   Vocalion K05142
   & E. Hobday pf

BRAHMS

(21) Hungarian Dances pf duet
   Hungarian dance No. 5, in f sharp arr. vln & pf "in g" Joachim
   with E. Hobday pf   Vocalion K05231
   Hungarian dance No. 8, in a arr. vln & pf Joachim
   with C. von Bos pf   145620–2   Columbia 5681, 03584, 2061M,
                                           DF251, J5035

Trio No. 2, in C, Op. 87 pf, vln & vlc
          CAX 7646–2, 7647/9–1, 7650/3–2   Columbia 68636/9D, (set M266),
   with M. Hess   70149/52D, LWX119/22,
   & G. Cassadó vlc   LX497/500

CORTI

Grave vln & pf
   with A. Bergh pf   148114   Columbia 2092M, 2203D, DB361

DELIBES

(Le) Roi S'Amuse (1882) – Incidental music orch.
   No. 6. Passepied arr. vln & pf Gruenberg
   with piano   148026   Columbia 2042D, 2084M,
                               2144M, DB108, DO150

DESPLANES

Intrada (Adagio) vln & c – arr. vln & pf Nachèz
   with piano   148027   Columbia 1774D, J5099

DESTOUCHES

Issé (1697) – opera
   Passepied arr. vln & pf Dandelot
   with E. Hobday pf   03875   Vocalion K05203

DIENZL

Spinnlied, Op. 46 vln & pf
   with E. Hobday pf   03564   Vocalion K05118

DRDLA

Souvenir vln & pf
   with A. Bergh pf   148115–2   Columbia 5681, 2203D, 2092M,
                               DF251

FALLA

(7) Canciones populares españolas (1914) v & pf
   No. 4. Jota arr. vln & pf Kochański
   with C. von Bos pf   Columbia 03582, J5034

FRASER

Cueca (1926) vln & pf – arr. 2 vlns & pf
   with A. Fachiri vln   M 0236X   Vocalion K05292
   & E. Hobday pf

GALUPPI

(12) Sonatas, Op. 1 hpsi
   Sonata No. 1, in C: Allegro giocoso (1st mvt) arr. cl or vln & pf Craxton
   with E. Hobday pf   03874   Vocalion K05203
   Sonata No. 3, in a: Largo (2nd mvt) arr. cl or vln & pf Craxton
   with E. Hobday pf   Vocalion K05203

GATTI

Bagatelle in D vln & pf
   with A. Bergh pf   147939   Columbia 2126D, 2144M, DB361

GLUCK

Orphée et Eurydice (1762) – opera
   Dance of the blessed spirits: Lento "Mélodie" (No. 2) arr. vln & pf
   Kreisler
   with C. von Bos pf   145610   Columbia 5427, 03582, 147M,
                               J5034

GODARD

(6) Duettini, Op. 18 2 vlns & pf
   No. 5. Minuit
   with A. Fachiri vln & E. Hobday pf   Vocalion K05260
   No. 6. Sérénade
   with A. Fachiri vln & E. Hobday pf   Vocalion K05260

HANDEL

(9) Sonatas, Op. 2 (1724) 2 vlns or obs & c
   Sonata No. 7, in g
   with A. Fachiri vln   04088/91   Vocalion K05222/3
   & E. Hobday pf

HUBAY

(6) Poèmes hongroise, Op. 27 vln & pf
   Poème hongrois No. 6, in B flat
   with C. von Bos pf   Columbia 03584, 2042D, 2084M

JOACHIM

   Romance in C vln & pf
   with E. Hobday pf   03563   Vocalion K05118

KELLY

Suite, Op. 7 fl & pf
   No. 5. Jig arr. vln & pf
   with E. Hobday pf   Vocalion R6141

KRAMER

Silhouette (O Kaiserstadt, du schöne) v & pf – arr. vln & pf
with C. von Bos pf   Columbia 50165D, 7281M, J7608

KREISLER

Rondino on a theme by Beethoven vln & pf
with C. von Bos pf   145629   Columbia 5427, 147M, J5035

Scherzo (Dittersdorf) vln & pf
with C. von Bos pf,   147931   Columbia 1774D, J5099

LECLAIR

(6) Sonatas, Op. 3 (1730) 2 vlns
Sonata No. 2, in a arr. 2 vlns & pf
with A. Fachiri vln & E. Hobday pf   Vocalion K05279

Sonata No. 4, in B flat arr. 2 vlns & pf
with A. Fachiri vln & E. Hobday pf   Vocalion X9877

(12) Sonatas, Op. 9 – Book IV (1738) vln & c
Sonata No. 3, in d: Sarabande (1st mvt); **Tambourin** (3rd mvt) arr. vln & pf Sarasate
with E. Hobday pf   03708   Vocalion K05168

MARSICK

(2) Pieces, Op. 6 vln & pf
No. 2. Scherzando
with E. Hobday pf   Vocalion X9525

MARTINI, G.B.

(12) Sonatas, Op. 2 (1741) hpsi
Sonata No. 2, in D: Allegro (1st mvt) arr. vln & pf Endicott
with E. Hobday pf   Vocalion X9525

MOZART

Concerto No. 3, in G, K216 vln & orch.*
with Aeolian   04020/4   Vocalion A0242/4
Orch. – Chapple

Divertimento No. 17, in D, K334 2 hrns & strs
Minuet (3rd mvt) arr. vln & pf Burmester
with E. Hobday pf   03296   Vocalion D02103

Serenade No. 7, in D, K250 "Haffner" orch.
Minuetto (3rd mvt)
with Aeolian   04025   Vocalion A0244
Orch. – Chapple

NARDINI

Concerto in e, vln & arch.
Andante cantabile (2nd mvt)
with piano   Columbia 50165D, 7281M

PAGANINI

(24) Caprices, Op. 1 (1801/7) solo vln
Caprice No. 24, in a arr. vln & pf Auer
with E. Hobday pf   03297   Vocalion D02103

PERGOLESI

Aria unid – arr. vln & pf Fachiri
with A. Bergh pf   151411   Columbia 2443D

PIANELLI

Villanelle arr. vln & pf Salmon
with E. Hobday pf   Vocalion K05231

*Cadenza omitted.

PUGNANI

(6) Sonatas, Op. 1 2 vlns & c
Sonata No. 6, in C (ed. Moffat)
     03560X, X 03710   Vocalion K05110 & K05142
with A. Fachiri vln & E. Hobday pf

PURCELL

(The) Indian Queen, Z630 (1695) – opera
Act tune "air" (Act IV) arr. vln & pf Lambert
with E. Hobday pf   03707   Vocalion K05168

(10) Sonatas, Z802/11 (1697) 4 parts – 2 vlns & c
Sonata No. 9, in F, Z810 "Golden Sonata"
with A. Fachiri vln   03872/3   Vocalion K05177
& E. Hobday pf

SAMMARTINI, G.B.

(12) Sonatas, Op. 1 2 vlns & c
Sonata No. 6, in D: Allegro (1st mvt) arr. vln & pf Endicott
with E. Hobday pf   Vocalion X9525

SCHUBERT

Trio No. 1, in B flat, Op. 99 (D898) pf, vln & vlc
     98414–5, 98415/6–2, 98417/8–3,   Columbia 9509/12, 67436/9D,
       98419–2, 98420–1, 98421–2   (set M91), J7269/72, L2103/6
with M. Hess pf & F. Salmond vlc

SCHUMANN

(12) Duets, Op. 85 pf – 4 hands
No. 3. gartenmelodie arr. vln & pf
with E. Hobday pf   Vocalion R6141

SINDING

Serenade No. 1, in G, Op. 56 2 vlns & pf
with A. Fachiri vln & E. Hobday pf   Vocalion K05270

SPOHR

(3) Duets, Op. 39 2 vlns
No. 1. Duet No. 1, in d: Adagio (2nd mvt)
with A. Fachiri vln   M0239   Vocalion K05292

(3) Duets, Op. 67 2 vlns
No. 2. Duet No. 2, in D: Larghetto (3rd mvt)
with A. Fachiri vln   M03490   Vocalion D02146

TARTINI

(12) Sonatas, Op. 3 2 vlns & c
Sonata No. 4, in F: Andante attacca (1st mvt); **Allegro** (2nd mvt)
with A. Fachiri   04092, 04093 X   Vocalion X9877
vln & E. Hobday pf

TCHAIKOVSKY

Quartet No. 1, in D, Op. 11 2 vlns, vla & vlc
Andante cantabile (2nd mvt) arr. vln & pf Kreisler
with C. von Bos pf   Columbia J7608

VITALI

Chaconne in g vln & c – arr. vln & pf Charlier
     98637–3, 98638–4   Columbia 9875, 02989, 50267D,
with C. von Bos pf   7289M, J7593

Ferenc ARANYI (1893–1966)

CUI

(12) Miniatures, Op. 20 pf
No. 8. Berceuse arr. vln & pf Carse
with piano   Anker 107

DVOŘÁK

(8) Slavonic Dances, Op. 46 pf duet; orch.
No. 2. Slavonic dance No. 2, in e arr. vln & pf "in g" Kreisler
with W. Liachowsky pf   Polydor 90079

GLUCK

Orphée et Eurydice (1762) – opera
Dance of the blessed spirits: Lento "Mélodie" (No. 2) arr. vln & pf
Kreisler
with M. Raucheisen pf   Brunswick 85049
                                Polydor 90044, 90079

GODARD

Jocelyn (1888) – opera
Cachés dans cet asile "Berceuse" arr. vln & pf
with piano   Anker 111

GOUNOD

Ave Maria (Méditation on Bach's "Prelude No. 1, in C" from Book I of
"Das Wohltemperirte Clavier") v & pf – arr. vln & pf
with piano   Anker 112
Sérénade (Quand tu chantes) v & pf – arr. vln & pf Hermann
with piano   Anker 113

HANDEL

Serse (1738) – opera
Ombra mai fu "Largo" arr. vln & pf
with piano   Anker 111

HANSEN

Wiegenlied vln & pf
with piano   Anker 113

HUMMEL

Waltz in A pf – arr. vln & pf Burmester
with M. Raucheisen pf   Polydor 90014

KREISLER

Caprice viennois, Op. 2 vln & pf
with M. Raucheisen pf   Polydor 95071
(La) Gitana vln & pf
with M. Raucheisen pf   Brunswick 85049
                                Polydor 90044, 90079
Tambourin chinois, Op. 3 vln & pf
with M. Raucheisen pf,   Polydor 95071
Tempo di minuetto (Pugnani) vln & pf
with M. Raucheisen pf   Polydor 90044

SAINT–SAËNS

(Le) Déluge, Op. 45 (1876) – oratorio
Prélude vln & orch. – arr. vln & pf Saint-Saëns
with piano   E4154 Anker 115
                                Da Capo 2013

SAINT–SAËNS – *Continued*

Samson et Dalila (1877) – opera
Selection arr. vln & pf as "Fantasia" by Aranyi
with piano   Anker 114

SIMONETTI

Madrigale pf – arr. vln & pf
with piano   Anker 107

VIEUXTEMPS

Ballade & Polonaise in G, Op. 38 vln & pf
Polonaise
with M. Raucheisen pf   Polydor 95114
(6) Morceaux de salon, Op. 22 vln & pf
No. 3. Rêverie
with piano   Anker 112

WAGNER

(Die) Meistersinger von Nürnberg (1868) – opera
Morgenlich leuchtend "Prize song" arr. vln & pf Wilhelmj
with piano   E4153 Anker 115
                                Da Capo 2013

WEBER

(6) Sonatas, Op. 10 (J99/104) (1810) vln & pf
Sonata No. 1, in F: Romanze (2nd mvt) J99 arr. vln & pf as "Larghetto"
by Kreisler
with M. Raucheisen pf   Polydor 90014

R. d'ARCO

PARADIES

Sicilienne vln & pf — arr. Dushkin
with A. d'Arco pf   Pléiade P105

SAINT–SAËNS

(Le) Carnaval des animaux (1886) small orch.
Le cygne arr. vln & pf
with A. d'Arco pf   Pléiade P105

SCHUBERT

(4) Lieder, Op. 3 (D257) v & pf
No. 3. Heidenröslein arr. vln & pf
with A. d'Arco pf   Pléiade P101

WEBER

(6) Sonatas, Op. 10 (J99/104) (1810) vln & pf
Sonata No. 1, in F: Romanze (2nd mvt) J99 arr. vln & pf as "Larghetto"
by Kreisler
with A. d'Arco pf   Pléiade P208

Hans–Georg ARLT

DVOŘÁK

(8) Humoresques, Op. 101 pf
No. 7. Humoresque No. 7, in G flat arr. vln & orch.
with Peter Cramer String Orch.   Polydor EPH21162

TOSELLI

Serenade, Op. 6 vln & pf
   with FFB orch. – Eisbrenner

   Baccarola 77873ZK
   Eurodisc 60024GE, S60025GE

Georges ARMAND

BACH

Concerto in d, BWV1043 2 vlns, strs & c
   with C. Cyroulnik vln & Toulouse
   Symphony Orch. – Auriacombe

   Counterpoint C610, CS5610

TELEMANN

Concerto in G vln & strs
   with Toulouse Chamber
   Orch. – Auriacombe

   Nonesuch H1066, H71066

VIVALDI

(12) Concerti, Op. 3 "L'Estro armonico" var. cbns & strs
   Concerto No. 8, in a, P.2 (F.I, No. 177) 2 vlns, strs & c
   with O. Giordano vln & Toulouse
   Chamber Orch. – Auriacombe

   Vega C30 A381, ST20008

   Concerto No. 10, in b, P.148 (F.IV, No. 10) 4 vlns, strs & c
   with A. Auriacombe vln, O. Giordano
   vln, K. Muhlberger vln & Toulouse
   Chamber Orch. – L. Auriacombe

   Electrola 1C053–10068
   Seraphim S60129

(12) Concerti, Op. 8 (1725) "Il Cimento dell' Armonia e dell' Invenzione"
   (Nos. 1/4: Le quattro Stagioni) vln & strs
   Concerto No. 1, in E, F.I, No. 22 "La Primavera"
   with Toulouse Chamber Orch. –
   Auriacombe

   Seraphim S60144

   Concerto No. 2, in B flat, F.I, No. 23 "L'Estate"
   with Toulouse Chamber
   Orch. – Auriacombe

   Seraphim S60144

   Concerto No. 3, in F, F.I, No. 24 "L'Autunno"
   with Toulouse Chamber
   Orch. – Auriacombe

   Seraphim S60144

   Concerto No. 4, in f, F.I, No. 25 "L'Inverno"
   with Toulouse Chamber
   Orch. – Auriacombe

   Seraphim S60144

William ARMON

HAYDN, M.

Concerto in A vln & orch.
   with Little Orch. of London – Jones

   Pye GSGC14131

Gabriella ARMUZZI–ROMEI

CORELLI

(12) Sonatas, Op. 5 vln & c
   Sonata No. 4, in F
   with L.F. Tagliavini hpsi

   Erato ERG4012
   Musical Heritage Society
   MHS937

FRESCOBALDI

(28) Canzoni da Sonara (1628) 1–4part–var. inst
   Canzona I "La Bonvisia" vln & c
   with L.F. Tagliavini org

   Erato ERG4012
   Musical Heritage Society
   MHS937

   Canzona II "La Bernardina" vln & c
   with L.F. Tagliavini org

   Erato ERG4012
   Musical Heritage Society
   MHS937

TORELLI

(12) Concerti, Op. 8 (1709) 1/6: 2 vlns, strs & c – 7/2: vln, strs & c
   Concerto No. 2, in a
   with C. Rossi vln, M. Mauriello hpsi
   & Teatro Comunale Orch.,
   Bologna – Gotti

   Musical Heritage Society
   MHS893

VITALI, G.B.

Artifici musicali, Op. 13 (1689) vln & c
   Caprice No. 1, in D
   with L.F. Tagliavini org

   Erato ERG4012
   Musical Heritage Society
   MHS937

   Caprice No. 2, in g
   with L.F. Tagliavini org

   Erato ERG4012
   Musical Heritage Society
   MHS937

(12) Sonatas, Op. 5 (1669) vln & c
   Sonata No. 1, in D
   with L.F. Tagliavini org

   Erato ERG4012
   Musical Heritage Society
   MHS937

VITALI, T.

Chaconne in g vln & c – ed. David
   with L.F. Tagliavini hpsi

   Erato ERG4012
   Musical Heritage Society
   MHS937

VIVIANI

(12) Capricci armonici, Op. 4 (1678) vln & c
   No. 2. Sinfonia
   with L.F. Tagliavini org

   Erato ERG4012
   Musical Heritage Society
   MHS937

   No. 4. Aria
   with L.F. Tagliavini org

   Erato ERG4012
   Musical Heritage Society
   MHS937

Sulo ARO (1904–   )

SIBELIUS

(4) Pieces, Op. 78 vln & pf
   No. 2. Romance in F
   with piano

   Rytmi 2125

ARSCHENSKY

DRIGO

(2) Airs de Ballet orch.
  No. 2. Valse bluette arr. vln & pf Auer
  with piano   Piccadilly 358

KREISLER

Caprice viennois, Op. 2 vln & pf
  with piano   Piccadilly 378

MASSENET

Thaïs (1894) – opera
  Méditation arr. vln & pf Marsick
  with piano   Piccadilly 358

RUSSELL

Serenade to Nicolette vln & pf
  with piano   Piccadilly 378

Danièle ARTUR

VIVALDI

Concerto in B flat, P.406 (F.XII, No. 16) vln, ob, strs & c
  with M. André tpt & Rouen Chamber   Philips 802710DXY, PHC9049
  Orch. – Beaucamp

Arve ARVESEN (1869–)

BACH

(3) Sonatas & 3 Partitas, BWV1001/6 solo vln
  Partita No. 1, in b: Sarabande (5th mvt) BWV1002
  (unaccompanied)   3372SM HMV V57, V7–87903

HALVORSEN

(4) Mosaïques (suite des morceaux caractéristiques) vln & pf
  No. 4. Chant de Veslemøy
  with orch.   302SM HMV 2–087901, M19
Norsk bryllupsmarsch vln & pf
  with piano   301SM HMV 2–087900, M19

HUBAY

(3) Transcriptions, Op. 3 vln & pf
  No. 2a. Crépuscule (Massenet)
  with piano   3371SM HMV V57, V7–87902

Shmuel ASHKENAZI (1941–)

BACH

(3) Sonatas & 3 Partitas, BWV1001/6 solo vln
  Sonata No. 3, in C, BWV1005
  (unaccompanied)   Mezhdunarodnaya Kniga
                  D10289

ERNST

(6) Mehrstimmige Studien solo vln
  No. 6. Etude No. 6, in G (Variations on "The last rose of summer")
  (à Bazzini)
  (unaccompanied)   Mezhdunarodnaya Kniga
                  D10290

PAGANINI

Concerto No. 1, in D, Op. 6 (cadenza by Sauret) vln & orch.
  with Vienna Symphony Orch. – Esser   Deutsche Grammophon
                               SLPM139424
Concerto No. 2, in b, Op. 7 (cadenza by Ashkenasi) vln & orch.
  with Vienna Symphony Orch. – Esser   Deutsche Grammophon
                               SLPM139424

TCHAIKOVSKY

Souvenir d'un lieu cher, Op. 42 vln & pf
  No. 3. Mélodie
  with piano   Mezhdunarodnaya Kniga
                  D010325/8

Eduardo Hernandez ASIAIN

SARASATE

Caprice basque, Op. 24 vln & pf
  with J. Galdea pf   Hispavox HH10–60
                  Music Hall MH14052

(8) Danzas españolas vln & pf
  No. 1. Malagueña, Op. 21, No. 1
  with J. Galdea pf   Hispavox HH10–60
                  Music Hall MH14052

  No. 2. Habañera, Op. 21, No. 2
  with J. Galdea pf   Hispavox HH10–60
                  Music Hall MH14052

  No. 3. Romanza andaluza, Op. 22, No. 1
  with J. Galdea pf   Hispavox HH10–60
                  Music Hall MH14052

  No. 6. Zapateado, Op. 23, No. 2
  with J. Galdea pf   Hispavox HH10–60, HH16–123
                  Music Hall MH14052

  No. 7. Danza española No. 7, in A, Op. 26, No. 1
  with J. Galdea pf   Hispavox HH10–60, HH16–124
                  Music Hall MH14052

Introduction & Tarantelle, Op. 43 vln & pf
  with J. Galdea pf   Hispavox HH10–60, HH16–124
                  Music Hall MH14052

Zigeunerweisen, Op. 20 vln & pf or orch.
  with J. Galdea pf   Hispavox HH10–60, HH16–123
                  Music Hall MH14052

André ASSELIN (1895–)

CLERAMBAULT

Prelude & Allegro in G hpsi – arr. vln & pf Dandelot
  with piano   HMV K5905

COOLS

Romance sans paroles vln & pf
  with piano   HMV K5480

HANDEL

(16) Suites (1720/33) hpsi
  Suite No. 7, in g: Passacaglia (6th mvt) arr. vln & vlc Halvorsen
  with P. Bazelaire vlc   Odeon 188971

MOZART

Sonata No. 33, in E flat, K481 vln & pf
with L. Descaves–Truc pf   HMV W1573/4

NIN

(20) Cantos de España (1923) v & pf
No. 15. Paño murciano arr. vln & pf as "Murciana" by Nin & Gautier
with piano   HMV L804
No. 16. Villancico Catalán arr. vln & pf as "Catalana" by Nin & Gautier
with piano   HMV L804

RAVEL

Pavane pour une infante défunte (1899) pf – arr. vln & Kochański
with piano   HMV L804

SAINT–SAËNS

(Le) Déluge, Op. 45 (1876) – oratorio
Prélude vln & orch. – arr. vln & pf Saint–Saëns
with piano   HMV K5480

SCHUMANN

Fantasiestücke, Op. 88 pf, vln & vlc
with L. Wurmser pf & P. Bazelaire vlc   Odeon 188926/8
Trio No. 3, in g, Op. 110 pf, vln & vlc
with L. Wurmser pf & P. Bazelaire vlc   Odeon 123858/60

VIVALDI

(12) Concerti, Op. 3 "L'Estro armonico" var. cbns & strs
Concerto No. 11, in d: Largo (3rd mvt) P.250 (F.IV, No. 11) 2 vlns, vlc, strs & c – arr. vln & orch. Dandelot
with piano   HMV K5905
(6) Sonatas, Op. 13 (1737) "Il Pastor Fido" fl, ob, vln strs & c
Sonata No. 4, in A: Pastorale (3rd mvt) F.XVI, No. 8 arr. vln, vlc & cha orch.
with P. Bazelaire vlc & Chamber   Odeon 123921
Orch.

Anita AST

DRDLA

Souvenir vln & pf
with E. Meller pf   Ve 1583   Odeon A186432

JUON

(4) Pieces, Op. 28 vln & pf
No. 3. Berceuse
with E. Meller pf   Ve 1584   Odeon A186432

RAFF

(6) Pieces, Op. 85 vln & pf
No. 3. Cavatina in D
with E. Meller pf   Ve 1582   Odeon A186431

SMETANA

From my Homeland (1878) vln & pf
No. 2. Andantino
with E. Meller pf   Ve 1581   Odeon A186431

Francesco ASTI (1894–1963)

d'AMBROSIO

Petit chanson, Op. 28 vln & pf
with piano   BE 2348[II]   HMV X3455
Serenade, Op. 4 vln & pf
with S. Frykberg pf   BE 1404   HMV X3086

CODA

Bimba mia v & pf – arr. vln & pf
with S. Frykberg pf   BE 1405   HMV X3086

DICK–STON

Reçuerdos (Argentine tango) vln & pf
with piano   BE 2353[II]   HMV X3455

DRDLA

Serenade No. 1, in A vln & pf
with S. Frykberg pf   BE 1420   HMV X3281

DRIGO

(Les) Millions d'Arlequin (1900) – ballet orch.
Sérénade arr. vln & pf Auer
with S. Frykberg pf   BE 2351[I]△   HMV X3456

HENTSCHEL

Illusion tango vln & pf
with S. Frykberg pf   BE 2354   HMV X3457

HUBAY

(Le) Luthier de Crémone, Op. 40 (1894) – opera
Intermezzo orch. – arr. vln & pf Hubay
with S. Frykberg pf   BE 2349[I] △   HMV X3456

MERIKANTO

Valse lente pf – arr. vln & pf Burmester
with S. Frykberg pf   BE 1421   HMV X3087

MOSZKOWSKI

(6) Klavierstücke,, Op. 15 pf – 4 hands
No. 1. Serenata arr. vln & pf Rehfeld
with S. Frykberg pf   BE 2352–II   HMV X3454

SAINT–SAËNS

(Le) Carnaval des animaux (1886) small orch.
Le cygne arr. vln & pf
with S. Frykberg pf   BE 1406   HMV X3281

SIBELIUS

(4) Pieces, Op. 78 vln & pf
No. 2. Romance in F
with Göteborg   CE 2282[I]△   HMV C2004, Z206
Symphony Orch. – Mann

SIMONETTI

Madrigale pf – arr. vln & pf
with S. Frykberg pf   BE 2350   HMV X3457

STENHAMMAR

(2) Sentimental romances, Op. 28 (1910) vln & orch.
Sentimental romance No. 1, in A
with Göteborg   CE 2281[I]△   HMV C2004, Z206
Symphony Orch. – Mann

TCHAIKOVSKY

Souvenir d'un lieu cher, Op. 42 vln & pf
No. 3. Mélodie
with S. Frykberg pf   BE 1422   HMV X3087

WESTERMANN

Resignation, Op. 27 vln & pf
with S. Frykberg pf   BE 2347–II HMV X3454

Yvonne ASTRUC (1889–)

BACH

Concerto No. 1, in a, BWV1041 vln, strs & c
      1068½GPP, 1070 GPP,   Decca CA8225/6
      1069½GPP & 1071½GPP Polydor 516636/7
with string orch. – Bret

BOULANGER, L.

Cortège (1919) vln & pf
with N. Boulanger pf   WL 2076[I] Columbia LF15
Nocturne in F (1911) vln & pf
with N. Boulanger pf   WL 2056[I] Columbia LF15

GLUCK

Orphée et Eurydice (1762) – opera
Dance of the blessed spirits: Lento "Mélodie" (No. 2) arr. vln & pf Kreisler
with piano   Columbia D15202

GRIEG

Sonata No. 3, in c, Op. 45 vln & pf
with M. Ciampi pf   Columbia LFX176/8

KREISLER

Tempo di minuetto (Pugnani) vln & pf
with piano   Columbia D15202

MILHAUD

Concertino de printemps (1934) vln & cha orch.
      1029¾GPP & 1030 GPP Decca CA8025
with orch. – Milhaud   Polydor 67147, 516616

NARDINI

(6) Sonatas, Op. 2 (1765) vln & c
Sonata No. 4, in E flat: Adagio (2nd mvt) arr. vln & pf Salmon
with piano   Columbia LF28

NOVAČEK

(8) Concert Caprices, Op. 5 vln & pf
No. 4. Perpetuum mobile
with piano   Columbia LF28

Michèle AUCLAIR (1931–)

BACH

(6) Sonatas, BWV1014/9 vln & clav
Sonata No. 1, in b, BWV1014
with M–C. Alain org   Discophiles français DF209
Sonata No. 2, in A, BWV1015
with M–C. Alain org   Discophiles français DF210

BACH – *Continued*

Sonata No. 3, in E, BWV1016
with M–C. Alain org   Discophiles français DF209
Sonata No. 4, in c, BWV1017
with M–C. Alain org   Discophiles français DF210
Sonata No. 5, in f, BWV1018
with M–C. Alain org   Discophiles français DF210
Sonata No. 6, in G, BWV1019
with M–C. Alain org   Discophiles français DF209

BRAHMS

Concerto in D, Op. 77 vln & orch.
with Vienna Symphony Orch. – van Otterloo   Fontana 697006EL, 200060WGL

BRANDL

(Der) Liebe Augustin – operetta
Du alter Stefansturm arr. vln & pf as "The old refrain" by Kreisler
with O. Schulhof pf   Remington R199–126

BRUCH

Concerto No. 1, in g, Op. 26 vln & orch.
with Austrian Symphony   Concerteum CR219
Orch. – Loibner   Remington R199–127
Kol Nidrei, Op. 47 vlc or vln & orch.
with Austrian Symphony   Concerteum CR219
Orch. – Loibner   Remington R199–127

CHAMINADE

Sérénade espagnole pf – arr. vln & pf Kreisler
with O. Schulhof pf   Remington R199–128

DEBUSSY

Sonata No. 3, in g (1917) vln & pf
with J. Bonneau pf   Discophiles français 525122

DVOŘÁK

(7) Gypsy songs,, Op. 55 v & pf
No. 4. Songs my mother taught me arr. vln & pf Kreisler
with O. Schulhof pf   Remington R199–128

FALLA

(La) Vida Breve (1913) – opera
Danza española orch. – arr. vln & pf Kreisler
with O. Schulhof pf   Remington R199–128

GLUCK

Orphée et Eurydice (1762) – opera
Dance of the blessed spirits: Lento "Mélodie" (No. 2) arr. vln & pf Kreisler
with O. Schulhof pf   Remington R199–128

HAYDN

Concerto No. 1, in C, H.VIIa, No. 1 (1765) vln & orch.
with Paris Conservatory   HMV W1579/80
Orch. – Thibaud

KREISLER

Caprice viennois, Op. 2 vln & pf
with O. Schulhof pf   Remington R199–126
Liebesfreud vln & pf
with O. Schulhof pf   Remington R199–126

KREISLER – *Continued*

Liebesleid vln & pf
  with O. Schulhof pf   Remington R199–126

Rondino on a theme by Beethoven vln & pf
  with O. Schulhof pf   Remington R199–128

Schön Rosmarin vln & pf
  with O. Schulhof pf   Remington R199–126

Tambourin chinois, Op. 3 vln & pf
  with O. Schulhof pf   Remington R199–126

Praeludium & Allegro (Pugnani) vln & pf
  with O. Schulhof pf   Remington R199–128

LECLAIR

(6) Concerti, Op. 7 (1737) vln & str orch.
  Concerto No. 6, in A
  with Saar Chamber Orch. – Ristenpart   Discophiles français 225116, 525116

(6) Concerti, Op. 10 (1744) vln & str orch.
  Concerto No. 6, in g
  with Saar Chamber Orch. – Ristenpart   Discophiles français 225116, 525116

MENDELSSOHN

Concerto in e, Op. 64 vln & orch.
  with Innsbruck Symphony
  Orch. – Wagner   Fontana 894037ZKY, SFON10509
       Mercury DS641901L, DS836901Y, MGW14048, SRW18048
       Philips 610807VL, 836901DSY, 838607VY, GL5815, SGL5815

MOZART

Concerto No. 4, in D, K218 vln & orch.
  with Stuttgart Philharmonic
  Orch. – Couraud   Fontana 200063WGL, 698087FL, 700161WGY, 894039ZKY, SFL14090

Concerto No. 5, in A, K219 "Turkish" vln & orch.
  with Stuttgart Philharmonic
  Orch. – Couraud   Fontana 200063WGL, 698087FL, 700161WGY, 894039ZKY, SFL14090

RAVEL

Sonata (1927) vln & pf
  with J. Bonneau pf   Discophiles français 525122

SCHUBERT

Fantasia in C, Op. 159 (D934) vln & pf
  with G. Joy pf   Erato LDE3236, STE50136
       Musical Heritage Society MHS606

Rondo brillante in b, Op. 70 (D895) vln & pf
  with G. Joy pf   Erato LDE3236, STE50136
       Musical Heritage Society MHS606

Sonata in A, Op. 162 (D574) vln & pf
  with G. Joy pf   Erato LDE3237, STE50137
       Musical Heritage Society MHS607

SCHUBERT – *Continued*

(3) Sonatinas, Op. 137 (D384, D385 & D408) vln & pf
  No. 1. Sonatina No. 1, in D, D384
  with G. Joy pf   Erato LDE3237, STE50137
       Musical Heritage Society MHS607

  No. 2. Sonatina No. 2, in A, D385
  with G. Joy pf   Erato LDE3237, STE50137
       Musical Heritage Society MHS607

  No. 3. Sonatina No. 3, in g, D408
  with G. Joy pf   Erato LDE3236, STE50136
       Musical Heritage Society MHS606

TCHAIKOVSKY

Concerto in D, Op. 35 vln & orch.
  with Austrian Symphony
  Orch. – Wöss   Concerteum CR247
       Masterseal MSLP5002
       Remington R199–20

Concerto in D, Op. 35 vln & orch.
  with Innsbruck Symphony
  Orch. – Wagner   Fontana 700211WGY, 894037ZKY, SFL14059, SFON10509
       Mercury DS641901L, DS836901Y, MGW14048, SRW18048
       Philips 610807VL, 836901DSY, 838607VY, GL5815, SGL5815

Leopold AUER (1845–1930)

BRAHMS

(21) Hungarian Dances pf duet
  Hungarian dance No. 1, in g arr. vln & pf Joachim
  with piano*   Asco A123
       Victor

TCHAIKOVSKY

Souvenir d'un lieu cher, Op. 42 vln & pf
  No. 3. Mélodie (arr. Wilhelmj)
  with piano*   Asco A123
       Victor

Aimée AURIACOMBE

VIVALDI

(12) Concerti, Op. 3 "L'Estro armonico" var. cbns & strs
  Concerto No. 10, in b, P.148 (F.IV, No. 10) 4 vlns, strs & c
  with G. Armand vln, O. Giordano vln,   Electrola 1C053–10068
  K. Muhlberger vln & Toulouse   Seraphim S60129
  Chamber Orch. – L. Auriacombe

*Recorded after his 75th birthday concert at Carnegie Hall on June 7, 1920. Five copies only were made of the two selections and one each were given to Heifetz, Zimbalist, Elman, Eddy Brown & F. Steinway. The discs state "Victor Special Record"; have no matrix numbers, but are "take" two. they are enscribed by Auer "To my musical children."

Leopold AVAKIAN

COWELL

Homage to Iran (1959) vln, pf & Persian drms
with M. Andrews pf & B. Bahar   Composers Recordings CRI173
Persian drms

Felix AYO

ABACO

(12) Sonatas, Op. 3 (1714) 2 vlns & c
Sonata No. 4, in G (rev. Riemann)
with A.M. Cotogni vln & M. de   Victor (in set ML40002)
Robertis hpsi

ALBINONI

(12) Concerti, Op. 9 (1722) var. cbns & strs
Concerto No. 1, in B flat vln, strs & c
with I Musici   Philips 802828LY, (in set
                                       SC71AX305), 6580 001

Concerto No. 4, in A vln, strs & c
with I Musici   Philips 802828LY, (in set
                                       SC71AX305)

Concerto No. 7, in D vln, strs & c
with I Musici   Philips 802829LY, (in set
                                       SC71AX305)

Concerto No. 8, in D vln, strs & c
with I Musici   Angel 35088
                                       Columbia CX1163, FCX305,
                                       QCX10039
                                       HMV LALP209

Concerto No. 10, in F vln, strs & c
with I Musici ,   Philips 802830LY, (in set
                                       SC71AX305)

BACH

Concerto No. 2, in E, BWV1042 vln strs & c
with I Musici   Epic BC1018, LC3553
                                       Philips 6580 021, 610106VL,
                                       835007AY, 839591VGY,
                                       A00519L, ABL3259, L09008L

Concerto in d, BWV1043 2 vlns strs & c*
with R. Michelucci vln & I Musici   Epic BC1018, LC3553
                                       Philips 6580 021, 610106VL,
                                       802736AY, (in set C71AX401),
                                       836217AY, A00519L, ABL3259,
                                       G05347R, L09008L

BOCCHERINI

(6) Quintets, Op. 30 (1780) 2 vlns, vla & 2 vlcs
No. 6. Quintet No. 6, in C "La Musica Notturna di Madrid" (rev.
Upmeyer)
with A.M. Cotogni vln, C. Ghedin vla, Victor (in set ML40002)
E. Altobelli vlc & M. Centurione vlc

* excerpts only on Epic BC1.

CORELLI

(12) Concerti grossi, Op. 6 orch.
Concerto grosso No. 1, in D rev. Negri
with A. Apostoli vln, E. Altobelli vlc Philips 802761LY, (in set
& I Musici   SC71AX304)

Concerto grosso No. 2, in F (rev. Negri)
with A. Apostoli vln, E. Altobelli vlc Philips 802761LY, (in set
& I Musici   SC71AX304)

Concerto grosso No. 3, in c (rev. Negri)
with A. Apostoli vln, E. Altobelli vlc Philips 802761LY, (in set
& I Musici   SC71AX304)

Concerto Grosso No. 4, in D
with W. Gallozzi vln, E. Altobelli vlc Philips A00787R ABR4069,
& I Musici   G03090L, GBL5621 L02246L

Concerto grosso No. 4, in D (rev. Negri)
with A. Apostoli vln, E. Altobelli vlc Philips 802761LY, (in set
& I Musici   SC71AX304)

Concerto grosso No. 5, in B flat
with W. Gallozzi vln, E. Altobelli vlc Philips S06081R, SBR6207
& I Musici

Concerto grosso No. 5, in B flat (rev. Negri)
with A. Apostoli vln, E. Altobelli vlc Philips 802762LY, (in set
& I Musici   SC71AX304)

Concerto grosso No. 6, in F (rev. Negri)
with A. Apostoli vln, E. Altobelli vlc Philips 802762LY, in set
& I Musici   SC71AX304)

Concerto grosso No. 7, in D
with W. Gallozzi vln, E. Altobelli vlc Philips A00787R, ABR4069
& I Musici

Concerto grosso No. 7 in D (rev. Negri)
with A. Apostoli vln, E. Altobelli vlc Philips 802762LY, (in set
& I Musici   SC71AX304)

Concerto grosso No. 8, in g Christmas Concerto"
with W. Gallozzi vln, E. Altobelli vlc Philips 400024AE, 835129AY,
& I Musici   (in set C71AX401) ABE10029,
                                        PHM500025, PHS900025,
                                        S06081R, SBR6207

Concerto grosso No. 8, in g "Christmas Concerto" (rev. Negri)
with A. Apostoli vln, E. Altobelli vlc Philips 802762LY, (in set
& I Musici   SC71AX304)

Concerto grosso No. 9, in F
with W. Gallozzi vln, E. Altobelli vlc Philips A00787R, ABR4069
& I Musici

Concerto grosso No. 9, in F (rev. Negri)
with A. Apostoli vln, E. Altobelli vlc Philips 802763LY, (in set
& I Musici   SC71AX304)

Concerto grosso No. 10, in C
with W. Gallozzi vln, E. Altobelli vlc Philips A00787R, ABR4069
& I Musici

Concerto grosso No. 10, in C (rev. Negri)
with A. Apostoli vln, E. Altobelli vlc Philips 802763LY, (in set
& I Musici   SC71AX304)

Concerto grosso No. 11, in B flat (rev. Negri)
with A. Apostoli vln, E. Altobelli vlc Philips 802763LY, (in set
& I Musici   SC71AX304)

Concerto grosso No. 12, in F rev. Negri
with A. Apostoli vln, E. Altobelli vlc Philips 802763LY, (in set
& I Musici   SC71AX304)

GEMINIANI

(6) Concerti grossi, , Op. 7 (1746) orch.
Concerto grosso no. 1, and in D
  with W. Gallozzi vln, B. Giuranna vla,   Philips 839304EGY, PHC9010
  E. Altobelli vlc & I Musici
Concerto grosso No. 2, in d
  with W. Gallozzi vln, B. Giuranna vla,   Philips 839304EGY, PHC9010
  E. Altobelli vlc & I Musici
Concerto grosso No. 3, in C
  with W. Gallozzi vln, B. Giuranna vla,   Philips 839304EGY, PHC9010
  E. Altobelli vlc & I Musici
Concerto grosso No. 5, in c
  with W. Gallozzi vln, B. Giuranna vla,   Philips 839304EGY, PHC9010
  E. Altobelli vlc & I Musici
Concerto grosso No. 6, in B flat
  with W. Gallozzi vln, B. Giuranna vla   Philips 839304EGY, PHC9010
  E. Altobelli vlc & I musici

HAYDN

Concerto No. 1, in C, H.VIIa, No. 1 (1765) (Cadenza by V. Negri Bryks)
  vln & orch.
  with I Musici
    Epic BC1150, LC3818
    Philips 835156LY, A02076L,
    L02275L, SFL7519

LOCATELLI

(12) Concerti grossi, Op. 1 (1721) 2 vlns, vla, vlc, strs & c
Concerto grosso No. 8, in f
  with A.M. Cotogni vln, B. Giuranna   Epic BC1029, LC3587
  vla, E. Altobelli vlc & I Musici   Philips 835025AY, 835129AY,
    A02023L, PHC9032
    PHM500025, PHS900025
Concerto grosso No. 9, in D
  with A.M. Cotogni vln, B. Giuranna   Epic BC1029, LC3587
  vla, E. Altobelli vlc & I Musici   Philips 835025AY, A02023L
Concerto grosso No. 11, in c
  with A.M. Cotogni vln, B. Giuranna   Epic BC1029, LC3587
  vla, E. Altobelli vlc & I Musici   Philips 835025AY, A02023L,
    PHC9032
Concerto grosso No. 12, in g
  with A.M. Cotogni vln, B. Giuranna   Epic BC1029, LC3587
  vla, E. Altobelli vlc & I Musici   Philips 835025AY, A02023L,
    PHC9032

PERGOLESI

(14) Sonatas (1770) 2 vlns & c
Sonata No. 5, in C (rev. Caffarelli)
  with A.M. Cotogni vln & M. de   Victor (in set ML40002)
  Robertis hpsi

SCHUBERT

Rondo in A, D438 vln & str orch.
  with I Musici
    Philips 835095AY, A02098L,
    PHS900177

TARTINI

(12) Sonatas, Op. 3 2 vlns & c
Sonata No. 1, in D (rev. Pente)
  with A.M. Cotogni vln, C. Ghedin vla   Victor (in set ML40002)
  & E. Altobelli vlc

TELEMANN

Concerto in F, T.II, No. 3 3 vlns, strs & c
  with A. Apostoli vln, I. Colandrea vln   Philips 802864LY, PHS900188,
  & I Musici   SAL3737

VIVALDI

(12) Concerti, Op. 4 "La Stravaganza" vln, strs & c
Concerto No. 1, in B flat, F.I, No. 180
  with M.T. Garatti hpsi & I Musici   Philips 820054DTY, 835209AY,
    A02331L, PHM500069, (in set
    PHM2–540), PHS900070, (in set
    PHS2–940)

Concerto No. 2, in E, F.I, No. 181
  with M.T. Garatti hpsi & I Musici   Philips 820054DTY, 835209AY,
    A02331L, PHM500069, (in set
    PHM2–540), PHS900069, (in set
    PHS2–940)

Concerto No. 3, in G, F.I, No. 182
  with M.T. Garatti hpsi & I Musici   Philips 820054DTY, 835209AY,
    A02331L, PHM500069, (in set
    PHM2–540), PHS900069, (in set
    PHS2–940)

Concerto No. 4, in a, F.I, No. 183
  with M.T. Garatti hpsi & I Musici   Philips 820054DTY, 835209AY,
    A02331L, PHM500070, (in set
    PHM2–540), PHS900070, (in set
    PHS2–940)

Concerto No. 5, in A, F.I, No. 184
  with M.T. Garatti hpsi & I Musici   Philips 820054DTY, 835209AY,
    A02331L, PHM500070, (in set
    PHM2–540), PHS 900070, (in set
    PHS2–1940)

Concerto No. 6, in g, F.I, No. 185
  with M.T. Garatti hpsi & I Musici   Philips 820054DTY, 835209AY,
    A02331L, PHM500070, (in set
    PHM2–540), PHS900070, (in set
    PHS2–940),

Concerto No. 7, in c, F.I, No. 186
  with M.T. Garatti hpsi & I Musici   Philips 820055DTY, 835210AY,
    A02332L, PHM500070, (in set
    PHM2–540), PHS900070, (in set
    PHS2–940)

Concerto No. 8, in d, F.I, No. 187
  with M.T. Garatti hpsi & I Musici   Philips 820055DTY, 835210AY,
    A02332L, PHM500070, (in set
    PHM2–540), PHS900070, (in set
    PHS2–940)

Concerto No. 9, in F, F.I, No. 188
  with M.T. Garatti hpsi & I Musici   Philips 820055DTY, 835210AY,
    A02332L, PHM500070, (in set
    PHM2–540), PHS900070, (in set
    PHS2–940)

Concerto No. 10, in c, F.I, No. 189
  with M.T. Garatti hpsi & I Musici   Philips 820055DTY, 835210AY,
    A02332L, PHM500069, (in set
    PHM2–540), PHS900069, (in set
    PHS2–940)

VIVALDI – *Continued*

Concerto No. 11, in D, F.I, No. 190
with M.T. Garatti hpsi & I Musici   Philips 820055DTY, 835210AY, A02332L, PHM500069, (in set PHM2–540), PHS900069, (in set PHS2–940)

Concerto No. 12, in G, F.I, No. 191
with M.T. Garatti hpsi & I Musici   Philips 820055DTY, 835210AY, A02332L, PHM500069, (in set PHM2–540), PHS900069, (in set PHS2–940)

(12) Concerti, Op. 8 (1725) "Il Cimento dell' Armonia e dell' Invenzione"
(Nos. 1/4: Le quattro Stagioni) vln & strs
Concerto No. 1, in E, F.I, No. 22 "La Primavera"
with I Musici   Epic BC1086, LC3704, (in set SC6029)
Philips SABL117

Concerto No. 1, in E, F.I, No. 22 "La Primavera"
with I Musici   Epic LC3216
Philips 400110AE, 835030AY, ABL3128, L00301L, PHC9104

Concerto No. 2, in g, F.I, No. 23 "L'Estate"
with I Musici   Epic BC1086, LC3704, (in set SC6029)
Philips SABL117

Concerto No. 2, in g, F.I, No. 23 "L'Estate"
with I Musici   Epic LC3216
Philips 400111AE, 835030AY, ABL3128, L00301L, PHC9104

Concerto No. 3, in F, F.I, No. 24 "L'Autunno"
with I Musici   Epic BC1086, LC3704, (in set SC6029)
Philips SABL117

Concerto No. 3, in F, F.I, No. 24 "L'Autunno"
with I Musici   Epic LC3216
Philips 400112AE, 835030AY, ABL3128, L00301L, PHC9104

Concerto No. 4, in f, F.I, No. 25 "L'Inverno"
with I Musici   Epic BC1086, LC3704, (in set SC6029)
Philips SABL117

Concerto No. 4, in f, F.I, No. 25 "L'Inverno"
with I Musici   Epic LC3216
Philips 400113AE, 835030AY, ABL3128, L00301L, PHC9104

Concerto No. 5, in B flat, F.I, No. 26 "La Tempesta di mare"
with I Musici   Epic LC3343, (in set SC6029)
Philips A00383L, A02220L, ABL3182

Concerto No. 6, in C, F.I, No. 27 "Il Piacere"
with I Musici   Epic LC3343, (in set SC6029)
Philips A00383L, A02220L, ABL3182

Concerto No. 7, in d, F.I, No. 28
with I Musici   Epic LC3343, (in set SC6029)
Philips A00383L, A02220L, ABL3182

VIVALDI – *Continued*

Concerto No. 8, in g, F.I, No. 16
with I Musici   Epic LC3343, (in set SC6029)
Philips A00383L, A02220L, ABL3182

Concerto No. 9, in d, F. VII, No. 1
with I Musici   Epic LC3443, (in set SC6029)
Philips A02221L, L00443L

Concerto No. 10, in B flat, F.I, No. 29 "La Caccia"
with I Musici   Epic LC3443, (in set SC6029)
Philips A02221L, L00443L

Concerto No. 11, in D, F.I, No. 30
with I Musici   Epic LC3443, (in set SC6029)
Philips A02221L, L00443L

Concerto No. 12, in C, F.I, No. 31
with I Musici   Epic LC3443, (in set SC6029)
Philips A02221L, L00443L

(12) Concerti, Op. 9 (1728) "La Cetra" vln, strs & c
Concerto No. 1, in C, P.9 (F.I, No. 47)
with E. Altobelli vlc, M.T. Garatti org & I Musici   Philips 835289AY, A02419L, PHM500114, (in set PHM3–553), PHS900114, (in set PHS3–993)

Concerto No. 2, in A, P.214 (F.I, No. 51)
with E. Altobelli vlc, M.T Garatti org & I Musici   Philips 835289AY, A02419L, PHM500114, (in set PHM3–553), PHS900114, (in set PHS3–993)

Concerto No. 3, in g, P.339 (F.I, No. 52)
with E. Altobelli vlc, M.T. Garatti org & I Musici   Philips 835289AY, A02419L, PHM500114, (in set PHM3–553), PHS900114, (in set PHS3–993)

Concerto No. 4, in E, P.242 (F.I, No. 48)
with E. Altobelli vlc, M.T. Garatti org & I Musici   Philips 835289AY, A02419L, PHM500114, (in set PHM3–553), PHS900114, (in set PHS3–993)

Concerto No. 5, in a, P.10 (F.I, No. 53)
with E. Altobelli vlc, M.T. Garatti org & I Musici   Philips 835290AY, A02420L, PHM500115, (in set PHM3–553), PHS900115, (in set PHS3–993)

Concerto No. 6, in A, P.215 (F.I, No. 54) with solo vln scordato
with E. Altobelli vlc, M.T. Garatti org & I Musici   Philips 835290AY, A02420L, PHM500115, (in set PHM3–553), PHS900115, (in set PHS3–993)

Concerto No. 7, in B flat, P.340 (F.I, No. 55)
with E. Altobelli vlc, M.T. Garatti org & I Musici   Philips 835290AY, A02420L, PHM500115, (in set PHM3–553), PHS900115, (in set PHS3–993)

Concerto No. 8, in d, P.260 (F.I, No. 56)
with E. Altobelli vlc, M.T. Garatti org & I Musici   Philips 835290AY, A02420L, PHM500115, (in set PHM3–553), PHS900115, (in set PHS3–993)

Concerto No. 9, in B flat, P.341 (F.I, No. 57) with 2nd vln obb
with A.M. Cotogni vln, E. Altobelli vlc, M.T. Garatti org & I Musici   Philips 835291AY, A02421L, PHM500116, (in set PHM3–553), PHS900116, (in set PHS3–993)

Concerto No. 10, in G, P.103 (F.I, No. 49)
with E. Altobelli vlc, M.T. Garatti org & I Musici   Philips 835291AY, A02421L, PHM500116, (in set PHM3–553), PHS900116, (in set PHS3–993)

VIVALDI – *Continued*

Concerto No. 11, in c, P.416 (F.I, No. 58)
with E. Altobelli vlc, M.T. Garatti org   Philips 835291AY, A02421L,
& I Musici   PHM500116, (in set PHM3–553),
                                          PHS900116, (in set PHS3–993)

Concerto No. 12, in b, P.154 (F.I, No. 50) with solo vln scordato
with E. Altobelli vlc, M.T. Garatti org   Philips 835291AY, A02421L,
& I Musici   PHM500116, (in set PHM3–553),
                                          PHS900116, (in set PHS3–993)

Concerto in a, P.28 (F.I, No. 61) 2 vlns, strs & c
with R. Michelucci vln & I Musici   Epic (in sets BSC111 & SC6040)
                                        Philips 838122AY, G04812L

Concerto in E, P.246 (F.I, No. 127) (Op. 35, No. 6) "L'Amoroso" vln,
strs & c
with I Musici   Epic BC1021, LC3486
                                        Philips 400108AY, 835002AY,
                                        A00476L, ABL3237, SAB102

Concerto in F, P.278 (F.I., No. 34) 3 vlns, strs & c – rev. Garatti)
with F. Tamponi vln, W. Gallozzi vln   Angel 35088
& I Musici   Columbia CX1163, FCX305,
                                        QCX10039
                                        HMV LALP209

Concerto in F, P.278 (F.I, No. 34) 3 vlns, strs & c – rev. Garatti)
with A.M. Cotogni vln, F. Tamponi   Philips 835211AY, A02333L,
vln & I Musici   PHM500147, PHS900147

Concerto in B flat, P.388 (F.IV, No. 2) (Op. 22, No. 2) vln, vlc, strs & c
with E. Altobelli vlc & I Musici   Epic LC3565
                                      Philips A00462L, ABL3233

Sol BABITZ (1911–   )

IVES

Sonata No. 2 (1910) vln & pf
In the barn (2nd mvt)
with I. Dahl pf   Alco AR101/3
The revival (3rd mvt)
with I. Dahl pf   Alco AR101/3

STRAVINSKY

In Memorian Dylan Thomas (1954) t, 4 tbns, 2 vlns, vla & vlc
with R. Robinson t, L. Ulyate tbn,   Columbia ML5107
H. Bohannon tbn, F. Howard tbn,   Philips A01493L, ABL3391
S. Zeldin tbn, I. Baker vln, C. Figelski
vla, G. Neikrug vlc, cond. Igor
Stravinsky

Tino BACCHETTA

MARCELLO, B.

(12) Concerti, Op. 1 (1708) vln, vlc obb & strs
Concerto No. 3, in E
with G. Ghetti vlc, M. Sorelli hpsi &   Amadeo AVR12101, AVRS5029,
I Solisti di Milano – Ephrikian   AVRS12101
                                        Arcophon AM653/4

Concerto No. 5, in b
with E. Miori vlc, M. Sorelli hpsi &   Amadeo AVRS5024
I Solisti di Milano – Ephrikian   Musical Heritage Society
                                        MHS924

MARCELLO, B. – *Continued*

Concerto No. 6, in B flat
with E. Miori vlc, M. Sorelli hpsi &   Amadeo AVRS5024
I Solisti di Milano – Ephrikian   Musical Heritage Society
                                        MHS924

Concerto No. 7, in f
with G. Ghetti vlc, M. Sorelli hpsi &   Amadeo AVR12101, AVRS5029,
I Solisti di Milano – Ephrikian   AVRS12101
                                        Arcophon AM653/4

Concerto No. 8, in F
with G. Ghetti vlc, M. Sorelli hpsi &   Amadeo AVR12101, AVRS5029,
I Solisti di Milano – Ephrikian   AVRS12101
                                        Arcophon AM653/4

Concerto No. 9, in A
with G. Ghetti vlc, M. Sorelli hpsi &   Amadeo AVR12101, AVRS5029,
I Solisti di Milano – Ephrikian   AVRS12101
                                        Arcophon AM653/4

Concerto No. 10, in C
with G. Ghetti vlc, M. Sorelli hpsi &   Amadeo AVR12101, AVRS5029,
I Solisti di Milano – Ephrikian   AVRS12101
                                        Arcophon AM653/4

Concerto No. 11, in E flat
with G. Ghetti vlc, M. Sorelli hpsi &   Amadeo AVR12101, AVRS5029,
I Solisti di Milano – Ephrikian   AVRS12101
                                        Arcophon AM653/4

Concerto No. 12, in G
with G. Ghetti vlc, M. Sorelli hpsi &   Amadeo AVRS5024
I Solisti di Milano – Ephrikian   Musical Heritage Society
                                        MHS924

VIVALDI

(12) Concerti, Op. 4 "La Stravaganza" vln, strs & c
Concerto No. 4, in a, F.I, No. 183
with I Solisti di Milano – Ephrikian   Arcophon AC651/2
                                        HMV ASDF840/1, FALP840/1,
                                        HQS1105/6

Concerto No. 5, in A, F.I, No. 184
with I Solisti di Milano – Ephrikian   Arcophon AC651/2
                                        HMV ASDF840/1, FALP840/1,
                                        HQS1105/6

Concerto No. 6, in g, F.I, No. 185
with I Solisti di Milano – Ephrikian   Arcophon AC651/2
                                        HMV ASDF840/1, FALP840/1,
                                        HQS1105/6

Concerto No. 10, in c, F.I, No. 189
with I Solisti di Milano – Ephrikian   Arcophon AC651/2
                                        HMV ASDF840/1, FALP840/1,
                                        HQS1105/6

Concerto No. 11, in D, F.I, No. 190
with I Solisti di Milano – Ephrikian   Arcophon AC651/2
                                        HMV ASDF840/1, FALP840/1,
                                        HQS1105/6

Concerto No. 12, in G, F.I, No. 191
with I Solisti di Milano – Ephrikian   Arcophon AC651/2
                                        HMV ASDF840/1, FALP840/1,
                                        HQS1105/6

VIVALDI – *Continued*

(12) Concerti, Op. 8 (1725) "Il Cimento dell' Armonia e dell' Invenzione"
(Nos. 1/4: Le quattro Stagioni) vln & strs
Concerto No. 1, in E, F.I, No. 22 "La Primavera"
with Sinfonia Ensemble – Witold   Contrepoint MC20108
         London TWV91157
         Mode MDINT9043

Concerto No. 2, in g, F.I, No. 23 "L'Estate"
with Sinfonia Ensemble – Witold   Contrepoint MC20108
         London TWV91157
         Mode MDINT9043

Concerto No. 3, in F, F.I, No. 24 "L'Autunno"
with Sinfonia Ensemble – Witold   Contrepoint MC20108
         London TWV91157
         Mode MDINT9043

Concerto No. 4, in f, F.I, No. 25 "L'Inverno"
with Sinfonia Ensemble – Witold   Contrepoint MC20108
         London TWV91157
         Mode MDINT9043

Grazyna BACEWICZ (1913–1969)

SZOPOWICZ

(4) Mazurkas, Op. 1 pf
No. 3. Mazurka No. 3, in A flat arr. vln & pf
with piano   Muza 1597

SZYMANOWSKI

(9) Preludes, Op. 1 (1900) pf
No. 1. Prelude No. 1, in b arr. vln & pf Bacewicz
with piano   Muza 1597

Alberto BACHMANN (1875–1963)

BACH

(3) Sonatas & 3 Partitas, BWV1001/6 solo vln
Partita No. 3, in E: Gavotte (3rd mvt) BWV1006
(unaccompanied)   1387–0   Favorite 1–4062E

BACHMANN

Danse hongrois No. 3 vln & pf
with piano   1390–0   Favorite 27, 1–4049E
Mazurka brillante No. 2 "L'abeille" vln & pf
with piano   1384-0   Favorite 1–4059E
Theme & Variations solo vln
(unaccompanied)   1384-0   Favorite 1–4059E
Zapateado vln & pf
with piano   1387–0   Favorite 1–4062E

CHOPIN

(3) Nocturnes, Op. 9 pf
No. 2. Nocturne No. 2, in E flat arr. vln & pf Sarasate
with piano   Favorite 1–4060D

DRDLA

Serenade No. 1, in A vln & pf
with piano   1383–0   Favorite 26, 1–4046E
         John Bull B118

KREISLER

Tambourin chinois, Op. 3 vln & pf
with piano   2132–1–28   Emerson 782

MASSENET

Thaïs (1894) – opera
Méditation arr. vln & pf Marsick
with piano   2159–1–21   Emerson 782

PAGANINI

(Le) Streghe (variations on a theme from Süssmeyer's opera "Il Noce di Benevento") Op. 8 (1813) vln & orch.*
with piano   1242–0   Favorite 26, 1–4045E

SAINT-SAËNS

(Le) Carnaval des animaux (1886) small orch.
Le cygne arr. vln & pf
with piano   2150–1   Emerson 769
(Le) Carnaval des animaux (1886) small orch.
Le cygne arr. vln & pf
with piano   1388–0   Favorite 27, 1–4063E

WIENIAWSKI

Souvenir de Moscou, Op. 6 vln & pf or orch.
with piano   Favorite 1–4050D

Edwin BACHMANN

CORELLI

(12) Concerti grossi, Op. 6 str orch.
Concerto grosso No. 1, in D
with D. Guilet vln, F. Miller vlc &   Vox (in sets PL7893 & VBX39)
Corelli Tri–Centenary
Orch. – Eckertsen
Concerto grosso No. 2, in F
with D. Guilet vln, F. Miller vlc &   Vox (in sets PL7893 & VBX39)
Corelli Tri–Centenary
Orch. – Eckertsen
Concerto grosso No. 3, in c
with D. Guilet vln, F. Miller vlc &   Vox (in sets PL7893 & VBX39)
Corelli Tri–Centenary
Orch. – Eckertsen
Concerto grosso No. 4, in D
with D. Guilet vln, F. Miller vlc &   Vox (in sets PL7893 & VBX39)
Corelli Tri–Centenary
Orch. – Eckertsen
Concerto grosso No. 5, in B flat
with D. Guilet vln, F. Miller vlc &   Vox (in sets PL7893 & VBX39)
Corelli Tri–Centenary
Orch. – Eckertsen
Concerto grosso No. 6, in F
with D. Guilet vln, F. Miller vlc &   Vox (in sets PL7893 & VBX39)
Corelli Tri–Centenary
Orch. – Eckertsen
Concerto grosso No. 7, in D
with D. Guilet vln F. Miller vlc &   Vox (in sets PL7893 & VBX39)
Corelli Tri–Centenary
Orch. – Eckertsen

* Abridged.

CORELLI - *Continued*

Concerto grosso No. 8, in g "Christmas Concerto"
with D. Guilet vln, F. Miller vlc &   Vox (in sets PL7893 & VBX39)
Corelli Tri–Centenary
Orch. – Eckertsen

Concerto grosso No. 9, in F
with D. Guilet vln, F. Miller vlc &   Vox (in sets PL7893 & VBX39)
Corelli Tri–Centenary
Orch. – Eckertsen

Concerto grosso No. 10, in C
with D. Guilet vln, F. Miller vlc &   Vox (in sets PL7893 & VBX39)
Corelli Tri–Centenary
Orch. – Eckertsen

Concerto grosso No. 11, in B flat
with D. Guilet vln, F. Miller vlc &   Vox (in sets PL7893 & VBX39)
Corelli Tri–Centenary
Orch. – Eckertsen

Concerto grosso No. 12, in F
with D. Guilet vln, F. Miller vlc &   Vox (in sets PL7893 & VBX39)
Corelli Tri–Centenary
Orch. – Eckertsen

VIVALDI

(12) Concerti, Op. 3 "L'Estro armonico" var. cbns & strs
Concerto No. 11, in d, P.250 (F.IV, No. 11) 2 vlns, vlc, strs & c
with A. Schneider vln,   KM 1/2 R   Keynote K2003
B. Greenhouse vlc, R. Kirkpatrick hpsi   Mercury MG10002
& Dumbarton Oaks Orch. – Schneider

Guéorgui BADER

PROKOFIEV

Sonata No. 1, in f, Op. 80 vln & pf
with N. Evrov pf   Harmonia Mundi (Balkanton)
                                         HMB102

Sonata No. 2, in D, Op. 94 bis vln & pf
with N. Evrov pf   Harmonia Mundi (Balkanton)
                                         HMB102

Israel BAKER (1919–   )

ANTHEIL

Sonata No. 2 (1947) vln & pf
with Y. Menuhin pf   Music Library MLR8–12,
                                         MLR7006

BERG

Chamber Concerto (1925) vln, pf & 13 w–wnds
with P. Kaufman pf & Wind   CBS BRG72027, SBRG72027
Ensemble – Kraft   Columbia ML5687,
                                         (in set M2L271), MS6287,
                                         (in set M2S620)

BRAHMS

Sextet No. 2, in G, Op. 36 2 vlns, 2 vlas & 2 vlcs
with J. Heifetz vln, W. Primrose, vla,   Victor (in sets LD6159 &
V. Majewski vla, G. Piatigorsky vlc &   LDS6159)
G. Rejto vlc

DUKE

Etude (1931) vln & bsn
with D. Christlieb bsn   Contemporary C6007, 8007
Sonata in D (1949) vln & pf
with V. Duke pf   Contemporary C6007, 8007

DVOŘÁK

Quintet in A, Op. 81 pf, 2 vlns, vla & vlc
with J. Lateiner pf, J. Heifetz vln,   Victor LM2985, LSC2985
J. De Pasquale vla & G. Piatigorsky
vlc

FRANCK

Quintet in f (1878/9) pf, 2 vlns, vla & vlc
with L. Pennario pf, J. Heifetz vln,   Victor (in sets LD6159 &
W. Primrose vla & G. Piatigorsky vlc   LDS6159)

LEKEU

Trio in c (1891) pf, vln & vlc
with N. Ryshna pf & A. Kaproff vlc   Society for Forgotten Music
                                         7023, SFM1004

MENDELSSOHN

Octet in E flat, Op. 20 4 vlns, 2 vlas & 2 vlcs
with J. Heifetz vln, A. Belnick vln,   Victor (in sets LD6159 &
J. Stepansky vln, W. Primrose vla,   LDS6159)
V. Majewski vla, G. Piatigorsky vlc &
G. Rejto vlc

MOZART

Quintet in C, K515 2 vlns, 2 vlas & vlc
with J. Heifetz vln, W. Primrose vla,   Victor LSC3048
V. Majewski vla & G. Piatigorsky vlc

Quintet in c, K516 2 vlns, 2 vlas & vlc
with J. Heifetz vln, W. Primrose vla,   Victor (in sets LD6159 &
V. Majewski vla & G. Piatigorsky vlc   LDS6159)

SCHOENBERG

Concerto, Op. 36 (1936) vln & orch.
with CBC Symphony Orch. – Craft   CBS SBRG72119
                                         Columbia ML5812,
                                         (in set M2L279), ML6439,
                                         MS6412, (in set M2S679),
                                         MS7039

Fantasy, Op. 47 (1949) vln & pf
with G. Gould pf   CBS 77220
                                         Columbia ML6436,
                                         (in set M2L367), MS7036,
                                         (in set M2S767)

Suite, Op. 29 (1927) pic, cl, bs–cl, vln, vla, vlc & pf
with G. Johnston pic, H. Raimondi cl,   Columbia ML5099
W. Ulyate bs–cl, S. Figelski vla,   Philips A01499L, ABL3397
G. Neikrug vlc, L. Stein pf – cond.
R. Craft

SCHUBERT

Quintet in C, Op. 163 (D. 956) 2 vlns, vla & 2 vlcs
with J. Heifetz vln, W. Primrose vla,   Victor (in sets LD6159 &
G. Piatigorsky vlc & G. Rejto vlc   LDS6159)

STRAVINSKY

Double Canon (1939) 2 vlns, vla & vlc
with O. Igleman vln, S. Schonbach vla,   CBS BRG72007, SBRG72007
G. Neikrug vlc, cond. Igor Stravinsky   Columbia ML5672, MS6272

(L') Histoire du Soldat (1918) narrators & tpt, cbs, tbn, cl, vln, bsn & pcn
with C. Brady tpt, R. Kelley cbs,   CBS BRG72007, SBRG72007
R. Marsteller tbn, R. d'Antonio cl,   Columbia ML5672, ML6493,
D. Christlieb bsn, W. Kraft pcn –   MS6272, MS7093
cond. Igor Stravinsky

In Memoriam Dylan Thomas (1954) t, 4 tbns, 2 vlns, vla & vlc
with R. Robinson t, L. Ulyate tbn,   Columbia ML5107
H. Bohannon tbn, F. Howard tbn,   Philips A01493L, ABL3391
S. Zeldin tbn, S. Babitz vln, C. Figelski
vla, G. Neikrug vlc – cond. Igor
Stravinsky

(3) Japanese Lyrics (1913) s, 2 fls, 2 cls, 2 vlns, vla, vlc & pf
with M. Nixon s, A. Gleghorn fl,   Columbia ML5107
A. Hoberman fl, H. Raimondi cl,   Philips A01493L, ABL3391
W. Ulyate cl, D. Albert vln, C.
Figelski vla, H. Coff vlc, S. Boyes pf –
cond. Igor Stravinsky

(2) Poems of Balmont (1911) s, 2 fls, 2 cls, 2 vlns, vla, vlc & pf
with M. Nixon s, A. Gleghorn fl,   Columbia ML5107
A. Hoberman fl, H. Raimondi cl,   Philips A01493L, ABL3391
W. Ulyate cl, D. Albert vln, C.
Figelski vla, H. Coff vlc, S. Boyes pf –
cond. Igor Stravinsky

VILLA–LOBOS

Chôros No. 7 (1924) fl, ob, cl, sax, bsn, vln & vlc
with H. Lewis fl, B. Gassman ob,   Capitol CTL7014
K. Bloch cl, J. Krechter sax, F. Moritz
bsn, G. Neikrug vlc, B. Mattinson
tam–tam – cond. W. Janssen

VIOTTI

(3) Quartets, Op. 22 fl & vln or 2 vlns, vla & vlc
No. 1. Quartet No. 1, in B flat
with A. Belnick vln, A. Neiman vla &   Society for Forgotten Music
A. Kaproff vlc   SFM1006
No. 3. Quartet No. 3, in c
with A. Belnick vln, A. Neiman vla &   Society for Forgotten Music
A. Kaproff vlc   SFM1006

ZEISL

Sonata (1949) "Brandeis" vln & pf
with Y. Menuhin pf   Society for Participating Artists
SPA10

Simon BAKMAN (1910–)

BRAHMS

Sonata (1853) "Frei aber Einsam" vln & pf
Allegro (Scherzo) in c (3rd mvt) "Sonatensatz"
with I. Karr pf   Golden Music Society GMS1201

DIETRICH

Sonata (1853) "Frei aber einsam" vln & pf
Allegro in a (1st mvt)
with I. Karr pf   Golden Music Society GMS1201

GEMINIANI

Introduction & Allegro vln & c – arr. vln & pf Corti
with I. Karr pf   Decca K28289

HINDEMITH

Nobilissima Visione (1938) – ballet orch.
Méditation arr. vln & pf
with I. Karr pf   Golden Music Society GMS1201

REGER

Suite in F, Op. 93 "Im alten stil" vln & pf
Prelude (1st mvt); **Largo** (2nd mvt)
with I. Karr pf   Golden Music Society GMS1201

SCHUMANN

Sonata (1853) "Frei aber einsam" vln & pf
Intermezzo (2nd mvt); **Finale** (4th mvt)
with I. Karr pf   Golden Music Society GMS1201

Zenon BAKOWSKI

VIVALDI

(12) Concerti, Op. 3 "L'Estro armonico" var. cbns & strs
Concerto No. 10, in b, P.148 (F. IV, No. 10) 4 vlns, strs & c
with I. Iwanow vln, E. Komosiński   Muza XL0504
vln, L. Radek vln, J. Dobrzański hpsi
& Warsaw Chamber
Orch. – Sutkowski

Jan BALACHOWSKI

BEETHOVEN

Concerto in D, Op. 61 (cadenzas by Joachim) vln & orch.*
with Berlin Symphony   Royale 1307
Orch. – Rubahn

Rae Eleanor BALL

ABBOTT

Wonderland of dreams v & pf – arr. vln & pf Ball
with J.L. Deppen pf   8232   Edison cylinder 4457
Edison Diamond Disc 50857

ANONYMOUS

Drink to me only with thine eyes (1762) traditional – arr. vln & pf Johnson
with piano   Victor 216477

BALL

Creole serenade vln & pf
with J.F. Burckhardt pf   8602   Edison cylinder 4715
Edison Diamond Disc 51050

Rufus on the Old Kent Road vln & pf
with piano   Edison Diamond Disc 51245

BARTLETT

(A) Dream (1895) v & pf – arr. vln & pf Ball
with piano   Victor 216364

* Rondo or 3rd mvt is also on Royale 1314

BEETHOVEN

(6) Minuets, G167 pf
  No. 2. Minuet No. 2, in G arr. vln & pf Burmester
  with H. Miro pf   Victor 216364

BERLIN

Always (1925) v & pf – arr. vln & pf
  with piano   Edison Diamond Disc 51708
Remember (1925) v & pf – arr. vln & pf
  with piano   Edison Diamond Disc 51708
What'll I do? (1924) v & pf – arr. vln & pf
  with piano   Edison Diamond Disc 51410

CONNOR

Rose of love v & pf – arr. vln & pf
  with piano   Edison Diamond Disc 51410

CONRAD

Lonesome & sorry (1926) v & pf – arr. vln & pf
  with J.F. Burckhardt pf   11141 Edison cylinder 5221
                              Edison Diamond Disc 51808

DRDLA

Souvenir vln & pf
  with H. Miro pf   Victor 216358, 216508

DRIGO

(2) Airs de Ballet orch.
  No. 2. Valse bluette arr. vln & pf Auer
  with piano   Victor 216469

DVOŘÁK

(8) Humoresques, Op. 101 pf
  No. 7. Humoresque No. 7, in G flat arr. vln & pf "in G" Kreisler
  with piano   Victor 216489

FISHER

Oh! how I miss you to–night v & pf – arr. vln & pf
  with piano   Edison Diamond Disc 51602

de FREYNE

Where the lazy Mississippi flows v & pf – arr. vln & pf
  with piano   Pathé 1500

GARDNER

(2) Pieces, Op. 5 vln & pf
  No. 1. From the canebrake
  with piano   Pathé 1500

GARREN

Just a girl that men forget v & pf – arr. vln & pf
  with piano   Edison Diamond Disc 51245

GLOGAU

Moonlight lane v & pf – arr. vln & pf
  with J.F. Burckhardt pf   18035 Edison Diamond Disc 52146

GREENE

Sing me to sleep v & pf –arr. vln & pf Ball
  with H. Miro pf   Victor 216364

HERBERT

(The) Fortune Teller (1898) – operetta
  Gypsy love song arr. vln & pf
  with piano   10927 Edison Diamond Disc 51742
  Gypsy love song arr. vln & pf
  with H. Maurice Jacquet pf   Victor 216403, 216509

LEONARD

Iyone, my own Iyone v & pf – arr. vln & pf
  with J.F. Burckhardt pf   11140 Edison Diamond Disc 51808

LEVY

That naughty waltz (1920) v & pf – arr. vln & pf
  with R. Gayler pf   7500 Edison Diamond Disc 50703

MacDOWELL

Woodland Sketches, Op. 51 pf
  No. 1. To a wild rose arr. v, vln & pf
  with R. Green s & piano   Victor 216468

MAGINE

Venetian moon v & pf – arr. vln & pf
  with R. Gayler pf   7501 Edison cylinder 4160
                          Edison Diamond Disc 50703

MASSENET

Élégie v & pf – arr. vln & pf
  with piano   Victor 216418
Thaïs (1894) – opera
  Méditation arr. vln & pf Marsick
  with H. Miro pf   Victor 216358, 216508

MATTULLATH

Cradle song (1915) v & pf – arr. v, vln & pf
  with R. Green s & piano   Victor 216468

MENDELSSOHN

(6) Gesänge, Op. 34 v & pf
  No. 2. Auf Flügeln des Gesanges arr. vln & pf Achron
  with piano   Victor 216425
(6) Songs without words Op. 62 pf
  No. 6. Song without words No. 30, in A "Spring song" arr. vln & pf
  with piano   N 69325 Pathé–Actuelle 10167

PANELLA

Carolina lullaby vln & pf
  with J.L. Deppen pf   8023 Edison cylinder 4440
                        Edison Diamond Disc 50816

ROMBERG

Blossom Time (1921) – operetta
  Song of love arr. vln & pf
  with H. Maurice Jacquet pf   Victor 216403, 216509

ROSE

Underneath Hawaiian skies v & pf – arr. vln & pf
  with J.L. Deppen pf   8022 Edison Diamond Disc 50816

RUBINSTEIN

(2) Melodies, Op. 3 pf
  No. 1. Melody in F arr. vln & pf Wilhelmj
  with piano   Victor 216418

RUBINSTEIN – *Continued*

No. 1. Melody in F arr. vln & pf Wilhelmj
with piano   N 69324   Pathé–Actuelle 10167

RUPP

Arizona stars v & pf – arr. vln & pf
with J.F. Burckhardt pf   9410   Edison Diamond Disc 51319

Just an ivy–covered shack v & pf – arr. vln & pf
with piano   Victor 216510

SAINT–SAËNS

Samson et Dalila, Op. 47 (1877) – opera
  Mon coeur s'ouvre à ta voix arr. vln & pf
  with piano   Victor 216467

SARASATE

Caprice basque, Op. 24 vln & pf
with piano   Victor 216474

SCHUBERT

(7) Gesänge (set to Scott's "Lady of the Lake") Op. 52 v & pf
  No. 6. Ave Maria, D839 arr. vln & pf Wilhelmj
  with piano   Victor 216425

SMITH

Havana moon v & pf – arr. vln & pf
with J.L. Deppen pf   8233   Edison cylinder 4482
                   Edison Diamond Disc 50857

de SYLVA

Arcady v & pf – arr. vln & pf
with J.F. Burckhardt pf   Edison Diamond Disc 51319

THOMÉ

Simple aveu, Op. 25 pf – arr. vln & pf
with piano   Victor 216474

WESTPHAL

Broken dreams v & pf – arr. vln & pf
with piano   Edison Diamond Disc 51602

WHITING

Song of Persia v & pf – arr. vln & pf
with J.F. Burckhardt pf   8601   Edison Diamond Disc 51050

WILHITE

Yesterday v & pf – arr. vln & pf
with J.F. Burckhardt pf   18036   Edison Diamond Disc 52146

WOOD

Roses of Picardy (1916) v & pf – arr. vln & pf
with piano   Victor 216477, 216510

Zlatko BALOKOVIĆ (1895–1965)

BACH

(6) Sonatas, BWV1014/9 vln & clav
  Sonata No. 1, in b, BWV1014
  with J. Murai pf   Jugoton LPY80

  Sonata No. 3, in E, BWV1016
  with J. Murai pf   Jugoton LPYV74

CHAUSSON

Poème, Op. 25 vln & orch. arr. vln & pf
with J. Murai pf   Jugoton LPYV74

SLAVENSKI

Sonata, Op. 5 vln & pf
with J. Murai pf   Jugoton LPY80

SMETANA

From my Homeland (1878) vln & pf
with J. Murai pf   Jugoton LPYV74

Gabriel BANAT

BARTOK

Sonata No. 2 (1922) vln & pf
with B. Smith pf   Cutty Wren CWR102

Sonata in g (1944) solo vln
(unaccompanied)   Cutty Wren CWR102

LEWIS

Toccata (1963) vln & pcn
with S. Goodman timp & pcn &   Composers Recordings CRI263
W. Rosenberger pcn

MIMAROGLU

Music plus one (1970) vln & electromagnetic tape
with electronic equipment   Turnabout TV34429

PAGANINI

Concerto No. 2, in b, Op. 7 vln & orch.
  Ronde à clochette (3rd mvt) "La Campanella" arr. vln & pf Kreisler
  with G. Parsons pf   Decca CEP5529, SEC5529

PENDERECKI

Miniatury (1959) vln & pf
with piano   Turnabout TV34429

RAVEL

Berceuse sur le nom de Gabriel Fauré (1922) vln & pf
with G. Parsons pf   Decca CEP5529, SEC5529

SARASATE

(8) Danzas españolas vln & pf
  No. 2. Habañera, Op. 21, No. 2
  with G. Parsons pf   Decca CEP5529, SEC5529

  No. 6. Zapateado, Op. 23, No. 2
  with G. Parsons pf   Decca CEP5529, SEC5529

Michael BANNER (1868–   )

BANNER

Fantasia (on themes by Léonard & Paganini) vln & pf
with piano   Edison cylinder 373

Nora Duesberg BARANOWSKI (1895–   )

AULIN

(4) Aquarelles vln & pf
No. 3. Vaggsång
with W. Baranowski pf   BS 2762–I   HMV X2912

(3) Gottländische Tänze, Op. 28 vln pf*
with W. Baranowski pf   BS 2763–II   HMV X2912

HENRIQUES

(4) Songs, Op. 3 v & pf
No. 4. Agnetes Vuggevise arr. vln & pf Henriques
with W. Baranowski pf   Sto 2891   Odeon A162505, D1013

SJÖGREN

Sonata No. 1, in g, op. 19 vln & pf
Andantino (2nd mvt)
with W. Baranowski pf   CS 2764–II   HMV Z186
Sonata No. 2, in e, Op. 24 vln & pf
Andante sostenuto (2nd mvt)
with W. Baranowski pf   CS 2765–II   HMV Z186

TCHAIKOVSKY

Souvenir d'un lieu cher, Op. 42 vln & pf
No. 3. Mélodie
with W. Baranowski pf   Sto 2890   Odeon A162505, D1013

Renato de BARBIERI (1920–   )

ACHRON

Hebrew melody, Op. 33 vln & pf – arr. Auer
with G. Guastalla pf   2BA 7185□ 2   HMV DB11326

Hebrew melody, Op. 33 vln & pf – arr. Auer
with T. Macoggi pf   HMV QCLP12023

BEETHOVEN

Sonata No. 9, in A, Op. 47 "Kreutzer" vln & pf
with T. Macoggi pf   HMV QCLP12022

BRUCH

Kol Nidrei, Op. 47 vlc or vln & orch.
with G. Guastalla pf   HMV S10518

CASTELNUOVO–TEDESCO

Alt–Wien (Rhapsody) (1923) pf
No. 1. Valse arr. vln & pf Corti
with T. Macoggi pf   HMV QCLP12023

DINICU

Hora staccato (1906) vln & pf – arr. Heifetz
with T. Macoggi pf   HMV QCLP12023

DVOŘÁK

(8) Slavonic Dances, Op. 72 pf duet; orch.
No. 8. Slavonic dance No. 16, in A flat arr. vln & pf "in G" Kreisler
with G. Guastalla pf   2BA 7184□ 2   HMV DB11326

* It is not known which of the three dances is on this recording.

DVOŘÁK – *Continued*

(8) Waltzes, Op. 54 pf
No. 1. Waltz No. 1, in D flat arr. vln & pf Příhoda
with G. Guastalla pf   HMV AW340

ELGAR

(La) Capricieuse, Op. 17 vln & pf
with T. Macoggi pf   HMV QCLP12023

FALLA

(7) Canciones populares españolas (1914) v & pf
No. 4. Jota arr. vln & pf Kochański
with G. Guastalla pf   OBA 7187   HMV DA11317

GRIEG

Sonata No. 3, in c, Op. 45 vln & pf
with G. Guastalla pf   HMV S10529/31

HUBAY

(6) Blumenleben, Op. 30 vln & pf
No. 5. Der Zephir
with G. Guastalla pf   HMV S10518

KREISLER

Schön Rosmarin vln & pf
with G. Guastalla pf   OBA 7181□ 2   HMV DA11313

MENDELSSOHN

(6) Gesänge, Op. 34 v & pf
No. 2. Auf Flügeln des Gesanges arr. vln & pf Achron
with G. Guastalla pf   2BA 7190□ 2   HMV DB11325

MOSZKOWSKI

(2) Stücke, Op. 45 pf
No. 2. Guitarre arr. vln & pf Sarasate
with T. Macoggi pf   HMV QCLP12023

NEGLIA

Capriccio–valse, Op. 19b vln & pf
with G. Guastalla pf   HMV AW342
Intermezzo, Op. 19a vln & pf
with G. Guastalla pf   HMV AW342

NOVAČÉK

(8) Concert caprices, Op. 5 vln & pf
No. 4. Perpetuum mobile
with G. Guastalla pf   2BA 7189□   HMV DB11325
No. 4 Perpetuum mobile
with T. Macoggi pf   HMV QCLP12023

PAGANINI

(24) Caprices, Op. 1 (1801/7) solo vln
Caprice No. 13, in B flat arr. vln & pf Kreisler
with G. Guastalla pf   HMV HN2353
Caprice No. 13, in B flat
(unaccompanied)   OBA 7619–3□   HMV DA11326
Caprice No. 14, in E flat
(unaccompanied)   OBA 7620□   HMV DA11326
Caprice No. 15, in A
(unaccompanied)   OBA 7621□   HMV DA11327

PAGANINI – *Continued*

Caprice No. 16, in a
(unaccompanied)   OBA 7622☐   HMV DA11327

Caprice No. 17, in E flat
(unaccompanied)   OBA 7623–2☐   HMV DA11328

Caprice No. 18, in C
(unaccompanied)   OBA 7624–3☐   HMV DA11328

Caprice No. 19, in E flat
(unaccompanied)   OBA 7625☐   HMV DA11329

Caprice No. 20, in D arr. vln & pf Kreisler
with G. Guastalla pf   HMV HN2353

Caprice No. 20, in D
(unaccompanied)   OBA 7626☐   HMV DA11329

Caprice No. 21, in A
(unaccompanied)   OBA 7627☐   HMV DA11330

Caprice No. 22, in F
(unaccompanied)   OBA 7628☐   HMV DA11330

Caprice No. 23, in E flat
(unaccompanied)   OBA 7630–2☐   HMV DA11331

Caprice No. 24, in a
(unaccompanied)   OBA 7629–3☐   HMV DA11331

(6) Sonatas, Op. 3 (1801/6) vln & gtr
No. 6. Sonata No. 12, in e arr. vln & pf
with G. Guastalla pf   HMV AW339

(Le) Streghe (variations on a theme from Süssmeyer's opera "Il Noce di Benevento") Op. 8 (1813) vln & orch. – arr. vln & pf Kreisler
with T. Macoggi pf   HMV QCLP12021

PARADIES

Sicilienne vln & pf – arr. Dushkin
with T. Macoggi pf   HMV QCLP12023

PRINCIPE

(El) Campielo (1932) vln & pf
with piano   2BA 5559   HMV AW341

PROKOFIEV

Sonata No. 1, in f, Op. 80 vln & pf
with T. Macoggi pf   HMV QCLP12021

RAVEL

Tzigane (Rapsodie de concert) (1924) vln & pf or orch.
with T. Macoggi pf   HMV QCLP12023

RIMSKY–KORSAKOV

Sadko (1898) – opera
Chant hindou arr. vln & pf Kreisler
with G. Guastalla pf   OBA 7188☐ 3   HMV DA11316

SAINT-SAËNS

(Le) Carnaval des animaux (1886) small orch.
Le cygne arr. vln & pf
with G. Guastalla pf   OBA 7182☐   HMV DA11313

Introduction & Rondo Capriccioso, Op. 28 vln & orch.
with T. Macoggi pf   HMV QCLP12021

SARASATE

(8) Danzas españolas vln & pf
No. 3. Romanza andaluza, Op. 22, No. 1
with G. Guastalla pf   HMV AW340

No. 6. Zapateado, Op. 23, No. 2
with G. Guastalla pf   OBA 7186☐ 3   HMV DA11317

SCHUBERT

(7) Gesänge (set to Scott's "Lady of the Lake") Op. 52 v & pf
No. 6. Ave Maria, D839 arr. vln & pf Wilhelmj
with piano   2BA 5558   HMV AW341

SCHUMANN

(13) Kinderscenen, Op. 15 pf
No. 7. Träumerei arr. vln & pf
with T. Macoggi pf   HMV QCLP12023

TARTINI

Sonata in g "Il Trillo del Diavolo" vln & c – arr. vln & pf Barbieri
with G. Guastalla pf   HMV AW338/9

TCHAIKOVSKY

Souvenir d'un lieu cher, Op. 42 vln & pf
No. 3. Mélodie arr. Wilhelmj
with G. Guastalla pf   OBA 7183☐ 2   HMV DA11316

WIENIAWSKI

Polonaise brillante No. 1, in D, Op. 4 vln & pf
with T. Macoggi pf   HMV QCLP12021

Luiz BARBOSA*

BARBOSA

Romance vln & pf
with piano   Polydor 67500

BAZZINI

(La) Ronde des lutins, Op. 25 vln & pf
with piano   Polydor 67500

COLAÇO

Um fado pf – arr. vln & pf
with piano   Polydor 49030

KIEL

Guitarra vln & pf
with piano   Polydor 49030

KREISLER

Andantino (Padre Martini) vln & pf
with piano   Polydor 47500

Praeludium & Allegro (Pugnani) vln & pf
with piano   Polydor 49022

Sicilienne & Rigaudon (Francoeur) vln & pf
with piano   Polydor 49024

* Barbosa also plays obbligato in several lighter works to the singing of Elsa Penchi Levy & Ruy Guedes. these are Pathé 42192 & 44152.

MONTI

Csárdas (1904) vln & pf
  with piano   Polydor 42227

NACHÈZ

(4) Danses Tziganes, Op. 14 vln & pf
  No. 1. Danse Tzigane No. 1, in a
  with piano   Polydor 49026

  No. 2. Danse Tzigane No. 2, in G
  with piano   Polydor 49026

REHFELD

(2) Konzertstücke, Op. 58 vln & pf
  No. 1. Spanish dance
  with piano   Polydor 47500

RIES

Suite No. 3, in G, Op. 34 vln & pf
  No. 5. Perpetuum mobile
  with piano   Polydor 42227

SCHUBERT, François

(12) Bagatelles, Op. 13 vln & pf
  No. 9. L'abeille
  with piano   Polydor 67500

TIRINDELLI

(6) Morceaux de concert, Op. 1 vln & pf
  No. 6. Pasquinade
  with piano   Polydor 49024

Stanislav BARCEWICZ (1858–1929)

DRIGO

(2) Airs de Ballet orch.
  No. 2. Valse bluette arr. vln & pf Auer
  with piano   Favorite 1–74544D

GLINKA

Farewell to Petersburg (1840) – 12 songs v & pf
  No. 10. The lark arr. vln, vlc & pf
  with E. Kochański vlc & W. Eszyk pf   Favorite 1–74564D

GODARD

Jocelyn (1888) – opera
  Cachés dans cet asile "Berceuse" arr. vln & pf
  with piano   Favorite 1–74545D

HUBAY

(14) Scènes de la Csárda vln & pf
  No. 4. Hejre Kati, Op. 32
  with piano   Favorite 1–74577D

KONTSKI

Mazurka No. 1, Op. 7 vln & pf
  with piano   Favorite 1–74567D

MASSENET

Thaïs (1894) – opera
  Méditation arr. vln & pf Marsick
  with piano   Favorite 1–74572D

MOSZKOWSKI

(5) Danzas españolas, Op. 12 pf – 4 hands
  No. 5. Danza española No. 5, in D arr. vln, vlc & pf
  with E. Kochański vlc & W. Eszyk pf   Favorite 1–74565D

PADEREWSKI

(7) Miscellanea, Op. 16 pf
  No. 2. Mélodie arr. vln & pf Barcewicz
  with L. Urstein pf   Gramophone & Typewriter
                         27942

(7) Miscellanea, Op. 16 pf
  No. 2. Mélodie arr. vln & pf Barcewicz
  with piano   Favorite 1–74566D

SARASATE

Faust Fantasia (on themes from the opera by Gounod) vln & pf or orch.*
  with piano   Favorite 1–74574D

Zigeunerweisen, Op. 20 vln & pf or orch.*
  with piano   Favorite 1–74573D

TCHAIKOVSKY

Concerto in D, Op. 35 vln & orch.
  Canzonetta (2nd mvt) arr. vln & pf
  with L. Urstein pf   Gramophone & Typewriter
                         27941

WIENIAWSKI

Mazurka in a, Op. 3 "Kujawiak" vln & pf
  with L. Urstein pf   Gramophone & Typewriter
                         27945

Reinhold BARCHET (1920–1962)

BACH, J.C.

Quintet in F, T. P311 (?1785) fl, ob, vla, vlc & hpsi
  with G. Lemmen vla,   Music Guild M14, MG104,
  H. Münch–Holland vlc,   MS104, S14
  H. Winschermann ob & I. Lechner
  hpsi

BACH, J.C.F.

Sextet in C 2 hrns, ob, vln, vlc & hpsi
  with M. Oheim hrn, O. Wunder hrn,   Music Guild M14, MG104,
  H. Winschermann ob,   MS104, S14
  H. Münch–Holland vlc & I. Lechner
  hpsi

BACH, J.S.

(6) Brandenburg Concerti, BWV1046/51 (1721) strs & c
Brandenburg Concerto No. 1, in F, BWV1046 vln, 3 obs, bsn, 2 hrns & strs
  with P. Valentin ob, H. Helaerts bsn,   Ace of Clubs ACL68
  E. Leloir hrn, A. Galetti hrn,   Decca LXT2540, LXT5198
  G. Vaucher–Clerc hpsi & Stuttgart   London CMA7211,
  Chamber Orch. – Münchinger   (in set CSA2301)

* Abridged.

BACH, J.S. – *Continued*

Brandenburg Concerto No. 1, in F, BWV1046 vln, 3 obs, bsn, 2 hrns & strs
with H. Schneider ob, M. Linder ob,   Eurodisc (in set S70107XK)
F. Strowitzky ob, H. Müller bsn,   Europa E170
K. Arnold hrn, W. Büttner hrn &   Marble Arch (in set MAL669)
Southwest German Chamber   Victor (in sets LM7038 &
Orch. – Tilegant   LSC7038)

Brandenburg Concerto No. 1, in F, BWV1046 vln, 3 obs, bsn, 2 hrns & strs
with P. Pierlot ob, L. Seifert ob,   Erato EFM8106, LDE3229,
W. Grimm ob, K. Richter hrn,   STE50129, STU70129
W. Beck hrn, K. Kolbinger bsn,
R. Veyron–Lacroix hpsi & Pro Arte
Chamber Orch., Munich – Redel

Brandenburg Concerto No. 2, in F, BWV1047 tpt, fl, ob, vln & strs
with P. Longinotti tpt, A. Pépin fl,   Ace of Clubs ACL69
P. Valentin ob, G. Vaucher–Clerc hpsi   Decca AWD8509, CEP559,
& Stuttgart Chamber   LX3029, LXT5199
Orch. – Münchinger   London CMA7211,
   (in set CSA2301)

Brandenburg Concerto No. 2, in F, BWV1047 tpt, fl, ob, vln & strs
with A. Scherbaum tpt, K. Redel fl,   Erato LDE3034
P. Pierlot ob, H. Priegnitz hpsi & Pro
Arte Chamber Orch., Munich – Redel

Brandenburg Concerto No. 2, in F, BWV1047 tpt, fl, ob, vln & strs
with W. Gleissle tpt, K.T. Dilloo fl,   Eurodisc (in set S70107XK)
H. Schneider ob & Southwest German   Europa E170
Chamber Orch. – Tilegant   Marble Arch (in set MAL669)
   Victor (in sets LM7038 &
   LSC7038)

Brandenburg Concerto No. 2, in F, BWV1047 tpt, fl, ob, vln & strs
with M. André tpt, K. Redel fl,   Erato EFM8106, LDE3229,
P. Pierlot ob, R. Veyron–Lacroix hpsi   STE50129, STU70129
& Pro Arte Chamber Orch., Munich –
Redel

Brandenburg Concerto No. 4, in G, BWV1049 vln, 2 fls & strs
with A. Pépin fl, A. Roy fl,   Ace of Clubs ACL69
G. Vaucher–Clerc hpsi–c & Stuttgart   Decca AX319/20, K23001/2,
Chamber Orch. – Münchinger   K28254/5, LXT2501, LXT5199
   London CMA7211,
   (in set CSA2301), LL144

Brandenburg Concerto No. 4, in G, BWV1049 vln, 2 fls & strs
with K. Redel fl, W. Schwegler fl,   Erato LDE3034
H. Priegnitz hpsi & Pro Arte Chamber
Orch., Munich – Redel

Brandenburg Concerto No. 4, in G, BWV1049 vln, 2 fls & strs
with K.T. Dilloo fl, H. Strebel fl &   Eurodisc (in set S70107XK)
Southwest German Chamber   Europa E171
Orch. – Tilegant   Marble Arch (in set MAL669)
   Victor (in sets LM7038 &
   LSC7038)

Brandenburg Concerto no. 4, in G, BWV1049 vln, 2 fls & strs
with K Redel fl, P. Meisen fl,   Erato EFM8017, LDE3230,
R. Veyron–Lacroix hpsi & Pro Arte   STE50130, STU70130
Chamber Orch., Munich – Redel

Brandenburg Concerto No. 5, in D, BWV1050 clav, fl, vln & strs
with A. Pépin fl, H. Vaucher–Clerc   Ace of Clubs ACL69
hpsi & Stuttgart Chamber   Decca LXT2540, LXT5199
Orch. – Münchinger   London CMA7211
   (in set CSA2301)

BACH, J.S. – *Continued*

Brandenburg Concerto No. 5, in D, BWV1050 clav, fl, vln & strs
with K. Redel fl, H. Priegnitz hpsi &   Erato LDE3034
Pro Arte Chamber Orch.,
Munich – Redel

Brandenburg Concerto No. 5, in D, BWV1050 clav, fl, vln & strs
with H. Werdermann hpsi, K.T. Dilloo   Eurodisc (in set S70107XK)
fl & Southwest German Chamber   Europa E171
Orch. – Tilegant   Marble Arch (in set MAL669)
   Victor (in sets LM7038 &
   LSC7038)

Brandenburg Concerto No. 5, in D, BWV1050 clav, fl, vln & strs
with R. Veyron–Lacroix hpsi,   Erato EFM8017, LDE3230,
K. Redel fl & Pro Arte Chamber   STE50130, STU70130
Orch., Munich – Redel

Cantata No. 21 (Ich hatte viel Bekümmernis) BWV21
with E. Selig s, G. Jelden t, E. Wenk   Christophorus CGLP75760
bs, R. Wehrle ob, J. Muckel vlc,   Columbia SMC95151
E. Holderlin org, – The Heinrich   Erato LDE3227, STE50127,
Schütz Chorale of Heilbronn & the   STU70127
Pforzheim Chamber Orch. – Werner

Cantata No. 43 (Gott faehret auf mit Jauchzen) BWV43
with F. Sailer s, C. Hellmann a,   Christophorus CGLP75765
H. Krebs t, E. Wenk bs, J. Stämpfli bs,   Columbia SMC95150
H. Strebel rec, P. Pierlot ob,   Erato STU70087
J. Chambon ob, P. Hongne bsn,   Musical Heritage Society
W. Gleissle tpt, – The Heinrich Schütz   MHS832
Chorale of Heilbronn & the Pforzheim
Chamber Orch. – Werner

Cantata No. 80 (Ein feste Burg ist unser Gott) BWV80
with I. Reichelt s, H. Töpper a,   Erato LDE3135, STE50043
H. Krebs t, F. Kelch bs, W. Gleissle
tpt, P. Pierlot ob, J. Chambon ob,
P. Hongne bsn, Heinrich Schütz
Chorale of Heilbronn & Pforzheim
Chamber Orch. – Werner

Cantata No. 85 (Ich bin ein guter Hirt) BWV85
with I. Reichelt s, H. Töpper a,   Electrola SME95156
H. Krebs t, F. Kelch bs, A. Wenzinger   Musical Heritage Society
vlc–picc, P. Pierlot ob, J. Chambon ob,   MHS823
P. Hongne bsn, M–C. Alain org,
M. Scheck–Wache hpsi, – The
Heinrich Schütz Chorale of Heilbronn
& the Pforzheim Chamber Orch. –
Werner

Cantata No. 87 (Bisher habt ihr nichts gebeten in meinem Namen) BWV87
with H. Töpper a, H. Krebs t,   Erato LDE3135, STE50043
F. Kelch bs, P. Pierlot ob, J. Chambon
ob, P. Hongne bsn, Heinrich Schütz
Chorale of Heilbronn & Pforzheim
Chamber Orch. – Werner

Cantata No. 130 (Herr Gott, dich loben alle wir) BWV130
with F. Sailer s, C. Hellmann a,   Erato LDE3205, STE50085,
H. Krebs t, J. Stämpfli bs, M. Larrieu   STU70085
fl, W. Gleissle tpt, E. Holderlin org,
J. Muckel vlc, Heinrich Schütz
Chorale of Heilbronn & Pforzheim
Chamber Orch. – Werner

BACH, J.S. – *Continued*

Cantata No. 140 (Wachet auf, ruft uns die Stimme) BWV140
  with I. Reichelt s, H. Töpper a,   Electrola SME95156
  H. Krebs t, F. Kelch bs, A. Wenzinger   Musical Heritage Society
  vlc–picc, P. Pierlot ob, J. Chambon ob, MHS823
  P. Hongne bsn, M–C. Alain org,
  M. Scheck–Wache hpsi, – The
  Heinrich Schütz Chorale of Heilbronn
  & the Pforzheim Chamber Orch. –
  Werner

Cantata No. 171 (Gott, wie dein Name, so ist dein Ruhm) BWV171
  with H. Wehrung s, E. Lisken a,   Cantate 641209, 651209
  G. Jelden t, J. Stämpfli bs, A.
  Scherbaum tpt, F. Milde ob & ob
  d'amore, T. von Schön cbs, –
  Southwest German Chamber Orch.,
  Pforzheim & Southwest German
  Madrigal Choir, Stuttgart –
  Gönnenwein

Cantata No. 182 (Himmelskönig, sei Willkommen) BWV182
  with C. Hellmann a, H. Krebs t,   Christophorus CGLP75765
  E. Wenk bs, H. Strebel rec, P. Pierlot Columbia SMC95150
  ob, J. Chambon ob, P. Hongne bsn,   Erato STU70087
  W. Gleissle tpt, – The Heinrich Schütz Musical Heritage Society
  Chorale of Heilbronn & the   MHS832
  Pforzheim Chamber Orch. – Werner

Concerto No. 1, in a, BWV1041 vln, strs & c
  with Pro Musica String Orch.,   Seven Seas SH5041
  Stuttgart – Davisson   Vox PL9150, (in set VBX25)

Concerto No. 1, in a, BWV1041 vln, strs & c
  with Southwest German Chamber   Ariola 11362K, 12332P
  Orch. – Tilegant   Qualiton BLP11462
                                          World Record Club T136

Concerto No. 2, in E, BWV1042 vln, strs & c
  with Pro Musica String Orch.,   Seven Seas SH5041
  Stuttgart – Davisson   Vox PL9150, (in set VBX25)

Concerto No. 2, in E, BWV1042 vln, strs & c
  with Southwest German Chamber   Ariola 11362K
  Orch. – Tilegant   Qualiton BLP11462
                                          World Record Club T136

Concerto in d, BWV1043 2 vlns, strs & c
  with W. Beh vln & Pro Musica String   Panthéon XPV1024
  Orch., Stuttgart – Davisson   Vox PL9150, (in set VBX25)

Concerto in d, BWV1043 2 vlns, strs & c
  with G. van der Mueren vln &
  Southwest German Chamber   Ariola 11362K
  Orch. – Tilegant   Qualiton BLP11462
                                          World Record Club T136

Concerto in a, BWV1044 fl, vln, clav, strs & c
  with K. Redel fl, H. Priegnitz hpsi &   Ducretet–Thomson 270C081
  Saite Symphony Orch. – Desarzens   Telefunken BLE14048

Concerto in c, BWV1060 vln, ob, strs & c
  with K. Kalmus ob & Pro Arte   Ducretet–Thomson 270C081
  Chamber Orch. – Redel   Telefunken TW30144

BACH, J.S. – *Continued*

Mass in b, BWV232 (1733/7) s, a, t, b, cho, strs & c
  with I. Reichelt s, E. Fellner s, R.   Erato LDE3073/5
  Gunther a, H. Krebs t, F. Kelch bs, P.
  Pierlot ob, J. Chambon ob d'amore, M.
  Larrieu fl, P. del Vescovo hrn, W.
  Gleissle tpt, – The Heinrich Schütz
  Chorale of Heilbronn, & Phorzheim
  Chamber Orch. – Werner

Mass in F, BWV233
  with A. Giebel s, F. Kelch bs, F.   Renaissance X44
  Milde ob, E. Hölderlin org, The
  Swabian Choral Singers, Stuttgart &
  Tonstudio Orch., Stuttgart – Grischkat

Matthaeus–Passion, BWV244 (1729)
  with A. Giebel s, R. Gunther a,   Erato LDE3101/4, STE50006/9
  H. Krebs t, F. Kelch bs, H.
  Werdermann bs, J–P. Rampal fl, M.
  Larrieu fl,
  P. Pierlot ob, J. Chambon ob d'amore,
  J. Chambon E–hrn, H. Strebel rec,
  G. Braun rec, J. Koch gamba,
  M–C. Alain org, – Boys Choir of the
  Robert–Mayer School, Heilbronn –
  Henrich Schütz Chorale, Heilbronn &
  Pforzheim Chamber Orch. – Werner

(Ein) Musikalisches Opfer, BWV1079 (1729) strs & c
  with G. Schmid vla, K. Redel fl,   Erato LDE3038
  R. Zartner hpsi, – soloists & Pro Arte
  Chamber Orch. – Redel

(6) Sonatas, BWV1014/9 vln & clav
Sonata No. 1, in b, BWV1014
  with R. Veyron–Lacroix hpsi   Columbia OS3310
                                         Erato LDE3169, STE50079,
                                         STU70079
                                         Musical Heritage Society
                                         MHS536

Sonata No. 2, in a, BWV1015
  with R. Veyron–Lacroix hpsi   Columbia OS3310
                                         Erato LDE3169, STE50079,
                                         STU70079
                                         Musical Heritage Society
                                         MHS536

Sonata No. 3, in E, BWV1016
  with R. Veyron–Lacroix hpsi   Columbia OS3310
                                         Erato LDE3169, STE50079,
                                         STU70079
                                         Musical Heritage Society
                                         MHS536

Sonata No. 4, in c, BWV1017
  with R. Veyron–Lacroix hpsi   Columbia OS3311
                                         Erato LDE3170, STE50080,
                                         STU70080
                                         Musical Heritage Society
                                         MHS563

Sonata No. 5, in f, BWV1018
  with R. Veyron–Lacroix hpsi   Columbia OS3311
                                         Erato LDE3170, STE50080,
                                         STU70080
                                         Musical Heritage Society
                                         MHS563

BACH, J.S. – *Continued*

Sonata No. 6, in G, BWV1019
with R. Veyron–Lacroix hpsi

Columbia OS3311
Erato LDE3170, STE50080,
STU70080
Musical Heritage Society
MHS563

Sonata in G, BWV1021 vln & c*
with R. Veyron–Lacroix hpsi &
J. Muckel vlc

Columbia OS3312
Erato LDE3189, STE50089
Musical Heritage Society
MHS628
World Record Club CM47,
SCM47

Sonata in F, BWV1022 vln & hpsi
with R. Veyron–Lacroix hpsi

Columbia OS3312
Erato LDE3189, STE50089
Musical Heritage Society
MHS628
World Record Club CM47,
SCM47

Sonata in e, BWV1023 vln & c*
with R. Veyron–Lacroix hpsi &
J. Muckel vlc

Columbia OS3312
Erato LDE3189, STE50089
Musical Heritage Society
MHS628
World Record Club CM47,
SCM47

Sonata in c, BWV1024 vln & c*
with R. Veyron–Lacroix hpsi &
J. Muckel vlc

Columbia OS3312
Erato LDE3189, STE50089
Musical Heritage Society
MHS628
World Record Club CM47,
SCM47

HANDEL

(6) Concerti, Op. 4 (1735/6) org, obs & strs
Concerto No. 3, in g
with W. Kraft org, S. Barchet vlc &　Vox PL7130
Pro Musica Chamber Orch.,
Stuttgart – Reinhardt

(12) Concerti grossi, Op. 6 (1739) 2 vlns, vlc & strs
Concerto grosso No. 1, in G
with S. Lautenbacher vln, M. Brun vlc,　Vox (in sets PL10043 &
R. Reinhardt hpsi & Pro Arte Orch.,　VBX22)
Munich – Redel

Concerto grosso No. 2, in F
with S. Lautenbacher vln, M. Brun vlc,　Vox (in sets PL10043 & VBX22)
R. Reinhardt hpsi & Pro Arte Orch.,
Munich – Redel

Concerto grosso No. 3, in c
with S. Lautenbacher vln, M. Brun vlc,　Vox (in sets PL10043 & VBX22)
R. Reinhardt hpsi & Pro Arte Orch.,
Munich – Redel

Concerto grosso No. 4, in a
with S. Lautenbacher vln, M. Brun vlc,　Vox (in sets PL10043 & VBX22)
R. Reinhardt hpsi & Pro Arte Orch.,
Munich – Redel

* Realization by Robert Veyron–Lacroix.

HANDEL – *Continued*

Concerto grosso No. 5, in D
with S. Lautenbacher vln, M. Brun vlc, Vox (in sets PL10043 & VBX22)
R. Reinhardt hpsi & Pro Arte Orch.,
Munich – Redel

Concerto grosso No. 6, in g
with S. Lautenbacher vln, M. Brun vlc, Vox (in sets PL10043 & VBX22)
R. Reinhardt hpsi & Pro Arte Orch.,
Munich – Redel

Concerto grosso No. 7, in B flat
with S. Lautenbacher vln, M. Brun vlc, Vox (in sets PL10043 & VBX22)
R. Reinhardt hpsi & Pro Arte Orch.,
Munich – Redel

Concerto grosso No. 8, in c
with S. Lautenbacher vln, M. Brun vlc, Vox (in sets PL10043 & VBX22)
R. Reinhardt hpsi & Pro Arte Orch.,
Munich – Redel

Concerto grosso No. 9, in F
with S. Lautenbacher vln, M. Brun vlc, Vox (in sets PL10043 & VBX22)
R. Reinhardt hpsi & Pro Arte Orch.,
Munich – Redel

Concerto grosso No. 10, in d
with S. Lautenbacher vln, M. Brun vlc, Vox (in sets PL10043 & VBX22)
R. Reinhardt hpsi & Pro Arte Orch.,
Munich – Redel

Concerto grosso No. 11, in A
with S. Lautenbacher vln, M. Brun vlc, Vox (in sets PL10043 & VBX22)
R. Reinhardt hpsi & Pro Arte Orch.,
Munich – Redel

Concerto grosso No. 12, in b
with S. Lautenbacher vln, M. Brun vlc, Vox (in sets PL10043 & VBX22)
R. Reinhardt hpsi & Pro Arte Orch.,
Munich – Redel

HAYDN

Concerto in F, H.XVIII, No. 6 (1765) clav, vln & orch.
with H. Elsner pf & Stuttgart Chamber Vox PL11130
Orch. – Reinhardt

Sinfonia concertante in B flat, Op. 84 (H.I, No. 105) ob, bsn, vln, vlc &
orch.
with F. Milde ob, H. Gehring bsn, S.　Festival CFR12–312
Barchet vlc & Pro Musica Chamber　Vox PL7390
Orch., Stuttgart – Reinhardt

MONTEVERDI

Vespers of the Blessed Virgin (1610) (ed. Redlich)
with M. Guilleaume s, F. Sailer s,　Vox (in sets PL7902 &
L. Wolf-Matthäus a, H. Marten t, W.　VUX2004)
Hohmann t, F. Kelch bs, – Swabian
Choral Society & Stuttgart Bach
Orch. – Grischkat

MOZART

Concerto No. 3, in G, K216 vln & orch.
with Pro Musica Orch.,　　　　　Vox PL10050
Stuttgart – Reinhardt

Concerto No. 4, in D, K218 (cadenzas by Joachim) vln & orch.
with Pro Musica Orch.,　　　　　Pathé–Vox PV250
Stuttgart – Reinhardt　　　　　　Vox PL7240

MOZART – *Continued*

Concerto No. 4, in D, K218 (cadenzas by Joachim) vln & orch.
  with Pro Musica Orch.,   Festival CFR12–82
  Stuttgart – Reinhardt   Vox PL10110

Concerto No. 5, in A, K219 "Turkish" vln & orch.
  with Pro Musica Orch.,   Vox GBY12070, PL10050
  Stuttgart – Reinhardt

Concerto No. 6, in E flat, K268 (cadenzas omitted) vln & orch.
  with Pro Musica Orch.,   Pathé–Vox PV250
  Stuttgart – Reinhardt   Vox PL7240

Concerto No. 6, in E flat, K268 (cadenzas omitted) vln & orch.
  with Pro Musica Orch.,   Festival CFR12–82
  Stuttgart – Reinhardt   Vox PL10110

Sinfonia concertante in E flat, K364 vln, vla & orch.
  with H. Kirchner vla & Pro Musica   Vox PL7320
  Orch., Stuttgart – Seegelken

NARDINI

Concerto in e vln & orch.
  with Südwestdeutsche Chamber   Ariola 13199
  Orch. – Tilegant

SCHUBERT

Nocturne in E flat, Op. 148 (D897) pf, vln & vlc
  with F. Wührer pf & H. Reimann vlc   Vox PL8970

TELEMANN

Suite in B flat, T.III, No. 1 2 obs, strs & c – arr. 2 vlns, ob, strs & c
  with S. Lautenbacher vln, F. Milde ob Vox PL10650
  & Südwestdeutsche Chamber
  Orch. – Zucca

TORELLI

(12) Concerti, Op. 8 (1709) 1/6: 2 vlns, strs & c – 7/12: vln, strs & c
  Concerto No. 1, in C
  with W. Beh vln, H. Elsner hpsi & Pro Vox (in set DL113)
  Musica Orch., Stuttgart – Reinhardt

  Concerto No. 2, in a
  with W. Beh vln, H. Elsner hpsi & Pro Vox (in set DL113)
  Musica Orch., Stuttgart – Reinhardt

  Concerto No. 3, in E
  with W. Beh vln, H. Elsner hpsi & Pro Vox (in set DL113)
  Musica Orch., Stuttgart – Reinhardt

  Concerto No. 4, in B flat
  with W. Beh vln, H. Elsner hpsi & Pro Vox (in set DL113)
  Musica Orch., Stuttgart – Reinhardt

  Concerto No. 5, in G
  with W. Beh vln, H. Elsner hpsi & Pro Vox (in set DL113)
  Musica Orch., Stuttgart – Reinhardt

  Concerto No. 6, in g "Christmas Concerto"
  with W. Beh vln, H. Elsner hpsi & Pro Vox (in set DL113)
  Musica Orch., Stuttgart – Reinhardt

  Concerto No. 7, in d
  with H. Elsner hpsi & Pro Musica   Vox (in set DL113)
  Orch., Stuttgart – Reinhardt

  Concerto No. 8, in c
  with H. Elsner hpsi & Pro Musica   Vox (in set DL113)
  Orch., Stuttgart – Reinhardt

TORELLI – *Continued*

  Concerto No. 9, in e
  with H. Elsner hpsi & Pro Musica   Vox (in set DL113)
  Orch., Stuttgart – Reinhardt

  Concerto No. 10, in A
  with H. Elsner hpsi & Pro Musica   Vox (in set DL113)
  Orch., Stuttgart – Reinhardt

  Concerto No. 11, in f
  with H. Elsner hpsi & Pro Musica   Vox (in set DL113)
  Orch., Stuttgart – Reinhardt

  Concerto No. 12, in D
  with H. Elsner hpsi & Pro Musica   Vox (in set DL113)
  Orch., Stuttgart – Reinhardt

VIVALDI

(12) Concerti, Op. 3 "L'Estro armonico" var. cbns & strs
  Concerto No. 1, in D, P.146 (F.IV, No. 7) 4 vlns, vlc, strs & c
  with A. Steffen–Wendling vln, H.   Pathé–Vox (in set PV273)
  Endres vln, F. Hopfner vln, S. Barchet Vox (in sets DL271, PL7243,
  vlc, H. Elsner hpsi & Pro Musica   PL7420 & VBX20)
  Orch., Stuttgart – Reinhardt

  Concerto No. 2, in g, P.326 (F.IV, No. 8) 2 vlns, strs & c
  with A. Steffen–Wendling vln, H.   Pathé–Vox (in set PV273)
  Elsner hpsi & Pro Musica Orch.,   Vox (in sets DL271, PL7243,
  Stuttgart – Reinhardt   PL7420 & VBX20)

  Concerto No. 3, in G, P.96 (F.I, No. 173) vln, strs & c
  with H. Elsner hpsi & Pro Musica   Pathé–Vox (in set PV273)
  Orch., Stuttgart – Reinhardt   Vox (in sets DL271, PL7243,
                       PL7420 & VBX20)

  Concerto No. 4, in e, P.97 (F.I, No. 174) 4 vlns, strs & c
  with A. Steffen–Wendling vln, H.   Pathé–Vox (in set PV273)
  Endres vln, F. Hopfner vln, H. Elsner Vox (in sets DL271, PL7243,
  hpsi & Pro Musica Orch.,   PL7420 & VBX20)
  Stuttgart – Reinhardt

  Concerto No. 5, in A, P.212 (F.I, No. 175) 2 vlns, strs & c
  with H. Endres vln, H. Elsner hpsi & Pathé–Vox (in set PV273)
  Pro Musica Orch.,   Vox (in sets DL271, PL7243,
  Stuttgart – Reinhardt   PL7420 & VBX20)

  Concerto No. 6, in a, P.1 (F.I, No. 176) vln, strs & c
  with H. Elsner hpsi & Pro Musica   Pathé–Vox (in set PV273)
  Orch., Stuttgart – Reinhardt   Vox (in sets DL271, PL7243,
                       PL7420 & VBX20)

  Concerto No. 7, in F, P.249 (F.IV, No. 9) 4 vlns, strs & c
  with A. Steffen–Wendling vln, H.   Pathé–Vox (in set PV273)
  Endres vln, F. Hopfner vln, H. Elsner Vox (in sets DL271, PL7243,
  hpsi & Pro Musica Orch.,   PL7420 & VBX20)
  Stuttgart – Reinhardt

  Concerto No. 8, in a, P.2 (F.I, No. 177) 2 vlns, strs & c
  with H. Endres vln, H. Elsner hpsi & Pathé–Vox (in set PV273)
  Pro Musica Orch., Stuttgart –   Vox (in sets DL271, PL7243,
  Reinhardt   PL7420 & VBX20)

  Concerto No. 9, in D, P.147 (F.I, No. 178) vln, strs & c*
  with H. Elsner hpsi & Pro Musica   Pathé–Vox (in set PV273)
  Orch., Stuttgart – Reinhardt   Vox (in sets DL271, PL7243,
                       PL7420 & VBX20)

* The allegro or 1st mvt is also on Turnabout TV34800 & Vox PL13010
  & STPL513010.

Concerto No. 10, in b, P.148 (F.IV, No. 10) 4 vlns, strs & c
with A. Steffen–Wendling vln, H.   Pathé–Vox (in set PV273)
Endres vln, F. Hopfner vln, H. Elsner   Vox (in sets DL271, PL7243,
hpsi & Pro Musica Orch.,   PL7420 & VBX20)
Stuttgart – Reinhardt

Concerto No. 11, in d, P.250 (F.IV, No. 11) 2 vlns, vlc, strs & c
with A. Steffen–Wendling vln, S.   Pathé–Vox (in set PV273)
Barchet vlc, H. Elsner hpsi & Pro   Vox (in sets DL271, PL7243,
Musica Orch., Stuttgart – Reinhardt   PL7420 & VBX20)

Concerto No. 12, in E, P.240 (F.I, No. 179) vln, strs & c
with H. Elsner hpsi & Pro Musica   Pathé–Vox (in set PV273)
Orch., Stuttgart – Reinhardt   Vox (in sets DL271, PL7243,
                                       PL7420 & VBX20)

(12) Concerti, Op. 4 "La Stravaganza" vln, strs & c
Concerto No. 1, in B flat, F.I, No. 180
with Pro Musica Orch.,   Vox (in sets DL103 & VBX31)
Stuttgart – Reinhardt

Concerto No. 2, in E, F.I, No. 181
with Pro Musica Orch.,   Vox (in sets DL103 &VBX31)
Stuttgart – Reinhardt

Concerto No. 3, in G, F.I, No. 182
with Pro Musica Orch.,   Vox (in sets DL103 & VBX31)
Stuttgart – Reinhardt

Concerto No. 4, in a, F.I, No. 183
with Pro Musica Orch.,   Vox (in sets DL103 & VBX31)
Stuttgart – Reinhardt

Concerto No. 5, in A, F.I, No. 184
with Pro Musica Orch.,   Vox (in sets DL103 & VBX31)
Stuttgart – Reinhardt

Concerto No. 6, in g, F.I, No. 185
with Pro Musica Orch.,   Vox (in sets DL103 & VBX31)
Stuttgart – Reinhardt

Concerto No. 7, in C, F.I, No. 186
with Pro Musica Orch.,   Vox (in sets DL103 & VBX31)
Stuttgart – Reinhardt

Concerto No. 8, in d, F.I, No. 187
with Pro Musica Orch.,   Vox (in sets DL103 & VBX31)
Stuttgart – Reinhardt

Concerto No. 9, in F, F.I, No. 188
with Pro Musica Orch.,   Vox (in sets DL103 & VBX31)
Stuttgart – Reinhardt

Concerto No. 10, in c, F.I, No. 189
with Pro Musica Orch.,   Vox (in sets DL103 & VBX31)
Stuttgart – Reinhardt

Concerto No. 11, in D, F.I, No. 190
with Pro Musica Orch.,   Vox (in sets DL103 & VBX31)
Stuttgart – Reinhardt

Concerto No. 12, in G, F.I, No. 191
with Pro Musica Orch.,   Vox (in sets DL103 & VBX31)
Stuttgart – Reinhardt

(12) Concerti, Op. 8 (1725) "Il Cimento dell' Armonia e dell' Invenzione"
(Nos. 1/4: Le quattro Stagioni) vln & strs
Concerto No. 1, in E, F.I, No. 22 "La Primavera"
with Stuttgart Chamber   Ace of Clubs ACL91
Orch., – Münchinger   Decca LXT2600, LXT5377
                               London LL386
                               Richmond R19056

Concerto No. 1, in E, F.I, No. 22 "La Primavera"
with Pro Musica Orch.,   Vox (in sets DL173 & VBX32)
Stuttgart – Reinhardt

Concerto No. 1, in E, F.I, No. 22 "La Primavera"
with Südwestdeutsche Chamber   Bärenreiter Musicaphon BM30
Orch. – Tilegant   SL1215
                               Nonesuch H1070, H71070
                               Vega 19012

Concerto No. 2, in g, F.I, No. 23 "L'Estate"
with Stuttgart Chamber   Ace of Clubs ACL91
Orch. – Münchinger   Decca LXT2600, LXT5377
                               London LL386
                               Richmond R19056

Concerto No. 2, in g, F.I, No. 23 "L'Estate"
with Pro Musica Orch.,   Turnabout TV34800
Stuttgart – Reinhardt   Vox PL13010, STPL513010, (in
                               sets DL173 & VBX32)

Concerto No. 2, in g, F.I, No. 23 "L'Estate"
with Südwestdeutsche Chamber   Bärenreiter Musicaphon BM30
Orch. – Tilegant   SL1215
                               Nonesuch H1070, H71070
                               Vega 19012

Concerto No. 3, in F, F.I, No. 24 "L'Autunno"
with Stuttgart Chamber   Ace of Clubs ACL91
Orch. – Münchinger   Decca LXT2600, LXT5377
                               London LL386
                               Richmond R19056

Concerto No. 3, in F, F.I, No. 24 "L'Autunno"
with Pro Musica Orch.,   Vox (in sets DL173 & VBX32)
Stuttgart – Reinhardt

Concerto No. 3, in F, F.I, No. 24 "L'Autunno"
with Südwestdeutsche Chamber   Bärenreiter Musicaphon BM30
Orch. – Tilegant   SL1215
                               Nonesuch H1070, H71070
                               Vega 19012

Concerto No. 4, in f, F.I, No. 25 "L'Inverno"
with Stuttgart Chamber   Ace of Clubs ACL91
Orch. – Münchinger   Decca LXT2600, LXT5377
                               London LL386
                               Richmond R19056

Concerto No. 4, in f, F.I, No. 25 "L'Inverno"
with Pro Musica Orch.,   Vox (in sets DL173 & VBX32)
Stuttgart – Reinhardt

Concerto No. 4, in f, F.I, No. 25 "L'Inverno"
with Südwestdeutsche Chamber   Bärenreiter Musicaphon BM30
Orch. – Tilegant   SL1215
                               Nonesuch H1070, H71070
                               Vega 19012

Concerto No. 5, in B flat, F.I, No. 26 "La Tempesta di mare"
with Pro Musica Orch.,   Vox (in sets DL173 & VBX32)
Stuttgart – Reinhardt

Concerto No. 6, in C, F.I, No. 27 "Il Piacere"
with Pro Musica Orch.,   Vox (in sets DL173 & VBX32)
Stuttgart – Reinhardt

Concerto No. 7, in d, F.I, No. 28
with Pro Musica Orch.,   Vox (in sets DL173 & VBX32)
Stuttgart – Reinhardt

VIVALDI – *Continued*

Concerto No. 8, in g, F.I, No. 16
with Pro Musica Orch.,   Vox (in sets DL173 & VBX32)
Stuttgart – Reinhardt

Concerto No. 9, in d, F.VII, No. 1
with Pro Musica Orch.,   Vox (in sets DL173 & VBX32)
Stuttgart – Reinhardt

Concerto No. 10, in B flat, F.I, No. 29 "La Caccia"
with Pro Musica Orch.,   Vox (in sets DL173 & VBX32)
Stuttgart – Reinhardt

Concerto No. 11, in D, F.I, No. 30
with Pro Musica Orch.,   Vox (in sets DL173 & VBX32)
Stuttgart – Reinhardt

Concerto No. 12, in C, F.I, No. 31
with Pro Musica Orch.,   Vox (in sets DL173 & VBX32)
Stuttgart – Reinhardt

(12) Concerti, Op. 9 (1728) "La Cetra" vln, strs & c
Concerto No. 1, in C, P.9 (F.I, No. 47)
with H. Elsner hpsi & Pro Musica   Vox (in sets DL203 & VBX30)
Orch., Stuttgart – Reinhardt

Concerto No. 2, in A, P.214 (F.I, No. 51)
with H. Elsner hpsi & Pro Musica   Vox (in sets DL203 & VBX30)
Orch., Stuttgart – Reinhardt

Concerto No. 3, in g, P.339 (F.I, No. 52)
with H. Elsner hpsi & Pro Musica   Vox (in sets DL203 & VBX30)
Orch., Stuttgart – Reinhardt

Concerto No. 4, in E, P.242 (F.I, No. 48)
with H. Elsner hpsi & Pro Musica   Vox (in sets DL203 & VBX30)
Orch., Stuttgart – Reinhardt

Concerto No. 5, in a, P.10 (F.I, No. 53)
with H. Elsner hpsi & Pro Musica   Vox (in sets DL203 & VBX30)
Orch., Stuttgart – Reinhardt

Concerto No. 6, in A, P.215 (F.I, No. 54)
with H. Elsner hpsi & Pro Musica   Vox (in sets DL203 & VBX30)
Orch., Stuttgart – Reinhardt

Concerto No. 7, in B flat, P.340 (F.I, No. 55)
with H. Elsner hpsi & Pro Musica   Vox (in sets DL203 & VBX30)
Orch., Stuttgart – Reinhardt

Concerto No. 8, in d, P.260 (F.I, No. 56)
with H. Elsner hpsi & Pro Musica   Vox (in sets DL203 & VBX30)
Orch., Stuttgart – Reinhardt

Concerto No. 9, in B flat, P.341 (F.I, No. 57) with 2nd vln obb
with A. Steffen–Wendling vln,   Vox (in sets DL203 & VBX30)
H. Elsner hpsi & Pro Musica Orch.,
Stuttgart – Reinhardt

Concerto No. 10, in G, P.103 (F.I, No. 49)
with H. Elsner hpsi & Pro Musica   Vox (in sets DL203 & VBX30)
Orch., Stuttgart – Reinhardt

Concerto No. 11, in c, P.416 (F.I, No. 58)
with H. Elsner hpsi & Pro Musica   Vox (in sets DL203 & VBX30)
Orch., Stuttgart – Reinhardt

Concerto No. 12, in b, P.154 (F.I, No. 50) with solo vln scordato
with H. Elsner hpsi & Pro Musica   Vox (in sets DL203 & VBX30)
Orch., Stuttgart – Reinhardt

Concerto in E, P.246 (F.I, No. 127) (Op. 35, No. 6) "L'Amoroso" vln, strs & c
  Allegro (1st mvt)
  with Pro Musica Orch.,   Turnabout TV34800
  Stuttgart – Reinhardt   Vox PL13010, STPL513010

Galina Vsevolodovna BARINOVA (1910–   )

ARENSKY

(4) Morceaux, Op. 30 vln & pf
  No. 2. Sérénade in G
  with piano   Mezhdunarodnaya Kniga
                                       D15830

AULIN

(4) Aquarelles vln & pf
  No. 2. Humoresque
  with A. Dedyukhin pf   Mezhdunarodnaya Kniga
                                       D022109/10

(4) Pieces, Op. 15 vln & pf
  No. 4. Gavotte & Musette
  with G. Zinger pf   Mezhdunarodnaya Kniga
                                       D022109/10

BACH

(6) Sonatas, BWV1014/9 vln & clav
  Sonata No. 2, in A, BWV1015
  with S. Richter pf   Mezhdunarodnaya Kniga D1124
  Sonata No. 3, in E, BWV1016
  with L. Roizman org   Mezhdunarodnaya Kniga
                                       D11017/8

Sonata in g, BWV1020 vln & clav
  with S. Richter pf   Mezhdunarodnaya Kniga D1123,
                                       D21412/5

Sonata in d, BWV1036 2 vlns & c
  with R. Sobolevsky vln, T. Nikolayeva   Mezhdunarodnaya Kniga
  pf & M. Rostropovich vlc   D01302

BARTÓK

(6) Rumanian folk dances (1915) pf – arr. vln & pf Székely
  with G. Zinger pf   Mezhdunarodnaya Kniga
                                       D6133/4

BRAHMS

Sonata (1853) "Frei aber Einsam" vln & pf
  Allegro (Scherzo) in c (3rd mvt) "Sonatensatz"
  with piano   Mezhdunarodnaya Kniga
                                       D023687/8

(16) Waltzes, Op. 39 pf duet
  No. 15. Waltz No. 15, in A flat arr. vln & pf "in A" Hochstein
  with piano   Mezhdunarodnaya Kniga
                                       D023687/8

CHAMINADE

Sérénade espagnole pf – arr. vln & pf Kreisler
  with piano   Mezhdunarodnaya Kniga D1186,
                                       D22054

CUI

Kaleidoscope, Op. 50 vln & pf
  No. 5. Berceuse russe
  with A. Dedyukhin pf   Mezhdunarodnaya Kniga 18561
  No. 9. Orientale
  with A. Dedyukhin pf   Mezhdunarodnaya Kniga D439,
                                       D18560

DELIUS

Légende in E flat (1892) vln & pf
with G. Zinger pf   Mezhdunarodnaya Kniga
     D022109/10

DVOŘÁK

(8) Slavonic Dances, Op. 46 pf duet; orch.
No. 2. Slavonic dance No. 2, in e arr. vln & pf "in g" Kreisler
with piano   Mezhdunarodnaya Kniga
     D00445

FIOCCO

Suite No. 1, in G hpsi
Allegro (10th mvt) arr. vln & pf Bent & O'Neill
with piano   Mezhdunarodnaya Kniga D1185

GLAZOUNOV

Raymonda, Op. 57 (1897) ballet orch.
Valse arr. vln & pf Pogozhev
with piano   Mezhdunarodnaya Kniga
     D15831

GLIÈRE

Romance in c, Op. 45, No. 3 vln & pf
with orch. – Glière   Mezhdunarodnaya Kniga
     D12954/5

HANDEL

(The) Messiah (1742) – oratorio
No. 20a. He shall feed His flock arr. vln & pf as "Aria" by Flesch
with G. Zinger pf   Mezhdunarodnaya Kniga
     D6133/4

(15) Sonatas, Op. 1 (?1731) fl or vln & c
Sonata No. 3, in A vln I
with G. Zinger pf   Mezhdunarodnaya Kniga
     D6133/4

JÄRNEFELT

Berceuse in g orch. – arr. vln & pf
with piano   Mezhdunarodnaya Kniga D1186

KARLOWICZ

Concerto in A, Op. 8 vln & orch.
with USSR State Symphony   Colosseum CRLP90
Orch. – Kondrashin   Mezhdunarodnaya Kniga
     D500/1
     Westminster XWN18535

KREISLER

Praeludium & Allegro (Pugnani) vln & pf
with piano   Mezhdunarodnaya Kniga D1185

LYSENKO

Trio in A 2 vlns & vla
with B. Goldstein vln & R. Barshai vla   Mezhdunarodnaya Kniga
     D02389

MANÉN

Turkey in the straw (Morceau sur un thème américain) vln & pf
with I. Kataev pf   Mezhdunarodnaya Kniga
     D022109/10

MASSENET

Thaïs (1894) – opera
Méditation arr. vln & pf Marsick
with piano   Mezhdunarodnaya Kniga
     D023687/8

MLYNARSKI

Mazurka in G, Op. 26 vln & pf
with piano   Mezhdunarodnaya Kniga
     D18686

MONASTERIO

Sierra Morena vln & pf
with piano   Mezhdunarodnaya Kniga
     D023687/8

PARADIES

Sicilienne vln & pf – arr. Dushkin
with piano   Mezhdunarodnaya Kniga D1185

PORUMBESCU

Ballade in e, Op. 29 vln & pf
with G. Zinger pf   Mezhdunarodnaya Kniga 6133/4

PROKOFIEV

Sonata in d, Op. 115 solo vln
(unaccompanied)   Mezhdunarodnaya Kniga
     D023687/8

SCHUBERT

Sonata in a, D821 (1824) "Arpeggione" arpeggione & pf – arr. vln & pf
with G. Zinger pf   Mezhdunarodnaya Kniga
     D022109/10

SMETANA

From my Homeland (1878) vln & pf
No. 2. Andantino
with piano   Mezhdunarodnaya Kniga
     D023687/8

STRAVINSKY

Mavra (1922) – opera
Russian maiden's song (Parasha's aria) arr. vln & pf Dushkin & Stravinsky
with piano   Mezhdunarodnaya Kniga
     D023687/8

Petrouchka (1911) – ballet orch.
Danse russe arr. vln & pf Dushkin & Stravinsky
with piano   Mezhdunarodnaya Kniga
     D023687/8

SUK

(7) Pieces, Op. 7 pf
No. 1. Love song arr. vln & pf Kocián
with A. Dedyukhin pf   Mezhdunarodnaya Kniga
     D00358, D21038/9

SZYMANOWSKI

(9) Preludes, Op. 1 (1900) pf
Prelude No. 1, in b arr. vln & pf Bacewicz
with piano   Mezhdunarodnaya Kniga
     D22053

TARTINI

(12) Sonatas, Op. 1 (1734) vln & c
Sonata No. 10, in g "Didone abbandonata"
with L. Roizman org   Mezhdunarodnaya Kniga
D11018

TCHAIKOVSKY

(12) Pieces (of moderate difficulty) Op. 40 pf
No. 2. Chanson triste arr. vln & pf
with piano   Mezhdunarodnaya Kniga D1186

No. 10 Russian dance arr. vln & pf
with A. Dedyuhkin pf   Mezhdunarodnaya Kniga D439,
D16746/7

Sérénade mélancolique in b flat, Op. 26 vln & orch.
with Moscow Radio Symphony   Mezhdunarodnaya Kniga D9878
Orch. - Anosov

Souvenir d'un lieu cher, Op. 42 vln & pf
No. 1. Méditation arr. vln & orch.
with Moscow Radio Symphony   Mezhdunarodnaya Kniga
Orch. - Anosov   D1390/1, D9877

No. 2. Scherzo arr. vln & orch.
with Moscow Radio Symphony   Mezhdunarodnaya Kniga
Orch. - Anosov   D1390/1, D9877, D022323

No. 3. Mélodie arr. vln & orch.
with Moscow Radio Symphony   Mezhdunarodnaya Kniga
Orch. - Anosov   D00444, D1390/1, D9878,
D022322

VIEUXTEMPS

(6) Divertissements d'Amateurs sur des Mélodies russes, Op. 24 vln & pf
No. 1. Romance (Otgadaj, moja rodnaja/Divine, ma bien–Aimée) (after Alexander Lvovich Guriloyov, 1803–1858)
with piano   Mezhdunarodnaya Kniga
D16838/9

WHITE

Bandanna Sketches, Op. 12 vln & pf
No. 1. Nobody knows de trouble I see (Negro spiritual)
with A. Dedyukhin pf   Mezhdunarodnaya Kniga
D022109/10

WIENIAWSKI

(L') École moderne, Op. 10 (10 Études) solo vln
No. 5. Etude No. 5, in E flat "alla Saltarella" arr. vln & pf Kreisler
with piano   Mezhdunarodnaya Kniga D1186,
D21817

Légende, Op. 17 vln & pf or orch.
with USSR State Symphony   Mezhdunarodnaya Kniga D438,
Orch. - Kondrashin   D020061/2

Mazurka in a, Op. 3 "Kujawiak" vln & pf
with piano   Mezhdunarodnaya Kniga
D00445

(2) Mazurkas, Op. 12 vln & pf
No. 1. Mazurka No. 1, in D "Sielanka"
with piano   Mezhdunarodnaya Kniga
D00357, D18685

No. 2. Mazurka No. 2, in g "Le Ménetrier"
with piano   Mezhdunarodnaya Kniga
D00357, D18685

WIENIAWSKI – Continued

(2) Mazurkas, Op. 19 vln & pf
No. 2. Mazurka No. 2, in D "Dudziarz"
with piano   Mezhdunarodnaya Kniga D1186,
D21816

Souvenir de Moscou, Op. 6 vln & pf or orch.
with Moscow Radio Symphony   Mezhdunarodnaya Kniga
Orch. - Kondrashin   D00829/30

ZARZYCKI

Mazurka in G, Op. 26 vln & pf
with G. Zinger pf   Mezhdunarodnaya Kniga
D6133/4

Charles Alvinus BARKEL (1898–)

AULIN

(4) Aquarelles vln & pf
No. 1. Idyll
with N. Broman pf   R 175   Rytmi R11

No. 2. Humoresque
with N. Broman pf   Sto 2777   Odeon A162442, D1002

No. 2. Humoresque
with N. Broman pf   R 176   Rytmi R11

No. 3. Vaggsang
with N. Broman pf   Sto 2778   Odeon*

No. 3. Vaggsang
with N. Broman pf   R 177   Rytmi R12
Telefunken A5205

No. 4. Polonaise
with N. Broman pf   R 178   Rytmi R12
Telefunken A5205

Concerto No. 3, in c, Op. 14 vln & orch.
with Göteborg Radio   R 274/6   Rytmi R40 (a, b & c)
Orch. - Mann

Concerto No. 3, in c, Op. 14 vln & orch.
RTJ 2156/60 & 2165/7   Radiotjanst RE718/21
with Stockholm Radio Symphony
Orch. - Mann

BÄCK

Quartet No. 2 (1947) 2 vlns, vla & vlc
with S. Karpe vln, S–V. Bäck vla & F.   HMV DB11046/7
Bramme vlc

JUON

Sonata in a, Op. 7 vln & pf
Romance (2nd mvt)
with N. Broman pf   HMV X2747

(2) Violinistücke, Op. 52 vln & pf
No. 1. Arietta
with N. Broman pf   HMV X2747

KREISLER

Grave (W.F. Bach) vln & pf
with N. Broman pf   XXSto 2780   Odeon*

* Unissued.

KREISLER – *Continued*

Praeludium & Allegro (Pugnani) vln & pf
with N. Broman pf   XXSto 2779   Odeon*

SINDING

(3) Pieces, Op. 89 vln & pf
No. 2. Alte Weise (Old melody)
with N. Broman pf   Odeon A162442, D1002

Karl BARLEBEN

SARASATE

(8) Danzas españolas vln & pf
No. 6. Zapateado, Op. 23, No. 2
with piano   Phono–Cut 5106

Issay BARMAS (1872–1946)

HALVORSEN

(4) Mosaïques (Suite des morceaux caractéristiques) vln & pf
No. 4. Chant de Veslemøy
with piano   Polydor 14012

HENRIQUES

Merry dance vln & pf
with piano   Polydor 14012

MOZART

(6) Deutsche Tänze, K600 orch.
No. 4. Deutscher Tanz No. 4, in C arr. vln & pf Burmester
with piano   Polydor 13650

PIERNÉ

Sérénade in A, Op. 7 (1875) pf – arr. vln & pf
with piano   Polydor 13644

REGER

(3) Pieces, Op. 79d vln & pf
No. 1. Wiegenlied in G
with piano   Polydor 13693
Romance in G vln & pf
with piano   Polydor 13693

SAINT-SAËNS

(Le) Carnaval des animaux (1886) small orch.
Le cygne arr. vln & pf
with piano   Polydor 13644

SCHUMANN

(4) Duets, Op. 78 s & t
No. 4. Wiegenlied arr. vln & pf
with piano   Polydor 14012
(12) Duets, Op. 85 pf – 4 hands
No. 12. Abendlied arr. vln & pf Joachim
with piano   Polydor 13650
(13) Kinderscenen, Op. 15 pf
No. 1. Von fremden Landern und Menschen arr. vln & pf
with piano   Polydor 14012

* unissued.

TCHAIKOVSKY

(12) Pieces (of moderate difficulty) Op. 40 pf
No. 2. Chanson triste arr. vln & pf
with piano   Polydor 13693

Rudolf BARNERT

BACH

Concerto in D, BWV1064 3 clavs, strs & c – arr. 3 vlns, strs & c
with W. Prystawski vln, T. Soh vln &   Deutsche Grammophon
Lucerne Festival   SLPM139432
Strings – Baumgartner

VIVALDI

(12) Concerti, Op. 3 "L'Estro armonico" var. cbns & strs
Concerto No. 4, in e, P.97 (F.I, No. 174) 4 vlns, strs & c
with W. Prystawski vln, G. Ribiero   Archive 2705 002, SAPM198469
vln, T. Soh vln & Lucerne Festival
Strings – Baumgartner
Concerto No. 7, in F, P.249 (F.IV, No. 9) 4 vlns, vlc, strs & c
with W. Prystawski vln, H. Scherz vln,   Archive SAPM198470
T. Soh vln, K. Heitz vlc & Lucerne
Festival Strings – Baumgartner
Concerto No. 10, in b, P.148 (F.IV, No. 10) 4 vlns, strs & c
with W. Prystawski vln, H. Scherz vln,   Archive SAPM198471
T. Soh vln, K. Heitz vlc & Lucerne
Festival Strings – Baumgartner

Vera BARSTOW (1891–)

BRANDL

(Der) Liebe Augustin – operetta
Du alter Stefansturm arr. vln & pf as "The old refrain" by Kreisler
with piano   Edison Diamond Disc 80573

SCHUBERT

Rosamunde von Cypern, Op. 26 (D797) (1823) – Incidental music orch.
No. 9. Ballet music II, in G arr. vln & pf Kreisler
with piano   Edison Diamond Disc 80573

Raoul BARTHALAY

RIMSKY–KORSAKOV

Sadko (1898) – opera
Chant hindou arr. v, vln & pf
with N. Vallin s & piano   Parlophone R20106

Wilhelm BARTHOLDY

BULL

Säterjentens søndag v & pf – arr. vln & pf Svendsen
with piano   HMV K87920

WIENIAWSKI

(2) Mazurkas, Op. 19 vln & pf
No. 1. Mazurka No. 1, in G "Obertass"
with piano   HMV K87921

Walter BARYLLI (1921–)

BACH

Concerto No. 1, in a, BWV1041 vln, strs & c
  with Vienna State Opera   Heliodor 466003
  Orch. – Scherchen   Westminster 21002, WL5318,
                 XWN18021

Concerto No. 2, in E, BWV1042 vln, strs & c
  with Vienna State Opera   Heliodor 466003
  Orch. – Scherchen   Westminster WL5318,
                 XWN18021

Matthaeus–Passion, BMV244 (1729)
  with M. Laszlo s, H. Roessel–Majdan   Nixa WLP6401
  a, P. Munteanu t, R. Standen bs, H.   Westminster (set WAL401),
  Cuenod t, H. Rehfuss bs, E. Wächter   XWN18304/7, (set XWN4402)
  bs, P. Lagger bs, E. Hofstätter s, W.
  Huebner vln, K. Reznicek fl, K.
  Mayerhofer ob, B. Seidlhofer org, F.
  Holetschek hpsi, B. Reichert gamba,
  K. Oehlberger bsn &
  Orch. & Chorus – Scherchen

BRAHMS

Trio in E flat, Op. 40 hrn, pf & vln
  with F. Koch hrn & F. Holetschek pf   Nixa WLP5146
                 Westminster W9017, WL5146,
                 XWN18449

(16) Waltzes, Op. 39 pf duet
  No. 15. Waltz No. 15, in A flat arr. vln & pf – "in A" – Hochstein
  with O.A. Graef pf   3139½ GN 8   Polydor 10660, D132

CHOPIN

(3) Nocturnes, Op. 9 pf
  No. 2. Nocturne No. 2, in E flat arr. vln & pf Sarasate
  with O.A. Graef pf   Polydor 15202

DVOŘÁK

(8) Humoresques, Op. 101 pf
  No. 7. Humoresque No. 7, in G flat arr. vln & pf "in G" – Kreisler
  with O.A. Graef pf   Polydor 10811

JANÁČEK

Concertino (1925) pf, 2 vlns, vla, cl, hrn & bsn – arr. vln & pf
  with F. Holetschek pf   HMV CLP1749
                 Westminster WL5333

Dumka (1880) vln & pf
  with F. Holetschek pf   HMV CLP1749
                 Westminister WL5333,
                 XWN18750

Sonata (1913/21) vln & pf*
  with F. Holetschek pf   Westminster WL5333,
                 XWN18750

MASSENET

Thaïs (1894) – opera
  Méditation arr. vln & pf Marsick
  with O.A. Graef pf   Polydor 10811

* Four versions exist of this work. The above version is unidentified.

MOZART

Exsultate, jubilate, K165 s & orch.
  with H. Gueden s & Vienna   Decca LX3103, VD557
  Philharmonic Orch. – Erede   London LS681

(Il) Re Pastore, K208 (1775) – opera
  No. 10. L'Amerò, sarò costante
  with H. Gueden s & Vienna   Decca LX3103, LXT5242
  Philharmonic Orch. – Erede   London LS681

Sinfonia concertante in E flat, K364 vln, vla & orch.
  with P. Doktor vla & Vienna State   Nixa WLP5107
  Opera Orch. – Prohaska   Westminster WL5107,
                 WLP20053, XWN18041
                 Whitehall WH20064

Sonata No. 17, in C, K296 vln & pf
  with P. Badura–Skoda pf   Nixa WLP5130
                 Westminster WL5145,
                 XWN18568

Sonata No. 18, in G, K301 vln & pf
  with P. Badura–Skoda pf   Nixa WLP5130
                 Westminster WL5130,
                 XWN18568

Sonata No. 20, in E flat, K58 (K.Anh.209) vln & pf
  with P. Badura–Skoda pf   Nixa WLP5145
                 Westminster WL5145,
                 XWN18567

Sonata No. 21, in e, K304 vln & pf
  with P. Badura–Skoda pf   Nixa WLP5130
                 Westminster WL5130,
                 XWN18568

Sonata No. 22, in A, K305 vln & pf
  with P. Badura–Skoda pf   Nixa WLP5145
                 Westminster WL5145,
                 XWN18567

Sonata No. 24, in F, K376 vln & pf
  with P. Badura–Skoda pf   Westminster WL5394,
                 XWN18569

Sonata No. 25, in F, K377 vln & pf
  with P. Badura–Skoda pf   Nixa WLP5145
                 Westminster WL5145,
                 XWN18567

Sonata No. 27, in G, K379 vln & pf
  with P. Badura–Skoda pf   Nixa WLP5109
                 Westminster WL5109,
                 XWN18570

Sonata No. 29, in A, K402 vln & pf
  with P. Badura–Skoda pf   Westminster WL5394,
                 XWN18569

Sonata No. 32, in B flat, K454 vln & pf
  with P. Badura–Skoda pf   Nixa WLP5109
                 Westminster WL5109,
                 XWN18570

Sonata No. 33, in E flat, K481 vln & pf
  with P. Badura–Skoda pf   Westminster WL5394,
                 XWN18569

PAGANINI

Sonata a preghièra "Moses Fantasia" (on the aria "Dal tuo stellato soglio"
  from Rossini's opera "Mosè in Egitto") Op. 24 (1818 or 1819) vln &
  orch.
  with O.A. Graef pf   3515/6 GN 8   Decca PO5127
                               Polydor 10810

REGER

Romance in G, vln & pf
  with O.A. Graef pf   3142½ GN 8   Polydor 10660, D132

REUTER

American melody vln & pf – arr. Graef
  with O.A. Graef pf   Polydor 10522

TCHAIKOVSKY

Concerto in D, Op. 35 vln & orch.
  Canzonetta (2nd mvt) arr. vln & pf
  with O.A. Graef pf   Polydor 10522
Suite No. 3, in G, Op. 55 orch.
  Theme & variations (4th mvt)
  with Vienna Philharmonic   Angel 35975
  Orch. – Kempe   HMV ALP1930, ASD494
                                            World Record Club ST763, T763

WIENIAWSKI

Scherzo–Tarantelle, Op. 16 vln & pf
  with O.A. Graef pf   Polydor 15202

René BAS

FAURÉ

Berceuse, Op. 16 vln & pf
  with piano   Parlophone 22730
Pelléas et Mélisande, Op. 80 (1898) – Incidental music orch.
  No. 2. Fileuses arr. vln & pf Auer
  with piano   Parlophone 22730

GRANADOS

(12) Danzas españolas, Op. 37 (1893) pf
  No. 5 – Danza española No. 5, in e "Andaluza" arr. vln & pf Kreisler
  with piano   Parlophone 22621, 44651

HONEGGER

Sonatina (1932) vln & vlc
  with R. Krabanski vlc   Elite ERT6009/10, ERT7062/3

MOZART

Divertimento No. 17, in D, K334 strs & 2 hrns
  Minuet (3rd mvt) arr. vln & pf Burmester
  with piano   Parlophone 22621, 44651

PIERNÉ

Sérénade in A, Op. 7 (1875) pf – arr. vln & pf
  with piano   Parlophone 22751

PURCELL

(10) Sonatas, Z802/11 (1697) 4 parts – 2 vlns & c
  Sonata No. 6, in g, Z807 "Chaconne"
  with A. Schwarz vln, I. Nef hpsi,   L'Oiseau–Lyre LD10
  & A. Navarra vlc

SAINT-SAËNS

(Le) Déluge, Op. 45 (1876) – oratorio
  Prélude vln & orch. – arr. vln & pf Saint-Saëns
  with piano   Parlophone 22751

E. BASTIDE

FAURÉ

Berceuse, Op. 16 vln & pf
  with Y. Lévy pf   Tri–Ergon 10305

Hans BASTIEN (1911–)

CORELLI

(12) Sonatas, Op. 3 2 vlns & c
  Sonata No. 4, in b
  (as leader of Hans Bastien Trio)   Kantorei 8
(12) Sonatas, Op. 5 vln & c
  Sonata No. 11, in E
  with organ   Kantorei 7

HANDEL

(12) Concerti grossi, Op. 6 (1739) 2 vlns, vlc & strs
  Concerto grosso No. 2, in F
  with S. Borries vln & Berlin   Electrola E60017
  Philharmonic Orch. – Matzerath   HMV WDLP527
  Concerto grosso No. 12, in b
  with S. Borries vln & Berlin   Electrola E60017
  Philharmonic Orch. – Matzerath   HMV WDLP527

Milan BAUER (1932—)

FERENCZY

Sonata vln & pf
  with M. Karin pf   Supraphon 1 11 0228

HANDEL

(15) Sonatas, Op. 1 (?1731) fl or vln & c
  Sonata No. 10 in g vln II
  with M. Karin pf   Supraphon DV6178, SUA10685,
                                            SUA ST50685, SV8292

  Sonata No. 12, in F vln III
  with M. Karin pf   Supraphon DV6178, SUA10685,
                                            SUA ST50685, SV8292

  Sonata No. 14, in A vln V
  with M. Karin pf   Supraphon DV6178, SUA10685,
                                            SUA ST50685, SV8292

  Sonata No. 15, in E vln VI
  with M. Karin pf   Supraphon DV6178, SUA10685,
                                            SUA ST50685, SV8292

JUROVSKÝ

Romance (1933) vln & pf
  with M. Karin pf   Supraphon 1 11 0228

MOYZES

Concerto, Op. 53 vln & orch.
  with Slovak Philharmonic   Supraphon SUA18652, SUA
  Orch. – Rajter   ST58652, SV8312
Suite poetique, Op. 35 vln & pf
  with M. Karin pf   Supraphon 1 11 0228

Rudolf BAUMGARTNER (1917–)

BACH

(6) Brandenburg Concerti, BWV1046/51 (1721) strs & c
Brandenburg Concerto No. 2, in F, BWV1047 tpt, fl, ob, vln & strs
with A. Scherbaum tpt, H.M. Linde   Archive APM14143, ARC3157,
rec, H. Winschermann ob,   ARC73157, SAPM198143
E. Kaufmann hpsi, C. Starck vlc,   Musique Royale 199007
H. Voerkel cbs & Lucerne Festival
Strings – Baumgartner

Brandenburg Concerto No. 4, in G, BWV1049 vln, 2 fls & strs
with H.M. Linde rec, T. von Sparr rec,   Archive APM14142, ARC3156,
C. Starck vlc, H. Voerkel cbs,   ARC73156, SAPM198142
E. Kaufmann hpsi & Lucerne Festival
Strings – Baumgartner

Brandenburg Concerto No. 5, in D, BWV1050 clav, fl, vln & strs
with R. Kirkpatrick hpsi, A. Nicolet fl   Archive APM14143, ARC3157,
& Lucerne Festival Strings –   ARC73157, SAPM198143
Baumgartner

Concerto in d, BWV1043 2 vlns, strs & c
with W. Schneiderhan vln & Lucerne   Archive APM14086, ARC3099
Festival Strings – Baumgartner

Concerto in a, BWV1044 fl, vln, hpsi, strs & c
with A. Nicolet fl, R. Kirkpatrick hpsi   Archive APM14189, ARC3176,
& Lucerne Festival   ARC73176, SAPM198189
Strings – Baumgartner

(Ein) Musikalisches Opfer, BWV1079 (1749) strs
with L. von Pfersmann fl, A.   Philips A00300L
d'Harnoncourt vln & vla, K. Theimer
vln & vla, N. d'Harnoncourt vlc
& I. Ahlgrimm hpsi

VIVALDI

(12) Concerti, Op. 3 "L'Estro armonico" var. cbns & strs
Concerto No. 11, in d, P.250 (F.IV, No. 11) 2 vlns, vlc, strs & c
with W. Schneiderhan vln, C. Starck   Archive APM14097, ARC3116,
vlc, E. Kaufmann hpsi & Lucerne   EPA37199, SEPA181199
Festival Strings – Baumgartner   Deutsche Grammophon 135024

Jiří BAXA (1930–)

JANÁČEK

Concertino (1925) pf, 2 vlns, vla, cl, hrn & bsn
with J. Paleníček pf, V. Koulouch vln,   Crossroads 22 16 0073, 22 16
J. Motlik vla, Z.K. Dlouhy cl,   0074
V. Kubat hrn & K. Vaček bsn   Supraphon SUA10416, SUA
   ST50416, SV8093

Gerald BEAL (1932–)

HANDEL

(9) Sonatas, Op. 2 (1724) fl, vln or 2 vlns & c
Sonata No. 3, in g
with W. Beal vln, & H. Wingreen pf   Monitor MC2008

HONEGGER

Sonatina (1920) 2 vlns
with W. Beal vln   Monitor MC2008

MILHAUD

Sonatina (1940) 2 vlns
with W. Beal vln   Monitor MC2008

TELEMANN

Trio in E flat, T.I, No. 4 2 vlns & c
with W. Beal vln & H. Wingreen pf   Monitor MC2008

Wilfred BEAL (1932–)

HANDEL

(9) Sonatas, Op. 2 (1724) fl, vln or 2 vlns & c
Sonata No. 3, in g
with G. Beal vln, & H. Wingreen pf   Monitor MC2008

HONEGGER

Sonatina (1920) 2 vlns
with G. Beal vln   Monitor MC2008

MILHAUD

Sonatina (1940) 2 vlns
with G. Beal vln   Monitor MC2008

TELEMANN

Trio in E flat, T.I, No. 4 2 vlns & c
with G. Beal vln & H. Wingreen pf   Monitor MC2008

Hugh Cecil BEAN (1929–)

ANONYMOUS

(The) Rakes of Mallow traditional – arr. vln & pf Moffat
with D. Parkhouse pf   HMV 7EG 8757

BACH

(6) Brandenburg Concerti, BWV1046/51 (1721) strs & c
Brandenburg Concerto No. 1, in F, BWV1046 vln, 3 obs, bsn, 2 hrns & strs
with A. Civil hrn, A. Woodburn hrn,   Angel 35845, (in set 3627)
S. Sutcliffe ob, S. Smith ob,   Columbia CX1763, FCX910,
P. Newbury ob, C. James bsn,   SAFX224, SAX2408
G. Malcolm hpsi & Philharmonia
Orch. – Klemperer

Brandenburg Concerto No. 1, in F, BWV1046 vln, 3 obs, bsn, 2 hrns & strs: Polacca (from 4th mvt) arr. vln & pf Forbes
with D. Parkhouse pf   HMV 7EG 8757

Brandenburg Concerto No. 2, in F, BWV1047 tpt, fl, ob, vln & strs
with A. Scherbaum tpt, G. Morris fl,   Angel 35845/6, (in set 3627)
S. Sutcliffe ob, G. Malcolm hpsi &   Columbia CX1763/4, FCX910/1,
Philharmonia Orch. – Klemperer   SAFX224/5, SAX2408/9

Brandenburg Concerto No. 4, in G, BWV1049 vln, 2 fls & strs
with G. Morris fl, A. Ackroyd fl,   Angel 35846, (in set 3627)
G. Malcolm hpsi & Philharmonia   Columbia CX1765, FCX911,
Orch. – Klemperer   SAFX225, SAX2409

Brandenburg Concerto No. 5, in D, BWV1050 clav, fl, vln & strs
with G. Morris fl, G. Malcolm hpsi &   Angel 35845, (in set 3627)
Philharmonia Orch. – Klemperer   Columbia CX1764, FCX910,
   SAFX224, SAX2408

BACH

Cantata No. 156 (Ich steh' mit einem Fuss im Grabe) BWV156
Sinfonia arr. vln & pf as "Arioso" by Franko
  with D. Parkhouse pf   Saga ERO8009, EROS8009

Matthaeus–Passion, BWV244 (1729)
  with D. Fischer–Dieskau b, P. Pears t,   Angel 35801/5, (set 3599)
  E. Schwarzkopf s, C. Ludwig m–s,   Columbia C91200/3,
  N. Gedda t, W. Berry bs, J.C. Case b,   CX1799/803, SAX2446/50,
  O. Kraus b, J. Baker a, G. Evans b,   QCXS10458/62, SAXQS7358/62,
  H. Watts a, W. Brown t, G. Morris fl,   STC91200/3
  A. Ackroyd fl, S. Sutcliffe ob, P.
  Newbury ob, B. Dekany vln, D. Dupré
  gamba, R. Downes org, G. Malcolm
  hpsi, V. Tunnard hpsi, R. Clark vlc,
  J.W. Merrett cbs, The Choir Boys of
  Hampstead Parish Church &
  Philharmonia Orch. – Klemperer

BEETHOVEN

(3) Sonatas, Op. 30 vln & pf
  No. 3. Sonata No. 8, in G
  with D. Parkhouse pf   Saga XID5232, STXID5232
Sonata No. 9, in A, Op. 47 "Kreutzer" vln & pf
  with D. Parkhouse pf   Saga XID5232, STXID5232
Trio No. 6, in B flat, Op. 97 "Archduke" pf vln & vlc
  with D. Parkhouse pf & E. Croxford   Saga XID5226
  vlc

CORELLI

Largo affettuoso unid – arr. vln & pf Moffat
  with D. Parkhouse pf   HMV 7EG 8756
(12) Sonatas, Op. 5 vln & c
  Sonata No. 9, in A: Preludio (Largo) (1st mvt) arr. vln & pf Forbes
  with D. Parkhouse pf   HMV 7EG 8757

DEBUSSY

Sonata No. 3, in g (1917) vln & pf
  with D. Parkhouse pf   Saga XID5255, STXID5255

DINICU

Hora staccato (1906) vln & pf – arr. Heifetz
  with D. Parkhouse pf   Saga ERO8009, EROS8009

ELGAR

(La) Capricieuse, Op. 17 vln & pf
  with D. Parkhouse pf   Saga ERO8009, EROS8009

KREISLER

Caprice viennois, Op. 2 vln & pf
  with D. Parkhouse pf   Saga ERO8009, EROS8009
Liebesfreud vln & pf
  with D. Parkhouse pf   Saga ERO8009, EROS8009
Liebesleid vln & pf
  with D. Parkhouse pf   Saga ERO8009, EROS8009
Schön Rosmarin vln & pf
  with D. Parkhouse pf   Saga ERO8009, EROS8009

MENDELSSOHN

(6) Gesänge, Op. 34 v & pf
  No. 2. Auf Flügeln des Gesanges arr. vln & pf Achron
  with D. Parkhouse pf   Saga ERO8009, EROS8009

MOSZKOWSKI

(2) Stücke, Op. 45 pf
  No. 2. Guitarre arr. vln & pf Sarasate
  with D. Parkhouse pf   Saga ERO8009, EROS8009

PONCE

Estrellita (1913) v & pf – arr. vln & pf Heifetz
  with D. Parkhouse pf   Saga ERO8009, EROS8009

RAVEL

Trio in a (1915) pf, vln & vlc
  with D. Parkhouse pf & E. Croxford   Saga XID5255, STXID5255
  vlc

RIMSKY–KORSAKOV

Capriccio espagnol, Op. 34 (1887) orch.
  with Philharmonia Orch. – Gamba   HMV CLP1848, CSD1592
Scheherazade, Op. 35 (1888) orch.
  with Philharmonia Orch. – Kletzki   HMV XLP20026, SXLP20026

SAINT–SAËNS

Danse macabre, Op. 40 (1874) orch.
  with Philharmonia Orch. – Gamba   HMV CLP1848, CSD1592

SARASATE

Jota aragonesa, Op. 27 vln & pf
  with D. Parkhouse pf   Saga ERO8009, EROS8009

STONE

(8) Pieces in the 3rd position vln & pf
  Festive dance
  with D. Parkhouse pf   HMV 7EG 8757
  March in D
  with D. Parkhouse pf   HMV 7EG 8756

TCHAIKOVSKY

Souvenir d'un lieu cher, Op. 42 vln & pf
  No. 3. Mélodie arr. Wilhelmj
  with D. Parkhouse pf   Saga ERO8009, EROS8009
Suite No. 3, in G, Op. 55 orch.
  Theme & variations (4th mvt)
  with New Philharmooia   Mercury MG50455, (in set OL3–
  Orch. – Dorati   118), SR90455, (in set SR3–9018)
        Philips 802790LY

VALLE

Ao pé da fogueira (Prelude XV) pf – arr. vln & pf Heifetz
  with D. Parkhouse pf   Saga ERO8009, EROS8009

VAUGHAN WILLIAMS

(The) Lark Ascending (1914) vln & orch.
  with New Philharmonia Orch. – Boult   Angel 36469
        HMV ALP2329, ASD2329

VIVALDI

(12) Cóncerti, Op. 8 (1725) "Il Cimento dell' Armonia e dell' Invenzione"
  (Nos. 1/4: Le quattro Stagioni) vln & strs
  Concerto No. 1, in E, F.I, No. 22 "La Primavera"
  with C. Spink hpsi & New   Decca LK4873, PSF4142
  Philharmonia Orch. – Stokowski   London SPC21015
  Concerto No. 2, in g, F.I, No. 23 "L'Estate"
  with C. Spink hpsi & New   Decca LK4873, PSF4142
  Philharmonia Orch. – Stokowski   London SPC21015

VIVALDI – *Continued*

Concerto No. 3, in F, F.I, No. 24 "L'Autunno"
with C. Spink hpsi & New   Decca LK4873, PSF4142
Philharmonia Orch. – Stokowski   London SPC21015
Concerto No. 4, in f, F.I, No. 25 "L'Inverno"
with C. Spink hpsi & New   Decca LK4873, PSF4142
Philharmonia Orch. – Stokowski   London SPC21015

WEBER

(18) Favoritenwalzer, J.143/60 (1812) pf
No 5. Waltz No. 5, in B flat, J.147 arr. vln & pf Moffat
with D. Parkhouse pf   HMV 7EG 8756

WIENIAWSKI

Scherzo–Tarantelle, Op. 16 vln & pf
with D. Parkhouse pf   Saga ERO8009, EROS8009

Arthur BECKWITH (1887–1928)

CHOPIN

(3) Nocturnes, Op. 9 pf
No. 2. Nocturne No. 2, in E flat arr. vln & pf Sarasate
with piano   HMV C909

COLERIDGE–TAYLOR

(4) African Dances, Op. 58 vln & pf
No. 4. Allegro energico
with piano   HO 4357 AF   HMV C976

CUI

Kaleidoscope, Op. 50 vln & pf
No. 11. Arioso
with piano   Bb 1530[I]   HMV B1395

DICKINSON

Berceuse (Baby dreams) vln & pf
with piano   HO 4356 AF   HMV C976

FOULKES

Sérénade d'amour vln & pf
with piano   Cc 1526[I]   HMV C1078

GERMAN

Berceuse pf – arr. vln & pf
with piano   Bb 885[I]   HMV B1321

HUBAY

(6) Blumenleben, Op. 30 vln & pf
No. 5. Der Zephir
with piano   Bb 886[II]   HMV B1321

KREISLER

Tambourin chinois, Op. 3 vln & pf
with piano   HMV C909

MOZART

Divertimento No. 17, in D, K334 strs & 2 hrns
Minuet (3rd mvt) arr. vln & pf Burmester
with piano   Cc 1527[I]   HMV C1078

RONALD

Garden of Allah (1921) – Incidental music orch.
In an eastern garden
with Royal Albert Hall   HMV D488
Orch. – Ronald
Prelude
with Royal Albert Hall   HMV D488
Orch. – Ronald

SVENDSEN

Romance in G, Op. 26 vln & orch. – arr. vln & pf Wilhelmj
with piano   HO 3291 ef   HMV C1014

VIEUXTEMPS

Ballade & Polonaise in G, Op. 38 vln & pf
with piano   HMV Z88

WIENIAWSKI

Légende, Op. 17 vln & pf or orch.
with piano   HO 3295 ef   HMV C1014

Liliane BEGUIN

TORELLI

(12) Concerti, Op. 8 (1709) 1/6: 2 vlns, strs & c – 7/12: vln, strs & c
Concerto No. 2, in a
with H. Fernandez vln &   Erato LDE3145
Jean–François Paillard Chamber
Orch. – Paillard

Will BEH

BACH

Concerto in d, BWV1043 2 vlns, strs & c
with R. Barchet vln & Pro Musica   Panthéon XPV1024
• Orch., Stuttgart – Davisson   Vox PL9150, (in set VBX25)
Concerto in c, BWV1060 vln & ob or 2 vlns, strs & c
with F. Milde ob & Pro Musica Orch.,   Panthéon XPV1024
Stuttgart – Reinhardt   Vox PL9580

TORELLI

(12) Concerti, Op. 8 (1709) 1/6: 2 vlns, strs & c – 7/12: vln, strs & c
Concerto No. 1, in C
with R. Barchet vln, H. Elsner hpsi &   Vox (in set DL113)
Pro Musica Orch.,
Stuttgart – Reinhardt
Concerto No. 2, in a
with R. Barchet vln, H. Elsner hpsi &   Vox (in set DL113)
Pro Musica Orch.,
Stuttgart – Reinhardt
Concerto No. 3, in E
with R. Barchet vln H. Elsner hpsi &   Vox (in set DL113)
Pro Musica Orch.,
Stuttgart – Reinhardt
Concerto No. 4, in B flat
with R. Barchet vln, H. Elsner hpsi &   Vox (in set DL113)
Pro Musica String Orch.,
Stuttgart – Reinhardt

TORELLI – *Continued*

Concerto No. 5, in G
with R. Barchet vln, H. Elsner hpsi &   Vox (in set DL113)
Pro Musica String Orch.,
Stuttgart – Reinhardt
Concerto No. 6, in g "Christmas Concerto"
with R. Barchet vln, H. Elsner hpsi &   Vox (in set DL113)
Pro Musica String Orch.,
Stuttgart – Reinhardt

Nina BEILINA

BARTÓK

(6) Rumanian folk dances (1915) pf – arr. vln & pf Székely
with L. Pecherskaya pf   Mezhdunarodnaya Kniga
                                D4272/3

BLOCH

Baal Shem (3 Pictures of Chassidic life) (1923) vln & pf
No. 2 Nigun (Improvisation)
with L. Pecherskaya pf   Mezhdunarodnaya Kniga
                                D4272/3

GLAZOUNOV

Méditation, Op. 32 vln & pf
with L. Pecherskaya pf   Mezhdunarodnaya Kniga
                                D4272/3

MARTINŮ

Sonata No. 1 (1930) vln & pf
with piano   Mezhdunarodnaya Kniga
                                D024725/6

MILHAUD

(12) Saudades do Brasil (1920/1) pf
No. 3. Leme arr. vln & pf Levy
with piano   Mezhdunarodnaya Kniga
                                D024725/6

No. 4. Copacabana arr. vln & pf Levy
with piano   Mezhdunarodnaya Kniga
                                D024725/6

No. 5. Ipanema arr. vln & pf Levy
with piano   Mezhdunarodnaya Kniga
                                D024725/6

No. 7. Corcavado arr. vln & pf Levy
with piano   Mezhdunarodnaya Kniga
                                D024725/6

No. 8. Tijuca arr. vln & pf Levy
with piano   Mezhdunarodnaya Kniga
                                D024725/6

No. 9. Sumare arr. vln & pf Levy
with piano   Mezhdunarodnaya Kniga
                                D024725/6

OVCHINNIKOV

Ballad vln & pf
with piano   Mezhdunarodnaya Kniga
                                D010325/8

PAGANINI

Cantabile in D, Op. 17 vln & gtr
with T. Merkulová pf   Mezhdunarodnaya Kniga
                                D018489/90

(24) Caprices, Op. 1 (1801/7) solo vln
Caprice No. 2, in b
(unaccompanied)   Mezhdunarodnaya Kniga
                                D10705/6

Caprice No. 2, in b
(unaccompanied)   Mezhdunarodnaya Kniga
                                D018489/90

Caprice No. 9, in E
(unaccompanied)   Mezhdunarodnaya Kniga
                                D10705/6

Caprice No. 9, in E
(unaccompanied)   Mezhdunarodnaya Kniga
                                D018489/90

Caprice No. 14, in E flat
(unaccompanied)   Mezhdunarodnaya Kniga
                                D018489/90

Caprice No. 24, in a
(unaccompanied)   Mezhdunarodnaya Kniga
                                D018489/90

Concerto No. 2, in b, Op. 7 vln & orch.
Ronde à la Clochette (3rd mvt) "La Campanella " arr. vln & pf Kreisler
with T. Merkulová pf   Mezhdunarodnaya Kniga
                                D018489/90

PROKOFIEV

(5) Melodies, Op. 35bis (1921) vln & pf
with piano   Mezhdunarodnaya Kniga
                                D10705/6

RACHMANINOV

(2) Pieces, Op. 6 vln & pf
No. 1. Romance in d
with L. Pecherskaya pf   Mezhdunarodnaya Kniga
                                D4272–3

RESPIGHI

Sonata in b (1917) vln & pf
with T. Merkulová pf   Mezhdunarodnaya Kniga
                                D018489/90

STRAVINSKY

Mavra (1922) – opera
Russian maiden's song (Parasha's aria) arr. vln & pf Dushkin &
Stravinsky
with piano   Mezhdunarodnaya Kniga
                                D024725/6

TCHAIKOVSKY

Sérénade mélancolique in b flat, Op. 26 vln & orch. – arr. vln & pf
Wilhelmj
with piano   Mezhdunarodnaya Kniga
                                D10705/6

Souvenir d'un lieu cher, Op. 42 vln & pf
with piano   Mezhdunarodnaya Kniga
                                D10705/6

TCHAIKOVSKY – *Continued*

Waltz–Scherzo, Op. 34 vln & orch.
  with piano
  Mezhdunarodnaya Kniga D10705/6

VAINBERG

Moldavian Rhapsody in g, Op. 47 vln & pf
  with L. Pecherskaya pf
  Mezhdunarodnaya Kniga D4272/3

VILLA–LOBOS

Sonata–Fantasia No. 1, in c (1912) "Désespérance" vln & pf
  with piano
  Mezhdunarodnaya Kniga D024725/6

Marcus BELAYEFF

BEETHOVEN

Concerto in D, Op 61 vln & orch.
  with Odessa Philharmonic Symphony Orch. – Shivesky
  Egmont EGM7025

MENDELSSOHN

Concerto in e, Op. 46 vln & orch.
  with Odessa Philharmonic Symphony Orch. – Bodenheim
  Egmont EGM7001

TCHAIKOVSKY

Concerto in D, Op. 35 vln & orch.
  with Odessa Philharmonic Symphony Orch. – Bodenheim
  Egmont EGM7001

Bruno BĚLČÍK (1924–)

BEETHOVEN

(3) Trios, Op. 1 pf, vln & vlc
  No. 1. Trio No. 1, in E flat
  with F. Rauch pf & F. Smetana vlc
  Crossroads 22 16 0123, 22 16 0124
  Supraphon SUA10639, SUAST50639

BRAHMS

Trio No. 1, in B, Op. 8 pf, vln & vlc
  with F. Rauch pf & F. Smetana vlc
  Supraphon SUA10147

Trio in E flat, Op. 40 hrn, pf & vln
  with M. Stefek hrn & F. Rauch pf
  Supraphon 011 0516, 111 0516

MARTINU

Concerto No. 2 (1943) vln & orch.
  with Prague Symphony Orch. – Neumann
  Artia ALP205, ALPS7205
  Supraphon SUA10386, SV8037

NOVÁK

Trio quasi una ballata in d, Op. 27 pf, vln & vlc
  with F. Rauch pf & F. Smetana vlc
  Supraphon SUB10092

SAINT-SAËNS

Concerto No. 3, in b, Op. 61 vln & orch.
  with Prague Symphony Orch. – Smetáček
  Supraphon LPV428

Danse macabre, Op. 40 (1874) orch.
  with Prague Symphony Orch. – Smetáček
  Supraphon SUK30095

SCHUMANN

Trio No. 2, in F, Op. 80 pf, vln & vlc
  with F. Rauch pf & F. Smetana vlc
  Crossroads 22 16 0123, 22 16 0124
  Supraphon SUA10639, SUAST50639

ŠEVČÍK

(6) Bohemian Dances, Op. 10 vln & pf
  No. 2. Dance in G
  with J. Maštalír pf
  Supraphon LPM197
  Ultraphon H24214

  No. 4. Fantasia in G
  with J. Maštalír pf
  Supraphon LPM197
  Ultraphon 5115C

ŽELEZNÝ

Concerto vln & orch.
  with Prague (FOK) Symphony Orch. – Rohan
  Supraphon SV8218

Arnold BELNICK (1924–)

GEMINIANI

(12) Sonatas (1739) vln & c
  Sonata in c arr. vln & pf David
  with V. Padwa pf
  Columbia 69794/5D, (in set X155), DOX679/80

MENDELSSOHN

Octet in E flat, Op. 20 4 vlns, 2 vlas & 2 vlcs
  with J. Heifetz vln, I. Baker vln, J. Stepansky vln, W. Primrose vla, V. Majewski vla, G. Piatigorsky vlc & G. Rejto vlc
  Victor (in sets LD6159 & LDS6159)

TARTINI

(12) Sonatas, Op. 1 (1734) vln & c
  Sonatas No. 1, in A: Allegro (1st mvt) arr. vln & pf as "Fugue" by Kreisler
  with V. Padwa pf
  Columbia 69795D, (in set X155), DOX680

VIOTTI

(3) Quartets, Op. 22 fl & vln or 2 vlns, vla & vlc
  No. 1. Quartet No. 1, in B flat
  with I. Baker vln, A. Neiman vla & A. Kaproff vlc
  Society for Forgotten Music SFM1006

  No. 3. Quartet No. 3, in c
  with I. Baker vln, A. Neiman vla & A. Kaproff vlc
  Society for Forgotten Music SFM1006

Joel BELOV

BACH

(4) Suites, BWV1066/9 strs & c
    Suite No. 3, in D: Air (2nd mvt) BWV1068 2 obs, 3 tpts, drms & strs –
    arr. vln & pf as "Air on the G–string" by Wilhelmj
    with R. Gayler pf   6289   Edison cylinder 4010
                                  Edison Diamond Disc 80419

BEETHOVEN

(6) Minuets, G167 pf
    No. 2. Minuet No. 2, in G arr. vln & pf Burmester
    with R. Gayler pf   6288   Edison Diamond Disc 80419

HANDEL

Serse (1738) – opera
    Ombra mai fu "Largo" arr. vln & pf
    with R. Gayler pf   6288   Edison Diamond Disc 80419

Andrew BENAC

CORELLI

(12) Concerti grossi, Op. 6 orch.
    Concerto grosso No. 1, in D
    with D. Zafer vln & CBC Toronto   CBC SM3
    String Orch. – B. Brott

VIVALDI

(12) Concerti, Op. 3 "L'Estro armonico" var. cbns & strs
    Concerto No. 8, in a P.2 (F.I, No. 177) 2 vlns, strs & c
    with D. Zafer vln & CBC Toronto   CBC SM3
    String Orch. – B. Brott

Jacques BENAVENTE

DRDLA

Serenade No. 1, in A vln & pf
    with piano   aR 291   Ideal 7005

MASCAGNI

Cavalleria Rusticana (1890) – opera
    Intermezzo orch. – arr. vln & pf
    with piano   aR 293   Ideal 7007

METCALF

Absent (1899) v & pf – arr. vln & pf
    with piano   aR 294   Ideal 7005

OFFENBACH

(Les) contes d'Hoffmann (1881) – opera
    Belle nuit, O nuit d'amour "Barcarolle" arr. vln & str qt
    with Scala Quartet   aR 277   Ideal 7007

PARTOS

Sonia (Russian ballad) v & pf – arr. vln & pf
    with piano   aR 292   Ideal 7008

TATE

Somewhere a voice is calling (1911) v & pf – arr. vln & str qt
    with Scala Quartet   aR 284   Ideal 7008

René BENEDETTI (1901–   )

BACH

(3) Sonatas & 3 Partitas, BWV1001/6 solo vln
    Partita No. 3, in E: Preludio (1st mvt)
    (unaccompanied)   Columbia 50322D, 5121M
                                LFX22

BAZZINI

(La) Ronde des lutins, Op. 25 vln & pf
    with M. Fauré pf   Columbia LFX175

BEETHOVEN

(3) Trios, Op. 1 pf, vln & vlc
    No. 3. Trio No. 3, in c
    with J. Benvenuti pf & A. Navarra vlc   Pathé PGT33/5

BRAHMS

(16) Waltzes, Op. 39 pf duet
    No. 15. Waltz No. 15, in A flat arr. vln & pf "in A" Hochstein
    with M. Fauré pf   Columbia D13037

CHAMINADE

Sérénade espagnole pf – arr. vln & pf Kreisler
    with M. Fauré pf   Columbia D13031

CHOPIN

(2) Nocturnes, Op. 27 pf
    No. 2. Nocturne No. 8, in D flat arr. vln & pf Sarasate
    with M. Fauré pf   Columbia LFX21

DEBUSSY

Petite Suite (1889) pf – 4 hands
    No. 3. Menuet arr. vln & pf Dushkin
    with M. Fauré pf   Columbia D2037

DVOŘÁK

(8) Slavonic Dances, Op. 46 pf duet; orch.
    No. 2. Slavonic dance No. 2, in e arr. vln & pf "in g" Kreisler
    with M. Fauré pf   Columbia D13030
(8) Slavonic Dances, Op. 72 pf duet; orch.
    No. 2. Slavonic Dance No. 10, in e arr. vln & pf Kreisler
    with M. Fauré pf   Columbia D13038

FALLA

(7) Canciones populares españolas (1914) v & pf
    No. 3. Asturiana arr. vln & pf Kochański
    with M. Fauré pf   LX 435–1   Columbia 9684, 67659D,
                                          D15049, J7528

    No. 4. Jota arr. vln & pf Kochański
    with M. Fauré pf   LX 436   Columbia 9684, 67659D,
                                          D15049, J7528

    No. 6. Canción arr. vln & pf Kochański
    with M. Fauré pf   LX 436   Columbia 9684, 67659D,
                                          D15049, J7528

    No. 7. Polo arr. vln & pf Kochański
    with M. Fauré pf   LX 435–1   Columbia 9684, 67659D,
                                          D15049, J7528

(La) Vida breve (1913) – opera
    Danza española orch. – arr. vln & pf Kreisler
    with M. Fauré pf   Columbia D13037

GUIRAUD

Piccolino (1879) – opera
  Mélodrame arr. vln & pf
  with M. Fauré pf   Columbia DF2145

KREISLER

Caprice viennois, Op. 2 vln & pf
  with M. Fauré pf   LX 121[1]   Columbia D15008, LNX154
Recitative & Scherzo–caprice, Op. 6 solo vln
  (unaccompanied)   Columbia 50322D, 5121M,
                               LFX22
Rondino on a theme by Beethoven vln & pf
  with M. Fauré pf   Columbia D13087
Tambourin chinois, Op. 3 vln & pf
  with M. Fauré pf   Columbia D2037, D15009
Chanson Louis XIII & Pavane (L. Couperin) vln & pf
  with M. Fauré pf   Columbia LFX175
Variations on a theme of Corelli (Tartini) vln & pf
  with M. Fauré pf   Columbia D13087

MILHAUD

Cinéma–Fantaisie (on "Le Boeuf sur le toit") (1919) (cadenza by Honegger)
  vln & orch.
  with J. Wiéner pf   Columbia D15074/5

MONTI

Csárdas (1904) vln & pf
  with M. Fauré pf   Columbia DF2145

MOSZKOWSKI

(2) Stücke, Op. 45 pf
  No. 2. Guitarre arr. vln & pf Sarasate
  with M. Fauré pf   Columbia 193M, D13031

MOZART

Divertimento No. 17, in D, K334 strs & 2 hrns
  Minuet (3rd mvt) arr. vln & pf Burmester
  with M. Fauré pf   Columbia D13088
Serenade No. 7, in D, K250 "Haffner" orch.
  Rondo (4th mvt) arr. vln & pf Kreisler
  with M. Fauré pf   Columbia 2507D, LF4
Sonata No. 23, in D, K306 vln & pf
  with V. Perlemuter pf   Pathé DTX195

PAGANETTI

Méditation vln & pf
  with M. Benvenuti pf & organ   Columbia LF121
Scherzo vln & pf
  with M. Benvenuti pf & organ   Columbia LF121

PAGANINI

Concerto No. 1, in D, Op. 6 (cadenza by Benedetti) vln & orch.
  with Lamoureux Orch. – Bigot   Pathé PDT45/8, (set M6)

RAVEL

Trio in a (1915) pf, vln & vlc
  with J. Benvenuti pf & A. Navarra vlc   Pathé PGT37/9

RIES

Suite No. 3, in G, Op. 34 vln & pf
  No. 5. Perpetuum mobile
  with M. Fauré pf   Columbia D13030

SAINT–SAËNS

(6) Études, Op. 52 pf
  No. 6. Étude No. 6, in D flat "Étude en forme de valse" arr. vln & pf
  Ysaÿe
  with M. Fauré pf   Columbia L2878, LF79

SARASATE

Carmen Fantasia (on themes from the opera by Bizet) Op. 25 vln & pf or
  orch.
  with M. Fauré pf   Columbia LFX31
(8) Danzas españolas vln & pf
  No. 1. Malagueña, Op. 21, No. 1
  with M. Fauré pf   LX 123[1]   Columbia D15008, LNX154
  No. 2. Habañera, Op. 21, No. 2
  with M. Fauré pf   Columbia D15009
  No. 6. Zapateado, Op. 23, No. 2
  with M. Fauré pf   Columbia LFX21

SCHUBERT

Rosamunde von Cypren, Op. 26 (D797) (1823) – Incidental music orch.
  No. 9. Ballet music II, in G arr. vln & pf Kreisler
  with M. Fauré pf   Columbia D13088
Trio No. 1, in B flat, Op. 99 (D898) pf, vln & vlc
  with J. Benvenuti pf & A. Navarra pf   Pathé PGT29/32
                                     Vox PL1770

SZYMANOWSKI

(3) Mythes, Op. 30 (1915) vln & pf
  No. 1. La Fontaine d'Aréthuse
  with M. Fauré pf   Columbia 2167D, 193M, D13038

WIENIAWSKI

Souvenir de Moscou, Op. 6 vln & pf or orch.
  with piano   Columbia D15033, JW142

Umberto BENEDETTI MICHELANGELI

VIVALDI

Concerto in a, P.28 (F.I, No. 61) 2 vlns, strs & c
  with R. Biffoli vln & Angelicum Orch.,   Angelicum LPA5993
  Milan – Martinotti   Musical Heritage Society
                                     MHS878
Concerto in C, P.84 (F.XII, No. 14) "Per la Solennità di St. Lorenzo" 2 fls,
  2 obs, 2 cls, 2 vlns, bsn, strs & c
  with T. Pasquali vln, P. Salvi vlc, A.   Angelicum STA9017
  Berruti hpsi & Angelicum Orch.,
  Milan – Martinotti
Concerto in G, P.132 (F.I, No. 6) 2 vlns, strs & c
  with R. Biffoli vln & Angelicum Orch.,   Angelicum LPA5993
  Milan – Martinotti   Musical Heritage Society
                                     MHS878

Sándor BENEŠ

GOUNOD

Ave Maria (Méditation on Bach's "Prelude No. 1, in C" from Book I of
  "Das Wohltemperirte Clavier") v & pf – arr. vln & orch.
  with Orch. – Schröder   Compania Generale del Disco
                                  PV1521

INNOCENZI

Dal pincio (Intermezzo) vln & orch.
 with orch.   Weinberger W8

SCHUBERT

(7) Gesänge (set to Scott's "Lady of the Lake") Op. 52 v & pf
 No. 6. Ave Maria, D839 arr. vln & orch.
  with orch. – Schröder   Compania Generale del Disco
            PV1520
(14) Schwanengesang, D957 (1828) v & pf
 No. 4. Ständchen "Serenade" arr. vln & orch.
  with orch. – Schröder   Compania Generale del Disco
            PV1520

Franz BENETER

LANGER

Grandmother, Op. 20 pf – arr. vln & orch.
 with orch.   Favorite 1–14192

MOSZKOWSKI

(6) Klavierstüke, Op. 15 pf – 4 hands
 No. 1. Serenata arr. vln & orch.
  with orch.   Favorite 1–14194

Mario BENVENUTI

VIVALDI

(12) Concerti, Op. 3 "L'Estro armonico" var. cbns & strs
 Concerto No. 1, in D, P.146 (F.IV, No. 7) 4 vlns, vlc, strs & c
  with F. Gulli vln, E. Malanotte vln,   HMV ALP1809, ASD391
  A. Poltronieri vln & Virtuosi di
  Roma – Fasano
 Concerto No. 4, in e, F.97 (F.I, No. 174) 4 vlns, strs & c
  with A. Stefanato vln, R. Ruotolo vln,   HMV ALP1809, ASD391
  F. Gulli vln & Virtuosi di
  Roma – Fasano
 Concerto No. 7, in F, P.249 (F.IV, No. 9) 4 vlns, strs & c
  with E. Malanotte vln, L. Ferro vln, F.   HMV ALP1810, ASD392
  Gulli vln & Virtuosi di
  Roma – Fasano

Henry BERCHMANN

CHOPIN

(3) Nocturnes, Op. 9 pf
 No. 2. Nocturne No. 2, in E flat arr. vln & pf Sarasate
 with piano   HMV 107925

GOUNOD

Ave Maria (Méditation on Bach's "Prelude No. 1, in C" from Book I of
 "Das Wohltemperirte Clavier") v & pf – arr. vln & pf
 with piano   HMV 107919

MLYNARSKI

Mazurka in G, Op. 26 vln & pf
 with piano   HMV 107920

SCHUMANN

(13) Kinderscenen, Op. 15 pf
 No. 7. Träumerei arr. vln & pf
  with piano   HMV 107924

Alexander BEREGOWSKY

BOULANGER, G.

Avant de mourir, Op. 17 vln & pf
 with orch.   Parlophone A7383, F1432

KOŠTÀL

Minuet vln & pf
 with orch.   Parlophone A7383, F1432

Maurits van der BERG (1898–)

BACH

(4) Suites, BWV1066/9 strs & c
 Suite No. 3, in D: Air (2nd mvt) BWV1068 2 obs, 3 tpts, drms &
  strs – arr. vln & pf as "Air on the G–string" by Wilhelmj
  wit B. Seidler–Winkler pf   Tri–Ergon 1114

BEETHOVEN

Sonata No. 5, in F, Op. 24 "Spring" vln & pf
 with B. Seidler–Winkler pf   Tri–Ergon 1122/4

DRDLA

Souvenir vln & pf
 with B. Seidler–Winkler pf   Tri–Ergon 5054

GOSSEC

Rosine (1786) – opera
 Gavotte arr. vln & pf Burmester
 with B. Seidler–Winkler pf   Tri–Ergon 5076

JUON

(6) Skizzen, Op. 1 vln & pf
 No. 3. Canzonetta
 with B. Seidler–Winkler pf   Tri–Ergon 5076

KREISLER

Aus Wien vln & pf
 with B. Seidler–Winkler pf   Tri–Ergon 5054
Caprice viennois, Op. 2 vln & pf
 with B. Seidler–Winkler pf   Tri–Ergon 1102
(La) Gitana vln & pf
 with B. Seidler–Winkler pf   Tri–Ergon 1113
Liebesfreud vln & pf
 with B. Seidler–Winkler pf   Tri–Ergon 5053
Liebesleid vln & pf
 with B. Seidler–Winkler pf   Tri–Ergon 1102
Rondino on a theme by Beethoven vln & pf
 with B. Seidler–Winkler pf   Tri–Ergon 1114
Schön Rosmarin vln & pf
 with B. Seidler–Winkler pf   Tri–Ergon 5053

SARASATE

(8) **Danzas españolas** vln & pf
    No. 3. Romanza andaluza, Op. 22, No. 1
      with B. Seidler–Winkler pf   Tri–Ergon 1113

VIEUXTEMPS

Ballade & Polonaise in G, Op. 38 vln & pf
    Ballade
      with orch.   Parlophone P1269

Fantasia–appassionata, Op. 35 vln & pf
    Largo
      with orch.   Parlophone P1269

VIVALDI

(12) **Concerti,** Op. 3 "L'Estro armonico" var. cbns & strs
    Concerto No. 10, in b: Largo (2nd mvt) P.148 (F.IV, No. 10) 4 vlns, strs
    & c
      with S. Frenkel vln, W. Hanke vln, R.   Telefunken SK1318, TF52
      Totenberg vln, G. Werthein hpsi &
      Berlin Philharmonic Orch. – Unger

Franz BERGER

HANDEL

(12) **Concerti grossi,** Op. 6 (1739) 2 vlns, vlc & strs
    Concerto grosso No. 1, in G
      with O. Büchner vln, H. Melzer vlc,   Archive AP13010, APM14091,
      K. Richter hpsi & Bamberg Symphony   ARC3084
      Orch. – Lehmann   Decca DL9692, (in set DX126)
           Deutsche Grammophon 16080/1,
           EPA37072, PV7405/6

    Concerto grosso No. 2, in F
      with O. Büchner vln, H. Melzer vlc,   Archive AP13010, APM14091,
      K. Richter hpsi & Bamberg Symphony   ARC3084
      Orch. – Lehmann   Decca DL9692, (in set DX126)
           Deutsche Grammophon 16080/1,
           EPA37088, PV7407

    Concerto grosso No. 3, in e
      with O. Büchner vln, H. Melzer vlc,   Archive AP13011, APM14092,
      K. Richter hpsi & Bamberg Symphony   ARC3085
      Orch. – Lehmann   Decca DL9693, (in set DX126)
           Deutsche Grammophon 16080/1,
           EPA37106, PV7405/6

    Concerto grosso No. 4, in a
      with O. Büchner vln, H. Melzer vlc,   Archive AP13011, APM14092,
      K. Richter hpsi & Bamberg Symphony   ARC3085
      Orch. – Lehmann   Decca DL9693, (in set DX126)
           Deutsche Grammophon 16080/1,
           EPA37117, PV7409

    Concerto grosso No. 5, in D
      with O. Büchner vln, H. Melzer vlc,   Archive AP13012, APM14092,
      K. Richter hpsi & Bamberg Symphony   ARC3086
      Orch. – Lehmann   Decca DL9694, (in set DX126)
           Deutsche Grammophon
           EPA37040

    Concerto grosso No. 6, in g
      with O. Büchner vln, H. Melzer vlc,   Archive AP13013, APM14094,
      K. Richter hpsi & Bamberg Symphony   ARC3087
      Orch. – Lehmann   Decca DL9695, (in set DX126)

    Concerto grosso No. 7, in B flat
      with O. Büchner vln, H. Melzer vlc,   Archive AP13013, APM14094,
      K. Richter hpsi & Bamber Symphony   ARC3087
      Orch. – Lehmann   Decca DL9695, (in set DX126)
           Deutsche Grammophon
           EPA37053

    Concerto grosso No. 8, in c
      with O. Büchner vln, H. Melzer vlc,   Archive AP13013, APM14094,
      K. Richter hpsi & Bamberg Symphony   ARC3087
      Orch. – Lehmann   Decca DL9695, (in set DX126)

    Concerto grosso No. 9, in F
      with O. Büchner vln, H. Melzer vlc,   Archive AP13012, APM14093,
      K. Richter hpsi & Bamberg Symphony   ARC3086
      Orch. – Lehmann   Decca DL9694, (in set DX126)

    Concerto grosso No. 10 in d
      with O. Büchner vln, H. Mezer vlc,   Archive AP13011, APM14092,
      K. Richter hpsi & Bamberg Symphony   ARC3085
      Orch. – Lehmann   Decca DL9693, (in set DX126)

    Concerto grosso No. 11, in A
      with O. Büchner vln, H. Melzer vlc,   Archive AP13010/1,
      K. Richter hpsi & Bamberg Symphony   APM14091/2, ARC3084/5
      Orch. – Lehmann   Decca DL9692/3, (in set DX126)

    Concerto grosso No. 12, in b
      with O. Büchner vln, H. Melzer vlc,   Archive AP13010, APM14091,
      K. Richter hpsi & Bamberg Symphony   ARC3084
      Orch. – Lehmann   Decca DL9692, (in set DX126)

Wilhelm G. BERGER (1929–)

BERGER

Sonata (1964) solo vln
    (unaccompanied)   Electrecord ECE0231

Arthur BERGH (1882–1962)

BERGH

Scherzo vln & pf
    with piano   3222   Columbia A204

GODARD

Jocelyn (1888) – opera
    Cachés dans cet asile "Berceuse" arr. vln & pf
      with piano   Columbia A216

HUBAY

(14) **Scènes de la Csárda** vln & pf
    No. 4. Hejre Kati, Op. 32
      with piano   Columbia A212

V. BERGS

MEDYNS

Poem in b vln & orch.
    with Latvian Radio Symphony   Mezhdunarodnaya Kniga
    Orch. – Vigner   D00010991/2

Harold BERKLEY (1896–1965)

BLOCH
Sonata No. 1 (1920) vln & pf
  with M. Berkley pf   Gamut GT12106/9

Frances BERKOVA

BACH
(4) Suites, BWV1066/9 strs & c
  Suite No. 3, in D: Air (2nd mvt) BWV1068 2 obs, 3 tpts, drms &
  strs – arr. vln & pf as "Air on the G–string" by Wilhemj,
  with piano   51302   Homochord B8441

CUI
Kaleidoscope, Op. 50 vln & pf
  No. 9. Orientale
  with piano   51241   Homochord B8439

DVOŘÁK
(8) Slavonic Dances, Op. 46 pf duet; orch.
  No. 2. Slavonic dance No. 2, in e arr. vln & pf "in g" Kreisler
  with piano   51304   Homochord B8608

KREISLER
Sicilienne & rigaudon (Francoeur) vln & pf
  with piano   51303   Homochord B8441

PADEREWSKI
(6) Humoresques de concert, Op. 14 pf
  No. 1. Minuet in G arr. vln & pf Kreisler
  with piano   51305   Homochord B6808

SARASATE
(8) Danzas españolas vln & pf
  No. 3. Romanza andaluza, Op. 22, No. 1
  with piano   51240   Homochord B8439

Leo BERLIN

BORNUM
Capriccioso vln & pf
  with L. Sellegren pf   Philips 401011AE

FRUMERIE
Trio No. 2 (1952) pf, vln & vlc
  with L. Sellergren pf & A. Olofsson   Discofil LT33129
  vlc

von KOCH
(4) Dances vln & pf
  with L. Sellergren pf   Nordiska Musikförlaget
                          AEP1103

ROMAN
Concerto No. 3, in d vln & orch.
  with Stockholm Philharmonic   Victor LM10029, LSC10029
  Chamber Orch.

SJÖGREN
Sonata No. 2, in e, Op. 24 vln & pf
  with L. Sellergren pf   Discofil LT33157

Claire BERNARD (1947–)

BARBER
Concerto, Op. 14 (1941) vln & orch.
  with Orch. National de l'Opéra de   Philips 835796LY, PHC9105
  Monte–Carlo – van Remoortel

GAVINIÈS
(6) Concerti, Op. 4 (1764) vln & orch.
  Concerto No. 2, in F (cadenzas by Chaynes)
  with Rouen Chamber   Philips 641765LL, 835765AY,
  Orch. – Beauchamp   PHC9039
  Concerto No. 5, in A (cadenzas by Chaynes)
  with Rouen Chamber   Philips 641765LL, 835765AY,
  Orch. – Beauchamp   PHC9039

HAYDN
Sonata No. 7, in F, H.III, No. 82 vln & hpsi
  with H. Dreyfus pf   Philips 835784AY

KHACHATURIAN
Concerto in D (1940) vln & orch.
  with Bucharest Symphony   Philips 741744LL, 835744AY,
  Orch. – Khachaturian   PHC9046

LECLAIR
(6) Concerti, Op. 7 (1737) vln & strs
  Concerto No. 1, in d (res. J–P Dautel)
  with Rouen Chamber   Philips 641765LL, 835765AY,
  Orch. – Beauchamp   839845GSY, PHC9039
  Concerto No. 5, in a (res. J–P. Dautel)
  with Rouen Chamber   Philips 641765LL, 835765AY,
  Orch. – Beauchamp   PHC9039

MILHAUD
Concerto No. 2 (1946) vln & orch.
  with Orch. National de l'Opéra de   Philips 835796LY, PHC9105
  Monte–Carlo – van Remoortel

MOZART
Sonata No. 2, in D, K7 vln & pf
  with H. Dreyfus pf   Philips 835784AY
Sonata No. 5, in e, K10 vln & pf
  with H. Dreyfus pf   Philips 835784AY
Sonata No. 13, in C, K28 vln & pf
  with H. Dreyfus pf   Philips 835784AY

PROKOFIEV
Concerto No. 1, in D, Op. 19 vln & orch.
  with Bucharest Symphony   Philips 641774LL, 835744AY,
  Orch. – Bugeanu   PHC9046

SARASATE
Carmen Fantasia (on themes from the opera by Bizet) Op. 25 vln & pf or
orch.
  with L'Orch. National de l'Opéra de   Philips 6525 006
  Monte Carlo – Gilbault
(8) Danzas españolas vln & pf
  No. 2. Habañera, Op. 21, No. 2
  with L'Orch. National de l'Opéra de   Philips 6525 006
  Monte–Carlo – Gibault

SARASATE – *Continued*

Faust Fantasia (on themes from the opera by Gounod) vln & pf or orch.
  with L'Orch. National de l'Opéra de   Philips 6525 006
  Monte Carlo – Gibault

Zigeunerweisen, Op. 20 vln & pf or orch.
  with L'Orch. National de l'Opéra de   Philips 6525 006
  Monte Varlo – Gibault

Minetti BERNARDI

FAURÉ

Berceuse, Op. 16 vln & pf
  with piano   HMV R9035

SVENDSEN

Romance in G, Op. 26 vln & orch. – arr. vln & pf Wilhelmj
  with piano   HMV R9035

Josef BERNSTEIN

BACH

Concerto No. 1, in a, BWV1041 vln, strs & c.
  with Concert Hall Ensemble   Classic CL6065
                                         Concert Hall CHS40

BEETHOVEN

(3) Sonatas, Op. 12 vln & pf
  No. 2. Sonata No. 2, in A
  with E. Goldstein pf   Concert Hall CHC34
Sonata No. 4, in a, Op. 23 vln & pf
  with E. Goldstein pf   Concert Hall CHC34
Sonata No. 5, in F, op. 24 "Spring" vln & pf
  with E. Goldstein pf   Concert Hall CHC17

DVOŘÁK

(5) Bagatelles, Op. 47 2 vlns, vlc & harmonium
  nos. 1/4 only
  with P. Rybar vln, W. Landshoff vlc & Pro Musica PMR112
  Alban pf   Treasury of Music T9

VIVALDI

(12) Concerti, Op. 3 "L'Estro armonico" var. cbns & strs
  Concerto No. 6, in a, P.1, (F.I, No. 176) vln, strs & c
  with Concert Hall Ensemble   Classic CL6065
                                         Concert Hall CHS40
(12) Sonatas, Op. 2 (1712) vln & c
  Sonata No. 2, in A, F.XIII, No. 30
  with R. Starer pf   Classic CL6065
                                         Classics Club X26
                                         Concert Hall CHS40

Lála BERTLOVÁ (–1961)

KUBELÍK, R.

Dumka (Dupák) vln & pf
  with R. Kubelík pf   Ultraphon G14181

Edith BERTSCHINGER

HAYDN

Concerto No. 2, in G, HVIIa, No. 4 (1761) (cadenza by A. Heiller) vln & orch.
  with E. Heiller hpsi & Collegium   Erato LDE2005
  Musicum Orch, Vienna – Heiller   Haydn Society HS9031,
                                         HSL1014
                                         Nixa HLP1014

Concerto No. 3, in A, H.VIIa, No. 3 (1765) "Melk" (cadenza by A. Heiller) vln & orch.
  with Collegium Musicum Orch.   Haydn Society, HSL1017
  Vienna – Heiller   Nixa HLP1017

Jiří BEZDEKOVSKÝ (1920–)

FOERSTER

From Shakespeare, Op. 76 (1909) vln & orch.
  with Prague Symphony Orch. – Jiráček Supraphon LPM383, SUA20337

Igor BEZRODNY (1930–)

BACH

(3) Sonatas & 3 Partitas, BWV1001/6 solo vln
  Partita No. 2, in d: Chaconne (5th mvt) BWV1004
  (unaccompanied)   Mezhdunarodnaya Kniga D4856

BARTÓK

(6) Rumanian folk dances (1915) pf – arr. vln & pf Székely
  with piano   Mezhdunarodnaya Kniga
                                         D00624

BEETHOVEN

Concerto in D, Op. 61 (cadenzas by Kreisler) vln & orch.
  with Moscow State Philharmonic   Eurodisc 74629KK, 80041ZK
  Symphony Orch. – Rozhdestvensky   Mezhdunarodnaya Kniga
                                         D012041/2, S0601/2

BLOCH

Baal Shem (3 Pictures of Chassidic life) (1923) vln & pf
  No. 2. Nigun (Improvisation)
  with A. Makarov pf   Mezhdunarodnaya Kniga D3401
                                         Monitor MC2028

BRAHMS

(21) Hungarian Dances pf duet
  Hungarian Dance No. 1, in g arr. vln & pf Joachim
  with V. Yampolsky pf   Mezhdunarodnaya Kniga
                                         D00922, D17425

  Hungarian Dance No. 20, in d arr. vln & pf "in e" Joachim
  with V. Yampolsky pf   Mezhdunarodnaya Kniga
                                         D17789

CASTELNUOVO-TEDESCO

(3) Songs of Shakespeare – Book VIII (1926) v & pf
  No. 3. Two maids wooing a man arr. vln & pf as "Tango" by Heifetz
  with piano   Mezhdunarodnaya Kniga
                                         D09239/40

CHAUSSON

Poème, Op. 25 vln & orch.
    with USSR State Radio Symphony   Mezhdunarodnaya Kniga, D2161
    Orch. – Kondrashin   Westminister, XWN18534

CHOPIN

(4) Mazurkas, Op. 67 pf
  No. 4. Mazurka No. 45, in a arr. vln & pf Kreisler
    with V. Vampolsky pf   MG 128846   Le Chant du Monde GA5072
Nocturne No. 19, in e Op. 72, No. 1 pf arr. vln & pf Auer
    with piano   Mezhdunarodnaya Kniga
         D09239/40

DEBUSSY

Petite Suite (1889) pf – 4 hands
  No. 1. En bateau arr. vln & pf Dushkin
    with A. Makarov pf   Monitor MC2028
Prélude à l'après-midi d'un faune (1894) orch arr. vln & pf Heifetz
    with piano   Mezhdunarodnaya Kniga
         D09239/40

ELGAR

Adieu pf arr. vln & pf Szigeti
    with A. Makarov pf   Mezhdunarodnaya Kniga
         D004854
         Monitor MC2028

ERNST

Fantasia brillante (on themes from Rossini's opera "Otello") Op. 11 vln & pf
    with A. Makarov pf   Mezhdunarodnaya Kniga D6282

FOERSTER

Concerto in C, Op. 88 (1926) vln & orch.
    with USSR State Symphony   Mezhdunarodnaya Kniga
    Orch. – Anasov   D2474/5
         Westminster XWN18534

FUCHS

Jota vln & pf
    with A. Makarov pf   Mezhdunarodnaya Kniga
         D004855
         Monitor MC2028

GERSHWIN

(3) Jazz Preludes (1936) pf
  No. 1. Prelude No. 1, in B flat arr. vln & pf Heifetz
    with A. Makarov pf   Mezhdunarodnaya Kniga D6281
         Monitor MC2028
  No. 2. Prelude No. 2, in c sharp arr. vln & pf Heifetz
    with A. Makarov pf   Mezhdunarodnaya Kniga D6281
         Monitor MC2028
  No. 3. Prelude No. 3, in E flat arr. vln & pf Heifetz
    with A. Makarov pf   Mezhdunarodnaya Kniga D6281
         Monitor MC2028

GLAZOUNOV

Raymonda, Op. 57 (1897) – ballet orch.
  Entr'acte No. 1 arr. vln & pf Pogozhev
    with S. Wakman pf   Philips S06048R

GLIÈRE

Romance in D, Op. 3 vln & pf
    with V. Yampolsky pf   M6 128845   Le Chant du Monde GA5072
         Mezhudnarodnaya Kniga
         D001284, D17788

HANDEL

(15) Sonatas, Op. 1 (?1731) fl or vln & c
  Sonata No. 13, in D vln IV
    with V. Petrashinsky pf   Mezhdunarodnaya Kniga D4857
  Sonata No. 15, in E: Adagio (1st mvt); **Allegro** (2nd mvt) vln VI
    with V. Yampolsky pf   Mezhdunarodnaya Kniga
         D18914/5

KABALEVSKY

Concerto in C, Op. 48 vln & orch.
  Andante cantabile (2nd mvt)
    with orch. – Straszynski   Muza 1553

KREISLER

Gypsy Caprice vln & pf
    with A. Makarov pf   Mezhdunarodnaya Kniga D3401
         Monitor MC2028
Variations on a theme of Corelli (Tartini) vln & pf
    with V. Yampolsky pf   Mezhdunarodnaya Kniga
         D00922, D17424

LOCATELLI

(12) Sonatas, Op. 6 (1737) vln & c
  Sonata No. 7, in f "Au Tombeau" arr. vln & pf Ysaÿe
    with A. Makarov pf   Mezhdunarodnaya Kniga D3400

MERIKANTO

Intermezzo vln & pf
    with A. Makarov pf   Mezhdunarodnaya Kniga D6281

MOMPOU

(5) Scènes d'enfants (1915/8) pf
  No. 5. Jeunes filles au jardin arr. vln & pf Szigeti
    with A. Makarov pf   Mezhdunarodnaya Kniga
         D004854
         Monitor MC2028

MOSZKOWSKI

(2) Stücke, Op. 45 pf
  No. 2. Guitarre arr. vln & pf Sarasate
    with piano   Mezhdunarodnaya Kniga
         D09239/40, D0009991/2

MOZART

Serenade No. 7, in D, K250 "Haffner" orch.
  Rondo (4th mvt) arr. vln & pf Kreisler
    with piano   Mezhdunarodnaya Kniga
         D017426/7
Trio No. 5, in C, K548 pf, vln & vlc
    with D. Bashkirov pf & M. Khomitser   Mezhdunarodnaya Kniga
    vlc   D021245/6, S01621/2

NAPOLITANO

Tristesse vln & pf
    with piano   Mezhdunarodnaya Kniga
         D09239/40

NORDQVIST

Entreaty vln & pf
  with A. Makarov pf   Mezhdunarodnaya Kniga
  D004855

PROKOFIEV

(The) Love for Three Oranges, Op. 33 (1919) – opera
  No. 3. March arr. vln & pf Heifetz
  with A. Makarov pf   Mezhdunarodnaya Kniga D3401
Peter & the Wolf, Op. 67 narrator & orch.
  Theme & processional arr. vln & pf Grunes
  with A. Makarov pf   Monitor MC2028
  Theme & processional arr. vln & pf Grunes
  with S. Wakman pf   Philips S06048R

RACHMANINOV

(2) Pieces, Op. 6 pf
  No. 1. Romance in d arr. vln & pf
  with A. Makarov pf   Mezhdunarodnaya Kniga
  D001284

  No. 1. Romance in d arr. vln & pf
  with S.Wakman pf   Philips S06048R

  No. 1. Romance in d arr. vln & pf
  with piano   Mezhdunarodnaya Kniga
  D09239/40, D0009991/2
(10) Preludes, Op. 23 pf
  No. 4. Prelude No. 4, in D arr. vln & pf Erdenko
  with A. Makarov pf   Mezhdunarodnaya Kniga
  D001284, D3401

RAVEL

Tzigane (Rapsodie de concert) (1924) vln & pf or orch.
  with S. Wakman pf   Philips N402049E

RESPIGHI

Berceuse vln & pf
  with A. Makarov pf   Mezhdunarodnaya Kniga
  D004855
  Monitor MC2028

RUBINSTEIN

(6) Soirées de Saint–Pétersbourg, Op. 44 pf
  No. 1. Romance in E flat arr. vln & pf Wieniawski
  with piano   Mezhdunarodnaya Kniga
  D00342

SHOSTAKOVICH

Trio No. 2, in e, Op. 67 "In memory of I.I. Sollertinsky" pf, vln & vlc
  with D. Bashkirov pf & M. Khomitser   Mezhdunarodnaya Kniga
  vlc   D021245/6, S01621/2

SIBELIUS

(2) Serenades, Op. 69 vln & orch.
  No. 1. Serenade No. 1, in d
  with USSR Radio Symphony   Mezhdunarodnaya Kniga D2162
  Orch. – Kondrashin
  No. 2. Serenade No. 2, in g
  with USSR Radio Symphony   Mezhdunarodnaya Kniga D2162
  Orch. – Kondrashin

SMETANA

From my Homeland (1878) vln & pf
  No. 2. Andantino
  with S. Wakman pf   Philips N402049E

SZYMANOWSKI

Notturno & Tarantelle, Op. 28 vln & pf
  with piano   Mezhdunarodnaya Kniga
  D09239/40

Romance in D, Op. 23 (1909) vln & pf
  with A. Makarov pf   Mezhdunarodnaya Kniga D6281

TANEIEV

Concert Suite, Op. 28 (1911) vln & orch.*
  with USSR State Symphony   Mezhdunarodnaya Kniga
  Orch. – Kondrashin   D0361/2
  Fairytale (3rd mvt)
  with S. Wakman pf   Philips S06048R

TCHAIKOVSKY

Trio in a, Op. 50 "To the memory of a great artist" pf, vln & vlc
  with D. Bashkirov pf & M. Khomitser   Mezhdunarodnaya Kniga
  vlc   D018209/10, S01353/4

TOWNSEND

Berceuse vln & pf
  with piano   Mezhdunarodnaya Kniga
  D09239/40, D0009991/2

TRIGGS

Danza brasiliana vln & pf
  with A. Makarov pf   Mezhdunarodnaya Kniga
  D004855
  Monitor MC2028

VILLA–LOBOS

(0) Canto do cysne negro (1917) vlc & pf – arr. vln & pf Villa–Lobos
  with A. Makarov pf   Mezhdunarodnaya Kniga
  D004854
  Monitor MC2028

VIVALDI

Adagio unid vln & c
  with piano   Mezhdunarodnaya Kniga
  D19681/2

VLADIGEROV

Danse, Op. 37 pf – arr. vln & pf
  with piano   Mezhdunarodnaya Kniga
  D09239/40

Vardar (Rapsody bulgare) Op. 16 vln & orch.
  with V. Yampolsky   MG 128847/8   Le Chant du Monde GA5073
  pf   Mezhdunarodnaya Kniga D372

WAGNER

Albumblatt in C (1861) pf – arr. vln & pf Wilhelmj
  with piano   Mezhdunarodnaya Kniga
  D00341

---

* Prelude or 1st mvt & Gavotte or 2nd mvt is also on Mezhdunarodnaya Kniga D021535/6 while Fairytale or 3rd mvt is on Mezhdunarodnaya Kniga D21420/1

YSAŸE

Berceuse in f, Op. 20 vln & pf
    with A. Makarov pf   Mezhdunarodnaya Kniga D3400

ZIMBALIST

Fantasia (on themes from Rimsky–Korsakov's opera "Le Coq d'Or") vln &
pf
    with V. Yampolsky pf   Mezhdunarodnaya Kniga
                              D00921, D17221/2

Mikhail BEZWIERCHNYI (1952–   )

SZYMANOWSKI

(3) Caprices (after Paganini) Op. 40 vln & pf
  No. 3. Caprice No. 24, in a
    with B. Rakowa pf   Muza XL0433

Walter BIEDERMANN

ANDRÉ

On the high Alps unid – arr. 2 vlns & pf
    with H. von Wegern vln   Columbia A746
    & piano

MENZEL

Romanze, Op. 40 "Sweet longing" fl & var. inst – arr. vln, fl & pf
    with M. Lufsky fl   30045–2   Columbia 30045, A5040
    & C.A. Prince pf

MUSIN

(2) Morceaux de concert, Op. 7 (1887) vln & pf
  No. 1. Mazurka de concert
    with L. Smith hp   Columbia A182

POTTER

Serenata amorosa unid – arr. 2 vlns & pf
    with G. Stehl vln   Columbia A775
    & piano

VOIGT

Abendgedanken "An meine Mutter" vln, vla & pf – arr. vln, fl & pf
    with M. Lufsky fl & C.A.   3506–1   Columbia 3506, A179
    Prince pf

Renato BIFFOLI

CORELLI

(12) Sonatas, Op. 5 vln & c – arr. as "Concerti grossi" by Geminiani
  Concerto grosso No. 1, in D
    with G. Magnani vln, N. Gasperini   Vox STDL500423,
    vlc, B. Canino hpsi & Gli Accademici   (in set VBX38)
    di Milano – Eckertsen
  Concerto grosso No. 2, in B flat
    with G. Magnani vln, N. Gasperini   Vox STDL50025,
    vlc, B. Canino hpsi & Gli Accademici   (in set VBX38)
    di Milano – Eckertsen
  Concerto grosso No. 3, in C
    with G. Magnani vln, N. Gasperini   Vox. (in set VBX38)
    vlc, B. Canino hpsi & Gli Accademici
    di Milano – Eckertsen

CORELLI – *Continued*

  Concerto grosso No. 4, in F
    with G. Magnani vln, N. Gasperini   Vox (in set VBX38)
    vlc, B. Canino hpsi & Gli Accademici
    di Milano – Eckertsen
  Concerto grosso No. 5, in g
    with G. Magnani vln, N. Gasperini   Vox (in set VBX38)
    vlc, B. Canino hpsi & Gli Accademici
    di Milano – Eckertsen
  Concerto grosso No. 6, in A
    with G. Magnani vln, N. Gasperini   Vox (in set VBX38)
    vlc, B. Canino hpsi & Gli Accademici
    di Milano – Eckertsen
  Concerto grosso No. 7, in d
    with G. Magnani vln, N. Gasperini   Vox (in set VBX38)
    vlc, B. Canino hpsi & Gli Accademici
    di Milano – Eckertsen
  Concerto grosso No. 8, in e
    with G. Magnani vln, N. Gasperini   Vox (in set VBX38)
    vlc, B. Canino hpsi & Gli Accademici
    di Milano – Eckertsen
  Concerto grosso No. 9, in A
    with G. Magnani vln. N. Gasperini   Vox (in set VBX38)
    vlc, B. Canino hpsi & Gli Accademici
    di Milano – Eckertsen
  Concerto grosso No. 10, in F
    with G. Magnani vln, N. Gasperini   Vox (in set VBX38)
    vlc, B. Canino hpsi & Gli Accademici
    di Milano – Eckertsen
  Concerto grosso No. 11, in E
    with G. Magnani vln, N. Gasperini   Vox (in set VBX38)
    vlc, B. Canino hpsi & Gli Accademici
    di Milano – Eckertsen
  Concerto grosso No. 12, in d "La Follia"
    with G. Magnani vln, N. Gasperini   Vox (in set VBX38)
    vlc, B. Canino hpsi & Gli Accademici
    di Milano – Eckertsen

GEMINIANI

(6) Concerti grossi, Op. 2 (1732) orch.
  Concerto grosso No. 1, in c
    with P. Giusto vln & Gli Accademici   Dover HCR5230
    di Milano – Eckertsen   Vox DL413, STDL500413
  Concerto grosso No. 2, in c
    with P. Giusto vln & Gli Accademici   Dover HCR5230
    di Milano – Eckertsen   Vox DL413, STDL500413
  Concerto grosso No. 3, in d
    with P. Giusto vln & Gli Accademici   Dover HCR5231
    di Milano – Eckertsen
  Concerto grosso No. 4, in D
    with P. Giusto vln & Gli Accademici   Dover HCR5231
    di Milano – Eckertsen
  Concerto grosso No. 5, in d
    with P. Giusto vln & Gli Accademici   Dover HCR5231
    di Milano – Eckertsen
  Concerto grosso No. 6, in A
    with P. Giusto vln & Gli Accademici   Dover HCR5231
    di Milano – Eckertsen

GEMINIANI – *Continued*

(6) Concerti grossi, Op. 4 (1739) orch.
Concerto grosso No. 1, in D
with P. Giusto vln & Gli Accademici Dover HCR5230
di Milano – Eckertsen Vox DL413, STDL500413

Concerto grosso No. 2, in b
with P. Giusto vln & Gli Accademici Dover HCR5230
di Milano – Eckertsen Vox DL413, STDL500413

Concerto grosso No. 3, in e
with P. Giusto vln & Gli Accademici Dover HCR5232
di Milano – Eckertsen

Concerto grosso No. 4, in a
with P. Giusto vln & Gli Accademici Dover HCR5232
di Milano – Eckertsen

Concerto grosso No. 5, in A
with P. Giusto vln & Gli Accademici Dover HCR5232
di Milano – Eckertsen

Concerto grosso No. 6, in c
with P. Giusto vln & Gli Accademici Dover HCR5232
di Milano – Eckertsen

MANFREDINI

(12) Concerti, Op. 3 (1718) 2 vlns, strs & c
Concerto No. 1, in F
with G. Magnani vln & I Musici Vox (in set PL242)
Virtuosi di Milano – Eckertsen

Concerto No. 2, in a
with G. Magnani vln & I Musici Vox (in set PL242)
Virtuosi di Milano – Eckertsen

Concerto No. 3, in e
with G. Magnani vln & I Musici Vox (in set PL242)
Virtuosi di Milano – Eckertsen

Concerto No. 4, in B flat
with G. Magnani vln & I Musici Vox (in set PL242)
Virtuosi di Milano – Eckertsen

Concerto No. 5, in d
with G. Magnani vln & I Musici Vox (in set PL242)
Virtuosi di Milano – Eckertsen

Concerto No. 6, in D
with G. Magnani vln & I Musici Vox (in set PL242)
Virtuosi di Milano – Eckertsen

Concerto No. 7, in G
with G. Magnani vln & I Musici Vox (in set PL242)
Virtuosi di Milano – Eckertsen

Concerto No. 8, in F
with G. Magnani vln & I Musici Vox (in set PL242)
Virtuosi di Milano – Eckertsen

Concerto No. 9, in D
with G. Magnani vln & I Musici Vox (in set PL242)
Virtuosi di Milano – Eckertsen

Concerto No. 10, in g
with G. Magnani vln & I Musici Vox (in set PL242)
Virtuosi di Milano – Eckertsen

Concerto No. 11, in c
with G. Magnani vln & I Musici Vox (in set PL242)
Virtuosi di Milano – Eckertsen

Concerto No. 12, in C "Christmas Concerto"
with G. Magnani vln & I Musici Vox (in set PL242)
Virtuosi di Milano – Eckertsen

TARTINI

(6) Concerti, Op. 2 vln & strs
Concerto No. 1, in G
with I Musici Virtuosi di Vox (in set DL373)
Milano – Eckertsen

Concerto No. 2, in C
with I Musici Virtuosi di Vox (in set DL373)
Milano – Eckertsen

Concerto No. 3, in b
with I Musici Virtuosi di Vox (in set DL373)
Milano – Eckertsen

Concerto No. 4, in F
with I Musici Virtuosi di Vox (in set DL373)
Milano – Eckertsen

Concerto No. 5, in C
with I Musici Virtuosi di Vox (in set DL373)
Milano – Eckertsen

Concerto No. 6, in E
with I Musici Virtuosi di Vox (in set DL373)
Milano – Eckertsen

VIVALDI

(12) Concerti, Op. 8 (1725) "Il Cimento dell' armonia e dell' Invenzione"
(Nos. 1/4: Le quattro Stagioni) vln & strs
Concerto No. 1, in E, F.I, No. 22 "La Primavera"
with Milan Chamber Vox GBY11480, STGBY511480
Orch. – Eckertsen

Concerto No. 2, in B flat, F.I, No. 23 "L'Estate"
with Milan Chamber Vox GBY11480, STGBY511480
Orch. – Eckertsen

Concerto No. 3, in F, F.I, No. 24 "L'Autunno"
with Milan Chamber Vox GBY11480, STGBY511480
Orch. – Eckertsen

Concerto No. 4, in f, F.I, No. 25 "L'Inverno"
with Milan Chamber Vox GBY11480, STGBY511480
Orch. – Eckertsen

Concerto in a, P.28 (F.I, No. 61) 2 vlns, strs & c
with U. Benedetti Michelangeli vln & Angelicum LPA5993
Angelicum Orch. Milan – Martinotti Musical Heritage Society
  MHS878

Concerto in G, P.132 (F.I, No. 6) 2 vlns, strs & c
with U. Benedetti Michelangeli vln & Angelicum LPA5993
Angelicum Orch. Milan – Martinotti Musical Heritage Society
  MHS878

Frank BILBE

BRAHMS

(21) Hungarian Dances pf duet
Hungarian dance No. 6, in D flat arr. vln & pf Joachim
with piano Aco G15871

WIENIAWSKI

Concerto No. 2, in d, Op. 22 vln & orch.
Romance (2nd mvt) arr. vln & pf
with piano Aco G15871

Max BILD

HUBAY

(14) Scènes de la Csarda vln & pf
No. 4. Hejre Kati, Op. 32
with piano   Gramophone & Typewriter
47952

MASSENET

Thaïs (1894) – opera
Méditation arr. vln & pr Marsick
with piano   945e   Gramophone & Typewriter
47950

SARASATE

Zigeunerweisen, Op. 20 vln & pf or orch.
with piano   946e V   Gramophone & Typewriter
47951

WAGNER

(Die) Meistersinger von Nürnberg (1868) – opera
Morgenlich leuchtend "Prize song" arr. vln & pf Wilhelmj
with piano   Gramophone & Typewriter
47949

K. BIRZNIEKS

KALNINS

Latvian folk song suite vln & orch.
with Latvian Radio Symphony   Mezhdunarodnaya Kniga
Orch. – Vigner   D11667

SKULTE

Symphonic pictures (from the film "Rainis") vln & orch. with cl obb
with M. Nikitin cl and Latvian Radio   Mezhdunarodnaya Kniga
Symphony Orch. – Vigner   D019957/8

Elizabeth BISCHOFF

EGK

Geigenmusik (1936) vln & orch.
with Berlin Radio Symphony   Urania URLP7022
Orch. – Egk

Charles BISTESI

d'INDY

Sonata in C, Op. 59 vln & pf
with A. Vidal pf   HMV L1069/72

Tibor von BISZTRICZKY

ALBÉNIZ

España (6 Feuilles d'album) Op. 165 pf
No. 2 Tango in D arr. vln & pf Kreisler
with F. Schröder pf   Electrola SME73854

CHAMINADE

Sérénade espagnole pf – arr. vln & pf Kreisler
with F. Schröder pf   Deutsche Grammophon
LPE17161, SLPM133008

DEBUSSY

(La) Boîte à joujoux (1913) – ballet orch.
Petite nigar arr. vln & pf Pascal
with F. Schröder pf   Deutsche Grammophon
LPM17161, SLPM133008

DVOŘÁK

(8) Humoresques, Op. 101 pf
No. 7. Humoresque No. 7, in G flat arr. vln & pf "in G" Kreisler
with piano   (untraced)
(8) Slavonic Dances, Op. 72 pf duet; orch
No 2. Slavonic Dance No. 10, in e arr. vln & pf Kreisler
with F. Schröder pf   Deutsche Grammophon
LPE17161, SLPM133008

FIBICH

Images, Impressions & Souvenirs, Op. 41 pf
No. 14. Poem (from "Souvenirs", Part IV) arr. vln & pf Kubelík
with piano   (untraced)

HUBAY

(6) Blumenleben, Op. 30 vln & pf
No. 5. Der Zephir
with piano   (untraced)
No. 5. Der Zephir
with F. Schröder pf   Polydor 57184
No. 5. Der Zephir
with F. Schröder pf   Deutsche Grammophon
LPE17161, SLPM133008

(14) Scènes de la Csárda vln & pf
No. 5. Hullámzó balaton, Op. 33
with F. Schröder pf   Imperial I 40909

KODÁLY

Epigramm (1954) vln & pf
with piano   (untraced)
Valsette (1907) pf – arr. vln & pf Telmányi
with F. Schröder pf   Deutsche Grammophon
LPE17161, SLPM133008

LISZT

(3) Valses oubliées, G215 (1881/3) pf
No. 1. Valse oubliée No. 1 arr. vln & pf Hubay
with F. Schröder pf   Deutsche Grammophon
LPE17161, SLPM133008

MASSENET

Thaïs (1894) – opera
Méditation arr. vln & pf Marsick
with piano   (untraced)

RACHMANINOV

(5) Pieces, Op. 3 pf
No. 1. Élégie arr. vln & pf Hubay
with F. Schröder pf   Deutsche Grammophon
LPE17161, SLPM133008

SAINT–SAËNS

(Le) Carnaval des animaux (1886) small orch.
  Le cygne arr. vln & pf
  with piano   (untraced)

SARASATE

(8) Danzas españolas vln & pf
  No. 3. Romanza andaluza, Op. 22, No. 1
  with piano   (untraced)

STRAUSS, R.

(3) Lieder, Op. 29 v & pf
  No. 1. Traum durch die Dämmerung arr. vln & pf Hubay
  with piano   (untraced)

TCHAIKOVSKY

(6) Pieces, Op. 51 pf
  No. 6. Valse sentimentale arr. vln & pf Grunes
  with F. Schröder pf   Deutsche Grammophon
                    LPE17161, SLPM133008

VECSEY

Valse triste vln & pf
  with F. Schröder pf   Imperial I 40909

ZSOLT

Dragonflies vln & pf
  with F. Schröder pf   Deutsche Grammophon
                    LPE17161, SLPM133008

Herbstblätter vln & pf
  with F. Schröder pf   Imperial I 40909

Satyre & Dryades vln & pf
  with piano   (untraced)

Micheline BLANCHARD

BACH

Concerto in d, BWV1043 2 vlns & orch.
  with H. Fernandez vln   Erato EFM1021, EFM42057
  & Jean–François Paillard Chamber
  Orch. – Paillard

SAINT–GEORGES

(2) Sinfonia concertantes, Op. 9 (1778) 2 vlns & strs
Sinfonia concertante No. 2, in G "Cadenza by Paillard)*
  with G. Raymond vln   Erato LDE3037
  & Jean–François Paillard Chamber
  Orch. – Paillard

VIVALDI

Concerto in d, P.281 (F.I, No. 100) 2 vlns, strs & c
  with H. Fernandez vln   Erato LDE3077
  & Jean–François Paillard Chamber
  Orch. – Paillard

* It is now generally accepted that the above sinfonia is actually from opus 13 which was composed in 1782.

Ulrich BLECHER

BACH

Concerto No. 1, in a, BWV1041 vln, strs & c
  with Nordwestdeutsche Philharmonic   Imperial ILP169
  – Schuchter

Concerto No. 2, in E, BWV1042 vln, strs & c
  with Nordwestdeutsche Philharmonic   Imperial ILP169
  – Schuchter

Sigmund BLEIER

PAGANINI

(24) Caprices, Op. 1 (1801/7) solo vln
  Caprice No. 20, in D arr. vln & pf Bleier
  with O.A. Graef pf   3448½ gn Polydor 10979

TCHAIKOVSKY

(3) Souvenirs de Hapsal, Op. 2 pf
  No. 3. Chant sans paroles in f arr. vln & pf Bleier
  with O.A. Graef pf   3447½ gn Polydor 10979

Jan BLEUMERS

d'AMBROSIO

Canzonetta, Op. 6 vln & pf
  with P. Palla pf   Philips NH17801, PE422011

KREIN, D.

Gypsy carnival vln & pf
  with Cosmopolitan Orch. – Cleber   Philips PH17195

KREISLER

Schön Rosmarin vln & pf
  with P. Palla pf   Philips NH17801, PE422011

MONTI

Csárdas (1904) vln & pf
  with P. Palla org   AA 17800. 1 H Philips NH17800, PE422011,
                              PF317800

RIMSKY–KORSAKOV

Sadko (1898) – opera
  Chant hindou arr. vln & orch.
  with Cosmopolitan Orch. – Cleber   Philips PR10055

TCHAIKOVSKY

(6) Songs, Op. 6 v & pf
  No. 6. None but the weary heart arr. vln & orch.
  with Cosmopolitan Orch. – Cleber   Philips P10064R, PR10055

TOSELLI

Serenade, Op. 6 vln & pf
  with P. Palla org   AA 17800. 2 H Philips NH17800, PE422011,
                              PF317800

Naume Samoilovitch BLINDER (1889–)

ELGAR

(La) Capricieuse, Op. 17 vln & pf
with V. Pavlowsky pf | Columbia 50118D, 5104M, J3058
Regal–Zonophone G30004

GODARD

Jocelyn (1888) – opera
Cachés dans cet asile "Berceuse" arr. vln & pf
with V. Pavlowsky pf | Columbia M247

KREISLER

Caprice viennois, Op. 2 vln & pf
with V. Pavlowsky pf | 98504–7 | Columbia 02773, 50127D, 5106M, DX7, J3075

Grave (W.F. Bach) vln & pf
with V. Pavlowsky pf | Columbia 11680D, 5075M

Variations on a theme of Corelli (Tartini) vln & pf
with V. Pavlowsky pf | Columbia 02773, 50127D, 5106M, J3075

NOVACÉK

(8) Concert caprices, Op. 5 vln & pf
No. 4. Perpetuum mobile
with V. Pavlowsky pf | Columbia 158M, J485

SCHUBERT

(7) Gesänge (set to Scott's "Lady of the Lake") Op. 52 v & pf
No. 6. Ave Maria, D839 arr. vln & pf Wilhelmj
with V. Pavlowsky pf | 98454–2 | Columbia 11680D, 5075M, DX7

(2) Lieder, Op. 98 (D498) v & pf
No. 2. Wiegenlied (Schlafe, holder süsser Knabe) arr. vln & pf
with V. Pavlowsky pf | Columbia 158M, J485, M247

TCHAIKOWSKY

Concerto in D, Op. 35 vln & orch.
Canzonetta (2nd mvt)
with V. Pavlowsky pf | Columbia 50118D, 5104M, J3058

Sérénade mélancolique in b flat, Op. 26 vln & orch. – arr. vln & pf
Wilhelmj
98485–2 & 98486–6 | Columbia 9692, 5077M, J3057
with V. Pavlowsky pf

Erling BLOCH (1904–)

BEETHOVEN

Sonata No. 5, in F, Op. 24 "Spring" vln & pf
with H. Lund– | 2CS 2139/44–1 | HMV DB14/6
Christiansen pf

(3) Sonatas, Op. 30 vln & pf
No. 3. Sonata No. 8, in G
with H. Lund– | 2CS 2347/50–1 | HMV DB5280/1
Christiansen pf

Sonata No. 9, in A, Op. 47 "Kreutzer" vln & pf
with H. Lund– | 2CS 2131/8–1 | HMV DB10/3
Christiansen pf

BEETHOVEN – *Continued*

(10) Variations (on "Ich bin der Schneider Kakadu") Op. 121a pf, vln & vlc
2CS 1077–4, 1078–6, 1079–3, 1080–6 | HMV DB5229/30
with H. Lund–Christiansen pf | Victor 17555/6, (set M729)
& T. Svendsen vlc

KUHLAU

Trio in G, Op. 119b fl, vln & pf
1st mvt
with G. Jespersen | 2CS 1069/70–1 | HMV DB5258/9
fl & H. Lund–Christiansen pf

MOZART

Sonata No. 28, in E flat, K380 vln & pf
with | 2CS 1734/7–3 | HMV DB5258/9
H. Lund–Christiansen pf

NIELSEN

Sonata No. 2, in g, Op. 35 vln & pf
2CS 839–4, 840–2, 841–4, 842–1 | HMV DB5219/20
with H. Lund–Christiansen pf

RIISAGER

Serenade, Op. 26b vln, fl & vlc
with G. Jespersen fl | 2CS 722/3–1 | HMV DB5205
& T. Svendsen vlc

SCHUBERT

Fantasia in C, Op. 159 (D934) vln & pf
2CS 1874/6–5, 1877–1, 1878–5 | HMV DB4/6
with H. Lund–Christiansen pf

WEBER

(6) Sonatas, Op. 10 (J99/104) (1810) vln & pf
Sonata No. 3, in D, J101 (arr. as "Thème russe & Rondo" by Szigeti)
with | 2CS 1940–1 | HMV DB6
H. Lund–Christiansen pf

Robert BLOCH

JANÁČEK

Sonata (1913/21) vln & pf*
with L. Brandwynne pf | Redwood RRES3

REBEL

(12) Sonatas (1712) 2 & 3 part with figured bs
Sonata No. 5, in D "La Pallas"
with S. Weiner vln, J. Lamy gamba & | Discophiles français DF730076,
A. Geoffroy–Dechaume hpsi | DF740076

Sonata No. 6, in g "L'Immortelle"
with S. Weiner vln, J. Lamy gamba & | Discophiles français DF730076,
A. Geoffroy–Dechaume hpsi | DF740076

SCHUBERT

Fantasia in C, Op. 159 (D934) vln & pf
with L. Brandwynne pf | Redwood RRES3

* Four versions exist of this work. The above version is not identified.

Dominique BLOT (1912–1947)

ANONYMOUS

Ariettes & airs 18th century – arr. s, 2 vlns & c
    with L. ben Sedira s, E. Ortmans–Bach HMV DB5023
    vln, C. Crussard hpsi & Y. Thibout vlc

BACH

Concerto in c, BWV1060 vln & ob or 2 vlns, strs & c – res. Crussard
    with S. Lovis vln & Ars Rediviva   La Boîte à Musique 38/9
    Ensemble – Crussard

Fugue in g, BWV578 "The Little G Minor" org – arr. str ens
    with E. Ortmans–Bach vln, G. Drouet   La Boîte à Musique 10
    vla, C. Crussard hpsi & Y. Thibout vlc

Sonata in e, BWV1023 vln & c
    with C. Crussard pf   La Boîte à Musique 9

Sonata in d, BWV1036 2 vlns & c
    with E. Ortmans–Bach vln, C.   La Boîte à Musique 18/9
    Crussard hpsi & Y. Thibout vlc

Sonata in C, BWV1037 2 vlns & c
    with E. Ortmans–Bach vln, C.   La Boîte à Musique 28/9
    Crussard hpsi & J. Alliaume vlc

COUPERIN, F.

Sonata No. 3, in g (1963) "L'Astrée" 2 vlns & c
    PARTX 6090/3–1   La Boîte à Musique 58/9
    with E. Ortmans–Bach vln, C.
    Crussard hpsi* & J. Alliaume vlc

FUNCK

Suite in g 2 vlns, vla & c – arr. Crussard
    with E. Ortmans–Bach vln, G. Drouet   La Boîte à Musique 10
    vla, C. Crussard hpsi & Y. Thibout vlc

HANDEL

(9) Sonatas, Op. 2 (1724) 2 vlns or obs & c
Sonata No. 2, in g
    with E. Ortmans–Bach vln, C.   La Boîte à Musique 24
    Crussard hpsi & Y. Thibout vlc

KRIEGER

(12) Sonatas, Op. 2 (1693) vln & c
Sonata No. 3, in e arr. 2 vlns & c
    with E. Ortmans–Bach vln, C.   La Boîte à Musique 5
    Crussard hpsi & Y. Thibout vlc

LECLAIR

(6) Concerti, Op. 7 (1737) vln & strs
Concerto No. 4, in F
    with C. Crussard hpsi & Ars Rediviva   HMV DB5133/4
    Ensemble – Crussard

(12) Sonatas, Op. 4 (1732) 2 vlns & c
Sonata No. 2, in B flat: Sicilienne
    with E. Ortmans–Bach vln, C.   HMV DB5108
    Crussard hpsi & Y. Thibout vlc

Sonata No. 4, in A (ed. Crussard)
    with E. Ortmans–Bach vln, C.   HMV DB5107/8
    Crussard hpsi & Y. Thibout vlc

---

* Claire, *not* Claude Crussard in this recording.

MARINI

Romance, Gaillarde & Courante vln, strs & c
    with E. Ortmans–Bach   PART 738   La Boîte à Musique 3
    vln, J. Godard vla, S. Meyrieu vlc, C.
    Crussard hpsi & Y. Thibout vlc

RAMEAU

(5) Pièces de Clavecin en Concerts (1741) hpsi, vln & vlc
Concert No. 4, in B flat: excerpt unid
    with E. Ortmans–Bach vln & C.   HMV DB5055
    Crussard hpsi   Victor 12490

ROSENMÜLLER

(12) Sonatas (1670) var. cbns
Sonata in e 2 vlns & c
    with E. Ortmans–   2LA 2542/3[1]   HMV DB5064
    Bach vln, M. de Lacour hpsi, N.   Victor 12489
    Pierront org – cond. Crussard

SCARLATTI, A.

Diana ed Endimioni (1680/5) cantata
Boschi voi ch' in silenzio
    with L. ben Sedira s, E. Ortmans–Bach La Boîte à Musique 20
    vln, S. Morand vla, C. Crussard hpsi &
    Y. Thibout vlc

(L') Emireno (1697) – opera
Col dire a me cosi
    with L. ben Sedira s, E. Ortmans–Bach HMV DB5023
    vln, C. Crussard hpsi & Y. Thibout vlc

Speranza del mio core
    with M. Castellazzi–Bovy s, E.   La Boîte à Musique 4
    Ortmans–Bach vln, S. Meyrieu vla, J.
    Godard vla, C. Crussard hpsi & Y.
    Thibout vlc

(La) Tua pena mi dispiace
    with M. Castellazzi–Bovy s, E.   La Boîte à Musique 4
    Ortmans–Bach vln, S. Meyrieu vla, J.
    Godard vla, C. Crussard hpsi & Y.
    Thibout vlc

Partirò, che più mi piace unid. aria
    with M. Castellazzi–Bovy s, E.   La Boîte à Musique 4
    Ortmans–Bach vln, S. Meyrieu vla, J.
    Godard vla, C. Crussard hpsi & Y.
    Thibout vlc

Preparati, O mio core – cantata
Quanto è dolce
    with L. ben Sedira s, E. Ortmans–Bach HMV DB5024
    vln, C. Crussard hpsi & Y. Thibout vlc

(La) Tua gradita fe unid. aria
    with L. ben Sedira s, E. Ortmans–Bach HMV DB5023
    vln, C. Crussard hpsi & Y. Thibout vlc

VIVALDI

Concerto in a, P.13 vln, strs & c – arr. Crussard
    with Ars Rediviva   2LA 2540/1–1□   HMV DB5065
    Ensemble – Crussard

(12) Sonatas, Op. 2 (1712) vln & c
Sonata No. 3, in d, F.XIII, No. 30 arr. Crussard
    with C. Crussard   2LA 2426/7–1□   HMV DB5056 – Victor 12491
    pf

VIVALDI – *Continued*

Sonata No. 11, in D, F.XIII, No. 39 arr. Crussard
with C. Crussard   PART 2203/4–1   La Boîte à Musique 30
hpsi

Sonata No. 12, in a: Prelude & Capriccio, F.XIII, No. 40 arr. Crussard
with C. Crussard hpsi   La Boîte à Musique 30

Sonata in c vln & c – arr. vln & hpsi Crussard
with C. Crussard   2LA 3065/6–1   HMV DB5092
hpsi   Victor 13484

Harry BLUESTONE

BRANDL

(Der) Liebe Augustin – operetta
Du alter Stefansturm arr. vln & pf as "The old refrain" by Kreisler
with M. Kaye pf   B 25281   Brunswick 8465
                                   Columbia 35720, C6038, DO2091

DVOŘÁK

(8) Humoresques, Op. 101 pf
No. 7. Humoresque No. 7, in G flat, arr. vln & pf "in G" Kreisler
with M. Kaye pf   B 25280   Brunswick 8465
                                   Columbia C6038, DO2091

FRIML

Rose Marie (1916) – operetta
Indian love call arr. vln & pf
with T. Saidenberg pf   LA1959   Columbia 36239, C6030

GOUNOD

Ave Maria (Méditation on Bach's "Prelude No. 1, in C" from Book I of
"Das Wohltemperirte Clavier") v & pf – arr. vln & pf
with T. Saidenberg pf   LA 1958   Brunswick 8462
                                   Columbia C6041, DO2057

KREISLER

Liebesfreud vln & pf
with M. Kaye pf   Brunswick 8481
                                   Columbia 35720

Liebesleid vln & pf
with M. Kaye pf   Brunswick 8476
                                   Columbia DO2143

Schön Rosmarin vln & pf
with M. Kaye pf   Brunswick 8476
                                   Columbia DO2143

NEVIN

Mighty lak' a rose (1901) v & pf – arr. vln & pf Banner
with T. Saidenberg pf   LA 1955   Columbia 36239, C6030

WAGNER

Tannhäuser (1845) – opera
O du mein holder Abendstern (Act III) arr. vln & pf Léonard
with T. Saidenberg pf   LA 1957   Brunswick 8462
                                   Columbia C6041, DO2057

Jules BOBBE

ANONYMOUS

Loch Lomond Traditional Scottish ballad – arr. vln & pf Bobbé
with piano   Zonophone 130

GOUNOD

Faust (1859) – opera
selection arr. vln & pf Bobbé
with piano   Odeon X40068

VERDI

(Il) Trovatore (1853) – opera
selection arr. vln & pf Bobbé
with piano   Odeon X44049

Constantin BOBESCU (1899–)

HANDEL

(15) Sonatas, Op. 1 (?1731) fl or vln & c
Sonata No. 14, in A vln V
with H. Gehann org   Electrecord ECE0351

NARDINI

Concerto in a vln & orch.
with M. Kabdebo pf   Electrecord ECE0351

PUGNANI

(6) Sonatas, Op. 8 vln & c
Sonata No. 3, in D: Largo expressivo (2nd mvt) arr. vln & pf Moffat
with H. Gehann org   Electrecord ECE0351

TARTINI

(12) Sonatas, Op. 1 (1734) vln & c
Sonata No. 10, in g "Didone abbandonata"
with H. Gehann org   Electrecord ECE0351

VITALI

Chaconne in g vln & c – arr. vln & pf Charlier
with M. Kabdebo pf   Electrecord ECE0351

Lola Anna–Maria BOBESCU (1920–)

BACH

Clavierübung – part III, BWV802/5 clav
Duetto No. 1, in e, BWV802 arr. vln & vla David
with F. Legrand vla   Alpha DB45
Duetto No. 2, in F, BWV803 arr. vln & vla David
with F. Legrand vla   Alpha DB45
Duetto No. 3, in G, BWV804 arr. vln & vla David
with F. Legrand vla   Alpha DB45
Concerto No. 1, in a, BWV1041 vln, strs & c
with Rumanian Radio Symphony   Electrecord ECE0143
Orch. – C. Bobescu
(6) Sonatas, BWV1014/9 vln & clav
Sonata No. 3, in E, BWV1016
with M. Kapdebo pf   Electrecord ECE0261

BARTÓK

(6) Rumanian folk dances (1915) pf – arr. vln & pf Székely
with S. Guttman pf   Alpha DB32

CROES

(7) Concerti
Concerto No. 7, in c vln, strs & c
with Solistes de Bruxelles   Alpha CL3016, DB82

EICHNER

(6) Duets, Op. 10 – Books I & II vln & vla
No. 3. Duet No. 3, in G – Book I
with F. Legrand vla   Alpha DB45

ESPEJO

(2) Pieces in ancient style vln & pf
with S. Guttman pf   Alpha DB32

FAURÉ

Berceuse, Op. 16 vln & pf
with S. Guttman pf   Alpha DB32
Sonata No. 1 in A, Op. 13 vln & pf
with J. Genty pf   Decca LX3057
London LL1549, LS327

FRANCK

Sonata in A (1886) vln & pf
with J. Genty pf   Decca K23139/42, LX3056
London LL1549, LS326

GOLESTAN

Chant du berceau (1941) vln & pf
with A.M. Ginisty–Brisson pf   HMV DB11237, L1078
(Le) Laoutar (1934) vlc or vln & pf or orch.
Danse moldave
with A.M. Ginisty–Brisson pf   HMV K8422
Fantaisie
with A.M. Ginisty–Brisson pf   HMV K8422
(3) Pièces concertantes (1943) vln & pf
No. 1. Romanesca
with A.M. Ginisty–Brisson pf   HMV L1079
Tzingarella (1943) vln & pf
with A.M. Ginisty–Brisson pf   HMV DB11237, L1078

HANDEL

(15) Sonatas, Op. 1 (?1731) fl or vln & c
Sonata No. 13, in D vln IV
with J. Genty pf   Alpha CL3008, CL4008
(16) Suites (1720/33) hpsi
Suite No. 7, in g: Passacaglia (6th mvt) arr. vln & vla Halvorsen
with F. Legrand vla   Alpha DB45

HERRANDO

(10) Pieces (1750) clav
No. 9. Movemento perpétuel arr. vln & pf Nin
with S. Guttman pf   Alpha DB32

LALO

Symphonie espagnole, Op. 21 vln & orch.*
with Lamoureux Orch. – Bigot   Columbia LFX610/3

* Including Intermezzo.

LECLAIR

Concerto in d "L'Enfant" vln, strs & c
with Ensemble d'Archets Eugèn   Deutsche Grammophon 135141,
Ysaÿe – Bobescu   2538 018
(12) Sonatas, Op. 9 – Book IV (1738) vln & c
Sonata No. 3, in D
with J. Genty pf   Alpha CL3008, CL4008

MARTINŮ

(3) Madrigals (1948) vln & vla
with F. Legrand vla   Alpha DB45

MOZART

Concerto No. 5, in A, K219 "Turkish" (Cadenzas by Joachim) vln & orch.
with Rumanian Radio Symphony   Electrecord ECE0143
Orch. – C. Bobescu
Duo No. 1, in G, K423 vln & vla
with F. Legrand vla   Alpha CL3010, CL4010
Da Camera SM92901
Musica Rara MUS47
Duo No. 2, in B flat, K424 vln & vla
with F. Legrand vla   Alpha CL3010, CL4010
Da Camera SM92901
Musica Rara MUS47
Sinfonia concertante in E flat, K364 vln, vla & orch.
with G. Cappone vla   Discophiles français 525118,
and Saar Chamber Orch. – Ristenpart   DF730037

NIN

(5) Comentarios (1929) vln & pf
with M. Kapdebo pf   Electrecord ECE0261
(5) Comentarios (1929) vln & pf
with S. Guttman pf   Alpha DB32

PARADIES

Sicilienne vln & pf – arr. Dushkin
with S. Guttman pf   Alpha DB32

PERGOLESI

(6) Concertinos str orch.
Concertino No. 2, in G
with Les Solistes de   Alpha DB143
Bruxelles – Bobescu

RAVEL

Pièce en forme d'Habanera v & pf – arr. vln & pf Catherine
with S. Guttman pf   Alpha DB32

SOURIS

(3) Ancient pieces vln & vla
with A. Souris vla   Alpha DB45

STRAVINSKY

Mavra (1922) – opera
Russian maiden's song (Parasha's aria) arr. vln & pf Dushkin &
Stravinsky
with S. Guttman pf   Alpha DB32
Suite Italienne (on themes of Pergolesi) (1933) vln & pf
with M. Kapdebo pf   Electrecord ECE0261

TARTINI

(12) Sonatas, Op. 1 (1734) vln & c
  Sonata No. 10, in g
  with J. Genty pf   Alpha CL3008, CL4008

VERACINI

(12) Sonatas, Op. 2 (1744) vln & c
  Sonata No. 11, in E
  with J. Genty pf   Alpha CL3008, CL4008

VIVALDI

(12) Concerti, Op. 8 (1725) "Il Cimento dell' Armonia e dell' Invenzione"
  (Nos. 1/4: Le quattro Stagioni) vln & strs
  Concerto No. 1, in E, F.I, No. 22 "La Primavera"
  with J. Genty hpsi   Da Camera SM91917
  & Heidelberg Chamber Orch. – Genty   Musica Rara MUS50
                            Oryx EXP11

  Concerto No. 2, in B flat, F.I, No. 23 "L'Estate"
  with J. Genty hpsi   Da Camera SM91917
  & Heidelberg Chamber Orch. – Genty   Musica Rara MUS50
                            Oryx EXP11

  Concerto No. 3, in F, F.I, No. 24 "L'Autunno"
  with J. Genty hpsi   Da Camera SM91917
  & Heidelberg Chamber Orch. – Genty   Musica Rara MUS50
                            Oryx EXP11

  Concerto No. 4, in f, F.I, No. 25 "L'Inverno"
  with J. Genty hpsi   Da Camera SM91917
  & Heidelberg Chamber Orch. – Genty   Musica Rara MUS50
                            Oryx EXP11

**Concerto in C, P.14 (F.I, No. 13) (Op. 54, No. 3) "Per la SS. Assunzione di
  Maria Vergine" vln, strs & c**
  with Les Solistes de Bruxelles – Ephrikian Arcophon AC672
                            Seraphim S60118

Concerto in C, P.58, vln, 2 vlcs & strs
  with soloists   Deutsche Grammophon LP8592
  & Les Solistes de Bruxelles – Bobescu Heliodor 89647

Concerto in D, P.146 (F.IV, No. 7) 4 vlns, vlc, strs & c
  with soloists & Ensemble d'Archets Deutsche Grammophon 135141,
  Eugèn Ysaÿe – Bobescu   2538 018

**Concerto in B flat, P.368 (F.I, No. 60) (Op. 28, No. 3) "Scordatura" vln, 2
  str choruses & c**
  with K. d'Hooghe & Les Solistes de Arcophon AC672
  Bruxelles – Ephrikian   HMV HQS1060
                            Seraphim S60118

Irina BOCHKOVÁ

BONPORTI

(10) Invenzioni (1712) solo vln
  Invenzione No. 4, in g
  (unaccompanied)   Mezhdunarodnaya Kniga
                            D024107/8

HINDEMITH

(2) Sonatas, Op. 31 (1924) solo vln
  Sonata No. 1
  (unaccompanied)   Mezhdunarodnaya Kniga
                            D024107/8

KABALEVSKY

Rondo in C, Op. 69 vln & pf
  with piano   Mezhdunarodnaya Kniga
                            DX11097/8

KREISLER

Chanson Louis XIII & Pavane (L. Couperin) vln & pf
  with piano   Mezhdunarodnaya Kniga
                            D11097/8

PAGANINI

(24) Caprices, Op. 1 (1801/7) solo vln
  Caprice No. 17, in E flat
  (unaccompanied)   Mezhdunarodnaya Kniga
                            D11097/8

PROKOFIEV

Cinderella, Op. 87 (1941/4) – opera
  Waltz arr. vln & pf Fichtenholz
  with piano   Mezhdunarodnaya Kniga
                            D11097/8

SARASATE

(8) Danzas españolas vln & pf
  No. 2. Habañera, Op. 21, No. 2
  with piano   Mezhdunarodnaya Kniga
                            D024107/8

SUK

(4) Pieces, Op. 17 vln & pf
  with piano   Mezhdunarodnaya Kniga
                            D024107/8

TCHAIKOVSKY

Sérénade mélancolique in b flat, Op. 26 vln & orch. – arr. vln & pf
  Wilhelmj
  with piano   Mezhdunarodnaya Kniga
                            D11097/8

WEBER

(6) Sonatas, Op. 10 (J99/104) (1810) vln & pf
  Sonata No. 1, in F: Romanze (2nd mvt) J99 arr. as "Larghetto" by
  Kreisler
  with piano   Mezhdunarodnaya Kniga
                            D11097/8

WIENIAWSKI

Scherzo–Tarantelle, Op. 16 vln & pf
  with piano   Mezhdunarodnaya Kniga
                            D010325/8, D11097/8

E. BODER

HANDEL

(12) Concerti grossi, Op. 6 (1739) 2 vlns, vlc & strs
  Concerto grosso No. 10, in d
  with L. Gozman vln, L. Fishkov vlc & Mezhdunarodnaya Kniga
  Leningrad Chamber Orch. – Gozman   S1911/2

VIVALDI

(12) Concerti, Op. 3 "L'Estro armonico" var. cbns & strs
  Concerto No. 10, in b, P.148 (F.IV, No. 10) 4 vlns, strs & c
  with K. Varenberg vln, M. Furer vln,   Mezhdunarodnaya Kniga
  Y. Milkis vln & Leningrad Chamber   D018097/8, S01319/20
  Orch. – Gozman

Elisabeth BOHN

BENTZON

Capriccietta, Op. 28 vln & pf
  with G. Gamborg pf   Metronome MCEP3069
V3, Op. 35 (1945) vln & pf
  with G. Gamborg pf   Metronome MCEP3069

Tamás BOKOR

JARDÁNYI

Variations (1955) 2 vlns & vlc
  with M. Szenthelyi vln & G. Éder vlc   Qualiton LPX1188

SUGÁR

Little Suite pf, vln & vlc
  with A. Fasang pf & G. Éder vlc   Qualiton LPX1188

J. B. BOLDI

BOLDI

Romance bohèmienne vln & pf
  with piano   Bettini Disc 2291

Leonid BOLOTINE

VIVALDI

Concerto in C, P.84 (F.XII. No. 14) "Per la Solennità di St. Lorenzo" 2 fls,
  2 obs, 2 cls, 2 vlns, bsn, strs & c
  with S. Baron fl, H. Jones fl, L. Arner   Library of Recorded
  ob, H. Smyles ob, W. Lewis cl, C.   Masterpeices Vol. 1, No. 3
  Paashaus cl, A. Checchia bsn, F.
  Galimir vln, E. Earle hpsi & New
  York Sinfonietta – Goberman
Concerto in F, P.273 (Op. 46, No. 2) vln, 2 obs, 2 hrns, bsn, strs & c
  with A. Goltzer ob, H. Smyles ob, F.   Library of Recorded
  Schwartz bsn, J. Singer hrn, A. Berv   Masterpeices Vol. 1, No. 1
  hrn, R. Conant hpsi & New York
  Sinfonietta – Goberman

Clara BONALDI

BARTÓK

Sonata No. 1 (1921) vln & pf
  with S. Billier pf   Harmonia Mundi HM30597,
    HMS30597
Sonata No. 2 (1922) vln & pf
  with S. Billier pf   Harmonia Mundi HM30597,
    HMS30597

FRANCOEUR

(12) Sonatas – Book I vln & c
  Sonata No. 5, in c
  With J–L. Petit hpsi & J. Lamy gamba   Decca SMD1517
    Société Française du Son 174155,
    SXL20155
  Sonata No. 6, in E
  with J–L. Petit hpsi & J. Lamy gamba   Decca SMD1517
    Société Française du Son 174155,
    SXL20155
(12) Sonatas – Book II (1733) vln & c
  Sonata No. 1, in A
  with J–L. Petit hpsi & J. Lamy gamba   Decca SMD1517
    Société Française du Son 174155,
    SXL20155
  Sonata No. 3, in e
  with J–L. Petit hpsi & J. Lamy gamba   Decca SMD1517
    Société Française du Son 174155,
    SXL20155

RAVEL

Sonata (1927) vln & pf
  with S. Billier pf   Harmonia Mundi HM30753
    Musical Heritage Society
    MHS1235
Trio in a (1915) pf, vln & vlc
  with S. Billier pf & P. Boufil vlc   Harmonia Mundi HM30753

SCHUMANN

Sonata No. 1, in a, Op. 105 vln & pf
  with S. Billier pf   Harmonia Mundi HM30568,
    HMS30568
Sonata No. 2, in d, Op. 121 vln & pf
  with S. Billier pf   Harmonia Mundi HM30568,
    HMS30568

TARTINI

(12) Sonatas, Op. 1 (1734) vln & c
  Sonata No. 3, in A
  with L. Sgrizzi hpsi   Eurodisc 79087KK
  Sonata No. 10, in g "Didone abbandonata"
  with L. Sgrizzi hpsi   Eurodisc 79087KK
  Sonata No. 12, in F
  with L. Sgrizzi hpsi   Eurodisc 79087KK
Sonata No. 13, in A "Pastorale" vln & c
  with L. Sgrizzi hpsi   Eurodisc 79087KK

Ladislav BONIS

CUI

Kaleidoscope, Op. 50 vln & pf
  No. 9. Orientale arr. vln, vlc & pf
  with J. Bonis vlc & V. Petrescu pf   Odeon 199264

FIBICH

Images, Impressions & Souvenirs, Op. 41 pf
  No. 14. Poem (from "Souvenirs", Part IV) arr. vln & pf Kubelík
  with V. Petrescu pf   Odeon 199273

GODARD

Jocelyn (1888) – opera
  Cachés dans cet asile "Berceuse"arr. vln & pf
  with V. Petrescu pf   Odeon 199273

GRIEG

(4) Norwegian Dances, Op. 35 (1881) pf duet; orch.
  No. 1. Norwegian dance No. 1, in d arr, vln, vlc & pf
  with J. Bonis vlc & V. Petrescu pf   Odeon 199264

SARASATE

Zigeunerweisen, Op. 20 vln & pf or orch.
  with V. Petrescu pf   Odeon 178507

SCHELBECK

Canzona del violino vln & pf
  with V. Petrescu pf   Odeon 199263

WIENIAWSKI

(2) Mazurkas, Op. 19 vln & pf
  No. 1. Mazurka No. 1, in G "Obertass"
  with V. Petrescu pf   Odeon 199263

Marcel BONNEMAIN

d'AMBROSIO

Canzonetta, Op. 6 vln & pf
  with piano   Marathon 334

FAURÉ

Berceuse, Op. 16 vln & pf
  with piano   Marathon 334

SIMONETTI

Madrigale pf – arr. vln & pf
  with piano   Marathon 359

TCHAIKOVSKY

(3) Souvenirs de Hapsal, Op. 2 pf
  No. 3. Chant sans paroles in f arr. vln & pf Kreisler
  with piano   Marathon 359

Christian BOR (1950–)

BACH

Concerto in d, BWV1043 2 vlns, strs & c
  with E. Verhey vln &   Philips 88129DY
  Kunstmaandorkest,
  Amsterdam – Kersjes

BEETHOVEN

Romance No. 1, in G, Op. 40 vln & orch.
  with Kunstmaandorkest,   Philips 88129DY
  Amsterdam – Kersjes

E. BORGANI

d'AMBROSIO

Serenade, Op. 4 vln & pf
  with piano   Pathé–Actuelle 11337

BEETHOVEN

Concerto in D, Op. 61 vln & orch
  Larghetto (2nd mvt)
  with piano   Pathé–Actuelle 15242

GOLDMARK

Concerto in a, Op. 28 vln & orch.
  Andante (2nd mvt) "Air"
  with piano   Pathé–Actuelle 15242

GRIEG

Sonata No. 3, in c, Op. 45 vln & pf
  Allegro molto ed appassionata (1st mvt)
  with piano   Pathé–Actuelle 15201
  Allegretto expressivo alla Romanza (2nd mvt)
  with piano   Pathé–Actuelle 15201

Oscar BORGERTH (1906–)

FIBICH

Images, Impressions & Souvenirs, Op. 41 pf
  No. 14. Poem (from "Souvenirs", Part IV) arr. vln & pf Kubelík
  with piano   Brazilian Continental 20102

MIGNONE

Berceuse vln & pf
  with F. Mignone pf   Odeon 0–3305
Cançao brasileira vln & pf
  with F. Mignone pf   Odeon C7280
Lenda Sertaneja No. 2 vln & pf
  with F. Mignone pf   Odeon C7280
Tango capriccio vln & pf
  with F. Mignone pf   Odeon 0–3305

TAVARES

Concerto No. 4, Op. 107 "em formas brasileiras" vln & orch.
  with orquestra Sinfónica   Rádio Ministério da Educaçao e
  Nacional – Tavares   Cultura DVX3080/1

VILLA–LOBOS

Chôros No. 1 (1920) gtr – arr. vln & vlc Villa–Lobos
  with I. Gomes–Grosso vlc   Victor 12203
Chôros No. 2 (1924) fl & cl – arr. vln & vlc Villa–Lobos
  with I. Gomes–Grosso vlc   Victor 12203
Fantasia de movimentos mixtos (1922) vln & pf
  with J.V. Brandao pf   Victor 12207/10

WIENIAWSKI

(2) Mazurkas, Op. 19 vln & pf
  No. 1. Mazurka No. 1, in G "Obertass"
  with piano   Brazilian Continental 20102

M. BORGO

VIVALDI

Concerto in F, P.278 (F.I, No. 34) 3 vlns, strs & c
  with M. Abbado vln, L. d'Annibale vln Columbia FCX370
  & Milan String Orch. – Abbado

VIVALDI – *Continued*

Concerto in B flat, P.367 (F.I, No. 59) 4 vlns, strs & c
with M. Abbado vln, E. Pasquali vln,   Columbia FCX369
L. d'Annibale vln & Milan String
Orch. – Abbado

Karl BORNFORS (1901–   )*

JÄRNEFELT

Berceuse in g orch. – arr. vln & pf
with J. Larento pf†   0260   Skandia SG1548

LABITZKY

(Der) Traum der Sennerin (Dream of the mountains – 'Idyll) Op. 45
orch. – arr. vln & pf
with J. Larento pf   0142   Skandia SV1519

LARENTO

Böljesang vln & pf
with J. Larento pf   0063   Skandia SV1502

Colibri –salon waltz vln & pf
with J. Larento pf   0065   Skandia SV1503

(Un) Mirage vln & pf
with J. Larento pf   0064   Skandia SV1503

Souvenir d'amour vln & pf
with J. Larento pf   0062   Skandia SV1502

SCHUMANN

(13) Kinderscenen, Op. 15 pf
No. 7. Träumerei arr. vln & pf
with J. Larento pf   Skandia SG1548, SV1537

SJÖBERG

Tonerna vln & pf
with J. Larento pf   0258   Skandia SG1548, SV1537

TOSELLI

Serenade, Op. 6 vln & pf
with J. Larento pf   0143   Skandia SV1519

Lajos BOROSS

ANONYMOUS

Paraszt–verbunkos (peasant recruiting dance) arr. solo vln‡
(unaccompanied)   Qualiton LPX1216

SARASATE

Zigeunerweisen, Op. 20 vln & pf or orch.
with Hungarian State Symphony   Columbia FP1052
Orch. – G. Boross

* Recorded under the pseudonym of Carl Carlier.
† Accompanied Bornfors under the pseudonym of Stig Hansson.
‡ 1757 manuscript.

Siegfried BORRIES (1912–   )

BACH

(6) Brandenburg Concerti, BWV1046/51 strs & c
  Brandenburg Concerto No. 5, in D: BWV1050 clav, fl, vln & strs
                              461/6½GS, 467GS   Decca LY6101/4
  with F. Rupp hpsi, F. Thomas fl &   Polydor 15073/6
  Berlin Philharmonic Orch. – Melichar

Cantata No. 208 (Was mir behagt, ist nur die muntre Jagd) BWV208
  with A. Kupper s, E. Köth a,   Electrola E70475, STE70475,
  F. Wunderlich t, D. Fischer–Dieskau   STE80823
  bs, St. Hedwig's Cathedral Choir &   HMV ALP1985, ASD534,
  Berlin Symphony Orch. – Forster   ASDF756, FALP756

Weihnachts–Oratorium, BWV248(1734)
  with G. Weber s, S. Wagner a,   Archive APM14101/3,
  H. Krebs t, H. Rehfuss bs, H. Bastien   ARC3079/81
  vln, F. Demmler fl, K. Steins, ob, K.   Polydor 14051/2
  Steins ob d'amore, H. Schlövogt ob
  d'amore, W. Meyer org, P. Steiner vlc
  – Berlin Motet Choir & RIAS
  Chamber Choir & Berlin Philharmonic
  Orch. – Lehmann*

BEETHOVEN

Concerto in D, Op. 61 vln & orch.
  with Munich Philharmonic   Michel–Ange 120
  Orch. – Rieger

Romance No. 1, in G, Op. 40 vln & orch.
              2EA 3782³□, 3783¹△   HMV DB4662
  with Berlin Philharmonic
  Orch. – Schüller

Romance No. 2, in F, Op. 50 vln & orch.
  with Berlin   2RA 3780/1¹□   HMV DB4661
  Philharmonic Orch. – Schüller

Romance No. 2, in F, Op. 50 vln & orch.
  with Northwest German Philharmonic   Mace M9015, SM9015
  Orch. – Jochum

Sonata No. 5, in F, Op. 24 "Spring" vln & pf
              2RA4774/6ᴵᴵ□, 4777¹□,   HMV DB5610/2
  with R. Schmid pf   4778/9ᴵᴵ□

BRAHMS

(16) Waltzes, Op. 39 pf duet
  No. 15. Waltz No. 15, in A flat arr. vln & pf "in A" Hochstein
  with B. Seidler–   ORA 4282ᴵ   HMV DA4471
  Winkler pf

BRUCH

Concerto No. 1, in g, Op. 26 vln & orch.
              2RA 5871¹□, 5872²□, 5873⁴□,   HMV DB7672/4
              5874³□, 5875⁴□, 5876⁵□
  with Prussian State Orch. – Zaun

BUSONI

Concerto in D, Op. 35a vln & orch.
  with Berlin Radio Symphony   Urania URLP7043
  Orch. – Rother

* Günther Arndt conducts on sides 5 & 6.

DVOŘÁK

(8) Humoresques, Op. 101 pf
    No. 7. Humoresque No. 7, in G flat arr. vln & pf "in G" Kreisler
    with B. Seidler–   ORA 3035[2]☐   HMV DA4444
    Winkler pf

FUCHS

Hungarian march vln & pf
    with B. Seidler–   2RA 3037[1]☐   HMV DB4591
    Winkler pf

HANDEL

(12) Concerti Grossi Op. 6 (1739) 2 vlns, vlc & strs
    Concerto grosso No. 2, in F
    with H. Bastien vln, & Berlin   Electrola E60017
    Philharmonic Orch. – Matzerath   HMV WDLP527
    Concerto grosso No. 12, in b
    with H. Bastien vln, & Berlin   Electrola E60017
    Philharmonic Orch. – Matzerath   HMV WDLP527

MENDELSSOHN

Concerto in e, Op. 64 vln & orch.
    with Berlin Philharmonic   HMV DB11516/9
    Orch. – Celibidache   Victor LBC1049, (set WBC1049),
                        WBC1021

PAGANINI

(6) Sonatas, Op. 3 (1801/6) vln & gtr
    No. 6. Sonata No. 12, in e
    with A. Stauss pf   HMV DA5415, DA5501

RICHARTZ

Romance, Op 79 vln & orch.
    with Berlin Philharmonic   Deutsche Grammophon
    Orch. – Richartz   EPL30148

RIES

(La) Capricciosa vln & pf
    with B. Seidler–   ORA 3039[2]☐   HMV DA4444
    Winkler pf

RIMSKY–KORSAKOV

Sadko (1898) – opera
    Chant hindou arr. vln & pf Kreisler
    with B. Seidler–Winkler pf   HMV DA4440
                        Victor JE213

SCHUBERT

(7) Gesänge (set to Scott's "Lady of the Lake") Op. 52 v & pf
    No. 6. Ave Maria, D839 arr. vln & pf Wilhelmj
    with orch. – Seidler   2RA 4344[1]☐   HMV DB5550
    –Winkler
Litaney auf das Fest aller Seelen, D343 v & pf – arr. vln & orch.
    with orch. – Seidler– 2RA 4345[1]☐   HMV DB5550
    Winkler
Sonata in A, Op. 162 (D574) "Duo" vln & pf
    with E. Michel pf   HMV DB11505/7
(3) Sonatinas, Op. 137 (D384, D385, & D408) vln & pf
    No. 1. Sonatina No. 1, in D: Andantino (2nd mvt) D384
    with E. Michel pf   HMV DB11507

SCHÜTZ

(20) Symphoniae sacrae, Op. 6 – Book I (1629)
    Concerto No. 9 (O quam tu pulchra es) SWV265 2 t's, 2 vlns & c
    with H. Krebs t, R. Kunz b,   Cantate 643257, T72088K
    J. Klapka vln, & continuo
    Concerto No. 10 (Veni de Libano) SWV266 2 t's, 2 vlns & c
    with H. Krebs t, R. Kunz b,   Cantate 643257, T72087F
    J. Klapka vln & continuo

SIMONETTI

Madrigale pf – arr. vln, fl & hp
    with H. Breider fl   ORA 2567[II]☐   HMV EG6248
    & M. Saal hp

SPOHR

Concerto No. 8, in a, Op. 47 "Gesangsscene" vln & orch.
    with Northwest German Philharmonic Mace M9015, SM9015
    Orch. – Jochum

STRAUSS, R.

Concerto in d, Op. 8 (1882) vln & orch.
    with Berlin Radio Orch. – Rother   Urania URLP7032
Don Quixote, Op. 35 (1897) vlc, vln, vla & orch.
    with P. Tortelier vlc, G. Cappone vla, Electrola E80438, STE80438
    & Berlin Philharmonic Orch. – Kempe HMV ALP1759, ASD326,
                                CSDW7054
                                Seraphim S60122
(Der) Rosenkavalier, Op. 59 (1910) – opera
    Waltzes (Act II) arr. vln & pf Příhoda
    with B. Seidler–   2RA 3040[6]☐   HMV DB4591
    Winkler pf
Till Eulenspiegels lustige Streiche, Op. 28 (1895) orch.
    with Berlin Philharmonic   Electrola E80438, STE80438
    Orch. – Kempe   HMV ALP1759, ASD326,
                                CSDW7054, WCLP567

SVENDSEN

(4) Melodies, Op. 24 v & pf
    No. 3. Venetian serenade arr. vln, fl & hp
    with H. Breider fl,   ORA 2566[1]☐   HMV EG6248
    & M. Saal hp

SZYMANOWSKI

(3) Caprices (after Paganini) Op. 40 vln & pf
    No. 2. Caprice No. 21, in A
    with B. Seidler–Winkler pf   HMV DA4440
                         Victor JE213

TCHAIKOVSKY

Romance in f, Op. 5 pf – arr. vln & pf
    with B. Seidler–   ORA 4288[2]☐   HMV DA4471
    Winkler pf
Romance in f, Op. 5 pf – arr. vln & pf
    with A. Stauss pf   HMV DA5415, DA5501

TELEMANN

Cantata No. 19 (Gott will Mensch und sterblich werden)
    with H. Krebs t, H. Bemmer vlc, G.   Cantate 642208, T72088K
    Zschenker cbs & A. Schönstedt org

Tibor BORSODY

MOZART

Concerto No. 3, in G, K.216 vln & orch.
  with orch.
  Top Classic (Metronome)
  TC9019

Concerto No. 4, in D, K.218 vln & orch.
  with orch.
  Top Classic (Metronome)
  TC9019

Natalie BOSHKO (1906–)

BEETHOVEN

(6) Minuets, G.167 pf
  No. 2 Minuet No. 2, in G arr. vln & pf Burmester
  with V. Boshko pf
  Victor 17934

DVOŘÁK

Sonatina in G, Op. 100 vln & pf
  Scherzo (3rd mvt)*
  with V. Boshko pf
  Victor 17934

Willi BOSKOVSKY (1909–)

BACH

(6) Brandenburg Concerti, BWV.1046/51 (1721) strs & c
Brandenburg Concerto No. 1, in F, BWV.1046 vln, 3 obs, bsn, 2 hrns & strs
  with J. Schaeftlein ob, K. Dvořák bsn,   Music Guild (in set MS6303)
  F. Koch hrn, F. Bachmaier hrn, F.   Westminster WST14114,
  Holetschek hpsi & Vienna State Opera   (in set WST307), XWN18932,
  Orch. – Scherchen   (in set XWN3316)
Brandenburg Concerto No. 2, in F, BWV.1047 tpt, fl, ob, vln & strs
  with A. Scherbaum tpt, C. Wanausek   Music Guild (in set MS6303)
  fl, J. Schaeftlein ob, R. Harand vlc, F.   Westminster WST14114,
  Holetschek hpsi & Vienna State Opera   (in set WST307), XWN18932,
  Orch. – Scherchen   (in set XWN3316)
Brandenburg Concerto No. 4, in G, BWV.1049 vln, 2 fls & strs
  with P. Angerer rec, K. Trötzmüller   Music Guild (in set MS6303)
  rec, F. Holetschek hpsi & Vienna State   Westminster WST14115,
  Opera Orch. – Scherchen   (in set WST307), XWN18933,
    (in set XWN3316)
Brandenburg Concerto No. 5, in D, BWV.1050 clav, fl, vln & strs
  with G. Malcolm hpsi, C. Wanausek fl,   Music Guild (in set MS6303)
  R. Harand vlc & Vienna State Opera   Westminster WST14115,
  Orch. – Scherchen   (in set WST307), XWN18933,
    (in set XWN3316)

Matthaeus–Passion, BWV.244 (1729)
  with T. Stich–Randall s, H. Rössl–   Amadeo AVRS6165/8
  Majdan a, W. Kmentt t, H. Braun b,   Bach Guild BG494/7,
  W. Berry bs & Vienna State Opera   BGS5022/5
  Orch. – Wöldike

BEETHOVEN

Romance No. 1, in G, Op. 40 vln & orch.
  with Vienna Mozart   Decca SXL6436, SXL21188
  Ensemble – Boskovsky   London CS6656

* Labelled: "Tyrolean dance."

BEETHOVEN – *Continued*

Romance No. 2, in F, Op. 50 vln & orch.
  with Vienna Mozart   Decca SXL6436, SXL21188
  Ensemble – Boskovsky   London CS6656
(3) Sonatas, Op. 12 vln & pf
No. 1. Sonata No. 1, in D
  with L. Kraus pf   Discophiles français DF167
No. 2. Sonata No. 2, in A
  with L. Kraus pf   Discophiles français DF167
No. 3. Sonata No. 3, in E flat
  with L. Kraus pf   Discophiles français DF167
Sonata No. 4, in a, Op. 23 vln & pf
  with L. Kraus pf   Discophiles français DF168
Sonata No. 5, in F, Op. 24 "Spring" vln & pf
  with L. Kraus pf   Discophiles français DF168
(3) Sonatas, Op. 30 vln & pf
No. 1. Sonata No. 6, in A
  with L. Kraus pf   Discophiles français DF169
No. 2. Sonata No. 7, in c
  with L. Kraus pf   Discophiles français DF170
No. 3. Sonata No. 8, in G
  with L. Kraus pf   Discophiles français DF168
Sonata No. 9, in A, Op. 47 "Kreutzer" vln & pf
  with L. Kraus pf   Discophiles français DF169
Sonata No. 10, in G, Op. 96 vln & pf
  with L. Kraus pf   Discophiles français DF170

MENDELSSOHN

Octet in E flat, Op. 20 4 vlns, 2 vlas & 2 vlcs
  with G. Swoboda vln, P. Matheis vln,   Decca LXT2858
  F. Leitermeier vln, G. Breitenbach vla,   London LL859
  F. Strangler vla, N. Hübner vlc & R.
  Harand vlc

MOZART

Concerto No. 1, in B flat, K207 vln & orch.
  with Vienna Konzerthaus Chamber   Discophiles français DF85
  Orch. – Boskovsky   Haydn Society HSLP9010
Concerto No. 3, in G, K216 vln & orch.
  with Vienna Konzerthaus Chamber   Discophiles français EX25051,
  Orch. – Boskovsky   KLDC50
Concerto No. 4, in D, K218 vln & orch.
  with Vienna Konzerthaus Chamber   Discophiles français DF85,
  Orch. – Boskovsky   EX25028, KLDC50
    Haydn Society HSLP9010

Idomeneo, K366 (1781) – opera
  Non temer, amato bene
  with H. Gueden s & Vienna   Decca LX3067
  Philharmonic Orch. – Krauss
Serenade No. 7, in D, K250 "Haffner" orch.
  Rondo (4th mvt)
      2VH 7060–2, 7061–1 HMV C3990
  with Vienna Philharmonic
  Orch. – Böhm
Serenade No. 7, in D, K250 "Haffner" orch.
  with Vienna Philharmonic   Decca BLK21025, LXT5632,
  Orch. – Münchinger   SXL2272, SXL21025
    London CM9283, CS6214

MOZART – *Continued*

Sonata No. 1, in C, K6 vln & pf
with L. Kraus pf
Alpha DB77
Discophiles français DF188

Sonata No. 12, in G, K27 vln & pf
with L. Kraus pf
Alpha DB77
Discophiles français DF188

Sonata No. 17, in F, K55 vln & pf
with L. Kraus pf
Alpha DB77
Discophiles français DF188

Sonata No. 17, in C, K296 vln & pf
with L. Kraus pf
Alpha DB72
Discophiles français DF123
Haydn Society HSLP133

Sonata No. 18, in C, K56 vln & pf
with L. Kraus pf
Alpha DB74
Discophiles français DF185

Sonata No. 18, in G, K301 vln & pf
with L. Kraus pf
Alpha DB70
Discophiles français DF121
Haydn Society HSLP131

Sonata No. 19, in F, K57 vln & pf
with L. Kraus pf
Alpha DB71
Discophiles français DF122
Haydn Society HSLP132

Sonata No. 19, in E flat, K302 vln & pf
with L. Kraus pf
Alpha DB70
Discophiles français DF121,
EX17055
Haydn Society HSLP131

Sonata No. 20, in E flat, K58 vln & pf
with L. Kraus pf
Alpha DB73
Discophiles français DF124
Haydn Society HSLP134

Sonata No. 20, in C, K303 vln & pf
with L. Kraus pf
Alpha DB70
Discophiles français DF121
Haydn Society HSLP131

Sonata No. 21, in c, K59 vln & pf
with L. Kraus pf
Alpha DB75
Discophiles français DF186

Sonata No. 21, in e, K304 vln & pf
with L. Kraus pf
Alpha DB70
Discophiles français DF121,
EX17054
Haydn Society HSLP131

Sonata No. 22, in e, K60 vln & pf
with L. Kraus pf
Alpha DB72
Discophiles français DF123
Haydn Society HSLP133

Sonata No. 22, in A, K305 vln & pf
with L. Kraus pf
Alpha DB71
Discophiles français DF122
Haydn Society HSLP132

Sonata No. 23, in D, K306 vln & pf
with L. Kraus pf
Alpha DB76
Discophiles français DF187

Sonata No. 24, in F, K376 vln & pf
with L. Kraus pf
Alpha DB75
Discophiles français DF186

MOZART – *Continued*

Sonata No. 25, in F, K377 vln & pf
with L. Kraus pf
Alpha DB75
Discophiles français DF186

Sonata No. 26, in B flat, K378 vln & pf
with L. Kraus pf
Alpha DB72
Discophiles français DF123,
EX25062
Haydn Society HSLP133

Sonata No. 27, in G, K379 vln & pf
with L. Kraus pf
Alpha DB73
Discophiles français DF124,
EX25061
Haydn Society HSLP134

Sonata No. 28, in E flat, K380 vln & pf
with L. Kraus pf
Alpha DB76
Discophiles français DF187

Sonata No. 29, in A, K402 vln & pf
with L. Kraus pf
Alpha DB75
Discophiles français DF186

Sonata No. 30, in C, K403 vln & pf
with L. Kraus pf
Alpha DB77
Discophiles français DF188

Sonata No. 31, in C, K404 vln & pf
with L. Kraus pf
Alpha DB76
Discophiles français DF187

Sonata No. 32, in B flat, K454 vln & pf
with L. Kraus pf
Alpha DB71
Discophiles français DF122,
EX25063
Haydn Society HSLP132

Sonata No. 33, in E flat, K481 vln & pf
with L. Kraus pf
Alpha DB73
Discophiles français DF124,
EX25064
Haydn Society HSLP134

Sonata No. 34, in A, K526 vln & pf
with L. Kraus pf
Alpha DB74
Discophiles français DF185

Sonata No. 35, in F, K547 vln & pf
with L. Kraus pf
Alpha DB74
Discophiles français DF185

Trio in d, K442 pf, vln & vlc
with L. Kraus pf & N. Hübner vlc
Discophiles français DF82,
EX25032
Haydn Society HSLP9004

Trio No. 1, in B flat, K254 pf, vln & vlc
with L. Kraus pf & N. Hübner vlc
Discophiles français DF83
Haydn Society HSLP9005

Trio No. 2, in G, K496 pf, vln & vlc
with L. Kraus pf & N. Hübner vlc
Discophiles français DF81,
EX25032
Haydn Society HSLP9003

Trio No. 3, in B flat, K502 pf, vln & vlc
with L. Kraus pf & N. Hübner vlc
Discophiles français DF81
Haydn Society HSLP9003

Trio No. 4, in E, K542 pf, vln & vlc
with L. Kraus pf & N. Hübner vlc
Discophiles français DF83
Haydn Society HSLP9005

MOZART – *Continued*

Trio No. 5, in C, K548 pf, vln & vlc
  with L. Kraus pf & N. Hübner vlc
                      Discophiles français DF82
                      Haydn Society HSLP9004

Trio No. 6, in G, K564 pf, vln & vlc
  with L. Kraus pf & N. Hübner vlc
                      Discophiles français DF83,
                      EX17052
                      Haydn Society HSLP9005

SCHUBERT

(3) Sonatinas, Op. 137 (D384, D385 & D408) vln & pf
  No. 1. Sonatina No. 1, in D, D384
  with L. Kraus pf
                      Discophiles français DF215
  No. 3. Sonatina No. 3, in g, D408
  with L. Kraus pf
                      Discophiles français DF215

STRAUSS, R.

Also sprach Zarathustra, Op. 30 (1896) orch.
  with Vienna Philharmonic   Ace of Diamonds ADD175,
  Orch. – von Karajan   SDD175
                      Decca LXT5524, SXL2154
                      London CM9236, CS6129

(Ein) Heldenleben, Op. 40 (1898) orch.
  with Vienna Philharmonic   Ace of Clubs ACL241
  Orch. – Krauss   Decca HD41, LXT2729
                      London LL659
                      Richmond B19108

VIVALDI

(12) Concerti, Op. 3 "L'Estro armonico" var. cbns & strs
  Concerto No. 1, in D, P.146 (F.IV, No. 7) 4 vlns, vlc, strs & c
  with J. Tomasow vln, P. Matheis vln,   Amadeo AVRS6088
  W. Hintermeyer vln, R. Harand vlc,   Bach Guild BG572, BGS5016
  H. Norberg hpsi & Vienna State Opera   I Classici della Musica Classica
  Chamber Orch. – Rossi   XAM4023
                      Qualiton LPX1095
                      Top Rank 35–073
                      Vanguard SRV143

  Concerto No. 2, in g, P.326 (F.IV, No. 8) 2 vlns, strs & c
  with J. Tomasow vln, H. Nordberg &   Amadeo AVRS6088
  Vienna State Opera Chamber   Bach Guild BG572, BGS5016
  Orch. – Rossi   I Classici della Musica Classica
                      XAM4023
                      Qualiton LPX1095
                      Top Rank 35–073
                      Vanguard SRV143

  Concerto No. 4, in e, P.97 (F.I, No. 174) 4 vlns, strs & c
  with J. Tomasow vln, P. Matheis vln,   Amadeo AVRS6088
  W. Hintermeyer vln, H. Nordberg hpsi   Bach Guild BG572, BGS5016
  & Vienna State Opera Chamber   I Classici della Musica Classica
  Orch. – Rossi   XAM4023
                      Qualiton LPX1095
                      Top Rank 35–073
                      Vanguard SRV143

VIVALDI – *Continued*

  Concerto No. 5, in A, P.212 (F.I, No. 175) 2 vlns, strs & c
  with J. Tomasow vln, H. Nordberg   Amadeo AVRS6089
  hpsi & Vienna State Opera Chamber   Bach Guild BG573, BGS5017
  Orch. – Rossi   I Classici della Musica Classica
                      XAM4024
                      Qualiton LPX1096
                      Top Rank 35–074
                      Vanguard SRV144

  Concerto No. 7, in F, P.249 (F.IV, No. 9) 4 vlns, strs & c
  with J. Tomasow vln, P. Matheis vln,   Amadeo AVRS6089
  W. Hintermeyer vln, H. Nordberg hpsi   Bach Guild BG573, BGS5017
  & Vienna State Opera Chamber   I Classici della Musica Classica
  Orch. – Rossi   XAM4024
                      Qualiton LPX1096
                      Top Rank 35–074
                      Vanguard SRV144

  Concerto No. 8, in A, P.2 (F.I, No. 177) 2 vlns, strs & c
  with J. Tomasow vln, H. Nordberg   Amadeo AVRS6089
  hpsi & Vienna State Opera Chamber   Bach Guild BG573, BGS5017
  Orch. – Rossi   I Classici della Musica Classica
                      XAM4024
                      Qualiton LPX1096
                      Top Rank 35–074
                      Vanguard SRV144

  Concerto No. 10, in b, P.148 (F.IV, No. 10) 4 vlns, strs & c
  with J. Tomasow vln, P. Matheis vln,   Amadeo AVRS6090
  W. Hintermeyer vln, H. Nordberg hpsi   Bach Guild BG574, BGS5018
  & Vienna State Opera Chamber   I Classici della Musica Classica
  Orch. – Rossi   XAM4025
                      Qualiton LPX1097
                      Top Rank 35–075
                      Vanguard SRV145

  Concerto No. 11, in d, P.250 (F.IV, No. 11) 2 vlns, vlc, strs & c
  with J. Tomasow vln, R. Harand vlc,   Amadeo AVRS6090
  H. Nordberg hpsi & Vienna State   Bach Guild BG574, BGS5018
  Opera Chamber Orch. – Rossi   I Classici della Musica Classica
                      XAM4025
                      Qualiton LPX1097
                      Top Rank 35–075
                      Vanguard SRV145

(12) Concerti, Op. 9 (1728) "La Certra" vln, strs & c
  Concerto No. 9, in B flat, P.341 (F.I, No. 57) with 2nd vln obb
  with P. Makanowitzky vln & Vienna   Amadeo AVRS6229
  State Opera Chamber   Bach Guild BG609, BGS5035
  Orch. – Golschmann

Wilfried BÖTTCHER

NARDINI

(6) Sonatas, Op. 2 (1765) vln & c
  Sonata in E flat: Adagio (2nd mvt)
  with H. Tachezi hpsi   Amadeo AVRS EP15137

Jules BOUCHERIT (1878–   )

BACH

(4) Suites, BWV1066/9 strs & c
  Suite No. 3, in D: Air (2nd mvt) BWV1068 2 obs, 3 tpts, drms
  & strs – arr. vln & pf as "Air on the G–string" by Wilhelmj
  with L. Diémer pf   5598–o   Zonophone X87912

CHOPIN

(3) Nocturnes, Op. 9 pf
  No. 2. Nocturne No. 2, in E flat arr. vln & pf Sarasate
  with L. Diémer pf   5597–o   HMV 8897, X77905
                       Zonophone X87911

DIÉMER

Caprice scherzando, Op. 48 vln & pf
  with L. Diémer pf   5595–o   Zonophone X87908
Romance, Op. 46 vln & pf
  with L. Diémer pf   5502–o   Zonophone X87902

FAURÉ

Berceuse, Op. 16 vln & pf
  with L. Diémer pf   5508–o   Zonophone X87905

HUBAY

(14) Scènes de la Csárda vln & pf
  No. 4. Hejre Kati, Op. 32
  with L. Diémer pf   5506–o   Zonophone X87904

LECLAIR

Gavotte ancienna unid – arr. solo vln
  (unaccompanied)   5500–o   HMV 8895
                       Zonophone X87901
(12) Sonatas, Op. 9 – Book IV (1738) vln & c
  Sonata No. 3, in D: Tambourin (3rd mvt)
  with L. Diémer pf   5503–o   Zonophone X87903

LEFORT

Danse mauresque vln & pf
  with L. Diémer pf   5592/30–0   HMV 8897, X77904
                       Zonophone X87910

MASSENET

Thaïs (1894) – opera
  Méditation arr. vln & pf Marsick
  with L. Diémer pf   5592–o   Gramophone & Typewriter
                       237902
                       Zonophone X87906

MOZART

Concerto No. 5, in A, K219 "Turkish" vln & orch.
  Tempo di menuetto (3rd mvt)
  with piano   5599   Gramophone & Typewriter
                       237903
Divertimento No. 17, in D, K334 2 hrns & strs
  Minuet (3rd mvt) arr. vln & pf Burmester
  with L. Diémer pf   Zonophone X87913

SAINT-SAËNS

(Le) Carnaval des animaux (1886) small orch.
  Le cygne arr. vln & pf
  with L. Diémer pf   5499–o   HMV 8895
                       Zonophone X87900

Gabriel Georges BOUILLON (1898–   )

d'AMBROSIO

Canzonetta, Op. 6 vln & pf
  with L. Petitjean pf   HMV K6917

BACH

(6) Brandenburg Concerti, BWV1046/51 (1721) strs & c
  Brandenburg Concerto No. 4, in G, BWV1049 vln, 2 fls & strs
  with R. Cortet fl, P. Morseau fl &   HMV DB2037/8
  École Normale Chamber   Victor 7915/6
  Orch. – Cortot
(3) Sonatas & 3 Partitas, BWV1001/6 solo vln
  Partita No. 3, in E: Gavotte, (3rd mvt) BWV1006 arr. vln & pf Kreisler
  with L. Petitjean pf   OPG 358–2   HMV K6824

BRAHMS

(16) Waltzes, Op. 39 pf duet
  No. 15. Waltz No. 15, in A flat arr. vln & pf "in A" Hochstein
  with M. Fauré pf   N 8647   Pathé X5444
  No. 15. Waltz No. 15, in A flat arr. vln & pf "in A" Hochstein
  with piano   Polydor 522912

DESPLANES

Intrada (Adagio) vln & c – arr. vln & pf Nachèz
  with L. Petitjean pf   HMV K6917

DVOŘÁK

(8) Slavonic Dances, Op. 72 pf duet; orch.
  No. 2. Slavonic dance No. 10, in e arr. vln & pf Kreisler
  with M. Fauré pf   N 8646   Pathé X5444

FALLA

(La) Vida Breve (1913) – opera
  Danza española orch. – arr. vln & pf Kreisler
  with M. Fauré pf   Pathé X5445

FIORILLO

(36) Étude–Caprices, Op. 3 solo vln
  Caprice No. 14, in g (Adagio) arr. vln & pf Bouillon
  with M. Fauré pf   Pathé X98027

KREISLER

Variations on a theme of Corelli (Tartini) vln & pf
  with M Fauré pf   Pathé X5445

NEVIN

(The) Rosary (1898) v & pf – arr. vln & pf Kreisler
  with L. Petitjean pf   OPG 359–2A   HMV K6824

SCHUBERT

Rosamude von Cypern, Op. 26 (D797) (1823) – Incidental music orch.
  No. 9. Ballet music II, in G arr. vln & pf Kreisler
  with M. Fauré pf   Pathé X98027

Michèle BOUISSINOT (1929–   )

AUBERT

(6) Concerti, Op. 12 vln & strs
  Concerto No. 2, in a
  with L. Boulay hpsi & Versailles   Contrepoint MC20135
  Chamber Orch. – Wahl   Mode CMDINT9504

AUBERT – *Continued*

(6) Concerti, Op. 17 (1734/5) 4 vlns & strs
Concerto No. 1, in D
with L. Boulay hpsi & Versailles
Chamber Orch. – Wahl   Contrepoint MC20135

BARTÓK

(2) Portraits, Op. 5 (1907) vln & orch.
with Paris Radio Symphony   Columbia FCS532
Orch. – Bruck

FAURÉ

Berceuse, Op. 16 vln & pf
with G. Defresne pf   Festival FLD84

HANDEL

(15) Sonatas, Op. 1 (?1731) fl or vln & c
Sonata No. 13, in D vln IV
          CPTX 947/50–2 P   Pathé PDT246/7
with M. Fauré pf

KREISLER

Andantino (Padre Martini) vln & pf
with G. Defresne pf   Festival FLD84
Variations on a theme of Corelli (Tartini) vln & pf
with G. Defresne pf   Festival FLD84

PAGANINI

(24) Caprices, Op. 1 (1801/7) solo vln
Caprice No. 9, in E
(unaccompanied)   Festival FLD84
Caprice No. 13, in B flat,
(unaccompanied)   Festival FLD84

POLDINI

(7) Marionnettes pf
No. 2. Poupée valsante arr. vln & pf Kreisler
with G. Defresne pf   Festival FLD84

RAVEL

Tzigane (Rapsodie de concert) (1924) vln & pf or orch.
with G. Defresne pf   Festival FLD84

SCHUBERT

(7) Gesänge (set to Scott's "Lady of the Lake") Op. 52 v & pf
No. 6. Ave Maria, D839 arr. vln & pf Wilhelmj
with G. Defresne pf   Festival FLD84

WIENIAWSKI

Polonaise brillante No. 1, in D, Op. 4 vln & pf
with G. Defresne pf   Festival FLD84

YSAŸE

(3) Mazurkas, Op. 11 vln & pf
No. 3. Mazurka No. 3, in b "Lointaine–passé"
with G. Defresne pf   Festival FLD84

Georges BOULANGER (1892–)

ANONYMOUS

Kol Nidrei Hebrew melody – arr. vln & pf Rosenfeld
with piano   1604 AA   Kristall 05055

BECCE

Légende d'amour, Op. 11 pf – arr. vln & pf
with O. Jerochnik pf   Odeon 0–25969

BOULANGER

African serenade vln & pf
with O. Jerochnik pf   Odeon 0–25901
                              Parlophone DP3, R2389

Alles dunkel vln & pf
with piano   Telefunken A1693

American vision vln & pf
with O. Jerochnik pf   Odeon 0–25901
                              Parlophone DP3, R2389

Auf der Hochzeitsreise (Heiteres Intermezzo) vln & pf
with W. Schmidt pf   Odeon 0–26141

Augustin – waltz vln & pf
with piano   Telefunken A1677

Avant de mourir, Op. 17 vln & pf
with piano   Telefunken A1693

Berceuse vln & pf
with piano   Telefunken A1759

Caprice roumain, Op. 33 vln & pf
with piano   Kristall 5051

Comme ci, comme ça vln & pf
with O. Jerochnik pf   Odeon 0–25622

Comme ci, comme ça vln & pf
with piano   Telefunken A1775

Einsam unterm Sternenzelt (Romance) vln & pf
with W. Schmidt pf   Odeon 0–26167

Enttäuschung (Romance) vln & pf
with W. Schmidt pf   Odeon 0–26167

Flageolet – waltz No. 1 vln & pf
with piano   Odeon 0–26402

Flageolet – waltz No. 1 vln & pf
with piano   Telefunken A1677

Mazurka de concert, Op. 34 vln & pf
with piano   Kristall 5051

Norinka serenade, Op. 24 vln & pf
with piano   Telefunken A1759

Pizzicato waltz vln & pf
with O. Jerochnik pf   Be 11825   Decca 216013
                              Odeon 0–25949, GO19351
                              Parlophone DP2, R2519

Pourquoi, Madame? vln & pf
with piano   Telefunken A1775

Sérénade Georgette vln & pf
with O. Jerochnik pf   Odeon 0–25969

Tarantelle vln & pf
with piano   Odeon GO19351

Tout égal! (Intermezzo) vln & pf
with W. Schmidt pf   Odeon 0–26141

Triolette vln & pf
with piano   Odeon 0–26402

BOULANGER – *Continued*

Valse–caprice vln & pf
with piano — Telefunken A1775

Vous êtes jolie, Madame vln & pf
with O. Jerochnik pf — Odeon 0–25624

ELGAR

Salut d'amour, Op. 12 orch. – arr. vln & pf Elgar
with O. Jerochnik pf — Odeon 0–25622

KREISLER

Liebesleid vln & pf
with piano — Telefunken A1776

POLIAKIN

(Le) Canari (Concert–polka) vln & pf
with O. Jerochnik pf — Odeon 0–25624

RIMSKY–KORSAKOV

Sadko (1898) – opera
Chant hindou arr. vln & pf Kreisler
with O. Jerochnik pf — Be 11822 — Decca 216013
Odeon 0–25949, GO19351
Parlophone DP2, R2519

SAINT–SAËNS

(Le) Carnaval des animaux (1886) small orch.
Le cygne arr. vln & orch.
with Bucharest Gypsy Orch. — Colosseum CRLP200

STRANSKY

Kaddisch vlc & pf – arr. vln & pf
with piano — 1651 AA — Kristall 05055

Paule BOUQUET

BEETHOVEN

Romance No. 2, in F, Op. 50 vln & orch.
with A. Collard pf — Odeon 123896

FALLA

(La) Vida Breve (1913) – opera
Danza española orch. – arr. vln & pf Kreisler
with A. Collard pf — Odeon 123897

INFANTE

Chanson gitane vln & pf
with A. Collard pf — Odeon 188952

RODRIGO

(2) Esbozas, Op. 1 (1923) vln & pf
with A. Collard pf — Odeon 123897

Giovanni BOZZINI

TARTINI

Concerto in a, D115 (C76) vln, strs & c
with B. Salvi vln, M. Ceradini vln &
Angelicum Orch., Milan – Abbado — Angelicum LPA5921

I. BRAILOVSKY

KOKOITI

Rhapsody vln & orch.
with North–Ossetian Philharmonic
Symphony Orch. – Yadykh — Mezhdunarodnaya Kniga D21071/2

Norbert BRAININ (1923–)

BEETHOVEN

(11) Wiener Tänze, WoO17 orch.
No. 1. Waltz in E flat
with members of London Baroque
Ensemble – Haas — Pye CEC32027
No. 3. Waltz in B flat
with members of London Baroque
Ensemble – Haas — Pye CEC32027
No. 11. Waltz in D
with members of London Baroque
Ensemble – Haas — Pye CEC32027

HOLST

(4) Songs, Op. 35 v & vln
with P. Pears t — Argo RG497, ZRG5497

MOZART

Duo No. 1, in G, K423 vln & vla
with P. Schidlof vla — Iramac 6528
Sinfonia concertante in E flat, K364 vln, vla & orch.
with P. Schidlof vla & London Mozart — HMV CLP1014, LALP355
Players – Blech
Sinfonia concertante in B flat, K364 vln, vla & orch.
with P. Schidlof vla & Netherlands — Iramac 6528
Chamber Orch. – Zinman

Thomas BRANDIS

GOLDBERG

Sonata No. 4, in a 2 vlns & c
with H. Rehm vln, K. Grebe hpsi & — Archive APM14195, ARC3195,
E. Koch vlc — ARC73195, SAPM198195,
SAPM199008

MOZART

Sinfonia concertante in E flat, K364 vln, vla & orch.
with G. Cappone vla & Berlin — Deutsche Grammophon
Philharmonic Orch. – Böhm — LPM39156, SLPM139156

TELEMANN

Quartet in G, T.I, No. 2 fl, ob, vln & c
with H–M. Linde fl, M. Piguet ob, E. — Musique Royale 199012
Müller hpsi & A. Wenzinger vlc

VIVALDI

Concerto in a, P.28 (F.I, No. 61) 2 vlns, strs & c
with E. Maas vln & Berlin — Deutsche Grammophon 2530 094
Philharmonic Orch. – Karajan
Concerto in D, P.208 (F.I, No. 10) (Op. 51, No. 1) "L'Inquietudine" vln,
strs & c
with Berlin Philharmonic — Deutsche Grammophon 2530 094
Orch. – Karajan

VIVALDI – *Continued*

Concerto in E, P.246 (F.I, No. 127) (Op. 35, No. 6) "L'Amoroso" vln, strs
& c
with Berlin Philharmonic   Deutsche Grammophon 2530 094
Orch. – Karajan

Karl BRANDT

CHAUSSON

Poème, Op. 25 vln & orch.
with Berlin Symphony   Royale 1339
Orch. – Rubahn

PAGANINI

Concerto No. 1, in D, Op. 6 (cadenza by Sauret) vln & orch.
Allegro maestoso (1st mvt) arr. Wilhelmj
with Berlin Symphony   Royale 1339
Orch. – Rubahn

Yovanovitch BRATZA (1904–)

BACH

Concerto No. 2 in E, BWV1042 vln, strs & c
Allegro (1st mvt)
with Bach Cantata   CA11098/9–2   Columbia DB504, (in set CHM2)
Club String Orch. – Scott

(3) Sonatas & 3 Partitas, BWV1001/6 solo vln
Partita No. 3, in E: Preludio (1st mvt) BWV1006 arr. vln & pf Kreisler
with piano   A 244   Columbia D1468
Partita No. 3, in E: Gavotte (3rd mvt) BWV1006 arr. vln & pf Kreisler
with piano   A 241   Columbia D1468

BOULANGER, L.

Nocturne in F (1911) vln & pf
with piano   WA 4958   Columbia 4824, 01050, D1574,
     DQ3389

BRAHMS

(16) Waltzes, Op. 39 pf duet
No. 15. Waltz No. 15, in A flat arr. vln & pf "in A" Hochstein
with S. Krish pf   A 240   Columbia D1467

CHAMINADE

Sérénade espagnole pf – arr. vln & pf Kreisler
with piano   A 3994   Columbia 5029, 01507, J5061

CORELLI

(12) Sonatas, Op. 5 vln & c
Sonata No. 12, in d "La Follia"
with F. Jackson hpsi   WA 11084/5   Columbia DB501, (in set CHM2)

DUNHILL

Polacaprice (Caprice alla polacca) Op. 61, No. 4 vln & pf
with piano   A 262   Columbia D1485
Sérénade basque, Op. 61, No. 1 vln & pf
with piano   WA 4957   Columbia 5029, 01507, J5061

DVOŘÁK

(4) Romantic Pieces, Op. 75 vln & pf
No. 2. Allegro maestoso
with piano   Columbia D1471
(8) Slavonic Dances, Op. 46 pf duet; orch.
No. 2. Slavonic dance No. 2, in e arr. vln & pf "in g" Kreisler
with piano   A 1729   Columbia D1524

ELGAR

(La) Capricieuse, Op. 17 vln & pf
with piano   A 650   Columbia D1485

FAURÉ

(3) Chansons, Op. 7 v & pf
No. 1. Après un rêve arr. vln & pf Elman
with piano   A 3993–4   Columbia 1857D

FIBICH

Images, Impressions & Souvenirs, Op. 41 pf
No. 14. Poem (from "Souvenirs", Part IV) arr. vln & pf Kubelík
with S. Krish pf   69884   Columbia D1433

GLUCK

Orphée et Eurydice (1762) – opera
Dance of the blessed spirits: Lento "Mélodie" (No. 2) ar. vln & pf
Kreisler
with piano   Columbia D1516

HANDEL

(15) Sonatas, Op. 1 (?1731) fl or vln & c
Sonata No. 5, in G: Menuetto (5th mvt) arr. vln & pf Burmester
with piano   Columbia D1529

JONGEN

(2) Aquarelles, Op. 59 vln & pf
No. 1. Légende naïve
with piano   AX 2511–1   Columbia 9358, 02608, 50112D

KREISLER

Liebesleid vln & pf
with S. Krish pf   A 242   Columbia D1467
Rondino on a theme by Beethoven vln & pf
with S. Krish pf   71812–2   Columbia D1445
Rondino on a theme by Beethoven vln & pf
with S. Krish pf   A 3982–4   Columbia 4823
Tambourin chinois, Op. 3 vln & pf
with S. Kirsh pf   AX 1947   Columbia 9357, 02607, L1461
Grave (W.F. Bach) vln & pf
with S. Krish pf   Columbia L1656
Variations on a theme of Corelli (Tartini) vln & pf
with piano   Columbia D1516

LECLAIR

(12) Sonatas, Op. 9 – Book IV (1738) vln & c
Sonata No. 3, in D: Tambourin (3rd mvt) arr. vln & pf Kreisler
with S. Krish pf   Columbia L1439

MENDELSSOHN

(6) Songs without words, Op.62 pf
No. 1. Song without words No. 25, in G "May breezes" arr. vln & pf
Kreisler
with piano   WA 5078   Columbia 4824, 01050, D1574

MOSZKOWSKI

(2) Stücke, Op. 45 pf
   No. 2. **Guitarre** arr. vln & pf Sarasate
   with S. Krish pf   71866   Columbia D1449

MOZART

Divertimento No. 17, in D, K334 2 hrns & strs
   Minuet (3rd mvt) arr. vln & pf Burmester
   with S. Krish pf   A 3986–4   Columbia 4822, 1857D, D1435

PALMGREN

Romance in G vln & pf
   with piano   Columbia D1471

RIES

Suite No. 3, in G, Op. 34 vln & pf
   No. 5. **Perpetuum mobile**
   with S. Krish pf   71008   Columbia D1429

RIMSKY–KORSAKOV

Sadko (1898) – opera
   Chant hindou arr. vln & pf Kreisler
   with S. Krish pf   71811   Columbia D1445
   Chant hindou arr. vln & pf Kreisler
   with S. Krish pf   A 3983–3   Columbia 4823

SARASATE

Carmen Fantasia (on themes from the opera by Bizet) Op. 25 vln & pf or orch.
   with piano   Columbia DOX297, DX339
Carmen Fantasia (on themes from the opera by Bizet) Op. 25 vln & pf or orch.
   Habañera
   with S. Krish pf   69831   Columbia D1433

SCHUBERT

(2) Lieder, Op. 98 (D498) v & pf
   No. 2. **Wiegenlied** (Schlafe, holder süsser Knabe) arr. vln & pf Elman
   with S. Krish pf   A 3987   Columbia 4822, D1435
(6) Moments musicaux, Op. 94 (D780) (1823/7) pf
   No. 3. **Moment musicale No. 3, in f** "Air russe" arr. vln & pf Kreisler
   with S. Krish pf   A 3984   Columbia 4821, D1430
Rosamunde von Cypern, Op. 26 (D797) (1823) – Incidental music orch.
   No. 5. **Entr'acte III, in B flat,** arr. vln & pf Kreisler
   with piano   Columbia D1529

ŠEVČÍK

(6) Bohemian Dances, Op. 10 vln & pf
   No. 5. **Czech song** (Bretislav)
   with S. Krish pf   71873   Columbia D1449

SMETANA

From my Homeland (1878) vln & pf
   No. 2. **Andantino**
   with S. Krish pf   Columbia L1656

SUK

(7) Pieces, Op. 7 pf
   No. 1. **Love song** arr. vln & pf Mařák
   with S. Krish pf   AX 1946   Columbia 9357, 02607, L1461

SUK – *Continued*

(4) Pieces, Op. 17 vln & pf
   No. 3. **Un Poco triste**
   with piano   A 1728   Columbia D1524

TARTINI

Sonata in g "Il Trillo del Diavolo" vln & c – arr. vln & pf Kreisler
   Allegro energico (2nd mvt)
   with S. Kirsh pf   69901   Columbia D1429

TCHAIKOVSKY

(12) Pieces (of moderate difficulty) Op. 40 pf
   No. 2. **Chanson triste** arr. vln & pf
   with S. Krish pf   A 3985   Columbia 4821, D1430

WIENIAWSKI

Concerto No. 2, in d, Op. 22 vln & orch.
   Romance (2nd mvt)
   with piano   AX 2510–1   Columbia 9358, 02608, 50112D

ZSOLT

Dragonflies vln & pf
   with S. Krish   Columbia D1439

H. de BRAYNE

ACCORDI

(La) Seduzione (Air de ballet) orch. – arr. vln & pf
   with A. Delacroix pf   Zonophone X87928

BRAGA

(7) Melodies (1867) v & pf
   No. 5. **La serenata "Angel's serenade"** arr. vln & pf
   with A. Delacroix pf   Zonophone X88020

BROUSTET

Airs populaires espagnols vln & pf
   with orch.   Zonophone X80508

GOUNOD

Ave Maria (Méditation on Bach's "Prelude No. 1, in C" from Book I of "Das Wohltemperirte Clavier") v & pf – arr. vln & pf
   with orch.   Zonophone X88021

RENARD

(2) Berceaux, Op. 20 vln & pf
   No. 2. **Berceuse No. 2, in F**
   with A. Delacroix pf   Zonophone X87942

ROCHE

Bandinage vln & pf
   with orch.   Zonophone X80507

SAINT-SAËNS

Oratorio de Noël, Op. 12 (1863) – oratorio
   No. 7. **Tecum principium** arr. vln & pf
   with A. Delacroix pf   Zonophone X88026

THOMÉ

Andante religioso, Op. 70 pf – arr. vln & pf
   with A. Delacroix pf   Zonophone X88027

THUILLER

(Le) Sommeil d'un ange – cantabile pf – arr. vln & pf
  with A. Delacroix pf   Zonophone X87927

VERBRUGGHEN

Berceuse (Sommeil d'un ange) vln & pf
  with A. Delacroix pf   Zonophone X87941

Elias BREESKIN (1895–1969)

d'AMBROSIO

Canzonetta, Op. 6 vln & pf
  with piano   5804 Edison Diamond Disc 80704

BEETHOVEN

(6) Minuets, G167 pf
  No. 2. Minuet No. 2, in G arr. vln & pf Burmester
  with R. Gruen pf   3432 Brunswick 5090, 13005

BRANDL

(Der) Liebe Augustin – operetta
  Du alter Stefansturm arr. vln & pf as "The old refrain" by Kreisler
  with A. Loesser pf   4642 Brunswick 13017

CHAMINADE

Sérénade espagnole pf – arr. vln & pf Kreisler
  with J. Bonime pf   Brunswick 13023

FOSTER

(The) Old folks at home "Swanee river" (1851) v & pf – arr. v, vln & orch.
  with V. Rea s & orch.   3598 Brunswick 2703, 10013

GARDNER

(2) Pieces, Op. 5 vln & pf
  No. 1. From the canebrake
  with piano   Brunswick 5126

PIERNÉ

Sérénade in A, Op. 7 (1875) pf – arr. vln & pf
  with R. Gruen pf   3579 Brunswick 13017

RAFF

(6) Pieces, Op. 85 vln & pf
  No. 3. Cavatina in D
  with R. Gruen pf   3654 Brunswick 13012

SCHINDLER

Souvenir poétique (Paraphrase on Fibich's "Poem" Op. 41, No. 14) vln & pf
  with R. Gruen pf   3593 Brunswick 5090, 13005

SCHUMANN

(13) Kinderscenen, Op. 15 pf
  No. 7. Träumerei arr. vln & pf
  with piano   Edison cylinder 2339
  Romance (unid) arr. vln & pf
  with piano   Edison cylinder 2339

THOMÉ

Simple aveu, Op. 25 pf – arr. vln & pf
  with piano   Brunswick 5126

VIEUXTEMPS

Caprice burlesque (Souvenir d'Amérique) Op. 17 "Yankee Doodle" vln & pf
  with R. Gruen pf   3651 Brunswick 13012

ZIMBALIST

(3) Slavonic Dances vln & pf
  No. 2. Hebrew melody & dance
  with R. Gruen   Brunswick 13023

Hyman BRESS (1931–)

ANHALT

Sonata (1954) vln & pf
  with C. Reiner pf   Victor CC1014, CCS1014

ARCHER

Trio No. 1 (1953/4) pf, vln & vlc
  with J. Newmark pf & W. Joachim vlc CBC Transcription Program 112
Trio No. 2 (1956/7) pf, vln & vlc
  with J. Newmark pf & W. Joachim vlc CBC Transcription Program 196

BACH

Concerto No. 1, in d, BWV1052 clav, strs & c – restored vln, strs & c as "Concerto in d" by Reitz – arr. Szigeti
  with Montréal Symphony   Mode MDINT9246
  Orch. – Bress

(Ein) Musikalisches Opfer, BWV1079 (1749)
  with M. Duchesnes fl, O. Joachim vla CBC Transcription Program 95
  & W. Joachim vlc

(3) Sonatas & 3 Partitas, BWV1001/6 solo vln
  Sonata No. 1, in g, BWV1001
  (unaccompanied)   Eurodisc 70868KK, S70869KK
                Mace M9056, MCS9056

  Sonata No. 1, in g, BWV1001 arr. vln & pf Schumann
  with K. Bergemann pf   CBS (in set 77325)

  Partita No. 1, in b, BWV1002
  (unaccompanied)   Eurodisc 70868KK, S70869KK
                Mace M9056, MCS9056

  Partita No. 1, in b, BWV1002 arr. vln & pf Schumann
  with K. Bergemann pf   CBS (in set 77325)

  Sonata No. 2, in a, BWV1003
  (unaccompanied)   Eurodisc 70870KK, S70871KK
                Mace M9057, MCS9057

  Sonata No. 2, in a BWV1003 arr. vln & pf Schumann
  with K. Bergemann pf   CBS (in set 77325)

  Partita No. 2, in d, BWV1004
  (unaccompanied)   Folkways FM3351

  Partita No. 2, in d, BWV1004
  (unaccompanied)   Eurodisc 70870KK, S70871KK
                Mace M9057, MCS9057

  Partita No. 2, in d, BWV1004 arr. vln & pf Schumann
  with K. Bergemann pf   CBS (in set 77325)

  Sonata No. 3, in C, BWV1005
  (unaccompanied)   Eurodisc 70872KK, S70873KK
                Mace M9058, MCS9058

  Sonata No. 3, in C, BWV1005 arr. vln & pf Schumann
  with K. Bergemann pf   CBS (in set 77325)

  Partita No. 3, in E, BWV1006
  (unaccompanied)   Eurodisc 70872KK, S70873KK
                Mace M9058, MCS9058

BACH – *Continued*

Partita No. 3, in E, BWV1006 arr. vln & pf Schumann
with K. Bergemann pf   CBS (in set 77325)

BARTÓK

Sonata No. 1 (1921) vln & pf
with C. Reiner pf   Victor LM2853, LSC2853,
          RB6650, SB6650

Sonata No. 2 (1922) vln & pf
with C. Reiner pf   Victor LM2853, LSC2853,
          RB6650, SB6650

Sonata in g (1944) solo vln
(unaccompanied)   Folkways FM3354

BEETHOVEN

Romance No. 2, in F, Op. 50 vln & orch.
with London Philharmonic World Record Club ST730, T730
Orch. – Boult

(3) Sonatas, Op. 30 vln & pf
No. 2. Sonata No. 7, in c
with C. Reiner pf   Folkways FM3352

BLOCH

Abodah (1929) vln & pf
with C. Reiner pf   Folkways FM3357

Baal Shem (3 Pictures of Chassidic Life) (1923) vln & pf
No. 1. Vidui (Contrition)
with C. Reiner pf   Folkways FM3357

No. 2. Nigun (Improvisation)
with C. Reiner pf   Folkways FM3354

No. 3. Simchas Torah (Rejoicing)
with C. Reiner pf   Folkways FM3357

Concerto in a (1938) vln & orch.
with Prague Symphony Orch. – Rohan Crossroads 22 16 0212
          Erato STU70427
          Supraphon SUA10881, SUA
          ST50881, SV8407

Fantasie (1899) vln & pf
with C. Reiner pf   Folkways FM3357

Sonata No. 1 (1920) vln & pf
with C. Reiner pf   Folkways FM3357

Suite Hébraïque (1951) vla or vln & orch.
with Prague Symphony Orch. – Rohan Crossroads 22 16 0212
          Erato STU70427
          Supraphon SUA10881, SUA
          ST50881, SV8407

Suite No. 1 (1958) solo vln
(unaccompanied)   Folkways FM3357

BRAHMS

(21) Hungarian Dances pf duet
Hungarian dance No. 1, in g arr. vln & pf Joachim
with C. Reiner pf   Folkways FM3353

Quintet in f, Op. 34 pf, 2 vlns, vla & vlc
with G. Gould pf, M. Goodman vln, CBC Transcription Program 140
O. Joachim vla & W. Joachim vlc

Sonata No. 1, in G, Op. 78 vln & pf
with C. Reiner pf   Victor CC1014, CCS1014

Sonata No. 3, in d, Op. 108 vln & pf
with C. Reiner pf   Folkways FM3353

BRESS

Fantasy electronique vln & tape recorder
with electronic sounds   Folkways FM3355

BUSONI

Sonata No. 1, in C, Op. 29 (1890) vln & pf
with B. Johnsson pf   L'Oiseau–Lyre OL296, SOL296

Sonata No. 2, in e, Op. 36a (1898) vln & pf
with B. Johnsson pf   L'Oiseau–Lyre OL296, SOL296

CHAMPAGNE

Quartet No. 1 (1954) 2 vlns, vla & vlc
with M. Goodman vln, O. Joachim vla CBC Transcription Program 143
& W. Joachim vlc

CORELLI

(12) Sonatas, Op. 5 vln & c
Sonata No. 12, in d "La Follia" (arr. Léonard)
with C. Reiner pf   Folkways FM3351

DEBUSSY

Sonata No. 3, in g (1917) vln & pf
with C. Reiner pf   Folkways FM3354

DVOŘÁK

(8) Slavonic Dances, Op. 46 pf duet; orch.
No. 2. Slavonic Dance No. 2, in e arr. vln & pf "in g" Kreisler
with C. Reiner pf   Folkways FM3353

FAURÉ

Berceuse, Op. 16 vln & pf
with C. Reiner pf   Folkways FM3353

FERRABOSCO

Allemande fl & 5 viols
with M. Duschenes fl, M. Goodman CBC Transcription Program 191
vln, O. Joachim vla, W. Joachim vlc &
N. Clair cbs

GOULD

Quartet No. 1 (1956) 2 vlns, vla & vlc
with M. Goodman vln, O. Joachim vla CBC Transcription Program 142
& W. Joachim vlc

HABA

Fantasy, Op. 9a (1921) solo vln
(unaccompanied)   Folkways FM3355

HAYDN

Quartet No. 83, in B flat, Op. 103 (H.III, No. 83) "Unfinished" 2 vlns, vla
& vlc
with M. Goodman vln, O. Joachim vla CBC Transcription Program 190
& W. Joachim vlc

JOACHIM, O.

Quartet No. 1 (1956) 2 vlns, vla & vlc
with M. Goodman vln, O. Joachim vla CBC Transcription Program 190
& W. Joachim vlc

JONES

Introduction & Fugue (1959) vln & pf
with C. Reiner pf   Victor CC1014, CCS1014

JONES – *Continued*

Suite fl & strs
    with M. Duschenes fl, M. Goodman   CBC Transcription Program 191
    vln, O. Joachim vla & W. Joachim vlc

KREISLER

Schön Rosmarin vln & pf
    with C. Reiner pf   Folkways FM3353

LECLAIR

Sonata (unid) vln & c
    with J. Newmark pf & W. Joachim vlc   CBC Transcription Program 112
(12) Sonatas, Op. 9 – Book IV (1738) vln & c
    Sonata No. 3, in D
    with A. Gibson pf   World Record Club T106
    Sonata No. 3, in D: Sarabande (1st mvt); **Tambourin** (3rd mvt)
    with C. Reiner pf   Folkways FM3351

MAGNARD

Sonata in G, Op. 13 vln & pf
    with O. Alain pf   Alpha CL4018

MATHIEU

Quintet No. 1 2 vlns, vla, vlc & pf
    with C. Sieb vln, O. Joachim vla, W.   CBC Transcription Program 123
    Joachim vlc & C. Reiner pf

MOZART

Concerto No. 4, in D, K218 (cadenzas by Joachim) vln & orch
    with English Chamber   World Record Club T106
    Orch. – Gibson
Concerto No. 7, in D, K271a (cadenzas by Bress) vln & orch
    with Montréal Symphony   Mode MDINT9246
    Orch. – Bress
Serenade No. 7, in D, K250 "Haffner" orch.
    Rondo (4th mvt)
    with English Chamber Orch. – Gibson   World Record Club T106
Sonata No. 21, in e, K304 vln & pf
    with C. Reiner pf   Folkways FM3352

PAGANINI

(24) Caprices, Op. 1 (1801/7) solo vln
    Caprice No. 5, in a
    (unaccompanied)   World Record Club T106
    Caprice No. 5, in a
    (unaccompanied)   Folkways FM3352
    Caprice No. 24, in a
    (unaccompanied)   Folkways FM3352

PENTLAND

Quartet No. 1 (1944) 2 vlns, vla & vlc
    with M. Goodman vln, O. Joachim vla   CBC Transcription Program 141
    & W. Joachim vlc

PERRAULT

Sextet (1955) 2 vlns, vla, vlc, cl & hp
    with M. Goodman vln, O. Joachim   CBC Transcription Program 125
    vla, W. Joachim vlc, R. Masella cl &
    D. Weldon hp
Trio (1954) pf, vln & vlc
    with J. Newmark pf & W. Joachim vlc   CBC Transcription Program 125

REGER

(7) Sonatas, Op. 91 solo vln
    Sonata No. 1, in a
    (unaccompanied)   Dover HCR–ST 7016,
        HCR–ST7267, HCR5267
    Sonata No. 3, in B flat
    (unaccompanied)   Dover HCR–ST 7016,
        HCR–ST7267, HCR5267
    Sonata No. 7, in a (with Chaconne)
    (unaccompanied)   Dover HCR–ST7016,
        HCR–ST7267, HCR5267

ROPARTZ

Sonata No. 3, in A vln & pf
    with O. Alain pf   Alpha CL4018

SARASATE

(8) Danzas españolas vln & pf
    No. 6. Zapateado, Op. 23, No. 2
    with C. Reiner pf   Folkways FM3353
Zigeunerweisen, Op. 20 vln & pf or orch.
    with London Philarmonic   World Record Club ST728, T728
    Orch. – Boult

SCHOENBERG

Concerto, Op. 36 (1936) vln & orch.
    with Prague Symphony   Supraphon 1 10 0231,
    Orch. – Rohan   SUA10878, SUA ST50878
Fantasy, Op. 47 (1949) vln & pf
    with C. Reiner pf   Folkways FM3354

SCHUBERT

(3) Sonatinas, Op. 137 (D384, D385 & D408) vln & pf
    No. 1. Sonatina No. 1, in D, D384
    with C. Reiner pf   Folkways FM3352

SCHUMANN

Quintet in E flat, Op. 44 pf, 2 vlns, vla & vlc
    with J. Newmark pf, M. Goodman vln,   CBC Transcription Program 91
    O. Joachim vla & W. Joachim vlc
Sonata No. 1, in a, Op. 105 vln & pf
    with C. Reiner pf   Baroque BC1833, BC2833
Sonata No. 2, in d, Op. 121 vln & pf
    with C. Reiner pf   Baroque BC1833, BC2833

SESSIONS

Sonata (1953) solo vln
    (unaccompanied)   Folkways FM3355

SPOHR

Concerto No. 8, in a, Op. 47 "Gesangsscene" vln & orch.
    with Symphony Orch. – Beck   L'Oiseau–Lyre OL278, SOL278
Concerto No. 9, in d, Op. 55 vln & orch.
    with Symphony Orch. – Beck   L'Oiseau–Lyre OL278, SOL278

STRAVINSKY

Concerto in D (1931) vln & orch.
    with Prague Symphony   Supraphon 1 10 0231 SUA10878,
    Orch. – Rohan   SUA ST50878,
Duo concertante (1932) vln & pf
    with C. Reiner pf   Folkways FM3356

STRAVINSKY – *Continued*

Suite Italienne (on themes of Pergolesi) (1933) vln & pf
  with C. Reiner pf   Folkways FM3356

TARTINI

Sonata in g "Il trillo del Diavolo" vln & c – arr. vln & pf Kreisler
  with C. Reiner pf   Folkways FM3351

TCHAIKOVSKY

Concerto in D, Op. 35 vln & orch.
  with London Philharmonic   Crossroads 22 16 0024
  Orch. – Boult   World Record Club ST728, T728
Souvenir d'un lieu cher, Op. 42 vln & pf
  No. 3. Mélodie
  with C. Reiner pf   Folkways FM3353

TOMKINS

Fantasy 2 vlns, vla & vlc
  with M. Goodman vln, O. Joachim vla CBC Transcription Program 191
  & W. Joachim vlc

VALLERAND

Quartet No. 1 2 vlns, vla & vlc
  with M. Goodman vln, O. Joachim vla CBC Transcription Program 141
  & W. Joachim vlc

VERACINI

(12) Sonatas, Op. 1 (1721) vln & c
  Sonata No. 1, in g
  with O. Alain hpsi & J. Schrick gamba Lyrichord LL138, LLST7138
  Sonata No. 2, in a
  with O. Alain hpsi & J. Schrick gamba Lyrichord LL138, LLST7138
  Sonata No. 3, in b
  with O. Alain hpsi & J. Schrick gamba Lyrichord LL140, LLST7140
  Sonata No. 4, in C
  with O. Alain hpsi & J. Schrick gamba Lyrichord LL138, LLST7138
  Sonata No. 5, in d
  with O. Alain hpsi & J. Schrick gamba Lyrichord LL139, LLST7139
  Sonata No. 6, in e
  with O. Alain hpsi & J. Schrick gamba Lyrichord LL139, LLST7139
  Sonata No. 7, in A
  with O. Alain hpsi & J. Schrick gamba Lyrichord LL139, LLST7139
  Sonata No. 8, in B flat
  with O. Alain hpsi & J. Schrick gamba Lyrichord LL138, LLST7138
  Sonata No. 9, in C
  with O. Alain hpsi & J. Schrick gamba Lyrichord LL139, LLST7139
  Sonata No. 10, in D
  with O. Alain hpsi & J. Schrick gamba Lyrichord LL140, LLST7140
  Sonata No. 11, in E
  with O. Alain hpsi & J. Schrick gamba Lyrichord LL140, LLST7140
  Sonata No. 12, in F
  with O. Alain hpsi & J. Schrick gamba Lyrichord LL140, LLST7140

VIVALDI

(12) Concerti, Op. 3 "L'Estro armonico" var. cbns & strs
  Concerto No. 6, in a, P.1 (F.I, No. 176) vln, strs & c
  with Sinfonia of Montréal – Bress Baroque BC1832, BC2832
  Concerto No. 12, in E, P.240 (F.I, No. 179) vln, strs & c
  with Sinfonia of Montréal – Bress Baroque BC1832, BC2832

VIVALDI – *Continued*

(12) Concerti, Op. 4 "La Stravaganza" vln, strs & c
  Concerto No. 6, in g, (F.I, No. 185)
  with Sinfonia of Montréal – Bress Baroque BC1832, BC2832
  Concerto in A, P.228 (F.I, No. 141) "Pisendel" vln, strs & c
  with Sinfonia of Montréal – Bress Baroque BC1832, BC2832
  Concerto in c. P.419 (F.I, No. 2) (Op. 51, No. 3) "Il Sospetto" vln,
  strs & c
  with Sinfonia of Montréal – Bress Baroque BC1832, BC2832

WEBERN

(4) Pieces, Op. 7 (1910) vln & pf
  with C. Reiner pf   Folkways FM3355

WIENIAWSKI

Scherzo–Tarantelle, Op. 16 vln & pf
  with C. Reiner pf   Folkways FM3353

YSAŸE

(6) Sonatas, Op. 27 solo vln
  Sonata No. 1, in g
  (unaccompanied)   Alpha DB132
  Sonata No. 2, in a
  (unaccompanied)   Alpha DB132
  Sonata No. 3, in d
  (unaccompanied)   Alpha DB132
  Sonata No. 4, in e
  (unaccompanied)   Alpha DB132
  Sonata No. 5, in G
  (unaccompanied)   Alpha DB132
  Sonata No. 6, in E
  (unaccompanied)   Alpha DB132

John S. BRIDGE

BACH

Concerto in d, BWV1043 2 vlns, strs & c
  with A. Catterall vln &   AX 395/9 Columbia 67066/8D, L1613/5
  orch. – Harty

SPOHR

(3) Duets, Op. 39 2 vlns
  No. 1. Duet No. 1, in d: Presto (3rd mvt)
  with A. Catterall vln   AX 408 Columbia 67068D, L1615

Robert BRINK (1924–)

BACH, C.P.E.

Sonata in B flat, W158 2 vlns & c
  with L. Schaefer fl & D. Pinkham hpsi Allegro ALG3037
                                         Lyrichord LL57

BACH, W.F.

Sextet in E flat cl, 2 hrns, vln, vla & vlc
  with G. Cioffi cl, H. Shapiro hrn, H. Boston B1006
  Meek hrn, J. de Pasquale vla & S.
  Mayes vlc

BACH, W.F. – *Continued*

Sonata in F fl, vln & c
with L. Schaefer fl & D. Pinkham hpsi   Allegro ALG3037
                                        Lyrichord LL57

BAVICCHI

Sonata, Op. 39 vln & hpsi
with D. Pinkham hpsi   Composers Recordings CRI138

BERGER

Serenade concertante (1944, rev. 1951) orch.
with Brandeis Festival   MGM E3245
Orch. – Solomon

BOISMORTIER

Diane et Actéon – cantata*
with H. Cuénod t, D. Pinkham hpsi &   Allegro ALG3010
A. Zighera gamba   Lyrichord LL44
                                       Nixa LLP8044

BUXTEHUDE

Aperite mihi portas justitiae – cantata a, t, bs, 2 vlns & c
with H. Cuénod t, R. Conrad t, M.   Music Guild M45, S45
Pearson bs, W. Hibbard vln, J.
Davidoff vlc & D. Pinkham org

Herr, auf dich traue ich – cantata s & strs
with H. Cuénod t, R. Conrad t, M.   Music Guild M45, S45
Pearson bs, W. Hibbard vln, J.
Davidoff vlc & D. Pinkham org

Jesu dulcis memoria – motet a, t, bs, 2 vlns & c
with H. Cuénod t, R. Conrad t, M.   Music Guild M45, S45
Pearson bs, W. Hibbard vln, J.
Davidoff vlc & D. Pinkham org

Salve Jesu – cantata
with H. Cuénod t, R. Conrad t, M.   Music Guild M45, S45
Pearson bs, W. Hibbard vln, J.
Davidoff vlc & D. Pinkham org

Singet dem Herrn – Cantata No. 1 s, vln & c
with H. Cuénod t, R. Conrad t, M.   Music Guild M45, S45
Pearson bs, W. Hibbard vln, J.
Davidoff vlc & D. Pinkham org

(7) Sonatas, Op. 1 (1696) vln & c
Sonata No. 1, in F
with D. Pinkham hpsi & J. Davidoff   Music Guild M57, S57
gamba

Sonata No. 2, in G
with D. Pinkham hpsi & J. Davidoff   Music Guild M57, S57
gamba

Sonata No. 3, in a
with D. Pinkham hpsi & J. Davidoff   Music Guild M57, S57
gamba

Sonata No. 4, in B flat
with D. Pinkham hpsi & J. Davidoff   Music Guild M57, S57
gamba

CORELLI

(12) Sonatas, Op. 5 vln & c
Sonata No. 3, in C
with D. Pinkham hpsi   Allegro ALX109

* Attributed to Rameau.

CORELLI – *Continued*

Sonata No. 6, in A
with D. Pinkham hpsi   Allegro ALX109
Sonata No. 10, in F
with D. Pinkham hpsi   Allegro ALX109
Sonata No. 12, in d "La Follia"
with D. Pinkham pf   Allegro ALX109

COUPERIN, F.

Audite, omnes (1706) – Motet
with H. Cuénod t, W. Waterhouse vln   Allegro ALG91, ALG3003,
& D. Pinkham hpsi   ALX3003, LEG9014

COWELL

Prelude (1955) vln & hpsi
with D. Pinkham hpsi   Composers Recordings CRI109

HOVHANESS

Duet (1954) vln & hpsi
with D. Pinkham hpsi   Composers Recordings CRI109

MONTEVERDI

Madrigals, Book VII (1619)
  I Lettera amorosa
  with H. Cuénod t, J. Davidoff gamba   Music Guild M27, MG109,
  & D. Pinkham hpsi   MS109, S27
Madrigals, Book IX (1651)
  La mia turca
  with H. Cuénod t, J. Davidoff gamba   Music Guild M27, MG109,
  & D. Pinkham hpsi   MS109, S27
  Ohimé ch'io cado
  with H. Cuénod t, J. Davidoff gamba   Music Guild M27, MG109,
  & D. Pinkham hpsi   MS109, S27
  Si dolce è il tormento
  with H. Cuénod t, J. Davidoff gamba   Music Guild M27, MG109,
  & D. Pinkham hpsi   MS109, S27
Scherzi musicali (1632)
  Et è pur dunque vero
  with H. Cuénod t, J. Davidoff gamba   Music Guild M27, MG109,
  & D. Pinkham hpsi   MS109, S27
  Quel sguardo sdegnosetto
  with H. Cuénod t, J. Davidoff gamba   Music Guild M27, MG109,
  & D. Pinkham hpsi   MS109, S27

PINKHAM

Cantilena (1956) vln & hpsi
with D. Pinkham hpsi   Composers Recordings CRI109
Capriccio (1956) vln & hpsi
with D. Pinkham hpsi   Composers Recordings CRI109
Concertante No. 1 (1954) vln, hpsi & strs
with C.J. Chiasson hpsi, E. Low cel &   Composers Recordings CRI143
Brandeis Festival Orch. – Solomon   MGM E3245

PURCELL

(The) Fairy Queen, Z629 (1692) – opera
  O let me weep "The plaint"
  with P. Curtin s, D. Pinkham hpsi &   Allegro ALY60
  vlc

Ilse BRIX–MEINERT

ALLEGRI

Symphonie à 4 2 vlns, vla d'amore & cbs d'amore
with W. Kägi vln, J. Ulsamer T–viol,   Archive APM14317, ARC3217,
H. Haferland cbs & K. Grebe hpsi   ARC73217, SAPM198317

BACH

Cantata No. 189 (Meine Seele rühmt und preist) BWV189
with W. Ludwig t, H. Töttcher ob, G.   Archive 2427/8, APM14028,
Scheck rec, A. Wenzinger vlc & R.   ARC3067
Noll hpsi – cond. Lehmann

BUXTEHUDE

(7) Sonatas, Op. 1 (1696) vln & c
Sonata No. 4, in B flat
with J. Koch gamba & W. Gerwig lute Archive APM14603, ARC3103,
                                     EPA37156

(7) Sonatas, Op. 2 (1696) vln, & c
Sonata No. 2, in D
with W. Gerwig chit, C. Garvin hpsi Archive APM14603, ARC3103,
& J. Koch gamba   EPA37152

HANDEL

(15) Sonatas, Op. 1 (?1731) fl or vln & c
Sonata No. 10, in g vln II
with J. Koch gamba & W. Gerwig lute Archive 7408, AP13035,
                                     EPA37107

HAYDN

(6) Quartets, Op. 1 (H.III, Nos. 1/6) 2 vlns, vla & vlc
No. 6. Quartet No. 6, in C, H.III, No. 6 arr. lute, vln & gamba as
"Cassation"
with W. Gerwig lute & J. Koch gamba Archive 4405, EPA37090

Ariana BRONNE

VIVALDI

(12) Concerti, Op. 8 (1725) "Il Cimento dell' Armonia e dell' Invenzione"
(Nos. 1/4: Le quattro Stagioni) vln & strs
Concerto No. 1, in E, F.I, No. 22 "La Primavera"
with New York   Library of Recorded
Sinfonietta – Goberman   Masterpieces Vol 1, No. 8
                         Odyssey 32 16 0131, 32 16 0132

Concerto in F, P.278 (F.I, No. 34) 3 vlns, strs & c
with S. Monosoff vln, N. Koutzen vln, Library of Recorded
E. Earle hpsi & New york   Masterpieces Vol 1, No. 10
Sinfonietta – Goberman   Odyssey 32 16 0053, 32 16 0054

Antonio BROSA (1896–)

DVOŘÁK

(7) Gypsy songs, Op. 55 v & pf
No. 4. Songs my mother taught me arr. t, vln & pf
with D. Borgioli t, &   CA 15113–2   Columbia LB22
I. Newton pf

MENDELSSOHN

Concerto in e, Op. 64 vln & orch.
Andante (2nd mvt)
                    2EA 5372[1] □, 5373[1A] □   HMV C2928
with symphony orch. – Goehr

STRAUSS, R.

(4) Lieder, Op. 27 v & pf
No. 4. Morgen arr. v, vln & pf
with D. Borgioli t &   CA 15114–2   Columbia LB22
I. Newton pf

TCHAIKOVSKY

Swan Lake, Op. 20 (1875/6) – ballet orch.
Dance of the Queen of the swans
with London   2B 3548–1   HMV C2620, DB4239, S10440
Philharmonic Orch. – Barbirolli   Victor 11667

C. BROSA

AULIN

(4) Aquarelles vln & pf
No. 3. Vaggsäng
with piano   DB 80–1   Duophone D519

FIOCCO

Suite No. 1, in G hpsi
Allegro (10th mvt) arr. vln & pf Bent & O'Neill
with piano   DB 81–2   Duophone D519

KREISLER

Liebesleid vln & pf
with piano   DB 79–2   Duophone D518

SCHUMANN

(20) Albumblätter, Op. 124 pf
No. 16. Schlummerlied arr. vln & pf
with piano   DB 78–2   Duophone D518

Henk BROUWER

VIVALDI

(12) Concerti, Op. 3 "L'Estro armonico" var, cbns & strs
Concerto No. 8, in a, P.2 (F.I, No. 177) 2 vlns, strs & c
with A. Rombouts vln, A. Elkgiers vlc Studio 33 20006
& Netherlands Cantory Instrumental
Ensemble – Kooy

Eddy BROWN (1895–)

ANONYMOUS

Sleep baby sleep v & pf – arr. vln & ens
with ensemble   S.R. 1561–1   Sonora 1058 (in set MS462)

Turkey in the Straw arr. vln & pf
with piano   Royale 1874

BACH

(3) Sonatas & 3 Partitas, BWV1001/6 solo vln
Partita No. 3, in E: Gavotte (3rd mvt) BWV1006 arr. vln & pf Kreisler
with piano   Columbia 97M

BARNBY

Sweet & Low mixed voices – arr. v, vln & ens
with J. Merrill v &   S.R. 1557–2 Sonora 1057, (in set MS462)
ensemble

BEETHOVEN

(6) Minuets, G167 pf
No. 2. Minuet No. 2, in G arr. vln & pf Burmester
with piano   Columbia 3M, A3801

van BIENE

Broken melody vlc & pf – arr. vln & pf Bonime
with J. Bonime pf   80253 Columbia A3656

BLAUFUSS

My isle of golden dreams (1919) v & pf – arr. vln & pf ·
with M. Terr pf   78958–1 Columbia A2924
Your eyes have told me so (1919) v & pf – arr. vln & pf
with M. Terr pf   79273 Columbia A2989

BOROWSKI

Adoration (1903) vln & pf
with J. Bonime pf   Columbia 30M, A3845

BRAHMS

(5) Lieder, Op. 49 v & pf
No. 4. Wiegenlied "Cradle song" arr. v, vln & ens
with J. Merrill v &   S.R. 1558–1 Sonora 1056, (in set MS462)
ensemble ·

BRANDL

(Der) Liebe Augustin – operetta
Du alter Stefansturm arr. vln & pf as "The old refrain" by Kreisler
with M. Terr pf   78322 Columbia A2882

BREAU

Humming v & pf – arr. vln & pf Henderson
with J. Bonime pf   79786–4 Columbia A3399

BROWN

Rondino (on a melody by J.B. Cramer) vln & pf
with M. Terr pf   78321 Columbia A2778

CHAMINADE

Sérénade espagnole pf – arr. vln & pf Kreisler
with J. Bonime pf   79912–4 Columbia 5M, A3449, J234

CHOPIN

Nocturne No. 19, in e, Op. 72, No. 1 pf – arr. vln & pf Auer
with piano   Columbia A5810

CLUTSAM

Ma curly–headed baby v & pf – arr. v, vln & ens
with C. Holland v &   S.R. 1555 Sonora 1055, (in set MS462)
ensemble

CUI

Kaleidoscope, Op. 50 vln & pf
No. 9. Orientale
with L.T. Gruenberg pf   49272–2 Columbia 5020M, A6012
No. 9. Orientale
with piano   Parlophone E10177

DAWES

Melody in A (1912) vln & pf
with J. Bonime pf   80013–2 Columbia A3656

DRDLA

Serenade No. 1, in A vln & pf
with M. Terr pf   78388 Columbia A2882

DURAND

Chaconne in a, Op. 62 pf – arr. vln & pf Brown
with J. Bonime pf   80225–2 Columbia 4M, A3616

GODARD

Jocelyn (1888) – opera
Cachés dans cet asile "Berceuse" arr. vln & ens
with ensemble   S.R. 1554 Sonora 1055, (in set MS462)

GORDON

One little dream of love v & pf – arr. vln & pf
with piano   Columbia

GRIEG

Peer Gynt (Suite No. 2) Op. 55 orch.
No. 4. Solveig's song arr. vln & pf Sitt
with J. Bonime pf   79898 Columbia 5M, A3449, J234
No. 4. Solveig's song arr. vln & pf Sitt
with piano   Royale 1875
Sonata No. 2, in G, Op. 13 vln & pf
with C. Adler pf   Royale 589/91, (set 31)

HANDEL

(7) Sonatas, Op. 5 (1739) 2 vlns & c
Sonata No. 5, in g
with R. Totenberg vln & E.V. Wolff   Royale 603
hpsi
(16) Suites (1720/33) hpsi
Suite No. 7, in g: Passacaglia (6th mvt) arr. vln & vla Halvorsen
with M. Katims vla   Royale 1840

HAYDN

Minuet in F unid – arr. vln & pf Burmester
with piano   Columbia 29M, A3483

HERBERT

Petite valse vln & pf
with piano   Columbia 3M, A3801

JACOBI

On Miami shore (1919) v & pf – arr. vln & pf
with M. Terr pf   78957–2 Columbia A2924

JAKOBOWSKY

Erminie – musical
Lullaby arr. v, vln & ens
with J. Merrill v, &   S.R. 1559 Sonora 1057, (in set MS462)
ensemble

KOSCHAT

Forsaken v & pf – arr. vln & pf Winternitz
with piano   Columbia 30M, A3845

KOŽELUH

(La) Ritrovata Figlia de Ottone, Op. 39 – ballet orch.
No. 22. Gavotte (Act IV) arr. vln & pf Kramer
with H. Kaufman pf   79788   Columbia 79788

KREISLER

(La) Gitana vln & pf
with piano   Columbia 97M
Variations on a theme of Corelli (Tartini) vln & pf
with G. Falkenstein pf   48616–1   Columbia A5859

KÜZDÖ

(2) Pieces, Op. 25 solo vln
No. 2. Witches' dance
(unaccompanied)   48617-1   Columbia A5859

LEO

Concerto in D 4 vlns & c
with R. Totenberg vln,   US 1244/7   Royale 1826/7
B. Rabinoff vln, B. Schwarz vln, E.V.
Wolff hpsi & 2 vlcs & cbs

LÉONARD

(5) Scènes humoristiques, Op. 61 vln & pf
No. 5. Sérénade du lapin belliqueux – arr. 3 vlns & pf
with M. Mischakoff vln, B. Rabinoff vln & J. Zayde pf
                                        Royale 583

LEVY

That naughty waltz (1920) v & pf – arr. vln & pf
with M. Terr pf   79274   Columbia A2989

MacDOWELL

Woodland Sketches, Op. 51 pf
No. 1. To a wild rose arr. vln & pf Hartmann
with M. Terr pf   78329   Columbia A2778
No. 1. To a wild rose arr. vln & pf Hartmann
with piano   Royale 1874

MANA-ZUCCA

Concerto in D, Op. 224 (1954) vln & orch
with Orch. de l'Association des   Brandime LD-MS 1501
Concerts Pasdeloup, Paris – Allain

MASON

(3) Pieces, Op. 13 fl, hp & str qt
with J. Wummer fl, E. Vito hp & vln,   Royale 1867/8
vla & vlc

MASSENET

Élégie v & pf – arr. vln & pf
with M.C. Rumsey pf   48881–5   Columbia A5904

MENDELSSOHN

Concerto in e, Op. 64 vln & orch.*
with Berlin State Opera orch.   Parlophone E10175/7

Quartet No. 1, in E flat, Op. 12 (1829) 2 vlns, vla & vlc
Canzonetta (2nd mvt) arr. vln & pf as "Capricietto" by Burmester
with J. Bonime pf   80284–6   Columbia 2M, A3766

---

* 1st & 3rd mvts. only. The 2nd mvt is played by Edith Lorand on
Parlophone E 10178.

MOLLOY

Love's old sweet song v & pf – arr. v, vln & ens
with C. Holland v &   S.R. 1556–2   Sonora 1056, (in set MS462)
ensemble

PADEREWSKI

(6) Humoresques de concert, Op. 14 pf
No. 1. Minuet in G arr. vln & pf Kreisler
with piano   49412–4   Columbia 5003M, A6057

POWELL

Sonata Virginianesque, Op. 7 vln & pf
with J. Powell pf   Royale 1870/2, (in set 29)

RACHMANINOV

(14) Songs, Op. 34 (1912) v & pf
No. 14. Vocalise arr. vln & pf Press
with C. Adler pf   Royale 591, (in set 31)

RAFF

(6) Pieces, Op. 85 vln & pf
No. 3. Cavatina in D
with M.C. Rumsey pf   48884–4   Columbia A5904

RIMSKY–KORSAKOV

(Le) Coq d'Or (1910) – opera
Hymn to the sun arr. vln & pf Kreisler
with J. Bonime pf   144595–6   Columbia 01090, 1M, 143M,
                                        A3545, J463

Sadko (1898) – opera
Chant hindou arr. vln & pf Brown
with J. Bonime pf   144596–6   Columbia 01090, 1M, 143M,
                                        A3545, J463

SAAR

(5) Klavierstücke, Op. 23 pf
No. 1. Intermezzo arr. vln & pf as "Gavotte–Intermezzo" by Brown
with piano   48622–5   Columbia A5940

SARASATE

Caprice basque, Op. 24 vln & pf
with piano   Columbia A5810

Navarra, Op. 33 2 vlns & pf or orch.
with R. Totenberg vln & string orch.   Royale 582
                 US 121206/7

SCHOENBERG

Darling unid – arr. vln & pf
with J. Bonime pf   79787–3   Columbia A3399

SCHUMANN

(9) Waldscenen, Op. 82 pf
No. 7. Vogel als Prophet arr. vln & pf Auer
with piano   Royale 1875
No. 7. Vogel als Prophet arr. vln & pf Auer
with piano   48737–6   Columbia A5940

SHANNON

That's an Irish lullaby (Too–ra–loo–ra–loo–ral) (1914) v & pf – arr. v, vln
& ens
with J. Merrill v &   S.R. 1560   Sonora 1058 (in set MS462)
ensemble

SINDING

Serenade No. 1, in G, Op. 56 2 vlns & pf
with R. Totenberg vln & J. Zayde pf   Royale 1809/10

STOESSEL

Suite antique (1922) 2 vlns & cha orch.
with A. Stoessel vln &   US 1388/92   Royale 1854/6, (set 28)
Sinfonietta – Schenkman

SVENDSEN

Romance in G, Op. 26 vln & orch.
with piano   Columbia 29M, A3483

THOMAS

Mignon (1866) – opera
Entr'acte (Gavotte) (Act II) orch. – arr. vln & pf Sarasate
with J. Bonime pf   80226–3   Columbia 2M, A3766

VALDEZ

Sérénade du Tzigane vln & pf
with J. Bonime pf   80237–4   Columbia 4M, A3616

VIVALDI

(12) Concerti, Op. 3 "L'Estro armonico" var. cbns & strs
Concerto No. 8, in a, P.2 (F.I, No. 177) 2 vlns, strs & c
    US 121127–2, 121128/9–1   Royale 577/8, (set 26)
with R. Totenberg vln & chamber
orch.

WIENIAWSKI

Concerto No. 2, in d, Op. 22 vln & orch.
Allegro con fuoco; Allegro moderato "alla Zingara" (3rd mvt)
with L.T. Gruenberg pf   49271–3   Columbia 5003M, A6012
Mazurka in a, Op. 3 "Kujawiak" vln & pf
with piano   49356–6   Columbia 5020M, A6057

Franz BRUCKBAUER

MOZART

Serenade No. 7, in D, K250 "Haffner" orch.
Rondo (4th mvt) arr. vln & pf Kreisler
with piano   Polydor 68280

Karl BRÜCKNER (1893–   )

DVOŘÁK

(8) Slavonic Dances, Op. 72 pf duet; orch.
No. 8. Slavonic dance No. 16, in A flat arr. vln & pf "in G" Kreisler
with O. Urack pf   Vox 06225

HEUBERGER

(Der) Opernball, Op. 40 (1898) – operetta
Im chambre séparée arr. vln & pf as "Midnight bells" by Kreisler
with O. Urack pf   Vox 6226

KREISLER

Rondino on a theme by Beethoven vln & pf
with O. Urack pf   Vox 6226

MASSENET

Thaïs (1894) – opera
Méditation arr. vln & pf Marsick
with O. Urack pf   Vox 06225

PAGANINI

Concerto No. 1, in D, Op. 6 vln & orch.
excerpt (unid)
with O. Urack pf   Vox 06232

WIENIAWSKI

Concerto No. 2, in d, Op. 22 vln & orch.
Romance (2nd mvt)
with O. Urack pf   Vox 06232

Anne BRUGMAN

BACKER–GRØNDAHL

Barntes Vaardag (cycle of 8 songs) Op. 42 v & pf
No. 7. Mot Kvaeld (At eventide) arr. vln & pf Backer–Grøndahl
with B. Linderud pf   Tono K8088

DRDLA

Souvenir vln & pf
with B. Linderud pf   Tono K8087

HENRIQUES

(4) Songs, Op. 3 v & pf
No. 4. Agnetes Vuggevise arr. vln & pf Henriques
with B. Linderud pf   Tono K8088

KREISLER

Tambourin chinois, Op. 3 vln & pf
with B. Linderud pf   Tono K8087

MONTI

Csárdas (1904) vln & pf
with B. Linderud pf   Tono A181

SARASATE

(8) Danzas españolas vln & pf
No. 3. Romanza andaluza, Op. 22, No. 1
with B. Linderud pf   Tono A181

Alfred Alphonse BRUN (1888–1963)

SAINT-SAËNS

(Le) Déluge, Op. 45 (1876) /oratorio
Prélude vln & orch.
with Paris Conservatory   49534–3   Columbia 49534, A6087
Orch. – Messager

Virgilio BRUN

BUSONI

Sonata No. 2, in e, Op. 36a (1898) vln & pf
with T. Zumaglini–Polimeni pf   Fonit LPU0041

FUGA

Sonata No. 5 vln & pf
with T. Zumaglini–Polimeni pf   Fonit LPU0041

GEMINIANI

(6) Concerti grossi, Op. 3 (1755) orch.
  Concerto grosso No. 2, in g
    2–70700, 2–70701/2 II, 2–70703 Cetra BB25112/3, CB20303/4,
    with A. Gramegna vln, A. Succo hpsi, LPC50021
    B. Francalanci vla, G. Ferrari vlc & Parlophone R30011/2
    E.I.A.R. String Orch. – Zecchi

MOZART

Sonata No. 17, in C, K296 vln & pf
  with T. Zumaglini–Polimeni pf Cetra LPC55035

Sonata No. 21, in e, K304 vln & pf
  with T. Zumaglini–Polimeni pf Cetra LPC55035

Sonata No. 22, in A, K305 vln & pf
  with T. Zumaglini–Polimeni pf Cetra LPC55035

Sonata No. 27, in G, K379 vln & pf
  with T. Zumaglini–Polimeni pf Cetra LPC55042

Sonata No. 29, in A, K402 vln & pf
  with T. Zumaglini–Polimeni pf Cetra LPC55035

Sonata No. 30, in C, K403 vln & pf
  with T. Zumaglini–Polimeni pf Cetra LPC55042

Sonata No. 32, in B flat, K454 vln & pf
  with T. Zumaglini–Polimeni pf Cetra LPC55042

TURINA

Sonata No. 2, Op. 82 (1934) "Sonata española" vln & pf
  with T. Zumaglini–Polimeni pf Cetra AT0149/50

Noël Brunet (1916-)

BRAHMS

Trio in E flat, Op. 40 hrn, vln & pf
  with J. Masella hrn & J. Newmark pf CBC Transcription Program 10

PAPINEAU–COUTURE

Concerto vln & orch.
  with CBC orch. – Waddington CBC Transcription Program 117

Sonata in G (1944) vln & pf
  with J–M. Beaudet pf CBC transcription Program 92

VALLERAND

Sonata (1950) vln & pf
  with J–M. Beaudet pf CBC Transcription Program 92

L. BRUSHTEIN

NYAGA

Sonata in b vln & pf
  with N. Lelchuk pf Mezhdunarodnaya Kniga
    D10997/8

POPOV

(2) Septets, Op. 2 fl, cl, bsn, tpt, vln, vlc & cbs
  Septet in a
    with Y. Shkylanko fl, V. Sokolov cl, V. Mezhdunarodnaya Kniga
    Popov bsn, L. Volodin tpt, M. D21501/2
    Nemerenesky vlc, L. Rakov
    cbs – conducted by Saidel

POPOV – *Continued*

  Septet in C
    with Y. Shkylanko fl, V. Sokolov cl, V. Mezhdunarpdnaya Kniga
    Popov bsn, L. Volodin tpt, M. D21501/2
    Nemerenesky vlc, L. Rakov
    cbs – conducted by Saidel

Anshel BRUSILOW (1929–   )

BARTÓK

(2) Portraits, Op. 5 vln & orch.
  with Philadelphia Orch. – Ormandy CBS BRG72445, SBRG72445
    Columbia ML6189, MS6789

MASSENET

Thaïs (1894) – opera
  Méditation
    with Philadelphia Orch. – Ormandy Columbia ML6503, MS7103

RIMSKY–KORSAKOV

Scheherazade, Op. 35 (1888) orch.
  with Philadelphia Orch. – Ormandy CBS BRG72075, S61044,
    SBRG72075
    Columbia ML5675, MS6365

SARASATE

Introduction & Tarantelle, Op. 43 vln & pf
  with Philadelphia Orch. – Ormandy CBS BRG71027, SBRG71027
    ʿumb' ML6191, MS6791

STRAUSS, R.

(Ein) Heldenleben, Op. 40 (1898) orch.
  with Philadelphia Orch. – Ormandy CBS BRG72030, SBRG72030
    Columbia ML5649, MS6249

VIVALDI

(12) Concerti, Op. 8 (1725) "Il Cimento dell' Armonia e dell' Invenzione"
(Nos. 1/4: Le quattro Stagioni) vln & strs
  Concerto No. 1, in E, F.I, No. 22 "La Primavera"
    with Philadelphia Orch. – Ormandy Columbia ML5595, MS6195
      Fontana 697208EL, EFL2522

  Concerto No. 2, in B flat, F.I, No. 23 "L'Estate"
    with Philadelphia Orch. – Ormandy Columbia ML5595, MS6195
      Fontana 697208EL, EFL2522

  Concerto No. 3, in F, F.I, No. 24 "L'Autunno"
    with Philadelphia Orch – Ormandy Columbia ML5595, MS6195
      Fontana 697208EL, EFL2522

  Concerto No 4, in f, F.I, No. 25 "L'Inverno"
    with Philadelphia Orch. – Ormandy Columbia ML5595, MS6195
      Fontana 697208EL, EFL2522

YARDUMIAN

Concerto vln & orch
  with Philadelphia Orch. – Ormandy Columbia ML4991

Elsa Maria BRUUN (1911–   )

BACH

Concerto in d, BWV1043 2 vlns, strs & c
        2CS 2554–1, 2555/6–2, 2557–1   HMV DB5289/90
  with J. Koppel vln & Royal Danish
  Chamber Orch. – Wöldike

Concerto in c, BWV1060 vln & ob or 2 vlns, strs & c
        2CS 2485/6–1, 2487/8–2   HMV DB5286/7
  with W. Wölsing ob & Royal Danish
  Chamber Orch. – Wöldike

BEETHOVEN

Serenade in D, Op. 25 fl, vln & vla
  with J. Bentzen fl & J. Koppel vla   Columbia LDX7020/2

BERNHARDT

Füchet euch Nicht – cantata s & strs
  with K. Heerup s, M. Wöldike hpsi & Gramophone Shop GSC32/3
  A. Medici vlc

BUXTEHUDE

Aperite mihi portas justitiae – cantata a, t, bs, 2vlns & c
  with E. Sigfuss a,   2CX2489/90^{II}□ HMV KBLP14, Z292
  A. Schiøtz t, H. Nørgaard bs, J.   Odeon MOAK2
  Koppel vln M. Wöldike hpsi & T.A. Victor 12–0533
  Svendsen vlc

O wie selig sind die Todten – cantata t, bs, 2 vlns & c
  with N. Brinker t, H. Nørgaard bs, J. Gramophone Shop GSC31,
  Koppel vln, M. Wöldike hpsi & A. (in set 5)
  Medici vlc

(7) Sonatas, Op. 2 (1696) vln & c
Sonata No. 6, in C arr. 2 vlns & c
  with J. Koppel   2CS 1778/9–1□ HMV DB5249
  vln, M. Wöldike hpsi & A. Medici vlc

Was mich auf dieser Welt Betrübt – cantata s, 2 vlns & c
  with A. Schiøtz t, J.   2CS 1618 HMV DB5240
  Koppel vln, M. Wöldike hpsi & A.
  Medici vlc

CORELLI

(12) Concerti grossi, Op. 6 orch.
Concerto grosso No. 7, in D
        OCS 2497/9–1, 2500–2 HMV DA5256/7
  with J. Koppel vln, T. A. Svendson vlc
  & Copenhagen Palace Chappel
  Chamber Orch. – Wöldike

HANDEL

(9) Deutschen Arien (1729) v, vln, fl or ob & c
No. 4. Süsse Stille, sanfte Quelle
  with M. Ribbing s, J.   2CS3267^1□ HMV DB10515
  Hansen vlc & L. Selbiger hpsi
No. 6. Meine Seele hört im Sehen
  with M. Ribbing s, J.   2CS3268^1□ HMV DB10515
  Hansen vlc & L. Selbiger hpsi

HOLMBOE

Quartet No. 3, Op. 48 2 vlns, vla & vlc
  with A. Thyregod vln, J. Koppel vla & Decca LXT5092
  J. Hansen vlc

LÜBECK

Willkommen, süsser Bräutigam "Christmas Cantata" s, a & strs
  with K. Heerup s, V. Garde a, J.   Gramophone Shop GSC34/6,
  Koppel vln, M. Wöldike hpsi & A. (in set 5)
  Medici vlc

MOZART

Quartet in F, K370 ob, vln, vla & vlc
  with M.S. Andreassen ob, J. Koppel HMV KBLP6
  vla & J. Hansen vlc

Sinfonia concertante in E flat, K364 vln, vla & orch.
  with J. Koppel vla & orch. – Wöldike HMV KBLP18

NIELSEN

Quartet No. 4, in F, Op. 44 (1906) 2 vlns, vla & vlc
  with A. Thyregod vln, J. Koppel vla & Decca LXT5092
  J. Hanson vlc

Otto BÜCHNER (1924–   )

BACH

Concerto in d, BWV1043 2 vlns, strs & c
  with K. Guntner vln & Munich Bach Archive APM14321, ARC3221,
  Orch. – Richter   ARC73221, SAPM198321

Concerto in d, BWV1060 vln, ob, strs & c
  with E. Shann ob & Munich Bach Archive APM14321, ARC3221,
  Orch. – Richter   ARC73221, SAPM198321
                        Musique Royale 199007

Concerto in c, BWV1060 vln & ob or 2 vlns, strs & c
  with E. Shann ob & Munich Bach Deustche Grammophon (in set
  Orch. – Richter   2705 013)

(Ein) Musikalisches Opfer, BWV1079 (1749) strs
  with G.A. Nicolet fl, K. Guntner vln, Archive APM14320, ARC3220,
  F. Kishai vlc, H. Bilgram hpsi, S. ARC73220, SAPM198320
  Meinecke vln & K. Richter hpsi

(3) Sonatas & 3 Partitas, BWV1001/6 solo vln
Partita No. 2, in d, BWV1004
(unaccompanied)   Calig CAL30403
Partita No. 3, in E, BWV1006
(unaccompanied)   Calig CAL30403

HANDEL

(12) Concerti grossi, Op. 6 (1739) 2 vlns, vlc & strs
Concerto grosso No. 1, in G
  with F. Berger vln, H. Melzer vlc, K. Archive AP13010, APM14091,
  Richter hpsi & Bamberg Symphony ARC3084
  Orch. – Lehmann   Decca DL9692, (in set DX126)
                        Deutsche Grammophon 16080/1,
                        EPA37072, PV7405/6

Concerto grosso No. 2, in F
  with F. Berger vln, H. Melzer vlc, K. Archive AP13010, APM14091,
  Richter hpsi & Bamberg Symphony ARC3084
  Orch. – Lehmann   Decca DL9692, (in set DX126)
                        Deutsche Grammophon 16080/1,
                        EPA37088, PV7407

Concerto grosso No. 3, in e
  with F. Berger vln, H. Mezler vlc, K. Archive AP13011, APM14092,
  Richter hpsi & Bamberg Symphony ARC3085
  Orch. – Lehmann   Decca DL9693, (in set DX126)
                        Deutsche Grammophon 16080/1,
                        EPA37106, PV7405/6

HANDEL – *Continued*

Concerto grosso No. 4, in a
with F. Berger vln, H. Melzer vlc, K.
Richter hpsi and Bamberg Symphony
Orch. – Lehmann

Archive AP13011, APM14092,
ARC3085
Decca DL9693, (in set DX126)
Deutsche Grammophon 16080/1,
EPA37117, PV7409

Concerto grosso No. 5, in D
with F. Berger vln, H. Melzer vlc, K.
Richter hpsi & Bamberg Symphony
Orch. – Lehmann

Archive AP13012, APM14092,
ARC3085
Decca DL9694, (in set DX126)
Deutsche Grammophon
EPA37040

Concerto grosso No. 6, in g
with F. Berger vln, H. Melzer vlc, K.
Richter hpsi & Bamberg Symphony
Orch. – Lehmann

Archive AP13013, APM14094,
ARC3087
Decca DL9695, (in set DX126)

Concerto grosso No. 7, in B flat
with F. Berger vln, H. Melzer vlc, K.
Richter hpsi & Bamberg Symphony
Orch. – Lehmann

Archive AP13013, APM14094,
ARC3087
Decca DL9695, (in set DX126)
Deutsche Grammophon
EPA37053

Concerto grosso No. 8, in c
with F. Berger vln, H. Melzer vlc, K.
Richter hpsi & Bamberg Symphony
Orch. – Lehmann

Archive AP13013, APM14094,
ARC3087
Decca DL9695, (in set DX126)

Concerto grosso No. 9, in F.
with F. Berger vln, H. Melzer vlc, K.
Richter hpsi & Bamberg Symphony
Orch. – Lehmann

Archive AP13012, APM14093,
ARC3086
Decca DL9694, (in set DX126)

Concerto grosso No. 10, in d
with F. Berger vln, H. Melzer vlc, K.
Richter hpsi & Bamberg Symphony
Orch. – Lehmann

Archive AP13011, APM14092,
ARC3085
Decca DL9693, (in set DX126)

Concerto grosso No. 11, in A
with F. Berger vln, H. Melzer vlc, K.
Richter hpsi & Bamberg Symphony
Orch. – Lehmann

Archive AP13010/1,
APM14091/2, ARC3084/5,
Decca DL9692/3, (in set DX
126)

Concerto grosso No. 12, in b
with F. Berger vln, H. Melzer vlc, K.
Richter hpsi & Bamberg Symphony
Orch. – Lehmann

Archive AP13010, APM14091,
ARC3084
Decca DL9692, (in set DX126)

MOZART

Concertone in C, K190 2 vlns, ob, vlc & orch.
with G.F. Hendel vln, P. Pierlot ob, R.
Dommisch vlc & Radiodiffusion
Chamber Orch. – Ristenpart

Erato LDE3362, STE50262,
STU70262

Sinfonia concertante in E flat, K364 vln, vla & orch.
with G. Schmid vla & Radiodiffusion
Chamber Orch. – Ristenpart

Erato LDE3362, STE50262,
STU70262

TELEMANN

(6) Suites fl, vln & c
Suite No. 6, in d
with K. Hausmann ob, W. Spilling
hpsi & J. Ulsamer gamba

Archive APM14198, ARC3198,
ARC73198, SAPM198698

VIVALDI

(12) Concerti, Op. 8 (1725) "Il Cimento dell' Armonia e dell' Invenzione"
(Nos. 1/4: Le quattro Stagioni) vln & strs
Concerto No. 1, in E, F.I, No. 22 "La Primavera"
with L. Heindersdorf hpsi & Pro Arte
Chamber Orch., Munich – Redel

Christophorus CGLP75787,
SCGLP75788
Erato LDE3172, STE50058
Musical Heritage Society
MHS579
World Record Club T737

Concerto No. 2, in B flat, F.I, No. 23 "L'Estate"
with L. Heindersdorf hpsi & Pro Arte
Chamber Orch., Munich – Redel

Christophorus CGLP75787,
SCGLP75788
Erato LDE3172, STE50058
Musical Heritage Society
MHS579
World Record Club T737

Concerto No. 3, in F, F.I, No. 24 "L'Autunno"
with L. Heindersdorf hpsi & Pro Arte
Chamber Orch., Munich – Redel

Christophorus CGLP75787,
SCGLP75788
Erato LDE3172, STE50058
Musical Heritage Society
MHS579
World Record Club T737

Concerto No. 4, in f, F.I, No. 25 "L'Inverno"
with L. Heindersdorf hpsi & Pro Arte
Chamber Orch., Munich – Redel

Christophorus CGLP75787,
SCGLP75788
Erato LDE3172, STE50058
Musical Heritage Society
MHS579
World Record Club T737

Jan BUCHTELE (1874–1941)

EBERHARDT

Dance of the water nymph vln & pf
with piano

HMV 941, 277901

GRIEG

(8) Lyric Pieces, Op. 38 – Book II pf
No. 1. Berceuse arr. vln & pf Sitt
with piano

HMV 943, 277904

LÉONARD

Fantaisie militaire, Op. 15 vln & pf
with piano

HMV 944, 277906/7

NEŠVERA

Wiegenlied, Op. 25 vln & pf
with piano

HMV 942, 277902

SCHUMANN

(4) Duets, Op. 78 s, t & pf
No. 4 Wiegenlied arr. vln & pf
with piano

HMV 942, 277903

(13) Kinderscenen, Op. 15 pf
No. 7. Träumerei arr. vln & pf
with piano

HMV 943, 277905

SIMONETTI

Madrigale pf – arr. vln & pf
with piano

HMV 946, 277910

SMETANA
From my Homeland (1878) vln & pf
  No. 2. Andantino
    with piano   HMV 941, 277900

TCHAIKOVSKY
Pique Dame, Op. 68 (1890) – opera
  Romance arr. vln & pf
    with piano   HMV 946, 277911

WIENIAWSKI
Concerto No. 2, in d, Op. 22 vln & orch.
  Romance (2nd mvt)
    with piano   HMV 945, 277904
  Mazurka in a, Op. 3 "Kujawiak" vln & pf
    with piano   HMV 945, 277908

Nicolas BUCIA

ANONYMOUS
(Le) Carnevale di Venizia – variations arr. vln & pf Thomas
  with piano   15273   Homochord B1372
(Le) Carnevale di Venizia – variations arr. vln & pf Thomas
  with G. Alexandrescu pf   Pathé 9601
                      Pathé–Actuelle 15153
Two guitars (Russian folksong) arr. vln & pf Bucia
  with G. Alexandrescu pf   Pathé 9602
                      Pathé–Actuelle 15153

BUCIA
Danse rumène vln & pf
  with G. Alexandrescu pf   Pathé 5746, 9602
Imitation de Cornemuse vln & pf
  with piano   15274   Homochord B1372
Imitation de Cornemuse vln & pf
  with G. Alexandrescu pf   Pathé 9603
                      Pathé–Actuelle 15141
Popular Rumanian dance vln & pf
  with G. Alexandrescu pf   Pathé 5746, 9601

KREISLER
Tambourin chinois, Op. 3 vln & pf
  with G. Alexandrescu pf   Pathé 9603
                      Pathé–Actuelle 15141

SMETANA
Quartet No. 1, in e (1876) "From my life" 2 vlns, vla & vlc
  Allegro moderato alla Polka (2nd mvt) arr. vln & pf
    with piano   Pathé 5780
  Largo sostenuto (3rd mvt) arr. vln & pf
    with piano   Pathé 5780

Irene BUCKINGHAM

MONTI
Csárdas (1904) vln & pf*
  with piano   44672   Columbia WT1627

* Test pressing – not issued commercially.

N. BUDOVSKY

KOSENKO
Trio, Op. 17 "Classical" pf, vln & vlc
  with D. Yudilevich pf & M. Kravtsov   Mezhdunarodnaya Kniga
  vlc   D6343/4

LYATOSHINSKY
Trio No. 2, Op. 41 pf, vln & vlc
  with D. Yudilevich pf & M. Kravtsov   Mezhdunarodnaya Kniga
  vlc   D6341/2

ZNOSKO–BOROWSKY
Concerto vln & orch.
  with orch.   Mezhdunarodnaya Kniga
                            D03752/3

E. BULAVINOV

MEDYNS, Janis
Prelude vln & pf
  with V. Cirule pf   Mezhdunarodnaya Kniga
                            D022008

Fred BULDRINI

VIVALDI
(12) Concerti, Op. 3 "L'Estro armonico" var. cbns & strs
  Concerto No. 10, in b, P.148 (F.IV, No. 10) 4 vlns, strs & c
    with A. Eidus vln, L. Graeler vln, S.   Allegro ALG3146
    Shulman vln & Stradivari Ensemble   Concerteum CS194
                               Stradivari STR604

Hans BUNTE

BACH
Concerto in C, BWV1064 3 clavs, strs & c – arr. 3 vlns, strs & c
  with G.F. Hendel vln, K. Schlupp vln   Nonesuch H1057, H71057
  & Saar Chamber Orch., – Ristenpart

BIBER
Serenade in C "Der Nachtwächter" bs–v, 2 vlns, 2 vlas & c
  with J. Stämpfli bs–v, G.F. Hendel vln,   Erato STU70318
  G. Karau hpsi & B. Hindrichs vlc   Musical Heritage Society
                             MHS938

BUXTEHUDE
(7) Sonatas, Op. 1 (1696) vln & c
  Sonata No. 7, in e
    with R. Dommisch gamba, R.   Nonesuch H1119, H71119
    Ristenpart hpsi & B. Hindrichs vlc

CALDARA
(12) Sonatas, Op. 1 2 vlns & c
  Sonata No. 9, in b
    with G.F. Hendel vln, G. Karau hpsi   Erato STU70318
    & B. Hindrichs vlc   Musical Heritage Society
                               MHS938

CORELLI

(12) Concerti grossi, Op. 6 orch.
Concerto grosso No. 9, in F
with G.F. Hendel vln, B. Hindrichs   Columbia C50585, C91101,
vlc, G. Karau hpsi & Saar Chamber   STC50585, STC91101
Orch. – Ristenpart

MUFFAT

(12) Concerti grossi (1701) 2 vlns, vlc, strs & c
Concerto grosso No. 11, in e "Delirium Amoris" (real. A. Garcin-Lauth)
with G.F. Hendel vln, G. Karau hpsi,   Erato STU70318
B. Hindrichs vlc & Saar Radio   Musical Heritage Society
Chamber Orch. – Ristenpart   MHS938

TELEMANN

Concerto in C 2 vlns, strs & c
with G.F. Hendel vln, G. Karau hpsi   Columbia SMC95067
& Saar Radio Chamber   Erato LDE3372, STE50272
Orch. – Ristenpart   Musical Heritage Society
    MHS751

VIVALDI

Concerto in F, P.278 (F.I, No. 34) 3 vlns, strs & c
with G.F. Hendel vln, K. Schlupp vln   Elite-Special SMLP5011
& Saar Chamber Orch. – Ristenpart   Nonesuch H1022, H71022

Richard BURGIN (1892–)

ABACO

(12) Sonatas, Op. 3 (1714) 2 vlns & c
Sonata No. 1, in C
with R. Posselt vln & E. Bodky hpsi   Kapp KL9024
    Unicorn UNLP1030

ALBINONI

(12) Sonatas, Op. 1 (1694) 2 vlns & c
Sonata No. 3, in A
with R. Posselt vln & E. Bodky hpsi   Kapp KL9024
    Unicorn UNLP1030

BACH

(6) Brandenburg Concerti, BWV1046/51 (1721) strs & c
Brandenburg Concerto No. 1, in F, BWV1046 vln, 3 obs, bsn, 2 hrns & strs
with J. Stagliano hrn, H. Shapiro hrn,   Victor (in set LSC6140),
R. Gomberg ob & Boston Symphony   LM2182, RB16074
Orch. – Munch

Brandenburg Concerto No. 2, in F, BWV.1047 tpt, fl, ob, vln & strs
with R. Voisin tpt, G. Laurent fl, F.   HMV DB6764/5
Gillet ob & Boston Symphony   Victor 11–9538/9 (set M1118)
Orch. – Koussevitzky

Brandenburg Concerto No. 2, in F, BWV1047 tpt, fl, ob, vln & strs
with R. Voisin tpt, D. Ewyer fl,   Victor (in set LSC6140),
R. Gomberg ob & Boston Symphony   LM2182, RB16074
Orch. – Munch

Brandenburg Concerto No. 4, in G, BWV1049 vln, 2 fls & strs
with G. Laurent fl, G. Madsen fl &   HMV DB6457/8, ED646/7
Boston Symphony   Victor 11–9158/9
Orch. – Koussevitzky

Brandenburg Concerto No. 4, in G, BWV1049 vln, 2 fls & strs
with D. Dwyer fl, J. Pappoulsakis fl &   Victor (in set LSC6140),
Boston Symphony Orch. – Munch   LM2198, RB16075

BACH – *Continued*

Brandenburg Concerto No. 5, in D, BWV1050 clav, fl, vln & strs
with L. Foss pf, G. Laurent fl &   Camden CAL147
Boston Symphony   HMV DB6765/7
Orch. – Koussevitzky   Victor 11–9539/41, (set M1118)

Brandenburg Concerto No. 5, in D, BWV1050 clav, fl, vln & strs
with L. Foss pf, D. Dwyer fl & Boston   Victor (in set LSC6140),
Symphony Orch. – Munch   LM2198, RB16075

BUSONI

Sonata No. 2, in e, Op. 36a (1898) vln & pf
with E. Weiss pf   Circle L51–104

MOZART

Divertimento No. 15, in B flat, K287 2 hrns & strs
with Fiedler Sinfonietta – Fiedler   Victor 4383/6s & 12168,
    (set M 434)

Quintet in E flat, K407 hrn, vln, 2 vlas & vlc
with J. Stagliano hrn, J. de Pasquale   Boston B201
vla, J. Cauhapé vla & S. Mayes vlc

Quintet in A, K581 cl & str qt
with B. Goodman cl, A. Krips vln, J.   Victor LM2073, RB16013
de Pasquale vla & S. Mayes vlc

STRAUSS, R.

Don Quixote, Op. 35 (1897) orch.
with G. Piatigorsky vlc, J. de Pasquale   HMV ALP1211
vla & Boston Symphony   Victor LM1781
Orch. – Munch

TCHAIKOVSKY

Quartet No. 3, in e flat, Op. 30 2 vlns, vla & vlc
with L. Panasevich vln, J. de Pasquale   Boston B206
vla & S. Mayes vlc

Willy BURMESTER (1869–1933)

BACH

(3) Sonatas & 3 Partitas, BWV1001/6 solo vln
Partita No. 3, in E: Gavotte (3rd mvt) BWV1006 arr. vln & pf Burmester
with piano   247 ac   Gramophone & Typewriter
    047917

(4) Suites, BWV1066/9 strs & c
Suite No. 3, in D: Air (2nd mvt) BWV1068 2 obs, 3 tpts, drms
& strs – arr. vln & pf Burmester
with piano   248 ac   Gramophone & Typewriter
    047918

DUSSEK

Minuet unid – arr. vln & pf Burmester
with piano   1735 ab   Gramophone & Typewriter
    47979

HANDEL

Arioso unid – arr. vln & pf Burmester
with piano   1734 ab   Gramophone & Typewriter
    47984
    HMV V171

HANDEL – *Continued*

(6) Concerti, Op. 4 (1735/6) org, obs & strs
Concerto No. 3, in g: Sarabande (3rd mvt) arr. vln & pf Burmester
with piano   245 ac   Gramophone & Typewriter
                                    047919

(15) Sonatas, Op. 1 (?1731) fl or vln & c
Sonata No. 5, in G: Minuet (5th mvt) arr. vln & pf Burmester
with piano   1736 ab   Gramophone & Typewriter
                                    47985
                                    HMV V171

RAMEAU

Castor et Pollux (1737) – opera
Gavotte (Act IV) arr. vln & pf Burmester
with piano   1733 ab   Gramophone & Typewriter
                                    47978

SINDING

(3) Elegiac Pieces, Op. 106 vln & pf
No. 3. Andante religioso (arr. Burmester)
with piano   246 ac   Gramophone & Typewriter
                                    047920

Adolf BUSCH (1891–1952)

BACH

(6) Brandenburg Concerti, BWV1046/51 (1721) strs & c
Brandenburg Concerto No. 1, in F, BWV1046 vln, 3 obs, bsn, 2 hrns & strs
with E. Rothwell   CAX 7625/9–1   Angel COLC13
ob, A. Brain hrn, F. Bradley hrn &   Columbia 68434/6D, (in set
Busch Chamber Orch. – Busch   M249), COLC13, LX436/8
Brandenburg Concerto No. 2, in F, BWV1047 tpt, fl, ob, vln & strs
with G. Eksdale   CAX 7640/3–1   Angel COLC13
tpt, M. Moyse fl, E. Rothwell ob &   Columbia 68437/8D, (in set
Busch Chamber Orch.– Busch   M249), COLC13, LX439/40
Brandenburg Concerto No. 4, in G, BWV1049 vln, 2 fls & strs
with M. Moyse fl,   CAX 7636/9–1   Angel COLC14
L. Moyse fl & Busch Chamber   Columbia 68440/1D, (in set
Orch. – Busch   M249), COLC14, LX441/2
Brandenburg Concerto No. 5, in D, BWV1050 clav, fl, vln & strs
    CAX 7616/8–1 & 7622/4–1   Angel COLC14
with R. Serkin pf, M. Moyse fl &   Columbia 68442/4D, (in set
Busch Chamber Orch. – Busch   M250), COLC14, LX444/6
                                    Seraphim (in set IC6043)
Brandenburg Concerto No. 6, in B flat, BWV1051 2 vlas, 2 gambas, vlc, cbs & strs
with R. Serkin pf   CAX 7630/5–1   Angel COLC13
& Busch Chamber Orch. – Busch   Columbia 68445/7D, (in set
                                    M250), COLC13, LX447/9
Concerto No. 2, in E, BWV1042 vln, strs & c
with Busch Chamber Players – Busch   Columbia 11911/3D, (set M530),
                                    ML4002
Concerto in d, BWV1043 2 vlns, strs & c
with F. Magnes vln & Busch Chamber   Columbia 71674/5D, (set X253),
Players – Busch   ML4002
(3) Sonatas & 3 Partitas, BWV1001/6 solo vln
Partita No. 2, in d, BWV1004
    CNB 335^{II}△ 336/7^I△ 338^{III}△   HMV DB1422/4, DB7193/5
(unaccompanied)   339^{IV}△ 340^{II}△   Victor 7557/9, (set M133)

BACH – *Continued*

Partita No. 3, in E: Gavotte en Rondeau (3rd mvt) BWV1006
(unaccompanied)   236 av   Polydor 65601, 65982
Partita No. 3, in E: Preludio (1st mvt) BWV1006
(unaccompanied)   Polydor 65981
(6) Sonatas, BWV1014/9 vln & clav
Sonata No. 3, in E, BWV1016
with R. Serkin pf   Victor (set M235)
Sonata No. 4, in c: Siciliano, BWV1017
with R. Serkin pf   CAX 7671–2   Columbia LX438, LX8203,
                                    SW57
Sonata in G, BWV1021 vln & c
with R. Serkin pf   CNR 808/9^{III}△   HMV DB1434
Sonata in e, BWV1023 vln & c
with A. Balsam pf   Columbia 71572D

BEETHOVEN

Concerto in D, Op..61 (Cadenza by Busch) vln & orch.
with New York Philharmonic   Brüder–Busch 12PAL 3902/3
Symphony Orch. – F. Busch
(3) Sonatas, Op. 12 vln & pf
No. 3. Sonata No. 3, in E flat
    2B 824^V△, 825/6^{II}△ & 827^{IV}△   HMV DB1519/20
with R. Serkin pf   Victor 7560/1
Sonata No. 5, in F, Op. 24 "Spring" vln & pf
    2B 6702^I▢, 6703/4^{II}▢, 6705^I▢   HMV DB1970/2, DB7534/6
with R. Serkin pf   & 6706/7^{II}▢   Victor 8351/3, (set M228)
(3) Sonatas, Op. 30 vln & pf
No. 2. Sonata No. 7, in c
    2B 3888^{II}▢, 3889^{III}▢, 3890^{IV}▢   HMV DB1973/5
, 3891^{II}▢ & 3892/3^I▢   Victor 8821/3, 8824/6, (set
with R. Serkin pf   M283)
Sonata No. 9, in A, Op. 47 "Kreutzer" vln & pf
    XCO 31974/6–1, 31977–2 &   Columbia 71344/7D, 71348/51D,
with R. Serkin pf   31978/81–1   (set M496), 266473/7, C15596/9,
                                      (set D106), SW16/9, (set J59)
                                      Seraphim (in set IC6044)
(2) Trios, Op. 70 pf, vln & vlc
No. 1. Trio No. 4, in D "Ghost"
with R. Serkin pf & H. Busch vlc   Columbia 72748/50D, (set
                                    MM804), CX1043, ML4128,
                                    QCX10035
                                    Odyssey 32 16 0361

BRAHMS

(21) Hungarian Dances pf duet
Hungarian dance No. 2, in d arr. vln & pf Joachim
with B. Seidler–Winkler pf   255at   Polydor 62355
Hungarian dance No. 5, in f sharp arr. vln & pf "in g" Joachim
with piano   Polydor 62982
Hungarian dance No. 20, in d arr. vln & pf Joachim
with B. Seidler–Winkler pf   256at   Polydor 62355
Sonata No. 1, in G, Op. 78 vln & pf
    2B 817^{III}△, 818^V△ & 819/22^{III}△   HMV DB1527/9
with R. Serkin pf   Victor 7487/9, (set M121)
Sonata No. 2, in A, Op. 100 vln & pf
    2B 3872/4^I▢, 3875^{II}▢   HMV COLH41, DB1805/6
with R. Serkin pf   Victor 8359/60

BRAHMS – *Continued*

Trio in E flat, Op. 40 hrn, pf & vln
2B 6708^V□, 6709/10^{IV}□, 6711 | HMV COLH41, DB2105/8,
^{III}□, 6712^{II}□, 6713^{III}□, 6714^{II}□ & | DB7610/3
with A. Brain hrn, & R.   6715^{III}□ | Seraphim (in set IC6044)
Serkin pf | Victor 7965/8, (set M199)

Trio No. 2, in C, Op. 87 pf, vln & vlc
with R. Serkin pf & H. Busch vlc | Odyssey 32 16 0361

CORELLI

(12) Sonatas, Op. 5 vln & c
Sonata No. 5, in g: Adagio (1st mvt) arr. vln & pf Busch
with piano | 233av Polydor 65601

DVOŘÁK

(8) Humoresques, Op. 101 pf
No. 7. Humoresque No. 7, in G flat arr. vln & pf "in G" Wilhelmj
with piano | Polydor 65979

(4) Romantic Pieces, Op. 75 vln & pf
No. 4. Larghetto (Adagio)
with B. Seidler–Winkler pf | 851at Polydor 62469, 67535

(8) Slavonic Dances, Op. 72 pf duet; orch.
No. 8. Slavonic Dance No. 16, in A flat arr. vln & pf "in G" Kreisler
with piano | Polydor 65979/80

GEMINIANI

(12) Sonatas (1739) vln & c
Sonata in c: Siciliano arr. vln & pf Busch
with R. Serkin pf | 2B829¹△ HMV DB1524
Siciliano arr. vln & pf Busch
with A. Balsam pf | XCO32860–1 Columbia 72005D, 72021D,
| (in set M685)

GOSSEC

Rosine (1786) – opera
Gavotte arr. vln & pf Burmester
with piano | Polydor 20074, 62470

HANDEL

(12) Concerti Grossi, Op. 6 (1739) 2 vlns, vlc & strs
Concerto grosso No. 1, in G
with E. Drucker   XCO 3669/71–1 | Columbia 71981/2D, 72006/8D,
vln, H. Busch vlc, M. Horszowski pf & | (in set M685), ML4210, (in set
Busch Chamber Players – Busch | SL158)
Concerto grosso No. 2, in F
with E. Drucker   XCO 35854/7–1 | Columbia 71982/4D, 72009/12D,
vln, H. Busch vlc, M. Horszowski pf, | (in set M685), ML4210, (in set
& Busch Chamber Players – Busch | SL158)
Concerto grosso No. 3, in e
with E. Drucker   XCO 35720/2–1 | Columbia 71984/5D, 72010/2D,
vln, H. Busch vlc, M. Horszowski pf & | (in set M685), ML4211, (in set
Busch Chamber Players – Busch | SL158)
Concerto grosso No. 4, in a
with E. Drucker   XCO 35746/9–1 | Columbia 71986/7D, 72006/9D,
vln, H. Busch vlc, M. Horszowski pf & | (in set M685), ML4211, (in set
Busch Chamber Players – Busch | SL158)
Concerto grosso No. 5, in D
with E. Drucker   XCO 35706/9–1 | Columbia 71988/9D, 72013/6D,
vln, H. Busch vlc, M. Horszowski pf & | (in set M685), ML4212, (in set
Busch Chamber Players – Busch | SL158)

HANDEL – *Continued*

Concerto grosso No. 6, in g
with E. Drucker   XCO 35672/5–1 | Columbia 71990/1D, 72017/20D,
vln, H. Busch vlc, M. Horszowski pf & | (in set M685), ML4212/3, (in set
Busch Chamber Players – Busch | SL158)
Concerto grosso No. 7, in B flat
with E. Drucker   XCO 35715/8–1 | Columbia 71992/3D, 72017/20D,
vln, H. Busch vlc, M. Horszowski pf & | (in set M685), ML4213, (in set
Busch Chamber Players – Busch | SL158)
Concerto grosso No. 8, in c
with E. Drucker   XCO 35676/9–1 | Columbia 71994/5D, 72013/6D,
vln, H. Busch vlc, M. Horszowski pf & | (in set M685), ML4213, (in set
Busch Chamber Players – Busch | SL158)
Concerto grosso No. 9, in F
XCO 35742–2, 35743/5–1, 35755–1 | Columbia 71996/8D, 72021/5D,
with E. Drucker | (in set M685), ML4212/3, (in set
vln, H. Busch vlc, M. Horszowski pf & | SL158)
Busch Chamber Players – Busch
Concerto grosso No. 10, in d
E. Drucker vln,   XCO 35723/6–1 | Columbia 71998/200D.
H. Busch vlc, M. Horszowski pf & | 72026/9D, (in set M685),
Busch Chamber Players – Busch | ML4212, (in set SL158)
Concerto grosso No. 11, in A
with E. Drucker   XCO 35750/4–1 | Columbia 72000/2D, 72022/6D,
vln, H. Busch vlc, M. Horszowski pf & | (in set M685), ML4211, (in set
Busch Chamber Players – Busch | SL158)
Concerto grosso No. 12, in b
with E. Drucker   XCO 35710/4–1 | Columbia 72003/5D, 72022/6D,
vln, H. Busch vlc, M. Horszowski pf & | (in set M685), ML4210, (in set
Busch Chamber Players – Busch | SL158)

KREISLER

Praeludium & Allegro (Pugnani) vln & pf
with piano | Polydor 65981

Scherzo (Dittersdorf) vln & pf
with piano | Polydor 20074, 62470

Variations on a theme of Corelli (Tartini) vln & pf
with piano | Polydor 65980

MOZART

Concerto No. 5, in A, K219 "Turkish" (cadenzas by Joachim) vln & orch
XCO 34649/55–1 | Columbia 71749/52D, 71753/6D,
with Busch Chamber Players – Busch | (set M609)

Serenade No. 6, in D, K239 "Serenata notturna" orch.
OEA 1186/9¹ □, 1190^{II} □ | HMV DA1673/4
with Busch Chamber Players – Busch

Sonata No. 25, in F, K377 vln & pf
with R. Serkin pf   2EA 5484/7¹ □ | HMV DB3373/4
| Victor 15175/6

PORPORA

Aria in E unid – arr. vln & pf Corti
with piano | Polydor 62469

REGER

Sonata No. 5, in f sharp, Op. 84 vln & pf
Allegretto (2nd mvt)
with R. Serkin pf | 2B 843¹△ HMV DB1523
| Victor 7562, (in set M132)

SCHUBERT

Fantasia in C, Op. 159 (D934) vln & pf
    2B 834/5^{III}△, 836^V△, 837^{II}△ &   HMV DB1521/3
with R. Serkin pf   838^{III}△   Victor 7562/4, (set M132)

Trio No. 2, in E flat, ⊖p. 100 (D929) pf, vln & vlc
with R. Serkin pf & H. Busch vlc   HMV COLH43, DB2676/80
          Victor 14464/8, (set M374)

Trio No. 2, in E flat, Op. 100 (D929) pf, vln & vlc
with R. Serkin pf & H. Busch vlc   Columbia ML4654

SCHUMANN

(13) Kinderscenen, Op. 15 pf
  No. 7. Träumerei arr. vln & pf
  with piano   Polydor 62468

Sonata No. 1, in a, Op. 105 vln & pf
  with R. Serkin pf   2EA 5480/3^1□ HMV DB3371/2
          Victor 15393/4, (set M551)

TARTINI

(12) Sonatas, Op. 2 vln & c
  Sonata No. 12, in G: Adagio arr. vln & pf as "Air" by Busch
  with piano   Polydor 62468
  Sonata No. 12, in G: Adagio arr. vln & str orch. as "Air" by Busch
  with Busch   XCO 34664–1 Columbia 71752D, 71753D,
  Chamber Players – Busch   (in set M609)

VIVALDI

(12) Sonatas, Op. 2 (1712) vln & c
  Sonata No. 2, in A, F.XIII, No. 30 arr. vln & pf Busch
  with R. Serkin pf   2B 828^{II}△ HMV DB1524

WILLY BUSCH

BONPORTI

(10) Concerti, Op. 11 strs
  Concerto No. 5, in F: Adagio (2nd mvt) "Recitativo"
  with Ensemble Benedetto Marcello   Columbia CXH4

DVOŘÁK

(7) Gypsy songs, Op. 55 v & pf
  No. 4. Songs my mother taught me arr. vln & pf Kreisler
  with P. Palla pf   Philips PR600313, XPY855818

ELLERTON

(8) Bagatelles, Op. 18 vln & pf
  No. 4. Rondino
  with J. Bonda pf   Parlophone PHD3

FESCH

(6) Concerti, Op. 5 2 vlns, strs & c
  Concerto No. 6, in E
  with Ensemble Benedetto Marcello   Columbia CHX3

FLOTOW

Martha (1847) – opera
Ach so fromm arr. vln, pf & vlc
  with P. Palla pf & W. Amende vlc   Philips XPY855818

HANDEL

Serse (1738) – opera
Ombra mai fu "Largo" arr. vln, pf & vlc
  with P. Palla pf & W. Amende vlc   Philips PR600313, XPY855818

PARADIES

Sicilienne vln & pf – arr. Dushkin
  with J. Bonda pf   Parlophone PHD3

SAMMARTINI, G.

(6) Sonatas, Op. 1 2 vlns & c
  Sonata No. 4, in A: Andante arr. vln & pf as "Canto amoroso" by Elman
  with J. Bonda pf   Columbia DH503

SARASATE

(8) Danzas españolas vln & pf
  No. 5. Playera, Op. 23, No. 1
  with J. Bonda pf   Columbia DH503

SCHUMANN

(20) Albumblätter, Op. 124 pf
  No. 16. Schlummerlied arr. vln, pf & vlc
  with P. Palla & W. Amende vlc   Philips XPY855818

THOMAS

Mignon (1866) – opera
  Entr'acte (Gavotte) (Act II) arr. vln, pf & vlc
  with P. Palla & W. Amende vlc   Philips XPY855818

Guila BUSTABO (1919–)

CHOPIN

(2) Nocturnes, Op. 27 pf
  No. 2. Nocturne No. 8, in D flat arr. vln & pf Wilhelmj
  with G. Moore pf   CAX 7578–2 Columbia LOX257, LX423

DEBUSSY

Petite Suite (1889) pf – 4 hands
  No. 1. En bateau arr. vln & pf Dushkin
  with G. Moore pf   CA 15145–1 Columbia LB26, LO12, LW15

DVOŘÁK

Symphony No. 9, in e, Op. 95 "From the New World" orch.
  Largo (2nd mvt) arr. vln & pf as "Negro spiritual melody" by Kreisler
  with G. Moore pf   CAX 7575–1 Columbia LOX257, LX423

FALLA

(El) Amor Brujo (1915) – ballet m–s & orch.
  No. 14. Pantomime arr. vln & pf Kochanski
  with H. Schröter pf   CRX 210^1 Columbia LWX363

KREISLER

Praeludium & Allegro (Pugnani) vln & pf
  with G. Moore pf   CAX 7562–1 Columbia LCX35, LOX245,
          LX401

MENDELSSOHN

(6) Gesänge, Op. 34 v & pf
  No. 2. Auf Flügeln des Gesanges arr. vln & pf Achron
  with G. Moore pf   CAX 7561–1 Columbia LCX35, LOX245,
          LX401

NOVAČÉK

(8) Concert caprices, Op. 5 vln & pf
  No. 4. Perpetuum mobile
  with G. Moore pf   CA 15112–1 Columbia LB23, LO14

PAGANINI

(24) Caprices, Op. 1 (1801/7) solo vln
Caprice No. 5, in a
(unaccompanied) CA 15146–1 Columbia LB26, LO12, LW15
Concerto No. 1, in D, Op. 6 vln & orch.
Allegro maestoso (1st mvt) arr. vln & orch. Wilhelmj
GRX 211[I], 212[II], 213[I] & 214[II] Columbia LWX354/5
with Berlin State Opera Orch. – Zaun

RUBINSTEIN

(6) Lieder, Op. 72 v & pf
No. 1. Es blinkt der Tau (The dew is sparkling) arr. vln & pf
with G. Moore pf CA 15171–1 Columbia LB23, LO14

SARASATE

(8) Danzas españolas vln & pf
No. 2. Habañera, Op. 21, No. 2
with H. Schröter pf CRX 209[I] Columbia LWX363
No. 6. Zapateado, Op. 23, No. 2
with H. Schröter pf CR 790[3] Columbia LW36

SIBELIUS

Concerto in d, Op. 47 vln & orch.
CRX 247[1], 248[2], 249[3], 250/1[1], Columbia LWX372/5
with Berlin State 252[2], 253[1] & 254[2]
Opera Orch. – Zaun

SUK

(4) Pieces, Op. 17 vln & pf
No. 4. Burleska
with H. Schröter pf CR 791[1] Columbia LW36

James Oliver BUSWELL IV (1947–)

BACH

(6) Sonatas, BWV1014/9 vln & clav
Sonata No. 1, in b, BWV1014
with F. Valenti hpsi Cardinal VCS10080
Sonata No. 2, in A, BWV1015
with F. Valenti hpsi Cardinal VCS10081
Sonata No. 3, in E, BWV1016
with F. Valenti hpsi Cardinal VCS10081
Sonata No. 4, in c, BWV1017
with F. Valenti hpsi Cardinal VCS10080/1
Sonata No. 5, in f, BWV1018
with F. Valenti hpsi Cardinal VCS10081
Sonata No. 6, in G, BWV1019
with F. Valenti hpsi Cardinal VCS10080

STARER

Variants vln & pf
with D. Glazer pf Desto DC7106

VAUGHAN WILLIAMS

Concerto in d (1925) "Concerto accademico" vln & orch.
with London Symphony Victor LSC3178, SB6801
Orch. – Previn

Enrico CAMPAJOLA (1899–)

DVOŘÁK

(8) Slavonic Dances, Op. 46 pf duet; orch.
No. 2. Slavonic Dance No. 2, in e arr. vln & pf "in g" Kreisler
with piano Columbia D15503

KREISLER

Concerto in C (Vivaldi) vln & strs
with chamber orch. Columbia D15502/3

TCHAIKOVSKY

Sérénade mélancolique in b flat, Op. 26 vln & orch. – arr. vln & pf
Wilhelmj
with E. Sarti pf Columbia CQX16621

Alfredo CAMPOLI (1906–)

ALBÉNIZ

Cantos d'España, Op. 232 pf
No. 4. Córdoba arr. vln & pf
with E. Gritton pf AR 13573–1 Decca D71065, X571
España (6 Feuilles d'album) Op. 165 pf
No. 2. Tango in D arr. vln & pf Dushkin
with piano GB 3130–ICJ Decca F2512
No. 2. Tango in D arr. vln & pf Kreisler
with E. Gritton pf Decca D71092, LW5180,
LXT5012
London LD9192, LL1171
Suite española, Op. 47 pf
No. 3. Sevillañas arr. vln & pf Heifetz
with E. Gritton pf AR 13243–2 Decca D71065, K23287, K28220,
X571
London T5221, (in set LA114)

ANONYMOUS

Deep river Negro spiritual – arr. vln & pf Heifetz
with E. Gritton pf Decca LW5242
London LL1461
Londonderry air Traditional Irish ballad – arr. vln & org Morris
with organ GB 6500–II Decca F3868

BACH

Cantata No. 156 (Ich steh' mit einem Fuss in Grabe) BWV156 (1730)
Sinfonia arr. vln & pf as "Arioso" by Franko
with E. Gritton pf AR 10243–2 Decca K1531, (in set EDA81)
(3) Sonatas & 3 Partitas, BWV1001/6 solo vln
Partita No. 2, in d, BWV1004
AR 12440/4–1 & 12445–4 Decca AK1955/7, LXT2596
(unaccompanied) London LL395
(4) Suites, BWV1066/9 strs & c
Suite No. 3, in D: Air (2nd mvt) BWV1068 2 obs, 3 tpts, drms & strs –
arr. vln & pf as "Air on the G–string" by Wilhelmj
with E. Gritton pf AR 10247–2 Decca K1533

BAZZINI

(La) Ronde des lutins, Op. 25 vln & pf
with piano GA 3705–2cJ Decca K639
(La) Ronde des lutins, Op. 25 vln & pf
with E. Gritton pf AR 11312–1 Decca K1799

BEETHOVEN

Concerto in D, Op. 61 (cadenzas by Kreisler) vln & orch.
    with London Symphony Orch. – Krips Decca LXT2674, LXT5352
                                 Eclipse ECS521
                                 London LL560
                                 Telefunken MD1005

Concerto in D, Op. 61 (cadenzas by Kreisler) vln & orch.
    with Royal Philharmonic   HMV XLP20043
    Orch. – Pritchard   Regal QRX9015

BLISS

Concerto (1953) vln & orch.
    with London Philharmonic   Ace of Clubs ACL317
    Orch. – Bliss   Decca LXT5166
                             London LL1398

Theme & Cadenza (1949) vln & orch.
    with London Philharmonic   Ace of Clubs ACL317
    Orch. – Bliss   Decca LXT5166
                             London LL1398

BRAHMS

Concerto in a. Op. 102 vln, vlc & orch.
    with A. Navarra vlc & Hallé   Pye GGC4009, GSGC14009
    Orch. – Barbirolli   Vanguard SRV136, SRV136SD

(21) Hungarian Dances pf duet
Hungarian dance No. 7, in A arr. vln & pf Joachim
    with E. Gritton pf   DR 13703–1 Decca F9396
Hungarian dance No. 20, in e arr. vln & pf "in d" Joachim
    with E. Gritton pf   DR 13702–1 Decca F9396

(16) Waltzes, Op. 39 pf duet
No 15. Waltz No. 15, in A flat arr. vln & pf "in A" Hochstein
    with G. Moore pf   OEA 8325[1] HMV B9023

BRUCH

Concerto No. 1, in g, Op. 26 vln & orch.
    CAX 8087–1, 8088/9–2, 8090–   Columbia 69243/5D, (set M332),
    1A, 8091–2A & 8092–1A   DX807/9, DX8120/2,
    with orch. – Goehr   DWX1604/6, GQX11039/41
Concerto No. 1, in g, Op. 26 vln & orch.*
    DAR 16053/4–1, 16055–1–3 & Ace of Clubs ACL64
    with New Symphony Orch. 16056/8–1 Decca AX558/60, K23239/41,
    – Kisch   LX3092, LXT2596, LXT2904
                             Eclipse ECM505, ECS505
                             London LL395, LL966
                             Richmond R19021

Scottish Fantasia, Op. 46 vln & orch.
    with London Symphony Orch. – Boult Decca LXT5453, SXL2026
                             London CS6047, STS15015

CHAMINADE

Sérénade espagnole pf – arr. vln & pf Kreisler
    with piano   GB 6054–1D Decca F6179, Y5148

CHOPIN

(3) Nocturnes, Op. 9 pf
No. 2. Nocturne No. 2, in E flat arr. vln & pf Sarasate
    with E. Gritton pf   AR 13705–2 Decca K2252, K23275

* adagio or 2nd mvt. on Decca VD 507.

CORELLI

(12) Sonatas, Op. 5, vln & c
Sonata No. 12, in d "La Follia" arr. vln & pf Léonard
    with E. Gritton pf   AR 11305/7–1 Decca K1670/1, (set EDA82)
                                London (set LA174)

DEBUSSY

(12) Préludes – Book I (1910) pf
No. 8. La Fille aux cheveux de lin arr. vln & pf Hartmann
    with E. Gritton pf   AR 12413–1 Decca K2183
                               London T5345

No. 12. Minstrels arr. vln & pf Hartmann
    with E. Gritton pf   Decca LW5242
                             London LL1461

DINICU

Hora Staccato (1906) vln & pf – arr. Heifetz
    with S. Crooke pf   CA 16951–1 Columbia DB1781, DO1923

DOHNÁNYI

Ruralia Hungarica, Op. 32A pf – arr. vln & pf Kreisler
    with G. Malcolm pf   Decca LX3115
                            London LS793

DRDLA

Souvenir vln & pf
    with piano   GB 3132–2DJ Decca F2454
Souvenir vln & pf
    with E. Gritton pf   Decca D71085, K23368, LW5180
                             London LL1461

DRIGO

(2) Airs de Ballet orch.
No. 2. Valse bluette arr. vln & pf Auer
    with piano   GB 3131–3DJ Decca F2454
No. 2. Valse bluette arr. vln & pf Auer
    with E. Gritton pf   Decca LW5243
                             London LL1461

DVOŘÁK

(7) Gypsy songs, Op. 55 v & pf
No. 4. Songs my mother taught me arr. vln & pf Kreisler
    with S. Crooke pf   CA 16809–1 Columbia DB1772

ELGAR

(La) Capricieuse, Op. 17 vln & pf
    with piano   GB 3703–3CJ Decca F3174
                             Odeon 286114

(La) Capricieuse, Op. 17 vln & pf
    with E. Gritton pf*   Decca K1843

(La) Capricieuse, Op. 17 vln & pf
    with E. Gritton pf   Decca D71085, LW5242
                             London LL1461

Concerto in b, Op. 61 vln & orch.
    with London Philharmonic   Ace of Clubs ACL312
    Orch. – Boult   Decca LXT5014
                             London LL1168

Salut d'amour, Op. 12 orch. – arr. vln & pf Elgar
    with piano   GB 3702–3CJ Decca F3174

* This entry is with Elsie and *not* Eric Gritton.

FALLA

(La) Vida Breve (1913) – opera
    Danza española orch. – arr. vln & pf Kreisler
      with E. Gritton pf*   Decca K1843

FIBICH

Images, Impressions & Souvenirs, Op. 41 pf
    No. 14. Poem (from "Souvenirs", Part IV) arr. vln & pf Kubelík
      with E. Gritton pf   Decca D71103, LW5180
                      London LD9192, LL1461

FIOCCO

Suite No. 1, in G hpsi
    Allegro (10th mvt) arr. vln & pf Bent & O'Neill
      with E. Gritton pf   Decca LW5180
                      London LD9192, LL1461

FISHER

(An) Old violin v & pf – arr. s, vln & pf
    with O. Groves s &   GB 3777–7DJ   Decca F2773
    piano

FOSTER

(The) Old folks at home "Swanee river" (1851) v & pf – arr. vln & pf
    Kreisler
      with E. Gritton pf   Decca LW5242
                      London LL1461

GARDNER

(2) Pieces, Op. 5 vln & pf
    No. 1. From the canebrake
      with E. Gritton pf   Decca LW5242
                      London LL1461

GRANADOS

(12) Danzas españolas, Op. 37 (1893) pf
    No. 5. Danza española No. 5, in e "Andaluza" arr. vln & pf Kreisler
      with E. Gritton pf   Decca LK40110, LW5218,
                      LXT5012
                      Eclipse ECS587
                      London LL1171

HAHN

Si mes vers avaient des aîles v & pf – arr vln & pf
    with S. Crooke pf   GB 7143–11   Decca F5638

HANDEL

Serse (1738) – opera
    Ombra mai fu "Largo" arr. vln & org Campoli
      with organ   GB 6502–1   Decca F5100

(15) Sonatas, Op. 1 (?1731) fl or vln & c
    Sonata No. 3, in A vln I
      with G. Malcolm hpsi   Decca LXT2751
                      London LL652

    Sonata No. 10, in g vln II
      with G. Malcolm hpsi   Decca LXT2751
                      London LL652

    Sonata No. 12, in F vln III
      with G. Malcolm hpsi   Decca LXT2751
                      London LL652

HANDEL – *Continued*

    Sonata No. 13, in D vln IV
      with G. Malcolm hpsi   Decca LW5077, LXT2751
                      London LD9090, LL652

    Sonata No. 14, in A vln V
      with G. Malcolm hpsi   Decca LXT2751
                      London LL652

    Sonata No. 15, in E vln VI
      with G. Malcolm hpsi   Decca LW5077, LXT2751
                      London LD9090, LL652

HEUBERGER

(Der) Opernball, Op. 40 (1898) – operetta
    Im chambre séparée arr. vln & pf as "Midnight bells" by Kreisler
      with S. Crooke pf   TB 1555 IV   Decca F5532
    Im chambre séparée arr. vln & pf as "Midnight bells" by Kreisler
      with E. Gritton pf   Decca LW5180
                      London LL1461

HUBAY

(6) Blumenleben, Op. 30 vln & pf
    No. 5. Der Zephir
      with E. Gritton pf   AR 11313–1   Decca K1799

(14) Scènes de la Csárda vln & pf
    No. 4. Hejre Kati, Op. 32
      with S. Crooke pf   TB 1553 III   Decca F5532

HUMMEL

Rondo in E flat, Op. 11 "Rondo favori" pf – arr. vln & pf Heifetz
    with E. Gritton pf   AR 12412–1   Decca K2183
                      London T5345

KING

Song of paradise pf – arr. vln & org
    with R. Foort org   OER 254[1]☐   HMV BD484, MH117

KREISLER

Caprice viennois, Op. 2 vln & pf
    with piano   GA 3704–2CJ   Decca K639
Caprice viennois, Op. 2 vln & pf
    with E. Gritton pf   Decca D71092, LW5218,
                      LXT5012
                      Eclipse ECS587
                      London LL1171

(La) Gitana vln & pf
    with E. Gritton pf   Decca LW5218, LXT5012
                      Eclipse ECS587
                      London LL1171

Liebesfreud vln & pf
    with G. Moore pf   OEA 8327[1]☐   HMV B9011
Liebesfreud vln & pf
    with E. Gritton pf   Decca D71076, CEP546,
                      LW5217, LXT5012
                      Eclipse ECS587
                      London LL1171

Liebesleid vln & pf
    with G. Moore pf   OEA 8326[1]☐   HMV B9011

---

* This entry is with Elsie and *not* Eric Gritton.

KREISLER – *Continued*

Liebesleid vln & pf
   with E. Gritton pf   Decca D71076, CEP546,
                                  LW5217, LXT5012
                                  Eclipse ECS587
                                  London LL1171

Polichinelle–serenade vln & pf
   with E. Gritton pf   Decca CEP546, LW5217,
                                  LXT5012
                                  Eclipse ECS587
                                  London LL1171

Rondino on a theme by Beethoven vln & pf
   with G. Moore pf   OEA 8324¹□   HMV B9023

Rondino on a theme by Beethoven vln & pf
   with E. Gritton pf   Decca LW5217, LXT5012
                                  Eclipse ECS587
                                  London LL1171

Schön Rosmarin vln & pf
   with S. Crooke pf   TB 1554–II   Decca F5192

Schön Rosmarin vln & pf
   with E. Gritton pf   Decca CEP546, LW5217,
                                  LXT5012
                                  Eclipse ECS587
                                  London LL1171

Tambourin chinois, Op. 3 vln & pf
   with piano   GB 3133–IDJ   Decca F2512

Tambourin chinois, Op. 3 vln & pf
   with E. Gritton pf   Decca CEP546, D71092,
                                  LW5217, LXT5012
                                  Eclipse ECS587
                                  London LL1171

(La) Chasse (Cartier) vln & pf
   with E. Gritton pf   Decca K23368, LW5217,
                                  LXT5012
                                  Eclipse ECS587
                                  London LL1171

Praeludium & Allegro (Pugnani) vln & pf
   with E. Gritton pf   Decca LW5217, LXT5012
                                  Eclipse ECS587
                                  London LL1171

Sicilienne & Rigaudon (Francoeur) vln & pf
   with S. Crooke pf   GB 6028–IIID   Decca F6594, Y5213

Variations on a theme of Corelli (Tartini) vln & pf
   with S. Crooke pf   GB 6055–ID   Decca F6594, Y5213

Variations on a theme of Corelli (Tartini) vln & pf
   with E. Gritton pf   Decca LW5218, LXT5012
                                  Eclipse ECS587
                                  London LL1171

LALO

Symphonie espagnole, Op. 21 vln & orch.*
   with London Philharmonic   Ace of Clubs ACL124
   Orch. – van Beinum   Decca LXT2801
                             London LL763

* Including Intermezzo.

LEHÁR

Frasquita (1923) – operetta
   Hab' ein blaues Himmelbett arr. vln & pf as "Serenade" by Kreisler
   with S. Crooke pf   GB 6023–1C   Decca F3625

LIEURANCE

By the waters of the Minnetonka (1914) v & pf – arr. s, vln & pf
   with O. Groves s &   GB 3778–NDJ   Decca F2773
   piano

LILIUCKALANI, Queen

Aloha Oe (1892) v & pf – arr. vln & pf Kreisler
   with S. Crooke pf   GB 6026–IIID   Decca F3708

LISZT

Duo Sonata (on Chopin's "Mazurka in c sharp, Op. 6, No. 2") R127
(1832/5) vln & pf
   with V. Tryon pf   Virtuoso TPLS13017

LOGAN

Pale moon (1920) v & pf – arr. vln & pf Kreisler
   with S. Crooke pf   GB 6024–IIID   Decca F3625

MASSENET

Thaïs (1894) – opera
   Méditation arr. vln & pf Marsick
   with E. Gritton pf   AR 13704–1A   Decca K2252, K23275

MENDELSSOHN

Concerto in e, Op. 64 vln & orch.
   with London   AR 13501/6–1   Ace of Clubs ACL4
   Philharmonic Orch. – van Beinum   Decca AX290/2, K23026/8,
                                  LX3001, LXT2904, NLK40103
                                  Eclipse ECM505, ECS505
                                  London LL966, LPS90, T5144/6,
                                  (in set LA98)
                                  Richmond R19021

Concerto in e, Op. 64 vln & orch.
   with London Philharmonic   Decca LXT5453, SXL2026
   Orch. – Boult   London CS6047, STS15015

(6) Gesänge, Op. 34 v & pf
   No. 2. Auf Flügeln des Gesanges arr. vln & pf Achron
   with piano   2EA 8328–1   HMV C3144, JOX16
   No. 2. Auf Flügeln des Gesanges arr. vln & pf Achron
   with E. Gritton pf   Decca LW5242
                                  London LL1461

MONK

Abide with me (1861) v & pf – arr. vln & org
   with organ   GB 6501–1   Decca F5100

MONTI

Csárdas (1904) vln & pf
   with S. Crooke pf   TB 1552–1   Decca F5192

MOSZKOWSKI

(6) Klavierstücke, Op. 15 pf – 4 hands
   No. 1. Serenata arr. vln & org
   with R. Foort org   OER 253¹   HMV BD484, MH117
(2) Stücke, Op. 45 pf
   No. 2. Guitarre arr. vln & pf Sarasate
   with piano   GB 6025–IIID   Decca F6179

PADEREWSKI

(6) Humoresques de concert, Op. 14 pf
  No. 1. Minuet in G arr. vln & pf Kreisler
  with S. Crooke pf   GB 6027–IIID   Decca F3708
  No. 1. Minuet in G arr. vln & pf Kreisler
  with E. Gritton pf   Decca LW5218, LXT5012
                           Eclipse ECS587
                           London LL1171

PAGANINI

(24) caprices, Op. 1 (1801/7) solo vln
  Caprice No. 13, in B flat arr. vln & pf Kreisler
  with G. Malcolm pf   Decca LX3115
                           London LS793
  Caprice No. 20, in D arr. vln & pf Kreisler
  with G. Malcolm pf   Decca LX3115
                           London LS793

Concerto No. 1, in D, Op. 6 vln & orch.
  Allegro maestoso (1st mvt) arr. Kreisler
      AR 10358–1, 10359–2, 10360–1 Decca AK1822/3
  with National Symphony & 10361–1A London T5544/5, (set LA182)
  Orch. – Olof
  Allegro maestoso (1st mvt) arr. Kreisler
  with London Symphony   Decca LXT5302
  Orch. – Gamba   London CM9182, CS6084,
                           LL1624

Concerto No. 2, in b, Op. 7 vln & orch.
  Ronde à la clochette (3rd mt) "La Campanella" arr. vln & pf Kreisler
  with E. Gritton pf   AR 10246–2 Decca K1533, K1671
                          London T5528, (in set LA174)
  Ronde à la clochette (3rd mvt) "La Campanella" arr. vln & pf Kreisler
  with G. Malcolm pf   Decca LX3115, VD507
                          London LS793

Moto perpetuo (Allegro di concert) Op. 11 (1830) vln & orch.
  with S. Crooke pf   CA 16952–1 Columbia DB1772

POLIAKIN

(Le) Canari (Concert–polka) vln & pf
  with S. Crooke pf   GB 7142–11 Decca F5638
                              Polydor 10796

PONCE

Estrellita (1913) v & pf – arr. vln & pf Heifetz
  with E. Gritton pf   Decca D71103, LW5180
                           London LL1461

POULENC

(3) Pieces (1934/5) pf
  No. 1. Presto in B flat arr. vln & pf Heifetz
  with E. Gritton pf   DR 13241–1 Decca M669

RAVEL

Pièce en forme d'Habanera v & pf – arr. vln & pf Catherine
  with E. Gritton pf   DR 13242–1 Decca M669

RIES

(La) Capricciosa vln & pf
  with S. Crooke pf   CA 16808–1 Columbia DB1781, DO1923

SAINT-SAËNS

Concerto No. 3, in b, Op. 61 vln & orch.
  with London Symphony   Decca LXT5302
  Orch. – Gamba   London CM9182, CS6084,
                           LL1624

Havanaise, Op. 83 vln & orch.
  with London Symphony   Ace of Clubs ACL64
  Orch. – Fistoulari   Decca LW5085
                         London CM9183, LL1625

Introduction & Rondo Capriccioso, Op. 28 vln & orch.
        CAX 8418–1 & ⱝ419–2 Columbia 264548, 69640D,
  with London Symphony   DOX621, DX902
  Orch. – Goehr
Introduction & Rondo Capriccioso, Op. 28 vln & orch.
  with London Symphony   Ace of Clubs ACL64
  Orch. – Fistoulari   Decca LW5085
                         London CM9183, LL1625

SARASATE

Zigeunerweisen, Op. 20 vln & pf or orch.
  with London Symphony   Decca LW5306
  Orch. – Gamba   London CM9183, LL1625

SCHUBERT, François

(12) Bagatelles, Op. 13 vln & pf
  No. 9. L'abeille
  with E. Gritton pf   Decca LW5180
                           London LL1461

SCHUBERT, Franz

(7) Gesänge (set to Scott's "Lady of the Lake") Op. 52 v & pf
  No. 6. Ave Maria, D839 arr. vln & pf Wilhelmj
  with piano   2EA 8329–2 HMV C3144, JOX16

SCOTT, Lady John

Annie Laurie (1838) v & pf – arr. vln & org Campoli
  with organ   GB 6499–111 Decca F3868

STRAUSS, R.

(4) Lieder, Op. 27 v & pf
  No. 4. Morgen arr. t, vln & pf
  with W. Booth t &   2EA 8080^{II}□ HMV C3418
  E. Lush pf
Sonata in E flat, Op. 18 vln & pf
  with V. Tryon pf   Virtuoso TPLS13017

TARTINI

(12) Sonatas, Op. 1 vln & c
  Sonata No. 10, in g "Didone abbandonata"
  with E. Gritton pf   AR 10240/2–2 Decca K1531/2, K28219/20,
                              (set EDA81)
  Sonata No. 10, in g "Didone abbandonata"
  with G. Malcolm pf   Decca LX3137
(12) Sonatas, Op. 5 vln & c
  Sonata No. 3, in B flat: Presto arr. vln & pf Bridgewater
  with E. Gritton pf   AR 13572–1 Decca AK2366
Sonata in g "Il Trillo del Diavolo" vln & c – arr. vln & pf Campoli
  with E. Gritton pf   AR 13238/40–1 Decca AK2366/7, K23286/7
                             London T5221/2, (set LA114)
Sonata in g "Il Trillo del Diavolo" vln & c – arr. vln & pf Campoli
  with G. Malcolm pf   Decca LX3137

TCHAIKOVSKY

Concerto in D, Op. 35 vln & orch.
with London Symphony
Orch. – Argenta

Decca LXT5313, SXL2029
London CM9190, CS6011,
LL1647
Richmond R19085, S29085

Swan Lake, Op. 20 (1875/6) – ballet orch.
Dance of the queen of the swans
with W. de Mont vlc & London
Symphony Orch. – Fistoulari

Ace of Clubs ACL100/1
Decca LW5289, LXT2681/2,
LXT5409
Eclipse ECM516, ECS516
London LL565/6, LL1768
Richmond R19084

Pas de deux (Andante: Act III)
with London Symphony
Orch. – Fistoulari

Ace of Clubs ACL100/1
Decca LXT2681/2, LXT5409
Eclipse ECM516, ECS516
London LL565/6, LL1768
Richmond R19084

TORCH

Dr. Watson meets Sherlock Holmes – Incidental music orch.
with orch. – Torch   Decca LK4164

WIENIAWSKI

(L') École moderne, Op. 10 (10 Études) solo vln
Étude No. 5, in E flat "alla Saltarella" arr. vln & pf Kreisler
with E. Gritton pf

Decca D71136, LK40110,
LW5218, LXT5012
Eclipse ECS587
London LL1171

(8) Étude–Caprices, Op. 18 solo vln & 2nd vln obb
Étude–Caprice No. 4, in a arr. vln & pf Kreisler
with E. Gritton pf

Decca D71136, LK40110,
LW5218, LXT5012
Eclipse ECS587
London LL1171

Légende, Op. 17 vln & pf or orch.
with London Symphony
Orch. – Gamba

Decca LW5306
London CM9183, LL1625

Miguel CANDELA (1914–   )

ALBÉNIZ

España (6 Feuilles d'album) Op. 165 pf
No. 2. Tango in D arr. vln & pf Kreisler
with M. Fauré pf   Columbia LF32

CHOPIN

(4) Mazurkas, Op. 67 pf
No. 4. Mazurka No. 45, in a arr. vln & pf Kreisler
with M. Fauré pf   Columbia LF32

DINICU

Hora Staccato (1906) vln & pf – arr. Heifetz
with J. Benvenuti pf   Columbia 4194M, LF127

DRDLA

Serenade No. 1, in A vln & pf
with M. Fauré pf   Columbia LF85

FAIRCHILD

Mosquitos vln & pf – arr. Dushkin
with J. Benvenuti pf   Columbia LF138, LW13

GLAZOUNOV

Concerto in a, Op. 82 vln & orch.
with Pierné Orch. – Désormière   Columbia LFX645/7

GROBET

(2) Gavottes vln & pf
No. 1. Gavotte
with M. Fauré pf   Columbia LF85

KUHLAU

Elverhøj (The Elves hill) Op. 100 (1828) – Incidental music orch.
No. 12. Menuetto in F (Act V) arr. vln & pf Burmester
with J. Benvenuti pf   Columbia LF137

LALO

Concerto in g, Op. 29 "Concerto russe" vln & orch.
Intermezzo (3rd mvt)
with J. Benvenuti   Columbia LF145

MENDELSSOHN

(6) Gesänge, Op. 34 v & pf
No. 2. Auf Flügeln des Gesanges arr. vln & pf Achron
with J. Benvenuti pf   Columbia LF127

NIN

(20) Cantos de España (1923) v & pf
No. 7. Granadina arr. vln & pf Kochański
with J. Nin pf   Columbia 4194M, LF145
No. 8. Saeta arr. vln & pf Kochański
with J. Nin pf   Columbia 4194M, LF145

PADEREWSKI

(6) Humoresques de Concert, Op. 14 pf
No. 1. Minuet in G arr. vln & pf Kreisler
with M. Fauré pf   Columbia LF82

PIERNÉ

Cydalise et le Chèvre–Pied (1923) – ballet orch.
Marche des petits faunes arr. vln & pf Dushkin
with M. Fauré pf   Columbia LF27

Sonata in D, Op. 36 (1900) vln & pf
with J.M. Darré pf   Columbia LFX758/60

POLDINI

(7) Marionnettes pf
No. 2. Poupée valsante arr. vln & pf Kreisler
with M. Fauré pf   Columbia 2109M, LF84

RANDEGGER

Pierrot sérénade, Op. 33, No. 1 vln & pf
with M. Fauré pf   Columbia 2109M, LF84

RIMSKY–KORSAKOV

(The) Tale of Tsar Saltan (1900) – opera
Flight of the bumblebee (Act III) orch. – arr. vln & pf Hartmann
with J. Benvenuti pf   Columbia LF138, LW13

SAINT–SAËNS

Concerto No. 3, in b, Op. 61 vln & orch.
    LX 180, 181–1, 182/3–2, 210/1–1   Columbia D15209/12
    with Paris   & 212/3–2
    Conservatory Orch. – Gaubert

Havanaise, Op. 83 vln & orch.
    with J. Benvenuti pf   Columbia LFX332

SCHUBERT

(6) Moments musicaux, Op. 94 (D780) (1823/7) pf
    No. 3. Moment musicale No. 3, in f "Air russe" arr. vln & pf by Kreisler
    with M. Fauré pf   Columbia LF27

(14) Schwanengesang, D957 (1828) v & pf
    No. 4 Ständchen "Serenade" arr. vln & pf Candéla
    with M. Fauré   Columbia LF82, LW14

TARTINI

(12) Sonatas, Op. 1 (1734) vln & c
    Sonata No. 10, in g: Largo (3rd mvt) "Didone abbandonata" arr. vln & pf Salmon
    with J. Benvenuti pf   Columbia LF138, LW13

Sonata in g "Il Trillo del Diavolo" vln & c – arr. vln & pf Kreisler
    with J.M. Damase pf   Columbia GFX144/5

TCHAIKOVSKY

(The) Months (12 Characteristic pieces) Op. 37a pf
    No. 10. Autumn song (October) arr. vln & pf von Seybold
    with J. Benvenuti pf   Columbia LF137

Frank CANTELL (1901–1963)

MOZART

Divertimento No. 17, in D, K334 2 hrns & strs
    Minuet (3rd mvt) arr. vln & pf Burmester
    with piano   Piccadilly 744

SCHUBERT

Octet in F, Op. 166 (D803) 2 vlns, vla, vlc, cbs, cl, bsn & hrn
    Adagio (2nd mvt) arr. vln & pf
    with piano   Piccadilly 744

William CANTRELLE (1888–)

DEBUSSY

(12) Préludes – Book I (1910) pf
    No. 8. La Fille aux cheveux de lin arr. vln & pf Hartmann
    with G. Andolfi pf   Pathé X9885

FRANCK

Sonata in A (1886) vln & pf
    with L. Descaves pf   HMV L745/8

GOSSEC

(Le) Camp du Grand Pré (1793) – opera
    Tambourin arr. vln & pf Burmester
    with G. Andolfi pf   Pathé X9820, X9885

KREISLER

Scherzo (Dittersdorf) vln & pf
    with G. Andolfi   Pathé X9820

SCHUBERT, François

(12) Bagatelles, Op. 13 vln & pf
    No. 9. L'abeille
    with G. Andolfi pf   Pathé X9820

WIENIAWSKI

Polonaise brillante No. 2, in A, Op. 21 vln & pf
    with G. Andolfi pf   Pathé X5503

Eugenio CAPONI

DRDLA

Souvenir vln & pf
    with piano   Fonotipia 152681
                Odeon 2017A

DVOŘÁK

(8) Humoresques, Op. 101 pf
    No. 7. Humoresque No. 7, in G flat arr. vln & pf "in G" Kreisler
    with piano   Fonotipia 152680
                Odeon 2017A

KREISLER

Caprice viennois, Op. 2 vln & pf
    with piano   Fonotipia 74256
                Odeon 4503D

SCHUBERT

(7) Gesänge (set to Scott's "Lady of the Lake") Op. 52 v & pf
    No. 6. Ave Maria, D839 arr. vln & pf Wilhelmj
    with piano   Fonotipia 74255
                Odeon 4503D

TIRINDELLI

(6) Morceaux de concert, Op. 1 vln & pf
    No. 6. Pasquinade
    with piano   Fonotipia 152679
                Odeon 2016A

VERACINI

(12) Sonatas, Op. 2 (1744) "Sonate accademiche" vln & c
    Sonata No. 6, in A: Largo arr. vln & pf Corti
    with piano   Fonotipia 152678
                Odeon 2016A

F. CAPOULADE

GODARD

Jocelyn (1888) – opera
    Cachés dans cet asile "Berceuse" arr. vln & pf
    with piano   HMV K5141

André CARAZZA

BEETHOVEN

Concerto in D, Op. 61 (cadenzas by Kreisler) vln & orch.
    with Orch. du Festival de   Guilde Européenne du
    Constance – Antony   Microsillon GEM89

Ginette CARLES

HANDEL

(12) Concerti grossi, Op. 6 2 vlns, vlc & strs

Concerto grosso No. 1, in G
with H. Fernandez vln, B. Fonteny vlc, A.–M. Beckensteiner hpsi & Jean–François Paillard Chamber Orch. – Paillard
Erato STU70319
Musical Heritage Society MHS806

Concerto grosso No. 2, in F
with H. Fernandez vln, B. Fonteny vlc, A.–M. Beckensteiner hpsi & Jean–François Paillard Chamber Orch. – Paillard
Erato STU70319
Musical Heritage Society MHS806

Concerto grosso No. 3, in e
with H. Fernandez vln, B. Fonteny vlc, A.–M. Beckensteiner hpsi & Jean–François Paillard Chamber Orch. – Paillard
Erato STU70319
Musical Heritage Society MHS807

Concerto grosso No. 4, in a
with H. Fernandez vln, B. Fonteny vlc, A.–M. Beckensteiner hpsi & Jean–François Paillard Chamber Orch. – Paillard
Erato STU70320
Musical Heritage Society MHS807

Concerto grosso No. 5, in D
with H. Fernandez vln, B. Fonteny vlc, A.–M. Beckensteiner hpsi & Jean–François Paillard Chamber Orch. – Paillard
Erato STU70320
Musical Heritage Society MHS808

Concerto grosso No. 6, in g
with H. Fernandez vln, B. Fonteny vlc, A.–M. Beckensteiner hpsi & Jean–François Paillard Chamber Orch. – Paillard
Erato STU70320
Musical Heritage Society MHS808

Concerto grosso No. 7, in B flat
with H. Fernandez vln, B. Fonteny vlc, A.–M. Beckensteiner hpsi & Jean–François Paillard Chamber Orch. – Paillard
Erato STU70321
Musical Heritage Society MHS809

Concerto grosso No. 8, in c
with H. Fernandez vln, B. Fonteny vlc, A.–M. Beckensteiner hpsi & Jean–François Paillard Chamber Orch. – Paillard
Erato STU70321
Musical Heritage Society MHS809

Concerto grosso No. 9, in F
with H. Fernandez vln, B. Fonteny vlc, A.–M. Beckensteiner hpsi & Jean–François Paillard Chamber Orch. – Paillard
Erato STU70321
Musical Heritage Society MHS809

Concerto grosso No. 10, in d
with H. Fernandez vln, B. Fonteny vlc, A.–M. Beckensteiner hpsi & Jean–François Paillard Chamber Orch. – Paillard
Erato STU70321
Musical Heritage Society MHS809

Concerto grosso No. 11, in A
with H. Fernandez vln, B. Fonteny vlc, A.–M. Beckensteiner hpsi & Jean–François Paillard Chamber Orch. – Paillard
Erato STU70319
Musical Heritage Society MHS808

HANDEL – *Continued*

Concerto grosso No. 12, in b
with H. Fernandez vln, B. Fonteny vlc, A.–M. Beckensteiner hpsi & Jean–François Paillard Chamber Orch. – Paillard
Erato STU70320
Musical Heritage Society MHS808

SAINT–GEORGES

(2) Sinfonia concertantes, Op. 9 (1778) 2 vlns & strs

Sinfonia concertante No. 2, in G
with H. Fernandez vln & Jean–François Paillard Chamber Orch. – Paillard
Erato STU70237

STRADELLA

(8) Sonatas "Sinfonias" 2 vlns & concertino

Sonata No. 1, in a 2 vlns, vlc, cbs, lute & hpsi
with H. Fernandez vln, B. Fonteny vlc, M. Schäffer lute & A.–M. Beckensteiner hpsi – cond. Paillard
Erato STU70368

Sonata No. 2, in G 2 vlns, vlc, strs & org
with H. Fernandez vln, B. Fonteny vlc, O. Alain org & Jean–François Paillard Chamber Orch. – Paillard
Erato STU70368

Sonata No. 3, in D 2 vlns, vlc, hpsi, 2 tpts, tbn & org
with H. Fernandez vln, B. Fonteny vlc, A–M Beckensteiner hpsi, E. Tarr tpt, H. Eichhorn tpt, H. Schmitt tbn & O. Alain org – cond. Paillard
Erato STU70368

Sonata No. 5, in F 2 vlns, vlc & lute
with H. Fernandez vln, B. Fonteny vlc, M. Schäffer lute, cond. Paillard
Erato STU70368

VIVALDI

(12) Concerti,* Op. 3 "L'Estro armonico" var. cbns & strs

Concerto No. 1, in D, P.146 (F.IV, No. 7) 4 vlns, vlc, strs & c
with G. Jarry vln, H. Déat vln, J–N. Molard vln & Jean–François Paillard Chamber Orch. – Paillard
Erato STU70641

Concerto No. 4, in e, P.97 (F.I, No. 174) 4 vlns, strs & c
with G. Jarry vln, H. Déat vln, J–N. Molard vln & Jean–François Paillard Chamber Orch. – Paillard
Erato STU70641

Concerto No. 7, in F, P.249 (F.IV, No. 9) 4 vlns, strs & c
with G. Jarry vln, H. Déat vln, J–N. Molard vln & Jean–François Paillard Chamber Orch. – Paillard
Erato STU70641

Concerto No. 10, in b, P.148 (F.IV, No. 10) 4 vlns, strs & c
with G. Jarry vln, H. Déat vln, J–N. Molard vln & Jean–François Paillard Chamber Orch. – Paillard
Erato STU70641

Concerto in G, P.135 (F.IV, No. 1) 2 vlns, 2 vlcs, strs & c
with H. Fernandez vln, B. Fonteny vlc, C. Maurelet vlc, A–M. Beckensteiner hpsi & Jean–François Paillard Chamber Orch. – Paillard
Erato LDE3293, STE50193, STU70193
World Record Club CM86, SCM86

* These concerti also have Monique Vallet as one of the soloists. However, it is not clear as to which concerto features her as soloist.

VIVALDI – *Continued*

Concerto in B flat, P.367 (F.I, No. 59) 4 vlns, strs & c
with G. Jarry vln, H. Déat vln, J–N.   Erato STU70641
Molard vln & Jean–François Paillard
Chamber Orch. – Paillard

Norman CAROL (1930–   )

BRANDL

(Der) Liebe Augustin – operetta
Du alter Stefansturm arr. vln & pf as "The old refrain" by Kreisler
with J. Levine pf   Camden CAL419
                           Victor LBC1155

CHOPIN

(4) Mazurkas, Op. 67 pf
No. 4. Mazurka No. 45, in a arr. vln & pf Kreisler
with J. Levine pf   Camden CAL419
                           Victor LBC1155

Nocturne No. 20, in c sharp, Op. posth pf – arr. vln & pf Milstein
with J. Levine pf   Camden CAL419
                           Victor LBC1155

FIOCCO

Suite No. 1, in G hpsi
Allegro (10th mvt) arr. vln & pf Bent & O'Neill
with J. Levine pf   Camden CAL419
                           Victor LBC1155

KREISLER

Liebesfreud vln & pf
with J. Levine pf   Camden CAL419
                           Victor LBC1155

Liebesleid vln & pf
with J. Levine pf   Camden CAL419
                           Victor LBC1155

Schön Rosmarin vln & pf
with J. Levine pf   Camden CAL419
                           Victor LBC1155

Tambourin chinois, Op. 3 vln & pf
with J. Levine pf   Camden CAL419
                           Victor LBC1155

Variations on a theme of Corelli (Tartini) vln & pf
with J. Levine pf   Camden CAL419
                           Victor LBC1155

MANCINI

Cameo vln & orch.
with Philadelphia Orch.   Victor LSC3106
Pops – Mancini

SARASATE

Zigeunerweisen, Op. 20 vln & pf or orch.
with J. Levine pf   Camden CAL419
                           Victor LBC1155

TARTINI

(12) Sonatas, Op. 5 vln & c
Sonata No. 3, in B flat: Presto arr. vln & pf Bridgewater
with J. Levine pf   Camden CAL419
                           Victor LBC1155

TELEMANN

Concerto in B flat 3 obs, 3 vlns, hpsi & strs
with J. de Lancie ob, S. Hewitt ob,   Victor LSC3057, SB6820
C.M. Morris ob, D. Madison vln,
W. de Pasquale vln, R.M. Scott cbs,
W. Smith hpsi & Philadelphia
Orch. – Ormandy

Giannino CARPI

MENDELSSOHN

(6) Songs without words, Op. 62 pf
No. 1. Song without words No. 25, in G "May breezes" arr. vln & pf
Kreisler
with K. Szreter pf   133693 Decca 20381
                                   Odeon 11879
                                   Parlophone R2047

Yvon CARRACILLY

VIVALDI

(12) Concerti, Op. 3 "L'Estro armonico" var. cbns & strs
Concerto No. 10, in b, P.148 (F.IV, No. 10) 4 vlns, strs & c
with J–P. Wallez vln, C. Jacquillat vln, Christophorus SCGLP75896
N. Lepinte vln, L. Boulay hpsi &   Critère CRD186, SCRD5186
Collegium Musicum, Paris – Douatte   Monitor MCS2102

Bernard Molique CARRODUS (1867–1936)

CARRODUS

Scottish airs vln & pf
with piano   Gramophone & Typewriter 7952

Scottish Rhapsody, Op. 6 vln & pf
with piano   1322 b   Gramophone & Typewriter 7949

GOUNOD

Ave Maria (Méditation on Bach's "Prelude No. 1, in C" from Book I of
"Das Wohltemperirte Clavier") v & pf – arr. vln & pf
with piano   Gramophone & Typewriter 7955

HYDE

Slumber song vln & pf
with piano   Gramophone & Typewriter 7950

MENDELSSOHN

Concerto in e, Op. 64 vln & orch.
Andante (2nd mvt)
with piano   1321   Gramophone & Typewriter 7948

THOMÉ

Simple aveu, Op. 25 pf – arr. vln & pf
with piano   4139   Berliner 7924

TOBANI

Hearts & flowers, Op. 245 (1899) v & pf – arr. vln & pf
with piano   4141   Berliner 7923

WIENIAWSKI

Mazurka in a, Op. 3 "Kujawiak" vln & pf
with piano   4140   Berliner 7925

WIENIAWSKI – *Continued*

(2) Mazurkas, Op. 12 vln & pf
  No. 2. Mazurka No. 2, in g "Le Ménetrier"
  with piano   Gramophone & Typewriter 7954
Souvenir de Moscou, Op. 6 vln & pf or orch.
  with piano   Gramophone & Typewriter 7953

T. CARTER

BACH

(6) Brandenburg Concerti, BWV1046/51 (1721) strs & c
  Brandenburg Concerto No. 3, in G, BWV1048 3 vlns, 3 vlas, 3 vlcs & cbs
  with M. Eitler vln, J. Pougnet vln,   Nixa WLP6309
  F. Riddle vla, E. Grainger vla,   Westminster XWN18366, (in set
  E. Hurwitz vla, V. Joseph vlc, A. Pini   XWN2211)
  vlc, R. Albin vlc, R. Watson cbs &   Whitehall WH20071
  R. Veyron–Lacroix hpsi of the London
  Baroque Ensemble – Haas

Marius Robert Max CASADESUS (1892–   )

ANONYMOUS

(2) Mélodies catalanes arr. vln & pf Casadesus
  with piano   Polydor 524272
Visage (Tambourin) arr. vln & pf Casadesus
  with piano   Polydor 524272

HANDEL

(15) Sonatas, Op. 1 (?1731) fl or vln & c
  Sonata No. 3, in A vln I
  with instrumental ensemble   Pléiade P3077
                                      Westminster XWN18459

  Sonata No. 10, in g vln II
  with instrumental ensemble   Pléiade P3077
                                      Westminster XWN18459

  Sonata No. 12, in F vln III
  with instrumental ensemble   Pléiade P3077
                                      Westminster XWN18459

  Sonata No. 13, in D vln IV
  with instrumental ensemble   Pléiade P3077
                                      Westminster XWN18459

  Sonata No. 14, in A vln V
  with instrumental ensemble   Pléiade P3077
                                      Westminster XWN18459

  Sonata No. 15, in E vln VI
  with instrumental ensemble   Pléiade P3077
                                      Westminster XWN18459

SAINT–GEORGES

(Les) Caquets (Rondeau en staccato) hpsi – arr. vln & pf Casadesus
  with piano   3024/5   Polydor 524271

José Francisco del CASTILLO

BLOCH

Baal Shem (3 Pictures of Chassidic life) (1923) vln & pf
  No. 2. Nigun (Improvisation)
  with M. Imaz pf   Fundacion Mito Juan Pro–
                                      Musica (Vol. I)

KABALEVSKY

Improvisation, Op. 21, No. 1 vln & pf
  with M. Imaz pf   Fundacion Mito Juan Pro–
                                      Musica (Vol. I)

LIPINSKI

(3) Caprices, Op. 29 solo vln
  Caprice No. 3, in D
  (unaccompanied)   Fundacion Mito Juan Pro–
                                      Musica (Vol. I)

WIENIAWSKI

Légende, Op. 17 vln & pf or orch.
  with M. Imaz pf   Fundacion Mito Juan Pro–
                                      Musica (Vol. I)

YSAŸE

(6) Sonatas, Op. 27 solo vln
  Sonata No. 2, in a
  (unaccompanied)   Fundacion Mito Juan Pro–
                                      Musica (Vol I)

Arthur CATTERALL (1883–1943)

ARBÓS

(3) Danzas españolas, Op. 1 pf, vln & vlc
  No. 3. Seguidillas gitanes
  with W. Murdoch pf &   76984   Columbia L1225
  W.H. Squire vlc

ARENSKY

(4) Morceaux, Op. 30 vln & pf
  No. 2. Serenade in G
  with piano   WA 2573 Columbia 4825, 01051, D1584,
                                      J5023

Trio No. 1, in d, Op. 32 pf, vln & vlc
  Scherzo (2nd mvt)
  with W. Murdoch pf &   AX 61   Columbia 67090D, L1567
  W.H. Squire vlc

Variations on a theme of Tchaikovsky, Op. 35a str orch. – arr. 2 vlns, vla
  & vlc
  (as leader of Catterall   Cc 184[II] HMV D560
  string quartet)

BACH

Cantata No. 68 (Also hat Gott die Welt geliebt) BWV68
  No. 2. Mein gläubiges Herz arr. str qt
  (as leader of Catterall   AX 2545 Columbia 9252
  string quartet)
Concerto in d, BWV1043 2 vlns, strs & c
  with J.S. Bridge vln &   AX 395/9 Columbia 67066/8D, L1613/5
  orch. – Harty

BEETHOVEN

(6) Quartets, Op. 18 2 vlns, vla & vlc
  No. 1. Quartet No. 1, in F
        Cc 2909^I, 2910/2^{IV}, 2913^{III} &   HMV D947/50
  (as leader of Catterall   1299^I
  string quartet)
  No. 2. Quartet No. 2, in G
  (as leader of Catterall string quartet)   HMV D997/9
  No. 5. Quartet No. 5, in A: Menuetto (2nd mvt)
        Cc 179^{II} HMV D562
Septet in E flat, Op. 20 cl, hrn, bsn, vln, vla, vlc & cbs
        2EA 3688/9 ^{I} □, 3690^{II} □, 3691   HMV DB3026/30, DB8311/5
        ^{I} □, 3692^{III} □, 3693 ^{II} □, 3694/6^I Victor 12450/4, (set M571)
  with F. Thurston cl,   □ & 3697^{II} □
  A. Thonger hrn, A. Camden bsn,
  B. Shore vla, A. Gauntlett vlc & E.
  Cruft cbs
Sonata No. 5, in F, Op. 24 "Spring" vln & pf
  with W. Murdoch pf   AX 65/8–1 Columbia 67161/2D, L1231/2
Sonata No. 9, in A, Op. 47 "Kreutzer" vln & pf*
  with W. Murdoch pf   AX 71/4 Columbia 67051/2D, L1210/1
(3) Trios, Op. 1 pf, vln & vlc
  No. 3. Trio No. 3, in c: Andante cantabile con variazioni (2nd mvt)
  with W. Murdoch pf &   76983   Columbia L1225
  W.H. Squire vlc
  No. 3. Trio No. 3, in c: Menuetto; Quasi Allegro (3rd mvt)
  with W. Murdoch pf &   AX 51   Columbia L1521
  W.H. Squire vlc

BOCCHERINI

(6) Quintets, Op. 13 2 vlns, vla & 2 vlcs
  No. 5. Quintet No. 5, in E: Minuetto (3rd mvt) "Bull" arr. str qt
  (as leader of Catterall   AX 2544 Columbia 9252
  string quartet)

BRAHMS

(21) Hungarian Dances pf duet
  Hungarian dance No. 2, in d arr. vln & pf Joachim
  with piano   AX 2307 Columbia 9439
  Hungarian dance No. 3, in F arr. vln & pf Joachim
  with piano   A 4621 Columbia 4832, D1579, J5012
(2) Quartets, Op. 51 2 vlns, vla & vlc
  No. 1. Quartet No. 1, in c: Allegro (1st mvt)
  (as leader of   Cc 3109/10^{II} HMV D791
  Catterall string quartet)
  No. 1. Quartet No. 1, in c: Finale: Allegro (4th mvt)
  (as leader of Catterall   Cc 3111/2^{II} HMV D794
  string quartet)
Quartet No. 3, in B flat, Op. 67 2 vlns, vla & vlc
  Agitato (3rd mvt)
  (as leader of Catterall   Cc 675^I HMV D594
  string quartet)
Sonata No. 3, in d, Op. 108 vln & pf
  with W. Murdoch pf   AX 59/60   Columbia 67133/5D, (set M24),
                                        L1535/7
Trio in E flat, Op. 40 hrn, pf & vln
  Scherzo (2nd mvt); **Finale** (4th mvt) arr. pf, vln & vlc
  with W. Murdoch pf &   AX 59/60 Columbia 67089D, L1602
  W.H. Squire vlc

* Abridged.

COLERIDGE–TAYLOR

Sonata in d, Op. 28 vln & pf
  with W. Murdoch pf   AX 77/80 Columbia L1396/7

DEBUSSY

Quartet in g, Op. 10 (1893) 2 vlns, vla & vlc
  Andantino doucement expressif (3rd mvt)
  (as leader of Catterall   Cc 1304^{II} HMV D651
  string quartet)

DITTERSDORF

Sonata in E flat vln & pf – arr. Catterall
  Allegro (1st mvt)
  with piano   WA 3443   Columbia 4825, 01051, D1584,
                                        J5023

DVOŘÁK

Trio No. 4, in e, Op. 90 "Dumky" 2 vlns, pf & vlc
  Lento maestoso (1st mvt);
  with W. Murdoch pf &   AX 57/8 Columbia 67090D, L1588
  W.H. Squire vlc

ELGAR

(2) Chansons, Op. 15 vln & pf
  No. 1. Chanson de nuit
  with piano   Cc 17119^{IV} △   HMV C1839
  No. 2. Chanson du matin
  with piano   Cc 17120 ^{II}△   HMV C1839

FRANCK

Sonata in A (1886) vln & pf
  Allegretto ben moderato (1st mvt)
  with W. Murdoch pf   AX 75   Columbia L1149
  Allegro (2nd mvt)
  with W. Murdoch pf   AX 76   Columbia L1149
Sonata in A (1886) vln & pf
        AX 229/34 & 413/4* Columbia 67164/7D, (set M33)
  with W. Murdoch pf

GLINKA

Quartet in F (1830) 2 vlns, vla & vlc
  Minuet (3rd mvt)
  (as leader of Catterall   Cc 676^I HMV D646
  string quartet)

GODARD

Concerto No. 1, Op. 35 "Concerto Romantique" vln & orch.
  Canzonetta (2nd mvt)
  with piano   Columbia D1458

GOLDMARK

Concerto in a, Op. 28 vln & orch.
  Adagio (2nd mvt) "Air"
  with piano   AX 2734   Columbia 9610

HAYDN

(6) Quartets, Op. 76 (H.III, Nos. 75/80) 2 vlns, vla & vlc
  No. 1. Quartet No. 75, in G: Allegro con spirito (1st mvt) H. III, No. 75
  (as leader of Catterall   Cc 674^{II} HMV D594
  string quartet)

* Matrix numbers not in sequence relative to sides.

HAYDN – *Continued*

No. 5. Quartet No. 79, in D: Largo (2nd mvt) H.III, No. 79
(as leader of Catterall   Cc 183[I]   HMV D562
string quartet)

(31) Trios, H.XV, Nos. 1/31 pf, vln & vlc
Trio No. 25, in G: Rondo all' ongarese (3rd mvt) H.XV, No. 25 (Op. 73, No. 2)
with W. Murdoch pf &   76990/1–A   Columbia 67014D, L1324
W.H. Squire vlc

HOWELLS

Lady Audrey's Suite, Op. 19 (1916) 2 vlns, vla & vlc
The little girl & the old shepherd
(as leader of Catterall   Cc 1305[II]   HMV D646
string quartet)

IRELAND

Sonata No. 2, in a (1917) vln & pf
with W. Murdoch pf   AX 81/4   Columbia L1322/3

KREISLER

Allegretto (Boccherini) vln & pf
with piano   71290   Columbia 3101

Sicilienne & Rigaudon (Francoeur) vln & pf
with piano   AX 2727   Columbia 9610

Tempo di minuetto (Pugnani) vln & pf
with piano   A 4620   Columbia 4832, D1579, J5012

LACROIX

Aubade d'avril pf, vln & vlc
with W. Murdoch pf &   76031   Columbia L1324
W.H. Squire vlc

LIADOV

(Les) Vendredis "Fridays" pf
No. 3. Polka in D
(as leader of Catterall string quartet)   Columbia 9156

MENDELSSOHN

Quartet No. 2, in a, Op. 13 2 vlns, vla & vlc
Intermezzo (3rd mvt)
(as leader of Catterall string quartet)   Columbia 50229D

Trio No. 1, in d, Op. 49 pf, vln & vlc
Andante con moto tranquillo (2nd mvt)
with W. Murdoch pf &   AX 53   Columbia 67097D, L1486
W.H. Squire vlc

Scherzo (3rd mvt)
with W. Murdoch pf &   AX 54   Columbia 67097D, L1486
W.H. Squire vlc

Trio No. 2, in c, Op. 66 pf, vln & vlc
Andante expressivo (2nd mvt); **Scherzo** (3rd mvt)
with W. Murdoch pf &   76987/8   Columbia L1343
W.H. Squire vlc

MOZART

Ave verum corpus, K618 cho – arr. str qt
(as leader of Catterall   AX 2541   Columbia 9244, 50075D, 5128M,
string quartet)   J3052

Concerto No. 5, in A, K219 "Turkish" vln & orch.
with Hallé   AX 400/7   Columbia 67055/8D, (set M11),
Orch. – Harty   L1592/5

MOZART – *Continued*

Divertimento No. 17, in D, K334 2 hrns & strs
   Minuet (3rd mvt) arr. vln & pf Burmester
   with piano   Bb 17121[II]△   HMV B3216, GW585

Quartet No. 14, in G, K387 2 vlns, vla & vlc
   Allegro vivace assai (1st mvt)
   (as leader of Catterall   Cc 182[II]   HMV D560
   string quartet)

Quartet No. 15, in d, K421 2 vlns, vla & vlc
   Menuetto allegretto (3rd mvt)
   (as leader of Catterall string quartet)   HMV D630

Sonata No. 34, in A, K526 vln & pf
   with H. Harty pf   76961/6   Columbia 67139/41D, L1494/6

Trio No. 4, in E, K542 pf, vln & vlc
   Andante grazioso (2nd mvt)
   with W. Murdoch pf &   AX 50   Columbia L1521
   W.H. Squire vlc

NOVÁČEK

(8) Concert Caprices, Op. 5 vln & pf
   No. 4. Perpetum mobile
   with piano   Columbia D1458

Quartet in e, Op. 10 2 vlns, vla & vlc
   Andante (2nd mvt)
   (as leader of Catterall string quartet)   HMV D630

PAGANINI

(24) Caprices, Op. 1 (1801/7) solo vln
   Caprice No. 13, in B flat, arr. vln & pf Catterall
   with piano   Bb 17374[I]   HMV B3216, GW585

RAFF

(6) Pieces, Op. 85 vln & pf
   No. 3. Cavatina in D
   with piano   AX 2726   Columbia 9439, 50089D

SCHUBERT

(6) Moments musicaux, Op. 94 (D780) (1823/7) pf
   No. 3. Moment musicale No. 3, in f "Air russe" arr. str qt
   (as leader of Catterall   AX 2542   Columbia 9244, 50075D, 5128M,
   string quartet)   J3052

Trio No. 1, in B flat, Op. 99 (D898) pf, vln & vlc
   Scherzo (3rd mvt)
   with W. Murdoch pf &   AX 52   Columbia L1567
   W.H. Squire vlc

SCHUMANN

Fantasiestücke, Op. 88 pf. vln & vlc
   Duett (3rd mvt); **Finale** (4th mvt)
   with W. Murdoch pf &   AX 55/6   Columbia 69097D, L1503
   W.H. Squire vlc

(13) Kinderscenen, Op. 15 pf
   No. 7. Träumerei arr. str qt
   (as leader of Catterall   AX 2542   Columbia 9244, 50075D, 5128M,
   string quartet)   J3052

(3) Quartets, Op. 41 2 vlns, vla & vlc
   No. 2. Quartet No. 2, in E: Andante, quasi variazioni (2nd mvt)
   (as leader of Catterall   Cc 678[II]   HMV D597
   string quartet)

SPOHR

(3) Duets, Op. 39 2 vlns
  No. 1. Duet No. 1, in D: Presto (3rd mvt)
  with J.S. Bridge vln   AX 408   Columbia 67068D, L1615

TANEIEV

Quartet No. 4, in a, Op. 11 2 vlns, vla & vlc
  Scherzo (3rd mvt)
  (as leader of Catterall   Cc 1303^I HMV D651
  string quartet)

TCHAIKOVSKY

Quartet No. 1, in D, Op. 11 2 vlns, vla & vlc
  Andante cantabile (2nd mvt)
            AX 1621 & 1627   Columbia 9203, J3024
  (as leader of Catterall string quartet)

Quartet No. 2, in F, Op. 22 2 vlns, vla & vlc
  Scherzo (2nd mvt)
  (as leader of Catterall   Cc 679^I HMV D597
  string quartet)

Quartet No. 2, in F, Op. 22 2 vlns, vla & vlc
  Scherzo (2nd mvt)
  (as leader of Catterall string quartet)   HMV D950

Trio in a, Op. 50 "To the memory of a great artist" pf, vln & vlc
  with W. Murdoch   WAX 2311/22 Columbia 67337/42D, (set M73),
  pf & W.H. Squire vlc   L1942/7, J7013/8

WIENIAWSKI

Légende, Op. 17 vln & pf or orch.
  with piano   AX 2724/5 Columbia 9359

Cesare CAVALCABO

GOUNOD

Ave Maria (Méditation on Bach's "Prelude No. 1, in C" from Book I of "Das Wohltemperirte Clavier") v & pf – arr. vln & org
  with W. Marti org   cd 141–T^I Antrochord AK10001

MASSENET

Thaïs (1894) – opera
  Méditation arr. vln & pf Marsick
  with W. Marti org   cd 142–T^{II} Antrochord AK10002

Jaroslav ČELEDA (1890–)

KUBELÍK

Canzonetta vln & pf
  with J. Heller pf   Ultraphon D23314

Minuet vln & pf
  with J. Heller pf   Ultraphon D23314

Margherita CERADINI

BONPORTI

(12) Sonatas, Op. 1 (1696) 2 vlns & vlc ob
  Sonata No. 3, in g (rev. Barblan)
  with A. Redditi vln & R. Caruana vlc   Carisch BCA7017

BRESCIANELLO

(12) Concerti 2 vlns & c
  Concerto No. 1, in B flat, (rev. Damerini)
  with A. Redditi vln, N. Poli hpsi &   Carisch BCA7017
  R. Caruana vlc

CORELLI

(12) Sonatas, Op. 2 (1685) 2 vlns & c
  Sonata No. 4, in e (rev. Allorto)
  with A. Redditi vln, N. Poli hpsi &   Carisch BCA7017
  R. Caruana vlc

MOZART

Serenade No. 6, in D, K239 "Serenata Notturna" orch.
  with A. Redditi vln & Angelicum   Angelicum LPA989
  Orch., Milan – Zecchi

TARTINI

Concerto in a, D115 (C76) 3 vlns, strs & c
  with B. Salvi vln, G. Bozzini vln &   Angelicum LPA5921
  Angelicum Orch., Milan – Abbado

Sinfonia pastorale in D vln & strs
  with Angelicum Orch. – Bruni   Angelicum LPA1059
                      Harmonia Mundi HM30106

TORELLI

(12) Concerti, Op. 8 (1709) Nos. 1/6: 2 vlns, strs & c – 7/12: vln, strs & c
  Concerto No. 1, in C
  with A. Redditi vln & Angelicum   Angelicum LPA1003
  Orch., Milan – Maderna
  Concerto No. 3, in E
  with A. Redditi vln & Angelicum   Angelicum LPA1003
  Orch., Milan – Maderna

VIOTTI

(3) Duets, Op. 29 2 vlns & orch.
  No. 2. Duo concertante No. 2, in d (arr. Quaranta)
  with N. Pignatelli vln & Angelicum   Angelicum LPA966
  Orch., Milan – Janes

VIVALDI

(12) Concerti, Op. 3 "L'Estro armonico" var. cbns & strs
  Concerto No. 10, in b, P.148 (F.IV, No. 10) 4 vlns, strs & c
  with B. Salvi vln, A. Stefanato vln, C.   Angelicum LPA5911, STA8911
  Ferraresi vln & Angelicum Orch.,   Harmonia Mundi HM30664
  Milan – Zedda

(12) Concerti, Op. 9 (1728) "La Cetra" vln, strs & c
  Concerto No. 3, in g, P.339 (F.I, No. 52)
  with Angelicum Orch., Milan – de   Angelicum LPA1061
  Stoutz

Concerto in D, P.188 (F.IV, No. 4) 2 vlns, 2 vlcs, strs & c
  with A. Redditi vln, R. Caruana vlc, S.   Angelicum LPA1066
  Busetto vlc & Angelicum Orch., Milan
  – Lupi

Concerto in d, F.XII, No. 31 (Op. 41, No. 1) 2 fls, 2 obs, bsn, 2 vlns, strs & c – rev. Malipiero
  with G. Tassinari fl, C. Hoogendoorn   Angelicum LPA5929
  fl, L. Caroli ob, G. Cappello ob, V.
  Menghini bsn, B. Salvi vln, &
  Angelicum Orch., Milan – Suvini

VIVALDI – *Continued*

Concerto in e vln, strs & c
    with Angelicum Orch. Milan – de   Angelicum LPA1061
    Stoutz

Friedrich CERHA (1926–   )

CERHA

Formation & Solution vln & pf
    with I. Eröd pf   Amadeo AVRS5019

Montserrat CERVERA

VIVALDI

(12) Concerti, Op. 3 "L'Estro armonico" var. cbns & strs
    Concerto No. 9, in D, P.147 (F.I, No. 178) vln, strs & c
    with I Musici   Angel 35087
    Columbia CX1170, FCX304,
    QCX10038
    HMV LALP210

Louis CESANO

BRAHMS

(16) Waltzes, Op. 39 pf duet
    No. 15. Waltz No. 15 in A flat arr. vln & pf "in A" Hochstein
    with G. Andolfi pf   Pathé PA495

TCHAIKOVSKY

(The) Months (12 Characteristic pieces) Op. 37a pf
    No. 6. Barcarolle (June) arr. vln & pf Forbes
    with G. Andolfi pf   Pathé PA495

TOSELLI

Serenade, Op. 6 vln & pf
    with orch.   Pathé 8021

TOSTI

(The) Last kiss (Dernier Baiser) v & pf – arr. vln & orch.
    with orch.   Pathé 8021

Eleves de Marcel CHAILLEY (1891–1936)

DESPLANES

Intrada (Adagio) vln & c – arr. vln & pf Nachèz
    with organ   Lumen 30063

PUGNANI

(6) Sonatas, Op. 8 vln & c
    Sonata No. 3, in D: Largo expressivo (2nd mvt) arr. vln & pf Moffat
    with organ   Lumen 30063

Albert CHAMBERLAND (1886–   )

BALL

Let the rest of the world go by (1919) v & pf – arr. vln & pf
    with piano   Victor 216243

HIRSCH

Mary (1920) – musical
    The love nest arr. vln & pf Kreisler
    with piano   Victor 216243

Jean CHAMPEIL (1910–   )

BACH

(3) Sonatas & 3 Partitas, BWV1001/6 solo vln
    Sonata No. 1, in g: Adagio (1st mvt); **Siciliano** (3rd mvt) BWV1001
    (unaccompanied)   Vega C30 S208
    Partita No. 1, in b: Allemande (1st mvt); **Sarabande** (5th mvt); **Bourrée**
    (7th mvt) BWV1002
    (unaccompanied)   Vega C30 S208
    Sonata No. 2, in a: Grave (1st mvt); **Andante** (3rd mvt) BWV1003
    (unaccompanied)   Vega C30 S208
    Partita No. 2, in d: Allemande (1st mvt); **Sarabande** (3rd mvt)
    BWV1004
    (unaccompanied)   Vega C30 S208
    Sonata No. 3, in C: Adagio (1st mvt); **Largo** (3rd mvt) BWV1005
    (unaccompanied)   Vega C30 S208
    Partita No. 3, in E: Preludio (1st mvt); **Loure** (2nd mvt); **Gavotte en**
    Rondeau (3rd mvt); **2 Menuets** (4th mvt) BWV1006
    (unaccompanied)   Vega C30 S208

RAVEL

Quartet in F (1910) 2 vlns, vla & vlc
    (as leader of Champeil string quartet)   Club français du Disque 32
SCHMITT   Saturn LP7001
Quartet, Op. 112 (1912) 2 vlns, vla & vlc
    (as leader of Champeil string quartet)   Pathé DTX232

VIVALDI

(12) Concerti, Op. 3 "L'Estro armonico" var. cbns & strs
    Concerto No. 1, in D, P.146 (F.IV, No. 8) 4 vlns, vlc, strs & c
    with L. Yordanoff vln, L. Gali vln,   Ducretet–Thomson LAG1014
    R. Gendre vln & Pro Musica
    Orch. – Saguer
    Concerto No. 7, in F, P.249 (F.IV, No. 9) 4 vlns, strs & c
    with L. Yordanoff vln, L. Gali vln,   Ducretet–Thomson LAG1014
    R. Gendre vln & Pro Musica Orch. –
    Saguer
    Concerto in B flat, P.349 vln, strs & c
    with Pro Musica Orch. – Saguer   Ducretet–Thomson LAG1014

Roland CHARMY (1908–   )

BARLOW

Sonatina fl, vln & pf
    with J–P. Rampal fl & G. Joy pf   Erato 20173

BERG

Chamber Concerto (1925) vln, pf & 13 w–wnds)
    M6–121893, 121702/3, 121803/4,   Classic C2107/12, CL6098
    121806, 121815/6, 121805, 121818,   Dial LP9
    with J. Monod pf & 121817 & 121819   Esquire TW4–004/9
    Paris Chamber Wind   Felsted L89004
    Ensemble – Leibowitz

BRAGA

(7) Melodies (1867) v & pf
  No. 5. La serenata "Angel's serenade" arr. vln & pf
  with piano   HMV K6135

CHOPIN

(3) Nocturnes, Op. 9 pf
  No. 2. Nocturne No. 2, in E flat arr. vln & pf Sarasate
  with piano   HMV L937

DRIGO

(Les) Millions d'Arlequin (1900) – ballet orch.
  Sérénade arr. vln & pf Auer
  with piano   HMV K6135

HAHN

O Mon bel Inconnu (1933)
  Est–ce qu'il est mal arr. s, vln & orch.
  with S. Simon s & orch. – Cariven   Columbia DF1357

HAYDN

Sinfonia concertante in B flat, Op. 84 (H.I, No. 105) (1792) vln, ob, vlc, bsn & orch.
  with M. Morel ob, A. Navarra vlc,   L'Oiseau–Lyre OL83/5
  F. Oubradous bsn & Paris
  Conservatory Orch. – Munch

IBERT

Trio (1944) vln, vlc & hp
  with C. Bartsch vlc & J. Ibert hp   Pathé DTX167

KREISLER

Sicilienne & Rigaudon (Francoeur) vln & pf
  with piano   HMV L937

MOZART

Sonata No. 21, in e, K304 vln & pf
  with V. Perlemuter pf   Pathé DTX196

SAINT–SAËNS

(Le) Déluge, Op. 45 (1876) – oratorio
  Prélude
  with Lamoureux Orch. – Wolff   Brunswick 90339
                                               Polydor 566164

Havanaise, Op. 83 vln & orch.
  with piano   HMV L850

SAUVEPLANE

Habanéra vln & pf
  with J. Manuel pf   Le Chant du Monde 518

STRAVINSKY

Ragtime (1918) fl, cl, hrn, tpt, tbn, cym, cymb, 2 vlns, vla & cbs
  with L. Lavailotte fl,   CLX 1810–1 Columbia 68300D, LFX357,
  Godeau cl, J. Deveny hrn, E. Foveau   LX382
  tpt, R. Tudesq tbn, . Racz cym,
  M. Morel ob, H. Volant vln, E. Ginot
  vla & . Juste cbs – cond. Stravinsky

Joachim CHASSMAN

GRIFFIS

Sonata (1931) vln & pf
  with E. Griffis pf   Educo 4008

CHAUSOW

VAUGHAN WILLIAMS

(The) Lark ascending (1914) vln & orch
  with Utah Symphony   Candide CE31052
  Orch. – Abravanel

Michel CHAUVETON (1929–)

BARTÓK

(6) Rumanian folk dances (1915) pf – arr. vln & pf Székely
  with B. Anderson pf   Lumen LD1–427

BRAHMS

(16) Waltzes, Op. 39 pf duet
  No. 15. Waltz No. 15, in A flat arr. vln & pf "in A" Hochstein
  with B. Anderson pf   Lumen LD1–426

DEBUSSY

Suite Bergamasque (1890) pf
  No. 3. Clair de lune arr. vln & pf Roelens
  with C. Masson pf   Lumen LD1–450

DVOŘÁK

(8) Humoresques, Op. 101 pf
  No. 7. Humoresque No. 7, in G flat arr. vln & pf "in G" Kreisler
  with B. Anderson pf   Lumen LD1–442

FAURÉ

Berceuse, Op. 16 vln & pf
  with B. Anderson   Lumen LD1–426

Sonata No. 1, in A, Op. 13 vln & pf
  with B. Smith pf   Allegro ALG3032

GLUCK

Orphée et Eurydice (1762) – opera
  Dance of the blessed spirits: Lento "Mélodie" (No. 2) arr. vln & pf
  Kreisler
  with B. Anderson pf   Lumen LD1–442

HANDEL

Serse (1738) – opera
  Ombra mai fu "Largo" arr. vln & pf
  with C. Masson pf   Lumen LD1–450

HAYDN

Concerto in F, H.XVIII, No. 6 (1765) clav, vln & orch.
  with R. Puyana hpsi & French   Lumen LD2444
  Chamber Orch. – Michon

KREISLER

Liebesfreud vln & pf
  with B. Anderson pf   Lumen LD1–442

Rondino on a theme by Beethoven vln & pf
  with C. Masson pf   Lumen LD1–450

KREISLER – *Continued*

Schön Rosmarin vln & pf
  with B. Anderson pf   Lumen LD1–425

LALO

Sonata in D, Op. 12 vln & pf
  with B. Smith pf   Allegro ALG3032

LEGUERNEY

Sonatina vln & pf
  with J–M. Damase pf   Lumen LD3441

MASSENET

Thaïs (1894) – opera
  Méditation arr. vln & pf Marsick
  with B. Anderson pf   Lumen LD1–425

MENDELSSOHN

(6) Songs without words, Op. 62 pf
  No. 1. Song without words No. 25, in G "May breezes" arr. vln & pf Kreisler
  with C. Masson pf   Lumen LD1–451
  No. 6. Song without words No. 30, in A "Spring song" arr. vln & pf
  with B. Anderson pf   Lumen LD1–426

MOZART

Divertimento No. 17, in D, K334 2 hrns & strs
  Minuet (3rd mvt) arr. vln & pf Burmester
  with C. Masson pf   Lumen LD1–451

POLDINI

(7) Marionnettes pf
  No. 2. Poupée valsante arr. vln & pf Kreisler
  with C. Masson pf   Lumen LD1–450

RIMSKY–KORSAKOV

Sadko (1898) – opera
  Chant hindou arr. vln & pf Kreisler
  with B. Anderson pf   Lumen LD1–442

SAINT–SAËNS

(Le) Déluge, Op. 45 (1876) – oratorio
  Prélude vln & orch. – arr. vln & pf Saint–Saëns
  with B. Anderson pf   Lumen LD1–425

SCHUBERT

(7) Gesänge (set to Scott's "Lady of the Lake") Op. 52 v & pf
  No. 6. Ave Maria, D839 arr. vln & pf Wilhelmj
  with C. Masson pf   Lumen LD1–451
(6) Moments musicaux, Op. 94 (D780) (1823/7) pf
  No. 3. Moment musicale No. 3, in f "Air russe" arr. vln & pf Kreisler
  with B. Anderson pf   Lumen LD1–426
Rosamunde von Cypern, Op. 26 (D797), (1823) – Incidental music orch.
  No. 9. Ballet music II, in G arr. vln & pf Kreisler
  with B. Anderson pf   Lumen LD1–442

SCHUMANN

(13) Kinderscenen, Op. 15 pf
  No. 7. Träumerei arr. vln & pf
  with B. Anderson pf   Lumen LD1–426
Sonata No. 1, in a, Op. 105 vln & pf
  with J–M. Damase pf   Lumen LD3441

TCHAIKOVSKY

(3) Souvenirs de Hapsal, Op. 2 pf
  No. 3. Chant sans paroles in f arr. vln & pf
  with B. Anderson pf   Lumen LD1–442

THOMÉ

Simple aveu, Op. 25 pf – arr. vln & pf
  with C. Masson pf   Lumen LD1–451

TOSELLI

Serenade, Op. 6 vln & pf
  with B. Anderson pf   Lumen LD1–425

Renée CHEMET (1888–   )

ACKERNLEY

(A) Dream song v & pf – arr. vln & pf
  with H. Craxton pf   Bb 1635[II]   HMV DA539

d'AMBROSIO

Romance in D, Op. 9 vln & pf
  with piano   HMV DB864
                                         Victor 6473

ANONYMOUS

(The) Holly bush traditional tune – arr. vln & pf Newton
  with I. Newton pf   HMV 5–7928, DA416

BACH

(3) Sonatas & 3 Partitas, BWV1001/6 solo vln
  Partita No. 1, in b: Bourrée (7th mvt) arr. vln & hpsi Moffat
  with M. Delcourt hpsi   HMV 5–7907
                                         Victor 66063

BARNS

Swing song vln & pf
  with I. Newton pf   HMV 5–7929

BARTLETT

(A) Dream (1895) v & pf – arr. vln & pf
  with piano   HMV DA1106

BEETHOVEN

Romance No. 1, in G, Op. 40 vln & orch.
  with piano   HMV DB760

BOROWSKI

Adoration (1903) vln & pf
  with piano   HMV DB864
                                         Victor 6473

Adoration (1903) vln & pf
  with A. Seidlova pf   HMV DB1444
                                         Victor 7253

CHABRIER

(5) Pièces posthumes (1891) pf
  No. 4. Feuillet d'album arr. vln & pf
  with M. Delcourt pf   Bb 8867[III]△   HMV DA812

CHOPIN

(3) Nocturnes, Op. 9 pf
  No. 2. Nocturne No. 2, in E flat arr. vln & pf Sarasate
  with piano   HMV DB686

DRDLA

Souvenir vln & pf
  with M. Delcourt pf   Bb 8898^{II}△   HMV DA811

DVOŘÁK

(7) Gypsy songs, Op. 55 v & pf
  No. 4. Songs my mother taught me arr. vln & pf Kreisler
  with M. Delcourt pf   Bb 2088^{III}   HMV DA539

FALLA

(7) Canciones populares españolas (1914) v & pf
  No. 1. El paño moruno arr. vln & pf Kochański
  with M. Delcourt pf   Bb 8887^{IV}△   HMV DA814
  No. 4. Jota arr. vln & pf Kochański
  with M. Delcourt pf   Bb 8890^I△   HMV DA814

FIBICH

Images, Impressions & Souvenirs, Op. 41 pf
  No. 14. Poem (from "Souvenirs" Part IV) arr. vln & pf Kubelík
  with H. Craxton pf   Bb 1636^{II}   HMV DA419

FIELD

Waltz unid pf – arr. vln & hp
  with harp   HMV 5–7908

FORSTER

Rose in the bud vln & pf
  with H. Kaufman pf   Victor 1132

GODARD

Jocelyn (1888) – opera
  Cachés dans cet asile "Berceuse" arr. vln & pf
  with piano   HMV DB855

GOLDMARK

Concerto in a, Op. 28 vln & orch.
  Andante (2nd mvt) "Air"
  with piano   HMV DB687

GORDON

One little dream of love v & pf – arr. vln & pf
  with H. Kaufman pf   Victor 1132

GROVLEZ

(6) Mélodies sur les poèmes de Henri Bataille pf
  No. 2. Berceuse arr. vln & pf
  with M. Delcourt pf   Bb 8868^{III}△   HMV DA812

HANDEL

(15) Sonatas, Op. 1 (?1731) fl or vln & c
  Sonata No. 3, in A: Andante (1st mvt); **Allegro** (2nd mvt) vln I
  with piano   HMV DB964
  Sonata No. 15, in E: Adagio (1st mvt); **Allegro** (2nd mvt) vln VI
  with piano   HMV DB855
                                                 Victor 6497

d'HARDELOT

Because (1902) v & pf – arr. vln & pf
  with A. Seidlova pf   HMV DA1231

HAYDN

Sonata No. 3, in C, H.XVI, No. 3 pf
  Minuet (3rd mvt) arr. vln & pf Hartmann
  with H. Kaufman pf   A 33771△   HMV DB888, DB910ª
                                              Victor 6609

Symphony No. 96, in D (1791) "Miracle" orch.
  Minuet (3rd mvt) arr. vln & pf Burmester
  with G. Moore pf   Bb 3262^{II}   HMV DA530

HERBERT

Bandinage pf – arr. vln & pf Chemet
  with piano   Victor 26602

(The) Fortune Teller (1898) – operetta
  Gypsy love song arr. vln & pf
  with A. Seidlova pf & cymbalam   Victor 1402

Mademoiselle Modiste (1905) – operetta
  Kiss me again arr. vln & pf
  with A. Seidlova pf & cymbalam   Victor 1402

Sweethearts (1913) – operetta
  Selection (unid) arr. vln & pf
  with piano   Victor 26602

de KOVEN

Oh! Promise me (1889) v & pf – arr. vln & pf
  with A. Seidlova pf   Victor 1328

KREISLER

Chanson Louis XIII et Pavane (L. Couperin) vln & pf
  with piano   HMV DB686

Praeludium & Allegro (Pugnani) vln & pf
  with M. Delcourt pf   HMV 3–07920, DB472

LALO

Concerto in F, Op. 20 (1872) vln & orch.
  Romance (2nd mvt)
  with H. Craxton pf   HMV 3–07935, DB474

Symphonie espagnole, Op. 21 vln & orch.
  Allegro non troppo (1st mvt)
  with H. Craxton pf   HMV 3–07937, DB473
  Scherzando (2nd mvt)
  with H. Craxton pf   HMV 3–07936, DB473
  Rondo allegro (5th mvt)
  with H. Craxton pf   HMV 3–07938, DB474

LIEURANCE

By the waters of the Minnetonka (1914) v & pf – arr. vln & pf
  with A. Seidlova pf   A 29428△   HMV DA871
                                              Victor 66259, 1015, 1228

MacMURROUGH

Macushla (1910) v & pf – arr. vln & pf
  with piano   HMV DA1106

MARSHALL

I hear you calling me v & pf – arr. vln & pf
  with piano   Victor 1291

MASSENET

Thaïs (1894) – opera
  Méditation arr. vln & pf Marsick
  with M. Delcourt pf   HMV 3–07939, DB472

MENDELSSOHN

(6) Songs without words, Op. 62 pf
  No. 6. Song without words No. 30, in A "Spring song" arr. vln & pf
  with A. Seidlova pf   Victor 1242

MIYAGI

Haru no umi (The sea in springtime) (1929) v & pf – arr. vln & pf Chemet
  with A. Seidlova pf   HMV DA1314

MOYA

(The) Song of songs (1914) v & pf – arr. vln & pf
  with A. Seidlova pf   HMV DA1231

MOZART

Concerto No. 6, in E flat, K268* vln & orch.
  with H. Craxton pf   HMV DB688 & DB692

Serenade No. 7, in D, K250 "Haffner" orch.
  Rondo (4th mvt) arr. vln & pf Kreisler
  with A. Loesser pf   HMV 3–07967, DB687
                            Victor 6497

  Rondo (4th mvt) arr. vln & pf Kreisler
  with A. Seidlova pf   HMV DB1444
                            Victor 7253

PIERNÉ

Sérénade in A, Op. 7 (1875) pf – arr. vln & pf Haddock
  with I. Newton pf   HMV 5–7930, DA418
Sérénade in A, Op. 7 (1875) pf – arr. vln & pf Haddock
  with A. Seidlova pf   A 41713△ HMV DA955
                            Victor 1302

POLDINI

(7) Marionnettes pf
  No. 2. Poupée valsante arr. vln & pf Kreisler
  with M. Delcourt pf   Bb 8899ᴵᴵᴵ△ HMV DA811

SAINT–SAËNS

Introduction & Rondo Capriccioso, Op. 28 vln & orch.
              Cc 6789ᴵ△ & 6790ᴵᴵ△ HMV DB887
  with H. Craxton pf   Victor 7587

SIMONETTI

Madrigale pf – arr. vln & pf
  with G. Moore pf   Bb 3361ᴵ HMV DA530

TARTINI

(12) Sonatas, Op. 1 (1734) vln & c
  Sonata No. 10, in g "Didone abbandonata"
  with M. Delcourt pf   HMV 3–07917, 3–07921,
                            & 5–7931, DA417, DB475
                            Victor 74751/2, 6349 & 66076,
                            613

* Abridged.

TCHAIKOVSKY

(6) Pieces, Op. 19 pf
  No. 4. Nocturne in c sharp arr. vln & pf Hartmann
  with H. Kaufman pf   A 33770△ HMV DB888, DB910
                            Victor 6609

THOMÉ

Sous la feuillée, Op. 29 pf – arr. vln & pf
  with A. Seidlova pf   A 29429△ HMV DA871
                            Victor 66260, 1015, 1228

TOSELLI

Serenade, Op. 6 vln & pf
  with A. Seidlova pf   A 41712△ HMV DA955
                            Victor 1302

VIEUXTEMPS

(6) Voix Intimes, Op. 45 vln & pf
  No. 5. Sérénité
  with H. Kaufman pf   Victor 1242

VIVALDI

(12) Concerti, Op. 3 "L'Estro armonico" var. cbns & strs
  Concerto No. 6, in a: Largo (2nd mvt) P.1 (F.I, No. 176) arr. vln & pf
  Nachèz
  with H. Craxton pf   HMV DA417
  Concerto No. 6, in a, P.1 (F.I, No. 176)
  with piano   HMV DB761

WEBER

(18) Favoritenwalzer, J.143/60 (1812) pf
  No. 5. Waltz No. 5, in B flat, J147 arr. vln & pf Burmester
  with M. Delcourt pf   HO 5783ᴵ AE HMV 5–7905
                            Victor 66043, 613

WIENIAWSKI

Polonaise brillante No. 1, in D, Op. 4 vln & pf
  with piano   HMV DB964

WOOD

Love's garden of roses v & pf – arr. vln & pf
  with A. Seidlova pf   Victor 1328
Roses of Piccardy (1916) v & pf – arr. vln & pf
  with A. Seidlova pf   Victor 1291

Ivan CHENSKI

DRDLA

Souvenir vln & pf
  with piano   Madison 14015

DVOŘÁK

(8) Humoresques, Op. 101 pf
  No. 7. Humoresque No. 7, in G flat arr. vln & pf "in G" Kreisler
  with piano   Madison 14015

Gregor CHERNIAVSKY

DRIGO

(2) Airs de Ballet orch.
  No. 2. Valse bluette arr. vln & pf Auer
with piano   Pathé 999

(Les) Millions d'Arlequin (1900) – ballet orch.
  Sérénade arr. vln & pf Auer
with piano   Pathé 999

DVOŘÁK

(8) Humoresques, Op. 101 pf
  No. 7. Humoresque No. 7, in G flat arr. vln & pf "in G" Kreisler
with piano   Pathé 82, 8920, 9546, 79073

RAFF

(6) Pieces, Op. 85 vln & pf
  No. 3. Cavatina in D
with piano   Pathé 999

TCHAIKOVSKY

Swan Lake, Op. 20 (1875/6) – ballet orch.
  Russian dance arr. vln & pf
with piano   Pathé 82, 8921, 9545, 79072

Leo CHERNIAVSKY (1890–)

d'AMBROSIO

Canzonetta, Op. 6 vln & pf
with piano   Pathé 506, 3200, 79319

BOHM

(6) Miniatures, Op. 187 vln & pf
  No. 4. Perpetuum mobile
with piano   Pathé 506, 3200, 79311
(6) Pieces, Op. 314 vln & pf
  No. 3. Gavotte
with piano   Pathé 506, 3200, 79311

BRAHMS

(16) Waltzes, Op. 39 pf duet
  No. 15. Waltz No. 15, in A flat arr. vln & pf "in A" Hochstein
with piano   Columbia 0894

CHAMINADE

Sérénade espagnole pf – arr. vln & pf Kreisler
with piano   Columbia 0804

CHERNIAVSKY

Mazurka No. 5 vln & pf
with piano   Pathé 507, 3171, 9527, 79314

DVOŘÁK

(8) Humoresques, Op. 101 pf
  No. 7. Humoresque No. 7, in G flat arr. vln & pf "in G" Wilhelmj
with piano   Pathé 3170, 19536, 79073

ELGAR

Salut d'amour, Op. 12 orch. – arr. vln & pf Elgar
with piano   Pathé 505, 5526, 6331, 79309

ESPERON

(La) Baerachita (Mexican song) v & pf – arr. vln & Cherniavsky
with piano   Columbia 0895

GARDNER

(2) Pieces, Op. 5 vln & pf
  No. 1. From the canebrake
with piano   Columbia 0894

GOSSEC

Rosine (1786) – opera
  Gavotte arr. vln & pf Burmester
with piano   Pathé 506, 3200, 79311

HUBAY

(14) Scènes de la Csárda vln & pf
  No. 4. Hejre Kati, Op. 32
with piano   Pathé 505, 6331

KREISLER

Caprice viennois, Op. 2 vln & pf
with piano   Columbia 0895

LEHÁR

Frasquita (1923) – operetta
  Hab' ein blaues Himmelbett arr. vln & pf as "Serenade" by Kreisler
with piano   Columbia 0921

PADEREWSKI

(6) Humoresques de concert, Op. 14 pf
  No. 1. Minuet in G arr. vln & pf Kreisler
with J. Cherniavsky pf   A 3973   Columbia 0848, 3360R

SARASATE

(8) Danzas españolas vln & pf
  No. 8. Danza española No. 8, in C, Op. 26, No. 2
with piano   Pathé 507, 3171, 9527, 79313

TCHAIKOVSKY

Swan Lake, Op. 20 (1875/6) – ballet orch.
  Russian dance arr. vln & pf
with piano   Pathé 3170/1, 19536, 79072

Mikhail CHERNYKHOVSKY

BARTÓK

Rhapsody No. 1, in G (1928) vln & orch.
  with Moscow Radio Symphony   Mezhdunarodnaya Kniga
  Orch. – Rozhdestvensky   D024846, SM02299
Rhapsody No. 2, in d (1928) vln & orch.
  with Moscow Radio Symphony   Mezhdunarodnaya Kniga
  Orch. – Rozhdestvensky   D024846, SM02299

PROKOFIEV

Suite of Waltzes, Op. 110 (1946) pf – arr. orch.
  No. 1. Since I met you
  with Moscow Radio Symphony   Melodiya–Angel SR40075
  Orch. – Rozhdestvensky   Mezhdunarodnaya Kniga
                             D021013/4, S01581/2

PROKOFIEV – *Continued*

No. 3. Mephisto waltz
with Moscow Radio Symphony   Melodiya–Angel SR40075
Orch. – Rozhdestvensky   Mezhdunarodnaya Kniga
    D021013/4, S01581/2

SAVELYEV

Sports Suite orch.
No. 2. Figure skating
with V. Simon vlc, & Moscow Radio   Mezhdunarodnaya Kniga
Symphony Orch. – Jansons   D020568, S01590
No. 3. Yachting at night
with V. Simon vlc, & Moscow Radio   Mezhdunarodnaya Kniga
Symphony Orch. – Jansons   D020568, S01590

STRAUSS, R.

(Ein) Heldenleben, Op. 40 (1898) orch.
with Moscow Radio Large Symphony   Mezhdunarodnaya Kniga
Orch. – Rozhdestvensky   SM01985/6

TCHAIKOVSKY

Swan Lake, Op. 20 (1875/6) – ballet orch.
with O. Erdeli hp, V. Simon vlc, S.   HMV (Melodiya) SLS795/1–3
Gevorkian tpt & Moscow Radio
Symphony Orch. – Rozhdestvensky

Levon CHILINGIRIAN

SCHUBERT

(3) Sonatinas, Op. 137 (D384, D385 & D408) vln & pf
No. 1. Sonatina No. 1, in D, D.384
with C. Benson pf   Pearl SHE503
No. 2. Sonatina No. 2, in a, D385
with C. Benson pf   Pearl SHE503
No. 3. Sonatina No. 3, in g, D408
with C. Benson pf   Pearl SHE503

Niels Simon CHRISTIANSEN

LUMBYE

Concert–polka (1863) 2 vlns & orch.
with E. Kjeldsen vln & Royal Danish   Mercury MG50461, SR90461
Orch. – Hammelboe   Philips 839828GSY

Nicolas CHUMACHENKO (1944–)

STRAVINSKY

(L') Histoire du Soldat (1918) narrators, tpt, cbs, tbn, cl, vln, bsn & pcn
with G. Carrat narrator &   Erato STU70620
Instrumental ensemble – Dutoit

Kyung–Wha CHUNG (1948–)

SIBELIUS

Concerto in d, Op. 47 vln & orch.
with London Symphony   Decca SXL6493
Orch. – Previn   London CS6710

TCHAIKOVSKY

Concerto in D, Op. 35 vln & orch.
with London Symphony Orch. –   Decca SXL6493
Previn   London CS6710

Carlo Felice CILLARIO (1915–)

BACH

(3) Sonatas & 3 Partitas, BWV1001/6 solo vln
Partita No. 3, in E: Preludio (1st mvt) BWV1006
(unaccompanied)   2BA 4519[II]   HMV DB5409

CASELLA

Serenata, Op. 50 (1927) cl, bsn, tpt, vln & vlc
No. 6. Finale (Vivacissimo, alla napoletana) arr. vln & pf
with G. Simoncelli pf   HMV GW1703

DINICU

Hora staccato (1906) vln & pf – arr. Heifetz
with piano   HMV DA5412

LOGAN

Pale moon (1920) v & pf – arr. vln & pf Kreisler
with piano   HMV GW1427

MOZART

Sonata No. 26, in B flat, K378 vln & pf
with C. Mola hpsi   HMV DB5364/5

PAGANINI

(24) Caprices, Op. 1. (1801/7) solo vln
Caprice No. 24, in a arr. vln & pf Pilati
with piano   HMV DB5410

ROSSELINI

(La) Fontanna malata (1930) vln & pf
with G. Simoncelli pf   HMV GW1703

SAMMARTINI, G.

(6) Sonatas, Op. 1 2 vlns & c
Sonata No. 4, in A: Andante (3rd mvt) arr. vln & pf as "Canto amoroso"
by Elman
with piano   HMV DA5412

SARASATE

(8) Danzas españolas vln & pf
No. 4. Jota Navarra, Op. 22, No. 2
with G. Simoncelli pf   HMV S10472

SZYMANOWSKI

(3) Mythes, Op. 30 (1915) vln & pf
No. 1. La Fontaine d'Aréthuse
with G. Simoncelli pf   HMV S10472

VERACINI

(12) Sonatas, Op. 2 (1744) "Sonate accademiche" vln & c
Sonata No. 6, in A: Largo (2nd mvt) (ed. Corti)
with piano   2BA 4518[II]   HMV DB5409

Georgio CIOMPI

CHOPIN

Nocturne No. 20, in c sharp, Op. posth. pf – arr. vln & pf Milstein
with W. Baracchi pf   Cetra AT0202, T17008

LECLAIR

(12) Sonatas, Op. 2 – Book II (1728) vln & c
Sonata No. 3, in C
with H. Chessid hpsi & L. Rostal vlc   Concert Hall H9

PURCELL

(10) Sonatas, Z802/11 (1697) 4 parts – 2 vlns & c
Sonata No. 1, in b, Z802
with W. Torkanowsky vln, H. Chessid   Contrepoint MC20053
hpsi & G. Koutzen vlc   Dover HCR5224
                                         Period SPL572

Sonata No. 2, in E flat, Z803
with W. Torkanowsky vln, H. Chessid   Contrepoint MC20053
hpsi & G. Koutzen vlc   Dover HCR5224
                                         Period SPL572

Sonata No. 4, in d, Z805
with W. Torkanowsky vln, H. Chessid   Contrepoint MC20053
hpsi & G. Koutzen vlc   Dover HCR5224
                                         Period SPL572

Sonata No. 7, in G, Z808
with W. Torkanowsky vln, H. Chessid   Contrepoint MC20053
hpsi & G. Koutzen vlc   Dover HCR5224
                                         Period SPL572

Sonata No. 8, in g, Z809
with W. Torkanowsky vln, H. Chessid   Contrepoint MC20053
hpsi & G. Koutzen vlc   Dover HCR5224
                                         Period SPL572

Sonata No. 9, in F, Z810 "Golden Sonata"
with W. Torkanowsky vln, H. Chessid   Contrepoint MC20053
hpsi & G. Koutzen vlc   Dover HCR5224
                                         Period SPL572

Sonata No. 10, in D, Z811
with W. Torkanowsky vln, H. Chessid   Contrepoint MC20053
hpsi & G. Koutzen vlc   Dover HCR5224
                                         Period SPL572

SCARLATESCU

Bagatelle (in Rumanian style) vln & pf
with W. Baracchi pf   Cetra AT0202, T17008

Volodymyr CISYK

FOMENKO

Legend vln & orch.
with symphony   Victor T55038*
orch. – Zadorozny

Herman CLEBANOFF (1917–)

BRAHMS

Trio No. 3, in c, Op. 101 pf, vln & vlc
with N.M. Minchin pf & K. Früh vlc   Pro Musica PMT201

---

* Private recording – not issued commercially

LOEILLET

(12) Sonatas, Op. 2 Nos 1/6: 2 vlns & c
Sonata No. 6, in c arr. vln, vlc & pf "in b" de Béon
with N.M. Minchin pf & K. Früh vlc   Pro Musica PMT201

PROVOST

Intermezzo (1940) vln & orch.
with Clebanoff strings   Mercury MPT7528

TCHEREPNIN

Trio in D, Op. 34 (1925) pf, vln & vlc
with N.M. Minchin pf & K. Früh vlc   Pro Musica PMT201

Hector CLOCKERS

d'AMBROSIO

Petit chanson, Op. 28 vln & pf
with piano   HMV F239

MOSZKOWSKI

(2) Stücke, Op. 45 pf
No. 2. Guitarre arr. vln & pf Sarasate
with piano   HMV F239

VIEUXTEMPS

Ballade & Polonaise in G, Op. 38 vln & pf
with piano   HMV AU23

Fantasia–appasionata, Op. 35 vln & pf
with piano   HMV AU24

Peggy COCHRANE (1907–)

ANONYMOUS

Cherry ripe (English folksong) arr. vln & pf Scott
with piano   Aco G16044

Swing low, sweet chariot (traditional Negro spiritual) arr. vln & pf
with piano   Aco G16157

BARNS

Swing song vln & pf
with piano   Aco G15517

CADMAN

Little firefly vln & pf
with piano   Aco G16089

CHAMINADE

Sérénade espagnole pf – arr. vln & pf Kreisler
with piano   Aco G15699

CHOPIN

(4) Mazurkas, Op. 67 pf
No. 4 Mazurka No. 45, in a arr. vln & pf Kreisler
with piano   Aco G15981

(3) Nocturnes, Op. 9 pf
No. 2. Nocturne No. 2, in E flat arr. vln & pf Wilhelmj
with piano   Broadcast 5016, B6013

CUI

Kaleidoscope, Op. 50 vln & pf
  No. 5. Berceuse russe
  with piano   Aco G16089

DRDLA

Serenade No. 1, in A vln & pf
  with piano   Aco G15410
Souvenir vln & pf
  with piano   Broadcast 5016, B6002
Vision, Op. 28 vln & pf
  with piano   Aco G15826

GANNE

(L') Estase–Rêverie pf – arr. vln & pf
  with piano   Aco G15739

GERMAN

Saltarelle vln & pf
  with piano   Aco G16089

HEUBERGER

(Der) Opernball, Op. 40 (1898) – operetta
  Im chambre séparée arr. vln & pf as "Midnight bells" by Kreisler
  with piano   Aco G16044

HUBAY

(14) Scènes de la Csárda vln & pf
  No. 4. Hejre Kati, Op. 32
  with piano   Piccadilly 5024

JÄRNEFELT

Berceuse in g orch. – arr. vln & pf
  with piano   Aco G15769

KREISLER

Liebesfreud vln & pf
  with piano   Broadcast 5025
Liebesleid vln & pf
  with piano   Aco G15410
Polichinelle–Serenade vln & pf
  with piano   Aco G15739
(Le) Précieuse (L. Couperin) vln & pf
  with piano   Aco G15826

LIEURANCE

By the waters of the Minnetonka (1914) v & pf – arr. vln & pf
  with piano   Aco G16157

MASSENET

Thaïs (1894) – opera
  Méditation arr. vln & pf Marsick
  with piano   Broadcast 5007

MENDELSSOHN

Concerto in e, Op. 64 vln & orch.
  Andante (2nd mvt)
  with piano   Broadcast 5042, B6013

PADEREWSKI

(6) Humoresques de concert, Op. 14 pf
  No. 1. Minuet in G arr. vln & pf Kreisler
  with piano   Aco G16089

RAFF

(6) Pieces, Op. 85 vln & pf
  No. 3. Cavatina in D
  with piano   Broadcast 5007, B6001

RESPIGHI

Valse caressante vln & pf
  with piano   Aco G16128

RIMSKY–KORSAKOV

(Le) Coq d'Or (1910) – opera
  Hymn to the sun arr. vln & pf Kreisler
  with piano   Piccadilly 5024
Sadko (1898) – opera
  Chant hindou arr. vln & pf Kreisler
  with piano   Broadcast 5042, B6002

SCHUMANN

(13) Kinderscenen, Op. 15 pf
  No. 7. Träumerei arr. vln & pf
  with piano   Broadcast 5025
(3) Romances, Op. 94 ob or vlc or vln or cl & pf
  Romance No. 2, in A arr. vln & pf Kreisler
  with piano   Aco G15769

SINIGAGLIA

(4) Kleine Stücke, Op. 25 vln & pf
  No. 2. Capriccio all 'antica
  with piano   Aco G16128

TCHAIKOVSKY

Souvenir d'un lieu cher, Op. 42 vln & pf
  No. 3. Mélodie
  with piano   Aco G15699
(3) Souvenirs de Hapsal, Op. 2 pf
  No. 3. Chant sans paroles in f arr. vln & pf Kreisler
  with piano   Aco G15981
  No. 3. Chant sans paroles in f arr. vln & pf Kreisler
  with piano   Broadcast 5072

THOMÉ

Simple aveu, Op. 25 pf – arr. vln & pf
  with piano   Broadcast 5072

WAGNER

(Die) Meistersinger von Nürnberg (1868) – opera
  Morgenlich leuchtend "Prize song" arr. vln & pf Wilhelmj
  with piano   Broadcast 5025, B6001

WOLSTENHOLME

Allegretto vln & pf
  with piano   Aco G15517

WOODFORDE–FINDEN

(4) Indian Love Lyrics (1903) orch.
  No. 1 The temple bells arr. vln & pf
  with piano   Aco G15919

WOODFORDE–FINDEN – *Continued*

No. 3. Kashmiri song arr. vln & pf
with piano   Aco G15919

(A) Lover in Damascus – song cycle v & pf
No. 1. Far across the desert sands arr. vln & pf
with piano   Aco G16220
No. 2. Where the Abana flows arr. vln & pf
with piano   Aco G15919
No. 3. Beloved in your absence arr. vln & pf
with piano   Aco G16220
No. 4. How many a lonely caravan arr. vln & pf
with piano   Aco G15919
No. 5. If in the great bazaars arr. vln & pf
with piano   Aco G16220
No. 6. Allah be with us arr. vln & pf
with piano   Aco G16220

Isidore COHEN

ANTES

(3) Trios, Op. 3 2 vlns & vlc
Trio No. 1, in E flat (ed. T. Johnson)
with W. Torkanowsky vln & S. Barab   New Records Inc. NRI2016
vlc   Society for the Preservation of
                                       the American Musical Heritage
                                       MIA99

Trio No. 2, in d (ed. T. Johnson)
with W. Torkanowsky vln & S. Barab   New Records Inc. NRI2016
vlc   Society for the Preservation of
                                       the American Musical Heritage
                                       MIA99

Trio No. 3, in C (ed. T. Johnson)
with W. Torkanowsky vln & S. Barab   New Records Inc. NRI2016
vlc   Society for the Preservation of
                                       the American Musical Heritage
                                       MIA99

BACH

(6) Brandenburg Concerti, BWV1046/51 (1721) strs & c
Brandenburg Concerto No. 5, in D, BWV1050 clav, fl, vln & strs
with S. Marlowe hpsi, S. Baron fl &   Decca DL10130, DL710130
Baroque Chamber Orch. – Saidenberg

MOZART

Quintet in A, K581 cl, 2 vlns, vla & vlc
with H. Wright cl, A. Schneider vln, S.   Columbia MS7447
Rhodes vla & L. Parnas vlc

SIEGMEISTER

Sonata No. 3 (1965) vln & pf
with A. Mandel pf   Desto DC6467

Raymond COHEN (1919–   )

ACHRON

Hebrew dance, Op. 35, No. 1 vln & pf
with A. Rael pf   Belcantodisc LR2

BLOCH

Baal Shem (3 Pictures of Chassidic Life) (1923) vln & pf
No. 2. Nigun (Improvisation)
with A. Rael pf   Belcantodisc LR2

DELIUS

Concerto (1916) vln, vlc & orch.
with G. Warburg vlc & Royal   Pye GGC4073, GSGC14073
Philharmonic Orch. – Del Mar

FARNON

Rhapsody vln & orch.
with London Festival Symphony   Delysé ECB3157
Orch. – Farnon

TCHAIKOVSKY

Swan Lake, Op. 20 (1875/6) – ballet orch.
Dance of the queen of the swans
with Royal Philharmonic   HMV XLP20024
Orch. – Weldon

Italo COLANDREA

TELEMANN

Concerto in F, T.II, No. 3 3 vlns, strs & c
with F. Ayo vln, A. Apostoli vln & I   Philips 802864LY, PHS900188,
Musici   SAL3737

VIVALDI

(12) Concerti, Op. 3 "L'Estro armonico" var. cbns & strs
Concerto No. 2, in g, P.326 (F.IV, No. 8) 2 vlns, strs & c
with R. Michelucci vln, E. Altobelli   Philips 835162AY, A02277L
vlc & I Musici
Concerto No. 5, in A P.212 (F.I. No. 175) 2 vlns, strs & c
with R. Michelucci vln and I Musici   Philips 835163AY, A02278L

Oliver COLBENTSON (1927–   )

BEETHOVEN

Sonata No. 9, in A, Op. 47 "Kreutzer" vln & pf
with D. Garvey pf   Classics Club X22
                                       Musical Masterpiece Society
                                       MMS18

BRAHMS

Sonata No. 3, in d, Op. 108 vln & pf
with E. Appel pf   Colosseum MST606

DEBUSSY

Sonata No. 3, in g (1917) vln & pf
with E. Ulmer pf   Chamber Music Society CM10
                                       Concert Hall H12
                                       Musical Masterpiece Society
                                       MMS103

FRANCK

Sonata in A (1886) vln & pf
with E. Appel pf   Colosseum MST606

RÓZSA

North Hungarian peasant songs & dances, Op. 5 (1929) vln & orch.
with Frankenland State Symphony MGM E3645
Orch. – Kloss

Derek COLLIER

BORTKIEWICZ

In 3/4 time, Op. 45, No. 5 pf – arr. vln & pf
with E. Lush pf HMV XLP20080, SXLP20080

COPLAND

Rodeo (1942) – ballet orch.
 No. 4. Hoe–down arr. vln & pf Copland
with E. Lush pf HMV XLP20080, SXLP20080

CROTHER

Gweedore brae vln & pf
with E. Lush pf HMV XLP20080, SXLP20080

DEBUSSY

(12) Préludes – Book I (1910) pf
 No. 8. La Fille aux cheveux de lin arr. vln & pf Hartmann
with E. Lush pf HMV XLP20080, SXLP20080

DVOŘÁK

(7) Gypsy songs, Op. 55 v & pf
 No. 4. Songs my mother taught me arr. vln & pf Kreisler
with E. Lush pf HMV XLP20080, SXLP20080

GADE

Canzonetta vln & pf
with E. Lush pf HMV XLP20080, SXLP20080

GRANADOS

(12) Danzas españolas, Op. 37 (1893) pf
 No. 5. – Danza española No. 5, in e "Andaluza" arr. vln & pf Kreisler
with E. Lush pf HMV XLP20080, SXLP20080

KREISLER

Liebesleid vln & pf
with E. Lush pf HMV XLP20080, SXLP20080

KROLL

Banjo & fiddle vln & pf
with E. Lush pf HMV XLP20080, SXLP20080

PONCE

Estrellita (1913) v & pf – arr. vln & pf Heifetz
with E. Lush pf HMV XLP20080, SXLP20080

PRINCIPE

(El) Campielo (1932) vln & pf
with E. Lush pf HMV XLP20080, SXLP20080

SCHUBERT

(4) Impromptus, Op. 90 (D899) (1827) pf
 No. 3. Impromptu No. 3, in G arr. vln & pf Heifetz
with E. Lush pf HMV XLP20080, SXLP20080

SGAMBATI

(2) Pieces, Op. 24 vln & pf
 No. 2. Serenata napoletana
with E. Lush pf HMV XLP20080, SXLP20080

TCHAIKOVSKY

Souvenir d'un lieu cher, Op. 42 vln & pf
 No. 3. Mélodie
with E. Lush pf HMV XLP20080, SXLP20080

WINTERNITZ

Dance of the marionettes vln & pf
with E. Lush pf HMV XLP20080, SXLP20080

Emilio COLOMBO (1874–1937)

d'AMBROSIO

Serenade, Op. 6 vln & pf
with piano Edison Bell 0208

ARDITI

(Il) Bacio (1859) v & pf – arr. vln & pf
with piano Edison Bell 0208

DRDLA

Serenade No. 1, in A vln & pf
with piano Edison Bell 0267
Souvenir vln & pf
with piano Edison Bell 0277

HEUBERGER

(Der) Opernball, Op. 40 (1898) – operetta
 Im chambre séparée arr. vln & pf as "Midnight bells" by Kreisler
with piano Edison Bell 0277

MOLLOY

Love's old sweet song v & pf – arr. vln & pf
with piano Edison Bell 0226

POLIAKIN

(Le) Canari (Concert–polka) vln & pf
with piano Edison Bell 0208

RIMSKY–KORSAKOV

Sadko (1898) – opera
 Chant hindou arr. vln & pf Kreisler
with piano Edison Bell 0267

Mlle. COMBARIEU

SAINT–SAËNS

Concerto No. 1, in A, Op. 20 "Konzertstück" vln & orch. – arr. vln
& pf Spiering
with piano Pathé 9552

Louis Gay de COMBES

ABACO

(12) Sonatas, Op. 3 (1714) 2 vlns & c
Sonata No. 2, in F

with A. Scrosoppi vln, L. Sgrizzi hpsi	Cycnus 30 CM009
& E. Roveda vlc	Eurodisc 70908MK, 70909MK
	Nonesuch (in sets H3008 &
	H73008)

BONPORTI

(10) Invenzioni (1712) solo vln
No. 4 Invenzione No. 4, in g arr. vln & hpsi

with L. Sgrizzi hpsi	Cycnus 30 CM009
	Eurodisc 70908MK, 70909MK
	Nonesuch (in sets HC3008 &
	HC73008)

PORPORA

(6) Sinfonias da camera, Op. 2 (1735) 2 vlns & c
No. 4. Sinfonia da camera No. 4, in D

with A. Scrosoppi vln & L. Sgrizzi	Eurodisc 70933MK, S70933MK
hpsi	

SCARLATTI, A.

Sonata in F rec, ob, vln & hpsi

with A. Zuppiger fl, A. Scrosoppi vln	Eurodisc 70933MK, S70933MK
& L. Sgrizzi hpsi	

TARTINI

Concerto in D, C78 vln & orch.

with I Solisti della Società cameristica	Cycnus 30 CM009
di Lugano	Eurodisc 70908MK, 70909MK

VIVALDI

(12) Concerti, Op. 8 (1725) "Il Cimento dell' Armonia e dell' Invenzione"
(Nos. 1/4: Le quattro Stagioni) vln & strs
Concerto No. 1, in E, F.I, No. 22 "La Primavera"

with L. Sgrizzi hpsi & Radio Suisse	Musidisc RC804
Italienne Orch. – Douatte	

Concerto No. 2, in B flat, F.I, No. 23 "L'Estate"

with L. Sgrizzi hpsi & Radio Suisse	Musidisc RC804
Italienne Orch. – Douatte	

Concerto No. 3, in F, F.I, No. 24 "L'Autunno"

with L. Sgrizzi hpsi & Radio Suisse	Musidisc RC804
Italienne Orch. – Douatte	

Concerto No. 4, in f, F.I, No. 25 "L'Inverno"

with L. Sgrizzi hpsi & Radio Suisse	Musidisc RC804
Italienne Orch. – Douatte	

Gonçal COMELLAS

CORELLI

(12) Sonatas, Op. 5 vln & c
Sonata No. 12, in d "La Follia" (arr. Léonard)

with M. Zanetti pf	Ensayo ENY41

HAYDN

Concerto No. 1, in C, H.VIIa, No. 1 (1765) vln & orch.

with Padova Chamber	Ensayo ENY30
Orch. – Scimone	

NARDINI

(6) Sonatas, Op. 2 (1765) vln & c
Sonata No. 5, in D arr. vln & pf Flesch

with M. Zanetti pf	Ensayo ENY41

TARTINI

Sonata in g "Il Trillo del Diavolo" vln & c – arr. vln & pf Kreisler

with M. Zanetti pf	Ensayo ENY41

VIVALDI

Sonata in D, F. XII, No. 6 vln & c – rev. Respighi

with M. Zanetti pf	Ensayo ENY41

Manuel COMPINSKY (1901–)

BACH

Concerto in c, BWV1060 vln & ob or 2 vlns, strs & c – arr. Schneider

with G. Schoneberg ob & Pacific	Alco AC202, Y1210
Sinfonietta – Van Den Burg	

RACHMANINOV

Trio No. 2, in d, Op. 9 "Trio élégiaque" pf, vln & vlc

(as leader of Compinsky trio)	Alco A4/8, (set A4), ALP1008

SHOSTAKOVICH

Trio No. 2, in e, Op. 67 (1944) "In memory of I.I. Sollertinsky" pf, vln & vlc

(as leader of Comprinsky trio)	Alco A7/9, (set A3), T103*

Henry CONDAMINE

BRUCH

Kol Nidrei, Op. 47 vlc or vln & orch.

with piano	Columbia J2390
	Odeon O–11210

GALLOS

(Le) Lac de Come – Nocturne pf – arr. vln & pf

with piano	Parlophone 22791

HUBAY

(6) Poèmes hongroise, Op. 27 vln & pf
Poème hongrois No. 6, in B flat

with piano	Columbia J2390
	Odeon O–11210

LEONCAVALLO

Mattinata (1904) v & pf – arr. vln & pf

with piano	Parlophone 22791

Trevor CONNAH

VIVALDI

(12) Concerti, Op. 3 "L'Estro armonico" var. cbns & strs
Concerto No. 10, in b, P.148 (F.IV, No. 10) 4 vlns, strs & c

with N. Marriner vln, N. Nelson vln,	L'Oiseau-Lyre OL276,
A. Howard vln & Academy of St.	SMO1520, SOL276
Martin-in-the-Fields – Marriner	

* experimental 16" LP

Mihai CONSTANTINESCU

BEETHOVEN
Romance No. 1, in G, Op. 40 vln & orch.
with Rumanian Film Orch. – Bugeanu Electrecord ECE0180

Romance No. 2, in F, Op. 50 vln & orch.
with Rumanian Film Orch. – Bugeanu Electrecord ECE0180

Sonata No. 5, in F, Op. 24 "Spring " vln & pf
with V. Stefănescu pf Electrecord ECE0180

MOZART
Concerto No. 6, in E flat, K268 vln & orch.
with Bucharest Chamber
Orch. – Cristescu Electrecord ECE058

Sonata No. 27, in G, K379 vln & pf
with M. Cardas pf Electrecord ECC768

Alexander CORES

ALBINONI
(12) Concerti, Op. 5 (1707) vln or ob, strs & c
Concerto No. 5, in a
with Telemann Society Orch. – Schulze Adès (Florilège) 13017
Counterpoint CPT621,
CPTS5621

d'AMBROSIO
Serenade, Op. 4 vln & pf
with S. Kagen pf Columbia 36350, (in set E6)

CORELLI
(12) Sonatas, Op. 5 vln & c
Sonata No. 1, in D: Grave (1st mvt) **& Allegro** (2nd mvt)
with S. Kagen pf Columbia 36349, (in set E6)

LULLY
Ballets du Roy (1659) – ballet orch.*
Gavotte en rondeau arr. vln & pf Burmester
with S. Kagen pf Columbia 35897, (in set E3)

NARDINI
Concerto in e vln & orch – arr. vln & pf Pente
with S. Kagen pf Columbia 36348/9, (in set E6)

PUGNANI
(6) Sonatas, Op. 8 vln & c
Sonata No. 3, in D: Largo espressivo (2nd mvt) arr. vln & pf Moffat
with S. Kagen pf Columbia 36350, (in set E6)

RAMEAU
Dardanus (1739) – opera
Rigaudon (Act I) arr. vln & pf Burmester
with S. Kagen pf Columbia 35897, (in set E3)

RIES
Suite No. 3, in G, Op. 34 vln & pf
No. 5. Perpetuum mobile
with S. Kagen pf Columbia 35895, (in set E3)

* Unidentified

TENAGLIA
Have pity, sweet eyes v & pf – arr. vln & pf as "Aria in f" by Ries
with S. Kagen pf Columbia 35895, (in set E3)

VIVALDI
(12) Concerti, Op. 3 "L'Estro armonico" var cbns & strs
Concerto No. 6, in a, P.1 (F.I, No.`176) vln, strs & c
with S. Kagen pf Columbia 35896/7, (in set E3)

John CORIGLIANO (1901–)

BEETHOVEN
Concerto in C, Op. 56 "Triple" vln, vlc, pf & orch.
with L. Rose vlc, W. Hendl pf & New Columbia 12986/9D, (set
York Philharmonic Symphony MM842), FC1002, ML2059,
Orch. – Walter ML5368, QC1002
Philips A01423L, ABL3290,
G05647R

Mass in D, Op. 123 "Missa solemnis"
with E. Farrell s, C. Smith a, CBS BRG72013/4,
R. Lewis t, K. Borg bs & New York SBRG72013/4
Philharmonic Symphony Columbia ML5699/700, (set
Orch. – Bernstein M2L270), MS6299/300, (set
M2S619)

CHAUSSON
Concerto in D, Op. 21 pf, vln & str qt
with R. Votapek pf & International Mace MC9074, MCS9074
Soloists String Quartet

CORIGLIANO, John (Jr.)
Sonata (1963) vln & pf
with R. Votapek pf Composers Recordings CRI215

KHACHATURIAN
Gayaneh (Suite No. 2) (1942) – ballet orch.
No. 11. Gayaneh's Adagio
with M. Rosenker vln, W. Lincer vla, Columbia CL714, DX1642,
L. Rose vlc, T. Cella hp – cond. Kurtz ML4030, SX1012
Masquerade (1939) – Incidental music to the ballet orch.
Nocturne
with New York Philharmonic Columbia CL758
Symphony Orch. – Kostelanetz Philips NBE11033, SBF118

MAHLER
Symphony No. 3, in d (1895) orch.
Comodo; Scherzando (3rd mvt)
with M. Lipton m–s, J. Ware CBS BRG72065/6,
p–hrn – Women's Chorus of the SBRG72065/6
Schola Cantorum directed by Hugh Columbia ML5734/5, (set
Ross – Boys' Choir of the Church of M2L275), MS6334/5, (set
the Transfiguration directed by Stuart M2S675)
Gardner & New York Philharmonic
Symphony Orch. – Bernstein

RIMSKY–KORSAKOV
Scheherazade, Op. 35 (1888) orch.
with New York Philharmonic Columbia ML5387, MS6069
Symphony Orch. – Bernstein Philips A01403L, ABL3266

SAINT-SAËNS

Danse macabre, Op. 40 (1874) orch.

with New York Philharmonic	Columbia 4–13150D
Symphony Orch. – Mitropoulos	Philips A01604R, ABE10008

STOLZ

(The) Melody that haunts my heart orch. – arr. vln & orch.

with orch. – Stolz	Brunswick 04096

TCHAIKOVSKY

(3) Souvenirs de Hapsal, Op. 2 pf
No. 3. Chant sans paroles in f arr. vln & orch.

with Decca Symphony	Decca (in set A90), DL5211,
Orch. – Mendoza	US223524

VIVALDI

(12) Concerti, Op. 8 (1725) "Il Cimento dell' Armonia e dell' Invenzione"
(Nos. 1/4: Le quattro Stagioni) vln & strs
Concerto No. 1, in E, F.I, No. 22 "La Primavera"

with New York Philharmonic	Columbia ML5044
Symphony Orch. – Cantelli	Philips A01224L, ABL3063,
	G03576L, GBL5599

Concerto No. 1, in E, F.I, No. 22 "La Primavera"

with New York Philharmonic	CBS BRG72363, SBRG72363
Symphony Orch. – Bernstein	Columbia ML6144, MS6744

Concerto No. 2, in B flat, F.I, No. 23 "L'Estate"

with New York Philharmonic	Columbia ML5044
Symphony Orch. – Cantelli	Philips A01224L, ABL3063,
	G03576L, GBL5599

Concerto No. 2, in B flat, F.I, No. 23 "L'Estate"

with New York Philharmonic	CBS BRG72363, SBRG72363
Symphony Orch. – Bernstein	Columbia ML6144, MS6744

Concerto No. 3, in F, F.I, No. 24 "L'Autunno"

with New York Philharmonic	Columbia ML5044
Symphony Orch. – Cantelli	Philips A01124L, ABL3063,
	G03576L, GBL5599

Concerto No. 3, in F, F.I, No. 24 "L'Autunno"

with New York Philharmonic	CBS BRG72363, SBRG72363
Symphony Orch. – Bernstein	Columbia ML6144, MS6744

Concerto No. 4, in f, F.I, No. 25 "L'Inverno"

with New York Philharmonic	Columbia ML5044
Symphony Orch. – Cantelli	Philips A01124L, ABL3063,
	G03576L, GBL5599

Concerto No. 4, in f, F.I, No. 25 "L'Inverno"

with New York Philharmonic	CBS BRG72363, SBRG72363
Symphony Orch. – Bernstein	Columbia ML6144, MS6744

Concerto in A gtr, vln, vla & vlc

with C. Romero gtr, D. Saltarelli vla	Mercury SR90487
& M. Bella vlc	

CORVINO

CHAMINADE

Sérénade espagnole pf – arr. vln & pf Kreisler

with piano	Columbia N1123

LESERNA

Arieta española del siglo XVIII v & pf – arr. vln & pf

with piano	Columbia N1123

Anna Maria COTOGNI

ABACO

(12) Sonatas, Op. 3 (1714) 2 vlns & c
Sonata No. 4, in G (rev. Riemann)

with F. Ayo vln & M. de Robertis hpsi	Victor (in set ML40002)

BOCCHERINI

(6) Quintets, Op. 30 (1780) 2 vlns, vla & 2 vlcs
No. 6. Quintet No. 6, in C "La Musica Notturna di madrid"
(rev. Upmeyer)

with F. Ayo vln, C. Ghedin vla, E.	Victor (in set ML40002)
Altobelli vlc & M. Centurione vlc	

CAZZATI

(6) Sonatas, Op. 55 (1670) vln & c
Sonata No. 1, in d (rev. Apel)

with M. de Robertis hpsi	Victor (in set ML40001)

CORELLI

(12) Sonatas, Op. 5 vln & c
Sonata No. 3, in C

with M. de Robertis hpsi	Victor (in set ML40001)

FONTANA

Sonata in C vln & c – rev. Torchi

with M. de Robertis hpsi	Victor (in set ML40001)

LOCATELLI

(12) Concerti grossi, Op. 1 (1721) 2 vlns, vla, vlc, strs & c
Concerto grosso No. 8, in f

with F. Ayo vln, B. Giuranna vla, E.	Epic BC1029, LC3587
Altobelli vlc & I Musici	Philips 835025AY, 835129AY,
	A02023L, PHM500025,
	PHS900025

Concerto grosso No. 9, in D

with F. Ayo vln, B. Giuranna vlc, E.	Epic BC1029, LC3587
Altobelli vlc & I Musici	Philips 835025AY, A02023L

Concerto grosso No. 11, in c

with F. Ayo vln, B. Giuranna vlc, E.	Epic BC1029, LC3587
Altobelli vlc & I Musici	Philips 835025AY, A02023L

Concerto grosso No. 12, in g

with F. Ayo vln, B. Giuranna vlc, E.	Epic BC1029, LC3587
Altobelli vlc & I Musici	Philips 835025AY, A02023L

MANFREDINI

(12) Concerti, Op. 3 (1718) 2 vlns, strs & c
Concerto No. 2, in a

with R. Michelucci vln & I Musici	Epic LC3514
	Philips A00448L

Concerto No. 3, in e

with R. Michelucci vln & I Musici	Epic LC3514
	Philips A00448L

Concerto No. 7, in G

with R. Michelucci vln & I Musici	Epic LC3514
	Philips A00448L

Concerto No. 8, in F

with R. Michelucci vln & I Musici	Epic LC3514
	Philips A00448L

Concerto No. 10, in g

with R. Michelucci vln & I Musici	Epic LC3514
	Philips A00448L

Concerto No. 12, in C
with R. Michelucci vln & I Musici   Epic LC3514
Philips 835129AY, A00448L,
PHM500025, PHS900025

PERGOLESI

(14) Sonatas (1770) 2 vlns & c
Sonata No. 5, in C (rev. Caffarelli)
with F. Ayo vln & M. de Robertis hpsi   Victor (in set ML40002)

TARTINI

(12) Sonatas, Op. 3 2 vlns & c
Sonata No. 1, in D (rev. Pente)
with F. Ayo vln, C. Ghedin vla & E.   Victor (in set ML40002)
Altobelli vlc

TORELLI

(12) Concerti, Op. 8 (1709) 1/6: 2 vlns, strs & c – 7/12: vln, strs & c
Concerto No. 2, in a
with R. Michelucci vln, M. Centurione   Epic LC3217
vlc & I Musici   Philips A00302L, ABL3153
Concerto No. 3, in E
with R. Michelucci vln, M. Centurione   Epic LC3217 Philips A00302L,
vlc & I Musici   ABL3153
Concerto No. 6, in g "Christmas Concerto"
with R. Michelucci vln, M. Centurione   Epic LC3217
vlc & I Musici   Philips 835129AY, A00302L,
ABL3153, PHM500025,
PHS900025

VIOTTI

(6) Duets, Op. 20 2 vlns
No. 3. Duet No. 3, in G
with R. Michelucci vln   Victor (in set ML40003)

VITALI

Sonata in D (1689) vln & c – rev. Torchi
with M. de Robertis hpsi   Victor (in set LM40001)

VIVALDI

(12) Concerti, Op. 3 "L'Estro armonico" var. cbns & strs
Concerto No. 1, in D, P.146 (F.IV, No. 7) 4 vlns, vlc, strs & c
with R. Michelucci vln, W. Gallozzi   Philips 835162AY, A02277L,
vln, L. Vicari vln & I Musici   PHC9111, (in set PHC3–017)
Concerto No. 4, in e, P.97 (F.I, No. 174) 4 vlns, strs & c
with R. Michelucci vln, W. Gallozzi   Philips 835162AY, A02277L,
vln, L. Vicari vln & I Musici   PHC9111, (in set PHC3–017)
Concerto No. 7, in F, P.249 (F.IV, No. 9) 4 vlns, strs & c
with R. Michelucci vln, W. Gallozzi   Philips 835163AY, A02278L,
vln, L. Vicari vln & I Musici   PHC9112, (in set PHC3–017)
Concerto No. 8, in a, P.2 (F.I, No. 177) 2 vlns, strs & c
with R. Michelucci vln & I Musici   Epic LC3563, (in set SC6040),
BSC111
Philips 400107AE, A00462L,
ABL3233
Concerto No. 8, in a, P.2 (F.I, No. 177) 2 vlns, strs & c
with R. Michelucci vln & I Musici   Philips 835163AY, A02278L,
PHC9112, (in set PHC3–017)
Concerto No. 10, in b, P.148 (F.IV, No. 10) 4 vlns, strs & c
with R, Michelucci vln, W. Gallozzi   Fontana 894075ZKY
vln, L. Vicari vln, E. Altobelli vlc & I   Philips 802735AY, (in set
Musici   C71AX401, 835164AY,
839526VGY, PHC9113, (in set
PHC3–017)

VIVALDI – *Continued*

Concerto No. 11, in d, P.250 (F.IV, No. 11) 2 vlns, vlc, strs & c
with R. Michelucci vln, E. Altobelli   Philips 835164AY, A02279L,
vlc & I Musici   PHC9113, (in set PHC3–017)
(12) Concerti, Op. 9 (1728) "La Cetra" vln, strs & c
Concerto No. 9, in B flat, P.341 (F.I, No. 57) with 2nd vln obb
with F. Ayo vln, E. Altobelli vlc, M.T.   Philips 835291AY, A02421L,
Garatti org & I Musici   PHM500116, (in set PHM3–553),
PHS900115, (in set PHS3–993)
Concerto in E, P.248 (F.I, No. 4) "Il Riposo" vln, strs & c
with I Musici   Epic BC1021, LC3486
Philips 835002AY, A00476L,
ABL3153
Concerto in F, P.278 (F.I, No. 34) 3 vlns, strs & c
with F. Ayo vln, F. Tamponi vln & I   Philips 835211AY, A02333L
Musici

Gert CRAFOORD

CARLSTEDT

(8) Duets 2 vlns
with M. Nordin vln   Telefunken LT43075

CRAVIO

GRIEG

(6) Lyric Pieces – Book III, Op. 43 pf
No. 6. To the spring arr. vln & pf Kreisler
with piano   Odeon 33670

Émile CRÉGUT

di CAPUA

Maria Mari v & pf – arr, vln & pf
with F. Gaveau pf   Kl 2705–2   Odeon 165819

DRIGO

(Les) Millions d'Arlequin (1900) – ballet orch.
Sérénade arr. vln & pf Auer
with F. Gaveau pf   Kl 2704–3   Odeon 165819

FRIML

Rose Marie (1916) – operetta
Indian love call arr. vln & pf
with F. Gaveau pf   Odeon 165818

RIMSKY–KORSAKOV

Sadko (1898) – opera
Chant hindou arr. vln & pf Kreisler
with F. Gaveau pf   Odeon 165820

TCHAIKOVSKY

(12) Pieces (of moderate difficulty) Op. 40 pf
No. 2. Chanson triste arr. vln & pf
with F. Gaveau pf   Odeon 165820

WOOD

Roses of Picardy (1916) v & pf – arr. vln & pf
with F. Gaveau pf   Odeon 165818

C. CRENNE

VIVALDI

(12) Concerti, Op. 3 "L'Estro armonico" var. cbns & strs
   Concerto No. 10, in b, P.148 (F.IV, No. 10) 4 vlns, strs & c
   with P. Diaz-Pelaz vln, A. Moglia   Classic 991062
   vln, N. Risner vln, M. Roche hpsi
   & Ensemble Instrumental de France – Hartemann

Michael CRON

BACH

Concerto in d, BWV1043 2 vlns, strs & c
   with P. Hofer vln & Disenhaus   Guilde Européenne du
   Concert Orch. – Disenhaus   Microsillon GEM1
      Lyrichord LLS5

PEPUSCH

Sonata in C fl, gamba, vln & org
   with M. Larrieu fl, R. Perulli gamba &   Harmonia Mundi HM30571
   M. Chapuis org   Oryx ORYX713

Sonata in d fl, gamba & c
   with M. Larrieu fl, R. Perulli gamba &   Harmonia Mundi HM30571
   M. Chapuis org   Oryx ORYX713

Erik Johan CRONVALL (1904–   )

KROHN

Nocturne vln & pf
   with E. Cronvall pf   Fennica ST20

SIBELIUS

(4) Pieces, Op. 78 vln & pf
   No. 2. Romance in F
   with piano   Columbia 17812

(5) Pieces, Op. 81 vln & pf
   No. 3. Valse
   with Helsinki Odeon Concert   Odeon A228490, PLD15
   Orch. – Andström

(The) Tempest, Op. 109 (1926) – Incidental music orch.
   with Finnish Radio Orch. – Jalas   Metronome MCEP3013

Maurice CRUT

BEETHOVEN

Sonata No. 9, in A, Op. 47 "Kreutzer" vln & pf
   with J.C. Englebert pf   Ducretet–Thomson 270C007
      Telefunken LB6123

DELVINCOURT

Sonata in d (1923) vln & pf
   with L. Descaves pf   Ducretet–Thomson 270C104,
      LPG8241

HONEGGER

Sonata No. 1, in c sharp (1916/8) vln & pf
   with A. Terrasse pf   Ducretet–Thomson 300C054,
      LPG8241

MOZART

Serenade No. 7, in D, K250 "Haffner" orch.
   Andante (2nd mvt)
   with orch. – Cébron   Lumen 30093, 206012

VIVALDI

(12) Concerti, Op. 3 "L'Estro armonico" var. cbns & strs
   Concerto No. 10, in b: largo (2nd mvt) P.148 (F.IV, No. 10) 4 vlns,
   strs & c
   with H. Merckel vln, L. Schwartz vln,   Polydor 540002, 566275
   J. Dumont vln & Pro Musica
   Orch. – Goldschmidt

Jerry CSABA (1940–   )

PAGANINI

Cantabile in D, Op. 17 vln & gtr
   with A. Nagytothy–Toth gtr   Baroque BC1827, BC2827

Sonata in A, Op. posth. vln & gtr
   with A. Nagytothy–Toth gtr   Baroque BC1827, BC2827

RODE

Trio in D vln, vla & gtr
   with J. Csaba vla & A. Nagytothy–   Baroque BC1827, BC2827
   Toth gtr

SPOHR

Trio in F, Op. 123 pf, vln & vlc – arr. gtr, vln & vla
   with J. Csaba vla &   Baroque BC1827, BC2827
   A. Nagytothy–Toth gtr   Janus–Pirouette JA19031

Alfred CSAMMER

DVOŘÁK

Ballade in d, Op. 15 vln & pf
   with S. Speidel pf   Corona 30003

Romance in f, Op. 11 vln & orch.
   with S. Speidel pf   Corona 30003

(4) Romantic pieces, Op. 75 vln & pf
   with S. Speidel pf   Corona 30003

GRIEG

Sonata No. 1, in F, Op. 8 vln & pf
   with S. Speidel pf   Corona 30003

Sascha CULBERTSON (1894–1944)

BAZZINI

(La) Ronde des lutins, Op. 25 vln & pf
   with H. Hamilton pf   Vocalion 70001

BRAHMS

(21) Hungarian dances pf duet
   Hungarian dance No. 5, in f sharp arr. vln & pf "in g" Joachim
   with piano   Vocalion 30140

(16) Waltzes, Op. 39 pf duet
   No. 15. Waltz No. 15, in A flat arr. vln & pf "in A" Hochstein
   with piano   Vocalion 60001

DRDLA

Souvenir vln & pf
with piano   Vocalion 30111

DRIGO

(2) Airs de Ballet orch.
 No. 2. Valse bluette arr. vln & pf Auer
with piano   Vocalion X9448

(Les) Millions d'Arlequin (1900) – ballet
 Sérénade arr. vln & pf Auer
with piano   Vocalion X9448

DVOŘÁK

(8) Humoresques, Op. 101 pf
 No. 7. Humoresque No. 7, in G flat arr. vln & pf "in G" Kreisler
with piano   Vocalion 30132

(8) Slavonic Dances, Op. 46 pf duet; orch.
 No. 2. Slavonic dance No. 2, in e arr. vln & pf "in g" Kreisler
with W. Schaeffer pf   Vocalion 30148

Sonatina in G, Op. 100 vln & pf
 Larghetto (2nd mvt) arr. vln & pf as "Indian lament" by Kreisler
with H. Hamilton pf 52006 Vocalion 70016, K05058

KREISLER

Caprice viennois, Op. 2 vln & pf
 with H. Hamilton pf 52019 Vocalion 70016

Liebesfreud vln & pf
with piano   Vocalion 30144

LILIUOKALANI

Aloha Oe (1892) v & pf – arr. v, vln & pf
 with M. Peterson s & pf Vocalion 30107

MASSENET

Thaïs (1894) – opera
 Méditation arr. vln & pf Marsick
with piano   Vocalion 70001

MOSZKOWSKI

(2) Stücke, Op. 45 pf
 No. 2. Guitarre arr. vln & pf Sarasate
with piano   Vocalion X9194

SARASATE

(8) Danzas españolas vln & pf
 No. 3. Romanza andaluza, Op. 22, No. 1
with piano   AM 10449 Vocalion D02143
 No. 6. Zapateado, Op. 23, No. 2
with piano   Vocalion 60002
 No. 6. Zapateado, Op. 23, No. 2
with piano   Vocalion X9194

SCHUBERT

(7) Gesänge (set to Scott's "Lady of the Lake") Op. 52 v & pf
 No. 6. Ave Maria, D839 arr. vln & pf Wilhelmj
with piano   Vocalion K05058

SCHUMANN

(13) Kinderscenen, Op. 15 pf
 No. 7. Träumerei arr. vln & pf
with piano   Vocalion 30114

WIENIAWSKI

Concerto No. 2, in d, Op. 22 vln & orch.
 Romance (2nd mvt)
with piano   AM 10451 Vocalion D02143

Yvonne CURTI

ABRAHAM

(Un) Chant d'amour v & pf – arr. vln & pf
 with G. Andolfi pf   Pathé PA282

ACCORDI

(La) Seduzione (Air de Ballet) orch. – arr. vln & pf
 with G. Andolfi pf   Pathé PA31

d'AMBROSIO

Primavera (Intermezzo) vln & pf
 with G. Andolfi pf   Pathé PA164

ANDOLFI

Berceuse vln & pf
 with G. Andolfi pf   Pathé X9834

Lorsque tu passes "Sérénade appassionata" vln & pf
 with G. Andolfi pf   Pathé PA812

ANONYMOUS

Song of the Volga boatman (traditional Russian folksong) arr. vln & pf Kreisler
 with G. Andolfi pf   Pathé X9755

BARNS

Humoresque vln & pf
 with G. Andolfi pf   Pathé X9834

BENATZKY

Im weissen Rössl – operetta
 Es muss was Wunderbares sein arr. vln & pf
with G. Andolfi pf   Pathé X98139

BILLI

Campane à sera vln or mand & pf
 with J. Benvenuti pf Columbia DF1549

BOCCHERINI

(6) Quintets, Op. 13 2 vlns, vla & 2 vlcs
 No. 5. Quintet No. 5, in E: Minuetto (3rd mvt) "Bull" arr. vln & pf Kreisler
with G. Andolfi pf   Pathé X98079

BOHM

(6) Miniatures, Op. 187 vln & pf
 No. 4. Perpetuum mobile
with G. van Parys pf Columbia 2149M, D19047, DF384

BOLDI

Chanson bohèmienne pf – arr. vln & pf
 with G. Andolfi pf   Pathé X9773

BONINCONTRO

Tes yeux (Sais – tu pourquoi?) v & pf – arr. vln & pf
 with J. Benvenuti pf Columbia DF1418

BOULANGER, G.

Avant de mourir, Op. 17 vln & pf
  with G. Andolfi pf   Pathé PA1057

CHOPIN

(12) Etudes, Op. 10 pf
  No. 3. Etude No. 3, in E arr. vln & pf Hamelle
  with G. Andolfi pf   Pathé X98104
  No. 5. Etude No. 5, in G flat arr. vln & pf
  with G. Andolfi pf   Pathé X98104
(3) Nocturnes, Op. 9 pf
  No. 2. Nocturne No. 2, in E flat arr. vln & pf Sarasate
  with G. Andolfi pf   N 9664 Pathé X9744

CUI

(12) Miniatures, Op. 20 vln & pf
  No. 8. Berceuse
  with G. Andolfi pf   Pathé X9746

DEBUSSY

Petite Suite (1889) pf – 4 hands
  No. 1. En bateau arr. vln & pf G. Choisnel
  with M. Fauré pf   Columbia DFX82

DEUTSCH

Chantez pour moi violons vln & pf*
  with G. Andolfi pf   Pathé X98178

DRDLA

Souvenir vln & pf
  with G. Andolfi pf   N 9677 Pathé X9745

DRIGO

(Les) Millions d'Arlequin (1900) – ballet orch.
  Sérénade arr. vln & pf Auer
  with G. Andolfi pf   Pathé X9721

DYFF

Scènes montagnardes (Morceau imitatif) vln & pf
  with G. Andolfi pf   Pathé X98190

ERWIN

I kiss your hand, madam (1929) v & pf – arr. vln & pf
  with G. Andolfi pf   Pathé X9835

FAIN

Prologues orch†
  Près de la cascade arr. vln & pf
  with G. Andolfi pf   Pathé PA163

FAURÉ

Berceuse, Op. 16 vln & pf
  with G. Andolfi pf   Pathé PA283, X9751
(3) Chansons, Op. 7 v & pf
  No. 1. Après un rêve arr. vln & pf
  with G. Andolfi pf   N 9678 Pathé X9745

* With Altman.
† Film music.

FAURÉ – *Continued*

(3) Chansons, Op. 23 v & pf
  No. 1. Les berceaux arr. vln & pf
  with G. Andolfi pf   Pathé X98156

FÉVRIER

Mélancolle vln & pf
  with G. Andolfi pf   Pathé X9835
(Le) Recitativo de Djalmar vln & pf
  with G. Andolfi pf   Pathé PA31

FRIML

Rose Marie (1916) – operetta
  Indian love call arr. vln & pf
  with G. Andolfi pf   301695–MC3 Pathé X9747, X98138

GADE

Jealousy (1927) vln & orch.
  with G. Andolfi pf   N 300542–A1 Pathé X9873

GILLET

Loin du Bal, Op. 36 – ballet orch.
  Intermezzo arr. vln & pf
  with J. Benvenuti pf   Columbia DF1549

GUGO–NORIS

Valse d'Or vln & pf
  with G. Andolfi pf   Pathé X98103

HAHN

Ciboulette (1923) – operetta
  Comme frère et soeur arr. vln & pf
  with G. Andolfi pf   Pathé X98121
Si mes vers avaient des aîles v & pf – arr. vln & pf
  with G. Andolfi pf   Pathé X98156

HEYMANN

Je ne sais v & pf – arr. vln & pf*
  with G. Andolfi pf   Pathé X98139

JURMANN & KAPER

Vivons l'amour, vivons la vie – Tango orch – arr. vln & pf
  with G. Andolfi pf   Pathé PA432

KÁLMÁN

Gräfin Mariza (1924) – operetta
  Komm' Zigany arr. vln & pf†
  with G. Andolfi pf   Pathé X98025

KERN

(The) Cat & the Fiddle (1931) – musical
  The night was made for love arr. vln & pf
  with G. Andolfi pf   Pathé PA282

KREISLER

Schön Rosmarin vln & pf
  with G. Andolfi pf   Pathé X98113

* From the film "Le rêve blond."
† A second selection is listed on label as "c'est pour un baiser."

LACAMBRA–MATÉO

Chant du soir (Rêverie) vln & pf
with G. Andolfi pf   Pathé PA1058

LEHÁR

Frasquita (1923) – operetta
 Hab' ein blaues Himmelbett arr. vln & pf as "Serenade" by Kreisler
 with G. Andolfi pf   Pathé X98178

(Das) Land des Lächelns (1923) – operetta
 Boston Walzer arr. vln & pf
 with G. Andolfi pf   Pathé X98120

 Dein ist mein ganzes Herz arr. vln & pf
 with G. Andolfi pf   Pathé X98120

Paganini (1925) – operetta
 Gern hab' ich die Frau'n geküsst arr. vln & pf
 with G. Andolfi pf   Pathé PA503, X9747

MASSENET

Thaïs (1894) – opera
 Méditation arr. vln & pf Marsick
 with G. Andolfi pf   N 9663   Pathé X9744

MEISEL

Maria–Louise (Sérénade) vln & pf
with G. Andolfi pf   Pathé PA164

de MESQUITA

Chanson de l'Esmeralda, Op. 104 vln & pf
with G. Andolfi pf   300543–A   Pathé X9873

MONTI

Aubade d'amour vln & pf
with G. Andolfi pf   Pathé X9721

Csárdas (1904) vln & pf
with G. Andolfi pf   Pathé X9721

Csárdas (1904) vln & pf
with G. van Parys pf   L 869   Columbia 5290, 01529, D19041, J704

OPENSHAW

Love sends a little gift of roses (1919) v & pf – arr. vln & pf
with J. Benvenuti pf   Columbia DF1418

PIERNÉ

Sérénade in A, Op. 7 (1875) pf – arr. vln & pf
with G. Andolfi pf   Pathé X9773

PIOT

Danza española vln & pf
with G. Andolfi pf   Pathé X98104

PUGNANI

(6) Sonatas, Op. 8 vln & c
 Sonata No. 3, in D: Largo espressivo (2nd mvt) arr. vln & pf Moffat
 with M. Fauré pf   Columbia 2149M, DF384

RACHMANINOV

(5) Pieces, Op. 3 (1892) pf
 No. 5. Mélodie arr. vln & pf Press
 with G. Andolfi pf   Pathé X9754

RAFF

(6) Pieces, Op. 85 vln & pf
 No. 3. Cavatina in D
 with G. Andolfi pf   Pathé X98079

RAVEL

Pavane pour une infante défunte (1899) pf – arr. vln & pf Kochański
with M. Fauré pf   Columbia DFX82

RAVINI

Serenade (Sans les étoiles) vln & pf
with G. Andolfi pf   Columbia DB1714
   Pathé PA813

RAY

Your gentle smile v & pf – arr. vln & pf
with G. Andolfi pf   Pathé PA1058

RENARD

(2) Berceaux, Op. 20 vln & pf
 No. 2. Berceuse in F
 with G. Andolfi pf   Pathé X9756

RICHEPIN

(Le) Sommeil d'Antinéa pf – arr. vln & pf
with G. Andolfi pf   Pathé PA1057

RIMSKY–KORSAKOV

(Le) Coq d'Or (1910) – opera
 Hymn to the sun arr. vln & pf Kreisler
 with M. Fauré pf   Columbia DF384
Sadko (1898) – opera
 Chant hindou arr. vln & pf Kreisler
 with G. Andolfi pf   301694 MC 1   Pathé X9754, X98138

ROBIN & RAINGER

Love in bloom (1934) v & pf – arr. vln & pf
with G. Andolfi pf   Pathé PA432

ROMBERG

(The) Rose of France – operetta
 Tango arr. vln & pf
 with G. Andolfi pf   Pathé X98202

ROUSSEAU

(Les) Promis v & pf – arr. vln & pf
with G. Andolfi pf   Pathé X9768

RUBINSTEIN

(2) Melodies, Op. 3 pf
 No. 1. Melody in F arr. vln & pf
 with G. Andolfi pf   Pathé PA502

SAINT–SAËNS

(Le) Carnaval des animaux (1886) small orch.
 Le cygne arr. vln & pf
 with G. Andolfi pf   Pathé X9755

SAMMARTINI, G.

(6) Sonatas, Op. 1 2 vlns & c
 Sonata No. 4, in a: Andante (3rd mvt) arr. vln & pf as "Canto amoroso" by Elman
 with G. van Parys pf   Columbia D19047

SCHMITT

(5) Pieces, Op. 19 vln or vlc & pf
No. 1. Chanson à bercer (Lullaby)
with G. Andolfi pf   Pathé X9768

SCHUBERT, François

(12) Bagatelles, Op. 13 vln & pf
No. 9. L'abeille
with M. Fauré pf   Columbia 2149M, D19047,
DF384

SIMONETTI

Madrigale pf – arr. vln & pf
with G. Andolfi pf   Pathé X9756
Madrigale pf – arr. vln & pf
with G. van Parys pf   L 870   Columbia 5290, 01529, D19041,
J704

SORBI

Fiori sparsi (Scattered flowers) arr. vln & pf
with G. Andolfi pf   Columbia DB1714
Pathé PA813

STOLZ

Donne–moi ton coeur ce soir v & pf – arr. vln & pf
with G. Andolfi pf   Pathé PA812

STRAUS, O.

(Ein) Walzertraum (1907) – operetta
Selection unid – arr. vln & pf
with G. Andolfi pf   Pathé X9720

STRAUSS, J. (II)

(Die) Fledermaus (1874) – operetta
Trinke Liebchen, trinke schnell
with G. Andolfi pf   Pathé PA163

SVENDSEN

Romance in G, Op. 26 vln & orch. – arr. vln & pf Wilhelmj
with G. Andolfi pf   Pathé X98078

SYLVIANO

Je n'ai que mon coeur v & pf – arr. vln & pf
with G. Andolfi pf   Pathé X98121

TCHAIKOVSKY

(12) Pieces (of moderate difficulty) Op. 40 pf
No. 2. Chanson triste arr. vln & pf
with G. Andolfi pf   Pathé X9746

THOMÉ

Simple aveu, Op. 25 pf – arr. vln & pf
with L. Petitjean pf   Columbia DF1040

TOSELLI

Serenade, Op. 6 vln & pf
with G. Andolfi pf   Pathé PA283, X9751
Serenade, Op. 6 vln & pf
with L. Petitjean pf   Columbia DF1040

WARREN

(The) Gold Diggers of 1933 – musical
The Gold Diggers song arr. vln & pf
with G. Andolfi pf   Pathé X98202

WAYNE

Ramona (1927) v & pf – arr. vln & pf
with G. Andolfi pf   Pathé X9762

WILLAUME

(La) Noce bretonne vln & pf
with G. Andolfi pf   Pathé X98190

WOOD

Roses of Picardy (1916) v & pf – arr. vln & pf
with G. Andolfi pf   Pathé PA503, X9762

Charles CYROULNIK

BACH

Concerto No. 1, in a, BWV1041 vln, strs & c
with Toulouse Symphony   Counterpoint C610, CS5610
Orch. – Auriacombe
Concerto No. 2, in E, BWV1042 vln, strs & c
with Toulouse Symphony   Counterpoint C610, CS5610
Orch. – Auriacombe
Concerto in d, BWV1043 2 vlns, strs & c
with G. Armand vln, & Toulouse   Counterpoint C610, CS5610
Symphony Orch. – Auriacombe

BEETHOVEN

Concerto in D, Op. 61 (cadenzas by Kreisler) vln & orch.
with L'Orch. des Concerts   Ducretet–Thomson CC506,
Colonne – Dervaux   SCC506
World Record Club ST310, T310

(3) Sonatas, Op. 12 vln & pf
No. 3. Sonata No. 3, in E flat
with A. Ciccolini pf   Vega C30 A314, C30 ST20014,
MT10139

Sonata No. 9, in A, Op. 47 "Kreutzer" vln & pf
with A. Ciccolini pf   Vega 10252, C30 A314, C30
ST20014, MT10139

DEBUSSY

Sonata No. 3, in g (1917) vln & pf
with J. Hubeau pf   Erato LDE3201, STE50091,
STU70091
Musical Heritage Society
MHS803

FRANCOEUR

(12) Sonatas – Book II (1733) vln & c
Sonata No. 6, in g
with M. Charbonnier hpsi & M–A.   Musica et litera 00346ALK
Mocquot gamba   Philips L00346L

LECLAIR

(6) Concerti, Op. 7 (1737) vln & strs
Concerto No. 6, in A
with chamber orch. – Hewitt   Musica et litera 00346ALK
Philips L00346L

MOZART

Sonata No. 26, in B flat, K378 vln & pf
  with A. Ciccolini pf   Vega C30 A319, C30 ST20015

Sonata No. 32, in B flat, K454 vln & pf
  with A. Ciccolini pf   Vega C30 A319, C30 ST20025

Richard CZERWONKY (1886–1949)

BACH

(3) Sonatas & 3 Partitas, BWV1001/6 solo vln
  Partita No. 2, in d: Chaconne (5th mvt) BWV1004
  (unaccompanied)   Christschall 146/7

BOROWSKI

Adoration (1903) vln & pf
  with piano   Edison cylinder 2475
    Edison Diamond Disc 80207

GOUNOD

Ave Maria (Méditation on Bach's "Prelude No. 1, in C" from Book I of
  "Das Wohltemperirte Clavier") v & pf – arr. vln & pf
  with H. Steiner pf   Christschall 150

KREISLER

Liebesfreud vln & pf
  with piano   Edison cylinder 2625
    Edison Diamond Disc 80207

MASSENET

Thaïs (1894) – opera
  Méditation arr. vln & pf Marsick
  with H. Steiner pf   Christschall 150

VIVALDI

(12) Concerti, Op. 3 "L'Estro armonico" var. cbns & strs
  Concerto No. 8, in a, P.2 (F.I, No. 177) 2 vlns, strs & c
  with C. Steiner vln & H. Steiner pf   Christschall 148/9

WIENIAWSKI

Légende, Op. 17 vln & pf or orch.
  with piano   Edison cylinder 2932
    Edison Diamond Disc 80207

Jan DAHMEN (1898–1957)

BACH

(3) Sonatas & 3 Partitas, BWV1001/6 solo vln
  Sonata No. 1, in g: Adagio (1st mvt); **Fugue** (2nd mvt) BWV1001
  (unaccompanied)   Telefunken E1671

(4) Suites, BWV1066/9 strs & c
  Suite No. 3, in D: Air (2nd mvt) BWV1068 2 obs, 3 tpts,
  drms & strs – arr. vln & pf as "Air on the G–string" by Wilhelmj
  with M. Raucheisen pf   19464   Telefunken A1608
    Ultraphon AP1243

KREISLER

Andantino (Padre Martini) vln & pf
  with piano   Telefunken A1555

Variations on a theme of Corelli (Tartini) vln & pf
  with M. Raucheisen pf   19466   Telefunken A1608
    Ultraphon AP1243

MOZART

Concerto No. 5, in A, K219 "Turkish" vln & orch.*
  2RA 3102ᴵᴬ☐, 3103ᴵᴵᴬ☐, 3104ᴵᴵ☐ HMV DB4578/81
  ☐, 3105ᴵᴵᴬ☐, 3106/7ᴵᴵ☐, 3108ᴵᴬ☐
  with Saxon State   & 3109ᴵᴬ☐
  Orch. – Böhm

RIES

(La) Capricciosa vln & pf
  with piano   Telefunken A1555

RIMSKY–KORSAKOV

Scheherazade, Op. 35 (1888) orch.
  with Concertgebouw Orch.,   Epic LC3300
  Amsterdam – van Beinum   Philips A00373L, ABL3194,
    G05407R

SIBELIUS

Concerto in d, Op. 47 vln & orch.
  with London Philharmonic   Decca LXT2813
  Orch. – van Beinum   London LL777

Bela DAJOS (1897–)

ANONYMOUS

O du Fröhliche, O du Selige (1819) v & pf – arr. vln & org
  with organ   Odeon 0–2624

BLAAUW

(The) Clock is playing pf – arr. vln & pf
  with M. Spoliansky pf   50283   Odeon 0–7230

BRAGA

(7) Melodies (1867) v & pf
  No. 5. La serenata "Angel's serenade" arr. vln, vlc & pf
  with G. Piatigorsky vlc   XXB 7634   Odeon AA68038
  & K. Szreter pf   Parlophone E10593

CHOPIN

(3) Nocturnes, Op. 9 pf
  No. 2. Nocturne No. 2, in E flat arr. vln & pf Sarasate
  with M. Spoliansky pf   57805   Odeon 0–7231

DVOŘÁK

(8) Humoresques, Op. 101 pf
  No. 7. Humoresque No. 7, in G flat arr. vln & pf "in G" Kreisler
  with orch.   XXB 7527–1   Odeon 3202, 0–6506, 212012AA

GLUCK

Orphée et Eurydice (1762) – opera
  Dance of the blessed spirits: Lento "Mélodie" (No. 2) arr. vln & pf
  Kreisler
  with M. Spoliansky pf   57806   Odeon 0–7231

GODARD

Jocelyn (1888) – opera
  Cachés dans cet asile "Berceuse" arr. vln, vlc & pf
  with G. Piatigorsky vlc   XXB 7633   Odeon AA68038
  & K. Szreter pf   Parlophone E10593

* Cadenza omitted.

KREISLER

Caprice Viennois, Op. 2 vln & pf
  with orch.   XXB 7530/2 Odeon 3202, 0–6506, 212012AA

Liebesfreud vln & pf
  with orch.   Odeon 0–6511

Liebesleid vln & pf
  with orch.   Odeon 0–6511

Andantino (Padre Martini) vln & pf
  with M. Spoliansky pf   57806 Odeon 0–7231

MICHAÏLOW

Gavotte, Op. 2 vln & pf
  with M. Spoliansky pf   50271 Odeon 0–7063

ROLF

Sehnsucht v & pf – arr. vln & pf Spoliansky
  with M. Spoliansky pf   50302 Odeon 0–7230

RUBINSTEIN

(2) Melodies, Op. 3 pf
  No. 1. Melody in F arr. vln, vlc & pf
  with G. Piatigorsky vlc,   XXB 7641 Odeon AA68034
  & K. Szreter pf

SAINT–SAËNS

(Le) Carnaval des animaux (1886) small orch.
  Le cygne arr. vln & pf
  with M. Spoliansky pf   50272 Odeon 0–7063

SCHUMANN

(13) Kinderscenen, Op. 15 pf
  No. 7. Träumerei arr. vln, vlc & pf
  with G. Piatigorsky vlc   XXB 7643 Odeon AA68034
  & K. Szreter pf

Indulis DALMANIS (1922–)

KEPITIS

Trio No. 3, in G pf, vln & vlc
  with J. Kepitis pf & E. Bertovsky vlc   Mezhdunarodnaya Kniga D6179

STURESTEP

(Le) Moulin (The mill) vln & pf
  with piano   Mezhdunarodnaya Kniga
                      D0009975/6

VITOL

Romance in d, Op. 15 vln & pf
  with piano   Mezhdunarodnaya Kniga
                      D0009975/6

Benone DAMIAN

GOLESTAN

(Le) Laoutar (1934) vlc or vln & pf or orch.
  Danse moldave
  with E. Vaida pf   Electrecord ECC699
  Fantaisie
  with E. Vaida pf   Electrecord ECC699

LAZÁR

(3) Bagatelles (1924) vln & pf
  with E. Vaida pf   Electrecord ECC699

Viktor DANCHENKO

BOCCHERINI

(6) Quintets, Op. 57 (1799) pf, 2 vlns, vla & vlc
  No. 1. Quintet No. 1, in D gtr, 2 vlns, vla & vlc
  with A. Ivanov–Kramsky gtr, E.   Mezhdunarodnaya Kniga
  Grach vln, V. Sitkovetsky vla & V. D014779/80, SM02347/8
  Simon vlc

CHAUSSON

Concerto in D, Op. 21 pf, vln & str qt
  with B. Davidovich pf, E. Grach vln, Mezhdunarodnaya Kniga
  G. Sosonsky vln, V. Sitkovetsky vla & D016507/8
  V. Simon vlc

DEBUSSY

(La) Plus que lente – valse (1910) pf – arr. vln & pf Heifetz
  with M. Muntyan pf   Mezhdunarodnaya Kniga
                      D17635/6

FALLA

(La) Vida Breve (1913) – opera
  Danza española orch. – arr. vln & pf Kreisler
  with M. Muntyan pf   Mezhdunarodnaya Kniga
                      D17635/6

GRIEG

Sonata No. 1, in F, Op. 8 vln & pf
  with A. Ginzburg pf   Mezhdunarodnaya Kniga
                      D021593

MEDTNER

Quintet in C (1950) pf, 2 vlns, vla & vlc
  with A. Bakhchiev pf, E. Grach vln, Mezhdunarodnaya Kniga
  V. Sitkovetsky vla & V. Simon vlc D016518

MENDELSSOHN, A.

Partita on a theme of Bach (1957) solo vln
  Prelude (1st mvt); **Fugue** (2nd mvt)
  (unaccompanied)   Mezhdunarodnaya Kniga
                      D021594

SHOSTAKOVICH

Quartet No. 4, in D, Op. 83 (1949) 2 vlns, vla & vlc
  Andantino arr. vln & pf Tziganov
  with M. Muntyan pf   Mezhdunarodnaya Kniga
                      D17635/6

STRAUSS, R.

Quartet in A, Op. 2 2 vlns, vla & vlc
  with E. Grach vln, V. Sitkovetsky vla Mezhdunarodnaya Kniga
  & V. Simon vlc   D017631/2

VIEUXTEMPS

(6) Morceaux de Salon, Op. 22 vln & pf
  No. 4. Tarantelle in a
  with M. Muntyan pf   Mezhdunarodnaya Kniga
                      D17635/6

YSAŸE

(3) Mazurkas, Op. 11 vln & pf
No. 1. Mazurka No. 1, in G "Danse souvenir"
with M. Khylstov pf — Mezhdunarodnaya Kniga
D021594

No. 2. Mazurka No. 2, in a
with M. Khylstov pf — Mezhdunarodnaya Kniga
D021594

No. 3. Mazurka No. 3, in b "Lointaine–passé"
with M. Khylstov pf — Mezhdunarodnaya Kniga
D021594

(6) Sonatas, Op. 27 solo vln
Sonata No. 1, in g
(unaccompanied) — Mezhdunarodnaya Kniga
D17635/6

Kaja DANCZOWSKA (1949–)

WIENIAWSKI

(L') École moderne, Op. 10 (10 Études) solo vln
No. 7. Étude No. 7, in A flat "La Cadenza"
(unaccompanied) — Muza XL0433

Scherzo–Tarantelle, Op. 16 vln & pf
with K. Kujawa pf — Muza XL0433

Julian DANEMAN

BEETHOVEN

Sextet in E flat, Op. 81 2 vlns, vla, vlc & 2 hrns
with V. Zhuk vln, M. Tolpygo vla, G. — Mezhdunarodnaya Kniga
Ivanov vlc, A. Demin — SM02453/4
hrn & B. Kharchenko hrn

Ruth DANZ

VIVALDI

(12) Concerti, Op. 3 "L'Estro armonico" var cbns & strs
Concerto No. 11. in d, P.250 (F.IV, No. 11) 2 vlns, vlc, strs & c
with F. Zepparoni vln, W. Hillringhaus Adès (Florilège) 13001
vlc & Augsbourg Chamber
Orch. – Deyle

Marcel DARRIEUX (1891–)

ALBÉNIZ

Canciòn catalan unid – arr. vln & pf
with Evard pf — Odeon 166196

ANONYMOUS

Londonderry air Traditional Irish ballad – arr. vln & pf Kreisler
with Mme. Darrieux pf — Odeon 166440

BEETHOVEN

Serenade in D, Op. 25 fl, vln & vla
with M. Moyse fl & J. Pasquier vla — Decca 25592/3, K582/3,
T10002/3

DEBUSSY

(12) Préludes – Book I (1910) pf
No. 8. La Fille aux cheveux de lin arr. vln & pf Hartmann
with Mme. Darrieux pf — Odeon 166197

DUSSEK

Minuet pf unid – arr. vln & pf Burmester
with Mme. Darrieux pf — Odeon 166322

ELGAR

Salut d'amour, Op. 12 orch. – arr. vln & pf Elgar
with Mme. Darrieux pf — Odeon 166385

FALLA

Concerto (1923/6) hpsi, fl, ob, cl, vln & vlc
with M. de Falla hpsi, M. Moyse fl, Columbia 266017/8, 67922/3D,
Bonneau ob, Godeau cl & Cruque vlc (set X9), LFX92/3

GODARD

(6) Morceaux, Op. 128 vln & pf
No. 5. Sérénade andalouse
with Mme. Darrieux pf — Odeon 166441

GUIRAUD

Piccolino (1879) – opera
Mélodrame arr. vln & pf
with Mme. Darrieux pf — Odeon 166440

JAQUES–DALCROZE

Danse frivole vln & pf
with Mme. Darrieux pf — Odeon 166323

KREISLER

Liebesleid vln & pf
with Mme. Darrieux pf — Odeon 166492

MASSENET

Thaïs (1894) – opera
Méditation arr. vln & pf Marsick
with Mme Darrieux pf — Odeon 166491

MONTI

Aubade d'amour vln & pf
with Mme Darrieux pf — Kl 3953[1] Odeon 166384

Csárdas (1904) vln & pf
with piano — Odeon 0–26149

PIERNÉ

Sérénade in A, Op. 7 (1875) pf – arr. vln & pf
with Mme. Darrieux pf — Odeon 166195

RAFF

(6) Pieces, Op. 85 vln & pf
No. 3. Cavatina in D
with Mme. Darrieux pf — Odeon 0–26228, 166441

RAVEL

Berceuse sur le nom de Gabriel Fauré (1922) vln & pf
with Mme. Darrieux pf — Odeon 0–26229, 166322

Pièce en forme d'Habanera v & pf – arr. vln & pf Catherine
with Mme. Darrieux pf — Odeon 0–26229, 166197

RICO

Primo Bachio vln & pf
    with Mme. Darrieux pf   Kl 3952[1]   Odeon 166384

SAINT–SAËNS

Oratorio de Noël, Op. 12 (1863) – oratorio
  No. 7. Tecum principium arr. vln, vlc, hp & org
    with J. Ibos vlc, L. Laskin hp & J.   Decca TF140
    Lemaire org

SCHUMANN

(12) Duets, Op. 85 pf – 4 hands
  No. 12. Abendlied arr. vln & pf Wilhelmj
    with Mme. Darrieux pf   Odeon 166323, 0–26227
(13) Kinderscenen, Op. 15 pf
  No. 7. Träumerei arr. vln & pf
    with Mme. Darrieux pf   Odeon 166195, 0–26227

SIMONETTI

Madrigale pf – arr. vln & pf
    with Mme. Darrieux pf   Odeon 166385, 0–26228

STRAVINSKY

(L') Histoire du Soldat (1918) narrators, tpt, cbs, tbn, cl, vln, bsn & pcn
  with E. Foveau tpt, Dellos tbn,   Columbia 68123/5D, (set M184),
  Godeau cl, Boussagol cbs, Dherin bsn   GQX10672/4, LFX263/5,
  & M. Morel pcn – cond. Stravinsky   LX197/9, LWX25/7

TOSELLI

Serenade, Op. 6 vln & pf
    with Mme. Darrieux pf   Odeon 166195

Henry DATYNER (1917–)

VAUGHAN WILLIAMS

Job (1930) orch.
  Elihu's dance of youth & beauty
    with London Philharmonic   Everest LPBR6019, SDBR3019
    Orch. – Boult

WOLPE

Piece (in 2 parts for 6 players) vln, cl, tpt, vlc, hp & pf
  with C. Bradbury cl, D. Mason tpt, C.   HMV ASD2388
  Tunnell vlc, M. Jefferies hp & K.
  Wolpe pf

Lukas DAVID

DAVID, J.N.

Concerto, Op. 45 (1952) vln & orch.
  with Munich Philharmonic   Deutsche Grammophon 803,
  Orch. – T.C. David   LP16403

GRAUNKE

Concerto vln & orch.
  with Graunke Symphony   Eurodisc 60176GK, 60177GK
  Orch. – Graunke

STADLMAIR

Concerto vln & strs
  with Munich Chamber   Amadeo AVRS5050
  Orch. – Stadlmair   Mace MXX9083

Rosalynd DAVIS

FRIML

Mélodie, Op. 27 vln & pf
  with B. Dann pf   7054   Edison Diamond Disc 80527

SAINT–SAËNS

(Le) Carnaval des animaux (1886) small orch.
  Le Cygne arr. vln & pf
    with B. Dann pf   7053   Edison Diamond Disc 80527

Arthur DAVISON

BERKELEY

Sonatina in A, Op. 17 (1942) vln & pf
  with R. Pratt pf   CBC Transcription Program 138

BRAHMS

Sonata (1853) "Frei aber einsam" vln & pf
Allegro (Scherzo) in c "Sonatensatz"
  with R. Pratt pf   CBC Transcription Program 138

MARAIS

(5) Danses anciennes vln & c
  with R. Pratt pf   CBC Transcription Program 138

Andrew DAWES

PAGANINI

Sonata concertante in A, Op. 61 (1804) vln & gtr
  with A. Lagoya gtr   Victor LSC3142

Huguette DEAT

VIVALDI

*(12) Concerti, Op. 3 "L'Estro armonico" var. cbns & strs
  Concerto No. 1, in D, P.146(F.IV, No. 7) 4 vlns, vlc, strs & c
    with G. Jarry vln, G. Carles vln J–N   Erato STU70641
    Molard vln & Jean–François Paillard
    Chamber Orch. – Paillard
  Concerto No. 4, in e, P.97 (F.I, No. 174) 4 vlns, strs & c
    with G. Jarry vln, G. Carles vln, J–N.   Erato STU70641
    Molard vln & Jean–François Paillard
    Chamber Orch. – Paillard
  Concerto No. 7, in F, P.249 (F.IV, No.9) 4 vlns, strs & c
    with G. Jarry vln, G. Carles vln, J–N.   Erato STU70641
    Molard vln & Jean–François Paillard
    Chamber Orch. – Paillard
  Concerto No. 10, in b, P.148 (F.IV, No. 10) 4 vlns, strs & c
    with G. Jarry vln, G. Carles vln, J–N.   Erato STU70641
    Molard vln & Jean–François Paillard
    Chamber Orch. – Paillard

* These five concerti also have Monique Vallet as one of the soloists.
  However, it is not clear as to which concerto features her as soloist.

VIVALDI – *Continued*

Concerto in B flat, P.367 (F.I, No. 59) 4 vlns, strs & c
  with G. Jarry vln, G. Carles vln, J–N.   Erato STU70641
  Molard vln & Jean–François Paillard
  Chamber Orch. – Paillard

Alexander DEBRUILLE

ALBÉNIZ

España (6 Feuilles d'album) Op. 165 pf
  No. 2. Tango in D arr. vln & pf Elman
    with G. Truc pf   Pathé–Actuelle 52048

BIZET

Agnus Dei v & pf – arr. v, vln & pf
  with C.M. Agussol s & piano   Odeon 33450
                                 Zonophone 1259

CHAMINADE

Sérénade espagnole pf – arr. vln & pf Kreisler
  with piano   Pathé 1585
                                 Pathé–Actuelle 10298

CUI

Kaleidoscope, Op. 50 vln & pf
  No. 9. Orientale
    with piano   Pathé 1585
                                 Pathé–Actuelle 10298

DRIGO

(2) Airs de Ballet orch.
  No. 2. Valse bluette arr. vln & pf Auer
    with G. Truc pf   Pathé–Actuelle 10270, 25036

DVOŘÁK

Sonatina in G, Op. 100 vln & pf
  Larghetto (2nd mvt) arr. vln & pf as "Indian lament" by Kreisler
    with G. Truc pf   Pathé–Actuelle 52049

KREISLER

Caprice viennois, Op. 2 vln & pf
  with G. Truc pf   Pathé–Actuelle 10525, 52048
Liebesfreud vln & pf
  with piano   Pathé 1606
                                 Pathé–Actuelle 10449
Liebesleid vln & pf
  with G. Truc pf   Pathé–Actuelle 52049
Schön Rosmarin vln & pf
  with piano   Pathé–Actuelle 10270

OPENSHAW

Love sends a little gift of roses (1919) v & pf – arr. vln & pf
  with piano   Pathé 1396
                                 Perfect 11529

RAFF

(6) Pieces, Op. 85 vln & pf
  No. 3. Cavatina in D
    with G. Truc pf   E 67210–1 Pathé 5629
                                    Pathé–Actuelle 52037

RIMSKY–KORSAKOV

Sadko (1898) – opera
  Chant hindou arr. vln & pf Kreisler
    with G. Truc pf   Pathé–Actuelle 25036

de ROSE

When you're gone I won't forget v & pf – arr. vln & pf
  with piano   Pathé 1396

SARASATE

(8) Danzas españolas vln & pf
  No. 1. Malagueña, Op. 21, No. 1
    with piano   Pathé 1606
                                 Pathé–Actuelle 10449

SCHUBERT, François

(12) Bagatelles, Op. 13 vln & pf
  No. 9. L'abeille
    with G. Truc pf   E 67201–2 Pathé 5629
                                    Pathé–Actuelle 52037

SCHUMANN

(26) Myrthen, Op. 25 v & pf
  No. 3. Der Nussbaum arr. vln & pf
    with piano   Pathé–Actuelle 10270

THOMAS

Mignon (1886) – opera
  Entr'acte (Gavotte) (Act II) orch. – arr. vln & pf Sarasate
    with G. Truc pf   Pathé 1122
                                 Pathé–Actuelle 25029
                                 Perfect 11529

THOMÉ

Simple aveu, Op. 25 pf – arr. vln & pf
  with G. Truc pf   Pathé 1122
                                 Pathé–Actuelle 25029

David DE GROOT (1881–1933)

d'AMBROSIO

Canzonetta, Op. 6 vln & pf
  with piano   Bb 2212ᵛ HMV B1483

ANONYMOUS

Auld Robin Gray (1780) traditional Scottish ballad – arr. vln & pf
  with piano   HMV B814
Bonnie Mary of Argyle traditional Scottish ballad – arr. vln & pf
  with piano   HMV B814
Drink to me only with thine eyes (1762) v & pf – arr. vln & org Calcott
  with H. Dawson org   Bb 19606ᴵᴵ△ HMV B3511

BEETHOVEN

(6) Minuets, G.167 pf
  No. 2. Minuet No. 2, in G arr. vln & pf Burmester
    with P. Kahn pf   HO 4296 ae HMV B989, X652

BOND

(A) Perfect day (1910) v & pf – arr. vln & org
   with H. Dawson org   Bb 19607^I△   HMV B3512

CLAY

I'll sing thee songs of Araby (1877) v & pf – arr. vln & org
   with H. Dawson org   Bb 19604^{III}△   HMV B3511

DRIGO

(Les) Millions d'Arlequin (1900) – ballet orch.
   Sérénade arr. vln & pf Auer
   with piano   HO 3277 ae   HMV B772

DVOŘÁK

(8) Humoresques, Op. 101 pf
   No. 7. Humoresque No. 7, in G flat arr. vln & pf "in G" Wilhelmj
   with piano   Bb 2213^{IX} HMV B1483

GOUNOD

Ave Maria (Méditation on Bach's "Prelude No. 1, in C" from Book I of
"Das Wohltemperirte Clavier") v & pf – arr. vln, pf & org
   with piano & organ   HMV B846, X645
Ave Maria (Méditation on Bach's "Prelude No. 1, in C" from Book I of
"Das Wohltemperirte Clavier") v & pf – arr. vln & org
   with E. O'Henry   BR 2785^{III}△   HMV B3489, HN451
   cinema org

d'HARDELOT

Because (1902) v & pf – arr. vln & org
   with H. Dawson org   Bb 19605^I△   HMV B3512

LALO

(Le) Roi d'Ys (1888) – opera
   Vainement, ma bien aimée (Aubade) arr. vln & pf Szigeti
   with P.B. Kahn pf   HO 4298 ae   HMV B989, X652

MASCAGNI

Cavalleria Rusticana (1890) – opera
   Intermezzo orch. – arr. vln, pf & org
   with piano & organ   HMV B846, X645
   Intermezzo orch. – arr. vln & org
   with E. O'Henry   BR 2786^{II}△   HMV B3489
   cinema org

MOLLOY

Love's old sweet song v & pf – arr. vln & org
   with H. Dawson org   OB 1528^{II}△   HMV B4185

MOSZKOWSKI

(6) Klavierstücke, Op. 15 pf – 4 hands
   No. 1. Serenata arr. vln & org
   with H. Dawson org   OB 1529^{II}△   HMV B4070

RAFF

(6) Pieces, Op. 85 vln & pf
   No. 3. Cavatina in D arr. vln & org
   with T. Casey org   BR 2181^{III}△   HMV B2920

RIMSKY–KORSAKOV

Sadko (1898) – opera
   Chant hindou arr. vln & pf Kreisler
   with piano   HMV B1922

SAINT–SAËNS

(Le) Carnaval des animaux (1886) small orch.
   Le cygne arr. vln & pf
   with piano   HO 3505 ae   HMV B1230
Samson et Dalila, Op. 47 (1877) – opera
   Mon coeur s'ouvre à ta voix arr. vln & org
   with H. Dawson org   OB 1526^{II}△   HMV B4070

SCHUMANN

(13) Kinderscenen, Op. 15 pf
   No. 7. Träumerei arr. vln, pf & org
   with piano & organ   b 20512 e   HMV B878

TCHAIKOVSKY

(12) Pieces (of moderate difficulty) Op. 40 pf
   No. 2. Chanson triste arr. vln & pf
   with P.B. Kahn pf   HO 3372 af   HMV C903

TOSTI

Parted v & pf – arr. vln & org
   with T. Casey org   BR 2087^{IIA}△   HMV B2920

WOOD

Love's garden of roses v & pf – arr. vln & org
   with H. Dawson org   OB 1527^{II}△   HMV B4185

YEARSLEY

Siesta v & pf – arr. vln & pf
   with piano   HMV C994

YRADIER

(La) Paloma (1877) v & pf – arr. vln, pf & org
   with piano & organ   b 20519 e   HMV B772

YSAŸE

Rêve d'enfant, Op. 14 vln & pf
   with P. B. Kahn pf   HO 3366 af   HMV C903

Frida DE GROOT

BRAGA

(7) Melodies (1867) v & pf
   No. 5. La serenata "Angel's serenade" arr. vln & pf
   with piano   Favorite 1–94089D

SIMONETTI

Madrigale pf – arr. vln & pf
   with piano   Favorite 1–94079D

Max DE GROOT

BRAHMS

(21) Hungarian Dances pf duet
   Hungarian Dance No. 5, in f sharp arr. vln & pf "in g" Joachim
   with piano   327 °   Favorite 1–14018E, 51
   Hungarian dance No. 5, in f sharp arr. vln & pf "in g" Joachim
   with piano   Beka 5180

DELIBES

Sylvia (1876) – ballet orch.
No. 16a. Pizzicato–scherzettino (Act III) arr. vln & pf
with piano   329 °   Favorite 1–14020E, 51

GOUNOD

Ave Maria (Méditation on Bach's "Prelude No. 1, in C" from Book I of "Das Wohltemperirte Clavier") v & pf – arr. vln & pf
with piano   Beka 5181

MONTI

Csárdas (1904) vln & pf
with piano   Marathon 310

WIENIAWSKI

Mazurka in a, Op. 3 "Kujawiak" vln & pf
with piano   Marathon 310

Jacques DEJEAN

RAVEL

Introduction & Allegro (1906) hp, str qt, fl & cl
with M–C. Jamet hp, P. Sanchez vln,   Erato LDE3173
C. Lequien vla, P. Degenne vlc, C.   Musical Heritage Society
Lardé fl & G. Deplus cl   MHS892

TELEMANN

Concerto in D 4 vlns, strs & c
with J. Pasquier vln, G. Gaunet vln, F.   Éditions phonographiques
Geyr vln & Paris Collegium Musette –   parisiennes (Allegro) APG125
Douatte

VIVALDI

(12) Concerti, Op. 3 "L'Estro armonico" var. cbns & strs
Concerto No. 8, in a, P.2 (F.I, No. 177) 2 vlns, strs & c
with R. Gendre vln & Paris Chamber   Lumen LD2–401
Orch. – Duvauchelle
Concerto No. 10, in b, P.148 (F.IV, No. 10) 4 vlns, strs & c
with R. Gendre vln, S. Plazonich vln,   La Boîte à Musique LD102
D. Marchand vln & Paris Chamber   Lumen 2–08011/3
Orch. – Davauchelle

Mary DELMOR

d'AMBROSIO

Petite chanson, Op. 28 vln & pf
with piano   Aco G15104

BARNS

Swing song vln & pf
with piano   Aco G15104

KREISLER

Rondino on a theme by Beethoven vln & pf
with piano   Aco G15273
Schön Rosmarin vln & pf
with piano   Aco G15273

Rudolf DEMAN

AMANI

(4) Pièces caractéristiques, Op. 7 pf
No. 2. Orientale arr. vln & pf Elman
with J. Heidenreich pf   Vox 06213

d'AMBROSIO

Canzonetta, Op. 6 vln & pf
with K. Szreter pf   Vox 06180
Canzonetta, Op. 6 vln & pf
with J. Heidenreich pf   51484   Homochord B8504

BRAHMS

(21) Hungarian Dances pf duet
Hungarian Dance No. 2, in d arr. pf, vln & vlc
with O. Urack pf & C. Dechert vlc   Vox 06071
Hungarian Dance No. 6, in E flat, arr. pf, vln & vlc
with O. Urack pf & C. Dechert vlc   Vox 06071

BRUCH

Kol Nidrei, Op. 47 vlc or vln & orch.
with J. Heidenreich pf   51483   Homochord B8527

CUI

Kaleidoscope, Op. 50 vln & pf
No. 9. Orientale
with K. Szreter pf   Vox 06180

DITTERSDORF

Quartet No. 5, in E flat, 2 vlns, vla & vlc
with E. Kornsand vln, K. Reitz vla &   Polydor 90048/50
C. Dechert vlc

DRDLA

Serenade No. 1, in A vln & pf
with O. Urack pf   Vox 06053
Serenade No. 1, in A vln & pf
with O. Urack pf   Vox 645, 06108
Souvenir vln & pf
with O. Urack pf   Vox 06108

DVOŘÁK

(8) Slavonic Dances, Op. 46 pf duet; orch.
No. 2. Slavonic Dance No. 2, in e arr. pf, vln & vlc
with O. Urack pf & C. Dechert vlc   Vox 6045
No. 6. Slavonic Dance No. 6, in D arr. pf, vln & vlc
with O. Urack pf & C. Dechert vlc   Vox 6045
(8) Slavonic Dances, Op. 72 pf duet; orch.
No. 4. Slavonic Dance No. 12, in D flat arr. pf, vln & vlc
with O. Urack pf & C. Dechert vlc   Vox 06072
No. 7. Slavonic Dance No. 15, in C arr. pf, vln & vlc
with O. Urack pf & C. Dechert vlc   Vox 06072

GLAZOUNOV

(5) Novellettes, Op. 15 (1888) 2 vlns, vla & vlc
No. 3. Interludium in modo Antico
with E. Kornsand vln, K. Reitz vla &   Polydor 95280
C. Dechert vlc
No. 4. Valse
with E. Kornsand vln, K. Reitz vla &   Polydor 95280
C. Dechert vlc

GLUCK

Orphée et Eurydice (1762) – opera
  Dance of the blessed spirits: Lento "Mélodie" (No. 2) arr. vln & pf
  Kreisler
    with J. Heidenreich pf   51481   Homochord B8526

KREISLER

Liebesfreud vln & pf
    with O. Urack pf   Vox 06076
Liebesleid vln & pf
    with O. Urack pf   Vox 06076
Polichinelle–Serenade vln & pf
    with J. Heidenreich pf   Vox 06222
Grave (W.F. Bach) vln & pf
    with J. Heidenreich pf   Vox 06231
(La) Précieuse (L. Couperin) vln & pf
    with J. Heidenreich pf   Vox 06222

LANGER

Grandfather, Op. 22 salon orch. – arr. vln & pf
    with K. Szreter pf   Vox 6181
Grandmother, Op. 20 pf – arr. vln & pf
    with K. Szreter pf   Vox 6181

LECLAIR

(12) Sonatas, Op. 9 – Book IV (1738) vln & c
  Sonata No. 3, in D: Tambourin (3rd mvt) arr. vln & pf Kreisler
    with J. Heidenreich pf   51482   Homochord B8526

MOSZKOWSKI

(6) Klavierstücke, Op. 15 pf – 4 hands
  No. 1. Serenata arr. vln & pf
    with O. Urack pf   Vox 645, 06053

MOZART

Divertimento No. 17, in D, K.334 2 hrns & strs
  Minuet (3rd mvt) arr. vln & pf Burmester
    with K. Szreter pf   Vox 06183
Quartet No. 19, in C, K.465 2 vlns, vla & vlc
    with E. Kornsand vln, K. Reitz vla &   Polydor 95301/4
    C. Dechert vlc

RIMSKY–KORSAKOV

Sadko (1898) – opera
  Chant hindou arr. vln & pf Kreisler
    with J. Heidenreich pf   51485   Homochord B8504

SCHUBERT

(5) Deutsche Tänze (Minuets) & 6 Trios, D89 (1813) orch.– arr 2 vlns, vla
  & vlc
    with E. Kornsand vln, K. Reitz vla &   Polydor 95220/1
    C. Dechert vlc
Quartet No. 10, in E flat, Op. 125 (D87) 2 vlns, vla & vlc
    with E. Kornsand vln, K. Reitz vla &   Polydor 90045/8
    C. Dechert vlc
Quartet No. 13, in a, Op. 29, No. 1 (D804) 2 vlns, vla & vlc
    with E. Kornsand vln, K. Reitz vla &   Polydor 95062/5
    C. Dechert vlc
Quartet No. 14, in d, D.810 "Death & the Maiden" 2 vlns, vla & vlc
    with E. Kornsand vln, K. Reitz vla &   Polydor 95135/9
    C. Dechert vlc

SCHUMANN

(12) Duets, Op. 85 pf – 4 hands
  No. 12. Abendlied arr. vln & pf Wilhelmj
    with O. Urack pf   Vox 06052
(13) Kinderscenen, Op. 15 pf
  No. 7. Träumerei arr. vln & pf
    with O. Urack pf   Vox 06052

STRAUSS, R.

Sonata in E flat, Op. 18 vln & pf
  Lento (2nd mvt)
    with K. Szreter pf   Vox 06183

VECSEY

Valse triste vln & pf
    with J. Heidenreich pf   51486   Homochord B8527

John DEMBECK

HANDEL

(15) Sonatas, Op. 1 (?1731) fl or vln & c
  Sonata No. 15, in E vln VI
    with L. Barkin pf   CBC Radio Canada SM27

HINDEMITH

(6) Sonatas, Op. 11
  Sonata No. 1, in E flat, (1920) vln & pf
    with L. Barkin pf   CBC Radio Canada SM27

YSAŸE

(6) Sonatas, Op. 27 solo vln
  Sonata No. 3, in d
  (unaccompanied)   CBC Radio Canada SM27

Dick DE REUS (1923–   )

DRESDEN

Trio (1943) pf, vln & vlc
    with G. Hengeveld pf & J. De Nobel   Radio Nederland RN508
    vlc

HANDEL

(15) Sonatas, Op. 1 (?1731) fl or vln & c
  Sonata No. 13, in D vln IV
    with A. de Klerk hpsi   Telefunken AWT8022

HENKEMANS

Concerto (1948) vln & orch
    with Hilversum Radio Philharmonic   Radio Nederland 109872
    Orch. – Travis

Edouard DERU (1875–1928)

KREISLER

Rondino on a theme by Beethoven vln & pf
    with piano   Pathé–Actuelle 52040

PIERNÉ

Sérénade in A, Op. 7 (1875) pf – arr. vln & pf
    with piano   Pathé–Actuelle 52040

George DESARZENS

FORNEROD
Concert 2 vlns & pf
  with V. Desarzens vln & J. Godard pf   Columbia DZX11/2

Victor DESARZENS (1908–)

FORNEROD
Concert 2 vlns & pf
  with G. Desarzens vln & J. Godard pf   Columbia DZX11/2

Bernhard DESSAU (1861–1923)

AULIN
(4) Aquarelles vln & pf
  No. 2. Humoresque
  with piano   HMV 2–47909

BACH
(3) Sonatas & 3 Partitas, BWV1001/6 solo vln
  Partita No. 1, in b: Sarabande (5th mvt) BWV1002
  (unaccompanied)   Gramophone & Typewriter
                                47937
  Partita No. 3, in E: Rondeau (3rd mvt) BWV1006
  (unaccompanied)   Gramophone & Typewriter
                                47939
(4) Suites, BWV1066/9 strs & c
  Suite No. 3, in D: Air (2nd mvt) BWV1068 2 obs, 3 tpts,
  drms & strs – arr. vln & pf as "Air on the G–string" by Wilhelmj
  with piano   Gramophone & Typewriter
                                47934

BECUCCI
Tesoro mio – waltz, Op. 228 orch. – arr. vln & pf
  with piano   Odeon 97561, X66943

BEETHOVEN
(3) Trios, Op. 1 pf, vln & vlc
  No. 1. Trio No. 1, in E flat: Adagio cantabile (2nd mvt)
  with M. Mayer–Mahr pf & H.   Polydor 19273
  Grünfeld vlc

BLECH
Alpenkönig und Menschenfiend, Op. 14 – opera
  Prelude orch. – arr. vln & pf Dessau
  with piano   HMV 2–47910

BOSC
Moss rose vln & pf
  with piano   Odeon 97560

BRAGA
(7) Melodies (1867) v & pf
  No. 5. La serenata "Angel's serenade" arr. vln & orch.
  with orch.   Odeon 36819
  No. 5. La serenata "Angel's serenade" arr. pf, vln & vlc
  with M. Mayer–Mahr pf & H.   Polydor 65307
  Grünfeld vlc

BRAHMS
(21) Hungarian Dances pf duet
  Hungarian dance No. 2, in d arr. vln & pf Joachim
  with piano   Gramophone & Typewriter
                                47936
  Hungarian dance No. 2, in d arr. vln & pf Joachim
  with piano   Odeon 51995, X50334
  Trio No. 3, in c, Op. 101 pf, vln & vlc
  Andante grazioso (3rd mvt)
  with M. Mayer–Mahr pf & H.   Polydor 19273
  Grünfeld vlc

CHOPIN
(3) Nocturnes, Op. 9 pf
  No. 2. Nocturne No. 2, in E flat arr. vln & pf Sarasate
  with piano   Gramophone & Typewriter
                                047901
  No. 2. Nocturne No. 2, in E flat arr. vln & pf Sarasate
  with piano   Odeon 51000, X50539

COUPERIN, F.
(La) Fleurie, ou la Tendre Nanette, I, No. 16 hpsi – arr. vln & orch
  with orch. – Kark   Odeon 51004, X50428

CRISTOFARO
Love's nocturne, Op. 27 mand & pf – arr. vln & orch.
  with orch.   Odeon 0616, X66900

DELIBES
Sylvia (1876) – ballet orch.
  No. 16a. Pizzicato–scherzettino (Act III) arr. vln & pf
  with piano   Gramophone & Typewriter
                                47919

DESSAU
Abendlied, Op. 47 vln & pf
  with piano   Gramophone & Typewriter
                                47933
Arioso in F, Op. 45 vln & pf
  with piano   Odeon 51003, X50425
Aus meinem Jugendgarten, Op. 53 (8 Charakterstücke) vln & pf
  No. 1b. Song without words in A
  with orch.   Odeon 51996, X50343
  No. 2d. Scherzo in G
  with piano   Gramophone & Typewriter
                                2–47904
  No. 2d. Scherzo in G
  with piano   Polydor 20075
(2) Fantasiestücke, Op. 19 vln & pf
  No. 2. Waltz
  with piano   Odeon 51998, X50384
Mazurka in g, Op. 26 vln & pf
  with piano   Gramophone & Typewriter
                                47935
Mazurka in g, Op. 26 vln & pf
  with piano   Odeon 51993, X50331
Mazurka No. 2, in e, Op. 11 vln & pf
  with piano   349 A   Gramophone & Typewriter
                                047900

DESSAU – *Continued*

Mazurka No. 2, in e, Op. 11 vln & pf
with piano   13635 R   Gramophone & Typewriter
2–47912

Mazurka No. 2, in e, Op. 11 vln & pf
with orch. – Kark   Odeon 51002, X50285

Minuet in A, Op. 35 vln & pf
with orch.   Odeon 51054, X50510

(2) Morceaux, Op. 20 vln & pf
     No. 2. Valse–caprice
with piano   Odeon 51994, X50342

Pastorale in G, Op. 25 vln & pf
with orch.   Odeon 51055, X50538

Suite in Dance Form, Op. 54 vln & pf
     No. 2. Ländler in F
with piano   Polydor 15803

     No. 3. Gavotte in D
with piano   Gramophone & Typewriter
47941
HMV 2–47903

     No. 3. Gavotte in D
with piano   Odeon 51997, X50382

     No. 3. Gavotte in D
with piano   Polydor 20075

(5) Vortragsstücke, Op. 57 vln & pf
     No. 4. Danse orientale
with piano   13634 R   Gramophone & Typewriter
2–47911

DONIZETTI

(La) Fille du Regiment (1840) – opera
     Tyrolienne arr. vln & pf
with piano   Polydor 20074, 61894

FIÉGIER

(Les) Stances v & pf – arr. vln & orch.
with orch.   Odeon 36823

GILLET

Babillage pf – arr. vln & pf
with piano   Odeon 60104

Loin du Bal, Op. 36 – Ballet orch.
     Intermezzo arr. vln & pf
with orch.   Odeon 60085

GODARD

Jocelyn (1888) – opera
     Cachés dans cet asile "Berceuse" arr. vln & orch.
with orch. – Kark   Odeon 51001, X50263

GOUNOD

Ave Maria (Méditiation on Bach's "Prelude No. 1, in C" from Book I of
"Das Wohltemperirte Clavier") v & pf – arr. vln & orch.
with orch.   Odeon 36838

Faust (1859) – opera
     Salut! Demeure chaste et pure arr. pf, vln & vlc
with M. Mayer–Mahr pf & H.   Polydor 65306
Grünfeld vlc

Hymne à Sainte–Cécile (1864) vln, org & pf – arr. vln & pf
with piano   1024 m   Polydor 15759, 0947907

GRIEG

(6) Lyric pieces – Book III, Op. 43 pf
     No. 6. To the spring arr. vln & orch.
with orch.   Odeon 0618, X66901

Peer Gynt (Suite No. 1) Op. 46 orch.
     No. 3. Anitra's dance arr. pf, vln & vlc
with M. Mayer–Mahr pf & H.   Polydor 65306
Grünfeld vlc

HUBAY

Hungarian fantasy "Kunok abrand" vln & pf
with piano   Odeon 97723

JENKINSON

(6) Lyrical pieces vln & pf
     No. 2. Elfentanz
with orch.   Odeon 67623

KREISLER

Liebesfreud vln & pf
with piano   2172 ak   HMV 2–47901, V172

Liebesfreud vln & pf
with piano   Polydor 20073

Liebesleid vln & pf
with piano   2173 ak   HMV 2–47902, V172

Liebesleid vln & pf
with piano   Polydor 20073

Scherzo (Dittersdorf) vln & pf
with piano   Polydor 20074, 61894

MENDELSSOHN

(6) Songs without words, Op. 62 pf
     No. 1. Song without words No. 25, in G "May breezes" arr. pf, vln & vlc
with M. Mayer–Mahr pf & H.   Polydor 61897
Grünfeld vlc

MOSZKOWSKI

(6) Klavierstücke, Op. 15 pf – 4 hands
     No. 1. Serenata arr. pf, vln & vlc
with M. Mayer–Mahr pf & H.   Polydor 61897
Grünfeld vlc

OFFENBACH

(La) Chanson de Fortunio (1861) – opéra–comedie
     No. 6bis. La chanson de fortunio (Si vous croyez que je vais dire)
with orch.   XP 3758   Odeon 60538

(La) Périchole (1868) – opéra–bouffe
     No. 3. La lettre (O mon cher amant, je te jure)
with orch.   Odeon 60583

RAFF

(6) Pieces, Op. 85 vln & pf
     No. 3. Cavatina in D
with piano   Gramophone & Typewriter
47938

RIES

Suite No. 3, in G, Op. 34 vln & pf
     No. 4. Gondoliera
with piano   Gramophone & Typewriter
47910

RUBINSTEIN

(12) Two–part songs, Op. 48 cho & pf
No. 5. Wanderess Nachtlied arr. pf, vln & vlc
with M. Mayer–Mahr pf & H.   Polydor 61896
Grünfeld vlc

SAINT–SAËNS

(Le) Déluge, Op. 45 (1876) – oratorio
Prélude vln & orch. – arr. vln & pf Saint–Saëns
with piano   Polydor 15803

SARASATE

Carmen Fantasia (on themes from the opera by Bizet) Op. 25.
vln & pf or orch.
with piano   Odeon 97736, X66942
(8) Danzas españolas vln & pf
No. 3. Romanza andaluza, Op. 22, No. 1
with piano   Odeon 51999, X50515
Faust Fantasia (on themes from the opera by Gounod) vln & pf or orch.
Valse
with orch.   Odeon 44068

SCHMALSTICH

Elfenreigen, Op. 54 vln & pf
with piano   HMV X947967

SCHUBERT

Litanei auf das Fest aller Seelen, D.343 v & pf – arr. pf, vln & vlc
with M. Mayer–Mahr pf & H.   Polydor 61896
Grünfeld vlc
(3) Marches militaires, Op. 51 (D.733) pf
No. 1. Marche militaire No. 1, in D arr. pf, vln & vlc
with M. Mayer–Mahr pf & H.   Polydor 65308
Grünfeld vlc
Octet in F, Op. 166 (D.803) cl, hrn, bsn, 2 vlns, vla, vlc & cbs
Adagio (2nd mvt) arr. pf, vln & vlc
with M. Mayer–Mahr pf & H.   Polydor 65308
Grünfeld vlc

SCHÜTT

(4) Morceaux, Op. 52 vln & pf
No. 2. Serenata
with piano   HMV 2–47907
No. 4. Mazurka
with piano   HMV 2–47908

SEIDLER–WINKLER

Gavotte in C vln & pf
with piano   HMV 2–47905
Scherzo in A vln & pf
with piano   HMV 2–47906
Wiegenliedchen vln & pf
with piano   HMV X947966

STRAUS, O.

Suite, Op. 4 pf, vln & vlc
Finale (4th mvt)
with M. Mayer–Mahr pf & H.   Polydor 65307
Grünfeld vlc

STRAUSS, R.

(Der) Rosenkavalier, Op. 59 (1911) – opera
Waltzes (Act II) arr. vln & pf
with piano   407 al & 408 al   HMV 047937/8

TCHAIKOVSKY

Trio in a, Op. 50 "To the memory of a great artist" pf, vln & vlc*
with M. Mayer–Mahr pf & H.   Polydor 19274/5
Grünfeld vlc

THOMAS

Mignon (1866) – opera
Entr'acte (Gavotte) (Act II) orch. – arr. vln & pf Sarasate
with orch.   Odeon 36829

TIRINDELLI

(6) Morceaux de concert, Op. 1 vln & pf
No. 4. Airs hongrois
with orch.   Odeon 37687/8

VERDI

(Il) Trovatore (1853) – opera
potpourri arr. vln & orch.
with orch.   Odeon 44049

WIENIAWSKI

Légende, Op. 17 vln & pf or orch.
with piano   36 Y Ao 2²   Gramophone & Typewriter 047902
(2) Mazurkas, Op. 19 vln & pf
No. 1. Mazurka No. 1, in G "Obertass"
with orch.   Odeon 67624

WILHELMJ

Parsifal Fantasia (on themes from the opera by Wagner) vln & pf
with piano   1025 m   Gramophone & Typewriter 0947906
     Polydor 15759

Emery DEUTSCH (1907–)

BRAHMS

(21) Hungarian Dances pf duet
Hungarian dance No. 1, in g arr. vln & pf Joachim
with piano   Bluebird 10340

Gioconda DE VITO (1907–)

BACH

(6) Brandenburg Concerti, BWV1046/51 (1721) strs & c
Brandenburg Concerto No. 5, in D, BWV1050 clav, fl, vln & strs
with C. Zecchi pf, A. Tassinari fl &   Cetra CB20159/61, CB20454/6,
Radio Italiana Orch. – Previtali   CC2061/3
Concerto No. 2, in E, BWV1042 vln, strs & c
     2EA 13608/9–1, 13616–2 &   HMV DB6884/6, DB9370/2
with London Chamber   13610/12–1
Orch. – Bernard

* Abridged.

BACH – *Continued*

Concerto No. 2, in E, BWV1042 vln, strs & c
with London Symphony   HMV ALP1856, ASD429
Orch. – Kubelík

Concerto in d, BWV1043 2 vlns, strs & c
with Y. Menuhin vln & Philharmonia   Electrola E70036
Orch. – Bernard   HMV BLP1046, FBLP1061,
                               GHLP1002, LBLP1017,
                               QBLP5028
                               Victor LHMV16

(3) Sonatas & 3 Partitas, BWV1001/6 solo vln
  Partita No. 2, in d, BWV1004
    2EA 12283–3, 12284–1, 12285/6   HMV DB6632/3 & DB21063 &
    –2, 14460–4, 14478–1, 14477–1C & DB21300
    (unaccompanied)   14479–1A

BEETHOVEN

Romance No. 2, in F, Op. 50 vln & orch.
    2EA 13030–2 & 13031–3   HMV DB6727
with Philharmonia Orch. – Erede

(3) Sonatas, Op. 30 vln & pf
  No. 2. Sonata No. 7, in c
    with T. Aprea pf   HMV ALP1521, QALP10226

Sonata No. 9, in A, Op. 47 "Kreutzer" vln & pf
    with T. Aprea pf   HMV ALP1319, QALP10149

BRAHMS

Concerto in D, Op. 77 (cadenza by Joachim) vln & orch.
with German Opera House   Polydor 68308/12
Orch. – van Kempen

Concerto in D, Op 77 (cadenza by Joachim) vln & orch.
with Philharmonia Orch. – Schwarz   Encore ENC110
                               HMV ALP1104
                               Music for Pleasure MFP2003

Concerto in a, Op. 102 "Double" vln, vlc & orch.
with A. Baldovino vlc & Philharmonia   HMV BLP1028, QBLP5017
Orch. – Schwarz   Victor LHMV1057

Sonata No. 1, in G, Op 78 vln & pf
with E. Fischer pf   Angel 35523
                               HMV ALP1282, LALP305,
                               QALP10131

Sonata No. 2, in A, Op. 100 vln & pf
    with T. Aprea pf   HMV ALP1521, QALP10226

Sonata No. 3, in d, Op. 108 vln & pf
with E. Fischer pf   Angel 35523
                               HMV ALP1282, LALP305,
                               QALP10131

di CAPUA

O sole mio v & pf – arr. v, vln & pf
    with B. Sarti t & piano   Edison Bell 0301

CARISSIMI

Cantata (unid)
  Piangete, ohimé, piangete arr. v, hpsi & str qt Paoli
  (leading str qt)   OEA 13621/2–1   HMV DA1945
  with G. Gatti (s) & M Silver hpsi

FRANCK

Sonata in A (1886) vln & pf
    with T. Aprea pf   HMV BLP1087

HANDEL

(15) Sonatas, Op. 1 (?1731) fl or vln & c
  Sonata No. 13, in D vln IV
    2EA 15845–2, 15846–4, 15847–2   HMV DB21420/1 . DB9696/7
  with G. Malcolm hpsi   & 15848–4

(9) Sonatas, Op. 2 (1724) 2 vlns or obs & c
  Sonata No. 8, in g
  with Y. Menuhin vln, R. Leppard hpsi   HMV ALP1462, 7ERL1429
  & J. Shinebourne vlc

(7) Sonatas, Op. 5 (1739) 2 vlns & c
  Sonata No. 2, in D
  with Y. Menuhin vln, G. Malcolm   Electrola E50554
  hpsi & J. Shinebourne vlc   HMV BLP1046, FBLP1060,
                                   LBLP1017, QBLP5028,
                                   7ERW9390
                                   Victor LHMV16

MASSENET

Élégie v & pf – arr. v, vln & pf
  with B. Sarti t & piano   Edison Bell 0279

MENDELSSOHN

Concerto in e, Op. 64 vln & orch.
with London Symphony   HMV BLP1008, QBLP5008,
Orch. – Sargent   VBLP807, WBLP1008

MOZART

Concerto No. 3, in G, K216 (cadenzas by Tovey) vln & orch
    2EA 13808/9–1, 13810–2A,   HMV DB9570/2, DB21177/9
    13811–1A, 13812–1 & 13813–2
with Royal Philharmonic
Orch. – Beecham

Concerto No. 3, in G, K216 (cadenzas by Principe & Marteau) vln & orch
with London Symphony   HMV ALP1856, ASD429
Orch. – Kubelík

PURCELL

(10) Sonatas, Z802/11 (1697) 4 parts – 2 vlns & c
  Sonata No. 9, in F, Z.810 "Golden Sonata"
  with Y. Menuhin vln, R. Leppard hpsi   HMV ALP1462, 7ERL1402
  & J. Shinebourne vlc

SCHREIER–BOTTERO

(30) Original Lieder v & pf
  No. 15. Tango of the roses arr. v, vln & pf Schreier–Bottero
  with B. Sarti t & piano   Edison Bell 0301

SPOHR

(3) Duets, Op. 67 2 vlns
  No. 2. Duet No. 2, in D: Larghetto (2nd mvt); **Rondo** (3rd mvt)
  with Y. Menuhin vln   HMV ALP1462

  No. 3. Duet No. 3, in g: Allegro (1st mvt)
  with Y. Menuhin vln   HMV ALP1462

TOSELLI

Serenade, Op. 6 vln & pf – arr. v, vln & pf
  with B. Sarti t & piano   Edison Bell 0279

VIOTTI

(3) Duets, Op. 2 2vlns
  No. 3. Duet No. 3, in G
  with Y. Menuhin vln   HMV ALP1462

VITALI

Chaconne in g vln & c – arr. vln, orch. & org Respighi
    2EA 13040/2–2 & 13084–1 HMV DB6936/7
  with H. Dawson org and Philharmonia
  Orch. – Erede

Gabrielle DEVRIÈS

BARTÓK

Sonata No. 1 (1921) vln & pf
  with N. Desouches pf   Pacific LDPC205

BEETHOVEN

Sonata No. 5, in F, Op. 24 "Spring" vln & pf
  with N. Desouches pf   Michel–Ange 14
                    Pacific LDPF187

CARRILLO

Horizontes (Poème symphonique) vln, vlc, hp & orch.
  with R. Flachhot vlc, M. Rollin hp & Philips 839272DSY
  Orch. des Concerts
  Lamoureux – Carrillo

Sextet in G (1902) 4 vlns, vla & vlc
  with R. Gendre vln, J. Ghestem vln, Sonido 9
  R. Flachot vln, S. Collot
  vla & R. Bex vlc

Sonata No. 1, in e solo vln
  (unaccompanied)   Sonido 8

Sonata No. 2, in D solo vln
  (unaccompanied)   Sonido 8

ROUSSEL

Sonata No. 2, in A Op. 28 vln & pf
  with I. Marika pf   La Boîte à Musique LD027

SCHUBERT

Sonata in A, Op. 162 (D574) "Duo" vln & pf
  with N. Desouches pf   Michel–Ange 14
                    Pacific LDPF187

STRAVINSKY

Duo concertante (1932) vln & pf
  with I. Marika pf   La Boîte à Musique LD027

Celso DIAZ

DIAZ

(La) Pilarica (Santa Cecilia) vln & pf
  with F. Queredo pf   HMV AF190

Viva mi pueblo (Jota populare) vln & pf
  with F. Queredo pf   HMV AF190

FREIRE

Ay, ay, ay v & pf – arr. vln & pf
  with F. Queredo pf   HMV AE2262

GOUNOD

Ave Maria (Méditation on Bach's "Prelude No. 1, in C" from Book I of
"Das Wohltemperirte Clavier") v & pf – arr. vln & pf
  with F. Queredo pf   HMV AE2262

Patrick DIAZ – PELAZ (see PELAZ)

Glenn DICHTEROW (1948–)

PAGANINI

(24) Caprices, Op. 1 (1801/7) solo vln
  Caprice No. 9, in E
  (unaccompanied)   Mezhdunarodnaya Kniga
                    D028103/4

Annegret DIEDRICHSEN

BEETHOVEN

(3) Trios, Op. 1 pf, vln & vlc
  No. 1. Trio No. 1, in E flat
  with L. Hokanson pf & W. Herzer vlc Orpheus OR326
  No. 2. Trio No. 2, in G
  with L. Hokanson pf & W. Herzer vlc Orpheus OR326
  No. 3. Trio No. 3, in c
  with L. Hokanson pf & W. Herzer vlc Orpheus OR327

Trio in B flat, Op. 11 cl, vlc & pf
  with L. Hokanson pf & W. Herzer vlc Orpheus OR328

(2) Trios, Op. 70 pf, vln & vlc
  No. 1. Trio No. 4, in D "Ghost"
  with L. Hokanson pf & W. Herzer vlc Orpheus OR328
  No. 2. Trio No. 5, in E flat
  with L. Hokanson pf & W. Herzer vlc Orpheus OR329

Trio No. 6, in B flat, Op. 97 "Archduke" pf, vln & vlc
  with L. Hokanson pf & W. Herzer vlc Orpheus OR330

Trio in E flat, G153 (WoO38) pf, vln & vlc
  with L. Hokanson pf & W. Herzer vlc Orpheus OR327

Trio in B flat, G154(WoO39) "In one mvt" pf, vln & vlc
  with L. Hokanson pf & W. Herzer vlc Orpheus OR330

(14) Variations in E flat, Op. 44 pf, vln & vlc
  with L. Hokanson pf & W. Herzer vlc Orpheus OR327

(10) Variations (on "Ich bin der Schneider Kakadu") Op. 121a pf, vln & vlc
  with L. Hokanson pf & W. Herzer vlc Orpheus OR329

MOZART

Sonata No. 26, in B flat, K378 vln & pf
  with L. Hokanson pf   Amadeo AVRS6362
                    Mace M9080, SMC9080

Trio No. 6, in G, K564 pf, vln & vlc
  with L. Hokanson pf & E. Finke vlc Amadeo AVRS6362
                    Mace M9080, SMC9080

Hanns Hermann DIENER (1897–1955)

BACH

Concerto in d, BWV1043 2 vlns, strs & c
    2RA 2960[V]☐, 2961[IV]☐ & HMV EH1217/8
  with C. Hampe vln and   2962/3[II]☐
  Collegium Musicum Orch.

Helga DIERCKS

BACH

Concerto in d, BWV1043 2 vlns, strs & c
  with W. Hansen vln and Hamburg Classics Club X3018
  Chamber Orch. – Walther

Grigoras DINICU (1889–1948)

ANONYMOUS

Hungarian potpourri arr. Dinicu
with orch.　　　A 7336　Columbia 5684

Romanta tiganesti vln & pf
with piano　　　H 1046　Columbia D8414

BIZET

(Les) Pêcheurs de Perles (1863) – opera
A cette voix ... Je crois entendre encore (Romance de Nadir) arr vln & pf
with piano　　　Columbia D8570

BURMESTER

Serenade vln & pf
with piano　　　Columbia D30702, OD14

DINICU

Hora Staccato vln & pf
with orch.　　　A 7335　Columbia 5684

DRDLA

Serenade No. 1, in A vln & pf
with piano　　　A7338　Columbia 14143, DO13

Souvenir vln & pf
with piano　　　A 7337　Columbia 14143, DO13

DVOŘÁK

(8) Humoresques, Op. 101 pf
No. 7. Humoresque No. 7, in G flat arr. vln & pf "in G" Wilhelmj
with piano　　　Columbia DC6, OD15

FREIRE

Ay–ay–ay v & pf – arr. vln & orch.
with orch.　　　Columbia DC6, OD15

GODARD

Jocelyn (1888) – opera
Cachés dans cet asile "Berceuse" arr. vln & pf
with piano　　　Columbia D8570

GOUNOD

Ave Maria (Méditation on Bach's "Prelude No. 1, in C" from Book I of "Das Wohltemperirte Clavier") v & pf – arr. vln & pf France
with piano　　　WA 7454–1　Columbia D30701, DV61

KREISLER

Scherzo (Dittersdorf) vln & pf
with piano　　　Columbia D30701

MARTINI (Il Tedesco)

Plaisir d'amour v & pf – arr. vln & pf
with piano　　　H 1047　Columbia D8414

NEAGA

Élégie vln & pf
with piano　　　Columbia D8572, OD16

POLIAKIN

(Le) Canari (Concert–polka) vln & pf
with orch.　　　Columbia DF130

SCHUBERT

(14) Schwanengesang, D957 v & pf
No. 4. ständchen "Serenade" arr. vln & pf
with piano　　　Columbia D30702, OD14

STRAUSS, J. (II)

Wiener Blut, Op. 354 orch. – arr. vln & orch
with orch.　　　Columbia DF130

TCHAIKOVSKY

Souvenir d'un lieu cher, Op. 42 vln & pf
No. 3. Mélodie
with piano　　　WA 7428　Columbia D30701, DV61

TOSELLI

Serenade, Op. 6 vln & pf
with piano　　　Columbia D8572, OD16

Nelly DIÓS

JÁRDÁNYI

Concertino (1953) vln & pf
with I. Szücs pf　　　Qualiton LPX1188

Mischa DOBRINSKI

BORIES

Consolation vln & pf
with Mme. Dobrinski pf　　　Columbia 0926

CLARK

Charmeuse arr. vln & pf Dobrinski
with Mme Dobrinski pf　　　Columbia 0926

DRDLA

Serenade No. 1, in A vln & pf
with Mme. Dobrinski pf　　　Columbia 0664

Souvenir vln & pf
with Mme. Dobrinski pf　　　Columbia 0622

DVOŘÁK

(8) Humoresques, Op. 101 pf
No. 7. Humoresque No. 7, in G flat arr. vln & pf "in g" Kreisler
with Mme Dobrinski pf　　　Columbia 0664

FRIML

Rose Marie (1916) – operetta
Door of my dreams arr. vln & pf Dobrinski
with G. Dech pf　　　Columbia 0582

Indian love call arr. vln & pf Dobrinski
with G. Dech pf　　　Columbia 0582

LEHÁR

(Die) Lustige Witwe (1905) – operetta
S'flüstern Geigen ... Lippen schweigen (waltz) arr. vln & pf Dobrinski
with G. Dech pf　　　Columbia 0999

PERGAMENT

Serenade vln or vlc & pf
with Mme Dobrinski pf　　　Columbia 0622

ROMBERG

(The) Student Prince (1924) – operetta
Deep in my heart, dear arr. vln & pf Dobrinski
with Mme. Dobrinski pf Columbia 0713

Sérénade arr. vln & pf Dobrinski
with Mme. Dobrinski pf Columbia 0713

SILÉSU

(A) Little love, a little kiss (1912) v & pf – arr. vln & org Dobrinski
with G. Dech org Columbia 0999

Max DOLIN

BALFE

(The) Bohemian Girl (1843) – opera
Then you'll remember me arr. vln & pf Dolin
with piano Victor 20048

DVOŘÁK

(7) Gypsy songs, Op. 55 v & pf
No. 4. Songs my mother taught me arr. vln & pf Kreisler
with piano Pathé 5407, 40178

FOSTER

I dream of Jeannie with the light brown hair v & pf – arr. vln & pf
with piano Paragon 9002

My old Kentucky home v & pf – arr. vln & pf
with piano Paragon 9002

GOUNOD

Ave Maria (Méditation on Bach's "Prelude No. 1, in C" from Book I of "Das Wohltemperirte Clavier") v & pf – arr. vln & pf
with piano Paragon 9001

ROMBERG

(The) Student Prince (1924) – operetta
Sérénade arr. vln & pf
with piano Victor 20048

TCHAIKOVSKY

Souvenir d'un lieu cher, Op. 42 vln & pf
No. 3. Mélodie
with piano Pathé 5407, 40178

TOSELLI

Serenade, Op. 6 arr. vln & pf
with piano Paragon 9001

Leonard DOMMETT (1929–)

HANDEL

(15) Sonatas, Op. 1 (?1731) fl or vln & c
Sonata No. 13, in D vln IV
with M. Cooke hpsi W & G WB–BS5175

MOZART

Sonata No. 27, in G, K379 vln & pf
with M. Cooke pf W & G WB–BS5175

Sonata No. 33, in E flat, K481 vln & pf
with M. Cooke hpsi W & G WB–BS5175

SCULTHORPE

Irkanda IV (1961) vln & orch.
with Melbourne Symphony
Orch. – Hopkins Foundation for the Recording of Australian Music FRAM1, SFRAM1
Odyssey 36 16 0150

Paul DONY

di CAPUA

O sole mio v & pf – arr. vln & pf
with piano Perfectaphone 3146

DRIGO

(Les) Millions d'Arlequin (1900) – ballet orch.
Sérénade arr. vln & pf Auer
with piano HMV K5012

FAURÉ

Berceuse, Op. 16 vln & pf
with piano Perfectaphone 3147

(3) Chansons, Op. 7 v & pf
No. 1. Après un rêve arr. vln & pf
with piano Perfectaphone 3147

GOLDBERG

Galante conversation v & pf – arr. vln & pf
with piano Perfectaphone 3153

HAHN

Paysage v & pf – arr. vln & pf
with piano Perfectaphone 3153

MASSON–KIEK

(En) Relisant vos lettres – Valse lente orch – arr. vln & pf
with piano HMV K5012

ROPP

I canto per te v & pf – arr. vln & pf
with piano Perfectaphone 3146

Michael DORÉ

ARENSKY

(4) Morceaux, Op. 30 vln & pf
No. 2. Sérénade in G
with S. Rosenbloom pf Columbia 2972

DRIGO

(Les) Millions d'Arlequin (1900) – ballet
Sérénade arr. vln & pf Auer
with S. Rosenbloom pf Columbia 2972

PRESSMANN

Caprice de la Balerine vln & pf
with S. Rosenbloom pf 69755 Columbia 2988

ROSENBLOOM

Gavotte in D vln & pf
with S. Rosenbloom pf 69752 Columbia 2988

Charles DORSON (1882–   )

DORSON

(La) Chanson du vent vln & pf
  with piano   Pathé 9627

Scherzando vln & pf
  with piano   Pathé 9627

Pierre DOUKAN

BACH

Fugue in g, BWV1026 vln & c
  with L. Boulay hpsi   Christophorus CLP75489

Sonata in G, BWV1038 fl, vln & c
  with C. Lardé fl & L. Boulay hpsi   Christophorus CLP75489
                                   Erato EFM42032

BERTHEAUME

(2) Sinfonia concertantes, Op. 6 (1787) 2 vlns & orch.
  Sinfonia concertante No. 1, in G
  with R. Gendre vln &   Pathé DTX230
  Orch. – Froment

CORELLI

(12) Concerti grossi, Op. 6 orch.
  Concerto grosso No. 3, in c
  with L. Yordanoff vln, A. Rémond vlc,   London EL93042
  M. de Lacour hpsi & Collegium   Ducretet Thomson LA1018
  Musicum, Paris – Douatte   Telefunken LB6091

EGK

(La) Tentation de Saint–Antoine (1945) b, 2 vlns, vla & vlc
  with B. Lefort b, G. Alès vln,   L'Oiseau–Lyre OL50134
  P. Ladhuite vla & R. Albin vlc

FAURÉ

Sonata No. 1, in A, Op. 13 vln & pf
  with T. Cochet pf   Erato LDE3061

Sonata No. 2, in e, Op. 108 vln & pf
  with T. Cochet pf   Erato LDE3061

FRANCK

Sonata in A (1886) vln & pf
  with T. Cochet pf   Erato LDE3091

GOSSEC

Rondo in D fl, vln, hp & orch.
  with J–P. Rampal fl, L. Laskin hp &   Pathé DTX230
  orch. – Froment

GRIEG

Sonata No. 3, in c, Op. 45 vln & pf
  with T. Cochet pf   Erato LDE3091

MANCINI

Concerto a quattro in e (1729) fl, 2 vlns & hpsi
  with J–P. Rampal fl, G. Alès vln, & R.   L'Oiseau–Lyre LD66, OL50009
  Gerlin hpsi

MANFREDINI

(12) Concerti, Op. 3 (1718) 2 vlns, strs & c
  Concerto No. 12, in C "Christmas Concerto"
  with L. Yordanoff vln, M. de Lacour   Ducretet Thomson LA1018
  hpsi, A. Rémond vlc & Collegium   London EL93043
  Musicum, Paris – Douatte   Telefunken LB6091

RAVEL

Berceuse sur le nom de Gabriel Fauré (1922) vln & pf
  with T. Cochet pf   Erato LDE3119

Sonata (1927) vln & pf
  with T. Cochet pf   Erato LDE3119

Tzigane (Rapsodie de concert) (1924) vln & pf or orch
  with T. Cochet pf   Erato LDE3119

ROUSSEL

Sonata No. 2, in A Op. 28 vln & pf
  with T. Cochet pf   Erato LDE3119

SCHUMANN

Sonata No. 1, in a, Op. 105 vln & pf
  with F. Petit pf   Erato LDE3048

Sonata No. 2, in d, Op. 121 vln & pf
  with F. Petit pf   Erato LDE3048

TORELLI

(12) Concerti, Op. 8 (1709) 1/6: 2 vlns, strs & c – 7/12: vln, strs & c
  Concerto No. 6, in g "Christmas Concerto"
  with L. Yordanoff vln, M. de Lacour   Ducretet Thomson LA1018
  hpsi, A. Rémond vlc & Collegium   London EL93042
  Musicum, Paris – Douatte   Telefunken LB6091

VIVALDI

(12) Concerti, Op. 3 "L'Estro armonico" var, cbns & strs
  Concerto No. 8, in a, P.2 (F.I, No. 177) 2 vlns, strs & c
  with R. Gendre vln & Chamber   Club National du Disque
  Orch. – Froment   CND1003

Franz DRDLA (1868–1944)

BRUCH

Concerto No. 1, in g, Op. 26 vln & orch.
  Allegro moderato (2nd mvt)*
  with piano   Audio Archives LP0079
                               Gramophone & Typewriter
                               47923

CHOPIN

(3) Nocturnes, Op. 9 pf
  No. 2. Nocturne No. 2, in E flat arr. vln & pf Sarasate
  with piano   949 X (Fo–2²)   Gramophone & Typewriter
                               47929
                               Pearl GEM102

DRDLA

Alt Wien (Alt Wiener weise) Op. 226 orch. – arr. vln & pf Drdla
  with piano   Polydor 20202

Berceuse in C, Op. 33 vln & pf
  with piano   3406 ar   Polydor 20200

* Abridged.

DRDLA – *Continued*

Chant d'amour (Valse–chanson in D) Op. 31 vln & pf
with piano   Polydor 20199

Fairytales (March) vln & pf
with E. Kris pf   3402 ar   Polydor 20197

Graziella vln & pf
with piano   Polydor 20198

Griselda, Op. 138 vln & pf
with E. Kris pf   3397 ar   Polydor 20195

Guitarerro, Op. 88 vln & pf
with piano   Odeon 327, 1190, 51057, 99784

(8) Hungarian Dances, Op. 30 vln & pf
   No. 1. Hej de Fényes
with E. Kris pf   3396 ar   Polydor 20194
   No. 2. Hamis babán
with E. Kris pf   3396 ar   Polydor 20194

Idylle in A, Op. 36 vln & pf
with piano   Polydor 20202

Illusion in A, Op. 48 vln & pf
with piano   Polydor 20201

Madrigale in A Op. 25 vln & pf
with piano   Odeon 2227, X25630

Mazurka No. 2, in G, Op. 23 vln & pf
with piano   Polydor 20201

Minuet in G, Op. 81 vln & pf
with piano   Polydor 20199

(3) Morceaux, Op. 37 vln & pf
   No. 3. Feu Follet in D
with piano   3398 ar   Polydor 20200

(2) Morceaux, Op. 52 vln & pf
   No. 2. Capriccio in G
with piano   3409 ar   Polydor 20200

Rano vln & pf
with piano   3401 ar   Polydor 20196

Romanze in A vln & pf
with piano   Gramophone & Typewriter 47943

Serenade No. 1, in A vln & pf
with piano   Gramophone & Typewriter 47922

Serenade No. 1, in A vln & pf
with piano   Odeon 51056

Serenade No. 1, in A vln & pf
with E. Kris pf   3400 ar   Polydor 20197

Serenade No. 3, in A vln & pf
with piano   Gramophone & Typewriter 047908

Song without words in D, Op. 147 vln & pf
with piano   Polydor 20193

Souvenir vln & pf
with E. Kris pf   3395 ar   Polydor 20194

Valse viennois vln & pf
with piano   Polydor 20198

Visione in E flat, Op. 28 vln & pf
with piano   Polydor 20193

Waltz–serenata, Op. 42 vln & pf
with E. Kris pf   3399 ar   Odeon 327, 1192, 99856
                           Polydor 20195

HERBERT

Suite in F, Op. 3 vln & pf
   No. 4. Serenade (Andante grazioso)
with piano   Gramophone & Typewriter 47916

LÉONARD

Fantaisie militaire, Op. 15 vln & pf
with piano   948 x (Fo–2^z)   Gramophone & Typewriter 47927

PIERNÉ

Sérénade in A, Op. 7 (1875) pf – arr. vln & pf
with piano   946 x (Fo–2^z)   Gramophone & Typewriter 47928

Helmut DRESCHER

BEETHOVEN

Sonata No. 5, in F, Op. 24 "Spring" vln & pf
with M. Huttner pf   Royale 1435, 1511

(3) Sonatas, Op. 30 vln & pf
   No. 3. Sonata No. 8, in G
with M. Huttner pf   Royale 1511

Sonata No. 9, in A, Op. 47 "Kreutzer" vln & pf
with M. Huttner pf   Royale 1526

BRUCH

Concerto No. 1, in g, Op. 26 vln & orch.
with Berlin Symphony   Royale 1435
Orch. – Schreiber

PROKOFIEV

Concerto No. 1. in D, Op. 19 vln & orch.
with Berlin Symphony   Royale 1483
Orch. – Schreiber

Concerto No. 2, in g, Op. 63 vln & orch.
with Berlin Symphony   Royale 1483
Orch. – Schreiber

Henry DRIFFIELD

SCHUBERT

(7) Gesänge (set to Scott's "Lady of the Lake") Op. 52 v & pf
   No. 6. Ave Maria, D839 arr. vln & pf Wilhelmj
with piano   Jumbo 806
                Odeon A22980

TCHAIKOVSKY

(3) Souvenirs de Hapsal, Op. 2 pf
   No. 3. Chant sans paroles in f arr. vln & pf Kreisler
with piano   Jumbo 806
                Odeon A22981

Eduard DROLC

PAGANINI

Trio in D, Op. 66 (1833) vln, vlc & gtr
with G. Donderer vlc & S. Behrend   Deutsche Grammophon
gtr   SLPM139370

Ernest DRUCKER

HANDEL

(12) Concerti Grossi, Op. 6 (1739) 2 vlns, vlc & strs

Concerto grosso No. 1, in G

with A. Busch vln, H. Busch vlc, M. Horszowski pf & Busch Chamber Players – Busch | XCO 35669/71–1 | Columbia 71981/2D, 72006/8D, (in set M685), ML4210, (in set SL158)

Concerto grosso No. 2, in F

with A. Busch vln, H. Busch vlc, M. Horszowski pf & Busch Chamber Players – Busch | XCO 35854/7–1 | Columbia 71982/4D, 72009/12D, (in set M685), ML4210, (in set SL158)

Concerto grosso No. 3, in e

with A. Busch vln, H. Busch vlc, M. Horszowski pf & Busch Chamber Players – Busch | XCO 35720/2–1 | Columbia 71984/5D, 72010/2D, (in set M685), ML4211, (in set SL158)

Concerto grosso No. 4, in a

with A. Busch vln, H. Busch vlc, M. Horszowski pf & Busch Chamber Players – Busch | XCO 35746/9–1 | Columbia 71986/7D, 72006/9D, (in set M685), ML4211, (in set SL158)

Concerto grosso No. 5, in D

with A. Busch vln, H. Busch vlc, M. Horszowski pf & Busch Chamber Players – Busch | XCO 35706/9–1 | Columbia 71988/9D, 72013/6D, (in set M685), ML4212, (in set SL158)

Concerto grosso No. 6, in g

with A. Busch vln, H. Busch vlc, M. Horszowski pf & Busch Chamber Players – Busch | XCO 35672/5–1 | Columbia 71990/1D, 72017/20D, (in set M685), ML4212/3, (in set SL158)

Concerto grosso No. 7, in B flat

with A. Busch vln, H. Busch vlc, M. Horszowski pf & Busch Chamber Players – Busch | XCO 35715/8–1 | Columbia 71992/3D, 72017/20D, (in set M685), ML4213, (in set SL158)

Concerto grosso No. 8, in c

with A. Busch vln, H. Busch vlc, M. Horszowski pf & Busch Chamber Players – Busch | XCO 35676/9–1 | Columbia 71994/5D, 72013/6D, (in set M685), ML4213, (in set SL158)

Concerto grosso No. 9, in F

with A. Busch vln, H. Busch vlc, M. Horszowski pf & Busch Chamber Players – Busch | XCO 35742–2, 35743/5–1 & 35755–1 | Columbia 71996/8D, 72021/5D, (in set M685), ML4212/3, (in set SL158)

Concerto grosso No. 10, in d

with A. Busch vln, H. Busch vlc, M. Horszowski pf & Busch Chamber Players – Busch | XCO 35723/6–1 | Columbia 71998/200D, 72026/90, (in set M685), ML4212, (in set SL158)

Concerto grosso No. 11, in A

with A. Busch vln, H. Busch vlc, M. Horszowski pf & Busch Chambers Players – Busch | XCO 35750/4–1 | Columbia 72000/2D, 72022/6D, (in set M685), ML4211, (in set SL158)

Concerto grosso No. 12, in b

with A. Busch vln, H. Busch vlc, M. Horszowski pf & Busch Chamber Players – Busch | XCO 35710/4–1 | Columbia 72003/5D, 72022/6D, (in set M685), ML4210, (in set SL158)

Rafael DRUIAN (1922–)

BARTÓK

Sonata No. 2 (1922) vln & pf

with J. Simms pf — Mercury MG50089, MG80000, MMA11047

Philips A04129, PHC9019, (in set PHC2–002)

BLOCH

Sonata No. 1 (1920) vln & pf

with J. Simms pf — Mercury MG50095, MMA11155, MRL2501

Sonata No. 2 (1924) "Poème mystique" vln & pf

with J. Simms pf — Mercury MG50095, MMA11155, MRL2501

BRAHMS

Sonata No. 2, in A, Op. 100 vln & pf

with J. Simms pf — Mercury MG50091, MG80002

BRANDL

(Der) Liebe Augustin – operetta

Du alter Stefansturm arr. vln & pf as "The old refrain" by Kreisler

with J. Simms pf — Mercury MG50119, MMA11007, XEP9017

DELIBES

Coppélia (1870) – ballet orch.

No. 5. Ballade de l'Épi (Act I)

with Minneapolis Symphony orch. – Dorati — Mercury MG50328, MMA11000, SR90328

DELIUS

Hassan (1920) – Incidental music orch.

Serenade arr. Beecham

with M. Dalton hp & Cleveland Sinfonietta – Lane — Columbia SCX3525, SX1640

Epic BC1275, LC3875

ENESCU

Sonata No. 3, in a, Op. 25 "In the popular Rumanian style" vln & pf

with J. Simms pf — Mercury MG50090, MG80001, MMA11040

Philips PHC9084

HEUBERGER

(Der) Opernball, Op. 40 (1898) – operetta

Im chambre séparée arr. vln & pf as "Midnight bells" by Kreisler

with J. Simms pf — Mercury MG50119, MMA11007, XEP9017

IVES

Sonata No. 1 (1903/8) vln & pf

with J. Simms pf — Mercury MG50096

Philips PHC9018, (in set PHC 2–002)

Sonata No. 2 (1910) vln & pf

with J. Simms pf — Mercury MG50097

Philips PHC8018, (in set PHC 2–002)

IVES – *Continued*

Sonata No. 3 (1914) vln & pf
  with J. Simms pf
                                    Mercury MG50097
                                    Philips PHC9019,
                                    (in set PHC 2–002)

Sonata No. 4 (1916) "Children's day at the camp meeting" vln & pf
  with J. Simms pf
                                    Mercury MG50097
                                    Philips PHC9018,
                                    (in set PHC2–002)

JANÁČEK

Sonata (1913/21) vln & pf
  with J. Simms pf
                                    Mercury MG50090, MG80001,
                                    MMA11040
                                    Philips PHC9084

KREISLER

Caprice viennois, Op. 2 vln & pf
  with J. Simms pf
                                    Mercury MG50119, MMA11007,
                                    XEP9017

Liebesfreud vln & pf
  with J. Simms pf
                                    Mercury MG50119, MMA11007,
                                    XEP9009

Liebesleid vln & pf
  with J. Simms pf
                                    Mercury MG50119, MMA11007,
                                    XEP9009

Schön Rosmarin vln & pf
  with J. Simms pf
                                    Mercury MG50119, MMA11007

Tambourin chinois, Op. 3 vln & pf
  with J. Simms pf
                                    Mercury MG50119, MMA11007,
                                    XEP9017

Andantino (Padre Martini) vln & pf
  with J. Simms pf
                                    Mercury MG50119, MMA11007

Chanson Louis XIII & Pavane (L. Couperin) vln & pf
  with J. Simms pf
                                    Mercury MG50119, MMA11007

Minuet (Porpora) vln & pf
  with J. Simms pf
                                    Mercury MG50119, MMA11007

Praeludium & Allegro (Pugnani) vln & pf
  with J. Simms pf
                                    Mercury MG50119, MMA11007,
                                    XEP9009

(Le) Précieuse (L. Couperin) vln & pf
  with J. Simms pf
                                    Mercury MG50119, MMA11007

Sicilienne & Rigaudon (Francoeur) vln & pf
  with J. Simms pf
                                    Mercury MG50119, MMA11007

MOZART

Divertimento No. 17, in D, K334 2 hrns & strs
  with Cleveland Orch. – Lane
                                    Columbia ML6324, MS6924

Sinfonia concertante in E flat, K364 vln, vla & orch.
  with A. Skernick vla and Cleveland
  Orch. members – Szell
                                    Columbia ML6025, MS6625,
                                    SAX5280
                                    Epic BC1352, LC3952

Sonata No. 17, in C, K296 vln & pf
  with G. Szell pf
                                    CBS S61055
                                    Columbia ML6464, MS7064

Sonata No. 18, in G, K301 vln & pf
  with G. Szell pf
                                    CBS S61055
                                    Columbia ML6464, MS7064

MOZART – *Continued*

Sonata No. 21, in e, K304 vln & pf
  with G. Szell pf
                                    CBS S61055
                                    Columbia ML6464, MS7064

Sonata No. 24, in F, K376 vln & pf
  with G. Szell pf
                                    CBS S61055
                                    Columbia ML6464, MS7064

PORTER

Sonata No. 2, in a (1929) vln & pf
  with J. Simms pf
                                    Mercury MG50096

RAVEL

Sonata (1927) vln & pf
  with J. Simms pf
                                    Mercury MG50089, MG80000,
                                    MMA11047

RIMSKY–KORSAKOV

Scheherazade, Op. 35 (1888) orch.
  with Minneapolis Symphony
  Orch. – Dorati
                                    Fontana 610801VL, 894027ZKY
                                    Mercury MG50009, MMA11022,
                                    MRL2503, SR90195
                                    MGW14008, SRW18008
                                    Philips 838501VY, GL5835,
                                    SGL5835

SCHUBERT

Fantasia in C, Op. 159 (D934) vln & pf
  with J. Simms pf
                                    Mercury MG50120

Sonata in A, Op. 162 (D574) "Duo" vln & pf
  with J. Simms pf
                                    Mercury MG50120

SCHUMANN

Sonata No. 1, in a, Op. 105 vln & pf
  with J. Simms pf
                                    Mercury MG50091, MG80002

STRAUSS, R.

Don Quixote, Op. 35 (1897) vln, vla, vlc & orch.
  with A. Skernick vla, P. Fournier vlc
  & Cleveland Orch. – Szell
                                    Columbia CX1853
                                    Epic BC1135, LC3786

(Ein) Heldenleben, Op. 40 (1898) orch.
  with Minneapolis Symphony
  Orch. – Dorati
                                    Mercury MG50012, MMA11069,
                                    MRL2545, SRW18014

TCHAIKOVSKY

Sleeping Beauty, Op. 66 (1888/9) – ballet
  with Minneapolis Symphony
  Orch. – Dorati
                                    Mercury MG50064/7,
                                    (set OL3–103), MMA11113/5,
                                    MRL2524–7

Swan Lake, Op. 20 (1875/6) – ballet
  with Minneapolis Symphony
  Orch. – Dorati
                                    Mercury MG50068/70, (set OL3–
                                    102), MG50118, XEP9010

VAUGHAN WILLIAMS

(The) Lark Ascending (1914) vln & orch.
  with Cleveland Sinfonietta – Lane
                                    Columbia SCX3525, SX1640
                                    Epic BC1275, LC3875

Irena DUBISKA (1899–   )

BACH, C.P.E.

Sonata in G, W.157 2 vlns & c
  with E. Umińska vln, K. Wilkomirska   Muza XL0287
  vlc & J. Lefeld hpsi

BACH, J.S.

Sonata in d, BWV1036 2 vlns & c
  with E. Umińska vln, K. Wilkomirska   Muza XL0287
  vlc & J. Lefeld hpsi

HANDEL

(9) Sonatas, Op. 2 (1724) 2 vlns or obs & c
  Sonata No. 7, in g
  with E. Umińska vln, K. Wilkomirska   Muza XL0287
  vlc & J. Lefeld hpsi

  Sonata No. 8, in g
  with E. Umińska vln, K. Wilkomirska   Muza XL0287
  vlc & J. Lefeld hpsi

SZYMANOWSKI

(12) Pieśni kurpiowskio (Kurpian songs) Op. 58 (1931/2) v & pf
  Polish folksong arr. vln & pf Kochański
  with L. Urstein pf   Columbia DM1931

Alfred DUBOIS (1898–1949)

d'AMBROSIO

Canzonetta, Op. 6 vln & pf
  with F. Goeyens pf   Columbia D13090

Serenade, Op. 4 vln & pf
  with F. Goeyens pf   Columbia D15175

(A) Ton reveil vln & pf
  with F. Goeyens pf   Columbia D13095, J5115

BACH

(6) Sonatas, BWV1014/9 vln & clav
  Sonata No. 2, in A: Andante un poco (3rd mvt) BWV1015
  with M. Maas pf   CLBX118–2   Columbia 68144D, (in set M186), LFX271, LX306

  Sonata No. 4, in c, BWV1017
  with M. Maas pf   CLBX 105/8–2   Columbia 68133/5D, (set M186), LFX267/8

  Sonata No. 5, in f, BWV1018
  with M. Maas pf   CLBX 109/13–2   Columbia 68142/4D, (set M187), LFX269/71, LX304/6, LX8096/8

  Sonata No. 6, in G, BWV1019
  with M. Maas pf   Columbia 68136/7D, LFX272/3

BEETHOVEN

(3) Sonatas, Op. 30 vln & pf
  No. 2. Sonata No. 7, in c
  with M. Maas pf   Columbia DFX195/7

DEBUSSY

(La) Plus que lente – valse (1910) pf – arr. vln & pf Roques
  with F. Goeyens pf   Columbia D19042

DEBUSSY – Continued

(12) Préludes – Book I (1910) pf
  No. 8. La Fille aux cheveux de lin arr. vln & pf Hartmann
  with F. Goeyens pf   Columbia D13095, J5115

Sonata No. 3, in g (1917) vln & pf
  with M. Maas pf   Columbia 68878/9D, (set X44), DFX198/9

FRANCK

Sonata in A (1886) vln & pf
  with M. Maas pf   Columbia 67928/31D, (set M158), LFX77/80

GOEYENS

Humoresque vln & pf
  with F. Goeyens pf   Columbia D13090

HANDEL

(15) Sonatas, Op. 1 (?1731) fl or vln & c
  Sonata No. 15, in E vln VI
  with G. Moore pf   Columbia LCX103

KREISLER

Recitative & Scherzo–caprice, Op. 6 solo vln
  (unaccompanied)   Columbia LF3

LECLAIR

(12) Sonatas, Op. 9 – Book IV (1738) vln & c
  Sonata No. 3, in D: Tambourin (3rd mvt) arr. vln & pf Kreisler
  with F. Goeyens pf   Columbia LF2

MOZART

Concerto No. 6, in E flat, K268 (K365b) vln & orch.
  with Brussels Conservatory   Columbia 68052/4D, (set M174),
  Orch. – Defauw   GQX10660/2, LFX201/3 Odeon 0–9405/7

Divertimento No. 17, in D, K334 2 hrns & strs
  Minuet (3rd mvt) arr. vln & pf Burmester
  with F. Goeyens pf   Columbia 68054D, (in set M174), GQX10662, LFX203 Odeon 0–9407

NARDINI

(6) Sonatas, 2 (1765) vln & c
  Sonata No. 3, in A: Adagio cantabile (2nd mvt) arr. vln & pf as "Aria" by Ysaÿe
  with F. Goeyens pf   Columbia 33026, LF2

VIEUXTEMPS

Concerto No. 5, in a, Op. 37 vln & orch.
  with Brussels Conservatory   Columbia LFX14/6
  Orch. – Defauw

VOGLER

Aria, Chasse & Minuetto vln & pf
  with M. Maas pf   Columbia 68879D, (in set X44), DFX199

YSAŸE

Rêve d'enfant, Op. 14 vln & pf
  with F. Goeyens pf   Columbia D15175

YSAŸE – *Continued*

(6) Sonatas, Op. 27 solo vln
Sonata No. 3, in d
(unaccompanied)   Columbia LCX104

Eugene DUBOIS

DVOŘÁK

(8) Humoresques, Op. 101 pf
No. 7. Humoresque No. 7, in G flat arr. vln & pf "in G" Kreisler
with piano   Silvertone 2022

RUBINSTEIN

(2) Melodies, Op. 3 pf
No. 1. Melody in F arr. vln & pf
with piano   Silvertone 2022

R. DUKSON

GRANADOS

(12) Danzas españolas, Op. 37 (1893) pf
No. 5. Danza española No. 5, in e "Andaluza" arr. vln & pf Dukson
with piano   Columbia JX1109

MENDELSSOHN

(6) Songs without words, Op. 62 pf
No. 1. Song without words No. 25, in G "May Breezes" arr. vln & pf
Kreisler
with piano
                    Columbia JX1109

Jacques DUMONT (1913–   )

BACH

(3) Sonatas & 3 Partitas, BWV1001/6 solo vln
Sonata No. 1, in g, BWV1001
(unaccompanied)   Belvedere ELY06130
Partita No. 1, in b, BWV1002
(unaccompanied)   Belvedere ELY06130
Sonata No. 2, in a, BWV1003
(unaccompanied)   Belvedere ELY06131
Partita No. 2, in d, BWV1004
(unaccompanied)   Belvedere ELY06131
Sonata No. 3, in C, BWV1005
(unaccompanied)   Belvedere ELY06132
Partita No. 3, in E, BWV1006
(unaccompanied)   Belvedere ELY06132
(4) Suites, BWV1066/9 strs & c
Suite No. 3, in D: Air (2nd mvt) BWV1068 2 obs, 3 tpts, drms &
strs – arr. vln & pf as "Air on the G–string" by Wilhelmj
with A. Collard pf   Pathé D106, PDT251

BEETHOVEN

Romance No. 1, in G, Op. 40 vln & orch.
with A. Collard pf   Pathé PDT267
Romance No. 2, in F, Op. 50 vln & orch.
with A. Collard pf   Pathé PDT266

CHARPENTIER, M–A.

Orphée descendant aux Enfers – cantata t, b, bs, vln, inst ens &
hpsi – trans. & real. Guy–Lambert
with J. Giraudeau t, J. Pruvost b,   Pathé DT1033
L. Noquera bs, F. Petit hpsi &
Instrumental Ensemble – Martini

DRDLA

Serenade No. 1, in A vln & pf
with piano   Odeon 282040
Souvenir vln & pf
with piano   Odeon 282040

MENDELSSOHN

(6) Songs without words, Op. 19 pf
No. 1. Song without words No. 1, in E "Sweet remembrance" arr. vln &
pf Heifetz
with A. Collard pf   Pathé FC5, PD134
(6) Songs without words, Op. 62 pf
No. 6. Song without words No. 30, in G "Spring song" arr. vln & pf
with A. Collard pf   Pathé FC5, PD134

MICHIELS

(6) Csárdas (on national Hungarian airs) vln & pf
No. 1. Csárda No. 1 "Piroska"
with piano   Odeon 282041

MONTI

Csárdas (1904) vln & pf
with piano   Odeon 282041

MOZART

Conterto in D, K315 "Unfinished" vln, pf & orch.
with R. Veyron–Lacroix pf, &   Pathé DTX191
Chamber Orch. – Oubradous
Divertimento No. 17, in D, K344 2 hrns & strs
Minuet (3rd mvt) arr. vln & pf Burmester
with A. Collard pf   Pathé D106, PDT251
Sonata No. 1, in C, K6 vln & pf
with R. Veyron–Lacroix hpsi   Pathé DTX191
Sonata No. 2, in D, K7 vln & pf
with R. Veyron–Lacroix hpsi   Pathé DTX191
Sonata No. 3, in B flat, K8 vln & pf
with R. Veyron–Lacroix hpsi   Pathé DTX191
Sonata No. 4, in G, K9 vln & pf
with R. Veyron–Lacroix hpsi   Pathé DTX191

PROKOFIEV

Quintet, Op. 39 ob, cl, vln, vla & cbs
with M. Goetgeluck ob, U. Delécluse   Nixa PLP512
cl, L. Pascal vla & M. Boussagol cbs   Pacific LDO–E51022
                            Period SPLP512

SCHUBERT

Quintet in A, Op. 114 (D667) "The Trout" pf, vln, vla, vlc & cbs
with M. Mercier pf, L. Pascal vla, R.   Pathé ADTX1806, DTX139
Salles vlc & H. Moreau cbs

VIVALDI

(12) Concerti, Op. 3 "L'Estro armonico" var. cbns & strs
Concerto No. 10, in b: Largo (2nd mvt) P.148 (F.IV, No. 10) 4 vlns, strs & c
with H. Merckel vln, L. Schwartz vln,   Polydor 540002, 566275
M. Crut vln & Pro Musica
Orch. – Goldschmidt

John DUNN (1866–1940)

BACH

(3) Sonatas & 3 Partitas, BWV1001/6 solo vln
Partita No. 3, in E: Gavotte (3rd mvt) BWV1006
(unaccompanied)   Odeon A143085
(4) Suites, BWV1066/9 strs & c
Suite No. 3, in D: Air (2nd mvt) BWV1068 2 obs, 3 tpts, drms & strs – arr. vln & pf as "Air on the G-string" by Wilhelmj
with piano   8164 D   Edison Bell 1089

BAZZINI

(La) Ronde des lutins, Op. 25 vln & pf
with piano   Edison Bell 536

CHOPIN

(3) Nocturnes, Op. 9 pf
No. 2. Nocturne No. 2, in E flat arr. vln & pf Sarasate
with piano   Odeon A143080
No. 2. Nocturne No. 2, in E flat arr. vln & pf Sarasate
with piano   X 1309   Edison Bell 614

DUNN

Berceuse vln & pf
with piano   Odeon A143087
Soliloquay vln & pf
with piano   X 1308   Edison Bell 614

GODARD

Jocelyn (1888) – opera
Cachés dans cet asile "Berceuse" arr. vln & pf
with piano   Edison Bell 1045

PAGANINI

(24) Caprices, Op. 1 (1801/7) solo vln
Caprice No. 13, in B flat arr. vln & pf
with piano   Odeon A143079

SARASATE

(8) Danzas españolas vln & pf
No. 3. Romanza andaluza, Op. 22, No. 1
with piano   Edison Bell 545
No. 6. Zapateado, Op. 23, No. 2
with piano   Odeon X86, XX72613
No. 7. Danza española No. 7, in a, Op. 26, No. 1
with piano   Edison Bell 545

SCHUBERT, François

(12) Bagatelles, Op. 13 vln & pf
No. 9. L' abeille
with piano   Edison Bell 1045

SCHUBERT, Franz

(7) Gesänge (set to Scott's "Lady of the Lake") Op. 52 v & pf
No. 6. Ave Maria, D839 arr. vln & pf Wilhelmj
with piano   Odeon X86, XX72614

WIENIAWSKI

(2) Mazurkas, Op. 19 vln & pf
No. 1. Mazurka No. 1, in G "Obertass"
with piano   8028 A   Edison Bell 1089

L. DUROSOIR

DUROSOIR

Berceuse vln & pf
with H. Magne pf   Durosoir SM503
Bretagne vln & pf
with H. Magne pf   Durosoir SM504
Chant élégiaque (in memory of Ginette Neveu) vln & pf
with H. Magne pf   Durosoir SM505
Prière à Marie vln & pf
with H. Magne pf   3662   Durosoir SM502

Samuel DUSHKIN (1898–   )

ALBÉNIZ

(2) Danzas españolas, Op. 164 pf
No. 1. Jota aragonesa arr. vln & pf Dushkin
with M. Pirani pf   Bb 12750^{II}△   HMV E523, P824
España (6 Feuilles d'album) Op. 165 pf
No. 2. Tango in D arr. vln & pf Dushkin
with M. Pirani pf   Bb 12752^{III}△   HMV E523, P824

GERSHWIN

Short story vln & pf
with piano   HMV ER261, P794

STRAVINSKY

(Le) Chant du rossignol (1919) – ballet orch.
Air arr. vln & pf Dushkin & Stravinsky
with I. Stravinsky pf   CLX 1706–1   Columbia 68334D, LFX335, LX383
Marche chinois arr. vln & pf Dushkin & Stravinsky
with I. Stravinsky pf   CLX 1705–1   Columbia 68334D, LFX335, LX383
Concerto in D (1931) vln & orch.
  767/8 ½ GEP, 769 GEP, 770 ½   Polydor 95500/2, 566173/5
with Lamoureux   GEP, 771/2 GEP   Vox 12014/6, (set 173), PL6340
Orch. – Stravinsky
Duo concertante (1932) vln & pf
  CL 4278/81–3 & CLX 1674–4   Columbia 17040/1D & 68238D,
with I. Stravinsky pf   (set M199), LB12/3 & LX290, LF131/2 & LFX334
Firebird (1910) – ballet orch.
No. 3. Jeu des princesses avec les pommes d'or (Scherzo) arr. vln & pf
Dushkin & Stravinsky
with I. Stravinsky pf   Columbia 17049D, LF130
No. 5. Berceuse arr. vln & pf Dushkin & Stravinsky
with I. Stravinsky pf   Columbia 17049D, LF130

STRAVINSKY – *Continued*

Pastorale (1908) v & pf – arr. vln & wnd qnt Dushkin & Stravinsky
with L. Gromer ob,   CL 4371–1   Columbia 292576, 17075D,
Durand E–hrn, A. Vacellier cl,   LB15, LF129
Grandmaison bsn, conducted by
Stravinsky

Pétrouchka (1911) – ballet orch.
   Danse russe arr. vln & pf 1933 Dushkin & Stravinsky
   with I. Stravinsky pf   CL 4377–4 Columbia 17075D, LB15, LF129

Suite Italienne (on themes of Pergolesi) (1933) vln & pf
   No. 2. Serenata
   with I. Stravinsky pf   CLX 1675–4 Columbia 68238D, (in set M199),
                                LFX334, LX290

   No. 5. Scherzino
   with I. Stravinsky pf   CLX 1675–4 Columbia 68238D, (in set M199),
                                LFX334, LX290

Spencer DYKE (1880–1946)

d'AMBROSIO

(2) Morceaux, Op. 17 vln & pf
   No. 1. Aubade rêverie
   with piano   016 X 7   Odeon 0159, 32868

Serenade, Op. 4 vln & pf
   with piano   Odeon 51667

BRAHMS

Quartet No. 3, in c, Op. 60 pf, vln, vla & vlc
   with O. Bloom pf, B. Shore vla &   National Gramophonic Society
   P. Parker vlc   NGS88/91

Sextet No. 1, in B flat, Op. 18 2 vlns, 2 vlas & 2 vlcs
   Rondo (4th mvt)
   with E. Quaife vln, E. Tomlinson vla,   National Gramophonic Society
   J. Lockyer vla, P. Parker vlc &   DD
   E. Robinson vlc

Sextet No. 2, in G, Op. 36 2 vlns, 2 vlas & 2 vlcs
   with E. Quaife vln, E. Tomlinson vla,   National Gramophonic Society
   J. Lockyer vla, P. Parker vlc &   NGS105/8
   E. Robinson vlc

Trio in E flat, Op. 40 hrn, pf & vln
   with A. Brain hrn, & Y. Bowen pf   National Gramophonic Society
                               NGS65/8

CHOPIN

(3) Nocturnes, Op. 9 pf
   No. 2. Nocturne No. 2, in E flat arr. vln & pf Sarasate
   with piano   116 X 7   Odeon 0159, 32869

DRDLA

Mazurka No. 2, in G, Op. 23 vln & pf
   with piano   Odeon 0157, 44282, 44306

Souvenir vln & pf
   with piano   Odeon 0157, 44282

DVOŘÁK

(8) Humoresques, Op. 101 pf
   No. 7. Humoresque No. 7, in G flat arr. vln & pf "in G" Kreisler
   with piano   Odeon 0154, 44931

DVOŘÁK – *Continued*

Quartet No. 6, in F Op. 96 "American" 2 vlns, vla & vlc
   (as leader of Spencer Dyke String   Vocalion K05132/4
   Quartet)

ELGAR

Salut d'amour, Op. 12 orch. – arr. vln & pf Elgar
   with piano   Odeon 0149, 44986

GODARD

Jocelyn (1888) – opera
   Cachés dans cet asile "Berceuse" arr. vln & pf
   with piano   Odeon 0155, 44600

HAYDN

(6) Quartets, Op. 64 (H.III, Nos. 63/8) 2 vlns, vla & vlc
   No. 5. Quartet No. 67, in D, H.III, No. 67 "The Lark"
   (as leader of Spencer Dyke String   Vocalion X9554/6
   Quartet)

JENKINSON

(6) Lyrical pieces vln & pf
   No. 2. Elfentanz
   with piano   Odeon X67623

MARCHETTI

Fascination (Valse tzigane) orch. – arr. vln & pf
   with piano   Odeon 788, 51646

MASCAGNI

Cavalleria Rusticana (1890) – opera
   Intermezzo orch. – arr. vln & pf
   with piano   Odeon 0153, 66060

   Selection arr. vln & pf as "Fantasia" by Dyke
   with piano   Odeon 0153, 66023

MENDELSSOHN

(3) Quartets, Op. 44 2 vlns, vla & vlc
   No. 2. Quartet No. 4, in c: Scherzo (2nd mvt)
   with E. Quaife vln, E. Tomlinson vla   National Gramoponic Society
   & P. Parker vlc   MMM

MEYER–HELMUND

Leaves & buds (Sérénade Rococo) (1896) 2 mands & pf – arr. vln & pf
   with piano   Odeon 788, 51647

MOSZKOWSKI

(6) Klavierstücke, Op. 15 pf – 4 hands
   No. 1. Serenata arr. vln & pf
   with piano   Odeon 0155, 32838

MOZART

Duo No. 1, in G, K423 vln & vla
   Adagio (2nd mvt)
   with E. Tomlinson vla   National Gramophonic Society
                              AAA

Quintet in A, K581 cl, 2 vlns, vla & vlc
   with C. Draper cl, E. Quaife vln,   National Gramophonic Society
   E. Tomlinson vla, & P. Parker vlc   AAA & XX/ZZ

RAFF

(6) Pieces, Op. 85 vln & pf
No. 3. Cavatina in D
  with piano   Odeon 0154, 44933

SCHUBERT

Quartet No. 13, in a, Op. 29, No. 1 (D804) 2 vlns, vla & vlc
  with E. Quaife vln, E. Tomlinson vla   National Gramophonic Society
  & P. Parker vlc   HHH, JJJ, KKK, LLL & MMM

THOMÉ

Andante religioso, Op. 70 pf – arr. vln & pf
  with piano   Odeon 51666

Simple aveu, Op. 25 pf – arr. vln & pf
  with piano   Odeon 0149, 44963

TOMLINSON

Lament 2 vlns, vla & vlc
  with E. Quaife vln, E. Tomlinson vla   National Gramophonic Society
  & P. Parker vlc   EE

WIENIAWSKI

(2) Mazurkas, Op. 19 vln & pf
No. 1. Mazurka No. 1, in G "Obertass"
  with piano   Odeon X67624

Georg EGGER

TELEMANN

Concerto in F, T.II, No. 2, 3 vlns, strs & c
  with S. Lautenbacher vln, A. Schäfer   Turnabout TV34288
  vln & Stuttgart solisten

Arnold EIDUS (1923–)

ACHRON

Stimmungen, Op. 32, vln & pf
  with G. Agostini hp   Period SPL748, PRST2748

d'AMBROSIO

Canzonetta, Op. 6 vln & pf
  with G. Agostini hp   Period SPL748, PRST2748

BEETHOVEN

Qaurtet No. 4 in E flat, Op. 16 pf, vln, vla & vlc
  with L. Mittman pf, D. Mankowitz vla   Contrepoint MC20062
  & G. Ricci vlc   Stradivari STR616

BRAHMS

Sonata No. 2, in A, Op. 100 vln & pf
  with L. Mittman pf   Contrepoint MC20056
                Stradivari STR611

CHOPIN

Nocturne No. 20, in c sharp, Op. posth pf – arr. vln & pf Milstein
  with G. Agostino hp   Period SPL748, PRST2748

DEBUSSY

(2) Danses (1904) hp & str qt
No. 1. Danse sacrée
  with E. Vito hp, A. Levin vln, J. de   Concerteum CS192
  Pasquale vla & G. Ricci vlc   Period SPL747, PRST2747
                Saga XID5240

No. 2. Danse profane
  with E. Vito hp, A. Levin vln, J. de   Concerteum CS192
  Pasquale vla & G. Ricci vlc   Period SPL747, PRST2747
                Saga XID5240

(12) Préludes – Book I (1910) pf
No. 8. La Fille aux cheveux de lin arr. vln & pf Hartmann
  with G. Agostini hp   Period SPL748, PRST2748

DOHNÁNYI

Quartet No. 2, in D flat, Op. 15 2 vlns, vla & vlc
  with A. Levin vln, D. Mankowitz vla   Contrepoint MC20061
  & G. Ricci vlc   Stradivari STR614

Serenade in C, Op. 10 vln, vla & vlc
  with D. Mankowitz vla & G. Ricci vlc   Contrepoint MC20061
                Stradivari STR614

DVOŘÁK

(8) Humoresques, Op. 101 pf
No. 7. Humoresque No. 7, in G flat arr. vln & pf "in G" Kreisler
  with G. Agostini pf   Period SLP748, PRST2748

Quartet No. 6, in F, Op. 96 "American" 2 vlns, vla & vlc
  with A. Levin vln, D. Mankowitz vla   Contrepoint MC20068
  & G. Ricci vlc   Stradivari STR613

Trio No. 4, in e, Op. 90 "Dumky" pf, vln & vlc
  with L. Mittman pf & G. Ricci vlc   Stradivari STR620

ELGAR

(La) Capricieuse, Op. 17 vln & pf
  with G. Moore pf   2EA 11718–2   HMV C3582

GLUCK

Orphée et Eurydice (1762) – opera
Dance of the blessed spirits: Lento "Mélodie" (No. 2) arr. vln & pf
Kreisler
  with G. Agostini hp   Period SPL748, PRST2748

GOUNOD

Ave Maria (Méditation on Bach's "Prelude No. 1, in C" from Book I of
"Das Wohltemperirte Clavier") v & pf – arr. vln & hp
  with G. Agostini hp   Period SPL748, PRST2748

GRANADOS

(12) Danzas españolas, Op. 37 (1893) pf
No. 5. Danza española No. 5, in e "Andaluza" arr. vln & pf Kreisler
  with G. Agostini hp   Period SPL748, PRST2748

KODÁLY

Duo, Op. 7 (1914) vln & vlc
  with J. Starker vlc   Period SPL720, (in set TE1093)

MASSENET

Élégie v & pf – arr. vln & pf
  with G. Agostini hp   Period SPL748, PRST2748

Thaïs (1894) – opera
Méditation arr. vln & pf Marsick
  with G. Agostini hp   Period SPL748, PRST2748

MOZART

Quintet in E flat, K407 hrn, vln, 2 vlas & vlc
  with O. De Rosa hrn, I. Zir vla, A. Concerteum CS268
  Levin vla & G. Ricci vlc Stradivari STR601

Quintet in A K581 cl, 2 vlns, vla & vlc
  with A. Duques cl, E. Green vln, Concerteum CS268
  I. Zir vla & G. Ricci vlc Stradivari STR601

PROKOFIEV

Sonata in C, Op. 56 2 vlns
  with L. Persinger vln Stradivari STR1001

PROVOST

Intermezzo (1940) vln & pf
  with G. Agostini hp Period SPL748, PRST2748

RAVEL

Introduction & Allegro (1906) hp, fl, cl & str qt
  with E. Vito hp, V. Just fl, A. Duques Concerteum CS192
  cl, A. Levin vln, J. de Pasquale vla & Period SHO301
  G. Ricci vlc Saga XID5240
  Stradivari STR1007

Pièce en forme d'Habanera v & pf – arr. vln & pf Catherine
  with G. Agostini hp Period SPL748, PRST2748

Sonata (1927) vln & pf
  with B. Smith pf Stradivari SLP1005

Trio in a (1915) pf, vln & vlc
  with B. Smith pf & G. Ricci vlc Stradivari SLP1005

SAINT–SAËNS

Fantaisie in A, Op. 124 (1907) vln & hp
  with E. Vito hp Concerteum CS192
  Period SPL747, PRST2747
  Saga XID5240

SARASATE

(8) Danzas españolas vln & pf
  No. 2. Habañera, Op. 21, No. 2
  with G. Moore pf 2EA 11717–1 HMV C3582

Zigeunerweisen, Op. 20 vln & pf or orch.
  with piano HMV SL114

SCHUBERT, François

(12) Bagatelles, Op. 13 vln & pf
  No. 9. L'abeille
  with G. Agostini hp Period SPL748, PRST2748

SIBELIUS

Concerto in d, Op. 47 vln & orch.
  with Vienna Orch. Society – Hummel Contrepoint MC20056
  Music Treasures of the World
  MT528
  Stradivari STR611

SMETANA

Quartet No. 1, in e (1876) "From my life" 2 vlns, vla & vlc
  with A. Levin vln, D. Mankowitz vla Stradivari STR613
  & G. Ricci vlc

Trio in g, Op. 15 pf, vln & vlc
  with L. Mittman pf & G. Ricci vlc Stradivari STR620

SPOHR

Nonet in F, Op. 31 fl, ob, cl, hrn, bsn, vln, vla, vlc & cbs
  with members of Stradivari Ensemble Stradivari STR609

TCHAIKOVSKY

Souvenir d'un lieu cher, Op. 42 vln & pf
  No. 3. Mélodie
  with G. Agostini pf Period SPL748, PRST2748

VIVALDI

(12) Concerti, Op. 3 "L'Estro armonico" var. cbns & strs
  Concerto No. 10, in b, P.148 (F.IV, No. 10) 4 vlns, strs & c
  with S. Shulman vln, F. Buldrini vln, Allegro ALG3146
  L. Graeler vln & Stradivari Ensemble Concerteum CS194
  Stradivari STR604

WIENIAWSKI

(L') École moderne, Op. 10 (10 Études) solo vln
  No. 5. Étude No. 5, in E flat "alla Saltarella" arr. vln & pf Kreisler
  with E. Flissler pf Concerteum CS275
  Guilde Européenne du
  Microsillon GEM34
  Stradivari SLP1003

(8) Étude–Caprices, Op. 18 solo vln & 2nd vln obb
  Étude–Caprice No. 4, in a arr. vln & pf Kreisler
  with E. Flissler pf Concerteum CS275
  Guilde Européenne du
  Microsillon GEM34
  Stradivari SLP1003

Polonaise brillante No. 1, in D, Op. 4 vln & pf
  with E. Flissler pf Concerteum CS275
  Guilde Européenne du
  Microsillon GEM34
  Stradivari SLP1003

Polonaise brillante No. 2, in A, Op. 21 vln & pf
  with E. Flissler pf Concerteum CS275
  Guilde Européenne du
  Microsillon GEM34
  Stradivari SLP1003

Scherzo–Tarantelle, Op. 16 vln & pf
  with E. Flissler pf Concerteum CS275
  Guilde Européenne du
  Microsillon GEM34
  Stradivari SLP1003

Souvenir de Moscou, Op. 6 vln & pf
  with L'Orch. des Concerts HMV DB11142
  Colonne – Fournet

Souvenir de Moscou, Op. 6 vln & pf
  with E. Flissler pf Concerteum CS275
  Guilde Européenne du
  Microsillon GEM34
  Stradivari SLP1003

Harold EISENBERG

CHOPIN

(3) Nocturnes, Op. 9 pf
  No. 2. Nocturne No. 2, in E flat arr. vln & pf Sarasate
  with piano Imperial 45481

GODARD

(3) Morceaux, Op. 78 – suite vln & pf
No. 2. Berceuse in G
with piano   Imperial 45480

VIEUXTEMPS

Ballade & Polonaise, in G Op. 38 vln & pf
Ballade
with piano   Imperial 45479

Marta EITLER (1922–   )

BACH

(6) Brandenburg Concerti, BWV1046/51 (1721) strs & c
Brandenburg Concerto No. 3, in G, BWV1048 3 vlns, 3 vlas, 3 vlcs & cbs
with T. Carter vln, J. Pougnet vln,   Nixa WLP6309
F. Riddle vla, E. Grainger vla,   Westminster XWN18366, (in set
E. Hurwitz vla, V. Joseph vlc, A. Pini   XWN2211)
vlc, R. Albin vlc, R. Watson cbs & R.   Whitehall WH20071
Veyron–Lacroix hpsi, of the London
Baroque Ensemble – Haas

SCHUBERT

Konzertstück in D, D345 (1816) vln & orch.
with London Baroque   Parlophone PMA1017 (unissued),
Ensemble – Haas   PMC1078

Peter ELBAEK

ALBINONI

(12) Sonatas, Op. 1 (1964) "Sinfonias"
Sonata No. 3, in A 2 vlns & c
with O. Kinch vln, B. Anker vlc   Bach Guild BG566
& J.E. Hansen vir   Metronome MCEP3021

LUMBYE

Concert Polka (1863) 2 vlns & orch.
with B. Madsen vln & Tivoli Gardens   Vox PL12840, STPL512840
Musikkorps – Felumb

Mischa ELMAN (1891–1967)

ACHRON

Hebrew melody, Op. 33, vln & pf – arr. Auer
with L. Mittman pf   Victor 11–9111

Hebrew melody, Op. 33 vln & pf – arr. Auer
with J. Seiger pf   London LL1467

Hebrew melody, Op. 33 vln & pf – arr. Auer
with J. Seiger pf   Vanguard VRS1099, VSD2137

ALBÉNIZ

España (6 Feuilles d'album) Op. 165 pf
No. 2. Tango in D arr. vln & pf Elman
with J. Bonime pf   Victor 64821, 610

No. 2. Tango in D arr. vln & pf Elman
with piano   HMV DB1460
                                 Victor 7195

d'AMBROSIO

Canzonetta, Op. 6 vln & pf
with orch.   A 25587   HMV 5–7949, DA197
                                      Victor 66008, 602

ANONYMOUS

Eili, Eili (Zionist hymn) – arr. vln & pf Elman
with E. Balaban pf   HMV DB233
                                 Victor 74732, 6098

Eili, Eili (Zionist hymn) – arr. vln & pf Elman
with J. Seiger pf   Vanguard VRS1099, VSD2137

Old Irish song & dance unid – arr. vln & pf
with L. Mittman pf   V–Disc 142

ARENSKY

(4) Morceaux, Op. 30 vln & pf
No. 2. Serenade in G arr. Elman
with piano   Pathé 8073, 8398, 8503
No. 2. Serenade in G arr. Elman
with J. Bonime pf   A 34462 △   HMV DA1094
                                 Victor 1434, 10–0018

No. 2. Serenade in G arr. Elman
with W. Rosé pf   Victor 10–1492, (in set
                                 DM1328), 49–0612, (in set
                                 WDM1328), LM83

On wings of dreams v & pf – arr. v, vln & pf
with R. Ponselle s & R. Romani pf   Camden (in set CBL1001),
                                       CDN1006
                                       Victor 16451

ASCHER

Alice, where art thou? (1861) v & pf – arr. vln & orch. Elman
with orch.   HMV DB232
                                 Victor 74724, 6097

AULIN

(4) Aquarelles vln & pf
No. 2. Humoresque
with piano   Pathé 5396, 8072, 8506

BACH

Concerto No. 2, in E, BWV1042 vln, strs & c
2B 4088[III] □, 4089[IV] □, 4090[IIIA]   HMV DB1871/3
       □, 4091[IV] □ & 4092[IIIA] □
with string orch. – Barbirolli

Concerto No. 2, in E, BWV1042 vln strs & c
with Vienna State Opera Orch. –   Vanguard (in set VSD701/2),
Golschmann   VRS1059, VSD2073

(3) Sonatas & 3 Partitas, BWV1001/6 solo vln
Sonata No. 2, in a: Allegro (4th mvt) BWV1003
(unaccompanied)   Pathé 5395, 8071, 8508
Partita No. 3, in E: Preludio (1st mvt) BWV1006
(unaccompanied)   2B 4348[I] □   HMV DB1873
Partita No. 3, in E: Gavotte (3rd mvt) BWV1006
(unaccompanied)   Pathé 5397, 8072, 8505, 9547
(4) Suites, BWV1066/9 strs & c
Suite No. 3, in D: Air (2nd mvt) BWV1068 2 obs, 3 tpts, drms & strs –
arr. vln & pf as "Air on the G–string" by Wilhelmj
with P.B. Kahn pf   A 9871   HMV 2–07972, DB226
                                     Victor 74292, 6101

BACH – *Continued*

Suite No. 3, in D: Air (2nd mvt) BWV1068 2 obs, 3 tpts, drms & strs – arr. vln & pf as "Air on the G–string" by Wilhelmj
with J. Bonime pf   Victor 7103

Suite No. 3, in D: Air (2nd mvt) BWV1068 2 obs, 3 tpts, drms & strs – arr. vln & pf as "Air on the G–string" by Wilhelmj
with J. Seiger pf   Decca LXT5303
                                           London LL1631

BALAKIREV

(20) Songs (1858) v & pf
No. 10. Oh, come to me arr. vln & pf Volpe
with L. Mittman pf   Victor 11–9423, 49–0972

BARNS

Swing song vln & pf
with P.B. Kahn pf   6654 HMV 3–7915, 37957
                                 Victor 61183

BEETHOVEN

Concerto in D, Op. 61 (candenzas by Elman) vln & orch.
with London Philharmonic   Decca LXT5068
Orch. – Solti   London LL1257

(12) Contretänze, G141 orch.
Contretanz No. 1, in C arr. vln & pf Elman
with A. Loesser pf   A 23436 HMV 5–7940, DA193
                                  Victor 64968, 597

Contretanz No. 1, in C arr. vln & pf Seiss
with M. van Gool pf   Bb 18456^{IIA}△ HMV DA1232

(6) Minuets, G167 pf
No. 2. Minuet No. 2, in G arr. vln & pf Burmester
with P.B. Kahn pf   HMV 3–7921, DA200
                           Victor 64121, 607

No. 2. Minuet No. 2, in G arr. vln & pf Burmester
with J. Bonime pf   A 53534 △ HMV DA1094
                                 Victor 1434, 10–0018

No. 2. Minuet No. 2, in G arr. vln & pf Burmester
with W. Rosé pf
                  Victor 10–1493, (in set
                  DM1328), 49–0613, (in set
                  WDM1328), 49–3444, 26035,
                  ERA29, LM83 & (in set
                  WEPR29)

No. 2. Minuet No. 2, in G arr. vln & pf Burmester
with J. Seiger pf   Vanguard VRS1051, VSD2048

Romance No. 1, in G, Op. 40 vln & orch.
         2B 4341^{III} △ & 4342^{II} △ HMV DB1846
with London Symphony Orch. –
Collingwood

Romance No. 2, in F, Op. 50 vln & orch.
         2B 4343^{I} △ & 4344^{II} △ HMV DB1847
with London Symphony Orch. –
Collingwood

(Die) Ruinen von Athen, Op. 113 – Incidental music orch.
No. 4. Marcia alla turca arr. vln & pf Auer
with J. Bonime pf   A 22637 HMV DA194
                               Victor 64915, 598

Sonata No. 5, in F, Op. 24 "Spring" vln & pf
with J. Seiger pf   Decca LXT5126
                           London LL1258

BEETHOVEN – *Continued*

Sonata No. 9, in A, Op. 47 "Kreutzer" vln & pf
with J. Seiger pf   Decca LXT5126
                           London LL1258

BENJAMIN

From San Domingo (1945) orch. – arr. vln & pf
with J. Seiger pf   Decca LXT5304
                           London LL1629

From San Domingo (1945) orch. – arr. vln & pf
with J. Seiger pf   Vanguard VRS1173, VSD71173

BLOCH

Baal Shem (3 Pictures of Chassidic life) (1923) vln & pf
No. 2. Nigun (Improvisation)
with V. Padwa pf   Victor 11–8575
No. 2. Nigun (Improvisation)
with J. Seiger pf   London LL1467
No. 2. Nigun (Improvisation)
with J. Seiger pf   Vanguard VRS1099, VSD2137

BOHM

(6) Miniatures, Op. 187 vln & pf
No. 4. Perpetuum mobile
with P.B. Kahn pf   8330½b Gramophone & Typewriter
                              37942, 47958
                              HMV 3–7908
                              Victor 61180

(6) Pieces, Op. 314 vln & pf
No. 3. Gavotte
with P.B. Kahn pf   HMV 3–7916
                           Victor 61184

BONIME

Danse Hébraïque vln & pf
with J. Seiger pf   Vanguard VRS1099, VSD2137

BRAGA

(7) Melodies (1867) v & pf
No. 5. La serenata "Angel's serenade" arr. v, vln & pf
with F. Alda s & F. La Forge pf   Victor 88523, 89130, 8001
No. 5. La serenata "Angel's serenade" arr. v, vln & pf
with J. Peerce t & W. Rosé pf   Victor (in set WDM1703),
                                  LM1703

BRAHMS

(21) Hungarian Dances pf duet
Hungarian dance No. 7, in A arr. vln & pf Joachim
with P.B. Kahn pf   A 14688 HMV 3–7977, DA193
                             Victor 64439, 597

Hungarian dance No. 17, in f sharp arr. vln & pf Joachim
with A. Loesser pf   HMV DA203
                           Victor 64977, 611

Sonata No. 2, in A, Op. 100 vln & pf
with J. Seiger pf   London LL1630

Sonata No. 3, in d, Op. 108 vln & pf
with W. Rosé pf   Victor 12–0414/6, (in set
                           DM1232), LM30

Sonata No. 3, in d, Op. 108 vln & pf
with J. Seiger pf   London LL1630

BRUCH

Concerto No. 1, in g, Op. 26 vln & orch.
with London Philharmonic   Decca LXT5222
Orch. – Boult   London LL1486
Concerto No. 2, in d, Op. 44, vln & orch.
with London Symphony   Decca LW5290
Orch. – Fistoulari
Kol Nidrei, Op. 47 vlc or vln & orch.
with J. Bonime pf   A 23443   HMV 3–07913, DB233
Victor 74601, 6098

Kol Nidrei, Op. 47 vlc or vln & orch.
with J. Seiger pf   Vanguard VRS1099, VSD2137

BRÜLL

(3) Morceaux, Op. 90 vln & pf
No. 1. Scène espagnole
with piano   724 c   Gramophone & Typewriter
07907, 037904, 047912
HMV 4420

Souvenir pf – arr. vln & pf
with piano   Gramophone & Typewriter
37954

CHAJES

(The) Chassid vln & pf
with J. Seiger pf   Vanguard VRS1099, VSD2137

CHOPIN

(3) Nocturnes, Op. 9 pf
No. 2. Nocturne No. 2, in E flat arr. vln & pf Sarasate
with piano   727 c   Gramophone & Typewriter
07906, 037903, 047911
HMV 4420
Victor 74052, 6099

No. 2. Nocturne No. 2, in E flat arr. vln & pf Sarasate
with P.B. Kahn pf   A 8813   HMV 07928, DB234
No. 2. Nocturne No. 2, in E flat arr. vln & pf Sarasate
with J. Seiger pf   Vanguard VRS1051, VSD2048
(2) Nocturnes, Op. 27 pf
No. 2. Nocturne No. 8, in D flat arr. vln & pf Wilhelmj
with P.B. Kahn pf   A 22640   HMV 2–07976, DB234
Victor 74590, 6099

No. 2. Nocturne No. 8, in D flat arr. vln & pf Wilhelmj
with M. van Gool pf   Cc 18458[IA] △   HMV DB1398

CUI

Kaleidoscope, Op. 50 vln & pf
No. 9. Orientale
with orch.   A 18963   HMV 4–7920, DA195
Victor 64639, 599

No. 9. Orientale
with orch.   A 18963 △   HMV DA1010
Victor 1354

No. 9. Orientale
with W. Rosé pf   Victor 10–1491, (in set
DM1328), 10–3299, 49–0611, (in
set WDM1328), 49–3299, LM83

No. 9. Orientale
with J. Seiger pf   Vanguard VRS1051, VSD2048

CUI – *Continued*

No. 21. Lettre d'amour arr. Elman
with J. Bonime pf   A 34461△   HMV DA802
Victor 1160

DEBUSSY

(La) Plus que lente – valse (1910) pf – arr. vln & pf Roques
with J. Seiger pf   Vanguard VRS1173, VSD71173
Sonata No. 3, in g (1917) vln & pf
with L. Mittman pf   Victor 11–8329/30, (set M938),
11–8428/9

DELIBES

(Le) Roi s'Amuse (1882) – Incidental music orch.
No. 6. Passépied arr. vln & pf Elman
with J. Bonime pf   Victor 64903, 606

DENZA

Si vous l'aviez compris! v & pf – arr. v, vln & pf
with E. Caruso t &   A 15682   HMV 2/032018, DK104
G. Scognamiglio pf   Victor 89084, 8008

DINICU

Hora staccato (1906) vln & pf – arr. Heifetz
with V. Padwa pf   Victor 2064

DITTERSDORF

Deutscher Tanz unid – arr. vln & pf Burmester
with piano   2356 f   Gramophone & Typewriter
07909
Victor 71039

Deutscher Tanz unid – arr. vln & pf Burmester
with P.B. Kahn pf   A 8820   HMV 07934, DB650
Victor 74164, 6424

Quartet No. 3, in G 2 vlns, vla & vlc
Andante (2nd mvt)
(as leader of Elman string   A 19169   HMV 08056, DB238
quartet)   Victor 74525, 6102
Quartet No. 5, in E flat 2 vlns, vla & vlc
Finale (4th mvt)
(as leader of Elman string quartet)   HMV 8195, DA174
Victor 64671, 612

DRDLA

Longing, Op. 228 vln & pf
with C. Hollister pf   A 69697△   HMV DA1233
Serenade No. 1, in A vln & pf
with piano   Victor 66048, 601
Serenade No. 1, in A vln & pf
with C. Hollister pf   A 67433△   HMV DA1214
Victor 1538

Souvenir vln & pf
with piano   8741 b   Gramophone & Typewriter
37911, 47959

Souvenir vln & pf
with P. Gordon pf   A 18966   HMV 4–7930, DA195
Victor 64644, 599

Souvenir vln & pf
with R. Bauman pf   A 18966 △   HMV DA1010
Victor 1354

DRDLA – *Continued*

Souvenir vln & pf
　with W. Rosé pf

Victor 10–1493, (in set DM1328), 10–3299, 49–0613, (in set WDM1328), 49–3299, LM83

DRIGO

(2) Airs de Ballet orch.
　No. 2. Valse bluette arr. vln & pf Auer
　　with J. Seiger pf

Vanguard VRS1051, VSD2048

(Les) Millions d'Arlequin (1900) – ballet orch.
　Sérénade arr. vln & pf Auer
　　with piano

Pathé 5397, 9547

　Sérénade arr. vln & pf Auer
　　with piano　　A 8821

HMV 3–7922

　Sérénade arr. vln & pf Auer
　　with piano　　A 8877

Gramophone & Typewriter 37956
HMV 3–7914
Victor 61185

　Sérénade arr. vln & pf Auer
　　with P.B. Kahn pf

HMV 4–7949, DA428
Victor 64123, 600

　Sérénade arr. vln & pf Auer
　　with C. Hollister pf　　A 67434 △

HMV DA1214
Victor 1538

　Sérénade arr. vln & pf Auer
　　with W. Rosé pf

Victor 10–1491, (in set DM1328), 49–0611, (in set WDM1328), 49–3444, LM83 & (in set WEPR29)

DVOŘÁK

(8) Humorsques, Op. 101 pf
　No. 7. Humoresque No. 7, in G flat arr. vln & pf "in G" Elman
　　with P.B. Kahn pf　　A 8799　HMV 07930, 2–07974, DB230
Victor 74163, 6095

　No. 7. Humoresque No. 7, in G flat arr. vln & pf "in G" Elman
　　with piano

HMV DB1269

　No. 7. Humoresque No. 7, in G flat arr. vln & pf "in G" Elman
　　with R. Bauman pf　　A 8799△　HMV DB1354
Victor 6836

　No. 7. Humoresque No. 7, in G flat arr. vln & pf "in G" Elman
　　with L. Mittman pf

Victor 11–8950, LM83

　No. 7. Humoresque No. 7, in G flat arr. vln & pf "in G" Elman
　　with J. Seiger pf

Vanguard VRS1051, VSD2048

(8) Slavonic Dances, Op. 46 pf duet; orch.
　No. 2. Slavonic dance No. 2, in e arr. vln & pf "in g" Kreisler
　　with J. Seiger pf

Philips A04308L, AL3423
Vanguard VRS1066, VSD2084

(8) Slavonic Dances, Op. 72 pf duet; orch.
　No. 2. Slavonic dance No. 10, in e arr. vln & pf Kreisler
　　with J. Seiger pf

Philips A04308L, AL3423
Vanguard VRS1066, VSD2084

ELMAN

In a gondola (Impromptu) vln & pf
　with W.H. Golde pf

HMV 4–7909, DA198
Victor 64530, 603

ELMAN – *Continued*

Tango vln & pf
　with W. Rosé pf

Victor (in set WDM1625)

Tango vln & pf
　with J. Seiger pf

Decca LXT5304
London LL1629

ESPEJO

Airs tziganes, Op. 11 (1926) vln & pf
　with M. van Gool pf　　2B 1131 III △

HMV DB1594
Victor 7574

Airs tziganes, Op. 11 (1926) vln & pf
　with J. Seiger pf

Decca LXT5304
London LL1629

Airs tziganes, Op. 11 (1926) vln & pf
　with J. Seiger pf

Vanguard VRS1173, VSD71173

FAURÉ

Berceuse, Op. 16 vln & pf
　with J. Seiger pf

Vanguard VRS1173, VSD71173

(3) Chansons, Op. 7 v & pf
　No. 1. Après un rêve arr. vln & pf Bachmann
　　with L. Mittman pf

Victor 11–8329, 11–8428, (in set M938)

Sonata No. 1, in A, Op. 13 vln & pf
　with L. Mittman pf

Victor 18351/3, 18354/6, (set M859)

Sonata No. 1. in A, Op. 13 vln & pf
　with J. Seiger pf

London LL1628

FRANCK

Sonata in A (1886) vln & pf*
　with piano

Pathé 9589/90

Sonata in A (1886) vln & pf
　with J. Seiger pf

London LL1628

FRIML

Au soir (at evening) pf – arr. vln & pf Kramer
　with J. Bonime pf　　A 34464△

HMV DA802
Victor 1160

GABRIEL–MARIE

(La) Cinquantaine (1894) pf duet – arr. vln & orch.
　with orch.　　A 25588　HMV 5–7970, DA197
Victor 66073, 603

GLUCK

Orphée et Eurydice (1762) – opera
　Dance of the blessed spirits: Lento "Mélodie" (No. 2) arr. vln & pf Wilhelmj
　　with W.H. Golde pf

HMV 2–07975, DB225
Victor 74459, 6090

　Dance of the blessed spirits: Lento "Mélodie" (No. 2) arr. vln & pf Wilhelmj
　　with piano

HMV DB1385
Victor 7654

Paride ed Elena (1770) – opera
　O del mio dolce ardor arr. vln & pf as "Largo" by Ries
　　with J. Seiger pf

Vanguard VRS1173, VSD71173

* Abridged.

GOLDFADEN

Raisins & almonds v & pf – arr. vln & pf Collins
  with J. Seiger pf   Vanguard VRS1099, VDS2137

GOSSEC

(Le) Camp du Grand pré (1793) – opera
  Tambourin arr. vln & pf Burmester
  with P. B. Kahn pf   A 10408   HMV 3–7936, 4–7943, DA506
     Victor 64198

Rosine (1786) – opera
  Gavotte arr. vln & pf Elman
  with piano   2356 f   Gramophone & Typewriter
     07909
     Victor 71039

  Gavotte arr. vln & pf Elman
  with P.B. Kahn pf   A 8820   HMV 07934, DB650
     Victor 74164, 6424

  Gavotte arr. vln & pf Elman
  with W. Rosé pf   Victor 10–1492, (in set
     DM1328), 49–0612, (in set
     WDM1328), LM83

  Gavotte arr. vln & pf Elman
  with J. Seiger pf   Vanguard VRS1051, VSD2048

GOUNOD

Ave Maria (Méditation on Bach's "Prelude No. 1, in C" from Book I of "Das Wohltemperirte Clavier") v & pf – arr. v, vln & pf
  with F. Alda s & F. La Forge pf   Victor 88522, 89129, 8001

GRÉTRY

Éphale et Procris (1773) – opera
  Gavotte arr. vln & pf Franko
  with P.B. Kahn pf   A 10408   HMV 4–7943, DA506
     Victor 64198

GRIEG

(4) Albumblätter, Op. 28 pf
  No. 3. Albumleaf in A arr. vln & pf Hartmann
  with L. Mittman pf   Victor (in set WEPR29), 26024,
     10–1271, ERA29

(6) Lyric Pieces – Book V, Op. 54 pf
  No. 4. Nocturne arr. vln & pf Elman
  with J. Bonime pf   HMV DB227
     Victor 74643, 6092

Sonata No. 1, in F, Op. 8 vln & pf
  with J. Seiger pf   Decca LXT5113
     London LL1253

Sonata No. 3, in c, Op. 45 vln & pf
  with J. Seiger pf   Decca LXT5113
     London LL1253

HANDEL

Cantata (unid)
  Dank sei dir, Herr "Arioso" arr. s, vln, vlc & pf
  with H. Lashanska s,   2A 031473 △   HMV DB3819
  E. Feuermann vlc & R. Serkin pf   Victor 15365

Serse (1738) – opera
  Ombra mai fu "Largo" arr. vln & pf Elman
  with H. Dawson org   HMV DB1853

HANDEL – *Continued*

(15) Sonatas, Op. 1 (?1731) fl or vln & c
  Sonata No. 13, in D vln IV
  with W. Rosé pf   Victor (in set WDM1590),
     LM1183

  Sonata No. 13, in D vln IV
  with J. Seiger pf   Decca LXT5303
     London LL1631

  Sonata No. 14, in A vln V
  with W. Rosé pf   Victor (in set WDM1590),
     LM1183

  Sonata No. 15, in E vln VI
  with W. Rosé pf   Victor (in set WDM1590),
     LM1183

(16) Suites (1720/33) hpsi
  Suite No. 14, in G: Gavotte (6th mvt) arr. vln & pf Moffat
  with W. Rosé pf   Victor (in set WDM1590)

HAYDN

Capriccietto–Presto unid – arr. vln & pf Burmester
  with piano   HMV DA1290

Minuet in F unid – arr. vln & pf Burmester
  with P.B. Kahn pf   A 8823   HMV 3–7923
     Victor 64135, 1060

(6) Quartets, Op. 76 (H.III, Nos. 75/80) 2 vlns, vla & vlc
  No. 2. Quartet No. 76, in d, H.III, No. 76 "Quinten"
  (as leader of Elman   A 37403/6△   HMV DB1146/7
  string quartet)   Victor 6701/2

  No. 3. Quartet No. 77, in C: Theme & variations (2nd mvt) H.III, No. 77 "Emperor"
  (as leader of Elman string   A 19169   HMV 08073, DB651
  quartet)   Victor 74516, 6103

  No. 3. Quartet No. 77, in C: Theme & variations (2nd mvt) H.III, No. 77 "Emperor"
  (as leader of Elman   A 19169△   HMV DB1055
  string quartet)   Victor 6634

Symphony No. 96, in D (1791) "Miracle" orch.
  Minuet (3rd mvt) arr. vln & pf Burmester
  with W.H. Golde pf   HMV 4–7946, DA200
     Victor 64538, 607

HERBERT

À la valse vln & pf
  with J. Bonime pf   Victor 1079

HOLLMAN

Chanson d'amour v & pf – arr. v, vln & pf
  with F. Alda s & F. La Forge pf   HMV 2–033083, DB516
     Victor 88521, 89128

HUBAY

(14) Scènes de la Csárda vln & pf
  No. 4. Hejre Kati, Op. 32
  with L. Mittman pf   Victor 11–9423, 49–0972

HUMMEL

Waltz in A pf – arr. vln & pf
  with piano   HMV DA202
     Victor 64829, 610

HUMMEL – *Continued*

Waltz in E flat pf – arr. vln & pf Burmester
with P.B. Kahn pf
    HMV 3–7957, DA198
    Victor 64336, 604

JOSTEN

Sonatina (1939) vln & pf
with J. Seiger pf
    London LL1467

KAHN

Ave Maria v & pf – arr. v, vln & pf
with E. Caruso t &   A 13004   HMV 02472, CSLP508, DK103
P.B. Kahn pf
    Victor 89065, 8007, 17–0127,
    LCT2, RCX1014, WCT7,
    WCT1121

KHACHATURIAN

Concerto in D (1940) vln & orch.
with Vienna State Opera
Orch. – Golschmann
    Amadeo AVRS6156
    I Classici della Musica Classica
    XAM4016
    Vanguard VRS1049, VSD2037

KOPYLOW

(14) Kleine Charakterstücke, Op. 52 pf
No. 9. Beim Einschlummern (To slumberland) arr. vln & pf Hartmann
with J. Bonime pf
    Victor 1079

KORNGOLD

Viel Lärmen um Nichts (Much ado about nothing) Op. 11 (1919) –
Incidental music orch. – arr. vln & pf as "Suite" by Korngold
with J. Seiger pf
    London LL1467

KREISLER

Caprice viennois, Op. 2 vln & pf
with J. Seiger pf
    Amadeo EP15136
    Philips A04308L, AL3423
    Vanguard VRS1066, VSD2084

(La) Gitana vln & pf
with J. Seiger pf
    Amadeo AVRS6215
    Philips A04308L, AL3423
    Vanguard VRS1066, VSD2084

Liebesfreud vln & pf
with J. Seiger pf
    Amadeo AVRS6215, EP15136
    Philips A04308L, AL3423
    Vanguard VRS1066, VSD2084

Liebesleid vln & pf
with piano   A 8950   HMV 07942

Liebesleid vln & pf
with J. Seiger pf
    Decca LXT5304
    London LL1629

Rondino on a theme by Beethoven vln & pf
with W.H. Golde pf
    HMV 4–7948, DA203
    Victor 64547, 611

Rondino on a theme by Beethoven vln & pf
with J. Seiger pf
    Amadeo AVRS6215, EP15136
    Philips A04308L, AL3423
    Vanguard VRS1066, VSD2084

KREISLER – *Continued*

Schön Rosmarin vln & pf
with J. Seiger pf
    Amadeo AVRS6215, EP15136
    Philips A04308L, AL3423
    Vanguard VRS1066, VSD2084

Slavonic Fantasy in b (on themes by Dvořák) vln & pf
with W. Rosé pf
    Victor 12–0241

Slavonic Fantasy in b (on themes by Dvořák) vln & pf
with J. Seiger pf
    Decca LXT5304
    London LL1629

Slavonic Fantasy in b (on themes by Dvořák) vln & pf
with J. Seiger pf
    Vanguard VRS1173, VSD71173

Allegretto (Boccherini) vln & pf
with J. Seiger pf
    Amadeo AVRS6215
    Philips A04308L, AL3423
    Vanguard VRS1066, VSD2084

Chanson Louis XIII & Pavane (L. Couperin) vln & pf
with W.H. Golde pf
    HMV 07999, DB650
    Victor 74340

Minuet (Porpora) vln & pf
with piano
    HMV DB230
    Victor 74394

Praeludium & Allegro (Pugnani) vln & pf
with J. Seiger pf
    Amadeo AVRS6215
    Philips A04308L, AL3423
    Vanguard VRS1066, VSD2084

(Le) Précieuse (L. Couperin) vln & pf
with J. Seiger pf
    Vanguard VRS1173, VSD71173

Preghièra (Padre Martini) vln & pf
with J. Seiger pf
    Amadeo AVRS6215
    Philips A04308L, AL3423
    Vanguard VRS1066, VSD2084

Scherzo (Dittersdorf) vln & pf
with piano
    HMV DA1290

Sicilienne & Rigaudon (Francoeur) vln & pf
with P.B. Kahn pf
    HMV 2–07979
    Victor 74308

Sicilienne & Rigaudon (Francoeur) vln & pf
with J. Seiger pf
    Amadeo AVRS6215
    Philips A04308L, AL3423
    Vanguard VRS1066, VSD2084

Variations on a theme of Corelli (Tartini) vln & pf
with J. Seiger pf
    Amadeo AVRS6215
    Philips A04308L, AL3423
    Vanguard VRS1066, VSD2084

KROLL

Juanita vln & pf
with J. Seiger pf
    Vanguard VRS1173, VSD71173

LALO

Symphonie espagnole, Op. 21 vln & orch.
Andante (4th mvt)
with A. Loesser pf   A 24772   HMV 3–07969, DB224
    Victor 74771, 6089

LALO – Continued

Symphonie espagnole, Op. 21 vln & orch.*
  with Vienna State Opera   Amadeo AVRS6155
  Orch. – Golschmann   I Classici della Musica Classica
                                   XAM4004
                                   Fontana BIG305, BIG405
                                   Vanguard VRS1050, VSD2047

LAVRY

(6) Jewish Dances, Op. 192 vln & pf
  No. 5. Yemenite wedding dance
  with J. Seiger pf   Vanguard VRS1099, VSD2137

LEONCAVALLO

Sérénade française v & pf – arr. v, vln & pf
  with E. Caruso t &   A 15683   HMV 2–032017, CSLP512,
  G. Scognamiglio pf   DK104
                                   Victor 89085, 8008, LM6127

Sérénade napolitaine v & pf – arr. v, vln & pf
  with E. Caruso t & G.   A 15683   HMV 2–032017, CSLP512,
  Scognamiglio pf   DK104
                                     Victor 89085, 8008, LM6127

MASSENET

Élégie v & pf – arr. v, vln & pf
  with E. Caruso t & P.B.   A 13005   HMV 2–032010, DK103
  Kahn pf   Victor 89066, 8007, LCT2,
                                   WCT7

Élégie v & pf – arr. v, vln & pf
  with R. Stevens m–s & B. Smith pf   Victor (in set WDM1703),
                                   LM1703

Thaïs (1894) – opera
  Méditation arr. vln & pf Marsick
  with P.B. Kahn pf   A 13186   HMV 07996, DB235
                                   Victor 74341, 6100

  Méditation arr. vln & pf Marsick
  with J. Bonime pf   A 49498△   HMV DB1537
                                   Victor 7392

  Méditation arr. vln & pf Marsick
  with L. Mittman pf   Victor (in set WEPR29), 11–
                                   8950, 26024, 49–0316, ERA29

  Méditation arr. vln & pf Marsick
  with J. Seiger pf   Vanguard VRS1051, VSD2048

MENDELSSOHN

Concerto in e, Op. 64 vln & orch.
  with Chicago Symphony   Victor (set WDM1196), 12–
  Orch. – Defauw   0128/31, (set M1196), 412R0116,
                                   LM9024, T16103

Concerto in e, Op. 64 vln & orch.
  with Vienna State Opera   Amadeo AVRS6155
  Orch. – Golschmann   I Classici della Musica Classica
                                     XAM4004
                                   Fontana BIG305, BIG405
                                   Vanguard VRS1050, VSD2047

Hymn: Hear my prayer "O for the wings of a dove" (Psalm 55) 1844) s,
mix–cho & org – arr. vln & pf Lucas
  with M. van Gool pf   Cc 18455ᴵᴵᴬ△   HMV DB1398

*Omitting Intermezzo.

MENDELSSOHN – Continued

Quartet No. 1, in E flat, Op. 12 2 vlns, vla & vlc
  Canzonetta (2nd mvt) arr. vln & pf as "Capriccietto" by Burmester
  with P.B. Kahn pf   HMV 4–7942, DA199
                                   Victor 64204, 605

(6) Songs without words, Op. 62 pf
  No. 1. Song without words No. 25, in G "May breezes" arr. vln & pf
  Kreisler
  with piano   Victor 74393

  No. 1. Song without words No. 25, in G "May breezes" arr. vln & pf
  Kreisler
  with V. Padwa pf   Victor 2064

  No. 1. Song without words No. 25, in G "May breezes" arr. vln & pf
  Kreisler
  with W. Rosé pf   Victor (in set WDM1196), 12–
                                   0131, (in set M1196)

  No. 1. Song without words No. 25, in G "May breezes" arr. vln & pf
  Kreisler
  with J. Seiger pf   Decca LXT5304
                                   London LL1629

(6) Songs without words, Op. 67 pf
  No. 6. Song without words No. 36, in E "Serenade" arr. vln & pf
  Kreisler
  with J. Bonime pf   HMV DB231
                                   Victor 74607, 6096

MILLER

Cubanaise (1951) vln & pf
  with J. Seiger pf   Decca LXT5304
                                   London LL1629

MILLÖCKER

(The) Blue lagoon v & pf – arr. vln & pf Winternitz
  with J. Bonime pf   Victor 66144, 900

MONSIGNY

Aline, Reine de Golconde (1776) – opera
  Rigaudon arr. vln & pf Franko
  with P.B. Kahn pf   HMV 4–7947
                                   Victor 64201, 606

MOORE

(The) Last rose of summer v & pf – arr. vln & pf Auer
  with A. Loesser pf   HMV DA313
                                   Victor 64958, 608

MOZART

Concerto No. 4, in D, K218 (cadenzas by Joachim) vln & orch.
  with New Symphony Orch. – Krips   Decca LXT5078
                                   Everest SDBR3298
                                   London LL1271

Concerto No. 5, in A, K219 "Turkish" (cadenzas by Joachim) vln & orch.
  with New Symphony Orch. – Krips   Decca LXT5078
                                     Everest SDBR3298
                                   London LL1271

Idomeneo, Re di Creta, K366 (1781) – opera
  Gavotte in G arr. vln & pf Auer
  with P.B. Kahn pf   A 8803   HMV 4–7944
                                   Victor 64140

MOZART – *Continued*

(6) Ländler, K606 orch.
  No. 1. Ländler No. 1, in B flat arr. vln & pf
  with J. Bonime pf   Victor 66151, 900
Quartet No. 15, d, K421 2 vlns, vla & vlc
  Minuet (3rd mvt)
  (as leader of Elman string quartet)   HMV 8171, DA174
                                             Victor 64661, 612
Quartet No. 16, in E flat, K428 2 vlns, vla & vlc
  Minuet (3rd mvt)
  (as leader of Elman string   A 21498   HMV 08099, DB238
  quartet)   Victor 74576, 6102
Sonata No. 4, in E flat, K282 pf
  Adagio (2nd mvt) arr. vln & pf Friedberg
  with J. Bonime pf   Victor 74837, 6424
Sonata No. 32, in B flat, K454 vln & pf
  with W. Rosé pf   Victor (set WDM1634), LM1208

NACHÈZ

Passacaglia on a theme of G.B. Sammartini vln & pf
  with J. Seiger pf   Decca LXT5303
                               London LL1631

NARDINI

Concerto in e vln & orch.
  with Vienna State Opera   Vanguard VRS1059, VSD2073
  Orch. – Golschmann

OFFENBACH

(Les) Contes d'Hoffmann (1881) – opera
  Belle Nuit, O nuit d'amour "Barcarolle" arr. v, vln & pf Bass
  with R. Stevens m–s & B. Smith pf   Victor 886–5011, LM1703, (in
                                       set WDM1703)

PAGANINI

(24) Caprices, Op. 1 (1801/7) solo vln
  Caprice No. 24, in a arr. vln & pf Elman
  with W. Rosé pf   Victor LM1208

PENTE

(2) Pieces, Op. 12 vln & pf
  No. 2. Les farfadets arr. Elman
  with P.B. Kahn pf   HMV 4–7945, DA507
                           Victor 64128

PERLMAN

Suite Hebraïque (1929) vln & pf
  No. 2. Dance of the Rebbitzen
  with J. Seiger pf   Vanguard VRS1099, VSD2137

PIASTRO–BORISOFF

Valse–staccato, Op. 60, No. 3 (based on "Étude mignonne" by J.H. Ravina)
  vln & pf
  with J. Bonime pf   Victor 1034

POPPER

(3) Stücke, Op. 64 vlc & pf
  No. 1. Wie einst in schönern Tagen (Fond recollections) arr. vln & pf
  with orch.   HMV DA506
                        Victor 66099, 608

RABEY

Dans tes yeux en pleurs v & pf – arr. v, vln & pf
  with F. Alda s & piano   A 15793   American Gramophone Society
                                       AGSA46
                                       HMV 7–33014, DA503
                                       Victor 87216, 87556, 3030

RACHMANINOV

(14) songs, Op. 34 (1912) v & pf
  No. 14. Vocalise arr. vln & pf Press
  with R. Bauman pf   A 45081△   HMV DA1033
                                       Victor 1364

RAFF

(6) Pieces, Op. 85 vln & pf
  No. 3. Cavatina in D
  with P.B. Kahn pf   A 13183   HMV 07994, DB224
                                      Victor 74336, 6093

  No. 3. Cavatina in D
  with J. Bonime pf   A 53557   HMV DB1354
                                      Victor 7461

RAVEL

Pièce en forme d'Habanera v & pf – arr. vln & pf Catherine
  with C. Hollister pf   Victor 1592

del RIEGO

O dry those tears v & pf – arr. v, vln & pf Bass
  with J. Peerce t & W. Rosé pf   Victor (in set WDM1703),
                                   LM1703

RIES

Suite No. 3, in G, Op. 34 vln & pf
  No. 4. Gondoliera
  with piano   HMV DB796
                        Victor 74893, 6457

RIMSKY–KORSAKOV

(Le) Coq d'Or (1910) – opera
  Hymn to the sun arr. vln & pf Franko
  with J. Bonime pf   HMV DB232
                           Victor 74897, 6100

  Hymn to the sun arr. vln & pf Franko
  with J. Bonime pf   HMV DB1324
                           Victor 7392

(La) Nuit de Mai (1880) – opera
  Selection arr. vln & pf Elman
  with piano   Victor 64536
(4) Songs, Op. 2 (1865/6) v & pf
  No. 2. Enslaved by the rose & the nightingale arr. v, vln & pf
  with R. Ponselle s & R. Romani pf   Victor 16451

RISSLAND

Valse caprice, Op. 16 vln & pf
  with piano   HMV 4–7929, DA507
                        Victor 64643, 604

RODE

(24) Caprices, Op. 22 solo vln
  Caprice No. 17, in A flat (Vivacissimo) arr. vln & pf Elman
  with J. Bonime pf   Victor 1060

RUBINSTEIN

(6) Lieder, Op. 72 v & pf
  No. 1. Es blinkt der Tau (The dew is sparkling) arr. vln & pf Elman
  with J. Bonime pf   HMV DA199
                                    Victor 64894, 605, 3030

(2) Melodies, Op. 3 pf
  No. 1. Melody in F arr. vln & pf Wilhelmj
  with piano   Pathé 5395, 8074, 8509

(6) Soirées de Saint–Pétersbourg, Op. 44 pf
  No. 1. Romance in E flat arr. vln & pf Bonime
  with J. Bonime pf   Victor 66205, 974

SAENGER

(3) Concert Miniatures, Op. 130 vln & pf
  No. 2. Scotch pastorale
  with J. Bonime pf   Victor 64884, 609

SAINT–SAËNS

(Le) Carnaval des animaux (1886) small orch.
  Le cygne arr. vln & pf
  with C. Hollister pf   A 62248△   HMV DA1143
                                      Victor 1592

Introduction & Rondo Capriccioso, Op. 28 vln & orch.
  with piano   Gramophone & Typewriter
                                    07908
                                    Victor 71038

Introduction & Rondo Capriccioso, Op. 28 vln & orch.
  with P.B. Kahn pf   A 8811   HMV 07932, DB651
                                      Victor 74165, 6089

Introduction & Rondo Capriccioso, Op. 28 vln & orch.
  with Vienna State Opera Orch. –   Amadeo AVRS6156
  Golschmann   I Classici della Musica Classica
                                    XAM4016
                                    Vanguard VRS1049, VSD2037

SAMMARTINI, G.

(6) Sonatas, Op. 1 2 vlns & c
  Sonata No. 4, in A: Andante (3rd mvt) arr. vln & pf as "Canto amoroso"
  by Elman
  with P.B. Kahn pf   HMV 2–07912, DB227
                                    Victor 74392, 6092

  Sonata No. 4, in A: Andante (3rd mvt) arr. vln & pf as "Canto amoroso"
  by Elman
  with J. Seiger pf   Decca LXT5304
                              London LL1629

SARASATE

Caprice basque, Op. 24 vln & pf
  with P.B. Kahn pf   A 8801   HMV 2–07973, DB229
                                      Victor 74176, 6094

(8) Danzas españolas vln & pf
  No. 3. Romanza andaluza, Op. 22, No. 1
  with W.H. Golde pf   A 16607   HMV 2–07941, DB229
                                      Victor 74455, 6094

Zigeunerweisen, Op. 20 vln & pf or orch.
  with C. Hollister pf   A 62242/3△   HMV DB1536
                                    Victor (in set WCT3), 7780,
                                  LCT1002

Zigeunerweisen, Op. 20 vln & pf or orch.
  with J. Seiger pf   Vanguard VRS1051, VSD2048

SCARLATTI

Sonata in E, L.375 pf – arr. vln & pf as "Capriccio" by Burmester
  with P. Gordon pf   A 18961   HMV 4–7928, DA196
                                    Victor 64642, 602

Sonata in e, L.413 pf – arr. vln & pf as "Pastorale" by Bridgewater
  with P. Gordon pf   HMV 4–7917, DA202
                                    Victor 64636, 609

SCHINDLER

Souvenir poetique (Paraphrase on Fibich's "Poem" Op. 41, No. 14) vln &
pf
  with J. Bonime pf   Victor 66206, 974

SCHUBERT

(16) Deutsche Tänze, Op. 33 (D783) (1824) orch.
  No. 3. Deutscher Tanz No. 3, in B flat arr. vln & pf as "Valse
  sentimentale" by Franko
  with J. Bonime pf   Victor 1034

  No. 3. Deutscher Tanz No. 3, in B flat arr. vln & pf as "Valse
  sentimentale" by Franko
  with C. Hollister pf   A 29888△   HMV DA1144
                                    Victor 1482

(7) Gesänge (set to Scott's "Lady of the Lake") Op. 52 v & pf
  No. 6. Ave Maria, D839 arr. vln & pf Wilhelmj
  with P.B. Kahn pf   A 13184   HMV 07995, DB226, DB425
                                    Pearl GEM101
                                    Victor 74339, 6101

  No. 6. Ave Maria, D839 arr. vln & pf Wilhelmj
  with J. Bonime pf   HMV DB1385
                                    Victor 7103, 7654

  No. 6. Ave Maria, D839 arr. vln & pf Wilhelmj
  with J. Seiger pf   Vanguard VRS1051, VSD2048

  No. 6. Ave Maria, D839 arr. v, vln & pf
  with R. Ponselle s & piano   HMV VB74

Litanie auf das Fest aller Seelen, D343 v & pf – arr. v, vln, vlc & pf
Pasternack
  with H. Lashanska s,   2A 031474△ HMV DB3819
  E. Feuermann vlc & R. Serkin pf   Victor 15365

(6) Moments musicaux, Op. 94 (D780) (1823/7) pf
  No. 3. Moment musicale No. 3, in f "Air russe" arr. vln & pf Auer
  with piano   8330½b Gramophone & Typewriter
                                    3–7908, 37942, 47958
                                    HMV DA200
                                    Victor 61180

  No. 3. Moment musicale No. 3, in f "Air russe" arr. vln & pf Auer
  with piano   Pathé 5398, 8074, 8502, K77942

Quartet No. 13, in a, Op. 29, No. 1 (D804) 2 vlns, vla & vlc
  Minuet (3rd mvt)
  (as leader of Elman string quartet)   HMV 08077, DB652
                                    Victor 74574

(14) Schwanengesang, D957 (1828) v & pf
  No. 4. Ständchen "Serenade" arr. vln & pf Elman
  with piano   Pathé 8504

  No. 4. Ständchen "Serenade" arr. vln & pf Elman
  with P.B. Kahn pf   A 8798   HMV 07927
                                      Victor 74167, 6095

  No. 4. Ständchen "Serenade" arr. vln & pf Elman
  with R. Bauman pf   HMV DB1854
                                    Victor 7461

SCHUMANN

(12) Duets, Op. 85 pf – 4 hands
No. 12. Abendlied arr. vln & pf Joachim
with piano   Pathé 5396, 8071, 8507

(13) Kinderscenen, Op. 15 pf
No. 7. Träumerei arr. vln & pf Hullweck
with P.B. Kahn pf   A 9052   HMV 3–7937, 4–7950, DA428
                                  Victor (in set WCT3), 64197,
                                  600, LCT1002

No. 7. Träumerei arr. vln & pf Hullweck
with piano   Pathé 8501, K77945

No. 7. Träumerei arr. vln & pf Hullweck
with M. van Gool pf   A 9952   HMV DA1144
                                  Victor 1482

No. 7. Träumerei arr. vln & pf Hullweck
with L. Mittman pf   Victor (in set WEPR29), 10–
                                  1271, 26024, ERA29

No. 7. Träumerei arr. vln & pf Hullweck
with J. Seiger pf   Vanguard VRS1051, VSD2048

(9) Waldscenen, Op. 82 pf
No. 7. Vogel als Prophet arr. vln & pf Auer
with P.B. Kahn pf   HMV 3–7976, DA313
                                  Victor 64438

No. 7. Vogel als Prophet arr. vln & pf Auer
with J. Seiger pf   Vanguard VRS1051, VSD2048

SIBELIUS

Kuolema, Op. 44 (1903) – Incidental music orch.
Valse triste arr. vln & pf Franko
with R. Bauman pf   45079   HMV DB1269
                                  Victor 6836

(5) Pieces, Op. 81 vln & pf
No. 1. Mazurka
with L. Mittman pf   Victor 11–9111

SINIGAGLIA

(4) Kleine Stücke, Op. 25 vln & pf
No. 2. Capriccio all'antica
with piano   8148 b   Gramophone & Typewriter
                                  3–7910, 37943, 47960
                                  Rococo 2001

No. 3. Bagatelle
with piano   8148 b   Gramophone & Typewriter
                                  3–7910, 37943, 47960
                                  Rococo 2001

SMETANA

From my Homeland (1878) vln & pf
No. 1. Moderato
with W. Rosé pf   Victor 12–0241

No. 2. Andantino (ed. Sitt)
with W. Rosé pf   OEA 14592/3–1   HMV DA1942

No. 2. Andantino (ed. Sitt)
with J. Seiger pf   Decca LXT5304
                                  London LL1629

No. 2. Andantino (ed. Sitt)
with J. Seiger pf   Vanguard VRS1173, VSD71173

STAINER

(The) Daughter of Jairus (1878) – oratorio
Love divine, all love excelling arr. 2 vlns, vla & vlc
(as leader of Elman string quartet)   Victor 74516

SULZER

Sarabande, Op. 8 vln or vlc & pf
with H. Dawson org   HMV DB1853

Sarabande, Op. 8 vln or vlc & pf
with J. Seiger pf   Vanguard VRS1051, VSD2048

TCHAIKOVSKY

Concerto in D, Op. 35 vln & orch.
     CR 2471[IIA]△, 2472[I]△, 2473[IIA]△,   HMV DB1405/8, DB7057/60
   2474[II]△, 2475[IIA]△, 2476[II]△, 2477[II]△   Victor 8186/9, (set M79)
with London Symphony   & 2478[I]△
Orch. – Barbirolli

Concerto in D, Op. 35 vln & orch.
with London Philharmonic   Ace of Clubs ACL25
Orch. – Boult   Decca LXT2970
                                  Eclipse ECS569
                                  London LL1073

(12) Pieces (of moderate difficulty) Op. 40 pf
No. 10. Russian dance arr. vln & pf Lange
with L. Mittman pf   V–Disc 142

No. 10. Russian dance arr. vln & pf Koutzen
with J. Seiger pf   Victor (in set WDM1740),
                                  A630277, LM1740

No. 10. Russian dance arr. vln & pf Koutzen
with J. Seiger pf   Vanguard VRS1173, VSD71173

(6) Pieces, Op. 51 pf
No. 6. Valse sentimentale arr. vln & pf Grunes
with J. Seiger pf   Victor (in set WDM1740),
                                  ERA97, LM1740

Quartet No. 1, in D, Op. 11 2 vlns, vla & vlc
Andante cantabile (2nd mvt)
(as leader of Elman string quartet)   HMV 08074, DB652
                                  Victor 74575, 6103

Andante cantabile (2nd mvt)
(as leader of Elman   A 21497△   HMV DB1055
string quartet)   Victor 6634

Andante cantabile (2nd mvt) arr. vln & pf Kreisler
with J. Seiger pf   Victor (in set WDM1740),
                                  A630277, LM1740

Serenade in C, Op. 48 str orch.
Valse (2nd mvt) arr. vln & pf Auer
with J. Seiger pf   Victor (in set WDM1740), 26035,
                                  A630277, ERA97, LM1740

Sérénade mélancolique in b flat, Op. 26 vln & orch.
with orch. – Shilkret   A 62395/6△   HMV DB1470
                                  Victor 7744

(6) Songs, Op. 6 v & pf
No. 6. None but the weary heart arr. vln & pf
with P.B. Kahn pf   A 8800   HMV 07926, 2–07977, DB226
                                  Victor 74178, 6091

No. 6. None but the weary heart arr. vln & org
with H. Dawson org   HMV DB1854

No. 6. None but the weary heart arr. vln & pf
with J. Seiger pf   Victor (in set WDM1740),
                                  A630277, LM1740

TCHAIKOVSKY – *Continued*

(3) Souvenirs de Hapsal, Op. 2 pf
No. 3. Chant sans paroles in f arr. vln & pf Kreisler
  with J. Seiger pf   Victor (in set WDM1740),
                            A630277, LM1740

Souvenir d'un lieu cher, Op. 42 vln & pf
No. 2. Scherzo
  with J. Seiger pf   Victor (in set WDM1740),
                            A630277, LM1740

No. 3. Mélodie
  with piano   725 c   Gramophone & Typewriter
                         07905, 047910

No. 3. Mélodie
  with P.B. Kahn pf   A 8812 HMV 07929, DB425
                            Victor 74053, 6091

No. 3. Mélodie
  with C. Hollister pf   A 62241 △ HMV DA1143

No. 3. Mélodie
  with J. Seiger pf   Vanguard VRS1051, VSD2048

THOMÉ

Simple aveu, Op. 25 pf – arr. vln & pf
  with P. Gordon pf   A 18965 HMV 2–07964, DB235
                            Victor 74515, 6097

Simple aveu, Op. 25 pf – arr. vln & pf
  with C. Hollister pf   A 69695 △ HMV DA1232

VITALI

Chaconne in g vln & c – arr. vln & pf David
  with J. Seiger pf   Decca LXT5303
                            London LL1631

VIVALDI

(6) Concerti, Op. 12 vln, strs & c
Concerto No. 1, in g, P.343 (F.I, No. 211) ed. Nachèz
  2B 1490^{II}△, 1491/2^{I}△ & 1493^{II}△ HMV DB1595/6
  with New Symphony   Victor 7585/6
  Orch. – Collingwood

Concerto No. 1, in g, P.343 (F.I, No. 211), ed. Nachèz
  with Vienna State Opera   Vanguard VRS1059, VSD2073
  Orch. – Golschmann

VOGRICH

Dans le Bois (based on "Caprice No. 9, in E" Op. 1 by Paganini) vln & pf
  with P.B. Kahn pf   HMV 2–07914, DB231
                        Victor 74395, 6096

WAGNER

Albumblatt in C (1861) pf – arr. vln & pf Wilhelmj
  with piano   HMV DB796
                   Victor 74892, 6457

Albumblatt in C (1861) pf – arr. vln & pf Wilhelmj
  with C. Hollister pf   HMV DB1460
                   Victor 7195

(Die) Meistersinger von Nürnberg (1868) – opera
Morgenlich leuchtend "Prize song" arr. vln & pf Wilhelmj
  with P.B. Kahn pf   A 8810 HMV 07925, 2–07978, DB225
                            Victor 74186, 6090

Morgenlich leuchtend "Prize song" arr. vln & pf Wilhelmj
  with C. Hollister pf   HMV DB1460
                   Victor 7649

WARNER

Serenade vln & pf
  with C. Hollister pf   A 69696△ HMV DA1233

WEBER

Contretanz in D (1815) orch. – arr. vln & pf Elman
  with W.H. Golde pf   A 18591 HMV 4–7910, DA194
                            Victor 64537, 598

WIENIAWSKI

Concerto No. 2, in d, Op. 22 vln & orch.
  with Robin Hood Dell   Victor 49–3126/8, (set
  Orch. – Hilsberg   WDM1504), A12R0116, LM53,
                          LM9024

Concerto No. 2, in d, Op. 22 vln & orch.
  with London Philharmonic   Decca LXT5222
  Orch. – Boult   Eclipse ECS569
                         London LL1486

(L') École moderne, Op. 10 (10 Études) solo vln
No. 5. Étude No. 5, in E flat "alla Saltarella" arr. vln & pf Kreisler
  with R. Bauman pf   A 45080 △ HMV DA1033,
                            Victor 1364

Fantaisie brillante (on themes from Gounod's "Faust") Op. 20 vln & orch.
Garden scene
  with piano   8772 b Gramophone & Typewriter
                         37912, 37955, 47961
                         Victor 61182

Garden scene
  with P.B. Kahn pf   A 8824 HMV 3 – 7924, DA196
                         Victor 64122, 601

Légende, Op. 17 vln & pf or orch.
  with C. Hollister pf   A 62244△ HMV DB1537
                         Victor 7649

Légende, Op. 17 vln & pf or orch.
  with J. Seiger pf   Victor (in set WDM1740),
                         A630277, LM1740

Mazurka in a, Op. 3 "Kujawiak" vln & pf
  with J. Seiger pf   Victor (in set WDM1740), 26035,
                       A630277, ERA97, LM1740

(2) Mazurkas, Op. 12 vln & pf
No. 2. Mazurka No. 2, in g "Le Ménetrier"
  with J. Seiger pf   Victor (in set WDM1740), 26035,
                       A630277, ERA97, LM1740

No. 2. Mazurka No. 2, in g "Le Ménetrier"
  with J. Seiger pf   Decca LXT5304
                         London LL1629

(2) Mazurkas, Op. 19 vln & pf
No. 2. Mazurka No. 2, in D "Dudziarz"
  with J. Seiger pf   Victor (in set WDM1740),
                         A630277, LM1740

Polonaise brillante No. 1, in D, Op. 4 vln & pf
  with J. Seiger pf   Victor A630277, LM1740

Souvenir de Moscou, Op. 6 vln & pf or orch.
  with piano   670 c Gramophone & Typewriter
                        07904, 047909

Souvenir de Moscou, Op. 6 vln & pf or orch.
  with P.B. Kahn pf   HMV 07933
                   Victor 74051, 6093

YSAŸE

Rêve d'enfant, Op. 14 vln & pf
  with M. van Gool pf   2B 1130^{II}△ HMV DB1594
                                      Victor 7574

Vittorio EMANUELE

VIVALDI

(12) Concerti, Op. 8 (1725) "Il Cimento dell' Armonia e dell' Invenzione"
(Nos. 1/4: Le quattro Stagioni) vln & strs
  Concerto No. 1, in E, F.I, No. 22 "La Primavera"*
  with Società Corelli   Victor (in set ML61002),
                                A430332, A640507, LM2424,
                                LSC2424, ML20026, SL20026

  Concerto No. 2, in B flat, F.I. No. 23 "L'Estate"
  with Società Corelli   Victor (in set ML61002),
                                A430332, A640507, LM2424,
                                LSC2424, ML20026, SL20026

  Concerto No. 3, in F, F.I. No. 24 "L'Autunno"
  with Società Corelli   Victor (in set ML61002),
                                  A430332, A640507, LM2424,
                                LSC2424, ML20026, SL20026

  Concerto No. 4, in f, F.I. No. 25 "L'Autunno"
  with Società Corelli   Victor (in set ML61002),
                                  A430332, A640507, LM2424,
                                LSC2424, ML20026, SL20026

Heinz ENDRES

BACH

Cantata No. 137 (Lobe den Herren, den mächtigen König der Ehren)
  BWV137
  with C. Owen s, G. Lutze t, K. Engen Telefunken AWD8907E
  bs, K. Kalmus ob, G. Donderer tpt,
  F. Ortner cbs & Munich Bach Choir &
  State Opera Orch. – Richter

Cantata No. 140 (Wachet auf, ruft uns die Stimme) BWV140
  with C. Owen s, G. Lutze t, K. Engen Telefunken AWD8902E
  bs, K. Kalmus ob, G. Donderer tpt,
  F. Ortner cbs & Munich Bach Choir &
  State Opera Orch. – Richter

Concerto in d, BWV1043 2 vlns, strs & c
  with W. Stross vln & Berlin Radio   Le Chant du Monde LDXA8008
  Chamber Orch. – Stross

(Ein) Musikalisches Opfer, BWV1079 (1749) strs
  with S. Lautenbacher vln,   Vox DL490, STDL500490
  J. Rottenfusser vln, F. Ruf vla,
  A. Schmidt vlc, K.H. Zöller fl, H.
  Weber hrn & M. Galling hpsi

Weihnachts–Oratorium, BWV248 (1734) – oratorio
  with G. Lutze t, C. Owen s,   Decca LXT2003/5
  H. Töpper a, H. Günter bs, K. Engen
  bs, G. Donderer tpt, W. Theurer fl,
  F. Sonnleitner vln, E. Shann ob &
  Munich Bach Choir & State Opera
  Orch. – Richter

* Allegro or 1st mvt. is also on Victor SPS 33–10.

HINDEMITH

Sonata No. 3, in E (1935) vln & pf
  with H. Steurer pf   Colosseum SM528

VIVALDI

(12) Concerti, Op. 3 "L'estro armonico" var. cbns & strs
  Concerto No. 1, in D, P.146 (F.IV, No. 7) 4 vlns, vlc, strs & c
  with R. Barchet vln,   Pathé–Vox (in set PV273)
  A. Steffen–Wendling vln,   Vox (in sets DL271, PL7243,
  F. Hopfner vln, H. Elsner hpsi & Pro PL7420 & VBX20)
  Musica Chamber Orch., Stuttgart –
  Reinhardt

  Concerto No. 4, in e, P.97 (F.I, No. 174) 4 vlns, strs & c
  with R. Barchet vln,   Pathé–Vox (in set PV273)
  A. Steffen–Wendling vln, F. Hopfner Vox (in sets DL271, PL7243,
  vln,   PL7420 & VBX20)
  H. Elsner hpsi & Pro Musica Chamber
  Orch., Stuttgart – Reinhardt

  Concerto No. 7, in F, P.249 (F.IV, No. 9) 4 vlns, strs & c
  with R. Barchet vln,   Pathé–Vox (in set PV273)
  A. Steffen–Wendling vln, F. Hopfner Vox (in sets DL271, PL7243,
  vln,   PL7420 & VBX20)
  H. Elsner hpsi & Pro Musica Chamber
  Orch., Stuttgart – Reinhardt

  Concerto No. 10, in b, P.148 (F. IV, No. 10) 4 vlns, strs & c
  with R. Barchet vln,   Pathé–Vox (in set PV273)
  A. Steffen–Wendling vln, F. Hopfner Vox (in sets DL271, PL7243,
  vln,   PL7420 & VBX20)
  H. Elsner hpsi & Pro Musica Chamber
  Orch., Stuttgart – Reinhardt

Georges ENESCU (1881–1955)

d'AMBROSIO

Serenade, Op. 4 vln & pf
  with E.C. Harris pf   81556–5 Columbia 7006, 20023D, 2008M

BACH

Concerto in d, BWV1043 2 vlns strs & c
             2L 370/2^{II} △ & 373^{I} △ HMV COLH77, DB1718/9,
  with Y. Menuhin vl & Paris   FJLP5018
  Conservatory Orch. – Monteux   Victor 7732/3, 11–18601/2,
                                    11–8603/4, (set M932),
                                    LCT1120, LVT1006

(3) Sonatas & 3 Partitas, BWV1001/6 solo vln
  Sonata No. 1, in g, BWV1001
  (unaccompanied)   Continental CLP104/6
                                Remington (no number: side 1)

  Partita No. 1, in b, BWV1002
  (unaccompanied)   Continental CLP104/6
                                  Remington (no number: side 4),
                                  PL1–149

  Sonata No. 2, in a, BWV1003
  (unaccompanied)
                                  Continental CLP104/6
                                  Remington (no number: side 2)

  Partita No. 2, in d, BWV1004
  (unaccompanied)
                                    Continental CLP104/6
                                  Remington (no number: side 5)

  Sonata No. 3, in C, BWV1005
  (unaccompanied)   Continental CLP104/6
                                  Remington (no number: side 3)

BACH – *Continued*

Partita No. 3, in E, BWV1006
(unaccompanied)

Continental CLP104/6
Remington (no number: side 6)

BEETHOVEN

(Die) Ruinen von Athen, Op. 113 – Incidental music orch.
No. 3. Chor der Derwische arr. vln & pf Auer
with piano   Columbia 7007, 20029D, 2026M
Sonata No. 9, in A, Op. 47 "Kreutzer" vln & pf
with C. Chailley–Richez pf   Columbia FC1058

CHAUSSON

Poème, Op. 25 vln & orch.
with S. Schlüssel pf   98621/4   Columbia 50273/4D, 5118/9M,
                            DVX5/6, LFX125/6, W252/3
                            Veritas VM111

CORELLI

(12) Sonatas, Op. 5 vln & c
Sonata No. 12, in d "La Follia"
with S. Schlüssel pf   Columbia 50161D, 5109M,
                            D41043
                            Veritas VM111

ENESCU

Sonata No. 2, in f, Op. 6 vln & pf
with C. Chailley–Richez pf   Remington RLP149–52
Sonata No. 2, in f, 9, Op. 6 vln & pf
with D. Lipatti pf   Electrecord ECD61
                          Monitor MC2049
Sonata No. 3, in a, Op. 25 "In the popular Rumanian style" vln & pf
with C. Chailley–Richez pf   Columbia GFX121/3
Sonata No. 3, in a, Op. 25 "In the popular Rumanian style" vln & pf
with D. Lipatti pf   Electrecord ECD95

HANDEL

(15) Sonatas, Op. 1 (?1731) fl or vln & c
Sonata No. 13, in D vln IV
with S. Schlüssel pf   98617/20   Columbia 50187/8D, 5110/1M,
                            J7632/3, W297/8, (set 80)
                            Veritas VM111

KREISLER

Aubade provençale (L. Couperin) vln & pf
with E.C. Harris pf   81530–3   Columbia 7006, 20023D, 2008M
Tempo di minuetto (Pugnani) vln & pf
with S. Schlüssel pf   Columbia 50235D, DFX145,
                            DVX7

PUGNANI

(6) Sonatas, Op. 8 vln & c
Sonata No. 3, in D: Largo expressivo (2nd mvt) arr. vln & pf Moffat
with S. Schlüssel pf   Columbia 50235D, DFX 145,
                            DVX7
                            Veritas VM111

SCHUMANN

Sonata No. 2, in d, Op. 121 vln & pf
with C. Chailley–Richez pf   Remington RLP149–50

WAGNER

Albumblatt in C (1861) pf – arr. vln & pf Wilhelmj
with piano   Columbia 7007, 20029D, 2026M

Hallvor ENGELBRETSON

BULL

I ensomme Stunde pf – arr. vln & pf
with piano   HMV X434, X7–287904
Säterjentens søndag v & pf – arr. vln & pf Svendsen
with piano   HMV X434, X7–287905

Wolfgang ENGELS

BEETHOVEN

Sonata No. 5, in F, Op. 24 "Spring" vln & pf
with H–E. Riebensahm pf   Intercord 709–05SB
Sonata No. 10. in G, Op. 96 vln & pf
with H–E. Riebensahm pf   Intercord 709–05SB

Folke ENGLUNG

BULL

Säterjentens søndag v & pf – arr. vln & pf Svendsen
with piano   Parlophone B41056

GRIEG

Peer Gynt (Suite No. 2) Op. 55 orch.
No. 4. Solveig's song arr. vln & pf Sitt
with piano   Parlophone B41056

Mikhail ERDENKO

CUI

Kaleidoscope, Op. 50 vln & pf
No. 9. Orientale
with piano   Mezhdunarodnaya Kniga
                  D14171

VIEUXTEMPS

(6) Divertissements d'Amateurs sur des mélodies russes, Op. 24 vln & pf
No. 2. Le Rossignol (after Alexander Alabiev, 1787–1851)
with piano   Mezhdunarodnaya Kniga
                  D14500

Ayla ERDURAN (1936–   )

BACH

(3) Sonatas & 3 Partitas, BWV1001/6 solo vln
Partita No. 2, in d: Chaconne (5th mvt) BWV1004
(unaccompanied)   Telefunken BLE14088

WIENIAWSKI

Polonaise brillante No. 1, in D, Op. 4 vln & pf
with I. Kollegorskaya pf   Muza L0223

L. ERENDI

RÄÄTS

Concerto, Op. 21 vln & cha orch.
  with* Tallinn Chamber Orch. – Jarvi   Mezhdunarodnaya Kniga
                                         D025161/2

Ivan ERICSON (1911–)

ÅKERLIND

Romance vln & orch.
  with Curt Åkerlind Orch. – Achatz   Odeon D6070

BJÖRKANDER

Cavatina vln & orch.
  with Swedish Radio   RTJ 3969–A   Rytmi
  Orch. – Rybrant

BLOMDAHL

Trio (1933) vln, vla & vlc
  with G. Finnström   2SB 3401/4   HMV DB11048/9
  vla & G. Lundqvist vlc

PERGAMENT

Dibbuk Fantasia vln & orch.
         1208 C RTJ 2682–C & 1248 A   Cupol 6017
  with Stockholm   RTJ 2741–A
  Concerto Society Orch. – Pergament

Broadus ERLE

BERGER

Duo No. 2 vln & pf
  with A. Berger pf   New Editions 4

FLANAGAN

Chaconne vln & pf
  with A. Berger pf   New Editions 4

Devy ERLIH (1928–)

ACHRON

Hebrew melody, Op. 33 vln & pf – arr. Auer
  with M. Bureau pf   Ducretet–Thomson 470C038

ALBÉNIZ

España (6 Feuilles d'album) Op. 165 pf
  No. 2. Tango in D arr. vln & pf Kreisler
  with M. Bureau pf   Ducretet–Thomson 255C052,
                                 470C036, DTL93106
  No. 3. Malagueña in b arr. vln & pf Kreisler
  with M. Bureau pf   HMV DB11252

ANONYMOUS

Eili, Eili (Zionist hymn) – arr. vln & pf Elman
  with M. Bureau pf   Ducretet–Thomson 470C037

* Estonian Radio.

BACH

Concerto No. 1, in a, BWV1041 vln, strs & c
  with Pro Arte Chamber Orch. – Redel   Ducretet–Thomson 270C080,
                                             DTL93067

Concerto in d, BWV1043 2 vlns, strs & c
  with H. Merckel vln & Pro Arte   Ducretet–Thomson 270C081,
  Chamber Orch. – Redel   DTL93067
                                             Telefunken TW30144

(3) Sonatas & 3 Partitas, BWV1001/6 solo vln
  Sonata No. 1, in g, BWV1001
  (unaccompanied)   Adès 13054
  Partita No. 1, in b, BWV1002
  (unaccompanied)   Adès 13054
  Sonata No. 2, in a, BWV1003
  (unaccompanied)   Adès 13055
  Partita No. 2, in d, BWV1004
  (unaccompanied)   Adès 13055
  Sonata No. 3, in C, BWV1005
  (unaccompanied)   Adès 13056
  Partita No. 3, in E, BWV1006
  (unaccompanied)   Adès 13056

BARTÓK

Rhapsody No. 1, in G (1928) vln & orch.
  with Orch. des Cento Soli,   Club Français du Disque 4
  Paris – Husa   Record Society RS2
Rhapsody No. 2, in d (1928) vln & orch.
  with Orch. des Cento Soli,   Club français du Disque 4
  Paris – Husa   Record Society RS2
(6) Rumanian folk dances (1915) pf – arr. vln & pf Székely
  Nos. 1, 5 & 6 only
  with M. Bureau pf   HMV DA5041
Sonata in g (1944) solo vln
  (unaccompanied)   Adès 15502

BEETHOVEN

Concerto in C, Op. 56 "Triple" vln, vlc, pf & orch.
  with G. Fallot vlc, M. Fallot pf &   Ducretet–Thomson 260C087
  Baden–Baden Symphony Orch. – Bour

BLOCH

Baal shem (3 Pictures of Chassidic life) (1923) vln & pf
  No. 2. Nigun (Improvisation)
  with M. Bureau pf   Ducretet–Thomson 470C038

BRAHMS

Concerto in a, Op. 102 "Double" vln, vlc & orch.
  with G. Fallot vlc & Baden–Baden   Ducretet–Thomson 270C110
  Symphony Orch. – Bour

FALLA

(La) Vida Breve (1913) – opera
  Danza española orch. – arr. vln & pf Kreisler
  with M. Bureau pf   Ducretet–Thomson 255C052,
                                 470C036, DTL93106

JOLIVET

Suite rapsodique (1965) solo vln
  (unaccompanied)   Adès 15502

KHACHATURIAN
Concerto in D (1940) vln & orch.
with Orch. des Cento Soli,
Paris – Baudo   Musidisc RC723
     Record Society RS8

KREISLER
Liebesleid vln & pf
with M. Bureau pf   Ducretet–Thomson 255C052,
     470C040

Tambourin chinois, Op. 3 vln & pf
with M. Bureau pf   Ducretet–Thomson 255C052,
     470C037

Praeludium & Allegro (Pugnani) vln & pf
with M. Bureau pf   Ducretet–Thomson 255C052,
     470C036, DTL93106

Sicilienne & Rigaudon (Francoeur) vln & pf
with M. Bureau pf   Ducretet–Thomson 255C052,
     470C040

LALO
Symphonie espagnole, Op. 21 vln & orch.*
with London Philharmonic
Orch. – Inghelbrecht   Ducretet–Thomson 320C124

LECLAIR
(12) Sonatas, Op. 9 – Book IV (1738) vln & c
Sonata No. 3, in D: Tambourin (3rd mvt) arr. vln & pf Kreisler
with M. Bureau pf   Ducretet–Thomson 255C052,
     470C037

MENDELSSOHN
Concerto in e, Op. 64 vln & orch.
with orch. – Bour   Ducretet–Thomson 255C048

MOZART
Concerto No. 1, in B flat, K207 (Cadenzas by Enescu) vln & orch.
with Lamoureux Orch. – Goldschmidt   HMV FALP152

Concerto No. 2, in D, K211 vln & orch.
with Lamoureux Orch. – Goldschmidt   HMV FALP152

MUSSORGSKY
Sorochintsy Fair (1911/23) – opera
Gopak (Act III) arr. vln & pf Dushkin
with M. Bureau pf   Ducretet–Thomson 470C037

PAGANINI
(24) Caprices, Op. 1 (1801/7) solo vln
Caprice No. 1, in E
(unaccompanied)   Adès (Florilège) 13025

Caprice No. 5, in a
(unaccompanied)   Adès (Florilège) 13025

Caprice No. 6, in g
(unaccompanied)   Adès (Florilège) 13025

Caprice No. 9, in E
(unaccompanied)   Adès (Florilège) 13025

Caprice No. 13, in B flat
(unaccompanied)   Adès (Florilège) 13025

Caprice No. 14, in E flat
(unaccompanied)   Adès (Florilège) 13025

* Including intermezzo.

PAGANINI – *Continued*

Caprice No. 15, in e
(unaccompanied)   Adès (Florilège) 13025

Caprice No. 17, in E flat
(unaccompanied)   Adès (Florilège) 13025

Caprice No. 19, in E flat
(unaccompanied)   Adès (Florilège) 13025

Caprice No. 20, in D
(unaccompanied)   Adès (Florilège) 13025

Caprice No. 21, in A
(unaccompanied)   Adès (Florilège) 13025

Caprice No. 24, in a
(unaccompanied)   Adès (Florilège) 13025

PARMEGIANI
Violostries vln & 4 channels
with Groupe de Recherches Musicales   Philips 836889DSY
de l'O.R.T.F.

PROKOFIEV
(The) Love for Three Oranges, Op. 33 (1919) – opera
No. 3. March arr. vln & pf Heifetz
with M. Bureau pf   Ducretet–Thomson 470C040

RAVEL
Pièce en forme d'Habanera v & pf – arr. vln & pf Catherine
with M. Bureau pf   Ducretet–Thomson 270C099,
     DTL93106

Sonata (1927) vln & pf
with M. Bureau pf   Ducretet–Thomson 270C099,
     DTL93106

Trio in a (1915) pf, vln & vlc
with C. Helffer pf & R. Albin vlc   Club français du Disque 32

Tzigane (Rapsodie de concert) (1924) vln & pf or orch.
with M. Bureau pf   Ducretet–Thomson 270C099,
     DTL93106

RIMSKY-KORSAKOV
(The) Tale of Tsar Saltan (1900) – opera
Flight of the bumblebee (Act III) orch. – arr. vln & pf Hartmann
with M. Bureau pf   Ducretet–Thomson 470C040

ROPARTZ
Sonata in D (1907) vln & pf
with M. Bureau pf   Ducretet–Thomson 300C023

SARASATE
(8) Danzas españolas vln & pf
No. 3. Romanza andaluza, Op. 22, No. 1
with A. Collard pf   Ducretet–Thomson 250C037
No. 4. Jota Navarra, Op. 22, No. 2
with A. Collard pf   Ducretet–Thomson 250C037
No. 5. Playera, Op. 23, No. 1
with A. Collard pf   Ducretet–Thomson 250C037
No. 6. Zapateado, Op. 23, No. 2
with M. Bureau pf   HMV DB11252
No. 6. Zapateado, Op. 23, No. 2
with M. Bureau pf   Ducretet–Thomson 250C037
Jota aragonesa, Op. 27 vln & pf
with A. Collard pf   Ducretet–Thomson 250C037

SARASATE – *Continued*

Zigeunerweisen, Op. 20 vln & pf or orch.
  with A. Collard pf   Ducretet–Thomson 250C037

SCHUBERT, François

(12) Bagatelles, Op. 13 vln & pf
  No. 9. L'abeille
  with M. Bureau pf   Ducretet–Thomson 470C040

SHOSTAKOVICH

(The) Age of Gold, Op. 22 (1930) – ballet orch.
  Polka arr. vln & pf Grunes
  with M. Bureau pf   HMV DA5041

STRAVINSKY

Élégie (1944) solo vla or vln
  (unaccompanied)   Adès 15502
Pastorale (1908) v & pf – arr. vln & pf 1933 Dushkin & Stravinsky
  with M. Bureau pf   HMV DA5049
Pétrouchka (1911) – ballet orch.
  Danse russe arr. vln & pf 1933 Dushkin & Stravinsky
  with M. Bureau pf   HMV DA5049

TCHAIKOVSKY

Concerto in D, Op. 35 vln & orch.
  with Südwestfunk Symphony Orch.,   Ducretet–Thomson 300C067,
  Baden–Baden – Somögyi   370C001
Concerto in D, Op. 35 vln & orch.
  with L'Orch. des Concerts   Ducretet–Thomson CC508,
  Colonne – Dervaux   SCC508

Toshita ETO (1927–)

BRAHMS

Sonata No. 1, in G, Op. 78 vln & pf
  with B. Smith pf   Decca DL10030, DL710030
Sonata No. 3, in d, Op. 108 vln & pf
  with B. Smith pf   Decca DL10030, DL710030

CORELLI

(12) Sonatas, Op. 5 vln & c
  Sonata No. 3, in C
  with V. Sokoloff pf   Decca DL10014, DL710014

MAMIYA

Concerto (1959) vln & orch.
  with Japan Philharmonic Symphony   Columbia OS433, OS10053
  Orch. – Watanabe

TARTINI

(12) Sonatas, Op. 1 (1734) vln & c
  Sonata No. 10, in g "Didone abbandonata"
  with V. Sokoloff pf   Decca DL10014, DL710014
Sonata in g "Il Trillo del Diavolo" vln & c – arr. vln & pf Kreisler
  with V. Sokoloff pf   Decca DL10014, DL710014

VIVALDI

(12) Sonatas, Op. 2 (1712) vln & c
  Sonata No. 2, in A, F.XIII, No. 30 ed. David
  with V. Sokoloff pf   Decca DL10014, DL710014

Grete EWELER

BACH

(3) Sonatas & 3 Partitas, BWV1001/6 solo vln
  Sonata No. 1, in g: Siciliano (3rd mvt) BWV1001
  (unaccompanied)   20598   Homochord 4–2981
  Partita No. 3, in E: Gavotte & Rondeau (3rd mvt) BWV1006
  (unaccompanied)   20599   Homochord 4–2981

BEETHOVEN

(6) Minuets, G167 pf
  No. 2. Minuet No. 2, in G arr. vln & pf Burmester
  with F. Günther pf   19063   Homochord 4–2365

BLUME

Valse–caprice "Schön Erika" vln & pf
  with chamber orch.   Homochord 4–3419

BRAHMS

(16) Waltzes, Op. 39 pf duet
  No. 15. Waltz No. 15, in A flat arr. vln & pf "in A" Hochstein
  with F. Günther pf   Homochord 4–3522

BRANDL

(Der) Liebe Augustin – operetta
  Du alter Stefansturm arr. vln & pf as "The old refrain" by Kreisler
  with F. Günther pf   19147   Homochord 4–2339

CZIBULKA

Gavotte (Stephanie) Op. 312 pf – arr. vln & orch.
  with salon orch. – Beregowsky   Homochord 4–2876

DELIBES

Coppélia (1870) – ballet orch.
  No. 1b. Valse lente arr. vln & orch.
  with chamber orch.   Homochord H3025
Sylvia (1876) – ballet orch.
  No. 16a. Pizzicato–scherzettino (Act III) arr. vln & orch.
  with chamber orch.   Homochord H3025

DRDLA

Serenade No. 1, in A vln & pf
  with chamber orch.   Homochord 4–2487

DVOŘÁK

(8) Humoresques, Op. 101 pf
  No. 7. Humoresque No. 7, in G flat arr. vln & pf "in G" Wilhelmj
  wiht F. Günther pf   19891   Homochord 4–2565

ELGAR

Salut d'amour, Op. 12 orch. – arr. vln & orch.
  with chamber orch.   19215   Homochord 4–2348

FELIX

(Die) Kätzchen (1890) – operetta
  Unter dem Lindenbaum arr. vln & pf
  with F. Günther pf   19138   Homochord 4–2374

FIBICH

Images, Impressions & Souvenirs, Op. 41 pf
  No. 14. Poem (from "Souvenirs", Part IV) arr. vln & orch.
  with chamber orch.   52344   Homochord 4–8948

FRIEDMAN

(6) Viennese Dances (on themes by E. Gärtner) pf
No. 1. Wiener Tanz No. 1, in G flat arr. vln & pf
with piano   Homochord 4–3121
No. 2. Wiener Tanz No. 2, in G arr. vln & pf
with piano   Homochord 4–3121

GANNE

(L') Extase – Rêverie pf – arr. vln & orch.
with chamber orch.   19165   Homochord 4–2332

GOUNOD

Ave Maria (Méditation on Bach's "Prelude No. 1, in C" from Book I of
"Das Wohltemperirte Clavier") v & pf – arr. vln & orch.
with chamber orch.   52207[1]   Homochord 4–8800
Hymne à Sainte–Cécile (1864) vln, org & pf – arr. vln, fl, hp & org
with A. Lichtenstein fl & harp &   Homochord 4–8800
organ

GRIEG

Peer Gynt (Suite No. 2) Op. 55 orch.
No. 4. Solveig's song arr. vln & orch.
with Berlin Symphony Orch. – Bohnke   Homochord 4–8841

HASLINDE

Abendwind in Sevilla vln & pf
with piano   Homochord 4–3523
(Die) Galanten vln & pf
with F. Günther pf   Homochord 4–3522

HAYDN

Trio No. 34, in D, H.XI, No. 34 baryton, vla & cbs
with E. Selin vla d'amore &   Homochord H4270
G. Packer vlc
Trio No. 78, in D, H.XI, No. 78 baryton, vla & cbs
with E. Selin vla d'amore &   Homochord H4270
G. Packer vlc

HEUBERGER

(Der) Opernball, Op. 40 (1898) – operetta
Im chambre séparée arr. vln & pf as "Midnight bells" by Kreisler
with F. Günther pf   19139   Homochord 4–2374

KAHN

Ave Maria v & pf – arr. vln & orch.
with chamber orch.   19166   Homochord 4–2348

KÖNIGSBERGER

Rêverie vln & pf
with chamber orch.   Homochord 4–3419

KORNGOLD

Viel Lärmen um Nichts, Op. 11 (1919) – Incidental music orch.
No. 3. Gartenszene arr. vln & pf
with F. Günther pf   Homochord 4–2598
No. 4. Mummenschanz arr. vln & pf
with F. Günther pf   Homochord 4–2598

KREISLER

Liebesfreud vln & pf
with F. Günther pf   19160   Homochord 4–2338

KREISLER – *Continued*

Liebesleid vln & pf
with F. Günther pf   19161   Homochord 4–2338
Schön Rosmarin vln & pf
with F. Günther pf   19159   Homochord 4–2339

LANGER

Grandmother, Op. 20 pf – arr. vln & orch.
with chamber orch.   Homochord 4–2406

LEHÁR

Friederike (1928) – operetta
selection arr. vln & orch.
with orch.   Homochord 4–8975
(Die) Lustige Witwe (1905) – operetta
Viljalied
with H.H. Bollmann t & Berlin   Homochord 4–8933
Symphony Orch. – Lehár

LUBBE

Erinnerung (Réminiscence) arr. vln & orch.
with chamber orch.   Homochord 4–2487

MOZART

Sonata No. 24, in F, K376 vln & pf
Allegro (1st mvt); **Rondo: Allegretto grazioso** (3rd mvt)
H–2–53076[2] & H–2–53077   Decca 25025
with A. Ehlers hpsi   Parlophone E11099

PADEREWSKI

(6) Humoresques de concert, Op. 14 pf
No. 1. Minuet in G arr. vln & pf Kreisler
with F. Günther pf   Homochord 4–2273
(7) Miscellanea, Op. 16 pf
No. 2. Mélodie arr. vln & pf
with F. Günther pf   Homochord 4–2273

PIERNÉ

Sérénade in A, Op. 7 (1875) pf – arr. vln & pf Haddock
with piano   Homochord 3523

PUCCINI

(La) Bohème (1896) – opera
Che gelida manina arr. vln & orch.
with chamber orch.   Homochord 4–2826
Tosca (1900) – opera
E lucevan le stelle arr. vln & orch.
with chamber orch.   Homochord 4–2826

RUBINSTEIN

(2) Melodies, Op. 3 pf
No. 1. Melody in F arr. vln & orch.
with salon orch. – Beregowsky   Homochord 4–2876

SAINT-SAËNS

Samson & Dalila, Op. 47 (1877) – opera
Mon coeur s'ouvre à ta voix arr. vln & orch.
with chamber orch.   52343   Homochord 4–8948

SCHUBERT

Scherzo in B flat, D953 pf – arr. vln & orch.
with chamber orch.   20389   Homochord 4–2489

SCHUBERT – *Continued*

(14) Schwanengesang, D957 (1828) v & pf
No. 4. Ständchen "Serenade" arr. vln & orch.
with chamber orch.　　　　20388　Homochord 4–2489

SCHUMANN

(13) Kinderscenen, Op. 15 pf
No. 7. Träumerei arr. vln & orch.
with chamber orch.　　　　Homochord 4–2486

SIBELIUS

(4) Pieces, Op. 78 vln & pf
No. 2. Romance in F
with M. Eweler pf　　　　Homochord 4–2861

SIMONETTI

Madrigale pf – arr. vln & pf
with F. Günther pf　　　19062　Homochord 4–2365

STRAUSS, R.

(4) Lieder, Op. 27 v & pf
No. 4. Morgen arr. vln & pf
with M. Eweler pf　　　　Homochord 4–2861

TCHAIKOVSKY

(12) Pieces (of moderate difficulty) **Op. 40** pf
No. 2. Chanson triste arr. vln & pf
with F. Günther pf　　　19890[1]　Homochord 4–2565

THOMAS

Mignon (1866) – opera
Connais–tu le pays? arr. vln & orch.
with chamber orch.　　　　Homochord 4–2847

selection arr. vln & orch. as "Fantasia"
with salon orch. – Lemeau　　　Homochord 4–8820

THOMÉ

Simple aveu, Op. 25 pf – arr. vln & orch.
with chamber orch.　　　19167　Homochord 4–2332

TOSELLI

Serenade, Op. 6 vln & pf
with chamber orch.　　　　Homochord 4–2406

VERDI

(La) Traviata (1853) – opera
aria unid – arr. vln & orch.
with chamber orch.　　　　Homochord 4–2847

WENINGER

Auf Wiederhören
selection arr. vln & orch.
with salon orch. – Lemeau
　　　　　　　　　　Homochord 4–8868

WIDOR

Serenade in B flat, Op. 10 orch. – arr. vln & orch.
with chamber orch.　　　　Homochord 4–2486

Carmine FABRIZIO

FAURÉ

Berceuse, Op. 16 vln & pf
with piano　　　　Edison Diamond Disc 80550

KREISLER

Liebesfreud vln & pf
with piano　　　　Phono–Cut 5058

WILHELMJ

Swedish melody vln & pf
with piano　　　　Edison Diamond Disc 80550

Pietro FABRONI

BÉRIOT

Concerto No. 7, in G, Op. 76 vln & orch.
Adagio (2nd mvt)
with piano　　　　Favorite 1–34005

WIENIAWSKI

(2) Mazurkas, Op. 19 vln & pf
No. 2. Mazurka No. 2, in D "Dudziarz"
with piano　　　　Favorite 1–34006

Adila FACHIRI (1888–1962)

BACH

Concerto in d, BWV1043 2 vlns, strs & c
with Y. d'Aranyi vln & orch. –　　Vocalion A0252/3
Chapple

Concerto in d, BWV1043 2 vlns, strs & c
Largo (2nd mvt)
　　　　　　03294 X & 03295　Vocalion D02107
with Y. d'Aranyi vln & E. Hobday pf

Concerto in c, BWV1060 vln & ob or 2 vlns, strs & c
Allegro (3rd mvt)
with Y. d'Aranyi vln & E.　　03559　Vocalion K05110
Hobday pf

(3) Sonatas & 3 Partitas, BWV1001/6 solo vln
Partita No. 1, in b: Sarabande (5th mvt) BWV1002
(unaccompanied)　　　　Vocalion K05173

Partita No. 3, in E: Gavotte en Rondeau (3rd mvt) BWV1006
with E. Hobday pf　　　　Vocalion K05247

(6) Sonatas, BWV1014/9 vln & clav
Sonata No. 2, in A: Adagio (1st mvt) BWV1015
with D.F. Tovey pf　　　National Gramophonic Society
　　　　　　　　　　NGS117

Sonata in C, BWV1037 2 vlns & c
Gigue (Presto) (4th mvt)
with Y. d'Aranyi vln & E.　　03489　Vocalion D02146
Hobday pf

BEETHOVEN

Sonata No. 10, in G, Op. 96 vln & pf
with D.F. Tovey pf　　　National Gramophonic Society
　　　　　　　　　　NGS114/7

BOCCHERINI

Sonata in c vla & pf
    Andante expressivo (2nd mvt) arr. 2 vlns & pf Moffat
    with Y. d'Aranyi vln & E.   03709   Vocalion K05142
    Hobday pf

BRAHMS

(21) Hungarian Dances pf duet
    Hungarian dance No. 2, in d arr. vln & pf Joachim
    with I. Newton pf   Vocalion R6138

CASTELNUOVO–TEDESCO

Capitan Fracassa (1921) vln & pf
    with E. Hobday pf   Vocalion K05198

COUPERIN, F.

(Les) Chérubins, XX, No. 3 hpsi – arr. vln & pf Slater
    with E. Hobday pf   Vocalion X9494

DEBUSSY

Rêverie (1890) pf – arr. vln & pf Bachmann
    with E. Hobday pf   Vocalion K05198

d'ERLANGER

Poème vln & pf
    with F. d'Erlanger pf   04522/3 Vocalion K05287

FRASER

Cueca (1926) vln & pf – arr. 2 vlns & pf
    with Y. d'Aranyi vln & E.   M 0236 Vocalion K05292
    Hobday pf

GODARD

(6) Duettini, Op. 18 2 vlns & pf
    No. 5. Minuit
    with Y. d'Aranyi vln & E. Hobday pf   Vocalion K05260
    No. 6. Sérénade
    with Y. d'Aranyi vln & E. Hobday pf   Vocalion K05260

GRANADOS

(12) Danzas españolas, Op. 37 (1893) pf
    No. 5. Danza española No. 5, in e "Andaluza" arr. vln & pf Kreisler
    with I. Newton pf   Vocalion K05173

HANDEL

(9) Sonatas, Op. 2 (1724) 2 vlns or obs & c
    Sonata No. 7, in g
    with Y. d'Aranyi vln &   04088/91 Vocalion K05222/3
    E. Hobday pf

HUBAY

(14) Scènes de la Csárda vln & pf
    No. 5. Hullámzó balaton, Op. 33
    with E. Hobday pf   04029 Vocalion K05226

KREISLER

Variations on a theme of Corelli (Tartini) vln & pf
    with E. Hobday pf   Vocalion X9494

LECLAIR

(6) Sonatas, Op. 3 (1730) 2 vlns
    Sonata No. 2, in A arr. 2 vlns & pf
    with Y. d'Aranyi vln & E. Hobday pf   Vocalion K05270

LECLAIR – *Continued*

    Sonata No. 4, in B flat arr. 2 vlns & pf
    with Y. d'Aranyi vln & E. Hobday pf   Vocalion X9877

MOZART

Divertimento No. 17, in D, K334 2 hrns & strs
    Adagio (4th mvt) arr. vln & pf
    with E. Hobday pf   Vocalion K05247

PUGNANI

(6) Sonatas, Op. 1 2 vlns & c
    Sonata No. 6, in C ed. Moffat
           ᵃ03560 X & ᵇ03710 Vocalion K05110ᵃ & K05142ᵇ
    with Y. d'Aranyi vln & E. Hobday pf

PURCELL

(10) Sonatas, Z802/11 (1697) 4 parts – 2 vlns & c
    Sonata No. 9, in F, Z810 "Golden Sonata"
    with Y. d'Aranyi vln & E.   03872/3 Vocalion K05177
    Hobday pf

SINDING

Serenade No. 1, in G, Op. 56 2 vlns & pf
    with Y. d'Aranyi vln & E. Hobday pf   Vocalion K05270

SPOHR

(3) Duets, Op. 39 2 vlns
    No. 1. Duet No. 1, in d: Adagio (2nd mvt)
    with Y. d'Aranyi vln   M 0239 Vocalion K05292
(3) Duets, Op. 67 2 vlns
    No. 2. Duet No. 2, in D: Larghetto (3rd mvt)
    with Y. d'Aranyi vln   03490 Vocalion D02146

TARTINI

(12) Sonatas, Op. 3 2 vlns & c
    Sonata No. 4, in F: Andante attacca (1st mvt); **Allegro** (2nd mvt)
         04092 & 04093 X Vocalion X9777
    with Y. d'Aranyi vln & E. Hobday pf

VIVALDI

(12) Concerti, Op. 3 "L'Estro armonico" var. cbns, strs & c
    Concerto No. 6, in a: Allegro (1st mvt) vln, strs & c – arr. vln & pf
    Nachèz
    with E. Hobday pf   04028 X Vocalion K05226

WEBER

(6) Sonatas, Op. 10 (J99/104) (1810) vln & pf
    Sonata No. 1, in F: Romanze (2nd mvt) J99 arr. vln & pf as "Larghetto"
    by Kreisler
    with I. Newton pf   Vocalion R6138

Lis FAGERLUND

SCARLATTI, A.

Sonata in F rec, ob, vln or 2 vlns & c
    with O. Kinch vln, M. Svendsen rec,   Bach Guild BG566
    J.E. Hansen virg & H.G. Petersen vlc   Haydn Society HS9011
                            Metronome MCEP3003

TELEMANN

Sonata in F rec, vln & c
  with O. Kinch vln, M. Svendsen rec,   Metronome MCEP3004
  J.E. Hansen virg & H.G. Petersen vlc

Roza FAIN (1929–)

BRAHMS

(21) Hungarian Dances pf duet
Hungarian dance No. 1, in g arr. vln & pf Joachim
  with I. Zaitseva pf   Mezhdunarodnaya Kniga
      D5572/3

Sonata No. 2, in A, Op. 100 vln & pf
  with E. Epstein pf   Mezhdunarodnaya Kniga
      D016595

GLUCK

Orphée et Eurydice (1762) – opera
Dance of the blessed spirits: Lento "Mélodie" (No. 2) arr. vln & pf
Kreisler
  with piano   Mezhdunarodnaya Kniga
      D10431/2

KREISLER

Liebesfreud vln & pf
  with I. Zaitseva pf   Mezhdunarodnaya Kniga
      D5572/3

(La) Précieuse (L. Couperin) vln & pf
  with piano   Mezhdunarodnaya Kniga
      D10431/2

LOCATELLI

(12) Sonatas, Op. 6 (1737) vln & c
Sonata No. 1, in g ed. David
  with E. Epstein pf   Mezhdunarodnaya Kniga
      D013935/6

MOZART

Concerto No. 4, in D, K218 (cadenza by David) vln & orch.
  with Moscow Philharmonic Symphony   Mezhdunarodnaya Kniga
  Orch. Soloists Ensemble – D. Oistrakh   D024847/8, SM02295/6
Rondo in C, K373 vln & orch.
  with Moscow Philharmonic Symphony   Mezhdunarodnaya Kniga
  Orch. Soloists Ensemble – D. Oistrakh   D024847/8, SM02295/6

PERGOLESI

Concerto in B flat vln & strs – ed. Dushkin
  with Moscow Philharmonic Symphony   Mezhdunarodnaya Kniga
  Orch. Soloists Ensemble – D. Oistrakh   D024847/8, SM02295/6

RACHMANINOV

(14) Songs, Op. 34 (1912) v & pf
No. 14. Vocalise arr. vln & pf Press
  with E. Epstein pf   Mezhdunarodnaya Kniga
      D016596

RAVEL

Sonata (1927) vln & pf
  with piano   Mezhdunarodnaya Kniga
      D10431/2

RAVEL – *Continued*

(Le) Tombeau de Couperin (1914/7) pf
No. 4. Rigaudon arr. vln & pf Dushkin
  with I. Zaitseva pf   Mezhdunarodnaya Kniga
      D5572/3

SAINT–SAËNS

Introduction & Rondo Capriccioso, Op. 28 vln & orch.
  with I. Kollegorskaya pf   Eterna 720110
      Muza L0223
      Telefunken BLE14088

Introduction & Rondo Capriccioso, Op. 28 vln & orch.
  with Moscow State Philharmonic   Mezhdunarodnaya Kniga
  Symphony Orch. – Kondrashin   D016148, S01004

SARASATE

Caprice basque, Op. 24 vln & pf
  with E. Epstein pf   Mezhdunarodnaya Kniga
      D013935/6

SCHELLING

Divertimento (1927) pf, 2 vlns, vla & vlc
No. 4. Irlandaise arr. vln & pf Kreisler
  with piano   Mezhdunarodnaya Kniga
      D10431/2

SCHUBERT

Fantasia in C, Op. 159 (D934) vln & pf
  with V. Petrashinsky pf   Mezhdunarodnaya Kniga
      D013935/6

TARTINI

Sonata in g "Il Trillo del Diavolo" vln & c – arr. vln & pf Kreisler
  with I. Kollegorskaya pf   Eterna 720110
      Muza XL0386
      Telefunken BLE14088

VIVALDI

Sonata in D, F.XII, No. 6 vln & c – arr. vln & pf Respighi
  with E. Epstein pf   Mezhdunarodnaya Kniga
      D016596

Sonata in d, Op. 18 vln & c
Adagio (2nd mvt) arr. vln & pf Nachèz
  with I. Zaitseva pf   Mezhdunarodnaya Kniga
      D5572/3

WIENIAWSKI

Concerto No. 2, in d, Op. 22 vln & orch.*
  with Polish State Philharmonic   Telefunken TW30214
  Symphony Orch. – Górzynski

Concerto No. 2, in d, Op. 22 vln & orch.
  with Moscow State Philharmonic   Mezhdunarodnaya Kniga
  Symphony Orch. – Kondrashin   D016147, S01003
(8) Étude–Caprices, Op. 18 solo vln & 2nd vln obb
Étude–Caprice No. 4, in a arr. vln & pf Kreisler
  with I. Zaitseva pf   Mezhdunarodnaya Kniga
      D5572/3

* Allegro moderato "à la Zingara" or 3rd mvt is also on Telefunken
BLE14088.

WIENIAWSKI – *Continued*

Polonaise brillante No. 1, in D, Op. 4 vln & pf
with E. Epstein pf   Mezhdunarodnaya Kniga
D016596

Scherzo–Tarantelle, Op. 16 vln & pf
with I. Kollegorskaya pf   Eterna 720110
Telefunken TW30214

Scherzo–Tarantelle, Op. 16 vln & pf
with piano   Mezhdunarodnaya Kniga
D10431/2

YSAŸE

Extase in E flat (Poème No. 4) Op. 21 vln & pf or orch.
with I. Zaitseva pf   Mezhdunarodnaya Kniga
D5572/3

Extase in E flat (Poème No. 4) Op. 21 vln & pf or orch.
with Moscow State Philharmonic   Mezhdunarodnaya Kniga
Symphony Orch. – Kondrashin   D016148, S01004

Harold FAIRHURST (1903–)

BRAHMS

(21) Hungarian Dances pf duet
Hungarian dance No. 1, in g
with piano   Metropole 1124

GLUCK

Orphée et Eurydice (1762) – opera
Dance of the blessed spirits: Lento "Mélodie" (No. 2) arr. vln & pf
Kreisler
with piano   Metropole 1157
Octacros 297

KREISLER

(La) Chasse (Cartier) vln & pf
with piano   Metropole 1124

SCHUBERT, François

(12) Bagatelles, Op. 13 vln & pf
No. 9. L'abeille
with piano   Metropole 1124

SCHUBERT, Franz

(6) Moments musicaux, Op. 94 (D780) (1823/7) pf
No. 3. Moment musicale No. 3, in f "Air russe" arr. vln & pf Kreisler
with piano   Metropole 1157
Octacros 297

TCHAIKOVSKY

Children's Album, Op. 39 pf
No. 22. Song of the lark arr. vln & pf Burmester
with piano   Metropole 1157
Octacros 297

Margeret FAIRLESS (1897–)

BACH

(4) Suites, BWV1066/9 strs & c
Suite No. 3, in D: Air (2nd mvt) BWV1068 2 obs, 3 tpts, drms & strs –
arr. vln & pf as "Air on the G–string" by Wilhelmj
with piano   HMV D34

WIENIAWSKI

Scherzo–Tarantelle, Op. 16 vln & pf
with piano   HMV D34

Jules FALK (1875–1928)

SARASATE

Zigeunerweisen, Op. 20 vln & pf or orch.*
with piano   39254   Columbia A1518

SCHUBERT

(7) Gesänge (set to Scott's "Lady of the Lake") Op. 52 v & pf
No. 6. Ave Maria, D839 arr. vln & pf Wilhelmj
with piano   Columbia A1110

SCHUMANN

(13) Kinderscenen, Op. 15 pf
No. 7. Träumerei arr. vln & pf
with piano   Columbia A1110

SIMONETTI

Madrigale pf – arr. vln & pf
with piano   39255   Columbia A1518

Franco FANTINI

MARCELLO

(12) Concerti, Op. 1 (1708) vln, vlc obb & strs
Concerto No. 1, in D
with G. Ghetti vlc, M. Sorelli hpsi & I   Amadeo AVRS5024
Solisti di Milano – Ephrikian   Arcophon AM653/4
Musical Heritage Society
MHS924

Concerto No. 2, in e
with G. Ghetti vlc, M. Sorelli hpsi & I   Amadeo AVRS5024
Solisti di Milano – Ephrikian   Arcophon AM653/4
Musical Heritage Society
MHS924

Concerto No. 4, in F
with G. Ghetti vlc, M. Sorelli hpsi & I   Amadeo AVRS5024
Solisti di Milano – Ephrikian   Musical Heritage Society
MHS924

VIVALDI

(12) Concerti, Op. 4 "La Stravaganza" vln, strs & c
Concerto No. 1, in B flat, F.I, No. 180
with I. Solisti di Milano – Ephrikian   Arcophon AC651/2
HMV ASDF840/1, FALP840/1,
HQS1105/6

* Abridged.

VIVALDI – *Continued*

Concerto No. 2, in E, F.I, No. 181
with I Solisti di Milano – Ephrikian

Arcophon AC651/2
HMV ASDF840/1, FALP840/1,
HQS1105/6

Concerto No. 3, in G, F.I, No. 182
with I Solisti di Milano – Ephrikian

Arcophon AC651/2
HMV ASDF840/1, FALP840/1,
HQS1105/6

Concerto No. 7, in C, F.I, No. 186
with I Solisti di Milano – Ephrikian

Arcophon AC651/2
HMV ASDF840/1, FALP840/1,
HQS1105/6

Concerto No. 8, in d, F.I, No. 187
with I Solisti di Milano – Ephrikian

Arcophon AC651/2
HMV ASDF840/1, FALP840/1,
HQS1105/6

Concerto No. 9, in F, F.I, No. 188
with I Solisti di Milano – Ephrikian

Arcophon AC651/2
HMV ASDF840/1, FALP840/1,
HQS1105/6

(6) Concerti, Op. 6 vln, strs & c
Concerto No. 4, in D, F.I., No. 195
with I Solisti di Milano – Ephrikian   Arcophon AC685

Concerto No. 5, in e, F.I, No. 196
with I Solisti di Milano – Ephrikian   Arcophon AC685

Concerto No. 6, in d, F.I, No. 197
with I Solisti di Milano – Ephrikian   Arcophon AC685

(12) Concerti, Op. 8 (1725) "Il Cimento dell' Armonia e dell' Invenzione"
(nos. 1/4: Le quattro Stagioni) vln & strs
Concerto No. 1, in E, F.I, No. 22 "La Primavera"
with I Solisti di Milano – Ephrikian   Arcophon AC675
Erato STU70380

Concerto No. 2, in B flat, F.I, No. 23 "L'Estate"
with I Solisti di Milano – Ephrikian   Arcophon AC675
Erato STU70380

Concerto No. 3, in F, F.I, No. 24 "L'Autunno"
with I Solisti di Milano – Ephrikian   Arcophon AC675
Erato STU70380

Concerto No. 4, in f, F.I, No. 25 "L'Inverno"
with I Solisti di Milano – Ephrikian   Arcophon AC675
Erato STU70380

(6) Concerti, Op. 12 vln, strs & c
Concerto No. 1, in g, P.343 (F.I, No. 211)
with I Solisti di Milano – Ephrikian   Arcophon AC683

Concerto No. 2, in d, F.I, No. 212
with I Solisti di Milano – Ephrikian   Arcophon AC683

Concerto No. 3, in D
with I Solisti di Milano – Ephrikian   Arcophon AC683

Concerto No. 4, in C, F.I, No. 213
with I Solisti di Milano – Ephrikian   Arcophon AC683

Concerto No. 5, in E flat, F.I, No. 86
with I Solisti di Milano – Ephrikian   Arcophon AC683

Concerto No. 6, in E flat, F.I, No. 214
with I Solisti di Milano – Ephrikian   Arcophon AC683

Concerto in D, P.164 (F.I, No. 62) "Per la S.S. Assunzione di Maria
Vergine" vln & 2 str choruses
with I Solisti di Milano – Ephrikian   Arcophon AC672
Seraphim S60118

Reno FANTUZZI

VIVALDI

Concerto in D, P.165 (F.I, No. 136) "Fatto per la solennità della S. Lingua
di S. Antonio" vln, strs & c
with Orch. Scuola Veneziana –
Ephrikian

Musidisc RC852
Period SPL740

Concerto in F P.273 (Op. 46, No. 2) vln, 2 obs, 2 hrns, bsn, strs & c
with Orch. Scuola Veneziana–
Ephrikian

Contrepoint MC20078
Period SPL740
Stradivari STR621

Concerto in B flat, P.385 (F.XII, No. 12) (Op. 41, No. 5) vln, strs & c
with Orch. Scuola Veneziana –
Ephrikian

Contrepoint MC20078
Period SPL740
Stradivari STR621

Harry FARBMANN

AULIN

(4) Aquarelles vln & pf
No. 2. Humoresque
with piano   Polydor 66019

BACH

(4) Suites, BWV1066/9 strs & c
Suite No. 3, in D: Air (2nd mvt) BWV1068 2 obs, 3 tpts, drms & strs –
arr. vln & pf as "Air on the G–string" by Wilhelmj
with piano   Polydor 62486

BEETHOVEN

(6) Minuets, G167 pf
No. 2. Minuet No. 2, in G arr. vln & pf Burmester
with piano   Polydor 66026

BRAHMS

Sonata No. 3, in d, Op. 108 vln & pf
Adagio (2nd mvt)
with piano   Polydor 66024

BURLEIGH

(8) Characteristic Pieces, Op. 6 vln & pf
No. 4. Indian snake dance
with piano   Polydor 66017

CHOPIN

(2) Nocturnes, Op. 27 pf
No. 2. Nocturne No. 8, in D flat arr. vln & pf Wilhelmj
with piano   Polydor 66018

CUI

Kaleidoscope, Op. 50 vln & pf
No. 9. Orientale
with piano   Polydor 62489

FAIRCHILD

Canzonetta vln & pf
with piano   Polydor 62488

GOSSEC

Rosine (1786) – opera
Gavotte arr. vln & pf Farbmann
with piano   Polydor 66023

GRIEG

Sonata No. 3, in c, Op. 45 vln & pf
  Allegro expressivo alla Romanza (2nd mvt)
  with piano   Polydor 66017

HANDEL

(15) Sonatas, Op. 1 (?1731) fl or vln & c
  Sonata No. 9, in b: Andante (6th mvt) arr. vln & pf as "Larghetto" by Hubay
  with piano   Polydor 66022
  Sonata No. 15, in E vln VI
  with piano   Polydor 66016

JUON

(4) Pieces, Op. 28 vln & pf
  No. 3. Berceuse
  with piano   Polydor 62490

KREISLER

Aus Wien vln & pf*
  with piano   Polydor 62484

Polichinelle–serenade vln & pf
  with piano   Polydor 62487

Schön Rosmarin vln & pf
  with piano   Polydor 62484

Tambourin chinois, Op. 3 vln & pf
  with piano   Polydor 66020

Sicilienne & Rigaudon (Francoeur) vln & pf
  with piano   Polydor 66020

MENDELSSOHN

Concerto in e, Op. 64 vln & orch.
  Andante (2nd mvt)
  with piano   Polydor 66027

MOSZKOWSKI

(2) Stücke, Op. 45 pf
  No. 2. Guitarre arr. vln & pf Sarasate
  with piano   Polydor 62485

PAGANINI

Concerto No. 2, in b, Op. 7 vln & orch.
  Ronde à clochette (3rd mvt) "La Campanella" arr. vln & pf Kreisler
  with piano   Polydor 66019

POWELL

Plantation melodies vln & pf
  with piano   Polydor 62485

RAFF

(6) Pieces, Op. 85 vln & pf
  No. 3. Cavatina in D
  with piano   Polydor 66018

RAMEAU

(Les) Fêtes d'Hébé (1739) – opera
  Tambourin arr. vln & pf Kreisler
  with piano   Polydor 66026

* Unidentified.

RIMSKY–KORSAKOV

Sadko (1898) – opera
  Chant hindou arr. vln & pf Kreisler
  with piano   Polydor 62487

SARASATE

Caprice basque, Op. 24 vln & pf
  with piano   Polydor 66021

(8) Danzas españolas vln & pf
  No. 1. Malagueña, Op. 21, No. 1
  with piano   Polydor 66023

Faust Fantasia (on themes from the opera by Gounod) vln & pf or orch.
  Valse
  with piano   Polydor 62490

Introduction & Tarantelle, Op. 43 vln & pf
  with piano   Polydor 66021

SCHUBERT

(7) Gesänge (set to Scott's "Lady of the Lake") Op. 52 v & pf
  No. 6. Ave Maria, D839 arr. vln & pf Wilhelmj
  with piano   Polydor 66022

(6) Moments musicaux, Op. 94 (D780) (1823/7) pf
  No. 3. Moment musicale No. 3, in f "Air russe" arr. vln & pf Kreisler
  with piano   Polydor 62488

(14) Schwanengesang, D957 (1828) v & pf
  No. 4. Ständchen "Serenade" arr. vln & pf
  with piano   Polydor 66024

SCHUMANN

(2) Albumblätter, Op. 124 pf
  No. 6. Wiegenliedchen arr. vln & pf
  with piano   Polydor 62489

(13) Kinderscenen, Op. 15 pf
  No. 1. Von fremden Ländern und Menschen arr. vln & pf
  with piano   Polydor 62489

SIMONETTI

Madrigale pf – arr. vln & pf
  with piano   Polydor 62486

TCHAIKOVSKY

Concerto in D, Op. 35 vln & orch.
  Canzonetta (2nd mvt)
  with piano   Polydor 66025

Eugene Onegin, Op. 24 (1877/88) – opera
  Faint echo of my youth (Lensky's aria) arr. vln & pf
  with piano   Polydor 66025

Swan Lake, Op. 20 (1875/6) – ballet orch.
  with St. Louis Symphony Orch. – Golschmann   Victor 11–8995/9, 11–9000/4, (set M1028), LM1003

WEBER

Contratanz in D (1815) orch. – arr. vln & pf Elman
  with piano   Polydor 66023

WIENIAWSKI

Concerto No. 2, in d, Op. 22 vln & orch.
  Romance (2nd mvt)
  with piano   Polydor 66026

Hedwing FASSBANDER (1897–1939)

FLIES

Wiegenlied (Schlafe, mein Prinzchen) v & pf – arr. 2 vlns
   with H. Rohr vln   HMV EG1639

LEHÁR

(Die) Lustige Witwe (1904) – operetta
   Ez waren zwei Königskinder arr. 2 vlns
   with H. Rohr vln   HMV EG1639

MOZART

Concerto No. 5, in A, K219 "Turkish" (cadenza omitted) vln & orch.*
   with orch.   Parlophone E10493/4, P1553 &
                   P1575

Stuart FASTOFSKY (1927–1964)

AMES

Dust of snow vln & pf
   with A. Sternklar pf   Dorian 1022

DELMAR

Sonata vln & pf
   with A. Sternklar pf   Dorian 1022

PAGANINI

(6) Sonatas, Op. 2 (1801/6) vln & gtr
   No. 2. Sonata No. 2, in C
   with C. Denys pf   Dorian 1022
   No. 5. Sonata No. 5, in D
   with C. Denys pf   Dorian 1022
   No. 6. Sonata No. 6, in a
   with C. Denys pf   Dorian 1022

RACHMANINOV

(5) Pieces, Op. 3 (1892) pf
   No. 5. Mélodie arr. vln & pf Altschuler
   with A. Sternklar pf   Dorian 1022

YSAŸE

Extase in E flat (Poème No. 4) Op. 21 vln & pf or orch.
   with C. Denys pf   Dorian 1022

Grigory FEIGIN

ARENSKY

Trio No. 1, in d, Op. 32 pf, vln & vlc
   with I. Zhukov pf & V. Feigin vlc   HMV 2C063–91079
                           Mezhdunarodnaya Kniga
                           D024821, SM02289

BEETHOVEN

(3) Sonatas, Op. 12 vln & pf
   No. 3. Sonata No. 3, in E flat
   with piano   Mezhdunarodnaya Kniga
                D025177/8

* Abridged.

BEETHOVEN – *Continued*

(3) Trios, Op. 1 pf, vln & vlc
   No. 1. Trio No. 1, in E flat
   with I. Zhukov pf & V. Feigin vlc   Mezhdunarodnaya Kniga
                           SM02173/4

(2) Trios, Op. 70 pf, vln & vlc
   No. 2. Trio No. 5, in E flat
   with I. Zhukov pf & V. Feigin vlc   Mezhdunarodnaya Kniga
                           D025721/2, S01919/20

Trio No. 6, in B flat, Op. 97 "Archduke" pf, vln & vlc
   with I. Zhukov pf & V. Feigin vlc   Mezhdunarodnaya Kniga
                           SM02241/2

Trio in E flat, G153 (WoO38) pf, vln & vlc
   with I. Zhukov pf & V. Feigin vlc   Mezhdunarodnaya Kniga
                           S01919/20

(14) Variations in E flat, Op. 44 pf, vln & vlc
   with I. Zhukov pf & V. Feigin vlc   Mezhdunarodnaya Kniga
                           SM02173/4

(10) Variations on "Ich bin der Schneider Kakadu", Op. 121a pf, vln & vlc
   with I. Zhukov pf & V. Feigin vlc   Mezhdunarodnaya Kniga
                           D025721/2

BRAHMS

Trio No. 1, in B, Op. 8 pf, vln & vlc
   with I. Zhukov pf & V. Feigin vlc   Mezhdunarodnaya Kniga
                           D018997, SM02405

GLINKA

Trio in d (1826/7) "Trio pathétique" pf, vln & vlc
   with I. Zhukov pf & V. Feigin vlc   HMV 2C063–91079
                           Mezhdunarodnaya Kniga
                           D024822, SM02290

GLUCK

Orphée et Eurydice (1762) – opera
   Dance of the blessed spirits: Lento "Mélodie" (No. 2) arr. vln & pf
   Kreisler
   with piano   Mezhdunarodnaya Kniga
                D025177/8

HAYDN

(31) Trios, H.XV, Nos. 1/31 pf, vln & vlc
   Trio No. 25, in G, H.XV, No. 25 (Op. 73, No. 2)
   with I. Zhukov pf & V. Feigin vlc   Mezhdunarodnaya Kniga
                           D018998, SM02406

HUMMEL

Rondo in E flat, Op. 11 "Rondo favori" pf – arr. vln & pf Heifetz
   with piano   Mezhdunarodnaya Kniga
                           D025177/8

KHACHATURIAN

Ballade, Op. 2 (1927) vln & pf
   with D. Sakharov pf   Mezhdunarodnaya Kniga
                           D17593/4

MOZART

Adagio in E, K261 vln & orch.
   with Y. Gushanskaya pf   Mezhdunarodnaya Kniga
                           D17593/4

OVCHINNIKOV

Melody vln & pf
with piano Mezhdunarodnaya Kniga
D025177/8

RAMEAU

(5) Pièces de Clavecin en Concerts (1741) hpsi, vln & vlc
No. 1. Concert No. 1, in c
with I. Zhukov hpsi & V. Feigin vlc Mezhdunarodnaya Kniga
D024605/6, S01877/8

No. 2. Concert No. 2, in G
with I. Zhukov hpsi & V. Feigin vlc Mezhdunarodnaya Kniga
D024605/6, S01877/8

No. 3. Concert No. 3, in A
with I. Zhukov hpsi & V. Feigin vlc Mezhdunarodnaya Kniga
D024605/6, S01877/8

No. 4. Concert No. 4, in B flat
with I. Zhukov hpsi & V. Feigin vlc Mezhdunarodnaya Kniga
D024593/4, S01879/80

No. 5. Concert No. 5, in d
with I. Zhukov hpsi & V. Feigin vlc Mezhdunarodnaya Kniga
D024593/4, S01879/80

RAVEL

Tzigane (Rapsodie de concert) (1924) vln & pf or orch.
with Y. Gushanskaya pf Mezhdunarodnaya Kniga
D17593/4

SHOSTAKOVICH

(3) Danses fantastiques, Op. 5, (1922) pf arr. vln & pf Glickman
with Y. Gushanskaya pf Mezhdunarodnaya Kniga
D17593/4

WIENIAWSKI

(8) Étude–Caprices, Op. 18 solo vln & 2nd vln obb
Étude–Caprice No. 3, in D
(playing both parts) Mezhdunarodnaya Kniga
D025177/8

ZIMBALIST

Fantasia (on themes from the opera "Le Coq d'or" by Rimsky–Korsakov)
vln & pf
with piano Mezhdunarodnaya Kniga
D025177/8

Hermann FEIK

NACHÈZ

Abendlied, Op. 18 vln & pf
with orch. – Strauss Pathé 54308

Rudolfo FELICANI (1902–   )

BACH

(6) Brandenburg Concerti, BWV1046/51 (1721) strs & c
Brandenburg Concerto No. 1, in F, BWV1046 vln, 3 obs, bsn, 2 hrns, strs
& c
playing violino piccolo with U. Baccelli Archive APM14011, APM14107,
hrn, C. Esposito Hrn, H. ARC3105/6
Winschermann hrn & Schola
Cantorium Basiliensis – Wenzinger

BACH – *Continued*

Brandenburg Concerto No. 4, in G, BWV1049 vln, 2 fls, strs & c
with J. Bopp fl, H. Haldemann fl & Epic LC3167
Basle Chamber Orch. – Sacher Fontana 695011KL
Philips 400047AE, ABE10065

Brandenburg Concerto No. 5, in D, BWV1050 clav, fl, vln, strs & c
with E. Müller hpsi, J. Bopp fl, H. Archive APM14012, APM14108,
Winschermann hrn & Schola ARC3106, 2422/3
Cantorium Basiliensis – Wenzinger Fontana 695011KL

Concerto in a, BWV1044 clav, fl, vln, strs & c
with E. Müller hpsi, J. Bopp fl & Archive AP13049
Schola Cantorium Basiliensis –
Wenzinger

Concerto in c, BWV1060 vln & ob or 2 vlns, strs & c
with E. Shann ob & Basle Chamber Philips A00719R, NBR6028
Orch. – Sacher

BOCCHERINI

(6) Quintets, Op. 56 (1797) pf, 2 vlns, vla & vlc
No. 1. Quintet No. 1, in e gtr, 2 vlns, vla & vlc
with F. Wörsching gtr, W. Neininger Archive APM14070, ARC3057
vln, M. Majer vla & A. Wenzinger vlc

PACHELBEL

Canon & Gigue in D 3 vlns & c
with R. Lahrs vln, I. Brix–Meinert vln, Archive EPA37056
H. Heintze hpsi & J. Koch gamba

Partita No. 6, in B flat 2 vlns & c
with I. Brix–Meinert vln, H. Heintze Archive EPA37056
hpsi & J. Koch gamba

TELEMANN

Quartet in e, T.III, No. 2 fl. vln gamba & c
with H–M. Linde fl, A. Wenzinger vlc, Archive APM14838, ARC3238,
E. Müller hpsi & H. Müller vlc ARC73238, SAPM198838
Musique Royale 199012

VOGLER

Sonata in C "The Matrimonial Tiff" 2 vlns, vla & c
with W. Kägi vln, M. Majer vla, F. Archive EPA37216, SEPA181216
Neumeyer pf & H. Müller vlc

Boris FELICIANT

MUSSORGSKY

Sorochintsy Fair (1911/23) – opera
Gopak (Act III) orch. – arr. vln & pf Dushkin
with piano OG 547^{II}△ HMV B4126, EK107

TCHAIKOVSKY

Concerto in D, Op. 35 vln & orch.
Canzonetta (2nd mvt)
with piano OG 546^{II}△ HMV B4126, EK107

Edmund Horace FELLOWES (1870–1951)

ANONYMOUS

Flowers o' the forest arr. vln & pf Moffat
with piano A 16166 HMV 3–7932, B388

ANONYMOUS – *Continued*

(The) Mason's apron – reel arr. vln & pf Moffat
   with piano   A 16166   HMV 3–7932, B388

Stumpie strathspey arr. vln & pf Moffat
   with piano   A 16166   HMV 3–7932, B388

HOLLAND

(4) Fancies, Op. 18 vln & pf
No. 1. poem
   with T.S. Holland pf   Edison Bell 1101/2
No. 2. Fireflies
   with T.S. Holland pf   Edison Bell 1101/2
No. 3. Nightfall
   with T.S. Holland pf   Edison Bell 1101/2
No. 4. Green lattice
   with T.S. Holland pf   Edison Bell 1101/2

SAINTON

Fantaisie Ecossaise, Op. 27 vln & pf
   with piano   Ac 4773 f   HMV 07949, C488

Lorand FENYVES (1918–)

BACH

Concerto in c, BWV1060 vln & ob or 2 vlns, strs & c
   with H. Holliger ob & Geneva   Monitor MC2088, MCS2088
   Baroque Orch. – Auberson

BARTÓK

Contrasts (1938) vln, cl & pf
   with R. Gugulz cl & L. Rev pf   Guilde Internationale du Disque
                                  SMS2491

(44) Duos (1931) 2 vlns
   with V. Martin vln   Ensayo ENY26

(2) Portraits, Op. 5 (1907) vln & orch.
   with L'Orch. de la Suisse Romande –   Decca LXT6121, SXL6121
   Ansermet   London CM9407, CS6407

(6) Rumanian folk dances (1915) pf – arr. vln & pf Székely
   with B. Siki pf   CBC Radio Canada SM26

Sonata No. 2 (1922) vln & pf
   with B. Siki pf   CBC Radio Canada SM44

Sonata in g (1944) solo vln
   (unaccompanied)   CBC Radio Canada SM26

BEETHOVEN

(3) Sonatas, Op. 30 vln & pf
No. 1. Sonata No. 6, in A
   with A. Kuerti pf   Victor LSC3146

Sonata No. 9, in A, Op. 47 "Kreutzer" vln & pf
   with A. Kuerti pf   Victor LSC3146

RIMSKY–KORSAKOV

Scheherazade, Op. 35 (1888) orch.
   with L'Orch. de la Suisse Romande –   Decca LXT5628, SXL2268
   Ansermet   London CM9281, CS6212,
                                   SLC1213

Huguette FERNANDEZ

AUBERT

(6) Concerti, Op. 17 (1734/5) 4 vlns & strs
Concerto No. 6, in g
   with Jean–François Paillard Chamber   Erato EFM8019
   Orch. – Paillard   Musical Heritage Society
                                 MHS521

BACH

Concerto No. 1, in a, BWV1041 vln, strs & c
   with Jean–François Paillard Chamber   Erato EFM8021, LDE3107
   Orch. – Paillard

Concerto No. 2, in E, BWV1042 vln, strs & c
   with Jean–François Paillard Chamber   Erato EFM8021, LDE3107
   Orch. – Paillard

Concerto in d, BWV1043 2 vlns, strs & c
   with M. Blanchard vln & Jean–   Erato EFM 8021, EFM42057
   François Paillard Chamber Orch. –
   Paillard

Concerto in a, BWV1044 clav, fl, vln, strs & c
   with A–M. Beckensteiner hpsi, C.   Musical Heritage Society
   Lardé fl & J–M. Leclair Instrumental   MHS1028
   Ensemble – Paillard .

Concerto in a, BWV1044 clav, fl, vln, strs & c
   with A–M. Beckensteiner hpsi, C.   Columbia SMC95054
   Lardé fl & Jean–François Paillard   Erato LDE3094, STE50003
   Chamber Orch. – Paillard   Musical Heritage Society
                                   MHS535

Concerto in c, BWV1060 vln & ob or 2 vlns – arr. vln & tpt, strs & c
   with M. André tpt & Jean–François   Electrola 1C065–28217
   Paillard Chamber Orch. – Paillard   Erato STU70511

Concerto in c, BWV1060 vln & ob or 2 vlns, strs & c
   with P. Lamacque vln & Jean–   Erato EFM42057
   François Paillard Chamber Orch. –
   Paillard

(6) Sonatas, BWV1014/9 vln & clav
Sonata No. 2, in A, BWV1015
   with A–M. Beckensteiner pf   Erato EFM42051
Sonata No. 3, in E, BWV1016
   with A–M. Beckensteiner pf   Erato EFM42051

BERNIER

Bacchus (Cantata) arr. L. Boulay
   with L.J. Rondeleux b, L. Boulay hpsi,   La Boîte à Musique LD047,
   M.A. Mocquot gamba & D. Gouarne   LDS5047
   hpsi

BERTHEAUME

(2) Sinfonia concertantes, Op. 6 (1787) 2 vlns & orch.
Sinfonia concertante No. 2, in E flat
   with G. Raymond vln, P. Pelvescovo   Erato LDE3037
   hrn & Jean–François Paillard Chamber
   Orch. – Paillard

BONPORTI

(10) Concerti, Op. 11 strs
Concerto No. 5, in F: Adagio (2nd mvt) "Recitativo"
   with Jean–François Paillard Chamber   Christophorus CLP75502
   Orch. – Paillard   Erato EFM8006, EFM42069,
                                  STE60002

CORELLI

(12) Concerti grossi, Op. 6 orch.
  Concerto grosso No. 8, in g "Christmas Concerto"
    with G. Raymond vln, P. Degenne vlc,   Erato EFM42042
    A–M. Beckensteiner hpsi & Jean–
    François Paillard Chamber Orch. –
    Paillard

COUPERIN, F.

(Les) Goûts réunis, ou Nouveaux Concerts unsp inst & c
  Concert No. 10, in a "La Tromba" vln, vla & c
    with R. Boulay vla L. Boulay hpsi &   La Boîte à Musique LD056,
    E. Pasquier vlc   LDS5056
(3) Leçons des Ténèbres v & c
    with N. Sautereau s, J. Collard a, N.   Erato DP23–1
    Pierront org, M–C. Misson vln, M–A.   Haydn Society HSL105
    Mocquot gamba, – cond L. Boulay
(Les) Nations – 4 Suites (1726) 2 vlns & c
  Suite No. 1, in e "La Françoise"
    with R. Gendre vln, R. Boulay vla, J–   Music Guild M21, MG108,
    P. Rampal fl, J. Pasquier vln & L.   MS108, S21
    Boulay hpsi
  Suite No. 2, in c "L'Espagnole"
    with R. Gendre vln, R. Boulay vla, J–   Music Guild M21, MG108,
    P. Rampal fl, J. Pasquier vln & L.   MS108, S21
    Boulay hpsi
  Suite No. 3, in d "L'Impériale"
    with R. Gendre vln, R. Boulay vla, J–   La Boîte à Musique LD056,
    P. Rampal fl, J. Pasquier vln & L.   LDS5056
    Boulay hpsi   Music Guild M21, MG108,
      MS108, S21
  Suite No. 4, in g "La Piémontoise"
    with R. Gendre vln, R. Boulay vla, J–   Music Guild M21, MG108,
    P. Rampal fl, J. Pasquier vln & L.   MS108, S21
    Boulay hpsi

DANDRIEU

(12) Trio–Sonatas, Op. 1 (1705), 2 vlns & c
  Sonata No. 6, in e
    with P. Lamacque vln, L. Boulay hpsi   Erato STU70314
    & J. Lamy gamba   Musical Heritage Society
      MHS930

HANDEL

(6) Concerti grossi, Op. 3 (1759) orch.
  Concerto grosso No. 3, in G
    with J–P. Rampal fl & Jean–François   Erato LDE3371, STE50271,
    Paillard Chamber Orch. – Paillard   STU70322
  Concerto grosso No. 7, in F*
    with G. Raymond vln, P. Degenne vlc,   Christophorus CGLP75741
    A–M. Beckensteiner hpsi & Jean–
    François Paillard Chamber Orch. –
    Paillard
(12) Concerti grossi, Op. 6 (1739) 2 vlns, vlc & strs
  Concerto grosso No. 1, in G
    with G. Carles vln, B. Fonteny vlc, A–   Erato STU70319
    M. Beckensteiner hpsi & Jean–François   Musical Heritage Society
    Paillard Chamber Orch. – Paillard   MHS806

* This is a reworking of thematic materials from the F Concerto No. 4 for
  organ which dates from 1734.

HANDEL – *Continued*

  Concerto grosso No. 2, in F
    with G. Carles vln, B. Fonteny vlc, A–   Erato STU70319
    M. Beckensteiner hpsi & Jean–François   Musical Heritage Society
    Paillard Chamber Orch. – Paillard   MHS806
  Concerto grosso No. 3, in e
    with G. Carles vln, B. Fonteny vlc, A–   Erato STU70319
    M. Beckensteiner hpsi & Jean–François   Musical Heritage Society
    Paillard Chamber Orch. – Paillard   MHS807
  Concerto grosso No. 4, in a
    with G. Carles vln, B. Fonteny vlc, A–   Erato STU70320
    M. Beckensteiner hpsi & Jean–François   Musical Heritage Society
    Paillard Chamber Orch. – Paillard   MHS807
  Concerto grosso No. 5, in D
    with G. Carles vln, B. Fonteny vlc, A–   Erato STU70320
    M. Beckensteiner hpsi & Jean–François   Musical Heritage Society
    Paillard Chamber Orch. – Paillard   MHS808
  Concerto grosso No. 6, in g
    with G. Carles vln, B. Fonteny vlc, A–   Erato STU70320
    M. Beckensteiner hpsi & Jean–François   Musical Heritage Society
    Paillard Chamber Orch. – Paillard   MHS808
  Concerto grosso No. 7, in B flat
    with G. Carles vln, B. Fonteny vlc, A–   Erato STU70321
    M. Beckensteiner hpsi & Jean–François   Musical Heritage Society
    Paillard Chamber Orch. – Paillard   MHS809
  Concerto grosso No. 8, in c
    with G. Carles vln, B. Fonteny vlc, A–   Erato STU70321
    M. Beckensteiner hpsi & Jean–François   Musical Heritage Society
    Paillard Chamber Orch. – Paillard   MHS809
  Concerto grosso No. 9, in F
    with G. Carles vln, B. Fonteny vlc, A–   Erato STU70321
    M. Beckensteiner hpsi & Jean–François   Musical Heritage Society
    Paillard Chamber Orch. – Paillard   MHS809
  Concerto grosso No. 10, in d
    with G. Raymond vln, P. Degenne vlc,   Christophorus CGLP75741
    A–M. Beckensteiner hpsi & Jean–
    François Paillard Chamber Orch. –
    Paillard
  Concerto grosso No. 10, in d
    with G. Carles vln, B. Fonteny vlc, A–   Erato STU70321
    M. Beckensteiner hpsi & Jean–François   Musical Heritage Society
    Paillard Chamber Orch. – Paillard   MHS809
  Concerto grosso No. 11, in A
    with G. Carles vln, B. Fonteny vlc, A–   Erato STU70319
    M. Beckensteiner hpsi & Jean–François   Musical Heritage Society
    Paillard Chamber Orch. – Paillard   MHS808
  Concerto grosso No. 12, in b
    with G. Carles vln, B. Fonteny vlc, A–   Erato STU70320
    M. Beckensteiner hpsi & Jean–François   Musical Heritage Society
    Paillard Chamber Orch. – Paillard   MHS808

LECLAIR

(6) Concerti, Op. 7 (1737) vln & strs
  Concerto No. 2, in D
    with Leclair Instrumental Ensemble –   Chiristophorus CGLP75815,
    Paillard   SCGLP75816
      Erato DP21–2, STU70134
      Haydn Society HS9059, HSL140
      Music Guild M56, MG148,
      MS148, S56

LECLAIR – *Continued*

(6) Concerti, Op. 10 (1744) vln & strs
Concerto No. 2, in A
with Leclair Instrumental Ensemble – Christophorus CGLP75815,
Paillard SCGLP75816
Erato DP21/1, STU70134
Haydn Society HSL103
Music Guild M56, MG148,
MS148, S56

Concerto No. 3, in D
with Leclair Instrumental Ensemble – Erato LPE1010
Paillard

Concerto No. 5, in e
with Leclair Instrumental Ensemble – Erato DP21-1
Paillard Haydn Society HS9059, HSL140

Concerto No. 6, in g
with Leclair Instrumental Ensemble – Christophorus CGLP75815,
Paillard SCGLP75816
Erato STU70134
Music Guild M56, MG148,
MS148, S56

(12) Sonatas, Op. 1 – Book I (1723) vln & c
Sonata No. 8, in G
with L. Boulay hpsi & J. Lamy vlc Erato LDE3328, STE50228

(12) Sonatas, Op. 5 – Book III (1734) vln & c
Sonata No. 4, in B flat
with L. Boulay hpsi & J. Lamy vlc Erato LDE3328, STE50228

(12) Sonatas, Op. 9 – Book IV (1738) vln & c
Sonata No. 4, in A
with L. Boulay hpsi & J. Lamy vlc Erato LDE3328, STE50228

(12) Sonatas, Op. 12 2 vlns c
Sonata No. 4, in B flat
with P. Lamacque vln, L. Boulay hpsi Erato LDE3328, STE50228
& J. Lamy vlc

LOCATELLI

(12) Concerti, Op. 3 (1733) "L'Arte del Violino" (with 24 solo caprices) vln & orch.
Concerto No. 2, in c
with Leclair Instrumental Ensemble – Erato DP31-1
Paillard Haydn Society HSL147

(12) Concerti, Op. 7 (1741) "Il pianto d'Arianna" strs & c
Concerto No. 6, in E flat vln, strs & c
with Leclair Instrumental Ensemble – Erato DP31-1
Paillard Haydn Society HSL147

MESSIAEN

Quartet (1940) "For the end of time" vln, cl, vlc & pf
with G. Deplus cl, J. Neilz vlc & M– Erato LDE3256, STE50156,
M. Petit pf STU70156
Musical Heritage Society
MHS978
Music Guild MS150

SAINT–GEORGES

(2) Sinfonia concertantes, Op. 9 2 vlns & orch.
Sinfonia concertante No. 2, in G
with G. Carles vln & Jean–François Erato STU70237
Paillard Chamber Orch. – Paillard

SCHUBERT

Rondo in A, D438 vln & str orch.
with Jean–François Paillard Chamber Erato EFM42094, LDE3117,
Orch. – Paillard STE60024
Musical Heritage Society
MHS585

SOLER

(6) Quintets 2 vlns, vla, vlc & org or pf
Quintet No. 6, in g
with G. Raymond vln, M–R. Guiet Erato DP501
vla, J. Deferrieux vlc & M–C. Alain Westminster XWN18754
org

STRADELLA

(8) Sonatas "Sinfonias" 2 vlns & concertino
Sonata No. 1, in a 2 vlns, vlc, cbs, lute & hpsi
with G. Carles vln, B. Fonteny vlc, M. Erato STU70368
Schäffer lute, A–M. Beckensteiner hpsi
– cond. Paillard

Sonata No. 2, in G 2 vlns, vlc, strs & org
with G. Carles vln, B. Fonteny vlc, O. Erato STU70368
Alain org & Jean–François Paillard
Chamber Orch. – Paillard

Sonata No. 3, in D 2 vlns, vlc, hpsi, 2 tpts, tbn & org
with G. Carles vln, B. Fonteny vlc, A– Erato STU70368
M. Beckensteiner hpsi, E. Tarr tpt, H.
Eichhorn tpt, H. Schimtt tbn & O.
Alain org – cond. Paillard

Sonata No. 5, in F 2 vlns, vlc & lute
with G. Carles vln, B. Fonteny vlc, M. Erato STU70368
Schäffer lute – cond. Paillard

TORELLI

(12) Concerti, Op. 8 (1709) 1/6: 2 vlns, strs & c; 7/12: vln, strs & c
Concerto No. 2, in a
with L. Beguin vln & Jean–François Erato LDE3145
Paillard Chamber Orch. – Paillard

Concerto No. 8, in c
with Jean–François Paillard Chamber Erato LDE3145
Orch. – Paillard

VIVALDI

(12) Concerti, Op. 8 (1725) "Il Cimento dell' Armonia e dell' Invenzione"
(nos. 1/4: Le quattro Stagioni) vln & strs
Concerto No. 10, in B flat, F.I, No. 29 "La Caccia"
with Jean–François Paillard Chamber Erato STU70234
Orch. – Paillard

(12) Concerti, Op. 9 (1728) "La Cetra" vln, strs & c
Concerto No. 12, in b, P.154 (F.I, No. 50) with solo vln scordato
with Jean–François Paillard Chamber Musical Heritage Society
Orch. – Paillard MHS570

Concerto in G, P.135 (F.IV, No. 1) 2 vlns, 2 vlcs, strs & c
with G. Carles vln, B. Fonteny vlc, C. Erato LDE3293, STE50193
Maurelet vlc & Jean–François Paillard World Record Club CM86,
Chamber Orch. – Paillard SCM86

Concerto in D, P.185 vln, strs & c
with Leclair Instrumental Ensemble – Erato EFM43031
Paillard

VIVALDI – *Continued*

Concerto in D, P.207 (F.XII, No. 25) fl, ob, vln, bsn & c
with M. Larrieu fl, J. Chambon ob, J.   Erato LDE3218, STE50118,
Louchez bsn A–M. Beckensteiner hpsi   STU70118
& B. Fonteny vlc

Concerto in F, P.274 (F.XII, No. 41) vln, org, strs & c
with M–C. Alain org, A–M.   Erato LDE3293, STE50193,
Beckensteiner hpsi & Jean–François   STU70193
Paillard Chamber Orch. – Paillard   World Record Club CM86,
   SCM86

Concerto in d, P.281 (F.I, No. 100) 2 vlns, strs & c
with M. Blanchard vln & Jean–   Erato LDE3077
François Paillard Chamber Orch. –
Paillard

Concerto in g, P.360 fl, ob, vln, bsn & c
with M. Larrieu fl, J. Chambon ob, J.   Erato LDE3218, STE50118,
Louchez bsn, A–M. Beckensteiner hpsi   STU70118
& B. Fonteny vlc

Concerto in g, P.383 (F.XII, No. 3) "Per l'orchestra di Dresda" vln, 2 fls, 2
obs, 2 bsns & c
with Leclair Instrumental Ensemble –   Erato DP31–1
Paillard

Concerto in B flat, P.406 (F.XII, No. 16) vln, ob, strs & c
with P. Pierlot ob, A–M. Beckensteiner   Erato LDE3293, STE50193,
hpsi & Jean–François Paillard   STU70193
Chamber Orch. – Paillard   World Record Club CM86,
   SCM86

(12) Sonatas, Op. 2 (1712) vln & c
Sonata No. 9, in e, F.XIII, No. 37
with A–M. Beckensteiner hpsi & B.   Erato LDE3218, STE50118,
Fonteny vlc   STU70118

Aldo FERRARESI (1906–)

ACHRON

Stimmungen,, Op. 32 vln & pf
with E. Galdieri pf   HMV QDLP6048

ARENSKY

Concerto in a, Op. 54 vln & orch.
Tempo di valse (2nd mvt) arr. vln & pf Heifetz
with E. Galdieri pf   HMV QCLP12025

BAZZINI

(La) Ronde des lutins, Op. 25 vln & pf
with P. Ferraresi pf   [1]BE 12205   Odeon 0–26264

BONPORTI

Aria – arr. vln & pf*
with G. Spinelli pf   Storia della Musica SdM015
   (Vol. 2, No. 2)

DEBUSSY

Images – Set I (1904) pf
No. 3. Mouvement arr. vln & pf
with E. Galdieri pf   HMV QCLP12025

(La) Plus que lente – valse (1910) pf arr. vln & pf Roques
with E. Galdieri pf   HMV QCLP12025

* Unidentified.

DEBUSSY – *Continued*

(12) Preludes – Book I (1910) pf
No. 8. La Fille aux cheveux de lin arr. vln & pf Hartmann
with E. Galdieri pf   HMV QCLP12025

DUNSCHEDE

Capriccio–valse, Op. 15 vln & pf
with G. Faveretto pf   HMV GW2015

DVOŘÁK

(7) Gypsy songs, Op. 55 v & pf
No. 4. Songs my mother taught me arr. vln & pf Kreisler
with E. Galdieri pf   HMV QDLP6048

(8) Slavonic Dances, Op. 72 pf duet; orch.
No. 8. Slavonic dance No. 16, in A flat arr. vln & pf "in G" Kreisler
with E. Galdieri pf   HMV QDLP6048

GERSHWIN

(3) Jazz Preludes (1936) pf
No. 3. Prelude No. 3, in E flat arr. vln & pf Heifetz
with E. Galdieri pf   HMV QCLP12025

Porgy & Bess (1935) – opera
It ain't necessarily so arr. vln & pf Heifetz
with E. Galdieri pf   HMV QDLP6048

My man's gone now arr. vln & pf Heifetz
with E. Galdieri pf   HMV QDLP6048

GLUCK

Orphée et Eurydice (1762) – opera
Dance of the blessed spirits: Lento "Mélodie" (No. 2) arr. vln & pf
Kreisler
with E. Galdieri pf   HMV QCLP12025

GODOWSKY

Triakontameron (30 moods & scenes in triple measure) (1920) pf
No. 11. Alt Wien arr. vln & pf Heifetz
with E. Galdieri pf   HMV QCLP12025

GOUNOD

Ave Maria (Méditation on Bach's "Prelude No. 1, in C" from Book I of
"Das Wohltemperirte Clavier") v & pf – arr. vln & pf
with C. Vidusso pf   CM 1191[II] △   HMV S10113

Ave Maria (Méditation on Bach's "Prelude No. 1, in C" from Book I of
"Das Wohltemperirte Clavier") v & pf – arr. v, vln & pf
with A. Albertini s & piano   HMV S10159

HUBAY

(6) Blumenleben, Op. 30 vln & pf
No. 5. Der Zephir
with G. Favaretto pf   HMV GW2015

KREISLER

Gypsy Caprice vln & pf
with E. Galdieri pf   HMV QCLP12025

Grave (W.F. Bach) vln & pf
with E. Galdieri pf   HMV QCLP12025

LISZT

(3) Liebesträume, G326 pf
No. 3. Liebestraum No. 3, in A flat arr. vln & pf
with G. Favaretto pf   2BA 4469 ☐   HMV S10493

MARINI

Sonata vln & c
  with G. Spinelli hpsi   Storia della Musica MdM015
                                 (Vol. 2, No. 2)

MASCAGNI

(L') Amico Fritz (1891) – opera
  Violinista arr. vln & pf Bufolari
  with C. Vidusso pf   HMV HN188

MASSENET

Thaïs (1894) – opera
  Méditation arr. vln & pf Marsick
  with C. Vidusso pf   HMV S10159

MENDELSSOHN

(6) Songs without words, Op. 62 pf
  No. 1. Song without words No. 25, in G "May breezes" arr. vln & pf Kreisler
  with E. Galdieri pf   HMV QDLP6048

MERULA

Canzone la Loda 2 vlns & c
  with G. Franzetti vln, G. Spinelli hpsi Storia della Musica MdM015
  & A. Riccardi gamga   (Vol. 2, No. 2)

NAPOLI

Aria vln & pf
  with E. Galdieri pf   HMV QDLP6048

PAGANINI

Nel cor più non mi sento "Sonata appassionata con variazioni" (on the aria from Paisiello's opera "La bella molinara") Op. 38 (1820 or 1821) solo vln
  (unaccompanied)   Storia della Musica SdM015
                                 (Vol. 2, No. 2)

(6) Sonatas, Op. 3 (1801/6) vln & gtr
  No. 6. Sonata No. 12, in e
  with P. Ferraresi pf   [1]BE 12204   Odeon 0–26264

(Le) Streghe (Variations on a theme from Süssmeyer's opera "Il Noce di Benevento") Op. 8 (1813) vln & orch. – arr. vln & pf Kreisler
  with C. Vidusso pf   CM 1276[1]△ HMV S10113

(Le) Streghe (variations on a theme from Süssmeyer's opera "Il Noce di Benevento") Op. 8 (1813) vln & orch. – arr. vln & pf Kreisler
  with G. Spinelli pf   Storia della Musica SdM015bis
                                 (Vol. 2, No. 2bis)

RAVEL

Sonatina in F sharp (1905) pf
  Menuet (2nd mvt) arr. vln & pf Roques
  with E. Galdieri pf   HMV QCLP12025

SARASATE

(8) Danzas españolas vln & pf
  No. 3. Romanza andaluza, Op. 22, No. 1
  with G. Spinelli pf   Storia della Musica SdM015bis
                                   (Vol. 2, No. 2bis)

  No. 6. Zapateado, Op. 23, No. 2
  with C. Vidusso pf   HMV HN188

STRAUSS, R.

(Der) Rosenkavalier, Op. 59 (1911) – opera
  Watzes (Act II, vln & pf Příhoda
  with G. Favaretto pf   2BA 4470 ☐ HMV S10493

STRAVINSKY

Mavra (1922) – opera
  Russian maiden's song (Parasha's aria) arr. vln & pf Dushkin & Stravinsky
  with E. Galdieri pf   HMV QCLP12025

SUK

(7) Pieces, Op. 7 pf
  No. 1. Love song arr. vln & pf Mařák
  with G. Favaretto pf   HMV GW2014

TARTINI

(50) Variations on a theme of Corelli solo vln
  Theme & 13th variation only arr. vln & pf Francescatti
  with G. Spinelli pf   Storia della Musica SdM015
                                 (Vol. 2, No. 2)

WEBER

(6) Sonatas, Op. 10 (J99/104) (1910) vln & pf
  Sonata No. 3, in D: Rondo (2nd mvt) J101 arr. Heifetz
  with E. Galdieri pf   HMV QCLP12025

Cesare FERRARESI (1918–   )

ALBINONI

(12) Concerti, Op. 9 (1722) var, cbns & strs
  Concerto No. 1, in B flat vln, strs & c
  with Italian Baroque Ensemble – Bryks Dover HCR5225
                                       Vox DL193

  Concerto No. 4, in A vln, strs & c
  with Italian Baroque Ensemble – Bryks Dover HCR5225
                                       Vox DL193

  Concerto No. 7, in D vln, strs & c
  with Italian Baroque Ensemble – Bryks Dover HCR5225
                                       Vox DL193

  Concerto No. 10, in F vln, strs & c
  with Italian Baroque Ensemble – Bryks Dover HCR5225
                                       Vox DL193

BONPORTI

(10) Concerti, Op. 11 strs
  Concerto No. 1, in A
  with Palladium Orch., Milan – Giulini Pacific LDP–E51020

  Concerto No. 4, in B flat
  with Palladium Orch., Milan – Giulini Pacific LDP–E51020

  Concerto No. 5, in F
  with Palladium Orch., Milan – Giulini Pacific LDP–E51020

  Concerto No. 8, in D
  with Palladium Orch., Milan – Giulini Pacific LDP–E51020

CIMA

(2) Concerti ecclesiastici (1610)
  Sonata No. 2, in a 2 vlns, gamba & org
  with F. Gulli vln, G. Caramia vlc & Angelicum LPA5947
  A. Berutti org   Musica Sacra AMS46

GASTOLDI

(3) Balletti (1594) fl, vln, gamba & lute
with N. Poli spin, E. Smith cbs & R. Rapp lute   Carisch MCA28019

LEGRENZI

(12) Sonatas, Op. 10 (1673) 2 vlns & c
Sonata No. 5, in D
with F. Gulli vln, A. Berutti org & G. Caramia vlc   Angelicum LPA5947
Musica Sacra AMS46

MARINI

(La) Gardana (1617) vln, cbs, spin & lute
with E. Smith cbs, N. Poli spin & R. Rapp lute   Carisch BCA7014, MCA28019

RUGGIERI

(10) Sonatas, Op. 3 (1693) 2 vlns & c
Sonata No. 5, in g
with F. Gulli vln, A. Berutti org & G. Caramia vlc   Angelicum LPA5947
Musica Sacra AMS46

TORELLI

(12) Sonatas, Op. 3 vln & c
Sonata No. 7, in e
with F. Gulli vln, A. Berutti org & G. Caramia vlc   Angelicum LPA5947
Musica Sacra AMS46

VERACINI

(12) Sonatas, Op. 1 (1721) vln & c
Sonata No. 3, in b
with L. Sgrizzi hpsi   Cycnus 30CM032, 60CS532
Nonesuch H3008, H73008

VITALI

(12) Concerti di Sonate, Op. 4 vln, vlc & c
Sonata No. 11, in b
with F. Gulli vln, A. Berutti org & G. Caramia vlc   Angelicum LPA5947
Musica Sacra AMS46

VIVALDI

(12) Concerti, Op. 3 "L'Estro armonico" var. cbns & strs
Concerto No. 8, in a, P.2 (F.I, No. 177) 2 vlns, strs & c
with A. Stefanato vln & Angelicum Orch. – Zedda   Angelicum LPA5958, SLPA5958
Concerto No. 10, in b, P.148 (F.IV, No. 10) 4 vlns, strs & c
with B. Salvi vln, A. Stefanato vln, M. Ceradini vln & Angelicum Orch. – Zedda   Angelicum LPA5911, STA8911
Harmonia Mundi HM30664
Sonata a quattro in E flat F.XVI, No. 2 (P.441) "Al Santo Sepolcro" 2 vlns, vla & c
with F. Gulli vln, B. Tosatti vla, A. Berutti hpsi & G. Caramia vlc   Angelicum LPA5958, SLPA5958
Electrola 1C053–02068

ZAVATERI

(12) Concerti, Op. 1 (1735) vln & orch.
Concerto No. 12 "La Tempesta di mare" rev. Giazotto
with Angelicum Orch. – Argento   Angelicum LPA969

Astorre FERRARI

ALBINONI

(12) Concerti, Op. 9 (1722) var. cbns & strs
Concerto No. 4, in A vln, strs & c
with I Solisti Veneti – Scimone   Electrola C063–28275
Erato STU70475
Musical Heritage Society HMS1074

VIVALDI

(12) Concerti, Op. 8 (1725) "Il Cimento dell' Armonia e dell' Invenzione" (nos. 1/4: Le quattro Stagioni) vln & strs
Concerto No. 1, in E, F.I, No. 22 "La Primavera"
with Stuttgart Chamber Orch. – Couraud   Fontana 700134WGY, 894013ZKY
Mercury MGW14041, SRW18041
Philips 610117VR, 836226VZ, G05424R
Concerto No. 2, in B flat, F.I, No. 23 "L'Estate"
with Stuttgart Chamber Orch. – Couraud   Fontana 700134WGY, 894013ZKY
Mercury MGW14041, SRW18041
Philips 610117VR, 836226VZ, G05424R
Concerto No. 3, in F, F.I, No. 24 "L'Autunno"
with Stuttgart Chamber Orch. – Couraud   Fontana 700134WGY, 894013ZKY
Mercury MGW14041, SRW18040
Philips 610117VR, 836226VZ, G05424R
Concerto No. 4, in f, F.I, No. 25 "L'Inverno"
with Stuttgart Chamber Orch. – Couraud   Fontana 700134WGY, 894013ZKY
Mercury MGW14041, SRW18041
Philips 610117VR, 836226VZ, G05424R

Concerto in C, P.16 (F.XII, No. 37) 2 mands, 2 obs, 2 fls, 2 cls, 2 vlns, vlc, strs & c
with B. Bianchi mand, A. Pitrelli mand, M. Schaffer ob, K. Gerwig ob, C. Larde fl, C. Scimone fl, A. Pecile cl, A. Gerbi cl, P. Toso vln, M. Cassoli vlc & I Solisti Veneti – Scimone   Musical Heritage Society MHS1100

Franco Claudio FERRARI

PAGANINI

(24) Caprices, Op. 1 (1801/7) solo vln
Caprice No. 5, in a
(unaccompanied)   HMV GW1427

Guido FERRARI

FERRARI, M.
Concerto vln & orch.
with orch.   Excelsius UN2801

Mario FERRARIS

VIVALDI

(6) Concerti, Op. 6 vln, strs & c
  Concerto No. 1, in g, F.I, No. 192
  with I Solisti di Milano – Ephrikian   Arcophon AC685
  Concerto No. 2, in E flat, F.I, No. 193
  with I Solisti di Milano – Ephrikian   Arcophon AC685
  Concerto No. 3, in g, F.I, No. 194
  with I Solisti di Milano – Ephrikian   Arcophon AC685

(12) Sonatas, Op. 1 2 vlns & c
  Sonata No. 1, in g, F.XIII, No. 17
  with E. Molinario vln, M. Sorelli hpsi   Arcophon AC677
  & A. Pocaterra vlc   HMV C063–90250/1
  Sonata No. 2, in e, F.XIII, No. 18
  with E. Molinario vln, M. Sorelli hpsi   Arcophon AC677
  & A. Pocaterra vlc   HMV C063–90250/1
  Sonata No. 3, in C, F.XIII, No. 19
  with E. Molinario vln, M. Sorelli hpsi   Arcophon AC677
  & A. Pocaterra vlc   HMV C063–90250/1
  Sonata No. 4, in E, F.XIII, No. 20
  with E. Molinario vln, M. Sorelli hpsi   Arcophon AC677
  & A. Pocaterra vlc   HMV C063–90250/1
  Sonata No. 5, in F, F.XIII, No. 21
  with E. Molinario vln, M. Sorelli hpsi   Arcophon AC677
  & A. Pocaterra vlc   HMV C063–90250/1
  Sonata No. 6, in D, F.XIII, No. 220
  with E. Molinario vln, M. Sorelli hpsi   Arcophon AC677
  & A. Pocaterra vlc   HMV C063–90250/1
  Sonata No. 7, in E flat, F.XIII, No. 23
  with E. Molinario vln, M. Sorelli hpsi   Arcophon AC677
  & A. Pocaterra vlc   HMV C063–90250/1
  Sonata No. 8, in d, F.XIII, No. 24
  with E. Molinario vln, M. Sorelli hpsi   Arcophon AC677
  & A. Pocaterra vlc   HMV C063–90250/1
  Sonata No. 9, in A, F.XIII, No. 25
  with E. Molinario vln, M. Sorelli hpsi   Arcophon AC677
  & A. Pocaterra vlc   HMV C063–90250/1
  Sonata No. 10 in B flat, F.XIII, No. 26
  with E. Molinario vln M. Sorelli hpsi   Arcophon AC677
  & A. Pocaterra vlc   HMV C063–90250/1
  Sonata No. 11, in b, F.XIII, No. 27
  with E. Molinario vln, M. Sorelli hpsi   Arcophon AC677
  & A. Pocaterra vlc   HMV C063–90250/1
  Sonata No. 12, in d, F.XIII, No. 28 "La Follia"
  with E. Molinario vln, M. Sorelli hpsi   Arcophon AC677
  & A. Pocaterra vlc   HMV C063–90250/1

Christian FERRAS (1933–   )

BACH

(6) Brandenburg Concerti, BWV1046/51 (1721) strs & c
  Brandenburg Concerto No. 5, in D, BWV1050 clav, fl, vln, strs & c
  with C. Chailley–Richez pf, J–P.   Decca FAT173530
  Rampal fl & Paris Chamber Orch. –
  Enescu

BACH – *Continued*

Concerto in d, BWV1043 2 vlns, strs & c
  with Y. Menuhin vln & Robert   Capitol G7210, SG7210
  Masters Chamber Orch. – Menuhin   Electrola E91025, STE91025
    HMV ALP1760, ASD346,
    ASDQ5267, ASDW346,
    CVB3510, FALP30222,
    QALP10278, WALP1760

Concerto in a, BWV1044 clav, fl, vln, strs & c
  with C. Chailley–Richez pf, J–P.   Decca FAT173530
  Rampal fl & Paris Chamber Orch. –
  Enescu

BANDO

Concerto hongrois vln & orch.
  with Orch. de la Société des Concerts   Pathé ASTX326, DTX326
  Colonne – Lombard

BEETHOVEN

Concerto in D, Op. 61 (cadenzas by Kreisler) vln & orch.
  with Royal Philharmonic Orch. –   HMV ASDF210, FALP648
  Sargent   Kristall SMVP8020
    Trianon CTRE6166
    World Record Club ST971

Concerto in D, Op. 61 (cadenzas by Kreisler) vln & orch.
  with Berlin Philharmonic Orch. –   Deutsche Grammophon
  Karajan   LPM39021, SLPM139021

Romance No. 1, in G, Op. 40 vln & orch.
  with Hamburg State Philharmonic   Telefunken EPTD9037,
  Orch. – Ludwig   TM68043, USK9206, UV114

Romance No. 2, in F, Op. 50 vln & orch.
  with Hamburg State Philharmonic   Telefunken EPTD9037,
  Orch. – Ludwig   TM68043, USK9206, UV114

(3) Sonatas, Op. 12 vln & pf
  No. 1. Sonata No. 1, in D
  with P. Barbizet pf   HMV FALP584/7
  No. 1 Sonata No. 1, in D
  with P. Barbizet pf   HMV ALP1999, ASD549,
    ASDF785, FALP785
    Seraphim S60048
    World Record Club ST699, T699
  No. 1. Sonata No. 1, in D
  with P. Barbizet pf   Guilde Internationale du Disque
    SMS2702/8
  No. 2. Sonata No. 2, in A
  with P. Barbizet pf   HMV FALP584/7
  No. 2. Sonata No. 2, in A
  with P. Barbizet pf   Guilde Internationale du Disque
    SMS2702/8
  No. 3. Sonata No. 3, in E flat
  with P. Barbizet pf   HMV FALP584/7
  No. 3. Sonata No. 3, in E flat
  with P. Barbizet pf   Guilde Internationale du Disque
    SMS2702/8

Sonata No. 4, in a, Op. 23 vln & pf
  with P. Barbizet pf   HMV FALP584/7

Sonata No. 4, in a, Op. 23 vln & pf
  with P. Barbizet pf   Guilde Internationale du Disque
    SMS2702/8

BEETHOVEN – *Continued*

Sonata No. 5, in F, Op. 24 "Spring" vln & pf
  with P. Barbizet pf   Telefunken LE6501, LGX66014,
                                        TW30011

Sonata No. 5, in F, Op. 24 "Spring" vln & pf
  with P. Barbizet pf   HMV FALP584/7

Sonata No. 5, in F, Op. 24 "Spring" vln & pf
  with P. Barbizet pf   Guilde Internationale du Disque
                                       SMS2702/8

(3) Sonatas, Op. 30 vln & pf
  No. 1. Sonata No. 6, in A
  with P. Barbizet pf   HMV FALP584/7

  No. 1. Sonata No. 6, in A
  with P. Barbizet pf   Guilde Internationale du Disque
                                       SMS2702/8

  No. 2. Sonata No. 7, in c
  with P. Barbizet pf   HMV FALP584/7

  No. 2. Sonata No. 7, in c
  with P. Barbizet pf   Guilde Internationale du Disque
                                       SMS2702/8

  No. 3. Sonata No. 8, in G
  with P. Barbizet pf   HMV FALP584/7

  No. 3. Sonata No. 8, in G
  with P. Barbizet pf   Guilde Internationale du Disque
                                       SMS2702/8

Sonata No. 9, in A, Op. 47 "Kreutzer" vln & pf
  with P. Barbizet pf   HMV FALP584/7

Sonata No. 9, in A, Op. 47 "Kreutzer" vln & pf
  with P. Barbizet pf   Guilde Internationale du Disque
                                       SMS2702/8

Sonata No. 10, in G, Op. 96 vln & pf
  with P. Barbizet pf   HMV FALP584/7

Sonata No. 10, in G, Op. 96 vln & pf
  with P. Barbizet pf   Guilde Internationale du Disque
                                       SMS2702/8

BERG

Chamber Concerto (1925) pf, vln & 13 w–wnds
  with P. Barbizet pf & Paris Wind   Angel 36171
  Instrumental Ensemble – Prêtre   Electrola E91305, STE91305
                                        HMV ASDF795, CVB1795,
                                        FALP795

Concerto (1935) vln & orch.
  with Paris Conservatory Orch. – Prêtre Angel 36171
                                        Electrola E91305, STE91305
                                        HMV ASDF795, CVB1795,
                                        FALP795

BLOCH

Baal Shem (3 Pictures of Chassidic Life) (1923) vln & pf
  No. 2. Nigun (Improvisation)
  with piano   Decca M635

BRAHMS

Concerto in D, Op. 77 (cadenza by Kreisler) vln & orch.
  with Vienna Philharmonic Orch. –   Ace of Clubs ACL17
  Schuricht   Decca LW50095, LXT2949,
                                        MD1025
                                        London LL1046
                                        Richmond R19018

BRAHMS – *Continued*

Concerto in D, Op. 77 (cadenza by Kreisler) vln & orch.
  with Berlin Philharmonic Orch. –   Deutsche Grammophon
  Karajan   LPM18930, SLPM138930

Concerto in a, Op. 102 "Double" vln, vlc & orch.
  with P. Tortelier vlc & Philharmonia   HMV ALP1999, ASD549,
  Orch. – Kletzki   ASDF785, FALP785
                                         Seraphim S60048
                                         World Record Club ST699, T699

Sonata No. 1, in G, Op. 78 vln & pf
  with P. Barbizet pf   Deutsche Grammophon 2538 105

Sonata No. 2, in A, Op. 100 vln & pf
  with P. Barbizet pf   Deutsche Grammophon 2538 105

Sonata No. 3, in d, Op. 108 vln & pf
  with P. Barbizet pf   Telefunken LE6501, LGX66014,
                                        TW30011

Sonata No. 3, in d, Op. 108 vln & pf
  with P. Barbizet pf   Deutsche Grammophon 2538 105

BRUCH

Concerto No. 1, in g, Op. 26 vln & orch.
  with Philharmonia Orch. – Susskind   Angel 35769
                                        Classics for Pleasure CFP107
                                        Electrola 1C053–00791
                                        HMV ALP1746, ASD314,
                                        FALP614

CHAMINADE

Sérénade espagnole pf – arr. vln & pf Kreisler
  with J–C. Ambrosini pf   Deutsche Grammophon 135133

CHAUSSON

Concerto in D, Op. 21 vln, pf & str qt
  with P. Barbizet pf & Parrenin string   HMV CVC2117
  quartet

Poème, Op. 25 vln & orch.
  with Belgian National Symphony   Decca LXT2827
  Orch. – Sébastian   London LL762

DEBUSSY

Sonata No. 3, in g (1917) vln & pf
  with P. Barbizet pf   Decca FAT173138,
                                        GAG15097/8, LXT2810
                                        Everest LPBR6140, SDBR3140
                                        London LL909

Sonata No. 3, in g (1917) vln & pf
  with P. Barbizet pf   Electrola E80749, STE80749
                                        HMV ALP1980, ASD531,
                                        ASDF769, CVA769, FALP769,
                                        QALP10374
                                        Mace M9045, MCS9045

DINICU

Hora staccato (1906) vln & pf – arr. Heifetz
  with J–C. Ambrosini pf   Deutsche Grammophon 135133

DVOŘÁK

(8) Humoresques, Op. 101 pf
  No. 7. Humoresque No. 7. in G flat arr. vln & pf "in G" Kreisler
  with J–C. Ambrosini pf   Deutsche Grammophon 135133

ELIZALDE

Concerto (1951) vln & orch.
  with London Symphony Orch. –
  Poulet   Decca AK1777/9, LX3116
           London LS564

ENESCU

Sonata No. 3, in a, Op. 25 "in the popular Rumanian style" vln & pf
  with P. Barbizet pf   Electrola E80749, STE80749
          HMV ALP1980, ASD531,
          ASDF769, CVA769, FALP769,
          QALP10374
          Mace M9045, MCS9045

FALLA

(La) Vida breve (1913) – opera
  Danza española orch. – arr. vln & pf Kreisler
  with J–C. Ambrosini pf   Deutsche Grammophon 135133

FAURÉ

Berceuse, Op. 16 vln & pf
  with P. Barbizet pf   Decca GAG15099
Berceuse, Op. 16 vln & pf
  with J–C. Ambrosini pf   Deutsche Grammophon 135133
Sonata No. 1, in A, Op. 13 vln & pf
  with P. Barbizet pf   HMV ALP1666, FALP420
Sonata No. 1, in A, Op. 13 vln & pf
  with P. Barbizet pf   HMV ASDF856, CVA856,
          FALP856
Sonata No. 2, in e, Op. 108 vln & pf
  with P. Barbizet pf   Decca FAT173138, LXT2810
          Everest LPBR6140, SDBR3140
          London LL909
Sonata No. 2, in e, Op. 108 vln & pf
  with P. Barbizet pf   HMV ASDF856, CVA856,
          FALP856

FRANCK

Sonata in A (1886) vln & pf
  with P. Barbizet pf   HMV ALP1666, FALP420
Sonata in A (1886) vln & pf
  with P. Barbizet pf   Deutsche Grammophon
          LPM39124, SLPM139124

HONEGGER

Sonata (1940) solo vln
  (unaccompanied)   Decca BAT133071, LW50171,
          LXT2827
          London LL762

KREISLER

Caprice viennois, Op. 2 vln & pf
  with J–C. Ambrosini pf   Deutsche Grammophon 135133
Liebesfreud vln & pf
  with J–C. Ambrosini pf   Deutsche Grammophon 135133
Liebesleid vln & pf
  with J–C. Ambrosini pf   Deutsche Grammophon 135133
Rondino on a theme by Beethoven vln & pf
  with J–C. Ambrosini pf   Deutsche Grammophon 135133
Praeludium & Allegro (Pugnani) vln & pf
  with E. Lush pf   AR 13005–1 Decca K2299
                London T5660

LALO

Symphonie espagnole, Op. 21 vln & orch.*
  with Philharmonia Orch. – Susskind   Angel 35769
          Classics for Pleasure CFP107
          HMV ALP1746, ASD314,
          FALP614
Symphonie espagnole, Op. 21 vln & orch.*
  with Orch. National de l'Opéra de
  Monte–Carlo – Klopfenstein   Guilde International du Disque
          SMA2675

LEKEU

Sonata in G (1892) vln & pf
  with P. Barbizet pf   Deutsche Grammophon
          LPM39124, SLPM139124

MASSENET

Thaïs (1894) – opera
  Méditation arr. vln & pf Marsick
  with P. Barbizet pf   Decca GAG15099
  Méditation arr. vln & pf Marsick
  with J–C. Ambrosini pf   Deutsche Grammophon 135133

MENDELSSOHN

Concerto in e, Op. 64 vln & pf
  with Philharmonia Orch. – Silvestri   Angel 35606
          Electrola 1C053–00791, E90896
          HMV ALP1543, ASD278,
          ASDQ5296, CVD1514,
          FALP514, LALP553,
          QALP10218, SXLP30122,
          WALP1543
(6) Songs without words, Op. 62 pf
  No. 1. Song without words No. 25, in G "May breezes" arr. vln & pf
  Kreisler
  with J–C. Ambrosini pf   Deutsche Grammophon 135133

MOZART

Concerto No. 3, in G, K216 vln & orch.
  with Stuttgart Chamber Orch. –
  Münchinger   Decca LW5272, LXT5044
          London LL1172
Concerto No. 4, in D, K218 (cadenzas by Joachim) vln & orch.
  with Paris Conservatory Orch. –
  Vandernoot   HMV ALP1858, ASDF189,
          QIM6344, SQIM6344
          Kristall SMVP8059
          Pathé DTX30227
Concerto No. 5, in A, K219 "Turkish" (cadenzas by Joachim) vln & orch.
  with Paris Conservatory Orch. –
  Vandernoot   HMV ALP1858, ASDF189,
          QIM6344, SQIM6344
          Kristall SMVP8059
          Pathé DTX30227
Concerto No. 6, in E flat, K268 vln & orch.†
  with Stuttgart Chamber Orch. –
  Münchinger   Decca LW50155, LXT5044
          London LL1172
Sonata No. 22, in A, K305 vln & pf
  with P. Barbizet pf   Decca LX3141
Sonata No. 24, in F, K376 vln & pf
  with P. Barbizet pf   Decca LX3141

* Omitting Intermezzo.
† Cadenzas omitted.

NIGG

Concerto (1960) vln & orch.
  with O.R.T.F. Philharmonic Orch. –
Bruck

Deutsche Grammophon
SLPM139171
Heliodor H25058, HS25058

RAVEL

Pavane pour une infante défunte (1899) pf – arr. vln & pf Kochański
  with P. Barbizet pf   Decca GAG15097

Tzigane (Rapsodie de concert) (1924) vln & pf or orch.
  with P. Barbizet pf   Decca GAG15100

Tzigane (Rapsodie de concert) (1924) vln & pf or orch.
  with Belgian National Symphony   Decca BAT133071, LW50171,
Orch. – Sébastian   LXT2827
     London LL762

Tzigane (Rapsodie de concert) (1924) vln & pf or orch.
  with P. Barbizet pf   Electrola E80749, STE80749
     HMV ALP1980, ASD531,
     ASDF769, CVA769, FALP769,
     QALP10374
     Mace M9045, MCS9045

RIMSKY–KORSAKOV

Sadko (1898) – opera
  Chant hindou arr. vln & pf Kreisler
  with J–C. Ambrosini pf   Deutsche Grammophon 135133

RODRIGO

Concerto (1943) vln & orch.
  with Paris Conservatory Orch. –   Decca LXT2678
Enescu   London LL546

SARASATE

(8) Danzas españolas vln & pf
  No. 3. Romanza andaluza, Op. 22, No. 1
  with E. Lush pf   AR 13004–1   Decca K2299
     London T5660

  No. 3. Romanza andaluza, Op. 22, No. 1
  with J–C. Ambrosini pf   Deutsche Grammophon 135133

SCHUBERT

(7) Gesänge (set to Scott's "Lady of the Lake") Op. 52 v & pf
  No. 6. Ave Maria, D839 arr. vln & pf
  with J–C. Ambrosini pf   Deutsche Grammophon 135133

SCHUMANN

(13) Kinderscenen, Op. 15 pf
  No. 7. Träumerei arr. vln & pf Catherine
  with J–C. Ambrosini pf   Deutsche Grammophon 135133

(3) Romances, Op. 94 ob or vln or vlc or cl & pf
  Romance No. 1, in a
  with P. Barbizet pf   Deutsche Grammophon
     LPM18998, SLPM138998

  Romance No. 2, in A
  with P. Barbizet pf   Deutsche Grammophon
     LPM18998, SLPM138998

  Romance No. 3, in a
  with P. Barbizet pf   Deutsche Grammophon
     LPM18998, SLPM138998

Sonata No. 1, in a, Op. 105 vln & pf
  with P. Barbizet pf   Deutsche Grammophon
     LPM18998, SLPM138998

SCHUMANN – *Continued*

Sonata No. 2, in d, Op. 121 vln & pf
  with P. Barbizet pf   Deutsche Grammophon
     LPM18998, SLPM138998

SEMENOFF

Concerto "Double" vln, pf & orch.
  with P. Barbizet pf & orch. – Semenoff   Decca LXT2678
     London LL546

SIBELIUS

Concerto in d, Op. 47 vln & orch.
  with Berlin Philharmonic Orch. –   Deutsche Grammophon
Karajan   LPM18961, SLPM138961

TCHAIKOVSKY

Concerto D, Op. 35 vln & orch.
  with Philharmonia Orch. – Silvestri   Angel 35606
     Electrola E90896
     HMV ALP1543, ASD278,
     ASDQ5296, CVD1514,
     FALP514, LALP553,
     QALP10218, SXLP30122,
     WALP1543

Concerto in D, Op. 35 vln & orch.
  with Berlin Philharmonic Orch. –   Deutsche Grammophon
Karajan   LPM39028, SLPM139028

Pierre FERRIT

PURCELL

(10) Sonatas, Z802/11 (1697), 4 parts – 2 vlns & c
  Sonata No. 9, in F, Z810 "Golden Sonata"
  with J. Pasquier vln, R. Gerlin hpsi &   L'Anthologie Sonore 22
E. Pasquier vlc

Luigi FERRO (1903–)

MARCHESELLI

Concerto No. 1, in D vln, ob, vlc & strs
  with R. Zanfini ob, B. Mazzacurati vlc   HMV ALP1641
& Virtuosi di Roma – Fasano

TARTINI

Concerto in E, D53 (C84) vln & orch.
  with Virtuosi di Roma – Fasano   Brunswick AXTL1004
     Decca DL9572, UAT273091
     Fonit LP1006

VALENTINI

(12) Concerti, Op. 6 orch.
  Concerto No. 3, in C
  with R. Zanfini ob & Virtuosi di Roma   HMV ALP1344, FALP436
– Fasano

VIVALDI

(12) Concerti, Op. 3 "L'Estro armonico" var. cbns & strs
  Concerto No. 2, in g, P.326 (F.IV, No. 8) 2 vlns, strs & c
  with G. Mozzato vln, B. Mazzacurati   Brunswick AXA4505
vlc & Virtuosi di Roma – Fasano   Decca DL9729, UAT273589

VIVALDI – *Continued*

Concerto No. 2, in g, P.326 (F.IV, No. 8) 2 vlns, strs & c
with G. Mozzato vln, B. Mazzacurati   HMV ALP1809, ASD391
vlc & Virtuosi di Roma – Fasano

Concerto No. 7, in F, P.249 (F.IV, No. 9) 4 vlns, strs & c
with E. Malanotte vln, F. Gulli vln, B.   HMV ALP1810, ASD392
Benvenuti vln & Virtuosi di Roma –
Fasano

Concerto No. 9, in D, P.147 (F.I, No. 178) vln, strs & c
with Virtuosi di Roma – Fasano   HMV ALP1811, ASD393

Concerto No. 10, in b, P.148 (F.IV, No. 10) 4 vlns, strs & c
with A. Gramegna vln, A. Pelliccia   Cetra BB25291/2
vln, E. Malanotte vln & Rome
Collegium Musicum – Fasano

Concerto No. 10, in b, P.148 (F.IV, No. 10) 4 vlns, strs & c
with E. Malanotte vln, A. Stefanato   HMV ALP1811, ASD393
vln, F. Gulli vln & Virtuosi di Roma –
Fasano

Concerto No. 11, in d, P.250 (F.IV, No. 11) 2 vlns, vlc, strs & c
with E. Malanotte vln, B. Mazzacurati   Angel 45030
vlc & Virtuosi di Roma – Fasano   Electrola E70380
    HMV ALP1629, WBLP552

Concerto No. 11, in d, P.250 (F.IV, No. 11) 2 vlns, vlc, strs & c
with E. Malanotte vln, B. Mazzacurati   HMV ALP1811, ASD393
vlc & Virtuosi di Roma – Fasano

Concerto No. 12, in E, P.240 (F.I, No. 179) vln, strs & c
with Virtuosi di Roma – Fasano   Brunswick AXA4505
    Decca DL9729, UAT273589

Concerto No. 12, in E, P.240 (F.I, No. 179) vln, strs & c
with Virtuosi di Roma – Fasano   HMV ALP1811, ASD393

(12) Concerti, Op. 8 (1725) "Il Cimento dell'Armonia e dell' Invenzione"
(nos. 1/4: Le quattro Stagioni) vln & strs
Concerto No. 1, in E, F.I, No. 22 "La Primavera"
with Virtuosi di Roma – Fasano   Brunswick AXTL1032
Concerto No. 1, in E, F.I, No. 22 "La Primavera"
with Virtuosi di Roma – Fasano   Electrola E90099, STE90099
    HMV ALP1234, ASDW306,
    WALP1234
Concerto No. 1, in E, F.I, No. 22 "La Primavera"
with Virtuosi di Roma – Fasano   Angel 35877, ASC5038, (in set
    3611)
    HMV ALP1786, ASD367
Concerto No. 3, in F, F.I, No. 24 "L'Autunno"
with Virtuosi di Roma – Fasano   Brunswick AXTL1032
Concerto No. 3, in F, F.I, No. 24 "L'Autunno"
with Virtuosi di Roma – Fasano   Electrola E90099, STE90099
    HMV ALP1234, ASDW306,
    WALP1234
Concerto No. 3, in F, F.I, No. 24 "L'Autunno"
with Virtuosi di Roma – Fasano   Angel 35877, (in set 3611),
    ASC5038
    HMV ALP1786, ASD367

Concerto in D "Accademico formato" vln, ob, vlc, strs & c
with R. Zanfini ob, B. Mazzacurati vlc   Angel 45028
& Virtuosi di Roma – Fasano

VIVALDI – *Continued*

Concerto in C, P.14 (F.I, No. 13) (Op. 54, No. 3) "Per la SS. Assunzione di
Maria Vergine" vln, strs & c
with Virtuosi di Roma – Fasano   Electrola E70034
    HMV BLP1042, FBLP1054,
    QBLP5019, WBLP1042

Mikhail FICHTENHOLZ (1920–   )

ALBÉNIZ

Ibéria – Book I (1906/9) pf
No. 6. Triana arr. vln & pf Fichtenholz
with L. Fichtenholz pf   Mezhdunarodnaya Kniga
    D013337/8

BACH

(3) Sonatas & 3 Partitas, BWV1001/6 solo vln
Sonata No. 2, in A, BWV1003
(unaccompanied)   Mezhdunarodnaya Kniga
    D019155

Partita No. 3, in E, BWV1006
(unaccompanied)   Mezhdunarodnaya Kniga
    D019156

Sonata in G, BWV1021 vln & clav
with N. Gureyeva org   Mezhdunarodnaya Kniga
    D023503

Sonata in e, BWV1023 vln & c
with N. Gureyeva org   Mezhdunarodnaya Kniga
    D023503

Sonata in c, BWV1024 vln & c
with N. Gureyeva org   Mezhdunarodnaya Kniga
    D023504

(4) Suites, BWV1066/9 strs & c
Suite No. 3, in D: Air (2nd mvt) BWV1068 2 obs, 3 tpts, drms, strs & c
– arr. vln & pf as "Air on the G–string" by Wilhelmj
with N. Gureyeva org   Mezhdunarodnaya Kniga
    D023504

BIZET

(L') Arlesienne (Suite No. 2) (1872) orch.
No. 7. Menuet arr. vln & pf Fichtenholz
with L. Fichtenholz pf   Mezhdunarodnaya Kniga
    D013337/8

FICHTENHOLZ

Paraphrase on themes of Waltzes by Johann Strauss II vln & pf
with L. Fichtenholz pf   Mezhdunarodnaya Kniga
    D013337/8

MOZART

Sonata No. 26, in B flat, K378 vln & pf
with L. Fichtenholz pf   Mezhdunarodnaya Kniga
    D013337/8

SCARLATTI

Sonata in G, L487 "Presto" hpsi – arr. vln & pf Fichtenholz
with L. Fichtenholz pf   Mezhdunarodnaya Kniga
    D013337/8

SCRIABIN

(12) Etudes, Op. 8 pf
Etude No. 11, in B flat arr. vln & pf Fichtenholz
with L. Fichtenholz pf   Mezhdunarodnaya Kniga
D013337/8

(8) Etudes, Op. 42 pf
Etude No. 7, in F sharp arr. vln & pf Fichtenholz
with L. Fichtenholz pf   Mezhdunarodnaya Kniga
D013337/8

Samuel FIDELMANN*

BACH

(3) Sonatas & 3 Partitas, BWV1001/6 solo vln
Partita No. 3, in E, BWV1006: **Gavotte** (3rd mvt)
(unaccompanied)   Anker E9193 (using a Guarneri)

Partita No. 3, in E: Gavotte (3rd mvt) BWV1006
(unaccompanied)   Anker E9421 (using a Guarneri)

DRDLA

Serenade No. 1, in A vln & pf
with piano   Anker E9192 (using the
"Crown" Stradivari)

FIBICH

Images, Impressions & Souvenirs, Op. 41 pf
No. 14. Poem (from "Souvenirs", Part IV) arr. vln & pf Kubelík
with piano   Anker E9408 (using the
"Sibirische" Stradivari)

PAGANINI

Nel cor più non mi sento "Sonata appassionata con variazioni" (on the aria
from Paisiello's opera "La bella molinara") Op. 38 (1820 or 1821) solo
vln
(unaccompanied)   Anker E9421 (using the
"Sibirische" Stradivari)

PIERNÉ

Sérénade in A, Op. 7 (1875) pf – arr. vln & pf Haddock
with piano   Anker E9408 (using a Stainer)

RAFF

(6) Pieces, Op. 85 vln & pf
No. 3. Cavatina in D
with piano   Anker E9192 (using a Stradivari
of 1690)

VIEUXTEMPS

Ballade & Polonaise in G, Op. 38 vln & pf
Ballade
with piano   Anker E9193 (using the
"Crown" Stradivari)

* playing on various famous violins.

Joan FIELD

BEETHOVEN

Romance No. 1, in G, Op. 40 vln & orch.
with Berlin Symphony Orch. – Rother   Telefunken C047–91082 GMA51,
LT43048, SLT43048, TC8046,
TCS18046

Romance No. 2, in F, Op. 50 vln & orch.
with Berlin Symphony Orch. – Rother   Telefunken C047–91082 GMA51,
LT43048, SLT43048, TC8046,
TCS18046

BRUCH

Concerto No. 1, in g, Op. 26 vln & orch.*
with Berlin Symphony Orch. – Albert   Telefunken C047–91084 GMA19,
LT43016, NT196, SLT43016,
STW30231, TCS18031, TW30231

DVOŘÁK

Concerto in a, Op. 53 vln & orch.
with Berlin Philharmonic Orch. –
Rother   Telefunken GMA51, LT43048,
SLT43048, TC8046, TCS18046

IVES

Sonata No. 1 (1903/8) vln & pf
with L. Mittman pf   Lyrichord LL17
Sonata No. 2 (1910) vln & pf
with L. Mittman pf   Lyrichord LL17

MENDELSSOHN

Concerto in e, Op. 64 vln & orch.†
with Berlin Symphony Orch. – Albert   Telefunken C047–91084 GMA44,
LT43040, NT196, SLT43040,
TC8044, TCS18044

MOZART

Concerto No. 5, in A, K219 "Turkish" vln & orch.
with Berlin Philharmonic Orch. –
Albert   Telefunken C047–91082 GMA44,
LT43040, NT259, SLT43030,
TC8044, TCS18044

SPOHR

Concerto No. 8, in a, Op. 47 "Gesangsscene" vln & orch.
with Berlin Symphony Orch. – Albert   Telefunken GMA19, TCS18031

Anton FIETZ (1926–)

BACH

Sonata in C, BWV1037 2 vlns & c
with P. Rybar vln & T. Sack hpsi   Concert Hall G15

CORELLI

(12) Sonatas, Op. 1 2 vlns & c
Sonata No. 9, in G
with P. Rybar vln, H. Andrae hpsi &   Concert Hall CHC29
A. Tusa gamba

* Adagio or 2nd mvt is also on Telefunken SUV404 & UV404.
† Andante or 2nd mvt is also on the Telefunken SUV404 & UV404.

HANDEL

(7) Sonatas, Op. 5 (1739) 2 vlns & c
Sonata No. 4, in G
with P. Rybar vln, H. Andrae hpsi &   Concert Hall (set G13)
H. Boschi vlc

MANFREDINI

(12) Concerti, Op. 3 (1718) 2 vlns, strs & c
Concerto No. 12, in C: Pastorale (1st mvt) "Christmas Concerto"
with L. Kaufman vln & Concert Hall   Concert Hall F17
String Ensemble – Dahinden

TELEMANN

Concerto in F, T.II, No. 3 3 vlns, strs & c
with L. Kaufman vln, P. Rybar vln &   Concert Hall DL12 (set D12)
Concert Hall String Orch. – Swoboda

VIVALDI

(12) Concerti, Op. 3 "L'Estro armonico" var. cbns & strs
Concerto No. 10, in b, P.148 (F.IV, No. 10) 4 vlns, strs & c
with L. Kaufman vln, P. Rybar vln,   Concert Hall E2
G. Piraccini vln & Winterthur
Chamber Orch. – Dahinden

Hermanos FIGUEROA

BRÉTON

(4) Escenas Andaluzas pf
No. 2. Polo gitano arr. vln & pf
with piano   Columbia AG7034

SCHUBERT

(7) Gesänge (set to Scott's "Lady of the Lake") Op. 52 v & pf
No. 6. Ave Maria, D839 arr. vln & pf Wilhelmj
with piano   Columbia AG7034

José C. FIGUEROA (1905–   )

BACH

(3) Sonatas & 3 Partitas, BWV1001/6 solo vln
Sonata No. 1, in g, BWV1001
(unaccompanied)   New Records Incorporated
NRLP408

Partita No. 1, in b, BWV1002
(unaccompanied)   New Records Incorporated
NRLP410

Sonata No. 2, in a, BWV1003
(unaccompanied)   New Records Incorporated
NRLP408

Partita No. 2, in d, BWV1004
(unaccompanied)   New Records Incorporated
NRLP410

Sonata No. 3, in C, BWV1005
(unaccompanied)   New Records Incorporated
NRLP411

Partita No. 3, in E, BWV1006
(unaccompanied)   New Records Incorporated
NRLP411

FRANCESCHINI

Trio Sonata in B flat 2 vlns & c
with J. Margolis vln, J. Saunders vlc &   New Records Incorporated
F. Valenti hpsi   NRLP2006
Society for the Preservation of
the American Musical Heritage
MIA113

PIERNÉ

Sonata in D, Op. 36 (1900) vln & pf
with P. Miguel pf   New Records Incorporated
NRLP401

REGER

Serenade in D, Op. 77a fl, vln & vla
with S. Caratelli fl, & di Piazza vla   New Records Incorporated
NRLP202

Serenade in G, Op. 141a fl, vln & vla
with S. Caratelli fl & di Piazza vla   New Records Incorporated
NRLP202

Trio in a, Op. 77b vln, vla & vlc
with di Piazza vla & J. Saunders vlc   New Records Incorporated
NRLP202

Trio in d, Op. 141b vln, vla & vlc
with di Piazza vla & J. Saunders vlc   New Records Incorporated
NRLP202

SARASATE

Jota aragonesa, Op. 27 vln & pf
with M. Figueroa pf   Victor 4550

STRAUSS, R.

Quartet in c, Op. 13 pf, vln, vla & vlc
with B. Ségall pf, F. Brieff vla & G.   New Records Incorporated
Ricci vlc   NRLP201

TURINA

Sonata No. 2, Op. 82 (1934) "Sonata española" vln & pf
with P. Miguel pf   New Records Incorporated
NRLP401

VIVALDI

(12) Sonatas, Op. 2 (1712) vln & c
Sonata No. 2, in A F.XIII, No. 30 (ed. David)
with M. Figueroa pf   Victor 4551

Simonne FILON

ALBÉNIZ

España (6 Feuilles d'album) Op. 165 pf
No. 2. Tango in D arr. vln & pf Kreisler
with piano   Polydor 524288

CHAMINADE

Sérénade espagnole pf – arr. vln & pf Kreisler
with piano   Polydor 522840

CHOPIN

(12) Etudes, Op. 10 pf
No. 3 Etude No. 3, in E arr. vln & pf Stone & Seidel
with piano   Polydor 522841

CUI

Kaleidoscope, Op. 50 vln & pf
  No. 5. Berceuse russe
  with piano   Polydor 522839

DEBUSSY

(La) Plus que lente – valse (1910) pf – arr. vln & pf Roques
  with piano   Polydor 522839

DVOŘÁK

(8) Humoresques, Op. 101 pf
  No. 7 Humoresque No. 7, in G flat arr. vln & pf "in G" Kreisler
  with piano   Polydor 522840

KREISLER

Caprice viennois, Op. 2 vln & pf
  with piano   Polydor 522840

LEMAIRE

Dansez Marquise vln & pf
  with piano   Polydor 522838

NEVIN

(The) Rosary (1898) v & pf – arr. vln & pf
  with piano   Polydor 524017

PUCCINI

(La) Bohème (1896) – opera
  Quando me'n vo soletta "Musetta's waltz song" arr. vln & pf Filon
  with piano   Polydor 522841

SAINT-SAËNS

Havanaise, Op. 83 vln & orch.
  with piano   Polydor 516591

SARASATE

Zigeunerweisen, Op. 20 vln & pf or orch.
  with M. Sohet pf   5715/6 BKP   Decca PO5103
                                 Polydor 10076, 522415

SCHMIDT

Désolance vln & pf
  with piano   Polydor 524017

SCHMIT

Emprise (Habañera) vln & pf
  with piano   Polydor 524288

THOMÉ

Simple aveu, Op. 25 pf – arr. vln & pf
  with piano   Polydor 522838

Ursula FIORITO

BERTHEAUME

(2) Sinfonia concertantes, Op. 6 (1787) 2 vlns & orch.
  Sinfonia concertante No. 1, in G
  with H. Kempler vln & Dresden   Baroque BU1806
  Chamber orch.

A. FISBERG

DRDLA

Souvenir vln & pf
  with piano   Silvertone 2109

RICE

Dear old pal of mine (1918) v & pf – arr. vln & pf
  with piano   Silvertone 2109

Jascha FISCHBERG

DRDLA

Serenade No. 1, in A vln & pf
  with piano   Dacapo 30, E4060
Souvenir vln & pf
  with piano   Dacapo 155, E4062

DRIGO

(Les) Millions d'Arlequin (1900) – ballet orch.
  Sérénade arr. vln & pf Auer
  with piano   Dacapo 155, E4061

FISCHBERG

Monte Cristo Waltz vln & pf
  with piano   Dacapo 156, E4066

GOUNOD

Ave Maria (Méditation on Bach's "Prelude No. 1, in C" from Book I of
  "Das Wohltemperirte Clavier") arr. vln & pf
  with piano   Dacapo 29, E4063

MOZART

Divertimento No. 17, in D, K334 2 hrns & strs
  Minuet (3rd mvt) arr. vln & pf Burmester
  with piano   Dacapo 156, E4065

TCHAIKOVSKY

Quartet No. 1, in D, Op. 11 2 vlns, vla & vlc
  Andante cantabile (2nd mvt) arr. vln & pf Kreisler
  with piano   Dacapo 30, E4059

WIENIAWSKI

(2) Mazurkas, Op. 19 vln & pf
  No. 1 Mazurka No. 1, in G "Obertass"
  with piano   Dacapo 29, E4064

Ethel FLEMING

BOROWSKI

Adoration (1903) vln & pf
  with M. Fleming pf   7181   Edison Diamond Disc 80538

MASSENET

Thaïs (1894) – opera
  Méditation arr. vln & pf Marsick
  with R. Gayler pf   6201   Edison Diamond Disc 80509

Carl FLESCH (1873–1944)

ANONYMOUS

(The) Foggy, foggy dew American folksong – arr. vln & pf Alexander
with H. Kaufman pf   9353   Edison Diamond Disc 82327

BACH

Concerto in d, BWV1043 2 vlns, strs & c
with J. Szigeti vln   CAX8060/3–1   Columbia 69109/10D, (set X90),
& orch. – Goehr   C15705/6, (set J12),
                                  GOX10887/8, LOX360/1,
                                  LX659/60
                                  HMV HQM1127

(3) Sonatas & 3 Partitas, BWV1001/6 solo vln
Partita No. 1, in b: Sarabande (5th mvt) BWV1002
(unaccompanied)   Odeon RX67780

BOHM

(6) Pieces, Op. 314 vln & pf
No. 2. Cavatina in D
with piano   Edison Diamond Disc 82348

BRANDL

(Der) Liebe Augustin – operetta
Du alter Stefansturm arr. vln & pf as "The old refrain" by Kreisler
with W. Liachowsky pf   9358   Edison Diamond Disc 82321

DAWES

Melody in A (1912) vln & pf
with piano   Edison Diamond Disc 82346

DOBROVEN

Melody hébraïque vln & pf
with piano   HMV EJ438

DVOŘÁK

(8) Slavonic Dances, Op. 46 pf duet; orch.
No. 2. Slavonic dance No. 2, in e arr. vln & pf "in g" Kreisler
with K. Ruhrseitz pf   Edison Diamond Disc 80878
No. 7. Slavonic dance No. 7, in c arr. vln & pf
with W. Liachowsky pf   9352   Edison Diamond Disc 82311

ERNST

Élégie in c, Op. 10 vln & pf
with piano   Edison Diamond Disc 82348

FALLA

(7) Canciones populares españolas (1914) v & pf
No. 1. El paño moruno arr. vln & pf Kochański
with piano   Edison Diamond Disc 80894
No. 4. Jota arr. vln & pf Kochański
with piano   Edison Diamond Disc 80894
No. 4. Jota arr. vln & pf Kochański
with piano   HMV EW68

FAURÉ

Berceuse, Op. 16 vln & pf
with piano   258 av   Polydor 65983, 68059
Berceuse, Op. 16 vln & pf
with piano   HMV EW68

FIORILLO

(36) Étude–Caprices, Op. 3 solo vln
Caprice No. 28, in D (Allegro assai) arr. vln & pf Randegger
with W. Liachowsky pf   9357   Edison Diamond Disc 82313

FRANCK

Panis angelicus (1872) t, org, hp, vlc & cbs – arr. v, vln & orch.
with P. De Haan–Manifarges s & orch. Odeon 30263

GÄRTNER

Aus Wien pf – arr. vln & pf Kreisler
with H. Kaufman pf   Edison Diamond Disc 82330

GRIEG

(4) Norwegian Dances, Op. 35 (1881) pf duet; orch.
No. 2. Norwegian dance No. 2, in A arr. vln & pf Flesch
with K. Ruhrseitz pf   Edison Diamond Disc 82349
No. 2. Norwegian dance No. 2, in A arr. vln & pf Flesch
with piano   Polydor 62471, 67532

HANDEL

(The) Choice of Hercules (1750) – secular chorale
There the brisk, sparkling nectar drain arr. vln & pf as "March" by Flesch
with R. Bauman pf   18324   Edison Diamond Disc 80889
There the brisk, sparkling nectar drain arr. vln & pf as "March" by Flesch
with piano   HMV EW67
Solomon (1748) – oratorio
No. 40. Beneath the vine arr. vln & pf as "Pastorale" by Flesch
with R. Bauman pf   Edison Diamond 80893
(15) Sonatas, Op. 1 (?1731) fl or vln & c
Sonata No. 13, in D: Allegro (2nd mvt) vln IV
with piano   Odeon RX67782
Sonata No. 14, in A vln V
with F. Dyck pf   Polydor 67178
Te Deum, Dettingen (1743) – cantata
No. 17. Gebet ('Verlieh uns Herr, zu schirmen ...) arr. vln & pf as "Prayer" by Flesch
with R. Bauman pf   18322   Edison Diamond Disc 80889
No. 17. Gebet ('Verlieh uns Herr, zu schirmen...) arr. vln & pf as "Prayer" by Flesch
with piano   HMV EW67

HEUBERGER

(Der) Opernball, Op. 40 (1898) – operetta
Im chambre séparée arr. vln & pf as "Midnight bells" by Kreisler
with H. Kaufman pf   Edison Diamond Disc 82330

HUBAY

(14) Scènes de la Csárda vln & pf
No. 4. Hejre Kati, Op. 32
with R. Bauman pf   Edison Diamond Disc 47001*

KREISLER

Rondino on a theme by Beethoven vln & pf
with K. Ruhrseitz pf   Edison Diamond Disc 80865
Rondino on a theme by Beethoven vln & pf
with piano   Polydor 65984, 68058

* Electrical recording.

LOTTI

Arminio (1714) – pasticcio
Pur dicesti arr. vln & pf as "Aria in A" by Flesch
with R. Bauman pf   Edison Diamond Disc 80893
Pur dicesti arr. vln & pf as "Aria in A" by Flesch
with piano   257 av   Polydor 65983, 68057
Pur dicesti arr. vln & pf as "Aria in A" by Flesch
with piano   Odeon RX67780

MARTINI, G.B.

(12) Sonatas, Op. 2 (1714) hpsi
Sonata No. 12, in F: Gavotte arr. vln & pf Burmester
with piano   Odeon RX67787

MENDELSSOHN

(6) Songs without words, Op. 62 pf
No. 1. Song without words No. 25, in G "May breezes" arr. vln & pf
Kreisler
with W. Liachowsky pf   9358   Edison Diamond Disc 82321

MOZART

Sonata No. 26, in B flat, K378 vln & pf
with F. Dyck pf   Polydor 67179/80

PAGANINI

(24) Caprices, Op. 1 (1801/7) solo vln
Caprice No. 13, in B flat arr. vln & pf
with piano   HMV EJ438

PIERNÉ

Sérénade in A, Op. 7 (1875) pf – arr. vln & pf
with piano   Odeon 2060, 30383, 8004X,
     RX67778

RUBINSTEIN

(6) Soirées de Saint–Pétersbourg, Op. 44 pf
No. 1. Romance in E flat arr. vln & pf Wieniawski
with piano   Edison Diamond Disc 82346

SARASATE

(8) Danzas españolas vln & pf
No. 1. Malagueña, Op. 21, No. 1
with H. Kaufman pf   9354   Edison Diamond Disc 82327

SCHUBERT

(7) Gesänge (set to Scott's "Lady of the Lake") Op. 52 v & pf
No. 6. Ave Maria, D839 arr. vln & pf Wilhelmj
with piano   2946   Edison Diamond Disc 82063

SCHUMANN

(13) Kinderscenen, Op. 15 pf
No. 7. Träumerei arr. vln & pf
with piano   Odeon 2060, 30383, 8004X,
     RX67779

SMETANA

From my Homeland (1878) vln & pf
No. 2. Andantino
with K. Ruhrseitz pf   Edison Diamond Disc 80865

TARTINI

(12) Sonatas, Op. 1 (1734) vln & c
Sonata No. 10, in g: Largo (3rd mvt) "Didone abbandonata"
with piano   Odeon 8005X, RX67787
Sonata in g vln & c
Larghetto affettuoso (1st mvt)
with piano   Odeon 8006X, RX67792

TCHAIKOVSKY

Concerto in D, Op. 35 vln & orch.
Canzonetta (2nd mvt)
with piano   Edison Diamond Disc 80878
Sérénade mélancolique in b flat, Op. 26 vln & orch. – arr. vln & pf
Wilhelmj
with piano   Polydor 65984, 68060

TENAGLIA

Have pity, sweet eyes v & c – arr. vln & pf as "Aria in f" by Ries
with piano   Odeon 8006X RX67791

TITL

Serenade arr. vln & pf Flesch
with W. Liachowsky pf   9355   Edison Diamond Disc 82313

VIEUXTEMPS

(6) Morceaux de salon, Op. 22 vln & pf
No. 3. Rêverie
with R. Bauman pf   Edison Diamond Disc 47001*
(3) Salonstücke, Op. 32 vln & pf
No. 2. Rondino
with H. Samuels pf   2943   Edison Diamond Disc 82072

WEBER

(6) Sonatas, Op. 10 (J99/104) (1810) vln & pf
Sonata No. 1, in F: Romanze (2nd mvt) J99 arr. as "Larghetto" by
Kreisler
with W. Liachowsky pf   9351   Edison Diamond Disc 82311
Sonata No. 1, in F: Romanze (2nd mvt) J99 arr. as "Larghetto" by
Kreisler
with piano   Polydor 62471, 67531

WIENIAWSKI

Légende, Op. 17 vln & pf or orch.
with K. Ruhrseitz pf   Edison Daimond Disc 82349
(2) Mazurkas, Op. 19 vln & pf
No. 2. Mazurka No. 2, in D "Dudziarz"
with H. Samuels pf   2939   Edison Diamond Disc 82072
No. 2. Mazurka No. 2, in D "Dudziarz"
with piano   Odeon 30382, 8005X, RX67788

Joyce FLISSLER (1929–)

PORTER

Sonata No. 2, in a (1929) vln & pf
with H. Wingreen pf   MK 1571
     Mezhdunarodnaya Kniga D4267,
     D07418

* Electrical recording.

PROKOFIEV

Sonata No. 1, in f, Op. 80 vln & pf
  with H. Wingreen pf

             MK 1571
             Mezhdunarodnaya Kniga
             D4264/5, D07417/8

FLORI

ALBÉNIZ

España (6 Feuilles d'album) Op. 165 pf
  No. 2. Tango in D arr. vln & pf Kreisler
  with piano
             HMV GW171

Gösta FOGELBERG

ANONYMOUS

Minuet unid – arr. vln & pf K. Edgardt
  with K. Edgardt pf   W 44023   Columbia 8416

KREISLER

Andantino (Padre Martini) vln & pf
  with K. Edgardt pf   W 44024   Columbia 8416

Béla FÖLDES

SCHMID

Wunderschöner Rosengarten pf – arr. vln & pf
  with piano   Favorite 1–14342

ZERKOVITZ

Schwalbe, wu fliegst du bin v & pf – arr. vln & pf
  with piano   Favorite 1–14343

Patrice FONTANAROSA (1943–)

CORELLI

(12) Sonatas, Op. 5 vln & c
  Sonata No. 12, in d "La Follia" arr. vln & gtr Dintrich
  with M. Dintrich gtr   Classic 991025

DEBUSSY

Sonata No. 3, in g (1917) vln & pf
  with D. Renault pf   Société Française de Productions
                  Phonographiques CVS20001

ENESCU

Sonata No. 3, in a, Op. 25 "In the popular Rumanian style" vln & pf
  with D. Renault pf   Société Française de Productions
                  Phonographiques CVS20001

FALLA

(El) Amor Brujo (1915) – ballet m–s & orch.
  No. 7. Danza rituel del fuego arr. vln & pf Kochański
  with M. Dintrich gtr   Classic 990009
(La) Vida breve (1913) – opera
  Danza española orch. – arr. vln & pf Kreisler
  with M. Dintrich gtr   Classic 990009

GIULIANI

Divertimento gtr & vln
  with M. Dintrich gtr   Classic 991025

GRANADOS

(12) Danzas españolas, Op. 37 (1893) pf
  No. 5. Danza española No. 5, in e "Andaluza" arr. vln & pf Kreisler
  with M. Dintrich gtr   Classic 990009

IBERT

Entr'acte fl or vln & gtr
  with M. Dintrich gtr   Classic 990009

LOEILLET, J.B.

(12) Sonatas, Op. 2 1/6: 2 vlns & c – 7/9: 2 fls & c – 10/12: ob, fl & c
  Sonata No. 2, in F
  with J. Ponticelli vln & J–L. Petit hpsi Decca 174141, SMD1513,
                                    SXL20141

  Sonata No. 5, in c
  with J. Ponticelli vln & J–L. Petit hpsi Decca 174141, SMD1513,
                                    SXL20141

  Sonata No. 6, in c
  with J. Ponticelli vln & J–L. Petit hpsi Decca 174141, SMD1513,
                                    SXL20141

  Sonata No. 9, in g
  with J. Ponticelli vln & J–L. Petit hpsi Decca 174141, SMD1513,
                                    SXL20141

Suite de danses vln & c – arr. vln & gtr
  with M. Dintrich gtr   Classic 991025

MOZART

Concerto No. 3, in G, K216 vln & orch.
  with Cologne Chamber Orch. – Müller Classic 991084
  –Brühl
Sinfonia concertante in E flat, K364 vln, vla & orch.
  with B. Pasquier vla & Cologne   Classic 991084
  Chamber Orch. – Müller–Brühl

PAGANINI

Sonata concertante in A, Op. 61 (1804) vln & gtr
  with M. Dintrich gtr   Classic 990009

SARASATE

(8) Danzas españolas vln & pf
  No. 3. Romanza andaluza, Op. 22, No. 1
  with M. Dintrich gtr   Classic 990009

SCHEIDLER

Sonata in D vln & gtr
  with M. Dintrich gtr   Classic 991025

VIVALDI

(12) Sonatas, Op. 2 (1712) vln & c
  Sonata No. 1, in g, F.XIII, No. 29
  with M. Dintrich gtr   Classic 990009

Léon FONTOVA (1875–)

WIENIAWSKI

(2) Mazurkas, Op. 19 vln & pf
No. 1. Mazurka No. 1, in G "Obertass"
with piano   Odeon 196131

Sverre FORCHHAMMER

VIVALDI

(12) Concerti, Op. 3 "L'Estro armonico" var. cbns & strs
Concerto No. 11, in d, P.250 (F.IV, No. 11) 2 vlns, vlc, strs & c
with E. Telmányi vln, J.   2561/4 D   Tono L28000/1
Friisholm vlc & Telmányi Chamber
Orch. – Telmányi

P. FÖRSTER

ANONYMOUS

Heart's confession v & pf – arr. vln & pf *
with piano   Scala 878

(A) Summer's night v & pf – arr. vln & pf *
with piano   Scala 394

BERLIN

Rememb'ring (Topsy & Eva) (1923) v & pf – arr. vln & pf
with piano   Scala 394

BOND

(A) Perfect day (1910) v & pf – arr. vln & cel
with K. Edmunds cel   Scala 894

de CURTIS

Torna a Sorrento v & pf – arr. vln & pf
with piano   Scala 1587

DRDLA

Souvenir vln & pf
with piano   Scala 485

HOLLMAN

Chanson d'amour v & pf – arr. vln & pf
with piano   Scala 878

LOHR

Little grey home in the west (1911) v & pf – arr. vln & pf
with piano   Scala 527

RUBINSTEIN

(2) Melodies, Op. 3 pf
No. 1. Melody in F arr. vln & pf Wilhelmj
with piano   Scala 485

SILÉSU

(A) Little love, a little kiss (1912) v & pf – arr. vln & pf
with piano   Scala 527

* Composers unidentified.

WOOD

Love's garden of roses v & pf – arr. vln & cel
with K. Edmunds cel   Scala 894

Jean FOURNIER (1913–)

ABACO

(12) Sonatas, Op. 3 (1714) 2 vlns & c
Sonata No. 2, in F
with J. Pasquier vln, E. Pasquier vlc &   L'Anthologie Sonore 46
R. Gerlin hpsi   Haydn Society AS13, HSLP13

ALBÉNIZ

España (6 Feuilles d'album) Op. 165 pf
No. 2. Tango in D arr. vln & pf Kreisler
with A. Collard pf   Vega C30A38

BACH, J.C.

(6) Quintets, Op. 11 (1772/7) (T.P 303/4) fl, ob, vln, vla & c
Quintet No. 6, in D
with G. Crunelle fl, L. Gromer ob, P.   L'Anthologie Sonore 50
Villain vla & P. Fournier vlc

BEETHOVEN

(3) Sonatas, Op. 12 vln & pf
No. 1. Sonata No. 1, in D
with G. Doyen pf   Westminster WL5176,
                             XWN18418

No. 2. Sonata No. 2, in A
with G. Doyen pf   Westminster WL5272,
                             XWN18418

No. 3. Sonata No. 3, in E flat
with G. Doyen pf   Westminster WL5247,
                             XWN18418

Sonata No. 4, in a, Op. 23 vln & pf
with G. Doyen pf   Westminster WL5164,
                             XWN18419

Sonata No. 5, in F, Op. 24 "Spring" vln & pf
with G. Doyen pf   Westminster WL5247,
                             XWN18419

(3) Sonatas, Op. 30 vln & pf
No. 1. Sonata No. 6, in A
with G. Doyen pf   Westminster WL5164,
                             XWN18420

No. 2. Sonata No. 7, in c
with G. Doyen pf   Westminster WL5292,
                             XWN18419

No. 3. Sonata No. 8, in G
with G. Doyen pf   Westminster WL5292,
                             XWN18419

Sonata No. 9, in A, Op. 47 "Kreutzer" vln & pf
with G. Doyen pf   Westminster WL5272,
                             XWN18421

Sonata No. 10, in G, Op. 96 vln & pf
with G. Doyen pf   Westminster WL5176,
                             XWN18421

(3) Trios, Op. 1 pf, vln & vlc
No. 1. Trio No. 1, in E flat
with P. Badura–Skoda pf & A. Janigro   Westminster W9007, XWN18232
vlc

BEETHOVEN – *Continued*

No. 3. Trio No. 3, in c
with P. Badura–Skoda pf & A. Janigro   Westminster W9006, XWN18030
vlc

Trio in B flat, Op. 11 cl, vlc & pf
with P. Badura–Skoda pf & A. Janigro   Westminster W9006, XWN18030
vlc

(2) Trios, Op. 70 pf, vln & vlc
No. 1. Trio No. 4, in D "Ghost"
with P. Badura–Skoda pf & A. Janigro   Westminster W9007, XWN18232
vlc

Trio No. 6, in B flat, Op. 97 "Archduke" pf, vln & vlc
with P. Badura–Skoda pf & A. Janigro   Heliodor 478060
vlc   Nixa WLP5131, WLP20018
                                        Westminster WL5131,
                                        XWN18270
                                        Whitehall WH20039

BLOCH

Baal Shem (3 Pictures of Chassidic Life) (1923) vln & pf
No 2. Nigun (Improvisation)
with A. Collard pf   Vega C30A32

BRAHMS

Concerto in a, Op. 102 "Double" vln, vlc & orch.
with A. Janigro vlc & Vienna State   Heliodor 476011
Opera Orch. – Scherchen   Nixa WLP5117, WLP20019
                                        Vega 19002
                                        Westminster W9712, WL5117,
                                        XWN18268

Trio No. 1, in B, Op. 8 pf, vln & vlc
with P. Badura–Skoda pf & A. Janigro   Heliodor 479042
vlc   Nixa WLP5237
                                        Vega C30A9
                                        Westminster PWN351, W9049,
                                        WL5237, XWN18450

CLÉRAMBAULT

Léandre et Héro (1710) – cantata
with M. Angelici s, G. Crunelle fl, V.   L'Anthologie Sonore 105/6
Clerget gamba & P. Aubert hpsi

DEBUSSY

(La) Plus que lente – valse (1910) pf – arr. vln & pf Roques
with P. Capdevielle pf   Pathé PDT59
Sonata No. 3, in g (1917) vln & pf
with P. Capdevielle pf   Pathé PDT58/9
Sonata No. 3, in g (1917) vln & pf
with G. Doyen pf
                                        Westminster W9054, WL5207,
                                        XWN18511

DVOŘÁK

Trio No. 2, in g, Op. 26 pf, vln & vlc
with P. Badura–Skoda pf & A. Janigro   Westminster W9024, XWN18398
vlc

Trio No. 4, in e, Op. 90 "Dumky" pf, vln & vlc
with P. Badura–Skoda pf & A. Janigro   Westminster W9024, XWN18398
vlc

FAURÉ

Sonata No. 1, in A, Op. 13 vln & pf
with G. Doyen pf   Vega C30A11
                                        Westminster W9072, WL5156,
                                        XWN18576

Sonata No. 2, in e, Op. 108 vln & pf
with G. Doyen pf   Vega C30A11
                                        Westminster W9072, WL5156,
                                        XWN18576

GLUCK

Orphée et Eurydice (1762) – opera
Dance of the blessed spirits: Lento "Melodie" (No. 2) arr. vln & pf
Kreisler
with A. Collard pf   Vega C30A38

HANDEL

(15) Sonatas, Op. 1 (?1731) fl or vln & c
Sonata No. 3, in A vln I
with G. Doyen pf   Vega C37A39
Sonata No. 10, in g vln II
with G. Doyen pf   Vega C30S182
Sonata No. 12, in F vln III
with G. Doyen pf   Vega C30S182
Sonata No. 13, in D vln IV
with G. Doyen pf   Vega C37A42
Sonata No. 14, in A vln V
with G. Doyen pf   Vega C30S182
Sonata No. 15, in E vln VI
with G. Doyen pf   Vega C30S182, C37A44

HAYDN

(31) Trios, H.XV, Nos. 1/31 pf, vln & vlc
Trio No. 1, in g, H.XV, No. 1 (Op. 70, No. 2)
with P. Badura–Skoda pf & A. Janigro   Heliodor 479050
vlc   Westminster W9026, XWN18054
Trio No. 4, in F, H.XV, No. 4 (Op. 40, No. 2)
with P. Badura–Skoda pf & A. Janigro   Nixa WLP5293
vlc   Westminster W9028, WL5293,
                                        XWN18611
Trio No. 5, in G, H.XV, No. 5 (Op. 40, No. 3)
with P. Badura–Skoda pf & A. Janigro   Nixa WLP5202
vlc   Westminster W9027, WL5202,
                                        XWN18610
Trio No. 12, in e, H.XV, No. 12 (Op. 57, No. 2)
with P. Badura–Skoda pf & A. Janigro   Westminster W9026, XWN18054
vlc
Trio No. 14, in A flat, H.XV, No. 14 (Op. 61)
with P. Badura–Skoda pf & A. Janigro   Heliodor 479050
vlc   Westminster W9026, XWN18054
Trio No. 16, in D, H.XV, No. 16 (Op. 63)
with P. Badura–Skoda pf & A. Janigro   Nixa WLP5202
vlc   Westminster W9027, WL5202,
                                        XWN18610
Trio No. 17, in F, H.XV, No. 17 (Op. 68)
with P. Badura–Skoda pf & A. Janigro   Nixa WLP5293
vlc   Westminster W9028, WL5293,
                                        XWN18611
Trio No. 22, in E flat, H.XV, No. 22 (Op. 75, No. 3)
with J. Février pf & P. Fournier vlc   L'Anthologie Sonore 55/6,
                                        3003LD

HAYDN – *Continued*

Trio No. 25, in G, H.XV, No. 25 (Op. 73, No. 2)
with P. Badura–Skoda pf & A. Janigro   Heliodor 479050
vlc   Nixa WLP5202
   Westminster W9027, WL5202,
   XWN18610

Trio No. 28, in E, H.XV, No. 28 (Op. 75, No. 2)
with P. Badura–Skoda pf & A. Janigro   Nixa WLP5293
vlc   Westminster W9028, WL5293,
   WXN18611

Trio No. 30, in E flat, H.XV, No. 30 (Op. 42, No. 3)
with P. Badura–Skoda pf & A. Janigro   Heliodor 479050
vlc   Nixa WLP5293
   Westminster W9028, WL5293,
   XWN18611

KREISLER

Caprice viennois, Op. 2 vln & pf
with A. Collard pf   Vega C30A38, 30MT1044

Chanson Louis XIII & Pavane (L. Couperin) vln & pf
with A. Collard pf   Vega C30A38

(La) Chasse (Cartier) vln & pf
with A. Collard pf   Vega C30A38

Grave (W.F. Bach) vln & pf
with A. Collard pf   Vega C30A38

Minuet (Porpora) vln & pf
with A. Collard pf   Vega C30A38

Praeludium & Allegro (Pugnani) vln & pf
with A. Collard pf   Vega C30A38

Sicilienne & Rigaudon (Francoeur) vln & pf
with A. Collard pf   Vega C30A38

Tempo di minuetto (Pugnani) vln & pf
with A. Collard pf   Vega C30A38

Variations on a theme of Corelli (Tartini) vln & pf
with A. Collard pf   Vega C30A38

MARTINON

Sonatina No. 5, Op. 32, No. 1 solo vln
(unaccompanied)   Vega C30A32

MOZART

Concerto No. 3, in G, K216 (cadenzas by Ysaÿe) vln & orch.
with Vienna State Opera Orch. –   Heliodor 480006
Horvath   Nixa WLP5187
   Westminster WL5187,
   XWN18549

Concerto No. 5, in A, K219 "Turkish" (cadenzas by Joachim) vln & orch.
with Vienna State Opera Orch. –   Heliodor 480006
Horvath   Nixa WLP5187
   Westminster WL5187,
   XWN18549

Serenade No. 7, in D, K250 "Haffner" orch.
Rondo (4th mvt) arr. vln & pf Kreisler
with A. Collard pf   Vega C30A38

Sonata No. 24, in F, K376 vln & pf
with G. Doyen pf   Pathé PDT256/7

Trio No. 1, in B flat, K254 pf, vln & vlc
with P. Badura–Skoda pf & A. Janigro   Westminster W9056, WL5284,
vlc   XWN18106

MOZART – *Continued*

Trio No. 2, in G, K496 pf, vln & vlc
with P. Badura–Skoda pf & A. Janigro   HMV XLP20077
vlc   Vega C30A15
   Westminster W9057, WL5242,
   XWN18107

Trio No. 3, in B flat, K502 pf, vln & vlc
with P. Badura–Skoda pf & A. Janigro   Vega C30A15
vlc   Westminster W9056, WL5242,
   XWN18106

Trio No. 4, in E, K542 pf, vln & vlc
with P. Badura–Skoda pf & A. Janigro   HMV XLP20077
vlc   Westminster W9057, WL5267,
   XWN18107

Trio No. 5, in C, K548 pf, vln & vlc
with P. Badura–Skoda pf & A. Janigro   HMV XLP20077
vlc   Westminster W9057, WL5267,
   XWN18107

Trio No. 6, in G, K564 pf, vln & vlc
with P. Badura–Skoda pf & A. Janigro   Westminster W9056, WL5284,
vlc   XWN18106

PAGANINI

(24) Caprices, Op. 1 (1801/7) solo vln
Caprice No. 13, in B flat arr. vln & pf Kreisler
with J. Vigne pf   Pathé PDT61

RAVEL

Ma Mère l'Oye (1908) pf duet; orch.
No. 2. Petit Poucet arr. vln & pf
with J. Vigne pf   Pathé PDT61

Tzigane (Rapsodie de concert) (1924) vln & pf or orch.
with Paris Radio Orch. – Fournet   Pathé PDT60/1

RICHTER

Trio No. 3, in A pf, vln & vlc
Larghetto (2nd mvt)
with J. Février pf & P. Fournier vlc   L'Anthologie Sonore 56

SCHMITT

Sonata, Op. 68 (1918/9) vln & pf
with G. Doyen pf   Vega C35A251

SCHUBERT

Rosamunde von Cypern, Op. 26 (D797) (1823) – Incidental music orch.
No. 9. Ballet music II, in G arr. vln & pf Kreisler
with A. Collard pf   Vega C30A38

Trio No. 1, in B flat, Op. 99 (D898) pf, vln & vlc
with P. Badura–Skoda pf & A. Janigro   Nixa WLP5188
vlc   Vega C30A24
   Westminster WL5188,
   XWN18481

Trio No. 2, in E flat, Op. 100 (D929) pf, vln & vlc
with P. Badura–Skoda pf & A. Janigro   Ducretet-Thomson LAG1046
vlc   Nixa WLP5121
   Vega C30A25
   Westminster WL5121,
   XWN18482

STAMITZ, K.

(6) Quartets, Op. 4 (1787) 2 vlns, vla & vlc
No. 4. Quartet No. 4, in F arr. vln, vla, vlc & gamba
with G. Figueroa vla, P. Fournier vlc   L'Anthologie Sonore 85
& E. Heinitz gamba

STRAVINSKY

Suite Italienne (on themes of Pergolesi) (1933) vln & pf
with A. Collard pf   Vega C30A32

SUK

(4) Pieces, Op. 17 vln & pf
with A. Collard pf   Vega C30A32

VIVALDI

(12) Concerti, Op. 3 "L'Estro armonico" var. cbns & strs
Concerto No. 9, in D, P.147 (F.I, No. 178) vln, strs & c
with string orch. –   AS 84/5–1   L'Anthologie Sonore 37, 2503LD
Sachs   Haydn Society HSLP31

Frederick FRADKIN (1892–1963)

ARNDT

Nola (1916) pf – arr. vln & orch.
with orch.   10150   Brunswick 2409, 4318

BASS

Chansonette v & pf – arr. vln & pf Kreisler
with F. Persson pf   Brunswick 2496

BEETHOVEN

(6) Minuets, G167 pf
No. 2. Minuet No. 2, in G arr. vln & pf Burmester
with piano   Brunswick 3119

BERLIN

Russian lullaby v & pf – arr. vln & pf
with piano   Brunswick 3119
What does it matter? (1927) v & pf – arr. vln & pf
with piano   Brunswick 3467

BIZET

Agnus Dei v & pf – arr. v, vln & pf
with M. Chamlee t & F.   X 9330[2]   Brunswick 50021
La Forge pf

BRAGA

(7) Melodies (1867) v & pf
No. 5. La serenata "Angel's serenade" arr. v, vln & pf
with E. Rethberg s & piano   Brunswick 10189

BRANDL

(Der) Liebe Augustin – operetta
Du alter Stefansturm arr. vln & pf as "The old refrain" by Kreisler
with H.E. Myers pf   Victor 26560, (in set P22)
Du alter Stefansturm arr. Mattullath
with M. Chamlee t & orch.   Brunswick 10121, A62577

BROCKMAN

Nightingale v & pf – arr. vln, bird imitations & orch.
with M. McKee bird imitations &   Brunswick 2675
orch.

BROWN

Wedding of the painted doll (1929) v & pf – arr. vln & pf
with piano   Brunswick 4461

COSLOW

One summer night v & pf – arr. vln & pf
with piano   Brunswick 3621

CUI

Kaleidoscope, Op. 50 vln & pf
No. 9. Orientale
with orch.   Brunswick 3911, 4097

DAVID

Tonight you belong to me (1926) v & pf – arr. vln & pf
with piano   Brunswick 3334

DAWES

Melody in A (1912) vln & pf
with F. Persson pf   Brunswick 2728

DONALDSON

My buddy (1922) v & pf – arr. vln & pf
with piano   Brunswick 2342

DRDLA

Serenade No. 1, in A vln & pf
with F. Persson pf   Brunswick 2728
Souvenir vln & pf
with H.E. Myers pf   Victor 26560, (in set P22)
Souvenir vln & pf
with L. Russotto pf   Brunswick 3262

DRIGO

(2) Airs de Ballet orch.
No. 2. Valse bluette arr. vln & pf Auer
with F. Persson pf   Brunswick 2593, 3911
No. 2. Valse bluette arr. vln & pf Auer
with D. Lieberfeld pf   Brunswick 4097
No. 2. Valse bluette arr. vln & pf Auer
with H.E. Myers pf   Victor 26558, (in set P22)

DVOŘÁK

(8) Humoresques, Op. 101 pf
No. 7. Humoresque No. 7, in G flat arr. vln & pf "in G" Kreisler
with orch.   Brunswick 20019
    Odeon 0774, A143005

ELGAR

Salut d'amour, Op. 12 orch. – arr. vln & pf Elgar
with piano   Odeon 0797, A143010

ENGEL

Nachtgesang, Op. 7 v & pf – arr. v, vln & pf
with M. Chamlee t & F. Persson pf   Brunswick 10123, 15080

FIBICH

Images, Impressions & Souvenirs, Op. 41 pf
No. 14. Poem (from "Souvenirs", Part IV) arr. vln & pf Kubelík
with F. Persson pf   Brunswick 2593
No. 14. Poem (from "Souvenirs", Part IV) arr. vln & pf Kubelík
with H.E. Myers pf   Victor 26559, (in set P22)

FIORITO

Sometime (1925) v & pf – arr. vln & pf
  with D. Lieberfeld pf   Brunswick 2987

FOSTER

(The) Old folks at home "Swanee River" (1851) v & pf – arr. v, vln & pf
  with F. Easton s & piano   Brunswick 10152

FRADKIN

Honey vln & pf
  with piano   Brunswick 4461

(The) Magic of moonlight & love "Natja" (adaptation of Tchaikovsky melodies by Hajos) vln & pf
  with piano   Brunswick 2860

FRIML

(L') Amour, toujours l'amour (1922) v & pf – arr. vln & pf
  with piano   Brunswick 3067

GARDNER

(2) Pieces, Op. 5 vln & pf
  No. 1. From the canebrake
  with piano   Brunswick 3193, 3689

GODARD

Jocelyn (1888) – opera
  Cachés dans cet asile "Berceuse" arr. t, vln & pf
  with M. Chamlee t & piano   Brunswick 10126, 15084

GOODMAN

Cherie, I love you (1926) v & pf – arr. vln & pf
  with piano   Brunswick 3467

GOUNOD

Ave Maria (Médiation on Bach's "Prelude No. 1, in C" from Book I of "Das Wohltemperirte Clavier") v & pf – arr. v, vln, hp & org
  with F. Easton s & harp   X 10821 [2]   Brunswick 50025
  & organ

de GRASSI

Berceuse vln & pf
  with orch.   10153   Brunswick 2409

GREENE

Sing me to sleep v & pf – arr. v, vln & pf
  with F. Easton s & piano   Brunswick 10100

HAGEMAN

Do not go, my love v & pf – arr. v, vln & pf
  with L. Melchior t & piano   Brunswick 10245

HANLEY

Just a cottage small by a waterfall (1925) v & pf – arr. vln & orch.
  with orch.   Brunswick 3142

HENDERSON

So blue v & pf – arr. vln & pf
  with piano   Brunswick 3565

HERBERT

(The) Fortune Teller (1898) – operetta
  Gypsy love song arr. vln & pf
  with piano   Brunswick 3505

HERBERT – *Continued*

Heart o' mine v & pf – arr. v, vln & pf
  with F. Easton s & piano   Brunswick 15076

Mademoiselle Modiste (1905) – operetta
  Kiss me again arr. vln & pf
  with piano   Brunswick 2279

Orange Blossoms (1922) – operetta
  A kiss in the dark arr. vln & pf
  with piano   Brunswick 2342

HIRSCH

Colorado v & pf – arr. vln & pf
  with piano   Brunswick 2771

KAHN

Ave Maria v & pf – arr. v, vln & pf
  with M. Chamlee t & F.   X 9331   Brunswick 50021
  La Forge pf

KLUPSCH

In a little rendezvous v & pf – arr. vln & pf
  with piano   Brunswick 2771

KREISLER

Caprice viennois, Op. 2 vln & pf
  with piano   Odeon 0724, 312484, A143004,
      UA42845

Liebesfreud vln & pf
  with piano   Odeon A42882, A143118,
      UA42846

Schön Rosmarin vln & pf
  with D. Lieberfeld pf   Brunswick 3121

LEDERER

Scène de la Csárda No. 1 vln & pf
  with piano   Odeon A42882, A143117

LEHÁR

Frasquita (1923) – operetta
  Hab' ein blaues Himmelbett arr. vln & pf as "Serenade" by Kreisler
  with piano   Brunswick 4528
  Hab' ein blaues Himmelbett arr. vln & pf as "Serenade" by Kreisler
  with H. E. Myers pf   Victor 26559, (in set P22)

LEIGH

Lovely Lucerne v & pf – arr. vln & pf
  with piano   Brunswick 2322

LOGAN

Missouri waltz (1914) v & pf – arr. vln & orch.
  with orch.   8309 [2]   Brunswick 2298

Pale moon (1920) v & pf – arr. vln & pf Kreisler
  with piano   Brunswick 3142

LORENZO & WHITING

Sleepytime gal (1925) v & pf – arr. vln & pf
  with D. Lieberfeld pf   Brunswick 2987

MacDOWELL

Woodland Sketches, Op. 51 pf
No. 1. To a wild rose arr. vln & pf
with piano   Brunswick 3689

MASSENET

Élégie v & pf – arr. v, vln & pf
with R. Rethberg s & piano   Brunswick 10189
Thaïs (1894) – opera
Méditation arr. vln & pf Marsick
with orch.   Brunswick 20019

MOORE

(The) Last rose of summer v & pf – arr. vln & pf Auer
with D. Lieberfeld pf   Brunswick 3121

NEVIN

Mighty lak' a rose (1901) v & pf – arr. vln & pf
with piano   Brunswick 3119
Mighty lak' a rose (1901) v & pf – arr. v, vln & pf
with F. Easton s & piano   Brunswick 10100

OLCOTT

My wild Irish rose (1899) v & pf – arr. vln & orch.
with orch.   8305 [1] Brunswick 2298

OPENSHAW

June brought the roses (1924) v & p – arr. vln & pf
with piano   Brunswick 3067

ROBERTS

Lonesome, that's all v & pf – arr. vln & pf
with piano   Brunswick 2467

ROBLEDO

Three o'clock in the morning (1922) v & pf – arr. vln & pf
with piano   Brunswick 2322

ROMBERG

(The) Student Prince (1924) – operetta
Deep in my heart, dear arr. vln & pf
with piano   Brunswick 2860

SAINT-SAËNS

(Le) Carnaval des animaux (1886) small orch.
Le Cygne arr. vln & pf
with H.E. Myers pf   Victor 26558, (in set P22)

SCHUBERT

(14) Schwanengesang, D957 (1828) v & pf
No. 4. Ständchen "Serenade" arr. v, vln & pf
with E. Rethberg s & piano   Brunswick 10134, A62597

SCHUMANN

(12) Duets, Op. 85 pf – 4 hands
No. 12. Abendlied arr. v, vln & pf
with C. Dux s & organ   Brunswick 10205
(13) Kinderscenen, Op. 15 pf
No. 7. Träumerei arr. vln & pf Hüllweck
with D. Lieberfeld pf   Brunswick 3262

SPIER & CONRAD

Memory lane (1924) v & pf – arr. vln & orch.
with orch.   Brunswick 2675

TCHAIKOVSKY

(6) Songs, Op. 6 v & pf
No. 5. Why?
with M. Chamlee t & F. Persson pf   Brunswick 10123, 15080
(3) Souvenirs de Hapsal, Op. 2 pf
No. 3. Chant sans paroles arr. vln & pf Kreisler
with piano   Odeon 0797, A143017

TOBIAS & TURK

Just another day wasted away (1927) v & pf – arr. vln & pf
with piano   Brunswick 3621

TOSELLI

Serenade, Op. 6 vln & pf – arr. Fradkin
with A. Jones hp   Brunswick 2496

WAYNE

In a little Spanish town v & pf – arr. vln & pf
with piano   Brunswick 3505

WHITTEMORE

In a little garden v & pf – arr. vln & pf
with piano   Brunswick 3334

WOOD

Roses of Picardy (1916) v & pf – arr. vln & pf
with piano   Brunswick 2279

YELLEN

I'm waiting for the ships that never come in v & pf – arr. vln & pf
with piano   Brunswick 2467

Vojtěch FRAIT (1894–)

ONDŘÍČEK

Fantasia (on themes from the opera "The Bartered Bride" by Smetana) Op. 9 vln & pf
with V. Polívka pf   3530/3   Esta K4006/7
Fantasia (on "Dance of the comedians" from the opera "The Bartered Bride" by Smetana) Op. 15 vln & pf
with V. Polívka pf   Esta H5041
               Supraphon H22800

Rapsodie bohème, Op. 21 vln & orch.
with Prague Radio   3771/2   Esta H5037/8
Symphony Orch. – Parík   Supraphon H22799
Scherzo Capriccio, Op. 18 vln & pf
with V. Polívka pf   Esta H5041
               Supraphon H22800

Zino FRANCESCATTI (1905–)

ALBÉNIZ

España (6 Feuilles d'album) Op. 165 pf
No. 2. Tango in D arr. vln & pf Kreisler
with A. Balsam pf   Columbia A1533, ML4310
            Philips N02101L, NBL5010,
            S06602R

ANONYMOUS

Londonderry air traditional Irish ballad – arr. vln & pf Kreisler
with A. Balsam pf   Columbia ML4534

Londonderry air traditional Irish ballad – arr. vln & pf Kreisler
with A. Balsam pf   Columbia ML5255

BACH

Concerto No. 2, in E, BWV1042 vln, strs & c
with Columbia Symphony Orch. –   Columbia ML4648
Szell

(3) Sonatas & 3 Partitas, BWV1001/6 solo vln
Partita No. 2, in d, BWV1004
(unaccompanied)   Columbia ML4935
Partita No. 3, in E: Preludio (1st mvt) BWV1006
(unaccompanied)   CLX 2476–1   Columbia LFX726
Partita No. 3, in E, BWV1006
(unaccompanied)   Columbia ML4935

(6) Sonatas, BWV1014/9 vln & clav
Sonata No. 2, in A, BWV1015
with R. Casadesus pf   American Library in Paris*

(4) Suites, BWV1066/9 strs & c
Suite No. 3, in D: Air (2nd mvt) BWV1068 2 obs, 3 tpts, drms, strs & c –
arr. vln & pf as "Air on the G–String" by Wilhelmj
with G. Becker pf   HMV K2087

BAZZINI

(La) Ronde des lutins, Op. 25 vln & pf
with M. Fauré pf   Columbia LFX192

BEETHOVEN

Concerto in D, Op. 61 (cadenzas by Kreisler) vln & orch.†
with Philadelphia Orch. – Ormandy   Columbia A1086, CX1011,
FCX126, LNX8058/62, ML4371,
QCX126
Philips G03577L, GBL5506

Concerto in D, Op. 61 (cadenzas by Kreisler) vln & orch.
with Columbia Symphony Orch. –   CBS BRG72006, S61001,
Walter   SBRG72006
Columbia ML5663, MS6263,
OL177, OS181
Odyssey Y30042

Romance No. 1, in G, Op. 40 vln & orch.
with Columbia Symphony Orch. –   Columbia ML4575
Morel   Philips 409009AE, ABE10003

Romance No. 2, in F, Op. 50 vln & orch.
with Columbia Symphony Orch. –   Columbia ML4575
Morel   Philips 409009AE, ABE10003

(3) Sonatas, Op. 12 vln & pf
No. 1. Sonata No. 1, in D
with R. Casadesus pf   CBS BRG72197, SBRG72197
Columbia ML5423, (in set
D4L324), MS6125, (in set
D4S724)

* Private unnumbered disc.
† Rondo or 3rd mvt is on Philips G03536L & GBL5534.

BEETHOVEN – *Continued*

No. 2. Sonata No. 2, in A
with R. Casadesus pf   CBS BRG72220, SBRG72220
Columbia ML5972, (in set
D4L324), MS6572, (in set
D4S724)

No. 3. Sonata No. 3, in E flat
with R. Casadesus pf   Columbia ML4478
Philips A01611R, ABR4025

No. 3. Sonata No. 3, in E flat
with R. Casadesus pf   CBS BRG72113, SBRG72113
Columbia ML5827, (in set
D4L324), MS6447, (in set
D4S724)

Sonata No. 4, in a, Op. 23 vln & pf
with R. Casadesus pf   Columbia ML4478
Philips A01611R, ABR4025

Sonata No. 4, in a, Op. 23 vln & pf
with R. Casadesus pf   CBS BRG72113, SBRG72113
Columbia ML5827, (in set
D4L324), MS6447, (in set
D4S724)

Sonata No. 5, in F, Op. 24 "Spring" vln & pf
with R. Casadesus pf   CBS BRG72113, SBRG72113
Columbia ML5827, (in set
D4L324), MS6447, (in set
D4S724), OS299

(3) Sonatas, Op. 30 vln & pf
No. 1. Sonata No. 6, in A
with R. Casadesus pf   CBS 8605, BRG72220,
SBRG72220
Columbia ML5972, (in set
D4L324), MS6572, (in set
D4S724)

No. 2. Sonata No. 7, in c
with R. Casadesus pf   Columbia ML4861
No 2. Sonata No. 7, in c
with R. Casadesus pf   CBS BRG72380, SBRG72380
Columbia ML6138, (in set
D4L324), MS6738, (in set
D4S724)

No. 3. Sonata No. 8, in G
with R. Casadesus pf   Columbia ML4861
No. 3. Sonata No. 8, in G
with R. Casadesus pf   CBS 8615, BRG72220,
SBRG72220
Columbia ML5972, (in set
D4L324), MS6572, (in set
D4S724)

Sonata No. 9, in A, Op. 47 "Kreutzer" vln & pf
with R. Casadesus pf   Columbia ML4327
Philips A01607R, ABR4007,
G05641R

Sonata No. 9, in A, Op. 47 "Kreutzer" vln & pf
with R. Casadesus pf   CBS BRG72197, SBRG72197
Columbia ML5423, (in set
D4L324), MS6125, (in set
D4S724), OS299

BEETHOVEN

Sonata No. 10, in G, Op. 96 vln & pf
  with R. Casadesus pf

    CBS BRG72380, SBRG72380
Columbia ML6138, (in set D4L324), MS6738, (in set D4S724)

BERNSTEIN

Serenade (1954) vln, hp, pcn & str orch.
  with New York Philharmonic
  Symphony Orch. – Bernstein

    Columbia ML6458, MS7058

BRAHMS

Concerto in D, Op. 77 (cadenza by Kreisler) vln & orch.*
  with Philadelphia Orch. – Ormandy

    Columbia ML5114
Philips A01376L, ABL3229

Concerto in D, Op. 77 (cadenza by Kreisler) vln & orch.
  with New York Philharmonic
  Symphony Orch. – Bernstein

    CBS BRG72130, SBRG72130
Columbia ML5871, MS6471

Concerto in a, Op. 102 "Double" vln, vlc & orch.
  with P. Fournier vlc & Columbia
  Symphony Orch. – Walter

    CBS BRG72087, SBRG72087
Columbia ML5493, MS6158
Philips 835559AY, A01466L, ABL3345

BRUCH

Concerto No. 1, in g, Op. 26 vln & orch.†
  with New York Philharmonic
  Symphony Orch. – Mitropoulos

    Columbia ML4575
Philips A01610R, ABR4011, L09410L, S06638R

Concerto No. 1, in g, Op. 26 vln & orch.
  with New York Philharmonic
  Symphony Orch. – Schippers

    CBS BRG72044, SBRG72044, S61061
Columbia ML5751, ML6131, MS6351, MS6731

BURMESTER

Contretanze (on a theme of Beethoven) vln & pf
  with G. Becker pf

    HMV K1762

CASADESUS, R.

Hommage à Chausson, Op. 51 vln & pf
  with R. Casadesus pf

    American Library in Paris‡

CHABRIER

Marche joyeuse pf – arr. vln & pf Dushkin
  with A. Balsam pf

    Columbia ML4534
Philips 409514NE, NBE11010

CHAUSSON

Concerto in D, Op. 21 vln, pf & str qt
  with R. Casadesus pf & Guilet String
  Quartet

    Columbia ML4998
Philips L01275L

---

* Adagio or 2nd mvt is on Philips G03536L & GBL5534.
† Adagio or 2nd mvt is on Philips G03536L & GBL5534.
‡ Private unnumbered disc.

CHAUSSON – *Continued*

Poème, Op. 25 vln & orch.
  with Philadelphia Orch. – Ormandy

    Columbia C1029, FC1029, ML2194, QC5012
Philips L01275L

Poème, Op. 25 vln & orch.
  with Columbia Symphony Orch. –
  Smith

    Columbia ML5253

Poème, Op. 25 vln & orch.
  with New York Philharmonic
  Symphony Orch. – Bernstein

    CBS BRG72247, SBRG72247
Columbia ML6017, MS6617

CHOPIN

(2) Nocturnes, Op. 27 pf
  No. 2. Nocturne No. 8, in D flat arr. vln & pf Wilhelmj
  with G. Becker pf

    CS 315[1] HMV L357

DEBUSSY

Preludes – Book I (1910) pf
  No. 8. La Fille aux cheveux de lin arr. vln & pf Hartmann
  with M. Lanner pf

    Columbia ML4310
Philips N02101L, NBL5010

  No. 12. Minstrels arr. vln & pf Hartmann
  with M. Lanner pf

    Columbia A1533, ML4310
Philips N02101L, NBL5010

Sonata No. 3, in g (1917) vln & pf
  with R. Casadesus pf

    Columbia 72045/6D, (set X280), CX1111, FCX125, ML4178

DRDLA

(2) Morceaux, Op. 52 vln & pf
  No. 2. Capriccio in G
  with G. Becker pf

    237946 HMV K1723

Vision, Op. 28 vln & pf
  with G. Becker pf

    HMV K2087

DRIGO

(2) Airs de Ballet orch.
  No. 2. Valse bluette arr. vln & pf Auer
  with M. Fauré pf

    Columbia P21

(Les) Millions d'Arlequin (1900) – ballet orch.
  Sérénade arr. vln & pf Auer
  with G. Becker pf

    HMV K2148

DVOŘÁK

(8) Humoresques, Op. 101 pf
  No. 7. Humoresque No. 7, in G flat arr. vln & pf "in G" Kreisler
  with G. Becker pf

    HMV K2298

  No. 7. Humoresque No. 7, in G flat arr. vln & pf "in G" Kreisler
  with M. Fauré pf

    Columbia LF91, P21

ECCLES

Sonata in g vln & c – arr. vln & pf Salmond
  with M. Fauré pf

    Columbia LF89

FAURÉ

Sonata No. 1, in A, Op. 13 vln & pf
  with R. Casadesus pf

    Columbia ML5049

Sonata No. 2, in e, Op. 108 vln & pf
  with R. Casadesus pf

    Columbia ML5049

FRANCK

Sonata in A (1886) vln & pf

        XCO 36066/9–2, 36070/1–3,   Columbia 72367/70D, (set
with R. Casadesus 36072–5 & 36073–4   MM717), C16112/5, (set D204),
pf   CX1111, FCX125, ML4178

HANDEL

(15) Sonatas, Op. 1 (?1731) fl or vln & c
  Sonata No. 13, in D: Larghetto (3rd mvt) vln IV
  with G. Becker pf   HMV K2972

KREISLER

Caprice viennois, Op. 2 vln & pf
  with piano   CK 2788[1]△ HMV L663

Caprice viennois, Op. 2 vln & pf
  with A. Balsam pf   XCO 37586–1 Columbia 72516D, LFX1015,
                                 LX1378, ML4219
                                 Philips 313469SF, SBF253

Caprice viennois, Op. 2 vln & pf
  with A. Balsam pf   Columbia ML5255

Caprice viennois, Op. 2 vln & pf
  with G. Becker pf   HMV K2148

(La) Gitana vln & pf
  with A. Balsam pf   XCO 37587–1A Columbia LX1422

Liebesfreud vln & pf
  with M. Fauré pf   Columbia DC87, GN109, LF44

Liebesfreud vln & pf
  with A. Balsam pf   Columbia 17560D, ML4219

Liebesfreud vln & pf
  with A. Balsam pf   CBS EP8516
                      Columbia ML5255

Liebesleid vln & pf
  with G. Becker pf   HMV K2298

Liebesleid vln & pf
  with M. Fauré pf   Columbia DC87, GN109, LF44

Liebesleid vln & pf
  with A. Balsam pf   Columbia 17560D, ML4219

Liebesleid vln & pf
  with A. Balsam pf   CBS EP8516
                      Columbia ML5255

Recitative & Scherzo–caprice, Op. 6 solo vln
  (unaccompanied)   XCO 37588–1A Columbia 72516D, LX1422,
                                ML4219

Recitative & Scherzo–caprice, Op. 6 solo vln
  (unaccompanied)   Columbia ML5255

Rondino on a theme by Beethoven vln & pf
  with G. Becker pf   HMV K1762

Rondino on a theme by Beethoven vln & pf
  with M. Fauré pf   WL 3142–1 Columbia LF90

Rondino on a theme by Beethoven vln & pf
  with M. Lanner pf   Columbia ML4310
                      Philips N02101L, NBL5010

Rondino on a theme by Beethoven vln & pf
  with A. Balsam pf   Columbia ML5255

Schön Rosmarin vln & pf
  with A. Balsam pf   Columbia ML4310
                      Philips N02101L, NBL5010

Schön Rosmarin vln & pf
  with A. Balsam pf   Columbia ML5255

KREISLER – *Continued*

Tambourin chinois, Op. 3 vln & pf
  with piano   CK 2789[1]△ HMV L663

Tambourin chinois, Op. 3 vln & pf
  with A. Balsam pf   XCO 37585–2 Columbia LFX1015, LX1378,
                                ML4219
                                Philips 313469SF, SBF253

Tambourin chinois, Op. 3 vln & pf
  with A. Balsam pf   Columbia ML5255

Allegretto (Boccherini) vln & pf
  with G. Becker pf   HMV K1690

Allegretto (Boccherini) vln & pf
  with A. Balsam pf   Columbia A1533, ML4534

Allegretto (Boccherini) vln & pf
  with A. Balsam pf   Columbia ML5255

Grave (W.F. Bach) vln & pf
  with A. Balsam pf   Columbia ML4534

Minuet (Porpora) vln & pf
  with A. Balsam pf   Columbia ML4534
                      Philips 409514NE, NBE11010

Minuet (Porpora) vln & pf
  with A. Balsam pf   Columbia ML5255

Praeludium & Allegro (Pugnani) vln & pf
  with A. Balsam pf   Columbia A1086, ML4534
                      Philips 409514NE, NBE11010

Praeludium & Allegro (Pugnani) vln & pf
  with A. Balsam pf   Columbia ML5255

(La) Précieuse (L. Couperin) vln & pf
  with G. Becker pf   HMV K1690

Variations on a theme of Corelli (Tartini) vln & pf
  with M. Fauré pf   WL 3141–1 Columbia LF90

LALO

Symphonie espagnole, Op. 21 vln & orch.*
  with Columbia   CLX 2473/80–1 Columbia 500236/9, LFX723/6
  Symphony Orch. – Cluytens

Symphonie espagnole, Op. 21 vln & orch.*
  with New York Philharmonic   CBS BRG72321
  Symphony Orch. – Mitropoulos   Columbia ML5184, OS300

Symphonie espagnole, Op. 21 vln & orch.*
  with Philadelphia Orch. – Ormandy   Columbia ML5601, MS6201
                                Philips A01480L, ABL3296,
                                SABL191

MASSENET

Thaïs (1894) – opera
  Méditation arr. vln & pf Marsick
  with A. Balsam pf   Columbia A1533, ML4534
                      Philips 409514NE, NBE11010

MENDELSSOHN

Concerto in e, Op. 64 vln & orch.†
  with New York Philharmonic   Columbia A1109, ML4965
  Symphony Orch. – Mitropoulos   Philips A01214L, ABL3159

* Omitting intermezzo.
† Andante or 2nd mvt is also on Philips G03536L & GBL5534.

MENDELSSOHN – *Continued*

Concerto in e, Op. 64 vln & orch.*
with Columbia Symphony Orch. –
Szell

    CBS BRG72044, S61061,
SBRG72044

    Columbia ML5751, ML6158,
MS6351, MS6758, OS300

MOZART

Concerto No. 2, in D, K211 vln & orch.
with Zürich Chamber Orch. – De
Stoutz

    Columbia MS7389

Concerto No. 3, in G, K216 (cadenzas by Ysaÿe) vln & orch.
with Columbia Symphony Orch. –
Walter

    CBS135308, BRG72323,
SBRG72323

    Columbia ML5381, MS6063

    Philips A01426L, ABL3287, C24,
SABL150

Concerto No. 4, in D, K218 (cadenzas by Joachim) vln & orch.
with Columbia Symphony Orch. –
Walter

    CBS135308, BRG72323,
SBRG72323

    Columbia ML5381, MS6063

    Philips A01426L, ABL3287, C24,
SABL150

Concerto No. 5, in A, K219 "Turkish" (cadenza by Joachim) vln & orch.
with Zürich Chamber Orch. – De
Stoutz

    Columbia MS7389

PAGANINI

(24) Caprices, Op. 1 (1801/7) solo vln
  Caprice No. 9, in E arr. vln & pf Pilati
  with A. Balsam pf

    Columbia 17571D, (in set
MM818), ML4219

    Philips 409030AE, ABE10160

  Caprice No. 13, in B flat arr. vln & pf Pilati
  with A. Balsam pf CO 39838–1 Columbia 30000, 17572D, (in set
MM818), LB89, ML4219

    Philips 409030AE, ABE10160

  Caprice No. 14, in E flat arr. vln & pf Pilati
  with A. Balsam pf

    Columbia 17574D, (in set
MM818), ML4219

    Philips 409030AE, ABE10160

  Caprice No. 15, in g arr. vln & pf Pilati
  with A. Balsam pf CO 39841–1 Columbia 17573D, (in set
MM818), LB102, LF283,
ML4219

  Caprice No. 20, in D arr. vln & pf Pilati
  with A. Balsam pf

    Columbia 17573D, (in set
MM818), ML4219

    Philips 409030AE, ABE10160

  Caprice No. 21, in A arr. vln & pf Pilati
  with A. Balsam pf CO 39843–1 Columbia 17572D, (in set
MM818), LB102, LF283,
ML4219

  Caprice No. 22, in F arr. vln & pf Pilati
  with A. Balsam pf CO 39844–1 Columbia 30000, 17572D, (in set
MM818), LB89, ML4219

PAGANINI – *Continued*

  Caprice No. 24, in a arr. vln & pf Pilati
  with A. Balsam pf

    Columbia 17574D, (in set
MM818), ML4219

    Philips 409030AE, ABE10160

(La) Carnevale di Venizia – variations, Op. 10 (1829) solo vln – arr. vln &
pf
with A. Balsam pf   Columbia PE19*

Concerto No. 1, in D, Op. 6 (cadenza by Ševčík) vln & orch.†
with Philadelphia XCO 42272/7 CBS BRG72151, SBRG72151
Orch. – Ormandy   Columbia A1006, (set MM936),
FCX140, LVX181/3, LZX274/6,
ML4315, MS6268

    Philips S04620L, SBL5219

    Supraphon 1 10 0219,
SUA10935, SUAST50935

God save the King – variations, Op. 9 (1829) vln & orch.
with M. Fauré pf   Columbia LFX192

(I) Palpiti (variations on the aria "Di tanti palpiti" (from Rossini's opera
"Tancredi") Op. 13 (1819) vln & orch.
with A. Balsam XCO 41203/4–1 Columbia 73042D, ML4310
pf   Philips N02101L, NBL5010,
S06602R

(I) Palpiti (variations on the aria "Di tanti palpiti" (from Rossini's opera
"Tancredi") Op. 13 (1819) vln & orch. – arr. Francescatti
with Zürich Chamber Orch. – De   CBS BRG72560, SBRG72560,
Stoutz   S75560

    Columbia ML6353, MS6953

POULENC

(3) Pieces (1934/5) pf
  No. 1. Presto in B flat arr. vln & pf Heifetz
  with A. Balsam pf   Columbia ML4534

PROKOFIEV

Concerto No. 2, in g, Op. 63 (1935) vln & orch.
with New York Philharmonic   Columbia ML4648
Symphony Orch. – Mitropoulos   Philips 641400AXL

RAVEL

Berceuse sur le nom de Gabriel Fauré (1922) vln & pf
with R. Casadesus pf   Columbia 72046D, (in set X280)

Berceuse sur le nom de Gabriel Fauré (1922) vln & pf
with A. Balsam pf   Columbia ML5058

(2) Mélodies hébraïques pf
  No. 1. Kaddisch arr. vln & pf Garban
  with A. Balsam pf   Columbia ML5058

Pièce en forme d'Habanera v & pf – arr. vln & pf Catherine
with A. Balsam pf   Columbia ML5058

Sonata (1927) vln & pf
with A. Balsam pf   Columbia ML5058

Tzigane (Rapsodie de concert) (1924) vln & pf or orch.
with M. Fauré pf WLX 1524/5–1 Columbia 264967, 68102D,
LFX191, LX258, W270

---

* The Columbia Symphony orch. is listed as the orch. on number ML5751
whereas ML6158 lists members of the Cleveland orch. The matrix
number XSM56320 establishes the performance as being identical as it
appears on the label of both discs.

* Limited edition.
† Allegro spiritoso or 1st mvt is also on Philips G03536L & GBL5534.

RAVEL – *Continued*

Tzigane (Rapsodie de concert) (1924) vln & pf or orch.
   with A. Balsam   XCO 37583/4–1   Columbia 72771D
   pf

Tzigane (Rapsodie de concert) (1924) vln & pf or orch.
   with A. Balsam pf   Columbia ML5058

Tzigane (Rapsodie de concert) (1924) vln & pf or orch.
   with New York Philharmonic   CBS BRG72247, SBRG72247
   Symphony Orch. – Bernstein   Columbia ML6017, MS6617

RIMSKY–KORSAKOV

(Le) Coq d'Or (1910) – opera
   Hymn to the sun arr. vln & pf Kreisler
   with M. Fauré pf   Columbia LF92

Scheherazade, Op. 35 (1888) orch.
   The young Prince & young Princesses (3rd mvt) arr. vln & pf as
   "Chanson arabe" by Kreisler
   with M. Fauré pf   Columbia LF92

SAINT–SAËNS

Concerto No. 3, in b, Op. 61 vln & orch.
   with New York   XCO 42286/91   CBS BRG72151, SBRG72151
   Philharmonic Symphony Orch. –   Columbia (set MM937),
   Mitropoulos   FCX140, LX1526/8, LX8910/2,
                             ML4315, MS6268
                             Philips S04620L, SBL5219
                             Supraphon 1 10 0219,
                             SUA10935, SUAST50935

Havanaise, Op. 83 vln & orch.
   with Philadelphia Orch. – Ormandy   Columbia C1029, QC5012

Havanaise, Op. 83 vln & orch.
   with Columbia Symphony Orch. –   Columbia ML5253
   Smith

Introduction & Rondo Capriccioso, Op. 28 vln & orch.
   with Philadelphia Orch. – Ormandy   Columbia C1029, ML2194
                             Philips S04643L, SBL5234

Introduction & Rondo Capriccioso, Op. 28 vln & orch.
   with Columbia Symphony Orch. –   Columbia ML5253
   Smith

Introduction & Rondo Capriccioso, Op. 28 vln & orch.
   with New York Philharmonic   CBS BRG72247, SBRG72247
   Symphony Orch. – Bernstein   Columbia ML6017, MS6617

SARASATE

Zigeunerweisen, Op. 20 vln & pf or orch.
   with G. Becker pf   CS 300[1]   HMV L357

Zigeunerweisen, Op. 20 vln & pf or orch.
   with M. Fauré pf   WLX 1272/3   Columbia DCX37, LFX43

Zigeunerweisen, Op. 20 vln & pf or orch.
   with Columbia Symphony Orch. –   CBS EP8516
   Smith   Columbia ML5253

SCHUBERT

Fantasia in C, Op. 159 (D934) vln & orch.
   with E. Bagnoli pf   CBS S75464
                            Columbia ML6229, MS6829

(7) Gesänge (set to Scott's "Lady of the Lake") Op. 52 v & pf
   No. 6. Ave Maria, D839 arr. vln & pf Wilhelmj
   with G. Becker pf   HMV K2203

SCHUBERT – *Continued*

(6) Moments musicaux, Op. 94 (D780) (1823/7) pf
   No. 3. Moment musicale No. 3, in f "Air russe" arr. vln & pf Kreisler
   with G. Becker   HMV K2203

(3) Sonatinas, Op. 137 (D384, D385 & D408) vln & pf
   No. 1. Sonatina No. 1. in D, D384
   with E. Bagnoli pf   CBS S75464
                            Columbia ML6229, MS6829

   No. 3. Sonatina No. 3, in g, D408
   with E. Bagnoli pf   CBS S75464
                            Columbia ML6229, MS6829

SCHUMANN

(9) Waldscenen, Op. 82 pf
   No. 7. Vogel als Prophet arr. vln & pf Auer
   with M. Lanner pf   Columbia 17406D, (in set M660),
                          ML4310
                          Philips N02101L, NBL5010

SHOSTAKOVICH

(The) Age of Gold, Op. 22 (1930) – ballet orch.
   Polka arr. vln & pf Grunes
   with M. Lanner pf   Columbia 17404D, (in set M660),
                          ML4310
                          Philips N02101L, NBL5010

SIBELIUS

Concerto in d, Op. 47 vln & orch.
   with New York Philharmonic   CBS BRG72351, SBRG72351
   Symphony Orch. – Bernstein   Columbia ML6131, MS6731

TARTINI

Concerto in d, D45 (C61) vln & orch.
   with Zürich Chamber Orch. – De   CBS BRG72560, SBRG72560,
   Stoutz   S75560
                          Columbia ML6353, MS6953

(50) Variations on a theme of Corelli solo vln – arr. vln & pf Francescatti[*]
   with M. Lanner pf   Columbia 17404D, (in set M660),
                          ML4310
                          Philips N02101L, NBL5010

TCHAIKOVSKY

Concerto in D, Op. 35 vln & orch.
   with New York Philharmonic   Columbia ML4965
   Symphony Orch. – Mitropoulos   Philips A01214L, A01615R,
                          ABL3159, G05615R, GBR6512

Concerto in D, Op. 35 vln & orch.
   with New York Philharmonic   Columbia ML6158, MS6758
   Symphony Orch. – Schippers

VALLE

Ao pé de fogueira (Prelude XV) pf – arr. vln & pf Heifetz
   with A. Balsam pf   Columbia ML4534

* Allegro moderato or 1st mvt is also on Philips G03536L & GBL5534
   while the Canzonetta or 2nd mvt is on Philips 412003AE.

VIEUXTEMPS

Concerto No. 4, in d, Op. 31 vln & orch.
with Philadelphia Orch. – Ormandy

CBS BRG72321
Columbia ML5184
Philips 641400AXL

VILLA–LOBOS

O canto do cysne negro (1917) vlc & pf – arr. vln & pf Villa–Lobos
with A. Balsam pf

Columbia ML4534

VITALI

Chaconne in g vln & c – arr. Charlier
with A. Balsam pf

Columbia ML4534

Chaconne in g vln & c – arr. vln & orch. Francescatti
with Zürich Chamber Orch. – De Stoutz

CBS BRG72560, SBRG72560, S75560
Columbia ML6353, MS6953

WALTON

Concerto (1939) vln & orch.
with Philadelphia Orch. – Ormandy

CBS BRG72351
Columbia ML5601, MS6201
Philips A01480L, ABL3296, SABL191

WIENIAWSKI

(8) Étude–Caprices, Op. 18 solo vln & 2nd vln obb
Étude–Caprice No. 4, in a arr. vln & pf Kreisler
with M. Lanner pf

Columbia 17406D, (in set M660), A1533, ML4310
Philips N02101L, NBL5010, S06602R

Souvenir de Moscou, Op. 6 vln & pf or orch.
with A. Balsam pf

Columbia ML4310
Philips A01610R, ABR4011, N02101L, NBL5010, S06602R

ZARZYCKI

Mazurka in G, Op. 26 vln & pf
with G. Becker pf

237945   HMV K1723

Karlheinz FRANKE

HAYDN

Sonata No. 1, in G, H.XV, No. 32 (1794) vln & hpsi
with P. von Schilhawsky pf

Da Camera SM93306
Musica Rara MUS55

MOZART, L.

Suite aus dem Jahre (1762) vln & hpsi
with P. von Schilhawsky pf

Da Camera SM93306
Musica Rara MUS55

MOZART, W.A.

Sonata No. 2, in D, K7 vln & pf
with P. von Schilhawsky pf

Da Camera SM93306
Musica Rara MUS55

Sonata No. 21, in e, K304 vln & pf
with P. von Schilhawsky pf

Da Camera SM93306
Musica Rara MUS55

Giulio FRANZETTI

LEGRENZI

(12) Sonatas, Op. 2 (1655) 2 vlns & c
Sonata in G "La Raspona"
with E. Porta vln, G. Spinelli hpsi & A. Riccardi gamba

Storia della Musica MdM014 (Vol. 2, No. 1)

MERULA

Canzone la Loda 2 vlns & c
with A. Ferraresi vln, G. Spinelli hpsi & A. Riccardi gamba

Storia della Musica MdM015 (Vol. 2, No. 2)

VITALI, G.B.

(12) Sonatas, Op. 5 (1669) vln & c
Sonata No. 1, in D
with G. Spinelli hpsi

Storia della Musica MdM014 (Vol. 2, No. 1)

Monique FRASCA–COLOMBIER

BACH

(6) Brandenburg Concerti, BWV1046/51 (1721) strs & c
Brandenburg Concerto No. 1, in F, BWV1046 vln, 3 obs, bsn 2 hrns & strs
with A. Fournier hrn, R. Navasse hrn & orch. – Kuentz

Club National du Disque CND1019

Brandenburg Concerto No. 2, in F, BWV1047 tpt, fl, ob, vln & strs
with A. Scherbaum tpt, C. Lardé fl & orch. – Kuentz

Club National du Disque CND1019

Brandenburg Concerto No. 3, in G, BWV1048 3 vlns, 3 vlas, 3 vlcs & cbs
with J–L. Hardy vlc & orch. – Kuentz

Club National du Disque CND1020

Brandenburg Concerto No. 4, in G, BWV1049 vln, 2 fls & strs
with C. Lardé fl & orch. – Kuentz

Club National du Disque CND1020

Brandenburg Concerto No. 5, in D, BWV1050 clav, fl, vln & strs
with F. Boudlot hpsi, C. Lardé fl & orch. – Kuentz

Club National du Disque CND1021

Concerto No. 1, in a, BWV1041 vln, strs & c
with orch. – Kuentz

Club National du Disque CND1051/2

Concerto in D, BWV1043 2 vlns, strs & c
with L. Garnier vln & orch. – Kuentz

Club National du Disque CND1051/2

Concerto in c, BWV1060 vln & ob or 2 vlns, strs & c
with L. Garnier vln & orch. – Kuentz

Club National du Disque CND1051/2

HANDEL

(15) Sonatas, Op. 1 (?1731) fl or vln & c
Sonata No. 10, in g vln II
with P. Kuentz hpsi & J–P. Hardy vlc

Club National du Disque CND12

Sonata No. 13, in D vln IV
with P. Kuentz hpsi & J–P. Hardy vlc

Club National du Disque CND12

Sonata No. 14, in A vln V
with P. Kuentz hpsi & J–P. Hardy vlc

Club National du Disque CND12

Sonata No. 15, in E vln VI
with P. Kuentz hpsi & J–P. Hardy vlc

Club National du Disque CND12

HAYDN

Concerto No. 1, in C, H.VIIa, No. 1 (1765) vln & orch.
  with chamber orch. – Kuentz   Trianon TRX6185

LECLAIR

(6) Concerti, Op. 7 (1737) vln & strs
  Concerto No. 2, in D
  with orch. – Kuentz   Club National du Disque
                               CND1014

  Concerto No. 3, in C
  with orch. – Kuentz   Club National du Disque
                               CND1014

VIVALDI

(12) Concerti, Op. 8 (1725) "Il Cimento dell' Armonia e dell' Invenzione"
(Nos. 1/4: Le quattro Stagioni) vln & strs
  Concerto No. 1, in E, F.I, No. 22 "La Primavera"
  with Paul Kuentz Chamber Orch. –   Heliodor 89813
  Kuentz

  Concerto No. 2, in B flat, F.I, No. 23 "L'Estate "
  with Paul Kuentz Chamber Orch. –   Heliodor 89813
  Kuentz

  Concerto No. 3, in F, F.I, No. 24 "L'Autunno"
  with Paul Kuentz Chamber Orch. –   Heliodor 89813
  Kuentz

  Concerto No. 4, in f, F.I, No. 25 "L'Inverno"
  with Paul Kuentz Chamber Orch. –   Heliodor 89813
  Kuentz

Wallace FREDERICKS

ANONYMOUS

Spanish dance – arr. vln & pf*
  with piano   Edison cylinder B402

BELLINI

(La) Sonnambula (1831) – opera
  excerpt – arr. vln & pf*
  with piano   Edison cylinder B393

BRAHMS

(21) Hungarian Dances pf duet
  Hungarian dance No. 5, in f sharp arr. vln & pf "in g" Joachim
  with piano   Edison cylinder B395

CHOPIN

Waltz pf – arr. vln & pf*
  with piano   Edison cylinder B384

DELIBES

Sylvia (1876) – ballet orch.
  No. 16a. Pizzicato–scherzettino (Act III) arr. vln & pf
  with piano   Edison cylinder B394

FOSTER

Old black Joe (1860) v & pf – arr. vln & pf
  with piano   Edison cylinder B403

* Unidentified.

SARASATE

Danza española vln & pf*
  with piano   Edison cylinder B385

WALLACE

Maritana (1845) – opera
  Scenes that are brightest arr. vln & pf
  with piano   Edison cylinder B396

WIENIAWSKI

(2) Mazurkas, Op. 19 vln & pf
  No. 2. Mazurka No. 2, in D "Dudziarz"
  with piano   Edison cylinder B404

Grace FREEMAN

HAUSER

(2) Lieder ohne Worte, Op. 11 vln & pf
  No. 2. Wiegenlied
  with R. Gayler pf   6106   Edison Diamond Disc 80733

Stefan FRENKEL (1902–   )

d'AMBROSIO

Canzonetta, Op. 6 vln & pf
  with piano   19721   Homochord 4–2693

BACH

Fugue in g, BWV1026 vln & c
  with E.V. Wolff hpsi & S. Hunkins vlc   Musicraft 1029, (in set 3)

Suite in A, BWV1025 vln & clav
  with E.V. Wolff hpsi   Musicraft 1026/9, (set 3)

BEETHOVEN

(25) Irish songs, G223 (1813) v, pf, vln & vlc
  No. 1. The return to Ulster
  with R. Dyer–Bennet t, I. Strasfogel pf   Concert Hall (in set AG)
  & J. Bernstein vlc pf

  No. 3. Once more I hail thee
  with R. Dyer–Bennet t, I. Strasfogel pf   Concert Hall (in set AG)
  & J. Bernstein vlc

  No. 4. The morning air
  with R. Dyer–Bennet t, I. Strasfogel pf   Concert Hall (in set AG)
  & J. Bernstein vlc

  No. 5. The massacre of Glencoe
  with R. Dyer–Bennet   CHS #90–3   Concert Hall 1090, (in set A9),
  t, I. Strasfogel pf & J. Bernstein vlc   CHC13

  No. 21. Morning a cruel turmoiler is
  with R. Dyer–Bennet t, I. Strasfogel pf   Concert Hall (in set AG)
  & J. Bernstein vlc

(20) Irish songs, G224 (1813) v, pf, vln & vlc
  No. 3. The British Light Dragoons
  with R. Dyer–Bennet   CHS #91–6   Concert Hall 1091, (in set A9),
  t, L. Strasfogel pf & J. Bernstein vlc   CHC13

(12) Irish songs, G225 (1813) v, pf, vln & vlc
  No. 4. The pulse of an Irishman
  with R. Dyer–Bennet t, I. Strasfogel pf   Concert Hall (in set AG)
  & J. Bernstein vlc

* Unidentified.

BEETHOVEN – *Continued*

No. 5. Oh! who, my dear Dermot
with R. Dyer–Bennet t, I. Strasfogel pf Concert Hall (in set AG)
& J. Bernstein vlc

(25) Scottish songs, Op. 108 (1815) v, pf, vln & vlc
No. 2. Sunset (The sun upon the Weirlaw Hill)
with R. Dyer–Bennet CHS #88–8 Concert Hall 1088, (in set A9),
t, I. Strasfogel pf & J. Bernstein vlc CHC13

No. 3. O sweet were the hours
with R. Dyer–Bennet CHS #86–8 Concert Hall 1086, (in set A9),
t, I. Strasfogel pf & J. Bernstein vlc CHC13

No. 7. Bonny laddie, highland laddie
with R. Dyer–Bennet Chs #92–5 Concert Hall 1095, (in set A9),
t, I. Strasfogel pf & J. Bernstein vlc CHC13

No. 8. The lovely lass of Inverness
with R. Dyer–Bennet CHS #87–5 Concert Hall 1087, (in set A9),
t, I. Strasfogel pf & J. Bernstein vlc CHC13

No. 14. O how can I be blithe & glad?
with R. Dyer–Bennet CHS #86–8 Concert Hall 1086, (in set A9),
t, I. Strasfogel pf & J. Bernstein vlc CHC13

No. 16. Could this ill world have been contrived?
with R. Dyer–Bennet CHS #87–5 Concert Hall 1087, (in set A9),
t, I. Strasfogel pf & J. Bernstein vlc CHC13

No. 17. O Mary, at thy window be
with R. Dyer–Bennet CHS #92–5 Concert Hall 1095, (in set A9),
t, I. Strasfogel pf & J. Bernstein vlc CHC13

No. 20. Faithful Johnny
with R. Dyer– CHS #85–14 Concert Hall 1085, (in set A9),
Bennet t, I. Strasfogel pf & J. CHC13
Bernstein vlc

No. 24. Again my lyre
with R. Dyer–Bennet CHS #89–7 Concert hall 1089, (in set A9),
t, I. Strasfogel pf & J. Bernstein vlc CHC13

CUI

Kaleidoscope, Op. 50 vln & pf
No. 9. Orientale
with F. Günther pf Homochord 4–3255

HANDEL

(15) Sonatas, Op. 1 (?1731) fl or vln & c
Sonata No. 12, in F vln III
with E.V. Wolff hpsi & S. Hunkins vlc Musicraft 1030/1

Sonata No. 14, in A vln V
with E.V. Wolff hpsi & S. Hunkins vlc Musicraft 1082

KERN, K.

Sarabande in c sharp vln & pf
with piano 20224 Homochord 4–2693

Sarabande in c sharp vln & pf
with piano Homochord 4–2742

KREISLER

Liebesleid vln & pf
with piano Kristall 5063

PURCELL

(10) Sonatas, Z802/11 (1697) 4 parts – 2 vlns & c
Sonata No. 6, in g "Chaconne"
with E.V. Wolff hpsi & S. Hunkins vlc Musicraft 1023

RATHAUS

Suite in f vln & orch.
Capriccio
with Orch. – Doll Homochord 9070

SUK

(4) Pieces, Op. 17 vln & pf
No. 3. Un poco triste
with piano Homochord 4–3255

No. 4. Burleska
with piano Homochord 4–2742

TIESSEN

Totentanz–Melodie, Op. 29 vln & pf
with orch. – Doll Homochord 9070

VIVALDI

(12) Concerti, Op. 3 "L'Estro armonico" var. cbns & orch.
Concerto No. 10, in b: Largo (2nd mvt) P.148 (F.IV, No. 10) 4 vlns, strs & c
with M. van der Berg vln, W. Hanke Telefunken SK1318, TF52
vln, R. Totenberg vln, G. Wertheim
hpsi & Berlin Philharmonic Orch. –
Unger

WEILL

Suite vln & pf
No. 1. Zuhälterballade
with piano Homochord 4–3988

No. 2. Seeräuber–Jenny
with piano Homochord 4–3988

No. 3. Polly's lied
with piano Homochord 4–3988

No. 4. Ruf aus der Grupt
with piano Homochord 4–3988

WIENIAWSKI

(2) Mazurkas, Op. 19 vln & pf
No. 1. Mazurka No. 1, in G "Obertass"
with piano Kristall 5063

Karl FREUND (1904–   )

BACH

Toccata, Adagio & Fugue in C, BWV564 org
Adagio (2nd mvt) arr. vln & pf
with piano Polydor 47307

BEETHOVEN

Concerto in D, Op. 61 (Cadenzas by Léonard) vln & orch.
580/1 GO, 802 GS[I], 803½ GS[I], Polydor 15205/9
804/5½ GS[I], 643 GO, 807/8½ GS[I]
with Berlin Philharmonic & 809 GS[I]
Orch. – Davisson

DVOŘÁK

Trio No. 4, in e, Op. 90 "Dumky" pf, vln & vlc
with B. von Pozniak pf & J. Schuster Polydor 66194/5
vlc

DVOŘÁK – Continued

Trio No. 4, in e, Op. 90 "Dumky" pf, vln & vlc
with P. von Pozniak pf & J. Bernstein   HMV AN715/7, C2384/6,
vlc   EH647/9

JUON

(9) Miniatures, Op. 18 "Satyre und Nymphen" pf
No. 3. Rêverie arr. pf, vln & vlc
with B. von Pozniak pf & J. Schuster   Polydor 62548
vlc

No. 6. Élégie arr. pf, vln & vlc
with B. von Pozniak pf & J. Schuster   Polydor 62549
vlc

No. 7. Humoresque arr. pf, vln & vlc
with B. von Pozniak pf & J. Schuster   Polydor 62548
vlc

(5) Neue Tanzrhytmen, Op. 24 vln & pf
No. 2. Danse fantastique arr. pf, vln & vlc
with B. von Pozniak pf & J. Schuster   Polydor 62549
vlc

KLETZKI

Trio in d, Op. 16 pf, vln & vlc
Adagio (2nd mvt)
with B. von Pozniak pf & J. Schuster   Polydor 66415
vlc

KORNAUTH

Trio in b, Op. 27 pf, vln & vlc
excerpt*
with B. von Pozniak pf & J. Schuster   Polydor 66415
vlc

RAMEAU

(6) Concerts on Sextuor 3 vlns, vla & 2 vlcs
Concert en Sextuor No. 5 arr. pf, vln & vlc
with B. von Pozniak pf & J. Schuster   Polydor 66197
vlc

SCHUBERT

Allegretto grazioso unid – arr. vln & pf
with piano   Polydor 47307

(3) Sonatinas, Op. 137 (D384, D385 & D408) vln & pf
No. 3. Sonatina No. 3, in g, D408
with S. Fischer pf   Polydor 47118/20

SMETANA

Trio in g, Op. 15 pf, vln & vlc
Allegro ma non agitato (2nd mvt)
with B. von Pozniak pf & J. Schuster   Polydor 66196
vlc

William FREY

POLIAKIN

(Le) Canari (Concert–polka) vln & pf
with orch.   Favorite 599, 1–14352E

* Unidentified.

SCHLESINGER

Gavotte – vln & pf
with orch.   Favorite 599, 1–14351E

Henrick FRIDHEIM

RIMSKY–KORSAKOV

Scheherazade, Op. 35 (1888) orch.
with USSR Symphony Orch. –   HMV ASD2520
Svetlanov   Melodiya–Angel SR40112
                                         Mezhdunarodnaya Kniga
                                         D024851/2

Erick FRIEDMAN (1940–   )

BACH

Concerto in d, BWV1043 2 vlns, strs & c
with J. Heifetz vln, T. Lofthouse hpsi   Victor LM2577, LSC2577,
& New Symphony Orch. of London –   LSC5015, RB16277, SB2146
Sargent

(3) Sonatas & 3 Partitas, BWV1001/6 solo vln
Partita No. 2, in d: Chaconne, BWV1004
(unaccompanied)   Victor A635036/7, A645036/7,
                                         (in set LSC7033)

(6) Sonatas, BWV1014/9 vln & clav
Sonata No. 1, in b, BWV1014
with B. Prince–Joseph hpsi   Victor A635036/7, A645036/7,
                                         (in set LSC7033)

Sonata No. 2, in A, BWV1015
with B. Prince–Joseph hpsi   Victor A635036/7, A645036/7,
                                         (in set LSC7033)

Sonata No. 3, in E, BWV1016
with B. Prince–Joseph hpsi   Victor A635036/7, A645036/7,
                                         (in set LSC7033)

Sonata No. 4, in c, BWV1017
with B. Prince–Joseph hpsi   Victor A635036/7, A645036/7,
                                         (in set LSC7033)

Sonata No. 5, in f, BWV1018
with B. Prince–Joseph hpsi   Victor A635036/7, A645036/7,
                                         (in set LSC7033)

Sonata No. 6, in G, BWV1019
with B. Prince–Joseph hpsi   Victor A635036/7, A645036/7,
                                         (in set LSC7033)

CASTELNUOVO–TEDESCO

(2) Etudes d'ondes pf – arr. vln & pf as "Sea Murmurs" by Heifetz
with B. Smith pf   Victor A635007, A645007,
                                         LM2671, LSC2671

CHAUSSON

Poème, Op. 25 vln & orch.
with London Symphony Orch. –   Victor A635021, A645021,
Sargent   LM2689, LSC2689

DEBUSSY

Sonata No. 3, in g (1917) vln & pf
with A. Previn pf   Victor A635068, A645068,
                                         LM2907, LSC2907, RB6688,
                                         SB6688

DINICU

Hora staccato vln & ens – arr. vln & pf Heifetz
with B. Smith pf — Victor A635007, A645007, LM2671, LSC2671

FALLA

(La) Vida breve (1913) – opera
Danza española orch. – arr. vln & pf Kreisler
with B. Smith pf — Victor A635007, A645007, LM2671, LSC2671

FRANCK

Sonata in A (1886) vln & pf
with A. Previn pf — Victor A635068, A645068, LM2907, LSC2907, RB6688, SB6688

KREISLER

Minuet (Porpora) vln & pf
with B. Smith pf — Victor A635007, A645007, LM2671, LSC2671

MENDELSSOHN

Concerto in e, Op. 64 vln & orch.
with London Symphony Orch. – Ozawa — Victor A635062, A645062, LM2865, LSC2865, RB6666, SB6666

MOZART

Rondo in C, K373 vln & orch.
with B. Smith pf — Victor A635007, A645007, LM2671, LSC2671

PAGANINI

(24) Caprices, Op. 1 (1801/7) solo vln
Caprice No. 17, in E flat
(unaccompanied) — Victor A635007, A645007, LM2671, LSC2671

Caprice No. 21, in A
(unaccompanied) — Victor A635753, A645753, LM2671, LSC2671

Concerto No. 1, in D, Op. 6 (cadenza by Friedman) vln & orch.
with Chicago Symphony Orch. – Hendl — Victor A635030, A645030, LM2610, LSC2610

PROKOFIEV

Concerto No. 1, in D, Op. 19 vln & orch.
with Boston Symphony Orch. – Leinsdorf — Victor A635030, A645030, LM2732, LSC2732, RB6597, SB6597

RAVEL

Tzigane (Rapsodie de concert) (1924) vln & pf or orch.
with London Symphony Orch. – Sargent — Victor A635021, A645021, LM2689, LSC2689

RIMSKY–KORSAKOV

(The) Tale of Tsar Saltan (1900) – opera
Flight of the bumblebee (Act III) orch. – arr. vln & pf Heifetz
with B. Smith pf — Victor A635007, A645007, LM2671, LSC2671

SAINT-SAËNS

Havanaise, Op. 83 vln & orch.
with London Symphony Orch. – Sargent — Victor A635021, A645021, LM2689, LSC2689

Introduction & Rondo Capriccioso, Op. 28 vln & orch.
with Chicago Symphony Orch. – Hendl — Victor A630753, LM2610, LSC2610, RB6514, SB6514

SARASATE

Zigeunerweisen, Op. 20 vln & pf or orch.
with London Symphony Orch. – Sargent — Victor A635021, A645021, LM2689, LSC2689

SZYMANOWSKI

Romance D, Op. 23 (1909) vln & pf
with B. Smith pf — Victor A635007, A645007, LM2671, LSC2671

TARTINI

(50) Variations on a theme of Corelli solo vln – arr. vln & pf Francescatti
with B. Smith pf — Victor A635007, A645007, LM2671, LSC2671

TCHAIKOVSKY

Concerto in D, Op. 35 vln & orch.
with London Symphony Orch. – Ozawa — Victor A635062, A645062, LM2865, LSB4016, LSC2865, RB6666, SB6666

Sérénade mélancolique in b flat, Op. 26 vln & orch. – arr. vln & pf Wilhelmj
with B. Smith pf — Victor A635007, A645007, LM2671, LSC2671

WIENIAWSKI

Légende, Op. 17 vln & pf or orch.
with London Symphony Orch. – Sargent — Victor A635021, A645021, LM2689, LSC2689

Scherzo–tarantelle, Op. 16 vln & pf
with B. Smith pf — Victor A635007, A645007, LM2671, LSC2671

Lilli FRIEDMANN

BACH

Sonata in G, BWV1021 vln & c
with F. Viderø hpsi & H. E. Deckert gamba — Haydn Society HSL95

CORELLI

(12) Sonatas, Op. 5 vln & c
Sonata No. 5, in g
with F. Viderø hpsi & H.E. Deckert gamba — Haydn Society HSL95

HANDEL

(15) Sonatas, Op. 1 (?1731) fl or vln & c
Sonata No. 14, in A vln V
with F. Viderø hpsi & H.E. Deckert gamba — Haydn Society HSL95

LECLAIR

(12) Sonatas, Op. 9 – Book IV (1738) vln & c
  Sonata No 3, in D
  with F. Viderø hpsi & H.E. Deckert   Haydn Society HSL95
  gamba

TELEMANN

(12) Fantasias (1735) solo vln
  Fantasia No. 8, in E
  (unaccompanied)   Polydor 4003
  Fantasia No. 12, in a
  (unaccompanied)   Polydor 4003

WALTHER

Sonata No. 2, in A (1676) vln & c
  with W. Gerwig lute & J. Koch gamba Polydor PV4401

Lavard FRIISHOLM (1912–   )

CORELLI

(12) Sonatas, Op. 3 2 vlns & c
  Sonata No. 1, in F
  with H. Kassow vln, S. Sørensen org & Metronome MCEP3070
  J. Friisholm vlc
  Sonata No. 5, in d
  with H. Kassow vln, S. Sørensen org & Metronome MCEP3070
  J. Friisholm vlc

HANDEL

(7) Sonatas, Op. 5 (1739) 2 vlns & c
  Sonata No. 1, in A
  with H. Kassow vln, S. Sørensen hpsi Haydn Society HSL85, (in set
  & J. Friisholm vlc   HSL–E)
  Sonata No. 2, in D
  with H. Kassow vln, S. Sørensen hpsi Haydn Society HSL85, (in set
  & J. Friisholm vlc   HSL–E)
  Sonata No. 3, in e
  with H. Kassow vln, S. Sørensen hpsi Haydn Society HSL85, (in set
  & J Friisholm vlc   HSL–E)
  Sonata No. 4, in G
  with H. Kassow vln, S. Sørensen hpsi Haydn Society HSL85, (in set
  & J. Friisholm vlc   HSL–E)
  Sonata No. 5, in g
  with H. Kassow vln, S. Sørensen hpsi Haydn Society HSL86, (in set
  & J. Friisholm vlc   HSL–E)
    Metronome MCEP3010
  Sonata No. 6, in F
  with H. Kassow vln, S. Sørensen hpsi Haydn Society HSL86, (in set
  & J. Friisholm vlc   HSL–E)
    Metronome MCEP3023
  Sonata No. 7, in B
  with H. Kassow vln, S. Sørensen hpsi Haydn Society HSL86, (in set
  & J. Friisholm vlc   HSL–E)
    Metronome MCEP3024

David FRISINA

STRAUSS, R.

(Ein) Heldenleben, Op. 40 (1898) orch.
  with Los Angeles Philharmonic Orch. Decca SXL6382
  – Mehta   London CS6608

Harry FRITZ–CRONE

BECCE

Légende d'amour, Op. 11 pf – arr. vln & pf
  with I. Fritz–Crone pf   BS 2901–1 HMV X2857

BULL

Säterjëntens Søntag v & pf – arr. vln & pf Svendsen
  with I. Fritz–Crone pf   Be 726[I] HMV X1658

DRDLA

Souvenir vln & pf
  with I. Fritz–Crone pf   BT 704–1 HMV X2269
Souvenir vln & pf
  with I. Fritz–Crone pf   BT 705 HMV*
Souvenir vln & pf
  with I. Fritz–Crone   BS2900 – III HMV X2857
  pf

FIBICH

Images, Impressions & Souvenirs, Op. 41 pf
  No. 14. Poem (from "Souvenirs", Part IV) arr. vln & pf Kubelík
  with I. Fritz–Crone pf   BT 1579–1 HMV X2269
  No. 14. Poem (from "Souvenirs", Part IV) arr. vln & pf Kubelík
  with I. Fritz–Crone pf   OSB 291 HMV X4598

GODARD

Jocelyn (1888) – opera
  Cachés dans cet asile "Berceuse" arr. vln & pf
  with I. Fritz–Crone pf   OSB 292 HMV X4597

GRIEG

(2) Elegiac melodies, Op. 34 str orch.
  No. 2. Spring arr. vln & pf
  with I. Fritz–Crone pf   OSB 289 HMV X4597

HANDEL

Serse (1738) – opera
  Ombra mai fu "Largo" arr. vln & pf
  with I. Fritz–Crone pf   BT 1581[I] HMV X2278

JÄRNEFELT

Berceuse in g orch. – arr. vln & pf
  with I. Fritz–Crone pf   BT 1580[I] HMV X2278

KREISLER

Liebesfreud vln & pf
  with I. Fritz–Crone pf   OT 532–1 HMV X3914
Liebesleid vln & pf
  with I. Fritz–Crone pf   OT 531–11 HMV X3914

* Unissued.

MASSENET

Élégie v & pf – arr. vln & pf
  with I. Fritz–Crone pf   Be 725[1]   HMV X1658

TOSELLI

Serenade, Op. 6 vln & pf
  with I. Fritz–Crone pf   OSB 290   HMV X4598

Igor FROLOV

ALMEIDA

Cuban dance arr. vln & pf Frolov
  with piano   Mezhdunarodnaya Kniga
                          SM02065/6

ANKERMANN

Cuban song vln & pf
  with piano   Mezhdunarodnaya Kniga
                          SM02065/6

BRAHMS

(21) Hungarian dances pf duet
Hungarian dance No. 17, in f sharp arr. vln & pf Kreisler
  with piano   Mezhdunarodnaya Kniga
                          SM02065/6

HANDEL

(15) Sonatas, Op. 1 (?1731) fl or vln & c
Sonata No. 13, in D vln IV
  with piano   Mezhdunarodnaya Kniga
                          SM02065/6

PONCE

Estrellita (1913) v & pf – arr. vln & pf Heifetz
  with piano   Mezhdunarodnaya Kniga
                          SM02065/6

PRATS

Maria's song vln & pf
  with paino   Mezhdunarodnaya Kniga
                          SM02065/6

VITALI

Chaconne in g vln & c
  with piano   Mezhdunarodnaya Kniga
                          SM02065/6

WIENIAWSKI

Légende, Op. 17 vln & pf or orch.
  with piano   Mezhdunarodnaya Kniga
                          SM02065/6

Mazurka in a, Op. 3 "Kujawiak" vln & pf
  with piano   Mezhdunarodnaya Kniga
                          SM02065/6

Elfriede FRÜH

LEO

Concerto in D 4 vlns, strs & c
  with D. Vorholz vln, G. Terebesi vln,   Archive APM14340, ARC3240,
  H. Schön vln & Berlin Chamber Music   ARC73240, SAPM198340
  Ensemble – Lange

Herbert FRÜHAUF

HAYDN

(6) Divertimenti, H.IV, Nos. 6/11 (Op. 100) fl, vln & vlc
Divertimento No. 1, in D, H.IV, No. 6 arr. vla d'amour, vln & vlc
  with K. Stumpf vla d'amour & H.   Amadeo AVRS6261
  Koller vlc

Lars FRYDÉN

BACH

Concerto in a, BWV1044 clav, fl, vln, strs & c
  with G. Leonhardt hpsi, J. Feltkamp fl   Telefunken AWT8404E
  & Baroque Ensemble – Leonhardt

(6) Sonatas, BWV1014/9 vln & clav
Sonata No. 1, in b, BWV1014
  with G. Leonhardt hpsi   Telefunken AWT9433,
                          SAWT9433, STEL16, TEL16

Sonata No. 2, in A, BWV1015
  with G. Leonhardt hpsi   Telefunken AWT9434,
                          SAWT9434, STEL17, TEL17

Sonata No. 3, in E, BWV1016
  with G. Leonhardt hpsi   Telefunken AWT9433,
                          SAWT9433, STEL16, TEL16

Sonata No. 4, in c, BWV1017
  with G. Leonhardt hpsi   Telefunken AWT9434,
                          SAWT9434, STEL17, TEL17

Sonata No. 5, in f, BWV1018
  with G. Leonhardt hpsi   Telefunken AWT9433,
                          SAWT9433, STEL16, TEL16

Sonata No. 6, in G, BWV1019
  with G. Leonhardt hpsi   Telefunken AWT9434,
                          SAWT9434, STEL17, TEL17

de MONDONVILLE

(6) Sonatas, Op. 3 vln & hpsi
Sonata No. 1, in g
  with G. Leonhardt hpsi   Telefunken AWT9497,
                          SAWT9497

Sonata No. 2, in F
  with G. Leonhardt hpsi   Telefunken AWT9497,
                          SAWT9497

Sonata No. 3, in B flat
  with G. Leonhardt hpsi   Telefunken AWT9497,
                          SAWT9497

Sonata No. 4, in C
  with G. Leonhardt hpsi   Telefunken AWT9497,
                          SAWT9497

Sonata No. 5, in G
  with G. Leonhardt hpsi   Telefunken AWT9497,
                          SAWT9497

de MONDONVILLE – *Continued*

Sonata No. 6, in A
with G. Leonhardt hpsi   Telefunken AWT9497,
SAWT9497

ROMAN

(6) Assaggi solo vln
Assaggio No. 6, in b, B324
(unaccompanied)   Sveriges Radio RELP5008

TELEMANN

Concerto in F, T.II, No. 3 3 vlns, orch & C
  with E. Mayer–Schierning vln, E.   Archive APM14837, ARC3237,
Melkus vln, O. Steinkopf hpsi &   ARC73237, SAPM198837
Schola Cantorum Basiliensis –
Wenzinger

Joseph Philip FUCHS (1900–   )

BACH

Cantata No. 140 (Wachet auf, ruft uns die Stimme) BWV140
  with S. Friel s, R. Russell t, P.   Victor 10–1351/4
Matthew bs, R. Bloom ob & RCA
Victor Chorus & Orch. – Shaw

Matthaeus–Passion, BWV244 (1729)
No. 47. Erbarme dich, mein Gott
  with M. Anderson a & Victor   Victor 11–9380, (in set M1087),
Chamber Orch. – Shaw   LCT1111, (in set WCT1111)

BEETHOVEN

Romance No. 1, in G, Op. 40 vln & orch.
  with Little Orch. Society – Scherman   Brunswick AXL2003
     Decca DL4004, UW333006

Romance No. 2, in F, Op. 50 vln & orch.
  with Little Orch. Society – Scherman   Brunswick AXL2003
     Decca DL4004, UW333006

Serenade in D, Op. 8 vln, vla & vlc
  with L. Fuchs vla & L. Rose vlc   Brunswick AXL2004
     Decca AK243075, DL9574,
     UA243075

Serenade in D, Op. 25 fl, vln & vla
  with J. Baker fl & L. Fuchs vla   Brunswick AXTL1033
     Decca DL7506, UAT273054

(3) Sonatas, Op. 12 vln & pf
No. 1. Sonata No. 1, in D
  with A. Balsam pf   Brunswick AXTL1045
     Decca DL9640, (in set DX150)

No. 2. Sonata No. 2, in A
  with A. Balsam pf   Brunswick AXTL1046
     Decca DL9641, (in set DX150)

No. 3. Sonata No. 3, in E flat
  with A. Balsam pf   Brunswick AXTL1050
     Decca DL9643, (in set DX150)

Sonata No. 4, in a, Op. 23 vln & pf
  with A. Balsam pf   Brunswick AXTL1057
     Decca DL9644, (in set DX150)

Sonata No. 5, in F, Op. 24 "Spring" vln & pf
  with A. Balsam pf   Brunswick AXTL1052
     Decca DL9642, (in set DX150)

BEETHOVEN – *Continued*

(3) Sonatas, Op. 30 vln & pf
No. 1. Sonata No. 6, in A
  with A. Balsam pf   Brunswick AXTL1050
     Decca DL9643, (in set DX150)

No. 2. Sonata No. 7, in c
  with A. Balsam pf   Brunswick AXTL1057
     Decca DL9644, (in set DX150)

No. 3. Sonata No. 8, in G
  with A. Balsam pf   Brunswick AXTL1052
     Decca DL9642, (in set DX150)

Sonata No. 9, in A, Op. 47 "Kreutzer" vln & pf
  with A. Balsam pf   Brunswick AXTL1045
     Decca DL9640, (in set DX150)

Sonata No. 10, in G, Op. 96 vln & pf
  with A. Balsam pf   Brunswick AXTL1046
     Decca DL9641, (in set DX150)

(3) Trios, Op. 1 pf, vln & vlc
No. 1. Trio No. 1, in E flat
  with E. Istomin pf & P. Casals vlc   Columbia ML5291
(3) Trios, Op. 9 vln, vla & vlc
No. 3. Trio No. 4, in c
  with L. Fuchs vla & H. Fuchs vlc   Brunswick AXTL1033
     Decca DL9574, UAT273054

(2) Trios Op. 70 pf, vln & vlc
No. 1. Trio No. 4, in D "Ghost"
  with E. Istomin pf & P. Casals vlc   Columbia ML5291

COPLAND

Sonata (1943) vln & pf
  with L. Smit pf   Brunswick AXTL1047
     Decca DL8503, UAT273048

DEBUSSY

Sonata No. 3, in g (1917) vln & pf
  with A. Balsam pf   Decca DL9836

DRIGO

(2) Airs de Ballet orch.
No. 2. Valse bluette arr. vln & pf Auer
  with piano   50776   Homochord B8144

DVOŘÁK

(7) Gypsy songs, Op. 55 v & pf
No. 4. Songs my mother taught me arr. v, vln & orch.
  with J. Novotna s & RCA Victor   Victor 11–9153
Orch. – Weissmann
Sonatina in G, Op. 100 vln & pf
Larghetto (2nd mvt) arr. vln & pf as "Indian lament" by Kreisler
  with piano   50770   Homochord B8142

ELGAR

(La) Capricieuse, Op. 17 vln & pf
  with piano   50769   Homochord B8141

FAURÉ

Sonata No. 1, in A, Op. 13 vln & pf
  with A. Balsam pf   Brunswick AXTL1083
     Decca DL9716, UMT263597
     Deutsche Grammophon
     LPEM19167

FRANCK

Sonata in A (1886) vln & pf
with A. Balsam pf

Brunswick AXTL1083
Decca DL9716, UMT263597
Deutsche Grammophon
LPEM19167

GRIEG

Sonata No. 1, in F, Op. 8 vln & pf
with F. Sheridan pf

Brunswick AXTL1017
Columbia CCL35020
Decca DL9571, UAT273081

Sonata No. 3, in c, Op. 45 vln & pf
with F. Sheridan pf

Brunswick AXTL1017
Columbia CCL35020
Decca DL9571, UAT273081

HINDEMITH

Concerto in D (1940) vln & orch.
with London Symphony Orch. –
Goossens

Everest LPBR6040, SDBR3040
World Record Club SCM33

KREISLER

Caprice viennois, Op. 2 vln & pf
with piano   50775 Homochord B8140
(La) Gitana vln & pf
with orch.   MGM 9504
Liebesleid vln & pf
with piano   50767 Homochord B8140
Tambourin chinois, Op. 3 vln & pf
with piano   50773 Homochord B8143
Variations on a theme of Corelli (Tartini) vln & pf
with piano   50768 Homochord B8141

LEONCAVALLO

Mattinata (1904) v & pf – arr. vln & pf
with piano   50774 Homochord B8143, B8144

LOPATNIKOFF

Sonata No. 2, Op. 32 vln & pf
with A. Balsam pf

Decca DL9541

MARTINŮ

(3) Madrigals (1948) vln & vla
with L. Fuchs vla

Brunswick AXTL1030
Decca DL8510, UAT273082

MENASCE

Sonata No. 1 (1940) vln & pf
with A. Balsam pf

Composers Recordings CRI154

MOZART

Adagio in E, K261 vln & orch.
with Aeterna Chamber Orch. –
Waldman

Brunswick AXTL1097, SXA4005
Decca DL10037, DL710037

Concerto No. 3, in G, K216 vln & orch.
with London Symphony Orch. –
Goossens

Everest LPBR6040, SDBR3040
World Record Club SCM33

Duo No. 1, in G, K423 vln & vla
with L. Fuchs vla

CBS S75590
Columbia ML5692, MS6292

MOZART – *Continued*

Duo No. 2, in B flat K424 vln & vla
with L. Fuchs vla

Brunswick AXTL1030
Decca DL8510, UAT273082

Duo No. 2, in B flat, K424 vln & vla
with L. Fuchs vla

CBS S75590
Columbia ML5692, MS6292

Rondo in C, K373 vln & orch.
with Aeterna Chamber Orch. –
Waldman

Brunswick AXTL1097, SXA4005
Decca DL10037, DL710037

Sinfonia concertante in B flat, K364 vln, vla & orch.
with L. Fuchs vla & Zimbler
Sinfonietta

Brunswick AXTL1018
Decca DL9596, UAT273050
Deutsche Grammophon LP16122

Sinfonia concertante in B flat, K364 vln, vla & orch.
with L. Fuchs vla & Aeterna Chamber
Orch. – Waldman

Brunswick AXTL1097, SXA4005
Decca DL10037, DL710037

PISTON

Sonata (1939) vln & pf
with A. Balsam pf

Decca DL9541

PROVOST

Intermezzo (1940) vln & pf
with MGM String Orch. – Marrow   MGM 30063

SARASATE

Zigeunerweisen, Op. 20 vln & pf or orch.
with piano   50765 Homochord B8139

SCHUBERT

Sonata in A, Op. 162 (D574) "Duo" vln & pf
with A. Balsam pf   Decca DL9922
(3) Sonatinas, Op. 137 (D384, D385 & D408) vln & pf
Sonatina No. 1, in D, D384
with A. Balsam pf   Decca DL9922
Sonatina No. 3, in g, D408
with A. Balsam pf   Decca DL9922

SCOTT

Lotus land, Op. 47, No. 1 (1905) pf – arr. vln & pf Kreisler
with MGM String Orch. – Marrow   MGM 30063

SMETANA

From my Homeland (1878) vln & pf
No. 2. Andantino
with piano   50771 Homochord B8142

STRAUSS, R.

Sonata in E flat, Op. 18 vln & pf
with A. Balsam pf

Decca DL9836

STRAVINSKY

Duo Concertante (1932) vln & pf
with L. Smit pf

Brunswick AXTL1047
Decca DL8503, UAT273048

TCHAIKOVSKY

(The) Months (12 Characteristic pieces) Op. 37a pf
  No. 10 Autumn song arr. vln & orch.
    with orch. – Camarata   Brunswick AXL2010
                                    Decca DL4082

Sérénade mélancolique in b flat, Op. 26 vln & orch.
  with orch. – Camarata   Brunswick AXL2010
                                    Decca DL4082

Souvenir d'un lieu cher, Op. 42 vln & pf
  No. 3. Mélodie arr. vln & orch.
    with orch. – Camarata   Brunswick AXL2010
                                    Decca DL4082

(3) Souvenirs de Hapsal, Op. 2 pf
  No. 3. Chant sans paroles in f arr. vln & orch.
    with orch. – Camarata   Brunswick AXL2010
                                    Decca DL4082

Swan Lake, Op. 20 (1875/6) – ballet orch.
  Pas de deux (Act II)
    with orch. – Camarata   Brunswick AXL2010
                                    Decca DL4082

THOMSON

Sonata (1930) vln & pf*
  with A. Balsam pf   Composers Recordings CRI207
                               Hi Fi Stereo Review †

VAUGHAN WILLIAMS

Concerto in d (1925) "Concerto accademico" vln & orch.
  with Zimbler Sinfonietta   Brunswick AXTL1006
                                Decca DL9625

WIENIAWSKI

Souvenir de Moscou, Op. 6 vln & pf or orch.
  with piano   50766   Homochord B8139

James de la FUENTE (1914–1963)

MOZART

Sonata No. 34, in A, K526 vln & pf
  with J. Goodman pf   Sound Recording Company 1

TARTINI

Sonata in g "Il Trillo del Diavolo" vln & c – arr. vln & pf Kreisler
  with J. Goodman pf   Sound Recording Company 1

Maurice FUERI

MIGOT

Sonata (1951) solo vln
  (unaccompanied)   Lumen LD3452

* Recorded at Town Hall, New York City on Dec. 18th 1961. Live
  performance.
† Special pressing.

Mayumi FUJIKAWA

BACH

Concerto No. 2, in E, BWV1042 vln, strs & c
  with Moscow Chamber Orch. –   Mezhdunarodnaya Kniga
  Barshai   SM02113/4

BARTÓK

(6) Rumanian folk dances (1915) pf – arr. vln & pf Székely
  with piano   Mezhdunarodnaya Kniga
                               D028103

BEETHOVEN

(3) Sonatas, Op. 12 vln & pf
  No. 1. Sonata No. 1, in D
    with E. Livshits pf   Mezhdunarodnaya Kniga
                               SM02113/4

TCHAIKOVSKY

Sérénade mélancolique in b flat, Op. 26 vln & orch.
  with E. Livshits pf   Mezhdunarodnaya Kniga
                               SM02113/4

Hideko FUKANO

HANDEL

(12) Concerti grossi, Op. 6 (1739) 2 vlns, vlc & strs
  Concerto grosso No. 5, in D
    with P. Nölting vln, H. Spengler vlc,   Da Camera HKO1001
    K. Preis hpsi & Heidelberg Chamber
    Orch. – Albert

M. FURER

VIVALDI

(12) Concerti, Op. 3 "L'Estro armonico" var. cbns & strs
  Concerto No. 10, in b, P.148 (F.IV, No. 10) 4 vlns, strs & c
    with K. Varenberg vln, E. Boder vln,   Mezhdunarodnaya Kniga
    Y. Milkis vln & Leningrad Chamber   D018097/8, S01319/20
    Orch. – Gozman

Shmuel Isaakovich FURER (1909–　)

ACHRON

Stimmungen, Op. 32 vln & pf
  with R. Branovskaya pf   Mezhdunarodnaya Kniga
                               D014078

ARENSKY

Concerto in a, Op. 54 vln & orch.
  with USSR Radio Symphony Orch. –   Monarch MWL322
  Smirnov

BEETHOVEN

(Die) Ruinen von Athen, Op. 113 – Incidental music orch.
  No. 3. Chor der Derwische arr. vln & pf Auer
    with piano   Mezhdunarodnaya Kniga
                               D5144/5

BLOCH

Baal Shem (3 Pictures of Chassidic life) (1923) vln & pf
  No. 2. Nigun (Improvisation)
  with E. Dyachenko pf
                Mezhdunarodnaya Kniga
                D014077

BRAHMS

(21) Hungarian Dances pf duet
  Hungarian dance No. 6, in D flat arr. vln & pf "in B flat" Joachim
  with L. Epshtein pf
                Mezhdunarodnaya Kniga
                D014077

DVOŘÁK

(8) Slavonic Dances, Op. 72 pf duet; orch.
  No. 3. Slavonic dance No. 11, in F arr. vln & pf Příhoda
  with piano
                Mezhdunarodnaya Kniga
                D5144/5

  No. 5. Slavonic dance No. 13, in B flat arr. vln & pf Press
  with piano
                Mezhdunarodnaya Kniga
                D18478

FIOCCO

Suite No. 1, in G hpsi
  Allegro (10th mvt) arr. vln & pf Bent & O'Neill
  with Y. Kaletsky pf
                Mezhdunarodnaya Kniga
                D014078

KREISLER

Recitative & Scherzo–caprice, Op. 6 solo vln
  (unaccompanied)
                Mezhdunarodnaya Kniga
                D014078

Shepherd's madrigal vln & pf
  with E. Seimovich pf
                Mezhdunarodnaya Kniga
                D014077

LOTKA

Croatian Rhapsody vln & pf
  with R. Branovskaya pf
                Mezhdunarodnaya Kniga
                D014078

MASSENET

Thaïs (1894) – opera
  Méditation arr. vln & pf Marsick
  with piano
                Mezhdunarodnaya Kniga
                D5144/5

MONASTERIO

Serenata andaluza vln & pf
  with L. Epshtein pf
                Mezhdunarodnaya Kniga
                D014078

PURCELL

Aria in a unid – arr. vln & pf Moffat
  with piano
                Mezhdunarodnaya Kniga
                D5144/5

RIMSKY–KORSAKOV

(The) Snow Maiden (1882) – opera
  Dance of the tumblers arr. vln & pf
  with Y. Kaletsky pf
                Mezhdunarodnaya Kniga
                D014077

STATKOVSKI

Cracovienne, Op. 7 "Krakowiak" vln & pf
  with piano
                Mezhdunarodnaya Kniga
                D5144/5

VALDEZ

Sérénade du Tzigane vln & pf
  with E. Dyachenko pf
                Mezhdunarodnaya Kniga
                D014077

VECSEY

Valse triste vln & pf
  with piano
                Mezhdunarodnaya Kniga
                D5144/5

VIEUXTEMPS

(6) Divertissements d'Amateurs sur des Mélodies russes, Op. 24 vln & pf
  No. 1. Romance (Otgadaj, moja rodnaja "Divine, ma bien–Aimée) (after
  Alexander Lvovich Gurilyov, 1803–1858)
  with piano
                Mezhdunarodnaya Kniga
                D5144/5

  No. 3. Romance (after Alexander Sergeyevich Dargomizhsky, 1813–1869)
  with E. Seimovich pf
                Mezhdunarodnaya Kniga
                D014078

ZARZYCKI

Mazurka in G, Op. 26 vln & pf
  with piano
                Mezhdunarodnaya Kniga
                D5144/5

FURNEY

SCHWARTZ

Aria No. 2 vln & drms
  with Thrailkill drms
                Advance FGR7

Arkady FUTER

CHULAKI

Improvisation & Fugue solo vln
  (unaccompanied)
                Mezhdunarodnaya Kniga
                D11055/6

KNIPPER

Concerto in D "Little" vln & str orch.
  with Moscow Radio Symphony Orch.
  Strings – Rozhdestvensky
                Mezhdunarodnaya Kniga
                D021817

ROUSSEL

Serenade in C, Op. 30 fl, vln, vla, vlc & hp
  with A. Korneyev fl, M. Miloslavsky
  vla, R. Furer vlc & O. Erdeli hp
                Mezhdunarodnaya Kniga
                D024119/20, S01831/2

Louis GABOWITZ

BIBER

(8) Sonatas (1681) vln & c
  Sonata No. 6, in c
  with A. Salerno pf
                Bruno BR14037, SBR32001

GRIEG

Sonata No. 3, in c, Op. 45 vln & pf
  with A. Salerno pf   Bruno BR14038, SBR32002

HAYDN

Sonata No. 1, in G, H.XV, No. 32 (1794) vln & hpsi
  with A. Salerno pf   Bruno BR14037, SBR32001

MOZART

Sonata No. 18, in G, K301 vln & pf
  with A. Salerno pf   Bruno BR14037, SBR32001

VIVALDI

Concerto in g, P.359 "Per S.A.R. di Sassonia" 3 obs, bsn, vln, 2 hrns, strs & c
  with L. Arner ob, H. Smyles ob, A.   Library of Recorded
  Laubin ob, A. Checchia bsn, J. Eger   Masterpieces Vol. 2, No. 2
  hrn, D. Corrado hrn, E. Earle hpsi &
  New York Sinfonietta – Goberman

(12) Sonatas, Op. 2 (1712) vln & c
  Sonata No. 2, in A, F.XIII, No. 30 (ed. David)
  with A. Salerno pf   Bruno BR14037, SBR32001

André GABRIËL

GLAZOUNOV

Concerto in a, Op. 82 vln & orch.
  with RIAS Symphony Orch. – Jochum   Remington RLP199–191

Jacob H. GADE

BEETHOVEN

(6) Minuets, G167 pf
  No. 2. Minuet No. 2, in G arr. vln & pf Burmester
  with piano   HMV X287990

GOSSEC

Rosine (1786) – opera
  Gavotte arr. vln & pf Burmester
  with piano   HMV X2–287903

KREISLER

Liebesleid vln & pf
  with piano   HMV X2–287902

RAMEAU

Castor et Pollux (1737) – opera
  Gavotte (Act IV) arr. vln & pf Burmester
  with piano   HMV X287991

Jules GAILLARD

TOSELLI

Serenade, Op. 6 vln & pf
  with piano   Parlophone E6201

Michael GAISER

HANDEL

(12) Concerti grossi, Op. 6 (1739) 2 vlns, vlc & strs
  Concerto grosso No. 1, in G
  with S. Lautenbacher vlc, R. Blees vlc,   Intercord (in set 973–09Z)
  M. Galling hpsi & Süddeutsche
  Chamber Philharmonic, Stuttgart –
  Wich

  Concerto grosso No. 2, in F
  with S. Lautenbacher vlc, T. Blees vlc,   Intercord (in set 973–09Z)
  M. Galling hpsi & Süddeutsche
  Chamber Philharmonic, Stuttgart –
  Wich

  Concerto No. 3, in e
  with S. Lautenbacher vlc, T. Blees vlc,   Intercord (in set 973–09Z)
  M. Galling hpsi & Süddeutsche
  Chamber Philharmonic, Stuttgart –
  Wich

  Concerto grosso No. 4, in a
  with S. Lautenbacher vlc, T. Blees vlc,   Intercord (in set 973–09Z)
  M. Galling hpsi & Süddeutsche
  Chamber Philharmonic, Stuttgart –
  Wich

  Concerto grosso No. 5, in D
  with S. Lautenbacher vlc, T. Blees vlc,   Intercord (in set 973–09Z)
  M. Galling hpsi & Süddeutsche
  Chamber Philharmonic, Stuttgart –
  Wich

  Concerto grosso No. 6, in g
  with S. Lautenbacher vlc, T. Blees vlc,   Intercord (in set 973–09Z)
  M. Galling hpsi & Süddeutsche
  Chamber Philharmonic, Stuttgart –
  Wich

  Concerto grosso No. 7, in B flat
  with S. Lautenbacher vlc, T. Blees vlc,   Intercord (in set 973–09Z)
  M. Galling hpsi & Süddeutsche
  Chamber Philharmonic, Stuttgart –
  Wich

  Concerto grosso No. 8, in c
  with S. Lautenbacher vlc, T. Blees vlc,   Intercord (in set 973–09Z)
  M. Galling hpsi & Süddeutsche
  Chamber Philharmonic, Stuttgart –
  Wich

  Concerto grosso No. 9, in F
  with S. Lautenbacher vlc, T. Blees vlc,   Intercord (in set 973–09Z)
  M. Galling hpsi & Süddeutsche
  Chamber Philharmonic, Stuttgart –
  Wich

  Concerto grosso No. 10, in d
  with S. Lautenbacher vlc, T. Blees vlc,   Intercord (in set 973–09Z)
  M. Galling hpsi & Süddeutsche
  Chamber Philharmonic, Stuttgart –
  Wich

  Concerto grosso No. 11, in A
  with S. Lautenbacher vlc, T. Blees vlc,   Intercord (in set 973–09Z)
  M. Galling hpsi & Süddeutsche
  Chamber Philharmonic, Stuttgart –
  Wich

HANDEL – *Continued*

Concerto grosso No. 12, in b
with S. Lautenbacher vlc, T. Blees vlc,   Intercord (in set 973–09Z)
M. Galling hpsi & Süddeutsche
Chamber Philharmonic, Stuttgart –
Wich

Lionel GALI

MASSENET

Thaïs (1894) – opera
  Méditation
  with orch. – Etcheverry   Vega C30A315/7

SAINT-SAËNS

Quintet in a, Op. 14 pf, 2 vlns, vla & vlc
  with J. Laforge pf, M. Noel vln, B.   HMV C063–10980
  Pasquier vla & R. Bex vlc

Septet in E flat, Op. 65 tpt, 2 vlns, vla, vlc, cbs & pf
  with A. Lagorce tpt, M. Noel vln, B.   HMV C063–10980
  Pasquier vla, R. Bex vlc, J. Cazauran
  cbs & J. Laforge pf

VIVALDI

(12) Concerti, Op. 3 "L'Estro armonico" var. cbns & strs
  Concerto No. 1, in D, P.146 (F.IV, No. 8) 4 vlns, vlc, strs & c
  with J. Champeil vln, R. Gendre vln,   Ducretet–Thomson LAG1014
  L. Yordanoff vln & Pro Musica Orch.
  – Saguer
  Concerto No. 7, in F, P.249 (F.IV, No. 9) 4 vlns, strs & c
  with J. Champeil vln, R. Gendre vln,   Ducretet–Thomson LAG1014
  L. Yordanoff vln & Pro Musica Orch.
  – Saguer

Felix GALIMIR

BACH

(6) Brandenburg Concerti, BWV1046/51 (1721) strs & c
  Brandenburg Concerto No. 3, in G, BWV1048 3 vlns, 3 vlas, 3 vlcs & cbs
  with N. Koutzen vln, H. Kwalwasser   Library of Recorded
  vln, B. Yokell vla, B. Zaslaw vla, B.   Masterpieces BB1
  Robbins vla, S. Hunkins vlc, A.   Odyssey 32 16 0190 (in set 32 26
  Kouguell vlc, J. Schneider vlc, J.   0014)
  Levine cbs, F. Rupp hpsi & New York
  Sinfonietta – Goberman

  Brandenburg Concerto No. 5, in D, BWV1050 clav, fl, vln & strs
  with J. Wummer fl, F. Rupp hpsi &   Library of Recorded
  New York Sinfonietta – Goberman   Masterpieces BB3
                    Odyssey 32 16 0188/90, (in set
                    32 26 0014)

BEETHOVEN

(6) Quartets, Op. 18 2 vlns, vla & vlc
  No. 1. Quartet No. 4, in c
  with E. Morini vln, W. Trampler vla   Westminster W9074, XWN18595
  & L. Varga vlc

BOCCHERINI

(6) Quintets, Op. 13 2 vlns, vla & 2 vlcs
  No. 5. Quintet No. 5, in E "Bull"
  with A. Schneider vln, M. Tree vla, D.   I Classici della Musica Classica
  Soyer vlc & L. Harrell vlc   SXVA4183
                    Philips GL5861, ŠGL5861
                    Vanguard VRS1147, VSD71147

(6) Quintets, Op. 57 (1799) pf, 2 vlns, vla & vlc
  No. 6. Quintet No. 6, in C, Op. 57 "La Ritirata di Madrid" gtr, 2 vlns,
  vla & vlc*
  with A. Diaz gtr, A. Schneider vln, M.   I Classici della Musica Classica
  Tree vla & D. Soyer vlc   SXVA4183
                    Philips GL5861, SGL5861
                    Vanguard VRS1147, VSD71147

DVOŘÁK

Quintet in A, Op. 81 pf, 2 vlns, vla & vlc
  with P. Serkin pf, A. Schneider vln,   Amadeo AVRS6008
  M. Tree vla & D. Soyer vlc   Philips GL5863, SGL5863
                    Vanguard SRV288SD, VRS1148,
                    VSD71148

HANDEL

(12) Concerti grossi, Op. 6 2 vlns, vlc & strs
  Concerto gorsso No. 1, in G
  with A. Schneider vln, C. McCracken   Victor (in set LSC6172)
  vlc, R. Conant hpsi & Chamber Orch.
  – Schneider

  Concerto grosso No. 2, in F
  with A. Schneider vln, C. McCracken   Victor (in set LSC6172)
  vlc, R. Conant hpsi & Chamber Orch.
  – Schneider

  Concerto grosso No. 3, in e
  with A. Schneider vln, C. McCracken   Victor (in set LSC6172)
  vlc, R. Conant hpsi & Chamber Orch.
  – Schneider

  Concerto grosso No. 4, in a
  with A. Schneider vln, C. McCracken   Victor (in set LSC6172)
  vlc, R. Conant hpsi & Chamber Orch.
  – Schneider

  Concerto grosso No. 5, in D
  with A. Schneider vln, C. McCracken   Victor (in set LSC6172)
  vlc, R. Conant hpsi & Chamber Orch.
  – Schenider

  Concerto grosso No. 6, in g
  with A. Schneider vln, C. McCracken   Victor (in set LSC6172)
  vlc, R. Conant hpsi & Chamber Orch.
  – Schneider

  Concerto grosso No. 7, in B flat
  with A. Schneider vln, C. McCracken   Victor (in set LSC6172)
  vlc, R. Conant hpsi & Chamber Orch.
  – Schneider

  Concerto grosso No. 8, in c
  with A. Schneider vln, C. McCracken   Victor (in set LSC6172)
  vlc, R. Conant hpsi & Chamber Orch.
  – Schneider

* Boccherini's own transcription of the piano quintets, Op. 57.

HANDEL – *Continued*

Concerto grosso No. 9, in F
with A. Schneider vln, C. McCracken   Victor (in set LSC6172)
vlc, R. Conant hpsi & Chamber Orch.
– Schneider

Concerto grosso No. 10, in d
with A. Schneider vln, C. McCracken   Victor (in set LSC6172)
vlc, R. Conant hpsi & Chamber Orch.
– Schneider

Concerto grosso No. 11, in A
with A. Schneider vln, C. McCracken   Victor (in set LSC6172)
vlc, R. Conant hpsi & Chamber Orch.
– Schneider

Concerto grosso No. 12, in b
with A. Schneider vln, C. McCracken   Victor (in set LSC6172)
vlc, R. Conant hpsi & Chamber Orch.
– Schneider

MOZART

Quartet No. 23, in F, K590 2 vlns, vla & vlc
with E. Morini vln, W. Trampler vla   Westminster W9074, XWN18595
& L. Varga vlc

VIVALDI

Concerto in a, P.77 (F.XII, No. 11) 2 vlns, fl, vlc, strs & c
with H. Kwalwasser vln, H. Jones fl,   Library of Recorded
C. McCracken vlc, E. Earle hpsi &   Masterpieces Vol. 2, No. 4
New York Sinfonietta – Goberman

Concerto in C, P.84 (F.XII, No. 14) "Per la Solennità di St. Lorenzo" 2 fls,
2 obs, 2 cls, 2 vlns, bsn, strs & c
with S. Baron fl, H. Jones fl, L. Arner   Library of Recorded
ob, H. Smyles ob, C. Paashaus cl, W.   Masterpieces Vol. 1, No. 3
Lewis cl, L. Bolotine vln, A. Checchia
bsn, E. Earle hpsi & New York
Sinfonietta – Goberman

Concerto in G, P.135 (F.IV, No. 1) 2 vlns, 2 vlcs, strs & c
with N. Koutzen vln, C. McCracken   Library of Recorded
vlc, T. Brys vlc, E. Earle hpsi & New   Masterpieces Vol. 1, No. 12
York Sinfonietta – Goberman

Concerto in B flat, P.406 (F.XII, No. 16) vln, ob, strs & c
with H. Shulman ob, E. Earle hpsi &   Library of Recorded
New York Sinfonietta – Goberman   Masterpieces Vol. 2, No. 5

Sonata in c, F.XVI, No. 1 (P.7, No. 1) (Op. 24) vln, vlc & c
with C. McCracken vlc, A. Checchia   Library of Recorded
bsn & E. Earle hpsi   Masterpieces Vol. 1, No. 11

Mario GALLI (–1937)

BECCE

Légende d'amour, Op. 11 pf – arr. vln & pf
with piano   4780 ar   Polyphon XS47510

DRDLA

Souvenir vln & pf
with piano   W 44890   Columbia 18396

DVOŘÁK

(8) Humoresques, Op. 101 pf
No. 7. Humoresque No. 7, in G flat arr. vln & pf "in G" Kreisler
with piano   W 44889   Columbia 18396

GALLI

Serenata veneziana vln & pf
with piano   Columbia 18421

HANDEL

Serse (1738) – opera
Ombra mai fu "Largo" arr. vln & pf
with piano   W 44547   Columbia 8657

HUBAY

(2) Mazurkas, Op. 45 vln & pf
No 1. Mazurka No. 1, in a "Madame Leopold Horowitz"
with piano   4781 ar   Polyphon XS47510

Nocturne in a, Op. 42 vln & pf
with piano   Columbia 18422

KÄMPE

Bagatelle vln & pf
with piano   W 44758   Columbia 18420

RAFF

(6) Pieces, Op. 85 vln & pf
No. 3. Cavatina in D
with piano   W 44548   Columbia 8657

RÜTHSTRÖM

(En) Gammal – waltz vln & pf
with piano   W 44759   Columbia 18420

SALESSKI

Rêverie triste vln & pf
with piano   Columbia 18422

SIMONETTI

Madrigale pf – arr. vln & pf
with piano   Columbia 18421

Walter GALLOZZI

CORELLI

(12) Concerti grossi, Op. 6 orch.
Concerto grosso No. 4, in D
with F. Ayo vln, E. Altobelli vlc & I   Epic LC3264
Musici   Philips A00787L, ABR4069,
G03090L, GBL5621, L02246L

Concerto grosso No. 5, in B flat
with F. Ayo vln, E. Altobelli vlc & I   Philips S06081R, SBR6207
Musici

Concerto grosso No. 7, in D
with F. Ayo vln, E. Altobelli vlc & I   Epic LC3264
Musici   Philips A00787L, ABR4069

Concerto grosso No. 8, in g "Christmas concerto"
with F. Ayo vln, E. Altobelli vlc & I   Epic LC3264
Musici   Fontana 894107ZKY
Philips 400024AE, 411946SE,
802734AY, (in set C71AX401),
835129AY, ABE10029,
PHM500025, PHS900025,
S06081R, SBR6207

CORELLI – *Continued*

Concerto grosso No. 9, in F
with F. Ayo vln, E. Altobelli vlc & I   Epic LC3264
Musici   Philips A00787L, ABR4069

Concerto grosso No. 10, in C
with F. Ayo vln, E. Altobelli vlc & I   Epic LC3264
Musici   Philips A00787L, ABR4069

GEMINIANI

(6) Concerti grossi, Op. 7 orch.
Concerto grosso No. 1, in D
with F. Ayo vln, B. Giuranna vla, E.   Philips 839304EGY, PHC9010
Altobelli vlc & I Musici

Concerto grosso No. 2, in d
with F. Ayo vln, B. Giuranna vla, E.   Philips 839304EGY, PHC9010
Altobelli vlc & I Musici

Concerto grosso No. 3, in C
with F. Ayo vln, B. Giuranna vla, E.   Philips 839304EGY, PHC9010
Altobelli vlc & I Musici

Concerto grosso No. 5, in c
with F. Ayo vln, B. Giuranna vla, E.   Philips 839304EGY, PHC9010
Altobelli vlc & I Musici

Concerto grosso No. 6, in B flat
with F. Ayo vln, B. Giuranna vla, E.   Philips 839304EGY, PHC9010
Altobelli vlc & I Musici

VIVALDI

(12) Concerti, Op. 3 "L'Estro armonico" var, cbns & strs
Concerto No. 1, in D, P.146 (F.IV, No. 8) 4 vlns, vlc, strs & c
with R. Michelucci vln, A–M. Cotogni   Philips 835162AY, A02277L,
vln, L. Vicari vln & I Musici   PHC9111, (in set PHC3–017)

Concerto No. 4, in e, P.97 (F.I, No. 174) 4 vlns, strs & c
with R. Michelucci vln, A–M. Cotogni   Philips 835162AY, A02277L,
vln, L. Vicari vln & I Musici   PHC9111, (in set PHC3–017)

Concerto No. 7, in F, P.249 (F.IV, No. 9) 4 vlns, strs & c
with R. Michelucci vln, A–M. Cotogni   Philips 835163AY, A02278L,
vln, L. Vicari vln & I Musici   PHC9112, (in set PHC3–017)

Concerto No. 10, in b, P.148 (F.IV, No. 10) 4 vlns, strs & c
with R. Michelucci vln, A–M. Cotogni   Fontana 894075ZKY
vln, L. Vicari vln & I Musici   Philips 802735AY, (in set
   71AX401), 835164AY,
   839526VGY, A02279L,
   PHC9113, (in set PHC3–017)

Concerto in D, P.208 (F.I, No. 10) (Op. 51, No. 1) "l'Inquietude" vln strs
& c
with I Musici   Epic BC1021, LC3486
   Philips 835002AY, 839839GSY,
   A00476L, ABL3237

Concerto in A, P.222 (F.I, No. 139) "L'eco in lontano" 2 vlns, strs & c
with F. Zampani vln & I Musici   Philips CXL15000

Concerto in F, P.278 (F.I, No. 34) 3 vlns, strs & c
with F. Ayo vln, F. Tamponi vln & I   Angel 35088
Musici   Columbia CX1163, FCX305,
   QCX10039
   HMV LALP209

Ettore GANDINI

BACH

(4) Suites, BWV1066/9 strs & c
Suite No. 3, in D: Air (2nd mvt) BWV1068 2 obs, 3 tpts, drms & strs
arr. vln & strs
with I.C.B.S. Orch. –   XXVAT 2   Musique au Vatican 1151
Antonelli

PORPORA

Aria in E unid – arr. vln & strs
with I.C.B.S. Orch. –   XXVAT 3   Musique au Vatican 1151
Antonelli

VERACINI

(12) Sonatas, Op. 2 (1744) "Sonate accademiche" vln & c
Sonata No. 6, in A: Largo (2nd mvt) arr. vln & strs
with I.C.B.S. Orch. –   XXVAT 30   Musique au Vatican 1152
Antonelli

Leonelli GANDINO

DRDLA

Souvenir vln & pf
with piano   5072²   Imperial 2015

MONTAVANI

Impromptu serenade vln & pf
with piano   5073²   Imperial 2015

S. GANIEV

BACH

Concerto No. 1, in a, BWV1041 vln, strs & c
with Azerbaijanian Radio Chamber   Mezhdunarodnaya Kniga
Orch. – Rzayev   D21767

KARAYEV

Sonata in d vln & pf
with Z. Adigezal–Zadeh pf   Mezhdunarodnaya Kniga
   D21768

Carl GARAGULY (1900–)

AULIN

(4) Aquarelles vln & pf
No. 2. Humoresque
with S. Frykberg pf   BE 1429   HMV X3089
No. 3. Vaggsång
with S. Frykberg pf   BE 1430   HMV X3282

BRAHMS

(21) Hungarian Dances pf duet
Hungarian dance No. 2, in d arr. vln & pf Joachim
with S. Frykberg pf   BE 1427   HMV X3089

GARAGULY

Csárdas vln & pf – arr. S. Erhardt
with T. Wiberg pf   CU 3028–A   Cupol 6039

GARAGULY – *Continued*

Hungarian fantasy vln & pf
with T. Wiberg pf   CU 3027–A   Cupol 6039

HANDEL

(15) Sonatas, Op. 1 (?1731) fl or vln & c
Sonata No. 9, in b: Andante (1st mvt) arr. vln & pf as "Larghetto" by Hubay
with S. Frykberg pf   BE 1415   HMV X3088

LULLY

Ballet du Roy (1659)
Gavotte arr. vln & pf
with S. Frykberg pf   BE 1416   HMV X3088

VECSEY

Valse triste vln & pf
with S. Frykberg pf   BE 1428   HMV X3282

Arthur GARAMI (1921–)

BARRAUD

Sonatina (1941) vln & pf
with C. Reiner pf   CBC Transcription Program 137

BARTÓK

(6) Rumanian folk dances (1915) pf – arr. vln & pf Székely
with G. Solchany pf   Pacific 3251, PIZ1574

DINICU

Hora staccato vln & ens – arr. vln & pf Heifetz
with G. Solchany pf   Pacific PIZ1571, PIZ6166

DOHNÁNYI

Ruralia Hungarica, Op. 32A pf – arr. vln & pf Kreisler
with G. Solchany pf   Pacific PIZ1568/9, PIZ6164/5

KASEMETS

Sonata vln & pf
with C. Reiner pf   CBC Transcription Program 137

PAGANINI

Moto perpetuo (Allegro di concert) Op. 11 (1830) vln & orch.
with G. Solchany pf   Pacific PIZ1571, PIZ6166

PARADIES

Sicilienne vln & pf – arr. Dushkin
with G. Solchany pf   Pacific PIZ6168

RIMSKY–KORSAKOV

(The) Tale of Tsar Saltan (1900) – opera
Flight of the bumblebee (Act III) orch. – arr. vln & pf Hartmann
with G. Solchany pf   Pacific PIZ6165

SCHUBERT, François

(12) Bagatelles, Op. 13 vln & pf
No. 9. L'abeille
with G. Solchany pf   Pacific PIZ6165

VITALI

Chaconne in g vln & c – arr. Charlier
with G. Solchany pf   Pacific PIZ 6167/8

György GARAY (1909–)

BARTÓK

Concerto No. 2 (1938) vln & orch.
with Leipzig Radio Symphony Orch. – Deutsche Grammophon
Kegel   LPM18786, SLPM138786
For Children (40 pieces) (1909) pf
nos. 6, 13, 18, 25, 31, 36 & 40 arr. vln & pf as "Hungarian folk tunes"
by Szigeti
with E. Petri pf   Qualiton SZN3054
Sonatina in D (on 3 Transylvanian peasant themes) (1915) pf – transc. vln & pf Gertler
with I. Hajdu pf   Qualiton EP3510

BERG

Concerto (1935) vln & orch.
with Leipzig Radio Symphony Orch. – Eterna 820538
Kegel   Heliodor 89786

BRAHMS

Sonata No. 3, in d, Op. 108 vln & pf
with A. Rakowski pf   Edition Rhodos ERS1205

DOHNÁNYI

Ruralia Hungarica, Op. 32A pf – arr. vln & pf Kreisler
with E. Petri pf   Qualiton HLP3501

GOLDMARK

Concerto in a, Op. 28 vln & orch.
with Hungarian State Concert Orch. – Qualiton HLPX1021
Bródy

HUBAY

(Le) Luthier de Crémone, Op. 40 (1894) – opera
Intermezzo orch. – arr. vln & pf Hubay
with E. Petri pf   Qualiton QKM5002

KÓKAY

Verbunkos rapszódia (Recruiting rhapsody) (1955) vln & pf
with E. Petri pf   Qualiton HLP3501

LEHÁR

Paganini (1925) – operetta
Zigeunerfest (Act II) arr. vln & orch.
with orch.   Qualiton QNM7031

LISZT

Duo Sonata (on Chopin's "Mazurka in c sharp", Op. 6 no. 2) R127 (1832/5) vln & pf
with A. Rakowski pf   Edition Rhodos ERS1205

PAGANINI

(24) Caprices, Op. 1 (1801/7) solo vln
Caprice No. 13, in B flat arr. vln & pf Petri
with E. Petri pf   Qualiton QKM5006

POLGÁR

Serenade (1924) vln & pf
with E. Petri pf   Qualiton QKM5006

TARTINI

Sonata in g "Il Trillo del Diavolo" vln & c – arr. vln & pf Kreisler
with E. Petri pf   Qualiton HLP3501

VECSEY

Valse triste vln & pf
with E. Petri pf — Qualiton QKM5007

VLADIGEROV

Vardar (Rapsodie bulgare) Op. 16 vln & orch.
with E. Petri pf — Qualiton SZN3005

ZSOLT

Berceuse in D flat (1908) vln & pf
with E. Petri pf — Qualiton QKM5002

Satyre et Dryades vln & pf
with E. Petri pf — Qualiton QKM5007

Mario GARDI

BRUCH

Concerto No. 1, in g, Op. 26 vln & orch.
Adagio (2nd mvt)
with Hamburg — 03039 LWS — Polydor 20047, 58605,
Philharmonic Orch. – Brückner– — EPH21170
Rüggeberg

SVENDSEN

Romance in G, Op. 26 vln & orch.
with Hamburg — 03038 LWS — Polydor 20047, 58605,
Philharmonic Orch. – Brückner– — EPH21170
Rüggeberg

Samuel GARDNER (1892–)

BAYLY

Long, long ago (1843) v & pf – arr. vln & orch.
with orch. — Victor 17888

BEETHOVEN

Sonata No. 12, in A flat, Op. 26 pf
Marcia funebra (3rd mvt) arr. vln & pf Gardner
with piano — Edison Diamond Disc 50205

BÉRIOT

Concerto No. 2, in b, Op. 32 vln & orch.
Andante (2nd mvt)
with orch. — Victor 18175

DVOŘÁK

(8) Humoresques, Op. 101 pf
No. 7. Humoresque No. 7, in G flat arr. vln & pf "in G" Wilhelmj
with piano — Edison Cylinder 2485

FOSTER

My old Kentucky home v & pf – arr. vln & orch.
with orch. — Victor 17756

FRIML

Mignonette, Op. 59 vln & pf
with piano — Edison Diamond Disc 50139

HANBY

Darling Nellie Gray (1856) v & pf – arr. vln & orch.
with orch. — Victor 17888

KREISLER

Sicilienne & Rigaudon (Francoeur) vln & pf
with piano — Edison Diamond Disc 50139

Variations on a theme of Corelli (Tartini) vln & pf
with piano — Edison Diamond Disc 50205

MOORE

Believe me if all those endearing young charms v & pf – arr. vln & orch.
with orch. — Victor 17871

(The) Last rose of summer v & pf – arr. vln & pf Auer
with orch. — Victor 17871

SCOTT, Lady John

Annie Laurie (Scottish ballad) (1838) v & pf – arr. vln, hp & orch.
with harp & orch. — Victor 17756

Liliane GARNIER

BACH

Concerto No. 2, in E, BWV1042 vln, strs & c
with orch. – Kuentz — Club National du Disque CND1051/2

Concerto in d, BWV1043 2 vlns, strs & c
with M. Frasca–Colombier vln & orch. — Club National du Disque
– Kuentz — CND1051/2

Concerto in c, BWV1060 vln & ob or 2 vlns, strs & c
with M. Frasca–Colombier vln & orch. — Club National du Disque
– Kuentz — CND1051/2

BARTÓK

(6) Rumanian folk dances (1915) pf – arr. vln & pf Székely
with A–M. Globenski pf — Victor CC1004, CCS1004,
LM2646, LSC2646

BEETHOVEN

Romance No. 2, in F, Op. 50 vln & orch.
with A–M. Globenski pf — Victor CC1004, CCS1004,
LM2646, LSC2646

DEBUSSY

(12) Préludes – Book I (1910) pf
No. 8. La Fille aux cheveux de lin arr. vln & pf Hartmann
with A–M. Globenski pf — Victor CC1004, CCS1004,
LM2646, LSC2646

DELVINCOURT

Sonata in d (1923) vln & pf
with J–P. Sevilla pf — Club National du Disque 3

KREISLER

Caprice viennois, Op. 2 vln & pf
with A–M. Globenski pf — Victor CC1004, CCS1004,
LM2646, LSC2646

Variations on a theme of Corelli (Tartini) vln & pf
with A–M. Globenski pf — Victor CC1004, CCS1004,
LM2646, LSC2646

PAGANINI

(24) Caprices, Op. 1 (1801/7) solo vln
Caprice No. 20, in D
(unaccompanied)　　　　　　　Victor CC1004, CCS1004,
　　　　　　　　　　　　　　　　LM2646, LSC2646

Concerto No. 2, in b, Op. 7 vln & orch.
Ronde à la clochette (2nd mvt) "La Campanella" arr. vln & pf Kreisler
　with piano　　　　　　　　　Club National du Disque
　　　　　　　　　　　　　　　　CND1046

Sonata a preghière "Moses Fantasia" (on the aria "Dal tuo stellato soglio"
　from Rossini's opera "Mosè in Egitto") Op. 24 (1818 or 1819) vln &
　orch.
　with piano　　　　　　　　　Club National du Disque
　　　　　　　　　　　　　　　　CND1046

RAVEL

Berceuse sur le nom de Gabriel Fauré (1922) vln & pf
　with R. Zugaro pf　　　　　　Club National du Disque
　　　　　　　　　　　　　　　　CND1029

Sonatina in f sharp (1905) pf
Menuet (2nd mvt) arr. vln & pf Roques
　with R. Zugaro pf　　　　　　Club National du Disque
　　　　　　　　　　　　　　　　CND1029

Tzigane (Rapsodie de concert) (1924) vln & pf or orch.
　with R. Zugaro pf　　　　　　Club National du Disque
　　　　　　　　　　　　　　　　CND1029

Tzigane (Rapsodie de concert) (1924) vln & pf or orch.
　with A–M. Globenski pf　　　Victor CC1004, CCS1004,
　　　　　　　　　　　　　　　　LM2646, LSC2646

WIENIAWSKI

Polonaise brillante No. 1, in D, Op. 4 vln & pf
　with piano　　　　　　　　　Club National du Disque
　　　　　　　　　　　　　　　　CND1046

Polonaise brillante No. 1, in D, Op. 4 vln & pf
　with A–M. Globenski pf　　　Victor CC1004, CCS1004,
　　　　　　　　　　　　　　　　LM2646, LSC2646

Scherzo–tarantelle, Op. 16 vln & pf
　with piano　　　　　　　　　Club National du Disque
　　　　　　　　　　　　　　　　CND1046

ZARZYCKI

Mazurka in G, Op. 26 vln & pf
　with piano　　　　　　　　　Club National du Disque
　　　　　　　　　　　　　　　　CND1046

Tibor GAŠPAREK (1913–　)

FREŠO

Capriccio (1948) vln & pf
　with M. Karin pf　　　　　　Supraphon 3892
Toccata, Op. 5 vln & pf
　with M. Karin pf　　　　　　Supraphon 3867

JUROVSKÝ

Romance (1933) vln & pf
　with M. Karin pf　　　　　　Supraphon 3864, 3879

MATÚŠKA

Variations vln & pf
　with M. Karin pf　　　　　　Supraphon 3879

MOYZES

Suite poetique, Op. 35 vln & pf
　with M. Karin pf　　　　　　Ultraphon H23473/5

OČENÁŠ

Children's Suite vln & pf
Nocturne
　with M. Karin pf　　　　　　Supraphon 3892

SUCHOŇ

Fantasy & Burlesque, Op. 7 vln & orch.
　with Slovak Philharmonic Orch. –　　Supraphon LPM79
　Rajter　　　　　　　　　　　　　Ultraphon H23608/11
Sonata, Op. 11 vln & pf
　with M. Karin pf　　　　　　Supraphon LPM458, SUG20362

G. GAUNET

TELEMANN

Concerto in D 4 vlns, strs & c
　with J. Dejean vln, F. Geyr vln, J.　　Éditions phonographiques
　Pasquier vln & Paris Collegium　　　parisiennes APG125
　Musette – Douatte

Jeanne GAUTIER (1898–　)

BAZZINI

(La) Ronde des lutins, Op. 25 vln & pf
　with F. Gaveau pf　　　　　　Odeon 166406

BRAHMS

(21) Hungarian Dances pf duet
Hungarian dance No. 5, in f sharp arr. vln & pf "in g" Joachim
　with F. Gaveau pf　　　　　　Odeon 166315
(16) Waltzes, Op. 39 pf duet
No. 15. Waltz No. 15, in A flat arr. vln & pf "in A" Hochstein
　with F. Gaveau pf　　　　　　Odeon 166455

BRUCH

Kol Nidrei, Op. 47 vlc or vln & orch.
　with F. Gaveau pf　　　　　　Odeon 171118

DEBUSSY

(La) Plus que lente – valse (1910) pf – arr. vln & pf Roques
　with J.D. Todd pf　　　　　　Columbia DOX671
(La) Plus que lente – valse (1910) pf – arr. vln & pf Roques
　with F. Gaveau pf　　　　　　Odeon 171104

DRDLA

Serenade No. 1, in A vln & pf
　with F. Gaveau pf　　　K 13356[1]　Odeon 166314, 0–26226
Souvenir vln & pf
　with F. Gaveau pf　　　K 12695[2]　Odeon 166227, 0–26226

DVOŘÁK

(8) Humoresques, Op. 101 pf
No. 7. Humoresque No. 7, in G flat arr. vln & pf "in G" Kreisler
　with F. Gaveau pf　　　　　　Odeon 166022, 221038A, 0–4043,
　　　　　　　　　　　　　　　　182649
　　　　　　　　　　　　　　　　Parlophone R275

FALLA

(7) Canciones populares españolas (1914) v & pf
  No. 1. El paño moruna arr. vln & pf Kochański
           PARTX 9261–22   Le Chant du Monde GA5062
  with N. Desouches pf
  No. 3. Asturiana arr. vln & pf Kochański
           PARTX 9262–22   Le Chant du Monde GA5062
  with N. Desouches pf
  No. 4 Jota arr. vln & pf Kochański
           PARTX 9263–22B   Le Chant du Monde GA5062
  with N. Desouches pf
  No. 5. Nana arr. vln & pf Kochański
           PARTX 9261–22   Le Chant du Monde GA5062
  with N. Desouches pf
  No. 6. Canción arr. vln & pf Kochański
           PARTX 9262–22   Le Chant du Monde GA5062
  with N. Desouches pf
  No. 7 Polo arr. vln & pf Kochański
           PARTX 9263–22B   Le Chant du Monde GA5063
  with N. Desouchs pf
(La) Vida breve (1913) – opera
  Danza española orch. – arr. vln & pf Kreisler
  with J.D. Todd pf   Columbia DOX671
  Danza española orch. – arr. vln & pf Kreisler
  with F. Gaveau pf   Odeon 171104

FAURÉ

Berceuse, Op. 16 vln & pf
  with F. Gaveau pf   Odeon 166039
Trio in d, Op. 120 pf, vln & vlc
  with G. Joy pf & A. Levy vlc   Prétoria CL8001

GAILLARD

Weekend vln & pf
  Blues
  with M–F. Gaillard pf   Odeon 166682
  Forestside
  with M–F. Gaillard pf   Odeon 166681
  Riverside
  with M–F. Gaillard pf   Odeon 166682
  Seaside
  with M–F. Gaillard pf   Odeon 166682

GERSHWIN

Short story vln & pf
  with J.D. Todd pf   Columbia DO2362

GLAZOUNOV

Méditation, Op. 32 vln & pf
  with F. Gaveau pf   Odeon 166227

GRANADOS

(12) Danzas españolas, Op. 37 (1893) pf
  No. 5. Danza española No. 5, in e "Andaluza" arr. vln & pf Kreisler
  with F. Gaveau pf   Odeon 166454

HANDEL

(15) Sonatas, Op. 1 (?1731) fl or vln & c
  Sonata No. 14, in A vln V
  with M. le Marc'Hadour pf   Odeon 188958

HUBAY

(6) Blumenleben, Op. 30 vln & pf
  No. 5. Der Zephir
  with F. Gaveau pf   Odeon 166125

KREISLER

Caprice viennois, Op. 2 vln & pf
  with F. Gaveau pf   Odeon 171118, 221038A
Liebesleid vln & pf
  with F. Gaveau pf   Odeon 166125
Rondino on a theme by Beethoven vln & pf
  with F. Gaveau pf   Ki 1722[2]   Decca G20270
                                        Odeon 166118
Tambourin chinois, Op. 3 vln & pf
  with F. Gaveau pf   Ki 1251[2]   Odeon O 4033, 166038, 182487
Allegretto (Boccherini) vln & pf
  with F. Gaveau pf   Odeon 166314
Andantino (Padre Martini) vln & pf
  with F. Gaveau pf   Odeon 166454
(La) Chasse (Cartier) vln & pf
  with F. Gaveau pf   Ki 1252[2]   Odeon O 4044, 166038, 182487
Praeludium & Allegro (Pugnani) vln & pf
  with F. Gaveau pf   Odeon 166230
Variations on a theme of Corelli (Tartini) vln & pf
  with F. Gaveau pf   Odeon 166406

LALO

Concerto in g, Op. 29 "Concerto russe" vln & orch.
  Chants russes (2nd mvt)
  with F. Gaveau pf   Odeon O 4043, 166022

LECLAIR

(12) Sonatas, Op. 9 – Book IV (1738) vln & c
  Sonata No. 3, in D: Tambourin (3rd mvt) arr. vln & pf Kreisler
  with F. Gaveau pf   Ki 1721[2]   Decca G20270
                                        Odeon 166118

MASCAGNI

Cavalleria Rusticana (1890) – opera
  Intermezzo orch. – arr. vln & pf
  with F. Gaveau pf   Ki 1037[1]   Odeon O 4045, 166018, 221039A
                                        Parlophone R270

MASSENET

Thaïs (1894) – opera
  Méditation arr. vln & pf Marsick
  with F. Gaveau pf   Odeon O 4046, 166019, 221040A
                                        Parlophone R275

NIN

(20) Cantos de España (1923) v & pf
  No. 1. Tonada de Valdovinos arr. vln & pf as "Vieja Castilla" by Nin & Gautier
  with J.D. Todd pf   Columbia DOX664
  No. 4. Montañesa arr. vln & pf Kochański
  with J. Nin pf   Ki 1603[2]   Odeon 166090, 183782
  No. 4. Montañesa arr. vln & pf Kochański
  with M. Orlov pf   PARTX 9259–1   Le Chant du Monde GA5061
  No. 5. Tonada del Conde Sol arr. vln & pf as "Tonada murciano" by Kochański
  with J. Nin pf   Odeon 166090

NIN – *Continued*

No. 7. Granadina arr. vln & pf Kochański
with J. Nin pf   Odeon 166091

No. 7. Granadina arr. vln & pf Kochański
with M. Orlov pf   PARTX 9259–1 Le Chant du Monde GA5061

No. 8. Saeta (Invocation) arr. vln & pf Kochański
with J. Nin pf   Kl 1604–2 Odeon 166091, 183782

No. 8. Saeta (Invocation) arr. vln & pf Kochański
with M. Orlov pf   PARTX 9260–1 Le Chant du Monde GA5061

No. 15. Paño murciano arr. vln & pf as "Murciana" by Nin & Gautier
with J.D. Todd pf   Columbia DOX664

No. 15. Paño murciano arr. vln & pf as "Murciana" by Nin & Gautier
with M. Orlov pf   PARTX 9260–1 Le Chant du Monde GA5061

No. 16. Villancico Catalán arr. vln & pf as "Catalana" by Nin & Gautier
with J.D. Todd pf   Columbia DOX664

No. 18. El Vito arr. vln & pf as "Andaluza" by Nin & Gautier
with J.D. Todd pf   Columbia DOX664

(5) Comentarios (1929) vln & pf
No. 1. Sobra un tema del Salinas
with M. Orlov pf   PARTX 9264–1 Le Chant du Monde GA5063

No. 2. Sobre un tema de José de Bassa
with J. Nin pf   Odeon 166228

No. 2. Sobre un tema de José de Bassa
with M. Orlov pf   PARTX 9264–1 Le Chant du Monde GA5063

No. 5. Sobra un aire de danza de Pablo Estève
with J. Nin pf   Odeon 166228

PIERNÉ

Sérénade in A, Op. 7 (1875) pf – arr. vln & pf
with F. Gaveau pf   Odeon 166455

POULENC

(3) Mouvements perpetuels (1918) pf
No. 1. Mouvement perpetuel No. 1, in C arr. vln & pf Heifetz
with J.D. Todd pf   Columbia DO2362

PURCELL

Sonata in g, Z780 vln & c
with M. le Marc'Hadour pf   Odeon 188955

RAVEL

Sonata (1922) vln & vlc
with A. Lévy vlc   Le Chant du Monde LDZM8145
Sonata (1927) vln & pf
                    PARTX 8684/7–1 Le Chant du Monde GA5056/7,
with Y. Lefébure pf   LDYA8115
Trio in a (1915) pf, vln & vlc
with G. Joy pf & A. Lévy vlc   Prétoria CL8001

RIMSKY–KORSAKOV

Sadko (1898) – opera
Chant hindou arr. vln & pf Kreisler
with F. Gaveau pf   Ki 1033⁴ Odeon 166018, 221039A, O 4045
                    Parlophone R270

SCHUBERT, François

(12) Bagatelles, Op. 13 vln & pf
No. 9. L'abeille
with F. Gaveau pf   Odeon 166039

SCHUBERT, Franz

(6) Moments musicaux, Op. 94 (D780) (1823/7) pf
No. 3. Moment musicale No. 3, in f "Air russe" arr. vln & pf Kreisler
with F. Gaveau pf   Odeon 166315

STRAVINSKY

(Le) Baiser de la Fée (1928) – ballet orch.
Ballade arr. vln & pf Dushkin & Stravinsky
with M. le Marc'Hadour pf   Odeon 123905
Élégie (1944) solo vla or vln
(unaccompanied)   Odeon 123905

TCHAIKOVSKY

(3) Souvenirs de Hapsal, Op. 2 pf
No. 3. Chant sans paroles in f arr. vln & pf Kreisler
with F. Gaveau pf   Odeon 166019, 221040A, O
                    4046, 182649

GAUVOVETSKAYA

CHOPIN

(The) Nightingale sings unid v & pf – arr. v, vln & pf
with M. Michailova s & piano   Gramophone & Typewriter
                    23442

Saschko GAVRILOV (1929–   )

BACH

Cantata No. 210 (O holder Tag, erwünschte Zeit) BWV210
with U. Buckel s, H. Winschermann   Cantate 641217, 651217
ob, K. Redel fl, A. Bauer vlc, A.
Schönstedt hpsi & Deutsche Bach–
Solisten – Winschermann

Concerto No. 5, in f, BWV1056 clav strs & c – arr. vln, strs & c in g
with Frankfurt Bach Orch. – Egel   Bärenreiter Musicaphon SL1206
                    BM30

BEETHOVEN

Concerto in D, Op. 61 vln & orch.
with Nordwestdeutsche Symphony   Alshire S821
Orch., Hamburg – Stein

Romance No. 1, in G, Op. 40 vln & orch.
with Nordwestdeutsche Symphony   Marble Arch MAL714
Orch., Hamburg – Stein   Somerset SM611

Romance No. 2, in F, Op. 50 vln & orch.
with Berlin Radio Symphony Orch. –   Eterna 120007
Guhl

Romance No. 2, in F, Op. 50 vln & orch.
with Nordwestdeutsche Symphony   Marble Arch MAL714
Orch., Hamburg – Stein   Somerset SM611

Sonata No. 5, in F, Op. 24 "Spring" vln & pf
with H. Kajiwara pf   Classics Club X87

BERG

Chamber Concerto (1925) vln, pf & 13 w–wnds
with D. Barenboim pf & BBC   CBS SBRG72614
Symphony Orch. Members – Boulez   Columbia MS7179

BERIO

(2) Pieces (1951) vln & pf
  with K. Schilde pf   Wergo WER319

DAVID

Sonata No. 2, Op. 58, No. 1 (1963) solo vln
  (unaccompanied)   Wergo WER70002

DEBUSSY

Sonata No. 3, in g (1917) vln & pf
  with M. Bergmann pf   Wergo WER60025

HANDEL

(12) Concerti grossi, Op. 6 (1739) 2 vlns, vlc & strs
  Concerto grosso No. 7, in B
  with H. Pietsch vln, W. Haupt vlc, E.   Eterna 121061/2
  Erthel ob, W. Watzig ob & Berlin
  Chamber Orch. – Guhl
  Concerto grosso No. 8, in c
  with H. Pietsch vln, W. Haupt vlc, E.   Eterna 121063/5, 520060
  Erthel ob, W. Watzig ob & Berlin
  Chamber Orch. – Guhl

LUENING

Sonata No. 3 (1945) vln & pf
  with K.P. Pietsch pf   Remington RLP199–211

MENDELSSOHN

Concerto in e, Op. 64 vln & orch.
  with Nordwestdeutsche Symphony   Alshire S821
  Orch., Hamburg – Stein   Marble Arch MAL714
                         Somerset SM611

RAKOV

Concerto in e (1948) vln & orch.
  with Berlin Radio Symphony Orch. –   Urania URLP7112
  Rothe

TCHAIKOVSKY

Concerto in D, Op. 35 vln & orch.
  with Pro Musica Orch., Hamburg   CBS 51067, S51067

VIVALDI

(12) Concerti, Op. 3 "L'Estro armonico" var. cbns & strs
  Concerto No. 1, in D, P.146 (F.IV, No. 8) 4 vlns, vlc, strs & c
  with S. Karolyi vln, E. Schilling vln,   Cetra LPU006
  K.A. Hermann vln & Frankfurt
  Chamber Orch. – Goehr
  Concerto No. 2, in g, P.326 (F.IV, No. 8) 2 vlns, strs & c
  with S. Karolyi vln & Frankfurt   Cetra LPU006
  Chamber Orch. – Goehr
  Concerto No. 3, in G, P.96 (F.I, No. 173) vln, strs & c
  with Frankfurt Chamber Orch. –   Cetra LPU006
  Goehr
  Concerto No. 4, in e, P.97 (F.I, No. 174) 4 vlns, strs & c
  with S. Karolyi vln, E. Schilling vln,   Cetra LPU007
  K.A. Hermann vln & Frankfurt
  Chamber Orch. – Goehr
  Concerto No. 5, in A, P.212 (F.I, No. 175) 2 vlns, strs & c
  with S. Karolyi vln & Frankfurt   Cetra LPU006
  Chamber Orch., – Goehr

VIVALDI – *Continued*

  Concerto No. 6, in a, P.1 (F.I, No. 176) vln, strs & c
  with Frankfurt Chamber Orch. –   Cetra LPU007
  Goehr
  Concerto No. 7, in F, P.249 (F.IV, No. 9) 4 vlns, strs & c
  with S. Karolyi vln, E. Schilling vln,   Cetra LPU007
  K.A. Hermann vln & Frankfurt
  Chamber Orch. – Goehr
  Concerto No. 8, in a, P.2 (F.I, No. 177) 2 vlns, strs & c
  with S. Karolyi vln & Frankfurt   Cetra LPU006
  Chamber Orch. – Goehr
  Concerto No. 9, in D, P.147 (F.I, No. 178) vln, strs & c
  with Frankfurt Chamber Orch. –   Cetra LPU007
  Goehr
  Concerto No. 10, in b, P.148 (F.IV, No. 10) 4 vlns, strs & c
  with S. Karolyi vln, E. Schilling vln,   Cetra LPU006
  K.A. Hermann vln & Frankfurt
  Chamber Orch. – Goehr
  Concerto No. 11, in d, P.250 (F.IV, No. 11) 2 vlns, vlc, strs & c
  with S. Karolyi vln & Frankfurt   Cetra LPU007
  Chamber Orch. – Goehr
  Concerto No. 12, in E, P.240 (F.I, No. 179) vln, strs & c
  with Frankfurt Chamber Orch. –   Cetra LPU007
  Goehr

YUN

Gaza (1963) vln & pf
  with B. Kontarsky pf   Wergo WER60034

Sylvia de GAY

BRAHMS

(16) Waltzes, Op. 39 pf duet
  No. 15. Waltz No. 15, in A flat arr. vln & pf "in A" Hochstein
  with piano   Edison Bell 5499

DVOŘÁK

(8) Slavonic Dances, Op. 72 pf duet; orch.
  No. 2. Slavonic dance No. 10, in e arr. vln & pf Kreisler
  with piano   Edison Bell 5510

KREISLER

Caprice viennois, Op. 2 vln & pf
  with piano   Edison Bell 5510
Tambourin chinois, Op. 3 vln & pf
  with piano   Edison Bell 5499

LAURICELLA

Duo Sonata (1962) 2 vlns
  with R. Lauricella vln   Apollo Sound AS1002

Barnabas von GECZY (1897–   )

HUBAY

(14) Scènes de la Csárda vln & pf
  No. 5. Hullámzo balaton, Op. 33
  with orch.   HMV EG3294

KASCHUBEC

Konzertstück in G vln & orch.
        2RA 3455[I]☐ & 3456[II]☐   HMV EH1251
  with orch.

SARASATE

Zigeunerweisen, Op. 20 vln & pf or orch.
  with orch.   HMV AL2280, EG3295

Martha GEISSMAR

BACH

(6) Sonatas, BWV1014/9 vln & clav
  Sonata No. 2, in A: Allegro (1st mvt) BWV1015
  with E. Bodky hpsi   38169 Decca 20166
                                     Parlophone B37032, R1026

HANDEL

(6) Trio–Sonatas (1696) 2 obs or 2 vlns & c
  Trio–sonata No. 3, in E flat: Adagio (3rd mvt)
  with G. Blumensart ob, E.   38171 Decca 20166
  Bodky hpsi, & P. Herman vlc   Parlophone B37032, R1026

A. GENDELMAN

AGUIRRE

(5) Tristes pf
  Triste No. 4, in B flat arr. vln & orch.
  with Argentine Symphony Orch. –   Odeon 56535, LDM302
  Artola

Robert GENDRE

BACH, J.C.

(6) Quartets, Op. 8 (?1775) (T. P 306) fl vln, vla & vlc
  Quartet No. 4, in F
  with J–P. Rampal fl, R. Lepauw vla &   L'Oiseau–Lyre OL50188,
  R. Bex vlc   SOL60018
(2) Quintets, Op. 22 (T. P 304) fl, ob, vln, vlc & hpsi
  Quintet No. 1, in D
  with J–P. Rampal fl, P. Pierlot ob, P.   La Boîte à Musique LD011
  Hongue bsn & R. Veyron–Lacroix hpsi Erato LDE3345, STE50245,
                                    STU70331
                                    Haydn Society HSLP117
                                    Musical Heritage Society
                                    MHS820

BEETHOVEN

(2) Trios, Op. 70 pf, vln & vlc
  No. 1. Trio No. 4, in D "Ghost"
  with N. Lee pf & R. Bex vlc   La Boîte à Musique LD058,
                                    LDS5058
  No. 2. Trio No. 5, in E flat
  with N. Lee pf & R. Bex vlc   La Boîte à Musique LD058,
                                    LDS5058
Trio in B flat, G154 (WoO39) "In one movement" pf, vln & vlc
  with R. Veyron–Lacroix pf & R. Bex   Musical Heritage Society
  vlc   MHS963

BERTHEAUME

(2) Sinfonia concertantes, Op. 6 (1787) 2 vlns & orch.
  Sinfonia concertante No. 1, in G
  with P. Doukan vln & orch. –   Pathé DTX230
  Froment

BOISMORTIER

(5) Sonatas, Op. 37 (1732) 2 fls & c
  Sonata No. 5, in c arr. fl. ob, vln, bsn & hpsi
  with J–P. Rampal fl, P. Pierlot ob, P.   La Boîte à Musique LD060,
  Hongue bsn & R. Veyron–Lacrois hpsi LDS5060
                                    Music Guild M32, MG111,
                                    MS111, S32

BRAHMS

Trio No. 2, in C, Op. 87 pf, vln & vlc
  with N. Lee pf & R. Bex vlc   La Boîte à Musique LD079
Trio No. 3, in c, Op. 101 pf, vln & vlc
  with N. Lee pf & R. Bex vlc   La Boîte à Musique LD079

CARRILLO

Concerto (1918) "Triple" vln, fl, vlc & orch.
  with J–P. Rampal fl, R. Bex vlc &   Sonido 3
  Lamoureux Orch. – Carrillo
Quartet "Spring" 2 vlns, vla & vlc
  with J. Ghestem vln, S. Collot vla & Sonido 7
  R. Bex vlc
Quartet "Tercer" 2 vlns, vla & vlc
  with J. Ghestem vln, S. Collot vla & Sonido 7
  R. Bex vlc
Sextet in G (1902) 4 vlns, vla & vlc
  with J. Ghestem vln, G. Devries vln, Sonido 9
  R. Flachot vln, S. Collot vla & R. Bex
  vlc

CORRETTE

(21) Concerti comique, Op. 8
  Concerto No. 6, in G "Le Plaisir du Dames" fl, ob, vln, bsn & hpsi
  with J–P. Rampal fl, P. Pierlot ob, P.   Erato STU70331
  Hongne bsn & R. Veyron–Lacroix hpsi Musical Heritage Society
                                    MHS820

COUPERIN, F.

(Les) Goûts réunis, ou Nouveaux Concerts unsp inst & c
  Concert No. 14, in d vln & c
  with E. Pasquier vlc & L. Boulay hpsi La Boîte à Musique LD056,
                                    LDS5056
(Les) Nations – 4 suites (1726) 2 vlns & c
  Suite No. 1, in e "La Françoise"
  with H. Fernandez vln, R. Boulay vla, Music Guild M21, MG108,
  J–P. Rampal fl, J. Pasquier vln & L.   MS108, S21
  Boulay hpsi
  Suite No. 2, in c "L'Espagnole"
  with H. Fernandez vln, R. Boulay vla, Music Guild M21, MG108,
  J–P. Rampal fl, J. Pasquier vln & L.   MS108, S21
  Boulay hpsi
  Suite No. 3, in d "L'Impériale"
  with H. Fernandez vln, R. Boulay vla, La Boîte à Musique LD056,
  J–P. Rampal fl, J. Pasquier vln & L.   LDS5056
  Boulay hpsi   Music Guild M21, MG108,
                                    MS108, S21

COUPERIN, F. – *Continued*

Suite No. 4, in g "La Piémontoise"
with H. Fernandez vln, R. Boulay vla,   Music Guild M21, MG108,
J–P. Rampal fl, J. Pasquier vln & L.   MS108, S21
Boulay hpsi

Sonata No. 3, in g (1693) "L'Astrée" 2 vlns & c – arr. fl, vln & c
with J–P. Rampal fl, L. Boulay hpsi &   La Boîte à Musique LD056,
E. Pasquier vlc   LDS5056

DEVIENNE

(6) Quatuors concertants, Op. 16 fl, vln, vla & vlc
Quartet No. 5, in G
with J–P. Rampal fl, R. Lepauw vla &   L'Oiseau–Lyre OL50188,
R. Bex vlc   SOL60018

ENESCU

Octet in C, Op. 7 4 vlns, 2 vlas & 2 vlcs
with D. Marchand vln, F. Geyre vln,   Remington R199–52
M.L. Ricros vln, M.T. Chailley vla, C.
Lequier vla, A. Rémond vlc & J.
Brizard vlc – cond. Enescu

HANDEL

(6) Trio–Sonatas (1696) 2 obs or 2 vlns & c
Trio–Sonata No. 3, in E flat
with P. Pierlot ob, P. Hongue bsn &   La Boîte à Musique LD011
R. Veyron–Lacroix hpsi   Haydn Society HSL117

HAYDN

(31) Trios, H.XV, Nos. 1/31 pf, vln & vlc
Trio No. 26, in f sharp, H.XV, No. 26 (Op. 73, No. 3)
with A. Krust pf & R. Bex vlc   Harmonia Mundi HM30526
Trio No. 28, in E, H.XV, No. 28 (Op. 75, No. 2)
with P. Duvauchelle pf & C. Bartsch   La Boîte à Musique 75/6
vlc
Trio No. 28, in E, H.XV, No. 28 (Op. 75, No. 2)
with A. Krust pf & R. Bex vlc   Harmonia Mundi HM30526
    Musique de tous les Temps EP16
(3) Trios, H.XVI, Nos. 40/2 (Op. 53) vln, vla & vlc
Trio No. 3, in D, H.XVI, No. 42
with A. Krust pf & R. Bex vlc   Harmonia Mundi HM30526

HONEGGER

Sonatina (1932) vln & vlc
with R. Bex vlc
    La Boîte à Musique LD059,
    LDS5059

LECLAIR

(6) Concerti, Op. 7 (1737) vln & strs
Concerto No. 6, in A
with Chamber Orch. – Oubradous   Orphée LDO–E51019
    Pacific LDO–E51019
(12) Sonatas, Op. 9 – Book IV (1738) vln & c
Sonata No. 3, in D
with R. Veyron–Lacroix hpsi
    La Boîte à Musique LD060,
    LDS5060
    Music Guild M32, MG111,
    MS111, S32

LULLY

Suite No. 3, in B orch.
with Chamber Orch. – Oubradous   Orphée LDO–E51019
    Pacific LDO–E51019

Suite No. 7, in g orch.
with Chamber Orch. – Oubradous   Orphée LDO–E51019
    Pacific LDO–E51019

de MONDONVILLE

Sonata in G fl, vln & clav
with J–P. Rampal fl & R. Veyron–   La Boîte à Musique LD060,
Lacroix hpsi   LDS5060
    Music Guild M32, MG111,
    MS111, S32

PLEYEL

(3) Quartets, Op. 17 – Book III fl, vln, vla & vlc
Quartet No. 1, in D
with J–P. Rampal fl, R. Lepauw vla &   L'Oiseau–Lyre OL50188,
R. Bex vlc   SOL60018

SCARLATTI, A.

Sonata in F 3 recs & c – ed. Veyron–Lacroix
with J–P. Rampal fl, P. Pierlot ob, P.   La Boîte à Musique LD011
Hongue bsn & R. Veyron–Lacroix hpsi   Haydn Society HSLP117

TAPRAY

Sinfonia concertante in E flat, Op. 9 hpsi, pf, vln & orch.
with H. Schoonbroodt hpsi, P. Houdy   Musica Mundi VMS2019
pf & Gérard Cartigny Chamber Orch.

TELEMANN

Concerto in A, T.I, No. 3 fl, vln, vlc, strs & c
with J–P. Rampal fl, J. Neilz vlc &   Critère CRD187, SCRD5187
Collegium Musicum, Paris – Douatte   Nonesuch H1124, H71124
Concerto in F, T.II, No. 3 3 vlns, strs & c
with J–P. Wallez vln, N. Laroque vln,   CBS S75563
L. Boulay hpsi & Collegium Musicum,   Eurodisc 74225KK
Paris – Douatte   Nonesuch H1109, H71109
Essercizii Musici (1721)
No. 9. Trio–sonata in E fl, vln & c
with J–P. Rampal fl, P. Hongue bsn &   Erato LDE3163, STE50263,
R. Veyron–Lacroix hpsi   STU70163
    Music Guild M54, S54
Quartet in d, T.II, No. 2 fl, vln, ob, bsn & hpsi
with J–P. Rampal fl, P. Pierlot ob, P.   Music Guild M54, S54
Hongue bsn & R. Veyron–Lacroix hpsi
Quartet in e (1733) fl, vln, bsn & hpsi
with J–P. Rampal fl, P. Hongue bsn &   Erato LDE3163, STE50263,
R. Veyron–Lacroix hpsi   STU70163
Quartet in G, T.I, No. 2 fl, ob, vln & c
with J–P. Rampal fl, P. Pierlot ob, P.   La Boîte à Musique LD011
Hongue bsn & R. Veyron–Lacroix hpsi   Haydn Society HSLP117
Quartet in G, T.I, No. 2 fl, ob, vln & c
with J–P. Rampal fl, P. Pierlot ob, P.   Erato LDE3163, STE50263,
Hongue bsn & R. Veyron–Lacroix hpsi   STU70163
    Music Guild M54, S54

TELEMANN – *Continued*

Trio–sonata in B flat rec, hpsi & c
with P. Pierlot ob & R. Veyron– | La Boîte à Musique LD06,
Lacroix hpsi | LD013
| Epic BC1344, LC3944
| Erato LDE3263, STE50163,
| STU70331
| Musical Heritage Society
| MHS820

VIOTTI

(3) Quartets, Op. 22 fl & vln or 2 vlns, vla & c
No. 3. Quartet No. 3, in c
with J–P. Rampal fl, R. Lepauw vla & | L'Oiseau–Lyre OL50188,
R. Bex vlc | SOL60018

VIVALDI

(12) Concerti, Op. 3 "L'Estro armonico" var. cbns & strs
Concerto No. 1, in D, P.146 (F.IV, No. 7) 4 vlns, vlc, strs & c
with J. Champeil vln, L. Yordanoff | Ducretet–Thomson LAG1014
vln, L. Gali vln & Pro Musica Orch. –
Saguer

Concerto No. 7, in F, P.249 (F.IV, No. 9) 4 vlns, strs & c
with J. Champeil vln, L. Yordanoff | Ducretet–Thomson LAG1014
vln, L. Gali vln & Pro Musica Orch. –
Saguer

Concerto No. 8, in a, P.2 (F.I, No. 177) 2 vlns, strs & c
with P. Doukan vln & Paris Chamber | Club National du Disque
Orch. – Froment | CND1003

Concerto No. 8, in a, P.2 (F.I, No. 177) 2 vlns, strs & c
with J. Dejean vln & Paris Chamber | Lumen LD2–401
Orch. – Duvauchelle

Concerto No. 10, in b, P.148 (F.IV, No. 10) 4 vlns, strs & c
with S. Plazonich vln, J. Dejean vln, | La Boîte à Musique LD102
D. Marchand vln & Paris Chamber | Lumen 2–08011/3
Orch. – Duvauchelle

Concerto in G, P.135 (F.IV, No. 1) 2 vlns, 2 vlcs, strs & c
with G. Alès vln, R. Albin vlc, A. | La Boîte à Musique LD84
Rémond vlc & L'Orch. de l'Oiseau– | Fontana 695300KL
Lyre – Froment | L'Oiseau–Lyre OL50124

Concerto in D, P.198 (F.XII, No. 7) vln, fl & c
with J–P. Rampal fl & R. Veyron– | La Boîte à Musique LD013
Lacroix hpsi | Epic BC1344, LC3944
| Erato STU70225
| Haydn Society HSLP116

Concerto in D, P.204 (F.XII, No. 29) "La Pastorella" fl, ob, vln, bsn & c
with J–P. Rampal fl, P. Pierlot ob, P. | Argo RG95
Hongne bsn & R. Veyron–Lacroix hpsi | La Boîte à Musique LD06,
| LD013
| Erato STU70331
| Haydn Society HSLP2
| Musical Heritage Society
| MHS820

Concerto in D, P.207 (F.XII, No. 25) fl, ob, vln, bsn & c
with J–P. Rampal fl, P. Pierlot ob, P. | La Boîte à Musique LD013
Hongne bsn & R. Veyron–Lacroix hpsi | Erato STU70225
| Haydn Society HSLP116

Concerto in d, P.310 (F.I, No. 11) "Senza cantin" vln, 2 fls, 2 obs & 2 bsns
with J–M. Rampal fl, P. Hongne bsn | Epic BC1344, LC3944
& R. Veyron–Lacroix hpsi | Erato STU70225

VIVALDI – *Continued*

Concerto in F, P.322 (F.XII, No. 21) fl, ob, vln & c
with J–P. Rampal fl, P. Hongne bsn & | Argo RG95
R. Veyron–Lacroix hpsi | La Boîte à Musique LD06
| Haydn Society HSLP82

Concerto in F, P.323 fl, ob, vln, bsn & c
with J–P. Rampal fl, P. Pierlot ob, P. | La Boîte à Musique LD013
Hongne bsn & R. Veyron–Lacroix hpsi | Haydn Society HSLP116

Concerto in g, P.360 fl, ob, vln, bsn & c
with J–P. Rampal fl, P. Pierlot ob, P. | La Boîte à Musique LD01,
Hongne bsn & R. Veyron–Lacroix hpsi | LD086
| Epic BC1344, LC3944
| Erato STU70225
| Haydn Society HSLP80

(12) Sonatas, Op. 1 2 vlns & c
Sonata No. 2, in e, F.XIII, No. 18
with P. Pierlot ob, P. Hongne bsn & | La Boîte à Musique LD013
R. Veyron–Lacroix hpsi | Haydn Society HSLP116

Alessandro GENESINI

MASCAGNI

(L') Amico Fritz (1891) – opera
Zingaresca arr. vln & pf
with S. Corttone pf | CON 699 | Gramophone & Typewriter
| 057900

GEORGE

MOZART

Concerto No. 4, in D, K218 vln & orch.
with Süddeutsches Kammerorchester – | CBS S51103
Peters
Concerto No. 5, in A, K219 "Turkish" vln & orch.
with Süddeutsches Kammerorchester – | CBS S51103
Peters

Nina GERARD

LEHÁR

Hungarian dance (unid) vln & pf
with orch. | Parlophone 80079

POLIAKIN

Marche des petits tambours vln & pf
with orch. | Parlophone 22596

ROSS

(Le) Chant du Rossignol v & pf – arr. vln & orch.
with orch. | Parlophone 22596

SCHUBERT

(14) Schwanengesang, D957 (1828) v & pf
No. 4. Ständchen "Serenade" arr. vln & orch.
with orch. | Parlophone 80079

Robert GERLE (1924–   )

BACH

(6) Sonatas, BWV1014/9 vln & clav
Sonata No. 1, in b, BWV1014
with A. Fuller hpsi

Decca DL10050, (in set DX168), DL710050, (in set DXS7168)

Sonata No. 2, in A, BWV1015
with A. Fuller hpsi

Decca DL10050, (in set DX168), DL710050, (in set DXS7168

Sonata No. 3, in E, BWV1016
with A. Fuller hpsi

Decca DL10050, (in set DX168), DL710050, (in set DXS7168)

Sonata No. 4, in c, BWV1017
with A. Fuller hpsi

Decca DL10051, (in set DX168), DL710051, (in set DXS7168)

Sonata No. 5, in f, BWV1018.
with A. Fuller hpsi

Decca DL10051, (in set DX168), DL710051, (in set DXS7168)

Sonata No. 6, in G, BWV1019
with A. Fuller hpsi

Decca DL10051, (in set DX168), DL710051, (in set DXS7168)

BARBER

Concerto, Op. 14 (1941) vln & orch.
with Vienna State Opera Orch. –
Zeller

Westminster WST17045, XWN19045
World Record Club CM59, SCM59

BARTÓK

(10) Easy Pieces (1908) pf
No. 5, Este á Székelyeknél arr. vln & pf
with R. Benoit pf

Westminster WST17150

For Children (40 pieces) (1909) pf
nos. 6, 13, 18, 25, 31, 36 & 40 arr. vln & pf as "3 Hungarian folk tunes"
by Szigeti
with R. Benoit pf

Westminster WST17150

(6) Rumanian folk dances (1915) pf – arr. vln & pf Székely
with R. Benoit pf

Westminster WST17150

Sonatina in D (on 3 Transylvanian peasant themes) (1915) pf – transc. vln & pf Gertler, 1931
with R. Benoit pf

Westminster WST17150

BEETHOVEN

(3) Sonatas, Op. 12 vln & pf
No. 1. Sonata No. 1, in D
with M. Neely pf

Westminster (in set WST404)

No. 2. Sonata No. 2, in A
with M. Neely pf

Westminster (in set WST404)

No. 3. Sonata No. 3, in E flat
with M Neely pf

Westminster (in set WST404)

Sonata No. 4, in a, Op. 23 vln & pf
with M. Neely pf

Westminster (in set WST404)

Sonata No. 5, in F, Op. 24 "Spring" vln & pf
with M. Neely pf

Westminster (in set WST404)

(3) Sonatas, Op. 30 vln & pf
No. 1. Sonata No. 6, in A
with M. Neely pf

Westminster (in set WST404)

No. 2. Sonata No. 7, in c
with M. Neely pf

Westminster (in set WST404)

BEETHOVEN – *Continued*

No. 3. Sonata No. 8, in G
with M. Neely pf

Westminster (in set WST404)

Sonata No. 9, in A, Op. 47 "Kreutzer" vln & pf
with M. Neely pf

Westminster (in set WST404)

Sonata No. 10, in G, Op. 96 vln & pf
with M. Neely pf

Westminster (in set WST404)

BRAHMS

(21) Hungarian Dances pf duet
Hungarian Dance No. 1, in g arr. vln & pf Joachim
with N. Shetler pf

Westminster WST17093, XWN19093

Hungarian Dance No. 2, in d arr. vln & pf Joachim
with N. Shetler pf

Westminster WST17093, XWN19093

Hungarian Dance No. 3, in F arr. vln & pf Joachim
with N. Shetler pf

Westminster WST17093, XWN19093

Hungarian Dance No. 4, in f arr. vln & pf "in b" Joachim
with N. Shetler pf

Westminster WST17093, XWN19093

Hungarian Dance No. 5, in f sharp arr. vln & pf "in g" Joachim
with N. Shetler pf

Westminster WST17093, XWN19093

Hungarian Dance No. 6, in D flat arr. vln & pf "in B flat" Joachim
with N. Shetler pf

Westminster WST17093, XWN19093

Hungarian Dance No. 7, in A arr. vln & pf Joachim
with N. Shetler pf

Westminster WST17093, XWN19093

Hungarian Dance No. 8, in a arr. vln & pf Joachim
with N. Shetler pf

Westminster WST17093, XWN19093

Hungarian Dance No. 9, in e arr. vln & pf Joachim
with N. Shetler pf

Westminster WST17093, XWN19093

Hungarian Dance No. 10, in E arr. vln & pf "in G" Joachim
with N. Shetler pf

Westminster WST17093, XWN19093

Hungarian Dance No. 11, in C arr. vln & pf Joachim
with N. Shetler pf

Westminster WST17093, XWN19093

Hungarian Dance No. 12, in d arr. vln & pf Joachim
with N. Shetler pf

Westminster WST17093, XWN19093

Hungarian Dance No. 13, in D arr. vln & pf Joachim
with N. Shetler pf

Westminster WST17093, XWN19093

Hungarian Dance No. 14, in d arr. vln & pf Joachim
with N. Shetler pf

Westminster WST17093, XWN19093

Hungarian Dance No. 15, in B flat arr. vln & pf "in A" Joachim
with N. Shetler pf

Westminster WST17093, XWN19093

Hungarian Dance No. 16, in f arr. vln & pf "in g" Joachim
with N. Shetler pf

Westminster WST17093, XWN19093

BRAHMS – *Continued*

Hungarian Dance No. 17, in f sharp arr. vln & pf Joachim
with N. Shetler pf   Westminster WST17093,
           XWN19093

Hungarian Dance No. 18, in D arr. vln & pf Joachim
with N. Shetler pf   Westminster WST17093,
           XWN19093

Hungarian Dance No. 19, in b arr. vln & pf "in a" Joachim
with N. Shetler pf   Westminster WST17093,
           XWN19093

Hungarian Dance No. 20, in e arr. vln & pf "in d" Joachim
with N. Shetler pf   Westminster WST17093,
           XWN19093

Hungarian Dance No. 21, in e arr. vln & pf Joachim
with N. Shetler pf   Westminster WST17093,
           XWN19093

COPLAND

Vitebsk (Study on a Jewish theme) (1929) pf, vln & vlc
with K. Wallingford pf & G. Magyar   University of Oklahoma 1
vlc

DELIUS

Concerto (1916) vln & orch.
with Vienna State Opera Orch. –   Westminster WST17045,
Zeller   XWN19045
           World Record Club CM59,
           SCM59

DOHNÁNYI

Ruralia Hungarica, Op. 32a pf – arr. vln & pf Kreisler
with R. Benoit pf   Westminster WST17150

HARRIS

Trio (1934) pf, vln & vlc
with K. Wallingford pf & G. Magyar   University of Oklahoma 1
vlc

HAYDN, Franz Josef

Concerto No. 3, in A, H.VIIa, No. 3 (1765) "Melk" (cadenzas by Gerle)
vln & orch.
with Vienna Radio Orch. – Zeller   Westminster WST17106,
           XWN19106

HAYDN, Michael

Concerto in B flat (1760) vln & orch.
with Vienna Radio Orch. – Zeller   Westminster WST17106,
           XWN19106

KERR

Trio in a (1941) pf, vln & vlc
with K. Wallingford pf & G. Magyar   University of Oklahoma 1
vlc

KODÁLY

Adagio in C (1905) vln & pf
with R. Benoit pf   Westminster WST17150

Háry János (1926) – opera
No. 10. Intermezzo orch. – arr. vln & pf Szigeti
with R. Benoit pf   Westminster WST17150

VIEUXTEMPS

Concerto No. 2, in f, Op. 19 vln & orch.
with Vienna Radio Orch. – Zeller   Westminster WST17123,
           XWN19123

VIVALDI

Concerto in B flat, P.112 (F.I, No. 163) "Posthorn" vln, strs & c
with Vienna Radio Orch. – Zeller   Westminster WST17123,
           XWN19123

Concerto in B flat, P.368 (F.I, No. 60) (Op. 28, No. 3) scordatura vln, 2 str
choruses & c
with Vienna Radio Orch. – Zeller   Westminster WST17123,
           XWN19123

Paul GERSHMAN

VIVALDI

Concerto in C, P.54 (F.XII, No. 17) 2 fls, 2 obs, bsn, 2 vlns, strs & c
with J. Baker fl, H. Bennett fl, L.   Library of Recorded
Arner ob, H. Smyles ob, E. Carmen   Masterpieces Vol. 1, No. 2
bsn, F. Manzella vln & New York
Sinfonietta – Goberman

Concerto in d, P.310 (F.I, No. 11) vln, strs & c – ed. Malipiero
with E. Earle hpsi & New York   Library of Recorded
Sinfonietta – Goberman   Masterpieces Vol. 1, No. 5
           Odyssey 32 16 0053, 32 16 0054

Concerto in g, P.383 (F.XII, No. 3) "Per l'orch. di Dresda" vln, 2 fls, 2
obs, 2 bsns, strs & c – ed. Ephrikian
with J. Baker fl, H. Bennett fl, L.   Library of Recorded
Arner ob, H. Smyles ob, E. Carmen   Masterpieces Vol. 1, No. 2
bsn, F. Schwartz bsn & New York   Odyssey 32 16 0053, 32 16 0054
Sinfonietta – Goberman

André GERTLER (1907–)

BACH

Concerto No. 1, in a, BWV1041 vln, strs & c
with Hungarian Radio Orch. – Lehel   Qualiton LPX1113, SLPX1113

BARTÓK

Concerto No. 1 (1908) Op. posthumous vln & orch.
with Brno State Philharmonic Orch. –   Crossroads (in sets 22 26 0011 &
Ferencsik   22 26 0012)
           Supraphon SUA10466,
           SUAST50466, SV8141

Concerto No. 2 (1938) vln & orch.
with Czech Philharmonic Orch. –   Bärenreiter Musicaphon
Ančerl   BM30SL1604
           Crossroads (in sets 22 26 0011 &
           22 26 0012)
           Supraphon SUA10696,
           SUAST50696, SV8301

Contrasts (1938) cl, vln & pf
with A. Prinz cl & E. Farnadi pf   HMV CLP1828, CSD1583
           Vega C30A436
           Westminster WST17064,
           XWN19064

Contrasts (1938) cl, vln & pf
with M. Etlik cl & D. Andersen pf   Supraphon SUA10740,
           SUAST50740, SV8323

BARTÓK – *Continued*

(44) Duos (1931) 2 vlns
  with J. Suk vln

Crossroads 22 16 0208
Supraphon SUA10770,
SUAST50770, SV8345

For Children (40 pieces) (1909) pf
  nos. 6, 13, 18, 25, 31, 36 & 40 arr. vln & pf as "3 Hungarian folk tunes"
by Szigeti
  with D. Andersen pf

Supraphon SUA10650,
SUAST50650, SV8307

Quartet No. 6, in D (1939) 2 vlns, vla & vlc
        AR 10168/73–2 & 10174–1 Decca AK1433/6
  with H. Chigo vln, R. Courte vla &
M. Louon vlc

Rhapsody No. 1, in G (1928) vln & orch.
  with Brno State Philharmonic Orch. –
Ferencsik

Crossroads (in sets 22 26 0011 &
22 26 0012)
Supraphon SUA10466,
SUAST50466, SV8141

Rhapsody No. 2, in d (1928) vln & orch.
  with Brno State Philharmonic Orch. –
Ferencsik

Crossroads (in sets 22 26 0011 &
22 26 0012)
Supraphon SUA10466,
SUAST50466, SV8141

Sonata (1903) vln & pf
  with D. Andersen pf

Supraphon SUA10740,
SUAST50740, SV8323

Sonata No. 1 (1921) vln & pf
  with E. Farnadi pf

Westminster WST17098,
XWN19098

Sonata No. 1 (1921) vln & pf
  with D. Andersen pf

Supraphon SUA10650,
SUAST50650, SV8307

Sonata No. 2 (1922) vln & pf
  with E. Farnadi pf

Westminster WST17098,
XWN19098

Sonata No. 2 (1922) vln & pf
  with D. Andersen pf

Artia ALP711, ALPS711
Supraphon SUA10481,
SUAST50481, SV8190

Sonata in g (1944) solo vln
(unaccompanied)

Angel 35091
Columbia C1046, FCX297

Sonata in g (1944) solo vln
(unaccompanied)

Artia ALP711, ALPS711
Supraphon SUA10481,
SUAST50481, SV8190

Sonatina in D (on Transylvanian peasant themes) (1915) pf – transc. vln &
pf Gertler, 1931
  with D. Andersen pf

Supraphon SUA10650,
SUAST50650, SV8307

BERG

Concerto (1935) vln & orch.
  with Philharmonia Orch. – Kletzki

Angel 35091
Columbia C1030, C70090,
FCX297, WC1030

ENESCU

Sonata No. 3, in a, Op. 25 "in the popular Rumanian style" vln & pf
  with D. Andersen pf   Supraphon SUA10483

FRANCK

Sonata in A (1886) vln & pf
  with E. Farnadi pf

HMV XLP20085
Westminster WST17054,
XWN19054

GRIEG

Sonata No. 3, in c, Op. 45 vln & pf
  with E. Farnadi pf

HMV XLP20085
Westminster WST17054,
XWN19054

HARTMANN

Concerto funèbre (1939) vln & str orch.
  with Czech Philharmonic Orch. –
Ančerl

Supraphon 0 10 0508, 1 10 0508

HAYDN

(3) Quartets, Op. 74 (H.III, Nos. 72/4) 2 vlns, vla & vlc
  No. 1. Quartet No. 72, in C: Menuetto (3rd mvt) H.III, No. 72
  with H. Chigo vln, R.   AR 10175–1 Decca AK1433
Courte vla & M. Louon vlc

HINDEMITH

Concerto in c sharp (1939) vln & orch.
  with Czech Philharmonic Orch. –
Ančerl

Supraphon 0 10 0508, 1 10 0508

HONEGGER

Sonata No. 2, in d (1919) vln & pf
  with A. Holeček pf

Supraphon LPM361, SUF20330

JACOBI

Concerto (1937) vln & orch.
  with Belgian National Orch. – André

Society of Participating Artists
SPA7

KÓKAI

Concerto (1950) vln & orch.
  with Hungarian Radio Orch. – Lehel

Qualition LPX1113, SLPX1113

LARSSON

Concerto, Op. 42 vln & orch.
  with Stockholm Radio Orch. –
Frykberg

Discofil TR11014
London TW91091

MILHAUD

Sonata No. 2 (1917) vln & pf
  with S. Askenaze pf   Muza L0047

Sonata No. 2 (1917) vln & pf
  with D. Andersen pf   Supraphon SUA10483

MOZART

Sonata No. 25, in F, K377 vln & pf
  with S. Askenaze pf   Muza L0047

TARTINI

Concerto in A, D95 vln & orch.
with Zürich Chamber Orch. – De Stoutz — Amadeo AVRS6302, Cetra LPU0069

Concerto in D, D24 vln & orch.
with Zürich Chamber Orch. – De Stoutz — Amadeo AVRS6301, Vanguard SRV213SD

Concerto in D, D30 vln & orch.
with Zürich Chamber Orch. – De Stoutz — Amadeo AVRS6302, Cetra LPU0069

Concerto in E, D53 (C84) vln & orch.
with Zürich Chamber Orch. – De Stoutz — Amadeo AVRS6301, Vanguard SRV213SD

Concerto in F, D68 vln & orch.
with Zürich Chamber Orch. – De Stoutz — Amadeo AVRS6301, Cetra LPU0069, Vanguard SRV213SD

Concerto in G, D75 vln & orch.
with Zürich Chamber Orch. – De Stoutz — Amadeo AVRS6302, Cetra LPU0069

Concerto in G, D83 vln & orch.
with Zürich Chamber Orch. – De Stoutz — Amadeo AVRS6301, Vanguard SRV213SD

VIVALDI

(6) Concerti, Op. 12 vln, strs & c
Concerto No. 1, in g, P.343 (F.I, No. 211) arr. Nachèz
with Hungarian State Orch. – Vaszy — Qualiton MK1556/7

Stefi GEYER (1893–1958)

BACH

(3) Sonatas & 3 Partitas, BWV1001/6 solo vln
Partita No. 3, in E: Loure (2nd mvt) BWV1006
(unaccompanied) — Columbia DCX10, LZX1

BEETHOVEN

Romance No. 1, in G, Op. 40 vln & orch.
with piano — Columbia DCX11, LZX2

BURKHARD

Quartet No. 2, Op. 68 (1943) "in one movement" 2 vlns, vla & vlc
(as leader of Geyer str qt) — Columbia LZX11/2

DVOŘÁK

(8) Slavonic Dances, Op. 72 pf duet; orch.
No. 2. Slavonic dance No. 10, in e arr. vln & pf Kreisler
with piano — Odeon D3558, Parlophone 64542, P9130

GOLDMARK

Concerto in a, Op. 28 vln & orch.
Andante (2nd mvt) "Air"
with piano — Odeon D3558, Parlophone 64542, P9130

HAYDN

Concerto No. 1, in C, H.VIIa, No. 1 (1765) vln & orch.
Adagio (2nd mvt)
with piano — Columbia DCX10, LZX1

HAYDN – *Continued*

Concerto No. 1, in C, H.VIIa, No. 1 (1765) (cadenza by Klengel) vln & orch.
with Zürich Collegium Musicum Orch. — Columbia LZX238/9 – Sacher

KREISLER

Schön Rosmarin vln & pf
with piano — WZ 302 — Columbia DC61, LZ1

Andantino (Padre Martini) vln & pf
with piano — WZ 303 — Columbia DC61, LZ1

MOZART

Adagio in E, K261 vln & orch.
with Zürich Collegium Musicum Orch. — Columbia LZX7 – Sacher

Divertimento in D, K136 str orch.
with Zürich Collegium Musicum Orch. — Columbia LZX6 – Sacher

REGER

Suite in a, Op. 103a vln & pf
Aria (3rd mvt)
with W. Schuldhess pf — XXB 7755 — Decca 25763, Odeon 9205, O–6573

SCHOECK

Concerto in B flat, Op. 21 (1911/2) vln & orch.
with Zürich Tonhalle Orch. – Andreae — Columbia LZX242/5

TARTINI

(12) Sonatas, Op. 1 (1734) vln & c
Sonata No. 1, in A: Allegro (1st mvt) arr. vln & pf as "Fugue" by Kreisler
with W. Schuldhess pf — XXB 7756 — Decca 25763, Odeon 9205, 0–6573

F. GEYR

TELEMANN

Concerto in D 4 vlns, strs & c
with J. Dejean vln, G. Gaunet vln, J. Pasquier vln & Paris Collegium Musette – Douatte — Éditions phonographiques parisiennes APG125

Manfred GEYRHALTER

CORELLI

(12) Sonatas, Op. 5 vln & c
Sonata No. 7, in d
with B. Zaczek gtr — Musical Heritage Society MHS819

Sonata No. 8, in e
with B. Zaczek gtr — Musical Heritage Society MHS819

LOCATELLI

Sonata in G (c1736) 2 vlns & c
with M. Kuhn vln, H. Langfort hpsi & R. Harand vlc — Musical Heritage Society MHS1037

TELEMANN

Concerto in F, T. II, No. 3 3 vlns, strs & c
with R. Kalup vln, T. Kakuska vln, H. Musical Heritage Society
Langfort hpsi & Austrian Tonkünstler MHS638
Orch., Vienna – Bernet

Stefan GHEORGHIU

BENTOIU

Concerto, Op. 9 vln & orch.
with Radioteleviziunii Romane Electrecord ECE0248
Symphony Orch. – Conta

CONSTANTINESCU

Concerto "Triple" vln, vlc, pf & orch.
with R. Aldulescu vlc, V. Gheorghiu Electrecord ECE0194
pf & Radioteleviziunii Romane
Symphony Orch. – Conta

ENESCU

Chamber Symphony vln, pf, ob, vla, vlc, cbs, fl, E.hrn, cbs, cl, hrn & tpt
with V. Gheorghiu pf, I. Danie ob, G. Electrecord ECE–L014
Popovici vla, R. Aldulescu vlc, V.
Damschin cbs N. Alexandru fl, P.
Tornea E.hrn, E. Biclea cbs, O. Popa
cl, I. Bandanoiu hrn & L. Obreja tpt

Impressions from childhood, Op. 28 vln & pf
with V. Gheorghiu pf Electrecord ECE–L076

Quartet No. 2, in d, Op. 30 pf, vln, vla & vlc
with V. Gheorghiu pf, G. Popovici vla Electrecord ECE014
& R. Aldulescu vlc

GHEORGHIU, V.

Trio in A pf, vln & vlc
with V. Gheorghiu pf & R. Aldulescu Supraphon 20Z69
vlc

SCHUMANN

Trio No. 1, in d, Op. 63 pf, vln & vlc
with V. Gheorghiu pf & R. Aldulescu Electrecord ECD1020
vlc

Jacques GHESTEM

ALBÉNIZ

España (6 Feuilles d'album) Op. 165 pf
No. 2. Tango in D arr. vln & pf Kreisler
with R. Gola pf Philips P76213R

BOCCHERINI

(6) Quintets, Op. 13 2 vlns, vla & 2 vlcs
Quintet No. 5, in E: Minuet (3rd mvt) "Bull" arr. vln & pf Kreisler
with R. Gola pf Philips P76161R

BRAHMS

(21) Hungarian dances pf duet
Hungarian dance No. 5, in f sharp arr. vln & pf "in g" Joachim
with R. Gola pf Philips P76172R
Hungarian dance No. 6, in D flat arr. vln & pf "in B flat" Joachim
with R. Gola pf Philips P76213R

BRAHMS – *Continued*

(5) Lieder, Op. 49 v & pf
No. 4. Wiegenlied "Cradle song" arr. vln & pf
with R. Gola pf Philips P76161R

(16) Waltzes, Op. 39 pf duet
No. 15. Waltz No. 15, in A flat arr. vln & pf "in A" Hochstein
with R. Gola pf Philips P76172R

CARRILLO

Quartet "Spring" 2 vlns, vla & vlc
with R. Gendre vln, S. Collot vla & R. Sonido 7
Bex vlc

Quartet "Tercer" 2 vlns, vla & vlc
with R. Gendre vln, S. Collot vla & R. Sonido 7
Bex vlc

Sextet in G (1902) 4 vlns, vla & vlc
with R. Gendre vln, G. Devries vln, R. Sonido 9
Flachot vln, S. Collot vla & R. Bex vlc

CHOPIN

(12) Études, Op. 10 pf
No. 3. Étude No. 3, in E arr. vln & pf
with R. Gola pf Philips P76161R

(3) Nocturnes, Op. 9 pf
No. 2. Nocturne No. 2, in E flat arr. vln & pf Sarasate
with R. Gola pf Philips P76172R

DRDLA

Souvenir vln & pf
with R. Gola pf Philips P76213R

DVOŘÁK

(8) Humoresques, Op. 101 pf
No. 7. Humoresque No. 7, in G flat arr. vln & pf "in G" Kreisler
with R. Gola pf Philips P76161R

GODARD

Jocelyn (1888) – opera
Cachés dans cet asile "Berceuse" arr. vln & pf
with R. Gola pf Philips P76213R

GOUNOD

Ave Maria (Méditation on Bach's "Prelude No. 1, in C" from Book I of
"Das Wohltemperirte Clavier") v & pf – arr. vln & pf
with R. Gola pf Philips P76172R

GRIEG

Peer Gynt (Suite No. 2) Op. 55 orch.
No. 4. Solveig's song arr. vln & pf Sitt
with R. Gola pf Philips P76172R

HANDEL

Serse (1738) – opera
Ombra mai fu "Largo" arr. vln & pf
with R. Gola pf Philips P76161R

KREISLER

Liebesfreud vln & pf
with R. Gola pf Philips P76213R

Liebesleid vln & pf
with R. Gola pf Philips P76213R

LULLY

(Le) Bourgeois Gentilhomme (1670) – Comédie–ballet orch.
   Menuet arr. vln & pf
     with R. Gola pf   Philips P76172R

MARTINI (Il Tedesco)

Plaisir d'amour v & pf – arr. vln & pf
   with R. Gola pf   Philips P76161R

MASSENET

Thaïs (1894) – opera
   Méditation arr. vln & pf Marsick
     with R. Gola pf   Philips P76213R

MENDELSSOHN

(6) Songs without words, Op. 62 pf
   No. 1. Song without words No. 25, in G "May breezes" arr. vln & pf
   Kreisler
     with R. Gola pf   Philips P76161R

MILHAUD

Septet (1964) 2 vlns, 2 vlas, 2 vlcs & cbs
   with G. Jarry vln, S. Collot vla, M.   Adès 15503
   Wales vla, M. Tournus vlc, M. Renard   Everest LPBR6176, SDBR3176
   vlc & J. Cazauran cbs

MOZART

Divertimento No. 17, in D, K334 2 hrns & strs
   Minuet (3rd mvt) arr. vln & pf Burmester
     with R. Gola pf   Philips P76172R

PONCE

Estrellita (1913) v & pf – arr. vln & pf Heifetz
   with R. Gola pf   Philips P76213R

RIMSKY–KORSAKOV

Sadko (1898) – opera
   Chant hindou arr. vln & pf Kreisler
     with R. Gola pf   Philips P76172R

RUBINSTEIN

(2) Melodies, Op. 3 pf
   No. 1. Melody in F arr. vln & pf Franko
     with R. Gola pf   Philips P76172R

SCHUBERT

(7) Gesänge (set to Scott's "Lady of the Lake") Op. 52 v & pf
   No. 6. Ave Maria, D839 arr. vln & pf Wilhelmj
     with R. Gola pf   Philips 76161R
(14) Schwanengesang, D957 (1828) v & pf
   No. 4. Ständchen "Serenade" arr. vln & pf
     with R. Gola pf   Philips P76172R

SCHUMANN

(13) Kinderscenen, Op. 15 pf
   No. 7. Träumerei arr. vln & pf Hüllweck
     with R. Gola pf   Philips P76161R

STRAVINSKY

(3) Pieces (1914) 2 vlns, vla & vlc
   with J. Parrenin vln, M. Walès vla &   Adès LA541, LA1003
   P. Penassou vlc

YRADIER

(La) Paloma (1877) v & pf – arr. vln & pf
   with R. Gola pf   Philips P76161R

Ercole GIACCONE

VIVALDI

Concerto in A, P.222 (F.I, No. 139) "L'eco in lontano" 2 vlns, strs & c –
arr. Molinari
   with A. Gramegna vln   2.70408/11   Cetra BB25047/8, CB20194/5,
   & E.I.A.R. Orch. – Ferrero   CC2217/8

Peter GIBBS (1921–)

PURCELL

(15) Fantasias, Z731/45 4 & 5 part – orig. viols
   Fantasia No. 1, in F, Z731 (?1679) 3 parts upon a ground
   with N. Marriner vln, G. Jones vln, G.   Top Rank XRK508
   Malcolm hpsi & D. Dupré gamba
(5) Pavanes, Z748/52 (pre–1680) Nos. 1/4: 3 part; No. 5: 4 part
   Pavane No. 5, in g, Z752 (?1677)
   with N. Marriner vln, G. Jones vln &   Top Rank XRK508
   D. Dupré gamba
   Pavane No. 5, in g, Z752 (?1677)
   with N. Marriner vln, C. Pini vln & T.   Argo RG113
   Dart org
(12) Sonatas, Z790/801 (1683) 3 part – 2 vlns & c
   Sonata No. 1, in g, Z790
   with N. Marriner vln, T. Dart org &   Argo RG84
   D. Dupré bs–viol   Bach Guild BG570, BGS70570
   Sonata No. 2, in B flat, Z791
   with N. Marriner vln, T. Dart org &   Argo RG84
   D. Dupré bs–viol   Bach Guild BG570, BGS70570
   Sonata No. 3, in d, Z792
   with N. Marriner vln, T. Dart org &   Argo RG84
   D. Dupré bs–viol   Bach Guild BG570, BGS70570
   Sonata No. 4, in F, Z793
   with N. Marriner vln, T. Dart org &   Argo RG84
   D. Dupré bs–viol   Bach Guild BG570, BGS70570
   Sonata No. 5, in a, Z794
   with N. Marriner vln, T. Dart org &   Argo RG84
   D. Dupré bs–viol   Bach Guild BG570, BGS70570
   Sonata No. 6, in C, Z795
   with N. Marriner vln, T. Dart org &   Argo RG84
   D. Dupré bs–viol   Bach Guild BG570, BGS70570
   Sonata No. 7, in e, Z796
   with N. Marriner vln, T. Dart org &   Argo RG85
   D. Dupré bs–viol   Bach Guild BG571, BGS70571
   Sonata No. 8, in G, Z797
   with N. Marriner vln, T. Dart org &   Argo RG85
   D. Dupré bs–viol   Bach Guild BG571, BGS70571
   Sonata No. 9, in c, Z798
   with N. Marriner vln, T. Dart org &   Argo RG85
   D. Dupré bs–viol   Bach Guild BG571, BGS70571
   Sonata No. 10, in A, Z799
   with N. Marriner vln, T. Dart org &   Argo RG85
   D. Dupré bs–viol   Bach Guild BG571, BGS70571

PURCELL – *Continued*

Sonata No. 11, in f, Z800
with N. Marriner vln, T. Dart org & Argo RG85
D. Dupré bs–viol Bach Guild BG571, BGS70571

Sonata No. 12, in D, Z801
with N. Marriner vln, T. dart org & Argo RG85
D. Dupré bs–viol Bach Guild BG571, BGS70571

(10) Sonatas, Z802/11 (1697) 4 parts – 2 vlns & c

Sonata No. 1, in b, Z802
with N. Marriner vln, T. Dart org & Argo RG112
D. Dupré bs–viol

Sonata No. 2, in E flat, Z803
with N. Marriner vln, T. Dart org & Argo RG112
D. Dupré bs–viol

Sonata No. 3, in a, Z804
with N. Marriner vln, T. Dart org & Argo RG112
D. Dupré bs–viol

Sonata No. 4, in d, Z805
with N. Marriner vln, T. Dart org & Argo RG112
D. Dupré bs–viol

Sonata No. 5, in d, Z806
with N. Marriner vln, T. Dart org & Argo RG112
D. Dupré bs–viol

Sonata No. 6, in g, Z807 "Chaconne"
with N. Marriner vln, T. Dart org & Argo RG112
D. Dupré bs–viol

Sonata No. 7, in G, Z808
with N. Marriner vln, T. Dart org & Argo RG113
D. Dupré bs–viol

Sonata No. 8, in g, Z809
with N. Marriner vln, T. Dart org & Argo RG113
D. Dupré bs–viol

Sonata No. 9, in F, Z810 "Golden Sonata"
with N. Marriner vln, T. Dart org & Argo RG113
D. Dupré bs–viol

Sonata No. 10, in D, Z811
with N. Marriner vln, T. Dart org & Argo RG113
D. Dupré bs–viol

Hans GIESELER

HINDEMITH

Symphonic Metamorphosis on themes by Weber "Four Temperaments"
(1946) orch.
with H. Otte pf & Berlin Philharmonic Decca DL9829
Orch. – Hindemith Deutsche Grammophon
LPM18301

VIVALDI

Concerto in g, P.383 (F.XII, No. 3) "Per l'orch. di Dresda" vln, 2 fls, 2
obs, 2 bsns & c
with Berlin Philharmonic Orch. – von Columbia C50584, C91105,
Benda STC50584

Elizaveta GILELS (1919–)

BACH

(6) Brandenburg Concerti, BWV1046/51 (1721) strs & c
Brandenburg Concerto No. 5, in D, BWV1050 clav, fl, vln, strs & c
with E. Gilels pf, N. Kharkovsky fl & Colosseum CRLP250
USSR State Symphony Orch. – Mezhdunarodnaya Kniga
Zanderling D1432/3

Concerto in d, BWV1043 2 vlns strs & c
with L. Kogan vln & Moscow Mezhdunarodnaya Kniga
Chamber Orch. – Barshai D05492

Concerto in d, BWV1043 2 vlns, strs & c
with L. Kogan vln & Philharmonia Angel 35343
Orch. – Ackermann Columbia C70427, CX1373,
WC530

BARTÓK

(6) Rumanian folk dances (1915) pf – arr. vln & pf Székely
with A. Makarov pf Ultraphon B15038

KABALEVSKY

Improvisation, Op. 21, No. 1 vln & pf
with A. Makarov pf Ultraphon F15036

KREISLER

Sicilienne & Rigaudon (Francoeur) vln & pf
with piano Mezhdunarodnaya Kniga
D001221

LECLAIR

(6) Sonatas, Op. 3 (1730) 2 vlns
Sonata No. 1, in G
with L. Kogan vln Columbia CX1887, FCX984,
SAX2531, SAXF984
Mezhdunarodnaya Kniga
D012691/2, S0719/20

Sonata No. 3, in C
with L. Kogan vln Columbia CX1887, FCX984,
SAX2531, SAXF984
Mezhdunarodnaya Kniga
D012691/2, S0719/20

PAGANINI

Concerto No. 1, in D, Op. 6 vln & orch.
Allegro maestoso (1st mvt) arr. Wilhelmj
with USSR State Symphony Orch. – Mezhdunarodnaya Kniga
Orlov D08786/7 & D08858/9

Concerto No. 2, in b, Op. 7 vln & orch.
Ronde à la clochette (3rd mvt) "La Campanella" arr. vln & pf Kreisler
with piano Mezhdunarodnaya Kniga
D5809/10

SCHUMANN

(3) Romances, Op. 94 ob or vlc, or vln or cl & pf
Romance No. 2, in A arr. vln & pf Kreisler
with USSR State Symphony Orch. – Mezhdunarodnaya Kniga
Orlov D09113

TCHAIKOVSKY

Sextet, Op. 70 "Souvenir de Florence" 2 vlns, 2 vlas & 2 vlcs
    with L. Kogan vln, G. Talalyan vla, R.   Le Chant du Monde LDX–
    Barshai vla, S. Knushevitsky vlc & M.   A8358
    Rostropovich vlc   Mezhdunarodnaya Kniga
                              D03310/1, D9645/6
                              Monitor MC2019

(3) Souvenirs de Hapsal, Op. 2 pf
    No. 3. Chant sans paroles in f arr. vln & pf Kreisler
    with A. Makarov pf   Ultraphon F15036

TELEMANN

(6) Sonatas, Op. 2 (1727) "Duets" 2 fls or vlns
    Sonata No. 1, in G "Canonic"
    with L. Kogan vln   Columbia CX1887, FCX984,
                              SAX2531, SAXF984
                              Mezhdunarodnaya Kniga
                              D012691/2, S0719/20

WIENIAWSKI

Capriccio–valse, Op. 7 vln & pf
    with piano   Mezhdunarodnaya Kniga
                              D001222

YSAŸE

Sonata No. 1, in C 2 vlns
    with L. Kogan vln   Columbia CX1887, FCX984,
                              SAX2531, SAXF984
                              Mezhdunarodnaya Kniga
                              D012691/2, S0719/20

Bronislaw GIMPEL (1911–)

ACHRON

Dance (Improvisation on a Hebrew folk tune) Op. 37 vln & pf
    with A. Balsam pf   VX 9071   Vox 663, (in set 616)
Hebrew dance, Op. 35, No. 1 vln & pf
    with A. Balsam pf   VX 9069/70   Vox 664, (in set 616)

BACH

(3) Sonatas & 3 Partitas, BWV1001/6 solo vln
    Sonata No. 1, in g, BWV1001
    (unaccompanied)   Dover HCR5229
    Partita No. 1, in b, BWV1002
    (unaccompanied)   Dover HCR5229
    Sonata No. 2, in a, BWV1003
    (unaccompanied)   Dover HCR5228
    Partita No. 2, in d, BWV1004
    (unaccompanied)   Dover HCR5212
    Sonata No. 3, in C, BWV1005
    (unaccompanied)   Dover HCR5228
    Partita No. 3, in E, BWV1006
    (unaccompanied)   Dover HCR5212

BARTÓK

(6) Rumanian folk dances (1915) pf – arr. vln & pf Székely
    with A. Balsam pf   VX 9065/6   Vox 662/3, (in set 616)

BEETHOVEN

Concerto in C, Op. 56 "Triple" vln, vlc, pf & orch.
    with J. Schuster vlc, F. Wührer pf &   Panthéon XPV1049
    Orch. – Davisson
Concerto in D, Op. 61 (cadenzas by Kreisler) vln & orch.
    with Bamberg Symphony Orch. –   Vox PL9340, VXL2*
    Hollreiser
Romance No. 1, in G, Op. 40 vln & orch.
    with Bamberg Symphony Orch. –   Panthéon XPV1007
    Hollreiser   Vox PL9340
Romance No. 2, in F, Op. 50 vln & orch.
    with Bamberg Symphony Orch. –   Panthéon XPV1007
    Hollreiser   Vox PL9340
Trio in B flat, G154 (WoO 39) pf, vln & vlc
    with J. Mannes pf & L. Silva vlc   Brunswick AXTL1019
                              Decca DL9555, UAT273071

BRAHMS

Concerto in D, Op. 77 vln & orch.
    with Berlin Symphony Orch. – Grüber   I Classici della Musica Classica
                              SXAE4092
                              Marble Arch MALS809

Concerto in a, Op. 102 "Double" vln, vlc & orch.
    with J. Schuster vlc & Stuttgart Orch.   Panthéon XPV1054
    – Davisson   VOX GBY11660
Quartet No. 2, in A, Op. 26 pf, vln, vla & vlc
    with H. Monath pf, F. Brieff vla & J.   Allegro AL19
    Bernstein vlc
Trio in E flat, Op. 40 hrn pf & vln
    with F. Klein hrn & L. Mittman pf   Renaissance X13

DVOŘÁK

Concerto in a, Op. 53 vln & orch.
    with Südwestdeutsche.Radio Orch.,   Vox PL10290
    Baden–Baden – Reinhardt

FALLA

(La) Vida Breve (1913) – opera
    Danza española orch. – arr. vln & pf Kreisler
    with Pro Musica Orch., Stuttgart –   Vox PL10950
    Cremer

GLAZOUNOV

Concerto in a, Op. 82 vln & orch.
    with Pro Musica Orch., Stuttgart –   Vox PL10450
    Eichwald

GOLDMARK

Concerto in a, Op. 28 vln & orch.
    with Südwestdeutsche Radio Orch.,   Vox PL10290
    Baden–Baden – Reinhardt

KREISLER

Caprice viennois, Op. 2 vln & pf
    with Pro Musica Orch., Stuttgart –   Vox PL10950
    Cremer
(La) Gitana vln & pf
    with Pro Musica Orch., Stuttgart –   Vox PL10950
    Cremer

*16 2/3 rpm

KREISLER – *Continued*

Liebesfreud vln & pf
    with Pro Musica Orch., Stuttgart –   **Vox PL10950**
    Cremer

Liebesleid vln & pf
    with Pro Musica Orch., Stuttgart –   **Vox PL10950**
    Cremer

Polichinelle–serenade vln & pf
    with Pro Musica Orch., Stuttgart –   **Vox PL10950**
    Cremer

Schön Rosmarin vln & pf
    with Pro Musica Orch., Stuttgart –   **Vox PL10950**
    Cremer

Tambourin chinois, Op. 3 vln & pf
    with Pro Musica Orch., Stuttgart –   **Vox PL10950**
    Cremer

Praeludium & Allegro (Pugnani) vln & pf
    with Pro Musica Orch., Stuttgart –   **Vox PL10950**
    Cremer

(La) Précieuse (L. Couperin) vln & pf
    with Pro Musica Orch., Stuttgart –   **Vox PL10950**
    Cremer

LALO

Symphonie espagnole, Op. 21 vln & orch.*
    with Munich Philharmonic Orch. –   Deutsche Grammophon
    Rieger   LPEM19071
    Heliodor 89544

MENDELSSOHN

Concerto in e, Op. 64 vln & orch.
    with Bamberg Symphony Orch., –   Eurodisc LP55010
    Schüller   Marble Arch MALS809

PAGANINI

Concerto No. 1, in D, Op. 6 (cadenza by Sauret) vln & orch.
    Allegro maestoso (1st mvt) arr. Wilhelmj
    with Pro Musica Orch., Stuttgart –   **Vox PL10450, VXL8†**
    Reinhardt

RACHMANINOV

(6) Songs, Op. 38 (1916) v & pf
    No. 3. Daisies arr. vln & pf as "Marguerite" by Kreisler
    with Pro Musica Orch., Stuttgart   **Vox PL10950**
    Cremer

RAVEL

Tzigane (Rapsodie de concert) (1924) vln & pf or orch.
    2EF 207/8–6A & 209–4A   HMV JOX7036/7, TK5/6
    with A. Kotowska pf

RIMSKY–KORSAKOV

Scheherazade, Op. 35 (1888) orch.
    The young Prince & young Princesses (3rd mvt) arr. vln & pf as
    "Chanson arabe" by Kreisler
    with Pro Musica Orch., Stuttgart –   **Vox PL10950**
    Cremer

* Including Intermezzo.
† 16 2/3 rpm.

SARASATE

(8) Danzas españolas vln & pf
    No. 4. Jota Navarra, Op. 22, No. 2
    with A. Balsam pf   **VX 9072   Vox 662, (in set 616)**

SCHUBERT

Nocturne in E flat, Op. 148 (D897) pf, vln & vlc
    with J. Mannes pf & L. Silva vlc   **Brunswick AXTL1014**
    Decca DL9604, UST253547

SCHUMANN, Clara

Trio in g, Op. 17 pf, vln & vlc
    with J. Mannes pf & L. Silva vlc   **Brunswick AXTL1019**
    Decca DL9555, UAT273071

SCHUMANN, Robert

Quintet in E flat, Op. 44 2 vlns, vla, vlc & pf
    with W. Szpilman pf, T. Wroński vln,   **Muza XL0270**
    S. Kamasa vla, A. Ciechański vlc
Trio No. 1, in d, Op. 63 pf, vln & vlc
    with J. Mannes pf & L. Silva vlc   **Brunswick AXTL1014**
    Decca DL9604, UST253547

SHOSTAKOVICH

Quintet in g, Op. 57 pf, 2 vlns, vla & vlc
    with W. Szpilman pf, T. Wroński vln,   **Muza XL0270**
    S. Kamasa vla & A. Ciechański vlc

SIBELIUS

Concerto in d, Op. 47 vln & orch.
    with Pro Musica Orch., Stuttgart –   **Panthéon XPV1031**
    Eichwald   **Vox PL16030**
(4) Humoresques, Op. 89 vln & orch.
    No. 2. Humoresque No. 4. in g
    with C. Szalkiewicz pf   **OBF 74–1A   HMV JO351, TJ21**
(4) Pieces, Op. 78 vln & pf
    No. 2. Romance in F
    with A. Kotowska pf   **2EF 210–3A   HMV JOX7036, TK5**
(5) Pieces, Op. 81 vln & pf
    No. 1. Mazurka
    with C. Szalkiewicz pf   **OBF 75–1A   HMV JO351, TJ21**

STRAVINSKY

Pétrouchka (1911) – ballet orch.
    Danse russe arr. vln & pf Dushkin & Stravinsky
    with A. Balsam pf   **VX 9067   Vox 664, (in set 616)**

TARTINI

(12) Sonatas, Op. 1 (1734) vln & c
    Sonata No. 1, in A: Allegro (1st mvt) arr. vln & pf as "Fugue" by
    Kreisler
    with Pro Musica Orch., Stuttgart –   **Vox PL10950**
    Cremer

TCHAIKOVSKY

Concerto in D, Op. 35 vln & orch.
    with Bamberg Symphony Orch. –   **Eurodisc LP55010**
    Schüller

WIENIAWSKI

Concerto No. 2, in d, Op. 22 vln & orch.
    with Pro Musica Orch., Stuttgart –   **Vox PL10450**
    Reinhardt

WIENIAWSKI – *Continued*

Fantaisie brillante (on themes from Gounod's "Faust") Op. 20 vln & orch.
    with Warsaw National Philharmonic   Bruno BR14076
    Orch., – Rezler   Muza XL0104

Légende, Op. 17 vln & pf or orch.
    with Warsaw National Philharmonic   Bruno BR14076
    Orch. – Rezler   Muza XL0104

Mazurka in a, Op. 3 "Kujawiak" vln & pf
    with Warsaw National Philharmonic   Bruno BR14076
    Orch. – Rezler   Muza XL0104

(2) Mazurkas, Op. 19 vln & pf
  Mazurka No. 1, in G "Obertass"
    with Warsaw National Philharmonic   Bruno BR14076
    Orch. – Rezler   Muza XL0104

  Mazurka No. 2, in D "Dudziarz"
    with A. Balsam pf   VX 9068 Vox 665, (in set 616)

  Mazurka No. 2, in D "Dudziarz"
    with Warsaw National Philharmonic   Bruno BR14076
    Orch. – Rezler   Muza XL0104

Polonaise brillante No. 1, in D, Op. 4 vln & pf
    with Warsaw National Philharmonic   Bruno BR14076
    Orch. – Rezler   Muza XL0104

Polonaise brillante No. 2, in A, Op. 21 vln & pf
    with Warsaw National Philharmonic   Bruno BR14076
    Orch. – Rezler   Muza XL0104

Scherzo–tarantelle, Op. 16 vln & pf
    with Warsaw National Philharmonic   Bruno BR14076
    Orch. – Rezler   Muza XL0104

ZAREBSKI

Quintet in g, Op. 34 (1885) pf, 2 vlns, vla & vlc
    with W. Szpilman pf, R. Wroński vln,   Muza XL0178
    S. Kamasa vla & A. Ciechański vlc

Josef GINGOLD (1909–)

BLOCH

Sonata No. 1 (1920) vln & pf
    with B. Rubinstein pf   Victor 12310/3S, (set M498)

FRANÇAIX

Sonatina in B (1934) vln & pf
    with L. Elman pf   GM 480/1 Friends of Chamber Music 25

HARRIS

Sonata (1941) vln & pf
    with J. Harris pf   Columbia ML4842

HAYDN

(Die) Sieben letzte Worte des Erlösers am Kreuze (1786) orch. – arr. str qt
    as "Quartet No. 50, in d, Op. 51, No. 1" by Haydn, 1787)
    with O. Shumsky vln, W. Primrose vla Victor 17786/94, (set M757)
    & H. Shapiro vlc

Oreste GIORDANO

VIVALDI

(12) Concerti, Op. 3 "L'Estro armonico" var. cbns & strs
  Concerto No. 8, in a, P.2 (F.I, No. 177) 2 vlns, strs & c
    with G. Armand vln & Toulouse   Vega C30A381, ST20008
    Chamber Orch. – Auriacombe

  Concerto No. 10, in b, P.148 (F.IV, No. 10) 4 vlns, strs & c
    with G. Armand vln, A. Auriacombe Electrola 1C053–10068
    vln, K. Muhlberger vln & Toulouse Seraphim S60129
    Chamber Orch. – L. Auriacombe

Hans GIRDACH

BARBER

Concerto, Op. 14 (1941) vln & orch.
    with Berlin Radio Symphony Orch. –   Regent 5024
    Schultz

GLAZOUNOV

Concerto in a, Op. 82 vln & orch.
    with Berlin Radio Symphony Orch. –   Festival CFR10–603
    Schultz   Regent 5021

Ivry GITLIS (1922–)

BARTÓK

Concerto No. 2 (1938) vln & orch.
    with Pro Musica Orch., Vienna –   Dover HCR5211
    Horenstein   Vox GBY12300, PL9020

Sonata in g (1944) solo vln
  (unaccompanied)   Dover HCR5211
    Vox PL9020

BERG

Chamber Concerto (1925) vln, pf & 13 w–wnds
    with C. Zelka pf & Pro Musica Wind Lyrichord LL94
    Ensemble, Vienna – Byrns   Vox PL8660

Concerto (1935) vln & orch.
    with Pro Musica Orch., Vienna –   Vox PL8660, PL10760
    Strickland

BRUCH

Concerto No. 1, in g, Op. 26 vln & orch.
    with Pro Musica Orch., Vienna –   Vox PL9660, STPL513090,
    Horenstein   VXL8*

HINDEMITH

Concerto in D (1940) vln & orch.
    with Westphalia Symphony Orch. –   Turnabout TV34276
    Reichert   Vox PL11980

MENDELSSOHN

Concerto in e, Op. 64 vln & orch.
    with Pro Musica Orch., Vienna –   Vox PL8840, STPL513090,
    Swarowsky   VSL8*

* 16 2/3 rpm.

PAGANINI

Cantabile in D, Op. 17 vln & gtr
  with T. Janopoulo pf
        Philips 6504 023, 835777LY

(24) Caprices, Op. 1 (1801/7) solo vln
  Caprice No. 13, in B flat arr. vln & pf Kreisler
  with T. Janopoulo pf
        Philips 6504 023, 835777LY
  Caprice No. 20, in D arr. vln & pf Kreisler
  with T. Janopoulo pf
        Philips 6504 023, 835777LY
  Caprice No. 24, in a arr. vln & pf Auer
  with T. Janopoulo pf
        Philips 6504 023, 835777LY

Concerto No. 1, in D, Op. 6 (cadenza by Sauret) vln & orch.
  Allegro maestoso arr. Wilhelmj
  with Austrian Symphony Orch. –   Remington RLP149–20
  Wöss

Concerto No. 1, in D, Op. 6 (cadenza by Sauret) vln & orch.
  with Warsaw National Philharmonic   Fourfront 4FM10006
  Orch. – Wislocki   Philips 835743LY
                          Turnabout TV34203

Concerto No. 2, in b, Op. 7 (cadenza by Gitlis) vln & orch.
  with Warsaw National Philharmonic   Fourfront 4FM10006
  Orch. – Wislocki   Philips 835743LY
                          Turnabout TV34203

Concerto No. 2, in b, Op. 7 vln & orch.
  Ronde à la clochette (3rd mvt) "La Campanella" arr. vln & pf Kreisler
  with T. Janopoulo pf
        Philips 6504 023, 835777LY

Minuet in F vln & pf
  with T. Janopoulo pf
        Philips 6504 023, 835777LY

(I) Palpiti (variations on the aria "Di tanti palpiti" from Rossini's opera "Tancredi") Op. 13 (1819) vln & orch.
  with T. Janopoulo pf
        Philips 6504 023, 835777LY

(6) Sonatas, Op. 3 (1801/6) vln & gtr
  No. 6. Sonata No. 12, in e
  with T. Janopoulo pf
        Philips 6504 023, 835777LY

SAINT–SAËNS

Concerto No. 2, in C, Op. 58 vln & orch.
  with Orch. National de l'Opéra de   Philips 837919LY
  Monte–Carlo – van Remoortel

(6) Études, Op. 52 pf
  No. 6. Étude No. 6, in D flat "Étude en forme de valse" arr. vln & orch. Ysaÿe
  with Orch. National de l'Opéra de   Philips 837919LY
  Monte–Carlo – van Remoortel

Morceau de concert, Op. 62 vln & orch.*
  with Orch. National de l'Opéra de   Philips 837919LY
  Monte–Carlo – van Remoortel

SIBELIUS

Concerto in d, Op. 47 vln & orch.
  with Pro Musica Orch., Vienna –   Vox PL9660
  Horenstein

STRAVINSKY

Concerto in D (1931) vln & orch.
  with L'Orch. des Concerts Colonne –   Dover HCR5208
  .Byrns   Turnabout TV34276
                        Vox PL9410, PL10760

* Concerto No. 4, in G "Unfinished."

STRAVINSKY – *Continued*

Duo concertante (1932) vln & pf
  with C. Zelka pf
        Dover HCR5208
        Vox PL9410

TCHAIKOVSKY

Concerto in D, Op. 35 vln & orch.
  with Pro Musica Orch., Vienna –   Vox PL8840, PL10350, VXL8*
  Hollreiser

WIENIAWSKI

Concerto No. 1, in f sharp, Op. 14 vln & orch.
  with Orch. National de l'Opéra de   Philips 6504 001
  Monte–Carlo – Casadesus

Concerto No. 2, in d, Op. 22 vln & orch.
  with Orch. National de l'Opéra de   Philips 6504 001
  Monte–Carlo – Casadesus

Frank GITTELSON (1896–   )

d'AMBROSIO

Canzonetta, Op. 6 vln & pf
  with C.A. Prince pf   46371–1   Columbia A2096

BOCCHERINI

(6) Quintets, Op. 13 2 vlns, vla & 2 vlcs
  No. 5. Quintet No. 5, in E: Minuet (3rd mvt) "Bull" arr. vln & pf Kreisler
  with C.A. Prince pf   46376–2   Columbia 46376, A2186

BRAGA

(7) Melodies (1867) v & pf
  No. 5. La serenata "Angel's serenade"
  with L Gates s & R.H.   49143–3   Columbia 49143, A5972
  Bowers pf

BRAHMS

(21) Hungarian Dances pf duet
  Hungarian dance No. 7, in A arr. vln & pf Joachim
  with C.A. Prince pf   46383–3   Columbia A2096

DRDLA

Souvenir vln & pf
  with C.A. Prince pf   46456–2   Columbia 46456, A2186

GREENE

Sing me to sleep v & pf – arr. v, vln & orch.
  with L. Gates s & orch.   49142–1   Columbia 49142, A5972

KREISLER

Caprice viennois, Op. 2 vln & pf
  with orch.   49167–2   Columbia A5988

MASSENET

Thaïs (1894) – opera
  Méditation arr. vln & pf Marsick
  with orch.   49166–2   Columbia A5988

*16 2/3 rpm.

RAFF

(6) Pieces, Op. 85 vln & pf
  No. 3. Cavatina in D
  with C.A. Prince pf   46377–1   Columbia A2029

TCHAIKOVSKY

Souvenir d'un lieu cher, Op. 42 vln & pf
  No. 3. Mélodie
  with C.A. Prince pf   46374–1   Columbia A2029

Pio GIUSTO

GEMINIANI

(6) Concerti grossi, Op. 2 (1732) orch.
  Concerto grosso No. 1, in c
  with R. Biffoli vln & Gli Accademici   Dover HCR5230
  di Milano – Eckertsen   Vox DL413, STDL500413
  Concerto grosso No. 2, in c
  with R. Biffoli vln & Gli Accademici   Dover HCR5230
  di Milano – Eckertsen   Vox DL413, STDL500413
  Concerto grosso No. 3, in d
  with R. Biffoli vln & Gli Accademici   Dover HCR5231
  di Milano – Eckertsen
  Concerto grosso No. 4, in D
  with R. Biffoli vln & Gli Accademici   Dover HCR5231
  di Milano – Eckertsen
  Concerto grosso No. 5, in d
  with R. Biffoli vln & Gli Accademici   Dover HCR5231
  di Milano – Eckertsen
  Concerto grosso No. 6, in A
  with R. Biffoli vln & Gli Accademici   Dover HCR5231
  di Milano – Eckertsen
(6) Concerti grossi, Op. 4 (1739) orch.
  Concerto grosso No. 1, in D
  with R. Biffoli vln & Gli Accademici   Dover HCR5230
  di Milano – Eckertsen   Vox DL413, STDL500413
  Concerto grosso No. 2, in b
  with R. Biffoli vln & Gli Accademici   Dover HCR5230
  di Milano – Eckertsen   Vox DL413, STDL500413
  Concerto grosso No. 3, in e
  with R. Biffoli vln & Gli Accademici   Dover HCR5232
  di Milano – Eckertsen
  Concerto grosso No. 4, in a
  with R. Biffoli vln & Gli Accademici   Dover HCR5232
  di Milano – Eckertsen
  Concerto grosso No. 5, in A
  with R. Biffoli vln & Gli Accademici   Dover HCR5232
  di Milano – Eckertsen
  Concerto grosso No. 6, in c
  with R. Biffoli vln & Gli Accademici   Dover HCR5232
  di Milano – Eckertsen

O.M. GLASE–SCHIRIN

LALO

Symphonie espagnole, Op. 21 vln & orch.*
  with Central Europe Symphony Orch.   Guilde Européenne du
  – von Berhányi   Microsillon GEM165

Peter GLATTE

BEETHOVEN

(12) Variations in F (on the aria "Se vuol ballare" from the opera "Le
  Nozze di Figaro" by Mozart) G156 (WoO.40) vln & pf
  with E. Ander pf   Eurodisc 80357XK
(6) Variations (on very easy themes) Op. 105 pf & vln or fl
  with E. Ander pf   Eurodisc 80357XK
(10) Variations (on national themes) Op. 107 pf, vln or fl
  with E. Ander pf   Eurodisc 80357XK

Carroll GLENN (1922–   )

BONPORTI

(10) Concerti, Op. 11 strs
  Concerto No. 4, in B flat
  with H. Langfort hpsi & Austrian   Musical Heritage Society
  Tonkünstler Orch., Vienna – Schaenen MHS652

HAYDN

Concerto in F, H.XVII, No. 6 (1765) vln, hpsi & orch.
  with E. List pf & Biedermeier Orch. – Musical Heritage Society
  K. List   MHS539

LISZT

Hungarian Rhapsody, G383 (paraphrase on N. Lenau's poem "Die Drei
  Zigeuner" by Hubay) vln & orch.
  with Vienna State Opera Orch. – Lehel HMV CLP1747, CSD1549
                                       Westminster WST17025,
                                       XWN19025

MARCELLO, B.

Concerto in D vln & orch.
  with H. Langfort hpsi & Austrian   Musical Heritage Society
  Tonkünstler Orch., Vienna – Schaenen MHS652

MENDELSSOHN

Concerto in d (1823) "Double" vln, pf & str orch.
  with E. List pf & Vienna Chamber   Westminster WST17166
  Orch. – Maerzendorfer

SAMMARTINI, G.B.

Concerto No. 2, in C vln & orch.
  with H. Langfort hpsi & Austrian   Musical Heritage Society
  Tonkünstler Orch., Vienna – schaenen MHS652

STRAUSS, R.

Concerto in d, Op. 8 (1882) vln & orch.
  with Vienna State Opera Orch. – List Amadeo AVRS6352
                                       Fourfront 848101VKY,
                                       4FM10004
                                       Odyssey 32 16 0312

* Including intermezzo.

STRAUSS, R. – *Continued*

Sonata in E flat, Op. 18 vln & pf
  with E. List pf   Amadeo AVRS6427

TORELLI

(12) Concerti, Op. 8 (1709) 1/6: 2 vlns, strs & c – 7/12: vln, strs & c
  Concerto No. 8, in c
    with H. Langfort hpsi & Austrian   Musical Heritage Society
    Tonkünstler Orch., Vienna – Schaenen   MHS652

VERACINI

Concerto in D vln & orch.
  with H. Langfort hpsi & Austrian   Musical Heritage Society
  Tonkünstler Orch., Vienna – Schaenen   MHS652

VIOTTI

Concerto in E flat "Double" pf, vln & str orch.
  with E. List pf & Biedermeier Orch. –   Musical Heritage Society
  K. List   MHS539

VIVALDI

Concerto in E, P.248 (F.I, No. 4) "Il Riposo" vln, strs & c
  with Pro Musica Chamber Orch. –   Classic CL6116
  Goldschmidt   Nixa SPLP514
                              Period SPLP514

Concerto in g, P.383 (F.XII, No. 3) "Per l'orch. di Dresda" vln, 2 fls, 2 obs & 2 bsns
  with Pro Musica Chamber Orch. –   Classic CL6116
  Goldschmidt   Nixa SPLP514
                              Period SPLP514

Concerto in g, P.383 (F.XII, No. 3) "Per l'orch. di Dresda" vln, 2 fls, 2 obs & 2 bsns
  with H. Grötzer vln, F. Opalensky fl,   Musical Heritage Society
  A. Hertel ob, K. Dworak bsn, G.   MHS539
  Zatschek vlc & E. List hpsi

Concerto in c, P.419 (F.I, No. 2) (Op. 51, No. 3) "Il Sospetto" vln, strs & c
  with Pro Musica Chamber Orch. –   Classic CL6116
  Goldschmidt   Nixa SPLP514
                              Period SPLP514

Max GOBERMAN (1911–1962)

BACH

(6) Brandenburg Concerti, BWV1046/51 (1721) strs & c
  Brandenburg Concerto No. 6, in B flat, BWV1051 2 vlas, 2 gambas, vlc & cbs
    playing vla, with B. Yokell vla, S.   Library of Recorded
    Hunkins gamba, B. Mueser gamba, A.   Masterpieces BB3
    Kouguell vlc, J. Levine cbs, F. Rupp   Odyssey 32 16 0187 (in set 32 26
    hpsi, of the New York Sinfonietta –   0013), 32 16 0188 (in set 32 26
    Goberman   0014)

CORELLI

(12) Sonatas, Op. 4 2 vlns & c
  Sonata No, 3, in A
    with M. Tree vln, E. Earle hpsi & J.   CBS–Odyssey 54028
    Schneider vlc   Library of Recorded
                              Masterpieces Vol. 2
                              Odyssey 32 16 0073, (in set 32
                              26 0005), 32 16 0074, (in set 32
                              26 0006)

CORELLI – *Continued*

  Sonata No. 4, in D
    with M. Tree vln, E. Earle hpsi & J.   CBS–Odyssey 54029
    Schneider vlc   Library of Recorded
                              Masterpieces Vol. 1
                              Odyssey 32 16 0075, (in set 32
                              26 0005), 32 16 0076, (in set 32
                              26 0006)

  Sonata No. 5, in a
    with M. Tree vln, E. Earle hpsi & J.   CBS–Odyssey 54029
    Schneider vlc   Library of Recorded
                              Masterpieces Vol. 3
                              Odyssey 32 16 0075, (in set 32
                              26 0005), 32 16 0076, (in set 32
                              26 0006)

  Sonata No. 6, in E
    with M. Tree vln, E. Earle hpsi & J.   CBS–Odyssey 54029
    Schneider vlc   Library of Recorded
                              Masterpieces Vol. 3
                              Odyssey 32 16 0075, (in set 32
                              26 0005), 32 16 0076, (in set 32
                              26 0006)

  Sonata No. 9, in B flat
    with M. Tree vln, E. Earle hpsi & J.   CBS–Odyssey 54029
    Schneider vlc   Library of Recorded
                              Masterpieces Vol. 2
                              Odyssey 32 16 0075, (in set 32
                              26 0005), 32 16 0076, (in set 32
                              26 0006)

  Sonata No. 10, in G
    with M. Tree vln, E. Earle hpsi & J.   CBS–Odyssey 54028
    Schneider vlc   Library of Recorded
                              Masterpieces Vol. 1
                              Odyssey 32 16 0073, (in set 32
                              26 0005), 32 16 0074, (in set 32
                              26 0006)

PROKOFIEV

Overture on Hebrew themes, Op. 34 (1919) cl, pf, 2 vlns, vla & vlc
  with F. Fuchs cl, K. Rapf pf, F.   Library of Recorded
  Miksovsky vln, D. van Ostheim vla &   Masterpieces LRM510
  D. Gurtler vlc   Odyssey 32 16 0083, 32 16 0084

TCHAIKOVSKY

Quartet No. 1, in D, Op. 11 2 vlns, vla & vlc
  with F. Miksovsky vln, D. van   Library of Recorded
  Ostheim vla & D. Gurtler vlc   Masterpieces LRM508

VIVALDI

(6) Concerti, Op. 10 fl, 2 vlns, vla, org & vlc
  Concerto No. 3, in D, P.155 (F.VI, No. 14)
    with J. Baker fl, H. Shulman ob, A.   Library of Recorded
    Checchia bsn, E. Earle hpsi–c & J.   Masterpieces Vol. 1, No. 5
    Schneider vlc, of the New York
    Sinfonietta – Goberman

Concerto in C, P.82 fl, ob, vln, bsn & c
  with J. Baker fl, H. Shulman ob, A.   Library of Recorded
  Checchia bsn, J. Schneider vlc & E.   Masterpieces Vol. 2, No. 1
  Earle hpsi, of the New York
  Sonfonietta – Goberman

VIVALDI – *Continued*

Concerto in G, P.105 fl, vln, ob, bsn & c
with J. Baker fl, H. Shulman ob, A. | Library of Recorded
Checchia bsn, E. Earle hpsi & J. | Masterpieces Vol. 2, No. 3
Schneider vlc, of the New York
Sinfonietta – Goberman

Concerto in D, P.204 (F.XII, No. 29) "La Pastorella" fl, ob, vln, bsn & c
with J. Baker fl, H. Shulman ob, A. | Library of Recorded
Checchia bsn, E. Earle hpsi–c & J. | Masterpieces Vol. 1, No. 7
Schneider vlc, of the New York
Sinfonietta – Goberman

Concerto in D, P.209 (F.XII, No. 15) 2 vlns, lute, strs & c – ed. Malipiero
with F. Manzella vln, J. Iadone lute, | Library of Recorded
E. Earle hpsi & J. Schneider vlc, of the | Masterpieces Vol. 1, No. 4
New York Sinfonietta – Goberman | Odyssey 32 16 0053, 32 16 0054

Concerto in F, P.323 fl, ob, vln, bsn & c
with J. Baker fl, H. Shulman ob, A. | Library of Recorded
Checchia bsn, E. Earle hpsi & J. | Masterpieces Vol. 1, No. 9
Schneider vlc, of the New York
Sinfonietta – Goberman

Concerto in g, P.360 fl, ob, vln, bsn & c
with J. Baker fl, H. Shulman ob, A. | Library of Recorded
Checchia bsn, E. Earle hpsi & J. | Masterpieces Vol. 1, No. 6
Schneider vlc, of the New York
Sinfonietta – Goberman

Concerto in g, P.403 (F.XII, No. 20) fl, ob, vln, bsn & c
with J. Baker fl, H. Shulman ob, A. | Library of Recorded
Checchia bsn, E. Earle hpsi & J. | Masterpieces Vol. 1, No. 10
Schneider vlc, of the New York
Sinfonietta – Goberman

(4) Sonatas, Op. 19 2 vlns & c
Sonata No. 1, in F
with F. Manzella vln & E. Earle hpsi | Library of Recorded
 | Masterpieces Vol. 1, No. 6

Sonata No. 2, in G
with F. Manzella vln & E. Earle hpsi | Library of Recorded
 | Masterpieces Vol. 1, No. 9

Sonata No. 3, in F
with F. Manzella vln & E. Earle hpsi | Library of Recorded
 | Masterpieces Vol. 1, No. 4

Sonata No. 4, in B flat
with F. Manzella vln & E. Earle hpsi | Library of Recorded
 | Masterpieces Vol. 1, No. 7

(2) Sonatas, Op. 55 lute, vln & c
Sonata No. 2, in C
with J. Iadone lute & E. Earle hpsi | Library of Recorded
 | Masterpieces Vol. 1, No. 5

Sonata a quattro in E flat, P.441 (F.XVI, No. 2) "Al Santo Sepolcro" 2
vlns, vla & c
with J. Baker fl, H. Shulman ob, A. | Library of Recorded
Checchia bsn, E. Earle hpsi–c & J. | Masterpieces Vol. 1, No. 5
Schneider vlc, of the New York
Sinfonietta – Goberman

Louis GODOWSKY (1900–   )

BRAHMS

(21) Hungarian Dances pf duet
Hungarian dance No. 5, in f sharp arr. vln & pf "in g" Joachim
with piano | Piccadilly 5040

DRDLA

Souvenir vln & pf
with piano | Dominion B22

DRIGO

(2) Airs de Ballet orch.
No. 2. Valse bluette arr. vln & pf Auer
with piano | XX 2078–2 Metropole 1207

DVOŘÁK

(7) Gypsy songs, Op. 55 v & pf
No. 4. Songs my mother taught me arr. vln & pf Kreisler
with piano | Dominion B27

ELGAR

(La) Capricieuse, Op. 17 vln & pf
with piano | Piccadilly 5040

KREISLER

Sicilienne & Rigaudon (Francoeur) vln & pf
with piano | Homochord H407

MENDELSSOHN

Concerto in e, Op. 64 vln & orch.
Allegro molto vivace (3rd mvt)
with piano | Dominion B27

MOSZKOWSKI

(2) Stücke, Op. 45 pf
No. 2. Guitarre arr. vln & pf Sarasate
with piano | Homochord H407

RUSSELL

Serenade to Nicolette vln & pf
with piano | M 3038–2 Metropole 1207

SARASATE

Caprice basque, Op. 24 vln & pf
with piano | Dominion B34

Caprice basque, Op. 24 vln & pf
with piano • | 3314–2 Piccadilly 5003

Zigeunerweisen, Op. 20 vln & pf or orch.
with piano | Dominion B22

STRAUSS, J. (II)

G'schichten aus dem Wiener Wald, Op. 325 orch. – arr. vln & pf Godowsky
with piano | Dominion B34

VOGLEIN

Old Viennese dance vln & pf
with piano | 3313–2 Piccadilly 5003

Paul GODWIN (1902–)

d'AMBROSIO

Canzonetta, Op. 6 vln & pf
with piano .... Polydor 22251

BACH, C.P.E.

Sonata in b, W143 fl, vln & c
with E. van Royen fl, C. van Leeuwen ..... Telefunken AWT9447,
Boomkamp vlc & G. van Royen hpsi SAWT9447

BACH, J.S.

(Ein) Musikalisches Opfer, BWV1079 (1749) strs & c
with E. van Royen fl, H. Stotijn ob, J. ..... Telefunken AWT9401
van Helden vla, C. van Leeuwen
Boomkamp vlc & G. van Royen hpsi–c

(6) Sonatas, BWV1014/9 vln & clav
Sonata No. 4, in c: Siciliano (2nd mvt) BWV1017
with piano .... Polydor 21969

BRAHMS

(21) Hungarian Dances pf duet
Hungarian Dance No. 2, in d arr. vln & pf Joachim
with piano .... Decca M32210

CUI

Kaleidoscope, Op. 50 vln & pf
No. 9. Orientale
with piano .... Polydor 22251

DRDLA

Serenade No. 1, in A vln & pf
with piano .... Polydor 20274

GODARD

Jocelyn (1888) – opera
Cachés dans cet asile "Berceuse" arr. vln & pf
with piano .... Decca K700
.... Polydor 19913

GRANADOS

(12) Danzas españolas, Op. 37 (1893) pf
No. 5 – Danza española No. 5, in e "Andaluza" arr. vln & pf Kreisler
with piano .... Polydor 19917

GRIEG

Sonata No. 2, in G, Op. 13 vln & pf
with A. Zakin pf .... Polydor 27064/5

HANDEL

Serse (1738) – opera
Ombra mai fu "Largo" arr. b, vln & orch.
with H. Schlusnus b & orch. – Prüwer ..... Decca CA8024
.... Polydor 66984, 67250

(15) Sonatas, Op. 1 (?1731) fl or vln & c
Sonata No. 9, in b: Andante (2nd mvt) arr. vln & pf as "Larghetto" by
Hubay
with organ .... Decca X10036
.... Polydor 21969

KREISLER

Liebesfreud vln & pf
with I. Rossiçan pf .... Fontana 494009EE

Liebesleid vln & pf
with I. Rossiçan pf .... Fontana 494009EE

Rondino on a theme by Beethoven vln & pf
with I. Rossiçan pf .... Fontana 494009EE

Schön Rosmarin vln & pf
with orch. .... Fontana 665002ER

Schön Rosmarin vln & pf
with I. Rossiçan pf .... Fontana 494009EE

LANGER

Grandmother, Op. 20 pf – arr. vln & pf
with piano .... Polydor 20274

MacBETH

Love in idleness vln & pf
with piano .... Polydor 22548

MASSENET

Thaïs (1894) – opera
Méditation arr. vln & pf Marsick
with piano .... Polydor 21970, 522688

PRAETORIUS

Es ist ein Rös' entsprungen Choral setting – arr. vln & pf
with piano .... Polydor 22251

RAFF

(6) Pieces, Op. 85 vln & pf
No. 3. Cavatina in D
with piano .... Polydor 19913, 21969

RIMSKY–KORSAKOV

Sadko (1898) – opera
Chant hindou arr. vln & pf Kreisler
with piano .... Decca M32210

SMETANA

From my Homeland (1878) vln & pf
No. 2. Andantino
with P. Palla pf .... Decca X10043, XP6004

WIENIAWSKI

(2) Mazurkas, Op. 19 vln & pf
No. 2 – Mazurka No. 2, in D "Dudziarz"
with piano .... Polydor 19917

YAMADA

Kismit (Orientale characteristique) vln & pf
with piano .... Polydor 22548

O. GOGGI

BAZZINI

(6) Morceaux lyriques, Op. 35 vln & pf
No. 1. Élégie
with piano .... Odeon A42810

CABRERA

Plaisanterie vln & pf
with piano .... Odeon A42809

DRDLA

Serenade No. 1, in A vln & pf
with piano   Odeon A42820, 0–82454

Souvenir vln & pf
with piano   Odeon 0–82455

PIERNÉ

Sérénade in A, Op. 7 (1875) pf – arr. vln & pf Haddock
with piano   Odeon 0–82451

VERDI

(I) Lombardi (1843) – opera
selection arr. vln & pf as "Fantasia" by Goggi
with piano   Odeon A42819, 0–82450

Maude GOLD

ANONYMOUS

Brunswick medley* arr. vln & pf
with piano   Brunswick 20056

Londonderry air Traditional Irish ballad – arr. vln & pf Kreisler
with piano   Brunswick 156

BACH

(4) Suites, BWV1066/9 strs & c
Suite No. 3, in D: Air (2nd mvt) BWV1068 2 obs, 3 tpts, drms & strs – arr. vln & pf as "Air on the G–string" by Wilhelmj
with piano   Brunswick 123

BRUCH

Kol Nidrei, Op. 47 vlc or vln & orch.
with piano   Brunswick 131

DRDLA

Souvenir vln & pf
with piano   Brunswick 121

KREISLER

Tambourin chonois, Op. 3 vln & pf
with piano   Brunswick 121

Variations on a theme of Corelli (Tartini) vln & pf
with piano   Brunswick 123

LECLAIR

(12) Sonatas, Op. 9 – Book IV (1738) vln & c
Sonata No. 3, in D: Sarabande (1st mvt); **Tambourin** (3rd mvt) arr. vln & pf Sarasate
with piano   Brunswick 156

* Selections unknown.

Szymon GOLDBERG (1909–)

BACH

(6) Brandenburg Concerti, BWV1046/51 (1721) strs & c
Brandenburg Concerto No. 1, in F, BWV1046 vln, 3 obs, bsn, 2 hrns & strs

691¾BE, 692½BE, 740½BE,	Decca LY6082/4
with G. Kern ob, 741 BE & 742½BE	Polydor 27313/5

P. Spörri tpt, A. Harzer fl, H. Bottermund vlc, E. Kruttge cem & Berlin Philharmonic Orch. – Melichar

Brandenburg Concerto No. 1, in F, BWV1046 vln, 3 obs, bsn, 2 hrns & strs
with H. Stotijn ob, A. Mater ob, W. Knip ob, T. de Klerk bsn, J. Bos hrn, I. Sveteman hrn & Netherlands Chamber Orch. – Goldberg
     Epic BC1043, (in set BSC105), LC3604, (in set SC6032) Philips G03018L, GBL5511

Brandenburg Concerto No. 2, in F, BWV1047 tpt, fl, ob, vln & strs

1251 BI & 1252/4½BI	Brunswick 90245/6
with P. Spörri tpt, A. Harzer fl, G.	Decca LY6061/2
Kern ob, H. Bottermund vlc, E.	Polydor 15236/7, 27293/4

Kruttge cem & Berlin Philharmonic Orch. – Melichar

Brandenburg Concerto No. 2, in F, BWV1047 tpt, fl, ob, vln & strs
with W. Groot tpt, H. Barwahser fl, H. Stotijn ob & Netherlands Chamber Orch. – Goldberg
     Epic BC1043, (in set BSC105), LC3604, (in set SC6032) Philips G03018L, GBL5511

Brandenburg Concerto No. 4, in G, BWV1049 vln, 2 fls & strs

699/700 BE & 701/3½ BE	Decca LY6069/71
& Berlin Philharmonic Orch. –	Polydor 27307/9

Melichar

Brandenburg Concerto No. 4, in G, BWV1049 vln, 2 fls & strs
with H. Barwahser fl, L. Oostdam fl & Netherlands Chamber Orch. – Goldberg
     Epic BC1044, (in set BSC105), LC3605, (in set SC6032) Philips G03019L, GBL5512

Brandenburg Concerto No. 5, in D, BWV1050 clav, fl, vln & strs
with J. van Wering hpsi, H. Barwahser fl & Netherlands Chamber Orch. – Goldberg
     Epic BC1045, (in set BSC105), LC3606, (in set SC6032) Philips G03019L, GBL5512

Brandenburg Concerto No. 6, in B flat, BWV1051 2 vlas, 2 gambas, vlc & cbs
playing vla, with M. Major vla, P. Lentz gamba, H. Bol gamba, H. Schrecker vlc, A. Woodrow cbs & J. van Wering hpsi, of the Netherlands Chamber Orch. – Goldberg
     Epic BC1045, (in set BSC105), LC3606, (in set SC6032) Philips G03019L, GBL5512

Concerto No. 1, in a, BWV1041 vln, strs & c

CXE 13526–5A, 13527–2B,	Parlophone SW8140/1
13528–1A & 13529–2A	

with Philharmonia Orch. – Susskind

Concerto No. 2, in E, BWV1042 vln strs & c
with Philharmonia Orch. – Susskind
     Decca DL7507
Odeon 123918/20, ODX104, OLAX1002
Parlophone PMA1007, PXO1064/6, R20582/4

BEETHOVEN

Quartet No. 4, in E flat, Op. 16 pf, vln, vla & vlc
with V. Babin pf, W. Primrose vla & N. Graudan vlc
     Victor (in set LSC6068), LM2200

BEETHOVEN – *Continued*

Serenade in D, Op. 8 vln, vla & vlc

	CAX 7067/72–2	Columbia 264923/5, 68307/9D,
with P. Hindemith vla & E. Feuermann vlc		(set M217), GQX10747/9, LX354/6, W31/3, (in set 10)

(3) Sonatas, Op. 12 vln & pf
No. 2. Sonata No. 2, in A

	CXE 7961–3, 7962–2, 7963–1 &	Decca 29033/4
with L. Kraus pf	7968–3	

Sonata No. 5, in F, Op. 24 "Spring" vln & pf

with L. Kraus pf	XXBb 1087/92	Columbia W149/51, (set 34)
		Decca 29026/8
		Odeon 123839/41, C7301/3

(3) Sonatas, Op. 30 vln & pf
No. 1. Sonata No. 6, in A

with L. Kraus pf	XXBb 1093/9	Decca 29035/7
		Odeon 177253/5

Sonata No. 9, in A, Op. 47 "Kreutzer" vln & pf

	CXE 7975/6–4, 7977–1, 7978/9–	Decca 29029/32
	3, 7980–2 & 7984/5–1	Odeon 123828/31, C7330/3
with L. Kraus pf		Parlophone R20478/81, SW8085/8

Sonata No. 10, in G, Op. 96 vln & pf

	CXE 8306/7–1, 8310–1, 8312–2	Columbia JW31/3
with L. Kraus pf	& 8313–1	Odeon 123825/7
		Parlophone AR1106/8, R20383/5

BERG

Concerto (1935) vln & orch.

with Pittsburgh Symphony Orch. – Steinberg	Pittsburgh Festival of Contemporary Music CB180

BRAHMS

Quartet No. 1, in g, Op. 25 pf, vln, vla & vlc

with V. Babin pf, W. Primrose vla & N. Graudan vlc	Victor LM2473, LSC2473, RB16265, SB2136

Quartet No. 3, in c, Op. 60 pf, vln, vla & vlc

with V. Babin pf, W. Primrose vla & N. Graudan vlc	Victor (in set LSC6068), LM2330, LSC2330

Sonata No. 1, in G, Op. 78 vln & pf

with A. Balsam pf	Brunswick AXTL1082
	Decca DL9720, UMT263601

Sonata No. 2, in A, Op. 100 vln & pf

with A. Balsam pf	Brunswick AXTL1082
	Decca DL9720, UMT263601

Sonata No. 3, in d, Op. 108 vln & pf

with A. Balsam pf	Decca DL9721

DVOŘÁK

(8) Slavonic Dances, Op. 46 pf duet; orch.
No. 2. Slavonic dance No. 2, in e arr. vln & pf "in g" Kreisler

with A. Sándor pf	Telefunken B1286
	Ultraphon BP1092

HANDEL

(15) Sonatas, Op. 1 (?1731) fl or vln & c
Sonata No. 13, in D vln IV

	CXE 11898/901–1	Decca DL8504
with G. Moore pf		Odeon 123900/1
		Parlophone PXO1043/4, R20568/9

HAYDN

Concerto No. 1, in C, H.VIIa, No. 1 (1765) (cadenza by Flesch) vln & orch.

	CXE 11875/80–1	Decca DL8504
with Philharmonia Orch. – Susskind		Odeon 520004/6, ODX104, OLAX1002
		Parlophone PMA1007, PXO1045/7, PXO7000/2, R20558/60

(31) Trios, H.XV, Nos. 1/31 pf, vln & vlc
Trio No. 26, in f sharp, H.XV, No. 26 (Op. 73, No. 3)

with L. Kraus pf	CXE 10064/7–1	Decca DL8507, (in set DX104)
& A. Pini vlc		Odeon 177272/3
		Parlophone SW21/2

Trio No. 27, in C, H.XV, No. 27 (Op. 75, No. 1)

	CXE 10057–2, 10062–1, 10063–2	Decca DL8507, (in set DX104)
with L. Kraus pf	& 10068–2	Odeon 177270/1
& A. Pini vlc		Parlophone SW23/4

Trio No. 29, in E flat, H.XV, No. 29 (Op. 75, No. 3)

	CXE 10069/72–1	Decca DL8508, (in set DX104)
with L. Kraus pf		Odeon 177270/1
& A. Pini vlc		Parlophone SW25/6

HINDEMITH

Trio No. 2 (1934) vln, vla & vlc

with P. Hindemith	CAX 7061/6–1	Columbia 68274/6D, (set M209),
vla & E. Feuermann vlc		72303/5D, J8501/3, LWX63/5, LX311/3

MILHAUD

Concertino de printemps (1934) vln & cha orch.

with Ensemble de Solistes des Concerts Lamoureux – Milhaud	Philips 839270DSY, A00575L

MOZART

Concerto No. 3, in G, K216 vln & orch.

with Philharmonia Orch. – Susskind	Decca DL9609
	Odeon ODX105
	Parlophone PMA1003

Concerto No. 4, in D, K218 (cadenzas by Joachim) vln & orch.

with Philharmonia Orch. – Susskind	Decca DL9609
	Odeon ODX105
	Parlophone PMA1003

Concerto No. 5, in A, K219 "Turkish" vln & orch.
Adagio (2nd mvt)

with Berlin Philharmonic Orch. – Kletzki	Telefunken SK1234, TE16
	Ultraphon FP1060

Duo No. 1, in G, K423 vln & vla

with F. Riddle	CXE 12286/9–1	Decca DL8523
vla		Parlophone R20576/7

Duo No. 2, in B flat, K424 vln & vla

	CAX 7057/60–1	Columbia 68285/6D, (set X46),
with P. Hindemith vla		LX291/2

MOZART – *Continued*

Serenade No. 7, in D, K250 "Haffner" orch.
  Rondo (4th mvt) arr. vln & pf Kreisler

XE 8804–2 & 8805–1	Columbia W268
with A.N. Other pf	Odeon 125140
	Parlophone PXO1037, R20373

Sonata No. 17, in C, K296 vln & pf

CXE 7259–1, 7260–2 & 7261/2–1	Columbia W29/30, (set 9)
with L. Kraus pf	Decca DL8500, (in set DX103)
	Odeon 0–8759/60
	Parlophone SW7/8, SW8000/3

Sonata No. 25, in F, K377 vln & pf

with L. Kraus pf CXE 8271/4–2	Decca DL8501, (in set DX103)
	Parlophone SW19/20, SW8007/10

Sonata No. 26, in B flat, K378 vln & pf

CXE 8277/8–2 & 8280/2–2	Decca DL8502, (in set DX103)
with L. Kraus pf	Parlophone SW14/6, SW8007/11

Sonata No. 27, in G, K379 vln & pf

CXE 7002/3–1, 7263–1 & 7264–2	Columbia W118/9, (set 24)
with L. Kraus pf	Decca DL8502, (in set DX103)
	Odeon 0–8761/2
	Parlophone SW9/10, SW8004/6

Sonata No. 28, in E flat, K380 vln & pf

CXE 8283/4–1 & 8289/91–1	Decca DL8501, (in set DX103)
with L. Kraus pf	Parlophone SW16/8, SW8011/3

Sonata No. 31, in C, K404 vln & pf

with L. Kraus pf CXE 8292–1	Decca DL8505
	Parlophone AR1112, R20407, SW8035

Sonata No. 33, in E flat, K481 vln & pf

CXE 7347/8–2, 7349/51–1 &	Columbia J8520/2
with L Kraus pf 7352–2	Decca DL8500, (in set DX103)
	Odeon 124010/2, 0–8382/4
	Parlophone SW11/3, SW8000/5

Trio No. 3, in B flat, K502 pf, vln & vlc
  with J. Graudan pf & N. Graudan vlc   Decca DL9722

Trio No. 5, in C, K547 pf, vln & vlc
  with J. Graudan pf & N. Graudan vlc   Decca DL9722

PARADIES

Sicilienne vln & pf – arr. Dushkin

with A. Sándor pf	Telefunken B1286
	Ultraphon BP1092

SCHUBERT

Quintet in A, Op. 114 (D667) "Trout" pf, vln, vla, vlc & cbs

with V. Babin pf, W. Primrose vla, N.	Camden Classics VCCS1399
Graudan vlc & S. Sankey cbs	Victor LM2147, LSC2147, VICS1399

SCHUMANN

Quartet in E flat, Op. 47 pf, vln, vla & vlc

with V. Babin pf, W. Primrose vla &	Victor (in set LSC6068), LM2200
N. Graudan vlc	

Sonata No. 1, in a, Op. 105 vln & pf

with A. Balsam pf	Decca DL9721

Milton GOLDIN

BACH

(3) Sonatas & 3 Partitas, BWV1001/6 solo vln
  Partita No. 3, in E: Gavotte (3rd mvt) BWV1006
  (unaccompanied)   Columbia M26

(4) Suites, BWV1066/9 strs & c
  Suite No. 3, in D: Air (2nd mvt) BWV1068 2 obs, 3 tpts, drms & strs – arr. vln & pf as "Air on the G–string" by Wilhelmj
  with piano   Columbia M26

BEETHOVEN

(6) Minuets, G167 pf
  No. 2. Minuet No. 2, in G arr. vln & pf Burmester
  with piano   Columbia M28

BOCCHERINI

(6) Quintets, Op. 13 2 vlns, vla & 2 vlcs
  No. 5. Quintet No. 5, in E: Minuet (3rd mvt) "Bull" arr. vln & pf Kreisler
  with piano   Columbia M49

BRAHMS

(21) Hungarian Dances pf duet
  Hungarian dance No. 5, in f sharp arr. vln & pf "in g" Joachim
  with piano   Columbia M49

(16) Waltzes, Op. 39 pf duet
  No. 15. Waltz No. 15, in A flat arr. vln & pf "in A" Hochstein
  with piano   Columbia M62

DRIGO

(Les) Millions d'Arlequin (1900) – ballet orch.
  Sérénade arr. vln & pf Auer
  with piano   Columbia M62

KREISLER

Rondino on a theme by Beethoven vln & pf
  with piano   Columbia M28

M. L. GOLDIS

GOUNOD

Ave Maria (Méditation on Bach's "Prelude No. 1, in C" from Book I of "Das Wohltemperirte Clavier") v & pf – arr. vln & pf
  with piano   Polydor 22681

SCHUMANN

(13) Kinderscenen, Op. 15 pf
  No. 7. Träumerei arr. vln & pf
  with piano   Polydor 22681

Boris GOLDSTEIN (1922–)

ALBÉNIZ

Suite española, Op. 47 pf
  No. 3. Savillanas arr. vln & pf Heifetz
  with E. Selkina pf   Mezhdunarodnaya Kniga D019480

ARENSKY

Concerto in a, Op. 54 vln & orch.
Tempo di valse (2nd mvt) arr. vln & pf Heifetz
with piano   Mezhdunarodnaya Kniga
D022579/80

BACH

Concerto No. 2, in E, BWV1042 vln, strs & c
with Moscow Conservatory Chamber Mezhdunarodnaya Kniga
Orch. – Terian   D022591/2

BALAKIREV

Polka in f sharp pf – arr. vln & pf Mostras
with piano   Mezhdunarodnaya Kniga
D022579/80

BEETHOVEN

(12) Contretänze, G141 orch.
Contratanz No. 1, in C arr. vln & pf Heifetz
with E. Selkina pf   Mezhdunarodnaya Kniga
D019480

(12) Deutsche Tänze, G140 (WoO.8) orch.
Deutscher Tanz No. 6, in G arr. vln & pf as "Folkdance" by Heifetz
with E. Selkina pf   Mezhdunarodnaya Kniga
D019480

Sonata No. 5, in F, Op. 24 "Spring" vln & pf
with G. Goldstein pf   Mezhdunarodnaya Kniga
D08289

BLOCH

Sonata No. 1, in a (1920) vln & pf
with E. Selkina pf
Mezhdunarodnaya Kniga
D025847/8

BRAHMS

(5) Lieder, Op. 105 v & pf
No. 1. Wie Melodien zieht es arr. vln & pf as "Contemplation" by Heifetz
with E. Selkina pf   Mezhdunarodnaya Kniga
D019480

CONUS

Concerto in e (1939) vln & orch.
with Moscow Philharmonic Symphony Mezhdunarodnaya Kniga
Orch. – Rozhdestvensky   D011747/8, S0575/6

DEBUSSY

(3) Chansons de Bilitis (1898) v & pf
No. 2. La Chevelure arr. vln & pf Heifetz
with E. Selkina pf   Mezhdunarodnaya Kniga
D019480

Children's Corner Suite (1908) pf
No. 6. Golliwogg's cake–walk arr. vln & pf Heifetz
with E. Selkina pf   Mezhdunarodnaya Kniga
D019479

Prélude à l'après–midi d'un faune (1894) orch. – arr. vln & pf Heifetz
with G. Goldstein pf   Mezhdunarodnaya Kniga
D08290

FELTZMAN

Concerto in e vln & orch.
with USSR State Symphony Orch. – Mezhdunarodnaya Kniga
Rakhlin   D011747/8, S0575/6

GERSHWIN

Porgy & Bess (1935) – opera
It ain't necessarily so arr. vln & pf Heifetz
with G. Goldstein pf   Mezhdunarodnaya Kniga
D08290

My man's gone now arr. vln & pf Heifetz
with G. Goldstein pf   Mezhdunarodnaya Kniga
D08290

GLIÈRE

Concerto in g, Op. 100 "Concert Allegro" vln & orch. – arr. Lyatoshinsky
with Moscow Philharmonic Symphony Mezhdunarodnaya Kniga
Orch. – Esipov   D12998, D024022, S776

GLINKA

Album leaf unid – arr. vln & pf
with piano   Mezhdunarodnaya Kniga
D022579/80

GLUCK

Orphée et Eurydice (1762) – opera
Dance of the blessed spirits: Lento "Mélodie" (No. 2) arr. vln & pf Kreisler
with piano   Mezhdunarodnaya Kniga
D0008819/20

HANDEL

Solomon (1748) – oratorio
No. 40. Am klaren Bach im stillen Tal arr. vln & pf as "Pastorale" by Flesch
with G. Goldstein pf   Mezhdunarodnaya Kniga
D08289

HAYDN

(3) Quartets, Op. 54 (H.III, Nos. 57/9) 2 vlns, vla & vlc
No. 2. Quartet No. 58, in C: Adagio–Presto (4th mvt) H.III, No. 58 arr. vln & pf Heifetz
with E. Selkina pf   Mezhdunarodnaya Kniga
D019480

HONEGGER

Sonata No. 1, in c sharp (1916/8) vln & pf
with E. Selkina pf   Mezhdunarodnaya Kniga
D019479

LIADOV

Fridays – Vol. II pf
No. 2. Sarabande in g arr. vln & pf Mostras
with piano   Mezhdunarodnaya Kniga
D022579/80

LYSENKO

Trio in A 2 vlns & vla
with G. Barinova vln & R. Barshai vla Mezhdunarodnaya Kniga
D02389

MENDELSSOHN

Concerto in e, Op. 64 vln & orch.
with Moscow Conservatory Chamber Mezhdunarodnaya Kniga
Orch. – Terian   D022591/2

MILHAUD

Scaramouche (1937) 2 pfs
No. 3. Brasileira arr. vln & pf Heifetz
with piano
Mezhdunarodnaya Kniga
D0008819/20

No. 3. Brasileira arr. vln & pf Heifetz
with E. Selkina pf
Mezhdunarodnaya Kniga
D019480

MUSSORGSKY

Sorochintsy Fair (1911/23) – opera
Gopak (Act III) orch. – arr. vln & pf Dushkin
with piano
Mezhdunarodnaya Kniga
D022579/80

POULENC

Sonata in d "In memory of Federico Garcia Lorca" (1943) vln & pf
with T. Merkulova pf   Mezhdunarodnaya Kniga D9039

PROKOFIEV

(4) Pieces, Op. 32 (1918) pf
No. 3. Gavotta arr. vln & pf Heifetz
with G. Goldstein pf
Mezhdunarodnaya Kniga
D08290

RACHANINOV

(2) Pieces, Op. 2 (1892) pf
No. 2. Danse oriental arr. vln & pf as "Oriental sketch" by Heifetz
with piano
Mezhdunarodnaya Kniga
D022579/80

(13) Preludes, Op. 32 pf
No. 5. Prelude No. 5, in G arr. vln & pf
with piano
Mezhdunarodnaya Kniga
D022579/80

(6) Songs, Op. 38 (1916) v & pf
No. 3. Daisies arr. vln & pf Heifetz
with piano
Mezhdunarodnaya Kniga
D022579/80

RZAYEV

Concerto No. 1, in a vln & orch.
with Moscow Philharmonic Symphony
Orch. – Yadykh
Mezhdunarodnaya Kniga
D15509/10

SCRIABIN

(2) Nocturnes, Op. 5 pf
Nocturne No. 1, in f sharp arr. vln & pf Moguilevsky
with G. Goldstein pf
Mezhdunarodnaya Kniga
D08290, D000819/20

STRAVINSKY

Divertissement vln & pf
with piano
Mezhdunarodnaya Kniga
D022579/80

SZYMANOWSKI

Sonata No. 1, in d, Op. 9 vln & pf
with E. Selkina pf
Mezhdunarodnaya Kniga
D025847/8

TCHAIKOVSKY

(6) Pieces, Op. 51 pf
No. 6. Valse sentimentale arr. vln & pf Grunes
with G. Goldstein pf
Mezhdunarodnaya Kniga
D0008819/20

(3) Souvenirs de Hapsal Op. 2 pf
No. 3. Chant sans paroles in f arr. vln & pf Kreisler
with G. Goldstein pf
Mezhdunarodnaya Kniga
D05834

Swan Lake, Op. 20 (1875/6) – ballet orch.
Russian dance (Act III) arr. vln & pf Koutzen
with piano
Mezhdunarodnaya Kniga
D022579/80

VLADIGEROV

(2) Bulgarian Paraphrases, Op. 18 vln & pf
No. 1. Choro
with G. Goldstein pf
Mezhdunarodnaya Kniga
D08290

Grisha GOLUBOFF

BRAHMS

(21) Hungarian Dances pf duet
Hungarian Dance No. 1, in g arr. vln & pf Joachim
with I. Newton pf   CA 16064–1   Columbia 17078D, DB1666, DW4529

DEBUSSY

(12) Préludes – Book I (1910) pf
No 8. La Fille aux cheveux de lin arr. vln & pf Hartmann
with I. Newton pf   CA 16066–1   Columbia 17078D, DB1666, DW4529

José Soler GOMEZ (1875–)

DVOŘÁK

(8) Humoresques, Op. 101 pf
No. 7. Humoresque No. 7, in G flat arr. vln & pf "in G" Wilhelmj
with piano
Favorite 1–64024
Homophone 134

GOMEZ

Habañera vln & pf
with piano   4463   Favorite 1–64020
Homophone 132

MASCAGNI

(L') Amico Fritz (1891) – opera
Air arr. vln & pf Gomez
with piano   4462   Favorite 1–64019
Homophone 131

MASSENET

Thaïs (1894) – opera
Méditation arr. vln & pr Marsick
with piano   Marathon 148

MOSZKOWSKI

(6) Klavierstücke, Op. 15 pf – 2 hands
No. 1. Serenata arr. vln & pf
with piano   4460 ·   Favorite 1–64017
                             Homophone 134

RAFF

(6) Pieces, Op. 85 vln & pf
No. 3. Cavatina in D
with piano   4457 ·   Favorite 1–64016
                             Homophone 130

No. 3. Cavatina in D
with piano   Marathon 148

SARASATE

Guernikako Arbola vln & pf
with piano   4464 ·   Favorite 1–64021
                             Homophone 132

SCHUMANN

(13) Kinderscenen, Op. 15 pf
No. 7. Träumerei arr. vln & pf
with piano   Favorite 1–64025
                             Homophone 134

YRADIER

(La) Paloma (1877) v & pf – arr. vln & pf
with piano   4461 ·   Favorite 1–64018
                             Homophone 131

Christeta GONI (1900–   )

d'AMBROSIO

(2) Morceaux, Op. 17 vln & pf
No. 1. Aubade rêverie
with piano   38284   Columbia 2360, A1250
(2) Morceaux, Op. 35 vln & pf
No. 2. Nocturne
with piano   Columbia 455, A5528

DRDLA

Serenade No. 1, in A vln & pf
with piano   Columbia 455, 2360, A1336,
                             E2215

LANGE

Flower song, Op. 39 vln & pf
with piano   38608   Columbia 2448, A1350

NACHÈZ

Rapsodie hongrois No. 1, Op. 16 vln & pf
with piano   Columbia 2398

SARASATE

(8) Danzas españolas vln & pf
No. 2. Habañera, Op. 21, No. 2
with piano   Columbia 2398, A1487
No. 3. Romanza andaluza, Op. 22, No. 1
with piano   Columbia 2448, A1487

Mildred GOODMAN

ARCHER

Sonata No. 1 (1956) vln & pf
with J. Newmark pf   CBC Transcription Program 196

CHAMPAGNE

Quartet No. 1 (1954) 2 vlns, vla & vlc
with H. Bress vln, O. Joachim vla &   CBC Transcription Program 143
W. Joachim vlc

FERRABOSCO

Allemande fl & 5 viols
with M. Duschenes fl, H. Bress vln, O. CBC Transcription Program 191
Joachim vla, W. Joachim vlc & N.
Clair cbs

GOULD

Quartet No. 1 (1956) 2 vlns, vla & vlc
with H. Bress vln, O. Joachim vla &   CBC Transcription Program 142
W. Joachim vlc

HAYDN

Quartet No. 83, in B flat, Op. 103 (H.III, No. 83) "Unfinished" 2 vlns, vla
& vlc
with H. Bress vln, O. Joachim vla &   CBC Transcription Program 190
W. Joachim vlc
(31) Trios, H.XV, Nos. 1/31 pf, vln & vlc
Trio No. 28, in E, H.XV, No. 28 (Op. 75, No. 2)
with J. Newmark pf & P. Rosemarin CBC Transcription Program 44
vlc

JOACHIM, O.

Quartet No. 1 (1956) 2 vlns, vla & vlc
with H. Bress vln, O. Joachim vla &   CBC Transcription Program 190
W. Joachim vlc

JONES

Suite fl & strs
with M. Duschenes fl, H. Bress vln, O. CBC Transcription Program 191
Joachim vla & W. Joachim vlc

MOZART

Trio No. 4, in E, K542 pf, vln & vlc
with J. Newmark pf & P. Rosemarin CBC Transcription Program 44
vlc.

PENTLAND

Quartet No. 1 (1944) 2 vlns, vla & vlc
with H. Bress vln, O. Joachim vla &   CBC Transcription Program 141
W. Joachim vlc

PERRAULT

Sextet (1955) 2 vlns, vla, vlc, cl & hp
with H. Bress vln, O. Joachim vla, W. CBC Transcription Program 125
Joachim vlc, R. Masella cl & D.
Weldon hp

SCHUMANN

Quintet in E flat, Op. 44 2 vlns, vla, vlc & pf
with H. Bress vln, O. Joachim vla, W. CBC Transcription Program 91
Joachim vlc & J. Newmark pf

TELEMANN

Essercizii musici (1721)
No. 9. Trio–sonata in E fl, vln & c
with M. Duschenes fl & pf & vlc Hallmark RS6

TOMKINS

Fantasy 2 vlns, vla & vlc
with H. Bress vln, O. Joachim vla & CBC Transcription program 191
W. Joachim vlc

VALLERAND

Quartet No. 1 2 vlns, vla & vlc
with H. Bress vln, O. Joachim vla & CBC Transcription Program 141
W. Joachim vlc

Derk GOOTJES

BEETHOVEN

(6) Minuets, G167 pf
No. 2 – Minuet No. 2, in G arr. vln & pf Burmester
with piano 44859 Columbia E3379

Jacques GORDON (1899–1948)

COPLAND

(2) Pieces (1926) vln & pf
No. 1. Nocturne
with A. Copland pf Columbia 68321D, (in set X48)
No. 2. Ukulele serenade
with A. Copland pf Columbia 68742D, (in set X68)

JANÁČEK

Concertino (1925) pf, 2 vlns, vla, cl, hrn & bsn
with R. Firkusny pf, U. Rossi vln, D. Concert Hall (set B10) CHS1076
Dawson vla, C. Brody B flat cl D.
Weber E flat cl, J. Barrows hrn & H.
Goltzer bsn

LOEFFLER

(10) Mélodies, Op. 10 v & pf
No. 2. Adieu pour jamais arr. vln & pf Gordon
with C. Deis pf Schirmer 2533, (in set 10)
No. 4. Les Paons arr. vln & pf Gordon
with L Pattison pf Columbia 68823D, (in set M275)
Partita (1930) vln & pf
with L. Pattison pf Columbia 68820/3D, (set M275)

Kenneth GORDON

DEBUSSY

(La) Plus que lente – valse (1910) pf – arr. vln & pf Roques
with H. Greenslade pf CE12950–1 Parlophone R3308

DRDLA

Souvenir vln & pf
with H. Greenslade CE 13115–2 Odeon X3368
pf Parlophone R3374

FALLA

(7) Canciones populares españolas (1914) v & pf
No 4. Jota arr. vln & pf Kochański
with H. Greenslade pf CE13118–1 Odeon X3368
  Parlophone R3374

KREISLER

Liebesleid vln & pf
with H. Greenslade CE 13116–1 Parlophone R3447
pf

Rondino on a theme by Beethoven vln & pf
with H. Greenslade CE 13117–1 Parlophone R3447
pf

KROLL

Banjo & fiddle vln & pf
with H. Greenslade CE 12949–1 Parlophone R3308
pf

Mayer GORDON

BAZZINI

(La) Ronde des lutins, Op. 25 vln & pf
with piano Columbia 9077

DRDLA

Serenade No. 1, in A vln & pf
with piano A 1622 Columbia 3692, J171
Souvenir vln & pf
with piano A 1624 Columbia 3692, J171

DVOŘÁK

(8) Slavonic Dances, Op. 72 pf duet; orch.
No. 2. Slavonic dance No. 10, in e arr. vln & pf Kreisler
with piano Columbia 9081

SAINT–SAËNS

(Le) Carnaval des animaux (1886) small orch.
Le cygne arr. vln & pf
with piano Columbia 3830, J277

THOMÉ

Simple aveu, Op. 25 pf – arr. vln & pf
with piano Columbia 3830, J277

VIEUXTEMPS

Ballade & Polonaise in G, Op. 38 vln & pf
Polonaise
with piano Columbia 9077

WIENIAWSKI

Scherzo–tarantelle, Op. 16 vln & pf
with piano Columbia 9081

Lev GORELIK

KAMINSKY

Concerto No. 2, in A vln & orch.
with Byelorussian State Symphony Mezhdunarodnaya Kniga
Orch. – Kataev D016598

Pavel GORELIK

PODKOVYROV

Concert–poème in G vln & orch.
with Byelorussian State Philharmonic
Society Orch. – Afanasyev
Mezhdunarodnaya Kniga
D3680/1

Eli GOREN (1923–)

BACH

Concerto in D, BWV1045 vln, tpts, strs & c
with London Baroque Ensemble –
Haas
Pye GGC4043, GSGC14043

MOZART

Concertone in C, K190 2 vlns, ob, vlc & orch.
with E. Hurwitz vln, P. Graem ob, T.
Weil vlc & English Chamber Orch. –
Davis
L'Oiseau–Lyre OL50199;
SOL60030

VIVALDI

(12) Concerti, Op. 3 "L'Estro armonico" var. cbns & strs
Concerto No. 10, in b, P.148 (F.IV, No. 10) 4 vlns, strs & c
with Y. Menuhin vln, R. Masters vln,
S. Humphreys vln & Bath Festival
Orch. – Menuhin
Angel 36103
Electrola E91219, STE91219
HMV ALP1949, ASD500,
ASDF283, FALP747,
QALP10356

Paul GORENSKY

BULL

Säterjëntens Søndag v & pf – arr. vln & pf Svendsen
with piano
HMV X6780

DRDLA

Souvenir vln & pf
with piano
OSB 2169–1S HMV X6773

DRIGO

(Les) Millions d'Arlequin (1900) – ballet orch.
Sérénade arr. vln & pf Auer
with piano
OSB 2170–IIS HMV X6773

GRIEG

Peer Gynt (Suite No. 2) Op. 55 orch.
No. 4. Solveig's song arr. vln & pf Sitt
with piano
HMV X6780

Alexei GOROKHOV

BRAHMS

(21) Hungarian Dances pf duet
Hungarian dance No. 17, in f sharp arr. vln & pf Kreisler
with piano
Mezhdunarodnaya Kniga
D6505/6

(16) Waltzes, Op. 39 pf duet
No. 15. Waltz No. 15, in A flat arr. vln & pf "in A" Kreisler
with piano
Mezhdunarodnaya Kniga
D11225/6

BRANDL

(Der) Liebe Augustin – operetta
Du alter Stefansturm arr. vln & pf as "The old refrain" by Kreisler
with piano
Mezhdunarodnaya Kniga
D6505/6

DEBUSSY

(L') Enfant prodigue (1884) – cantata v, cho & orch.
Prélude arr. vln & pf Heifetz
with piano
Mezhdunarodnaya Kniga
D6505/6

Petite Suite (1889) pf – 4 hands
No. 1. En bateau arr. vln & pf Kreisler
with piano
Mezhdunarodnaya Kniga
D11225/6

DVOŘÁK

Sonatina in g, Op. 100 vln & pf
Larghetto (2nd mvt) arr. as "Indian lament" by Kreisler
with piano
Mezhdunarodnaya Kniga
D6505/6

HUBAY

(6) Blumenleben, Op. 30 vln & pf
No. 5. Der Zephir
with piano
Mezhdunarodnaya Kniga
D11225/6

KOŽELUH

(La) Ritrovata Figlia de Ottone, Op. 39 – ballet orch.
No. 22. Gavotte (Act IV) arr. vln & pf Kramer
with piano
Mezhdunarodnaya Kniga
D11225/6

KREISLER

Schön Rosmarin vln & pf
with piano
Mezhdunarodnaya Kniga
D22275

Chanson Louis XIII & Pavane (L. Couperin) vln & pf
with piano
Mezhdunarodnaya Kniga
D11225/6

Scherzo (Dittersdorf) vln & pf
with piano
Mezhdunarodnaya Kniga
D11225/6

LECLAIR

(12) Sonatas, Op. 9 – Book IV (1738) vln & c
Sonata No. 3, in D: Tambourin (3rd mvt) arr. vln & pf Kreisler
with piano
Mezhdunarodnaya Kniga
D22274

MENDELSSOHN

(6) Songs without words, Op. 62 pf
No. 1. Song without words No. 25, in G "May breezes" arr. vln & pf Kreisler
with piano
Mezhdunarodnaya Kniga
D11225/6

NEVIN

(The) Rosary (1898) v & pf – arr. vln & pf Kreisler
with piano
Mezhdunarodnaya Kniga
D11225/6

PAGANINI

(24) Caprices, Op. 1 (1801/7) solo vln
  Caprice No. 2, in b
  (unaccompanied)   Mezhdunarodnaya Kniga
                                       D6505/6

SCHUBERT

Sonata No. 17, in D, Op. 53 (D850) pf
  Rondo (4th mvt) arr. vln & pf Friedberg
  with piano   Mezhdunarodnaya Kniga
                                       D6505/6

SCHUMANN

(3) Romances, Op. 94 ob or vlc, or vln or cl & pf
  Romance No. 2, in A arr. vln & pf Kreisler
  with piano   Mezhdunarodnaya Kniga
                                       D6505/6

SCOTT

Lotus land, Op. 47, No. 1 (1905) pf – arr. vln & pf Kreisler
  with piano   Mezhdunarodnaya Kniga
                                       D11225/6

SHTOGARENKO

Trio "Youth" pf, vln & vlc
  with V. Sechkin pf & V. Chernov vlc Mezhdunarodnaya Kniga
                                       D13741/2

Nell GOTKOVSKY (1939–   )

BARTÓK

(44) Duos (1931) 2 vlns
  Nos. 28, 31, 33, 36, 41, 42 & 44
  with Y. Menuhin vln   Angel 36026, 36360
                                       Electrola SME91491
                                       HMV ALP2281, ASD2281,
                                       CVB912

HAYDN

Concerto No. 1, in C, H.VIIa, No. 1 (1765) (cadenzas by Flesch) vln & orch.
  with Toulouse Chamber Orch. –   Electrola SME91743
  Auriacombe   HMV ASDQ5431, CVB1107
                                       Nonesuch H71185
                                       World Record Club ST968

Concerto No. 3, in A, H.VIIa, No. 3 "Melk" (1765) (cadenzas by Gotkovsky) vln & orch.
  with Toulouse Chamber Orch. –   Electrola SME91743
  Auriacombe   HMV ASDQ5431, CVB1107
                                       Nonesuch H71185
                                       World Record Club ST968

Hugo GOTTESMANN

BRAHMS

Sonata (1853) "Frei aber Einsam" vln & pf*
  Allegro (Scherzo) in c (3rd mvt) "Sonatensatz"
  with A. Baller pf   American Record Society 210/4

DIETRICH

Sonata (1853) "Frei aber Einsam" vln & pf*
  Allegro in a (1st mvt)
  with A. Baller pf   American Record Society 210/4

SCHUMANN

Sonata (1853) "Frei aber Einsam" vln & pf*
  Intermezzo (2nd mvt); **Finale** (4th mvt)
  with A. Baller pf   American Record Society 210/4

F. GOVERNALE

RAFF

(6) Pieces, Op. 85 vln & pf
  No. 3. Cavatina in D
  with Curti's Mexican Orch.   Columbia 5416, A148

L. GOZMAN

HANDEL

(12) Concerti grossi, Op. 6 (1739) 2 vlns, vlc & strs
  Concerto grosso No. 4, in a
  with V. Selitsky vln, I. Ziss vlc & Mezhdunarodnaya Kniga
  Leningrad Chamber Orch. – Gozman   D18357/8, S1307/8
  Concerto grosso No. 10, in d
  with E. Boder vln, L. Fishkov vlc, & Mezhdunarodnaya Kniga
  Leningrad Chamber Orch. – Gozman   S1911/2

HINDEMITH

Schulwerk, Op. 44 (1927) var. inst
  No. 4. 5 Pieces in first position for more advanced players
  with Leningrad Chamber Orch. –   Mezhdunarodnaya Kniga
  Gozman   D021085/6

MOZART

(Ein) Musikalischer Spass in F, K522 strs & 2 hrns
  with Leningrad Chamber Orch. –   Mezhdunarodnaya Kniga
  Gozman   SM01951/2

VIVALDI

(12) Concerti, Op. 3 "L'Estro armonico" var. cbns & strs
  Concerto No. 11, in d, P.250 (F.IV, No. 11) 2 vlns, vlc, strs & c
  with K. Varenberg vln, & Leningrad Mezhdunarodnaya Kniga
  Chamber Orch. – Gozman   D018097/8, S01319/20

J. GRABOWSKA

FRANCOEUR

(12) Sonatas – Book II (1733) vln & c
  Sonata No. 6, in g: Adagio; Allemande
  with P. Aubert hpsi   M6–93415   L'Antholgie Sonore 74, AS166

SENAILLIÉ

(10) Sonatas – Book I (1710) vln or fl & c
  Sonata No. 4, in E
  with P. Aubert hpsi   M6–93416   L'Anthologie Sonore 74, AS167

* From a WQXR New York radio broadcast – April 5th 1941.

Eduard GRACH

AFANASYEV

Concerto vln & orch.
with USSR State Symphony Orch. – Ivanov — Mezhdunarodnaya Kniga D3062

AKBAROV

Concerto No. 1, in G vln & orch.
with Moscow Radio Symphony Orch. – Aronovich — Mezhdunarodnaya Kniga D021911

BALTIN

Concerto in g (1964) vln & orch.
with Moscow Radio Symphony Orch. – Rabinovich — Mezhdunarodnaya Kniga D19909

BEETHOVEN

Rondo in G, G155 vln & pf
with A. Maloletkova pf — Mezhdunarodnaya Kniga D17481

(3) Trios, Op. 9 vln, vla & vlc
No. 2. Trio No. 3, in D
with V. Sitkovetsky vla & V. Simon vlc — Mezhdunarodnaya Kniga D021595

Trio in B flat, Op. 11 cl, vlc & pf – arr. vln, vlc & pf
with N. Shakhovskaya vlc & Y. Malinin pf — Mezhdunarodnaya Kniga D020377, SM02263

Trio No. 6, in B flat, Op. 97 "Archduke" pf, vln & vlc
with Y. Malinin pf & N. Shakhovskaya vlc — Mezhdunarodnaya Kniga D020377

BOCCHERINI

(6) Quintets, Op. 57 (1799) pf, 2 vlns, vla & vlc
No. 1. Quintet No. 1, in D gtr, 2 vlns, vla & vlc*
with A. Ivanov–Kramskoi gtr, V. Danchenko vln, V. Sitkovetsky vla & V. Simon vlc — Mezhdunarodnaya Kniga D014799/80, SM02347/8

BRAHMS

Sonata No. 3, in d, Op. 108 vln & pf
with I. Chernyshev pf — Mezhdunarodnaya Kniga D05132

CASSADÓ

Danse du diable vert vln & pf
with piano — Mezhdunarodnaya Kniga D11077/8

CHAUSSON

Concerto in D, Op. 21 vln, pf & str qt
with B. Davidovich pf, V. Danchenko vln, G. Sosonsky vln, V. Sitkovetsky vla & V. Simon vlc — Mezhdunarodnaya Kniga D016507/8

DEBUSSY

(La) Plus que lente – valse (1910) pf – arr. vln & pf Roques
with A. Makarov pf — Mezhdunarodnaya Kniga D8305

Suite Bergamasque (1890) pf
No. 3. Clair de lune arr, vln & pf Roelens
with M. stern pf — Mezhdunarodnaya Kniga D2789

* Boccherini's own transcriptions of the piano quintets, Op. 57.

DELANNOY

Suite à danser orch.
No. 6. Danse des négrillons arr. vln & pf
with A. Makarov pf — Mezhdunarodnaya Kniga D8306

DVOŘÁK

(8) Humoresques, Op. 101 pf
No. 7. Humoresque No. 7, in G flat arr. vln & pf "in G" Kreisler
with M. Stern pf — Mezhdunarodnaya Kniga D021393

(8) Slavonic Dances, Op. 72 pf duet; orch.
No. 8. Slavonic dance No. 16, in A flat arr. vln & pf "in G" Kreisler
with A. Makarov pf — Mezhdunarodnaya Kniga D8306

ESHPAI

Concerto (1956) vln & orch.
with USSR Radio Symphony Orch. – Svetlanov — Le Chant du Monde LDXS8279
Mezhdunarodnaya Kniga D3968/9

Hungarian melodies (1958) vln & orch.
with Moscow Philharmonic Symphony Orch. – Rozhdestvensky — Mezhdunarodnaya Kniga D19910, D028816

Sonata in B flat (1963) vln & pf*
with piano — Mezhdunarodnaya Kniga D025857/8

FALLA

(La) Vida breve (1913) – opera
Danza española orch. – arr. vln & pf Kreisler
with A. Makarov pf — Mezhdunarodnaya Kniga D8306

FRANCAIX

Sonatina in B (1934) vln & pf
with piano — Mezhdunarodnaya Kniga D025857/8

GERSHWIN

Short story vln & pf – arr. Dushkin
with piano — Mezhdunarodnaya Kniga D11077/8

GODARD

Concerto No. 1, Op. 35 "Concerto Romantique" vln & orch.
Canzonetta (2nd mvt)
with A. Makarov pf — Mezhdunarodnaya Kniga D8305

HAYDN

(6) Quartets, Op. 2 (H.III, Nos. 7/12) 2 vlns, vla & vlc
No. 2. Quartet No. 8, in E, H.III, No. 8 arr. gtr, vln, vla & vlc in D – Z. Berenda
with A. Ivanov–Kramskoi gtr, V. Sitkovetsky vla & V. Simon vlc — Mezhdunarodnaya Kniga D017632

HINDEMITH

Trauermusik (for the death of King George V) (1936) vla – arr. vln & str orch.
with A. Maloletkova pf — Mezhdunarodnaya Kniga D17482

* 1st edition.

HINDEMITH – *Continued*

Trio No. 2 (1934) vln, vla & vlc
with V. Sitkovetsky vla & V. Simon vlc   Mezhdunarodnaya Kniga D021591/2

HUMMEL

Rondo in E flat, Op. 11 "Rondo favori" pf – arr. vln & pf Heifetz
with M. Stern pf   Mezhdunarodnaya Kniga D021394

KREISLER

Berceuse romantique, Op. 9 vln & pf
with piano   Mezhdunarodnaya Kniga D11077/8

Caprice viennois, Op. 2 vln & pf
with I. Chernyshev pf   Mezhdunarodnaya Kniga D03487

(La) Gitana vln & pf
with I. Chernyshev pf   Mezhdunarodnaya Kniga D03487

Gypsy Caprice vln & pf
with I. Chernyshev pf   Mezhdunarodnaya Kniga D03486

Liebesfreud vln & pf
with I. Chernyshev pf   Mezhdunarodnaya Kniga D03487

Liebesleid vln & pf
with I. Chernyshev pf   Mezhdunarodnaya Kniga D03487

Marche miniature viennoise vln & pf
with I. Chernyshev pf   Mezhdunarodnaya Kniga D03487

Marche miniature viennoise vln & pf
with piano   Mezhdunarodnaya Kniga D11077/8

Negro folk tune (unid) vln & pf*
with I. Chernyshev pf   Mezhdunarodnaya Kniga D03486

Polichinelle (serenade) vln & pf
with A. Makarov pf   Mezhdunarodnaya Kniga D8305

Recitative & Scherzo – Caprice, Op. 6 solo vln
(unaccompanied)   Mezhdunarodnaya Kniga D03486

Rondino on a theme by Beethoven vln & pf
with I. Chernyshev pf   Mezhdunarodnaya Kniga D03486

Schön Rosmarin vln & pf
with I. Chernyshev pf   Mezhdunarodnaya Kniga D03487

Syncopation vln & pf
with I. Chernyshev pf   Mezhdunarodnaya Kniga D03487

Tambourin chinois, Op. 3 vln & pf
with I. Chernyshev pf   Mezhdunarodnaya Kniga D03486

* May be Negro spiritual melody "Largo" from Dvořák's 5th Symphony or Foster's Old folks at home.

KREISLER – *Continued*

Grave (W.F. Bach) vln & pf
with piano   Mezhdunarodnaya Kniga D025857/8

(La) Précieuse (L. Couperin) vln & pf
with I. Chernyshev pf   Mezhdunarodnaya Kniga D03486

Sicilienne et Rigaudon (Francoeur) vln & pf
with A. Makarov pf   Mezhdunarodnaya Kniga D8305

MacDOWELL

Woodland Sketches, Op. 51 pf
  No. 1. To a wild rose arr. vln & pf Ilyevich
  with piano   Mezhdunarodnaya Kniga D11077/8

  No. 7. From uncle Remus arr. vln & pf Ilyevich
  with piano   Mezhdunarodnaya Kniga D11077/8

MATCHAVARIANI

Doluri solo vln
(unaccompanied)   Mezhdunarodnaya Kniga D17481

MATTHESON

(12) Suites (1714) hpsi
  Suite No. 5, in c: Air arr. vln & pf Burmester
  with A. Maloletkova pf   Mezhdunarodnaya Kniga D17481

MEDTNER

Quintet in C (1950) pf, 2 vlns, vla & vlc
with A. Bakhchiev pf, V. Danchenko vln, V. Sitkovetsky vla & V. Simon vlc   Mezhdunarodnaya Kniga D016518

PAGANINI

Cantabile e valzer in E, Op. 19 (1823 or 1824) vln & gtr
with A. Ivanov–Kramskoi gtr   Mezhdunarodnaya Kniga D015371

(24) Caprices, Op. 1 (1801/7) solo vln
  Caprice No. 13, in B flat
  (unaccompanied)   Mezhdunarodnaya Kniga D2788

  Caprice No. 21, in A
  (unaccompanied)   Mezhdunarodnaya Kniga D2788

  Caprice No. 23, in E flat
  (unaccompanied)   Mezhdunarodnaya Kniga D2788

(18) Centone di sonate, Op. 64 (1828) vln & gtr
  Sonata No. 1, in A
  with A. Ivanov–Kramskoi gtr   Mezhdunarodnaya Kniga D015371

  Sonata No. 2, in D
  with A. Ivanov–Kramskoi gtr   Mezhdunarodnaya Kniga D015371

  Sonata No. 3, in C
  with A. Ivanov–Kramskoi gtr   Mezhdunarodnaya Kniga D015372

  Sonata No. 4, in A
  with A. Ivanov–Kramskoi gtr   Mezhdunarodnaya Kniga D015372

PAGANINI – *Continued*

(3) Quartets, Op. 4 (1806/16) vln, vla, vlc & gtr
Quartet No. 2, in C
with V. Sitkovetsky vla, V. Simon vlc   Mezhdunarodnaya Kniga
& A. Ivanov–Kramskoi gtr   D014779/80, SM02347/8

(6) Sonatas, Op. 3 (1801/6) vln & gtr
No. 4. Sonata No. 10, in a
with A. Ivanov–Kramskoi gtr   Mezhdunarodnaya Kniga
   D015372

PEIKO

Fantasia on Finnish folk themes vln & orch.
with USSR State Symphony Orch. –   Mezhdunarodnaya Kniga D3063
Kondrashin

PROKOFIEV

(The) Duenna (Betrothal in the Monastery) Op. 86 (1940/1) – opera
Andantino arr. vln & pf Feigin
with piano   Mezhdunarodnaya Kniga
   D11077/8

Moment musicale arr. vln & pf Feigin
with piano   Mezhdunarodnaya Kniga
   D11077/8

Serenade arr. vln & pf Feigin
with piano   Mezhdunarodnaya Kniga
   D11077/8

Sonata No. 2, in D, Op. 94bis vln & pf
with I. Chernyshev pf   Mezhdunarodnaya Kniga
   D05133

RAVEL

Tzigane (Rapsodie de concert) (1924) vln & pf or orch.
with A. Maloletkova pf   Mezhdunarodnaya Kniga
   D17482

SAINT–SAËNS

Havanaise, Op. 83 vln & orch.
with M. Stern pf   Mezhdunarodnaya Kniga D2789

SCOTT

(5) Impressions from the Jungle Book (1912) pf
No. 2. Dawn arr. vln & pf Mostras
with piano   Mezhdunarodnaya Kniga
   D11077/8

SHCHEDRIN

(The) Hump–backed Horse (1959) – ballet orch.
No. 1. Balalaika arr. vln & pf Snitkovsky
with piano   Mezhdunarodnaya Kniga
   D025857/8

STRAUSS, R.

Quartet in A, Op. 2 2 vlns, vla & vlc
with V. Danchenko vln, V. Sitkovetsky   Mezhdunarodnaya Kniga
vla & V. Simon vlc   D017631/2

Quartet in c, Op. 13 pf, vln, vla & vlc
with A. Bakhchiev pf, V. Sitkovetsky   Mezhdunarodnaya Kniga
vla & V. Simon vlc   D014559/60

STRAVINSKY

Mavra (1922) – opera
Russian maiden's song (Parasha's aria) arr. vln & pf Dushkin &
Stravinsky
with A. Makarov pf   Mezhdunarodnaya Kniga D8306

Suite Italienne (on themes of Pergolesi) (1933) vln & pf
with piano   Mezhdunarodnaya Kniga
   D025857/8

SVIRIDOV

Trio in a (1945 – ed. 1955) pf, vln & vlc
with Y. Malinin pf & N.   Mezhdunarodnaya Kniga
Shakhovskaya vlc   D020378, SM022634

TELEMANN

Suite No. 1, in a (1725) 2 vlns, vla & c – ed. A. Schering
with A. Kaptsan vln, V. Sitkovetsky   Mezhdunarodnaya Kniga
vla, A. Bakhchiev & V. Simon vlc   D021591/2

Suite No. 2, in g (1730) 2 vlns, vla & c – ed. A. Schering
with A. Kaptsan vln, V. Sitkovetsky   Mezhdunarodnaya Kniga
vla, A. Bakhchiev pf & V. Simon vlc   D021591/2

TSINTSADZE

Melody vln & pf
with piano   Mezhdunarodnaya Kniga
   D11077/8

VLADIGEROV

Suite bulgare, Op. 21 pf
No. 2. Chant arr. vln & pf Vladigerov
with A. Maloletkova pf   Mezhdunarodnaya Kniga
   D17481

V. GRADOV

PROKOFIEV

(5) Melodies, Op. 35bis (1921) vln & pf
with A. Makarov pf   Mezhdunarodnaya Kniga
   D21835/6

Sonata No. 2, in D, Op. 94bis vln & pf
with A. Makarov pf   Mezhdunarodnaya Kniga
   D21835/6

Louis GRAELER

VIVALDI

(12) Concerti, Op. 3 "L'Estro armonico" var. cbns & strs
Concerto No. 10, in b, P.148 (F.IV, No. 10) 4 vlns, strs & c
with F. Buldrini vln, A. Eidus vln, S.   Allegro ALG3146
Shulman vln & Stradivari Ensemble   Concerteum CS194
   Stradivari STR604

Victor GRADSKY

LALO

Symphonie espagnole, Op. 21 vln & orch.*
with Versailles Symphony Orch. – de   Festival FES4549
Ghistelles

* Including intermezzo.

Sophie–Carmen GRAMATTE (1902–   )

BACH

(3) Sonatas & 3 Partitas, BWV1001/6 solo vln
Partita No. 2, in d: Chaconne (5th mvt) BWV1004
           P XXAU 689/92   Decca 25820/1
(unaccompanied)   Odeon 0–6977/8
                               Parlophone E11293/4

GRAMATTE

Concerto in a (1925) vln & orch.
with orch.   Odeon 0–6973/6

Armando GRAMEGNA

GEMINIANI

(6) Concerti grossi, Op. 3 (1755) orch.
Concerto grosso No. 2, in g
    2–70700, 2–70701/2[II] & 2–70703   Cetra BB25112/3, CB20303/4
with V. Brun vln, A. Succo cem, B.   Cetra–Soria LP50021
Francalanci vla, G. Ferrari vlc &   Parlophone R30011/2
E.I.A.R. Orch. – Zecchi

MASSENET

Thaïs (1894) – opera
Méditation arr. vln & pf Marsick
with A. Salerno pf   Cetra CB20484, CC2059

RIMSKY–KORSAKOV

Scheherazade, Op. 35 (1888) orch.
with E.I.A.R. Orch. – Ferrero   Cetra BB25137/41
                             Tempo TT2030

SAINT–SAËNS

Danse macabre, Op. 40 (1874) orch.
with Italian Radio Orch. – Basile   Cetra AT0137

SARASATE

(8) Danzas españolas vln & pf
No. 3. Romanza andaluza, Op. 22, No. 1
with A. Salerno pf   Cetra CB20484, CC2059

VIVALDI

(12) Concerti, Op. 3 "L'Estro armonico" var. cbns & strs
Concerto No. 10, in b, P.148 (F.IV, No. 10) 4 vlns, strs & c
with L. Ferro vln, E. Malanotte vln,   Cetra BB25291/2
A. Pelliccia vln & Collegium Musicum,
Rome – Fasano
Concerto in A, P.222 (F.I, No. 139) "L'eco in lontano" 2 vlns, strs & c –
arr. Molinari
with E. Giaccone vln &   2.70408/11   Cetra BB25047/8, CB20194/5,
E.I.A.R. Orch. – Ferrero   CC2217/8
Concerto in E, P.248 (F.I, No. 4) "Il Riposo" vln, strs & c – arr. Fanna
with Collegium Musicum, Rome –   Cetra BB25264
Fasano   Cetra–Soria LP50022

Arthur GRAMM

DRDLA

Souvenir vln & pf
with piano   38919   Columbia A1502
                             Regal G6771

GRAMM

Prelude vln & pf
with piano   38920   Columbia A1502

REHFELD

(2) Konzertstücke, Op. 58 vln & pf
No. 1. Spanish dance
with piano   Columbia E1552
                             Regal G6771

SAINT–SAËNS

(Le) Déluge, Op. 45 (1876) – oratorio
Prélude vln & orch. – arr. vln & pf Saint–Saëns
with piano   Columbia E1552

Endre GRÁNÁT

BACH

(3) Sonatas & 3 Partitas, BWV1001/6 solo vln
Partita No. 2, in d: Chaconne (5th mvt) BWV1004
(unaccompanied)   Da Camera HBE2402. SV3301
                             Musica Rara MUR35

Marco GRANCHI

ALBÉNIZ

España (6 Feuilles d'album) Op. 165 pf
No. 2. Tango in D arr. vln & pf Kreisler
with J. Da Costa pf   Odeon GO19092

MENDELSSOHN

(6) Gesänge, Op. 34 v & pf
No. 2. Auf Flügeln des Gesanges arr. vln & pf Achron
with J. Da Costa pf   Odeon GO19075

PAGANINI

(6) Sonatas, Op. 3 (1801/6) vln & gtr
No. 6. Sonata No. 12, in e arr. vln & pf Alard
with L. Finza pf   Odeon GO19091

SARASATE

Zigeunerweisen, Op. 20 vln & pf or orch.
with J. Da Costa pf   Odeon GO19075

SCHUBERT

(7) Gesänge (set to Scott's "Lady of the Lake") Op. 52 v & pf
No. 6. Ave Maria, D839 arr. vln & pf Wilhelmj
with L. Finza pf   Odeon GO19091
(6) Moments musicaux, Op. 94 (D780) (1823/7) pf
No. 3. Moment musicale No. 3, in f "Air russe" arr. vln & pf Kreisler
with J. Da Costa pf   Odeon GO19092

Antonio de GRASSI (1880–)

GRIEG

(6) Lyric pieces – Book III, Op. 43 pf
No. 6. To the spring arr. vln & pf Kreisler
  with G. Steele pf   SCM–W–2 Harmony Music 73

SÖDERMAN

Swedish wedding march, Op. 12 vln & pf
  with G. Steele pf   SCM–W–1 Harmony Music 73

Jean–René GRAVOIN

AUBERT

(6) Concerti, Op. 17 (1734/5) 4 vlns & strs
Concerto No. 4, in e
  with J. Manzone vln & Jean–Louis   Decca LXT20118, SMD1507,
  Petit Chamber Orch. – Petit   SXL20118
                          Société Française du Son 174118,
                          SXL20118

BARTÓK

(44) Duos (1931) 2 vlns
  with J–F. Manzone vln   Société Française de Production
                     Phonographiques CVS20002

LECLAIR

(12) Sonatas, Op. 2 – Book II (1728) vln & c
Sonata No. 9, in E flat
  with J–L. Petit hpsi   Decca LXT20106, SMD1504,
                  SXL20106
                  Société Française du Son 174106,
                  SXL20106

(12) Sonatas, Op. 5 – Book III (1734) vln & c
Sonata No. 3, in e
  with J–L. Petit hpsi   Decca LTX20106, SMD1504,
                  SXL20106
                  Société Française du Son 174106,
                  SXL20106

Sonata No. 10, in C
  with J–L. Petit hpsi   Decca LXT20106, SMD1504,
                  SXL20106
                  Société Française du Son 174106,
                  SXL20106

(12) Sonatas, Op. 9 – Book IV (1738) vln & c
Sonata No. 9, in E*
  with J–L. Petit hpsi   Decca LXT20106, SMD1504,
                  SXL20106
                  Société Française du Son 174106,
                  SXL20106

RAMEAU

(Les) Paladins (1760) – opera
Ballet suites 1 & 2 ed. Désormière
  with Jean–Louis Petit Chamber Orch. Ace of Diamonds ADD149,
  – Petit   SDD149
                  Société Française du Son 174078,
                  SXL20521

* Adagio only is on Société Française du Son. SGS1.

Karol GREGOROWICZ (1867–1920)

d'AMBROSIO

Madrigal, Op. 26 vln & pf
  with piano   Gramophone & Typewriter
         27952

BACH

(4) Suites, BWV1066/9 strs & c
Suite No. 3, in D: Air (2nd mvt) BWV1068 2 obs, 3 tpts, drms & strs –
arr. vln & pf as Air on the G–string" by Wilhelmj
  with piano   Gramophone & Typewriter
         27950

SCHUBERT, François

(12) Bagatelles, Op. 13 vln & pf
No. 9. L'abeille
  with piano   Gramophone & Typewriter
         27953

WIENIAWSKI

(2) Mazurkas, Op. 19 vln & pf
No. 1. Mazurka No. 1, in G "Obertass"
  with piano   Gramophone & Typewriter
         27949

Souvenir de Moscou, Op. 6 vln & pf or orch.
  with piano   Gramophone & Typewriter
         027900

Ulrich GREHLING (1917–)

BACH, C.P.E.

(2) Duets fl & vln or 2 vlns
Duet No. 1, in e, W140
  with K. Redel fl   L'Oiseau–Lyre LD53, OL50017
Sonata in b, W143 fl, vln & c
  with K. Redel fl & I. Lechner hpsi L'Oiseau–Lyre LD53, OL50017
Sonata in d, W145 fl, vln & c
  with H.U. Niggemann fl, K.H. Lautner Archive APM14819, ARC3219,
  hpsi & G. Niggemann gamba   ARC72319, SAPM198819

BACH. J.C.

(6) Quintets, Op. 11 (1772/7) (T. P 303/4) fl, ob, vln, vla & c
Quintet No. 1, in F
  with H. Winschermann ob, G. Schmid L'Oiseau–Lyre LD55, OL50046
  vla, I. Lechner hpsi & M. Bochmann
  vlc
Quintet No. 2, in E flat
  with K. Redel fl, H. Winschermann L'Oiseau–Lyre LD55, OL50046
  ob, G. Schmid vla, M. Bochmann vlc
  & I. Lechner hpsi
Quintet No. 3, in D
  with K. Redel fl, H. Winschermann L'Oiseau–Lyre LD55, OL50046
  ob, G. Schmid vla, M. Bochmann vlc
  & I. Lechner hpsi

BACH, J.C.F.

Septet in E flat (1794) fl, ob, vln, vla, 2 hrns & c
  with K. Redel fl, H. Winschermann L'Oiseau–Lyre LD54
  ob, G. Schmid vla, M. Bochmann vlc
  & I. Lechner hpsi

BACH, J.S.

Cantata No. 84 (Ich bin vergnügt mit meinem Glücke) BWV84
with A. Giebel s, H. Winschermann ob Cantate 641212, 651212
& Ensemble

Cantata No. 158 (Der Friede sei mit dir) BWV158
with H. Günter b, H. Töttcher ob, J.   Archive APM14099, EPA37020
Koch gamba, H. Stöhr cbs, C. Gorvin
org & Hannover Academy Chamber
Choir – Gorvin

Concerto No. 1, in a, BWV1041 vln, strs & c
with Saar Chamber Orch. – Ristenpart Discophiles Français DF127

Concerto No. 2, in E, BWV1042 vln, strs & c
with Saar Chamber Orch. – Ristenpart Discophiles Français DF127,
                                                                        EX25017

Concerto in d, BWV1043 2 vlns, strs & c
with G–F. Hendel vln & Saar   Discophiles Français DF127
Chamber Orch. – Ristenpart

Concerto No. 5, in f, BWV1056 clav, strs & c – arr. vln, strs & c as
"Concerto in g" by Szigeti – res. Reitz
with Saar Chamber Orch. – Ristenpart Discophiles Français EX17050

Concerto in c, BWV1060 vln & ob or 2 vlns, strs & c
with P. Pierlot ob & Saar Chamber   Discophiles Français DF165,
Orch. – Ristenpart   EX17024

Sonata in G, BWV1021 vln & c
with I. Lechner hpsi   L'Oiseau–Lyre LD52, OL50015

Sonata in G, BWV1038 fl, vln & c
with K. Redel fl, I. Lechner hpsi & M. L'Oiseau–Lyre LD52, OL50015
Bochmann vlc

BIBER

(16) Biblical Sonatas "Mysterien" vln & c
Sonata No. 6, in c "Christ on the Mount of Olives"
with J. Koch gamba, W. Gerwig lute   Harmonia Mundi HM25145
& R. Ewerhart org

Sonata No. 9, in a "Christ on the way to Calvary"
with J. Koch gamba, W. Gerwig lute   Harmonia Mundi HM25145
& R. Ewerhart org

Sonata No. 10, in g "The Crucifixion"
with J. Koch gamba, W. Gerwig lute   Harmonia Mundi HM25145
& R. Ewerhart org

BOISMORTIER

Diane et Actéon – Cantata (att. Rameau)
with E. Verlooy s, J. Koch gamba &   Archive APM14116, ARC3123,
R. Ewerhart hpsi   ARC73123, SAPM198001

CORELLI

(12) Concerti grossi, Op. 6 orch.
Concerto grosso No. 1, in D
with D. Vorholz vln, R. Ewerhart org, Harmonia Mundi HM25140
K. Storck vlc & Collegium Musicum
Orch.

Concerto grosso No. 3, in c
with D. Vorholz vln, R. Ewerhart org, Harmonia Mundi HM25140
K. Storck vlc & Collegium Musicum
Orch.

Concerto grosso No. 8, in g "Christmas Concerto"
with O. Schärnack vln & Cappella   Archive AP13046, EPA37062
Coloniensis – Wenzinger

CORELLI – *Continued*

(12) Sonatas, Op. 5 vln & c
Sonata No. 12, in d "La Follia"
with F. Neumeyer hpsi & A.   Archive APM14024, ARC3008,
Wenzinger vlc   EPA37035

GRAUN

Trio–Sonata in F (1741) ob, vln & c
with H–U. Niggemann fl, G.   Archive APM14819, ARC3219,
Niggemann gamba & K.H. Lautner   ARC73219, SAPM198819
hpsi

HANDEL

Concerto in C (1736) "Alexander's Feast" 2 vlns, 2 obs & strs
with G. Scheck rec, H.M. Linde rec, Archive APM14140, ARC3140,
H. Schneider ob, F. Fest ob, O.   ARC73140, EPA17195
Steinkopf bsn, H. Göldner bsn, F.
Neumeyer hpsi, H. Münch–Holland
vlc, H. Müller vlc, E. Müller hpsi &
Capella Coloniensis – Wenzinger

(6) Concerti grossi, Op. 3 (1759) orch.
Concerto grosso No. 1, in B flat
with G. Scheck rec, H.M. Linde rec, Archive APM14139, ARC3139,
H. Schneider ob, F. Fest ob, O.   ARC73139, EPA37210,
Steinkopf bsn, H. Göldner bsn, F.   SAPM198217
Neumeyer hpsi, E. Müller hpsi &
Cappella Coloniensis – Wenzinger

Concerto grosso No. 2, in B flat
with D. Vorholz vln, H. Schneider ob, Archive APM14139, ARC3139,
H. Münch–Holland vlc, H. Müller vlc, ARC73139, SAPM198217
F. Neumeyer hpsi, E. Müller hpsi &
Cappella Coloniensis – Wenzinger

Concerto grosso N. 3, in G
with H. Winschermann ob, F.   Archive APM14139, ARC3139,
Neumeyer hpsi, E. Müller hpsi &   ARC73139, SAPM198217
Cappella Coloniensis – Wenzinger

Concerto grosso No. 4, in F
with H. Winschermann ob, H.   Archive APM14139, ARC3139,
Schneider ob, H. Münch–Holland vlc, ARC73139, SAPM198217
F. Neumeyer hpsi, E. Müller hpsi &
Cappella Coloniensis – Wenzinger

(12) Concerti grossi, Op. 6 (1739) 2 vlns, vlc & strs
Concerto grosso No. 1, in G
with W. Neininger vln, H. Müller vlc, Archive APM14846, ARC3246,
E. Müller hpsi & Schola Cantorum   ARC73246, SAPM198846
Basiliensis – Wenzinger

Concerto grosso No. 2, in F
with W. Neininger vln, H. Müller vlc, Archive APM14846, ARC3246,
E. Müller hpsi & Schola Cantorum   ARC73246, SAPM198846
Basiliensis – Wenzinger

Concerto grosso No. 3, in e
with W. Neininger vln, H. Müller vlc, Archive APM14847, ARC3247,
E. Müller hpsi & Schola Cantorum   ARC73247, SAPM198847
Basiliensis – Wenzinger

Concerto grosso No. 4, in a
with W. Neininger vln, H. Müller vlc, Archive APM14847, ARC3247,
E. Müller hpsi & Schola Cantorum   ARC73247, SAPM198847
Basiliensis – Wenzinger

HANDEL – *Continued*

Concerto grosso No. 5, in D
with W. Neininger vln, H. Müller vlc, E. Müller hpsi & Schola Cantorum Basiliensis – Wenzinger
Archive APM14847, ARC3247, ARC73247, SAPM198847

Concerto grosso No. 6, in g
with W. Neininger vln, H. Müller vlc, E. Müller hpsi & Schola Cantorum Basiliensis – Wenzinger
Archive APM14848, ARC3248, ARC73248, SAPM198848

Concerto grosso No. 7, in B flat
with W. Neininger vln, H. Müller vlc, E. Müller hpsi & Schola Cantorum Basiliensis – Wenzinger
Archive APM14848, ARC3248, ARC73248, SAPM198848

Concerto grosso No. 8, in c
with W. Neininger vln, H. Müller vlc, E. Müller hpsi & Schola Cantorum Basiliensis – Wenzinger
Archive APM14847, ARC3247, ARC73247, SAPM198847

Concerto grosso No. 9, in F
with W. Neininger vln, H. Müller vlc, E. Müller hpsi & Schola Cantorum Basiliensis – Wenzinger
Archive APM14848, ARC3248, ARC73248, SAPM198848

Concerto grosso No. 10, in d
with W. Neininger vln, H. Müller vlc, E. Müller hpsi & Schola Cantorum Basiliensis – Wenzinger
Archive APM14846, ARC3246, ARC73246, SAPM198846,

Concerto grosso No. 11, in A
with W. Neininger vln, H. Müller vlc, E. Müller hpsi & Schola Cantorum Basiliensis – Wenzinger
Archive APM14846, ARC3246, ARC73246, SAPM198846

Concerto grosso No. 12, in b
with W. Neininger vln, H. Müller vlc, E. Müller hpsi & Schola Cantorum Basiliensis – Wenzinger
Archive APM14848, ARC3248, ARC73248, SAPM198848

(9) Deutschen Arien (1729) v, vln, fl or ob & c
No. 2. Das zitternde Glänzen der spielenden Wellen
with M. Guilleaume s, A. Wenzinger vlc & F. Neumeyer hpsi
Archive APM14031, ARC3042

No. 7. Die ihr aus dunklen Grüften
with M. Guilleaume s, A. Wenzinger vlc & F. Neumeyer hpsi
Archive APM14031, ARC3042

No. 9. Flammende Rose, zierde der Erden
with M. Guilleaume s, A. Wenzinger vlc & F. Neumeyer hpsi
Archive APM14031, ARC3042

HAYDN

Cassation in G, H.II, No. 9 2 vlns, 2 obs, 2 hrns, 2 vlas, vlc & cbs
with F–J. Maier vln, A. Sous ob, H. Hucke ob, G. Seifert hrn, E. Penzel hrn, G. Lemmen vla, U. Koch vla, R.J. Buhl vlc & J. Koch cbs
Harmonia Mundi HM30643, HMST530643

Cassation in F, H.II, No. 20 2 vlns, 2 obs, 2 hrns, 2 vlas, vlc & cbs
with F–J. Maier vln, A. Sous ob, H. Hucke ob, G. Seifert hrn, E. Penzel hrn, G. Lemmen vla, U. Koch vla, R.J. Buhl vlc & J. Koch cbs
Harmonia Mundi HM30643, HMST530643

LECLAIR

(12) Sonatas, Op. 5 – Book III (1734) vln & c
Sonata No. 6, in c
with F. Neumeyer hpsi & K. Storck vlc
Archive EPA37159
Heliodor H25018, HS25018

MOZART

Divertimento No. 10, in F, K247 2 hrns & strs
with F–J. Maier vln, E. Penzel hrn, G. Seifert hrn, G. Lemmen vla, R.J. Buhl vlc & J. Koch cbs
Harmonia Mundi HM30646, HMST530646

Divertimento No. 11, in D, K251 2 hrns, ob & strs
with H. Hucke ob, F–J. Maier vln, E. Penzel hrn, G. Seifert hrn, G. Lemmen vla, R.J. Buhl vlc & J. Koch cbs
Harmonia Mundi HM30646, HMST530646

Duo No. 1, in G, K423 vln & vla
with U. Koch vla
Harmonia Mundi HM30168

Duo No. 2, in B flat, K424 vln & vla
with U. Koch vla
Harmonia Mundi HM30168

Serenade No. 4, in D, K203 orch.
with Cappella Coloniensis of Radio Cologne (WDR) – Leitner
Archive APM14363, ARC3263, ARC73263, SAPM198363

PACHELBEL

Canon & Gigue in D 3 vlns & c
with S. Lautenbacher vln, D. Wolff–Malm vln, R.J. Buhl vlc & F. Neumeyer hpsi
Archive EPA37256, SEPA181256

Partita No. 2 in c 2 vlns & c
with S. Lautenbacher vln, R.J. Buhl vlc & F. Neumeyer hpsi
Archive EPA37256, SEPA 181256

RAMEAU

Orphée (1721) – cantata
with E. Verlooy s, J. Koch gamba & R. Ewerhart hpsi
Archive APM14116, ARC3123, ARC73123, SAPM198001

STAMITZ, K.

Sinfonia concertante in D vln, vla & orch.
with U. Koch vla & Collegium aureum – Reinhardt
Harmonia Mundi HM30645, HMST530645

Sinfonia in E flat vln, vla & orch.
with U. Koch vla & Collegium aureum – Reinhardt
Harmonia Mundi HM30645, HMST530645

Emily GRESSER (1894–   )

BRAHMS

(21) Hungarian Dances pf duet
Hungarian Dance No. 2, in d arr. vln & pf Joachim
with piano
Pathé 5555, 52031

CHOPIN

(4) Mazurkas, Op. 67 pf
No. 4. Mazurka No. 45, in a arr. vln & pf Kreisler
with piano
Pathé 25019

DRDLA

Serenade No. 1, in A vln & pf
with piano
Pathé–Actuelle 10236, 020584

DRDLA – *Continued*

Souvenir vln & pf
with piano   Pathé–Actuelle 10236, 020584

KREISLER

Polichinelle (serenade) vln & pf
with piano   Pathé 25019

RIMSKY-KORSAKOV

(Le) Coq d'Or (1910) – opera
Hymn to the sun arr. vln & pf Kreisler
with piano   Pathé 5555, 52031

Frederick GREY

DVOŘÁK

(8) Humoresques, Op. 101 pf
No. 7. Humoresque No. 7, in G flat arr. vln & pf "in G" Kreisler
with piano   Aco G15142

Tatyana GRINDENKO

TCHAIKOVSKY

Souvenir d'un lieu cher, Op. 42 vln & pf
No. 3. Mélodie
with piano   Mezhdunarodnaya Kniga
     D028103

Frederick GRINKE (1911–)

BACH

(6) Brandenburg Concerti, BWV1046/51 (1721) strs & c
Brandenburg Concerto No. 2, in F, BWV1047 tpt, fl, ob, vln & strs
     AR 10403–3, 10404–2, 10405–1   Decca (set EDA27), K1550/1,
with G. Eskdale tpt, A.   & 10406–2   Z886/7
Cleghorn fl & Boyd Neel String Orch.
– Neel

Brandenburg Concerto No. 4, in G, BWV1049 vln, 2 fls & strs
     AR 9515/7–2 & 9518–1   Decca K1616/7
with A. Cleghorn fl, G. Morris fl &
Boyd Neel String Orch. – Neel

Brandenburg Concerto No. 5, in D, BWV1050 clav, fl, vln & strs
with K. Long pf,   AR 11885/90–1   Decca AK1889/91
G. Morris fl & Boyd Neel String Orch.   London (set LA191)
– Neel

Clavierübung – part 3, BWV802/5 clav – arr. vln & vla as "4 Duetti" by David
Duetto No. 1, in e, BWV802
with W. Forbes vla   AR 5583–3   Decca K1072, Z850

Duetto No. 2, in F, BWV803
with W. Forbes vla   AR 5583–3   Decca K1072, Z850

Duetto No. 3, in G, BWV804
with W. Forbes vla   AR 5584–3   Decca K1072, Z850

Duetto No. 4, in a, BWV805
with W. Forbes vla   AR 5584–3   Decca K1072, Z850

BARTÓK

Contrasts (1938) cl, vln & pf
with J. Brymer cl & W. Parry pf   Argo RG89
     La Boîte à Musique LD033
     Westminster XWN18425

BEETHOVEN

(2) Trios, Op. 70 pf, vln & vlc
No. 2. Trio No. 5, in E flat
     AR 6132–3, 6133–1, 6134/6–3 &   Decca K1069/71
with K. Taylor pf & F.   6137–4
Hooton vlc

BENJAMIN

Sonatina (1925) vln & pf
with A. Benjamin pf   Decca LXT5143
     London LL1382

BERKELEY

Sonatina in A, Op. 17 (1942) vln & pf
with L. Berkeley pf   Decca LXT2978
     London LL1055

Theme & Variations, Op. 33, No. 1 solo vln
(unaccompanied)   Decca LXT2978
     London LL1055

BOULANGER, L.

Nocturne in F (1911) vln & pf
with I. Newton pf   DR 7332–2   Decca M570

BRIDGE

Trio in c (1908) "Phantasie" pf, vln & vlc
     AR 4401–1, 4402–3 & 4403/4–1   Decca K945/6
with K. Taylor pf & F. Hooton vlc

DALE

(3) Pieces, Op. 10 (1916/20) vln & pf
No. 1. English dance
with I. Newton pf   DR 7079/80–1   Decca M530

DVOŘÁK

Ballade in d, Op. 15 vln & pf
with G. Moore pf   AR 5934–1   Decca K1017

(4) Romantic Pieces, Op. 75 vln & pf
with G. Moore pf   AR 5931/3–1   Decca K1016/7

Sonatina in G, Op. 100 vln & pf
     AR 5927–1, 5928–2 & 5929/30–1   Decca K1006/7
with K. Taylor pf

Terzetto in C, Op. 74 2 vlns & vla
     AR 5616/8–1, 5619–2, 5620–1 &   Decca K981/3
with D. Martin vln & W.   5621–2
Forbes vla

GURNEY

(The) Apple orchard vln & pf
with I. Newton pf   DR 7083–2   Decca M539

HANDEL

(12) Concerti grossi, Op. 6 (1739) 2 vlns, vlc & strs
  Concerto grosso No. 10, in d
    DTA 3586–1, 3587/8–2 & 3589–1 Decca X138/9
  with D. Martin vln, J. Whitehouse
  vlc, A. Goldsbrough hpsi & Boyd Neel
  String Orch. – Neel
  Concerto grosso No. 12, in b
    AR 3018–2, 3019–1, 3020–2 & Decca X142/3
  with D. Martin vln, J. 3021–1
  Whitehouse vlc, A. Goldsbrough hpsi
  & Boyd Neel String Orch. – Neel

(16) Suites (1720/33) hpsi
  Suite No. 11, in b: Sarabande (2nd mvt) arr. vln & vla Halvorsen
      AR 3985–2 3986–3 Decca K917, Z807
  with W. Forbes vla

IRELAND

Sonata No. 1, in d (1909) vln & pf
    AR 9839/41–2, 9843–1 & 9844/6–2 Decca K1400/3
  with J. Ireland pf
Trio No. 1, in a (1908) "Phantasy–Trio" pf, vln & vlc
    AR 3105–3, 3106–2, 3107–3 & Decca K899/900
  with K. Taylor pf & F. 3108–1
  Hooton vlc
Trio No. 3, in E (1938) pf, vln & vlc
  with K. Taylor pf & F. Hooton vlc
    Decca X242/4, Z799/801

LIEURANCE

By the waters of the Minnetonka (1914) v & pf – arr. v, vln & pf
  with J. Hammond s CA 18460–1 Columbia DB2015
  & G. Moore pf

MOZART

Concerto No. 5, in A, K219 "Turkish" (cadenzas by Joachim) vln & orch.
    AR 9507–3, 9508/10–4, 9511–1 Decca K1268/71
  with Boyd Neel Orch. – & 9512/4–2
  Neel
Duo No. 1, in G, K423 vln & vla
    AR 3642–6 & 3643/4–2 Decca K910/1
  with W. Forbes vla
Duo No. 2, in B flat, K424 vln & vla
    AR 3645–3, 3646–2 & 3647–3 Decca K911/2
  with W. Forbes vla
Sonata No. 32, in B flat, K454 vln & pf
  with K. Taylor pf Decca LXT2802
    London LL739
Sonata No. 34, in A, K526 vln & pf
  with K. Taylor pf Decca LXT2802
    London LL739

NOVAČEK

(8) Concert Caprices, Op. 5 vln & pf
  No. 4. Perpetuum mobile
  with I. Newton pf DR 7131–3 Decca M570

PURCELL

Sonata in g, Z780 vln & c – arr. vln & pf Goldsbrough
  with A. AR 9958/9–2 Decca K1404
  Goldsbrough pf London T5443

PURCELL – *Continued*

(10) Sonatas, Z802/11 (1697) 4 parts – 2 vlns & c
  Sonata No. 3, in a, Z804
      CA 7383–2 & 7384–1 vln Decca 25615, K809
  with J. Pougnet vln & B. Ord hpsi
  Sonata No. 9, in F, Z810 "Golden Sonata"
  with J. Pougnet vln CA 7381/2–1 Decca 25614, K778
  & B. Ord hpsi Polydor 45252

QUILTER

(3) Pastoral songs, Op. 22 v, vln, vlc & pf
  No. 2. Cherry valley
  with M. Raphael b, CA 14804–3 Columbia DB1648, RO78
  H. Withers vlc & R. Quilter pf
(3) Shakespeare songs, Op. 6 v, vln, vlc & pf
  No. 1, Come away death
  with M. Raphael b, M. Gilbert vla, H. Columbia 225M, RO73
  Withers vlc & R. Quilter pf
(5) Shakespeare songs, Op. 23 v, vln, vlc & pf
  No. 4. Take, o take those lips away
  with M. Raphael b, CA 14800–4 Columbia DB1629, DO1567
  M. Gilbert vla, H. Withers vlc & R.
  Quilter pf

RACHMANINOV

(5) Pieces, Op. 3 pf
  No. 5. Serenade arr. vln & pf Press
  with I. Newton pf DR 7130–1 Decca M539

RICHARDSON

Dreaming spires vln & pf
  with I. Newton pf DR 7129–2 Decca M551
Sonnet vln & pf
  with I. Newton pf DR 7128–2 Decca M551

RUBBRA

Sonata No. 2, Op. 31 (1931) vln & pf
  with E. Rubbra pf Decca LXT2978
    London LL1055

SMETANA

From my Homeland (1878) vln & pf
  No. 2. Andantino
  with I. Newton pf DR 7081/2–4 Decca M564

VAUGHAN WILLIAMS

Concerto in d (1925) "Concerto accademico" vln & orch.
    AR 3563–1, 3564/5–2 & 3566–1 Decca X248/9
  with Boyd Neel String Orch. – Neel
(The) Lark ascending (1914) vln & orch.
  with Boyd Neel AR 4405/8–2 Decca X259/60, Z812/3
  String Orch. – Neel
On Wenlock edge – song cycle (1909) t, 2 vlns, vla, vlc & pf
  with G. Maran t, L. Bentley vln, K. Decca LW5233
  Cummings vla, D. Cameron vlc & I.
  Newton pf
Sonata in a vln & pf
  with M. Mulliner pf Decca LXT5143
    London LL1382

Robert GROSS (1914–)

HUMEL

Sonata "Journey to Praha" vln & pf
with P. Hewitt pf　　　　　　　　Composers Recordings CRI 237

Einar GROTH (1903–)

BULL

Säterjëntens søndag v & pf – arr. vln & pf Svendsen
with R. Svensson　　　　Sto 7135　Odeon*
Hammond org

GROTH

Till rosorna vln & pf
with R. Svensson　　　　Sto 7134　Odeon*
Hammond org

GROTHE

Illusion – waltz vln & pf
with W. Lind org　　　6560–S–S–C　Sonora 6001

GULLMAR

Mon amour vln & pf
with R. Svensson　　　　Sto 7137　Odeon D5138
Hammond org

KING

Song of paradise pf – arr. vln & org
with R. Svensson org　　6430–S–S–C　Sonora 6000

MALDEREN

(Le) Tango de rêve vln & pf
with W. Lind org　　　6559–S–S–C　Sonora 6001

MOYA

(The) Song of songs (1914) v & pf – arr. vln & org
with R. Svensson org　　6431–S–S–C　Sonora 6000

WINTER

Inga orkideer v & pf – arr. vln & org
with R. Svensson　　　　Sto 7136　Odeon D5138
Hammond org

Hans GRÖTZER

SARASATE

Zigeunerweisen, Op. 20 vln & pf or orch.
with Vienna State Opera Orch. –　　Reader's Digest
Desarzens

VIVALDI

Concerto in g, P.383 (F.XII, No. 3) "Per l'orch. di Dresda" vln, 2 fls, 2 obs
& 2 bsns
with C. Glenn vln, F. Opalensky fl, A.　Musical Heritage Society
Hertel ob, K. Dworak bsn, G.　　　MHS539
Zatschek vlc & E. List hpsi

* Unissued.

Erich GRUENBERG (1924–)

BEETHOVEN

(2) Trios, Op. 70 pf, vln & vlc
No. 1. Trio No. 4, in D "Ghost"
with E. Rubbra pf & W. Pleeth vlc　　Argo ARS1005, RG5

DRIGO

(Les) Millions d'Arlequin (1900) – ballet orch.
Pas de trois
with London Symphony Orch. –　Decca MET254, SET254
Bonynge　　　　　London CS6342, (in set
　　　　　　　　　CSA2213), (in set CMA7213)

GEMINIANI

(6) Concerti grossi, Op. 3 (1755) orch.
Concerto grosso No. 3, in e
with J. Rothstein vln, C. Aronowitz　L'Oiseau–Lyre OL50129
vla, B. Rickelman vlc, T. Dart hpsi &
Boyd Neel Orch. – Dart

HAYDN

(31) Trios, H.XV, Nos. 1/31 pf, vln & vlc
Trio No. 26, in f sharp: Adagio (2nd mvt) H.XV, No. 26 (Op. 73, No. 3)
with E. Rubbra pf　　2EA 16647–3A　HMV HLP19, HMS81
& W. Pleeth vlc　　　　　Victor (in set LM6137)

LOVENSKJOLD

(La) Sylphide (1836) – ballet orch.
Scène de la Sylphide (Act II)
with London Symphony Orch. –　Decca MET254, SET254
Bonynge　　　　　London CS6342, (in set
　　　　　　　　　CSA2213), (in set CMA7213)

MINKUS

(La) Bayadère (1877) – ballet orch.
Grand pas de deux (Act IV)
with London Symphony Orch. –　Decca MET254, SET254
Bonynge　　　　　London CS6342, (in set
　　　　　　　　　CSA2213), (in set CMA7213)

MOZART

Trio No. 2, in G, K496 pf, vln & vlc
with E. Rubbra pf & W. Pleeth vlc　　Argo ARS1005, RG5

PUGNI

Pas de quatre (1845) – ballet orch. – arr. MacDermott
with London Symphony Orch. –　Decca MET255, SET255
Bonynge　　　　　London CS6343, (in set
　　　　　　　　　CSA2213), (in set CMA7213)

RIMSKY–KORSAKOV

Scheherazade, Op. 35 (1888) orch.
with London Symphony Orch. –　Decca PFS4062, SMD1074
Stokowski　　　　　London PM55002, SPC21005
Scheherazade, Op. 35 (1888) orch.
with London Symphony Orch. –　Philips 835160AY, A02284L,
Markevitch　　　　　AL3437, SAL3437

RUBBRA

Trio, Op. 68 "In one movement" pf, vln & vlc
with E. Rubbra pf & W. Pleeth vlc　　Argo ARS1005, RG5

SCARLATTI, A.

Concerto No. 1, in f 2 vlns, vla, vlc, strs & c
with J. Rothstein vln, C. Aronowitz   L'Oiseau–Lyre OL50129
vla, B. Rickelman vlc, T. Dart hpsi &
Boyd Neel Orch. – Dart

SCHUMANN

Trio No. 2, in F, Op. 80 pf, vln & vlc
  Sehr lebhaft (1st mvt)
            2EA 18046/7–3C   HMV HLP23, HMS97
with E. Rubbra pf & W. Pleeth vlc   Victor (in set LM6153)

STRAVINSKY

Orphée (1947) – ballet orch.
with London Symphony Orch. – Davis   Philips 835242LY, L02363L,
PHM500153, PHS900153

TCHAIKOVSKY

Swan Lake, Op. 20 (1875/6) – ballet orch.
  Pas de deux (Act III) "The black swan"
with London Symphony Orch. –   Decca MET255, SET255
Bonynge   London CS6343, (in set
CSA2213), (in set CMA7213)

Arthur GRUMIAUX (1921–)

ALBÉNIZ

España (6 Feuilles d'album) Op. 165 pf
  No. 2. Tango in D arr. vln & pf Kreisler
with I. Hajdu pf   Philips A02294L

BACH

Concerto No. 1, in a, BWV1041 vln, strs & c
with Vienna Symphony Orch. – Moralt   Philips A00750L

Concerto No. 1, in a, BWV1041 vln, strs & c
with chamber orch. – Guller   Epic LC3342
                  Fontana 695023KL
                  Philips A00782L, G05326R,
                  NBR6032

Concerto No. 1, in a, BWV1041 vln strs & c
with English Chamber Orch. –   Philips 835254AY, 839557VGY,
Leppard   A02376L, AL3489, PHM500075,
                  PHS900075, SAL3489,
                  SFM23022

Concerto No. 2, in E, BWV1042 vln, strs & c
with chamber orch. – Guller   Epic LC3342
                  Fontana 695023KL
                  Philips A00782L, G05326R,
                  NBR6032

Concerto No. 2, in E, BWV1042 vln, strs & c
with English Chamber Orch. –   Philips 802823AY, 835254AY,
Leppard   839557VGY, (in set
                  SC71AX403), A02376L,
                  A02823L, (in set C71AX403),
                  AL3489, PHM500075,
                  PHS900075, SAL3489,
                  SFM23022

Concerto in d, BWV1043 2 vlns, strs & c
with J. Pougnet   CAX 9503/6–1   Columbia DOX854/5,
vln & Philharmonia Orch. – Susskind   DX1276/7, GFX124/5,
                  GQX11320/1

BACH – *Continued*

Concerto in d, BWV1043 2 vlns, strs & c
with K. Toyoda vln, P. Ledger hpsi & Philips 6500 119
New Philharmonia Orch. – de Waart

Concerto in c, BWV1060 vln & ob or 2 vlns, strs & c
with H. Holliger ob, P. Ledger hpsi & Philips 6500 119
New Philharmonia Orch. – de Waart

(3) Sonatas & 3 Partitas, BWV1001/6 solo vln
  Sonata No. 1, in g, BWV1001
  (unaccompanied)   Philips 835198AY, A00205L,
                  AL3472, PHM500005, (in set
                  PHM2–500), PHS900005, (in set
                  PHS2–900)

  Partita No. 1, in b, BWV1002
  (unaccompanied)   Philips 835198AY, A00205L,
                  AL3472, PHM500005/6, (in set
                  PHM2–500), PHS900005/6, (in
                  set PHS2–900)

  Sonata No. 2, in a, BWV1003
  (unaccompanied)   Philips 835199AY, A00206L,
                  AL3473, PHM500006, (in set
                  PHM2–500), PHS900006, (in set
                  PHS2–900)

  Partita No. 2, in d: Chaconne (5th mvt) BWV1004
  (unaccompanied)   Argo RG109
                  Boston B202

  Partita No. 2, in d, BWV1004
  (unaccompanied)   Philips 835199AY, A00206L,
                  AL3473, PHM500006, (in set
                  PHM2–500), PHS900006, (in set
                  PHS2–900)

  Sonata No. 3, in C, BWV1005
  (unaccompanied)   Philips 835200AY, A00207L,
                  AL3474, PHM500005, (in set
                  PHM2–500), PHS900005, (in set
                  PHS2–900)

  Partita No. 3, in E, BWV1006
  (unaccompanied)   Philips 835200AY, A00207L,
                  AL3474, PHM500005, (in set
                  PHM2–500), PHS900005, (in set
                  PHS2–900)

(6) Sonatas, BWV1014/9 vln & clav
  Sonata No. 1, in b, BWV1014
  with E. Giordani–Sartori hpsi   Philips 835227AY, A02349L,
                  AL3487, PHM500143, (in set
                  PHM2–597), PHS900143, (in set
                  PHS2–997), SAL3487

  Sonata No. 2, in A, BWV1015
  with E. Giordani–Sartori hpsi   Philips 835227AY, A02349L,
                  AL3487, PHM500143, (in set
                  PHM2–597), PHS900143, (in set
                  PHS2–997), SAL3487

  Sonata No. 3, in E, BWV1016
  with E. Giordani–Sartori hpsi   Philips 835227AY, A02349L,
                  AL3487, PHM500143, (in set
                  PHM2–597), PHS900143, (in set
                  PHS2–997), SAL3487

BACH – *Continued*

Sonata No. 4, in c, BWV1017
with E. Giordani–Sartori hpsi
Philips 835228AY, A02350L, AL3488, PHM500144, (in set PHM2–597), PHS900144, (in set PHS2–997), SAL3488

Sonata No. 5, in f, BWV1018
with E. Giordani–Sartori hpsi
Philips 835228AY, A02350L, AL3488, PHM500144, (in set PHM2–597), PHS900144, (in set PHS2–997), SAL3488

Sonata No. 6, in G, BWV1019
with E. Giordani–Sartori hpsi
Philips 835228AY, A02350L, AL3488, PHM500144, (in set PHM2–597), PHS900144, (in set PHS2–997), SAL3488

BARTÓK

(6) Rumanian folk dances (1915) pf – arr. vln & pf Székely
with P. Ulanowsky pf
Boston B203

BEETHOVEN

Concerto in D, Op. 61 (cadenzas by Kreisler) vln & orch.
with Concertgebouw Orch., Amsterdam – van Beinum
Epic LC3420
Eterna 820126
Fontana 894048ZKY
Philips L00434L

Concerto in D, Op. 61 (cadenzas by Kreisler) vln & orch.
with New Philharmonia Orch. – Galliera
Philips 802719LY, 802822LY, A02822L, AL3616, (in set S–C71 AX403), L02719L, PHS900222, SAL3616, SBAL32

Romance No. 1, in G, Op. 40 vln & orch.
with Concertgebouw Orch., Amsterdam – Haitink
Epic LC3762, BC1120
Fontana 894069ZKY
Philips 400211AE, ABE10268, G05406R, SABE2028

Romance No. 1, in G, Op. 40 vln & orch.
with New Philharmonia Orch. – de Waart
Philips 6580 047

Romance No. 2, in F, Op. 50 vln & orch.
with Concertgebouw Orch., Amsterdam – Haitink
Epic LC3762, BC1120
Fontana 894069ZKY
Philips 400211AE, ABE10268, G05406R, SABE2028

Romance No. 2, in F, Op. 50 vln & orch.
with New Philharmonia Orch. – de Waart
Philips 6580 047

Serenade in D, Op. 8 vln, vla & vlc
with G. Janzer vla & E. Czako vlc
Philips 802896LY, (in set S–C 71 AX309), 6500 167 AXS3007/2, PHS900227

Serenade in D, Op. 25 fl, vln & vla
with M. Larrieu fl & G. Janzer vla
Philips 802896LY, (in set S–C 71 AX 309), 6500 167 AXS3007/2, PHS900227

(3) Sonatas, Op. 12 vln & pf
No. 1. Sonata No. 1, in D
with C. Haskil pf
Epic LC3400, (in set SC6030)
Philips 836962DSY, A00409L, ABL3204

BEETHOVEN – *Continued*

No. 2. Sonata No. 2, in A
with C. Haskil pf
Epic LC3488, (in set SC6030)
Philips 836961DSY, A00400L, ABL3199, GL5857

No. 3. Sonata No. 3, in E flat
with C. Haskil pf
Epic LC3488, (in set SC6030)
Philips 836961DSY, A00400L, ABL3199

Sonata No. 4, in a, Op. 23 vln & pf
with C. Haskil pf
Epic LC3400, (in set SC6030)
Philips 836962DSY, A00409L, ABL3204

Sonata No. 5, in F, Op. 24 "Spring" vln & pf
with C. Haskil pf
Epic LC3400, (in set SC6030)
Fontana 695073KL
Philips 6580 032 836962DSY, A00409L, ABL3204

(3) Sonatas, Op. 30 vln & pf
No. 1. Sonata No. 6, in A
with C. Haskil pf
Epic LC3458, (in set SC6030)
Philips 836963DSY, A00430L, ABL3226, GL5860

No. 2. Sonata No. 7, in c
with C. Haskil pf
Epic LC3381, (in set SC6030)
Philips 836963DSY, A00412L, ABL3207,

No. 3. Sonata No. 8, in G
with C. Haskil pf
Epic LC3488, (in set SC6030)
Philips 836961DSY, A00400L, ABL3199, GL5857

Sonata No. 9, in A, Op. 47 "Kreutzer" vln & pf
with C. Haskil pf
Epic LC3458, (in set SC6030)
Fontana 695073KL
Philips 6580 032 836964DSY, A00430L, ABL3226, G05351R, GBR6536, GL5860

Sonata No. 10, in G, Op. 96 vln & pf
with C. Haskil pf
Epic LC3381, (in set SC6030)
Philips 836963DSY, A00412L, ABL3207

Trio No. 1, in E flat, Op. 3 vln, vla & vlc
with G. Janzer vla & E. Szako vlc
Philips 6500 168, 802897LY, (in set SC 71 AX 309), AXS3007/3

(3) Trios, Op. 9 vln, vla & vlc
No. 1. Trio No. 2, in G
with G. Janzer vla & E. Czako vlc
Philips 802895LY, (in set S–C 71 AX 309), 6500 168, AXS3007/1, PHS900226

No. 2. Trio No. 3, in D
with G. Janzer vla & E. Czako vlc
Philips 802897LY, (in set S–C 71 AX 309), AXS3007/3, PHS900226

No. 3. Trio No. 4, in c
with G. Janzer vla & E. Czako vlc
Philips 802895LY, (in set S–C 71 AX 309), AXS3007/1, PHS900226

BERG

Concerto (1935) vln & orch.
with Concertgebouw Orch.,
Amsterdam – Markevitch

Philips 802785LY, PHS900194,
SAL3650

BERLIOZ

Rêverie & Caprice, Op. 8 (1839) vln & orch.
with New Philharmonia Orch. – de
Waart

Philips 6580 047

BRAHMS

Concerto in D, Op. 77 (cadenza by Joachim) vln & pf
with Concertgebouw Orch.,
Amsterdam – van Beinum

Epic BC1017, LC3552
Philips 802823AY, (in set S–C 71
AX403), 835234LY, 836255VZ,
A02356L, A02823L, AL3526,
G05461R, SABL141, SAL3526,
SBAL32, SFL7726

Sonata No. 2, in A, Op. 100 vln & pf
(accompanying himself at the piano)

Philips 802839LY, A02078L,
C40

Trio in E flat, Op. 40 pf, vln & hrn
with G. Tucker pf & J. Stagliano hrn

Boston B209

BRUCH

Concerto No. 1, in g, Op. 26 vln & orch.
with Vienna Symphony Orch. –
Lescovich

Epic LC3365

Concerto No. 1, in g, Op. 26 vln & orch.
with Concertgebouw Orch.,
Amsterdam – Haitink

Fontana 894100ZKY
Philips 6580 022 610124VR,
835234LY, 838127DXY,
A02356L, AL3526, SAL3526

CHAUSSON

Poème, Op. 25 vln & orch.
with Lamoureux Orch. – Fournet

Epic LC3082
Fontana 695092KL
Philips A00228L, ABL3126,
G03032L

Poème, Op. 25 vln & Orch.
with Lamoureux Orch. – Rosenthal

Philips 802708LY, AL3587
PHS900195, SAL3587

CORELLI

(12) Sonatas, Op. 5 vln & c
Sonata No. 12, in d "La Follia"
with R. Castagnone pf

Epic LC3414
Philips A00380L

DEBUSSY

Sonata No. 3, in g (1917) vln & pf
with P. Ulanowsky pf

Boston B203

Sonata No. 3, in g (1917) vln & pf
with R. Castagnone pf

Epic LC3667
Philips L00348L

Sonata No. 3, in g (1917) vln & pf
with I. Hajdu pf

Philips 802770LY, 835174AY,
A02264L, AL3644, SAL3644

FALLA

(7) Canciones populares españolas (1914) v & pf
No. 4. Jota arr. vln & pf Kochański
with L. Degraux pf   CA 20153–5   Columbia DB2557, DC422

(La) Vida Breve (1913) – opera
Danza española orch. – arr. vln & pf Kreisler
with L. Degraux pf   CAX 9643–1   Columbia DCX74, DX1634,
GQX16631

FAURÉ

(3) Chansons, Op. 23 v & pf
No. 1. Les berceaux arr. vln & pf
with I. Hajdu pf

Philips A02294L

Sonata No. 1, in A, Op. 13 vln & pf
with I. Hajdu pf

Philips 835174AY, A02264L

FIOCCO

Suite No. 1, in G hpsi
Allegro (10th mvt) arr. vln & pf Bent & O'Neill
with H. Greenslade pf   CA 20150–1   Columbia DB2488

Allegro (10th mvt) arr. vln & pf Bent & O'Neill
with G. Tucker pf

Argo RG109
Boston B202

Allegro (10th mvt) arr. vln & pf Bent & O'Neill
with I. Hajdu pf

Philips A02294L

FRANCK

Sonata in A (1886) vln & pf
with I. Hajdu pf

Philips 835342LY, A02236L,
SAL3738, SFL7603

GRANADOS

(12) Danzas españolas, Op. 37 (1893) pf
No. 5. Danza española No. 5, in e "Andaluza" arr. vln & pf Kreisler
with L. Degraux pf   CAX 9642–1   Columbia DCX74, DX1634,
GQX16631

No. 5. Danza española No. 5, in e "Andaluza" arr. vln & pf Kreisler
with I. Hajdu pf

Philips A02294L

GRIEG

Sonata No. 3, in c, Op. 45 vln & pf
with I. Hajdu pf

Philips 835342LY, A02236L,
SAL3738, SFL7603

HANDEL

(15) Sonatas, Op. 1 (?1731) vln or fl & c
Sonata No. 3, in A vln I
with R. Veyron–Lacroix hpsi

Philips 835389AY, SAL3687

Sonata No. 10, in g vln II
with R. Veyron–Lacroix hpsi

Philips 835389AY, SAL3687

Sonata No. 12, in F vln III
with R. Veyron–Lacroix hpsi

Philips 835389AY, SAL3687

Sonata No. 13, in D vln IV
with R. Veyron–Lacroix hpsi

Philips 835389AY, SAL3687

Sonata No. 14, in A vln V
with R. Veyron–Lacroix hpsi

Philips 835389AY, SAL3687

Sonata No. 15, in E vln VI
with R. Veyron–Lacroix hpsi

Philips 835389AY, SAL3687

HAYDN

Concerto No. 1, in C, H.VIIa, No. 1 (1765) vln & orch.
  with English Chamber Orch. –   Philips 802781DXY, 835254AY,
  Leppard   839557VGY, A02376L, AL3489,
                                PHM500075, PHS900075,
                                SAL3489, SFM23022

Concerto No. 2, in G, H.VIIa, No. 4 (1768) vln & orch.
  with New Philharmonia Orch. –   Philips 802848LY, SAL3660
  Leppard

(3) Trios, Op. 53 (H.XVI, Nos. 40/2) vln, vla & vlc
  No. 1. Trio No. 1, in G, H.XVI, No. 40
  with G. Janzer vla & E. Szako vlc   Philips 802905LY
  No. 2. Trio No. 2, in B flat, H.XVI, No. 41
  with G. Janzer vla & E. Szako vlc   Philips 802905LY
  No. 3. Trio No. 3, in D, H.XVI, No. 42
  with G. Janzer vla & E. Szako vlc   Philips 802905LY

HAYDN, M.

Concerto in A (cadenza by Grumiaux) vln & orch.*
  with Concertgebouw Orch.,   Philips 6515 002, 839757LY,
  Amsterdam – de Waart   SAL3804

HOFFMEISTER

(3) Duets, Op. 6 vln & vla
  No. 3. Duet No. 3, in G
  with A. Pelliccia vla   Philips 839747LY

JONGEN

Serenata vln & pf
  with L. Degraux pf   CA 20306–2   Columbia DC421

KREISLER

Caprice viennois, Op. 2 vln & pf
  with R. Castagnone pf   Epic LC3592
                          Philips G05372R

Liebesfreud vln & pf
  with R. Castagnone pf   Epic LC3592
                          Philips G05372R

Liebesleid vln & pf
  with R. Castagnone pf   Epic LC3592
                          Philips G05372R

Rondino on a theme by Beethoven vln & pf
  with I. Hajdu pf   Philips A02294L

Schön Rosmarin vln & pf
  with R. Castagnone pf   Epic LC3592
                          Philips G05372R

Tambourin chinois, Op. 3 vln & pf
  with R. Castagnone pf   Epic LC3592
                          Philips G05372R

LALO

Symphonie espagnole, Op. 21 vln & orch. †
  with Lamoureux Orch. – Fournet   Epic LC3082
                          Fontana 695091KL
                          Philips A00228L, ABL3126

* Discovered 1964.
† Omitting intermezzo.

LALO – *Continued*

Symphonie espagnole, Op. 21 vln & orch.*
  with Lamoureux Orch. – Rosenthal   Philips 802824AY, (in set S–C 71
                          AX403), 835184LY, L02309L,
                          PHC9140, SBAL32, SFL7680

LEKEU

Sonata in G (1892) vln & pf
  with R. Castagnone pf   Epic LC3667
                          Philips L00348L

MENDELSSOHN

Concerto in e, Op. 64 vln & orch.
  with Philharmonia Orch. – Galliera   Columbia DZX25/8S,
                          GQX11126/9S

Concerto in e, Op. 64 vln & orch.
  with Vienna Symphony Orch. – Moralt   Epic LC3173
                          Fontana 695015KL
                          Philips C31, G03001L,
                          GBL5582, S06112R

Concerto in e, Op. 64 vln & orch.
  with Concertgebouw Orch.,   Philips 6580 022, 610103BL,
  Amsterdam – Haitink   802821AY, (in set S–C 71
                          AX403), 835055LY, 836201VZ,
                          A02051L, A02821L, ABL3337,
                          SABL176, SBAL32

MOZART

Adagio in E, K261 vln & orch.
  with New Philharmonia Orch. –   Philips 802848LY, SAL3660
  Leppard

Concerto No. 1, in B flat, K207 vln & orch.
  with Vienna Symphony Orch. –   Epic LC3230
  Paumgartner   Fontana, 695035KL,
                          894105ZKY,
                          Philips A00313L, ABL3147

Concerto No. 1, in B flat, K207 (cadenzas by Grumiaux) vln & orch.
  with London Symphony Orch. – Davis   Philips 6580 009, 835136AY,
                          A02253L, AL3440, PHS900236,
                        SAL3440

Concerto No. 2, in D, K211 (cadenzas by Grumiaux) vln & orch.
  with Vienna Symphony Orch. –   Epic LC3157
  Paumgartner   Fontana 695071KL
                          Philips A00258L, ABL3099

Concerto No. 2, in D, K211 (cadenzas by Grumiaux) vln & orch.
  with London Symphony Orch. – Davis   Philips 835256LY, AL3492,
                          L02378L, PHM500130,
                        PHS900130, SAL3492

Concerto No. 3, in G, K216 (cadenzas by Ysaÿe) vln & orch.
  with Vienna Symphony Orch. – Moralt   Epic LC3060
                          Eterna 820132
                          Fontana 695048KL
                          Philips A00199L, ABL3040,
                          G05343R

Concerto No. 3, in G, K216 (cadenzas by Ysaÿe) vln & orch.
  with London Symphony Orch. – Davis   Philips 610130VR, 835112AY,
                          836245VZ, A02224L,
                        PHM500012, PHS900012

* Omitting intermezzo.

MOZART – *Continued*

Concerto No. 4, in D, K218 vln & orch.*
with Vienna Symphony Orch. – Moralt
Epic LC3060
Eterna 820132
Fontana 695035KL, 894105ZKY
Philips A00199L, ABL3040,
G05344R

Concerto No. 4, in D, K218 vln & orch.
with London Symphony Orch. – Davis
Philips 6580 009, 835136AY,
A02253L, AL3440, PHS900236,
SAL3440

Concerto No. 5, in A, K219 "Turkish" (cadenzas by Joachim & Grumiaux) vln & orch.
with Vienna Symphony Orch. –
Paumgartner
Epic LC3157
Fontana 695048KL
Philips A00258L, ABL3099,
FL5555, G05345R

Concerto No. 5, in A, K219 "Turkish" (cadenzas by Joachim & Grumiaux) vln & orch.
with London Symphony Orch. – Davis
Philips 610128VR, 802781DXY,
835112AY, 836240VZ, A02224L,
PHM500012, PHS900012

Concerto No. 7, in D, K271a (cadenzas by Enescu) vln & orch.
with Vienna Symphony Orch. –
Paumgartner
Epic LC3230
Fontana 695071KL
Philips A00313L, ABL3147,
FL5555

Divertimento in E flat, K563 vln, vla & vlc
with G. Janzer vla & E. Czako vlc
Philips 802803LY, PHS900173,
SAL3664

Duo No. 1, in G, K423 vln & vla
with A. Pelliccia vla
Philips 839747LY

Duo No. 2, in B flat, K424 vln & vla
with A. Pelliccia vla
Philips 839747LY

Quartet No. 1, in D, K285 fl, vln, vla & vlc
with W. Bennett fl, G. Janzer vla & E.
Szako vlc
Philips 6500 034

Quartet No. 2, in G, K285a fl, vln, vla & vlc
with W. Bennett fl, G. Janzer vla & E.
Szako vlc
Philips 6500 034

Quartet No. 3, in C, K285b fl, vln, vla & vlc
with W. Bennett vl, G. Janzer vla & E.
Szako vlc
Philips 6500 034

Quartet No. 4, in A, K298 fl, vln, vla & vlc
with W. Bennett fl, G. Janzer vla & E.
Szako vlc
Philips 6500 034

Rondo in C, K373 vln & orch.
with New Philharmonia Orch. –
Leppard
Philips 802848LY, SAL3660

Serenade No. 7, in D, K250 "Haffner" orch.
Rondo (4th mvt) arr. vln & pf Kreisler
with I. Hajdu pf
Philips A02294L

Sinfonia concertante in E flat, K364 vln, vla & orch.
with A. Pelliccia vla & London
Symphony Orch. – Davis
Philips 835256LY, AL3492,
L02378L, PHM500130,
PHS900130, SAL3492

* Rondo, or 3rd mvt only is also on Philips S06100R & SBR6200.

MOZART – *Continued*

Sonata No. 18, in G, K301 vln & pf
with G. Tucker pf
Argo RG109
Boston B202

Sonata No. 18, in G, K301 vln & pf
with C. Haskil pf
Epic BC1034, LC3602
Philips 835103LY, A00432L

Sonata No. 21, in e, K304 vln & pf
with G. Tucker pf
Argo RG109
Boston B202

Sonata No. 21, in e, K304 vln & pf
with C. Haskil pf
Epic BC1034, LC3602
Philips 835103LY, A00432L

Sonata No. 24, in F, K376 vln & pf
with C. Haskil pf
Epic BC1034, LC3602
Philips 835103LY, A00432L

Sonata No. 26, in B flat, K378 vln & pf
with C. Haskil pf
Epic BC1034, LC3602
Philips 835103LY, A00432L

Sonata No. 32, in B flat, K454 vln & pf
with C. Haskil pf
Epic LC3299
Philips A00338L, ABL3144

Sonata No. 33, in E flat, K481 vln & pf
(accompanying himself at the piano)
Philips 802839LY, A02078L,
C40

Sonata No. 34, in A, K526 vln & pf
with C. Haskil pf
Epic LC3299
Philips A00338L, ABL3144

MUSSORGSKY

Sorochintsy Fair (1911/23) – opera
Gopak orch. – arr. vln & pf Dushkin
with L. Degraux pf   CA 20152–3   Columbia DB2557, DC422

PAGANINI

Concerto No. 4, in d (1829) (cadenza by Grumiaux) vln & orch.
with Lamoureux Orch. – Gallini
Columbia 50004/7
Epic LC3143
Fontana 894017ZKY
Philips 836931VZ, A00741L,
ABR4024, G03062L, G05327R,
GBL5576, L00465L

(I) Palpiti (variations on the aria "Di tanti palpiti" from Rossini's opera "Tancredi") Op. 13 (1819) vln & orch.
with R. Castagnone pf
Epic LC3592
Philips G03062L, G05372R,
GBL5576

(Le) Streghe (variations on a theme from Süssmeyer's opera "Il Noce di Benevento") Op. 8 (1813) vln & orch. – arr. vln & pf Kreisler
with R. Castagnone pf
Epic LC3592
Philips G05372R

RAVEL

Pièce en forme d'Habanera v & pf – arr. vln & pf Catherine
with L. Degraux pf   CA 20151–3   Columbia DB2488, DC421

Pièce en forme d'Habanera v & pf – arr. vln & pf Catherine
with P. Ulanowsky pf
Boston B203

Pièce en forme d'Habanera v & pf – arr. vln & pf Catherine
with I. Hajdu pf
Philips A02294L

RAVEL – *Continued*

Sonata (1927) vln & pf
with I. Hajdu pf   Philips 835174AY, A02264L

Tzigane (Rapsodie de concert) (1924) vln & pf or orch.
with Lamoureux Orch. – Fournet   Epic LC3082
Philips A00228L, ABL3126

Tzigane (Rapsodie de concert) (1924) vln & pf or orch.
with P. Ulanowsky pf   Boston B203

Tzigane (Rapsodie de concert) (1924) vln & pf or orch.
with Lamoureux Orch. – Rosenthal   Fontana 695092KL
Philips 6580 031, 802708LY,
AL3587, PHS900195, SAL3587

Tzigane (Rapsodie de concert) (1924) vln & pf or orch.
with I. Hajdu pf   Philips A02294L

SAINT–SAËNS

Concerto No. 3, in b, Op. 61 vln & orch.
with Lamoureux Orch. – Fournet   Epic LC3399
Fontana 695091KL
Philips L00465L

Concerto No. 3, in b, Op. 61 vln & orch.
with Lamoureux Orch. – Rosenthal   Philips 835253LY, 836931VR,
AL3493, L02375L, PHC9109,
PHM500061, PHS900061,
SAL3493, SFL7820

Havanaise, Op. 83 vln & orch.
with Lamoureux Orch. – Fournet   Epic LC3399
Philips G05406R
Fontana 695092KL

Havanaise, Op. 83 vln & orch.
with Lamoureux Orch. – Rosenthal   Fontana 894100ZKY
Philips 835184LY, 838127DXY,
839831GSY, L02309L,
PHC9140, SFL7680

Introduction & Rondo Capriccioso, Op. 28 vln & orch.
with Lamoureux Orch. – Fournet   Epic LC3399
Fontana 695092KL
Philips G03032L, G05406R

Introduction & Rondo Capriccioso, Op. 28 vln & orch.
with Lamoureux Orch. – Rosenthal   Fontana 894100ZKY
Philips 835184LY, 838127DXY,
839831GSY, L02309L,
PHC9140, SFL7680

SARASATE

Zigeunerweisen, Op. 20 vln & pf or orch.
with I. Hajdu pf   Philips A02294L

SCHUBERT

Quintet in A, Op. 114 (D667) pf, vln, vla, vlc & cbs
with I. Haebler pf, G. Janzer vla, E.   Philips 802757LY, SAL3621
Szako vlc & J. Cazauran cbs

Rondo in A, D438 vln & orch.
with New Philharmonia Orch. –   Philips 802848LY, SAL3660
Leppard

Sonata in A, Op. 162 (D574) "Duo" vln & pf
with R. Castagnone pf   Epic LC3609
Philips A00499L, PHC9103,
S06082R, SBR6230

SCHUBERT – *Continued*

(3) Sonatinas, Op. 137 (D384, D385 & D408) vln & pf
Sonatina No. 1, in D, D384
with R. Castagnone pf   Epic LC3609
Philips A00499L, PHC9103,
S06082R, SBR6230

Sonatina No. 2, in a, D385
with R. Castagnone pf   Epic LC3609
Philips A00499L, PHC9103

Sonatina No. 3, in g, D408*
with R. Castagnone pf   Epic LC3609
Philips A00499L, PHC9103

Trio in B flat, D471 ("Sonata" in one movement) vln, vla & vlc
with G. Janzer vla & E. Szako vlc   Philips 802905LY

Trio in B flat, D581 vln, vla & vlc
with G. Janzer vla & E. Szako vlc   Philips 802905LY

STRAVINSKY

Concerto in D (1931) vln & orch.
with Concertgebouw Orch.,   Philips 802785LY, PHS900194,
Amsterdam – Bour   SAL3650

SVENDSEN

Romance in G, Op. 26 vln & orch.
with New Philharmonia Orch. – de   Philips 6580 047
Waart

SZYMANOWSKI

Notturno & Tarantella, Op. 28 vln & pf
CAX 9321–1 & 9322–3   Columbia DX1199
with G. Moore pf

TARTINI

Sonata in g "Il Trillo del Diavolo" vln & c – arr. vln & pf Kreisler
with R. Castagnone pf   Epic LC3414
Philips A00380L, ABE10090

TCHAIKOVSKY

Concerto in D, Op. 35 vln & orch.
with Vienna Symphony Orch. –   Epic LC3365
Lescovich

Concerto in D, Op. 35 vln & orch.
with Concertgebouw Orch.,   Epic BC1109, LC3745
Amsterdam – Haitink   Philips 802821AY, (in set S–C 71
AX 403), 835055LY, A02051L,
ABL3337, C31, SABL176,
SBAL32

Sérénade mélancolique in b flat, Op. 26 vln & orch.
with New Philharmonia Orch. – de   Philips 6580 047
Waart

TELEMANN

(12) Fantasias (1735) solo vln
Fantasia No. 1, in b
(unaccompanied)   Philips 6500 106

Fantasia No. 2, in G
(unaccompanied)   Philips 6500 106

Fantasia No. 3, in f
(unaccompanied)   Philips 6500 106

* Allegro giusto (1st mvt) on Philips S06082R & SBR6230.

TELEMANN – *Continued*

Fantasia No. 4, in D
(unaccompanied)   Philips 6500 106

Fantasia No. 5, in A
(unaccompanied)   Philips 6500 106

Fantasia No. 6, in e
(unaccompanied)   Philips 6500 106

Fantasia No. 7, in E flat
(unaccompanied)   Philips 6500 106

Fantasia No. 8, in E
(unaccompanied)   Philips 6500 106

Fantasia No. 9, in b
(unaccompanied)   Philips 6500 106

Fantasia No. 10, in D
(unaccompanied)   Philips 6500 106

Fantasia No. 11, in F
(unaccompanied)   Philips 6500 106

Fantasia No. 12, in a
(unaccompanied)   Philips 6500 106

VERACINI

(12) Sonatas, Op. 1 (1721) vln & c
Sonata No. 7, in A
with R. Castagnone pf   Epic LC3414
                                   Philips A00380L

VIEUXTEMPS

Concerto No. 4, in d, Op. 31 vln & orch.
with Lamoureux Orch. – Rosenthal   Philips 802708LY, A02824L,
                                   AL3587, PHS900195, SAL3587

Concerto No. 5, in a, Op. 37 vln & orch.
with Lamoureux Orch. – Rosenthal   Philips 802824AY, (in set S–C 71
                                   AX 403), 835253LY, AL3493,
                                   L02375L, PHC9109,
                                   PHM500061, PHS900061,
                                   SAL3493, SBAL32, SFL7820

VIOTTI

Concerto No. 22, in a (cadenza by Grumiaux) vln & orch.
with Concertgebouw Orch.,   Philips 6515 002, 839757LY,
Amsterdam – de Waart   SAL3804

VITALI

Chaconne in g vln & c – arr. vln & pf Charlier
with R. Castagnone pf   Epic LC3414
                                   Philips A00380L

VIVALDI

(12) Concerti, Op. 3 "L'Estro armonico" var. cbns & strs
Concerto No. 6, in a, P.I (F.I, No. 176) vln, strs & c
with P. Ledger hpsi & New   Philips 6500 119
Philharmonia Orch. – de Waart

WIENIAWSKI

Concerto No. 2, in d, Op. 22 vln & orch.
Romance (2nd mvt)
with New Philharmonia Orch. – de   Philips 6580 047
Waart

Légende, Op. 17 vln & pf or orch.
with New Philharmonia Orch. – de   Philips 6580 047
Waart

WIENIAWSKI – *Continued*

Souvenir de Moscou, Op. 6 vln & pf or orch.
with I. Hajdu pf   Philips A02294L

Nora GRUMLÍKOVÁ (1930–)

BLOCH

Baal Shem (3 Pictures of Chassidic life) (1923) vln & pf
No. 1. Vidui (Contrition)
with J. Kolář pf   Supraphon 1 41 0117,
                                   SUA10708, SUAST50708

Suite No. 2 solo vln
(unaccompanied)   Supraphon SUA10520, SV8252

BRITTEN

Concerto No. 1, in d, Op. 15 (1939 – rev. 1958) vln & orch.
with Prague Symphony Orch. – Maag Supraphon 1 10 0233,
                                   SUA10959, SUAST50959

FAURÉ

Berceuse, Op. 16 vln & pf
with J. Kolář pf   Supraphon 1 41 0117,
                                   SUA10708, SUAST50708

Sonata No. 1, in A, Op. 13 vln & pf
with J. Kolář pf   Supraphon SUA10686,
                                   SUAST50686, SV8339

FELD

Rhapsody vln & orch.
with Prague Symphony Orch. (FOK) – Supraphon SV8218
Turnovský

GLUCK

Orphée et Eurydice (1762) – opera
Dance of the blessed spirits: Lento "Mélodie" (No. 2.) arr. vln & pf
Kreisler
with J. Kolář pf   Supraphon 1 41 0117,
                                   SUA10708, SUAST50708

GRIEG

Sonata No. 2, in g, Op. 13 vln & pf
with J. Kolář pf   Supraphon SUA10686,
                                   SUAST50686, SV8339

KABALEVSKY

Improvisation, Op. 21, No. 1 vln & pf
with J. Kolář pf   Supraphon 1 41 0117,
                                   SUA10708, SUAST50708

MENDELSSOHN

(6) Gesänge, Op. 34 v & pf
No. 2. Auf Flügeln des Gesanges arr. vln & pf Achron
with J. Kolář pf   Supraphon 1 41 0117, SUA
                                   10708, SUAST50708

PARADIES

Sicilienne vln & pf – arr. Dushkin
with J. Kolář pf   Supraphon 1 41 0117,
                                   SUA10708, SUAST50708

PROKOFIEV

Cinderella, Op. 87 (1941/4) – ballet orch.
  Winter fairytale arr. vln & pf Fichtenholz
    with J. Kolář pf   Supraphon 1 41 0117,
                                SUA10708, SUAST50708

REGER

(7) Sonatas, Op. 91 solo vln
  Sonata No. 1, in a
  (unaccompanied)   Supraphon SUA10520, SV8252

SARASATE

(8) Danzas españolas vln & pf
  No. 2. Habañera, Op. 21, No. 2
    with J. Kolář pf   Supraphon 1 41 0117,
                                SUA10708, SUAST50708

  No. 3. Romanza andaluza, Op. 22, No. 1
    with J. Kolář pf   Supraphon 1 41 0117,
                                SUA10708, SUAST50708

SCHUMANN

(3) Romances, Op. 94 ob or vlc, or vln or cl & pf
  No. 2. Romance No. 2, in A arr. vln & pf Kreisler
    with J. Kolář pf   Supraphon 1 41 0117,
                                SUA10708, SUAST50708

Sonata No. 1, in a, Op. 105 vln & pf
  with J. Kolář pf   Supraphon SUA10686,
                                SUAST50686, SV8339

SUK

(4) Pieces, Op. 17 vln & pf
  No. 4. Burleska
    with J. Kolář pf   Supraphon 1 41 0117,
                                SUA10708, SUAST50708

VAUGHAN WILLIAMS

Concerto in d (1925) "Concerto accademico" vln & orch.
  with Prague Symphony Orch. – Maag   Supraphon 1 10 0233,
                                        SUA10959, SUAST50959

YSAŸE

(6) Sonatas, Op. 27 solo vln
  Sonata No. 2, in a
  (unaccompanied)   Supraphon SUA10520, SV8252

Anne-Maria GRÜNDER

BARTÓK

(44) Duos (1931) 2 vlns
  15 only unid
    with G. Lengyel vln   Ducretet–Thomson LAP1008,
                                    LPG8192

FORNEROD

Concert 2 vlns & pf
  with A. Wachsmuth–Loew vln & R.   Communauté de travail pour la
  Dobos pf   diffusion de la musique suisse.
                                    CT64–24

Josef GRÜNFARB (1920–)

BLOMDAHL

Concerto (1947) vln & orch.
  Finale (3rd mvt)
    with Stockholm Radio   RTJ 2562/3   Cupol 4118
    Orch. – Blomdahl

Gian Mario GUARINO (1920–)

CHOPIN

(2) Nocturnes, Op. 27 pf
  No. 1. Nocturne No. 7, in c sharp arr. vln & pf
    with A. Satamato pf   Columbia GQ7225
  Nocturne No. 20, in c sharp, Op. posth. pf – arr. vln & pf Milstein
    with A. Satamato pf   Columbia GQ7225

DEBUSSY

(12) Préludes – Book I (1910) pf
  No. 12. Minstrels arr. vln & pf Hartmann
    with A. Satamato pf   Columbia GQ7225

RAVEL

Pièce en forme d'Habanera v & pf – arr. vln & pf Catherine
  with piano   HMV GW1645

VERACINI

(12) Sonatas, Op. 2 (1744) "Sonate accademiche" vln & c
  Sonata No. 6, in A: Largo (2nd mvt) ed. Corti
    with piano   HMV GW1645

Giovanni GUGLIELMO

ALBINONI

(12) Sonatas, Op. 4 (1704) vln, vlc & c
  Sonata No. 3, in F
    with M. de Robertis hpsi   Victor (in set ML40002)

BONPORTI

(10) Concerti, Op. 11 strs
  Concerto No. 5, in F
    with Solisti Veneti String Orch. –   Victor (in set ML40002)
    Scimone

MARTINI, G.B.

Concerto in F vln & strs – rev. Desderi
  with M. de Robertis hpsi & Solisti   Victor (in set ML40002)
  Veneti String Orch. – Scimone

VERACINI

(12) Sonatas, Op. 1 (1721) vln & c
  Sonata No. 8, in B flat rev. Gallico
    with M. de Robertis hpsi   Victor (in set ML40002)

VIVALDI

Concerto in D, P.188 (F.IV, No. 4) 2 vlns, 2 vlcs, strs & c – rev. Galli
  with P. Toso vln, M. Cassoli vlc, G.   Victor (in set ML40002)
  Chiampan vlc & Solisti Veneti String
  Orch. – Scimone

Scipione GUIDI (1884–1966)

BEETHOVEN

(6) Minuets, G167 pf
No. 2. Minuet No. 2, in G arr. vln & pf Burmester
with piano   Gennett 10081

BRAHMS

(21) Hungarian Dances pf duet
Hungarian dance No. 5, in f sharp arr. vln & pf "in g" Joachim
with piano   Gennett 10081

CUI

Kaleidoscope, Op. 50 vln & pf
No. 9. Orientale
with piano   Gennett 10077

DVOŘÁK

(8) Humoresques, Op. 101 pf
No. 7. Humoresque No. 7, in G flat arr. vln & pf "in G" Wilhelmj
with piano   8084   Gennett 9310, 10070

GOUNOD

Ave Maria (Méditation on Bach's "Prelude No. 1, in C" from Book I of
"Das Wohltemperirte Clavier") v & pf – arr. vln & pf
with L. Abbott pf   7508a   Gennett 4738, 9140

GRANADOS

(12) Danzas españolas, Op. 37 (1893) pf
No. 5. Danza española No. 5, in e "Andaluza" arr. vln & pf Kreisler
with piano   Gennett 10078

KREISLER

Caprice viennois, Op. 2 vln & pf
with piano   Gennett 2601
Liebesfreud vln & pf
with piano   7746   Gennett 9213, 10056
Schön Rosmarin vln & pf
with piano   7745   Gennett 9213, 10056
Tambourin chinois, Op. 3 vln & pf
with piano   8038   Gennett 9302, 10066

MacDOWELL

Woodland Sketches, Op. 51 pf
No. 1. To a wild rose arr. vln & pf
with piano   8037   Gennett 9302, 10066

MASSENET

Thaïs (1894) – opera
Méditation arr. vln & pf Marsick
with piano   Gennett 2601

MENDELSSOHN

(6) Songs without words, Op. 62 pf
No. 6. Song without words No. 30, in A "Spring song" arr. vln & pf
with T. Griselle pf   8034a   Gennett 9183, 10068

MOSZKOWSKI

(6) Klavierstücke, Op. 15 pf – 4 hands
No. 1. Serenata arr. vln & pf
with piano   Gennett 10078

NEVIN

(The) Rosary (1898) v & pf – arr. vln & pf
with piano   8083   Gennett 9310, 10070

RIMSKY–KORSAKOV

Sadko (1898) – opera
Chant hindou arr. vln & pf Kreisler
with piano   Gennett 10077

SCHUBERT

(6) Moments musicaux, Op. 94 (D780) (1823/7) pf
No. 3. Moment musicale No. 3, in f "Air russe" arr. vln & pf Kreisler
with T. Griselle pf   8044b   Gennett 9183, 10068
(14) Schwanengesang, D957 (1828) v & pf
No. 4. Ständchen "Serenade" arr. vln & pf
with L. Abbott pf   7507a   Gennett 4738, 9140

SCHUMANN

Quintet in E flat, Op. 44 2 vlns, vla, vlc & pf
with E.R. Schmitz pf, A. Lichstein vln,   Edison Diamond Disc 80885/6
L.E. Barzin vla & O. Mazzucchi vlc

STRAUSS, R.

(Ein) Heldenleben, Op. 40 (1898) orch.
with New York Philharmonic   Camden CAL337
Symphony Orch. – Mengelberg   HMV AB586/90, D1711/5
                             Victor 6982/6, (set M44)

WAGNER

Siegfried (1876) – opera
Gönntest du mir wohl (Waldweben) (Act II)
with New York Philharmonic   Victor 7192
Symphony Orch. – Mengelberg

Daniel GUILET (1899–   )

BARTÓK

Contrasts (1938) cl, vln & pf
with H. Tichman cl   Concert Hall G8
& R. Budnevich pf   Musical Masterpiece Society
                             MMS89

BEETHOVEN

(3) Trios, Op. 1 pf, vln & vlc
No. 1. Trio No. 1, in E flat
with A. Balsam pf & A. Navarra vlc   Concert Hall DL11
No. 2. Trio No. 2, in G
with A. Balsam pf & A. Navarra vlc   Concert Hall CHC27
Trio in B flat, G154 (WoO39) "In one movement" pf, vln & vlc
with A. Balsam pf & A. Navarra vlc   Concert Hall DL11

CASADESUS, R.

Sonata No. 2, in A, Op. 34 vln & pf
with G. Casadesus pf   MGM E3521

CORELLI

(12) Concerti grossi, Op. 6 orch.
Concerto grosso No. 1, in D
with E. Bachmann vln, F. Miller vlc &   Vox (in sets PL7893 & VBX39)
Corelli Tri–Centenary Orch. –
Eckertsen

CORELLI – *Continued*

Concerto grosso No. 2, in F
with E. Bachmann vln, F. Miller vlc &   Vox (in sets PL7893 & VBX39)
Corelli Tri–Centenary Orch. –
Eckertsen

Concerto grosso No. 3, in c
with E. Bachmann vln, F. Miller vlc &   Vox (in sets PL7893 & VBX39)
Corelli Tri–Centenary Orch. –
Eckertsen

Concerto grosso No. 4, in D
with E. Bachmann vln, F. Miller vlc &   Vox (in sets PL7893 & VBX39)
Corelli Tri–Centenary Orch. –
Eckertsen

Concerto grosso No. 5, in B flat
with E. Bachmann vln, F. Miller vlc &   Vox (in sets PL7893 & VBX39)
Corelli Tri–Centenary Orch. –
Eckertsen

Concerto grosso No. 6, in F
with E. Bachmann vln, F. Miller vlc &   Vox (in sets PL7893 & VBX39)
Corelli Tri–Centenary Orch. –
Eckertsen

Concerto grosso No. 7, in D
with E. Bachmann vln, F. Miller vlc &   Vox (in sets PL7893 & VBX39)
Corelli Tri–Centenary Orch. –
Eckertsen

Concerto grosso No. 8, in g
with E. Bachmann vln, F. Miller vlc &   Vox, (in sets PL7893 & VBX39)
Corelli Tri–Centenary Orch. –
Eckertsen

Concerto grosso No. 9, in F
with E. Bachmann vln, F. Miller vlc &   Vox (in sets PL7893 & VBX39)
Corelli Tri–Centenary Orch. –
Eckertsen

Concerto grosso No. 10, in C
with E. Bachmann vln, F. Miller vlc &   Vox (in sets PL7893 & VBX39)
Corelli Tri–Centenary Orch. –
Eckertsen

Concerto grosso No. 11, in B flat
with E. Bachmann vln, F. Miller vlc &   Vox (in sets PL7893 & VBX39)
Corelli Tri–Centenary Orch. –
Eckertsen

Concerto grosso No. 12, in F
with E. Bachmann vln, F. Miller vlc &   Vox (in sets PL7893 & VBX39)
Corelli Tri–Centenary Orch. –
Eckertsen

DVOŘÁK

Trio No. 4, in e, Op. 90 "Dumky" pf, vln & vlc
with M. Pressler pf   Guilde Internationale du Disque
& B. Greenhouse vlc   M2323

FAURÉ

Sonata No. 2, in e, Op. 108 vln & pf
with G. Casadesus pf   Concerteum CLP197
Delta 12009
Nixa QLP4008
Polymusic PR1008

Trio in d, Op. 120 pf, vln & vlc
with M. Pressler pf & B. Greenhouse   Parlophone PMC1035
vlc

MENDELSSOHN

Quartet No. 1, in c, Op. 1 pf, vln, vla & vlc
with A. Balsam pf, W. Schoen vla &   Concert Hall E13
D. Soyer vlc

Sonata in f, Op. 4 vln & pf
with A. Balsam pf   Classic CL6230
Concert Hall CHS1095

Trio No. 1, in d, Op. 49 pf, vln & vlc
with M. Pressler pf & B. Greenhouse   Guilde Internationale du Disque
vlc   M2323

RAVEL

Trio in a (1915) pf, vln & vlc
with M. Pressler pf & B. Greenhouse   Parlophone PMC1035
vlc

STRAUSS, R.

Don Quixote, Op. 35 (1897) orch.
with F. Miller vlc, C. Cooley vla &   HMV ALP1493
NBC Symphony Orch. – Toscanini   Victor LM2026

Daniel GUILEVITCH

CHOPIN

(12) Etudes, Op. 10 pf
Etude No. 3, in E arr. vln & pf
with L. Petitjean pf   Polydor 524611

TCHAIKOVSKY

(12) Pieces (of moderate difficulty) Op. 40 pf
No. 2. Chanson triste arr. vln & pf
with L. Petitjean pf   Polydor 524611

Franco GULLI (1926–   )

BACH

(3) Sonatas & 3 Partitas, BWV1001/6 solo vln
Sonata No. 1, in g, BWV1001
(unaccompanied)   Angelicum LPA5952

BEETHOVEN

Concerto in D, Op. 61 (cadenzas by Kreisler) vln & orch.
with Lamoureux Orch. – Albert   Record Society RS72, RSS20

(3) Sonatas, Op. 12 vln & pf
No. 1. Sonata No. 1, in D
with E. Cavallo pf   Angelicum CALP18, STA9005
Musidisc RC724
Orpheus ORB–267

No. 2. Sonata No. 2, in A
with E. Cavallo pf   Angelicum CALP18, STA9005
Musidisc RC724
Orpheus ORB–267

No. 3. Sonata No. 3, in E flat
with E. Cavallo pf   Angelicum CALP19, STA9006
Musidisc RC725
Orpheus ORB–268

Sonata No. 4, in a, Op. 23 vln & pf
with E. Cavallo pf   Angelicum CALP19, STA9006
Musidisc RC725
Orpheus ORB–268

BEETHOVEN – *Continued*

Sonata No. 5, in F, Op. 24 "Spring" vln & pf
with E. Cavallo pf   Record Society RS25
Sonata No. 5, in F, Op. 24 "Spring" vln & pf
with E. Cavallo pf   Angelicum CALP20, STA9007
     Musidisc RC726
     Orpheus ORB–269

(3) Sonatas, Op. 30 vln & pf
No. 1. Sonata No. 6, in A
with E. Cavallo pf   Angelicum CALP20, STA9007
     Musidisc RC726
     Orpheus ORB–269

No. 2. Sonata No. 7, in c
with E. Cavallo pf   Angelicum CALP21, STA9008
     Musidisc RC727
     Orpheus ORB–270

No. 3. Sonata No. 8, in G
with E. Cavallo pf   Angelicum CALP21, STA9008
     Musidisc RC727
     Orpheus ORB–270

Sonata No. 9, in A, Op. 47 "Kreutzer" vln & pf
with E. Cavallo pf   Angelicum CALP22, STA9009
     Musidisc RC728
     Orpheus ORB–271

Sonata No. 10, in G, Op. 96 vln & pf
with E. Cavallo pf   Record Society RS25
Sonata No. 10, in G, Op. 96 vln & pf
with E. Cavallo pf   Angelicum CALP22, STA9009
     Musidisc RC728
     Orpheus ORB–271

CHOPIN

(4) Mazurkas, Op. 67 pf
No. 4. Mazurka No. 45, in a arr. vln & pf Kreisler
with G. Vidusso pf   Adam C111
     Celson NY2000

CIMA

(2) Concerti ecclesiastica (1610)
Sonata No. 2, in a 2 vlns, gamba & org
with C. Ferraresi vln, G. Caramia vlc   Angelicum LPA5947
& A. Berutti org   Musica Sacra AMS46

CURCI

Concerto No. 1, Op. 21 "Concerto romantico" vln & orch.
with orch. – Capuana   Curci LP110
Concerto No. 2, Op. 30 vln & orch.
with orch. – Capuana   Curci LP110
Concerto No. 3, Op. 33 vln & orch.
with Orch. – Capuana   Curci LP120
Suite italiana, Op. 34 vln & orch.
with orch. – Capuana   Curci LP120

DVOŘÁK

Sonatina in G, Op. 100 vln & pf
Larghetto (2nd mvt) arr. vln & pf as "Indian lament" by Kreisler
with G. Vidusso pf   Adam C112
     Celson NY2000
     Classic C2008

HAYDN

Sinfonia concertante in B flat, Op. 84 (H.I, No. 105) vln, ob, vlc, bsn & orch.
with E. Ovcinnekoff ob, G. Caramia vlc, U. Benedettelli bsn & Orch. of Naples – Vaughan   Victor (in sets LM6805 & LSC6805)

KREISLER

Tambourin chinois, Op. 3 vln & pf
with G. Vidusso pf   Adam C111
     Celson NY2001

LEGRENZI

(12) Sonatas, Op. 10 (1673) 2 vlns & c
Sonata No. 5, in D
with C. Ferraresi vln, A. Berutti org & G. Caramia vlc   Angelicum LPA5947
     Musica Sacra AMS46

MENDELSSOHN

Concerto in d (1823) "Double" vln, pf & strs
with E. Cavallo pf & Angelicum Chamber Orch., Milan – Urbini   Angelicum LPA5978
     Musica Mundi VMS2011
     Orpheus OR359

Concerto in e, Op. 64 vln & orch.
with La Fenice Theatre Orch., Venice – Gracis   Record Society RS59

Sonata in F (1838) vln & pf
with E. Cavallo pf   Angelicum LPA5978
     Musica Mundi VMS2011
     Orpheus OR359

MOZART

Concerto No. 3, in G, K216 (cadenzas by Franko) vln & orch.
with Angelicum Orch., Milan – Gulli   Angelicum LPA5962
Concerto No. 3, in G, K216 (cadenzas by Franko) vln & orch.
with Lausanne Chamber Orch. – Jordan   Guilde International du Disque SMS2649
Concerto No. 4, in D, K218 (cadenzas by Joachim) vln & orch.
with Angelicum Orch., Milan – Gulli   Angelicum LPA5962
Concerto No. 5, in A, K219 "Turkish" (cadenzas by Joachim) vln & orch.
with Lausanne Chamber Orch. – Jordan   Guilde International du Disque SMS2649
Divertimento in E flat, K563 vln, vla & vlc
with B. Giuranna vla & G. Caramia vlc   Deutsche Grammophon LPM39150, SLPM139150
Duo No. 2, in B flat, K424 vln & vla
with B. Giuranna vla   Angelicum LPA5990, STA8990
     Musical Heritage Society MHS1020

(Ein) Musikalischer Spass in F, K522 strs & 2 hrns
with San Pietro Orch. – Ruotolo   Decca DL10068, DL710068
Sinfonia concertante in E flat, K364 vln, vla & orch.
with B. Giuranna vla & Angelicum Orch., Milan – Galliera   Angelicum LPA5990, STA8990
     Musical Heritage Society MHS1020

PAGANINI

Cantabile in D, Op. 17 vln & gtr
with E. Cavallo pf   Angelicum LPA7015
     Decca DL10081, DL710081
     Musical Heritage Society DRM110

PAGANINI – *Continued*

(24) Caprices, Op. 1 (1801/7) solo vln
Caprice No. 13, in B flat
(unaccompanied)　　　　　　　Angelicum LPA5952
Caprice No. 16, in g
(unaccompanied)　　　　　　　Angelicum LPA5933, LPA7015
　　　　　　　　　　　　　　　Musical Heritage Society
　　　　　　　　　　　　　　　DRM110
　　　　　　　　　　　　　　　Storia della Musica SdM054
　　　　　　　　　　　　　　　(Vol. 5, No. 2)
Caprice No. 17, in E flat
(unaccompanied)　　　　　　　Angelicum LPA5933, LPA7015
　　　　　　　　　　　　　　　Musical Heritage Society
　　　　　　　　　　　　　　　DRM110
　　　　　　　　　　　　　　　Storia della Musica SdM054
　　　　　　　　　　　　　　　(Vol. 5, No. 2)
Caprice No. 20, in D
(unaccompanied)　　　　　　　Angelicum LPA5952
Concerto No. 5, in a (1830) vln & orch.
with Angelicum Chamber Orch., Milan　　Angelicum LPA5933
– Rosada　　　　　　　　　　Decca DL710081
　　　　　　　　　　　　　　　Harmonia Mundi HM30663
　　　　　　　　　　　　　　　Musical Heritage Society
　　　　　　　　　　　　　　　DRM110
(I) Palpiti (variations on the aria "Di tanti palpiti" from Rossini's opera
"Tancredi") Op. 13 (1819) vln & orch.
with E. Cavallo pf　　　　　　Angelicum LPA5933, LPA7015
　　　　　　　　　　　　　　　Decca DL710081
　　　　　　　　　　　　　　　Musical Heritage Society
　　　　　　　　　　　　　　　DRM110
　　　　　　　　　　　　　　　Storia della Musica SdM054,
　　　　　　　　　　　　　　　(Vol. 5, No. 2)

RUGGIERI

(10) Sonatas da chiesa, Op. 3 (1693) 2 vlns & c
Sonata No. 5, in g
with C. Ferraresi vln, A. Berutti org &　Angelicum LPA5947
G. Caramia vlc　　　　　　　　Musica Sacra AMS46

SCARLATESCU

Bagatelle (in Rumanian style) vln & pf
with G. Vidusso pf　　　　　　Adam C112
　　　　　　　　　　　　　　　Celson NY2001
　　　　　　　　　　　　　　　Classic C2008

SCHUBERT

Sonata in A, Op. 162 (D574) "Duo" vln & pf
with E. Cavallo pf　　　　　　Record Society RS18
(3) Sonatinas, Op. 137 (D384, D385 & D408) vln & pf
Sonatina No. 2, in a, D385
with E. Cavallo pf　　　　　　Record Society RS18

STRADELLA

(2) Sonatas "Sinfonias" vln, vlc & bs
Sonata No. 1, in d vln & c
with A. Berutti org & G. Caramia vlc　Angelicum LPA5947
　　　　　　　　　　　　　　　Musica Sacra AMS46

TARTINI

Concerto in D, D15 (C79) vln & orch. – rev. Abbado
with Angelicum Orch., Milan –　　Angelicum LPA5921
Abbado　　　　　　　　　　　Music Guild M33, S33
Concerto in F, C63 vln & orch.
with Angelicum Orch., Milan –　　Angelicum LPA5921
Abbado　　　　　　　　　　　Music Guild M33, S33
Sonata in g "Il Trillo del Diavolo" vln & c – arr. vln & pf Cavallo
with E. Cavallo pf　　　　　　Angelicum LPA5952
　　　　　　　　　　　　　　　Storia della Musica SdM018
　　　　　　　　　　　　　　　(Vol. 2, No. 5)

TORELLI

(12) Sonatas, Op. 3 vln & c
Sonata No. 7, in e
with C. Ferraresi vln, A. Berutti org &　Angelicum LPA5947
G. Caramia vlc　　　　　　　　Musica Sacra AMS46

VIEUXTEMPS

(7) Romances sans paroles, Op. 7 vln & pf
No. 2. Romance No. 2, in c "Désespoir"
with E. Cavallo pf　　　　　　Angelicum LPA5952

VIOTTI

Concerto No. 3, in A pf, vln, obb & strs
with E. Cavallo pf & Angelicum　Angelicum LPA5977, STA8977
Orch., Milan – Urbini　　　　　Musical Heritage Society
　　　　　　　　　　　　　　　MHS1132
(3) Duets, Op. 29 2 vlns
No. 3. Duo concertante No. 3, in D
(playing both solo parts)
　　　　　　　　　　　　　　　Angelicum LPA5977, STA8977
　　　　　　　　　　　　　　　Musical Heritage Society
　　　　　　　　　　　　　　　MHS1132

VITALI

(12) Concerti di Sonate, Op. 4 vln, vlc & c
Sonata No. 11, in b
with C. Ferraresi vln, A. Berutti org &　Angelicum LPA5947
G. Caramia vlc　　　　　　　　Musica Sacra AMS46

VIVALDI

(12 Concerti, Op. 3 "L'Estro armonico" var. cbns & strs
Concerto No. 1, in D, P.146 (F.IV, No. 7) 4 vlns, vlc, strs & c
with E. Malanotte vln, M. Benvenuti　HMV ALP1809, ASD391
vln, A. Poltronieri vln & Virtuosi di
Roma – Fasano
Concerto No. 3, in G, P.96 (F.I, No. 173) vln, strs & c
with Virtuosi di Roma – Fasano　HMV ALP1809, ASD391
Concerto No. 4, in e, P.97 (F.I, No. 174) 4 vlns, strs & c
with A. Stefanato vln, R. Ruotolo vln,　AMV ALP1809, ASD391
M. Benvenuti vln & Virtuosi di Roma
– Fasano
Concerto No. 6, in a, P.I (F.I, No. 176) vln, strs & c
with Virtuosi di Roma – Fasano　HMV ALP1810, ASD392
Concerto No. 7, in F, P.249 (F.IV, No. 9) 4 vlns, strs & c
with E. Malanotte vln, L. Ferro vln,　HMV ALP1810, ASD392
M. Benvenuti vln & Virtuosi di Roma
– Fasano
Concerto No. 8, in a, P.2 (F.I, No. 177) 2 vlns, strs & c
with E. Malanotte vln & Virtuosi di　HMV ALP1810, ASD392
Roma – Fasano

VIVALDI – *Continued*

Concerto No. 10, in b, P.148 (F.IV, No. 10) 4 vlns, strs & c
with E. Malanotte vln, A. Stefanato   Electrola E70435, STE70435
vln, L. Ferro vln & Virtuosi di Roma   HMV ALP1811, ASD393
– Fasano

(12) Concerti, Op. 8 (1725) "Il Cimento dell'Armonia e dell' Invenzione"
(Nos. 1/4: Le quattro Stagioni) vln & strs
Concerto No. 1, in E, F.I, No. 22 "La Primavera"
with Angelicum Orch. – Ceccato   Angelicum LPA5949
    Audio Fidelity FSC50032
    Charlin SLC23

Concerto No. 2, in B flat, F.I, No. 23 "L'Estate"
with Angelicum Orch. – Ceccato   Angelicum LPA5949
    Audio Fidelity FSC50032
    Charlin SLC23

Concerto No. 3, in F, F.I, No. 24 "L'Autunno"*
with Angelicum Orch. – Ceccato   Angelicum LPA5949
    Audio Fidelity FSC50032
    Charlin SLC23

Concerto No. 4, in f, F.I, No. 25 "L'Inverno"
with Vivaldi Academy Orch. –   Discophiles Français EDC34
Amaducci

Concerto No. 4, in f, F.I, No. 25 "L'Inverno"
with Angelicum Orch. – Ceccato   Angelicum LPA5949
    Audio Fidelity FSC50032
    Charlin SLC23

Concerto No. 7, in d, F.I, No. 28
with Virtuosi di Roma – Fasano   Angel 35878, (in set 3611),
    ASC5039
    Electrola E70435, STE70435
    HMV ALP1787, ASD368,
    BSDW8009, QALP10296,
    WBLP570

Concerto No. 8, in g, F.I, No. 16
with Virtuosi di Roma – Fasano   Angel 35878, (in set 3611),
    ASC5039
    HMV ALP1787, ASD368,
    QALP10296

Concerto No. 11, in D, F.I, No. 30
with Virtuosi di Roma – Fasano   Angel 35879, (in set 3611),
    ASC5040
    HMV ALP1788, ASD369,
    QALP10297

Concerto in G, P.132 (F.I, No. 6) 2 vlns, strs & c
with E. Malanotte vln & Virtuosi di   HMV ALP1344
Roma – Fasano

Concerto in A, P.238 vln, vlc strs & c
with B. Mazzacurati vlc & Virtuosi di   Electrola E90147
Roma – Fasano   HMV ALP1439, QALP10113,
    WALP1439

(6) Sonatas, Op. 5 "Fatte per Monsieur Pisendel" vln & c
Sonata No. 1, in F
with V. Luccini hpsi & A. Pocaterra   Arcophon AC711
vlc

Sonata No. 2, in A
with V. Luccini hpsi & A. Pocaterra   Arcophon AC711
vlc

* Also on Angelicum LPA5958 & Audio Fidelity FSC50036.

VIVALDI – *Continued*

Sonata No. 3, in B flat
with V. Luccini hpsi & A. Pocaterra   Arcophon AC711
vlc

Sonata No. 4, in e
with V. Luccini hpsi & A. Pocaterra   Arcophon AC711
vlc

Sonata No. 5, in E flat
with V. Luccini hpsi & A. Pocaterra   Arcophon AC711
vlc

Sonata No. 6, in g
with V. Luccini hpsi & A. Poçaterra   Arcophon AC711
vlc

Sonata a quattro in E flat, P.441 (F.XVI, No.2) "Al Santo Sepolcro" 2
vlns, vla & c
with C. Ferraresi vln, B. Tosatti vla,   Angelicum LPA5958
A. Berruti hpsi & G. Caramia vlc   Electrola 1C053–02068

Robert GUNDERSEN

MASSENET

Thaïs (1894) – opera
Méditation vln & orch.
with Boston "Pops"   2A 92827△   HMV C2838, EH970, S10533
Orch. – Fiedler   Victor 11887

SCHÜTZ

(27) Symphoniae sacrae, Op. 10 (1647)
Concerto No. 6 (Ich werde nicht sterben) SWV346 s, 2 vlns & c
    T 1524 A/B & 1525 A   Technichord TC11/2, (in set T2)
with H. Cuénod t, C.J. Chiasson hpsi,
G. Elcus vln & J. Langendoen vlc

Max GÜNTHER

BACH

Concerto in c, BWV1060 vln & ob or 2 vlns, strs & c
with H. Ortmann ob & Classics Club   Classics Club X1008
Chamber Orch. – Friedmann

Kurt GUNTNER

BACH

Concerto in d, BWV1043 2 vlns, strs & c
with O. Büchner vln & Munich Bach   Archive APM14321, ARC3221,
Orch. – Richter   ARC73221, SAPM198321
    Musique Royale 199007

(Ein) Musikalisches Opfer, BWV1079 (1749) strs
with O. Büchner vln, G.A. Nicolet fl,   Archive APM14320, ARC3220,
F. Kiskalt vlc, H. Bilgram hpsi, S.   ARC73220, SAPM198320
Meinecke vln & K. Richter hpsi

Michel GUSIKOFF (1895–)

ANONYMOUS

Wee bit o' heart arr. vln & orch.
with orch.   Victor 19538

HAYS

Molly darling (1871) v & pf – arr. vln & orch.
   with orch.   Victor 18987

MacDOWELL

Woodland Sketches, Op. 51 pf
  No. 1. To a wild rose arr. vln & orch.
    with orch.   Victor 18144
                     Zonophone 2800

  No. 1. To a wild rose arr. vln & orch.
    with orch.   Victor 19892

MARKS

When dreams come true v & pf – arr. vln & orch.
    with orch.   Victor 19538

PIERNÉ

Sérénade in A, Op. 7 (1875) pf – arr. vln & pf Haddock
    with orch.   Victor 16051

SCHINDLER

Souvenir poétique (Paraphrase on Fibich's "Poem" Op. 41, No. 14) vln & pf
    with orch.   Victor 18144
                     Zonophone 2800

Souvenir poétique (Paraphrase on Fibich's "Poem" Op. 41, No. 14) vln & pf
    with R. Bourdon pf   Victor 19892

WESTENDORF

I'll take you home again Kathleen (1876) v & pf – arr. vln & orch.
    with orch.   Victor 18987

Boris GUTNIKOV (1931–)

BACH

Concerto No. 1, in a, BWV1041 vln, strs & c
  with Leningrad Philharmonic   Mezhdunarodnaya Kniga
  Symphony Orch. – Gozman   D014449, SM02287
Concerto in d, BWV1043 2 vlns, strs & c
  with M. Vaiman vln & Leningrad   Mezhdunarodnaya Kniga
  Philharmonic Symphony Orch. –   D014449/50, SM02288
  Gozman
(6) Sonatas, BWV1014/9 vln & clav
  Sonata No. 1, in b, BWV1014
    with L. Pecherskaya pf   Mezhdunarodnaya Kniga
                          D010223

BRAHMS

Sonata No. 2, in A, Op. 100 vln & pf
  with L. Pecherskaya pf   Mezhdunarodnaya Kniga
                         D014729

Sonata No. 3, in d, Op. 108 vln & pf
  with L. Pecherskaya pf   Mezhdunarodnaya Kniga
                         D014730

BRITTEN

Suite, Op. 6 vln & pf
  with L. Pecherskaya pf   Mezhdunarodnaya Kniga
                         D16333

FRANCK

Sonata in A (1886) vln & pf
  with L. Pecherskaya pf   Mezhdunarodnaya Kniga
                         D013707/8

GERSHWIN

Porgy & Bess (1935) – opera
  Bess, you is my woman arr. vln & pf Heifetz
    with L. Pecherskaya pf   Mezhdunarodnaya Kniga D4697

GLAZOUNOV

Raymonda, Op. 57 (1897) – ballet orch.
  Entr'acte No. 1 arr. vln & pf Rodionov
    with L. Pecherskaya pf   Mezhdunarodnaya Kniga
                         D04469

HANDEL

Solomon (1748) – oratorio
  No. 40. Am klaren Bach im stiller Tal arr. vln & pf as "Pastorale" by
  Flesch
    with L. Pecherskaya pf   Mezhdunarodnaya Kniga D4696
(15) Sonatas, Op. 1 (?1731) fl or vln & c
  Sonata No. 13, in D vln IV
    with L. Pecherskaya pf   Mezhdunarodnaya Kniga
                         D04468

  Sonata No. 15, in E vln VI
    with L. Pecherskaya pf   Mezhdunarodnaya Kniga
                         D013707/8

HINDEMITH

(6) Sonatas, Op. 11
  No. 1. Sonata No. 1, in E flat (1920) vln & pf
    with L. Pecherskaya pf   Mezhdunarodnaya Kniga
                         D013707/8

KABALEVSKY

Rondo in C, Op. 69 vln & pf
  with L. Pecherskaya pf   Mezhdunarodnaya Kniga
                         D010224, D010325/8

KREISLER

(La) Gitana vln & pf
  with L. Pecherskaya pf   Mezhdunarodnaya Kniga D4697
                         Supraphon SUF20006
                         Ultraphon DM5528

MOZART

Serenade No. 7, in D, K250 "Haffner" orch.
  Rondo (4th mvt) arr. vln & pf Kreisler
    with L. Pecherskaya pf   Mezhdunarodnaya Kniga
                         D010223, D010367/8,
                         D00010549/50

ONDŘIČEK

Scherzo–Capriccio, Op. 18 vln & pf
  with L. Pecherskaya pf   Mezhdunarodnaya Kniga D4696

PROKOFIEV

(10) Pieces (from the ballet "Romeo & Juliet") Op. 75 (1937) pf
  No. 5. Masques arr. vln & pf Grunes
    with L. Pecherskaya pf   Mezhdunarodnaya Kniga D4696
                         Supraphon SUF20006
                         Ultraphon DM5528

PROKOFIEV – *Continued*

Romeo & Juliet, Op. 64b (1935/6) – 2nd ballet suite orch.
No. 4. Danse de Jeunes antillaises arr. vln & pf Grunes
with L. Pecherskaya pf   Mezhdunarodnaya Kniga D4696
                                Supraphon SUF20006
                                Ultraphon DM5528

RAVEL

Pièce en forme d'Habanera v & pf – arr. vln & pf Catherine
with L. Pecherskaya pf   Mezhdunarodnaya Kniga D4697

SAINT–SAËNS

Introduction & Rondo Capriccioso, Op. 28 vln & orch.
with L. Pecherskaya pf   Mezhdunarodnaya Kniga
                                D04469

SCOTT

Lotus land, Op. 47, No. 1 (1905) pf – arr. vln & pf Kreisler
with L. Pecherskaya pf   Mezhdunarodnaya Kniga
                                D04468
                                Supraphon SUF20006, SUL30043
                                Ultraphon DM5528

SHOSTAKOVICH

(24) Preludes, Op. 34 (1932/3) pf
Prelude No. 2, in a arr. vln & pf Tziganov
with L. Pecherskaya pf   Mezhdunarodnaya Kniga
                                D16334

Prelude No. 6, in b arr. vln & pf Tziganov
with L. Pecherskaya pf   Mezhdunarodnaya Kniga
                                D16334

Prelude No. 10, in c sharp arr. vln & pf Tziganov
with L. Pecherskaya pf   Mezhdunarodnaya Kniga
                                D16334

Prelude No. 12, in g sharp arr. vln & pf Tziganov
with L. Pecherskaya pf   Mezhdunarodnaya Kniga
                                D16334

Prelude No. 13, in F sharp arr. vln & pf Tziganov
with L. Pecherskaya pf   Mezhdunarodnaya Kniga
                                D16334

Prelude No. 15, in D flat arr. vln & pf Tziganov
with L. Pecherskaya pf   Mezhdunarodnaya Kniga
                                D16334

Prelude No. 16, in b flat arr. vln & pf Tziganov
with L. Pecherskaya pf   Mezhdunarodnaya Kniga
                                D16334

Prelude No. 17, in A flat arr. vln & pf Tziganov
with L. Pecherskaya pf   Mezhdunarodnaya Kniga
                                D16334

Prelude No. 18, in f arr. vln & pf Tziganov
with L. Pecherskaya pf   Mezhdunarodnaya Kniga
                                D16334

Prelude No. 19, in E flat arr. vln & pf Tziganov
with L. Pecherskaya pf   Mezhdunarodnaya Kniga
                                D16334

Prelude No. 20, in c arr. vln & pf Tziganov
with L. Pecherskaya pf   Mezhdunarodnaya Kniga
                                D16334

SHOSTAKOVICH – *Continued*

Prelude No. 21, in B flat arr. vln & pf Tziganov
with L. Pecherskaya pf   Mezhdunarodnaya Kniga
                                D16334

Prelude No. 22, in g arr. vln & pf Tziganov
with L. Pecherskaya pf   Mezhdunarodnaya Kniga
                                D16334

Prelude No. 24, in d arr. vln & pf Tziganov
with L. Pecherskaya pf   Mezhdunarodnaya Kniga
                                D010223

SLAVÍK

Concerto No. 2, in a "Unfinished" vln & orch.
Allegro (1st mvt)
with Prague Symphony Orch. –   Suprahon LPM429, SUF20356
Smetácek   Ultraphon DM5528

SMETANA

From my Homeland (1878) vln & pf
No. 2. Andantino
with L. Pecherskaya pf   Mezhdunarodnaya Kniga
                                D04468

TCHAIKOVSKY

Concerto in D, Op. 35 vln & orch.
with Moscow Philharmonic Orch. –   Mezhdunarodnaya Kniga
Rozhdestvensky   D10711/2, S0653/4
Souvenir d'un lieu cher, Op. 42 vln & pf
No. 1. Méditation
with L. Pecherskaya pf   Mezhdunarodnaya Kniga
                                D04469
                                Supraphon SUF20006
                                Ultraphon DM5528

No. 1. Méditation
with L. Pecherskaya pf   Mezhdunarodnaya Kniga
                                D010224

Waltz–Scherzo, Op. 34 vln & pf or orch.
with L. Pecherskaya pf   Mezhdunarodnaya Kniga
                                D010224, D00010549/50

TELEMANN

Quartet in e (1733) fl, vln, vlc & c
with L. Perepyolkin fl, V. Morozov vlc   Mezhdunarodnaya Kniga
& I. Braudo hpsi   D019631, S01375

WAGNER

Albumblatt in C (1861) pf – arr. vln & pf Wilhelmj
with L. Pecherskaya pf   Mezhdunarodnaya Kniga D4697
                                Supraphon SUF20006
                                Ultraphon DM5528

YSAŸE

(6) Sonatas, Op. 27 solo vln
Sonata No. 3, in d
(unaccompanied)   Mezhdunarodnaya Kniga
                                D010224, D010325/8

ZARZYCKI

Mazurka in G, Op. 26 vln & pf – arr. Dubiska
with L. Pecherskaya pf   Supraphon SUF20006
                                Ultraphon DM5528

Ibolyka GYARFAS

BRAHMS

(21) Hungarian Dances pf duet
Hungarian dance unid – arr. vln & pf Hubay
with piano   26162   Polydor 16044

Hungarian Dance No. 5, in f sharp arr. vln & pf "in g" Joachim
with piano   19042 L   HMV 2–47915
Polydor 20076, 62186

CARRI

Elfentanz (Concert etude) Op. 8 vln & pf
with W. Scholz pf   79564   Odeon 0–6076

DRIGO

(Les) Millions d'Arlequin (1900) – ballet orch.
Sérénade arr. vln & pf Auer
with O. Urack pf   Vox 06070

GOSSEC

Rosine (1786) – opera
Gavotte arr. vln & pf Burmester
with O. Urack pf   314 B   Vox 6012

Gavotte arr. vln & pf Burmester
with J. Simon pf   51059   Homochord B8223

Gavotte arr. vln & pf Burmester
with piano   26165   Polydor 16045

HUBAY

(Le) Luthier de Crémone, Op. 40 (1894) – opera
Intermezzo orch. – arr. vln & pf Hubay
with J. Simon pf   51058   Homochord B8615

(2) Mazurkas, Op. 45 vln & pf
No. 1. Mazurka No. 1, in a "Madame Leopold Horowitz"
with piano   19043 L   HMV 2–47916
Polydor 20076, 62186

(14) Scènes de la Csárda vln & pf
No. 4. Hejre Kati, Op. 32
with B. Seidler-Winkler   19044/5 L   Polydor 20077, 62289
pf

No. 4. Hejre Kati, Op. 32
with W. Scholz pf   79556/7   Odeon 0–6003

HUMMEL

Waltz in A pf – arr. vln & pf Burmester
with O. Urack pf   Vox 6017

Waltz in A pf – arr. vln & pf Burmester
with J. Simon pf   51062   Homochord B8223

KREISLER

Caprice viennois, Op. 2 vln & pf
with O. Urack pf   Vox 06011

Schön Rosmarin vln & pf
with O. Urack pf   315 B   Vox 6012

(La) Chasse (Cartier) vln & pf
with W. Scholz pf   79559   Odeon 0–6223

Variations on a theme of Corelli (Tartini) vln & pf
with piano   Polydor 15955

MOZART

(6) Deutsche Tänze, K600 orch.
No. 1. Deutscher Tanz No. 1, in C "Ländler" arr. vln. & pf Ries
with W. Scholz pf   79563   Odeon 0–6223

PADEREWSKI

(6) Humoresques de concert, Op. 14 pf
No. 1. Minuet in G arr. vln. & pf Kreisler
with O. Urack pf   Vox 06011

RIMSKY–KORSAKOV

Sadko (1898) – opera
Chant hindou arr. vln & pf Kreisler
with W. Scholz pf   79558   Odeon 0–6076

SCHUBERT

(7) Gesänge (set to Scott's "Lady of the Lake") Op. 52 v & pf
No. 6. Ave Maria, D839 arr. vln & pf Wilhelmj
with O. Urack pf   Vox 06070

(6) Moments musicaux, Op. 94 (D780) (1823/7) pf
No. 3 – Moment musicale No. 3, in f "Air russe" arr. vln & pf Burmester
with O. Urack pf   Vox 6017

No. 3 – Moment musicale No. 3, in f "Air russe" arr. vln & pf
Burmester
with piano   26164   Polydor 16045

SEIDLER–WINKLER

Gavotte in C vln & pf
with piano   26163   Polydor 16044

WIENIAWSKI

Mazurka in a, Op. 3 "Kujawiak" vln & pf
with J. Simon pf   51060   Homochord B8615

Vera GYARMATI (1936–)

BRAHMS

Sonata (1853) "Frei aber Einsam" vln & pf
Allegro (Scherzo) in c (3rd mvt) "Sonatensatz"
with A. Katona pf   Qualiton LPX1152

LECLAIR

(12) Sonatas, Op. 9 – Book IV (1738) vln & c
Sonata No. 3, in D
with A. Katona pf   Qualiton LPX1152

MOZART

Adagio in E, K261 vln & orch.
with A. Katona pf   Qualiton LPX1152

RAVEL

Pièce en forme d'Habanera v & pf – arr. vln & pf Catherine
with A. Katona pf   Qualiton LPX1152

SCHUBERT, François

(12) Bagatelles, Op. 13 vln & pf
No. 9. L'abeille
with A. Katona pf   Qauliton LPX1152

YSAŸE

(6) Sonatas, Op. 27 solo vln
   Sonata No. 3, in d
   (unaccompanied)

Qualiton LPX1152

Ota GYGI

DRDLA

Serenade No. 1, in A vln & pf
   with piano

15032   Applaudando 1317

GODARD

Jocelyn (1888) – opera
   Cachés dans cet asile "Berceuse" arr. vln & pf
   with piano

15034   Applaudando 1318

MOZART

Divertimento No. 17, in D, K334 2 hrns & strs
   Minuet (3rd mvt) arr. vln & pf Burmester
   with piano

15031   Applaudando 1317

PIERNÉ

Sérénade in A, Op. 7 (1875) pf – arr. vln & pf
   with piano

15033   Applaudando 1318

SARASATE

Faust Fantasia (on themes from the opera by Gounod) vln & pf or orch.
   with piano

32078/9   Applaudando 31319

Hanno HAAG

BOECKE

Romanze in g vln & pf
   with A. Schlicker pf

Da Camera SM93310

DALBERG

Sonata in F, Op. 28 vln & pf
   Largo ma non tanto (2nd mvt)
   with A. Schlicker pf

Da Camera SM93302
Musica Rara MUS14

EDELMANN

(3) Sonatas, Op. 2 vln & pf
   Sonata No. 1, in c
   with A. Schlicker pf

Da Camera SM93310

EICHNER

(3) Sonatas, Op. 2 vln & c
   Sonata No. 1, in A
   with A. Schlicker pf

Da Camera SM93302
Musica Rara MUS14

GUGEL

Ballo vln & pf
   with A. Schlicker pf

Da Camera SM93310

HÜLLMANDEL

(3) Sonatas, Op. 6 vln & pf
   Sonata No. 3, in B
   with A. Schlicker pf

Da Camera SM93310

KRAMER

Adagio in g vln & pf
   with A. Schlicker pf

Da Camera SM93310

KRAUS

Sonata No. 2, in D vln & pf
   with A. Schlicker pf

Da Camera SM93310

LACHNITH

Rondo in F vln & pf
   with A. Schlicker pf

Da Camera SM93302
Musica Rara MUS14

LANG, J.G.

Aria & Menuette vln & pf
   with A. Schlicker pf

Da Camera SM93310

(6) Sonatas, Op. 6 vln & c
   Sonata No. 6 in A
   with A. Schlicker pf

Da Camera SM93302
Musica Rara MUS14

MOZART

Sonata No. 1, in C, K6 vln & pf
   with A. Schlicker pf

Da Camera SM93304
Musica Rara MUS48

Sonata No. 6, in G, K11 vln & pf
   with A. Schlicker pf

Da Camera SM93304
Musica Rara MUS48

Sonata No. 8, in F, K13 vln & pf
   with A. Schlicker pf

Da Camera SM93304
Musica Rara MUS48

Sonata No. 11, in E flat, K26 vln & pf
   with A. Schlicker pf

Da Camera SM93304
Musica Rara MUS48

Sonata No. 13, in C, K28 vln & pf
   with A. Schlicker pf

Da Camera SM93304
Musica Rara MUS48

Sonata No. 15, in F, K30 vln & pf
   with A. Schlicker pf

Da Camera SM93302
Musica Rara MUS14

Sonata No. 22, in e, K60 vln & pf
   with A. Schlicker pf

Da Camera SM93304
Musica Rara MUS48

SCHMOLL

(6) Sonatas, Op. 1 cem obb & vln & vlc ad libitum
   Sonata No. 3, in E flat
   with A. Schlicker pf

Da Camera SM93302
Musica Rara MUS14

TELEMANN

Quartet in g fl, vln, vlc, bsn & hpsi
   with G. Kuhn fl, H. Broszinski vlc, E.
   Prappacher bsn & K. Preis hpsi

Da Camera HBE92006, M2001
Musica Rara MUR6

VOGLER

Caprice in E flat vln & pf
   with A. Schlicker pf

Da Camera SM93302
Musica Rara MUS14

WEBER

(6) Sonatas, Op. 10 (J99/104) (1810) vln & pf
Sonata No. 1, in F, J99
with A. Schlicker pf | Da Camera SM93305

Sonata No. 2, in G, J100
with A. Schlicker pf | Da Camera SM93305

Sonata No. 3, in D, J101
with A. Schlicker pf | Da Camera SM93305

Sonata No. 4, in E flat, J102
with A. Schlicker pf | Da Camera SM93305

Sonata No. 5, in A, J103
with A. Schlicker pf | Da Camera SM93305

Sonata No. 6, in C, J104
with A. Schlicker pf | Da Camera SM93305

Ingebret HAALAND (1878–1934)

ANONYMOUS

Aa Ola, min Ola Norwegian melody – arr. vln & pf Haaland
with piano | HMV X1387, X287958

Je vet e lita Jente Norwegian melody – arr. vln & pf Haaland
with piano | HMV X1387, X287957

Paal paa Haugen traditional Norwegian melody – arr. vln & pf Haaland
with piano | HMV X1387, X287957

BULL

Säterjëntens Søndag v & pf – arr. vln & pf Halvorsen
with piano | HMV X1246, X287944

ELLING

Huldra v & pf – arr. vln & pf Haaland
with piano | HMV X1379, X287947

HAALAND

Bøn vln & pf
with piano | HMV X1246, X287943

Norsk dance No. 1 vln & pf
with piano | HMV X1379, X287948

THRANE

Fjeldeventyret (1824) – dramatic scene
Aagots Fjeldsang arr. vln & pf Haaland
with piano | HMV X1387, X287958

Paul HADJAJE

BRAHMS

(16) Waltzes, Op. 39 pf duet
No. 15, Waltz No. 15, in A flat arr. vln & pf "in A" Hochstein
with M. Etcheverry hp | Pacific 150020

Ida HAENDEL (1928–   )

ACHRON

Hebrew melody, Op. 33 vln & pf – arr. Auer
with A. Haendel pf | AR 7145–2 | Decca K1047

ALBÉNIZ

España (6 Feuilles d'album) Op. 165 pf
No. 3. Malagueña in b arr. vln & pf Kreisler
with N. Mewton – | AR 5537–1 | Decca K1073
Wood pf | | Odeon 263772

BACH

(3) Sonatas & 3 Partitas, BWV1001/6 solo vln
Partita No. 2, in D: Chaconne (5th mvt) BWV1004
(unaccompanied) | Mezhdunarodnaya Kniga D07287

BARTÓK

(6) Rumanian folk dances (1915) pf – arr. vln & pf Székely
AR 11129–1 & 11130–3 | Decca K1873
with I. Newton pf | London T5409

(6) Rumanian folk dances (1915) pf – arr. vln & pf Székely
with G. Moore pf | Angel SCBAE6504
HMV CLP1021, 7EP7013, 7ERL1113

(6) Rumanian folk dances (1915) pf – arr. vln & pf Székely
with V. Yampolsky pf | Mezhdunarodnaya Kniga D07288

BAZZINI

(La) Ronde des lutins, Op. 25 vln & pf
with A. Kotowska pf | DR 4931–1 | Decca F7659

BEETHOVEN

Concerto in D, Op. 61 (cadenzas by Joachim) vln & orch.
2EA 14172/3–1, 14174–1B, | HMV C4126/31S, C7879/84S,
14175–1, 14176–1A, 14177/9–1, | EH1409/14, EH2001/6,
14180–1A & 14181/2–1 | FBLP138
with Philharmonia Orch. – Kubelík | Victor (in set WBC1003), LBC1003

(3) Sonatas, Op. 30 vln & pf
No. 3. Sonata No. 8, in G
AR 5379/81–1 & 5382–2 | Decca K959/60
with N. Mewton–Wood pf

BLOCH

Abodah (God's worship) (1929) vln & pf
AR 6776–2 & 6777–1 | Decca K1076
with A. Kotowska pf

Baal Shem (3 Pictures of Chassidic life) (1923) vln & pf
No. 2. Nigun (Improvisation)
with G. Moore pf | HMV CLP1021, EPG525, 7EP7011

BRAHMS

Concerto in D, Op. 77 (cadenza by Joachim) vln & orch.
with London Symphony Orch. – | HMV CLP1032, QALP12011
Celibidache | Victor (set WBC1011), LBC1051

(21) Hungarian Dances pf duet
Hungarian dance No. 17, in f sharp arr. vln & pf Kreisler
with G. Moore pf | 2EA 13271–1 | HMV C3818
Victor (in set WBC1013), LBC1013

Hungarian dance No. 17, in f sharp arr. vln & pf Kreisler
with A. Holeček pf | Supraphon SUA10465, SUAST50465, SV8091

BRAHMS – *Continued*

(16) Waltzes, Op. 39 pf duet
No. 15, Waltz No. 15, in A flat arr. vln & pf "in A" Hochstein
with A. Kotowska pf   DR 4949–1   Decca M495
No. 15. Waltz No. 15, in A flat arr. vln & pf "in A" Hochstein
with G. Moore pf   HMV CLP1021, 7EP7040,
                   7ERL1297

BRUCH

Concerto No. 1, in g, Op. 26 vln & orch.
            2EA 13310/1–1, 13312–5 &   HMV C3802/4, C7733/5, GB7/9
with Philharmonia Orch. – 13313/5–1   Victor (in set WBC1013),
Kubelík   LBC1013

COPLAND

Rodeo (1942) – ballet orch.
No. 4. Hoe–down arr. vln & pf Copland
with G. Moore pf   OEA 14714–2   HMV B9994

CORELLI

(12) Sonatas, Op. 5 vln & c
Sonata No. 12, in d "La Follia" arr. Léonard
with V. Yampolsky pf   Mezhdunarodnaya Kniga
                       D07288

DINICU

Hora staccato vln & ens – arr. vln & pf Heifetz
with A. Kotowska pf   AR 6777–1   Decca K1076

DVOŘÁK

Concerto in a, Op. 53 vln & orch.
            AR 11472/3–1, 11474/5–2,   Decca (set EDA77), K1744/7
            11476–1 & 11477/9–2
with National Symphony Orch. –
Rankl
(8) Humoresques, Op. 101 pf
No. 7. Humoresque No. 7, in G flat arr. vln & pf "in G" Kreisler
            XYZ DR 4950–1   Decca M521
with A. Kotowska pf
(8) Slavonic Dances, Op. 46 pf duet; orch.
No. 2. Slavonic Dance No. 2, in e arr. vln & pf "in g" Kreisler
with G. Moore pf   2EA 18053–1C   HMV C4262, CLP1021
(8) Slavonic Dances, Op. 72 pf duet; orch.
No. 2. Slavonic dance No. 10, in e arr. vln & pf Kreisler
with A. Kotowska pf   DR 4930–1   Decca M495
No. 2. Slavonic dance No. 10, in e arr. vln & pf Kreisler
with G. Moore pf   HMV CLP1021, 7P151

ELGAR

(La) Capricieuse, Op. 17 vln & pf
with G. Moore pf   HMV CLP1021, 7EP7040,
                     7ERL1297

FALLA

(El) Sombrero de Tre Picos (1919) – ballet orch.
Danza del Molinero arr. vln & pf Szigeti
with A. Kotowska pf   DR 10769–1   Decca M603
(La) Vida breve (1913) – opera
Danza española orch. – arr. vln & pf Kreisler
with A. Kotowska pf   AR 6790–4   Decca K1073

FALLA – *Continued*

Danza española orch. – arr. vln & pf Kreisler
with A. Kotowska pf   AR 10114–2   Decca K1214
Danza española orch. – arr. vln & pf Kreisler
with G. Moore pf   2EA 18052–1C   HMV C4262, CLP1021,
                     7EP7040, 7ERL1297, 7P151

GLAZOUNOV

Concerto in a, Op. 82 vln & orch.
with Prague Symphony Orch. –   Supraphon SUA10687,
Smetacek   SUAST50687, SV8295

GRIEG

(6) Moods, Op. 73 pf
No. 2. Scherzo–Impromptu arr. vln & pf Achron
with G. Moore pf   OEA 14709–1   HMV B10135

HANDEL

Solomon (1748) – oratorio
No. 40. Am klaren Bach im stillen Tal arr. vln & pf as "Pastorale" by Flesch
with V. Yampolsky pf   Mezhdunarodnaya Kniga
                       D07287

IBERT

(10) Histoires pf
No. 2. Le Petit àne blanc arr. vln & pf Hoèrès
with A. Kotowska pf   DR 10770–1   Decca M603

KREISLER

Caprice viennois, Op. 2 vln & pf
with A. Kotowska pf   DR 4951–1   Decca M521
Schön Rosmarin vln & pf
with A. Kotowska pf   DR 4948–1   Decca M520
Schön Rosmarin vln & pf
with G. Moore pf   HMV CLP1021, 7EP7040,
                     7ERL1297
Tambourin chinois, Op. 3 vln & pf
with A. Kotowska pf   DR 4947–1   Decca M520
Praeludium & Allegro (Puganini) vln & pf
with G. Moore pf   2EA 14650–1   HMV C4021, 7P121, 7RW118
                     Victor LBC1013
Praeludium & Allegro (Pugnani) vln & pf
with A. Holeček pf   Supraphon SUA10465,
                     SUAST50465, SV8091
Sicilienne & Rigaudon (Francoeur) vln & pf
with G. Moore pf   OEA 14713–1   HMV B9994

KROLL

Banjo & fiddle vln & pf
with G. Moore pf   2EA 14648–1   HMV C4021, 7P121
                     Victor LBC1013

Banjo & fiddle vln & pf
with A. Holeček pf   Supraphon SUA10465,
                     SUAST50465, SV8091

LALO

Symphonie espagnole, Op. 21 vln & orch.*
with National Symphony Orch. –   Decca K1275/7
Jordá

Symphonie espagnole, Op. 21 vln & orch.*
with Czech Philharmonic Orch. –   Classic 990003
Ančerl   Parliament PLP620, PLPS620
                                      Supraphon SUA10615,
                                      SUAST50615, SV8195

LECLAIR

(12) Sonatas, Op. 9 – Book IV (1738) vln & c
Sonata No. 3, in D: Sarabande (1st mvt); **Tambourin** (3rd mvt) arr.
Sarasate
with A. Kotowska pf   DR 4946–1   Decca F7727

MASSENET

Thaïs (1894) – opera
Méditation arr. vln & pf Marsick
with A. Kotowska pf   DR 4944–1   Decca F7659

MENDELSSOHN

Concerto in e, Op. 64 vln & orch.
with National Symphony Orch. –   Decca K1377/80
Sargent

(6) Gesänge, Op. 34 v & pf
No. 2. Auf Flügeln des Gesanges arr. vln & pf Achron
with G. Moore pf   2EA 14649–1   HMV C3994
                                     Victor LBC1013

PAGANINI

(24) Caprices, Op. 1 (1801/7) solo vln
Caprice No. 24, in a arr. vln & pf Auer
with G. Moore pf   Angel SCBAE6504
                                     HMV CLP1021, 7EP7013,
                                     7ERL1113

Sonata a preghière "Moses Fantasia" (on the aria "Dal tuo stellato soglio"
from Rossini's opera "Mosè in Egitto") Op. 24 (1818 or 1819) vln &
orch.
with G. Moore pf   HMV CLP1021

Sonata a preghière "Moses Fantasia" (on the aria "Dal tuo stellato soglio"
from Rossini's opera "Mosè in Egitto") Op. 24 (1818 or 1819) vln &
orch.
with A. Holeček pf   Suprahon SUA10465,
                                     SUAST50465, SV8091

RAVEL

Pièce en forme d'Habanera v & pf – arr. vln & pf Catherine
with G. Moore pf   OEA 14712–1   HMV B10135

Pièce en forme d'Habanera v & pf – arr. vln & pf Catherine
with A. Holeček pf   Supraphon SUA10465,
                                     SUAST50465, SV8091

Tzigane (Rapsodie de concert) (1924) vln & pf or orch.
with I. Newton pf   AR 5893/4–1   Decca K1013

Tzigane (Rapsodie de concert) (1924) vln & pf or orch.
with Czech Philharmonic Orch. –   Classic 990003
Ančerl   Parliament PLP620, PLPS620
                                     Supraphon SUA10615,
                                     SUAST50615, SV8195

* Omitting Intermezzo.

SAINT-SAËNS

Introduction & Rondo Capriccioso, Op. 28 vln & orch.
             AR 9368–1 & 9369–3   Decca K1171
with National Symphony Orch. –
Cameron

SARASATE

Carmen Fantasia (on themes from the opera by Bizet) Op. 25 vln & pf or
orch.
    DR 5978/9–1, 5980–2 & 5981–1   Decca M501/2, Y5837/8
with A. Kotowska pf

(8) Danzas españolas vln & pf
No. 6. Zapateado, Op. 23, No. 2
with A. Kotowska pf   DR 4945–II   Decca F7727

Zigeunerweisen, Op. 20 vln & pf or orch.
             AR 4952–1 & 4953–2   Decca K940
with A. Kotowska pf

Zigeunerweisen, Op. 20 vln & pf or orch.
             AR 11381–1 & 11382–2   Decca K1842
with I. Newton pf   London T5368

Zigeunerweisen, Op. 20 vln & pf or orch.
with A. Holeček pf   Supraphon SUA10465,
                                     SUAST50465, SV8091

SCHUBERT

(7) Gesänge (set to Scott's "Lady of the Lake") Op. 52 v & pf
No. 6. Ave Maria, D839 arr. vln & pf Wilhelmj
with G. Moore pf   2EA 14708–1   HMV C3994
                                     Victor (in set WBC1013),
                                     LBC1013

No. 6. Ave Maria, D839 arr. vln & pf Wilhelmj
with V. Yampolsky pf   Mezhdunarodnaya Kniga
                                     D07288

Rosamunde von Cypern, Op. 26 (D797) (1823) – Incidental music orch.
No. 9. Ballet music II, in G arr. vln & pf Kreisler
with A. Kotowska pf   AR 6775–4   Decca K1075

(3) Sonatinas, Op. 137 (D384, D385 & D408) vln & pf
Sonatina No. 3, in g, D408
             AR 6224/5–4 & 6226–6   Decca K1074/5
with A. Kotowska pf

STRAVINSKY

Divertissement vln & pf
with I. Newton pf   Decca K1930/2

Divertissement vln & pf
with A. Holeček pf   Supraphon SUF20036

Pétrouchka (1911) – ballet orch.
Danse russe arr. vln & pf 1933 Dushkin & Stravinsky
with I. Newton pf   Decca K1932

Danse russe arr. vln & pf 1933 Dushkin & Stravinsky
with G. Moore pf   HMV CLP1021

Danse russe arr. vln & pf 1933 Dushkin & Stravinsky
with V. Yampolsky pf   Mezhdunarodnaya Kniga
                                     D07288

SZYMANOWSKI

King Roger, Op. 46 (1926) – opera
Chant de Roxane arr. vln & pf Kochański
with A. Kotowska pf   AR 10113–1   Decca K1214

SZYMANOWSKI – *Continued*

Notturno & Tarantella, Op. 28 vln & pf
  with A. Kotowska   AR 10767/8–1   Decca K1651
  pf   London T5461

TARTINI

(12) Sonatas, Op. 5 vln & c
  Sonata No. 3, in B flat: Presto arr. vln & pf Bridgewater
  with G. Moore pf   HMV CLP1021, 7EP7011,
                                       7EPQ525

(12) Sonatas, Op. 7 vln & c
  Sonata No. 5, in g: Andante arr. vln & pf Bridgewater
  with G. Moore pf   HMV CLP1021, 7EP7011,
                                       7EPQ525

Sonata in g "Il Trillo del Diavolo" vln & c – arr. vln & pf Kreisler
  with A. Holeček pf   Supraphon SUA10465,
                                       SUAST50465, SV8091

TCHAIKOVSKY

Concerto in D, Op. 35 vln & orch.
       AR 9356–3, 9357–2, 9358–4,   Decca K1444/7
  9359/60–2, 9361–3 & 9362/3–2
  with National Symphony Orch. –
  Cameron

Concerto in D, Op. 35 vln & orch.
  with Royal Philharmonic Orch. –   HMV DLP1190
  Goossens

WIENIAWSKI

Concerto No. 2, in d, Op. 22 vln & orch.
  with Prague Symphony Orch. –   Supraphon SUA10687,
  Smetacek   SUAST50687, SV8295

Polonaise brillante No. 1, in D, Op. 4 vln & pf
  with G. Moore pf   2EA 13272–1   HMV C3818

Polonaise brillante No. 2, in A, Op. 21 vln & pf
             AR 10111–1 & 10112–3   Decca K1213
  with A. Kotowska pf

Scherzo–Tarantelle, Op. 16 vln & pf
  with A. Kotowska pf   AR 6228–4   Decca K1047

Scherzo–Tarantelle, Op. 16 vln & pf
  with A. Holeček pf   Supraphon SUA10465,
                                       SUAST50465, SV8091

Sophie HAGEMANN

HALACZINSKY

Canzoni da sonas, Op. 39 (1968) vln & pf
  with E. Gröschel pf   Colosseum MST608

(7) Stücke vln & pf
  with E. Gröschel pf   Colosseum MST608

HEILMANN

Sonata No. 1 vln & pf
  with E. Gröschel pf   Colosseum MST608

JARNACH

(3) Rhapsodies, Op. 20 (1927) vln & pf
  with E. Gröschel pf   Colosseum M603

KLEBE

Sonata, Op. 14 vln & pf
  with E. Gröschel pf   Colosseum M603

SCHIBLER

Danses concertantes, Op. 38 vln & pf
  with E. Gröschel pf   Colosseum M603

SCHOENBERG

Fantasy, Op. 47 (1949) vln & pf
  with E. Gröschel pf   Colosseum M603

SIMBRIGER

Sonata, Op. 110 (1965) vln & pf
  with E. Gröschel pf   Colosseum MST608

WEBERN

(4) Pieces, Op. 7 (1910) vln & pf
  with E. Gröschel pf   Colosseum M603

Betty–Jean HAGEN (1930–   )

BEETHOVEN

(3) Sonatas, Op. 12 vln & pf
  No. 2. Sonata No. 2, in A
  with J. Newmark pf   CBC Transcription Program 245

BRAHMS

(21) Hungarian Dances pf duet
  Hungarian dance No. 2, in d arr. vln & pf Joachim
  with J. Newmark pf   CBC Transcription Program 245
  Hungarian dance No. 3, in F arr. vln & pf Joachim
  with J. Newmark pf   Ace of Diamonds SDD2157
                                       CBC Transcription Program 245
  Hungarian dance No. 6, in D flat arr. vln & pf Joachim
  with L. Barkin pf   CBC Radio Canada SM82
  Hungarian dance No. 7, in A arr. vln & pf Joachim
  with J. Newmark pf   Ace of Diamonds SDD2157
                                       CBC Transcription Program 245
  Hungarian dance No. 8, in a arr. vln & pf Joachim
  with J. Newmark pf   Ace of Diamonds SDD2157
                                       CBC Transcription Program 245

Sonata No. 3, in d, Op. 108 vln & pf
  with L. Barkin pf   CBC Transcription Program 195

MOZART

Serenade No. 7, in D, K250 "Haffner" orch.
  Rondo (4th mvt) arr. vln & pf Kreisler
  with L. Barkin pf   CBC Transcription Program 195

PAPINEAU–COUTURE

Aria (1946) solo vln
  (unaccompanied)   CBC Transcription Program 245

SCHUBERT

Sonata in A, Op. 162 (D574) "Duo" vln & pf
  with L. Barkin pf   Ace of Diamonds SDD2157
                                       CBC Radio Canada SM82

SCHUMANN

Sonata No. 1, in a, Op. 105 vln & pf
   with L. Barkin pf   Ace of Diamonds SDD2157
                                      CBC Radio Canada SM82

SZYMANOWSKI

Notturno & Tarantelle, Op. 28 vln & pf
   with J. Newmark pf   CBC Transcription Program 245

Frederick W. HAGER (1841–1927)*

ANONYMOUS

Gypsy dance unid – arr. vln & pf
   with piano   Edison cylinder 6702

Irish medley unid – arr. vln & pf
   with piano   Edison cylinder 6704

BEETHOVEN

(2) Sonatas, Op. 27 pf
   No. 2. Sonata No. 14, in c sharp: Adagio sostenuto (2nd mvt)
   "Moonlight" arr. vln & pf
   with piano   Edison cylinder 7208

BÉRIOT

Concerto No. 2, in b, Op. 32 vln & orch.
   Andante (2nd mvt)
   with piano   Edison cylinder 7194
Scène de Ballet (Fantaisie–ballet No. 1) Op. 100 vln & orch.
   with piano   Edison cylinder 6708

GODARD

Contemplation in F, Op. 4, No. 28 v & pf – arr. vln & pf
   with piano   Edison cylinder 7209

GOUNOD

Ave Maria (Méditation on Bach's "Prelude No. 1, in C" from Book I of
   "Das Wohltemperirte Clavier") v & pf – arr. vln & pf
   with piano   Edison cylinder 6701

HELF

(A) Picture no artist can paint (1899) v & pf – arr. vln & pf
   with piano   Edison cylinder 7528

MASCAGNI

Cavalleria Rusticana (1890) – opera
   Intermezzo orch. – arr. vln & pf
   with piano   Edison cylinder 6703

MENDELSSOHN

(6) Songs without words, Op. 62 pf
   No. 6. Song without words No. 30, in A "Spring song" arr. vln & pf
   with piano   Edison cylinder 7195

RUBINSTEIN

(2) Melodies, Op. 3 pf
   No. 1. Melody in F arr. vln & pf Wilhelmj
   with piano   Edison cylinder 6706

* Pseudonym for Wallace Fredericks.

SCHUBERT

(14) Schwanengesang, D957 (1828) v & pf
   No. 4. Ständchen "Serenade" arr. vln & pf
   with piano   Edison cylinder 7192

SCHUMANN

(13) Kinderscenen, Op. 15 pf
   No. 7. Träumerei arr. vln & pf
   with piano   Edison cylinder 6707

SCOTT, Lady John

Annie Laurie (1838) v & pf – arr. vln & pf
   with piano   Edison cylinder 6700

WINNER

(The) Mocking bird vln & orch.
   with orch.   Edison cylinder 6705

P. HAIKALA

RIMSKY–KORSAKOV

Sadko (1898) – opera
   Chant hindou arr. vln & pf Kreisler
   with piano   Polydor 26098

Mieczyslaw HALIK (1902–)

WIENIAWSKI

Concerto No. 2, in d, Op. 22 vln & orch.
   Romance (2nd mvt)
   with Symphony Orch. – Straszynski   Muza 1435

Bernard HALL

BRAGA

(7) Melodies (1867) v & pf
   No. 5. La serenata "Angel's serenade" arr. vln & pf
   with piano   Diamond 050

ELGAR

Salut d'amour, Op. 12 orch. – arr. vln & pf Elgar
   with piano   Diamond 0191

KREISLER

Schön Rosmarin vln & pf
   with piano   Diamond 015

MASCAGNI

Cavalleria Rusticana (1890) – opera
   Intermezzo orch. – arr. vln & pf
   with piano   Diamond 0191

MASSENET

Thaïs (1894) – opera
   Méditation arr. vln & pf Marsick
   with piano   Diamond 015

MILES

Idyll vln & pf
   with piano   Diamond 050

MENDELSSOHN

(6) Songs without words, Op. 62 pf
No. 6. Song without words No. 30, in A "Spring song" arr. vln & pf Kreisler
with piano   Diamond 0190

TCHAIKOVSKY

(3) Souvenirs de Hapsal Op. 2 pf
No. 3. Chant sans paroles arr. vln & pf Kreisler
with piano   Diamond 0190

Marie HALL (1884–1947)

d'AMBROSIO

Canzonetta, Op. 6 vln & pf
with piano   Gramophone & Typewriter 7996
           HMV 3–7974, E15

Romance in D, Op. 9 vln & pf
with piano   HMV 2–07938, D78

Serenade, Op. 4 vln & pf
with piano   HMV 4–7935, E15

de ANGELIS

Gigue, Op. 2 vln & pf
with piano   Gramophone & Typewriter
           07903
           HMV 07973

ANONYMOUS

(A) Borée traditional – arr. vln & pf Moffat
with piano   HMV E2

AULIN

(4) Aquarelles vln & pf
No. 2. Humoresque
with piano   HO 2961 ae   HMV 4–7924, E17

BACH

(3) Sonatas & 3 Partitas, BWV1001/6 solo vln
Partita No. 3, in E: Gavotte (3rd mvt) BWV1006
(unaccompanied)   Ak 17707 e HMV 3–7971, E16

BEETHOVEN

(6) Minuets, G167 pf
No. 2. Minuet No. 2, in G arr. vln & pf Burmester
with piano   Bb 4241^I HMV 3–7945, E18

CUI

(12) Miniatures, Op. 20 pf
No. 8. Berceuse arr. vln & pf Carse
with piano   HMV E2

DVOŘÁK

(8) Humoresques, Op. 101 pf
No. 7. Humoresque No. 7, in G flat arr. vln & pf "in G" Wilhelmj
with piano   6404 b Gramophone & Typewriter 7988
No. 7. Humoresque No. 7, in G flat arr. vln & pf "in G" Wilhelmj
with piano   HO 2096 ab   HMV 4–7931, E16
No. 7. Humoresque No. 7, in G flat arr. vln & pf "in G" Wilhelmj
with piano   Gramophone & Typewriter
          07905
          HMV 07975

ELGAR

Concerto in b, Op. 61 vln & orch.*
with Symphony   HO 2408/12 af HMV 2–07942/5, D79/80
Orch. – Elgar   Pearl GEM112

FIOCCO

Suite No. 1, in G hpsi
Allegro (10th mvt) arr. vln & pf Bent & O'Neill
with piano   HMV 3–7947

GOOSSENS

Old Chinese folksong, Op. 4, No. 1 vln & pf
with piano   Bb 4236^{III}   HMV 6–7937, E348

HANDEL

Bourrée unid – arr. vln & pf Schmidt
with piano   z 6490 f Gramophone & Typewriter
          07904
          HMV 07974, D76
          Pearl GEM102

HOLST

Valse–Étude vln & pf
with piano   Bb 4237^I   HMV 6–7938, E348

KREISLER

Minuet (Porpora) vln & pf
with piano   HMV 3–7950

(La) Précieuse (L. Couperin) vln & pf
with piano   Bb 4299^I   HMV 3–7973, E18

LECLAIR

(12) Sonatas, Op. 9 – Book IV (1738) vln & c
Sonata No. 3, in D: Sarabande (1st mvt); **Tambourin** (3rd mvt) arr. vln & pf Sarasate
with piano   HMV 2–07953, D78

MENDELSSOHN

Concerto in e, Op. 64 vln & orch.
Allegretto non troppo; Allegro molto vivace (3rd mvt)
with piano   6408 b Gramophone & Typewriter 7990,
           47977

Concerto in e, Op. 64 vln & orch.
Allegretto non troppo; Allegro molto vivace (3rd mvt)
with piano   438 c Gramophone & Typewriter
          07903
          Pearl GEM102

MOZART

Divertimento No. 17, in D, K334 2 hrns & strs
Minuet (3rd mvt) arr. vln & pf Burmester
with piano   6405 b Gramophone & Typewriter 7991,
          37951, 47969

PAGANINI

Moto perpetuo (Allegro di concert) Op. 11 (1830) vln & orch.
with piano   Al 7960 f HMV 2–07916, D77
          Rococo 2001

*Abridged.

RAFF

(6) Pieces, Op. 85 vln & pf
  No. 3. Cavatina in D
    with piano   z 6489 f   Gramophone & Typewriter
                                      07902
                                        HMV 07972, D77
                                        Pearl GEM102

RIES

Suite No. 3, in G, Op. 34 vln & pf
  No. 5. Perpetuum mobile
    with piano   6407 b   Gramophone & Typewriter 7989,
                                          47976

SAINT-SAËNS

(Le) Carnaval des animaux (1886) small orch.
  Le cygne arr. vln & pf
    with piano   5135   Gramophone & Typewriter 7962,
                                          47968

  Le cygne arr. vln & pf
    with piano   HO 2092 ab   HMV 3-7972, E17

SARASATE

Jota aragonesa, Op. 27 vln & pf
  with piano   HMV 2-07953, D76

SCHUBERT, François

(12) Bagatelles, Op. 13 vln & pf
  No. 9. L'abeille
    with piano   z 6490 f   Gramophone & Typewriter
                                          07904
                                          HMV 07974, D76

SCHUBERT, Franz

(6) Moments musicaux, Op. 94 (D780) (1823/7) pf
  No. 3. Moment musicale No. 3, in f "Air russe" arr. vln & pf Auer
    with piano   Gramophone & Typewriter
                                          07903

SINDING

(2) Romances, Op. 79 vln & pf
  No. 1. Romance No. 1
    with piano   Bb 4227[I]   HMV E340

SINIGAGLIA

(4) Kleine Stücke, Op. 25 vln & pf
  No. 2. Capriccio all'antica
    with piano   Bb 4233[III]   HMV E340

Leif Fritjof HALVORSEN (1887–)

GRIEG

(2) Élégiac mélodies, Op. 34 str orch.
  No. 2. Spring arr. vln & pf
    with piano   HMV X2201
Peer Gynt (Suite No. 2) Op. 55 orch.
  No. 4. Solveig's song arr. vln & pf Sitt
    with piano   HMV X2202

HALVORSEN

(3) Danses norvègiennes (1914)
  Danse norvègienne No. 1, in D
    with piano   HMV X2201

HALVORSEN – *Continued*

  Danse norvègienne No. 2, in A
    with piano   HMV X2202

Bernhard HAMANN (1909–)

BACH

(6) Brandenburg Concerti, BWV1046/51 (1721) strs & c
  Brandenburg Concerto No. 1, in F, BWV1046 vln, 3 obs, bsn, 2 hrns &
  strs (playing violino piccolo)
    with Hamburg Chamber Orch. –   Pathé DMX105
    Schüchter

  Brandenburg Concerto No. 2, in F, BWV1047 tpt, fl, ob, vln & strs
    with A. Scherbaum tpt, G. Otto fl, H.   Pathé DMX105, EMD10059
    Eggers ob & Hamburg Chamber Orch.
    – Schüchter

  Brandenburg Concerto No. 4, in G, BWV1049 vln, 2 fls & strs
    with F. Conrad fl, H-M. Linde fl &   Pathé DMX106
    Hamburg Chamber Orch. – Schüchter

  Brandenburg Concerto No. 5, in D BWV1050, clav, fl, vln & strs
    with H. Bernstein hpsi, G. Otto fl &   Pathé DMX106
    Hamburg Chamber Orch. – Schüchter

Concerto in d, BWV1043 2 vlns, strs & c
  with M. Kayser vln & North West   HMV QFLP4078
  German Philharmonic Orch. –
  Schüchter

CORELLI

(12) Concerti grossi, Op. 6 orch.
  Concerto grosso No. 8, in g "Christmas Concerto"
    with M. Kayser vln, S. Palm vlc &   Electrola I 41399, J60277
    North West German Philharmonic   Imperial ILP132, IPE1027
    Orch. – Schüchter

JARNACH

Musik zum Gedächtnis der Einsamen (1952) 2 vlns, vla & vlc
  with F. Köhnsen vln, F. Lang vla & S.   Deutsche Grammophon 603,
  Palm vlc   LPM18403

HAMOWETSKAYA

GODARD

Jocelyn (1888) – opera
  Cachés dans cet asile "Berceuse" arr. v, vln & pf
    with M.A. Michailova s &   28491   Gramophone & Typewriter
    piano   23476
                                          Victor 61139

GOUNOD

Ave Maria (Méditation on Bach's "Prelude No. 1, in C" from Book I of
  "Das Wohltemperirte clavier") v & pf – arr. v, vln & pf
    with M.A. Michailova s & piano   Gramophone & Typewriter
                                          23477
                                          HMV 2-43068
                                          Victor 61131, 790

Charlotte HAMPE (1910–)

BACH

Concerto in d, BWV1043 2 vlns, strs & c

    2RA 2960^V ☐, 2961^{IV} ☐ &   HMV EH1217/8

with H. Diener vln &   2962/3^{II} ☐

Collegium Musicum Orch. – Diener

Gheorghe HAMZA

CAPOIANU

Concerto (1957) vln & orch.

  with Radiotelevision Symphony Orch.   Electrecord ECE0224

  – Elenescu

KREISLER

Sicilienne et Rigaudon (Francoeur) vln & pf

  with M. Kapdebo pf   Electrecord ECC732

POLDINI

(7) Marionnettes pf

  No. 2. Poupée valsante arr. vln & pf Kreisler

  with M. Kapdebo pf   Electrecord ECC732

SCARLATESCU

Bagatelle (in Rumanian style) vln & pf

  with M. Kapdebo pf

    Electrecord ECC732

SCHUBERT

Quartet No. 14, in d, D810 "Death & the maiden" 2 vlns, vla & vlc

  with C. Costache vln, C. Buicâ vla &   Electrecord ECE0260

  R. Sladek vlc

SCHUMANN

(3) Romances, Op. 94 ob or vlc, or vln or cl & pf

  Romance No. 2, in A arr. vln & pf Kreisler

  with M. Kapdebo pf

    Electrecord ECC732

Winnifred HANKE

BEETHOVEN

Mass in D, Op. 123 "Missa Solemnis"

  with Bruno Kittel Choir & Berlin   Brunswick 90020/30

  Philharmonic Orch. – Kittel   Decca CA8069/79

SCHUBERT

Quintet in A, Op. 114 (D667) "Trout" pf, vln, vla, vlc & cbs

  with A. Aeschbacher pf, F. Lang vla,   Polydor 68012/6

  B. Günther vlc & L. Wilhelm cbs

VIVALDI

(12) Concerti, Op. 3 "L'Estro armonico" var. cbns & strs

  Concerto No. 10, in b: Largo (2nd mvt) P.148 (F.IV, No. 10) 4 vlns, strs & c

  with M. van der Berg vln, S. Frenkel   Telefunken SK1318, TF52

  vln, R. Totenberg vln, hpsi & Berlin

  Philharmonic Orch. – Unger

Arvo HANNIKAINEN (1897–1942)

HANNIKAINEN

Spring wagon vln & pf

  with piano   HMV X3133

    Victor V4083

MERIKANTO

Valse lente pf – arr. vln & pf Hannikanen

  with piano   HMV X3133

    Victor V4083

PALMGREN

(7) Compositions, Op. 78 vln & pf

  No. 5. Finnish romance

  with piano   HMV X3133

    Victor V4083

Karel HANOUSEK (1902–)

HANOUSEK

Capriccietto vln & pf

  with V. Trojan pf   41436*   Supraphon A22712

Valse–Caprice vln & pf

  with V. Trojan pf   41437   Supraphon A22712

Cecilia HANSEN (1898–)

ARENSKY

(4) Morceaux, Op. 30 vln & pf

  No. 2. Serenade in g arr. Elman

  with B. Zakharoff pf   HMV DA764

BRAHMS

(21) Hungarian Dances pf duet

  Hungarian Dance No. 4, in f arr. vln & pf "in b" Auer

  with B. Zakharoff pf   HMV DB742

    Victor 74877, 6447

CUI

(12) Miniatures, Op. 20 pf

  No. 8. Berceuse arr. vln & pf Carse

  with B. Zakharoff pf   HMV DA657

    Victor 1035

HUBAY

(14) Scènes de la Csárda vln & pf

  No. 4. Hejre Kati, Op. 32

  with B. Zakharoff pf   HMV DB906

    Victor 6550

JÄRNEFELT

Berceuse in g orch. – arr. vln & pf

  with B. Zakharoff pf   HMV DA657

    Victor 1035

* Label differs from above matrix. It reads 41584.

VIEUXTEMPS

(3) Salonstücke, Op. 32 vln & pf
No. 2. Rondino
with B. Zakharoff pf   HMV DB742
                                    Victor 74878, 6447

WEBER

Ländlichen Tanz (unid) arr. vln & pf
with B. Zakharoff pf   HMV DA764

WIENIAWSKI

Mazurka in a, Op. 3 "Kujawiak" vln & pf
with B. Zakharoff pf   HMV DB906
                                    Victor 6550

(2) Mazurkas, Op. 19 vln & pf
No. 1. Mazurka No. 1, in G "Obertass"
with B. Zakharoff pf   HMV DA764

Leo HANSEN (1911–)

BACH

(6) Brandenburg Concerti, BWV1046/51 (1721) strs & c
Brandenburg Concerto No. 1, in F, BWV1046 vln, 3 obs, bsn, 2 hrns & strs
with W. Wolsing   2CS2952/6¹☐   HMV DB20140/2
ob, I. Michelsen hrn K.E. Olsen hrn &
Danish State Radio Chamber Orch. –
Wöldike

Brandenburg Concerto No. 2, in F, BWV1047 tpt, fl, ob, vln & strs
            2CS 2908/10–2A & 2911–3A   HMV C7848/9
with K. Hovaldt tpt, P. Birkelund fl,   Victor LHMV1048
W. Wolsing ob, A. Medici vlc, S.
Sorensen hpsi & Danish State Radio
Chamber Orch. – Wöldike

Brandenburg Concerto No. 4, in G BWV1049 vln, 2 fls & strs
            2CS 2718/9–4, 2720–4, 2721–6 &   HMV C4073/5, DB20109/11
with P. Birkelund fl,   2722–4   Victor LHMV1048
J. Bentzon fl, H. Kopple hpsi, &
Danish State Radio Chamber Orch. –
Wöldike

Brandenburg Concerto No. 5, in D, BWV1050 clav, fl, vln & strs
            2CS 2819–2, 2820–3, 2821/2–2,   HMV DB20118/20
with H. Koppel   2823–3 & 2824–2   Victor LHMV1048
hpsi, P. Birkelund fl & Danish State
Radio Chamber Orch. – Wöldike

BEETHOVEN

Septet in E flat, Op. 20 cl, hrn, bsn, vln, vla, vlc & cbs
            PCX 1315/6–1 & 1317/24–2   Columbia LDX7006/10
with P.A. Erichsen cl, I. Michelsen
hrn, C. Bloch bsn, G. Frederiksen vla,
V. Norup vlc & E. Hansen cbs

BUXTEHUDE

Wenn ich, Herr Jesu, habe dich – Cantata a, vln & c
with V. Garde a, N.   2CS 2647–1   HMV Z335
Borre vln, A. Medici vlc & M.
Wöldike hpsi

CORELLI

(12) Sonatas Op. 3 2 vlns & c
Sonata No. 7, in e
with C. Senderovitz vln, V. Norup vlc   Haydn Society HSLP2073
& M. Wöldike org

GRIEG

Sonata No. 2, in G, Op. 13 vln & pf
with F. Jensen pf   Columbia LDX7011/3

HAYDN

Sinfonia concertante in B flat, Op. 84 (H.I, No. 105) vln, vlc, ob, bsn & orch.
            2CS 2914/6–2A & 2918/9–3A   HMV C4122/4, C7876/8,
with A. Medici vlc, W. Wolsing ob, C.   DB20134/6
Bloch bsn & Danish State Radio
Chamber Orch. – Busch

LUMBYE

Concert–polka (1863) 2 vlns & orch.
with L. Preil vln & Copenhagen Radio   Odeon D6429
Orch. – Hammelboe

SCHÜTZ

(21) Symphoniae Sacrae, Op. 12 (1650)
Concerto No. 5 (O Herr, hilf) a, s, t, vln & c
with V. Garde a, E. Brems s,   Haydn Society HSL2072,
A. Schiøtz t, C. Senderovitz vln, V.   HS9038
Norup vlc & M. Wöldike org   Metronome MCEP3055

TARP

Serenade, Op. 28b fl, vln, vla & vlc
with E. Thomsen fl, G. Frederiksen vla   Tono A122
& L. Jensen vlc

Marius HANSEN

GRIEG

Peer Gynt (Suite No. 2) Op. 55 orch.
No. 4. Solveig's song arr. vln & pf Sitt
with piano   144484   Odeon 689A

HENRIQUES

(4) Songs Op. 3 v & pf
No. 4. Agnetes Vuggevise arr. vln & pf Henriques
with piano   144464   Odeon 689A

MOZART

Divertimento No. 17, in D, K334 2 hrns & strs
Minuet (3rd mvt) arr. vln & pf Burmester
with piano   144465   Odeon 676A

SARASATE

Zigeunerweisen, Op. 20 vln & pf or orch.
with piano   144486   Odeon 676A

SCHUMANN

(12) Duets, Op. 85 pf – 4 hands
No. 12. Abendlied arr. vln & pf Wilhelmj
with piano   144485   Odeon 624A

WIENIAWSKI

Légende, Op. 17 vln & pf or orch.
with piano   144483   Odeon 624A

Werner HANSEN

BACH

Concerto in d, BWV1043 2 vlns, strs & c
with H. Diercks vln & Hamburg   Classics Club X3018
Chamber Orch. – Walther

Rosemary HARBISON

WOLPE

Pieces (in 2 parts) solo vln
(unaccompanied)   Acoustic Research AR5

Alice HARNONCOURT

BACH

(6) Brandenburg Concerti, BWV1046/51 (1721) strs & c
Brandenburg Concerto No. 1, in F, BWV1046 3 obs, vln, bsn, 2 hrns & strs
with J. Schaeftlein ob, K. Gruber ob,   Telefunken SAWT9459
B. Klebel ob, O. Fleischmann bsn H.
Rohrer hrn, H. Fischer hrn, G. Fischer
hpsi & Concentus Musicus, Wien – N.
Harnoncourt

Brandenburg Concerto No. 2, in F, BWV1047 tpt, fl, ob, vln & strs
with W. Holy tpt, L. Stastny rec, J.   Telefunken SAWT9460
Schaeftlein ob, N. Harnoncourt vlc, G.
Fischer hpsi & Concentus Musicus,
Wien – N. Harnoncourt

Brandenburg Concerto No. 4, in G, BWV1049 vln, 2 fls & strs
with J. Schaeftlein rec, L. Stastny rec,   Telefunken SAWT9449
G. Fischer hpsi & Concentus Musicus,
Wien – N. Harnoncourt

Brandenburg Concerto No. 5, in D, BWV1050 clav, fl, vln & strs
with G. Fischer hpsi, L. Stastny rec &   Telefunken SAWT9460
Concentus Musicus, Wien – N.
Harnoncourt

Concerto No. 1, in a, BWV1041 vln, strs & c
with Concentus Musicus, Wien – N.   Telefunken SAWT9508
Harnoncourt

Concerto No. 2, in E, BWV1042 vln, strs & c
with Concentus Musicus, Wien – N.   Telefunken SAWT9508
Harnoncourt

Concerto in d, BWV1043 2 vlns, strs & c
with W. Pfeiffer vln & Concentus   Telefunken SAWT9508
Musicus, Wien – N. Harnoncourt

Concerto in D, BWV1045 vln, tpts, strs & c
with Vienna Concentus Musicus – N.   Telefunken SAWT9557
Harnoncourt

Concerto in c, BWV1060 vln & ob or 2 vlns, strs & c
with J. Schaeftlein ob & Vienna   Telefunken SAWT9557
Concentus Musicus – N. Harnoncourt

BACH – Continued

(Ein) Musikalisches Opfer, BWV1079 strs
with L. von Pfersmann fl, R.   Philips A00300L
Baumgartner vln, K. Theimer vln &
vla, N. Harnoncourt vlc & I.
Ahlgrimm hpsi

BIBER

(7) Partitas "Harmonia artificiosa–ariosa" 2 vlns & c
Partita No. 1, in d
with W. Pfeiffer vln, N. Harnoncourt   Amadeo AVRS6413
gamba & H. Tachezi hpsi   Musical Heritage Society
                                MHS1092

Partita No. 3, in a
with W. Pfeiffer vln, N. Harnoncourt   Amadeo AVRS6413
gamba & H. Tachezi hpsi   Musical Heritage Society
                                MHS1092

Partita No. 5, in g
with W. Pfeiffer vln, N. Harnoncourt   Amadeo AVRS6413
gamba & H. Tachezi hpsi   Musical Heritage Society
                                MHS1092

Partita No. 6, in D
with W. Pfeiffer vln, N. Harnoncourt   Amadeo AVRS6413
gamba & H. Tachezi hpsi   Musical Heritage Society
                                MHS1092

HANDEL

(9) Sonatas, Op. 2 (1724) 2 vlns or obs & c
Sonata No. 1B, in b fl, vln & c
with F. Brüggen fl, H. Tachezi hpsi &   Telefunken SAWT9559
N. Harnoncourt vlc

Sonata No. 3, in F* 2 vlns & c
with W. Pfeiffer vln, H. Tachezi hpsi   Telefunken SAWT9559
& N. Harnoncourt vlc

Sonata No. 5, in F rec, vln & c
with F. Brüggen rec, H. Tachezi hpsi   Telefunken SAWT9559
& N. Harnoncourt vlc

Sonata in d ob, vln & c
with J. Schaeftlein ob, H. Tachezi hpsi   Telefunken SAWT9559
& N. Harnoncourt vlc

MARAIS

Sonnerie de Sainte Geneviève du Mont de Paris (1723) vln, gamba & hpsi
with N. Harnoncourt gamba & H.   Musical Heritage Society
Tachezi hpsi   MHS964

MOZART

Sonata in F, K244 2 vlns & c
with W. Pfeiffer vln, H. Tachezi org &   Telefunken SAWT9555
N. Harnoncourt vlc

Sonata in C, K328 2 vlns & c
with W. Pfeiffer vln, H. Tachezi org &   Telefunken SAWT9555
N. Harnoncourt vlc

TELEMANN

Concerto in G 4 vlns & orch.
with W. Pfeiffer vln, P. Schuberwalter   Telefunken SAWT9483
vln, K. Theiner vln & Concentus
Musicus, Wien – N. Harnoncourt

* Listed as Op. 2, No. 2, in d.

TELEMANN – *Continued*

Suite in F "Konzertsuite" 2 hrns, 2 vlns & c
with H. Rohrer hrn, H. Fischer hrn,   Telefunken SAWT9483
W. Pfeiffer vln & Concentus Musicus,
Wien – N. Harnoncourt

Margaret HARRISON

BURLEIGH
Plantation sketches, Op. 36 vln & pf
with piano   Bb 18461[I]△   HMV B3475

CORELLI
(12) Sonatas, Op. 5 vln & c
Sonata No. 1, in D: Adagio (4th mvt) arr. pf, vln & vlc as "O Sanctissima" by Kreisler
with B. Harrison vlc   Bb 17330[I]△   HMV B3471
& piano

SMETANA
From my Homeland (1878) vln & pf
No. 2. Andantino
with piano   Bb 18462[IIA]△   HMV B3475

STRAUSS, R.
(4) Lieder, Op. 27 v & pf
No. 4. Morgen arr. pf, vln & vlc
with B. Harrison vlc   Bb 17331[II]△   HMV B3471
& piano

May HARRISON (1891–1959)

DELIUS
Sonata No. 1 (1892) vln & pf
          Cc 15823[IIA]△, 15824[II]△, 15825   HMV C1749/50
with A. Bax pf   [IV]△ & 15826[III]△

Sydney HARTH (1925–   )

BEN-HAIM
Sonata in G vln & pf
with A. Loesser pf   Iramac 6519
                            Musical Heritage Society
                            MHS1298

BLOCH
Baal Shem (3 Pictures of Chassidic life) (1923) vln & pf
No. 2. Nigun (Improvisation)
with H. Szperka pf   Muza XL0045, XL0386
No. 2. Nigun (Improvisation)
with S. Anschütz pf   Iramac 6523

BRAHMS
Sonata No. 1, in G, Op. 78 vln & pf
with A. Loesser pf   Iramac 6519
                            Musical Heritage Society
                            MHS1297

BRAHMS – *Continued*
Sonata No. 3, in d, Op. 108 vln & pf
with A. Loesser pf   Iramac 6518
                            Musical Heritage Society
                            MHS1297

CHOPIN
Nocturne No. 20 in c sharp, Op. posth pf – arr. vln & pf Milstein
with S. Anschütz pf   Iramac 6523

ELWELL
Concert Suite (1957) vln & orch.
with Louisville Orch. – Whitney   Louisville LOU593

FAURÉ
Sonata No. 1, in A, Op. 13 vln & pf
with A. Loesser pf   Iramac 6523

FAWICK
Musicale (1969) 2 vlns*
with T. Testa vln   143583   Pride

GLUCK
Orphée et Eurydice (1762) – opera
Dance of the blessed spirits: Lento "Mélodie" (No. 2) arr. vln & pf Kreisler
with H. Szperka pf   Muza XL0045

KREISLER
Recitative & Scherzo–caprice, Op. 6 solo vln
(unaccompanied)   Iramac 6518
                         Musical Heritage Society
                         MHS1298

MOZART
Adagio in E, K261 vln & orch.
with H. Szperka pf   Muza XL0045, XL0386

NOVÁČEK
(8) Concert Caprices, Op. 5 vln & pf
No. 4. Perpetuum mobile
with H. Szperka pf   Muza XL0045

PAGANINI
(6) Sonatas, Op. 3 (1801/6) vln & gtr
No. 6. Sonata No. 12, in e
with H. Szperka pf   Muza XL0045

RIEGGER
Variations, Op. 71 (1959) vln & orch.
with Louisville Orch. – Whitney   Louisville LOU601

RIMSKY-KORSAKOV
Scheherazade, Op. 35 (1888) orch.
with Chicago Symphony Orch. –   Victor LM2446, LSC2446,
Reiner   VICS1480

* Variously scored for solo vln, vln & pf, 2 vlns.,

ROSENBERG

Concerto (1955) "Louisville" vln & orch.
　with G. Whitney pf, V. Schneider vla　Louisville LOU561
　& Louisville Orch. – Whitney

RUBBRA

Improvisation, Op. 89 (1955) vln & orch.
　with Louisville Orch. – Whitney　　Louisville LOU576

SCHUBERT

Sonata in A, Op. 162 (D574) "Duo" vln & pf
　with A. Loesser pf　　　　　Iramac 6518
　　　　　　　　　　　　　　Musical Heritage Society
　　　　　　　　　　　　　　MHS1298

(3) Sonatinas, Op. 137 (D384, D385 & D408) vln & pf
　Sonatina No. 1, in D, D384
　　with D. Handman pf　　　Guilde Internationale du Disque
　　　　　　　　　　　　　SMS2651

　Sonatina No. 2, in a, D385
　　with D. Handman pf　　　Guilde Internationale du Disque
　　　　　　　　　　　　　SMS2651

　Sonatina No. 3, in g, D408
　　with D. Handman pf　　　Guilde Internationale du Disque
　　　　　　　　　　　　　SMS2651

TELEMANN

(6) Sonatas, Op. 2 (1727) "Duets" 2 fls or vlns
　Sonata No. 1, in G "Canonic"
　　with T. Testa vln　　　　Allegro ALG3039
　Sonata No. 2, in b
　　with T. Testa vln　　　　Allegro ALG3039
　Sonata No. 4, in b
　　with T. Testa vln　　　　Allegro ALG3039
　Sonata No. 6, in E
　　with T. Testa vln　　　　Allegro ALG3039

YSAŸE

(6) Sonatas, Op. 27 solo vln
　Sonata No. 3, in d
　(unaccompanied)　　　　　Iramac 6523

Joseph HASSID (1924–1946)

ACHRON

Hebrew melody, Op. 33 vln & pf – arr. Auer
　with G. Moore pf　　2EA 9051[I]　HMV C3219

DVOŘÁK

(8) Humoresques, Op. 101 pf
　No. 7. Humoresque No. 7, in G flat arr. vln & pf "in G" Kreisler
　　with G. Moore pf　　2EA9052[I]　HMV C3219

ELGAR

(La) Capricieuse, Op. 17 vln & pf
　with G. Moore pf　　OEA 8803[I]　HMV B9074, EA3286

KREISLER

Caprice viennois, Op. 2 vln & pf
　with G. Moore pf　　2EA 8900[I]　HMV C3208

MASSENET

Thaïs (1894) – opera
　Méditation arr. vln & pf Marsick
　　with G. Moore pf　　　2EA 9053[I]　HMV C3208

SARASATE

(8) Danzas españolas vln & pf
　No. 5. Playera, Op. 23, No. 1
　　with G. Moore pf　　　2EA 8801[III]　HMV C3185
　No. 6. Zapateado, Op. 23, No. 2
　　with G. Moore pf　　　2EA 8802[I]　HMV C3185

TCHAIKOVSKY

Souvenir d'un lieu cher, Op. 42 vln & pf
　No. 3. Mélodie
　　with G. Moore pf　　　OEA 8550[I]　HMV B9074, EA3286

Gustav HAVEMANN (1882–1960)

BLEYLE

Quartet in a, Op. 37 (1925) 2 vlns, vla & vlc
　Cavatina; Scherzo
　　with W. Steiner vln, H. Mahlke vla &　Polydor 27285
　　A. Steiner vlc

JUON

Humoresque, Op. 72 vln & pf
　with piano　　　　　　　Parlophone P1657

(2) Violinstücke, Op. 52 vln & pf
　No. 2. Arva "Valse mignonne"
　　with piano　　　　　　　Parlophone P1657

REGER

(14) Lose Blätter, Op. 13 pf
　No. 5. Petite caprice in b flat arr. vln & pf "in g"
　　with K. Ruhrseitz pf　　　Parlophone P1577

(3) Pieces, Op. 79d vln & pf
　No. 1. Wiegenlied in G
　　with K. Ruhrseitz pf　　　Parlophone P1577

RIES

Suite No. 3, in G, Op. 34 vln & pf
　No. 3. Adagio
　　with K. Ruhrseitz pf　　　Parlophone P1584

SINIGAGLIA

Rapsodie piemontese, Op. 26 vln & pf
　with K. Ruhrseitz pf　　　Parlophone P1584

TCHAIKOVSKY

Souvenir d'un lieu cher, Op. 42 vln & pf
　No. 3. Mélodie
　　with K. Ruhrseitz pf　　　Parlophone P1577

A. Stroud HAXTON

BLAKE

I'm just wild about Harry (1921) v & pf – arr. vln, pf & effects
　with M. Darewski pf & sound effects　Zonophone 2292

di CAPUA

O sole mio v & pf – arr. vln & pf
with piano   L 02742 p[II]   Jumbo 189, A22017
                             Scala 1023

CONFREY

You tell 'em ivories pf – arr. vln, pf & effects
with M. Darewski pf & sound effects   Zonophone 2336

DAREWSKI, M.

I might have known v & pf – arr. vln, pf & effects
with M. Darewski pf & sound effects   Zonophone 2292

I want a girl to foxtrot v & pf – arr. vln, pf & effects
with M. Darewski pf & sound effects   Zonophone 2364

(The) Nine O'Clock Revue – revue
   Shadow man
   with M. Darewski pf &   yy 2399[1]   Zonophone 2317, X48084
   sound effects

Snowball song v & pf – arr. vln, pf & effects
with M. Darewski pf & sound effects   Zonophone 2336

That's the time v & pf – arr. vln, pf & effects
with M. Darewski pf & sound effects   Zonophone 2364

Ting–ling (Me lovee you) v & pf – arr. vln, pf & effects
with M. Darewski pf & sound effects   Zonophone 2304

DRDLA

Serenade No. 1, in A vln & pf
with piano   Pathé L55617

Souvenir vln & pf
with piano   Beka 767
                             Parlophone E5053

Souvenir vln & pf
with piano   Phoenix 0128

Souvenir vln & pf
with piano   Columbia 1113

Souvenir vln & pf
with piano   L 0335   Jumbo 157, A22042
                             Odeon 2230, A42938

ELGAR

Salut d'amour, Op. 12 orch. – arr. vln & pf Elgar
with piano   L 2741[2]   Jumbo 157, A22050
                             Odeon 2231, A42939

Salut d'amour, Op. 12 orch. – arr. vln & pf Elgar
with piano   Phoenix 019

GALLATLY

Fall o' day vln & pf
with piano   Beka 786

GILLET

Coeur Brisé pf – arr. vln & pf
with piano   Beka 739
                             Scala 395

GODARD

Jocelyn (1888) – opera
   Cachés dans cet asile "Berceuse" arr. vln & pf
   with piano   Columbia 1391
                             Regal G6220

GODARD – *Continued*

   Cachés dans cet asile "Berceuse" arr. vln & pf
   with piano   Phoenix 019

GOUNOD

Ave Maria (Méditation on Bach's "Prelude No. 1, in C" from Book I of "Das Wohltemperirte Clavier") v & pf – arr. vln & pf
with piano   26926   Columbia 1203, J163
                             Regal G6218

Ave Maria (Méditaion on Bach's "Prelude No. 1, in C" from Book I of "Das Wohltemperirte Clavier") v & pf – arr. vln & pf
with piano   Jumbo 72, A22006
                             Odeon 2228

GRIEG

Peer Gynt (Suite No. 2) Op. 55 orch.
   No. 4. Solveig's song arr. vln & pf Sitt
   with piano   Pathé K55616

d'HARDELOT

I know a lovely garden v & pf – arr. vln & pf
with piano   26670   Rena 1222

JOHNSON

Intermezzo (Marcella) v & pf – arr. vln & pf
with piano   Edison cylinder 3149

Intermezzo (Marcella) v & pf – arr. vln & pf
with piano   Zonophone 462, X47913

KERN

Ka–lu–a v & pf – arr. vln, pf & effects
with M. Darewski pf & sound effects   Zonophone 2304

LASSEN

(6) Lieder, Op. 85 v & pf
   No. 3. Allerseelen "All souls day" arr. vln & pf
   with piano   26669   Rena 1222

LOHR

Little grey home in the west (1911) v & pf – arr. vln & pf
with piano   Beka 786

MASCAGNI

Cavalleria Rusticana (1890) – opera
   Intermezzo orch. – arr. vln & pf
   with piano   Jumbo 72, A22009
                             Odeon 2229, A42931

   Intermezzo orch. – arr. vln & pf
   with piano   Pathé K78005

MASCHERONI

Eternamente (1891) v & pf – arr. vln & pf
with piano   Columbia 168

MASSENET

Thaïs (1894) – opera
   Méditation arr. vln & pf Marsick
   with piano   26928   Columbia J164
                             Rena 1652

MENDELSSOHN

(6) Songs without words, Op. 62 pf
No. 6. Song without words No. 30, in A "Spring song" arr. vln & pf
Kreisler
with piano   26924   Columbia 1391
                 Regal G6220

NEVIN

Mighty lak' a rose (1901) v & pf – arr. vln & pf
with piano   Beka 692
                 Scala 395

Mighty lak' a rose (1901) v & pf – arr. vln & pf
with piano   Parlophone E5053

PAGANINI

(La) Carnevale di Venizia – variations, Op. 10 (1829) solo vln
with piano   Columbia 1378
                 Regal G6219

PAPINI

(2) Morceaux de salon "Souvenir di Sorrento", Op. 55 vln & pf
No. 2. Saltarella
with piano   L 0333 M³   Jumbo 189, A22044
                 Scala 1023

No. 2. Saltarella*
with piano   8703 e   Zonophone 166, T5135

PIERNÉ

Sérénade in A, Op. 7 (1875) pf – arr. vln & pf Haddock
with piano   Beka 767
Sérénade in A, Op. 7 (1875) pf – arr. vln & pf Haddock
with piano   Pathé K78004

POLIAKIN

(Le) Canari (Concert–polka) vln & pf
with piano   Columbia 1113
(Le) Canari (Concert–polka) vln & pf
with piano   Zonophone 137

RAFF

(6) Pieces, Op. 85 vln & pf
No. 3. Cavatina in D
with piano   Columbia 1412
                 Regal G6221

No. 3. Cavatina in D
with piano   144926   Jumbo 71, A22007
                 Odeon A42932
                 Skandia 237R

ROBLEDO

Three o'clock in the morning (1922) v & pf – arr. vln, pf & effects
with M. Darewski pf &   yy 2398III   Zonophone 2317, X48083
sound effects

RUBINSTEIN

(2) Melodies, Op. 3 pf
No. 1. Melody in F arr. vln & pf
with piano   Beka 739

* Labelled "Souvenir de Sorrento" with composer omitted.

RUBINSTEIN – *Continued*

No. 1. Melody in F arr. vln & pf
with piano   Columbia 1203, J163
                 Regal G6218

No. 1. Melody in F arr. vln & pf
with orch.   Pathé 945, 78909

SCHUMANN

(13) Kinderscenen, Op. 15 pf
No. 7. Träumerei arr. vln & pf
with piano   144927   Jumbo 71, A22008
                 Odeon A42933
                 Skandia 237R

No. 7. Träumerei arr. vln & pf
with piano   Columbia J164
No. 7. Träumerei arr. vln & pf
with piano   26927   Rena 1652

SILÉSU

(A) Little love, a little kiss (1912) v & pf – arr. vln & pf
with piano   Beka 692

TOBANI

Hearts & flowers, Op. 245 (1899) v & pf – arr. vln & pf
with piano   Columbia 1378
                 Regal G6219

Hearts & flowers, Op. 245 (1899) v & pf – arr. vln & orch.
with orch.   Pathé 945, 78808

Hearts & flowers, Op. 245 (1899) v & pf – arr. vln & pf
with piano   Zonophone 462, X47912

TOSTI

My dreams v & pf – arr. vln & pf
with piano   Columbia 168

VERDI

Rigoletto (1851) – opera
Caro nome arr. vln & pf Haxton
with piano   Columbia 1412
                 Regal G6221

Marjorie HAYWARD (1885–1953)

d'AMBROSIO

Canzonetta, Op. 6 vln & pf
with piano   HO 3099 ae   HMV 4–7901, B705
Canzonetta, Op. 6 vln & pf
with K. Markwell pf   Bb 7191¹△   HMV B2534
Petite Suite, Op. 37 vln & pf
No. 3. Valse
with piano   HMV B1926

ANONYMOUS

(The) Admiral's galliard arr. vln & pf Moffat
with piano   Bb 3606IV   HMV B1754
(A) Donegal air traditional – arr. vln & pf Coleman
with piano   Bb 3603III   HMV B1754
(An) Island sheiling song traditional – arr. vln & pf Fraser
with piano   HMV B1169

ANONYMOUS – *Continued*

Londonderry air traditional Irish ballad – arr. 2 vlns, vla & vlc Bridge
with E. Virgo vln, R.   Cc 10528[IV]△   HMV C1470
Jeremy vla & C. Sharpe vlc

Molly on the shore traditional – arr. 2 vlns, vla & vlc Grainger
with E. Virgo vln, R.   Bb 11204[II]△   HMV B2589
Jeremy vla & C. Sharpe vlc

My love is like a red, red rose traditional – arr. v, vln, vlc & pf
with J. Hislop t, C.   Bb 10966[II]△   HMV DA901
Sharpe vlc & P.B. Kahn pf

(The) Rope dancer traditional – arr. vln & pf Moffat
with piano   Bb 1033[III]   HMV B1395

(The) Skye fisher's song traditional – arr. vln & pf Fraser
with piano   HMV B1169

(4) Welsh tunes arr. vln & pf Davies*
with W. Davies pf†   Cc 956[II]   HMV C1069

(4) Welsh tunes arr. vln & pf Davies‡
with W. Davies pf†   Cc 957[IV]   HMV C1069

BEETHOVEN

(6) Quartets, Op. 18 2 vlns, vla & vlc
No. 6. Quartet No. 6, in B flat
    Cc 9742[II]△, 9743[I]△, 9761[III]△,   HMV D1206/9, D7430/3
    9762[IV]△, 9763[III]△ & 9785/6[II]△
with E. Virgo vln, R. Jeremy vla & C.
Sharpe vlc

(3) Quartets, Op. 59 "Rasumovsky" 2 vlns, vla & vlc
No. 2. Quartet No. 8, in e
    Cc 4540[V], 4614[VI], 4615/6[I], 4617   HMV D953/6
    [II], 4690[III], 4691[II] & 4692[III]
with E. Virgo vln, R. Jeremy vla & C.
Sharpe vlc

No. 3. Quartet No. 9, in C
    Cc 8583[V]△, 8584/5[IV]△, 8651[III]   HMV D1202/5, D7426/9
    △, 8652[V]△, 8727[III]△ & 8728[IV]△
with E. Virgo vln, R. Jeremy vla & C.
Sharpe vlc

Quartet No. 12, in E flat, Op. 127 2 vlns, vla & vlc
with E. Virgo vln, R. Jeremy vla & C.   HMV D1183/7
Sharpe vlc

Sonata No. 8, in c, Op. 13 "Pathétique" pf
Adagio cantabile (2nd mvt) arr. vln & pf
with L. Lawrence pf   HMV X600

Sonata No. 9, in A, Op. 47 "Kreutzer" vln & pf.§
    HO 3092 ef, 3094 ef & 3096/7 ef   HMV C844 & C854, L558/9,
with U. Bourne pf   Z78/9

Sonata No. 10, in G, Op. 96 vln & pf
Adagio expressivo (2nd mvt)
with W. Davies pf   Cc 16842[I]△   HMV C1765

* Written by schoolchildren.
† From "Lecture Illustrations."
‡ Written by summer school students.
§ Abridged.

BEETHOVEN – *Continued*

(3) Trios, Op. 1 pf, vln & vlc
No. 1. Trio No. 1, in E flat: Presto (4th mvt)
with W. Davies pf & C. Sharpe vlc   HMV C1767

No. 2. Trio No. 2, in G: Presto (4th mvt)
with M. Hambourg pf & C. Warwick   HMV 08075
Evans vlc

Trio in B flat, Op. 11 cl, vlc & pf – arr. pf, vln & vlc
Adagio (2nd mvt)
with W. Davies pf & C. Sharpe vlc   HMV C1766

BORODIN

Quartet No. 2, in D (1881/5) 2 vlns, vla & vlc
Notturno (3rd mvt)
with E. Virgo vln, R.   Cc 12033[II]△   HMV C2271
Jeremy vla & C. Sharpe vlc

BRAGA

(7) Melodies (1867) v & pf
No. 5. La serenata "Angel's serenade" arr. vln & pf
with piano   HO 3096 ae   HMV 4–7902, B705

No. 5. La serenata "Angel's serenade" arr. vln & pf
with K. Markwell pf   Bb 7186[III]△   HMV B2534

No. 5. La serenata "Angel's serenade" arr. v, vln & pf
with E. Danieli s &   Bb 17134[II]△   HMV B3108
piano

BRAHMS

(21) Hungarian Dances pf duet
Hungarian dance No. 3, in F arr. vln & pf Joachim
with orch.   y 21859 E   Zonophone GO47, X47953

Hungarian dance No. 5, f sharp arr. vln & pf "in g" Joachim
with orch.   y 21860 E   Zonophone GO53, X47964

BRIDGE

Gondoliera (1911) vln & pf
with piano   Cc 1032[II]   HMV C1057

(3) Idylls (1906) 2 vlns, vla & vlc
    Cc 4728/9[I] & 4730/1[II]   HMV D915/6
with E. Virgo vln, R. Jeremy vla & C.
Sharpe vlc

No. 1. Adagio molto espressivo
with E. Virgo vln,   Cc 13540/1[II]△   HMV C1593
R. Jeremy vla & C. Sharpe vlc

(3) Novelettes (1904) 2 vlns, vla & vlc
Novelette No. 3
with E. Virgo vln, R.   Cc 16240[I]△   HMV C1663
Jeremy vla & C. Sharpe vlc   Victor 9379

Serenade (1910) vln & pf
with piano   Bb 4780[I]   HMV B1871

CADMAN

At dawning, Op. 29 No. 1 v & pf – arr. v, vln, vlc & pf
with J. Hislop t, C.   Bb 9218[IA]△   HMV DA819
Sharpe vlc & P.B. Kahn pf

CILEA

Adriana Lecouvreur (1902) – opera
Intermezzo orch. – arr. vln & orch.
with orch.   Zonophone 2663

COATES

I heard you singing v & pf – arr. v, vln, vlc & pf
with J. Hislop t, C.   Bb 9219[IIIA] △   HMV DA818
Sharpe vlc & P.B. Kahn pf

COLERIDGE–TAYLOR

(4) Characteristic Waltzes, Op. 22 orch.
   No. 3. Valse de la Reine arr. vln & pf
   with piano   HMV B2692

COLLINS

(A) Moorish interlude vln & pf
   with orch.   Zonophone 2534

CUI

Kaleidoscope, Op. 50 vln & pf
   No. 5. Berceuse russe
   with piano   HO 5126 ae   HMV B1277

DEBUSSY

Quartet in g, Op. 10 (1893) 2 vlns, vla & vlc
    Cc 6690[II]△, 6691[V]△, 6692[VII]△,   HMV D1058/61, D7482/5
    6711/2[III]△, 6713[II]△ & 6891[IV]△
   with E. Virgo vln, R. Jeremy vla & C.
   Sharpe vlc

DENZA

Si vous l'aviez compris! v & pf – arr. v, vln & pf
with B. Mummery t   Bb 11270[III]△   HMV B2756
& G. Moore pf

DITTERSDORF

Quartet No. 5, in E flat 2 vlns, vla & vlc
   Minuet (2nd mvt)
   with E. Virgo vln, R. Jeremy vla & C.   HMV D1187
   Sharpe vlc

DRDLA

Serenade No. 1, in A vln & pf
   with piano   Bb 6724[III]△   HMV B2140

DVOŘÁK

(7) Gypsy songs, Op. 55 v & pf
   No. 4. Songs my mother taught me arr. vln & pf Kreisler
   with orch.   Zonophone 2663

ELGAR

Bavarian Highlands, Op. 27 cho & orch.
   No. 2. In Hammersbach arr. vln & pf
   with K. Markwell pf   Bb 9198[VI]△   HMV B2511
Sonata in e, Op. 82 vln & pf*
    HO 4118 af, 4115 af & HO 4116   HMV C957 & C980
   with U. Bourne pf   af, 4117 af

FIBICH

Images, Impressions & Souvenirs, Op. 41 pf
   No. 14. Poem (from "Souvenirs", Part IV) arr. vln & pf Kubelík
   with G. Moore pf   Bb 14382[III]△   HMV B2938

* Abridged.

FRANCK

Quartet in D (1889) 2 vlns, vla & vlc
    Cc 5588[IV], 5589[II], 5595[II],   HMV D1006/11
    5596/7[IV], 5622[II], 5623[I], 5624[II], 5625
   with E. Virgo   [I], 5892[IV] & 5893/4[II]
   vln, R. Jeremy vla & C. Sharpe vlc
Sonata in A (1886) vln & pf*
    HO 3558 af, 3560 af & HO 3563   HMV C895 & C898
   with U. Bourne pf   af, 3565 af

FRIML

Romance, Op. 17 vln & pf
   with piano   HMV B1926

GARDNER

(2) Pieces, Op. 5 vln & pf
   No. 1. From the canebrake
   with K. Markwell pf   Bb 12867[II]△   HMV B2832

GEEHL

For you alone (1909) v & pf – arr. v, vln, vlc & pf
   with J. Hislop t, C.   Bb 9220[IIA]△   HMV DA819
   Sharpe vlc & P.B. Kahn pf

GERMAN

Henry VIII (1892) – Incidental music orch.
   Morris dance arr. vln & pf
   with piano   HO 2105 ef   HMV C722
   Shepherd's dance arr. vln & pf
   with piano   HO 2107½ ef   HMV C722
   Torch dance arr. vln & pf
   with piano   HO 2105 ef   HMV C722

GLAZOUNOV

(5) Novellettes, Op. 15 (1888) 2 vlns, vla & vlc
   No. 2. Orientale
   with E. Virgo vln, R.   Bb 10526[V]△   HMV B2784
   Jeremy vla & C. Sharpe vlc

GLUCK

Orphée et Eurydice (1762) – opera
   Dance of the blessed spirits: Lento "Mélodie" (No. 2) arr. vln & pf
   Kreisler
   with K. Markwell pf   Bb 12868[I]△   HMV B2832

GODARD

Concerto No. 1, Op. 35 "Concerto Romantique" vln & orch.
   Canzonetta (2nd mvt)
   with orch.   Zonophone GO59
Jocelyn (1888) – opera
   Cachés dans cet asile "Berceuse" arr. v, vln & pf
   with L. Gowings t &   Cc 8179[X]△   HMV C1444
   piano

GOSSEC

(Le) Camp du Grand Pré (1793) – opera
   Tambourin arr. str qt Sharpe
   with E. Virgo vln,   Bb 10527[IV]△   HMV B2589
   R. Jeremy vla & C. Sharpe vlc
Rosine (1786) – opera
   Gavotte arr. vln & pf Burmester
   with orch.   Zonophone GO45

* Abridged.

GOUNOD

Ave Maria (Méditation on Bach's "Prelude No. 1, in C" from Book I of "Das Wohltemperirte Clavier") v & pf – arr. v, vln & pf
with E. Suddaby s &   Cc 16912^{III}△   HMV C1733
piano

Faust (1859) – opera
Salut! Demeure chaste et pure
with T. Davies t & orch.   Cc 3165^I HMV D739
– Goossens

Salut! Demeure chaste et pure
with J. Hislop t & orch.   HMV DB944

GRIEG

Quartet in g, Op. 27 2 vlns, vla & vlc
Romance (2nd mvt); **Intermezzo** (3rd mvt)
with E. Virgo vln, R. Jeremy vla & C.   HMV C1635
Sharpe vlc

Sonata No. 3, in c, Op. 45 vln & pf
Cc 6812^{IV}△, 6813^{VI}△, 6814^{VIII}△,   HMV C1388/90
7008/9^V△, & 7010^{III}△,
with U. Bourne pf

HANDEL

Berenice (1737) – opera
Minuet arr. vln & pf
with piano   HMV B1003
Minuet arr. vln & pf Davies*
with W. Davies pf   Cc 960^I HMV C1070
Minuet arr. vln & pf Davies
with W. Davies pf   Cc 16841^I HMV C1765

Messiah (1742) – oratorio
No. 2. Comfort ye my people arr. vln & pf
with piano   HMV C883
No. 3. Every valley shall be exalted arr. vln & pf
with piano   HMV C883

Ottone, re di Germania (1723) – opera*
Overture arr. vln & pf as "Gavotte" by Davies
with W. Davies pf   Cc 959^V HMV C1070

Rinaldo (1711) – opera*
Overture arr. vln & pf as "Gigue" by Davies
with W. Davies pf   Cc 959^V HMV C1070
Suite (melodies from "Alcina, Alexander's Feast & Ottone, re di Germania") arr. vln, pf & vlc Davies
with W. Davies pf & C. Sharpe vlc   HMV C1766

HARRISON

Widdicombe Fair, Op. 22 "Humoresque" 2 vlns, vla & vlc
with E. Virgo vln,   Bb 12032^{III}△   HMV B3137
R. Jeremy vla & C. Sharpe vlc

HAYDN

(6) Quartets, Op. 3 (H.III, Nos. 13/8) 2 vlns, vla & vlc
No. 5. Quartet No. 17, in F, H.III, No. 17: Andante Cantabile "Serenade" (2nd mvt)
with E. Virgo vln, R.   Bb 13919^{II}△   HMV B3137
Jeremy vla & C. Sharpe vlc   Victor 26511, (in set P12)

* From "Lecture Illustrations."

HAYDN – *Continued*

(3) Quartets, Op. 74 (H.III, Nos. 72/4) 2 vlns, vla & vlc
No. 1. Quartet No. 72, in C, H.III, No. 72: Allegro moderato (1st mvt)
with E. Virgo vln, R.   Cc 8729^{VI}△   HMV D1205, D7429
Jeremy vla & C. Sharpe vlc

(6) Quartets, Op. 76 (H.III, Nos. 75/80) 2 vlns, vla & vlc
No. 3. Quartet No. 77, in C, H.III, No. 77 "Emperor": Poco adagio cantabile (theme & variations) (2nd mvt)
with E. Virgo vln, R.   Cc 12030^I△   HMV C1470
Jeremy vla & C. Sharpe vlc

HUBAY

(Le) Luthier de Crémone, Op. 40 (1894) – opera
Intermezzo orch. – arr. vln & pf Hubay
with K. Markwell pf   Bb 7722^I△   HMV B2511

(14) Scènes de la Csárda vln & pf
No. 4. Hejre Kati, Op. 32
with orch.   y 21869 E   Zonophone GO47, X47954

IRELAND

Bagatelle (1911) vln & pf
with piano   Bb 6723^I△   HMV B2648

JÄRNEFELT

Berceuse in g orch. – arr. vln & pf
with orch.   y 21862 E   HMV X872
Zonophone GO49, X47956

JOHNSON

Intermezzo (Marcella) vln & pf
with orch.   y 21740 e   Zonophone GO53, X47963

LANGE

Flower song, Op. 39 vln & pf
with L. Lawrence pf   HMV X600

LANGER

Grandmother, Op. 20 pf – arr. vln & pf
with L. Lawrence org   HMV X600

MASSENET

Élégie v & pf – arr. v, vln & pf
with E. Danieli s &   Bb 17135^{IA}△   HMV B3108
piano

Thaïs (1894) – opera
Méditation arr. vln & pf Marsick
with G. Moore pf   Bb 14381^{III}△   HMV B2938

MENDELSSOHN

Elijah, Op. 70 (1846) – oratorio
No. 31. O rest in the Lord arr. vln & pf
with piano   HMV C883

(3) Quartets, Op. 44 2 vlns, vla & vlc
No. 3. Quartet No. 5, in E flat: Scherzo (Assai leggiero vivace) (2nd mvt)
with E. Virgo vln, R.   Cc 7021^I△   HMV D1061, D7485
Jeremy vla & C. Sharpe vlc

(6) Songs without words, Op. 62 pf
No. 6. Song without words No. 30, in A "Spring song" arr. vln & pf Kreisler
with piano   HO 3094 ae   HMV B858

MONTI

Csárdas (1904) vln & pf
with Cremona String   y 21738 e   Zonophone GO43, X47947
Quartet
Csárdas (1904) vln & pf
with orch.   Zonophone GO47

MOZART

(Il) Re Pastore, K208 (1775) – opera
No. 10. L'amerò, sarò costante
with E. Schumann s & orch.   HMV DB1011, HQM1187
Sonata No. 26, in B flat, K378 vln & pf
Cc 7233^I△, 7234^{II}△, 7492^{II} &   HMV C1247/8, L613/4
with U. Bourne pf   7493^{III}△
Sonata No. 32, in B flat, K454 vln & pf*
Allegretto (3rd mvt)
with W. Davies pf   Cc 961/2^I HMV C1071

NASH

(A) Sleepy tune vln & pf
with piano   Bb 9602^{VI}△   HMV B2648

OFFENBACH

(Les) Contes d'Hoffmann (1881) – opera
Belle Nuit, O nuit d'amour "Barcarolle" arr. vln & orch.
with orch.   Zonophone GO45

ONDŘÍČEK

Fantasia (on "Dance of the comedians" from the opera "The Bartered
Bride" by Smetana) Op. 15 vln & pf
with piano   Cc 1034^{II} HMV C1057

POLDINI

(7) Marionnettes pf
No. 2. Poupée valsante arr. vln & pf Kreisler
with K. Markwell pf   Bb 7187^{III}△   HMV B2289
No. 2. Poupée valsante arr. vln & str qt
with Cremona String   y 21742 e   Zonophone GO43, X47948
Quartet

PURCELL

(10) Sonatas, Z802/11 (1697) 4 parts – 2 vlns & c
Sonata No. 8, in g, Z809 arr. vln & pf Moffat
with Mme. Adami   HO 3907/8 af   HMV D935, Z84
pf

QUILTER

Where the Rainbow Ends (1911) – Incidental music orch.
Fairy frolic arr. vln & pf
with piano   Bb 4781^{II} HMV B1871
Rosamund arr. vln & pf
with piano   Bb 4781^{II} HMV B1871

RAVEL

Introduction & Allegro (1906) hp, fl, cl, 2 vlns, vla & vlc
Cc 15828^I△, 15829^{III}△ & 15830   HMV C1662/3
with J. Cockerill hp, ^{IIA}△   Victor 9738/9
R. Murchie fl, C. Draper cl, E. Virgo
vln, R. Jeremy vla & C. Sharpe vlc

* From "Lecture Illustrations."

RAVEL – *Continued*

Quartet in F (1910) 2 vlns, vla & vlc
Cc 16241/4^{II}△ & 16361/2^{II}△   HMV C2268/70
with E. Virgo vln, R. Jeremy vla & C.
Sharpe vlc

RICHARDSON

Mary v & pf – arr. v, vln, vlc & pf
with J. Hislop t, C.   Bb 10965^{IV}△   HMV DA901
Sharpe vlc & P.B. Kahn pf

ROBINSON

(The) Snowy–breasted pearl v & pf – arr. vln & pf
with K. Markwell pf   Bb 7192^{II}△   HMV B2289

RONALD

Summertime – 4 songs (1901) v & pf
No. 4. O lovely night arr. v, vln & pf
with W. Glynne t &   Bb 8690^{II}△   HMV B2395
piano

SAINT–SAËNS

Quartet in B flat, Op. 41 pf, vln, vla & vlc
Scherzo (3rd mvt)
with M. Hambourg pf, F. Bridge vla &   HMV 08054, D62
C. Warwick Evans vlc

SANDERSON

Until (1918) v & pf – arr. v, vln & pf
with W. Glynne t &   Bb 15959^I△   HMV B3005
piano

SCHUBERT

Litanei auf das Fest aller Seelen, D343 v & pf – arr. v, vln & pf
with E. Gerhardt m–s   Cc 7912^I△   HMV D1462
& P. Hegner pf
(6) Moments musicaux, Op. 94 (D780) (1823/7) pf
No. 3. Moment musicale No. 3, in f "Air russe" arr. str qt
with E. Virgo vln, R.   Cc 9787^{III}△   HMV D1209, D7433
Jeremy pf & C. Sharpe vlc   Victor 11494

SCHUMANN

(12) Duets, Op. 85 pf – 4 hands
No. 3. Gartenmelodie arr. vln & pf Taylor
with piano   HO 3922 ae   HMV B1245
Quintet in E flat, Op. 44 pf, 2 vlns, vla & vlc
Scherzo: Molto vivace (3rd mvt)
with M. Hambourg pf, H. Kinze vln,   HMV 08053, D62
F. Bridge vla & C. Warwick Evans vlc

SCOTT

Valse triste, Op. 73, No. 3 vln & pf
with piano   Bb 6725^{II}△   HMV B2140

SIMONETTI

Madrigale pf – arr. vln & pf
with piano   HMV B748, X640

SINDING

(6) Pieces, Op. 32 pf
No. 3. Frühlingsrauschen "Rustle of spring" arr. vln & pf Varney
with orch.   Zonophone GO59

STEANE

Love's pleading v & pf – arr. vln & orch.
with orch.   y 21870 E   HMV X872
                          Zonophone GO49, X47955

TCHAIKOVSKY

(2) Pieces, Op. 10 pf
No. 2. Humoresque in G arr. vln & pf Kreisler
with piano   HO 3924 ae   HMV B1245
Quartet No. 1, in D, Op. 11 2 vlns, vla & vlc
with E. Virgo vln, R. Jeremy vla & C.   HMV D865/8
Sharpe vlc
(3) Souvenirs de Hapsal, Op. 2 pf
No. 3. Chant sans paroles in f arr. vln & pf Kreisler
with piano   HMV B2692
Trio in a, Op. 50 "To the memory of a great artist" pf, vln & vlc
Tema con variazioni: Andante con moto (2nd mvt)
with M. Hambourg pf & C. Warwick   HMV 08068
Evans vlc

THOMAS

Mignon (1866) – opera
Entr'acte (Gavotte) (Acte II) orch. – arr. str qt Kaiser
with E. Virgo vln, R.   Bb 12051^{III} HMV B2784
Jeremy vla & C. Sharpe vlc

THOMÉ

(L') Extase pf – arr. vln & pf
with piano   HMV B748, X640
Simple aveu, Op. 25 pf – arr. vln & pf
with piano   HMV B1003

WILHELMJ

Swedish melody vln & pf
with orch.   Zonophone 2534

WOOD

(2) Little pieces vln & pf
No. 1. Slumber song
with piano   HO 5128 ae   HMV B1277

NOTE: Miss Hayward has also participated in a musical appreciation series called "Twelve talks on Melody" on HMV numbers C 1759/64. An older version of the same series is on HMV numbers C 1063/8*. The narrative in both sets is by Walfred Davies. Miss Hayward has also recorded as a member of the English String Quartet. The above ensemble listed as E. Virgo, R. Jeremy & C. Sharpe were, with Miss Hayward, known as the **Virtuoso String Quartet.**

Richard HEBER

BACH

(6) Sonatas, BWV1030/5 nos. 1/3 fl & clav; nos. 4/6 fl & c
Sonata No. 2, in E flat: Siciliano (2nd mvt) BWV1031 arr. vln & pf Auer
with K. Grosse org   Polydor 21969
(4) Suites, BWV1066/9 strs & c
Suite No. 3, in D: Air (2nd mvt) BWV1068 2 obs, 3 tpts, drms & strs – arr. vln & pf as "Air on the G–string" by Wilhelmj
with K. Grosse org   Polydor 21842

* C 1063 Cc 958^{I} 1052^{III} c 1064 C 1065 Cc 1238^{I} C 1066 Cc 1039^{V} 1394^{II} C 1067 Cc 1395^{I} 1240^{IV} C 1068 Cc 1035^{V} 1393^{V}

HANDEL

Serse (1738) – opera
Ombra mai fu "Largo" arr. vln & org
with K. Grosse org   Polydor 21969

KREISLER

Andantino (Padre Martini) vln & pf
with K. Grosse org   Polydor 21843

MATTHESON

(12) Suites (1714) hpsi
Suite No. 5, in c: Air arr. vln & pf Burmester
with K. Grosse org   Polydor 21843

SCHUMANN

(13) Kinderscenen, Op. 15 pf
No. 7. Träumerei arr. vln & org
with K. Grosse org   Polydor 21842

Hugo HEERMANN (1844–1935)

d'AMBROSIO

Canzonetta, Op. 6 vln & pf
with orch. – Kark   2–513   Beka M30, M513
                        Parlophone E10034, P218

BACH

(3) Sonatas & 3 Partitas, BWV1001/6 solo vln
Partita No. 3, in E: Preludio (1st mvt) BWV1006
(unaccompanied) 514   Parlophone P217

ERNST

Nocturne, Op. 8 vln & pf – arr. Heermann
with orch. – Kark   511   Parlophone P217

FELIX

(Die) Kätzchen (1890) – operetta
Unter dem Lindenbaum arr. vln & orch.
with orch.   Parlophone 7314

HUBAY

(14) Scènes de la Csárda vln & pf
No. 4. Hejre Kati, Op. 32
with orch. – Kark   2–512   Beka M30, M512
                        Parlophone E10034, P218

LEONCAVALLO

Mattinata (1904) v & pf – arr. vln & orch.
with orch.   Parlophone 7314

WIENIAWSKI

(2) Mazurkas, Op. 19 vln & pf
No. 1. Mazurka No. 1, in G "Obertass"
with orch. – Kark   509   Beka M39, M509
                        Parlophone P216

No. 2. Mazurka No. 2, in D "Dudziarz"
with orch. – Kark   510   Beka M39, M510
                        Parlophone P216

Ferenc HEGEDUS

BACH, J.C.

Sinfonia concertante in E flat, T. P284 (1770) 2 vlns, 2 fls, 2 hrns, strs & c
  with P. Riemann vln, K. Mayrhofer ob   Bach Guild BG504
  & Vienna Symphony Orch. – Günther   Decca UMT263022
                                       Nixa BLP304

Anna HEGNER (1881–1963)

BRAHMS

(21) Hungarian Dances pf duet
  Hungarian dance No. 5, in f sharp arr. vln & pf "in g" Joachim
  with O. Urack pf   Vox 6031
  Hungarian dance No. 7, in A arr. vln & pf Joachim
  with O. Urack pf   Vox 6031

KREISLER

Liebesleid vln & pf
  with O. Urack pf   Vox 06030
Scherzo (Dittersdorf) vln & pf
  with O. Urack pf   Vox 06032
Sicilienne & Rigaudon (Francoeur) vln & pf
  with O. Urack pf   Vox 06030

SARASATE

(8) Danzas españolas vln & pf
  No. 7. Danza española No. 7, in a, Op. 26, No. 1
  with O. Urack pf   Vox 06032

Jascha HEIFETZ (1899–   )

ACHRON

Hebrew dance, Op. 35, No. 1 vln & pf – rev. Auer
  with I. Achron pf   A 30931   HMV DB838
                                     Rococo 2025
                                     Victor 6491
Hebrew lullaby, Op. 35, No. 2 vln & pf – rev. Auer
  with S. Chotzinoff pf   A 27034   HMV 6–7926, DA596
                                     Victor 66201, 970
Hebrew melody, Op. 33 vln & pf – arr. Auer
  with orch.   A 21268   HMV 2–07981, DB291
                                     Rococo 2025
                                     Victor 74568, 6160
Hebrew melody, Op. 33 vln & pf – arr. Auer
  with I. Achron pf   A 38949 △ HMV DB1048
                                     Victor 6695
Hebrew melody, Op. 33 vln & pf – arr. Auer
  with E. Bay pf   HMV DB6469
                                     Victor 11–9572, 49–0668,
                                     LSC3233
Stimmungen, Op. 32 vln & pf
  with I. Achron pf   A 30936   HMV DA659
                                     Victor 1048

AGUIRRE

Huella (Canción argentina) Op. 49 orch. – arr. vln & pf Heifetz
  with E. Bay pf   Brunswick LAT8020
                                     Decca DL8521

ALBÉNIZ

Suite española, Op. 47 pf
  No. 3. Savillanas arr. vln & pf Heifetz
  with A. Sándor pf   2B 6056[II]□   HMV DB2220

d'AMBROSIO

Serenade, Op. 4 vln & pf
  with S. Chotzinoff pf   A 23405   HMV 5–7957, DA247
                                     Victor 66022, 676

ANONYMOUS

Deep river Negro spiritual – arr. vln & pf Heifetz
  with M. Kaye pf   Brunswick AXL2017
                                     Decca 23387, (in set A385),
                                     DL9780, UA243086
                                     Odeon 288917

Gentle maiden English folksong – arr. vln & pf Scott
  with I. Achron pf   Victor 1082

ARENSKY

Concerto in a, Op. 54 vln & orch.
  Tempo di valse (2nd mvt) arr. vln & pf Heifetz
  with E. Bay pf   HMV ALP1206, FALP248
                                     Victor 10–1344, (in set MO1158),
                                     49–1221, (in set WDM1158),
                                     ERA57, LM1166

Trio No. 1, in d, Op. 32 pf, vln & vlc
  with L. Pennario pf & G. Piatigorsky   Victor LM2867, LSC2867,
  vlc   RB6665, SB6665

BACH

Concerto No. 1, in a, BWV1041 vln, strs & c
  with Los Angeles Philharmonic Orch.   HMV BLP1070
  – Wallenstein   Victor A630223, ERA9698,
                                         LM1818, LM9810

Concerto No. 2, in E, BWV1042 vln strs & c
  with Los Angeles Philharmonic Orch.   HMV BLP1070
  – Wallenstein   Victor A630223, LM1818,
                                         LM9810

Concerto in d, BWV1043 2 vlns, strs & c
  (playing both solo parts)
  with Victor Chamber Orch. – Waxman   HMV DB6892/3
                                        Victor (set WDM1136), 11–
                                        9648/9, 11–9650/1, (set
                                        DM1136), LM1051

Concerto in d, BWV1043 2 vlns strs & c
  with E. Friedman vln & New   Victor LM2577, LSC2577,
  Symphony Orch. of London – Sargent   LSC3234, LSC5015, RB16277,
                                        SB2146

(6) English Suites, BWV806/11 clav
  English Suite No. 3, in g: Gavottes 1 & 2 (5th mvt) BWV808 arr. vln &
  pf as "Gavotte & Musette" by Heifetz
  with A. Sándor pf   OB 6041[1]□   HMV DA1568
  English Suite No. 6, in d: Gavottes 1 & 2 (6th mvt) BWV811 arr. vln &
  pf Heifetz
  with E. Bay pf   D6–RB–3101   HMV ALP1206, DA2001,
                                        EC176, FALP248, 7RF249
                                        Victor 10–1342, (in set MO1158),
                                        49–1219, (in set WDM1158),
                                        A95225, ERA214, LM1166

BACH – *Continued*

(15) Sinfonias – 3–part Inventions, BWV787/801 clav
Sinfonia No. 3, in D, BWV789 arr. vln, vla & vlc Heifetz, Primrose & Piatigorsky
with W. Primrose vla & G. Piatigorsky Victor LM2563, LSC2563
vlc
Sinfonia No. 4, in d, BWV790 arr. vln, vla & vlc Heifetz, Primrose & Piatigorsky
with W. Primrose vla & G. Piatigorsky Victor LM2563, LSC2563
vlc
Sinfonia No. 9, in f, BWV795 arr. vln, vla & vlc Heifetz, Primrose & Piatigorsky
with W. Primrose vla & G. Piatigorsky Victor LM2563, LSC2563
vlc

(3) Sonatas & 3 Partitas, BWV1001/6 solo vln
Sonata No. 1, in g, BWV1001
(unaccompanied) HMV DB2721/2*
RS RS691†
Victor JD769/70

Sonata No. 1, in g, BWV1001
(unaccompanied) HMV ALP1449
Victor (in sets LM6105 & WDM6105), A630372, A12R0051/3, LM1976

Partita No. 1, in b, BWV1002‡
(unaccompanied) HMV. ALP1449
Victor (in sets LM6105 & WDM6105), A12R0051/3, RB16218

Sonata No. 2, in a, BWV1003
(unaccompanied) HMV ALP1450
Victor (in sets LM6105 & WDM6105), A12R0051/3, LM2115

Partita No. 2, in d, BWV1004
2EA 2584/5[II], 2586[III], 2591[II] & HMV DB2723/6*
(unaccompanied) 2592/4[I] RS RS691†
Victor JD1593/6S, (set JAS759)

Partita No. 2, in d, BWV1004§
(unaccompanied) HMV ALP1450
Victor (in sets LM6105 & WDM6105), A630372, A12R0051/3, LM1976

Partita No. 2, in d: Chaconne (5th mvt) BWV1004
(unaccompanied) Victor LSC3205
Sonata No. 3, in C, BWV1005
(unaccompanied) HMV DB2726/8*

* Unissued.
† Private edition by Robert Staub.
‡ Bourrée or 7th mvt is also on Victor LSC5015.
§ Chaconne or 5th mvt is also on Victor ERA1976/1 & ERA9544.

BACH – *Continued*

Sonata No. 3, in C, BWV1005
(unaccompanied) HMV ALP1451
Victor (in sets LM6105 & WDM6105), A12R0051/3, LM2210, RB16218

Partita No. 3, in E: 2 Minuettos (4th mvt) BWV1006
(unaccompanied) A 34072 △ HMV DB945
Partita No. 3, in E, BWV1006 *
(unaccompanied) HMV ALP1451
Victor (in sets LM6105 & WDM6105), A12R0051/3, LM2115

BAX
Mediterranean (1921) pf; orch. – arr. vln & pf Heifetz
with E. Bay pf HMV EC193
Victor 10–1293, (in set M1126)

BAZZINI
(La) Ronde des lutins, Op. 25 vln & pf
with A. Benoist pf A 21271 HMV 2–07962, DB290
Pearl GEM109
Victor 74570, 6159

(La) Ronde des lutins, Op. 25 vln & pf
with E. Bay pf 2EA 4895[1]☐ HMV DB3214, DB3535
Victor 15813, 18329

BEETHOVEN
Concerto in D, Op. 61 (cadenzas by Auer/Joachim) vln & orch.†
with NBC Symphony Orch. – HMV DB5724/8S, DB6065/9S,
Toscanini DB8821/5S, DB11140/4,
CSLP507, ED53/7S, FJLP5017
Victor 17441/5S, 17451/5S, (set M705), (in set DPS2006), LCT1010, ND44/8, (set JAS9)

Concerto in D, Op. 61 (cadenzas by Auer/Joachim) vln & orch.
with Boston Symphony Orch. – HMV ALP1437
Munch Victor (in set VCM(S)7087), A644502, LM1992, LSC1992, RB16124, SB2047

(12) Deutsche Tänze, G140 (WoO8) orch.
Deutscher Tanz No. 6, in G arr. vln & pf as "Folkdance" by Heifetz
with E. Bay pf D6–RB–3102 HMV ALP1206, DA2001, FALP248
Victor 10–1347, (in set MO1158), 49–1219, (in set WDM1158), ERA184, LM1166

Romance No. 1, in G, Op. 40 vln & orch.
E1–RC–2414–2A & 2415–1A HMV BLP1022, DB21471,
with Victor Symphony Orch. – FALP270, QBLP5011,
Steinberg VBLP808, 7ER5035, 7ERF102, 7ERQ103, 7RF167
Victor (in sets DPS2006, VCM(S)7067 & WEPR9), 26001, 49–3611, LM9014

* Prelude or 1st mvt and Gavotte en rondeau or 3rd mvt is also on Victor LSC5015.
† Rondo or 3rd mvt is also on Victor 11–9236 which is in set M1064.

BEETHOVEN – *Continued*

Romance No. 2, in F, Op. 50 vln & orch.
E1–RC–2416/7–1   HMV BLP1022, BD21600,
with Victor Symphony Orch. –   FALP270, QBLP5011,
Steinberg   VBLP808, 7ER5035, 7ERF102,
7ERQ103, 7RF168
Victor (in sets DPS2006,
VCM(S)7067 & WEPR9), 26001,
49–3612, LM9014

(Die) Ruinen von Athen, Op. 113 – Incidental music orch.
No. 3. Chor der Derwische arr. vln & pf Auer
with A. Benoist pf   A 21073   HMV 4–7939, DA242
Victor 64759, 671

No. 4. Marcia alla turca arr. vln & pf Auer
with A. Benoist pf   A 21074   HMV 4–7941, DA242
Victor 64770, 671

Serenade in D, Op. 8 vln, vla & vlc
with W. Primrose vla & G. Piatigorsky   Victor A630640, LM2550,
vlc   LSC2550

(3) Sonatas, Op. 12 vln & pf
No. 1. Sonata No. 1, in D
with E. Bay pf   HMV ALP1422, BD9489/90
Victor 12–0511/2, (in set
DM1254), 49–0438/41, (in set
WDM1254), A630792, LM1015,
(in sets LM6701 & LVT5000)

No. 2. Sonata No. 2, in A
with E. Bay pf   HMV ALP1422, DB9491/2
Victor 12–0513/4, (in set
DM1254), 49–0438/41, (in set
WDM1254), A630792, LM1015,
(in sets LM6701 & LVT5000)

No. 3. Sonata No. 3, in E flat
with E. Bay pf   Victor 18327/9S, (set M852)
No. 3. Sonata No. 3, in E flat
with E. Bay pf   HMV ALP1423
Victor A630796, LM1912, (in
sets LM6701 & LVT5000)

Sonata No. 4, in a, Op. 23 vln & pf
with E. Bay pf   HMV ALP1423
Victor A630796, LM1842,
LVT1040, (in sets LM6701 &
LVT5000)

Sonata No. 5, in F, Op. 24 "Spring" vln & pf
with E. Bay pf   D7–RC 6978/81   HMV ALP1424, DB21030/1
Victor 12–0725/6, (set DM1283),
LM1022, (in sets LM6701,
LVT5000 & WDM1283)

(3) Sonatas, Op. 30 vln & pf
No. 1. Sonata No. 6, in A
with E. Bay pf   HMV ALP1424
Victor LM1912, (in sets LM6701
& LVT5000)

No. 2. Sonata No. 7, in c
with E. Bay pf   HMV ALP1425
Victor 49–3172/4, (set
WDM1499), LM60, LM1842,
LVT1040, (in sets LM6701 &
LVT5000)

BEETHOVEN – *Continued*

No. 3. Sonata No. 8, in G
with E. Bay pf   Victor 15457/9S, (set M570)
No. 3. Sonata No. 8, in G
with E. Bay pf   HMV ALP1425
Victor LM1914, (in sets LM6701
& LVT5000)

Sonata No. 9, in A, Op. 47 "Kreutzer" vln & pf
with B. Moiseiwitsch pf   HMV ALP1093, ALP1426,
LBLP1011
Victor LM1193, (in sets
LM6701, LVT5000 &
WDM1612)

Sonata No. 9, in A, Op. 47 "Kreutzer" vln & pf
with B. Smith pf   Victor (in sets DPS2006 &
VCM(S)7067), LM2577,
LSC2577, RB16277, SB2146

Sonata No. 10, in G, Op. 96 vln & pf
with E. Bay pf   HMV ALP1426
Victor LM1914, (in sets LM6701
& LVT5000)

(3) Trios, Op. 1 vln, vlc & pf
No. 1. Trio No. 1, in E flat
with J. Lateiner pf & G. Piatigorsky   Victor A635029, A645029,
vlc   LM2770, LSC2770

Trio No. 1, in E flat, Op. 3 vln, vla & vlc
with W. Primrose vla, & G.   Victor LM2180
Piatigorsky vlc

(3) Trios, Op. 9 vln, vla & vlc
No. 1. Trio No. 2, in G
with W. Primrose vla & G. Piatigorsky   Victor LM2180
vlc

No. 2. Trio No. 3, in D
with W. Primrose vla & G. Piatigorsky   Victor LM2563, LSC2563
vlc

No. 3. Trio No. 4, in c
with W. Primrose vla & G. Piatigorsky   Victor LM2186
vlc

Trio No. 6, in B flat, Op. 97 "Archduke" pf, vln & vlc
with A. Rubinstein pf & E. Feuermann   HMV ALP1184
vlc   Victor 11–8477/81, (set M949),
L17041, LCT1020

BENJAMIN

(2) Jamaican pieces (1940) orch.
No. 2. Jamaican rumba arr. vln & pf Heifetz
VP 1196–D5–TC–139 – 1D   V–Disc 422
with orch. – Voorhees

No. 2. Jamaican rumba arr. vln & pf Heifetz
with M. Kaye pf   Brunswick 03740, AXL2017,
LAT8066
Decca 23385, (in set A385),
DL5214, DL9760, UA243086,
UAT273572

Romantic Fantasy (1935) vln, vla & orch.
with W. Primrose vla & RCA Victor   Victor LM2149, LM2767,
Orch. – Solomon   LSC2767, RB6605, SB6605

BENNETT

Hexapoda (5 Studies in Jitteroptera) (1941) vln & pf
  with E. Bay pf
                                      Brunswick LAT8066
                                        Decca 23659/60, (in set DA454), DL9760, ED3509

(A) Song Sonata vln & pf
  with B. Smith pf   Victor LM2382, RB16243

BERLIN

White Christmas (1942) v & pf – arr. vln & pf Heifetz
  with orch. – Camarata   Decca 23376, 45–72461

BLOCH

Sonata No. 1 (1920) vln & pf
  with E. Bay pf   Victor LM1861
Sonata No. 2 (1924) "Poème mystique" vln & pf
  with B. Smith pf   Victor LM2089, RB16020

BOCCHERINI

Sonata in D vln & vlc
  with G. Piatigorsky vlc   Victor LSC3009

BOULANGER, L.

Cortège (1919) vln & pf
  with I. Achron pf   Victor 1082
Nocturne in F (1911) vln & pf
  with I. Achron pf   Victor 1082

BRAHMS

Concerto in D, Op. 77 (cadenza by Auer – arr. Heifetz) vln & orch.
  with Boston Symphony Orch. – Koussevitzky   HMV DB5738/42S, DB8874/8S
                                   Victor (set WCT71), 15526/30S, (set M581), LCT1043

Concerto in D, Op. 77 (cadenza by Heifetz) vln & orch.*
  with Chicago Symphony Orch. – Reiner   HMV ALP1334
                                     Victor (in set VCS7088), A630299, A12R1070, L17013, LM1903, LSC1903, RB16117

Concerto in a, Op. 102 "Double" vln, vlc & orch.
  with E. Feuermann vlc & Philadelphia Orch. – Ormandy   HMV DB6120/3, DB8929/32, DB11131/4, ED376/9
                                   Victor 18132/5, (set M815), LCT1016

Concerto in a, Op. 102 "Double" vln, vlc & orch.
  with G. Piatigorsky vlc & RCA Victor Orch. – Wallenstein   Victor LD2513, LDS2513, LM9891, LSC3228, LSC9891, RB16270

(21) Hungarian Dances pf duet
  Hungarian dance No. 1, in g arr. vln & pf Joachim
  with S. Chotzinoff pf   HMV DA245
                             Victor 66123, 675

  Hungarian Dance No. 7, in A arr. vln & pf Joachim/Heifetz
  with E. Bay pf   Columbia CCL35032
                             Decca 24131, (in set A592), DL9780, ED3501, EUA108503

  Hungarian dance No. 7, in A arr. vln & pf Joachim–Heifetz
  with Los Angeles Philharmonic Orch.   Victor LSC3232
  – Wallenstein

* Allegro giocoso ma non troppo vivace or 3rd mut is also on Victor LSC5234.

BRAHMS – *Continued*

Hungarian dance No. 11, in d arr. vln & pf Joachim
  with B. Smith pf   Victor A630588, LM2382, RB16243
Hungarian dance No. 17, in f sharp arr. vln & pf Kreisler
  with B. Smith pf   Victor A630588, LM2382, RB16243
Hungarian dance No. 20, in e arr. vln & pf "in d" Joachim
  with B. Smith pf   Victor A630588, LM2382, RB16243

Quartet No. 3, in c, Op. 60 pf, vln, vla & vlc
  with J. Lateiner pf, S. Schonbach vla   Victor LSC3009
  & G. Piatigorsky vlc

Sextet No. 2, in G, Op. 36 2 vlns, 2 vlas & 2 vlcs
  with I. Baker vln, W. Primrose vla, V.   Victor A640761/3, (in sets
  Majewski vla, G. Rejto vlc & G.   LD6159 & LDS6159), LM2739,
  Piatigorsky vlc   LSC2739, SOR630761/3, RB6652, SB6652

Sonata No. 2, in A, Op. 100 vln & pf
  with E. Bay pf   Victor 18339/41S, 18342/4S, (set M856)

Sonata No. 3, in d, Op. 108 vln & pf
  with W. Kapell pf   Victor A630815, A12R0003, LM71, LM2836

Trio No. 1, in B, Op. 8 pf, vln & vlc
  with A. Rubinstein pf & E. Feuermann   HMV BLP1056, ED324/7
  vlc   Victor 16212/5, 18513/6, 18517/20, (set M883), 17–0123/6, (set WCT30), A630778, LM1022, LVT1001

BRUCH

Concerto No. 1, in g, Op. 26 vln & orch.
  with London Symphony Orch. –   HMV ALP1124
  Sargent   Victor (set WDM9007), LM9007
Concerto No. 1, in g, Op. 26 vln & orch.
  with New Symphony Orch. of London   Victor A630767, LM2652,
  – Sargent   LSC2652, LSC4011, RB6527, SB6527

Concerto No. 2, in d, Op. 44 vln & orch.
  with RCA Victor Symphony Orch. –   HMV ALP1362
  Solomon   Victor LM1931
Scottish Fantasy, Op. 46 vln & orch.
  with Victor Symphony Orch. –   HMV ALP1288
  Steinberg   Victor 12–0008/10, (set DM1183), (set V11), 18–0084/6, 18–0087/9, 49–0447/9, (set WDM1183), LM4, LM9016

Scottish Fantasy, Op. 46 vln & orch.
  with O. Ellis hp & New Symphony   Victor A630720, A640720,
  Orch. of London – Sargent   LM2603, LSC2603, LSC3205

BURLEIGH

Natures Voices, Op. 44 vln & pf
  No. 1. Giant hills
  with E. Bay pf   Columbia CCL35032
                             Decca 24131, (in set A592), DL9780, ED3501, EUA108503

BURLEIGH – *Continued*

(4) Small concert pieces, Op. 21 vln & pf
No. 4. Moto perpetuo
with E. Bay pf
Columbia CCL35032
Decca 24131, (in set A592),
DL9780, ED3501, EUA108503

CASTELNUOVO–TEDESCO
Alt–Wien (Rhapsody) (1923) pf
No. 1. Valse arr. vln & pf Corti
with A. Sándor pf   OB 6044ᴵᴵ☐   HMV DA1377
Concerto No. 2 (1933) "I Profeti" vln & orch.
with Los Angeles Philharmonic Orch.   Victor LM2050
– Wallenstein
(2) Études d'ondes pf – arr. vln & pf as "Sea murmurs" by Heifetz
with A. Sándor pf   Victor 1645
(2) Études d'ondes pf – arr. vln & pf as "Sea murmurs" by Heifetz
D6–RB–3107–1A   HMV DA2037, 7RF171
with E. Bay pf   Victor 10–1328, 49–1294
Figaro (paraphrase on the aria "Largo al factotum" from the opera "Il Barbiere di Siviglia" by Rossini) vln & pf
with E. Bay pf
Brunswick 0156, LAT8066
Decca 29153, DL9760, ED3502,
UAT273572
(The) Lark (Poème en forme de Rondeau) vln & pf
with E. Bay pf   Victor LM2074
(3) Songs of Shakespeare – Book VIII (1926) v & pf
No. 3. Two maids wooing a man arr. vln & pf as "Tango" by Heifetz
with E. Bay pf
HMV EC193
Victor 10–1293, (in set M1126)

CHAUSSON
Concerto in D, Op. 21 vln, pf & str qt
with J.M. Sanromà pf & Musical Art   Victor 18487/90, (set M877),
string quartet   LCT1113
Poème, Op. 25 vln & orch.
with RCA Victor Symphony Orch. –   HMV BLP1072
Solomon   Victor A630202, LM2069,
LM7017, LSC3232

CHOPIN
(3) Nocturnes, Op. 9 pf
No. 2. Nocturne No. 2, in E flat arr. vln & pf Sarasate
with A. Benoist pf   Victor 74616, 6156
(2) Nocturnes, Op. 27 pf
No. 2. Nocturne No. 8, in D flat arr. vln & pf "in D" Wilhelmj
with S. Chotzinoff pf   A 27038   HMV 3–07974, DB292
Rococo 2025
Victor 74811, 6161
(2) Nocturnes, Op. 55 pf
No. 2. Nocturne No. 16, in E flat arr. vln & pf Heifetz
with E. Bay pf
Brunswick LAT8020
Decca DL8521
Nocturne No. 19, in e, Op. 72, No. 1 pf – arr. vln & pf Auer
with E. Bay pf
HMV DB6865
Victor 11–9573

CLÉRAMBAULT
Largo in c hpsi – arr. vln & pf – G–string – Dandelot
with A. Sándor pf   2B 6052ᴵᴵ☐   HMV DB2219
Victor 14369

CONUS
Concerto in e (1939) vln & orch.
with RCA Victor Symphony Orch. –   HMV BLP1072
Solomon   Victor A630202, LM2069,
LM7017

COUPERIN, F.
(Les) Petits moulins à vent, XVII, No. 2 hpsi – arr. vln & pf Heifetz
with I. Achron pf   A 34072 △   HMV DB945

CROTHER
Gweedore Brae vln & pf
with M. Kaye pf
Brunswick 0156
Columbia CCL35032
Decca 29153, DL9780, ED3502

DEBUSSY
(6) Ariettes oubliées (1888/1903) v & pf
No. 2. Il pleure dans mon coeur arr. vln & pf Hartmann
with E. Bay pf   HMV ALP1206
Victor 10–1341, (in set MO1158),
49–1218, (in set WDM1158),
LM1166
Beau soir (1878) v & pf – arr. vln & pf Heifetz
with M. Kaye pf
Brunswick AXL2017
Columbia CCL35032
Decca 23386, (in set A385),
UA243086
Odeon 288917
Beau soir (1878) v & pf – arr. vln & pf Heifetz
with B. Smith pf
Victor A635051, A645051,
LM2856, LSC2856, RB6644,
SB6644
(3) Chansons de Bilitis (1898) v & pf
No. 2. La Chevelure arr. vln & pf Heifetz
with E. Bay pf   HMV DA1914, 7EB6001
Victor 10–1295, (in set M1126),
ERA71, (in set WDM1126)
No. 2. La Chevelure arr. vln & pf Heifetz
with B. Smith pf
Victor A635051, A645051,
LM2856, LSC2856, RB6644,
SB6644
Children's Corner Suite (1908) pf
No. 6. Golliwogg's cake–walk arr. vln & pf Heifetz
with E. Bay pf
Brunswick 03691
Columbia CCL35032
Decca 23498, 60257, DL9780,
ED3502
Odeon 288884
No. 6. Golliwogg's cake–walk arr. vln & pf Heifetz
with B. Smith pf
Victor A635051, A645051,
LM2856, LSC2856, LSC5017,
RB6644, SB6644
(L') Enfant Prodigue (1884) – cantata v, cho & orch.
Prélude orch. – arr. vln & pf Heifetz
with A. Sándor pf   OB 6055ᴵᴵ☐   HMV DA1376
Victor 1694
(La) Plus que lente – valse (1910) pf – arr. vln & pf Roquès
with I. Achron pf   A 34070 △   HMV DB945, DB1049
Victor 6622

DEBUSSY – *Continued*

(La) Plus que lente – valse (1910) pf – arr. vln & pf Roques
with E. Bay pf   HMV ALP1206, DB6469,
                                                            FALP248
                                                            Victor 11–9571, 49–0301,
                                                            LM1166, LSC3233, LSC5017

(12) Préludes – Book I (1910) pf
No. 8. La fille aux cheveux de lin arr. vln & pf Hartmann
with I. Achron pf   A 37290 △   HMV DB1049, DB1246
                                        Victor 6622
No. 8. La Fille aux cheveux de lin arr. vln & pf Hartmann
                    EO–RB 6209–1A   HMV DA2058, 7RF172
with E. Bay pf   Victor 10–1324, 10–3312, 49–
                                    0626, 49–3312, ERA126,
                                    LM2382, LSC5017, RB16243
No. 8. La Fille aux cheveux de lin arr. vln & pf Hartmann
with B. Smith pf   Victor LSC3205
Sonata No. 3, in g (1917) vln & pf
with E. Bay pf   HMV FALP165, QALP165
                                    Victor (set WDM1515), LM1184,
                                    LVT1034

Suite Bergamasque (1890) pf
No. 3. Clair de lune arr. vln & pf Heifetz
with E. Bay pf   Brunswick 03691
                                    Columbia CCL35032
                                    Decca 23498, 60257, DL9780,
                                    ED3502
                                    Odeon 288884

DINICU

Hora staccato vln & ens – arr. vln & pf Heifetz
with E. Bay pf   OEA 4894–1   HMV DA1568, DA1702
                                      Victor 1864

Hora staccato vln & ens – arr. vln & pf Heifetz
                    EO–RB–6208–1A   HMV DA2058, 7EB6001,
with E. Bay pf   7RF172
                                     Victor 10–3312, 49–3312,
                                     ERA71, LM2382, LSC3233,
                                     RB16207, RB16243

DOHNÁNYI

Ruralia Hungarica, Op. 32A pf
No. 6. Adagio arr. vln & pf as "Gypsy Andante" by Kreisler
with A. Sándor pf   2B 6102 III □   HMV DB2220
No. 6. Adagio arr. vln & pf as "Gypsy Andante" by Kreisler
            VP–1267 D5–TC–228–1A   V–Disc 471
with orch. – Barlow
Serenade in C, Op. 10 vln, vla & vlc
with W. Primrose vla & E. Feuermann   HMV DB6143/5, DB8947/9
vlc   Victor 11–8176/8, 11–8179/81,
                                        (set M903), A630291, LCT1160,
                                        LVT1017

DRIGO

(2) Airs de Ballet orch.
No. 2. Valse bluette arr. vln & pf Auer
with A. Benoist pf   A 21068   HMV 4–7938, DA244
                                   Victor 64758, 673
No. 2. Valse bluette arr. vln & pf Auer
with I. Achron pf   A 21068 △   HMV DA984
                                    Victor 1332

DRIGO – *Continued*

No. 2. Valse bluette arr. vln & pf Auer
with E. Bay pf   Victor 10–1345, 49–0278,
                                    ERA240, LSC3233

DVOŘÁK

(8) Humoresques, Op. 101 pf
No. 7. Humoresque No. 7, in G flat arr. vln & pf "in G" Heifetz
with M. Kaye pf   Brunswick 03617, AXL2017
                                    Columbia CCL35032
                                    Decca 23384, (in set A385),
                                    DL5214, DL9780, UA233086
                                    Odeon 288889

Quintet in A, Op. 81 pf, 2 vlns, vla & vlc
with J. Lateiner pf, I. Baker vln, J. de   Victor LM2985, LSC2985,
Pasquale vla & G. Piatigorsky vlc   RB6745, SB6745
(8) Slavonic Dances, Op. 46 pf duet; orch.
No. 2. Slavonic dance No. 2, in e arr. vln & pf "in g" Kreisler
with S. Chotzinoff pf   A 23411   HMV 6–7904, DA247
                                     Victor 66139, 675

(8) Slavonic Dances, Op. 72 pf duet; orch.
No. 2. Slavonic dance No. 10, in e arr. vln & pf Kreisler
with S. Chotzinoff pf   HMV DB110
                                    Victor 74820, 6376

No. 8. Slavonic dance No. 16, in A flat arr. vln & pf "in G" Kreisler
with S. Chotzinoff pf   HMV DB110
                                    Victor 74821, 6376

Trio No. 4, in e, Op. 90 "Dumky" pf, vln & vlc
with J. Lateiner pf & G. Piatigorsky   Victor LSC3068
vlc

DYER

(An) Outlandish Suite (1924) vln & pf
No. 2. Florida night song
with E. Bay pf   73168   Brunswick LAT8066
                                 Decca 23659, DL9760, ED3509

ELGAR

(La) Capricieuse, Op. 17 vln & pf
with A. Benoist pf   A 21075   HMV 4–7951, DA243
                                   Victor 64760, 672

(La) Capricieuse, Op. 17 vln & pf
with A. Sándor pf   OB 6059 II   HMV DA1378
Concerto in b, Op. 61 vln & orch.
            2EA 13929/31–2, 13932/3–1,   HMV ALP1014, DB9533/7,
            13934–2, 13935–4A, 13936/7–1 &   DB21056/60, QALP10019
with London Symphony   13938–2   Victor 49–1268/72, (set
Orch. – Sargent   WDM1385), LM1090, LM1385,
                                        LM2919, LSB4022, LVT1030

FALLA

(El) Amor Brujo (1915) – ballet m–s & orch.
No. 14. Pantomime arr. vln & pf Kochański
with E. Bay pf   HMV ALP1206, FALP248
                                    Victor 10–1343, (in set MO1158),
                                    49–1220, (in set WDM1158),
                                    LM1166

(7) Canciones populares españolas (1914) v & pf
No. 4. Jota arr. vln & pf Kochański
with I. Achron pf   A 43960 △   HMV DB1216
                                    Victor 6848

FALLA – *Continued*

No. 4. Jota arr. vln & pf Kochański
with E. Bay pf   Victor 10–1324

No. 4. Jota arr. vln & pf Kochański
with B. Smith pf   Victor LM2978, LSC2978

No. 5. Nana arr. vln & pf Kochański
with B. Smith pf   Victor LM2978, LSC2978

(La) Vida breve (1913) – opera
Danza española orch. – arr. vln & pf Kreisler
with E. Bay pf   2EA 2581^{III}□   HMV DB2846, DB3535
                                                         Victor 14625

FAURÉ

Sonata No. 1, in A, Op. 13 vln & pf
with E. Bay pf   HMV DB3176/8
                                                        Victor 14195/7, 14198/200, (set
                                                        M328)

Sonata No. 1, in A, Op. 13 vln & pf
with B Smith pf   Victor LM2074

FERGUSON

Sonata No. 1, Op. 2 (1931) vln & pf
with L. Steuber pf   Victor LM2909, LSC2909

FOSTER

I dream of Jeannie with the light–brown hair v & pf – arr. vln & pf Heifetz
with E. Bay pf   Brunswick LAT8020
                                                       Decca DL8521

(The) Old folks at home "Swanee River" (1851) v & pf – arr. vln & pf
Heifetz
with E. Bay pf   Brunswick LAT8020
                                                       Decca DL8521

FRANCAIX

Trio in C (1933) vln, vla & vlc
with J. de Pasquale vla & G.   Victor LM2985, LSC2985,
Piatigorsky vlc   RB6745, SB6745

FRANCK

Quintet in f (1878/9) pf, 2 vlns, vla & vlc
with L. Pennario pf, I. Baker vln, W.   Victor (in sets LD6159 &
Primrose vla & G. Piatigorsky vlc   LDS6159), A640761/3, LM2739,
                                                       RB6652, SB6652, SOR630761/3

Sonata in A (1886) vln & pf
with A.   2EA 4883/8^I□   HMV DB3206/8, DB8362/4
Rubinstein pf   Victor 14895/7, (set M449),
                                                       16398/400, LCT1122, LVT1007

GARDNER

(2) Pieces, Op. 5 vln & pf
No. 1. From the canebrake
with M. Kaye pf   Brunswick AXL2017, LAT8066
                                                       Decca 23386, (in set A385),
                                                       DL9760, UA243086

GERSHWIN

(3) Jazz Preludes (1936) pf
No. 1. Prelude No. 1, in B flat arr. vln & pf Heifetz
with E. Bay pf   W 73177 B   Brunswick LAT8066
                                      Decca 23522, (in set A435),
                                      DL7003, DL9760, UAT273572,
                                      UM233070

No. 1. Prelude No. 1, in B flat arr. vln & pf Heifetz
with B. Smith pf   Victor A635051, A645051,
                                     LM2856, LSC2856, RB6644,
                                     SB6644

No. 2. Prelude No. 2, in c sharp arr. vln & pf Heifetz
with E. Bay pf   W 73178 A1 Brunswick LAT8066
                                      Decca 23523, (in set A435),
                                      DL7003, DL9760, UAT273572,
                                      UM233070

No. 2. Prelude No. 2, in c sharp arr. vln & pf Heifetz
with B. Smith pf   Victor A635051, A645051,
                                     LM2856, LSC2856, RB6644,
                                     SB6644

No. 3. Prelude No. 3, in E flat, arr. vln & pf Heifetz
with E. Bay pf   W 73179   Brunswick LAT8066
                                      Decca 23523, (in set A435),
                                      DL7003, DL9760, UAT273572,
                                      UM233070

No. 3. Prelude No. 3, in E flat arr. vln & pf Heifetz
with B. Smith pf   Victor A635051, A645051,
                                     LM2856, LSC2856, RB6644,
                                     SB6644

Porgy & Bess (1935) – opera
Bess, you is my woman arr. vln & pf Heifetz
with E. Bay pf   W 73174 C   Brunswick LAT8066
                                      Decca 23522, (in set A435),
                                      DL7003, DL9760

Bess, you is my woman arr. vln & pf Heifetz
with B. Smith pf   Victor A635051, A645051,
                                     LM2856, LSC2856, RB6644,
                                     SB6644

It ain't nescessarily so arr. vln & pf Heifetz
with E. Bay pf   W 73173 A   Brunswick LAT8066
                                      Decca 23521, (in set A435),
                                      DL7003, DL9760, UAT273572

It ain't nescessarily so arr. vln & pf Heifetz
with B. Smith pf   Victor A635051, A645051,
                                     LM2856, LSC2856, RB6644,
                                     SB6644

It ain't nescessarily so arr. vln & pf Heifetz
with B. Smith pf   Victor LSC3205

My man's gone now arr. vln & pf Heifetz
with E. Bay pf   W 73176 A   Brunswick LAT8066
                                      Decca 29195, (in set A435),
                                      DL7003, DL9760, UAT273572

My man's gone now arr. vln & pf Heifetz
with B. Smith pf   Victor A635051, A645051,
                                     LM2856, LSC2856, RB6644,
                                     SB6644

Summertime arr. vln & pf Heifetz
with E. Bay pf   W 73172 A   Brunswick LAT8066
                                      Decca 29195, (in set A435),
                                      DL7003, DL9760

GERSHWIN – *Continued*

Summertime arr. vln & pf Heifetz
with B. Smith pf   Victor A635051, A645051,
                                                 LM2856, LSC2856, RB6644,
                                                 SB6644

Tempo di blues arr. vln & pf Heifetz
with E. Bay pf   W 73175 A   Brunswick LAT8066
                                     Decca 23521, (in set A435),
                                     DL7003, DL9760

Tempo di blues arr. vln & pf Heifetz
with B. Smith pf   Victor A635051, A645051,
                                                 LM2856, LSC2856, RB6644,
                                                 SB6644

(A) Woman is a sometime thing arr. vln & pf Heifetz
with E. Bay pf   W 73172 A   Brunswick LAT8066
                                     Decca 29195, (in set A435),
                                     DL7003, DL9760, UAT273572

(A) Woman is a sometime thing arr. vln & pf Heifetz
with B. Smith pf   Victor A635051, A645051,
                                                 LM2856, LSC2856, RB6644,
                                                 SB6644

GLAZOUNOV

Concerto in a, Op. 82 vln & orch.
          2B 6853^{II}☐, 6854^{I}☐, 6855^{II}☐   HMV DB2196/8, DB7696/8
with London   & 6856/7^{1}☐   Victor 8296/8, 8302/4, (set
Philharmonic Orch. – Barbirolli   M218)

Concerto in a, Op. 82 vln & orch.
with RCA Victor Orch. – Hendl   Victor LSC2734, LSC4011

Méditation, Op. 32 vln & pf
with A. Benoist pf   A 21269   HMV 4–7940, DA246
                                     Victor 64769, 676

Méditation, Op. 32 vln & pf
with A. Sándor pf   2B 6103^{II}☐   HMV DB2198, DB7698
                                     Victor 8298, 8304, 14323, (in set
                                     M218), 18197, (in set M831)

Raymonda, Op. 57 (1897) – ballet orch.
  Grand Adagio arr. vln & pf Zimbalist
with S. Chotzinoff pf   A 27033   HMV 6–7925, DA596
                                     Victor 66200, 970

  Valse arr. vln & pf Heifetz
with S. Chotzinoff pf   A 24471   HMV 3–07940, DB288, S870
                                     Victor 74660, 6158

GLUCK

Orphée et Eurydice (1762) – opera
  Dance of the blessed spirits: Lento "Mélodie" (No. 2) arr. vln & pf
  Kreisler
with E. Bay pf   Columbia CCL35032
                                     Decca 24139, (in set A592),
                                     DL9780, ED3501, EUA108503

GODARD

Jocelyn (1888) – opera
  Cachés dans cet asile "Berceuse" arr. v, vln & orch.
with B. Crosby v &   L 4227 A   Brunswick 03938
orch. – Young   Decca 40012

GODOWSKY

(12) Impressions (1916) pf
  No. 8. Waltz in D arr. vln & pf Heifetz
with S. Chotzinoff pf   A 24477   HMV DA659
                                     Victor 1048

  No. 12. Viennese arr. vln & pf Heifetz
with M. Kaye pf   Brunswick 03740, AXL2017
                                     Columbia CCL35032
                                     Decca 23385, (in set A385),
                                     DL9780, UA243086

Triakontameron (30 moods & scenes in triple measure) (1920) pf
  No 11. Alt Wien arr. vln & pf Heifetz
with A. Sándor pf   Victor 1645
  No. 11. Alt Wien arr. vln & pf Heifetz
with E. Bay pf   D6–RB–3111   HMV ALP1206, DA2037,
                                     EC208, FALP248
                                     Victor 10–1345, 49–0278,
                                     LM1166, LSC3233

GOLDMARK

Concerto in a, Op. 28 vln & orch.
  Andante (2nd mvt) "Air"
with orch.   A 24476   HMV 3–07968, DB289
                                     Pearl GEM109
                                     Victor 74764, 6157

GRANADOS

(12) Danzas españolas, Op. 37 (1893) pf
  No. 5. Danza española No. 5, in e "Andaluza" arr. vln & pf Kreisler
with S. Chotzinoff pf   HMV DA245
                                     Victor 66110, 674

GRASSE

Wellenspiel (Waves at play) pf – arr. vln & pf Heifetz
with E. Bay pf   Brunswick LAT8020
                                     Decca DL8521

GRIEG

(7) Lyric pieces – Book X, Op. 71 pf
  No. 3. Puck (Småtrold) arr. vln & pf Achron
with I. Achron pf   A 43960 △ HMV DB1206, DB1216
                                     Victor 6848

(6) Moods, Op. 73 pf
  No. 2. Scherzo–Impromptu arr. vln & pf Achron
with I. Achron pf   A 37290 △ HMV DB1049, DB1246
                                     Victor 6622

Sonata No. 2, in G, Op. 13 vln & pf
with E. Bay pf   HMV ED283/5S
                                     Victor 17611/3S, 17617S/9, (set
                                     M735)

Sonata No. 2, in G, Op. 13 vln & pf
with B. Smith pf   Victor LM2089, RB16020

GRUENBERG

Concerto, Op. 47 vln & orch.
with San Francisco Symphony Orch. –   Victor 11–9333/6, 11–9337/40,
Monteux   (set M1079), A630291, LCT1160,
                                     LVT1017

HALFFTER–ESCRICHE

Sonatina (1928) – ballet orch.
No. 4. Danza de la gitana arr. vln & pf Heifetz
with E. Bay pf   Victor 10–1296, (in set M1126)

HANDEL

(15) Sonatas, Op. 1 (?1731) fl or vln & c
Sonata No. 15, in E vln VI
with E. Bay pf   Victor LM1861

(16) Suites (1720/33) hpsi
Suite No. 7, in g: Passacaglia (6th mvt) arr. vln & vla Halvorsen
     2A 065639[III] Δ & 065640[II] Δ   HMV DB6170, ED357
with W. Primrose vla   Victor 11–8151, LCT1150,
     LVT1014

HAYDN

(6) Quartets, Op. 64 (H.III, nos. 63/8) 2 vlns, vla & vlc
No. 5. Quartet No. 67, in D: Vivace (4th mvt) H.III, No. 67 "The Lark"
arr. vln & pf Auer
with S. Chotzinoff pf   Victor 66273, 1024

HERBERT

À la valse vln & pf
with M. Kaye pf   Brunswick LAT8066
     Decca 23376, 45–72461, DL9760

HUMMEL

Rondo in E flat, Op. 11 "Rondo favori" pf – arr. vln & pf Heifetz
with A. Sándor pf   2B 6043[II]☐   HMV DB2449
     Victor 8420

IBERT

(10) Histoires pf
No. 2. Le Petit âne blanc arr. vln & pf Hoérès
with B. Smith pf   Victor A635051, A645051,
     LM2856, LSC2856, RB6644,
     SB6644

JUON

(4) Pieces, Op. 28 vln & pf
No. 3. Berceuse
with S. Chotzinoff pf   A 24471   HMV 3–07940, DB288
     Victor 74660, 6158

KHACHATURIAN, A.

Gayaneh (Suite No. 1) (1942) – ballet orch.
No. 1. Sabre dance arr. vln & pf Heifetz
with B. Smith pf   Victor A630588, ERA240,
     LM2382, LSC3233, RB16243

KHACHATURIAN, K.

Sonata in g, Op. 1 vln & pf
with L. Steuber pf   Victor LM2909, LSC2909

KODÁLY

Duo, Op. 7 (1914) vln & vlc
with G. Piatigorsky vlc   Victor A630640, LM2550,
     LSC2550

KORNGOLD

Concerto in D, Op. 35 vln & orch.
with Los Angeles Philharmonic Orch.   HMV ALP1233
– Wallenstein   Victor LM1782

KORNGOLD – *Continued*

Viel Lärmen um Nichts (Much ado about nothing) Op. 11 (1919) –
Incidental music orch.
No. 2. Hozapfel und Schlehwein arr. vln & pf Heifetz
with A. Sándor pf   OB 6054[II]☐   HMV DA1378
     Victor 1864
No. 2. Holzapfel und Schlehwein arr. vln & pf Heifetz
with E. Bay pf   Victor 10–1314, 49–0626
No. 3. Gartenszene arr. vln & pf Heifetz
with E. Bay pf   HMV DB6878
     Victor 12–0430, 18–0168, 49–
     0668

KREIN

Dance No. 4 vln & pf
with E. Bay pf   Brunswick LAT8020
     Decca DL8521

KREISLER

Minuet (Porpora) vln & pf
with A. Benoist pf   A 22275   HMV 5–7901, DA244
     Victor 64856, 673

Sicilienne & Rigaudon (Francoeur) vln & pf
with A. Benoist pf   A 22271   HMV 5–7925, DA246
     Victor 64917, 674

KROLL

Banjo & Fiddle vln & pf
with E. Bay pf   HMV DB6878
     Victor 12–0430, 18–0168, 49–
     0668, LM2382, LSC3233,
     RB16243

LALO

Symphonie espagnole, Op. 21 vln & orch.
Andante (4th mvt)
with orch.   HMV DB287
     Victor 74646, 6156

Symphonie espagnole, Op. 21 vln & orch.*
with RCA Victor Symphony Orch. –   HMV BLP1029, FALP252,
Steinberg   FBLP1019, VBLP809
     Victor (set WDM1603), LM127,
     LM1782

LOHR

Where my caravan has rested (1909) v & pf – arr. v, vln & orch.
with B. Crosby v &   L 4228 A   Brunswick 03938
orch. – Young   Decca 40012

MARTINŮ

Duo No. 1 (1927) vln & vlc
with G. Piatigorsky vlc   Victor LM2867, LSC2867,
     RB6665, SB6665

MEDTNER

(2) Fairy tales, Op. 20 (1910) pf
Fairy tale No. 1, in b flat arr. vln & pf Heifetz
with E. Bay pf   HMV DA1914
     Victor 10–1295, (in set M1126)

* Omitting Intermezzo.

MENDELSSOHN

Concerto in e, Op. 64 vln & orch.
  Allegro molto vivace (3rd mvt)
  with S. Chotzinoff pf   A 24472   HMV 3–07953, DB288
                                    Victor 74721, 6157

Concerto in e, Op. 64 vln & orch.
    2EA 13947–2T, 13948–1, 13949–   HMV DB6956/8, DB9413/5,
    2, 13950–1, 13951–4A & 13952–1   FALP136, LALP140, QALP136
  with Royal Philharmonic Orch. –   Plaisir Musical 30257
  Beecham   Seraphim 60162
                                  Victor (sets DM1356 &
                                  WDM1356), LM18, LM9016

Concerto in e, Op. 64 vln & orch.
  with Boston Symphony Orch. –   Victor (in set VCS7058),
  Munch   LM2314, LSC2314, LSC4012,
                                    RB16182, SB2066*1

(6) Gesänge, Op. 34 v & pf
  No. 2. Auf flügeln des Gesanges arr. vln & pf Achron
  with A. Benoist pf   A 22272   HMV 2–07982, DB283
                                  Pearl GEM109
                                  Victor 74583, 6152

  No. 2. Auf flügeln des Gesanges arr. vln & pf Achron
  with I. Achron pf   A 22272 △   HMV DB1206, DB1216, DB1246
                                  Victor 8648

  No. 2. Auf flügeln des Gesanges arr. vln & pf Achron
  with E. Bay pf   HMV ALP1206, FALP248
                                  Victor 12–0963, 49–0453,
                                  A95225, ERA126, LM1166,
                                  LSC3233

Octet in E flat, Op. 20 4 vlns, 2 vlas & 2 vlcs
  with I. Baker vln, A. Belnick vln, J.   Victor (in sets LD6159 &
  Stepansky vln, W. Primrose vla, V.   LDS6159), A640761/3, LM2738,
  Majewski vla, G. Piatigorsky vlc & G.   LSC2738, SHP2322,
  Rejto vlc   SOR630761/3

(6) Songs without words, Op. 19 pf
  No. 1. Song without words No. 1, in E "Sweet remembrance" arr. vln &
  pf Heifetz
  with E. Bay pf   HMV ALP1206, FALP248,
                                  7EB6001, 7EBW6001, 7RF267,
                                  7RQ267
                                  Victor 10–1457, 49–0540,
                                  ERA71, LM1166

Trio No. 1, in d, Op. 49 pf, vln & vlc
  Scherzo (3rd mvt) arr. vln & pf Heifetz
  with E. Bay pf   HMV ALP1206, FALP248
                                  Victor 10–1344, (in set MO1158),
                                  49–1221, (in set WDM1158),
                                  A95225, ERA214, LM1166

Trio No. 1, in d, Op. 49 pf, vln & vlc
  with A. Rubinstein pf & G.   HMV ALP1009, FALP111,
  Piatigorsky vlc   QALP10029
                                    Victor 49–3115/7, (set
                                  WDM1487), LM1119

Trio No. 2, in c, Op. 66 pf, vln & vlc
  with L. Pennario pf & G. Piatigorsky   Victor LSC3048
  vlc

* Allegro molto vivace or 3rd mvt is also on Victor LSC3234.

MILHAUD

(12) Saudades do Brasil (1920/1) pf
  No. 7. Corcavado arr. vln & pf Lévy
  with E. Bay pf   HMV ALP1206, FALP248,
                                    7RF250
                                  Victor 10–1343, (in set MO1158),
                                  49–1220, (in set WDM1158),
                                  LM1166

  No. 9. Sumaré arr. vln & pf Lévy
  with A. Sándor pf   OB 6053^III □   HMV DA1375

MOSZKOWSKI

(2) Stücke, Op. 45 pf
  No. 2. Guitarre arr. vln & pf Sarasate
  with A. Benoist pf   A 22270   HMV 4–7952, DA243
                                    Victor 64823, 672

  No. 2. Guitarre arr. vln & pf Sarasate
  with A. Sándor pf   OB 6045^V □   HMV DA1377
                                      Victor 1694

MOZART

Concerto No. 4, in D, K218 (cadenzas by Heifetz) vln & orch.
    2EA 12521–1 12522/5–2 12526–1   HMV DB6678/80, DB9336/8,
  with Royal Philharmonic Orch. –   FALP136, LALP140, QALP136
  Beecham   Plaisir Musical 30257
                                  Seraphim 60162
                                  Victor 12–0625/7, (set DM1267),
                                  49–0444/6, (set WDM1267),
                                  LM1051

Concerto No. 4, in D, K218 (cadenzas by Heifetz) vln & orch.
  with New Symphony Orch. of London   Victor A630767, LM2652,
  – Sargent   LSC2652, RB6527, SB6527

Concerto No. 5, in A, K219 "Turkish" (cadenzas by Joachim) vln & orch.
    2B 6801/3^I □, 6804^II □, 6805^I □   HMV DB2199/202, DB7692/5
    , 6806^II □ & 6807/8^I □   Victor 8601/4, (set M254)
  with London Philharmonic Orch. –
  Barbirolli

Concerto no. 5, in A, K219 "Turkish" (cadenzas by Joachim) vln & orch.
  with London Symphony Orch. –   HMV ALP1124, DB21472/5
  Sargent   Victor (set WDM9014), LM9014

Concerto No. 5, in A, K219 "Turkish" (cadenzas by Joachim) vln & orch.
  with chamber orch. – Heifetz   Victor LM2957, LSC2957,
                                    RB6715, SB6715

Divertimento in E flat, K563 vln, vla & vlc
  with W. Primrose vla & E. Feuermann   Victor 11–8546/9, 11–8550/3,
  vlc   (set M959), LCT1150, LVT1014

Divertimento No. 17, in D, K334 2 hrns & strs
  Minuet (3rd mvt) arr. vln & pf Burmester
  with S. Chotzinoff pf   Victor 66233, 997

  Minuet (3rd mvt) arr. vln & pf Burmester/Heifetz
  with E. Bay pf   HMV ALP1206, FALP248,
                                  7RF249
                                  Victor 12–0786, (in set
                                  DM1290), 12–0963, 49–0453,
                                  LM1166

Duo No. 2, in B flat, K424 vln & vla
  with W. Primrose vla   HMV DB8944S/6*
                                    Victor 18195/7S, (set M831),
                                  LCT1150, LVT1014

* Unissued.

MOZART – *Continued*

Quintet in C, K515 2 vlns, 2 vlas & vlc
with I. Baker vln, W. Primrose vla, H.　Victor LSC3048
Majewski vla & G. Piatigorsky vlc

Quintet in g, K516 2 vlns, 2 vlas & vlc
with I. Baker vln, W. Primrose vla, H.　Victor (in sets LD6159 &
Majewski vla & G. Piatigorsky vlc　　LDS6159), A640761/3, LM2738,
　　LSC2738, SHP2322,
　　SOR630761/3

Serenade No. 7, in D, K250 "Haffner" orch.
　Rondo (4th mvt) arr. vln & pf Kreisler
　with S. Chotzinoff pf　　A 24469　HMV 3–07964, DB292
　　　Rococo 2025
　　　Victor 74750, 6161

　Rondo (4th mvt) arr. vln & pf Kreisler
　with B. Smith pf
　　　Victor LSC3205

Sinfonia concertante in E flat, K354 vln, vla & orch.
with W. Primrose vla & RCA Victor　Victor LM2149, LSC2734,
Orch. – Solomon　　LSC3228

Sonata No. 17, in C, K296 vln & pf
with E. Bay pf
　　　Victor 12–0786/7, (set DM1290),
　　　(set WDM1290), LM1022

Sonata No. 26, in B flat, K378 vln & pf
with E. Bay pf
　　　HMV DB6050/1
　　　Victor 14326/7, 14331/4, (in set
　　　M343)

Sonata No. 26, in B flat, K378 vln & pf
with B. Smith pf
　　　HMV ALP1331
　　　Victor LM1958

Sonata No. 32, in B flat, K454 vln & pf
with E. Bay pf
　　　HMV DB6052/4
　　　Victor (set JAS238), 14328/30,
　　　14331/5, (in set M343)

Sonata No. 32, in B flat, K454 vln & pf
with B. Smith pf
　　　HMV ALP1331
　　　Victor LM1958

NIN

(20) Cantos de España (1923) v & pf
　No. 14. Asturiana arr. vln & pf as "Cantilène asturienne" by Lévy)
　with E. Bay pf
　　　HMV ALP1206, FALP248,
　　　7RF250
　　　Victor 10–1343, (in set MO1158),
　　　49–1220, (in set WDM1158),
　　　LM1166

PAGANINI

(24) Caprices, Op. 1 (1801/7) solo vln
　Caprice No. 13, in B flat arr. vln & pf Kreisler
　with S. Chotzinoff pf
　　　HMV DA241
　　　Victor 66037, 670

　Caprice No. 13, in B flat arr. vln & pf Kreisler
　with A. Sándor pf　　OB 6105 □ II　HMV DA1376, DA1761
　　　Victor 1697

　Caprice No. 13, in B flat arr. vln & pf Kreisler
　with B. Smith pf
　　　Victor A630588, LM2382,
　　　RB16243

　Caprice No. 20, in D arr. vln & pf Kreisler
　with A. Benoist pf
　　　HMV DA241
　　　Victor 64833, 670

PAGANINI – *Continued*

　Caprice No. 20, in D arr. vln & pf Kreisler
　with A. Sándor pf　　OB 6104[II] □　HMV DA1375, DA1761
　　　Victor 1697

　Caprice No. 20, in D arr. vln & pf Kreisler
　with B. Smith pf
　　　Victor A630588, LM2382,
　　　RB16243

　Caprice No. 24, in a arr. vln & pf Auer
　　　2B 6057[II] □ & 6058[I] □　HMV DB2218
　with A. Sándor pf　　Victor 8828

Moto perpetuo (Allegro di concert) Op. 11 (1880) vln & orch.
　with A. Benoist pf　　A 22267　HMV 2–07963, DB287
　　　Victor 74581

POLDOWSKI

Tango vln & pf
　with E. Bay pf
　　　HMV ALP1206
　　　Victor 10–1341, (in set MO1158),
　　　49–1218, (in set WDM1158),
　　　A95225, LM1166

PONCE

Estrellita (1913) v & pf – arr. vln & pf Heifetz
　with I. Achron pf　　A 43945　HMV DA984, DA1702
　　　Victor 1332

Estrellita (1913) v & pf – arr. vln & pf Heifetz
　with E. Bay pf
　　　Victor 10–1314, 49–0626,
　　　A95225, LSC3233

POULENC

(3) Mouvements perpétuels (1918) pf
　Mouvement perpétuel No. 1, in C arr. vln & pf Heifetz
　with E. Bay pf　　HMV DB3213*

　Mouvement perpétuel No. 1, in C arr. vln & pf Heifetz
　with B. Smith pf
　　　Victor A635051, A645051,
　　　LM2856, LSC2856, RB6644,
　　　SB6644

(3) Pieces (1934/5) pf
　No. 1. Presto in B flat arr. vln & pf Heifetz
　with E. Bay pf
　　　HMV DA1915
　　　Victor 10–1294, (in set M1126),
　　　ERA126, LSC3233

PROKOFIEV

Concerto No. 2, in g, Op. 63 (1935) vln & orch.
　with Boston　　2A 014400/05 △　HMV DB3604/6, DB8554/6
　Symphony Orch. – Koussevitzky　Victor 14907/9, (set M450),
　　　LCT6

Concerto No. 2, in g, Op. 63 (1935) vln & orch.†
　with Boston Symphony Orch. –　Victor LM2314, LSC2314,
　Munch　　LSC4010

(The) Love for Three Oranges, Op. 33 (1919) – opera
　No. 3. March arr. vln & pf Heifetz
　with E. Bay pf
　　　Brunswick LAT8020
　　　Decca DL8521

* Unissued.
† Andante assai or 2nd mvt. is also on Victor LSC3234.

PROKOFIEV – *Continued*

No. 3. March arr. vln & pf Heifetz
with B. Smith pf   Victor LSC3205

(10) Pieces, Op. 12 (1908/13) pf
No. 1. March in f arr. vln & pf Heifetz
with E. Bay pf   Victor 10–1355

(4) Pieces, Op. 32 (1918) pf
No. 3. Gavotta arr. vln & pf Heifetz
with E. Bay pf   Victor 10–1355

(10) Pieces (from the ballet "Romeo & Juliet") Op. 75 (1937) pf
No. 5. Masques arr. vln & pf Heifetz
with E. Bay pf   Columbia CCL35032
                                    Decca 24130, (in set A592),
                                    DL9780

RACHMANINOV

(9) Études–Tableaux, Op. 39 pf
No. 2. Étude–tableau No. 2, in a (Lento assai) arr. vln & pf Heifetz
with E. Bay pf   Victor 10–1296, (in set M1126)

(2) Pieces, Op. 2 (1892) pf
No. 2. Danse orientale arr. vln & pf as "Oriental sketch" by Heifetz
with E. Bay pf   Victor 10–1355

No. 2. Danse orientale arr. vln & pf as "Oriental sketch" by Heifetz
with B. Smith pf   Victor LM2978, LSC2978

(14) Songs, Op. 34 (1912) v & pf
No. 14. Vocalise arr. vln & pf Press
with E. Bay pf   Victor 26034, 12–0765, 49–0884,
                                    ERA94, LSC3233

(6) Songs, Op. 38 (1916) v & pf
No. 3. Daisies arr. vln & pf Heifetz
with E. Bay pf   Victor 10–1355

No. 3. Daisies arr. vln & pf Heifetz
with B. Smith pf   Victor LM2978, LSC2978

No. 3. Daisies arr. vln & pf Heifetz*
with B. Smith pf   Victor SPS33–565

RAVEL

Pièce en forme d'Habanera v & pf – arr. vln & pf Catherine
with M. Kaye pf   Brunswick 03617, AXL2017
                                    Columbia CCL35032
                                    Decca 23384, (in set A385),
                                    DL9780

Sonatina in f sharp (1905) pf
Menuet (2nd mvt) arr. vln & pf Roques
with E. Bay pf   Victor 12–0765, 49–0884,
                                    A630588, LM2382, RB16243

Trio in a (1915) pf, vln & vlc
                  EO–RC–386/9–1A,   HMV ALP1009, DB9620/2,
with A. Rubinstein pf & G. 390–IC & DB21294/6, FALP111,
Piatigorsky vlc   391–1A   QALP10029
                                    Victor 49–3112/4, (set
                                    WDM1486), LM1119

Tzigane (Rapsodie de concert) (1924) vln & pf or orch.
with A. Sándor pf   Victor 8411

Tzigane (Rapsodie de concert) (1924) vln & pf or orch.
with Los Angeles Philharmonic Orch. Victor A12R0153, A630815,
– Wallenstein   LM1832, LM2836

RAVEL – *Continued*

(7) Valses nobles et sentimentales (1911) pf
Nos. 6 & 7 arr. vln & pf Heifetz
with E. Bay pf   HMV DA1915
                                    Victor 10–1294, (in set M1126)

Nos. 6 & 7 arr. vln & pf Heifetz
with B. Smith pf   Victor A635051, A645051,
                                    LM2856, LSC2856, RB6644,
                                    SB6644

RESPIGHI

Sonata in b (1917) vln & pf
with E. Bay pf   HMV FALP165
                                    Victor (set WDM1576), LM1184,
                                    LVT1034

RIMSKY–KORSAKOV

(Le) Coq d'Or (1910) – opera
Hymn to the sun arr. vln & pf Kreisler
with E. Bay pf   Columbia CCL35032
                                    Decca 24129, (in set A592),
                                    DL9780, ED3501, EUA108503

(The) Tale of Tsar Saltan (1900) – opera
Flight of the bumblebee (Act III) orch. – arr. vln & pf Heifetz
with A. Sándor pf   Victor 1645

Flight of the bumblebee (Act III) orch. – arr. vln & pf Heifetz
                  D6–RB–3107–1A   HMV DA2037, EC208, 7RF171
with E. Bay pf   Victor 10–1328, 49–0540, 49–
                                    1294, ERA126

ROZSA

Concerto, Op. 24 vln & orch.
with Dallas Symphony Orch. – Hendl Victor LM2027, LM2767,
                                    LSC2767, RB6605, RB16009,
                                    SB6605

Concerto (1964) "Double" vln, vlc & orch.
Tema con variazioni (2nd mvt)
with G. Piatigorsky vlc & chamber   Victor A635029, A645029,
orch.   LM2770, LSC2770

SAINT–SAËNS

(Le) Carnaval des animaux (1886) small orch.
Le cygne arr. vln & pf Heifetz
with E. Bay pf   Brunswick LAT8020
                                    Decca DL8521

Le cygne arr. vln & pf Heifetz
with B. Smith pf   Victor A635051, A645051,
                                    LM2856, LSC2856, RB6644,
                                    SB6644

Havanaise, Op. 83 vln & orch.
with I. Achron pf   HMV DB866
                                    Victor 6510

Havanaise, Op. 83 vln & orch.
with London   2EA 4744/5¹ᴬ☐ HMV DB3211, ED89
Symphony Orch. – Barbirolli   Victor 15347

---

* Recorded September 15th & 16th 1970 at ORTE Studio 102, Paris.

SAINT–SAËNS – *Continued*

Havanaise, Op. 83 vln & orch.
E1–RC–2420–3A & 2421–1A
with RCA Victor Symphony Orch. –
Steinberg

HMV BLP1022, DB21552,
FALP252, QBLP5011,
VBLP808, 7RF169
Victor 49–3634, (in set
WDM1642), LM163, LM2382,
LSC3232, RB16243

Introduction & Rondo Capriccioso, Op. 28 vln & orch.
with London   2EA 1450/1ᴵᴵ□   HMV DB2580, DB3212
Philharmonic Orch. – Barbirolli   Victor 14115

Introduction & Rondo Capriccioso, Op. 28 vln & orch.
E1–RC–2422/3–2A
with RCA Victor Symphony Orch. –
Steinberg

HMV BLP1022, DB21516,
ED1236, FALP252, QBLP5011,
VBLP808, WBLP1022, 7R133,
7RF161, 7RQ161
Victor 12–3443, (in set
WDM1642), ERB7055, LSC3232

Sonata No. 1, in d, Op. 75 vln & pf
with E. Bay pf   Victor (set WDM1658), LM9007
Sonata No. 1, in d, Op. 75 vln & pf
with B. Smith pf   Victor LM2978, LSC2978

SARASATE

Carmen Fantasia (on themes from the opera by Bizet) Op. 25 vln & pf or
orch.
with I. Achron pf   HMV DB866
Victor 6510

(8) Danzas españolas vln & pf
No. 1. Malagueña, Op. 21, No. 1
with A. Benoist pf   A 21270   HMV 2–07966, DB285
Pearl GEM109
Rococo 2025
Victor 74569, 6154

No. 2. Habañera, Op. 21, No. 2
with I. Achron pf   A 27046   HMV DB838
Rococo 2025
Victor 6491

No. 3. Romanza andaluza, Op. 22, No. 1
with E. Bay pf   HMV DB6865
Victor 26034, 11–9573, ERA94

No. 3. Romanza andaluza, Op. 22, No. 1
with orch. –   J–584 USS 1006   V–Disc 848
Voorhees

No. 6. Zapateado, Op. 23, No. 2
with A. Benoist pf   A 22273   HMV 5–7982
Pearl GEM109
Victor 66097

No. 6. Zapateado, Op. 23, No. 2
with I. Achron pf   A 22273 △   HMV DB1048
Rococo 2025
Victor 6695

No. 6. Zapateado, Op. 23, No. 2
with E. Bay pf   HMV 7EB6001, 7EBW6001,
7RF171
Victor 10–1328, 49–1294,
ERA71, LSC3233

No. 6. Zapateado, Op. 23, No. 2
with orch. –   J 585 USS 1024   V–Disc 857
Voorhees

SARASATE – *Continued*

Introduction & Tarantelle, Op. 43 vln & pf
with A. Benoist pf   HMV DB285
Rococo 2025
Victor 74626, 6154

Zigeunerweisen, Op. 20 vln & pf or orch.
A 23407 & A 23410   HMV 3–07945 & 3–07947,
with S. Chotzinoff pf   DB284, S868 & S898
Pearl GEM109
Rococo 2025
Victor 74689 & 74694, 6153

Zigeunerweisen, Op. 20 vln & pf or orch.
with London   2EA 4746/7ᴵᴵ□   HMV DB3212
Symphony Orch. – Barbirolli   Victor 15246

Zigeunerweisen, Op. 20 vln & pf or orch.
E1–RC–2418/9–1A
with RCA Victor Symphony Orch. –
Steinberg

HMV DB21560, FALP252,
7RF225, 7RQ225
Victor 12–3782, 49–3782, (in set
WDM1642), ERB7055, LM163,
LM2069, LRM7055, LSC3232

SCHUBERT

Fantasia in C, Op. 159 (D934) vln & pf
with B. Smith pf   Victor LSC3109

(7) Gesänge (set to Scott's "Lady of the Lake") Op. 52 v & pf
No. 6. Ave Maria, D839 arr. vln & pf Wilhelmj
with A. Benoist pf   A 21072   HMV 2–07980, DB283
Victor 74563, 6152

No. 6. Ave Maria, D839 arr. vln & pf Wilhelmj
with I. Achron pf   A 21072   HMV DB1047
Victor 6691

No. 6. Ave Maria, D839 arr. vln & pf Wilhelmj
with E. Bay pf   HMV ALP1206, FALP248,
7RF267, 7RQ267
Victor 11–9571, 49–0301,
ERA184, LM1166, LSC3233

(4) Impromptus, Op. 90 (D899) pf
No. 3. Impromptu No. 3, in G arr. vln & pf Heifetz
with A. Sándor pf   2A 78974 △   HMV DB3215
Victor 8420

No. 3. Impromptu No. 3, in G arr. vln & pf Heifetz
VP–1546–D5–TC–1343–1E   V–Disc 547
with orch. – Voorhees

Quintet in C, Op. 163 (D956) 2 vlns, vla & 2 vlcs
with I. Baker vln, W. Primrose vla, G.   Victor (in sets LD6159 &
Piatigorsky vlc & G. Rejto vlc   LDS6159)

Sonata No. 17, in D, Op. 53 (D850) pf
Rondo (4th mvt) arr. vln & pf Friedberg
with I. Achron pf   A 38948   HMV DB1047, DB11114
Victor 6691

Rondo (4th mvt) arr. vln & pf Friedberg
with E. Bay pf   HMV DB6894
Victor 11–9572, ERA240

(3) Sonatinas, Op. 137 (D384, D385 & D408) vln & pf
Sonatina No. 3, in g, D408
with E. Bay pf   Victor A12R0159, LM1861

Trio No. 1, in B flat, Op. 99 (D898) pf, vln & vlc
with A. Rubinstein pf & E. Feuermann   HMV ED360/3
vlc   Victor 11–8274/7, 11–8394/7,
(set M923), A630778, LVT1000

SCHUBERT – *Continued*

Trio in B flat, D471 ("Sonata" in one movement) vln, vla & vlc
with W. Primrose vla & G. Piatigorsky Victor LM2563, LSC2563
vlc

SCHUMANN
(26) Myrthen, Op. 25 v & pf
No. 1. Widmung arr. vln & pf Auer
with S. Chotzinoff pf   Victor 66234, 997
(9) Waldscenen, Op. 82 pf
No. 7. Vogel als Prophet arr. vln & pf Auer
with E. Bay pf   Brunswick LAT8020
Decca DL8521

SCOTT
Danse nègre, Op. 58, No. 5 pf – arr. vln & pf Kramer
with E. Bay pf   HMV DB3213*

Tallahassee Suite, Op. 73 (1910) vln & pf
No. 1. Bygone memories
VP 1196–D5–TC–139–1D   V–Disc 422
with orch. – Voorhees

SGAMBATI
(2) Pieces, Op. 24 vln & pf
No. 2. Serenata napoletana
with B. Smith pf   Victor ERA240, LM2382,
RB16243

SHOSTAKOVICH
(3) Danses fantastiques, Op. 5 (1922) pf
No. 1. Allegretto arr. vln & pf Glickman
with E. Bay pf   HMV 7RF250
Victor 10–1457, 49–0450,
A630588, LM2382, RB16243
(24) Preludes, Op. 34 (1932/3) pf
Prelude No. 10, in c sharp arr. vln & pf Tziganov
with E. Bay pf   Columbia CCL35032
Decca 24129, (in set A592),
DL9780
Prelude No. 15, in D flat arr. vln & pf Tziganov
with E. Bay pf   Columbia CCL35032
Decca 24129, (in set A592),
DL9780

SHULMAN
Suite American "Folksong suite" vln & pf
Cod liver 'ile
with B. Smith pf   Victor LM2382, RB16243

SIBELIUS
Belshazzar's Feast, Op. 51 – Incidental music orch.
No. 3. Nocturne "Night song" arr. vln & pf Press
with B. Smith pf   Victor LM2978, LSC2978
Concerto in d, Op. 47 vln & orch.
2EA 2818ᴵᴵ☐, 2819/20ᴵ☐, 2821   HMV DB2791/4
ᴵᴵ☐, 2822ᴵᴵᴵ☐, 2823–3A☐, 2824ᴵᴵᴵ☐   Victor 14016/9, (set M309),
with London   & 2825ᴵᴵᴬ☐   16728/31, LCT1113, (set
Philharmonic Orch. – Beecham   WCT1113)

* Unissued.

SIBELIUS – *Continued*
Concerto in d, Op. 47 vln & orch.
with Chicago Symphony Orch. –   Victor A630827, LM2435,
Hendl   LSC2435, LSC4010, RB16229,
SB2101

SINDING
Suite in a, Op. 10 vln & orch.
with Los Angeles Philharmonic Orch.   Victor A630815, LM1832,
– Wallenstein   LM2836

SPOHR
Concerto No. 8, in a, Op. 47 "Gesangsscene" vln & orch.
with RCA Victor Symphony Orch. –   Victor LM2027, LM2860,
Solomon   RB6665, RB16009
Quartet No. 1, in d, Op. 65 "Double Quartet" 4 vlns, 2 vlas & 2 vlcs
with I. Baker vln, P. Amoyal vln, P.   Victor LSC3068
Rosenthal vln, M. Thomas vla, A.
Harshman vla, G. Piatigorsky vlc & L.
Lesser vlc

STRAUSS, R.
Sonata in E flat, Op. 18 vln & pf
with A. Sándor pf   Victor 7974/7S, 7978/81S, (set
M200), LCT1122, LVT1007
Sonata in E flat, Op. 18 vln & pf
with B. Smith pf   Victor LM2050, LM2860,
RB6665
(5) Stimmungsbilder, Op. 9 pf
No. 2. An einsamer Quelle arr. vln & pf Heifetz
with A. Sándor pf   2B 6042ᴵᴵᴵ☐   HMV DB3214
Victor 14369

STRAVINSKY
Firebird (1910) – ballet suite orch.
No. 5. Berceuse arr. vln & pf Dushkin & Stravinsky
with E. Bay pf   HMV 7RF250
Victor 10–1457, 49–0450,
A630588, ERA94, LM2382,
RB16243

SZYMANOWSKI
King Roger, Op. 46 (1926) – opera
Chant de Roxane arr. vln & pf Kochański
with E. Bay pf   2EA 2580ᴵ☐   HMV DB2846
Victor 14625

TANSMAN
(5) Pieces vln & pf or small orch.
No. 3. Mouvement perpétuel
with E. Bay pf   Victor 12–0765, 49–0884

TCHAIKOVSKY
Concerto in D, Op. 35 vln & orch.
Canzonetta (2nd mvt)
with orch.   A 24475   HMV 3–07941, DB289
Pearl GEM109
Victor 74678, 6158

TCHAIKOVSKY – *Continued*

Concerto in D, Op. 35 vln & orch.
with London   2EA 4709/16[1]☐   HMV DB3159/62
Philharmonic Orch. – Barbirolli   Victor 14401/4, 14405/8, (set M356), 16756/9, ND85/8, (set JAS21)

Concerto in D, Op. 35 vln & orch.
     2EA 14804–3A, 14805–1A,   HMV BLP1012, DB21228/31,
14806–1B, 14807–3, 14808–1, 14809   FBLP1008, LBLP1046,
–3A, 14810–3 & 14811–1D   QBLP1008
with Philharmonia Orch. – Susskind   Victor 49–3033/6, (set WDM1442), A12R0153, LM1111, LM1832

Concerto in D, Op. 35 vln & orch.*
with Chicago Symphony Orch. –   Victor (in sets VCS7058 &
Reiner   VCS7086), A630641, LM2129, LM6803, LSC2129, LSC4012, LSC5020, LSC6803, RB16038, SB2002

Serenade in C, Op. 48 str orch.
   Valse (2nd mvt) arr. vln & pf Auer
with orch.   A 23409   HMV 3–07928, DB286
Victor 74635, 6155

Serenade in C, Op. 48 str orch.
   Valse (2nd mvt) arr. vln & pf Auer
with chamber orch.   Victor LSC3109

Sérénade mélancolique in b flat, Op. 26 vln & orch.
with orch.   A 24478   HMV 3–07950, DB286
Victor 74711, 6155

Sérénade mélancolique in b flat, Op. 26 vln & orch.
with Los Angeles Philharmonic Orch.   Victor LM2027, LM2860,
– Wallenstein   RB6665, RB16009

Sérénade mélancolique in b flat, Op. 26 vln & orch.
with chamber orch.   Victor LSC3109

Souvenir d'un lieu cher, Op. 42 vln & pf
   No. 2. Scherzo
with S. Chotzinoff pf   Victor 66191, 1024
   No. 3. Mélodie
with E. Bay pf   Brunswick LAT8020
Decca DL8521

Trio in a, Op. 50 "To the memory of a great artist" pf, vln & vlc
with A. Rubinstein pf & G.   HMV FALP166, QALP166
Piatigorsky vlc   Victor 49–3121/5, (set WDM1488), A630639, L16212, LM1120

TOCH

(2) Divertimenti, Op. 37
   Divertimento No. 2 vln & vla
with G. Piatigorsky vlc   Victor LM3009, LSC3009

TURINA

Trio No. 1, in d, Op. 35 pf, vln & vlc
with L Pennario pf & G. Piatigorsky   Victor LM2957, LSC2957
vlc

* Allegro moderato or 1st mvt is also on Victor LSC3234.

VALLE

Ao pé da fogueira (Prelude XV) pf – arr. vln & pf Heifetz
with E. Bay pf   Brunswick LAT8020
Decca DL8521

VIEUXTEMPS

Concerto No. 4, in d, Op. 31 vln & orch.
     2EA 1444/6[1]☐, 1447[1]☐ &   HMV DB2444/6
with London Philharmonic 1448/9[II]☐   Victor 8913/5, 8916/8, (set
Orch. – Barbirolli   M297), 16941/3

Concerto No. 5, in a, Op. 37 vln & orch.
with London   2EA 1213/6 ☐   HMV ALP1124, DB6547/8,
Symphony Orch. – Sargent   FALP270
Victor (set WDM1240), 12–0381/2, (set DM1240), LM1121, LVT1033

Concerto No. 5, in a, Op. 37 vln & orch.
with New Symphony Orch. of London   Victor A630720, A640720,
– Sargent   LM2603, LSC2603, RB6503, SB6503

VITALI

Chaconne in g vln & c – arr. Respighi
with R. Ellsasser org   HMV DB4320, 7RF170
Victor 49–3305, LM2074

VIVALDI

Concerto in B flat, P.388 (F.IV, No.2) (Op. 22, No. 2) vln, vlc, strs & c
with G. Piatigorsky vlc, M. Hamilton   Victor LM2867, LSC2867,
hpsi & chamber orch.   RB6665, SB6665

(12) Sonatas, Op. 2 (1712) vln & c
   Sonata No. 2, in A, F.XIII, No. 30 arr. vln & pf Busch
with A. Sándor pf   HMV DA1370
Victor 1810

WALTON

Concerto (1939) vln & orch.
with Cincinnati Symphony Orch. –   HMV DB5953/5, DB8911/3,
Goossens   ED217/9
Victor 18414/6, 18417/9, (set M868)

Concerto (1939) vln & orch.
     2EA 14847/9–1, 14850–1A,   HMV BLP1047, DB21257/9,
with   14851–1 & 14852–1B   DB9611/3, QBLP5027
Philharmonia Orch. – Walton   Victor LM1121, LVT1033

WAXMAN

Carmen Fantasia (on themes from the opera by Bizet) vln & orch.
with RCA Victor Symphony Orch. –   Victor 11–9422, 49–0130, (in set
Voorhees   WDM1642), LM163, L16285, LSC3232

WEILL

(Die) Dreigroschenoper (1928) – opera
   Morität arr. vln & pf as "Moderato assai" by Heifetz
with E. Bay pf   Brunswick LAT8020
Decca DL8521

WHITE

Levee dance (based on "Go down Moses") Op. 27, No. 2 vln & pf
  with M. Kaye pf
    Brunswick AXL2017
    Columbia CCL35032
    Decca 23387, (in set A385),
    DL9780, UA243086
    Odeon 288889

WIENIAWSKI

Capriccio–valse, Op. 7 vln & pf
  with B. Smith pf   Victor LM2978, LSC2978
Concerto No. 2, in d, Op. 22 vln & orch.
  Romance (2nd mvt)
  with A. Benoist pf   A 22266 HMV 3–07912, DB291
    Pearl GEM109
    Rococo 2025
    Victor 74600, 6160

Concerto No. 2, in d, Op. 22 vln & orch.
  2EA 1452^{II}□, 1453^{I}□, 1454^{II}□ HMV DB2447/9, DB7866/8
  with London   & 1455/6^{I}□ Victor 8757/9, (set M275),
  Philharmonic Orch. – Barbirolli 16991/3
Concerto No. 2, in d, Op. 22 vln & orch.
  with RCA Victor Symphony Orch. – HMV ALP1362
  Solomon   Victor LM1931
Polonaise brillante No. 1, in D, Op. 4 vln & pf
  with E. Bay pf   2EA 4856^{II}□ HMV DB3215
    Victor 15813, 17613, (in set
    M735)
Polonaise brillante No. 1, in D, Op. 4 vln & pf
  with E. Bay pf   Victor ERA57
Scherzo–Tarantelle, Op. 16 vln & pf
  with A. Benoist pf   A 21069 HMV 2–07961, DB290
    Pearl GEM109
    Rococo 2025
    Victor 74562, 6159

Scherzo–Tarantelle, Op. 16 vln & pf
  with a. Sándor pf   2B 6067^{II}□ HMV DB2219
    Victor 16991, 18341, (in set
    M856)
Scherzo–Tarantelle, Op. 16 vln & pf
  with E. Bay pf   Victor 26034, ERA94, LSC3233

Adolf HEINEMANN

BACH

(6) Brandenburg Concerti, BWV1046/51 (1721) strs & c
  Brandenburg Concerto No. 2, in F, BWV1047 tpt, fl, ob, vln & strs
  with J. Flugel tpt, C. Fischer fl, O. Classics Club X3005
  Bruch ob & Nordwestdeutsche
  Chamber Orch. – Friedmann
  Brandenburg Concerto No. 4, in G, BWV1049 vln, 2 fls & strs
  with C. Fischer fl, H. Vogel fl & Classic Club X3006
  Nordwestdeutsche Chamber Orch. –
  Friedmann
  Brandenburg Concerto No. 5, in D, BWV1050 clav, fl, vln & strs
  with F. Neumann hpsi, C. Fischer fl & Classics Club X3006
  Nordwestdeutsche Chamber Orch. –
  Friedmann

BACH – Continued

Concerto in d, BWV1043 2 vlns, strs & c
  with O. Schmidt vln & Classics Club Classics Club X1008
  Chamber Orch. – Friedmann

Hans HEKKING

SVENDSEN

Romance in G, Op. 26 vln & orch.
  with Scandinavian Symphony Orch. – Maestro OAT25008
  Johannesen   Vega MT10194

Amely HELLER

NEŠVERA

Wiegenlied, Op. 25 vln & pf
  with piano   LX 809^{2} G Odeon 32802

SCHUMANN

(12) Duets, Op. 85 pf – 4 hands
  No. 12. Abendlied arr. vln & pf
  with piano   LX 810 G Odeon 32803

Ferdinand HELLMANN

BACH

Concerto in d, BWV1043 2 vlns, strs & c
  with L. Zimmermann vln &   Decca K20043/4
  Concertgebouw Orch., Amsterdam –
  Mengelberg

VIVALDI

(12) Concerti, Op. 3 "L'Estro armonico" var. cbns & strs
  Concerto No. 8, in a, P.2 (F.I, No. 177) 2 vlns, strs & c
  with L. Zimmermann vln & orch. – Telefunken SK2401/2
  Mengelberg

Ruth HELLMANN

BACH

Cantata No. 129 (Gelobet sei der Herr) BWV129
  with U. Buckel s, M. Conrad a, C–H. Da Camera SM94019
  Müller bs, H. Zickler tpt, H. Thal tpt,
  F. Kelber tpt, W. Richter fl, F.
  Mohrmann ob, H. Bogacki ob d'amore,
  G. Schuldt bsn, W. Taube vlc, M.
  Schuster org & Bach Choir & Orch.,
  Mainz – Hellmann

Georg Friedrich HENDEL

ALBINONI

Adagio in g strs & org
  with Saar Chamber Orch. – Ristenpart Columbia SMC95047
    Erato STU70231

BACH

Concerto in d, BWV1043 2 vlns, strs & c
  with U. Grehling vln & Saar Chamber   Discophiles Français DF127
  Orch. – Ristenpart

Concerto in a, BWV1044 clav, fl, vln, strs & c
  with S. Kind hpsi, K. Cromm fl &   Nonesuch H1057, H71057
  Saar Chamber Orch. – Ristenpart

Concerto in c, BWV1060 vln & ob or 2 vlns, strs & c
  with H. Winschermann ob & German   Bärenreiter Musicaphon BM30
  Bach Soloists – Winschermann   SL1201
    Cantate 047702, 057702
    Oryx 3C308

Concerto in C, BWV1064 3 clavs, strs & c – arr. fl, ob, vln, strs & c "in D"
  with H–J. Möhring fl, H.   Bärenreiter Musicaphon BM30
  Winschermann ob & German Bach   SL1201
  Soloists – Winschermann

Concerto in C, BWV1064 3 clavs, strs & c – arr. 3 vlns, strs & c "in D"
  with K. Schlupp vln, H. Bünte vln &   Nonesuch H1057, H71057
  Saar Chamber Orch. – Ristenpart

(6) Sonatas, BWV1014/9 vln & clav
  Sonata No. 1, in b, BWV1014
  with H. Dreyfus hpsi   Valois MB815
  Sonata No. 2, in A, BWV1015
  with H. Dreyfus hpsi   Valois MB815
  Sonata No. 3, in E, BWV1016
  with H. Dreyfus hpsi   Valois MB815
  Sonata No. 4, in c, BWV1017
  with H. Dreyfus hpsi   Valois MB815
  Sonata No. 5, in f, BWV1018
  with H. Dreyfus hpsi   Valois MB816
  Sonata No. 6, in G, BWV1019
  with H. Dreyfus hpsi   Valois MB816

Sonata in C, BWV1037 2 vlns & c
  with K. Schlupp vln, R. Christensen   Christophorus CGLP75841/2,
  hpsi & B. Hindrichs vlc   SDGLP75843/4
    Erato STU70189
    Musical Heritage Society
    MHS657

Sonata in G, BWV1038 fl, vln & c*
  with M. Larrieu fl, R. Christensen hpsi   Christophorus CGLP75841/2,
  & B. Hindrich vlc   SDGLP75843/4
    Erato STU70189
    Musical Heritage Society
    MHS657

BIBER

Serenade in C "Der Nachtwächter" bs–v, 2 vlns, 2 vlas & c
  with J. Stämpfli bs, H. Bünte vln, G.   Erato STU70318
  Karau hpsi & B. Hindrich vlc   Musical Heritage Society
    MHS938

CALDARA

(12) Sonatas, Op. 1 2 vlns & c
  Sonata No. 9, in b
  with H. Bünte vln, G. Karau hpsi &   Erato STU70318
  B. Hindrichs vlc   Musical Heritage Society
    MHS938

* Doubtful.

CORELLI

(12) Concerti grossi, Op. 6 orch.
  Concerto grosso No. 9, in F
  with H. Bünte vln, G. Karau hpsi, B.   Columbia C91101, EPC50585,
  Hindrichs vlc & Saar Chamber Orch. –   EPSTC50585, STC91101
  Ristenpart

HANDEL

(12) Concerti grossi, Op. 6 2 vlns, vlc & strs
  Concerto grosso No. 6, in g
  with E. Mayer–Schierning vln, A.   Cantate 047705, 057705
  Bauer vlc & German Bach Soloists –
  Stephani

HAYDN

Sinfonia concertante in B flat, Op. 84 (H.I, No. 105) vln, vlc, ob, bsn & orch.
  with B. Hindrichs vlc, H.   Music Guild M35, S35
  Winschermann ob, J. Haultier bsn &   Nonesuch H1024, H71024
  Saar Chamber Orch. – Ristenpart

MOZART

Adagio in E, K261 vln & orch.
  with Saar Chamber Orch. – Ristenpart   Erato STU70318
    Musical Heritage Society
    MHS938

Concerto in G, K250 vln & orch.
  with Saar Radio Chamber Orch. –   Erato EGR4008
  Ristenpart   Musical Heritage Society
    MHS921

Concerto No. 3, in G, K216 (cadenzas by Franko) vln & orch.
  with Saar Radio Chamber Orch. –   Erato EGR4008
  Ristenpart   Musical Heritage Society
    MHS921

Concertone in C, K290 2 vlns, ob, vlc & orch.
  with P. Makanowitzky vln & Saar   Club Français du Disque
  Chamber Orch. – Ristenpart

Concertone in C, K190 2 vlns, ob, vlc & orch.
  with O. Büchner vln, P. Pierlot ob, R.   Erato LDE3362, STE50262,
  Dommisch vlc & Radiodiffusion   STU70262
  Chamber Orch. – Ristenpart

Rondo in C, K373 vln & orch.
  with Saar Radio Chamber Orch. –   Erato EGR4008
  Ristenpart   Musical Heritage Society
    MHS921

Serenade No. 7, in D, K250 "Haffner" orch.
  with Saar Radio Chamber Orch. –   Erato LDE3357, STE50257,
  Ristenpart   STU70257
    Musical Heritage Society
    MHS756

MUFFAT

(12) Concerti grossi (1701) 2 vlns, vlc, strs & c
  Concerto grosso No. 11, in e "Delirium Amoris" (real. A. Garcin–Lauth)
  with H. Bünte vln, G. Karau hpsi, B.   Erato STU70318
  Hindrichs vlc & Saar Radio Chamber   Musical Heritage Society
  Orch. – Ristenpart   MHS938

STAMITZ, K.

Sinfonia concertante in D vln, vla & orch.
  with P. Makanowitzky vln & Saar   Nonesuch H1014, H71014
  Chamber Orch. – Ristenpart

TELEMANN

Concerto in C 2 vlns, strs & c
    with H. Bünte vln, G. Karau hpsi &
    Saar Radio Chamber Orch. –
    Ristenpart

Columbia SMC95067
Erato LDE3372, STE50272,
STU70272
Musical Heritage Society
MHS751

TOËSCHI

Concerto in D vln & orch.
    with Saar Radio Chamber Orch. –
    Ristenpart

Columbia C91103, STC91103

VIVALDI

(12) Concerti, Op. 3 "L'Estro armonico" var. cbns & strs
    Concerto No. 6, in a, P.1 (F.I, No. 176) vln, strs & c
    with Saar Radio Chamber Orch. –
    Ristenpart

Nonesuch H1022, H71022

Concerto in D, P.189 (F.I, No. 41) 2 vlns, strs & c
    with K. Schlupp vln & Saar Radio
    Chamber Orch. – Ristenpart

Elite Special SMLP5011
Nonesuch H9, H79, H1022,
H71022

Concerto in F, P.278 (F.I, No. 34) 3 vlns, strs & c
    with K. Schlupp vln, H. Bünte vln &
    Saar Radio Chamber Orch. –
    Ristenpart

Elite Special SMLP5011
Nonesuch H1022, H71022

Concerto in B flat, P.406 (F.XII, No. 16) vln, ob, strs & c
    with J. Chambon ob & Saar Chamber
    Orch. – Ristenpart

Nonesuch H1104, H71104

M. HENDRIKS

BACH

Concerto in c, BWV1060 vln & ob or 2 vlns, strs & c
    with H. Töttcher ob & Berlin Radio
    Symphony Orch.

Urania RS7–31

William H. HENLEY (1874–1957)

HENLEY

Variations hongroises, Op. 55 vln & pf
    with piano

Beka 87, 40567

Variations on the Austrian hymn, Op. 33, No. 1 vln & pf
    with piano

Beka 87, 40566

MOSZKOWSKI

(6) Klavierstücke, Op. 15 pf – 4 hands
    No. 1. Serenata arr. vln, vlc & pf
    with Lebell vlc & H.E. Geehl pf

Beka 40564, M18

TCHAIKOVSKY

(12) Pieces (of moderate difficulty) Op. 40 pf
    No. 2. Chanson triste arr. vln, vlc & pf
    with Lebell vlc & H.E. Geehl pf

Beka 40565, M18

Fini Valdemar HENRIQUES (1867–1940)

BACH

(3) Sonatas & 3 Partitas, BWV1001/6 solo vln
    Partita No. 3, in E: 2 Minuettos (4th mvt) BWV1006 arr. vln & pf
    Henriques
    with piano

451 ak HMV 7–87907, V73

BEETHOVEN

Élégie unid pf – arr. vln & pf Henriques
    with piano

837 aj HMV 2–087903, M24

GABRINSKY

Petite polonaise vln & pf
    with piano

3957 ah HMV 7–87906, V73

GODARD

Concerto No. 1, Op. 35 "Concerto Romantique" vln & orch.
    Canzonetta (2nd mvt) arr. vln & pf Henriques
    with piano

3192 ab HMV X1621

GOSSEC

Rosine (1786) – opera
    Gavotte arr. vln & pf Burmester
    with piano

116047 Odeon 2235, 257X

GOUNOD

Ave Maria (Méditation on Bach's "Prelude No. 1, in C" from Book I of "Das Wohltemperirte Clavier") v & pf – arr. v, vln & pf
    with E. Wilton s &
    piano

BW 1490^{II}△ HMV 7–53129, V192

Noël v & pf – arr. v, vln & pf
    with P. Cornelius t &
    piano

4064 ah HMV 7–82044, V66, X1942

HENRIQUES

Canzonetta, Op. 27 vln & pf
    with piano

3977 ah HMV K87905, V58

Det døende barn (The dying child) (1899) v & pf – arr. v, vln & pf
    Henriques*
    with E. Wilton s &
    piano

BW 1489^I△ HMV V195

(5) Erotic pieces, Op. 15 pf
    No. 4. Petite romance arr. vln & pf Henriques
    with piano

3976 ah HMV K87904, V58

Myggedans (Gnat's dance) Op. 20, No. 5 vln & pf
    with piano

3197 ab HMV K87923, X1623

Myggedans (Gnat's dance) Op. 20, No. 5 vln & pf
    with B. Rosenbaum pf

OCS 456–2 HMV X4834

(10) Pieces pf
    No. 3. Bryllupsdans (Gavotte) arr. vln & pf Henriques
    with piano

3976 ah HMV K87904, V58

Romance in D, Op. 43 vln & pf – arr. 2 vlns & pf Henriques
    with K. Pedersen vln &
    piano

1281 ak HMV K88022, V101

Sammenspil (10 character pieces) Op. 22 vln & pf
    No. 6. Vuggesang
    with piano

3196 ab HMV X1623

* Music set to a poem by H.C. Andersen.

HENRIQUES – *Continued*

(4) Songs, Op. 3 v & pf
No. 4. Agnetes Vuggevise arr. v, vln & pf Henriques
with E. Wilton s &   BW 1489¹△   HMV V195
piano

No. 4. Agnetes Vuggevise arr. vln & pf Henriques
with B. Rosenbaum pf   OCS 457–1   HMV X4834

To maa man vaere (There must be two) (1920) v & pf – arr. v, vln & pf
Henriques*
with E. Wilton s &   BW 569¹△   HMV V185
piano

Wiegenlied vln & pf
with piano   3195 ab   HMV K87922

JÄRNEFELT

Berceuse in g orch. – arr. vln & pf Henriques
with piano   3194 ab   HMV K87927, X1622

LECLAIR

(12) Sonatas, Op. 9 – Book IV (1738) vln & c
Sonata No. 3, in D: Sarabande (1st mvt) arr. vln & pf Sarasate
with piano   3197 ab   HMV K87923, X1623

LENZ

Concert mazurka vln & pf
with piano   116045   Odeon 1194, 413X

LOTTI

Arminio (1714) – pasticcio
Pur dicesti arr. vln & pf Henriques
with piano   3198 ab   HMV X1622

PRUME

Fantaisie & variations sur un thème d'Hérold, Op. 9 vln & pf – arr. Henriques
with piano   4 AR   HMV 2–087904, M24

RAFF

(6) Pieces, Op. 85 vln & pf
No. 3. Cavatina in D
with piano   116044   Odeon 1193, 413X

No. 3. Cavatina in D arr. 2 vlns & pf Henriques
with J.F. Henriques vln &   3954 ah   HMV K7–88000, V59, X2046
piano

SCHUMANN

(12) Duets, Op. 85 pf – 4 hands
No. 12. Abendlied arr. vln & pf
with piano   3193 ab   HMV K87926, X1621

No. 12. Abendlied arr. 2 vlns & pf Henriques
with J.F. Henriques vln &   3955 ah   HMV K7–88001, V59, X2046
piano

(13) Kinderscenen, Op. 15 pf
No. 7. Träumerei arr. vln & pf
with piano   116048   Odeon 2232, 235X

* Music set to a poem by H. Rantzau.

SINDING

Serenade No. 1, in G, Op. 56 2 vlns & pf
with J.F. Henriques vln &   3956 ah   HMV K88021, V101
piano

SIVORI

(2) Romanzas senza paroles, Op. 23 vln & pf*
with piano   116046   Odeon 2234, 257X

SVENDSEN

Romance in G, Op. 26 vln & orch.
with orch.   426 ac   HMV M087900, Z152

WIENIAWSKI

Capriccio–valse, Op. 7 vln & pf
with piano   429 ac   HMV M087901, Z152

Mazurka in a, Op. 3 "Kujawiak" vln & pf
with piano   116049   Odeon 2233, 235X

Johan Fini HENRIQUES (1892–)

FLÉGIER

(Les) Stances v & pf – arr. v, vln & pf
with T. Frederiksen s &   41 ¹¹ AR   HMV 2–083005, M35
piano

NICHOLLS

(The) Heart of a rose vln & pf
with piano   651 AX   Polydor 47500

PIERNÉ

Sérenade in A, Op. 7 (1875) pf – arr. vln & pf Haddock
with piano   652 AX   Polydor 47501

RAFF

(6) Pieces, Op. 85 vln & pf
No. 3. Cavatina in D arr. 2 vlns & pf Henriques
with F. V. Henriques vln   3954 ah   HMV K7–88000, V59, X2046
& piano

SAINT-SAËNS

(Le) Carnaval des animaux (1886) small orch.
Le cygne arr. vln & pf
with piano   3975 ah   HMV AL727, X437, X7–287911

SCHUMANN

(12) Duets, Op. 85 pf – 4 hands
No. 12. Abendlied arr. 2 vlns & pf Henriques
with F.V. Henriques vln &   3955 ah   HMV K7–88001, V59, X2046
piano

SINDING

Serenade No. 1, in G, Op. 56 2 vlns & pf
with F.V. Henriques vln &   3956 ah   HMV K88021, V101
piano

TOSELLI

Serenade, Op. 6 vln & pf
with piano   3974 ah   HMV AL727, X437, X7–287910

* Unidentified.

Charles HERMAN

d'AMBROSIO

Canzonetta No. 3, Op. 47 vln & pf
with piano   Pathé X9807

Introduction & Humoresque, Op. 25 vln & pf
with orch.   Pathé 9537

ASSEMMACHES

Divertissement vln & pf
with piano   Pathé X9847

BRAHMS

(21) Hungarian Dances pf duet
Hungarian dance No. 5, in f sharp arr. vln & pf "in g" Joachim
with piano   Pathé 8514, 9539, 40128
                                             Pathé–Actuelle 15240

CHOPIN

(3) Nocturnes, Op. 9 pf
No. 2. Nocturne No. 2, in E flat arr. vln & pf Sarasate
with orch.   Pathé 9540

ERLANGER

Aphrodite (1905) – opera
Prélude orch. – arr. vln & orch.
with orch.   Pathé 9545

FLAMENT

Aubade No. 5 vln & pf
with piano   Pathé X9847

GODARD

Concerto No. 1, Op. 35 "Concerto Romantique" vln & orch
Canzonetta (2nd mvt)
with piano   Pathé X9807

LALO

Concerto in g, Op. 29 "Concerto Russe" vln & orch.
Chants russes (2nd mvt)
with orch.   Pathé 9544

MENDELSSOHN

(6) Songs without words, Op. 62 pf
No. 6. Song without words No. 30, in A "Spring song" arr. vln & pf
with piano   Pathé 8534, 9542, 40147

MOSZKOWSKI

(6) Nachtstücke, Op. 56 vln & pf
No. 2. Sarabande
with piano   Pathé 9541

No. 3. Passepied
with piano   Pathé 9541

MUSIN

(2) Morceaux de concert, Op. 7 (1887) vln & pf
No. 1. Mazurka de concert
with orch.   Pathé 9538

No. 2. Valse de concert
with orch.   Pathé 9538

PAGANINI

(24) Caprices, Op. 1 (1801/7) solo vln
Caprice No. 13, in B flat arr. vln & pf Herman
with piano   Pathé 8513, 9537, 40128

Caprice No. 24, in a arr. vln & pf Herman
with piano   Pathé X9808

PROVINCIALI

Aubade vln & pf
with piano   Pathé 8519, 9542

RUBINSTEIN

(6) Soirées de Saint–Pétersbourg, Op. 44 pf
No. 1. Romance in E flat arr. vln & pf Wieniawski
with piano   Pathé 9541, 9643, 40147

SAINT–SAËNS

(Le) Déluge, Op. 45 (1876) – oratorio
Prélude, vln & orch.
with orch.   Pathé 9545

SCHUMANN

(13) Kinderscenen, Op. 15 pf
No. 7. Träumerei arr. vln & orch.
with orch.   Pathé 9543

TCHAIKOVSKY

(3) Souvenirs de Hapsal, Op. 2 pf
No. 3. Chant sans paroles in f arr. vln & pf Kreisler
with orch.   Pathé 9543

VIVALDI

(12) Sonatas, Op. 2 (1712) vln & c
Sonata No. 2, in A, F.XIII, No. 30 (ed.David)
with piano   Pathé 9540, 9643

WIENIAWSKI

Concerto No. 2, in d, Op. 22 vln & orch.
Romance (2nd mvt)
with orch.   Pathé 9544

ZARZYCKI

Mazurka in G, Op. 26 vln & pf
with piano   Pathé 8515, 9539
                                             Pathé–Actuelle 15240

K. A. HERMANN

VIVALDI

(12) Concerti, Op. 3 "L'Estro armonico" var. cbns & strs
Concerto No. 1, in D, P.146 (F.IV, No. 8) 4 vlns, vlc, strs & c
with S. Gavrilov vln, S. Karolyi vln, E.   Cetra LPU006
Schilling vln & Frankfurt Chamber
Orch. – Goehr

Concerto No. 4, in e, P.97 (F.I, No. 174) 4 vlns, strs & c
with S. Gavrilov vln, S. Karolyi vln, E.   Cetra LPU007
Schilling vln & Frankfurt Chamber
Orch. – Goehr

Concerto No. 7, in f, P.249 (F.IV, No. 9) 4 vlns, strs & c
with S. Gavrilov vln, S. Karolyi vln, E.   Cetra LPU007
Schilling vln & Frankfurt Chamber
Orch. – Goehr

VIVALDI – *Continued*

Concerto No. 10, in b, P.148 (F.IV, No. 10) 4 vlns, strs & c
with S. Gavrilov vln, S. Karolyi vln, E. Cetra LPU006
Schilling vln & Frankfurt Chamber
Orch. – Goehr

Yeala HERTZ

HAYDN

Concerto in F, H.XVIII, No. 6 (1765) vln, hpsi & orch.
with K. Gilbert hpsi & McGill   CBC Radio Canada SM18
Chamber Orch. – Brott

Max HERZL

HANDEL

Serse (1738) – opera
Ombra mai fu "Largo" arr. vln & pf
with piano   Pathé 19849

WIENIAWSKI

Mazurka in a, Op. 3 "Kujawiak" vln & pf
with piano   Pathé 19848

Gerhard HETZEL

LOUIS FERDINAND (Prince of Prussia)

Suite romantique vln & orch.
with Chamber Orch. – von Benda   Eurodisc 41190CK, 41191CK

Yvonne HEURTEVANT

LALO

Symphonie espagnole, Op. 21 vln & orch.*
with Vienna Tonkunstler Symphony   Plymouth P12–46
Orch.

Marta HIDY

ADASKIN

Canzona & Rondo (1949) vln & pf
with C. Duncan pf   Victor CC1015, CCS1015

BARTÓK

(6) Rumanian folk dances (1915) pf – arr. vln & pf Székely
with L. Barkin pf   CBC Radio Canada SM28

BLOCH

Baal Shem (3 Pictures of Chassidic life) (1923) vln & pf
No. 2. Nigun (Improvisation)
with L. Barkin pf   CBC Radio Canada SM28

DEBUSSY

Sonata No. 3, in g (1917) vln & pf
with L. Barkin pf   CBC Radio Canada SM54

* Including Intermezzo.

GRIEG

Sonata No. 3, in c, Op. 45 vln & pf
with L. Barkin pf   CBC Radio Canada SM54

KODÁLY

Adagio in C (1905) vln & pf
with L. Barkin pf   CBC Radio Canada SM28

MORAWETZ

Duo (1946) vln & pf
with L. Barkin pf   CBC Radio Canada SM28

PROKOFIEV

(The) Love for Three Oranges, Op. 33 (1919) – opera
No. 3. March arr. vln & pf Heifetz
with L. Barkin pf   CBC Radio Canada SM28

SOMERS

Sonata No. 1 (1953) vln & pf
with C. Duncan pf   Victor CC1015, CCS1015

Alexander HILSBERG (1900–1961)

SAINT-SAËNS

Danse macabre, Op. 40 (1874) orch.
with Philadelphia Orch. – Stokowski   HMV DB3077
                                        Victor 14162

STRAUSS, R.

Don Quixote, Op. 35 (1897) orch.
with Philadelphia Orch. – Ormandy   Camden CAL202
                                        HMV ED269/73
                                        Victor 17529/33, (set M720)

(Ein) Heldenleben, Op. 40 (1898) orch.
with Philadelphia Orch. – Ormandy   HMV ED334/8
                                        Victor 15666/70, 15661/5, (set
                                        M610)

Jessie HINCHLIFFE

RAWSTHORNE

Theme & variations (1927) 2 vlns
            DTA 3569–3, 3570–4, 3571–3 & Decca K884/5
with K. Washbourne vln   3572–4

Walter HINTERMEYER (1892–   )

CORELLI

(12) Concerti grossi, Op. 6 orch.
Concerto grosso No. 1, in D
with E. Melkus vln, G. Zatschek vlc,   Library of Recorded
C. Landon hpsi, J. Nebois hpsi &   Masterpieces Vol. 1
Vienna Sinfonietta – Goberman   Odyssey (in set 32 36 0001/2)
Concerto grosso No. 2, in F
with E. Melkus vln, G. Zatschek vlc,   Library of Recorded
C. Landon hpsi, J. Nebois hpsi &   Masterpieces Vol. 2
Vienna Sinfonietta – Goberman   Odyssey (in set 32 36 0001/2)

CORELLI – *Continued*

Concerto grosso No. 3, in c
with E. Melkus vln, G. Zatschek vlc,   Library of Recorded
C. Landon hpsi, J. Nebois hpsi &   Masterpieces Vol. 3
Vienna Sinfonietta – Goberman   Odyssey (in set 32 36 0001/2)

VIVALDI

(12) Concerti, Op. 3 "L'Estro armonico" var. cbns & strs
Concerto No. 1, in D, P.146 (F.IV, No. 7) 4 vlns, vlc, strs & c
With W. Boskovsky vln, P. Matheis   Amadeo AVRS6088
vln, J. Tomasow vln, R. Harand vlc,   Bach Guild BG572, BGS5016
H. Nordberg hpsi & Vienna State   I Classici della Musica Classica
Opera Chamber Orch. – Rossi   XAM4023
    Qualiton LPX1095
    Top Rank 35–073
    Vanguard SRV143

Concerto No. 4, in e, P.97 (F.I, No. 174) 4 vlns, strs & c
with W. Boskovsky vln, P. Matheis   Amadeo AVRS6088
vln, J. Tomasow vln, H. Nordberg hpsi   Bach Guild BG572, BGS5016
& Vienna State Opera Chamber Orch.   I Classici della Musica Classica
– Rossi   XAM4023
    Qualiton LPX1095
    Top Rank 35–073
    Vanguard SRV143

Concerto No. 7, in F, P.249 (F.IV, No. 9) 4 vlns, strs & c
with W. Boskovsky vln, P. Matheis   Amadeo AVRS6089
vln, J. Tomasow vln, H. Nordberg hpsi   Bach Guild BG573, BGS5017
& Vienna State Opera Chamber Orch.   I Classici della Musica Classica
– Rossi   XAM4024
    Qualiton LPX1096
    Top Rank 35–074
    Vanguard SRV144

Concerto No. 10, in b, P.148 (F.IV, No. 9) 4 vlns, strs & c
with W. Boskovsky vln, P. Matheis   Amadeo AVRS6090
vln, J. Tomasow vln, H. Nordberg hpsi   Bach Guild BG574, BGS5018
& Vienna State Opera Chamber Orch.   I Classici della Musica Classica
– Rossi   XAM4025
    Qualiton LPX1097
    Top Rank 35–075
    Vanguard SRV145

Eva HITZKER

HAYDN

Concerto No. 3, in A, H.VIIa, No. 3 (1765) "Melk" (cadenzas by Paul
Angerer) vln & orch.
with Vienna Chamber Orch. – Zecchi   Amadeo AVRS6355
    Musical Heritage Society
    MHS625

MOZART

Concerto No. 5, in A, K219 "Turkish" (cadenzas by Joachim) vln & orch.
with Salzburg Festival Orch. –   Plymouth P10–30
Weidlich   Remington RLP149–37

Libor HLAVÁČEK (1926–   )

BACH

Concerto No. 1, in a, BWV1041 vln, strs & c
with Czech Philharmonic Orch. –   Supraphon LPV487, SUA10155
Chalabala

DRDLA

Serenade No. 1, in A vln & pf
with A. Holeček pf   Supraphon SUL30043

DVOŘÁK

(8) Humoresques, Op. 101 pf
No. 7. Humoresque No. 7, in G flat arr. vln & pf – "in G" – Kreisler
with J. Hála pf   Supraphon LPV114, SUA10226
Mazurka in e, Op. 49 vln & pf
with J. Hála pf   Supraphon LPV114, SUA10226,
    SUEC802

NOVÁK

Quintet in a, Op. 12 pf, 2 vlns, vla & vlc
with A. Holeček pf, D. Pandula vln, J.   Supraphon SUB10092
Podjukl vla & J. Chovanec vlc

OSTRCIL

Sonatina, Op. 22 (1925) vln, vla & pf
with A. Hyksa vla & A. Holeček pf   Supraphon SUB10376

SCHMELZER

(13) Sonatas (1672) var. inst
Sonata in g tbn, bsn, vln & c
with Z. Pulec tbn, J. Meszáros bsn,   Supraphon SUA10683,
V.J. Sýkora hpsi & F. Pošta gamba   SUAST50683

TOSELLI

Serenade, Op. 6 vln & pf
with A. Holeček pf   Supraphon SUL30043

Marie HLOUŇOVÁ (1912–   )

DOUBRAVA

Sonata (1943) vln & pf
with J. Pǎnenkǎ pf   Supraphon G22835/6
    Ultraphon G15137/8

NEJEDLÝ

Petite Suite, Op. 11 vln & pf
with V. Řepková pf   Supraphon G22984
    Ultraphon G15208, H15177

David HOCHSTEIN (1892–   )

BRAHMS

(16) Waltzes, Op. 39 pf duet
No. 15. Waltz No. 15, in A flat arr. vln & pf "in A" Hochstein
with piano   2417-1-7 Emerson 7147

CUI

Kaleidoscope, Op. 50 vln & pf
No. 9. Orientale
with piano   2604 Emerson 7215

KREISLER

Liebesleid vln & pf
with piano   2418–1–10   Emerson 7147

Georg HØEBERG

BACH

(4) Suites, BWV1066/9 strs & c
  Suite No. 3, in D: Air (2nd mvt) BWV1068 2 obs, 3 tpts, drms & strs –
  arr. vln & pf as "Air on the G–string" by Wilhelmj
  with piano   Pathé cylinder 459

BULL

Säterjëntens sondag v & pf – arr. vln & pf Svendsen
  with piano   Pathé cylinder 457

RAFF

(6) Pieces, Op. 85 vln & pf
  No. 3. Cavatina in D
  with piano   Pathé cylinder 458

WIENIAWSKI

Mazurka in a, Op. 3 "Kujawiak" vln & pf
  with piano   Pathé cylinder 460

Pierre HOFER

BACH

Concerto in d, BWV1043 2 vlns strs & c
  with M. Cron vln & Disenhaus   Guilde Européenne de
  Concert Orch. – Disenhaus   Microsillon GEM1
       Lyrichord LLS5

Michel HOFFMAN

BRAHMS

(21) Hungarian Dances pf duet
  Hungarian dance No. 1, in g arr. vln & pf Joachim
  with piano   Gennett 10027

MOORE

The Last rose of Summer v & pf – arr. vln & pf Auer
  with piano   Gennett 10027

P. HOFFNER

BACH

Concerto in d, BWV1043 2 vlns, strs & c
  with M. Korn vln & orch. – Disenhaus Melomanes français MF2506

Ralph Francis HOLMES (1937–)

TCHAIKOVSKY

Concerto in D, Op. 35 vln & orch.
  with Nürnberg Symphony Orch. –   Great Musicians Vol. 8
  Maga

Henry HOLST (1899–)

BAX

Ballad (1916) vln & pf
  with F. Merrick pf   Frank Merrick Society FMS18
Legend (1915) vln & pf
  with F. Merrick pf   Frank Merrick Society FMS21
Sonata No. 1, in E (1910/5) vln & pf
  with F. Merrick pf   Concert Artist LPA1099
       Revolution RCB20
Sonata No. 2, in D (1915) vln & pf
  with F. Merrick pf   Frank Merrick Society FMS18
Sonata No. 3, in g (1927) vln & pf
  with F. Merrick pf   Frank Merrick Society FMS18

BEETHOVEN

Trio No. 6, in B flat, Op. 97 "Archduke" pf, vln & vlc
  2EA 10028^V□, 10029^{VI}□, 10030   HMV C3362/6, C7588/92,
  ^{V}□, 10031^{IV}□, 10032^{III}□, 10033^V□,   ED310/4
       10036/8^V□ & 10039^{VI}□
  with C. Solomon pf & A. Pini vlc

DELIUS

Légende in E flat (1893) vln & pf
  with G. Moore pf   CAX 9032/3–1   Columbia DOX373, DX1094
Sonata No. 2 (1924) vln & pf
  with F. Merrick pf   Concert Artist LPA1099

DVOŘÁK

Trio No. 4, in e, Op. 90 "Dumky" pf, vln & vlc
  CAX 8861/2–1, 8863/5–2, 8866–   Columbia DX1017/20
  with L. Kentner   1, 8867–2 & 8868–1
  pf & A. Pini vlc

FRUMERIE

Sonata No. 1, in a (1934) vln & pf
  with F. Merrick pf   Frank Merrick Society FMS23
Sonata No. 2, in c sharp (1944) vln & pf
  with F. Merrick pf   Frank Merrick Society FMS23

HAYDN

(31) Trios, H.XV, Nos. 1/31 pf, vln & vlc
  Trio No. 25, in G, H.XV, No. 25 (Op. 73, No. 2)
  with E. Joyce pf   CAX 8956/9–1   Columbia DX1054/5
  & A. Pini vlc

ISAACS

Sonata in A vln & pf
  2nd mvt only
  with F. Merrick pf   Frank Merrick Society FMS21

PROKOFIEV

(5) Melodies, Op. 35bis (1921) vln & pf
  with F. Merrick pf   Frank Merrick Society FMS19

PURCELL

Sonata in g, Z780 vln & c – real. Merrick
  with F. Merrick pf   Frank Merrick Society FMS21

REGER

Sonata No. 5, in f sharp, Op. 84 vln & pf
  with F. Merrick pf   Frank Merrick Society FMS19

REGER – *Continued*

Suite in F, Op. 93 "In olden style" vln & pf
with F. Merrick pf   Frank Merrick Society FMS19

RUBBRA

Sonata No. 2, Op. 31 (1931) vln & pf
with F. Merrick pf   Frank Merrick Society FMS21

SARASATE

Zigeunerweisen, Op. 20 vln & pf or orch.
with orch.   Clangor M9241/2
       Telefunken A728
       Tri–Ergon 1022
       Ultraphon AP273

SCHUBERT

Trio No. 1, in B flat, Op. 99 (D898) pf, vln & vlc
with V. Schioler pf & E.B. Bengtsson   HMV BLP1077
vlc

SIBELIUS

Sonatina in E, Op. 80 vln & pf
with F. Merrick pf   Frank Merrick Society FMS23

STEVENS

Fantasia on a theme of Dowland, Op. 23 (1953) vln & pf
with F. Merrick pf   Frank Merrick Society FMS21

Jacques HOLTMAN

BEETHOVEN

(6) Minuets, Wo09 2 vlns & cbs
  Minuet No. 1, in E flat
  with J. Schröder vln & A. Woodrow   Saba MPS13001
  cbs
  Minuet No. 2, in G
  with J. Schröder vln & A. Woodrow   Saba MPS13001
  cbs
  Minuet No. 3, in C
  with J. Schröder vln & A. Woodrow   Saba MPS13001
  cbs
  Minuet No. 4, in F
  with J. Schröder vln & A. Woodrow   Saba MPS13001
  cbs
  Minuet No. 5, in D
  with J. Schröder vln & A. Woodrow   Saba MPS13001
  cbs
  Minuet No. 6, in G
  with J. Schröder vln & A. Woodrow   Saba MPS13001
  cbs

TELEMANN

Concerto in F, T.II, No. 3 3 vlns, strs & c
with J. Schröder vln, M. Leonhardt   Telefunken SAWT9452
vln, G. Leonhard hpsi & Concerto
Amsterdam – Brüggen

Trio in E flat, T.I, No. 4 2 vlns & c
with J. Schröder vln, A. Bylsma vlc &   Telefunken SAWT9450
G. Leonhardt hpsi

VIVALDI

(12) Concerti, Op. 3 "L'Estro armonico" var. cbns & strs
  Concerto No. 11, in d P.250 (F.IV, No. 11) 2 vlns, vlc, strs & c
  with J. Krachmalnick vln, J. de Nobel   Telefunken AWT9426,
  vlc & Amsterdam Chamber Orch. –   SAWT9426
  van der Horst

Antoinette van den HOMBERGH

ANONYMOUS

Allemande No. 2* 2 vlns & rec
with M. Leonhardt vln & M. Ferguson   Radio Nederland 109773
rec

Allemande No. 4* 2 vlns & rec
with M. Leonhardt vln & M. Ferguson   Radio Nederland 109776
rec

HACQUART

Sonata 2 vlns & c†
with M. Leonhardt vln, M. Smit–   Radio Nederland 109775
Sibinga hpsi & V. Hampe gamba

TURINI

Madrigali ... con alcune Sonate, Libro Primo (1624)
  Sonata in a 2 vlns & c
  with M. Leonhardt vln, G. Leonhardt   Telefunken SAWT9461
  hpsi & D. Koster vlc

Florence HOOD

KREISLER

Caprice viennois, Op. 2 vln & pf
with P. French pf   Victor 216461

SAINT–SAËNS

(Le) Carnaval des animaux (1886) small orch.
  Le cygne arr. vln & pf
  with P. French pf   Victor 216461

Franz HOPFNER

VIVALDI

(12) Concerti, Op. 3 "L'Estro armonico" var. cbns & strs
  Concerto No. 1, in D, P.146 (F.IV, No. 7) 4 vlns, vlc, strs & c
  with R. Barchet vln, A. Steffen–   Pathé–Vox (in set PV273)
  Wendling vln, H. Endres vln, S.   Vox (in sets DL271, PL7243,
  Barchet vlc, H. Elsner hpsi & Pro   PL7420 & VBX20)
  Musica Orch., Stuttgart – Reinhardt
  Concerto No. 4, in e, P.97 (F.I, No. 174) 4 vlns, strs & c
  with R. Barchet vln, A. Steffen–   Pathé–Vox (in set PV273)
  Wendling vln, H. Endres vln, H.   Vox (in sets DL271, PL7243,
  Elsner hpsi & Pro Musica Orch.,   PL7420 & VBX20)
  Stuttgart – Reinhardt

* From the volume "The Excellent Cabinet."
† From the volume "Harmonia Parnassia".

VIVALDI – *Continued*

Concerto No. 7, in F, P.249 (F.IV, No. 9) 4 vlns, strs & c
  with R. Barchet vln, A. Steffen– Pathé–Vox (in set PV273)
  Wendling vln, H. Endres vln, H. Vox (in sets DL271, PL7243,
  Elsner hpsi & Pro Musica Orch., PL7420 & VBX20)
  Stuttgart – Reinhardt

Concerto No. 10, in b, P.148 (F.IV, No. 10) 4 vlns, strs & c
  with R. Barchet vln, A. Steffen– Pathé–Vox (in set PV273)
  Wendling vln, H. Endres vln, H. Vox (in sets DL271, PL7243,
  Elsner hpsi & Pro Musica Orch., PL7420 & VBX20)
  Stuttgart – Reinhardt

Masafumi HORI

TELEMANN

Concerto in C 4 vlns, strs & c
  with O. Kortner vln, P. Nägele vln, G. Da Camera SM91017
  Ohnheiser vln & Heidelburg Chamber
  Orch.

Johan HORVATH

ANONYMOUS

O du Fröhliche, o du Selige (1819) v & pf – arr. vln, vlc & orch.
  with H. Metzler vlc & string orch. – Decca D18091, LW50053
  Carste

GRUBER

Stille Nacht, heilige Nacht (1818) v & pf – arr. vln, vlc & orch.
  with H. Metzler vlc & string orch. – Decca D18091, LW50053
  Carste

HUBAY

(14) Scènes de la Csárda vln & pf
  No. 4. Hejre Kati, Op. 32
  with Berlin Symphony Orch. – Liebe Odeon 0–28059

OFFENBACH

Orphée aux Enfers (1858) – opera
  Overture
  with Berlin Symphony Orch. – Parlophone DPX41
  Bushkotter

TOSELLI

Serenade, Op. 6 vln & pf
  with Berlin Symphony Orch. – Liebe Odeon 0–28059

Robert HOSSELET

RASSE

Concerto in C vln & orch.
  with Belgian National Orch. – Decca BA133183
  Defossez London W91063

Herbert HÖVER

MOZART

Serenade No. 6, in D, K239 "Serenata Notturna" orch.
  with W. Prystawski vln, R. Weber vla, Deutsche Grammophon
  R. Frei cbs & Lucerne Festival Strings LPEM19480, SLPEM136480
  – Baumgartner

MÜLLER–ZÜRICH

Concerto, Op. 61 2 vlns, cem & strs
  with W. Prystawski vln & Rome Philips G04401L
  Philharmonic Orch. – Fauré

VIVALDI

Concerto in A, P.222 (F.I, No. 139) "L'eco in lontano" 2 vlns & strs
  with W. Prystawski vln & Lucerne Deutsche Grammophon
  Festival Strings – Baumgartner LPM18947, SLPM138947

Anthony HOWARD

VIVALDI

(12) Concerti, Op. 3 "L'Estro armonico" var. cbns & strs
  Concerto No. 10, in b, P.148 (F.IV, No. 10) 4 vlns, strs & c
  with N. Marriner vln, N. Nelson vln, L'Oiseau–Lyre OL276,
  T. Connah vln & Academy of St. SMO1520, SOL276
  Martin–in–the–Fields – Marriner

Dragutin HRDJOK

CORELLI

(12) Concerti grossi, Op. 6 orch.
  Concerto grosso No. 8, in g "Christmas Concerto"
  with J. Stanič–Krek vln, A. Heiller Bach Guild BG569, BGS5006
  hpsi, Z. Pomykato vlc & I Solisti di Top Rank 40–003, TR5002
  Zagreb – Janigro

Jenö HUBAY (1858–1937)

BACH

(4) Suites, BWV1066/9 strs & c
  Suite No. 3, in D: Air (2nd mvt) BWV1068 2 obs, 3 tpts, drms & strs –
  arr. vln & pf as "Air on the G–String" by Wilhelmj
  with Budapest Conservatory Orch. – HMV AN418
  Szolt

HANDEL

(15) Sonatas, Op. 1 (?1731) fl or vln & c
  Sonata No. 9, in b: Andante (1st mvt) arr. vln & pf as "Larghetto" by
  Hubay
  with Budapest Conservatory Orch. – HMV AN418
  Szolt

HUBAY

(Le) Luthier de Crémone, Op. 40 (1894) – opera
  Intermezzo orch. – arr. vln & pf Hubay
  with O. Herz pf Cw 2046^{II}△ HMV AN217
   Victor 9642

HUBAY – *Continued*

(10) Poèmes caractéristiques, Op. 79 vln & pf
No. 9 Berceuse
with O. Herz pf   Cw 2047¹△   HMV AN217
                                           Victor 9642

(6) Poèmes hongroise, Op. 27 vln & pf
Poème hongrois No. 6, in B flat
with piano   Dacapo 8805/6
                                 Premier 8805/6

(14) Scènes de la Csárda vln & pf
No. 5. Hullámzó balaton, Op. 33
with O. Herz pf   HMV AM1691
No. 12. Piczi tubiczám (Little dove) Op. 83
with Budapest   CV 696/7¹△   HMV AN442
Conservatory Orch. – Zsolt

Ugy–e Jani (Clever Jack) Op. 92 v, pf & vln obb
with M. Basilides a &   CV 804¹△   HMV AN454
O. Herz pf

Bronisláw HUBERMAN (1882–1947)*

BACH

Concerto No. 1, in a, BWV1041 vln, strs & c
        WHAX 20–2, 21–1, 22–2 & 23–1   Columbia 68277/8D, (set X45),
with Vienna Philharmonic Orch. –   LX329/30
Dobrowen

Concerto No. 2, in E, BWV1042 vln, strs & c
        WHAX 15–5, 16/8–2 & 19–4   Columbia 68376/8D, (set M235),
with Vienna Philharmonic Orch. –   LFX411/3, LX408/10,
Dobrowen   LX8183/5

Orgelbüchlein, BWV599/644 org
No. 1. Nun komm', der Heiden Heiland, BWV599 arr. vln & pf
Huberman
with S. Schultze pf   CAX 7428–3   Columbia LOX315, LX531

(3) Sonatas & 3 Partitas, BWV1001/6 solo vln
Partita No. 1, in b: Sarabande & double (3rd mvt) BWV1002
(unaccompanied)   WHAX 45–2   Columbia GQX 10992, LX513
                                         Rococo 2008

Sonata No. 2, in a: Andante sostenuto (3rd mvt) BWV1003
(unaccompanied)   WHAX 46–2   Columbia LFX413, LX410,
                                         LX8185
                                         Rococo 2008

(4) Suites, BWV1066/9 strs & c
Suite No. 3, in D: Air (2nd mvt) BWV1068 2 obs, 3 tpts, drms & strs –
arr. vln & pf as "Air on the G–String" by Wilhelmj
with P. Frenkel pf   Brunswick 30027
Suite No. 3, in D: Air (2nd mvt) BWV1068 2 obs, 3 tpts, drms & strs –
arr. vln & pf as "Air on the G–String" by Wilhelmj
with S. Schultze pf   WAX 5007–7   Columbia LX107, W92
                                         Decca 25305
                                         Fonotipia 172167
                                         Odeon 6674N, 0–8746
                                         Parlophone P 9898
                                         Rococo 2008

* See also Fritz MALACHOWSKY, a pseudonym.

BAZZINI

(La) Ronde des lutins, Op. 25 vln & pf
with P. Frenkel pf   Brunswick 15022, A62625

BEETHOVEN

Concerto in D, Op. 61 (cadenzas by Joachim) vln & orch.
         WHAX 30/1–4, 32/3–2, 34–1,   Columbia LX509/13,
with Vienna   35–2 & 36/8–3   LX8256/60, ML4769
Philharmonic Orch. – Szell

Sonata No. 9, in A, Op. 47 "Kreutzer" vln & pf
with S. Schultze pf   Brunswick 50062/4

Sonata No. 9, in A, Op. 47 "Kreutzer" vln & pf
        WAX 5730–1, 5731–3, 5732–4,   Columbia LFX95/8, LOX75/8,
  5733–3, 5736–2, 5737/8–1 & 5739–2   LX72/5, (set M160), W114/7,
with I. Friedman pf   (set 23)
                                         Decca 25505/8
                                         Fonotipia 172149/52
                                         Muza XL0148
                                         Odeon 0–8908/11, 6670/3N,
                                         LP60794

BRAHMS

Concerto in D, Op. 77 vln & orch.*
with New York Philharmonic   Rococo 2007
Symphony Orch. – Walter

(21) Hungarian Dances pf duet
Hungarian dance No. 1, in g arr. vln & pf Joachim
with P. Frenkel pf   Brunswick 15022, A62625

Hungarian dance No. 1, in g arr. vln & pf Joachim
with S. Schultze pf   IDWA 9155–5   Columbia GQ7175, LB8, LF108
                                         Decca 20363
                                         Odeon 16001M, 6674N, 0–4830
                                         Rococo 2008

Hungarian dance No. 5, f sharp arr. vln & pf "in g" Joachim
with S. Schultze pf   Polydor 590008

Hungarian dance No. 7, in A arr. vln & pf Joachim
with P. Frenkel pf   10048⁸   Brunswick 15063
                                         Rococo 2008

(16) Waltzes, Op. 39 pf duet
No. 15. Waltz No. 15, in A flat arr. vln & pf "in A" Hochstein
with S. Schultze pf   WAX 5012–5   Columbia 68310D, LX107, W92
                                         Decca 25305
                                         Fonotipia 172167
                                         Odeon 123769, 0–8746
                                         Rococo 2008

BRUCH

Kol Nidrei, Op. 47 vlc or vln & orch.
with P. Frenkel pf   X 9241 ⁷   Brunswick 50022, A73046

Kol Nidrei, Op. 47 vlc or vln & orch.
with S. Schultze pf   WAX 5949–3   Columbia LFX315, LOX318,
                                         LX155, W91
                                         Odeon 24000N

CHOPIN

(3) Nocturnes, Op. 9 pf
No. 2. Nocturne No. 2, in E flat arr. vln & pf Sarasate
with piano   Gramophone & Typewritier
                                         47901/2

* From a 1937 radio broadcast.

CHOPIN – *Continued*

No. 2. Nocturne No. 2, in E flat arr. vln & pf Sarasate
with P. Frenkel pf   6586 Brunswick 30023

No. 2. Nocturne No. 2, in E flat arr. vln & pf Sarasate
with S. Schultze pf   CAX 7427–1 Columbia LOX315, LX531

(16) Waltzes, Op. 64 pf
  No. 2. Waltz No. 7, in c sharp arr. vln & pf Huberman
  with S. Schultze pf   CA 11131–2 Columbia LB8, LF108, LO7
                           Decca 20363
                           Odeon 0–4830

  No. 2. Waltz No. 7, in c sharp arr. vln & pf Huberman
  with S. Schultze pf   WAX 4672–2 Columbia GQX10516, LX137
                           Fonotipia 172206
               . Odeon 217828, 6679N, 0–8748
                           Parlophone P9882*
                           Rococo 2008

(3) Waltzes, Op. 70 pf
  No. 1. Waltz No. 11, in G flat arr. vln & pf Huberman
  with S. Schultze pf   CA 14912–1 Columbia LB25, LO20
                           Odeon 16001M
                           Parlophone P9882

ELGAR

(La) Capricieuse, Op. 17 vln & pf
  with P. Frenkel pf   X 6589[1] Brunswick 30024
                           Rococo 2008

(La) Capricieuse, Op. 17 vln & pf
  with S. Schultze pf   WAX 5951–2 Columbia GQX10516, LX137
                           Fonotipia 172206
                           Odeon 217828, 6679N, 0–8748
                           Parlophone P9882

GLUCK

Orphée et Eurydice (1762) – opera
  Dance of the blessed spirits: Lento "Mélodie" (No. 2) arr. vln & pf
  Wilhelmj
  with P. Frenkel pf   10049 [9] Brunswick 15063
                           Rococo 2008

LALO

Symphonie espagnole, Op. 21 vln & orch.
  Andante (4th mvt)
  with P. Frenkel pf   X 9993 Brunswick 50041, A73049
  Rondo (5th mvt)
  with P. Frenkel pf   X 9994 Brunswick 50041, A73049
Symphonie espagnole, Op. 21 vln & orch. †
        WHAX 39–3, 40/1–2, 42–1, 43– Columbia 68288/90D, (set
  with Vienna Philharmonic   3 & 44–1   M214), LFX370/2, LGX201/3,
  Orch. – Szell   LX347/9 LX8129/31, W11/3,
                           (set 4)
                           Rococo 2002

MENDELSSOHN

Concerto in e, Op. 64 vln & orch.
  Andante (2nd mvt)
  with S. Schultze pf   Brunswick 50049, A73030
                           Polydor 27242

* Matrix no. 2–21816.
† Omitting Intermezzo.

MENDELSSOHN – *Continued*

  Allegro molto vivace (3rd mvt)
  with S. Schultze pf   Brunswick 50049, A73030
                           Polydor 27242

MOZART

Concerto No. 3, in G, K216 (cadenzas by Huberman) vln & orch.
        WHAX 24/5–5, 26–3, 27–1 & Columbia 68548/50D, 70137/9D,
  with Vienna Philharmonic   28/9–3 (Set M258), LOX319/21,
  Orch. – Dobrowen   LX494/6, LX8243/5

PAGANINI

Concerto No. 2, in b, Op. 7 vln & orch.
  Ronde à la clochette "La Campanella" (3rd mvt) arr. vln & pf Wilhelmj
  with P. Frenkel pf   X 9643 [8] Brunswick 50026, A73047
                           Polydor 595010
                           Rococo 2008

SARASATE

Carmen Fantasia (on themes from the opera by Bizet) Op. 25 vln & pf or
orch.
  with S. Schultze pf   Brunswick 10220, 10254, A62601
                           Polydor 62601

(8) Danzas españolas vln & pf
  No. 3. Romanza andaluza, Op. 22, No. 1
  with S. Schultze pf   XXB 8477 Brunswick 50051, A73050
                           Odeon 0–8744
                           Rococo 2008

  No. 3. Romanza andaluza, Op. 22, No. 1
  with S. Schultze pf   Columbia 264769, J7549, L2332,
                           W23
                           Decca 25748
                           Fonotipia 172125
                           Odeon 123769, 6667N
                           Parlophone P9877
                           Qualiton QNM7041

  No. 4. Jota Navarra, Op. 22, No. 2
  with S. Schultze pf   Brunswick 50051, A73050
                           Rococo 2008

SCHUBERT

(7) Gesänge (set to Scott's "Lady of the Lake") Op. 52 v & pf
  No. 6. Ave Maria, D839 arr. vln & pf Wilhelmj
  with S. Schultze pf   WAX 5950–1 Columbia 264943, LFX314,
                           LOX318, LX155, W91
                           Odeon 0–8758, 24000N

(6) Moments musicaux, Op. 94 (D780) (1823/7) pf
  No. 3. Moment musicale No. 3, in f "Air russe" arr. vln & pf Auer
  with S. Schultze pf   CA 14914–1 Columbia LB25, LO20

TCHAIKOVSKY

Concerto in D, Op. 35 vln & orch.
  Canzonetta (2nd mvt)
  with P. Frenkel pf   X 9564[9] Brunswick 50026, A73047

TCHAIKOVSKY – *Continued*

Concerto in D, Op. 35 vln & orch.
WAX 4509–2, 4510/1–1, 4512–2,   Columbia 67726/9D, (set M131),
with Berlin State   4513/4 & 4515–2   GQX10585/8, J7550/3, L2335/8,
Opera Orch. – Steinberg   W145/8, (set 33)
Decca 25470/3
Fonotipia 172058/61
Odeon 0–8737/40, 6652/5N
Parlophone P9855/8
Rococo 2002

Souvenir d'un lieu cher, Op. 42 vln & pf
No. 3. Mélodie
with P. Frenkel pf   Brunswick 15002, A70724
No. 3. Mélodie
with S. Schultze pf   WAX 4671–1   Columbia 67729D, (in set M131)
J7553, L2338, W148, (in set 33)
Decca 25473
Odeon 0–8740, 0–8758
Parlophone P9858

VIEUXTEMPS

Ballade & Polonaise in G, Op. 38 vln & pf
with P. Frenkel   X 9140³ & 9138³   Brunswick 50019
pf   Rococo 2008

WIENIAWSKI

Capriccio–valse, Op. 7 vln & pf
with P. Frenkel pf   X 9641   Brunswick 50031, A73048
Concerto No. 2, in d, Op. 22 vln & orch.
Romance (2nd mvt)
with P. Frenkel pf   X 9965   Brunswick 50031, A73048
(2) Mazurkas, Op. 19 vln & pf
No. 2. Mazurka No. 2, in D "Dudziarz"
with P. Frenkel pf   Brunswick 15002, A70724

ZARZYCKI

Mazurka in G, Op. 26 vln & pf
X 9244¹⁰, XXB 8478 or B   Brunswick 50022, A73046
with P. Frenkel pf   27669*   Odeon 0–8744

Mazurka in G, Op. 26 vln & pf
with S. Schultze pf   WAX 5011–1   Columbia 68310D, J7549, L2332
Decca 25748
Fonotipia 172125
Odeon 123769, 6667N, 0–8744
Parlophone P9877
Qualiton QNM7041

Václav HUDEČEK (1953–)

HANDEL

(15) Sonatas, Op. 1 (?1731) fl or vln & c
Sonata No. 3, in A vln I
with J. Hála hpsi & F. Sláma vlc   Panton 01 0230, 11 0230

* Possibly separate performances.

PAGANINI

Concerto No. 1, in D, Op. 6 (cadenza by Kubelík) vln & orch.
Allegro maestoso (1st mvt) arr. vln & orch. Wilhelmj
with Orch. of Prague Symphonists –   Panton 01 0230, 11 0230
Nohejl

RAVEL

Tzigane (Rapsodie de concert) (1924) vln & pf or orch.
with J. Hála pf   Panton 01 0230, 11 0230

Sydney HUMPHREYS (1926–)

VIVALDI

(12) Concerti, Op. 3 "L'Estro armonico" var. cbns & strs
Concerto No. 10, in b, P.148 (F.IV, No. 10) 4 vlns, strs & c
with Y. Menuhin vln, E. Goren vln, R.   Angel 36103
Masters vln & Bath Festival Chamber   Electrola E91219, STE91219
Orch. – Menuhin   HMV ALP1949, ASD500,
ASDF283, FALP747,
QALP10356

Hugo HUNDT

DRDLA

Serenade No. 1, in A vln & pf
with piano   Albion 1117
Beka 88, G40503

MLYNARSKI

Mazurka in G, Op. 26 vln & pf
with piano   Albion 1117
Beka 88, G40505

Heinz HUPPERTZ

ALBÉNIZ

España (6 Feuilles d'album) Op. 165 pf
No. 2. Tango in D arr. vln & pf Kreisler
with piano   Odeon 0–25214
Parlophone C7918, B97033

BOHM

(143) Lieder, Op. 326 v & pf
No 27. Still wie die Nacht arr. vln & hp
with harp   Odeon 0–25352

BOND

(A) Perfect day (1910) v & pf – arr. vln & org
with M. Palotti org   Odeon 0–11913

BOSC

Moss rose v & pf – arr. vln, org & pf
with M. Palotti org &   P Be 10612²   Odeon 0–25128
piano   Parlophone R1875

DENZA

Si vous l'aviez compris v & pf – arr. vln & org
with M. Palotti org   Odeon 0–11940

FELIX

(Die) Kätzchen (1890) – operetta
Unter dem Lindenbaum arr. vln & org
with M. Palotti org   Odeon 0–11996

FIBICH

Images, Impressions & Souvenirs, Op. 41 pf
No. 14. Poem (from "Souvenirs", Part IV) arr. vln & pf Kubelík
with M. Palotti org &   P Be 10613   Odeon 0–25128
piano   Parlophone R1875

GODARD

Jocelyn (1888) – opera
Cachés dans cet asile "Berceuse" arr. vln & org
with M. Palotti pf   Odeon 0–11996

GOUNOD

Ave Maria (Méditation on Bach's "Prelude No. 1, in C" from Book I of
"Das Wohltemperirte Clavier") v & pf – arr. vln & org
with M. Palotti org   Odeon 0–11924

GRUBER, L.

Mei' Muatterl war a Wienerin, Op. 1000 v & pf – arr. vln & org
with M. Palotti org   Odeon 0–26136

GRUBER

Viennese song unid v & pf – arr. vln & org
with M. Palotti org   Odeon 0–11957

HEUBERGER

(Der) Opernball, Op. 40 (1898) – operetta
Im chambre séparée arr. vln & pf as "Midnight Bells" by Kreisler
with M. Palotti org   Odeon 0–11957

KREISLER

Marche miniature viennois vln & pf
with M. Palotti org   Odeon 0–25214
                                       Parlophone B97033, C7918

MASCAGNI

Cavalleria Rusticana (1890) – opera
Intermezzo orch. – arr. vln & pf
with M. Palotti pf   Odeon 0–25164
                                       Parlophone R1927

MEYER–HELMUND

(3) Lieder, Op. 21 v & pf
No. 2. Das Zauberlied arr. vln & org
with M. Palotti org   Odeon 0–25352

NEVIN

(The) Rosary (1898) v & pf – arr. vln & org
with M. Palotti org   Odeon 0–11924

STRECKER

Drunt' in der Lobau v & pf – arr. vln & orch.
with chamber orch.   Odeon 0–26136

TOSTI

For a kiss (Pour un baiser) v & pf – arr. vln & org
with M. Palotti org   Odeon 0–11913, 0–11940

YRADIER

(La) Paloma (1877) v & pf – arr. vln & pf
with M. Palotti pf   Odeon 0–25164
                                       Parlophone R1927

Sulo HURSTINEN

PALMGREN

Illusion solo vln
(unaccompanied)   Columbia DY165

Emanuel HURWITZ (1919–   )

AVISON

(12) Concerti, Op. 6 2 vlns, strs & c
Concerto No. 1, in g
with I. McMahon vln, C. Spinks hpsi   L'Oiseau–Lyre SOL318
& Hurwitz Chamber Ensemble –
Hurwitz

Concerto No. 2, in B flat
with I. McMahon vln, C. Spinks hpsi   L'Oiseau–Lyre SOL318
& Hurwitz Chamber Ensemble –
Hurwitz

Concerto No. 6, in D
with I. McMahon vln, C. Spinks hpsi   L'Oiseau–Lyre SOL318
& Hurwitz Chamber Ensemble –
Hurwitz

Concerto No. 8, in e
with I. McMahon vln, C. Spinks hpsi   L'Oiseau–Lyre SOL318
& Hurwitz Chamber Ensemble –
Hurwitz

Concerto No. 9, in D
with I. McMahon vln, C. Spinks hpsi   L'Oiseau–Lyre SOL318
& Hurwitz Chamber Ensemble –
Hurwitz

Concerto No. 12, in A
with I. McMahon vln, C. Spinks hpsi   L'Oiseau–Lyre SOL318
& Hurwitz Chamber Ensemble –
Hurwitz

BACH

Sonata in C, BWV1037 2 vlns & c
with N. Liddell vln, C. Spinks hpsi & L'Oiseau–Lyre SOL319
T. Weil vlc

HANDEL

(12) Concerti grossi, Op. 6 2 vlns, vlc & strs
Concerto grosso No. 1, in G (rev. Negri)
with R. Keenlyside vln, K. Harvey vlc Philips 802766AY, (in set SC71
& English Chamber Orch. – Leppard   AX302)

Concerto grosso No. 2, in F (rev. Negri)
with R. Keenlyside vln, K. Harvey vlc Philips 802766AY, (in set SC71
& English Chamber Orch. – Leppard   AX302)

Concerto grosso No. 3, in e (rev. Negri)
with R. Keenlyside vln, K. Harvey vlc Philips 802766AY, (in set SC71
& English Chamber Orch. – Leppard   AX302)

Concerto grosso No. 4, in a (rev. Negri)
with R. Keenlyside vln, K. Harvey vlc Philips 802766AY, (in set SC71
& English Chamber Orch. – Leppard   AX302)

HANDEL – *Continued*

Concerto grosso No. 5, in D (rev. Negri)
with R. Keenlyside vln, K. Harvey vlc   Philips 802767AY, (in set SC71
& English Chamber Orch. – Leppard   AX302)

Concerto grosso No. 6, in g (rev. Negri)
with R. Keenlyside vln, K. Harvey vlc   Philips 802767AY, (in set SC71
& English Chamber Orch. – Leppard   AX302)

Concerto grosso No. 7, in B flat (rev. Negri)
with R. Keenlyside vln, K. Harvey vlc   Philips 802767AY, (in set SC71
& English Chamber Orch. – Leppard   AX302)

Concerto grosso No. 8, in c (rev. Negri)
with R. Keenlyside vln, K. Harvey vlc,   Philips 802767AY, (in set SC71
& English Chamber Orch. – Leppard   AX302)

Concerto grosso No. 9, in F (rev. Negri)
with R. Keenlyside vln, K. Harvey vlc   Philips 802768AY, (in set SC71
& English Chamber Orch. – Leppard   AX302)

Concerto grosso No. 10, in d (rev. Negri)
with R. Keenlyside vln, K. Harvey vlc   Philips 802768AY, (in set SC71
& English Chamber Orch. – Leppard   AX302)

Concerto grosso No. 11, in A (rev. Negri)
with R. Keenlyside vln, K. Harvey vlc   Philips 802768AY, (in set SC71
& English Chamber Orch. – Leppard   AX302)

Concerto grosso No. 12, in b (rev. Negri)
with R. Keenlyside vln, K. Harvey vlc   Philips 802768AY, (in set SC71
& English Chamber Orch. – Leppard   AX302)

(7) Sonatas, Op. 5 (1739) 2 vlns & c
Sonata No. 2, in D
with N. Liddell vln, C. Spinks hpsi &   L'Oiseau–Lyre SOL319
T. Weil vlc

HAYDN

Sinfonia concertante in B flat, Op. 84 (H.I, No. 105) vln, vlc, ob, bsn &
orch.
with K. Harvey vlc, P. Graeme ob, M.   Electrola 1C063–01900
Gatt bsn & English Chamber Orch. –   HMV ASD2462
Barenboim

HOLST

Concerto, Op. 49 (1929) 2 vlns & orch.
with K. Sillito vln & English Chamber   Lyrita SRCS44
Orch. – I. Holst

MOZART

Concertone in C, K190 2 vlns, ob, vlc & orch.
with E. Goren vln, P. Graem ob, T.   L'Oiseau–Lyre OL50199,
Weil vlc & English Chamber Orch. –   SOL60030
Davis

PURCELL

(12) Sonatas, Z790/801 (1683) 3 part – 2 vlns & c
Sonata No. 4, in F, Z793
with N. Liddell vln, C. Spinks hpsi &   L'Oiseau–Lyre SOL319
T. Weil vlc

Sonata No. 9, in c, Z798
with N. Liddell vln, C. Spinks hpsi &   L'Oiseau–Lyre SOL319
T. Weil vlc

(10) Sonatas, Z802/11 (1697) 4 parts – 2 vlns & c
Sonata No. 6, in g, Z807 "Chaconne"
with N. Liddell vln, C. Spinks hpsi &   L'Oiseau–Lyre SOL319
T. Weil vlc

HUTTENBACH

KREISLER

Andantino (Padre Martini)
with piano   Odeon GO19093

PAGANINI

(24) Caprices, Op. 1 (1801/7) solo vln
Caprice No. 20, in D arr. vln & pf
with piano   Odeon GO19093

Mariuccia IACOVINO

GUARNIERI

Sonata No. 4 (1956) vln & pf
with A. Estrella pf   Musica Brasileira SLP1

VILLA–LOBOS

Sonata–Fantasia No. 1, in c (1912) "Déspespérance" vln & pf
with A. Estrêla pf   Classic RSCL4005

Sonata–Fantasia No. 2 (1914) vln & pf
with A. Estrêla pf   Classic RSCL4005

Sonata–Fantasia No. 3 (1915) vln & pf
with A. Estrêla pf   Classic RSCL4005

Mischa IGNATIEFF (1910–)

CHOPIN

(3) Waltzes, Op. 64 pf
No. 2. Waltz No. 7, in c sharp arr. vln & pf Huberman
with piano   HMV EG3310

WIENIAWSKI

Mazurka in a, Op. 3 "Kujawiak" vln & pf
with piano   HMV EG3310

Anja IGNATIUS–HIRVENSALO (1911–)

PALMGREN

Berceuse in A flat vln & pf
with T. Mikkilä pf   OSB 1034[II]☐   HMV X6341

SCHUMANN

(9) Waldscenen, Op. 82 pf
No. 7. Vogel als Prophet arr. vln & pf Heifetz
with T. Mikkilä pf   OSB 1033[II]☐   HMV X6342

SIBELIUS

(4) Compositions, Op. 115 vln & pf
No. 1. Moods of the moor
with T. Mikkilä pf   OSB 1035[II]☐   HMV X6342

Concerto in d, Op. 47 vln & orch.
with Berlin State Opera   2084½GS, 2085GS, 2086¾GS &   Polydor 68046/9
Orch. – Järnefelt   2087/91½GS

(4) Pieces, Op. 78 vln & pf
No. 2. Romance in F
with J. Jalas pf   Rytmi R6146

SIBELIUS – *Continued*

(5) Pieces, Op. 81 vln & pf
No. 1. Mazurka
with T. Mikkilä pf — OSB 1036[II]☐ — HMV X6341
No. 1. Mazurka
with J. Jalas pf — Rytmi R6146

Alfred INDIG

SAINT–SAËNS

Samson et Dalila, Op. 47 (1877) – opera
Mon coeur s'ouvre ta voix arr. vln & pf
with piano — F 11 — Columbia D9729

THOMAS

Mignon (1866) – opera
selection arr. vln & pf as "Fantasia" by Sarasate
with piano — F 10 — Columbia D9729

C. van INGEN–WERTS

BOUVY

Élégie vln & pf
with piano — Odeon A42901

GOUNOD

Ave Maria (Méditation on Bach's "Prelude No. 1, in C" from Book I of "Das Wohltemperirte Clavier") v & pf – arr. vln & pf
with piano — Odeon A42907

HANDEL

(15) Sonatas, Op. 1 (?1731) fl or vln & c
Sonata No. 9, in b: Andante (1st mvt) arr. vln & pf as "Larghetto" by Hubay
with piano — Odeon A42908

NARDINI

(7) Sonatas vln & c*
Sonata No. 7, in B flat: larghetto (2nd mvt)
with piano — Odeon A42905

A. INZAURRAGA

AGUIRRE

(2) Aires criollos vln & pf
Aire criollo No. 1 arr. Gaos
with piano — Victor P91

Gica IONESCU †

ALEXANDRI

My thoughts (Trecui pe langa cruce) vln & pf
with E. Ionescu pf — Brunswick 3181

* No opus number.
† Violinist of the Royal Concert Orch. of Queen marie of Rumania.

IONESCU, C.

Dream of roses (Visul florilor) vln & pf
with E. Ionescu pf — Brunswick 3182
Russian Gypsy romance (Malerco) vln & pf
with E. Ionescu pf — Brunswick 3181

PADUREANO

Eyes of sin (Sund Ochii Adinci ca un pacat) vln & pf
with E. Ionescu pf — Brunswick 3182

Hermann IRMER

MLYNARSKI

Mazurka in G, Op. 7 vln & pf
with piano — Gramophone & Typewriter 47921

VIEUXTEMPS

Concerto No. 4, in d, Op. 31 vln & orch.
Adagio religioso (2nd mvt)
with piano — Gramophone & Typewriter 47920

Lila ISAACS

RAFF

(6) Pieces, Op. 85 vln & pf
No. 3. Cavatina in D
with piano — Columbia A1180, E2215; Regal G6731

WIENIAWSKI

Concerto No. 2, in d, Op. 22 vln & orch.
Romance (2nd mvt)
with piano — Columbia A1180; Regal G6731

Liana ISAKADZE (1946–)

BACH

Concerto in C, BWV1064 3 clavs, strs & c – arr. 3 vlns & strs "in D" R. Baumgartner
with O. Kagen vln, M. Lubotsky vln, G. Rozhdestvensky hpsi & Moscow Radio Large Symphony Orch. Chamber Group – Rozhdestvensky — Mezhdunarodnaya Kniga S01867/8

BEETHOVEN

(3) Sonatas, Op. 30 vln & pf
No. 2. Sonata No. 7, in c
with piano — Mezhdunarodnaya Kniga D025147/8

BRAHMS

Sonata No. 1, in G, Op. 78 vln & pf
with J. Kollegorskaya pf — Mezhdunarodnaya Kniga D021449/50

DEBUSSY

Suite Bergamasque (1890) pf
No. 3. Clair de lune arr. vln & pf Roelens
with piano   Mezhdunarodnaya Kniga
            D025147/8

No. 4. Passepied arr. vln & pf Caramba
with piano   Mezhdunarodnaya Kniga
            D025147/8

FALLA

(La) Vida breve (1913) – opera
Danza española orch. – arr. vln & pf Kreisler
with piano   Mezhdunarodnaya Kniga
            D025147/8

FAURÉ

Berceuse, Op. 16 vln & pf
with piano   Mezhdunarodnaya Kniga
            D025147/8

PAGANINI

Cantabile in D, Op. 17 vln & gtr
with J. Kollegorskaya pf
         Mezhdunarodnaya Kniga
         D021449/50

SAINT–SAËNS

(6) Études, Op. 52 pf
No. 6. Étude No. 6, in D flat "Étude en forme de valse" arr. vln & pf
Ysaÿe
with piano   Mezhdunarodnaya Kniga
            D025147/8

SARASATE

Caprice basque, Op. 24 vln & pf
with J. Kollegorskaya pf
         Mezhdunarodnaya Kniga
         D021449/50

TCHAIKOVSKY

Waltz–scherzo, Op. 34 vln & pf or orch.
with piano   Mezhdunarodnaya Kniga
            D028104

YSAŸE

(6) Sonatas, Op. 27 solo vln
Sonata No. 2, in a
(unaccompanied)   Mezhdunarodnaya Kniga
            D021449/50

Marito IWAMOTO (1926–   )

BACH

(6) Sonatas, BWV1014/9 vln & clav
Sonata No. 1, in b, BWV1014
with U. Nobechi pf   Columbia G146/7

BEETHOVEN

Romance No. 1, in G, Op. 40 vln & orch.
with Tokyo Symphony Orch. – Saito   Victor NH2018
Romance No. 2, in F, Op. 50 vln & orch.
with Tokyo Symphony Orch. – Saito   Victor NH2019

KIYOSE

(2) Movements (1959) vln & pf
with S. Tsubota pf   Toshiba JSC3009

LEKEU

Sonata in G (1891) vln & pf
with U. Nobechi pf   Columbia G33/6

MITSUKURI

Sonata in F vln & pf
with S. Tsubota pf   Toshiba JSC3009

SCHUMANN

(13) Kinderscenen, Op. 15 pf
No. 7. Träumerei arr. vln & pf
with U. Nobechi pf   Columbia G40

Igor IWANOW

LIPINSKI

Concerto No. 2, in D, Op. 21 "Military" vln & orch.
with Polish National Philharmonic   Muza XL0176
Orch. – Rowicki

MIELCZEWSKI

Canzona 2 vlns & c
with Z. Murawski vln, L. Zawistowski   Veriton XV704
vlc & J. Borzym hpsi

VIVALDI

(12) Concerti, Op. 3 "L'Estro armonico" var. cbns & strs
Concerto No. 10, in b, P.148 (F.IV, No. 10) 4 vlns, strs & c
with Z. Bakowski vln, E. Komosiński   Muza XL0504
vln, L. Radek vln, J. Dobrzanski hpsi
& Warsaw Chamber Orch. –
Sutkowski
Concerto in B flat, F.I, No. 40 2 vlns, strs & c
with J. Kucharski vln, J. Dobrzański   Muza XL0504
hpsi & Warsaw Chamber Orch. –
Sutkowski

Joseph JACOB

MacKENZIE

(6) Pieces, Op. 37 vln & pf
No. 3. Benedictus
with orch.   Beka 346, 40802

MENDELSSOHN

(6) Songs without words, Op. 62 pf
No. 6. Song without words No. 30, in A "Spring song" arr. vln & pf
with piano   Beka 346, 40888

George JACOBS (1880–   )

DELIBES

Sylvia (1876) – ballet orch.
No. 16a. Pizzicato–scherzettino (Act III) arr. vln & pf Jacobs
with piano   Berliner 7921

ELGAR

Salut d'amour, Op. 12 orch. – arr. vln & pf Elgar
with piano   Gramophone & Typewriter 7941

GODARD

Jocelyn (1888) – opera
 Cachés dans cet asile "Berceuse" arr. vln & pf
with piano   Berliner 7903
       Gramophone & Typewriter 7943

GOUNOD

Faust (1859) – opera
 selection arr. vln & pf Jacobs
with piano   Berliner 7919

MASCAGNI

Cavalleria Rusticana (1890) – opera
 Intermezzo orch. – arr. vln & pf
with piano   Berliner 7915

MENDELSSOHN

Concerto in e, Op. 64 vln & orch.
 Allegro molto vivace (3rd mvt)
with piano   Berliner 7917

MOSZKOWSKI

(6) Klavierstücke, Op. 15 pf – 4 hands
 No. 1. Serenata arr. vln & pf Rehfeld
with piano   Berliner 7920
       Gramophone & Typewriter 7945

SAINT–SAËNS

Introduction & Rondo Capriccioso, Op. 28 vln & orch.
with piano   Berliner 7909

SARASATE

Zigeunerweisen, Op. 20 vln & pf or orch.
with piano   Berliner 7906

SCHUBERT

(7) Gesänge (set to Scott's "Lady of the Lake") Op. 52 v & pf
 No. 6. Ave Maria, D839 arr. vln & pf Wilhelmj
with piano   Berliner 7904

STRAUSS, R.

(8) Lieder, Op. 10 v & pf
 No. 8. Allerseelen arr. vln & pf
with piano   Berliner 7914

THOMÉ

Simple aveu, Op. 25 pf – arr. vln & pf
with piano   Berliner 7910

TOBANI

Hearts & flowers, Op. 245 (1899) v & pf – arr. vln & pf
with piano   Berliner 7911

WIENIAWSKI

Légende, Op. 17 vln & pf or orch.
with piano   Berliner 7912 & 7918
(2) Mazurkas, Op. 19 vln & pf
 No. 1. Mazurka No. 1, in G "Obertass"
with piano   Berliner 7908

WIENIAWSKI – *Continued*

 No. 2. Mazurka No. 2, in D "Dudziarz"
with piano   Berliner 7909
Polonaise brillante No. 2, in A, Op. 21 vln & pf
with piano 131– VX^1– 4h Berliner 7913
       Gramophone & Typewriter 7944,
       7946

Sascha JACOBSEN (1895–   )

BERGH

Evening vln & pf
with piano   Columbia 01147, J554

BERLIN

Russian lullaby v & pf – arr. vln & pf
with piano   Columbia 133M, J308

BLACK

Dardanella (1919) pf – arr. vln & orch.
with orch.   78979 Columbia A2912

BOISDEFFRE

Au bord, du ruisseau (Sérénade champêtre) Op. 52 vln & pf
with piano   Columbia 01165, 7M, 177M,
      A3820, J735

CADDIGAN & STOREY

Blue diamonds v & pf – arr. vln & pf
with piano   79203 Columbia A2977

CADMAN

At dawning, Op. 29, No. 1 v & pf – arr. vln & pf Jacobsen
with piano   Columbia 0793, 4536, A3484

DAREWSKI, H.

As you were – revue
 If you could care arr. vln & pf
with E. Balaban pf 78984 Columbia A2912

DRDLA

Guitarerro, Op. 88 vln & pf
with piano   Columbia 20008D, 9M
Souvenir vln & pf
with S. Chotzinoff pf 78061 Columbia A2779

DRIGO

(2) Airs de Ballet orch.
 No. 2. Valse bluette arr. vln & pf Auer
with piano   Columbia 9M, A3485
(Les) Millions d'Arlequin (1900) – ballet orch.
 Sérénade arr. vln & pf Auer
with S. Chotzinoff pf 78065 Columbia A2779

DVOŘÁK

(7) Gypsy songs, Op. 55 v & pf
 No. 4. Songs my mother taught me arr. vln & pf Kreisler
with piano   Columbia A3866

FAURÉ

Berceuse, Op. 16 vln & pf
 with piano   Columbia 01147, 177M, J735

de FREYNE

Where the lazy Mississippi flows v & pf – arr. vln & pf
 with E. Balaban pf   79837   Columbia A3419

FRIML

(The) Vagabond King (1925) – operetta
 Only a rose arr. vln & pf Hooker
 with piano   141920   Columbia 125M

GABRIEL–MARIE

(La) Cinquantaine (1894) pf duet – arr. vln & pf
 with E. Balaban pf   81032   Columbia 100M, J123

GARDNER

(2) Pieces, Op. 5 vln & pf
 No. 1. From the canebrake
 with A. Bergh pf   145882   Columbia 01148, 7M, 161M,
          A3820, J635

GODARD

Jocelyn (1888) – opera
 Cachés dans cet asile "Berceuse" arr. vln & pf
 with E. Balaban pf   79817   Columbia 8M, A3597

GOODEVE

Fiddle & I v & pf – arr. v, vln & pf
 with H. Lashanska s & orch.   78392   Columbia 78392, 33037D, 34M,
          X259

GORDON

Far–away bells v & pf – arr. vln & pf
 with piano   Columbia 0779, 133M, J308

GOUNOD

Ave Maria (Méditation on Bach's "Prelude No. 1, in C" from Book I of
 "Das Wohltemperite Clavier") v & pf – arr. v, vln & pf
 with H. Lazaro t & R.   49350   Columbia 49350, 8931M
 Romani pf

GRIEG

(6) Lyric Pieces – Book III, Op. 43 pf
 No. 6. To the spring arr. vln & pf Kreisler
 with S. Chotzinoff pf   81461   Columbia 20019D, 10M

HANDEL

(15) Sonatas, Op. 1 (?1731) fl or vln & c
 Sonata No. 9, in b: Andante (1st mvt) arr. vln & pf as "Larghetto" by
 Hubay
 with C.A. Baker pf   Victor 17415

HANLEY

Just a cottage small by a waterfall (1925) v & pf – arr. vln & pf
 with piano   141918   Columbia 0779, 125M

HERBERT

Suite in F, Op. 3 vln & pf
 No. 4. Serenade
 with S. Chotzinoff pf   78021   Columbia A2753

HEUBERGER

(Der) Opernball, Op. 40 (1898) – operetta
 Im chambre séparée arr. vln & pf as "Midnight bells" by Kreisler
 with piano   Columbia 01148, J554

HIRSCH

Mary (1920) – musical
 The love nest arr. vln & pf
 with piano   79190   Columbia A2977

JONES

Indiana moon (1923) v & pf – arr. vln & pf
 with piano   Columbia 20001D

KRAMER

Chant nègre, Op. 32, No. 1 vln & pf
 with A. Bergh pf   146251   Columbia 01165, 20008D, 161M,
          J635

KREISLER

Liebesleid vln & pf
 with piano   Columbia A3485

Tambourin chinois, Op. 3 vln & pf
 with S. Chotzinoff pf   49470   Columbia 5001M, A6093

LOGAN

Pale moon (1920) v & pf – arr. vln & pf Kreisler
 with piano   Columbia 01146, 20001D, 8M,
          152M, J653

MacDOWELL

Woodland Sketches, Op. 51 pf
 No. 1. To a wild rose arr. vln & pf
 with piano   Columbia 01146, 152M, J653

MASSENET

Élégie v & pf – arr. v, vln & pf
 with R. Stracciari b & piano   49333   Columbia 49333, 68070D, 9902M

Thaïs (1894) – opera
 Méditation arr. vln & pf Marsick
 with S. Chotzinoff pf   49389   Columbia A6093

MENDELSSOHN

(6) Songs without words, Op. 62 pf
 No. 6. Song without words No. 30, in A "Spring song" arr. vln & pf
 with piano   Columbia 28M, A3495

MERKUR & DAVIS

I lost my heart to you v & pf – arr. vln & pf
 with E. Balaban pf   79836   Columbia A3419

MOSZKOWSKI

(5) Danzas españolas, Op. 12 pf – 4 hands
 No. 5. Danza española No. 5, in D (Con spirito) arr. vln & pf
 with E. Balaban pf   79822   Columbia 100M, J123

MOYA

(The) Song of songs (1914) v & pf – arr. vln & pf
 with piano   A 5776   Columbia 0792, 4771

NEVIN

(The) Rosary (1898) v & pf – arr. vln & pf
 with piano   Columbia 0792, 4536

PIERNÉ

Sérénade in A, Op. 7 (1875) pf – arr. vln & pf Haddock
with piano   Columbia 28M, A3495

POLDINI

(7) Marionnettes pf
No. 2. Poupée valsante arr. vln & pf Kreisler
with piano   A 5788   Columbia 0793, 4771

RAFF

(6) Pieces, Op. 85 vln & pf
No. 3. Cavatina in D
with R. Bauman pf   98144–3   Columbia 60007D, 5002M

RENARD

(2) Berceaux, Op. 20 vln & pf
No. 2. Berceuse in F
with C.A. Baker pf   Victor 17385

RICE

Dear old pal of mine (1918) v & pf – arr. vln & pf
with S. Chotzinoff pf   78389   Columbia A2753

SAINT–SAËNS

Introduction & Rondo Capriccioso, Op. 28 vln & orch.
with R. Bauman pf   98145–3   Columbia 60007D, 5002M

SARASATE

(8) Danzas españolas vln & pf
No. 1. Malagueña, Op. 21, No. 1
with E. Balaban pf   49959   Columbia A6223

SCHUBERT

(2) Lieder, Op. 98 (D498) v & pf
No. 2. Wiegenlied (Schlafe, holder süsser Knabe) arr. vln & pf Elman
with piano   Columbia A3484

SCHUMANN

(13) Kinderscenen, Op. 15 pf
No. 7. Träumerei arr. vln & pf
with C.A. Baker pf   Victor 17385

TCHAIKOVSKY

Concerto in D, Op. 35 vln & orch.
Canzonetta (2nd mvt)
with orch.   49948   Columbia 5001M, A6223

TOSELLI

Serenade, Op. 6 vln & pf
with E. Balaban pf   80183   Columbia A3597

WIENIAWSKI

Capriccio–valse, Op. 7 vln & pf
with S. Chotzinoff pf   81473   Columbia 20019D, 10M

Fantaisie brillante (on themes from Gounod's "Faust") Op. 20 vln & orch.
with piano   Columbia A3866

Cécile JACQUILLAT

VIVALDI

(12) Concerti, Op. 3 "L'Estro armonico" var. cbns & strs
Concerto No. 10, in b, P.148 (F.IV, No. 10) 4 vlns, strs & c
with J–P. Wallez vln, N. Lepinte vln,   Christophorus SCGLP75896
Y. Carracilly vln, L. Boulay hpsi &   Critère CRD186, SCRD5186
Collegium Musicum, Paris – Douatte   Monitor MC2102, MCS2102

Jörg–Wolfgang JAHN

BACH

(6) Brandenburg Concerti, BWV1046/51 (1721) strs & c
Brandenburg Concerto No. 4, in G, BWV1049 vln, 2 fls & strs
with G. Höller rec, M. Peters rec &   Da Camera SM91922
Heidelberg Chamber Orch. – Göttsche

BUXTEHUDE

(7) Sonatas, Op. 1 (1696) vln & c
Sonata No. 3, in a
with H. Schmidt hpsi & J. Wolf gamba   Da Camera SM92104
Sonata No. 4, in B flat
with H. Schmidt hpsi & J. Wolf gamba   Da Camera SM92104
Sonata No. 5, in C
with H. Schmidt hpsi & J. Wolf gamba   Da Camera SM92104
(7) Sonatas, Op. 2 (1696) vln & c
Sonata No. 6, in E
with H. Schmidt hpsi & J. Wolf gamba   Da Camera SM92104

DEBUSSY

(2) Danses (1904) hp & strs
No. 1. Danse sacrée
with G. Herbert hp & Heidelberg   Da Camera SM91011
Chamber Orch. – Würtz
No. 2. Danse profane
with G. Herbert hp & Heidelberg   Da Camera SM91011
Chamber Orch. – Würtz

DUSSEK

Sonata in B vln, hp & vlc
with G. Herbert hp & W. Jaksch vlc   Da Camera SM91011

IBERT

(2) Interludes fl, vln & hp
with J. Starke fl & G. Herbert hp   Da Camera SM91011

PERGOLESI

(14) Sonatas (1770) 2 vlns & c
Sonata No. 1, in G
with N. Araki vln, M.G. Schneider   Da camera SM92207
hpsi & G. Reith vlc
Sonata No. 2, in B
with N. Araki vln, M.G. Schneider   Da Camera SM92207
hpsi & G. Reith vlc
Sonata No. 3, in c
with N. Araki vln, M.G. Schneider   Da Camera SM92207
hpsi & G. Reith vlc
Sonata No. 4, in G
with N. Araki vln, M.G. Schneider   Da Camera SM92207
hpsi & G. Reith vlc

PERGOLESI – *Continued*

Sonata No. 5, in C
with N. Araki vln, M.G. Schneider   Da Camera SM92207
hpsi & G. Reith vlc

Sonata No. 6, in D
with N. Araki vln, M.G. Schneider   Da Camera SM92207
hpsi & G. Reith vlc

Sonata No. 7, in g
with N. Araki vln, M.G. Schneider   Da Camera SM92208
hpsi & G. Reith vlc

Sonata No. 8, in E flat
with N. Araki vln, M.G. Schneider   Da Camera SM92208
hpsi & G. Reith vlc

Sonata No. 9, in A
with N. Araki vln, M.G. Schneider   Da Camera SM92208
hpsi & G. Reith vlc

Sonata No. 10, in F
with N. Araki vln, M.G. Schneider   Da Camera SM92208
hpsi & G. Reith vlc

Sonata No. 11, in d
with N. Araki vln, M.G. Schneider   Da Camera SM92208
hpsi & G. Reith vlc

Sonata No. 12, in E
with N. Araki vln, M.G. Schneider   Da Camera SM92208
hpsi & G. Reith vlc

Sonata No. 13, in g
with N. Araki vln, M.G. Schneider   Da Camera SM92208
hpsi & G. Reith vlc

Sonata No. 14, in C
with N. Araki vln, M.G. Schneider   Da Camera SM92208
hpsi & G. Reith vlc

TELEMANN

(6) Quartets "Paris" fl, vln, vlc & c
Quartet No. 1, in D
with J. Starke fl, J. Wolf vlc & H. Ruf Da Camera SM92007
hpsi

Quartet No. 3, in G
with J. Starke fl, J. Wolf vlc & H. Ruf Da Camera SM92007
hpsi

Quartet No. 4, in b
with J. Starke fl, J. Wolf vlc & H. Ruf Da Camera SM92007
hpsi

Quartet No. 6, in e "Chaconne"
with J. Starke fl, J. Wolf vlc & H. Ruf Da Camera SM92007
hpsi

Krzysztof JAKOWICZ (1939–   )

BACH

Concerto No. 2, in E, BWV1042 vln, strs & c
with Warsaw Philharmonic Orch. –   Muza SXL0622
Teutsch

SZYMANOWSKI

(3) Mythes, Op. 30 (1915) vln & pf
with M. Jurasz pf   Muza SXL0522

VIVALDI

Concerto in B flat, P.112 (F.I, No. 163) "Posthorn" vln, strs & c
with Warsaw Philharmonic Orch. –   Muza SXL0622
Teutsch

YSAŸE

(6) Sonatas, Op. 27 solo vln
Sonata No. 2, in a
(unaccompanied)   Muza SXL0522
Sonata No. 3, in d
(unaccompanied)   Muza SXL0522

Augusto JANCOWICH (1878–1937)

d'AMBROSIO

Serenade, Op. 4 vln & pf
with E. Curellich pf   17052 u HMV 947914

BACH

(4) Suites, BWV1066/9 strs & c
Suite No. 3, in D: Air (2nd mvt) BWV1068 2 obs, 3 tpts, drms & strs –
arr. vln & pf as "Air on the G–String" by Wilhelmj
with E. Curellich pf   HMV 947916

MOSZKOWSKI

(2) Stücke, Op. 45 pf
No. 2. Guitarre arr. vln & pf Sarasate
with E. Curellich pf   HMV 947915

PIERNÉ

Sérénade in A, Op. 7 (1875) pf – arr. vln & pf Haddock
with E. Curellich pf   17051 u HMV 947913

Rigo JANESI (1863–1927)

DRIGO

(Les) Millions d'Arlequin (1900) – ballet orch.
Sérénade arr. vln & pf Auer
with piano   Imperial 1247
                                    Regal 9349

Piotr JANOWSKI (1951–   )

BACEWICZ

Concerto No. 7 vln & orch.
with Warsaw National Philharmonic   Muza XW1184
Symphony Orch. – Markowski   Polskie Nagrania 239

GEMINIANI

(6) Sonatas, Op. 5 (1738) solo vln
Sonata in B flat (ed. Corti)
(unaccompanied)   Muza XL0433

MOZART

Concerto No. 4, in D, K218 vln & orch.
with Warsaw National Philharmonic   Muza XL0518
Symphony Orch. – Wislocki

SZYMANOWSKI

Concerto No. 1, in a, Op. 35 (1922) vln & orch.
  with Warsaw National Philharmonic   Muza XL0518
  Symphony Orch. – Wislocki

WIENIAWSKI

Polonaise brillante No. 2, in A, Op. 21 vln & pf
  with Z. Vogtman pf   Muza XL0433

Gérard JARRY

AMY

Trajectories (1965/6) vln & orch.
  with Orch. National de l'O.R.T.F. –   Erato STU70593
  Amy

BACH

Concerto No. 1, in a, BWV1041 vln, strs & c
  with l'O.R.T.F. Chamber Orch. –   Victor A640005
  Girard

Concerto No. 2, in E, BWV1042 vln, strs & c
  with l'O.R.T.F. Chamber Orch. –   Victor A640005
  Girard

(3) Sonatas & 3 Partitas, BWV1001/6 solo vln
  Partita No. 3, in E: Preludio (1st mvt) BWV1006
  (unaccompanied)   Club National du Disque CND40

BARTÓK

(6) Rumanian folk dances (1915) pf – arr. vln & pf Székely
  with J. Klauffer pf   Club National du Disque CND40

BEETHOVEN

Serenade in D, Op. 8 vln, vla & vlc
  with S. Collet vla & M. Tournus vlc   Decca DL10116, DL710116
     Discophile Français DF730086,
     DF740086

Serenade in D, Op. 25 fl, vln & vla
  with J–P. Rampal fl & S. Collet vla   Decca DL10116, DL710116
     Discophile Français DF730086,
     DF740086

Sonata No. 5, in F, Op. 24 "Spring" vln & pf
  excerpts
  with J. Klauffer pf   Club National du Disque CND40

Trio No. 6, in B flat, Op. 97 "Archduke" pf, vln & vlc
  with C. Helffer pf & R. Albin vlc   Club National du Disque CND31
     Trianon TRX6194

BRAHMS

(16) Waltzes, Op. 39 pf duet
  No. 15. Waltz No. 15, in A flat arr. vln & pf "in A" Kreisler
  with M. Etcheverry hp   Pacific 150020

FALLA

(La) Vida breve (1913) – opera
  Danza española orch. – arr. vln & pf Kreisler
  with A. Collard pf   Columbia FCX222

FAURÉ

Berceuse, Op. 16 vln & pf
  with J. Klauffer pf   Club National du Disque CND40

HANDEL

Sonata in B flat (1710) vln, strs & c
  with Jean–François Paillard Chamber   Erato STU70579
  Orch. – Paillard   Musical Heritage Society
     MHS1221

HAYDN

Concerto in F, H.XVIII, No. 6 (1765) vln, hpsi & orch.
  with R. Veyron–Lacroix hpsi &   HMV C063–10981
  Toulouse Chamber Orch. –
  Auriacombe

(6) Divertimenti, H.II, Nos. 9/14 (Op. 5) fl, vln, vla & vlc
  Quartet No. 1, in D, H.II, No. 9
  with J–P. Rampal fl, S. Collot vla &   Angel 36226
  M. Tournus vlc

  Quartet No. 2, in G, H.II, No. 10
  with J–P. Rampal fl, S. Collot vla &   Angel 36226
  M. Tournus vlc

  Quartet No. 3, in D, H.II, No. 11
  with J–P. Rampal fl, S. Collot vla &   Angel 36226
  M. Tournus vlc

  Quartet No. 4, in G, H.II, No. 12
  with J–P. Rampal fl, S. Collot vla &   Angel 36226
  M. Tournus vlc

  Quartet No. 5, in D, H.II, No. 13
  with J–P. Rampal fl, S. Collot vla &   Angel 36226
  M. Tournus vlc

  Quartet No. 6, in C, H.II, No. 14
  with J–P. Rampal fl, S. Collot vla &   Angel 36226
  M. Tournus vlc

Sonata in B flat, Op. 4 (H.XIV, No. 1) "Divertimento" 2 hrns, vln, vlc & hpsi
  with G. Barboteu hrn, G. Coursier   HMV C063–10981
  hrn, M. Tournus vlc & R. Veyron–
  Lacroix hpsi

KREISLER

Tambourin chinois, Op. 3 vln & pf
  with A. Collard pf   Columbia FCX222, LD7

Sicilienne & Rigaudon (Francoeur) vln & pf
  with A. Collard pf   Columbia FCX222

Variations on a theme of Corelli (Tartini) vln & pf
  with A. Collard pf   Columbia FCX222

MASSENET

Thaïs (1894) – opera
  Méditation arr. vln & pf Marsick
  with M. Etcheverry hp   Mode MDINT9442
     Pacific 150020

MENDELSSOHN

Trio No. 1, in d, Op. 49 pf, vln & vlc
  with C. Helffer pf & R. Albin vlc   Club National du Disque
     CND1026

MILHAUD

Aspen–Serenade (1957) fl, ob, cl, bsn, tpt, vln, vla, vlc & cbs
  with J–P. Rampal fl, P. Pierlot ob, J.   Adès 15503
  Lancelot cl, P. Hongne bsn, P.   Everest LPBR6176, SDBR3176
  Thibaud tpt, S. Collot vla, M. Tournus
  vlc & J. Cazauran cbs, cond. Milhaud

MILHAUD – *Continued*

Septet (1964) 2 vlns, 2 vlas, 2 vlcs & cbs
with J. Ghestem vln, S. Collot vla, M. Adès 15503
Wales vla, M. Tournus vlc, M. Renard Everest LPBR6176, SDBR3176
vlc & J. Cazauran cbs

Suite de quatrains (1962) narrator, fl, a–sax, bs–cl, hp, vln, vlc & cbs
with M. Milhaud narrator, J–P. Adès 15503
Rampal fl, D. Deffayet a–sax, L. Everest LPBR6176, SDBR3176
Montaigne bs–cl, F. Pierre hp, M.
Tournus vlc & J. Cazauran cbs, cond.
Milhaud

MOZART

Divertimento in E flat, K563 vln, vla & vlc
with S. Collot vla & M. Tournus vlc Discophile Français DF730080,
 DF740080
 Nonesuch H1102, H71102

Serenade No. 7, in D, K250 "Haffner" orch.
 Rondo (4th mvt) arr. vln & pf Kreisler
 with A. Collard pf Columbia FCX222

Sonata No. 24, in F, K376 vln & pf
 excerpts
 with J. Klauffer pf Club National du Disque CND40

PAGANINI

(24) Caprices, Op. 1 (1801/7) solo vln
 Caprice (unid)
 (unaccompanied) Club National du Disque CND40

PARADIES

Sicilienne arr. vln & pf Dushkin
 with N. Nova pf Columbia LFX1036

POUSSEUR

Madrigal III (1962) cl, vln, vlc, 2 pcn & pf
with G. Deplus cl, M. Tournus vlc, D. Adès 15005
Masson pcn, J–C. François pcn, F. Everest LPBR6170, SDBR3170
Boury pf – cond Boulez

RAVEL

Pièce en forme d'Habanera v & pf – arr. vln & pf Catherine
 with A. Collard pf Columbia FCX222

RIES

Suite No. 3, in G, Op. 34 vln & pf
 No. 5. Perpetuum mobile
 with A. Collard pf Columbia FCX222

SAINT–SAËNS

(le) Carnaval des animaux (1886) small orch.
 Le cygne arr. vln & hp
 with M. Etcheverry hp Pacific 150020

SCHOENBERG

Trio, Op. 45 (1946) vln, vla & vlc
with S. Collot vla & M. Tournus vlc Electrola 1C063–28368/71

SCHUBERT, François

(12) Bagatelles, Op. 13 vln & pf
 No. 9. L'abeille
 with A. Collard pf Columbia FCX222

SCHUMANN

Sonata No. 1, in a, Op. 105 vln & pf
 excerpts
 with J. Klauffer pf Club National du Disque CND40

TARTINI

Sonata in g "Il Trillo del Diavolo" vln & c
 excerpts
 with J. Klauffer pf Club National du Disque CND40

VIVALDI

*(12) Concerti, Op. 3 "L'Estro armonico" var. cbns & strs
 Concerto No. 1, in D, P.146 (F.IV, No. 7) 4 vlns, vlc, strs & c
 with G. Carles vln, H. Déat vln, J–N. Erato STU70641
 Molard vln & Jean–François Paillard
 Chamber Orch. – Paillard

 Concerto No. 4, in e, P.97 (F.I, No. 174) 4 vlns, strs & c
 with G. Carles vln, H. Déat vln, J–N. Erato STU70641
 Molard vln & Jean–François Paillard
 Chamber Orch. – Paillard

 Concerto No. 7, in F, P.249 (F.IV, No. 9) 4 vlns, strs & c
 with G. Carles vln, H. Déat vln, J–N. Erato STU70641
 Molard vln & Jean–François Paillard
 Chamber Orch. – Paillard

 Concerto No. 10, in b, P.148 (F.IV, No.10) 4 vlns, strs & c
 with G. Carles vln, H. Déat vln, J–N. Erato STU70641
 Molard vln & Jean–François Paillard
 Chamber Orch. – Paillard

(12) Concerti, Op. 8 (1725) "Il Cimento dell' Armonia e dell' Invenzione"
(Nos. 1/4: Le quattro Stagioni) vln & strs
 Concerto No. 1, in E, F.I, No. 22 "La Primavera"
 with Jean–François Paillard Chamber Electrola SHZEL94
 Orch. – Paillard Erato EFM8041

 Concerto No. 2, in B flat, F.I, No. 23 "L'Estate"
 with Jean–François Paillard Chamber Electrola SHZEL94
 Orch. – Paillard Erato EFM8041

 Concerto No. 3, in F, F.I, No. 24 "L'Autunno"
 with Jean–François Paillard Chamber Electrola SHZEL94
 Orch. – Paillard Erato EFM8041

 Concerto No. 4, in f, F.I, No. 25 "L'Inverno"
 with Jean–François Paillard Chamber Electrola SHZEL94
 Orch. – Paillard Erato EFM8041

*Concerto in B flat, P.367 (F.I, No. 59) 4 vlns, strs & c
with G. Carles vln, H. Déat vln, J–N. Erato STU70641
Molard vln & Jean–François Paillard
Chamber Orch. – Paillard

WEBERN

(4) Pieces, Op. 7 vln & pf
 with C. Ivaldi pf Electrola 1C063–28368/71

Trio, Op. posthumous vln, vla & vlc
 with S. Collot vla & M. Tournus vlc Electrola 1C063–28368/71

Trio, Op. 20 vln, vla & vlc
 with S. Collot vla & M. Tournus vlc Electrola 1C063–28368/71

WIENIAWSKI

Polonaise brillante No. 2, in A, Op. 21 vln & pf
 with A. Collard pf Columbia FCX222

---

* These five concerti also has Monique Vallet as one of the soloists.
However, it is not clear as to which concerto features her as soloist.

WIENIAWSKI – *Continued*

Scherzo–Tarantelle, Op. 16 vln & pf
  with A. Collard pf   Columbia FCX222

Gerald JARVIS

RIMSKY–KORSAKOV

Scheherazade, Op. 35 (1888) orch.
  with Bournemouth Symphony Orch. –   Capitol P8678, SP8678
  Silvestri   Studio Two STWO167

Ladislav JÁSEK (1929–   )

BACH

Concerto in d, BWV1043 2 vlns, strs & c
  with J. Suk vln & Prague Symphony   Crossroads 22 16 0037, 22 16
  Orch. – Smetáček   0038
                                       Supraphon SUA10672,
                                       SUAST50672, SV8396

BLOCH

Baal Shem (3 Pictures of Chassidic life) (1923) vln & pf
  No. 2. Nigun (Improvisation)
  with F. Maxián pf   Supraphon SUEC834, SUK30305

BOŘKOVEC

Sonata No. 2 (1956) vln & pf
  with A. Holeček pf   Supraphon MNB9, SUA18178

BRITTEN

Suite, Op. 6 vln & pf
  with J. Hála pf   Supraphon SUA10707,
                                       SUAST50707, SV8300

CHAUSSON

Poème, Op. 25 vln & orch.
  with Czech Philharmonic Orch. –   Supraphon LPV500, SUB10021
  Jiráček

DALLAPICCOLA

Tartiniana No. 1 (1951) vln & pf
  with J. Hála pf   Supraphon SUA10707,
                                       SUAST50707, SV8300

DOUBRAVA

Sonata No. 2 "In memoriam B. Martinů" vln & pf
  with J. Hála pf   Supraphon SV8344

DVOŘÁK

Sonatina in G, Op. 100 vln & pf
  with Z. Lochmanová pf   Le Chant du Monde LDZP8153

FALLA

(La) Vida breve (1913) – opera
  Danza española orch. – arr. vln & pf Kreisler
  with J. Hála pf   Supraphon LPV467

GEMINIANI

(12) Sonatas (1739) vln & c
  Sonata in d "Sonata Impetuosa"
  with J. Hála pf   Supraphon LPV467

HANDEL

(15) Sonatas, Op. 1 (?1731) fl or vln & c
  Sonata No. 13, in D vln IV
  with J. Hála pf   Supraphon LPV467

MARTINŮ

Sonatina (1938) vln & pf
  with J. Hála pf   Supraphon SV8344

PROKOFIEV

Concerto No. 2, in g, Op. 63 vln & orch.
  with Prague Symphony Orch. –   Artia ALP713, ALPS713
  Turnovský   Supraphon SUA10676,
                                       SUAST50676, SV8263

Sonata in d, Op. 115 solo vln
  (unaccompanied)   Supraphon SUA10707,
                                       SUAST50707, SV8300

RAVEL

Tzigane (Rapsodie de concert) (1924) vln & pf or orch.
  with J. Hála pf   Supraphon LPV467

SOMMER

Concerto in g, Op. 10 vln & orch.
  with Czech Philharmonic Orch. –   Supraphon SUB10021
  Jiráček

SZYMANOWSKI

Concerto No. 2, Op. 61 (1932/3) vln & orch.
  with Prague Symphony Orch. –   Artia ALP713, ALPS713
  Turnovský   Supraphon SUA10676,
                                       SUAST50676, SV8263

Notturno & Tarantella, Op. 28 vln & pf
  with J. Hála pf   Supraphon LPV467

WIENIAWSKI

Polonaise brillante No. 1, in D, Op. 4 vln & pf
  with F. Maxián pf   Supraphon SUEC834, SUK30305

Åke JELVING (1908–   )

BACKER–GRØNDAHL

Barntes Vaardag (cycle of 8 songs) Op. 42 v & pf
  No. 7. Mot Kvaeld (At eventide) arr. vln & org
                    M–2–B. RTJ 1216–B   Musica A8551
  with W. Ringstrand (Wurlitzer org)

FRIML

(L') Amour, toujours l'amour (1922) v & pf – arr. vln & org
  with R. Svenssen org   6737–SSC Sonora 6019

HENTSCHEL

Illusion tango vln & pf
  with R. Svenssen org   6739–SSB Sonora 6015

HERBERT

Naughty Marietta (1910) – operetta
  Ah! Sweet mystery of life arr. vln & org
  with R. Svenssen org   6736–SSB Sonora 6019

HEUBERGER

(Der) Opernball, Op. 40 (1898) – operetta
  Im chambre séparée arr. vln & pf as "Midnight bells" Kreisler
  with S. Carlberg gtr   M 3167–F Musica A3139

KING

Song of paradise pf – arr. vln & org
            M–3–D. RTJ 1217–D Musica A8551
  with W. Ringstrand Wurlitzer org

NEVIN

(The) Rosary (1898) v & pf – arr. vln & org
  with R. Svenssen   8195–S–S–C Sonora 7817
  Hammond org

PROVOST

Intermezzo (1940) vln & pf
  with S. Carlberg gtr   M 3168–C Musica A3139

ROBERTSON

Violin d'amour vln & pf
  with orch. – Waldimir   8030–SSB Sonora 9030

SIECZYNSKI

Wien, mina drömmars stad v & pf – arr. vln & org
  with R. Svenssen   8196–S–S–B Sonora 7817
  Hammond org

SJÖGREN

Sonata No. 2, in e, Op. 24 vln & pf
  with N. Broman pf   RTJ 1710/7 Radiotjänst RE705/8

WOOD

Roses of Picardy (1916) v & pf – arr. vln & org
  with R. Svenssen org   6738–SSC Sonora 6015

François JERNOU

GLUCK

Orphée et Eurydice (1762) – opera
  Dance of the blessed spirits: Lento "Mélodie"(No. 2) arr. vln & pf
  Kreisler
  with piano   Filmophone 183

KREISLER

Liebesleid vln & pf
  with piano   Filmophone 183

Alfred JILKA

BACH

(6) Brandenburg Concerti, BWV1046/51 (1721) orch.
  Brandenburg Concerto No. 3, in G, BWV1048 3 vlns, 3 vlas, 3 vlcs & cbs
  with R. Streng vln, J. Tomasow vln, Amadeo AVRS6043
  R. Harand vlc, G. Weis vlc, L. Beinl Bach Guild BG541
  vlc, W. Hübner vla, E. Rab vla, E.
  Kriss vla, O. Rühm cbs & A. Heiller
  hpsi

Joseph JOACHIM (1831–1907)

BACH

(3) Sonatas & 3 Partitas, BWV1001/6 solo vln
  Sonata No. 1, in g: Adagio (1st mvt) BWV1001
  (unaccompanied)   204y Gramophone & Typewriter
                          047903
                          Pearl GEM101

  Partita No. 1, in b: Bourrée (7th mvt) BWV1002
  (unaccompanied)   205y Gramophone & Typewriter
                          047904

BRAHMS

(21) Hungarian Dances pf duet
  Hungarian dance No. 1, in g arr. vln & pf Joachim
  with piano   219y Asco A123
                          Gramophone & Typewriter
                          047907
                          Pearl GEM101

  Hungarian dance No. 2, in d arr. vln & pf Joachim
  with piano   217y Asco A123
                          Audio Archives LP0079
                          Delta TQD3035
                          Gramophone & Typewriter
                          047905
                          HMV D88, D803

JOACHIM

Romance in C vln & pf
  with piano   218y Delta TQD3035
                          Gramophone & Typewriter
                          047906

Jim JOHANNESSEN

BULL

Concerto in e vln & orch.
  Adagio (2nd mvt)
  with piano   HMV AL2117, X3637

Et Säterbesøg (Fantasy) vln & pf
  with piano   HMV AL2118, X3601

I ensomme Stunde pf – arr. vln & pf Bull
  with piano   HMV AL2117, X3637

DUSSEK

Minuet unid pf – arr. vln & pf
  with piano   HMV X3566

Rondo unid pf – arr. vln & pf
  with piano   HMV X3566

HALVORSEN

(3) Danses norvègiennes (1914) vln & pf
  No. 1. Danse norvègienne No. 1, in D
  with piano   Artiphone 11288

(4) Mosaïques (Suite des morceaux caractéristiques) vln & pf
  No. 4. Chant de Veslemoy
  with piano   Artiphone 11289/90

RAMEAU

Castor et Pollux (1737) – opera
    Gavotte (Act IV) arr. vln & pf Burmester
    with piano   HMV X3566

Willy JOHANSEN

ANONYMOUS

Du grønne glitrende Tre vln & pf
    with piano   HMV AL2159
Et barn er født i Betlehem vln & pf
    with piano   HMV AL2159
Jeg er sa glad hver julekveld vln & pf
    with piano   HMV AL2159
Jeg synger julekvad arr. vln & pf
    with piano   HMV AL2159

BULL

Säterjentens søndag v & pf – arr. vln & pf Svendsen
    with piano   HMV AL2262

GRIEG

Peer Gynt (Suite No. 2) Op. 55 orch.
    No. 4. Solveig's song arr. vln & pf Sitt
    with piano   HMV AL2262

HAALAND

Bøn vln & pf
    with piano   HMV AL2356
Serenade vln & pf
    with piano   HMV AL2356

Granville JONES (1922–1968)

PURCELL

(15) Fantasias, Z731/45 4 & 5 part – orig. viols
    Fantasia No. 1, in F, Z731 (3 parts upon a ground) (?1679)
    with P. Gibbs vln, N. Marriner vln, G. Top Rank XRK508
    Malcolm hpsi & D. Dupré gamba
(5) Pavanes, Z748/52 (pre–1680) (Nos. 1/4: 3 part; No. 5: 4 part)
    Pavane No. 5, in g, Z752
    with P. Gibbs vln, N. Marriner vln &   Top Rank XRK508
    D. Dupré gamba

Charles JONGEN

BACH, J.C.

Sinfonia concertante in E flat, T. P284 (1770) 2 vlns, 2 fls, 2 hrns, strs & c
    with E. Koch vln, A. Antoine ob &   Erato STU70383
    Les Solistes de Liège – Lemaire   Musical Heritage Society
                                   MHS891

JOSEPH

KERR

Sonata (1955) vln & pf
    with C. Eschenbach pf   Century 31380

Wolfgang JOSEPHI

ANONYMOUS

O du Fröhliche, o du Selige v & pf – arr. vln & org
    with W. Fischer org   Polydor 19583

GRUBER

Stille Nacht, heilige Nacht v & pf – arr. vln & org
    with W. Fischer org   Polydor 19583

HANDEL

Serse (1738) – opera
    Ombra mai fu "Largo" arr. vln & org
    with W. Fischer org   Polydor 19584, 69015

HASSE

Abendlied vln & hpsi – arr. vln & org
    with W. Fischer org   Polydor 19584

SCHUMANN

(12) Duets, Op. 85 pf – 4 hands
    No. 12. Abendlied arr. vln & pf Joachim
    with W. Fischer org   Polydor 19585, 69015
(13) Kinderscenen, Op. 15 pf
    No. 7. Träumerei arr. vln & org
    with W. Fischer org   Polydor 19585, 69015

Milan–Braca JOVANOVIĆ (1904–   )

BOULANGER, L.

Nocturne in F (1911) vln & pf
    with piano   Columbia 4824

KREISLER

Rondino on a theme by Beethoven vln & pf
    with piano   Columbia 4823

MENDELSSOHN

(6) Songs without words, Op. 62 pf
    No. 1. Song without words No. 25, in G "May breezes" arr. vln & pf Kreisler
    with piano   Columbia 4824

MOZART

Divertimento No. 17, in D, K334 2 hrns & strs
    Minuet (3rd mvt) arr. vln & pf Burmester
    with piano   Columbia 4822

RIMSKY–KORSAKOV

Sadko (1898) – opera
    Chant hindou arr. vln & pf Kreisler
    with piano   Columbia 4821

SCHUBERT

(2) Lieder, Op. 98 (D498) v & pf
    No. 2. Wiegenlied (Schlafe, holder süsser Knabe) arr. vln & pf Elman
    with piano   Columbia 4822
(6) Moments musicaux, Op. 94 (D780) (1823/7) pf
    No. 3. Moment musicale No. 3, in f "Air russe" arr. vln & pf Kreisler
    with piano   Columbia 4821

TCHAIKOVSKY

(12) Pieces (of moderate difficulty) Op. 40 pf
No. 2. Chanson triste arr. vln & pf
with piano — Columbia 4821

Jo JUDA (1909–)

BADINGS

Sonata (1940) solo vln
Allegretto (3rd mvt)
(unaccompanied) — Radio Nederland 109569

Sonata (1940) solo vln
Allegro (1st mvt)
(unaccompanied) — Radio Nederland DR109046, RN512

Sonata No. 2 (1939) vln & pf
with H. Dercksen pf — Radio Nederland 109570

DRESDEN

Concerto No. 2 (1942) vln & orch.
with Concertgebouw Orch.,
Amsterdam – Haitink — Donemus DAVS6702

MAHLER

Symphony No. 3, in d (1895) orch.
with Amsterdam Women's Chorus –
Boys Chorus of St. Wilibrord Church,
Amsterdam, K. Kos tpt, H. Maasen
tbn, M. Forrester s & Concertgebouw
Orch., Amsterdam – Haitink — Philips 802711/2LY, PHM500136/7, (set PHM2–596), PHS900136/7, (set PHS2–996)

MENDELSSOHN

Sonata in f, Op. 4 vln & pf
with G. Hengeveld pf — Radio Nederland RN512

REGER

(4) Sonatas, Op. 42 solo vln
Sonata No. 2, in A
(unaccompanied) — Radio Nederland DR109270

Wolde JUSSILA

KONDOR

Vanha mustalainen (The old Gypsy) v & pf – arr. vln & pf Jussila &
Koskimies
with A–L. Koskimies pf — Finlandia PEP66

WIENIAWSKI

Légende, Op. 17 vln & pf or orch.
with A–L. Koskimies pf — Finlandia PEP66

Oleg KAGEN (1946–)

BACH

Concerto in C, BWV1064 3 clavs strs & c – arr. 3 vlns & strs "in D"
Baumgartner
with L. Isakadze vln, M. Lubotsky vln,
G. Rozhdestvensky hpsi & Moscow
Radio Large Symphony Orch.
Chamber Group – Rozhdestvensky — Mezhdunarodnaya Kniga S01867/8

BARTÓK

Sonata No. 1 (1921) vln & pf
with A. Lyubimov pf — Mezhdunarodnaya Kniga SM02159/60

DEBUSSY

Sonata No. 3, in g (1917) vln & pf
with A. Lyubimov pf — Mezhdunarodnaya Kniga SM02159/60

MOZART

Concerto No. 3, in G, K216 (cadenza by D. Oistrakh) vln & orch.
with Moscow Philharmonic Symphony
Orch. Chamber Group – D. Oistrakh — Le Chant du Monde LDX78455 Mezhdunarodnaya Kniga S01917/8

Concerto No. 5, in A, K219 "Turkish" (cadenza by Joachim) vln & orch.
with Moscow Philharmonic Symphony
Orch. Chamber Group – D. Oistrakh — Le Chant du Monde LDX78455 Mezhdunarodnaya Kniga S01917/8

Walter KÄGI (1901–)

ALLEGRI

Symphonie à 4 2 vlns, vla d'amore & cbs d'amore
with I. Brix–Meinert vln, J. Ulsamer
t–viol, H. Haferland cbs & K. Grebe
hpsi — Archive ARC3217, ARC73217, APM14317, SAPM198317

CIMA

Sonata in g vln & c
with J. Ulsamer bs–gamba & K. Grebe
hpsi — Archive APM14317, ARC3217, ARC73217, SAPM198317

Thomas KAKUSKA

TELEMANN

Concerto in F, T.II, No. 3 3 vlns, strs & c
with R. Kalup vln, M. Geyrhalter vln,
H. Langfort hpsi & Austrian
Tonkünstler Orch., Vienna – Bernet — Musical Heritage Society MHS638

Hans KALAFUSZ

BACH

Concerto No. 1, in a, BWV1041 vln, strs & c
with Süddeutsche Chamber
Philharmonic, Stuttgart — Intercord 939–09Z

Concerto No. 2, in E, BWV1042 vln, strs & c
with Süddeutsche Chamber
Philharmonic, Stuttgart — Intercord 939–09Z

Concerto in d, BWV1043 2 vlns, strs & c
with W. Rösch vln & Süddeutsche
Chamber Philharmonic, Stuttgart — Intercord 939–09Z

Concerto in c, BWV1060 vln & ob or 2 vlns, strs & c
with W. Schnell ob & Süddeutsche
Chamber Philharmonic, Stuttgart — Intercord 939–09Z

BRAHMS

(16) Waltzes, Op. 39 pf duet
No. 15. Waltz No. 15, in A flat arr. vln & pf "in A" Kreisler
with K. Wildemann pf   CBS S51121

DVOŘÁK

(8) Humoresques, Op. 101 pf
No. 7. Humoresque No. 7, in G flat arr. vln & pf "in G" Kreisler
with K. Wildemann pf   CBS S51121

MENDELSSOHN

(6) Songs without words, Op. 62 pf
No. 6. Song without words No. 30, in A "Spring song" arr. vln & pf
with K. Wildemann pf   CBS S51121

MOZART

Concerto No. 2, in D, K211 vln & orch.
with Kurpfälzische Chamber Orch. –   Intercord 935–09Z
Hofmann

PAGANINI

(6) Sonatas, Op. 3 (1801/6) vln & gtr
No. 6. Sonata No. 12, in e
with K. Wildemann pf   CBS S51121

RUBINSTEIN

(2) Melodies, Op. 3 pf
No. 1. Melody in F arr. vln & pf Wilhelmj
with K. Wildemann pf   CBS S51121

SVENDSEN

Romance in G, Op. 26 vln & orch.
with K. Wildemann pf   CBS S51121

TCHAIKOVSKY

Waltz–scherzo, Op. 34 vln & pf or orch.
with K. Wildemann pf   CBS S51121

VIEUXTEMPS

(7) Romances sans paroles, Op. 7 vln & pf
No. 1. Romance No. 1, in D flat "Chant d'amour"
with K. Wildemann pf   CBS S51121

E. KALINAUSKAITE

GROUDIS

Oriental dance vln & pf
with piano   Mezhdunarodnaya Kniga D009587/8

LAUMENSKENE

Recollection vln & pf
Mazurka
with piano   Mezhdunarodnaya Kniga D009587/8

Tarantella
with piano   Mezhdunarodnaya Kniga D009587/8

Simon KALINOVSKY

GLAZOUNOV

Raymonda, Op. 57 (1897) – ballet orch.
Grand Adagio
with Bolshoi Theatre Orch. – Faier   Mezhdunarodnaya Kniga D23898/9

GLIÈRE

(The) Red Poppy, Op. 70 (1926/7) – ballet orch.
Romance
with Bolshoi Theatre Orch. – Faier   Mezhdunarodnaya Kniga D00011775

RIMSKY–KORSAKOV

Scheherazade, Op. 35 (1888) orch.
with Bolshoi Theatre Orch. – Melik–Pashaev   Mezhdunarodnaya Kniga D04406/7

TCHAIKOVSKY

Swan Lake, Op. 20 (1875/6) – ballet orch.
with Bolshoi Theatre Orch. – Faier   Le Chant du Monde LDX–S8254/6
Mezhdunarodnaya Kniga D04984/9

Max KALKI

HAYDN

(6) Quartets, Op. 3 (H.III, Nos. 13/8) 2 vlns, vla & vlc
No. 5. Quartet No. 17, in F, H.III, No. 17
with F. Wehmeyer vln, A. von der Höh vla & W. Rebhahn vlc   Telefunken LGM65014

(6) Quartets, Op. 64 (H.III, Nos. 63/8) 2 vlns, vla & vlc
No. 5. Quartet No. 67, in D, H.III, No. 67 "The Lark"
with F. Wehmeyer vln, A. von der Höh vla & W. Rebhahn vlc   Telefunken LGM65014

MASSENET

Thaïs (1894) – opera
Méditation
with Berlin Municipal Orch. – Otto   Telefunken FT270 TC044, LA6066, U45559

RAFF

(6) Pieces, Op. 85 vln & pf
No. 3. Cavatina in D
with Berlin Municipal Orch. – Otto   Telefunken FT270 TC044, LA6066, U45559

Lilla KÁLMÁN

ACHRON

Hebrew lullaby, Op. 35, No. 2 vln & pf
with O. Urack pf   Vox 6038

d'AMBROSIO

Sonnet allègre, Op. 53 vln & pf
with O. Urack pf   Vox 6037

CUI

(12) Miniatures, Op. 20 pf
No. 8. Berceuse arr. vln & pf Carse
with O. Urack pf   Vox 6038

GRANADOS

(12) Danzas españolas, Op. 37 (1893) pf
No. 5. Danza española No. 5, in e "Andaluza" arr. vln & pf Kreisler
with O. Urack pf   Vox 06036

RIMSKY–KORSAKOV

Sadko (1898) – opera
Chant hindou arr. vln & pf Kreisler
with O. Urack pf   Vox 6037

WIENIAWSKI

Scherzo–Tarantelle, Op. 16 vln & pf
with O. Urack pf   Vox 06036

Henry KALMER

KREISLER

Praeludium & Allegro (Pugnani) vln & pf
with piano   Aco F33040

PADEREWSKI

(6) Humoresques de concert, Op. 14 pf
No. 1 Minuet in G arr. vln & pf Kreisler
with piano   Aco G15211

SCHUBERT

(7) Gesänge (set to Scott's "Lady of the Lake") Op. 52 v & pf
No. 6. Ave Maria, D839 arr. vln & pf Wilhelmj
with piano   Aco F33040

THOMÉ

Simple aveu, Op. 25 pf – arr. vln & pf
with piano   Aco G15211

Percy KALT

BACH

Cantata No. 1 (Wie schön leuchtet der Morgensten!) BWV1
No. 1. Chorus
with P. Pierlot ob. J. Chambon hrn, G.   Erato STU70284
Terebesi vln, E. Hölderlin hpsi, J.
Muckel vlc, – Heinrich Schütz Chorale
of Heilbronne & Pforzheim Chamber
Orch. – Werner
No. 5. Aria
with G. Jeldin t, G. Terebesi vln, E.   Erato STU70284
Hölderlin hpsi, J. Muckel vlc &
Pforzheim Chamber Orch. -- Werner
Cantata No. 7 (Christ unser Herr zum Jordan kam) BWV7
No. 4. Aria
with G. Jelden t, G. Terebesi vln, E.   Erato STU70342
Hölderlin hpsi & J. Muckel vlc

BACH – *Continued*

Markus–Passion, BWV247
No. 6. Aria
with E. Lisken a. G. Terebesi vln, H.   Erato LDE3346, STE50246
Haferland gamba, A. Lessing gamba,
E. Hölderlin org & J. Muckel vlc

Rudolf KALUP

MOZART

Serenade No. 3, in D, K185 "Andretter" orch.
with Tonkünstler Orch. – Schaenen   Amadeo AVRS6420
       Philips 906420ASY

TELEMANN

Concerto in F, T.II, No. 3 3 vlns, strs & c
with M. Geyrhalter vln, T. Kakuska   Musical Heritage Society
vln, H. Langfort hpsi & Austrian   MHS638
Tonkünstler Orch., Vienna – Bernet
Solo in A, T.II, No. 5 vln & c
with J. Luitz vlc & H. Langfort hpsi   Musical Heritage Society
       MHS637

VIVALDI

Concerto in C, P.87 (F.XII, No. 23) 2 fls, ob, E.hrn, 2 tpts, vln, 2 vlas & 2 hpsi
with H. Riessberger fl, J. Futschik fl,   Amadeo AVRS6416
A. Dutka ob, E. Krall E.hrn, J.   Musical Heritage Society
Spindler tpt, M. Idinger tpt, T.   MHS588
Guschlbauer hpsi, H. Langfort hpsi, of
the Austrian Tonkünstler Orch.,
Vienna – Seipenbusch
(12) Sonatas, Op. 1 2 vlns & c
Sonata No. 1, in g, F.XIII, No. 17
with Z. Topolski vln, H. Langfort hpsi   Musical Heritage Society
& R. Harand vlc   MHS804
Sonata No. 2, in e, F.XIII, No. 18
with Z. Topolski vln, H. Langfort hpsi   Musical Heritage Society
& R. Harand vlc   MHS804
Sonata No. 3, in C, F.XIII, No. 19
with Z. Topolski vln, H. Langfort hpsi   Musical Heritage Society
& R. Harand vlc   MHS804
Sonata No. 4, in E, F.XIII, No. 20
with Z. Topolski vln, H. Langfort hpsi   Musical Heritage Society
& R. Harand vlc   MHS804
Sonata No. 5, in F, F.XIII, No. 21
with Z. Topolski vln, H. Langfort hpsi   Musical Heritage Society
& R. Harand vlc   MHS804
Sonata No. 6, in D, F.XIII, No. 22
with Z. Topolski vln, H. Langfort hpsi   Musical Heritage Society
& R. Harand vlc   MHS804

Emil KAMILAROV

TARTINI

(12) Sonatas, Op. 1 (1734) vln & c
Sonata No. 10, in g "Didone abbandonata"
with N. Duneva-Nemechek pf   Mezhdunarodnaya Kniga D4262

WIENIAWSKI

Polonaise brillante No. 2, in A, Op. 21 vln & pf
with N. Duneva–Nemechek pf   Mezhdunarodnaya Kniga D4263

ZLATEV–CHERKIN

Svevdana, Op. 28 vln & pf
with N. Duneva–Nemechek pf   Mezhdunarodnaya Kniga D4263

Anton KAMPER

SCHUBERT

Rondo in A, D438 vln & str orch.
with Vienna Konzerthaus String   Westminster WL5223,
Quartet   XWN18480
Trio in B flat, D471 ("Sonata" in one movement) vln, vla & vlc
with E. Weiss vla & F. Kwarda vlc   Westminster XWN18480
Trio in B flat, D581 vln, vla & vlc
with E. Weiss vla & F. Kwarda vlc   Westminster WL5223,
                                      XWN18480

Julius KANTROVITCH

MONTI

Csárdas (1904) vln & pf
with piano   2025   Metropole 1165

WIENIAWSKI

(2) Mazurkas, Op. 19 vln & pf
No. 1. Mazurka No. 1, in G "Obertass" arr. Wilhelmj
with piano   2024   Metropole 1165

Lisbeth KÄPPELI

VIVALDI

(12) Concerti, Op. 3 "L'Estro armonico" var. cbns & strs
Concerto No. 1, in D, P.146 (F.IV, No. 8) 4 vlns, vlc, strs & c
with H. Scherz vln, B. Seeger vln, T.   Archive SAPM198469
Soh vln, K. Heitz vlc & Lucerne
Festival Strings – Baumgartner

A. KAPTSAN

TELEMANN

Suite No. 1, in a (1725) 2 vlns, vla & c
with E. Grach vln, V. Sitkovetsky vla,   Mezhdunarodnaya Kniga
A. Bakhchiev pf & V. Simon vlc   D021591/2
Suite No. 2, in g (1730) 2 vlns, vla & c
with E. Grach vln, V. Sitkovetsky vla,   Mezhdunarodnaya Kniga
A. Bakhchiev pf & V. Simon vlc   D021591/2

Sándor KAROLYI

VIVALDI

(12) Concerti, Op. 3 "L'Estro armonico" var. cbns & strs
Concerto No. 1, in D, P.146 (F.IV, No. 7) 4 vlns, vlc, strs & c
with S. Gavrilov vln, E. Schilling vln, Cetra LPU006
K.A. Hermann vln & Frankfurt
Chamber Orch. – Goehr

VIVALDI – *Continued*

Concerto No. 2, in g, P.326 (F.IV, No. 8) 2 vlns, strs & c
with S. Gavrilov vln & Frankfurt   Cetra LPU006
Chamber Orch. – Goehr
Concerto No. 4, in e, P.97 (F.I, No. 174) 4 vlns, strs & c
with S. Gavrilov vln, E. Schilling vln,   Cetra LPU007
K.A. Hermann vln & Frankfurt
Chamber Orch. – Goehr
Concerto No. 5, in A, P.212 (F.I, No. 175) 2 vlns, strs & c
with S. Gavrilov vln & Frankfurt   Cetra LPU006
Chamber Orch. – Goehr
Concerto No. 7, in F, P.249 (F.IV, No. 9) 4 vlns, strs & c
with S. Gavrilov vln, E. Schilling vln,   Cetra LPU007
K.A. Hermann vln & Frankfurt
Chamber Orch. – Goehr
Concerto No. 8, in a, P.2 (F.I, No. 177) 2 vlns, strs & c
with S. Gavrilov vln & Frankfurt   Cetra LPU006
Chamber Orch. – Goehr
Concerto No. 10, in b, P.148 (F.IV, No. 10) 4 vlns, strs & c
with S. Gavrilov vln, E. Schilling vln,   Cetra LPU006
K.A. Hermann vln & Frankfurt
Chamber Orch. – Goehr
Concerto No. 11, in d, P.250 (F.IV, No. 11) 2 vlns, vlc, strs & c
with S. Gavrilov vln & Frankfurt   Cetra LPU007
Chamber Orch. – Goehr

Sven KARPE (1908–   )

BÄCK

Quartet No. 2 (1947) 2 vlns, vla & vlc
with C. Barkel vln, S–V. Bäck vla &   HMV DB11046/7
F. Bramme vlc

HAQUINIUS

Sonata in c sharp vln & pf
with C. Kinberg pf   DFT 5368–A   Discofil A64
Svensk dans vln & pf
with C. Kinberg pf   DFT 5369–A   Discofil A64

von KOCH

(4) Dances vln & pf
Dance No. 2, in A
with E. von Koch pf   OSB 879–1   HMV X6214

NORDQVIST

Bøn pf – arr. vln & pf Karpe
with G. Nordqvist pf   OSB 880–1   HMV X6214

WIRÉN

Suite miniature, Op. 8a vlc & orch. – arr. vln & pf
with D. Wirén pf   Discofil A65

Daniel KARPILOWSKI

BEETHOVEN

Concerto in D, Op. 61 vln & orch.
  Larghetto (2nd mvt)
  with orchestra   Vox 06342

BEETHOVEN – *Continued*

Rondo (3rd mvt)
with orchestra — Vox 06343

Sonata No. 5, in F, Op. 24 "Spring" vln & pf
with Biber pf — Vox 06344/6

KARPILOWSKI

Berceuse vln & pf
with piano — Vox 6323

RIMSKY–KORSAKOV

Sadko (1898) – opera
Chant hindou arr. vln & pf Kreisler
with piano — Vox 6323

Günther KARPINSKI

VIVALDI

(12) Concerti, Op. 3 "L'Estro armonico" var. cbns & strs
Concerto No. 8, in a, P.2 (F.I, No. 177) 2 vlns, strs & c
with F. Wührer vln & Wührer — Somerset 554
Chamber Orch. – Wührer

Eugene KASH (1912–)

BLOCH

Baal Shem (3 Pictures of Chassidic life) (1923) vln & pf
No. 1. Vidui (Contrition)
with J. Newmark pf — CBC Transcription Program 9

MORAWETZ

Duo (1946) vln & pf
with J. Newmark pf — CBC Transcription Program 9

POULENC

Sonata in d (1943) "In memory of Federico Garcia Lorca" vln & pf
with J. Newmark pf — CBC Transcription Program 9

REGER

Trio in b, Op. 2 pf, vln & vla
with J. Newmark pf & S. Kondaks vla — CBC Transcription Program 45

Hans KASSOW (1902–)

CORELLI

(12) Sonatas, Op. 3 2 vlns & c
Sonata No. 1, in F
with L. Friisholm vln, S. Sørenson org — Metronome MCEP3070
& J. Friisholm vlc

Sonata No. 5, in d
with L. Friisholm vln, S. Sørenson org — Metronome MCEP3070
& J. Friisholm vlc

HANDEL

(7) Sonatas, Op. 5 (1739) 2 vlns & c
Sonata No. 1, in A
with L. Friisholm vln, J. Friisholm vlc — Haydn Society HSL85, (in set
& S. Sørenson hpsi — HSL–E)

HANDEL – *Continued*

Sonata No. 2, in D
with L. Friisholm vln, J. Friisholm vlc — Haydn Society HSL85, (in set
& S. Sørenson hpsi — HSL–E)

Sonata No. 3, in e
with L. Friisholm vln, J. Friisholm vlc — Haydn Society HSL85, (in set
& S. Sørenson hpsi — HSL–E)

Sonata No. 4, in G
with L. Friisholm vln, J. Friisholm vlc — Haydn Society HSL85, (in set
& S. Sørenson hpsi — HSL–E)

Sonata No. 5, in g
with L. Friisholm vln, J. Friisholm vlc — Haydn Society HSL86, (in set
& S. Sørenson hpsi — HSL–E)
Metronome MCEP3010

Sonata No. 6, in F
with L. Friisholm vln, J. Friisholm vlc — Haydn Society HSL86, (in set
& S. Sørenson hpsi — HSL–E)
Metronome MCEP3023

Sonata No. 7, in B
with L. Friisholm vln, J. Friisholm vlc — Haydn Society HSL86, (in set
& S. Sørenson hpsi — HSL–E)
Metronome MCEP3024

Louis KAUFMAN (1905–)

ACHRON

Stimmungen, Op. 32 vln & pf
with T. Saidenberg pf — Concert Hall CHC58

ANONYMOUS

Londonderry air traditional Irish ballad – arr. vln & pf Kreisler
with P. Ulanowsky pf — Capitol CCL7513, L8165

BACH

Concerto No. 2, in E, BWV1042 vln, strs & c
with Bach Chamber Group – Kaufman — Tempo 4600, MTT2044

(3) Sonatas & 3 Partitas, BWV1001/6 solo vln
Partita No. 1, in b: Sarabande (5th mvt) BWV1002
(unaccompanied) — Tempo MTT2044

BARBER

Concerto, Op. 14 (1941) vln & orch.
with Concert Hall Symphony Orch. – — Concert Hall CHS1253, H1653,
Goehr — (set E9)
Musical Masterpiece Society
MMS105

BENNETT

Hexapoda (5 Studies in Jitteroptera) (1941) vln & pf
with R.R. Bennett pf — Columbia 70727D

(A) Song Sonata vln & pf
with T. Saidenberg pf — Concert Hall CHS1062

BLOCH

Sonata No. 1 (1920) vln & pf
with P. Pozzi pf — Concert Hall H18

BRAHMS

Sonata No. 1, in G, Op. 78 vln & pf
  with H. Pignari pf

Classics Club X83
Musical Masterpiece Society
MMS109

CHAUSSON

Concerto in D, Op. 21 vln, pf & str qt
  with A. Balsam pf & Pascal string
  quartet

Classic CL6217
Concert Hall CHS1071
Nixa CLP1071

COPLAND

(2) Pieces (1926) vln & pf
  No. 1. Nocturne
  with A. Copland pf

Concert Hall 96, (in set C10),
CHS1140

  No. 2. Ukulele serenade
  with A. Kaufman pf   VX 8102–3

Concert Hall CHC57, CHS1140
Vox 668, (in set 627)

Rodeo (1942) – ballet orch.
  No. 4. Hoe–down arr. vln & pf Copland
  with A. Kaufman pf   VX 8100–5

Concert Hall CHC58, CHS1140
Vox 668, (in set 627)

Sonata (1943) vln & pf
  with A. Copland pf

Concert Hall 96/8, (set C10)

DELIUS

Sonata No. 1 (1892) vln & pf
  with T. Saidenberg pf

Concert Hall 124/5, (set A0),
CHS1062

DOWLING

Little log cabin of dreams (1927) v & pf – arr. vln & pf
  with L. Spielman pf   18462 Edison Diamond Disc 52301

DRDLA

Souvenir vln & pf
  with P. Ulanowsky pf

Capitol CCL7513, L8165

DVOŘÁK

(8) Humoresques, Op. 101 pf
  No. 7. Humoresque No. 7, in G flat arr. vln & pf "in G" Kreisler
  with P. Ulanowsky pf

Capitol CCL7513, CEC004,
FAP8208, L8165

(4) Romantic Pieces, Op. 75 vln & pf
  with A. Balsam pf

Capitol CCL7506, L8112,
LCB8112

Trio No. 3, in f, Op. 65 pf, vln & vlc
  with A. Balsam pf & M. Cervera vlc

Classic CL6248
Classics Club X69
Concert Hall CHS1117

FRANCK

Sonata in A (1886)
  with H. Pignari pf

Classics Club X83
Musical Masterpiece Society
MMS103

GLINKA

Quartet in F (1830) 2 vlns, vla & vlc
  with J. Stepansky vln, L. Kievman vla
  & G. Neikrug vlc

Society for Forgotten Music
SFM1001

GUARNIERI

Sonata No. 2 (1947) vln & pf
  with A. Balsam pf

Concert Hall DL17, (set D17)

HELM

Comment on 2 spirituals vln & pf
  with A. Kaufman pf   VX 8103–3

Concert Hall CHC58
Vox 666, (in set 627)

HINDEMITH

(6) Sonatas, Op. 11
  Sonata No. 2, in D (1920) vln & pf
  with A. Balsam pf

Capitol CTL7001, P8063

KHACHATURIAN

Concerto in D (1940) vln & orch.
                              CHS 171–1, 173/8–1 & 180–1
  with Santa Monica Symphony Orch. –
  Rachmilovich

Concert Hall 126/9, (in set AN),
1173/80, CHC2

KODÁLY

Adagio in C (1905) vln & pf
  with T. Saidenberg pf

Concert Hall CHC58

MANFREDINI

(12) Concerti, Op. 3 (1718) 2 vlns, strs & c
  Concerto No. 12, in C: Pastorale (1st mvt) "Christmas Concerto"
  with A. Fietz vln & Concert Hall
  String Ensemble – Dahinden

Concert Hall F17

MARTINŮ

(5) Pièces Brèves (1930) vln & pf
  No. 2. Andante
  with P. Pozzi pf

Concert Hall E12

  No. 5. Allegro
  with P. Pozzi pf

Concert Hall E12

Sonata (1932) 2 vlns & pf
  with P. Rybar vln & P. Pozzi pf

Concert Hall E12

MASSENET

Thaïs (1894) – opera
  Méditation arr. vln & pf Marsick
  with P. Ulanowsky pf

Capitol CCL7513, L8165

McBRIDE

Aria & Toccata in Swing (1946) vln & pf
  with A. Kaufman pf   VX 8105–2

Concert Hall CHC58, CHS1140
Vox 666, (in set 627)

MATTHESON

(12) Sonatas (1720) fl or vln & clav
  Sonata No. 6, in e
  with A. Geoffroy-Dechaume hpsi

Eurochord LPG627
Lyrichord LL8

MENDELSSOHN

Concerto in e, Op. 64 vln & orch.
    with Netherlands Philharmonic Orch.   Classic LP11001
    – Ackermann   Classics Club X71
                                     Musical Masterpiece Society
                                     MMS7
                                     Nixa MLPY7

Quartet No. 1, in E flat, Op. 12 2 vlns, vla & vlc
    with J. Stepansky vln, L. Kievman vla   Society for Forgotten Music
    & G. Neikrug vlc   SFM1001

MILHAUD

Concertino de printemps (1934) vln & orch.
                 5337–1 & 5338–3   Capitol 8–86013, CTL7005,
    with French National Radiodiffusion   P8071
    Orch. – Milhaud

Concerto No. 2 (1946) vln & orch.
    with French National Radiodiffusion   Capitol 6F87027/9, (set
    Orch. – Milhaud   ECL8072), CTL7005, P8071

Danses de Jacarémirim (1921) vln & pf
    with A. Balsam pf   Capitol CTL7005, P8071

(12) Saudades do Brasil (1920/1) pf
    No. 5. Ipanema arr. vln & pf Levy
    with T. Saidenberg pf   Concert Hall CHC58

MOZART

Concerto in D, KAnH 294a "Princess Adelaide" vln & orch.
    with Netherlands Philharmonic Orch.   Concert Hall G10
    – Ackermann

PORTER

Sonata No. 2, in a (1929) vln & pf
    with A. Balsam pf   Concert Hall DL16, (set D16)

POULENC

Sonata in d (1943) "In memory of Federico Garcia Lorca" vln & pf
    with A. Balsam pf   Capitol CTL7001, P8063

PROKOFIEV

Cinderella, Op. 87 (1941/4) – ballet orch.
    Gavotte arr. vln & pf Fichtenholz
    with T. Saidenberg pf   Concert Hall CHC58

RAVEL

Sonata (1927) vln & pf
    with A. Balsam pf   Concert Hall E6

RESPIGHI

Sonata in b (1917) vln & pf
    with T. Saidenberg pf   Tempo MTT2078

RIMSKY–KORSAKOV

(Le) Coq d'Or (1910) – opera
    Hymn to the sun arr. vln & pf Kreisler
    with P. Ulanowsky pf   Capitol CCL7513, L8165

SAINT–SAËNS

Concerto No. 3, in b, Op. 61 vln & orch.
    with Santa Monica Symphony Orch. –   Disc 4120/2, (set 805)
    Rachmilovich   Tempo MTT2078

SAINT–SAËNS – *Continued*

Concerto No. 3, in b, Op. 61 vln & orch.
    with Netherlands Philharmonic Orch.   Musical Masterpiece Society
    – van den Berg   MMS62

Havanaise, Op. 83 vln & orch.
    with Netherlands Philharmonic Orch.   Musical Masterpiece Society
    – van den Berg   MMS62

SCHUBERT

(7) Gesänge (set to Scott's "Lady of the Lake") Op. 52 v & pf
    No. 6. Ave Maria, D839 arr. vln & pf Wilhelmj
    with P. Ulanowsky pf   Capitol CCL7513, L8165

Sonata in A, Op. 162 (D574) "Duo" vln & pf
    with P. Pozzi pf   Concert Hall H14

SCHUMANN

(13) Kinderscenen, Op. 15 pf
    No. 7. Träumerei arr. vln & pf
    with P. Ulanowsky pf   Capitol CCL7513, CEC004,
                                L8165

Sonata No. 1, in a, Op. 105 vln & pf
    with A. Balsam pf   Capitol CCL7506, L8112
                                Telefunken NLSB8112

SIBELIUS

(2) Pieces, Op. 2 vln & pf
    No. 2. Epilogue
    with T. Saidenberg pf   Concert Hall CHC58

SMETANA

Trio in g, Op. 15 pf, vln & vlc
                 VX 8106–6, 8107/8–2, 8109/10–   Celson DC1009/11
    with R. Firkusny   3 & 8111–2   Vox 669/71, (set 628)
    pf & W. van der Berg vlc

STILL

Carmela arr. vln & pf Kaufman
    with A. Kaufman pf   Orion ORS7152

Lenox Avenue Suite (1937) orch.
    Blues arr. vln & pf Kaufmann
    with A. Kaufman pf   VX 8101–2   Concert Hall CHC57, CHS1140
                                   Vox 667, (in set 627)

    Blues arr. vln & pf Kaufman
    with A. Kaufman pf   Orion ORS7152

    Here's one (Negro spiritual) arr. vln & pf Kaufman
    with A. Kaufman pf   VX 8104–4   Concert Hall CHC58, CHS1140
                                   Vox 667, (in set 627)

    Here's one (Negro spiritual) arr. vln & pf Kaufman
    with A. Kaufman pf   Orion ORS7152

Pastorela (1946) vln & orch. – arr. vln & pf Kaufman
    with A. Kaufman pf   Orion ORS7152

Suite (1943) vln & pf – ed. Kaufman
    with A. Kaufman pf   Orion ORS7152

(3) Visions (1936) pf
    No. 2. Summerland arr. vln & pf
    with A. Kaufman pf   Orion ORS7152

STRAUSS, R.

Sonata in E flat, Op. 18 vln & pf
    with A. Balsam pf   Concert Hall F15

STRAVINSKY

Duo concertante (1932) vln & pf
with H. Pignari pf — Musical Masterpiece Society
MMS107

TARTINI

Sonata in B flat vln & c
with A. Geoffroy–Dechaume hpsi — Eurochord LPG627
Lyrichord LL8

TCHAIKOVSKY

Quartet No. 1, in D, Op. 11 2 vlns, vla & vlc
Andante cantabile (2nd mvt) arr. vln & pf Kreisler
with P. Ulanowsky pf — Capitol CCL7513, L8165

Trio in a, Op. 50 "To the memory of a great artist" pf, vln & vlc
with T. Saidenberg pf & K. Reher vlc — Vox PL6530

TELEMANN

Concerto in F vln & strs
with Concert Hall Chamber Orch. – Stevens — Concert Hall G17

Concerto in F, T.II, No. 3 3 vlns, strs & c
with P. Rybar vln, A. Fietz vln & Concert Hall String Orch. – Swoboda — Concert Hall (set D12), DL12

Sonata in a vln & c
with A. Geoffroy–Dechaume hpsi — Eurochord LPG627
Lyrichord LL8

Sonata in g vln & c
with A. Geoffroy–Dechaume hpsi — Eurochord LPG627
Lyrichord LL8

Suite in D, T.II, No. 1 ob, tpt, strs & c
with S. Zilverberg ob, F. Hausdorfer tpt & Concert Hall Chamber Orch. – Stevens — Concert Hall G17

TOCH

Quartet in D flat, Op. 18 (1909) 2 vlns, vla & vlc
with J. Stepansky vln, L. Kievman vla & G. Neikrug vlc — Contemporary C6002

Serenade in G, Op. 25 (1917) 2 vlns & vla
with G. Manasevitch vln & R. Menhennick vla — Vox 16081/2, (set 177)

Serenade in G, Op. 25 (1917) 2 vlns & vla
with J. Stepansky vln & L. Kievman vla — Contemporary C6002

TORELLI

(12) Concerti, Op. 8 (1709) 1/6: 2 vlns, strs & c – 7/12: vln, strs & c
Concerto No. 1, in C
with G. Alès vln, R. Albin vlc, R. Gerlin hpsi & L'Oiseau–Lyre Ensemble – Kaufman — L'Oiseau–Lyre LD115, OL50089

Concerto No. 2, in a
with G. Alès vln, R. Albin vlc, R. Gerlin hpsi & L'Oiseau–Lyre Ensemble – Kaufman — L'Oiseau–Lyre LD115, OL50089

Concerto No. 3, in E
with anonymous violinist & string orch. – Dahinden — Concert Hall F17

TORELLI – *Continued*

Concerto No. 3, in E
with G. Alès vln, R. Albin vlc, R. Gerlin hpsi & L'Oiseau–Lyre Ensemble – Kaufman — L'Oiseau–Lyre LD115, OL50089

Concerto No. 4, in B flat
with G. Alès vln, R. Albin vlc, R. Gerlin hpsi & L'Oiseau–Lyre Ensemble – Kaufman — L'Oiseau–Lyre LD116, OL50090

Concerto No. 5, in G
with G. Alès vln, R. Albin vlc, R. Gerlin hpsi & L'Oiseau–Lyre Ensemble – Kaufman — L'Oiseau–Lyre LD116, OL50090

Concerto No. 6, in g "Christmas Concerto"
with G. Alès vln, R. Albin vlc, R. Gerlin hpsi & L'Oiseau–Lyre Ensemble – Kaufman — L'Oiseau–Lyre LD116, OL50090

Concerto No. 7, in d
with R. Albin vlc, R. Gerlin hpsi & L'Oiseau–Lyre Ensemble – Kaufman — L'Oiseau–Lyre LD116, OL50090

Concerto No. 8, in c
with R. Albin vlc, R. Gerlin hpsi & L'Oiseau–Lyre Ensemble – Kaufman — L'Oiseau–Lyre LD115, OL50089

Concerto No. 9, in e
with R. Albin vlc, R. Gerlin hpsi & L'Oiseau–Lyre Ensemble – Kaufman — L'Oiseau–Lyre LD115, OL50089

Concerto No. 10, in A
with R. Albin vlc, R. Gerlin hpsi & L'Oiseau–Lyre Ensemble – Kaufman — L'Oiseau–Lyre LD116, OL50090

Concerto No. 11, in F
with R. Albin vlc, R. Gerlin hpsi & L'Oiseau–Lyre Ensemble – Kaufman — L'Oiseau–Lyre LD116, OL50090

Concerto No. 12, in D
with R. Albin vlc, R. Gerlin hpsi & L'Oiseau–Lyre Ensemble – Kaufman — L'Oiseau–Lyre LD115, OL50089

TRIGGS

Danza brasiliana vln & pf
with A. Kaufman pf — VX 8104–4 Concert Hall CHC58
Vox 667, (in set 627)

VAUGHAN WILLIAMS

Concerto in d (1925) "Concerto accademico" vln & orch.
with Zürich Radio Symphony Orch. – Dahinden — Concert Hall CHS1253, F8

VIVALDI

(12) Concerti, Op. 3 "L'Estro armonico" var. cbns & strs
Concerto No. 10, in b, P.148 (F.IV, No. 10) 4 vlns, strs & c
with P. Rybar vln, A. Fietz vln, G. Piraccini vln & Winterthur Symphony Orch. – Dahinden — Concert Hall E2

(12) Concerti, Op. 4 "La Stravagnanza" vln, strs & c
Concerto No. 6, in C, F.I, No. 185
with orch. – Dahinden — Musical Masterpiece Society MMS104

Concerto No. 7, in c, F.I, No. 186
with orch. – Dahinden — Musical Masterpiece Society MMS104

VIVALDI – *Continued*

Concerto No. 9, in F, F.I, No. 188
with orch. – Dahinden   Musical Masterpiece Society
     MMS104

Concerto No. 11, in D, F.I, No. 190
with orch. – Dahinden   Musical Masterpiece Society
     MMS104

(12) Concerti, Op. 8 (1725) "Il Cimento dell' Armonia e dell' Invenzione"
(Nos. 1/4: Le quattro Stagioni) vln & strs
Concerto No. 1, in E, F.I, No. 22 "La Primavera"
with E. Weiss–Mann hpsi, E. Nies–   Amphion AD381/6, (set A1)
Berger org & Concert Hall Orch. –   Classics Club X65
Swoboda   Concert Hall 79/84, (set AR),
     CHC1, CHC1001
     Musical Masterpiece Society
     MMS56

Concerto No. 1, in E, F.I, No. 22 "La Primavera"
with orch. – Dahinden   Classic CL6054/5

Concerto No. 2, in B flat, F.I, No. 23 "L'Estate"
with E. Weiss–Mann hpsi, E. Nies–   Amphion AD381/6, (set A1)
Berger org & Concert Hall Orch. –   Classics Club X65
Swoboda   Concert Hall 79/84, (set AR),
     CHC1, CHC1001
     Musical Masterpiece Society
     MMS56

Concerto No. 2, in B flat, F.I, No. 23 "L'Estate"
with orch. – Dahinden   Classic CL6054/5

Concerto No. 3, in F, F.I, No. 24 "L'Autunno"
with E. Weiss–Mann hpsi, E. Nies–   Amphion AD381/6, (set A1)
Berger org & Concert Hall Orch. –   Classics Club X65
Swoboda   Concert Hall 79/84, (set AR),
     CHC1, CHC1001
     Musical Masterpiece Society
     MMS56

Concerto No. 3, in F, F.I, No. 24 "L'Autunno"
with orch. – Dahinden   Classic CL6054/5

Concerto No. 4, in f, F.I, No. 25 "L'Inverno"
with E. Weiss–Mann hpsi, E. Nies–   Amphion AD381/6, (set A1)
Berger org & Concert Hall Orch. –   Classics Club X65
Swoboda   Concert Hall 79/84, (set AR),
     CHC1, CHC1001
     Musical Masterpiece Society
     MMS56

Concerto No. 4, in f, F.I, No. 25 "L'Inverno"
with orch. – Dahinden   Classic CL6054/5

Concerto No. 5, in E flat, F.I, No. 26 "La Tempesta di mare"
with Concert Hall Chamber Orch. –   Concert Hall CHC1064
Dahinden   Nixa CLP1064

Concerto No. 6, in C, F.I, No. 27 "Il Piacere"
with Concert Hall Chamber Orch. –   Concert Hall CHC1064
Dahinden   Nixa CLP1064

Concerto No. 7, in d, F.I, No. 28
with Concert Hall Chamber Orch. –   Concert Hall CHC1064
Dahinden   Nixa CLP1064

Concerto No. 8, in g, F.I, No. 16
with Concert Hall Chamber Orch. –   Concert Hall CHC1064
Dahinden   Nixa CLP1064

Concerto No. 9, in d, F.VII, No. 1
with Concert Hall Chamber Orch. –   Concert Hall CHC1064
Dahinden   Nixa CLP1064

VIVALDI – *Continued*

Concerto No. 10, in B flat, F.I, No. 29 "La Caccia"
with Concert Hall Chamber Orch. –   Concert Hall CHC1064
Dahinden   Nixa CLP1064

Concerto No. 11, in D, F.I, No. 30
with Concert Hall Chamber Orch. –   Concert Hall CHC1064
Dahinden   Nixa CLP1064

Concerto No. 12, in C, F.I, No. 31
with Concert Hall Chamber Orch. –   Concert Hall CHC1064
Dahinden   Nixa CLP1064

(12) Concerti, Op. 9 (1728) "La Cetra" vln, strs & c
Concerto No. 1, in C, P.9 (F.I, No. 47)
with French National Radio String   Concert Hall (set CHS1134)
Orch. – Kaufman

Concerto No. 2, in A, P.214 (F.I, No. 51)
with French National Radio String   Concert Hall (set CHS1134)
Orch. – Kaufman

Concerto No. 3, in g, P.339 (F.I, No. 52)
with French National Radio String   Concert Hall (set CHS1134)
Orch. – Kaufman

Concerto No. 4, in E, P.242 (F.I, No. 48)
with French National Radio String   Concert Hall (set CHS1134)
Orch. – Kaufman

Concerto No. 5, in a, P.10 (F.I, No. 53)
with French National Radio String   Concert Hall (set CHS1134)
Orch. – Kaufman

Concerto No. 6, in A, P.215 (F.I, No. 54) with solo vln scordato
with French National Radio String   Concert Hall (set CHS1134)
Orch. – Kaufman

Concerto No. 7, in B flat, P.340 (F.I, No. 55)
with French National Radio String   Concert Hall (set CHS1134)
Orch. – Kaufman

Concerto No. 8, in d, P.260 (F.I, No. 56)
with French National Radio String   Concert Hall (set CHS1134)
Orch. – Kaufman

Concerto No. 9, in B flat, P.341 (F.I, No. 57) with 2nd vln obb
with French National Radio String   Concert Hall (set CHS1134)
Orch. – Kaufman

Concerto No. 10, in G, P.103 (F.I, No. 49)
with French National Radio String   Concert Hall (set CHS1134)
Orch. – Kaufman

Concerto No. 11, in c, P.416 (F.I, No. 58)
with French National Radio String   Concert Hall (set CHS1134)
Orch. – Kaufman

Concerto No. 12, in b, P.154 (F.I, No. 50) with solo vln scordato
with French National Radio String   Concert Hall (in set CHS1134)
Orch. – Kaufman

Concerto (unid) 2 vlns, strs & c
with unid. vln & French National   Capitol (in set KCM8091)
Radio Orch. – Désormière

Concerto in D, P.159 vlns, strs & c
with P. Rybar vln & Winterthur   Concert Hall E2
Chamber Orch. – Dahinden   Musical Masterpiece Society
     MMS84

Concerto in d, P.310 (F.I, No. 11) "Senza cantin" vln, 2 fls, 2 obs & 2 bsns
with French National Radio Orch. –   Capitol 6F87036/8, (in set
Désormière   KCM8076)

VIVALDI – *Continued*

Concerto in g, P.383 (F.XII, No. 3) "Per l'orch. di Dresda" vln, 2 fls, 2
obs, 2 bsns & c
with French National Radio Orch. –   Capitol 6F87036/8, (in set
Désormière   KCM7076)

Concerto in E flat, P.429 (Op. 33, No. 1) vln, strs & c
with French National Radio Orch. –   Capitol (in set KCM8091)
Désormière   Telefunken E3801/2

WAYNE

Ramona (1927) v & pf – arr. vln & pf
with L. Spielman pf   18463   Edison cylinder 5537
                                       Edison Diamond Disc 52301

Adolf KAUFMANN

BEETHOVEN

(6) Minuets, G167 pf
No. 2. Minuet No. 2, in G arr. vln & pf Burmester
with piano   Artiphon D3024

BRAHMS

(5) Lieder, Op. 49 v & pf
No. 4. Wiegenleid (Cradle song) arr. vln & pf
with piano   Artiphon D3020

DVOŘÁK

(8) Humoresques, Op. 101 pf
No. 7. Humoresque No. 7, in G flat arr. vln & pf "in G" Kreisler
with piano   Artiphon D3023

POLIAKIN

(Le) Canari (Concert–Polka) vln & pf
with piano   Artiphon D3021

RAFF

(6) Pieces, Op. 85 vln & pf
No. 3. Cavatina in D
with piano   Artiphon D3022

RICHARDS

(La) Canzone degli Uccelletti v & pf – arr. vln & pf
with piano   Artiphon D3013

Erich KAUFMANN

BAKALEINIKOV

Litosc miej! (Habe mitleid mit mir) v & pf – arr. vln & pf
with piano   Vox 6048

BENATZKY

Angoisse d'amour (Einmal kommt der Tag) orch. – arr. vln & pf
with piano   Vox 6047

GREENE

Sing me to sleep v & pf – arr. vln & pf
with piano   Vox 6047

WOLF

Vom Sekt sind die Geigen berauscht v & pf – arr. vln & pf
with piano   Vox 6048

Paul KAUL (1902–)

BEETHOVEN

Romance No. 2, in F, Op. 50 vln & orch.
             CPTX 206–2 & 207–3☐   Columbia DX741
with G. Andolfi pf   Pathé PAT47

(3) Sonatas, Op. 12 vln & pf
No. 1. Sonata No. 1, in D
with N. Radisse pf   Saturn LDG8005
No. 3. Sonata No. 3, in E flat
with N. Radisse pf   Pathé PDT173/4

Sonata No. 5, in F, Op. 24 "Spring" vln & pf
with N. Radisse pf   Saturn LDG8005

SVENDSEN

Romance in G, Op. 26 vln & orch. – arr. vln & pf Wilhelmj
with piano   Parlophone 80659

Ivan KAWACIUK (1913–)

DEBUSSY

(La) Plus que lente – valse (1910) pf – arr. vln & pf Roques
with F. Vrána pf   047731   Supraphon H23994, LPM135
                                     Ultraphon 5185C

DVOŘÁK

Concerto in a, Op. 53 vln & orch.
with Prague Symphony Orch. – Klima   Odeon 0–9162/5

FIBICH

Images, Impressions & Souvenirs, Op. 41 pf
No. 14. Poem (from "Souvenirs", Part IV) arr. vln & pf Kubelík
with F. Maxián pf   42517   Supraphon A22273
                                     Ultraphon A12258

KREISLER

Tambourin chinois, Op. 3 vln & pf
with F. Vrána pf   Supraphon H23993, LPM135
                                     Ultraphon 5185C

MONTI

Csárdas (1904) vln & pf
with F.O.K. Orch. –   44266   Suprahon C22393
Smetaček

NEDBAL

Valse triste (1902) pf – arr. vln & pf Meyer
with F. Maxián pf   42518   Supraphon A22273
                                     Ultraphon A12258

PAGANINI

(24) Caprices, Op. 1 (1801/7) solo vln
Caprice No. 1, in E
(unaccompanied)   Supraphon SUA10059
Caprice No. 2, in b
(unaccompanied)   Supraphon SUA10059

PAGANINI – *Continued*

Caprice No. 3, in e
(unaccompanied) Supraphon SUA 10059

Caprice No. 4, in c
(unaccompanied) Supraphon SUA 10059

Caprice No. 5, in a
(unaccompanied) Supraphon SUA 10059

Caprice No. 6, in g
(unaccompanied) Supraphon SUA 10059

Caprice No. 7, in a
(unaccompanied) Supraphon SUA 10059

Caprice No. 8, in E flat
(unaccompanied) Supraphon SUA 10059

Caprice No. 9, in E
(unaccompanied) Supraphon SUA 10059

Caprice No. 10, in g
(unaccompanied) Supraphon SUA 10059

Caprice No. 11, in C
(unaccompanied) Supraphon SUA 10059

Caprice No. 12, in A flat
(unaccompanied) Supraphon SUA 10059

Caprice No. 13, in B flat
(unaccompanied) Supraphon SUA 10060

Caprice No. 14, in E flat
(unaccompanied) Supraphon SUA 10060

Caprice No. 15, in e
(unaccompanied) Supraphon SUA 10060

Caprice No. 16, in g
(unaccompanied) Supraphon SUA 10060

Caprice No. 17, in E flat
(unaccompanied) Supraphon SUA 10060

Caprice No. 18, in C
(unaccompanied) Supraphon SUA 10060

Caprice No. 19, in E flat
(unaccompanied) Supraphon SUA 10060

Caprice No. 20, in D
(unaccompanied) Supraphon SUA 10060

Caprice No. 21, in A
(unaccompanied) Supraphon SUA 10060

Caprice No. 22, in F
(unaccompanied) Supraphon SUA 10060

Caprice No. 23, in E flat
(unaccompanied) Supraphon SUA 10060

Caprice No. 24, in a
(unaccompanied) Supraphon SUA 10060

Sonata a preghière "Moses Fantasia" (on the aria "Dal tuo stellato soglio" from Rossini's opera "Mosè in Egitto" Op. 24) (1818 or 1819) vln & orch. – arr. vln & pf Kawaciuk
with F. Vrána pf Supraphon H23993, LPM135
Ultraphon 5185C

PROVAZNIK

Hindoo song, Op. 140 vln & pf
with F. Vrána pf 047732 Supraphon H23994, LPM135

SARASATE

(8) Danzas españolas vln & pf
No. 3. Romanza andaluza, Op. 22, No. 1
with R. Kubínský pf 032960 Supraphon E22329
Ultraphon E11917

ŠEVČÍK

(6) Bohemian Dances, Op. 10 vln & pf
No. 1. Blue–eyed maiden (Holka Modrooká)
with R. Kubínský pf 32961 Supraphon E22329
Ultraphon E11917

No. 1. Blue–eyed maiden (Holka modrooká)
with F. Vrána pf Supraphon LPM135
Ultraphon 5115C

No. 5. Czech song (Bretislav)
with F. Vrána pf Supraphon LPM135
Ultraphon 5115C

SMETANA

From my Homeland (1878) vln & pf
with F. Maxián pf 042728/9 Ultraphon E12364

SUK

(7) Pieces, Op. 7 pf
No. 1. Love song arr. vln & pf Mařák
with F. Maxián pf Ultraphon A12251

TOSELLI

Serenade, Op. 6 vln & pf
with F.O.K. orch. – 44267 Supraphon C22393
Smetáček

TROJAN

(The) Emperor's Nightingale (1948) vln & orch.
with F.O.K. orch. – Parík Supraphon H23822/4, LPM199

Max KAYSER

BACH

Concerto in d, BWV1043 2 vlns, strs & c
with B. Hamann vln & HMV QFLP4078
Nordwestdeutsche Philharmonic Orch.
– Schüchter

BOHM

(143) Lieder, Op. 326 v & pf
No. 27. Still wie die Nacht arr. v, vln & orch.
with R. Schock t & orch. – Eisbrenner Electrola E30006
HMV 7PW506

BRUCH

Concerto No. 1, in g, Op. 26 vln & orch.*
with Nordwestdeutsche Philharmonic Gloria SMGL14016
Orch. – Schüchter HMV QFLP4094
Imperial ILP115

* Adagio or 2nd mvt. is also on Odeon BOEW3003.

CORELLI

(12) Concerti grossi, Op. 6 orch.
Concerto grosso no. 8, in g "Christmas Concerto"
with B. Hamann vln, S. Palm vlc &   Electrola I41399, J60277
Nordwestdeutsche Philharmonic Orch.   Imperial ILP132, IPE1027
– Schüchter

DVOŘÁK

(8) Slavonic Dances, Op. 72 pf duet; orch.
No. 2. Slavonic dance No. 10, in e – arr. vln & pf Kreisler
with Nordwestdeutsche Philharmonic   Imperial ILP115
Orch. – Schüchter   Odeon OLAL1012

GADE

(3) Noveletten in A, Op. 29 pf, vln & vlc
with H. Göbel pf & G. Schmidt–   Da Camera SM92107
Enders vlc

GODARD

Trio in g, Op. 32 pf, vln & vlc
with H. Göbel pf & G. Schmidt–   Da Camera SM92107
Enders vlc

HAYDN

(6) Quartets, Op. 64 (H.III, Nos. 63/8) 2 vlns, vla & vlc
No. 5. Quartet No. 67, in D "Lark"
with M. Brosch vln, R. Kayser vla &   Electrola J60258
H. Naumann vlc   Imperial ILP112
(6) Quartets, Op. 76 (H.III, Nos. 75/80) 2 vlns, vla & vlc
No. 3. Quartet No. 77, in C "Emperor"
with M. Brosch vln, R. Kayser vla &   Electrola J60258
H. Naumann vlc   Imperial ILP112

KREUTZER, C.

(Das) Nachtlager in Granada (1834) – opera
Ein Schutz' bin ich
with H. Prey b & Berlin Symphony   Electrola C60156, E80675,
Orch. – Stein   SCXW7535, STE80675
                           HMV WS521, WSX618

MOZART

Concerto No. 5, in A, K219 "Turkish" (cadenzas by Joachim) vln & orch.
with Nordwestdeutsche Philharmonic   HMV QFLP4094
Orch. – Schüchter

SITT

(3) Trios, Op. 63 pf, vln & vlc
No. 1. Trio No. 1, in G
with H. Göbel pf & G. Schmidt–   Da Camera SM92107
Enders vlc

SVENDSEN

Romance in G, Op. 26 vln & orch.
with Nordwestdeutsche Philharmonic   HMV QFLP4094
Orch. – Schüchter   Imperial ILP115
                           Odeon BEOW3003, OLAL1012

TCHAIKOVSKY

Sérénade mélancolique in b flat, Op. 26 vln & orch.
with Nordwestdeutsche Philharmonic   Imperial ILP115
Orch. – Schüchter   Odeon OLAL1012

TOSELLI

Serenade, Op. 6 vln & pf – arr. v, vln & orch. Bohm
with R. Schock t & orch. – Eisbrenner   Electrola E20036, E40060,
                                E60003
                                HMV 7EGW8365, EG580,
                                WDLP507

Raymond KEENLYSIDE

HANDEL

(12) Concerti grossi, Op. 6 2 vlns, vlc & strs
Concerto grosso No. 1, in G (rev. Negri)
with E. Hurwitz vln, K. Harvey vlc &   Philips 802766AY, (in set SC71
English Chamber Orch. – Leppard   AX302)
Concerto grosso No. 2, in F (rev. Negri)
with E. Hurwitz vln, K. Harvey vlc &   Philips 802766AY, (in set SC71
English Chamber Orch. – Leppard   AX302)
Concerto grosso No. 3, in e (rev. Negri)
with E. Hurwitz vln, K. Harvey vlc &   Philips 802766AY, (in set SC71
English Chamber Orch. – Leppard   AX302)
Concerto grosso No. 4, in a (rev. Negri)
with E. Hurwitz vln, K. Harvey vlc &   Philips 802766AY, (in set SC71
English Chamber Orch. – Leppard   AX302)
Concerto grosso No. 5, in D (rev. Negri)
with E. Hurwitz vln, K. Harvey vlc &   Philips 802767AY, (in set SC71
English Chamber Orch. – Leppard   AX302)
Concerto grosso No. 6, in g (rev. Negri)
with E. Hurwitz vln, K. Harvey vlc &   Philips 802767AY, (in set SC71
English Chamber Orch. – Leppard   AX302)
Concerto grosso No. 7, in B flat (rev. Negri)
with E. Hurwitz vln, K. Harvey vlc &   Philips 802767AY, (in set SC71
English Chamber Orch. – Leppard   AX302)
Concerto grosso No. 8, in c (rev. Negri)
with E. Hurwitz vln, K. Harvey vlc &   Philips 802767AY, (in set SC71
English Chamber Orch. – Leppard   AX302)
Concerto grosso No. 9, in F (rev. Negri)
with E. Hurwitz vln, K. Harvey vlc &   Philips 802768AY, (in set SC71
English Chamber Orch. – Leppard   AX302)
Concerto grosso No. 10, in d (rev. Negri)
with E. Hurwitz vln, K. Harvey vlc &   Philips 802768AY, (in set SC71
English Chamber Orch. – Leppard   AX302)
Concerto grosso No. 11, in A (rev. Negri)
with E. Hurwitz vln, K. Harvey vlc &   Philips 802768AY, (in set SC71
English Chamber Orch. – Leppard   AX302)
Concerto grosso No. 12, in b (rev. Negri)
with E. Hurwitz vln, K. Harvey vlc &   Philips 802768AY, (in set SC71
English Chamber Orch. – Leppard   AX302)

Gunter KEHR (1920–)

CORRETTE

Sonata in D "Les jeux olympiques" vln & hpsi
with H. Ruf hpsi   Turnabout TV4010, TV34010

HAYDN

(6) Quartets, Op. 2 (H.III, Nos. 7/12) 2 vlns, vla & vlc
No. 2. Quartet No. 8, in E, H.III, No. 8 arr. gtr, vln, vla & vlc
with K.H. Böttner gtr, G. Lemmen vla   Vox DL1010, STDL501010
& S. Palm vlc

HESSENBERG

Trio, Op. 48 (1949) vln, vla & vlc
with G. Schmid vla & H. Münch–
Holland vlc
Deutsche Grammophon 603,
LPM18403

MOZART

(6) Adagios & 6 Fugues, K404a vln, vla & vlc
Adagio No. 6, in f
with G. Schmid vla & H. Münch–
Holland vlc
Vox PL9560

Divertimento in E flat, K563 vln, vla & vlc
with G. Schmid vla & H. Münch–
Holland vlc
Vox PL9560

Quartet No. 1, in D, K285 fl, vln, vla & vlc
with A. Nicolet fl, G. Schmid vla & H.
Münch–Holland vlc
Telefunken GMA37, LGX66065,
TW30225, UV451

Quartet in F, K370 ob, vln, vla & vlc
with H. Winschermann ob, G. Schmid
vla & H. Münch–Holland vlc
Telefunken GMA37, LGX66065,
TW30225, UV451

Erich KELLER

MOZART

Sonata No. 18, in C, K56 vln & pf
with E. Schwarz pf
Da Camera SM93303
Musica Rara MUS19

Sonata No. 19, in F, K57 vln & pf
with E. Schwarz pf
Da Camera SM93303
Musica Rara MUS19

(12) Variations (on "La Bergère Célimène") K359 vln & pf
with E. Schwarz pf
Da Camera SM93303
Musica Rara MUS19

(6) Variations (on "Hélas j'ai perdu mon amant") K360 vln & pf
with E. Schwarz pf
Da Camera SM93303
Musica Rara MUS19

REGER

(3) Pieces, Op. 79d vln & pf
No. 1. Wiegenlied in G
with E. Schwarz pf
Da Camera SM92704
Musica Rara MUS37

No. 2. Capriccio in b
with E. Schwarz pf
Da Camera SM92704
Musica Rara MUS37

No. 3. Burla in a
with E. Schwarz pf
Da Camera SM92704
Musica Rara MUS37

(8) Preludes & Fugues, Op. 117 solo vln
Prelude & Fugue No. 7, in a
(unaccompanied)
Da Camera SM92704
Musica Rara MUS37

Suite in F, Op. 93 "Im alten stil" vln & pf
with E. Schwarz pf
Da Camera SM92704
Musica Rara MUS37

Trio in a, Op. 77b vln, vla & vlc
with F. Schessl vla & M. Braun vlc
Da Camera SM92705

Raphael KELLERT

BENATZKY

Angoisse d'amour (Einmal kommt der Tag) orch. – arr. vln & pf
with M. Kellert pf
Victor 216520 .

BLAAUW

(The) Clock is playing pf – arr. vln & pf Hänsch
with M. Kellert pf
Victor 216517

BOROWSKI

Adoration (1903) vln & pf
with M. Kellert pf
Victor 216520

POLIAKIN

(Le) Canari (Concert–polka) vln & pf
with M. Kellert pf
Victor 216517

Edith KELLY–LANGE

DANCLA

Boléro & Romance, Op. 50 vln & pf
with piano
Parlophone E5382

HARTY

Irish Fantasia vln & pf
with piano
HMV B2419

Werner KELTSCH

BACH

Sonata in d, BWV1036 2 vlns & c
with R. Kussmaul vln, W. Taube vlc
& L. Praetorius hpsi
Bach 303
Da Camera HBE92204

Sonata in C, BWV1037 2 vlns & c
with R. Kussmaul vln, W. Taube vlc
& L. Praetorius hpsi
Bach 303
Da Camera HBE92204

Sonata in G, BWV1038 fl, vln & c
with H. Strebel fl, W. Taube vlc, & L.
Praetorius hpsi
Bach 303
Da Camera HBE92204

MOZART

Concertone in C, K190 2 vlns, ob, vlc & orch.
with S. Lautenbacher vln, A. Sous ob,
H. Beckedorf vlc & Stuttgart Bach
Kollegium – Rilling
Turnabout TV4098, TV34098

SCHÜTZ

(20) Symphoniae sacrae, Op. 6 (1629)
Concerto No. 5 (Venite ad me) SWV261 t, 2 vlns & c
with K. Huber t, S. Lautenbacher vln,
M. Galling hpsi & P. Buck vlc
Bärenreiter Musicaphon BM30
SL1323
Nonesuch H1160, H71160

Concerto No. 9 (O quam tu pulchra es) SWV265 2 t's, 2 vlns & c
with K. Huber t, W. Jochims t, S.
Lautenbacher vln, M. Galling hpsi &
P. Buck vlc
Bärenreiter Musicaphon BM30
SL1323
Nonesuch H1160, H71160

Concerto No. 10 (Veni de Libano) SWV266 2 t's, 2 vlns & c
with K. Huber t, W. Jochims t, S.
Lautenbacher vln, M. Galling hpsi &
P. Buck vlc
Bärenreiter Musicaphon BM30
SL1323
Nonesuch H1160, H71160

SCHÜTZ – *Continued*

(27) Symphoniae sacrae, Op. 10 (1647)
Concerto No. 2 (Singet dem Herren ein neues Lied) SWV342 t, 2 vlns, & c

with H.J. Rotzsch t, S. Lautenbacher vln, M. Galling hpsi & H. Michel vlc	Bärenreiter Musicaphon BM30 SL1324 Nonesuch H71196

Concerto No. 6, (Ich werde nicht sterben) SWV346 s, 2 vlns & c

with H.J. Rotzsch t, S. Lautenbacher vln, M. Galling hpsi & H. Michel vlc	Bärenreiter Musicaphon BM30 SL1324 Nonesuch H71196

Concerto No. 7 (Ich danke dir, Herr) SWV347 s, 2 vlns & c

with E. Speiser s, S. Lautenbacher vln, M. Galling hpsi & H. Michel vlc	Bärenreiter Musicaphon BM30 SL1324 Nonesuch H71196

Concerto No. 8 (Herzlich lieb hab ich dich, o Herr) SWV348 a, 2 vlns or obs & c

with M. Lehane a, S. Lautenbacher vln, M. Galling hpsi & H. Michel vlc	Bärenreiter Musicaphon BM30 SL1324 Nonesuch H71196

Concerto No. 27 (Freuet euch des Herrn, ihr Gerechten) SWV367 2 t's, bs, 2 vlns & c

with K. Huber t, H.J. Rotzsch t, W. Pommerien bs, S. Lautenbacher vln, M. Galling hpsi & H. Michel vlc	Bärenreiter Musicaphon BM30 SL1324 Nonesuch H71196

G. KEMLIN

SHOSTAKOVICH

(The) Gadfly – film music orch.
Romance

with USSR Cinema Symphony Orch. – Khachaturian	Mezhdunarodnaya Kniga D00018303

Hans KEMPLER

BERTHEAUME

(2) Sinfonia concertantes, Op. 6 (1787) 2 vlns & orch
Sinfonia concertante No. 1, in G

with U. Fiorito vln & Dresden Chamber Orch.	Baroque BU1806

HAYDN

Concerto No. 1, in C, H.VIIa, No. 1 (1765) vln & orch.

with Dresden Chamber Orch.	Baroque BU1806

Concerto No. 2, in G, H.VIIa, No. 4 (1768) (cadenzas by Heiller) vln & orch.

with Haydn Sinfonietta	Baroque BC1841, BC2841

MOZART

Serenade No. 3, in D, K185 "Andretter" orch.

with Baroque Chamber Ensemble – Bernard	Baroque BC1840, BC2840

Serenade No. 4, in D, K203 orch.

with Baroque Chamber Ensemble – Bernard	Baroque BC1840, BC2840

VIVALDI

(12) Concerti, Op. 3 "L'Estro armonico" var. cbns & strs
Concerto No. 3, in G, P.96 (F.I, No. 173) vln, strs & c

with Baroque Chamber Ensemble – Kempler	Baroque BU1822

Concerto in B flat, P.388 (F.IV, No. 2) (Op. 22, No. 2) vln, vlc, strs & c

with Baroque Chamber Ensemble – Kempler	Baroque BU1809

Daisy KENNEDY (1893–)

d'AMBROSIO

Canzonetta, Op. 6 vln & pf

with piano	65831	Columbia D1371

ANONYMOUS

Londonderry air Traditional Irish ballad – arr. vln & pf O'Connor Morris

with piano	Dc 7592^{3}X	Duophone GS7005

BACH

(3) Sonatas & 3 Partitas, BWV1001/6 solo vln
Partita No. 3, in E: Preludio (1st mvt) arr. vln & pf Kreisler

with piano	Duophone GS7006

(4) Suites, BWV1066/9 strs & c
Suite No. 3, in D: Air (2nd mvt) BWV1068 2 obs, 3 tpts, drms & strs – arr. vln & pf as "Air on the G–string" by Wilhelmj

with piano	Columbia D1406

BARNS

Swing song vln & pf

with piano	Columbia 2697

BEETHOVEN

Romance No. 1, in G, Op. 40 vln & orch.

with H. Harty pf	Columbia L1340

BRAHMS

(21) Hungarian Dances pf duet
Hungarian dance No. 2, in d arr. vln & pf Joachim

with piano	Duophone GS7004

Sonata No. 3, in d, Op. 108 vln & pf
Adagio (2nd mvt)

with H. Harty pf	76511	Columbia L1337

Sonata (1853) "Frei aber Einsam" vln & pf
Allegro (Scherzo) in c (3rd mvt) "Sonatensatz"

with H. Harty pf	76512	Columbia L1337

BRANDL

(Der) Liebe Augustin – Operetta
Du alter Stefansturm arr. vln & pf as "The old refrain" by Kreisler

with piano	Duophone GS7004

CRAMER

Waltz pf – arr. vln & pf Burmester

with piano	Duophone GS7006

DRDLA

Danse, Op. 96 vln & pf

with piano	Columbia 2697

GRIEG

Sonata No. 1, in F, Op. 8 vln & pf
Allegro con brio (1st mvt)
with H. Harty pf — Columbia L1440

Allegro molto vivace (3rd mvt)
with H. Harty pf — Columbia L1440

Sonata No. 2, in G, Op. 13 vln & pf
Allegretto tranquillo (2nd mvt)
with H. Harty pf — Columbia L1336

Allegro animato (3rd mvt)
with H. Harty pf — Columbia L1336

KOSLOFF

Idylle finnoise, Op. 5 vln & pf
with piano — Columbia 2698

Mélodie tartare vln & pf
with piano — 65832 Columbia D1371

KREISLER

Liebesfreud vln & pf
with piano — Columbia D1373

MILANDRE

Minuetto unid – arr. vln & pf Burmester
with piano — 69479 Columbia D1409

MISTOWSKI

Suite of 6 pieces vln & pf
Hornpipe
with piano — Columbia D1412

ROSENBLOOM

Lament vln & pf
with piano — Columbia 2747

Waltz–Scherzo vln & pf
with piano — Columbia D1412

SAINT–SAËNS

Introduction & Rondo Capriccioso, Op. 28 vln & orch.
with H. Harty pf — Columbia L1335

SCHUBERT

(2) Lieder, Op. 98 (D498) v & pf
No. 2. Wiegenlied (Schlafe, holder süsser Knabe) arr. vln & pf Elman
with piano — Columbia 2747

Octet in F, Op. 166 (D803) cl, hrn, bsn, 2 vlns, vla, vlc & cbs
Andante un poco mosso (2nd mvt) arr. vln & pf as "Preghiera"
with piano — 69480 Columbia D1409

SCHUMANN

Sonata No. 1, in a, Op. 105 vln & pf
Mit leidenschaftlichem Ausdruck (1st mvt)
with H. Harty pf — Columbia L1338/9

Allegretto (2nd mvt)
with H. Harty pf — Columbia L1338/9

SCOTT

Danse nègre, Op. 58, No. 5 pf – arr. vln & pf Kramer
with piano — Dc 7859 Duophone GS7005

ZARZYCKI

Mazurka in G, Op. 26 vln & pf
with H. Harty pf — 76564 Columbia L1339

ZIMBALIST

(3) Slavonic Dances vln & pf
No. 1. Russian dance
with piano — Columbia D1373

No. 2. Hebrew melody & dance
with piano — Columbia 2698

ZSOLT

Dragonflies vln & pf
with piano — Columbia D1406

Duci de KEREKJARTO (1900–1962)

BEETHOVEN

(6) Minuets, G167 pf
No. 2. Minuet No. 2, in G arr. vln & pf Burmester
with M. Eisner — 142394 Columbia 128M, J226

(2) Sonatas, Op. 27 pf
No. 2. Sonata No. 14, in c sharp: (2nd mvt) "Moonlight" arr. vln & pf Kerekjarto
with piano — Columbia 80802, 20010D, 11M

BISHOP

Clari (1823) – opera
Home, sweet home arr. vln & pf Kerekjarto
with piano — Columbia 20026D

BRAHMS

(21) Hungarian Dances pf duet
Hungarian dance No. 6, in D flat arr. vln & pf "in D" Hubay
with piano — Columbia 20005D

CHOPIN

(2) Nocturnes, Op. 27 pf
No. 2. Nocturne No. 8, in D flat, arr. vln & pf Wilhelmj
with M. Eisner pf — 49901–4 Columbia 49901, 60003D

DRDLA

Serenade No. 1, in A vln & pf
with M. Eisner pf — 79577 Columbia 79577, 20006D, J226

Serenade No. 1, in A vln & pf
with piano — 142395 Columbia 128M

Souvenir vln & pf
with F. Moore pf — 49708 Columbia 49708, 20007D, 32M

DVOŘÁK

(8) Humoresques, Op. 101 pf
No. 7. Humoresque, No. 7, in G flat arr. vln & pf "in G" Wilhelmj
with F. Moore pf — 49912 Columbia 49912, 60003D

GRANADOS

(12) Danzas españolas, Op. 37 (1893) pf
No. 5. Danza española No. 5, in e "Andaluza" arr. vln & pf Kreisler
with piano — Columbia 81024, 31M

HUBAY

(14) Scènes de la Csárda vln & pf
  No. 2. Scène de la Csárda, Op. 13
  with piano   49899 Columbia 49899, 60002D, 5076M

KEREKJARTO

Child's dream vln & pf
  with piano   Columbia 20026D

MOSZKOWSKI

(6) Klavierstücke, Op. 15 pf – 4 hands
  No. 1. Serenata arr. vln & pf
  with D. D'Antalfy pf   79749 Columbia 79749, 20010D, 11M

RIES

Suite No. 3, in G, Op. 34 vln & pf
  No. 5. Perpetuum mobile
  with F. Moore pf   79721 Columbia 79721, 20014D

SAINT-SAËNS

(Le) Déluge, Op. 45 (1876) – oratorio
  Prélude vln & orch. – arr. vln & pf Saint-Saëns
  with M. Eisner pf   80783–1 Columbia 20020D

SAMMARTINI, G.

(6) Sonatas, Op. 1 2 vlns & c
  Sonata No. 4, in A: (3rd mvt) arr. vln & pf as "Canto amoroso" by Elman
  with M. Eisner pf   79457 Columbia 79457, 20007D, 32M

SARASATE

(8) Danzas españolas vln & pf
  No. 3. Romanza andaluza, Op. 22, No. 1
  with M. Eisner pf   49900–2 Columbia 49900, 60004D
  No. 6. Zapateado, Op. 23, No. 2 arr. Kerekjarto
  with M. Eisner pf   79456 Columbia 79456, 20005D
Jota de Pablo, Op. 52 vln & pf
  with M. Eisner pf   49903 Columbia 49903, 60004D, 5076M
Muiñeira, Op. 32 vln & pf
  with F. Moore pf   49931–4 Columbia 49931, 60002D

TCHAIKOVSKY

(3) Souvenirs de Hapsal, Op. 2 pf
  No. 3. Chant sans paroles in f arr. vln & pf Kreisler
  with M. Eisner pf   80801–7 Columbia 20020D

VANDERSLOAT

Dreamy Hawaii v & pf – arr. vln & pf
  with F. Moore pf   79718 Columbia 79718, 20006D

WIENIAWSKI

Légende, Op. 17 vln & pf or orch.
  with M. Eisner pf   98052–4 Columbia 60001D
Mazurka in a, Op. 3 "Kujawiak" vln & pf
  with M. Eisner pf   81055 Columbia 81055, 20014D, 31M
Souvenir de Moscou, Op. 6 vln & pf or orch.
  with M. Eisner pf   98090–3 Columbia 60001D

Albert KERRY

PROVOST

Intermezzo (1940) vln & pf
  with M. Nadelle pf   67864 Decca 3275, 25276
     Rex 9880

WHITING

'Till we meet again
  Where was I? v & pf – arr. vln & pf
  with M. Nadelle pf   67865 Decca 3275, 25276
     Rex 9880

Eda KERSEY (1904–1944)

ANONYMOUS

Gentle maiden English folksong – arr. vln & pf Scott
  with piano   MB 1042–2A Decca F1692

BRAHMS

(21) Hungarian Dances pf duet
  Hungarian dance No. 2, in d arr. vln & pf Joachim
  with piano   MB 1490–3A Decca F1824
(16) Waltzes, Op. 39 pf duet
  No. 15. Waltz No. 15, in A flat arr. vln & pf "in A" Hochstein
  with piano   MB 1489–1A Decca F1824

HUBAY

(Le) Luthier de Crémone, Op. 40 (1894) – opera
  Intermezzo orch. – arr. vln & pf Hubay
  with piano   MB 1041–2A Decca F2061

KREISLER

Liebesleid vln & pf
  with piano   Duophone D518

MONSIGNY

Aline, Reine de Golconde (1766) – opera
  Rigaudon arr. vln & pf Franko
  with piano   MB 1043–2A Decca F1692

MOZART

Idomeneo, Re di Creta, K366 (1781) – opera
  Gavotte in G arr. vln & pf Auer
  with piano   MB 1488–2A Decca F2061

SCHUMANN

(20) Albumblätter, Op. 124 pf
  No. 16. Schlummerlied arr. vln & pf
  with piano   Duophone D518

Young Uck KIM (1947–)

BACH

(3) Sonatas & 3 Partitas, BWV1001/6 solo vln
  Partita No. 1, in b, BWV1002
  (unaccompanied)   Deutsche Grammophon 2555 002

BEETHOVEN

(3) Sonatas, Op. 12 vln & pf
No. 3. Sonata No. 3, in E flat
  with K. Engel pf   Deutsche Grammophon 2555 002

Beryl KIMBER

NIN

(20) Cantos de España (1923) v & pf
No. 4. Montañesa arr. vln & pf Kochański
  with R. Branovskaya pf   Mezhdunarodnaya Kniga D4266
No. 5. Tonada del Conde Sol arr. vln & pf as "Tonada murciana" by
Kochański
  with R. Branovskaya pf   Mezhdunarodnaya Kniga D4266
No. 7. Granadina arr. vln & pf Kochański
  with R. Branovskaya pf   Mezhdunarodnaya Kniga D4266
No. 8. Saeta (Invocation) arr. vln & pf Kochański
  with R. Branovskaya pf   Mezhdunarodnaya Kniga D4266

RAVEL

Tzigane (Rapsodie de concert) (1924) vln & pf or orch.
  with R. Branovskaya pf   Mezhdunarodnaya Kniga D4271

TCHAIKOVSKY

Sérénade mélancolique in b flat, Op. 26 vln & orch. – arr. vln & pf
Wilhelmj
  with R. Branovskaya pf   Mezhdunarodnaya Kniga D4270
Souvenir d'un lieu cher, Op. 42 vln & pf
No. 3. Mélodie
  with R. Branovskaya pf   Mezhdunarodnaya Kniga D4270

Ole KINCH

ALBINONI

(12) Sonatas, Op. 1 (1694) "Sinfonias"
Sonata No. 3, in A 2 vlns & c
  with P. Elbaek vln, J.E. Hansen virg &   Bach Guild BG566
  B. Anker vlc   Metronome MCEP3021
(12) Sonatas, Op. 6 (1711) "Trattenimenti armonia" vln & c
Sonata No. 11, in A
  with J.E. Hansen virg & H. G.   Metronome MCEP3003
  Petersen vlc

SCARLATTI, A.

Sonata in F rec, ob, vln or 2 vlns & c
  with M. Svendsen rec, L. Fagerlund   Bach Guild BG566
  vln, J.E. Hansen virg & H.G. Petersen   Haydn Society HS9011
  vlc   Metronome MCEP3003

TELEMANN

Sonata in F rec, vln & c
  with M. Svendsen rec, L. Fagerlund   Metronome MCEP3004
  vln, J.E. Hansen virg & H.G. Petersen
  vlc

VIVALDI

(12) Sonatas, Op. 2 (1712) vln & c
Sonata No. 9, in e, F.XIII, No. 37
  with B. Anker vlc & J.E. Hansen virg   Bach Guild BG566
     Metronome MCEB3021

Willi KIRCH

TELEMANN

Concerto in D 4 vlns, strs & c
  with R. Schulz vln, G. Silzer vln, H–J.   Archive APM14609. ARC3109
  Westphal vln & Chamber Orch. –
  Seiler

Fritz KIRMSE

MALIPIERO

Concerto (1932) vln & orch.
  with Leipzig Radio Orch. – Kleinert   Urania URLP7112

Robert KITAIN

BRAHMS

Sonata No. 3, in d, Op. 108 vln & pf
  with A. Kitain pf   MGM E3103

FRANCK

Sonata in A (1886) vln & pf
  with A. Kitain pf   MGM E3103

Eyvind KJELDSEN

LUMBYE

Concert–polka (1863) 2 vlns & orch.
  with N.S. Christiansen vln & Royal   Mercury MG50461, SR90461
  Danish Orch. – Hammelboe   Philips 839828GSY

WAlter KLASINC (1924–)

KOHAUT

Divertimento vln, gtr & vlc
  with M. Bäuml gtr & H. Schwarz vlc   Columbia SMC80971

LOCATELLI

Tema con Variazione vln, gtr & vlc
  with M. Bäuml gtr & H. Schwarz vlc   Columbia SMC80971

PAGANINI

Grande Sonata in A, Op. 39 gtr with vln acc
  with M. Bäuml gtr   Columbia C80696, QCX10500,
     STC80696
     Mace M9025, SM9025

Sonata concertante in A, Op. 61 (1804) vln & gtr
  with M. Bäuml gtr   Columbia C80696, QCX10500,
     STC80696
     Mace M9025, SM9025

Sonata in A, Op. posth. vln & gtr
  with M. Bäuml gtr   Columbia C80696, QCX10500,
     STC80696
     Mace M9025, SM9025

RUST

Sonata in G vln & gtr
  with M. Bäuml gtr   Columbia SMC80971

SCHEIDLER
Sonata in D vln & gtr
with M. Bäuml gtr   Columbia SMC80971

Wilhelm KLEPPER

BEETHOVEN
Concerto in D, Op. 61 vln & orch.
with Nürnberg Symphony Orch. –   Audio Fidelity FCS50048
Deaky

Nap de KLIJN (1909–)

BEETHOVEN
Sonata No. 5, in F, Op. 24 "Spring" vln & pf
with A. Heksch pf   Philips A00234L
(3) Sonatas, Op. 30 vln & pf
No. 1. Sonata No. 6, in A
with A. Heksch pf   Philips A00234L
Sonata No. 9, in A, Op. 47 "Kreutzer" vln & pf
with A. Heksch pf   Elite 7074/7

BRAHMS
Sonata No. 3, in d, Op. 108 vln & pf
with A. Heksch pf   Elite 7071/3

CORELLI
(12) Sonatas, Op. 5 vln & c
Sonata No. 9, in A
with R. Jansen pf   Iramac 6516

HANDEL
(15) Sonatas, Op. 1 (?1731) fl or vln & c
Sonata No. 13, in D vln IV
with R. Jansen pf   Iramac 6509

LOCATELLI
(12) Sonatas, Op. 6 (1737) vln & c
Sonata No. 1, in g ed David
with R. Jansen pf   Iramac 6516

MOZART
Adagio in E, K261 vln & orch.
with Vienna Symphony Orch. –   Epic LC3197
Paumgartner   Philips A00299L
Quartet in F, K370 ob, vln, vla & vlc
with J. Stotijn ob, P. Godwin vla & C.   Philips ABE10012, G05379L
van Leeuwen Boomkamp vlc
Quartet No. 20, in D, K499 2 vlns, vla & vlc
with J. Schröder vln, P. Godwin vla &   Epic LC3100
C. van Leeuwen Boomkamp vlc   Philips A00232L, ABL3080
Quartet No. 22, in B flat, K589 "King of Prussia" 2 vlns, vla & vlc
with J. Schröder vln, P. Godwin vla &   Epic LC3100
C. van Leeuwen Boomkamp vlc   Philips A00232L, ABL3080
Rondo in B flat, K269 vln & orch.
with Vienna Symphony Orch. –   Epic LC3197
Paumgartner   Philips A00299L
Rondo in C, K373 vln & orch.
with Vienna Symphony Orch. –   Epic LC3197
Paumgartner   Philips A00299L

MOZART – *Continued*
Sinfonia concertante in E flat, K364 vln, vla & orch.
with P. Godwin vla, & Vienna   Epic LC3197
Symphony Orch. – Paumgartner   Philips A00299L
Sonata No. 6, in G, K11 vln & pf
with A. Heksch pf   11155 ½G Epic LC3131
                                Philips A11155G
Sonata No. 18, in G, K301 vln & pf
with A. Heksch pf   Epic LC3034
                           Philips A00112R, S04012L
Sonata No. 21, in e, K304 vln & pf
with A. Heksch pf   Epic LC3034
                           Philips A00112R, S04012L
Sonata No. 23, in D, K306 vln & pf
with A. Heksch pf   Epic LC3131
                           Philips A00691R, ABR4028
Sonata No. 26, in B flat, K378 vln & pf
with A. Heksch pf   Epic LC3034
                           Philips A00614R, S04012L
Sonata No. 27, in G, K379 vln & pf
with A. Heksch pf   Epic LC3034
                           Philips A00614R, S04012L
Sonata No. 33, in E flat, K481 vln & pf
with A. Heksch pf   Epic LC3131
                           Philips A00691R, ABR4028
Sonata No. 34, in A, K526 vln & pf
with A. Heksch pf   4404/7 Elite 7069/70
(6) Variations (on "Hélas, j'ai perdu mon amant") K360 vln & pf
with A. Heksch pf   Epic LC3131
                           Philips A11246G

SCHUBERT
Quintet in A, Op. 114 (D.667) "Trout" pf, vln, vla, vlc & cbs
with G. van Renessee pf, P. Godwin   Epic LC3046
vla, C. van Leeuwen Boomkamp vlc &   Philips 610138VR, 836254VZ,
L. Groen cbs   G03041L, GBL5543

SENAILLIÉ
(10) Sonatas – Book I (1710) vln or fl & c
Sonata No. 9, in g
with R. Jansen pf   Iramac 17–01, 6509

SHOSTAKOVICH
Quartet No. 1, in C, Op. 49 2 vlns, vla & vlc
Allegro molto (3rd mvt)
with D. Vos vln, P.   AR 11119–1 Decca AK1789
Godwin vla & M. Franck vlc

SMETANA
Quartet No. 1, in e (1876) "From my life" 2 vlns, vla & vlc
with D. Vos vln,   AR 11106/12–1 Decca AK1789/92
P. Godwin vla & M. Franck vlc

TARTINI
(12) Sonatas, Op. 1 (1734) vln & c
Sonata No. 10, in g "Didone abbandonata"
with R. Jansen pf   Iramac 6509

VERACINI

(12) Sonatas, Op. 2 (1744) "Sonate accademiche" vln & c
Sonata No. 8, in e
  with R. Jansen pf   Iramac 6516

VITALI

Chaconne in g vln & c – arr. vln & pf Charlier
  with R. Jansen pf   Iramac 6509

VIVALDI

(12) Sonatas, Op. 2 (1712) vln & c
Sonata No. 2, in A, F.XIII, No. 30 ed. Corti
  with R. Jansen pf   Iramac 6516

WIJDEVELD

Sonata (1952) vln & pf
  with G. Frid pf   Radio Nederland RN507

Josip KLIMA (1927–)

BACH

Concerto in c, BWV1060 vln & ob or 2 vlns, strs & c – arr. "in d"
  with A. Lardrot ob, A. Heiller hpsi &   Amadeo AVRS6052
  I Solisti di Zagreb – Janigro   Bach Guild BG562
         I Classici della Musica Classica
         XAM4036
         Vanguard PVL7031

Valery KLIMOV (1931–)

BABAJANIAN

Sonata in b flat vln & pf
  with piano   Mezhdunarodnaya Kniga
         D023507/8

BACH

(6) Sonatas, BWV1014/9 vln & clav
Sonata No. 3, in E, BWV1016
  with V. Yampolsky pf   Mezhdunarodnaya Kniga
         D05981
         MK MK1560

BEETHOVEN

Concerto in D, Op.61 (cadenzas by Kreisler) vln & orch.
  with USSR Symphony Orch. – Zecchi   Mezhdunarodnaya Kniga
         SM02077/8

(3) Sonatas, Op. 12 vln & pf
No. 3. Sonata No. 3, in E flat
  with V. Yampolsky pf   Mezhdunarodnaya Kniga
         D08863/4

Sonata No. 9, in A, Op. 47 "Kreutzer" vln & pf
  with piano   Mezhdunarodnaya Kniga
         D022625

BRAHMS

(21) Hungarian Dances pf duet
Hungarian dance No. 1, in g arr. vln & pf Joachim
  with V. Yampolsky pf   Mezhdunarodnaya Kniga
         D005591

BRAHMS – *Continued*

Hungarian dance No. 17, in f sharp arr. vln & pf Kreisler
  with piano   Mezhdunarodnaya Kniga
         D022626

DEBUSSY

Suite Bergamasque (1890) pf
No. 3. Clair de lune arr. vln & pf Roelens
  with piano   Mezhdunarodnaya Kniga
         D022626

DVOŘÁK

(7) Gypsy songs, Op. 55 v & pf
No. 4. Songs my mother taught me arr. vln & pf Kreisler
  with piano   Mezhdunarodnaya Kniga
         D05054/5

ESPÉJO

(2) Pieces in ancient style vln & pf
  with piano   Mezhdunarodnaya Kniga
         D022625/6

FRANCK

Sonata in A (1886) vln & pf
  with V. Yampolsky pf   Mezhdunarodnaya Kniga
         D5600/1

HANDEL

(15) Sonatas, Op. 1 (?1731) fl or vln & c
Sonata No. 13, in D vln IV
  with V. Yampolsky pf   Mezhdunarodnaya Kniga
         D05982
         MK MK1560

MENDELSSOHN

Concerto in e, Op. 64 vln & orch.
  with USSR Symphony Orch. – M.   Eurodisc 80022KK
  Shostakovich   HMV 1–063–91039
         Mezhdunarodnaya Kniga
         D021100, S01596

MOZART

Concerto No. 3, in G, K216 (cadenzas by D. Oistrakh) vln & orch.
  with USSR Symphony Orch. – M.   Eurodisc 80022KK
  Shostakovich   HMV 1–063–91039
         Mezhdunarodnaya Kniga
         D021099, S01595

PROKOFIEV

(10) Pieces (from the ballet "Romeo & Juliet") Op. 75 (1937) pf
No. 5. Masques arr. vln & pf Heifetz
  with piano   Mezhdunarodnaya Kniga
         D023507/8

Romeo & Juliet, Op. 64b (1935/6) – 2nd ballet suite orch.
No. 1. Montagues & Capulets arr. vln & pf
  with piano   Mezhdunarodnaya Kniga
         D023507/8

No. 4. Danse de jeunes antillaises arr. vln & pf
  with piano   Mezhdunarodnaya Kniga
         D023507/8

PROKOFIEV – *Continued*

Sonata No. 2, in D, Op. 94bis vln & pf
  with I. Kalegorskaya pf
              Supraphon SUF20004
              Ultraphon DM5541

SARASATE

Caprice basque, Op. 24 vln & pf
  with piano
              Mezhdunarodnaya Kniga
              D05055

Jota aragonesa, Op. 27 vln & pf
  with piano
              Mezhdunarodnaya Kniga
              D023507/8

SCHUBERT

Fantasia in C, Op. 159 (D934) vln & pf
  with V. Yampolsky pf
              Mezhdunarodnaya Kniga
              D08863/4

(4) Impromptus, Op. 90 (D899) pf
  No. 3. Impromtu No. 3, in G arr. vln & pf Heifetz
  with piano
              Mezhdunarodnaya Kniga
              D023507/8

SCHUMANN

Fantasia in C, Op. 131 vln & orch. – arr. vln & pf Kreisler
  with piano
              Mezhdunarodnaya Kniga
              D05055

SCOTT

Lotus land, Op. 47, No. 1 (1905) pf – arr. vln & pf Kreisler
  with piano
              Mezhdunarodnaya Kniga
              D023507/8

SHOSTAKOVICH

(24) Preludes, Op. 34 (1932/3) pf
  Prelude No. 10, in c sharp arr. vln & pf Tziganov
  with I. Kalegorskaya pf
              Mezhdunarodnaya Kniga
              D04443
              Supraphon SUF20004
              Ultraphon DM5541

  Prelude No. 10, in c sharp arr. vln & pf Tziganov
  with piano   Mezdunarodnaya Kniga D05054

  Prelude No. 15, in D flat arr. vln & pf Tziganov
  with I. Kalegorskaya pf
              Mezhdunarodnaya Kniga
              D04443
              Supraphon SUF20004
              Ultraphon DM5541

  Prelude No. 15, in D flat arr. vln & pf Tziganov
  with piano
              Mezhdunarodnaya Kniga
              D05054

  Prelude No. 16, in b flat arr. vln & pf Tziganov
  with piano
              Mezhdunarodnaya Kniga
              D05054

  Prelude No. 24, in d arr. vln & pf Tziganov
  with piano
              Mezhdunarodnaya Kniga
              D05054

TANEIEV

Concert suite, Op. 28 vln & orch.
  Fairytale (3rd mvt)
  with piano
              Mezhdunarodnaya Kniga
              D05054

TCHAIKOVSKY

Concerto in D, Op. 35 vln & orch.
  with Moscow State Philharmonic
  Orch. – Eliasberg
              Mezhdunarodnaya Kniga
              D04302/3
              MK MK1502

Souvenir d'un lieu cher, Op. 42 vln & pf
  No. 1. Méditation
  with V. Yampolsky pf
              Mezhdunarodnaya Kniga
              D005590

Waltz–scherzo, Op. 34 vln & pf or orch.
  with V. Yampolsky pf
              Mezhdunarodnaya Kniga
              D005591

YSAŸE

(6) Sonatas, Op. 27 solo vln
  Sonata No. 6, in E
  (unaccompanied)
              Supraphon SUF20004
              Ultraphon DM5541

Paul KLING

BEETHOVEN

Sonata No. 4, in a, Op. 23 vln & pf
  with H. Kahn pf
              Concerteum CR222
              Remington R199–113

Sonata No. 5, in F, Op. 24 "Spring" vln & pf
  with O. Schulhof pf
              Concerteum CR222
              Remington R199–113

BLACKWOOD

Concerto, Op. 21 vln & orch.
  with Louisville Orch. – Mester   Louisville LOU694, LS694

BRITTEN

Concerto No. 1, in d, Op. 15 (1939 – rev. 1958) vln & orch.
  with Louisville Orch. – Whitney   Louisville LOU626

KRAFT

Concerto grosso (1962) fl, bsn, vln, vlc & orch.
  with F. Fuge fl, D. Nelson bsn, G.   Louisville LOU653
  Whitney vlc & Louisville Orch. –
  Whitney

MARTIN

Concerto (1951) vln & orch.
  with Louisville Orch. – Whitney   Louisville LOU636

Karl KLINGLER (1879–1971)

BEETHOVEN

Serenade in D, Op. 25 vl, vln & vla
    2RA 1887/8 II □, 1889 I □, 1890 II HMV EH1073/5
        □, 1891 I □ & 1892 II □
  with G. Scheck fl & F. Klingler vla

MOZART

Duo No. 2, in B flat, K424 vln & vla
  Andante cantabile (2nd mvt)
  with F. Klingler vla   2RA 1735 II □ HMV EH1031

REGER

Serenade in D, Op. 77a fl, vln & vla
　　　2RA 1729/30[II] □ & 1731/3[1] □　HMV EH1029/31
　　with G. Scheck fl & F. Klingler vla

Trio in a, Op. 77b vln, vla & vlc
　　with F. Klingler vla & unid vlc　　HMV EH950/2

Rok KLOPČIĆ (1933–　)

MOZART

Sonata No. 21, in e, K304 vln & pf
　　with M. Lipovšek pf　　Jugoton 26380

Franz KNEISEL (1865–1926)

BRAHMS

(21) Hungarian Dances pf duet
　　Hungarian dance unid – arr. vln & pf Joachim
　　with piano　　Bettini disc 2203

KNEISEL

Mazurka, Op. 27 vln & pf
　　with piano　　Bettini disc 2201
Mazurka, Op. 27 vln & pf
　　with piano　　Bettini disc 2207
Serenade, Op. 28 vln & pf
　　with piano　　Bettini disc 2212

SINGALÉE

Fantasia (on themes from Bellini's opera "I Lombardi") Op. 28 "Jérusalem Fantaisie" vln & pf
　　with piano　　Bettini disc 2208

SIVORI

(2) Romanzas senza paroles, Op. 23 vln & pf*
　　with piano　　Bettini disc 2202

TARTINI

Sonata in g "Il Trillo del Diavolo" vln & c – arr. vln & pf†
　　with piano　　Bettini disc 2206

WIENIAWSKI

Légende, Op. 17 vln & pf or orch.
　　with piano　　Bettini disc 2210

NOTE: The composers of the following works have not been identified: Air Roumain, apparently two Bettini discs 2204 & 2209; Danse & pastorale, Bettini disc 2211; Le Réveil du Lion, Bettini disc 2205.

Georgi KNELLER

PROKOFIEV

(5) Melodies, Op. 35bis (1921) vln & pf
　　Melody No. 5
　　with piano　　Mezhdunarodnaya Kniga
　　　　　　　　D028103

* Unidentified.
† Abridged.

Georg KNIESTAEDT

BACH

(4) Suites, BWV1066/9 strs & c
　　Suite No. 3, in D: Air (2nd mvt) BWV1068 2 obs, 3 tpts, drms & strs – arr. vln & pf as "Air on the G–string" by Wilhelmj
　　with H–M. Theopold pf　　Clangor M9317

BEETHOVEN

Romance No. 1, in G, Op. 40 vln & orch.
　　with Berlin State Opera Orch.　　Clangor MD1699

BRAHMS

(21) Hungarian Dances pf duet
　　Hungarian dance No. 2, in d arr. vln & pf Joachim
　　with H–M. Theopold pf　　Clangor M9319

CHOPIN

(3) Nocturnes, Op. 9 pf
　　No. 2. Nocturne No. 2, in E flat arr. vln & pf Sarasate
　　with organ, harp & double 　16491　Belvox 510
　　quintet　　　　　　　　　　　　　Ultraphon AP364
　　No. 2. Nocturne No. 2, in E flat arr. vln & pf Sarasate
　　with orch.　　Clangor M1738

DRDLA

Serenade No. 1, in A vln & pf
　　with piano　　Polydor 15968
Serenade No. 1, in A vln & pf
　　with S. Grosz pf　　10926　Supraphon A22283
　　　　　　　　　　　　　　　　　　Ultraphon A485, AP751

Souvenir vln & pf
　　with S. Grosz pf　　10927　Supraphon A22283
　　　　　　　　　　　　　　　　　　Ultraphon A485, AP751

DVOŘÁK

(8) Humoresques, Op. 101 pf
　　No. 7. Humoresque No. 7, in G flat arr. vln & pf "in G" Kreisler
　　with K. Rockstroh pf　　LA 4285　Kalliope K1118
　　No. 7. Humoresque No. 7, in G flat arr. vln & pf "in G" Kreisler
　　with H–M. Theopold pf　　Clangor M9320

HANDEL

Cantata unid
　　Dank sei Dir, Herr "Arioso" arr. vln, org, hp & double qnt
　　with organ, harp & double 　11031　Clangor M9244
　　quintet　　　　　　　　　　　　　Telefunken A522
　　　　　　　　　　　　　　　　　　Ultraphon AP240

Serse (1738) – opera
　　Ombra mai fu "Largo" arr. vln, org, hp & double qnt
　　with organ, harp & double 　11028　Clangor M9243
　　quintet　　　　　　　　　　　　　Telefunken A522
　　　　　　　　　　　　　　　　　　Ultraphon AP240

HUBAY

(14) Scènes de la Csárda vln & pf
　　No. 4. Hejre Kati, Op. 32
　　with piano　　Polydor 14355

HUERT

Mon coeur vln & pf
　　with orch.　　6600　Adler 5299

KREISLER

Caprice viennois, Op. 2 vln & pf
  with piano   Polydor 15912

Schön Rosmarin vln & pf
  with piano   Polydor 14355

Schön Rosmarin vln & pf
  with piano   Broadcast B1319

MOZART

Concerto No. 4, in D, K218 vln & orch.
  with Berlin State Opera Orch. –   Clangor MD327/9
  Steiner

PATÁKY

Auf dem Flusse v & pf – arr. vln & pf
  with orch.   6649   Adler 5299

RAFF

(6) Pieces, Op. 85 vln & pf
  No. 3. Cavatina in D
  with piano & string quartet   16488   Kalliope K542
                               Ultraphon A3647, AP874

RIES

(La) Capricciosa vln & pf
  with piano & string quartet   16489   Kalliope K542
                               Ultraphon A3647, AP874

(La) Capricciosa vln & pf
  with H–M. Theopold pf   Clangor M9318

SCHUBERT

(14) Schwanengesang, D957 (1828) v & pf
  No. 4. Ständchen "Serenade" arr. vln & pf Elman
  with piano   Polydor 15968
  No. 4. Ständchen "Serenade" arr. vln, org hp & double qnt
  with organ, harp & double   16490   Belvox 510
  quintet   Ultraphon AP364

SCHUMANN

(12) Duets, Op. 85 pf – 4 hands
  No. 12. Abendlied arr. vln & pf Wilhelmj
  with harmonium   Polydor 14408
(13) Kinderscenen, Op. 15 pf
  No. 7. Träumerei arr. vln & pf
  with harmonium   Polydor 14408

SCHUURMANN

Vision vln & pf
  witn piano   Polydor 19017

STRAUSS, H.

Frühlings–serenade, Op. 52 vln & pf
  with piano   Polydor 15912

STRAUSS, R.

Don Juan, Op. 20 (1888) orch.
  with E. Mainardi vlc, K. Reitz vla &   Decca CA8126/7
  Berlin State Opera Orch. – Strauss   Fonit 91083/4
                                  Polydor 66902/3

TOSELLI

Serenade, Op. 6 vln & pf
  with piano   Polydor 19017

VIOTTI

Concerto No. 22, in a vln & orch.
  Adagio (2nd mvt)
  with Berlin State Opera Orch.   Clangor MD1700

WIENIAWSKI

Mazurka in a, Op. 3 "Kujawiak" vln & pf
  with piano   Broadcast B1319
(2) Mazurkas, Op. 19 vln & pf
  No. 2. Mazurka No. 2, in D "Dudziarz"
  with K. Rockstroh pf   LA 4286   Kalliope K1118

Gustav KNIESTAEDT

BRAHMS

(21) Hungarian Dances pf duet
Hungarian Dance No. 5, in f sharp arr. vln & pf "in g" Joachim
  with orch.   Telefunken M22275
Hungarian Dance No. 6, in D flat arr. vln & pf "in B flat" Joachim
  with orch.   Telefunken M22275

Joseph KNITZER (1913–1967)

VAUGHAN WILLIAMS

Serenade to Music (1937/8) soloists, cho & orch.
  with N. Jaynes s, W. Anderson t, J.M.   Victor LM2807, LSC2807
  Ousley bsn & the Interlochen Arts
  Festival Chorus – Cliburn

Anatol KNORRE

d'AMBROSIO

Canzonetta, Op. 6 vln & pf
  with piano   Polydor 27079

KIRMAN

Chanson palestinienne pf – arr. vln & pf Dushkin
  with piano   Polydor 27078

PURCELL

(10) Sonatas, Z802/11 (1697) 4 parts – 2 vlns & c
  Sonata No. 5, in d: (2nd mvt) Z806 arr. vln & pf Moffat
  with piano   Polydor 27078

RACHMANINOV

(14) Songs, Op. 34 (1912) v & pf
  No. 14. Vocalise arr. vln & pf Press
  with piano   Polydor 27079

Clifford KNOWLES

ALBINONI

Adagio in g strs & org
  with C. Jarvis org & Royal Liverpool   HMV 7P405
  Philharmonic Orch. – Groves

Gunnar KNUDSEN (1907–   )

BULL
Säterjëntens sondag v & pf – arr. vln & pf Svendsen
  with R. Riefling pf — Columbia GN196

ECCLES
Sonata in g vln & c – arr. vln & pf Salmond
  with E. García pf — Music Library MLR5002

FAURÉ
(3) Chansons, Op. 7 v & pf
  No. 1. Après un rêve arr. vln & pf Bachmann
  with piano — HMV AL2883
  No. 1. Après un rêve arr. vln & pf Bachmann
  with E. García pf — Music Library MLR42,
    MLR5003

GJERSTROM
(The) Myth vln & pf – arr. Knudsen
  with E. García pf — Music Library MLR5002

GRIEG
(4) Norwegian Dances, Op. 35 pf duet; orch.
  Norwegian dance No. 2, in A arr. vln & pf Flesch
  with R. Riefling pf — Columbia GN195
Peer Gynt (Suite No. 2) Op. 55 orch.
  No. 4. Solveig's song arr. vln & pf Sitt
  with R. Riefling pf — Columbia GN196
  No. 4. Solveig's song arr. vln & pf Sitt
  with piano — Columbia GN1222
Sonata No. 3, in c, Op. 45 vln & pf
  with R. Riefling pf — 2NA 704/8–1 — HMV DB11900/2

HALVORSEN
(4) Mosaïques (Suite des morceaux caractéristiques) vln & pf
  No. 4. Chant de Veslemøy
  with R. Riefling pf — Columbia GN195
  No. 4. Chant de Veslemøy
  with piano — Columbia GN1222
  No. 4. Chant de Veslemøy
  with E. García pf — Music Library MLR5003

HAYDN
(6) Quartets, Op. 33 (H.III, nos. 37/42) 2 vlns, vla & vlc
  No. 2. Quartet No. 38, in E flat: Scherzando (2nd mvt) H.III, No. 38
  arr. vln & pf Knudsen
  with E. García pf — Music Library MLR41,
    MLR5003

KNUDSEN
Norwegian Rhapsody vln & pf
  with E. García pf — Music Library MLR5002
Reflections vln & pf*
  with E. García pf — Music Library MLR5003

PROKOFIEV
(5) Melodies, Op. 35bis (1921) vln & pf
  No. 1. Melody
  with E. García pf — Music Library MLR5003

* Composed jointly with Eva García.

REGER
Suite in a, Op. 103a vln & pf
  Aria (3rd mvt) arr. Barmas
  with E. García pf — Music Library MLR5002

SVENDSEN
Romance in G, Op. 26 vln & orch. – arr. vln & pf Wilhelmj
  with R. Levin pf — HMV AL3013

TVEITT
Baldurs draumar – ballet orch.
  with E. García pf — Music Library MLR5003

Kenji KOBAYASHI

WOLFF
Duo vln & pf
  with D. Tudor pf — Time 58009, S8009
Summer 2 vlns, vla & vlc
  with M. Raimondi vln, W. Trampler — Time 58009, S8009
  vla & D. Soyer vlc

Daniel KOBIALKA

BAVICCHI
Sonata No. 1 (1956) vln & pf
  with M. Press pf — Medea 1002

BRANT
Hieroglyphics (1966) solo vln
  (unaccompanied) — Advance 6

CHENEY
Rhapsody (1941) vln & pf
  with M. Press pf — Medea 1002

FRANCHETTI
Chamber Concertino (1965) vln & cha ens
  with Hartt Chamber Players – Larsen — Ars Nova/Ars Antiqua AN1002

KIRCHNER
Duo (1947) vln & pf
  with M. Press pf — Medea 1002

MARTINO
Fantasy variations solo vln
  (unaccompanied) — Advance 6

ROCHBERG
Duo concertante (1955 – rev. 1959) vln & vlc
  with J. Kobialka vlc — Advance 6

SCHOENBERG
Fantasy, Op. 47 (1949) vln & pf
  with M. Press pf — Ars Nova/Ars Antiqua AN1002

SYDEMAN
Trio (1958) fl, vln & cbs
  with N. Turetzky fl & B. Turetzky cbs — Medea 1001

Otto KOBIN

AULIN

(4) Aquarelles vln & pf
No. 2. Humoresque
with piano   Vox 6175

CRAMER

Waltz pf – arr. vln & pf Burmester
with piano   Vox 06177

FIBICH

Images, Impressions & Souvenirs, Op. 41 pf
No. 14. Poem (from "Souvenirs", Part IV) arr. vln & pf Kubelík
with piano   Vox 6176

HUBAY

(14) Scènes de la Csárda vln & pf
No. 5. Hullámzó balaton, Op. 33
with piano   Vox 06177

SIMON

(2) Pieces, Op. 17 vln & pf
No. 2. Berceuse
with piano   Vox 6175

WEBER

(18) Favoritenwalzer, J143/60 (1812) pf
No. 5. Waltz No. 5, in B flat, J147 arr. vln & pf "in D" Burmester
with piano   Vox 6176

Emmanuel KOCH

BACH

Sinfonia concertante in E flat, T. P284 (1770) 2 vlns, 2 fls, 2 hrns & orch.
with C. Jongen vln, A. Antoine ob &   Erato STU70363
Les Solistes de Liège – Lemaire   Musical Heritage Society
                                   MHS891

de CROES

(7) Concerti
Concerto No. 6, in B flat fl, vln & strs
with A. Isselée fl, M. Koch–Pichon   Erato STU70317
hpsi & Les Solistes de Liège – Lemaire   Musical Heritage Society CC11,
                                   MHS793

PIELTAIN

Concerto in G vln & orch.
with Les Solistes de Liège – Lemaire   Alpha DB120
                                   Oryx ORYX733

YSAŸE

Harmonies du soir, Op. 31 2 vlns, vla, vlc & strs
with H. Koch vln, P. Lambert vla, G.   Alpha CL3007, CL4007
Mallach vlc & Les Solistes de Liège –
Lemaire

Henri KOCH

FRANCK

Sonata in A (1886) vln & pf
with A. Dumortier pf   Alpha CL3002, DB30

LEKEU

Quartet in b (1893) "Unfinished" pf, vln, vla & vlc
     2217 BMP, 2218½ BMP, 2219   Decca LY6195/7
         BMP & 2220/2½ BMP   Polydor 516555/7
with C. van Lancker pf, J. Rogister vla
& L. Rogister vlc
Sonata in G (1892) vln & pf
     2183/9½ BMP & 2190¾ BMP   Decca LY6182/5
with C. Van Lancker pf   Polydor 516549/52
Sonata in G (1892) vln & pf
with A. Dumortier pf   Alpha CL3002, DB30

ROGISTER

Concerto in G (1945) vln & orch.
with Liège Symphony Orch. – Quinet   Decca FAT173312

YSAŸE

Harmonies du soir, Op. 31 2 vlns, vla, vlc & strs
with E. Koch vln, P. Lambert vla, G.   Alpha CL3007, CL4007
Mallach vlc & Les Solistes de Liège –
Lemaire

Walter KOCH

BIBER

(16) Biblical Sonatas "Mysterien" vln & c
Sonata No. 1, in d "The annunciation of the birth of Christ"
with O. Sailer hpsi   Da Camera WK4712
Sonata No. 2, in A "Visit of Mary to Elizabeth"
with O. Sailer hpsi   Da Camera WK4712
Sonata No. 3, in b "Birth of Christ"
with O. Sailer hpsi   Da Camera WK4713
Sonata No. 4, in d "Christ in the temple"
with O. Sailer hpsi   Da Camera WK4713

Paul KOCHAŃSKI (1887–1934)

BRAHMS

(21) Hungarian Dances pf duet
Hungarian Dance No. 1, in g arr. vln & pf Joachim
with J. Kochański pf   Vocalion X9433
Sonata No. 3, in d, Op. 108 vln & pf
     2B 2298¹¹ 𝔉, 2B 2299¹ 𝔉 & 2B   HMV DB1728/30, DB7249/51
with A. Rubinstein pf   2300/03¹¹ 𝔉   Victor 8483/5, (set M241)

KREISLER

(La) Gitana vln & pf
with J. Kochański pf   Vocalion X9433

PIERNÉ

Sérénade in A, Op. 7 (1875) pf – arr. vln & pf Haddock
with J. Kochański pf   Vocalion X9632

RACHMANINOV

(14) Songs, Op. 34 (1912) v & pf
No. 14. Vocalise arr. vln & pf Press
with F. Tresselt pf   Vocalion 70009

RAFF

(6) Pieces, Op. 85 vln & pf
  No. 3. Cavatina in D
  with J. Kochański pf   Vocalion X9632

SARASATE

(8) Danzas españolas vln & pf
  No. 1. Malagueña, Op. 21, No. 1
  with J. Kochański pf   Vocalion 70005, K05084

TCHAIKOVSKY

Souvenir d'un lieu cher, Op. 42 vln & pf
  No. 3. Mélodie
  with J. Kochański pf   Vocalion 60062, X9480

(3) Souvenirs de Hapsal, Op. 2 pf
  No. 3. Chant sans paroles in f arr. vln & pf Kreisler
  with J. Kochański pf   Vocalion 60062, X9480

WAGNER

(Die) Meistersinger von Nürnberg (1868) – opera
  Morgenlich leuchtend "P ize song" arr. vln & pf Wilhelmj
  with F. Tresselt pf   Vocalion 70009

WIENIAWSKI

(Le) Carnaval russe (on the Russian air "Po ulicy mostovoj") Op. 11 vln & pf
  with J. Kochański pf   Vocalion 70005, K05084

Jaroslav KOCIÁN (1883–1950)

d'AMBROSIO

Canzonetta, Op. 6 vln & pf
  with piano   Columbia 1423

PIERNÉ

Sérénade in A, Op. 7 (1875) pf – arr. vln & pf Haddock
  with piano   Columbia 1422, A206

SPIES

Elfentanz in D, Op. 62 vln & pf
  with piano   Columbia 1458, A609

Albert KOCSIS

BACH

(3) Sonatas & 3 Partitas, BWV1001/6 solo vln
  Sonata No. 1, in g, BWV1001
  (unaccompanied)   Qualiton LPX1148

  Partita No. 2, in d, BWV1004
  (unaccompanied)   Qualiton LPX1148

GIULIANI, M.

Sonata Grande, Op. 25 gtr & vln
  with L. Szendrei Karper gtr   Qualiton LP1568

PAGANINI

(6) Sonatas, Op. 2 (1801/6) vln & gtr
  Sonata No. 1, in A
  with L. Szendrei Karper gtr   Qualiton LP1568

  Sonata No. 2, in C
  with L. Szendrei Karper gtr   Qualiton LP1568

PAGANINI – *Continued*

  Sonata No. 4, in A
  with L. Szendrei Karper gtr   Qualiton LP1568

YSAŸE

(6) Sonatas, Op. 27 solo vln
  Sonata No. 4, in e
  (unaccompanied)   Qualiton LPX1148

Rudolf KOECKERT (1913–   )

BACH

Mass in b, BWV232 (1733/7) s,a,t, b, cho, strs & c*
  with L. Marshall s, H. Töpper a, P.   Epic BC1031/3, (in set BSC102),
  Pears t, K. Borg bs, K. Benzinger tpt,   LC3502/3, (in set SC6027)
  M. Scharitzer hpsi, A. Nowakowski   Fontana 698002/3CL,
  org, K. Richter hrn, F. Höger cbs, J.   875041/2CY, CFL1028/9
  Merz vlc, K. Kalmus ob, d'amore, W.
  Grimm ob, d'amore & Bavarian Radio
  Chorus & Orch. – Jochum

BEETHOVEN

Romance No. 1, in G, Op. 40 vln & orch.
  with Bamberg Symphony Orch. –   Deutsche Grammophon 72432,
  Leitner   EPL30050, LPEM19012,
     LPX29257
     Heliodor 478135

Romance No. 2, in F, Op. 50 vln & orch.
  with Bamberg Symphony Orch. –   Deutsche Grammophon 72432,
  Leitner   EPL30050, LPEM19012,
     LPX29257
     Heliodor 478135

MOZART

Serenade No. 7, in D, K250 "Haffner" orch.
  with Bavarian Radio Symphony Orch.   Deutsche Grammophon
  – Kubelík   LPM18869, SLPM138869

SPOHR

Concerto No. 8, in a, Op. 47 "Gesangsscene" vln & orch.
  with Bavarian Radio Symphony Orch.   Deutsche Grammophon
  – Lehmann   LPEM19012

STRAUSS, R.

Sonata in E flat, Op. 18 vln & pf
  with E. Frieser pf   Da Camera SM93709

Francis KOENE (1900–1935)

d'AMBROSIO

Canzonetta, Op. 6 vln & pf
  with M. van Ijzer pf   Columbia D17191

BEETHOVEN

Romance No. 1, in G, Op. 40 vln & orch.
  with M. van Ijzer pf   Columbia D17187

* Excerpts on Fontana 663009ER & CFE15016.

BLOCH

Baal Shem (3 Pictures of Chassidic life) (1923) vln & pf
No. 1. Vidui (Contrition)
  with M. van Ijzer pf   Columbia D17188

DUSSEK

Minuet pf – arr. vln & pf Burmester
  with organ   Columbia D17189

FALLA

(7) Canciones populares españolas (1914) v & pf
No. 3. Asturiana arr. vln & pf Kochański
  with M. van Ijzer pf   Columbia D17188

KREISLER

Polichinelle–serenade vln & pf
  with M. van Ijzer pf   Columbia D9994
Schön Rosmarin vln & pf
  with M. van Ijzer pf   Columbia D9994
Andantino (Padre Martini) vln & pf
  with M. van Ijzer pf   Columbia D17190
Scherzo (Dittersdorf) vln & pf
  with M. van Ijzer pf   Columbia D17190

MILHAUD

(12) Saudades do Brasil (1920/1) pf
No. 3. Leme arr. vln & pf Lévy
  with M. van Ijzer pf   Columbia D9995
No. 5. Ipanema arr. vln & pf Lévy
  with M. van Ijzer pf   Columbia D9995

NIN

(20) Cantos de España (1923) v & pf
No. 5. Tonada del Conde Sol arr. vln & pf as "Tonada murciano" by Kochański
  with M. van Ijzer pf   Columbia D17188
No. 15. Paño murciano arr. vln & pf as "Murciana" by Nin & Gautier
  with M. van Ijzer pf   Columbia D17187

RAMEAU

Castor et Pollux (1737) – opera
Gavotte (Act IV) arr. vln & pf Burmester
  with M. van Ijzer pf   Columbia D17187

TCHAIKOVSKY

Concerto in D, Op. 35 vln & orch.
Canzonetta (2nd mvt)
  with M. van Ijzer pf   Columbia D17191

I. KOGAN

KURMANGAZY

Balbraun vln & pf
  with S. Kogan pf   Mezhdunarodnaya Kniga
                               D00019063/4

Sary–arka arr. vln & pf I. Kogan
  with S. Kogan pf   Mezhdunarodnaya Kniga
                               D00019711

Leonid Borisovich KOGAN (1924–)

ACHRON

Hebrew melody, Op. 33 vln & pf – arr. Auer
  with N. Walter pf   Le Chant du Monde LDX–S8370
                               Mezhdunarodnaya Kniga
                               D013064, S0746

ALBÉNIZ

Ibéria – Book I (1906/9) pf
No. 2. El puerto arr. vln & pf Zimbalist
  with A. Mitnik pf   Bruno BR14015
                               Mezhdunarodnaya Kniga
                               D012171/2
                               Westminster XWN18229

Suite española, Op. 47 pf
No. 3. Savillanas arr. vln & pf Heifetz
  with A. Mitnik pf   Bruno BR14015
                               Mezhdunarodnaya Kniga
                               D004537, D012171/2
                               Westminster XWN18229

BACH

(6) Brandenburg concerti, BWV1046/51 (1721) strs & c
Brandenburg Concerto No. 1, in F, BWV1046 vln, 3 obs, bsn, 2 hrns & strs
  with A. Petrov ob, A. Yankelevich   Mezhdunarodnaya Kniga
  hrn, S. Yankelevich hrn & USSR State D2540/1
  Symphony Orch. – Ginsburg
Concerto No. 2, in E, BWV1042 vln, strs & c
  with Moscow Chamber Orch. –   Mezhdunarodnaya Kniga
  Barshai   D05493
                               Trianon TRX6133
Concerto No. 2, in E, BWV1042 vln, strs & c
  with Philharmonia Orch. – Ackermann Angel 35343
                               Columbia C70427, CX1373,
                               WC530
Concerto in d, BWV1043 2 vlns, strs & c
  with E. Gilels vln & Moscow Chamber Mezhdunarodnaya Kniga
  Orch. – Barshai   D05492
                               Trianon TRX6133
Concerto in d, BWV1043 2 vlns, strs & c
  with E. Gilels vln & Philharmonia   Angel 35343
  Orch. – Ackermann   Columbia C70427, CX1373,
                               WC530
(3) Sonatas & 3 Partitas, BWV1001/6 solo vln
Partita No. 1, in b, Sarabande (5th mvt) BWV1002
  (unaccompanied)   Angel 35343
                               Columbia C70427, CX1373,
                               WC530
Sonata No. 3, in C, BWV1005
  (unaccompanied)   Janus–Pirouette J19018,
                               JAS19018
(6) Sonatas, BWV1014/9 vln & clav
Sonata No. 4, in c, BWV1017
  with G. Ginsburg pf   Mezhdunarodnaya Kniga
                               D028611

BEETHOVEN

Concerto in D, Op. 61 (cadenzas by Joachim) vln & orch.
  with Moscow State Radio Symphony   Mezhdunarodnaya Kniga
  Orch. – Nebolsin   D022752/61

BEETHOVEN – *Continued*

Concerto in D, Op. 61 (cadenzas by Jaochim) vln & orch.
with USSR State Symphony Orch. –
Kondrashin
 Lion CL40001
 Mezhdunarodnaya Kniga
 D04422/3
 Telefunken LT6622

Concerto in D, Op. 61 (cadenzas by Joachim) vln & orch.
with Paris Conservatory Orch. –
Silvestri
 Classics for Pleasure CFP139
 Columbia CX1738, QCX10411,
 SAX2386, SAXQ7308,
 SMC91333
 HMV CVD850

Concerto in D, Op. 61 (cadenzas by Joachim) vln & orch.
with USSR Symphony Orch. –
Svetlanov
 Eurodisc 80079KK
 Mezhdunarodnaya Kniga
 D025831/2, S01665/6

Romance No. 1, in G, Op. 40 vln & orch.
with Moscow Chamber Orch. –
Barshai
 Eurodisc 73637KK
 Mezhdunarodnaya Kniga S01310

Romance No. 2, in F, Op. 50 vln & orch.
with Moscow State Radio Symphony
Orch. – Aranowitch
 Eurodisc 73637KK
 Mezhdunarodnaya Kniga S01310

(Die) Ruinen von Athen, Op. 113 – Incidental music orch.
No. 4. Marcia alla turca arr. vln & pf Auer
with A. Mitnik pf
 Mezhdunarodnaya Kniga
 D08311, D0008921/2, D15902

(3) Sonatas, Op. 12 vln & pf
No. 1. Sonata No. 1, in D
with G. Ginsburg pf
 Mezhdunarodnaya Kniga
 D07293
 Qualiton LP1575
 Vanguard VRS 6029

No. 3. Sonata No. 3, in E flat
with G. Ginsburg pf
 Mezhdunarodnaya Kniga
 D07294
 Vanguard VRS6029

(3) Sonatas, Op. 30 vln & pf
No. 2. Sonata No. 7, in c
with A. Mitnik pf
 Le Chant du Monde LDA8129
 Monitor MC2011

Sonata No. 9, in A, Op. 47 "Kreutzer" vln & pf
with A. Mitnik pf MGM GC30003
Trio No. 1, in E flat, Op. 3 vln, vla & vlc
with R. Barshai vla & M.
Rostropovich vlc
 MGM GC30007
 Mezhdunarodnaya Kniga
 D03458/9

(3) Trios, Op. 9 vln, vla & vlc
No. 1. Trio No. 2, in G
with R. Barshai vla & M.
Rostropovich vlc
 Artia ALP164
 Mezhdunarodnaya Kniga
 D4560/1, D027315

No. 3. Trio No. 4, in c
with R. Barshai vla & M.
Rostropovich vlc
 Artia ALP164
 Mezhdunarodnaya Kniga
 D4434/5, D027316

(2) Trios, Op. 70 pf, vln & vlc
No. 2. Trio No. 5, in E flat
with E. Gilels pf & M. Rostropovich
vlc
 Colosseum CRLP255
 Mezhdunarodnaya Kniga D1234
 Monitor MC2005

BEETHOVEN – *Continued*

Trio No. 6, in B flat, Op. 97 "Archduke" pf, vln & vlc
with E. Gilels pf & M. Rostropovich
vlc
 Mezhdunarodnaya Kniga
 D03456/7
 Monitor MC2010
 Telefunken BLE14110

Trio in E flat, G153 WoO38) pf, vln & vlc
with E. Gilels pf & M. Rostropovich
vlc
 Mezhdunarodnaya Kniga
 D028117/8

BERG

Concerto (1935) vln & orch.
with Moscow Radio Symphony Orch.
– Rozhdestvensky
 Mezhdunarodnaya Kniga
 D021401/2, S01839/40

BLOCH

Baal Shem (3 Pictures of Chassidic life) (1923) vln & pf
No. 2. Nigun (Improvisation) arr. Achron
with A. Mitnik pf
 Mezhdunarodnaya Kniga
 D08312

No. 2. Nigun (Improvisation) arr. Achron
with A. Mitnik pf
 Victor LM2250

BORODIN

Petite Suite (1878/85) pf
No. 6. Sérénade arr. vln & pf Heifetz
with A. Mitnik pf
 Mezhdunarodnaya Kniga
 D02889

BRAHMS

Concerto in D, Op. 77 (cadenza by Joachim) vln & orch.
with Paris Conservatory Orch. – Bruck Angel 35412
 Columbia CX1506, FCX404

Concerto in D, Op. 77 (cadenza by Joachim) vln & orch.
with Philharmonia Orch. – Kondrashin Angel 35690
 Columbia CX1692, QCX10385,
 SAX2307, SAXQ7276
 Electrola 1C047–50512
 HMV XLP30063, SXLP30063
 Kristall SMVP8036
 Regal SREG1095
 Seraphim S60059

Concerto in D, Op. 77 (cadenza by Joachim) vln & orch.
with Moscow Philharmonic Symphony
Orch. – Kondrashin
 Le Chant du Monde LDX78421
 Eurodisc 77837KK
 Mezhdunarodnaya Kniga
 D021409/10, S01635/6

(21) Hungarian Dances pf duet
Hungarian dance No. 1, in g arr. vln & pf Joachim
with A. Mitnik pf
 Mezhdunarodnaya Kniga
 D02889
 Westminster XWN18629

Hungarian dance No. 2, in d arr. vln & pf Auer
with A. Mitnik pf
 Mezhdunarodnaya Kniga
 D005167, D012171/2, D15059,
 D17412

Hungarian dance No. 4, in f arr. vln & pf "in b" Joachim
with A. Mitnik pf
 Mezhdunarodnaya Kniga
 D08312, D0008921/2

BRAHMS – *Continued*

Hungarian dance No. 16, in f arr. vln & pf "in g" Joachim
with A. Mitnik pf
Mezhdunarodnaya Kniga
D02889
Westminster XWN18629

Hungarian dance No. 17, in f sharp arr. vln & pf Joachim
with A. Mitnik pf
Mezhdunarodnaya Kniga
D17411

Sonata No. 1, in G, Op. 78 vln & pf
with A. Mitnik pf
Mezhdunarodnaya Kniga
D05500

Sonata No. 1, in G, Op. 78 vln & pf
with A. Mitnik pf
Angel 35332
Columbia CX1381
HMV LALP374

Sonata No. 2, in A, Op. 100 vln & pf
with A. Mitnik pf
Angel 35332
Columbia CX1381
HMV LALP374

Sonata (1853) "Frei aber Einsam" vln & pf
Allegro (Scherzo) in c (3rd mvt) "Sonatensatz"
with N. Walter pf
Hall of Fame HOF515
Mezhdunarodnaya Kniga
D014823/4, SM02227/8

Trio in E flat, Op. 40 hrn, pf & vln
with Y. Shapiro hrn & E. Gilels pf
Bruno BR14010
Colosseum CRLP258
Mezhdunarodnaya Kniga
D1746/7
Westminster XWN18181

CASTELNUOVO–TEDESCO

Figaro (Paraphrase on the aria "Largo al factotum" from the opera "Il Barbiere di Siviglia" by Rossini) vln & pf
with N. Walter pf
Le Chant du Monde LDX–S8370
Mezhdunarodnaya Kniga
D013064, D00015715/6, S0746

CHOPIN

(2) Nocturnes, Op. 27 pf
No. 2. Nocturne No. 8, in D flat arr. vln & pf Balakirev
with A. Mitnik pf
Mezhdunarodnaya Kniga
D001264, D005167, D012171/2
Telefunken TW30221

DEBUSSY

(6) Ariettes oubliées (1888/1903) v & pf
No. 2. Il pleure dans mon coeur arr. vln & pf Hartmann
with A. Mitnik pf
Mezhdunarodnaya Kniga
D02889
Telefunken UV199
Westminster XWN18629

Beau soir (1878) v & pf – arr. vln & pf Heifetz
with N. Walter pf
Le Chant du Monde LDX–S8370
Hall of Fame HOF515
Mezhdunarodnaya Kniga
D013063, S0745

Prélude à l'après–midi d'un faune (1894) orch. – arr. vln & pf Heifetz
with A. Mitnik pf
Mezhdunarodnaya Kniga
D08312, D0008921/2

DEBUSSY – *Continued*

Suite Bergamasque (1890) pf
No. 3. Clair de lune arr. vln & pf Roelens
with A. Mitnik pf
Victor LM2250

DVOŘÁK

(8) Humoresques, Op. 101 pf
No. 7. Humoresque No. 7, in G flat arr. vln & pf "in G" Heifetz
with N. Walter pf
Le Chant du Monde LDX–S8370
Mezhdunarodnaya Kniga
D013063, S0745

(8) Slavonic dances, Op. 72 pf duet; orch.
No. 2. Slavonic dance No. 10, in e arr. vln & pf Kreisler
with piano
Mezhdunarodnaya Kniga
D027563/4

No. 8. Slavonic dance No. 16, in A flat arr. vln & pf "in G" Kreisler
with A. Mitnik pf
Mezhdunarodnaya Kniga D5073

FALLA

(7) Canciones populares españolas (1914) v & pf
No. 1. El paño moruno arr. vln & pf Kochański
with N. Walter pf
Mezhdunarodnaya Kniga
D014823/4, SM02227/8

No. 3. Asturiana arr. vln & pf Kochański
with N. Walter pf
Mezhdunarodnaya Kniga
D014823/4, SM02227/8

No. 4. Jota arr. vln & pf Kochański
with N. Walter pf
Mezhdunarodnaya Kniga
D014823/4, SM02227/8

No. 5. Nana arr. vln & pf Kochański
with N. Walter pf
Mezhdunarodnaya Kniga
D014823/4, SM02227/8

No. 6. Canción arr. vln & pf Kochański
with N. Walter pf
Mezhdunarodnaya Kniga
D014823/4, SM02227/8

FAURÉ

Quartet No. 1, in c, Op. 15 pf, vln, vla & vlc
with E. Gilels pf, R. Barshai vla & M. Rostropovich vlc
Mezhdunarodnaya Kniga
D04572/3

GERSHWIN

(3) Jazz Preludes (1936) pf
No. 1 Prelude No. 1, in B flat arr. vln & pf Heifetz
with N. Walter pf
Le Chant du Monde LDX–S8370
Mezhdunarodnaya Kniga
D013063, D00015715/6, S0745

Porgy & Bess (1935) – opera
Tempo di blues arr. vln & pf Heifetz
with N. Walter pf
Le Chant du Monde LDX–S8370
Mezhdunarodnaya Kniga
D013063, D00015715/6, S0745

GLAZOUNOV

Méditation, Op. 32 vln & pf
witn A. Mitnik pf
Mezhdunarodnaya Kniga
D02888

Raymonda, Op. 57 (1897) – ballet orch.
Entr'acte No. 1 arr. vln & pf Pogozhev
with A. Mitnik pf
Mezhdunarodnaya Kniga
D022761

GLAZOUNOV – *Continued*

Entr'acte No. 1 arr. vln & pf Pogozhev
with A. Mitnik pf   Victor LM2250

Grand Adagio arr. vln & pf Zimbalist
with A. Mitnik pf   Mezhdunarodnaya Kniga
           D00127, D7864, D004612/3,
           D0008375/6
           Westminster XWN18229

Valse arr. vln & pf Pogozhev
with A. Mitnik pf   Mezhdunarodnaya Kniga
           D00127, D004612/3, D7864,
           D0008375/6
           Westminster XWN18229

GODOWSKY

Triakontameron (30 moods & scenes in triple measure) (1920) pf
 No. 11. Alt Wien arr. vln & pf Heifetz
 with N. Walter pf   Le Chant du Monde LDX–S8370
           Mezhdunarodnaya Kniga
           D013063, D00015715/6, S0745

GOLDENWEISER

Trio in e, Op. 31 pf, vln & vlc
 with A. Goldenweiser pf & M.   Mezhdunarodnaya Kniga
 Rostropovich vlc   D9123/4

GRANIANI

Duet in A vln & gtr
 with A. Ivanov–Kramskoi gtr Mezhdunarodnaya Kniga
           D005078/9, D027559/60

GRIEG

Sonata No. 1, in F, Op. 8 vln & pf
 with G. Ginsburg pf   Mezhdunarodnaya Kniga
           D028513

Sonata No. 3, in c, Op. 45 vln & pf
 with G. Ginsburg pf   Mezhdunarodnaya Kniga
           D028514

HANDEL

Cantata unid
 Dank sei Dir, Herr "Arioso" arr. vln & pf
 with A. Mitnik pf   Mezhdunarodnaya Kniga
           D15901

(15) Sonatas, Op. 1 (?1731) fl or vln & c
 Sonata No. 15, in E vln VI
 with N. Walter pf   Mezhdunarodnaya Kniga
           D014823/4, SM02227/8

(16) Suites (1720/33) hpsi
 Suite No. 7, in g: Passacaglia (6th mvt) arr. vln & vla Halvorsen
 with M. Rostropovich vlc Mezhdunarodnaya Kniga
           D007353, D027559/60

HAYDN

Sonata No. 4, in A, H.XVI, No. 26 vln & pf*
 with G. Ginsburg pf   Mezhdunarodnaya Kniga
           D028611/2

* Arrangement of piano sonata – ed. David.

HAYDN – *Continued*

(31) Trios, H.XV, Nos. 1/31 pf, vln & vlc
 Trio No. 16, in D, H.XV, No. 16 (Op. 63)
 with E. Gilels pf & M. Rostropovich Mezhdunarodnaya Kniga
 vlc   D19102/7, D028563
           Saga XID5311
           Westminster XWN18181

 Trio No. 19, in g, H.XV, No. 19 (Op. 70, No. 2)
 with E. Gilels pf & M. Rostropovich Colosseum CRLP248
 vlc   Mezhdunarodnaya Kniga D1233,
           D028117/8
           Saga XID5311

KHACHATURIAN

Chanson poème in e (1929) vln & pf
 with N. Walter pf   Le Chant du Monde LDX–S8370
           Mezhdunarodnaya Kniga
           D013064, S0746

Concerto in D (1940) (cadenza by Khachaturian) vln & orch.
 with Moscow Radio Symphony Orch. Le Chant du Monde LDA8051
 – Khachaturian   Concert Hall CHS1300
           Mezhdunarodnaya Kniga
           D0548/9
           Whitehall 5024

Concerto in D (1940) (cadenza by Khachaturian) vln & orch.
 with Boston Symphony Orch. – Vega MT10226
 Monteux   Victor LM2220, VIC1153,
           VICS1153

Concerto–Rhapsody vln & orch.
 with Moscow Philharmonic Symphony Mezhdunarodnaya Kniga
 Orch. – Kondrashin   D026587/8

Gayaneh (Suite No. 1) (1942) – ballet orch.
 No. 1. Sabre dance arr. vln & pf Heifetz
 with A. Mitnik pf   Colosseum CRLP179
           Mezhdunarodnaya Kniga
           D00128, D08311, D0008375/6,
           D18567

 No 2. Dance of Ayshe arr. vln & pf Heifetz
 with A. Mitnik pf   Mezhdunarodnaya Kniga
           D08311, D0008375/6, D18568

 No. 2. Dance of Ayshe arr. vln & pf Heifetz
 with A. Mitnik pf   Victor LM2250

Gayaneh (Suite No. 2) (1942) – ballet orch.
 No. 11. Gayaneh's Adagio arr. vln & pf
 with A. Mitnik pf   Colosseum CRLP179
           Mezhdunarodnaya Kniga
           D00128

Masquerade (1939) – Incidental music (Suite) orch.
 Mazurka arr. vln & pf
 with A. Mitnik pf   Mezhdunarodnaya Kniga
           D022638/9, D22644/5

 Nocturne arr. vln & pf
 with A. Mitnik pf   Le Chant du Monde LDY8126
           Mezhdunarodnaya Kniga
           D01475

KHANDOSHKIN

Variations on Russian themes vln & vlc
 with M. Rostropovich vlc Mezhdunarodnaya Kniga
           D007354, D027559/60
           Monitor MC2019

KHRENNIKOV

Concerto in C, Op. 14 vln & orch.
with USSR Radio Symphony Orch. –
Kondrashin

Le Chant du Monde LDX–
A8339
Mezhdunarodnaya Kniga
D06095, D07426
MK MK1574

Concerto in C, Op. 14 vln & orch.
with Leningrad Philharmonic Orch. –
Sanderling

Baroque BC1866, BC2866

KREIN

Dance No. 4 vln & pf
with N. Walter pf

Le Chant du Monde LDX–S8370
Mezhdunarodnaya Kniga
D013063, S0745

KREISLER

Caprice viennois, Op. 2 vln & pf
with A. Mitnik pf

Mezhdunarodnaya Kniga
D02888

Caprice viennois, Op. 2 vln & pf
with A. Mitnik pf

Victor LM2250

Cavatina vln & pf
with A. Mitnik pf

Mezhdunarodnaya Kniga
D08311

(La) Gitana vln & pf
with A. Mitnik pf

Mezhdunarodnaya Kniga
D02888
Telefunken UV199
Westminster XWN18629

LALO

Symphonie espagnole, Op. 21 vln & orch.*
with Paris Conservatory Orch. – Bruck

Angel 35503
Columbia C1059, C70384,
FCX403, WC1059
HMV LALP480

Symphonie espagnole, Op. 21 vln & orch.*
with Philharmonia Orch. – Kondrashin

Angel 35721
Columbia C70432, CX1683,
SAX2329, SBOW8502,
STC70432
World Record Club ST562, T562

LECLAIR

(6) Sonatas, Op. 3 2 solo vlns
Sonata No. 1, in G
with E. Gilels vln

Columbia CX1887, FCX984,
SAX2531, SAXF984
Mezhdunarodnaya Kniga
D012691/2, S0719/20

Sonata No. 3, in C
with E. Gilels vln

Columbia CX1887, FCX984,
SAX2531, SAXF984
Mezhdunarodnaya Kniga
D012691/2, S0719/20

* Including Intermezzo.

LISZT

Soirées italiennes (6 amusements sur des motifs de Mercadante) G411
(1838) pf
No. 1. La primavera arr. vln & pf as "Canzonetta"
with A. Mitnik pf

Mezhdunarodnaya Kniga
D18626

LOCATELLI

(12) Sonatas, Op. 6 (1737) vln & c
Sonata No. 7, in f "Au Tombeau" arr. vln & pf Ysaÿe
with A. Mitnik pf

Angel 35444
Columbia CX1546, FC1052
HMV 7ERL1398, LALP30010

MENDELSSOHN

Concerto in e, Op. 64 vln & orch.
with Paris Conservatory Orch. –
Silvestri

Columbia CX1744, SAX2304

(6) Songs without words, Op. 62 pf
No. 1. Song without words No. 25, in G "May breezes" arr. vln & pf
Kreisler
with A. Mitnik pf

Victor LM2250

MILHAUD

(12) Saudades do Brasil (1920/1) pf
No. 7. Corcovado arr. vln & pf Lévy
with A. Mitnik pf

Mezhdunarodnaya Kniga
D02888
Westminster XWN18629

No. 9. Sumare arr. vln & pf Lévy
with A. Mitnik pf

Mezhdunarodnaya Kniga
D02888
Telefunken UV199
Westminster XWN18629

MOZART

Concerto No. 3, in G, K216 (cadenzas by D. Oistrakh) vln & orch.
with Philharmonia Orch. – Ackermann Angel 35344
Columbia C70378, CX1395,
WC523
Trianon TRX6132

Concerto No. 3, in G, K216 (cadenzas by Franko) vln & orch.
with Paris Conservatory Orch. –
Silvestri

Columbia C70460, CX1744,
SAX2304, SBOW8503,
STC70460

Concerto No. 3, in G, K216 (cadenzas by Franko) vln & orch.
with Leningrad Philharmonic Orch. –
Sanderling

Baroque BC1866, BC2866

Concerto No. 5, in A, K219 "Turkish" (cadenzas by Joachim) vln & orch.
with Moscow Chamber Orch. –
Barshai

Eurodisc 73637KK
Mezhdunarodnaya Kniga
D06527/8, D07425, S0319/20
MK MK1574

Concerto No. 5, in A, K219 "Turkish" (cadenzas by Joachim) vln & orch.
with l'Orch. de la Société des Concerts Trianon TRX6132
Colonne – Vandernoot

Concerto No. 5, in A, K219 "Turkish" (cadenzas by Joachim) vln & orch.
with Moscow Radio Symphony Orch. Mezhdunarodnaya Kniga
– Rozhdestvensky D021401/2, S01839/40

Sonata No. 24, in F, K376 vln & pf.
with G. Ginsburg pf

Monitor MC2011

MOZART – *Continued*

Trio No. 6, in G, K564 pf, vln & vlc
   with E. Gilels pf & M. Rostropovich
   vlc

Kingsway KL261
Mezhdunarodnaya Kniga
D028564
Que LP2006
Record Hunter TRH1

NARDINI

(6) Sonatas, Op. 2 (1765) vln & c
Sonata in E flat: Adagio (2nd mvt)
   with A. Mitnik pf

Victor LM2250

PAGANINI

Cantabile in D, Op. 17 vln & gtr
   with A. Mitnik pf

Angel 35502
Columbia CX1562, FCX402,
QCX10300

(24) Caprices, Op. 1 (1801/7) solo vln
Caprice No. 9, in E
(unaccompanied)

Mezhdunarodnaya Kniga
D005166, D012171/2
Westminster XWN18629

Caprice No. 23, in E flat
(unaccompanied)

Mezhdunarodnaya Kniga
D005166, D012171/2
Westminster XWN18629

Concerto No. 1, in D, Op. 6 (cadenza by Sauret) vln & orch
   with Moscow State Radio Orch. –
   Nebolsin

Mezhdunarodnaya Kniga
D06391/2, D20199/206
Musidisc RC857
Telefunken BLE14117

Concerto No. 1, in D, Op. 6 (cadenza by Sauret) vln & orch.
   with Paris Conservatory Orch. – Bruck

Angel 35502
Bruno BR14022*
Columbia CX1562, FCX402,
QCX10300

Nel cor più non mi sento "Sonata appassionata con variazioni" (on the aria from Paisiello's opera "La bella molinara") Op. 38 (1820 or 1821) solo vln
(unaccompanied)

Bruno BR14022
Mezhdunarodnaya Kniga D5073,
D028067/8
Westminster XWN18229

(I) Palpiti (variations on the aria "Di tanti palpiti" from Rossini's opera "Tancredi") Op. 13 (1819) vln & orch.
   with A. Mitnik pf

Bruno BR14022
Westminster XWN18229

(6) Sonatas, Op. 2 (1801/6) vln & gtr
No. 1. Sonata No. 1, in A
   with A. Ivanov–Kramskoi gtr

Mezhdunarodnaya Kniga
D027559/60

* Label states USSR orch. conducted by Nebolsin, but recording checked is that of the Paris Conservatory Orch. conducted by Charles Bruck.

PONCE

Estrellita (1913) v & pf – arr. vln & pf Heifetz
   with A. Mitnik pf

Mezhdunarodnaya Kniga
D02888, D5146/7
Telefunken UV199
Westminster XWN18629

POULENC

(3) Pieces (1934/5) pf
No. 1. Presto in B flat arr. vln & pf Heifetz
   with N. Walter pf

Le Chant du Monde LDX–S8370
Mezhdunarodnaya Kniga
D013063, S0745

PROKOFIEV

Concerto No. 2, in g, Op. 63 vln & orch.
   with USSR State Symphony Orch. –
   Kondrashin

Bruno BR14002
Le Chant du Monde LDM8202
Decca LXT2009
Mezhdunarodnaya Kniga
D3190/1
Monitor MC2002

Concerto No. 2, in g, Op. 63 vln & orch.
   with London Symphony Orch. –
   Cameron

Angel 35344
Columbia C70378, CX1395
HMV LALP428

(10) Pieces, Op. 12 (1908/13) pf
No. 1. March in f arr. vln & pf Heifetz
   with N. Walter pf

Le Chant du Monde LDX–S8370
Mezhdunarodnaya Kniga
D013063/4, S0745/6

(10) Pieces (from the ballet "Romeo & Juliet") Op. 75 (1937) pf
No. 5. Masques arr. vln & pf Heifetz
   with A. Mitnik pf

Mezhdunarodnaya Kniga
D02888
Westminster XWN18629

No. 5. Masques arr. vln & pf Heifetz
   with A. Mitnik pf

Victor LM2250

Romeo & Juliet, Op. 64b (1935/6) – 2nd ballet suite orch.
No. 1. Montagues & Capulets arr. vln & pf Grunes
   with A. Mitnik pf

Mezhdunarodnaya Kniga
D005157, D08312

Sonata No. 2, in D, Op. 94bis vln & pf
   with N. Walter pf

Mezhdunarodnaya Kniga
D014823/4, SM02227/8

Sonata No. 2, in D, Op. 94bis vln & pf
   with E. König pf

Janus–Pirouette J19018,
JAS19018

RAMEAU

(6) Concerts en Sextuor 3 vlns, vla & 2 vlcs
Concert No. 6, in g arr. vln & strs
   with Moscow Chamber Orch. –
   Barshai

Mezhdunarodnaya Kniga D3578
Monitor MC2018

RAVEL

Pièce en forme d'Habanera v & pf – arr. vln & pf Catherine
   with A. Mitnik pf

Mezhdunarodnaya Kniga
D5146/7, D02889
Westminster XWN18629

RAVEL – *Continued*

Tzigane (Rapsodie de concert) (1924) vln & pf or orch.
with Bolshoi Theatre Orch. –   Hall of Fame HOF515
Kondrashin   Mezhdunarodnaya Kniga
    D06528

RIMSKY–KORSAKOV

Scheherazade, Op. 35 (1888) orch.
with USSR State Symphony orch. –   Mezhdunarodnaya Kniga
Svetlanov   S01767/8

SAINT–SAËNS

(Le) Carnaval des animaux (1886) small orch.
    Le cygne arr. vln & pf Heifetz
    with N. Walter pf   Mezhdunarodnaya Kniga
    D013063, S0745

Havanaise, Op. 83 vln & orch.
with USSR State Symphony Orch. –   Eurodisc 78425ZK
Kondrashin   Hall of Fame HOF515
    Mezhdunarodnaya Kniga
    D03098, D011074
    Telefunken TW30221

Havanaise, Op. 83 vln & orch.
with Boston Symphony Orch. –   Vega MT10226
Monteux   Victor LM2220, VIC1153,
    VICS1153

Introduction & Rondo Capriccioso, Op. 28 vln & orch.
with Moscow Radio Symphony Orch.   Eurodisc 78425ZK
– Gauk   Mezhdunarodnaya Kniga D149,
    D004629, D010627
    Monitor MC2076, MCS2076
    Westminster XWN18228

SARASATE

Caprice basque, Op. 24 vln & pf
with A. Mitnik pf   Bruno BR14015
    Mezhdunarodnaya Kniga D2294,
    D004613, D22868/9, D028067/8
    Westminster XWN18229

Caprice basque, Op. 24 vln & pf
with A. Mitnik pf   Victor LM2250

Carmen Fantasia (on themes from the opera by Bizet) Op. 25 vln & pf or orch.
with Moscow State Radio Orch. –   Bruno BR14015
Nebolsin   Le Chant du Monde LD8010
    Mezhdunarodnaya Kniga
    D839/40, D03099, D17980/3
    Monitor MC2076, MCS2076
    Westminster XWN18228

(8) Danzas españolas vln & pf
    No. 1. Malagueña, Op. 21, No. 1
    with A. Mitnik pf   Mezhdunarodnaya Kniga D2294,
    D028067/8

    No. 3. Romanza andaluza, Op. 22, No. 1
    with A. Mitnik pf   Mezhdunarodnaya Kniga
    D02889, D5146/7
    Westminster XWN18629

SARASATE – *Continued*

    No. 6. Zapateado, Op. 23, No. 2
    with N. Walter pf   Le Chant du Monde LDX–S8370
    Hall of Fame HOF515
    Mezhdunarodnaya Kniga
    D013064, D00015715/6, S0746

SCHUBERT

(4) Impromptus, Op. 90 (D899) pf
    No. 3. Impromptu No. 3, in G arr. vln & pf Heifetz
    with A. Mitnik pf   Mezhdunarodnaya Kniga
    D08312

SCHUMANN

Fantasia in C, Op. 131 vln & orch. – arr. vln & pf Kreisler
with A. Mitnik pf   MGM GC30003
    Mezhdunarodnaya Kniga D2293,
    D027563/4

Trio No. 1, in d, Op. 63 pf, vln & vlc
with E. Gilels pf & M. Rostropovich   Mezhdunarodnaya Kniga
vlc   D4564/5, D028117/8

SHOSTAKOVICH

Concerto No. 1, in a, Op. 99 (1955) vln & orch.
with Moscow Philharmonic Orch. –   Hall of Fame HOF512
Kondrashin   Mezhdunarodnaya Kniga
    D8451/2, S201/2
    Supraphon SV8224

(24) Preludes, Op. 34 (1932/3) pf
    Prelude No. 10, in c sharp arr. vln & pf Tziganov
    with D. Shostakovich pf   Mezhdunarodnaya Kniga D3037,
    D005157

    Prelude No. 10, in c sharp arr. vln & pf Tziganov
    with A. Mitnik pf   Victor LM2250

    Prelude No. 15, in D flat arr. vln & pf Tziganov
    with D. Shostakovich pf   Mezhdunarodnaya Kniga D3037,
    D005157

    Prelude No. 15, in D flat arr. vln & pf Tziganov
    with A. Mitnik pf   Victor LM2250

    Prelude No. 16, in b flat arr. vln & pf Tziganov
    with D. Shostakovich pf   Mezhdunarodnaya Kniga D3037,
    D005157

    Prelude No. 16, in b flat arr. vln & pf Tziganov
    with A. Mitnik pf   Victor LM2250

    Prelude No. 24, in d arr. vln & pf Tziganov
    with D. Shostakovich pf   Mezhdunarodnaya Kniga D3037,
    D005157

    Prelude No. 24, in d arr. vln & pf Tziganov
    with A. Mitnik pf   Victor LM2250

STRAUSS, R.

Sonata in E flat, Op. 18 vln & pf
with A. Mitnik pf   Mezhdunarodnaya Kniga
    D05501

SZYMANOWSKI

Notturno & Tarantella, Op. 28 vln & pf
with A. Mitnik pf   Mezhdunarodnaya Kniga
    D5146/7, D012171/2

TANEIEV

Concert Suite, Op. 28 vln & orch.
  Gavotte (2nd mvt)
  with orch.   Mezhdunarodnaya Kniga
                         D21420/1

TCHAIKOVSKY

Concerto in D, Op. 35 vln & orch.
  with USSR Radio Symphony Orch. –   Kingsway KL241
  Nebolsin   Mezhdunarodnaya Kniga
                         D01237/8, D022752/60
                         Que LP2005
                         Saga XID5022

Concerto in D, Op. 35 vln & orch.
  with Paris Conservatory Orch. –   Angel 35444
  Vandernoot   Columbia C70377, CX1546,
                         WC522
                         HMV LALP30010, LBLP1035

Concerto in D, Op. 35 vln & orch.
  with Paris Conservatory Orch. –   Columbia CX1711, QCX10413,
  Silvestri   SAX2323, SAXQ7310
                         Seraphim S60075

Sérénade mélancolique in b flat, Op. 26 vln & orch.
  with USSR State Symphony Orch. –   Eurodisc 78425ZK
  Kondrashin   Hall of Fame HOF515
                         Mezhdunarodnaya Kniga
                         D004628, D010627
                         Telefunken TW30221

Sérénade mélancolique in b flat, Op. 26 vln & orch. – arr. vln & pf
  Wilhelmj
  with A. Mitnik pf   Eterna LPM1011

Sérénade mélancolique in b flat, Op. 26 vln & orch.
  with Philharmonia Orch. – Kondrashin   Columbia CX1683, SAX2329
                         World Record Club ST562, T562

Sextet, Op. 70 "Souvenir de Florence" 2 vlns, 2 vlas & 2 vlcs
  with E. Gilels vln, G. Talalyan vla, R.   Le Chant du Monde LDX–
  Barshai vla, S. Knushevitsky vlc & M.   A8358
  Rostropovich vlc   Mezhdunarodnaya Kniga
                         D03310/1, D9645/6
                         Monitor MC2019

Souvenir d'un lieu cher, Op. 42 vln & pf
  No. 1. Méditation
  with A. Mitnik pf   Mezhdunarodnaya Kniga D7864,
                         D027563/4

  No. 1. Méditation
  with Paris Conservatory Orch. –   Columbia CX1711, QCX10413,
  Silvestri   SAX2323, SAXQ7310
                         Seraphim S60075

Swan Lake, Op. 20 (1875/6) – ballet orch.
  Russian dance arr. vln & pf
  with orch.   8569/2   Mezhdunarodnaya Kniga
                         D08569

Trio in a, Op. 50 "to the memory of a great artist" pf, vln & vlc
  with E. Gilels pf & M. Rostropovich   A 440 AC1202
  vlc   Le Chant du Monde LDX–
                         A8040
                         Heritage 1203
                         Mezhdunarodnaya Kniga
                         D0289/90
                         Monarch MWL332

TCHAIKOVSKY – *Continued*

Waltz–scherzo, Op. 34 vln & pf
  with USSR Radio Symphony Orch. –   Eurodisc 78425ZK
  Gauk   Kingsway KL241
                         Mezhdunarodnaya Kniga
                         D010627
                         Que LP2005
                         Saga XID5022

TELEMANN

(6) Sonatas, Op. 2 (1727) "Duets" 2 fls or vlns
  Sonata No. 1, in G "Canonic"
  with E. Gilels vln   Columbia CX1887, FCX984,
                         SAX2531, SAXF984
                         Mezhdunarodnaya Kniga
                         D012691/2, S0719/20

VAINBERG

Concerto in g, Op. 67 vln & orch.
  with Moscow Philharmonic Orch. –   Mezhdunarodnaya Kniga
  Kondrashin   D8529/30, S203/4

VIEUXTEMPS

Concerto No. 5, in a, Op. 37 vln & orch.
  with Moscow State Symphony Orch. –   Mezhdunarodnaya Kniga
  Kondrashin   D01445
                         Monitor MC2076, MCS2076
                         Westminster XWN18228

(3) Salonstücke, Op. 32 vln & pf
  No. 2. Rondino
  with V. Yampolsky pf   Mezhdunarodnaya Kniga D7863,
                         D028067/8

  No. 2. Rondino
  with A. Mitnik pf   Victor LM2250

VIVALDI

(6) Concerti, Op. 12 vln, strs & c
  Concerto No. 1, in g, P.343 (F.I, No. 211)
  with Moscow Chamber Orch. –   Bruno BR14019
  Barshai   Mezhdunarodnaya Kniga
                         D03450
                         Monitor MC2018

  Concerto No. 1, in g, P.343 (F.I, No. 211)
  with Paris Conservatory Orch. –   Angel 35444
  Vandernoot   Columbia CX1546, FC1052
                         HMV LALP30010

WAXMAN

Carmen Fantasia (on themes from the opera by Bizet) vln & orch.
  with USSR State Symphony Orch. –   Eurodisc 78425ZK
  Kondrashin   Mezhdunarodnaya Kniga
                         D03098, D011074
                         Telefunken TW30221

WEBER

(6) Sonatas, Op. 10 (J99/104) (1810) vln & pf
  Sonata No. 1, in F, J99
  with G. Ginsburg pf   Mezhdunarodnaya Kniga
                         D028611/2

  Sonata No. 2, in G, J100
  with G. Ginsburg pf   Mezhdunarodnaya Kniga
                         D028611/2

WEBER – *Continued*

Sonata No. 5, in A, J103
with G. Ginsburg pf
Mezhdunarodnaya Kniga
D028611/2

WIENIAWSKI

Adagio élégiaque in A, Op. 5 vln & pf
with A. Mitnik pf
Mezhdunarodnaya Kniga
D001263, D5146/7, D012171/2

Fantaisie brillante (on themes from the opera "Faust" by Gounod) Op. 20 vln & orch.
with USSR State Symphony Orch. –
Degtarenko
Mezhdunarodnaya Kniga
D001445

Légende, Op. 17 vln & pf or orch.
with Moscow Radio Symphony Orch.
– Gauk
Eterna 520065, LPM1011
Eurodisc 78425ZK
Mezhdunarodnaya Kniga
D011074

(2) Mazurkas, Op. 19 vln & pf
No. 1. Mazurka No. 1, in G "Obertass"
with A. Mitnik pf
Eterna LPM1011

No. 1. Mazurka No. 1, in G "Obertass"
with A. Mitnik pf
Mezhdunarodnaya Kniga
D08311, D18627

No. 2. Mazurka No. 2, in D "Dudziarz"
with A. Mitnik pf
Mezhdunarodnaya Kniga
D08311

Polonaise brillante No. 2, in A, Op. 21 vln & pf
with A. Kaplan pf
Mezhdunarodnaya Kniga
D004536, D012171/2
Westminster XWN18229

Variations in A (on an original theme) Op. 15 vln & pf
with A. Kaplan pf
Mezhdunarodnaya Kniga D5072,
D20017/20, D027563/4

YSAŸE

(3) Mazurkas, Op. 11 vln & pf
Mazurka No. 2, in a
with A. Mitnik pf
Festival FLD84
Mezhdunarodnaya Kniga D5072,
D028117/8

Scène au rouet (Poème No. 2) Op. 13 vln & pf or orch.
with A. Mitnik pf
Mezhdunarodnaya Kniga D7863,
D028117/8

Sonata No. 1, in C 2 vlns
with E. Gilels vln
Columbia CX1887, FCX984,
SAX2531, SAXF984
Mezhdunarodnaya Kniga
D012691/2, S0719/20

Harold KOHON

BERNIER

Agréable Caffé "Coffee cantata" (1703) v, vln & c
with J. Wheeler s & D. Walters hpsi   Vox PL14000, STPL514000

LECLAIR

(12) Sonatas, Op. 4 (1732) 2 vlns & c
Sonata No. 4, in A
with R. Weinstock vln & D. Walters
hpsi
Vox PL14000, STPL514000

PAGANINI

(6) Sonatas, Op. 2 (1801/6) vln & gtr
No. 1. Sonata No. 1, in A
with R. Shaughnessy gtr   Orion ORS6907

No. 2. Sonata No. 2, in C
with R. Shaughnessy gtr   Orion ORS6907

No. 3. Sonata No. 3, in d
with R. Shaughnessy gtr   Orion ORS6907

No. 4. Sonata No. 4, in A
with R. Shaughnessy gtr   Orion ORS6907

No. 5. Sonata No. 5, in D
with R. Shaughnessy gtr   Orion ORS6907

No. 6. Sonata No. 6, in a
with R. Shaughnessy gtr   Orion ORS6907

(6) Sonatas, Op. 3 (1801/6) vln & gtr
No. 1. Sonata No. 7, in A
with R. Shaughnessy gtr   Orion ORS6907

No. 2. Sonata No. 8, in G
with R. Shaughnessy gtr   Orion ORS6907

No. 3. Sonata No. 9, in D
with R. Shaughnessy gtr   Orion ORS6907

No. 4. Sonata No. 10, in a
with R. Shaughnessy gtr   Orion ORS6907

No. 5. Sonata No. 11, in A
with R. Shaughnessy gtr   Orion ORS6907

No. 6. Sonata No. 12, in e
with R. Shaughnessy gtr   Orion ORS6907

SCARLATTI, A.

Sonata in F rec, ob, vln or 2 vlns & c
with R. Schulze rec, T. Schulze ob &
D. Walters hpsi
Vox PL16260, STPL516260

TELEMANN

Concerto in a rec, ob, vln, hpsi & strs
with R. Schulze rec, T. Schulze ob, A.
Makas hpsi & Telemann Society Orch.
– Schulze
Counterpoint CPTS5622,
CPT622

VIVALDI

(6) Sonatas, Op. 13 (1737) "Il Pastor Fido" fl, ob, vln, strs & c
Sonata No. 4, in A, F.XVI, No. 8
with R.F. Capon rec, R. Shaughnessy
gamba & C.H. Smith hpsi
Turnabout TV34228

Sonata No. 6, in g, F.XVI, No. 10
with R.F. Capon rec, R. Shaughnessy
Gamba & C.H. Smith hpsi
Turnabout TV34228

Zdeněk KOLÁŘSKÝ (1898–   )

von HOOP

Etude in e vln & pf
with V. Polivka pf
Ultraphon F12512

MOZART
Sonata No. 26, in B flat, K378 vln & pf
 Andantino Sostenuto e cantabile (2nd mvt)
  with V. Polivka pf   Ultraphon F12512

Byron KOLASSIS (1922–   )

KALOMIRIS
Oblivion v, 2 vlns, vla, vlc & pf
  with N. Frangia m–s, & E. Nicolaidou   Philips N00247L
  pf (as member of string quartet)

KONSTANTINIDIS
Suite (on Greek themes of the Dodecanese) vln & pf
  with A. Kounadis pf   Philips N00743R

SKAKOTTAS
(4) Greek dances vln & pf
  with Y. Papadopoulos pf   Philips N00247L

VARVOGLIS
Pastoral Suite 2 vlns, vla & vlc
  (as member of string quartet)   Philips N00247L

Hugo KOLBERG (1898–   )

BACH
(6) Brandenburg Concerti, BWV1046/51 (1721) strs & c
Brandenburg Concerto No. 1, in F, BWV1046 vln, 3 obs, bsn, 2 hrns & strs
  with W. Wilbur hrn, R. Bloom ob &   Columbia ML4281, RL3104
  Instrumental Ensemble – Reiner   Harmony HL7062
Brandenburg Concerto No. 4, in G, BWV1049 vln, 2 fls & strs
  with J. Baker fl, R. Eichar fl &   Columbia ML4282, RL3105
  Instrumental Ensemble – Reiner   Harmony HL7063
Brandenburg Concerto No. 5, in D, BWV1050 clav, fl, vln & strs
  with S. Marlowe hpsi, J. Baker fl &   Columbia ML4283, RL3106
  Instrumental Ensemble – Reiner   Harmony HL7064

BEETHOVEN
Sonata No. 5, in F, Op. 24 "Spring" vln & pf
  with F. Rupp pf   Odeon 0–7771/3

CROTHER
Gweedore Brae vln & pf
  with F. Schröder pf   Mace MXX9089
                Odeon 0–80610, OLAX1027

HUBAY
(14) Scènes de la Csárda vln & pf
 No. 5. Hullámzó balaton, Op. 33
  with P. Vladigerov pf   Polydor 24307

KROLL
Banjo & fiddle vln & pf
  with F. Schröder pf   Mace MXX9089
                Odeon 0–80610, OLAX1027

MASSENET
Thaïs (1894) – opera
 Méditation arr. vln & pf Marsick
  with piano   Polydor 27266

MOZART.
Divertimento No. 17, in D, K334 2 hrns & strs
 Minuet (3rd mvt) arr. vln & pf Burmester
  with P. Vladigerov pf   Polydor 24307

NACHÈZ
(4) Danses Tziganes, Op. 14 vln & pf
 No. 1. Danse Tzigane No. 1, in a
  with piano   Polydor 24634

PISTON
Concerto (1939) vln & orch.
  with Berlin Symphony Orch. –   Mace MXX9089
  Matzerath   Odeon 0–80610, OLAX1027

SHOSTAKOVICH
Satirical dance vln & pf
  with F. Schröder pf   Mace MXX9089
                Odeon 0–80610, OLAX1027

SUK
(4) Pieces, Op. 17 vln & pf
 No. 4. Burleska
  with F. Schröder pf   Mace MXX9089
                Odeon 0–80610, OLAX1027

VIVALDI
Sonata in D, F.XII, No. 6 vln & c – arr. vln & pf Respighi
  with F. Schröder pf   Mace MXX9089
                Odeon 0–80610, OLAX1027

WAGNER
Albumblatt in C (1861) pf – arr. vln & pf Wilhelmj
  with piano   Polydor 24634

WIENIAWSKI
Scherzo–Tarantelle, Op. 16 vln & pf
  with piano   Polydor 27266

Adolf KOLDOFSKY (1905–1951)

SCHOENBERG
Fantasia, Op. 49a (1949) vln & pf
  with E. Steuermann pf   Dial LP14

Václav KOLOUCH

JANÁČEK
Concertino (1925) pf, 2 vlns, vla, cl, hrn & bsn
  with J. Baxa vln, J. Palenicek pf, J.   Crossroads 22 16 0073, 22 16
  Motlik vla, Z.K. Dlouhy cl, V. Kubat   0074
  hrn & K. Vacek bsn   Supraphon SUA10416,
                SUAST50416, SV8093

VIOTTI

Duet No. 2 unid – 2 vlns
  with R. Novosad vln   Supraphon SUA10741

Mark KOMISSAROV (1928–   )

ALBÉNIZ

Love song unid – arr. vln & pf
  with piano   Mezhdunarodnaya Kniga

AULIN

(4) Aquarelles vln & pf
  No. 2. Humoresque
  with T. Fidler pf   Mezhdunarodnaya Kniga D3279

BACEWICZ

Sonata No. 4 vln & pf
  with T. Fidler pf   Mezhdunarodnaya Kniga
                                 D025593/4

BARTÓK

Sonatina in D (on 3 Transylvanian peasant themes) (1915) pf – transc. vln & pf Gertler, 1931
  with T. Fidler pf   Mezhdunarodnaya Kniga
                                 D016417

BRAHMS

(21) Hungarian Dances pf duet
  Hungarian dance No. 1, in g arr. vln & pf Joachim
  with T. Fidler pf   Mezhdunarodnaya Kniga
                                 D17949/50

COTTENET

Chanson méditation vln & pf
  with T. Fidler pf   Mezhdunarodnaya Kniga D3279

DEBUSSY

(La) Plus que lente – valse (1910) pf – arr. vln & pf Roques
  with T. Fidler pf   Mezhdunarodnaya Kniga
                                 D17949/50

ELGAR

(La) Capricieuse, Op. 17 vln & pf
  with T. Fidler pf   Mezhdunarodnaya Kniga D3279

HINDEMITH

(6) Sonatas, Op. 11 var cbns
  Sonata No. 2, in D (1920) vln & pf
  with T. Fidler pf   Mezhdunarodnaya Kniga
                                 D016417

MENDELSSOHN

(6) Gesänge, Op. 34 v & pf
  No. 2. Auf Flügeln des Gesanges arr. vln & pf Achron
  with T. Fidler pf   Mezhdunarodnaya Kniga
                                 D17949/50

MOZART

Sonata No. 34, in A, K526 vln & pf
  with T. Fidler pf   Mezhdunarodnaya Kniga
                                 D025593/4

PROKOFIEV

(The) Love for Three Oranges, Op. 33 (1919) – opera
  No. 3. March arr. vln & pf Heifetz
  with T. Fidler pf   Muza XL0045
(5) Melodies, Op. 35bis (1921) vln & pf
  with T. Fidler pf   Mezhdunarodnaya Kniga D3278
                                 Muza L0223

SAINT-SAËNS

(6) Études, Op. 52 pf
  No. 6. Étude No. 6, in D flat "Étude en forme de valse" arr. vln & pf Ysaÿe
  with piano   Mezhdunarodnaya Kniga
Sonata No. 1, in d, Op. 75 vln & pf
  with T. Fidler pf   Mezhdunarodnaya Kniga
                                 D016418

SARASATE

Adios montañas mias, Op. 37 vln & pf
  with piano   Mezhdunarodnaya Kniga

SCHUBERT

(12) Walzer, D145 (1815/21) pf
  No. 3. Waltz No. 3, in a arr. vln & pf Sher
  with T. Fidler pf   Mezhdunarodnaya Kniga
                                 D17949/50

SCHUMANN

Sonata No. 1, in a, Op. 105 vln & pf
  with T. Fidler pf   Mezhdunarodnaya Kniga
                                 D027157/8

Sonata No. 2, in d, Op. 121 vln & pf
  with T. Fidler pf   Mezhdunarodnaya Kniga
                                 D027157/8

SHER

Fantasia (on themes from Prokofiev's opera "War & Peace") vln & pf
  with T. Fidler pf   Mezhdunarodnaya Kniga
                                 D17949/50

SZYMANOWSKI

(3) Mythes, Op. 30 (1915) vln & pf
  No. 1. La Fontaine d'Aréthuse
  with T. Fidler pf   Muza XL0045, XL0386

VERACINI

(12) Sonatas, Op. 2 (1744) "Sonate accademiche" vln & c
  Sonata No. 8, in e
  with T. Fidler pf   Eterna 720102
                                 Muza XL0045

Peter KOMLÓS (1935–   )

BRAHMS

Sonata No. 2, in A, Op. 100 vln & pf
  with G. Miklós pf   Qualiton LPX1117

FRANCK

Sonata in A (1886) vln & pf
  with G. Miklós pf   Qualiton LPX1226, SLPX1226

RAVEL

Sonata (1927) vln & pf
  with G. Miklós pf   Qualiton LPX1226, SLPX1226

SCHUBERT

Quintet in A, Op. 114 (D667) "Trout" pf, vln, vla, vlc & cbs
  with M. Frager pf, G. Németh vla, K.   Qualiton LPX11342, SLPX11342
  Botvay vlc & Z. Tibay cbs

(3) Sonatinas, Op. 137 (D384, D385 & D408) vln & pf
  No. 1. Sonatina No. 1, in D, D384
  with G. Miklós pf   Qualiton LPX1226, SLPX1226

TARTINI

Sonata in g "Il Trillo del Diavolo" vln & c – arr. vln & pf Kreisler
  with G. Miklós pf   Qualiton LPX1117

Edmund KOMOSIŃSKI

VIVALDI

(12) Concerti, Op. 3 "L'Estro armonico" var. cbns & strs
  Concerto No. 10, in b, P.148 (F.IV, No. 10) 4 vlns, strs & c
  with Z. Bakowski vln, I. Iwanow vln,   Muza XL0504
  L. Radek vln, J. Dobrzański hpsi &
  Warsaw Chamber Orch. – Sutkowski

Kees KOOPER

BARTÓK

(6) Rumanian folk dances (1915) pf – arr. vln & pf Székely
  with piano   20th Century Fox TFM4006

BLOCH

Baal Shem (3 Pictures of Chassidic life) (1923) vln & pf
  No. 2. Nigun (Improvisation)
  with piano   20th Century Fox TFM4006

BRAHMS

(21) Hungarian Dances pf duet
  Hungarian dance No. 6, in D flat arr. vln & pf "in B flat" Joachim
  with piano   20th Century Fox TFM4006

DESPLANES

Intrada (Adagio) vln & c – arr. vln & pf Nachèz
  with piano   20th Century Fox TFM4006

FALLA

(7) Canciones populares españolas (1914) v & pf
  No. 1. El paño moruno arr. vln & pf Kochański
  with M.L. Böhm pf   Dot DLP3040
  No. 3. Asturiana arr. vln & pf Kochański
  with M.L. Böhm pf   Dot DLP3040
  No. 4. Jota arr. vln & pf Kochański
  with M.L. Böhm pf   Dot DLP3040
  No. 5. Nana arr. vln & pf Kochański
  with M.L. Böhm pf   Dot DLP3040
  No. 6. Canción arr. vln & pf Kochański
  with M.L. Böhm pf   Dot DLP3040

(La) Vida breve (1913) – opera
  Danza española orch. – arr. vln & pf Kreisler
  with M.L. Böhm pf   Dot DLP3040

FALLA – *Continued*

  Danza española orch. – arr. vln & pf Kreisler
  with piano   20th Century Fox TFM4006

KREISLER

Caprice viennois, Op. 2 vln & pf
  with piano   20th Century Fox TFM4006

Polichinelle–serenade vln & pf
  with piano   20th Century Fox TFM4006

MARAIS

(5) Danses anciennes vln & c
  No. 5. Le basque arr. vln & pf Aldis & Rowe
  with piano   20th Century Fox TFM4006

RAVEL

Berceuse sur le nom de Gabriel Fauré (1922) vln & pf
  with piano   20th Century Fox TFM4006

SCHUBERT

(7) Gesänge (set to Scott's "Lady of the Lake") Op. 52 v & pf
  No. 6. Ave Maria, D839 arr. vln & pf Wilhelmj
  with piano   20th Century Fox TFM4006

SOLER

(3) Sonatas vln & pf*
  with M.L. Böhm pf   Dot DLP3040

NOTE: Other works on Dot DLP 3040 include compositions by Herrando, Falla, etc., but remain unidentified.

Julius KOPPEL (1910–)

BACH

Concerto in d, BWV1043 2 vlns, strs & c
        2CS 2554–1, 2555/6–2 & 2557–1   HMV DB5289/90
  with E.M. Bruun vln & Royal Danish
  Chamber Orch. – Wöldike

BEETHOVEN

Serenade in D, Op. 25 fl, vln & vla
        CCX 1473–3C, 1474–1C, 1475–   Columbia LDX7020/2
        3A, 1476/7–1A & 1478–2B
  playing vla,
  with J. Bentzen fl & E.M. Bruun vln

BUXTEHUDE

Aperite mihi portas justitiae – cantata a, t, bs, 2 vlns & c
        2CX 2489/90ᴵᴵ☐   HMV KBLP14, Z292
  with E. Sigfuss a, A. Schiotz t,   Odeon MOAK2
  H. Norgaard bs, E.M. Bruun vln, M.   Victor 12–0533
  Wöldike hpsi & T.A. Svendsen vlc

O wie selig sind die Todten – cantata t, bs, 2 vlns & c
  with N. Brinker t,   GSC 52–2 Gramophone Shop GSC31, (in
  H. Norgaard bs, E.M. Bruun vln, M.   set 5)
  Wöldike hpsi & A. Medici vlc

(7) Sonatas, Op. 2 (1696) vln & c
  Sonata No. 6, in C arr. 2 vlns & c
  with E.M. Bruun   2CS 1778/9–1   HMV DB5249
  vln, M. Wöldike hpsi & A. Medici vlc

* Unidentified.

BUXTEHUDE – *Continued*

Was mich auf dieser Welt betrübt – cantata s, 2 vlns & c
with A. Schiotz t, E.M.   2CS 1618 HMV DB5240
Bruun vln, M. Wöldike hpsi & A.
Medici vlc

CORELLI

(12) Concerti grossi, Op. 6 orch.
Concerto grosso No. 7, in D
with E.M. Bruun vlc, T.A. Svendsen   HMV DA5256/7
vlc & Copenhagen Palace Chappel
Chamber Orch. – Wöldike

LÜBECK

Willkommen, süsser Bräutigam "Christmas Cantata" s, a & strs
   GSC42–1, 49/50–1 & 51–2 Gramophon Shop GSC34/6, (in
with K. Heerup s, V. Garde a, E.M. set 5)
Bruun vln, M. Wöldike hpsi & A.
Medici vlc

MOZART

Quartet in F, K370 ob, vln, vla & vlc
playing vla, with M.S. Andreassen ob, HMV KBLP6
E.M. Bruun vln & J. Hansen vlc

Sinfonia concertante in E flat, K364 vln, vla & orch.
playing vla, with E.M. Bruun vln & HMV KBLP18
orch. – Wöldike

TELEMANN

(12) Fantasies (1735) solo vln
Fantasia No. 4, in D
(unaccompanied)   Haydn Society HSE9103

M. KORN

BACH

Concerto in d, BWV1043 2 vlns, strs & c
with P. Hoffner vln & orch. – Melomanes français MF2506
Disenhaus

André KORSAKOV

SHOSTAKOVICH

(24) Preludes, Op. 34 (1932/3) pf
Prelude No. 10, in c sharp arr. vln & pf Tziganov
with piano   Mezhdunarodnaya Kniga
   D028103/4

Prelude No. 15, in D flat arr. vln & pf Tziganov
with piano   Mezhdunarodnaya Kniga
   D028103/4

Prelude No. 16, in b flat arr. vln & pf Tziganov
with piano   Mezhdunarodnaya Kniga
   D028103/4

Prelude No. 24, in d arr. vln & pf Tziganov
with piano   Mezhdunarodnaya Kniga
   D028103/4

Ottavia KORTNER

TELEMANN

Concerto in C 4 vlns, strs & c
with P. Nägele vln, G. Ohnheiser vln, Da Camera SM91017
M. Hori vln & Heidelberg Chamber
Orch.

Hugo KORTSCHAK (1884–1957)

BRAHMS

(21) Hungarian Dances pf duet
Hungarian Dance No. 2, in d arr. vln & pf Joachim
with piano   481 ak[II] Polydor 13210

DRDLA

Souvenir vln & pf
with J. Ring pf   S–71–339 C Okey 4833

DVOŘÁK

(8) Humoresques, Op. 101 pf
No. 7. Humoresque No. 7, in G flat arr. vln & pf "in G" Kreisler
with J. Ring pf   S–71–340 B Okey 4833

MASSENET

Thaïs (1894) – opera
Méditation arr. vln & pf Marsick
with piano   480 ak[II] Polydor 13210

Lásló KÓTÉ (1941–)

RAVEL

Tzigane (Rapsodie de concert) (1924) vln & pf or orch.
with Hungarian State Orch. – Qualiton LPX11366, SLPX11366
Oberfrank

SAINT–SAËNS

Introduction & Rondo Capriccioso, Op. 28 vln & orch.
with Hungarian State Orch. – Qualiton LPX11366, SLPX11366
Oberfrank

SIBELIUS

Concerto in d, Op. 47 vln & orch.
with Hungarian State Orch. – Qualiton LPX11366, SLPX11366
Oberfrank

Boris KOUTZEN (1901–1966)

BACH

(3) Sonatas & 3 Partitas, BWV1001/6 solo vln
Partita No. 3, in E: Preludio (1st mvt) BWV1006
(unaccompanied)   Vox 06163
(6) Sonatas, BWV1014/9 vln & clav
Sonata No. 4, in c: Largo (1st mvt) BWV1017 arr. vln & pf Auer
with W. Scholz pf   Vox 06193

BRAHMS

(16) Waltzes, Op. 39 pf duet
No. 15. Waltz No. 15, in A flat arr. vln & pf "in A" Hochstein
with W. Scholz pf   Vox 06144

DVOŘÁK

(8) Humoresques, Op. 101 pf
    No. 7. Humoresque No. 7, in G flat arr. vln & pf "in G" Wilhelmj
    with W. Scholz pf   Vox 06193
(8) Slavonic Dances, Op. 72 pf duet; orch.
    No. 2. Slavonic Dance No. 10, in e arr. vln & pf Kreisler
    with W. Scholz pf   Vox 06142

GLUCK

Orphée et Eurydice (1762) – opera
    Dance of the blessed spirits: Lento "Mélodie" (No. 2) arr. vln & pf
    Wilhelmj
    with W. Scholz pf   Vox 6147

HANDEL

(15) Sonatas, Op. 1 (?1731) fl or vln & c
    Sonata No. 9, in b: Andante (1st mvt) arr. vln & pf as "Larghetto" by
    Hubay
    with W. Scholz pf   Vox 06163

KREISLER

Schön Rosmarin vln & pf
    with W. Scholz pf   Vox 6145
Tambourin chinois, Op. 3 vln & pf
    with V. Padwa pf   Vox 06114
Allegretto (Boccherini) vln & pf
    with W. Scholz pf   Vox 6147
(La) Précieuse (L.Couperin) vln & pf
    with W. Scholz pf   Vox 06143
Sicilienne & Rigaudon (Francoeur) vln & pf
    with W. Scholz pf   Vox 06143

MOZART

Divertimento No. 17, in D, K334 2 hrns & orch.
    Minuet (3rd mvt) arr. vln & pf Burmester
    with W. Scholz pf   Vox 6146
Idomeneo, Re di Creta, K366 (1781) – opera
    Gavotte in G arr. vln & pf Auer
    with V. Padwa pf   Vox 06114
    Gavotte in G arr. vln & pf Auer
    with W. Scholz pf   Vox 6146

SARASATE

(8) Danzas españolas vln & pf
    No. 1. Malagueña, Op. 21, No. 1
    with W. Scholz pf   Vox 06142

SCHUBERT

(6) Moments musicaux, Op. 94 (D780) (1823/7) pf
    No. 3. Moment musicale No. 3, in f "Air russe" arr. vln & pf Auer
    with W. Scholz pf   Vox 06144

SCHUMANN

(9) Waldscenen, Op. 82 pf
    No. 7. Vogel als Prophet arr. vln & pf Auer
    with W. Scholz pf   Vox 6145

WIENIAWSKI

Capriccio–valse, Op. 7 vln & pf
    with W. Scholz pf   Vox 6145

Nadia KOUTZEN

BACH

(6) Brandenburg Concerti, BWV1046/51 (1721) strs & c
    Brandenburg Concerto No. 3, in G, BWV1048 3 vlns, 3 vlas, 3 vlcs & cbs
    with F. Galimir vln, H. Kwalwasser   Library of Recorded
    vln, B. Yokell vla, B. Zaslav vla, B.   Masterpieces BB1
    Robbins vla, S. Hunkins vlc, A.   Odyssey 32 16 0190, (in set 32
    Kouguell vlc, J. Schneider vlc, J.   26 0014)
    Levine cbs & F. Rupp hpsi, of the
    New York Sinfonietta – Goberman

VIVALDI

(12) Concerti, Op. 8 (1725) "Il Cimento dell' Armonia e dell' Invenzione"
    (nos. 1/4: Le quattro Stagioni) vln & strs
    Concerto No. 4, in f, F.I, No. 25 "L'Inverno"
    with New York Sinfonietta –   Library of Recorded
    Goberman   Masterpieces Vol. 1, No. 8
        Odyssey 32 16 0132

Concerto in G, P.135 (F.IV, No. 1) 2 vlns, 2 vlcs, strs & c
    with F. Galimir vln, C. McCracken   Library of Recorded
    vlc, T. Brys vlc, E. Earle hpsi & New   Masterpieces Vol. 1, No. 12
    York Sinfonietta – Goberman

Concerto in F, P.278 (F.I, No. 34) 3 vlns, strs & c
    with S. Monosoff vln, A. Bronne vln,   Library of Recorded
    E. Earle hpsi & New York Sinfonietta   Masterpieces Vol. 1, No. 10
    – Goberman   Odyssey 32 16 0053, 32 16 0054

Concerto in c, P.436 (F.I, No. 12) 2 vlns, strs & c
    with H. Kwalwasser vln, E. Earle hpsi   Library of Recorded
    & New York Sinfonietta – Goberman   Masterpieces Vol. 2, No. 1

Dénes KOVÁCS (1930–)

BARTÓK

Concerto No. 1, Op. posth. (1908) vln & orch.
    with Budapest Philharmonic Orch. –   Qualiton LPX11314, SLPX11314
    Koródy
Concerto No. 2 (1938) vln & orch.
    with Budapest Philharmonic Orch. –   Qualiton LPX1068
    Koródy
Rhapsody No. 1, in G (1928) vln & orch.
    with H. Boschi pf   Le Chant du Monde LDZM8155

BEETHOVEN

Concerto in D, Op. 61 (cadenzas by Joachim) vln & orch.
    with Hungarian State Orch. –   Hungaroton SHLX90006
    Ferencsik   Qualiton LPX1143
Romance No. 1, in G, Op. 40 vln & orch.
    with Hungarian State Orch. – Melles   Qualiton EP1563
Sonata No. 4, in a, Op. 23 vln & pf
    with M. Bächer pf   Dover HCR–ST7281
        Qualiton LPX1134
Sonata No. 9, in A, Op. 47 "Kreutzer" vln & pf
    with M. Bächer pf   Dover HCR–ST7281
        Qualiton LPX1134

HAYDN

(6) Sonatas, H.VI, Nos. 1/6 vln & vla
    Sonata No. 1, in C, H.VI, No. 1
    with G. Németh vla   Qualiton LPX11426

HAYDN – *Continued*

Sonata No. 2, in A, H.VI, No. 2
with G. Németh vla   Qualiton LPX11426

Sonata No. 3, in E flat, H.VI, No. 3
with G. Németh vla   Qualiton LPX11426

Sonata No. 4, in F, H.VI, No. 4
with G. Németh vla   Qualiton LPX11426

Sonata No. 5, in D, H.VI, No. 5
with G. Németh vla   Qualiton LPX11426

Sonata No. 6, in B flat, H.VI, No. 6
with G. Németh vla   Qualiton LPX11426

HIDAS

Concertino (1957) vln & orch.
with Hungarian Radio & Television   Qualiton LPX1273
Orch. – Lehel

KODÁLY

Adagio in C (1905) vln & pf
with H. Boschi pf   Le Chant du Monde LDZM8155

MENDELSSOHN

Concerto in e, Op. 64 vln & orch.
with Hungarian State Orch. – Németh   Qualiton LPX1191

MIHÁLY

Concerto (1959) vln, orch. & pf obb
with E. Petri pf & Hungarian Radio   Qualiton LPX1068
Symphony Orch. – Lukács

MOZART

Concerto No. 5, in A, K219 "Turkish" (cadenzas by Joachim) vln & orch.
     Hungaroton SHLX90014
with Hungarian State Concert Orch. –   Qualiton LPX1003
Lehel

Duo No. 1, in G, K423 vln & vla
with G. Németh vla   Qualiton LPX11427

Duo No. 2, in B flat, K424 vln & vla
with G. Németh vla   Qualiton LPX11427

Sonata in E flat, K293b vln & pf
with M. Bächer pf   Qualiton LPX1039

Sonata in G, K373a vln & pf
with M. Bächer pf   Qualiton LPX1039

Sonata No. 17, in C, K296 vln & pf
with M. Bächer pf   Dover HCR5279, HCR–ST7279
     Qualiton LPX1039

Sonata No. 18, in G, K301 vln & pf
with M. Bächer pf   Dover HCR5277, HCR–ST7277
     Qualiton LPX1122

Sonata No. 19, in E flat, K302 vln & pf
with M. Bächer pf   Dover HCR5279, HCR–ST7279

Sonata No. 24, in F, K376 vln & pf
with M. Bächer pf   Dover HCR5277, HCR–ST7277
     Qualiton LPX1122

Sonata No. 27, in G, K379 vln & pf
with M. Bächer pf   Dover HCR5279, HCR–ST7279

Sonata No. 32, in B flat, K454 vln & pf
with M. Bächer pf   Dover HCR5277, HCR–ST7277
     Qualiton LPX1122

VIVALDI

(12) Concerti, Op. 8 (1725) "Il Cimento dell' Armonia e dell' Invenzione"
(nos. 1/4: Le quattro Stagioni) vln & strs
Concerto No. 1, in E, F.I, No. 22 "La Primavera"
with Hungarian Radio Orch. –   Qualiton LPX1102, SLPX1102
Gardelli

Concerto No. 2, in B flat, F.I, No. 23 "L'Estate"
with Hungarian Radio Orch. –   Qualiton LPX1102, SLPX1102
Gardelli

Concerto No. 3, in F, F.I, No. 24 "L'Autunno"
with Hungarian Radio Orch. –   Qualiton LPX1102, SLPX1102
Gardelli

Concerto No. 4, in f, F.I, No. 25 "L'Inverno"
with Hungarian Radio Orch. –   Qualiton LPX1102, SLPX1102
Gardelli

(12) Sonatas, Op. 2 (1712) vln & c
Sonata No. 1, in g, F.XIII, No. 29
with J. Sebestyén hpsi & M. Frank vlc   Qualiton LPX11387, SLPX11387

Sonata No. 2, in A, F.XIII, No. 30
with J. Sebestyén hpsi & M. Frank vlc   Qualiton LPX11387, SLPX11387

Sonata No. 3, in d, F.XIII, No. 31
with J. Sebestyén hpsi & M. Frank vlc   Qualiton LPX11387, SLPX11387

Sonata No. 4, in F, F.XIII, No. 32
with J. Sebestyén hpsi & M. Frank vlc   Qualiton LPX11387, SLPX11387

Sonata No. 5, in b, F.XIII, No. 33
with J. Sebestyén hpsi & M. Frank vlc   Qualiton LPX11387, SLPX11387

Sonata No. 6, in C, F.XIII, No. 34
with J. Sebestyén hpsi & M. Frank vlc   Qualiton LPX11387, SLPX11387

Sonata No. 7, in c, F.XIII, No. 35
with J. Sebestyén hpsi & M. Frank vlc   Qualiton LPX11388, SLPX11388

Sonata No. 8, in G, F.XIII, No. 36
with J. Sebestyén hpsi & M. Frank vlc   Qualiton LPX11388, SLPX11388

Sonata No. 9, in e, F.XIII, No. 37
with J. Sebestyén hpsi & M. Frank vlc   Qualiton LPX11388, SLPX11388

Sonata No. 10, in f, F.XIII, No. 38
with J. Sebestyén hpsi & M. Frank vlc   Qualiton LPX11388, SLPX11388

Sonata No. 11, in D, F.XIII, No. 39
with J. Sebestyén hpsi & M. Frank vlc   Qualiton LPX11388, SLPX11388

Sonata No. 12, in a, F.XIII, No. 40
with J. Sebestyén hpsi & M. Frank vlc   Qualiton LPX11388, SLPX11388

Varuzhan KOZIGYAN

BACH

(3) Sonatas & 3 Partitas, BWV1001/6 solo vln
Partita No. 2, d: Chaconne (5th mvt) BWV1004
(unaccompanied)   Mezhdunarodnaya Kniga D4268

PROKOFIEV

Cinderella, Op. 87 (1941/4) – ballet orch.
Gavotte arr. vln & pf Fichtenholz
with E. Seidel pf   Mezhdunarodnaya Kniga D4269

Waltz arr. vln & pf Fichtenholz
with E. Seidel pf   Mezhdunarodnaya Kniga D4269

RAVEL

Pièce en forme d'Habanera v & pf – arr. vln & pf Catherine
with E. Seidel pf   Mezhdunarodnaya Kniga D4269

Marina KOZOLUPOVA (1918–)

BRAHMS

(21) Hungarian Dances pf duet
Hungarian dance No. 1, in g arr. vln & pf Joachim
with I. Kozolupova pf   Mezhdunarodnaya Kniga
                                  D10724

Hungarian dance No. 17, in f sharp arr. vln & pf Joachim
with I. Kozolupova pf   Mezhdunarodnaya Kniga D9295

DAQUIN

Pièces de clavecin – Book I (1735) hpsi*
Le coucou arr. vln & pf Manén
with A. Porter pf   Mezhdunarodnaya Kniga 5522

DVOŘÁK

(8) Slavonic Dances, Op. 72 pf duet; orch.
No. 2. Slavonic dance No. 10, in e arr. vln & pf Kreisler
with I. Kozolupova pf   Mezhdunarodnaya Kniga D9294

HANDEL

Solomon (1748) – oratorio
No. 40. Am klaren Bach im stillen Tal arr. vln & pf as "Pastorale" by
Flesch
with L. Fichtenholz pf   Mezhdunarodnaya Kniga
                                  D05796

KABALEVSKY

Improvisation, Op. 21, No. 1 vln & pf
with piano   Mezhdunarodnaya Kniga
                                  D14211/2

KREISLER

Andantino (Padre Martini) vln & pf
with piano   Mezhdunarodnaya Kniga
                                  D22276

MOZART

Concerto No. 5, in A, K219 "Turkish" (cadenzas by Joachim) vln & orch.
with USSR State Philharmonic Orch. –   Mezhdunarodnaya Kniga
Anosov   D0751/2

NARDINI

(6) Sonatas, Op. 2 (1765) vln & c
Sonata No. 5, in D arr. vln & pf Ysaÿe
with L. Fichtenholz pf   Mezhdunarodnaya Kniga
                                  D05796

RIMSKY–KORSAKOV

Fantasia on Russian themes, Op. 33 vln & orch.
with USSR State Radio Orch. –   Westminster XWN18120
Anosov

SAMMARTINI, G.

(6) Sonatas, Op. 1 2 vlns & c
Sonata No. 4, in A (3rd mvt) arr. vln & pf as "Canto amoroso" by
Elman
with piano   Mezhdunarodnaya Kniga
                                  D22277

* Recorded in Moscow for the New York World Fair, 1939, to highlight
Kozolupova as being a Laureate of International & U.S.S.R. competitions.

SCHUBERT

(3) Sonatinas, Op. 137 (D384, D385 & D408) vln & pf
Sonatina No. 1, in D, D384
with L. Fichtenholz pf   Mezhdunarodnaya Kniga
                                  D05797

TCHAIKOVSKY

Concerto in D, Op. 35 vln & orch.
Canzonetta (2nd mvt)
with piano   Mezhdunarodnaya Kniga
                                  D16816/7

VITALI

Chaconne in g vln & c – arr. vln & pf Charlier
with L. Fichtenholz pf   Mezhdunarodnaya Kniga
                                  D05797

WAGNER

Albumblatt in C (1861) pf – arr. vln & pf Wilhelmj
with I. Kozolupova pf   Colosseum CRLP179
                                  Mezhdunarodnaya Kniga
                                  D10723

Jacob KRACHMALNICK (1922–)

BEETHOVEN

Romance No. 2, in F, Op. 50 vln & orch.
with Philadelphia Orch. – Ormandy   Columbia ML4629

HAYDN

Sinfonia concertante in B flat, Op. 84 (H.I, No. 105) vln, vlc, ob, bsn &
orch.
with L. Munroe vlc, J. de Lancie ob,   CBS BRG75586, SBRG75586
B. Garfield bsn & Philadelphia Orch. –   Columbia ML5374, MS6061
Ormandy

JANÁČEK

Concertino (1925) pf, 2 vlns, vla, cl, hrn & bsn
with R. Firkusny pf, O. Madison vlc,   Columbia ML4995
S. Lifschey vla & Philadelphia   Philips A01642R, ABR4057
Woodwind Quintet – Ormandy

STRAUSS, R.

(Ein) Heldenleben, Op. 40 (1898) orch.
with Philadelphia Orch. – Ormandy   Columbia ML4887
                                  Philips A01148L, ABL3061

VIVALDI

(12) Concerti, Op. 3 "L'Estro armonico" var cbns & orch.
Concerto No. 11, in d P.250 (F.IV, No. 11) 2 vlns, vlc, strs & c
with J. Holtman vln, J. de Nobel vlc &   Telefunken AWT9426,
Amsterdam Chamber Orch. – van der   SAWT9426
Horst

Curt KRÄMER (1904–1963)

ERHARDT

Marfa vln & pf
with orch. – Erhardt   25794   Telefunken A10330
Rumanian rhapsody vln & pf
with orch. – Erhardt   25797   Telefunken A10330

Louis KRASNER (1903–)

BERG

Concerto (1935) vln & orch.
with Cleveland   XCO 29764/9   Columbia 11589/91D, (set
Symphony Orch. – Rodzinski   M465), C15561/3, (set D98),
LOX594/6, ML4857

PISTON

Sonata (1939) vln & pf
with W. Piston pf   Columbia 71121/2D, 71123/4D,
(set X199)

SCHOENBERG

Concerto, Op. 36 (1936) vln & orch.
with New York Philharmonic   Columbia ML4857
Symphony Orch. – Mitropoulos

Serenade, Op. 24 (1924) b, cl, bs-cl, vln, vlc, mand, & vla
with W. Galjour b, C. Brody cl, E.   Counterpoint CPT501
Simon bs-cl, S. Barab vlc, S. Piccardi   Esoteric ES501
mand, J. Smith gtr, R. Hersh vla, –
cond. Mitropoulos

Herman KREBBERS (1923–)

ALBINONI

(12) Concerti, Op. 5 (1707) vln or ob & strs
Concerto No. 7, in D
with L. van der Lee hpsi &   CBS S51127
Amsterdam Chamber Orch. –
Voorberg

BACH, C.P.E.

(2) Duets fl & vln or 2 vlns
Duet No. 2, in C, W142
with T. Olof vln   Radio Nederland DR109276
Duet No. 2, in C, W142
with T. Olof vln   Telefunken AWT9447,
SAWT9447, STEL15, TEL15

BACH, J.S.

Cantata No. 206 (Schleicht, spielende Wellen) BWV206
with I. Jacobeit s, W. Matthès a, T.   Telefunken AWT9425,
Brand t, J. Villisech bs, soloists & the   SAWT9425
Monteverdi Choir, Hamburg &
Amsterdam Chamber Orch. – Rieu
Cantata No. 208 (Was mir behagt, ist nur die muntre Jagd) BWV208
"Hunting Cantata"
with E. Spoorenberg s, I. Jacobeit s, T.   Telefunken AWT9427,
Brand t, J. Villisech bs, soloists & the   SAWT9427
Monteverdi Choir, Hamburg &
Amsterdam Chamber Orch. – Rieu
Concerto in d, BWV1043 2 vlns strs & c
with T. Olof vln & Hague Residentie   Epic LC3036
Orch. – van Otterloo   Mercury MGW14044,
SRW18044
Philips A00140L

BACH, J.S. – *Continued*

Mattheus–Passion, BWV244 (1729)
with T. Brand t, L. Bogtman bs, G.   Telefunken LT6598/601,
Hoekman bs, E. Spoorenberg s, A.   BLE14074*
Hermes a, A. Blanken t, C. Stotijn ob,
– The Netherlands Bach Choir,
Amsterdam Boys' Choir & Hague Residente
Orch. – van der Horst

BADINGS

Capriccio (1952) vln & 2 soundtracks
& tape recorder   Radio Nederland DR109270
Concerto (1954) 2 vlns & orch.
with T. Olof vln & Residentie Orch. –   Philips A02242L
van Otterloo
Sonata No. 1 (1928) 2 vlns
with T. Olof vln   Radio Nederland DR109276

BARTÓK

(44) Duos (1931) 2 vlns
with T. Olof vln   Philips N00209L

BEETHOVEN

Concerto in D, Op. 61 vln & orch.
with Hague Residentie Orch. –   Epic LC3023
van Otterloo   Fontana 675000KR, 695027KL
Philips A00132L, S04000L,
SBL5221

Romance No. 2, in F, Op. 50 vln & orch.
with Hague Residentie Orch. –   Epic LC3036
van Otterloo   Fontana 200031WGL,
675011KR, 695027KL
Mercury MGW14044,
SRW18044
Philips A00140L, S06000R,
SBF102

BONPORTI

(12) Concerti, Op. 11 strs
Concerto No. 5, in F: Adagio (2nd mvt) "Recitativo"
with L. van der Lee hpsi &   CBS S51126
Amsterdam Chamber Orch. –
Voorberg

BRAHMS

Concerto in D, Op. 77 (cadenza by Joachim) vln & orch.
with Brabant Philharmonic Orch. –   Fontana 200137WGL,
Jordans   700137WGY, SFL14033

BRUCH

Concerto No. 1, in g, Op. 26 vln & orch.
with Brabant Philharmonic Orch. –   Fontana 200130WGL,
Jordans   700130WGY

FAURÉ

Berceuse, Op. 16 vln & pf
with F. de Nobel pf   Radio Nederland DR109270

* excerpts only

HAYDN

Concerto No. 1, in C, H.VIIa, No. 1 (1765) vln & orch.
  with Amsterdam Chamber Orch. –   CBS S54051
  Rieu   Crossroads 22 16 0206
Concerto No. 2, in G, H.VIIa, No. 4 (1768) vln & orch.
  with Amsterdam Chamber orch. –   CBS S54051
  Rieu   Crossroads 22 16 0206

LOCATELLI

(12) Concerti grossi, Op. 1 (1721) strs
  Concerto grosso No. 2, in c: Adagio (1st mvt)
    with L. van der Lee hpsi &   CBS S51126
    Amsterdam Chamber Orch. –
    Voorberg

MANFREDINI

(12) Concerti, Op. 3 (1718) 2 vlns, strs & c
  Concerto No. 9, in D
    with J.L. Stuurop vln, L. van der Lee   CBS S51127
    hpsi & Amsterdam Chamber Orch. –
    Voorberg

MARCELLO

(12) Concerti, Op. 1 (1708) vln, vlc obb & strs
  Concerto No. 4, in F
    with L. van der Lee hpsi &   CBS S51127
    Amsterdam Chamber Orch. –
    Voorberg
  Introduzione, Aria & Presto vln & strs
    with L. van der Lee hpsi &   CBS S51127
    Amsterdam Chamber Orch. –
    Voorberg

NARDINI

(6) Concerti, Op. 1 vln & orch.
  Concerto No. 1, in A
    with G. Leonhardt hpsi & Amsterdam   Telefunken AWT9415,
    Chamber Orch. – Rieu   SAWT9415

PAGANINI

Concerto No. 1, in D, Op. 6 (cadenza by Ševčík) vln & orch.
  with Vienna Symphony Orch. – van   Epic LC3143
  Otterloo   Fontana 894017ZKY
                                        Philips A00263L

PERGOLESI

(6) Concertini "Concerti armonici" str orch.
  Concertino No. 1, in G: Grave (2nd mvt)
    with L. van der Lee hpsi &   CBS S51126
    Amsterdam Chamber Orch. –
    Voorberg

POULENC

(3) Pieces (1934/5) pf
  No. 1. Presto in B flat arr. vln & pf Heifetz
    with F. de Nobel pf   Radio Nederland DR109270

SAINT–SAËNS

Danse macabre, Op. 40 orch.
  with Concertgebouw Orch.,   Philips 835166AY, A02286L,
  Amsterdam – Haitink   PHC9139
Havanaise, Op. 83 vln & orch.
  with Residentie Orch. – van Otterloo Philips SBL5236

SAINT–SAËNS – *Continued*

Introduction & Rondo Capriccioso, Op. 28 vln & orch.
  with Residentie Orch. – van Otterloo Philips N09049S, N11234G

STRAUSS, R.

(Ein) Heldenleben, Op. 40 (1898) orch.
  with Concertgebouw Orch.,   Philips 6500 048
  Amsterdam – Haitink

SVENDSEN

Romance in G, Op. 26 vln & orch.
  with Hague Philharmonic Orch. – van   Fontana 494025EE
  Otterloo

VALENTINI

(12) Sonatas, Op. 8 (1714) "Alletamenti" vln & c
  Sonata in D
    with D. Dechenne pf   Artone EPDE6612

VERACINI

(12) Sonatas, Op. 2 (1744) "Sonate accademiche" vln & c
  Sonata No. 6, in A: Largo (2nd mvt)
    with L. van der Lee hpsi &   CBS S51126, S51127
    Amsterdam Chamber Orch. –
    Voorberg

VIEUXTEMPS

Concerto No. 4, in d, Op. 31 vln & orch.
  with Residentie Orch. – van Otterloo Philips A00263L

VIVALDI

(12) Concerti, Op. 3 "L'Estro armonico" var. cbns & strs
  Concerto No. 11, in d, P.250 (F.IV, No. 11) 2 vlns, vlc, strs & c*
    with J.L. Stuurop vln, K. Schouten CBS S51125
    vla, H. Secrete vlc, L. van der Lee hpsi
    & Amsterdam Chamber Orch. –
    Voorberg
(12) Concerti, Op. 8 (1725) "Il Cimento dell' Armonia e dell' Invenzione"
  (Nos. 1/4: Le quattro Stagioni) vln & strs
  Concerto No. 1, in E: Largo (2nd mvt) F.I, No. 22 "La Primavera"
    with L. van der Lee hpsi &   CBS S51126
    Amsterdam Chamber Orch. –
    Voorberg
  Concerto No. 3, in F: Adagio molto (2nd mvt) F.I, No. 24 "L'Autunno"
    with L. van der Lee hpsi &   CBS S51126
    Amsterdam Chamber Orch. –
    Voorberg
  Concerto No. 4, in F: Largo (2nd mvt) F.I, No. 25 "L'Inverno"
    with L. van der Lee hpsi &   CBS S51126
    Amsterdam Chamber Orch. –
    Voorberg
Concerto in C, P.74 (F.XII, No. 4) vln, rec, strs & c
  with F. Brüggen rec, G. Leonhardt   Telefunken AWT9426,
  hpsi & Amsterdam Chamber Orch. –   SAWT9426
  Rieu
Concerto in B flat, F.XI, No. 5 (P.342) vln, strs & c
  with L. van der Lee hpsi &   CBS S51125
  Amsterdam Chamber Orch. –
  Voorberg

* The Largo or 2nd mvt. is on CBS S51126.

VIVALDI – *Continued*

Concerto in g, F.XI, No. 21 vln, strs & c
with L. Van der Lee hpsi &   CBS S51125
Amsterdam Chamber Orch. –
Voorberg

Concerto in F, F.XI, No. 29 vln, strs & c
with L. van der Lee hpsi &   CBS S51125
Amsterdam Chamber Orch. –
Voorberg

Concerto in g, F.XII, No. 6 vln, strs & c
with L. van der Lee hpsi &   CBS S51125
Amsterdam Chamber Orch. –
Voorberg

Concerto in e, F.XII, No. 13 vln, strs & c
with L. van der Lee hpsi &   CBS S51125
Amsterdam Chamber Orch. –
Voorberg

Fritz KREISLER (1875–1962)

ALBÉNIZ

España (6 Feuilles d'album) Op. 165 pf
No. 2. Tango in D arr. vln & pf Kreisler
with C. Lamson pf   A 38221△ Camden CAL518, CDN1026
            HMV DA1009, DA1354
            Victor 1339, A430378

No. 3. Malagueña in b arr. vln & pf Kreisler
with C. Lamson pf   A 38220△ Camden CAL518, CDN1026
            HMV DA1354, EC84
            Victor 1244, A430378

ANONYMOUS

Cherry ripe English folksong – arr. vln & pf Kreisler
with C. Lamson pf   Victor 66196, 966

I saw from the beach folksong – arr. v, vln & pf Hughes
with J. McCormack t & Bb 5119–1 HMV4–2041, DA636, IR1010
piano

Londonderry air traditional Irish ballad – arr. vln, vlc & pf Kreisler
with H. Kreisler vlc & V. O'Brien pf Victor 87577, 3017

Londonderry air traditional Irish ballad – arr. vln & pf Kreisler
with F. Rupp pf   OEA 6107–2 Angel GR11
            Electrola E60800
            HMV COLH19, CSLP506,
            DA1622, WDLP700, XLP30009
            Victor (in set WCT80), 2164,
            LCT1049

Londonderry air traditional Irish ballad – arr. vln & pf Kreisler
with M. Raucheisen CLR 6063III△ HMV DB2117
pf

Londonderry air traditional Irish ballad – arr. vln & pf Kreisler
with Victor Symphony Orch. – Victor 10–1204, (in set M1044)
Voorhees

Molly on the shore traditional Irish ballad – arr. vln & pf Kreisler
with C. Lamson pf   Victor 1075

Song of the Volga boatman traditional Russian folksong – arr. vln & pf
Kreisler
with C. Lamson pf   HMV DA1182
            Victor 1122

BACH

Concerto in d, BWV1043 2 vlns, strs & c
with E. Zimbalist vln & A 15560/2 HMV 2–07918 & 2–07920 & 2–
string quartet   07922, DB587/8
            Rococo 2005
            Victor (in set LM6099),
            76028/30, 8040/1, A430569,
            RB6525

Notenbüchlein für Anna Magdalena Bach (1725) clav
No. 4. Minuet in G, BWV.Anh114 arr. vln & pf Winternitz
with C. Lamson pf   A 31940△ HMV DA777
            Victor 1136

No. 5. Minuet in g, BWV.Anh115 arr. vln & pf Winternitz
with C. Lamson pf   A 31940△ HMV DA777
            Victor 1136

(3) Sonatas & 3 Partitas, BWV1001/6 solo vln
Sonata No. 1, in g: Adagio (1st mvt) BWV1001
(unaccompanied)   CwR 642IA△ HMV DB995
            Rococo 2006
            Victor 8079, (in set M13)

Partita No. 3, in E: Preludio (1st mvt) BWV1006 arr. vln & pf Kreisler
with piano   Gramophone & Typewriter
            47946

Partita No. 3, in E: Preludio (1st mvt) BWV1006 arr. vln & pf Kreisler
with G. Falkenstein pf A 12728 HMV 07985, DB669
            Victor 74332

Partita No. 3, in E: Gavotte (3rd mvt) BWV1006 arr. vln & pf Kreisler
with G. Falkenstein pf   HMV DA262
            Victor 64132, 712

Partita No. 3, in E: Gavotte (3rd mvt) BWV1006 arr. vln & pf Kreisler
with C. Lamson pf   A 5705 Delta TQD3031
            HMV 07968, DB669

Partita No. 3, in E: Gavotte (3rd mvt) BWV1006 arr. vln & pf Kreisler
with F. Rupp pf   OEA 6097I□ Angel GR11
            Electrola E60800
            HMV COLH19, DA1628,
            WDLP700, XLP30009
            Victor 10–1022, LCT1142

(4) Suites, BWV1066/9 strs & c
Suite No. 3, in D: Air (2nd mvt) BWV1068 2 obs, 3 tpts, drms & strs –
arr. vln & pf as "Air on the G–string" by Wilhelmj
with piano   2087 X Gramophone & Typewriter
            37953, 47947
            Pearl GEM102

BALOGH

Caprice antique pf – arr. vln & pf Kreisler
with C. Lamson pf   Victor 1093

Dirge of the north pf – arr. vln & pf Kreisler
with C. Lamson pf   Victor 1043

BASS

Chansonnette v & pf – arr. vln & pf Kreisler
with C. Lamson pf   A 29844 HMV DA737
            Victor 1062

BEETHOVEN

Andante in F, G170 "Andante favori" pf – arr. vln, vlc & pf Kreisler
with H. Kreisler vlc & piano Victor 3037

BEETHOVEN – *Continued*

Concerto in D, Op. 61 (cadenzas by Kreisler) vln & orch.
        CwR 631^{IA}△, 632^{II}△, 633^{IA}△,   Electrola 1 C047–01243 M
  634^{IVA}△, 635^{II}△, 636^{IIIA}△, 637^{IIA}△,   HMV DB990/5
  638^{II}△, 639^{IIIA}△, 640^{II}△ & 641^{IIA}△   Rococo 2006
with Berlin State Opera Orch. – Blech   Victor 8074/9, (set M13)

Concerto in D, Op. 61 (cadenzas by Kreisler) vln & orch.
    2EA 2974^I☐, 2975–Ia☐, 2976   Angel COLH11
^{IIA}☐, 2977^{IIIA}☐, 2978^{IA}☐, 2979^{IIIA} Electrola E80486
☐, 2980^{IIA}☐, 2981^{IIIA}☐, 2982^{IIA}☐,   HMV DB2927/31, DB8210/5
          2983^{IA}☐ & 2984^{IIIA}☐   Victor 14163/8, (set M325)
with London Philharmonic Orch. –   World Record Club H101
Barbirolli

(6) Minuets, G167 pf
  No. 2. Minuet No. 2, in G arr. vln, vlc & pf Kreisler
  with H. Kreisler vlc & piano   Victor 3037

(3) Sonatas, Op. 12 vln & pf
  No. 1. Sonata No. 1, in D
      2EA 1377^{IV}☐, 1378/9^{II}☐ &   HMV COLH6, DB2554/6,
  with F. Rupp pf   1380/1^I☐   DB7892/6
  No. 2. Sonata No. 2, in A
      2EA 1382^{II}☐, 1383/4^I☐, 1385^{II} HMV COLH6, DB2556/8,
  with F. Rupp pf   ☐ & 1386^{III}☐   DB7892/4 & DB7897/8
  No. 3. Sonata No. 3, in E flat
      2EA 1387^{II}☐, 1388^{III}☐, 1389^I HMV COLH7, DB2559/60,
  with F. Rupp pf   ☐ & 1390^{IV}☐   DB7895/8, LALP519

Sonata No. 4, in a, Op. 23 vln & pf
      2EA 1396^V☐, 1397^I☐, 1398^{III} HMV COLH7, DB2781/3,
      ☐, 1399^V☐ & 1400^{III}☐   DB8054/5 & DB8058/60
with F. Rupp pf

Sonata No. 5, in F, Op. 24 "Spring" vln & pf
      2EA 1391/3^{IV}☐, 1394^{VII}☐ &   HMV COLH8, DB2783/5,
  with F. Rupp pf   1395^V☐   DB8056/60, HQM1214

(3) Sonatas, Op. 30 vln & pf
  No. 1. Sonata No. 6, in A
      2EA 3081^{III}☐, 3082^{II}☐, 3083/4   HMV COLH8, DB3296/8,
  with F. Rupp pf ^{I}☐ & 3085/6^{III}☐   DB8349/54
  No. 2. Sonata No. 7, in c
      2EA 3091/2^{II}☐, 3093/4^{III}☐,   HMV COLH9, DB3068/70,
  with F. Rupp pf 3095^{II}☐ & 3096^I☐   DB8235/40
  No. 3. Sonata No. 8, in G
      A 41759/61△ & 41763△   HMV DB1463/4
  with S. Rachmaninov pf   Victor 8163/4, (in set LM6099),
          A430569, RB6525, RB16154
  No. 3. Sonata No. 8, in G
      2EA 3087^{III}☐, 3088^{II}☐, 3089^I HMV COLH10, DB2786/7,
  with F. Rupp pf   ☐ & 3090^{III}☐   DB8054/7

Sonata No. 9, in A, Op. 47 "Kreutzer" vln & pf
      2EA 3705^I☐, 3706^{III}☐, 3707/9^I HMV COLH10, DB3071/4,
  with F. Rupp pf   ☐ & 3713/5^I☐   DB8235/41, HQM1214

Sonata No. 10, in G, Op. 96 vln & pf
  with F. Rupp pf   2EA 3716/21^I☐   HMV COLH9, DB3299/301,
          DB8349/54

BERLIN

Blue skies (1927) v & pf – arr. vln & pf Kreisler
  with C. Lamson pf   A 38215△   HMV DA880
          Victor 1233

BIZET

(L') Arlésienne (Suite No. 1) (1872) orch.
  No. 3. Adagietto arr. vln & pf Kreisler
  with string quartet   A 17755   HMV 4–7964, DA264
          Victor 64601, 715

(L') Arlésienne (Suite No. 2) (1872) orch.
  No. 2. Intermezzo arr. vln, vlc & pf Kreisler
  with H. Kreisler vlc   Cw 1238^{II}△   HMV DB1166
  & M. Raucheisen pf   Victor (in set LM6099), 8090,
          A430569, RB6525

BOCCHERINI

(6) Quintets, Op. 13 2 vlns, vla & 2 vlcs
  No. 5. Quintet No. 5, in E: Minuet (3rd mvt) "Bull" arr. vln & pf Kreisler
  with string quartet   A 17753   HMV 4–7965, DA267
          Victor 64614, 718

BOHM

(143) Lieder, Op. 326 v & pf
  No. 27. Still wie die Nacht arr. v, vln & pf
  with J. McCormack t &   A 16093   Everest SDBR3258
  piano   HMV 4–2699, DA460
          Victor 87233, 87550, 3023

BRAGA

(7) Melodies (1867) v & pf
  No. 5. La serenata "Angel's serenade" arr. v, vln & pf
  with J. McCormack t &   A 14623   HMV 02540, DB578
  V. O'Brien pf   Victor 88479, 89103, 8033

BRAHMS

Concerto in D, Op. 77 (cadenza by Kreisler) vln & orch.
      CwR 1355/6^{III}△, 1357^I△, 1366^{II} HMV DB1120/4 (set 58)
  △, 1367^{IV}△, 1368/9^{II}△ & 1376^V△   Victor 8098/102 (set M36)
  with Berlin State Opera Orch. – Blech

Concerto in D, Op. 77 (cadenza by Kreisler) vln & orch.
      2EA 2986^{IA}☐, 2987/8^{IIA}☐,   HMV COLH35, DB2915/9,
  2989^I☐, 2990/2^{IA}☐ & 2997/8^{IV}☐   DB8127/31, (set 261), LALP487
  with London Philharmonic Orch. –   Victor 14588/92, (set M402)
  Barbirolli   World Record Club SH115

(21) Hungarian Dances pf duet
  Hungarian dance No. 5, in f sharp arr. vln & pf "in g" Joachim
  with piano   A 5703   Delta TQD3031
          HMV 07966
          Pearl GEM102

  Hungarian dance No. 5, in f sharp arr. vln & pf "in g" Joachim
  with G. Falkenstein pf   A 8969   HMV 3–7928, DA262
          Victor 64131, 712

  Hungarian dance No. 17, in f sharp arr. vln & pf Kreisler
  with C. Lamson pf   Victor 6706

(16) Waltzes, Op. 39 pf duet
  No. 15, Waltz No. 15, in A flat arr. vln & pf "in A" Kreisler
  with C. Lamson pf   A 24188   HMV 5–7961, DA282
          Victor 66041, 726

  No. 15, Waltz No. 15, in A flat arr. vln & pf "in A" Kreisler
  with F. Rupp pf   OEA 6104^{II}☐   HMV DA1631, EC102

BRANDL

(Der) Liebe Augustin – operetta

Du alter Stefansturm arr. vln & pf as "The old refrain" by Kreisler
with C. Lamson pf   HMV 3–7968, DA269
           Victor (in set WCT3), 64529,
           720, 17–0012, LCT1002

Du alter Stefansturm arr. vln & pf as "The old refrain" by Kreisler
with M. Raucheisen   BLR 6061^{III}△   HMV DA1138
pf   Victor 1465, VIC1372

Du alter Stefansturm arr. vln & pf as "The old refrain" by Kreisler
with Victor Symphony Orch. –   Victor 10–1202, (in set M1044)
Voorhees

BRUCH

Concerto No. 1, in g, Op. 26 vln & orch.
with Royal Albert Hall Orch. –   HMV*
Goossens

CADMAN

(4) American Indian Songs, Op. 45 v & pf

No. 1. From the land of the sky–blue water arr. vln & pf Kreisler
with C. Lamson pf   A 29812△   HMV 7–7903, DA745
           Victor 66269, 1021, 1115

At dawning, Op. 29, No. 1 v & pf – arr. vln & pf Rissland
with C. Lamson pf.   Victor 1165

Legend of the canyon vln & pf
with C. Lamson pf   Victor 1093

CHAMINADE

Sérénade espagnole pf – arr. vln & pf Kreisler
   with C. Lamson pf   HMV DA280
           Victor 64503, 724

CHOPIN

(4) Mazurkas, Op. 33 pf

No. 2. Mazurka No. 23, in D arr. vln & pf Kreisler
with C. Lamson pf   A.27726   HMV 6–7917, DA511
           Victor 66157, 947

(4) Mazurkas, Op. 67 pf

No. 4. Mazurka No. 45, in a arr. vln & pf Kreisler
with C. Lamson pf   A 15940   HMV 3–7995, DA282
           Victor 64504, 726

No. 4. Mazurka No. 45, in a arr. vln & pf Kreisler
with F. Rupp pf   OEA 6096^{I}□   HMV DA1631, EC102
           Victor 2164

CORELLI

(12) Sonatas, Op. 5 vln & c

Sonata No. 1, in D: Adagio (4th mvt) arr. vln, vlc & pf as "O Sanctissima" by Kreisler
with H. Kreisler vlc   Cw 1237^{IV}△   HMV DB1166
& M. Raucheisen pf   Victor (in set LM6099), 8090,
           A430569, RB6525

COTTENET

Chanson méditation vln & pf
with G. Falkenstein pf   A 5701   HMV 07964, DB321
           Victor 74330, 6188

---

* Recorded at Hayes, Middlesex on December 29th & 30th 1924 & January 2nd 1925, but unissued due to the standardization of the electrical process.

de CURTIS

Carmé v & pf – arr. v, vln & orch.
with J. McCormack t &   A 16091   Everest SDBR3258
orch.   HMV 7–52075, DA455, IR1006
           Victor 87231, 87548, 3018

DAWES

Melody in A (1912) vln & pf
with C. Lamson pf   A 25130   HMV 5–7911, DA281
           Victor 64961, 725

DEBUSSY

Petite Suite (1889) pf

No. 1. En bateau arr. vln & pf Kreisler
with C. Lamson pf   A 40358△   Camden CAL518, CDN1026
           HMV DA1026
           Victor 1358, A430378, LCT1142

(12) Préludes – Book I (1910) pf

No. 8. La Fille aux cheveux de lin arr. vln & pf Hartmann
with C. Lamson pf   A 31939△   Camden CAL518, CDN1026
           HMV DA1026
           Victor 1358, A430378, LCT1142

DOHNÁNYI

Ruralia Hungarica, Op. 32A pf – arr. vln & pf Kreisler*
      A 41598△, 42401△, 41599△ &   HMV DA1148/9
with C. Lamson pf   42400△   Victor 1428/9

DRDLA

Souvenir vln & pf
with C. Lamson pf   A 25134   HMV 5–7941, DA265
           Victor 64974, 716

Souvenir vln & pf
with C. Lamson pf   A 25134△   HMV DA975
           Victor 1325

DVOŘÁK

(7) Gypsy songs, Op. 55 v & pf

No. 4. Songs my mother taught me arr. vln & pf Kreisler
with C. Lamson pf   HMV 4–7961, DA283
           Victor 64563, 727

No. 4. Songs my mother taught me arr. vln & pf Kreisler
with C. Lamson pf   A 49148△   Camden CAL518, CDN1026
           HMV DA1057
           Victor 1414

(8) Humoresques, Op. 101 pf

No. 7. Humoresque No. 7, in G flat arr. vln & pf "in G" Kreisler
with orch.   A 22887   HMV 07939, DB314

No. 7. Humoresque No. 7, in G flat arr. vln & pf "in G" Kreisler
with G. Falkenstein pf   Victor 74180, 6181

No. 7. Humoresque No. 7, in G flat arr. vln & pf "in G" Kreisler
with C. Lamson pf   A 8941   HMV DB1091
           Victor 6692

No. 7. Humoresque No. 7, in G flat arr. vln & pf "in G" Kreisler
with F. Rupp pf   2EA 6100^{I}□   Angel GR11
           Electrola E60800
           HMV COLH19, CSLP506,
           DB3443, WDLP700, XLP30009
           Victor 15217, (in set WCT80),
           LCT1049, VIC1372

---

* Number 6 or Adagio is also on Victor VIC1372.

DVOŘÁK – Continued

(8) Slavonic Dances, Op. 46 pf duet; orch.
No. 2. Slavonic dance No. 2, in e arr. vln & pf "in g" Kreisler
with piano   HMV 3–7982, DA279
                                      Victor 64488, 723

No. 2. Slavonic dance No. 2, in e arr. vln & pf "in g" Kreisler
with C. Lamson pf   A 15738△   Camden CAL518, CDN1026
                                     HMV DA1057
                                     Victor 1414, A430378, VIC1372

(8) Slavonic Dances, Op. 72 pf duet; orch.
No. 2. Slavonic dance No. 10, in e arr. vln & pf Kreisler
with C. Lamson pf   A 15742   HMV 2–07985, DB316
                                       Victor 74437, 6183

No. 8. Slavonic dance No. 16, in A flat arr. vln & pf "in G" Kreisler
with C. Lamson pf   A 15737△   Camden CAL518, CDN1026
                                       HMV DB1445
                                       Victor 7225, A430378, VIC1372

Sonatina in G, Op. 100 vln & pf
Larghetto (2nd mvt) arr. vln & pf as "Indian lament" by Kreisler
with V. O'Brien pf   Everest SDBR3258
                                       HMV 2–07910, DB319
                                       Victor 74387, 6186

Larghetto (2nd mvt) arr. vln & pf as "Indian lament" by Kreisler
with C. Lamson pf   A 14653△   Camden CAL518, CDN1026
                                       HMV DB1445
                                       Victor 7225, A430378, VIC1372

Symphony No. 9, in e, Op. 95 "From the New World" orch.
Largo (2nd mvt) arr. vln & pf as "Negro spiritual melody" by Kreisler
with C. Lamson pf   Victor 66270, 1021

Largo (2nd mvt) arr. vln & pf as "Negro spiritual melody" by Kreisler
with C. Lamson pf   HMV DA1182
                                       Victor 1122

EARL

Beautiful Ohio (1918) v & pf – arr. vln & pf Kreisler
with orch.   A 22863   HMV 4–7953, DA273
                                       Victor 64817, 707

FALLA

(7) Canciones populares españolas (1914) v & pf
No. 4. Jota arr. vln & pf Kochański
with M. Raucheisen   BLR 6065III△   HMV DA1157, HMQ1104
pf   Victor 1504, A430378

No. 6. Canción arr. vln & pf Kochański
with C. Lamson pf   Camden CAL518, CDN1026
                                       HMV DA905
                                       Victor 1244, A430378

(La) Vida breve (1913) – opera
Danza española orch. – arr. vln & pf Kreisler
with C. Lamson pf   A 40359△   Camden CAL518, CDN1026
                                       HMV DA1009
                                       Victor 1339, A430378

Danza española orch. – arr. vln & pf Kreisler
with F. Rupp pf   OEA 6106IIA☐   Angel GR11
                                     Electrola E60800
                                     HMV COLH19, DA1630,
                                     WDLP700, XLP30009
                                     Victor 1891, LCT1142

FOSTER

(The) Old folks at home (1851) "Swanee River" v & pf – arr. vln & pf Kreisler
with G. Falkenstein pf   HMV 4–7957, DA278
                                       Victor 64130, 722

(The) Old folks at home (1851) "Swanee River" v & pf – arr. vln & pf Kreisler
with C. Lamson pf   A 8939   HMV CSLP506, DA975
                                       Victor 1325, LCT1049

FRIEDBERG

Old French Gavotte vln & pf
with C. Lamson pf   Victor 66251, 1010

FRIML

Dance of the maidens, Op. 48 pf – arr. vln & pf Kreisler
with C. Lamson pf   A 38216△   HMV DA880, DA992

Rose Marie (1916) – operetta
Indian love call arr. vln & pf Kreisler
with C. Lamson pf   A 34704△   HMV DA785
                                       Victor 1151

GÄRTNER

Aus Wien pf – arr. vln & pf Kreisler
with C. Lamson pf   HMV 3–7970, DA529
                                       Victor 64406, 910

GLAZOUNOV

(2) Pieces, Op. 20 vlc & pf
No. 2. Sérénade espagnole arr. vln & pf Kreisler
with M. Raucheisen   BLR 6062III△   HMV DA1157, HQM1104
pf   Victor 1504

GLUCK

Orphée et Eurydice (1762) – opera
Dance of the blessed spirits: Lento "Mélodie" (No. 2) arr. vln & pf Kreisler
with piano   HMV 3–7952
                                       Victor 64313

GODARD

Jocelyn (1888) – opera
Cachés dans cet asile "Berceuse" arr. v, vln & pf
with J. McCormack t &   A 14626   Everest SDBR3258
V. O'Brien pf   HMV 02542, DB577
                                       Victor 88483, 89106, 8032,
                                       A430569, RB6525, (in set
                                       LM6099)

GODOWSKY

(12) Impressions (1916) pf
No. 12. Viennese arr. vln & pf Kreisler
with C. Lamson pf   HMV 2–07986, DB320
                                       Victor 74463, 6187

GOUNOD

Ave Maria (Méditation on Bach's "Prelude No. 1, in C" from Book I of "Das Wohltemperirte Clavier") v & pf – arr. v, vln & pf
with J. McCormack t &   A 14624   Camden CAL635
V. O'Brien pf   HMV 02541, DB577
                                       Victor 88481, 89104, 8032

GRANADOS

(12) Danzas españolas, Op. 37 (1893) pf
 No. 5. Danza española No. 5, in e "Andaluza" arr. vln & pf Kreisler
 with C. Lamson pf   HMV DA280
                                                Victor 64556, 724

GRIEG

(6) Lyric Pieces – Book III, Op. 43 pf
 No. 6. To the spring arr. vln & pf Kreisler
 with C. Lamson pf   HMV DA283
                                                Victor 64993, 727

Sonata No. 3, in c, Op. 45 vln & pf
 CL 4511/4^V△, 4515^{VI}△ & 4516^V HMV DB1259/61
 with S. Rachmaninov pf   △ Victor (set WCT1128), 8112/4,
                                                (set M45), LCT1128, LVT1009,
                                                RB16154

HANDEL

Serse (1738) – opera
 Ombra mai fu "Largo" arr. vln & pf Kreisler
 with C. Lamson pf   A 14342 HMV 2–07906, DB488
                                                Victor 74384, 6184

HAYDN

(6) Quartets, Op. 76 (H.III, nos. 75/80) 2 vlns, vla & vlc
 No. 3. Quartet No. 77, in C: Theme & variations (2nd mvt) "Emperor"
 arr. vln & pf Kreisler
 with C. Lamson pf   Victor 64408, 910
Symphony No. 96, in D "Miracle" orch.
 Minuet (3rd mvt) arr. vln & pf Friedberg
 with C. Lamson pf   Victor 66250, 1010
(31) Trios, H.XV, Nos. 1/31 pf, vln & vlc
 Trio No. 25, in G: Rondo all' ongarese (3rd mvt) H.XV, No. 25 (Op. 73,
 No. 2) arr. vln & pf Kreisler
 with Victor Symphony Orch. –   Victor 10–1204, (in set M1044)
 Voorhees

HERBERT

Orange Blossoms (1922) – operetta
 A kiss in the dark arr. vln & pf Kreisler
 with C. Lamson pf   Victor 1029

HEUBERGER

(Der) Opernball, Op. 40 (1898) – operetta
 Im chambre séparée arr. vln & pf as "Midnight bells" by Kreisler
 with piano   HMV DA266
                                                Victor 66149, 717

 Im chambre séparée arr. vln & pf as "Midnight bells" by Kreisler
 with M. Raucheisen   BLR 6066^{III} HMV DA1138
 pf   Victor 1465

 Im chambre séparée arr. vln & pf as "Midnight bells" by Kreisler
 with Victor Symphony Orch. –   Victor 10–1203, (in set M1044)
 Voorhees

HIRSCH

Mary (1920) – musical
 Love nest arr. vln & pf Kreisler
 with orch.   A 24713 HMV 5–7926, DA263
                                                Victor 64924, 714

HUBBELL

(The) Big Show (1916) – musical
 Poor butterfly arr. vln & pf Kreisler
 with orch.   A 19322 HMV 4–7959, DA263
                                                Rococo 2005
                                                Victor 64655, 714

JACOBI

On Miami shore (1919) v & pf – arr. vln & orch.
 with orch.   A 24186 HMV 5–7936, DA273
                                                Victor 64947, 707

JERAL

Sérénade viennois, Op. 18 vln & pf – arr. vln, vlc & pf Kreisler
 with H. Kreisler vlc & M. Raucheisen   Victor 87579, 3017
 pf

JOHNSON

Since you went away v & pf – arr. v, vln & pf
 with J. McCormack t &   A 24037 HMV 5–2318, DA459, DA520
 E. Schneider pf   Victor 87573, 3022

KORNGOLD

(Die) Tote Stadt, Op. 12 (1920) – opera
 Meine sehnen, mein Wähnen (Pierrotlied) arr. vln & pf as "Pierrot's
 dance song" by Kreisler
 with C. Lamson pf   Victor 1062

KOSCHAT

Forsaken v & pf – arr. vln & pf Winternitz
 with orch.   HMV DA274
                                                Victor 64873, 708

KOŽELUH

(La) Ritrovata Figlia de Ottone, Op. 39 – ballet orch.
 No. 22. Gavotte (Act IV) arr. vln & pf Kramer
 with C. Lamson pf   A 31975△ HMV DA777
                                                Victor 1136

KRAKAUER

Im Paradies (1926) pf – arr. vln & pf Kreisler
 with orch.   A 22865 HMV 5–7958, DA281
                                                Victor 66023, 725

KRAMER

Entr'acte, Op. 46, No. 2 vln & pf
 with C. Lamson pf   A 27725 HMV 6–7924, DA737
                                                Victor 66197, 966

(The) Last hour v & pf – arr. v, vln & pf
 with J. McCormack t &   A 24036 HMV 5–2505, DA460
 piano   Victor 87576, 3023

KREISLER

Apple Blossoms (1919) – operetta
 Who can tell? arr. vln & pf Kreisler
 with orch.   HMV DA268
                                                Victor 64902

Aucassin & Nicolette (Canzonetta medievale) vln & pf
 with C. Lamson pf   HMV DA266
                                                Victor 66104, 717

KREISLER – *Continued*

Berceuse romantique, Op. 9 vln & pf
with C. Lamson pf   HMV 4–7954, DA261
Rococo 2005
Victor 64565, 711

Caprice viennois, Op. 2 vln & pf
with G. Falkenstein pf   A 8940   Delta TQD3031
Everest SDBR3258
HMV 07935, DB314
Supraphon 0 11 0436
Victor 74197, 6181

Caprice viennois, Op. 2 vln & pf
with piano   A 5697[8]   HMV 07960

Caprice viennois, Op. 2 vln & pf
with C. Lamson pf   A 8940△   HMV DB1091
Victor 6692, RB16268, VIC1372

Caprice viennois, Op. 2 vln & pf
with F. Rupp pf   2RA 1484[III]□   HMV DB3050
Victor 14690

Caprice viennois, Op. 2 vln & pf
     VP–813–D4–TC–257–1B   V–Disc 304
with orch. – Voorhees

Caprice viennois, Op. 2 vln & pf
with Victor Symphony Orch. –   HMV CSLP506
O'Connell   Victor (in set WCT63), 11–8230,
(in set M910), LCT1049

(La) Gitana vln & pf
with orch.   A 22866   HMV 4–7998, DA275
Victor 64842, 709

(La) Gitana vln & pf
with F. Rupp pf   OEA 6103[I]□   Angel GR11
Electrola E60800
HMV COLH19, DA1629,
WDLP700, XLP30009

(La) Gitana vln & pf
with Victor Symphony Orch. –   HMV CSLP506
O'Connell   Victor (in set WCT63), 11–8232,
(in set M910), LCT1049

Gypsy Caprice vln & pf
with C. Lamson pf   A 37461△   HMV DB1110
Victor 6712, VIC1372

(The) King Steps Out – film
Stars in my eyes arr. vln & pf Kreisler
with Victor Symphony Orch. –   Victor 10–1395
Voorhees

Liebesfreud vln & pf
with G. Falkenstein pf   A 5700   Delta TQD3031
Everest SDBR3258
HMV 07963, DB479
Victor (in set WCT3), 74196,
6182, LCT1002

Liebesfreud vln & pf
with C. Lamson pf   A 8951△   HMV DB985
Victor 6608, VIC1372

Liebesfreud vln & pf
with F. Rupp pf   OEA 6111[IA]□   Angel GR11
Electrola E60800
HMV COLH19, DA1630,
WDLP700, XLP30009
Victor 1891, RB16207

KREISLER – *Continued*

Leibesfreud vln & pf
with Victor Symphony Orch. –   HMV CSLP506, DB10127
O'Connell   Victor (in set WCT63), 11–8231,
(in set M910), LCT1049

Liebesleid vln & pf
with G. Falkenstein pf   A 8950   Delta TQD3031
HMV 07942, DB315
Victor (in set WCT3), 74333,
6182, LCT1002

Liebesleid vln & pf
with C. Lamson pf   A 8950△   HMV DB985
Victor 6608, VIC1372

Liebesleid vln & pf
with F. Rupp pf   OEA 6110[I]□   Angel GR11
Electrola E60800
HMV COLH19, DA1629,
WDLP700, XLP30009
Victor 1950

Liebesleid vln & pf
with Victor Symphony Orch. –   HMV CSLP506, DB10127
O'Connell   Victor (in set WCT63), 11–8231,
(in set M910), LCT1049

Marche miniature viennoise vln & pf – arr. vln, vlc & pf Kreisler
with H. Kreisler vlc   Bw 1240[III]△   HMV DA961
& M. Raucheisen pf   Victor 3035

Marche miniature viennoise vln & pf
with Victor Symphony Orch. –   Victor 10–1202, (in set M1044)
Voorhees

Polichinelle–serenade vln & pf
with G. Falkenstein pf   HMV 4–7958, DA277
Victor 64731, 721

Polichinelle–serenade vln & pf
with M. Raucheisen   BLR 6064[III]△   HMV DA1215
pf   Victor 1501

Quartet in a (1919) 2 vlns, vla & vlc
   2EA 1370[I]□, 1371/2[II]□, 1373[I]   HMV DB2483/6
   □, 1374[II]□, 1375[I]□ & 1376[II]□   Victor 14249/52, (set M335)
with T. Petrie vln, W. Primrose vla &
L. Kennedy vlc

Rondino on a theme by Beethoven vln & pf
with string quartet   A 17754   HMV 4–7966, DA264
Victor 64600, 64575, 715

Rondino on a theme by Beethoven vln & pf
with C. Lamson pf   A 16985△   Camden CAL518, CDN1026
HMV DA1044
Victor 1386, A430378

Rondino on a theme by Beethoven vln & pf
with F. Rupp pf   OEA 6098[I]□   Angel GR11
Electrola E60800
HMV COLH19, DA1628,
WDLP700, XLP30009
Victor 10–1022, LCT1142

Rondino on a theme by Beethoven vln & pf
with Victor Symphony Orch. –   Victor 10–1203, (in set M1044)
Voorhees

Schön Rosmarin vln & pf
with G. Falkenstein pf   HMV 3–7953, DA277
Victor 64314, 721

KREISLER – *Continued*

Schön Rosmarin vln & pf
with C. Lamson pf   A 12730△   HMV DA1044
Victor 1386, VIC1372

Schön Rosmarin vln & pf
with F. Rupp pf   OEA 6109–I   Angel GR11
Electrola E60800
HMV COLH19, DA1627,
WDLP700, XLP30009

Schön Rosmarin vln & pf
with Victor Symphony Orch. –   HMV CSLP506
O'Connell   Victor (in set WCT63), 11–8232,
(in set M910), LCT1049

Shepherd's madrigal vln & pf
with C. Lamson pf   A 38219△   HMV DB1110
Victor 6712, VIC1372

Slavonic Fantasia in b (on themes by Dvořák) vln & pf
with G. Falkenstein pf   Victor 74172, 6188

Syncopation vln & pf – arr. vln, vlc & pf Kreisler
with H. Kreisler vlc   Bw 1239^{IV}△   HMV DA961
& M. Raucheisen pf   Victor 3035

Tambourin chinois, Op. 3 vln & pf
with C. Lamson pf   A 15745   HMV 07961, 2–07926, DB318
Delta TQD3031
Everest SDBR3258
Victor 74203, 6185

Tambourin chinois, Op. 3 vln & pf
with C. Lamson pf   A 15743△   HMV DB1207
Victor 6844, VIC1372

Tambourin chinois, Op. 3 vln & pf
with F. Rupp pf   2RA 1485^{1}□   HMV DB3050
Victor 14690

Tambourin chinois, Op. 3 vln & pf
with Victor Symphony Orch. –   HMV CSLP506
O'Connell   Victor (in set WCT63), 11–8230,
(in set M910), LCT1049

Toy soldier's march vln & pf
with C. Lamson pf   HMV DA284
Victor 66137, 728

Viennese Rhapsodic Fantasietta vln & orch.
with Victor Symphony Orch. –   Victor 11–9952
Voorhees

Allegretto (Boccherini) vln & pf
with G. Falkenstein pf   A 5696   Delta TQD3031
HMV 07959, DB488

Andantino (Padre Martini) vln & pf
with G. Falkenstein pf   HMV 3–7954, DA276
Victor 64315, 710

Aubade provençale (L. Couperin) vln & pf
with G. Falkenstein pf   A 14414   HMV 3–7941, DA521
Victor 64202, 713

Chanson Louis XIII & Pavane (L. Couperin) vln & pf
with G. Falkenstein pf   A 5704   Delta TQD3031
HMV 07967, DB479

Chanson Louis XIII & Pavane (L. Couperin) vln & pf
with G. Falkenstein pf   Victor 64292, 713

Chanson Louis XIII & Pavane (L. Couperin) vln & pf
with M. Raucheisen   BLR 6069^{II}△   HMV DA1139, HQM1104
pf   Victor 1503, VIC1372

KREISLER – *Continued*

Chanson Louis XIII & Pavane (L. Couperin) vln & pf
with Victor Symphony Orch. –   Victor 11–9265, 11–9266, (in set
Voorhees   M1070)

(La) Chasse (Cartier) vln & pf
with piano   HMV 3–7942, DA521

Concerto in C (Vivaldi) vln & strs
with Victor String Orch. – Voorhees   Victor 11–9264/5, 11–9266/7,
(set DM1070), LCT1142

(La) Précieuse (L. Couperin) vln & pf
with piano   A 5692   Delta TQD3031
HMV 07957

(La) Précieuse (L. Couperin) vln & pf
with M. Raucheisen   BLR 6068^{III}△   HMV DA1139, HQM1104
pf   Victor 1503

Scherzo (Dittersdorf) vln & pf
with G. Falkenstein pf   A 5694   Delta TQD3031
HMV 07958, DB320
Victor 64568, 74294, 6187

Scherzo (Dittersdorf) vln & pf – arr. str qt
with T. Petrie vln,   2EA 2001^{IV}□   HMV DB2486
W. Primrose vla & L. Kennedy vlc   Victor 14252, 14256

Variations on a theme of Corelli (Tartini) vln & pf
with G. Falkenstein pf   Delta TQD3031
HMV 3–7927, DA276
Rococo 2005
Victor 64156, 710

LARCHET

Padraic the fiddler v & pf – arr. v, vln & pf
with J. McCormack t &   Bb 5118–2   HMV 6–2040, DA636, IR1010
V. O'Brien pf

LEHÁR

Frasquita (1923) – operetta
Hab' ein blaues Himmelbett arr. vln & pf as "Serenade" by Kreisler
with C. Lamson pf   HMV DA792, DA815
Victor 1158

LEMARE

Andantino, Op. 83, No. 2 pf – arr. vln & pf Saenger
with C. Lamson pf   A 35121   HMV 3–7954, DA803
Victor 1165

LEROUX

(Le) Nil v & pf – arr. v, vln & pf
with J. McCormack t &   A 14625   HMV 2–032016, IRX1012
V. O'Brien pf   Rococo 5301
Victor 88482, 89105

LILIUOKALANI, Queen

Aloha Oe (1892) v & pf – arr. vln & pf Kreisler
with C. Lamson pf   A 33189△   HMV DA745
Victor 1115

LOGAN

Pale moon (1920) v & pf – arr. vln & pf Kreisler
with G. Falkenstein pf   HMV DA284
Victor 66127, 728

MASCAGNI

Cavalleria Rusticana (1890) – opera
Intermezzo orch. – arr. v, vln & pf*
with J. McCormack t &   A 14652   HMV 4–2471, DA458
V. O'brien pf   Victor 87192, 87546, 3021

MASSENET

Thaïs (1894) – opera
Méditation arr. vln & pf Marsick
with G. Falkenstein pf   Everest SDBR3258
                                          HMV 2–07983, DB319
                                          Victor 74182, 6186

Méditation arr. vln & pf Marsick
with C. Lamson pf   A 8944   HMV CSLP506, DB1207
                                          Victor (in set WCT80), 6844,
                                          LCT1049

MATTEI

Non è ver v & pf – arr. v, vln & pf
with J. McCormack t &   A 17651   Victor†
piano

MENDELSSOHN

Concerto in e, Op. 64 vln & pf
          CwR 614^{IIA}△, 615/7^{IA}△, 618/9   HMV DB997/1000
with Berlin State ^{IIA}△ & 620^{IIIA}△   Rococo 2005
Opera Orch. – Blech   Victor 8080/3, (set M19)

Concerto in e, Op. 64 vln & orch.
          2EA 1465^{IVA}□, 1466^{IIA}□, 1467   HMV DB2460/2, DB7889/91,
^{IA}□, 1468^{IIA}□, 1469^{IA}□ & 1470^{IV}□   HQM1104
with London Philharmonic Orch. –   Seraphim (in set IC6044)
Ronald   Victor 8786/8, 16689/91, (set
                                          M277), LCT1117

(6) Songs without words, Op. 62 pf
No. 1. Song without words No. 25, in G "May breezes" arr. vln & pf
Kreisler
with G. Falkenstein pf   HMV 3–7969, DA529
                                          Victor 64542

No. 1. Song without words No. 25, in G "May breezes" arr. vln & pf
Kreisler
with A. Sándor pf   Cw 622^{IIA}△   HMV DB1000, DB2117
                                          Victor 8083

MEYER–HELMUND

(3) Lieder, Op. 73 v & pf
No. 2. Ballgeflüster "Flirtation" arr. v, vln & pf
with J. McCormack t &   A 16092   HMV 4–2730, DA459
piano   Victor 87232, 87549, 3022

MOSZKOWSKI

(6) Klavierstücke, Op. 15 pf – 4 hands
No. 1. Serenata arr. v, vln & orch.
with J. McCormack t &   A 16090   HMV 4–2700, DA455
orch.   Victor 87230, 87547, 3018

* Entitled "Ave Maria".
† Unissued.

MOZART

Concerto No. 4, in D, K218 (cadenzas by Kreisler) vln & orch.
          Cc 5396^{II}, 5397^{I}, 5398^{III}, 5399^{I},   HMV DB815/8
with London   5400/01^{II} & 5408/9^{I} Victor 6516/9, 6520/3
Philharmonic Orch. – Ronald

Concerto No. 4, in D, K218 (cadenzas by Kreisler) vln & orch.
          2EA 6212^{III}□, 6213^{IV}□, 6214^{II} HMV DB3734/6, DB8637/9
          □, 6215^{III}□ & 6216/7^{IV}□   Victor 15759/61, (set M623),
with London Philharmonic Orch. –   LCT1117
Sargent

Serenade No. 7, in D, K250 "Haffner" orch.
Rondo (4th mvt) arr. vln & pf Kreisler
          2EA 6101^{IIA}□ & 6102^{I}□   HMV DB3731, HQM1104
with F. Rupp pf   Victor 17220

NEVIN

Mighty lak' a rose (1901) v & pf – arr. v, vln & orch.
with G. Farrar s & orch.   A 16043   HMV 03677, DB173
– Rogers   Victor (in set LM6099), 88537,
                                          89108, 8024, A430569, RB6525

Mighty lak' a rose (1901) v & pf – arr. vln & pf Kreisler
with C. Lamson pf   Victor 1320

(The) Rosary (1898) v & pf – arr. vln & pf Kreisler
with C. Lamson pf   HMV 4–7960, DA269
                                          Victor 64502, 720

(The) Rosary (1898) v & pf – arr. vln & pf Kreisler
with C. Lamson pf   A 13937△   HMV DA992
                                          Victor 1320

(The) Rosary (1898) v & pf – arr. vln & pf Kreisler
with Victor Symphony Orch. –   HMV CSLP506
Voorhees   Victor 10–1395

OFFENBACH

(Les) Contes d'Hoffmann (1881) – opera
Belle Nuit, O nuit d'amour "Barcarolle" arr. v, vln & pf
with J. McCormack t &   A 17655   HMV 5–2153, DA456
E. Schneider pf   Victor 87245, 87551, 3019

OPENSHAW

Love sends a little gift of roses (1919) v & pf – arr. vln & pf Kreisler
with C. Lamson pf   Victor 66231, 994

OWEN

Invocation pf – arr. vln & pf Kreisler
with C. Lamson pf   Victor 1209

PADEREWSKI

(6) Humoresques de concert, Op. 14 pf
No. 1. Minuet in G arr. vln & pf Kreisler
with string quartet   A 20333   HMV 4–7955, DA267
                                          Victor 64709, 718

(7) Miscellanea, Op. 16 pf
No. 2. Mélodie arr. vln & pf Kreisler
with C. Lamson pf   A 27727   HMV 6–7918, DA511
                                          Victor 66176, 947

PAGANINI

Concerto No. 1, in D, Op. 6 vln & orch.
Allegro maestoso (1st mvt) arr. Kreisler
with Philadelphia Orch. – Ormandy   HMV DB3234/5
                                          Victor 14420/1, (set M361),
                                          LCT1142, SP33–555

PERGOLESI

Tre giorni son che Nina v & c – arr. vln, vlc & pf Kreisler
with H. Kreisler vlc & M. Raucheisen   Victor 3036
pf

POLDINI

(7) Marionnettes pf
No. 2. Poupée valsante arr. vln & pf Kreisler
with C. Lamson pf   Victor 1029

No. 2. Poupée valsante arr. vln & pf Kreisler
with F. Rupp pf   OEA 6105–1A   Angel GR11
                                      Electrola E60800
                                      HMV COLH19, DA1622,
                                      WDLP700, XLP30009
                                      Victor 1981

RACHMANINOV

(6) Songs, Op. 4 v & pf
No. 3. In the silent night* arr. v, vln & pf
with J. McCormack t &   A 23905   Everest SDBR3258
E. Schneider pf   HMV 5–2263, DA457, IR1009
                                    Victor (in set LM6099), 87571,
                                    3020, A430569, RB6525

No. 4. O cease thy singing, maiden fair arr. v, vln & pf
with J. McCormack t &   A 23906   HMV 5–2377, DA457
E. Schneider pf   Victor (in set LM6099), 87574,
                                    3020, A430569, RB6525

(12) Songs, Op. 21 v & pf
No. 7. How fair this spot arr. v, vln & pf
with J. McCormack t &   Bb 5101–1 HMV 6–2038, DA680,
piano   HQM1176

(15) Songs, Op. 26 (1906) v & pf
No. 7. To the children arr. v, vln & pf
with J. McCormack t &   Bb 5117–2 HMV 6–2114, DA680,
piano   HQM1176

No. 10. Before my window arr. v, vln & pf
with J. McCormack t &   Bb 5116   HMV 6–2039, DA644
piano

(6) Songs, Op. 38 (1916) v & pf
No. 3. Daisies arr. vln & pf as "Albumblatt–Marguerite" by Kreisler
with C. Lamson pf   HMV DA815
                                    Victor 1170, LCT1142

RAFF

Serenade, Op. 1 pf – arr. v, vln & pf Rosier
with J. McCormack t &   A 17654   HMV 4–2953, DA456
E. Schneider pf   Victor 87258, 87552, 3019

RAMEAU

(Les) Fêtes D'Hébé (1739) – opera
Tambourin orch. – arr. vln & pf Kreisler
with M. Eisner pf   A 8945   HMV 2–07984, DB318
                                    Victor 74202, 6185

RIMSKY–KORSAKOV

(Le) Coq d'Or (1910) – opera
Hymn to the sun arr. vln & pf Kreisler
with C. Lamson pf   A 25133   HMV 3–07954, DB316
                                    Victor 74720, 6183

* Entitled "When night descends".

Hymn to the sun arr. vln & pf Kreisler
with F. Rupp pf   2EA 6108¹☐ Angel GR11
                                     Electrola E60800
                                     HMV COLH19, DB3444,
                                     WDLP700, XLP30009
                                     Victor 15487, LCT1142

Sadko (1898) – opera
Chant hindou arr. vln & pf Kreisler
with orch.   A 22869   HMV 5–7915, DA272
                                     Victor 64890, 706

Chant hindou arr. vln & pf Kreisler
with F. Rupp pf   OEA 6094¹☐ Angel GR11
                                     Electrola E60800
                                     HMV COLH19, DA1627,
                                     WDLP700, XLP30009
                                     Victor 1981

Scheherazade, Op. 35 (1888) orch.
The young Prince & the young Princesses (3rd mvt) arr. vln & pf as "Chanson arabe" by Kreisler
with C. Lamson pf   A 26425   HMV 5–7976, DA272
                                     Victor 66079, 706

Festival at Baghdad (4th mvt) arr. vln & pf as "Danse orientale" by Kreisler
with C. Lamson pf   Victor 1075

(4) Songs, Op. 2 (1865/6) v & pf
No. 2. Enslaved by the rose & the nightingale arr. vln & pf as "Oriental romance" by Gordon
with C. Lamson pf   HMV DA857
                                     Victor 1209

ROMBERG

(The) Student Prince (1924) – operetta
Deep in my heart, dear arr. vln & pf Kreisler
with C. Lamson pf   A 34703△   HMV DA785
                                    Victor 1151

SCHUBERT, François

(12) Bagatelles, Op. 13 vln & pf
No. 9. L'abeille
with piano   2085 X   Gramophone & Typewriter
                                    47945
                                    Rococo 2005

SCHUBERT, Franz

(7) Gesänge (set to Scott's "Lady of the Lake") Op. 52 v & pf
No. 6. Ave Maria, D839 arr. v, vln & pf
with J. McCormack t &   A 14633   Camden CAL635
V. O'Brien pf   HMV 02543, DB578
                                    Victor 88484, 89107, 8033

(6) Moments musicaux, Op. 94 (D780) (1823/7) pf
No. 3. Moment musicale No. 3, in f "Air russe" arr. vln & pf Kreisler
with M. Eisner pf   A 8943   HMV 2–07984, DB318
                                    Victor 64555, 74202, 6185

Rosamunde von Cypern, Op. 26 (D797) (1823) – Incidental music orch.
No. 9. Ballet music II, in G arr. vln & pf Kreisler
with orch.   A 19328   HMV 4–7962, DA279
                                    Victor 64670, 723

No. 9. Ballet music II, in G arr. vln & pf Kreisler
with M. Raucheisen   BLR 6067ᴵᴵᴵ△ HMV DA1137, HQM1104
pf   Victor 1505, 26573

SCHUBERT, Franz – *Continued*

(14) Schwanengesang, D957 (1828) v & pf
No. 4. Ständchen "Serenade" arr. v, vln & pf
with J. McCormack t & A 14651 HMV 4–2470, DA458
V. O'Brien pf   Victor 87191, 87545, 3021

Sonata in A, Op. 162 (D574) "Duo" vln & pf
with S. Rachmaninov A 49280/5△ HMV DB1465/7
pf   Victor (in set WCT1128),
             8216/8, (set M107), (in set
             LM6099), LCT1128, LVT1009,
             RB16154

SCHUMANN

(12) Duets, Op. 85 pf – 4 hands
No. 12. Abendlied arr. vln, vlc & pf Kreisler
with H. Kreisler vlc & M. Raucheisen Victor 3036
pf

(3) Romances, Op. 94 ob or vlc, or vln or cl & pf
Romance No. 2, in A arr. vln & pf Kreisler
with M. Raucheisen Cw 1434ᴵᴵᴵ△ HMV DB1122
pf   Victor 8102

SCHÜTT

(3) Morceaux, Op. 53 vln & pf
No. 1. Élégie slave arr. as "Slavonic lament" by Friedberg
with C. Lamson pf   Victor 1043

SCOTT, Cyril

Lotus land, Op. 47, No. 1 (1905) pf – arr. vln & pf Kreisler
with A. Sándor pf   Victor 6706

Lotus land, Op. 47, No. 1 (1905) pf – arr. vln & pf Kreisler
with F. Rupp pf 2EA 6099ᴵᴬ☐ Angel GR11
          HMV DB3444, XLP30009
          Victor 15487

SCOTT, Lady John

Annie Lauri (1838) v & pf – arr. v, vln & orch.
with G. Farrar s & orch. A 16046 Victor*

SEITZ

(The) World is waiting for the sunrise (1919) v & pf – arr. vln & pf
Kreisler
with C. Lamson pf   Victor 66232, 994

SMETANA

From my Homeland (1878) vln & pf
No. 2. Andantino
with G. Falkenstein pf   Everest SDBR3258
          HMV DB321
          Victor 74172

SPENCER

Underneath the stars v & pf – arr. vln & pf Pasternack
with orch.   HMV 4–7963, DA268
          Victor 64660, 719

* Unissued.

STRAUSS, R.

(4) Lieder, Op. 27 v & pf
No. 4. Morgen arr. v, vln & pf
with J. McCormack t & Bb 5115 HMV 7–42089, DA644
piano

SULZER

Sarabande, Op. 8 vln or vlc & pf
with piano   2085 X Gramophone & Typewriter
          47945
          Rococo 2005

TCHAIKOVSKY

(2) Pieces, Op. 10 pf
No. 2. Humoresque in G arr. vln & pf Kreisler
with C. Lamson pf A 31872△ HMV DA803, DA815
          Victor 1170, LCT1142

Quartet No. 1, in D, Op. 11 2 vlns, vla & vlc
Andante cantabile (2nd mvt) arr. vln & pf Kreisler
with string quartet A 17671 HMV 2–07987, DB588
          Victor 74487, 6184

Andante cantabile (2nd mvt) arr. vln & pf Kreisler
with F. Rupp pf 2EA 6095ᴵ☐ Electrola E60800
          HMV COLH19, CSLP506,
          DB3443, WDLP700, XLP30009
          Victor (in set WCT80), 15217,
          LCT1049

(3) Souvenirs de Hapsal, Op. 2 pf
No. 3. Chant sans paroles in f arr. vln & pf Kreisler
with piano   2084 X Gramophone & Typewriter
          37952, 47944

No. 3. Chant sans paroles in f arr. vln & pf Kreisler
with G. Falkenstein pf A 5702 HMV 07965, DB315

No. 3. Chant sans paroles in f arr. vln & pf Kreisler
with G. Falkenstein pf A 8952 Delta TQD3031
          HMV 3–7926, DA265
          Supraphon 0 11 0436
          Victor 64142, 716

THOMAS

Mignon (1866) – opera
Connais–tu le pays?
with G. Farrar s & orch. A 16045 Belcantodisc BC241
– Rogers   HMV 2–033054, DB173
          Victor (in set LM6099), 88538,
          89104, 8024, A430569, RB6525

TOSTI

(La) Serenata v & pf – arr. v, vln, hp & str qt
with G. Farrar s, F.J. Lapitino hp & Victor 88535*
string quartet

TOWNSEND

Berceuse vln & pf
with G. Falkenstein pf A 12727 HMV 3–7956, DA261
          Victor 64319, 711

* Unissued.

VALDEZ

Sérénade du Tzigane vln & pf
with orch.
    A 22868   HMV 5–7902, DA275
                          Victor 64857, 709

WEBER

(6) Sonatas, Op. 10 (J99/104) (1810) vln & pf
  Sonata No. 1, in F: Romanze (2nd mvt) arr. vln & pf as "Larghetto" by Kreisler
  with piano
                    HMV DA437
  Sonata No. 1, in F: Romanze (2nd mvt) arr. vln & pf as "Larghetto" by Kreisler
  with M. Raucheisen   BLR 6070¹△   HMV DA1137, HQM1104
  pf   Victor 1505, 26573

WHITE

Bandana Sketches, Op. 12 vln & pf
  No. 1. Nobody knows de trouble I see (Negro spiritual)
  with orch.
                    HMV 4–7956, DA278
                    Victor 64824, 722

WINTERNITZ

Dance of the marionettes vln & pf
  with C. Lamson pf   A 41758   HMV DA1215
                                  Victor 1501

Dream of youth vln & pf
  with orch.
                    HMV DA274
                    Victor 64730, 708

Guidon KREMER (1947–)

CHAUSSON

Poème, Op. 25 vln & orch.
  with Y. Smirnov pf
                    Mezhdunarodnaya Kniga
                    SM02035/6

CORELLI

(12) Sonatas, Op. 5 vln & c
  Sonata No. 1, in D (ed. A. Tony)
  with Y. Smirnov pf
                    Mezhdunarodnaya Kniga
                    SM02035/6

ERNST

(6) Mehrstimmige Studien solo vln
  No. 6. Etude No. 6, in G (Variations on "The last rose of summer") (à Bazzini)
  (unaccompanied)
                    Mezhdunarodnaya Kniga
                    D028103/4

GEMINIANI

(6) Sonatas, Op. 5 (1739) solo vln
  Sonata in B flat (ed. Corti)
  (unaccompanied)
                    Melodisc 80896K
                    Mezhdunarodnaya Kniga
                    D022629/30, SM02387/8

HAYDN

Sonata No. 3, in E flat, H.XVI, No. 25 (1773) vln & hpsi
  with Y. Smirnov pf
                    Mezhdunarodnaya Kniga
                    SM02035/6

KREISLER

Rondino on a theme by Beethoven vln & pf
  with H. Braun pf
                    Melodisc 80896K
                    Mezhdunarodnaya Kniga
                    D022629/30, SM02387/8

LOCATELLI

(12) Sonatas, Op. 6 (1737) vln & c
  Sonata No. 7 in f "Au Tombeau" arr. vln & pf Ysaÿe
  with H. Braun pf
                    Melodisc 80896K
                    Mezhdunarodnaya Kniga
                    D022629/30, SM02387/8

PAGANINI

Cantabile in D, Op. 17 vln & gtr
  with H. Braun pf
                    Melodisc 80896K
                    Mezhdunarodnaya Kniga
                    D022629/30, SM02387/8

(24) Caprices, Op. 1 (1801/7) solo vln
  Caprice No. 4, in c
  (unaccompanied)
                    Melodisc 80896K
                    Mezhdunarodnaya Kniga
                    D022629/30, SM02387/8

  Caprice No. 17, in E flat
  (unaccompanied)
                    Mezhdunarodnaya Kniga
                    D028737/8

SHCHEDRIN

In imitation of Albéniz pf – arr. vln & pf Tziganov
  with H. Braun pf
                    Melodisc 80896K
                    Mezhdunarodnaya Kniga
                    D022629/30, SM02387/8

TCHAIKOVSKY

Concerto in D, Op. 35 vln & orch.
  with USSR Symphony Orch. – Temirkanov
                    Eurodisc (in set 80979XK)
                    Mezhdunarodnaya Kniga
                    D028737/8

Waltz–scherzo, Op. 34 vln & pf or orch.
  with Y. Smirnov pf
                    Mezhdunarodnaya Kniga
                    D028737/8

WIENIAWSKI

(8) Étude–Caprices, Op. 18 solo vln & 2nd vln obb
  Étude–Caprice No. 4, in a arr. vln & pf Kreisler
  with H. Braun pf
                    Melodisc 80896K
                    Mezhdunarodnaya Kniga
                    D022629/30, SM02387/8

Variations in A, (on an original theme) Op. 15 vln & pf
  with Y. Smirnov pf
                    Mezhdunarodnaya Kniga
                    SM02035/6

Editha KRENGEL

DVOŘÁK

(8) Humoresques, Op. 101 pf
  No. 7. Humoresque No. 7, in G flat arr. vln & pf "in G" Wilhelmj
  with piano   Vox 6116

RAFF

(6) Pieces, Op. 85 vln & pf
No. 3. Cavatina in D
with piano   Vox 6117

TCHAIKOVSKY

Souvenir d'un lieu cher, Op. 42 vln & pf
No. 3. Mélodie
with piano   Vox 6117

WIENIAWSKI

Mazurka in a, Op. 3 "Kujawiak" vln & pf
with piano   Vox 6116

Robert KRETTLY (1891-   )

LÉONARD

(5) Scènes humoristiques, Op. 61 vln & pf
No. 1. Coq et poules
with string quartet   Columbia 2972D, LF87
No. 3. Chatte et souris
with string quartet   Columbia 2972D, LF87

Alfred KRIPS

DELIBES

Coppélia (1870) – ballet orch.
excerpts
with Boston Symphony Orch. – Monteux   Victor (in set LM6113), A630218, A12R0131, LM1913
Sylvia (1876) – ballet orch.
excerpts
with Boston Symphony Orch. – Monteux   Victor (in set LM6113), A630219, A12R0131, LM1913

GADE

Jealousy (1927) orch. – arr. vln & orch.
with Boston "Pops" Orch. – Fiedler   Victor LM2810, LSC2810

GROFÉ

Grand Canyon Suite (1931) orch.
On the trail (3rd mvt)
with L. Litwin cel & Boston "Pops" Orch. – Fiedler   Victor LM2810, LSC2789, LSC2810

KREISLER

Caprice viennois, Op. 2 vln & pf
with Boston "Pops" Orch. – Fiedler   Victor ERB7047, LM1910, LRM7047
(La) Gitana vln & pf
with Boston "Pops" Orch. – Fiedler   Victor ERB7047, LM1910, LRM7047

LUMBYE

Concert-Polka (1863) 2 vlns & orch.
with G. Zazofsky vln & Boston "Pops" Orch. – Fiedler   Victor LM2885, LSC2885

MOZART

Quintet in A, K581 cl, 2 vlns, vla & vlc
with B. Goodman cl, R. Burgin vln, J. de Pasquale vla & S. Mayes vlc   Victor LM2173, RB16013

WAGNER

(5) Gedichte "Wesendonck–Lieder" v & pf
No. 5. Träume arr. vln & orch.
with Boston "Pops" Orch. – Fiedler   Victor INTS1035, LSC3023

William KROLL (1901-   )

BACH

Concerto in a, BWV1044 clav, fl, vln strs & c
     2A 021641△, 021642^{II}△,&   HMV DB3796/8
with Y. Pessl hpsi, F.   021649/52 △,   Victor 15330/2, (set M534)
Blaisdell fl & string orch. – Bamberger

BEETHOVEN

Sonata No. 9, in A, Op. 47 "Kreutzer" vln & pf
with G. Johannesen pf   Golden Crest CR4072

ENGEL

Triptych (1920) vln & pf
with F. Sheridan pf   Schirmer 15

MOZART

Sonata No. 17, in C, K296 vln & pf
with A. Balsam pf   L'Oiseau–Lyre OL50213, SOL60044

Sonata No. 21, in e, K304 vln & pf
with A. Balsam pf   L'Oiseau–Lyre OL50212, SOL60043

Sonata No. 22, in A, K305 vln & pf
with A. Balsam pf   L'Oiseau–Lyre OL50213, SOL60044

Sonata No. 27, in G, K379 vln & pf
with A. Balsam pf   L'Oiseau–Lyre OL50212, SOL60043

Sonata No. 32, in B flat, K454 vln & pf
with A. Balsam pf   L'Oiseau–Lyre OL50213, SOL60044

Sonata No. 33, in E flat, K481 vln & pf
with A. Balsam pf   L'Oiseau–Lyre OL50212, SOL60043

RIEGGER

Trio, Op. 1 (1920) pf, vln & vlc
with J. Covelli pf & A. Kouguell vlc   Columbia ML5589, MS6189

TURNER

Serenade for Icarus (1960) vln & pf
with G. Johannesen pf   Golden Crest CR4072

Werner KROTZINGER

BACH

(6) Brandenburg Concerti, BWV1046/51 (1721) strs & c
Brandenburg Concerto No. 1, in F, BWV1046 vln, 3 obs, bsn, 2 hrns & strs

with F. Fischer ob, H. Weber ob, F. Schweinfurter ob, H. Anton bsn, K. Krumbein hrn, H. Irmscher hrn, I. Lechner hpsi & Stuttgart Chamber Orch. – Münchinger	Decca LXT5512, SXL2125 London CHA7211, (in set CSA2301)

Brandenburg Concerto No. 2, in F, BWV1047 tpt, fl, ob, vln & strs

with A. Scherbaum tpt, W. Glas fl, F. Fischer ob, S. Barchet vlc, I. Lechner hpsi & Stuttgart Chamber Orch. – Münchinger	Decca BR3081, CEP635, LXT5513, SAWD8530, SXL2126 London CHA7212, (in set CSA2301)

Brandenburg Concerto No. 4, in G, BWV1049 vln, 2 fls & strs

with W. Glas fl, K.F. Mess fl, S. Barchet vlc, I. Lechner hpsi & Stuttgart Chamber Orch. – Münchinger	Decca BR3081, LXT5513, SXL2127 London CHA7212, (in set CSA2301)

Brandenburg Concerto No. 5, in D, BWV1050 clav, fl, vln & strs

with I. Lechner hpsi, W. Glas fl, S. Barchet vlc & Stuttgart Chamber Orch. – Münchinger	Decca BR3007, LW50166, LXT5513, SLW50166, SXL2126 London CHA7212, (in set CSA2301)

Cantata No. 202 (Weichet nur, betrübte Schatten) BWV202

with S. Danco s, F. Fischer ob, G. Vaucher–Clerc hpsi & Stuttgart Chamber Orch. – Münchinger	Decca LXT2926 London LL993

(Ein) Musikalisches Opfer, BWV1079 (1749) strs

with W. Glas fl, S. Barchet vlc, U. Strauss vla, H–P. Weber ob & hrn, I. Lechner hpsi & Stuttgart Chamber Orch. – Münchinger	Decca LXT5036, SXL2204 London CM9127, CS6142, LL1181

VIVALDI

(12) Concerti, Op. 8 (1725) "Il Cimento dell' Armonia e dell' Invenzione" (nos. 1/4: Le quattro Stagioni) vln & strs
Concerto No. 1, in E, F.I, No. 22 "La Primavera"

with Stuttgart Chamber Orch. – Münchinger	Decca CEP622, LXT5519, SEC5038, SMD1143, SXL2019 Eclipse ECM506, ECS506 London CM9037, CS6044 Telefunken SAWD9919

Concerto No. 2, in B flat, F.I, No. 23 "L'Estate"

with Stuttgart Chamber Orch. – Münchinger	Decca CEP622, LXT5519, SMD1143, SEC5038, SXL2019 Eclipse ECM506, ECS506 London CM9037, CS6044 Telefunken SAWD9919

Concerto No. 3, in F, F.I, No. 24 "L'Autunno"

with Stuttgart Chamber Orch. – Münchinger	Decca CEP622, LXT5519, SEC5038, SMD1143, SXL2019 Eclipse ECM506, ECS506 London CM9037, CS6044 Telefunken SAWD9919

VIVALDI – *Continued*

Concerto No. 4, in f, F.I, No. 25 "L'Inverno"

with Stuttgart Chamber Orch. – Münchinger	Decca CEP622, LXT5519, SEC5038, SMD1143, SXL2019 Eclipse ECM506, ECS506 London CM9037, CS6044 Telefunken SAWD9919

Boris KROYT (1897–1969)*

CHOPIN

Nocturne No. 19, in e, Op. 72, No. 1 pf – arr. vln & pf Auer

with C. Stabernack pf	Parlophone P1371

DRDLA

Serenade No. 1, in A vln & pf

with piano	Vox 06150

Souvenir vln & pf

with piano	Vox 06150

KREISLER

Grave (W.F. Bach) vln & pf

with C. Stabernack Mustel org	Parlophone P1371

Oleg KRYSA (1942–   )

BEETHOVEN

(3) Sonatas, Op. 30 vln & pf
No. 2. Sonata No. 7, in c

with I. Kollegorskaya pf	Mezhdunarodnaya Kniga D017943/4

BRAHMS

Sonata No. 1, in G, Op. 78 vln & pf

with I. Kollegorskaya pf	Mezhdunarodnaya Kniga D017619/20

HINDEMITH

(6) Sonatas, Op. 11 var. cbns
Sonata No. 1, in E flat (1920) vln & pf

with I. Kollegorskaya pf	Mezhdunarodnaya Kniga D017943/4

MOZART

Adagio in E, K261 vln & orch.

with I. Kollegorskaya pf	Mezhdunarodnaya Kniga D017943/4

PAGANINI

Cantabile in D, Op. 17 vln & gtr

with I. Kollegorskaya pf	Mezhdunarodnaya Kniga D017943/4

RAVEL

Tzigane (Rapsodie de concert) (1924) vln & pf or orch.

with I. Kollegorskaya pf	Mezhdunarodnaya Kniga D017619/20

* Also violist with Budapest string quartet.

SIBELIUS

Novelette, Op. 102 vln & pf – arr. Press
  with I. Kollegorskaya pf   Mezhdunarodnaya Kniga
                                    D017619/20

Pan & Echo, Op. 53 orch.
  No. 3. Nocturne arr. vln & pf Press
  with I. Kollegorskaya pf   Mezhdunarodnaya Kniga
                                    D017619/20

TCHAIKOVSKY

Souvenir d'un lieu cher, Op. 42 vln & pf
  No. 1. Méditation
  with I. Kollegorskaya pf   Mezhdunarodnaya Kniga
                                    D017619/20

WIENIAWSKI

Concerto No. 1, in f sharp, Op. 14 vln & orch.
  with Polish National Philharmonic   Muza XL0168
  Orch. – Satanowski

Jan KUBELÍK (1880–1940)

d'AMBROSIO

Serenade, Op. 4 vln & pf
  with piano   XPh 271[1]   Fonotipia 39191, F978
                                     Odeon 2239, 8008FXB, LX99984

ANONYMOUS*

Etude unid – vln & pf
  with piano   XPh 2229   Fonotipia†

BACH

(3) Sonatas & 3 Partitas, BWV1001/6 solo vln
  Partita No. 3, in E: Preludio (1st mvt)
  (unaccompanied)   XPh 2230   Fonotipia†
(4) Suites, BWV1066/9 strs & c
  Suite No. 3, in d: Air (2nd mvt) BWV1068 2 obs, 3 tpts, drms & strs –
  arr. vln & pf as "Air on the G–string" by Wilhelmj
  with G. Falkenstein pf   HMV 3–7966, S924
                              Victor 64390

BAZZINI

(La) Ronde des lutins, Op. 25 vln & pf
  with piano   XPh 295[2]   Fonotipia 39195, 72306, F980
                                 Odeon 8012FXC
                                 Okey 72306

(La) Ronde des lutins, Op. 25 vln & pf
  with piano   Asco A123
                                 Delta TQD3035
                                 Gramophone & Typewriter 07901

DRDLA

Berceuse, Op. 56 vln & pf
  with piano   Fonotipia 62574
                                 Odeon 8015FXC

* Composer unidentified.

† Unissued.

DRDLA – *Continued*

Serenade No. 1, in A vln & pf*
  with piano   XPh 284[4]   Fonotipia 39193, F977
                                 Odeon 2238, 8007FXB,
                                 8013FXC, LX99982, RX98113
                                 Okey 72301

Serenade No. 1, in D vln & pf
  with piano   Fonotipia 39193**

Serenade No. 1, in A vln & pf
  with piano   2701b   Gramophone & Typewriter 7956,
                                 47952
                                 Victor 5029, 88674, 91024

Serenade No.1, in D vln & pf
  with piano   Fonotipia 39193†

Souvenir vln & pf ‡
  with piano   XPh 270   Fonotipia 39162, F977
                                 Odeon 2236, 8007FXB,
                                 LX99981, RX98112
                                 Okey 72303

Souvenir vln & pf
  with piano   Fonotipia 39162§

Souvenir vln & pf
  with piano   HO 674 m   HMV 07980, DB496, S940

Visione, Op. 28 vln & pf
  with piano   XPh 2401   Fonotipia 62037, 72302, F982
                                 Odeon 8014FXC, LX99992
                                 Okey 72302

DVOŘÁK

(8) Humoresques, Op. 101 pf
  No. 7. Humoresque No. 7, in G flat arr. vln & pf "in G" Kreisler
  with piano   Ho 676 m   HMV 07981, S948
  No. 7. Humoresque No. 7, in G flat arr. vln & pf "in G" Kubelík
  with A. Holeček   031843   Supraphon G22326
  pfembossed.   Telefunken C22326
                                 Ultraphon G11386//

FIBICH

Images, Impressions & Souvenirs, Op. 41 pf
  No. 14. Poem (from "Souvenirs", Part IV) arr. vln & pf Kubelík
  with piano   xxPh 4552   Fonotipia 62573
                                 Odeon 8015FXC
                                 Pearl GEM102

  No. 14. Poem (from "Souvenirs", Part IV) arr. vln & pf Kubelík
  with A. Holeček pf   031843   Supraphon G22326
                                 Telefunken C22326
                                 Ultraphon G11386//

* Also matrix XPh 4307.

** Matrix XPh 4307 – Take IV. Catalog number unchanged.

† Matrix XPh 284[2] – Take II. Catalog number unchanged.

‡ Also matrix XPh 2402[2].

§ Matrix XPh 2402[2] – Take II. Catalog number unchanged.

// Matrix number 014843 is printed on the label while 031843 is embossed.

FIORILLO

(36) Étude–Caprices, Op. 3 solo vln
Caprice No. 28, in D (Allegro assai) arr. vln & pf Randegger
with piano   z 7329 f   HMV 07987, DB673

GLUCK

Orphée et Eurydice (1762) – opera
Dance of the blessed spirits: Lento "Mélodie" (No. 2) arr. vln & pf Wilhelmj
with piano   Ho 671 m   HMV 07978, DB674, S950

GOUNOD

Ave Maria (Méditation on Bach's "Prelude No. 1, in C" from Book I of "Das Wohltemperirte Clavier") v & pf – arr. v, vln & pf
with N. Melba s & G.   A 13897   HMV 03033, DK112
Lapierre pf   Victor 89073

Faust (1859) – opera
Nous nous retrouverons (Act II) arr. vln & pf as "Variazioni sulla ballata di Mefisto" by Kubelík
with piano   XPh 273²   Fonotipia 39164, F979
     Odeon 2240, 8009FXB

HANDEL

(15) Sonatas, Op. 1 (?1731) fl or vln & c
Sonata No. 15, in E: Adagio (1st mvt); **Allegro** (2nd mvt) vln VI
with G. Falkenstein pf   A 13876   HMV 2–07902, DB674
     Victor 74368

HUBAY

(6) Blumenleben, Op. 30 vln & pf
No. 5. Der Zephir
with piano   XPh 2228   Fonotipia 39925, 72304, F981
     Odeon 2243, 8010FXB
     Okey 72304

No. 5. Der Zephir
with A. Holeček pf   14845   Supraphon C22444
     Ultraphon C11384

KUBELÍK

Burlesque vln & pf
with A. Holeček pf   031844   Supraphon G22443

Canzonetta vln & pf
with A. Holeček pf   14842   Supraphon C22444
     Ultraphon C11384

MOZART

(Il) Re Pastore, K208 (1775) – opera
No. 10. L'Amerò, sarò costante
with N. Melba s & G.   z 7322 f   HMV 2–053083, DK112
Lapierre pf   Victor 89074

Romance in A flat, K.Anh.205 pf – arr. vln & pf Kubelík*
with piano   Ho 668 m   HMV 07976, DB490, S936
     Victor 88673

NACHÈZ

Danse hongrois No. 1, in G vln & pf
with piano   XPh 272²   Fonotipia 39163, F978
     Odeon 2238, 8008FXB, LX99983
     Rococo 2001

* Not by Mozart.

PAGANINI

(24) Caprices, Op. 1 (1801/7) solo vln
Caprice No. 6, in g
(unaccompanied)   XXR 4558   Fonotipia 74085
     Odeon 8019FXXE
     Rococo 2001

Concerto No. 1, in D, Op. 6 vln & orch.
Cadenza arr. Kubelík
(unaccompanied)   Fonotipia 74086
     Odeon 8019FXXE
     Okey 52301
     Rococo 2001

God save the King – variations, Op. 9 (1829) vln & orch.
with piano   XXPh 275   Fonotipia 69013, F984
     Odeon 8016FXC

Moto perpetuo (Allegro di concert) Op. 11 (1830) vln & orch.
with piano   XPh 276²   Fonotipia 39192, F980
     Odeon 8012FXC
     Pearl GEM102

Nel cor più non mi sento "Sonata appassionata con variazioni" (on the aria from Paisiello's opera "La bella molinara") Op. 38 (1820 or 1821) solo vln*
(unaccompanied)   4605b   Gramophone & Typewriter 7961
     Rococo 2001

RAFF

(6) Pieces, Op. 85 vln & pf
No. 3. Cavatina in D
with piano   XPh 2400²   Fonotipia 62036, F982
     Odeon 8014FXC, LX99986

RANDEGGER

Pierrot Sérénade, Op. 33, No. 1 vln & pf
with piano   XPh 4559   Fonotipia 62603
     Odeon 8013FXC

Pierrot Sérénade, Op. 33, No. 1 vln & pf
with piano   5123 f   HMV 07951, DB673, S934
     Victor 74256

RIES

Suite No. 3, in G, Op. 34 vln & pf
No. 5. Perpetuum mobile
with piano   5128 f   HMV 07954, S932
     Victor 74257

RUBINSTEIN

(6) Soirées de Saint–Pétersbourg, Op. 44 pf
No. 1. Romance in E flat arr. vln & pf Wilhelmj
with G. Falkenstein pf   z 7330 f   HMV 07986, DB675, S944
     Opera Disc 07986
     Victor 74365

ST. LUBIN

Sextet (from the opera "Lucia di Lammermoor" by Donizetti) Op. 56 solo vln
(unaccompanied)   2703   Gramophone & Typewriter 7957, 47953
     Rococo 2001
     Victor 5030, 91025

* Theme & pizzicato variations only.

ST. LUBIN – Continued

Sextet (from the opera "Lucia di Lammermoor" by Donizetti) Op. 56 solo vln
(unaccompanied)   Fonotipia 69010, F983
               Odeon 8016FXC

SAINT–SAËNS

(Le) Carnaval des aninaux (1886) small orch.
 Le cygne arr. vln & pf
 with piano   Fonotipia 62497
            Odeon 8017FXC
            Okey 72305

SARASATE

Carmen Fantasia (on themes from the opera by Bizet) Op. 25 vln & pf or orch.
 with piano   4601/2 Gramophone & Typewriter
           7967/8, 47954/5
           Rococo 2001*

(8) Danzas españolas vln & pf
 No. 3. Romanza andaluza, Op. 22, No. 1
 with G. Falkenstein pf   HMV 2–07904, DB675, S938
           Victor 74367

 No. 6. Zapateado, Op. 23, No. 2
 with piano   XPh 4305 Delta TQD3035
           Fonotipia 74083
           Odeon 8011FXXE, 0–9033
           Okey 52302

 No. 6. Zapateado, Op. 23, No. 2
 with piano   5126 f HMV 07953, DB676, S946
           Victor 74255

 No. 8. Danza española No. 8, in a, Op. 26, No. 2
 with G. Falkenstein pf z 7328 f HMV 07988, DB676, S926
           Opera Disc 72510
           Victor 74366

Zigeunerweisen, Op. 20 vln & pf or orch.
 with piano   XPh 2402 Fonotipia 74084
           Odeon 0–9033, 8011FXXE,
           LXX76993
           Pearl GEM102

Zigeunerweisen, Op. 20 vln & pf or orch.
 with piano   Ho 677 m HMV 07982, DB496, S930
           Opera Disc 72508
           Victor 88675

SCHUBERT

(7) Gesänge (set to Scott's "Lady of the Lake") Op. 52 v & pf
 No. 6. Ave Maria, D839 arr. vln & pf Wilhelmj
 with piano   XXPh 2404 Fonotipia†

 No. 6. Ave Maria, D839 arr. vln & pf Wilhelmj
 with A. Holeček pf 031846 Supraphon G22443

SCHUMANN

(13) Kinderscenen, Op. 15 pf
 No. 7. Träumerei arr. vln & pf
 with piano   XPh 285 Fonotipia 39194, F979
           Odeon 2241, LX99985

* Chanson bohème only is on Rococo 2001.
† Unissued.

SGAMBATI

(2) Pieces, Op. 24 vln & pf
 No. 2. Serenata napoletana
 with piano   Fonotipia 62496
           Odeon 8017FXC

SUK

(4) Pieces, Op. 17 vln & pf
 No. 4. Burleska
 with A. Holeček pf 031847 Supraphon G22326
           Telefunken C22326
           Ultraphon G11386*

TCHAIKOVSKY

Concerto in D, Op. 35 vln & orch.
 Canzonetta (2nd mvt)
 with G. Lapierre pf Ho 672 m HMV 07979, DB490, S922
           Victor 88672

WIENIAWSKI

Concerto No. 2, in d, Op. 22 vln & orch.
 Allegro con fuoco: Allegro moderato (a la Zingara) (3rd mvt)
 with G. Lapierre pf z 7326 f HMV 07989, DB672, S928
           Victor 74370

(2) Mazurkas, Op. 19 vln & pf
 No. 2. Mazurka No. 2, in D "Dudziarz"
 with piano   5124 f HMV 07952, DB672, S942

Scherzo–Tarantelle, Op. 16 vln & pf
 with piano   XPh 2231 Fonotipia 39884, F981
           Odeon 2242
           Pearl GEM102

Yoko KUBO

DVOŘÁK

(8) Humoresques, Op. 101 pf
 No. 7. Humoresque No. 7, in G flat arr. vln & pf "in G" Wilhelmj
 with piano   Mezhdunarodnaya Kniga
           D10075/6

IKENOUCHI

Sonatina No. 2 vln & pf
 Interlude & Finale
 with piano   Mezhdunarodnaya Kniga
           D10075/6

MOZART

Serenade No. 7, in D, K250 "Haffner" orch.
 Rondo (4th mvt) arr. vln & pf Kreisler
 with piano   Mezhdunarodnaya Kniga
           D10075/6

SAINT–SAËNS

Introduction & Rondo Capriccioso, Op. 28 vln & orch.
 with piano   Mezhdunarodnaya Kniga
           D10075/6

* Matrix number 014847 is printed on the label while 031843 is embossed.

SCHUBERT

(7) Gesänge (set to Scott's "Lady of the Lake") Op. 52 v & pf
No. 6. Ave Maria, D839 arr. vln & pf Wilhelmj
with piano   Mezhdunarodnaya Kniga
                              D10075/6

TCHAIKOVSKY

Souvenir d'un lieu cher, Op. 42 vln & pf
No. 2. Scherzo
with piano   Mezhdunarodnaya Kniga
                              D010325/8

Janusz KUCHARSKI

VIVALDI

Concerto in B flat, F.I, No. 40 2 vlns, strs & c
with I. Iwanow vln, J. Dobrzański hpsi Muza XL0504
& Warsaw Chamber Orch. –
Sutkowski

Manfred KUHN

LOCATELLI

Sonata in G (c1736) 2 vlns & c
with M. Geyrhalter vln, H. Langfort   Musical Heritage Society
hpsi & R. Harand vlc   MHS1037

Sigiswald KUIJKEN

BERTALI

Sonata in E 2 vlns & c
with J. Rubinlicht vln, R. Kohnen hpsi Telefunken SAWT9542
& W. Kuijken gamba

CASTILLO

Sonata concertante (1629)
Sonata in c 2 vlns & c
with J. Rubinlicht vln, R. Kohnen hpsi Telefunken SAWT9542
& W. Kuijken gamba

CAVALLI

Musiche Sacre Concernenti ... (1656)
Sonata in a 2 vlns & c
with J. Rubinlicht vln, R. Kohnen hpsi Telefunken SAWT9542
& W. Kuijken gamba

CIMA

(2) Concerti ecclesiastici (1610)
Sonata No. 1, in f vln, gamba & org
with W. Kuijken gamba & R. Kohnen   Telefunken SAWT9542
org

Sonata No. 2, in a 2 vlns, gamba & org
with J. Rubinlicht vln, W. Kuijken   Telefunken SAWT9542
gamba & R. Kohnen org

FARINA

(Il) Terzo libro primo della Pavane, Gagliarde ... (1626)
Sonata in f 2 vlns & c
with J. Rubinlicht vln, R. Kohnen hpsi Telefunken SAWT9542
& W. Kuijken gamba

ROSSI

Sonata in f (1613) 2 vlns & hpsi
with J. Rubinlicht vln & R. Kohnen   Telefunken SAWT9542
hpsi

VIVALDI

(12) Sonatas, Op. 1 2 vlns & c
Sonata No. 3, in C, F.XIII, No. 19
with F–J. Maier vln, G. Leonhardt   Harmonia Mundi CVH333,
hpsi & H. Beckendorf vlc   HMS30881

Georg KULENKAMPFF (1898–1948)

ADAM

Cantique de Noël v & pf – arr. vln & orch.
with orch.   Ultraphon B148

ALBÉNIZ

España (6 Feuilles d'album) Op. 165 pf
No. 2. Tango in D arr. vln & pf Kreisler
with F. Rupp pf   18890   Telefunken A2551, B1319
                                 Ultraphon BP1106

d'AMBROSIO

Canzonetta, Op. 6 vln & pf
with piano   Ultraphon B131, BP301

BACH

Concerto No. 2, in E, BWV1042 vln, strs & c
Adagio (2nd mvt)
with Berlin Philharmonic   018451/2   Supraphon F22450
Orch. – Kletzki   Telefunken F1193

(3) Sonatas & 3 Partitas, BWV1001/6 solo vln
Partita No. 3, in E: Gavotte & Rondeau (3rd mvt) BWV1006
(unaccompanied)   022726   Telefunken E2398

(4) Suites, BWV1066/9 strs & c
Suite No. 3, in D: Air (2nd mvt) BWV1068 2 obs, 3 tpts, drms & strs –
arr. vln & pf as "Air on the G–string" by Wilhelmj
with piano   Telefunken E1827

BEETHOVEN

Concerto in D, Op. 61 (cadenzas by Kreisler) vln & orch.
with Berlin   021284/94   Capitol P8099
Philharmonic Orch. – Schmidt–   Supraphon 70004/9, F22550/5
Isserstedt   Telefunken E2016/21, HT6,
                                    LGX66017, LE6507, TE496/501,
                                    (in set KT110081/2)

Romance No. 1, in G, Op. 40 vln & orch.
with German Opera   024168/9   Telefunken E2904, HT6
House Orch. – Rother

Romance No. 2, in F, Op. 50 vln & orch.
with Berlin Philharmonic 018453/4   Supraphon F22349, FP1111
Orch. – Kletzki   Telefunken (in set KT110081/2),
                                     F1142, HT6

Sonata No. 5, in F, Op. 24 "Spring" vln & pf
              025024–I & 025025/9   Telefunken E3124/6, HT15
with S. Schultze pf

BEETHOVEN – *Continued*

Sonata No. 9, in A, Op. 47 "Kreutzer" vln & pf
505/9½GS & 518/20½GS   Decca CA8207/10
    with W. Kempff pf   Deutsche Grammophon
                                         LPE17153
                                         Heliodor 2548 712
                                         Polydor 35017/20, 67062/5,
                                         516621/4

Sonata No. 9, in A, Op. 47 "Kreutzer" vln & pf
    with S. Schultze pf   Telefunken E3108/11, HT15

Sonata No. 9, in A, Op. 47 "Kreutzer" vln & pf
    with G. Solti pf   Decca K28119/22
                                      London CM9507, (in set
                                      CHA7218)

BRAHMS

Concerto in D, Op. 77 vln & orch.
    Adagio (2nd mvt)
    with Berlin Philharmonic   019184/5   Supraphon G22455
    Orch. – van Kempen   Telefunken E22455, F1423,
                                           TF161
                                           Ultraphon FP1156, FP1198

Concerto in D, Op. 77 (cadenza by Joachim) vln & orch.
    with Berlin   021389/97   Supraphon F22556/60
    Philharmonic Orch. – Schmidt–   Telefunken E2074/8, TE528/32
    Isserstedt

Concerto in a, Op. 102 "Double" vln, vlc & orch.
        SAR 274/9–1, 280–2 & 281–1   Decca AK2025/8, (set EDA94)
    with E. Mainardi vlc & Suisse   London (set LA147)
    Romande Orch. – Schuricht

(21) Hungarian Dances pf duet
    Hungarian dance No. 5, in f sharp arr. vln & pf "in g" Joachim
    with F. Rupp pf   907 bd   Brunswick 7006
                                        Polydor 90017

    Hungarian dance No. 7, in A arr. vln & pf Joachim
    with F. Rupp pf   Polydor 62749

Sonata No. 1, in G, Op. 78 vln & pf
        ARS 76–2 & 77/81–1   Ace of Clubs ACL250
    with G. Solti pf   Decca AK1705/7, K23013/5
                             London CM9506, (in set
                             CHA7218)

Sonata No. 2, in A, Op. 100 vln & pf
    with G. Solti pf   SAR 346/51–1   Ace of Clubs ACL250
                                      Decca K2083/5
                                      London CM9506, (in set
                                      CHA7218)

Sonata No. 3, in d, Op. 108 vln & pf
    with G. Solti pf   Ace of Clubs ACL250
                             Decca K2112/4
                             London CM9506, (in set
                             CHA7218)

BRUCH

Concerto No. 1, in g, Op. 26 vln & orch.
    Adagio (2nd mvt)
    with Berlin Philharmonic   019182/3   Telefunken E1492
    Orch. – van Kempen

Concerto No. 1, in g, Op. 26 vln & orch.
        ARS 70–1, 71/2–2, 73/4–3 & 75   Decca AK1603/5
    with Zürich Tonhalle Orch. –   –1   London (set LA223)
    Schuricht

BRUCH – *Continued*

Concerto No. 1, in g, Op. 26 vln & orch.
    with Berlin Philharmonic Orch. –   Telefunken SK3172/4
    Keilberth

CORELLI

(12) Sonatas, Op. 5 vln & c
    Sonata No. 12, in d "La Follia"
    with orch. – Meyrowitz   30096/7   Ultraphon F137

DEBUSSY

Petite Suite (1889) pf
    No. 3. Menuet arr. vln & pf Dushkin
    with F. Rupp pf   481 GS   Polydor 15095

DESPLANES

Intrada (Adagio) vln & c – arr. vln & pf Nachèz
    with piano   Telefunken A1730

DVOŘÁK

Concerto in a, Op. 53 vln & orch.
    with Berlin   T 025925/32   Capitol P8052
    Philharmonic Orch. – Jochum   Telefunken 310TC008, HT26,
                                        LGX66020, LSK7004,
                                        SK3237/40
                                        Ultraphon G18033/6

(8) Humoresques, Op. 101 pf
    No. 7. Humoresque No. 7, in G flat arr. vln & pf "in G" Kreisler
    with F. Rupp pf   375 be   Polydor 95074

Sonatina in G, Op. 100 vln & pf
    Larghetto (2nd mvt) arr. vln & pf as "Indian lament" by Kreisler
    with orch.   10133   Ultraphon B153

FRANCK

Sonata in A (1886) vln & pf
    with S. Schultze pf   Telefunken E3268/71

GLUCK

Orphée et Eurydice (1762) – opera
    Dance of the blessed spirits: Lento "Mélodie" (No. 2) arr. vln & pf
    Kreisler
    with piano   Telefunken B131
                                       Ultraphon B131, BP301

GOSSEC

(Le) Camp du Grand Pré (1793) – opera
    Tambourin arr. vln & pf Burmester
    with F. Rupp pf   20175–2   Telefunken A1794

GRIEG

Sonata No. 3, in c, Op. 45 vln & pf
    with S. Schultze pf   Telefunken E3284/6

GRUBER

Stille Nacht, heilige Nacht (1818) v & pf – arr. vln & orch.
    with orch.   Ultraphon B148

IBERT

Jeux Sonatina (1926) fl & pf – arr. vln & pf
    with piano   23261   Telefunken A2653

KREISLER

Tambourin chinois, Op. 3 vln & pf
  with piano
    Telefunken B1319
    Ultraphon BP1106

Allegretto (Boccherini) vln & pf
  with F. Rupp pf   908 bd   Brunswick 7006
    Polydor 90017

LULLY

Ballets du Roy (1659)*
Gavotte & Rondeau arr. vln & pf Burmester
  with F. Leitner pf   C 23266   Supraphon B22210
    Telefunken A2625, TA766
    Ultraphon B18052

MENDELSSOHN

Concerto in e, Op. 64 vln & orch.
  with Berlin Philharmonic Orch. –
  Schmidt–Isserstedt   Telefunken E1824/7

MOZART

Adagio in E, K261 vln & orch.
  with F. Rupp pf   374 be   Brunswick 90269
    Decca X211
    Polydor 67156, 95075, 566188

Adagio in E, K261 vln & orch.
  with H. Hoppe pf   Polydor 90007

Adagio in E, K261 vln & orch.
  with Berlin Philharmonic   021295   Supraphon F22550
  Orch. – Schmidt–Isserstedt   Telefunken E2021

Concerto No. 5, in A, K219 "Turkish" (cadenzas by Joachim) vln & orch.
  with German Opera   024137/44   Telefunken (in set KT110081/2),
  House Orch. – Rother   E3044/7, HT5

(6) Deutsche Tänze, K600 orch.
No. 1. Deutscher Tanz No. 1, in C "Ländler" arr. vln & pf Ries
  with F. Rupp pf   20176   Telefunken A1794

Sonata No. 32, in B flat, K454 vln & pf
  with G. Solti pf   SAR 352/7–1   Decca (set EDA108), AK2101/3,
    K23056/8
    London CM9507, (in set
    CHA7218)

PARADIES

Sicilienne vln & pf – arr. Dushkin
  with piano
    Telefunken A1730

RAVEL

Sonatina in f sharp (1905) pf
Menuet (2nd mvt) arr. vln & pf Roques
  with piano   23265   Telefunken A2653

REGER

(7) Sonatas, Op. 91 solo vln
Sonata No. 1, in a: Andante sostenuto (2nd mvt)
  (unaccompanied)   021604   Supraphon F22556
    Telefunken E2078, TE532

Suite in a, Op. 103a vln & pf
Praeludium (1st mvt)
  with H. Hoppe pf   Polydor 95018

* Unidentified.

RIES

(La) Capricciosa vln & pf
  with H. Hoppe pf   Polydor 95018
(La) Capricciosa vln & pf
  with F. Rupp pf   Polydor 95073

SCHUBERT, François

(12) Bagatelles, Op. 13 vln & pf
No. 9. L'abeille
  with F. Rupp pf   20175–2   Telefunken A1794

SCHUBERT, Franz

(7) Gesänge (set to Scott's "Lady of the Lake") Op. 52 v & pf
No. 6. Ave Maria, D839 arr. vln & pf Wilhelmj
  with F. Rupp pf   371 be   Polydor 95074
No. 6. Ave Maria, D839 arr. vln & pf Wilhelmj
  with F. Rupp pf   1759 GS   Brunswick 90332
    Polydor 95229

SCHUMANN

Concerto in d (1853) vln & orch.
  022686–11, 022687–1, 022688–11,   Telefunken (set KT110081/2),
  022689/91 & 022692–1   E2395/8, HT5, TE655/8
  with Berlin Philharmonic Orch. –
  Schmidt–Isserstedt

(12) Duets, Op. 85 pf – 4 hands
No. 12. Abendlied arr. vln & pf Wilhelmj
  with Berlin Philharmonic   020777   Telefunken E1849
  Orch. – Schmidt–Isserstedt

SCOTT

(2) Preludes, Op. 57 (1914) vln & pf
No. 2. Danse
  with F. Rupp pf   Polydor 95073

SIBELIUS

Concerto in d, Op. 47 vln & orch.*
  with Berlin Philharmonic Orch. –
  Furtwängler   Unicorn UNI107

SMETANA

From my Homeland (1878) vln & pf
No. 1. Moderato
  with F. Rupp pf   Polydor 10383, 62749

SPOHR

Concerto No. 8, in a, Op. 47 "Gesangsscene" vln & orch.
  with Berlin Philharmonic   020772/6   Telefunken E1847/9
  Orch. – Schmidt–Isserstedt

SVENDSEN

Romance in G, Op. 26 vln & orch. – arr. vln & pf Wilhelmj
  with F. Leitner pf   23264   Supraphon B22210
    Telefunken A2625
    Ultraphon B18052, TA766

TARTINI

(12) Sonatas, Op. 1 (1734) vln & c
Sonata No. 1, in A: Allegro (1st mvt) arr. vln & pf as "Fugue" by Kreisler
  with F. Rupp pf   Polydor 90269, 95075

* From a German Radio Broadcast of 1943.

415

TCHAIKOVSKY

Concerto in D, Op. 35 vln & orch.
with German Opera House Orch. –   Telefunken E3010/3, HT26,
Rother   LE6512
     Ultraphon F18094/7

(The) Months (12 characteristic pieces) Op. 37b pf
    No. 2. Carnival time (February) arr. vln & pf as "Neapolitan" by
    Burmester
    with F. Rupp pf   19188   Telefunken A1535 A2551

WAGNER

Albumblatt in C (1861) pf – arr. vln & pf Wilhelmj
    with F. Rupp pf   479 GS   Polydor 15095

WIENIAWSKI

(2) Mazurkas, Op. 19 vln & pf
    No. 2. Mazurka No. 2, in D "Dudziarz"
    with orch.   10132   Ultraphon B153

Konstanty KULKA (1947–)

BACH

(3) Sonatas & 3 Partitas, BWV1001/6 solo vln
    Sonata No. 1, in g, BWV1001
    (unaccompanied)   Muza XL0483
     Telefunken SMT1229

    Partita No. 3, in E, BWV1006
    (unaccompanied)   Muza XL0483
     Telefunken SMT1229

GLAZOUNOV

Concerto in a, Op. 82 vln & orch.
with Warsaw National Philharmonic   Musical Heritage Society
Symphony Orch. – Katlewicz   DRM111
     Muza XL0416
     Telefunken SAT22518

LALO

Symphonie espagnole, Op. 21 vln & orch.
with Polish Radio Symphony Orch. –   Muza XL0497
Kord   Telefunken SLT43119

MENDELSSOHN

Concerto in e, Op. 64 vln & orch.
with Warsaw National Philharmonic   Musical Heritage Society
Symphony Orch. – Katlewicz   DRM111
     Muza XL0416
     Telefunken SAT22518

SAINT–SAËNS

Introduction & Rondo Capriccioso, Op. 28 vln & orch.
with Polish Radio Symphony Orch. –   Muza XL0497
Kord   Telefunken SLT43119

Arpad KUN

GODARD

Jocelyn (1888) – opera
    Cachés dans cet asile "Berceuse" arr. vln & pf
    with piano   261 ab   Gramophone & Typewriter
     47970

GODARD – *Continued*

    Cachés dans cet asile "Berceuse" arr. vln & pf
    with piano   Odeon 2226, X25631

KUN

Romance vln & pf
    with piano   Gramophone & Typewriter
     47986

SCHUMANN

(13) Kinderscenen, Op. 15 pf
    No. 7. Träumerei arr. vln & pf
    with piano   98 ab   Gramophone & Typewriter
     47971

B. KUPIEV

BACH

Concerto in a, BWV1044 clav, fl, vln, strs & c
with S. Dizhur hpsi, L. Mironovich fl   Mezhdunarodnaya Kniga
& Moscow Chamber Orch. – Barshai   D014065

Yuriko KURONUMA

HAYASHI

Rhapsody "Winter on 72nd Street" vln & pf
    with H. Hayashi pf   Victor SJX1024

MARTINŮ

(5) Madrigal Stanzas (1943) vln & pf
    with A. Holeček pf   Supraphon 0 11 0575, 1 11 0575
Sonata No. 3 (1944) vln & pf
    with A. Holeček pf   Supraphon 0 11 0575, 1 11 0575

MIYOSHI

Sonata vln & pf
    with A. Miyoshi pf   Victor SJX1024

I. KUSHNIR

SHAMO

Sinfoniette—Concerto vln, pf, bayan, cel & cha orch.
with I. Shamo pf, V. Besfamilnov   Mezhdunarodnaya kniga
bayan, V. Shevchenko cel & Chamber   D021847/8
Orch. – Kozharsky

Rainer KUSSMAUL

ABEL

(6) Quartets, Op. 12 fl or ob, vln, vla & vlc
    Quartet No. 2, in A
    with G. Kuhn fl, J. Kussmaul vla &   Da Camera HBE2501
    H. Lissok vlc   Musica Rara MUR36

ALBINONI

(12) Concerti, Op. 5 (1707) vln or ob & strs
    Concerto No. 5, in a
    with Heidelberg Chamber Orch.   Da Camera SM91013

ALBINONI – *Continued*

Concerto in C (1718) vln or ob & strs
with Heidelberg Chamber Orch.   Da Camera SM91013

(12) Sonatas, Op. 6 (1711) "Trattenimenti armonia" vln & c
Sonata No. 11, in A
with Heidelberg Chamber Orch.   Da Camera SM91013

BACH, C.P.E.

Sonata in B flat, W161, No. 2 2 vlns & c or fl, vln & hpsi
with H. Strebel fl & L. Praetorius hpsi   Da Camera SM92205
    Musica Rara MUR12, MUS12

BACH, J.C.

(4) Sonatas (1785) clav, vln, vla & vlc
Sonata No. 4, in G, P.310 arr. as "Quartet in G"
with G. Krieger pf, J. Kussmaul vla &   Da Camera HBE2401
H. Lissok vlc   Musica Rara MUR35

BACH, J.S.

(6) Brandenburg Concerti, BWV1046/51 (1721) strs & c
Brandenburg Concerto No. 1, in F vln, 3 obs, bsn, 2 hrns & strs
with H. Hickel ob, M. Kühn ob, K.   Da Camera SM91921
Germann ob, E. Prappacher bsn, K.
Dannhausen hrn, H. Warné hrn, M.
Scheurich hpsi & Heidelberg Chamber
Orch. – Göttsche

Brandenburg Concerto No. 2, in F, BWV1047 tpt, fl, ob, vln & strs
with H. Zickler tpt, K. Behrmann fl,   Da Camera SM91008, SM91921
A. Meidhof ob, M. Scheurich hpsi &
Heidelberg Chamber Orch. – von
Websky

Brandenburg Concerto No. 5, in D, BWV1050 clav, fl, vln & strs
with M. Scheurich clav, J. Starke fl &   Da Camera SM91922
Heidelberg Chamber Orch.

Concerto No. 2, in E, BWV1042 vln & orch.
with Heidelberg Chamber Orch.   Oryx EXP14
    Sastruphon SM007 010

Sonata in d, BWV1036 2 vlns & c
with W. Offner vln, K. Pries hpsi & J.   Da Camera HBE2202, HBE2203
Wolf vlc

Sonata in d, BWV1036 2 vlns & c
with W. Keltsch vln, L. Praetorius   Bach 303
hpsi & W. Taube vlc   Da Camera HBE92204

Sonata in C, BWV1037 2 vlns & c
with W. Keltsch vln, L. Praetorius   Bach 303
hpsi & W. Taube vlc   Da Camera HBE92204

Sonata in G, BWV1038 fl, vln & c
with H. Strebel fl, L. Praetorius hpsi &   Bach 303
J. Wolf vlc   Da Camera HBE92204

BRAHMS

Trio No. 1, in B, Op. 8 pf, vln & vlc
with M. Leonhard pf & P. Hahn vlc   Intercord 989–09K

BUXTEHUDE

(7) Sonatas, Op. 1 (1696) vln & c
Sonata No. 1, in f
with M. Scheurich hpsi & J. Wolf   Da Camera SM92103
gamba   Musica Rara MUS5

BUXTEHUDE – *Continued*

Sonata No. 2, in G
with M. Scheurich hpsi & J. Wolf   Da Camera SM92103
gamba   Musica Rara MUS5

Sonata No. 7, in e
with M. Scheurich hpsi & J. Wolf   Da Camera SM92103
gamba   Musica Rara MUS5

(7) Sonatas, Op. 2 (1696) vln & c
Sonata No. 2, in D
with M. Scheurich hpsi & J. Wolf   Da Camera SM92103
gamba   Musica Rara MUS5

CORELLI

(12) Sonatas, Op. 5 vln & c
Sonata No. 12, in d "La Follia"
with L. Praetorius hpsi   Da Camera SC3402
    Musica Rara MUR7

COUPERIN, F.

(4) Concerts Royaux (1722) 2 vlns, vla, fl & c
Concert Royale No. 1, in G
with J. Starke fl, K. Preis hpsi & H.   Da Camera SM92102
Lissok vlc   Musica Rara MUS3

Concert Royale No. 2, in D
with J. Starke fl, K. Preis hpsi & H.   Da Camera SM92102
Lissok vlc   Musica Rara MUS3

Concert Royale No. 3, in A
with J. Starke fl, K. Preis hpsi & H.   Da Camera SM92102
Lissok vlc   Musica Rara MUS3

Concert Royale No. 4, in e
with J. Starke fl, K. Preis hpsi & H.   Da Camera SM92102
Lissok vlc   Musica Rara MUS3

DEVIENNE

(3) Quartets, Op. 73 bsn, vln, vla & vlc
Quartet No. 1, in C
with E. Prappacher bsn, J. Kussmaul   Da Camera HBE2503
vla & J. Wolf vlc

KRAUS

Quintet in D fl, 2 vlns, vla & vlc
with W. Löhrich fl, U. Wichenhäuser   Da Camera HBE2701
vln, J. Kussmaul vla & J. Wolf vlc

MOZART

Quintet in A, K581 cl, 2 vlns, vla & vlc
with W. Gärtner cl, H. Mebert vln, J.   Sastruphon SM007 009
Kussmaul vla & J. Wolf vlc

SCHUBERT

Quintet in A, Op. 114 (D667) "Trout" pf, vln, vla, vlc & cbs
with R. Laugs pf, J. Kussmaul vla, J.   Oryx EXP10
Wolf vlc & W. Nestle cbs

STAMITZ, K.

(6) Duets, Op. 18 vln & vla
No. 5. Duet No. 5, in F
with J. Kussmaul vla   Da Camera SM92305

STAMITZ, K. – *Continued*

(4) Quartets, Op. 8 ob or cl, vln, vla & vlc
No. 4. Quartet No. 4, in E flat
with W. Gärtner cl, J. Kussmaul vla &   Da Camera SM92305
J. Wolf vlc
Quartet No. 4, in E flat
with G. Koch ob, J. Kussmaul vla &   Da Camera HBE2304
J. Wolf vlc   Musica Rara MUR18, MUR36
(3) Trios, Op. 14 fl, vln & c
No. 1. Trio No. 1, in G
with W. Richter fl, J. Nerokas hpsi &   Da Camera SM92305
J. Wolf vlc

TELEMANN

Quartet in b fl, vln, vlc, bsn & hpsi
with J. Starke fl, J. Wolf vlc, E.   Da Camera HBE92006
Prappacher bsn & K. Preis hpsi   Musica Rara MUS54
Quartet in b fl, vln, vlc, bsn & hpsi
with J. Starke fl, J. Wolf vlc, E.   Da Camera HBE2005,
Prappacher bsn & K. Preis hpsi   HBE92006
                                         Musica Rara MUR6
Quartet in D fl, vln, vlc, bsn & hpsi
with J. Starke fl, H. Adomeit vlc, E.   Da Camera HBE2004
Prappacher bsn & K. Preis hpsi   Musica Rara MUS54
Quartet in e (1733) fl, vln, vlc & c
with G. Kuhn fl, K. Hirzel vlc, E.   Da Camera HBE2002,
Prappacher bsn & K. Preis hpsi   HBE92006
                                         Musica Rara MUR6

Samuel KUTCHER (1899–)

FIBICH

Images, Impressions & Souvenirs, Op. 41 pf
No. 14. Poem (from "Souvenirs", Part IV) arr. vln & pf Kubelík
with piano   Vocalion X9803

KREISLER

Liebesleid vln & pf
with piano   Vocalion X9803
Polichinelle–serenade vln & pf
with piano   Vocalion X9893

WOOD

(2) Little Pieces vln & pf
No. 1. Slumber song
with piano   Vocalion X9893

Emmanuel KUTSOVSKY

RAUTIO

Sonatina in c vln & pf
with N. Vilchinskaya pf   Mezhdunarodnaya Kniga
                                         D10176

Michael KUTTNER

BARTÓK

(44) Duos (1931) 2 vlns
with V. Aitay vln   Bartók BRS907

Helen KWALWASSER (1927–)

BACH

(6) Brandenburg Concerti, BWV1046/51 (1721) strs & c
Brandenburg Concerto No. 1, in F, BWV1046 vln, 3 obs, bsn, 2 hrns & strs
playing vln pic with J. Eger hrn, D.   Library of Recorded
Corrado hrn, L. Arner ob, H. Smyles   Masterpieces BB1
ob, A. Laubin ob, A. Checchia bsn, E.   Odyssey 32 16 0188, (in set 32
Earle hpsi & New York Sinfonietta –   26 0014)
Goberman
Brandenburg Concerto No. 2, in F, BWV1047 tpt, fl, ob, vln & strs
with M. Broiles tpt, L. Davenport rec,   Library of Recorded
L. Arner ob, E. Earle hpsi & New   Masterpieces BB2
York Sinfonietta – Goberman   Odyssey 32 16 0190, (in set 32
                                         26 0014)
Brandenburg Concerto No. 3, in G, BWV1048 3 vlns, 3 vlas, 3 vlcs & cbs
with F. Galimir vln, N. Koutzen vln,   Library of Recorded
B. Yokell vla, B. Zaslav vla, B.   Masterpieces BB1
Robbins vla, S. Hunkins vlc, A.   Odyssey 32 16 0190, (in set 32
Kouguell vlc, J. Schneider vlc, J.   26 0014)
Levine cbs, F. Rupp hpsi, of the New
York Sinfonietta – Goberman
Brandenburg Concerto No. 4, in G, BWV1049 vln, 2 fls & strs
with L. Davenport rec, M. Bixler rec,   Library of Recorded
E. Earle hpsi & New York Sinfonietta   Masterpieces BB2
– Goberman   Odyssey 32 16 0190, (in set 32
                                         26 0014)

VIVALDI

(12) Concerti, Op. 8 (1725) "Il Cimento dell' Armonia e dell' Invenzione"
(nos. 1/4: Le quattro Stagioni) vln & strs
Concerto No. 3, in F, F.I, No. 24 "L'Autunno"
with New York Sinfonietta –   Library of Recorded
Goberman   Masterpieces Vol. 1, No. 8
                                         Odyssey 32 16 0132
Concerto in a, P.77 (F.XII, No. 11) 2 vlns, fl, vlc, strs & c
with F. Galimir vln, H. Jones fl, C.   Library of Recorded
McCracken vlc, E. Earle hpsi & New   Masterpieces Vol. 2, No. 4
York Sinfonietta – Goberman
Concerto in D, P.206 vln, fl, bsn, strs & c
with H. Jones fl, A. Checchia bsn, C.   Library of Recorded
McCracken vlc, E. Earle hpsi & New   Masterpieces Vol 2, No. 2
York Sinfonietta – Goberman
Concerto in A, P.236 (F.I, No. 5) vln, strs & c
with E. Earle hpsi & New York   Library of Recorded Masterpices
Sinfonietta – Goberman   Vol. 2, No. 3
Concerto in g, P.404 (F.XII, No. 8) vln, fl, bsn, strs & c
with H. Jones fl, A. Checchia bsn, C.   Library of Recorded
McCracken vlc, E. Earle hpsi & New   Masterpieces Vol 2, No. 5
York Sinfonietta – Goberman
Concerto in c, P.436 (F.I, No. 12) 2 vlns, strs & c
with N. Koutzen vln, E. Earle hpsi &   Library of Recorded
New York Sinfonietta – Goberman   Masterpieces Vol. 2, No. 1

Otto KYNDEL (1904–   )

BERWALD

Quartet No. 3, in E flat (1849) 2 vlns, vla & vlc
   with S–E. Bäck vln,   2SB 2367/71   HMV DB11000 & DB11002/3,
   G. Brodin vla & G. Gröndahl vlc   DBS11060/2

Quintet No. 1, in c, Op. 5 pf, 2 vlns, vla & vlc
           RTJ 2031/3 & 2040/2   Radiotjänst RD524/6
   with B. Hjort pf, G. Brodin vln, S.
   Broman vla & G. Narrby vlc

ERIKSSON

Concerto in g (1932) vln & orch.
   Scherzo
   with Radiotjänst Orch.   RTJ 2733–c   Cupol 4127
   – Rybrant

MOZART

Sonata No. 18, in G, K301 vln & pf
   with S. Frykberg pf   RTJ 1989/92   Classic C2121/2
                         Cupol 6000/1
                         Mayor 504/5

PROVOST

Intermezzo (1940) vln & pf
   with S. Waldimir pf   OSB 342–2   HMV AL2360, B9026, X4653
Intermezzo (1940) vln & pf
   with piano   OSB 2255   HMV X7018

SKÖLD

Melodi vln & pf
   with S. Waldimir pf   OSB 343–2   HMV AL2360, B9026, X4653

STENHAMMAR

(2) Sentimental romances, Op. 28 (1910) vln & orch.
   Sentimental romance No. 2, in f
   with Stockholm Radio   RTJ 1385/6   Radiotjänst RC303
   Light Orch. – Frykberg

SYLVAIN

Canzonetta vln & pf
   with Radiotjänst   RTJ 2484–C   Cupol 4107
   Orch. – Waldimir
Rêverie de Printemps vln & pf
   with Radiotjänst   RTJ 2483–D   Cupol 4107
   Orch. – Waldimir

TCHAIKOVSKY

Romance in f, Op. 5 pf – arr. vln & pf
   with S. Waldimir pf   OSB 2256   HMV X7018

WIRÉN

Quartet No. 2, in C, Op. 9 (1936) 2 vlns, vla & vlc
   with S–E. Bäck vln,   2SB 2361/4   HMV DB11007 & DB11010/1,
   G. Brodin vla & G. Gröndahl vlc   DB11063/5

Alexander LABKO

MEDTNER

Sonata No. 3, in e, Op. 57 (1936) "Sonata epica" vln & pf
   with Y. Svetlanov pf   Mezhdunarodnaya Kniga
                            D025861/2

SVETLANOV

(2) Sonatinas vln & pf
   Sonatina No. 1, in C
   with Y. Svetlanov pf   Mezhdunarodnaya Kniga
                            D025866

   Sonatina No. 2, in e
   with Y. Svetlanov pf   Mezhdunarodnaya Kniga
                            D025866

Fredell LACK

COPLAND

Sonata (1943) vln & pf
   with L. Hambro pf   Allegro AL33, LEG9001

CORELLI

(12) Sonatas, Op. 5 vln & c
   Sonata No. 1, in D
   with F. Valenti hpsi   Allegro AL94
   Sonata No. 8, in e
   with F. Valenti hpsi   Allegro AL94

HINDEMITH

(6) Sonatas, Op. 11
   Sonata No. 2, in D (1920) vln & pf
   with L. Hambro pf   Allegro AL33, LEG9001

JACOBI

Ballade (1942) vln & pf
   with I. Jacobi pf   Composers Recordings CRI146

MENDELSSOHN

Concerto in e, Op. 64 vln & orch.
   with New York Stadium Concerts
   Orch. – Smallens   Music Appreciation Records
                            MAR92
                            World Record Club T5

SCHUBERT

Sonata in A, Op. 162 (D574) "Duo" vln & pf
   with L. Hambro pf   Allegro 4042, AL22

TARTINI

(12) Sonatas, Op. 1 (1734) vln & c
   Sonata No. 1, in A
   with F. Valenti hpsi   Allegro AL94
   Sonata No. 10, in g "Didone abbandonata"
   with F. Valenti hpsi   Allegro AL94

J. LACROUTS

LECLAIR

(12) Sonatas, Op. 4 (1732) 2 vlns & c
   Sonata No. 3, in d
   with G. Raymond vln, A–M.   Erato 21–1
   Beckensteiner hpsi & J. Deferrieux vlc   Haydn Society HSLP103

Max LADSCHECK (1889–   )

d'AMBROSIO

Canzonetta, Op. 6 vln & pf
with piano   Polydor 21382

DRDLA

Souvenir vln & pf
with piano   Cetra LL3013

ELGAR

Salut d'amour, Op. 12 orch. – arr. vln & pf Elgar
with A. Preuss pf   6001 GD 8   Polydor 10239

LADSCHECK

Méditation (based on Schumann's "Kleine Studie") vln & pf
with piano   107 br   Polydor 21383

MONTI

Csárdas (1904) vln & pf
with A. Preuss pf   6002 GD 8   Polydor 10239

MOZART

Divertimento No. 17, in D, K334 2 hrns & strs
  Minuet (3rd mvt) arr. vln & pf Burmester
  with piano   Polydor 10266

POLDINI

(7) Marionnettes pf
  No. 2. Poupée valsante arr. vln & pf Kreisler
  with A. Preuss pf   Polydor 10505

SCHUMANN

(20) Albumblätter, Op. 124 pf
  No. 16. Schlummerlied arr. vln & pf
  with piano   105 br   Polydor 21383

SIBELIUS

Belshazzar's Feast, Op. 51 – Incidental music orch.
  No. 3. Nocturne "Night song" arr. vln & pf Press
  with A. Preuss pf   Polydor 10505

SIMONETTI

Madrigale pf – arr. vln & pf
with piano   Cetra LL3013
    Polydor 10266

TCHAIKOVSKY

Souvenir d'un lieu cher, Op. 42 vln & pf
  with R. Dahlgrün   02251/2 LWH   Polydor 72046
  pf

VALENSIN

Symphony No. 1, in G orch.
  Minuet arr. vln & pf A. Rüdinger
  with piano   Polydor 21382

Rosemarie LAHRS

PACHELBEL

Canon & Gigue in D 3 vlns & c
  with I. Brix–Meinert vln, R. Felicani   Archive EPA37056
  vln, H. Heintze hpsi & J. Koch gamba

Philippe LAMACQUE

ALBINONI

Adagio in g strs & org
  with D. Gouarne org & Symphonic   I Classici della Musica Classica
  Instrumental Ensemble – Witold   SXVG4126
    Contrepoint EXTP1005

(12) Concerti, Op. 5 (1707) vln or ob & strs
  Concerto No. 3, in D
  with G. Nucci org & Symphonic   Editions phonographiques
  Instrumental Ensemble – Witold   parisiennes SLP1

  Concerto No. 9, in e
  with D. Gouarne hpsi & Symphonic   Contrepoint MC20101,
  Instrumental Ensemble – Witold   STMC20101
    Nonesuch H1005, H71005

  Concerto No. 12, in C
  with D. Gouarne hpsi & Symphonic   Period SPL723
  Instrumental Ensemble – Witold

  Concerto No. 12, in C
  with D. Gouarne hpsi & Symphonic   Contrepoint MC20101,
  Instrumental Ensemble – Witold   STMC20101
    Nonesuch H1005, H71005

(12) Concerti, Op. 7 (1716) vln or ob & strs
  Concerto No. 1, in D
  with D. Gouarne hpsi & Symphonic   Period SPL723
  Instrumental Ensemble – Witold

Concerto in C (1718) vln or ob & strs
  with Symphonic Instrumental   Period SPL723
  Ensemble – Witold

BACH

Concerto in c, BWV1060 vln & ob or 2 vlns, strs & c
  with H. Fernandez vln & Jean–   Erato EFM42057
  François Paillard Chamber Orch. –
  Paillard

DANDRIEU

(12) Trio–sonatas, Op. 1 (1705) 2 vlns & c
  Sonata No. 6, in e
  with H. Fernandez vln, L. Boulay hpsi   Erato STU70314
  & J. Lamy gamba   Musical Heritage Society
    MHS930

LECLAIR

(12) Sonatas, Op. 12 2 vlns & c
  Sonata No. 4, in B flat
  with H. Fernandez vln, L. Boulay hpsi   Erato LDE3328, STE50228
  & J. Lamy vlc

TELEMANN

Quartet in e, T.III, No. 2 fl, vln, gamba & c
  with J–P. Rampal fl, C. Brion vlc &   Contrepoint EXTP1017,
  Symphonic Instrumental Ensemble –   MC20100
  Witold

Suite in B flat, T.III, No. 1 2 obs, strs & c
  with J–P. Rampal fl, C. Brion vlc &   Contrepoint MC20100
  Symphonic Instrumental Ensemble –
  Witold

VIVALDI

(12) Concerti, Op. 4 "La Stravaganza" vln, strs & c
Concerto No. 4, in a, F.I, No. 183
with C. Brion vlc, P. Degenne vlc, D.   Contrepoint MC20043
Gouarne hpsi & Symphonic   London TWV91052
Instrumental Ensemble – Witold

Concerto in B flat, P.391 2 vlns, strs & c
with F. Oguse vln & Symphonic   Contrepoint MC20043
Instrumental Ensemble – Witold   London TWV91052

LAMBERT

d'AMBROSIO

Canzonetta, Op. 6 vln & pf
with piano   Odeon 12176

RAFF

(6) Pieces, Op. 85 vln & pf
No. 3. Cavatina in D
with piano   Odeon 42309

RENARD

(2) Berceaux, Op. 20 vln & pf
No. 2. Berceuse in F
with piano   Odeon 12176

RIES

Suite No. 3, in G, Op. 34 vln & pf
Adagio (3rd mvt)
with piano   Odeon X51433

SAINT–SAËNS

(Le) Carnaval des animaux (1886) small orch.
Le cygne arr. vln & pf
with piano   Odeon 42309
Le cygne arr. vln & pf
with piano   Odeon X51434

Brenton LANGBEIN (1928–)

ALBICASTRO

(9) Trio–sonatas, Op. 5 vln & c
Trio–sonata in B
with H. Steinbeck ob, W. Gohl hpsi &   Fono FLG25–4316
M. Sax bsn

ANONYMOUS*

Concerto in A vln, fl, ob d'amore & c
with M. Wendel fl, H. Steinbeck ob   Fono FGL25–4316
d'amore, W. Gohl hpsi & M. Sax bsn

BANKS

Trio hrn, vln & pf
with B. Tuckwell hrn & M. Jones pf   Argo RG475, ZRG5475

FRITZ

(6) Solos, Op. 2 vln & c
Solo No. 4, in e
with W. Gohl hpsi   Fono GFL25–4316

* 18th century.

MOZART

Cassation No. 1, in G, K63 orch.
Adagio (5th mvt)
with Collegium Musicum, Zürich –   Turnabout TV34373
Sacher

Sonata No. 21, in e, K304 vln & pf
with M. Jones pf   Decca LXT2944
   London LL1069

Sonata No. 23, in D, K306 vln & pf
with M. Jones pf   London LL1173

Sonata No. 26, in B flat, K378 vln & pf
with M. Jones pf   Decca LXT2944
   London LL1069

Sonata No. 33, in E flat, K481 vln & pf
with M. Jones pf   Decca LXT2944
   London LL1069

Sonata No. 34, in A, K526 vln & pf
with M. Jones pf   London LL1173

Vladimir LANTSMAN (1942–)

FRANCK

Sonata in A (1886) vln & pf
with A. Mishchenko pf   Mezhdunarodnaya Kniga
   SM02461

PAGANINI

(24) Caprices, Op. 1 (1801/7) solo vln
Caprice No. 15, in e
(unaccompanied)   Mezhdunarodnaya Kniga
   D16682

(6) Sonatas, Op. 2 (1801/6) vln & gtr
No. 4. Sonata No. 4, in A
with S. Chernyakhovskaya pf   Mezhdunarodnaya Kniga
   D16682

No. 6. Sonata No. 6, in a
with S. Chernyakhovskaya pf   Mezhdunarodnaya Kniga
   D16682

PASCAL

Sonata No. 2, in A (1963) vln & pf
with A. Levina pf   Mezhdunarodnaya Kniga
   D16681

RAVEL

Pièce en forme d'Habanera v & pf – arr. vln & pf Catherine
with A. Levina pf   Mezhdunarodnaya Kniga
   D16681

SCHUBERT

Rondo brillante in b, Op. 70 (D895) vln & pf
with A. Mishchenko pf   Mezhdunarodnaya Kniga
   SM02462

SHOSTAKOVICH

(24) Preludes, Op. 34 (1932/3) pf
Prelude No. 1, in C arr. vln & pf Tziganov
with S. Chernyakhovskaya pf   Mezhdunarodnaya Kniga
   D16682

Prelude No. 3, in G arr. vln & pf Tziganov
with S. Chernyakhovskaya pf   Mezhdunarodnaya Kniga
   D16682

SHOSTAKOVICH – *Continued*

Prelude No. 5, in D arr. vln & pf Tziganov
with S. Chernyakhovskaya pf   Mezhdunarodnaya Kniga
    D16682

Prelude No. 8, in f sharp arr. vln & pf Tziganov
with S. Chernyakhovskaya pf   Mezhdunarodnaya Kniga
    D16682

Prelude No. 11, in B arr. vln & pf Tziganov
with S. Chernyakhovskaya pf   Mezhdunarodnaya Kniga
    D16682

George LAPENSON

ASSALY

Sonata in A (1951) vln & pf
with E. Assaly pf   CBC Transcription Program 115

BROTT

Invocation & Dance (1941) vln & pf
with E. Assaly pf   CBC Transcription Program 115

Jean–Louis LARDINOIS

BACH

Sonata in d, BWV1036 2 vlns & c
with G. Altmann vln & J. Louel pf   Decca FAT173454

Sonata in C, BWV1037 2 vlns & c
with G. Altmann vln & J. Louel pf   Decca FAT173454

Sonata in G, BWV1038 fl, vln & c
with G. Altmann vln & J. Louel pf   Decca FAT173454

Sonata in G, BWV1039 2 fls or vlns & c
with G. Altmann vln & J. Louel pf   Decca FAT173454

BARTÓK

(44) Duos (1931) 2 vlns
with G. Altmann vln   Decca FAT173400
    London–Globe GLB1022

Jaime LAREDO (1941–)

BACH

Concerto No. 1, in a, BWV1041 vln strs & c
with Boston Symphony Orch. –   Victor SMR8001, VIC1129,
Munch   VICS1129

(3) Sonatas & 3 Partitas, BWV1001/6 solo vln
Partita No. 3, in E, BWV1006
(unaccompanied)   Victor LM2414, LSC2414

(4) Suites, BWV1066/9 strs & c
Suite No. 3, in D: Air (2nd mvt) BWV1068 2 obs, 3 tpts, drms, strs & c
– arr. vln & pf as "Air on the G–string" by Wilhelmj
with V. Sokoloff pf   Victor LM2373, LSC2373,
    RB16191

BEETHOVEN

Concerto in C, Op. 56 "Triple" vln, vlc, pf & orch.
with L. Parnas vlc, R. Serkin pf &   CBS BRG72202, SBRG72202
Marlboro Festival Orch. – Schneider   Columbia ML5964, MS6564

BRAHMS

Sonata No. 3, in d, Op. 108 vln & pf
with V. Sokoloff pf   Victor LM2414, LSC2414

BRUCH

Concerto No. 1, in g, Op. 26 vln & orch.*
with National Symphony Orch. –   Victor KV25, LM2472,
Mitchell   LSC2472, VIC11, VIC1033,
    VICS1033

DEBUSSY

(12) Préludes – Book I (1910) pf
No. 8. La Fille aux cheveux de lin arr. vln & pf Hartmann
with V. Sokoloff pf   Victor LM2373, LSC2373,
    RB16191

FALLA

(7) Canciones populares españolas (1914) v & pf
No. 4. Jota arr. vln & pf Kochański
with V. Sokoloff pf   Victor LM2373, LSC2373,
    RB16191

Nana arr. vln & pf Kochański
with V. Sokoloff pf   Victor LM2373, LSC2373,
    RB16191

MENDELSSOHN

Concerto in e, Op. 64 vln & orch.
with Boston Symphony Orch. –   Victor KV25, VIC11, VIC1033,
Munch   VICS1033

Octet in E flat, Op. 20 4 vlns, 2 vlas & 2 vlcs
with A. Schneider vln, A. Steinhardt   CBS BRG72473, SBRG72473
vln, J. Dalley vln, M. Tree vla, S.   Columbia ML6248, MS6848
Rhodes vla, L. Parnas vlc & D. Soyer
vlc

MOZART

Concerto No. 3, in G, K216 (cadenzas by Franko) vln & orch.
with National Symphony Orch. –   Victor LM2472, LSC2472,
Mitchell   SMR8001, VIC1129, VICS1129

Concertone in C, K190 2 vlns, ob, vlc & orch.
with M. Tree vln & Marlboro Festival   CBS BRG72435, SBRG72435
Orch. – Schneider   Columbia ML6248, MS6848

Trio No. 3, in B flat, K502 pf, vln & vlc
with R. Serkin pf & M. Foley vlc   Columbia MS7447

PAGANINI

(24) Caprices, Op. 1 (1801/7) solo vln
Caprice No. 13, in B flat
(unaccompanied)   Victor LM2373, LSC2373,
    RB16191

PARADIES

Sicilienne vln & pf – arr. Dushkin
with V. Sokoloff pf   Victor LM2373, LSC2373,
    RB16191

* The Adagio or 2nd mvt is also on Victor ECS9042 & ERA9042.

SARASATE

Carmen Fantasia (on themes from the opera by Bizet) Op. 25 vln & pf or orch. – arr. Zimbalist
  with V. Sokoloff pf   Victor LM2373, LSC2373, RB16191

SCHOENBERG

Serenade, Op. 24 (1924) 2 cls, gtr, mand, vln, vla, vlc & cbs
  with H. Wright cl, D. Stewart cl, S.   Marlboro Recording Society
  Silverman gtr, J. Glick mand, S.   MRS3
  Rhodes vla, M. Foley vlc & T. Paul
  cbs – cond. Kirchner

Suite, Op. 29 (1927) bs–cl, vln, vla, vlc & pf
  with J. Corwin cl, H. Wright cl, D.   Marlboro Recording Society
  Stewart cl, S. Rhodes vla, M. Foley   MRS2
  vlc, R. Laredo pf – cond. Kirchner

SCHUBERT

Quintet in A, Op. 114 (D667) "Trout" pf, vln, vla, vlc & cbs
  with R. Serkin pf, P. Nägele vla, L.   CBS BRG72640, SBRG72640
  Parnas vlc & J. Levine cbs   Columbia ML6467, MS7067

VIVALDI

(12) Sonatas, Op. 2 (1712) vln & c
Sonata No. 2, in A, F.XIII, No. 30 (ed. David)
  with V. Sokoloff pf   Victor LM2373, LSC2373, RB16191

WIENIAWSKI

Scherzo–Tarantelle, Op. 16 vln & pf
  with V. Sokoloff pf   Victor LM2373, LSC2373, RB16191

Fanfulla LARI (1876–1931)

BRAHMS

(21) Hungarian Dances pf duet
Hungarian Dance No. 5, in f sharp arr. vln & pf "in g" Joachim
  with piano   Odeon 110243

BROGI

Mazurka vln & pf
  with piano   Odeon 110178

(2) Morceaux, Op. 34 vln & pf
No. 2. Arietta all'antica
  with piano   Odeon 110247

CHOPIN

(3) Nocturnes, Op. 9 pf
No. 2. Nocturne No. 2, in E flat arr. vln & pf Sarasate
  with piano   Odeon 110177

FRANCI

Emma–Gavotte, Op. 60 vln & pf
  with piano   Odeon 110248

HAUSER

Rapsodie hongrois No. 1, in d, Op. 43 vln & pf
  with piano   Odeon 110244

SCHUMANN

(12) Duets, Op. 85 pf – 4 hands
No. 12. Abendlied arr. vln & pf Wilhelmj
  with piano   Odeon 110245

SIVORI

(2) Romanzas senza paroles, Op. 23 vln & pf*
  with piano   Odeon 110246

TARTINI

Sonata in g "Il Trillo del Diavolo" vln & c – arr. Léonard†
  with piano   Odeon 110176

TIRINDELLI

(6) Morceaux de concert, Op. 1 vln & pf
No. 6. Pasquinade
  with piano   Odeon 110175

Reginald LARNER

VIVALDI

Concerto in F, P.278 (F.I, No. 34) 3 vlns, strs & c
  with N. Roth vln, S. Rozsa vln &   Morgan M100IL
  London Soloists Ensemble

Nicole LAROQUE

CORELLI

(12) Concerti grossi, Op. 6 orch.
Concerto grosso No. 8, in g "Christmas Concerto"
  with J.P. Wallez vln, A. Queille vla,   Critère CRD186, SCRD5186
  H. Martinerie vlc, L. Boulay hpsi &
  Collegium Musicum, Paris – Douatte

TELEMANN

Concerto in F, T.II, No. 3 3 vlns, strs & c
  with R. Gendre vln, J.P. Wallez vln,   CBS SBRG75563
  L. Boulay hpsi & Collegium Musicum,   Eurodisc 74225KK
  Paris – Douatte   Nonesuch H1109, H71109

Bjarne LARSEN (1922–)

BRUSTAD

Capricci vln & vla
  with A. Sletsje vla   Philips 839249AY

GRIEG

Sonata No. 1, in F, Op. 8 vln & pf
  with I. Johnsen pf   Triola RNLP1

Sonata No. 2, in G, Op. 13 vln & pf
  with I. Johnsen pf   Triola RNLP1

SVENDSEN

Romance in G, Op. 26 vln & orch.
  with Oslo Philharmonic Orch. –   Philips A631096L
  Grüner–Hegge

---

* It is not clear whether number 1 or number 2 is on this disc.
† Abridged.

Jørgen Fischer LARSEN

NIELSEN

Prelude & Presto, Op. 52 solo vln
   (unaccompanied)   Odeon MOAK18, PASK2003
Prelude & Theme with Variations, Op. 48 solo vln
   (unaccompanied)   Odeon MOAK18, PASK2003

Eduard LARYSZ

RAFF

(6) Pieces, Op. 85 vln & pf
   No. 3. Cavatina in D
   with Vienna Solisten Orch. – Grell   Philips G03138L

Johannes Michael LASOWSKI (1894–   )

BRAGA

(7) Melodies (1867) v & pf
   No. 5. La serenata "Angel's serenade" arr. vln & orch.
   with Beka Orch.   Parlophone B6575

GOUNOD

Ave Maria (Méditation on Bach's "Prelude No. 1, in C" from Book I of
   "Das Wohltemperirte Clavier" v & pf – arr. vln & orch.
   with Beka Orch.   Parlophone B6575

MENDELSSOHN

(6) Songs without words, Op. 62 pf
   No. 6. Song without words No. 30, in A "Spring song" arr. vln & orch.
   with orch. – Lorand   Parlophone 22294

MOSZKOWSKI

(6) Klavierstücke, Op. 15 pf – 4 hands
   No. 1. Serenata arr. vln & pf
   with piano   Parlophone 22120

RAFF

(6) Pieces, Op. 85 vln & pf
   No. 3. Cavatina in D arr. v, vln & orch.
   with E. Bettendorf s & orch.   Parlophone P2076

Joseph LASOWSKI

BACH

(4) Suites, BWV1066/9 orch.
   Suite No. 3, in D: Air (2nd mvt) BWV1068 2 obs, 3 tpts, drms & strs –
   arr. vln & pf as "Air on the G–string" by Wilhelmj
   with J. Bukowski org   Gloria GO27175

DRDLA

Souvenir vln & pf
   with J. Bukowski org   Gloria GO27175

Boris LASS

ANONYMOUS

Harusame Japanese air – arr. vln & pf Lass
   with piano   Columbia J5096

Irish folksong arr. vln & pf Yamada
   with piano   Columbia J5100
Japanese mother's lullaby Japanese air – arr. vln & pf Yamada
   with piano   Columbia J5100
Oshoro Takashima arr. vln & pf Yamada
   with piano   Columbia J5096
Uruwashiki Tennen arr. vln & pf Yamada
   with piano   Columbia J5089

BEETHOVEN

Sonata No. 9, in A, Op. 47 "Kreutzer" vln & pf
   with M. Shapiro pf   Columbia J55015/8

BRAHMS

(16) Waltzes, Op. 39 pf duet
   No. 15. Waltz No. 15, in A flat arr. vln & pf "in A" Hochstein
   with piano   Columbia J5107

BRANDL

(Der) Liebe Augustin – operetta
   Du alter Stefansturm arr. vln & pf as "The old refrain" by Kreisler
   with piano   Columbia J5073

DRDLA

Souvenir vln & pf
   with piano   Columbia J5062

DRIGO

(Les) Millions d'Arlequin (1900) – ballet
   Sérénade arr. vln & pf Auer
   with piano   Victor 216536
   Sérénade arr. vln & pf Auer
   with piano   Columbia J5062

DVOŘÁK

(8) Humoresques, Op. 101 pf
   No. 7. Humoresque No. 7, in G flat arr. vln & pf "in G" Kreisler
   with piano   Victor 216536
   No. 7. Humoresque No. 7, in G flat arr. vln & pf "in G" Kreisler
   with piano   Columbia J5055
Sonatina in G, Op. 100 vln & pf
   Larghetto (2nd mvt) arr. vln & pf as "Indian lament" by Kreisler
   with piano   Columbia J5070

GHRDEN

Mashiroki fujino ne arr. vln & pf Sugita
   with M. Lass pf   Columbia 28644

GODARD

Jocelyn (1888) – opera
   Cachés dans cet asile "Berceuse" arr. vln & pf
   with piano   Columbia J5122

HANDEL

Serse (1738) – opera
   Ombra mai fu "Largo" arr. vln & pf
   with piano   Columbia J5054

HIROTA

Chikuma–Gawa Ryojo no Uta vln & pf
with piano   Columbia J5071

Shikararete arr. vln & pf Lass
with piano   Columbia J5105

KOSCKI

Sendo Kawaiya – Variations vln & pf – arr. Sugita
with M. Lass pf   Columbia 28644

KREISLER

Caprice viennois, Op. 2 vln & pf
with piano   Columbia J5073

LASS

Song of Nara vln & pf
with piano   Columbia J5105

MASSENET

Thaïs (1894) – opera
 Méditation arr. vln & pf Marsick
 with piano   Columbia J5055

MOSZKOWSKI

(6) Klavierstücke, Op. 15 pf – 4 hands
 No. 1. Serenata arr. vln & pf
 with piano   Columbia J5250

NACHÈZ

(4) Danses Tziganes, Op. 14 vln & pf
 No. 1. Danse Tzigane No. 1, in a
 with piano   Columbia 28293

RIMSKY–KORSAKOV

(Le) Coq d'Or (1910) – opera
 Hymn to the sun arr. vln & pf Kreisler
 with piano   Victor 216538
 Hymn to the sun arr. vln & pf Kreisler
 with piano   Columbia J5054

Sadko (1898) – opera
 Chant hindou arr. vln & pf Kreisler
 with piano   Victor 216538
 Chant hindou arr. vln & pf Kreisler
 with piano   Columbia J5083

SARASATE

(8) Danzas españolas vln & pf
 No. 3. Romanza andaluza, Op. 22, No. 1
 with piano   Columbia J5070

Zigeunerweisen, Op. 20 vln & pf or orch.
with piano   Columbia J5078

SIMONETTI

Madrigale pf – arr. vln & pf
with piano   Columbia J5122

SUGIYAMA

Debune arr. vln & pf Lass
with piano   Columbia J5095

TAKI

Kojo No Tsuki v & pf – arr. vln & pf Yamada*
with piano   Columbia J5053

TCHAIKOVSKY

(6) Pieces, Op. 19 pf
 No. 4. Nocturne in c sharp arr. vln & pf Hartmann
 with orch. – Yamada   Columbia J5250

VIEUXTEMPS

(6) Divertissements d'Amateurs sur des Mélodies russes, Op. 24 vln & pf
 No. 2. Le rossignol (after Alexander Alabiev, 1787–1851)
 with piano   Columbia 28293

WHITE

Bandanna Sketches, Op. 12 vln & pf
 No. 1. Nobody knows de trouble I see (Negro spiritual)
 with piano   Columbia J5107

WIENIAWSKI

Concerto No. 2, in d, Op. 22 vln & orch.
 Romance (2nd mvt)
 with piano   Columbia J5083

YAMADA

Karatachi no Hana vln & pf
with piano   Columbia J5123

Nobara vln & pf
with piano   Columbia J5089

Suite Japonaise vln & pf
with piano   Columbia J5123

Tomari–bune vln & pf
with piano   Columbia J5071

Yuko Haru vln & pf
with piano   Columbia J5100

Malcolm LATCHEM

BARTÓK

Contrasts (1938) cl, vln & pf
with G. Dobrée cl & G. Watson pf   Argo ATM1002, TM9

HANDEL

(12) Concerti grossi, Op. 6 2 vlns, vlc & strs
 Concerto grosso No. 1, in G
 with N. Marriner vln, K. Heath vlc,   Decca LXT6369, SXL6369
 T. Dart hpsi, A. Davis org &   London CS6595, (in set
 Academy of Saint–Martin–in–the–   CSA2309)
 Fields – Marriner

 Concerto grosso No. 2, in F
 with N. Marriner vln, K. Heath vlc,   Decca LXT6369, SXL6369
 T. Dart hpsi, A. Davis org &   London CS6595, (in set
 Academy of Saint–Martin–in–the–   CSA2309)
 Fields – Marriner

 Concerto grosso No. 3, in e
 with N. Marriner vln, K. Heath vlc,   Decca LXT6369, SXL6369
 T. Dart hpsi, A. Davis org &   London CS6595, (in set
 Academy of Saint–Martin–in–the–   CSA2309)
 Fields – Marriner

* "Song of the ruined castle".

HANDEL – *Continued*

Concerto grosso No. 4, in a
with N. Marriner vln, K. Heath vlc,
T. Dart hpsi, A. Davis org &
Academy of Saint–Martin–in–the–
Fields – Marriner

Decca LXT6369, SXL6369
London CS6595, (in set CSA
2309)

Concerto grosso No. 5, in D
with N. Marriner vln, K. Heath vlc,
T. Dart hpsi, A. Davis org &
Academy of Saint–Martin–in–the–
Fields – Marriner

Decca LXT6370, SXL6370
London CS6596, (in set
CSA2309)

Concerto grosso No. 6, in g
with N. Marriner vln, K. Heath vlc,
T. Dart hpsi, A. Davis org &
Academy of Saint–Martin–in–the–
Fields – Marriner

Decca LXT6370, SXL6370
London CS6596, (in set
CSA2309)

Concerto grosso No. 7, in B flat
with N. Marriner vln, K. Heath vlc,
T. Dart hpsi, A. Davis org &
Academy of Saint–Martin–in–the–
Fields – Marriner

Decca LXT6370, SXL6370
London CS6596, (in set
CSA2309)

Concerto grosso No. 8, in c
with N. Marriner vln, K. Heath vlc,
T. Dart hpsi, A. Davis org &
Academy of Saint–Martin–in–the–
Fields – Marriner

Decca LXT6370, SXL6370
London CS6596, (in set
CSA2309)

Concerto grosso No. 9, in F
with N. Marriner vln, K. Heath vlc,
T. Dart hpsi, A. Davis org &
Academy of Saint–Martin–In–the–
Fields – Marriner

Decca LXT6371, SXL6371
London CS6597, (in set
CSA2309)

Concerto grosso No. 10, in d
with N. Marriner vln, K. Heath vlc,
T. Dart hpsi, A. Davis org &
Academy of Saint–Martin–in–the–
Fields – Marriner

Decca LXT6371, SXL6371
London CS6597, (in set
CSA2309)

Concerto grosso No. 11, in A
with N. Marriner vln, K. Heath vlc,
T. Dart hpsi, A. Davis org &
Academy of Saint–Martin–in–the–
Fields – Marriner

Decca LXT6371, SXL6371
London CS6597, (in set
CSA2309)

Concerto grosso No. 12, in b
with N. Marriner vln, K. Heath vlc,
T. Dart hpsi, A. Davis org &
Academy of Saint–Martin–in–the–
Fields – Marriner

Decca LXT6371, SXL6371
London CS6597, (in set
CSA2309)

O. LAUE

ANONYMOUS

Sehnsuchtsträume arr. vln & orch.
with orch. – Kark

Beka G41295

GODARD

Jocelyn (1888) – opera
Cachés dans cet asile "Berceuse" arr. vln & orch.
with orch. – Kark

Beka G14028

MEYER–HELMUND

Intermezzo, Op. 28 pf – arr. vln & orch.
with orch. – Kark

Beka G13908

Waltz, Op. 14 pf – arr. vln & orch.
with orch. – Kark

Beka G13908

SCHUBERT

(14) Schwanengesang, D957 (1828) v & pf
No. 4. Ständchen "Serenade" arr. vln & orch.
with orch. – Kark

Beka G13882

Marcel LAURANE

TCHAIKOVSKY

Concerto in D, Op. 35 vln & orch.
with Europa Symphony Orch. –
Westermann

Fontana 200031WGL

Jacques LAURENT

HANDEL

Concerto grosso in C (1736) "Alexander's Feast" orch.
with N. Petrovic vln, A. Bauer vlc &
the Masterplayers – Schumacher

Amadeo AVRS6175

PERGOLESI

Concerto in B flat vln & strs – ed. Lualdi
with Collegium Musicum, Paris –
Douatte

Les Quatre Saisons AR2

Remo LAURICELLA

LAURICELLA

Duo Sonata (1962) 2 vlns
with S. de Gay vln

Apollo Sound AS1002

Sonata (1955) vln & pf
with B. Raikin pf

Apollo Sound AS1002

Kai LAURSEN

NIELSEN

Prelude & Presto, Op. 52 solo vln
(unaccompanied)

Metronome MCLP85305
Washington WR462, WS9462

Prelude & Theme with Variations, Op. 48 solo vln
(unaccompanied)

Metronome MCLP85305
Washington WR462, WS9462

Sonata No. 2, in g, Op. 35 (1912) vln & pf
with E. Moller pf

Metronome MCLP85305
Washington WR462, WS9462

Suzanne LAUTENBACHER (1932–)

BACH

(6) Brandenburg Concerti, BWV1046/51 (1721) strs & c
Brandenburg Concerto No. 1, in F, BWV1046 vln, 3 obs, bsn, 2 hrns, strs & c
with W. Schnell ob, D. Keller ob, G.   Turnabout TV4044, TV34044
Steinert ob, E. Thieme bsn, E. Penzel
hrn, H. Irmscher hrn, M. Galling hpsi
& Württemberg Chamber Orch. –
Faerber

Brandenburg Concerto No. 2, in F, BWV1047 tpt, fl, ob, vln, strs & c
with A. Scherbaum tpt, K.F. Mess fl &   Columbia ML5351/2, (in set
Stuttgart Baroque Ensemble – Couraud   M2L259), (in set M2S605)
                            Fontana 663500ER

Brandenburg Concerto No. 2, in F, BWV1047 tpt, fl, ob, vln, strs & c
with H. Schneidewind tpt, H. Strebel   Turnabout TV4044, TV34044
fl, W. Schnell ob, P. Buck vlc, M.
Galling hpsi & Württemberg Chamber
Orch. – Faerber

Brandenburg Concerto No. 4, in G, BWV1049 vln, 2 fls, strs & c
with K.F. Mess fl, J. Starke fl &   Columbia ML5351/2, (in set
Stuttgart Baroque Ensemble – Couraud   M2L259), (in set M2S605)
                            Fontana 697102EL, EFL2514,
                            EFR2028

Brandenburg Concerto No. 4, in G, BWV1049 vln, 2 fls, strs & c
with H. Strebel fl, G. Braun fl, M.   Turnabout TV4045, TV34045
Galling hpsi & Württemberg Chamber
Orch. – Faerber

Brandenburg Concerto No. 5, in D, BWV1050 clav, fl, vln, strs & c
with M. Galling hpsi, K.F. Mess fl &   Columbia ML5351/2, (in set
Stuttgart Baroque Ensemble – Couraud   M2L259), (in set M2S605)
                            Fontana 697102EL, EFL2514

Brandenburg Concerto No. 5, in D, BWV1050 clav, fl, vln, strs & c
with M. Galling hpsi, H. Steinkraus fl,   Turnabout TV4045, TV34045
P. Buck vlc & Württemberg Chamber
Orch. – Faerber

Cantata No. 208 (Was mir behagt ist nur die muntre Jagd) BWV208
"Hunting Cantata"
with H. Donath s, E. Speiser s, W.   Bärenreiter Musicaphon BM30
Jochims t, J. Stämpfli bs, E. Penzel   SL135
hrn, G. Hauke hrn, H. Strebel rec, G.   Nonesuch H1147, H71147
Braun rec, A. Sous ob, H. Hucke ob,
I. Goritzki E–hrn, M. Galling hpsi, B.
Haferland gamba, G. Hörtnagel cbs,
M. Schaeffer lute, H. Haferland gamba,
– Choir of Gedächtniskirche &
Chamber Ensemble of the Bach
Collegium, Stuttgart – Rilling

Concerto No. 1, in a, BWV1041 vln, strs & c
with Mainz Chamber Orch. – Kehr   Vox (in sets SVBX567 &
                            VBX67), PL11540, STDL511540

Concerto No. 2, in E, BWV1042 vln, strs & c
with Mainz Chamber Orch. – Kehr   Vox (in sets SVBX567 &
                            VBX67), PL11540, STDL511540

Concerto in d, BWV1043 2 vlns, strs & c
with D. Vorholz vln & Mainz   Vox (in sets SVBX567 &
Chamber Orch. – Kehr   VBX67), PL11540, STDL511540

Concerto in a, BWV1044 clav, fl, vln, strs & c
with H. Elsner hpsi, K.F. Mess fl &   Vox PL10730
Pro Musica Orch., Stuttgart –
Reinhardt

Concerto in a, BWV1044 clav, fl, vln, strs & c
with M. Galling hpsi, H.J. Möhring fl   Turnabout TV4219, TV34219
& Stuttgart Soloists

(Ein) Musikalisches Opfer, BWV1079 (1749) strs & c
with H. Endres vln, J. Rottenfusser   Vox DL490, STDL500490
vln, F. Ruf vla, A. Schmidt vlc, K.H.
Zöller fl, H. Weber hrn & M. Galling
hpsi

Ostern–Oratorium, BWV249 (1736)
with F. Sailer s, M. Bence a, W.S.   Epic BC1244, LC3844
Braun t, A. Messthaler bs, F. Milde ob   Philips 835498AY, L77416L
d'amore, M. Galling hpsi & Pro
Musica Orch., Stuttgart – Couraud

(3) Sonatas & 3 Partitas, BWV1001/6 solo vln
Sonata No. 1, in g, BWV1001
(unaccompanied)   Bärenreiter Musicaphon BM30
                            L1504

Partita No. 1, in b, BWV1002
(unaccompanied)   Bärenreiter Musicaphon BM30
                            L1504

Sonata No. 2, in a, BWV1003
(unaccompanied)   Bärenreiter Musicaphon BM30
                            L1505

Partita No. 2, in d, BWV1004
(unaccompanied)   Bärenreiter Musicaphon BM30
                            L1505

Sonata No. 3, in C, BWV1005
(unaccompanied)   Bärenreiter Musicaphon BM30
                            L1506

Partita No. 3, in E, BWV1006
(unaccompanied)   Bärenreiter Musicaphon BM30
                            L1506

(6) Sonatas, BWV1014/9 vln & clav
Sonata No. 1, in b, BWV1014
with M. Galling hpsi   Vox (in sets VUX2027 &
                            SVUX52027)

Sonata No. 2, in A, BWV1015
with M. Galling hpsi   Vox (in sets VUX2027 &
                            SVUX52027)

Sonata No. 3, in E, BWV1016
with M. Galling hpsi   Vox (in sets VUX2027 &
                            SVUX52027)

Sonata No. 4, in c, BWV1017
with M. Galling hpsi   Vox (in sets VUX2027 &
                            SVUX52027)

Sonata No. 5, in f, BWV1018
with M. Galling hpsi   Vox (in sets VUX2027 &
                            SVUX52027)

Sonata No. 6, in G, BWV1019
with M. Galling pf   Vox (in sets VUX2027 &
                            SVUX52027)

BEETHOVEN

Concerto in D, Op. 61 (cadenzas by Kreisler) vln & orch.
with Westphalia Symphony Orch. –　　Vox GBY11170, PL11170,
Reichert　　　　　　　　　　　　　　STGBY511170, STPL511170

Romance No. 1, in G, Op. 40 vln & orch.
with Badische Staatskapelle – Cremer　Vox GBY11170, PL11170,
　　　　　　　　　　　　　　　　　　STGBY511170, STPL511170

Romance No. 2, in F, Op. 50 vln & orch.
with Badische Staatskapelle – Cremer　Vox GBY11170, PL11170,
　　　　　　　　　　　　　　　　　　STGBY511170, STPL511170

Serenade in D, Op. 8 vln, vla & vlc
with U. Koch vla & T. Blees vlc　　　Intercord (in set 710–09Z)
　　　　　　　　　　　　　　　　　　Vox (in set SVBX599)

(3) Sonatas, Op. 12 vln & pf
　No. 1. Sonata No. 1, in D
　with M. Galling pf　　　　　　　　Intercord 713–09MH
　No. 2. Sonata No. 2, in A
　with M. Galling pf　　　　　　　　Intercord 713–09MH

Sonata No. 5, in F, Op. 24 "Spring" vln & pf
with R. Reinhardt pf　　　　　　　　Vox XPV30050

Sonata No. 9, in A, Op. 47 "Kreutzer" vln & pf
with R. Reinhardt pf　　　　　　　　Vox XPV30050

Trio No 1, in E flat, Op. 3 vln, vla & vlc
with U. Koch vla & T. Blees vlc　　　Intercord (in set 710–09Z)
　　　　　　　　　　　　　　　　　　Vox (in set SVBX599)

(3) Trios, Op. 9 vln, vla & vlc
　No. 1. Trio No. 2, in G
　with U. Koch vla & T. Blees vlc　　Intercord (in set 710–09Z)
　　　　　　　　　　　　　　　　　　Vox (in set SBVX599)

　No. 2. Trio No. 3, in D
　with U. Koch vla & T. Blees vlc　　Intercord (in set 710–09Z)
　　　　　　　　　　　　　　　　　　Vox (in set SVBX599)

　No. 3. Trio No. 4, in c
　with U. Koch vla & T. Blees vlc　　Intercord (in set 710–09Z)
　　　　　　　　　　　　　　　　　　Vox (in set SVBX599)

BIBER

(16) Biblical Sonatas "Mysterien" vln & c
　Sonata No. 1, in d "The annunciation of the birth of Christ"
　with R. Ewerhart org & J. Koch　　Vox (in sets VBX52 &
　gamba　　　　　　　　　　　　　　SVBX552)

　Sonata No. 2, in A "Visit of Mary to Elizabeth"
　with R. Ewerhart org & J. Koch　　Vox (in sets VBX52 &
　gamba　　　　　　　　　　　　　　SVBX552)

　Sonata No. 3, in b "Birth of Christ"
　with R. Ewerhart hpsi & J. Koch　　Vox (in sets VBX52 &
　gamba　　　　　　　　　　　　　　SVBX552)

　Sonata No. 4, in d "Christ in the temple"
　with R. Ewerhart org & J. Koch　　Vox (in sets VBX52 &
　gamba　　　　　　　　　　　　　　SVBX552)

　Sonata No. 5, in A "The twelve–year–old Jesus in the temple"
　with R. Ewerhart hpsi & J. Koch　　Vox (in sets VBX52 &
　gamba　　　　　　　　　　　　　　SVBX552)

　Sonata No. 6, in c "Christ on the Mount of Olives"
　with R. Ewerhart org　　　　　　　Vox (in sets VBX52 &
　　　　　　　　　　　　　　　　　　SVBX552)

　Sonata No. 7, in F "The Flagellation of Christ"
　with R. Ewerhart org & J. Koch　　Vox (in sets VBX52 &
　gamba　　　　　　　　　　　　　　SVBX552)

BIBER – *Continued*

　Sonata No. 8, in B flat "Christ's crowning with thorns"
　with R. Ewerhart hpsi & J. Koch　　Vox (in sets VBX52 &
　gamba　　　　　　　　　　　　　　SVBX552)

　Sonata No. 9, in a "Christ on the way to Calvary"
　with R. Ewerhart org & J. Koch　　Vox (in sets VBX52 &
　gamba　　　　　　　　　　　　　　SVBX552)

　Sonata No. 10, in g "The Crucifixion"
　with R. Ewerhart org & J. Koch　　Vox (in sets VBX52 &
　gamba　　　　　　　　　　　　　　SVBX552)

　Sonata No. 11, in G "The Resurrection"
　with R. Ewerhart org　　　　　　　Vox (in sets VBX52 &
　　　　　　　　　　　　　　　　　　SVBX552)

　Sonata No. 12, in C "The Ascension"
　with R. Ewerhart hpsi & J. Koch　　Vox (in sets VBX52 &
　gamba　　　　　　　　　　　　　　SVBX552)

　Sonata No. 13, in d "The Emanation of the Holy Ghost"
　with R. Ewerhart hpsi & J. Koch　　Vox (in sets VBX52 &
　gamba　　　　　　　　　　　　　　SVBX552)

　Sonata No. 14, in D "The Ascension of the Holy Virgin"
　with R. Ewerhart org　　　　　　　Vox (in sets VBX52 &
　　　　　　　　　　　　　　　　　　SVBX552)

　Sonata No. 15, in C "Coronation of the Virgin"
　with R. Ewerhart org & J. Koch　　Vox (in sets VBX52 &
　gamba　　　　　　　　　　　　　　SVBX552)

　Sonata No. 16, in g "The Guardian Angel"*
　(unaccompanied)　　　　　　　　　Vox (in sets VBX52 &
　　　　　　　　　　　　　　　　　　SVBX552)

BRAHMS

Concerto in D, Op. 77 (cadenza by Joachim) vln & orch.
with Innsbruck Symphony Orch. –　　Great Musicians TGM03
Wagner　　　　　　　　　　　　　　Vox GBY12260, STGBY512260

COUPERIN, F.

(Les) Nations – 4 suites (1726) 2 vlns & c
　Suite No. 3, in d "L'Impériale"
　with M. Galling hpsi, P. Buck vlc &　Philips 835491AY, C37
　Stuttgart Chamber Orch. – Couraud

(Le) Parnasse, ou l'Apothéose de Corelli (1725) 2 vlns & c
with M. Galling hpsi, P. Buck vlc &　Philips 835491AY, C37
Stuttgart Chamber Orch. – Couraud

DEVIENNE

(3) Quartets, Op. 73 bsn, vln, vla & vlc
　Quartet No. 1, in C
　with G. Zukerman bsn, F. Beyer vla &　Turnabout TV34304
　T. Blees vlc

DURANTE

(8) Quartetti concertanti 2 vlns, vla & c
　Concerto No. 1, in f
　with F–J. Maier vln, G. Schmid vla,　Harmonia Mundi HM30619
　A. May vlc & Collegium Aurem –
　Reinhardt

* Known as "Passacaglia".

DURANTE – *Continued*

Concerto No. 2, in g
with F–J. Maier vln, G. Schmid vla,
A. May vlc & Collegium Aurem –
Reinhardt — Harmonia Mundi HM30619

Concerto No. 4, in e
with F–J. Maier vln, G. Schmid vla,
A. May vlc & Collegium Aurem –
Reinhardt — Harmonia Mundi HM30619

Concerto No. 7, in C
with F–J. Maier vln, G. Schmid vla,
A. May vlc & Collegium Aurem –
Reinhardt — Harmonia Mundi HM30619

HANDEL

(6) Concerti grossi, Op. 3 (1759) orch.
Concerto grosso No. 1, in B flat
with A. Sous ob, W. Schnell ob, A.
Lutz vlc, M. Galling hpsi &
Süddeutsche Chamber Philharmonic,
Stuttgart – Wich — Intercord (in set 928–09Z)

Concerto grosso No. 2, in B flat
with A. Sous ob, W. Schnell ob, A.
Lutz vlc, M. Galling hpsi &
Süddeutsche Chamber Philharmonic,
Stuttgart – Wich — Intercord (in set 928–09Z)

Concerto grosso No. 3, in G
with A. Sous ob, W. Schnell ob, A.
Lutz vlc, M. Galling hpsi &
Süddeutsche Chamber Philharmonic,
Stuttgart – Wich — Intercord (in set 928–09Z)

Concerto grosso No. 4, in F
with A. Sous ob, W. Schnell ob, A.
Lutz vlc, M. Galling hpsi &
Süddeutsche Chamber Philharmonic,
Stuttgart – Wich — Intercord (in set 928–09Z)

Concerto grosso No. 5, in d
with A. Sous ob, W. Schnell ob, A.
Lutz vlc, M. Galling hpsi &
Süddeutsche Chamber Philharmonic,
Stuttgart – Wich — Intercord (in set 928–09Z)

Concerto grosso No. 6, in D
with A. Sous ob, W. Schnell ob, A.
Lutz vlc, M. Galling hpsi &
Süddeutsche Chamber Philharmonic,
Stuttgart – Wich — Intercord (in set 928–09Z)

(12) Concerti grossi, Op. 6 (1739) 2 vlns, vlc & strs
Concerto grosso No. 1, in G
with R. Barchet vln, R. Reinhardt
hpsi, M. Brun vlc & Pro Arte Orch.,
Munich – Redel — Vox (in sets PL10043 & VBX22)

Concerto grosso No. 1, in G
with M. Gaiser vln, T. Blees vlc, M.
Galling hpsi & Süddeutsche Chamber
Philharmonic, Stuttgart – Wich — Intercord (in set 973–09Z)

Concerto grosso No. 2, in F
with R. Barchet vln, R. Reinhardt
hpsi, M. Brun vlc & Pro Arte Orch.,
Munich – Redel — Vox (in sets PL10043 & VBX22)

HANDEL – *Continued*

Concerto grosso No. 2, in F
with M. Gaiser vln, T. Blees vlc, M.
Galling hpsi & Süddeutsche Chamber
Philharmonic, Stuttgart – Wich — Intercord (in set 973–09Z)

Concerto grosso No. 3, in e
with R. Barchet vln, R. Reinhardt
hpsi, M. Brun vlc & Pro Arte Orch.,
Munich – Redel — Vox (in sets PL10043 & VBX22)

Concerto grosso No. 3, in e
with M. Gaiser vln, T. Blees vlc, M.
Galling hpsi & Süddeutsche Chamber
Philharmonic, Stuttgart – Wich — Intercord (in set 973–09Z)

Concerto grosso No. 4, in a
with R. Barchet vln, R. Reinhardt
hpsi, M. Brun vlc & Pro Arte Orch.,
Munich – Redel — Vox (in sets PL10043 & VBX22)

Concerto grosso No. 4, in a
with M. Gaiser vln, T. Blees vlc, M.
Galling hpsi & Süddeutsche Chamber
Philharmonic, Stuttgart – Wich — Intercord (in set 973–09Z)

Concerto grosso No. 5, in D
with R. Barchet vln, R. Reinhardt
hpsi, H. Brun vlc & Pro Arte Orch.,
Munich – Redel — Vox (in sets PL10043 & VBX22)

Concerto grosso No. 5, in D
with M. Gaiser vln, T. Blees vlc, M.
Galling hpsi & Süddeutsche Chamber
Philharmonic, Stuttgart – Wich — Intercord (in set 973–09Z)

Concerto grosso No. 6, in g
with R. Barchet vln, R. Reinhardt
hpsi, M. Brun vlc & Pro Arte Orch.,
Munich – Redel — Vox (in sets PL10043 & VBX22)

Concerto grosso No. 6, in g
with M. Gaiser vln, T. Blees vlc, M.
Galling hpsi & Süddeutsche Chamber
Philharmonic, Stuttgart – Wich — Intercord (in set 973–09Z)

Concerto grosso No. 7, in B flat
with R. Barchet vln, R. Reinhardt
hpsi, M. Brun vlc & Pro Arte Orch.,
Munich – Redel — Vox (in sets PL10043 & VBX22)

Concerto grosso No. 7, in B flat
with M. Gaiser vln, T. Blees vlc, M.
Galling hpsi & Süddeutsche Chamber
Philharmonic, Stuttgart – Wich — Intercord (in set 973–09Z)

Concerto grosso No. 8, in c
with R. Barchet vln, R. Reinhardt
hpsi, M. Brun vlc & Pro Arte Orch.,
Munich – Redel — Vox (in sets PL10043 & VBX22)

Concerto grosso No. 8, in c
with M. Gaiser vln, T. Blees vlc, M.
Galling hpsi & Süddeutsche Chamber
Philharmonic, Stuttgart – Wich — Intercord (in set 973–09Z)

Concerto grosso No. 9, in F
with R. Barchet vln, R. Reinhardt
hpsi, M. Brun vlc & Pro Arte Orch.,
Munich – Redel — Vox (in sets PL10043 & VBX22)

HANDEL – *Continued*

Concerto grosso No. 9, in F
with M. Gaiser vln, T. Blees vlc, M.　Intercord (in set 973–09Z)
Galling hpsi & Süddeutsche Chamber
Philharmonic, Stuttgart – Wich

Concerto grosso No. 10, in d
with R. Barchet vln, R. Reinhardt　Vox (in sets PL10043 & VBX22)
hpsi, M. Brun vlc & Pro Arte Orch.,
Munich – Redel

Concerto grosso No. 10, in d
with M. Gaiser vln, T. Blees vlc, M.　Intercord (in set 973–09Z)
Galling hpsi & Süddeutsche Chamber
Philharmonic, Stuttgart – Wich

Concerto grosso No. 11, in A
with R. Barchet vln, R. Reinhardt　Vox (in sets PL10043 & VBX22)
hpsi, M. Brun vlc & Pro Arte Orch.,
Munich – Redel

Concerto grosso No. 11, in A
with M. Gaiser vln, T. Blees vlc, M.　Intercord (in set 973–09Z)
Galling hpsi & Süddeutsche Chamber
Philharmonic, Stuttgart – Wich

Concerto grosso No. 12, in b
with R. Barchet vln, R. Reinhart hpsi,　Vox (in sets PL10043 & VBX22)
M. Brun vlc & Pro Arte Orch.,
Munich – Redel

Concerto grosso No. 12, in b
with M. Gaiser vln, T. Blees vlc, M.　Intercord (in set 973–09Z)
Galling hpsi & Süddeutsche Chamber
Philharmonic, Stuttgart – Wich

(15) Sonatas, Op. 1 (?1731) fl or vln & c
Sonata No. 3, in A vln I
with H. Ruf hpsi & J. Koch gamba　Bärenreiter Musicaphon BM30
L1518, BM30 SL1518
Nonesuch (in set H71238)

Sonata No. 10, in g vln II
with H. Ruf hpsi & J. Koch gamba　Bärenreiter Musicaphon BM30
L1518, BM30 SL1518
Nonesuch (in set H71238)

Sonata No. 12, in F vln III
with H. Ruf hpsi & J. Koch gamba　Bärenreiter Musicaphon BM30
L1518, BM30 SL1518
Nonesuch (in set H71238)

Sonata No. 13, in D vln IV
with H. Ruf hpsi & J. Koch gamba　Bärenreiter Musicaphon BM30
L1519, BM30 SL1519
Nonesuch (in set H71238)

Sonata No. 14, in D vln V
with H. Ruf hpsi & J. Koch gamba　Bärenreiter Musicaphon BM30
L1519, BM30 SL1519
Nonesuch (in set H71238)

Sonata No. 15, in E vln VI
with H. Ruf hpsi & J. Koch gamba　Bärenreiter Musicaphon BM30
L1519, BM30 SL1519
Nonesuch (in set H71238)

HAYDN

(6) Divertimenti, H.II, Nos. 9/14 (Op. 5) fl, vln, vla & vlc
No. 3. Divertimento No. 3, in D, H.II, No. 11
with H. Steinkraus fl, W. Schnell ob,　Turnabout TV34237
A. Schaefer vln, T. Blees vlc, G.
Krueger cbs & M. Galling hpsi

Sextet "Divertimento" in E flat, H.II, No. 39 "Echo" 4 vlns & 2 vlcs
with R. Nielen–Wagner vln, J.　Turnabout TV34237
Rottenfusser vln, W. Forchert vln, H.
Beckedorf vlc & H. Michel vlc

Sinfonia Concertante in B flat, Op. 84 (H.I, No. 105) vln, vlc, ob, bsn &
orch.
with P. Schwarzl vlc, W. Liebermann　Eurodisc 70094KK, 70095KK
ob, H. Bär bsn & Bamberg Symphony
Orch. – Kertész

Sinfonia concertante in B flat, Op. 84 (H.I, No. 105) vln, vlc, ob, bsn &
orch.
with P. Buck vlc, F. Milde ob, H.　Turnabout TV34418
Anton bsn & Württemburg Chamber
Orch., Heilbronn – Faerber

HUMMEL

Concerto in G, Op. 17 "Le Grande" vln, pf & orch.
with M. Galling pf & Stuttgart　Turnabout TV4028, TV34028
Philharmonic Orch. – Paulmüller　Vox DL1370

LOCATELLI

(12) Concerti, Op. 3 (1733) "L'Arte del Violino" (with 24 Caprices) vln &
strs
Concerto No. 1, in D
with Mainz Chamber Orch. – Kehr　Vox (in sets VBX40 &
SVBX540), DL500–2

Concerto No. 2, in c
with Mainz Chamber Orch. – Kehr　Vox (in sets VBX40 &
SVBX540)

Concerto No. 3, in F
with Mainz Chamber Orch. – Kehr　Vox (in sets VBX40 &
SVBX540)

Concerto No. 4, in E
with Mainz Chamber Orch. – Kehr　Vox (in sets VBX40 &
SVBX540), DL500–2

Concerto No. 5, in C
with Mainz Chamber Orch. – Kehr　Vox (in sets VBX40 &
SVBX540)

Concerto No. 6, in g
with Mainz Chamber Orch. – Kehr　Vox (in sets VBX40 &
SVBX540)

Concerto No. 7, in B flat
with Mainz Chamber Orch. – Kehr　Vox (in sets VBX 41 &
SVBX541)

Concerto No. 8, in e
with Mainz Chamber Orch. – Kehr　Vox (in sets VBX41 &
SVBX541)

Concerto No. 9, in G
with Mainz Chamber Orch. – Kehr　Vox (in sets VBX41 &
SVBX541)

Concerto No. 10, in F
with Mainz Chamber Orch. – Kehr　Vox (in sets VBX41 &
SVBX541)

LOCATELLI – *Continued*

Concerto No. 11, in A
with Mainz Chamber Orch. – Kehr   Turnabout TV4047, TV34047
Vox (in sets VBX41 &
SVBX541)

Concerto No. 12, in D
with Mainz Chamber Orch. – Kehr   Turnabout TV4047, TV34047
Vox (in sets VBX41 &
SVBX541)

MOZART

Concertone in C, K190 2 vlns, ob, vlc & orch.
with W. Keltsch vln, A. Sous ob, H.   Turnabout TV4098, TV34098
Beckendorf vlc & Stuttgart Bach
Kollegium – Rilling

Serenade No. 4, in D, K203 orch.
with Süddeutsche Chamber   Intercord 947–09K
Philharmonic, Stuttgart – Wich

Serenade No. 7, in D, K250 "Haffner" orch.
with Württemberg State Orch. –   Turnabout TV4013, TV34013
Leitner   Vox PL12960, STPL512960

Sinfonia concertante in E flat, K364 vln, vla & orch.
with U. Koch vla & Bamberg   Eurodisc 70094KK, 70095KK
Symphony Orch. – Kertész   Nonesuch H1074, H71074

Sinfonia concertante in E flat, K364 vln, vla & orch.
with U. Koch vla & Stuttgart Bach   Turnabout TV4098, TV34098
Kollegium – Rilling

PACHELBEL

Canon & Gigue in D 3 vlns & c
with U. Grehling vln, D. Wolff–Malm   Archive EPA37256, SEPA181256
vln, F. Neumeyer hpsi & R. Buhl vlc

Partita No. 2, in c 2 vlns & c
with U. Grehling vln, F. Neumeyer   Archive EPA37256, SEPA181256
hpsi & R. Buhl vlc

PEPUSCH

Sonata in a vln, gamba & c
with J. Koch gamba, H. Ruf hpsi &   Bärenreiter Musicaphon BM30
H. Haferland gamba   SL1536

PFITZNER

Concerto in b, Op. 34 (1923) vln & orch.
with Philharmonia Hungarica – Wich   Candide CE31026
Intercord 978–09K

RAMEAU

(5) Pièces de Clavecin en Concerts (1741) hpsi, vln & c
No. 1. Concert No. 1, in c
with M. Galling hpsi, P. Buck vlc &   Philips C37
Stuttgart Chamber Orch. – Couraud
No. 4. Concert No. 4, in B flat
with M. Galling hpsi, P. Buck vlc &   Philips C37
Stuttgart Chamber Orch. – Couraud

SCHUBERT

Fantasia in C, Op. 159 (D934) vln & pf
with M. Galling pf
    Bärenreiter Musicaphon BM30
L1531

SCHUBERT – *Continued*

Sonata in A, Op. 162 (D574) "Duo" vln & pf
with M. Galling pf   Bärenreiter Musicaphon BM30
L1531

SCHÜTZ

(20) Symphoniae sacrae, Op. 6 (1629)
Concerto No. 3 (In te, Domine, speravi) SWV259 a, vln, tbn & c
with M. Rauter–Edzart a, R. Zettler   Bärenreiter Musicaphon BM30
tbn, M. Galling hpsi & P. Buck vlc   SL1323
Nonesuch H1160, H71160

Concerto No. 5 (Venite ad me) SWV261 t, 2 vlns & c
with K. Huber t, W. Keltsch vln, M.   Bärenreiter Musicaphon BM30
Galling hpsi & P. Buck vlc   SL1323
Nonesuch H1160, H71160

Concerto No. 9 (O quam tu pulchra es) SWV265 2 t's, 2 vlns & c
with K. Huber t, W. Jochims t, W.   Bärenreiter Musicaphon BM30
Keltsch vln, M. Galling hpsi & P.   SL1323
Buck vlc   Nonesuch H1160, H71160

Concerto No. 10 (Veni de Libano) SWV266 2 t's, 2 vlns & c
with K. Huber t, W. Jochims t, W.   Bärenreiter Musicaphon BM30
Keltsch vln, M. Galling hpsi & P.   SL1323
Buck vlc   Nonesuch H1160, H71160

(27) Symphoniae sacrae, Op. 10 (1647)
Concerto No. 2 (Singet dem Herren ein neues Lied) SWV342 t,
2 vlns & c
with H.J. Rotzsch t, W. Keltsch vln,   Bärenreiter Musicaphon BM30
M. Galling hpsi & H. Michel vlc   SL1324
Nonesuch H71196

Concerto No. 6 (Ich werde nicht sterben) SWV346 s, 2 vlns & c
with E. Speiser s, W. Keltsch vln, M.   Bärenreiter Musicaphon BM30
Galling hpsi & H. Michel vlc   SL1324
Nonesuch H71196

Concerto No. 7 (Ich danke dir, Herr) SWV347 s, 2 vlns & c
with E. Speiser s, W. Keltsch vln, M.   Bärenreiter Musicaphon BM30
Galling hpsi & H. Michel vlc   SL1324
Nonesuch H71196

Concerto No. 8 (Herzlich lieb hab ich dich, o Herr) SWV348 a, 2 vlns or
obs & c
with M. Lehane a, W. Keltsch vln, M.   Bärenreiter Musicaphon BM30
Galling hpsi & H. Michel vlc   SL1324
Nonesuch H71196

Concerto No. 27 (Freuet euch des Herrn, ihr Gerechten) SWV367 2 t's,
bs, 2 vlns & c
with K. Huber t, H.J. Rotzsch t, W.   Bärenreiter Musicaphon BM30
Pommerien bs, W. Keltsch vln, M.   SL1324
Galling hpsi & H. Michel vlc   Nonesuch H71196

SPOHR

Concerto No. 8, in a, Op. 47 "Gesangsscene" vln & orch.
with Hamburg Symphony Orch. –   Candide CE31043
Springer

Grand Duo in e, Op. 13 vln & vla
with U. Koch vla   Candide CE31043

(2) Potpourris (on airs from the opera "Jessonda") Op. 64 vln, vlc & orch.
with T. Blees vlc & Hamburg   Candide CE31043
Symphony Orch. – Springer

STAMITZ K.

Sinfonia concertante in D vln, vla & orch.
   with E. Wallfisch vla & Stuttgart   Turnabout TV4221, TV34221
   Soloisten

TELEMANN

Concerto in F, T.II, No. 3 3 vlns, strs & c
   with A. Schäfer vln, G. Egger vln &   Turnabout TV34288
   Stuttgart Solisten

Essercizii Musici (1721)
   No. 3. Trio–sonata in F vln, gamba & c
   with J. Koch gamba, H. Ruf hpsi &   Bärenreiter Musicaphon BM30
   H. Haferland gamba   SL1536

(6) Partitas var. cbns
   Partita No. 3, in c vln & c
   with H. Ruf hpsi & J. Koch gamba   Bärenreiter Musicaphon BM30
    SL1539

   Partita No. 6, in E flat vln & c
   with H. Ruf hpsi & J. Koch gamba   Bärenreiter Musicaphon BM30
    SL1540

Suite in B flat, T.III, No. 1 2 obs, strs & c
   with R. Barchet vln, F. Milde ob &   Vox PL10650
   Südwestdeutsche Chamber Orch. –
   Zucca

VIOTTI

Concerto in E flat "Double" pf, vln & str orch.
   with M. Galling pf & Berlin   Turnabout TV4229, TV34229
   Symphony Orch. – Bünte

Concerto No. 22, in a (cadenza by Ysaÿe) vln & orch.
   with Berlin Symphony Orch. – Bünte   Turnabout TV4229, TV34229

VIVALDI

(12) Concerti, Op. 8 (1725) "Il Cimento dell' Armonia e dell' Invenzione"
(Nos. 1/4: Le quattro Stagioni) vln & strs
   Concerto No. 1, in E, F.I, No. 22 "La Primavera"
   with Württemberg Chamber Orch. –   Intercord 061–09K
   Faerber   Turnabout TV4040, TV34040

   Concerto No. 2, in B flat, F.I, No. 23 "L'Estate"
   with Württemberg Chamber Orch. –   Intercord 061–09K
   Faerber   Turnabout TV4040, TV34040

   Concerto No. 3, in F, F.I, No. 24 "L'Autunno"
   with Württemberg Chamber Orch. –   Intercord 061–09K
   Faerber   Turnabout TV4040, TV34040

   Concerto No. 4, in f, F.I, No. 25 "L'Inverno"
   with Württemberg Chamber Orch. –   Intercord 061–09K
   Faerber   Turnabout TV4040, TV34040

Concerto in A, P.222 (F.I, No. 139) "L'eco in lontano" 2 vlns, strs & c –
arr. Molinari
   with E. Mampaey vln & Emil Seiler   Archive APM14318, ARC3218,
   Chamber Orch. – Hofman   ARC73218, SAPM198318
    Musique Royale 199010

Marjorie LAVERS

CROFT

Sonata in b vln & c
   with R. Elliott hpsi & J. Ryan gamba   Oryx ORYX730

Sonata in g vln & c
   with R. Elliott hpsi & J. Ryan gamba   Oryx ORYX730

Mary LAW (1890–1919)

ANONYMOUS

Londonderry air traditional Irish ballad – arr. vln & str qt O'Connor
   Morris
   with piano & string   y 21004 e   Gramophone & Typewriter
   quartet   47939
    Zonophone GO35

BACH

(3) Sonatas & 3 Partitas, BWV1001/6 solo vln
   Partita No. 3, in E: Gavotte (3rd mvt) BWV1006 arr. vln & pf Kreisler
   with piano   Zonophone A151

BALFE

(The) Bohemian Girl (1843) – opera
   selection arr. vln & pf as "Fantasia"
   with piano   Zonophone A231

BÉRIOT

Concerto No. 7, in G, Op. 76 vln & orch.
   Allegro moderato (1st mvt)
   with piano   HMV C802
Scène de Ballet (Fantaisie–ballet No. 1) Op. 100 vln & orch.
   with piano   HMV C873

CHOPIN

(3) Nocturnes, Op. 9 pf
   No. 2. Nocturne No. 2, in E flat arr. vln & pf Sarasate
   with piano & string   y 21011 e   Gramophone & Typewriter
   quartet   47938
    HMV X773
    Zonophone GO30

DONIZETTI

(La) Fille du Regiment (1840) – opera
   selection arr. vln & pf as "Fantasia"
   with piano   z 8399 f   Gramophone & Typewriter
    047923
    Zonophone A94

DRDLA

Serenade No. 1, in A vln & pf
   with piano   Zonophone A81

DVOŘÁK

(8) Humoresques, Op. 101 pf
   No. 7. Humoresque No. 7, in G flat arr. vln & pf "in G" Wilhelmj
   with piano   Zonophone A123

FLOTOW

Martha (1847) – opera
   selection arr. vln & pf as "Fantasia"
   with piano   AL 8352 f   Gramophone & Typewriter
    047924
    Zonophone A194

HUBAY

(6) Blumenleben, Op. 30 vln & pf
   No. 5. Der Zephir
   with piano   Zonophone A141

HUBAY – *Continued*

(14) Scènes de la Csárda vln & pf
No. 4. Hejre Kati, Op. 32
with piano
Gramophone & Typewriter
047900
Zonophone A71

KREISLER

Variations on a theme of Corelli (Tartini) vln & pf
with piano   z 6805 f Gramophone & Typewriter
047905
Zonophone A98

MASSENET

Thaïs (1894) – opera
Méditation arr. vln & pf Marsick
with piano   Zonophone A199

MENDELSSOHN

Concerto in e, Op. 64 vln & orch.
Andante (2nd mvt)
with piano   Zonophone A131

Allegro non troppo; Allegro molto vivace (3rd mvt)
with piano   z 6804 f Gramophone & Typewriter
047904
Zonophone A98

MOSZKOWSKI

(6) Klavierstücke, Op. 15 pf – 4 hands
No. 1. Serenata arr. vln, pf & str qt
with piano & string   y 21479 e Gramophone & Typewriter
quartet   47942
Zonophone GO40

RAFF

(6) Pieces, Op. 85 vln & pf
No. 3. Cavatina in D
with piano   Zonophone A81

RAMEAU

Andante* arr. vln & pf
with piano   AL 8295 f Gramophone & Typewriter
047918
Zonophone A166

Castor et Pollux (1737) – opera
Gavotte (Act IV) arr. vln & pf Burmester
with piano   AL 8295 f Gramophone & Typewriter
047918
Zonophone A166

RIES

Suite No. 3, in G, Op. 34 vln & pf
Gondoliera (4th mvt)
with piano   Zonophone A151

* Unidentified.

ROSSINI

Guillaume Tell (1829) – opera
selection arr. vln & pf as "Fantasia"
with piano   z 8398 f Gramophone & Typewriter
047921
Zonophone A187

SAINT–SAËNS

(Le) Carnaval des animaux (1886) small orch.
Le cygne arr. vln & pf
with piano   Zonophone A141

SARASATE

Zigeunerweisen, Op. 20 vln & pf or orch.
with piano   Gramophone & Typewriter
047901
Zonophone A71

SCHUBERT, François

(12) Bagatelles, Op. 13 vln & pf
No. 9. L'abeille
with piano   Zonophone A141

SCHUBERT, Franz

(6) Moments musicaux, Op. 94 (D780) (1823/7) pf
No. 3. Moment musicale No. 3, in f "Air russe" arr. vln & pf Kreisler
with piano   HMV C802

SIBELIUS

Kuolema, Op. 44 – Incidental music orch.
Valse triste arr. vln & pf Franko
with piano & string   y 21006 e Gramophone & Typewriter
quartet   47937
HMV X773
Zonophone GO30

SULLIVAN

(The) Gondoliers (1889) – operetta
selection arr. vln & pf as "Fantasia"
with piano   Zonophone A227

Iolanthe (1882) – operetta
selection arr. vln & pf as "Fantasia"
with piano   z 8649 f Zonophone A235

(The) Mikado (1885) – operetta
selection arr. vln & pf as "Fantasia"
with piano   z 8654 f Zonophone A235

(The) Pirates of Penzance (1880) – operetta
selection arr. vln & pf as "Fantasia"
with piano   Zonophone A227

Ruddigore (1887) – operetta
selection arr. vln & pf as "Fantasia"
with piano   Zonophone A239

Yeomen of the Guard (1888) – operetta
selection arr. vln & pf as "Fantasia"
with piano   Zonophone A239

TCHAIKOVSKY

(12) Pieces (of moderate difficulty) Op. 40 pf
No. 2. Chanson triste arr. vln & pf
with piano   Zonophone A211

TCHAIKOVSKY – *Continued*

(3) Souvenirs de Hapsal, Op. 2 pf
No. 3. Chant sans paroles in f arr. vln & pf Kreisler
with piano & string   y 21057 e   Gramophone & Typewriter
quartet   47940
                                       Zonophone GO35

THOMAS

Mignon (1866) – opera
Entr'acte (Gavotte) (Act II) arr. vln & pf Sarasate
with piano & string   y 21477 e   Gramophone & Typewriter
quartet   47941
                                       Zonophone GO40

THOMÉ

Andante religioso, Op. 70 pf – arr. vln & pf
with piano   Zonophone A211

VERDI

Aïda (1871) – opera
selection arr. vln & pf as "Fantasia"
with piano   Zonophone A199
Rigoletto (1851) – opera
selection arr. vln & pf as "Fantasia"
with piano   z 8393 f   Gramophone & Typewriter
                                      047922
                                      Zonophone A187
(La) Traviata (1853) – opera
selection arr. vln & pf as "Fantasia"
with piano   AL 8354 f   Gramophone & Typewriter
                                      047920
                                      Zonophone A177
(Il) Trovatore (1853) – opera
selection arr. vln & pf as "Fantasia"
with piano   AL 8350 f   Gramophone & Typewriter
                                      047919
                                      Zonophone A177

VIEUXTEMPS

Ballade & Polonaise in G, Op. 38 vln & pf
Polonaise
with piano   AL 8294 f   Gramophone & Typewriter
                                      047917
                                      Zonophone A166
Concerto No. 4, in d, Op. 31 vln & orch.
Adagio religioso (2nd mvt)
with piano   HMV C873

WALLACE

Maritana (1845) – opera
selection arr. vln & pf as "Fantasia"
with piano   Zonophone A231

WIENIAWSKI

Concerto No. 2, in d, Op. 22 vln & orch.
Romance (2nd mvt)
with piano   Zonophone A112
Allegro con fuoco; Allegro moderato "a la Zingara" (3rd mvt)
with piano   Zonophone A131
Légende, Op. 17 vln & pf or orch.
with piano   Zonophone A123

WIENIAWSKI – *Continued*

Mazurka in a, Op. 3 "Kujawiak" vln & pf
with piano   HMV C802
Souvenir de Moscou, Op. 6 vln & pf or orch.
with piano   Zonophone A112

Arthur LEBLANC (1906–)

ARCHER
Prelude & Allegro (1954) vln & pf
with C. Reiner pf   CBC Transcription Program 136

CHAMPAGNE
Danse villageoise (1930) vln & pf
with C. Reiner pf   Acadia 3000CB

FRASER
Élégie vln & pf
with C. Reiner pf   CBC Transcription Program 136

GRATTON
Danse Canadiénne No. 4, (inspired from Canadian folklore) (1935) vln & pf
with C. Reiner pf   CBC Transcription Program 136

LEBLANC
Petite Suite Canadienne vln & pf
with C. Reiner pf   CBC Transcription Program 136

Deszö LEDERER (1858–)

BACH
(4) Suites, BWV1066/9 strs & c
Suite No. 3, in D: (2nd mvt) BWV1068 2 obs, 3 tpts, drms, strs & c –
arr. vln & pf as "Air on the G–string" by Wilhelmj
with piano   1402 f   Favorite 4028E
                                  Homophone 25

GOUNOD
Ave Maria (Méditation on Bach's "Prelude No. 1, in C" from Book I of
"Das Wohltemperirte Clavier") v & pf – arr. v, vln & pf
with M. Agussol s & piano   Favorite 1–14020E

LEDERER
Mélodie, Op. 15 vln & pf
with piano   Favorite 1–14018E

MASSENET
Thaïs (1894) – opera
Méditation arr. vln & Marsick
with piano   1400 f   Favorite 4027E
                                  Homophone 25

LEDRU

FLOTOW
Martha (1847) – opera
selection arr. vln & pf as "Fantasia" by Ledru
with orch.   15881 u   HMV 30741

MASCAGNI

Cavalleria Rusticana (1890) – opera
  Intermezzo orch. – arr. vln & orch. Ledru
  with orch.   15495 u   HMV 30726

Ulrich LEHMANN (1928–   )

BACH

(6) Brandenburg Concerti, BWV1046/51 (1721) strs & c
  Brandenburg Concerto No. 2, in F, BWV1047 tpt, fl, ob, vln, strs & c
  with A. Scherbaum tpt, A. Jaunet fl,   Amadeo AVRS206
  A. Raoult ob & Zürich Chamber Orch.
  – de Stoutz

Concerto in c, BWV1060 vln & ob or 2 vlns, strs & c
  with A. Lardrot ob & Zürich Chamber Amadeo AVRS6363
  Orch. – de Stoutz   Philips 906363ASY
                                Vanguard SRV198SD

HARTMANN, K.A.

Concerto funèbre (1939) vln & str orch.
  with Zürich Chamber Orch. – de   Amadeo AVRS6242
  Stoutz   Record Society RS70, RSS19

MARTINŮ

Concerto da camera (1941) vln, pf, pcn & strs
  with Zürich Chamber Orch. – de   Amadeo AVRS6242
  Stoutz   Record Society RS70, RSS19

SCHOECK

Concerto in B flat, Op. 21 (1911/2) vln & orch.
  with Zürich Chamber Orch. – de
  Stoutz   Amadeo AVRS5042

Géry LEMAIRE

PASQUINI

Arietta vln & str orch.
  with Les Solistes de Liège – Lemaire   Alpha CL3006, CL4006

Bouw LEMKES

GILTAY

Concerto (1967) 2 vlns & orch.
  with J. Lemkes vln & Utrecht   Radio Nederland 109870
  Symphony Orch. – Hupperts

Jeanne LEMKES

GILTAY

Concerto (1967) 2 vlns & orch.
  with B. Lemkes vln & Utrecht   Radio Nederland 109870
  Symphony Orch. – Hupperts

Valère LENAERTS

BOECK

Concerto vln & orch.
  with Belgian National Orch. – Louël   Cultura 5066-2

Jenö LENER (1894–1948)

BEETHOVEN

Sonata No. 5, in F, Op. 24 "Spring" vln & pf
             CAX 8305-2 & 8306/10-1   Columbia 266111/3, 69843/5D,
  with L. Kentner pf   (in set MM404), 70329/31D,
                                  LX759/61

(3) Sonatas, Op. 30 vln & pf
  No. 1. Sonata No. 6, in A
             CAX 8480/1-2, 8482/3-1, 8484–
  with L. Kentner pf   5 & 8485-3   Columbia LOX424/6, LX827/9

Gabrielle LENGYEL (1920–   )

BARTÓK

(44) Duos (1931) 2 vlns
  15 only*
  with A–M. Gründer vln   Ducretet-Thomson LAP1008,
                                    LPG8192

Jean LENSEN

DEQUIN

Brise argentine – waltz pf – arr. vln & orch.
  with orch.   01562 v   Gramophone & Typewriter
                                    037917, 047931

DICK–STON

Désire vln & pf
  with orch.   01561 v   Gramophone & Typewriter
                                    037916, 047930

DVOŘÁK

(8) Humoresques, Op. 101 pf
  No. 7. Humoresque No. 7, in G flat arr. vln & pf "in G" Wilhelmj
  with piano   01323 v   Gramophone & Typewriter
                                    037914, 047926

LEONCAVALLO

(I) Pagliacci (1892) – opera
  selection arr. vln & pf as "Paraphrase" by Lensen
  with piano   01324 v   Gramophone & Typewriter
                                    027901, 037915

PADEREWSKI

(6) Humoresques de concert, Op. 14 pf
  No. 1. Minuet in G arr. vln & pf Kreisler
  with piano   Gramophone & Typewriter
                                    047925

Boris LENSKY

BECCE

Serenata Mignonne pf – arr. vln & pf
  with piano   Columbia 198M

* Unidentified.

FIBICH

Images, Impressions & Souvenirs, Op. 41 pf
  No. 14. Poem (from "Souvenirs", Part IV) arr. vln & pf Kubelík
    with cinema organ   Columbia D9911, OD17

d'HARDELOT

Wait v & pf – arr. vln & org
  with cinema organ   Columbia D9909

HERMITE

(The) Nights of Erzeroum v & pf – arr. vln & org
  with cinema organ   Columbia D9905

KLICKMANN

Waters of the Perkiomen (1925) v & pf – arr. vln & org
  with cinema organ   Columbia D9905

KREISLER

Schön Rosmarin vln & pf
  with cinema organ   Columbia D9910

LOHR

Little grey home in the west (1911) v & pf – arr. vln & org
  with cinema organ   Columbia D9907

MONTI

Csárdas (1904) vln & pf
  with piano   Columbia D10084

NICKLAS–KEMPNER

Csárdas vln & pf
  with piano   Columbia 198M, D10084

PETRIE

(Los) Seemans v & pf – arr. vln & org Martell
  with cinema organ   Columbia D9910

SANDERS

Once v & pf – arr. vln & org
  with cinema organ   Columbia D9911, OD17

SCHERTZINGER

Marchéta (1913) v & pf – arr. vln & org
  with cinema organ   Columbia D9906

SILÉSU

Star of my life v & pf – arr. vln & org
  with cinema organ   Columbia D9908

WOOD

Love's garden of roses v & pf – arr. vln & org
  with cinema organ   Columbia D9906
Roses of Picardy (1916) v & pf – arr. vln & org
  with cinema organ   Columbia D9907
World of love v & pf – arr. vln & org
  with cinema organ   Columbia D9908

ZAMECNIK

Only a smile v & pf – arr. vln & org
  with cinema organ   Columbia D9909

Augustin LEON–ARA (1936–   )

ALBÉNIZ

España (6 Feuilles d'album) Op. 165 pf
  No. 3. Malagueña in b arr. vln & pf Kreisler
    with F. Lavilla pf   Decca LXT29014

FALLA

(La) Vida Breve (1913) – Opera
  Danza española orch. – arr. vln & pf Kreisler
    with F. Lavilla pf   Decca LXT29014

LOCATELLI

(12) Sonatas, Op. 6 (1737) vln & c
  Sonata No. 7, in f "Au Tombeau" arr. vln & pf Ysaÿe
    with T. Fidler pf   Eterna 720102
                         Muza XL0386
                         Telefunken BLE14088

PAGANINI

Concerto No. 2, in b, Op. 7 vln & orch.
  Ronde à la clochette "La Campanella" (3rd mvt) arr. vln & pf Kreisler
    with T. Fidler pf   Eterna 720102
                         Muza L0223

RODRIGO

Capriccio (1944) "Ofrenda a Sarasate" solo vln
  (unaccompanied)   Decca LXT29014
(2) Esbozas, Op. 1 (1923) vln & pf
  No. 1. La enamorada junto al pequeño surtidor
    with F. Lavilla pf   Decca LXT29014
  No. 2. Pequeña ronda
    with F. Lavilla pf   Decca LXT29014
Sonata Pimpante "Homage to Joaquin Turina" vln & pf
  with M. Zanetti pf   Tempo TIL001

SARASATE

Caprice basque, Op. 24 vln & pf
  with M. Zanetti pf   Tempo TIL001
(8) Danzas españolas vln & pf
  No. 2. Habanera, Op. 21, No. 2
    with M. Zanetti pf   Tempo TIL001
  No. 3. Romanza andaluza, Op. 22, No. 1
    with F. Lavilla pf   Decca LXT29014
  No. 4. Jota Navarra, Op. 22, No. 2
    with M. Zanetti pf   Tempo TIL001
  No. 6. Zapateado, Op. 23, No. 2
    with M. Zanetti pf   Tempo TIL001
Introduction & Tarantella, Op. 43 vln & pf
  with F. Lavilla pf   Decca LXT29014

TURINA

Sonata No. 1, in d, Op. 51 (1929) vln & pf
  with F. Lavilla pf   Decca LXT29014

Marie LEONHARDT

ALBICASTRO

Trio–sonata unid – vln & c
  with M. Ferguson rec, M. Smit–   Radio Nederland 109775
  Sibinga hpsi & V. Hampe gamba

ANONYMOUS

Allemande No. 2 2 vlns & rec*
with A. van den Hombergh vln & M.   Radio Nederland 109773
Ferguson rec

Allemande No. 4 2 vlns & rec*
with A. van den Hombergh vln & M.   Radio Nederland 109776
Ferguson rec

BACH

Concerto in a, BWV1044 clav, fl, vln, strs & c
with G. Leonhardt hpsi, A.   Telefunken SAWT9552
Uittenbosch fl & Leonhardt Consort

HACQUART

Sonata 2 vlns & c†
with A. van den Hombergh vln, M.   Radio Nederland 109775
Smit–Sibinga hpsi & V. Hampe gamba

TELEMANN

Concerto in F, T.II, No. 3 3 vlns, strs & c
with J. Schröder vln, J. Holtman vln,   Telefunken SAWT9452
G. Leonhardt hpsi & Concerto
Amsterdam – Brüggen

TURINI

Madrigali ... con alcune Sonate, Libro Primo (1624)
Sonata in a 2 vlns & c
with A. van den Hombergh vln, G.   Telefunken AWT9461,
Leonhardt hpsi & D. Koster vlc   SAWT9461

Leon LEONIDOFF (1895–   )

CHOPIN

(3) Nocturnes, Op. 9 pf
No. 2. Nocturne No. 2, in E flat arr. vln & pf Sarasate
with piano   Polydor 57805

GLUCK

Orphée et Eurydice (1762) – opera
Dance of the blessed spirits: Lento "Mélodie" (no. 2) arr. vln & pf
Kreisler
with piano   Polydor 57806

KREISLER

Andantino (Padre Martini) vln & pf
with piano   Polydor 57806

Reginald LEOPOLD

ANONYMOUS

Greensleeves traditional English ballad – arr. vln & strs
with Reginald Kilbey & his strings   Capitol SP8691

BIZET

Agnus Dei v & pf – arr. vln & strs
with Reginald Kilbey & his strings   Capitol SP8691

* From the volume "The Excellent Cabinet."
† From the volume "Harmonia Parnassia."

BOCCHERINI

(6) Quintets, Op. 13 2 vlns, vla & 2 vlcs
No. 5. Quintet No. 5, in E: Minuet (3rd mvt) "Bull" arr. vln & strs
with Reginald Kilbey & his strings   Capitol SP8691

DVOŘÁK

(8) Humoresques, Op. 101 pf
No. 7. Humoresque No. 7, in G flat arr. vln & strs
with Reginald Kilbey & his strings   Capitol SP8691

HANDEL

Serse (1738) – opera
Ombra mai fu "Largo" arr. vln & strs
with Reginald Kilbey & his strings   Capitol SP8691

LISZT

(3) Liebesträume, G326 pf
No. 3. Liebestraum No. 3, in A flat arr. vln & strs
with Reginald Kilbey & his strings   Capitol SP8691

MacDOWELL

Woodland sketches, Op. 51 pf
No. 1. To a wild rose arr. vln & strs
with Reginald Kilbey & his strings   Capitol SP8691

SULLIVAN

(The) Lost chord (1877) v & pf – arr. vln & strs
with Reginald Kilbey & his strings   Capitol SP8691

Nicole LEPINTE

VIVALDI

(12) Concerti, Op. 3 "L'Estro armonico" var. cbns & strs
Concerto No. 10, in b, P.148 (F.IV, No. 10) 4 vlns, strs & c
with J–P. Wallez vln, C. Jacquillat vln,   Christophorus SCGLP75896
Y. Carracilly vln, L. Boulay hpsi &   Critère CRD186, SCRD5186
Collegium Musicum, Paris – Douatte   Monitor MCS2102

Marcelle LEROY

ALBINONI

Adagio in g strs & org
with P. Berthier org & Netherlands   Fontana 200030WGL
Chamber Orch. – Goldberg

HANDEL

Serse (1738) – opera
Ombra mai fu "Largo" arr. vln, org & strs
with P. Berthier org & Netherlands   Fontana 675402KR
Chamber Orch. – Goldberg

Boyan LESHEV

KAZANDJIEV

Sonata solo vln
(unaccompanied)   Balkanton 396

PIPKOV

Sonata (1929) vln & pf
with S. Gulubova pf   Balkanton 396

Bernard LESSMANN

DRDLA
Serenade No. 1, in A vln & pf
   with Chamber Orch.   24817   Telefunken A10140, TA928

Souvenir vln & pf
   with Chamber Orch.   24818   Telefunken A10140, TA928

HUBAY
(14) Scènes de la Csárda vln & pf
   No. 4. Hejre Kati, Op. 32
        26014–1 & 26015   Telefunken A10469
   with German Opera House Orch. –
   Lutze

JÄRNEFELT
Berceuse in g orch. – arr. vln & orch.
   with Chamber Orch.   Telefunken A10177

KOBIN
(Die) Quelle vln & pf
   with Chamber Orch.   Telefunken A10177

SARASATE
Zigeunerweisen, Op. 20 vln & pf or orch.
        025257 & 025258–1   Telefunken E3127, TE963
   with German Opera House Orch. –
   Lutze

SCHUMANN
(12) Duets, Op. 85 pf – 4 hands
   No. 12. Abendlied
   with Chamber Orch.   Telefunken A10157

(13) Kinderscenen, Op. 15 pf
   No. 7. Träumerei arr. vln & orch.
   with Chamber Orch.   Telefunken A10157

Ivan LETH

FORSMAN
Andantino Carino vln & pf
   with V. Borggaard pf   4916   Tono K8100

HENRIQUES
Ballerina vln & pf
   with V. Borggaard pf   4915   Tono K8100

MORTENSEN
Humoresque vln & pf
   with V. Borggaard pf   Tono K8099

TCHAIKOVSKY
(3) Pieces, Op. 9 pf
   No. 3. Mazurka de salon in d arr. vln & pf Artemieff
   with V. Borggaard pf   Tono K8099

Christopher LEUTJENS

DELARUE
Bébe à Jésus cho – arr. vln & orch.
   with orch.   Pathé 5903, 6512

LEUTJENS
Caresse de fleurs (Intermezzo) vln & pf
   with piano   1334 °   Favorite 28, 1–4053E
Caresse de fleurs (Intermezzo) vln & pf
   with orch.   Pathé 959, 5900, 9503
Chant de brise (valse lente) vln & pf
   with orch.   Pathé 5907
Charme secret (valse lente) vln & pf
   with orch.   Pathé 959, 5901, 9503
Heimliche Reize vln & pf
   with orch.   Pathé 1097, 9501
Intermezzo (waltz) vln & pf
   with orch.   Pathé 1097, 5900
Simple aubade vln & pf
   with orch.   Pathé 9505

MASSENET
Thaïs (1894) – opera
   Méditation arr. vln & pf Marsick
   with orch.   Pathé 8906

MATHÉ
(Le) Petit savoyard vln & pf
   with orch.   Pathé 5905, 9501

MONIUSZKO
Halka (1854) – opera
   Air unid – arr. vln & orch.
   with orch.   Pathé 26707
   The wind whistles (Jontek's aria) arr. vln & orch.
   with orch.   Pathé 26708

TELLAM
(En) Sourdine sur les motifs d'une sérénade de J. Tellam vln & pf
   with orch.   Pathé 9505

THOMÉ
Simple aveu, Op. 25 pf – arr. vln & pf
   with orch.   Pathé 5103

Michel LEVAN

VIVALDI
(12) Concerti, Op. 8 (1725) "Il Cimento dell' Armonia e dell' Invenzione"
(Nos. 1/4: Le quattro Stagioni) vln & strs
Concerto No. 5, in E flat, F.I, No. 26 "La Tempesta di mare"
   with Instrumental Ensemble –   Mercury MG50401, SR90401
   Duhamel

James LEVEY (1887–1955)

BACH
(4) Suites, BWV1066/9 strs & c
   Suite No. 3, in D: Air (2nd mvt) BWV1068 2 obs, 3 tpts, drms, strs & c
   – arr. vln & pf as "Air on the G–string" by Wilhelmj
   with piano   69476   Columbia 3149

DRDLA
Souvenir vln & pf
   with piano   Aco G15016

FAURÉ

Berceuse, Op. 16 vln & pf
  with piano   Columbia 3163

FIOCCO

Suite No. 1, in G hpsi
  Allegro (10th mvt) arr. vln & pf Bent & O'Neill
  with piano   71731 Columbia 3149

GODARD

Concerto No. 1, Op. 35 "Concerto Romantique" vln & orch.
  Canzonetta (2nd mvt)
  with piano   Aco G15016

KINZE

Canzonetta vln & pf
  with piano   Columbia 2958

KREISLER

Andantino (Padre Martini) vln & pf
  with piano   Columbia 2955
Tempo di minuetto (Pugnani) vln & pf
  with piano   Columbia 2955

MASSENET

Thaïs (1894) – opera
  Méditation arr. vln & pf Marsick
  with piano   Aco G15009

PIERNÉ

Sérénade in A, Op. 7 (1875) pf – arr. vln & pf Haddock
  with piano   Aco G15009

SCHUMANN

(13) Kinderscenen, Op. 15 pf
  No. 7. Träumerei arr. vln & pf
  with piano   Columbia 2958

SCOTT

Lullaby, Op. 57, No. 2 v & pf – arr. vln & pf
  with piano   Columbia 3163

SQUIRE

Fantaisie hongrois vlc & pf – arr. vln & pf
  with piano   Aco F33009

SVENDSEN

Romance in G, Op. 26 vln & orch. – arr. vln & pf Wilhelmj
  with piano   C 43 Aco F33008

TCHAIKOVSKY

(3) Souvenirs de Hapsal, Op. 2 pf
  No. 3. Chant sans paroles in f arr. vln & pf Kreisler
  with piano   Aco F33029

WARNER

Intermezzo vln & pf
  with piano   Columbia 2936
Lullaby vln & pf
  with piano   Columbia 2936

Anatoli LEVIN

SHOSTAKOVICH

Pirogov (Suite from music to the film) Op. 76a orch.
  No. 1. Introduction
  with L. Zaks vln & Bolshoi Theatre   Melodiya Angel SR40160
  Orch. – M. Shostakovich   Mezhdunarodnaya Kniga
                                   D020135/6
Zoya (Suite from music to the film) Op. 64a orch.
  No. 1. Introduction (Song about Zoya)
  with L. Zaks vln & Bolshoi Theatre   Melodiya Angel SR40160
  Orch. – M. Shostakovich   Mezhdunarodnaya Kniga
                                   D020135/6

D. LEVIN

DINICU

Hora staccato vln & pf – arr. vln & orch. Vladigerov
  with orch.   Mezhdunarodnaya Kniga
                                 D15562

Theodore LEVY

STRANGE

Birds in the forest pf – arr. 2 vlns & fl
  with H. Rattay vln & D. Lyons fl   Victor 16296

THOMAS

Mignon (1866) – opera
  Entr'acte (Gavotte) (Act II) orch. – arr. str qt
  with H. Rattay vln, L.   B 6617 Victor 16323
  Heine vla & . Francillo vlc

Philip LEWIS

GOUNOD

Ave Maria (Méditation on Bach's "Prelude No. 1, in C" from Book I of
  "Das Wohltemperirte Clavier") v & pf – arr. vln & pf
  with piano   Grammavox 6001, C12

SCHUMANN

(13) Kinderscenen, Op. 15 pf
  No. 7. Träumerei arr. vln & pf
  with piano   Grammavox 6002, C9
                       Popular P36

SVENDSEN

Romance in G, Op. 26 vln & orch. – arr. vln & pf Wilhelmj
  with piano   Edison Bell 3703

THOMÉ

(L') Extase pf – arr. vln & pf
  with piano   Grammavox 6003, C7
                       Popular P35

WOOD

(2) Little pieces vln & pf
  No. 1. Slumber song
  with piano   Edison Bell 3703

Henri LEWKOWITZ

ALBÉNIZ

(2) Danzas españolas, Op. 164 pf
No. 1. Jota aragonesa arr. vln & pf Dushkin
with P. Vallribera pf   Columbia RG16150

BEETHOVEN

Romance No. 2, in F, Op. 50 vln & orch.
with P. Vallribera pf   Columbia RG16178

BLOCH

Baal Shem (3 Pictures of Chassidic life) (1923) vln & pf
No. 2. Nigun (Improvisation)
with P. Vallribera pf   Columbia RG16160

BRUCH

Concerto No.1, in g, Op. 26 vln & orch.
Adagio (2nd mvt)
with Bamberg Symphony Orch. –   Telefunken GMA109, SLE14450,
Wöss   SMA109

DAQUIN

Pièces de clavecin – Book I (1735) hpsi
Le coucou arr. vln & pf Manén
with P. Vallribera pf   Columbia RG16154

DVOŘÁK

(8) Slavonic Dances, Op. 72 pf duet; orch.
No. 2. Slavonic dance No. 10, in e arr. vln & pf Kreisler
with P. Vallribera pf   Columbia RG16154

GOLESTAN

Tzingarella (1943) vln & pf
with P. Vallribera pf   Decca 215766, CCL38005

HINDEMITH

(2) Sonatas, Op. 31 (1924) solo vln
Sonata No. 2
(unaccompanied)   Decca 215766, CCL38005

MILHAUD

(Le) Printemps (1921) vln & pf
with P. Vallribera pf   Decca 215766, CCL38005

PAGANINI

Moto perpetuo (Allegro di concert) Op. 11 (1830) vln & orch.
with P. Vallribera pf   Decca 215766, CCL38005

RAVEL

Berceuse sur le nom de Gabriel Fauré (1922) vln & pf
with P. Vallribera pf   Decca 215766, CCL38005

Pièce en forme d'Habanera v & pf – arr. vln & pf Catherine
with P. Vallribera pf   Columbia RG16154

SARASATE

Caprice basque, Op. 24 vln & pf
with P. Vallribera pf   Decca 215766, CCL38005

STRAVINSKY

Mavra (1922) – opera
Russian maiden's song arr. vln & pf Dushkin & Stravinsky
with P. Vallribera pf   Decca 215766, CCL38005

SZYMANOWSKI

(3) Mythes, Op. 30 (1915) vln & pf
No. 1. La Fontaine d'Aréthuse
with P. Vallribera pf   Columbia RG16160

No. 1. La Fontaine d'Aréthuse
with P. Vallribera pf   Decca 215766, CCL38005

TCHAIKOVSKY

Quartet No. 1, in D, Op. 11 2 vlns, vla & vlc
Andante cantabile (2nd mvt) arr. vln & pf Kreisler
with P. Vallribera pf   Columbia RG16150

WIENIAWSKI

Polonaise brillante No. 1, in D, Op. 4 vln & pf
with P. Vallribera pf   Decca 215766, CCL38005

Viktor LIBERMAN

ALBINONI

Concerto in C (1718) vln or ob & strs – ed. W. Upmeyer
with Leningrad Chamber Orch. –   Mezhdunarodnaya Kniga
Serebryakov   D023615/6, S01881/2

BRAHMS

(21) Hungarian Dances pf duet
Hungarian dance No. 2, in d arr. vln & pf Auer
with piano   Mezhdunarodnaya Kniga
          D4398/9

PAGANINI

(24) Caprices, Op. 1 (1801/7) solo vln
Caprice No. 17, in E flat
(unaccompanied)   Mezhdunarodnaya Kniga
          D4398/9

PREDIERI

Concerto in C vln & strs
with Leningrad Chamber Orch. –   Mezhdunarodnaya Kniga
Serebryakov   D023615/6, S01881/2

SCHUBERT

Sonata No. 17, in D, Op. 53 (D850) pf
Rondo (4th mvt) arr. vln & pf Friedberg
with piano   Mezhdunarodnaya Kniga
          D4398/9

SCRIABIN

(2) Nocturnes, Op. 5 pf
No. 1. Nocturne No. 1, in f sharp arr. vln & pf Moguilevsky
with piano   Mezhdunarodnaya Kniga
          D4398/9

TANEIEV

Concert Suite, Op. 28 vln & orch.
Fairytale (3rd mvt)
with piano   Mezhdunarodnaya Kniga
          D4398/9

TORELLI

(12) Concerti, Op. 8 (1709) 1/6: 2 vlns, strs & c – 7/12: vln, strs & c
Concerto No. 8, in c (ed. Paumgartner)
with Leningrad Chamber Orch. –   Mezhdunarodnaya Kniga
Serebryakov   D023615/6, S01881/2
Concerto No. 9, in e (ed. Paumgartner)
with Leningrad Chamber Orch. –   Mezhdunarodnaya Kniga
Serebryakov   D023615/6, S01881/2

VIVALDI

(12) Concerti, Op. 3 "L'Estro armonico" var. cbns & strs
Concerto No. 6, in a, P.1 (F.I, No. 176) vln, strs & c
with Leningrad Chamber Orch. –   Mezhdunarodnaya Kniga
Serebryakov   D023615/6, S01881/2

WIENIAWSKI

Polonaise brillante No. 2, in A, Op. 21 vln & pf
with piano   Mezhdunarodnaya Kniga
                              D4398/9

Leopold LICHTENBERG (1861–1935)

DRIGO

(2) Airs de Ballet orch.
No. 2. Valse bluette arr. vln & pf Auer
with piano   744   Paramount 33087
                            Puritan 744

SCHUBERT

(14) Schwanengesang, D957 (1828) v & pf
No. 4. Ständchen "Serenade" arr. vln & pf
with piano   742   Banner 2012
                            Puritan 9082
                            Regal 9468

SCHUMANN

(13) Kinderscenen, Op. 15 pf
No. 7. Träumerei arr. vln & pf
with orch.   743   Banner 2012
                            Puritan 9082
                            Regal 9468

Nona LIDDELL

BACH

Sonata in C, BWV1037 2 vlns & c
with E. Hurwitz vln, C. Spinks hpsi &   L'Oiseau–Lyre SOL319
T. Weil vlc

HANDEL

(7) Sonatas, Op. 5 (1739) 2 vlns & c
Sonata No. 2, in D
with E. Hurwitz vln, C. Spinks hpsi &   L'Oiseau–Lyre SOL319
T. Weil vlc

PURCELL

(12) Sonatas, Z790/801 (1683) 3 parts – 2 vlns & c
Sonata No. 4, in F, Z793
with E. Hurwitz vln, C. Spinks hpsi &   L'Oiseau–Lyre SOL319
T. Weil vlc

PURCELL – *Continued*

Sonata No. 9, in c, Z798
with E. Hurwitz vln, C. Spinks hpsi &   L'Oiseau–Lyre SOL319
T. Weil vlc
(10) Sonatas, Z802/11 (1697) 4 parts – 2 vlns & c
Sonata No. 6, in g, Z807 "Chaconne"
with E. Hurwitz vln, C. Spinks hpsi &   L'Oiseau–Lyre SOL319
T. Weil vlc

Maria LIDKA

FRICKER

Sonata, Op. 12 vln & pf
with M. Kitchin pf   Argo ATC1002, RG6

Alice LIEBMAN

HAUSER

Rapsodie hongrois No. 1, in d, Op. 43 vln & pf – arr. Sitt
with piano   Odeon 0147, 44196

RAFF

(6) Pieces, Op. 85 vln & pf
No. 3. Cavatina in D
with piano   Odeon 0147, 44154

Mats LILJEFORS

ROMAN

Concerto No. 3, in b vln & orch.
with Cologne Chamber Orch. – Müller Musica Mundi VMS2031
–Brühl

Yu LI–NA

HO

Concerto (1960) "Butterfly lovers" vln & orch.
with Shanghai Symphony Orch. – Fan Chung Kuo Ch'ang–P'ien Ch'ang
                                          M043

Alice LINDBLOM

DVOŘÁK

(8) Humoresques, Op. 101 pf
No. 7. Humoresque No. 7, in G flat arr. vln & pf "in G" Kreisler
with piano   Be 716[1]   HMV X1626

KREISLER

Schön Rosmarin vln & pf
with piano   Be 717[1]   HMV X1626

Gustav LINK (1894–   )

JUON
(8) Bagatellen, Op. 36 vln & pf
No. 8. Swedish airs
with piano   Polydor 21353

MOSZKOWSKI
Tanz–Momente, Op. 89 pf
No. 2. Valse mignonne arr. vln & pf
with piano   Polydor 21355

RAMEAU
Castor et Pollux (1737) – opera
Gavotte (Act IV) arr. vln & pf Burmester
with piano   Polydor 21354

SCOTT
Valse triste, Op. 73, No. 3 vln & pf
with piano   Polydor 21355

SINDING
(4) Pieces, Op. 61 vln & pf
No. 1. Prelude
with piano   Polydor 21352
No. 2. Elegy
with piano   Polydor 21352

SITT
Souvenir Suite, Op. 105 vln & pf
Saltarella (4th mvt)
with piano   Polydor 21353

VECSEY
(A) Toi vln & pf
with piano   Polydor 21354

Marta LINZ (1898–   )

HUBAY
(14) Scènes de la Csárda vln & pf
No. 4. Hejre Kati, Op. 32
with K. Szreter pf   Be 5820[2]   Odeon 0–2223, 221041A
Parlophone R135

KREISLER
Caprice viennois, Op. 2 vln & pf
with K. Szreter pf   Be 5819[2]   Odeon 0–2223, 221041A
Sicilienne & Rigaudon (Francoeur) vln & pf
with K. Szreter pf   Odeon 0–2472

SARASATE
(8) Danzas españolas vln & pf
No. 3. Romanza andaluza, Op. 22, No. 1
with K. Szreter pf   Odeon 0–2472
Parlophone R135

Endel LIPPUS*

MÄGI
Serenade vln & orch.
with Estonian Radio Symphony Orch.   Mezhdunarodnaya Kniga
– Matsov   D05907

George LIPSCHULTZ

CADMAN
At dawning, Op. 29, No. 1 v & pf – arr. vln & pf Rissland
with piano   Columbia 904D

HERBERT
Mademoiselle Modiste (1905) – operetta
Kiss me again arr. vln & pf
with piano   Columbia 1218D

LIEURANCE
By the waters of the Minnetonka (1914) v & pf – arr. vln & pf
with piano   Columbia 1218D

PONCE
Estrellita (1913) v & pf – arr. vln & pf Heifetz
with piano   Columbia 1795D, J776

SERRADELL
(La) Golondrina v & pf – arr. vln & pf
with piano   Columbia 1795D, J776

TOSELLI
Serenade, Op. 6 vln & pf
with piano   Columbia 904D

Alexander LIPSKY (1900–   )

CHAVEZ
Sonatina (1924) vln & pf
with Lipsky pf   New Music Quarterly Recordings
1/4, 1012

Karl LIST (1902–   )

MENDELSSOHN
Concerto in e, Op. 64 vln & orch.
with orch. – Berendt   Allegro ALG3068
Pacific LDAD53

TCHAIKOVSKY
Concerto in D, Op. 35 vln & orch.
with orch. – Berendt   Allegro ALG3054
Pacific LDAD53, MIC7

* Also 2nd vln in Estonian Philharmonic String Quartet.

Alexandras LIVONTAS

AUSTER

Tijna – ballet orch.
  Tijna's dance arr. vln & pf
  with piano
        Mezhdunarodnaya Kniga
        D23563/4

  Tijna's plaint arr. vln & pf
  with piano
        Mezhdunarodnaya Kniga
        D23563/4

BAJORAS

Dance vln & pf
  with piano
        Mezhdunarodnaya Kniga
        D23563/4

BALSYS

Concerto No. 1, in a vln & orch.
  with Moscow State Philharmonic
  Orch. – Zhiuraitis
        Mezhdunarodnaya Kniga
        D3676/7

Concerto No. 2, in c vln & orch.
  with Moscow Radio Symphony Orch.
  – Klenickis
        Mezhdunarodnaya Kniga
        D16645

Dramatic frescoes vln, pf & orch.
  with O. Steinbergaite pf & Lithuanian
  SSR Philharmonic Symphony Orch. –
  Domarkas
        Mezhdunarodnaya Kniga
        D017272

Eglé, the Queen of Grass Snakes (1960) – ballet orch.
  Adagio arr. vln & pf
  with piano
        Mezhdunarodnaya Kniga
        D23563/4

  No. 1. Lament arr. vln & pf
  with O. Steinbergaite pf
        Mezhdunarodnaya Kniga
        D16646

  No. 2. Dryabulite, a naughty girl arr. vln & pf
  with O. Steinbergaite pf
        Mezhdunarodnaya Kniga
        D16646

  No. 3. Dance of little fishes arr. vln & pf
  with O. Steinbergaite pf
        Mezhdunarodnaya Kniga
        D16646

  No. 4. The mermaid arr. vln & pf
  with O. Steinbergaite pf
        Mezhdunarodnaya Kniga
        D16646

  No. 5. March arr. vln & pf
  with O. Steinbergaite pf
        Mezhdunarodnaya Kniga
        D16646

BARKAUSKAS

Partita solo vln
  (unaccompanied)
        Mezhdunarodnaya Kniga
        D027057/8

BRAZINSKAS

Sonata, Op. 7 vln & pf
  with O. Steinbergaite pf
        Mezhdunarodnaya Kniga
        D16709/10

BRUCH

Kol Nidrei, Op. 47 vlc or vln & orch.
  with piano
        Mezhdunarodnaya Kniga
        D23563/4

BURINSKAS

Scherzino vln & pf
  with B. Vasiliauskas pf
        Mezhdunarodnaya Kniga
        D17313/4

DVARIONAS

Concerto (1949) vln & orch.*
  with USSR State Symphony Orch. –
  Dvarionas
        Mezhdunarodnaya Kniga
        D2189/90

GLUCK

Orphée et Eurydice (1762) – opera
  Dance of the blessed spirits: Lento "Mélodie" (no. 2) arr. vln & pf
  Kreisler
  with B. Vasiliauskas pf
        Mezhdunarodnaya Kniga
        D17313/4

KARNAVIČIUS

(2) Caprices vln & pf
  with B. Vasiliauskas pf
        Mezhdunarodnaya Kniga
        D17313/4

KAROSAS

Sonata "Legend of the sea" vln & pf
  with O. Steinbergaite pf
        Mezhdunarodnaya Kniga
        D16709/10

Suite vln & pf
  Allegro vivo
  with O. Steinbergaite pf
        Mezhdunarodnaya Kniga
        D16994, D19592

KLOVA

Nocturne Prelude vln & pf
  with B. Vasiliauskas pf
        Mezhdunarodnaya Kniga
        D17313/4

KREISLER

(La) Précieuse (L. Couperin) vln & pf
  with B. Vasiliauskas pf
        Mezhdunarodnaya Kniga
        D17313/4

MASSENET

Thaïs (1894) – opera
  Méditation arr. vln & pf Marsick
  with piano
        Mezhdunarodnaya Kniga
        D23563/4

PAKALNIS

(The) Bride – ballet orch.
  Grand Adagio arr. vln & pf
  with B. Vasiliauskas pf
        Mezhdunarodnaya Kniga
        D17313/4

RIES

(La) Capricciosa vln & pf
  with piano
        Mezhdunarodnaya Kniga
        D23563/4

* 2nd mvt only is on Mezhdunarodnaya Kniga D16991/3.

VAINIUNAS

Rhapsody on Lithuanian themes, Op. 30 vln & orch.
with Moscow Radio Symphony Orch.   Mezhdunarodnaya Kniga D3675
– Klenickis

VIVALDI

Sonata in D, F.XII, No. 6 vln & c – arr. vln & pf Respighi
with B. Vasiliauskas pf   Mezhdunarodnaya Kniga
                                D17313/4

Ilja LIVSCHAKOFF

BORSCHEL

Danse petite vln & pf
with orch.   Polydor 47076

BRAGA

(7) Melodies (1867) v & pf
  No. 5. La serenata "Angel's serenade" arr. vln, fl & hp
with A. Harzer fl & M. Saal hp   Polydor 23882

GODARD

Jocelyn (1888) – opera
  Cachés dans cet asile "Berceuse" arr. vln, fl & hp
with A. Harzer fl & M. Saal hp   Polydor 23880

GRIEG

Peer Gynt (Suite No. 1) Op. 46 orch.
  No. 3. Anitra's dance arr. vln, fl & hp
with A. Harzer fl & M. Saal hp   Polydor 23879

HUBAY

(14) Scènes de la Csárda vln & pf
  No. 4. Hejre Kati, Op. 32 arr. Lindemann
with orch.   Polydor 10326

OFFENBACH

(Les) Contes d'Hoffmann (1881) – opera
  Belle Nuit, O nuit d'amour "Barcarolle" arr. vln, fl & hp
with A. Harzer fl & M. Saal hp   Polydor 23879

REGER

(60) Schlichte Weisen – 6 Books, Op. 76 v & pf
  No. 52. Maria–Wiegenlied arr. vln & pf
with piano   Polydor 47076

SCHUBERT

(14) Schwanengesang, D957 (1828) v & pf
  No. 4. Ständchen "Serenade" arr. vln, fl & hp
with A. Harzer fl & M. Saal hp   Polydor 23880

TOSTI

(La) Serenata v & pf – arr. vln, fl & hp
with A. Harzer fl & M. Saal hp   Polydor 23882

VERDI

(La) Forza del Destino (1862) – opera
  Solenn in quest'ora arr. vln & orch. Atzler
with orch.   Polydor 10326

Albert LOCATELLI

COUPERIN, F.

(Les) Chérubins, XX, No. 3 hpsi – arr. vln & pf Salmon
with piano   Odeon 238037

DRDLA

Serenade No. 1, in A vln & pf
with piano   Decca 20269
                               Odeon 238036

DVOŘÁK

(8) Slavonic Dances, Op. 46 pf duet; orch.
  No. 2. Slavonic dance No. 2, in e arr. vln & pf "in g" Kreisler
with piano   Columbia DF2000

GOUNOD

Jeanne d'Arc (1873) – Incidental music orch.
  Vision de Jeanne d'Arc orch. – arr. vln & pf
with piano   Kl 6144–1   Odeon 0–250499

HONEGGER

Petite Suite (1936) 2 fls, cl, sax, vln & pf
with M. Moyse fl, L. Moyse fl, G.   Le Chant du Monde 519
Hamelin cl, F. L'Homme sax & J.
Manuel pf

KREISLER

Polichinelle–serenade vln & pf
with piano   Decca 20269
                               Odeon 238036

(La) Précieuse (L. Couperin) vln & pf
with piano   Odeon 250500

LALO

Arlequin vln & pf
with piano   Odeon 238037

MASSENET

(La) Vierge (1880) – oratorio
  Le Dernier sommeil de la Vierge orch. – arr. vln & pf
with piano   Kl 6145–1   Odeon 250499

SARASATE

(8) Danzas españolas vln & pf
  No. 3. Romanza andaluza, Op. 22, No. 1
with piano   Columbia DF2062

Elizabeth LOCKHART (1921–)

CHAUSSON

Poème, Op. 25 vln & orch.
with London Symphony Orch. –   MGM E3041
Fistoulari

RAVEL

Tzigane (Rapsodie de concert) (1924) vln & pf or orch.
with London Symphony Orch. –   MGM E3041
Fistoulari

Abram LOFT

SMITH, W.O.
Ecloque vln & pf
  with B. Weiser pf   New Editions 4

Edith LORAND

ARCADELT
Ave Maria cho – arr. vln & pf
  with piano   Parlophone E10217, P1555

BEETHOVEN
(6) Minuets, G167 pf
  No. 2. Minuet No. 2, in G arr. vln & pf Burmester
  with F. S. Weissmann pf   5952 Parlophone E10202, P1405
  No. 2. Minuet No. 2, in G arr. vln & pf Burmester
  with piano   2–20018 Decca 25769
                            Parlophone E10549
Sonata No. 5, in F, Op. 24 "Spring" vln & pf
  with M. Raucheisen pf   2–8311/6 Parlophone E10414/6

BRAHMS
(21) Hungarian Dances pf duet
  Hungarian dance No. 1, in g arr. vln & pf Joachim
  with piano   Parlophone 57086
Sonata No. 2, in A, Op. 100 vln & pf
  with M. Raucheisen pf   Parlophone E10457/9

BRANDL
(Der) Liebe Augustin –operetta
  Du alter Stefansturm arr. vln & pf as "The old refrain" by Kreisler
  with orch.   133154 Decca G20267
                        Parlophone B48020, P9041
  Du alter Stefansturm arr. vln & pf as "The old refrain" by Kreisler
  with piano   2–20017 Parlophone E10549, E10667,
                                P1661

CHOPIN
(3) Waltzes, Op. 64 pf
  No. 2. Waltz No. 7, in c sharp arr. vln & pf Huberman
  with piano   Parlophone B48122

DRDLA
(8) Hungarian Dances, Op. 30 vln & pf
  Hungarian dance*
  with piano   Parlophone E10248

DRIGO
(2) Airs de Ballet orch.
  No. 2. Valse bluette arr. vln & pf Auer
  with piano   Parlophone E10360

FALLA
(7) Canciones populares españolas (1914) v & pf
  No. 3. Asturiana arr. vln & pf Kochański
  with piano   Parlophone E10654
  No. 4. Jota arr. vln & pf Kochański
  with piano   Parlophone E10654

* Unidentified.

FALLA – *Continued*
  No. 4. Jota arr. vln & pf Kochański
  with M. Raucheisen pf   2–20843 Parlophone E10779
  No. 6. Canción arr. vln & pf Kochański
  with piano   Parlophone E10654
(La) Vida Breve (1913) – opera
  Danza espanola orch. – arr. vln & pf Kreisler
  with M. Raucheisen pf   2–21310² Columbia 50298D
  Danza española orch. – arr. vln & pf Kreisler
  with piano   Decca 25016
                    Parlophone 57050

FIBICH
Images, Impressions & Souvenirs, Op. 41 pf
  No. 14. Poem (from "Souvenirs", Part IV) arr. vln & pf Kubelík
  with piano   Columbia 2657D
  No. 14. Poem (from "Souvenirs", Part IV) arr. vln & pf Kubelík
  with piano   Parlophone P1449

FOSTER
(The) Old folks at home (1851) "Swanee river" v & pf – arr. vln & pf
Kreisler
  with piano   2–20160 Parlophone E10667

GILLET
(Au) Village pf – arr. vln & pf
  with piano   Parlophone E10113

GOLDMARK
Trio in e, Op. 33 pf, vln & vlc
  Scherzo; Andantino grazioso (2nd mvt)
  with M. Raucheisen pf &   2–20036 Decca 25137
  G. Piatigorsky vlc   Parlophone E10639

GOUNOD
Ave Maria (Méditation on Bach's "Prelude No. 1, in C" from Book I of
"Das Wohltemperirte Clavier") v & pf – arr. vln & pf
  with piano   Parlophone P1555

GRANADOS
(12) Danzas españolas, Op. 37 (1893) pf
  No. 5. Danza española No. 5, in e "Andaluza" arr. vln & pf Kreisler
  with piano   Columbia 50298D
  No. 5. Danza española No. 5, in e "Andaluza" arr. vln & pf Kreisler
  with piano   2–20431 Parlophone E10667
  No. 5. Danza española No. 5, in e "Andaluza" arr. vln & pf Kreisler
  with M. Raucheisen pf   2–20842 Decca 25016
                    Parlophone 57050, E10779

GRIEG
Peer Gynt (Suite No. 2) Op. 55 orch.
  No. 4. Solveig's song arr. pf, vln & vlc
  with M. Raucheisen pf & E. Stegmann Beka 6129
  vlc

HANDEL
Serse (1738) – opera
  Ombra mai fu "Largo" arr. vln & pf Hermann
  with piano   Parlophone 57000

HANDEL – *Continued*

(15) Sonatas, Op. 1 (?1731) fl or vln & c
Sonata No. 9, in b: Andante (1st mvt) arr. vln & pf as "Larghetto" by
Hubay
with piano   Parlophone 57000

HENTSCHEL, E.

Liebesreigen–serenade vln & pf
with piano   Parlophone P1489

HUBAY

(6) Poèmes hongroise, Op. 27 vln & pf
Poème hongrois No. 3, in A
with piano   7853–3   Parlophone E10361
Poème hongrois No. 4, in a
with piano   7853–3   Parlophone E10361
Poème hongrois No. 6, in B flat
with B. Weyersberg pf   2–2969   Parlophone P1216
(14) Scènes de la Csárda vln & pf
No. 4. Hejre Kati, Op. 32
with orch.   Decca 20488
                                Odeon 0–25058
                                Parlophone R2103

HUMMEL

Waltz in A pf – arr. vln & pf Burmester
with B. Weyersberg pf   2–2968   Parlophone P1216, P1415

KREISLER

Caprice viennois, Op. 2 vln & pf
with piano   Parlophone E10033, P1488
Liebesfreud vln & pf
with F. S. Weissmann pf   5950   Parlophone E10537, P1359,
                                P9055
Liebesfreud vln & pf – arr. Roberts
with orch.   Decca 20266
                                Parlophone B27122
Liebesleid vln & pf
with F. S. Weissmann pf   5850   Parlophone E10537, P1359,
                                P9055
Marche miniature viennois vln & pf arr. vln, vlc & pf
with G. Piatigorsky vlc &   2–20435   Decca 25787
M. Raucheisen pf   Parlophone E11023
Paraphrase on 2 Russian folksongs vln & pf
with M. Raucheisen pf   2–20163   Decca 25787
                                Parlophone E11023
Schön Rosmarin vln & pf
with piano   2–20018   Decca 25769
                                Parlophone E10549
Schön Rosmarin vln & pf
with orch.   Decca 20266
Slavonic Fantasia in b (on themes by Dvořák) vln & pf
with orch.   38469   Decca G20267
                                Odeon 0–25062
Tambourin chinois, Op. 3 vln & pf
with orch.   Decca 20265
Praeludium & Allegro (Pugnani) vln & pf
with piano   Odeon 0–25011
                                Parlophone B49795

KREISLER – *Continued*

Praeludium & Allegro (Pugnani) vln & pf
with orch.   Decca 20265

LANGE

Ave Maria (based on Bach's "Prelude No. 1, in C" from Book I of "Das
Wohltemperirte Clavier") v & pf – arr. vln & pf
with piano   Parlophone E10217

LIADOV

Prelude unid – arr. vln & orch.
with orch.   A 3131 B¹   Odeon 3131
Prelude unid – arr. vln & pf
with piano   Parlophone P1554

MASCAGNI

Cavalleria Rusticana (1890) – opera
selection arr. vln & pf Lorand
with piano   Parlophone E5154

MASSENET

Scènes pittoresques (1874) orch. – arr. vln & pf
with piano   Parlophone E10274
Thaïs (1894) – opera
Méditation arr. vln & pf Marsick
with piano   Decca 25079
                                Parlophone E10889

MENDELSSOHN

Concerto in e, Op. 64 vln & orch.
Andante (2nd mvt)
with Berlin State Opera   6646/7   Parlophone E10178, P1676
Orch. – Hildebrandt
Trio No. 1, in d, Op. 49 pf, vln & vlc
Andante con moto tranquillo (2nd mvt)
with M. Raucheisen pf & G.   Parlophone E10563
Piatigorsky vlc

MOSZKOWSKI

(5) Danzas españolas, Op. 12 pf – 4 hands
No. 5. Danza española No. 5, in D (con spirito) arr. vln & pf
with piano   Parlophone 80189
(6) Klavierstücke, Op. 15 pf – 4 hands
No. 1. Serenata arr. vln & pf
with piano   Parlophone E10033, P1488

MOZART

Divertimento No. 17, in D, K334 2 hrns & strs
Minuet (3rd mvt) arr. vln & pf Burmester
with orch.   Decca G20297
                                Parlophone 80516, B48122,
                                R1696
Serenade No. 7, in D, K250 "Haffner" orch.
Rondo (4th mvt) arr. vln & pf Kreisler
with orch.   Decca G20540
                                Parlophone B48140, R2432

NICKLAS–KEMPNER

Zigeuner–Sehnsucht orch. – arr. vln & orch.
with orch.   Parlophone P1489

PADEREWSKI

(6) Humoresques de concert, Op. 14 pf
  No. 1. Minuet in G arr. vln & pf Kreisler
  with orch.   Decca 25769

POPY

Suite orientale vln & pf
  with piano   Parlophone E10427

PUCCINI

(La) Bohème (1896) – opera
  selection arr. vln & pf Lorand
  with piano   Parlophone E5154

Tosca (1900) – opera
  selection arr. vln & pf Lorand
  with piano   Parlophone E5246

PUGNANI

(6) Sonatas, Op. 8 vln & c
  Sonata No. 3, in D: Largo expressivo (2nd mvt) arr. vln & pf Moffat
  with P. Kiss pf   7851 Parlophone E10468, P1878

RAMEAU

Castor et Pollux (1737) – opera
  Gavotte (Act IV) arr. vln & pf Burmester
  with orch.   Parlophone B48130

RIMSKY–KORSAKOV

(Le) Coq d'Or (1910) – opera
  Hymn to the sun arr. vln & pf Kreisler
  with piano   Columbia 50298D
  Hymn to the sun arr. vln & pf Kreisler
  with piano   Decca G20296
                  Parlophone 57049, P1661, R2331

Sadko (1898) – opera
  Chant hindou arr. vln & pf Kreisler
  with piano   A 3131 A¹ Odeon 3131

RUBINSTEIN

(2) Melodies, Op. 3 pf
  No. 1. Melody in F arr. vln, vlc & pf
  with G. Piatigorsky vlc & 2–20161 Decca 25137
  M. Raucheisen pf   Parlophone E10639

SAINT–SAËNS

Samson et Dalilah, Op. 47 (1877) – opera
  Mon coeur s'ouvre ta voix arr. vln & pf Lorand
  with piano   Decca G20296
                  Parlophone E5205

SARASATE

Zigeunerweisen, Op. 20 vln & pf or orch.
  with orch.   Parlophone B48269, R2078

SCHARWENKA

(5) Polish Dances, Op. 3 pf
  No. 1. Polish dance No. 1, in E flat arr. vln & pf
  with piano   Parlophone E10190

SCHUBERT

(7) Gesänge (set to Scott's "Lady of the Lake") Op. 52 v & pf
  No. 6. Ave Maria, D839 arr. vln & pf Wilhelmj
  with piano   Parlophone E10889

SCHUBERT – *Continued*

Quartet No. 14, in d, D810 "Death & the maiden" 2 vlns, vla & vlc
  (as leader of Lorand str qt)   Parlophone E10464/8
Quintet in A, Op. 114 (D667) "Trout" pf, vln, vla, vlc & cbs
  with M. Raucheisen pf, K. Reitz vla, Odeon 76000/4
  K. Wendel vln, A. Liebermann vlc & Parlophone P9287/8 & P9218/9
  M. Skibicki cbs   & P9304
Rosamunde von Cypern, Op. 26 (D797) (1823) – Incidental music orch.
  No. 9. Ballet music II, in G arr. vln & pf Kreisler
  with piano   Odeon 0–9245

SGAMBATI

(2) Pieces, Op. 24 vln & pf
  No. 2. Serenata napoletana
  with piano   Parlophone P1449

SPENDIAROV

(2) Stücke, Op. 3 orch.
  No. 2. Berceuse arr. vln & pf
  with piano   Parlophone P1554

SUK

(4) Pieces, Op. 17 vln & pf
  No. 3. Un poco triste
  with M. Raucheisen pf   2–21309 Columbia 50298D
  No. 3. Un poco triste
  with piano   Parlophone 57049

TCHAIKOVSKY

(The) Months (12 Characteristic pieces) Op. 37a pf
  No. 6. Barcarolle (June) arr. vln, vlc & pf
  with G. Piatigorsky vlc & M.   Parlophone E10459
  Raucheisen pf
(3) Pieces, Op. 9 pf
  No. 3. Mazurka de salon in d arr. vln & pf Artemieff
  with piano   Parlophone E10121

TELESFOR

Hungarian song unid – arr. vln & pf
  with piano   6938–1 Parlophone E10361

THOMAS

Mignon (1866) – opera
  selection arr. vln & pf Lorand
  with piano   Parlophone E5246

TOSELLI

Serenade, Op. 6 vln & pf – arr. vln, vlc & pf
  with E. Stegmann vlc & M.   Beka 6129
  Raucheisen pf

VALDEZ

Sérénade du Tzigane vln & pf
  with piano   Parlophone E10134

VITALI

Chaconne in g vln & c – arr. vln, strs & org Charlier
  with string orch. & organ   Parlophone E10523

WIENIAWSKI

Fantaisie brillante (on themes from the opera "Faust" by Gounod) Op. 20
vln & orch.
with orch.　　　　　2–20121/2　Parlophone E10579, P9091

Ferry LORÁNT

BRANDL

(Der) Liebe Augustin – operetta
Du alter Stefansturm arr. vln & pf as "The old refrain" by Kreisler
with piano　　　　　50385　Homochord B8365

CHOPIN

(3) Nocturnes, Op. 9 pf
No. 2. Nocturne No. 2, in E flat arr. vln & pf Sarasate
with piano　　　　　50382　Homochord B8364

GÄRTNER

Aus Wien pf – arr. vln & pf Kreisler
with piano　　　　　50384　Homochord B8365

GODARD

Jocelyn (1888) – opera
Cachés dans cet asile "Berceuse" arr. vln & pf
with piano　　　　　50383　Homochord B8364

KREISLER

Liebesleid vln & pf
with piano　　　　　50401　Homochord B8363
Rondino on a theme by Beethoven vln & pf
with piano　　　　　50386　Homochord B8366
Variations on a theme of Corelli (Tartini) vln & pf
with piano　　　　　50387　Homochord B8366

PAGANINI

Sonata a preghièra "Moses Fantasia" (on the aria "Dal tuo stellato soglio"
from Rossini's opera "Mosè in Egitto") Op. 24 (1818 or 1819) vln &
orch.
with piano　　　　　50402　Homochord B8363

SARASATE

(8) Danzas españolas vln & pf
No. 3. Romanza andaluza, Op. 22, No. 1
with orch.　　　　　50399　Homochord B8362
No. 7. Danza española No. 7, in a, Op. 26, No. 1
with orch.　　　　　50400　Homochord B8362

TCHAIKOVSKY

Souvenir d'un lieu cher, Op. 42 vln & pf
No. 3. Mélodie
with orch.　　　　　50389　Homochord B8361

WAGNER

Albumblatt in C (1861) pf – arr. vln & pf Wilhelmj
with orch.　　　　　50388　Homochord B8361

Margaret LORENZO

d'AMBROSIO

Petit Chanson, Op. 28 vln & pf
with piano　　　　　Imperial 1225

BARNS

Swing song vln & pf
with piano　　　　　Banner 2058
　　　　　　　　　　Imperial 1224
　　　　　　　　　　Regal 9334

BOISDEFFRE

Au bord, du ruisseau (Sérénade champêtre) Op. 52 vln & pf
with piano　　　　　Banner 2058
　　　　　　　　　　Imperial 1225
　　　　　　　　　　Regal 9334

DRDLA

Souvenir vln & pf
with piano　　　　　Banner 2046
　　　　　　　　　　Regal 9104

DRIGO

(2) Airs de Ballet orch.
No. 2. Valse bluette arr. vln & pf Auer
with piano　　　　　Banner 2046
　　　　　　　　　　Regal 9104

KREISLER

Liebesfreud vln & pf
with piano　　　　　Imperial 1247

Isaak LOSOWSKY

FIBICH

Images, Impressions & Souvenirs, Op. 41 pf
No. 14. Poem (from "Souvenirs", Part IV) arr. vln & pf Kubelík
with piano　　　　　Beltona 6057

SARASATE

(8) Danzas españolas vln & pf
No. 6. Zapateado, Op. 23, No. 2
with piano　　　　　Beltona 6059

SCHUMANN

(13) Kinderscenen, Op. 15 pf
No. 7. Träumerei arr. vln & pf
with piano　　　　　Beltona 6059

ZSOLT

Dragonflies vln & pf
with piano　　　　　Beltona 6057

Alan Raymond LOVEDAY (1928–)

BACH

Concerto No. 2, in E, BWV1042 vln & orch.
with Royal Danish Orch. – Hurst　　Forum F7009
　　　　　　　　　　　　　　　　Saga XID5024

(3) Sonatas & 3 Partitas, BWV1001/6 solo vln
Partita No. 3, in E, BWV1006
(unaccompanied)　　　Forum F7009
　　　　　　　　　　Saga XID5024

BEETHOVEN

Concerto in D, Op. 61 (cadenzas by Kreisler) vln & orch.
  with Royal Danish Orch. – Hurst   Forum F7006
                   Saga STXID5025, XID5025

Sonata No. 5, in F, Op. 24 "Spring" vln & pf
  with L. Cassini pf   Fidelio ATL4060, TLS6011
                   Revolution RCB9
                   Saga STXID5316

(3) Sonatas, Op. 30 vln & pf
No. 2. Sonata No. 7, in c
  with L. Cassini pf   Fidelio ATL4109
                   Saga STXID5316

No. 3. Sonata No. 8, in G
  with L. Cassini pf   Fidelio ATL4109

Sonata No. 9, in A, Op. 47 "Kreutzer" vln & pf
  with L. Cassini pf   Fidelio ATL4060, TLS6011
                   Revolution RCB9

Trio No. 6, in B flat, Op. 97 "Archduke" pf, vln & vlc
  with L. Cassini pf & A. Fleming vlc   Fidelio ATL4110

BRAHMS

Sonata No. 1, in G, Op. 78 vln & pf
  with L. Cassini pf   Fidelio ATL4174
                   Revolution RCB16

Sonata No. 2, in A, Op. 100 vln & pf
  with L. Cassini pf   Fidelio ATL4174
                   Revolution RCB16

Sonata No. 3, in d, Op. 108 vln & pf
  with L. Cassini pf   Fidelio ATL4175
                   Revolution RCB16

ELGAR

Sonata in e, Op. 82 vln & pf
  with L. Cassini pf   Delta DEL12016
                   Dover HCR5259, HCRST7011,
                   HCRST7259

FRANCK

Sonata in A (1886) vln & pf
  with L. Cassini pf   Fidelio ATL4175

GRIEG

Sonata No. 1, in F, Op. 8 vln & pf
  with L. Cassini pf   Saga STXID5296, XID5296
Sonata No. 2, in G, Op. 13 vln & pf
  with L. Cassini pf   Saga STXID5296, XID5296
Sonata No. 3, in c, Op. 45 vln & pf
  with L. Cassini pf   Saga STXID5296, XID5296

HAYDN

(6) Quartets, Op. 2 (H.III, nos. 7/12) 2 vlns, vla & vlc
No. 2. Quartet No. 8, in E, H.III, No. 8*
  with J. Williams gtr, C. Aronowitz vla   CBS SBRG72678
  & A. Fleming vlc   Columbia MS7163

IRELAND

Sonata No. 1, in d (1909) vln & pf
  with L. Cassini pf   Revolution RCB5
                   Summit LSU3081

* Arr. lute, vln, vla & vlc – authenticity of lute transcription is uncertain.

MARTINŮ

Sonata No. 1 (1930) vln & pf
  with L. Cassini pf   Delta DEL12016

PAGANINI

Trio in D, Op. 66 (1833) vln, vlc & gtr
  with A. Fleming vlc & J. Williams gtr   CBS SBRG72678
                   Columbia MS7163

RIMSKY–KORSAKOV

Scheherazade, Op. 35 (1888) orch.
  with Royal Philharmonic Orch. –   Classics for Pleasure CFP174
  Kempe   Crossroads 22 16 0220
                   World Record Club ST657, T657

VIVALDI

(12) Concerti, Op. 8 (1725) "Il Cimento dell' Armonia e dell' Invenzione"
  (Nos. 1/4: Le quattro Stagioni) vln & strs
Concerto No. 1, in E, F.I, No. 22 "La Primavera"
  with Academy of Saint–Martin–in–the–   Argo ZRG654
  Fields – Marriner   Decca SXL21202
Concerto No. 2, in B flat, F.I, No. 23 "L'Estate"
  with Academy of Saint–Martin–in–the–   Argo ZRG654
  Fields – Marriner   Decca SXL21202
Concerto No. 3, in F, F.I, No. 24 "L'Autunno"
  with Academy of Saint–Martin–in–the–   Argo ZRG654
  Fields – Marriner   Decca SXL21202
Concerto No. 4, in f, F.I, No. 25 "L'Inverno"
  with Academy of Saint–Martin–in–the–   Argo ZRG654
  Fields – Marriner   Decca SXL21202

Sonia LOVIS (1924–1947)

BACH

Concerto in c, BWV1060 vln & ob or 2 vlns, strs & c
  with D. Blot vln & Ars Rediviva –   La Boîte à Musique 38/9
  Crussard

Carmenzita LOZADA

DVOŘÁK

Concerto in a, Op. 53 vln & orch.
  with Berlin Symphony Orch. – Conz   Eurodisc 80180PK

RAVEL

Tzigane (Rapsodie de concert) (1924) vln & pf or orch.
  with Berlin Symphony Orch. – Conz   Eurodisc 80180PK

Lea LUBOSHUTZ (1889–1965)

ARENSKY

(4) Morceaux, Op. 30 vln & pf
No. 2. Serenade in G
  with piano   6875 r   Gramophone & Typewriter
                   27954

CUI

Kaleidoscope, Op. 50 vln & pf
No. 12. Perpetuum mobile
with piano   6875 r Gramophone & Typewriter
           27954

POPPER

Elfentanz, Op. 39 vlc & pf – arr. vln & pf Halír
with piano
         Gramophone & Typewriter
         27951

Mark LUBOTSKY

BACH

Concerto in C, BWV1064 3 clavs, strs & c – arr. 3 vlns, strs & c "in D"
Baumgartner
with L. Isakadze vln, O. Kagen vln, G. Mezhdunarodnaya Kniga
Rozhdestvensky hpsi & Moscow Radio S01867/8
Large Symphony Orch. Chamber
Group – Rozhdestvensky

(6) Sonatas, BWV1014/9 vln & clav
Sonata No. 1, in b, BWV1014
with L. Yedlina pf   Mezhdunarodnaya Kniga
         D022701/4

Sonata No. 2, in A, BWV1015
with L. Yedlina pf   Mezhdunarodnaya Kniga
         D022701/4

Sonata No. 3, in E, BWV1016
with L. Yedlina pf   Mezhdunarodnaya Kniga
         D022701/4

Sonata No. 4, in c, BWV1017
with L. Yedlina pf   Mezhdunarodnaya Kniga
         D022701/4

Sonata No. 5, in f, BWV1018
with L. Yedlina pf   Mezhdunarodnaya Kniga
         D022701/4

Sonata No. 6, in G, BWV1019
with L. Yedlina pf   Mezhdunarodnaya Kniga
         D022701/4

BALAKIREV

Octet in c, Op. 3 pf, fl, ob, hrn, vln, vla, vlc & cbs
with D. Paperno pf, A. Korneyev fl, S. Mezhdunarodnaya Kniga
Trubashkin ob, B. Afanasyev hrn, F. D16327
Druzhinin vla, V. Simon vlc & L.
Andreyev cbs

BRAHMS

Sonata (1853) "Frei aber Einsam" vln & pf
Allegro (Scherzo) in c (3rd mvt) "Sonatensatz"
with piano   Mezhdunarodnaya Kniga
         D014587/8

BRITTEN

Concerto No. 1, in d, Op. 15 (1939 – rev. 1958) vln & orch.
with Moscow Philharmonic Symphony Mezhdunarodnaya Kniga
Orch. – Kondrashin   S1623/4

Concerto No. 1, in d, Op. 15 (1939 – rev. 1958) vln & orch.
with English Chamber Orch. – Britten Decca SXL6512
         London CS6723

CHAUSSON

Concerto in D, Op. 21 vln, pf & str qt
with L. Yedlina pf & Borodin String D025849/50, SM02335/6
Quartet

DOHNÁNYI

Ruralia Hungarica, Op. 32A pf – arr. vln & pf Kreisler
with piano   Mezhdunarodnaya Kniga
         D014587/8

GLUCK

Concerto in G vln & orch.
with Moscow Radio Large Symphony Mezhdunarodnaya Kniga
Orch. Chamber Group –   S01867/8
Rozhdestvensky

HAYDN

Sonata No. 7, in F, H.III, No. 82 vln & hpsi
with L. Yedlina pf   Mezhdunarodnaya Kniga
         D020371

MOZART

Sonata No. 21, in e, K304 vln & pf
with H. Mirvisz pf   Mezhdunarodnaya Kniga D4370

RAVEL

Berceuse sur le nom de Gabriel Fauré (1922) vln & pf
with piano   Mezhdunarodnaya Kniga
         D014587/8

SCHUBERT

(3) Sonatinas, Op. 137 (D384, D385 & D408) vln & pf
No. 3. Sonatina No. 3, in g, D408
with piano   Mezhdunarodnaya Kniga
         D014587/8

SHNITKE

Sonata (1962) vln & pf
with L. Yedlina pf   Mezhdunarodnaya Kniga
         D020372

TCHAIKOVSKY

Souvenir d'un lieu cher, Op. 42 vln & pf
No. 3. Mélodie
with V. Yampolsky pf   Mezhdunarodnaya Kniga D4371

TORELLI

(12) Concerti, Op. 8 (1709) 1/6: 2 vlns, strs & c – 7/12: vln, strs & c
Concerto No. 8, in c
with N. Muntyan hpsi & Moscow Mezhdunarodnaya Kniga
Radio Large Symphony Orch. S01867/8
Chamber Group – Rozhdestvensky

VITALI

Chaconne in g vln & c – arr. vln & pf Charlier
with L. Yedlina pf   Mezhdunarodnaya Kniga
         D020371

WIENIAWSKI

Polonaise brillante No. 1, in D, Op. 4 vln & pf
with V. Yampolsky pf   Mezhdunarodnaya Kniga D4371

YSAŸE

(6) Sonatas, Op. 27 solo vln
  Sonata No. 3, in d
  (unaccompanied)   Mezhdunarodnaya Kniga D4371
  Sonata No. 6, in E
  (unaccompanied)   Mezhdunarodnaya Kniga
                                     D014587/8

Georg LUBOW

ANONYMOUS

O du Fröhliche, O du Selige (1819) v & pf – arr. vln & pf
  with piano   Polydor 19257

GRUBER

Stille Nacht, heilige Nacht (1818) v & pf – arr. vln & pf
  with piano   Polydor 19257

Godfrey R. LUDLOW (1893–1956)

ALBÉNIZ

España (6 Feuilles d'album) Op. 165 pf
  No. 2. Tango in D arr. vln & pf Elman
  with piano   Aco G15191

DICKINSON

Memories vln & pf
  with W. Golde pf   Vocalion 15378

KREISLER

Tambourin chinois, Op. 3 vln & pf
  with piano   Aco F33025

LEMARE

Andantino, Op. 83, No. 2 pf – arr. vln & pf Ludlow
  with piano   Brunswick 4165

LEYBACH

Nocturne No. 5, in A flat, Op. 52 pf – arr. vln & pf
  with piano   Brunswick 4165

LOHR

Star of the east v & pf – arr. vln & pf
  with piano   Aco G15191

OTEO

Mi viejo amour v & pf – arr. vln & pf
  with L. Gainsborg pf   Brunswick 3647

PONCE

Estrellita (1913) v & pf – arr. vln & pf Heifetz
  with L. Gainsborg pf   Brunswick 3647

ROBINSON

(The) Snowy–breasted pearl v & pf – arr. vln & pf
  with piano   Aco F33025

ZSOLT

Dragonflies vln & pf
  with W. Golde pf   Vocalion 15378

Fernand LUQUIN

BÉRIOT

Scène de Ballet (Fantaisie–ballet No. 1) Op. 100 vln & orch.
  with piano   Pathé cylinder 70153

KREISLER

Variations on a theme of Corelli (Tartini) vln & pf
  with piano   Pathé cylinder 70152

MASSENET

Thaïs (1894) – opera
  Méditation arr. vln & pf Marsick
  with piano   Pathé cylinder 70150

THOMÉ

Simple aveu, Op. 25 pf – arr. vln & pf
  with piano   Pathé cylinder 70154

WIENIAWSKI

Mazurka in a, Op. 3 "Kujawiak" vln & pf
  with piano   Pathé cylinder 70151

Milan LUSK (1898–)

ANONYMOUS

Slovenske a Ceske pisne unid – arr. vln & pf
  with piano   Edison cylinder 9869
Smes Cesko (Slavic song) unid – arr. vln & pf
  with piano   Edison cylinder 9868

DRDLA

Souvenir vln & pf
  with Mme Voguckova–Welch pf   Emerson 02005X

DRIGO

(2) Airs de Ballet orch.
  No. 2. Valse bluette arr. vln & pf Auer
  with Mme Voguckova–Welch pf   Emerson 02007X

DVOŘÁK

(8) Humoresques, Op. 101 pf
  No. 7. Humoresque No. 7, in G flat arr. vln & pf "in G" Kreisler
  with piano   Banner 2057
                                     Regal 9335

GRANADOS

(12) Danzas españolas, Op. 37 (1893) pf
  No. 5. Danza española No. 5, in e "Andaluza" arr. vln & pf Kreisler
  with Mme Voguckova–Welch pf   Emerson 02007X

MASSENET

Thaïs (1894) – opera
  Méditation arr. vln & pf Marsick
  with piano   Banner 2057
                                     Regal 9335

SCHUMANN

(13) Kinderscenen, Op. 15 pf
  No. 7. Träumerei arr. vln & pf
  with Mme Voguckova–Welch pf   Emerson 02005X

ŠKROUP

Kde domov muj (1834) v & pf – arr. vln & pf*
  with piano   Edison cylinder 9871

SMETANA

(The) Bartered Bride (1866) – opera
  No. 28, Think it over, Marenka arr. vln & pf Lusk
  with piano   Edison cylinder 9870

Andrej LÜTSCHG

TARTINI

(12) Sonatas, Op. 1 (1734) vln & c
  Sonata No. 10, in g "Didone abbandonata"
  with B. Billeter hpsi & C. Stark vlc   Tudor TUD0711

Sonata in c vln & c
  with B. Billeter hpsi & C. Stark vlc   Tudor TUD0711

Sonata in g "Il Trillo del Diavolo" vln & c
  with B. Billeter hpsi & C. Stark vlc   Tudor TUD0711

Sonata No. 13, in A "Pastorale" vln & c
  with B. Billeter hpsi & C. Stark vlc   Tudor TUD0711

Grigori LUTSKY

GLINKA

Sextet in E flat pf, 2 vlns, vla, vlc & cbs
  with T. Fidler pf, V. Ovcharek vln, V.   Mezhdunarodnaya Kniga
  Solovyov vla, I. Levinzon vlc & S.   D029887
  Akopov cbs

HAYDN

(6) Quartets, Op. 3 (H.III, Nos. 13/18) 2 vlns, vla & vlc
  No. 5. Quartet No. 17, in F, H.III, No. 17
  with V. Ovcharek vln, V. Solovyov vla   Mezhdunarodnaya Kniga
  & B. Morozov vlc   D21803

KOSHA

Trio (1946) 2 vlns & vla
  with V. Ovcharek vln & V. Solovyov   Mezhdunarodnaya Kniga
  vla   D022065/6, S01902

SABO

Trio (1927) 2 vlns & vla
  with V. Ovcharek vln & V. Solovyov   Mezhdunarodnaya Kniga
  vla   D21804

TANEIEV

Trio in D, Op. 21 2 vlns & vla
  with V. Ovcharek vln & V. Solovyov   Mezhdunarodnaya Kniga
  vla   D029888

Albert LYNCH

GRIEG

(6) Lyric Pieces – Book III, Op. 43 pf
  No. 6. To the spring arr. vln & pf Kreisler
  with piano   Columbia 01237

* Czech National anthem.

WHITE

Bandanna Sketches, Op. 12 vln & pf
  No. 1. Nobody Knows de trouble I see (Negro spiritual)
  with piano   Columbia 01237

Peder LYNGED (1886–   )

GOUNOD

Faust (1859) – opera
  Salut! demeure chaste et pure
  with M. Jacobsen t & orch.   HMV 32–1922

LUMBYE

Concert–polka (1863) 2 vlns & orch.
  with C. Andersen vln & Royal Opera   London T5039
  House Orch. – Høeberg   Polyphon Z60130

Alberto LYSY

ALBINONI

(12) Sonatas, Op. 1 (1694) "Sinfonias"
  Sonata No. 11, in c 2 vlns & c
  with M. Westergaard vln, L. Cerroni   I Classici della Musica Classica
  hpsi & G. Selmi vlc   XAC4049

BLOCH

Suite No. 1 solo vln
  (unaccompanied)   I Classici della Musica Classica
                          XAC4050

CORELLI

(12) Sonatas, Op. 1 2 vlns & c
  Sonata No. 7, in C
  with M. Westergaard vln, L. Cerroni   I Classici della Musica Classica
  hpsi & G. Selmi vlc   XAC4049

MENDELSSOHN

Sonata in F (1838) vln & pf
  with J. Hopkins pf   I Classici della Musica Classica
                          XAC4050

MOZART

Concertone in C, K190 2 vlns, ob, vlc & orch.
  with Y. Menuhin vln & Bath Festival   Angel 36240
  Orch. – Menuhin   Electrola E91331, SME18006,
                          STE91331
                          HMV ALP2043, ASD592,
                          ASDF830, CVB1830, FALP830

PURCELL

(5) Pavanes, Z748/52 (pre–1680) (Nos. 1/4: 3 part – No. 5: 4 part)
  Pavane No. 5, in g, Z752 (?1677)
  with Y. Menuhin vln, R. Masters vln,   Angel 36270
  A. Gauntlett gamba & R. Jesson cha   HMV ALP2088, ASD635,
  org   ASDF867, FALP867
(12) Sonatas, Z790/801 (1683) 3 part – 2 vlns & c
  Sonata No. 6, in C, Z795
  with Y. Menuhin vln, A. Gauntlett   Angel 36270
  gamba & R. Jesson hpsi   HMV ALP2088, ASD635,
                          ASDF867, FALP867

PURCELL – *Continued*

Sonata No. 8, in G, Z797
with Y. Menuhin vln, A. Gauntlett — Angel 36270
gamba & R. Jesson hpsi — HMV ALP2088, ASD635, ASDF867, FALP867

(10) Sonatas, Z802/11 (1697) 4 part – 2 vlns & c
Sonata No. 6, in g, Z807 "Chaconne"
with Y. Menuhin vln, A. Gauntlett — Angel 36270
gamba & R. Jesson hpsi — HMV ALP2088, ASD635, ASDF867, FALP867

TARTINI

(12) Sonatas, Op. 1 (1734) vln & c
Sonata No. 10, in g "Didone abbandonata"
with P. Saenz hpsi — Odyssey 32 16 0310

TELEMANN

(12) Fantasies (1735) solo vln
Fantasia No. 1, in b
(unaccompanied) — I Classici della Musica Classica XAC4050

(6) Sonatas, Op. 2 (1727) "Duets" 2 fls or 2 vlns
Sonata No. 4, in b
with G. Levy fl — I Classici della Musica Classica XAC4049

VIVALDI

(12) Sonatas, Op. 1 2 vlns & c
Sonata No. 8, in d, F.XIII, No. 24
with M. Westergaard vln, L. Cerroni — I Classici della Musica Classica
hpsi & G. Selmi vlc — XAC4049

Madeleine MacGUIGAN

SCHROEDER

Do you hear me calling? v & pf – arr. vln & pf MacGuigan
with piano — Edison Diamond Disc 80687

Ivor McMAHON

AVISON

(12) Concerti, Op. 6 2 vlns, strs & c
Concerto No. 1, in g
with E. Hurwitz vln, C. Spinks hpsi & — L'Oiseau–Lyre SOL318
Hurwitz Chamber Ensemble – Hurwitz

Concerto No. 2, in B flat
with E. Hurwitz vln, C. Spinks hpsi & — L'Oiseau–Lyre SOL318
Hurwitz Chamber Ensemble – Hurwitz

Concerto No. 6, in D
with E. Hurwitz vln, C. Spinks hpsi & — L'Oiseau–Lyre SOL318
Hurwitz Chamber Ensemble – Hurwitz

Concerto No. 8, in e
with E. Hurwitz vln, C. Spinks hpsi & — L'Oiseau–Lyre SOL318
Hurwitz Chamber Ensemble – Hurwitz

Concerto No. 9, in D
with E. Hurwitz vln, C. Spinks hpsi & — L'Oiseau–Lyre SOL318
Hurwitz Chamber Ensemble – Hurwitz

Francis MacMILLEN (1885–   )

BEETHOVEN

(6) Minuets, G167 pf
No. 2. Minuet No. 2, in G arr. vln & pf Burmester
with N. Schneer pf — 77101 Columbia A2337, D1410

DAWES

Improvisation vln & pf
with piano — HMV 3–7933

DRDLA

Souvenir vln & pf
with R. Hageman pf — 47365 Columbia A2337, D1410

GOLDMARK

Concerto in a, Op. 28 vln & pf
Andante "Air" (2nd mvt)
with orch. – Pitt — 4260 f Gramophone & Typewriter 07924, 047933

HENRI

Légende amoureuse (Mélodie sentimentale) vln & pf
with piano — 5121 f HMV 07950, M0130

LEDERER

(2) Poèmes hongroise, Op. 16 vln & pf
No. 1. Poème hongrois No. 1, in e
with piano — 5121 f HMV 07950

MacMILLEN

Barcarolle vln & pf
with R. Hageman pf — 49057 Columbia 49057, A5964

Causerie "Prairy flowers" vln & pf
with piano — Gramophone & Typewriter 07922

Causerie "Prairy flowers" vln & pf
with orch. — 49121 Columbia 49121, A5964

MASSENET

Italian Christmas Pastorale unid – arr. vln & pf MacMillen
with piano — 4280 f HMV 07947

MOZART

Divertimento No. 17, in D, K334 2 hrns & orch.
Minuet (3rd mvt) arr. vln & pf Burmester
with piano — HMV 3–7944, C146, E152

PIERNÉ

Sérénade à Colombine, Op. 32 (1894) pf – arr. vln & pf
with piano — HMV 3–7935, E152

RANDEGGER

Bohemian dance, Op. 22 vln & pf
with piano — Gramophone & Typewriter 07923

Saltarello–caprice, Op. 17, No. 2 vln & pf
with piano — Gramophone & Typewriter 07945

WIENIAWSKI

Concerto No. 2, in d, Op. 22 vln & orch.
  Romance (2nd mvt)
  with piano   HMV 07970

L. McMORROW

CHOPIN

(3) Nocturnes, Op. 9 pf
  No. 2. Nocturne No. 2, in E flat arr. vln & orch.
  with orch.   Columbia GL513

Frederick MacMURRAY

ASCHER

Alice, where art thou? (1861) v & pf – arr. vln & orch. MacMurray
  with orch.   6296   Edison Diamond Disc 80733

BLAND

Carry me back to old Virginny (1878) v & cho – arr. vln & orch.
  MacMurray
  with orch.   Edison cylinder 4546

Emil MAAS

VIVALDI

Concerto in a, P.28 (F.I, No. 61) 2 vlns, strs & c
  with T. Brandis vln & Berlin   Deutsche Grammophon 2530 094
  Philharmonic Orch. – Karajan

Lorin MAAZEL (1930–)

MOZART

Concerto No. 3, in G, K216 vln & orch.
  with English Chamber Orch. – Maazel Electrola SHZE310
Concerto No. 5, in A, K219 "Turkish" vln & orch.
  with English Chamber Orch. – Maazel Electrola SHZE310

S. MADATOV

BARTÓK

Élégie vln & orch.
  with Moscow Philharmonic Orch. –   Mezhdunarodnaya Kniga
  Zecchi   D05450/1

Alexander Peter MADLE (1928–)

PAGANINI

(6) Sonatas, Op. 3 (1801/7) vln & gtr
  No. 6. Sonata No. 12, in e
  with F. Maxián pf   Ultraphon B12793

SCHUBERT, François

(12) Bagatelles, Op. 13 vln & pf
  No. 9. L'abeille
  with F. Maxián pf   Ultraphon B12793

TUREČEK

Menuet vln & pf
  with F. Maxián pf   Ultraphon B12793

Borge MADSEN

LUMBYE

Concert–polka (1863) 2 vlns & orch.
  with P. Elbaek vln & Tivoli Gardens   Vox PL12840, STPL512840
  Musikkorps – Felumb

Elliot MAGAZINER

IVES

Sonata No. 2 (1910) vln & pf
  with F. Glazer pf   Polymusic PR1001
Trio (1901/3) vln, cl & pf
  Largo
  with D. Weber cl & F. Glazer pf   Polymusic PR1001

VIVALDI

Concerto in D, P.88 (F.I, No. 3) vln, strs & c
  with Paris Symphony Orch. – Bruck   Concerteum CR196
                        Polymusic PR1006

Concerto in B flat, P.405 vln, strs & c
  with Paris Symphony Orch. – Bruck   Concerteum CR196
                        Polymusic PR1006

Giuseppe MAGNANI

CORELLI

(12) Sonatas, Op. 5 vln & c – arr. orch. as "Concerti grossi" by Geminiani
  Concerto grosso No. 1, in D
  with R. Biffoli vln, N. Gasperini vlc,   Vox STDL500423, (in set
  B. Canino hpsi & Gli Accademici di   VBX38)
  Milano – Eckertsen

  Concerto grosso No. 2, in B flat
  with R. Biffoli vln, N. Gasperini vlc,   Vox STDL500425, (in set
  B. Canino hpsi & Gli Accademici di   VBX38)
  Milano – Eckertsen

  Concerto grosso No. 3, in C
  with R. Biffoli vln, N. Gasperini vlc,   Vox (in set VBX38)
  B. Canino hpsi & Gli Accademici di
  Milano – Eckertsen

  Concerto grosso No. 4, in F
  with R. Biffoli vln, N. Gasperini vlc,   Vox (in set VBX38)
  B. Canino hpsi & Gli Accademici di
  Milano – Eckertsen

  Concerto grosso No. 5, in g
  with R. Biffoli vln, N. Gasperini vlc,   Vox (in set VBX38)
  B. Canino hpsi & Gli Accademici di
  Milano – Eckertsen

  Concerto grosso No. 6, in A
  with R. Biffoli vln, N. Gasperini vlc,   Vox (in set VBX38)
  B. Canino hpsi & Gli Accademici di
  Milano – Eckertsen

CORELLI – *Continued*

Concerto grosso No. 7, in d
with R. Biffoli vln, N. Gasperini vlc,   Vox (in set VBX38)
B. Canino hpsi & Gli Accademici di
Milano – Eckertsen

Concerto grosso No. 8, in e
with R. Biffoli vln, N. Gasperini vlc,   Vox (in set VBX38)
B. Canino hpsi & Gli Accademici di
Milano – Eckertsen

Concerto grosso No. 9, in A
with R. Biffoli vln, N. Gasperini vlc,   Vox (in set VBX38)
B. Canino hpsi & Gli Accademici di
Milano – Eckertsen

Concerto grosso No. 10, in F
with R. Biffoli vln, N. Gasperini vlc,   Vox (in set VBX38)
B. Canino hpsi & Gli Accademici di
Milano – Eckertsen

Concerto grosso No. 11, in E
with R. Biffoli vln, N. Gasperini vlc,   Vox (in set VBX38)
B. Canino hpsi & Gli Accademici di
Milano – Eckertsen

Concerto grosso No. 12, in d
with R. Biffoli vln, N. Gasperini vlc,   Vox (in set VBX38)
B. Canino hpsi & Gli Accademici di
Milano – Eckertsen

MANFREDINI

(12) Concerti, Op. 3 (1718) 2 vlns, strs & c
Concerto No. 1, in F
with R. Biffoli vln & I Musici Virtuosi   Vox (in set PL242)
di Milano – Eckertsen

Concerto No. 2, in a
with R. Biffoli vln & I Musici Virtuosi   Vox (in set PL242)
di Milano – Eckertsen

Concerto No. 3, in e
with R. Biffoli vln & I Musici Virtuosi   Vox (in set PL242)
di Milano – Eckertsen

Concerto No. 4, in B flat
with R. Biffoli vln & I Musici Virtuosi   Vox (in set PL242)
di Milano – Eckertsen

Concerto No. 5, in d
with R. Biffoli vln & I Musici Virtuosi   Vox (in set PL242)
di Milano – Eckertsen

Concerto No. 6, in D
with R. Biffoli vln & I Musici Virtuosi   Vox (in set PL242)
di Milano – Eckertsen

Concerto No. 7, in G
with R. Biffoli vln & I Musici Virtuosi   Vox (in set PL242)
di Milano – Eckertsen

Concerto No. 8, in F
with R. Biffoli vln & I Musici Virtuosi   Vox (in set PL242)
di Milano – Eckertsen

Concerto No. 9, in D
with R. Biffoli vln & I Musici Virtuosi   Vox (in set PL242)
di Milano – Eckertsen

Concerto No. 10, in g
with R. Biffoli vln & I Musici Virtuosi   Vox (in set PL242)
di Milano – Eckertsen

MANFREDINI – *Continued*

Concerto No. 11, in c
with R. Biffoli vln & I Musici Virtuosi   Vox (in set PL242)
di Milano – Eckertsen

Concerto No. 12, in C "Christmas Concerto"
with R. Biffoli vln & I Musici Virtuosi   Vox (in set PL242)
di Milano – Eckertsen

Frances MAGNES (1922–   )

BACH

Concerto in d, BWV1043 2 vlns, strs & c
with A. Busch vln & Busch Chamber   Columbia 71674/5D, (set X253),
Players – Busch   ML4002

SERLY

Sonata (1947) "in Modus Lascivus" solo vln
(unaccompanied)   Bartók BRS908

STRAVINSKY

Suite Italienne (on themes of Pergolesi) (1933) vln & pf
with D. Garvey pf   Bartók BRS908

WOLPE

Sonata (1949) vln & pf
with D. Tudor pf   Esoteric ES530

Hugh MAGUIRE (1926–   )

MOZART

Serenade No. 6, in D, K239 "Serenata Notturna" orch.
with N. Marriner vln, S. Streatfield   Decca LXT5570, SMD1097,
vla, S. Knussen cbs & London   SXL2196
Symphony Orch. – Maag   London CM9133, CS6133

RIMSKY–KORSAKOV

Capriccio espagnole, Op. 34 (1887) orch.
with London Symphony Orch. –   Victor RB16233, SB2105
Martinon

Scheherazade, Op. 35 (1888) orch.
with London Symphony Orch. –   Everest LPBR6026, SDBR3026
Goossens   Hallmark HM512

Scheherazade, Op. 35 (1888) orch.
with London Symphony Orch. –   Victor RB16077, VIC1013
Monteux

STRAUSS, R.

(Ein) Heldenleben, Op. 40 (1898) orch.
with London Symphony Orch. –   Everest LPBR6038, SDBR3038
Ludwig   Top Rank BUY003
                                World Record Club T163

STRAVINSKY

(L') Histoire du Soldat (1918) narrators, tpt, cbs, tbn, cl, vln, bsn & pcn
with D. Clift tpt, S. Knussen cbs, D.   Everest LPBR6017, SDBR3017
Wick tbn, G. de Peyer cl, W.
Waterhouse bsn, C. Donaldson pcn &
London Symphony Orch. – Carewe

TCHAIKOVSKY

Swan Lake, Op. 20 (1875/6) – ballet orch.
No. 5. Pas de deux (Andante)
with London Symphony Orch. –   Philips 835142LYS, A02261L
Martinon

No. 13b. Dance of the Queen of the Swans (1st dance)
with London Symphony Orch. –   Philips 835142LYS, A02261L
Martinon

Tamás MAGYAR (1913–   )

ALBÉNIZ

España (6 Feuilles d'album) Op. 165 pf
No. 2. Tango in D arr. vln & pf Kreisler
with W. Hielkema pf   Philips S06049R

BACH

(3) Sonatas & 3 Partitas, BWV1001/6 solo vln
Partita No. 2, in d, BWV1004
(unaccompanied)   Philips N00238L
Partita No. 3, in E, BWV1006
(unaccompanied)   Philips N00238L

BARTÓK

For Children (40 pieces) (1909) pf
Nos. 6, 13, 18, 25, 31, 36 & 40 arr. vln & pf as "Hungarian folk tunes"
by Szigeti
with W. Hielkema pf   Philips N00700R
(6) Rumanian folk dances (1915) pf – arr. vln & pf Székely
with W. Hielkema pf   Philips N00700R

BLOCH

Baal Shem (3 Pictures of Chassidic life) (1923) vln & pf
No. 2. Nigun (Improvisation)
with W. Hielkema pf   Philips N00125R

DOHNÁNYI

Ruralia Hungarica, Op. 32A pf – arr. vln & pf Kreisler
with W. Hielkema pf   Philips N00700R

DVOŘÁK

Concerto in a, Op. 53 vln & orch.
with Vienna Symphony Orch. –   Epic LC3173
Loibner   Philips A00751R

FALLA

(La) Vida Breve (1913) – opera
Danza española orch. – arr. vln & pf Kreisler
with W. Hielkema pf   Philips S06049R

GLAZOUNOV

Concerto in a, Op. 82 vln & orch.
with Hague Residentie Orch. – van   Epic LC3184
Otterloo   Philips A00269L

GOUNOD

Ave Maria (Méditation on Bach's "Prelude No. 1, in C" from Book I of
"Das Wohltemperirte Clavier") v & pf – arr. vln & pf
with W. Hielkema pf   Philips N00605R, N09043S,
N11227G

GRANADOS

(12) Danzas españolas, Op. 37 (1893) pf
No. 5. Danza española No. 5, in e "Andaluza" arr. vln & pf Kreisler
with W. Hielkema pf   Philips S06049R

HANDEL

Te Deum, Dettingen (1743)
No. 17. Gebet ('Verlieh uns Herr, zu Schirmen ...) arr. vln & pf as
"Prayer" by Flesch
with W. Hielkema pf   Philips N00605R, N09045S,
N11230G

KHACHATURIAN

Concerto in D (1940) vln & orch.
with Vienna Symphony Orch. – Moralt Epic LC3080
Philips A00684R

KREISLER

Caprice viennois, Op. 2 vln & pf
with W. Hielkema pf   Philips N00605R, N09044S,
N11226G, SBF217

Liebesfreud vln & pf
with W. Hielkema pf   Philips N00605R, N09042S,
N11228G, N402001E

Liebesleid vln & pf
with W. Hielkema pf   Philips N00605R, N09042S,
N11228G, N402001E

Tambourin chinois, Op. 3 vln & pf
with W. Hielkema pf   Philips N00605R, N09044S,
N11226G, N402010E, SBF217

Praeludium & Allegro (Pugnani) vln & pf
with W. Hielkema pf   Philips N00125R

Sicilienne & Rigaudon (Francoeur) vln & pf
with W. Hielkema pf   AA11194 2G   Philips N09013S, N11194G

Variations on a theme of Corelli (Tartini) vln & pf
with W. Hielkema pf   Philips N09009S, N11157G

MASSENET

Thaïs (1894) – opera
Méditation arr. vln & pf Marsick
with W. Hielkema pf   Philips N00605R, N09043S,
N11227G

NIN

Rapsodie ibérica (1930) vln & pf
with W. Hielkema pf   Philips S06049R

PARADIES

Sicilienne vln & pf – arr. Dushkin
with W. Hielkema   AA 11194 1G   Philips N09013S, N11194G
pf

RAVEL

Pièce en forme d'Habanera v & pf – arr. vln & pf Catherine
with W. Hielkema pf   Philips N00125R, N09009S,
N11157G

Tzigane (Rapsodie de concert) (1924) vln & pf or orch.
with W. Hielkema pf   Philips N00125R

RIMSKY–KORSAKOV

(Le) Coq d'Or (1910) – opera
Hymn to the sun arr. vln & pf Kreisler
with W. Hielkema pf   Philips N00605R, N09045S,
                          N11230G

SARASATE

(8) Danzas españolas vln & pf
No. 1. Malagueña, Op. 21, No. 1
with W. Hielkema pf   Philips S06049R

SIBELIUS

Concerto in d, Op. 47 vln & orch.
with Hague Residentie Orch. – van   Epic LC3184
Otterloo   Philips A00269L

TARTINI

(12) Sonatas, Op. 1 (1734) vln & c
Sonata No. 10, in g "Didone abbandonata"
with W. Hielkema pf   Philips N09046S, N11231G

Hans MAHLKE

DRDLA

Souvenir vln & pf
with K. Rockstroh pf   4611   Kalliope K1170

GOUNOD

Ave Maria (Méditation on Bach's "Prelude No. 1, in C" from Book I of
"Das Wohltemperirte Clavier") v & pf – arr. vln & pf
with K. Rockstroh pf   4614   Kalliope K1269

GRIEG

(8) Lyric Pieces – Book I, Op. 12 pf
No. 6. Norwegian melody arr. vln & pf Sitt
with E. Künnecke pf   Odeon 79176/9
No. 7. Albumblatt arr. vln & pf Sitt
with E. Künnecke pf   Odeon 79176/9
(8) Lyric Pieces – Book II, Op. 38 pf
No. 1. Berceuse arr. vln & pf Sitt
with E. Künnecke pf   Odeon 1191, 79176/9
No. 6. Élégie arr. vln & pf Sitt
with E. Künnecke pf   Odeon 1195, 79176/9
No. 7. Waltz arr. vln & pf Sitt
with E. Künnecke pf   Odeon 1195, 79176/9
(6) Lyric Pieces – Book III, Op. 43 pf
No. 2. Lonely wanderer arr. vln & pf Sitt
with E. Künnecke pf   Odeon 1191, 79176/9
(7) Lyric Pieces – Book IV, Op. 47 pf
No. 3. Melody arr. vln & pf Sitt
with E. Künnecke pf   Odeon 79176/9
Peer Gynt (Suite No. 2) Op. 55 orch.
No. 4. Solveig's song arr. vln & pf Sitt
with K. Rockstroh pf   4612   Kalliope K1269

RAFF

(6) Pieces, Op. 85 vln & pf
No. 3. Cavatina in D
with K. Rockstroh pf   4613[2]   Kalliope K1170

Frederic L. MAHN

RAFF

(6) Pieces, Op. 85 vln & pf
No. 3. Cavatina in D
with piano   Phono–Cut 5106

Franz–Josef MAIER (1925–   )

BACH, J.C.

Sinfonia concertante in A, T. P284 (1770) vln, vlc & orch.
with A. May vlc & Collegium Aureum Harmonia Mundi HM30695
– Peters

BACH, J.S.

(6) Brandenburg Concerti, BWV1046/51 (1721) strs & c
Brandenburg Concerto No. 1, in F, BWV1046 vln, 3 obs, bsn, 2 hrns, strs
& c
playing vln–pic with A. Sous ob, H.   Camden Classics (in set
Hucke ob, I. Goritzki ob, W.   VCCS6023)
Mauruschat bsn, E. Penzel hrn, G.   Victor (in set VICS6023)
Seifert hrn, G. Leonhardt hpsi &
Collegium Aureum

Brandenburg Concerto No. 2, in F, BWV1047 tpt, fl, ob, vln, strs & c
with E.H. Tarr tpt, H–M. Linde rec,   Camden Classics (in set
H. Hucke ob, G. Leonhardt hpsi &   VCCS6023)
Collegium Aureum   Victor (in set VICS6023)

Brandenburg Concerto No. 3, in G, BWV1048 3 vlns, 3 vlas, 3 vlcs & cbs
with W. Neuhaus vln, B. Seeger vln,   Camden Classics (in set
G. Lemmen vla, F. Beyer vla, D. Wolff VCCS6023)
–Malm vla, R.J. Buhl vlc, R.   Victor (in set VICS6023)
Mandalka vlc, H. Beckedorf vlc, P.
Breuer cbs & G. Leonhardt hpsi, of
the Collegium Aureum

Brandenburg Concerto No. 4, in G, BWV1049 vln, 2 fls, strs & c
with H–M. Linde rec, G. Höller rec &   Camden Classics (in set
Collegium Aureum   VCCS6023)
                                       Victor (in set VICS6023)

Brandenburg Concerto No. 5, in D, BWV1050 clav, fl, vln, strs & c
with G. Leonhardt hpsi, H–M. Linde   Camden Classics (in set
fl & Collegium Aureum   VCCS6023)
                                       Victor (in set VICS6023)

HAYDN

Cassation in G, H.II, No. 9 2 vlns, 2 vlas, 2 obs, 2 hrns & cbs
with U. Grehling vln, U. Koch vla, G.   Harmonia Mundi HM30643,
Lemmen vla, A. Sous ob, H. Hucke   HMST530643
ob, G. Seifert hrn, E. Penzel hrn, R.J.
Buhl vlc & J. Koch viol

Cassation in F, H.II, No. 20 2 vlns, 2 vlas, 2 obs, 2 hrns & cbs
with U. Grehling vln, U. Koch vla, G.   Harmonia Mundi HM30643,
Lemmen vla, A. Sous ob, H. Hucke   HMST530643
ob, G. Seifert hrn, E. Penzel hrn, R.J.
Buhl vlc & J. Koch viol

LECLAIR

(6) Concerti, Op. 7 (1737) vln & strs
Concerto No. 2, in D
with Collegium Aureum – Peters   Harmonia Mundi HM30699,
                                     HMST530699

LOCATELLI

(12) Concerti, Op. 7 (1741) "Il pianto d'Arianna" strs & c
Concerto No. 12, in F 4 vlns, strs & c
    with W. Neuhaus vln, B. Seeger vln,   Harmonia Mundi HMS30887
    G. Vollmer vln & Collegium Aureum

MOZART

Divertimento No. 10, in F, K247 2 hrns & strs
    with G. Seifert hrn, E. Penzel hrn, U.   Harmonia Mundi HM30646,
    Grehling vln, G. Lemmen vla, R.J.   HMST530646
    Buhl vlc & J. Koch viol

Divertimento No. 11, in D, K251 2 hrns & strs
    with G. Seifert hrn, E. Penzel hrn, U.   Harmonia Mundi HM30646,
    Grehling vln, G. Lemmen vla, R.J.   HMST530646
    Buhl vlc & J. Koch viol

STAMITZ, K.

Sinfonia concertante in A vln, vla, vlc & orch.
    with F. Beyer vla, T. Blees vlc &   Harmonia Mundi HMS30840
    Collegium Aureum   Victor VICS1339

VIVALDI

Concerto in E flat, F.I, No. 231 "Il Ritiro" vln, strs & c
    with Collegium Aureum   Harmonia Mundi HMS30887
Concerto in E flat, P.423 (F.I, No. 101) 2 vlns, strs & c
    with D. Vorholz vln & Collegium   Harmonia Mundi CVH333,
    Aureum – Reinhardt   HM30644
(12) Sonatas, Op. 1 2 vlns & c
    Sonata No. 3, in C, F.XIII, No. 19
    with S. Kuijken vln, G. Leonhardt   Harmonia Mundi CVC333,
    hpsi & H. Beckedorf vlc   HMS30881

Paul MAKANOWITZKY (1920–   )

BACH

(6) Sonatas, BWV1014/9 vln & clav
    Sonata No. 1, in b, BWV1014
    with N. Lee pf   Lumen LD3–437

    Sonata No. 2, in A, BWV1015
    with N. Lee pf   Lumen LD3–437

    Sonata No. 3, in E, BWV1016
    with N. Lee pf   Lumen LD3–437

    Sonata No. 4, in c, BWV1017
    with N. Lee pf   Lumen LD3–438

    Sonata No. 5, in f, BWV1018
    with N. Lee pf   Lumen LD3–438

    Sonata No. 6, in G, BWV1019
    with N. Lee pf   Lumen LD3–438

BEETHOVEN

(3) Sonatas, Op. 12 vln & pf
    No. 1. Sonata No. 1, in D
    with N. Lee pf   Lumen LD3–419

    No. 2. Sonata No. 2, in A
    with N. Lee pf   Lumen LD3–419

    No. 3. Sonata No. 3, in E flat
    with N. Lee pf   Lumen LD3–416
Sonata No. 4, in a, Op. 23 vln & pf
    with N. Lee pf   Lumen LD3–418
                    Vanguard VRS1038

BEETHOVEN – *Continued*

Sonata No. 5, in F, Op. 24 "Spring" vln & pf
    with N. Lee pf   Lumen LD3–418
                    Vanguard VRS1038

(3) Sonatas, Op. 30 vln & pf
    No. 1. Sonata No. 6, in A
    with N. Lee pf   Lumen LD3–417
                    Vanguard VRS1039

    No. 2. Sonata No. 7, in c
    with N. Lee pf   Lumen LD3–417
                    Vanguard VRS1039

    No. 3. Sonata No. 8, in G
    with N. Lee pf   Lumen LD3–418
                    Vanguard VRS1038

Sonata No. 9, in A, Op. 47 "Kreutzer" vln & pf
    with N. Lee pf   Lumen LD3–416
Sonata No. 10, in G, Op. 96 vln & pf
    with N. Lee pf   Lumen LD3–419

BRAHMS

Sonata No. 1, in G, Op. 78 vln & pf
    with N. Lee pf   Lumen LD3–428
Sonata No. 2, in A, Op. 100 vln & pf
    with N. Lee pf   Lumen LD3–428
Sonata No. 3, in d, Op. 108 vln & pf
    with N. Lee pf   Lumen LD3–429
Trio in E flat, Op. 40 hrn, pf & vln
    with P. Delvescovo hrn & N. Lee pf   Lumen LD3–429

MOZART

Concertone in C, K190 2 vlns, ob, vlc & orch.
    with G.F. Hendel vln & Saar Chamber   Nonesuch H1068, H71068
    Orch. – Ristenpart
Concerto No. 3, in G, K216 vln & orch.
    with Saar Chamber Orch. – Ristenpart   Nonesuch H1056, H71056
Concerto No. 4, in D, K218 vln & orch.
    with Saar Chamber Orch. – Ristenpart   Nonesuch H1056, H71056

STAMITZ, K.

Sinfonia concertante in D vln & vla or 2 vlns & orch.
    with G.F. Hendel vln & Saar Chamber   Nonesuch H1014, H71014
    Orch. – Ristenpart

VIVALDI

(12) Concerti, Op. 9 (1728) "La Cetra" vln, strs & c
    Concerto No. 1, in C, P.9 (F.I, No. 47)
    with Vienna State Opera Chamber   Amadeo AVRS6227
    Orch. – Golschmann   Bach Guild BG607, BGS5033
                    I Classici della Musica Classica
                    XAM4071

    Concerto No. 2, in A, P.214 (F.I, No. 51)
    with Vienna State Opera Chamber   Amadeo AVRS6227
    Orch. – Golschmann   Bach Guild BG607, BGS5033
                    I Classici della Musica Classica
                    XAM4071

    Concerto No. 3, in g, P.399 (F.I, No. 52)
    with Vienna State Opera Chamber   Amadeo AVRS6227
    Orch. – Golschmann   Bach Guild BG607, BGS5033
                    I Classici della Musica Classica
                    XAM4071

VIVALDI – *Continued*

Concerto No. 4, in E, P.242 (F.I, No. 48)
with Vienna State Opera Chamber   Amadeo AVRS6227
Orch. – Golschmann   Bach Guild BG607, BGS5033
    I Classici della Musica Classica
    XAM4071

Concerto No. 5, in a, P.10 (F.I, No. 53)
with Vienna State Opera Chamber   Amadeo AVRS6228
Orch. – Golschmann   Bach Guild BG608, BGS5034
    I Classici della Musica Classica
    XAM4072

Concerto No. 6, in A, P.215 (F.I, No. 54) with solo vln scordato
with Vienna State Opera Chamber   Amadeo AVRS6228
Orch. – Golschmann   Bach Guild BG608, BGS5034
    I Classici della Musica Classica
    XAM4072

Concerto No. 7, in B flat, P.340 (F.I, No. 55)
with Vienna State Opera Chamber   Amadeo AVRS6228
Orch. – Golschmann   Bach Guild BG608, BGS5034
    I Classici della Musica Classica
    XAM4072

Concerto No. 8, in d, P.260 (F.I, No. 56)
with Vienna State Opera Chamber   Amadeo AVRS6228
Orch. – Golschmann   Bach Guild BG608, BGS5034
    I Classici della Musica Classica
    XAM4072

Concerto No. 9, in B flat, P.341 (F.I, No. 57) with 2nd vln obb
with W. Boskovsky vln & Vienna   Amadeo AVRS6229
State Opera Chamber Orch. –   Bach Guild BG609, BGS5035
Golschmann   I Classici della Musica Classica
    XAM4073

Concerto No. 10, in G, P.103 (F.I, No. 49)
with Vienna State Opera Chamber   Amadeo AVRS6229
Orch. – Golschmann   Bach Guild BG609, BGS5035
    I Classici della Musica Classica
    XAM4073

Concerto No. 11, in c, P.416 (F.I, No. 58)
with Vienna State Opera Chamber   Amadeo AVRS6229
Orch. – Golschmann   Bach Guild BG609, BGS5035
    I Classici della Musica Classica
    XAM4073

Concerto No. 12, in b, P.154 (F.I, No. 50) with solo vln scordato
with Vienna State Opera Chamber   Amadeo AVRS6229
Orch. – Golschmann   Bach Guild BG609, BGS5035
    I Classici della Musica Classica
    XAM4073

Fritz MALACHOWSKY*

MENDELSSOHN

Concerto in e, Op. 64 vln & orch.
  with Berlin Symphony Orch. – Balzer   Royale 1286

TCHAIKOVSKY

Concerto in D, Op. 35 vln & orch.
  with Berlin Symphony Orch. – Balzer   Royale 1265

* Pseudonym for Bronislaw Huberman. Both works listed above are derived
from air checks. Excerpts from concerti by Brahms, Mendelssohn &
Tchaikovsky, via air checks, are on Royale 1314.

Edmondo MALANOTTE (1912–)

CORELLI

(12) Concerti grossi, Op. 6 orch.
  Concerto grosso No. 4, in D
  with G. Mozzato vln & Virtuosi di   HMV BLP1041
  Roma – Fasano

VIVALDI

(12) Concerti, Op. 3 "L'Estro armonico" var. cbns & strs
  Concerto No. 1, in D, P.146 (F.IV, No. 7) 4 vlns, vlc, strs & c
  with F. Gulli vln, M. Benvenuti vln,   HMV ALP1809, ASD391
  A. Poltronieri vln & Virtuosi di Roma
  – Fasano

  Concerto No. 7, in F, P.249 (F.IV, No. 9) 4 vlns, strs & c
  with L. Ferro vln, F. Gulli vln, M.   HMV ALP1810, ASD392
  Benvenuti vln & Virtuosi di Roma –
  Fasano

  Concerto No. 8, in a, P.2 (F.I, No. 177) 2 vlns, strs & c
  with G. Mozzato vln & Virtuosi di   Brunswick AXA4505
  Roma – Fasano   Decca DL9729, UAT273589

  Concerto No. 8, in a, P.2 (F.I, No. 177) 2 vlns, strs & c
  with F. Gulli vln & Virtuosi di Roma   HMV ALP1810, ASD392
  – Fasano

  Concerto No. 10, in b, P.148 (F.IV, No. 10) 4 vlns, strs & c
  with L. Ferro vln, A. Gramegna vln,   Cetra BB25291/2
  A. Pelliccia vln & Collegium Musicum
  Italicum – Fasano

  Concerto No. 10, in b, P.148 (F.IV, No. 10) 4 vlns, strs & c
  with L. Ferro vln, A. Stefanato vln, F.   HMV ALP1811, ASD393
  Gulli vln & Virtuosi di Roma –
  Fasano

  Concerto No. 11, in d, P.250 (F.IV, No. 11) 2 vlns, vlc, strs & c
  with L. Ferro vln, B. Mazzacurati vlc   Angel 45030
  & Virtuosi di Roma – Fasano   Electrola E70380
    HMV ALP1629, WBLP552

  Concerto No. 11, in d, P.250 (F.IV, No. 11) 2 vlns, vlc, strs & c
  with L. Ferro vln, B. Mazzacurati vlc   HMV ALP1811, ASD393
  & Virtuosi di Roma – Fasano

(12) Concerti, Op. 4 "La Stravaganza" vln, strs & c
  Concerto No. 5, in A, F.I, No. 184
  with Virtuosi di Roma – Fasano   HMV QALP10113
    Victor LHMV26

(12) Concerti, Op. 8 (1725) "Il Cimento dell' Armonia e dell' Invenzione"
  (Nos. 1/4: Le quattro Stagioni) vln & strs
  Concerto No. 5, in E flat, F.I, No. 26 "La Tempesta di mare"
  with Virtuosi di Roma – Fasano   Electrola E90147
    HMV ALP1439, WALP1439

  Concerto No. 5, in E flat, F.I, No. 26 "La Tempesta di mare"
  with Virtuosi di Roma – Fasano   Angel 35878, (in set 3611),
    ASC5039
    HMV ALP1787, ASD368

  Concerto No. 10, in B flat, F.I, No. 29 "La Caccia"
  with Virtuosi di Roma – Fasano   Electrola E70435, STE70435
    HMV BSDW8009, WBLP570

  Concerto No. 10, in B flat, F.I, No. 29 "La Caccia"
  with Virtuosi di Roma – Fasano   Angel 35879, (in set 3611),
    ASC5040
    HMV ALP1788, ASD369

VIVALDI – *Continued*

Concerto in a, P.28 (F.I, No. 61) 2 vlns, strs & c – arr. Casella
with F. Scaglia vln & Collegium Cetra LPC50045
Musicum Italicum – Fasano   Cetra–Soria CS546
Concerto in G, P.132 (F.I, No. 6) 2 vlns, strs & c
with F. Gulli vln & Virtuosi di Roma HMV ALP1344
– Fasano

Vladimir MALININ (1935–)

BACH

(6) Sonatas, BWV1014/9 vln & clav
Sonata No. 3, in E, BWV1016
with M. Stern pf   Mezhdunarodnaya Kniga
        D012957/8

BALASANYAN

Shakuntala – ballet orch.
Lyric dance arr. vln & pf Vladimirsky
with M. Stern pf   Mezhdunarodnaya Kniga
        D026390

Shakuntala's variations arr. vln & pf Vladimirsky
with M. Stern pf   Mezhdunarodnaya Kniga
        D026390

BEETHOVEN

Romance No. 1, in G, Op. 40 vln & orch.
with piano   Mezhdunarodnaya Kniga D6014

FALLA

(La) Vida Breve (1913) – opera
Danza española orch. – arr. vln & pf Kreisler
with piano   Mezhdunarodnaya Kniga D6014

KHACHATURIAN

Chanson poème in e (1929) vln & pf
with piano   Mezhdunarodnaya Kniga
       D11055/6

MEDTNER

(4) Fairytales, Op. 34 pf
No. 2. Fairytale No. 2, in e arr. vln & pf Vladimirsky
with M. Stern pf   Mezhdunarodnaya Kniga
        D016139

Sonata No. 1, in b, Op. 21 vln & pf
with M. Stern pf   Mezhdunarodnaya Kniga
        D016139

MIRZOYEV

Adagio & waltz–scherzo vln & pf
with M. Stern pf   Mezhdunarodnaya Kniga
        D026390

MOZART

Sonata No. 22, in A, K305 vln & pf
with M. Stern pf   Mezhdunarodnaya Kniga
        D026389

Sonata No. 32, in B flat, K454 vln & pf
with M. Stern pf   Mezhdunarodnaya Kniga
        D012957/8

PROKOFIEV

(4) Pieces, Op. 32 (1918) pf
No. 3. Gavotta arr. vln & pf Heifetz
with M. Stern pf   Mezhdunarodnaya Kniga
        D026390

SARASATE

Caprice basque, Op. 24 vln & pf
with M. Stern pf   Mezhdunarodnaya Kniga
        D026389

SCHUBERT

Sonata No. 17, in D, Op. 53 (D850) pf
Rondo (4th mvt) arr. vln & pf Friedberg
with M. Stern pf   Mezhdunarodnaya Kniga
        D026389

SCRIABIN

(9) Mazurkas, Op. 25 pf
No. 1. Mazurka No. 1, in f arr. vln & pf Tziganov
with M. Stern pf   Mezhdunarodnaya Kniga
        D016140

(2) Nocturnes, Op. 5 pf
No. 1. Nocturne No. 1, in f sharp arr. vln & pf Moguilevsky
with M. Stern pf   Mezhdunarodnaya Kniga
        D016140

(3) Pieces, Op. 45 (1907) pf
No. 1. Album leaf in E flat arr. vln & pf Yamada
with M. Stern pf   Mezhdunarodnaya Kniga
        D016140

Waltz in A flat, Op. 38 pf – arr. vln & pf Yampolsky
with M. Stern pf   Mezhdunarodnaya Kniga
        D016140

SHCHEDRIN

Humoresque pf – arr. vln & pf Tziganov
with M. Stern pf   Mezhdunarodnaya Kniga
        D026390

In imitation of Albéniz pf – arr. vln & pf Tziganov
with M. Stern pf   Mezhdunarodnaya Kniga
        D026390

SHOSTAKOVICH

(24) Preludes, Op. 34 (1932/3) pf
Prelude No. 2, in a arr. vln & pf Tziganov
with M. Stern pf   Mezhdunarodnaya Kniga
        D016140

Prelude No. 6, in b arr. vln & pf Tziganov
with M. Stern pf   Mezhdunarodnaya Kniga
        D016140

Prelude No. 12, in g sharp arr. vln & pf Tziganov
with M. Stern pf   Mezhdunarodnaya Kniga
        D016140

Prelude No. 13, in F sharp arr. vln & pf Tziganov
with M. Stern pf   Mezhdunarodnaya Kniga
        D016140

Prelude No. 17, in A flat arr. vln & pf Tziganov
with M. Stern pf   Mezhdunarodnaya Kniga
        D016140

Prelude No. 18, in f arr. vln & pf Tziganov
with M. Stern pf   Mezhdunarodnaya kniga
        D016140

SHOSTAKOVICH – *Continued*

Prelude No. 19, in E flat arr. vln & pf Tziganov
with M. Stern pf
Mezhdunarodnaya Kniga
D016140

Prelude No. 20, in c arr. vln & pf Tziganov
with M. Stern pf
Mezhdunarodnaya Kniga
D016140

Prelude No. 21, in B flat arr. vln & pf Tziganov
with M. Stern pf
Mezhdunarodnaya Kniga
D016140

Prelude No. 22, in g arr. vln & pf Tziganov
with M. Stern pf
Mezhdunarodnaya Kniga
D016140

Quartet No. 4, in D, Op. 83 2 vlns, vla & vlc
Andantino (2nd mvt) arr. vln & pf Tziganov
with M. Stern pf
Mezhdunarodnaya Kniga
D026390

VIEUXTEMPS

(6) Morceaux de salon, Op. 22 vln & pf
No. 4. Tarantelle in a
with piano
Mezhdunarodnaya Kniga D6014

YSAŸE

(6) Sonatas, Op. 27 solo vln
Sonata No. 4, in e
(unaccompanied)
Mezhdunarodnaya Kniga D6013

Ernesto MAMPAEY

VIVALDI

Concerto in A, P.222 (F.I, No. 139) "L'eco in lontano" 2 vlns, strs & c –
arr. Molinari
with S. Lautenbacher vln & Emil
Seiler Chamber Orch. – Hofman
Archive APM14318, ARC3218,
ARC73218, SAPM198318
Musique Royale 199010

N. T. MANASEVICH

AUER

Romance, Op. 4 vln & pf
with piano
Gramophone & Typewriter
27948

CUI

(5) Little Duets, Op. 56 fl, vln & pf
No. 2. Berceuse
with V.F. Stepanov fl & piano
Gramophone & Typewriter
28013

No. 4. Nocturne
with V.F. Stepanov fl & piano
Gramophone & Typewriter
28014

No. 5. Valse
with V.F. Stepanov fl & piano
Gramophone & Typewriter
28015

DENZA

Reviens v & pf – arr. v, vln & pf
with N.A. Bolshakov t & piano
Pathé 24336

GLINKA

Doubt (1838) v & pf – arr. pf, vln & vlc
with P. Gross pf & Y. Butkovsky vlc
Gramophone & Typewriter
28016

Élégie unid – arr. pf, vln & vlc
with P. Gross pf & Y. Butkovsky vlc
Gramophone & Typewriter
28017

RUBINSTEIN

Trio No. 3, in B flat, Op. 52 pf, vln & vlc
Andante (2nd mvt)
with P. Gross pf & Y. Butkovsky vlc
Gramophone & Typewriter
28010

Grete MANCKE

GOUNOD

Ave Maria (Méditation on Bach's "Prelude No. 1, in C" from Book I of
"Das Wohltemperirte Clavier") v & pf – arr. vln & orch.
with Edith Lorand's Orch.
Parlophone P1586

Henri MANDEL

FAURÉ

Sonata No. 2, in e, Op. 108 vln & pf
with E. König pf
Baroque BC1845, BU2845

FRANCK

Sonata in A (1886) vln & pf
with R. Cabiri pf
Baroque BC1845, BU2845

Juan MANÉN (1883–   )

BACH

(4) Suites, BWV1066/9 strs & c
Suite No. 3, in D: Air (2nd mvt) BWV1068 2 obs, 3 tpts, drms, strs & c
– arr. vln & pf as "Air on the G–string" by Wilhelmj
with E. Künnecke pf
Favorite 1–14373

BECCE

Légende d'amour, Op. 11 pf – arr. vln, hp & org
with harp & Mustel organ
Parlophone E10094

BRUCH

Concerto No. 1, in g, Op. 26 vln & orch.
Allegro moderato (1st mvt)
Cc 795–II & 796–III   HMV 067935/6, M72
with orch.
Allegro moderato (1st mvt)
with string orch.   122–C   Favorite 2–14012
Adagio (2nd mvt)
with orch.   Cc 797/8–II   HMV 067937/8, M79
Adagio (2nd mvt)
with string orch.   123–C   Favorite 2–14013
Concerto No 1, in g, Op. 26 vln & orch
with orch.
HMV AB 24, 27 & 28

CHOPIN

(3) Nocturnes, Op. 9 pf
  No. 2. Nocturne No. 2, in E flat arr. vln & pf Sarasate
  with E. Künnecke pf   Favorite 1–14375

DAQUIN

Pièces de clavecin – Book I (1735) hpsi
  Le coucou arr. vln & pf Manén
  with wind sextet   Favorite 1–14377
  Le coucou arr. vln & pf Manén
  with orch.   Parlophone P212
  Le coucou arr. vln & pf Manén
  with piano   HMV AA7

DRDLA

Serenade No. 1, in A vln & pf
  with piano   Scala 5010
Serenade No. 1, in A vln & pf
  with orch. – Kark   1–2044 Parlophone P210

GLUCK

Orphée et Eurydice (1762) – opera
  Dance of the blessed spirits: Lento "Mélodie" (No. 2) arr. vln & pf
  Wilhelmj
  with wind sextet   Favorite 1–14377
  Dance of the blessed spirits: Lento "Mélodie" (No. 2) arr. vln & pf
  Kreisler
  with piano   HMV AA7

HÉROLD

(Le) Pré aux Clercs (1832) – opera
  Jours de mon enfance
  with H. Francillo–Kaufmann 5059 Anker 9921
  s & Berlin Symphony Orch. –   Coliseum 4011
  Weyersberg   International Record Collectors
                    Club 3103

  O Dieu du jeune âge
  with H. Francillo–Kaufmann 5060 Anker 9921
  s & Berlin Symphony Orch. –   Coliseum 4011
  Weyersberg   International Record Collectors
                    Club 3103

MANÉN

Chanson–Adagietto, Op. A–8, No. 1 vln & pf
  with piano   HMV AB151
Toccata vln & pf
  with piano   Parlophone P212

MARTINI, G.B.

(12) Sonatas, Op. 2 (1741) hpsi
  Sonata No. 12, in F: Gavotte arr. vln & pf Manén
  with E. Künnecke pf   Favorite 1–14373

MENDELSSOHN

Concerto in e, Op. 64 vln & orch
      s 03139v, s 03122v, s 03123v, s HMV 067905/10
      03140v & s 03125/6v
  with Barcelona Orch. – Gelabert
Concerto in e, Op. 64 vln & orch.
      Cc 805–III & 806/10–II HMV 067927/32, M80/2
  with orch.

MENDELSSOHN – *Continued*

Concerto in e, Op. 64 vln & orch.
  Allegretto non troppo; Allegro molto vivace (3rd mvt)
  with orch.   Parlophone E10032, P213

PAGANINI

Moto perpetuo (Allegro di concert) Op. 11 (1830) vln & orch.
  with piano   Scala 5010
Moto perpetuo (Allegro di concert) Op. 11 (1830) vln & orch.
  with orch. – Kark   2043 Parlophone E10105, P211

SARASATE

Jota aragonesa, Op. 27 vln & pf
  with orch. – Kark   2046 Parlophone E10105, P211
Jota aragonesa, Op. 27 vln & pf
  with piano   HMV AB151

SCHUMANN

(13) Kinderscenen, Op. 15 pf
  No. 7. Träumerei arr. vln & pf
  with E. Künnecke pf   Favorite 1–14375

WIENIAWSKI

Légende, Op. 17 vln & pf or orch.
  with orch. – Kark   1–2047 Parlophone P210

André Louis MANGEOT (1883–1970)

DEBUSSY

Sonata No. 3, in g (1917) vln & pf
  with L. Barbour pf   National Gramophonic Society
                    NGS127/8

GOOSSENS

Sonata No. 1, in e, Op. 21 (1918) vln & pf
  Molto adagio (2nd mvt)
  with E. Goossens pf   National Gramophonic Society
                    NGS56

VAUGHAN WILLIAMS

Quintet (1914) "Phantasy" 3 vlns, vla & vlc
  with B. Pecker vln, J. Pougnet vln, National Gramophonic Society
  H.J. Berley vla & J. Barbirolli vlc 54/5

Gerhard MANKE (1910–)

BRAHMS

Concerto in D, Op. 77 vln & orch.
  with Leipzig Radio Orch. – Abendroth Urania RS7–24

Robert MANN (1920–)

BARTÓK

Contrasts (1938) cl, vln & pf
  with S. Drucker cl & L. Hambro pf Bartók BRS916
Sonata No. 1 (1921) vln & pf
  with L. Hambro pf   Bartók BRS922
Sonata in g (1944) solo vln
  (unaccompanied)   Bartók BRS916

KOHS

Chamber Concerto (1949) vln, vla & strs
  with F. Molnar vla & string ensemble   Columbia ML4492

SCHOENBERG

Trio, Op. 45 (1946) vln, vla & vlc
  with R. Hillyer vla & C. Adam vlc   Columbia ML6436, (in set
M2L367), MS7036, (in set
M2S767)

Sydney MANN

BOYCE

Concerto in b "Double" 2 vlns & strs – transcr & ed. D. Stevens
  with N. Roth vln & London Soloists'   CBS SBRG72541
  Ensemble – Roth

Julius Maria von MÁNNOK

BECUCCI

Tesoro mio – waltz, Op. 228 orch. – arr. vln & orch.
  with orch.   HMV 1115

BRAHMS

(21) Hungarian Dances pf duet
  Hungarian dance No. 2, in d arr. vln & pf Joachim
  with piano   HMV 12771

DVOŘÁK

(8) Humoresques, Op. 101 pf
  No. 7. Humoresque No. 7, in G flat arr. vln & pf "in G" Wilhelmj
  with piano   HMV 12603
  No. 7. Humoresque No. 7, in G flat arr. vln & pf "in G" Wilhelmj
  with orch.   HMV 1115

FIBICH

Images, Impressions & Souvenirs, Op. 41 pf
  No. 14. Poem (from "Souvenirs", Part IV) arr. vln & pf Kubelík
  with piano   HMV 12603

GOUNOD

Ave Maria (Méditation on Bach's "Prelude No. 1, in C" from Book I of
"Das Wohltemperirte Clavier") v & pf – arr. vln & pf
  with piano   HMV 1977

MOSZKOWSKI

(6) Klavierstücke, Op. 15 pf – 4 hands
  No. 1. Serenata arr. vln & pf
  with piano   HMV 12771

NICOLAI

(Die) Lustigen Weiber von Windsor (1849) – opera
  Mondnacht und Elfreigen arr. vln & pf
  with piano   HMV 12999

REGER

Ukolé bavka unid
  with piano   HMV 1977

SMETANA

(The) Bartered Bride (1866) – opera
  No. 5. As my mother blessed me ... Faithful love arr. vln & pf
  with piano   HMV 12999

Annúnzio Paulo MANTOVANI (1905–)

COATES

By the sleepy lagoon v & pf – arr. vln & org
  with S. Torch. org   DR 4855–1   Decca F7563

DVOŘÁK

(7) Gypsy songs, Op. 55 v & pf
  No. 4. Songs my mother taught me arr. vln & pf Kreisler
  with H. Smart org   DR 13151–2   London R10070, (in set LA71)

FIELD

North star vln & pf
  with H. Smart org   DR 13158–2   Decca F9092

GODARD

Jocelyn (1888) – opera
  Cachés dans cet asile "Berceuse" arr. vln & org
  with H. Smart org   DR 13154–1   London R10071, (in set LA71)

HERBERT

Naughty Marietta (1910) – operetta
  Ah! sweet mystery of life arr. vln & org
  with H. Smart org   DR 13153–2   London R10071, (in set LA71)

LIEURANCE

By the waters of the Minnetonka (1914) v & pf – arr. vln & org
  with H. Smart org   DR 13155–2   London R10072, (in set LA71)

MacDOWELL

Woodland Sketches, Op. 51 pf
  No. 1. To a wild rose arr. vln & org
  with H. Smart org   DR 13152–3   London R10070, (in set LA71)

MARTIN

Evensong v & pf – arr. vln & org
  with S. Torch org   DR 5100–2   Decca F7757

MASCAGNI

Cavalleria Rusticana (1890) – opera
  Intermezzo orch. – arr. vln & org
  with S. Torch org   DR 5098–1   Brunswick SA817

OFFENBACH

(Les) Contes d'Hoffmann (1888) – opera
  Belle Nuit, O nuit d'amour "Barcarolle" arr. vln & org
  with S. Torch org   DR 5097–1   Brunswick SA817

POLDINI

(7) Marionnettes pf
  No. 2. Poupée valsante arr. vln & pf Kreisler
  with H. Smart org   DR 13156–III   London R10072, (in set LA71)

PROVOST

Intermezzo (1940) vln & pf
  with S. Torch org   DR 4852–1   Decca F7563

PROVOST – *Continued*

Intermezzo (1940) vln & pf
  with H. Smart org   DR 13157–1   Decca F9092, LF1025

SCHUMANN

(13) Kinderscenen, Op. 15 pf
  No. 7. Träumerei arr. vln & pf
  with piano   WA 7666   Columbia J866
                                    Regal–Zonophone G9193

SILÉSU

(A) Little love, a little kiss (1912) v & pf – arr. vln & org
  with S. Torch org   DR 5099–1   Decca F7757

MANUELLO

BRAHMS

(21) Hungarian Dances pf duet
  Hungarian dance No. 1, in g arr. vln & pf Joachim
  with piano   68932   Regal G7821
  Hungarian dance No. 2, in d arr. vln & pf Joachim
  with piano   68933   Regal G7821

DENZA

If you have loved me v & pf – arr. vln & pf
  with piano   16305   Regal G8075

DRDLA

Serenade No. 1, in A vln & pf
  with piano   Columbia J514

DVOŘÁK

(8) Humoresques, Op. 101 pf
  No. 7. Humoresque No. 7, in G flat arr. vln & pf "in G" Kreisler
  with piano   69409   Columbia J270
                                    Regal G7757

GABRIEL–MARIE

Sérénade badine pf – arr. vln & pf
  with piano   16302   Regal G8075

GLUCK

Orphée et Eurydice (1762) – opera
  Dance of the blessed spirits: Lento "Mélodie" (No. 2) arr. vln & pf Kreisler
  with piano   A 2049   Regal G8408

HERMITE

Evening in the desert v & pf – arr. vln & pf
  with piano   Regal G9243

KLICKMANN

Waters of the Perkiomen (1925) v & pf – arr. vln & org
  with organ   F 382   Regal G9044

KREISLER

Caprice viennois, Op. 2 vln & pf
  with piano   A 2047   Regal G8408

LEONCAVALLO

Mattinata (1904) v & pf – arr. vln & pf Manuello
  with piano   16298   Regal G8030

MASCAGNI

Cavalleria Rusticana (1890) – opera
  selection arr. vln & pf as "Fantasia" by Manuello
  with piano   75671   Regal G1018

PERGOLESI

Tre giorni son che Nina v & pf – arr. vln & pf
  with piano   Regal

PIERNÉ

Sérénade in A, Op. 7 (1875) pf – arr. vln & pf Haddock
  with piano   Columbia J514

PUCCINI

(La) Bohème (1896) – opera
  selection arr. vln & pf as "Fantasia" by Manuello
  with piano   75673   Regal G1020

RAFF

(6) Pieces, Op. 85 vln & pf
  No. 3. Cavatina in D
  with piano   69407   Columbia J270
                                    Regal G7757

SANDERS

Once v & pf – arr. vln & pf
  with piano   Regal G9243

SCHERTZINGER

Marchéta (1913) v & pf – arr. vln & org
  with organ   F 384   Regal G9044

SCHUBERT

Rosamunde von Cypern, Op. 26 (D797) (1823) – Incidental music orch.
  No. 5. Entr'acte III, in B flat arr. vln & pf Kreisler
  with piano   Regal G8729
  No. 9. Ballet music II, in G arr. vln & pf Kreisler
  with piano   Regal G8729

STRAUSS, J. (II)

An der schönen, blauen Donau – waltz, Op. 314 orch. – arr. vln & pf
  with piano   Regal G1038
Morgenblätter – waltz, Op. 279 orch. – arr. vln & pf
  with piano   Regal G1038

SULZER

Sarabande, Op. 8 vln & pf
  with piano   65929   Regal G7790

THOMÉ

Simple aveu, Op. 25 pf – arr. vln & pf
  with piano   69369   Regal G7790

TOSELLI

Serenade, Op. 6 vln & pf
  with piano   Regal

TOSTI

Ideale (1884) v & pf – arr. vln & pf
  with piano   16290   Regal G8030

VERDI

(La) Traviata (1853) – opera
  selection arr. vln & pf as "Fantasia" by Manuello
  with piano   75670   Regal G1020

(Il) Trovatore (1853) – opera
  selection arr. vln & pf as "Fantasia" by Manuello
  with piano   75672   Regal G1018

WIENIAWSKI

(2) Mazurkas, Op. 19 vln & pf
  No. 1. Mazurka No. 1, in G "Obertass"
  with piano   Regal

WOOD

Love's garden of roses v & pf – arr. vln & pf
  with piano   Regal

Roses of Picardy (1916) v & pf – arr. vln & pf
  with piano   Regal

Fred MANZELLA

VIVALDI

Concerto in C, P.54 (F.XII, No. 17) 2 fls, 2 obs, bsn, 2 vlns, strs & c
  with J. Baker fl, H. Bennett fl, L.   Library of Recorded
  Arner ob, H. Smyles ob & New York Masterpieces Vol. 1, No. 2
  Sinfonietta – Goberman

Concerto in D, P.209 (F.XII, No. 15) 2 vlns, lute & c
  with M. Goberman vln, J. Iadone lute, Library of Recorded
  E. Earle hpsi & J. Schneider vlc   Masterpieces Vol 1, No. 4
                               Odyssey 32 16 0053, 32 16 0054

Concerto in F, P.301 vln, ob, strs & c
  with H. Smyles ob & New York   Library of Recorded
  Sinfonietta – Goberman   Masterpieces Vol. 1, No. 2
                               Odyssey 32 16 0214

(4) Sonatas, Op. 19 2 vlns & c
  Sonata No. 1, in F
  with M. Goberman vln & E. Earle Library of Recorded
  hpsi   Masterpieces Vol. 1, No. 6
  Sonata No. 2, in G
  with M. Goberman vln & E. Earle Library of Recorded
  hpsi   Masterpieces Vol. 1, No. 9
  Sonata No. 3, in F
  with M. Goberman vln & E. Earle Library of Recorded
  hpsi   Masterpieces Vol. 1, No. 4
  Sonata No. 4, in B flat
  with M. Goberman vln & E. Earle Library of Recorded
  hpsi   Masterpieces Vol. 1, No. 7

Sonata a quattro in E flat, F.XVI, No. 2 (P.441) "Al Santo Sepolcro"
2 vlns, vla & c
  with M. Goberman vln, B. Yokell vla, Library of Recorded
  E. Earle hpsi & J. Schneider vlc   Masterpieces Vol. 1, No. 4

Jacques–Francis MANZONE

AUBERT

Concerto No. 13, in e "du Carillon" vln & strs
  with Jean–Louis Petit Chamber Orch. Decca LXT20118, SMD1507,
  – Petit   SXL20118
                               Société Française du Son 174118,
                               SXL20118

BARTÓK

(44) Duos (1931) 2 vlns
  with J–R. Gravoin vln   Société Française de Productions
                               Phonographiques CVS20002

CORELLI

(12) Sonatas, Op. 5 vln & c
  Sonata No. 1, in D
  with N. Pillet–Wiener hpsi & P. Decca 7602/4
  Degenne vlc
  Sonata No. 2, in B flat
  with N. Pillet–Wiener hpsi & P. Decca 7602/4
  Degenne vlc
  Sonata No. 3, in C
  with N. Pillet–Wiener hpsi & P. Decca 7602/4
  Degenne vlc
  Sonata No. 4, in F
  with N. Pillet–Wiener hpsi & P. Decca 7602/4
  Degenne vlc
  Sonata No. 5, in g
  with N. Pillet–Wiener hpsi & P. Decca 7602/4
  Degenne vlc
  Sonata No. 6, in A
  with N. Pillet–Wiener hpsi & P. Decca 7602/4
  Degenne vlc
  Sonata No. 7, in d
  with N. Pillet–Wiener hpsi & P. Decca 7602/4
  Degenne vlc
  Sonata No. 8, in e
  with N. Pillet–Wiener hpsi & P. Decca 7602/4
  Degenne vlc
  Sonata No. 9, in A
  with N. Pillet–Wiener hpsi & P. Decca 7602/4
  Degenne vlc
  Sonata No. 10, in F
  with N. Pillet–Wiener hpsi & P. Decca 7602/4
  Degenne vlc
  Sonata No. 11, in E
  with N. Pillet–Wiener hpsi & P. Decca 7602/4
  Degenne vlc
  Sonata No. 12, in d "La Follia"
  with N. Pillet–Wiener hpsi & P. Decca 7602/4
  Degenne vlc

HAYDN

Concerto in F, H.XVIII, No. 6 (1765) vln, hpsi & orch.
  with F. Petit hpsi & Henri–Claude Baroque BC1876, BUS2876
  Fantapié Chamber Orch. – Fantapié Société Française de Productions
                               Phonographiques CVS30002

Renée MARCEL

TCHAIKOVSKY

Concerto in D, Op. 35 vln & orch.
with Europa Symphony Orch.

Gramophone (RCA) 2058
Plymouth P12–121
Varsity 2058

Jean MARCU

d'AMBROSIO

Canzonetta, Op. 6 vln & pf
with piano   12061 C   Edison Bell 5132, 5671

RIMSKY–KORSAKOV

Sadko (1898) – opera
Chant hindou arr. vln & pf Kreisler
with piano   12062 C   Edison Bell 5132

Jacques MARGOLIES

FRANCESCHINI

Trio–sonata in B flat 2 vlns & c
with J. Figueroa vln, F. Valenti hpsi &   New Records Inc. NRLP2006
J. Saunders vlc   Society for the Preservation of
the American Musical Heritage
MIA113

MARIANI

SCHUBERT

(7) Gesänge (set to Scott's "Lady of the Lake") Op. 52 v & pf
No. 6. Ave Maria, D839 arr. vln & org Mariani
with M. Springher org   Fonit 13148

SCHUMANN

(13) Kinderscenen, Op. 15 pf
No. 7. Träumerei arr. vln & org Mariani
with M. Springher org   Fonit 13148

Albert MARKOV (1933–   )

BACH

(15) Inventions – 2 part, BWV772/86 clav
Invention No. 2, in G, BWV773 arr. vln & pf
with O. Yablonskaya pf   Mezhdunarodnaya Kniga
D08265/6

BRAHMS

(21) Hungarian Dances pf duet
Hungarian dance No. 17, in f sharp arr. vln & pf Kreisler
with piano   Mezhdunarodnaya Kniga
D6549/50

CORELLI

(12) Sonatas, Op. 5 vln & c
Sonata No. 12, in d "La Follia" arr. vln & pf Kreisler
with S. Chernyakhovskaya pf   Mezhdunarodnaya Kniga
D013339/40

ERKIN

Concerto vln & orch.
with USSR Cinema Symphony Orch. –   Mezhdunarodnaya Kniga
Niyazi   D011583

FALLA

(La) Vida Breve (1913) – opera
Danza española orch. – arr. vln & pf Kreisler
with S. Chernyakhovskaya pf   Mezhdunarodnaya Kniga
D013339/40

HANDEL

(15) Sonatas, Op. 1 (?1731) fl or vln & c
Sonata No. 10, in g vln II
with S. Chernyakhovskaya pf   Mezhdunarodnaya Kniga
D013339/40

KABALEVSKY

Improvisation, Op. 21, No. 1 vln & pf
with S. Chernyakhovskaya pf   Mezhdunarodnaya Kniga
D013339/40

KHACHATURIAN

Chanson poème in e (1929) vln & pf
with S. Chernyakhovskaya pf   Mezhdunarodnaya Kniga
D013339/40

KREISLER

(La) Gitana vln & pf
with O. Yablonskaya pf   Mezhdunarodnaya Kniga
D08265/6

Gypsy Caprice vln & pf
with S. Chernyakhovskaya pf   Mezhdunarodnaya Kniga
D013339/40

Allegretto (Boccherini) vln & pf
with piano   Mezhdunarodnaya Kniga
D6549/50

KVERNADZE

Concerto (1956) vln & orch.
with Moscow Radio Symphony Orch.   Mezhdunarodnaya Kniga
– Khurodze   D4826/7

MARKOV

Variations on a theme of Paganini's "La Carnevale di Venizia" vln & pf
with A. Mitnik pf   Mezhdunarodnaya Kniga
D027550

PAGANINI

(24) Caprices, Op. 1 (1801/7) solo vln
Caprice No. 7, in a
(unaccompanied)   Mezhdunarodnaya Kniga
D013339/40

Concerto No. 2, in b, Op. 7 vln & orch.
with Moscow Radio Symphony Orch.   Mezhdunarodnaya Kniga
– Rozhdestvensky   D15351/2

(6) Sonatas, Op. 2 (1801/6) vln & gtr
No. 2. Sonata No. 2, in C arr. vln & pf O. Agarkov
with A. Mitnik pf   Mezhdunarodnaya Kniga
D027550

PAGANINI – *Continued*

No. 6. Sonata No. 6, in a arr. vln & pf O. Agarkov
with A. Mitnik pf   Mezhdunarodnaya Kniga
         D027550

(6) Sonatas, Op. 3 (1801/6) vln & gtr
No. 4. Sonata No. 10, in a
with piano   Mezhdunarodnaya Kniga
         D6549/50

No. 4. Sonata No. 10, in a arr. vln & pf O. Agarkov
with A. Mitnik pf   Mezdunarodnaya Kniga D027550

(Le) Streghe (variations on a theme from Süssmeyer's opera "Il noce di Benevento") Op. 8 (1813) vln & orch. – arr. vln & pf Kreisler
with piano   Mezhdunarodnaya Kniga
         D6549/50

PROKOFIEV

Sonata in d, Op. 115 solo vln
(unaccompanied)   Mezhdunarodnaya Kniga
         D08265/6

SARASATE

(8) Danzas españolas vln & pf
No. 5. Playera, Op. 23, No. 1
with O. Yablonskaya pf Mezhdunarodnaya Kniga
         D08265/6

No. 6. Zapateado, Op. 23, No. 2
with O. Yablonskaya pf Mezhdunarodnaya Kniga
         D08265/6

SCHUBERT

(7) Gesänge (set to Scott's "Lady of the Lake") Op. 52 v & pf
No. 6. Ave Maria, D839 arr. vln & pf Wilhelmj
with A. Mitnik pf   Mezhdunarodnaya Kniga
         D027549

Sonata No. 17, in D, Op. 53 (D850) pf
Rondo (4th mvt) arr. vln & pf Friedberg
with A. Mitnik pf   Mezhdunarodnaya Kniga
         D027549

(3) Sonatinas, Op. 137 (D384, D385 & D408) vln & pf
No. 1. Sonatina No. 1, in D, D384
with A. Mitnik pf   Mezhdunarodnaya Kniga
         D027549

SCOTT

Lotus land, Op. 47, No. 1 (1905) pf – arr. vln & pf Kreisler
with piano   Mezhdunarodnaya Kniga
         D6549/50

WEBER

(6) Sonatas, Op. 10 (J99/105) vln & pf
Sonata No. 1, in F: Romanze (2nd mvt) J99 arr. vln & pf as "Larghetto" by Kreisler
with piano   Mezhdunarodnaya Kniga
         D6549/50

YSAŸE

Poème élégiaque in d (Poème No. 1) Op. 12 vln & pf or orch.
with O. Yablonskaya pf Mezhdunarodnaya Kniga
         D08265/6

Vladimir MARKOVIČ (1917–)

BARTÓK

(6) Rumanian folk dances (1915) pf – arr. vln & pf Székely
with A. Preger pf   Jugoton 26331

FALLA

(La) Vida Breve (1913) – opera
Danza española orch. – arr. vln & pf Kreisler
with A. Preger pf   Jugoton 26331

SUK

(4) Pieces, Op. 17 vln & pf
No. 3. Un poco triste
with A. Preger pf   Jugoton 26330

No. 4. Burleska
with A. Preger pf   Jugoton 26330

VIVALDI

Sonata in D, F.XII, No. 6 vln & c – arr. vln & pf Respighi
with A. Preger pf   Jugoton 26330

Neville MARRINER (1924–)

CARISSIMI

Jonas – oratorio s, a, 2 t's, 2 b's & cho
Justus es, Domine
with W. Herbert t, 2EA 14424–1B HMV HLP12, HMS50
W. Roberts vln, A. Goldsbrough org &
T. Weil vlc

COLEMAN

Caprice vln & pf
with E. Brook pf   Herald RPL607

Happy landscape vln & pf
with E. Brook pf   Herald RPL607

Romance vln & pf
with E. Brook pf   Herald RPL607

Scherzo vln & pf
with E. Brook pf   Herald RPL607

Sonata in A "Pastoral" vln & pf
with E. Brook pf   Herald RPL607

CORELLI

(12) Sonatas, Op. 3 2 vlns & c
Sonata No. 9, in f
     2EA 14422–2E & 14423–3C HMV HLP15, HMS65
with W. Roberts vln, A. Goldsbrough Victor (in set LM6031)
org; & T. Weil vlc

COUPERIN, F.

(Les) Nations – 4 suites (1726) 2 vlns & c
Suite No. 1, in e "La Françoise"
with C. Pini vln, T. Dart hpsi & D. L'Oiseau–Lyre OL251
Dupré gamba

Suite No. 2, in c "L'Espagnole"
with C. Pini vln, T. Dart hpsi & D. L'Oiseau–Lyre OL251
Dupré gamba

Suite No. 3, in d "L'Impériale"
with C. Pini vln, T. Dart hpsi & D. L'Oiseau–Lyre OL251
Dupré gamba

COUPERIN, F. – *Continued*

Suite No. 4, in g "La Piémontoise"
with C. Pini vln, T. Dart hpsi & D.   L'Oiseau–Lyre OL251
Dupré gamba

HANDEL

(12) Concerti grossi, Op. 6 (1739) 2 vlns, vlc & strs
Concerto grosso No. 1, in G
with M. Latchem vln, K. Heath vlc,   Decca LXT6369, SLX6369
T. Dart hpsi, A. Davis org &   London CS6595, (in set
Academy of Saint–Martin–in–the–   CSA2309)
Fields – Marriner

Concerto grosso No. 2, in F
with M. Latchem vln, K. Heath vlc,   Decca LXT6369, SXL6369
T. Dart hpsi, A. Davis org &   London CS6595, (in set
Academy of Saint–Martin–in–the–   CSA2309)
Fields – Marriner

Concerto grosso No. 3, in e
with M. Latchem vln, K. Heath vlc,   Decca LXT6369, SXL6369
T. Dart hpsi, A. Davis org &   London CS6595, (in set
Academy of Saint–Martin–in–the–   CSA2309)
Fields – Marriner

Concerto grosso No. 4, in a
with M. Latchem vln, K. Heath vlc,   Decca LXT6369, SXL6369
T. Dart hpsi, A. Davis org &   London CS6595, (in set
Academy of Saint–Martin–in–the–   CSA2309)
Fields – Marriner

Concerto grosso No. 5, in D
with M. Latchem vln, K. Heath vlc,   Decca LXT6370, SXL6370
T. Dart hpsi, A. Davis org &   London CS6596, (in set
Academy of Saint–Martin–in–the–   CSA2309)
Fields – Marriner

Concerto grosso No. 6, in g
with M. Latchem vln, K. Heath vlc,   Decca LXT6370, SXL6370
T. Dart hpsi, A. Davis org &   London CS6596, (in set
Academy of Saint–Martin–in–the–   CSA2309)
Fields – Marriner

Concerto grosso No. 7, in B flat
with M. Latchem vln, K. Heath vlc,   Decca LXT6370, SXL6370
T. Dart hpsi, A. Davis org &   London CS6596, (in set
Academy of Saint–Martin–in–the–   CSA2309)
Fields – Marriner

Concerto grosso No. 8, in c
with M. Latchem vln, K. Heath vlc,   Decca LXT6370, SXL6370
T. Dart hpsi, A. Davis org &   London CS6596, (in set
Academy of Saint–Martin–in–the–   CSA2309)
Fields – Marriner

Concerto grosso No. 9, in F
with M. Latchem vln, K. Heath vlc,   Decca LXT6371, SXL6371
T. Dart hpsi, A. Davis org &   London CS6597, (in set
Academy of Saint–Martin–in–the–   CSA2309)
Fields – Marriner

Concerto grosso No. 10, in d
with M. Latchem vln, K. Heath vlc,   Decca LXT6371, SXL6371
T. Dart hpsi, A. Davis org &   London CS6597, (in set
Academy of Saint–Martin–in–the–   CSA2309)
Fields – Marriner

HANDEL – *Continued*

Concerto grosso No. 11, in A
with M. Latchem vln, K. Heath vlc,   Decca LXT6371, SXL6371
T. Dart hpsi, A. Davis org &   London CS6597, (in set
Academy of Saint–Martin–in–the–   CSA2309)
Fields – Marriner

Concerto grosso No. 12, in b
with M. Latchem vln, K. Heath vlc,   Decca LXT6371, SXL6371
T. Dart hpsi, A. Davis org &   London CS6597, (in set
Academy of Saint–Martin–in–the–   CSA2309)
Fields – Marriner

Concerto grosso in C (1736) "Alexander's Feast" 2 vlns, 2 obs & strs
with C. Pini vln, T. Dart hpsi, J. Hall   L'Oiseau–Lyre OL50181,
vlc & Philomusica of London – Jones   SOL60013

MOZART

Serenade No. 6, in D, K239 "Serenata Notturna" orch.
with H. Maguire vln, S. Streatfield vla,   Decca LXT5570, SMD1097,
S. Knussen cbs & London Symphony   SXL2196
Orch. – Maag   London CM9133, CS6133

PURCELL

(15) Fantasias, Z731/45 4 & 5 part – orig. viols
Fantasia No. 1, in F, Z731 (3 parts upon a ground) (?1679)
with P. Gibbs vln, G. Jones vln, G.   Top Rank XRK508
Malcolm hpsi & D. Dupré gamba

Fantasia No. 1, in F, Z731 (3 parts upon a ground) (?1679)
with C. Pini vln & T. Dart hpsi   Argo EAF16, RG113

(5) Pavanes, Z748/52 (pre–1680) (nos. 1/4: 3 part; No. 5: 4 part)
Pavane No. 5, in g, Z752 (?1677)
with P. Gibbs vln, G. Jones vln & D.   Top Rank XRK508
Dupré gamba

Pavane No. 5, in g, Z752 (?1677)
with P. Gibbs vln, C. Pini vln & T.   Argo RG113
Dart org

Sonata in g, Z780 vln & c
with G. Malcolm hpsi   Bach Guild BG570/1,
                                            BGS70570/1
                                            Top Rank 15–001, XRK509

(12) Sonatas, Z790/801 (1683) 3 part – 2 vlns & c
Sonata No. 1, in g, Z790
with P. Gibbs vln, T. Dart org & D.   Argo RG84
Dupré bs–viol   Bach Guild BG570, BGS70570

Sonata No. 2, in B flat, Z791
with P. Gibbs vln, T. Dart org & D.   Argo RG84
Dupré bs–viol   Bach Guild BG570, BGS70570

Sonata No. 3, in d, Z792
with P. Gibbs vln, T. Dart org & D.   Argo RG84
Dupré bs–viol   Bach Guild BG570, BGS70570

Sonata No. 4, in F, Z793
with P. Gibbs vln, T. Dart org & D.   Argo RG84
Dupré bs–viol   Bach Guild BG570, BGS70570

Sonata No. 5, in a, Z794
with P. Gibbs vln, T. Dart org & D.   Argo RG84
Dupré bs–viol   Bach Guild BG570, BGS70570

Sonata No. 6, in C, Z795
with P. Gibbs vln, T. Dart org & D.   Argo RG84
Dupré bs–viol   Bach Guild BG570, BGS70570

PURCELL – *Continued*

Sonata No. 7, in e, Z796
with P. Gibbs vln, T. Dart org & D.   Argo RG85
Dupré bs–viol   Bach Guild BG571, BGS70571

Sonata No. 8, in G, Z797
with P. Gibbs vln, T. Dart org & D.   Argo RG85
Dupré bs–viol   Bach Guild BG571, BGS70571

Sonata No. 9, in c, Z798
with P. Gibbs vln, T. Dart org & D.   Argo RG85
Dupré bs–viol   Bach Guild BG571, BGS70571

Sonata No. 10, in A, Z799
with P. Gibbs vln, T. Dart org & D.   Argo RG85
Dupré bs–viol   Bach Guild BG571, BGS70571

Sonata No. 11, in f, Z800
with P. Gibbs vln, T. Dart org & D.   Argo RG85
Dupré bs–viol   Bach Guild BG571, BGS70571

Sonata No. 12, in D, Z801
with P. Gibbs vln, T. Dart org & D.   Argo RG85
Dupré bs–viol   Bach Guild BG571, BGS70571

(10) Sonatas, Z802/11 (1697) 4 parts – 2 vlns & c

Sonata No. 1, in b, Z802
with P. Gibbs vln, T. Dart org & D.   Argo RG112
Dupré bs–viol

Sonata No. 2, in E flat, Z803
with P. Gibbs vln, T. Dart org & D.   Argo RG112
Dupré bs–viol

Sonata No. 3, in a, Z804
with P. Gibbs vln, T. Dart org & D.   Argo RG112
Dupré bs–viol

Sonata No. 4, in d, Z805
with P. Gibbs vln, T. Dart org & D.   Argo RG112
Dupré bs–viol

Sonata No. 5, in d, Z806
with P. Gibbs vln, T. Dart org & D.   Argo RG112
Dupré bs–viol

Sonata No. 6, in g Z807 "Chaconne"
with P. Gibbs vln, T. Dart org & D.   Argo RG112
Dupré bs–viol

Sonata No. 7, in G, Z808
with P. Gibbs vln, T. Dart org & D.   Argo RG113
Dupré bs–viol

Sonata No. 8, in g, Z809
with P. Gibbs vln, T. Dart org & D.   Argo RG113
Dupré bs–viol

Sonata No. 9, in F, Z810 "Golden Sonata"
with P. Gibbs vln, T. Dart org & D.   Argo RG113
Dupré bs–viol

Sonata No. 10, in D, Z811
with P. Gibbs vln, T. Dart org & D.   Argo RG113
Dupré bs–viol

VIVALDI

(12) Concerti, Op. 3 "L'Estro armonico" var. cbns & strs
Concerto No. 10, in b, P.148 (F.IV, No. 10) 4 vlns, strs & c
with N. Nelson vln, A. Howard vln,   L'Oiseau–Lyre OL276,
T. Connah vln & Academy of St.   SMO1520, SOL276
Martin–in–the–Fields – Marriner

Wolfgang MARSCHNER (1926–)

BACH

(Ein) Musikalisches Opfer, BWV1079 (1749) strs & c
with K. Redel fl, W. Schneller vlc, L.   Erato LDE3038, STU70197
Hokanson hpsi & Pro Arte Orch.,
Munich – Redel

BEETHOVEN

Concerto in D, Op. 61 vln & orch.
with Südwestdeutsche Philharmonic –   Intercord 716–05SB
Neidlinger

Romance No. 1, in G, Op. 40 vln & orch.
with Südwestdeutsche Philharmonic –   Intercord 700–09MH
Neidlinger

Romance No. 2, in F, Op. 50 vln & orch.
with Südwestdeutsche Philharmonic –   Intercord 700–09MH
Neidlinger

Serenade in D, Op. 25 fl, vln & vla
with N. Delius fl & U. Koch vla   Christophorus SCGLP75911

Sonata No. 5, in F, Op. 24 "Spring" vln & pf
with K. Elsner pf   Christophorus SCGLX75955

Sonata No. 9, in A, Op. 47 "Kreutzer" vln & pf
with K. Elsner pf   Christophorus SCGLX75955

KREISLER

Caprice viennois, Op. 2 vln & pf
with W. Neuhaus pf   Ducretet–Thomson 205TC025

Liebesfreud vln & pf
with W. Neuhaus pf   Ducretet–Thomson 205TC025

Liebesleid vln & pf
with W. Neuhaus pf   Ducretet–Thomson 205TC025

Schön Rosmarin vln & pf
with W. Neuhaus pf   Ducretet–Thomson 205TC025

MENDELSSOHN

Concerto in e, Op. 64 vln & orch.
with Südwestdeutsche Philharmonic –   Intercord 700–09MH
Neidlinger

PAGANINI

(Le) Streghe (variations on a theme from Süssmeyer's opera "Il noce di Benevento") Op. 8 (1813) vln & orch. – arr. vln & pf Kreisler
with W. Neuhaus pf   Ducretet–Thomson 205TC025
   Telefunken UV184

SARASATE

Zigeunerweisen, Op. 20 vln & pf or orch.
with W. Neuhaus pf   Ducretet–Thomson 205TC025
   Telefunken UV184

SCHOENBERG

Concerto, Op. 36 (1936) vln & orch.
with Südwestdeutsche Radio Orch. –   Turnabout TV4051, TV34051
Gieler   Vox PL10530

SVENDSEN

Romance in G, Op. 26 vln & orch.
with Nordmark Symphony Orch. –   Deutsche Grammophon
Steiner   LPE121678, LPEM19482,
   SLPEM136482

Henri Marteau (1874–1934)

BACH

(3) Sonatas & 3 Partitas, BWV1001/6 solo vln
Sonata No. 1, in g: Presto (4th mvt) BWV1001
(unaccompanied)   Bettini cylinder
Partita No. 3, in E: Bourrée (5th mvt) BWV1006
(unaccompanied)   Bettini cylinder
Partita No. 3, in E, BWV1006
(unaccompanied)   Gramophone & Typewriter
47993/7

(4) Suites, BWV1006/9 strs & c
Suite No. 3, in D: Air (2nd mvt) BWV1068 2 obs, 3 tpts, drms, strs & c
– arr. vln & pf as "Air on the G–string" by Wilhelmj
with P. Vladigerov pf   HMV EH397

BOCCHERINI

(6) Quintets, Op. 13 2 vlns, vla & 2 vlcs
No. 5. Quintet No. 5, in E: Minuet (3rd mvt) "Bull" arr. vln & pf
Marteau
with piano   2481 ah   Gramophone & Typewriter
47998
No. 5. Quintet No. 5, in E: Minuet (3rd mvt) "Bull" arr. vln & pf
Marteau
with P. Vladigerov pf   HMV EH244

BRAHMS

(21) Hungarian Dances pf duet
Hungarian dance No. 6, in D flat arr. vln & pf "in B flat" Joachim
with P. Vladigerov pf   HMV EH248

GODARD

(6) Morceaux, Op. 128 vln & pf
No. 3. Adagio pathétique arr. Marteau
with P. Vladigerov pf   HMV EH244

HEGAR

(6) Waltzes, Op. 14 vln & pf
No. 2. Waltz No. 2
with piano   2482 ah   HMV K47991
No. 4. Waltz No. 4
with piano   15041 L   HMV K47992

MASSENET

(Les) Erinnyes (1873) – Incidental music orch.
Entr'acte arr. vln & pf
with piano   Bettini cylinder

SAINT-SAËNS

(Le) Déluge, Op. 45 (1876) – oratorio
Prélude vln & orch. – arr. vln & pf Saint–Saëns
with piano   Bettini cylinder

SARASATE

Carmen Fantasia (on themes from the opera by Bizet) Op. 25 vln & pf or
orch.
with P. Vladigerov pf   HMV EH104

SARASATE – *Continued*

Carmen Fantasia (on themes from the opera by Bizet) Op. 25 vln & pf or
orch.
CLR 4702[11] & CNR 741[11]   HMV EH413
with P. Vladigerov pf*

(8) Danzas españolas vln & pf
No. 2. Habañera, Op. 21, No. 2
with P. Vladigerov pf   HMV EH248

SCHUBERT

(14) Schwanengesang, D957 (1828) v & pf
No. 4. Ständchen "Serenade" arr. vln & pf Rémenyi
with P. Vladigerov pf   HMV EH397

David MARTIN

DVOŘÁK

Terzetto in C, Op. 74 2 vlns & vla
with F. Grinke vln & W. Forbes vla   Decca K981/3

HANDEL

(12) Concerti grossi, Op. 6 (1739) 2 vlns, vlc & strs
Concerto grosso No. 10, in d
with F. Grinke vln, J. Whitehouse vlc,   Decca X138/9
A. Goldsbrough hpsi & Boyd Neel
String Orch. – Neel
Concerto grosso No. 12, in b
with F. Grinke vln, J. Whitehouse vlc,   Decca X142/3
A. Goldsbrough hpsi & Boyd Neel
String Orch. – Neel

Victor MARTIN (1940–)

BARTÓK

(44) Duos (1931) 2 vlns
with L. Fenyves vln   Ensayo ENY26

HALFFTER

Concerto (1939/40) vln & orch.
with Orquestra Philharmonia de   Columbia SCLL14083
España – Frühbeck de Burgos   Decca 7110

HAYDN

Symphony No. 6, in D "Le Matin" orch.
with Cologne Chamber Orch. – Müller Musica Mundi VMS2007
–Brühl
Symphony No. 7, in C "Le Midi" orch.
with Cologne Chamber Orch. – Müller Musica Mundi VMS2007
–Brühl
Symphony No. 8, in G "Le Soir" orch.
with Cologne Chamber Orch. – Müller Musica Mundi VMS2007
–Brühl

KODÁLY

Duo, Op. 7 (1914) vln & vlc
with M. Scano vlc   Ensayo ENY8

---

* Clemens Schmalstich is the pianist on side two.

RAVEL

Berceuse sur le nom de Gabriel Fauré (1922) vln & pf
with M. Zanetti pf   Ensayo ENY4

Sonata (1927) vln & pf
with M. Zanetti pf   Ensayo ENY4

Sonata (1922) vln & vlc
with M. Scano vlc   Ensayo ENY4

SARASATE

(8) Danzas españolas vln & pf
No. 1. Malagueña, Op. 21, No. 1
with M. Zanetti pf   Ensayo ENY3
No. 2. Habañera, Op. 21, No. 2
with M. Zanetti pf   Ensayo ENY3
No. 3. Romanza andaluza, Op. 22, No. 1
with M. Zanetti pf   Ensayo ENY3
No. 4. Jota navarra, Op. 22, No. 2
with M. Zanetti pf   Ensayo ENY3
No. 5. Playera, Op. 23, No. 1
with M. Zanetti pf   Ensayo ENY3
No. 6. Zapateado, Op. 23, No. 2
with M. Zanetti pf   Ensayo ENY3
No. 7. Danza española No. 7, in a, Op. 26, No. 1
with M. Zanetti pf   Ensayo ENY3
No. 8. Danza española No. 8, in C, Op. 26, No. 2
with M. Zanetti pf   Ensayo ENY3
Miramar–Zortzico, Op. 42 vln & pf
with M. Zanetti pf   Ensayo ENY3

STRAVINSKY

(L') Histoire du Soldat (1918) narrators & tpt, cbs, tbn, cl, vln, bsn & pcn
with J. Foriscot tpt, F. Sala cbs, M.   Ensayo ENY20
Badia tbn, J. Pañella cl, J.M. Franquet
bsn, R. Armengol pcn – cond.
Guinjoan

TCHAIKOVSKY

Trio in a, Op. 50 "To the memory of a great artist" pf, vln & vlc
with J. Bolet pf & M. Scano vlc   Christophorus SCGLX 73736
  Ensayo ENY2

TURINA

Sonata No. 1, in d, Op. 51 (1929) vln & pf
with E. Sánchez pf   Ensayo ENY22
Sonata No. 2, Op. 82 (1934) "Sonata española" vln & pf
with E. Sánchez pf   Ensayo ENY22
Trio No. 1, in d, Op. 35 pf, vln & vlc
with E. Sánchez pf & J. Trotta vlc   Ensayo ENY22

Johanna MARTZY (1924–)

BACH

(3) Sonatas & 3 Partitas, BWV1001/6 solo vln
Sonata No. 1, in g, BWV1001
(unaccompanied)
  Angel 35280
  Columbia C90452, CX1286

Partita No. 1, in b, BWV1002
(unaccompanied)
  Angel 35280
  Columbia C90452, CX1286

BACH – *Continued*

Sonata No. 2, in a, BWV1003
(unaccompanied)
  Angel 35281
  Columbia C90453, CX1287

Partita No. 2, in d, BWV1004
(unaccompanied)
  Angel 35281
  Columbia C90453, CX1287

Sonata No. 3, in C, BWV1005
(unaccompanied)
  Angel 35282
  Columbia C90454, CX1288

Partita No. 3, in E, BWV1006
(unaccompanied)
  Angel 35282
  Columbia C90454, CX1288

BEETHOVEN

Romance No. 1, in G, Op. 40 vln & orch.
with Philharmonia Orch. – Kletzki   Angel 35236
  Columbia C90910, CX1497

Romance No. 2, in F, Op. 50 vln & orch.
with Philharmonia Orch. – Kletzki   Angel 35236
  Columbia C90910, CX1497

(3) Sonatas, Op. 30 vln & pf
No. 3. Sonata No. 8, in G
with J. Antonietti pf   Deutsche Grammophon
  LPM18075

BRAHMS

Concerto in D, Op. 77 (cadenza by Joachim) vln & orch.
with Philharmonia Orch. – Kletzki   Angel 35137
  Columbia CX1165, QCX10102

DVOŘÁK

Concerto in a, Op. 53 vln & orch.*
with RIAS Symphony Orch. – Fricsay   Decca DL9858
  Deutsche Grammophon
  LPE17178, LPM18152
  Heliodor 89804, 478428

FALLA

(La) Vida Breve (1913) – opera
Danza española orch. – arr. vln & pf Kreisler
with J. Antonietti pf   Deutsche Grammophon 36015,
  LP16017, LPEM19126

MENDELSSOHN

Concerto in e, Op. 64 vln & orch.
with Philharmonia Orch. – Kletzki   Angel 35236
  Columbia C90910, CX1210,
  CX1497

MILHAUD

(12) Saudades do Brasil (1920/1) pf
No. 5. Ipanema arr. vln & pf Lévy
with J. Antonietti pf   Deutsche Grammophon 36015,
  LP16017, LPEM19126

* Allegro giocoso, ma non troppo, or 3rd mvt, is also on Deutsche
Grammophon LPEM 19017.

MOZART

Concerto No. 3, in G, K216 vln & orch.
  with Philharmonia Orch. – Kletzki   Columbia CX1210

Concerto No. 4, in D, K218 vln & orch.
  with Bavarian   04326/9 LWN   Deutsche Grammophon 72323/4,
  Radio Chamber Orch. – Jochum   LP16119, LP29307, LPX29251
                 Heliodor 89620, 478133

Sonata No. 24, in F, K376 vln & pf
  with J. Antonietti pf   Deutsche Grammophon
             36035/6S, LPM18075

RAVEL

Berceuse sur le nom de Gabriel Fauré (1922) vln & pf
  with J. Antonietti pf   Deutsche Grammophon 36015,
             LP16017, LPEM19126

Pièce en forme d'Habanera v & pf – arr. vln & pf Catherine
  with J. Antonietti pf   Deutsche Grammophon 36015,
             LP16017, LPEM19126

SCHUBERT

Fantasia in C, Op. 159 (D934) vln & pf
  with J. Antonietti pf   Angel 35366
             Columbia CX1372

Rondo brillante in b, Op. 70 (D895) vln & pf
  with J. Antonietti pf   Angel 35366
             Columbia C80758, CX1372
             Mace M9013

Sonata in A, Op. 162 (D574) "Duo" vln & pf
  with J. Antonietti pf   Angel 35365
             Columbia C80758, CX1399
             Mace M9013

(3) Sonatinas, Op. 137 (D384, D385 & D408) vln & pf
  No. 1. Sonatina No. 1, in D, D384
  with J. Antonietti pf   Angel 35364
             Columbia C80757, C70079,
             CX1359
             Mace M9012

  No. 2. Sonatina No. 2, in a, D385
  with J. Antonietti pf   Angel 35364
             Columbia C80757, CX1359
             Mace M9012

  No. 3. Sonatina No. 3, in g, D408
  with J. Antonietti pf   Angel 35365
             Columbia C70079, C80757,
             CX1399
             Mace M9012

SZYMANOWSKI

Notturno & Tarantella, Op. 28 vln & pf
  with J. Antonietti pf   Deutsche Grammophon 36015,
             LP16017, LPEM19126,
             SLPEM136316

Marguerite MARX

HANDEL

Serse (1738) – opera
  Ombra mai fu "Largo" arr. vln, vlc & hp
  with J. Marx vlc & G. Marx hp   Pathé 9510

WIDOR

Serenade in B flat, Op. 10 orch. – arr. vln, vlc & hp
  with J. Marx vlc & G. Marx hp   Pathé 9510

Frances MASON

ELGAR

Quartet in e, Op. 83 2 vlns, vla & vlc
  with H. Bean vln, C. Wellington vla &   HMV HQS1252
  E. Croxford vlc

ROBERTS

Capriccio vln & pf
  with C. Bradbury pf   Music in our Time MIOT LP3

Joan MASSIA

BACH

(6) Sonatas, BWV1014/9 vln & clav
  Sonata No. 3, in E: Adagio ma non tanto (3rd mvt) BWV1016
  with B. Selva pf   Columbia LFX108

BEETHOVEN

Sonata No. 5, in F, Op. 24 "Spring" vln & pf
  with B. Selva pf   Columbia LFX105/8

FRANCK

Sonata in A (1886) vln & pf
             WLX 1378/9, 1380–1, 1381   Columbia DOX209/12,
             1388/9–1, 1390 & 1391–1   DX239/42, LFX100/3
  with B. Selva pf

Robert Henderson MASTERS (1917–   )

BRAHMS

Sextet No. 1, in B flat, Op. 18 2 vlns, 2 vlas & 2 vlcs
  with Y. Menuhin vln, C. Aronowitz   Angel 36234, (in set 3727)
  vla, E. Wallfisch vla, M. Gendron vlc   Electrola E80758, STE80758
  & D. Simpson vlc   HMV ALP2038, ASD587,
             CVA819, FALP819

Sextet No. 2, in G, Op. 36 2 vlns, 2 vlas & 2 vlcs
  with Y. Menuhin vln, C. Aronowitz   Electrola E80903, SME80903
  vla, E. Wallfisch vla, M. Gendron vlc   HMV ALP2096, ASD643,
  & D. Simpson vlc   ASDF871, CVA871, FALP871,
             QALP10406

CORELLI

(12) Concerti grossi, Op. 6 orch.
  Concerto grosso No. 2, in F
  with Y. Menuhin vln, D. Simpson vlc   Angel 36303
  & Bath Festival Orch. – Menuhin   Electrola SME91462
             HMV ALP2090, ASD637

HANDEL

(12) Concerti grossi, Op. 6 (1739) 2 vlns, vlc & strs
  Concerto grosso No. 1, in G
  with Y. Menuhin vln, D. Simpson vlc,   Angel 36201, (in set 3647)
  G. Malcolm hpsi, R. Jesson org &   Electrola E91371, STE91371
  Bath Festival Orch. – Menuhin   HMV ALP2055, ASD604,
             ASDF827, CVA827, FALP827

HANDEL – *Continued*

Concerto grosso No. 2, in F
with Y. Menuhin vln, D. Simpson vlc,
G. Malcolm hpsi, R. Jesson org &
Bath Festival Orch. – Menuhin

Angel 36201/2, (in set 3647)
Electrola E91371, STE91371
HMV ALP2055, ASD604,
ASDF827, CVA827, FALP827

Concerto grosso No. 3, in e
with Y. Menuhin vln, D. Simpson vlc,
G. Malcolm hpsi, R. Jesson org &
Bath Festival Orch. – Menuhin

Angel 36203, (in set 3647)
Electrola E91372, STE91372
HMV ALP2049, ASD598,
ASDF827, CVA827, FALP827

Concerto grosso No. 4, in a
with Y. Menuhin vln, D. Simpson vlc,
G. Malcolm hpsi, R. Jesson org &
Bath Festival Orch. – Menuhin

Angel 36203, (in set 3647)
Electrola E91371, STE91371
HMV ALP2055, ASD604,
ASDF827, CVA827, FALP827

Concerto grosso No. 5, in D
with Y. Menuhin vln, D. Simpson vlc,
K. Anderson hpsi, R. Jesson org &
Bath Festival Orch. – Menuhin

Angel 36203/4, (in set 3647)
Electrola E91371, STE91371
HMV ALP2055, ASD604,
ASDF828, CVA828, FALP828

Concerto grosso No. 6, in g
with Y. Menuhin vln, D. Simpson vlc,
K. Anderson hpsi, R. Jesson org &
Bath Festival Orch. – Menuhin

Angel 36204, (in set 3647)
Electrola E91372, STE91372
HMV ALP2049, ASD598,
ASDF828, CVA828, FALP828

Concerto grosso No. 7, in B flat
with Y. Menuhin vln, D. Simpson vlc,
K. Anderson hpsi, R. Jesson org &
Bath Festival Orch. – Menuhin

Angel 36204, (in set 3647)
Electrola E91220, E91373,
STE91373
HMV ALP1927, ASD491,
ASDF828, CVA828, FALP828,
QALP10353

Concerto grosso No. 8, in c
with Y. Menuhin vln, D. Simpson vlc,
K. Anderson hpsi, R. Jesson org &
Bath Festival Orch. – Menuhin

Angel 36203/4, (in set 3647)
Electrola E91220, E91373,
STE91373
HMV ALP1927, ASD491,
ASDF828, CVA828, FALP828,
QALP10353

Concerto grosso No. 9, in F
with Y. Menuhin vln, D. Simpson vlc,
K. Anderson hpsi, R. Jesson org &
Bath Festival Orch. – Menuhin

Angel 36203, (in set 3647)
Electrola E91220, E91373,
STE91373
HMV ALP1827, ASD491,
ASDF829, FALP829,
QALP10353

Concerto grosso No. 10, in d
with Y. Menuhin vln, D. Simpson vlc,
K. Anderson hpsi, R. Jesson org &
Bath Festival Orch. – Menuhin

Angel 36202, (in set 3647)
Electrola E91372, STE91372
HMV ALP2049, ASD598,
ASDF829, FALP829

Concerto grosso No. 11, in A
with Y. Menuhin vln, D. Simpson vlc,
K. Anderson hpsi, R. Jesson org &
Bath Festival Orch. – Menuhin

Angel 36201/2, (in set 3647)
Electrola E91220, E91373,
STE91373
HMV ALP1927, ASD491,
ASDF829, FALP829,
QALP10353

HANDEL – *Continued*

Concerto grosso No. 12, in b
with Y. Menuhin vln, D. Simpson vlc,
K. Anderson hpsi, R. Jesson org &
Bath Festival Orch. – Menuhin

Angel 36201, (in set 3647)
Electrola E91372, STE91372
HMV ALP2049, ASD598,
ASDF829, FALP829

PURCELL

(15) Fantasias, Z731/45 4 & 5 part – orig. viols
Fantasia No. 8, in d, Z739 (1680)
with Y. Menuhin vln, C. Aronowitz
vla & D. Simpson vlc

Angel 36270
HMV ALP2088, ASD635,
ASDF867, FALP867

Fantasia No. 11, in G, Z742 (1680)
with Y. Menuhin vln, C. Aronowitz
vla & D. Simpson vlc

Angel 36270
HMV ALP2088, ASD635,
ASDF867, FALP867

Fantasia No. 15, in F, Z745 (?1679) "Upon one note"
with Y. Menuhin vln, C. Aronowitz
vla, W. Gerhard vla & D. Simpson vlc

Angel 36270
HMV ALP2088, ASD635,
ASDF867, FALP867

(5) Pavanes, Z748/52 (pre–1680) (Nos. 1/4: 3 part; No. 5: 4 part)
Pavane No. 5, in g, Z752 (?1677)
with Y. Menuhin vln, A. Lysy vln, R.
Jesson cha org & A. Gauntlett gamba

Angel 36270
HMV ALP2088, ASD635,
ASDF867, FALP867

SKALKOTTAS

(8) Variations on a Greek folk tune (1938) vln, vlc & pf
with D. Simpson vlc & M. Gazelle pf   HMV ALP2289, ASD2289

TIPPETT

Fantasia concertante on a theme of Corelli (1953) 2 vlns, vlc & strs
with Y. Menuhin vln, D. Simpson vlc
& Bath Festival Orch. – Tippett

Angel 36303
Electrola SME91462
HMV ALP2090, ASD637

VIVALDI

(12) Concerti, Op. 3 "L'Estro armonico" var. cbns & strs
Concerto No. 10, in b, P.148 (F.IV, No. 1) 4 vlns, strs & c
with Y. Menuhin vln, E. Goren vln, S.
Humphreys vln & Bath Festival
Chamber Orch. – Menuhin

Angel 36103
Electrola E91219, STE91219
HMV ALP1949, ASD500,
ASDF283, FALP747,
QALP10356

Karl MASTNY

KUTSCHERA

(Die) Granen Augen v & pf – arr. vln & pf
with piano   Favorite 1–24176

TICHÝ

Walzer–Zauber (Intermezzo) Op. 66 vln & pf
with piano   Favorite 1/24177

Sandro MATERASSI (1904–   )

DALLAPICCOLA

(2) Studies (1947) vln & pf
No. 1. Sarabanda
with L. Dallapiccola pf   Durium E11

No. 2. Fanfara e fuga
with L. Dallapiccola pf   Durium E11

Tartiniana No. 2 (1955) vln & pf
with L. Dallapiccola pf   Durium E11

Blain MATHE (1907–1967)

DEBUSSY

Suite Bergamasque (1890) pf
No. 3. Clair de lune arr. vln & org
with K. Stokes org   Victor 56–0004, (in set CP2)

Philipp MATHEIS

MENDELSSOHN

Octet in E flat, Op. 20 4 vlns, 2 vlas & 2 vlcs
with W. Boskovsky vln, G. Swoboda   Decca LXT2858
vln, F. Leitermeier vln, G. Breitenbach   London LL859
vla, F. Strangler vla, N. Hübner vlc &
R. Harand vlc

VIVALDI

(12) Concerti, Op. 3 "L'Estro armonico" var. cbns & strs
Concerto No. 1, in D, P.146 (F.IV, No. 7) 4 vlns, vlc, strs & c
with W. Boskovsky vln, W.   Amadeo AVRS6088
Hintermeyer vln, J. Tomasow vln, R.   Bach Guild BG572, BGS5016
Harand vlc, H. Nordberg hpsi &   I Classici della Musica Classica
Vienna State Opera Chamber Orch. –   XAM4023
Rossi   Qualiton LPX1095
          Top Rank 35–073
          Vanguard SRV143

Concerto No. 4, in e, P.97 (F.I, No. 174) 4 vlns, strs & c
with W. Boskovsky vln, W.   Amadeo AVRS6088
Hintermeyer vln, J. Tomasow vln, H.   Bach Guild BG572, BGS5016
Nordberg hpsi & Vienna State Opera   I Classici della Musica Classica
Chamber Orch. – Rossi   XAM4023
          Qualiton LPX1095
          Top Rank 35–073
          Vanguard SRV143

Concerto No. 7, in F, P.249 (F.IV, No. 9) 4 vlns, strs & c
with W. Boskovsky vln, W.   Amadeo AVRS6089
Hintermeyer vln, J. Tomasow vln, H.   Bach Guild BG573, BGS5017
Nordberg hpsi & Vienna State Opera   I Classici della Musica Classica
Chamber Orch. – Rossi   XAM4024
          Qualiton LPX1096
          Top Rank 35–074
          Vanguard SRV144

Concerto No. 10, in b, P.148 (F.IV, No. 10) 4 vlns, strs & c
with W. Boskovsky vln, W.   Amadeo AVRS6090
Hintermeyer vln, J. Tomasow vln, H.   Bach Guild BG574, BGS5018
Nordberg hpsi & Vienna State Opera   I Classici della Musica Classica
Chamber Orch. – Rossi   XAM4025
          Qualiton LPX1097
          Top Rank 34–075
          Vanguard SVR145

Thomas MATTHEWS (1907–1969)

DOHNÁNYI

Sonata in c sharp, Op. 21 vln & pf
with E. Ralph pf   Columbia DO2571/3

SCHUBERT

(3) Sonatinas, Op. 137 (D384, D385 & D408) vln & pf
No. 3. Sonatina No. 3, in g, D408
with E. Ralph pf   Columbia DO2574/5

Yoko MATSUDA

WILSON

Music for Violin & Violoncello (1969) vln & vlc
with F. Sherry vlc   Composers Recordings CRI271

H. MAURICE

BRAHMS

(21) Hungarian Dances pf duet
Hungarian dance No. 5, in f sharp arr. vln & pf "in g" Joachim
with piano   Jumbo 728, A22131
          Odeon A22131

BULL

Säterjëntens søndag v & pf – arr. vln & pf Svendsen
with piano   Jumbo 665, A22132
          Odeon A22132

DVOŘÁK

(8) Humoresques, Op. 101 pf
No. 7. Humoresque No. 7, in G flat arr. vln & pf "in G" Wilhelmj
with piano   Jumbo 773, A22222
          Odeon A22222

GODARD

Jocelyn (1888) – opera
Cachés dans cet asile "Berceuse" arr. vln & pf
with piano   42981 Jumbo 368, A22092
          Odeon 4070A, A22092

GOSSEC

(Le) Camp du Grand Pré (1793) – opera
Tambourin arr. vln & pf Burmester
with piano   Odeon A22114

Rosine (1786) – opera
Gavotte arr. vln & pf Burmester
with piano   Odeon A22113

GOUNOD

Sérénade (Quand tu chantes) v & pf – arr. vln & pf Hermann
with piano   Jumbo 728, A22135
          Odeon A22135, A42981

GRIEG

Peer Gynt (Suite No. 2) Op. 55 orch.
No. 4. Solveig's song arr. vln & pf Sitt
with piano   42982 Jumbo A22093, 368
          Odeon 4070A, A22093, A42982

LASSEN

(6) Lieder, Op. 85 v & pf
No. 3. Allerseelen "All souls day" arr. vln & pf
with piano   Odeon A22219

MENDELSSOHN

(6) Songs without words, Op. 62 pf
No. 6. Song without words No. 30, in A "Spring song" arr. vln & pf
Kreisler
with piano   42985   Jumbo 542, A22110
                                        Odeon 4071, A22110

MICHIELS

(6) Csárdas (on national Hungarian airs) vln & pf
No. 1 Csárda No. 1 "Piroska"
with piano   Odeon A22220

PIERNÉ

Sérénade in A, Op. 7 (1875) pf – arr. vln & pf Haddock
with piano   42999   Jumbo 589, A22137
                                        Odeon 4069A, A22136, A42999

RUBINSTEIN

(2) Melodies, Op. 3 pf
No. 1. Melody in F arr. vln & pf Wilhelmj
with piano   42800   Jumbo 773, A22223
                                        Odeon 4069A, A22223

SIMON

(2) Pieces, Op. 17 vln & pf
No. 2. Berceuse
with piano   Jumbo 773, A22223
                                        Odeon A22223

SIMONETTI

Madrigale pf – arr. vln & pf
with piano   42986   Jumbo 542, A22111
                                        Odeon 4071A, A22111

TCHAIKOVSKY

(3) Souvenirs de Hapsal, Op. 2 pf
No. 3. Chant sans paroles in f arr. vln & pf Kreisler
with piano   42991   Jumbo 194, A22112
                                        Odeon 4072A, A22112

THOMAS

Mignon (1866) – opera
Entr'acte (Gavotte) (Act II) orch. – arr. vln & pf Sarasate
with piano   Jumbo 665, A22134
                                        Odeon A22134

THOMÉ

Simple aveu, Op. 25 pf – arr. vln & pf
with orch.   42992   Jumbo 194, A22115
                                        Odeon 4072A, A22115

Ariodante MAY

ALASSIO

Montecarlo – march, Op. 515 mand & pf – arr. vln & pf May
with piano   Pathé 19560, 80689

ANONYMOUS

(La) Ballo Lola (La seduzione) arr. vln & pf
with piano   1886 II   Zonophone X1886

BECUCCI

Tesoro mio – waltz, Op. 228 orch. – arr. vln & pf
with piano   Pathé 168, 82131

COSTA

Frangesa march v & pf – arr. vln & pf
with piano   Pathé 169, 19560, 80687

DONIZETTI

Lucrezia Borgia (1833) – opera
La Gloriosa bandiera arr. vln & pf May
with piano   Pathé 169, 1097, 82124, 82133

GOUNOD

Ave Maria (Méditation on Bach's "Prelude No. 1, in C" from Book I of
"Das Wohltemperirte Clavier") v & pf – arr. vln & pf
with piano   Pathé 82122

MASCAGNI

(L') Amico Fritz (1891) – opera
selection arr. vln & pf as "Fantasia" by May
with piano   Pathé 19554, 82123

PIERNÉ

Scherzo de concert, Op. 29bis pf – arr. vln & pf
with piano   Pathé 80743
Sérénade in A, Op. 7 (1875) pf – arr. vln & pf Haddock
with piano   Pathé 166

SARASATE

Faust Fantasia (on themes from the opera by Gounod) vln & pf or orch.
with piano   Pathé 82129

THOMAS

Mignon (1866) – opera
Je suis Titania "Polonaise" arr. vln & pf
with piano   HMV S77900
selection arr. vln & pf as "Fantasia" by May
with piano   Pathé 80746

VERDI

(La) Traviata (1853) – opera
selection arr. vln & pf as "Fantasia" by May
with piano   Pathé 82126
Waltz orch. & cho – arr. vln & pf May
with piano   Pathé 82130
(Il) Trovatore (1853) – opera
selection arr. vln & pf as "Fantasia" by May
with piano   Pathé 19554, 82128

WALDTEUFEL

Estudiantina, Op. 191 orch. – arr. vln & pf Lacombe
with piano   Pathé 82132

Ernst MAYER-SCHIERNING

HANDEL

(12) Concerti grossi, Op. 6 (1739) 2 vlns, vlc & strs
Concerto grosso No. 6, in g
with G.F. Hendel vln, A. Bauer vlc &   Cantate 047705, 057705
German Bach Soloists – Stephani

STAMITZ, K.

Concerto in D vln, vla, ob & orch.
with P. Schroer vla, W. Schulz ob &   Mace M9031, SM9031
Cologne Soloists Ensemble – Müller–   Odeon 0 80620, STO80620
Brühl

TELEMANN

Concerto in a vln, strs & c
with Cologne Soloists Ensemble –   Christophorus SCGLP75909
Müller–Brühl   Critère CRD185, SCRD5185
                                        Nonesuch H1078, H71078

Concerto in D tpt, vln, strs & c
with H. Schneidewind tpt & Cologne   Musica Mundi VMS2010
Chamber Orch. – Müller–Brühl

Concerto in F, T.II, No. 3 3 vlns, strs & c
with E. Melkus vln, L. Frydén vln, O.   Archive APM14837, ARC3237,
Steinkopf hpsi & Schola Cantorum   ARC73237, SAPM198368,
Basiliensis – Wenzinger   SAPM198837

TORELLI

(12) Concerti, Op. 8 (1709) 1/6: 2 vlns, strs & c – 7/12: vln, strs & c
Concerto No. 2, in a
with B. Seeger vln & Cologne Soloists   Mace M9031, SM9031
Ensemble – Müller–Brühl   Odeon 0 80620, STO80620

MAZZIONETTA

LABITZKY

(Der) Traum der Sennerin (Dream of the mountains – Idyll) Op. 45 orch. –
arr. vln, fl & orch.
with Hess fl &   11462–A 1152 HMV V28121
orch.

Mehli MEHTA (1908–)

DEBUSSY

(L') Enfant Prodigue (1884) – cantata v, cho & orch.
Prélude arr. vln & pf Heifetz
with piano   HMV P30005

FALLA

(El) Amor Brujo (1915) – ballet m–s & orch.
No. 7. Danza rituel del fuego arr. vln & pf
with piano   HMV P30005

SUK

(7) Pieces, Op. 7 pf
No. 1. Love song arr. vln & pf Mařák
with piano   HMV N4461, P30004

WAGNER

Albumblatt in C (1861) pf – arr. vln & pf Wilhelmj
with piano   HMV N4461, P30004

Eugene MEIER (1880–)

CHOPIN

(3) Nocturnes, Op. 9 pf
No. 2. Nocturne No. 2, in E flat arr. vln & pf Sarasate
with piano   413–1 V   Marathon 198

GODARD

Jocelyn (1888) – opera
Cachés dans cet asile "Berceuse" arr. vln & pf
with piano   412–1 V   Marathon 198

MASCAGNI

Cavalleria Rusticana (1890) – opera
selection unid – arr. vln & pf
with piano   28498   Regal G6068

Gustav MEINE

EHRICH

Liebesfrühling – Ländler, Op. 32 pf & 2 vlns
with A. Sens vln   1560 ak   HMV AL501, X287965

GREEL

Laurbaer & Roser v & pf – arr. 2 vlns
with A. Sens vln   HMV X287953

GUNGL

Oberländler (Country sounds) Op. 31 pf – arr. 2 vlns
with A. Sens vln   HMV 1297

LANGER

Grandmother, Op. 20 pf – arr. 2 vlns
with A. Sens vln   15279 b   HMV X287927

MASSENET

Thaïs (1894) – opera
Méditation arr. 2 vlns & pf
with A. Sens vln & piano   Polydor 12650

MELCHERT

Raslende Solv, brusende Bolge v & pf – arr. 2 vlns
with A. Sens vln   HMV X287954

MENDELSSOHN

(6) Duets, Op. 63 2 v's & pf
No. 1. Ich wollt' meine Lieb' arr. 2 vlns
with A. Sens vln   1561 ak   HMV AL501, X287966

OFFENBACH

(Les) Contes d'Hoffmann (1881) – opera
Belle Nuit, O nuit d'amour "Barcarolle" arr. 2 vlns
with A. Sens vln   15278½ b   HMV X287928

SEIDLER-WINKLER

Romance in G vln & pf – arr. 2 vlns & pf
with A. Sens vln & piano   Polydor 12650

Ferdinand MEISEL

SVENDSEN

Romance in G, Op. 26 vln & orch.
with Berlin Symphony Orch. – Guhl   Urania URLP7166
Romance in G, Op. 26 vln & orch.
with Berlin Radio Orch. – Dobrindt   Eterna 520187

Wilhelm MELCHER

BRUCH

Concerto No. 1, in g, Op. 26 vln & orch.
with Hamburg Symphony Orch. –
Ötvös   Joker M1007

MENDELSSOHN

Concerto in e, Op. 64 vln & orch.
with Hamburg Symphony Orch. –
Ötvös   Joker M1007

MOZART

Sonata No. 2, in D, K7 vln & pf
with C. Eschenbach hpsi   Deutsche Grammophon LPEM19052

Sonata No. 12, in G, K27 vln & pf
with C. Eschenbach hpsi   Deutsche Grammophon LPEM19052

Eduard MELKUS

BACH

Concerto No. 1, in a, BWV1041 vln, strs & c
with Capella Academica Wien – Melkus   Archive 2533 075

Concerto No. 2, in E, BWV1042 vln, strs & c
with Capella Academica Wien – Melkus   Archive 2533 075

Concerto in d, BWV1043 2 vlns, strs & c
with S. Rantos vln & Capella Academica Wien – Melkus   Archive 2533 075

BIBER

(16) Biblical Sonatas "Mysterien" vln & c
Sonata No. 1, in d "The annunciation of the birth of Christ"
with L. Rogg org, K. Scheit lute, G. Sonneck gamba & A. Planyavsky cbs   Archive SAPM198422/3, (in set 2714 002)

Sonata No. 2, in A "Visit of Mary to Elizabeth"
with L. Rogg org, K. Scheit lute, G. Sonneck gamba & A. Planyavsky cbs   Archive SAPM198422/3, (in set 2714 002)

Sonata No. 3, in b "Birth of Christ"
with H. Dreyfus hpsi, K. Scheit lute, G. Sonneck gamba & A. Planyavsky cbs   Archive SAPM198422/3, (in set 2714 002)

Sonata No. 4, in d "Christ in the temple"
with H. Dreyfus hpsi, K. Scheit lute, G. Sonneck gamba & A. Planyavsky cbs   Archive SAPM198422/3, (in set 2714 002)

Sonata No. 5, in A "The 12 year–old Jesus in the temple"
with H. Dreyfus hpsi, K. Scheit lute, A. Planyavsky cbs & H–J. Lange bsn   Archive SAPM198422/3, (in set 2714 002)

BIBER – Continued

Sonata No. 6, in c "Christ on the Mount of Olives"
with L. Rogg org   Archive SAPM198422/3, (in set 2714 002)

Sonata No. 7, in F "The Flagellation of Christ"
with L. Rogg org, K. Scheit lute, A. Planyavsky cbs & H–J. Lange bsn   Archive SAPM198422/3, (in set 2714 002)

Sonata No. 8, in B flat "Christ's crowning with thorns"
with H. Dreyfus hpsi, K. Scheit lute, G. Sonneck gamba & A. Planyavsky cbs   Archive SAPM198422/3, (in set 2714 002)

Sonata No. 9, in a "Christ on the way to Calvary"
with L. Rogg org, K. Scheit lute, G. Sonneck gamba & A. Planyavsky cbs   Archive SAPM198422/3, (in set 2714 002)

Sonata No. 10, in g "The Crucifixion"
with L. Rogg org, K. Scheit lute, A. Planyavsky cbs & H–J. Lange bsn   Archive SAPM198422/3, (in set 2714 002)

Sonata No. 11, in G "The Resurrection"
with L. Rogg org   Archive SAPM198422/3, (in set 2714 002)

Sonata No. 12, in C "The Ascension"
with H. Dreyfus hpsi, K. Scheit lute, A. Planyavsky cbs & H–J. Lange bsn   Archive SAPM198422/3, (in set 2714 002)

Sonata No. 13, in d "The Emanation of the Holy Ghost"
with H. Dreyfus hpsi, K. Scheit lute, G. Sonneck gamba & A. Planyavsky cbs   Archive SAPM198422/3, (in set 2714 002)

Sonata No. 14, in D "The Ascension of the Holy Virgin"
with L. Rogg org   Archive SAPM198422/3, (in set 2714 002)

Sonata No. 15, in C "Coronation of the Virgin"
with L. Rogg org, K. Scheit lute, A. Planyavsky cbs & H–J. Lange bsn   Archive SAPM198422/3, (in set 2714 002)

Sonata No. 16, in g "The Guardian angel"*
(unaccompanied)   Archive SAPM198422/3, (in set 2714 002)

CALDARA

(La) Clemenza di Tito – opera
Balletto in G vln, vlc, hpsi & positiv org
with P. Grümmer vlc, V. Schwarz hpsi & R. Clemencic positiv org   Amadeo AVRS5060
Musical Heritage Society MHS864

Morte e Sepultura di Gesu Christo – oratorio
Magdalen's recitative & aria
with A. Hückl s, V. Schwarz hpsi & P. Grümmer vlc   Amadeo AVRS5060
Musical Heritage Society MHS864

(12) Sonatas, Op. 2 2 vlns & c
Sonata No. 6, in C†
with R. Clemencic rec, V. Schwarz hpsi & P. Grümmer vlc   Amadeo AVRS5060
Musical Heritage Society MHS864

* Known as "Passacaglia".
† Original key: A Major.

CALDARA – *Continued*

Sonata in F vln & c
with V. Schwarz hpsi & P. Grümmer   Amadeo AVRS5060
vlc   Musical Heritage Society
    MHS864

Sonata No. 5, in C vln & c
with V. Schwarz hpsi & P. Grümmer   Amadeo AVRS5060
vlc   Musical Heritage Society
    MHS864

CORELLI

(12) Concerti grossi, Op. 6 orch.
  Concerto grosso No. 1, in D
  with W. Hintermeyer vln, G. Zatschek Library of Recorded
  vlc, C. Landon hpsi, J. Nebois hpsi & Masterpieces Vol. 1
  Vienna Sinfonietta – Goberman Odyssey (in sets 32 36 0001/2)
  Concerto grosso No. 2, in F
  with W. Hintermeyer vln, G. Zatschek Library of Recorded
  vlc, C. Landon hpsi, J. Nebois hpsi & Masterpieces Vol. 2
  Vienna Sinfonietta – Goberman Odyssey (in sets 32 36 0001/2)
  Concerto grosso No. 3, in c
  with W. Hintermeyer vln, G. Zatschek Library of Recorded
  vlc, C. Landon hpsi, J. Nebois hpsi & Masterpieces Vol. 3
  Vienna Sinfonietta – Goberman Odyssey (in sets 32 36 0001/2)

COUPERIN, F.

(L') Apothéose de Lully (1725) 2 vlns & c
with S. Rantos vln, F. Stradner fl, B.   Archive 2533 067
Klebel ob, J. Koch gamba, L. Cermak
bsn & H. Dreyfus hpsi

(Le) Parnasse, ou l'Apothéose de Corelli (1725) 2 vlns & c
with S. Rantos vln, F. Stradner fl, B.   Archive 2533 067
Klebel ob, J. Koch gamba, L. Cermak
bsn & H. Dreyfus hpsi

HANDEL

Adagio–Allegro in A (1750 or 1751) vln & org
with E. Müller org   Archive SAPM198475

(15) Sonatas, Op. 1 (?1731) fl or vln & c
  Sonata No. 1, in d*
  with E. Müller org, A. Wenzinger vlc Archive SAPM198475
  & K. Scheit lute

  Sonata No. 3, in A vln I
  with E. Müller hpsi & A. Wenzinger Archive SAPM198475
  vlc

  Sonata No. 6, in g
  with K. Scheit lute & A. Wenzinger Archive SAPM198475
  vlc

  Sonata No. 10, in g vln II
  with E. Müller org, A. Wenzinger vlc Archive SAPM198474
  & K. Scheit lute

  Sonata No. 12, in F vln III
  with E. Müller hpsi & A. Wenzinger Archive SAPM198475
  vlc

  Sonata No. 13, in D vln IV
  with E. Müller hpsi & A. Wenzinger Archive SAPM198474
  vlc

* Opus 1, No. 1b.

HANDEL – *Continued*

  Sonata No. 14, in A vln V
  with E. Müller hpsi & A. Wenzinger Archive SAPM198474
  vlc

  Sonata No. 15, in E vln VI
  with E. Müller hpsi   Archive SAPM198475

Sonata in G vln & hpsi*
with E. Müller hpsi   Archive SAPM198474

HAYDN

Concerto in F, H.XVIII, No. 6 (1765) vln, hpsi & orch.
with V. Schwarz hpsi & Capella Musica Mundi VMS2028
Academica Wien – Müller–Brühl

Concerto No. 2, in G, H.VIIa, No. 4 (1768) vln & orch.
with Capella Academica Wien – Musica Mundi VMS2023,
Müller–Brühl VMS5001–3

(31) Trios, H.XV, Nos. 1/31 pf, vln & vlc
  Trio No. 24, in D, H.XV, No. 24 (Op. 73, No. 1)
  with H. Dreyfus pf & E. Vogt vlc Valois MB879
  Trio No. 25, in G, H.XV, No. 25 (Op. 73, No. 2)
  with H. Dreyfus pf & E. Vogt vlc Valois MB879
  Trio No. 26, in f sharp, H.XV, No. 26 (Op. 73, No. 3)
  with H. Dreyfus pf & E. Vogt vlc Valois MB879
  Trio No. 31, in e flat, H.XV, No. 31
  with H. Dreyfus pf & E. Vogt vlc Valois MB879

LECLAIR

(12) Sonatas, Op. 5 – Book III (1734) vln & c
  Sonata No. 6, in c "Le Tombeau"
  with H. Dreyfus hpsi & J. Koch Archive 2533 067
  gamba

MONN

Concertino fugato in G (1742) vln & strs
with Capella Academica Wien – Archive 2533 048
Melkus

MOZART

Sonata No. 27, in G, K379 vln & pf
with P. Badura–Skoda pf Harmonia Mundi HM30630

Sonata No. 32, in B flat, K454 vln & pf
with P. Badura–Skoda pf Harmonia Mundi HM30630

(6) Variations (on "Hélas, j'ai perdu mon amant") K360 vln & pf
with P. Badura–Skoda pf Harmonia Mundi HM30630

NARDINI

Concerto in E flat (1765) vln, strs & 2 hrns
with Capella Academica Wien – Archive APM14870, ARC3270,
Winzinger ARC73270, SAPM198370

PISENDEL

Concerto in D vln, 2 obs, strs & c
with Pro Arte Chamber Orch. – Redel Archive APM14866, ARC3266,
  ARC73266, SAPM198866

* Attributed to Handel.

RUGGIERI

(10) Sonatas, Op. 3 (1693) 2 vln & c

Sonata No. 1, in e
with E. Steinbauer vln, E. Knava
gamba, A. Planyavsky cbs, K. Rapf
org & K. Scheit gtr
Society of Participating Artists
SPA18

Sonata No. 2, in b
with E. Steinbauer vln, E. Knava
gamba, K. Rapf hpsi & A. Planyavsky
cbs
Society of Participating Artists
SPA18

Sonata No. 3, in B flat
with E. Steinbauer vln, E. Knava
gamba, K. Scheit lute & A. Planyavsky
cbs
Society of Participating Artists
SPA18

Sonata No. 4, in F
with E. Steinbauer vln, E. Knava
gamba, A. Planyavsky cbs, K. Rapf
org & K. Scheit gtr
Society of Participating Artists
SPA18

Sonata No. 5, in g
with E. Steinbauer vln, E. Knava
gamba, K. Scheit lute & A. Planyavsky
cbs
Society of Participating Artists
SPA19

Sonata No. 6, in A
with E. Steinbauer vln, E. Knava
gamba, K. Scheit gtr & A. Planyavsky
cbs
Society of Participating Artists
SPA19

Sonata No. 7, in a
with E. Steinbauer vln, E. Knava vlc,
K. Rapf pf & A. Planyavsky cbs
Society of Participating Artists
SPA18

Sonata No. 8, in G
with E. Steinbauer vln, E. Knava
gamba, K. Rapf hpsi & A. Planyavsky
cbs
Society of Participating Artists
SPA19

Sonata No. 9, in d
with E. Steinbauer vln, E. Knava vlc,
K. Rapf pf & A. Planyavsky cbs
Society of Participating Artists
SPA18

Sonata No. 10, in D
with E. Steinbauer vln, E. Knava
gamba, K. Rapf hpsi & A. Planyavsky
cbs
Society of Participating Artists
SPA19

TARTINI

Concerto in D, D15 (C79) vln & orch.
with Capella Academica Wien –
Wenzinger
Archive APM14870, ARC3270,
ARC73270, SAPM198370

Concerto in G, D75 vln & orch.
with Capella Academica Wien –
Wenzinger
Archive APM14870, ARC3270,
ARC73270, SAPM198370

TELEMANN

Concerto in B flat "Polonaise" 2 vlns, vla, hpsi & c
with S. Rantos vln, K. Hart vla, I.
Ahlgrimm hpsi, V. Schwarz hpsi & S.
Ladwig vlc
Archive SAPM198467

Concerto in E flat 2 fls, ob, vln, strs & c
with B. Walter fl, F. Kirschner fl, M.
Clément ob & Pro Arte Orch., Munich
– Redel
Philips 641750LL, 835750LY

TELEMANN – *Continued*

Concerto in F, T.II, No. 3 3 vlns, strs & c
with L. Frydén vln, E. Mayer-
Schierning vln, O. Steinkopf hpsi &
Schola Cantorum Basiliensis –
Wenzinger
Archive APM14837, ARC3237,
ARC73237, SAPM198368

Concerto in G "alla Polonaise" 2 vlns, vla, hpsi & c
with S. Rantos vln, K. Hart vla, I.
Ahlgrimm hpsi, V. Schwarz hpsi & S.
Ladwig vlc
Archive SAPM198467

Polonaise in B flat "Partie" 2 vlas, vlc, violone & hpsi
playing vla with C. Barrus vla, G.
Sonneck violone & I. Ahlgrimm hpsi
Archive SAPM198467

Solo in A, T.II, No. 5 vln & c
with E. Müller hpsi & A. Wenzinger
vlc
Archive APM14837, ARC3237,
ARC73237, SAPM198368

Sonata No. 1, in a "Sonata Polonaise" 2 vlns & c
with K. Hart vla, I. Ahlgrimm hpsi &
S. Ladwig vlc
Archive SAPM198467

Sonata No. 2, in a "Sonata Polonaise" 2 vlns & c
with S. Rantos vln, C. Barrus vla, I.
Ahlgrimm hpsi & S. Ladwig vlc
Archive SAPM198467

TOMASINI

Concerto in A vln, 2 hrns & strs
with Capella Academica Wien –
Müller–Brühl
Musica Mundi VMS2023

VIVALDI

Concerto in g, P.383 (F.XII, No. 3) "Per l'orch. di Dresda" vln, 2 fls, 2
obs, 2 bsns & c
with Instrumental Soloists of the
Munich Chamber Orch. – Stadlmair
Archive 2533 044

WELLESZ

Concerto, Op. 84 (1962) vln & orch.
with Austrian Radio Orch., Vienna –
Zillig
Amadeo AVRS5022

Albert MELL

SCARLATTI, A.

Sonata in F rec, ob, vln, or 2 vlns & c
with A. Mann rec, L. Mann ob & E.
Weiss–Mann hpsi
Westminster WL5214

TELEMANN

Sonata in e 2 vlns & c
with A. Mann rec, L. Mann ob & E.
Weiss–Mann hpsi
Westminster WL5214

Daniel MELSA (1892–1952)

FALLA

(La) Vida Breve (1913) – opera
Danza española orch. – arr. vln & pf Kreisler
with piano   L 0442   Broadcast 5151, 6039

HUBAY

(14) Scènes de la Csárda vln & pf
No. 4. Hejre Kati, Op. 32
with piano   Broadcast 5130

KREISLER

Caprice viennois, Op. 2 vln & pf
with piano   L 0352 x   Broadcast 5110

Tambourin chinois, Op. 3 vln & pf
with piano   L 0440   Broadcast 5151, 6039

PAGANINI

(24) Caprices, Op. 1 (1801/7) solo vln
Caprice*
with piano   Edison Diamond Disc 80194

SARASATE

(8) Danzas españolas vln & pf
No. 6. Zapateado, Op. 23, No. 2
with piano   L 0353   Broadcast 5110

Zigeunerweisen, Op. 20 vln & pf or orch.
with piano   Broadcast 5130

WIENIAWSKI

Fantaisie brillante (on themes from the opera "Faust" by Gounod) Op. 20
vln & orch.
with piano   Edison Diamond Disc 80194

Franz MELSER

LALO

Symphonie espagnole, Op. 21 vln & orch.†
with Berlin Symphony Orch. –   Classic Record Club AACMP19
Schartner   Music Treasures of the World
  MTW538
  Urania RS7–13, URLP7156 •

Émile MENDELS

ACCORDI

(La) Seduzione (Air de ballet) orch. – arr. vln & orch.
with orch.   Pathé 171, 1092, 5509, 9551

BACH

(4) Suites, BWV1066/9 strs & c
Suite No. 3, in D: Air (2nd mvt) BWV1068 2 obs, 3 tpts, drms, strs & c
– arr. vln & pf as "Air on the G–string" by Wilhelmj
with Pathé Symphony Orch.   Pathé 1093, 5179, 5517, 9546

BAZZINI

(La) Ronde des lutins, Op. 25 vln & pf
with piano   Pathé 9592

BECUCCI

Tesoro mio – waltz, Op. 228 orch. – arr. vln & orch.
with orch.   Pathé 171, 1087, 9511, 40121

* Unidentified.
† Including Intermezzo.

BRAGA

(7) Melodies (1867) v & pf
No. 5. La serenata "Angel's serenade" arr. vln & pf
with piano   Pathé 9519

FAURÉ

Berceuse, Op. 16 vln & pf
with orch.   Pathé 9501

GODARD

Jocelyn (1888) – opera
Cachés dans cet asile "Berceuse" arr. vln & orch.
with orch.   Pathé 9502

MASSENET

Thaïs (1894) – opera
Méditation arr. vln & pf Marsick
with orch.   Pathé 9501, 40121

MENDELSSOHN

Concerto in e, Op. 64 vln & orch.
Andante (2nd mvt)
with orch.   Pathé 9512

OFFENBACH

(Les) Contes d'Hoffmann (1881) – opera
Belle Nuit, O nuit d'amour "Barcarolle" arr. vln & pf
with piano   Pathé 5559, 40080

PAGANINI

(La) Carnevale di Venizia – variations, Op. 10 (1829) solo vln – arr. vln &
orch.
with Pathé Symphony Orch.   Pathé 170, 1087, 5510, 9551

PIERNÉ

Sérénade in A, Op. 7 (1875) pf – arr. vln & pf Haddock
with piano   Pathé 9591

SAINT–SAËNS

(Le) Carnaval des animaux (1886) small orch.
Le cygne arr. vln & orch.
with orch.   Pathé 1092, 5508

(Le) Déluge, Op. 45 (1876) – oratorio
Prélude vln & orch.
with Pathé Symphony Orch.   Pathé 170, 1088, 5508, 9546

SARASATE

Zigeunerweisen, Op. 20 vln & pf or orch.
with Pathé Symphony Orch.   Pathé 1093, 5179, 5516

SINGALÉE

Fantasia (on themes from Hérold's opera "Le Pré aux Clercs") Op. 24 vln
& pf
with Pathé Symphony Orch.   Pathé 172, 1088, 5512

TCHAIKOVSKY

(The) Months (12 characteristic pieces) Op. 37a pf
No. 6. Barcarolle (June) arr. vln & pf
with piano   Pathé 9591

THOMAS

Mignon (1866) – opera
Entr'acte (Gavotte) (Act II) arr. vln & pf Sarasate
with piano   Pathé 5554, 9519, 40080

THOMÉ

Simple aveu, Op. 25 pf – arr. vln & pf
with piano   Pathé 172, 5511, 9511

TOSELLI

Serenade, Op. 6 vln & pf
with piano   Pathé 9592

WIENIAWSKI

Légende, Op. 17 vln & pf or orch.
with orch.   Pathé 9502
(2) Mazurkas, Op. 19 vln & pf
No. 1. Mazurka No. 1, in G "Obertass"
with piano   Pathé 9518
Polonaise brillante No. 1, in D, Op. 4 vln & pf
with piano   Pathé 9518

Isolde MENGES (1893–)

ACHRON

Hebrew lullaby, Op. 35, No. 2 vln & pf – arr. Auer
with E. Beattie pf   Bb 1106^{III} HMV E258

BACH

Matthaeus–Passion, BWV244 (1729)
No. 47. Erbarme dich, mein Gott
        Cc 7744^{I} & 7745^{II} HMV DB907
with M. Offers a & Orch. – Sargent Victor 11143
(3) Sonatas & 3 Partitas, BWV1001/6 solo vln
Sonata No. 1, in G: Fugue (2nd mvt) BWV1001
        Bb 1103^{V} & 1104^{VI} HMV E269
(unaccompanied)
Partita No. 2, in d: Chaconne (5th mvt) BWV1004
(unaccompanied)   HMV D875/6
Partita No. 3, in E: Gavotte (3rd mvt) BWV1006 arr. vln & pf Kreisler
with E. Beattie pf   Bb 17124^{II}△ HMV B3465
(6) Sonatas, BWV1014/9 vln & clav
Sonata No. 3, in E, BWV1016
        Cc 13604^{IVA}△, 13803^{III}△, 13805 HMV C1632/3
with H. Samuel pf ^{II}△ & 13806^{III}△
(4) Suites, BWV1066/9 strs & c
Suite No. 3, in D: Air (2nd mvt) BWV1068 2 obs, 3 tpts, drms, strs & c
arr. vln & pf as "Air on the G–string" by Wilhelmj
with E. Beattie pf   Cc 10976^{I}△ HMV D1288, EJ186

BEETHOVEN

Concerto in D, Op. 61 (cadenzas by Joachim) vln & orch.
        Cc 3392^{I}, 3398/9^{II}, 3400^{III}, HMV D767/71, W518/22
3401^{II}, 3406/7^{II}, 3408^{III} & 3413/4^{V}
with Royal Albert Hall Orch. –
Ronald
Sonata No. 9, in A, Op. 47 "Kreutzer" vln & pf
        Cc 6780^{VII}△, 6881^{IV}△, 6782^{IV}△, HMV D1066/9, D7434/7
6783^{V}△, 7086^{III}△, 7087/8^{V}△ & 7089 Victor 9001/4, (set M2)
with A. de Greef pf ^{I}△

BOYD

Samoan lullaby vln & pf
with T. Boyd pf   Bd 448^{III} HMV E245
Serenade vln & pf
with T. Boyd pf   HMV D581
Valse capricieuse vln & pf
with E. Beattie pf   Bb 687^{V} HMV E258

BRAHMS

(21) Hungarian Dances pf duet
Hungarian dance No. 2, in d arr. vln & pf Joachim
with H. Harty pf   HMV 2–07935, D354
Hungarian dance No. 5, in f sharp arr. vln & pf "in g" Joachim
with E. Beattie pf   Bb 11730^{II}△ HMV E496
Hungarian dance No. 7, in A arr. vln & pf Joachim
with H. Harty pf   HO 2127 ab HMV 3–7999, E153
Hungarian dance No. 7, in A arr. vln & pf Joachim
with E. Beattie pf   Bb 18546^{II}△ HMV B3465
Hungarian dance No. 20, in e arr. vln & pf "in d" Joachim
with E. Beattie pf   HO 2125 ab HMV E206
Hungarian dance No. 20, in e arr. vln & pf "in d" Joachim
with E. Beattie pf   Bb 11729^{I}□ HMV E496
Sonata No. 2, in A, Op. 100 vln & pf
        Bb 16979^{III}△, 16980^{II}△, 16981^{IA} HMV B3098/100
  △, 16982^{III}△, 16983^{IV}△ & 16984^{II}△
with H. Samuel pf
Sonata No. 3, in d, Op. 108 vln & pf
        Cc 18434^{III}△, 18435^{IIA}△, 18436 HMV C1923/5, C7213/5
with H. Samuel pf ^{V}△ & 18437/9^{II}△
(16) Waltzes, Op. 39 pf duet
No. 15. Waltz No. 15, in A flat arr. vln & pf "in A" Boyd
with T. Boyd pf   Bb 565^{II} HMV E245
No. 15. Waltz No. 15, in A flat arr. vln & pf "in A" Hochstein
with E. Beattie pf   BR 66^{II}△ HMV E508

CHOPIN

(3) Nocturnes, Op. 9 pf
No. 2. Nocturne No. 2, in E flat arr. vln & pf Sarasate
with E. Beattie pf   Cc 10979^{I}△ HMV D1288, EJ186
(2) Nocturnes, Op. 27 pf
No. 2. Nocturne No. 8, in D flat arr. vln & pf Wilhelmj
with piano   HMV D529
Nocturne No. 19, in e, Op. 72, No. 1 pf – arr. vln & pf Auer
with H. Harty pf   HMV 2–07933, D355

DVOŘÁK

Quartet No. 8, in G, Op. 106 2 vlns, vla & vlc
        AR 5481/5–1, 5895/6–1, 5605–1, Decca K1000/4
with B. Carelle vln, 5606–2 & 5607–1
J.Y. Dyer vla & I. James vlc
Sextet in A, Op. 48 2 vlns, 2 vlas & 2 vlcs
        AR 5451/6–1 & 5457/8–3 Decca K963/6
with B. Carelle vln, J.Y. Dyer vla, I.
James vlc, A. de Reyghere vla & H.
Just vlc

ELGAR

Salut d'amour, Op. 12 orch. – arr. vln & pf Elgar
with E. Beattie pf   Cc 10978^{II}△ HMV D1313

FALLA

(La) Vida Breve (1913) – opera
  Danza española orch. – arr. vln & pf Kreisler
  with E. Beattie pf   Bb 11731^{II}△ HMV E508

FAURÉ

Berceuse, Op. 16 vln & pf
  with piano   Cc 3490^{IV} HMV D861

Berceuse, Op. 16 vln & pf
  with E. Beattie pf   CR 65^{II}△ HMV D1099, W735

FIBICH

Images, Impressions & Souvenirs, Op. 41 pf
  No. 14. Poem (from "Souvenirs", Part IV) arr. vln & pf Kubelík
  with E. Beattie pf   Bb 18545^{I}△ HMV B3749

FIOCCO

Suite No. 1, in G hpsi
  Allegro (10th mvt) arr. vln & pf Bent & O'Neill
  with E. Beattie pf   Bb 3469^{II} HMV E373

GODARD

(6) Morceaux, Op. 128 vln & pf
  No. 6. Staccato–valse
  with H. Harty pf   HMV 2–07925

GOUNOD

Ave Maria (Méditation on Bach's "Prelude No. 1, in C" from Book I of "Das Wohltemperirte Clavier") v & pf – arr. v, vln, hp & org
  with G. Ljungberg s   CR 1368^{III}△ HMV DB962
  & harp & organ

HANDEL

Minuet in F unid – arr. vln & pf Harty
  with piano   HO 3133 ae HMV E206

(15) Sonatas, Op. 1 (?1731) fl or vln & c
  Sonata No. 3, in A vln I
  with E. Beattie pf   Cc 7544/5^{IX}△ HMV D1371

  Sonata No. 13, in D vln IV
    Bb 688^{I}, 862^{II}, 883^{II} & 884^{I} HMV E279/80
  with piano

Suite vln & pf
  No. 1. Rigaudon
  with E. Beattie pf   Cc 6348^{V}△ HMV D1023, W729

  No. 3. Hornpipe
  with E. Beattie pf   Cc 6348^{V}△ HMV D1023, W729

  No. 4. Passacaglia
  with E. Beattie pf   Cc 6349^{IV}△ HMV D1023, W729

HUBAY

(6) Blumenleben, Op. 30 vln & pf
  No. 5. Der Zephir
  with E. Beattie pf   Bb 18544^{I}△ HMV B3749

(14) Scènes de la Csárda vln & pf
  No. 4. Hejre Kati, Op. 32
  with E. Beattie pf   Cc 9503^{IIIA} HMV D1223

MACKENZIE

(6) Pieces, Op. 37 (1888) vln & pf
  No. 3. Benedictus
  with piano   HMV 2–07939, D354

MASSENET

Thaïs (1894) – opera
  Méditation arr. vln & pf Marsick
  with E. Beattie pf   Cc 9502^{II}△ HMV D1223

PURCELL

(10) Sonatas, Z802/11 (1697) 4 parts – 2 vlns & c
  Sonata No. 9, in F, Z810 "Golden Sonata"
    Cc 4393^{IV} & 4394^{VI} HMV D889
  with W. Primrose vln &.H.J.
  Templeman pf

  Sonata No. 9, in F, Z810 "Golden Sonata"
  with W. Primrose   CAX 7598/9–1 Columbia 11098D, (in set M315),
  vln, A. Ticehurst hpsi & A. Gauntlett ROX133
  gamba

RIMSKY–KORSAKOV

(Le) Coq d'Or (1910) – opera
  Hymn to the sun arr. vln & pf Kreisler
  with piano   HMV D581

  Hymn to the sun arr. vln & pf Kreisler
  with E. Beattie pf   Bb 8240^{IV}△ HMV E444, P755

Sadko (1898) – opera
  Chant hindou arr. vln & pf Kreisler
  with E. Beattie pf   Bb 8239^{VII}△ HMV E444, P755

SARASATE

(8) Danzas españolas vln & pf
  No. 1. Malagueña, Op. 21, No. 1
  with piano   Cc 3491^{IV} HMV D861

  No. 1. Malagueña, Op. 21, No. 1
  with E. Beattie pf   CR 63^{II}△ HMV D1099, W735

SCHUBERT

(7) Gesänge (set to Scott's "Lady of the Lake") Op. 52 v & pf
  No. 6. Ave Maria, D839 arr. vln & pf Wilhelmj
  with E. Beattie pf   Cc 10977^{III}△ HMV D1313

(3) Sonatinas, Op. 137 (D384, D385 & D408) vln & pf
  No. 3. Sonatina No. 3, in g, D408
    Cc 12130^{I}△ & 12131/3^{II}△ HMV D1398/9
  with A. de Greef pf

SCHUMANN

(12) Duets, Op. 85 pf – 4 hands
  No. 12. Abendlied arr. vln & pf Joachim
  with E. Beattie pf   Bb 4050^{II} HMV E373

STANFORD

(4) Irish Dances, Op. 89 vln & pf
  No. 3. Leprechaun's dance
  with E. Beattie pf   Cc 13814^{II}△ HMV C1623

STRAUSS, R.

(4) Lieder, Op. 27 v & pf
  No. 4. Morgen arr. v, vln & orch.
  with E. Schumann s &   Cc 9888^{II}△ HMV COLH102, DB1010
  orch.

SVENDSEN

Romance in G, Op. 26 vln & orch. – arr. vln & pf Wilhelmj
  with piano   Cc 686^{I} HMV D712

VAUGHAN WILLIAMS

(The) Lark Ascending (1914) vln & orch.
  Cc 12857[IIA], 12858[IA] & 12859[IIA]   HMV C1622/3
  with orch. – Sargent

WIENIAWSKI

Concerto No. 2, in d, Op. 22 vln & orch.
  Allegro moderato (1st mvt)
  with piano   HMV D529
Polonaise brillante No. 1, in D, Op. 4 vln & pf
  with piano   HMV 2–07923, D355

ZARZYCKI

Mazurka in G, Op. 26 vln & pf
  with piano   Cc 1873[1]   HMV D712

Yehudi MENUHIN (1916–)

ANONYMOUS

Drink to me only with thine eyes (1762) traditional – arr. solo vln
  (unaccompanied)   Capitol HBZ21002
                Electrola E70469, STE70469
                HMV ASDF274, CLP1523,
                FALP738, 7EG8672, 7EGY150

(La) Romanesca (16th Century gaillarde) arr. vln & pf Achron*
  with L. Persinger pf   Pc 42093   HMV DB1267
                    Victor 6841

Song of the Volga boatmen traditional – arr. solo vln
  (unaccompanied)   Capitol HBZ21002
                Electrola E70469, STE70469
                HMV ASDF274, CLP1523,
                FALP738, 7EG8672, 7EGY150

BACH

(6) Brandenburg Concerti, BWV1046/51 (1721) strs & c
Brandenburg Concerto No. 1, in F, BWV1046 vln, 3 obs, bsn, 2 hrns, strs & c
  playing vln–pic, with B. Tuckwell hrn,   Capitol (in sets GBR7217 &
  J. Quaife hrn, J. Craxton ob, M.   SGBR7217)
  Dobson ob, R. Morgan ob, A. Camden   Electrola E91026, SME91678,
  bsn, K. Anderson hpsi & Bath Festival   STE91026
  Chamber Orch. – Menuhin   HMV ALP1755, ASD327,
                    ASDQ5272, ASDW327,
                    CVB3511, FALP30220,
                    QALP10268, WALP1755

Brandenburg Concerto No. 2, in F, BWV1047 tpt, fl, ob, vln, strs & c
  with D. Clift tpt, C. Taylor rec, J.   Capitol (in sets GBR7217 &
  Craxton ob, K. Anderson hpsi & Bath   SGBR7217)
  Festival Chamber Orch. – Menuhin   Electrola E50553, E91026,
                    SME91678, STE50553,
                    STE91026
                    HMV ALP1755, ASD327,
                    ASDQ5272, ASDW327,
                    CVB3511, FALP30220,
                    QALP10268, RESQ1009,
                    RESW4277, WALP1755,
                    7ER5180, 7ERQ246, 7ERW5180
                    Seraphim (in set S6061)

BACH – *Continued*

Brandenburg Concerto No. 4, in G, BWV1049 vln, 2 fls, strs & c
  with C. Taylor rec, R. Taylor rec, K.   Capitol (in sets GBR7217 &
  Anderson hpsi–c & Bath Festival   SGBR7217)
  Chamber Orch. – Menuhin   Electrola E91027, SME91679,
                    STE91027
                    HMV ALP1756, ASD327,
                    ASDQ5273, ASDW328,
                    FALP30221, QALP10269,
                    WALP1756, CVB3512

Brandenburg Concerto No. 5, in D, BWV1050 clav, fl, vln, strs & c
  with G. Malcolm hpsi, E. Shaffer fl &   Capitol (in sets GBR7217 &
  Bath Festival Chamber Orch. –   SGBR7217)
  Menuhin   Electrola E91027, SME91679,
                    STE91027
                    HMV ALP1756, ASD328,
                    ASDQ5273, ASDW328,
                    CVB3512, FALP30221,
                    QALP10269, WALP1756

Brandenburg Concerto No. 6, in B flat, BWV1051 2 vlas, 2 gambas, vlc & cbs
  playing vla, with P. Ireland vla, A.   Capitol (in sets GBR7217 &
  Gautlett gamba, D. Nesbitt gamba, of   SGBR7217)
  the Bath Festival Chamber Orch. –   Electrola E91027, SME91679,
  Menuhin   STE91027
                    HMV ALP1756, ASD328,
                    ASDQ5273, ASDW328,
                    CVB3512, QALP10269,
                    WALP1756

Concerto No. 1, in a, BWV1041 vln, strs & c
  with Paris   2LA 915/8[1]☐   HMV COLH77, DB2911/2
  Symphony Orch. – Enescu   Victor 14370/1

Concerto No. 1, in a, BWV1041 vln, strs & c
  with Robert Masters Chamber Orch. –   Capitol G7210, SG7210
  Menuhin   Electrola E50559, E70462,
                    E91025, SME91677, STE70462,
                    STE91025
                    Eterna 820513
                    HMV ALP1760, ASD346,
                    ASDQ5267, CVB3510,
                    FALP30222, QALP10278,
                    7ERW5392

Concerto No. 2, in E, BWV1042 vln, strs & c
    2PG 859/60[II△], 861[1△] & 862/3   HMV COLH77, DB2003/5,
  with Paris Symphony Orch. –   [II△]   DB7586/8, ED684/6
  Enescu   Victor 8367/9, 8370/2, (set
                    M221), 17091/3

Concerto No. 2, in E, BWV1042 vln, strs & c
  with Robert Masters Chamber Orch. –   Capitol G7210, SG7210
  Menuhin   Electrola E70462, E91025,
                    SME91677, (in set SME2035/6),
                    STE70462, STE91025
                    Eterna 820513
                    HMV ALP1760, ASD346,
                    ASDQ5267, ASDW346,
                    BSDW8007, CVB3510,
                    FALP30222, QALP10278,
                    WALP1760, WBLP568

---

* Excerpts only on Electrola E91475 & HMV FALP896 & HQM1018.

BACH – *Continued*

Concerto in d, BWV1043 2 vlns, strs & c*
2L 370/2 II △ & 373 I △ HMV COLH77, DB1718/9,
with G. Enescu vln & Paris FJLP5018
Conservatory Orch. – Monteux Victor 7732/3, 11–8601/2, 11–
8603/4, (set M932), LCT1120,
LVT1006

Concerto in d, BWV1043 2 vlns, strs & c
with G. De Vito vln & Philharmonia Electrola E70036
Orch. – Bernard HMV BLP1046, FBLP1061,
GHLP1002, LBLP1017,
QBLP5028
Victor LHMV16

Concerto in d, BWV1043 2 vlns, strs & c
with C. Ferras vln & Robert Masters Capitol G7210, SG7210
Chamber Orch. – Menuhin Electrola E91025, SME91677,
STE91025
HMV ALP1760, ASD346,
ASDQ5267, ASDW346,
CVB3510, FALP30222,
QALP10278, WALP1760

Concerto in a, BWV1044 clav, fl, vln, strs & c
with G. Malcolm hpsi, W. Bennett fl Angel 36336
& Bath Festival Orch. – Menuhin Columbia SMC91476
HMV 2C063–01854, ALP2267,
ASD2267, CVA908

Concerto in c, BWV1060 vln & ob or 2 vlns, strs & c
with L. Goossens ob & Bath Festival Angel 36103
Chamber Orch. – Menuhin Electrola E91219, SME91219,
STE91219
HMV 2C063/01854, ALP1949,
ASD500, ASDF283, FALP747,
QALP10356

(Ein) Musikalisches Opfer, BWV1079 (1749) strs & c – arr. Boyling
with E. Shaffer fl, K. Anderson hpsi, Angel 35731
A. Camden bsn–c & members of the Electrola E91153, STE91153
Bath Festival Chamber Orch. – Eterna 820435
Menuhin HMV ALP1839, ASD414,
ASDW414, WALP1839

(3) Sonatas & 3 Partitas, BWV1001/6 solo vln
Sonata No. 1, in g, BWV1001†
(unaccompanied) 2PG 883/6 I △ HMV DB2007/8
Victor 8361/2

Sonata No. 1, in g, BWV1001
(unaccompanied) HMV DB2869/70

Sonata No. 1, in g, BWV1001
(unaccompanied) M 191/4–I Victor SD3034/5, (set JAS200)

Sonata No. 1, in g, BWV1001
(unaccompanied) Electrola E90897
Eterna 820494
HMV ALP1512, FALP450,
WALP1512

* Excerpt from Vivace or 1st mvt also on Electrola E91475 & HMV
FALP896 & HQM1018.

† Extract from Adagio or 1st mvt. on Electrola E91475 & HMV FALP896
& HQM1018.

Partita No. 1, in b: Sarabande (5th mvt) BWV1002
(unaccompanied) 2PG 882 I △ HMV DB2005
Victor 8369, (in set M221),
15126, (in set M488), 16269

Partita No. 1, in b, BWV1002
(unaccompanied) HMV DB2816/9
Victor 15116/9, (set M487)

Partita No. 1, in b, BWV1002
(unaccompanied) Electrola E90897
Eterna 820494
HMV ALP1512, FALP450,
WALP1512

Partita No. 1, in b: Bourrée (7th mvt) BWV1002*
(unaccompanied) Electrola E70469, STE70469
HMV ASDF274, CLP1523,
FALP738, 7EG8672

Sonata No. 2, in a: Andante (3rd mvt) BWV1003**
(unaccompanied) 2B 2353 I HMV DB1738, DB7157
Victor 7737, 14324, (in set
M231), JD47, (in set JAS503)

Sonata No. 2, in a, BWV1003
(unaccompanied) HMV DB2824/6†

Sonata No. 2, in a, BWV1003
(unaccompanied) Electrola E90898
Eterna 820495
HMV ALP1531, FALP451,
WALP1531

Partita No. 2, in d, BWV1004
2PG 1622 I □, 1623/4 II □, 1625 HMV DB2287/90
III □, 1626 I □ & 1627/9 II □ Victor 8395/8, 8399/402, (set
(unaccompanied) M232), 17071/4

Partita No. 2, in d: Sarabande (3rd mvt) BWV1004
(unaccompanied) Victor SD3041

Partita No. 2, in d, BWV1004‡
(unaccompanied) Electrola E90898
Eterna 820495
HMV ALP1531, FALP451,
WALP1531

Partita No. 2, in d: Chaconne (5th mvt) BWV1004§
(unaccompanied) B & C Recording Inc BC13228

* Excerpt only.

** Two "takes" were issued under the same catalog number. The other
"take" number is 2LA 856.

† Unissued.

‡ Chaconne or 5th mvt on Electrola E50526, SHZE103 & HMV 7ERQ247
& 7ERW5383.

§ Spoken analysis is by Menuhin.

BACH – *Continued*

Partita No. 2, in d: Chaconne (5th mvt) BWV1004*
(unaccompanied)   Capitol HBZ21002
                               Electrola E70469, STE70469
                               HMV ASDF274, CLP1523,
                               FALP738, 7EG8672, 7EGY150

Sonata No. 3, in C, BWV1005
Cc 18165/6[II]△, 18167[I]△, 18168   HMV DB1368/70
[II]△, 18169[I]△ & 18170[II]△   Victor 7615/7, (set M148)
(unaccompanied)

Sonata No. 3, in C, BWV1005
(unaccompanied)   HMV DB2284/6
                               Victor 8830/2, 8833/5, (set
                               M284), 16966/8

Sonata No. 3, in C, BWV1005
(unaccompanied)   Electrola E90889
                               Eterna 820496
                               HMV ALP1532, FALP452,
                               WALP1532

Partita No. 3, in E, BWV1006
2LA 859[II]□ & 860/3[I]□   HMV DB2829/31
(unaccompanied)   Victor 15124/6S, 15127/9S, (set
                               M488), 16269/71

Partita No. 3, in E, BWV1006
(unaccompanied)   Victor SD3039/41

Partita No. 3, in E: Preludio (1st mvt) BWV1006
(unaccompanied)   2EA 9989[I]□ HMV DB5801, DB6156, 7P221,
                               7R112, 7RQ3054, 7RW120
                               Victor 15323, (in set M531), 11–
                               8736, 11–8782, (in set M987)

Partita No. 3, in E, BWV1006
(unaccompanied)   Electrola E90899
                               Eterna 820496
                               HMV ALP1532, FALP452,
                               WALP1532

(6) Sonatas, BWV1014/9 vln & clav
Sonata No. 1, in b, BWV1014
with L. Kentner pf   Electrola E70028
                               HMV BLP1026, DB9607/8,
                               DB21292/3, WBLP1026
                               Victor LHMV1016

Sonata No. 1, in b, BWV1014
with G. Malcolm hpsi & A. Gauntlett   Angel 35916, (in set 3629)
gamba   HMV ALP1924, ASD489,
                               CVB1740

Sonata No. 2, in A, BWV1015
with L. Kentner pf   Electrola E70028
                               HMV BLP1026, DB21328†,
                               DB9638, WBLP1026
                               Victor LHMV1016

Sonata No. 2, in A, BWV1015
with G. Malcolm hpsi & A. Gauntlett   Angel 35917, (in set 3629)
gamba   HMV ALP1925, ASD490,
                               CVB1741

* Excerpts only.

† Unissued.

BACH – *Continued*

Sonata No. 3, in E, BWV1016
with H. Menuhin   2EA 6184/7[I]□   HMV DB3501/2, ED827/8
pf   Victor 18531/2, 18533/4, (set
                               M887)

Sonata No. 3, in E, BWV1016
with W. Landowska hpsi   HMV DB6681/3
                               Victor 11–9049/51, 11–9052/4,
                               (set M1035), LCT1120,
                               LVT1006, WCT1120

Sonata No. 3, in E, BWV1016
2EA 15332/4–2, 15335/6–1 &   HMV DB9740/2, DB21435/7,
with L. Kentner pf   15337–4 FJLP5018
                               Victor LHMV1016

Sonata No. 3, in E, BWV1016
with G. Malcolm hpsi & A. Gauntlett   Angel 35916, (in set 3629)
gamba   HMV ALP1925, ASD490,
                               CVB1741

Sonata No. 4, in c, BWV1017
2EA 15559–6C & 15560/2–2   HMV DB9761/2, DB21514/5*,
with L. Kentner pf   Victor LHMV1017

Sonata No. 4, in c, BWV1017
with G. Malcolm hpsi & A. Gauntlett   Angel 35916/7, (in set 3629)
gamba   HMV ALP1924, ASD489,
                               CVB1740

Sonata No. 5, in f, BWV1018
with L Kentner pf   Victor LHMV1017

Sonata No. 5, in f, BWV1018
with G. Malcolm hpsi & A. Gauntlett   Angel 35916/7, (in set 3629)
gamba   HMV ALP1925, ASD490,
                               CVB1741

Sonata No. 6, in G, BWV1019
with L. Kentner pf   Victor LHMV1017

Sonata No. 6, in G, BWV1019
with G. Malcolm hpsi & A. Gauntlett   Angel 35917, (in set 3629)
gamba   HMV ALP1924, ASD489,
                               CVB1740

(4) Suites, BWV1066/9 strs & c
Suite No. 3, in D: Air (2nd mvt) BWV1068 2 obs, 3 tpts, drms, strs & c
– arr. vln & pf in original key
with M. Gazelle pf   2EA 9986[II]□   HMV DB6156, 7P221, 7R112,
                               7RQ3054, 7RW120

BARTÓK

Concerto No. 1, Op. posth (1908) vln & orch.
with New Philharmonia Orch. – Angel 36438
Dorati   Electrola 1C063–00333
                               HMV ALP2323, ASD2323,
                               ASDQ5347, CVB2059

Concerto No. 2 (1938) vln & orch.
with Dallas Symphony Orch. – Dorati   HMV DB6361/5, DB9291/5
                               Victor 11–9552/6, 11–9557/61,
                               (Set DM1120)

* Unissued.

BARTÓK – *Continued*

Concerto No. 2 (1938) vln & orch.
with Philharmonia Orch. –
Furtwängler

Electrola E90070
Eterna 820547
HMV ALP1121, FALP313,
LALP151, QALP10158,
WALP1121
Victor LHMV3

Concerto No. 2 (1938) vln & orch.
with Minneapolis Symphony Orch. –
Dorati

Mercury MG50140, MGW14104,
SR90003, SRW18104

Concerto No. 2 (1938) vln & orch.
with New Philharmonia Orch. –
Dorati

Angel 36360
Electrola 1C063–00303,
SME91491
HMV ALP2281, ASD2281,
CVB912

Concerto (1945) vln & orch.
playing vla with New Philharmonia
Orch. – Dorati

Angel 36438
Electrola 1C063–00331
HMV ALP2323, ASD2323,
ASDQ5347, CVB2059

(44) Duos (1931) 2 vlns
nos. 28, 31, 33, 36, 41 & 42
with N. Gotkovsky vln

Angel 36026, 36360
Electrola 1C063–00303,
HMV ALP2281, ASD2281,
CVB912

Rhapsody No. 1, in G (1928) vln & orch.
with BBC Symphony Orch. – Boulez

Electrola SME91789
HMV 2C063–01855, ASD2449

Rhapsody No. 2, in d (1928) vln & orch.
with BBC Symphony Orch. – Boulez

Electrola SME91789
HMV 2C063–01855, ASD2449

(6) Rumanian folk dances (1915) pf – arr. vln & pf Székely
2EA 10293^{III}□ & 10294^{II}□
with M. Gazelle pf

HMV DB6178, 7RF217
Victor 12–1061, 49–1796

(6) Rumanian folk dances (1915) pf – arr. vln & pf Székely
with A. Baller pf

Victor LM1742

(6) Rumanian folk dances (1915) pf – arr. vln & pf Székely
with G. Moore pf

HMV 7EP7178

Sonata No. 1 (1921) vln & pf
with A. Baller pf

Victor 12–1748/51, (set
DM1286), 49–0320/3, (set
WDM1286), LM1009, LM1087

Sonata No. 1 (1921) vln & pf
with H. Menuhin pf

Electrola E80544
HMV ALP1705, WCLP666

Sonata No.1 (1921) vln & pf
with H. Menuhin pf

HMV ASD2602

Sonata in g (1944) solo vln
2EA 12078/9–1 12080–2
(unaccompanied) 12089/91–2

HMV DB6533/5, DB9231/3
Victor (set WDM1350), 12–
1082/4, (set DM1350), LM1087

Sonata in g (1944) solo vln
(unaccompanied)

Electrola E80544
HMV ALP1705, FALP265,
WCLP666

BAZZINI

(La) Ronde des lutins, Op. 25 vln & pf*
with M. Gazelle pf   2LA 25□I

HMV DB2414, DB5395
Orion OR7271
Victor 8695

BEETHOVEN

Concerto in D, Op. 61 (cadenzas by Kreisler) vln & orch.†
2ZA 31–4, 32–3, 33–2, 34–1,
35/6–2, 37–1C, 38–2, 39–1, 40–3 &
with Lucerne Festival Orch. –   41–1
Furtwängler

HMV DB6574/9S, DB9198/203S

Concerto in D, Op. 61 (cadenzas by Kreisler) vln & orch.
with Philharmonia Orch. –
Furtwängler

Electrola 1C047–00117, 1C047–
50514, E90065
HMV ALP1100, FALP314,
FALP30041, LALP113,
QALP10056, VALP537,
WALP1100
Victor LHMV3, LHMV1061
Seraphim 60135

Concerto in D, Op. 61 (cadenzas by Kreisler) vln & orch.
with Vienna Philharmonic Orch. –
Silvestri

Capitol G7229, SG7229
Electrola E91082, STE91082
Eterna 820450
HMV 2C053–00186, ALP1799,
ASD377, ASDQ5295,
ASDW377, QALP10302,
WALP1799

Concerto in D, Op. 61 (cadenzas by Kreisler) vln & orch.
with New Philharmonia Orch. –
Klemperer

Angel 36369, (in set 3727)
Electrola 1C063–00307,
SME91621
HMV ALP2285, ASD2285,
CVA921

(6) Minuets, G167 pf
No. 2. Minuet No. 2, in G arr. vln & pf Burmester
with M. Gazelle pf

Victor LM2014

Romance No. 1, in G, Op. 40 vln & orch.
with Philharmonia Orch. –
Furtwängler

Angel LPC11582
Electrola E41131, E41686,
E50513, E90074
HMV ALP1135, FALP312,
LALP125, QALP10071,
7EGW8597, 7ERL1427,
7ERW5371
Plaisir Musical 25051
Seraphim 60135

Romance No. 1, in G, Op. 40 vln & orch.
with Philharmonia Orch. – Pritchard

Electrola BSDW8015,
GESW7039, STE41148,
STE70476

Romance No. 1, in G, Op. 40 vln & orch.
with Philharmonia Orch. – Pritchard

Capitol P8667, SP8667
HMV ALP2070, ASD618,
ASDF847, CVA847, FALP847

---

* Extract on Electrola E91475 & HMV FALP896 & HQM1018.

† Extract from Allegro ma non troppo or 1st mvt. is on Electrola E91475
& HMV FALP896 & HQM1018, while an extract from the Allegro or
3rd mvt. is Electrola E91475 & HMV FALP896.

BEETHOVEN – *Continued*

Romance No. 2, in F, Op. 50 vln & orch.
with Philharmonia Orch. –
Furtwängler

Angel LPC11582
Electrola E41686, E50513,
E90074
HMV ALP1135, FALP312,
LALP125, QALP10071,
7ERL1391, 7ERW5371
Plaisir Musical 25051
Seraphim 60135

Romance No. 2, in F, Op. 50 vln & orch.
with Philharmonia Orch. – Pritchard

Electrola BSDW8015,
GESW7039, STE41148,
STE70476, (in set SME2035/6)

Romance No. 2, in F, Op. 50 vln & orch.
with Philharmonia Orch. – Pritchard

Capitol P8667, SP8667
HMV ALP2070, ASD618,
ASDF847, CVA847, FALP847

Rondo in G, G155 vln & pf
with H. Menuhin pf   2EA 6176[II]□

HMV DB3506*
Victor 11–8843, 11–8844, (in set M1008)

Rondo in G, G155 vln & pf
with W. Kempff pf

Deutsche Grammophon 643669,
(in set 2720 018)

(Die) Ruinen von Athen, Op. 113 – Incidental music orch.
No. 4. Marcia alla turca arr. vln & pf Auer
with M. Gazelle pf   OLA 844[I]□   HMV DA1494

(3) Sonatas, Op. 12 vln & pf
No. 1. Sonata No. 1, in D
Cc 18160/2[II]△, 18163[IIA]△ &   HMV DB1365/7
with H. Giesen pf   18164[II]△   Victor 7360/2, (set M91)

No. 1. Sonata No. 1, in D
with L. Kentner pf

Electrola E90047
HMV ALP1050, FALP421,
QALP10026
Victor (set WHMV1037),
LHMV1037

No. 1. Sonata No. 1, in D
with W. Kempff pf

Deutsche Grammophon 643669,
(in set 2720 018)

No. 2. Sonata No. 2, in A
with L. Kentner pf

Electrola E90138
HMV ALP1338, FALP421

No. 2. Sonata No. 2, in A
with W. Kempff pf

Deutsche Grammophon 643669,
(in set 2720 018)

No. 3. Sonata No. 3, in E flat
with H. Menuhin pf

HMV DB5802/4S

No. 3. Sonata No. 3, in E flat
with L. Kentner pf

Electrola E90047
HMV ALP1050, FALP422,
QALP10026

No. 3. Sonata No. 3, in E flat
with W. Kempff pf

Deutsche Grammophon 643670,
(in set 2720 018)

* Unissued.

BEETHOVEN – *Continued*

Sonata No. 4, in a, Op. 23 vln & pf
with L. Kentner pf

Electrola E90138
HMV ALP1338, FALP422

Sonata No. 4, in a, Op. 23 vln & pf
with W. Kempff pf

Deutsche Grammophon 643670,
(in set 2720 018)

Sonata No. 5, in F, Op. 24 "Spring" vln & pf
with L. Kentner pf

Electrola E90068
HMV ALP1105, FALP423,
QALP10164
Victor LHMV1053

Sonata No. 5, in F, Op. 24 "Spring" vln & pf
with H. Menuhin pf

Capitol G7246, SG7246
Electrola 1C063–00170, (in set
SME2035/6), E80549, STE80549
Eterna 820491
HMV ASD389, ASDQ5301,
CSDW7070, QALP10311,
WCLP701

Sonata No. 5, in F, Op. 24 "Spring" vln & pf
with W. Kempff pf

Deutsche Grammophon 643671,
(in set 2720 018)

(3) Sonatas, Op. 30 vln & pf
No. 1. Sonata No. 6, in A
with L. Kentner pf

Electrola E90140
HMV ALP1354, FALP423,
QALP10154

No. 1. Sonata No. 6, in A
with W. Kempff pf

Deutsche Grammophon 643671,
(in set 2720 018)

No. 2. Sonata No. 7, in c
with H. Menuhin pf   2EA 6177/83[I]

HMV DB3503/6*
Victor 11–8840/3, 11–8844/7,
(set M1008)

No. 2. Sonata No. 7, in c
with L. Kentner pf

Electrola E90140
HMV ALP1354, FALP424,
QALP10154

No. 2. Sonata No. 7, in c
with H. Menuhin pf

Electrola E80562, STE80562
HMV ALP1959, ASD510,
ASDF281, FALP745

No. 2. Sonata No. 7, in c
with W. Kempff pf

Deutsche Grammophon 643672,
(in set 2720 018)

No. 3. Sonata No. 8, in G: Allegro vivace (3rd mvt)
with H. Menuhin pf   HMV DB2834
No. 3. Sonata No. 8, in G
with L. Kentner pf

Electrola E90144
HMV ALP1376, FALP425,
QALP10178

No. 3. Sonata No. 8, in G
with W. Kempff pf

Deutsche Grammophon 2530
135, (in set 2720 018)

* Unissued.

BEETHOVEN – *Continued*

Sonata No. 9, in A, Op. 47 "Kreutzer" vln & pf
2EA 553☐, II 554–5, 555[1]☐,   HMV DB2409/12, DB7815/8
556☐, II 557–3A, 558[II]☐ & 559/60   Victor 8642/5, 8646/9, (set
with H. Menuhin pf   ☐II M260), 17007/10

Sonata No. 9, in A, Op. 47 "Kreutzer" vln & pf
with L. Kentner pf   Electrola E90144
                            HMV ALP1376, FALP425,
                            QALP10178
                            Victor LHMV10

Sonata No. 9, in A, Op. 47 "Kreutzer" vln & pf
M 177/83–I & 184–II   Victor SD3042/5, (set JAS218)
with A. Baller pf

Sonata No. 9, in A, Op. 47 "Kreutzer" vln & pf*
with H. Menuhin pf   Capitol G7246, SG7246
                            Electrola 1C063–00170, E80549,
                            STE80549
                            Eterna 820491
                            HMV ALP1739, ASD389,
                            ASDQ5301, CSDW7070,
                            QALP10311, WCLP701

Sonata No. 9, in A, Op. 47 "Kreutzer" vln & pf
with W. Kempff pf   Deutsche Grammophon 2530
                            135, 2810 008, (in set 2720 018)

Sonata No. 10, in G, Op. 96 vln & pf
with H. Menuhin   2EA 6623/8[1]☐   HMV DB3585/7
pf

Sonata No. 10, in G, Op. 96 vln & pf
with H. Menuhin   2EA 11812/7–1   HMV DB6495/7, DB9234/6
pf

Sonata No. 10, in G, Op. 96 vln & pf
with L. Kentner pf   Electrola E90068
                            HMV ALP1105, FALP424,
                            QALP10164

Sonata No. 10, in G, Op. 96 vln & pf
with H. Menuhin pf   Electrola E80562, STE80562
                            HMV ALP1959, ASD510,
                            ASDF281, FALP745

Sonata No. 10, in G, Op. 96 vln & pf
with W. Kempff pf   Deutsche Grammophon 643672,
                            (in set 2720 018)

(2) Trios, Op. 70 pf, vln & vlc
No. 1. Trio No. 4, in D "Ghost"
2LA 973/7[1]☐ & 978[II]☐   HMV DB2879/81
with H. Menuhin pf & M. Eisenberg   Victor 14442/4, 14445/7, (set
vlc   M370)

No. 1. Trio No. 4, in D "Ghost"
with H. Menuhin pf & M. Gendron   Electrola SME80905
vlc   HMV ALP2258, ASD2258,
                                  ASDF880, FALP880

No. 2. Trio No. 5, in E flat
with H. Menuhin pf & M. Gendron   Electrola SME80905
vlc   HMV ALP2258, ASD2258,
                                  ASDF880, FALP880

(12) Variations in F (on the aria "Se vuol ballare" from the opera "Le
Nozze di Figaro" by Mozart) G156 vln & pf
with W. Kempff pf   Deutsche Grammophon 643669,
                           (in set 2720 018)

* Presto or 3rd mvt is on Electrola SHZE103.

BERG
Concerto (1935) vln & orch.
with BBC Symphony Orch. – Boulez   Electrola SME91789
                                   HMV 2C063–01855, ASD2449

BERLIOZ
Harold in Italy, Op. 16 vla & orch.
playing vla with Philharmonia orch. –   Angel 36123
Davis   Electrola E91309, STE91309
                                         HMV ALP1986, ASD537,
                                         ASDF782, FALP782,
                                         QALP10370

Rêverie & Caprice, Op. 8 vln & orch.
with Philharmonia Orch. – Pritchard   Capitol P8667, SP8667
                                      HMV ALP2070, ASD618,
                                      ASDF847, CVA847, FALP847

BLOCH
Abodah (1929) "God's worship" vln & pf*
with H. Endt pf   2EA 7659[1]☐   HMV DB3782, DB6139
                                   Victor 15887

Baal Shem (3 Pictures of Chassidic life) (1923) vln & pf
No. 2. Nigun (Improvisation)
with L. Persinger pf   A 49849/50△   HMV DB1283
                                     Victor 7108

BOULANGER, L.
Cortège (1919) vln & pf
with C. Curzon pf   HMV CVC2077

Nocturne in F (1911) vln & pf
with C. Curzon pf   HMV CVC2077

(D') Un Matin de printemps (1922) vln or fl & pf
with C. Curzon pf   HMV CVC2077

BRAHMS
Concerto in D, Op. 77 (cadenza by Kreisler) vln & orch.
with Lucerne   2ZA 63/71–1A   Electrola E90013
Festival Orch. – Furtwängler   HMV DB9444/8S, DB21000/4S,
                                    FALP122, FALP30001,
                                    QALP122, WLP524
                                    Plaisir Musical 30001
                                    Victor 12–1161/5, (set DM1361),
                                    49–1077/81, (set WDM1361),
                                    LM1142, LS2002

Concerto in D, Op. 77 (cadenza by Kreisler) vln & orch.
with Berlin Philharmonic Orch. –   Capitol PAO8410, SG7173
Kempe   Electrola E90017, STE90017
                                   HMV ALP1568, ASD264,
                                   ASDL758, ASDQ5275,
                                   CVB1595, FALP595, FALP758,
                                   QALP10284, WALP528,
                                   WDLP528

(21) Hungarian Dances pf duet
Hungarian dance No. 1, in g arr. vln & pf Joachim
with M. Gazelle pf   OLA 837[1]☐   HMV DA1491
                                   Victor 2010

Hungarian dance No. 4, in f sharp arr. vln & pf "in b" Joachim
with M. Gazelle pf   2LA 927[1]☐   HMV DB2922
                                   Victor 14905

* Excerpts on Electrola E91475 & HMV FLAP896 & HQM1018.

BRAHMS – *Continued*

Hungarian dance No. 4, in f sharp arr. vln & pf "in b" Joachim
with T. Saidenberg pf
Victor 12–1161, (in set
DM1361), 49–1077, (in set
WDM1361)

Hungarian dance No. 5, in f sharp arr. vln & pf "in g" Joachim
with A. Baller pf
Victor SF703

Hungarian dance No. 6, in D flat arr. vln & pf "in B flat" Joachim
with M. Gazelle pf   2EA 562[II]□   HMV DB2413
Victor 8866

Hungarian dance No. 7, in A arr. vln & pf Joachim
with M. Gazelle pf   OLA 839[I]□   Electrola E91475
HMV DA1482, FALP89
HQM1018

Hungarian dance No. 11, in d arr. vln & pf Joachim
with F. Webster pf   2EA 6150[I]□   HMV DB3500

Hungarian dance No. 12, in d arr. vln & pf Joachim
with F. Webster pf   OEA 6149[III]□   HMV DA1636

Hungarian dance No. 17, in f sharp arr. vln & pf Joachim
with M. Gazelle pf   OLA 838[II]□   HMV DA1491
Victor 2010

Sextet No. 1, in B flat, Op. 18 2 vlns, 2 vlas & 2 vlcs
with R. Masters vln, C. Aronowitz vla,   Angel 36234, (in set 3727)
E. Wallfisch vla, M. Gendron vlc & D.   Electrola 1C061–00234, E80758,
Simpson vlc   STE80758
HMV ALP2038, ASD587,
ASDF819, ASDQ5417, CVA819,
FALP819

Sextet No. 2, in G, Op. 36 2 vlns, 2 vlas & 2 vlcs
with R. Masters vln, C. Aronowitz vla,   Electrola E80903, SME80903
E. Wallfisch vla, M. Gendron vlc & D.   HMV ALP2096, ASD643,
Simpson vlc   ASDF871, CVA871, FALP871,
QALP10406

Sonata No. 1, in G, Op. 78 vln & pf
with H. Menuhin pf
HMV DB5798/801
Victor 11–8732/5, 11–8736/9,
(set M987)

Sonata No. 1, in G, Op. 78 vln & pf
with L. Kentner pf
Capitol (in set GBR7142)
Electrola E80563, STE80563
HMV ALP1906, ASD474

Sonata No. 2, in A, Op. 100 vln & pf
with H. Menuhin pf
Victor SD3001/3, (set JAS164)

Sonata No. 2, in A, Op. 100 vln & pf
with L. Kentner pf
Capitol (in set GBR7142)
Electrola E80563, STE80563
HMV ALP1906, ASD474

Sonata No. 3, in d, Op. 108 vln & pf
with H. Menuhin pf
HMV DB2832/4

Sonata No. 3, in d, Op. 108 vln & pf
  2EA 11785–2, 11786/7–1, 11788   HMV DB6441/3, DB9103/5
with H. Menuhin pf –2 & 11789/90–1

Sonata No. 3, in d, Op. 108 vln & pf
with L. Kentner pf
Capitol (in set GBR7142)
HMV ALP1907, ASD475

Sonata No. 3, in d, Op. 108 vln & pf
with H. Menuhin pf
Capitol G7215, SG7215

BRAHMS – *Continued*

Sonata (1853) "Frei aber Einsam" vln & pf
Allegro (Scherzo) in c (3rd mvt) "Sonatensatz"
with H. Menuhin pf
Angel 36234, (in set 3727)
Electrola 1C061–00234, E80758,
STE80758
HMV ALP2038, ASD587,
ASDF819, CVA819, FALP819

Trio No. 2, in C, Op. 87 pf, vln & vlc
with H. Menuhin pf & M. Gendron
vlc
Angel 36472
Electrola SME91714
HMV ALP2354, ASD2354

Trio in E flat, Op. 40 hrn, pf & vln
with A. Civil hrn & H. Menuhin pf
Angel 36472
Electrola SME91714
HMV ALP2354, ASD2354

BRANDL

(Der) Liebe Augustin – operetta
Du alter Stefansturm arr. vln & pf as "The old refrain" by Kreisler
with A. Baller pf
Victor ERA259

BRUCH

Concerto No. 1, in g, Op. 26 vln & orch.
  2B 2022/3[II], 2024–3 & 2025/7[I]   HMV DB1611/3, DB7230/2
with London Symphony Orch. –   Victor 7509/11, 7512/4, (set
Ronald   M124), 16574/6

Concerto No. 1, in g, Op. 26 vln & orch.
with San Francisco Symphony Orch. –   Victor 11–8951/3, 11–8954/6,
Monteux   (set M1023)

Concerto No. 1, in g, Op. 26 vln & orch.
with Boston Symphony Orch. –   HMV DB21415/7, FBLP1016
Munch   Victor (set WDM1547), LM122,
LM1797

Concerto No. 1, in g, Op. 26 vln & orch.*
with Philharmonia Orch. – Susskind   Capitol G7148, SG7148
Electrola 1C063–00156, E70423,
E91055, STE91055
Eterna 820463
HMV ALP1669, ASD334,
ASDQ5293, ASDW334,
CVB612, FALP612, QALP10257

CHAUSSON

Concerto in D, Op. 21 vln, pf & str qt
with L. Kentner pf & Pascal String   HMV ALP1285, FALP353
Quartet   Victor LHMV30

Poème, Op. 25 vln & orch.
with Paris   2PG 855/8[II]△   HMV DB1961/2
Symphony Orch. – Enescu   Victor 7913/4

Poème, Op. 25 vln & orch.
  2EA 16299–4C, 16300–3D,   HMV DB9759/60, DB21512/3
16301–2C & 16302–4C
with London Philharmonic Orch. –
Boult

* Adagio or 2nd mvt is on Electrola E41131, SHZE103 & HMV
7EGW8597.

CHAUSSON – *Continued*

Poème, Op. 25 vln & orch.
  with Philharmonia Orch. – Pritchard   Capitol P8667, SP8667
       Electrola (in set SME2035/6)
       HMV ALP2070, ASD618,
       ASDF847, CVA847, FALP847

COPLAND

Sonata (1943) vln & pf
  Lento (2nd mvt)
  with M. Gazelle pf   2EA 18804–1   HMV HLP27, HMS113
       Victor (in set LM6092)

CORELLI

(12) Concerti grossi, Op. 6 orch.
  Concerto grosso No. 2, in F
  with R. Masters vln, D. Simpson vlc &   Angel 36303
  Bath Festival Orch. – Menuhin   Electrola SME91462
       HMV ALP2090, ASD637

(12) Sonatas, Op. 5 vln & c
  Sonata No. 12, in d "La Follia" arr. vln & pf Léonard
       Cc 20557^{III}△ & 20558^{I}△   HMV DB1501
  with H. Giesen pf
  Sonata No. 12, in d "La Follia" arr. vln & pf Léonard
  with G. Moore pf   Victor LHMV10

DEBUSSY

(12) Préludes – Book I (1910) pf
  No. 8. La Fille aux cheveux de lin arr. vln & pf Hartmann
  with M. Gazelle pf   OLA 787^{I}□   HMV DA1499
  No. 8. La Fille aux cheveux de lin arr. vln & pf Hartmann
  with A. Baller pf   Victor 10–1220
  No. 8. La Fille aux cheveux de lin arr. vln & pf Hartmann
  with G. Moore pf   OEA 16859–1A   Angel 292705
       HMV DA2023
       Victor LHMV22
  No. 8. La Fille aux cheveux de lin arr. vln & pf Hartmann
  with G. Moore pf   Angel 36640, 1C065–01961
       HMV SAN255
  No. 12. Minstrels arr. vln & pf Hartmann
  with A. Balsam pf   OL 325^{I}△   HMV DA1280

DELIBES

Coppélia (1870) – ballet orch.
  No. 5. Ballade de l'Épi (Act I)
  with Philharmonia Orch. – Irving   Capitol G7245, SG7245
       HMV ALP1869, ASD439

Sylvia (1876) – ballet orch.
  Pas de deux (Act III)
  with Philharmonia Orch. – Irving   Capitol G7245, SG7245
       HMV ALP1869, ASD439

DELIUS

Hassan (1920) – Incidental music orch.
  Serenade arr. vln & pf
  with M. Gazelle pf   Victor LM2014

DINICU

Hora staccato vln & pf – arr. Heifetz
  with H. Endt pf   OEA 7661^{III}□   HMV DA1685

DVOŘÁK

Concerto in a, Op. 53 vln & orch.
       2LA 935/8^{I}□ & 947/9^{I}□   HMV DB2838/41, DB8074/7
  with Paris Conservatory Orch. –   Victor 14518/21S, 14522/5S, (set
  Enescu   M387)

(7) Gypsy songs, Op. 55 v & pf
  No. 4. Songs my mother taught me arr. vln & pf Persinger
  with M. Gazelle pf   OLA 786^{II}□   HMV DA1499
  No. 4. Songs my mother taught me arr. vln & pf Kreisler
  with G. Moore pf   2EA 17745–1C   HMV DB21608, 7R176,
       7RQ3035

(8) Slavonic Dances, Op. 46 pf duet; orch.
  No. 2. Slavonic dance No. 2, in e arr. vln & pf "in g" Kreisler
  with M. Gazelle pf   OLA 925^{I}□   HMV DA1506
  No. 2. Slavonic dance No. 2, in e arr. vln & pf "in g" Kreisler
  with A. Baller pf   Victor EP3043, LS2004, SD3038,
       (in set JAS206)

(8) Slavonic Dances, Op. 72 pf duet; orch.
  No. 2. Slavonic dance No. 10, in e arr. vln & pf Kreisler
  with M. Gazelle pf   2LA 926^{I}□   HMV DB2922
       Victor 14905

Symphony No. 9, in e, Op. 95 "From the New World" orch.
  Largo (2nd mvt) arr. vln & pf as "Negro spiritual melody" by Kreisler
  with M. Gazelle pf   2LA 791^{II}□   HMV DB2856
       Victor 15369
  Largo (2nd mvt) arr. vln & pf as "Negro spiritual melody" by Kreisler
  with M. Gazelle pf   2EA 9991^{I}□   HMV DB6158
  Largo (2nd mvt) arr. vln & pf as "Negro spiritual melody" by Kreisler
  with A. Baller pf   Victor (in set WDM1742),
       EP3043, LM1742, LS2004,
       SD3046

ELGAR

Concerto in b, Op. 61 vln & orch.*
     2B 2968/9^{IIA}, 2970^{IA}, 2971^{IIA},   Electrola E80480
  2972^{IA}, 2973^{IIA}, 2974/5^{IA}, 2976^{IIA},   HMV ALP1456, DB1751/6,
     2977^{IA}, 2978^{I}& 2979^{II} DB7175/80, WCLP609
  with London Symphony Orch. – Elgar   Victor 7747/52, 7753/8, (set
       M174), 17156/61

Concerto in b, Op. 61 vln & orch.
  with New Philharmonia Orch. – Boult   Angel 36330
       HMV ALP2259, ASD2259

Salut d'amour, Op. 12 orch. – arr. vln & pf Elgar
  with A. Baller pf   Victor 10–1220

ENESCU

Sonata No. 3, in a, Op. 25 (1926) "In the popular Rumanian style" vln &
  pf†
       2LA 799/803–1□ & 804–2□   HMV DB2739/41
  with H. Menuhin pf   Victor 14107/9, 14110/2, (set
       M318), 16892/4

---

* Extract from Allegro or 1st mvt. on Electrola E91475 & HMV FALP896
   & HQM1018.

† Extract from Moderato malinconico or 1st mvt. on Electrola E91475 &
   HMV FALP896 & HQM1018.

ENESCU – *Continued*

Sonata No. 3, in a, Op. 25 (1926) "In the popular Rumanian style" vln & pf
  with H. Menuhin pf
Angel 36418
Electrola 1C061–00774, SHZE230
HMV ALP2294, ASD2294, CVA925, CVB1925

FALLA

(La) Vida Breve (1913) – opera
  Danza española orch. – arr. vln & pf Kreisler
  with A. Balsam pf   OL 324^{II}△   HMV DA1280
Orion OR7271

  Danza española orch. – arr. vln & pf Kreisler
  with G. Moore pf
Victor LHMV22

FAURÉ

Andante in B flat, Op. 75 vln & pf
  with J. Menuhin pf   HMV HQS1245
Berceuse, Op. 16 vln & pf
  with J. Menuhin pf   HMV HQS1245
Quartet No. 1, in c, Op. 15 pf, vln, vla & vlc
  with J. Menuhin pf, E. Wallfisch vla &   HMV HQS1245
  M. Gendron vlc
Sonata No. 1, in A, Op. 13 vln & pf
  Allegro molto (1st mvt)
  with M. Gazelle pf   2EA 18802/3–1   HMV HLP24, HMS98
Victor (in set LM6153)

FIOCCO

Suite No. 1, in G hpsi
  Allegro (10th mvt) arr. vln & pf Bent & O'Neill
  with L. Persinger pf   PB 42091△   HMV DA1003
Victor 1329

FRANCK

Sonata in A (1886) vln & pf*
  2LA 805/9^I□, 810^{II}□ & 811/2^I   HMV DB2742/5, DB8035/8
  with H. Menuhin pf   □
Sonata in A (1886) vln & pf
  with L. Kentner pf
Electrola E70043
HMV BLP1082, WBLP1082
Sonata in A (1886) vln & pf
  with H. Menuhin pf
Capitol G7215, SG7215
Electrola 1C061–00774

GRANADOS

(12) Danzas españolas, Op. 37 (1893) pf
  No. 5. Danza española No. 5, in e "Andaluza" arr. vln & pf Kreisler
  with F. Webster pf   2EA 6152^I□   HMV DB3500
Orion OR7271

  No. 5. Danza española No. 5, in e "Andaluza" arr. vln & pf Kreisler
  with G. Moore pf
Victor LM1742

  No. 5. Danza española No. 5, in e "Andaluza" arr. vln & pf Kreisler
  with A. Baller pf
Victor LS2004, SD3049, (in set JAS230)

* Extract from Allegretto poco mosso or 4th mvt. on Electrola E91475 & HMV FALP896 & HQM1018.

GREEN

Romance (on a theme by Paganini) (1946) vln & pf*
  with G. Moore pf   OEA 10535–1   HMV DA1861, 7R104, 7RW121
Victor 10–1459

GRIEG

Sonata No. 1, in F, Op. 8 vln & pf
  with R. Levin pf   HMV ALP1712
Sonata No. 2, in G, Op. 13 vln & pf
  with R. Levin pf   HMV ALP1712
Sonata No. 3, in c, Op. 45 vln & pf
  with R. Levin pf   HMV ALP1712

HANDEL

(12) Concerti grossi, Op. 6 (1739) 2 vlns, vlc & strs
  Concerto grosso No. 1, in G
  with R. Masters vln, D. Simpson vlc,
  G. Malcolm hpsi, R. Jesson org &
  Bath Festival Orch. – Menuhin
Angel 36201, (in set 3647)
Electrola E91371, STE91371
HMV ALP2055, ASD604, ASDF827, CVA827, FALP827

  Concerto grosso No. 2, in F
  with R. Masters vln, D. Simpson vlc,
  G. Malcolm hpsi, R. Jesson org &
  Bath Festival Orch. – Menuhin
Angel 36201/2, (in set 3647)
Electrola E91371, STE91371
HMV ALP2055, ASD604, ASDF827, CVA827, FALP827

  Concerto grosso No. 3, in e
  with R. Masters vln, D. Simpson vlc,
  G. Malcolm hpsi, R. Jesson org &
  Bath Festival Orch. – Menuhin
Angel 36202, (in set 3647)
Electrola E91372, STE91372
HMV ALP2049, ASD598, ASDF827, CVA827, FALP827
World Record Club ST944

  Concerto grosso No. 4, in a
  with R. Masters vln, D. Simpson vlc,
  G. Malcolm hpsi, R. Jesson org &
  Bath Festival Orch. – Menuhin
Angel 36203, (in set 3647)
Electrola E91371, STE91371
HMV ALP2055, ASD604, ASDF827, CVA827, FALP827

  Concerto grosso No. 5, in D
  with R. Masters vln, D. Simpson vlc,
  K. Anderson hpsi, R. Jesson org &
  Bath Festival Orch. – Menuhin
Angel 36203/4, (in set 3647)
Electrola E91371, STE91371
HMV ALP2055, ASD604, ASDF828, CVA828, FALP828

  Concerto grosso No. 6, in g
  with R. Masters vln, D. Simpson vlc,
  K. Anderson hpsi, R. Jesson org &
  Bath Bestival Orch. – Menuhin
Angel 36204, (in set 3647)
Electrola E91372, STE91372
HMV ALP2049, ASD598, ASDF828, CVA828, FALP828
World Record Club ST944

  Concerto grosso No. 7, in B flat
  with R. Masters vln, D. Simpson vlc,
  K. Anderson hpsi, R. Jesson org &
  Bath Festival Orch. – Menuhin
Angel 36204, (in set 3647)
Electrola E91220, E91373, STE91373
HMV ALP1927, ASD491, ASDF828, CVA828, FALP828, QALP10353

* Theme from the 1st mvt. of Paganini's Concerto No. 1, in D. Featured in the 1946 J. Arthur Rank film "The Magic Bow".

HANDEL – *Continued*

Concerto grosso No. 8, in c
with R. Masters vln, D. Simpson vlc,
K. Anderson hpsi, R. Jesson org &
Bath Festival Orch. – Menuhin

Angel 36203/4, (in set 3647)
Electrola E91220, E91373,
STE91373
HMV ALP1927, ASD491,
ASDF828, CVA828, FALP828,
QALP10353

Concerto grosso No. 9, in F
with R. Masters vln, D. Simpson vlc,
K. Anderson hpsi, R. Jesson org &
Bath Festival Orch. – Menuhin

Angel 36203, (in set 3647)
Electrola E91220, E91373,
STE91373
HMV ALP1927, ASD491,
ASDF829, CVA829, FALP829,
QALP10353

Concerto grosso No. 10, in d
with R. Masters vln, D. Simpson vlc,
K. Anderson hpsi, R. Jesson org &
Bath Festival Orch. – Menuhin

Angel 36202, (in set 3647)
Electrola E91372, STE91372
HMV ALP2049, ASD598,
ASDF829, CVA829, FALP829
World Record Club ST944

Concerto grosso No. 11, in A
with R. Masters vln D. Simpson vlc,
K. Anderson hpsi, R. Jesson org &
Bath Festival Orch. – Menuhin

Angel 36201/2, (in set 3647)
Electrola E91220, E91373,
STE91373
HMV ALP1927, ASD491,
ASDF829, CVA829, FALP829,
QALP10353

Concerto grosso No. 12, in b
with R. Masters vln, D. Simpson vlc,
K. Anderson hpsi, R. Jesson org &
Bath Festival Orch. – Menuhin

Angel 36201, (in set 3647)
Electrola E91372, STE91372
HMV ALP2049, ASD598,
ASDF829, CVA829, FALP829
World Record Club ST944

Concerto in B flat vln, strs & c
with Menuhin Festival Orch. –
Menuhin

Angel 36604
Electrola 1C063–01962
HMV ASD2485

Serse (1738) – opera
Ombra mai fu "Largo" arr. v, vln & pf
with R. Merrill b & C. Hollister pf

Victor (in set WDM1703),
LM1703

(15) Sonatas, Op. 1 (?1731) fl or vln & c
Sonata No. 3, in A vln I
with G. Malcolm hpsi & A. Gauntlett
gamba

HMV ALP2384, ASD2384,
CVB2176

Sonata No. 10, in g vln II
with G. Malcolm hpsi & A. Gauntlett
gamba

HMV ALP2384, ASD2384,
CVB2176

Sonata No. 12, in F vln III
with G. Malcolm hpsi & A. Gauntlett
gamba

HMV ALP2384, ASD2384,
CVB2176

Sonata No. 13, in D vln IV
2EA 10289^{III}□, 10290^{II}□;   HMV DB6175/6, ED427/8
10291^{I}□ & 10292^{II}□
with M. Gazelle pf

Sonata No. 13, in D: Largo (1st mvt); **Allegro** (2nd mvt) vln IV
with G. Moore pf   HMV 7EP7178

HANDEL – *Continued*

Sonata No. 13, in D vln IV
with G. Malcolm hpsi & A. Gauntlett
gamba

HMV ALP2384, ASD2384,
CVB2176

Sonata No. 14, in A vln V
with G. Malcolm hpsi & A. Gauntlett
gamba

HMV ALP2384, ASD2384,
CVB2176

Sonata No. 15, in E vln VI
2EA 7657^{III}□ & 7658–2   HMV DB3816
with H. Endt pf   Victor 16450

Sonata No. 15, in E vln VI
with G. Malcolm hpsi & A. Gauntlett
gamba

HMV ALP2384, ASD2384,
CVB2176

(9) Sonatas, Op. 2 (1724) 2 vlns or 2 obs & c
Sonata No. 8, in g
with G. De Vito vln, R. Leppard hpsi   HMV ALP1462, 7ERL1429
& J. Shinebourne vlc

(7) Sonatas, Op. 5 (1739) 2 vlns & c
Sonata No. 2, in D
with G. De Vito vln, G. Malcolm hpsi   Electrola E50554
& J. Shinebourne vlc   HMV BLP1046, FBLP1061,
                              LBLP1017, QBLP5028,
                              7ERW5390
                              Victor LHMV16

Te Deum, Dettingen (1743)
No. 17. Gebet ('Verlich uns Herr, zu schirmen ...) arr. vln & pf as
"Prayer" by Flesch
with L. Persinger pf   A 49847△   HMV DB1284
                              Victor 6951

No. 17. Gebet ('Verlich uns Herr, zu schirmen ...) arr. vln & pf as
"Prayer" by Flesch
with G. Moore pf   OEA 16858–2A   Angel 292705
                              HMV DA2023
                              Victor LM2014

HAYDN

Concerto No. 1, in C, H.VIIa, No. 1 (1765) (cadenzas by Menuhin) vln &
orch.
with Bath Festival Orch. – Menuhin   Angel 36190
                              Electrola E91243, STE91243
                              HMV ALP2017, ASD567,
                              ASDF791, FALP791

HINDEMITH

Schulwerk, Op. 44 (1927) var. inst
No. 4. 5 Pieces in the first position for more advanced players*
with Bath Festival Orch. – Menuhin   Angel 36335
                              Electrola SME91474
                              HMV ALP2255, ASD2255

KREISLER

Caprice viennois, Op. 2 vln & pf
with M. Gazelle pf   OLA 924^{1}□   HMV DA1506
                              Victor 26572

Caprice viennois, Op. 2 vln & pf
with M. Gazelle pf   OEA 9992^{1}□   HMV DA1832

* 5th piece only – "Lebhaft".

KREISLER – *Continued*

Caprice viennois, Op. 2 vln & pf
with A. Baller pf   Victor (in set WDM1742),
ERA259, LM1742, SD3049, (in
set JAS230)

Liebesleid vln & pf
with A. Baller pf   Victor ERA259

Recitative & Scherzo–Caprice, Op. 6 solo vln
(unaccompanied)   2B 2354[II]   HMV DB1787

Schön Rosmarin vln & pf
with M. Gazelle pf   OLA 788[III]☐   Electrola E91475
HMV DA1489, FALP896,
HQM1018

Schön Rosmarin vln & pf
with A. Baller pf   Victor ERA259

Tambourin chinois, Op. 3 vln & pf
with M. Gazelle pf   OLA 792[I]☐   HMV DA1489

(La) Chasse (Cartier) vln & pf
with M. Gazelle pf   OLA 785[II]☐   HMV DA1494

Praeludium & Allegro (Pugnani) vln & pf
OLA 842[II]☐ & 843[I]☐   HMV DA1490
with M. Gazelle pf   Victor 1863

Sicilienne & Rigaudon (Francoeur) vln & pf
with A. Balsam pf   OL 321[II]△   HMV DA1282

LALO

Symphonie espagnole, Op. 21 vln & pf*
   2PG 847[II]△, 848[III]△, 849/50[II]△   HMV DB1999/2002, DB7582/5
with Paris   851[I], & 852/4[II],   Victor 7943/6, 7947/50, (set
Symphony Orch. – Enescu   M136), 16577/80

Symphonie espagnole, Op. 21 vln & orch.*
   2LA 4894–2, 4895–1, 4901–2,   HMV DB6608/11, DB9209/12,
   4896–3 & 4897/900–1   FALP107
with L'Orchestre des Concerts Colonne   Victor 12–0210/3, 12–0214/7,
– Fournet   (set DM1207), LM1011,
LVT1022, (set WDM1207)

Symphonie espagnole, Op. 21 vln & orch.*
with Philharmonia Orch. – Goossens   Capitol G7108, SG7108
HMV ALP1571, ASD290,
CVA556

LECLAIR

(12) Sonatas, Op. 9 – Book IV (1738) vln & c
Sonata No. 3, in D: Sarabande (1st mvt); **Tambourin** (3rd mvt) arr. vln &
pf Sarasate
with L. Persinger pf   A 49852△   HMV DB1295
Victor 7182

LEKEU

Sonata in G (1892) vln & pf
with H. Menuhin   2EA 6164/71[I]☐   HMV DB3492/5
pf   Victor 15488/91, 15492/5, (set
M579), 16073/6

Sonata in G (1892) vln & pf
with M. Gazelle pf   Victor LM2014

* Including Intermezzo.

LOCATELLI

(24) Caprices, Op. 3 solo vln
Caprice No. 23, in D "Il laberinto armonico" arr. vln & pf as "Le
Labyrinthe" by David
with F. Webster pf   OEA 6151[I]☐   HMV DA1636

MENDELSSOHN

Concerto in d (1822) vln & strs
with RCA Victor String Orch. –   Victor (set WDM1720), LM1720
Menuhin

Concerto in d (1822) vln & strs
with Philharmonia Orch. – Boult   Angel LPC11546
Electrola E90057
HMV ALP1085, FALP300,
LALP545

Concerto in e, Op. 64 vln & orch.
with L'Orchestre   2LA 2466/72[I]☐   HMV DB3555/8, DB8586/9,
des Concerts Colonne – Enescu   DB6012/5S
Victor 15320/3S, 15321/4, (set
M531), 16169/72

Concerto in e, Op. 64 vln & orch.
with Berlin Philharmonic Orch. –   Angel LPC11582
Furtwängler   Electrola E60546
HMV ALP1135, FALP312,
LALP125, QALP10071,
WDLP602
Kristal SMVP8040
Victor LM1720, (set WDM1720)

Concerto in e, Op. 64 vln & orch.
with London Philharmonic Orch. –   Capitol G7148, SG7148
Kurtz   Electrola 1C063–00156, (in set
SME2035/6), E70423, E91055,
STE91055
Eterna 820430
HMV ALP1669, ASD334,
ASDW334, CVB612, FALP612

Sonata in F (1838) vln & pf
with G. Moore pf   Angel LPC11546
Electrola E90057
HMV ALP1085, FALP300,
LALP545, WALP1085
Victor LHMV1071

MONASTERIO

Sierra Morena vln & pf
with L. Persinger pf   Pc 42090△   HMV DB1267
Victor 6841

MONSIGNY

Aline, Reine de Golconde (1766) – opera
Rigaudon arr. vln & pf Franko
with H. Giesen pf   Bb 20556△[II]   HMV DA1196

MOSZKOWSKI

(2) Stücke, Op. 45 pf
No. 2. Guitarre arr. vln & pf Sarasate
with A. Balsam pf   OL 317[II]△   HMV DA1282

MOZART

Concerto No. 1, in B flat, K207 (cadenzas by Menuhin) vln & orch.
with Bath Festival Orch. – Menuhin   Angel 36231
Electrola E91142, SME18003,
STE91142
HMV ALP2042, ASDF823,
ASD591, CVB1823, FALP823

Concerto No. 2, in D, K211 (cadenzas by Menuhin) vln & orch.
with Bath Festival Orch. – Menuhin   Angel 36231
Electrola E91142, SME18003,
STE91142
HMV ALP2042, ASD591,
ASDF823, CVB1823, FALP823

Concerto No. 3, in G, K216 vln & orch.
Adagio (2nd mvt)
with L. Persinger pf   A 49851△   HMV DB1295
Victor 7182

Concerto No. 3, in G, K216 (cadenzas by Franko) vln & orch.
2LA 773/4[1]☐, 775[II]☐, 776[I]☐   HMV DB2729/31, DB8184/6
with Paris Symphony   & 777/8[II]☐   Victor 15078/80, 15081/3, (set
Orch. – Enescu   M485), 16283/5

Concerto No. 3, in G, K216 vln & orch.
Adagio (2nd mvt)*
(unaccompanied)   Capitol HBZ21002
Electrola E70469, STE70469
HMV ASDF274, CLP1523,
FALP738, 7EG8672, 7EGY150

Concerto No. 3, in G, K216 (cadenzas by Franko) vln & orch.
with Bath Festival Orch. – Menuhin   Angel 35745
Electrola E91140, SME18004,
STE91140
Eterna 820462
HMV ALP1905, ASD473,
ASDF736, ASDW473, CVB1736,
FALP736, WALP1905

Concerto No. 4, in D, K218 (cadenzas by Menuhin) vln & orch.
with Liverpool   2ER 701/6–1☐   HMV DB6146/8, DB8950/2
Philharmonic Orch. – Sargent

Concerto No. 4, in D, K218 (cadenzas by Menuhin) vln & orch.
with Philharmonia Orch. – Pritchard   Electrola E90112
HMV ALP1281, LALP30002
Victor LM1961
World Record Club T584

Concerto No. 4, in D, K218 (cadenzas by Menuhin) vln & orch.
with Bath Festival Orch. – Menuhin   Angel 36152
Electrola E91141, SME18004,
SME91791, STE91141
HMV ALP1982, ASD533,
ASDF780, CVB1780, FALP780,
QALP10366

Concerto No. 5, in A, K219 "Turkish" (cadenzas by Franko) vln & orch.
with Philharmonia Orch. – Pritchard   Electrola E90112
HMV ALP1281, LALP30002
Victor LM1961
World Record Club T584

* Excerpts only.

MOZART – *Continued*

Concerto No. 5, in A, K219 "Turkish" (cadenzas by Menuhin) vln & orch.
with Bath Festival Orch. – Menuhin   Angel 35745
Electrola E91140, SME18005,
SME91791, STE91140
Eterna 820463
HMV ALP1905, ASD473,
ASDF272, ASDW473, CVB1736,
FALP736, WALP1905

Concerto No. 6, in E flat, K268 (Anh.656)* vln & orch.
with Bath Festival Orch. – Menuhin   Angel 36240
Electrola E91331, SME18005,
STE91331
HMV ALP2043, ASD592,
ASDF830, CVB1830, FALP830

Concerto No. 7, in D, K271a (cadenzas by Enescu) vln & orch.
with orch. – Enescu   2L 374/80[1]△   HMV DB1735/8, DB7157/60
Victor 7734/7, 7738/41, (set
M168), 17075/8

Concerto No. 7, in D, K271a (cadenzas by Enescu) vln & orch.
with Bath Festival Orch. – Menuhin   Angel 36152
Electrola E91141, SME18006,
STE91141
Eterna 820462
HMV ALP1982, ASD533,
ASDF780, CVB1780, FALP780,
QALP10366

Concerto in D, K.Ahn.294a "Princess Adelaide" (cadenzas by Hindemith)
vln & orch.
2PG 1602[II]☐, 1603[1]☐, 1604/6[II]☐   HMV DB2268/70, DB7723/5
with Paris Symphony   ☐ & 1607[1]☐   Victor 8389/91, 8392/4, (set
Orch. – Monteux   M246), 17047/9

Concertone in C, K190 2 vlns, ob, vlc & orch.
with A. Lysy vln & Bath Festival   Angel 36240
Orch. – Menuhin   Electrola E91331, SME18006,
STE91331
HMV ALP2043, ASD592,
ASDF830, CVB1830, FALP830

Divertimento No. 17, in D, K334 2 hrns & strs
Minuet (3rd mvt) arr. vln & pf Kross
with G. Moore pf   OEA 10536–1   HMV DA1861, 7R104, 7RW121
Victor 10–1459

Quartet No. 1, in g, K478 pf, vln, vla & vlc
with F. Ts'ong pf, W. Gerhardt vla &   HMV ALP2319, ASD2319,
G. Cassadó vlc   CVA898

Quartet No. 2, in E flat, K493 pf, vln, vla & vlc
with F. Ts'ong pf, W. Gerhardt vla &   HMV ALP2319, ASD2319,
G. Cassadó vlc   CVA898

Serenade No. 7, in D, K250 "Haffner" orch.
with Bath Festival Orch. – Menuhin   Electrola SME91405
HMV ALP2079, ASD627,
ASDF854, FALP854

Sinfonia concertante in E flat, K364 (cadenzas by Mozart) vln, vla & orch.
with R. Barshai vla & Bath Festival   Angel 36190
Orch. – Menuhin   Electrola E91243, STE91243
HMV ALP2017, ASD567,
ASDF791, FALP791

* Cadenza omitted.

MOZART – *Continued*

Sonata No. 17, in C, K296 vln & pf
Andante sostenuto (2nd mvt)
  with H. Giesen pf   Cc 18171^{II}△   HMV DB1367
                                          Victor 7362

Sonata No. 18, in G, K301 vln & pf
Allegro con spirito (1st mvt)
  with H. Menuhin pf   2EA 6622^I□   HMV DB3582, DB5801
                                          Victor 16106

Sonata No. 20, in C, K303 vln & pf
Tempo di menuetto (2nd mvt)
  with J. Menuhin pf   Electrola E91475
                                          HMV FALP896, HQM1018

Sonata No. 24, in F, K376 vln & pf
               2EA 6172^{II}□ & 6173/5^I□   HMV DB3552/3, ED342/3
  with H. Menuhin pf   Victor 18054/5, 18056/7, (set
                                            M791)

Sonata No. 26, in B flat, K378 vln & pf
Andantino sostenuto e cantabile (2nd mvt)*
  with Y. Menuhin   2EA 6621^{III}□   HMV DB3558, DB8586
  pf   Victor 16106

Sonata No. 32, in B flat, K454 vln & pf
  with L. Kentner pf   Victor LHMV1053

Sonata No. 32, in B flat, K454 vln & pf
  with L. Kentner pf   Capitol G7123
                                          HMV ALP1547

Sonata No. 34, in A, K526 vln & pf
               2PG 878^{IV}△, 879^{VI}△, 880^{III}△ & HMV DB2057/8
  with H. Menuhin pf   881^{VII}△   Victor 8442/3

Sonata No. 34, in A, K526 vln & pf
  with L. Kentner pf   Capitol G7123
                                          HMV ALP1547

Trio No. 4, in E, K542 pf, vln & vlc
  with L. Kentner pf & G. Cassadó vlc   Angel 35630
                                          HMV ALP1849, ASD423

NIELSEN

Concerto in D, Op. 33 (1911) vln & orch.
  with Danish State Radio Orch. –   HMV BLP1025, FBLP1066,
  Woldike   KBLP1
                                          Music for Pleasure MFP2079
                                          Odeon MOAK7
                                          Victor LHMV22

NIN

(20 Cantos de España (1923) v & pf
No. 7. Granadina arr. vln & pf Kochański
  with G. Moore pf   HMV 7EB6017, 7ERL1117
                                          Victor LM2014

No. 18. El Vito arr. vln & pf as "Andaluza" by Kochański
  with H. Endt pf   OEA 7662^I□   HMV DA1685

NOVÁČEK

(8) Concert caprices, Op. 5 vln & pf
No. 4. Perpetuum mobile
  with H. Giesen pf   Bb 20554^{II}△   HMV DA1196

---

* Excerpt on Electrola E91475 & HMV FALP896 & HQM1018.

NOVÁČEK – *Continued*

No. 4. Perpetuum mobile
  with Paris   2PG 1601^{III}□   HMV DB2283, DB7737
  Symphony Orch. – Monteux   Victor 8383, (in set M230),
                                         17079

No. 4. Perpetuum mobile
  with A. Baller pf   Victor LM1742, SF703

No. 4. Perpetuum mobile
  with G. Moore pf   HMV 7EB6017, 7ERL1117

PAGANINI

(24) Caprices, Op. 1 (1801/7) solo vln
Caprice No. 6, in g arr. vln & pf Enescu
  with G. Enescu pf   2LA 919^I□   HMV DB2841
                                          Victor 14228

Caprice No. 6, in g
(unaccompanied)   2EA 18972–2   HMV HLP24, HMS100
                                          Victor (in set LM6153)

Caprice No. 9, in E
(unaccompanied)   2LA 864^{II}□   HMV DB2831*
                                          Victor 14228, 14916, (in set
                                          M451), 16376

Caprice No. 13, in B flat arr. vln & pf Kreisler
  with M. Gazelle pf   OLA 841^I□   HMV DA1500
Caprice No. 20, in D arr. vln & pf Kreisler
  with M. Gazelle pf   OLA 840^I□   HMV DA1500
Caprice No. 23, in E flat
(unaccompanied)   HMV DB2826*

Caprice No. 24, in a arr. vln & pf Kreisler
              OL 318^{II}△ & 320^{II}△   HMV DA1281
  (unaccompanied)   Victor 1650

Concerto No. 1, in D, Op. 6 (cadenza by Sauret) vln & orch.†
                   2PG 1592/600^I□   HMV DB2279/83, DB7737/41
  with Paris Symphony Orch. – Monteux   Victor 8379/83, 8384/8, (set
                                         M230), 17079/83

Concerto No. 1, in D, Op. 6 (cadenza by Sauret) vln & orch.
  with London Symphony Orch. –   Electrola E90139
  Fistoulari   HMV ALP1350, FALP440
                                          Victor LM1946

Concerto No. 1, in D, Op. 6 (cadenza by Sauret) vln & orch.‡
  with Royal Philharmonic Orch. –   Electrola 1C063–00194, E91183,
  Erede   STE91183
                                          HMV ALP1872, ASD440,
                                          CVB1718, WALP1872

Concerto No. 2, in b, Op. 7 vln & orch.
Ronde à la clochette (2nd mvt) "La Campanella" arr. vln & pf Wilhelmj
  with H. Giesen pf   Cc 20553^I△   HMV DB1638, DB5394
                                         Orion OR7271
                                         Victor 7599

---

* Unissued.

† Excerpt from Rondo allegro spiritoso or 3rd mvt. on Electrola E91475 &
  HMV FALP896 & HQM1018.

‡ Allegro maestoso or 1st mvt. is on Electrola SHZE103.

PAGANINI – *Continued*

Concerto No. 2, in b, Op. 7 (cadenza by Baller) vln & orch.*

2EA 15080/5–1 15086–2	Electrola E70026
with Philharmonia Orch. – Fistoulari	HMV BLP1018, DB21245/8S, DB9588S/91, FBLP1006, FBLP25064, LBLP1049, VBLP804, WBLP1018
	Victor LHMV1015

Concerto No. 2, in b, Op. 7 (cadenza by Baller) vln & orch.

with Royal Philharmonic Orch. – Erede	Electrola 1C063–00194, E91183, STE91183
	Eterna 820430
	HMV ALP1872, ASD440, CVB1718, WALP1872

Moto perpetuo (Allegro di concert), Op. 11 (1830) vln & orch.

with M. Gazelle pf 2LA 26□[III]	HMV DB2414
	Orion OR7271
	Victor 8866

Nel cor più non mi sento "Sonata appassionata con variazioni" (on the aria from Paisiello's opera "La bella molinara") Op. 38 (1820 or 1821) solo vln†

(unaccompanied)	
	Capitol HBZ21002
	Electrola E70469, STE70469, STE81475
	HMV ASDF274, CLP1523, FALP738, 7EG8672, 7EGY150

Nel cor più non mi sento "Sonata appassionata con variazioni" (on the aria from Paisiello's opera "La bella molinara") Op. 38 (1820 or 1821) solo vln‡

(unaccompanied)	
	Electrola E91475
	HMV FALP896, HQM1018

Sonata a preghièra "Moses Fantasia" (on the aria "Dal tuo stellato soglio" from Rossini's opera "Mosè in Egitto") Op. 24 (1818 or 1819) vln & orch.

2EA 6147[I]□ & 6148[II]□	HMV DB3499, ED370
with F. Webster pf	Victor 17730

PIZZETTI

Sonata No. 1, in A (1918) vln & pf

with H. Menuhin pf	HMV DB3579/82
	Victor 15721/4S, 15725/8S, (set M615), 16001S/4

PROKOFIEV

Sonata No. 1, in f, Op. 80 (1938/46) vln & pf

2EA 13298–3, 13299–2, 13300–3	HMV DB6845/7, DB9376/8,
with M. Gazelle pf & 13301/3–1	FALP265
	Victor (set DM1403), (set WDM1403)

* Ronde à la clochette or 3rd mvt "La Campanella" is on HMV DB20406.
† Excerpts only.
‡ Opening extract as recorded in 1945 for the film "The Magic Bow". Menuhin recorded the complete Nel cor più for HMV at the height of the film's popularity, but it was not released.

PURCELL

(15) Fantasias, Z731/45 4 & 5 part – orig. viols

Fantasia No. 4, in g, Z735 (1680)

with C. Aronowitz vla, W. Gerhard	Angel 36270
vla & D. Simpson vlc	HMV ALP2088, ASD635, ASDF867, FALP867

Fantasia No. 7, in c, Z738 (1680)

with C. Aronowitz vla, W. Gerhard	Angel 36270
vla & D. Simpson vlc	HMV ALP2088, ASD635, ASDF867, FALP867

Fantasia No. 8, in d, Z739 (1680)

with R. Masters vln, C. Aronowitz vla	Angel 36270
& D. Simpson vlc	HMV ALP2088, ASD635, ASDF867, FALP867

Fantasia No. 11, in G, Z742 (1680)

with R. Masters vln, C. Aronowitz vla	Angel 36270
& D. Simpson vlc	HMV ALP2088, ASD635, ASDF867, FALP867

Fantasia No. 15, in F, Z745 (?1679) "Upon one note"

with R. Masters vln, C. Aronowitz vla,	Angel 36270
W. Gerhard vla & D. Simpson vlc	HMV ALP2088, ASD635, ASDF867, FALP867

(5) Pavanes, Z748/52 (pre–1680) (Nos. 1/4: 3 part: No. 5: 4 part)

Pavane No. 5, in g, Z752 (?1677)

with R. Masters vln, A. Lysy vln, R.	Angel 36270
Jesson cha org & A. Gauntlett gamba	HMV ALP2088, ASD635, ASDF867, FALP867

(12) Sonatas, Z790/801 (1683) 3 part – 2 vlns & c

Sonata No. 6, in C, Z795

with A. Lysy vln, R. Jesson hpsi & A.	Angel 36270
Gauntlett gamba	HMV ALP2088, ASD635, ASDF867, FALP867

Sonata No. 8, in G, Z797

with A. Lysy vln, R. Jesson hpsi & A.	Angel 36270
Gauntlett gamba	HMV ALP2088, ASD635, ASDF867, FALP867

(10) Sonatas, Z802/11 (1697) 4 part – 2 vlns & c

Sonata No. 6, in g, Z807

with A. Lysy vln, R. Jesson hpsi & A.	Angel 36270
Gauntlett gamba	HMV ALP2088, ASD635, ASDF867, FALP867

Sonata No. 9, in F, Z810 "Golden Sonata"

with G. De Vito vln, R. Leppard hpsi	HMV ALP1462, 7ERL1402
& J. Shinebourne vlc	

RACHMANINOV

(6) Songs, Op. 4 v & pf

No. 3. In the silent night arr. v, vln & pf

with R. Merrill b & C. Hollister pf	Victor (in set WDM1703), LM1703

RAVEL

(2) Mélodies hébraïques v & pf

No. 1. Kaddisch arr. vln & pf Garban

with M. Gazelle pf 2LA 928[I]□	HMV DB2873, DB6139
	Victor 15887

No. 1. Kaddisch arr. vln & pf Garban

with G. Moore pf	Victor LHMV 22

Pièce en forme d'Habanera v & pf – arr. vln & pf Catherine

with M. Gazelle pf OEA 9987[I]□	HMV DA1832

RAVEL – *Continued*

Pièce en forme d'Habanera v & pf – arr. vln & pf Catherine
   with A. Baller pf   Victor LM1742, SD3046

Pièce en forme d'Habanera v & pf – arr. vln & pf Catherine
   with G. Moore pf   Angel 36640, 1C065–01961
                          HMV SAN255

Trio in a (1915) pf, vln & vlc
   with L. Kentner pf & G. Cassadó vlc   Angel 35630
                          Electrola E60700, STE60700
                          HMV ALP1849, ASD423,
                          DSDW6032, WDLP692

Tzigane (Rapsodie de concert) (1924) vln & pf or orch.
           2L 316^{II}△ & 319^{II}△   HMV DB1785
   with A. Balsam pf   Victor 7810

RIES

(La) Capricciosa vln & pf
   with L. Persinger pf   PB 42092 △   HMV DA1003
                              Victor 1329

RIMSKY–KORSAKOV

(The) Tale of Tsar Saltan (1900) – opera
   Flight of the bumblebee (Act III) orch. – arr. vln & pf Hartmann
   with A. Balsam pf   OL 325^{I}△   HMV DA1280
                          Orion OR7271

   Flight of the bumblebee (Act III) orch. – arr. vln & pf Hartmann
   with M. Gazelle pf   Victor LM2014

(The) Tsar's Bride (1899) – opera
   Haste thee, mother mine arr. vln & pf as "Song of the bride" by Franko
   with H. Giesen pf   Cc 20555^{II}△   HMV DB1638
                          Victor 7599

SAENGER

(3) Concert Miniatures, Op. 130 vln & pf
   No. 2. Scotch pastorale
   with L. Persinger pf   A 49848△   HMV DB1284
                          Victor 6951

SAINT–SAËNS

Concerto No. 3, in b, Op. 61 vln & orch.
   with Philharmonia Orch. – Poulet   HMV ALP1241, FBLP25041
                                  Victor LHMV1071

Havanaise, Op. 83 vln & orch.
   with Philharmonia Orch. – Goossens   Capitol G7108, SG7108
                                   HMV ALP1571, ASD290,
                                   CVA556
                                   Plaisir Musical 25051

Introduction & Rondo Capriccioso, Op. 28 vln & orch.
   with Philharmonia Orch. – Goossens   Capitol G7108, SG7108
                                   HMV ALP1571, ASD290,
                                   CVA556
                                   Plaisir Musical 25051

SAMAZEUILH

Chant d'Espagne vln & pf
   with L. Persinger pf   A 49853△   HMV DB1301
                          Victor 7317

SARASATE

Caprice basque, Op. 24 vln & pf
   with M. Gazelle pf   2LA 789^{II}□   HMV DB2856
                          Victor 15369, 14531, (in set
                          M388)

(8) Danzas españolas vln & pf
   No. 1. Malagueña, Op. 21, No. 1
   with H. Endt pf   2EA 7660^{IV}□   HMV DB3782
                            Victor 15823

   No. 1. Malagueña, Op. 21, No. 1
   with A. Baller pf   Victor SD3047, (in set JAS230),
                            LS2004

   No. 1. Malagueña, Op. 21, No. 1
   with G. Moore pf   2EA 17597–3B   HMV DB21595, 7EB6017,
                            7ERL1117
                          Victor (in set WDM1742),
                          LM1742

   No. 2. Habañera, Op. 21, No. 2
   with M. Gazelle pf   2LA 790^{II}□   HMV DB2873*
                          Victor 15823

   No. 2. Habañera, Op. 21, No. 2
   with G. Moore pf   2EA 12491   HMV DB6704
                          Victor 12–0922, 49–0404

   No. 2. Habañera, Op. 21, No. 2
   with A. Baller pf   Victor SD3047, (in set JAS230),
                          LS2004

   No. 2. Habañera, Op. 21, No. 2
   with G. Moore pf   2EA 17596–3A   HMV DB21595, 7RF224
                          Victor (in set WDM1742),
                          LM1742

   No. 2. Habañera, Op. 21, No. 2†
   (unaccompanied)   Capitol HBZ21002
                          Electrola E70469, STE70469
                          HMV ASDF274, CLP1523,
                          FALP738, 7EG8672, 7EGY150

   No. 3. Romanza andaluza, Op. 22, No. 1
   with M. Gazelle pf   2EA 561^{II}□   HMV DB2413, DB5395
                          Victor 8695

   No. 3. Romanza andaluza, Op. 22, No. 1
   with A. Baller pf   Victor SD3048, (in set JAS230),
                          LS2004

   No. 3. Romanza andaluza, Op. 22, No. 1
   with A. Baller pf   Victor (in set WDM1742),
                          LM1742

   No. 6. Zapateado, Op. 23, No. 2‡
   with M. Gazelle pf   OLA 836^{I}□   HMV DA1482
                          Victor 26572

SCHUBERT

Fantasia in C, Op. 159 (D934) vln & pf
   with L. Kentner pf   Capitol (in set GBR7142)
                          HMV ALP1907, ASD475

* Unissued.

† Excerpts only.

‡ Excerpts on Electrola E91475 & HMV FALP896 & HQM1018.

SCHUBERT – *Continued*

(7) Gesänge (set to Scott's "Lady of the Lake") Op. 52 v & pf
No. 6. Ave Maria, D839 arr. vln & pf Wilhelmj
with A. Balsam pf   2L 323^{II}△   HMV DB1788, DB5394
           Victor JD86

No. 6. Ave Maria, D839 arr. vln & pf Menuhin
with M. Gazelle pf   2EA 9990^{I}☐   HMV DB6158

No. 6. Ave Maria, D839 arr. vln & pf Menuhin
with G. Moore pf   2EA 17746–3B   HMV DB21608, 7R176,
           7RQ3055

Nocturne in E flat, D897 pf, vln & vlc
with H. Menuhin pf & M. Gendron   Electrola 1C063–01927
vlc   HMV ASD2536

Rondo brillante in b, Op. 70 (D895) vln & pf
with H. Menuhin   2EA 6617/20^{I}☐   HMV DB3583/4
pf   Victor 11–8182/3, 11–8184/5,
           (set M901)

Sonata in B, D28 pf, vln & vlc
with H. Menuhin pf & M. Gendron   Angel 36614
vlc   Electrola 1C063–01926

Sonata in A, Op. 162 (D574) "Duo" vln & pf
with A. Baller pf   Victor (set WDM1593), LM140

(3) Sonatinas, Op. 137 (D384, D385 & D408) vln & pf
No. 1. Sonatina No. 1, in D: Andantino (2nd mvt) D384
with A. Baller pf   Victor (in set WDM1593)

Trio in B flat, D471 ("Sonata" in one movement) vln, vla & vlc
with C. Aronowitz vla & D. Simpson   Electrola E80903, SME80903
vlc   HMV ALP2096, ASD643,
           ASDF871, FALP871,
           QALP10406

Trio No. 1, in B flat, Op. 99 (D898) pf, vln & vlc
with H. Menuhin pf & M. Gendron   Angel 36614
vlc   Electrola 1C063–01926

Trio No. 2, in E flat, Op. 100 (D929) pf, vln & vlc
with H. Menuhin pf & M. Gendron   Electrola 1C063–01927
vlc   HMV ASD2536

SCHUMANN

Concerto in d (1853) vln & orch.
with New York   2A 018860/6△   HMV DB3435/8, DB8448/51
Philharmonic Symphony Orch. –   Victor 14913/6, (set M451),
Barbirolli   16373/6

(3) Romances, Op. 94 ob or vlc or vln or cl & pf
Romance No. 2, in A arr. vln & pf Kreisler
with F. Webster pf   2EA 6146^{I}☐   HMV DB3438
           Orion OR7271

Sonata No. 2, in d, Op. 121 vln & pf
     2PG 1614^{VII}☐, 1615^{III}☐, 1616^{V}
☐, 1617^{II}☐, 1618^{I}☐ & 1619/21^{III}☐   HMV DB2264/7, DB7780/3
     Victor 8403/6, (set M225)
with H. Menuhin pf

SCOTT

Danse nègre, Op. 58, No. 5 pf – arr. vln & pf Kramer
with H. Endt pf   OEA 7662^{I}☐   HMV DA1685

SERRANO

(La) Canción del Olvido (1916) – zarzuela
Canción de Marinella arr. vln & pf Persinger
with L. Persinger pf   A 49854 △   HMV DB1301
           Victor 7317

SHANKAR

Prabhāti (based on Rāga Gunkali) vln & tabla*
with A. Rakha tabla   Angel 36418
           HMV ALP2294, ASD2294,
           CVA925, CVB1925

Rāga Piloo vln, sitar & tabla†
with R. Shankar sitar, A. Rakha tabla   Angel 36026
& K. Chakravarti tamboura   Electrola SHZE247

Swara-Kākāli (based on Rāga Tilang) vln & sitar*
with R. Shankar sitar   Angel 36418
           HMV ALP2294, ASD2294,
           CVA925, CVB1925

SIBELIUS

Concerto in d, Op. 47 vln & orch.
with London Philharmonic Orch. –   Electrola E90139
Boult   HMV ALP1350, FALP440
           Victor LM1946

SPOHR

(3) Duets, Op. 39 2 vlns
No. 1. Duet No. 1, in d: Rondo (3rd mvt) arr. vln & pf Persinger
with L. Persinger pf   A 49854 △   HMV DB1301
           Victor 7317

(3) Duets, Op. 67 2 vlns
No. 2. Duet No. 2, in D: Larghetto (2nd mvt); **Rondo** (3rd mvt)
with G. De Vito vln   HMV ALP1462

No. 3. Duet No. 3, in g: Allegro (1st mvt)
with G. De Vito vln   HMV ALP1462

SZYMANOWSKI

Notturno & Tarantella, Op. 28 vln & pf
with M. Gazelle pf   2LA 781/2^{I}☐   HMV DB2871
           Victor 14383

TARTINI

Sonata in g "Il Trillo del Diavolo" vln & c – arr. vln & pf Kreisler
     2L 313/4^{II}△ & 315–1△   HMV DB1786/7
with A. Balsam pf

Sonata in g "Il Trillo del Diavolo" vln & c – arr. vln & pf Kreisler
with G. Moore pf   Victor (in set WDM1742),
           LM1742

Sonata in g "Il Trillo del Diavolo" vln & c – arr. vln & pf Kreisler
with A. Baller pf   Victor SD3037/8, (set JAS206)

TCHAIKOVSKY

Sleeping Beauty, Op. 66 (1888/9) – ballet orch.
Aurora's variations (Acts I & III)
with Philharmonia Orch. – Kurtz   HMV ALP1790, ASD371,
           CVA681
           Seraphim (in set 6011)

---

* Cadenza in 2nd mvt improvised by Menuhin.

† Composed for the United Nations Human Rights Day concert, December 10th 1967 where it was first performed by Shankar & Menuhin.

TCHAIKOVSKY – *Continued*

Swan Lake, Op. 20 (1875/6) – ballet orch.
  Dance of the queen of the swans
    with Philharmonia Orch. – Kurtz — Capitol G7188, SG7188
      HMV ALP1644, ASD271,
      CVA603
      Seraphim (in set 6011)

  Pas de deux (Act III) "The black swan"
    with Philharmonia Orch. – Kurtz — Capitol G7188, SG7188
      HMV ALP1644, ASD271,
      CVA603
      Seraphim (in set 6011)

  Russian dance
    with Philharmonia Orch. – Kurtz — Capitol G7188, SG7188
      HMV ALP1644, ASD271,
      CVA603
      Seraphim (in set 6011)

Trio in a, Op. 50 "To the memory of a great artist" pf, vln & vlc
      2LA 961/6[1]☐, 967[II]☐ & — HMV DB2887/92S, DB8439/44S
    with H. Menuhin pf   968/71[1]☐ — Victor 14526/31S, 14532/7S, (set
    & M. Eisenberg vlc — M388), 16552S/7

Trio in a, Op. 50 "To the memory of a great artist" pf, vln & vlc
    with H. Menuhin pf & M. Gendron — Electrola 1C063–12082
    vlc — HMV ASD2594

TIPPETT

Fantasia concertante on a theme of Corelli (1953) 2 vlns, vlc & strs
    with R. Masters vln, D. Simpson vlc & — Angel 36303
    Bath Festival Orch. – Tippett — Electrola SME91462
      HMV ALP2090, ASD637

VIEUXTEMPS

Concerto No. 4, in d, Op. 31 vln & orch.
      2EA 15585–5, 15586–3, 15587–2, — HMV DB21307/9, DB9653/5,
        15588–4 & 15589/90–2A — BLP1005, FBLP1026, QBLP1036
    with Philharmonia Orch. – Susskind — Victor (set WHMV1015),
      LHMV1015

Concerto No. 5, in a, Op. 37 vln & orch.
    with Philharmonia Orch. – Pritchard — HMV ALP1241
      Victor LHMV30

VIOTTI

(3) Duets, Op. 2 2 vlns
  No. 3. Duet No. 3, in G
    with G. De Vito vln — HMV ALP1462

VIVALDI

(12) Concerti, Op. 3 "L'Estro armonico" var. cbns & strs
  Concerto No. 10, in b, P.148 (F.IV, No. 10) 4 vlns, strs & c
    with R. Masters vln, E. Goren vln, S. — Angel 36103
    Humphreys vln & Bath Festival — Electrola E91219, STE91219
    Chamber Orch. – Menuhin — HMV ALP1949, ASD500,
      ASDF283, FALP747,
      QALP10356

(12) Concerti, Op. 8 (1725) "Il Cimento dell' Armonia e dell' Invenzione"
    (Nos. 1/4: Le quattro Stagioni) vln & strs
  Concerto No. 6, in C, F.I, No. 27 "Il Piacere"
    with Philharmonia Orch. – Boult — Victor LHMV16

WALTON

Concerto (1929) vla & orch.
    playing vla with New Philharmonia — Angel 36719
    Orch. – Walton — HMV ASD2542

Concerto (1939) vln & orch.
    with London Symphony Orch. – — Angel 36719
    Walton — HMV ASD2542

Sonata (1939) vln & pf*
      2EA 14640/4–1 & 14645–1A — HMV DB9513/5, DB21156/8
    with L. Kentner pf — Victor LHMV1037

WIENIAWSKI

Légende, Op. 17 vln & pf or orch.
    with L'Orchestre   2LA 2473/4[1]☐ — HMV DB3653
    des Concerts Colonne – Enescu — Orion OR7271
      Victor 15423

Légende, Op. 17 vln & pf or orch.
    with Philharmonia Orch. – Pritchard — Capitol P8667, SP8667
      HMV ALP2070, ASD618,
      ASDF847, CVA847, FALP847

Scherzo–Tarantelle, Op. 16 vln & pf
    with A. Balsam pf   2L 322[III]△ — HMV DB1788
      Victor JD86

Scherzo–Tarantelle, Op. 16 vln & pf
    with G. Moore pf   2EA 12492 — HMV DB6704
      Victor 12–0922, 49–0404

Scherzo–Tarantelle, Op. 16 vln & pf
    with G. Moore pf — HMV 7EB6017, 7ERL1117,
      7RF224
      Victor (in set WDM1742),
      LM1742

Scherzo–Tarantelle, Op. 16 vln & pf
    with A. Baller pf — Victor SD3048, (in set JAS230),
      LS2004

Souvenir de Moscou, Op. 6 vln & pf or orch.
      2LA 783[1]☐ & 784[III]☐ — HMV DB2872
    with M. Gazelle pf — Victor 14352

Emöke MENYHERT

HAJDÚ

Little Suite 2 vlns & vlc
  Rondo & Serenade
    with I. Párkányi vln & I. Záhorszky — Qualiton LPX1188
    vlc

Henri MERCKEL (1897–)

BACH, J.C.

(6) Trio–Sonatas, Op. 4 (?1765) (T. P314) 2 vlns & vlc
  Sonata No. 3, in E flat
    with B. Schwarz vln   PART 1443/6 — L'Oiseau–Lyre OL118/9
    & A. Navarra vlc

* Extract from Tema con 7 variazione or 2nd mvt is on Electrola E91475 &
  HMV FALP896 & HQM1018.

BACH, J.S.

(6) Brandenburg Concerti, BWV1046/51 (1721) strs & c
Brandenburg Concerto No. 4, in G, BWV1049 vlns, 2 fls, strs & c
with Pro Musica Orch. – Klemperer　　Polydor 566216/7
　　　　　　　　　　　　　　　　　　Vox (set 622), PL6200

Brandenburg Concerto No. 5, in D, BWV1050 clav, fl, vln, strs & c
with M. Roesgen–Champion hpsi, R.　　Polydor 566218/20
Cortet fl & Pro Musica Orch. –　　　Vox (set 622)
Klemperer

Concert No. 2, in E, BWV1042 vln, strs & c
with Pro Arte Orch. – Redel　　Ducretet–Thomson 270C080,
　　　　　　　　　　　　　　　DTL93067
　　　　　　　　　　　　　　　Telefunken PLB6153

Concerto in d, BWV1043 2 vlns, strs & c
with D. Erlih vln & Pro Arte Orch. –　Ducretet–Thomson 270C081,
Redel　　　　　　　　　　　　　　DTL93067
　　　　　　　　　　　　　　　　Telefunken TW30144

Concerto in a, BWV1044 clav, fl, vln, strs & c
with A. van de Wiele hpsi, F. Caratgé　Amphion AD762/7, (set A4)
fl & string orch. – Swoboda　　　　Concert Hall (set D10), DL10

(3) Sonatas & 3 Partitas, BWV1001/6 solo vln
Sonata No. 1, in g: Adagio (1st mvt) BWV1001
(unaccompanied)　　WLX 1427–3　Columbia DFX81, DX713
Partita No. 3, in E: Menuets I & II (4th mvt) BWV1006
(unaccompanied)　　WLX 1426–3　Columbia DVX81, DX713

(6) Sonatas, BWV1014/9 vln & clav
Sonata No. 1, in b, BWV1014
with I. Nef hpsi　　L'Oiseau–Lyre OL195/200

Sonata No. 2, in A, BWV1015
with I. Nef hpsi　　L'Oiseau–Lyre OL195/200

Sonata No. 3, in E, BWV1016
with I. Nef hpsi　　L'Oiseau–Lyre OL195/200

BEETHOVEN

Concerto in D, Op. 61 (cadenzas by Léonard) vln & orch.
with Lamoureux Orch. – Bigot　　HMV W1508/12

BOZZA

Rapsodie niçoise vln & orch.
with orch. – Bozza　　Florilège 46, HP2051/2

COUPERIN, F.

(L') Apothéose de Lully (1725) 2 vlns & c
with G. Alès vln, M. Frécheville vlc,　L'Oiseau–Lyre OL LD1
R. Gerlin hpsi & M. Morel ob

(4) Concerts Royaux (1714/5) 2 vlns, vla, fl & c
Concert Royale No. 4, in e
with R. Cortet fl,　　PART 1276/9　L'Oiseau–Lyre OL51/2, OL LD1
M. Morel ob, F. Oubradous bsn, R.
Gerlin hpsi & M. Frécheville vlc

(Les) Goûts–réunis, ou Nouveaux Concerts unsp inst & c
Concert No. 9, in E "Ritratto del' Amore"
with J. Goetghelück　　PART 1311/4　L'Oiseau–Lyre OL73/4
ob, F. Oubradous bsn, I. Nef hpsi, A.
Navarra vlc cond. Désormière

(La) Létiville, XVI, No. 7 hpsi – arr. vln & hpsi
with I. Nef hpsi　　PART 1306–1　L'Oiseau–Lyre OL55

(La) Parnasse, ou l'Apothéose de Corelli (1725) 2 vlns & c
　　　　　Part 1280–1, 1281–2 & 1283/3　L'Oiseau–Lyre OL57/8
with G. Alès vln, R. Gerlin hpsi & M.
Frécheville vlc

DELANNOY

Sérénade concertante (1938) vln & orch.
with Paris Conservatory Orch. –　　HMV DB5184/6
Munch

FAURÉ

Berceuse, Op. 16 vln & pf
with Pasdeloup Orch. – Coppola　　HMV L1015

Quartet No. 1, in c, Op. 15 pf, vln, vla & vlc
with E. Zurfluh–　　2PG 1268/76[I]△　HMV DB2106/9, DB7869/72,
Tenroc pf, A. Merckel vla & G.　　　　　　　L973/6
Marchesini vlc　　　　　　　　Victor 12481/4, (set M594)

HINDEMITH

Concerto in C sharp (1939) vln & orch.
with Lamoureux　　2LA 5451/7–1　HMV DB11212/5S
Orch. – Désormière

(2) Sonatas, Op. 31 (1924) solo vln
Sonata No. 1
(unaccompanied)　　Pathé ED24

HONEGGER

Sonata (1940) solo vln
(unaccompanied)　　Pathé ED25

Sonata (1940) solo vln
2 mvts only*
(unaccompanied)　　Festival FLD5

HUBEAU

Concerto in C (1938) vln & orch.
with Lamoureux Orch. – Bigot　　HMV W1503/5

LALO

Concerto in g, Op. 29 "Concerto russe" vln & orch.
Intermezzo (3rd mvt)
with Pasdeloup Orch. – Coppola　　HMV L1015

Symphonie espagnole, Op. 21 vln & orch.†
　　　　2W 1271[I]△, 1272[II]△, 1273[III]△,　HMV C2459/62, L923/6
　　　　1278[II]△, 1274/5[II]△, 1276[III]△ &　Victor 11275/8
with Pasdeloup Orch. –　　1277[II]△
Coppola

MARTINON

Sonatina No. 5, Op. 32, No. 1 solo vln
(unaccompanied)　　Polydor 566323

MOZART

Sonata No. 32, in B flat, K454 vln & pf
with J. Hubeau pf　　L'Anthologie Sonore 111/3,
　　　　　　　　　　AS528

PAGANINI

(24) Caprices, Op. 1 (1801/7) solo vln
Caprice No. 9, in E
(unaccompanied)　　Vega C30 S244

Caprice No. 13, in B flat
(unaccompanied)　　Vega C30 S244

* Unidentified.
† Including Intermezzo.

PIERNÉ

Impressions de Music Hall (1927) – ballet suite orch. – arr. vln & pf Pierné
with M.L. Pugnet–   2LA 4472/5–1   HMV DB11126/7
Gaillard pf

POULENC

(Le) Bal masqué (1932) – secular cantata b, septet & pcn
with P. Baritone b & Instrumental   Vega C35 A35
Ensemble – Fremaux

PURCELL

(12) Sonatas, Z790/801 (1683) 3 part – 2 vlns & c
   Sonata No. 1, in g, Z790
                    0111³ GCP & 0112² GCP   L'Oiseau–Lyre 207/8, (in set
   with G. Alès vln, I. Nef hpsi & A.   OLP1)
   Navarra vlc
   Sonata No. 2, in B flat, Z791
   with G. Alès vln, I.   0113/4² GCP   L'Oiseau–Lyre 209/10, (in set
   Nef hpsi & A. Navarra vlc   OLP1)
   Sonata No. 3, in d, Z792
   with G. Alès vln, I.   0115/6² GCP   L'Oiseau–Lyre 211/2, (in set
   Nef hpsi & A. Navarra vlc   OLP1)
   Sonata No. 4, in F, Z793
                    0117³ GCP & 0118² GCP   L'Oiseau–Lyre 211/2, (in set
   with G. Alès vln, I. Nef hpsi & A.   OLP1)
   Navarra vlc
   Sonata No. 5, in a, Z794
                    0119² GCP & 0120³ GCP   L'Oiseau–Lyre 209/10, (in set
   with G. Alès vln, I. Nef hpsi & A.   OLP1)
   Navarra vlc
   Sonata No. 6, in C, Z795
                    0121² GCP & 0122⁴ GCP   L'Oiseau–Lyre 207/8, (in set
   with G. Alès vln, I. Nef hpsi & A.   OLP1)
   Navarra vlc
   Sonata No. 7, in e, Z796
                    0123³ GCP & 0124² GCP   L'Oiseau–Lyre 213/4, (in set
   with G. Alès vln, I. Nef hpsi & A.   OLP1)
   Navarra vlc
   Sonata No. 8, in G, Z797
   with G. Alès vln, I.   0125/6² GCP   L'Oiseau–Lyre 215/6, (in set
   Nef hpsi & A. Navarra vlc   OLP1)
   Sonata No. 9, in c, Z798
   with G. Alès vln, I.   0129/30³ GCP   L'Oiseau–Lyre 217/8, (in set
   Nef hpsi & A. Navarra vlc   OLP1)
   Sonata No. 10, in A, Z799
                    0131² GCP & 0132¹ GCP   L'Oiseau–Lyre 217/8, (in set
   with G. Alès vln, I. Nef hpsi & A.   OLP1)
   Navarra vlc
   Sonata No. 11, in f, Z800
                    0133² GCP & 0134³ GCP   L'Oiseau–Lyre 215/6 (in set
   with G. Alès vln, I. Nef hpsi & A.   OLP1)
   Navarra vlc
   Sonata No. 12, in D, Z801
                    0127² GCP & 0128¹ GCP   L'Oiseau–Lyre 213/4, (in set
   with G. Alès vln, I. Nef hpsi & A.   OLP1)
   Navarra vlc

RAVEL

(L') Enfant et les Sortilèges (1925) – opera–ballet
   Pastourelle arr. vln & pf
   with M.L. Pugnet–Gaillard pf   Polydor A6346

RAVEL – *Continued*

Sonata (1927) vln & pf
   with M.L. Pugnet–Gaillard pf   Polydor A6346/8
Trio in a (1915) pf, vln & vlc
   with E. Zurfluh–   2G 443/8ᴵᴵ△   HMV DB4803/5
   Tenroc pf & M. Marcelli–Herson vlc   Victor 11243/5, (set M129)

ROESGEN–CHAMPION

Pièces vln & pf
   with M. Roesgen–Champion pf   HMV DA4937

SAINT–SAËNS

Concerto No. 3, in b, Op. 61 vln & orch.
                    2LA 427–3, 428–5, 429–3, 430–2,   HMV L1000/2
   with Pasdeloup   431–3 & 432–4
   Orch. – Coppola
Danse macabre, Op. 40 (1874) orch.
                    WLX 1325² & 1326¹   Columbia DFX205, DX121,
   with symphony orch. – Gaubert   LFX44, LGX192

SARASATE

Zigeunerweisen, Op. 20 vln & pf or orch.
   with orch.   Pathé X98187

SCHUBERT

Sonata in A, Op. 162 (D574) "Duo" vln & pf
   with M.L. Pugnet–Gaillard pf   HMV DA5016/8
(3) Sonatinas, Op. 137 (D384, D385 & D408) vln & pf
   No. 1. Sonatina No. 1, in D: Allegro Molto (1st mvt) D384
   with M.L. Pugnet–Gaillard pf   HMV DA5018

SCHUMANN

Trio No. 1, in d, Op. 63 pf, vln & vlc
   with J. Hubeau pf & P. Tortelier vlc   Erato LDE3153
Trio No. 3, in g, Op. 110 pf, vln & vlc
   with J. Hubeau pf & P. Tortelier vlc   Erato LDE3153

VIVALDI

(12) Concerti, Op. 3 "L'Estro armonico" var cbns & strs
   Concerto No. 10, in b: Largo (2nd mvt) P.148 (F.IV, No. 10) 4 vlns, strs
   & c
   with L. Schwartz vln, J. Dumont vln,   Polydor 540002, 566275
   M. Crut vln & Pro Musica Orch. –
   Goldschmidt

Petr MESSIEREUR (1937–   )

BARTÓK

Sonata No. 2 (1922) vln & pf
   with J. Kozderková pf   Qualiton LPX1168/71

HINDEMITH

(6) Sonatas, Op. 11 var. cbns
   Sonata No. 1, in E flat (1920) vln & pf
   with J. Kozderková pf   Supraphon SUA10693,
                              SUAST50693, SV9318

SCHOENBERG

Fantasy, Op. 47 (1949) vln & pf
   with J. Kozderková pf   Supraphon SUA10693,
                              SUAST50693, SV8318

STRAVINSKY

Duo concertante (1932) vln & pf
  with J. Kozderková pf   Supraphon SUA10693,
             SUAST50693, SV8318

WEBERN

(4) Pieces, Op. 7 (1910) vln & pf
  with J. Kozderková pf   Qualiton LPX1168/71

(4) Pieces, Op. 7 (1910) vln & pf
  with J. Kozderková pf   Supraphon SUA10693,
             SUAST50693, SV8318

Claud de MEYER

BACH

(4) Suites, BWV1066/9 strs & c
  Suite No. 3, in D: Air (2nd mvt) BWV1068 2 obs, 3 tpts, drms, strs & c
  – arr. vln & pf as "Air on the G–string" by Wilhelmj
  with M–L. Girod org   Deva M12

DESPLANES

Intrada (Adagio) vln & c – arr. vln & pf Nachèz
  with E. Pache pf   Deva 45AL

FIOCCO

Suite No. 1, in G hpsi
  Allegro (10th mvt) arr. vln & pf Bent & O'Neill
  with E. Pache pf   Deva 45AL

GOUNOD

Ave Maria (Méditation on Bach's "Prelude No. 1, in C" from Book I of
  "Das Wohltemperirte Clavier") v & pf – arr. vln & pf
  with E. Pache pf   Deva 45H

HANDEL

Serse (1738) – opera
  Ombra mai fu "Largo" arr. vln & org
  with M–L. Girod org   Deva M12

MASSENET

Thaïs (1894) – opera
  Méditation arr. vln & pf Marsick
  with E. Pache pf   Deva 45H

MOZART

Divertimento No. 17, in D, K334 2 hrns & strs
  Minuet (3rd mvt) arr. vln & pf Burmester
  with E. Pache pf   Deva 45AL

PORPORA

Aria in E arr. vln & pf Corti*
  with M–L. Girod org   Deva M12

SAINT-SAËNS

(Le) Carnaval des animaux (1886) small orch.
  Le cygne arr. vln & pf
  with E. Pache pf   Deva 45AL

* Unidentified.

SCHUBERT

(7) Gesänge (set to Scott's "Lady of the Lake") Op. 52 v & pf
  No. 6. Ave Maria, D839 arr. vln & pf Wilhelmj
  with E. Pache pf   Deva 45H

VIVALDI

(12) Concerti, Op. 3 "L'Estro armonico" var. cbns & strs
  Concerto No. 6, in a, P.1 (F.I, No. 176) vln, strs & c
  with M–L. Girod org   Deva M12

William MEYER

WIENIAWSKI

(2) Mazurkas, Op. 19 vln & pf
  No. 2. Mazurka No. 2, in D "Dudziarz"
  with piano   Bettini cylinder

Ernest MICHAELIAN

DELIUS

Sonata No. 3 (1930) vln & pf
  with V.L. Hagopian pf   Music Library MLR7047

DOHNÁNYI

Sonata in c sharp, Op. 21 vln & pf
  with V.L. Hagopian pf   Music Library MLR7047

GOOSSENS

Sonata No. 1, in e, Op. 21 vln & pf
  with V.L. Hagopian pf   Music Library MLR7068

LOCATELLI

(12) Sonatas, Op. 6 (1737) vln & c
  Sonata No. 7, in f "Au Tombeau" arr. vln & pf Ysaÿe
  with V.L. Hagopian pf   Music Library MLR7068

MARTINŮ

(5) Madrigal Stanzas (1943) vln & pf
  with V.L. Hagopian pf   Music Library MLR7068

Geoffrey MICHAELS

PAGANINI

(24) Caprices, Op. 1 (1801/7) solo vln
  Caprice No. 5, in a
  (unaccompanied)   Mezhdunarodnaya Kniga
             D028103/4

Max MICHAÏLOW

BEETHOVEN

(6) Minuets, G167 pf
  No. 2. Minuet No. 2, in G arr. vln & pf Burmester
  with piano   Okey 4435

BRANDL

(Der) Liebe Augustin – operetta
  Du alter Stefansturm arr. vln & pf as "The old refrain" by Kreisler
  with E. Milzkott pf   Telefunken A10944

BUTTING

Kleine Kammermusik, Op. 70 fl, E.hrn, vln & vlc
with E. Milzkott fl, E. Erthel E.hrn &   Eterna 120041/2, 520030
W. Haupt vlc

CHOPIN

(3) Nocturnes, Op. 9 pf
No. 2. Nocturne No. 2, in E flat arr. vln & pf Sarasate
with piano   Okey 4450

DENZA

Si vous l'aviez compris! v & pf – arr. vln & orch.
with orch.   Parlophone P1319

Si vous l'aviez compris! v & pf – arr. vln, vlc & pf
with 'cello & piano   B 3095 A[1]   Odeon 3095

DIETRICH, P.

Abendlied v & pf – arr. vln & pf
with piano   Polydor 99010

DRDLA

Souvenir vln & pf
with orch.   Parlophone E10216, P1325

DRIGO

(Les) Millions d'Arlequin (1900) – ballet orch.
Précieuse arr. vln & orch.
with orch.   Parlophone E10089, P1491
Sérénade arr. vln & orch.
with orch.   2–6323   Parlophone E10035, P1490
Valse des Alouettes arr. vln & orch.
with orch.   2–6295   Parlophone E10035, P1490

DVOŘÁK

(8) Humoresques, Op. 101 pf
No. 7. Humoresque No. 7, in G flat arr. vln & pf "in G" Kreisler
with piano   Polydor 16042

FIBICH

Images, Impressions & Souvenirs, Op. 41 pf
No. 14. Poem (from "Souvenirs", Part IV) arr. vln & pf Kubelík
with piano   Okey 3006
                               Parlophone P1040
                               Polydor 16043
No. 14. Poem (from "Souvenirs", Part IV) arr. vln & pf Kubelík
with E. Milzkott pf   Telefunken A10941

FIELD

Waltz pf – arr. vln & pf Burmester
with piano   Okey 4449

GANNE

(L') Extase – Rêverie pf – arr. vln & pf
with piano   Polydor 67512

GILLET

Polonaise vln & pf
with orch.   Parlophone E10089, P1491
Précieuse vln & pf
with orch.   A 3095 B[4]   Odeon 3095

GLINKA

Farewell to Petersburg (1840) – 12 songs v & pf
No. 10. The lark arr. vln & pf Zimbalist
with piano   Parlophone P1356

GLUCK

Orphée et Eurydice (1762) – opera
Danse of the blessed spirits: Lento "Mélodie" (No. 2) arr. vln & pf
Kreisler
with E. Milzkott pf   Telefunken A10860

GOSSEC

Rosine (1786) – opera
Gavotte arr. vln & pf Burmester
with piano   Okey 4449

GRIEG

(4) Danish songs, Op. 5 v & pf
No. 3. Jeg elsker dig (Ich liebe dich) arr. vln & pf
with piano   Polydor 99514
Peer Gynt (Suite No. 2) Op. 55 orch.
No. 4. Solveig's song arr. vln & pf Sitt
with piano   Okey 3006
                               Parlophone P1040
No. 4. Solveig's song arr. vln & pf Sitt
with piano   Polydor 67508
No. 4. Solveig's song arr. vln & pf Sitt
with piano   Telefunken A10942

HANDEL

(15) Sonatas, Op. 1 (?1731) fl or vln & c
Sonata No. 12, in F vln III
with E. Milzkott hpsi   Le Chant du Monde LPA8019

HAYDN

(6) Quartets, Op. 20 (H.III, Nos. 31/6) 2 vlns, vla & vlc
No. 4. Quartet No. 34, in D, H.III, No. 34
with H. Pietsch vln, H. Fricke vla &   Eterna 820016
W. Haupt vlc

KREISLER

(La) Gitana vln & pf
with E. Milzkott pf   Telefunken A10948
Liebesleid vln & pf
with E. Milzkott pf   Telefunken A10944
Schön Rosmarin vln & pf
with E. Milzkott pf   Telefunken A10860
Sicilienne & Rigaudon (Francoeur) vln & pf
with E. Milzkott pf   Telefunken A10941

LANGER

Grandmother, Op. 20 pf – arr. vln & orch.
with orch.   Parlophone P1340

MANÉN

Chanson–Adagietto, Op. A–8, No. 1 vln & pf
with E. Milzkott pf   Telefunken A10948

MARCHETTI

Coeur affolé! ... andante appassionato pf – arr. vln & orch.
with orch.   Parlophone P1450

MEYER–HELMUND

(3) Lieder, Op. 21 v & pf
  No. 2. Das Zauberlied arr. vln & pf
  with piano   Polydor 67508

MICHAÏLOW

(La) Carnevale di Venizia (Italian folksong)
  with piano   Polydor 16042

(La) Carnevale di Venizia (Italian folksong)
  with piano   Okey 4435

Gavotte, Op. 2 vln & pf
  with piano   Parlophone P1340

MONTI

Csárdas (1904) vln & pf
  with piano   56751   Diadal D1217
                      Parlophone 44590, E5052

MOSZKOWSKI

(6) Klavierstücke, Op. 15 pf – 4 hands
  No. 1. Serenata arr. vln & pf
  with piano   Polydor 99514

MOZART

Quartet No. 18, in A, K464 2 vlns, vla & vlc
  with H. Pietsch vln, H. Fricke vla &   Eterna 720011
  W. Haupt vlc

Quartet No. 21, in D, K575 2 vlns, vla & vlc
  with H. Pietsch vln, H. Fricke vla &   Eterna 820016
  W. Haupt vlc

PUCCINI

(La) Bohème (1896) – opera
  Quando m'en vo soletta "Musetta's waltz song" arr. vln & pf Michaïlow
  with piano   Parlophone E10216

Tosca (1900) – opera
  selection arr. vln & pf as "Fantasy" by Michaïlow
  with piano   Polydor 67510

RIMSKY–KORSAKOV

Sadko (1898) – opera
  Chant hindou arr. vln & pf Kreisler
  with E. Milzkott pf   Telefunken A10942

ROUSSEAU, L.J.

Incanto valse pf – arr. vln & orch.
  with orch.   Parlophone P1325

RUBINSTEIN

(6) Soirées de Saint–Pétersbourg, Op. 44 pf
  No. 1. Romance in E flat arr. vln & pf Wieniawski
  with piano   Okey 4394

SCHUBERT

(14) Schwanengesang, D957 (1828) v & pf
  No. 4. Ständchen "Serenade" arr. vln & pf
  with piano   56748   Diadal D1217
                      Parlophone 44590, E5052

SCHUMANN

(13) Kinderscenen, Op. 15 pf
  No. 1. Träumerei arr. vln & pf
  with piano   Okey 4450
                      Polydor 16043

SINDING

(6) Pieces, Op. 32 pf
  No. 3. Frühlingsrauschen "Rustle of spring" arr. vln & pf
  with piano   Polydor 99010

THOMÉ

Simple aveu, Op. 25 pf – arr. vln & orch.
  with orch.   Parlophone P1450

TOSTI

For a kiss (Pour un baiser) v & pf – arr. vln & pf
  with piano   Parlophone P1356

(La) Serenata v & pf – arr. vln & orch.
  with orch.   Parlophone P1319

WAGNER

(Die) Walküre (1870) – opera
  Winterstürme wichen dem Wonnemond arr. vln & pf
  with piano   Polydor 67512

WALDTEUFEL

Rendezvous – valse, Op. 172 orch. – arr. vln & orch.
  with orch.   Parlophone P1425

Ted MICHEL

HUBAY

(14) Scènes de la Csárda vln & pf
  No. 2. Scène de la Csárda, Op. 13
  with Gypsy Ensemble – Michel   Romany RR5

  No. 3. Maros vize, Op. 18
  with Gypsy Ensemble – Michel   Romany RR5

  No. 6. Sárga Cserebogár, Op. 34
  with Gypsy Ensemble – Michel   Romany RR5

  No. 7. Kossuth–Nóta, Op. 41
  with Gypsy Ensemble – Michel   Romany RR5

PAGANINI

(6) Sonatas, Op. 2 (1801/6) vln & gtr
  No. 1. Sonata No. 1, in A
  with A. Malakoff gtr   Romany LP1501

  No. 2. Sonata No. 2, in C
  with A. Malakoff gtr   Romany LP1501

  No. 3. Sonata No. 3, in d
  with A. Malakoff gtr   Romany LP1501

  No. 4. Sonata No. 4, in A
  with A. Malakoff gtr   Romany LP1501

  No. 5. Sonata No. 5, in D
  with A. Malakoff gtr   Romany LP1501

  No. 6. Sonata No. 6, in a
  with A. Malakoff gtr   Romany LP1501

(6) Sonatas, Op. 3 (1801/6) vln & gtr
  No. 1. Sonata No. 7, in A
  with A. Malakoff gtr   Romany LP1501

PAGANINI – *Continued*

No. 2, Sonata No. 8, in G
with A. Malakoff gtr | Romany LP1501

No. 3. Sonata No. 9, in D
with A. Malakoff gtr | Romany LP1501

No. 4. Sonata No. 10, in a
with A. Malakoff gtr | Romany LP1501

No. 5. Sonata No. 11, in A
with A. Malakoff gtr | Romany LP1501

No. 6. Sonata No. 12, in e
with A. Malakoff gtr | Romany LP1501

Roberto MICHELUCCI

ALBINONI

(12) Concerti, Op. 9 (1722) var. cbns & strs
Concerto No. 4, in A vln & strs
with I Musici | Epic BC1076, LC3682
Philips 835029AY, 839839GSY, A00539L, ABL3321, SABL158, SFL7571

Concerto No. 10, in F vln & strs
with I Musici | Epic BC1076, LC3682
Philips 835029AY, A00539L, ABL3321, G05397R, SABL158, SFL7571, SFM23030

(12) Concerti, Op. 10 vln, strs & c
Concerto No. 1, in B flat
with I Musici | Philips 839723LY, (in set SC71 AX308), AXA3006/1

Concerto No. 2, in g
with I Musici | Philips 839723LY, (in set SC71 AX308), AXA3006/1

Concerto No. 3, in C
with I Musici | Philips 839723LY, (in set SC71 AX308), AXA3006/1

Concerto No. 4, in G
with I Musici | Philips 839724LY, (in set SC71 AX308), AXA3006/2

Concerto No. 5, in A
with I Musici | Philips 839724LY, (in set SC71 AX308), AXA3006/2

Concerto No. 6, in D
with I Musici | Philips 839724LY, (in set SC71 AX308), AXA3006/2

Concerto No. 7, in F
with I Musici | Philips 839724LY, (in set SC71 AX308), AXA3006/2

Concerto No. 8, in g
with I Musici | Philips 839724LY, (in set SC71 AX308), AXA3006/2, 6580 001

Concerto No. 9, in C
with I Musici | Philips 839725LY, (in set SC71 AX308), AXA3006/3

Concerto No. 10, in F
with I Musici | Philips 839725LY, (in set SC71 AX308), AXA3006/3

ALBINONI – *Continued*

Concerto No. 11, in E flat
with I Musici | Philips 839725LY, (in set SC71 AX308), AXA3006/3

Concerto No. 12, in B flat
with I Musici | Philips 839725LY, (in set SC71 AX308), AXA3006/3

BACH

Concerto No. 1, in a, BWV1041 vln, strs & c
with I Musici | Epic BC1018, LC3553
Philips 8580 021, 835007AY, 839591VGY, A00519L, ABL3259, L09008L

Concerto in d, BWV1043 2 vlns, strs & c*
with F. Ayo vln & I Musici | Epic BC1018, LC3553
Philips 6580 021, 610106VR, 802736AY, (in set C71 AX401), 836217AY, 839591VGY, A00519L, ABL3259, G05347R, L09008L

Concerto in a, BWV1044 clav, fl, vln, strs & c
with M.T. Garatti hpsi, S. Gazzelloni fl & I Musici | Philips 802736AY, (in set C71 AX401), 835074AY, A02077L, ABL3380, PHM500008, PHS900008

Concerto in c, BWV1060 vln & ob or 2 vlns, strs & c
with L. Driehuys ob & I Musici | Philips 835074AY, A02077L, ABL3380, PHM500008, PHS900008

BARTÓK

(6) Rumanian folk dances (1915) pf – arr. vln & pf Székely
with I Musici | Philips 835096AY, A02099L, ABL3411, PHM500001, PHS900001, SABL216

BONPORTI

(10) Concerti, Op. 11 strs
Concerto No. 4, in B flat
with I Musici | Epic LC3542
Philips A00449L

Concerto No. 4, in B flat
with I Musici | Philips 6500 182

Concerto No. 5, in F
with I Musici | Epic LC3542
Philips A00449L

Concerto No. 6, in F
with I Musici | Epic LC3542
Philips A00449L

Concerto No. 8, in D
with I Musici | Epic LC3542
Philips A00449L

Concerto no. 8, in D
with I Musici | Philips 6500 182

Concerto No. 9, in E
with I Musici | Philips 6500 182

* Excerpts only on Epic BC1.

LOCATELLI

(12) Concerti, Op. 3 (1733) "L'Arte del Violino" (with 24 Caprices) vln & strs

Concerto No. 1, in D
with I Musici

Epic BC1155, LC3827
Philips 6580 035, 411945SE,
802734AY, (in set C71 AX401),
835060LY, L02056L
Fontana 894075 ZKY

Concerto No. 8, in e
with I Musici

Epic BC1155, LC3827
Philips 6580 035, 835060LY,
L02056L

Concerto No. 9, in G
with I Musici

Epic BC1155, LC3827
Philips 6580 035, 835060LY,
L02056L

MANFREDINI

(12) Concerti, Op. 3 (1718) 2 vlns, strs & c

Concerto No. 2, in a
with A–M. Cotogni vln & I Musici

Epic LC3514
Philips A00448L

Concerto No. 3, in e
with A–M. Cotogni vln & I Musici

Epic LC3514
Philips A00448L

Concerto No. 7, in G
with A–M. Cotogni vln & I Musici

Epic LC3514
Philips 400103AE, A00448L

Concerto No. 8, in F
with A–M. Cotogni vln & I Musici

Epic LC3514
Philips 400103AE, A00448L

Concerto No. 10, in g
with A–M. Cotogni vln & I Musici

Epic LC3514
Philips A00448L

Concerto No. 12, in C
with A–M. Cotogni vln & I Musici

Epic LC3514
Philips 835129AY, A00448L,
PHM500025, PHS900025

MENDELSSOHN

Concerto in d (1822) vln & strs
with I Musici

Philips 6500 099

TORELLI

(12) Concerti, Op. 8 (1709) 1/6: 2 vlns, strs & c – 7/12: vln, strs & c

Concerto No. 2, in a
with A–M. Cotogni vln, M. Centurione
vlc & I Musici

Epic LC3217
Philips A00302L, ABL3153

Concerto No. 3, in E
with A–M. Cotogni vln, M. Centurione
vlc & I Musici

Epic LC3217
Philips A00302L, ABL3153

Concerto No. 6, in g "Christmas Concerto"
with A–M. Cotogni vln, M. Centurione
vlc & I Musici

Epic LC3217
Philips 835129AY, A00302L,
ABL3153, PHM500025,
PHS900025

Concerto No. 9, in e
with I Musici

Epic LC3217
Philips A00302L, ABL3153

TORELLI – *Continued*

Concerto No. 12, in D
with I Musici

Epic LC3217
Philips A00302L, ABL3153

VIOTTI

(6) Duets, Op. 20 2 vlns
No. 3. Duet No. 3, in G
with A–M. Cotogni vln

Victor (in set ML40003)

VIVALDI

(12) Concerti, Op. 3 "L'Estro armonico" var. cbns & strs

Concerto No. 1, in D, P.146 (F.IV, No. 7) 4 vlns, vlc, strs & c
with W. Gallozzi vln, A–M Cotogni
vln, L. Vicari vln & I Musici

Philips 835162AY, A02277L,
PHC9111, (in set PHC3–017)

Concerto No. 2, in g, P.326 (F.IV, No. 8) 2 vlns, strs & c
with I. Colandrea vln, E. Altobelli vlc
& I Musici

Philips 835162AY, A02277L,
PHC9111, (in set PHC3–017)

Concerto No. 3, in G, P.96, (F.I, No. 173) vln, strs & c
with I Musici

Philips 835162AY, A02277L,
PHC9111, (in set PHC3–017)

Concerto No. 4, in e, P.97 (F.I, No. 174) 4 vlns, strs & c
with W. Gallozzi vln, A–M. Cotogni
vln, L. Vicari vln & I Musici

Philips 835162AY, A02277L,
PHC9111, (in set PHC3–017)

Concerto No. 5, in A, P.212 (F.I, No. 175) 2 vlns, strs & c
with I. Colandrea vln & I Musici

Philips 835163AY, A02278L,
PHC9112, (in set PHC3–017)

Concerto No. 6, in a, P.1 (F.I, No. 176) vln, strs & c
with I Musici

Philips 835163AY, A02278L,
PHC9112, (in set PHC3–017)

Concerto No. 7, in F, P.249 (F.IV, No. 9) 4 vlns, strs & c
with W. Gallozzi vln, A–M. Cotogni
vln, L. Vicari vln, E. Altobelli vlc & I
Musici

Philips 835163AY, A02278L,
PHC9112, (in set PHC3–017)

Concerto No. 8, in a, P.2 (F.I, No. 177) 2 vlns, strs & c
with A–M. Cotogni vln & I Musici

Epic (in set BSC111), LC3565,
(in set SC6040)
Philips 400107AE, A00462L,
ABL3233, C7

Concerto No. 8, in a, P.2 (F.I, No. 177) 2 vlns, strs & c
with A–M. Cotogni vln & I Musici

Philips 835163AY, A02278L,
PHC9112, (in set PHC3–017)

Concerto No. 9, in D, P.147 (F.I, No. 178) vln, strs & c
with I Musici

Philips 835164AY, A02279L,
PHC9113, (in set PHC3–017)

Concerto No. 10, in b, P.148 (F.IV, No. 10) 4 vlns, strs & c
with W. Gallozzi vln, A–M. Cotogni
vln, L. Vicari vln, E. Altobelli vlc & I
Musici

Fontana 894075ZKY
Philips 802735AY, (in set C71
AX401), 835164AY, A02279L,
PHC9113, (in set PHC3–017)

Concerto No. 11, in d, P.250 (F.IV, No. 11) 2 vlns, vlc, strs & c
with A–M. Cotogni vln, E. Altobelli
vlc & I Musici

Philips 835164AY, A02279,
PHC9113, (in set PHC3–017)

Concerto No. 12, in E, P.240 (F.I, No. 179) vln, strs & c
with I Musici

Philips 835164AY, A02279L,
PHC9113, (in set PHC3–017)

(12) Concerti, Op. 8 (1725) "Il Cimento dell' Armonia e dell' Invenzione" (Nos. 1/4: Le quattro Stagioni) vln & strs

Concerto No. 1, in E, F.I, No. 22 "La Primavera"
with I Musici

Philips 6500 017

VIVALDI – *Continued*

Concerto No. 2, in B flat, F.I, No. 23 "L'Estate"
with I Musici   Philips 6500 017

Concerto No. 3, in F, F.I, No. 24 "L'Autunno"
with I Musici   Philips 6500 017

Concerto No. 4, in f, F.I, No. 25 "L'Inverno"
with I Musici   Philips 6500 017

(6) Concerti, Op. 11 vln, strs & c
Concerto No. 2, in e P.106 (F.I, No. 208) "Il Favorito"
with I Musici   Epic BC1021, LC3486
       Philips 802735AY, (in set C71
       AX401), 88186DY, A00476L,
       A02246L, ABL3237, GBL5621,
       SABL102

Concerto in a, P.28 (F.I, No. 61) 2 vlns, strs & c – arr. Casella
with F. Ayo vln & I Musici   Epic (in set BSC111), (in set
       SC6040)
       Philips 838122AY, G04812L

Alexei MIKHLIN (1938–   )

KHACHATURIAN, K.

Sonata in g, Op. 1 vln & pf
with piano   Mezhdunarodnaya Kniga
       D15353/4

PROKOFIEV

(The) Love for Three Oranges, Op. 33 (1919) – opera
  No. 3. March arr. vln & pf Heifetz
with Y. Seidel pf   Mezhdunarodnaya Kniga
       D019332

(4) Pieces, Op. 32 (1918) pf
  No. 3. Gavotta arr. vln & pf Heifetz
with Y. Seidel pf   Mezhdunarodnaya Kniga
       D019332

SHOSTAKOVICH

(24) Preludes, Op. 34 (1932/3) pf
  Prelude No. 1, in C arr. vln & pf Tziganov
with piano   Mezhdunarodnaya Kniga
       D15353/4

  Prelude No. 3, in G arr. vln & pf Tziganov
with piano   Mezhdunarodnaya Kniga
       D15353/4

  Prelude No. 5, in D arr. vln & pf Tziganov
with piano   Mezhdunarodnaya Kniga
       D15353/4

  Prelude No. 8, in f sharp arr. vln & pf Tziganov
with piano   Mezhdunarodnaya Kniga
       D15353/4

  Prelude No. 10, in c sharp arr. vln & pf Tziganov
with Y. Seidel pf   Mezhdunarodnaya Kniga
       D019332

  Prelude No. 11, in B arr. vln & pf Tziganov
with piano   Mezhdunarodnaya Kniga
       D15353/4

  Prelude No. 15, in D flat arr. vln & pf Tziganov
with Y. Seidel pf   Mezhdunarodnaya Kniga
       D019332

SHOSTAKOVICH – *Continued*

  Prelude No. 16, in B flat arr. vln & pf Tziganov
with Y. Seidel pf   Mezhdunarodnaya Kniga
       D019332

  Prelude No. 24, in d arr. vln & pf Tziganov
with Y. Seidel pf   Mezhdunarodnaya Kniga
       D019332

VAINBERG

Sonatina in d, Op. 46 vln & pf
with Y. Seidel pf   Mezhdunarodnaya Kniga
       D019332

VERACINI

(12) Sonatas, Op. 2 (1744) "Sonate accademiche" vln & c
Sonata No. 6, in A: Largo (2nd mvt) ed. Corti
with piano   Mezhdunarodnaya Kniga
       D15353/4

YSAŸE

Poème élégiaque in d (Poème No. 1) Op. 12 vln & pf or orch.
with Y. Seidel pf   Mezhdunarodnaya Kniga
       D019331

(6) Sonatas, Op. 27 solo vln
Sonata No. 2, in a
(unaccompanied)   Mezhdunarodnaya Kniga
       D019331

Sonata No. 6, in E
(unaccompanied)   Mezhdunarodnaya Kniga
       D15353/4

Friedrich MIKSOVSKY

PROKOFIEV

Overture on Hebrew themes, Op. 34 (1919) cl, pf, 2 vlns, vla & vlc
with F. Fuchs cl, K. Rapf pf, M.   Library of Recorded
Goberman vln, D. Gurtler vlc & D.   Masterpieces LRM510
van Ostheim vla   Odyssey 32 16 0083, 32 16 0084

TCHAIKOVSKY

Quartet No. 1, in D, Op. 11 2 vlns, vla & vlc
  Andante cantabile (2nd mvt)
with M. Goberman vln, D. van   Library of Recorded
Ostheim vla & D. Gurtler vlc   Masterpieces LRM508

Stoika MILANOVA (1946–   )

VIVALDI

(12) Concerti, Op. 8 (1725) "Il Cimento dell' Armonia e dell' Invenzione"
(Nos. 1/4: Le quattro Stagioni) vln & strs
Concerto No. 1, in E, F.I, No. 22 "La Primavera"
with Sofia Chamber Orch. –   Harmonia Mundi (Balkanton)
Kazandjiev   HMB107

Concerto No. 2, in B flat, F.I, No. 23 "L'Estate"
with Sofia Chamber Orch. –   Harmonia Mundi (Balkanton)
Kazandjiev   HMB107

Concerto No. 3, in F, F.I, No. 24 "L'Autunno"
with Sofia Chamber Orch. –   Harmonia Mundi (Balkanton)
Kazandjiev   HMB107

VIVALDI – *Continued*

Concerto No. 4, in f, F.I, No. 25 "L'Inverno"
with Sofia Chamber Orch. –   Harmonia Mundi (Balkanton)
Kazandjiev   HMB107

Y. MILKIS

VIVALDI

(12) Concerti, Op. 3 "L'Estro armonico" var. cbns & strs
Concerto No. 10, in b, P.148 (F.IV, No. 60) 4 vlns, strs & c
with K. Varenberg vln, E. Boder vln,   Mezhdunarodnaya Kniga
M. Furer vln & Leningrad Chamber   D018097/8, S01319/20
Orch. – Gozman

Nathan MILSTEIN (1904–   )

BACH

Concerto No. 1, in a, BWV1041 vln, strs & c
with Festival Orch. – Blech   Capitol K80326, P8362
                              Pickwick PC4013, SPC4013

Concerto No. 1, in a, BWV1041 vln, strs & c
with strings & harpsichord – Milstein Angel 36010
                              Columbia SAX5285
                              Electrola SME91683

Concerto No. 2, in E, BWV1042 vln, strs & c
with strings & harpsichord – Milstein Angel 36010
                              Columbia SAX5285
                              Electrola SME91683

Concerto in d, BWV1043 2 vlns, strs & c
with E. Morini vln & Chamber Orch. Angel 36006
– Milstein   Columbia CX1940, FCX1050,
                              SAX2579, SAXF1050
                              Electrola SME91683

(3) Sonatas & 3 Partitas, BWV1001/6 solo vln
  Sonata No. 1, in g: Adagio (1st mvt) BWV1001
(unaccompanied)   XCO 18475–4 Columbia 68477D, (in set X61),
                              LX522

  Sonata No. 1, in g, BWV1001
(unaccompanied)   Capitol (in set PCR8370),
                              CTL7088, P8298, P30270

  Partita No. 1, in b, BWV1002
(unaccompanied)   Capitol (in set PCR8370),
                              P30271

  Sonata No. 2, in a, BWV1003
(unaccompanied)   Capitol (in set PCR8370),
                              P30272

  Partita No. 2, in d, BWV1004
        XCO 18452–3, 18453–1, 18460/1 Columbia 68514/6SD,
(unaccompanied)   –2 & 18462–3 70198/200D, (set M276),
                              GQX10990/2, LX619/21S

  Partita No. 2, in d, BWV1004*
(unaccompanied)   Capitol (in set PCR8370),
                              CTL7088, P8298, P30272

  Sonata No. 3, in C, BWV1005
(unaccompanied)   Capitol (in set PCR8370),
                              P30271

* The Chaconne or 5th mvt only is also on Capitol CCL7526 & L8297.

BACH – *Continued*

Partita No. 3, in E, BWV1006
(unaccompanied)   Capitol (in set PCR8370),
                              P30270

Sonata in C, BWV1037 2 vlns & c
with E. Morini vln & B. Fischer pf   Angel 36006
                              Columbia CX1940, FCX1050,
                              SAX2579, SAFX1050

(4) Suites, BWV1066/9 strs & c
Suite No. 3, in D: Air (2nd mvt) BWV1068 2 obs, 3 tpts, drms, strs & c
– arr. vln & pf as "Air on the G–string" by Wilhelmj
with L. Pommers pf   Capitol P8396

BEETHOVEN

Concerto in D, Op. 61 (cadenzas by Milstein) vln & orch.
with Pittsburgh Symphony Orch. –   Capitol K80374, P8313
Steinberg   Music for Pleasure MFP2098

Concerto in D, Op. 61 (cadenzas by Milstein) vln & orch.
with Philharmonia Orch. – Leinsdorf Angel 35783, (in sets 3664 &
                              3712)
                              Columbia FCX995, SAXF995

Romance No. 2, in F, Op. 50 vln & orch.
with Concert Arts Orch. – Susskind Capitol P8528, SP8528

Sonata No. 5, in F, Op. 24 "Spring" vln & pf
with A. Balsam pf   Victor (in set WDM1594),
                              LM134

Sonata No. 5, in F, Op. 24 "Spring" vln & pf
with R. Firkusny pf   Capitol (in sets PBR8502 &
                              SPBR8502)

(3) Sonatas, Op. 30 vln & pf
No. 3. Sonata No. 8, in G
with L. Mittman pf   Columbia 69623/4D, (set X137)
No. 3. Sonata No. 8, in G
with A. Balsam pf   Capitol P8430, PAO8430
                              Pickwick PC4017, SPC4017

Sonata No. 9, in A, Op. 47 "Kreutzer" vln & pf
with A. Balsam pf   Capitol P8430, PAO8430
                              Pickwick PC4017, SPC4017

BLOCH

Baal Shem (3 Pictures of Chassidic life) (1923) vln & pf
No. 2. Nigun (Improvisation)
with L. Mittman pf   Columbia 17134D
No. 2. Nigun (Improvisation)
with C. Bussotti pf   Capitol CTL7058, P8259

BRAHMS

Concerto in D, Op. 77 (cadenza by Milstein) vln & orch.
with Pittsburgh Symphony Orch. –   Capitol CTL7070, K80308,
Steinberg   P8271

Concerto in D, Op. 77 (cadenza by Milstein) vln & orch.
with Philharmonia Orch. – Fistoulari Angel 36000, (in sets 3664 &
                              3712)
                              Capitol P8560, SP8560
                              Electrola 1C053–00624
                              World Record Club T597

Concerto in a, Op. 102 "Double" vln, vlc & orch.
with G. Piatigorsky vlc & Robin Hood HMV FALP171
Dell Orch. – Reiner   Victor (set WDM1609),
                              A12R0094, LM1191

BRAHMS – *Continued*

(21) Hungarian Dances pf duet
Hungarian dance No. 2, in d arr. vln & pf Joachim
with A. Balsam pf   CO 32781–1   Columbia 17352D

Hungarian dance No. 2, in d arr. vln & pf Joachim
with L. Pommers pf   Capitol FAP1–20468, P8339

Sonata No. 3, in d, Op. 108 vln & pf
with V. Horowitz pf   HMV QBLP1026
    Victor (set WDM1551), LM106

Sonata (1853) "Frei aber Einsam" vln & pf
Allegro (Scherzo) in c (3rd mvt) "Sonatensatz"
with C. Bussotti pf   Capitol CTL7058, P8259

(16) Waltzes, Op. 39 pf duet
No. 15. Waltz No. 15, in A flat arr. vln & pf "in A" Hochstein
with L. Pommers pf   Capitol P8536, SP8536

BRUCH

Concerto No. 1, in g, Op. 26 vln & orch.
    XCO 32668/73–1   Columbia 11855/7D, 11858/60D,
with New York Philharmonic   (set M517), C15655/7, (set
Symphony Orch. – Barbirolli   D120), ML2003, RL6631
    Harmony HL7083

Concerto No. 1, in g, Op. 26 vln & orch.
with Pittsburgh Symphony Orch. –   Capitol CTL7059, K80306,
Steinberg   P8243
    Pickwick PC4023, SPC4023

Concerto No. 1, in g, Op. 26 vln & orch.
with Philharmonia Orch. – Barzin   Angel 35730
    Capitol P8518, SP8518
    Electrola SHZE210

CHAUSSON

Poème, Op. 25 vln & orch.
with Philharmonia Orch. – Fistoulari   Angel 36005
    Columbia CCA1029, FCX1029,
    SAXF1029

CHOPIN

Nocturne No. 20, in c sharp, Op. posth pf – arr. vln & pf Milstein
with L. Mittman pf   XCO18463–2   Columbia 266244, 68480D,
    LCX34, LOX499, LX595

Nocturne No. 20, in c sharp, Op. posth pf – arr. vln & pf Milstein
with L. Pommers pf   Capitol P8339

CORELLI

(12) Sonatas, Op. 5 vln & c
Sonata No. 12, in d "La Follia" arr. vln & pf Léonard
with L. Pommers pf   Capitol FAP3–8481, P8481,
    SFP3–8481, SP8481

DEBUSSY

(12) Préludes – Book I (1910) pf
No. 8. La Fille aux cheveux de lin arr. vln & pf Hartmann
with L. Pommers pf   Capitol P8396

No. 12. Minstrels arr. vln & pf Hartmann
with L. Pommers pf   Capitol (in sets PBR8502 &
    SPBR8502)

DVOŘÁK

Concerto in a, Op. 53 vln & orch.
with Minneapolis Symphony Orch. –   HMV FALP158, FALP241
Dorati   Victor (set WDM1537), LM1147

Concerto in a, Op. 53 vln & orch.
with Pittsburgh Symphony Orch. –   Capitol K80306, P8382, SP8382
Steinberg

Concerto in a, Op. 53 vln & orch.
with New Philharmonia Orch. –   Angel 36011
Frühbeck de Burgos   Electrola SME91694
    HMV ALP2365, ASD2365,
    ASDQ5429, CVB2090

(8) Humoresques, Op. 101 pf
No. 7. Humoresque No. 7, in G flat arr. vln & pf "in G" Kreisler
with L. Mittman pf   Columbia 17337D

FALLA

(7) Canciones populares españolas (1914) v & pf
No. 3. Asturiana arr. vln & pf Kochański
with L. Mittman pf   Columbia 292540, 17111D

No. 3. Asturiana arr. vln & pf Kochański
with L. Pommers pf   Capitol P8396

No. 4. Jota arr. vln & pf Kochański
with L. Pommers pf   Capitol P8396

FAURÉ

(3) Chansons, Op. 7 v & pf
No. 1. Après un rêve arr. vln & orch. Anderson
with Boston "Pops" Orch. – Fiedler   Victor 26009, ERA77, LM77

No. 1. Après un rêve arr. vln & pf
with L. Pommers pf   Capitol (in sets PBR8502 &
    SPBR8502)

FOSTER

(The) Old folks at home (1851) "Swanee River" v & pf – arr. vln & orch.
Anderson
with Boston "Pops" Orch. – Fiedler   Victor 26009, LM77

GEMINIANI

(12) Sonatas, Op. 4 vln & c
Sonata No. 10, in A
with L. Pommers pf   Capitol P8481, SP8481

GLAZOUNOV

Concerto in a, Op. 82 vln & orch.
    D9–RC–939/40–1A, 941–1B &   HMV DB9480/2, DB21085/7,
with Victor Symphony   942/3–1A   FALP241, QALP241
Orch. – Steinberg   Victor 12–0965/7, (set DM1315),
    LM1064

Concerto in a, Op. 82 vln & orch.
with Pittsburgh Symphony Orch. –   Capitol K80328, P8382, SP8382,
Steinberg   STK80328

Concerto in a, Op. 82 vln & orch.
with New Philharmonia Orch. –   Angel 36011
Frühbeck de Burgos   Electrola SME91694
    HMV ALP2365, ASD2365,
    ASDQ5429, CVB2090

Meditation, Op. 32 vln & pf
with A. Balsam pf   D9–RC–969–1A   HMV DB9480, DB21087,
    7RF279
    Victor 12–0965, (in set DM1315)

GLAZOUNOV – *Continued*

Meditation, Op. 32 vln & pf – arr. vln & orch. Jones
with orch. – Irving
Angel 36002
Columbia CCA1028, CX1922,
FCX1028, QCX10488, SAX2563,
SAXF1028

GLUCK

Orphée et Eurydice (1762) – opera
Dance of the blessed spirits: Lento "Mélodie" (No. 2) arr. vln & pf
Kreisler
with A. Balsam pf   CO 32875–1   Columbia 17408D
Dance of the blessed spirits: Lento "Mélodie" (No. 2) arr. vln & pf
Kreisler
with L. Pommers pf   Capitol P8339

GOLDMARK

Concerto in a, Op. 28 vln & orch.
with Philharmonia Orch. – Blech   Capitol P8414

HANDEL

(15) Sonatas, Op. 1 (?1731) fl or vln & c
Sonata No. 9, in b: Andante (1st mvt) arr. vln & pf as "Larghetto" by
Hubay
with L. Pommers pf   Capitol P8536, SP8536
Sonata No. 13, in D vln IV
with A. Balsam pf   Capitol K80316, P8315

KODÁLY

(7) Zongoramuzsika, Op. 11 (1908/10) pf
No. 3. It is raining in the village arr. vln & pf Milstein
with L. Mittman pf   Columbia 292540, 17111D
No. 3. It is raining in the village arr. vln & pf Milstein
with L. Pommers pf   Capitol P8339

KREISLER

Rondino on a theme by Beethoven vln & pf
with A. Balsam pf   CO 32783–1   Columbia 17408D
Praeludium & Allegro (Pugnani) vln & pf
with L. Pommers pf   Capitol P8536, SP8536
Sicilienne & Rigaudon (Francoeur) vln & pf
with L. Pommers pf   Capitol P8536, SP8536

LALO

Symphonie espagnole, Op. 21 vln & orch.*
            XCO 33852/5–1, 33856–3 &   Columbia 12064/6D, (set M564),
with Philadelphia Orch. –   33857–2   C15845/7, (set D131)
Ormandy
Symphonie espagnole, Op. 21 vln & orch.*
with St. Louis Symphony Orch. –   Capitol CTL7095, P8303
Golschmann

LECLAIR

(12) Sonatas, Op. 9 – Book IV (1738) vln & c
Sonata No. 3, in D: Tambourin (3rd mvt) arr. vln & pf Kreisler
with L. Pommers pf   Capitol P8536, SP8536

* Omitting Intermezzo.

LISZT

(6) Consolations, G172 (1849/50) "Tröstungen" pf
No. 3. Consolation No. 3, in D flat arr. vln & pf "in E flat" Milstein
with L. Mittman pf   XCO 18476–5   Columbia 68479D, LX558

MASSENET

Thaïs (1894) – opera
Méditation arr. vln & pf Marsick
with A. Balsam pf   XCO 32753[1]   Columbia 71400D, LX993
Méditation arr. vln & pf Marsick
            VP–646–D4– TC–151–1A   V–Disc 251
with A. Balsam pf
Méditation arr. vln & pf Marsick
with L. Pommers pf   Capitol P8339

MENDELSSOHN

Concerto in e, Op. 64 vln & orch.
            XCO 34739/46–1   Columbia 12142/5D, (set M577),
with New York Philharmonic   30–5385/8, C15947/50, (set
Symphony Orch. – Walter   D157), ML4001
                V–Disc 696/7
Concerto in e, Op. 64 vln & orch.
with Pittsburgh Symphony Orch. –   Capitol CLCX046, CTL7059,
Steinberg   K80306, P8243
                Pickwick PC4023, SPC4023
Concerto in e, Op. 64 vln & orch.
with Philharmonia Orch. – Barzin   Angel 35730
                Capitol P8518, SP8518
                Electrola SHZE210
(6) Gesänge, Op. 34 v & pf
No 2. Auf Flügeln des Gesanges arr. vln & orch. Anderson
with Boston "Pops" Orch. – Fiedler   HMV 7RF183
                Victor 49–1280, LM77
(6) Songs without words, Op. 62 pf
No. 1. Song without words No. 25, in G "May breezes" arr. vln & pf
Kreisler
with L. Pommers pf   Capitol P8536, SP8536

MILSTEIN

Paganiniana solo vln
(unaccompanied)   Capitol CCL7526, CTL7058,
                L8297, P8259

MOZART

Adagio in E, K261 vln & orch.
with Victor Symphony Orch. –   HMV 7RF187
Golschmann   Victor (in sets DM1393 &
                WEPR11), LM1064
Adagio in E, K261 vln & orch.
with Concert Arts Orch. – Susskind   Capitol P8528, SP8528
Concerto No. 4, in D, K218 (cadenzas by Milstein) vln & orch.
with Philharmonia Orch. – Milstein   Angel 36007
                Columbia CCA1081, CX5254,
                SAX5254
                Electrola 1C053–80278
Concerto No. 5, in A, K219 "Turkish" (cadenzas by Milstein) vln & orch.
with Festival Orch. – Blech   Capitol P8362, K80326
                Pickwick PC4013, SPC4013

MOZART – *Continued*

Concerto No. 5, in A, K219 "Turkish" (cadenzas by Milstein) vln & orch.
  with Philharmonia Orch. – Milstein   Angel 36007
     Columbia CCA1081, CX5254,
     SAX5254
     Electrola 1C053–80278

Rondo in C, K373 vln & orch.
  with Victor Symphony Orch. –   HMV ERF106, ERQ106,
  Golschmann   7RF230
     Victor (in sets DM1393 &
     WEPR11), LM1064

Rondo in C, K373 vln & orch.
  with Concert Arts Orch. – Susskind   Capitol P8528, SP8528

Sonata No. 17, in C, K296 vln & pf
  with A. Balsam pf   Columbia 266268/9, 69683/4D,
     (set X143)

Sonata No. 17, in C, K296 vln & pf
  with L. Pommers pf   Capitol P8452

Sonata No. 18, in G, K301 vln & pf
  with L. Pommers pf   Capitol P8452

Sonata No. 24, in e, K304 vln & pf
  with L. Pommers pf   Capitol P8452

MUSSORGSKY

(La) Coutourière (Scherzino) (1871) pf – arr. vln & pf Milstein
  with L. Mittman pf   Columbia 17111D
Sorochintsy Fair (1911/23) – opera
  Gopak (Act III) orch. – arr. vln & orch. Jones
  with orch. – Irving   Angel 36002
     Columbia CCA1028, CX1922,
     FCX1028, QCX10488, SAX2563,
     SAXF1028

NARDINI

(7) Sonatas vln & c
  Sonata No. 7, in B flat: Larghetto (2nd mvt)
  with L. Mittman pf   XCO 22346–1   Columbia 264644, 69179D,
     LOX517, LX724

  Sonata No. 7, in B flat: Larghetto (2nd mvt)
  with L. Pommers pf   Capitol P8339

NOVAČEK

(8) Concert Caprices, Op. 5 vln & pf
  No. 4. Perpetuum mobile
  with L. Pommers pf   Capitol P8396

  No. 4. Perpetuum mobile
  with Concert Arts Orch. – Susskind   Capitol P8528, SP8528

PAGANINI

Concerto No. 2, in b Op. 7 vln & orch.
  Ronde à la clochette (3rd mvt) "La Campanella" arr. vln & pf Kreisler
  with L. Mittman pf   XCO 18477–1   Columbia 68479D, LOX499,
     LX595

PARADIES

Sicilienne vln & pf – arr. Dushkin
  with L. Pommers pf   Capitol P8339

PERGOLESI

(14) Sonatas (1770) 2 vlns & c
  Sonata No. 12, in E arr. vln & pf
  with L. Mittman pf   XCO 20895–1   Columbia 69179D, LOX517,
     LX724

  Sonata No. 12, in E arr. vln & pf
  with C. Bussotti pf   Capitol CTL7058, P8259

PIZZETTI

(3) Canti ad una giovane fidanzata (1924) vln & pf
  No. 1. Affettuoso
  with L. Mittman pf   Columbia 266172, 69398D
  No. 1. Affettuoso
  with L. Pommers pf   Capitol (in sets PBR8502 &
     SPBR8502

POLDINI

(7) Marionnettes pf
  No. 2. Poupée valsante arr. vln & orch. Anderson
  with Boston "Pops" Orch. – Fiedler   HMV 7RF183
     Victor 49–1280, LM77

  No. 2. Poupée valsante arr. vln & pf Kreisler
  with L. Pommers pf   Capitol P8536, SP8536

PROKOFIEV

Concerto No. 1, in D, Op. 19 (1913) vln & orch.
  with St. Louis Symphony Orch. –   Capitol CTL7095, P8303
  Golschmann

Concerto No. 1, in D, Op. 19 (1913) vln & orch.
  with Philharmonia Orch. – Giulini   Angel 36009
     Columbia CCA1089, CX5275,
     SAX5275

Concerto No. 2, in g, Op. 63 (1935) vln & orch.
  with New Philharmonia Orch. –   Angel 36009
  Frühbeck de Burgos   Columbia CCA1089, CX5275,
     SAX5275

Sonata No. 2, in D, Op. 94bis (1944) vln & pf
  with A. Balsam pf   Capitol K80316, P8315

RACHMANINOV

(14) Songs, Op. 34 (1912) v & pf
  No. 14. Vocalise arr. vln & orch.
  with orch. – Irving   Angel 36002
     Columbia CCA1028, CX1922,
     FCX1028, QCX10488, SAX2563,
     SAXF1028

RAVEL

Berceuse sur le nom de Gabriel Fauré (1922) vln & pf
  with L. Pommers pf   Capitol P8396

RIES

Suite No. 3, in G, Op. 34 vln & pf
  No. 5. Perpetuum mobile
  with L. Pommers pf   Capitol P8339

RIMSKY-KORSAKOV

Fantasia on Russian themes, Op. 33 vln & orch. – arr. Kreisler
  with orch. – Irving   Angel 36002
     Columbia CCA1028, CX1922,
     FCX1028, QCX10488, SAX2563,
     SAXF1028

RIMSKY-KORSAKOV – *Continued*

(The) Tale of Tsar Saltan (1900) – opera
Flight of the bumblebee orch. – arr. vln & pf Hartmann
with A. Balsam pf   CO 32782–1   Columbia 17352D
Flight of the bumblebee orch. – arr. vln & pf Hartmann
        VP–647–D4–TC–152–1   V–Disc 251
with A. Balsam pf
Flight of the bumblebee orch. – arr. vln & pf Hartmann
with L. Pommers pf   Capitol P8339, P8426, PAO8426

SAINT–SAËNS

Concerto No. 3, in b, Op. 61 vln & orch.
with Philharmonia Orch. – Fistoulari   Angel 36005
        Columbia CCA1029, FCX1029,
        SAXF1029
Introduction & Rondo Capriccioso, Op. 28 vln & orch.
with Concert Arts Orch. – Susskind   Capitol P8528, SP8528

SARASATE

(8) Danzas españolas vln & pf
No. 3. Romanza andaluza, Op. 22, No. 1
with A. Balsam pf   XCO 32811[1]   Columbia 71400D, LX993
No. 3. Romanza andaluza, Op. 22, No. 1
with L. Pommers pf   Capitol FAP1–20468, P8396
Introduction & Tarantelle, Op. 43 vln & pf
with L. Pommers pf   Capitol (in sets PBR8502 &
        SPBR8502)

SCHUBERT

(14) Schwanengesang, D957 (1828) v & pf
No. 4. Ständchen "Serenade" arr. vln & orch. Anderson
with Boston "Pops" Orch. – Fiedler   HMV 7RF210
        Victor 26009, LM77

SCHUMANN

(12) Duets, Op. 85 pf – 4 hands
No. 12. Abendlied arr. vln & pf Wilhelmj
        VP–647–D4–TC–152–1   V–Disc 251
with A. Balsam pf
No. 12. Abendlied arr. vln & pf Wilhelmj
with L. Pommers pf   Capitol P8536, SP8536
(13) Kinderscenen, Op. 15 pf
No. 7. Träumerei arr. vln & pf Hüllweck
with L. Mittman pf   Columbia 17337D
No. 7. Träumerei arr. vln & pf Hüllweck
with L. Pommers pf   Capitol FAP1–20468, P8396
Sonata (1853) "Frei aber Einsam" vln & pf
Intermezzo (2nd mvt)
with C. Bussotti pf   Capitol CTL7058, P8259

SMETANA

From my Homeland (1878) vln & pf
No. 2. Andantino
with L. Mittman pf   XCO 18478–1   Columbia 68408D, LCX34,
        LX558
No. 2. Andantino
with L. Pommers pf   Capitol P8339

STAMITZ, K.

Concerto in B flat vln & orch.
Adagio (2nd mvt); **Rondo** (3rd mvt)
        XCO 28938–1 & 28939–2   Columbia 70747D
with A. Balsam pf

STRAVINSKY

Firebird (1910) – ballet suite orch.
No. 5. Berceuse arr. vln & pf Dushkin & Stravinsky
with L. Mittman pf   Columbia 17115D
No. 5. Berceuse arr. vln & pf Dushkin & Stravinsky
with Concert Arts Orch. – Susskind   Capitol P8528, SP8528
Mavra (1922) – opera
Russian maiden's song (Parasha's aria) arr. vln & pf Dushkin &
Stravinsky
with A. Balsam pf   Victor 12–1017
Russian maiden's song (Parasha's aria) arr. vln & pf Dushkin &
Stravinsky
with L. Pommers pf   Capitol P8339

SUK

(4) Pieces, Op. 17 vln & pf
No. 4. Burleska
with A. Balsam pf   XCO 29048–1   Columbia 71498D
No. 4. Burleska
with C. Bussotti pf   Capitol CTL7058, P8259

SZYMANOWSKI

(3) Mythes, Op. 30 (1915) vln & pf
No. 1. La Fontaine d'Aréthuse
with L. Pommers pf   Capitol (in sets PBR8502 &
        SPBR8502)
Notturno & Tarantella, Op. 28 vln & pf
Tarantelle
with L. Mittman pf   Columbia 69398D
Notturna & Tarantella, Op. 28 vln & pf
with L. Pommers pf   Capitol P8536, SP8536

TARTINI

Sonata in g "Il Trillo del Diavolo" vln & c – arr. vln & pf Kreisler
        XCO 22347/8–2, 22349–1 &   Columbia 264745/6, 69196/7D,
with L. Mittman pf   22350–5   (set X98), LX825/6
Sonata in g "Il Trillo del Diavolo" vln & c – arr. vln & pf Kreisler
with L. Pommers pf   Capitol FAP1–8481, P8481,
        SFP1–8481, SP8481

TCHAIKOVSKY

Concerto in D, Op. 35 vln & orch.
with Chicago Symphony Orch. – Stock   Columbia 30–5015/8, 11276/9D,
        (set M413), C20044/7, (set D46),
        JS126/9, LX25014/7, ML4013,
        RL6631
        Harmony HL7083
Concerto in D, Op. 35 vln & orch.
with Boston Symphony Orch. –
Munch   HMV FBLP1045
        Victor A630243, LM1760,
        VIC1003

TCHAIKOVSKY – *Continued*

Concerto in D, Op. 35 vln & orch.
with Pittsburgh Symphony Orch. –   Angel 35686, (in set 3712)
Steinberg   Capitol (in sets PBR8502 &
     SPBR8502), P8512, SP8512
     Electrola SHZE214
     World Record Club ST574, T574

(6) Songs, Op. 6 v & pf
    No. 6. None but the weary heart
    with E. Pinza bs & G. King pf   Victor (in set WDM1703),
     LM1703, RB6506

Souvenir d'un lieu cher, Op. 42 vln & pf
    No. 1. Méditation arr. vln & orch. Glazounov
    with orch. – Irving   Angel 36002
     Columbia CCA1028, CX1922,
     FCX1028, QCX10488, SAX2563,
     SAXF1028

    No. 2. Scherzo
    with L. Mittman pf   Columbia 17115D

    No. 2. Scherzo arr. vln & orch. Glazounov
    with orch. – Irving   Angel 36002
     Columbia CX1922, FCX1028,
     QCX10488, SAX2563,
     SAXF1028

    No. 3. Mélodie
    with L. Pommers pf   Capitol P8396

Waltz–scherzo, Op. 34 vln & pf or orch.
    with orch. – Irving   Angel 36002
     Columbia CCA1028, CX1922,
     FCX1028, QCX10488, SAX2563,
     SAXF1028

VITALI

Chaconne in g vln & c – arr. vln & pf Charlier
     XCO 18464/5–2 & 18466–3   Columbia 68476/7D, (set X61),
with L. Mittman pf   LX521/2

Chaconne in g vln & c – arr. vln & pf Charlier
    with A. Balsam pf   Capitol K80316, P8315

VIVALDI

(12) Concerti, Op. 3 "L'Estro armonico" var. cbns & strs
    Concerto No. 11, in d, P.250 (F.IV, No. 11) 2 vlns, vlc, strs & c
    with E. Morini vln, H. Shapiro vlc &   Angel 36006
    Chamber Orch. – Milstein   Columbia CX1940, FCX1050,
     SAX2579, SAXF1050

(12) Concerti, Op. 8 (1725) "Il Cimento dell' Armonia e dell' Invenzione"
(Nos. 1/4: Le quattro Stagioni) vln & strs
    Concerto No. 7, in d, P.258 (F.I, No. 28)
    with strings & harpsichord – Milstein   Angel 36010
     Columbia SAX5285

Concerto in C, P.88 (F.I, No. 3) vln, strs & c – real. Maderna
    with Chamber Orch. – Milstein   Angel 36001
     Columbia CX1874, FCX990,
     QCX10457, SAX2517, SAXF990,
     SAXQ7357

Concerto in D, P.163 (F.I, No. 133) vln, strs & c – real. Malipiero
    with R. Conant hpsi & Chamber Orch.   Angel 36004
    – Milstein   Columbia CX5264, QCX7376,
     SAX5264, SAXQ7376

VIVALDI – *Continued*

Concerto in D, P.195 (F.I, No. 162) vln, strs & c – real. Malipiero
    with R. Conant hpsi & Chamber Orch.   Angel 36004
    – Milstein   Columbia CX5264, QCX7376,
     SAX5264, SAXQ7376

Concerto in D, P.208 (F.I, No. 10) (Op. 51, No. 1) "L'Inquietudine" vln,
strs & c – real. Ephrikian
    with R. Conant hpsi & Chamber Orch.   Angel 36004
    – Milstein   Columbia CX5264, QCX7376,
     SAX5264, SAXQ7376

Concerto in A, P.228 (F.I, No. 141) "Pisendel" vln, strs & c – real.
Malipiero
    with R. Conant hpsi & Chamber Orch.   Angel 36004
    – Milstein   Columbia CX5264, QCX7376,
     SAX5264, SAXQ7376

Concerto in A, P.229 (F.I, No. 39) vln, strs & c
    with strings & harpsichord – Milstein   Angel 36010
     Columbia SAX5285

Concerto in A, P.234 (F.I, No. 106) vln, strs & c – real. Malipiero
    with Chamber Orch. – Milstein   Angel 36001
     Columbia CX1874, FCX990,
     QCX10457, SAX2518, SAXF990,
     SAXQ7357

Concerto in A, P.236 (F.I, No. 5) vln, strs & c – real Maderna
    with Chamber Orch. – Milstein   Angel 36001
     Columbia CX1874, FCX990,
     QCX10457, SAX2518, SAXF990,
     SAXQ7357

Concerto in c, P.419 (F.I, No. 2) (Op. 51, No. 3) "Il Sospetto" vln, strs & c
    with Chamber Orch. – Milstein   Angel 36001
     Columbia CX1874, FCX990,
     QCX10457, SAX2518, SAXF990,
     SAXQ7357

Concerto in E flat, F.I, No. 231 "Il Ritiro" vln, strs & c
Siciliano
    with L. Pommers pf   Capitol P8339

(12) Sonatas, Op. 2 (1712) vln & c
    Sonata No. 2, in A, F.XIII, No. 30 ed. David
     CO 19064–2 & 19065–1   Columbia 17070D, LB34
    with L. Mittman pf

    Sonata No. 2, in A, F.XIII, No. 30 ed. David
    with L. Pommers pf   Capitol P8481, SP8481

Sonata in D, F.XII, No. 6 vln & c – arr. vln & pf Respighi
     XCO 18704[1] & 18705[3]   Columbia 68478D, GQX10886,
with L. Mittman pf   LOX516, LX543

WIENIAWSKI

Concerto No. 2, in d, Op. 22 vln & orch.
    Romance (2nd mvt)
    with L. Mittman pf   XCO 20896–3   Columbia 69032D, LFX529,
     LOX366, LX676

Légende, Op. 17 vln & pf or orch.
    with Concert Arts Orch. – Susskind   Capitol P8528, SP8528

(2) Mazurkas, Op. 19 vln & pf
    No. 2. Mazurka No. 2, in D "Dudziarz"
    with A. Balsam pf   HMV 7RF279
     Victor 12–1017

    No. 2. Mazurka No. 2, in D "Dudziarz"
    with L. Pommers pf   Capitol P8339

WIENIAWSKI – *Continued*

Polonaise brillante No. 1, in D, Op. 4 vln & pf
with L. Mittman pf   XCO 18706–3   Columbia 69032D, LFX529,
LOX366, LX676

Polonaise brillante No. 1, in D, Op. 4 vln & pf
with L. Pommers pf   Capitol P8396

Scherzo–Tarantelle, Op. 16 vln & pf
with A. Balsam pf   XCO 32876–1   Columbia 71498D

Scherzo–Tarantelle, Op. 16 vln & pf
with L. Pommers pf   Capitol P8396

Enrico MINETTI (1900–)

VIVALDI

Concerto in E flat, P.429 (Op. 33, No. 1) vln, strs & c
with La Scala String Orch., Milan –   Colosseum CRLP1015
Valdinoci

Lisa MINGHETTI (1912–)

BRAHMS

(21) Hungarian Dances pf duet
Hungarian dance No. 2, in d arr. vln & pf Joachim
with piano   HMV EG2344

PARADIES

Sicilienne vln & pf – arr. Dushkin
with piano   HMV EG2344

REGER

Romance in G vln & pf
with piano   HMV EG2344

Mischa MISCHAKOFF (1895–)

BACH

(6) Brandenburg Concerti, BWV1046/51 (1721) strs & c
Brandenburg Concerto No. 2, in F, BWV1047 tpt, fl, ob, vln, strs & c
with J. Baker fl, J. Wummer fl, R.   Musicians Foundation of
Bloom ob & NBC Symphony Orch. –   America 3
Leinsdorf

BEETHOVEN

Concerto in D, Op. 61 vln & orch.
Rondo (3rd mvt)
with Victor Symphony Orch. –   Victo. (in set DM1428), LM1101
Leinsdorf

BRAHMS

Concerto in D, Op. 77 vln & orch.
Allegro giocoso (3rd mvt)
with Victor Symphony Orch. –   Victor (in set DM1428), LM1101
Leinsdorf

Concerto in a, Op. 102 "Double" vln, vlc & orch.
with F. Miller vlc & NBC Symphony   Victor LM2178, RB16066
Orch. – Toscanini

BRUCH

Concerto No. 1, in g, Op. 26 vln & orch.
Allegro moderato (1st mvt)
with Victor Symphony Orch. –   Victor (in set DM1428), LM1101
Leinsdorf

LALO

Symphonie espagnole, Op. 21 vln & orch.
Intermezzo (3rd mvt)
with Victor Symphony Orch. –   Victor (in set DM1428), LM1101
Leinsdorf

LÉONARD

(5) Scènes humoristiques, Op. 61 vln & pf
No. 5. Sérénade du lapin belliqueux – arr. 3 vlns & pf
with E. Brown vln, B. Rabinoff   Royale 583
vln & J. Zayde pf

MENDELSSOHN

Concerto in e, Op. 64 vln & orch.
Allegro appassionato (1st mvt)
with Victor Symphony Orch. –   Victor (in set DM1428), LM1101
Leinsdorf

MOZART

Concerto No. 3, in G, K216 vln & orch.
Rondo allegro (3rd mvt)
with Victor Symphony Orch. –   Victor (in set DM1428), LM1101
Leinsdorf

SCHUBERT

(3) Sonatinas, Op. 137 (D384, D385 & D408) vln & pf
No. 1. Sonatina No. 1, in D, D384
with E. Balogh pf   Eurochord LPG626
Lyrichord LL7

No. 2. Sonatina No. 2, in a, D385
with E. Balogh pf   Eurochord LPG626
Lyrichord LL7

No. 3. Sonatina No. 3, in g, D408
with E. Balogh pf   Eurochord LPG626
Lyrichord LL7

TCHAIKOVSKY

Concerto in D, Op. 35 vln & orch.
Canzonetta (2nd mvt)
with Victor Symphony Orch. –   Victor (in set DM1428), LM1101
Leinsdorf

WIENIAWSKI

Concerto No. 2, in d, Op. 22 vln & orch.
Romance (2nd mvt)
with Victor Symphony Orch. –   Victor (in set DM1428), LM1101
Leinsdorf

Issay MITNITZKY (1887–)

BACH

(3) Sonatas & 3 Partitas, BWV1001/6 solo vln
Partita No. 3, in E; Preludio (1st mvt) BWV1006 arr. vln & pf Saint-
Saëns
with piano   Columbia DN246

BRAHMS

(21) Hungarian Dances pf duet
Hungarian Dance No. 2, in d arr. vln & pf Joachim
with piano   Columbia DN244

(16) Waltzes, Op. 39 pf duet
No. 15. Waltz No. 15, in A flat arr. vln & pf "in A" Hochstein
with piano   Columbia DN245

FIORILLO

(36) Étude–Caprices, Op. 3 solo vln
Étude–Caprice No. 14, in g (Adagio) arr. vln & pf "G string" Mistowzky
with piano   Columbia DN246

GRAM

Canzonetta vln & pf
with piano   Columbia DN244

REGER

(60) Schlichte Weisen – 6 Books, Op. 76 v & pf
No. 52. Maria–Wiegenlied arr. vln & pf
with piano   Columbia DN245

Bronisław MITTMANN

d'AMBROSIO

Romance in D, Op. 9 vln & pf
with piano   16493   Homochord B32

DRDLA

Serenade No. 1, in A vln & pf
with piano   16484   Homochord B16
Souvenir vln & pf
with piano   16485   Homochord B16

LANGER

Grandfather, Op. 22 salon orch. – arr. vln & pf
with orch.   16473   Homochord B9
Grandfather, Op. 22 salon orch. – arr. vln & pf
with orch.   50516   Homochord B8036
Grandmother, Op. 20 pf – arr. vln & pf
with orch.   16466   Homochord B9
Grandmother, Op. 20 pf – arr. vln & pf
with orch.   50517   Homochord B8036

MOZART

Divertimento No. 17, in D, K334 2 hrns & strs
Minuet (3rd mvt) arr. vln & pf Burmester
with piano   16494   Homochord B37

RIMSKY–KORSAKOV

Sadko (1898) – opera
Chant hindou arr. vln & pf Kreisler
with piano   61037   Homochord B37

TOSELLI

Serenade, Op. 6 vln & pf
with piano   16492   Homochord B32
Serenade, Op. 6 vln & pf
with orch.   50518   Homochord B8056

Max MODERN

BÉRIOT

Concerto No. 9, in a, Op. 104 vln & orch.
Adagio (2nd mvt)
with piano   15020   Applaudando 1319

DELIBES

Coppélia (1870) – ballet orch.
No. 1b. Valse lente arr. vln & pf
with piano   15019   Applaudando 1319

HANDEL

Serse (1738) – opera
Ombra mai fu "Largo" arr. vln & pf
with piano   15022   Applaudando 1320

HUBAY

(14) Scènes de la Csárda vln & pf
No. 4. Hejre Kati, Op. 32
with piano   32034   Applaudando 31318

KREISLER

Schön Rosmarin vln & pf
with piano   32035   Applaudando 31318

RAFF

(6) Pieces, Op. 85 vln & pf
No. 3. Cavatina in D
with piano   32032   Applaudando 31317

SCHUMANN

(13) Kinderscenen, Op. 15 pf
No. 7. Träumerei arr. vln & pf
with piano   15021   Applaudando 1320

THOMÉ

Andante religioso, Op. 70 pf – arr. vln & pf
with piano   32033   Applaudando 31317

Alain MOGLIA

BACH

Concerto in d, BWV 1043 2 vlns, strs & c
with J–P. Wallez vln & Ensemble   Classic 991081
Instrumental de France – Wallez

VIVALDI

(12) Concerti, Op. 3 "L'Estro armonico" var. cbns & strs
Concerto No. 10, in b, P.148 (F.IV, No. 10) 4 vlns, strs & c
with C. Crenne vln, P.D. Pelaz vln, J–   Classic 991062
P. Wallez vln, M. Roche hpsi &
Ensemble Instrumental de France –
Wallez

A. MOGUILEVSKI

BEETHOVEN

Sonata No. 5, in F, Op. 24 "Spring" vln & pf
with L. Kreutzer pf   Polydor 5027/9

CORELLI

(12) Sonatas, Op. 5 vln & c
Sonata No. 12, in d arr. vln & pf Moguilevski
with piano   Columbia JW264/5

CUI

Kaleidoscope, Op. 50 vln & pf
No. 9. Orientale
with piano   Polydor 1142

DEBUSSY

Children's Corner Suite (1908) pf
No. 5. The little shepherd arr. vln & pf Durand
with piano   Columbia JD6028

Suite Bergamasque (1890) pf
No. 3. Clair de lune arr. vln & pf Roelens
with piano   Columbia JW553

FALLA

(7) Canciones populares españolas (1914) v & pf
No. 1. El paño moruno arr. vln & pf Kochański
with piano   Columbia J5631/2

No. 3. Asturiana arr. vln & pf Kochański
with piano   Columbia J5631/2

No. 4. Jota arr. vln & pf Kochański
with piano   Columbia J5631/2

No. 5. Nana arr. vln & pf Kochański
with piano   Columbia J5631/2

No. 6. Canción arr. vln & pf Kochański
with piano   Columbia J5631/2

FAURÉ

(3) Chansons, Op. 7 v & pf
No. 1. Après un rêve arr. vln & pf
with piano   Columbia JD6028

GLAZOUNOV

(2) Pieces, Op. 20 vlc & pf
No. 2. Sérénade espagnole arr. vln & pf Kreisler
with piano   Columbia J5626

KRAKAUER

Im Paradies (1926) pf – arr. vln & pf Kreisler
with piano   Columbia J5640

KREISLER

Paraphrase on 2 Russian folksongs vln & pf
with piano   Columbia J5640

MELARTIN

(2) Songs, Op. 3 v & pf
No. 2. Élégie arr. vln & pf
with piano   Columbia JW553

PALMGREN

Jugend (6 lyric pieces) Op. 28 pf
No. 5. Der Schwan arr. vln & pf Sandby
with piano   Columbia JD6012

SIBELIUS

Pan & Echo, Op. 53 orch.
No. 3. Nocturne arr. vln & pf Press
with piano   Columbia JD6012

TCHAIKOVSKY

Concerto in D, Op. 35 vln & orch.
Canzonetta (2nd mvt)
with piano   Columbia JW265

Sérénade mélancolique in b flat, Op. 26 vln & orch. – arr. vln & pf
Wilhelmj
with A. Abaza pf   Columbia JW683

VECSEY

Valse triste vln & pf
with piano   Columbia J5626

VERACINI

(12) Sonatas, Op. 2 (1744) "Sonate accademiche" vln & c
Sonata No. 8, in e
with A. Abaza pf   Columbia JW635/6

Sonata No. 11, in E: Minuet; Gavotte
with A. Abaza pf   Columbia JW636

Villi MOKATSYAN

ALTUNYAN

Concerto–Symphony vln, vla & orch.
with R. Altunyan vla & Armenian   Mezhdunarodnaya Kniga
Radio Symphony Orch. – Davtyan   D25159

BABAJANIAN

Concerto in a (1949) vln & orch.
with Armenian SSR Symphony Orch.   Mezhdunarodnaya Kniga
– Maluntsyan   D023029

Jean–Noël MOLARD

VIVALDI

*(12) Concerti, Op. 3 "L'Estro armonico" var. cbns & strs
Concerto No. 1, in D, P.146 (F.IV, No. 7) 4 vlns, vlc, strs & c
with G. Carles vln, H. Déat vln, G.   Erato STU70641
Jarry vln & Jean–François Paillard
Chamber Orch. – Paillard

Concerto No. 4, in e, P.97 (F.I, No. 174) 4 vlns, strs & c
with G. Carles vln, H. Déat vln, G.   Erato STU70641
Jarry vln & Jean–François Paillard
Chamber Orch. – Paillard

Concerto No. 7, in F, P.249 (F.IV, No. 9) 4 vlns, strs & c
with G. Carles vln, H. Déat vln, G.   Erato STU70641
Jarry vln & Jean–François Paillard
Chamber Orch. – Paillard

Concerto No. 10, in b, P.148 (F.IV, No. 10) 4 vlns, strs & c
with G. Carles vln, H. Déat vln, G.   Erato STU70641
Jarry vln & Jean–François Paillard
Chamber Orch. – Paillard

* These five concerti also has Monique Vallet as one of the soloists.
However, it is not clear as to which concerto features her as soloist.

VIVALDI – *Continued*

Concerto in B flat, P367 (F.I, No. 59) 4 vlns, strs & c
with G. Carles vln, H. Déat vln, G.   Erato STU70641
Jarry vln & Jean–François Paillard
Chamber Orch. – Paillard

Bernardino MOLINARI

VIVALDI

(12) Concerti, Op. 8 (1725) "Il Cimento dell' Armonia e dell' Invenzione"
(Nos. 1/4: Le quattro Stagioni) vln & strs
Concerto No. 1, in E, F.I, No. 22 "La Primavera"
with Orch. Santa Cecilia Roma –   Cetra LPU0016
Molinari

Concerto No. 2, in B flat, F.I, No. 23 "L'Estate"
with Orch. Santa Cecilia Roma –   Cetra LPU0016
Molinari

Concerto No. 3, in F, F.I, No. 24 "L'Autunno"
with Orch. Santa Cecilia Roma – .   Cetra LPU0016
Molinari

Concerto No. 4, in f, F.I, No. 25 "L'Inverno"
with Orch. Santa Cecilia Roma –   Cetra LPU0016
Molinari

Ermanno MOLINARIO

VIVALDI

(12) Sonatas, Op. 1 2 vlns & c
Sonata No. 1, in g, F.XIII, No. 17
with M. Ferraris vln, M. Sorelli hpsi & Arcophon AC677
A. Pocaterra vlc   HMV C063–90250/1

Sonata No. 2, in e, F.XIII, No. 18
with M. Ferraris vln, M. Sorelli hpsi & Arcophon AC677
A. Pocaterra vlc   HMV C063–90250/1

Sonata No. 3, in C, F.XIII, No. 19
with M. Ferraris vln, M. Sorelli hpsi & Arcophon AC677
A. Pocaterra vlc   HMV C063–90250/1

Sonata No. 4, in E, F.XIII, No. 20
with M. Ferraris vln, M. Sorelli hpsi & Arcophon AC677
A. Pocaterra vlc   HMV C063–90250/1

Sonata No. 5, in F, F.XIII, No. 21
with M. Ferraris vln, M. Sorelli hpsi & Arcophon AC677
A. Pocaterra vlc   HMV C063–90250/1

Sonata No. 6, in D, F.XIII, No. 22
with M. Ferraris vln, M. Sorelli hpsi & Arcophon AC677
A. Pocaterra vlc   HMV C063–90250/1

Sonata No. 7, in E flat, F.XIII, No. 23
with M. Ferraris vln, M. Sorelli hpsi & Arcophon AC677
A. Pocaterra vlc   HMV C063–90250/1

Sonata No. 8, in d, F.XIII, No. 24
with M. Ferraris vln, M. Sorelli hpsi & Arcophon AC677
A. Pocaterra vlc   HMV C063–90250/1

Sonata No. 9, in A, F.XIII, No. 25
with M. Ferraris vln, M. Sorelli hpsi & Arcophon AC677
A. Pocaterra vlc   HMV C063–90250/1

Sonata No. 10, in B flat, F.XIII, No. 26
with M. Ferraris vln, M. Sorelli hpsi & Arcophon AC677
A. Pocaterra vlc   HMV C063–90250/1

VIVALDI – *Continued*

Sonata No. 11, in b, F.XIII, No. 27
with M. Ferraris vln, M. Sorelli hpsi & Arcophon AC677
A. Pocaterra vlc   HMV C063–90250/1

Sonata No. 12, in d, F.XIII, No. 28 "La follia"
with M. Ferraris vln, M. Sorelli hpsi & Arcophon AC677
A. Pocaterra vlc   HMV C063–90250/1

David MOLL

STEIN

Sonata solo vln
(unaccompanied)   Music Library MLR7115
Sonata vln & pf
with C. Siegel pf   Music Library MLR7115

MOLLER*

BOSC

Moss rose v & pf – arr. vln & pf
with piano   Bettini cylinder
Bettini disc 2158

BRAHMS

(21) Hungarian Dances pf duet
Hungarian dance arr. vln & pf Joachim†
with piano   Bettini cylinder
Bettini disc 2155

di CAPUA

Marie Mari v & pf – arr. vln & pf
with piano   Bettini disc 2177

CHÂTEAU–THIERRY

Frou–Frou – valse orch. – arr. vln & pf
with piano   Bettini cylinder

CZIBULKA

Loin du Pays – valse pf – arr. vln & pf
with piano   Bettini cylinder

DESPRET

Sourire d'Avril – valse pf – arr. vln & pf
with piano   Bettini cylinder

GCKI–ALBI

(L') Ours – valse orch. – arr. vln & pf
with piano   Bettini cylinder

GILLET

Loin du Bal, Op. 36 – ballet orch.
Intermezzo arr. vln & pf
with piano   Bettini cylinder

*The Moller cylinders date from 1898 and most were listed in Bettini's
catalog No. 11 on page 18, issued June 1901. It may be that the discs are
different "takes" and not dubbings from the cylinders as they were issued
several years later.

† Unidentified.

GILLET – *Continued*

Rêve après le Bal – valse pf – arr. vln & pf
with piano   Bettini cylinder

HAUSER

Rapsodie hongrois No. 1, in d, Op. 43 vln & pf
with piano   Bettini cylinder

HUBAY

(14) Scènes de la Csárda vln & pf
   Scène de la Csárda*
with piano   Bettini cylinder
                         Bettini disc 2160

KERKER

(The) Belle of New York (1897) – musical
   I'm the Belle of New York arr. vln & pf
with piano   Bettini cylinder
                         Bettini disc 2154

KETLAR

Monte Cristo – valse tzigane orch. – arr. vln & pf Rouveirolis
with piano   Bettini cylinder
                         Bettini disc 2157

LEONCAVALLO

(I) Pagliacci (1892) – opera
   Vesti la giubba arr. vln & pf
with piano   Bettini cylinder
                         Bettini disc 2152

MARGIS

Valse bleu vln & pf
with piano   Bettini cylinder

MASCAGNI

Cavalleria Rusticana (1890) – opera
   Intermezzo orch – arr. vln & pf
with piano   Bettini cylinder

MASSENET

Thaïs (1894) – opera
   Méditation arr. vln & pf Marsick
with piano   Bettini cylinder

MEZZACCAPO

Sympathie – valse pf – arr. vln & pf
with piano   Bettini cylinder

NERUDA

Berceuse slave d'après un chant polonaise, Op. 11 vln & pf
                         Bettini cylinder
                         Bettini disc 2176

PUCCINI

(La) Bohème (1896) – opera
   selection
with piano   Bettini cylinder
                         Bettini disc 2151

* Unidentified.

RAFF

(6) Pieces, Op. 85 vln & pf
   No. 3. Cavatina in D
with piano   Bettini cylinder
                         Bettini disc 2159

SAINT-SAËNS

Samson et Dalila, Op. 47 (1877) – opera
   Mon coeur s'ouvre à ta voix arr. vln & pf
with piano   Bettini cylinder
                         Bettini disc 2153

SARASATE

Zigeunerweisen, Op. 20 vln & pf or orch.*
with piano   Bettini cylinder

SCHUMANN

(13) Kinderscenen, Op. 15 pf
   No. 7. Träumerei arr. vln & pf
with piano   Bettini cylinder
                         Bettini disc 2156

WIENIAWSKI

(2) Mazurkas, Op. 19 vln & pf
   No. 1. Mazurka No. 1, in G "Obertass"
with piano   Bettini cylinder
                         Bettini disc 2161

ZELLER

(Der) Vogelhändler (1891) – operetta
   Der Schmoller arr. vln & pf
with piano   Bettini cylinder
   Mir scheint, ich Kenn' dich spröde Fee (Waltz) arr. vln & pf
with piano   Bettini cylinder

Peder MØLLER

BACH

(4) Suites, BWV 1066/9 strs & c
   Suite No. 3, in D; Air (2nd mvt) BWV 1068 2 obs, 3 tpts, drms, strs & c
   – arr. vln & pf as "Air on the G–string" by Wilhelmj
with piano   Polyphon 47504

HANDEL

(15) Sonatas, Op. 1 (?1731) fl or vln & c
   Sonata No. 9, in b: Andante (1st mvt) arr. vln & pf as "Larghetto" by
   Hubay
with piano   Polyphon 47508

KREISLER

Praeludium & Allegro (Pugnani) vln & pf
with piano   Polyphon 47504

MASSENET

Thaïs (1894) – opera
   Méditation arr. vln & pf Marsick
with piano   Polyphon 47508

* Abridged.

Grischa MONASEVITCH

TOCH

Serenade in G, Op. 25 (1917) 2 vlns & vla
   with L. Kaufman vln & R.   Vox 16081/2, (set 177)
   Menhennick vla

Ferdinand de MONGE

GILLET

(Le) Lettre de Manon – valse pf – arr. vln & orch.
   with orch.   Odeon 2244, 60501

HÉROLD

(Le) Pré aux Clercs (1832) – opera
   Cadenza arr. vln & orch. de Monge
   with orch.   Odeon 60503

SAINT–SAËNS

(Le) Carnaval des animaux (1886) small orch.
   Le cygne arr. vln & orch.
   with orch.   Odeon X67654
Samson et Dalila, Op. 47 (1877) – opera
   Selection arr. vln & pf as "Fantasia" by de Monge
   with orch.   Odeon 60503

SCHUBERT

(7) Gesänge (set to Scott's "Lady of the Lake") Op. 52 v & pf
   No. 6. Ave Maria, D839 arr. vln & pf Wilhelmj
   with harp & orch.   Odeon X67655

STEWART

(La) Lettre d'amour – valse tzigane vln & pf
   with orch.   Odeon 2245, 60501

THOMÉ

Sous la feuillée, Op. 29 pf – arr. vln & orch.
   with orch.   Odeon 60500

VERDI

Rigoletto (1851) – opera
   Selection arr. vln & pf as "Fantasia" by de Monge
   with orch.   Odeon 60500

Sonya MONOSOFF

BACH

(6) Sonatas, BWV1014/9 vln & clav
   Sonata No. 1, in b, BWV1014
      with K. Weaver hpsi   Cambridge (in set CRS2822)
   Sonata No. 2, in A, BWV1015
      with K. Weaver hpsi   Cambridge (in set CRS2822)
   Sonata No. 3, in E, BWV1016
      with K. Weaver hpsi   Cambridge (in set CRS2822)
   Sonata No. 4, in c, BWV1017
      with K. Weaver hpsi   Cambridge (in set CRS2822)
   Sonata No. 5, in f, BWV1018
      with K. Weaver hpsi   Cambridge (in set CRS2822)
   Sonata No. 6, in G, BWV1019
      with K. Weaver hpsi   Cambridge (in set CRS2822)

BACH – *Continued*

Sonata in G, BWV1021 vln & c
   with K. Weaver hpsi & J. Davidoff   Cambridge (in set CRS2822)
   gamba
Sonata in e, BWV1023 vln & c
   with K. Weaver hpsi & J. Davidoff   Cambridge (in set CRS2822)
   gamba

BIBER

(16) Biblical Sonatas "Mysterien" vln & c
   Sonata No. 1, in d "The annunciation of the birth of Christ"
      with M. Smith org & J. Scholz gamba   Cambridge (in set CRM811 &
                                                CRS1811)
   Sonata No. 2, in A "Visit of Mary to Elizabeth"
      with M. Smith org & J. Scholz gamba   Cambridge (in sets CRM811 &
                                                CRS1811)
   Sonata No. 3, in b "Birth of Christ"
      with M. Smith hpsi & J. Scholz gamba   Cambridge (in sets CRM811 &
                                                CRS1811)
   Sonata No. 4, in d "Christ in the temple"
      with M. Smith hpsi & J. Scholz gamba   Cambridge (in sets CRM811 &
                                                CRS1811)
   Sonata No. 5, in A "The 12 year–old Jesus in the temple"
      with M. Smith hpsi & J. Miller bsn   Cambridge (in sets CRM811 &
                                                CRS1811)
   Sonata No. 6, in c "Christ on the Mount of Olives"
      with M. Smith org   Cambridge (in sets CRM811 &
                                                CRS1811)
   Sonata No. 7, in F "The Flagellation of Christ"
      with M. Smith org & J. Miller bsn   Cambridge (in sets CRM811 &
                                                CRS1811)
   Sonata No. 8, in B flat "Christ's crowning with thorns"
      with M. Smith hpsi & J. Scholz gamba   Cambridge (in sets CRM811 &
                                                CRS1811)
   Sonata No. 9, in a "Christ on the way to Calvary"
      with M. Smith org & J. Scholz gamba   Cambridge (in sets CRM811 &
                                                CRS1811)
   Sonata No. 10, in g "The Crucifixion"
      with M. Smith org & J. Miller bsn   Cambridge (in sets CRM811 &
                                                CRS1811)
   Sonata No. 11, in G "The Resurrection"
      with M. Smith org   Cambridge (in sets CRM811 &
                                                CRS1811)
   Sonata No. 12, in C "The Ascension"
      with M. Smith hpsi & J. Miller bsn   Cambridge (in sets CRM811 &
                                                CRS1811)
   Sonata No. 13, in d "The Emanation of the Holy Ghost"
      with M. Smith hpsi & J. Scholz gamba   Cambridge (in sets CRM811 &
                                                CRS1811)
   Sonata No. 14, in D "The Ascension of the Holy Virgin"
      with M. Smith org   Cambridge (in sets CRM811 &
                                                CRS1811)
   Sonata No. 15, in C "Coronation of the Virgin"
      with M. Smith org & J. Miller bsn   Cambridge (in sets CRM811 &
                                                CRS1811)

BIBER – *Continued*

Sonata No. 16, in g "The Guardian Angel" solo vln*
(unaccompanied)   Cambridge (in sets CRM811 &
                                   CRS1811)
(8) Sonatas (1681) vln & c
  Sonata No. 1, in A
  with M. Smith hpsi & J. Scholz gamba Cambridge CRM812, CRS1812
  Sonata No. 2, in d
  with M. Smith hpsi & J. Scholz gamba Cambridge CRM812, CRS1812
  Sonata No. 3, in F
  with M. Smith hpsi & J. Scholz gamba Cambridge CRM812, CRS1812
  Sonata No. 4, in D
  with M. Smith hpsi & J. Scholz gamba Cambridge CRM812, CRS1812
  Sonata No. 5, in e
  with M. Smith hpsi & J. Scholz gamba Cambridge CRM812, CRS1812
  Sonata No. 6, in c
  with M. Smith hpsi & J. Scholz gamba Cambridge CRM813, CRS1813
  Sonata No. 7, in g
  with M. Smith hpsi & J. Scholz gamba Cambridge CRM813, CRS1813
  Sonata No. 8, in A
  with M. Smith hpsi & J. Scholz gamba Cambridge CRM813, CRS1813

CORELLI

(12) Sonatas, Op. 5 vln & c
  Sonata No. 1, in D
  with S. Lincoln hpsi & S. Hunkins vlc   Library of Recorded
                                          Masterpieces Vol. 2
  Sonata No. 3, in C
  with S. Lincoln hpsi & S. Hunkins vlc   Library of Recorded
                                          Masterpieces Vol. 3
  Sonata No. 8, in e
  with S. Lincoln hpsi & S. Hunkins vlc   Library of Recorded
                                          Masterpieces Vol. 1

VIVALDI

(12) Concerti, Op. 8 (1725) "Il Cimento dell' Armonia e dell' Invenzione"
(Nos. 1/4: Le quattro Stagioni) vln & strs
  Concerto No. 2, in B flat, F.I. No. 23 "L'Estate"
  with New York Sinfonietta –   Library of Recorded
  Goberman   Masterpieces Vol. 1, No. 8
                                        Odyssey 32 16 0132
Concerto in F, P.278 (F.I. No. 34) 3 vlns, strs & c
  with N. Koutzen vln, A. Bronne vln,   Library of Recorded
  E. Earle hpsi & New York Sinfonietta Masterpieces Vol. 1, No. 8
  – Goberman   Odyssey 32 16 0053, 32 16 0054

Raymond Gallois MONTBRUN (1918–)

FAURÉ

Sonata No. 1, in A, Op. 13 vln & pf
  with J. Hubeau pf   Erato STU70550
Sonata No. 2, in e, Op. 108 vln & pf
  with J. Hubeau pf   Erato STU70550

MILHAUD

Sonata No. 2 (1917) vln & pf
  with K. Yasukawa pf
                                        Victor SD3076/7, (set JAS276)

* Known as "Passacaglia"

MONTBRUN

Symphonie concertante in E (1951) vln & orch.
  with Tokyo Symphony Orch. – Ueda   Victor SD3069/72, (set JAS244)

PAGANINI

(24) Caprices, Op. 1 (1801/7) solo vln
  Caprice No. 6, in g arr. vln & pf
  with G. Joy pf   Victor SD3078
  Caprice No. 9, in E arr. vln & pf
  with G. Joy pf   Victor SD3078

RAVEL

Sonata (1927) vln & pf
  with G. Joy pf   Victor SD3081/2, (set JAS250)

Placidus MORASCH

STRAUSS, R.

(Ein) Heldenleben, Op. 40 (1898) orch.
  with Bavarian State Orch. – Strauss   Decca DL9602
                                        Deutsche Grammophon (set 30)
                                        Polydor 67756/60, 69840/4

Egon MORBITZER (1927–)

BRAHMS

Quintet in b, Op. 115 cl, 2 vlns, vla & vlc
  with O. Michallik cl, W. Martens vln, Eterna 820366
  W. Buchholz vla & B. Günther vlc   Philips 6580 057
Sonata No. 1, in G Op. 78 vln & pf
  with D. Zechlin pf   Eterna 820241

BRUCH

Concerto No. 1, in g, Op. 26 vln & orch.
  with Berlin Staatskapelle Orch. –   Eterna 720107
  Konwitschny   Realm RM222
Concerto No. 1, in g, Op. 26 vln & orch.*
  with Grosses Symphony Orch.   Baccarola 60160UK

DEBUSSY

Suite Bergamasque (1890) pf
  No. 3. Clair de lune arr. vln & orch.
  with Leipzig Radio Symphony Orch. –   Fontana 88478DY, (in set K71
  Hanell   BC801)

DRDLA

Serenade No. 1, in A vln & pf
  with Berlin Radio Orch. – Dobrindt   Amiga 740007
Souvenir vln & pf
  with Berlin Radio Orch. – Dobrindt   Amiga 740007
Souvenir vln & pf
  with Grosses Orch. des   Fontana 88484DY, (in set K71
  Deutschlandsenders – Hanell   BC801)

* Adagio or 2nd mvt is on Baccarola 77873ZK.

DVOŘÁK

(8) Humoresques, Op. 101 pf
No. 7. Humoresque No. 7, in G flat arr. vln & orch.
with Leipzig Radio Symphony Orch. – Fontana 88482DY, (in set K71
Hanell BC801)

FIBICH

Images, Impressions & Souvenirs, Op. 41 pf
No. 14. Poem (from "Souvenirs", Part IV) arr. vln & orch.
with Grosses Orch. des Fontana 88480DY, (in set K71
Deutschlandsenders – Hanell BC801)

GODARD

Jocelyn (1888) – opera
Cachés dans cet asile "Berceuse" arr. vln & orch.
with Grosses Orch. des Fontana 88484DY, (in set K71
Deutschlandsenders – Hanell BC801)

GOUNOD

Ave Maria (Méditation on Bach's "Prelude No. 1, in C" from Book I of
"Das Wohltemperirte Clavier") v & pf – arr. v, vln & orch.
with E. Ebert s, S. Stöckigt pf, H. Otto Fontana 88484DY, (in set K71
org & Leipzig Radio Symphony Orch. BC801)
– Hanell

HAYDN

(6) Quartets, Op. 76 (H.III, Nos. 75/80) 2 vlns, vla & vlc
No. 2. Quartet No. 76, in d, H.III, No. 76
with W. Martens vln, W. Buchholz vla Eterna 120032, 720005
& B. Günther vlc

HUBAY

(14) Scènes de la Csárda vln & pf
No. 4. Hejre Kati, Op. 32
with Berlin Radio Orch. – Dobrindt Amiga 740007

KOCHAN

Concerto in D, Op. 1 vln & orch.
with Berlin Radio Orch. – Lange Eterna 120035/7

KREISLER

Caprice viennois, Op. 2 vln & pf
with Berlin Radio Orch. – Dobrindt Amiga 740007
Caprice viennois, Op. 2 vln & pf
with Dresden Philharmonic Symphony Fontana 88478DY, (in set K71
Orch. – Masur BC801)
Liebesfreud vln & pf
with Berlin Radio Orch. – Dobrindt Amiga 740007
Liebesfreud vln & pf
with Dresden Philharmonic Symphony Fontana 88478DY, (in set K71
Orch. – Masur BC801)
Liebesleid vln & pf
with Berlin Radio Orch. – Dobrindt Amiga 740007
Liebesleid vln & pf
with Dresden Philharmonic Symphony Fontana 88478DY, (in set K71
Orch. – Masur BC801)
Schön Rosmarin vln & pf
with Berlin Radio Orch. – Dobrindt Amiga 740007
Schön Rosmarin vln & pf
with Dresden Philharmonic Symphony Fontana 88478DY, (in set K71
Orch. – Masur BC801)

MASSENET

Thaïs (1894) – opera
Méditation
with Dresden Philharmonic Symphony Fontana 88480DY, (in set K71
Orch. – Masur BC801), (in set 6736 003)

MONTI

Csárdas (1904) vln & pf
with Grosses Orch. des Fontana 88484DY, (in set K71
Deutschlandsenders – Hanell BC801)

RAFF

(6) Pieces, Op. 85 vln & pf
No. 3. Cavatina in D
with Leipzig Radio Symphony Orch. – Fontana 88479DY, (in set K71
Hanell BC801)

SCHUMANN

Sonata No. 1, in a, Op. 105 vln & pf
with D. Zechlin pf Eterna 820241

SVENDSEN

Romance in G, Op. 26 vln & orch.
with Berlin Staatskapelle Orch. – Eterna 720107
Konwitschny Realm RM222
Romance in G, Op. 26 vln & orch.
with Dresden Philharmonic Symphony Fontana 88480DY, (in set K71
Orch. – Masur BC801), (in set 6736 003)

MORENA

GOUNOD

Faust (1859) – opera
Valse (Act II) orch. – arr. vln & pf as "Waltz Fantasy" by Morena
with piano Columbia 1171
Regal G6223

VERDI

(Il) Trovatore (1853) – opera
Miserere arr. vln & pf Morena
with piano Columbia 1171
Regal G6223

V. MORGAGNI

BRAHMS

(21) Hungarian Dances pf duet
Hungarian dance No. 5, in f sharp arr. vln & pf "in g" Joachim
with piano Cantoria MD206

MONTI

Csárdas (1904) vln & pf
with piano Cantoria MD206

Harold MORGAN

d'AMBROSIO

Canzonetta, Op. 6 vln & pf
with piano yy 1228[II] Ariel 1048

MORGAN

Variations on the Austrian Hymn vln & pf
with piano   ab 14384   Ariel 1048

Erica MORINI (1906–   )

ANONYMOUS

Londonderry air Traditional Irish ballad – arr. vln & pf Kreisler
with M. Raucheisen pf   98¾ be   Polydor 67024, 69861

BACH

Cantata No. 156 (Ich steh' mit einem Fuss im Grabe) BWV156 (1730)
Sinfonia arr. vln & pf as "Arioso" by Franko
with L. Kentner pf   BLR 5868^{II}△T   HMV DA1103

Concerto No. 1, in a, BWV1041 vln, strs & c
with Princeton Chamber Orch. –   Decca DL10134, DL710134
Harsányi

Concerto No. 2, in E, BWV1042 vln, strs & c
with Aeterna Chamber Orch. –   Decca DL10053, DL710053
Waldman

Concerto in d, BWV1043 2 vlns, strs & c
with N. Milstein vln & Chamber Orch.   Angel 36006
– Milstein   Columbia CX1940, FCX1050,
                                       SAX2579, SAXF1050
                                       Electrola SME91683

Sonata in C, BWV1037 2 vlns & c
with N. Milstein vln & B. Fischer pf   Angel 36006
                                       Columbia CX1940, FCX1050,
                                       SAX2579, SAXF1050

BEETHOVEN

(6) Quartets, Op. 18 2 vlns, vla & vlc
No. 4. Quartet No. 4, in c
with F. Galimir vln, W. Trampler vla   Westminster W9074, XWN18595
& L. Varga vlc

Sonata No. 5, in F, Op. 24 "Spring" vln & pf
        Bw 1210^I△, 1211/2^{II}△, 1213^{III}   HMV E499/501, E7006/8,
with N. Schwalb pf   △ & 1214/5^{II}△   EW38/40

Sonata No. 5, in F, Op. 24 "Spring" vln & pf
with R. Firkusny pf   Decca DL10045, DL710045

(3) Sonatas, Op. 30 vln & pf
No. 2. Sonata No. 7, in c
with R. Firkusny pf   Decca DL10045, DL710045

No. 3. Sonata No. 8, in G
with R. Firkusny pf   Decca DL10065, DL710065

BRAHMS

Concerto in D, Op. 77 (cadenza by Joachim) vln & orch.
with London Philharmonic Orch. –   Heliodor 428003, 478015
Rodzinski   Westminster (in set WM1011),
                                       P281, PWS705, WST14037,
                                       XWN18600
                                       Whitehall WH20047, WHS40047

(21) Hungarian Dances pf duet
Hungarian dance No. 1, in g arr. vln & pf Joachim
with A. Balsam pf   Camden CAE180, CAL207,
                                       CAL351
                                       Victor 10–1215, (in set M1053)

Hungarian dance No. 5, in f sharp arr. vln & pf "in g" Joachim
with A. Balsam pf   Camden CAE129, CAL207
                                       Victor 10–1214, (in set M1053)

Hungarian dance No. 6, in D flat arr. vln & pf "in B flat" Joachim
with A. Balsam pf   Camden CAE129, CAL207
                                       Victor 10–1213, (in set M1053)

Hungarian dance No. 7, in A arr. vln & pf Joachim
with A. Balsam pf   Camden CAE129, CAL207
                                       Victor 10–1214, (in set M1053)

Hungarian dance No. 8, in a arr. vln & pf Joachim
with M. Raucheisen pf   225½ bg   Polydor 67023, 69825

Hungarian dance No. 8, in a arr. vln & pf Joachim
with A. Balsam pf   Camden CAE180, CAL207
                                       Victor 10–1215, (in set M1053)

Hungarian dance No. 17, in f sharp arr. vln & pf Joachim
with A. Balsam pf   Camden CAE129, CAL207
                                       Victor 10–1213, (in set M1053)

Sonata No. 2, in A, Op. 100 vln & pf
with L. Pommers pf   Westminster XWN18592

Sonata No. 3, in d, Op. 108 vln & pf
with L. Pommers pf   Westminster XWN18592

Sonata No. 3, in d, Op. 108 vln & pf
with R. Firkusny pf   Decca DL10065, DL710065

(16) Waltzes, Op. 39 pf duet
No. 15. Waltz No. 15, in A flat arr. vln & pf "in A" Hochstein
with M. Raucheisen pf   227½ bg   Polydor 67023, 69825

BRANDL

(Der) Liebe Augustin – operetta
Du alter Stefansturm arr. vln & pf as "The old refrain" by Kreisler
with M. Raucheisen pf   795 bh IV   Decca LY6085
                                     Polydor 62658

Du alter Stefansturm arr. vln & pf as "The old refrain" by Kreisler
with piano   553 bi IV   Polydor 66822

BRUCH

Concerto No. 1, in g, Op. 26 vln & orch.
with Berlin Radio Symphony Orch. –   Deutsche Grammophon
Fricsay   DGM12029, DGS712029,
                                       LPM18577, SLPM138044

CHAMINADE

Sérénade espagnole pf – arr. vln & pf Kreisler
with M. Raucheisen pf   Polydor 67022, 69824

Sérénade espagnole pf – arr. vln & pf Kreisler
with L. Pommers pf   Westminster (in set WM1011),
                                       XWN18087

DVOŘÁK

(8) Slavonic Dances, Op. 72 pf duet; orch.
No. 2. Slavonic dance No. 10, in e arr. vln & pf Kreisler
with N. Schwalb pf   Cw 1219^{III}   HMV D1397, EJ237

FALLA

(La) Vida Breve (1913) – opera
Danza española orch. – arr. vln & pf Kreisler
with L. Kentner pf   HMV ER250, EW37, P751

FOSTER

(The) Old folks at home (1851) "Swanee river" v & pf – arr. vln & pf
Kreisler
with M. Raucheisen pf   550½ bi   Decca LY6085
Polydor 66822

FRANCK

Sonata in A (1886) vln & pf
with R. Firkusny pf   Decca DL10038, DL710038

GLAZOUNOV

Concerto in a, Op. 82 vln & orch.
with Berlin Radio Symphony Orch. –
Fricsay   Deutsche Grammophon
DGM12029, DGS712029,
LPM18577, SLPM138044

GLUCK

Orphée et Eurydice (1762) – opera
Dance of the blessed spirits: Lento "Mélodie" (No. 2) arr. vln & pf
Kreisler
with M. Raucheisen pf   97½ be   Polydor 67024, 69861
Dance of the blessed spirits: Lento "Mélodie" (No. 2) arr. vln & pf
Kreisler
with L. Pommers pf   Westminster (in set WM1011),
XWN18087

GODARD

Concerto No. 1, Op. 35 "Concerto Romantique" vln & orch.
Canzonetta (2nd mvt)
with E. Balaban pf   A 25724   HMV DA338
Victor 66038, 792

Canzonetta (2nd mvt)
with L. Pommers pf   Westminster (in set WM1011),
XWN18087

GOLDMARK

Concerto in a, Op. 28 vln & orch.
Andante (2nd mvt) "Air"
with N. Schwalb pf   Cw 1222[II]   HMV D1397, EJ237

GRANADOS

(12) Danzas españolas, Op. 37 (1893) pf
No. 5. Danza española No. 5, in e "Andaluza" arr. vln & pf Kreisler
with L. Kentner pf   HMV EW37
No. 5. Danza española No. 5, in e "Andaluza" arr. vln & pf Kreisler
with M. Raucheisen pf   551 bi IV   Polydor 66823

HANDEL

(15) Sonatas, Op. 1 (?1731) fl or vln & c
Sonata No. 9, in b: Andante (1st mvt) arr. vln & pf as "Larghetto" by
Hubay
with M. Raucheisen pf   231½ bg   Brunswick 95046
Polydor 67021, 69823, 69872

HEUBERGER

(Der) Opernball, Op. 40 (1898) – operetta
Im chambre séparée arr. vln & pf as "Midnight bells" by Kreisler
with L. Pommers pf   Westminster (in set WM1011),
XWN18087

HUBAY

(6) Blumenleben, Op. 30 vln & pf
No. 5. Der Zephir
with L. Kentner pf   HMV DA1104

JUON

(4) Pieces, Op. 28 vln & pf
No. 3. Berceuse
with M. Raucheisen pf   797½ bh IV   Polydor 62659

KOSCHAT

Forsaken v & pf – arr. vln & pf Winternitz
with M. Raucheisen pf   100½ be   Brunswick 80011
Polydor 67025, 69862

KREISLER

Caprice viennois, Op. 2 vln & pf
with L. Pommers pf   Westminster (in set WM1011),
XWN18087

Liebesleid vln & pf
with L. Pommers pf   Westminster (in set WM1011),
XWN18087

Paraphrase on 2 Russian folksongs vln & pf
with L. Kentner pf   HMV EJ236, ES335

Rondino on a theme by Beethoven vln & pf
with L. Kentner pf   HMV ER250, EW37, P751

Schön Rosmarin vln & pf
with M. Raucheisen pf   793½ bh IV   Polydor 62658

Schön Rosmarin vln & pf
with L. Pommers pf   Westminster (in set WM1011),
XWN18087

Praeludium & Allegro (Pugnani) vln & pf
   BLR 5869/70[1]△T   HMV DA1109
with L. Kentner pf

(La) Précieuse (L. Couperin) vln & pf
with M. Raucheisen pf   794½ bh IV   Decca DE7028
Polydor 62657

Variations on a theme of Corelli (Tartini) vln & pf
with M. Raucheisen pf   228 bg   Brunswick 95046
Polydor 67021, 69823

Variations on a theme of Corelli (Tartini) vln & pf
with L. Pommers pf   Westminster (in set WM1011),
XWN18087

LALO

Symphonie espagnole, Op. 21 vln & orch.
Andante (4th mvt)
with M. Reicheisen pf   Polydor 67022, 69824

LANGE

Flower song, Op. 39 vln & pf
with K. Hetzel pf   HMV DB803
Victor 74888, 6454

LULLY

Ballets du Roy (1659)*
  Gavotte arr. vln & pf Burmester
  with M. Raucheisen pf   271½bd   Brunswick 7001
                                                    Decca DE7030
                                                    Polydor 62699, 68519

MOZART

Concerto No. 4, in D, K218 vln & orch.
  with Princeton Chamber Orch. –   Decca DL10134, DL710134
  Harsányi

Concerto No. 5, in A, K219 "Turkish" vln & orch.
  with Perpignan Festival Orch. – Casals   Columbia ML4565, (in set
                                                    SL167)

Concerto No. 5, in A, K219 "Turkish" vln & orch.
  with Aeterna Chamber Orch. –   Decca DL10053, DL710053
  Waldman

Divertimento No. 17, in D, K334 2 hrns & strs
  Minuet (3rd mvt) arr. vln & pf Kross
  with M. Raucheisen pf   272½bd   Brunswick 7001
                                                    Decca DE7030
                                                    Polydor 62699, 68519

  Minuet (3rd mvt) arr. vln & pf Burmester
  with L. Pommers pf   Westminster (in set WM1011),
                                                  XWN18087

Quartet No. 23, in F, K590 2 vlns, vla & vlc
  with F. Galimir vln, W. Trampler vla   Westminster W9074, XWN18595
  & L. Varga vlc

Sonata No. 32, in B flat, K454 vln & pf
     CLR 5872/3ᴵᴵ△T, 5874/6ᴵ△T &   HMV DB1429/31
  with L. Kentner pf   5877ᴵᴵ△T   Victor 7722/4, (set M164)

Sonata No. 33, in E flat, K481 vln & pf
  with R. Firkusny pf   Decca DL10038, DL710038

NACHÈZ

(4) Danses Tziganes, Op. 14 vln & pf
  Danse Tzigane No. 3, in G
  with M. Raucheisen pf   99¾be   Brunswick 80011
                                                    Polydor 67025, 69862

NARDINI

(7) Sonatas vln & c
  Sonata No. 2, in D
  with L. Pommers pf   Decca DL10102, DL710102

PARADIES

Sicilienne vln & pf – arr. Dushkin
  with L. Pommers pf   Westminster (in set WM1011),
                                                  XWN18087

PERGOLESI

(14) Sonatas (1770) 2 vlns & c
  Sonata No. 1, in G: Andantino arr. vln & pf
  with L. Pommers pf   Decca DL10102, DL710102

RAVEL

Pièce en forme d'Habanera v & pf – arr. vln & pf Catherine
  with M. Lanner pf   Camden CAE180, CAL207
                                                  Victor 10–1011

* Unidentified.

SARASATE

Carmen Fantasia (on themes from the opera by Bizet) Op. 25 vln & pf or orch.
  with orch.   Victor 74869, 6445

(8) Danzas españolas vln & pf
  No. 3. Romanza andaluza, Op. 22, No. 1
  with A. Morini pf   Victor 74692, 6226
  No. 3. Romanza andaluza, Op. 22, No. 1
  with C. Keith pf   Cc 12796ᴵᴵ△   HMV D1445, EJ314, W960

Faust Fantasia (on themes from the opera by Gounod) vln & pf or orch.
  Waltz
  with A. Morini pf   HMV DA338
                                                  Victor 64979, 791

  Waltz
  with M. Lanner pf   Camden CAE180, CAL207
                                                  Victor 10–1011

  Waltz
  with L. Pommers pf   Westminster (in set WM1011),
                                                  XWN18087

Introduction & Tarantelle, Op. 43 vln & pf
  with C. Keith pf   Cc 12798ᴵ△   HMV D1445, EJ314, W960

SCHUBERT

(16) Deutsche Tänze, Op. 33 (D783) pf
  No. 3. Deutscher Tanz No. 3, in B flat arr. vln & pf as "Valse
  sentimentale" by Franko)
  with E. Balaban pf   Victor 66086, 792

(7) Gesänge (set to Scott's "Lady of the Lake") Op. 52 v & pf
  No. 6. Ave Maria, D839 arr. vln & pf Wilhelmj
  with L. Pommers pf   Westminster (in set WM1011),
                                                  XWN18087

(2) Lieder, Op. 98 (D498) v & pf
  No. 2. Wiegenlied (Schlafe, holder süsser Knabe) arr. vln & pf Elman
  with M. Raucheisen pf   796½bh IV   Polydor 62659

SCHUMANN

(12) Duets, Op. 85 pf – 4 hands
  No. 9. Am Springbrunnen arr. vln & pf
  with E. Balaban pf   Victor 66074, 791

SVENDSEN

Romance in G, Op. 26 vln & orch. – arr. vln & pf Wilhelmj
  with A. Morini pf   Victor 74797, 6226

TARTINI

(12) Sonatas, Op. 1 (1734) vln & c
  Sonata No. 10, in g "Didone abbandonata"
  with L. Pommers pf   Westminster W9070, XWN18594
  Sonata No. 10, in g "Didone abbandonata"
  with L. Pommers pf   Decca DL10102, DL710102

Sonata in g "Il Trillo del Diavolo" vln & c – arr. vln & pf Kreisler
  with L. Pommers pf   Westminster W9070, XWN18594

TCHAIKOVSKY

Concerto in D, Op. 35 vln & orch.
  with Chicago Symphony Orch. –   Victor (in sets DM1168 &
  Defauw   WBC1061), LBC1061

Concerto in D, Op. 35 vln & orch.
  with London Philharmonic Orch. –   Westminster (in set WM1011),
  Rodzinski   P321, WST14017, XWN18397

TCHAIKOVSKY – *Continued*

(The) Months (12 Characteristic pieces) Op. 37a pf
No. 2. Carnival time (February) arr. vln & pf as "Neapolitan" by Burmester
with L. Pommers pf
    Westminster (in set WM1011), XWN18087

No. 6. Barcarolle (June) arr. vln & pf
with A. Morini pf
    HMV DA560
    Victor 66186, 957

(2) Pieces, Op. 10 pf
No. 2. Humoresque in G arr. vln & pf Kreisler
with L. Kentner pf
    HMV DA1104

(3) Souvenirs de Hapsal, Op. 2 pf
No. 3. Chant sans paroles in f arr. vln & pf Sweet
with M. Raucheisen pf   792½bh VI   Decca DE7028
    Polydor 62657

No. 3. Chant sans paroles in f arr. vln & pf Sweet
with L. Pommers pf
    Westminster (in set WM1011, XWN18087

TOBANI

Hearts & flowers, Op. 245 (1899) v & pf – arr. vln & pf
with N. Shilkret pf
    HMV DB803
    Victor 74889, 6454

TOSELLI

Serenade, Op. 6 vln & pf
with S. Vas pf
    Victor 66153, 957

VALDEZ

Sérénade du Tzigane vln & pf
with L. Kentner pf   BLR 5871ᴵᴵ△T   HMV DA1103

VIOTTI

Concerto No. 22, in a vln & orch.
Adagio (2nd mvt)
with L. Kentner pf
    HMV EJ236, ES335

VIVALDI

(12) Concerti, Op. 3 "L'Estro armonico" var. cbns & strs
Concerto No. 11, in d, P.250 (F.IV, No. 11) 2 vlns, vlc, strs & c
with N. Milstein vln, H. Shapiro vlc & Angel 36006
Chamber Orch. – Milstein   Columbia CX1940, FCX1050, SAX2579, SAXF1050

Sonata in D, F.XII, No. 6 vln & c – arr. vln & pf Respighi
with M. Lanner pf
    Camden CAL207
    Victor 11–8671

Sonata in D, F.XII, No. 6 vln & c – arr. vln & pf Respighi
with L. Pommers pf
    Decca DL10102, DL710102

WIENIAWSKI

Capriccio–valse, Op. 7 vln & pf
with A. Morini pf
    HMV DB372
    Victor 74686, 6227

Capriccio–valse, Op. 7 vln & pf
with M. Raucheisen pf   552½bi   Polydor 66823

Capriccio–valse, Op. 7 vln & pf
with M. Lanner pf
    Camden CAL207
    Victor 11–8731

WIENIAWSKI – *Continued*

Concerto No. 2, in d, Op. 22 vln & orch.
Romance (2nd mvt)
with E. Balaban pf   A 25127   HMV 3–07955, DB372
    Victor 74717, 6227

Romance (2nd mvt)
with M. Lanner pf
    Victor 11–8731

ZARZYCKI

Mazurka in G, Op. 26 vln & pf
with E. Balaban pf   A 25126   HMV 3–07958
    Victor 74727, 6445

Giulietta MORINO

ANONYMOUS

Night of joy arr. vln & pf*
with piano
    Regal Zonophone EE341

Red butterfly – mazurka arr. vln & pf*
with piano
    Regal Zonophone EE341

BRAGA

(7) Melodies (1867) v & pf
No. 5. La serenata "Angel's serenade" arr. vln & orch.
with orch.   Victor V47

di CAPUA

O sole mio v & pf – arr. vln & orch. Cibelli
with orch. & flute
    HMV AL1035, EG1949
    Regal Zonophone T5358
    Victor 150009, V3

DRIGO

(Les) Millions d'Arlequin (1900) – ballet orch.
Sérénade arr. vln & gtr
with guitar   Victor 21225

GOUNOD

Ave Maria (Méditation on Bach's "Prelude No. 1, in C" from Book I of "Das Wohltemperirte Clavier") v & pf – arr. vln & orch.
with orch.   Victor V47

POGGIS

Amor v & pf – arr. vln & pf
with piano
    HMV GW586
    Victor 80239

Laura v & pf – arr. vln & pf
with piano
    HMV GW586
    Victor 80239

POLLACK & RAPÉE

Diane (1927) v & pf – arr. vln & gtr
with guitar   Victor 21225

VORREI

Could I? v & pf – arr. vln & pf
with piano
    Victor 81229

* Unidentified.

WAYNE

Ramona (1927) v & pf – arr. vln & pf
  with piano   Victor 81229

YRADIER

(La) Paloma (1877) v & pf – arr. vln & orch. Cibelli
  with orch. & flute   HMV AL1035, EG1949
                             Regal Zonophone T5358
                             Victor 150009, V3

Eugen MORIS

BRUCH

Concerto No. 2, in d, Op. 44 vln & orch.
  with Berlin Symphony Orch. –   Urania URLP7166
  Kleinert

Marie Dawson MORRELL

CUI

Kaleidoscope, Op. 50 vln & pf
  No. 9. Orientale
  with F. Tresselt pf   Vocalion 14391

ELMAN

In a gondola (Impromptu) vln & pf
  with F. Tresselt pf   Vocalion 14391

FORSTER

Rose in the bud vln & pf
  with F. Tresselt pf   Vocalion 14802, X9457

HERBERT

(The) Fortune Teller (1898) – operetta
  Gypsy love song arr. vln & pf
  with F. Tresselt pf   Vocalion 14570

Mademoiselle Modiste (1905) – operetta
  Kiss me again arr. vln & pf
  with F. Tresselt pf   Vocalion 14802, X9457

MacDOWELL

Woodland Sketches, Op. 51 pf
  No. 1. To a wild rose arr. vln & pf
  with F. Tresselt pf   Vocalion 14234, X9100

SEITZ

(The) World is waiting for the sunrise (1919) v & pf – arr. vln & pf
  with F. Tresselt pf   Vocalion 14570

VALDEZ

Sérénade du Tzigane vln & pf
  with F. Tresselt pf   Vocalion 14234, X9100

Earl Williams MORSE

LOCATELLI

(12) Sonatas, Op. 6 (1737) vln & c
  Sonata (unid)
  with piano   79292   Odeon 3286AA

TENAGLIA

Have pity, sweet eyes v & c – arr. vln & pf as "Aria in f" by Ries
  with piano   79293   Odeon 3286AA

VIEUXTEMPS

Concerto No. 4, in d, Op. 31 vln & orch.
  Adagio religioso (2nd mvt)
  with piano   79295   Odeon 3366AA

(6) Morceaux de salon, Op. 22 vln & pf
  No. 4. Tarantelle in a
  with piano   79294   Odeon 3366AA

Isadore MOSKOWITZ

d'AGOSTINO

Flower of Italy (Mazurka brillante No. 2) Op. 10 vln & pf
  with piano   Edison cylinder 2729
                       Edison Diamond Disc 50958

DVOŘÁK

(8) Humoresques, Op. 101 pf
  No. 7. Humoresque No. 7, in G flat arr. vln & pf "in G" Wilhelmj
  with orch.   3098   Edison cylinder 5393
                       Edison Diamond Disc 80181

  No. 7. Humoresque No. 7, in G flat arr. vln & pf "in G" Wilhelmj
  with orch.   3822   Edison Diamond Disc 80181

GOUNOD

Ave Maria (Méditation on Bach's "Prelude No. 1, in C" from Book I of "Das Wohltemperirte Clavier") v & pf – arr. v, vln & orch.
  with C. Kirwan s & orch.   Edison Diamond Disc 80290

Sérénade (Quand tu chantes) v & pf – arr. v, vln & orch.
  with C. Arden a & orch.   Edison Diamond Disc 80572

RUBINSTEIN

(2) Melodies, Op. 3 pf
  No. 1. Melody in F arr. vln & pf Wilhelmj
  with orch.   3101   Edison cylinder 2818
                       Edison Diamond Disc 80181

  No. 1. Melody in F arr. vln & pf Wilhelmj
  with orch.   3887   Edison Diamond Disc 80181

SARASATE

(8) Danzas españolas vln & pf
  No. 3. Romanza andaluza, Op. 22, No. 1
  with American Symphony   3100   Edison Diamond Disc 80097
  Orch.

  No. 3. Romanza andaluza, Op. 22, No. 1
  with orch.   1522   Edison Diamond Disc 82019

TCHAIKOVSKY

Ye who have yearned alone v & pf – arr. v, vln & orch.
  with C. Arden a & orch.   Edison Diamond Disc 80572

Raymond MOSLEY

BACH

(4) Suites, BWV1066/9 orch.
Suite No. 3, in D: Air (2nd mvt) BWV1068 2 obs, 3 tpts, drms, strs & c
– arr. vln & pf as "Air on the G–string" by Wilhelmj
with G. Tristram org — Ryemuse SALR1202

CROTHER

Gweedore Brae vln & pf
with G. Tristram org — Ryemuse SALR1202

ELGAR

(2) Chansons, Op. 15 vln & pf
No. 2. Chanson du matin
with G. Tristram org — Ryemuse SALR1202

KREISLER

Praeludium & Allegro (Pugnani) vln & pf
with G. Tristram org — Ryemuse SALR1202
Variations on a theme by Corelli (Tartini) vln & pf
with G. Tristram org — Ryemuse SALR1202

SVENDSEN

Romance in G, Op. 26 vln & orch. – arr. vln & pf Wilhelmj
with G. Tristram org — Ryemuse SALR1202

TCHAIKOVSKY

Souvenir d'un lieu cher, Op. 42 vln & pf
No. 3. Mélodie
with G. Tristram org — Ryemuse SALR1202

WIENIAWSKI

Concerto No. 2, in d, Op. 22 vln & orch.
Romance (2nd mvt)
with G. Tristram org — Ryemuse SALR1202

Marshall MOSS

BRAHMS

Sonata No. 1, in G, Op. 78 vln & pf
with A. Mekler pf — Lizard C20105
Sonata No. 2, in A, Op. 100 vln & pf
with A. Mekler pf — Lizard C20105
Sonata No. 3, in d, Op. 108 vln & pf
with A. Mekler pf — Lizard C20105

CORELLI

(12) Sonatas, Op. 5 vln & c
Sonata No. 9, in A
with N. Roberts hpsi — Golden Crest RE7032

COUPERIN, A–L.

(6) Sonates en Pièce Clavecin, Op. 2 (1765) hpsi & vln obb
Sonata No. 2, in D
with N. Roberts hpsi — Golden Crest RE7032

HANDEL

(15) Sonatas, Op. 1 (?1731) fl or vln & c
Sonata No. 13, in D vln IV
with N. Roberts hpsi — Golden Crest RE7032

LISZT

Hungarian Rhapsody, G383 (paraphrase on N. Lenau's poem "Die Drei Zigeuner" by Hubay) vln & orch.
with A. Mekler pf — Lizard C20105

MOZART

Sonata No. 26, in B flat, K378 vln & pf
with A. Mekler pf — Lizard C20105
Sonata No. 32, in B flat, K454 vln & pf
with A. Mekler pf — Lizard C20105

Max MOSSEL (1871–1929)

d'AMBROSIO

Canzonetta, Op. 6 vln & pf
with piano — Gramophone & Typewriter 3–7900
Madrigale, Op. 26 vln & pf
with piano — 3532 e — Gramophone & Typewriter 7998

AULIN

(4) Aquarelles vln & pf
No. 3. Vaggsang
with piano — Columbia 2777

FAURÉ

Berceuse, Op. 16 vln & pf
with piano — Columbia 657

KREISLER

Andantino (Padre Martini) vln & pf
with piano — Columbia 657

MERIKANTO

Valse lente pf – arr. vln & pf Burmester
with piano — Columbia 2809

MLYNARSKI

Mazurka in G, Op. 26 vln & pf
with piano — 3117 e — Gramophone & Typewriter 7999, 27963

SAINT-SAËNS

Sérénade, Op. 15 pf or vln & vla – arr. vln & pf
with piano — 3533 e — Gramophone & Typewriter 3–7909, 27964

SIMONETTI

Madrigale pf – arr. vln & pf
with piano — Columbia 2777

WIENIAWSKI

Mazurka in a, Op. 3 "Kujawiak" vln & pf
with piano — Columbia 2809

Alexander M. MOSZKOWSKI (1851–1934)

CHOPIN

(3) Nocturnes, Op. 9 pf
No. 2. Nocturne No. 2, in E flat arr. vln & pf Sarasate
with O. Moszkowski pf — Kristall 21135

HUBAY

(6) Blumenleben, Op. 30 vln & pf
No. 5. Der Zephir
  with O. Moszkowski pf   Kristall 21133

RUYNEMAN

Sonata in G vln & pf
  with O. Moszkowski pf   Kristall 021132

TCHAIKOVSKY

Souvenir d'un lieu cher, Op. 42 vln & pf
No. 3. Mélodie
  with O. Moszkowski pf   Kristall 21133

WIENIAWSKI

(2) Mazurkas, Op. 19 vln & pf
No. 1. Mazurka No. 1, in G "Obertass"
  with O. Moszkowski pf   Kristall 21135

Aladár MÓŽI (1923–)

KOLMAN

Monumento per 6,000,000 orch.
  with Bratislava Radio Symphony Orch. Supraphon 012 0472, 112 0472
  – Režucha

SARASATE

Zigeunerweisen, Op. 20 vln & pf or orch.
  with orch.   Ultraphon H23834

SCHUBERT

Quintet in A, Op. 114 (D667) "Trout" pf, vln, vla, vlc & cbs
  with M. Karin pf, R. Hoffmann vla, Supraphon LPV165
  A. Berky vlc & F. Gabriel cbs

Guido MOZZATO

BONPORTI

(10) Concerti, Op. 11 strs
Concerto No. 5, in F: Adagio (2nd mvt) "Recitativo"
  with Virtuosi di Roma – Fasano Brunswick AXTL1042
                          Decca DL9674, UAT273583
                          Fonit LP3005

CORELLI

(12) Concerti grossi, Op. 6 orch.
Concerto grosso No. 4, in D
  with E. Malanotte vln & Virtuosi di HMV BLP1041
  Roma – Fasano

VIVALDI

(12) Concerti, Op. 3 "L'Estro armonico" var. cbns & strs
Concerto No. 2, in g, P.326 (F.IV, No. 8) 2 vlns, strs & c
  with L. Ferro vln, B. Mazzacurati vlc Brunswick AXA4505
  & Virtuosi di Roma – Fasano   Decca DL9729, UAT273589
Concerto No. 2, in g, P.326 (F.IV, No. 8) 2 vlns, strs & c
  with L. Ferro vln, B. Mazzacurati vlc HMV ALP1809, ASD391
  & Virtuosi di Roma – Fasano

VIVALDI – *Continued*

Concerto No. 5, in A, P.212 (F.I, No. 175) 2 vlns, strs & c
  with R. Ruotolo vln & Virtuosi di Angel 45030
  Roma – Fasano   Electrola E70380
                          HMV ALP1629, WBLP552
Concerto No. 8, in a, P.2 (F.I, No. 177) 2 vlns, strs & c
  with L. Ferro vln, B. Mazzacurati vlc Brunswick AXA4505
  & Virtuosi di Roma – Fasano   Decca DL9729, UAT273589
(12) Concerti, Op. 8 (1725) "Il Cimento dell' Armonia e dell' Invenzione"
  (Nos. 1/4: Le quattro Stagioni) vln & strs
Concerto No. 2, in B flat, F.I, No. 23 "L'Estate"
  with Virtuosi di Roma – Fasano Electrola E90099, STE90099
                          HMV ALP1234, ASDW306,
                          WALP1234
Concerto No. 2, in B flat, F.I, No. 23 "L'Estate"
  with Virtuosi di Roma – Fasano Angel 35877, (in set 3611),
                          ASC5038
                          HMV ALP1786, ASD367
Concerto No. 4, in f, F.I, No. 25 "L'Inverno"
  with Virtuosi di Roma – Fasano Electrola E90099, STE90099
                          HMV ALP1234, ASDW306,
                          WALP1234, 7EPQ644
Concerto No. 4, in f, F.I, No. 25 "L'Inverno"
  with Virtuosi di Roma – Fasano Angel 35877, (in set 3611),
                          ASC5038
                          HMV ALP1786, ASD367

Guido van der MUEREN

BACH

Concerto in d, BWV1043 2 vlns, strs & c
  with R. Barchet vln &   Ariola 11362K
  Sudwestdeutsche Chamber Orch. – Telefunken BLP11462
  Tilegant   World Record Club T136

Klaus MUHLBERGER

VIVALDI

(12) Concerti, Op. 3 "L'Estro armonico" var. cbns & strs
Concerto No. 10, in b, P.148 (F.IV, No. 10) 4 vlns, strs & c
  with G. Armand vln, A. Auriacombe Electrola 1C053–10068
  vln, O. Giordano vln & Toulouse Seraphim S60129
  Chamber Orch. – L. Auriacombe

Peter MUNN

BACH

Concerto in d, BWV1043 2 vlns, strs & c
  with J. Petiot vln & String Orch. – Saga XID5252
  Montserrat

Zygmunt MURAWSKI

MIELCZEWSKI

Canzona 2 vlns & c
  with I. Iwanow vln, J. Borzym hpsi & Veriton XV704
  L. Zawistowski vlc

Abel MUS

AGUIRRE

(2) Aires criollos vln & pf – arr. Gaos
with D. Colacelli pf   C 17321/2¹   Odeon 56022

GRANADOS

Goyescas (1916) – opera
Intermezzo orch. – arr. vln & pf
with D. Colacelli pf   Odeon 66033

HIERRO

Jota capricho vln & pf
with D. Colacelli pf   Odeon 56024

RODRIGO

(2) Esbozas, Op. 1 (1923) vln & pf
No. 1. La enamorado junto al pequeño surtidor
with J. Rodrigo pf   Odeon 66033

SAMMARTINI, G.

(6) Sonatas, Op. 1 2 vlns & c
Sonata No. 4, in A: Andante (3rd mvt) arr. vln & pf as "Canto amoroso"
by Elman
with D. Colacelli pf   Odeon 57008

SARASATE

(8) Danzas españolas vln & pf
No. 3. Romanza andaluza, Op. 22, No. 1
with D. Colacelli pf   Odeon 64003
No. 5. Playera, Op. 23, No. 1
with D. Colacelli pf   Odeon 64003
Miramar–Zortzico, Op. 42 vln & pf
with D. Colacelli pf   Odeon 57008

Ovide MUSIN (1854–1929)

MUSIN

Berceuse et Prière, Op. 9 vln & pf
with piano   Belgian Conservatory of Music
                    Inc. 4002

Nightingale (paraphrase on 2 Russian folk Themes) Op. 24 vln & pf
with piano   Belgian Conservatory of Music
                    Inc. 4004

Tivadár NACHÈZ (1859–1930)

NACHÈZ

(4) Danses Tziganes, Op. 14 vln & pf
No. 1. Danse Tzigane No. 1, in a
with piano   HMV 07993
No. 2. Danse Tzigane No. 2, in G
with piano   HMV 07992

SCHUMANN

(13) Kinderscenen, Op. 15 pf
No. 7. Träumerei arr. vln & pf
with piano   z 6910 f HMV 07991, C488

David NADIEN (1928–   )

BEETHOVEN

(6) Minuets, G167 pf
No. 2. Minuet No. 2, in G arr. vln & pf Burmester
with B. Barere pf   Kapp KL1342, KS3342

BRAHMS

(16) Waltzes, Op. 39 pf duet
No. 15. Waltz No. 15, in A flat arr. vln & pf "in A" Kreisler
with B. Barere pf   Kapp KL1342, KS3342

DEBUSSY

Sonata No. 3, in g (1917) vln & pf
with D. Hancock pf   Monitor MC2017

DRDLA

Souvenir vln & pf
with B. Barere pf   Kapp KL1342, KS3342

DVOŘÁK

(8) Humoresques, Op. 101 pf
No. 7. Humoresque No. 7, in G flat arr. vln & pf "in G" Kreisler
with B. Barere pf   Kapp KL1342, KS3342

ELGAR

Salut d'amour, Op. 12 orch. – arr. vln & pf Elgar
with B. Barere pf   Kapp KL1342, KS3342

FAURÉ

Berceuse, Op. 16 vln & pf
with D. Hancock pf   Monitor MC2017

FRANCK

Sonata in A (1886) vln & pf
with D. Hancock pf   Monitor MC2017

KREISLER

Recitative & Scherzo–Caprice, Op. 6 solo vln
(unaccompanied)   Kapp KC9060, KCL9060
Praeludium & Allegro (Pugnani) vln & pf
with B. Barere pf   Kapp KC9060, KCL9060
Variations on a theme of Corelli (Tartini) vln & pf
with B. Barere pf   Kapp KC9060, KCL9060

MASSENET

Thaïs (1894) – opera
Méditation arr. vln & pf Marsick
with B. Barere pf   Kapp KL1342, KS3342

MENDELSSOHN

(6) Gesänge, Op. 34 vln & pf
No. 2. Auf Flügeln des Gesanges arr. vln & pf Achron
with B. Barere pf   Kapp KL1342, KS3342

PAGANINI

(24) Caprices, Op. 1 (1801/7) solo vln
Caprice No. 20, in D arr. vln & pf Kreisler
with B. Barere pf   Kapp KC9060, KCL9060
Moto perpetuo (Allegro di concert), Op. 11 (1830) vln & orch.
with B. Barere pf   Kapp KC9060, KCL9060

PROKOFIEV

Sonata in C, Op. 56 2 vlns
 with R. Ricci vln   Decca DL710177
             MCA MACS3478

RAFF

(6) Pieces, Op. 85 vln & pf
 No. 3. Cavatina in D
 with B. Barere pf   Kapp KL1342, KS3342

RAVEL

Pièce en forme d'Habanera v & pf – arr. vln & pf Catherine
 with D. Hancock pf   Monitor MC2017

RUBINSTEIN

(2) Melodies, Op. 3 pf
 No. 1. Melody in F arr. vln & pf Wilhelmj
 with B. Barere pf   Kapp KL1342, KS3342

SAINT–SAËNS

Danse macabre, Op. 40 (1874) orch.
 with New York Philharmonic   Columbia (in set D3S785),
 Symphony Orch. – Bernstein   MS7165, MS7246, MS7522

SARASATE

Caprice basque, Op. 24 vln & pf
 with B. Barere pf   Kapp KC9060, KCL9060
(8) Danzas españolas vln & pf
 No. 2. Habañera, Op. 21, No. 2
 with B. Barere pf   Kapp KC9060, KCL9060
 No. 6. Zapateado, Op. 23, No. 2
 with B. Barere pf   Kapp KC9060, KCL9060
Introduction & Tarantelle, Op. 43 vln & pf
 with B. Barere pf   Kapp KC9060, KCL9060

SCHUBERT

(7) Gesänge (set to Scott's "Lady of the Lake") Op. 52 v & pf
 No. 6. Ave Maria, D839 arr. vln & pf Wilhelmj
 with B. Barere pf   Kapp KL1342, KS3342
(14) Schwanengesang, D957 (1828) v & pf
 No. 4. Ständchen "Serenade" arr. vln & pf
 with B. Barere pf   Kapp KL1342, KS3342

SCHUMANN

(13) Kinderscenen, Op. 15 pf
 No. 7. Träumerei arr. vln & pf
 with B. Barere pf   Kapp KL1342, KS3342

STRAUSS, R.

Also sprach Zarathustra, Op. 30 (1896) orch.
 with New York Philharmonic   CBS 72941
 Symphony Orch. – Bernstein   Columbia M30443
Don Quixote, Op. 35 (1897) orch.
 with L. Munroe vlc, W. Lincer vla &   Columbia M30067
 New York Philharmonic Symphony
 Orch. – Bernstein

VERACINI

(12) Sonatas, Op. 2 (1744) "Sonate accademiche" vln & c
 Sonata No. 6, in A: Largo (2nd mvt) (ed. Corti)
 with B. Barere pf   Kapp KC9060, KCL9060

VIEUXTEMPS

(3) Feuilles d'album, Op. 40 vln & pf
 No. 2. Regrets
 with B. Barere pf   Kapp KC9060, KCL9060

VIVALDI

(12) Concerti, Op. 8 (1725) "Il Cimento dell' Armonia e dell' Invenzione"
 (Nos. 1/4: Le quattro Stagioni) vln & strs
 Concerto No. 1, in E, F.I, No. 22 "La Primavera"
 with Kapp Sinfonietta – Vardi   Kapp KC9056, KCL9056
 Concerto No. 2, in B flat, F.I, No. 23 "L'Estate"
 with Kapp Sinfonietta – Vardi   Kapp KC9056, KCL9056
 Concerto No. 3, in F, F.I, No. 24 "L'Autunno"
 with Kapp Sinfonietta – Vardi   Kapp KC9056, KCL9056
 Concerto No. 4, in f, F.I, No. 25 "L'Inverno"
 with Kapp Sinfonietta – Vardi   Kapp KC9056, KCL9056

WIENIAWSKI

Scherzo–Tarantelle, Op. 16 vln & pf
 with B. Barere pf   Kapp KC9060, KCL9060

Philipp NÄGELE

DVOŘÁK

(4) Romantic pieces, Op. 75 vln & pf
 with G. Krieger pf   Da Camera SM93308
Sonata in F, Op. 57 vln & pf
 with G. Krieger pf   Da Camera SM93308
Sonatina in G, Op. 100 vln & pf
 with G. Krieger pf   Da Camera SM93308

TELEMANN

Concerto in C 4 vlns, strs & c
 with G. Ohnheiser vln, M. Hori vln,   Da Camera SM91017
 O. Kortner vln & Heidelburg Chamber
 Orch.

Yfrah NEAMAN (1924–)

BACH

(4) Suites, BWV1066/9 strs & c
Suite No. 3, in D: Air (2nd mvt) BWV1068 2 obs, 3 tpts, drms strs & c –
 arr. vln & pf as "Air on the G–string" by Wilhelmj
 with J. Wills pf   Manhattan SRO108

BLOCH

Baal Shem (3 Pictures of Chassidic life) (1923) vln & pf
      AR 9259–1 & 9260/2–2   Decca K1192/3
 with I. Newton pf

DEBUSSY

Suite Bergamasque (1890) pf
 No. 3. Clair de lune arr. vln & pf Roelens
 with J. Wills pf   Manhattan SRO80

DINICU

Hora Staccato vln & pf – arr. Heifetz
 with J. Wills pf   Manhattan SRO108

FALLA

(La) Vida Breve (1913) – opera
  Danza española orch. – arr. vln & pf Kreisler
  with J. Wills pf   Manhattan SRO80

GADE

Jealousy (1927) orch. – arr. vln & orch.
  with New Symphony Orch. of London   Reader's Digest 1
  – Leibowitz

GLUCK

Orphée et Eurydice (1762) – opera
  Dance of the blessed spirits: Lento "Mélodie" (No. 2) arr. vln & pf
  Kreisler
  with J. Wills pf   Manhattan SRO80

GODARD

Jocelyn (1888) – opera
  Cachés dans cet asile "Berceuse" arr. vln & pf
  with J. Wills pf   Manhattan SRO108

IBERT

(10) Histoires pf
  No. 2. Le petit âne blanc arr. vln & pf Hoèrès
  with J. Wills pf   Manhattan SRO108

KREISLER

Liebesleid vln & pf
  with J. Wills pf   Manhattan SRO108
Praeludium & Allegro (Pugnani) vln & pf
  with J. Wills pf   Manhattan SRO80

MOZART

Sonata No. 32, in B flat, K454 vln & pf
      AR 9320-2, 9321-1, 9322/3–4 &   Decca AK1417/9
  with H. Ferguson pf   9324/5–2

PROKOFIEV

(The) Love for Three Oranges, Op. 33 (1919) – opera
  No. 3. March arr. vln & pf Heifetz
  with J. Wills pf   Manhattan SRO108

RAVEL

Pièce en forme d'Habanera v & pf – arr. vln & pf Catherine
  with J. Wills pf   Manhattan SRO80

WEBER

(6) Sonatas, Op. 10 (J99/104) (1810) vln & pf
  Sonata No. 1, in F: Romanze (2nd mvt) J99 arr. vln & pf as "Larghetto"
  by Kreisler
  with J. Wills pf   Manhattan SRO80

Wolfgang NEININGER

BOCCHERINI

(6) Quintets, Op. 56 (1797) pf, 2 vlns, vla & vlc
  No. 1. Quintet No. 1, in e
  with F. Wörsching gtr, R. Felicani vln,   Archive APM14070, ARC3057
  M. Majer vla & A. Wenzinger vlc

HANDEL

(12) Concerti grossi, Op. 6 (1739) 2 vlns, vlc & strs

Concerto grosso No. 1, in G with U. Grehling vln, H. Müller vlc, E. Müller hpsi & Schola Cantorum Basiliensis – Wenzinger	Archive APM14846, ARC3246, ARC73246, SAPM198846
Concerto grosso No. 2, in F with U. Grehling vln, H. Müller vlc, E. Müller hpsi & Schola Cantorum Basiliensis – Wenzinger	Archive APM14846, ARC3246, ARC73246, SAPM198846
Concerto grosso No. 3, in e with U. Grehling vln, H. Müller vlc, E. Müller hpsi & Schola Cantorum Basiliensis – Wenzinger	Archive APM14847, ARC3247, ARC73247, SAPM198847
Concerto grosso No. 4, in a with U. Grehling vln, H. Müller vlc, E. Müller hpsi & Schola Cantorum Basiliensis – Wenzinger	Archive APM14847, ARC3247, ARC73247, SAPM198847
Concerto grosso No. 5, in D with U. Grehling vln, H. Müller vlc, E. Müller hpsi & Schola Cantorum Basiliensis – Wenzinger	Archive APM14847, ARC3247, ARC73247, SAPM198847
Concerto grosso No. 6, in g with U. Grehling vln, H. Müller vlc, E. Müller hpsi & Schola Cantorum Basiliensis – Wenzinger	Archive APM14848, ARC3248, ARC73248, SAPM198848
Concerto grosso No. 7, in B flat with U. Grehling vln, H. Müller vlc, E. Müller hpsi & Schola Cantorum Basiliensis – Wenzinger	Archive APM14848, ARC3248, ARC73248, SAPM198848
Concerto grosso No. 8, in c with U. Grehling vln, H. Müller vlc, E. Müller hpsi & Schola Cantorum Basiliensis – Wenzinger	Archive APM14847, ARC3247, ARC73247, SAPM198847
Concerto grosso No. 9, in F with U. Grehling vln, H. Müller vlc, E. Müller hpsi & Schola Cantorum Basiliensis – Wenzinger	Archive APM14848, ARC3248, ARC73248, SAPM198848
Concerto grosso No. 10, in d with U. Grehling vln, H. Müller vlc, E. Müller hpsi & Schola Cantorum Basiliensis – Wenzinger	Archive APM14846, ARC3246, ARC73246, SAPM198846
Concerto grosso No. 11, in A with U. Grehling vln, H. Müller vlc, E. Müller hpsi & Schola Cantorum Basiliensis – Wenzinger	Archive APM14846, ARC3246, ARC73246, SAPM198846
Concerto grosso No. 12, in b with U. Grehling vln, H. Müller vlc, E. Müller hpsi & Schola Cantorum Basiliensis – Wenzinger	Archive APM14848, ARC3248, ARC73248, SAPM198848

Norman NELSON

VIVALDI

(12) Concerti, Op. 3 "L'Estro armonico" var. cbns & strs
  Concerto No. 10, in b, P.148 (F.IV, No. 10) 4 vlns, strs & c
  with N. Marriner vln, A. Howard vln,   L'Oiseau–Lyre OL276,
  T. Connah vln & Academy of St.   SMO1520, SOL276
  Martin–in–the–Field – Marriner

Mary NEMET

BRITTEN

Suite, Op. 6 vln & pf
  with R. Wruble pf   Pye GGC4111, GSGC14111

HAYDN

Sonata No. 1, in G, H.XV, No. 32 (1794) vln & hpsi
  with R. Wruble pf   Pye GGC4106, GSGC14106
Sonata No. 2, in D, H.XVI, No. 24 (1773) vln & hpsi
  with R. Wruble pf   Pye GGC4106, GSGC14106
Sonata No. 3, in E flat, H.XVI, No. 25 (1773) vln & hpsi
  with R. Wruble pf   Pye GGC4106, GSGC14106
Sonata No. 5, in G, H.XVI, No. 43 (1785) vln & hpsi
  with R. Wruble pf   Pye GGC4106, GSGC14106

PROKOFIEV

Sonata No. 2, in D, Op. 94bis vln & pf
  with R. Wruble pf   Pye GSGC14123

SZYMANOWSKI

Sonata No. 1, in d, Op. 9 vln & pf
  with R. Wruble pf   Pye GSGC14123

WALTON

Sonata (1939) vln & pf
  with R. Wruble pf   Pye GGC4111, GSGC14111

Pierre NERINI (1915–   )

BEETHOVEN

Sonata No. 5, in F, Op. 24 "Spring" vln & pf
  with J. Nerini pf   Pacific PIZ1518/20

DELIBES

Sylvia (1876) – ballet orch.
  No. 12b. Rentrée de Sylvia (Act II)
  with Paris Conservatory Orch. –   Ace of Clubs ACL74
  Désormière   Decca AX411/3, K23101/3,
                     LM4502
                     London LL846, LPS184
                     Richmond B19045

DOHNÁNYI

Ruralia Hungarica, Op. 32A pf – arr. vln & pf Kreisler
  with J. Nerini pf   Columbia LF184/5

FALLA

Concerto in D (1926) hpsi, fl, ob, cl, vln & vlc
  with G. Soriano hpsi, M. Cebost fl, R.   Angel 36131
  Casier ob, A. Boutard cl, R. Cordier   Electrola E91310, STE91310
  vlc, – cond. Frühbeck de Burgos   HMV ALP1994, ASD545,
                                             CVA778, QALP10380

PAGANINI

Concerto No. 2, in b, Op. 7 vln & orch.
  Ronde à la clochette (2nd mvt) "La Campanella" arr. vln & pf Kreisler
  with J. Nerini pf   Pacific PIZ1517

RIMSKY–KORSAKOV

Scheherazade, Op. 35 (1888) orch.
  with Paris Conservatory Orch. –   Ace of Clubs ACL153
  Ansermet   Decca LXT5082, SXL2086
                    London LL1162
                    Richmond B19086, S29086

SARASATE

(8) Danzas españolas vln & pf
  No. 6. Zapateado, Op. 23, No. 2
  with J. Nerini pf   Pacific PIZ1544

TCHAIKOVSKY

Suite No. 3, in G, Op. 55 orch.
  Theme & Variations
  with Paris Conservatory Orch. – Boult Ace of Clubs ACL89
                    Decca LXT5099
                    London CM9143, CS6140

Carlo van NESTE (1914–   )

ALPAERTS

Concerto (1948) vln & orch.
  with Belgium National Orch. – Louel   Decca FA143234

BOURGUIGNON

Concerto, Op. 86 vln & orch.
  with Belgium National Orch. –   Decca FM133104
  Weemaels

BRAHMS

(16) Waltzes, Op. 39 pf duet
  No. 15. Waltz No. 15, in A flat arr. vln & pf "in A" Hochstein
  with Mme. van Neste pf   Columbia D11066

HUYBRECHTS

Sonata in G (1925) vln & pf
  with N. Sluszny pf   2EF 154/7–1 HMV DB4700/1

KREISLER

Variations on a theme of Corelli (Tartini) vln & pf
  with Mme. van Neste pf   Columbia D11066

LOCATELLI

(24) Caprices, Op. 3 solo vln
  Caprice No. 24, in D
  (unaccompanied)   2EF 163–1 HMV DB4702

MOZART

Sonata No. 23, in D, K306 vln & pf
                    2EF 159–2 & 160/2–1 HMV DB4703/4
  with N. Sluszny pf

SCHUBERT, François

(12) Bagatelles, Op. 13 vln & pf
  No. 9. L'abeille
  with Mme. van Neste pf   Columbia D11066

STRAVINSKY

Mavra (1922) – opera
Russian maiden's song (Parasha's aria) arr. vln & pf Dushkin & Stravinsky
with N. Sluszny pf   2EF 158–1   HMV DB4702

VOCHT

Concerto in E vln & orch.
with Belgium National Orch. – de Vocht   Decca FM133018

Werner NEUHAUS

BACH

(6) Brandenburg Concerti, BWV1046/51 (1721) strs & c
Brandenburg Concerto No. 3, in G, BWV1048 3 vlns, 3 vlas, 3 vlcs & cbs
with F–J. Maier vln, B. Seeger vln, G. Lemmen vla, F. Beyer vla, D. Wolff–Malm vla, R.J. Buhl vlc, R. Mandalka vlc, H. Beckedorf vlc, P. Breuer cbs & G. Leonhardt hpsi, of the Collegium Aureum   Camden Classics (in set VCCS6023)   Victor (in set VICS6023)

HAYDN

Sinfonia concertante in B flat, Op. 84 (H.I, No. 105) vln, vlc, ob, bsn & orch.
with H. Plümmacher vlc, H. Hucke ob, W. Mauruschat bsn & Consortium musicum – Lehan   Columbia SMC91383   HMV SXLP20069, XLP20069   Mace M9040, MCS9040

KRIEGER, A.

Aria: Ich will es nicht achten, ich will es nicht tun v & strs
with C. Ocker b, H. Thoene vln, H. Jopen vla, E. Seiler vla, H. Hedler gamba, A. Lessing gamba & W. Thoene spin   Columbia C91111, STC91111

LOCATELLI

(12) Concerti, Op. 7 (1741) "Il pianto d'Arianna" strs & c
Concerto No. 12, in F 4 vlns, strs & c
with F–J. Maier vln, B. Seeger vln, G. Vollmer vln & Collegium Aureum   Harmonia Mundi HMS30887

ROSENMÜLLER

Sinfonia undecima 2 vlns, 2 vlas, 2 gambas, lute & hpsi
with H. Thoene vln, H. Jopen vla, E. Seiler vla, H. Hedler t–gamba, A. Lessing bs–gamba, E. Müller–Dombois lute & W. Thoene spin   Columbia C91111, STC91111

WALTHER

Aria in e (1676) vln & c
with H. Naumann gamba & E.M. Dombois theorbe*   Columbia C91113, STC91113

* Large lute.

Laszlo NEUMANN

BRAHMS

(21) Hungarian Dances pf duet
Hungarian dance No. 1, in g arr. vln & pf Joachim
with J. Doyen pf   Ultraphon AP578
(16) Waltzes, Op. 39 pf duet
No. 15. Waltz No. 15, in A flat arr. vln & pf "in A" Hochstein
with O. Herz pf   Edison Bell SH1154

DVOŘÁK

(8) Humoresques, Op. 101 pf
No. 7. Humoresque No. 7, in G flat arr. vln & pf "in G" Kreisler
with O. Herz pf   Edison Bell SH1153

KREISLER

(La) Gitana vln & pf
with O. Herz pf   Edison Bell SH1153

SCHUMANN

(13) Kinderscenen, Op. 15 pf
No. 7. Träumerei arr. vln & pf
with O. Herz pf   Edison Bell SH1153

WIENIAWSKI

Mazurka in a, Op. 3 "Kujawiak" vln & pf – arr. Marteau
with J. Doyen pf   Ultraphon AP578

Adolphe NEURI

ELGAR

Salut d'amour, Op. 12 orch. – arr. vln & pf Elgar
with piano   Beka 853

GOUNOD

Ave Maria (Méditation on Bach's "Prelude No. 1, in C" from Book I of "Das Wohltemperirte Clavier") v & pf – arr. vln & pf
with piano   Beka 853

Ginette NEVEU (1919–1949)

BACH. W.F.

Air vln & clav*
with B. Seidler–Winkler pf   HMV DB4577

BRAHMS

Concerto in D, Op. 77 (cadenza by Joachim) vln & orch.
with Philharmonia Orch. – Dobrowen   2EA 11172/4–2, 11175/6–1, 11177–2, 11178/9–1 & 11180–3   HMV COLH80, DB6415/9S, DBS9126/30, DB11145/9S

CHAUSSON

Poème, Op. 25 vln & orch.
with Philharmonia Orch. – Dobrowen   Angel 35128   HMV ALP1520, FJLP5037

CHOPIN

Nocturne No. 20, in c sharp, Op. posth pf – arr. vln & pf Rodionov
with B. Seidler–Winkler pf   HMV DB4514

* Unidentified.

CHOPIN – *Continued*

Nocturne No. 20, in c sharp, Op. posth pf – arr. vln & pf Rodionov
with J. Neveu pf   2EA 10941–4   HMV DB6908

DEBUSSY

Sonata No. 3, in g (1917) vln & pf
with J. Neveu pf   Angel 35128
Electrola E60052
HMV ALP1520, FJLP5037,
WDLP567

DINICU

Hora staccato vln & pf – arr. Heifetz
with J. Neveu pf   OEA 11157–1   HMV DA1865, 7RF132

FALLA

(La) Vida Breve (1913) – opera
  Danza española orch. – arr. vln & pf Kreisler
with J. Neveu pf   OEA 11164–1   HMV DA1865, 7RF132

GLUCK

Orphée et Eurydice (1762) – opera
  Dance of the blessed spirits: Lento "Mélodie" (No. 2) arr. vln & pf
  Kreisler
with B. Seidler–   ORA 2841[1]☐,   HMV DA4453
Winkler pf

KREISLER

Variations on a theme of Corelli (Tartini) vln & pf
with G. Beck pf   2RA 3839[II]☐,   HMV DB4666

PARADIES

Sicilienne vln & pf – arr. Dushkin
with B. Seidler–   ORA 2842[1]☐,   HMV DA4453
Winkler pf

RAVEL

Pièce en forme d'Habanera v & pf – arr. vln & pf Catherine
with J. Neveu pf   OEA 11162–1   HMV DA1871, 7ER5099

Tzigane (Rapsodie de concert) (1924) vln & pf or orch.
     2EA 10938–1, 10939–7 & 10940–4   Angel 35128
with J. Neveu pf   Electrola E60052
HMV ALP1520, DB6907/8,
FJLP5037, WDLP567, 7ER5099

SCARLATESCU

Bagatelle (in Rumanian style) vln & pf
with J. Neveu pf   OEA 11163–1   HMV DA1871

SIBELIUS

Concerto in d, Op. 47 vln & orch.
    2EA 10675[1]☐, 10766[II]☐, 10767[1]☐,   Angel 35129, LPC11575
    10768[II]☐, 10771[II]☐, 10772[1]☐, &   Electrola E60586
                    10769/70[1]☐,   HMV ALP1479, DB6244/7,
with Philharmonia Orch. – Susskind   DB9007/10, FJLP5036,
WDLP622

STRAUSS, R.

Sonata in E flat, Op. 18 vln & pf
    2RA 3832[1]☐, 3833[II]☐, 3834/7[1]   HMV DB4663/6
with G. Beck pf   ☐, & 3838[II]☐,

SUK

(4) Pieces, Op. 17 vln & pf
  No. 2. Appassionata
  with B. Seidler–Winkler pf   HMV DB4514
  No. 3. Un poco triste
  with B. Seidler–Winkler pf   HMV DB4577
(4) Pieces, Op. 17 vln & pf
    2EA 11168/9–2, 11170–1 &   Angel 35129, LPC11575
with J. Neveu pf   11171–2   HMV ALP1479, DB6359/60,
FJLP5036, WDLP622
Victor 11–9840 & 12–0154

Heinrich NEWE

MARTINI, G.B.

(12) Sonatas, Op. 2 (1741) hpsi
  Sonata No. 12, in F: Gavotte arr. vln & pf Manén
  with piano   51728   Ekophon NS1726

SCHUMANN

(13) Kinderscenen, Op. 15 pf
  No. 7. Träumerei arr. vln & pf
  with G. Enders pf   653 "KA 690"   Pax 2

WILHELMJ

Berceuse vln & pf
  with piano   51727   Ekophon NS1726

Tibor NEY (1906–)

BARTÓK

Rhapsody No. 1, in G (1928) vln & orch.
  with E. Petri pf   Qualiton LP1583
Sonata No. 2 (1922) vln & pf
  with E. Szegedi pf   Qualiton LP1552

SOPRONI

Ovidii Metamorphoses v, vln, cho & orch.
  with E. Sziklay s & Hungarian Radio   Qualiton LPX1298, SLPX1298
  & TV Chorus & orch. – Erdélyi

G. NIAGA (1922–)

MULYAR

(6) Miniatures vln & pf
  with G. Strakhilevich pf   Mezhdunarodnaya Kniga
D29538

RIVILIS

Suite, Op. 9 vln & pf
  with G. Strakhilevich pf   Mezhdunarodnaya Kniga
D29537

Ellen Birgithe NIELSEN (1924–)

BACH

(4) Suites, BWV1066/9 strs & c
  Suite No. 3, in D: Air (2nd mvt) BWV1068 2 obs, 3 tpts, drms, strs & c
  – arr. vln & pf as "Air on the G–string" by Wilhelmj
  with K. Browall pf   2CS 2374¹□, HMV DB5284

DVOŘÁK

(7) Gypsy songs, Op. 55 v & pf
  No. 4. Songs my mother taught me arr. vln & pf S. Hansen
  with K. Browall pf   OCS 2363¹□, HMV DA5250
  No. 4. Songs my mother taught me arr. vln & pf S. Hansen
  with K.L.   OCS 3007–3A HMV DA5267
  Christiansen pf

KREISLER

Liebesfreud vln & pf
  with K.L.   OCS 3005–3A HMV DA5266
  Christiansen pf
Liebesleid vln & pf
  with K.L.   OCS 3003–3A HMV DA5266
  Christiansen pf

PARADIES

Sicilienne vln & pf – arr. Dushkin
  with K. Browall pf   OCS 2362¹□, HMV DA5250
Sicilienne vln & pf – arr. Dushkin
  with K.L.   OCS 3004–2A HMV DA5265
  Christiansen pf

PORPORA

Aria in E arr. vln & pf Corti*
  with K.L.   OCS 3006–1A HMV DA5265
  Christiansen pf

RAVEL

Pièce en forme d'Habanera v & pf – arr. vln & pf Catherine
  with K.L.   OCS 3002–4A HMV DA5268
  Christiansen pf
Tzigane (Rapsodie de concert) (1924) vln & pf or orch.
  with K. Browall pf   2CS 2322/3–1 HMV DB5277

SCHUBERT

(7) Gesänge (set to Scott's "Lady of the Lake") Op. 52 v & pf
  No. 6. Ave Maria, D839 arr vln & pf Wilhelmj
  with K. Browall pf   2CS 2374¹□, HMV DB5284

SIBELIUS

(5) Pieces, Op. 81 vln & pf
  No. 1. Mazurka
  with K.L.   OCS 3000–3A HMV DA5267
  Christiansen pf

STRAVINSKY

Mavra (1922) – opera
  Russian maiden's song (Parasha's aria) arr. vln & pf Dushkin &
  Stravinsky
  with K.L.   OCS 3001–1A HMV DA5268
  Christiansen pf

* Unidentified.

TCHAIKOVSKY

(6) Songs, Op. 6 v & pf
  No. 6. None but the weary heart arr. vln & pf Tolhurst
  with K. Browall pf   OCS 2376¹□, HMV DA5251
Souvenir d'un lieu cher, Op. 42 vln & pf
  No. 3. Mélodie
  with K. Browall pf   OCS 2375¹□, HMV DA5251

Olaf NIELSEN (1898–)

BROMAN

Romance vln & pf
  with, N. Broman pf   OSB 595/6ᴵᴵ□, HMV X4921

PETERSON–BERGER

Fyra danspoem (1900) pf
  Serenade arr. vln & pf
  with piano   OT 550–II HMV*

Thorvald NIELSEN (1891–)

KREISLER

Rondino on a theme by Beethoven vln & pf
  with piano   HMV X2255

NIELSEN

Sonata No. 2, in g, Op. 35 (1912) vln & pf
  with C. Christiansen pf   Tono LPA35004, X25186/7

SCHUBERT

Litanei auf das Fest aller Seelen, D343 v & pf – arr. vln, vlc & pf Alex
Hildingsen
  with G. Hye–Knudsen vlc & piano   HMV X2255

Wacław NIEMCZYK (1907–)

FALLA

(La) Vida Breve (1913) – opera
  Danza española orch. – arr. vln & pf Kreisler
  with piano   Ultraphon BP1329

GRANADOS

(12) Danzas españolas, Op. 37 (1893) pf
  No. 5. Danza española No. 5, in e "Andaluza" arr. vln & pf Kreisler
  with piano   Ultraphon BP1330

MOZART

Serenade No. 7, in D, K250 "Haffner" orch.
  Rondo (4th mvt) arr. vln & pf Kreisler
  with piano   Ultraphon BP1458

PADEREWSKI

(6) Polish Dances, Op. 9 – Book II pf
  No. 5. Krakowiak in A arr. vln & pf
  with L. Urstein pf   WJ 389 Columbia DM1721

* Unissued.

SZYMANOWSKI

(La) Berceuse d'Aitacho Enia, Op. 52 (1925) vln & pf
  with L. Urstein pf   WJ 388   Columbia DM1721

TARTINI

Sonata in g "Il Trillo del Diavolo" vln & c – arr. vln & pf Kreisler
  with J. Sulikowski pf   P 76735/6   Ultraphon BP1188

Piet NIJLAND

FESCH

(12) Sonatas, Op. 12 (1748) 2 fls or vlns & c
  Sonata No. 2, in g
  with W. Noske vln, J. van Wering hpsi Radio Nederland 109775
  & C. van Leeuwen Boomkamp vlc

HACQUART

(10) Sonatas, Op. 2 2 vlns, vlc & c
  Sonata No. 8, in e
  with W. Noske vln, C. van Leeuwen   Radio Nederland 109774
  Boomkamp vlc, J. van Wering hpsi &
  L. Goossens vlc

MAHAUT

Duets, Op. 4 2 vlns
  Duet No. 6
  with W. Noske vln   Radio Nederland 109776

Johann NILSSON (1893–)

BULL

Säterjentens søndag v & pf – arr. vln & pf Svendsen
  with piano   Bw 239^{I}△ HMV X2367

HØEBERG

Romance in G, Op. 3 vln & pf
  with piano   Bw 244^{I}△ HMV X2368

KUHLAU

Elverhoj (The Elves hill) Op. 100 (1828) – Incidental music orch.
  No. 12. Menuetto in F (Act V) arr. vln & pf Burmester
  with piano   Bw 242^{II}△ HMV X2367

SCHUBERT

(7) Gesänge (set to Scott's "Lady of the Lake") Op. 52 v & pf
  No. 6. Ave Maria, D839 arr. vln & pf Wilhelmj
  with piano   Polyphon 47506

Litanei auf das Fest aller Seelen, D343 v & pf – arr. vln & pf
  with piano   Polyphon 47506

(14) Schwanengesang, D957 (1828) v & pf
  No. 4. Ständchen "Serenade" arr. vln & pf Elman
  with piano   Bw 243^{II}△ HMV X2368

Miwako NINOMIYA

OPRAEM

Benedictus in E flat bs, vln, hrn & strs
  with K. Engen bs, J. Meredith hrn &   Musica Bavarica MB202
  Chamber Orch. – Kirchberger

Ebba NISSEN

FIBICH

Images, Impressions & Souvenirs, Op. 41 pf
  No. 14. Poem (from "Souvenirs", Part IV) arr. vln & pf Kubelík
  with piano   4105–S–B Sonora 1100

KREISLER

Liebesleid vln & pf
  with piano   4106–S–A Sonora 1100

Sylvain NOACK (1881–1953)

SCHUBERT, François

(12) Bagatelles, Op. 13 vln & pf
  No. 9. L'abeille
  with piano   Phono–Cut 5058

Jean NOCETI

BEETHOVEN

(6) Minuets, G167 pf
  No. 2. Minuet No. 2, in G arr. vln & pf Noceti
  with piano   HMV K5777

MOZART

Divertimento No. 17, in D, K334 2 hrns & strs
  Minuet (3rd mvt) arr. vln & pf Noceti
  with piano   HMV K5789

NOCETI

Canzonetta vln & pf
  with piano   HMV K5777

PERGOLESI

Aria arr. vln & pf Noceti*
  with piano   HMV K5789

Peter NÖLTING

HANDEL

(12) Concerti grossi, Op. 6 (1739) 2 vlns, vlc & strs
  Concerto grosso No. 5, in D
  with H. Fukano vln, H. Spengler vlc, Da Camera HKO1001
  K. Preis hpsi & Heidelberg Chamber
  Orch. – Albert

STAMITZ, K.

Trio in G 2 fls & vlc
  with G. Kuhn fl, H. Lissok vlc & K. Da Camera HBE2301/2
  Preis hpsi

Mona NORDIN

CARLSTEDT

(8) Duets 2 vlns
  with G. Crafoord vln   Telefunken LT43075

* Unidentified.

Willem NOSKE (1918–)

DVOŘÁK

(4) Romantic Pieces, Op. 75 vln & pf
No. 1. Allegro moderato
with H. Schouwman pf   Radio Nederland DR109269
No. 2. Allegro maestoso
with H. Schouwman pf   Radio Nederland DR109269
No. 3. Allegro appassionato
with H. Schouwman pf   Radio Nederland DR109269

FESCH

(12) Concerti, Op. 3a (1716/7) var. cbns
Concerto No. 6, in a 4 vlns, ob & c
with Netherlands Chamber Orch. –   Donemus DAVS6802
Hupperts
Concerto No. 6, in a 4 vlns, ob & c
with Amsterdam Chamber Orch. –   Radio Nederland 109773
Rieu
(12) Sonatas, Op. 12 (1748) 2 fls or vlns & c
Sonata No. 2, in g
with P. Nijland vln, J. van Wering   Radio Nederland 109775
hpsi & C. van Leeuwen Boomkamp vlc

GRONEMANN

(12) Sonatas, Op. 1 vln & c
Sonata No. 12, in G
with J. van Wering hpsi & C. van   Radio Nederland 109774
Leeuwen Boomkamp vlc

HACQUART

(10) Sonatas, Op. 2 2 vlns, vlc & c
Sonata No. 8, in e
with P. Nijland vln, C. van Leeuwen   Radio Nederland 109774
Boomkamp vlc, J. van Wering hpsi &
L. Goossens vlc

HEINSIUS

(6) Concerti vln & strs
Concerto in G
with Amsterdam Chamber Orch. –   Radio Nederland 109775
Rieu

HELLENDAAL

(6) Sonatas, Op. 1 vln & c
Sonata No. 3, in g
with H. Schouwman hpsi & C. van   Radio Nederland DR109269
Leeuwen Boomkamp vlc

MAHAUT

Duets, Op. 4 2 vlns
Duet No. 6
with P. Nijland vln   Radio Nederland 109776

PETERSEN

Sonata in d vln & c
with J. van Wering hpsi & C. van   Radio Nederland 109773
Leeuwen Boomkamp vlc

Jiří NOVÁK (1924–)

DVOŘÁK

Sonatina in G, Op. 100 vln & pf
with P. Štěpán pf   Electrola SME91446
    HMV CVB2014

MARTINŮ

(3) Madrigals (1948) vln & vla
with M. Škampa vla   Supraphon SUA10191

MOZART

Concerto No. 4, in D, K218 vln & orch.
with Czech Philharmonic Orch. –   Elite CSLP6005
Talich   Parliament PLP104
    Supraphon LPV326, SUA10291
Duo No. 1, in G, K423 vln & vla
with M. Škampa vla   Supraphon SUA10677,
    SUAST50677, SV8265

PAGANINI

Concerto No. 1, in D, Op. 6 (cadenza by Kubelík) vln & orch.
Allegro maestoso (1st mvt) arr. Wilhelmj
with Prague Symphony Orch. –   Supraphon SUB10030
Smetáček   Ultraphon H24462/4

Franco NOVELLO (1929–)

ALBÉNIZ

España (6 Feuilles d'album) Op. 165 pf
No. 2. Tango in D arr. vln & pf Kreisler
with M. Gachet pf   Cetra LPC55040, LPU0031

BACH

Concerto in d, BWV1043 2 vlns, strs & c
with V. Příhoda vln & RIA Symphony   Cetra LPC55021, LPU0027
Orch., Turin – Gerelli

COPLAND

(2) Pieces (1926) vln & pf
No. 1. Nocturne
with M. Gachet pf   Cetra LPC55040, LPU0031
No. 2. Ukulele serenade
with M. Gachet pf   Cetra LPC55040, LPU0031

DINICU

Hora staccato vln & pf – arr. Heifetz
with M. Gachet pf   Cetra LPC55040, LPU0031

DVOŘÁK

Symphony No. 9, in e, Op. 95 "From the New World" orch.
Largo (2nd mvt) arr. vln & pf as "Negro spiritual melody" by Kreisler
with M. Gachet pf   Cetra LPC55040, LPU0031

NOVELLO

Malinconia vln & pf
with M. Gachet pf   Cetra LPC55040, LPU0031

PAGANINI

Concerto No. 1, in D, Op. 6 vln & orch.
Adagio espressivo (2nd mvt)
with M. Gachet pf   Cetra LPC55040, LPU0031

PŘÍHODA

Caprice in E (1926) vln & pf
with M. Gachet pf
Cetra LPC55040, LPU0031

Waltz in A vln & pf
with M. Gachet pf
Cetra LPC55040, LPU0031

VIOTTI

(3) Duets, Op. 29 2 vlns & orch.
No. 1. Duo concertante No. 1, in g arr. Quaranta – cadenza by Příhoda
with V. Příhoda vln & RIA Symphony Cetra LPU0059, LPV45009
Orch., Turin – Gerelli

Rudolf NOVOSAD

VIOTTI

Duet No. 2 unid 2 vlns
with V. Kolouch vln
Supraphon SUA10741

Georges OCTORS (1923–)

VIEUXTEMPS

Ballade & Polonaise in G, Op. 38 vln & pf
with Belgian Radio Orch. – Doneux   Gramola GLP2510

YSAŸE

(6) Sonatas, Op. 27 solo vln
Sonata No. 1, in g
(unaccompanied)   Gramola GLP2510

Riccardo ODNOPOSOFF (1914–)

BACH

Concerto No. 2, in E, BWV1042 vln, strs & c
with Netherlands Philharmonic Orch.   Musical Masterpiece Society
– Goehr   MMS54

(3) Sonatas & 3 Partitas, BWV1001/6 solo vln
Partita No. 2, in d: Chaconne (5th mvt) BWV1004
(unaccompanied)   Musical Masterpiece Society
MMS54

BEETHOVEN

Concerto in C, Op. 56 "Triple" vln, vlc, pf & orch.
CHAX 7008–1, 7009–2A, 7010–   Columbia 266408/12, 69163/7D,
3, 7011–3A, 7012–2A, 7013–1, 7014–   (set M327), GQX10915/9,
with S. Auber vlc, A.   2 & 7015/6–1   LFX518/22S, LVX27/31S,
Morales pf & Vienna Philharmonic   LX671/5S, LX8353/7S, ML2218
Orch. – Weingartner

Sonata No. 4, in a, Op. 23 vln & pf
with O. Herz pf   Allegro ALG3047

(3) Sonatas, Op. 30 vln & pf
No. 3. Sonata No. 8, in G
with O. Herz pf   Allegro ALG3047

BRAHMS

Concerto in D, Op. 77 (cadenza by Kreisler) vln & orch.
with Frankfurt Opera Orch. –   Concert Hall M145
Bamberger   Crowell–Collier Record Guild
CCRG121

BRANDL

(Der) Liebe Augustin – operetta
Du alter Stefansturm arr. vln & pf as "The old refrain" by Kreisler
with J. Antonietti pf   Musical Masterpiece Society
POP8

BRUCH

Concerto No. 1, in g, Op. 26 vln & orch.
with Netherlands Philharmonic Orch.   Musical Masterpiece Society
– Goehr   MMS40

CHAUSSON

Poème, Op. 25 vln & orch.
with Geneva Radio Symphony Orch. –   Musical Masterpiece Society
Rivoli   MMS2250

CHOPIN

Waltz No. 14, in e, Op. posth pf – arr. vln & pf Ysaÿe
with piano   Odeon 195125, A3281

DEBUSSY

Sonata No. 3, in g (1917) vln & pf
with L. Hambro pf   Allegro ALG3025

DVOŘÁK

Concerto in a, Op. 53 vln & orch.
with Les Concerts de Paris Symphony   Musical Masterpiece Society
Orch.   MMS21

FALLA

(7) Canciones populares españolas (1914) v & pf
No. 1. El paño moruno arr. vln & pf Kochański
with J. Antonietti pf   Concert Hall CHS1175
No. 3. Asturiana arr. vln & pf Kochański
with J. Antonietti pf   Concert Hall CHS1175
No. 4. Jota arr. vln & pf Kochański
with J. Antonietti pf   Concert Hall CHS1175
No. 5. Nana arr. vln & pf Kochański
with J. Antonietti pf   Concert Hall CHS1175
No. 6. Canción arr. vln & pf Kochański
with J. Antonietti pf   Concert Hall CHS1175

GEMINIANI ·

(12) Sonatas, Op. 4 vln & c
Sonata No. 10, in A
with B. Oren hpsi & L. Rostal vlc   Fonit LPU005
(6) Sonatas, Op. 5 (1738) solo vln
Sonata in B flat (ed Corti)
(unaccompanied)   Concert Hall CHS1170

GLAZOUNOV

Concerto in a, Op. 82 vln & orch.
with Les Concerts de Paris Symphony   Musical Masterpiece Society
Orch.   MMS21

GRANADOS

(12) Danzas españolas, Op. 37 (1893) pf
No. 5. Danza española No. 5, in e "Andaluza" arr. vln & pf Kreisler
with J. Antonietti pf   Musical Masterpiece Society
MMS915

KREISLER

Caprice viennois, Op. 2 vln & pf
  with J. Antonietti pf
  Musical Masterpiece Society
  POP8

Liebesfreud vln & pf
  with J. Antonietti pf
  Musical Masterpiece Society
  POP8

Liebesleid vln & pf
  with J. Antonietti pf
  Musical Masterpiece Society
  POP8

Recitative & Scherzo–caprice, Op. 6 solo vln
  (unaccompanied)
  Musical Masterpiece Society
  MMS915

Schön Rosmarin vln & pf
  with J. Antonietti pf
  Musical Masterpiece Society
  POP8

Variations on a theme of Corelli (Tartini) vln & pf
  with J. Antonietti pf
  Musical Masterpiece Society
  MMS915

LALO

Symphonie espagnole, Op. 21 vln & orch.*
  with Utrecht Symphony Orch. –
  Goehr
  Musical Masterpiece Society
  MMS14

MENDELSSOHN

Concerto in e, Op. 64 vln & orch.
  with Geneva Radio Symphony Orch. –
  Rivoli
  Concert Hall M2205
  Fonit LPU0011

NIN

(20) Cantos de España (1923) v & pf
  No. 4. Montañesa arr. vln & pf Kochański
    with J. Antonietti pf
    Concert Hall CHS1175
  No. 5. Tonada murciana arr. vln & pf Kochański
    with J. Antonietti pf
    Concert Hall CHS1175
  No. 7. Granadina arr. vln & pf Kochański
    with piano
    Odeon 195125, A3281
  No. 7. Granadina arr. vln & pf Kochański
    with J. Antonietti pf
    Concert Hall CHS1175
  No. 8. Saeta (Invocation) arr. vln & pf Kochański
    with piano
    Odeon 195125, A3281
  No. 8. Saeta (Invocation) arr. vln & pf Kochański
    with J. Antonietti pf
    Concert Hall CHS1175

NOVAČEK

(8) Concert Caprices, Op. 5 vln & pf
  No. 4. Perpetuum mobile
    with O. Herz pf
    Victor 10–1228

PAGANINI

Concerto No. 1, in D, Op. 6 vln & orch.
  with Geneva Radio Symphony Orch. –
  Rivoli
  Concert Hall M2205
  Fonit LPU0011
  Musical Masterpiece Society
  MMS2205

* Including Intermezzo.

PAGANINI – *Continued*

Concerto No. 2, in b, Op. 7 vln & orch.
  Ronde à clochette (2nd mvt) "La Campanella" arr. vln & pf Kochański
    with V. Pavlovsky pf
    HMV ED470
    Victor 11–8849
Concerto No. 2, in b, Op. 7 (cadenza by Baller) vln & orch.*
  with Utrecht Symphony Orch. –
  Hupperts
  Concert Hall G13

PROKOFIEV

Concerto No. 1, in D, Op. 19 vln & orch.
  with Zürich Radio Symphony Orch. –
  Hollreiser
  Classic CL6151
  Concert Hall CHS1160
  Musical Masterpiece Society
  MMS61
  Nixa CLP1160

Peter & the Wolf, Op. 67 narrator & orch.
  Theme & processional arr. vln & pf Grunes
    with V. Pavlovsky pf
    HMV ED470
    Victor 11–8849

SAINT–SAËNS

Havanaise, Op. 83 vln & orch.
  with Geneva Radio Symphony Orch. –
  Rivoli
  Musical Masterpiece Society
  MMS2250

Introduction & Rondo Capriccioso, Op. 28 vln & orch.
  with Geneva Radio Symphony Orch. –
  Rivoli
  Musical Masterpiece Society
  MMS2250

SARASATE

(8) Danzas españolas vln & pf
  No. 1. Malagueña, Op. 21, No. 1
    with G. Ashman pf
    Victor 11–9495
  No. 2. Habañera, Op. 21, No. 2
    with G. Ashman pf
    Victor 11–9495
Zigeunerweisen, Op. 20 vln & pf or orch.
  with Geneva Radio Symphony Orch. –
  Rivoli
  Musical Masterpiece Society
  MMS2250

SMETANA

From my Homeland (1878) vln & pf
  No. 2. Andantino
    with piano
    HMV C2967

TARTINI

Sonata in g "Il Trillo del Diavolo" vln & c – arr. vln & pf Kreisler
  with H. Wehrle hpsi
  Concert Hall CHS1170

TCHAIKOVSKY

Concerto in D, Op. 35 vln & orch.
  with Netherlands Philharmonic
  Symphony Orch. – Goehr
  Musical Masterpiece Society
  MMS34
  Nixa MLPY34

VILLA–LOBOS

(O) Canto do cysne negro (1917) vlc & pf – arr. vln & pf Villa-Lobos
  with O. Herz pf
  Victor 10–1228

* Ronde à la clochette or 3rd mvt. "La Campanella" is also on Musical
  Masterpiece Society MMS40.

VILLA–LOBOS – *Continued*

Sonata–Fantasia No. 3 (1915) vln & pf
 with L. Hambro pf   Allegro ALG3025

VITALI

Chaconne in g vln & c – arr. vln & orch. Charlier
 with H. Wehrle org   Concert Hall CHS1170

Chaconne in g vln & c – arr. vln & org Respighi
 with H. Wehrle org   Fonit LPU005

VIVALDI

(12) Sonatas, Op. 2 (1712) vln & c
 Sonata No. 2, in A, F.XIII, No. 30
 with B. Oren hpsi & L. Rostal vlc   Fonit LPU005

YSAŸE

(3) Mazurkas, Op. 11 vln & pf
 No. 3. Mazurka No. 3, in b "Lointaine–passé"
 with piano   2VH 7008^I ☐, HMV C2966

Rêve d'enfant, Op. 14 vln & pf
 with piano   2VH 7004^{II} ☐, HMV C2966

(6) Sonatas, Op. 27 solo vln
 Sonata No. 3, in d
 (unaccompanied)   Concert Hall CHS1175

 Sonata No. 4, in e
 (unaccompanied)   OVH 7000/3^{II} HMV*

 Sonata No. 4, in e
 (unaccompanied)   Concert Hall CHS1175

OEHLER

BEETHOVEN

Sonata No. 5, in F, Op. 24 "Spring" vln & pf
 with Heim pf   CBS S51111

Sonata No. 9, in A, Op. 47 "Kreutzer" vln & pf
 with Heim pf   CBS S51111

Werner OFFNER

BACH

Sonata in d, BWV1036 2 vlns & c
 with R. Kussmaul vln, K. Preis hpsi & Da Camera HBE2203
 J. Wolf vlc

Francis OGUSE

TELEMANN

Suite in B flat, T.III, No. 1 2 obs, strs & c
 with J–P. Rampal fl, C. Brion vlc &   Contrepoint MC20100
 Symphonic Instrumental Ensemble –
 Witold

VIVALDI

Concerto in B flat, P.391 2 vlns, strs & c
 with P. Lamacque vln & Symphonic   Contrepoint MC20043
 Instrumental Ensemble – Witold   London TWV91052

* Unpublished. Recorded 1938/9.

Gerhard OHNHEISER

TELEMANN

Concerto in C 4 vlns, strs & c
 with M. Hori vln, O. Kortner vln, P.   Da Camera SM91017
 Nägele vln & Heidelberg Chamber
 Orch.

David Fedorovich OISTRAKH (1908–   )

ALBÉNIZ

Love song unid – arr. vln & pf
 with V. Yampolsky pf   Colosseum CRLP249
                    Mezhdunarodnaya Kniga D1201,
                    D028807/8
                    Monitor MC2003

Love song unid – arr. vln & pf
 with D. Topilin pf   Colosseum CRLP 10050
                    Mezhdunarodnaya Kniga
                    D10497

BABAJANIAN

Trio in f sharp (1952) pf, vln & vlc
 with A. Babajanian pf & S.   Le Chant du Monde LDZA8103
 Knushevitsky vlc   Colosseum CRLP247
                    Mezhdunarodnaya Kniga
                    D1372/3
                    Monarch MWL367

BACH

(6) Brandenburg Concerti, BWV1046/51 (1721) strs & c
 Brandenburg Concerto No. 4, in G, BWV1049 vln, 2 fls, strs & c
 with A. Korneyev fl, N. Seidel fl &   Mezhdunarodnaya Kniga D4433,
 Moscow Chamber Orch. – Barshai   D026219/20
                    Monitor MC2037
                    Parlophone PMB1013

Concerto No. 1, in a, BWV1041 vln, strs & c
 with Moscow Chamber Orch. –   Artia ALP165
 Barshai   Bruno BR14058
                    Eurodisc 78351ZK
                    Mezhdunarodnaya Kniga D5082,
                    D08801, D026219/20

Concerto No. 1, in a, BWV1041 vln, strs & c
 with Vienna Philharmonic Orch. –   Deutsche Grammophon
 Oistrakh   LPM18820, SLPM138820, (in set
                    2705 013)

Concerto No. 2, in E, BWV1042 vln, strs & c
 with USSR State Philharmonic Orch. – Bruno BR14008
 Kondrashin   Colosseum CRLP254

Concerto No. 2, in E, BWV1042 vln, strs & c
 with Moscow Chamber Orch. –   Eurodisc 78427ZK, (in set
 Barshai   80569XK)
                    Mezhdunarodnaya Kniga
                    D08801
                    Musidisc RC856

Concerto No. 2, in E, BWV1042 vln, strs & c
 with Philadelphia Orch. – Ormandy   Columbia ML5087
                    Philips 409086AE, A01239L,
                    ABE10075, ABL3138, G05650R

BACH – *Continued*

Concerto No. 2, in E, BWV1042 vln, strs & c
with Vienna Philharmonic Orch. –
Oistrakh

Deutsche Grammophon
LPM18820, SLPM138820, (in set
2705 013)

Concerto in d, BWV1043 2 vlns, strs & c
with I. Oistrakh vln & Moscow
Chamber Orch. – Barshai

Bruno BR14008
Le Chant du Monde LDX–S8319
Eurodisc 78351ZK
Hall of Fame HOF516
Mezhdunarodnaya Kniga D5083,
D026219/20
Monitor MC2009
Musidisc RC856

Concerto in d, BWV1043 2 vlns, strs & c
with I. Oistrakh vln & Leipzig
Gewandhaus Orch. – Konwitschny

Decca DL9950
Deutsche Grammophon
LPE17160, LPM18393
Eterna 720031

Concerto in d, BWV1043 2 vlns, strs & c
with I. Oistrakh vln & Royal
Philharmonic Orch. – Goossens

Deutsche Grammophon
LPM18714, LPM18820,
SLPM138714, SLPM138820
Eterna 720162

(3) Sonatas & 3 Partitas, BWV1001/6 solo vln
Sonata No. 1, in g, BWV1001
(unaccompanied)

Mezhdunarodnaya Kniga
D04044

(6) Sonatas, BWV1014/9 vln & clav
Sonata No. 1, in b, BWV1014
with H. Pischner hpsi

Deutsche Grammophon
LPM39312, SLPM139312

Sonata No. 2, in A, BWV1015
with H. Pischner hpsi

Deutsche Grammophon
LPM18989, SLPM138989

Sonata No. 3, in E, BWV1016
with H. Pischner hpsi

Deutsche Grammophon
LPM18989, SLPM138989

Sonata No. 4, in c, BWV1017
with H. Pischner hpsi

Deutsche Grammophon
LPM39312, SLPM139312

Sonata No. 5, in f, BWV1018
with L. Oborin pf

Bruno BR14058
Le Chant du Monde LDYA8108
Colosseum CRLP193
Kingsway KL261
Mezhdunarodnaya Kniga
D06335
Monarch MWL3311
Que LP2006
Record Hunter TRH1
Saga STXID5253, XID5253

Sonata No. 5, in f, BWV1018
with H. Pischner hpsi

Deutsche Grammophon
LPM18677, SLPM138677

Sonata No. 6, in G, BWV1019
with V. Yampolsky pf

Bruno BR14058
Mezhdunarodnaya Kniga
D03822/3
Monitor MC2009

BACH – *Continued*

Sonata No. 6, in G, BWV1019
with H. Pischner hpsi

Deutsche Grammophon
LPM18677, SLPM138677

Sonata in C, BWV1037 2 vlns & c
with I. Oistrakh vln & V. Yampolsky
pf

Bruno BR14008
Le Chant du Monde LDY8138
Colosseum CRLP246
Mezhdunarodnaya Kniga
D004962/3, D015349
Monitor MC2005

Sonata in C, BWV1037 2 vlns & c
with I. Oistrakh vln & H. Pischner
hpsi

Decca DL9950
Deutsche Grammophon
LPM18393
Eterna 820283
Heliodor 89561, H25009

BARTÓK

Concerto No. 1, Op. posth (1908) vln & orch.
with Moscow Radio Orch. –
Rozhdestvensky

Le Chant du Monde LDXA8333,
LDXA48333
Mezhdunarodnaya Kniga
D010977, S0661/2
Period SHO342, SHOST2342

For Children (40 pieces) (1909) pf
Nos. 6, 13, 18, 25, 31, 36 & 40 arr. vln & pf as "Hungarian folk tunes"
by Szigeti
with V. Yampolsky pf

Colosseum CRLP249
Mezhdunarodnaya Kniga
D00905/6, D028113/4

6 Rumanian folk dances (1915) pf – arr. vln & pf Székely
with V. Yampolsky pf

Mezhdunarodnaya Kniga
D14653/4
Parliament PLP118
Supraphon LPM237, SUEC807

BEETHOVEN

Concerto in C, Op. 56 "Triple" vln, vlc, pf & orch.
with S. Knushevitsky vlc, L. Oborin pf
& Bolshoi Theatre Orch. – Golovanov

Colosseum CRLP10200
Eurodisc 80533ZK
Musidisc RC824
Period SHO327, SPL590

Concerto in C, Op. 56 "Triple" vln, vlc, pf & orch.
with S. Knushevitsky vlc, L. Oborin pf
& USSR State Philharmonic Orch. –
Kondrashin

Bruno BR14039

Concerto in C, Op. 56 "Triple" vln, vlc, pf & orch.
with S. Knushevitsky vlc, L. Oborin pf
& Philharmonia Orch. – Sargent

Angel 35697
Columbia C1062, C70387,
QCX10351, SAXQ7312,
SBO2753, SBOW2753,
SQIMX7033, STC70387
HMV SXLP30080, XLP30080
Regal SREG1098

Concerto in C, Op. 56 "Triple" pf, vln, vlc & orch.
with L. Oborin pf, S. Knushevitsky vlc
& Moscow Radio Symphony Orch. –
Orlov

Mezhdunarodnaya Kniga
D026327/8

BEETHOVEN – *Continued*

Concerto in C, Op. 56 "Triple" pf, vln, vlc & orch.
with S. Richter pf, M. Rostropovich
vlc & Berlin Philharmonic Orch. –
Karajan

Angel 36727
Electrola 1C065–02042
HMV ASD2582

Concerto in D, Op. 61 (cadenzas by Kreisler) vln & orch.
with USSR State Radio Orch. – Gauk

Bruno BR14020
Colosseum CRLP155
Concert Hall CHS1303, M2017
Design DLP122
Fidelio ATL4022
Gala GLP353
Guilde International du Disque
M2017
Mezhdunarodnaya Kniga
D019230/41, D0498/9
Musical Masterpiece Society
MMS2017
Musidisc RC812
Period SHO316, SPL598 , (in set
TE1163)
Supermajestic BBH1070
Vox GBY16150, (in set VSPS3)
Whitehall 5013

Concerto in D, Op. 61 (cadenzas by Kreisler) vln & orch.
with Stockholm Festival Orch. –
Ehrling

Angel 35162
Columbia CX1194, FCX354,
FCX30077, QCX10120
HMV LALP231

Concerto in D, Op. 61 (cadenzas by Kreisler) vln & orch.
with L'Orch. National de la
Radiodiffusion Française – Cluytens

Angel 35780
Columbia C91051, CX1672,
FCX817, QCX10384, SAX2315,
SAXQ7275, SAXW2315,
STC91051, WCX1672
Electrola SHZE143

(6) Minuets, G167 pf
No. 2. Minuet No. 2, in G arr. vln & pf Burmester
with S. Topilin pf

Mezhdunarodnaya Kniga D7591

Quartet No. 10, in E flat, Op. 74 "Harp" 2 vlns, vla & vlc
with P. Bondarenko vln, M. Terian vla
& S. Knushevitsky vlc

Mezhdunarodnaya Kniga
D021241/50

Romance No. 1, in G, Op. 40 vln & orch.
with USSR State Symphony Orch. –
Kondrashin

Eurodisc 80533ZK
Mezhdunarodnaya Kniga
D001224

Romance No. 1, in G, Op. 40 vln & orch.
with Royal Philharmonic Orch. –
Goossens

Deutsche Grammophon 135039,
EPL30586, LPM18714,
SEPL121586, SLPM138714
Mezhdunarodnaya Kniga
D08285/6, S0155/6

Romance No. 2, in F, Op. 50 vln & orch.
with Czech Philharmonic Orch. –
Ančerl

Eterna 820565
Supraphon LPV244, SUA10127,
SUN40074

Romance No. 2, in F, Op. 50 vln & orch.
with Moscow Chamber Orch. –
Barshai

Period SHO343, SHOST2343
Vedette VSC4020

BEETHOVEN – *Continued*

Romance No. 2, in F, Op. 50 vln & orch.
with Royal Philharmonic Orch. –
Goossens

Deutsche Grammophon 135039,
EPL30586, LPM18714,
SEPL121586, SLPM138714
Mezhdunarodnaya Kniga
D08285/6, S0155/6

Romance No. 2, in F, Op. 50 vln & orch.
with USSR Symphony Orch. –
Kondrashin

Mezhdunarodnaya Kniga
D026328

Serenade in D, Op. 25 fl, vln & vla
with G. Madatov fl & M. Terian vla

Mezhdunarodnaya Kniga
D7549/50

(3) Sonatas, Op. 12 vln & pf
No. 1. Sonata No. 1, in D
with V. Yampolsky pf

Eterna 820565
Supraphon LPV244, SUA10127

No. 1. Sonata No. 1, in D
with L. Oborin pf

Le Chant du Monde LDXA8301
Mezhdunarodnaya Kniga
D010763/4, S0477/8
Philips 835150AY, A02269L,
AL3416, PHM500032, (in set
PHM4–590), PHS900032, (in set
PHS4–990), SAL3416

No. 2. Sonata No. 2, in A
with L. Oborin pf

Le Chant du Monde LDXA8301
Mezhdunarodnaya Kniga
D010763/4, S0477/8
Philips 835151AY, A02270L,
AL3417, PHM500033, (in set
PHM4–590), PHS900033, (in set
PHS4–990), SAL3417

No. 3. Sonata No. 3, in E flat
with V. Yampolsky pf

Angel 35331
Columbia CX1580, FCX581,
QCX10324
HMV LALP365

No. 3. Sonata No. 3, in E flat
with L. Oborin pf

Le Chant du Monde LDXA8301
Mezhdunarodnaya Kniga
D010765/6, S0479/80
Philips 835152AY, A02271L,
AL3418, PHM500033, (in set
PHM4–590), PHS900033, (in set
PHS4–990), SAL3418

Sonata No. 4, in a, Op. 23 vln & pf
with A. Goldenweiser pf

Mezhdunarodnaya Kniga
D07893

Sonata No. 4, in a, Op. 23 vln & pf
with L. Oborin pf

Le Chant du Monde LDXA8302
Mezhdunarodnaya Kniga
D010765/6, S0479/80
Philips 835152AY, A02271L,
AL3418, PHM500033, (in set
PHM4–590), PHS900033, (in set
PHS4–990), SAL3418

BEETHOVEN – *Continued*

Sonata No. 5, in F, Op. 24 "Spring" vln & pf
with L. Oborin pf

Le Chant du Monde LDZA8110
Colosseum CRLP152
Dover HCR5245
Mezhdunarodnaya Kniga
D18882/9, D07894, D1296/7
Period SPL573

Sonata No. 5, in F, Op. 24 "Spring" vln & pf
with L. Oborin pf

Le Chant du Monde LDXA8302
Mezhdunarodnaya Kniga
D010767/8, S0481/2
Philips 835154AY, 835259AY,
A02273L, A02381L, AL3420,
FL5627, PHM500030, (in set
PHM4–590), PHS900030, (in set
PHS4–990), SAL3420

(3) Sonatas, Op. 30 vln & pf
No. 1. Sonata No. 6, in A
with L. Oborin pf

Le Chant du Monde LDXA8303
Mezhdunarodnaya Kniga
D010767/8, S0481/2
Philips 835154AY, A02273L,
AL3420, PHM500032, (in set
PHM4–590), PHS900032, (in set
PHS4–990), SAL3420

No. 2. Sonata No. 7, in c
with L. Oborin pf

Mezhdunarodnaya Kniga
D07637

No. 2. Sonata No. 7, in c
with L. Oborin pf

Le Chant du Monde LDXA8303
Mezhdunarodnaya Kniga
D010765/6, S0483/4
Philips 835152AY, A02271L,
AL3418, PHM500030, (in set
PHM4–590), PHS900030, (in
set PHS4–990), SAL3418

No. 3. Sonata No. 8, in G
with L. Oborin pf

Mezhdunarodnaya Kniga
D017293/6, D07638

No. 3. Sonata No. 8, in G
with L. Oborin pf

Le Chant du Monde LDXA8304
Mezhdunarodnaya Kniga
D010769/70, S0483/4
Philips 835150AY, A02269L,
AL3416, PHM500033, (in set
PHM4–590), PHS900033, (in set
PHS4–990), SAL3416

Sonata No. 9, in A, Op. 47 "Kreutzer" vln & pf
with L. Oborin pf

Le Chant du Monde LDA8077
Colosseum CRLP153
Mezhdunarodnaya Kniga
D03894/5
Vanguard VRS6024

Sonata No. 9, in A, Op. 47 "Kreutzer" vln & pf
with L. Oborin pf

Columbia C1047, C70100,
WC1047
HMV LBLP1050

BEETHOVEN – *Continued*

Sonata No. 9, in A, Op. 47 "Kreutzer" vln & pf
with L. Oborin pf

Le Chant du Monde LDXA8305
Mezhdunarodnaya Kniga
D010771/2, S0485/6
Philips 835153AY, 835259AY,
A02272L, A02381L, AL3419,
FL5627, PHM500031, (in set
PHM4–590), PHS900031, (in set
PHS4–990), SAL3419

Sonata No. 10, in G, Op. 96 vln & pf
with V. Yampolsky pf

Columbia ML5096
Monitor MC2042

Sonata No. 10, in G, Op. 96 vln & pf
with L. Oborin pf

Le Chant du Monde LDXA8304
Mezhdunarodnaya Kniga
D010769/70, S0487/8
Philips 835151AY, A02270L,
AL3417, PHM500031, (in set
PHM4–590), PHS900031, (in set
PHS4–990), SAL3417, SEL7634

(3) Trios, Op. 1 pf, vln & vlc
No. 3. Trio No. 3, in c
with L. Oborin pf & S. Knushevitsky
vlc

Mezhdunarodnaya Kniga
D015359/60

(2) Trios, Op. 70 pf, vln & vlc
No. 1. Trio No. 4, in D "Ghost"
with L. Oborin pf & S. Knushevitsky
vlc

Mezhdunarodnaya Kniga
D015359/60

Trio No. 6, in B flat, Op. 97 "Archduke" pf, vln & vlc
with L. Oborin pf & S. Knushevitsky
vlc

Angel 35704
Columbia C80542, CX1643,
QCX10337, SAXQ7300,
SCXW7518, SMC80542,
STC80542, WSX552
Music for Pleasure MFP2117

BENDA, J.

Trio–Sonata in E 2 vlns & c
with I. Oistrakh vln & V. Yampolsky
pf

Decca DL9962
Deutsche Grammophon
EPL30294, LP16136
Eterna 820283
Heliodor 89561, 478132, H25009

BRAHMS

Concerto in D, Op. 77 (cadenza by Kreisler) vln & orch.
with USSR State Radio Symphony
Orch. – Kondrashin

Bruno BR14004
Le Chant du Monde LDA8106
Colosseum CRLP150
Hall of Fame HOF508
Mezhdunarodnaya Kniga
D021868/77, D0857/8
Monarch MWL310
Musidisc RC853
Period SHO336, SHOST2336, (in
set TE1163)
Telefunken BLE14109
Vanguard VRS6018
Vox PL16380, (in set VSPS3)

BRAHMS – *Continued*

Concerto in D, Op. 77 (cadenza by Kreisler) vln & orch.
  with Saxon State Orch. – Konwitschny Decca DL9754, (in set DX141)
                                          Deutsche Grammophon
                                          LPM18199
                                          Eterna 820003, LPM1015
                                          Heliodor 89609, 478137,
                                          HS25091

Concerto in D, Op. 77 (cadenza by Kreisler) vln & orch.
  with L'Orch. National de la   Angel 35836
  Radiodiffusion Française – Klemperer Columbia C91134, CX1765,
                                          QCX10447, SAXQ7347,
                                          SAXW9542, STC91134,
                                          WCX560

Concerto in D, Op. 77 (cadenza by Kreisler) vln & orch.
  with Cleveland Orch. – Szell   Angel 36033
                                          Eurodisc 80184PK
                                          HMV Co69–02008, SLS786/1–2

Concerto in a, Op. 102 "Double" vln, vlc & orch.
  with M. Sadlo vlc & Czech   Bruno BR14039
  Philharmonic Orch. – Ancerl   Classic Editions SR8
                                          Colosseum CRLP120,
                                          CRLP10200
                                          Eurochord TAI738/41
                                          Supraphon G23282/5
                                        Symphonic SR8
                                        Ultraphon G15430/3

Concerto in a, Op. 102 "Double" vln, vlc & orch.
  with S. Knushevitsky vlc & USSR Mezhdunarodnaya Kniga
  Symphony Orch. – Eliasberg   D4848/9
                                          Monarch MWL333
                                        Period SHO336, SHOST2336

Concerto in a, Op. 102 "Double" vln, vlc & orch.
  with P. Fournier vlc & Philharmonia Angel 35353
  Orch. – Galliera   Columbia C70383, CX1487,
                                          QCX10378, SAX2264,
                                          SAXQ7264, SBOW8501,
                                        STC70383, WC520
                                        HMV LALP498

Concerto in a, Op. 102 "Double" vln, vlc & orch.
  with M. Rostropovich vlc & Cleveland Angel 36032
  Orch. – Szell   Electrola C063–02009
                                          HMV SLS786/1–2

(21) Hungarian Dances pf duet
  Hungarian dance No. 3, in F arr. vln & pf Joachim
  with V. Yampolsky pf   Mezhdunarodnaya Kniga D5872,
                                          D15059

  Hungarian dance No. 5, in f sharp arr. vln & pf "in g" Joachim
  with I. Yampolsky pf   Bruno BR14004
                                          Colosseum CRLP149
                                        Mezhdunarodnaya Kniga D1202,
                                          D15058
                                        Monarch MWL333
                                        Supraphon LPM184
                                        Ultraphon 5166C
                                        Vanguard VRS6020

Hungarian dance No. 8, in a arr. vln & pf Joachim
  with I. Yampolsky pf   Bruno BR14004
                                          Colosseum CRLP149
                                        Mezhdunarodnaya Kniga D1202,
                                          D15059, D029743/4
                                        Monarch MWL333
                                        Supraphon LPM184
                                        Ultraphon 5166C
                                        Vanguard VRS6020

Hungarian dance No. 9, in e arr. vln & pf Joachim
  with I. Yampolsky pf   Bruno BR14004
                                          Colosseum CRLP149
                                        Mezhdunarodnaya Kniga D1202,
                                          D22332, D029743/4
                                        Monarch MWL333
                                        Supraphon LPM184
                                        Ultraphon 5166C
                                        Vanguard VRS6020

Hungarian dance No. 11, in d arr. vln & pf Joachim
  with I. Yampolsky pf   Bruno BR14004
                                          Colosseum CRLP249
                                        Columbia ML5096
                                          Mezhdunarodnaya Kniga D1202,
                                          D22333, D029743/4

Hungarian dance No. 12, in d arr. vln & pf Joachim
  with V. Yampolsky pf   Mezhdunarodnaya Kniga D1202

Hungarian dance No. 20, in e arr. vln & pf "in d" Joachim
  with I. Yampolsky pf   Mezhdunarodnaya Kniga D1202,
                                          D10462
                                        Supraphon LPM184
                                      Ultraphon 5166C

(5) Lieder, Op. 49 v & pf
No. 4. Wiegenlied "Cradle song" arr. vln & pf Oistrakh
  with V. Yampolsky pf   Columbia ML5096
                                          Monitor MC2042

(2) Quartets, Op. 51 2 vlns, vla & vlc
No. 1. Quartet No. 1, in c
  with P. Bondarenko vln, M. Terian vla Mezhdunarodnaya Kniga
  & S. Knushevitsky vlc   D07281/2

Quintet in b, Op. 115 cl, 2 vlns, vla & vlc
  with V. Sorokin cl, P. Bondarenko vln, Bruno BR14062
  M. Terian vlc & S. Knushevitsky vlc Mezhdunarodnaya Kniga
                                          D03074/5

Sonata No. 3, in d, Op. 108 vln & pf
  with V. Yampolsky pf   046247/52   Colosseum CRLP148
                                          Supraphon H23324/6
                                        Ultraphon G15451/3
                                        Victor LS2025

Sonata No. 3, in d, Op. 108 vln & pf
  with V. Yampolsky pf   Angel 35331
                                          Columbia CX1580, FCX581,
                                          QCX10324
                                          HMV LALP365

BRAHMS – *Continued*

Sonata No. 3, in d, Op. 108 vln & pf*
with S. Richter pf
Le Chant du Monde MEL78444
Eurodisc 80080KK
HMV ASD2618
Melodiya–Angel SR40121
Mezhdunarodnaya Kniga
D025827/8, SM02257/8

Sonata (1853) "Frei aber Einsem" vln & pf
Allegro (Scherzo) in c (3rd mvt) "Sonatensatz"
with L. Oborin pf
Colosseum CRLP105,
CRLP10050
Mezhdunarodnaya Kniga
D13249/50

BRUCH

Concerto No. 1, in g, Op. 26 vln & orch.
with USSR State Symphony Orch. –
Gauk
Bruno BR14003
Colosseum CRLP225

Concerto No. 1, in g, Op. 26 vln & orch.
with London Symphony Orch. – von
Matacic
Angel 35243
Columbia C60548, CX1268,
FC25119, FCX419, QCX10240,
WS523
Electrola 1C047–50510
HMV LALP255, XLP30109
Kristall SMVP8028

Scottish Fantasia, Op. 46 vln & orch.
with O. Ellis hp & London Symphony
Orch. – Horenstein
Decca LXT6035, SXL6035
London CM9337, CS6337

CATOIRE

Élégie vln & pf
with V. Yampolsky pf
Mezhdunarodnaya Kniga D1408

Sonata No. 1, in b, Op. 15 vln & pf
with A. Goldenweiser pf
Mezhdunarodnaya Kniga
D026217

Sonata No. 2, in D, Op. 20 "Poem" vln & pf
with A. Goldenweiser pf
Mezhdunarodnaya Kniga
D026218

CHAUSSON

Poème, Op. 25 vln & orch.
with USSR State Symphony Orch. –
Kondrashin
Bruno BR14009
Le Chant du Monde LDM8173,
LDX–S8359
Colosseum CRLP253
Eurodisc 78705ZK, (in set
80569XK)
Mezhdunarodnaya Kniga
D03041
Monitor MC2073
Westminster XWN18177

Poème, Op. 25 vln & orch.
with Boston Symphony Orch. –
Munch
HMV ALP1460
Victor A630356, LM1988,
RB16166, VICS1058

* Recorded at the Moscow Conservatory Large Hall, December 1968.

CHOPIN

(4) Mazurkas, Op. 67 pf
No. 4. Mazurka No. 45, in a arr. vln & pf Kreisler*
with A. Dyakov pf
Mezhdunarodnaya Kniga 5521

(3) Nocturnes, Op. 9 pf
No. 2. Nocturne No. 2, in E flat arr. vln & pf Sarasate
with A. Makarov pf
Le Chant du Monde GA5002
Colosseum CRLP110
Mercury 16025, (in set DM27),
EP1–5008, MG10035
Mezhdunarodnaya Kniga
D12456
Supraphon G22207
Ultraphon G14742

Nocturne No. 19, in e, Op. 72, No. 1 pf – arr. vln & pf Auer
with V. Yampolsky pf
Mezhdunarodnaya Kniga
D017370

Nocturne No. 20, in c sharp, Op. posth pf – arr. vln & pf Rodionov
with V. Yampolsky pf
Mezhdunarodnaya Kniga
D017370

Trio in g, Op. 8 pf, vln & vlc
with L. Oborin pf & S. Knushevitsky vlc
Bruno BR14012
Colosseum CRLP251
Westminster XWN18174

DEBUSSY

Sonata No. 3, in g (1917) vln & pf
with F. Bauer pf
Le Chant du Monde LDX–
S78362
Philips 802727AY, AL3589,
PHM500112, PHS900112,
SAL3589

Suite Bergamasque (1890) pf
No. 3. Clair de lune arr. vln & pf Roelens
with V. Yampolsky pf
Bruno BR14018
Victor LS2026

No. 3. Clair de lune arr. vln & pf Roelens
with V. Yampolsky pf
Angel 35354
Columbia CX1466, ESL6252,
ESLQ1007, SAX2253, SEBQ219,
SEL1577, WSX604
Electrola SHZEL60

DVOŘÁK

Concerto in a, Op. 53 vln & orch.
with USSR State Symphony Orch. –
Kondrashin
Bruno BR14021
Le Chant du Monde LDA8111,
LDX–S8360
Colosseum CRLP137
Mezhdunarodnaya Kniga
D03064
Vanguard VRS6016, VRS6027

Trio No. 3, in f, Op. 65 pf, vln & vlc
with L. Oborin pf & S. Knushevitsky vlc
Mezhdunarodnaya Kniga
D03560/1
Monitor MCS2071
Westminster XWN18176

* This is the 10 inch 78 rpm disc that was recorded in Moscow for the New York World Fair, 1939, to highlight Oistrakh as being a Laureate of International and U.S.S.R. competitions.

545

DVOŘÁK – *Continued*

Trio No. 4, in e, Op. 90 "Dumky" pf, vln & vlc
  with L. Oborin pf & S. Knushevitsky
  vlc
  Bruno BR14009
  Colosseum CRLP253
  Eurodisc 78419ZK
  Mezhdunarodnaya Kniga
  D03562/3, D028561
  Westminster XWN18175

FALLA

(7) Canciones populares españolas (1914) v & pf
  No. 1. El paño moruna arr. vln & pf Kochański
    with V. Yampolsky pf   Mezhdunarodnaya Kniga D2164,
                            D028807/8

  No. 3. Asturiana arr. vln & pf Kochański
    with V. Yampolsky pf   Mezhdunarodnaya Kniga D2164,
                            D028807/8

  No. 4. Jota arr. vln & pf Kochański
    with V. Yampolsky pf   Mezhdunarodnaya Kniga
                            D00544
                            Victor LS2025

  No. 4. Jota arr. vln & pf Kochański
    with V. Yampolsky pf   Mezhdunarodnaya Kniga D2164,
                            D028807/8

  No. 4. Jota arr. vln & pf Kochański
    with V. Yampolsky pf   Angel 35354
                            Columbia CX1466, ESL6252,
                            ESLQ1007, SAX2253, SEBQ219,
                            SEL1577, WSX604
                            Electrola SHZEL60

  No. 5. Nana arr. vln & pf Kochański
    with V. Yampolsky pf   Mezhdunarodnaya Kniga D2164,
                            D028807/8

  No. 6. Canción arr. vln & pf Kochański
    with V. Yampolsky pf   Mezhdunarodnaya Kniga D2164,
                            D028807/8

(La) Vida Breve (1913) – opera
  Danza española orch. – arr. vln & pf Kreisler
    with V. Yampolsky pf   Monitor MC2003

FOSTER

(The) Old folks at home (1851) "Swanee River" v & pf – arr. vln & pf
  Kreisler
    with A. Makarov pf   Colosseum CRLP10050
                            Mezhdunarodnaya Kniga
                            D12458

FRANCK

Sonata in A (1886) vln & pf
  with L. Oborin pf
                            Le Chant du Monde LDA8112
                            Colosseum CRLP151
                            Mezhdunarodnaya Kniga
                            D20574/83, D349/50
                            Vanguard VRS6019

Sonata in A (1886) vln & pf
  with V. Yampolsky pf
                            Angel 35163
                            Columbia CX1201, FCX355,
                            QCX10160
                            HMV LALP497

FRANCK – *Continued*

Sonata in A (1886) vln & pf*
  with S. Richter pf
                            Le Chant du Monde MEL78444
                            Eurodisc 80080KK
                            HMV ASD2618
                            Melodiya–Angel SR40121
                            Mezhdunarodnaya Kniga
                            D025827/8, SM02257/8

GLAZOUNOV

Concerto in a, Op. 82 vln & orch.
  with USSR State Symphony Orch. –
  Kondrashin
                            Bruno BR14013
                            Le Chant du Monde LDA8041
                            Classics Club X1037
                            Colosseum CRLP137
                            Design DLP134
                            Eurodisc 78705ZK
                            Gala GLP372
                            Mezhdunarodnaya Kniga
                            D03040/7, D012939/40
                            Period SHO316, SPL598
                            Supraphon LPM7
                            Ultraphon H23871/3

Mazurka–Oberek in D orch. – arr. vln & orch. Glazounov
  with USSR State Symphony Orch. –
  Yudin
                            Bruno BR14012
                            Colosseum CRLP251
                            Mezhdunarodnaya Kniga
                            D026211/2, SM02445/6
                            Westminster XWN18177

Méditation, Op. 32 vln & pf
  with V. Yampolsky pf
                            Colosseum CRLPX011
                            Mezhdunarodnaya Kniga D1408
                            Vanguard VRS6020

GLIÈRE

(The) Bronze Horseman (1948/9) – ballet orch.
  excerpt† arr. vln & orch.
    with Bolshoi Theatre Orch. – Glière
                            Colosseum CRLP179
                            Mezhdunarodnaya Kniga
                            D16342
                            Supraphon B40116/7

Romance in c, Op. 45, No. 3 vln & orch.
  with USSR State Symphony Orch. –
  Kondrashin
                            Colosseum CRLP149
                            Mezhdunarodnaya Kniga
                            D026211/2
                            Vanguard VRS6016

GLINKA

Ruslan & Ludmila (1842) – opera
  Persian song arr. vln & pf Zimbalist
    with S. Topilin pf   Colosseum CRLP105,
                            CRLP10050
                            Mezhdunarodnaya Kniga
                            D10500

* Recorded at the Moscow Conservatory Large Hall, December 1968.
† Unidentified.

GLINKA – *Continued*

Trio in d (1926/7) "Trio pathétique" pf, vln & vlc
  with L. Oborin pf & S. Knushevitsky
  vlc   Colosseum CRLP10040
                             Concert Hall CHS1306
                             Monitor MCS2068

GODARD

Concerto No. 1, Op. 35 "Concerto Romantique" vln & orch.
  Canzonetta (2nd mvt)
  with S. Topilin pf   Colosseum CRLP105,
                             CRLP10050
                             Mezhdunarodnaya Kniga
                             D10497

  Canzonetta (2nd mvt)
  with USSR Symphony Orch. –
  Kondrashin   Mezhdunarodnaya Kniga
                             D026212

GRIEG

Sonata No. 1, in F, Op. 8 vln & pf
  with L. Oborin pf   Bruno BR14038
                             MGM GC30004
                             Mezhdunarodnaya Kniga
                             D012866

Sonata No. 2, in G, Op. 13 vln & pf
  with L. Oborin pf   Eurodisc 78437ZK
                             Mezhdunarodnaya Kniga
                             D04881

HANDEL

(9) Sonatas, Op. 2 (1724) 2 vlns & c
Sonata No. 7, in g
  with I. Oistrakh vln & V. Yampolsky   Decca DL9962
  pf   Deutsche Grammophon
                             EPL30287, LP16136
                             Eterna 820283
                             Heliodor 89561, 478132, H25009
                             Mezhdunarodnaya Kniga D5671

Sonata No. 7, in g
  with I. Oistrakh vln & A. Ginzburg pf   Hall of Fame HOF516
                             Mezhdunarodnaya Kniga
                             D015349

HAYDN

(3) Duos, H.III, Nos. 25/7 (1769) vln & vlc
No. 3. Duo No. 3, in B flat, H.III, No. 27 arr. 2 vlns
  with I. Oistrakh vln   Le Chant du Monde LDXA8280
                             Concert Hall SMSC201
                             Mezhdunarodnaya Kniga
                             D14141/2, S0579/80
                             Monitor MC2058

(31) Trios, H.XV, Nos. 1/31 pf, vln & vlc
Trio No. 21, in C: Presto (3rd mvt) H.XV, No. 21 (op. 75, No. 1)
  with L. Oborin pf & S. Knushevitsky   Mezhdunarodnaya Kniga
  vlc   D08005/6
Trio No. 21, in C, H.XV, No. 21 (Op. 75, No. 1)
  with L. Oborin pf & S. Knushevitsky   Colosseum CRLP248
  vlc   Mezhdunarodnaya Kniga
                             D03822/3
                             Monitor MCS2071
                             Westminster XWN18176

HAYDN – *Continued*

Trio No. 28, in E, H.XV, No. 28 (Op. 75, No. 2)
  with L. Oborin pf & S. Knushevitsky   Mezhdunarodnaya Kniga D1311
  vlc

HINDEMITH

Concerto in D (1940) vln & orch.
  with London Symphony Orch. –   Decca LXT6035, SXL6035
  Hindemith   London CM9337, CS6337
Concerto in D (1940) vln & orch.
  with USSR State Symphony Orch. –   Le Chant du Monde LDXA8333,
  Rozhdestvensky   LDXA48333
                             Mezhdunarodnaya Kniga
                             D010978

(6) Sonatas, Op. 11 var. cbns
Sonata No. 1, in E flat (1920) vln & pf
  with V. Yampolsky pf   Mezhdunarodnaya Kniga
                             D03822/3
                             Monitor MC2009

HONEGGER

Sonatina (1920) 2 vlns
  with I. Oistrakh vln   Le Chant du Monde LDXA8280
                             Concert Hall SMSC201
                             Mezhdunarodnaya Kniga
                             D14141/2, S0579/80
                             Monitor MC2058

HUBAY

(6) Blumenleben, Op. 30 vln & pf
No. 5. Der Zephir
  with S. Topilin pf   Colosseum CRLP105,
                             CRLP10050
                             Mezhdunarodnaya Kniga
                             D10499

JANÁČEK

Sonata (1913/21) vln & pf
  with F. Bauer pf   Le Chant du Monde LDX78489
                             Eurodisc 79289PK

KABALEVSKY

Concerto in C, Op. 48 vln & orch.
  with USSR State Symphony Orch. –   Bruno BR14001
  Kabalevsky   Le Chant du Monde LDYA8082
                             Colosseum CRLP123
                             Mezhdunarodnaya Kniga D489,
                             D014029, D17231/6
                             Monarch MWL330
                             Supraphon C23941/3
                             Vanguard VRS6002

Improvisation, Op. 21, No. 1 vln & pf
  with V. Yampolsky pf   Mezhdunarodnaya Kniga
                             D022226

KHACHATURIAN

Chanson poème in e (1929) vln & pf
  with V. Yampolsky pf   Le Chant du Monde LDA8075
                             Colosseum CRLP110, CRLP249
                             Eurodisc 40444CK
                             Supraphon C24112

KHACHATURIAN – *Continued*

Chanson poème in e (1929) vln & pf
  with L. Oborin pf — Vanguard VRS6020

Chanson poème in e (1929) vln & pf
  with A. Makarov pf — Mezhdunarodnaya Kniga D14246/7
  Supraphon B40040

Concerto in D (1940) (cadenza by D. Oistrakh) vln & orch.
  with USSR State Philharmonic Orch. – Gauk — KMR 014151/60 Colosseum CRLPX001
  Decca K1082/6
  Mercury 14000/4, (in set DM10), MG10000
  Mezhdunarodnaya Kniga D014151/60
  Supraphon B40058/62

Concerto in D (1940) (cadenza by D. Oistrakh) vln & orch.
  with USSR State Philharmonic Orch. – Khachaturian — Bruno BR14001
  Period SPL739

Concerto in D (1940) (cadenza by D. Oistrakh) vln & orch.
  with Philharmonia Orch. – Khachaturian — Angel 35244
  Columbia C90466, CX1303, FCX511, QCX10188, WCX1303
  HMV LALP427

Concerto in D (1940) (cadenza by D. Oistrakh) vln & orch.
  with Moscow Radio Symphony Orch. – Khachaturian — Eurodisc 74011KK
  HMV ASD2472
  Melodiya–Angel SR40002
  Mezhdunarodnaya Kniga D016483/4, S01115/6

Dance in B flat (1927) vln & pf
  with V. Yampolsky pf — Colosseum CRLP105, CRLP10050, CRLP249
  Eurodisc 40444CK

Dance in B flat (1927) vln & pf
  with A. Makarov pf — Mezhdunarodnaya Kniga D14248/9

Dance in B flat (1927) vln & pf
  with L. Oborin pf — Le Chant du Monde LDA8075
  Vanguard VRS6020

KHACHATURIAN, K.

Sonata in g, Op. 1 vln & pf
  with V. Yampolsky pf — Angel 35306
  Columbia CX1342, FCX514, QCX10202
  HMV LALP30012

KODÁLY

Kallo (1952) orch.
(3) Hungarian dances arr. vln & pf Feigin
  with V. Yampolsky pf — Colosseum CRLP249
  Mezhdunarodnaya Kniga D5029, D029743/4
  Parliament PLP118
  Supraphon LPM237, SUEC807

(3) Hungarian dances arr. vln & pf Feigin
  with N. Walter pf — Eterna 120021, 520026, 720048, LPM1023
  Saga EFID1005

KODÁLY – *Continued*

(3) Hungarian dances arr. vln & pf Feigin
  with V. Yampolsky pf — Angel 35354
  Columbia CX1466, SAX2253, WSX604
  Electrola SHZEL60

KREISLER

(La) Gitana vln & pf
  with V. Yampolsky pf — Le Chant du Monde LDA8175, LDXSP1801
  Decca DL9882

Rondino on a theme by Beethoven vln & pf
  with S. Topilin pf — Mezhdunarodnaya Kniga D7592

Variations on a theme of Corelli (Tartini) vln & pf
  with A. Makarov pf — 044732 Colosseum CRLP110
  Mercury 16025, (in set DM27), MG10035
  Supraphon G22207
  Ultraphon G14742

Variations on a theme of Corelli (Tartini) vln & pf
  with V. Yampolsky pf — Victor LS2025

LALO

Symphonie espagnole, Op. 21 vln & orch.*
  with USSR State Philharmonic Orch. – Kondrashin — Bruno BR14003
  Colosseum CRLP179
  Delta TQD3002
  Design DLP151
  Hall of Fame HOF502
  Mezhdunarodnaya Kniga D015565/72
  Musidisc RC818
  Period SHO312, (in set TE1163)
  Supraphon H24094/7

Symphonie espagnole, Op. 21 vln & orch.*
  with Philharmonia Orch. – Martinon — Angel 35205
  Columbia CX1246, FCX427, QCX10151
  HMV XLP30109

LECLAIR

(12) Sonatas, Op. 9 – Book IV (1738) vln & c
Sonata No. 3, in D
  with V. Yampolsky pf — Le Chant du Monde LDA8075, LDXSP1801
  Concert Hall M2226
  Eurodisc 70600EK
  Guilde International du Disque M2226
  Mezhdunarodnaya Kniga D5605, D028113/4

Sonata No. 3, in D
  with N. Walter pf — Eterna 120022/3, 520001, 720048, LPM1023

Sonata No. 3, in D
  with V. Yampolsky pf — HMV ALP1411
  Victor A630358, LM1987, LS2026, RCX1041, VICS1058

* Including Intermezzo.

LEVITIN

Sonata in c, Op. 43 vln & pf
with J. Levitin pf

Mezhdunarodnaya Kniga
D05622

LOCATELLI

(12) Sonatas, Op. 6 (1737) vln & c
Sonata No. 7, in f "Au Tombeau" arr. vln & pf Ysaÿe
with V. Yampolsky pf

Colosseum CRLP248

Sonata No. 7, in f "Au Tombeau" arr. vln & pf Ysaÿe
with V. Yampolsky pf

HMV ALP1411
Victor A630358, LM1987,
LS2025, RCX1017, VICS1058

MEDTNER

(3) Nocturnes, Op. 16 vln & pf
No. 1. Nocturne No. 1, in f sharp
with V. Yampolsky pf '

Monitor MC2003

Sonata No. 3, in e, Op. 57 (1936) "Sonata epica" vln & pf
with A. Goldenweiser pf

Eurodisc 79839ZK
Mezhdunarodnaya Kniga
D05596/7

MENDELSSOHN

Concerto in e, Op. 64 vln & orch.
with USSR State Symphony Orch. –
Kondrashin

Bruno BR14011
Colosseum CRLP225
Delta TQD3002
Design DLP134
Eurodisc 78439ZK, (in set
80569XK)
Gala GLP372
Hall of Fame HOF503
Mezhdunarodnaya Kniga
D017327/33, D1167/8,
D012939/40
Musidisc RC812
Period SHO312, (in set TE1163)
Supermajestic BBH1060
Tap T301
Vox (in set VSPS3)

Concerto in e, Op. 64 vln & orch.
with USSR State Symphony Orch. –
Gauk

Fidelio ATL4007
Vox GBY10160

Concerto in e, Op. 64 vln & orch.
with Philadelphia Orch. – Ormandy

Columbia ML5085
HMV CVD1514
Philips A01249L, ABL3145,
G05602R, GBR6507

(6) Gesänge, Op. 34 v & pf
No. 2. Auf Flügeln des Gesanges arr. vln & pf Achron
with V. Yampolsky pf

Columbia ML5096
Mezhdunarodnaya Kniga
D017548
Monitor MC2042

Quartet No. 1, in E flat, Op. 12 2 vlns, vla & vlc
Canzonetta (2nd mvt)
with P. Bondarenko vln, M. Terian vla
& S. Knushevitsky vlc

Mezhdunarodnaya Kniga
D018328/9

MENDELSSOHN – *Continued*

Trio No. 1, in d, Op. 49 pf, vln & vlc
Molto allegro ed agitato (1st mvt)
with L. Oborin pf & S. Knushevitsky
vlc

Mezhdunarodnaya Kniga
D18776/8

Trio No. 1, in d, Op. 49 pf, vln & vlc
with L. Oborin pf & S. Knushevitsky
vlc

Mezhdunarodnaya Kniga S02087

Trio No. 2, in c, Op. 66 pf, vln & vlc
with L. Oborin pf & S. Knushevitsky
vlc

Bruno BR14053
Colosseum CRLP247
Mezhdunarodnaya Kniga
D01750/1

Trio No. 2, in c, Op. 66 pf, vln & vlc
with L. Oborin pf & S. Knushevitsky
vlc

Mezhdunarodnaya Kniga S02088

MEYER

Concerto (1963/4) vln & orch.
with Staatskapelle Orch., Berlin –
Suitner

Eterna 820363

MIASKOVSKY

Concerto in d, Op. 44 (1938) vln & orch.
with USSR State Symphony Orch. –
Gauk

Colosseum CRLP149
Decca X272/6
Mezhdunarodnaya Kniga
D09660/3
Music Hall LP9014
Period SPL539
Ultraphon H23885/9

MOZART

Concerto No. 1, in B flat, K207 vln & orch.
with L'Orch. des Concerts Lamoureux,
Paris – Haitink

Mezhdunarodnaya Kniga
D013725, S0865
Philips 835190AY, A02315L,
AL3455, PHM500050,
PHS900050, SAL3455

Concerto No. 3, in G, K216 (cadenzas by D. Oistrakh) vln & orch.
with Czech Philharmonic Orch. –
Ančerl

Eterna 820565
Supraphon LPV244, SUA10127

Concerto No. 3, in G, K216 (cadenzas by D. Oistrakh) vln & orch.
with USSR State Philharmonic Orch. –
Kondrashin

Bruno BR14023

Concerto No. 3, in G, K216 (cadenzas by D. Oistrakh) vln & orch.
with Philharmonia Orch. – Oistrakh

Angel 35714
Columbia CX1660, FC25125,
QCX10355, SAX2304,
SAXQ7315
Electrola 1C047–50510,
SHZEL52
HMV SXLP30086, XLP30086
Kristall SMVP8028
Regal SREG1090

Concerto No. 3, in G, K216 (cadenzas by D. Oistrakh) vln & orch.
with Moscow Chamber Orch. –
Barshai

Artia ALP156
Eurodisc 76605ZK, (in set
80569XK)
Mezhdunarodnaya Kniga
D06129, S6655/6

MOZART – *Continued*

Concerto No. 4, in D, K218 vln & orch.
with USSR State Symphony Orch. –
Kondrashin

Bruno BR14023
Colosseum CRLP246
Mezhdunarodnaya Kniga
D1562/3

Concerto No. 4, in D, K218 vln & orch.
with Philadelphia Orch. – Ormandy

Columbia ML5085
Philips A01249L, ABL3145,
G05601R, GBR6506, S06633R

Concerto No. 5, in A, K219 "Turkish" vln & orch.
with Bolshoi Theatre Orch. –
Golovanov

Colosseum CRLP154
Period SHO327, SPL590

Concerto No. 5, in A, K219 "Turkish" vln & orch.
with Moscow Philharmonic Orch. –
Gauk

Musidisc RC822

Concerto No. 5, in A, K219 "Turkish" vln & orch.
with Saxon State Orch. – Konwitschny

Decca DL9766, (in set DX141)
Deutsche Grammophon
LP16101, LPE17159
Eterna 720030, 820004,
LPM1016
Heliodor 89593, 478132, H25017,
HS25017

Concerto No. 7, in D, K271a (cadenzas by Enescu) vln & orch.
with USSR State Philharmonic Orch. –
Kondrashin

Classic Editions CE2, CE3002
Colosseum CRLP154
Mezhdunarodnaya Kniga
D1562/3

Duo No. 1, in G, K423 vln & vla
playing vla, with I. Oistrakh vln

Decca LXT6088, SXL6088
London CM9377, CS6377

Quartet No. 11, in E flat, K171 2 vlns, vla & vlc – arr. fl, vln, vla & vlc
"in C"
with G. Madatov fl, M. Terian vla &
S. Knushevitsky vlc

Mezhdunarodnaya Kniga
D012849

Sinfonia concertante in E flat, K364 vln, vla & orch.
with R. Barshai vla & Moscow
Chamber Orch. – Barshai

Artia ALP165
Le Chant du Monde LDX–S8319
Eurodisc 77293ZK
Mezhdunarodnaya Kniga
D05236/7
Musidisc RC859
Period SHO343, SHOST2343
Recital Hall (in set RH301)
Vedette VSC4020

Sinfonia Concertante in E flat, K364 vln, vla & orch.
playing vla, with I. Oistrakh vln &
Moscow Philharmonic Orch. –
Kondrashin

Decca LXT6088, SXL6088
London CM9377, CS6377

Sonata No. 27, in G, K379 vln & pf
with L. Oborin pf

Colosseum CRLP194
Monarch MWL334

Sonata No. 27, in G, K379 vln & pf
with L. Oborin pf

Mezhdunarodnaya Kniga
D012850

MOZART – *Continued*

Sonata No. 32, in B flat, K454 vln & pf
with I. Yampolsky pf

Colosseum CRLP194
Mezhdunarodnaya Kniga
D06336
Monarch MWL334
Monitor MC2005

Sonata No. 32, in B flat, K454 vln & pf
with V. Yampolsky pf

Angel 35356
Columbia CX1415, QCX10306
HMV LALP475

Sonata No. 32, in B flat, K454 vln & pf
with V. Yampolsky pf

Mezhdunarodnaya Kniga
D012865

PAGANINI

(24) Caprices, Op. 1 (1801/7) solo vln
Caprice No. 13, in B flat, arr. vln & pf Kreisler
with V. Yampolsky pf

Colosseum CRLP179
Mezhdunarodnaya Kniga
D16339
Period SPL710

Caprice No. 17, in E flat
(unaccompanied)

Colosseum CRLP179
Mezhdunarodnaya Kniga
D16258
Period SPL710

Sonata a preghièra "Moses fantasia" (on the aria "Dal tuo stellato soglio"
from Rossini's opera "Mosè in Egitto") Op. 24 (1818 or 1819) vln &
orch.
with V. Yampolsky pf

Le Chant du Monde LDA8175,
LDXSP1801
Classics Club SMP101
Concert Hall M2226
Decca DL9882
Guilde International du Disque
M2226
Mezhdunarodnaya Kniga
D04045
Musidisc RC858

PROKOFIEV

Cinderella, Op. 87 (1941/4) – ballet orch.
Gavotte arr. vln & pf Fichtenholz
with V. Yampolsky pf

Colosseum CRLPX011
Mezhdunarodnaya Kniga
D02795, D22517
Monarch MEL707
Vanguard VRS6020

Gavotte arr. vln & pf Fichtenholz
with N. Walter pf

Ariola AR16395D
Eterna 120025

Mazurka arr. vln & pf Fichtenholz
with V. Yampolsky pf

Colosseum CRLPX011,
CRLP110
Mezhdunarodnaya Kniga
D02795, D22518
Monarch MEL707
Supraphon 11500, G23287
Vanguard VRS6020

PROKOFIEV – *Continued*

Mazurka arr. vln & pf Fichtenholz
with N. Walter pf
Ariola AR16395D
Eterna 120025
Eurodisc 40442CK
Saga EFID1003

Passepied arr. vln & pf Fichtenholz
with V. Yampolsky pf
Colosseum CRLPX011
Mezhdunarodnaya Kniga
D02795
Monarch MEL707
Vanguard VRS6020

Waltz arr. vln & pf Fichtenholz
with V. Yampolsky pf
Colosseum CRLPX011,
CRLP110
Mezhdunarodnaya Kniga
D02795
Monarch MEL707
Supraphon G23287
Vanguard VRS6020

Winter fairytale arr. vln & pf Fichtenholz
with V. Yampolsky pf
Colosseum CRLPX011,
CRLP110
Mezhdunarodnaya Kniga
D02795
Monarch MEL707
Supraphon G23287
Vanguard VRS6020

Winter fairytale arr. vln & pf Fichtenholz
with N. Walter pf
Ariola AR16395D
Eterna 120025
Eurodisc 40442CK
Saga EFID1003

Concerto No. 1, in D, Op. 19 vln & orch.
with USSR State Symphony Orch. –
Kondrashin
Bruno BR14002
Le Chant du Monde LDXA8333,
LDXA48333
Classics Club X1027
Colosseum CRLP123
Contrepoint MC20078
Eurodisc 78439ZK
Mezhdunarodnaya Kniga
D015181/5, D026326/31,
D03040
Monitor MCS2073
Period SHO338, SHOST2338,
SPL539, SPL739
Supraphon B40015/7, H23947/9
Westminster XWN18178

Concerto No. 1, in D, Op. 19 vln & orch.
with London Symphony Orch. – von
Matacic
Angel 35243
Columbia C70430, C91395,
CX1268, FCX419, QCX10240,
WC531
HMV LALP255

Concerto No. 1, in D, Op. 19 vln & orch.
with Moscow Radio Symphony Orch.
– Rozhdestvensky
HMV ASD2472

Concerto No. 2, in g, Op. 63 vln & orch.
with USSR State Symphony Orch. –
Kondrashin
Mezhdunarodnaya Kniga
D03041

PROKOFIEV – *Continued*

Concerto No. 2, in g, Op. 63 vln & orch.
with Philharmonia Orch. – Galliera
Angel 35714
Columbia CX1660, QCX10355,
SAX2304, SAXQ7315

(The) Love for Three Oranges, Op. 33 (1919) – opera
No. 3. March arr. vln & pf Heifetz
with V. Yampolsky pf
Monitor MC2003
Parliament PLP118
Supraphon LPM237, SUEC807

(5) Melodies, Op. 35bis (1921) vln & pf
No. 2.
with A. Makarov pf
Mezhdunarodnaya Kniga
D14633/4

No. 3.
with A. Makarov pf   044729
Le Chant du Monde GA5002
Colosseum CRLP110
Mercury 16026, (in set DM27),
EP1–5008, MG10035
Mezhdunarodnaya Kniga
D14633/4
Supraphon 11051, G22206
Telefunken E22206
Ultraphon G14741

(5) Melodies, Op. 35bis (1921) vln & pf
with F. Bauer pf
Le Chant du Monde LDX–
S78362
Philips 802727AY, AL3589,
PHM500112, PHS900112,
SAL3589

Sonata in C, Op. 56 2 vlns
with I. Oistrakh vln
Mezhdunarodnaya Kniga D5670

Sonata in C, Op. 56 2 vlns
with I. Oistrakh vln
Mezhdunarodnaya Kniga
D015350

Sonata in C, Op. 56 2 vlns
with I. Oistrakh vln
Le Chant du Monde LDXA8280
Concert Hall SMSC201
Mezhdunarodnaya Kniga
D14141/2, S0579/80
Monitor MCS2058

Sonata No. 1, in f, Op. 80 vln & pf
with V. Yampolsky pf
Bruno BR14006

Sonata No. 1, in f, Op. 80 vln & pf
with L. Oborin pf
Le Chant du Monde LDA8078
Mezhdunarodnaya Kniga
D5552/3
Vanguard VRS6019

Sonata No. 1, in f, Op. 80 vln & pf
with V. Yampolsky pf
HMV ALP1411
Victor A630358, LM1987,
RB16166

Sonata No. 1, in f, Op. 80 vln & pf
with F. Bauer pf
Le Chant du Monde LDX78489
Eurodisc 79289PK

Sonata No. 2, in D, Op. 94bis vln & pf
with V. Yampolsky pf
Bruno BR14006
Colosseum CRLP252

PROKOFIEV – *Continued*

Sonata No. 2, in D, Op. 94bis vln & pf
  with L. Oborin pf

Mezhdunarodnaya Kniga
D014963/70

Sonata No. 2, in D, Op. 94bis vln & pf
  with V. Yampolsky pf

Angel 35306
Columbia CX1342, FCX514,
QCX10202
HMV LALP30012
Victor LS2026

RACHMANINOV .

(2) Pieces, Op. 6 vln & pf
  No. 1. Romance in d
  with V. Yampolsky pf

Mezhdunarodnaya Kniga D1409,
D17367/8

(14) Songs, Op. 34 (1912) v & pf
  No. 14. Vocalise arr. vln & pf Press
  with I. Kollegorskaya pf

Colosseum CRLPX011
Mercury EP1-5008
Vanguard VRS6020

(6) Songs, Op. 38 (1916) v & pf
  No. 3. Daisies arr. vln & pf Kreisler
  with V. Yampolsky pf

Mezhdunarodnaya Kniga D1409,
D17371

Trio No. 2, in d, Op. 9 "Trio élégiaque" pf, vln & vlc
  with L. Oborin pf & S. Knushevitsky
  vlc

Bruno BR14077
Mezhdunarodnaya Kniga
D04436/7

RAKOV

Concerto in e (1948) vln & orch.
  with USSR State Symphony Orch. –
  Kondrashin

Griffon 1004
Mezhdunarodnaya Kniga
D015368/74

Concerto in e (1948) vln & orch.
  with USSR State Radio Symphony
  Orch. – Rakov

Colosseum CRLP2
Gallery LP12001
Mezhdunarodnaya Kniga
D2685/6
Period SLP709

Poem in e vln & pf
  with N. Rakov pf

Mezhdunarodnaya Kniga
D05623, D16477/8

Sonata in e (1951) vln & pf
  with N. Rakov pf

Mezhdunarodnaya Kniga
D02794

RAVEL

Sonata (1927) vln & pf
  with F. Bauer pf

Le Chant du Monde LDX–
S78362
Philips 802727AY, AL3589,
PHM500112, PHS900112,
SAL3589

RAVEL – *Continued*

Trio in a (1915) pf, vln & vlc
  with L. Oborin pf & S. Knushevitsky
  vlc

Le Chant du Monde LDM8146
Colosseum CRLP252
Mezhdunarodnaya Kniga
D2165/6
Monarch MWL367
Westminster XWN18174

Tzigane (Rapsodie de concert) (1924) vln & pf or orch.
  with USSR State Symphony Orch. –
  Kondrashin

Bruno BR14009
Le Chant du Monde LDM8173,
LDX–S8359
Eurodisc 78705ZK, (in set
80569XK)
Mezhdunarodnaya Kniga
D03041
Monitor MCS2073
Westminster XWN18177

RIMSKY–KORSAKOV

Scheherazade, Op. 35 (1888) orch.
  with USSR State Radio Symphony
  Orch. – Golovanov

Colosseum CRLP135
Mezhdunarodnaya Kniga
D014691/702
Supraphon B40099/104,
H23935/40

Trio in c (1897) pf, vln & vlc
  with L. Oborin pf & S. Knushevitsky
  vlc

Concert Hall CHS1306
Mezhdunarodnaya Kniga
D04524/5, D05542/3
Monarch MWL317

SAINT–SAËNS

(6) Études, Op. 52 pf
  No. 6. Étude No. 6, in D flat "Étude en forme de valse" arr. vln & pf
  Ysaÿe
  with V. Yampolsky pf

Bruno BR14018
Colosseum CRLP249
Fondation Eugèn Ysaÿe
FEY3001
Mezhdunarodnaya Kniga
D021961/2, D04045, D1202,
D2163
Monitor MC2003

Introduction & Rondo Capriccioso, Op. 28 vln & orch.
  with USSR State Symphony Orch. –
  Kondrashin

Bruno BR14018, SBR32002
Colosseum CRLP249
Mezhdunarodnaya Kniga
D016274/5
Supraphon H24271

Introduction & Rondo Capriccioso, Op. 28 vln & orch.
  with Boston Symphony Orch. –
  Munch

HMV ALP1460
Victor A630356, LM1988,
RB16166, VICS1058

SARASATE

Carmen Fantasia (on themes from the opera by Bizet) Op. 25 vln & pf or
orch.
  with A. Makarov pf

Colosseum CRLP105,
CRLP10050
Compass (in set C204)

SARASATE – *Continued*

(8) Danzas españolas vln & pf
 No. 1. Malagueña, Op. 21, No. 1
  with V. Yampolsky pf
   Mezhdunarodnaya Kniga
   D021759, D1188

 No. 2. Habañera, Op. 21, No. 2
  with V. Yampolsky pf
   Mezhdunarodnaya Kniga
   D021758, D1188

 No. 6. Zapateado, Op. 23, No. 2
  with V. Yampolsky pf
   Colosseum CRLP105,
   CRLP10050
   Mezhdunarodnaya Kniga
   D12457

Navarra, Op. 33 2 vlns & pf or orch.
 with I. Oistrakh vln & V. Yampolsky
 pf
   Bruno BR14015
   Hall of Fame HOF516
   Mezhdunarodnaya Kniga
   D17637/8, D6369/70,
   D029743/4
   Monitor MC2009

Navarra, Op. 33 2 vlns & pf or orch.
 with I. Oistrakh vln & Leipzig
 Gewandhaus Orch. – Konwitschny
   Decca DL9962
   Deutsche Grammophon
   EPL30286
   Eterna 520119, 720048
   Heliodor 89688, 478437

Zortzico, Op. 39 vln & pf
 with V. Yampolsky pf
   Le Chant du Monde LDM8185,
   LDXSP1801
   Colosseum CRLP249
   Decca DL9882
   Mezhdunarodnaya Kniga
   D19538, D1201, D028807/8

SCHUBERT

Fantasia in C, Op. 159 (D934) vln & pf
 with F. Bauer pf
   Le Chant du Monde LDX78479
Octet in F, Op. 166 (D803) cl, hrn, bsn, 2 vlns, vla, vlc & cbs
 Scherzo (3rd mvt)
 with V. Sorokin cl, J. Shapiro hrn, I.
 Stydel bsn, P. Bondarenko vln, M.
 Terian vla, S. Knushevitsky vlc & J.
 Gertovich cbs
   Mezhdunarodnaya Kniga
   D04926/7, D18661/2
Octet in F, Op. 166 (D803) cl, hrn, bsn, 2 vlns, vla, vlc & cbs
 with V. Sorokin cl, J. Shapiro hrn, I.
 Stydel bsn, P. Bondarenko vln, M.
 Terian vla, S. Knushevitsky vlc & J.
 Gertovich cbs
   Angel 35362, AB7007
   Columbia CX1423
   HMV LALP349
Sonata in A, Op. 162 (D574) "Duo" vln & pf
 with L. Oborin pf
   Le Chant du Monde LDZA8109
   Colosseum CRLP151
   Dover HCR5245
   Eurodisc 78437ZK
   Hall of Fame HOF503
   Mezhdunarodnaya Kniga
   D04880
   Monarch MWL311
   Period SPL573
   Saga STXID5253, XID5253
Sonata in A, Op. 162 (D574) "Duo" vln & pf
 with F. Bauer pf
   Le Chant du Monde LDX78479

SCHUBERT – *Continued*

Trio No. 1, in B flat, Op. 99 (D898) pf, vln & vlc
 with L. Oborin pf & S. Knushevitsky
 vlc
   Angel 35713
   Columbia C80543, CX1627,
   SAX2281, SCXW7519,
   STC80543, WSX553
   World Record Club CM88,
   SCM88
Trio No. 2, in E flat, Op. 100 (D929) pf, vln & vlc
 with L. Oborin pf & S. Knushevitsky
 vlc
   Mezhdunarodnaya Kniga
   D05018/9

SCRIABIN

(12) Etudes, Op. 8 pf
 No. 10. Etude No. 10, in D flat "Etude in thirds" arr. vln & pf Szigeti
   RR 5525/1 r 058 Decca M545
  with A. Giakov pf
   Disc 4008
(2) Nocturnes, Op. 5 pf
 No. 1. Nocturne No. 1, in f sharp arr. vln & pf Moguilevsky
   RR 5526/3 r 058 Decca M545
  with A. Giakov pf
   Disc 4008
 No. 1. Nocturne No. 1, in f sharp arr. vln & pf Moguilevsky
  with V. Yampolsky pf
   Mezhdunarodnaya Kniga D5028,
   D028807/8
   Monitor MC2003
 No. 1. Nocturne No. 1, in f sharp arr. vln & pf Moguilevsky
  with A. Makarov pf   044728 Colosseum CRLP110
   Mercury 16026, (in set DM27),
   EP1–5008, MG10035
   Supraphon G22206
   Telefunken E22206
   Ultraphon G14741

SHOSTAKOVICH

Concerto No. 1, in a, Op. 99 (1955) vln & orch.
 with Leningrad Philharmonic Orch. –
 Mravinsky
   Bruno BR14017
   Le Chant du Monde LDX–S8342
   Eurodisc 79829ZK
   Mezhdunarodnaya Kniga
   D5540/1, D03658/9
   Monitor MC2014
   Parlophone PMB1014
   Period SHO342, SHOST2342
   Telefunken TW30213
Concerto No. 1, in a, Op. 99 (1955) vln & orch.
 with New York Philharmonic
 Symphony Orch. – Mitropoulos
   Columbia ML5077
   Philips A01238L, ABL3101
Concerto No. 2, in c sharp, Op. 129 (1967) vln & orch.
 with Moscow Philharmonic Symphony
 Orch. – Kondrashin
   Eurodisc 78045KK
   HMV ASD2447
   Melodiya–Angel SR40064
   Mezhdunarodnaya Kniga
   D021405, C01627
Sonata, Op. 134 vln & pf*
 with S. Richter pf
   HMV ASD2718
   Mezhdunarodnaya Kniga
   D027313/4, SM02355/6

* Recording of the première performance at the Moscow Conservatory
 Large Hall, May 1969.

SHOSTAKOVICH – *Continued*

Trio No. 2, in e, Op. 67 "In memory of I. I. Sollertinsky" pf, vln & vlc
with D. Shostakovich pf & M. Sadlo vlc

Colosseum CRLPX011
Eurochord TAI721/3
Mercury MG10045
Supraphon G22667/9
Ultraphon G14927/9

SIBELIUS

Concerto in d, Op. 47 vln & orch.
with USSR State Philharmonic Orch. – Kondrashin

Bruno BR14021
Colosseum CRLP172

Concerto in d, Op. 47 vln & orch.
with Stockholm Festival Orch. – Ehrling

Angel 35315
Columbia C1036, C91395, C70094, FC1035, HC102, QC5025, WC1036
HMV LBLP1031

Concerto in d, Op. 47 vln & orch.
with Philadelphia Orch. – Ormandy

CBS S61041
Columbia ML5492, MS6157, OS412
Philips 835570AY, A01484L, ABL3366, SABL195

Concerto in d, Op. 47 vln & orch.
with Moscow Radio Symphony Orch. – Rozhdestvensky

Eurodisc 74111KK
Melodiya–Angel SR40020
Mezhdunarodnaya Kniga D016279/80, S01077/8

(2) Humoresques, Op. 87b vln & orch.
No. 1. Humoresque No. 1, in d
with Moscow Radio Symphony Orch. – Rozhdestvensky

Eurodisc 74111KK
Melodiya–Angel SR40020
Mezhdunarodnaya Kniga D016280, S01078

No. 2. Humoresque No. 2, in D
with Moscow Radio Symphony Orch. – Rozhdestvensky

Eurodisc 74111KK
Melodiya–Angel SR40020
Mezhdunarodnaya Kniga D016280, S01078

SMETANA

Trio in g, Op. 15 pf, vln & vlc
with L. Oborin pf & S. Knushevitsky vlc

Mezhdunarodnaya Kniga D028545/6
Westminster XWN18175

SPOHR

(3) Duets, Op. 67 2 vlns
No. 3. Duet No. 3, in g
with I. Oistrakh vln

Le Chant du Monde LDXA8280
Concert Hall SMSC201
Mezhdunarodnaya Kniga D14141/2, S0579/80
Monitor MC2058

STRAVINSKY

Concerto in D (1931) vln & orch.
with L'Orchestre des Concerts Lamoureux – Haitink

Mezhdunarodnaya Kniga D013726, S0866
Philips 6585 003, 835190AY, A02315L, AL3455, PHM500050, PHS900050, SAL3455

SUK

(7) Pieces, Op. 7 pf
No. 1. Love song arr. vln & pf Kocián
with V. Yampolsky pf

Colosseum CRLP105
Mezhdunarodnaya Kniga D5029, D10497, D028562, D029743/4
Monitor MC2003
Parliament PLP118
Supraphon C24409, LPM237

No. 1. Love song arr. vln & pf Kocián
with V. Yampolsky pf

Angel 35354
Columbia CX1466, SAX2253, SEB3515, WSX604
Electrola SHZEL60

No. 1. Love song arr. vln & pf Kocián
with N. Walter pf

Ariola AR16395D
Eurodisc 40442CK

(4) Pieces, Op. 17 vln & pf
No. 1. Quasi ballata
with I. Kollegorskaya pf

Mezhdunarodnaya Kniga D028562

No. 3. Un poco triste
with A. Makarov pf

Mezhdunarodnaya Kniga D028562

No. 4. Burleska
with A. Makarov pf

Mezhdunarodnaya Kniga D028562

SZYMANOWSKI

Concerto No. 1, in a, Op. 35 (1922) vln & orch.
with Leningrad State Philharmonic Orch. – Sanderling

Artia ALP156
Bruno BR14043
Eurodisc 79843ZK
Mezhdunarodnaya Kniga D05180/1

(3) Mythes, Op. 30 (1915) vln & pf
No. 1. La Fontaine d'Aréthuse
with V. Yampolsky pf

Bruno BR14043
Le Chant du Monde LDA8175
Concert Hall M2226
Guilde International du Disque M2226
Mezhdunarodnaya Kniga D2163, D029743/4
Monarch MEL707
Monitor MC2003
Parliament PLP118
Supraphon LPM237

Sonata No. 1, in d, Op. 9 vln & pf
with V. Yampolsky pf

Bruno BR14043
Colosseum CRLP190
MGM GC30004
Mezhdunarodnaya Kniga D05180/1

SZYMANOWSKI – *Continued*

Sonata No. 1, in d, Op. 9 vln & pf
  with V. Yampolsky pf

Angel 35163
Columbia CX1201, FCX355,
QCX10160
HMV LALP497

TAKTAKISHVILI

Concertino vln & orch.
  with USSR State Symphony Orch. –
  Taktakishvili

Mezhdunarodnaya Kniga
D04944/5

TANEIEV

Concert Suite, Op. 28 vln & orch.
  with USSR State Philharmonic Orch. –
  Kondrashin

Bruno BR14013

Concert Suite, Op. 28 vln & orch.
  with Philharmonia Orch. – Malko

Angel 35355
Columbia CX1390

Romance vln & pf
  with V. Yampolsky pf

Mezhdunarodnaya Kniga
D17372

Trio in D, Op. 21 2 vlns & vla
  with P. Bondarenko vln & M. Terian
  vla

Mezhdunarodnaya Kniga
D028625/6

Trio in D, Op. 22 pf, vln & vlc
  with L. Oborin pf & S. Knushevitsky
  vlc

Mezhdunarodnaya Kniga
D01458/9, D028545/6
Monitor MCS2068
Westminster XWN18679

TARTINI

(12) Sonatas, Op. 3 2 vlns & c
  Sonata No. 4, in F
  with I. Oistrakh vln & V. Yampolsky
  pf

Bruno BR14019
Mezhdunarodnaya Kniga D5671

  Sonata No. 4, in F
  with I. Oistrakh vln & H. Pischner
  hpsi

Decca DL9950
Deutsche Grammophon
LPM18393
Eterna 820283
Heliodor 89561, H25009

  Sonata No. 4, in F
  with I. Oistrakh vln & A. Ginzburg pf

Hall of Fame HOF516
Mezhdunarodnaya Kniga
D015350

Sonata in g "Il Trillo del Diavolo" vln & c – arr. vln & pf Kreisler
  with V. Yampolsky pf

Bruno BR14019
Le Chant du Monde LDYM8068
Colosseum CRLP148
Dover HCR5245
Mezhdunarodnaya Kniga
D017901/4, D508/9, D5604,
D028113/4
Musidisc RC858
Period SLP573

Sonata in g "Il Trillo del Diavolo" vln & c – arr. vln & pf Kreisler
  with V. Yampolsky pf

Angel 35356
Columbia CX1415, QCX10306
HMV LALP475

TCHAIKOVSKY

Concerto in D, Op. 35 vln & orch.
  with USSR State Philharmonic Orch. –
  Gauk

Bruno BR14016
Colosseum CRLP10010
Fidelio ATL4067
Golden Music Society LP3505
Hall of Fame HOF501
Mezhdunarodnaya Kniga
D06451/6
Musidisc RC812
Period SHO307, (in set TE1163),
SPL710
Supermajestic BBH1060
Supraphon B40105/9,
H24077/81
Vox (in set VSPS3), GBY16160

Concerto in D, Op. 35 vln & orch.
  with USSR State Symphony Orch. –
  Kondrashin

Le Chant du Monde LDS8167
Eurodisc 70185XK
Mezhdunarodnaya Kniga
D03820/1
Tap T301
Telefunken TW30170
Trophy LP9001

Concerto in D, Op. 35 vln & orch.
  with Saxon State Orch. – Konwitschny

Decca DL9755, (in set DX141)
Deutsche Grammophon
LPE17163, LPM18196
Eterna 820002, LPM1014
Heliodor 89688, 478437, H25071,
HS25071

Concerto in D, Op. 35 vln & orch.
  with Philadelphia Orch. – Ormandy

Columbia ML5698, MS6298,
OS412
CBS BRG72064, SBRG72064
HMV CVD1514
Odyssey Y30312
Philips 610305VR, 836402VZ
Supraphon 1 10 0217,
SUA10934, SUAST50934

Concerto in D, Op. 35 vln & orch.*
  with Moscow Philharmonic Symphony
  Orch. – Kondrashin

Le Chant du Monde
LDX78419/20
Eurodisc 73614KK, 77297ZK
Mezhdunarodnaya Kniga
D14619/20

Concerto in D, Op. 35 vln & orch.†
  with Moscow Philharmonic Symphony
  Orch. – Rozhdestvensky

Mezhdunarodnaya Kniga
D024141/2, S01779/80

Quartet No. 1, in D, Op. 11 2 vlns, vla & vlc
  Andante cantabile (2nd mvt)
  with P. Bondarenko vln, M. Terian vla
  & S. Knushevitsky vlc

Mezhdunarodnaya Kniga
D018266/7, D1054

* Recorded from a live concert.

† Recorded at a performance at the Moscow Conservatory Large Hall,
September 27th 1968.

TCHAIKOVSKY – *Continued*

Quartet No. 1, in D, Op. 11 2 vlns, vla & vlc
with P. Bondarenko vln, M. Terian vla & S. Knushevitsky vlc — Colosseum CRLP10190
Mezhdunarodnaya Kniga D019979/96, D295/8, D4180/1, D022793/4

Sérénade mélancolique in b flat, Op. 26 vln & orch.
with USSR State Symphony Orch. – Kondrashin — Colosseum CRLP110, CRLP10010
Compass 12982/5, (in set C202)
Mezhdunarodnaya Kniga D12982/5
Supraphon B40002/3

Souvenir d'un lieu cher, Op. 42 vln & pf
No. 1. Méditation
with V. Yampolsky pf — Classics Club SMP101
Colosseum CRLP110, CRLP10010
Mezhdunarodnaya Kniga D016044/5, D393, D6369/70, D022794
Musidisc RC858
Syrena 8599
Vanguard VRS6020
Victor LS2025

No. 1. Méditation
with N. Walter pf — Eterna 520026, LPM1023
Saga EFID1005

No. 3. Mélodie
with V. Yampolsky pf — Mezhdunarodnaya Kniga D5876

Trio in a, Op. 50 "To the memory of a great artist" pf, vln & vlc
with L. Oborin pf & S. Knushevitsky vlc — Mezhdunarodnaya Kniga D015696/707
Supraphon H24125/30

Waltz–Scherzo, Op. 34 vln & orch. – arr. vln & pf Bezékirsky
with V. Yampolsky pf — Le Chant du Monde LDA8075
Colosseum CRLP149
Concert Hall M2226
Eurodisc 40446CK
Guilde International du Disque M2226
Mezhdunarodnaya Kniga D6369/70, D9881/2, D16046/7
Musidisc RC858
Vanguard VRS6020

Waltz–Scherzo, Op. 34 vln & orch. – arr. vln & pf Bezékirsky
with V. Yampolsky pf — Angel 35354
Columbia CX1466, ESL6252, ESLQ1007, SAX2253, SEBQ219, SEL1577, WSX604
Electrola SHZEL60

VAINBERG

Moldavian Rhapsody in g, Op. 47 vln & pf
with M. Vainberg pf — Classic Editions CE3002
Colosseum CRLPX011
Mezhdunarodnaya Kniga D05623

VIEUXTEMPS

(6) Morceaux de salon, Op. 20 vln & pf
No. 4. Souvenir
with V. Yampolsky pf — Mezhdunarodnaya Kniga D19537

(7) Romances sans paroles, Op. 7 vln & pf
No. 2. Romance No. 2, in c "Désespoir"
with V. Yampolsky pf — Bruno BR14018
Le Chant du Monde LDA8175, LDXSP1801
Concert Hall, M2226
Decca DL9882
Guilde International du Disque M2226
Mezhdunarodnaya Kniga D5029, D028807/8
Musidisc RC858

No. 3. Romance No. 3, in C "Reminiscence"
with V. Yampolsky pf — Bruno BR14018
Le Chant du Monde LDA8175
Decca DL9882
Mezhdunarodnaya Kniga D5029, D028807/8
Musidisc RC858

VIOTTI

Concerto No. 22, in a vln & orch.
with USSR Symphony Orch. – Kondrashin — Mezhdunarodnaya Kniga D026211/2

VITALI

Chaconne in g vln & c – arr. vln & pf Charlier
with V. Yampolsky pf — Columbia ML5096
Mezhdunarodnaya Kniga D028113/4
Monitor MC2042

VIVALDI

(12) Concerti, Op. 3 "L'Estro armonico" var. cbns & strs
Concerto No. 8, in a, P.2 (F.I, No. 177) 2 vlns, strs & c
with I. Oistrakh vln & USSR State Philharmonic Orch. – Kondrashin — Bruno BR14019

Concerto No. 8, in a, P.2 (F.I, No. 177) 2 vlns, strs & c
with I. Oistrakh vln & Leipzig Gewandhaus Orch. – Konwitschny — Decca DL9950
Deutsche Grammophon LPE17160, LPM18393
Eterna 720031

Concerto No. 8, in a, P.2 (F.I, No. 177) 2 vlns, strs & c
with I. Stern vln & Philadelphia Orch. – Ormandy — Columbia ML5087
Philips 409020AE, A01239L, ABE10181, ABL3138, G05650R

Concerto No. 8, in a, P.2 (F.I, No. 177) 2 vlns, strs & c
with I. Oistrakh vln & Royal Philharmonic Orch. – Oistrakh — Deutsche Grammophon LPM18714, SLPM138714
Eterna 720162

Concerto in D, P.189 (F.I, No. 41) 2 vlns, strs & c
with I. Stern vln W.R. Smith hpsi & Philadelphia Orch. – Ormandy — CBS BRG72082, SBRG72082
Columbia ML5604, MS6204
Fontana 699061CL, 876008EZ, CFL1070, SCFL136
Supraphon SUA10932, SUAST50932

VIVALDI – *Continued*

Concerto in d, P.281 (F.I, No. 100) 2 vlns, strs & c
with I. Stern vln, W.R. Smith hpsi &
Philadelphia Orch. – Ormandy   CBS BRG72082, SBRG72082
Columbia ML5604, MS6204
Fontana 494100EE, 699061CL,
876008EZ, CFL1070, SCFL136
Supraphon SUA10932,
SUAST50932

Concerto in g, P.366 (F.I, No. 98) 2 vlns, strs & c
with I. Stern vln, W.R. Smith hpsi &
Philadelphia Orch. – Ormandy   CBS BRG72082, SBRG72082
Columbia ML5604, MS6204
Fontana 699061CL, 876008EZ,
CFL1070, SCFL136
Supraphon SUA10932,
SUAST50932

Concerto in c, P.436 (F.I, No. 12) 2 vlns, strs & c
with I. Stern vln, W.R. Smith hpsi &
Philadelphia Orch. – Ormandy   CBS BRG72082, SBRG72082
Columbia ML5604, MS6204
Fontana 699061CL, 876008EZ,
CFL1070, SCFL136
Supraphon SUA10932,
SUAST50932

VLADIGEROV

(2) Bulgarian Paraphrases, Op. 18 vln & pf
No. 1. Choro
with V. Yampolsky pf   Classic Editions CE3002
Colosseum CRLP153
Mezhdunarodnaya Kniga
D6369/70, D028113/4
Parliament PLP118
Supraphon LPM237

Vardar (Rapsodie bulgare) Op. 16 vln & orch.
with V. Yampolsky pf   Mezhdunarodnaya Kniga
D19026/8

WAGNER

Albumblatt in C (1861) pf – arr. vln & pf Wilhelmj
with V. Yampolsky pf   Mezhdunarodnaya Kniga
D5028/9
Monitor MC2003
Victor LS2026

WIENIAWSKI

(L') École moderne, Op. 10 (10 Études) solo vln
No. 5. Étude No. 5, in E flat "alla Saltarella" arr. 2 vlns
with I. Oistrakh vln   Decca DL9962
Deutsche Grammophon
EPL30286
Eterna 520119, 720048
Heliodor 69688, 478437

(8) Étude–Caprices, Op. 18 solo vln & 2nd vln obb
Étude–Caprice No. 5, in a
with I. Oistrakh vln   Decca DL9962
Deutsche Grammophon
EPL30286
Eterna 520119. 720048
Heliodor 69688, 478437

WIENIAWSKI – *Continued*

Étude–Caprice No. 5, in E flat
with I. Oistrakh vln   Decca DL9962
Deutsche Grammophon
EPL30286
Eterna 520119, 720048
Heliodor 69688, 478437

Étude–Caprice No. 5, in E flat arr. vln & pf Kreisler
with V. Yampolsky pf   Decca DL9882
Mezhdunarodnaya Kniga D1263,
D029743/4

Légende, Op. 17 vln & pf or orch.
with I. Yampolsky pf   Bruno SBR32002
Le Chant du Monde LDA8175,
LDX–S8360
Concert Hall M2226
Colosseum CRLP251
Decca DL9882
Guilde International du Disque
M2226
Mezhdunarodnaya Kniga D2163,
D029743/4
Monarch MEL707

Légende, Op. 17 vln & pf or orch.
with V. Yampolsky pf   Angel 35354
Columbia CX1466, SAX2253,
SEB3515, WSX604
Electrola SHZEL60

Scherzo–Tarantelle, Op. 16 vln & pf
with V. Yampolsky pf   Mezhdunarodnaya Kniga
D022227

YSAŸE

Extase in E flat (Poème No. 4) Op. 21 vln & pf or orch.
with V. Yampolsky pf   Bruno BR14018

Extase in E flat (Poème No. 4) Op. 21 vln & pf or orch.
with V. Yampolsky pf   Angel 35354
Capitol ZST44001
Columbia CX1466, SAX2253,
WSX604
Electrola SHZEL60

Poème élégiaque in d (Poème No. 1) Op. 12 vln & pf or orch.
with V. Yampolsky pf   Bruno BR14018
Decca DL9882
Fondation Eugèn Ysaÿe
FEY3001
Mezhdunarodnaya Kniga D5028,
D028807/8

(6) Sonatas, Op. 27 solo vln
Sonata No. 3, in d
(unaccompanied)   Le Chant du Monde LDA8075
Colosseum CRLP150
Eurodisc 70600EK
Europaische Fonoclub 2043
Parlophone 1175
Supraphon 18900, E23327
Vanguard VRS6024

Sonata No. 3, in d
(unaccompanied)

Le Chant du Monde LDX–
S78362
Philips 802727AY, AL3589,
PHM500112, PHS900112,
SAL3589

ZARZYCKI

Mazurka in G, Op. 26 vln & pf
with V. Yampolsky pf

Bruno SBR32002
Le Chant du Monde LDA8175
Decca DL9882
Guilde International du Disque
M2226
Mezhdunarodnaya Kniga
D04045
Monitor MC2003

Mazurka in G, Op. 26 vln & pf
with V. Yampolsky pf

Angel 35354
Columbia CX1466, SAX2253,
WSX604
Electrola SHZEL60

Igor Davidovich OISTRAKH (1931–   )

BACH

Concerto No. 2, in E, BWV1042 vln, strs & c
with Leipzig Gewandhaus Orch. –
Konwitschny

Decca DL9875
Deutsche Grammophon
LPM18328
Eterna 820027
Heliodor 89560

Concerto in d, BWV1043 2 vlns, strs & c
with D. Oistrakh vln & Moscow
Chamber Orch. – Barshai

Bruno BR14008
Le Chant du Monde LDX–S8319
Eurodisc 78351ZK
Hall of Fame HOF516
Mezhdunarodnaya Kniga D5083,
D026219/20
Monitor MC2009
Musidisc RC856

Concerto in d, BWV1043 2 vlns, strs & c
with D. Oistrakh vln & Leipzig
Gewandhaus Orch. – Konwitschny

Decca DL9950
Deutsche Grammophon
LPE17160, LPM18393
Eterna 720031

Concerto in d, BWV1043 2 vlns, strs & c
with D. Oistrakh vln & Royal
Philharmonic Orch. – Goossens

Deutsche Grammophon
LPM18714, LPM18820,
SLPM138714, SLPM138820
Eterna 720162

Concerto No. 5, in f, BWV1056 clav, strs & c – arr. vln, strs & c as
"Concerto in g" by Szigeti – res. Reitz
with Moscow Chamber Orch. –
Barshai

Eurodisc 78431ZK, (in set
80572XK)
Mezhdunarodnaya Kniga
D08802

(3) Sonatas & 3 Partitas, BWV1001/6 solo vln
Sonata No. 1, in g, BWV1001
(unaccompanied)

Le Chant du Monde LDA8092
Colosseum CRLP193
Eurodisc 70600EK
Vanguard VRS461

Sonata in C, BWV1037 2 vlns & c
with D. Oistrakh vln & V. Yampolsky
pf

Bruno BR14008
Le Chant du Monde LDY8138
Colosseum CRLP246
Mezhdunarodnaya Kniga
D004962/3, D015349
Monitor MC2005

Sonata in C, BWV1037 2 vlns & c
with D. Oistrakh vln & H. Pischner
hpsi

Decca DL9950
Deutsche Grammophon
LPM18393
Eterna 820283
Heliodor 89561, H25009

BARTÓK

Concerto No. 2 (1938) vln & orch.
with Moscow State Philharmonic
Orch. – Rozhdestvensky

Eurodisc 74495KK
Mezhdunarodnaya Kniga
D08405/6, S0161/2
Period SHO338, SHOST2338, (in
set TE1163)
Recital Hall (in set RH301)

For Children (40 pieces) (1909) pf
Nos. 6, 13, 18, 25, 31, 36 & 40 arr. vln & pf as "Hungarian folk tunes"
by Szigeti
with N. Zertsalova pf

Mezhdunarodnaya Kniga
D08831/2, S0225/6

BEETHOVEN

Concerto in D, Op. 61 (cadenzas by Kreisler) vln & orch.
with Pro Art Orch. – Schüchter

Angel 35516
Columbia CX1514
Trianon TRX6105

Concerto in D, Op. 61 vln & orch.
with Vienna Symphony Orch. – D.
Oistrakh

Melodiya–Eurodisc 80458PK

Romance No. 1, in G, Op. 40 vln & orch.
with Leipzig Gewandhaus Orch. –
Konwitschny

Decca DL9875
Deutsche Grammophon
EPL30246, LPM18328
Eterna 820027
Heliodor 89599, H25071,
HS25071

Romance No. 2, in F, Op. 50 vln & orch.
with Leipzig Gewandhaus Orch. –
Konwitschny

Decca DL9875
Deutsche Grammophon
EPL30246, LPM18328
Eterna 820027
Heliodor 89599, H25071,
HS25071

BEETHOVEN – *Continued*

(3) Sonatas, Op. 12 vln & pf
No. 1. Sonata No. 1, in D
with N. Zertsalova pf

Eurodisc (in set 80154XK)
HMV C153–91562/5
Mezhdunarodnaya Kniga S01851

No. 2. Sonata No. 2, in A
with N. Zertsalova pf

Eurodisc (in set 80154XK)
HMV C153–91562/5
Mezhdunarodnaya Kniga
S01851/2

No. 3. Sonata No. 3, in E flat
with N. Zertsalova pf

Eurodisc (in set 80154XK)
HMV C153–91562/5
Mezhdunarodnaya Kniga S01853

Sonata No. 4, in a, Op. 23 vln & pf
with N. Zertsalova pf

Eurodisc (in set 80154XK)
HMV C153–91562/5
Mezhdunarodnaya Kniga
S01853/4

Sonata No. 5, in F, Op. 24 "Spring" vln & pf
with N. Zertsalova pf

Eurodisc (in sets 80154XK &
80572XK)
HMV C153–91562/5
Mezhdunarodnaya Kniga S01854

(3) Sonatas, Op. 30 vln & pf
No. 1. Sonata No. 6, in A
with N. Zertsalova pf

Eurodisc (in set 80154XK)
HMV C153–91562/5
Mezhdunarodnaya Kniga S01852

No. 2. Sonata No. 7, in c
with N. Zertsalova pf

Eurodisc (in set 80154XK)
HMV C153–91562/5
Mezhdunarodnaya Kniga S01855

No. 3. Sonata No. 8, in G
with N. Zertsalova pf

Eurodisc (in set 80154XK)
HMV C153–91562/5
Mezhdunarodnaya Kniga S01858

Sonata No. 9, in A, Op. 47 "Kreutzer" vln & pf
with N. Zertsalova pf

Mezhdunarodnaya Kniga
D015363/4

Sonata No. 9, in A, Op. 47 "Kreutzer" vln & pf
with N. Zertsalova pf

Eurodisc (in set 80154XK)
HMV C153–91562/5
Mezhdunarodnaya Kniga
S01857/8

Sonata No. 10, in G, Op. 96 vln & pf
with B. Davidovich pf

Mezhdunarodnaya Kniga
D08843

Sonata No. 10, in G, Op. 96 vln & pf
with N. Zertsalova pf

Eurodisc (in set 80154XK)
HMV C153–91562/5
Mezhdunarodnaya Kniga S01856

BENDA, J.
Trio–Sonata in E 2 vlns & c
with D. Oistrakh vln & V. Yampolsky
pf

Decca DL9962
Deutsche Grammophon
EPL30294, LP16136
Eterna 820283
Heliodor 89561, 478132, H25009

BRAHMS
Concerto in D, Op. 77 (cadenza by Kreisler) vln & orch.
with Moscow Radio Symphony Orch.
– D. Oistrakh

Eurodisc 73606KK, 77303ZK
Mezhdunarodnaya Kniga
D07387/8

(21) Hungarian Dances pf duet
Hungarian dance No. 1, in g arr. vln & pf Joachim
with piano

Mezhdunarodnaya Kniga D5877

Sonata No. 1, in G, Op. 78 vln & pf
with A. Ginzburg pf

Mezhdunarodnaya Kniga
D06135
Recital Hall (in set RH301)

Sonata No. 1, in G, Op. 78 vln & pf
with A. Ginzburg pf

Columbia CX1740

Sonata No. 2, in A, Op. 100 vln & pf
with A. Ginzburg pf

Eurodisc 78431ZK, (in set
80572XK)
Mezhdunarodnaya Kniga
D06136
Recital Hall (in set RH301)

Sonata No. 2, in A, Op. 100 vln & pf
with A. Ginzburg pf

Columbia CX1740

Sonata No. 3, in d, Op. 108 vln & pf
with N. Zertsalova pf

Eterna 820357

Sonata (1853) "Frei aber Einsam" vln & pf
Allegro (Scherzo) in c (3rd mvt) "Sonatensatz"
with G. Ginzburg pf

Supraphon LPM347
Ultraphon DM5319

BRUCH
Concerto No. 1, in g, Op. 26 vln & orch.
with Royal Philharmonic Orch. – D.
Oistrakh

Deutsche Grammophon 135039
Mezhdunarodnaya Kniga
D08285/6, S0155/6

CHAUSSON
Poème, Op. 25 vln & orch.
with Moscow Radio Symphony Orch.
– Rozhdestvensky

Melodiya–Angel S40077
Mezhdunarodnaya Kniga
D021415/6, S01617/8

CHOPIN
(4) Mazurkas, Op. 67 pf
No. 4. Mazurka No. 45, in a arr. vln & pf Kreisler
with G. Ginzburg pf

Supraphon LPM347
Ultraphon DM5319

DEBUSSY
Petite Suite (1889) pf – 4 hands
No. 1. En bateau arr. vln & pf Kreisler
with G. Ginzburg pf

Supraphon LPM347
Ultraphon 16421, DM5319

FRANCK
Sonata in A (1886) vln & pf
with G. Ginzburg pf   Fontana 663025ER

GLAZOUNOV
Raymonda, Op. 57 (1897) – ballet orch.
Grand Adagio arr. vln & pf Pogozhev
with I. Kollegorskaya pf   Mezhdunarodnaya Kniga D3158

GLIÈRE
Romance in c, Op. 45, No. 3 vln & pf
with piano   Mezhdunarodnaya Kniga D00121

HANDEL
(9) Sonatas, Op. 2 (1724) 2 vlns & c
Sonata No. 7, in g
with D. Oistrakh vln & V. Yampolsky pf   Decca DL9962
Deutsche Grammophon EPL30287, LP16136
Eterna 820283
Heliodor 89561, 478132, H25009
Mezhdunarodnaya Kniga D5671

Sonata No. 7, in g
with D. Oistrakh vln & A. Ginzburg pf   Hall of Fame HOF516
Mezhdunarodnaya Kniga D015349

HAYDN
(3) Duos, H.III, Nos. 25/7 (1769) vln & vlc
No. 3. Duo No. 3, in B flat, H.III, No. 27 arr. 2 vlns
with D. Oistrakh vln   Le Chant du Monde LDXA8280
Concert Hall SMSC201
Mezhdunarodnaya Kniga D14141/2, S0579/80
Monitor MC2058

HINDEMITH
(4) Kammermusik, Op. 36 var. cbns
No. 3. Kammermusik No. 4 (1925) vln & cha orch.
with Moscow Radio Symphony Orch. – Rozhdestvensky   Melodiya–Angel S40068
Mezhdunarodnaya Kniga D021417/8, S01575/6

Sonata No. 3, in E (1935) vln & pf
with N. Zertsalova pf   Mezhdunarodnaya Kniga D08831/2, S0225/6

HONEGGER
Sonatina (1920) 2 vlns
with D. Oistrakh vln   Le Chant du Monde LDXA8280
Concert Hall SMSC201
Mezhdunarodnaya Kniga D14141/2, S0579/80
Monitor MC2058

KAVALEVSKY
Improvisation, Op. 21, No. 1 vln & pf
with I. Kollegorskaya pf   Mezhdunarodnaya Kniga D3159
Vanguard VRS461

Improvisation, Op. 21, No. 1 vln & pf
with piano   Mezhdunarodnaya Kniga D11055/6

KHACHATURIAN
Chanson poème in e (1929) vln & pf
with I. Kollegorskaya pf   Mezhdunarodnaya Kniga D001211
Westminster XWN18508

Concerto in D (1940) (cadenza by D. Oistrakh) vln & orch.
with Philharmonia Orch. – Goossens   Angel 35100
Columbia CX1141, QCX10126
Music for Pleasure MFP2050

KREISLER
Grave (W.F. Bach) vln & pf
with I. Kollegorskaya pf   Westminster XWN18508

LALO
Symphonie espagnole, Op. 21 vln & orch.*
with Moscow Radio Symphony Orch. – D. Oistrakh   Mezhdunarodnaya Kniga D11727/8, D012355/6, S565/6, S0649/50

MENDELSSOHN
Concerto in e, Op. 64 vln & orch.
with Leipzig Gewandhaus Orch. – Konwitschny   Decca DL9842
Deutsche Grammophon LPM18329
Eterna 820019
Heliodor 89599

MOZART
Duo No. 1, in G, K423 vln & vla
with R. Barshai vla   Mezhdunarodnaya Kniga D3161

Duo No. 1, in G, K423 vln & vla
with D. Oistrakh vla   Decca LXT6088, SXL6088
London CM9377, CS6377

Duo No. 2, in B flat, K424 vln & vla
with R. Barshai vla   Mezhdunarodnaya Kniga D3226/7

Serenade No. 7, in D, K250 "Haffner" orch.
Rondo (4th mvt) arr. vln & pf Kreisler
with A. Makarov pf   Le Chant du Monde LDA8092
Colosseum CRLP194
Eurodisc 40446CK
Vanguard VRS461

Rondo (4th mvt) arr. vln & pf Kreisler
with I. Kollegorskaya pf   Decca VD559
Mezhdunarodnaya Kniga D3158
Westminster XWN18508

Sinfonia concertante in E flat, K364 vln, vla & orch.
with D. Oistrakh vla & Moscow Philharmonic Orch. – Kondrashin   Decca LXT6088, SXL6088
London CM9377, CS6377

Sonata No. 26, in B flat, K378 vln & pf
with N. Zertsalova pf   Mezhdunarodnaya Kniga D015363/4

NIKOLAYEV
Sonata in C, Op. 18 vln & pf
with N. Zertsalova pf   Mezhdunarodnaya Kniga D18445/6

* Including Intermezzo

PROKOFIEV

Concerto No. 1, in D, Op. 19 vln & orch.
with Moscow Radio Symphony Orch.   HMV ASD2472
– Rozhdestvensky   Melodiya–Angel S40068
    Mezhdunarodnaya Kniga
    D021417/8, S01575/6

(5) Melodies, Op. 35bis (1921) vln & pf
with N. Zertsalova pf   Eterna 820357
Sonata in C, Op. 56 2 vlns
with D. Oistrakh vln   Mezhdunarodnaya Kniga D5670
Sonata in C, Op. 56 2 vlns
with D. Oistrakh vln   Mezhdunarodnaya Kniga
    D015350
Sonata in C, Op. 56 2 vlns
with I. Oistrakh vln   Le Chant du Monde LDXA8280
    Concert Hall SMSC201
    Mezhdunarodnaya Kniga
    D14141/2, S0579/80
    Monitor MCS2058

RAKOV

Concerto in e (1948) vln & orch.
with USSR Radio Symphony Orch. –   Bruno BR14017
Rakov   Mezhdunarodnaya Kniga
    D2685/6
    Parlophone PMA1039
    Westminster XWN18508

(5) Pieces 2 vlns & pf
with V. Pikaizen vln & N. Rakov pf   Mezhdunarodnaya Kniga
    D11055/6
Poem in e vln & pf
with I. Kollegorskaya pf   Westminster XWN18508

RAVEL

Tzigane (Rapsodie de concert) (1924) vln & pf or orch.
with Moscow Radio Symphony Orch.   Melodiya–Angel S40077
– Rozhdestvensky   Mezhdunarodnaya Kniga
    D021415/6, S01617/8

SAINT–SAËNS

Havanaise, Op. 83 vln & orch.
with Moscow Radio Symphony Orch.   Melodiya–Angel S40077
– Rozhdestvensky   Mezhdunarodnaya Kniga
    D021415/6, S01617/8

Introduction & Rondo Capriccioso, Op. 28 vln & orch.
with I. Kollegorskaya pf   Muza X2059, XL0385
Introduction & Rondo Capriccioso, Op. 28 vln & orch.
with G. Ginzburg pf   Supraphon LPM347
    Ultraphon 16303, DM5319
Introduction & Rondo Capriccioso, Op. 28 vln & orch.
with Pro Arte Orch. – Schüchter   Angel 35517
    Columbia CX1594
Introduction & Rondo Capriccioso, Op. 28 vln & orch.
with Moscow Radio Symphony Orch.   Melodiya–Angel S40077
– Rozhdestvensky   Mezhdunarodnaya Kniga
    D021415/6, S01617/8

SARASATE

Navarra, Op. 33 2 vlns & pf or orch.
with D. Oistrakh vln & V. Yampolsky   Bruno BR14015
pf   Hall of Fame HOF516
    Mezhdunarodnaya Kniga
    D17637/8, D6369/70,
    D029743/4
    Monitor MC2009

Navarra, Op. 33 2 vlns & pf or orch.
with D. Oistrakh vln & Leipzig   Decca DL9962
Gewandhaus Orch. – Konwitschny   Deutsche Grammophon
    EPL30286
    Eterna 520119, 720048
    Heliodor 89688, 478437

SCHUBERT

Sonata in A, Op. 162 (D574) "Duo" vln & pf
with B. Davidovich pf   Mezhdunarodnaya Kniga
    D08844

SCRIABIN

(12) Etudes, Op. 8 pf
No. 11. Etude No. 11, in B flat arr. vln & pf
with I. Kollegorskaya pf   Muza X2060, XL0385
    Westminster XWN18508

SPOHR

(3) Duets, Op. 67 2 vlns
No. 3. Duet No. 3, in g
with D. Oistrakh vln   Le Chant du Monde LDXA8280
    Concert Hall SMSC201
    Mezhdunarodnaya Kniga
    D14141/2, S0579/80
    Monitor MC2058

STRAVINSKY

Suite Italienne (on themes of Pergolesi) (1933) vln & pf
with N. Zertsalova pf   Mezhdunarodnaya Kniga
    D08831/2, S0225/6
Suite Italienne (on themes of Pergolesi) (1933) vln & pf
with N. Zertsalova pf   Eterna 820357

SZYMANOWSKI

(3) Mythes, Op. 30 (1915) vln & pf
No. 1. La Fontaine d'Aréthuse
with I. Kollegorskaya pf   Mezhdunarodnaya Kniga D3159
    Vanguard VRS461

TARTINI

(12) Sonatas, Op. 3 2 vlns & c
Sonata No. 4, in F
with D. Oistrakh vln & V. Yampolsky   Bruno BR14019
pf   Mezhdunarodnaya Kniga D5671
Sonata No. 4, in F
with D. Oistrakh vln & H. Pischner   Decca DL9950
hpsi   Deutsche Grammophon
    LPM18393
    Eterna 820283
    Heliodor 89561, H25009
Sonata No. 4, in F
with D. Oistrakh vln & A. Ginzburg   Hall of Fame HOF516
pf   Mezhdunarodnaya Kniga
    D015350

TCHAIKOVSKY, B.

Sonata in A vln & pf
  with N. Zertsalova pf   Mezhdunarodnaya Kniga
                                      D18445/6

TCHAIKOVSKY, P.

Concerto in D, Op. 35 vln & orch.
  with Pro Arte Orch. – Schüchter   Angel 35517
                                      Columbia CX1594

Concerto in D, Op. 35 vln & orch.*
  with Moscow Philharmonic Symphony   Eurodisc 76619IK
  Orch. – D. Oistrakh   Melodiya–Angel SR40009
                                      Mezhdunarodnaya Kniga
                                      D017433/4, S01243/4

Waltz–Scherzo, Op. 34 vln & orch. – arr. vln & pf Bezékirsky
  with I. Kollegorskaya pf   Decca VD559
                                      Mezhdunarodnaya Kniga D3158

VIEUXTEMPS

(6) Morceaux de salon, Op. 22 vln & pf
  No. 5. Tarantella in a
  with I. Kollegorskaya pf   Mezhdunarodnaya Kniga D3159
                                      Vanguard VRS461

VITALI

Chaconne in g vln & c – arr. vln & pf Charlier
  with A. Makarov pf   Le Chant du Monde LDA8092
                                      Colosseum CRLP193
                                      Eurodisc 70600EK
                                      Vanguard VRS461

VIVALDI

(12) Concerti, Op. 3 "L'Estro armonico" var. cbns & strs
  Concerto No. 8, in a, P.2 (F.I, No. 177) 2 vlns, strs & c
  with D. Oistrakh vln & USSR State   Bruno BR14019
  Philharmonic Orch. – Kondrashin

  Concerto No. 8, in a, P.2 (F.I, No. 177) 2 vlns, strs & c
  with D. Oistrakh vln & Leipzig   Decca DL9950
  Gewandhaus Orch. – Konwitschny   Deutsche Grammophon
                                        LPE17160, LPM18393
                                        Eterna 720031

  Concerto No. 8, in a, P.2 (F.I, No. 177) 2 vlns, strs & c
  with D. Oistrakh vln & Royal   Deutsche Grammophon
  Philharmonic Orch. – D. Oistrakh   LPM18714, SLPM138714
                                        Eterna 720162

WIENIAWSKI

Concerto No. 2, in d, Op. 22 vln & orch.
  with Leipzig Gewandhaus Orch. –   Decca DL9842, LXT2009
  Konwitschny   Deutsche Grammophon
                                        LPM18329
                                        Eterna 820019
                                        Heliodor 89867

Concerto No. 2, in d, Op. 22 vln & orch.
  with USSR State Philharmonic Society   Mezhdunarodnaya Kniga
  Orch. – Rozhdestvensky   D06130

* 1st mvt. in set Eurodisc 80572XK.

WIENIAWSKI – *Continued*

(L') École moderne, Op. 10 (10 Études) solo vln
  No. 5. Étude No. 5, in E flat "alla Saltarella" arr. 2 vlns
  with D. Oistrakh vln   Decca DL9962
                                      Deutsche Grammophon
                                      EPL30286
                                      Eterna 520119, 720048
                                      Heliodor 89688, 478437

(8) Étude–Caprices, Op. 18 solo vln & 2nd vln obb
  Étude–Caprice No. 4, in a
  with D. Oistrakh vln   Decca DL9962
                                      Deutsche Grammophon
                                      EPL30286
                                      Eterna 520119, 720048
                                      Heliodor 89688, 478437

  Étude–Caprice No. 5, in E flat
  with D. Oistrakh vln   Decca DL9962
                                      Deutsche Grammophon
                                      EPL30286
                                      Eterna 520119, 720048
                                      Heliodor 89688, 478437

Polonaise brillante No. 1, in D, Op. 4 vln & pf
  with G. Ginzburg pf   Supraphon LPM347
                                      Ultraphon 16421, DM5319

Scherzo–Tarantelle, Op. 16 vln & pf
  with I. Kollegorskaya pf   Muza X2060, XL0385
                                      Mezhdunarodnaya Kniga D3159
                                      Vanguard VRS461

YSAŸE

(3) Mazurkas, Op. 11 vln & pf
  No. 3. Mazurka No. 3, in b "Lointaine–passé"
  with N. Zertsalova pf   Mezhdunarodnaya Kniga
                                      D08831/2, S0225/6

(6) Sonatas, Op. 27 solo vln
  Sonata No. 3, in d
  (unaccompanied)   Mezhdunarodnaya Kniga
                                      D08831/2, S0225/6

Julian OLEVSKY (1927–   )

BACH

(3) Sonatas & 3 Partitas, BWV1001/6 solo vln
  Sonata No. 1, in g, BWV1001
  (unaccompanied)   Westminster WL5306,
                                      XWN18023, (in set OPW3311)

  Partita No. 1, in b, BWV1002
  (unaccompanied)   Westminster XWN18827, (in set
                                      OPW3311)

  Sonata No. 2, in a, BWV1003
  (unaccompanied)   Westminster XWN18072, (in set
                                      OPW3311)

  Partita No. 2, in d, BWV1004
  (unaccompanied)   Westminster WL5306,
                                      XWN18023, (in set OPW3311)

  Sonata No. 3, in C, BWV1005
  (unaccompanied)   Westminster XWN18827, (in set
                                      OPW3311)

BACH – *Continued*

Partita No. 3, in E, BWV1006
(unaccompanied)

Westminster XWN18072, (in set
OPW3311)

BRAHMS

Concerto in D, Op. 77 (cadenza by Kreisler) vln & orch.
with National Symphony Orch. –
Mitchell

Nixa WLP5273
Westminster WL5273,
XWN18439

BRANDL

(Der) Liebe Augustin – Operetta
Du alter Stefansturm arr. vln & pf as "The old refrain" by Kreisler
with W. Rose pf

Nixa WLP5346
Westminster WL5346,
XWN18438

BRUCH

Concerto No. 1, in g, Op. 26 vln & orch.
with Vienna State Opera Orch. –
Rudel

Heliodor 428018, 478065
Music for Pleasure MFP2106
Westminster P251, PWS701,
WST14080, XWN18860
Whitehall WH20041, WHS20041

HANDEL

(15) Sonatas, Op. 1 (?1731) fl or vln & c
Sonata No. 1, in e
with F. Valenti hpsi & M. Ormandy
vlc

Westminster W9064,
XWN18872, (in set OPW3314)

Sonata No. 2, in g
with F. Valenti hpsi & M. Ormandy
vlc

Westminster W9064,
XWN18872, (in set OPW3314)

Sonata No. 3, in A vln I
with F. Valenti hpsi & M. Ormandy
vlc

Westminster W9064,
XWN18872, (in set OPW3314)

Sonata No. 4, in a
with F. Valenti hpsi & M. Ormandy
vlc

Westminster W9064,
XWN18872, (in set OPW3314)

Sonata No. 5, in G
with F. Valenti hpsi & M. Ormandy
vlc

Westminster W9064,
XWN18872, (in set OPW3314)

Sonata No. 6, in g
with F. Valenti hpsi & M. Ormandy
vlc

Westminster W9064,
XWN18872, (in set OPW3314)

Sonata No. 7, in C
with F. Valenti hpsi & M. Ormandy
vlc

Westminster W9065,
XWN18873, (in set OPW3314)

Sonata No. 8, in c
with F. Valenti hpsi & M. Ormandy
vlc

Westminster W9065,
XWN18873, (in set OPW3314)

Sonata No. 9, in b
with F. Valenti hpsi & M. Ormandy
vlc

Westminster W9065,
XWN18873, (in set OPW3314)

Sonata No. 10, in g vln II
with F. Valenti hpsi & M. Ormandy
vlc

Westminster W9065,
XWN18873, (in set OPW3314)

Sonata No. 11, in F
with F. Valenti hpsi & M. Ormandy
vlc

Westminster W9065,
XWN18873, (in set OPW3314)

HANDEL – *Continued*

Sonata No. 12, in F vln III
with F. Valenti hpsi & M. Ormandy
vlc

Westminster W9066,
XWN18874, (in set OPW3314)

Sonata No. 13, in D vln IV
with F. Valenti hpsi & M. Ormandy
vlc

Westminster W9066,
XWN18874, (in set OPW3314)

Sonata No. 14, in A vln V
with F. Valenti hpsi & M. Ormandy
vlc

Westminster W9066,
XWN18874, (in set OPW3314)

Sonata No. 15, in E vln VI
with F. Valenti hpsi & M. Ormandy
vlc

Westminster W9066,
XWN18874, (in set OPW3314)

KREISLER

Caprice viennois, Op. 2 vln & pf
with W. Rose pf

Nixa WLP5346
Westminster WL5346,
XWN18438

Liebesfreud vln & pf
with W. Rose pf

Nixa WLP5346
Westminster WL5346,
XWN18438

Liebesleid vln & pf
with W. Rose pf

Nixa WLP5346
Westminster WL5346,
XWN18438

Romance, Op. 4 vln & pf
with W. Rose pf

Nixa WLP5346
Westminster WL5346,
XWN18438

Rondino on a theme by Beethoven vln & pf
with W. Rose pf

Nixa WLP5346
Westminster WL5346,
XWN18438

Schön Rosmarin vln & pf
with W. Rose pf

Nixa WLP5346
Westminster WL5346,
XWN18438

Tambourin chinois, Op. 3 vln & pf
with W. Rose pf

Nixa WLP5346
Westminster WL5346,
XWN18438

Chanson Louis XIII & Pavane (L. Couperin) vln & pf
with W. Rose pf

Nixa WLP5346
Westminster WL5346,
XWN18438

Praeludium & Allegro (Pugnani) vln & pf
with W. Rose pf

Nixa WLP5346
Westminster WL5346,
XWN18438

(La) Précieuse (L. Couperin) vln & pf
with W. Rose pf

Nixa WLP5346
Westminster WL5346,
XWN18438

Sicilienne & Rigaudon (Francoeur) vln & pf
with W. Rose pf

Nixa WLP5346
Westminster WL5346,
XWN18438

LALO

Symphonie espagnole, Op. 21 vln & orch.*
  with Vienna State Opera Orch. –
  Rudel

Vega MT10105
Westminster PWS745,
WST14121, XWN18938

MENDELSSOHN

Concerto in e, Op. 64 vln & orch.
  with Vienna State Opera Orch. –
  Rudel

Heliodor 428018, 478065
Music for Pleasure MFP2106
Westminster P251, PWS701,
WST14080, XWN18860
Whitehall WH20041, WHS20041

SCARLATTI, D.

(8) Sonatas vln & hpsi–c
  Sonata No. 1, in c
  with F. Valenti hpsi

Westminster W9046, XWN18113

  Sonata No. 2, in d
  with F. Valenti hpsi

Westminster W9046, XWN18113

  Sonata No. 3, in F
  with F. Valenti hpsi

Westminster W9046, XWN18113

  Sonata No. 4, in e
  with F. Valenti hpsi

Westminster W9046, XWN18113

  Sonata No. 5, in g
  with F. Valenti hpsi

Westminster W9046, XWN18113

  Sonata No. 6, in d
  with F. Valenti hpsi

Westminster W9046, XWN18113

  Sonata No. 7, in d
  with F. Valenti hpsi

Westminster W9046, XWN18113

  Sonata No. 8, in G
  with F. Valenti hpsi

Westminster W9046, XWN18113

VIVALDI

(12) Concerti, Op. 8 (1725) "Il Cimento dell' Armonia e dell' Invenzione"
(Nos. 1/4: Le quattro Stagioni) vln & strs
  Concerto No. 1, in E, F.I, No. 22 "La Primavera"
  with Vienna State Opera Orch. –
  Scherchen

Music for Pleasure MFP2118
Vega MT10197
Westminster P323, PWS757,
WST14087, XWN18913, (in set
OPW3315)

  Concerto No. 2, in B flat, F.I, No. 23 "L'Estate"
  with Vienna State Opera Orch. –
  Scherchen

Music for Pleasure MFP2118
Vega MT10197
Westminster P323, PWS757,
WST14087, XWN18913, (in set
OPW3315)

  Concerto No. 3, in F, F.I, No. 24 "L'Autunno"
  with Vienna State Opera Orch. –
  Scherchen

Music for Pleasure MFP2118
Vega MT10197
Westminster P323, PWS757,
WST14087, XWN18913, (in set
OPW3315)

* Omitting Intermezzo.

VIVALDI – *Continued*

Concerto No. 4, in f, F.I, No. 25 "L'Inverno"
  with Vienna State Opera Orch. –
  Scherchen

Music for Pleasure MFP2118
Vega MT10197
Westminster P323, PWS757,
WST14087, XWN18913, (in set
OPW3315)

Concerto No. 5, in E flat, F.I, No. 26 "La Tempesta di mare"
  with Vienna State Opera Orch. –
  Scherchen

Westminster XWN18914, (in set
OPW3315)

Concerto No. 6, in C, F.I, No. 27 "La Piacere"
  with Vienna State Opera Orch. –
  Scherchen

Westminster XWN18914, (in set
OPW3315)

Concerto No. 7, in d, F.I, No. 28
  with Vienna State Opera Orch. –
  Scherchen

Westminster XWN18914, (in set
OPW3315)

Concerto No. 8, in g, F.I, No. 16
  with Vienna State Opera Orch. –
  Scherchen

Westminster XWN18914, (in set
OPW3315)

Concerto No. 9, in d, F.VII, No. 1
  with Vienna State Opera Orch. –
  Scherchen

Westminster XWN18915, (in set
OPW3315)

Concerto No. 10, in B flat, F.I, No. 29 "La Caccia"
  with Vienna State Opera Orch. –
  Scherchen

Westminster XWN18915, (in set
OPW3315)

Concerto No. 11, in D, F.I, No. 30
  with Vienna State Opera Orch. –
  Scherchen

Westminster XWN18915, (in set
OPW3315)

Concerto No. 12, in C, F.I, No. 31
  with Vienna State Opera Orch. –
  Scherchen

Westminster XWN18915, (in set
OPW3315)

WIENIAWSKI

Concerto No. 2, in d, Op. 22 vln & orch.
  with Vienna State Opera Orch. –
  Rudel

Westminster PWS745,
WST14121, XWN18938

Theo OLOF (1924–   )

BACH, C.P.E.

(2) Duets fl & vln
  Duet No. 1, in G, W140 arr. 2 vlns
  with H. Krebbers vln

Radio Nederland DR109276

  Duet No. 1, in G, W140 arr. 2 vlns
  with H. Krebbers vln

Telefunken AWT9447,
SAWT9447, STEL15, TEL15

BACH, J.S.

Concerto in d, BWV1043 2 vlns, strs & c
  with H. Krebbers vln & Hague
  Residentie Orch. – van Otterloo

Epic LC3026
Philips A00140L

(3) Sonatas & 3 Partitas, BWV1001/6 solo vln
  Partita No. 2, in d: Allemande (1st mvt); **Sarabande** (3rd mvt); **Gigue**
  (4th mvt) BWV1004
  (unaccompanied)

Radio Nederland DR109269

BADINGS

Concerto (1954) 2 vlns & orch.
  with H. Krebbers vln & Hague
  Residentie Orch. – van Otterloo

Philips L02242L

564

BADINGS – *Continued*

Sonata 2 vlns
  with H. Krebbers vln
     Radio Nederland DR109276

BARTÓK

(44) Duos (1931) 2 vlns
  with H. Krebbers vln
     Philips N00209L

BEETHOVEN

Romance No. 1, in G, Op. 40 vln & orch.
  with Hague Residentie Orch. – van
  Otterloo
     Epic LC3036
     Fontana 200031WGL
     Philips 675011KR, A00140L,
     S06000R

BLOCH

Baal Shem (3 Pictures of Chassidic life) (1923) vln & pf
  No. 2. Nigun (Improvisation)
  with G. Moore pf
     HMV B9665

BRAHMS

Sonata No. 2, in A, Op. 100 vln & pf
  with D. Wayenberg pf
     Iramac 6510

FRANCK

Sonata in A (1886) vln & pf
  with D. Wayenberg pf
     Iramac 6505

van HEMEL

Concerto (1943/4) vln & orch.
  with Utrecht Symphony Orch. –
  Hupperts
     Radio Nederland 109220/1

HENKEMANS

Concerto (1954) vln & orch.
  with Concertgebouw Orch.,
  Amsterdam – van Beinum
     Columbia ML4937
     Epic LC3093
     Philips A00219L

JANÁČEK

Sonata (1921) vln & pf
  with D. Wayenberg pf
     Iramac 6510

KOX

Concerto (1963) vln & orch.
  with Utrecht Philharmonic Symphony
  Orch. – Hupperts
     Radio Nederland 109512,
     DR109533

MOZART

Concerto No. 5, in A, K219 "Turkish" (cadenzas by Joachim) vln & orch.
  with Symphony Orch. – Goehr
     Classics Club X67
     Musical Masterpiece Society
     MMS2003

Sonata No. 21, in e, K304 vln & pf
  with D. Wayenberg pf
     Iramac 6505

PIJPER

Concerto (1939) vln & orch.
  with Radio Nederland Philharmonic
  Orch., Hilversum – Haitink
     Radio Nederland 109217

WIJDEVELD

Sonata (1952) vln & pf
  with W. Wijdeveld pf
     Radio Nederland 109570

J. OLOWSKI

DINICU

Hora staccato vln & pf – arr. Heifetz
  with piano
     Odeon 55030

ELGAR

(La) Capricieuse, Op. 17 vln & pf
  with piano
     Odeon 55030

Henrik Gotthardt OLSEN

TELEMANN

Trio–sonata in d rec, vln & c
  with I.K. Mathiesen rec & A.H.
  Mathiesen hpsi
     Nonesuch H1065, H71065

Goran OLSSON–FÖLLINGER (1886–)

AULIN

(4) Aquarelles vln & pf
  No. 1. Idyll
  with piano
     19727 b HMV X2–287913
  No. 3. Vaggsång
  with piano
     19725 b HMV*

  No. 4. Polonaise
  with piano
     19726 b HMV X2–287912

BULL

Nocturne, Op. 2 vln & pf
  with piano
     19728 b HMV*

HANDEL

Arioso unid – arr. vln & pf Burmester
  with piano
     19710 b HMV 2–287914

(15) Sonatas, Op. 1 (?1731) fl or vln & c
  Sonata No. 5, in G: Minuet (5th mvt) arr. vln & pf Burmester
  with piano
     19729 b HMV 2–287915†

OLSSON–FÖLLINGER

(3) Karaktärsstycke vln & pf
  No. 1. Polska (Lapp Nils)‡
  with piano
     19712 b HMV*

  No. 2. Polska
  with piano
     19712 b HMV*

  No. 3. Gammal bondmarsch (Lapp Nils' "Jämtland")
  with piano
     19713 b HMV*

Nejlikan vln & pf
  with piano
     19709 b HMV 287998

* Unissued.

† Also matrix 19711 b; same catalog number.

‡ Folk specialist Nils Jonasson, 1804–1870.

OLSSON–FÖLLINGER – *Continued*

Spelmansvals vln & pf
  with piano   19712 b*   HMV 287999

Spelmansvals
  with piano   19709 b*   HMV†

Maurice ONDERET (1899–   )

CHOPIN

(2) Waltzes, Op. 69 pf
  No. 2. Waltz No. 10, in b arr. vln & pf Spalding
  with E.M. Hawkin pf   Victor 130839

FRANCK

Sonata in A (1886) vln & pf
  with W. Stevens pf   Select SSC13016

SARASATE

(8) Danzas españolas vln & pf
  No. 3. Romanza andaluza, Op. 22, No. 1
  with W. Stevens pf   Select SSC13016

TANGUAY

Romance vln & pf
  with E.M. Hawkin pf   Victor 130839

WIENIAWSKI

Légende, Op. 17 vln & pf or orch.
  with W. Stevens pf   Select SSC13016

František ONDŘÍČEK (1857–1922)

ONDŘÍČEK

(15) Etudes solo vln
  Etude No. 2
  (unaccompanied)   Pathé 6041

SCHUMANN

(12) Duets, Op. 85 pf – 4 hands
  No. 12. Abendlied arr. vln & pf Wilhelmj
  with piano   Pathé 6041

Victor OPFERMANN

ANONYMOUS

Bonnie Mary of Argyle traditional Scottish ballad – arr. vln & pf
  with piano   Edison Bell 10056

BISHOP

Clari (1823) – opera
  Home, sweet home arr. vln & pf
  with piano   Edison Bell 2440

DANBÉ

Berceuse, Op. 17 vln & pf
  with piano   202–1 V   Marathon 105

* Duplicative matrix numbers as yet unclear.

† unissued.

DRDLA

Serenade No. 1, in A vln & pf
  with piano   Edison Bell 1044

Souvenir vln & pf – arr. fl, vln & pf
  with A. Richards fl & piano   Marathon 106

DVOŘÁK

(8) Humoresques, Op. 101 pf
  No. 7. Humoresque No. 7, in G flat arr. vln & pf "in G" Wilhelmj
  with piano   201–1 V Marathon 105
  No. 7. Humoresque No. 7, in G flat arr. vln & pf "in G" Wilhelmj
  with piano   Edison Bell 1045

ELGAR

Salut d'amour, Op. 12 orch. – arr. vln & pf Elgar
  with piano   Odeon 0148, 33023, 33587

Salut d'amour, Op. 12 orch. – arr. vln & pf Elgar
  with orch.   Edison Bell 1043, 10297

GODARD

Jocelyn (1888) – opera
  Cachés dans cet asile "Berceuse" arr. vln & pf
  with piano   Edison Bell 888

GOUNOD

Faust (1859) – opera
  Selection unid – arr. vln & pf
  with piano   Odeon 0148, 33024

PADEREWSKI

(6) Humoresques de Concert, Op. 14 pf
  No. 1. Minuet in G arr vln & pf Kreisler
  with piano   Edison Bell 2440

RAFF

(6) Pieces, Op. 85 vln & pf
  No. 3. Cavatina in D
  with orch.   Edison Bell 10297

SAINT–SAËNS

(Le) Carnaval des animaux (1886) small orch.
  Le Cygne arr. vln & pf
  with piano   Edison Bell 1044

SCHUBERT

(7) Gesänge (set to Scott's "Lady of the Lake") Op. 52 v & pf
  No. 6. Ave Maria, D839 arr. vln & pf Wilhelmj
  with piano   Edison Bell 10066

(14) Schwanengesang, D957 (1828) v & pf
  No. 4. Ständchen "Serenade" arr. vln, fl & pf
  with A. Richards fl & piano   Marathon 106

THOMÉ

Simple aveu, Op. 25 pf – arr. vln & pf
  with piano   Edison Bell 1045

VERDI

(Il) Trovatore (1853) – opera
  Selection arr. vln & pf as "Fantasie" by Opfermann
  with piano   Edison Bell 1043

WIENIAWSKI

(2) Mazurkas, Op. 12 vln & pf
No. 2. Mazurka No. 2, in g "Le Ménetrier"
with piano   Edison Bell 107

WOOD

(2) Little Pieces vln & pf
No. 1. Slumber song
with piano   Edison Bell 108

Eugene ORMANDY (1899–   )

DRDLA

Souvenir vln & pf
with S.G. Ormandy hp   401086 E   Okey 41147

DVOŘÁK

(8) Humoresques, Op. 101 pf
No. 7. Humoresque No. 7, in G flat arr. vln & pf "in G" Kreisler
with S.G. Ormandy hp   401085 E   Okey 41147

RIMSKY–KORSAKOV

(Le) Coq d'Or (1910) – opera
Hymn to the sun arr. vln & pf Kreisler
with W. Axt pf   707   Lincoln 2225
Sadko (1898) – opera
Chant hindou arr. vln & pf Kreisler
with W. Axt pf   708   Lincoln 2225

Harold ORMOND

GOUNOD

Ave Maria (Méditation on Bach's "Prelude No. 1, in C" from Book I of
"Das Wohltemperirte Clavier") v & pf – arr. vln & pf
with piano   Bell 1134

MENDELSSOHN

(6) Songs without words, Op. 62 pf
No. 6. Song without words No. 30, in A "Spring song" arr. vln & pf
Kreisler
with piano   Bell 1134

Edgar ORTENBERG

BACH

(3) Sonatas & 3 Partitas, BWV1001/6 solo vln
Partita No. 2, in d: Sarabande (3rd mvt) BWV1004 arr. vln & org
with organ   Artiphon D03026
(4) Suites, BWV1066/9 strs & c
Suite No. 3, in D: Air (2nd mvt) BWV1068 2 obs, 3 tpts, drms, strs & c
– arr. vln & pf as "Air on the G–string" by Wilhelmj
with organ   Artiphon D03027

BLUME

Florida "Serenata lirica" vln & pf
with organ   Artiphon D03019
Valse–caprice "Schön Erika" vln & pf
with organ   Artiphon D03063

BRAHMS

(16) Waltzes, Op. 39 pf duet
No. 15. Waltz No. 15, in A flat arr. vln & pf "in A" Hochstein
with organ   Artiphon D03061

FOSS

Dedication vln & pf
with L. Foss pf   Hargail (in set MW300)

HINDEMITH

Sonata No. 3, in E (1935) vln & pf
with L. Foss pf   Hargail (set MW300)

KARK

Bramosia vln & pf
with organ   Artiphon D03061

Edmée ORTMANS–BACH (1896–1947)

ANONYMOUS

Ariettes & Airs (18th century) arr. s, 2 vlns & c
with L. ben Sedira s, D. Blot vln, C.   HMV DB5023
Crussard hpsi & Y. Thibout vlc

BACH

Fugue in g, BWV578 "The Little G Minor" org – arr. strs ens
with D. Blot vln, G. Drouet vla, C.   La Boîte à Musique 10
Crussard hpsi & Y. Thibout vlc
Sonata in d, BWV1036 2 vlns & c
with D. Blot vln, C. Crussard hpsi &   La Boîte à Musique 18/9
Y. Thibout vlc
Sonata in C, BWV1037 2 vlns & c
with D. Blot vln, C. Crussard hpsi &   La Boîte à Musique 28/9
J. Alliaume vlc

COUPERIN, F.

Sonata No. 3, in g (1693) "L'Astrée" 2 vlns & c
                    PARTX 6090/3–1 La Boîte à Musique 58/9
with D. Blot vln, C. Crussard hpsi* &
J. Alliaume vlc

FUNCK

Suite in g 2 vlns, vla & c – arr. Crussard
with D. Blot vln, G. Drouet vla, C.   La Boîte à Musique 10
Crussard hpsi & Y. Thibout vlc

HANDEL

(9) Sonatas, Op. 2 (1724) 2 vlns or obs & c
Sonata No. 2, in g
with D. Blot vln, C. Crussard hpsi &   La Boîte à Musique 24
Y. Thibout vlc

KRIEGER

(12) Sonatas, Op. 2 (1693) vln & c
Sonata No. 3, in e arr. 2 vlns & c
with D. Blot vln, C. Crussard hpsi &   La Boîte à Musique 5
Y. Thibout vlc

* Claire, *not* Claude Crussard in this recording.

LECLAIR

(12) Sonatas, Op. 4 (1732) 2 vlns & c
 Sonata No. 2, in B flat: Sicilienne
 with D. Blot vln, C. Crussard hpsi &   HMV DB5108
 Y. Thibout vlc
 Sonata No. 4, in A (ed. Crussard)
 with D. Blot vln, C. Crussard hpsi &   HMV DB5107/8
 Y. Thibout vlc

MARINI

Romance, Gaillarde & Courante vln, strs & c
 with D. Blot vln, J.   PART 738   La Boîte à Musique 3
 Godard vla, S. Maynieu vlc, C.
 Crussard hpsi & Y. Thibout vlc

RAMEAU

(5) Pièces de Clavecin en Concerts (1741) hpsi, vln & c
 No. 4. Concert No. 4, in B flat*
 with D. Blot vln & C. Crussard hpsi   HMV DB5055
                                        Victor 12490

ROSENMÜLLER

(12) Sonatas (1670) var. cbns
 Sonata in e arr. 2 vlns & c Crussard
 with D. Blot vln, M.   2LA 2542/3[1] HMV DB5064
 de Lacour hpsi, N. Pierront org, cond. Victor 12489
 Crussard

SCARLATTI, A.

Diana ed Endimioni (1680/5) – cantata
 Boschi voi ch' in silenzio
 with L. ben Sedira s, D. Blot vln, S.   La Boîte à Musique 20
 Morand vla, C. Crussard hpsi & Y.
 Thibout vlc
(L') Emireno (1697) – opera
 Col dire a me cosi
 with L. ben Sedira s, D. Blot vln, C.   HMV DB5023
 Crussard hpsi & Y. Thibout vlc
 La tua pena mi dispiace
 with M. Castellazzi–Bovy s, D. Blot   La Boîte à Musique 4
 vln, S. Meyrieu vla, J. Godard vla, C.
 Crussard hpsi & Y. Thibout vlc
 Speranza del mio core
 with M. Castellazzi–Bovy s, D. Blot   La Boîte à Musique 4
 vln, S. Meyrieu vla, J. Godard vla, Y.
 Thibout vlc & C. Crussard hpsi
 Partirò, che più mi piace†
 with M. Castellazzi–Bovy s, D. Blot   La Boîte à Musique 4
 vln, S. Mayrieu vla, J. Godard vla, C.
 Crussard hpsi & Y. Thibout vlc
Preparati, O mio core – cantata
 Quanto è dolce
 with L. ben Sedira s, D. Blot vln, C.   HMV DB5024
 Crussard hpsi & Y. Thibout vlc
(La) Tua gradita fe'
 with L. ben Sedira s, D. Blot vln, C.   HMV DB5023
 Crussard hpsi & Y Thibout vlc

* Excerpt only
† Unidentified aria.

L. OSKOTSKY

BACH, J.C.

Sinfonia concertante in E flat, T. P 284 (1770) 2 vlns, 2 fls, 2 hrns & orch.
 with L. Shinder vln & Leningrad   Mezhdunarodnaya Kniga
 Philharmonic Chamber Orch. –   SM02197/8
 Dmitriev

Fredy OSTROVSKY (1922–   )

GEMINIANI

(6) Sonatas, Op. 5 (1738) solo vln
 Sonata in B flat
 (unaccompanied)   Classic Editions CE1029

OSTROVSKY

Capriccio orientale solo vln
 (unaccompanied)   Classic Editions CE1029
Impromptu solo vln
 (unaccompanied)   Classic Editions CE1029
Je pense à mon amour solo vln
 (unaccompanied)   Classic Editions CE1029

PAGANINI

Cantabile in D, Op. 17 vln & gtr
 with E. Calabria gtr   Boston B213, BST1013
(18) Centone di Sonate, Op. 64 (1828) vln & gtr
 Sonata No. 1, in A
 with E. Calabria gtr   Boston B213, BST1013
 Sonata No. 2, in D
 with E. Calabria gtr   Boston B213, BST1013
 Sonata No. 3, in C
 with E. Calabria gtr   Boston B213, BST1013
 Sonata No. 4, in A
 with E. Calabria gtr   Boston B213, BST1013
 Sonata No. 5, in E
 with E. Calabria gtr   Boston B213, BST1013
 Sonata No. 6, in A
 with E. Calabria gtr   Boston B213, BST1013

STRAVINSKY

Élégie (1944) solo vla or vln
 (unaccompanied)   Classic Editions CE1029

Vladimir OVCHAREK

BACH, W.F.

Sextet in E flat cl, 2 hrns, vln, vla & vlc
 with A. Veinblat cl, V. Ivanov hrn, S.   Mezhdunarodnaya Kniga
 SedrISTY hrn, V. Solovyov vla & B.   D022065/6, S01901
 Morozov vlc

GLINKA

Sextet in E flat pf, 2 vlns, vla, vlc & cbs
 with T. Fidler pf, B. Lutsky vln, V.   Mezhdunarodnaya Kniga
 Solovyov vla, I. Levinzon vlc & S.   D029887
 Akopov cbs

HAYDN

(6) Quartets, Op. 3 (H.III, Nos. 13/18) 2 vlns, vla & vlc
No. 5. Quartet No. 17, in F, H.III, No. 17
with G. Lutsky vln, V. Solovyov vla &   Mezhdunarodnaya Kniga
B. Morozov vlc   D21803

KOSHA

Trio (1946) 2 vlns & vla
with G. Lutsky vln & V. Solovyov vla   Mezhdunarodnaya Kniga
D022065/6, S01902

MARTINŮ

Round dances 2 vlns, pf, ob, cl, bsn & tpt
with L. Shinder vln, G. Talrosé pf, V.   Mezhdunarodnaya Kniga
Grigorovich ob, A. Veinblat cl, A.   D22045/6, S1845/6
Topol bsn & G. Krylov tpt

MOZART

Concertone in C, K190 2 vlns, ob, vlc & orch.
with L. Shinder vln & Leningrad   Mezhdunarodnaya Kniga
Philharmonic Chamber Orch. –   D021255/6, S01597/8
Rabinovich

SABO

Trio (1927) 2 vlns & vla
with G. Lutsky vln & V. Solovyov vla   Mezhdunarodnaya Kniga
D21804

TANEIEV

Trio in D, Op. 21 2 vlns & vla
with G. Lutsky vln & V. Solovyov vla   Mezhdunarodnaya Kniga
D029888

Igor OZIM (1931–)

BEETHOVEN

Concerto in D, Op. 61 (cadenzas by Kreisler) vln & orch.
with Zagreb Philharmonic Symphony   Fontana 700154WGY, SFL14085
Orch. – Horvat   Jugoton 2209, 213112
Philips 610803VL, 838603VY
Wing WL1141

Romance No. 1, in G, Op. 40 vln & orch.
with Zagreb Philharmonic Symphony   Fontana 200130WGL,
Orch. – Horvat   700130WGY
Jugoton EP22206

Romance No. 2, in F, Op. 50 vln & orch.
with Zagreb Philharmonic Symphony   Fontana 200130WGL,
Orch. – Horvat   700130WGY
Jugoton EP22206

BRAHMS

Concerto in a, Op. 102 "Double" vln, vlc & orch.
with S. Palm vlc & Vienna Opera   Concert Hall SMCS2551
House Orch. – Atzmon

Sonata No. 3, in d, Op. 108 vln & pf
with piano   Argo ARL1015

DEBUSSY

(La) Plus que lente – valse (1910) pf – arr. vln & pf Roques
with M. Lipovšek pf   Jugoton 26300

LIPOVŠEK

Rhapsody vln & pf
with M. Lipovšek pf   Jugoton 0202

RAVEL

(2) Mélodies hébraïques v & pf
No. 1. Kaddisch arr. vln & pf Garban
with M. Lipovšek pf   Jugoton 26300

Pièce en forme d'Habanera v & pf – arr. vln & pf Catherine
with M. Lipovšek pf   Jugoton 26300

SCHUBERT

Rondo in A, D438 vln & str orch.
with Vienna Opera House Orch. –   Concert Hall SMCS2551
Atzmon

TCHAIKOVSKY

Concerto in D, Op. 35 vln & orch.
with Zagreb Philharmonic Symphony   Jugoton 2233, 213143
Orch. – Horvat

VITALI

Chaconne in g vln & c – arr. vln & pf Charlier
with M. Lipovšek pf   Jugoton 26301

VIVALDI

(12) Concerti, Op. 8 (1725) "Il Cimento dell' Armonia e dell' Invenzione"
(Nos 1/4: Le quattro Stagioni) vln & strs
Concerto No. 1, in E, F.I, No. 22 "La Primavera"
with Collegium Academicum de   Guilde International du Disque
Genève – Josefowitz   (in set SMS2676)

Concerto No. 2, in B flat, F.I, No. 23 "L'Estate"
with Collegium Academicum de   Guilde International du Disque
Genève – Josefowitz   (in set SMS2676)

Concerto No. 3, in F, F.I, No. 24 "L'Autunno"
with Collegium Academicum de   Guilde International du Disque
Genève – Josefowitz   (in set SMS2676)

Concerto No. 4, in f, F.I, No. 25 "L'Inverno"
with Collegium Academicum de   Guilde International du Disque
Genève – Josefowitz   (in set SMS2676)

Concerto No. 5, in E flat, F.I, No. 26 "La Tempesta di mare"
with Collegium Academicum de   Guilde International du Disque
Genève – Josefowitz   (in set SMS2676)

Concerto No. 6, in C, F.I, No. 26 "Il piacere"
with Collegium Academicum de   Guilde International du Disque
Genève – Josefowitz   (in set SMS2676)

Concerto No. 7, in d, F.I, No. 28 (P.258)
with Collegium Academicum de   Guilde International du Disque
Genève – Josefowitz   (in set SMS2676)

Concerto No. 8, in g, F.I, No. 16
with Collegium Academicum de   Guilde International du Disque
Genève – Josefowitz   (in set SMS2676)

Concerto No. 9, in d, F.VII, No. 1
with Collegium Academicum de   Guilde International du Disque
Genève – Josefowitz   (in set SMS2676)

Concerto No. 10, in B flat, F.I, No. 29 "La Caccia"
with Collegium Academicum de   Guilde International du Disque
Genève – Josefowitz   (in set SMS2676)

Concerto No. 11, in D, F.I, No. 30
with Collegium Academicum de   Guilde International du Disque
Genève – Josefowitz   (in set SMS2676)

VIVALDI – *Continued*

Concerto No. 12, in C, F.I, No. 31
with Collegium Academicum de   Guilde International du Disque
Genéve – Josefowitz   (in set SMS2676)

Joseph PACH

BACH
(6) Sonatas, BWV1014/9 vln & clav
Sonata No. 3, in E, BWV1016
with A. Nimmons pf   CBC Transcription Program 244

JONES
Introduction & Fugue (1959) vln & pf
with A. Nimmons pf   CBC Transcription Program 244

MORAWETZ
Duo (1946) vln & pf
with A. Nimmons pf   CBC Transcription Program 244

SOMERS
Rhapsody (1948) vln & pf
with A. Nimmons pf   CBC Transcription Program 244

Emanuel PAGANI

GOUNOD
Ave Maria (Méditation on Bach's "Prelude No. 1, in C" from Book I of
"Das Wohltemperirte Clavier") v & pf – arr. vln & pf
with piano   2929 Janus 1451

VERDI
(La) Traviata (1853) – opera
Prelude (Act I or III) orch. – arr. vln & pf
with piano   2930 Janus 1451

David PAGET

BOHM
(6) Miniatures, Op. 187 vln & pf
No. 4. Perpetuum mobile
with piano   Pathé 79255

IVANOVICI
Valurile Dunării "Danube waves" orch. – arr. vln & pf
with piano   Pathé 81, 79254

KREISLER
Andantino (Padre Martini) vln & pf
with piano   Pathé 79252

MASCAGNI
Cavalleria Rusticana (1890) – opera
Intermezzo orch. – arr. vln & pf
with piano   Pathé 81

SCHUMANN
(13) Kinderscenen, Op. 15 pf
No. 7. Träumerei arr. vln & pf
with piano   Pathé 79253

Ferenc PALINKO

GRIEG
Peer Gynt (Suite No. 1) Op. 46 orch.
No. 3. Anitra's dance arr. vln & pf Sitt
Peer Gynt (Suite No. 2) Op. 55 orch.   (untraced)
No. 4. Solveig's song arr. vln & pf Sitt
                                             (untraced)

Henryk PALULIS (1920–)

DVOŘÁK
(8) Slavonic Dances, Op. 72 pf duet; orch.
No. 2. Slavonic dance No. 10, in e – arr. vln & pf Kreisler
with J. Lefeld pf   Muza L0183

FALLA
(La) Vida Breve (1913) – opera
Danza española orch. – arr. vln & pf Kreisler
with J. Lefeld pf   Muza L0183

KREISLER
Liebesfreud vln & pf
with J. Lefeld pf   Muza L0183
Liebesleid vln & pf
with J. Lefeld pf   Muza L0183

SARASATE
Zigeunerweisen, Op. 20 vln & pf or orch.
with J. Lefeld pf   Muza L0183

SZYMANOWSKI
Concerto No. 2, Op. 61 (1932/3) vln & orch.*
with Moscow Radio Symphony Orch.   Mezhdunarodnaya Kniga
– Satanowski   D015055/6

TCHAIKOVSKY
Souvenir d'un lieu cher, Op. 42 vln & pf
No. 3. Mélodie
with J. Lefeld pf   Muza L0183

Manoug PARIKIAN (1920–)

BACH
(6) Brandenburg Concerti, BWV1046/51 (1721) strs & c
Brandenburg Concerto No. 2, in F, BWV1047 tpt, fl, ob, vln & strs
with H. Jackson tpt, G. Morris fl, S.   HMV ALP1084, FALP308
Sutcliffe ob, R. Clark vlc, E. Fischer pf Victor LHMV8
& Philharmonia orch. – Fischer

Brandenburg Concerto No. 5, in D, BWV1050 clav, fl, vln & strs
with E. Fischer pf, G. Morris fl, R.   HMV ALP1084, FALP308
Clark vlc   Victor LHMV8
& Philharmonic orch. – Fischer

Concerto No. 1, in a, BWV1041 vln, strs & c
with Baden Chamber Orch. –   Concert Hall M2148
Holtmann

Concerto No. 2, in E, BWV1042 vln, strs & c
with Baden Chamber Orch. –   Concert Hall M2148
Holtmann

* Recorded during an actual performance.

BACH – *Continued*

Mass in b, BWV232 (1733/7) s, a, t, b, cho, strs & c
with E. Schwarzkopf s, M. Höffgen a,   Angel 35015/7, (in set 3500)
N. Gedda t, H. Rehfuss bs, D. Brain   Columbia C80527, CX1121/3,
hrn, S. Sutcliffe ob, P. Newbury ob, G.   WSX544
Morris fl & Chorus & Orch. of the
Gesellschaft der Musikfreunde, Vienna
– von Karajan

Sonata in e, BWV1023 vln & c
with H. Holtmann hpsi & A. Molzahn   Concert Hall M2148
vlc

BERKELEY

Trio in e, Op. 19 (1952) vln, hrn & pf
with D. Brain hrn & C. Horsley pf   Capitol G7175
   HMV CLP1029, HQM1007
   Seraphim S60073

CROSSE

Concerto da camera, Op. 6 (1962) vln, w–wnds & pcn
with C. Hyde–Smith fl, P. Graeme ob,   HMV ALP2333, ASD2333
G. de Peyer cl, A. Jennings bs–cl, N.
Sanders hrn, J. Buck hrn, W.
Waterhouse bsn, D. Mason tpt, P.
Jones tpt, A. Flaszinski tbn, T. Fry
pcn, J. Lees pcn, cond. Downes

HANDEL

(12) Concerti grossi, Op. 6 (1739) 2 vlns, vlc & strs
  Concerto grosso No. 5, in D
with M. Salpeter   2EA 14480/3–1   HMV C7852/3
vln, R. Clark vlc, E. Lush hpsi &
Philharmonia Orch. – Markevitch

HOLST

St. Paul's Suite (1913) orch.
  Intermezzo
with Philharmonia Orch. – Weldon   Columbia S1100, SED5572

MASSENET

Thaïs (1894) – opera
  Méditation
with Philharmonia Orch. – von   Angel 35207
Karajan   Columbia CX1265, FCX407,
   QCX10150
   HMV LALP271, 7ERL1111

MOZART

Concerto No. 1, in B flat, K207 vln & orch.
with Amsterdam Philharmonic Society   Concert Hall CM2206, M2206
– Goehr

Concerto No. 3, in G, K216 vln & orch.
with Hamburg Chamber Orch. –   Concert Hall CM2092, M2092
Goehr   Harmony HL7174

Concerto No. 4, in D, K218 (cadenzas by Joachim) vln & orch.
with Hamburg Chamber Orch. –   Concert Hall CM2092, M2092
Goehr   Harmony HL7174

Concerto No. 5, in A, K219 "Turkish" vln & orch.
with Amsterdam Philharmonic Society   Concert Hall CM2206, M2206
– Goehr

MOZART – *Continued*

Serenade No. 6, in D, K239 "Serenata Notturna" orch.
with D. Wise vln, H. Downes vla, J.E.   Angel 35401
Merrett cbs & Philharmonia Orch. –   Columbia C90540, CX1438
Klemperer   HMV CLP1061, LALP539,
   7ERL1426

MUSGRAVE

Colloquy (1960) vln & pf
with L. Crowson pf   Argo RG328, ZRG5328

RAWSTHORNE

Sonata (1959) vln & pf
with L. Crowson pf   Argo RG328, ZRG5328

RIMSKY–KORSAKOV

Scheherazade, Op. 35 (1888) orch.
with Philharmonia Orch. – Stokowski   HMV ALP1339
   Victor LM1732

VIVALDI

(12) Concerti, Op. 8 (1725) "Il Cimento dell' Armonia e dell' Invenzione"
(Nos. 1/4: Le quattro Stagioni) vln & strs
  Concerto No. 1, in E, F.I, No. 22 "La Primavera"
with Philharmonia Orch. – Giulini   Angel 35216
   Columbia CX1365, FCX525
   HMV XLP30058

  Concerto No. 2, in B flat, F.I, No. 23 "L'Estate"
with Philharmonia Orch. – Giulini   Angel 35216
   Columbia CX1365, FCX525
   HMV XLP30058

  Concerto No. 3, in F, F.I, No. 24 "L'Autunno"
with Philharmonia Orch. – Giulini   Angel 35216
   Columbia CX1365, FCX525
   HMV XLP30058

  Concerto No. 4, in f, F.I, No. 25 "L'Inverno"
with Philharmonia Orch. – Giulini   Angel 35216
   Columbia CX1365, FCX525
   HMV XLP30058

István PÁRKÁNYI

HAJDÚ

Little Suite 2 vlns & vlc
  Rondo & Serenade
with E. Menyhért vln & I. Záhorszky   Qualiton LPX1188
vlc

Olgar PARKHOMENKO

KOSENKO

Sonata, Op. 18 vln & pf
with L. Levina pf   Mezhdunarodnaya Kniga D6833

MOZART

Concerto No. 5, in A, K219 "Turkish" (cadenzas by Joachim) vln & orch.
with Moscow Radio Symphony Orch.   Mezhdunarodnaya Kniga
– Gauk   D04166/7

PROKOFIEV

Cinderella, Op. 87 (1941/4) – ballet orch.
  Mazurka arr. vln & pf Fichtenholz
  with L. Levina pf   Mezhdunarodnaya Kniga D6398,
                   D6834

  Waltz arr. vln & pf Fichtenholz
  with L. Levina pf   Mezhdunarodnaya Kniga D6398,
                   D6834

REVUTSKY

Intermezzo vln & pf
  with L. Levina pf   Mezhdunarodnaya Kniga D6834

STATKOVSKI

Cracovienne, Op. 7 "Krakowiak" vln & pf
  with L. Levina pf   Mezhdunarodnaya Kniga D6834

Kathleen PARLOW (1890–1963)

ARENSKY

(4) Morceaux, Op. 30 vln & pf
  No. 2. Serenade in G
  with orch.   36920–2   Columbia A5588, L1070

BACH

(3) Sonatas & 3 Partitas, BWV1001/6 solo vln
  Partita No. 3, in E: Gavotte (3rd mvt) BWV1006
  (unaccompanied)   36920–2   Columbia A5588, L1070
(4) Suites, BWV1066/9 strs & c
  Suite No. 3, in D: Air (2nd mvt) BWV1068 2 obs, 3 tpts, drms, strs & c
  – arr. vln & pf as "Air on the G–string" by Wilhelmj
  with piano   HMV 3–7918

BEETHOVEN

(6) Minuets, G167 pf
  No. 2. Minuet No. 2, in G arr. vln & pf Burmester
  with piano   Edison cylinder 28192
  No. 2. Minuet No. 2, in G arr. vln & pf Burmester
  with orch.   19910–2   Columbia A1199
  No. 2. Minuet No. 2, in G arr. vln & pf Burmester
  with orch.   46684–2   Columbia A2162, D1360

CHOPIN

(3) Nocturnes, Op. 9 pf
  No. 2. Nocturne No. 2, in E flat, arr. vln & pf Sarasate
  with R. Gayler pf   Edison cylinder 28142
  No. 2. Nocturne No. 2, in E flat arr. vln & pf Sarasate
  with orch.   36391–1   Columbia A5431, D17701, L1081
  No. 2. Nocturne No. 2, in E flat arr. vln & pf Sarasate
  with C.A. Prince pf   48706–2   Columbia A5992
(2) Nocturnes, Op. 27 pf
  No. 2. Nocturne No. 8, in D flat arr. vln & pf Wilhelmj
  with piano   HMV 07920

DRIGO

(2) Airs de Ballet orch.
  No. 2. Valse bluette arr. vln & pf Auer
  with R. Gayler pf   Edison cylinder 28192
  No. 2. Valse bluette arr. vln & pf Auer
  with orch.   Columbia A1241, D1364

DRIGO – *Continued*

  No. 2. Valse bluette arr. vln & pf Auer
  with C.A. Prince pf   46722–2   Columbia A2162
(Les) Millions d'Arlequin (1900) – ballet orch.
  Sérénade arr. vln & pf Auer
  with C.A. Prince pf   48604–2   Columbia 48604, A5798, L1181

DVOŘÁK

(8) Humoresques, Op. 101 pf
  No. 7. Humoresque No. 7, in G flat arr. vln & pf "in G" Wilhelmj
  with orch.   36392–1   Columbia A5412, L1080
Sonatina in G, Op. 100 vln & pf
  Larghetto (2nd mvt) arr. vln & pf as "Indian lament" by Kreisler
  with C.A. Prince pf   48607–4   Columbia 48607, A5798, L1181

FREEDMAN

(5) Pieces (1949) 2 vlns, vla & vlc
  with S. Hersenhoren vln, S. Solomon   CBC Transcription Program 43
  vla & I. Mamott vlc

HALVORSEN

(3) Danses norvègiennes (1914) vln & pf
  Danse norvègienne*
  with piano   HMV 07919

(4) Mosaïques (Suite des morceaux caractéristiques) vln & pf
  No. 4. Chant de Veslemøy
  with piano   HMV 07919

KREISLER

Liebesfreud vln & pf
  with orch.   36379–3   Columbia A5431, D17701, L1081
Tambourin chinois, Op. 3 vln & pf
  with C.A. Prince pf   48608–2   Columbia A5819

MASCAGNI

Cavalleria Rusticana (1890) – opera
  Intermezzo orch. – arr. vln & orch.
  with orch.   48663–3   Columbia A5908, L1224

MASSENET

Thaïs (1894) – opera
  Méditation arr. vln & pf Marsick
  with C.A. Prince pf   48606–1   Columbia A5843

MENDELSSOHN

Concerto in e, Op. 64 vln & orch.
  Andante (2nd mvt)
  with orch.   48665–1   Columbia A5843

MOORE

(The) Last rose of summer v & pf – arr. vln & pf Auer
  with orch.   Columbia A1241
(The) Last rose of summer v & pf – arr. vln & pf Auer
  with orch.   46692–1   Columbia A2121, D1360

PAGANINI

Moto perpetuo (Allegro di concert) Op. 11 (1830) vln & orch.
  with piano   HMV 3–7917

* Unidentified.

REGER

Quartet No. 5, in F sharp, Op. 121 2 vlns, vla & vlc
Allegro expressivo
with S. Hersenhoren vln, S. Solomon   CBC Transcription Program 43
vla & I. Mamott vlc

RUBINSTEIN

(2) Melodies, Op. 3 pf
No. 1. Melody in F arr. vln & pf Wilhelmj
with orch.   36393–1–3   Columbia A5588, L1080

SARASATE

Carmen Fantasia (on themes from the opera by Bizet) Op. 25 vln & pf or
orch.
with C.A. Prince pf   48705–1   Columbia A5992
                          Rococo 2001

SCHUBERT

(6) Moments musicaux, Op. 94 (D780) (1823/7) pf
No. 3. Moment musicale No. 3, in f "Air russe" arr. vln & pf Auer
with orch.   19863–1   Columbia A1199
No. 3. Moment musicale No. 3, in f "Air russe" arr. vln & pf Kreisler
with orch.   46685–1   Columbia A2121, D1366

SVENDSEN

Romance in G, Op. 26 vln & orch. – arr. vln & pf Wilhelmj
with C.A. Prince pf   48700–2   Columbia A5819

TCHAIKOVSKY

Souvenir d'un lieu cher, Op. 42 vln & pf
No. 3. Mélodie
with R. Gayler pf   4624   Edison cylinder 29038
                        Edison Diamond Disc 80326
No. 3. Mélodie
with orch.   36378–1   Columbia A5412, L1070

WIENIAWSKI

Fantasia brillante (on themes from the opera "Faust" by Gounod) Op. 20
vln & orch.
Garden scene
with orch.   48662–4   Columbia A5908, L1224

Sascha PARNES (1909–   )

ACHRON

Hebrew melodie, Op. 33 vln & pf – arr. Auer
with J. Páleníček pf   44921   Supraphon C22581

BEN–HAIM

Berceuse vln & pf
with J. Páleníček pf   44920   Supraphon C22581
                        Ultraphon A24369

MARTINŮ

Sonata No. 2 (1933) vln & pf
with J. Páleníček pf   Ultraphon G14895/6

POLIAKIN

(Le) Canari (Concert–polka) vln & pf
with J. Páleníček pf   Ultraphon A24369

G. PARSHIN

DZUTOYEV

Elegy vln & orch.
with North Ossetian Radio Orch. –   Mezhdunarodnaya Kniga
Ovechkin   D00018316

André PASCAL (1894–   )

ANONYMOUS

Christ Kindel (Austrian carol) v & ₁f
with E. Rokyta s   PART 1406   L'Oiseau–Lyre OL89

HONEGGER

(La) Danse des Morts (1938) – oratorio
Lamento
with C. Panzéra b & Gouverné Chorus   HMV DB5136
& Conservatory Orch. – Munch

SAINT–SAËNS

Sonata No. 1, in d, Op. 75 vln & pf
       CPTX 73/5–1, 77–1 & 80/1–1   Columbia 71211/3D, 71214/6D,
with I. Philipp pf   (set M471)
                                       Pathé PAT15/7

T. PASQUALI

VIVALDI

Concerto in C, P.84 (F.XII, No. 14) "Per la Solennità di St. Lorenzo" 2 fls,
2 obs, 2 cls, 2 vlns, bsn, strs & c
with U. Benedetti Michelangeli vln, P.   Angelicum STA9017
Salvi vlc, A. Berruti hpsi & Angelicum
Orch., Milan – Martinotti
Concerto in B flat, P.367 (F.I, No. 59) 4 vlns, strs & c
with M. Abbado vln, L. d'Annibale   Columbia FCX369
vln, M. Borgo vln & Milan String
Orch. – Abbado

Jean PASQUIER (1903–   )

ABACO

(12) Sonatas, Op. 3 (1714) 2 vlns & c
Sonata No. 2, in F
with J. Fournier vln, R.   AS 95/6–1   L'Anthologie Sonore 46
Gerlin hpsi & E. Pasquier vlc   Haydn Society HSLP13

BACH

Concerto No. 1, in a, BWV1041 vln, strs & c
Andante (2nd mvt)
with orch. – Cébron   Lumen 30088, 206011

COUPERIN, F.

(Les) Nations – 4 Suites (1726) 2 vlns & c
Suite No. 1, in e "La Françoise"
with H. Fernandez vln, R. Boulay vla,   Music Guild M21, MG108,
J–P. Rampal fl, R. Gendre vln & L.   MS108, S21
Boulay hpsi

COUPERIN, F. – Continued

Suite No. 2, in c "L'Espagnole"
with H. Fernandez vln, R. Boulay vla,   Music Guild M21, MG108,
J–P. Rampal fl, R. Gendre vln & L.   MS108, S21
Boulay hpsi

Suite No. 3, in d "L'Impériale"
with H. Fernandez vln, R. Boulay vla,   Music Guild M21, MG108,
J–P. Rampal fl, R. Gendre vln & L.   MS108, S21
Boulay hpsi

Suite No. 4, in g "La Piémontoise"
with H. Fernandez vln, R. Boulay vla,   Music Guild M21, MG108,
J–P. Rampal fl, R. Gendre vln & L.   MS108, S21
Boulay hpsi

HAYDN

(6) Divertimenti, H.IV, Nos. 6/11x) (Op. 100) fl, vln & vlc
  Divertimento No. 1, in D, H.IV, No. 6
  with R. le Roy fl & E. Pasquier vlc   Musicraft 1071/4, (in set 17)
  Divertimento No. 2, in G, H.IV, No. 7
  with R. le Roy fl & E. Pasquier vlc   Musicraft 1071/4, (in set 17)
  Divertimento No. 4, in G, H.IV, No. 9
  with R. le Roy fl & E. Pasquier vlc   Musicraft 1071/4, (in set 17)
  Divertimento No. 6, in D, H.IV, No. 11
  with R. le Roy fl & E. Pasquier vlc   Musicraft 1071/4, (in set 17)
  Divertimento No. 6, in D, H.IV, No. 11
  with J–P. Rampal fl & E. Pasquier vlc   La Boîte à Musique 203

MESSIAEN

Quartet (1940) "For the end of time" pf, cl, vln & vlc
with O. Messiaen pf, A. Vacellier cl &   Record Society RS14
E. Pasquier vlc

MOZART

Duo No. 1, in G, K423 vln & vla
          PART 1769/72–1   Discophiles français 21/2, (in set
with P. Pasquier vla   4)

Duo No. 2, in B flat, K424 vln & vla
with P. Pasquier   PART 1773/6–1   Discophiles français 23/4, (in set
vla   4)

(Il) Re Pastore, K208 (1775) – opera
  No. 10. L'amerò, sarò costante
  with M. angelici s & orch. – Cébron   L'Anthologie Sonore 118

PURCELL

(10) Sonatas, Z802/11 (1697) 4 parts – 2 vlns & c
  Sonata No. 9, in F, Z810 "Golden Sonata"
  with P. Ferret vln, R.   AS 52/3   L'Anthologie Sonore 22
  Gerlin hpsi & E. Pasquier vlc

RAMEAU

(5) Pièces de Clavecin en Concerts (1741) hpsi, vln & c
  Concert No. 5, in d
  with P. Aubert hpsi &   AS 78/9–1   L'Anthologie Sonore 30
  E. Heinitz gamba

TELEMANN

Concerto in D 4 vlns, strs & c
with J. Dejean vln, G. Gaunet vln, F.   Éditions phonographiques
Geyr vln & Paris Collegium Musette –   parisiennes APG125
Douatte

Régis PASQUIER (1914–)

BACH

Concerto in a, BWV1044 clav, fl, vln, strs & c
with R. Gerlin hpsi, M. Larrieu fl &   Critère CRD181, SCRD5181
Collegium Musicum, Paris – Douatte   Eurodisc S73495KK
  Nonesuch (in sets HE3001 &
  HE73001

LEHÁR

Paganini (1925) – operetta
  Zigeunerfest (Act II)
  with Orch. de la Société des Concerts   Pathé ASTX130501, DTX30501
  du Conservatoire – Pourcel

PAGANINI

(18) Centone di Sonate, Op. 64 (1828) vln & gtr
  Sonata No. 1, in A
  with O. Ghiglia gtr   HMV ASDF848, FALP848
  Sonata No. 2, in D
  with O. Ghiglia gtr   HMV ASDF848, FALP848
  Sonata No. 3, in C
  with O. Ghiglia gtr   HMV ASDF848, FALP848
  Sonata No. 4, in A
  with O. Ghiglia gtr   HMV ASDF848, FALP848
  Sonata No. 5, in E
  with O. Ghiglia gtr   HMV ASDF848, FALP848
  Sonata No. 6, in A
  with O. Ghiglia gtr   HMV ASDF848, FALP848

Grande Sonata in A, Op. 39 gtr with vln acc
with O. Ghiglia gtr   HMV ASDF849, CLP3511,
  CSD3511, CVA849, FALP849

(6) Sonatas, Op. 3 (1801/6) vln & gtr
  No. 1. Sonata No. 7, in A
  with O. Ghiglia gtr   HMV ASDF849, CLP3511,
  CSD3511, CVA849, FALP849
  No. 2. Sonata No. 8, in G
  with O. Ghiglia gtr   HMV ASDF849, CLP3511,
  CSD3511, CVA849, FALP849
  No. 3. Sonata No. 9, in D
  with O. Ghiglia gtr   HMV ASDF849, CLP3511,
  CSD3511, CVA849, FALP849
  No. 4. Sonata No. 10, in a
  with O. Ghiglia gtr   HMV ASDF849, CLP3511,
  CSD3511, CVA849, FALP849
  No. 5. Sonata No. 11, in A
  with O. Ghiglia gtr   HMV ASDF849, CLP3511,
  CSD3511, CVA849, FALP849
  No. 6. Sonata No. 12, in e
  with O. Ghiglia gtr   HMV ASDF849, CLP3511,
  CSD3511, CVA849, FALP849

Tarantella in a, Op. 33 vln & orch.
with O. Ghiglia gtr   HMV ASDF849, CLP3511,
  CSD3511, CVA849, FALP849

György PAUK (1936–)

BARTÓK

Contrasts (1938) cl, vln & pf
  with B. Kovács cl & P. Frankl pf — Erato EFM42060
Qualiton LP3509

MOZART

Concerto No. 4, in D, K218 (cadenzas by Joachim) vln & orch.
  with Württemberg Chamber Orch. – Supermajestic SBBH1860
  Faerber — Turnabout TV4186, TV34186

Concerto No. 5, in A, K219 "Turkish" (cadenzas by Joachim) vln & orch.
  with Württemberg Chamber Orch. – The Great Musicians TGM12
  Faerber — Supermajestic SBBH1860
Turnabout TV4186, TV34186

Sonata No. 17, in C, K296 vln & pf
  with P. Frankl pf — Vox (in sets SVBX546 & VBX46)

Sonata No. 18, in G, K301 vln & pf
  with P. Frankl pf — Vox (in sets SVBX546 & VBX46)

Sonata No. 19, in E flat, K302 vln & pf
  with P. Frankl pf — Vox (in sets SVBX546 & VBX46)

Sonata No. 20, in C, K303 vln & pf
  with P. Frankl pf — Vox (in sets SVBX546 & VBX46)

Sonata No. 21, in e, K304 vln & pf
  with P. Frankl pf — Vox (in sets SVBX 546 & VBX46)

Sonata No. 22, in A, K305 vln & pf
  with P. Frankl pf — Vox (in sets SVBX546 & VBX46)

Sonata No. 23, in D, K306 vln & pf
  with P. Frankl pf — Vox (in sets SVBX546 & VBX46)

Sonata No. 24, in F, K376 vln & pf
  with P. Frankl pf — Vox (in sets SVBX546 & VBX46)

Sonata No. 25, in F, K377 vln & pf
  with P. Frankl pf — Vox (in sets SVBX546 & VBX46)

Sonata No. 26, in B flat, K378 vln & pf
  with P. Frankl pf — Vox (in sets SVBX546 & VBX46)

Sonata No. 27, in G, K379 vln & pf
  with P. Frankl pf — Vox (in sets SVBX547 & VBX47)

Sonata No. 28, in E flat, K380 vln & pf
  with P. Frankl pf — Vox (in sets SVBX547 & VBX47)

Sonata No. 29, in A, K402 vln & pf
  with P. Frankl pf — Vox (in sets SVBX547 & VBX47)

Sonata No. 32, in B flat, K454 vln & pf
  with P. Frankl pf — Vox (in sets SVBX547 & VBX47)

Sonata No. 33, in E flat, K481 vln & pf
  with P. Frankl pf — Vox (in sets SVBX547 & VBX47)

MOZART – *Continued*

Sonata No. 34, in A, K526 vln & pf
  with P. Frankl pf — Vox (in sets SVBX547 & VBX47)

Sonata No. 35, in F, K547 vln & pf
  with P. Frankl pf — Vox (in sets SVBX547 & VBX47)

(12) Variations (on "La Bergere Célimène") K359 vln & pf
  with P. Frankl pf — Vox (in sets SVBX547 & VBX47)

(6) Variations (on "Hélas, j'ai perdu mon amant") K360 vln & pf
  with P. Frankl pf — Vox (in sets SVBX547 & VBX47)

SCHUBERT

Fantasia in C, Op. 159 (D934) vln & pf
  with P. Frankl pf — Vox (in sets SVBX569 & VBX69)

Rondo brillante in b, Op. 70 (D895) vln & pf
  with P. Frankl pf — Vox (in sets SVBX569 & VBX69)

Sonata in A, Op. 162 (D574) "Duo" vln & pf
  with P. Frankl pf — Vox (in sets SVBX569 & VBX69)

(3) Sonatinas, Op. 137 (D384, D385 & D408) vln & pf
No. 1. Sonatina No. 1, in D, D384
  with P. Frankl pf — Vox (in sets SVBX569 & VBX69)

No. 2. Sonatina No. 2, in A, D385
  with P. Frankl pf — Vox (in sets SVBX569 & VBX69)

No. 3. Sonatina No. 3, in g, D408
  with P. Frankl pf — Vox (in sets SVBX569 & VBX69)

SCHUMANN

Quintet in E flat, Op. 44 pf, 2 vlns, vla & vlc
  with P. Frankl pf, J. Szekács vln, E. Deutsche Grammophon
  Schiffer vla & A. Szász vlc — LPE17132

TCHAIKOVSKY

Concerto in D, Op. 35 vln & orch.
  with London Philharmonic Orch. – Mode MD9051
  Stern — Pye GGL0119
Somerset SM544
Stereo Fidelity 14500

Eugenius PAULAUSKAS

FRANCK

Sonata in A (1886) vln & pf
  with T. Nikolayeva pf — Mezhdunarodnaya Kniga
D17957/8

GROUDIS

(3) Dances vln & pf
  with piano — Mezhdunarodnaya Kniga
D009587/8

GROUDIS – *Continued*

Sonata in d vln & pf
with G. Trinkunas pf   Mezhdunarodnaya Kniga
D016880

JUZELIUNAS
Concerto vln, org & orch.
with L. Digris org & Lithuanian SSR   Mezhdunarodnaya Kniga
Philharmonic Chamber Orch. –   D017271
Sondeckis

Benedetto PAVELLA

VIVALDI
(12) Concerti, Op. 8 (1725) "Il Cimento dell' Armonia e dell' Invenzione"
(Nos. 1/4: Le quattro Stagioni) vln & strs
Concerto No. 1, in E, F.I, No. 22 "La Primavera"
with Parma Collegium Musicum –   Classics Club X4004
Pervido

Concerto No. 2, in B flat, F.I, No. 23 "L'Estate"
with Parma Collegium Musicum –   Classics Club X4004
Pervido

Concerto No. 3, in F, F.I, No. 24 "L'Autunno"
with Parma Collegium Musicum –   Classics Club X4004
Pervido

Concerto No. 4, in f, F.I, No. 25 "L'Inverno"
with Parma Collegium Musicum –   Classics Club X4004
Pervido

Aleksandar PAVLOVIČ (1929–)

BLOCH
Baal Shem (3 Pictures of Chassidic life) (1923) vln & pf*
with R. Levin pf   Jugoton 212

DEBUSSY
Sonata No. 3, in g (1917) vln & pf
with R. Levin pf   Jugoton 211

DVOŘÁK
Sonatina in G, Op. 100 vln & pf†
with R. Levin pf   Jugoton 212

SLAVENSKI
Sonata, Op. 5 vln & pf
with R. Levin pf   Jugoton 211

Knud PEDERSEN

HENRIQUES
Romance in D, Op. 43 vln & pf – arr. 2 vlns & pf Henriques
with F.V. Henriques vln &   1281 ak   HMV K88022, V101
piano

---

* Nigun or 2nd mvt is also on Jugoton 26350.
† Larghetto or 2nd mvt is also on Jugoton 26350.

Edith PEINEMANN (1937–)

DVOŘÁK
Concerto in a, Op. 53 vln & orch.
with Czech Philharmonic Orch. –   Deutsche Grammophon
Maag   LPM39120, SLPM139120

RAVEL
Tzigane (Rapsodie de concert) (1924) vln & pf or orch.
with Czech Philharmonic Orch. –   Deutsche Grammophon 135147,
Maag   LPM39120, SLPM139120

P. D. PELAZ

VIVALDI
(12) Concerti, Op. 3 "L'Estro armonico" var. cbns & strs
Concerto No. 10, in b, P.148 (F.IV, No. 10) 4 vlns, strs & c
with C. Crenne vln, A. Moglia vln, J–   Classic 991062
P. Wallez vln, M. Roche hpsi & Paris
Instrumental Ensemble – Wallez

Arrigo PELLICCIA (1912–)

ALBINONI
(12) Concerti, Op. 9 (1722) var. cbns & strs
Concerto No. 7, in D vln & strs
with Virtuosi di Roma – Fasano   Brunswick AXTL1023
Decca DL9598, UAT273581
Fonit LP3003

BEETHOVEN
Trio in B flat, Op. 11 cl, vlc & pf – arr. pf, vln & vlc
with O. Santoliquido pf & M.   Fonit LPU0014
Amfitheatrof vlc

(2) Trios, Op. 70 pf, vln & vlc
No. 1. Trio No. 4, in D "Ghost"
with O. Santoliquido pf & M.   Deutsche Grammophon
Amfitheatrof vlc   LPM18044
Heliodor 478142

Trio No. 6, in B flat, Op. 97 "Archduke" pf, vln & vlc
with O. Santoliquido pf & M.   Fonit LPU0014
Amfitheatrof vlc

(10) Variations (on "Ich bin der Schneider Kakadu") Op. 121a pf, vln & vlc
with O. Santoliquido pf & M.   Deutsche Grammophon
Amfitheatrof vlc   LPM18044

BONPORTI
(10) Concerti, Op. 11 strs
Concerto No. 5, in F: Adagio (2nd mvt) "Recitativo"
with Naples Royal Conservatory   HMV DB05351
Chamber Orch. – Lauldi

BRAHMS
Quartet No. 1, in g, Op. 25 pf, vln, vla & vlc
with O. Santoliquido pf, B. Giuranna   Deutsche Grammophon
vla & M. Amfitheatrof vlc   LPM18529, SLPM138014

Quartet No. 2, in A, Op. 26 pf, vln, vla & vlc
with O. Santoliquido pf, B. Giuranna   Deutsche Grammophon
vla & M. Amfitheatrof vlc   LPM18529, SLPM138014

BRAHMS – *Continued*

Quartet No. 3, in c, Op. 60 pf, vln, vla & vlc
  with O. Santoliquido pf, B. Giuranna   Deutsche Grammophon 135001,
  vla & M. Amfitheatrof vlc   LPE17180

DINICU

Hora staccato vln & pf – arr. vln & orch.
  with chamber orch.   T1503   Durium A9209

MENDELSSOHN

Trio No. 1, in d, Op. 49 pf, vln & vlc
  with O. Santoliquido pf & M.   Deutsche Grammophon LP16107
  Amfitheatrof vlc

PERGOLESI

Concerto in B flat vln & strs – ed. Lualdi
  with Naples Royal Conservatory   HMV DB05350/1
  Chamber Orch. – Lualdi

Tre giorni son che Nina v & c – arr. vln, vlc & cha orch.
  with G. Menegozzi vlc &   T 1504   Durium A9209
  chamber orch.

SCHUBERT

Trio No. 1, in B flat, Op. 99 (D898) pf, vln & vlc
  with O. Santoliquido pf & M.   Deutsche Grammophon
  Amfitheatrof vlc   LPM18261
                           Heliodor 478142

VIVALDI

(12) Concerti, Op. 3 "L'Estro armonico" var. cbns & strs
  Concerto No. 10, in b, P.148 (F.IV, No. 10) 4 vlns, strs & c
  with A. Gremegna vln, L. Ferro vln,   Cetra BB25291/2
  E. Malanotte vln & Rome Collegium
  Musicum – Fasano

Concerto in C, P.58 vln, 2 vlcs, strs & c
  with M. Amfitheatrof vlc, B.   Brunswick AXTL1061
  Mazzacurati vlc & Virtuosi di Roma –   Decca DL9679
  Fasano   Fonit LP3002

Concerto in B flat, P.388 (F.IV, No. 2) (Op. 22, No. 1) vln, vlc, strs & c
  with M. Amfitheatrof vlc & Virtuosi di   Columbia CCL35012
  Roma – Fasano   Decca DL9684, UAT273574

Concerto in B flat, P.406 (F.XII, No. 16) vln, ob, strs & c
  with R. Zanfini ob & Virtuosi di Roma   Columbia CCL35012
  – Fasano   Decca DL9684, UAT273574

Concerto in c, P.419 (F.I, No. 2) (Op. 51, No. 3) "Il Sospetto" vln, strs & c
  with Virtuosi di Roma – Fasano   Brunswick AXA4505
                      Decca DL9729, UAT273589

Manuel PEREDIAZ

HALFFTER–ESCRICHE

Sonatina (1928) – ballet orch.
  No. 4. Danza de la gitana arr. vln & pf Manso
  with N. Figueroa pf   Pathé PAT83

SARASATE

(8) Danzas españolas vln & pf
  No. 3. Romanza andaluza, Op. 22, No. 1
  with N. Figueroa pf   Pathé PAT83

Antonio PEREZ (1936–)

BUCCHI

Concerto lirico (1959) vln & orch.
  with Orchestra da Camera Accademia   Golden Crest CR4078
  Musicale Napoletana – Guarino

PERGOLESI

Sonata (in the style of a Concerto) vln & strs – arr. Caffarelli
  with Orchestra da Camera Accademia   Golden Crest CR4078
  Musicale Napoletana – Guarino

Itzhak PERLMAN (1945–)

BRAHMS

Trio in E flat, Op. 40 hrn, pf & vln
  with V. Ashkenazy pf & B. Tuckwell   Decca SXL6408
  hrn   London CS6628

DVOŘÁK

Romance in f, Op. 11 vln & orch.
  with Boston Symphony Orch. –   Victor LM3014, LSC3014,
  Leinsdorf   SB6768

FRANCK

Sonata in A (1886) vln & pf
  with V. Ashkenazy pf   Decca SXL6408
                    London CS6628

LALO

Symphonie espagnole, Op. 21 vln & orch.*
  with London Symphony Orch. –   Victor LSC3073, SB6800
  Previn

PROKOFIEV

Concerto No. 2, in g, Op. 63 vln & orch.
  with Boston Symphony Orch. –   Victor LM2962, LSC2962,
  Leinsdorf   RB6722, SB6722

Sonata No. 1, in f, Op. 80 vln & pf
  with V. Ashkenazy pf   Victor LSC3118

Sonata No. 2, in D, Op. 94bis vln & pf
  with V. Ashkenazy pf   Victor LSC3118

RAVEL

Tzigane (Rapsodie de concert) (1924) vln & pf or orch.
  with London Symphony Orch. –   Victor LSC3073, SB6800
  Previn

SIBELIUS

Concerto in d, Op. 47 vln & orch.
  with Boston Symphony Orch. –   Victor LM2962, LSC2962,
  Leinsdorf   RB6722, SB6722

TCHAIKOVSKY

Concerto in D, Op. 35 vln & orch.
  with Boston Symphony Orch. –   Victor LM3014, LSC3014,
  Leinsdorf   SB6768

* Including Intermezzo.

Louis PERSINGER (1887–1967)

HANDEL
(16) Suites (1720/33) hpsi
  Suite No. 7, in g: Passacaglia (6th mvt) arr. vln & vla Halvorsen
  with R. Persinger vla   Contrepoint MC20076
         Stradivari STR608

MENDELSSOHN
Concerto in e, Op. 64 vln & orch.*
  with piano   Period STR101

MOZART
Duo No. 1, in G, K423 vln & vla
  with R. Persinger vla   Stradivari SLP1002

PROKOFIEV
Sonata in C, Op. 56 2 vlns
  with A. Eidus vln   Stradivari SLP1002

VILLA–LOBOS
Duo (1946) vln & vla
  with R. Persinger vla   Contrepoint MC20076
         Stradivari STR608

Robert PERUTZ (1886–   )

BARNS
Swing song vln & pf
  with T.P. Williams pf   11822   Gennett C3

GARDNER
(2) Pieces, Op. 5 vln & pf
  No. 1. From the canebrake
  with T.P. Williams pf   11822   Gennett C3

WIENIAWSKI
Capriccio–valse, Op. 7 vln & pf
  with T.P. Williams pf   11819   Gennett C3

Josef PEŠKA (1906–   )

BEETHOVEN
Quartet No. 15, in a, Op. 132 2 vlns, vla & vlc
  with F. Vohanka vln, J. Svoboda vla & Supraphon LPV172
  J. Háša vlc

BURIAN
Quartet No. 2 (1929) 2 vlns, vla & vlc
  with F. Vohanka vln, J. Svoboda vla & Ultraphon G14899/900
  J. Háša vlc

Quartet No. 3 (1940) 2 vlns, vla & vlc
  with F. Vohanka vln, J. Svoboda vla & Supraphon G22833/4
  J. Háša vlc   Ultraphon G14444/5
Sonata romantica (1938) vln & pf
  with J.H. Tichy pf   Ultraphon G14484/5

* Lecture illustration by Persinger.

ERKIN
Quartet 2 vlns, vla & vlc
  with F. Vohanka vln, J. Svoboda vla & Supraphon G22960/1
  J. Háša vlc

HÁBA
Fantasy, Op. 9a (1921) solo vln
  (unaccompanied)   40445/6   Supraphon B22160
         Ultraphon B11067

JEŽEK
Sonata vln & pf
  with V. Holzknecht pf   Supraphon 4350/1, G23301/2
         Ultraphon G14880/1

NEJEDLŸ
Quartet, Op. 12 2 vlns, vla & vlc
  with F. Vohanka vln, J. Svoboda vla & Supraphon G22983/4
  J. Háša vlc   Ultraphon G15207/8

SCHULHOFF
Quartet No. 1 2 vlns, vla & vlc
  with F. Vohanka vln, J. Svoboda vla & Supraphon G22833/4
  J. Háša vlc   Ultraphon G15127/8

Carlos PESSINA (1897–   )

CHOPIN
(3) Nocturnes, Op. 9 pf
  No. 2. Nocturne No. 2, in E flat arr. vln & pf Sarasate
  with R. Locatelli pf   Victor 13791

FALLA
(El) Sombrero de Tre Picos (1919) – ballet orch.
  No. 2. Danza del molinero arr. vln & pf Szigeti
  with orch.   Odeon 57016

GILARDI
Aires pampeanos vln & pf
  with R. Gonzalez pf   Victor 10–1108

MASSENET
Thaïs (1894) – opera
  Méditation
  with Colon Theatre Orch. – Martini   Odeon 66020, BSOA4003,
         BSOAE4513

MENDELSSOHN
(3) Quartets, Op. 44 2 vlns, vla & vlc
  No. 2. Quartet No. 4, in e: Scherzo (2nd mvt)
  (as leader of Pessina String Quartet)   Odeon 66046, LDC510

PANIZZA
Quartet in c 2 vlns, vla & vlc
  (as leader of Pessina String Quartet)   Odeon LDC527

RAFF
(3) Quartets, Op. 192 2 vlns, vla & vlc
  No. 2. Quartet No. 7, in D "The Mill"
  (as leader of Pessina String Quartet)   Odeon 66060, LDC510

SAINT–SAËNS

(Le) Carnaval des animaux (1886) small orch.
    Le cygne arr. vln & orch.
    with Colon Theatre Orch. – Martini   Odeon 66020

(Le) Déluge, Op. 45 (1876) – oratorio
    Prélude vln & orch.
    with Colon Theatre Orch. – Martini   Odeon BSOA4003, BSOAE4513

SCHUBERT

(16) Deutsche Tänze, Op. 33 (D783) pf
    No. 3. Deutscher Tanz No. 3, in B flat arr. vln & pf as "Valse sentimentale" by Franko
    with piano   Odeon 57016

TROIANI

Estilo, de Motivos de la sierra y la llanura vln & pf
    with R. Gonzalez pf   Victor 10–1108

TURINA

Sonata No. 2, Op. 82 (1934) "Sonata española" vln & pf
    with R. Locatelli pf   Victor 10–1026/8

UGARTE

Sonata (1928) vln & pf
    with R. Locatelli pf   Victor 4541/3

WILLIAMS

Sonata No. 2, in d, Op. 51 vln & pf
    with A. Fasoli pf   Odeon 66045

Reinhard PETERS

MOZART

Sonata No. 32, in B flat, K454 vln & pf
    with C. Rosen pf   Decca FST153035
                London LL674

Sonata No. 33, in E flat, K481 vln & pf
    with C. Rosen pf   Decca FST153035
                London LL674

Frederick Schnedler PETERSEN

GOSSEC

Rosine (1786) – opera
    Gavotte arr. vln & pf Burmester
    with piano   HMV X287977

HARTMANN, E.

Agnetes Vuggevise pf – arr. vln & pf Sitt
    with piano   HMV X287976

Jeanne PETIOT

BACH

Concerto in d, BWV1043 2 vlns, strs & c
    with P. Munn vln & string orch. –   Saga XID5252
    Montserrat

Leo PETRONI (1903–   )

FALLA

(7) Canciones populares españolas (1914) v & pf
    No. 4. Jota arr. vln & pf Petroni
    with G. Favaretto pf   HMV AV44

HAYDN

Minuet in E flat unid – arr. vln & pf Petroni
    with M. Raucheisen   2RA 3607[1]☐. HMV EH1236
    pf

LOTTI

Arminio (1714) – pasticcio
    Pur dicesti arr. vln & pf Bonelli
    with piano   20828   Telefunken A1912

MOZART

(6) Deutsche Tänze, K600 orch.
    No. 4. Deutscher Tanz No. 4, in C arr. vln & pf Burmester
    with piano   20827   Telefunken A1912

RAVEL

Pièce en forme d'Habanera v & pf – arr. vln & pf Catherine
    with G. Favaretto pf   HMV AV44

SCHUMANN

Sonata No. 1, in a, Op. 105 vln & pf
    with M.   2RA 3603/6[1]☐. HMV EH1237/8, S10482/3
    Raucheisen pf

TCHAIKOVSKY

(3) Souvenirs de Hapsal, Op. 2 pf
    No. 3. Chant sans paroles in f arr. vln & pf Kreisler
    with M. Raucheisen   2RA 3608[1]☐. HMV EH1236
    pf

Frédéric PETRONIO

BRUCH

Concerto No. 1, in g, Op. 26 vln & orch.
    with Belgian State Radio Orch. –   Maestro OAT25002
    Glière

DEFOSSEZ

Concerto (1951) vln & orch.
    with Belgian National Orch. –   Decca FM133011
    Defossez

(Le) Violoneux savant vln & pf
    with piano   Alpha DB34

HANDEL

(15) Sonatas, Op. 1 (?1731) fl or vln & c
    Sonata No. 14, in A vln V
    with piano   Alpha DB34

KHACHATURIAN

Chanson poème in e (1929) vln & pf
    with piano   Alpha DB34

KREISLER

Chanson Louis XIII & Pavane (L. Couperin) vln & pf
   with piano   Alpha DB34

LECLAIR

(12) Sonatas, Op. 9 – Book IV (1738) vln & c
  Sonata No. 3, in D
    with piano   Alpha DB34

MENDELSSOHN

Concerto in e, Op. 64 vln & pf
  with Belgian State Radio Orch. –   Maestro OAT25002
  Glière

SAINT–SAËNS

Havanaise, Op. 83 vln & orch.
  with Belgian State Radio Orch. –   Maestro OAT25006
  Doneux

Introduction & Rondo Capriccioso, Op. 28 vln & orch.
  with Belgian State Radio Orch. –   Maestro OAT25006
  Doneux

VLADIGEROV

Suite bulgare, Op. 21 pf
  No. 2. Chant arr. vln & pf Vladigerov
    with piano   Alpha DB34

YSAŸE

(6) Sonatas, Op. 27 solo vln
  Sonata No. 6, in E
  (unaccompanied)   Alpha DB34

Isabella PETROSYAN

BEETHOVEN

Sonata No. 4, in a, Op. 23 vln & pf
  with piano   Mezhdunarodnaya Kniga
                                      D024381/2

HINDEMITH

(2) Sonatas, Op. 31 (1924) solo vln
  Sonata No. 2
  (unaccompanied)   Mezhdunarodnaya Kniga
                                      D024381/2

MOZART

Adagio in E, K261 vln & orch. – arr. vln & pf Germann
  with piano   Mezhdunarodnaya Kniga
                                    D024381/2

SALINEN

Cadenza solo vln
  (unaccompanied)   Mezhdunarodnaya Kniga
                                    D024381/2

YSAŸE

Poème élégiaque in d (Poème No. 1) Op. 12 vln & pf or orch.
  with piano   Mezhdunarodnaya Kniga
                                    D024381/2

Nikola PETROVIK

HANDEL

Concerto in C (1736) "Alexander's Feast" 2 vlns, 2 obs & strs
  with J. Laurent vln, A. Bauer vlc &   Amadeo AVRS6175
  the Masterplayers – Schumacher

NARDINI

Concerto in e vln & orch.
  with the Masterplayers – Schumacher   Amadeo AVRS6206
                                              Cetra LPU0070

VIVALDI

(12) Concerti, Op. 3 "L'Estro armonico" var. cbns & strs
  Concerto No. 8, in a, P.2 (F.I, No. 177) 2 vlns, strs & c
  with R. Schumacher vln & the   Amadeo AVRS6206
  Masterplayers – Schumacher   Cetra LPU0070

Alexander PETSCHNIKOFF (1873–1949)

CUI

Suite concertante, Op. 25 vln & orch.
  No. 3. Cavatina
  with orch.   **05014–1**   Anker E9780

NARDINI

Concerto in e vln & orch.
  Allegro (1st mvt)
    with piano   Scala 4001
  Andante cantabile (2nd mvt)
    with piano   Scala 4001

SAINT–SAËNS

(Le) Carnaval des animaux (1886) small orch.
  Le cygne
    with B. Weyersberg pf   Anker E9553
  Le cygne
    with piano   5003   Tower 1010

STRAUSS, J. (II)

Vienna waltz song unid – arr. vln & pf
  with piano   5004   Tower 1010

TCHAIKOVSKY

Concerto in D, Op. 35 vln & orch.
  Canzonetta (2nd mvt)
    with Berlin Symphony Orch. –   Anker E9554
    Weyersberg
Souvenir d'un lieu cher, Op. 42 vln & pf
  No. 3. Mélodie
    with Berlin Symphony Orch. –   Anker E9554
    Weyersberg

VIEUXTEMPS

Fantasia–appassionata, Op. 35 vln & pf
  with Berlin Symphony Orch. –   Anker E9553
  Weyersberg

Romano PEZZANI

VIVALDI

(12) Concerti, Op. 3 "L'Estro armonico" var. cbns & strs
Concerto No. 8, in a, P.2 (F.I, No. 177) 2 vlns, strs & c
with B. Salvi vln & Angelicum Orch.   Angelicum LPA5961
Concerto No. 11, in d, P.250 (F.IV, No. 11) 2 vlns, vlc, strs & c
with B. Salvi vln, R. Caruana vlc &   Angelicum LPA5961
Angelicum Orch.

Walter PFEIFFER

BACH

Concerto in d, BWV1043 2 vlns, strs & c
with A. Harnoncourt vln & Concentus   Telefunken SAWT9508
Musicus, Vienna – N. Harnoncourt

BIBER

(7) Partitas "Harmonia artificiosa–ariosa" 2 vlns & c
Partita No. 1, in d
with A. Harnoncourt vln, H. Tachezi   Amadeo AVRS6413
hpsi & N. Harnoncourt gamba   Musical Heritage Society
MHS1092

Partita No. 3, in a
with A. Harnoncourt vln, H. Tachezi   Amadeo AVRS6413
hpsi & N. Harnoncourt gamba   Musical Heritage Society
MHS1092

Partita No. 5, in g
with A. Harnoncourt vln, H. Tachezi   Amadeo AVRS6413
hpsi & N. Harnoncourt gamba   Musical Heritage Society
MHS1092

Partita No. 6, in D
with A. Harnoncourt vln, H. Tachezi   Amadeo AVRS6413
hpsi & N. Harnoncourt gamba   Musical Heritage Society
MHS1092

HANDEL

(9) Sonatas, Op. 2 (1724) 2 vlns or obs & c
Sonata No. 3, in F 2 vlns & c
with A. Harnoncourt vln, H. Tachezi   Telefunken SAWT9559
hpsi & N. Harnoncourt vlc

MOZART

Sonata in F, K244 2 vlns & c
with A. Harnoncourt vln, H. Tachezi   Telefunken SAWT9555
org & N. Harnoncourt vlc
Sonata in C, K328 2 vlns & c
with A. Harnoncourt vln, H. Tachezi   Telefunken SAWT9555
org & N. Harnoncourt vlc

TELEMANN

Concerto in G 4 vlns, strs & c
with A. Harnoncourt vln, K. Theiner   Telefunken SAWT9483
vln, P. Schuberwalter vln & Concentus
Musicus, Vienna – N. Harnoncourt
Suite in F "Konzertsuite" 2 hrns, 2 vlns & c
with H. Rohrer hrn, H. Fischer hrn,   Telefunken SAWT9483
A. Harnoncourt vln & Concentus
Musicus, Vienna – N. Harnoncourt

PHAL

FLOTOW

Martha (1847) – opera
M'appari arr. vln & pf
with piano   Odeon 3726

MASSENET

Thaïs (1894) – opera
Méditation arr. vln & pf Marsick
with piano   Odeon 3724
(La) Vierge (1880) – oratorio
La Dernier sommeil de la Vierge orch. – arr. vln & pf
with piano   Odeon 3725

SAINT–SAËNS

(Le) Carnaval des animaux (1886) small orch.
Le cygne arr. vln & pf
with piano   Odeon 3724
(Le) Déluge, Op. 45 (1876) – oratorio
Prélude vln & orch. – arr. vln & pf Saint–Saëns
with piano   Odeon 3725

Georges PHILIPPOT

CHOPIN

(3) Nocturnes, Op. 9 pf
No. 2. Nocturne No. 2, in E flat arr. vln & pf Sarasate
with piano   1297   Perfectaphone 1136

MONTI

Csárdas (1904) vln & pf
with piano   1296   Perfectaphone 1136

Mischel PIASTRO (1892–1970)

ANONYMOUS

(La) Romanesca 16th Century gaillarde – arr. vln & pf Achron
with M. List pf   Brunswick 10268

ARENSKY

(4) Morceaux, Op. 30 vln & pf
No. 2. Serenade in G arr. Elman
with M. Nadelle pf   Brunswick 10209

BEETHOVEN

(Die) Ruinen von Athen, Op. 113 – Incidental music orch.
No. 4. Marcia alla turca arr. vln & pf Auer
with J. Veissi pf   Brunswick 15220

BIZET

(Les) Pêcheurs de Perles (1863) – opera
A cette voix ... Je crois entendre encore (Romance de Nadir) arr. vln &
pf Piastro
with piano   Brunswick 10150, 10262

DRIGO

(Les) Millions d'Arlequin (1900) – ballet orch.
Sérénade arr. vln & pf Auer
with M. List pf   Brunswick 10155, 10269

FIBICH

Images, Impressions & Souvenirs, Op. 41 pf
  No. 14. Poem (from "Souvenirs", Part IV) arr. vln & pf Kubelík
  with J. Veissi pf   Brunswick 15221

FRANKO

Irish lament vln & pf
  with M. Nadelle pf   Brunswick 10209

GRIEG

(6) Lyric Pieces – Book III, Op. 43 pf
  No. 2. Lonely wanderer arr. vln & pf Piastro
  with F. Black pf   Brunswick 15165

HANDEL

(15) Sonatas, Op. 1 (?1731) fl or vln & c
  Sonata No. 9, in b: Andante (1st mvt) arr. vln & pf as "Larghetto" by Hubay
  with J. Veissi pf   Brunswick 15220

MOZART

(Il) Re Pastore, K208 (1775) – opera
  No. 10. L'amerò, sarò costante
  with L. Pons s & orch. – Walter   Columbia 71696D

RIMSKY–KORSAKOV

Capriccio espagnole, Op. 34 (1887) orch.
  with New York Philharmonic   Columbia 264689/90, 11477/8D,
  Symphony Orch. – Barbirolli   11479/80D, (set MX185),
                            C15335/6

(Le) Coq d'Or (1910) – opera
  Hymn to the sun arr. vln & pf Kreisler
  with orch.   Brunswick 10155, 10269

SAINT–SAËNS

Introduction & Rondo Capriccioso, Op. 28 vln & orch.
  with Longine Symphonette – Piastro   Harmony HL7156
                           Longine LW121

SARASATE

Zigeunerweisen, Op. 20 vln & pf or orch.
  with piano   Brunswick 10267

SCHUBERT

Horch! Horch! die Lerch, D889 (1826) v & pf – arr. vln & pf
  with J. Veissi pf   Brunswick 15221

STRAUSS, R.

Don Quixote, Op. 35 (1897) orch.*
  with A. Wallenstein vlc, R. Pollain vla Victor 7589/93, (set M144)
  & New York Philharmonic Symphony Columbia LX186/90
  Orch. – Beecham

WIENIAWSKI

(Le) Carnaval russe (on the Russian air "Po ulicy mostovoj") Op. 11 vln & pf
  with F. Black pf   Brunswick 15165

Fantaisie brillante (on themes from the opera "Faust" by Gounod) Op. 20 vln & orch.
  with piano   Brunswick 10262, 15150

* Also on Victor transcription disc L11633.

WIENIAWSKI – *Continued*

Souvenir de Moscou, Op. 6 vln & pf or orch.
  with M. List pf   Brunswick 10268

Josef PIASTRO–BORISOFF (1889–)

DRDLA

Souvenir vln & pf
  with piano   204   Cameo S264

DRIGO

(Les) Millions d'Arlequin (1900) – ballet orch.
  Sérénade arr. vln & pf Auer
  with piano   203   Cameo S264

KREISLER

(La) Gitana vln & pf
  with M. Nadelle pf   7925   Edison cylinder 4798
                                Edison Diamond Disc 80693

MUSIN

(2) Morceaux de concert, Op. 7 (1887) vln & pf
  No. 1. Mazurka de concert
  with M. Nadelle pf   8047   Edison Diamond Disc 80693

Vladimir PIATKOWSKI

CORELLI

(12) Concerti grossi, Op. 6 orch.
  Concerto grosso No. 1, in D
  with B. Warchal vln, M. Capka vlc & Supraphon SUA10571,
  Slovak Chamber Orch. – Warchal   SUAST50571, SV8183

  Concerto grosso No. 2, in F
  with B. Warchal vln, M. Capka vlc & Supraphon SUA10808,
  Slovak Chamber Orch. – Warchal   SUAST50808, 140 0102

  Concerto grosso No. 3, in c
  with B. Warchal vln, M. Capka vlc & Supraphon SUA10571,
  Slovak Chamber Orch. – Warchal   SUAST50571, SV8183

  Concerto grosso No. 4, in D
  with B. Warchal vln, M. Capka vlc & Supraphon SUA10911,
  Slovak Chamber Orch. – Warchal   SUAST50911, 140 0106

  Concerto grosso No. 5, in B flat
  with B. Warchal vln, M. Capka vlc & Supraphon SUA10808,
  Slovak Chamber Orch. – Warchal   SUAST50808, 140 0102

  Concerto grosso No. 6, in F
  with B. Warchal vln, M. Capka vlc & Supraphon SUA10571,
  Slovak Chamber Orch. – Warchal   SUAST50571, SV8183

  Concerto grosso No. 7, in D
  with B. Warchal vln, M. Capka vlc & Supraphon SUA10571,
  Slovak Chamber Orch. – Warchal   SUAST50571, SV8183

  Concerto grosso No. 8, in g "Christmas Concerto"
  with B. Warchal vln, M. Capkal vlc & Supraphon SUA10808,
  Slovak Chamber Orch. – Warchal   SUAST50808, 140 0102

  Concerto grosso No. 9, in F
  with B. Warchal vln, M. Capka vlc & Supraphon SUA10808,
  Slovak Chamber Orch. – Warchal   SUAST50808, 140 0102

  Concerto grosso No. 10, in C
  with B. Warchal vln, M. Capka vlc & Supraphon SUA10911,
  Slovak Chamber Orch. – Warchal   SUAST50911, 140 0106

CORELLI – *Continued*

Concerto grosso No. 11, in B flat
with B. Warchal vln, M. Capka vlc   Supraphon SUA10911,
Slovak Chamber Orch. – Warchal   SUAST50911, 140 0106

Concerto grosso No. 12, in F
with B. Warchal vln, M. Capka vlc   Supraphon SUA10911,
Slovak Chamber Orch. – Warchal   SUAST50911, 140 0106

Günter PICHLER

GIULIANI, G.F.

Quartet No. 1, in A mand, vln, vla & lute
with E. Bauer–Slais mand, A. Baierle   Turnabout TV4016, TV34016
vla & V. Hladky lute

HOFFMANN, J.

Quartet in F mand, vln, vla & lute – arr. Hladky
with E. Kunschak mand, A. Baierle   Turnabout TV4016, TV34016
vla & V. Hladky lute

TORELLI

Concerto in D vln, gtr & strs
with K. Scheit gtr & Wiener Solisten –   Amadeo AVR12104, AVRS6236
Böttcher   Bach Guild BG618, BGS5043

Enrico PIERANGELI

BRAHMS

(21) Hungarian Dances pf duet
Hungarian dance No. 1, in g arr. vln & pf Joachim
with A. Mussato pf   Parlophone P56107
Hungarian dance No. 5, in f sharp arr. vln & pf "in g" Joachim
with A. Mussato pf   Parlophone P56107

FIGUEIREDO

Idilio amoroso iterrumpido por un aquelarre vln & pf
with A. Mussato pf   Cetra AT0214, TI7056

KREISLER

Grave (W.F. Bach) vln & pf
with A. Mussato pf   Parlophone P56107

SCHUBERT

Rondo brillante in b, Op. 70 (D895) vln & pf
with A. Mussato pf   Cetra AT0203/4, TI7020/1

SIMONETTI

Recitativo, Chorale & Cadenza vln & pf
with A. Mussato pf   Cetra AT0205, TI7022

TARTINI

(12) Sonatas, Op. 1 (1734) vln & c
Sonata No. 1, in A: Allegro (1st mvt) arr. vln & pf as "Fugue" by
Kreisler
with A. Mussato pf   Cetra PE135

VIVALDI

(12) Concerti, Op. 3 "L'Estro armonico" var. cbns & strs
Concerto No. 8, in a: Largetto (2nd mvt) P.2 (F.I, No. 177) 2 vlns, strs
& c – arr. vln & pf Gentili
with A. Mussato pf   Cetra PE135

Nilla PIERROU

PETERSON–BERGER

Concerto in f sharp (1928) vln & orch.
with Swedish Radio Orch. –   HMV CSDS1083
Westerberg
Romance (1915) vln & orch.
with Swedish Radio Orch. –   HMV CSDS1083
Westerberg

H. PIETSCH

HANDEL

(12) Concerti grossi, Op. 6 (1739) 2 vlns, vlc & strs
Concerto grosso No. 7, in B flat
with S. Gavrilov vln, W. Haupt vlc, E.   Eterna 121061/2
Erthel ob, W. Watzig ob & Berlin
Chamber Orch. – Guhl
Concerto grosso No. 8, in c
with S. Gavrilov vln, W. Haupt vlc, E.   Eterna 121063/5, 520060
Erthel ob, W. Watzig ob & Berlin
Chamber Orch. – Guhl

HAYDN

(6) Quartets, Op. 20 (H.III, nos. 31/6) 2 vlns, vla & vlc
No. 4. Quartet No. 34, in D, H.III, No. 34
with M. Michaïlow vln, H. Fricke vla   Eterna 820016
& W. Haupt vlc

MOZART

Quartet No. 18, in A, K464 2 vlns, vla & vlc
with M. Michaïlow vln, H. Fricke vla   Eterna 720011
& W. Haupt vlc
Quartet No. 21, in D, K575 2 vlns, vla & vlc
with M. Michaïlow vln, H. Fricke vla   Eterna 720011
& W. Haupt vlc

N. PIGNATELLI

VIOTTI

(3) Duets, Op. 29 2 vlns & orch.
No. 2. Duo concertante No. 2, in d arr. Quaranta
with M. Ceradini vln & Angelicum   Angelicum LPA966
Orch. – Janes

Viktor Alexandrovich PIKAIZEN (1933–)

BARTÓK

Contrasts (1938) cl, vln & pf
with L. Mikhailov cl & M. Yedlina pf   Mezhdunarodnaya Kniga
D016509/10, SM02443

BARTÓK – *Continued*

Sonata in g (1944) solo vln
(unaccompanied)   Mezhdunarodnaya Kniga
D016509/10

BRAHMS

(21) Hungarian Dances pf duet
  Hungarian dance No. 8, in a arr. vln & pf Joachim
  with I. Kollegorskaya pf   Mezhdunarodnaya Kniga D4255

DVOŘÁK

Concerto in a, Op. 53 vln & orch.
  with Moscow Philharmonic Symphony Le Chant du Monde LDX78441
  Orch. – D. Oistrakh   Eurodisc 78463KK
        Melodiya–Angel SR40185
        Mezhdunarodnaya Kniga
        D023101/2

GEMINIANI

(6) Sonatas, Op. 5 (1738) solo vln
  Sonata in B flat (ed. Corti)
  (unaccompanied)   Mezhdunarodnaya Kniga D2806

KNIPPER

Concert scherzo vln & pf
  with S. Chernyakhovskaya pf   Mezhdunarodnaya Kniga
        D29656

LAUB

Polonaise in G, Op. 8 vln & pf
  with V. Yampolsky pf   Supraphon SUEC860, SUK30328
        Ultraphon 04083

LEVITIN

Variations, Op. 45 solo vln
  (unaccompanied)   Mezhdunarodnaya Kniga D4254

MAKAROVA

Melody, Op. 18, No. 1 vln & pf
  with N. Makarova pf   Mezhdunarodnaya Kniga
        D21195/6

Scherzo in B flat, Op. 18, No. 2 vln & pf
  with N. Makarova pf   Mezhdunarodnaya Kniga
        D21195/6

MENDELSSOHN

Concerto in e, Op. 64 vln & orch.
  with Moscow Radio Large Symphony Erato LDX78484
  Orch. – Rozhdestvensky   Mezhdunarodnaya Kniga
        SM02073/4

MOSTRAS

Caprice, Recitative & Toccata vln & pf
  with I. Kollegorskaya pf   Mezhdunarodnaya Kniga D4254

PAGANINI

(24) Caprices, Op. 1 (1801/7) solo vln
  Caprice No. 1, in E
  (unaccompanied)   Le Chant du Monde LDX78397
        Mezhdunarodnaya Kniga
        D020345, SM02341

PAGANINI – *Continued*

Caprice No. 2, in b
(unaccompanied)   Supraphon SUEC860, SUK30328
        Ultraphon 04083

Caprice No. 2, in b
(unaccompanied)   Le Chant du Monde LDX78397
        Mezhdunarodnaya Kniga
        D020345, SM02341

Caprice No. 3, in e
(unaccompanied)   Le Chant du Monde LDX78397
        Mezhdunarodnaya Kniga
        D020345, SM02341

Caprice No. 4, in c
(unaccompanied)   Le Chant du Monde LDX78397
        Mezhdunarodnaya Kniga
        D020345, SM02341

Caprice No. 5, in a
(unaccompanied)   Le Chant du Monde LDX78397
        Mezhdunarodnaya Kniga
        D020345, SM02341

Caprice No. 6, in g
(unaccompanied)   Le Chant du Monde LDX78397
        Mezhdunarodnaya Kniga
        D020345, SM02341

Caprice No. 7, in a
(unaccompanied)   Le Chant du Monde LDX78397
        Mezhdunarodnaya Kniga
        D020346, SM02342

Caprice No. 8, in E flat
(unaccompanied)   Le Chant du Monde LDX78397
        Mezhdunarodnaya Kniga
        D020346, SM02342

Caprice No. 9, in E
(unaccompanied)   Le Chant du Monde LDX78397
        Mezhdunarodnaya Kniga
        D020346, SM02342

Caprice No. 10, in g
(unaccompanied)   Le Chant du Monde LDX78397
        Mezhdunarodnaya Kniga
        D020346, SM02342

Caprice No. 11, in C
(unaccompanied)   Le Chant du Monde LDX78397
        Mezhdunarodnaya Kniga
        D020346, SM02342

Caprice No. 12, in A flat
(unaccompanied)   Le Chant du Monde LDX78397
        Mezhdunarodnaya Kniga
        D020346, SM02342

Caprice No. 13, in B flat
(unaccompanied)   Le Chant du Monde LDX78398
        Mezhdunarodnaya Kniga
        D020347, SM02343

Caprice No. 14, in E flat
(unaccompanied)   Le Chant du Monde LDX78398
        Mezhdunarodnaya Kniga
        D020347, SM02343

Caprice No. 15, in e
(unaccompanied)   Le Chant du Monde LDX78398
        Mezhdunarodnaya Kniga
        D020347, SM02343

PAGANINI – *Continued*

Caprice No. 16, in g
(unaccompanied)
Le Chant du Monde LDX78398
Mezhdunarodnaya Kniga
D020347, SM02343

Caprice No. 17, in E flat
(unaccompanied)
Le Chant du Monde LDX78398
Mezhdunarodnaya Kniga
D020347, SM02343

Caprice No. 18, in C
(unaccompanied)
Le Chant du Monde LDX78398
Mezhdunarodnaya Kniga
D020347, SM02343

Caprice No. 19, in E flat
(unaccompanied)
Le Chant du Monde LDX78398
Mezhdunarodnaya Kniga
D020348, SM02344

Caprice No. 20, in D
(unaccompanied)
Le Chant du Monde LDX78398
Mezhdunarodnaya Kniga
D020348, SM02344

Caprice No. 21, in A
(unaccompanied)
Le Chant du Monde LDX78398
Mezhdunarodnaya Kniga
D020348, SM02344

Caprice No. 22, in F
(unaccompanied)
Le Chant du Monde LDX78398
Eurodisc 78463KK
Mezhdunarodnaya Kniga
D020348, SM02344

Caprice No. 23, in E flat
(unaccompanied)
Mezhdunarodnaya Kniga D2806

Caprice No. 23, in E flat
(unaccompanied)
Le Chant du Monde LDX78398
Eurodisc 78463KK
Mezhdunarodnaya Kniga
D020348

Caprice No. 24, in a
(unaccompanied)
Le Chant du Monde LDX78398
Eurodisc 78463KK
Mezhdunarodnaya Kniga
D020348, SM02344

Concerto No. 1, in D, Op. 6 vln & orch.
Allegro maestoso (1st mvt) arr. vln & orch. Wilhelmj
with Moscow State Philharmonic
Orch. – Kondrashin
Mezhdunarodnaya Kniga
D04535

RAKOV

(5) Pieces 2 vlns & pf
with I. Oistrakh vln & N. Rakov pf
Mezhdunarodnaya Kniga
D11055/6

SARASATE

(8) Danzas españolas vln & pf
No. 2. Habañera, Op. 21, No. 2
with S. Chernyakhovskaya pf
Mezhdunarodnaya Kniga
D29656

No. 3. Romanza andaluza, Op. 22, No. 1
with S. Chernyakhovskaya pf
Mezhdunarodnaya Kniga
D29656

SARASATE – *Continued*

Zigeunerweisen, Op. 20 vln & pf or orch.
with I. Kollegorskaya pf
Mezhdunarodnaya Kniga D2807

SCRIABIN

(12) Etudes, Op. 8 pf
No. 11. Etude No. 11, in B flat arr. vln & pf
with I. Kollegorskaya pf
Mezhdunarodnaya Kniga D4255
(2) Nocturnes, Op. 5 pf
No. 1. Nocturne No. 1, in f sharp arr. vln & pf Moguilevsky
with V. Yampolsky pf
Supraphon SUEC860, SUK30328
Ultraphon 04083

SMETANA

From my Homeland (1878) vln & pf
No. 2. Andantino
with I. Kollegorskaya pf
Mezhdunarodnaya Kniga
D17144/5

STRAVINSKY

Duo concertante (1932) vln & pf
with M. Yedlina pf
Mezhdunarodnaya Kniga
D011391

TCHAIKOVSKY

Waltz–Scherzo, Op. 34 vln & orch. – arr. vln & pf Bezékirsky
with I. Kollegorskaya pf
Mezhdunarodnaya Kniga D4255,
D04443

WIENIAWSKI

Concerto No. 1, in f sharp, Op. 14 vln & orch.
with Moscow Radio Large Symphony
Orch. – Rozhdestvensky
Erato LDX78484
Melodiya–Angel SR40185
Mezhdunarodnaya Kniga
SM02073/4

YSAŸE

(3) Mazurkas, Op. 11 vln & pf
No. 3. Mazurka No. 3, in b "Lointaine–passé"
with I. Kollegorskaya pf
Mezhdunarodnaya Kniga D2807

No. 3. Mazurka No. 3, in b "Lointaine–passé"
with Moscow Philharmonic Symphony
Orch. – D. Oistrakh
Le Chant du Monde LDX78441
Mezhdunarodnaya Kniga
D023102

Imre PILLITZ

CHOPIN

(3) Nocturnes, Op. 9 pf
No. 2. Nocturne No. 2, in E flat arr. vln & pf Sarasate
with orch.
60433   Odeon 60433

RAFF

(6) Pieces, Op. 85 vln & pf
No. 3. Cavatina in D
with orch.
60434   Odeon 60434

SARASATE

Zigeunerweisen, Op. 20 vln & pf or orch.
with orch.
60435[2]   Odeon 60435, UX52118

WIENIAWSKI

Scherzo–Tarantelle, Op. 16 vln & pf
with orch.   60436   Odeon 60436, UX52119

Maximilian PILZER (1890–1958)

BRUCH

Kol nidrei, Op. 47 vlc or vln & orch.
with orch.   Victor 68366

DRDLA

Souvenir vln & pf
with piano   Victor 35399

DVOŘÁK

(8) Humoresques, Op. 101 pf
No. 7. Humoresque No. 7, in G flat arr. vln & pf "in G" Wilhelmj
with orch.   Victor 35306

KREISLER

Caprice viennois, Op. 2 vln & pf
with piano   Vocalion 46000

Rondino on a theme by Beethoven vln & pf
with piano   Vocalion A24006

MASSENET

Thaïs (1894) – opera
Méditation
with orch.   HMV Z0287904
                              Victor 35306

Méditation arr. vln & pf Marsick
with piano   Vocalion 46000

MENDELSSOHN

(6) Songs without words, Op. 62 pf
No. 6. Song without words No. 30, in A "Spring song" arr. vln & pf
Kreisler
with orch.   Victor 17395

REHFELD

(2) Konzertstücke, Op. 58 vln & pf
No. 1. Spanish dance
with orch.   Victor 17206

No. 1. Spanish dance
with piano   Vocalion A24006

SGAMBATI

(2) Pieces, Op. 24 vln & pf
No. 2. Serenata napoletana
with R. Bourdon pf   Victor 18175

Marc PINCHERLE (1888–   )

CORELLI

(12) Sonatas, Op. 5 vln & c
Sonata No. 6, in A: Grave (1st mvt)
with M. Delcourt hpsi   Columbia 19234

M. J. PINELL

BERNIAUX

Wenn ich dein Herz gewonnen vln & pf
with orch.   Odeon A42804

GUGO–NORIS

Valse d'Or vln & pf
with orch.   Odeon A42995/6

WALDTEUFEL

Estudiantina, Op. 191 orch. – arr. vln & orch. Lacombe
with orch.   Odeon A42803

Carl PINI

BACH

(6) Brandenburg Concerti, BWV1046/51 (1721) strs & c
Brandenburg Concerto No. 1, in F, BWV1046 vln, 3 obs, bsn, 2 hrns, strs & c
playing vln–pic, with P. Graeme ob, R. Wells ob, N. Black ob, V. Elliott bsn, D. Clift tpt, S. Ellison tpt & Philomusica of London – Dart   L'Oiseau–Lyre OL50167, SOL60005 Telefunken AWD9902, SAWD9902

Concerto in d, BWV1043 2 vlns, strs & c
with G. Jones vln & London Philharmonic Orch. – Dart   L'Oiseau–Lyre OL50160

(6) Sonatas, BWV1014/9 vln & clav
Sonata No. 1, in b, BWV1014
with C. Tilney hpsi & D. Nesbitt gamba   Philharmonic 0103

Sonata No. 2, in A, BWV1015
with C. Tilney hpsi & D. Nesbitt gamba   Philharmonic 0104

Sonata No. 3, in E, BWV1016
with C. Tilney hpsi & D. Nesbitt gamba   Philharmonic 0103

Sonata No. 4, in c, BWV1017
with C. Tilney hpsi & D. Nesbitt gamba   Philharmonic 0103

Sonata No. 5, in f, BWV1018
with C. Tilney hpsi & D. Nesbitt gamba   Philharmonic 0104

Sonata No. 6, in G, BWV1019
with C. Tilney hpsi & D. Nesbitt gamba   Philharmonic 0104

COUPERIN, F.

(Les) Nations – 4 suites (1726) 2 vlns & c
Suite No. 1, in e "La Française"
with N. Marriner vln, T. Dart hpsi & D. Dupré gamba   L'Oiseau–Lyre OL251

Suite No. 2, in c "L'Espagnole"
with N. Marriner vln, T. Dart hpsi & D. Dupré gamba   L'Oiseau–Lyre OL251

Suite No. 3, in d "L'Impériale"
with N. Marriner vln, T. Dart hpsi & D. Dupré gamba   L'Oiseau–Lyre OL251

Suite No. 4, in g "La Piémontoise"
with N. Marriner vln, T. Dart hpsi & D. Dupré gamba   L'Oiseau–Lyre OL251

HANDEL

Concerto in C (1736) "Alexander's Feast" 2 vlns, 2 obs & strs
  with N. Marriner vln, T. Dart hpsi–c,   L'Oiseau–Lyre OL50181,
  J. Hall vlc & Philomusica of London –   SOL60013
  Jones

PURCELL

(15) Fantasias, Z731/45 4 & 5 part – orig. viols
  Fantasia No. 1, in F, Z731 (3 parts upon a ground) (?1679)
  with N. Marriner vln & T. Dart org   Argo EAF16, RG113

(5) Pavanes, Z748/52 (pre–1680) (Nos. 1/4: 3 part; No. 5: 4 part)
  Pavane No. 5, in g, Z752 (?1677)
  with N. Marriner vln, P. Gibbs vln &   Argo RG113
  T. Dart org

(12) Sonatas, Z790/801 (1683) 3 part – 2 vlns & c
  Sonata No. 1, in g, Z790
  with J. Tunnell vln, H. Lester hpsi &   Musical Heritage Society
  A. Pini vlc   MHS942

  Sonata No. 2, in B flat, Z791
  with J. Tunnell vln, H. Lester hpsi &   Musical Heritage Society
  A. Pini vlc   MHS942

  Sonata No. 3, in d, Z792
  with J. Tunnell vln, H. Lester hpsi &   Musical Heritage Society
  A. Pini vlc   MHS942

  Sonata No. 4, in F, Z793
  with J. Tunnell vln, H. Lester hpsi &   Musical Heritage Society
  A. Pini vlc   MHS943

  Sonata No. 5, in a, Z794
  with J. Tunnell vln, H. Lester hpsi &   Musical Heritage Society
  A. Pini vlc   MHS943

  Sonata No. 6, in C, Z795
  with J. Tunnell vln, H. Lester hpsi &   Musical Heritage Society
  A. Pini vlc   MHS943

  Sonata No. 7, in e, Z796
  with J. Tunnell vln, H. Lester hpsi &   Musical Heritage Society
  A. Pini vlc   MHS943

  Sonata No. 8, in G, Z797
  with J. Tunnell vln, H. Lester hpsi &   Musical Heritage Society
  A. Pini vlc   MHS943

  Sonata No. 9, in c, Z798
  with J. Tunnell vln, H. Lester hpsi &   Musical Heritage Society
  A. Pini vlc   MHS943

  Sonata No. 10, in A, Z799
  with J. Tunnell vln, H. Lester hpsi &   Musical Heritage Society
  A. Pini vlc   MHS942

  Sonata No. 11, in f, Z800
  with J. Tunnell vln, H. Lester hpsi &   Musical Heritage Society
  A. Pini vlc   MHS942

  Sonata No. 12, in D, Z801
  with J. Tunnell vln, H. Lester hpsi &   Musical Heritage Society
  A. Pini vlc   MHS942

(10) Sonatas, Z802/11 (1697) 4 parts – 2 vlns & c
  Sonata No. 1, in b, Z802
  with J. Tunnell vln, H. Lester hpsi &   Musical Heritage Society
  A. Pini vlc   MHS944

  Sonata No. 2, in E flat, Z803
  with J. Tunnell vln, H. Lester hpsi &   Musical Heritage Society
  A. Pini vlc   MHS944

PURCELL – *Continued*

  Sonata No. 3, in a, Z804
  with J. Tunnell vln, H. Lester hpsi &   Musical Heritage Society
  A. Pini vlc   MHS944

  Sonata No. 4, in d, Z805
  with J. Tunnell vln, H. Lester hpsi &   Musical Heritage Society
  A. Pini vlc   MHS945

  Sonata No. 5, in d, Z806
  with J. Tunnell vln, H. Lester hpsi &   Musical Heritage Society
  A. Pini vlc   MHS945

  Sonata No. 6, in g, Z807 "Chaconne"
  with J. Tunnell vln, H. Lester hpsi &   Musical Heritage Society
  A. Pini vlc   MHS945

  Sonata No. 7, in G, Z808
  with J. Tunnell vln, H. Lester hpsi &   Musical Heritage Society
  A. Pini vlc   MHS945

  Sonata No. 8, in g, Z809
  with J. Tunnell vln, H. Lester hpsi &   Musical Heritage Society
  A. Pini vlc   MHS945

  Sonata No. 9, in F, Z810 "Golden Sonata"
  with J. Tunnell vln, H. Lester hpsi &   Musical Heritage Society
  A. Pini vlc   MHS945

  Sonata No. 10, in D, Z811
  with J. Tunnell vln, H. Lester hpsi &   Musical Heritage Society
  A. Pini vlc   MHS944

Sonata in g, Z780 vln & c
  with H. Lester hpsi   Musical Heritage Society
                                            MHS944

VIVALDI

(12) Concerti, Op. 9 (1728) "La Cetra" vln, strs & c
  Concerto No. 1, in C, P.9 (F.I, No. 47)
  with Orch. of the Accademia   Orpheus OR334
  Monteverdiana – Stevens

  Concerto No. 2, in A, P.214 (F.I, No. 51)
  with Orch. of the Accademia   Orpheus OR334
  Monteverdiana – Stevens

  Concerto No. 3, in g, P.339 (F.I, No. 52)
  with Orch. of the Accademia   Orpheus OR334
  Monteverdiana – Stevens

  Concerto No. 4, in E, P.242 (F.I, No. 48)
  with Orch. of the Accademia   Orpheus OR334
  Monteverdiana – Stevens

  Concerto No. 5, in a, P.10 (F.I, No. 53)
  with Orch. of the Accademia   Orpheus OR335
  Monteverdiana – Stevens

  Concerto No. 6, in A, P.215 (F.I, No. 54) with solo vln scordato
  with Orch. of the Accademia   Orpheus OR335
  Monteverdiana – Stevens

  Concerto No. 7, in B flat, P.340 (F.I, No. 55)
  with Orch. of the Accademia   Orpheus OR335
  Monteverdiana – Stevens

  Concerto No. 8, in d, P.260 (F.I, No. 56)
  with Orch. of the Accademia   Orpheus OR335
  Monteverdiana – Stevens

  Concerto No. 9, in B flat, P.341 (F.I, No. 57) with 2nd vln obb
  with J. Tunnell vln & Orch. of the   Orpheus OR336
  Accademia Monteverdiana – Stevens

VIVALDI – *Continued*

Concerto No. 10, in G, P.103 (F.I, No. 49)
with Orch. of the Accademia   Orpheus OR336
Monteverdiana – Stevens

Concerto No. 11, in c, P.416 (F.I, No. 58)
with Orch. of the Accademia   Orpheus OR336
Monteverdiana – Stevens

Concerto No. 12, in b, P.154 (F.I, No. 50) with solo vln scordato
with Orch. of the Accademia   Orpheus OR336
Monteverdiana – Stevens

Ivan PINKAVA (1912–)

BACH

Concerto in a, BWV1044 clav, fl, vln, strs & c
with A. Heiller hpsi, W. Tripp fl & I   Amadeo AVRS6052
Solisti di Zagreb – Janigro   Bach Guild BG562
                             I Classici della Musica Classica
                             XAM4036
                             Vanguard PVL7031

TORELLI

(12) Concerti, Op. 8 (1709) 1/6: 2 vlns, strs & c – 7/12: vln, strs & c
Concerto No. 6, in g "Christmas Concerto"
with J. Stanič–Krek vln, A. Heiller   Bach Guild BG569, BGS5006
hpsi, Z. Pomykalo vlc & I Solisti di   Top Rank 40–003, TR5002
Zagreb – Janigro

G. PIRACCINI

VIVALDI

(12) Concerti, Op. 3 "L'Estro armonico" var. cbns & strs
Concerto No. 10, in b, P.148 (F.IV, No. 10) 4 vlns, strs & c
with A. Fietz vln, L. Kaufman vln, P.   Concert Hall E2
Rybar vln & Winterthur Chamber
Orch. – Dahinden

Armando di PIRAMO

BILLI

Campane à sera vln or mand & pf
with piano   Pathé 16100

Cintia vln or mand & pf
with piano   Columbia CQ235

Serenata alle rondini vln or mand & pf
with piano   Columbia CQ262

Topsy "Arabesca" vln or mand & pf
with piano   Columbia CQ193

CIOCIANO

Serenata Intermezzo vln & pf
with piano   Columbia CQ234

CORTOPASSI

Canzone d'Aprile vln & pf
with piano   Columbia CQ192

FREIRE

Ay, ay, ay v & pf – arr. vln & hp
with harp   Columbia 5621

GILLET

(Le) Lettre de Manon – valse pf – arr. vln & pf
with piano   Pathé 16122, 86668

MARGUTTI

Canzone appassionata vln & pf
with piano   Columbia CQ234

MARSAGLIA

Pas du cygne vln & pf
with piano   Columbia CQ192

MASCAGNI

(L') Amico Fritz (1891) – opera
Serenade arr. vln & pf
with piano   Pathé 16100

MASCHERONI

Cavezze (Melodia) vln & pf
with piano   Columbia CQ235

MICHELI

Rêverie vln & pf
with piano   Columbia CQ262

Serenata vln & pf
with piano   Columbia CQ193

SADAN

Serenade to Spring vln & pf
with piano   Pathé 16122, 86890

SILVESTRI

Sérénade d'autrefois pf – arr. vln & pf
with piano   Pathé 16101, 86665/6

Konstantin PLAEINITZ

BRAHMS

(21) Hungarian Dances pf duet
Hungarian dance No. 17, in f sharp arr. vln & pf Joachim
with U. Bogdanski pf   Kaskade 8002

DVOŘÁK

(4) Romantic pieces, Op. 75 vln & pf
No. 1. Allegro moderato
with U. Bogdanski pf   Kaskade 8002

(8) Slavonic Dances, Op. 46 pf duet; orch.
No. 2. Slavonic dance No. 2, in e arr. vln & pf "in g" Kreisler
with U. Bogdanski pf   Kaskade 8002

(8) Slavonic Dances, Op. 72 pf duet; orch.
No. 2. Slavonic dance No. 10, in e arr. vln & pf Kreisler
with U. Bogdanski pf   Kaskade 8002

Sonatina in G, Op. 100 vln & pf
with U. Bogdanski pf   Kaskade 8002

SARASATE

(8) Danzas españolas vln & pf
No. 3. Romanza andaluza, Op. 22, No. 1
with U. Bogdanski pf   Kaskade 8002

WIENIAWSKI

(2) Mazurkas, Op. 12 vln & pf
No. 2. Mazurka No. 2, in g "Le Ménetrier"
with U. Bogdanski pf   Kaskade 8002

Ernest Gill PLAMONDON (1896–)

DRIGO

(2) Airs de Ballet orch.
No. 2. Valse bluette arr. vln & pf Auer
with piano   Starr (Gennett) 591

DVOŘÁK

(8) Humoresques, Op. 101 pf
No. 7. Humoresque No. 7, in G flat arr. vln & pf "in G" Kreisler
with piano   Apex 567

SCHUMANN

(13) Kinderscenen, Op. 15 pf
No. 7. Träumerei arr. vln & pf
with piano   Apex 567

Alexander PLOCEK (1914–)

BEETHOVEN

Romance No. 1, in G, Op. 40 vln & orch.
with Czech Philharmonic Orch. –   Supraphon LPM263, SUH20284
Sejna   Ultraphon 5166C
Romance No. 2, in F, Op. 50 vln & orch.
with Czech Philharmonic Orch. –   Supraphon LPM263, SUH20284
Sejna   Ultraphon 5166C
(3) Sonatas, Op. 12 vln & pf
No. 2. Sonata No. 2, in A
with J. Páleníček pf   Supraphon LPV350, SUA10304

No. 3. Sonata No. 3, in E flat
with J. Páleníček pf   Supraphon SUA10149

Sonata No. 4, in a, Op. 23 vln & pf
with J. Páleníček pf   Supraphon SUA10149

Sonata No. 5, in F, Op. 24 "Spring" vln & pf
with J. Páleníček pf   Supraphon LPM129
                                   Ultraphon 5114C

(3) Sonatas, Op. 30 vln & pf
No. 2. Sonata No. 7, in c
with J. Páleníček pf   Supraphon LPM128
                                   Ultraphon 5113C

No. 3. Sonata No. 8, in G
with J. Páleníček pf   Supraphon SUA10149

Sonata No. 9, in A, Op. 47 "Kreutzer" vln & pf
with J. Páleníček pf   Supraphon LPM116, SUF20234
                                   Ultraphon 5099C

Sonata No. 10, in G, Op. 96 vln & pf
with J. Páleníček pf   Supraphon LPV350, SUA10304

DVOŘÁK

Trio No. 3, in f, Op. 65 pf, vln & vlc
with J. Páleníček pf & M. Sádlo vlc   Supraphon LPV58
Trio No. 4, in e, Op. 90 "Dumky" pf, vln & vlc
with J. Páleníček pf & M. Sádlo vlc   Supraphon LPM64

FRANCK

Sonata in A (1886) vln & pf
with J. Páleníček pf   Supraphon LPM115, SUF20233
                                   Ultraphon 5090C

JANÁCEK

Quartet No. 2 (1927/8) "Intimate pages" 2 vlns, vla & vlc
(as member of Černý string quartet)   Ultraphon G12968/70
Sonata (1913/21) vln & pf
with J. Páleníček pf   Esta H5156/7

MARTINŮ

Sonata No. 3 (1944) vln & pf
with J. Páleníček pf   Supraphon LPM301, SUF20305

MOZART

Sonata No. 18, in G, K301 vln & pf
with J. Páleníček pf   Supraphon LPV365
Sonata No. 21, in e, K304 vln & pf
with J. Páleníček pf   Supraphon LPV365
Sonata No. 32, in B flat, K454 vln & pf
with J. Páleníček pf   Supraphon LPV365

RAVEL

Trio in a (1915) pf, vln & vlc
with J. Páleníček pf & M. Sádlo vlc   Supraphon SUA10019

SCHUBERT

Trio No. 2, in E flat, Op. 100 (D929) pf, vln & vlc
with J. Páleníček pf & S. Vectomov vlc Eterna 820059

SHOSTAKOVICH

Trio No. 2, in e, Op. 67 "In memory of I.I. Sollertinsky" pf, vln & vlc
with J. Páleníček pf & M. Sádlo vlc   Supraphon SUA10019

SLAVÍK

Concerto No. 2, in a "Unfinished" vln & orch.
Allegro (1st mvt) (cadenza by Páleníček)*
with Czech Radio Orch.   044361/4 Supraphon G22096/7
– Stupka   Ultraphon G14206/7

SMETANA

From my Homeland (1878) vln & pf†
with F. Holeček pf   045026/7 Ultraphon G14893/4

Trio in g, Op. 15 pf, vln & vlc
with J. Páleníček pf & M. Sádlo vlc   Ultraphon G14890/3

SUK

Fantasy in g, Op. 24 vln & orch.
with Czech Philharmonic Orch. –   Supraphon LPV232, SUB10260
Ančerl   Ultraphon 5183C

* Also on Ultraphon MBA13046/7; cadenza omitted.
† Andantino only is on Supraphon G23243.

Stanley PLUMMER

CORELLI

(12) Sonatas, Op. 5 vln & c

Sonata No. 1, in D
with M. Hamilton hpsi & J. Kessler vlc — Everest (in sets LPBR6163 & SDBR3163)

Sonata No. 2, in B flat
with M. Hamilton hpsi & J. Kessler vlc — Everest (in sets LPBR6163 & SDBR3163)

Sonata No. 3, in C
with M. Hamilton hpsi & J. Kessler vlc — Everest (in sets LPBR6163 & SDBR3163)

Sonata No. 4, in F
with M. Hamilton hpsi & J. Kessler vlc — Everest (in sets LPBR6163 & SDBR3163)

Sonata No. 5, in g
with M. Hamilton hpsi & J. Kessler vlc — Everest (in sets LPBR6163 & SDBR3163)

Sonata No. 6, in A
with M. Hamilton hpsi & J. Kessler vlc — Everest (in sets LPBR6163 & SDBR3163)

Sonata No. 7, in d
with M. Hamilton hpsi & J. Kessler vlc — Everest (in sets LPBR6163 & SDBR3163)

Sonata No. 8, in e
with M. Hamilton hpsi & J. Kessler vlc — Everest (in sets LPBR6163 & SDBR3163)

Sonata No. 9, in A
with M. Hamilton hpsi & J. Kessler vlc — Everest (in sets LPBR6163 & SDBR3163)

Sonata No. 10, in F
with M. Hamilton hpsi & J. Kessler vlc — Everest (in sets LPBR6163 & SDBR3163)

Sonata No. 11, in E
with M. Hamilton hpsi & J. Kessler vlc — Everest (in sets LPBR6163 & SDBR3163)

Sonata No. 12, in d "La Follia"
with M. Hamilton hpsi & J. Kessler vlc — Everest (in sets LPBR6163 & SDBR3163)

DUKE, L.B.

Sonata No. 4, Op. 21 vln & pf
with Vallecillo pf — Byron 5

LAZAROF

Rhapsody (1966) vln & pf
with V. Steinhardt pf — Everest LPBR6160, SDBR3160

Tempi concertati (1964) vln, vla, fl, vibes, xylo, hp, pf, hpsi & cel
with M. Johnson vla, G. Shanley fl, E. Richards vibes & xylo, D. Remsen hp, G. Akst pf, hpsi & cel – cond. Lazarof — Everest LPBR6160, SDBR3160

Paavo POHJOLA

HJELT

(6) Eteläpohjalaisia tansse, Op. 17a vln & pf
with L. Pohjola pf — Kuula Levyt TK–S103

Leonid POLEESS

JANÁČEK

Concertino (1925) pf, 2 vlns, vla, cl, hrn & bsn
with J. Páleníček pf, A. Abramenkov vln, G. Talalyan vla, V. Tupikin cl, B. Afanasyev hrn & Y. Kurpekov bsn — Mezhdunarodnaya Kniga D06267

TELEMANN

Concerto in B flat 3 obs, 3 vlns, hpsi & strs
with E. Nepalo ob, P. Dubrov ob, S. Trubashnik ob, A. Abramenkov vln, R. Barshai vln & Moscow Chamber Orch. – Barshai — Angel 36264, Le Chant du Monde LDX–A8340, LDX–A48348, Electrola E91415, SME91415, Mezhdunarodnaya Kniga D022145/6

Juan POLINSKI

BEETHOVEN

(6) Minuets, G167 pf
No. 2. Minuet No. 2, in G arr. vln & pf Burmester
with piano — Famous 750

KREISLER

Caprice viennois, Op. 2 vln & pf
with piano — Famous 750

J. POLLAK

MOZART

Sinfonia concertante in E flat, K364 vln, vla & orch.
with W.L. van Rostock vla & Saxon State Orch. – Elsner — Colosseum CLPS1052

Robert POLLAK (1880–1962)

d'AMBROSIO

Canzonetta, Op. 6 vln & pf
with piano — 50697 Homochord B8104

ANONYMOUS

(Die) Gute alte Zeit Old Viennese song – arr. vln & pf Pollack
with F. Günther pf — 19423 Homochord 4–2417

Neuer Wien Old Viennese song – arr. vln & pf Pollack
with F. Günther pf — 19424 Homochord 4–2417

BEETHOVEN

(6) Minuets, G167 pf
No. 2. Minuet No. 2, in G arr. vln & pf Burmester
with piano — 50696 Homochord E8103

(3) Sonatas, Op. 12 vln & pf
No. 1. Sonata No. 1, in D: Tema con variazione (2nd mvt)
with E. Korngold pf — Homochord HB2091

JERAL

Sérénade viennois, Op. 18 vln & pf
with piano — 50695 Homochord E8103

KORNGOLD

(Die) Tote Stadt, Op. 12 (1920) – opera
  Mein sehnen, mein Wähnen (Pierrotlied) arr. vln & pf as "Pierrot's dance song" by Kreisler
  with E. Korngold pf   Homochord HB2097
Viel Lärmen um Nichts (Much ado about nothing) Op. 11 (1919) – Incidental music orch.
  No. 2. Holzapfel und Schlehwein arr. vln & pf
  with E. Korngold pf   Homochord HB2097 & HB2112
  No. 3. Gartenszene arr. vln & pf
  with E. Korngold pf   Homochord HB2097 & HB2112
  No. 4, Mummenschanz (Hornpipe) arr. vln & pf
  with E. Korngold pf   Homochord HB2097 & HB2112

LECLAIR

(12) Sonatas, Op. 1 – Book I (1723) vln & c
Sonata No. 8, in G: Musette, affettuosa (3rd mvt)
  with F. Günther pf   19422 Homochord 4–2484
(12) Sonatas, Op. 9 – Book IV (1738) vln & c
Sonata No. 3, in D: Tambourin (3rd mvt) arr. vln & pf Kreisler
  with piano   T 5036 Homochord P5001

LULLY

Ballet du Roy (1659)*
  Gavotte arr. vln & pf Burmester
  with piano   16772 Homochord B171

MENDELSSOHN

(6) Songs without words, Op. 19 pf
  No. 6. Song without words No. 6, in g "Venezianisches Gondellied" arr. vln & pf
  with F. Günther pf   19426 Homochord 4–2485
(6) Songs without words, Op. 62 pf
  No. 6. Song without words No. 30, in A "Spring song" arr. vln & pf
  with F. Günther pf   19425 Homochord 4–2485

MOZART

Divertimento No. 17, in D, K334 2 hrns & strs
  Minuet (3rd mvt) arr. vln & pf Burmester
  with piano   Homochord HB2129

PAGANINI

Gavotte variata unid – arr. vln & pf Corti
  with piano   T 5029 Homochord P5001

SAINT-SAËNS

(Le) Carnaval des animaux (1886) small orch.
  Le cygne arr. vln & pf
  with piano   50698 Homochord B8104

SARASATE

(8) Danzas españolas vln & pf
  No. 3. Romanza andaluza, Op. 22, No. 1
  with piano   Homochord HB2129

SCHUBERT, François

(12) Bagatelles, Op. 13 vln & pf
  No. 9. L'abeille
  with piano   50697 Homochord B8104

* Unidentified.

SIMONETTI

Madrigale pf – arr. vln & pf
  with piano   Homochord

TENAGLIA

Have pity, sweet eyes v & c – arr. vln & pf as "Aria in f" by Ries
  with F. Günther pf   19427 Homochord 4–2484

WIENIAWSKI

Légende, Op. 17 vln & pf or orch.
  with piano   Homochord
Mazurka unid – vln & pf
  with piano   Homochord

Max POLLIKOFF

LUENING

Gargoyles (1962) vln & synthesized sound
  with synthesized sound   Columbia ML5966, MS6566

RIMSKY–KORSAKOV

Scheherazade, Op. 35 (1888) orch.
  with Symphony Orch. – Gould   Victor LM1956, VICS1444

SYDEMAN

Concerto da camera No. 1 (1958) vln & orch.
  with CRI Chamber Ensemble – Wolfe   Composers Recordings CRI158

Enrico POLO (1868–1953)

BAZZINI

(6) Morceaux lyriques, Op. 35 vln & pf
  No. 1. Élégie
  with piano   Pathé 19559, 84098

BÉRIOT

Scène de Ballet (Fantaisie–ballet No. 1) Op. 100 vln & orch.
  with piano   Pathé 84101

COSTA

Frangesa march v & pf – arr. vln & pf
  with piano   Pathé 80687

GODARD

Jocelyn (1888) – opera
  Cachés dans cet asile "Berceuse" arr. vln & pf
  with piano   Pathé 84094

HERMANN

Boléro sur des motifs espagnols, Op. 52 vln & pf
  with piano   Pathé 84100

MENDELSSOHN

(6) Songs without words, Op. 62 pf
  No. 6. Song without words No. 30, in A "Spring song" arr. vln & pf
  with piano   Pathé 84093

RAFF

(6) Pieces, Op. 85 vln & pf
  No. 3. Cavatina in D
  with piano   Pathé 19559, 84099

Alberto POLTRONIERI (1892–)

BACH

(Ein) Musikalisches Opfer, BWV1079 (1749) strs & c – arr. Casella
2B 4764^{II} □, 4765^{I} □, & 4766/7^{II} HMV DB2168/9
with A. Casella pf   □, Victor 8710/1
& A. Bonucci vlc

BEETHOVEN

(2) Trios, Op. 70 pf, vln & vlc
No. 1. Trio No. 4, in D "Ghost"
WBX 997–1, 998/9 & 1027   Columbia GQX10132/3
with A. Casella pf & A. Bonucci vlc

BÉRIOT

Adagio unid – vln & pf*
with piano   Columbia GQX10062

BRAHMS

Trio No. 2, in C, Op. 87 pf, vln & vlc
with A. Casella pf & A. Bonucci vlc
Columbia GQX10523/5

CHAMINADE

Sérénade espagnole pf – arr. vln & pf Kreisler
with piano   Columbia GQ7021

DVOŘÁK

(8) Slavonic Dances, Op. 46 pf duet; orch.
No. 2. Slavonic dance No. 2, in e arr. vln & pf "in g" Kreisler
with piano   Odeon GO12896

FALLA

(7) Canciones populares españolas (1914) v & pf
No. 4. Jota arr. vln & pf Kochański
with piano   Odeon GO12896

HARRIS

Trio (1934) pf, vln & vlc
with A. Casella pf & A. Bonucci vlc   Columbia 68247/9D, (set M282)

JUON

(2) Violinstücke, Op. 52 vln & pf
No. 2. Arva "Valse mignonne"
with piano   Columbia GQX10062

KREISLER

Liebesleid vln & pf
with piano   Odeon GO12897

Andantino (Padre Martini) vln & pf
with piano   Columbia GQ7021

NIN

(2) Cantos de España (1923) v & pf
No. 4. Montañesa arr. vln & pf Kochański
with piano   Odeon GO12896

No. 8. Saeta (Invocation) arr. vln & pf Kochański
with piano   Odeon GO12897

PIZZETTI

Aria in D (1906) vln & pf
with I. Pizzetti pf
Columbia D14557, JW312

* Possibly the 2nd mvt from the "Concerto No. 7, in G" Op. 76.

PIZZETTI – *Continued*

(3) Canti ad una giovane fidanzata (1924) vln & pf
with I. Pizzetti pf   Columbia D14556/7, JW311/2

SCHUBERT

(2) Lieder, Op. 98 (D498) v & pf
No. 2. Wiegenlied (Schlafe, holder süsser Knabe) arr. vln & pf Elman
with piano   Columbia GQ7019

SGAMBATI

(2) Pieces, Op. 24 vln & pf
No. 2. Serenata napoletana
with piano   Columbia GQ7019

VIVALDI

(12) Concerti, Op. 3 "L'Estro armonico" var. cbns & strs
Concerto No. 1, in D, P.146 (F.IV, No. 8) 4 vlns, vlc, strs & c
with F. Gulli vln, E. Malanotte vln,   HMV ALP1809, ASD391
M. Benvenuti vln & Virtuosi di Roma
– Fasano

Arthur POLSON (1934–)

BRAHMS

Sonata No. 3, in d, Op. 108 vln & pf
with W. Aide pf   CBC Radio Canada SM64

LECLAIR

(12) Sonatas, Op. 9 – Book IV (1738) vln & c
Sonata No. 3, in D
with W. Aide pf   CBC Radio Canada SM64

POLSON

Fantasy "Dracula" vln & pf
with W. Aide pf   CBC Radio Canada SM64

Myron POLYAKIN (1895–1939)

BEETHOVEN

Sonata No. 9, in A, Op. 47 "Kreutzer" vln & pf
with A. Dyakov pf   Mezhdunarodnaya Kniga
D6527/30 & D8286/90 &
D8350/1

BRAHMS

(21) Hungarian Dances pf duet
Hungarian dance No. 20, in e arr. vln & pf "in d" Joachim
with D. Makarov pf   Mezhdunarodnaya Kniga
D10462

GLAZOUNOV

Concerto in a, Op. 82 vln & orch.
with USSR State Symphony Orch. –   Mezhdunarodnaya Kniga
Orlov   D09893/8

SARASATE

(8) Danzas españolas vln & pf
No. 2. Habañera, Op. 21, No. 2
with A. Dyakov pf   Mezhdunarodnaya Kniga
D8284/5

SARASATE – *Continued*

Zigeunerweisen, Op. 20 vln & pf or orch.
  with D. Makarov pf   Mezhdunarodnaya Kniga
                              D10460/1

SCHUBERT

(16) Deutsche Tänze, Op. 33 (D783) pf
  No. 3. Deutscher Tanz No. 3, in B flat arr vln & pf as "Valse
  sentimentale" by Franko
  with A. Dyakov pf   Mezhdunarodnaya Kniga D8349

TCHAIKOVSKY

Waltz–scherzo, Op. 34 vln & pf or orch. – arr. Bezékirsky
  with D. Makarov pf   Mezhdunarodnaya Kniga
                              D9881/2

TOWNSEND

Berceuse vln & pf
  with D. Makarov pf   Mezhdunarodnaya Kniga
                              D10459

Joseph PONTICELLI

LOEILLET, J.B.

(12) Sonatas, Op. 2 1/6: 2 vlns & c – 7/9: 2 fls & c – 10/12: ob, fl & c
  Sonata No. 2, in F
  with P. Fontanarosa vln & J–L. Petit   Decca 174141, SMD1513,
  hpsi   SXL20141
  Sonata No. 5, in c
  with P. Fontanarosa vln & J–L. Petit   Decca 174141, SMD1513,
  hpsi   SXL20141
  Sonata No. 6, in c
  with P. Fontanarosa vln, & J–L. Petit   Decca 174141, SMD1513,
  hpsi   SXL20141
  Sonata No. 9, in g
  with P. Fontanarosa vln & J–L. Petit   Decca 174141, SMD1513,
  hpsi   SXL20141

Enzo PORTA

LEGRENZI

(12) Sonatas, Op. 2 (1655) 2 vlns & c
  Sonata in G "La Raspona"
  with G. Franzetti vln, G. Spinelli hpsi   Storia della Musica MdM014
  & A. Riccardi gamba   (Vol. 2, No. 1)

José PORTA (1890–

ARBÓS

Cubana vln & pf
  with piano   Polydor 19240, 65633

BACH

(3) Sonatas & 3 Partitas, BWV1001/6 solo vln
  Partita No. 2, in d: Sarabande (3rd mvt) BWV1004
  (unaccompanied)   Parlophone 20078
                              Polydor 62377

KREISLER

Minuet (Porpora) vln & pf
  with piano   Polydor 19240, 65633

PAGANINI

(24) Caprices, Op. 1 (1801/7) solo vln
  Caprice No. 16, in a arr. vln & pf
  with piano   710 at   Parlophone 20079
                                 Polydor 62378

  Caprice No. 17, in E flat arr. vln & pf
  with piano   709 at   Parlophone 20079
                                 Polydor 62378

SCHUBERT, François

(12) Bagatelles, Op. 13 vln & pf
  No. 9. L'abeille
  with piano   Parlophone 20078
                              Polydor 62377

Vassilij PORTNOFF

PORTNOFF

(La) Danseuse vln & pf
  with M. Portnoff pf   Skandia SG1547
Serenade vln & pf
  with M. Portnoff pf   Skandia SG1547

Ruth POSSELT (1914–   )

ABACO

(12) Sonatas, Op. 3 (1714) 2 vlns & c
  Sonata No. 1, in C
  with R. Burgin vln & E. Bodky hpsi   Kapp KL9024
                                       Unicorn UNLP1030

ALBINONI

(12) Sonatas, Op. 1 (1694) "Sinfonias" 2 vlns & c
  Sonata No. 3. in A
  with R. Burgin vln & E. Bodky hpsi   Kapp KL9024
                                       Unicorn UNLP1030

ARBÓS

(3) Danzas españolas, Op. 6 vln & pf
  No. 3. Tango
  with A. Sly pf   Academy ALP304

BACH

Sonata in G, BWV1038 fl, vln & c
  with P. Kaplan fl, E. Bodky hpsi & S.   Allegro 4400, AL89
  Mayes vlc   Allegro–Elite 4004

BEETHOVEN

(3) Trios, Op. 1 pf, vln & vlc
  No. 2. Trio No. 2, in G
  with A. Bogin pf & S. Mayes vlc   Allegro ALG3026
                                    Allegro–Elite LDAD79

(2) Trios, Op. 9 vln, vla & vlc
  No. 1. Trio No. 2, in G
  with J. de Pasquale vla & S. Mayes vlc   Brunswick AXTL1056
                                           Decca DL9635, UAT273543

BEETHOVEN – *Continued*

No. 2. Trio No. 3, in D
with J. de Pasquale vla & S. Mayes vlc   Brunswick AXTL1056
    Decca DL9635, UAT273543

(2) Trios, Op. 70 pf, vln & vlc
No. 1. Trio No. 4, in D "Ghost"
with A. Bogin pf & S. Mayes vlc   Allegro ALG3026
    Allegro–Elite LDAD79

DALLAPICCOLA

Tartiniana No. 1 (1951) vln & pf
with Columbia Symphony Orch. –   Columbia ML4996
Bernstein

FAURÉ

Sonata No. 2, in e, Op. 108 vln & pf
with J. Rezits pf   Festival FLP70203

FIBICH

Images, Impressions & Souvenirs, Op. 41 pf
No. 14. Poem (from "Souvenirs", Part IV) arr. vln & pf Kubelík
with G. Posselt pf   HMV AV26
    Victor 4184

HAYDN

(3) Duos, H.III, Nos. 28/30 (1769) vln & vlc
No. 1. Duo No. 4, in D, H.III, No. 28
with S. Mayes vlc   Festival FLP70203

Sonata No. 51, in D, Op. 93 (H.XVI, No. 51) pf – arr. vln & vlc
with S. Mayes vlc   Festival FLP70203

HINDEMITH

Sonata No. 3, in E (1935) vln & pf
with A. Sly pf   Academy ALP304
    Esquire TW14005

MARTINŮ

Duo No. 1 (1927) vln & vlc
with S. Mayes vlc   Festival FLP70203

MOZART

Divertimento in E flat, K563 vln, vla & vlc
with J. de Pasquale vla & S. Mayes vlc Brunswick AXTL1031
    Decca DL9659, UAT273578

Trio No. 3, in B flat, K502 pf, vln & vlc
with A. Bogin pf & S. Mayes vlc   Allegro ALG3014
    Allegro–Elite LDAD73

Trio No. 4, in E, K542 pf, vln & vlc
with A. Bogin pf & S. Mayes vlc   Allegro ALG3014
    Allegro–Elite LDAD73

PROKOFIEV

(5) Melodies, Op. 35bis (1921) vln & pf
with A. Sly pf   Esquire TW14005

STICH

Quartet hrn, vln, vla & vlc
with J. Stagliano hrn, J. de Pasquale   Boston B209
vla & S. Mayes vlc

VILLA–LOBOS

Sonata–Fantasia No. 1, in c (1912) "Déspespérance" vln & pf
with A. Sly pf   Academy ALP304
    Esquire TW14005

WIENIAWSKI

(2) Mazurkas, Op. 12 vln & pf
No. 1. Mazurka No. 1, in D "Sielanka"
with G. Posselt pf   HMV AV26
    Victor 4184

Herman POST (1880–)

GODARD

Jocelyn (1888) – opera
Cachés dans cet asile "Berceuse" arr. vln & hp
with F. Post hp   Odeon 311879

GOUNOD

Ave Maria (Méditation on Bach's "Prelude No. 1, in C" from Book I of "Das Wohltemperirte Clavier") v & pf – arr. vln & hp
with F. Post hp   Odeon 311893

PRUME

(La) Mélancolie (Pastorale) Op. 1 vln & pf
with F. Post hp   Odeon 311879

SCHUBERT

(7) Gesänge (set to Scott's "Lady of the Lake") Op. 52 v & pf
No. 6. Ave Maria, D839 arr. vln & pf Wilhelmj
with F. Post hp   Odeon 311893

Jean POUGNET (1907–1968)

BACH

(6) Brandenburg Concerti, BWV1046/51 (1721) strs & c
Brandenburg Concerto No. 3, in G, BWV1048 3 vlns, 3 vlas, 3 vlcs & cbs
with T. Carter vln, M. Eitler vln, F.   Nixa WLP6309
Riddle vla, E. Grainger vla, E.   Westminster XWN18366, (in set
Hurwitz vla, V. Joseph vlc, A. Pini   XWN2211)
vlc, R. Albin vlc, R. Watson cbs & R.   Whitehall WH20071
Veyron–Lacroix hpsi of the London
Baroque Ensemble – Haas

Brandenburg Concerto No. 5, in D, BWV1050 clav, fl, vln, strs & c
with R. Veyron–Lacroix hpsi, R.   Nixa WLP6309
Adeney fl & London Baroque   Westminster XWN18366, (in set
Ensemble – Haas   XWN2211)
    Whitehall WH20071

Cantata No. 202 (Weichet nur, betrübte Schatten) BWV202
with J. Delman s & London Baroque   Parlophone PMA1023
Ensemble – Haas

Concerto in d, BWV1043 2 vlns, strs & c
with A. Grumiaux   CAX 9503/6–1   Columbia DOX854/5,
vln & Philharmonia Orch. – Susskind   DX1276/7, GFX124/5,
    GQX11320/1

BARTÓK

(2) Portraits, Op. 5 vln & orch.
with New Symphony Orch. – Autori   Bartók BRS303, BRS304

BEETHOVEN

Serenade in D, Op. 8 vln, vla & vlc
with F. Riddle vla & A. Pini vlc   Nixa WLP5219
Westminster (in sets WM1017 & WMS1017), XWN18412, WL5219

Trio No. 1, in E flat, Op. 3 vln, vla & vlc
with F. Riddle vla & A. Pini vlc   Westminster (in sets WM1017 & WMS1017), XWN18410, WL5226

(3) Trios, Op. 9 vln, vla & vlc
No. 1. Trio No. 2, in G
with F. Riddle vla & A. Pini vlc   Nixa WLP5198
Westminster (in sets WM1017 & WMS1017), XWN18411, WL5198

No. 2. Trio No. 3, in D
with F. Riddle vla & A. Pini vlc   Nixa WLP5198
Westminster (in sets WM1017 & WMS1017), XWN18411, WL5198

No. 3. Trio No. 4, in c
with F. Riddle vla & A. Pini vlc   Nixa WLP5219
Westminster (in sets WM1017 & WMS1017), XWN18412, WL5219

BERKELEY

Trio (1944) vln, vla & vlc
with F. Riddle vla & A. Pini vlc   Nixa WLP20017
Westminster XWN18515, WL5316

BOCCHERINI

(6) Quintets, Op. 45 fl, 2 vlns, vla & vlc
No. 5. Quintet No. 5, in E flat
with R. Adeney fl, K. Sturdy vln, H. Danks vla & J. Whitehead vlc   Nixa WLP5080
Westminster XWN18058, WL5080

CASELLA

Serenata, Op. 50 (1927) cl, bsn, tpt, vln & vlc
No. 6. Finale (Vivacissimo, alla napoletana)*
with R. Kell cl,   CA 16221–1   Columbia DB1788
P. Draper bsn, G. Eskdale tpt & A. Pini vlc

CHERUBINI

Pater Noster org & strs – arr. vln & strs Cherubini
with London Baroque Ensemble – Haas   Decca DL4081
Parlophone R20618

DELIUS

Concerto (1916) vln & orch.
     2EA 11329–3, 11330–2, 11331–1,   HMV ALP1890, DB6369/71,
with Royal   11332–3 & 11333–1   DB9092/4
Philharmonic Orch. – Beecham

* Called "Tarantella" on the record label.

DENZA

Si vous l'aviez compris v & pf – arr. v, vln & pf
with W. Booth t &   2EA 8082[1]   HMV C3116
E. Lush pf

DITTERSDORF

Concerto in G (1767) vln, strs & c
with L. Salter hpsi & London Baroque   Parlophone PMA1004
Ensemble – Haas

DOHNÁNYI

Serenade in C, Op. 10 vln, vla & vlc
with F. Riddle vla & A. Pini vlc   Nixa WLP20017
Westminster XWN18515, WL5316

FRANCAIX

Trio in C (1933) vln, vla & vlc
with F. Riddle vla & A. Pini vlc   Nixa WLP20017
Westminster XWN18515, WL5316

HAYDN

Concerto in F, H.XVIII, No. 6 (1765) vln, hpsi & orch.
     CXE 13422/3–2, 13424–3, 13425   Decca DL9661
with L. Salter hpsi & –2A & 13426–1   Parlophone PMA1012,
London Baroque Ensemble– Haas   R20594/6, SW8126/8
(3) Trios, H.XVI, Nos. 40/2 (Op. 53) vln, vla & vlc
Trio No. 1, in G, H.XVI, No. 40
with F. Riddle vla & A. Pini vlc   Westminster XWN18609, W9033, WL5295

Trio No. 2, in B flat, H.XVI, No. 41
with F. Riddle vla & A. Pini vlc   Westminster XWN18609, W9033, WL5295

Trio No. 3, in D, H.XVI, No. 42
with F. Riddle vla & A. Pini vlc   Westminster XWN18609, W9033, WL5295

HAYDN, M.

Divertimento in C, P99 vln, vlc & cbs
with J. Whitehead vlc & J. Merrett cbs   Nixa WLP5080
Westminster XWN18058, WL5080

HINDEMITH

Trio No. 1, Op. 34 (1924) vln, vla & vlc
with F. Riddle vla & A. Pini vlc   Nixa WLP5299
Westminster XWN18593, W9067, WL5299

Trio No. 2 (1934) vln, vla & vlc
with F. Riddle vla & A. Pini vlc   Nixa WLP5299
Westminster XWN18593, W9067, WL5299

KREISLER

Caprice viennois, Op. 2 vln & pf
with orch. – Torch   CXE 13636–1   Parlophone E11497

(La) Gitana vln & pf
with orch. – Torch   Parlophone CGEP7, R3556

Liebesfreud vln & pf
with orch. – Torch   Parlophone CGEP7, R3556

KREISLER – *Continued*

Concerto in C (Vivaldi) vln & strs
          CAX 8541/3–1 & 8606–1 Columbia DOX722/3, DX963/4
with Symphony Orch. – Goehr

Praeludium & Allegro (Pugnani) vln & pf
  with orch. – Torch   CXE 13635–3C Parlophone E11497

Praeludium & Allegro (Pugnani) vln & pf*
  with M. Sargent pf   2EA 12132–3 HMV C3619

LECLAIR

(12) Sonatas, Op. 2 – Book II (1728) vln & c
Sonata No. 5, in G
  with A. Goldsbrough hpsi & J.   HMV HLP15, HMS63
  Whitehead gamba   Victor (in set LM6031)

MOERAN

Trio in G (1931) vln, vla & vlc
  with F. Riddle vla   CAX 8851/6–1 Columbia DOX700/2,
  & A. Pini vlc   DX1014/6, DX8153/5

MOZART

Adagio in E, K261 vln & orch.
  with Symphony   CAX 8539/40–1 Columbia DX957
  Orch. – Goehr

Divertimento in E flat, K563 vln, vla & vlc
  with F. Riddle vla & A. Pini vlc   Heliodor 479048
                                     Nixa WLP5191
                                     Vega C30 A13
                                     Westminster XWN18551,
                                     W9068, WL5191

Rondo in C, K373 vln & orch.
          CAX 8071–2 & 8072–2A Columbia 69125D, DOX556,
  with Symphony Orch. – Goehr   DX769

Serenade No. 6, in D, K239 "Serenata Notturna" orch.
  with London Baroque Ensemble – Parlophone PMB1005
  Haas

PURCELL

(10) Sonatas, Z802/11 (1697) 4 parts – 2 vlns & c
Sonata No. 3, in a, Z804
          CA 7383–II & 7384–I Decca 25615, K809
  with F. Grinke vln & B. Ord hpsi
Sonata No. 9, in F, Z810 "Golden Sonata"
  with F. Grinke vln   CA 7381/2–1 Decca 25614, K778
  & B. Ord hpsi   Polydor 45252

RAVEL

Introduction & Allegro (1906) hp, fl, cl, 2 vlns, vla & vlc
          CAX 9630–2 & 9631/2–1 Columbia DX1310/1, RL3055
  with J. Cockerill hp, A. Gleghorn fl,
  R. Kell cl, D. Martin vln, F. Riddle
  vla & J. Whitehead vlc

STICH

Quintet 3 fls, vln & vlc
  with G. Gilbert fl, G. Crozier fl, L. Argo RG74
  Soloman fl & F. Gabarro vlc

* Abridged.

VAUGHAN WILLIAMS

(The) Lark ascending (1914) vln & orch.
  with London Philharmonic Orch. – Parlophone PMB1003
  Boult

Quintet (1914) "Phantasy" 3 vlns, vla & vlc
  with B. Pecker vln, A. Mangeot vln, National Gramophonic Society
  H.J. Berley vla & J. Barbirolli vlc 54/5

WILTON

(6) Trios (1783) vln, vla & vlc
Trio No. 1, in A
  with F. Riddle vla & A. Pini vlc   Westminster XWN18586,
                                       W9034, WL5296

Trio No. 3, in C
  with F. Riddle vla & A. Pini vlc   Westminster XWN18586,
                                       W9034, WL5296

Trio No. 6, in F
  with F. Riddle vla & A. Pini vlc   Westminster XWN18586,
                                       W9034, WL5296

Gérard Georges POULET (1938–)

FAURÉ

Romance in A, Op. 69 vlc & pf – arr. vln & pf
  with Lacoaref pf   Deva 45A2

KREISLER

Caprice viennois, Op. 2 vln & pf
  with Lacoaref pf   Deva M17

Tambourin chinois, Op. 3 vln & pf
  with Lacoaref pf   Deva M17

Praeludium & Allegro (Pugnani) vln & pf
  with Lacoaref pf   Deva M17

MOZART

Concerto No. 3, in G, K216 vln & orch.
  with Austrian Symphony Orch. – Concerteum CR292
  Poulet   Remington R199–131

Concerto No. 4, in D, K218 (cadenzas by Herrmann) vln & orch.
  with Austrian Symphony Orch. – Concerteum CR292
  Poulet   Remington R199–131

Concertone in C, K190 2 vlns, ob, vlc & orch.
  with H. Szeryng vln, R. Morgan ob, Philips 6500 038, (in set 6707
  N. Jones vlc & New Philharmonia 011)
  Orch. – Gibson

PAGANINI

(24) Caprices, Op. 1 (1801/7) solo vln
Caprice No. 9, in E
  (unaccompanied)   Deva M17

Caprice No. 13, in B flat
  (unaccompanied)   Deva M17

Caprice No. 24, in a
  (unaccompanied)   Deva M17

TCHAIKOVSKY

Romance in f, Op. 5 pf – arr. vln & pf
  with Lacoaref pf   Deva 45A2

WAGNER

Albumblatt in C (1861) pf – arr. vln & pf Wilhelmj
  with Lacoaref pf   Deva 45A2

Maud POWELL (1868–1920)

ANONYMOUS

Arkansas traveller Traditional American folksong – arr. vln & pf Guion
  with G. Falkenstein pf   Victor 64211
Little red lark arr. vln & pf
  with G. Falkenstein pf   Victor 64208
Molly on the shore Traditional Irish ballad – arr. vln & pf
  with A. Loesser pf   HMV 4–7976, DA341
                                          Victor 64611, 811

BACH

(3) Sonatas & 3 Partitas, BWV1001/6 solo vln
  Partita No. 1, in b: Bourrée (7th mvt) BWV1002
  (unaccompanied)   A 13731   HMV 2–07989, DB656
                                          Victor 74357
(6) Sonatas, BWV1014/9 vln & clav
  Sonata No. 4, in c: Largo (1st mvt); **Allegro** (2nd mvt) BWV1017
  with G. Falkenstein pf   HMV 4–7981/2, DA345
                                          Victor 64618/9

BEETHOVEN

(6) Minuets, G167 pf
  No. 2. Minuet No. 2, in G arr. vln & pf Powell
  with A. Loesser pf   A 17793   HMV 4–7974, DA341
                                          Pearl GEM101
                                          Victor 64620, 804

BÉRIOT

Concerto No. 7, in G, Op. 76 vln & orch.
  with A. Loesser pf   HMV 2–07932 & 2–07903/4,
                                          DB391 & DB394
                                          Victor 74446 & 74492/3, 6257 &
                                          6378

BOCCHERINI

(6) Quintets, Op. 13 2 vlns, vla & 2 vlcs
  No. 5. Quintet No. 5, in E: Minuet (3rd mvt) "Bull" arr. vln & pf
  Kreisler
  with G. Falkenstein pf   A 13727   HMV 3–07900, DB395
                                          Victor 74354

BOISDEFFRE

Au bord, du ruisseau (Sérénade champêtre) Op. 52 vln & pf
  with harp   HMV 4–7967, DA343
                                          Victor 64103, 801

BOROWSKI

Adoration (1903) vln & pf
  with G. Falkenstein pf   Victor*

BRUCH

Kol Nidrei, Op. 47 vlc or vln & orch.
  with G. Falkenstein pf   HMV 2–07999
                                          Victor 74355, 6256

* Unissued test pressing. Dated September 8th 1913.

CADMAN

Little firefly vln & pf
  with G. Falkenstein pf   Victor 64705

CHOPIN

(17) Polish songs, Op. 74 vln & pf
  No. 1. Zyczenie "The maiden's wish" arr. vln & pf MacMillen
  with G. Falkenstein pf   A 20024   HMV 2–07993, DB642
                                          Victor 74548, 6257
(3) Waltzes, Op. 64 pf
  No. 1. Waltz No. 6, in D flat "Minute waltz" arr. vln & pf
  with G. Falkenstein pf   A 4171   HMV 4–7968, DA551
                                          Victor 64076, 810

COLERIDGE–TAYLOR

(24) Negro Melodies, Op. 59 pf
  No. 10. Deep river arr. vln & pf Powell
  with G. Falkenstein pf   Victor 74246, 6253

DANKS

Silver threads among the gold (1873) v & pf – arr. vln & pf
  with G. Falkenstein pf   Victor 64459, 808

DRDLA

Guitarerro, Op. 88 vln & pf
  with A. Loesser pf   HMV 4–7971
                                          Victor 64621, 803
Souvenir vln & pf
  with G. Falkenstein pf   HMV 3–7964
                                          Victor 64074, 808

DVOŘÁK

(8) Humoresques, Op. 101 pf
  No. 7. Humoresque No. 7, in G flat arr. vln & pf "in G" Wilhelmj
  with A. Loesser pf   Victor 74494, 6255

ELGAR

Salut d'amour, Op. 12 orch. – arr. vln & pf Elgar
  with G. Falkenstein pf   A 13728   HMV 3–7980, DA346
                                          Victor 64373, 802

EMMETT

Dixie (1861) v & pf – arr. solo vln
  (unaccompanied)   Victor 64143

FOSTER

My old Kentucky home v & pf – arr. vln & orch. Powell
  with orch.   HMV 2–07997, DB390
                                          Victor 74547, 6253
Old black Joe (1860) v & pf – arr. vln & orch. Powell
  with orch.   HMV 2–07997, DB390
                                          Victor 74547, 6253

GILBERT

Marionettes (Scherzo) vln & pf
  with G. Falkenstein pf   Victor 64300

GLUCK

Orphée et Eurydice (1762) – opera
  Dance of the blessed spirits: Andante (No. 1) arr. vln & pf
  with G. Falkenstein pf   A 13731   HMV 2–07989, DB656
                                          Victor 74357

GLUCK – *Continued*

Dance of the blessed spirits: Lento "Mélodie" (No. 2) arr. vln & pf
Wilhelmj
with piano   HMV 4–7973
                                             Victor 64075, 807

GODARD

Jocelyn (1888) – opera
Cachés dans cet asile "Berceuse" arr. vln & pf
with piano   Victor 64435

GRIEG

(6) Lyric Pieces – Book III, Op. 43 pf
No. 6. To the spring arr. vln & pf Kreisler
with G. Falkenstein pf   HMV 4–7984, DA343
                                             Victor 64264, 810

HANDEL

Serse (1738) – opera
Ombra mai fu "Largo" arr. vln & orch.
with orch.   A 10540   HMV 2–07927, DB395
                                           Victor 74412, 6249

Ombra mai fu "Largo" arr. vln & pf
with W. Liachowsky pf   Victor 64227, 804

HERBERT

Petite valse vln & pf
with A. Loesser pf   HMV 4–7977
                                             Victor 64617

HUBAY

(6) Blumenleben, Op. 30 vln & pf
No. 5. Der Zephir
with G. Falkenstein pf   Victor 74188

(14) Scènes de la Csárda vln & pf
No. 4. Hejre Kati, Op. 32
with piano   A 12427   HMV 2–07992, DB393
                                           Victor 74324, 6258

(3) Transcriptions, Op. 3 vln & pf
No. 2a. Crépuscule (Massenet) arr. vln & hp as "Twilight" by Powell
with F.J. Lapitino hp   A 14995   HMV 3–07906
                                           Victor 74408

LECLAIR

(12) Sonatas, Op. 9 – Book IV (1738) vln & c
Sonata No. 3, in D: Tambourin (3rd mvt) arr. vln & pf Sarasate
with piano   HMV 4–7983
                                         Victor 64520

LEYBACH

Nocturne No. 5, in A flat, Op. 52 pf – arr. vln & orch.
with orch.   HMV 2–07995
                                         Victor 74531, 6251

MARTINI (Il Tedesco)

Plaisir d'amour v & pf – arr. vln & pf Powell
with A. Loesser pf   Victor 64615

MASSENET

Élégie v & pf – arr. vln & pf
with G. Falkenstein pf   A 20024   HMV 2–07993, DB642
                                           Victor 74548, 6257

MASSENET – *Continued*

Thaïs (1894) – opera
Méditation vln & orch.
with orch.   HMV 2–07900
                                         Victor 74135, 6255

MENDELSSOHN

Concerto in e, Op. 64 vln & orch.
Allegretto non troppo; Allegro molto vivace (3rd mvt)
with G. Falkenstein pf   A 1911   HMV 2–07996, DB391
                                           Victor 74026, 6252, 85040

MOSZKOWSKI

(6) Klavierstücke, Op. 15 pf – 4 hands
No. 1. Serenata arr. vln & pf
with piano   A 12396   HMV 3–7965, DA346
                                           Victor 64281, 807

MOZART

Divertimento No. 17, in D, K334 2 hrns & strs
Minuet (3rd mvt) arr. vln & pf Burmester
with piano   HMV 4–7975
                                         Victor 64073, 805

NERUDA

Berceuse slave d'après un chant polonaise, Op. 11 vln & pf
with piano   HMV 4–7969
                                       Victor 64027, 809, 81051

OFFENBACH

(Les) Contes d'Hoffmann (1881) – opera
Belle Nuit, O nuit d'amour "Barcarolle" arr. vln, hp & pf
with harp & piano   HMV 3–7978, DA344
                                       Victor 64457, 802

OGAREW

Caprice in a, Op. 51, No. 2 vln & pf
with G. Falkenstein pf   HMV 4–7970
                                     Victor 64301, 806

POLDINI

(7) Marionnettes pf
No. 2. Poupée valsante arr. vln & pf Hartmann
with G. Falkenstein pf   HMV 4–7979
                                     Victor 64784, 806

PUCCINI

(La) Bohème (1896) – opera
selection arr. vln & pf Powell
with piano   Victor 74546

RAFF

(6) Pieces, Op. 85 vln & pf
No. 3. Cavatina in D
with G. Falkenstein pf   HMV 2–07991
                                     Victor 74283, 6251

SAAR

(6) Klavierstücke, Op. 52 pf
No. 4. Gondoliera arr. vln & pf
with piano   HMV 4–7906
                                     Victor 64521

SAINT–SAËNS

(Le) Carnaval des animaux (1886) small orch.
    Le cygne arr. vln & pf
    with W. Liachowsky pf   Victor 64265, 801

SARASATE

(8) Danzas españolas vln & pf
    No. 8. Danza española No. 8, in C, Op. 26, No. 2
    with W. Liachowsky pf   HMV 3–07905
                                   Victor 74259, 6254

Zigeunerweisen, Op. 20 vln & pf or orch.*
    with W. Liachowsky pf   Victor 64262, 811

SAURET

(4) Morceaux, Op. 40 vln & pf
    No. 3. Farfalla–caprice "Will–o–the–wisp"
    with G. Falkenstein pf   HMV 2–07994, DB390
                                   Victor 74183, 6258

SCHMITT

(5) Pieces, Op. 19 vln or vlc & pf
    No. 1. Chanson à bercer (Lullaby)
    with piano   HMV 3–7981
                                   Victor 64458

SCHOOLCRAFT

Shine on v & pf – arr. vln & orch. Powell
    with orch.   HMV 2–07997, DB390
                                   Victor 74547, 6253

SCHUBERT, François

(12) Bagatelles, Op. 13 vln & pf
    No. 9. L'abeille
    with G. Falkenstein pf   A 4171   HMV 4–7968, DA551
                                     Victor 64076, 810

SCHUBERT, Franz

(7) Gesänge (set to Scott's "Lady of the Lake") Op. 52 v & pf
    No. 6. Ave Maria, D839 arr. vln & pf Wilhelmj
    with harp & string   A 15014   HMV 2–07988, DB396
    quartet   Victor 74177, 6249

Rosamunde von Cypern, Op. 26 (D797) (1823) – Incidental music orch.
    No. 5. Entr'acte III, in B flat arr. vln & pf Kreisler
    with G. Falkenstein pf   Victor 74447

SCHUMANN

(13) Kinderscenen, Op. 15 pf
    No. 7. Träumerei arr. vln & pf
    with G. Falkenstein pf   Victor 64134

SIBELIUS

King Christian ll, Op. 27 – Incidental music orch.
    Musette arr. vln & pf Powell
    with G. Falkenstein pf   A 14995   HMV 3–07906, DB642
                                     Victor 74408

Kuolema, Op. 44 – Incidental music orch.
    Valse triste arr. vln & pf Franko
    with G. Falkenstein pf   A 14999   HMV 2–07919, DB396
                                     Victor 74402, 6256

* Abridged.

TENAGLIA

Have pity, sweet eyes v & pf – arr. vln & pf as "Aria in f" by Ries
    with G. Falkenstein pf   HMV 2–07998
                                     Victor 74325, 6378

THOMAS

Mignon (1866) – opera
    Entr'acte (Gavotte) (Act II) arr. vln & pf Sarasate
    with G. Falkenstein pf   HMV 3–7979, DA344
                                     Victor 64454, 803

VIEUXTEMPS

Ballade & Polonaise in G, Op. 38 vln & pf
    Polonaise
    with G. Falkenstein pf   HMV 4–7978
                                     Victor 64028, 809, 81052

(6) Bouquet Américain, Op. 33 solo vln
    No. 2. La Fête de St. Patrice
    (unaccompanied)   Victor 74025, 6254, 85039

WIENIAWSKI

Capriccio–valse, Op. 7 vln & pf
    with G. Falkenstein pf   HMV 2–07990
                                     Victor 74173, 6250

Concerto No. 2, in d, Op. 22 vln & pf
    Romance (2nd mvt)
    with G. Falkenstein pf   A 9009   HMV 3–07902, DB656
                                     Victor 74179, 6252

Mazurka in a, Op. 3 "Kujawiak" vln & pf
    with G. Falkenstein pf   A 12398 HMV 2–07901, DB393
                                     Victor 74326, 6250

(2) Mazurkas, Op. 19 vln & pf
    No. 2. Mazurka No. 2, in D "Dudziarz"
    with G. Falkenstein pf   A 12398 HMV 2–07901, DB393
                                     Victor 74326, 6250

WORK

Kingdom coming v & pf – arr. vln & orch. Powell
    with orch.   HMV 2–07997, DB390
                                     Victor 74547, 6253

ZARZYCKI

Mazurka in G, Op. 26 vln & pf
    with G. Falkenstein pf   A 7097   HMV 4–7972, DA551
                                     Victor 64104, 805

Albert PRATZ (1914–)

ANONYMOUS

Gentle maiden English folksong – arr. Cyril Scott
    with orch. – Hyslop   Ace of Diamonds SDD2118

CHAMINADE

Sérénade espagnole pf – arr. vln & pf Kreisler
    with G. Kushner pf   CBC Transcription Program 42

CHOPIN

Nocturne No. 20, in c sharp, Op. posth pf – arr. vln & pf Milstein
    with orch. – Hyslop   Ace of Diamonds SDD2118

GLAZOUNOV

Raymonda, Op. 57 (1897) – ballet orch.
  Grand Adagio arr. vln & pf Zimbalist
  with orch. – Hyslop   Ace of Diamonds SDD2118

LULLY

Ballets du Roy (1659)*
  Gavotte arr. vln & pf Burmester
  with orch. – Hyslop   Ace of Diamonds SDD2118

MORAWETZ

Duo (1946) vln & pf
  with L. Barkin pf   CBC Transcription Program 124
Sonata No. 1 (1956) vln & pf
  with L. Barkin pf   CBC Transcription Program 194

MOSZKOWSKI

(2) Stücke, Op. 45 pf
  No. 2. Guitarre arr. vln & pf Sarasate
  with orch. – Hyslop   Ace of Diamonds SDD2118

PROKOFIEV

Cinderella, Op. 87 (1941/4) – ballet orch.
  Winter fairytale arr. vln & pf Fichtenholz
  with G. Gould pf   Hallmark RS3

SCARLATESCU

Bagatelle (in Rumanian style) vln & pf
  with orch. – Hyslop   Ace of Diamonds SDD2118

SHOSTAKOVICH

(3) Danses fantastiques, Op. 5 (1922) pf – arr. vln & pf Glickman
  with G. Gould pf   Hallmark RS3

SZYMANOWSKI

King Roger, Op. 46 (1926) – opera
  Chant de Roxane arr. vln & pf Kochański
  with G. Kushner pf   CBC Transcription Program 42

TAILLEFERRE

Pastorale vln & pf
  with orch. – Hyslop   Ace of Diamonds SDL2118

TANEIEV

(10) Immortelles, Op. 26 (1909) v & pf
  No. 1. Birth of a harp arr. vln & pf Hartmann
  with G. Gould pf   Hallmark RS3

TANSMAN

(5) Pieces vln & pf or small orch.
  No. 3. Mouvement perpétuel
  with orch. – Hyslop   Ace of Diamonds SDD2118

TURNER

Sonata (1956) vln & pf
  with P. Souvairan pf   CBC Transcription Program 194

WEINZWEIG

Concerto (1954) vln & orch.
  with CBC Symphony Orch. –   CBC Transcription Program 183
  Waddington

* Unidentified.

WHITE

Bandanna Sketches, Op. 12 vln & pf
  No. 1. Nobody knows de trouble I see (Negro spiritual)
  with orch. – Hyslop   Ace of Diamonds SDD2118

WILLAN

Sonata No. 1, in e (1922) vln & pf
  with G. Kushner pf   CBC Transcription Program 42
Sonata No. 1, in e (1922) vln & pf
  with L. Barkin pf   CBC Transcription Program 124

Louis PREIL (1901–)

LUMBYE

Concert–Polka (1863) 2 vlns & orch.
  with L. Hansen vln & Copenhagen   Odeon D6429
  Radio Orch. – Hammelboe

Giuseppe PRENCIPE

VIOTTI

Concerto No. 3, in a (cadenzas by Prencipe) vln & orch.
  with Orch. Rossini di Napoli –   Decca LXT6179, SMD1082,
  Caracciolo   SXL6179
                          London CM9445, CS6445

Michael PRESS (1872–1938)

COUPERIN, F.

(Les) Petits moulins à vent, XVII, No. 2 hpsi – arr. vln & pf Press
  with piano   Vox 06097

CUI

Kaleidoscope, Op. 50 vln & pf
  No. 9. Orientale
  with piano   Vox 06096

DAQUIN

Pièces de Clavecin – Book I (1735)
  Le coucou arr. vln & pf Press
  with piano   Vox 06096

DVOŘÁK

(8) Slavonic Dances, Op. 46 pf duet; orch.
  No. 8. Slavonic dance No. 8, in g arr. vln & pf Press
  with piano   Vox 06097

SCHUBERT

Rosamunde von Cypern, Op. 26 (D797) (1823) – Incidental Music orch.
  No. 9. Ballet music II, in G arr. vln & pf Kreisler
  with piano   Vox 06097

SCHUMANN

Wie glücklich sie wardeln arr. vln & pf as "Aria" by Press*
  with piano   Vox 06095

* Unidentified.

SIBELIUS

Belshazzar's Feast, Op. 51 – Incidental music orch.
No. 3. Nocturne "Night song" arr. vln & pf Press
    with piano   Vox 06095

WILHELMJ

Swedish melody vln & pf
    with piano   Vox 06069

Rudolf PRICK

GOUNOD

Ave Maria (Méditation on Bach's "Prelude No. 1, in C" from Book I of "Das Wohltemperirte Clavier") v & pf – arr. vln & orch.
    with Hamburg State Philharmonic   Telefunken SLE14271, UV243
    Orch. – Hertel

HANDEL

Serse (1738) – opera
Ombra mai fu "Largo" arr. vln & orch.
    with Hamburg State Philharmonic   Telefunken SLE14271, UV223
    Orch. – Hertel

MASSENET

Thaïs (1894) – opera
Méditation
    with Hamburg State Philharmonic   Telefunken UV223
    Orch. – Hertel

SCHUBERT

(7) Gesänge (set to Scott's "Lady of the Lake") Op. 52 v & pf
No. 6. Ave Maria, D839 arr. vln & orch.
    with Hamburg State Philharmonic   Telefunken UV243
    Orch. – Hertel

Váša PŘÍHODA (1900–1960)

ANONYMOUS

Eili, Eili Zionist hymn – arr. vln & pf Příhoda
    with C. Cerné pf   Polydor 95370

BACH

Concerto in d, BWV1043 2 vlns, strs & c
    with F. Novello vln & RAI Symphony   Cetra LPC55021
    Orch. Turin – Gerelli

(3) Sonatas & 3 Partitas, BWV1001/6 solo vln
Sonata No. 3, in C: Adagio (1st mvt); **Fugue** (2nd mvt) BWV1005
    (unaccompanied)   Polydor 68282/3

(4) Suites, BWV1066/9 strs & c
Suite No. 3, in D: Air (2nd mvt) BWV1068 2 obs, 3 tpts, drms, strs & c – arr. vln & pf as "Air on the G–string" by Wilhelmj
    with C. Cerné pf   Fonotipia 74965
                      Odeon 6536N, RXX80638
                      Polydor 66486, 95371

BAZZINI

(La) Ronde des lutins, Op. 25 vln & pf
    with A. Doubravska pf   7753   Edison Diamond Disc 82227
(La) Ronde des lutins, Op. 25 vln & pf
    with O.A. Graef pf   6329½ GR   Deutsche Grammophon 25703

BEETHOVEN

(6) Minuets, G167 pf
No. 2. Minuet No. 2, in G arr. vln & pf Burmester
    with C. Cerné pf   Polydor 62532

(Die) Ruinen von Athen, Op. 113 – Incidental music orch.
No. 4. Marcia alla turca arr. vln & pf Auer
    with piano   Edison Diamond Disc 82293
No. 4. Marcia alla turca arr. vln & pf Auer
    with C. Cerné pf   Polydor 62494

BRAHMS

(16) Waltzes, Op. 39 pf duet
No. 15. Waltz No. 15, in A flat arr. vln & pf "in A" Hochstein
    with C. Cerné pf   Polydor 66219

BUCHBINDER

Příhoda–serenade vln & pf
    with C. Cerné pf   Polydor 66061

CAPRI

Rêverie vln & pf
    with B. Seidler–Winkler pf   885 av   Polydor 65990
                               Rococo 2010

CERNÉ

Serenata (1928) vln & pf
    with C. Cerné pf   Polydor 90164

CHAMINADE

Sérénade espagnole pf – arr. vln & pf Kreisler
    with B. Seidler–Winkler pf   1169 at   Polydor 62472

CHOPIN

Berceuse in D flat, Op. 57 pf – arr. vln & pf Cerné
    with C. Cerné pf   Brunswick 25032
                      Fonotipia 74964, 74993
                      Odeon 6535N, 6556N,
                      08594XX
                      Polydor 66220, 66413

(3) Nocturnes, Op. 9 pf
No. 1. Nocturne No. 1, in b flat arr. vln & pf Příhoda
    with C. Cerné pf   Polydor 66487
No. 2. Nocturne No. 2, in E flat arr. vln & pf Sarasate
    with C. Cerné pf   1798 as   Polydor 66057

CORELLI

(12) Sonatas, Op. 5 vln & c
Sonata No. 12, in d "La Follia"
        924½ av & 925/7 av   Polydor 65996/7
    with B. Seidler–Winkler org

DAWES

Melody in A (1912) vln & pf
    with B. Seidler–Winkler pf   1166 at   Polydor 62473, 67545

DRDLA

Guitarerro, Op. 88 vln & pf
    with B. Seidler–Winkler pf   884 av   Polydor 65990
                               Rococo 2010

Madrigale in A Op. 25 vln & pf
    with b. Siedler – Winkler pf   1168 at   Polydor 62475

DRDLA – *Continued*

Souvenir vln & pf
  with B. Seidler–Winkler pf   1106 at Polydor 62475
Souvenir vln & pf
  with O.A. Graef pf   6325½ GR 8 Cetra LL3003
                            Polydor 47067
Souvenir vln & pf
  with C. Cerné pf   2377 BR II Decca DE7003
                            Polydor 90161

DRIGO

(Les) Millions d'Arlequin (1900) – ballet orch.
  Sérénade arr. vln & pf Auer
    with C. Cerné pf   1794 as Polydor 66060, 66063
  Sérénade arr. vln & pf Auer
    with O.A. Graef pf   6328 GR Deutsche Grammophon 25703

DVOŘÁK

Concerto in a, Op. 53 vln & orch.
  with Berlin State Symphony Orch. –   Polydor 68201/5S
  van Kempen
(7) Gypsy songs, Op. 55 v & pf
  No. 4. Songs my mother taught me arr. vln & pf Powell
    with A. Doubravska pf   7861 Edison Diamond Disc 82236
  No. 4. Songs my mother taught me arr. vln & pf Powell
    with C Cerné pf   1795 as Polydor 66060
(8) Humoresques, Op. 101 pf
  No. 7. Humoresque No. 7, in G flat arr. vln & pf "in G" Wilhelmj
    with A. Doubravska pf   7820 Edison Diamond Disc 82228
  No. 7. Humoresque No. 7, in G flat arr. vln & pf "in G" Wilhelmj
    with C. Cerné pf   619 Bi IV Polydor 66885
  No. 7. Humoresque No. 7, in G flat arr. vln & pf "in G" Wilhelmj
    with C. Cerné pf   3592 GN 8 Cetra LL3003
                            Decca CA8088
                            Polydor 30033, 48379, 66187
(8) Slavonic Dances, Op. 46 pf duet; orch.
  No. 2. Slavonic dance No. 2, in e arr. vln & pf "in g" Kreisler
    with C. Cerné pf   Polydor 66487
(8) Slavonic Dances, Op. 72 pf duet; orch.
  No. 2. Slavonic dance No. 10, in e arr. vln & pf Kreisler
    with C. Cerné pf   Cetra OR5041
                            Polydor 48379, 65985, 66487,
                            66886
  No. 2. Slavonic dance No. 10, in e arr. vln & pf Kreisler
    with O.A. Graef pf   562½ GS Polydor 57086
  No. 7. Slavonic dance No. 15, in C arr. vln & pf Příhoda
    with C. Cerné pf   Polydor 65994
  No. 8. Slavonic dance No. 16, in A flat arr. vln & pf "in G" Kreisler
    with I. Orlovetsky pf   Cetra LPU0053, LPV45018
Sonatina in G, Op. 100 vln & pf
  Larghetto (2nd mvt) arr. vln & pf as "Indian lament" by Kreisler
    with C. Cerné pf   1797 as Polydor 66058
Sonatina in G, Op. 100 vln & pf
  with M. Raucheisen pf   Heliodor 2548 712
                        Polydor 68284/6
Symphony No. 9, in e, Op. 95 "From the New World" orch.
  Largo (2nd mvt) arr. vln & pf Příhoda
    with C. Cerné pf   Polydor 67879

DVOŘÁK – *Continued*

(8) Waltzes, Op. 54 pf
  No. 7. Waltz No. 7, in d arr. vln & pf Mařák
    with A. Doubravska pf   7754 Edison Diamond Disc 80681
  No. 7. Waltz No. 7, in d arr. vln & pf Příhoda
    with C. Cerné pf   Fonotipia 74966, 74993
                        Odeon 6536N, 6556N
                        08594XX

ELGAR

(La) Capricieuse, Op. 17 vln & pf
  with C. Cerné pf   886 av Polydor 65986
                        Rococo 2010
(La) Capricieuse, Op. 17 vln & pf
  with C. Cerné pf   1177 BH IV Polydor 30034, 62672
Salut d'amour, Op. 12 orch. – arr. vln & pf Elgar
  with C. Cerné pf   366 BS II Polydor 95369
Salut d'amour, Op. 12 orch. – arr. vln & pf Elgar
  with C. Cerné pf   3591 GN 8 Polydor 30033, 48379

FIBICH

Images, Impressions & Souvenirs, Op. 41 pf
  No. 14. Poem (from "Souvenirs", Part IV) arr. vln & pf Kubelík
    with A. Doubravska pf   7861 Edison Diamond Disc 82236
  No. 14. Poem (from "Souvenirs", Part IV) arr. vln & pf Kubelík
    with C. Cerné pf   Polydor 62495

FIELD

Waltz pf – arr. vln & pf Burmester
  with C. Cerné pf   1795 as Polydor 66060

FRANZ

(6) Gesänge, Op. 17 v & pf
  No. 2. Ständchen (Der Mond ist schlafen 'gangen) arr. v, vln & pf
    with S. Kurz s & B. Seidler–Winkler Polydor 72852
    pf

FREIRE

Ay–ay–ay v & pf – arr. vln & pf Příhoda
  with C. Cerné pf   Polydor 62567

GODARD

Jocelyn (1888) – opera
  Cachés dans cet asile "Berceuse" arr. vln & pf
    with C. Cerné pf   363 BS II Polydor 95371
  Cachés dans cet asile "Berceuse" arr. v, vln & pf
    with S. Kurz s & B.   1289 as Polydor 72850
    Seidler–Winkler pf

GOLDMARK

Concerto in a, Op. 28 vln & orch.
  Andante (2nd mvt) "Air"
    with C. Cerné pf   Polydor 95370

GOSSEC

Rosine (1786) – opera
  Gavotte arr. vln & pf Burmester
    with O.A. Graef pf   6313½GR Polydor 47051, 90164

GOUNOD

Ave Maria (Méditation on Bach's "Prelude No. 1, in C" from Book I of "Das Wohltemperirte Clavier") v & pf – arr. v, vln & pf
  with S. Kurz s & B. Seidler–Winkler   Polydor 70673
pf

Sérénade (Quand tu chantes) v & pf
  with S. Kurz s & B. Seidler–Winkler   Polydor 72852
pf

GUERRA

Capricho brasileiro vln & pf
  with C. Cerné pf   Polydor 62531

HANDEL

Serse (1738) – opera
  Ombra mai fu "Largo" arr. vln & pf
    with B. Seidler–Winkler pf   1105 at   Polydor 62474
  Ombra mai fu "Largo" arr. vln & pf
    with C. Cerné pf   2379 BR [II]   Polydor 90163
  Ombra mai fu "Largo" arr. vln & pf
    with O.A. Graef pf   6333 GR 8   Cetra LL3001
                                     Deutsche Grammophon 25721,
                                     47030

HUBAY

(6) Blumenleben, Op. 30 vln & pf
  No. 5. Der Zephir
    with I. Orlovetsky pf   Cetra LPU0059, LPV45018

KOCIÁN

(2) Pieces, Op. 17 vln & pf
  No. 2. Humoresque
    with A. Doubravska pf   7802   Edison Diamond Disc 80681
                                    Rococo 2010

KREISLER

Caprice viennois, Op. 2 vln & pf
  with A. Doubravska pf   7821   Edison Diamond Disc 82227
Caprice viennois, Op. 2 vln & pf
  with C. Cerné pf   1791 as   Polydor 66058
Caprice viennois, Op. 2 vln & pf – arr. v, vln & pf
  with S. Kurz s & B.   1290 as   Polydor 72852
  Seidler–Winkler pf
Liebesfreud vln & pf
  with O.A. Graef pf   6330 GR 8   Decca DE7060
                                     Polydor 524191
Liebesfreud vln & pf
  with C. Cerné pf   Polydor 47036
Liebesleid vln & pf
  with B. Seidler–Winkler pf   1104 at   Polydor 62474, 67542
Liebesleid vln & pf
  with O.A. Graef pf   6327 GR 8   Decca DE7060
                                     Polydor 62556, 90162, 524191
Liebesleid vln & pf
  with C. Cerné pf   2382 BR [II]   Brunswick 7002
                                     Polydor 47036
Schön Rosmarin vln & pf
  with C. Cerné pf   Polydor 62492, 62495
Variations on a theme of Corelli (Tartini)
  with C. Cerné pf   Cetra OR5098
                                     Polydor 35091, 66482

LALO

Symphonie espagnole, Op. 21 vln & orch.
  Andante (4th mvt)
    with piano   Edison Diamond Disc 82293
  Andante (4th mvt)
    with C. Cerné pf   Fonotipia 74981
                                   Odeon 6538N
  Andante (4th mvt)
    with O.A. Graef pf   Polydor 47030
  Rondo (5th mvt)
    with C. Cerné pf   Fonotipia 74982
                                     Odeon 6538N

MACHO

Staccato–serenade, Op. 10 vln & pf
  with C. Cerné pf   Polydor 62493

MASSENET

Thaïs (1894) – opera
  Méditation arr. vln & pf Marsick
    with C. Cerné pf   Polydor 40011, 66059, 66485

MATTHESON

(12) Suites (1714) hpsi
  Suite No. 5, in c: Air arr. vln & pf Burmester
    with piano   Edison Diamond Disc 82293

MENDELSSOHN

Concerto in e, Op. 64 vln & orch.
  Allegro molto vivace (1st mvt)
    with piano   Edison Diamond Disc 80884
  Andante (2nd mvt)
    with piano   Edison Diamond Disc 80884
(6) Gesänge, Op. 34 v & pf
  No 2. Auf Flügeln des Gesanges arr. vln & pf Achron
    with A. Doubravska pf   7862   Edison Diamond Disc 82236
  No. 2. Auf Flügeln des Gesanges arr. vln & pf Achron
    with O.A. Graef pf   Polydor 66062
  No. 2. Auf Flügeln des Gesanges arr. vln & pf Achron
    with C. Cerné pf   68 bi   Decca CA8093
                                     Polydor 66484
(6) Songs without words, Op. 67 pf
  No. 6. Song without words No. 36, in E arr. vln & pf Cerné
    with C. Cerné pf   Polydor 62565

MOSZKOWSKI

(3) Stücke, Op. 29 vlc & pf
  No. 3. Berceuse in F arr. vln & pf Cerné
    with C. Cerné pf   Polydor 62531

MOZART

Concerto No. 3, in G, K216 (cadenzas by Příhoda) vln & orch.
  with RAI Symphony Orch., Turin –   Cetra LPC55021, LPU0026
  Gerelli
Concerto No. 4, in D, K218 vln & orch.
  Andante cantabile (2nd mvt)
    with C. Cerné pf   Fonotipia 74988
                                     Odeon 6539N, RXX80637
                                     Polydor 66485

MOZART – *Continued*

Concerto No. 4, in D, K218 (cadenzas by Príhoda) vln & orch.
with RAI Symphony Orch., Turin –   Cetra LPC55021, LPU0026
Gerelli

Divertimento No. 17, in D, K334 orch.
Minuet (3rd mvt) arr. vln & pf Burmester
with B. Seidler–Winkler pf   922 av Polydor 68090
Minuet (3rd mvt) arr. vln & pf Burmester
with C. Cerné pf   Polydor 65994

Sonata No. 11, in A, K331 pf
Rondo alla turca (3rd mvt) arr. vln & pf Cerné
with C. Cerné pf   168 bg Brunswick 25020
                             Polydor 27643, 66221, 69848
                             Rococo 2010

NOCETI

Waltz in F vln & pf
with C. Cerné pf   Polydor 62532

PAGANINI

Concerto No. 1, in D, Op. 6 (cadenza by Sauret) vln & orch.
Allegro maestoso (1st mvt) arr. vln & orch. Wilhelmj
with C. Cerné pf   Polydor 65991/2

Nel cor più non mi sento "Sonata appassionata con variazioni" (on the aria
from Paisiello's opera "La bella molinara") Op. 38 (1820 or 1821) solo
vln – arr. vln & pf Příhoda
with C. Cerné pf   Cetra OR5098
                        Polydor 66492/3

Nel cor più non mi sento "Sonata appassionata con variazioni" (on the aria
from Paisiello's opera "La bella molinara") Op. 38 (1820 or 1821) solo
vln – arr. vln & pf Příhoda
            825½GS i & 826 GS i Deutsche Grammophon
with O.A. Graef pf   EPL30549
                                  Polydor 35091

Nel cor più non mi sento "Sonata appassionata con variazioni" (on the aria
from Paisiello's opera "La bella molinara") Op. 38 (1820 or 1821) solo
vln
(unaccompanied)   Cetra LPC55022, LPU0027

(I) Palpiti (variations on the aria "Di tanti palpiti" from Rossini's opera
"Tancredi") Op. 13 (1819) vln & orch.
with C. Cerné pf   Polydor 65987

(6) Sonatas, Op. 3 (1801/6) vln & gtr
No. 6. Sonata No. 12, in e arr. vln & pf Příhoda
with C. Cerné pf   920 av Polydor 65995, 67879
                             Rococo 2010
No. 6. Sonata No. 12, in e arr. vln & pf Příhoda
with C. Cerné pf   Polydor 66463
No. 6. Sonata No. 12, in e arr. vln & pf Příhoda
with I. Orlovetsky pf   Cetra LPC55022, LPU0027

(Le) Streghe (variations on a theme from Süssmeyer's opera "Il Noce di
Benevento") Op. 8 (1813) vln & orch.
with piano   Edison Diamond Disc 82318

(Le) Streghe (variations on a theme from Süssmeyer's opera "Il Noce di
Benevento") Op. 8 (1813) vln & orch.
with C. Cerné pf   169/70 bg Cetra OR5098
                                Fonotipia 74979/80
                                Odeon 5572N, 6537N, 0–9031
                                Polydor 66222
                                Rococo 2001

PERGOLESI

Aria unid – arr. vln & pf Příhoda
with O.A. Graef pf   Cetra LL3011

PŘÍHODA

Caprice in E (1926) vln & pf
with C. Cerné pf   Polydor 66220

Minuet in olden style vln & pf
with M. Raucheisen   1763½GS 9 Polydor 67880
pf

Romance élégiaque vln & pf
with C. Cerné pf   171 bg Fonotipia 74987
                               Odeon 6539N, 0–8560XX
                               Polydor 66221

Serenata vln & pf
with I. Orlovetsky pf   Cetra LPU0059, LPV45018

Slavonic melody vln & pf
            936¾ GE 9 & 937½ GE 9 Cetra OR5052
with O.A. Graef pf   Polydor 35092

Slavonic melody vln & pf
with I. Orlovetsky pf   Cetra LPU0059, LPV45018

Waltz in A vln & pf
with O.A. Graef pf   9389½GD 9 Cetra LL3010
                                  Polydor 30039

PROHASKA

Arietta vln & pf
with C. Cerné pf   Polydor 62493

PROVAZNÍK

Caprice d'une femme vln & pf
with C. Cerné pf   Polydor 66061

Hindou song, Op. 140 vln & pf
with C. Cerné pf   Polydor 66190

Valse joyeuse, Op. 137 vln & pf
with O.A. Graef pf   3390½GD 9 Polydor 30039, 66063

Valse triste vln & pf
with C. Cerné pf   Polydor 66190

Valzer con brio vln & pf
with O.A. Graef pf   Cetra LL3010

RAFF

(6) Pieces, Op. 85 vln & pf
No. 3. Cavatina in D
with M. Raucheisen pf 1759 GS 9 Polydor 67880

No. 3. Cavatina in D
with C. Cerné pf   367 BS [II] Polydor 95371

REHFELD

(2) Konzertstücke, Op. 58 vln & pf
No. 1. Spanish dance
with O. Eisen pf   8286 Edison Diamond Disc 82255
                              Rococo 2010

RIMSKY-KORSAKOV

(Le) Coq d'Or (1910) – opera
Hymn to the sun arr. vln & pf Kreisler
with piano   Edison Diamond Disc 82318
Hymn to the sun arr. vln & pf Kreisler
with C. Cerné pf   Polydor 66486, 95061

RIMSKY–KORSAKOV – *Continued*

Sadko (1898) – opera
Chant hindou arr. vln & pf Kreisler
   with C. Cerné pf   1176 BH [IV]   Cetra OR5042
                                   Polydor 62473, 62672

Chant hindou arr. vln & pf Kreisler
   with C. Cerné pf   622 Bi [IV]   Polydor 95369

RUBINSTEIN

(6) Soirées de Saint–Pétersbourg, Op. 44 pf
No. 1. Romance in E flat arr. vln & pf Příhoda
   with C. Cerné pf   2376 BR [II]   Polydor 90163

SAINT–LUBIN

Sextet (from the opera "Lucia di Lammermoor" by Donizetti) Op. 56 solo
vln
(unaccompanied)   7786   Edison Diamond Disc 82225

SAINT–SAËNS

(Le) Carnaval des animaux (1886) small orch.
Le cygne arr. vln & pf
   with C. Cerné pf   172 bg   Brunswick 80002
                                     Polydor 66223

SARASATE

(8) Danzas españolas vln & pf
No. 3. Romanza andaluza, Op. 22, No. 1
   with C. Cerné pf   921 av   Polydor 65995
                                     Rococo 2010

No. 3. Romanza andaluza, Op. 22, No. 1
   with O.A. Graef pf   561 GS   Cetra OR5042
                                     Polydor 57086

No. 4. Jota navarra, Op. 22, No. 2
   with C. Cerné pf   Polydor 66062, 66886

No. 4. Jota navarra, Op. 22, No. 2
   with M. Raucheisen   1761¾ GS 9 Polydor 57392, 68045
   pf

No. 4. Jota navarra, Op. 22, No. 2
   with I. Orlovetsky pf   Cetra LPC55022, LPU0027

Introduction & Tarantelle, Op. 43 vln & pf
   with C. Cerné pf   173½ bg Brunswick 80002
                                     Fonotipia 74963
                                     Odeon 6535N, 0–8560XX
                                     Polydor 66223

Jota de Pablo, Op. 52 vln & pf
   with A. Doubravska pf   7787   Edison Diamond Disc 82228
                                      Rococo 2010

Zigeunerweisen, Op. 20 vln & pf or orch.
   with B. Seidler–Winkler pf 892 av   Polydor 68085

Zigeunerweisen, Op. 20 vln & pf or orch.
   with C. Cerné pf   Polydor 65993, 66481

Zigeunerweisen, Op. 20 vln & pf or orch.
   with O.A. Graef pf   6331/2 GR Cetra LL3000
                                     Polydor 30016, 62908, 524290

SCHUBERT

(7) Gesänge (set to Scott's "Lady of the Lake") Op. 52 v & pf
No. 6. Ave Maria, D839 arr. vln & pf Wilhelmj
   with B. Seidler–Winkler pf 887 av Polydor 68080

SCHUBERT – *Continued*

No. 6. Ave Maria, D839 arr. vln & pf Wilhelmj
   with C. Cerné pf   66 bi   Decca CA8093
                                  Polydor 40011, 65989, 66484

No. 6. Ave Maria, D839 arr. vln & pf Wilhelmj
   with O.A. Graef pf   564 GS Cetra OR5041
                                  Polydor 57030, 66589

(2) Lieder, Op. 98 (D498) v & pf
No. 2. Wiegenlied (Schlafe, holder süsser Knabe) arr. vln & pf Cerné
   with C. Cerné pf   Brunswick 7003
                                  Polydor 62564

Litanei auf das Fest aller Seelen, D343 v & pf – arr. vln & pf Příhoda
   with O.A. Graef pf   563½ GS Polydor 57030

(6) Moments musicaux, Op. 94 (D780) (1823/7) pf
No. 3. Moment musicale No. 3, in f "Air russe" arr. vln & pf Kreisler
   with C. Cerné pf   Brunswick 7003
                                  Polydor 62492, 62564

Rosamunde von Cypern, Op. 26 (D797) (1823) – Incidental music orch.
No. 9. Ballet music II, in G arr. vln & pf Kreisler
   with B. Seidler–Winkler pf 1102 at Polydor 62472, 67540

No. 9. Ballet music II, in G arr. vln & pf Kreisler
   with C. Cerné pf   Brunswick 7002
                                  Polydor 62566

SCHUMANN

(12) Duets, Op. 85 pf, 4–hands
No. 12. Abendlied arr. vln & pf Wilhelmj
   with C. Cerné pf   Cetra LL3011

(13) Kinderscenen, Op. 15 pf
No. 7. Träumerei arr. vln & pf
   with C. Cerné pf   Polydor 62564

No. 7. Träumerei arr. vln & pf
   with O.A. Graef pf   6334 GR 8 Cetra LL3001, LL3009, OL6013
                                    Deutsche Grammophon 25721,
                                    47030

SIMONETTI

Madrigale pf – arr. vln & pf
   with C. Cerné pf   2380 BR [II] Polydor 30034, 90162

SMETANA

From my Homeland (1878) vln & pf
No. 2. Andantino
   with O.A. Graef pf   8387/8½ GD 9 Deutsche Grammophon
                                    EPL30549
                                    Heliodor 2548 712
                                    Polydor 30038

STRAUSS, R.

(Der) Rosenkavalier, Op. 59 (1911) – opera
Waltzes (Act II) arr. vln & pf Příhoda
   with O.A. Graef pf   6316/7½ GR Cetra LL3002
                                    Polydor 47185

Waltzes (Act II) arr. vln & pf Příhoda
   with I. Orlovetsky pf   Cetra LPU0053, LPV45018

SUK

(7) Pieces, Op. 7 pf
No. 5. Dumka arr. vln & pf Ondříček
   with A. Doubravska pf   7801   Edison Diamond Disc 82225

SUK – *Continued*

No. 5. Dumka arr. vln & pf Ondříček
with C. Cerné pf   Polydor 66219

SVENDSEN

Romance in G, Op. 26 vln & orch. – arr. vln & pf Wilhelmj
with C. Cerné pf   1790 as   Polydor 66057

TARTINI

Sonata in g "Il Trillo del Diavolo" vln & c – arr. vln & pf Příhoda
       838/40½GE9 & 841⅞GE9   Cetra OR5049/50
with O.A. Graef pf   Polydor 15470/1, 57099/100

Sonata in g "Il Trillo del Diavolo" vln & c – real. Vieuxtemps
with Trio di archi*   Cetra LPU0053, LPV45008

TCHAIKOVSKY

(The) Months (12 characteristic pieces) Op. 37b pf
No. 10. Autumn song "October" arr. vln & pf Burmester
with C. Cerné pf   621 Bi [IV]   Decca CA8088
                                    Polydor 66834, 66885

Romance in f, Op. 5 pf – arr. vln & pf
with M. Raucheisen   1762½GS 9   Polydor 57392, 68045
pf

Romance in f, Op. 5 pf – arr. vln & pf
with C. Cerné pf   Polydor 68240

Serenade in C, Op. 48 str orch.
Valse (2nd mvt) arr. vln & pf Auer
with C. Cerné pf   Polydor 68240

TOSELLI

Serenade, Op. 6 vln & pf
with C. Cerné pf   2381 BR [II]   Cetra LL3009
                                    Decca DE7003

Serenade, Op. 6 vln & pf
with O.A. Graef pf   6326 GR   Cetra OL6013
                                    Polydor 47067

Serenade, Op. 6 vln & pf – arr. v, vln & pf
with S. Kurz s & B.   1288 as   Polydor 72850
Seidler-Winkler pf

VALDEZ

Sérénade du Tzigane vln & pf
with O. Eisen pf   8285   Edison Diamond Disc 82255
                                    Rococo 2010

Sérénade du Tzigane vln & pf
with C. Cerné pf   Polydor 66059

VIEUXTEMPS

Concerto No. 4, in d, Op. 31 vln & orch.
  Andante (1st mvt)
  with C. Cerné pf   Polydor 66188

  Adagio religioso (2nd mvt)
  with O. Eisen pf   8274   Edison Diamond Disc 82261
                                    Rococo 2010

  Adagio religioso (2nd mvt)
  with C. Cerné pf   Polydor 66189

* Lughi, vln – Francalanci, vla – Ferrari, vlc.

VIEUXTEMPS – *Continued*

  Allegro – Finale (4th mvt)
  with O. Eisen pf   8275   Edison Diamond Disc 82261
                                    Rococo 2010

VIOTTI

(3) Duets, Op. 29 2 vlns & orch.
No. 1. Duo concertante No. 1, in g arr. Quaranta – cadenza by Příhoda
with F. Novello vln & RAI Symphony   Cetra LPU0059, LPV45009
Orch., Turin – Gerelli

VITALI

Chaconne in g vln & c – arr. vln & pf Charlier
with B. Seidler-Winkler   881/4 av   Polydor 65988/9
org

Chaconne in g vln & c – arr. Respighi
with RAI Chamber Orch., Turin –   Cetra LPU0053, LPV45008
Gramegna

VOLKMANN

Waltz vln & pf – arr. Příhoda
with O.A. Graef pf   6319½GR   Polydor 47051, 62494, 90164

WAGNER

Albumblatt in C (1861) pf – arr. vln & pf Wilhelmj
with C. Cerné pf   Polydor 65997

WIENIAWSKI

Concerto No. 2, in d, Op. 22 vln & orch.
with C. Cerné pf   Polydor 65998/9

Fantaisie brillante (on themes from the opera "Faust" by Gounod) Op. 20
vln & orch.
with C. Cerné pf   Polydor 66186/7

Scherzo–Tarantelle, Op. 16 vln & pf
with C. Cerné pf   878 av   Polydor 65986
                                    Rococo 2010

William PRIMROSE (1904–   )

ARENSKY

(4) Morceaux, Op. 30 vln & pf
No. 2. Serenade in G arr. Elman
with piano   Columbia 4633, J461

BACH

(3) Sonatas & 3 Partitas, BWV1001/6 solo vln
Partita No. 3, in E: Gavotte (3rd mvt) BWV1006 arr. vln & pf Kreisler
with piano   AX 2817   Columbia 9258

(6) Sonatas, BWV1014/9 vln & clav
Sonata No. 2, in A, BWV1015
with H.J. Templeman pf   HMV D939/40

CHOPIN

(3) Nocturnes, Op. 9 pf
No. 2. Nocturne No. 2, in E flat arr. vln & pf Sarasate
with piano   AX 2816   Columbia 9258

DRIGO

(2) Airs de Ballet orch.
No. 2. Valse bluette arr. vln & pf Auer
with piano   MB 481   Decca F1597

KREISLER

Tempo di minuetto (Pugnani) vln & pf
with piano   MB 482   Decca F1597

MENDELSSOHN

Quartet No. 1, in E flat, Op. 12 2 vlns, vla & vlc
  Canzonetta (2nd mvt) arr. vln & pf as "Capriccietto" by Burmester
with piano   Columbia 4633, J461

PURCELL

(10) Sonatas, Z802/11 (1697) 4 parts – 2 vlns & c
  Sonata No. 9, in F, Z810 "Golden Sonata"
             Cc 4393^{IV} & 4394^{VI}   HMV D889
with I. Menges vln & H.J. Templeman
pf

  Sonata No. 9, in F, Z810 "Golden Sonata"
with I. Menges   CAX 7598/9–1   Columbia 11098D, (in set M315),
vln, A. Ticehurst hpsi & A. Gauntlett   ROX133
gamba

SAINT–SAËNS

Introduction & Rondo Capriccioso, Op. 28 vln & orch.
           Cc 3934^{II} & 3935^{III}   HMV D796
with G. O'Connor Morris pf

Remy PRINCIPI (1889–)

BEETHOVEN

Allegretto unid – arr. vln & pf Principi
with L. Ferrari–Trecate pf   Odeon GO12703
(6) Minuets, G167 pf
  No. 2. Minuet No. 2, in G arr. vln & pf Burmester
with L. Ferrari–Trecate pf   Odeon GO12704

DEBUSSY

(12) Préludes – Book I (1910) pf
  No. 8. La Fille aux cheveux de lin arr. vln & pf Hartmann
with L. Ferrari–Trecate pf   Odeon GO12703

FERRARI–TRECATE

(Il) Prode Anselmo vln & pf
with L. Ferrari–Trecate pf   Odeon GO12705

PRINCIPI

(El) Campielo vln & pf
with L. Ferrari–Trecate pf   Odeon GO12705
Canti siciliani vln & pf
with L. Ferrari–Trecate pf   Odeon GO12704

TARTINI

Concerto in d, D45 (C61) vln & orch.
  Grave (2nd mvt)
with I.C.B.S. Quartet   Musique au Vatican 1176

Ernst PRINZ

BRAHMS

Concerto in a, Op. 102 "Double" vln, vlc & orch.
with W. Kunlantz vlc & Rhineland   Regent 5027
Symphony Orch. – Federer

Victor PROVINSKY

CZERWONKY

Waltz vln & pf
with orch.   924   Banner 924
                            Triangle 15055

DRDLA

Souvenir vln & pf
with piano   Banner 928

DVOŘÁK

(8) Humoresques, Op. 101 pf
  No. 7. Humoresque No. 7, in G flat arr. vln & pf "in G" Kreisler
with piano   Banner 929

SAENGER

Improvisation vln & pf
with piano   Banner 927

Walter PRYSTAWSKI

BACH

Concerto in D, BWV1064 3 clavs, strs & c – arr. 3 vlns, strs & c
with R. Barnert vln, T. Soh vln &   Deutsche Grammophon
Lucerne Festival Strings –   SLPM139432
Baumgartner

DIETHELM

Sonata solo vln
(unaccompanied)   Fono FGLS30–4701

MOZART

Serenade No. 6, in D, K239 "Serenata Notturna" orch.
with H. Höver vln, R. Weber vla, R.   Deutsche Grammophon
Frei cbs & Lucerne Festival Strings –   LPEM19480, SLPEM136480
Baumgartner

MÜLLER–ZÜRICH

Concerto, Op. 61 2 vlns, cem & strs
with H. Höver vln & Rome   Philips G04401L
Philharmonic Orch. – Fauré

VIVALDI

(12) Concerti, Op. 3 "L'Estro armonico" var. cbns & strs
  Concerto No. 2, in g, P.326 (F.IV, No. 8) 2 vlns, strs & c
with H. Scherz vln, K. Heitz vlc &   Archive SAPM198469
Lucerne Festival Strings –
Baumgartner
  Concerto No. 3, in G, P.96 (F.I, No. 173) vln, strs & c
with Lucerne Festival Strings –   Archive 2705 002, SAPM198469
Baumgartner
  Concerto No. 4, in e, P.97 (F.I, No. 174) 4 vlns, strs & c
with R. Barnert vln, G. Ribeiro vln, T.   Archive 2705 002, SAPM198469
Soh vln & Lucerne Festival Strings –
Baumgartner
  Concerto No. 5, in A, P.212 (F.I, No. 175) 2 vlns, strs & c
with H. Scherz vln & Lucerne Festival   Archive 2705 002, SAPM198470
Strings – Baumgartner
  Concerto No. 6, in a, P.1 (F.I, No. 176) vln, strs & c
with Lucerne Festival Strings –   Archive 2705 002, SAPM198470
Baumgartner

VIVALDI – *Continued*

Concerto No. 7, in F, P.249 (F.IV, No. 9) 4 vlns, strs & c
with R. Barnert vln, H. Scherz vln, T.   Archive SAPM198470
Soh vln & Lucerne Festival Strings –
Baumgartner

Concerto No. 8, in a, P.2 (F.I, No. 177) 2 vlns, strs & c
with T. Soh vln & Lucerne Festival   Archive SAPM198470
Strings – Baumgartner

Concerto No. 9, in D, P.147 (F.I, No. 178) vln, strs & c
with Lucerne Festival Strings –   Archive SAPM198471
Baumgartner

Concerto No. 10, in b, P.148 (F.IV, No. 10) 4 vlns, strs & c
with R. Barnert vln, H. Scherz vln, T.   Archive SAPM198471
Soh vln, K. Heitz vlc & Lucerne
Festival Strings – Baumgartner

Concerto No. 11, in d, P.250 (F.IV, No. 11) 2 vlns, vlc, strs & c
with H. Scherz vln, K. Heitz vlc &   Archive SAPM198471
Lucerne Festival Strings –
Baumgartner

Concerto in A, P.222 (F.I, No. 139) "L'eco in lontano" 2 vlns, strs & c
with H. Höver vln & Lucerne Festival   Deutsche Grammophon
Strings – Baumgartner   LPM18947, SLPM138947

Eldon PUCCI

NARDINI

Concerto in e vln & orch.
with Nardini Chamber Orch. – Etto   Pan PAN6008, SPAN6008

Roland PUIG (1919–   )

BRAHMS

(16) Waltzes, Op. 39 pf duet
No 15. Waltz No. 15, in A flat arr. vln & pf "in A" Hochstein
with R. Boutry pf   Pathé EA162

RIMSKY-KORSAKOV

Sadko (1898) – opera
Chant hindou arr. vln & pf Kreisler
with R. Boutry pf   Pathé EA162

SCHUBERT

(7) Gesänge (set to Scott's "Lady of the Lake") Op. 52 v & pf
No. 6. Ave Maria, D839 arr. vln & pf Wilhelmj
with R. Boutry pf   Pathé EA162

Rosamunde von Cypern, Op. 26 (D797) (1823) – Incidental music orch.
No. 9. Ballet music II, in G arr. vln & pf Kreisler
with R. Boutry pf   Pathé EA162

Marcel PUJOL

COATES

Bird songs at eventide v & pf – arr. vln & pf
with piano   Pathé PA77

DARCY

Doleo v & pf – arr. vln & pf
with piano   Pathé PA77

Walter PUSCHACHER

VIVALDI

(12) Concerti, Op. 8 (1725) "Il Cimento dell' Armonia e dell' Invenzione"
(Nos. 1/4: Le quattro Stagioni) vln & strs
Concerto No. 1, in E, F.I, No. 22 "La Primavera"
with Vienna Chamber Orch. –   Michel–Ange 2
Lindenberg   Orphée LDP–D50001, LDP–
    D60001
    Pacific LDP–D50001, LDP–
    D60001

Concerto No. 2, in B flat, F.I, No. 23 "L'Estate"
with Vienna Chamber Orch. –   Michel–Ange 2
Lindenberg   Orphée LDP–D50001, LDP–
    D60001
    Pacific LDP–D50001, LDP–
    D60001

Concerto No. 3, in F, F.I, No. 24 "L'Autunno"
with Vienna Chamber Orch. –   Michel–Ange 2
Lindenberg   Orphée LDP–D50001, LDP–
    D60001
    Pacific LDP–D50001, LDP–
    D60001

Concerto No. 4, in f, F.I, No. 25 "L'Inverno"
with Vienna Chamber Orch. –   Michel–Ange 2
Lindenberg   Orphée LDP–D50001, LDP–
    D60001
    Pacific LDP–D50001, LDP–
    D60001

Joseph PUTTERS

WOESTIJNE

Concerto vln & 12 solo inst
with Belgian National Orch. – Gras   Decca FA143250

Lucien QUATTROCCHI

BACH

(4) Suites, BWV1066/9 strs & c
Suite No. 3, in D: Air (2nd mvt) BWV1068 2 obs, 3 tpts, drms, strs & c
– arr. vln & pf as "Air on the G–string" by Wilhelmj
with piano   HMV K5186

DRDLA

Serenade No. 1, in A vln & pf
with piano   N 8875–1   Omnia 27902

Visione, in E flat, Op. 28 vln & pf
with piano   HMV K5186

DRIGO

(Les) Millions d'Arlequin (1900) – ballet orch.
Sérénade arr. vln & pf Auer
with J. de la Houssaye pf   89497 L   Edison Bell F452

Sérénade arr. vln & pf Auer
with piano   HMV K5141

MENDELSSOHN

(6) Songs without words, Op. 62 pf
No. 6. Song without words No. 30, in A "Spring song" arr. vln & pf
with piano   N 8874–1   Omnia 27902

MONTI

Aubade d'amour vln & pf
    with J. de la Houssaye pf   89496 L   Edison Bell F452

Robert QUATTROCCHI

ALIPRANDI

Esquisses pyrénéennes vln & c
    with C. Eloffe pf   Voix des Nôtres MLP111

Fantasia vln & c
    with C. Eloffe pf   Voix des Nôtres MLP111

KREISLER

Tambourin chinois, Op. 3 vln & pf
    with C. Eloffe pf   Voix des Nôtres MLP111

PAGANINI

(24) Caprices, Op. 1 (1801/7) solo vln
  Caprice No. 13, in B flat arr. vln & pf Kreisler
    with C. Eloffe pf   Voix des Nôtres MLP111

SARASATE

(8) Danzas españolas vln & pf
  No. 2. Habañera, Op. 21, No. 2
    with C. Eloffe pf   Voix des Nôtres MLP111
  No. 6. Zapateado, Op. 23, No. 2
    with C. Eloffe pf   Voix des Nôtres MLP111

Riele QUELING

BACH

(3) Sonatas & 3 Partitas, BWV1001/6 solo vln
  Sonata No. 3, in C: Allegro assai (4th mvt) BWV1005
  (unaccompanied)   Parlophone B27002

BEETHOVEN

Concerto in D, Op. 61 vln & orch.
  Larghetto (2nd mvt)
    with orch. –   XXB7944/5   Odeon 0–6636
    Weissmann

Concerto in D, Op. 61 (cadenzas by Kreisler) vln & orch.
    with Berlin State Opera Orch. –   Odeon 0–6951/5
    Gurlitt

HAYDN

(6) Quartets, Op. 64 (H.III, Nos. 63/8) 2 vlns, vla & vlc
  No. 5. Quartet No. 67, in D, H.III, No. 67 "The lark"
  (as member of Queling string quartet)   HMV EH1248/9

MOZART

Concerto No. 4, in D, K218 (cadenzas by Joachim) vln & orch.
    with orch.   Parlophone E10383/5

REGER

Romance in G vln & pf
    with piano   Parlophone B27002

SCHUMANN

(12) Duets, Op. 85 pf – 4 hands
  No. 3. Gartenmelodie arr. vln & pf
    with piano   Parlophone 44600, B6456

SCHUMANN – *Continued*

  No. 12. Abendlied arr. vln & pf Wilhelmj
    with piano   Parlophone 44600, B6456

Robert QUICK

VIVALDI

Concerto in A, P.228 (F.I, No. 141) "Pisendel" vln, strs & c
    with Manuel–Williamson Ensemble   Musicraft 1147/8, (set 48)

(6) Sonatas, Op. 13 (1737) "Il Pastor Fido" fl, ob, vln, strs & c
  Sonata No. 4, in A: Pastorale (3rd mvt) F.XVI, No. 8
    with Manuel–Williamson Ensemble   Musicraft 1148, (in set 48)

Manuel QUIROGA (1890–1961)

ALBÉNIZ

España (6 Feuilles d'album) Op. 165 pf
  No. 2. Tango in D arr. vln & pf Kreisler
    with M. Quiroga pf   Pathé X9938

BACH

(4) Suites, BWV1066/9 strs & c
  Suite No. 3, in D: Air (2nd mvt) BWV1068 2 obs, 3 tpts, drms & strs –
  arr. vln & pf as "Air on the G–string" by Wilhelmj
    with piano   HMV X287973

BAZZINI

(La) Ronde des lutins, Op. 25 vln & pf
    with piano   17180 u   Gramophone & Typewriter
        237929

di CAPUA

O sole mio v & pf – arr. vln & pf
    with piano   HMV Z0287900

CHAMINADE

Sérénade espagnole pf – arr. vln & pf Kreisler
    with M. Quiroga pf   Pathé X98002

FALLA

(7) Canciones populares españolas (1914) v & pf
  No. 4. Jota arr. vln & pf Kochański
    with M. Quiroga pf   Pathé X9938

GODARD

Jocelyn (1888) – opera
  Cachés dans cet asile "Berceuse" arr. vln & pf
    with piano   HMV Z0287901

HUBAY

(6) Blumenleben, Op. 30 vln & pf
  No. 5. Der Zephir
    with piano   HMV 6–7908

KREISLER

Rondino on a theme by Beethoven vln & pf
    with M. Quiroga pf   Pathé X98001

LEHÁR

Frasquita (1923) – operetta
Hab' ein blaues Himmelbett arr. vln & pf as "Serenade" by Kreisler
with M. Quiroga pf   Pathé X98001

MOSZKOWSKI

(2) Stücke, Op. 45 pf
No. 2. Guitarre arr. vln & pf Sarasate
with piano   HMV X287972

QUIROGA

Canto amoroso vln & pf
with M. Quiroga pf   Victor 1336

Danza española vln & pf
with M. Quiroga pf   Victor 1336

Rondalla (Jota) vln & pf
with M. Quiroga pf   Victor 1341

Segunda Guajira vln & pf
with M. Quiroga pf   Victor 1341

SARASATE

(8) Danzas españolas vln & pf
No. 4. Jota navarra, Op. 22, No. 2
with piano   17283 u   HMV X287964

No. 4. Jota navarra, Op. 22, No. 2
with piano   Victor 65330

No. 4. Jota navarra, Op. 22, No. 2
with M. Quiroga pf   Pathé X5528

No. 6. Zapateado, Op. 23, No. 2
with M. Quiroga pf   Pathé X98002

Jota aragonesa, Op. 27 vln & pf
with M. Quiroga pf   Pathé X5528

Miramar-Zortzico, Op. 42 vln & pf
with piano   Victor 65330

WIENIAWSKI

Souvenir de Moscou, Op. 6 vln & pf or orch.
with piano   17179 u   HMV 6–7909, X287963

Michael RABIN (1936–1972)

BACH

(3) Sonatas & 3 Partitas, BWV1001/6 solo vln
Sonata No. 3, in C, BWV1005
(unaccompanied)   Angel 35305

BRANDL

(Der) Liebe Augustin – operetta
Du alter Stefansturm arr. vln & pf as "The old refrain" by Kreisler)
with Hollywood Bowl Symphony   Capitol K60690, P8510, SP8510,
Orch. – Slatkin   SP8653, STK60690
                    Seraphim S60199

BRUCH

Scottish Fantasia, Op. 46 vln & orch.
with Philharmonia Orch. – Boult   Angel 35484
                    Columbia C90964, CX1538

CHOPIN

(2) Nocturnes, Op. 27 pf
No. 2. Nocturne No. 8, in D flat arr. vln & pf Wilhelmj
with L. Pommers pf   Capitol P8506

DEBUSSY

(La) Plus que lente – valse (1910) pf – arr. vln & pf Roques
with L. Pommers pf   Capitol P8506

DINICU

Hora staccato vln & pf – arr. Heifetz
with Hollywood Bowl Symphony   Capitol K60690, P8510, SP8653,
Orch. – Slatkin   STK60690, SP8510
                    Seraphim S60199

DVOŘÁK

(8) Slavonic Dances, Op. 72 pf duet; orch.
No. 2. Slavonic dance No. 10, in e arr. vln & pf Kreisler
with A. Balsam pf   Columbia AAL30

ELGAR

(La) Capricieuse, Op. 17 vln & pf
with L. Pommers pf   Capitol P8506

ENGEL

Sea shells v & pf – arr. vln & pf Zimbalist
with A. Balsam pf   Columbia AAL30

Sea shells v & pf – arr. vln & pf Zimbalist
with L. Pommers pf   Capitol P8506

GLAZOUNOV

Concerto in a, Op. 82 vln & orch.
with Philharmonia Orch. – von   Angel 35259
Matacic   Columbia CX1281
                    HMV LALP526

KREISLER

Caprice viennois, Op. 2 vln & pf
with Hollywood Bowl Symphony   Capitol K60690, P8510, SP8510,
Orch. – Slatkin   STK60690
                    Seraphim S60199

(La) Chasse (Cartier) vln & pf
with A. Balsam pf   Columbia AAL30

KROLL

Banjo & fiddle vln & pf
with A. Balsam pf   Columbia AAL30

MASSENET

Thaïs (1894) – opera
Méditation vln & orch.
with Hollywood Bowl Symphony   Capitol K60690, P8510, SP8510,
Orch. – Slatkin   STK60690
                    Seraphim S60199

MENDELSSOHN

Concerto in e, Op. 64 vln & orch.*
with Philharmonia Orch. – Boult   Angel 35572
                    Columbia CX1597
                    Trianon TRX6183

* The Andante or 2nd mvt is also on Columbia CX1394.

MOMPOU

(5) Scènes d'enfants (1915/8) pf
No. 5. Jeunes filles au jardin arr. vln & pf Szigeti
with L. Pommers pf   Capitol P8506

NOVAČEK

(8) Concert Caprices, Op. 5 vln & pf
No. 4. Perpetuum mobile
with Columbia Symphony Orch. –   Columbia AAL38
Voorhees   Philips 409007AE, NBE11003

PAGANINI

(24) Caprices, Op. 1 (1801/7) solo vln
Caprice No. 1, in E
(unaccompanied)   Columbia ML2168, RL6633
Philips S06616R

Caprice No. 1, in E
(unaccompanied)   Capitol (in sets PBR8477 & SPBR8477), K80339

Caprice No. 2, in b
(unaccompanied)   Capitol (in sets PBR8477 & SPBR8477), K80339

Caprice No. 3, in e
(unaccompanied)   Capitol (in sets PBR8477 & SPBR 8477), K80339

Caprice No. 4, in c
(unaccompanied)   Capitol (in sets PBR8477 & SPBR8477), K80339

Caprice No. 5, in a
(unaccompanied)   Columbia ML2168, RL6633
Philips S06616R

Caprice No. 5, in a
(unaccompanied)   Capitol (in sets PBR8477 & SPBR8477), K80339

Caprice No. 6, in g
(unaccompanied)   Capitol (in sets PBR8477 & SPBR8477), K80339

Caprice No. 7, in a
(unaccompanied)   Capitol (in sets PBR8477 & SPBR8477), K80339

Caprice No. 8, in E flat
(unaccompanied)   Capitol (in sets PBR8477 & SPBR8477), K80339

Caprice No. 9, in E
(unaccompanied)   Columbia ML2168, RL6633
Philips S06616R

Caprice No. 9, in E
(unaccompanied)   Capitol (in sets PBR8477 & SPBR8477), K80339

Caprice No. 10, in g
(unaccompanied)   Capitol (in sets PBR8477 & SPBR8477), K80339

Caprice No. 11, in C
(unaccompanied)   Columbia ML2168, RL6633
Philips S06616R

Caprice No. 11, in C
(unaccompanied)   Capitol (in sets PBR8477 & SPBR8477), K80339

Caprice No. 12, in A flat
(unaccompanied)   Capitol (in sets PBR8477 & SPBR8477), K80339

Caprice No. 13, in B flat
(unaccompanied)   Columbia ML2168, RL6633
Philips S06616R

Caprice No. 13, in B flat
(unaccompanied)   Capitol (in sets PBR8477 & SPBR8477), K80340

Caprice No. 14, in E flat
(unaccompanied)   Columbia ML2168, RL6633
Philips S06616R

Caprice No. 14, in E flat
(unaccompanied)   Capitol (in sets PBR8477 & SPBR8477), K80340

Caprice No. 15, in e
(unaccompanied)   Capitol (in sets PBR8477 & SPBR8477), K80340

Caprice No. 16, in g
(unaccompanied)   Columbia ML2168, RL6633
Philips S06616R

Caprice No. 16, in g
(unaccompanied)   Capitol (in sets PBR8477 & SPBR8477), K80340

Caprice No. 17, in E flat
(unaccompanied)   Columbia ML2168, RL6633
Philips S06616R

Caprice No. 17, in E flat
(unaccompanied)   Capitol (in sets PBR8477 & SPBR8477), K80340

Caprice No. 18, in C
(unaccompanied)   Columbia ML2168, RL6633
Philips S06616R

Caprice No. 18, in C
(unaccompanied)   Capitol (in sets PBR8477 & SPBR8477), K80340

Caprice No. 19, in E flat
(unaccompanied)   Capitol (in sets PBR8477 & SPBR8477), K80340

Caprice No. 20, in D
(unaccompanied)   Capitol (in sets PBR8477 & SPBR8477), K80340

Caprice No. 21, in A
(unaccompanied)   Columbia ML2168, RL6633
Philips S06616R

Caprice No. 21, in A
(unaccompanied)   Capitol (in sets PBR8477 & SPBR8477), K80340

Caprice No. 22, in F
(unaccompanied)   Capitol (in sets PBR8477 & SPBR8477), K80340

Caprice No. 23, in E flat
(unaccompanied)   Capitol (in sets PBR8477 & SPBR8477), K80340

Caprice No. 24, in a
(unaccompanied)   Columbia ML2168, RL6633
Philips S06616R

PAGANINI – *Continued*

Caprice No. 24, in a
(unaccompanied)

Capitol (in sets PBR8477 &
SPBR8477), K80340

Concerto No. 1, in D, Op. 6 (cadenza by Flesch) vln & orch.
with Philharmonia Orch. – von
Matacic

Angel 35259
Columbia CX1281
HMV LALP526

Concerto No. 1, in D, Op. 6 (cadenza by Flesch) vln & orch.
with Philharmonia Orch. – Goossens

Capitol K70434, P8534, SP8534

Moto perpetuo (Allegro di concert) Op. 11 (1830) vln & orch.
with Columbia Symphony Orch. –
Voorhees

Columbia AAL38
Philips 409007AE, NBE11003

Moto perpetuo (Allegro di concert) Op. 11 (1830) vln & orch.
with Hollywood Bowl Symphony
Orch. – Slatkin

Capitol K60690, P8510, SP8510,
STK60690
Seraphim S60199

PROKOFIEV

(The) Love for Three Oranges, Op.33 (1919) – opera
No. 3. March arr. vln & pf Heifetz
with L. Pommers pf

Capitol P8506

RAVEL

Pièce en forme d'Habanera v & pf – arr. vln & pf Catherine
with L. Pommers pf

Capitol P8506

Tzigane (Rapsodie de concert) (1924) vln & pf or orch.
with Philharmonia Orch. – Boult

Angel 35572
Columbia CX1597

RIMSKY–KORSAKOV

(The) Tale of Tsar Saltan (1900) – opera
Flight of the bumblebee (Act III) orch. – arr. vln & pf Hartmann
with Hollywood Bowl Symphony
Orch. – Slatkin

Capitol (in sets ABO8496 &
SABO8496), K60690, P8510,
SP8510, STK60690
Seraphim S60199

SAINT–SAËNS

Havanaise, Op. 83 vln & orch.
with Philharmonia Orch. – Boult

Angel 35572
Columbia CX1597

Introduction & Rondo Capriccioso, Op. 28 vln & orch.
with Philharmonia Orch. – Galliera

Angel 35388
Columbia CX1422
Music for Pleasure MFP2002

Introduction & Rondo Capriccioso, Op. 28 vln & orch.
with Hollywood Bowl Symphony
Orch. – Slatkin

Capitol K60690, P8510, SP8510,
STK60690
Seraphim S60199

SARASATE

Carmen Fantasia (on themes from the opera by Bizet) Op. 25 vln & pf or
orch.
Finale
with A. Balsam pf

Columbia AAL30

(8) Danzas españolas vln & pf
No. 2. Habañera, Op. 21, No. 2
with L. Pommers pf

Capitol P8506

No. 6. Zapateado, Op. 23, No. 2
with L. Pommers pf

Capitol P8506

SARASATE – *Continued*

Zigeunerweisen, Op. 20 vln & pf or orch.
with Columbia Symphony Orch. –
Voorhees

Columbia AAL38
Philips 409007AE, NBE11003,
SBF225

Zigeunerweisen, Op. 20 vln & pf or orch.
with Hollywood Bowl Symphony
Orch. – Slatkin

Capitol K60690, P8510, SP8510,
STK60690
Seraphim S60199

SCRIABIN

(12) Etudes, Op. 8 pf
No. 10. Etude No. 10, in D flat arr. vln & pf as "Etude in Thirds" by
Szigeti
with L. Pommers pf

Capitol P8506

SUK

(4) Pieces, Op. 17 vln & pf
No. 4. Burleska
with L. Pommers pf

Capitol P8506

TCHAIKOVSKY

Concerto in D, Op. 35 vln & orch.
with Philharmonia Orch. – Galliera

Angel 35388
Columbia CX1422
Music for Pleasure MFP2002
Trianon TRX6183

WIENIAWSKI

Concerto No. 1, in f sharp, Op. 14 vln & orch.
with Philharmonia Orch. – Boult

Angel 35484
Columbia CX1538

Concerto No. 2, in d, Op. 22 vln & orch.
with Philharmonia Orch. – Goossens

Capitol K70434, P8534, SP8534

(8) Étude–Caprices, Op. 18 solo vln & 2nd vln obb
Étude–Caprice No. 4, in a arr. vln & pf Kreisler
with A. Balsam pf

Columbia AAL30

Étude–Caprice No. 4, in a arr. vln & pf Kreisler
with L. Pommers pf

Capitol P8506

YSAŸE

(6) Sonatas, Op. 27 solo vln
Sonata No. 3, in d
(unaccompanied)

Angel 35305

Sonata No. 4, in e
(unaccompanied)

Angel 35305

Benno RABINOFF (1910–   )

ALBÉNIZ

España (6 Feuilles d'album) Op. 165 pf
No. 2. Tango in D arr. vln & pf Kreisler
with S. Rabinoff pf

Decca DL4039, DL10101

BRAHMS

(21) Hungarian Dances pf duet
Hungarian dance No. 20, in e arr. vln & pf "in d" Joachim
with S. Rabinoff pf

Decca DL4040, DL10101

DVOŘÁK

(8) Slavonic Dances, Op. 46 pf duet; orch.
  No. 2. Slavonic dance No. 2, in e arr. vln & pf "in g" Kreisler
    with S. Rabinoff pf   Decca DL4039, DL10101

FALLA

(7) Canciones populares españolas (1914) v & pf
  No. 4. Jota arr. vln & pf Kochański
    with S. Rabinoff pf   Decca DL4040, DL10101

GRANADOS

(12) Danzas españolas, Op. 37 (1893) pf
  No. 5. Danza española No. 5, in e "Andaluza" arr. vln & pf Kreisler
    with S. Rabinoff pf   Decca DL4040, DL10101

KREISLER

(La) Gitana vln & pf
    with S. Rabinoff pf   Decca DL4040, DL10101

Gypsy Caprice vln & pf
    with S. Rabinoff pf   Decca DL4040, DL10101

LEO

Concerto in D 4 vlns & strs
    with E. Brown vln, R.   US 1244/7   Royale 1826/7
    Totenberg vln, B. Schwarz vln, E.V.
    Wolff hpsi & vlcs & cbs

LÉONARD

(5) Scènes humoristiques, Op. 61 vln & pf
  No. 5. Sérénade du lapin belliqueux – arr. 3 vlns & pf
    with E. Brown vln, M. Mischakoff   Royale 583
    vln & J. Zayde (pf)

RAVEL

Tzigane (Rapsodie de concert) (1924) vln & pf or orch.
    with S. Rabinoff pf   Decca DL4039, DL10101

SARASATE

Introduction & Tarantelle, Op. 43 vln & pf
    with S. Rabinoff pf   Decca DL4040, DL10101

Zigeunerweisen, Op. 20 vln & pf or orch.
    with S. Rabinoff pf   Decca DL4039, DL10101

Ludwik RADEK

VIVALDI

(12) Concerti, Op. 3 "L'Estro armonico" var. cbns & strs
  Concerto No. 10, in b, P.148 (F.IV, No. 10) 4 vlns, strs & c
    with Z. Bakowski vln, I. Iwanow vln,   Muza XL0504
    E. Komosiński vln, J. Dobrzański hpsi
    & Warsaw Chamber Orch. –
    Sutkowski

Lou RADERMAN

FRANCK

Trio in f sharp Op. 1, No. 1 (1841) pf, vln & vlc
    with T. Saidenberg pf   CA 207/12   Co–Art 5049/51, (set A–101)
    & K. Levienne vlc   Griffon LP1001

HERBERT

Babes in Toyland (1903) – musical comedy
  Toyland
    with Capitol Symphony Orch. –   Capitol SP8575
    Dragon

JÄRNEFELT

Berceuse in g orch.
    with Capitol Symphony Orch. –   Capitol SP8575
    Dragon

RAVEL

Pavane pour une infante défunte (1899) orch.
    with Capitol Symphony Orch. –   Capitol SP8575
    Dragon

Béla RADICS (1867–1930)

ANONYMOUS

Réponse unid – arr. vln & pf as "Fantasia" by Radics
    with piano   Odeon A41983

SAINT-SAËNS

Samson et Dalila, Op. 47 (1877) – opera
  selection arr. vln & orch. Radics
    with orch.   Odeon A41982

Matthew RAIMONDI

AREL

For Violin & Piano (1966) vln & pf
    with R. Miller pf   Composers Recordings
                                  CRI SD264

FALLA

Concerto in D (1926) hpsi, fl, ob, cl, vln & vlc
    with S. Marlowe hpsi, S. Baron fl, R.   Decca DL10108, DL710108
    Roseman ob, D. Glazer cl & A.
    Kouguell vlc

FELDMAN

Extensions I (1951) vln & pf
    with D. Tudor pf   Columbia MS6090
                                  Odyssey 32 16 0302

(3) Pieces (1954/6) 2 vlns, vla & vlc
    with J. Rabushka vln, W. Trampler vla   Columbia MS6090
    & S. Barab vlc   Odyssey 32 16 0302

Projection IV (1951) vln & pf
    with D. Tudor pf   Columbia MS6090
                                  Odyssey 32 16 0302

Structures (1951) 2 vlns, vla & vlc
    with J. Rabushka vln, W. Trampler vla   Columbia MS6090
    & S. Barab vlc   Odyssey 32 16 0302

LAYTON

(5) Studies, Op. 1 vln & pf
    with Y. Wyner pf   Composers Recordings CRI257

MOSS

Sonata (1959) vln & pf
   with Y. Wyner pf   Composers Recordings CRI186

SHAPEY

Evocation (1959) vln, pf & pcn
   with Y. Wyner pf & P. Price pcn   Composers Recordings CRI141

WOLFF

Summer 2 vlns, vla & vlc
   with K. Kobayashi vln, W. Trampler   Time 8009, 58009
   vla & D. Soyer vlc

WYNER

Concert Duo (1956) vln & pf
   with Y. Wyner pf   Composers Recordings CRI161

Erwin RAMOR

BARTÓK

(2) Portraits, Op. 5 (1907) vln & orch.
   with Philharmonia Hungarica – Dorati   Mercury AMS16068, MG50183,
                          MMA11121, SR90183

I. RANNAP

LEPNURM

Variations vln & org
   with R. Uusväli org   Mezhdunarodnaya Kniga
                      D22277/8

Spiros RANTOS

BACH

Concerto in d, BWV1043 2 vlns, strs & c
   with E. Melkus vln & Capella   Archive 2533 075
   Academica Wien – Melkus

COUPERIN, F.

(L') Apothéose de Lully (1725) 2 vlns & c
   with E. Melkus vln, F. Stradner fl, B.   Archive 2533 067
   Klebel ob, J. Koch gamba, L. Cermak
   bsn & H. Dreyfus hpsi

(Le) Parnasse, ou l'Apothéose de Corelli (1725) 2 vlns & c
   with E. Melkus vln, F. Stradner fl, B.   Archive 2533 067
   Klebel ob, J. Koch gamba, L. Cermak
   bsn & H. Dreyfus hpsi

TELEMANN

Concerto in B flat "alla Polonaise" 2 vlns, vla, hpsi & c
   with E. Melkus vln, K. Hart vla, I.   Archive SAPM198467
   Ahlgrimm hpsi, V. Schwarz hpsi & S.
   Ladwig vlc

Concerto in G "alla Polonaise" 2 vlns, vla, hpsi & c
   with E. Melkus vln, K. Hart vla, I.   Archive SAPM198467
   Ahlgrimm hpsi, V. Schwarz hpsi & S.
   Ladwig vlc

Sonata No. 2, in a "Sonata Polonaise" 2 vlns & c
   with E. Melkus vln, C. Barrus vla, I.   Archive SAPM198467
   Ahlgrimm hpsi & S. Ladwig vlc

Virgilio RANZATO (1883–1937)

d'AMBROSIO

Canzonetta, Op. 6 vln & pf
   with piano   yy 1228[11] Zonophone 464, X47907,
                        X97902*

BACH

(4) Suites, BWV1066/9 strs & c
   Suite No. 3, in D: Air (2nd mvt) BWV1068 2 obs, 3 tpts, drms, strs & c
   – arr. vln & pf as "Air on the G–string" by Wilhelmj
   with piano   Pathé 1479, 19545

BEETHOVEN

Sonata No. 8, in c, Op. 13 "Pathétique" pf
   Adagio (2nd mvt) arr. vln & pf
   with piano   11066 b HMV 247900
                        Victor 120555
                        Zonophone X97908

   Adagio (2nd mvt) arr. vln & pf
   with piano   Pathé 80491

BELLINI

(La) Sonnambula (1831) – opera
   Prendi l'anel ti dono (Act I) arr. vln & pf Ranzato
   with piano   HMV 7-257911, R 9033
   Prendi l'anel ti dono (Act I) arr. vln & pf Ranzato
   with piano   Pathé 19566, 80484

BOCCHERINI

(6) Quintets, Op. 13 2 vlns, vla & 2 vlcs
   No. 5. Quintet No. 5, in E: Minuet (3rd mvt) "Bull" arr. vln & pf
   Kreisler
   with piano   Victor 120555
   No. 5. Quintet No. 5, in E: Minuet (3rd mvt) "Bull" arr. vln & pf
   Kreisler
   with piano   Pathé 3249, 19569, 80487

BRAGA

Meditazione vlc or vln & pf
   with piano   Zonophone X97902
Meditazione vlc or vln & pf
   with piano   Pathé 156, 1090, 3246, 19558
(7) Melodies (1867) v & pf
   No. 5. La serenata "Angel's serenade" arr. vln & pf
   with piano   HMV 7-257903, R 9025
   No. 5. La serenata "Angel's serenade" arr. vln & pf Pollitzer
   with piano   Pathé 156, 80496
   No. 5. La serenata "Angel's serenade" arr. vln & pf Pollitzer
   with piano   Columbia D5471
   No. 5. La serenata "Angel's serenade" arr. v, vln, hp & org
   with C. Boninsegna (s) & hp & org   Pathé 3271, 84347

BRAHMS

(21) Hungarian Dances pf duet
   Hungarian dance No. 5 in f sharp arr. vln & pf "in g" Joachim
   with piano   HMV 7-257918, R 9039
   Hungarian dance No. 7, in A arr. vln, vlc & pf
   with   Berti vlc &   Moroni pf   Pathé–Actuelle 15185

* Matrix number 7129 b for Zonophone 464 indicates a 2nd version.

BRAHMS – *Continued*

(5) Lieder, Op. 49 v & pf
No. 4. Wiegenlied "Cradle song" arr. vln & pf
with piano   HMV 7-257915, R 9037

CAROSIO

Mandolinata–notturno mand or vln & pf
with piano   Pathé 6336, 80690

CILEA

Serenata v & pf – arr. vln & pf
with piano   Pathé 163, 1095, 3255, 19557, 80531

CORELLI

(12) Sonatas, Op. 5 vln & c
Sonata No. 1, in D: Adagio (4th mvt)
with piano   HMV HN475
Sonata No. 12, in d "La Follia"
with piano   Pathé 3247

DELIBES

Sylvia (1876) – ballet orch.
selection arr. vln & pf Ranzato*
with piano   Pathé 160, 6332, 19532, 80638

DRIGO

(Les) Millions d'Arlequin (1900) – ballet orch.
Sérénade arr. vln & pf Auer
with piano   Pathé 16098
Sérénade arr. vln & pf Auer
with piano   Columbia D5474

DVOŘÁK

(8) Humoresques, Op. 101 pf
No. 7. Humoresque No. 7, in G flat arr. vln & pf "in G" Wilhelmj
with piano   Pathé 1380
     Pathé–Actuelle 10649

EILENBERG

Russian Guard's Parade, Op. 231 pf
Sérénade des mandolines (Pizzicato) arr. vln & pf
with piano   Pathé 6336, 80686

FAURÉ

(3) Romances sans paroles, Op. 17 pf
No. 3. Romance sans paroles No. 3, in A flat arr. vln & pf
with piano   Pathé 19576

FERRONI

Angelo pallido vln & orch
with piano   HMV 7-257924, R 9045

GILLET

Babillage pf – arr. vln & pf
with piano   Pathé 159, 3253, 19570, 80682
Babillage pf – arr. vln & pf
with piano   Pathé 19576

* Including Pizzicato.

GILLET – *Continued*

(La) Lettre de Manon – valse pf – arr. vln & pf
with piano   HMV C950, X287967
Loin du Bal, Op. 36 – ballet orch.
Intermezzo arr. vln & pf
with piano   HMV C950
Intermezzo arr. vln & pf
with piano   Pathé 159, 1092, 3253, 80510
(6) Morceaux strs & pf
No. 2. Douce Caresse arr. vln & pf
with piano   Pathé 3258, 19558, 80654

GLAZOUNOV

Méditation, Op. 32 vln & pf
with piano   HMV 7-257922, R 9043

GLOVIRITZ

Polka brillante vln & pf
with piano   Pathé 3258, 80716

GODARD

Jocelyn (1888) – opera
Cachés dans cet asile "Berceuse" arr. vln & pf
with piano   HMV C949, X287978
Cachés dans cet asile "Berceuse" arr. vln & pf
with piano   Columbia D5967
Cachés dans cet asile "Berceuse" arr. vln, org & hp
with organ & harp   Pathé 3306, 19565
Cachés dans cet asile "Berceuse" arr. v, vln, org & hp
with B. Lenzi s & organ & harp   Pathé 80074, 84353
     Pathé–Actuelle 10192

GOUNOD

Ave Maria (Méditation on Bach's "Prelude No. 1, in C" from Book I of "Das Wohltemperirte Clavier") v & pf – arr. vln & pf
with piano   HMV 7-257902, R 9025
Ave Maria (Méditation on Bach's "Prelude No. 1, in C" from Book I of "Das Wohltemperirte Clavier") v & pf – arr. vln & pf
with piano   HMV HN475, R11082
Ave Maria (Méditation on Bach's "Prelude No. 1, in C" from Book I of "Das Wohltemperirte Clavier") v & pf – arr. vln & pf
with piano   Columbia D5473
Ave Maria (Méditation on Bach's "Prelude No. 1, in C" from Book I of "Das Wohltemperirte Clavier") v & pf – arr. v, vln, org & hp
with C. Boninsegna s & organ & hp   Pathé 0443, 3271, 84346
     Pathé–Actuelle 10298

GRIEG

(6) Lyric pieces – Book III, Op. 43 (pf)
No. 5. Erotik arr. vln & pf
with piano   HMV 7-257901, R 9023
Peer Gynt, Op. 23 – opera
Solveig's song (Act I) arr. v, vln, org & hp
with E. Burzio s & organ & hp   Pathé 3326, 13003, 84482
Peer Gynt (Suite No. 2) Op. 55 orch.
No. 4. Solveig's song arr. vln & pf Sitt
with piano   Pathé 3260, 80683
No. 4. Solveig's song arr. vln & pf Sitt
with piano   Columbia D5958

GUGO–NORIS

Valse d'Or vln & pf
with piano　　　　　　　　　　　　Pathé 162, 1093/4, 3254,
　　　　　　　　　　　　　　　　　　80528/9

HANDEL

Serse (1738) – opera
Ombra mai fu "Largo" arr. vln & pf
with piano　　　　　　　　　　　　Pathé 155, 80492

HUBAY

(3) Morceaux, Op. 10 vln & pf
No. 2. Danse diabolique
with piano　　　　　　　1904 c　HMV 097901, 0277900, C5539

LAFON

(La) Voluttuosa – valse pf – arr. vln & pf
with piano　　　　　　　　　　　　Pathé 80656

LEHÁR

Libellentanz (1922) – operetta
Intermezzo orch. – arr. vln & pf
with piano　　　　　　　　　　　　Edison Bell F147
Intermezzo orch. – arr. vln & pf
with piano　　　　　　　　　　　　Pathé 16129
　　　　　　　　　　　　　　　　　　Pathé–Actuelle 10895
Intermezzo orch. – arr. vln & pf
with piano　　　　　　　　　　　　Columbia D5471

LEONCAVALLO

Mattinata (1904) v & pf – arr. vln & pf
with piano　　　　　　　　　　　　Pathé 165, 19562, 80534

LORET

Berceuse vln & pf
with piano　　　　　　　　　　　　Pathé 165, 80674

LULLY

Ballets du Roy (1659)*
Gavotte arr. vln & pf Burmester
with piano　　　　　　　　　　　　HMV C948
　　　　　　　　　　　　　　　　　　Zonophone X97906
Gavotte arr. vln & pf Burmester
with piano　　　　　　　　　　　　Pathé 164, 1095, 80532

LUZZI

Ave Maria, Op. 80 v & pf – arr. vln & pf
with piano　　　　　　　　　　　　Pathé 158, 3250, 3252, 80664

MARENCO

(La) Incognito – mazurka pf – arr. vln & pf
with piano　　　　　　　　　　　　Pathé 80658

MARIANI

(L') Abbandono, voce del core mand or vln & pf
with piano　　　　　　　　　　　　Columbia CQ479

MASCAGNI

(L') Amico Fritz (1891) – opera
Violinista arr. vln & pf
with piano　　　　　　　　　　　　Pathé–Actuelle 15189

* Unidentified.

MASCAGNI – *Continued*

Violinista arr. vln & pf
with piano　　　　　　　　　　　　Columbia D5957
Cavalleria Rusticana (1890) – opera
Intermezzo orch. – arr. vln & pf
with piano　　　　　　yy 986[11]　HMV HN476
　　　　　　　　　　　　　　　　　　Zonophone 464, X47906,
　　　　　　　　　　　　　　　　　　X97906*
Siciliana arr. vln & pf
with piano　　　　　　　　　　　　Pathé–Actuelle 15189

MASSENET

Thaïs (1894) – opera
Méditation arr. vln & pf Marsick
with orch. – Stefani　　　1883 c　HMV 090500
Méditation arr. vln & pf Marsick
with piano　　　　　　　　　　　　HMV 7–257910, R 9033
Méditation arr. vln & pf Marsick
with piano　　　　　　　　　　　　Pathé 157, 1091, 3251, 6334,
　　　　　　　　　　　　　　　　　　9613, 19531, 80499
　　　　　　　　　　　　　　　　　　Pathé–Actuelle 15189
Méditation arr. vln & pf Marsick
with piano　　　　　　　　　　　　Columbia D5472, DQ428

MENDELSSOHN

(6) Songs without words, Op. 62 pf
No. 6. Song without words No. 30, in A "Spring song" arr. vln & pf
with piano　　　　　　　　　　　　HMV 7–257907, R 9029

MONTI

(Il) Natale di Pierrot orch. – mime drama
Serenata arr. vln & pf
with piano　　　　　　　　　　　　Columbia D5967

MOZART

Divertimento No. 17, in D, K334 2 hrns & strs
Minuet (3rd mvt) arr. vln & pf Burmester
with piano　　　　　　　　　　　　HMV 7–257921, R 9043
Minuet (3rd mvt) arr. vln & pf Burmester
with piano　　　　　　　　　　　　HMV C947, V277912
　　　　　　　　　　　　　　　　　　Zonophone X97904
Minuet (3rd mvt) arr. vln & pf Burmester
with piano　　　　　　　　　　　　Pathé 1479, 9578, 19534, 30138
Minuet (3rd mvt) arr. vln & pf Burmester
with piano　　　　　　　　　　　　Edison Bell F147
Minuet (3rd mvt) arr. vln & pf Burmester
with piano　　　　　　　　　　　　Columbia D5472, DQ429

NEGLIA

Minuet (in olden style) vln & pf – arr. Ranzato
with R. Bossi pf　　　　　　　　　HMV AW343
Romance, Op. 40 vln & pf – arr. Ranzato
with R. Bossi pf　　　　　　　　　HMV AW343

NERUDA

Berceuse slave d'après un chant polonaise, Op. 11 vln & pf
with piano　　　　　　　　　　　　HMV 7–257914, R 9037

* Matrix number 7131 b for Zonophone 464 indicates a 2nd version.

NERUDA – *Continued*

Berceuse slave d'après un chant polonaise, Op. 11 vln & pf
with piano   Pathé 19545

PACCHIEROTTI

(L') Albatro
  Assollo arr. vln & pf
  with piano   Pathé 3259, 6333, 19570, 80665

  Danza delle Algho
  with piano   Pathé 19563, 80719/20

(Il) Re Olaf v & pf
  Ballata arr. vln & pf
  with piano   Pathé 155, 1089, 3250, 80495

PAGANINI

(6) Sonatas, Op. 3 (1801/6) vln & gtr
  No. 6. Sonata No. 12, in e
  with piano   Pathé 1380
                Pathé–Actuelle 10649

Sonata in A, Op. posth vln & gtr
  with piano   Pathé 3259, 9613, 80672

PARELLI

(L') Alba nascente v & pf – arr. vln & pf
  with piano   Columbia D5474

PIERNÉ

Sérénade in A, Op. 7 (1875) pf – arr. vln & pf Haddock
  with piano   7130 b   HMV 257905, C949
                          Zonophone 107934, X27906,
                          X97901

Sérénade in A, Op. 7 (1875) pf – arr. vln & pf Haddock
  with piano   Pathé 2037

PINSUTI

(Il) Libro santo v & pf – arr. v, vln, org & hp
  with B. Lenzi s & organ & harp   Pathé 13046, 84359

PUCCINI

(La) Bohème (1896) – opera
  Quando m'en vo soletta "Musetta's waltz song" arr. vln & pf Ranzato
  with piano   Pathé 1424
Madama Butterfly (1904) – opera
  Un bel di, vedremo arr. vln & pf Ranzato
  with piano   Pathé 1424
                Pathé–Actuelle 10895

RAFF

(6) Pieces, Op. 85 vln & pf
  No. 3. Cavatina in D
  with piano   HMV AL613

RANZATO

Allegro alla zingareska vln & pf
  with piano   HMV 7–257900, R 9023
Berceuse vln & pf
  with piano   14023 b   HMV 247901
Cin–ci–la (Romanza) vln & pf
  with piano   Columbia D5979
Citta' Rosa (Romanza) vln & pf
  with piano   Columbia D5979

RANZATO – *Continued*

(Il) Cuculo vln & pf
  with piano   HMV 7–257905, R 9027
(La) Danza del Globo vln & pf
  with piano   Columbia D6010
(La) Danza di nonnina vln & pf
  with piano   HMV HN478
(La) Danza di nonnina vln & pf
  with piano   Columbia CQ480
(La) Duchessa di Hollywood vln & pf
  with piano   Columbia CQ478
(A) Galoppo vln & pf
  with piano   HMV C948
                Zonophone X97907

(A) Galoppo vln & pf
  with piano   Pathé 160, 1092, 6332, 19532,
                80514

Mazurka–caprice vln & pf
  with piano   Pathé 3248, 80666
(I) Monelle fiorentini vln & pf
  with piano   Columbia CQ478
(4) Morceaux, Op. 12 vln & pf
  No. 3. Berceuse
  with piano   HMV 97909

  No. 3. Berceuse
  with piano   Pathé 161, 1093, 80527
(L') Organetto di Barberia vln & pf
  with piano   Columbia D5958
(Il) Paese dei Campanelli (Romanza di Nola) vln & pf
  with piano   Columbia D6010
Pasquinade vln & pf
  with piano   Pathé 3249
(La) Pattuglia delgli tzigani vln & pf
  with piano   Columbia D5473
(La) Prieghiera della sera vln & pf
  with piano   Pathé 3306, 19565
Rapsodie russe vln & pf
  with piano   Pathé 19576
Romanza sans paroles vln & pf
  with piano   Pathé 161, 3248, 6335, 80515
Scherzo in d vln & pf
  with piano   HMV 7–257908, R 9031
Scherzo in e vln & pf
  with piano   1903 c   HMV 097900, 0277901, C5539
Scherzo in e vln & pf
  with piano   Pathé 19534, 30138
Serenata vln & pf
  with piano   HMV C947
                Zonophone X97904

Serenata vln & pf
  with piano   Pathé 3260, 19563, 80718
Serenata galante vln & pf
  with piano   HMV 7–257909, R 9031
Serenata galante vln & pf
  with piano   Pathé 2037, 6335, 19576
Valse des diamants vln & pf
  with piano   Pathé 80671

RANZATO – *Continued*

Valse des rubis vln & pf
  with piano   Pathé 155, 1089, 3250, 80495

RESKE

Amor segrets v & pf – arr. vln & pf
  with piano   Pathé 164

RIMSKY–KORSAKOV

Sadko (1898) – opera
  Chant hindou arr. vln & pf Kreisler
  with piano   Pathé 9615

ROSSINI

Stabat Mater (1842)
  No. 2. Cujus animam arr. vln & pf
  with piano   Pathé 158, 1091, 3252, 80507

SAINT–SAËNS

(Le) Carnaval des animaux (1886) small orch.
  Le cygne arr. vln & pf
  with piano   HMV 7–257906, R 9029
  Le cygne arr. vln & pf
  with piano   Pathé 19573

SCASSERRA

Élégie vln & pf
  with piano   P 14070 b   Zonophone X97910, X287979

SCHUBERT

(7) Gesänge (set to Scott's "Lady of the Lake") Op. 52 v & pf
  No. 6. Ave Maria, D.839 arr. vln & pf Wilhelmj
  with piano   HMV 7–257904, R 9027
(6) Moments musicaux, Op. 94 (D780) (1823/7) pf
  No. 3. Moment musical No. 3, in f "Air russe" arr. vln & pf Kreisler
  with piano   P 14067 b   HMV C947, V287913
                              Zonophone X97911
(14) Schwanengesang, D957 (1828) v & pf
  No. 4. Ständchen "Serenade" arr. vln & pf Corti
  with piano   HMV HN478

SCHUMANN

(13) Kinderscenen, Op. 15 pf
  No. 7. Träumerei arr. vln & pf
  with piano   Pathé 3246, 9615, 19571
  No. 7. Träumerei arr. vln & pf
  with piano   Columbia D5957, DQ431

SILVESTRI

Serenata medioevale pf – arr. vln & pf
  with piano   Columbia CQ479

SIMON

(2) Pieces, Op. 17 vln & pf
  No. 2. Berceuse
  with piano   Pathé 80645

SIMONETTI

Madrigale pf – arr. vln & pf
  with piano   Pathé 163, 728, 1094, 3255,
                                      80530

SIMONETTI – *Continued*

Madrigale pf – arr. v, vln, org & hp
  with E. Burzio s & organ & harp   Pathé 3326, 13003, 84483

STRADELLA

Preghiera v & viols – arr. vln & pf
  with piano   Pathé 80652

SVENDSEN

Romance in G, Op. 26 vln & orch. – arr. vln & pf Wilhelmj
  with piano   1905 c   HMV 097902
Romance in G, Op. 26 vln & orch. – arr. vln & pf Wilhelmj
  with piano   Pathé 156, 1090, 3246, 80498

TARENGHI

(5) Morceaux, Op. 51 pf
  No. 3. Berceuse arr. vln, vlc & pf
  with   Berti vlc &   Moroni pf   Pathé–Actuelle 15185

TARTINI

Sonata in g "Il Trillo del Diavolo" vln & c – arr. vln & pf*
  with piano   Pathé 19544

TCHAIKOVSKY

Concerto in D, Op. 35 vln & orch
  Canzonetta (2nd mvt)
  with piano   HMV 7–257917, R 9039
(The) Months (12 Characteristic pieces) Op. 37a pf
  No. 6. Barcarolle (June) arr. vln & pf
  with piano   HMV 7–257920, R 9041

THOMAS

Mignon (1866) – opera
  Connais–tu le pays? arr. vln & pf
  with piano   Pathé 166, 728, 1096, 3256,
                                      80535

TIRINDELLI

Mistica in G vln & pf – arr. v, vln, org & hp
  with B. Lenzi s & organ & harp   Pathé 13046, 84360
(6) Morceaux de concert, Op. 1 vln & pf
  No. 3. Histoire
  with piano   Pathé 19571
Serenata vln & pf
  with piano   Pathé 6333, 19569, 80485

TOSELLI

Serenade, Op. 6 vln & pf
  with piano   Pathé 9578, 16129, 19573

VERDI

(La) Forza del Destino (1862) – opera
  selection arr. vln & pf Ranzato
  with organ & orch.   Pathé 157, 3251, 6334, 19531,
                                      19566, 80513

(I) Lombardi (1843) – opera
  Prelude (Act III) orch. – arr. vln & pf Ranzato
  with piano   Columbia D5968

* Abridged.

VERDI – *Continued*

Rigoletto (1851) – opera
  Caro nome arr. vln & pf Ranzato
  with piano   Pathé 1096, 3256, 80533

VIEUXTEMPS

(4) Romances, Op. 8 vln & pf
  No. 4. Air savoyard
  with piano   HMV 257906

WAGNER

(Die) Meistersinger von Nürnberg (1868) – opera
  Morgenlich leuchtend "Prize song" arr. vln & pf Wilhelmj
  with piano   Columbia CQ480
  Morgenlich leuchtend "Prize song" arr. vln & pf Wilhelmj
  with piano   HMV AL613

WALDTEUFEL

Estudiantina, Op. 191 orch. – arr. vln & pf Ranzato
  with piano   Pathé 168

WIENIAWSKI

(2) Mazurkas, Op. 19 vln & pf
  No. 1. Mazurka No. 1, in G "Obertass"
  with piano   HMV 7–257923, R 9045
  No. 1. Mazurka No. 1, in G "Obertass"
  with piano   7128 b   HMV V27907
                       Zonophone 107935, X97903
  No. 2. Mazurka No. 2, in D "Dudziarz"
  with piano   HMV 7–257919, R 9041

Maurice RASKIN (1906–)

ABSIL

Chaconne, Op. 69 (1949) solo vln
  (unaccompanied)   Decca FA143347
Fantaisie concertante, Op. 99 (1959) vln & orch.
  with orch. – Defossez   Decca FA143347

DEBUSSY

Sonata No. 3, in g (1917) vln & pf
  with N. Lee pf   Valois MB438, MB938

FAURÉ

Quartet No. 2, in g, Op. 45 pf, vln, vla & vlc
        AR 8905–2, 8906–1, 8907/8–2,   Decca K1183/6
            8909/10–1 & 8911/2–2
  with M. Gazelle pf, L. Ardenois vla &
  R. Soiron vlc

RAVEL

Sonata (1927) vln & pf
  with J–C. Richard pf   Valois MB467, MB967
Sonata (1922) vln & vlc
  with H. Honegger vlc   Valois MB467, MB967
Tzigane (Rapsodie de concert) (1924) vln & pf or orch.
  with J–C. Richard pf   Valois MB467, MB967

SCHUBERT

Quintet in A, Op. 114 (D667) "Trout" pf, vln, vla, vlc & cbs
  with M. Gazelle pf, L. Ardenois vla,   Decca K1366/9
  R. Soiron vlc & H. Lodge cbs

YSAŸE

Poème élégiaque in d (Poème No. 1) Op. 12 vln & pf or orch.
  with Belgian National Orch. –   Decca FA143337
  Defossez
(6) Sonatas, Op. 27 solo vln
  Sonata No. 3, in d
  (unaccompanied)   Decca FA143337

Fern RAŠKOVIČ

SARASATE

Introduction & Tarantelle, Op. 43 vln & pf
  with Z. Mihailovič pf   Jugoton LPY–V643

Howard RATTAY

ADAMS

(The) Holy city (1892) v & pf – arr. vln & pf
  with piano   Victor 16191

BOROWSKI

Adoration (1903) vln & pf
  with piano   Victor 35024

BRAGA

(7) Melodies (1867) v & pf
  No. 5. La serenata "Angel's serenade" arr. vln, vlc & orch.
  with R. Bourdon vlc & orch.   Victor 16410*

DVOŘÁK

(7) Gypsy songs, Op. 55 v & pf
  No. 4. Songs my mother taught me arr. v, vln & orch. Heyduk
  with G. Farrar s & orch.   Victor 87350

GILLESPIE

When you look in the heart of a rose v & pf – arr. v, vln & orch.
  with G. Farrar s & orch. – Pasternack   Victor 22652

HANDEL

Serse (1738) – opera
  Ombra mai fu "Largo" arr. vln & orch.
  with orch.   Victor 16313

HILDACH

(2) Lieder, Op. 15 v & pf
  No. 1. Der Spielmann
  with R. Fornia s & orch.   Victor 74227

LEYBACH

Nocturne No. 5, in A flat, Op. 52 pf – arr. vln & orch.
  with orch.   Victor 5404, 16410

* On Victor 16410, takes 1 & 2 were with Bourdon while take 3 had L. Heine as 'cellist.

MASSENET
Thaïs (1894) – opera
  Méditation arr. vln & pf Marsick
  with piano   Victor 35147

MENZEL
Romanze, Op. 40 "Sweet longing" fl & var. inst – arr. vln & orch.
  with orch.   Victor 31455, 35087

MOSZKOWSKI
(6) Klavierstücke, Op. 15 pf – 4 hands
  No. 1. Serenata arr. vln & pf
  with piano   Victor 5480

MURATORI
Amore (T'amo perchè sei bella) v, pf & vln – arr. vln, vlc & orch.
  with L. Heine vlc & orch.   Victor 16338

NEMEROVSKY
Meditation in a, Op. 8 vln & pf
  with piano   Victor 5469

PINSUTI
When life is brightest v & pf – arr. vln, fl & orch.
  with D. Lyons fl & orch.   Victor 35021

RAFF
(6) Pieces, Op. 85 vln & pf
  No. 3. Cavatina in D
  with orch.   Victor 4191, 16051

REHFELD
(2) Konzertstücke, Op. 58 vln & pf
  No. 1. Spanish dance
  with piano   Victor 5548

SARASATE
Zigeunerweisen, Op. 20 vln & pf or orch.
  with orch.   Victor 5436 & 31701

SCHUMANN
(13) Kinderscenen, Op. 15 pf
  No. 7. Träumerei arr. vln & pf
  with piano   Victor 16050

SIMONETTI
Madrigale pf – arr. vln & pf
  with piano   Victor 16027

STRANGE
Birds in the forest pf – arr. 2 vlns & fl
  with T. Levy vln & D. Lyons fl   Victor 16296

TCHAIKOVSKY
(6) Songs, Op. 6 v & pf
  No. 6. None but the weary heart
  with G. Farrar s & orch.   HMV DA469
                          Victor 623, 87357

THOMAS
Mignon (1866) – opera
  Entr'acte (Gavotte) (Act II) orch. – arr. str qt
  with T. Levy vln, L. Heine   B 6617   Victor 16323
  vla & Francillo vlc

Germaine RAYMOND

BERTHEAUME
(2) Sinfonia concertantes, Op. 6 (1787) 2 vlns & orch.
  Sinfonia concertante No. 2, in E flat
  with H. Fernandez vln, P. Pelvescovo   Erato LDE3037
  hrn & Jean-François Paillard Chamber
  Orch. – Paillard

BOISMORTIER
(5) Sonatas, Op. 37 (1732) 2 fls & c
  Sonata No. 5, in e arr. fl, vln, ob, bsn & c
  with J. Rocheblave fl, A. Lardrot ob,   Erato 21–1
  J. Charpentier bsn, A–M.   Haydn Society HSL103
  Beckensteiner hpsi & M-A. Mocquot
  gamba

CORELLI
(12) Concerti grossi, Op. 6 orch.
  Concerto grosso No. 8, in g "Christmas Concerto"
  with H. Fernandez vln, P. Degenne   Erato EFM42042
  vlc, A–M. Beckensteiner hpsi & Jean-
  François Paillard Chamber Orch. –
  Paillard

HANDEL
(6) Concerti grossi, Op. 3 (1759) orch.
  Concerto grosso No. 7, in C
  with H. Fernandez vln, P. Degenne   Christophorus CGLP75741
  vlc, A–M. Beckensteiner hpsi & Jean-
  François Paillard Chamber Orch. –
  Paillard
(12) Concerti grossi, Op. 6 (1739) 2 vlns, vlc & strs
  Concerto grosso No. 10, in d
  with H. Fernandez vln, P. Degenne   Christophorus CGLP75741
  vlc, A–M. Beckensteiner hpsi & Jean-
  François Paillard Chamber Orch. –
  Paillard

LECLAIR
(6) Concerti, Op. 7 (1737) vln & strs
  Concerto No. 5, in a
  with Leclair Instrumental Ensemble –   Erato 21–2
  Paillard   Haydn Society HSL140
(6) Concerti, Op. 10 (1744) vln & strs
  Concerto No. 1, in B flat
  with Leclair Instrumental Ensemble –   Erato 21–2
  Paillard   Haydn Society HSL140
(12) Sonatas, Op. 9 – Book IV (1738) vln & c
  Sonata No. 3, in D
  with J. Lacrouts vln, A–M.   Erato 21–1
  Beckensteiner hpsi & J. Deferrieux vlc   Haydn Society HSL140

SAINT–GEORGES

(2) Sinfonia concertantes, Op. 9 (1778) 2 vlns & strs
Sinfonia concertante No. 2, in G (cadenza by Paillard)
with M. Blanchard vln & Jean–   Erato LDE3037
François Paillard Chamber Orch. –
Paillard

SOLER

(6) Quintets 2 vlns, vla, vlc & org or pf
Quintet No. 6, in g
with H. Fernandez vln, M–R. Guiet   Erato DP501
vla, J. Deferrieux vlc & M–C. Alain   Westminster XWN18754
org

Gladys RAYMOND

LEDERER

(2) Poèmes hongroise, Op. 16 vln & pf
No. 2. Poème hongrois No. 2, in D
with piano   Pathé 8286, 78795

LULLY

(Le) Bourgeois Gentilhomme (1670) – comédie–ballet orch.
Menuet arr. vln & pf
with piano   Pathé 8286, 78794

RAFF

(6) Pieces, Op. 85 vln & pf
No. 3. Cavatina in D
with piano   Pathé 879, 78792

TCHAIKOVSKY

(3) Souvenirs de Hapsal, Op. 2 pf
No. 3. Chant sans paroles in f arr. vln & pf Kreisler
with piano   Pathé 879, 78793

Aldo REDDITI

BONPORTI

(12) Sonatas, Op. 1 (1696) 2 vlns & vlc obb
Sonata No. 3, in g (rev. Barblan)
with M. Ceradini vln &   Carisch BCA7017
R. Caruana vlc

BRESCIANELLO

(12) Concerti 2 vlns & c
Concerto No. 1, in B flat
with M. Ceradini vln, N. Poli hpsi &   Carisch BCA7017
R. Caruana vlc

CAMBINI

Sinfonia concertante in F vln, vlc & strs
with R. Caruana vlc & Angelicum   Angelicum LPA978
Orch. – Argento

CORELLI

(12) Sonatas, Op. 2 (1685) 2 vlns & c
Sonata No. 4, in e (rev. Allorto)
with M. Ceradini vln, N. Poli hpsi &   Carisch BCA7017
R. Caruana vlc

HAYDN, M.

Divertimento in D, P93 2 vlns, vla & cbs
with Angelicum Orch. – Kloss   Angelicum LPA988

MARTINI, G.B.

Sinfonia concertante vln, hpsi & strs
with G.F. Spinelli hpsi & Angelicum   Angelicum LPA978
Orch. – Argento

MOZART

Serenade No. 6, in D, K239 "Serenata Notturna" orch.
with M. Ceradini vln & Angelicum   Angelicum LPA989
Orch. – Zecchi

SALIERI

Concerto in D "Triple" vln, ob, vlc & orch.
with S. Possidoni ob, R. Caruana vlc   Angelicum LPA1069
& Angelicum Orch. – Kloss

TARTINI

Concerto in e vln & orch.
with Angelicum Orch. – Janes   Angelicum LPA1063
Concerto in F vln & orch.
with Angelicum Orch. – Janes   Angelicum LPA1063

TORELLI

(12) Concerti, Op. 8 (1709) 1/6: 2 vlns, strs & c – 7/12: vln, strs & c
Concerto No. 1, in C
with M. Ceradini vln & Angelicum   Angelicum LPA1003
Orch. – Maderna
Concerto No. 3, in E
with M. Ceradini vln & Angelicum   Angelicum LPA1003
Orch. – Maderna
Concerto No. 7, in d
with Milan Chamber Orch. – Jenkins   Washington WR405, WS9405
Concerto No. 7, in d
with Angelicum Orch. – Maderna   Angelicum LPA1003
Concerto No. 9, in e
with Angelicum Orch. – Maderna   Angelicum LPA1003

VIVALDI

(12) Concerti, Op. 3 "L'Estro armonico" var. cbns & strs
Concerto No. 1, in D, P.146 (F.IV, No. 7) 4 vlns, vlc, strs & c
with soloists & Società Corelli   Victor (in set ML61003)
Concerto No. 2, in g, P.326 (F.IV, No. 8) 2 vlns, strs & c
with anon vln & Società Corelli   Victor (in set ML61003)
Concerto No. 3, in G, P.96 (F.I, No. 173) vln strs & c
with Società Corelli   Victor (in set ML61003)
Concerto No. 4, in e, P.97 (F.I, No. 174) 4 vlns, strs & c
with soloists & Società Corelli   Victor (in set ML61003)
Concerto No. 5, in A, P.212 (F.I, No. 175) 2 vlns, strs & c
with anon vln & Società Corelli   Victor (in set ML61003)
Concerto No. 6, in a, P.1 (F.I, No. 176) vln, strs & c
with Società Corelli   Victor (in set ML61003)
Concerto No. 7, in F, P.249 (F.IV, No. 9) 4 vlns, strs & c
with soloists & Società Corelli   Victor (in set ML61003)
Concerto No. 8, in a, P.2 (F.I, No. 177) 2 vlns, strs & c
with anon vln & Società Corelli   Victor (in set ML61003)
Concerto No. 9, in D, P.147 (F.I, No. 178) vln, strs & c
with Società Corelli   Victor (in set ML61003)

VIVALDI – *Continued*

Concerto No. 10, in b, P.148 (F.IV, No. 10) 4 vlns, strs & c
with soloists & Società Corelli   Victor (in set ML61003)

Concerto No. 11, in d, P.250 (F.IV, No. 11) 2 vlns, vlc, strs & c
with soloists & Società Corelli   Victor (in set ML61003)

Concerto No. 12, in E, P.240 (F.I, No. 179) vln, strs & c
with Società Corelli   Victor (in set ML61003)

(12) Concerti, Op. 8 (1725) "Il Cimento dell' Armonia e dell' Invenzione"
(Nos. 1/4: Le quattro Stagioni) vln & strs
Concerto No. 5, in E flat, F.I, No. 26 "La Tempesta di mare"
with Società Corelli   Victor (in sets MLD61002,
MLDS61002), A630791,
A640791, LM2743, LSC2743

Concerto No. 6, in C, F.I, No. 27 "Il piacere"
with Società Corelli   Victor (in sets MLD61002,
MLDS61002)

Concerto No. 7, in d, P.258 (F.I, No. 28)
with Società Corelli   Victor (in sets MLD61002,
MLDS61002)

Concerto No. 8, in g, F.I, No. 16
with Società Corelli   Victor (in sets MLD61002,
MLDS61002), A630791,
A640791, LM2743, LSC2743

Concerto No. 9, in d, F.VII, No. 1
with Società Corelli   Victor (in sets MLD61002,
MLDS61002)

Concerto No. 10, in B flat, F.I, No. 29 "La Caccia"
with Società Corelli   Victor (in sets MLD61002,
MLDS61002)

Concerto No. 11, in D, F.I, No. 30
with Società Corelli   Victor (in sets MLD61002,
MLDS61002)

Concerto No. 12, in C, F.I, No. 31
with Società Corelli   Victor (in sets MLD61002,
MLDS61002)

Concerto in C, P.14 (F.I, No. 13) (Op. 54, No. 3) "Per la SS. Assunzione di
Maria Vergine" vln, strs & c
with Angelicum Orch. – Maderna   Angelicum LPA1062

Concerto in D, P.188 (F.IV, No. 4) 2 vlns, 2 vlcs, strs & c
with M. Ceradini vln, R. Caruana   Angelicum LPA1066
vlc, S. Busetto vlc & Angelicum Orch.
– Lupi

Concerto in B flat, P.368 (F.I, No. 60) (Op. 28, No. 3) "Scordatura" vln, 2
str choruses & c
with Milan Chamber Orch. – Jenkins   Washington WR405, WS9405

Sonata in C "Mauro Foà" lute, vln & c – rev. Rapp
with R. Rapp lute, N. Poli hpsi & R.   Carisch BCA7017
Caruana vlc

William Henry REED (1876–1942)

ELGAR

Nursury Suite (1931) orch.
  Cadenza
  with London   2B 561^IIA△   HMV D1999
  Symphony Orch. – Elgar

HOLST

(4) Songs, Op. 35 v, vln & pf
  No. 1. Jesu sweet
  with D. Labbette s & piano   Columbia L1590
  No. 2. I sing of a maid
  with D. Labbette s & piano   Columbia L1590
  No. 3. My soul has nought but fire & ice
  with D. Labbette s & piano   Columbia L1590
  No. 4. My leman is so true of love
  with D. Labbette s & piano   Columbia L1590

Helga REHM

GOLDBERG

Sonata No. 4, in a 2 vlns & c
with T. Brandis vln, K. Grebe hpsi &   Archive APM14195, ARC3195,
E. Koch vlc   ARC73195, SAPM198195

Bernard REILLIE

BEETHOVEN

(6) Minuets, G167 pf
  No. 2. Minuet No. 2, in G arr. vln & pf Burmester
  with piano   A 2967   Columbia 3985, J187

DAVIES

Psalm XXIII (The Lord is my shepherd) Op. 8 (1900) t, 2 vlns, vla, vlc &
hp – arr. t, vln & pf
with A. Jordan t & piano   Columbia 9026

FRANCK

Ave Maria (1863) s, t, bs & org – arr. t, vln & pf
with A. Jordan t & piano   Columbia 9026

MASSENET

Thaïs (1894) – opera
  Méditation arr. vln & pf Marsick
  with piano   Columbia L1647

RAFF

(6) Pieces, Op. 85 vln & pf
  No. 3. Cavatina in D
  with piano   WA 11492   Columbia DB627

RIMSKY-KORSAKOV

Sadko (1898) – opera
  Chant hindou arr. vln & pf Kreisler
  with piano   A 2968   Columbia 3985, J187

SCHUMANN

(13) Kinderscenen, Op. 15 pf
  No. 7. Träumerei arr. vln & pf
  with piano   WA 11491   Columbia DB627

Folke REINHOLDSSON

SKÖLD

Canzonetta vln & pf
  with piano   1387 D   Cupol*

Lamy REIS

SARASATE

(8) Danzas españolas vln & pf
No. 5. Playera, Op. 23, No. 1
  with J. Silva pf   Polydor 47503

TOSELLI

Serenade, Op. 6 vln & pf
  with J. Silva pf   Polydor 47503

Pierre REITTINGER

AUBERT, L.

Vieille chanson espagnole v & hpsi – arr. vln & pf Reittinger
  with piano   Pathé X98081

BRAHMS

(21) Hungarian Dances pf duet
Hungarian dance No. 2, in d arr. vln & pf Joachim
  with piano   Pathé X98081

Ossy RENARDY (1921–1953)

BACH

(3) Sonatas & 3 Partitas, BWV1001/6 solo vln
Sonata No. 1, in g, BWV1001
(unaccompanied)   Decca LM4542
                      London LPS423
Sonata No. 3, in C, BWV1005
(unaccompanied)   AR 15043/8–1   Decca AK2378/80, LX4536
                      London LPS259

BRAHMS

Concerto in D, Op. 77 (cadenza by Joachim) vln & orch.
        HAR 41–3, 42/4–2, 45–1, 46–3   Decca AK2055/9, LXT2566
  with Amsterdam   & 47/50–2   London T5097/101, (set LA87),
  Philharmonic Orch. – Munch   LLP1
Sonata (1853) "Frei aber Einsam" vln & pf
Allegro (Scherzo) in c (3rd mvt) "Sonatensatz"
  with W. Robert pf   Victor 18032

BRANDL

(Der) Liebe Augustin – operetta
Du alter Stefansturm arr. vln & pf as "The old refrain" by Kreisler
  with E. Lush pf   London R10135

BURMESTER

Serenade vln & pf
  with W. Robert pf   Columbia 17132D

* Unissued.

CHAMINADE

Sérénade espagnole pf – arr. vln & pf Kreisler
  with E. Lush pf   DR 13764–1A   London R10137

CORELLI

(12) Sonatas, Op. 5 vln & c
Sonata No. 8, in e
  with L. Taubman   XCO 22498/9–1   Columbia 69152D, DX854
pf

DVOŘÁK

Ballade in d, Op. 15 vln & pf
  with W. Robert pf   Victor 18294
(8) Slavonic Dances, Op. 46 pf duet; orch.
No. 8. Slavonic dance No. 8, in g arr. vln & pf Press
  with W. Robert pf   XCO 24285–1   Columbia 69544D, (in set X129),
                      C15765, (in set J49)
Sonatina in G, Op. 100 vln & pf
        XCO 23968/9–2 & 23970–1   Columbia 69543/4D, (set X129),
  with W. Robert pf   C15765/6, (set J49)

ERNST

Airs hongrois variés in A, Op. 22 vln & pf
  with W. Robert pf   Victor 11–8113

FRANCK

Sonata in A (1886) vln & pf
  with E. List pf   Concerteum CR285
                  Remington R199–148

HANDEL

Te Deum, Dettingen (1743)
No. 17. Gebet ('Verlieh uns Herr, zu schirmen ...) arr. vln & pf as
"Prayer" by Flesch
  with W. Robert pf   Columbia 17119D

KREISLER

Caprice viennois, Op. 2 vln & pf
  with E. Lush pf   Decca LK4024
                  London LL159, R10134
Liebesfreud vln & pf
  with E. Lush pf   Decca LK4024
                  London LL159, R10136
Liebersleid vln & pf
  with E. Lush pf   Decca LK4024
                  London LL159, R10136
Schön Rosmarin vln & pf
  with E. Lush pf   London R10135
Tambourin chinois, Op. 3 vln & pf
  with E. Lush pf   Decca LK4024
                  London LL159, R10134

MOZART

Adagio in E, K261 vln & orch.
  with W. Robert pf   Victor 18032

NOVACÉK

(8) Concert Caprices, Op. 5 vln & pf
No. 4. Perpetuum mobile
  with E. Lush pf   DR 13765–1A   London R10137

PAGANINI

(24) Caprices, Op. 1 (1801/7) solo vln

Caprice No 1, in E arr. vln & pf with W. Robert pf	HMV ED132 Victor 16276, (in set M672)
Caprice No. 1, in E arr. vln & pf with E. Helmer pf	Remington R199–146
Caprice No. 2, in b arr. vln & pf with W. Robert pf	HMV ED132 Victor 16276, (in set M672)
Caprice No. 2, in b arr. vln & pf with E. Helmer pf	Remington R199–146
Caprice No. 3, in e arr. vln & pf with W. Robert pf	HMV ED132 Victor 16276, (in set M672)
Caprice No. 3, in e arr. vln & pf with E. Helmer pf	Remington R199–146
Caprice No. 4, in c arr. vln & pf with W. Robert pf	HMV ED132 Victor 16276, (in set M672)
Caprice No. 4, in c arr. vln & pf with E. Helmer pf	Remington R199–146
Caprice No. 5, in a arr. vln & pf with W. Robert pf	HMV ED133 Victor 16277, (in set M672)
Caprice No. 5, in a arr. vln & pf with E. Helmer pf	Remington R199–146
Caprice No. 6, in g arr. vln & pf with W. Robert pf	HMV ED133 Victor 16277, (in set M672)
Caprice No. 6, in g arr. vln & pf with E. Helmer pf	Remington R199–146
Caprice No. 7, in a arr. vln & pf with W. Robert pf	HMV ED133 Victor 16277, (in set M672)
Caprice No. 7, in a arr. vln & pf with E. Helmer pf	Remington R199–146
Caprice No. 8, in E flat arr. vln & pf with W. Robert pf	HMV ED133 Victor 16277, (in set M672)
Caprice No. 8, in E flat arr. vln & pf with E. Helmer pf	Remington R199–146
Caprice No. 9, in E arr. vln & pf with W. Robert pf	HMV ED134 Victor 16278, (in set M672)
Caprice No. 9, in E arr. vln & pf with E. Helmer pf	Remington R199–146
Caprice No. 10, in g arr. vln & pf with W. Robert pf	HMV ED134 Victor 16278, (in set M672)
Caprice No. 10, in g arr. vln & pf with E. Helmer pf	Remington R199–146
Caprice No. 11, in C arr. vln & pf with W. Robert pf	HMV ED134 Victor 16278, (in set M672)
Caprice No. 11, in C arr. vln & pf with E. Helmer pf	Remington R199–146

PAGANINI – *Continued*

Caprice No. 12, in A flat arr. vln & pf with W. Robert pf	HMV ED134 Victor 16278, (in set M672)
Caprice No. 12, in A flat arr. vln & pf with E. Helmer pf	Remington R199–146
Caprice No. 13, in B flat arr. vln & pf with W. Robert pf	Victor 17636, (in set M738)
Caprice No. 13, in B flat arr. vln & pf with E. Helmer pf	Remington R199–152
Caprice No. 14, in E flat arr. vln & pf with W. Robert pf	Victor 17636, (in set M738)
Caprice No. 14, in E flat arr. vln & pf with E. Helmer pf	Remington R199–152
Caprice No. 15, in e arr. vln & pf with W. Robert pf	Victor 17636, (in set M738)
Caprice No. 15, in e arr. vln & pf with E. Helmer pf	Remington R199–152
Caprice No. 16, in g arr. vln & pf with W. Robert pf	Victor 17636, (in set M738)
Caprice No. 16, in g arr. vln & pf with E. Helmer pf	Remington R199–152
Caprice No. 17, in E flat arr. vln & pf with W. Robert pf	Victor 17636, (in set M738)
Caprice No. 17, in E flat arr. vln & pf Fuchs with E. Lush pf AR 13763–1A	Decca LK4024 London LL159, T5266
Caprice No. 17, in E flat arr. vln & pf with E. Helmer pf	Remington R199–152
Caprice No. 18, in C arr. vln & pf with W. Robert pf	Victor 17636, (in set M738)
Caprice No. 18, in C arr. vln & pf with E. Helmer pf	Remington R199–152
Caprice No. 19, in E flat arr. vln & pf with W. Robert pf	Victor 17637, (in set M738)
Caprice No. 19, in E flat arr. vln & pf with E. Helmer pf	Remington R199–152
Caprice No. 20, in D arr. vln & pf with W. Robert pf	Victor 17637, (in set M738)
Caprice No. 20, in D arr. vln & pf with E. Helmer pf	Remington R199–152
Caprice No. 21, in A arr. vln & pf with W. Robert pf	Victor 17637, (in set M738)
Caprice No. 21, in A arr. vln & pf with E. Helmer pf	Remington R199–152
Caprice No. 22, in F arr. vln & pf with W. Robert pf	Victor 17637, (in set M738)
Caprice No. 22, in F arr. vln & pf with E. Helmer pf	Remington R199–152
Caprice No. 23, in E flat arr. vln & pf with W. Robert pf	Victor 17637, (in set M738)
Caprice No. 23, in E flat arr. vln & pf with E. Helmer pf	Remington R199–152
Caprice No. 24, in a arr. vln & pf with W. Robert pf	Victor 17638, (in set M738)

PAGANINI – *Continued*

Caprice No. 24, in a arr. vln & pf Flesch
with E. Lush pf   AR 13762–1A   Decca LK4024
    London LL159, T5266

Caprice No. 24, in a arr. vln & pf
with E. Helmer pf   Remington R199–152

(6) Sonatas, Op. 3 (1801/6) vln & gtr
No. 6. Sonata No. 12, in e
with W. Robert pf   Columbia 17132D

Sonata in A, Op. posth vln & gtr
with W. Robert pf   Victor 17638, (in set M738)

(Le) Streghe (variations on a theme from Süssmeyer's opera "Il Noce di Benevento") Op. 8 (1813) vln & orch. – arr. vln & pf Wilhelmj
with E. Lush pf   AR 13760/1–2B   Decca K2355, LK4024
    London LL159

PLATTI

(6) Sonatas, Op. 3 (1743) fl & c
Sonata No. 1, in e arr. vln & pf Jarnach
with W. Robert pf   XCO 22498/9   Columbia 69655D

RAVEL

Sonata (1927) vln & pf
with E. List pf   Concerteum CR285
    Remington R199–148

SAINT–SAËNS

Concerto No. 1, in A, Op. 20 "Konzertstück" vln & orch. – arr. vln & pf Spiering
with W. Robert pf   HMV ED277
    Victor 17479

SARASATE

Adios montañas mias, Op. 37 vln & pf
with W. Robert pf   XCO 24284–1   Columbia 69622D, (in set X134), 72114D, (in set MX134)

(8) Danzas españolas vln & pf
No. 3. Romanza andaluza, Op. 22, No. 1
with W. Robert pf   XCO 23595–3   Columbia 69621D, (in set X134), 72113D, (in set MX134)

No. 4. Jota navarra, Op. 22, No. 2
with W. Robert pf   XCO 23596–3   Columbia 69621D, (in set X134), 72113D, (in set MX134)

No. 6. Zapateado, Op. 23, No. 2
with W. Robert pf   XCO 24286–1   Columbia 69622D, (in set X134), 72114D, (in set MX134)

SCHUBERT

(7) Gesänge (set to Scott's "Lady of the Lake") Op. 52 v & pf
No. 6. Ave Maria, D839 arr. vln & pf Wilhelmj
with E. Lush pf   AR 13771–1A   Decca K2288, K23186, LK4024
    London LL159

(3) Sonatinas, Op. 137 (D384, D385 & D408) vln & pf
No. 1. Sonatina No. 1, in D, D384
    XCO 23551–1, 23552–2 & 23553   Columbia 69403/4D, (set X116),
with W. Robert pf   –1   C15709/10, (set J14)

No. 3. Sonatina No. 3, in g: Minuetto (3rd mvt); **Allegro moderato** (4th mvt) D408
with W. Robert pf   XCO 23505–2   Columbia 69404D, (in set X116), C15709, (in set J14)

VECSEY

Caprice No. 2 "La Cascade" vln & pf
with W. Robert pf   Columbia 17119D

WIENIAWSKI

Scherzo–Tarantelle, Op. 16 vln & pf
with E. Lush pf   DAR 13766–2B   Decca K2288, K23186, LK4024
    London LL159

ZARZYCKI

Mazurka in G, Op. 26 vln & pf
with W. Robert pf   Victor 18294

Ròzsy RÈTY

d'AMBROSIO

Canzonetta, Op. 6 vln & pf
with K. Rockstroh pf   5699   Kalliope K1582

DENZA

Si vous l'aviez compris! v & pf – arr. vln & pf
with K. Rockstroh pf   5849   Kalliope K1618

NEVIN

(6) Water Scenes, Op. 13 pf
No. 4. Narcissus arr. vln & pf
with K. Rockstroh pf   5850   Kalliope K1618

VECSEY

Valse triste vln & pf
with K. Rockstroh pf   Kalliope K1582

Georg RETYI

BACH

Concerto in c, BWV1060 vln & ob or 2 vlns, strs & c
with P. Pierlot ob, L. Hokanson hpsi   Erato EFM8027, EFM42088,
& Pro Arte Chamber Orch., Munich –   STE60018
Redel

TELEMANN

Concerto in E fl, ob d'amore, vla d'amore, strs & c
with K. Redel fl, W. Grimm ob   Christophorus CGLP75792,
d'amore & Pro Arte Chamber Orch.,   SCGLP75793
Munich – Redel   Erato LDE3243, STE50143,
    STU70143

Concerto in G 2 vlns, strs & c
with J. Steinhäusler vln & Pro Arte   Christophorus CGLP75792,
Chamber Orch., Munich – Redel   SCGLP75793
    Columbia SMC95066
    Erato LDE3243, STE50143,
    STU70143
    Westminster WST17042,
    XWN19042

VIVALDI

(12) Concerti, Op. 3 "L'Estro armonico" var. cbns & strs
Concerto No. 10, in b, P.148 (F.IV, No. 10) 4 vlns, strs & c
with soloists & Pro Arte Chamber   Christophorus CGLP75732
Orch., Munich – Redel   Musical Heritage Society
    MHS593

VIVALDI – *Continued*

(12) Concerti, Op. 4 "La Stravaganza" vln, strs & c
Concerto No. 2, in E, F.I, No. 181
with Pro Arte Chamber Orch., Munich   Christophorus CGLP75732
– Redel   Musical Heritage Society
MHS593

Florizel von REUTER (1893–   )

ANONYMOUS

Negro folksongs unid – arr. vln & pf Reuter
with P. Vladigerov pf   Polydor 95249

DVOŘÁK

Trio No. 4, in e, Op. 90 "Dumky" pf, vln & vlc
482/3½GS, 484¾GS &   Decca LY6109/12
with E. Ney pf &   485/8½GS
Hoelscher vlc

HAYDN

(31) Trios, H.XV, Nos. 1/31 pf, vln & vlc
Trio No. 25, in G: Rondo all' ongarese (3rd mvt) H.XV, No. 25 (Op. 73,
No. 2)
with E. Ney pf &   499¾GS   Decca CA8214
Hoelscher vlc   Deutsche Grammophon (in set
27)
Polydor 15090, 67071

LOCATELLI

(24) Caprices, Op. 3 solo vln
Caprice No. 23, in D "Il laberinto armonico" arr. vln & pf Reuter
with piano   Polydor 90036

MOZART

Trio No. 6, in G, K564 pf, vln & vlc
Allegretto (3rd mvt)
with E. Ney pf &   489½GS   Decca LY6112
Hoelscher vlc

PAGANINI

(24) Caprices, Op. 1 (1801/7) solo vln
Caprice No. 9, in E arr. vln & pf Reuter
with P. Vladigerov pf   590½Bi^{IV} Decca CA8097
Polydor 95250
Caprice No. 13, in B flat arr. vln & pf Reuter
with piano   Polydor 90036
Caprice No. 24, in a
(unaccompanied)   Polydor 95184
Concerto No. 2, in b, Op. 7 vln & orch.
Ronde à clochette (3rd mvt) "La Campanella" arr. vln & pf Wilhelmj
with piano   516 BI^{IV} Polydor 95185
Sonata a preghièra "Moses Fantasia" (on the aria "Dal tuo stellato soglio"
from Rossini's opera "Mosè in Egitto") Op. 24 (1818 or 1819) vln &
orch. – arr. vln & pf Reuter
with P. Vladigerov pf   589 Bi^{IV} Decca CA8097
Polydor 95250

SAINT–LUBIN

Sextet (from the opera "Lucia di Lammermoor" by Donizetti) Op. 56 solo
vln
(unaccompanied)   Polydor 95184

SARASATE

(Le) Chant du rossignol, Op. 29 vln & pf
with P. Vladigerov pf   Polydor 95249
(8) Danzas españolas vln & pf
No. 4. Jota navarra, Op. 22, No. 2
with piano   513 Bi^{IV} Polydor 95185

SCHUMANN

Quartet in E flat, Op. 47 pf, vln, vla & vlc
492 GS, 493½GS, 494/6 GS,   Decca CA8213/6
with E. Ney pf, 497½GS & 498 GS   Deutsche Grammophon (set 27)
W. Trampler vla & L. Hoelscher vlc   Polydor 15087/90

TARTINI

Sonata in g "Il Trillo del Diavolo" vln & c – arr. vln & pf
with piano   90/1 bo^{IV} Polydor 95183

Karl REUTER

BEETHOVEN

(6) Minuets, G167 pf
No. 2. Minuet No. 2, in G arr. vln & pf Burmester
with piano   Supertone S2154

LEYBACH

Nocturne No. 5, in A flat, Op. 52 pf – arr. vln & pf
with piano   Supertone S2154

Barbara REUTER–RAU

REUTER, F.

Sonata in e "Lausitzer Sonata" vln & pf
with R. Reuter pf   Eterna 820465

Julian REYENTOVICH

VLASOV

Asel – ballet orch.
No. 1. Introduction & Asel's 1st variation
with USSR Bolshoi Theatre Orch. –   Mezhdunarodnaya Kniga
Ziuraitis   D020571/2, S01541/2
No. 7. Asel's grief (Asel's Adagio with friends)
with USSR Bolshoi Theatre Orch. –   Mezhdunarodnaya Kniga
Ziuraitis   D020571/2, S01541/2
No. 10. Optimistic Allegro & Adagio of Baitemir & Asel
with USSR Bolshoi Theatre Orch. –   Mezhdunarodnaya Kniga
Ziuraitis   D020571/2, S01541/2

Angel REYES (1919–   )

BARRAUD

Sonatina (1941) vln & pf
with J. de Menasce pf   Amphion (set B9)
Concert Hall E17

Marcel REYNAL

CORELLI

(12) Sonatas, Op. 5 vln & c
  Sonata No. 11, in E: Allegro (2nd mvt)
    with R. Lopez pf   L'Encyclopédie Sonore 320E822

MOZART

Sonata No. 32, in B flat, K454 vln & pf
    with R. Lopez pf   L'Encyclopédie Sonore 320E822

André de RIBAUPIERRE (1893-1955)

TARTINI

Concerto in E, D53 (C84) vln & orch – ed. Scherchen
    with Winterthur Municipal Orch. –   HMV DB6093/4
    Scherchen

Gerardo RIBEIRO

VIVALDI

(12) Concerti, Op. 3 "L'Estro armonico" var. cbns & strs
  Concerto No. 4, in e, P.97 (F.I, No. 174) 4 vlns, strs & c
    with R. Barnert vln, W. Prystawski   Archive 2705 002, SAPM198469
    vln, T. Soh vln & Lucerne Festival
    Strings – Baumgartner

RICCI

ANONYMOUS

Piquant stories unid – arr. vln & pf
    with piano   Scala 322
Romance in C unid – arr. vln, fl & pf
    with E. Dearing fl & piano   Scala 87
Romance in F unid – arr. vln, fl & pf
    with E. Dearing fl & piano   Scala 87
(The) Waltz wizard unid – arr. vln & pf
    with piano   Scala 322

DELIBES

Sylvia (1876) – ballet orch.
  No. 16a. Pizzicato–scherzettino (Act III) arr. vln & pf
    with piano   Scala 90

FELIX

(Die) Kätzchen (1890) – operetta
  Unter dem Lindenbaum arr. vln & pf
    with piano   Scala 1555, DL92

HANDEL

Serse (1738) – opera
  Ombra mai fu "Largo" arr. vln & pf
    with piano   Scala 92

HUBAY

Romance, Op. 25 vln & pf or orch.
    with chamber orch.   Beka G45790
                                        Scala 93

HUBAY – *Continued*

Variations sur un thème hongrois, Op. 72 vln & pf
    with chamber orch.   Beka G45791
                                        Scala 93

LEONCAVALLO

Mattinata (1904) v & pf – arr. vln & pf
    with piano   Scala 1555, DL92

MASCAGNI

Cavalleria Rusticana (1890) – opera
  Intermezzo orch. – arr. vln, fl & pf
    with E. Dearing fl & piano   Scala 90

MOZART

Ave verum corpus, K618 cho – arr. vln & pf
    with piano   Scala 92

OFFENBACH

(Les) Contes d'Hoffmann (1881) – opera
  Belle Nuit, O nuit d'amour "Barcarolle" arr. vln, fl & pf
    with E. Dearing fl & piano   Scala 91

RUBENS

(The) Blue Moon – musical
  Mother dear arr. 2 vlns & pf
    with B. Mazzone vln & piano   Scala 88

Ruggiero RICCI (1918–   )

ACHRON

Hebrew melody, Op. 33 vln & pf – arr. Auer
    with E. Lush pf   Decca LXT5460
                                        Eclipse ECS595
                                        London CS6039, STS15049

BACH

Concerto No. 1, in a, BWV1041 vln, strs & c
    with City of London Chamber   Unicorn UNS202
    Ensemble – Ricci
Concerto No. 2, in E, BWV1042 vln, strs & c
    with Lamoureux Orch. – Bigot   Polydor 566239/41
                                        Vox PL6630
Concerto No. 2, in E, BWV1042 vln, strs & c
    with City of London Chamber   Unicorn UNS202
    Ensemble – Ricci
Concerto No. 1, in d, BWV1052 clav, strs & c – arr. vln, strs & c Reitz
    with City of London Chamber   Unicorn UNS202
    Ensemble – Ricci
(3) Sonatas & 3 Partitas, BWV1001/6 solo vln
  Sonata No. 1, in g, BWV1001
  (unaccompanied)   London LL1706
  Sonata No. 1, in g, BWV1001
  (unaccompanied)   Decca DL10142, DL710142
                                        MCA MUC103, MUCS103
  Partita No. 1, in b, BWV1002
  (unaccompanied)   Decca DL10142, DL710142
                                        MCA MUC103, MUCS103
  Sonata No. 2, in a, BWV1003
  (unaccompanied)   8007/10   Vox 12039/40, (set 187)

BACH – *Continued*

Sonata No. 2, in a, BWV1003
(unaccompanied) — Decca DL10151, DL710151

Partita No. 2, in d, BWV1004*
(unaccompanied) — Vox (set 638)

Partita No. 2, in d, BWV1004
(unaccompanied) — London LL1706

Partita No. 2, in d, BWV1004
(unaccompanied) — Decca DL10151, DL710151

Sonata No. 3, in C, BWV1005
(unaccompanied) — Decca DL10152, DL710152
MCA MUC122, MUCS122

Partita No. 3, in E, BWV1006
(unaccompanied) — Decca DL10152, DL710152
MCA MUC122, MUCS122

BARTÓK

Sonata in g (1944) solo vln
(unaccompanied) — Decca LXT5595, SXL2240
Eurodisc 70704KK, 70705KK
London CM9261, CS6193,
SLC1287

BAZZINI

(La) Ronde des lutins, Op. 25 vln & pf
with E. Lush pf — Decca CEP600, LXT5460,
SEC5022
Eclipse ECS595
London CS6039, STS15049

BEETHOVEN

Concerto in D, Op. 61 (cadenzas by Kreisler) vln & orch.
with London Philharmonic Orch. –
Boult — Ace of Clubs ACL5
Decca LXT2750
London LL562
Richmond R19034

(Die) Ruinen von Athen, Op. 113 – Incidental music orch.
No. 3. Chor der Derwische arr. vln & pf Auer
with L. Persinger pf — Vox 16047, (in set 196)

(3) Sonatas, Op. 30 vln & pf
No. 2. Sonata No. 7, in c
with F. Gulda pf — Decca LXT2942
London LL1004

Sonata No. 10, in G, Op. 96 vln & pf
with F. Gulda pf — Decca LXT2942
London LL1004

BOTTESINI

Grand duo concertante in a vln, cbs & orch.
with F. Petracchi cbs & Royal
Philharmonic Orch. – Bellugi — CBS 72995
Columbia M30574
Unicorn RHS304

* Chaconne or 5th mvt is on Vox VIP45360.

BRAHMS

(21) Hungarian Dances pf duet
Hungarian dance No. 17, in f sharp arr. vln & pf Joachim
with L. Pommers pf — Decca DXE179, DXSE7179,
SMU1104
Deutsche Grammophon
LPEM19464, SLPEM136464

Hungarian dance No. 20, in e arr. vln & pf "in d" Joachim
with L. Pommers pf — Decca DXE179, DXSE7179,
SMU1104
Deutsche Grammophon
LPEM19464, SLPEM136464

Sonata No. 2, in A, Op. 100 vln & pf
with J. Katchen pf — Decca LXT5270
London LL1569

Sonata No. 3, in d, Op. 108 vln & pf
with J. Katchen pf — Decca LXT5270
London LL1569

BRANDL

(Der) Liebe Augustin – operetta
Du alter Stefansturm arr. vln & pf as "The old refrain" by Kreisler
with B. Smith pf — Brunswick AXA4501, SXA4501
Decca DL10052, DL710052

BRUCH

Concerto No. 1, in g, Op. 26 vln & pf
with London Symphony Orch. –
Gamba — Decca LW5352, LW50075,
LXT5334, MD1026, SPA88,
SXL2006
London CM9194, CS6010,
LL1684

CHOPIN

(12) Études, Op. 25 pf
No. 8. Étude No. 20, in D flat arr. vln & pf Ricci
with L. Persinger pf — Vox 16047, (in set 196)

Nocturne No. 20, in c sharp, Op. posth pf – arr. vln & pf Milstein
with E. Lush pf — Decca LXT5460
Eclipse ECS595
London CS6039, STS15049

DESPLANES

Intrada (Adagio) vln & c – arr. vln & pf Nachèz
with L. Pommers pf — Decca DXE179, DXSE7179,
SMU1104
Deutsche Grammophon
LPEM19464, SLPEM136464

DOHNÁNYI

Sonata in c sharp, Op. 21 vln & pf
with F. Rados pf — Qualiton LPX–S1165

DVOŘÁK

Concerto in a, Op. 53 vln & orch.
with London Symphony Orch. –
Sargent — Ace of Diamonds ADD126,
SDD126
Decca LXT5641, ND373,
SXL2279
London CM9284, CS6215

ELGAR

(La) Capricieuse, Op. 17 vln & pf
with E. Lush pf

Decca CEP600, LXT5460,
SEC5022
Eclipse ECS595
London CS6039, STS15049

ERNST

Airs hongrois in A, Op. 22 vln & pf
with L. Pommers pf

Decca DL710172

(6) Mehrstimmige Studien solo vln
No. 6. Étude No. 6, in G (Variations on "The last rose of summer") (à
Bazzini)
(unaccompanied)

Decca DL710172

FALLA

(7) Canciones populares españolas (1914) v & pf
No. 1. El paño moruno arr. vln & pf Kochański
with F. Rados pf

Qualiton EP1620

No. 3. Asturiana arr. vln & pf Kochański
with F. Rados pf

Qualiton EP1620

No. 4. Jota arr. vln & pf Kochański
with F. Rados pf

Qualiton EP1620

No. 5. Nana arr. vln & pf Kochański
with F. Rados pf

Qualiton EP1620

No. 6. Canción arr. vln & pf Kochański
with F. Rados pf

Qualiton EP1620

HANDEL

(15) Sonatas, Op. 1 (?1731) fl or vln & c
Sonata No. 9, in b: Andante (1st mvt) arr. vln & pf as "Larghetto"by
Hubay
with L. Pommers pf

Decca DXE179, DXSE7179,
SMU1104
Deutsche Grammophon
LPEM19464, SLPEM136464

HINDEMITH

(2) Sonatas, Op. 31 (1924) solo vln
Sonata No. 1
(unaccompanied)

Decca LXT5595, SXL2240
Eurodisc 70704KK, 70705KK
London CM9261, CS6193,
SLC1287

Sonata No. 2
(unaccompanied)

Vox 639/40, (in set 603)

Sonata No. 2
(unaccompanied)

Decca LXT5595, SXL2240
Eurodisc 70704KK, 70705KK
London CM9261, CS6193,
SLC1287

Sonata No. 3, in E (1935) vln & pf
with L. Persinger pf

Vox 639/40, (in set 603)

HUBAY

(6) Blumenleben, Op. 30 vln & pf
No. 5 Der Zephir
with L. Persinger pf

Vox 16048, (in set 196),
VIP45340

HUBAY – Continued

No. 5. Der Zephir
with E. Lush pf

Decca LXT5460
Eclipse ECS595
London CS6039, STS15049

(Le) Luthier de Crémone, Op. 40 (1894) – opera
Intermezzo orch. – arr. vln & pf Hubay
with L. Pommers pf

Decca DXE179, DXSE7179,
SMU1104
Deutsche Grammophon
LPEM19464, SLPEM136464

KABALEVSKY

Improvisation, Op. 21, No. 1 vln & pf
with L. Pommers pf

Decca DXE179, DXSE7179,
SMU1104
Deutsche Grammophon
LPEM19464, SLPEM136464

KHACHATURIAN

Concerto in D (1940) (cadenza by D. Oistrakh) vln & orch.
with London Symphony Orch. –
Fistoulari

Decca LXT5259
London LL1537

KREISLER

Caprice viennois, Op. 2 vln & pf
with B. Smith pf

Brunswick AXA4501, SXA4501
Decca DL10052, DL710052,
SMU1122
Deutsche Grammophon
LPEM19389, SLPEM136389

(La) Gitana vln & pf
with B. Smith pf

Brunswick AXA4501, SXA4501
Decca DL10052, DL710052,
SMU1122
Deutsche Grammophon
LPEM19389, SLPEM136389

Liebesfreud vln & pf
with B. Smith pf

Brunswick AXA4501, SXA4501
Decca DL10052, DL710052,
SMU1122
Deutsche Grammophon
LPEM19389, SLPEM136389

Liebesleid vln & pf
with B. Smith pf

Brunswick AXA4501, SXA4501
Decca DL10052, DL710052,
SMU1122
Deutsche Grammophon
LPEM19389, SLPEM136389

Recitative & Scherzo–caprice, Op. 6 solo vln
(unaccompanied)

Polydor 566244
Vox 649, (in set 659)

Recitative & Scherzo–caprice, Op. 6 solo vln
(unaccompanied)

Brunswick AXA4501, SXA4501
Decca DL10052, DL710052,
SMU1122
Deutsche Grammophon
LPEM19389, SLPEM136389

KREISLER – *Continued*

Rondino on a theme by Beethoven vln & pf
    with B. Smith pf
        Brunswick AXA4501, SXA4501
        Decca DL10052, DL710052,
        SMU1122
        Deutsche Grammophon
        LPEM19389, SLPEM136389

Schön Rosmarin vln & pf
    with B. Smith pf
        Brunswick AXA4501, SXA4501
        Decca DL10052, DL710052,
        SMU1122
        Deutsche Grammophon
        LPEM19389, SLPEM136389

Tambourin chinois, Op. 3 vln & pf
    with B. Smith pf
        Brunswick AXA4501, SXA4501
        Decca DL10052, DL710052,
        SMU1122
        Deutsche Grammophon
        LPEM19389, SLPEM136389

Chanson Louis XIII & Pavane (L. Couperin) vln & pf
    with B. Smith pf
        Brunswick AXA4501, SXA4501
        Decca DL10052, DL710052,
        SMU1122
        Deutsche Grammophon
        SLPEM136389

(La) Chasse (Cartier) vln & pf
    with B. Smith pf
        Brunswick AXA4501, SXA4501
        Decca DL10052, DL710052,
        SMU1122
        Deutsche Grammophon
        SLPEM136389

Praeludium & Allegro (Pugnani) vln & pf
    with B. Smith pf
        Brunswick AXA4501, SXA4501
        Decca DL10052, DL710052,
        SMU1122
        Deutsche Grammophon
        SLPEM136389

Sicilienne & Rigaudon (Francoeur) vln & pf
    with B. Smith pf
        Brunswick AXA4501, SXA4501
        Decca DL10052, DL710052,
        SMU1122
        Deutsche Grammophon
        SLPEM136389

Variations on a theme of Corelli (Tartini) vln & pf
    with L. Persinger pf
        Vox 16046, (in set 196),
        VIP45340

Variations on a theme of Corelli (Tartini) vln & pf
    with B. Smith pf
        Brunswick AXA4501, SXA4501
        Decca DL10052, DL710052,
        SMU1122
        Deutsche Grammophon
        SLPEM136389

KROLL

Banjo & fiddle vln & pf
    with E. Lush pf
        Decca CEP600, LXT5460,
        SEC5022
        Eclipse ECS595
        London CS6039, STS15049

LALO

Symphonie espagnole, Op. 21 vln & orch.*
    with Suisse Romande Orch. –
    Ansermet
        Decca LXT5527, SXL2155
        Eurodisc 70547KK
        London CS6134, CM9016

LOCATELLI

(24) Caprices, Op. 3 solo vln

Caprice No. 23, in D "Il laberinto armonico"
(unaccompanied)
        Decca DL710172

MATTHESON

(12) Suites (1714) hpsi

Suite No. 5, in c: Air arr. vln & pf Burmester
with C. Fürstner pf   DRA 3406[II]☐   HMV DA4467

MENDELSSOHN

Concerto in e, Op. 64 vln & orch.
    with London Symphony Orch. –
    Gamba
        Decca LXT5334, LW50078,
        MD1026, SLW50078, SPA88,
        SXL2006
        London CM9194, CS6010,
        LL1684

(6) Songs without words, Op. 62 pf

No. 1. Song without words No. 25, in G "May breezes" arr. vln & pf Kreisler
    with L. Pommers pf
        Decca DXE179, DXSE7179,
        SMU1104
        Deutsche Grammophon
        LPEM19464, SLPEM136464

MOSZKOWSKI

(2) Stücke, Op. 45 pf

No. 2. Guitarre arr. vln & pf Sarasate
    with E. Lush pf
        Decca LXT5460
        Eclipse ECS595
        London CS6039, STS15049

MOZART

Sonata No. 4, in E flat, K282 pf

Adagio (2nd mvt) arr. vln & pf Friedberg
    with L. Pommers pf
        Decca DXE179, DXSE7179,
        SMU1104
        Deutsche Grammophon
        LPEM19464, SLPEM136464

Sonata No. 26, in B flat, K378 vln & pf
    with G. d'Attili pf   Vox PL6400

NARDINI

(7) Sonatas vln & c

Sonata No. 7, in B flat: Larghetto (2nd mvt)
    with L. Pommers pf
        Decca DXE179, DXSE7179,
        SMU1104
        Deutsche Grammophon
        LPEM19464, SLPEM136464

* Including Intermezzo.

PAGANINI

Cantabile e valzer in E, Op. 19 (1823 or 1824) vln & gtr
with L. Pommers pf
Decca DXE179, DXSE7179,
SMU1104
Deutsche Grammophon
LPEM19464, SLPEM136464

(24) Caprices, Op. 1 (1801/7) solo vln
Caprice No. 1, in E
(unaccompanied)
Decca LK4025
Everest SDBR3313
London LL264

Caprice No. 1, in E
(unaccompanied)
Decca LXT5569, SXL2194,
SXL21007
London CM9244, CS6163

Caprice No. 2, in b
(unaccompanied)
Decca LK4025
Everest SDBR3313
London LL264

Caprice No. 2, in b
(unaccompanied)
Decca LXT5569, SXL2194,
SXL21007
London CM9244, CS6163

Caprice No. 3, in e
(unaccompanied)
Decca LK4025
Everest SDBR3313
London LL264

Caprice No. 3, in e
(unaccompanied)
Decca LXT5569, SXL2194,
SXL21007
London CM9244, CS6163

Caprice No. 4, in c
(unaccompanied)
Decca LK4025
Everest SDBR3313
London LL264

Caprice No. 4, in c
(unaccompanied)
Decca LXT5569, SXL2194,
SXL21007
London CM9244, CS6163

Caprice No. 5, in a
(unaccompanied)
Decca LK4025
Everest SDBR3313
London LL264

Caprice No. 5, in a
(unaccompanied)
Decca LXT5569, SXL2194,
SXL21007
London CM9244, CS6163

Caprice No. 6, in g
(unaccompanied)
Decca LK4025
Everest SDBR3313
London LL264

Caprice No. 6, in g
(unaccompanied)
Decca LXT5569, SXL2194,
SXL21007
London CM9244, CS6163

Caprice No. 7, in a
(unaccompanied)
Decca LK4025
Everest SDBR3313
London LL264

PAGANINI – *Continued*

Caprice No. 7, in a
(unaccompanied)
Decca LXT5569, SXL2194,
SXL21007
London CM9244, CS6163

Caprice No. 8, in E flat
(unaccompanied)
Decca LK4025
Everest SDBR3313
London LL264

Caprice No. 8, in E flat
(unaccompanied)
Decca LXT5569, SXL2194,
SXL21007
London CM9244, CS6163

Caprice No. 9, in E
(unaccompanied)
Decca LK4025
Everest SDBR3313
London LL264

Caprice No. 9, in E
(unaccompanied)
Decca LXT5569, SXL2194,
SXL21007
London CM9244, CS6163

Caprice No. 10, in g
(unaccompanied)
Decca LK4025
Everest SDBR3313
London LL264

Caprice No. 10, in g
(unaccompanied)
Decca LXT5569, SXL2194,
SXL21007
London CM9244, CS6163

Caprice No. 11, in C
(unaccompanied)
Decca LK4025
Everest SDBR3313
London LL264

Caprice No. 11, in C
(unaccompanied)
Decca LXT5569, SXL2194,
SXL21007
London CM9244, CS6163

Caprice No. 12, in A flat
(unaccompanied)
Decca LK4025
Everest SDBR3313
London LL264

Caprice No. 12, in A flat
(unaccompanied)
Decca LXT5569, SXL2194,
SXL21007
London CM9244, CS6163

Caprice No. 13, in B flat arr. vln & pf Kreisler
with L. Persinger pf
Vox 615, (in set 614), VIP45420
Caprice No. 13, in B flat
(unaccompanied)
Decca LXT2588
Everest SDBR3313
London LL252

Caprice No. 13, in B flat
(unaccompanied)
Decca CEP693, LXT5569,
SEC5085, SXL2194, SXL21007,
SVD810, VD810
London CM9244, CS6163

Caprice No. 14, in E flat
(unaccompanied)
Decca LXT2588
Everest SDBR3313
London LL252

PAGANINI – *Continued*

Caprice No. 14, in E flat
(unaccompanied)

Decca CEP693, LXT5569,
SEC5085, SXL2194, SXL21007,
SVD810, VD810
London CM9244, CS6163

Caprice No. 15, in e
(unaccompanied)

Decca LXT2588
Everest SDBR3313
London LL252

Caprice No. 15, in e
(unaccompanied)

Decca LXT5569, SXL2194,
SXL21007
London CM9244, CS6163

Caprice No. 16, in g
(unaccompanied)

Decca LXT2588
Everest SDBR3313
London LL252

Caprice No. 16, in g
(unaccompanied)

Decca CEP693, LXT5699,
SEC5085, SXL2194, SXL21007,
SVD810, VD810
London CM9244, CS6163

Caprice No. 17, in E flat
(unaccompanied)

Decca LXT2588
Everest SDBR3313
London LL252

Caprice No. 17, in E flat
(unaccompanied)

Decca LXT5569, SXL2194,
SXL21007
London CM9244, CS6163

Caprice No. 18, in C
(unaccompanied)

Decca LXT2588
Everest SDBR3313
London LL252

Caprice No. 18, in C
(unaccompanied)

Decca LXT5569, SXL2194,
SXL21007
London CM9244, CS6163

Caprice No. 19, in E flat
(unaccompanied)

Decca LXT2588
Everest SDBR3313
London LL252

Caprice No. 19, in E flat
(unaccompanied)

Decca LXT5569, SXL2194,
SXL21007
London CM9244, CS6163

Caprice No. 20, in D arr. vln & pf Kreisler
with L. Persinger pf
Vox 615, (in set 614), VIP45420

Caprice No. 20, in D
(unaccompanied)

Decca LXT2588
Everest SDBR3313
London LL252

Caprice No. 20, in D
(unaccompanied)

Decca LXT5569, SXL2194,
SXL21007
London CM9244, CS6163

PAGANINI – *Continued*

Caprice No. 21, in A
(unaccompanied)

Decca LXT2588
Everest SDBR3313
London LL252

Caprice No. 21, in A
(unaccompanied)

Decca CEP693, LXT5569,
SEC5085, SVD810, SXL2194,
SXL21007, VD810
London CM9244, CS6163

Caprice No. 22, in F
(unaccompanied)

Decca LXT2588
Everest SDBR3313
London LL252

Caprice No. 22, in F
(unaccompanied)

Decca LXT5569, SXL2194,
SXL21007
London CM9244, CS6163

Caprice No. 23, in E flat
(unaccompanied)

Decca LXT2588
Everest SDBR3313
London LL252

Caprice No. 23, in E flat
(unaccompanied)

Decca LXT2588, SXL2194,
SXL21007
London CM9244, CS6163

Caprice No. 24, in a
(unaccompanied)

Decca LXT2588
Everest SDBR3313
London LL252

Caprice No. 24, in a
(unaccompanied)

Decca CEP693, LXT5569,
SEC5085, SVD810, SXL2194,
SXL21007, VD810
London CM9244, CS6163

Concerto No. 1, in D, Op. 6 (cadenza by Sauret) vln & orch.
    Allegro maestoso (1st mvt) arr. vln & orch. Wilhelmj
    with Lamoureux Orch. – Bigot
Festival CFR12–292
Polydor 566242/4
Vox 647/9, (set 659), PL6490

Concerto No. 1, in D, Op. 6 (cadenza by Sauret) vln & orch.
    with London Symphony Orch. –
    Collins
Decca LXT5075, LW5344,
MD1049
London CM9131, LL1215

Concerto No. 2, in b, Op. 7 vln & orch.
    Ronde à la clochette (3rd mvt) "La Campanella" arr. vln & pf Kochański
    with L. Persinger pf
Vox 614, (in set 614), PL6490,
VIP45420

    Ronde à la clochette (3rd mvt) "La Campanella" arr. vln & pf Kochański
    with K. Fürstner pf   2RA 3411[2]☐ HMV DB4619

    Ronde à la clochette (3rd mvt) "La Campanella" arr. vln & pf Kochański
    with L. Persinger pf
Decca 18174, 71066, LXT2808
Eclipse ECS585
London CM9099, LL1005

Concerto No. 2, in b, Op. 7 (cadenza by Balsam) vln & orch.
    with London Symphony Orch. –
    Collins
Decca LXT5075, MD1049
London CM9131, LL1215

PAGANINI – *Continued*

Concerto No. 2, in b, Op. 7 (cadenza by Balsam) vln & orch.
with Cincinnati Symphony Orch. –
Rudolf

	Brunswick AXA4529, SXA4529
	Decca 410004, DL10106,
	DL710106, SMU1103
	Deutsche Grammophon
	LPEM19478, SLPEM136478

Concerto No. 4, in d (1829) vln & orch.
with Royal Philharmonic Orch. –
Bellugi

	Columbia M30574
	CBS 72995
	Unicorn RHS304

God save the King – variations, Op. 9 (1829) vln & orch.
with L. Persinger pf

	Decca LXT2808
	Eclipse ECS585
	London CM9099, LL1005

God save the King – variations, Op. 9 (1829) vln & orch.
(unaccompanied)

| | Decca DL710172 |

Moto perpetuo (Allegro di concert) Op. 11 (1830) vln & orch.
with L. Persinger pf

| | Polydor 566257 |
| | Vox 615, (in set 614), PL6490 |

Moto perpetuo (Allegro di concert) Op. 11 (1830) vln & orch.
with L. Persinger pf

	Decca 18174, 71066, LXT2808
	Eclipse ECS585
	London CM9099, LL1005

Nel cor più non mi sento "Sonata appassionata con variazioni" (on the aria from Paisiello's opera "La bella molinara") Op. 38 (1820 or 1821) solo vln
(unaccompanied)

	Decca LXT2808
	Eclipse ECS585
	London CM9099, LL1005

Nel cor più non mi sento "Sonata appassionata con variazioni" (on the aria from Paisiello's opera "La bella molinara") Op. 38 (1820 or 1821) solo vln
(unaccompanied)

| | Decca DL710172 |

(I) Palpiti (variations on the theme "Di tanti palpiti" from Rossini's opera "Tancredi") Op. 13 (1819) vln & orch. – arr. vln & pf Kreisler
with L. Persinger pf

	Decca LXT2808
	Eclipse ECS585
	London CM9099, LL1005

(6) Sonatas, Op. 3 (1801/6) vln & gtr
No. 6. Sonata No. 12, in e
with L. Persinger pf

	Decca LXT2808
	Eclipse ECS585
	London CM9099, LL1005

No. 6. Sonata No. 12, in e
with R. Valdés–Blain gtr

| | Decca DL710177 |
| | MCA MACS3478 |

Sonata a preghièra "Moses Fantasia" (on the aria "Dal tuo stellato soglio" from Rossini's opera "Mosè in Egitto") Op. 24 (1818 or 1819) vln & orch.
with L. Persinger pf

| | Polydor 566257 |
| | Vox 614, (in set 614), PL6490 |

Sonata a preghièra "Moses Fantasia" (on the aria "Dal tuo stellato soglio" from Rossini's opera "Mosè in Egitto") Op. 24 (1818 or 1819) vln & orch.
with K. Fürstner pf   2RA 3410[3]☐   HMV DB4619

PAGANINI – *Continued*

Sonata a preghièra "Moses Fantasia" (on the aria "Dal tuo stellato soglio" from Rossini's opera "Mosè in Egitto") Op. 24 (1818 or 1819) vln & orch.
with L. Persinger pf

	Decca LXT2808
	Eclipse ECS585
	London CM9099, LL1005

Sonata con Variazioni (on the theme "Prig ch'io l'impegno" from Weigl's opera "L'Amor marinaro") (1828) vln & orch.
with L. Pommers pf

| | Decca DL710172 |

(Le) Streghe (variations on a theme from Süssmeyer's opera "Il Noce di Benevento") Op. 8 (1813) vln & orch. – arr. vln & pf Kreisler
with L. Persinger pf

| | Vox 616, (in set 614), PL6490 |

(Le) Streghe (variations on a theme from Süssmeyer's opera "Il Noce di Benevento") Op. 8 (1813) vln & orch. – arr. vln & pf Kreisler
with L. Persinger pf

	Decca LXT2808
	Eclipse ECS585
	London CM9099, LL1005

(Le) Streghe (variations on a theme from Süssmeyer's opera "Il Noce di Benevento") Op. 8 (1813) vln & orch.
with Royal Philharmonic Orch. –
Bellugi

	CBS 72995
	Columbia M30574
	Unicorn RHS304

PARADIES

Sicilienne vln & pf – arr. Dushkin
with L. Pommers pf

	Decca DXE179, DXSE7179,
	SMU1104
	Deutsche Grammophon
	LPEM19464, SLPEM136464

PROKOFIEV

Concerto No. 1, in D, Op. 19 vln & orch.
with Suisse Romande Orch. –
Ansermet

| | Decca LXT5446 |
| | London CM9006, CS6059 |

Concerto No. 2, in g, Op. 63 vln & orch.
with Suisse Romande Orch. –
Ansermet

| | Decca LXT5446 |
| | London CM9006, CS6059 |

Sonata in d, Op. 115 solo vln
(unaccompanied)

	Decca LXT5595, SXL2240
	Eurodisc 70704KK, 70705KK
	London CM9261, CS6193,
	SLC1287

Sonata No. 2, in D, Op. 94bis vln & pf
with C. Bussotti pf

| | Decca LXT2818 |
| | London LL770 |

Sonata in C, Op. 56 2 vlns
with D. Nadien vln

| | Decca DL710177 |
| | MCA MACS3478 |

RACHMANINOV

(14) Songs, Op. 34 (1912) v & pf
No. 14. Vocalise arr. vln & pf Press
with L. Persinger pf   2RA 3329[1]☐   HMV DB4622

RAVEL

Tzigane (Rapsodie de concert) (1924) vln & pf or orch.
with Lamoureux Orch. –
Bigot

	0.048/9–2	Celson DC1005
		Polydor 566248
		Vox PL6240

RAVEL – *Continued*

Tzigane (Rapsodie de concert) (1924) vln & pf or orch.
with Suisse Romande Orch. –   Decca LXT5527, SXL2155
Ansermet   Eurodisc 70547KK
    London CM9016, CS6134

SAINT–SAËNS

Concerto No. 1, in A, Op. 20 "Konzertstück" vln & orch.
with Cincinnati Symphony Orch. –   Brunswick AXA4529, SXA4529
Rudolf   Decca 410004, DL10106,
    DL710106, SMU1103
    Deutsche Grammophon
    LPEM19478, SLPEM136478

Concerto No. 3, in b, Op. 61 vln & orch.
with Lamoureux Orch. – Bigot   Celson DC1002/4
    Polydor 566245/7
    Vox PL6240

Fantaisie in A, Op. 124 (1907) vln & hp
with G. Agostini hp   Decca DL710177
    MCA MACS3478

Havanaise, Op. 83 vln & orch.
with London Symphony Orch. –   Decca LXT5571, SXL2197
Gamba   London CM9245, CS6165

Introduction & Rondo Capriccioso, Op. 28 vln & orch.
with London Symphony Orch. –   Decca LXT5571, SXL2197
Gamba   London CM9245, CS6165

SARASATE

Caprice basque, Op. 24 vln & pf
with L. Persinger pf   Decca LXT2930
    London CM9090, LL962

Caprice basque, Op. 24 vln & pf
with B. Smith pf   Decca DL10044, DL710044
    MCA MUCS134

Carmen Fantasia (on themes from the opera by Bizet) Op. 25 vln & pf or orch.
with London Symphony Orch. –   Decca LXT5571, SXL2197
Gamba   London CM9245, CS6165

(8) Danzas españolas vln & pf
No. 1. Malagueña, Op. 21, No. 1
with L. Persinger pf   Decca LXT2930
    London CM9090, LL962

No. 1. Malagueña, Op. 21, No. 1
with B. Smith pf   Decca DL10044, DL710044
    MCA MUCS134

No. 2. Habañera, Op. 21, No. 2
with L. Persinger pf   2RA 3333[II]   HMV DB4598
No. 2. Habañera, Op. 21, No. 2
with L. Persinger pf   Decca LXT2930
    London CM9090, LL962

No. 2. Habañera, Op. 21, No. 2
with B. Smith pf   Decca DL10044, DL710044
    MCA MUCS134

No. 3. Romanza andaluza, Op. 22, No. 1
with L. Persinger pf   Decca LXT2930, VD526
    London CM9090, LL962

No. 3. Romanza andaluza, Op. 22, No. 1
with B. Smith pf   Decca DL10044, DL710044
    MCA MUCS134

SARASATE – *Continued*

No. 4. Jota navarra, Op. 22, No. 2
with L. Persinger pf   Decca LXT2930
    London CM9090, LL962

No. 4. Jota navarra, Op. 22, No. 2
with B. Smith pf   Decca DL10044, DL710044
    MCA MUCS134

No. 5. Playera, Op. 23, No. 1
with L. Persinger pf   Decca LXT2930
    London CM9090, LL962

No. 5. Playera, Op. 23, No. 1
with B. Smith pf   Decca DL10044, DL710044
    MCA MUCS134

No. 6. Zapateado, Op. 23, No. 2
with L. Persinger pf   Decca LXT2930, VD526
    London CM9090, LL962

No. 6. Zapateado, Op. 23, No. 2
with B. Smith pf   Decca DL10044, DL710044
    MCA MUCS134

No. 7. Danza española No. 7, in A, Op. 26, No. 1
with L. Persinger pf   Decca LXT2930
    London CM9090, LL962

No. 7. Danza española No. 7, in A, Op. 26, No. 1
with B. Smith pf   Decca DL10044, DL710044
    MCA MUCS134

No. 8. Danza española No. 8, in C, Op. 26, No. 2
with L. Persinger pf   Decca LXT2930
    London CM9090, LL962

No. 8. Danza española No. 8, in C, Op. 26, No. 2
with B. Smith pf   Decca DL10044, DL710044
    MCA MUCS134

Introduction & Tarantelle, Op. 43 vln & pf
with L. Persinger pf   2RA 3332[I]   HMV DB4598
Introduction & Tarantelle, Op. 43 vln & pf
with L. Persinger pf   Decca LXT2930
    London CM9090, LL962

Introduction & Tarantelle, Op. 43 vln & pf
with B. Smith pf   Decca DL10044, DL710044
    MCA MUCS134

Jota aragonesa, Op. 27 vln & pf
with E. Lush pf   Decca LXT5460
    Eclipse ECS595
    London CS6039, STS15049

Serenata andaluza, Op. 28 vln & pf
with B. Smith pf   Decca DL10044, DL710044
    MCA MUCS134

Zigeunerweisen, Op. 20 vln & pf or orch.
    2RA 3408[2] & 3409[3]   HMV DB4673
with K. Fürstner pf
Zigeunerweisen, Op. 20 vln & pf or orch.
with L. Persinger pf   Decca LXT2930, VD526
    London CM9090, LL962

Zigeunerweisen, Op. 20 vln & pf or orch.
with London Symphony Orch. –   Decca LXT5571, SXL2197
Gamba   London CM9245, CS6165

SCHUMANN

(3) Romances, Op. 94 ob or vlc or vln or cl & pf
Romance No. 2, in A arr. vln & pf Kreisler
with L. Pommers pf   Decca DXE179, DXSE7179,
SMU1104
Deutsche Grammophon
LPEM19464, SLPEM136464

SIBELIUS

Concerto in d, Op. 47 vln & orch.
with London Symphony Orch. –
Fjelstad   Ace of Diamonds SDD276
Decca SXL2077
London CS6067

SMETANA

From my Homeland (1878) vln & pf
No. 2. Andantino
with E. Lush pf   Decca LXT5460
Eclipse ECS595
London CS6039, STS15049

STRAUSS, R.

Sonata in E flat, Op. 18 vln & pf
with C. Bussotti pf   Decca LXT2818
London LL770

Sonata in E flat, Op. 18 vln & pf
with F. Rados pf   Qualiton LPX–S1165

STRAVINSKY

Élégie (1944) solo vla or vln
(unaccompanied)   Decca LXT5595, SXL2240
Eurodisc 70704KK, 70705KK
London CM9261, CS6193,
SLC1287

SUK

(4) Pieces, Op. 17 vln & pf
No. 4. Burleska
with K. Fürstner pf   DRA 3405[1]☐   HMV DA4467
No. 4. Burleska
with E. Lush pf   Decca LXT5460
Eclipse ECS595
London CS6039, STS15049

TCHAIKOVSKY

Concerto in D, Op. 35 vln & orch.
    AR 14550–2, 14551/3–1, 14554–
    2, 14555/6–1 & 14557–2
with New Symphony Orch. – Sargent   Decca AX336/9, BR3110,
LXT5373, X53035/8
London LL172
Richmond R19011

Concerto in D, Op. 35 vln & orch.
with London Symphony Orch. –
Sargent   Ace of Diamonds ADD126,
SDD126
Decca LXT5641, ND373,
SXL2279

Sérénade mélancolique in b flat, Op. 26 vln & orch.
with London Symphony Orch. –
Fjelstad   Ace of Diamonds SDD276
Decca SXL2077
London CS6067

TCHAIKOVSKY – *Continued*

Souvenir d'un lieu cher, Op. 42 vln & pf
No. 2. Scherzo
with London Symphony Orch. –
Fjelstad   Ace of Diamonds SDD276
Decca SXL2077
London CS6067

No. 3. Mélodie
with L. Pommers pf   Decca DXE179, DXSE7179,
SMU1104
Deutsche Grammophon
LPEM19464, SLPEM136464

Suite No. 3, in G, Op. 55 orch.
with L'Orchestre de la Suisse
Romande – Ansermet   Decca SXL6311
London CM9543, CS6543

Suite No. 4, in G, Op. 61 "Mozartiana" orch.
with L'Orchestre de la Suisse
Romande – Ansermet   Decca SXL6312
London CM9542, CS6542

VECSEY

Caprice No. 1 "Le Vent" vln & pf
with L. Persinger pf   Vox 16046, (in set 196),
VIP45420

Caprice No. 1 "Le Vent" vln & pf
with E. Lush pf   Decca CEP600, LXT5460,
SEC5022
Eclipse ECS595
London CS6039, STS15049

Caprice No. 1 "Le Vent" vln & pf
with L. Pommers pf   Decca DL710172

VERACINI

(12) Sonatas, Op. 2 (1744) "Sonate accademiche" vln & c
Sonata No. 6, in A: Largo (2nd mvt)
with L. Pommers pf   Decca DXE179, DXSE7179,
SMU1104
Deutsche Grammophon
LPEM19464, SLPEM136464

Sonata No. 11, in E: Minuet; Gavotte
with L. Persinger pf   Vox 16048, (in set 196),
VIP45420

VILLA–LOBOS

Suite (1923) v & vln
with L. Venora s   Decca DL710177
MCA MACS3478

VIVALDI

(12) Concerti, Op. 8 (1725) "Il Cimento dell' Armonia e dell' Invenzione"
(Nos. 1/4: Le quattro Stagioni) vln & strs
Concerto No. 1, in E, F.I, No. 22 "La Primavera"
with Stradivarius Chamber Orch. –   Decca DL9423, DL79423
Ricci   MCA MUC115, MUCS115
Concerto No. 2, in B flat, F.I, No. 23 "L'Estate"
with Stradivarius Chamber Orch. –   Decca DL9423, DL79423
Ricci   MCA MUC115, MUCS115
Concerto No. 3, in F, F.I, No. 24 "L'Autunno"
with Stradivarius Chamber Orch. –   Decca DL9423, DL79423
Ricci   MCA MUC115, MUCS115
Concerto No. 4, in f, F.I, No. 25 "L'Inverno"
with Stradivarius Chamber Orch. –   Decca DL9423, DL79423
Ricci   MCA MUC115, MUCS115

VIVALDI – *Continued*

(12) Sonatas, Op. 2 (1712) vln & c
  Sonata No. 2, in A, F.XIII, No. 30
    with K. Cooper hpsi   Decca DL710177
                               MCA MACS3478
  Sonata No. 7, in c: Preludio (1st mvt) F.XIII, No. 35
    with L. Pommers pf   Decca DXE179, DXSE7179,
                               SMU1104
                               Deutsche Grammophon
                               LPEM19464, SLPEM136464

WEBER

(6) Sonatas, Op. 10 (J99/104) (1810) vln & pf
  Sonata No. 1, in F, J99
    with C. Bussotti pf   Decca LXT2959
                               London LL1006
  Sonata No. 2, in G, J100
    with C. Bussotti pf   Decca LXT2959
                               London LL1006
  Sonata No. 3, in d, J101
    with C. Bussotti pf   Decca LXT2959
                               London LL1006
  Sonata No. 4, in E flat, J102
    with C. Bussotti pf   Decca LXT2959
                               London LL1006
  Sonata No. 5, in A, J103
    with C. Bussotti pf   Decca LXT2959
                               London LL1006
  Sonata No. 6, in C, J104
    with C. Bussotti pf   Decca LXT2959
                               London LL1006

WIENIAWSKI

(L')École moderne, Op. 10 (10 Études) solo vln
  No. 4. Étude No. 4, in A "Le Staccato" arr. vln & pf
    with L. Persinger pf   Vox 16047, (in set 196)
Scherzo–Tarantelle, Op. 16 vln & pf
  with E. Lush pf   Decca LXT5460
                               Eclipse ECS595
                               London CS6039, STS15049
Variations in G (on the Austrian National Anthem) (1853) solo vln
  (unaccompanied)   Decca DL710172

YSAŸE

Rêve d'enfant, Op. 14 vln & pf
  with K. Fürstner pf   2RA 3407[1]☐   HMV DB4622

Louis RICH

BARTLETT

(A) Dream (1895) v & pf –arr. vln & pf
  with piano   Pathé 70120

BEETHOVEN

(6) Minuets, G167 pf
  No. 2. Minuet No. 2, in G arr. vln & pf Burmester
    with piano   Pathé 70120

BOND

(A) Perfect day (1910) vln & pf –arr. vln & pf
  with F. Banta pf   Pathé 30274

RICH

Venetian love dance vln & pf
  with F. Banta pf   Pathé 30274

Thaddeus RICH (1884–1969)

FAURÉ

Berceuse, Op. 16 vln & pf
  with piano   Okey 4015

RAFF

(6) Pieces, Op. 85 vln & pf
  No. 3. Cavatina in D
    with piano   Okey 4015

Irene RICHARDS (1911–1964)

BOULANGER, L.

Cortège (1919) vln & pf
  with Y. Fisher pf   Croydon CX2

HANDEL

(16) Suites (1720/33) hpsi
  Suite No. 7, in G: Passacaglia (6th mvt) arr. vln & pf Harty
    with Y. Fisher pf   Croydon CX2

PARADIES

Sicilienne vln & pf – arr. Dushkin
  with Y. Fisher pf   Croydon CX2

Paul RICHARTZ

RESPIGHI

Concerto Gregoriano (1922) vln & orch.
  with Berlin Municipal   2110/6½GS   Polydor 15511/4S, 59000/3S, (in
  Orch. – Heger   set DGS19)

Karl Arthur RICHTER (1883–1957)

DVOŘÁK

(8) Humoresques, Op. 101 pf
  No. 7. Humoresque No. 7, in G flat arr. vln & pf "in G" Kreisler
    with piano   Decca F40318

Rolf RICHTER

ANONYMOUS

O du Fröhliche, o du Selige (1819) arr. vln & org
  with organ   Polydor 19124

GRUBER

Stille Nacht, heilige Nacht (1818) v & pf – arr. vln & org
  with organ   Polydor 19124

MASCAGNI

Cavalleria Rusticana (1890) – opera
  Intermezzo orch. – arr. vln & org
    with organ   Polydor 14706

SCHUMANN

(13) Kinderscenen, Op. 15 pf
  No. 7. **Träumerei** arr. vln & org
    with organ   Polydor 14706

Christa RICHTER–STEINER (1903–   )

MOZART

Cassation No. 1, in G, K63 orch.
  with Salzburg Mozarteum Orch. –   Columbia C91106
  Paumgartner

Sinfonia concertante in E flat, K364 vln, vla & orch.
  with P. Doktor vla & Salzburg   Club Français du Disque 16
  Mozarteum Orch. – Paumgartner

Paul RIEMANN

BACH, J.C.

Sinfonia concertante in E flat, T. P284 (1770) 2 vlns, 2 fls, 2 hrns & orch.
  with F. Hegedüs vln, K. Mayrhofer ob   Bach Guild BG504
  & Vienna Symphony Orch. – Günther   Nixa BLP304

O. RITHÈRE

MARTINŮ

Duo No. 1 (1927) vln & vlc
  with M. Huvelin vlc   Columbia DFX1/2

Melvin RITTER

BARTÓK

Contrasts (1938) cl, vln & pf
  with R. Kell cl & J. Rosen pf   Decca DL9740

MILHAUD

Suite (1936) vln, cl & pf
  with R. Kell cl & J. Rosen pf   Decca DL9740

Tessa ROBBINS (1930–   )

DINICU

Hora staccato vln & pf – arr. Heifetz
  with R. Wood pf   Embassy WLP6022

DRDLA

Souvenir vln & pf
  with R. Wood pf   Embassy WLP6022

DRIGO

(2) Airs de Ballet orch.
  No. 2. **Valse bluette** arr. vln & pf Auer
  with R. Wood pf   Embassy WLP6022

ELGAR

Salut d'amour, Op. 12 orch. – arr. vln & pf Elgar
  with R. Wood pf   Embassy WLP6022

GRANADOS

(12) Danzas españolas, Op. 37 (1893) pf
  No. 5. **Danza española No. 5, in e** "Andaluza" arr. vln & pf Kreisler
  with R. Wood pf   Embassy WLP6022

HUBAY

(14) Scènes de la Csárda vln & pf
  No. 4. **Hejre Kati,** Op. 32
  with R. Wood pf   Embassy WLP6022

IRELAND

Sonata No. 2, in a (1917) vln & pf
  with A. Rowlands pf   Saga XID5206

KREISLER

Caprice viennois, Op. 2 vln & pf
  with R. Wood pf   Embassy WLP6022

Schön Rosmarin vln & pf
  with R. Wood pf   Embassy WLP6022

MASSENET

Élégie v & pf – arr. vln & pf
  with R. Wood pf   Embassy WLP6022

MENDELSSOHN

(6) Gesänge, Op. 34 v & pf
  No. 2. **Auf Flügeln des Gesanges** arr. vln & pf Achron
  with R. Wood pf   Embassy WLP6022

MONTI

Csárdas (1904) vln & pf
  with R. Wood pf   Embassy WLP6022

PROVOST

Intermezzo (1940) vln & pf
  with R. Wood pf   Embassy WLP6022

RIMSKY–KORSAKOV

Scheherazade, Op. 35 (1888) orch.
  with Embassy Symphony Orch. –   Embassy WLP5001
  Freedman

Winifred ROBERTS

BACH

(6) Sonatas, BWV1014/9 vln & clav
Sonata No. 2, in A, BWV1015
  with G. Jones hpsi   Baroque BC2868

BIBER

(8) Sonatas (1681) vln & c
  Sonata No. 4, in D: Introduction & Presto (1st mvt); **Gigue** (2nd mvt)
  with G. Jones hpsi   2EA 15351–4A   HMV HLP15, HMS62
                                          Victor (in set LM6031)

CARISSIMI

Jonas – oratorio s, a, 2 t's, 2 b's & cho
  Justus es, Domine
    with W. Herbert t,   2EA 14424–1B   HMV HLP12, HMS50
    N. Marriner vln, A. Goldsbrough org   Victor (in set LM6030)
    & T. Weil vlc

CORELLI

(12) Sonatas, Op. 3 2 vlns & c
  Sonata No. 9, in f
    2EA 14422–2E & 14423–3C   HMV HLP15, HMS65
    with N. Marriner vln, A. Goldsbrough   Victor (in set LM6031)
    org & T. Weil vlc

MOZART

Sonata No. 17, in C, K296 vln & pf
  with G. Jones hpsi   Baroque BC2868

TARTINI

Sonata in a vln & c
  with G. Jones hpsi   Baroque BC2868

VIVALDI

Concerto in B flat, P.406 (F.XII, No. 16) vln, ob, strs & c
    2EA 14950–4A & 14951–3A   HMV HLP16, HMS68
    with L. Brain ob & Goldsbrough Orch.   Victor (in set LM6031)
    – Goldsbrough

José ROCABRUNA (1870–   )

JORDÁ

Romántica mazurca vln & pf
  with piano   Edison cylinder 22140

LUCANTONI

Tarantelle vln & pf
  with piano   Edison cylinder 1877

SCHUBERT

Romance unid – arr. vln & pf
  with piano   Edison cylinder 1877

Joseph ROCHE

DVOŘÁK

Sonatina in G, Op. 100 vln & pf
  with R. Zgodava pf   Ampria*

SCHUBERT

(3) Sonatinas, Op. 137 (D384, D385 & D408) vln & pf
  No. 1. Sonatina No. 1, in D, D384
    with R. Zgodava pf   Ampria*
  No. 2. Sonatina No. 2, in A, D385
    with R. Zgodava pf   Ampria*
  No. 3. Sonatina No. 3, in g, D408
    with R. Zgodava pf   Ampria*

* Private limited edition.

Alfredo RODE (1905–   )

BAZZINI

(La) Ronde des lutins, Op. 25 vln & pf
  with piano   Bb 9585^{II}△   HMV B2436

PAGANINI

Concerto No. 2, in b, Op. 7 vln & orch.
  Ronde à la clochette (3rd mvt) "La Campanella" arr. vln & pf Wilhelmj
    with piano   Bb 9584^{II}△   HMV B2436

RODE

(La) Carnevale di Venizia – variations vln & pf
  with piano   Cc 9586^{I}△   HMV AN101, C1380

SARASATE

Zigeunerweisen, Op. 20 vln & pf or orch.
  with piano   Cc 9583^{III}△   HMV AN101, C1380

Sofie ROEDER

d'AMBROSIO

Romance in D, Op. 9 vln & pf
  with piano   Zonophone X67903

GODARD

Concerto No. 1, Op. 35 "Concerto Romantique" vln & orch.
  Canzonetta (2nd mvt)
    with piano   Zonophone X67904

SCHUBERT

(7) Gesänge (set to Scott's "Lady of the Lake") Op. 52 v & pf
  No. 6. Ave Maria, D839 arr. vln & pf Wilhelmj
    with piano   2769-1   Zonophone X67906

THOMÉ

Simple aveu, Op. 25 pf – arr. vln & pf
  with piano   2768   Gramophone & Typewriter
    27938

WIENIAWSKI

Mazurka in a, Op. 3 "Kujawiak" vln & pf
  with piano   2766-1 Zonophone X67905

Andreas RÖHN (1945–   )

BRAHMS

Sonata No. 1, in G, Op. 78 vln & pf
  with K. Bergemann pf   Deutsche Grammophon 642103

DEBUSSY

Sonata No. 3, in g (1917) vln & pf
  with K. Bergemann pf   Deutsche Grammophon 642103

HANDEL

(15) Sonatas, Op. 1 (?1731) fl or vln & c
  Sonata No. 13, in D vln IV
    with K. Bergemann pf   Deutsche Grammophon 642103

Erich RÖHN (1910–)

BEETHOVEN

Romance No. 1, in G, Op. 40 vln & orch.
with Berlin State Philharmonic Orch. – Imperial 014080
Schüler

Romance No. 1, in G, Op. 40 vln & orch.
with Munich   01819 LKK   Deutsche Grammophon 5007,
Philharmonic Orch. – Leitner   72005

Romance No. 2, in F, Op. 50 vln & orch.
with Berlin State   K–C 0419/20   Imperial 014079
Philharmonic Orch. – Schüler

Romance No. 2, in F, Op. 50 vln & orch.
with Munich   01818 LKK   Deutsche Grammophon 5007,
Philharmonic Orch. – Leitner   72005

Serenade in D, Op. 8 vln, vla & vlc
with R. Wolf vla &   03104/7 LKK   Deutsche Grammophon 72006/7,
A. Tröster vlc   LP16087

BERKELEY

Trio (1944) vln, vla & vlc
with R. Wolf vla & A. Tröster vlc   Polydor 68333/4

DVOŘÁK

Trio No. 4, in e, Op. 90 "Dumky" pf, vln & vlc
with C. Hansen pf & A. Tröster vlc   Telefunken LB6122, LGM65034

RAVEL

Tzigane (Rapsodie de concert) (1924) vln & pf or orch.
with Hamburg State Philharmonic   Telefunken TM68052, TW30032
Orch. – Martin

SCHUBERT

Rondo in A, D438 vln & str orch.
with Hamburg State Philharmonic   Telefunken TM68052, TW30032
Orch. – Martin

Trio No. 2, in E flat, Op. 100 (D929) pf, vln & vlc
with C. Hansen pf & A. Tröster vlc   Telefunken LE6523, LGX66039

Hanns RÖHR

FLIES

Wiegenlied (Schlafe, mein Prinzchen) v & pf – arr. 2 vlns
with H. Fassbander vln   HMV EG1639

LEHÁR

(Die) Lustige Witwe (1905) – operetta
Ez waren zwei Königskinder
with H. Fassbander vln   HMV EG1639

Stephan ROMASCANO

MOZART

Sinfonia concertante in E flat, K364 vln, vla & orch.
with M–R. Guiet vla & Lausanne   Westminster WST17036,
Chamber Orch. – Desarzens   XWN19036

Josef ROMBERG

JÄRNEFELT

Berceuse in g orch. – arr. vln & pf
with piano   G 1425   Duophone B5043

MASSENET

Thaïs (1894) – opera
Méditation arr. vln & pf Marsick
with piano   G 1424   Duophone B5043

Ad ROMBOUTS

VIVALDI

(12) Concerti, Op. 3 "L'Estro armonico" var. cbns & strs
Concerto No. 8, in a, P.2 (F.I, No. 177) 2 vlns, strs & c
with H. Brouwer vln, A. Elkgiers vlc   Studio 33 20006
& Netherlands Cantory Instrumental
Ensemble – Kooy

Aaron ROSAND (1929–)

BACH

(4) Suites, BWV1066/9 strs & c
Suite No. 3, in D: Air (2nd mvt) BWV1068 2 obs, 3 tpts, drms, strs & c
– arr. vln & pf as "Air on the G–string" by Wilhelmj
with M. Walevski pf   Vox PL12850, STPL512850

BEETHOVEN

(6) Allemandes, G171 (WoO42) vln & pf
Allemande No. 1, in F
with E. Flissler pf   Vox (in sets SVBX518 & VBX18)

Allemande No. 2, in D
with E. Flissler pf   Vox (in sets SVBX518 & VBX18)

Allemande No. 3, in F
with E. Flissler pf   Vox (in sets SVBX518 & VBX18)

Allemande No. 4, in A
with E. Flissler pf   Vox (in sets SVBX518 & VBX18)

Allemande No. 5, in D
with E. Flissler pf   Vox (in sets SVBX518 & VBX18)

Allemande No. 6, in G
with E. Flissler pf   Vox (in sets SVBX518 & VBX18)

Rondo in G, G155 vln & pf
with E. Flissler pf   Vox (in sets SVBX518 & VBX18)

(3) Sonatas, Op. 12 vln & pf
No. 1. Sonata No. 1, in D
with E. Flissler pf   Vox (in sets SVBX517 & VBX17)

No. 2. Sonata No. 2, in A
with E. Flissler pf   Vox (in sets SVBX517 & VBX17)

BEETHOVEN – *Continued*

No. 3. Sonata No. 3, in E flat
with E. Flissler pf — Vox (in sets SVBX517 & VBX17)

Sonata No. 4, in a, Op. 23 vln & pf
with E. Flissler pf — Vox (in sets SVBX517 & VBX17)

Sonata No. 5, in F, Op. 24 "Spring" vln & pf
with E. Flissler pf — Vox (in sets SVBX517 & VBX17), GBL11340, GBY11340, STGBY511340

(3) Sonatas, Op. 30 vln & pf
No. 1. Sonata No. 6, in A
with E. Flissler pf — Vox (in sets SVBX517 & VBX17)

No. 2. Sonata No. 7, in c
with E. Flissler pf — Vox (in sets SVBX518 & VBX18)

No. 3. Sonata No. 8, in G
with E. Flissler pf — Vox (in sets SVBX518 & VBX18)

Sonata No. 9, in A, Op. 47 "Kreutzer" vln & pf
with E. Flissler pf — Vox (in sets SVBX518 & VBX18), GBL11340, GBY11340, STGBY511340

Sonata No. 10, in G, Op. 96 vln & pf
with E. Flissler pf — Vox (in sets SVBX518 & VBX18)

(12) Variations in F (on the aria "Se vuol ballare" from the opera "Le Nozze di Figaro" by Mozart) G156 vln & pf
with E. Flissler pf — Vox (in sets SVBX518 & VBX18)

BERLIOZ

Rêverie & Caprice, Op. 8 vln & orch.
with Sudwestdeutsche Radio Orch. – Reinhardt — The Great Musicians TGM024, Turnabout TV34466, Vox PL10470

BRAHMS

Sonata No. 1, in G, Op. 78 vln & pf
with E. Flissler pf — Vox PL10090

Sonata No. 2, in A, Op. 100 vln & pf
with E. Flissler pf — Vox PL10090

CHAUSSON

Poème, Op. 25 vln & orch.
with Sudwestdeutsche Radio Orch. – Reinhardt — Turnabout TV34466, Vox PL10470, STPL510470

DRDLA

Souvenir vln & pf
with M. Walevski pf — Vox PL12850, STPL512850

ERNST

Concerto in f sharp, Op. 23 vln & orch.
with Radio Luxembourg Symphony Orch. – Froment — Candide CE31054

GODARD

Concerto No. 1, Op. 35 "Concerto romantique" vln & orch.
with Radio Luxembourg Symphony Orch. – Froment — Turnabout TV34466

HUBAY

Concerto No. 3, in g, Op. 99 vln & orch.
with Radio Luxembourg Symphony Orch. – Froment — Candide CE31054

KREISLER

Caprice viennois, Op. 2 vln & pf
with M. Walevski pf — Vox PL12850, STPL512850

Liebesfreud vln & pf
with M. Walevski pf — Vox PL12850, STPL512850

Liebesleid vln & pf
with M. Walevski pf — Vox PL12850, STPL512850

Schön Rosmarin vln & pf
with M. Walevski pf — Vox PL12850, STPL512850

Tambourin chinois, Op. 3 vln & pf
with M. Walevski pf — Vox PL12850, STPL512850

LALO

Symphonie espagnole, Op. 21 vln & orch.*
with Sudwestdeutsche Radio Orch. – Szöke — Vox PL11590, STPL511590

NOVAČEK

(8) Concert Caprices, Op. 5 vln & pf
No. 4 Perpetuum mobile
with M. Walevski pf — Vox PL12850, STPL512850

RAVEL

Tzigane (Rapsodie de concert) (1924) vln & pf or orch.
with Sudwestdeutsche Radio Orch. – Reinhardt — Turnabout TV34462, Vox PL10470

SAINT-SAËNS

Concerto No. 3, in b, Op. 61 vln & orch.
with Sudwestdeutsche Radio Orch. – Szöke — Vox PL11590, STPL511590

Havanaise, Op. 83 vln & orch.
with Sudwestdeutsche Radio Orch. – Reinhardt — Turnabout TV34462, Vox PL10470, STPL510470

Introduction & Rondo Capriccioso, Op. 28 vln & orch.
with Sudwestdeutsche Radio Orch. – Reinhardt — Turnabout TV34462, Vox PL10470, STPL510470

SARASATE

Caprice basque, Op. 24 vln & pf
with M. Walevski pf — Vox PL12760, STPL512760

Carmen Fantasia (on themes from the opera by Bizet) Op. 25 vln & pf or orch.
with Sudwestdeutsche Radio Orch. – Szöke — Super Majestic BBH1880, Turnabout TV34462, Vox GBY11600, PL11600, STPL511600

* Omitting Intermezzo

SARASATE – *Continued*

(8) Danzas españolas vln & pf
  No. 1. Malagueña, Op. 21, No. 1
  with M. Walevski pf

Super Majestic BBH1880
Turnabout TV34462
Vox PL12760, STPL512760

  No. 2. Habañera, Op. 21, No. 2
  with M. Walevski pf

Super Majestic BBH1880
Vox PL12760, STPL512760

  No. 3. Romanza andaluza, Op. 22, No. 1
  with M. Walevski pf

Vox PL12760, STPL512760

  No. 4. Jota navarra, Op. 22, No. 2
  with M. Walevski pf

Vox PL12760, STPL512760

  No. 5. Playera, Op. 23, No. 1
  with M. Walevski pf

Vox PL12760, STPL512760

  No. 6. Zapateado, Op. 23, No. 2
  with M. Walevski pf

Vox PL12760, STPL512760

  No. 7. Danza española No. 7, in a, Op. 26, No. 1
  with M. Walevski pf

Super Majestic BBH1880
Vox PL12760

  No. 8. Danza española No. 8, in C, Op. 26, No. 2
  with M. Walevski pf

Super Majestic BBH1880
Turnabout TV34462
Vox PL12760

Introduction & Tarantelle, Op. 43 vln & pf
  with M. Walevski pf

Vox PL12760, STPL512760

Navarra, Op. 33 2 vlns & pf or orch.
  (playing both parts) with M. Walevski
  pf

Super Majestic BBH1880
Turnabout TV34462
Vox PL12760, STPL512760

Zigeunerweisen, Op. 20 vln & pf or orch.
  with Sudwestdeutsche Radio Orch. –
  Szöke

Super Majestic BBH1880
Turnabout TV34462
Vox GBY11600, PL11600,
STPL511600

SCHUBERT

(7) Gesänge (set to Scott's "Lady of the Lake") Op. 52 v & pf
  No. 6. Ave Maria, D839 arr. vln & pf Wilhelmj
  with M. Walevski pf

Vox PL12850, STPL512850

SCHUMANN

(13) Kinderscenen, Op. 15 pf
  No. 7. Träumerei arr. vln & pf
  with M. Walevski pf

Vox PL12850, STPL512850

SIBELIUS

(2) Humoresques, Op. 87b vln & orch.
  No. 1. Humoresque No. 1, in d
  with Sudwestdeutsche Radio Orch. –
  Szöke

Turnabout TV34182
Vox GBY11600, PL11600,
STPL511600

  No. 2. Humoresque No. 2, in D
  with Sudwestdeutsche Radio Orch. –
  Szöke

Turnabout TV34182
Vox GBY11600, PL11600,
STPL511600

SIBELIUS – *Continued*

(4) Humoresques, Op. 89 vln & orch.
  No. 1. Humoresque No. 3, in g
  with Sudwestdeutsche Radio Orch. –
  Szöke

Turnabout TV34182
Vox GBY11600, PL11600,
STPL511600

  No. 2. Humoresque No. 4, in g
  with Sudwestdeutsche Radio Orch. –
  Szöke

Turnabout TV34182
Vox GBY11600, PL11600,
STPL511600

  No. 3. Humoresque No. 5, in E flat
  with Sudwestdeutsche Radio Orch. –
  Szöke

Turnabout TV34182
Vox GBY11600, PL11600,
STPL511600

  No. 4. Humoresque No. 6, in g
  with Sudwestdeutsche Radio Orch. –
  Szöke

Turnabout TV34182
Vox GBY11600, PL11600,
STPL511600

TCHAIKOVSKY

Sérénade mélancolique in b flat, Op. 26 vln & orch.
  with Sudwestdeutsche Radio Orch. –
  Szöke

Vox GBY11600, PL11600,
STPL511600

YSAYE

Chant d'Hiver, Op. 15 vln & cha orch.
  with Radio Luxembourg Symphony
  Orch. – Froment

Candide CE31054

Wolfgang RÖSCH

BACH

Concerto in d, BWV1043 2 vlns, strs & c
  with H. Kalafusz vln & Süddeutsche
  Chamber Philharmonic, Stuttgart

Intercord 939–09Z

Alma Maria ROSE (1905–)

BACH

Concerto in d, BWV1043 2 vlns, strs & c
          CA 43/4^{II}△, 45/6^{I}△ & 47△
  with A. Rose vln & chamber orch.

HMV D2014/6, ES663/5
Victor 7502/4, (set M123)

Arnold Josef ROSE (1863–1946)

BACH

Concerto in d, BWV1043 2 vlns, strs & c
          CA 43/4^{II}△, 45/6^{I}△ & 47△
  with A.M. Rose vln & chamber orch.

HMV D2014/6, ES663/5
Victor 7502/4, (set M123)

(3) Sonatas & 3 Partitas, BWV1001/6 solo vln
  Sonata No. 1, in g: Adagio (1st mvt) BWV1001
  (unaccompanied)   CA 48^{II}△

HMV D2016, ES665
Victor 7504, (in set M123)

(4) Suites, BWV1066/9 strs & c
  Suite No. 3, in D: Air (2nd mvt) BWV1068 2 obs, 3 tpts, drms, strs & c
  – arr. vln & pf as "Air on the G–string" by Wilhemj
  with piano   14680 u

Gramophone & Typewriter
47972
HMV 61889

BEETHOVEN

Romance No. 2, in F, Op. 50 vln & orch.

with piano   14682 u   Gramophone & Typewriter 37930, 47975
HMV 61871

BRAHMS

(21) Hungarian Dances pf duet
Hungarian dance No. 5, in f sharp arr. vln & pf "in g" Joachim
with piano   Gramophone & Typewriter 47915

Hungarian dance No. 5, in f sharp arr. vln & pf "in g" Joachim
with piano   14681 u^{II} Gramophone & Typewriter 47973
HMV 61890

CHOPIN

(3) Nocturnes, Op. 9 pf
No. 2. Nocturne No. 2, in E flat arr. vln & pf Wilhelmj
with piano   15098 b   Gramophone & Typewriter 47987

DVOŘÁK

Romance in f, Op. 11 vln & orch.
with piano   15099 b   Gramophone & Typewriter 47988

ERNST

Fantasia brillante (on themes from the opera "Otello" by Rossini) Op. 11 vln & pf
with piano   Gramophone & Typewriter 47926

Fantasia brillante (on themes from the opera "Otello" by Rossini) Op. 11 vln & pf
with piano   01213 v   Gramophone & Typewriter 047923

GOLDMARK

Concerto in a, Op. 28 vln & orch.
Allegro moderato (1st mvt)
with piano   2095 c   Gramophone & Typewriter 047928

Andante (2nd mvt) "Air"
with piano   Gramophone & Typewriter 47980

MENDELSSOHN

Concerto in e, Op. 64 vln & orch.
Andante (2nd mvt)
with piano   2096 c   Gramophone & Typewriter 047929

NARDINI

(7) Sonatas vln & pf
Sonata No. 7, in B flat: Larghetto (2nd mvt)
with piano   15096 b   Gramophone & Typewriter 47989

Sonata No. 7, in B flat: Rondo allegro (3rd mvt)
with piano   15097 b   Gramophone & Typewriter 47990

POPPER

Nocturne, Op. 22 vlc & pf – arr. vln & pf Rose
with piano   01214 v   Gramophone & Typewriter 047924

Nocturne, Op. 22 vlc & pf – arr. vln & pf Rose
with piano   Gramophone & Typewriter 47931

RUBINSTEIN

(6) Soirées de Saint–Pétersbourg, Op. 44 pf
No. 1. Romance in E flat arr. vln & pf Wieniawski
with piano   Gramophone & Typewriter 47974

SARASATE

(8) Danzas españolas vln & pf
No. 8. Danza española No. 8, in C, Op. 26, No. 2
with piano   910 x   Gramophone & Typewriter 47925

Faust Fantasia (on themes from the opera by Gounod) vln & pf or orch.
Waltz
with piano   Gramophone & Typewriter 47981

Zigeunerweisen, Op. 20 vln & pf or orch.*
with piano   2406 b   Gramophone & Typewriter 47917

Zigeunerweisen, Op. 20 vln & pf or orch.
with piano   Gramophone & Typewriter 047921

SCHUMANN

(13) Kinderscenen, Op. 15 pf
No. 7. Träumerei arr. vln & pf
with piano   15412 L   Gramophone & Typewriter 047922

SIMONETTI

Madrigale pf – arr. vln & pf
with piano   2403 b   Gramophone & Typewriter 47924
Rococo 2001

Madrigale pf – arr. vln & pf
with piano   15232 u   Gramophone & Typewriter 47982

STRAUSS, R.

(Der) Rosenkavalier: Suite (Überreichung der Silber–Rose) orch. – arr. Nambuat
with Vienna Philharmonic Orch. –   HMV AN722/3, C2294/5
Alwin   Victor 11217/8

WIENIAWSKI

Polonaise brillante No. 1, in D, Op. 4 vln & pf
with piano   15233 u   Gramophone & Typewriter 47983

* Abridged.

Max ROSEN (1900–1956)

ANONYMOUS

Eili, Eili (Zionist hymn) arr. vln & pf Shalitt
with R. Wilens pf   Brunswick 15206

BRAGA

(7) Melodies (1867) v & pf
No. 5. La serenata "Angel's serenade"
with E. Rethberg s & F. Persson pf   Brunswick 10253, A62600

BRUCH

Kol Nidrei, Op. 47 vlc or vln & orch.
with R. Wilens pf   Brunswick 15206

CHOPIN

(4) Mazurkas, Op. 67 pf
No. 4. Mazurka No. 45, in a arr. vln & pf Kreisler
with piano   Brunswick 10032, 15006

(3) Waltzes, Op. 64 pf
No. 2. Waltz No. 7, in c sharp arr. vln & pf Huberman
with R. Wilens pf   Brunswick 15187

CUI

Kaleidoscope, Op. 50 vln & pf
No. 9. Orientale
with piano   Brunswick 10029

DOBROVEN

Fairytale vln & pf
with piano   Brunswick 50164

DRDLA

Souvenir vln & pf
with F. Persson pf   3443   Brunswick 01841, 10012, 15003,
                                    A8712
                                    Decca 152

DRIGO

(Les) Millions d'Arlequin (1900) – ballet orch.
Sérénade arr. vln & pf Auer
with G. Hampson pf   3446   Brunswick 01841, 10011, 15005
                                    Decca 152

DVOŘÁK

(8) Humoresques, Op. 101 pf
No. 7. Humoresque No. 7, in G flat arr. vln & pf "in G" Wilhelmj
with piano   Brunswick 30002, 50005, 50108,
                                    50110
                                    Decca 15005

ELGAR

Salut d'amour, Op. 12 orch. – arr. vln & pf Elgar
with piano   Brunswick 15212

ERWIN

I kiss your hand, madam (1929) v & pf – arr. vln & pf
with piano   Brunswick 15203

FALLA

(La) Vida Breve (1913) – opera
Danza española orch. – arr. vln & pf Kreisler
with piano   Brunswick 50164

GOUNOD

Ave Maria (Méditation on Bach's "Prelude No. 1, in C" from Book I of
"Das Wohltemperirte Clavier") v & pf – arr. v, vln & orch.
with F. Easton s & orch.   X 5545[5] Brunswick 30011

GRANADOS

(12) Danzas españolas, Op. 37 (1893) pf
No. 5. Danza española No. 5, in e "Andaluza" arr. vln & pf Kreisler
with F. Persson pf   5604   Brunswick 10041, 15005

JOSEPH

Hebrew legend vln & pf
with piano   2734   Brunswick 10010

KREISLER

(La) Gitana vln & pf
with F. Persson pf   3881   Brunswick 10015, 15003,* 15217,
                                    A8712

MASSENET

Élégie v & pf
with E. Rethberg s & F. Persson pf   Brunswick 10253, A62600
Thaïs (1894) – opera
Méditation
with orch.   X 5512[2] Brunswick 30021, 50005, 50108,
                                    50110
                                    Decca 15005

ROMBERG

Blossom Time (1921) – operetta
Song of love arr. vln & pf Rosen
with R. Wilens pf   Brunswick 15203

SCHUBERT

(7) Gesänge (set to Scott's "Lady of the Lake") Op. 52 v & pf
No. 6. Ave Maria, D839 arr. vln & pf Wilhelmj
with piano   Brunswick 30003
No. 6. Ave Maria, D839 arr. v, vln & pf
with C. Dux s & F. Persson pf   Brunswick 10249

SCHUMANN

(13) Kinderscenen, Op. 15 pf
No. 7. Träumerei arr. vln & pf
with F. Persson pf   5455   Brunswick 10039, 15006

TCHAIKOVSKY

Souvenir d'un lieu cher, Op. 42 vln & pf
No. 3. Mélodie
with piano   Brunswick 15212

VALDEZ

Sérénade du Tzigane vln & pf
with F. Persson pf   Brunswick 10043

WAYNE

Chiquita (1928) v & pf – arr. vln & pf Rosen
with R. Wilens pf   Brunswick 15187

* The matrix number for Brunswick 15003 is 4513.

Paul ROSENTHAL (1942–)

DELLO–JOIO

Variations & Capriccio (1948) vln & pf
  with piano   Mezhdunarodnaya Kniga
                               D028103/4

Elliott ROSOFF

BARTÓK

Contrasts (1938) cl, vln & pf
  with G. Silfies cl & S. Thomas pf   CBS S51157
                                Mace M9055, MCS9055

(6) Rumanian folk dances (1915) pf – arr. vln & pf Székely
  with R. Eaton pf   CBS S51157
                                Mace M9055, MCS9055

BEETHOVEN

Duet in E flat, WoO32 (1796) "2 obbligato eyeglasses" vla – arr. vln & vlc
  with S. Rosoff vlc   Mace M9041, MCS9041

GLIÈRE

(8) Pieces, Op. 39 (1909) vln & vlc
  No. 1. Prelude
  with S. Rosoff vlc   Mace M9041, MCS9041
  No. 3. Lullaby
  with S. Rosoff vlc   Mace M9041, MCS9041
  No. 5. Intermezzo
  with S. Rosoff vlc   Mace M9041, MCS9041
  No. 7. Scherzo
  with S. Rosoff vlc   Mace M9041, MCS9041

HINDEMITH

Sonata No. 3, in E (1935) vln & pf
  with R. Eaton pf   CBS S51157
                                Mace M9055, MCS9055

PLEYEL

(6) Duets, Op. 24 vln & vla
  Duet No. 1, in C
  with H. Coletta vla   Mace M9041, MCS9041
  Duet No. 2, in g
  with H. Coletta vlc   Mace M9041, MCS9041

Christiano ROSSI

TORELLI

(12) Concerti, Op. 8 (1709) 1/6: 2 vlns, strs & c – 7/12: vln, strs & c
  Concerto No. 2, in a
  with G. Armuzzi–Romei vln, M.   Musical Heritage Society
  Mauriello hpsi & Teatro Comunale   MHS893
  Orch., Bologna – Gotti

Max ROSTAL (1905–)

AMANI

(4) Pièces caractéristiques, Op. 7 pf
  No. 2. Orientale
  with piano   Vox 06291

BACH

Sonata in e, BWV1023 vln & c
  with F. Pelleg hpsi & A. Tusa vlc   Classic CL6187
                               Concert Hall CHS1174

BARTÓK

Concerto No. 2 (1938) vln & orch.
  with London Symphony Orch. –   Decca K23104/8, LXT2574
  Sargent   London LL362

BAZZINI

(La) Ronde des lutins, Op. 25 vln & pf
  with piano   Vox 06281

BEETHOVEN

Romance No. 1, in G, Op. 40 vln & orch.
  with Winterthur Symphony Orch. –   Concert Hall G1
  Goehr   Musical Masterpiece Society
                                MMS917

Romance No. 2, in F, Op. 50 vln & orch.
  with Winterthur Symphony Orch. –   Concert Hall G1
  Goehr   Musical Masterpiece Society
                                MMS917

Rondo in G, G155 vln & pf
  with F. Osborn pf   AR 12006–1   Decca AK1950, LK4034
                                London (in set LA170), LL162

(3) Sonatas, Op. 12 vln & pf
  No. 2. Sonata No. 2, in A
      AR 12434–1, 12435–2 & 12436/7   Decca AK1958/9
  with F. Osborn pf   –1   London (set LA137)

Sonata No. 4, in a, Op. 23 vln & pf
  with F. Osborn pf   Decca LXT2752
                                London LL471

Sonata No. 5, in F, Op. 24 "Spring" vln & pf
      AR 10484–3 10485/8–2 & 10489–3   Decca K1817/9
  with F. Osborn pf

(3) Sonatas, Op. 30 vln & pf
  No. 1. Sonata No. 6, in A
      AR 12306/7–1, 12308–4, 12309–   Decca AK2220/2
  with F. Osborn pf   3 & 12310/1–1   London (set LA154)
  No. 2. Sonata No. 7, in c
      AR 14410/4–1A & 14415/7–1   Decca AK2356/9, LK4034
  with F. Osborn pf   London LL162
  No. 3. Sonata No. 8, in G
  with F. Osborn pf   Decca LXT2752
                                  London LL471

Sonata No. 9, in A, Op. 47 "Kreutzer" vln & pf
  with F. Osborn pf   Decca LXT2732
                                London LL575

Sonata No. 10, in G, Op. 96 vln & pf
             AR 11999/12005–1   Decca AK1950/3
  with F. Osborn pf   London (set LA170)

BIBER

(16) Biblical Sonatas "Mysterien" vln & c
  Sonata No. 16, in g "The Guardian Angel" solo vln
  (unaccompanied)   Classic CL6187
                                Concert Hall CHS1174

BRAHMS

Sonata (1853) "Frei aber Einsam" vln & pf
 Allegro (Scherzo) in c (3rd mvt) "Sonatensatz"
 with F. Osborn pf   Decca LK4034
                                        London LL162

BUSONI

Sonata No. 2, in e, Op. 36a (1898) vln & pf
 with N. Mewton–Wood pf   Argo ARS1014, RG14

CUI

Kaleidoscope, Op. 50 vln & pf
 No. 9. Orientale
 with piano   Vox 06219

DANKS

Silver threads among the gold (1873) v & pf – arr. vln & pf
 with piano   Vox 6296

DEBUSSY

Sonata No. 3, in g (1917) vln & pf
 with C. Horsley pf   HMV CLP1124

DELIUS

Sonata No. 2 (1924) vln & pf
 with C. Horsley pf   Argo RG47
                                 Westminster XWN18133

DVOŘÁK

(8) Slavonic Dances, Op. 46 pf duet; orch.
 No. 2. Slavonic dance No. 2, in e arr. vln & pf "in g" Kreisler
 with piano   Vox 06219
(8) Slavonic dances, Op. 72 pf duet; orch.
 No. 8. Slavonic dance No. 16, in A flat arr. vln & pf "in G" Kreisler
 with piano   Vox 06291

ELGAR

Sonata in e, Op. 82 vln & pf
 with C. Horsley pf   Argo TM49

FRANKEL

Sonata, Op. 13 solo vln
             AR 8581/2–2, 8583–1 & 8584–2 Decca K1178/9
 (unaccompanied)

KORNGOLD

Viel Lärmen um Nichts (Much ado about nothing) Op. 11 (1919) –
 Incidental music orch.
 No. 1. Mädchen im Brautgemach arr. vln & pf Korngold
 with piano   Vox 06172
 No. 2. Holzapfel und Schlehwein arr. vln & pf Korngold
 with piano   Vox 06172
 No. 3. Gartenszene arr. vln & pf Korngold
 with piano   Vox 06173
 No. 4. Mummenschanz arr. vln & pf Korngold
 with piano   Vox 06173

KREISLER

Caprice viennois, Op. 2 vln & pf
 with piano   Vox 06315
Recitative & Scherzo–caprice, Op. 6 solo vln
 (unaccompanied)   Vox 06309

KREISLER – *Continued*

Schön Rosmarin vln & pf
 with piano   Vox 06281
Chanson Louis XIII & Pavane (L. Couperin) vln & pf
 with piano   Vox 06218

MIHALOVICI

Sonata No. 2, Op. 45 vln & pf
 with M. Haas pf   Deutsche Grammophon
                                 LPM18520, SLPM138016

MOZART

Serenade No. 7, in D, K.250 "Haffner" orch
 Rondo (4th mvt) arr. vln & pf Kreisler
 with piano   Vox 06308

MUSSORGSKY

(Das) Alte Schloss v & pf – arr. vln & pf Rostal
 with piano   Vox 06308

ORR

Sonatine (1948) vln & pf
 with F. Osborn pf   AR 8579/80–2   Decca K1112

PADEREWSKI

(6) Humoresques de concert, Op. 14 pf
 No. 1. Minuet in G arr. vln & pf Kreisler
 with piano   Vox 6296
 No. 1. Minuet in G arr. vln & pf Kreisler
 with piano   Vox 06315

PAGANINI

Moto perpetuo (Allegro di concert) Op. 11 (1830) vln & orch
 with K. Szreter pf   Vox 06247

RAVEL

Sonata (1927) vln & pf
 with M. Haas pf   Deutsche Grammophon
                                 LPM18520, SLPM138016

REGER

Suite in a, Op. 103a vln & pf
 No. 3. Aria
 with K. Szreter pf   Vox 06247

REIZENSTEIN

Prologue, Variations & Finale (1939) vln & pf
 with F. Reizenstein   AR 9187/93–2   Decca AK1187/90
 pf   London T5415/8, (set LA155)
Suite (1936) pf
 No. 5. Marcia barbara arr. vln & pf Reizenstein
 with F. Reizenstein pf   AR 9600–2   Decca AK1187
                                 London T5415, (in set LA155)

 No. 6. Lullaby arr. vln & pf Reizenstein
 with F. Reizenstein pf   AR 9600–2   Decca AK1187
                                 London T5415, (in set LA155)

SARASATE

(8) Danzas españolas vln & pf
 No. 1. Malagueña, Op. 21, No. 1
 with piano   Vox 06286

SARASATE – *Continued*

No. 2. Habañera, Op. 21, No. 2
with piano   Vox 06286

SCHUBERT

Fantasia in C, Op. 159 (D984) vln & pf
with C. Horsley pf   HMV CLP1112, OCLP7501

Rondo brillante in b, Op. 70 (D895) vln & pf
with C. Horsley pf   HMV CLP1112

Rosamunde von Cypern, Op. 26 (D797) (1823) – Incidental music orch
No. 9. Ballet music II, in G arr. vln & pf Kreisler
with piano   Vox 06309

Sonata in A, Op. 162 (D574) "Duo" vln & pf
with C. Horsley pf   HMV CLP1113

(3) Sonatinas, Op. 137 (D384, D385 & D408) vln & pf
No. 1. Sonatina No. 1, in D, D384
with C. Horsley pf   HMV CLP1112

No. 2. Sonatina No. 2, in a, D385
with C. Horsley pf   HMV CLP1112

No. 3. Sonatina No. 3, in g, D408
with C. Horsley pf   HMV CLP1112

SCHUMANN

Sonata No. 1, in d, Op. 105 vln & pf
with C. Horsley pf   HMV CLP1124

STRAVINSKY

Duo concertante (1932) vln & pf
with C. Horsley pf   HMV CLP1124

TARTINI

Concerto in g, D86 (C6) vln & orch.
with Winterthur Symphony Orch. –   Classic CL6187
Goehr   Concert Hall CHS1174

Sonata in g "Il Trillo del Diavolo" vln & c
with piano   Vox 06284/5

WALTON

Sonata (1939) vln & pf
with C. Horsley pf   Argo RG48
                                             Westminster XWN18024

WIENIAWSKI

Scherzo–Tarantelle, Op. 16 vln & pf
with piano   Vox 06218

Feri ROTH (1899–1969)

MOZART

Divertimento No. 17, in D, K334 2 hrns & strs
Minuet (3rd mvt) arr. vln & pf Burmester
with piano   Odeon 5682A

Sonata No. 21, in e, K304 vln & pf
with H. Cumpson pf   Columbia

Sonata No. 22, in A, K305 vln & pf
with H. Cumpson pf   Columbia

VECSEY

Valse triste vln & pf
with piano   Odeon 5682A

Nicholas ROTH (1910–   )

BOYCE

Concerto "Double" 2 vlns & orch.
with S. Mann vln & London Soloists'   CBS BRG72541, SBRG72541
Ensemble – Roth

MARCELLO, B.

Concerto in D vln & orch.
with London Soloists Ensemble   Morgan M100 IL

TELEMANN

Concerto in a vln, strs & c
with London Soloists' Ensemble –   Nonesuch H1052, H71052
Roth

Concerto in B flat "Pisendel" vln, strs & c
with London Soloists' Ensemble –   CBS BRG72541, SBRG72541
Roth

VIVALDI

Concerto in F, P.278 (F.I, No. 34) 3 vlns, strs & c
with R. Larner vln, S. Rozsa vln &   Morgan M100 IL
London Soloists Ensemble

Suzanne ROZSA

VIVALDI

Concerto in F, P.278 (F.I, No. 34) 3 vlns, strs & c
with R. Larner vln, N. Roth vln &   Morgan M100 1L
London Soloists Ensemble

Roman RUBATO*

BRANDL

(Der) Liebe Augustin – operetta
Du alter Stefansturm arr. vln & pf as "The old refrain" by Kreisler
with B. Ritorno pf   Philips S06024R

DRDLA

Serenade No. 1, in A vln & pf
with B. Ritorno pf   Philips S06072R

DVOŘÁK

(7) Gypsy songs, Op. 55 v & pf
No. 4. Songs my mother taught me arr. vln & pf Kreisler
with B. Ritorno pf   Philips S06072R

ELGAR

Salut d'amour, Op. 12 orch. – arr. vln & pf Elgar
with B. Ritorno pf   Philips S06072R

ESPÉJO

Airs tziganes, Op. 11 (1926) vln & pf
with B. Ritorno pf   Philips S06024R

FIBICH

Images, Impressions & Souvenirs, Op. 41 pf
No. 14 Poem (from "Souvenirs", Part IV) arr. vln & pf Kubelík
with B. Ritorno pf   Philips S06072R

* Pseudonym for Herman Krebbers.

GOENS

Scherzo, Op. 12, No. 2 vln & pf
   with B. Ritorno pf   Philips S06072R

HEUBERGER

(Der) Opernball, Op. 40 (1898) – operetta
  Im chambre séparée arr. vln & pf as "Midnight bells" by Kreisler
   with B. Ritorno pf   Philips S06024R

PONCE

Estrellita (1913) v & pf – arr. vln & pf Heifetz
   with B. Ritorno pf   Philips S06024R

PROVOST

Intermezzo (1940) vln & pf
   with B. Ritorno pf   Philips S06024R

TOSELLI

Serenade, Op. 6 vln & pf
   with B. Ritorno pf   Philips S06072R

VECSEY

Valse triste vln & pf
   with B. Ritorno pf   Philips S06024R

WIENIAWSKI

Capriccio–valse, Op. 7 vln & pf
   with B. Ritorno pf   Philips S06072R

WINTERNITZ

Dance of the marionettes vln & pf
   with B. Ritorno pf   Philips S06024R

Karl RUBENS

DVOŘÁK

(8) Humoresques, Op. 101 pf
  No. 7 Humoresque No. 7, in G flat arr. vln & pf "in G" Kreisler
  with piano   Oriole 403

MENDELSSOHN

(6) Songs without words, Op. 62 pf
  No. 6. Song without words No. 30, in A "Spring song" arr. vln & pf
  with piano   Oriole 403

RUBINSTEIN

(2) Melodies, Op. 3 pf
  No. 1. Melody in F arr. vln & pf Wilhelmj
  with piano   Oriole 405

SCHUBERT

(7) Gesänge (set to Scott's "Lady of the Lake") Op. 52 v & pf
  No. 6. Ave Maria, D839 arr. vln & pf Wilhelmj
  with piano   Oriole 404
(14) Schwanengesang, D957 (1828) v & pf
  No. 4. Ständchen "Serenade" arr. vln & pf
  with piano   Oriole 404

SCHUMANN

(13) Kinderscenen, Op. 15 pf
  No. 7. Träumerei arr. vln & pf
  with piano   Oriole 405

Lida RUBENS

MEDYNS, Jekabs

Concert polka vln & pf – arr. Sturstep
  with piano   Mezhdunarodnaya Kniga D5422
Lettish caprice vln & pf
  with piano   Mezhdunarodnaya Kniga D5284
Romance vln & pf
  with piano   Mezhdunarodnaya Kniga D5423
Rondino vln & pf
  with piano   Mezhdunarodnaya Kniga D5283

Jerrold RUBENSTEIN

BACH

Concerto No. 2, in E, BWV1042 vln, strs & c
  with Brussels Chamber Orch. –   Alpha CM9
  Bonnaerens

Nathan RUBIN

BARTÓK

Rhapsody No. 1, in G (1928) vln & orch.
  with San Francisco Little Symphony – Fantasy 5003, 8009
  Miller
Rhapsody No. 2, in d (1928) vln & orch.
  with San Francisco Little Symphony – Fantasy 5003, 8009
  Miller

KIRCHNER

Trio (1954) pf, vln & vlc
  with L. Kirchner pf & G. Neikrug vlc Epic LC3306

POULENC

Sonata in d (1943) "In memory of Federico Garcia Lorca" vln & pf
  with N. Sparrow pf   Fantasy 85021

RAVEL

Sonata (1927) vln & pf
  with N. Sparrow pf   Fantasy 85021

SATIE

Choses vues à droite et à gauche (sans lunettes) (1914) vln & pf
  with N. Sparrow pf   Fantasy 85021

SMITH, L.

Trio vln, vla & vlc
  with M. James vla & B. Hampton vlc Fantasy 5010

SMITH, W.O.

Capriccio (1952) vln & pf
  with A. Previn pf   Contemporary 7015, C6001
Suite (1952) vln & cl
  with W.O. Smith cl   Contemporary 7015, C6001

Jan RUBINI (1900–   )

DELIBES

Sylvia (1876) – ballet orch.
   No. 16a. Pizzicato–scherzettino (Act III) arr. vln & pf
   with piano   Pathé 20244

DRDLA

Serenade No. 1, in A vln & pf
   with piano   Pathé 40074

Souvenir vln & pf
   with piano   Pathé 20288

ELLIOTT

There's a long, long trail (1913) v & pf – arr. vln & pf
   with piano   Pathé 20181

GREENE

Sing me to sleep v & pf – arr. vln & pf
   with piano   Pathé 20255

LOTH

Firelight fancies v & pf – arr. vln & pf
   with piano   Pathé 20346

MASCAGNI

Cavalleria Rusticana (1890) – opera
   Intermezzo orch.– arr. vln & pf
   with piano   Pathé 20165

MOSZKOWSKI

(6) Klavierstücke, Op. 15 pf–4 hands
   No. 1 Serenata arr. vln & pf
   with piano   Pathé 20244

MOZART

Don Giovanni, K527 (1787) – opera
   No. 14. Minuet orch. – arr. vln & pf
   with piano   Pathé 20165

O'HARA

(The) Blush rose v & pf – arr. vln & pf
   with piano   Pathé 20288

QUINN

Souvenir de Venise vln & pf
   with piano   Pathé 20346

RAY

(The) Sunshine of your smile (1915) v & pf – arr. vln & pf
   with piano   Pathé 40074

SANTLY

Hawaiian butterfly v & pf – arr. vln & pf
   with piano   Pathé 20181

SILÉSU

Love here is my heart v & pf – arr. vln & pf
   with piano   Pathé 20255

Janine RUBINLICHT

BERTALI

Sonata in E 2 vlns & c
   with S. Kuijken vln, R. Kohnen hpsi   Telefunken SAWT9542
   & W. Kuijken gamba

CASTILLO

Sonata concertante (1629)
   Sonata in c 2 vlns & c
   with S. Kuijken vln, R. Kohnen hpsi   Telefunken SAWT9542
   & W. Kuijken gamba

CAVALLI

Musiche Sacre Concernenti ..." (1656)
   Sonata in a 2 vlns & c
   with S. Kuijken vln, R. Kohnen hpsi   Telefunken SAWT9542
   & W. Kuijken gamba

CIMA

(2) Concerti ecclesiastici (1610)
   Sonata No. 2, in a 2 vlns, gamba & org
   with S. Kuijken vln, W. Kuijken   Telefunken SAWT9542
   gamba & R. Kohnen org

FARINA

(Il) Terzo libro primo della Pavane, Gagliarde ... (1626)
   Sonata in f 2 vlns & c
   with S. Kuijken vln R. Kohnen hpsi &   Telefunken SAWT 9542
   W. Kuijken gamba

ROSSI

Sonata in f (1613) 2 vlns & hpsi
   with S. Kuijken vln & R. Kohnen hpsi   Telefunken SAWT9542

Jan RUDÉNYI (–1914)

d'AMBROSIO

Canzonetta, Op. 6 vln & pf
   with piano   Pathé 5631, 5755, 6318

Serenade, Op. 4 vln & pf
   with piano   Pathé 5164, 5488, 6314, 30114

BEETHOVEN

Concerto in D, Op. 61 vln & orch.
   Larghetto (2nd mvt)
   with piano   Pathé 2101, 5059, 9551, 70014
   Rondo (3rd mvt)
   with piano   Pathé 2101, 5059, 9551, 70014

BENEDICT

(La) Carnevale di Venizia – variations v & pf – arr. vln & pf
   with piano   Pathé 3207, 79370

(La) Carnevale di Venizia – variations v & pf – arr. vln & pf
   with piano   13730 e   Zonophone 731, X47920

BRAGA

(7) Melodies (1867) v & pf
   No. 5. La serenata "Angel's serenade" arr. vln & pf
   with piano   Pathé 5162, 5630, 6321, 40090

BRUCH

Concerto No. 1, in g, Op. 26 vln & orch.
  Adagio (2nd mvt)
  with orch.   Pathé 2100, 5585, 9554,
  Allegro energico (3rd mvt)
  with orch.   Pathé 2100, 5585, 9554

(15) Swedish dances, Op. 63 vln & pf
  No. 1. Swedish dance No. 1, in d
  with orch.   Pathé 2131, 5336, 70024
  No. 2. Swedish dance No. 2, in D
  with orch.   Pathé 2131, 5336, 70024
  No. 3. Swedish dance No. 3, in d
  with orch.   Pathé 2131, 5336, 70024
  No. 5. Swedish dance No. 5, in g
  with orch.   Pathé 2131, 5336, 70024
  No. 6. Swedish dance No. 6, in E flat
  with orch.   Pathé 2131, 5336, 70024
  No. 7. Swedish dance No. 7, in B flat
  with orch.   Pathé 2131, 5336, 70024

CHOPIN

(3) Nocturnes, Op. 9 pf
  No. 2. Nocturne No. 2, in E flat arr. vln & pf Sarasate
  with orch.   Pathé 2157, 5491, 70027, 92283

DRDLA

Serenade No. 1, in A vln & pf
  with orch.   Pathé 2128, 5255, 8913, 9553, 9559, 70022
Souvenir vln & pf
  with orch.   Pathé 2128, 5255, 5528, 8918, 9553, 9559, 70022

ELGAR

Salut d'amour, Op. 12 orch. – arr. vln & pf Elgar
  with piano   Pathé 5589, 5755, 6320

ERNST

(La) Carnevale di Venizia – variations, Op. 18 vln & pf
  with orch.   Pathé 210, 3207, 8910
Élégie in c, Op. 10 vln & pf
  with piano   Pathé 25, 9558

GOLDMARK

Concerto in a, Op. 28 vln & pf
  Andante (2nd mvt) "Air"
  with orch.   Pathé 2102, 8920

GOSSEC

Rosine (1786) – opera
  Gavotte arr. vln & pf Burmester
  with piano   Pathé 5489, 9555

GRIEG

Sonata No. 3, in c, Op. 45 vln & pf
  Allegro molto ed appassionata (1st mvt)
  with piano   Pathé 2123, 5489
  Allegretto expressivo alla Romanza (2nd mvt)
  with piano   Pathé 2123, 5489

KREISLER

Liebesleid vln & pf
  with piano   Pathé 5162, 5630, 6321, 40090
Schön Rosmarin vln & pf
  with piano   Pathé 5164, 5488, 6321, 30114
Variations on a theme of Corelli (Tartini) vln & pf
  with piano   Pathé 5489

KRYL

(La) Carnevale di Venizia – variations tpt & pf – arr. vln & pf
  with piano   Beka 502, 41267

LÉONARD

Austrian Hymn – variations "Souvenir de Haydn" Op. 2 vln & pf
  with piano   Pathé 5198, 19514
Austrian Hymn – variations "Souvenir de Haydn" Op. 2 vln & pf
  with piano   Zonophone 768, X47922

MARCO

Humoresque vln & pf
  with orch.   Pathé 319, 3197, 8917, 79264

MASCAGNI

Cavalleria Rusticana (1890) – opera
  Intermezzo orch. – arr. vln & pf
  with piano   Pathé 376, 6320, 10060

MASSENET

Thaïs (1894) – opera
  Méditation arr. vln & pf Marsick
  with piano   Pathé 513, 30026

MENDELSSOHN

Concerto in e, Op. 64 vln & orch.
  Andante (2nd mvt)
  with orch.   Pathé 2062, 5054, 5490, 70008
  Allegro molto vivace (3rd mvt)
  with orch.   Pathé 2062, 5054, 5490, 70008
(6) Songs without words, Op. 62 pf
  No. 6. Song without words No. 30, in A "Spring song" arr. vln & pf
  with piano   Pathé 376, 6323, 10060

MILES

Idyll vln & pf
  with orch.   Pathé 626, 3198, 5444, 9556, 79276

MOSZKOWSKI

(6) Klavierstücke, Op. 15 pf–4 hands
No. 1. Serenata arr. vln & pf
       Pathé 3192, 3198, 5198, 19514, 79276, 79613
  with piano

MUSIN

(2) Morceaux de concert, Op. 7 (1887) vln & pf
  No. 1. Mazurka de concert
  with piano   Pathé 5436
  No. 1. Mazurka de concert
  with piano   13727 e   Zonophone 640, X47918

PAGANINI

Concerto No. 1, in D, Op. 6 vln & orch.*
  Allegro maestoso (1st mvt)
  with orch.   Pathé 2102, 8921, 9513

PECHOTSCH

Caprice vln & pf
  with piano   Pathé 5590, 6312, 30455

Cradle song vln & pf
  with orch.   Pathé 202

Cradle song vln & pf
  with piano   Zonophone 871, X47925

Légende vln & pf
  with piano   Pathé 5487, 30113

Rapsodie hongrois vln & pf
  with piano   Pathé 5487, 6314, 30113

Serenade vln & pf
  with orch.   Pathé 513, 3199, 20004, 30026, 79266

Tarantella romantique vln & pf
  with piano   Pathé 5590, 6312, 30408

Wiegenlied vln & pf
  with piano   Pathé 3195, 3199, 79266

PIERNÉ

Sérénade in A, Op. 7 (1875) pf – arr. vln & pf Haddock
  with piano   Pathé 25
                          Pathé–Actuelle 10759

RAFF

(6) Pieces, Op. 85 vln & pf
  No. 3. Cavatina in D
  with 'cello & harp   Pathé 5589, 6318, 30455
                          Pathé–Actuelle 10759

  No. 6. Tarantella
  with piano   Pathé 26, 6319

RUBINSTEIN

(2) Melodies, Op. 3 pf
  No. 1. Melody in F arr. vln & pf Wilhelmj
  with L. Bryant pf   Pathé 3316, 92628

RUDÉNYI

Chanson de Venise vln & pf
  with L. Bryant pf   Pathé 3316, 5339, 92082

Fantaisie hongrois vln & pf
  with piano   Pathé 626, 3198/9, 5526, 8913, 79267

Rêverie vln & pf
  with piano   Zonophone 768, X47923

Romance in A (Chant à Mélisande) vln & pf
  with piano   13732 e   Zonophone 731, X47921

Sérénade amoureuse vln & pf
  with piano   Pathé 5436, 6316, 9541

Sérénade d'amour vln & pf
  with piano   13726 e   Zonophone 640, X47919

* Abridged.

SAINT–SAËNS

(Le) Carnaval des animaux (1886) small orch.
  Le cygne arr. vln & pf
  with piano   Pathé 5631, 6319

SARASATE

Zigeunerweisen, Op. 20 vln & pf or orch.
  with orch.   Pathé 5256, 9552

SCHUMANN

(13) Kinderscenen, Op. 15 pf
  No. 7. Träumerei arr. vln & pf
  with piano   Zonophone 968

SCOTT, Lady

Annie Laurie (1838) v & pf – arr. vln & pf Rudényi
  with piano   Beka 502

Annie Laurie (1838) v & pf – arr. vln & pf Rudényi
  with orch.   Pathé 210, 3207, 9555, 79371

SVENDSEN

Romance in G, Op. 26 vln & orch.
  with orch.   Pathé 5256, 5528, 6323, 8918, 9552

TCHAIKOVSKY

Sérénade mélancolique in b flat, Op. 26 vln & orch. – arr. vln & pf Wilhelmj
  with piano   Pathé 378

(3) Souvenirs de Hapsal, Op. 2 pf
  No. 3. Chant sans paroles in f arr. vln & pf Kreisler
  with piano   Pathé 378

Souvenir d'un lieu cher, Op. 42 vln & pf
  No. 3. Mélodie
  with piano   Pathé 5339, 5444, 6316

THOMAS

Mignon (1866) – opera
  Entr'acte (Gavotte) (Act II) orch. – arr. vln & pf Sarasate
  with piano   Pathé 513, 3199

THOMÉ

Andante religioso, Op. 70 pf – arr. vln & pf
  with piano   Pathé 24

Simple aveu, Op. 25 pf – arr. vln & pf
  with piano   Pathé 24

TITL

Serenade arr. vln & pf Flesch
  with piano   Pathé 3195, 79211

VIEUXTEMPS

(6) Bouquet Américain, Op. 33 vln & pf
  No. 2. La Fête de St. Patrice
  with orch.   Pathé 202, 9556
  No. 2. La Fête de St. Patrice
  with piano   Zonophone 871, X47924

Caprice burlesque (Souvenir d'Amérique) Op. 17 "Yankee Doodle" vln & pf
  with orch.   Pathé 319, 3197, 8917, 79265

Concerto No. 4, in d, Op. 31 vln & orch.
  Adagio religioso (2nd mvt)
  with orch. & harp   Pathé 2063, 5055, 9557, 70009

VIEUXTEMPS – *Continued*

Andante (Finale) (4th mvt)
with orch. & harp   Pathé 2063, 5055, 70009

WIENIAWSKI

Capriccio–valse, Op. 7 vln & pf
with piano   Pathé 9557

Légende, Op. 17 vln & pf or orch.
with orch.   Pathé 2157, 5491, 70027, 92282

Souvenir de Moscou, Op. 6 vln & pf or orch.*
with piano   Pathé 26, 9558

Astolfi RUGGERO

GRANADOS

(12) Danzas españolas, Op. 37 (1893) pf
No. 5. Danza española No. 5, in e "Andaluza" arr. vln & pf Kreisler
with M. Gino Moroni pf   Odeon GO12450

VERACINI

(12) Sonatas, Op. 2 (1744) "Sonate accademiche" vln & c
Sonata No. 6, in A: Largo (2nd mvt) (ed. Corti)
with M. Gino Moroni pf   Odeon GO12450

Stefan RUHA (1931–)

BARTÓK

Rhapsody No. 1, in G (1928) vln & orch.
with F. Weiss pf   Electrecord ECD1054

CHOPIN

(4) Mazurkas, Op. 67 pf
No. 4. Mazurka No. 45, in a arr. vln & pf Kreisler
with E. Sinka pf   Mezhdunarodnaya Kniga
D04305

CONSTANTINESCU

Sonatina in a vln & pf
with F. Weiss pf   Electrecord ECD1054

DVOŘÁK

(8) Slavonic Dances, Op. 72 pf duet; orch.
No. 8. Slavonic dance No. 16, in A flat arr. vln & pf "in G" Kreisler
with F. Weiss pf   Electrecord ECD1054

HANDEL

(15) Sonatas, Op. 1 (?1731) fl or vln & c
Sonata No. 10, in g vln II
with E. Sinka pf   Mezhdunarodnaya Kniga
D04304

JORA

Quartet in c, Op. 9 (1926) 2 vlns, vla & vlc
with V. Horvath vln, V. Fülöp vla &   Electrecord ECE0251
I. Dula vlc

* Introduction & theme only.

KREISLER

Rondino on a theme by Beethoven vln & pf
with F. Weiss pf   Electrecord ECD1054

PAGANINI

(24) Caprices, Op. 1 (1801/7) solo vln
Caprice No. 14, in E flat
(unaccompanied)   Electrecord ECD1054
Concerto No. 1, in D, Op. 6 (cadenza by Sauret) vln & orch.
with Cluj Philharmonic Symphony   Electrecord ECD1037
Orch. – Wislocki

SARASATE

Caprice basque, Op. 24 vln & pf
with F. Weiss pf   Electrecord ECD1054

TCHAIKOVSKY

Concerto in D, Op. 35 vln & orch.
with Rumanian Radio Symphony   Electrecord ECD50
Orch. – Basarab

Sérénade mélancolique in b flat, Op. 26 vln & orch. – arr. vln & pf
Wilhelmj
with E. Sinka pf   Mezhdunarodnaya Kniga
D04305

Souvenir d'un lieu cher, Op. 42 vln & pf
No. 1. Méditation
with E. Sinka pf   Mezhdunarodnaya Kniga
D04305

No. 2. Scherzo
with E. Sinka pf   Mezhdunarodnaya Kniga
D04305, D04442

VITALI

Chaconne in g vln & c – arr. vln & pf Charlier
with E. Sinka pf   Mezhdunarodnaya Kniga
D04304

VIVALDI

(12) Concerti, Op. 8 (1725) "Il Cimento dell' Armonia e dell' Invenzione"
(Nos. 1/4: Le quattro Stagioni) vln & strs
Concerto No. 1, in E, F.I, No. 22 "La Primavera"
with Cluj Philharmonic Symphony   Electrecord ECE0326
Orch. – Cristescu   Select CC15048
Concerto No. 2, in B flat, F.I, No. 23 "L'Estate"
with Cluj Philharmonic Symphony   Electrecord ECE0326
Orch. – Cristescu   Select CC15048
Concerto No. 3, in F, F.I, No. 24 "L'Autunno"
with Cluj Philharmonic Symphony   Electrecord ECE0326
Orch. – Cristescu   Select CC15048
Concerto No. 4, in f, F.I, No. 25 "L'Inverno"
with Cluj Philharmonic Symphony   Electrecord ECE0326
Orch. – Cristescu   Select CC15048

Angelika RÜMAN

HAYDN

Concerto No. 1, in C, H.VIIa, No. 1 (1765) vln & orch.
with orch. – Graunke   Mercury MG10056

Mario RUMINELLI (1907–   )

KREISLER

Andantino (Padre Martini) vln & pf
with piano   HMV GW1679

PAGANINI

(6) Sonatas, Op. 3 (1801/6) vln & gtr
No. 6. Sonata No. 12, in e
with piano   HMV GW1679

Axel RUNNQVIST (1880–1947)

AULIN

(4) Aquarelles vln & pf
No. 3. Vaggsång
with N. Broman pf   802 am   HMV X845
(3) Gottländische Tänze, Op. 28 vln & pf
with N. Broman pf   1098 am   HMV X1008

DEBUSSY

Petite Suite (1889) pf – 4 hands
No. 1. En bateau arr. vln & pf
with N. Broman pf   804 am   HMV X845

HAQUINIUS

Svensk dans vln & pf
with N. Broman pf   1117 am   HMV X1008

Renato RUOTOLO (1912–   )

VIVALDI

(12) Concerti, Op. 3 "L'Estro armonico" var. cbns & strs
Concerto No. 4, in e, P.97 (F.I, No. 174) 4 vlns, strs & c
with M. Benvenuti vln, F. Gulli vln,   HMV ALP1809, ASD391
A. Stefanato vln & Virtuosi di Roma –
Fasano

Concerto No. 5, in A, P.212 (F.I, No. 175) 2 vlns, strs & c
with G. Mozzato vln & Virtuosi di   Angel 45030
Roma – Fasano   Electrola E70380
                                      HMV ALP1629, WBLP552
Concerto No. 5, in A, P.212 (F.I, No. 175) 2 vlns, strs & c
with A. Stefanato vln & Virtuosi   HMV ALP1810, ASD392
Roma – Fasano

(12) Concerti, Op. 8 (1725) "Il Cimento dell' Armonia e dell' Invenzione"
(Nos. 1/4: Le quattro Stagioni) vln & strs
Concerto No. 6, in C, F.I, No. 27 "Il piacere"
with Virtuosi di Roma – Fasano   Angel 35878, (in set 3611),
                                   ASC5039
                                   HMV ALP1787, ASD368

Christa RUPPERT

MENDELSSOHN

Concerto in e, Op. 64 vln & orch.
with Hamburg Symphony Orch. –   Rondolette SA103
Schmidt

Miroslav RUSIN

HONEGGER

Sonata No. 2, in d (1919) vln & pf
with I. Chernyshov pf   Mezhdunarodnaya Kniga
                                   D18501

SZYMANOWSKI

(3) Mythes, Op. 30 (1915) vln & pf
No. 1. La Fontaine d'Aréthuse
with M. Muntyan pf   Mezhdunarodnaya Kniga
                                   D18501

No. 2. Narcisse
with M. Muntyan pf   Mezhdunarodnaya Kniga
                                   D18502

No. 3. Dryades et Pan
with M. Muntyan pf   Mezhdunarodnaya Kniga
                                   D18502

Julius RÜTHSTRÖM (1877–1944)

AULIN

(2) Charakterstücke vln & pf
No. 2. Mazurka No. 2, in e
with A. Hillern–   XXSto 3246–II   Odeon A210243, D6062
Dunbar pf

ERIKSSON, J.

Aria, Op. 15 vln & pf
with A. Hillern–   XXSto 3245–II   Odeon A210243, D6062
Dunbar pf

GLUCK

Orphée et Eurydice (1762) – opera
Dance of the blessed spirits: Lento "Mélodie" (No. 2) arr. vln & pf
Kreisler
with piano   Sto 3241   Odeon*

SIBELIUS

Concerto in d, Op. 47 vln & orch.
Adagio di molto (2nd mvt)
with piano   Sto 3243/4   Odeon*

TARTINI

Concerto in E, D53 (C84) vln & orch.
Andante (2nd mvt)
with piano   Sto 3242   Odeon*

Peter RYBAR (1913–   )

BACH

(6) Brandenburg Concerti, BWV1046/51 (1721) strs & c
Brandenburg Concerto No. 4, in G, BWV1049 vln, 2 fls, strs & c
with P.L. Graf fl, W. Klemm fl &   Classic CL11009
Winterthur Symphony Orch. – Goehr   Musical Masterpiece Society
                                      MMS13
                                      Nixa MLPY13

* Unissued.

BACH – *Continued*

Brandenburg Concerto No. 5, in D, BWV1050 clav, fl, vln, strs & c
with F. Pelleg hpsi, P. Graf fl &   Classic CL11009
Winterthur Symphony Orch. – Goehr   Musical Masterpiece Society
    MMS13
    Nixa MLPY13

Concerto in d, BWV1043 2 vlns, strs & c
with H. Szeryng vln & Collegium   Mercury MG50466, SR90466
Musicum, Winterthur – Szeryng   Philips (in set 6830 004),
    835331LY, AL3540, L02462L,
    SAL3540

Concerto No. 5, in f BWV1056 clav, strs & c – arr. vln, strs & c as
"Concerto in g" – res. Schreck
with Winterthur Symphony Orch. –   Concert Hall G15
Dahinden

Concerto in c, BWV1060 vln & ob or 2 vlns, strs & c
with E. Parolari ob & Winterthur   Concert Hall G15
Symphony Orch. – Dahinden   Musical Masterpiece Society
    MMS77

Sonata in c, BWV1024 vln & c
with T. Sack hpsi & A. Tusa vlc   Concert Hall G15

Sonata in C, BWV1037 2 vlns & c
with A. Fietz vln & T. Sack hpsi   Concert Hall G15

BEETHOVEN

Quartet No. 10, in E flat, Op. 74 "Harp" 2 vlns, vla & vlc
with C. Dahinden vln, H. Wigand vla   Classics Club X28
& A. Tusa vlc

BRAHMS

Concerto in D, Op. 77 (cadenza by Kreisler) vln & orch.
with West Austrian Radio Symphony   Classic CL6215
Orch. – Moltkau   Classics Club X31
    Concert Hall CHS1113
    Musical Masterpiece Society
    MMS2007
    Nixa CLP1113
    Whitehall 5023

Quintet in f, Op. 34 2 vlns, vla, vlc & pf
with C. Dahinden vln, H. Wigand vla,   Nixa CLP46
A. Tusa vlc & C. Haskil pf

Sonata (1853) "Frei aber Einsam" vln & pf
Allegro (Scherzo) in c (3rd mvt) "Sonatensatz"
with H. Boschi pf   Le Chant du Monde LDXS8143

CORELLI

(12) Sonatas, Op. 1 2 vlns & c
Sonata No. 9, in G
with A. Fietz vln, H. Andrae hpsi &   Concert Hall CHC29
A. Tusa gamba

DVOŘÁK

(5) Bagatelles, Op. 47 2 vlns, vlc & harmonium
1/4 only
with J. Bernstein vln, W. Landschoff   Pro Musica PMR112
vlc &   . Alban pf   Treasury of music T9

Quartet No. 2, in E flat, Op. 87 pf, vln, vla & vlc
with A. Balsam pf, O. Kromer vla &   Concert Hall (set D2), DL2
A. Tusa vlc

DVOŘÁK – *Continued*

(4) Romantic Pieces, Op. 75 vln & pf
with F. Holetschek pf   Vega C30A84
    Westminster WL5015,
    XWN18066

Sonata in F, Op. 57 vln & pf
with F. Holetschek pf   Vega C30A84
    Westminster WL5015,
    XWN18066

GOLDMARK

Concerto in a, Op. 28 vln & orch.
with Vienna Symphony Orch. –   Nixa WLP5010
Swoboda   Westminster WL5010,
    XWN18454

HANDEL

(12) Concerti grossi, Op. 6 (1739) 2 vlns, vlc & strs
  Concerto grosso No. 6, in g
with J. Diggleman hpsi & Classics   Classics Club CCHN21, X21
Club Chamber Orch. – Dahinden
  Concerto grosso No. 12, in b
with J. Diggleman hpsi & Classics   Classics Club CCHN21, X21
Club Chamber Orch. – Dahinden

(9) Deutschen Arien (1729) v & var acc
  No. 4. Süsse Stille, sanfte Quelle v, fl & c
with R. Ginster s & K. Matthaei org   HMV DB10102

(7) Sonatas, Op. 5 (1739) 2 vlns & c
  Sonata No. 4, in G
with A. Fietz vln, H. Andreae hpsi &   Concert Hall (set C13)
H. Boschi vlc

HAYDN

Concerto in F, H.XVIII, No. 6 (1765) (cadenzas by Schultze) vln, hpsi & orch.
with H. Andreae hpsi & Concert Hall   Amphion 520/5, (set B3)
Chamber Orch. – Swoboda   Classic CL6156
    Concert Hall 103/5, (set C2),
    CHS1081

HESS

Quartet, Op. 50 2 vlns, vla & vlc
with C. Dahinden vln, H. Wigand vla   Elite Special TLPE6002
& A. Tusa vlc

HINDEMITH

(4) Kammermusik, Op. 36 var. cbns
  No. 3. Kammermusik No. 4 (1925) vln & cha orch.
with Winterthur Symphony Orch. –   Heliodor 479060
Swoboda   Nixa WLP5074
    Westminster WL5074,
    XWN18716

MARTINŮ

Sonata (1932) 2 vlns & pf
with L. Kaufman vln & P. Pozzi pf   Concert Hall E12

MENDELSSOHN

Concerto in e, Op. 64 vln & orch.
with Vienna Festival Orch. –   Whitehall WH20003, WHS40003
Desarzens

MOZART

Serenade No. 7, in D, K250 "Haffner" orch.
with Winterthur Symphony Orch. –	Concert Hall E1
Busch

NARDINI

Concerto in e vln & orch.
with Winterthur Symphony Orch. –	Westminster WL5049,
Dahinden	XWN18192

REGAMEY

Quartet No. 1 (1949) 2 vlns, vla & vlc
with C. Dahinden vln, H. Wigand vla	Decca LXT2849
& A. Tusa vlc	London LL893

SCHIBLER

Quartettsatz 2 vlns, vla & vlc
with C. Dahinden vln, O. Kromer vla	Odeon A208464/5
& A. Tusa vlc

SCHUBERT

(2) Quartets, Op. 125 2 vlns, vla & vlc
No. 2. Quartet No. 11, in E, D353
with C. Dahinden vln, O. Kromer vla	Classics Club X45
& A. Tusa vlc	Concert Hall D15
Quartet No. 12, in c, D703 "Quartettsatz" 2 vlns, vla & vlc
with C. Dahinden vln, O. Kromer vla	Classics Club X45
& A. Tusa vlc	Concert Hall D15
Quintet in A, Op. 114 (D667) "Trout" pf, vln, vla, vlc & cbs
with P. Pozzi pf, H. Wigand vla, A.	Classics Club X40
Tusa vlc & F. Jacquillard cbs	Musical Masterpiece Society
MMS39

SCHUMANN

Concerto in d (1853) vln & orch.
with Lausanne Symphony Orch. –	Classic CL6224
Desarzens	Concert Hall CHS1128
Nixa CLP1128
(3) Fantasiestücke, Op. 73 cl & pf – arr. vln & pf
with H. Boschi pf	Le Chant du Monde LDXA8144
(3) Quartets, Op. 41 2 vlns, vla & vlc
No. 3. Quartet No. 3, in A
with C. Dahinden vln, H. Wigand vla	Concert Hall CHS38
& A. Tusa vlc
Sonata (1853) "Frei aber Einsam" vln & pf
Intermezzo (2nd mvt); **Finale** (4th mvt)
with H. Boschi pf	Le Chant du Monde LDXS8143
Sonata No. 1, in a, Op. 105 vln & pf
with H. Boschi pf	Le Chant du Monde LDXA8144
Sonata No. 2, in d, Op. 121 vln & pf
with H. Boschi pf	Le Chant du Monde LDXA8144

STURZENEGGER

Quartet (1940) 2 vlns, vla & vlc
with C. Dahinden vln, H. Wigand vla	Edition Modern TLPE6000
& A. Tusa vlc	Elite Special TLPE6000

SUK

Fantasy in g, Op. 24 (1903) vln & orch.
with Vienna Symphony Orch. –	Westminster WL5011,
Swoboda	XWN18649

SUTER

Quartet No. 1 2 vlns, vla & vlc
with C. Dahinden vln, H. Wigand vla	Edition Modern TLPE6000
& A. Tusa vlc	Elite Special TLPE6000

TARTINI

Concerto in d, D45 (C61) (cadenzas by Rybar) vln & orch.
with Winterthur Symphony Orch. –	Westminster WL5118,
Dahinden	XWN18192
(12) Sonatas, Op. 3 2 vlns & c
Sonata No. 7, in g
with F. Holetschek hpsi	Nixa WLP5141
Westminster WL5141,
XWN18172
Sonata in a vln & c
with F. Holetschek hpsi	Nixa WLP5141
Westminster WL5141,
XWN18172
Sonata in b, P14 vln & c
with F. Holetschek hpsi	Nixa WLP5141
Westminster WL5141,
XWN18172
Sonata in D vln & c
with F. Holetschek hpsi	Nixa WLP5141
Westminster WL5141,
XWN18172
Sonata in E vln & c
with F. Holetschek hpsi	Westminster WL5118
Sonata in e vln & c
with F. Holetschek hpsi	Westminster WL5118

TCHAIKOVSKY

Concerto in D, Op. 35 vln & orch.
with Vienna Symphony Orch. –	Whitehall WH20004, WHS40004
Desarzens

TELEMANN

Concerto in F, T.II, No. 3 3 vlns, strs & c
with L. Kaufman vln, A. Fietz vln &	Concert Hall (set D12), DL12
Concert Hall String Orch. – Swoboda

VIOTTI

Concerto No. 22, in a (cadenzas by Ysaÿe) vln & orch.
with Winterthur Symphony Orch. –	Westminster WL5049,
Dahinden	XWN18192

VIVALDI

(12) Concerti, Op. 3 "L'Estro armonico" var. cbns & strs
Concerto No. 10, in b, P.148 (F.IV, No. 10) 4 vlns, vlc, strs & c
with L. Kaufman vln, A. Fietz vln, G.	Concert Hall E2
Piraccini vln & Winterthur Chamber
Orch. – Dahinden
(6) Concerti, Op. 12 vln, strs & c
Concerto No. 1, in g, P.343 (F.I, No. 211)
with Vienna Symphony Orch. – Moralt	Ducretet-Thomson LPG8318
Westminster WL5006,
XWN18718
Concerto in D, P.159 2 vlns, strs & c
with L. Kaufman vln & Winterthur	Concert Hall E2
Chamber Orch. – Dahinden	Musical Masterpiece Society
MMS84

VIVALDI – *Continued*

Concerto in E flat, P.428 (Op. 33, No. 1) vln, strs & c
with Vienna Symphony Orch. – Moralt Ducretet–Thomson LPG8318
Westminster WL5006,
XWN18718

WEBER

Quintet in B flat, Op. 34 cl, 2 vlns, vla & vlc
with G. Coutelen cl, C. Dahinden vln, Concert Hall CHS1244
H. Wigand vla & A. Tusa vlc

Henryk SACHSENSKJÖLD

BRAHMS

(16) Waltzes, Op. 39 pf duet
No. 15. Waltz No. 15, in A flat arr. vln & pf "in A" Hochstein
with piano HMV X6827

DEBUSSY

(12) Préludes – Book I (1910) pf
No. 8. La Fille aux cheveux de lin arr. vln & pf Hartmann
with F. Jensen pf Tono K8026

FALLA

(La) Vida Breve (1913) – opera
Danza española orch. – arr. vln & pf Kreisler
with F. Jensen pf Tono K8026

KREISLER

Rondino on a theme by Beethoven vln & pf
with piano HMV X6827

Georg SADLER

d'AMBROSIO

Canzonetta, Op. 6 vln & pf
with orch. P 1221 Odeon 6295

GILLET

Babillage pf – arr. vln & orch.
with orch. Odeon 60085
Loin du Bal, Op. 36 – ballet orch.
Intermezzo arr. vln & orch.
with orch. Odeon 60085

TCHAIKOVSKY

(3) Souvenirs de Hapsal, Op. 2 pf
No. 3. Chant sans paroles in f arr. vln & pf Kreisler
with piano Odeon X51431

VIEUXTEMPS

(3) Feuilles d'album, Op. 40 vln & pf
No. 1. Romance
with piano Odeon X51432

Fryderyk SADOWSKI

BONONCINI

Mario fuggitivo (1708) – opera
Più non ti voglio credere
with S. Woytowicz s & Warsaw Muza XL0243
Philharmonic Chamber Orch. –
Teutsch

CESTI

(I) Casti amori d'Orontea (1649) – opera
S'io non vedo Alidoro
with S. Woytowicz s & Warsaw Muza XL0243
Philharmonic Chamber Orch. –
Teutsch

CORELLI

(12) Concerti grossi, Op. 6 orch.
Concerto grosso No. 3, in c
with E. Sieja vln, A. Ciechánski vlc & Muza XL0191
Warsaw National Philharmonic
Chamber Orch. – Teutsch

Concerto grosso No. 8, in g "Christmas Concerto"
with E. Sieja vln, A. Ciechánski vlc & Muza XL0191
Warsaw National Philharmonic
Chamber Orch. – Teutsch

HANDEL

Amadigi di Gaula (1715) – opera
Ah! Spietato!
with S. Woytowicz s & Warsaw Muza XL0243
Philharmonic Chamber Orch. –
Teutsch

Armida abbandonata (Cantata No. 13) s, strs & c
Dietro l'orme fugacci
with S. Woytowicz s & Warsaw Muza XL0243
Philharmonic Chamber Orch. –
Teutsch

PASQUINI

Erminia in riva del Giordano – aria v & c
with S. Woytowicz s & Warsaw Muza XL0243
Philharmonic Chamber Orch. –
Teutsch

SCARLATTI, A.

Clearco in Negroponte (1686) – opera
Vengo a stringerti
with S. Woytowicz s & Warsaw Muza XL0243
Philharmonic Chamber Orch. –
Teutsch

STEFFANI

Enrico Leone (1689) – opera
Lo consolo i cori amanti
with S. Woytowicz s & Warsaw Muza XL0243
Philharmonic Chamber Orch. –
Teutsch

TORELLI

Ricercate, o mie speranze – aria v & c
    with S. Woytowicz s & Warsaw   Muza XL0243
    Philharmonic Chamber Orch. –
    Teutsch

Carmela SAGI

ENGEL

Elegy solo vln
    (unaccompanied)   CBS*

Herman SALOMON

PIJPER

Sonata No. 2 (1922) vln & pf
    with M. Stroo pf   Radio Nederland 109571

Max SALPETER (1910–   )

CHOPIN

(2) Nocturnes, Op. 27 pf
    No. 2. Nocturne No. 8, in D flat arr. vln & pf Wilhelmj
    with Philharmonia Orch. – Kurtz   Encore ENC121
                                           HMV ALP1301, 7ER5070

DELIBES

Sylvia (1876) – ballet orch.
    No. 16a. Pizzicato–scherzettino (Act III) orch. – arr. vln & pf
    with M. Sargent pf   Decca LXT5573

HANDEL

(12) Concerti grossi, Op. 6 (1739) 2 vlns, vlc & strs
    Concerto grosso No. 5, in D
    with M. Parikian   2EA 14480/3–1   HMV C7852/3
    vln, E. Lush hpsi, R. Clark vlc &
    Philharmonia Orch. – Markevitch

KREISLER

Praeludium & Allegro (Pugnani) vln & pf
    with M. Sargent pf   Decca LXT5573

Bruno SALVI

SAMMARTINI, G.

Concerto in F vln, strs & c
    with Angelicum Orch. – Jenkins   Angelicum LPA1701, SLPA1701

TARTINI

Concerto in a, D115 (C76) vln, strs & c
    with M. Ceradini vln, G. Bozzini vln   Angelicum LPA5921
    & Angelicum Orch., Milan – Abbado

* Japanese.

VIVALDI

(12) Concerti, Op. 3 "L'Estro armonico" var. cbns & strs
    Concerto No. 3, in G, P.96 (F.I, No. 173) vln, strs & c
    with Angelicum Orch. – Zedda   Angelicum LPA5911, STA8911
                                           Harmonia Mundi HM30664

    Concerto No. 8, in a, P.2 (F.I, No. 177) 2 vlns, strs & c
    with R. Pezzani vln & Angelicum   Angelicum LPA5961
    Orch. – Zedda

    Concerto No. 10, in b, P.148 (F.IV, No. 10) 4 vlns, strs & c
    with A. Stefanato vln, C. Ferraresi vln, Angelicum LPA5911, STA8911
    M. Ceradini vln & Angelicum Orch. –   Harmonia Mundi HM30664
    Zedda

    Concerto No. 11, in d, P.250 (F.IV, No. 11) 2 vlns, vlc, strs & c
    with R. Pezzani vln, R. Caruana vlc & Angelicum LPA5961
    Angelicum Orch. – Zedda

(12) Concerti, Op. 7 vln, strs & c
    Concerto No. 11, in D
    with Angelicum Orch. – Zedda   Angelicum LPA5958
                                           Audio Fidelity FSC50036

Concerto in C, P.54 (F.XII, No. 17) 2 fls, 2 obs, bsn, 2 vlns, strs & c – rev.
    Malipiero
    with G. Tassinari fl, C. Hoogendoorn   Angelicum LPA5929
    fl, L. Caroli ob, G. Cappello ob, V.
    Menghini bsn, L. Vianelli vln &
    Angelicum Chamber Orch. – Suvini

Concerto in g, P.383 (F.XII, No. 3) "Per l'orchestra di Dresda" vln, 2 fls, 2
    obs, 2 bsns & c – rev. Ephrikian
    with G. Tassinari fl, C. Hoogendoorn   Angelicum LPA5929
    fl, L. Caroli ob, G. Cappello ob, V.
    Menghini bsn, O. Danzi bsn &
    Angelicum Chamber Orch. – Suvini

Concerto in B flat P.388 (F.IV, No. 2) (Op. 22, No. 2) vln, vlc, strs & c –
    rev. Ephrikian
    with R. Caruana vlc & Angelicum   Angelicum LPA5929
    Chamber Orch. – Suvini

Concerto in d, F.XII, No. 31 (Op. 41, No. 1) 2 fls, 2 obs, bsn, 2 vlns, strs &
    c – rev. Malipiero
    with G. Tassinari fl, C. Hoogendoorn   Angelicum LPA5929
    fl, L. Caroli ob, G. Cappello ob, V.
    Menghini bsn, M. Ceradini vln &
    Angelicum Chamber Orch. – Suvini

Toscha SAMAROFF

FIBICH

Images, Impressions & Souvenirs, Op. 41 pf
    No. 14. Poem (from "Souvenirs", Part IV) arr. vln & pf Kubelík
    with orch. – René   D7–FB–2954   HMV JO102

Kanny SAMBLEBEN

CORELLI

(12) Concerti grossi, Op. 6 orch.
    Concerto grosso No. 1, in D
    with J. Thomsen vln, I. Hermann vlc,   Bach Guild BG584
    J.E. Hansen hpsi & Societas Musica
    Chamber Orch., Copenhagen – Hansen

TORELLI

(12) Concerti, Op. 8 (1709) 1/6: 2 vlns, strs & c – 7/12: vln, strs & c
Concerto No. 2, in a
with J. Thomsen vln, J.E. Hansen hpsi Bach Guild BG584
& Societas Musica Chamber Orch.,
Copenhagen – Hansen

Leon SAMETINI (1886–)

BACH

(4) Suites, BWV1066/9 strs & c
Suite No. 3, in D: Air (2nd mvt) BWV1068 2 obs, 3 tpts, drms, strs & c
– arr. vln & pf as "Air on the G–string" by Wilhelmj
with piano   Beka 292, G40806

DRIGO

(2) Airs de Ballet orch.
No. 2. Valse bluette arr. vln & pf Auer
with piano   Beka 292, G40807

Albert SAMMONS (1886–1953)

d'AMBROSIO

Petite Suite, Op. 37 vln & pf
No. 1. Chanson napolitaine arr. pf, vln & vlc
with W. Murdoch pf &   DR 5230–1 Decca F7821
C. Sharpe vlc

ANONYMOUS

Cherry ripe English folksong – arr. vln & pf Bridge
with piano   Columbia D1509
(The) Faithful bird Welsh air – arr. vln & pf Sammons
with H.M. Grenadier Guards   6961 Columbia L1106
– Williams
(The) Faithful bird Welsh air – arr. vln & pf Sammons
with E. Hobday pf   03236 X Vocalion D02136
Londonderry air Traditional Irish air – arr. vln & pf Sammons
with piano   WA 3886 Columbia 4820, 01049, D1586,
                                J5014
Molly on the shore Traditional Irish ballad – arr. vln & pf Sammons
with piano   WA 3885 Columbia 4820, 01049, D1586,
                                J5014
Old English songs & dances arr. vln & pf Randall
Nos. 5 & 6
with E. Hobday pf   Vocalion R6118

ARBÓS

(3) Danzas españolas, Op. 1 pf, vln & vlc
No. 1. Boléro española
with W. Murdoch pf & W.H. Squire   Columbia L1073
vlc

ARENSKY

(4) Morceaux, Op. 30 vln & pf
No. 2. Sérénade in G
with E. Hobday pf   01684 Vocalion R6005
No. 2. Sérénade in G
with G. Moore pf   DR 4547–2 Decca F7533, Y5655

BEETHOVEN

(6) Minuets, G167 pf
No. 2. Minuet No. 2, in G arr. vln & pf Burmester
with E. Hobday pf   Vocalion R6014
No. 2. Minuet No. 2, in G arr. vln & pf Burmester
with G. Moore pf   DR 4539 Decca F7529
Sonata No. 5, in F, Op. 24 "Spring" vln & pf
with W. Murdoch pf   AX 65/8 Columbia L1231/2
Sonata No. 9, in A, Op. 47 "Kreutzer" vln & pf
with W. Murdoch   WRAX 2288/97 Columbia 9352/6, 02602/6,
pf   67261/5D, (set M53), J7151/5,
                                L1884/8
(3) Trios, Op. 1 pf, vln & vlc
No. 2. Trio No. 2, in G: Presto (4th mvt)
with W. Murdoch pf &   75432 Columbia L1164
W.H. Squire vlc
Trio No. 6, in B flat, Op. 97 "Archduke" pf, vln & vlc
with W. Murdoch pf   WAX 2170/9 Columbia 67256/60D, (set M52),
& W.H. Squire vlc   J7146/50, L1851/5
Trio in B flat, G154 (WoO39) "In one movement" pf, vln & vlc
Allegretto
with W. Murdoch pf   76977 (6901) Columbia L1133
& W.H. Squire vlc

BRAHMS

(21) Hungarian Dances pf duet
Hungarian dance No. 6, in D flat arr. vln & pf "in D" Hermann
with E. Hobday pf   Vocalion R6118
Hungarian dance No. 8, in a arr. vln & pf Joachim
with pf   65423 Columbia D1350
(16) Waltzes, Op. 39 pf duet
No. 15. Waltz No. 15, in A flat arr. vln & pf "in A" Hochstein
with E. Hobday pf   03038 Vocalion R6102

BRIDGE

(9) Miniatures pf, vln & vlc
No. 1. Minuet
with W. Murdoch pf &   76982–3 Columbia L1198
W.H. Squire vlc
No. 8. Hornpipe
with W. Murdoch pf &   76982–3 Columbia L1198
W.H. Squire vlc

BRUCH

Concerto No. 1, in g, Op. 26 vln & orch.
with orch. – Harty   AX 1001/6 Columbia 67152/4D, (set 30),
                                L1680/2

CATHIE

Valse lente vln & pf
with E. Hobday pf   03238 Vocalion D02136

CHOPIN

(3) Nocturnes, Op. 9 pf
No. 2. Nocturne No. 2, in E flat arr. vln & pf Sarasate
with H.M. Grenadier Guards   6962 Columbia L1106
Band – Williams
No. 2. Nocturne No. 2, in E flat arr. vln & pf Sammons
with E. Hobday pf   01213 Vocalion K05111

CHOPIN – *Continued*

(2) Nocturnes, Op. 27 pf
  No. 2. Nocturne No. 8, in D flat arr. vln & pf Wilhelmj
  with E. Hobday pf   Vocalion D02061

COTTENET

Chanson méditation vln & pf
  with E. Hobday pf   Vocalion D02081

DELIUS

Concerto (1916) vln & orch.
      CAX 9191/2–1, 9193–2 & Columbia 71946/8D, (set M672),
  with Liverpool   9194/6–1   DX1160/2
  Philharmonic Orch. – Sargent
Sonata No. 2 (1924) vln & pf
  with E. Howard–Jones A 1369/72 Columbia D1500/1
  pf
Sonata No. 3 (1930) vln & pf
    DR 8076–2, 8077–1, 8078/9–2 & Decca M557/9
  with K. Long pf   8080–1 Odeon 285504/6

DRDLA

Souvenir vln & pf
  with E. Hobday pf   01216 Vocalion R6020
Souvenir vln & pf
  with G. Moore pf   DR 4544–1 Decca F7532

DUNHILL

Phantasy–Trio in E flat, Op. 36 pf, vln & vla
  with F. St. Leger pf & L. Tertis vla Vocalion R6027

DVOŘÁK

(5) Bagatelles, Op. 47 2 vlns, vlc & harmonium – arr. pf, vln & vla Tertis
  with E. Hobday pf [1]02759 & 02762 Vocalion D02083 & D02111
  & L. Tertis vla
(7) Gypsy songs, Op. 55 v & pf
  No. 4. Songs my mother taught me arr. vln & pf Kreisler
  with G. Moore pf CA 12846–2 Columbia DB911, OD79
(8) Humoresques, Op. 101 pf
  No. 7. Humoresque No. 7, in G flat arr. vln & pf Rehfeld
  with E. Hobday pf 01124 Vocalion D02009
  No. 7. Humoresque No. 7, in G flat arr. vln & pf Rehfeld
  with G. Moore pf CA 12845–2 Columbia DB1008
(8) Slavonic Dances, Op. 46 pf duet; orch.
  No. 2. Slavonic dance No. 2, in e arr. vln & pf "in g" Kreisler
  with E. Hobday pf 02479 X Vocalion X9611
(8) Slavonic Dances, Op. 72 pf duet; orch.
  No. 2. Slavonic dance No. 10, in e arr. vln & pf Kreisler
  with E. Hobday pf 03239 Vocalion K05111
Sonatina in G, Op. 100 vln & pf
  Larghetto (2nd mvt) arr. vln & pf as "Indian lament" by Kreisler
  with piano WAX 3337 Columbia 9484, J7569

ELGAR

Concerto in b, Op. 61 vln & orch.*
  with New Queen's Hall 6780/3 Columbia L1071/2
  Orch. – Wood

* abridged

ELGAR – *Continued*

Concerto in b, Op. 61 vln & orch.
    WAX 4785/94 & 4846/7 Columbia J7639/44, L2346/51,
  with New Queen's Hall Orch. – Wood (set 127)
          HMV HLM7011
Salut d'amour, Op. 12 orch. – arr. vln & pf Elgar
  with G. Moore pf DR 4542 Decca F7530
Sonata in e, Op. 82 vln & pf
    CHAX 7421–2, 7422/5–1 & Columbia 68392/4D, (set M241),
  with W. Murdoch pf 7426–2 LX379/81, LX8163/5

FAURÉ

Sonata No. 1, in A, Op. 13 vln & pf
    CTPX 4918/9 & 4894–1 HMV JG60/2
  with E. Miller pf

FIBICH

Images, Impressions & Souvenirs, Op. 41 pf
  No. 14. Poem (from "Souvenirs", Part IV) arr. vln & pf Kubelík
  with G. Moore pf DR 4540–2 Decca F7531

FUCHS

Duet, Op. 60 vln & vla
  with L. Tertis vla   Vocalion D02019

GADE, N.V.

Trio in F, Op. 42 pf, vln & vlc
  Scherzo (3rd mvt)
  with W. Murdoch pf & 76978 Columbia L1133
  W.H. Squire vlc

GANNE

(L') Extase – Rêverie pf – arr. pf, vln & vlc
  with W. Murdoch pf & 75427 Columbia L1198
  W.H. Squire vlc

GARDNER

(2) Pieces, Op. 5 vln & pf
  No. 1. From the canebrake
  with E. Hobday pf 03632 Vocalion X9611
  No. 1. From the canebrake
  with G. Moore pf A 9509 Columbia 5682, 2282D, 2146M

GLUCK

Orphée et Eurydice (1762) – opera
  Dance of the blessed spirits: Lento "Mélodie" (No. 2) arr. vln & pf
  Kreisler
  with piano   Vocalion D02061

GODARD

(6) Duettini, Op. 18 2 vlns & pf
  No. 1. Souvenir de campagne
  with L. Tertis vla & F.B. 02288 Vocalion R6063
  Kiddle pf
  No. 5. Minuit
  with L. Tertis vla 02289 Vocalion R6063

GRIEG

Sonata No. 2, in G, Op. 13 vln & pf
  with W. Murdoch pf AX 934/9 Columbia 67155/7D, (set M31),
          L1661/3

GRIEG – *Continued*

Sonata No. 3, in c, Op. 45 vln & pf
  Allegro molto ed appassionata (1st mvt)
  with W. Murdoch pf   6863   Columbia L1079
  Allegro molto ed appassionata (1st mvt)
  with F. St. Leger pf   Vocalion A0113
  Allegro molto ed appassionata (1st mvt)
  with F. St. Leger pf   01947 Vocalion D02066
  Allegretto expressivo alla Romanza (2nd mvt)
  with W. Murdoch pf   6864   Columbia L1079
  Allegretto expressivo alla Romanza (2nd mvt)
  with F. St. Leger pf   Vocalion A0113
  Allegretto expressivo alla Romanza (2nd mvt)
  with F. St. Leger pf   01949 Vocalion D02066

HANDEL

(15) Sonatas, Op. 1 (?1731) fl or vln & c
  Sonata No. 12, in F vln III
  with E. Hobday pf   03630/1 Vocalion K05155
(9) Sonatas, Op. 2 (1724) 2 vlns or obs & c
  Sonata No. 8, in g: Andante (1st mvt); **Allegro** (3rd mvt)
  with L. Tertis vla & F.B. Kiddle pf Vocalion D02023
(16) Suites (1720/33) hpsi
  Suite No. 7, in g: Passacaglia (6th mvt) arr. vln & vla Halvorsen
  with L. Tertis vla   Vocalion D02019
  Suite No. 7, in g: Passacaglia (6th mvt) arr. vln & vla Halvorsen
  with L. Tertis vla   WAX 4947/8 Columbia 9351, 67784D, J7625,
                                  L2364
                                  HMV HQM1055

HARTLEY

Sérénade mélancolique vln & pf
  with E. Hobday pf   03221 Vocalion R6114

HAYDN

(31) Trios, H.XV, Nos. 1/31 pf, vln & vlc
  Trio No. 25, in G: Rondo all' ongarese (3rd mvt) H.XV, No. 25 (Op. 73, No. 2)
  with W. Murdoch pf & DR 5231–1 Decca F7821
  C. Sharpe vlc

HUBAY

(14) Scènes de la Csárda vln & pf
  No. 4. Hejre Kati, Op. 32
  with piano   75901 Columbia L1218
  No. 4. Hejre Kati, Op. 32
  with E. Hobday pf   Vocalion D02040

JUON

(2) Violonstücke, Op. 52 vln & pf
  No. 2. Arva "Valse mignonne"
  with piano   Columbia D1509

KREISLER

Caprice viennois, Op. 2 vln & pf
  with E. Hobday pf   01216 Vocalion 38019, D02002
(La) Gitana vln & pf
  with E. Hobday pf   02498 Vocalion R6086
Liebesleid vln & pf
  with G. Moore pf   CA 12847–1 Columbia DB911, OD79

KREISLER – *Continued*

Tambourin chinois, Op. 3 vln & pf
  with E. Hobday pf   01215 Vocalion 38019, D02002
Praeludium & Allegro (Pugnani) vln & pf
  with piano   75472 Columbia L1170

LALO

Symphonie espagnole, Op. 21 vln & orch.
  Allegro non troppo (1st mvt)
  with New Queen's Hall Orch. – Wood Columbia L1365
  Andante (4th mvt)
  with New Queen's Hall Orch. – Wood Columbia L1365

LECLAIR

(12) Sonatas, Op. 9 – Book IV (1738) vln & c
  Sonata No. 3, in D: Sarabande (1st mvt) arr. vln & pf Sarasate
  with piano   6638   Columbia L1018

MASCAGNI

Cavalleria Rusticana (1890) – opera
  Intermezzo orch. – arr. vln & pf
  with G. Moore pf   DR 4546–2 Decca F7533, Y5655

MASSENET

Élégie v & pf – arr. vln & pf
  with G. Moore pf   AX 3338 Columbia 9415, 02687, J7346
Élégie v & pf – arr. v, vln & pf
  with V. Rosing t & piano   Vocalion A0210
Thaïs (1894) – opera
  Méditation arr. vln & pf Marsick
  with piano   6637   Columbia L1012
  Méditation arr. vln & pf Marsick
  with E. Hobday pf   Vocalion D02040
  Méditation arr. vln & pf Marsick
  with G. Moore pf   AX 3336 Columbia 9415, 02687, J7346

MENDELSSOHN

(6) Songs without words, Op. 62 pf
  No. 6. Song without words No. 30, in A "Spring song" arr. vln, fl & hp
  with G. Ackroyd fl & W. Barker hp Odeon 0788, 143031
Trio No. 1, in d, Op. 49 pf, vln & vlc
  with E. Hobday pf & C. 02525/8 Vocalion D02044 & D02054
  Warwick–Evans vlc
Trio No. 2, in c, Op. 66 pf, vln & vlc
  with L. Tertis vla & WAX 1190/7 Columbia 67212/5D, (set M43),
  W. Murdoch pf   L1755/8
Trio No. 2, in c, Op. 66 pf, vln & vlc
  with W. Murdoch pf AR 5222/9–1 Decca K950/3
  & C. Sharpe vlc

MOLLOY

Love's old sweet song v & pf – arr. vln, fl & hp
  with G. Ackroyd fl & W. Barker hp Odeon 0805, 143039

MOZART

Serenade No. 7, in D, K250 "Haffner" orch.
  Rondo (4th mvt) arr. vln & pf Kreisler
  with E. Hobday pf   02482 Vocalion D02047

MOZART – *Continued*

Sinfonia concertante in E flat, K364 (cadenzas by Mozart) vln, vla & orch.
CAX 6824/9–2 & 6830/1–1   Columbia 68148/51D, (set
with L. Tertis vla & London   M188), DX478/81, DX8041/4,
Philharmonic Orch. – Harty   (set 148)
HMV HQM1055

Trio in E flat, K498 pf, cl & vla – arr. pf, vln & vla
^I01784/5 & ^{II}01782   Vocalion D02015^I & D02064^{II}
with F. St. Leger pf & L. Tertis vla

Trio No. 4, in E, K542 pf, vln & vlc – arr. pf, vln & vla Tertis
^I02539 & ^{II}02540/1   Vocalion D02064^I & D02091^{II}
with E. Hobday pf & L. Tertis vla

Trio No. 5, in C, K548 pf, vln & vlc – arr. pf, vln & vla Tertis
with E. Hobday pf & L.   ^I03301/2   Vocalion D02150^I & K05174
Tertis vla

Trio No. 6, in G, K564 pf, vln & vlc – arr. pf, vln & vla Tertis*
with E. Hobday pf & L. Tertis vla   Vocalion D02023

NACHÈZ

Passacaglia on a theme of G.B. Sammartini vln & pf†
with piano   WAX 1882/3   Columbia 02601, L1834

PHILLIPS

Chanson Tzigane vln & pf
with E. Hobday pf   03219   Vocalion R6114

PONCE

Estrellita (1913) v & pf – arr. vln & pf Heifetz
with G. Moore pf   A 9508   Columbia 5682, 2282D, 2146M

RIMSKY–KORSAKOV

(Le) Coq d'Or (1910) – opera
Hymn to the sun arr. vln & pf Kreisler
with E. Hobday pf   02481   Vocalion D02047

Sadko (1898) – opera
Chant hindou arr. vln & pf Kreisler
with E. Hobday pf   02480   Vocalion R6086

Chant hindou arr. vln & pf Kreisler
with G. Moore pf   DR 4538   Decca F7530

Scheherazade, Op. 35 (1888) orch.
Danse orientale arr. vln & pf Kreisler
with E. Hobday pf   Vocalion D02100

RUBBRA

Sonata No. 2, Op. 31 (1932) vln & pf
with G. Moore pf   2EA 10975/8–2   HMV C3547/8, HQM1069

SAINT–SAËNS

Trio No. 1, in F, Op. 18 pf, vln & vlc
Andante (2nd mvt)
with W. Murdoch pf &   75430   Columbia L1169
W.H. Squire vlc

SAMMONS

Bagatelle vln & pf
with piano   6639   Columbia L1018

* abridged

† Theme is from the 1st 16 measures of the Ciacona from Sammartini's 4th
Sonata of opus 3 for 2 vlns & c.

SAMMONS – *Continued*

Bourrée, Op. 12 vln & pf
with piano   WAX 1889   Columbia 9484, J7569

Canzonetta, Op. 20 vln & pf
with E. Hobday pf   03037   Vocalion R6102

Cradle song (Berceuse) Op. 6 vln & pf
with E. Hobday pf   02174   Vocalion R6020

Danse hongrois vln & pf
with E. Hobday pf   Vocalion D02038

Fantasia on Irish airs vln & pf
with piano   65421/2   Columbia D1348

Humoresque vln & pf
with E. Hobday pf   Vocalion R6014

Intermezzo vln & pf
with E. Hobday pf   Vocalion D02100

Rêve d'enfant vln & pf
with piano   65424   Columbia D1350

Theme & Variations in the olden style vln & pf
with piano   75903   Columbia L1218

SCHUBERT

(3) Marches militaires, Op. 51 (D733) pf duet
No. 1. Marche militaire No. 1, in D arr. pf, vln & vlc
with W. Murdoch pf & W.H. Squire   Columbia L1073
vlc

(6) Moments musicaux, Op. 94 (D780) (1823/7) pf
No. 3. Moment musicale No. 3, in f "Air russe" arr. vln & pf Kreisler
with E. Tuckfield pf   69374   Columbia D1420

No. 3. Moment musicale No. 3, in f "Air russe" arr. vln & pf Kreisler
with E. Hobday pf   01687   Vocalion R6005

Rosamunde von Cypern, Op. 26 (D797) (1823) – Incidental music orch.
No. 5. Entr'acte III, in B flat arr. vln & pf Brunet
with G. Moore pf   CA 12848–2   Columbia DB1008

(14) Schwanengesang, D957 (1828) v & pf
No. 4. Ständchen "Serenade" arr. vln, fl & hp
with G. Ackroyd fl & W. Barker hp   Odeon 0788, 143030

(3) Sonatinas, Op. 137 (D384, D385 & D408) vln & pf
No. 1. Sonatina No. 1, in D, D384
with W. Murdoch pf   A 6744/9   Columbia 4794/6, 01098/100,
17010/2D, (set M94)

No. 3. Sonatina No. 3, in g: Allegro moderato (4th mvt)
with K. Long pf   DR 8081–2   Decca M559
Odeon 285506

Trio No. 1, in B flat, Op. 99 (D898) pf, vln & vlc – arr. pf, vln & vla Tertis
^I02538 & 02585, ^{II}02586 X &   Vocalion D02050^I & D02060^{II}
with E. Hobday pf & L. Tertis   02587
vla

SCHUMANN

(4) Duets, Op. 34 s, t & pf
No. 1. Liebesgarten arr. pf, vln & vlc
with W. Murdoch pf   6899 (76978)   Columbia L1126
& W.H. Squire vlc

(12) Duets, Op. 85 pf – 4 hands
No. 3. Gartenmelodie arr. vln & pf Taylor
with piano   75473   Columbia L1170

(13) Kinderscenen, Op. 15 pf
No. 7. Träumerei arr. vln & pf
with G. Moore pf   DR 4541   Decca F7529

SCHÜTT

(3) Marches, Op. 54 vln & pf
  No. 3. Waltz (Allegro vivace) arr. pf, vln & vlc
  with W. Murdoch pf &   75431   Columbia L1169
  W.H. Squire vlc

SINIGAGLIA

Rapsodie piemontese, Op. 26 vln & pf
  with E. Hobday pf   Vocalion D02081

SVENDSEN

Romance in G, Op. 26 vln & orch. – arr. vln & pf Wilhelmj
  with piano   75900   Columbia L1197
Romance in G, Op. 26 vln & orch. – arr. vln & pf Wilhelmj
  with piano   WA 3897/8   Columbia 4954, D1577

TARTINI

Sonata in g "Il Trillo del Diavolo" vln & c
  Allegro assai (3rd mvt)
  with piano   75902   Columbia L1197
Sonata in g "Il Trillo del Diavolo" vln & c – arr. vln & pf Kreisler
  with W. Murdoch pf   WA 3887/90   Columbia 4818/9, 01047/8,
                            17001/2D, D1559/60, X4818/9

TCHAIKOVSKY

(12) Pieces (of moderate difficulty) Op. 40 pf
  No. 2. Chanson triste arr. vln & pf
  with E. Tuckfield pf   69672   Columbia D1420
Trio in a, Op. 50 "To the memory of a great artist" pf, vln & vlc
  Tema con variazioni (2nd mvt)
  with W. Murdoch pf &   75429   Columbia L1164
  W.H. Squire vlc

THOMÉ

Simple aveu, Op. 25 pf – arr. vln, fl & hp
  with G. Ackroyd fl & W. Barker hp   Odeon 0805, 143050
Simple aveu, Op. 25 pf – arr. vln & pf
  with E. Hobday pf   01119   Vocalion D02009
Simple aveu, Op. 25 pf – arr. vln & pf
  with G. Moore pf   DR 4543–2   Decca F7531

TURINA

Sonata No. 1, in d, Op. 51 (1929) vln & pf
  with E. Miller pf   CP 1053/6   Private Recording*

VIEUXTEMPS

Ballade & Polonaise in G, Op. 38 vln & pf
  with H.M. Grenadier   6963/4   Columbia L1165
  Guards Band – Williams

VITALI

Chaconne in g vln & c – arr. vln & pf Charlier
  with piano   Columbia 17000/1D, D1496/7

WIDOR

Serenade in B flat, Op. 10 orch. – arr. pf, vln & vlc
  with W. Murdoch pf   6898 (76975)   Columbia L1126
  & W.H. Squire vlc

* Pressed by Decca.

WIENIAWSKI

Légende, Op. 17 vln & pf or orch.
  with piano   6636   Columbia L1012

José SANCHEZ

FRANCAIX

Quintet (1934) fl, vln, vla, vlc & hp
  with C. Lardé fl, C. Lequien vla, P.   Musical Heritage Society
  Degenne vlc & M–C. Jamet hp   MHS883

IBERT

Trio (1944) vln, vlc & hp
  with P. Degenne vlc & M–C. Jamet hp Erato ERG4004
                                Musical Heritage Society
                                MHS883

JOLIVET

Chant de linos (1944) fl, vln, vla, vlc & hp
  with C. Lardé fl, C. Lequien vla, P.   Erato ERG4004
  Degenne vlc & M–C. Jamet hp   Musical Heritage Society
                                  MHS883

Pépito SANCHEZ

BAZZINI

(La) Ronde des lutins, Op. 25 vln & pf
  with F. Doreau pf   Saturn M508

MONTI

Csárdas (1904) vln & pf
  with F. Doreau pf   Saturn M509

POLIAKIN

(Le) Canari (Concert–polka) vln & pf
  with F. Doreau pf   Saturn M508

RAVEL

Introduction & Allegro (1906) hp, fl, cl, 2 vlns, vla & vlc
  with M–C. Jamet hp, C. Lardé fl, G.   Musical Heritage Society
  Deplus cl, J. Dejean vln, C. Lequien   MHS892
  vla & P. Degenne vlc

RIMSKY–KORSAKOV

(Le) Coq d'Or (1910) – opera
  Hymn to the sun arr. vln & pf Kreisler
  with F. Doreau pf   Saturn M509
(The) Tale of Tsar Saltan (1900) – opera
  Flight of the bumblebee orch. – arr. vln & pf Hartmann
  with F. Doreau pf   Saturn M509

ROUSSEL

Serenade in C, Op. 30 fl, vln, vla, vlc & hp
  with C. Lardé fl, C. Lequien vla P.   Musical Heritage Society
  Degenne vlc & M–C. Jamet hp   MHS892

SCHMITT

Suite en rocaille, Op. 84 fl, vln, vla, vlc & hp
  with C. Lardé fl, C. Lequien vla,   Musical Heritage Society
  P. Degenne vlc & M–C. Jamet hp   MHS892

Alex SANDER

FRIML

Rose Marie (1924) – operetta
Door of my dreams arr. vln & pf
with piano   A 2169   Columbia 3696
         Harmony 21H

Indian love call arr. vln & pf
with piano   A 2168   Columbia 3696
         Harmony 21H

Robert SANDFORD

GODARD

Concerto No. 1, Op. 35 "Concerto romantique" vln & orch.
Canzonetta (2nd mvt)
with piano   992   Citizen 622

MASSENET

Thaïs (1894) – opera
Méditation arr. vln & pf Marsick
with piano   993   Citizen 622

Albert SANDLER (1906–1948)

ANONYMOUS

Eili, Eili Zionist hymn – arr. pf, vln & vlc Bor
with J. Byfield pf &   CA 15393–1   Columbia DB1625
R. Kilbey vlc

Kol Nidrei Hebrew melody – arr. pf, vln & vlc Bor
with J. Byfield pf &   CA 15392–1   Columbia DB1625
R. Kilbey vlc

Londonderry air Traditional Irish ballad – arr. vln & pf Kreisler
with J. Byfield pf   Vocalion K05271

Londonderry air Traditional Irish ballad – arr. vln & pf Kreisler
with S. Torch org   CA 13586–2   Columbia DB1223, FB1594

BENATZKY

Ich muss wieder einmal in Grinzing sein (Walzerlied) v & pf – arr. pf, vln & vlc
with J. Byfield pf &   CA 14650–1   Columbia DB1428
R. Kilbey vlc

BROWN

Paradise v & pf – arr. pf, vln & vlc
with J. Byfield pf &   CA 13136–1   Columbia DB980
M. Zimbler vlc

di CAPUA

O sole mio v & pf – arr. vln & pf
with J. Byfield pf   CA 14580–2   Columbia DB1423

DELIBES

Sylvia (1876) – ballet orch.
No. 16a. Pizzicato–scherzettino (Act III) arr. pf, vln & vlc
with J. Byfield pf &   CA 14703–1   Columbia DB1567
R. Kilbey vlc

DRIGO

(Les) Millions d'Arlequin (1900) – ballet orch.
Sérénade arr. vln & pf Woodhouse
with J. Byfield pf   Broadcast 5258

Sérénade arr. vln & pf Woodhouse
with J. Byfield pf   Vocalion X9915

Sérénade arr. vln & pf Woodhouse
with J. Byfield pf   CA. 10985–3   Columbia DB563, M195

DVOŘÁK

(7) Gypsy songs, Op. 55 v & pf
No. 4. Songs my mother taught me arr. vln & pf Kreisler
with piano   Pathé-Actuelle 11144

No. 4. Songs my mother taught me arr. vln & pf Kreisler
with J. Byfield pf   Vocalion X10006

ELGAR

(2) Chansons, Op. 15 vln & pf
No. 1. Chanson de nuit arr. vln & orch.
with Palm Court   CA 19933–1   Columbia DB2203
Orch.

No. 2. Chanson du matin
with Palm Court   CA 19934–1   Columbia DB2203
Orch.

FIOCCO

Suite No. 1, in G hpsi
Allegro (10th mvt) arr. vln & pf Bent & O'Neill
with J. Byfield pf   CA 13138–1   Columbia DB1038

FISHER

(An) Old violin v & pf – arr. v, vln & pf
with O. Groves s & J.   CA 12332–1   Columbia DB737
Melville pf

GANNE

(L') Extase – Rêverie pf – arr. pf, vln & vlc
with J. Byfield pf & J.   CA 14006–2   Columbia DB1423
Samehtini vlc

HAHN

(7) Chansons grises v & pf
No. 5. L'Heure exquise arr. pf, vln & vlc
with J. Byfield pf & J.   CA 14579–2   Columbia DB1493
Samehtini vlc

HANDEL

Serse (1738) – opera
Ombra mai fu "Largo" arr. vln & org
with S. Torch org   CA 13584–3   Columbia DB1223, FB1594

d'HARDELOT

Wait v & pf – arr. vln & pf
with J. Byfield pf   Vocalion X10006

HEUBERGER

(Der) Opernball, Op. 40 (1898) – operetta
Im chambre séparée arr. vln & pf as "Midnight bells" by Kreisler
with J. Byfield pf   Vocalion X9965

HEYKENS

(The) Child & his dancing doll orch. – arr. pf, vln & vlc
  with J. Byfield pf & J.   CA 14003–1   Columbia DB1307
  Samehtini vlc

Spanish serenade orch. – arr. pf, vln & vlc
  with J. Byfield pf & J.   CA 14004–2   Columbia DB1307
  Samehtini vlc

KETÈLBEY

Algerian scene orch. – arr. vln & pf Ketèlbey
  with A.W. Ketèlbey pf   AX 4643   Columbia 9863, J3106

Phantom melody orch. – arr. vln & pf Ketèlbey
  with A.W. Ketèlbey pf   AX 4642   Columbia 9863, J3106

KING

Daybreak pf – arr. pf, vln & vlc
  with R. King pf & R.   CA 14648–1   Columbia DB1480
  Kilbey vlc

Melody at dusk pf – arr. pf, vln & vlc
  with R. King pf & R.   CA 14649–1   Columbia DB1480
  Kilbey vlc

Song of paradise pf – arr. vln & org
  with S. Torch org   CA 14561–1   Columbia DB1411

KREISLER

Rondino on a theme by Beethoven vln & pf
  with J. Byfield pf   Vocalion X9915

Rondino on a theme by Beethoven vln & pf
  with J. Byfield pf   Broadcast 5258

Schön Rosmarin vln & pf
  with J. Byfield pf   M 0130   Vocalion X9934

Tambourin chinois, Op. 3 vln & pf
  with J. Byfield pf   04462 X   Vocalion X9818

LISZT

(3) Liebesträume, G326 pf
  No. 3. Liebestraum No. 3, in A flat arr. pf, vln & vlc
  with J. Byfield pf &   CAX 7201–3   Columbia DX621
  R. Kilbey vlc

LOGAN

Pale moon (1920) v & pf – arr. vln & pf Kreisler
  with J. Byfield pf   CA 13011–3   Columbia DB1038

Pale moon (1920) v & pf – arr. vln & pf Kreisler
  with piano   Vocalion X9839

MASSENET

Thaïs (1894) – opera
  Méditation arr. vln & pf Marsick
  with J. Byfield pf   CAX 7202–3   Columbia DX621, GQX16581

MELFI

Remembrance pf – arr. pf, vln & vlc
  with J. Byfield pf &   CA 14651–1   Columbia DB1428
  R. Kilbey vlc

MOLLOY

Love's old sweet song v & pf – arr. vln & pf
  with J. Byfield pf   M 0129   Vocalion X9934

MONK

Abide with me (1861) v & pf – arr. vln & org
  with S. Torch org   CA 13585–1   Columbia 2570D, DB1153,
    FB1411

MONTI

Csárdas (1904) vln & pf
  with piano   Pathé–Actuelle 11144

Csárdas (1904) vln & pf
  with J. Byfield pf   Vocalion X9965

MOORE

(The) Last rose of summer v & pf – arr. pf, vln & vlc
  with J. Byfield pf &   CA 13137–1   Columbia DB980
  M. Zimbler vlc

MOSZKOWSKI

(6) Klavierstücke, Op. 15 pf – 4 hands
  No. 1. Serenata arr. vln & pf
  with piano   Vocalion X9856

RUBENS

I love the moon v & pf – arr. vln & pf
  with piano   Vocalion X9856

Tina – musical
  The violin song arr. vln & pf
  with J. Byfield pf   Vocalion K05271

  The violin song arr. pf, vln & vlc
  with J. Byfield pf & J.   CA 14578–1   Columbia DB1493
  Samehtini vlc

RUBINSTEIN

Bal costumé (20 pieces) Op. 103 pf duet
  No. 7. Toréador et Andalouse arr. pf, vln & vlc Bor
  with J. Byfield pf &   CA 14704–3   Columbia DB1567
  R. Kilbey vlc

SAINT–SAËNS

(Le) Carnaval des animaux (1886) small orch.
  Le cygne arr. vln & pf
  with J. Byfield pf   04461   Vocalion X9818

SANDERSON

Looking for you v & pf – arr. v, vln & pf
  with O. Groves s & J.   CA 12333   Columbia DB737
  Melville pf

Until (1918) v & pf – arr. vln & pf
  with piano   Vocalion X9839

SCHUBERT

(14) Schwanengesang, D957 (1828) v & pf
  No. 4. Ständchen "Serenade" arr. vln & pf
  with S. Ffoulkes pf   CA 10984–2   Columbia DB563

SIMONS

Marta (1931) v & pf – arr. pf, vln & vlc
  with J. Byfield pf &   CA 13137–1   Columbia DB980
  M. Zimbler vlc

SMITH

Puritan Lullaby – musical
  Always arr. vln & org
  with S. Torch org   CA 14560–4   Columbia DB1411

TOSELLI
Serenade, Op. 6 vln & pf
   with piano   Columbia M195

TOSTI
Parted v & pf – arr. vln & org
   with S. Torch org   CA 13587–3   Columbia DB1153, FB1411

WALDTEUFEL
Dolores – waltz, Op. 170 orch. – arr. vln & pf
   with S. Ffoulkes pf   WA 10986–1   Columbia 2570D, DB362,
                                          FB1537

Estudiantina – waltz, Op. 191 orch. – arr. vln & pf
   with S. Ffoulkes pf   WA 10987–1   Columbia 2570D, DB362,
                                          FB1537

Myron SANDLER

COPLAND
Sonata (1943) vln & pf
   with L. Maury pf   Crystal S631

IVES
Sonata No. 2 (1910) vln & pf
   with L. Maury pf   Crystal S631

MAURY
Sonata "In memory of the Korean War dead" (1952) vln & pf
   with L. Maury pf   Crystal S631

Georg SÁNDOR

HUBAY
(Le) Luthier de Crémone, Op. 40 (1894) – opera
   Intermezzo orch. – arr. vln & pf Hubay
   with orch.   H–68191   Homochord 4–76726

(6) Poèmes hongroise, Op. 27 vln & pf
   Poème hongrois (unid)
   with orch.   H–68190   Homochord 4–76726

Bruno SÄNGER

BRAGA
(7) Melodies (1867) v & pf
   No. 5. La serenata "Angel's serenade" arr. vln & pf
   with piano   Odeon 0–28299

FIBICH
Images, Impressions & Souvenirs, Op. 41 pf
   No. 14. Poem (from "Souvenirs", Part IV) arr. vln & pf Kubelík
   with orch.   Odeon 0–28365

GOUNOD
Ave Maria (Méditation on Bach's "Prelude No. 1, in C" from Book I of
   "Das Wohltemperirte Clavier") v & pf – arr. vln & pf
   with H. Rothmüller pf   Odeon 0–28276

HANDEL
Serse (1738) – opera
   Ombra mai fu "Largo" arr. vln & org
   with H. Rothmüller org   Odeon 0–28276

JÄRNEFELT
Berceuse in g orch. – arr. vln & orch.
   with orch.   Odeon 0–28365

NEVIN
(The) Rosary (1898) v & pf – arr. vln & pf Sliel
   with piano   Odeon 0–28299

SCHUBERT
(14) Schwanengesang, D957 (1828) v & pf
   No. 4. Ständchen "Serenade" arr. vln & pf
   with B. Seidler–   ORA 4207[1] HMV EG7005
   Winkler pf

SCHUMANN
(20) Albumblätter, Op. 124 pf
   No. 16. Schlummerlied arr. vln & pf
   with B. Seidler–   ORA 4208[2] HMV EG7005
   Winkler pf

STRAUSS, R.
(4) Lieder, Op. 27 v & pf
   No. 4. Morgen arr. v, vln & pf
   with P. Lohmann b & M. Raucheisen   Odeon 0–25562
   pf

Ferruccio SANGIORGI

VIVALDI
Concerto in B flat, P.367 (F.I, No. 59) 4 vlns, strs & c
   with P. Toso vln, R. Valpreda vln, F.   CBS 32 11 0003, 32 11 0004,
   Zampieri vln & I Solisti Veneti –   BRG72057, SBRG72057
   Scimone

Alfredo SAN–MALO (1898–   )

FERNÁNDEZ
Trio brasileiro (1924) pf, vln & vlc
   Danza
   with N. Slonimsky pf & F. Magg vlc   Columbia 70714D, (in set M437)

RIMSKY–KORSAKOV
(The) Tale of Tsar Saltan (1900) – opera
   Flight of the bumblebee orch. – arr. vln & pf Hartmann
   with piano   Victor 4163

SARASATE
(8) Danzas españolas vln & pf
   No. 3. Romanza andaluza, Op. 22, No. 1
   with piano   Victor 4163

VILLA–LOBOS
Chôros No. 1 (1920) gtr – arr. vln & vlc Villa–Lobos
   with F. Magg vlc   Columbia 70714D, (in set M437)
Chôros No. 2 (1924) fl & cl – arr. vln & vlc Villa–Lobos
   with F. Magg vlc   Columbia 70714D, (in set M437)

Pablo de SARASATE (1844–1908)

BACH

(3) Sonatas & 3 Partitas, BWV1001/6 solo vln
Partita No. 3, in E: Preludio (1st mvt) BWV1006
(unaccompanied)   4258 o   Asco A123
            Audio Archives, LP0079
            Delta TQD3035
            Gramophone & Typewriter
            37931
            HMV E183, EW3

CHOPIN

(3) Nocturnes, Op. 9 pf
No. 2. Nocturne No. 2, in E flat arr. vln & pf Sarasate
with piano   4259 o   Asco A123
            Gramophone & Typewriter
            37938

SARASATE

Caprice basque, Op. 24 vln & pf
with piano   4262 o   Asco A123
            Audio Archives LP0079
            Delta TQD3035
            Gramophone & Typewriter
            37929, 47966
            Victor 63168

(8) Danzas españolas vln & pf
No. 2. Habañera, Op. 21, No. 2
with piano   4265 o   Asco A123
            Audio Archives LP0079
            Delta TQD3035
            Gramophone & Typewriter
            37936, 47967
            Victor 52707, 62110, 17–4001

No. 6. Zapateado, Op. 23, No. 2
with piano   4266 o   Gramophone & Typewriter
            37937
            Pearl GEM101

Introduction & Caprice–Jota, Op. 41 vln & pf*
with piano   Delta TQD3035
            Gramophone & Typewriter
            37932

Introduction & Tarantelle, Op. 43 vln & pf†
with piano   4260 o   Asco A123
            Audio Archives LP0079
            Delta TQD3035
            Gramophone & Typewriter
            37933, 47965
            Historical Record Society 1071
            HMV E183, EW3
            Pearl GEM101
            Victor 62111

* Caprice–Jota only.
† Tarantelle only.

SARASATE – *Continued*

Miramar–Zortzico, Op. 42 vln & pf
with piano   4261 o   Delta TQD3035
            Gramophone & Typewriter
            37934, 47964
            Historical Record Society 1071
            Victor 52708, 62110, 17–4001

Zigeunerweisen, Op. 20 vln & pf or orch.
with piano   4263/4 o   Audio Archives LP0079
            Delta TQD3035
            Gramophone & Typewriter
            37930 & 37935, 47962/3
            HMV E329
            Pearl GEM101
            Victor 63167

A. SARKISYAN

KHAITBAYEV

Concerto vln & orch.
  2nd mvt only
  with Uzbek State Philharmonic   Mezhdunarodnaya Kniga
  Symphony Orch. – Kozlovsky   D008324

Mircea SAULESCO

ALFVÉN

Sonata in c, Op. 1 vln & pf
  with J. Solyom pf   HMV 4E061–34024

ATTERBERG

Suite No. 3, in c sharp, Op. 19, No. 1 vln, vla & orch.
  with G. Roehr vla & Swedish Radio   Discofil SLT33167
  Orch. – Westerberg

STENHAMMAR

Sonata in a, Op. 19 vln & pf
  with J. Solyom pf   HMV SCLP1058

Feruccio SCAGLIA (1921–)

VIVALDI

Concerto in a, P.28 (F.I, No. 61) 2 vlns, strs & c – arr. Casella
  with E. Malanotte vln & Collegium   Cetra LPC50045
  Musicum Italicum – Fasano   Cetra–Soria CS546

Ralph SCHAEFFER

WEBERN

(4) Pieces, Op. 7 (1910) vln & pf
  with L. Stein pf   Columbia KL5020, (in set
                     K4L232)

Adelheid SCHÄFER

TELEMANN

Concerto in F, T.II, No. 3 3 vlns, strs & c
with S. Lautenbacher vln, G. Egger   Turnabout TV34288
vln & Stuttgart Solisten

Otto SCHÄRNACK

CIMA

Sonata in d vln & c
with K. Grebe hpsi & H. Haferland   Archive APM14317, ARC3217,
bs–gamba   ARC73217, SAPM198317

Josef SCHELZ

DRDLA

Serenade No. 1, in A vln & pf
with piano   Favorite 1–24054

SARASATE

Faust Fantasia (on themes from the opera by Gounod) vln & pf or orch.
Valse
with piano   Favorite 1–25055

Herbert SCHERZ

VIVALDI

(12) Concerti, Op. 3 "L'Estro armonico" var. cbns & strs
Concerto No. 1, in D, P.146 (F.IV, No. 7) 4 vlns, vlc, strs & c
with L. Käppeli vln, B. Seeger vln, T.   Archive SAPM198469
Soh vln & Lucerne Festival Strings –
Baumgartner
Concerto No. 2, in g, P.326 (F.IV, No. 8) 2 vlns, strs & c
with W. Prystawski vln, K. Heitz vlc   Archive SAPM198469
& Lucerne Festival Strings –
Baumgartner
Concerto No. 5, in A, P.212 (F.I, No. 175) 2 vlns, strs & c
with W. Prystawski vln & Lucerne   Archive 2705 002, SAPM198470
Festival Strings – Baumgartner
Concerto No. 7, in F, P.249 (F.IV, No. 9) 4 vlns, strs & c
with R. Barnert vln, W. Prystawski   Archive SAPM198470
vln, H. Soh vln & Lucerne Festival
Strings – Baumgartner
Concerto No. 10, in b, P.148 (F.IV, No. 10) 4 vlns, strs & c
with R. Barnert vln, W. Prystawski   Archive SAPM198471
vln, T. Soh vln, K. Heitz vlc &
Lucerne Festival Strings –
Baumgartner
Concerto No. 11, in d, P.250 (F.IV, No. 11) 2 vlns, vlc, strs & c
with W. Prystawski vln, K. Heitz vlc   Archive SAPM198471
& Lucerne Festival Strings –
Baumgartner

Benjamin SCHERZER

KREISLER

Caprice viennois, Op. 2 vln & pf
with piano   Apex 541

LUZ

(The) Four Horsemen of the Apocalypse – musical
I have a rendezvous with you arr. vln & pf
with piano   Starr (Gennett) 540

NEVIN

Mighty lak' a rose (1901) v & pf – arr. vln & pf
with piano   Starr (Gennett) 540

ROMBERG

Blossom Time (1921) – operetta
Song of love arr. vln & orch.
with orch.   Starr (Gennett) 591

SCHUBERT

(14) Schwanengesang, D957 (1828) v & pf
No. 4. Ständchen "Serenade" arr. vln & pf
with piano   Apex 541

Manfred SCHERZER (1933–   )

BRAHMS

Sonata No. 2, in A, Op. 100 vln & pf
with A. Webersinke pf   Eterna 820516

Trio in E flat, Op. 40 hrn, pf & vln
with A. Webersinke pf & P. Damm   Eterna 820516
hrn

Gian Piero SCHIAVINA

HINDEMITH

(6) Sonatas, Op. 11
Sonata No. 2, in D (1920) vln & pf
with D. Brunetta pf   Cetra LPU0058
(2) Sonatas, Op. 31 (1924) solo vln
Sonata No. 2
(unaccompanied)   Cetra LPU0058
Sonata No. 3, in C (1940) vln & pf
with D. Brunetta pf   Cetra LPU0058

E. SCHILLING

VIVALDI

(12) Concerti, Op. 3 "L'Estro armonico" var. cbns & strs
Concerto No. 1, in D, P.146 (F.IV, No. 7) 4 vlns, vlc, strs & c
with S. Gavrilov vln, K.A. Hermann   Cetra LPU006
vln, S. Karolyi vln & Frankfurt
Chamber Orch. – Goehr
Concerto No. 4, in e, P.97 (F.I, No. 174) 4 vlns, strs & c
with S. Gavrilov vln, K.A. Hermann   Cetra LPU007
vln, S. Karolyi vln & Frankfurt
Chamber Orch. – Goehr
Concerto No. 7, in F, P.249 (F.IV, No. 9) 4 vlns, strs & c
with S. Gavrilov vln, K.A. Hermann   Cetra LPU007
vln, S. Karolyi vln & Frankfurt
Chamber Orch. – Goehr

VIVALDI – *Continued*

Concerto No. 10, in b, P.148 (F.IV, No. 10) 4 vlns, strs & c
with S. Gavrilov vln, K.A. Hermann   Cetra LPU006
vln, S. Karolyi vln & Frankfurt
Chamber Orch. – Goehr

Marie Louise SCHIØLER

ANONYMOUS

Värmelands Pris Swedish folkmelody – arr. vln & pf
with piano   HMV AL86, X287981

DRIGO

(Les) Millions d'Arlequin (1900) – ballet orch.
Sérénade arr. vln & pf Auer
with piano   HMV AL86, X287980

Klaus SCHLUPP

BACH

Concerto in C, BWV1064 3 clavs, strs & c – arr. 3 vlns, strs & c "in D"
with G.F. Hendel vln, H. Bünte vln & Nonesuch H1057, H71057
Saar Chamber Orch. – Ristenpart

Sonata in C, BWV1037 2 vlns & c
with G.F. Hendel vln, R. Christensen Christophorus CGLP75841/2,
hpsi & B. Hindrichs vlc   SDGLP75843/4
                                      Erato STU70189
                                      Musical Heritage Society
                                      MHS657

BUXTEHUDE

(7) Sonatas, Op. 2 (1696) vln & c
Sonata No. 2, in D
with R. Mommisch gamba, R.   Nonesuch H1119, H71119
Ristenpart hpsi & B. Hindrichs vlc

LECLAIR

(12) Sonatas, Op. 2 – Book II (1728) vln & c
Sonata No. 8, in D
with T. Kempen vla, R. Ristenpart   Nonesuch H1119, H71119
hpsi & B. Hindrichs vlc

VIVALDI

Concerto in D, P.189 (F.I, No. 41) 2 vlns, strs & c
with G.F. Hendel vln & Saar Chamber   Elite Special SMLP5011
Orch. – Ristenpart   Nonesuch H9, H79, H1022,
                                      H71022

Concerto in F, P.278 (F.I, No. 34) 3 vlns, strs & c
with G.F. Hendel vln, H. Bünte vln & Elite Special SMLP5011
Saar Chamber Orch. – Ristenpart   Nonesuch H1022, H71022

Gustav SCHMAHL (1929–   )

HINDEMITH

(2) Sonatas, Op. 31 (1924) solo vln
Sonata No. 1
(unaccompanied)   Eterna 825936

KHACHATURIAN

Concerto in D (1940) (cadenza by D. Oistrakh) vln & orch.
with Leipzig Gewandhaus Orch. –   Eterna 820385
Pflüger   Heliodor 89783

REGER

(8) Preludes & Fugues, Op. 117 solo vln
No. 7. Prelude & Fugue No. 7, in a
(unaccompanied)   Eterna 825936

ROSENFELD

Concerto (1963) vln & orch.
with Dresden Philharmonic Symphony Eterna 820501
Orch. – Förster

STRAVINSKY

Duo concertante (1932) vln & pf
with G. Kootz pf   Eterna 825936

Alexander SCHMIDT

BARNBY

Sweet & low mixed voices – arr. vln & pf
with M. Eaver pf   Victor 22160

BRAHMS

(5) Lieder, Op. 49 v & pf
No. 4. Wiegenlied "Cradle song" arr. vln & pf
with M. Eaver pf   Victor 22160

(14) Volkskinderlieder (1858) v & pf
No. 4. Sandmännchen arr. vln & pf
with M. Eaver pf   Victor 22160

CHOPIN

(3) Waltzes, Op. 64 pf
No. 1. Waltz No. 6, in D flat "Minute waltz" arr. vln & pf
with M. Eaver pf   Victor 20614

FLIES

Wiegenlied (Schlafe, mein Prinzchen) v & pf – arr. vln & pf
with M. Eaver pf   Victor 22160

FRANZ

O Holy God, we praise Thy name! v & pf – arr. v, vln & pf
with J. McCormack t &   A 29870–2 American Gramophone Society
piano   AGSA46

FRIEDBERG

Old French gavotte vln & pf
with M. Eaver pf   Victor 24528

HANDEL

Serse (1738) – opera
Ombra mai fu "Largo" arr. vln & pf
with M. Eaver pf   Victor 24529

KOŽELUH

(La) Ritrovata Figlia de Ottone, Op. 39 – ballet orch.
No. 22. Gavotte (Act IV) arr. vln & pf Kramer
with M. Eaver pf   Victor 22167

KREISLER

Aubade provençale (L. Couperin) vln & pf
with M. Eaver pf   Victor 24531

LEYBACH

Nocturne No. 5, in A flat, Op. 52 pf – arr. vln & pf
with M. Eaver pf   Victor 22328

MOZART

(6) Ländler, K606 orch.
  No. 1. Ländler No. 1, in B flat arr. vln & pf
  with M. Eaver pf   Victor 24528
  No. 3. Ländler No. 3, in B flat arr. vln & pf
  with M. Eaver pf   Victor 24528

OGAREW

Caprice in a, Op. 51, No. 2 vln & pf
with M. Eaver pf   Victor 20614

RAFF

(6) Pieces, Op. 85 vln & pf
  No. 3. Cavatina in D
  with M. Eaver pf   Victor 22328

ROUSSEAU

Berceuse (Hush, my baby) v & pf – arr. vln & pf
with M. Eaver pf   Victor 22160

SCHUBERT, François

(12) Bagatelles, Op. 13 vln & pf
  No. 9. L'abeille
  with M. Eaver pf   Victor 20614

SCHUBERT, Franz

(2) Lieder, Op. 98 (D498) v & pf
  No. 2. Wiegenlied (Schlafe, holder süsser Knabe) arr. vln & pf
  with M. Eaver pf   Victor 22160

TCHAIKOVSKY

Quartet No. 1, in D, Op. 11 2 vlns, vla & vlc
  Andante cantabile (2nd mvt) arr. vln & pf Kreisler
  with M. Eaver pf   Victor 24529

WIENIAWSKI

Souvenir de Moscou, Op. 6 vln & pf or orch.
with M. Eaver pf   Victor 24531

Otto SCHMIDT

BACH

Concerto in d, BWV1043 2 vlns, strs & c
with A. Heinemann vln & Classics   Classics Club X1008
Club Chamber Orch. – Friedmann

Jaro SCHMIED

BOCCHERINI

(6) Quintets, Op. 13 2 vlns, vla & 2 vlcs
  No. 5. Quintet No. 5, in E: Minuet (3rd mvt) "Bull" arr. vln & pf
  Kreisler
  with piano   Columbia FPX158

BRAHMS

(5) Lieder, Op. 49 v & pf
  No. 4. Wiegenlied "Cradle song" arr. vln & pf Elman
  with piano   Columbia FPX158
(16) Waltzes, Op. 39 pf duet
  No. 15. Waltz No. 15, in A flat arr. vln & pf "in A" Hochstein
  with piano   Columbia FPX158

CHOPIN

(3) Nocturnes, Op. 9 pf
  No. 2. Nocturne No. 2, in E flat arr. vln & pf Sarasate
  with piano   Columbia FPX158

DRDLA

Souvenir vln & pf
with H. Nordberg pf   OVH 567-1   HMV GA5073

DVOŘÁK

(8) Humoresques, Op. 101 pf
  No. 7. Humoresque No. 7, in G flat arr. vln & pf "in G" Kreisler
  with H. Nordberg pf   OVH 568-3   HMV GA5073
  No. 7. Humoresque No. 7, in G flat arr. vln & pf "in G" Kreisler
  with piano   Columbia FPX158

EISENSTEIN

Romance vln & orch.
with Great Vienna Broadcasting Orch.   Concert Classics CC4151
– Varady

FALLA

(La) Vida Breve (1913) – opera
  Danza española orch. – arr. vln & pf Kreisler
  with piano   Columbia FPX158

GOUNOD

Ave Maria (Méditation on Bach's "Prelude No. 1, in C" from Book I of "Das Wohltemperirte Clavier") v & pf – arr. vln & pf
  with piano   Columbia FPX 158

KREISLER

Schön Rosmarin vln & pf
with ensemble   Telefunken M5119
Schön Rosmarin vln & pf
with piano   Columbia FPX158

MASSENET

Thaïs (1894) – opera
  Méditation arr. vln & pf Marsick
  with piano   Columbia FPX158

POLIAKIN

(Le) Canari (Concert–polka) vln & pf
with ensemble   Telefunken M5119

SAINT–SAËNS

Introduction & Rondo Capriccioso, Op. 28 vln & orch.
with orch.   Vienöla LPR1031

SARASATE

Zigeunerweisen, Op. 20 vln & pf or orch.
with orch.   Vienöla LPR1031

SCHUMANN

(3) Kinderscenen, Op. 15 pf
No. 7. Träumerei arr. vln & pf
with piano   Columbia FPX158

SIBELIUS

Kuolema, Op. 44 – Incidental music orch.
Valse triste arr. vln & pf Franko
with piano   Columbia FPX158

TOSELLI

Serenade, Op. 6 vln & pf
with piano   Columbia FPX158

WIENIAWSKI

Mazurka in a, Op. 3 "Kujawiak" vln & pf
with orch.   Vienöla LPR1031

Alexander SCHMULLER (1880–1933)

BRAHMS

(21) Hungarian Dances pf duet
Hungarian dance No. 3, in F arr. vln & pf Joachim
with piano   3106 Polydor 12123
Hungarian dance No. 13, in D arr. vln & pf Joachim
with piano   3108 Polydor 12124
Hungarian dance No. 19, in b arr. vln & pf Joachim
with piano   3108 Polydor 12123

HUBAY

(4) Scènes de la Csárda vln & pf
No. 4. Hejre Kati, Op. 32
with piano   3107 Polydor 12123, 12124

Hansheinz SCHNEEBERGER (1926–   )

BACH

(6) Brandenburg Concerti, BWV1046/51 (1721) strs & c
Brandenburg Concerto No. 1, in F, BWV1046 vln, 3 obs, bsn, 2 hrns, strs & c
with M. Clement ob, K. Kolbinger   Archive 104971, SAPM198438
bsn, H. Bilgram hpsi & Munich Bach
Orch. – Richter

Brandenburg Concerto No. 2, in F, BWV1047 tpt, fl, ob, vln, strs & c
with P. Thibaud tpt, H–M. Linde rec,   Archive 104972, SAPM198439
M. Clement ob, H. Bilgram hpsi &
Munich Bach Orch. – Richter

Brandenburg Concerto No. 3, in G, BWV1048 3 vlns, 3 vlas, 3 vlcs & cbs
with H. Bilgram hpsi & Munich Bach   Archive 104971, SAPM198438
Orch. – Richter

Brandenburg Concerto No. 4, in G, BWV1049 vln, 2 fls, strs & c
with H–M. Linde rec, G. Höller rec,   Archive 104972, SAPM198439
H. Bilgram hpsi & Munich Bach Orch.
– Richter

Brandenburg Concerto No. 5, in D, BWV1050 clav, fl, vln, strs & c
with K. Richter hpsi, A. Nicolet fl &   Archive 104972, SAPM198439
Munich Bach Orch. – Richter

BACH – *Continued*

(6) Sonatas, BWV1014/9 vln & clav
Sonata No. 1, in b, BWV1014
with E. Müller hpsi   Bärenreiter–Musicaphon BM25
                                   R901
                                   Nonesuch (in set HB73017)

Sonata No. 2, in A, BWV1015
with E. Müller hpsi   Bärenreiter–Musicaphon BM25
                                   R901
                                   Nonesuch (in set HB73017)

Sonata No. 3, in E, BWV1016
with E. Müller hpsi   Bärenreiter–Musicaphon BM25
                                   R902
                                   Nonesuch (in set HB73017)

Sonata No. 4, in c, BWV1017
with E. Müller hpsi   Bärenreiter–Musicaphon BM25
                                   R902
                                   Nonesuch (in set HB73017)

Sonata No. 5, in f, BWV1018
with E. Müller hpsi   Bärenreiter–Musicaphon BM25
                                   R903
                                   Nonesuch (in set HB73017)

Sonata No. 6, in G, BWV1019
with E. Müller hpsi   Bärenreiter–Musicaphon BM25
                                   R903
                                   Nonesuch (in set HB73017)

BEETHOVEN

(2) Trios, Op. 70 pf, vln & vlc
No. 1. Trio No. 4, in D "Ghost"
with K. Engel pf & G. Fallot vlc   Victor LSC3139

BURKHARD

Concerto, Op. 69 (1943) vln & orch.
with Lausanne Chamber Orch. –   Communauté de travail pour la
Desarzens   diffusion de la musique suisse
                                   CTS42

GAGNEBIN

Trio in D (1957) fl, vln & pf
with G. Aurèle fl & W. Lang pf   Decca LX3148
                                   London LD9224

HONEGGER

Petite Suite (1936) 2 fls, cl, sax, vln & pf – arr. fl, vln & pf
with G–A. Nicolet fl & P. Souvairan   Decca LXT2849
pf   London LL893

HUBER

Quartet "Waldlieder" pf, vln, vla & vlc
with F–J. Hirt pf, W. Kägi vla & R.   Communauté de travail pour la
Looser vlc   diffusion de la musique suisse
                                   CT64/6

MENDELSSOHN

Trio No. 1, in d, Op. 49 pf, vln & vlc
with K. Engel pf & G. Fallot vlc   Victor LSC3139

MOESCHINGER

Sonata No. 1, Op. 62 vln & pf
with P. Souvairan pf   Decca LXT2849
                                   London LL893

Alexander SCHNEIDER (1908–)

BACH

(6) Brandenburg Concerti, BWV1046/51 (1721) orch.
Brandenburg Concerto No. 1, in F, BWV1046 vln, 3 obs, bsn, 2 hrns, strs & c
with J. Mack ob, R. Richards ob, P. Christ ob, M. Bloom hrn, R. Johnson hrn, D. MacCourt bsn, R. Serkin pf & Marlboro Festival Orch. – Casals — CBS BRG72396, SBRG72396 Columbia ML6183, (in set M2L331), MS6783, (in set M2S731), MS7376, (in set D3S816)

Brandenburg Concerto No. 2, in F, BWV1047 tpt, fl, ob, vln, strs & c
with J. Wummer fl, M. Tabuteau ob & Prades Festival Orch. – Casals — Columbia ML4345

Brandenburg Concerto No. 2, in F, BWV1047 tpt, fl, ob, vln, strs & c
with R. Nagel tpt, O. Gulbransen fl, J. Mack ob, L. Parnas vlc, P. Serkin hpsi & Marlboro Festival Orch. – Casals — CBS BRG72396, SBRG72396 Columbia ML6183, (in set M2L331), MS6783, (in set M2S731), MS7376, (in set D3S816)

Brandenburg Concerto No. 4, in G, BWV1049 vln, 2 fls, strs & c
with O. Gulbransen fl, N. Dalley fl, R. Serkin pf & Marlboro Festival Orch. – Casals — CBS BRG72397, SBRG72397 Columbia ML6184, (in set M2L331), MS6783, (in set M2S731), MS7376/7, (in set D3S816)

Brandenburg Concerto No. 5, in D, BWV1050 clav, fl, vln, strs & c
with R. Serkin pf, O. Gulbransen fl & Marlboro Festival Orch. – Casals — CBS BRG72397, SBRG72397 Columbia ML6184, (in set M2L331), MS6784, (in set M2S731), MS7377, (in set D3S816)

Concerto in d, BWV1043 2 vlns, strs & c
with I. Stern vln & Prades Festival Orch. – Casals — Columbia FCX155, ML4351, QCX155

Concerto in a, BWV1044 clav, fl, vln, strs & c
with M. Horszowski pf, J. Wummer fl & Prades Festival Orch. – Casals — Columbia CX1113, FCX326, ML4352 Philips L01511L

(3) Sonatas & 3 Partitas, BWV1001/6 solo vln
Sonata No. 1, in g, BWV1001*
(unaccompanied) — Classic CL6285 Mercury MG10017, (in set MGL1)

Partita No. 1, in b, BWV1002†
(unaccompanied) — Classic CL6001, CL6287 Mercury MG10018, (in set MGL1)

Sonata No. 2, in a, BWV1003§
(unaccompanied) — Classic CL6285 Mercury MG10017, (in set MGL1)

* Siciliano or 3rd mvt is also on Mercury EP1–5059 & MEP14514.
† Bourrée or 7th mvt & Sarabande or 5th mvt is also on Mercury EP1–5061 & MEP14514; Courante or 3rd mvt is also on Mercury EP1–5059 & MEP14519.
§ Andante or 3rd mvt is also on Mercury EP1–5061 & MEP14514.

Partita No. 2, in d, BWV1004*
(unaccompanied) — Classic CL6002, CL6288 Mercury MG10019, (in set MGL1)

Sonata No. 3, in C, BWV1005
(unaccompanied) — Classic CL6289 Mercury MG10020, (in set MGL1)

Partita No. 3, in E, BWV1006†
(unaccompanied) — Classic CL6003, CL6289 Mercury MG10020, (in set MGL1)

(6) Sonatas, BWV1014/9 vln & clav
Sonata No. 1, in b, BWV1014
with R. Kirkpatrick hpsi — Columbia 72400/3D, (in set MM719), ML2109

Sonata No. 2, in A, BWV1015
with R. Kirkpatrick hpsi — Columbia 72404/6D, (in set MM719), ML2109

Sonata No. 3, in E, BWV1016
with R. Kirkpatrick hpsi — Columbia 72400/5D, (in set MM719), ML2110

Sonata No. 4, in c, BWV1017
with R. Kirkpatrick hpsi — Columbia 72407/11D, (in set MM719), ML2110

Sonata No. 5, in f, BWV1018
with R. Kirkpatrick hpsi — Columbia 72411/3D, (in set MM719), ML2111

Sonata No. 6, in G, BWV1019
with R. Kirkpatrick hpsi — Columbia 72047/50D, (in set MM719), ML2111

Sonata in c, BWV1079 fl, vln & c
with J. Wummer fl & L. Mannes pf — Columbia ML4347

BEETHOVEN

Serenade in D, Op. 25 fl, vln & vla
with J. Wummer fl & L. Mannes pf — Columbia ML2124

(3) Trios, Op. 1 pf, vln & vlc
No. 2. Trio No. 2, in G
with E. Istomin pf & P. Casals vlc — Columbia ML4573, (in set SL170)

Trio in B flat, Op. 11 cl, vlc & pf – arr. vln, vlc & pf
with P. Casals vlc & E. Istomin pf — Columbia ML4571, (in set SL170) Philips L01458L

(2) Trios, Op. 70 pf, vln & vlc
No. 2. Trio No. 5, in E flat
with E. Istomin pf & P. Casals vlc — Columbia ML4571, (in set SL170) Philips L01458L

Trio No. 6, in B flat, Op. 97 "Archduke" pf, vln & vlc
with E. Istomin pf & P. Casals vlc — Columbia ML4574, (in set SL169) Philips G03601L, GBL5639

* Chaconne or 5th mvt is also on Mercury EP1–5060 & MEP14518.
† Preludio or 1st mvt & Gavotte or 3rd mvt is also on Mercury EP1–5059 & MEP14519.

BOCCHERINI

(6) Quintets, Op. 13 2 vlns, vla & 2 vlcs
No. 5. Quintet No. 5, in E "Bull"
with F. Galimir vln, M. Tree vla, D.
Soyer vlc & L. Harrell vlc

I Classici della Musica Classica
SXVA4183
Philips GL5861, SGL5861
Vanguard VRS1147, VSD71147

(6) Quintets, Op. 57 (1799) pf, 2 vlns, vla & vlc
No. 6. Quintet No. 6, in C "La Ritirata di Madrid" gtr, 2 vlns, vla & vlc
with A. Diaz gtr, F. Galimir vln, M.
Tree vla & D. Soyer vlc

I Classici della Musica Classica
SXVA4183
Philips GL5861, SGL5861
Vanguard VRS1147, VSD71147

BRAHMS

Quartet No. 1, in g, Op. 25 pf, vln, vla & vlc
with M. Horszowski pf, M. Katims vla
& F. Miller vlc

Classic C2116/9
Mercury MG10011

Quartet No. 3, in c, Op. 60 pf, vln, vla & vlc
with M. Horszowski pf, M. Katims vla
& F. Miller vlc

Classic C2123/6, CL6031
Mercury (set DM9), MG10010

Quintet No. 2, in G, Op. 111 2 vlns, 2 vlas & vlc
with I. Stern vln, M. Katims vla, M.
Thomas vla & P. Tortelier vlc

Columbia ML4701, (in set
SL185), ML4711, (in set SL182)
Philips A01282L, ABL3184,
L01294L

Sextet No. 1, in B flat, Op. 18 2 vlns, 2 vlas & 2 vlcs
with I. Stern vln, M. Katims vla, M.
Thomas vla, P. Casals vlc & M. Foley
vlc

CBS BRG72324
Columbia ML4703, (in set
SL185), ML4713, (in set SL182)
Fontana 409118AE
Philips A01170L, ABL3085,
G03599L, GBL5623

Trio in E flat, Op. 40 hrn, vln & pf
with M. Jones hrn & M. Horszowski
pf

Columbia ML4892
Philips 699054CL, A01176L,
ABL3121

DVOŘÁK

Quintet in A, Op. 81 pf, 2 vlns, vla & vlc
with R. Serkin pf, F. Galimir vln, M.
Tree vla & D. Soyer vlc

Amadeo 66008
Philips GL5863, SGL5863
Vanguard SRV288SD, VRS1148,
VSD71148

FALLA

Concerto in D (1926) hpsi, fl, ob, cl, vln & vlc
with R. Kirkpatrick hpsi, M. Miller
ob, S. Baron fl, H. Freeman cl & B.
Greenhouse vlc

Classic C2026/7, CL6030
Mercury (set DM5), MG10012

HANDEL

(12) Concerti grossi, Op. 6 2 vlns, vlc & strs
Concerto No. 1, in G
with F. Galimir vln, C. McCracken
vlc, R. Conant hpsi & chamber orch. –
Schneider

Victor (in set LSC6172)

Concerto grosso No. 2, in F
with F. Galimir vln, C. McCracken
vlc, R. Conant hpsi & chamber orch. –
Schneider

Victor (in set LSC6172)

HANDEL – *Continued*

Concerto grosso No. 3, in e
with F. Galimir vln, C. McCracken
vlc, R. Conant hpsi & chamber orch. –
Schneider

Victor (in set LSC6172)

Concerto grosso No. 4, in a
with F. Galimir vln, C. McCracken
vlc, R. Conant hpsi & chamber orch. –
Schneider

Victor (in set LSC6172)

Concerto grosso No. 5, in D
with F. Galimir vln, C. McCracken
vlc, R. Conant hpsi & chamber orch. –
Schneider

Victor (in set LSC6172)

Concerto grosso No. 6, in g
with F. Galimir vln, C. McCracken
vlc, R. Conant hpsi & chamber orch. –
Schneider

Victor (in set LSC6172)

Concerto grosso No. 7, in B flat
with F. Galimir vln, C. McCracken
vlc, R. Conant hpsi & chamber orch. –
Schneider

Victor (in set LSC6172)

Concerto grosso No. 8, in c
with F. Galimir vln, C. McCracken
vlc, R. Conant hpsi & chamber orch. –
Schneider

Victor (in set LSC6172)

Concerto grosso No. 9, in F
with F. Galimir vln, C. McCracken
vlc, R. Conant hpsi & chamber orch. –
Schneider

Victor (in set LSC6172)

Concerto grosso No. 10, in d
with F. Galimir vln, C. McCracken
vlc, R. Conant hpsi & chamber orch. –
Schneider

Victor (in set LSC6172)

Concerto grosso No. 11, in A
with F. Galimir vln, C. McCracken
vlc, R. Conant hpsi & chamber orch. –
Schneider

Victor (in set LSC6172)

Concerto grosso No. 12, in b
with F. Galimir vln, C. McCracken
vlc, R. Conant hpsi & chamber orch. –
Schneider

Victor (in set LSC6172)

(15) Sonatas, Op. 1 (?1731) fl or vln & c
Sonata No. 3, in A vln I
with R. Kirkpatrick hpsi & F. Miller
vlc

Columbia ML2149, ML4787

Sonata No. 10, in g vln II
with R. Kirkpatrick hpsi & F. Miller
vlc

Columbia ML2149, ML4787

Sonata No. 12, in F vln III
with R. Kirkpatrick hpsi & F. Miller
vlc

Columbia ML2150, ML4787

Sonata No. 13, in D vln IV
with R. Kirkpatrick hpsi & F. Miller
vlc

Columbia ML2150, ML4787

Sonata No. 14, in A vln V
with R. Kirkpatrick hpsi & F. Miller
vlc

Columbia ML2151, ML4787

Sonata No. 15, in E vln VI
with R. Kirkpatrick hpsi & F. Miller
vlc

Columbia ML2151, ML4787

MENDELSSOHN

Octet in E flat, Op. 20 4 vlns, 2 vlas & 2 vlcs
with J. Laredo vln, A. Steinhardt vln,   CBS BRG72473, SBRG72473
J. Dalley vln, M. Tree vla, S. Rhodes   Columbia ML6248, MS6848
vla, L. Parnas vlc & D. Soyer vlc

Trio No. 1, in d, Op. 49 pf, vln & vlc
with M. Horszowski pf & P. Casals vlc   CBS BRG72035
   Columbia KL5726

MOZART

Concerto No. 4, in D, K218 (cadenzas by Joachim) vln & orch.
with Dumbarton Oaks Chamber Orch.   Erato LDE3001
– Schneider   Haydn Society HSLP1040
   Nixa HLP1040

Divertimento No. 11, in D, K251 2 hrns, ob & strs
with M. Tabuteau ob &   KM 3/8   Classic C2029/31
soloists & Dumbarton Oaks Chamber   Mercury 10008/10, (set DM4),
Orch. – Schneider   MG10002

Quartet No. 1, in D, K285 fl, vln, vla & vlc
playing vla, with I. Stern vln, J–P.   Columbia M30233
Rampal fl & L. Rose vlc

Quartet No. 1, in g, K478 pf, vln, vla & vlc
with P. Serkin pf, M. Tree vla & D.   Philips GL5862, SGL5862
Soyer vlc   Vanguard VRS1140, VSD71140

Quartet No. 2, in G, K258a fl, vln, vla & vlc
playing vla, with I. Stern vln, J–P.   Columbia M30233
Rampal fl & L. Rose vlc

Quartet No. 2, in E flat, K493 pf, vln, vla & vlc – arr. pf, 2 vlns & vla
with I. Stern vln, M. Katims vla & E.   Columbia ML5237
Istomin pf

Quartet No. 2, in E flat, K493 pf, vln, vla & vlc
with P. Serkin pf, M. Tree vla & D.   Philips GL5862, SGL5862
Soyer vlc   Vanguard VRS1140, VSD71140

Quartet No. 3, in C, K285b fl, vln, vla & vlc
playing vla, with I. Stern vln, J–P.   Columbia M30233
Rampal fl & L. Rose vlc

Quartet No. 4, in A, K298 fl, vln, vla & vlc
playing vla, with I. Stern vln, J–P.   Columbia M30233
Rampal fl & L. Rose vlc

Quintet in A, K581 cl, 2 vlns, vla & vlc
with H. Wright cl, I. Cohen vln, S.   Columbia MS7447
Rhodes vla & L. Parnas vlc

Sonata No. 17, in C, K296 vln & pf
with R.   XCO 35464/7–1   Columbia 71860/1D, (in set
Kirkpatrick hpsi   MM650), C16006/9, (in set
   D176), ML4113/4, (in set
   SL152)

Sonata No. 19, in E flat, K302 vln & pf
with R. Kirkpatrick hpsi   Columbia 72778/81D, (in set
   MM811), ML4113/4, (in set
   SL152)

Sonata No. 22, in A, K305 vln & pf
with R. Kirkpatrick hpsi   Columbia ML4617

Sonata No. 23, in D, K306 vln & pf
with R. Kirkpatrick hpsi   Columbia 72778/81D, (in set
   MM811), ML4113/4, (in set
   SL152)

Sonata No. 24, in F, K376 vln & pf
with R. Kirkpatrick hpsi   Columbia ML4617

MOZART – *Continued*

Sonata No. 26, in B flat, K378 vln & pf
   XCO 35468/71–1   Columbia 71862/3D, (in set
with R. Kirkpatrick hpsi   MM650), C16010/1, (in set
   D176), ML4113/4, (in set
   SL152)

Sonata No. 27, in G, K379 vln & pf
with R.   XCO 35472/5–1   Columbia 71864/5D, (in set
Kirkpatrick hpsi   MM650), C16006/9, (in set
   D176), ML4113/4, (in set
   SL152)

Sonata No. 34, in A, K526 vln & pf
with R. Kirkpatrick hpsi   Columbia ML4617

PISTON

Sonatina (1945) vln & hpsi
with R. Kirkpatrick hpsi   Columbia ML4495

SCHUBERT

Quintet in A, Op. 114 (D667) "Trout" pf, vln, vla, vlc & cbs
with P. Serkin pf, M. Tree vla, D.   Philips GL5867, SGL5867
Soyer vlc & J. Levine cbs   Vanguard VRS1145, VSD71145

Quintet in C, Op. 163 (D956) 2 vlns, vla & 2 vlcs
with I. Stern vln, M. Katims vla, P.   Columbia ML4714, (in set
Casals vlc & P. Tortelier vlc   SL183)
   Philips A01188L, ABL3100,
   G03600L, GBL5624

Rondo brillante in b, Op. 70 (D895) vln & pf
with P. Serkin pf   Vanguard VRS1146, VSD71146,
   VSL11015

Sonata in A, Op. 162 (D574) "Duo" vln & pf
with P. Serkin pf   Vanguard VRS1146, VSD71146,
   VSL11015

(3) Sonatinas, Op. 137 (D384, D385 & D408) vln & pf
No. 1. Sonatina No. 1, in D, D384
with P. Serkin pf   Vanguard VRS1128, VSD71128
No. 2. Sonatina No. 2, in a, D385
with M. Horszowski pf   Columbia ML5237
No. 2. Sonatina No. 2, in a, D385
with P. Serkin pf   Vanguard VRS1128, VSD71128
No. 3. Sonatina No. 3, in g, D408
with P. Serkin pf   Vanguard VRS1128, VSD71128

Trio No. 1, in B flat, Op. 99 (D898) pf, vln & vlc
with E. Istomin pf & P. Casals vlc   Columbia ML4715, (in set
   SL185)
   Philips A01645R, ABR4059,
   G03589L, GBL5611

Trio No. 2, in E flat, Op. 100 (D929) pf, vln & vlc
with M. Horszowski pf & P. Casals vlc   Columbia ML4716, (in set
   SL183)
   Philips A01107L, ABL3009,
   G03581L, GBL5602

SCHUMANN

Quartet in E flat, Op. 47 pf, vln, vla & vlc
with M. Horszowski pf, M. Katims vla   Columbia ML4892
& F. Miller vlc   Philips 699054CL, A01176L,
   ABL3121

SCHUMANN – *Continued*

Quintet in E flat, Op. 44 2 vlns, vla, vlc & pf
with I. Stern vln, M. Thomas vla, P.   Columbia ML4701, (in set
Tortelier vlc & M. Hess pf   SL185), ML4711, (in set SL182)
Philips A01282L, ABL3184

Trio No. 1, in d, Op. 63 pf, vln & vlc
with M. Horszowski pf & P. Casals vlc   Columbia ML4708, (in set
SL185), ML4718, (in set SL184)
Philips L01369L

STRAVINSKY

(L') **Histoire du Soldat** (1918) narrators & tpt, cbs, tbn, cl, vln, bsn & pcn
with R. Nagel tpt, J. Levine cbs, E.   Columbia ML4964
Price tbn, D. Oppenheim cl, L.   Philips A01193L, ABL3065
Glickman bsn, A. Howard pcn, cond.
Igor Stravinsky

TELEMANN

Cantata No. 19 (Gott will Mensch und sterblich werden)
with R. Oberlin c–t, D. Williams hpsi   Decca DL9414, DL79414
& B. Meuser gamba

VILLA–LOBOS

Trio (1945) vln, vla & vlc
with M. Katims vla & F. Miller vlc   Columbia ML2214

VIVALDI

(12) Concerti, Op. 3 "L'Estro armonico" var. cbns & strs
Concerto No. 11, in d, P.250 (F.IV, No. 11) 2 vlns, vlc, strs & c
with E. Bachmann vln,   KM 1/2 R   Keynote K2003
R. Kirkpatrick hpsi, B. Greenhouse vlc   Mercury MG10002
& Dumbarton Oaks Orch. – Schneider

Walther SCHNEIDERHAN (1901–)

BACH, C.P.E.

Sonata in B flat, W161, No. 2 2 vlns & c or fl, vln & hpsi
with C. Wanausek fl & H. Schnabel pf   Society of Participating Artists
SPA37

BACH, J.C.

Sinfonia concertante in A, T. P. 284 (1770) vln, vlc & orch.
with N. Hubner vlc, G. Leonhardt   Columbia ML4869
hpsi & Vienna Symphony Orch. –   Philips 839310EGY, A00675R,
Sacher   ABR4029

BACH, J.S.

Concerto No. 1, in a, BWV1041 vln, strs & c
with Vienna Baroque Orch. – Atzmon   Concert Hall SMSA2552

Concerto No. 2, in E, BWV1042 vln, strs & c
with Vienna Baroque Orch. – Atzmon   Concert Hall SMSA2552

Matthäus–Passion, BWV244 (1729)
No. 47. Erbarme dich, mein Gott
with A. Heynis a & Vienna Symphony   Philips A00460L, ABL3410
Orch. – Gillesberger

Sonata in C, BWV1037 2 vlns & c
with G. Swoboda vln, F. Holetschek   Ducretet–Thomson LPG8717
hpsi & S. Benesch vlc   Westminster WL5036

BEETHOVEN

Romance No. 1, in G, Op. 40 vln & pf
with Vienna Symphony Orch.   Fontana 494000EE

Romance No. 2, in F, Op. 50 vln & pf
with Vienna Symphony Orch.   Fontana 494000EE

(3) Sonatas, Op. 12 vln & pf
No. 2. Sonata No. 2, in A
with H. Berg pf   Concerteum CR225
Remington R199–95

(3) Sonatas, Op. 30 vln & pf
No. 2. Sonata No. 7, in c
with H. Berg pf   Concerteum TCR270
Remington RLP149–35

Sonata No. 9, in A, Op. 47 "Kreutzer" vln & pf
with E. Berg pf   Merit 200–21
Plymouth P12–21

BOCCHERINI

(6) Trios, Op. 34 2 vlns & vlc
No. 1. Trio No. 1, in f
with G. Swoboda vln & S. Benesch vlc   Westminster W9012, WL5046,
XWN18050

No. 2. Trio No. 2, in G
with G. Swoboda vln & S. Benesch vlc   Westminster W9012, WL5042,
XWN18050

No. 3. Trio No. 3, in E flat
with G. Swoboda vln & S. Benesch vlc   Westminster W9013, WL5046,
XWN18051

No. 4. Trio No. 4, in D
with G. Swoboda vln & S. Benesch vlc   Westminster W9013, WL5042,
XWN18051

No. 5. Trio No. 5, in C
with G. Swoboda vln & S. Benesch vlc   Westminster W9014, WL5042,
XWN18052

No. 6. Trio No. 6, in E
with G. Swoboda vln & S. Benesch vlc   Westminster W9014, WL5046,
XWN18052

BRAHMS

Concerto in D, Op. 77 vln & orch.
with Bamberg Symphony Orch. – van   Fidelio ATL4128
Remoortel   Super Majestic BBH1170
Vox PL16010, VP410

HANDEL

(7) Sonatas, Op. 5 (1739) 2 vlns & c
Sonata No. 6, in F
with G. Swoboda vln, F. Holetschek   Ducretet–Thomson LPG8717
hpsi & S. Benesch vlc   Westminster WL5036

HAYDN, F.J.

Trio in E flat, H.IV, No. 5 (1767) hrn, vln & vlc
with F. Koch hrn & N. Hübner vlc   Haydn Society HSLP1044
Nixa HLP1044

HAYDN, M.

Concerto in B flat (1760) vln & orch.
with J. Nebois hpsi & Vienna Orch.   Unicorn UNLP1018
Society – Adler

MAHLER

Symphony No. 3, in d (1895) soloists, cho & orch.
  with H. Rössl–Majdan a, E. Körner   Harmonia Mundi HM30501/2
  hrn, Women's Chorus of the Vienna   Society of Participating Artists
  State Opera & Vienna State   SPA70/1
  Philharmonic Orch. – Adler

MENDELSSOHN

Concerto in e, Op. 64 vln & orch.
  with Austrian Symphony Orch. –   Concerteum TCR259
  Scherman   Festival CFR30
     Merit 1–14
     Plymouth P12–78
     Remington RLP149–14

Concerto in e, Op. 64 vln & orch.
  with Bamberg Symphony Orch. – van   Great Musicians TGM35
  Remoortel

MOZART

Quartet No. 1, in D, K285 fl, vln, vla & vlc
  with C. Wanausek fl, J. de Sordi vla &   Philips ABE10017
  V. Gorlich vlc

Sinfonia concertante in E flat, K364 vln, vla & orch.
  with P. Angerer vla & Vienna Festival   World Record Club SC8
  Orch. – Litschauer

RIMSKY–KORSAKOV

Scheherazade, Op. 35 (1888) orch.
  with Vienna Symphony Orch. –   Fontana 200062WGL,
  Fournet   697007EL, SCFL110

SCHOENBERG

Pierrot Lunaire, Op. 21 (1912) speaker & inst ens
  with I. Steingruber s, B. Reichert vlc,   Philips 838201AY, A04301L
  H. Graf pf, R. Eichler cl & bs–cl, L.   Vanguard VRS1082, VSD2108
  Pfersmann fl & pic – cond.
  Golschmann

TARTINI

Concerto in F, D67 vln & orch.
  with Vienna State Philharmonic Orch.   Record Society RS51
  – Adler   Society of Participating Artists
     SPA46

Concerto in a, D115 (C76) vln & orch.
  with Vienna State Philharmonic Orch.   Record Society RS51
  – Adler   Society of Participating Artists
     SPA46

TELEMANN

Sonata No. 1, in a "Sonata Polonaise" 2 vlns & c
  with G. Swoboda vln, F. Holetschek   Ducretet–Thomson LPG8717
  hpsi & S. Benesch vlc   Westminster WL5036,
     XWN18031

Sonata No. 3, in E 2 vlns & c
  with G. Swoboda vln, F. Holetschek   Ducretet–Thomson LPG8717
  hpsi & S. Benesch vlc   Westminster WL5036,
     XWN18031

Wolfgang SCHNEIDERHAN (1915–)

d'AMBROSIO

Serenade, Op. 4 vln & pf
  with O. Schulhof pf   WHAX 11–3   Columbia 5124M, DX477

BACH

(6) Brandenburg Concerti, BWV1046/51 (1721) strs & c
Brandenburg Concerto No. 1, in F, BWV1046 vln, 3 obs, bsn, 2 hrns, strs
& c
  with H. Winschermann ob, C. Esposito   Archive APM14142, ARC3156,
  hrn, G. Schlund hrn & Lucerne   SAPM198142
  Festival Strings – Baumgartner

Cantata No. 202 (Weichet nur, betrübte Schatten) BWV202
  with I. Seefried s, A. Lardrot ob, C.   Deutsche Grammophon
  Starck vlc & Lucerne Festival Orch. –   LPM18606, SLPM138086
  Baumgartner

Concerto No. 1, in a, BWV1041 vln, strs & c
  with Zürich   05264/5 LKN   Archive EPA37025, PV2462
  Collegium Orch. – Sacher

Concerto No. 1, in a, BWV1041 vln, strs & c
  with Lucerne Festival Orch. –   Archive APM14086, ARC3099
  Baumgartner

Concerto No. 2, in E, BWV1042 vln, strs & c
  with Lucerne Festival Orch. –   Archive APM14086, ARC3099
  Baumgartner   Deutsche Grammophon
     LPM18460

Concerto in d, BWV1043 2 vlns, strs & c
  with R. Baumgartner vln & Lucerne   Archive APM14086, ARC3099
  Festival Strings – Baumgartner

(3) Sonatas & 3 Partitas, BWV1001/6 solo vln
Partita No. 2, in d: Chaconne (5th mvt) BWV1004
     CAX 10070–1, 10071–2, 10072–1   Columbia LVX41/2
  (unaccompanied)   & 10073–2

Partita No. 2, in d, BWV1004*
  (unaccompanied)   Archive AP13029

(6) Sonatas, BWV1014/9 vln & clav
Sonata No. 2, in A, BWV1015
  with S. Richter pf   Archive SAPM199008

BARTÓK

(6) Rumanian folk dances (1915) pf – arr. vln & pf Székely
  with A. Hirsch pf   Deutsche Grammophon
     EPL30334

Sonata No. 2 (1922) vln & pf
  with C. Seemann pf   Decca DL9980
     Deutsche Grammophon
     LPM18400

BEETHOVEN

Concerto in C, Op. 56 "Triple" pf, vln, vlc & orch.
  with G. Anda pf, P. Fournier vlc &   Deutsche Grammophon
  Berlin Radio Symphony Orch. –   LPEM19236, SLPEM136236
  Fricsay

* Chaconne or 5th mvt is also on Archive EPA37051 & Heliodor H25030
  & HS25030.

BEETHOVEN – *Continued*

Concerto in D, Op. 61 (cadenzas by Joachim) vln & orch.
with Berlin Philharmonic Orch. – van Kempen   Decca DL9784
Deutsche Grammophon 72366/8, LPM18099
Eterna 820005
Heliodor 88024

Concerto in D, Op. 61 cadenzas by Beethoven – arr. vln Schneiderhan vln & orch.
with Berlin Philharmonic Orch. – Jochum   Deutsche Grammophon LPM18824, SLPM138824, SLPM138999

Quartet No. 11, in f, Op. 95 2 vlns, vla & vlc
with O. Strasser   CHAX 464/7–1   Columbia LFX9333/4, LX8727/8
vln, K. Moravetz vla & R. Krotschak vlc

Romance No. 1, in G, Op. 40 vln & orch.
with Bayerische State Opera Orch., Munich – Heger   Electrola SHZE281

Romance No. 2, in F, Op. 50 vln & orch.
with Bayerische State Opera Orch., Munich – Heger   Electrola SHZE281

(3) Sonatas, Op. 12 vln & pf
No. 1. Sonata No. 1, in D
with W. Kempff pf   Deutsche Grammophon LPM18083

No. 1. Sonata No. 1, in D
with C. Seemann pf   Deutsche Grammophon LPM18621, SLPM138121

No. 2. Sonata No. 2, in A
with W. Kempff pf   Deutsche Grammophon LPM18083

No. 2. Sonata No. 2, in A
with C. Seemann pf   Deutsche Grammophon LPM18621, SLPM138121

No. 3. Sonata No. 3, in E flat
with W. Kempff pf   Deutsche Grammophon LPM18138

No. 3. Sonata No. 3, in E flat
with C. Seemann pf   Deutsche Grammophon LPM18622, SLPM138122

Sonata No. 4, in a, Op. 23 vln & pf
with W. Kempff pf   Deutsche Grammophon LPM18138

Sonata No. 4, in a, Op. 23 vln & pf
with C. Seemann pf   Deutsche Grammophon LPM18622, SLPM138122

Sonata No. 5, in F, Op. 24 "Spring" vln & pf
with W. Kempff pf   Deutsche Grammophon 72312/3, LPE17164, LPM18082

Sonata No. 5, in F, Op. 24 "Spring" vln & pf
with C. Seemann pf   Deutsche Grammophon 135148, LPM18620, SLPM138128

(3) Sonatas, Op. 30 vln & pf
No. 1. Sonata No. 6, in A
with W. Kempff pf   Deutsche Grammophon LPM18082

BEETHOVEN – *Continued*

No. 1. Sonata No. 6, in A
with C. Seemann pf   Deutsche Grammophon LPM18622, SLPM138122

No. 2. Sonata No. 7, in c
   CHAX 362/4–1, 365–2, 366–1 &   Columbia LX1190/3
with F. Wührer pf   373/4–1

No. 2. Sonata No. 7, in c
with W. Kempff pf   Deutsche Grammophon 72353/4, LPM18209

No. 2. Sonata No. 7, in c
with C. Seemann pf   Deutsche Grammophon LPM18623, SLPM138123

No. 3. Sonata No. 8, in G
with W. Kempff pf   Deutsche Grammophon LPM18144

No. 3. Sonata No. 8, in G
with C. Seemann pf   Deutsche Grammophon LPM18621, SLPM138121

Sonata No. 9, in A, Op. 47 "Kreutzer" vln & pf
with W. Kempff pf   Deutsche Grammophon LPM18092

Sonata No. 9, in A, Op. 47 "Kreutzer" vln & pf
with C. Seemann pf   Deutsche Grammophon 135148, LPM18620, SLPM138120

Sonata No. 10, in G, Op. 96 vln & pf
with W. Kempff pf   Deutsche Grammophon 72376/7, LPM18209

Sonata No. 10, in G, Op. 96 vln & pf
with C. Seemann pf   Deutsche Grammophon LPM18623, SLPM138123

BRAHMS

Concerto in D, Op. 77 (cadenza by Winkler) vln & orch.
   CRX 115[3], 116[2], 117[1], 118[2], 119   Columbia LWX331/5
with Saxon State   [1] & 120/3–2
Symphony Orch. – Böhm

Concerto in D, Op. 77 (cadenza by Winkler) vln & orch.
with Berlin Philharmonic Orch. – Fricsay   Deutsche Grammophon LPM18132

Concerto in D, Op. 77 (cadenza by Winkler) vln & orch.
with Berlin Philharmonic Orch. – van Kempen   Heliodor 89519

Concerto in a, Op. 102 "Double" vln, vlc & orch.
with J. Starker vlc & Berlin Radio Symphony Orch. – Fricsay   Deutsche Grammophon LPE17237, LPM18753, SLEP133237, SLPM138753

Concerto in a, Op. 102 "Double" vln, vlc & orch.
with J. Starker vlc & Berlin Radio Symphony Orch. – Fricsay   Deutsche Grammophon LPM39126, SLPM139126

(21) Hungarian Dances pf duet
Hungarian dance No. 5, in f sharp arr. vln & pf "in g" Joachim
with O. Schulhof pf   WHA 488–1   Columbia DB1084

Hungarian dance No. 5, in f sharp arr. vln & pf "in g" Joachim
with A. Hirsch pf   Deutsche Grammophon EPL30336

Sonata No. 1, in G, Op. 78 vln & pf
with F. Wührer pf   Deutsche Grammophon 72175/6, LP16027

BRAHMS – *Continued*

Sonata No. 1, in G, Op. 78 vln & pf
    with C. Seemann pf   Deutsche Grammophon
                                    LPM18696, SLPM138696

Sonata No. 2, in A, Op. 100 vln & pf
    with C. Seemann pf   Deutsche Grammophon
                                    LPM18633, SLPM138633

Sonata No. 3, in d, Op. 108 vln & pf
    with F. Wührer pf   Deutsche Grammophon
                                    LPM18144

Sonata No. 3, in d, Op. 108 vln & pf
    with C. Seemann pf   Deutsche Grammophon
                                    LPM18696, SLPM138696

Sonata (1853) "Frei aber Einsam" vln & pf
Allegro (Scherzo) in c (3rd mvt) "Sonatensatz"
    with C. Seemann pf   Deutsche Grammophon
                                    LPM18633, SLPM138633

BRANDL

(Der) Liebe Augustin – operetta
Du alter Stefansturm arr. vln & pf as "The old refrain" by Kreisler
    with E. Werba pf   Electrola SHZE281

BRUCH

Concerto No. 1, in g, Op. 26 vln & orch.
    with Bamberg   03723/5 LWN   Deutsche Grammophon
    Symphony Orch. – Leitner   72232/3S, LPE17028,
                                    LPEM19124, LPM18036
                                    Heliodor 2458 024

CHOPIN

(3) Nocturnes, Op. 9 pf
No. 2. Nocturne No. 2, in E flat arr. vln & pf Sarasate
    with A. Hirsch pf   Deutsche Grammophon
                                    EPL30337

DESPLANES

Intrada (Adagio) vln & c – arr. vln & pf Nachèz
    with H. Priegnitz pf   3914 KN   Deutsche Grammophon 32047,
                                      36084

DVOŘÁK

Sonatina in G, Op. 100 vln & pf
    with W. Klien pf   Deutsche Grammophon
                                    LPM39163, SLPM139163

ELGAR

(La) Capricieuse, Op. 17 vln & pf
    with A. Hirsch pf   Deutsche Grammophon
                                    EPL30336

FALLA

(La) Vida Breve (1913) – opera
Danza española orch. – arr. vln & pf Kreisler
    with A. Hirsch pf   Deutsche Grammophon
                                    EPL30337

FIBICH

Images, Impressions & Souvenirs, Op. 41 pf
No. 14. Poem (from "Souvenirs", Part IV) arr. vln & pf Kubelík
    with O. Schulhof pf   CHA 485–2   Columbia DB1058, DW4171,
                                      GN108

FRANCK

Sonata in A (1886) vln & pf
    with C. Seemann pf   Deutsche Grammophon
                                    LPM18633, SLPM138633

HENZE

Concerto (1948) vln & orch.
    with Bavarian Radio Symphony Orch.   Deutsche Grammophon
    – Henze   SLPM139382

HINDEMITH

Sonata No. 3, in C (1940) vln & pf
    with C. Seemann pf   Decca DL9980
                                    Deutsche Grammophon
                                    LPM18400

KLASEN

Berceuse, Op. 18 pf – arr. vln & pf
    with W. Klasen pf   HMV X2718

Mazurka, Op. 14 pf – arr. vln & pf
    with W. Klasen pf   HMV X2718

KREISLER

Caprice viennois, Op. 2 vln & pf
    with A. Hirsch pf   Deutsche Grammophon
                                    EPL30335

Caprice viennois, Op. 2 vln & pf
    with E. Werba pf   Electrola SHZE281

Liebesfreud vln & pf
    with A. Hirsch pf   Deutsche Grammophon
                                    EPL30335

Liebesleid vln & pf
    with A. Hirsch pf   Deutsche Grammophon
                                    EPL30335

Liebesleid vln & pf
    with E. Werba pf   Electrola SHZE281

Schön Rosmarin vln & pf
    with E. Werba pf   Electrola SHZE281

MARTIN

Concerto (1951) vln & orch.
    with Suisse Romande Orch. –   Decca LX3146
    Ansermet   London LD9213

Concerto (1951) vln & orch.
    with Luxembourg Radio Symphony   Candide CE31055
    Orch. – Martin

MARTINŪ

(7) Études rhythmiques (1931) vln & pf
No. 4. Étude rhythmique No. 4
    with A. Hirsch pf   Deutsche Grammophon
                                    EPL30337

MENDELSSOHN

Concerto in e, Op. 64 vln & orch.
    with Berlin Radio Symphony Orch. –   Deutsche Grammophon
    Fricsay   LPE17085, LPEM19124
                                    Heliodor 2458 024

MOZART

Adagio in E, K261 vln & orch.
with Berlin Philharmonic Orch. – Schneiderhan
Deutsche Grammophon SLPM139350/2, SLPM139464

Concerto No. 1, in B flat, K207 (cadenzas by Schneiderhan) vln & orch.
with Berlin Philharmonic Orch. – Schneiderhan
Deutsche Grammophon SLPM139350/2, SLPM139464

Concerto No. 2, in D, K211 (cadenzas by Schneiderhan) vln & orch.
with Berlin Philharmonic Orch. – Schneiderhan
Deutsche Grammophon SLPM139350/2, SLPM139445

Concerto No. 3, in G, K216 (cadenzas by Schneiderhan) vln & orch.
with Berlin Philharmonic Orch. – Schneiderhan
Deutsche Grammophon SLPM139350/2, SLPM139445

Concerto No. 4, in D, K218 (cadenzas by Schneiderhan) vln & orch.
with Berlin Philharmonic Orch. – Rosbaud
Decca DL9857
Deutsche Grammophon LPM18314

Concerto No. 4, in D, K218 (cadenzas by Schneiderhan) vln & orch.
with Berlin Philharmonic Orch. – Schmidt–Isserstedt
Deutsche Grammophon LPE17255, LPM18678, SLPM138678

Concerto No. 4, in D, K218 (cadenzas by Schneiderhan) vln & orch.
with Berlin Philharmonic Orch. – Schneiderhan
Deutsche Grammophon SLPM139350/2

Concerto No. 5, in A, K219 "Turkish" (cadenzas by Joachim) vln & orch.
with Vienna Symphony Orch. – Leitner
Decca DL9857
Deutsche Grammophon LP16060

Concerto No. 5, in A, K219 "Turkish" (cadenzas by Joachim) vln & orch.
with Hamburg Radio Symphony Orch. – Schmidt–Isserstedt
Deutsche Grammophon LPM18678, SLPM138678

Concerto No. 5, in A, K219 "Turkish" (cadenzas by Schneiderhan) vln & orch.
with Berlin Philharmonic Orch. – Schneiderhan
Deutsche Grammophon SLPM139350/2

Idomeneo, re di Creta, K366 (1781) – opera
Non temer, amato bene
with I. Seefried s & Vienna Symphony Orch. – Leitner
Deutsche Grammophon EPL30045

(Il) Re Pastore, K208 (1775) – opera
No. 10. L'amerò sarò costante
with I. Seefried s & Vienna Symphony Orch. – Leitner
Decca DL9768
Deutsche Grammophon 72351, EPL30045

Rondo in B flat, K269 vln & orch.
with Berlin Philharmonic Orch. – Schneiderhan
Deutsche Grammophon SLPM139350/2, SLPM139464

Rondo in C, K373 vln & orch.
with Berlin Philharmonic Orch. – Schneiderhan
Deutsche Grammophon SLPM139350/2, SLPM139464

Sonata No. 17, in C, K296 vln & pf
with C. Seemann pf
Deutsche Grammophon LPM18307

Sonata No. 18, in G, K301 vln & pf
with C. Seemann pf
Decca DL9886
Deutsche Grammophon LPM18323

Sonata No. 21, in e, K304 vln & pf
with C. Seemann pf
Decca DL9886
Deutsche Grammophon LP16092, LPM18323

MOZART – *Continued*

Sonata No. 22, in A, K305 vln & pf
with C. Seemann pf
Deutsche Grammophon LPM18316

Sonata No. 24, in F, K376 vln & pf
with C. Seemann pf
Deutsche Grammophon LPM18316

Sonata No. 25, in F, K377 vln & pf
with C. Seemann pf
Decca DL9862
Deutsche Grammophon LPM18250

Sonata No. 26, in B flat, K378 vln & pf
with C. Seemann pf
Deutsche Grammophon LPM18260

Sonata No. 27, in G, K379 vln & pf
with C. Seemann pf
Deutsche Grammophon LPM18260

Sonata No. 28, in E flat, K380 vln & pf
with C. Seemann pf
Decca DL9886
Deutsche Grammophon LP16092, LPM18323

Sonata No. 32, in B flat, K454 vln & pf
with C. Seemann pf
Decca DL9862
Deutsche Grammophon LPM18250

Sonata No. 33, in E flat, K481 vln & pf
with C. Seemann pf
Deutsche Grammophon LPM18307

Sonata No. 34, in A, K526 vln & pf
with C. Seemann pf
Deutsche Grammophon LPM18250

MUSSORGSKY

Hebrew song (1867) v & pf – arr. vln & pf Hartmann
with H. von Nordberg pf
CHA 1054   Columbia LB88, LV12

Hebrew song (1867) v & pf – arr. vln & pf Hartmann
with A. Hirsch pf
Deutsche Grammophon EPL30337

Sorochintsy Fair (1911/23) – opera
Gopak (Act III) orch. – arr. vln & pf Dushkin
with A. Hirsch pf
Deutsche Grammophon EPL30337

NASH

Minuet in D vln & pf
with O. Schulhof pf
WHA 488–1   Columbia DB1084

Minuet in D vln & pf
with H. Priegnitz pf
3917 LKN   Deutsche Grammophon 32047, 36084

PROKOFIEV

Sonata No. 2, in D, Op. 94bis vln & pf
with C. Seemann pf
Deutsche Grammophon LPM18794, SLPM138794

REGER

(3) Pieces, Op. 79d vln & pf
No. 1. Wiegenlied in G
with H. von   CHA 1055–1   Columbia LB88, LV12
Nordberg pf
No. 1. Wiegenlied in G
with A. Hirsch pf   Deutsche Grammophon
EPL30336

(60) Schlichte Weisen – 6 Books, Op. 76 v & pf
No. 52. Maria–Wiegenlied arr. v, vln & pf
with I. Seefried s & E. Werba pf   Deutsche Grammophon 62893

RIES

Suite No. 3, in G, Op. 34 vln & pf
No. 5. Perpetuum mobile
with O. Schulhof pf   WHAX 12–1   Columbia 5124M, DX477
No. 5. Perpetuum mobile
with A. Hirsch pf   Deutsche Grammophon
EPL30336

SAINT–SAËNS

(Le) Carnaval des animaux (1886) small orch.
Le cygne arr. vln & pf
with O. Schulhof pf   WHA 487–1   Columbia DB1058, DW4171,
GN108

Le cygne arr. vln & pf
with H. Priegnitz pf   3917 LKN   Deutsche Grammophon 32047,
36084

Le cygne arr. vln & pf
with A. Hirsch pf   Deutsche Grammophon
EPL30335

SCHUBERT, François

(12) Bagatelles, Op. 13 vln & pf
No. 9. L'abeille
with A. Hirsch pf   Deutsche Grammophon
EPL30336

SCHUBERT, Franz

Fantasia in C, Op. 159 (D934) vln & pf
with W. Klien pf   Deutsche Grammophon
LPM39164, SLPM139164

Octet in F, Op. 166 (D803) cl, hrn, bsn, 2 vlns, vla, vlc & cbs
with L. Wlach cl, G. van Freiberg hrn,   Columbia LWX364/9
K. Öhlberger bsn, O. Strasser vln, K.
Moravetz vla, R. Krotschak vlc & O.
Rühm cbs

Rondo brillante in b, Op. 70 (D895) vln & pf
with W. Klien pf   Deutsche Grammophon
LPM39164, SLPM139164

Sonata in A, Op. 162 (D574) "Duo" vln & pf
with C. Seemann pf   Deutsche Grammophon
LPM18241

Sonata in A, Op. 162 (D574) "Duo" vln & pf
with W. Klien pf   Deutsche Grammophon
LPM39164, SLPM139164

(3) Sonatinas, Op. 137 (D384, D385 & D408) vln & pf
No. 1. Sonatina No. 1, in D, D384
with C. Seemann pf   Deutsche Grammophon
LP16085, LPM18502

SCHUBERT, Franz – *Continued*

No. 1. Sonatina No. 1, in D, D384
with W. Klien pf   Deutsche Grammophon
LPM39101, SLPM139101

No. 2. Sonatina No. 2, in a, D385
with C. Seemann pf   Deutsche Grammophon
LPM18241

No. 2. Sonatina No. 2, in a, D385
with W. Klien pf   Deutsche Grammophon
LPM39101, SLPM139101

No. 3. Sonatina No. 3, in g, D408
with C. Seemann pf   Deutsche Grammophon
LP16085, LPM18502

No. 3. Sonatina No. 3, in g, D408
with W. Klien pf   Deutsche Grammophon
LPM39101, SLPM139101

SCHUMANN

Sonata No. 1, in a, Op. 105 vln & pf
Allegretto (2nd mvt)
with F. Wührer pf   CHAX 382–1   Columbia LX1193
Sonata No. 1, in a, Op. 105 vln & pf
with C. Seemann pf   Deutsche Grammophon
EPL30206, LPM18502

STRAUSS, R.

Sonata in E flat, Op. 18 vln & pf
with W. Klien pf   Deutsche Grammophon
LPM39163, SLPM139163

STRAVINSKY

Concerto in D (1931) vln & orch.
with Berlin Philharmonic Orch. –   Deutsche Grammophon 135155,
Ančerl   LPM18794, SLPM138794
Duo concertante (1932) vln & pf
with C. Seemann pf   Decca DL9980
Deutsche Grammophon
LPM18400

Mavra (1922) – opera
Russian maiden's song (Parasha's aria) arr. vln & pf Dushkin &
Stravinsky
with A. Hirsch pf   Deutsche Grammophon
EPL30334

Pétrouchka (1911) – ballet orch.
Danse russe arr. vln & pf Dushkin & Stravinsky
with A. Hirsch pf   Deutsche Grammophon
EPL30334

TARTINI

Concerto in d, D45 (C61) vln & orch.
with Lucerne Festival Orch. –   Archive APM14115, ARC3117
Baumgartner

VIVALDI

(12) Concerti, Op. 3 "L'Estro armonico" var. cbns & strs
Concerto No. 11, in d, P.250 (F.IV, No. 11) 2 vlns, vlc, strs & c
with R. Baumgartner vln, E.   Archive APM14097, ARC3116,
Kaufmann hpsi, C. Starck vlc &   EPA37199, SEPA181199
Lucerne Festival Strings –   Deutsche Grammophon 135024
Baumgartner

VIVALDI – *Continued*

(12) Concerti, Op. 8 (1725) "Il Cimento dell' Armonia e dell' Invenzione" (Nos. 1/4: Le quattro Stagioni) vln & strs
Concerto No. 1, in E, F.I, No. 22 "La Primavera"
with Lucerne Festival Strings –
Baumgartner
Archive AP13076, ARC3141,
ARC73141, SAP195008
Deutsche Grammophon 135024

Concerto No. 2, in B flat, F.I, No. 23 "L'Estate"
with Lucerne Festival Strings –
Baumgartner
Archive AP13076, ARC3141,
ARC73141, SAP195008
Deutsche Grammophon 135024

Concerto No. 3, in F, F.I, No. 24 "L'Autunno"
with Lucerne Festival Strings –
Baumgartner
Archive AP13076, ARC3141,
ARC73141, SAP195008
Deutsche Grammophon 135024

Concerto No. 4, in f, F.I, No. 25 "L'Inverno"
with Lucerne Festival Strings –
Baumgartner
Archive AP13076, ARC3141,
ARC73141, SAP195008
Deutsche Grammophon 135024

WOLF

Italienische Serenade in G 2 vlns, vla & vlc
with O. Strasser   CHAX 389/90–1   Columbia LVX45, LX1168
vln, K. Moravetz vla & R. Krotschak
vlc

Dina SCHNEIDERMANN

NENOV

Sonata vln & pf
with I. Zhekov pf   Balkanton 439

STOYANOV

Sonata vln & pf
with I. Zhekov pf   Balkanton 439

Michael SCHNITZER

HAYDN

Sinfonia concertante in B flat, Op. 84 (H.I, No. 105) vln, vlc, ob, bsn & orch.
with W. Herzer vlc, J. Schaeftlein ob,   Westminster WST17100,
L. Cermak bsn & Vienna Radio Orch.   XWN19100
– Scherchen

MOZART

Serenade No. 5, in D, K204 orch.
with Wiener Solisten – Böttcher
Amadeo AVRS6404
Philips 906404ASY

Alice SCHOENFELD

HONEGGER

Sonatina (1932) vln & vlc
with E. Schoenfeld vlc
Everest SDBR3243

RAVEL

Sonata (1922) vln & vlc
with E. Schoenfeld vlc
Everest SDBR3243

VILLA–LOBOS

Chôros No. 2 (1924) fl & cl – arr. vln & vlc Villa–Lobos
with E. Schoenfeld vlc   Everest SDBR3243

WAGNER, J.F.

Concert piece (1966) vln & vlc
with E. Schoenfeld vlc   Orion ORS7036
Preludes & Toccata (1964) hp, vln & vlc
with S. McDonald hp & E. Schoenfeld   Orion ORS7036
vlc

Alejandro SCHOLZ

RIMSKY–KORSAKOV

(The) Tale of Tsar Saltan (1900) – opera
Flight of the bumblebee orch. – arr. vln & pf Hartmann
with D. Colacelli pf   Odeon 66030

TCHAIKOVSKY

(6) Pieces, Op. 51 pf
No. 6. Valse sentimentale arr. vln & pf Franko
with D. Colacelli pf   Odeon 66030

WILLIAMS

En la sierra, Op. 32 pf
No. 4. El Rancho abandonado arr. vln & pf
with D. Colacelli pf   Odeon 66030

Helga SCHÖN

HANDEL

(6) Concerti grossi, Op. 3 (1759) orch.
Concerto grosso No. 3, in G
with H. Töttcher ob & Bach Orch.,   Archive AP13044
Berlin – Gorvin

LEO

Concerto in D 4 vlns & strs
with D. Vorholz vln, E. Früh vln, G.   Archive APM14340, ARC3240,
Terebesi vln & Berlin Chamber Music   ARC73240, SAPM198340
Ensemble – Lange

Rudolf SCHÖNE

WAGNER

Albumblatt in C (1861) pf – arr. vln & orch.
with Munich   2RA 4501² □   HMV DB5573
Philharmonic Orch. – Kabasta
(5) Gedichte "Wesendonck–Lieder" v & pf
No. 5. Träume arr. vln & orch.
with Munich   2RA 4500² □   HMV DB5573
Philharmonic Orch. – Kabasta

Joseph SCHRÖCKSNADEL

MOZART

Serenade No. 3, in D, K185 "Andretter" orch.
with Mozarteum Orch., Salzburg   Eurodisc 72273KK

Jaap SCHRÖDER (1925–   )

ANDRIESSEN

(3) Inventions vln & vlc
with A. Blylsma vlc   Radio Nederland RN510

BEETHOVEN

(6) Minuets, WoO.9 2 vlns & cbs
Minuet No. 1, in E flat
with J. Holtmann vln & A. Woodrow   Saba MPS13001
cbs

Minuet No. 2, in G
with J. Holtmann vln & A. Woodrow   Saba MPS13001
cbs

Minuet No. 3, in C
with J. Holtmann vln & A. Woodrow   Saba MPS13001
cbs

Minuet No. 4, in F
with J. Holtmann vln & A. Woodrow   Saba MPS13001
cbs

Minuet No. 5, in D
with J. Holtmann vln & A. Woodrow   Saba MPS13001
cbs

Minuet No. 6, in G
with J. Holtmann vln & A. Woodrow   Saba MPS13001
cbs

HAYDN

Concerto in F, H.XVIII, No. 6 (1765) vln, hpsi & orch.
with G. Leonhardt hpsi & Amsterdam   Telefunken AWT9429,
Chamber Orch. – Rieu   SAWT9429
Concerto No. 3, in A, H.VIIa, No. 3 "Melk" vln & orch.
with Concerto Amsterdam   Telefunken SAWT9529

HAYDN, M.

Concerto in B flat (1760) vln & orch.
with Concerto Amsterdam   Musik Production Schwarzwerk
                               (BASF) CRO837

LOCATELLI

(12) Concerti, Op. 3 (1733) "L'Arte del Violino" vln & strs
Concerto No. 1, in D
with Concerto Amsterdam – Schröder   Telefunken AWT9499,
                                   SAWT9499

PISENDEL

Concerto in D, vln, 2 obs, strs & c
with Concerto Amsterdam   Musik Production Schwarzwerk
                               (BASF) CRO837

TELEMANN

Concerto in A rec, vln, strs & c
with F. Vester rec, A. Bylsma vlc, G.   Telefunken SAWT9450
Leonhardt hpsi & Concerto
Amsterdam – Brüggen
Concerto in B flat "Pisendel" vln, strs & c
with Concerto Amsterdam   Musik Production Schwarzwerk
                               (BASF) CRO837
Concerto in F, T.II, No. 3 3 vlns, strs & c
with J. Holtman vln, M. Leonhardt   Telefunken SAWT9452
vln, G. Leonhardt hpsi & Concerto
Amsterdam – Brüggen

TELEMANN – *Continued*

Quartet in G rec, vln, vlc & c
with F. Vester rec, A. Bylsma vlc &   Telefunken SAWT9449
G. Leonhardt hpsi
Solo in A, T.II, No. 5 solo vln
(unaccompanied)   Telefunken SAWT9452
Suite in F vln, strs & c
with Concerto Amsterdam – Brüggen   Telefunken SAWT9541

VIVALDI

(12) Concerti, Op. 8 (1725) "Il Cimento dell' Armonia e dell' Invenzione"
(Nos. 1/4: Le quattro Stagioni) vln & strs
Concerto No. 1, in E, F.I, No. 22 "La Primavera"
with Concerto Amsterdam   Saba MPS13002
Concerto No. 2, in B flat, F.I, No. 23 "L'Estate"
with Concerto Amsterdam   Saba MPS13002
Concerto No. 3, in F, F.I, No. 24 "L'Autunno"
with Concerto Amsterdam   Saba MPS13002
Concerto No. 4, in f, F.I, No. 25 "L'Inverno"
with Concerto Amsterdam   Saba MPS13002

Rolf SCHRODER (1901–   )

BACH

(3) Sonatas & 3 Partitas, BWV1001/6 solo vln
Sonata No. 1, in g, BWV1001
(unaccompanied)   Columbia ML4743, (in set
                               SL189)

Partita No. 1, in b, BWV1002
(unaccompanied)   Columbia ML4743, (in set
                               SL189)

Sonata No. 2, in a, BWV1003
(unaccompanied)   Columbia ML4744, (in set
                               SL189)

Partita No. 2, in d, BWV1004
(unaccompanied)   Columbia ML4744, (in set
                               SL189)

Sonata No. 3, in C, BWV1005
(unaccompanied)   Columbia ML4745, (in set
                               SL189)

Partita No. 3, in E, BWV1006
(unaccompanied)   Columbia ML4745, (in set
                               SL189)

Peter SCHUBERWALTER

TELEMANN

Concerto in G 4 vlns, strs & c
with W. Pfeiffer vln, K. Theiner vln,   Telefunken SAWT9483
A. Harnoncourt vln & Concentus
Musicus Wien – N. Harnoncourt

Rudolph SCHULZ (1911–)

BACH

Concerto No. 2, in E, BWV1042 vln, strs & c*
　　with Berlin Radio Symphony Orch. –　Le Chant du Monde LDXA8008
　　Hering

BARTÓK

(2) Portraits, Op. 5 vln & orch.
　　with RIAS Symphony Orch. – Fricsay　Decca DL9748
　　　　　　　　　　　　　　　　　Deutsche Grammophon 72248,
　　　　　　　　　　　　　　　　　LPE16054

CHOPIN

(3) Waltzes, Op. 64 pf
　　No. 2. Waltz No. 7, in c sharp arr. vln & orch.
　　with symphony orch. – Steinkopf　　Clangor M1057

SHOSTAKOVICH

Quartet No. 2, in A, Op. 69 2 vlns, vla & vlc
　　(as leader of Schulz String Quartet)　Urania URLP7040

SPOHR

Concerto No. 7, in e, Op. 38 vln & orch.
　　with Berlin Radio Symphony Orch. –　Urania URLP7049
　　Heger

TCHAIKOVSKY

Concerto in D, Op. 35 vln & orch.
　　with Leipzig Radio Symphony Orch. –　Urania RS7–17
　　Abendroth

TELEMANN

Concerto in B flat 3 obs, 3 vlns, hpsi & strs
　　with H. Töttcher ob, F. Fest ob, F.　Archive APM14609, ARC3109
　　Wagner ob, G. Silzer vln, E. Seiler vln,
　　J. Wojciechowski bsn, W. Lutz vlc, G.
　　Zschenker cbs & W. Meyer hpsi
Concerto in D 4 vlns, strs & c
　　with W. Kirch vln, H–J. Westphal vln,　Archive APM14609, ARC3109
　　G. Silzer vln & Chamber Orch. –
　　Seiler

Paul SCHUMACHER

DRDLA

Serenade No. 1, in A vln & pf
　　with piano　　　　　1355–o–　Favorite 1–4057E, 29
Souvenir vln & pf
　　with piano　　　　　1356–o–　Favorite 1–4058E, 29

ELGAR

Salut d'amour, Op. 12 orch. – arr. vln & pf Elgar
　　with piano　　　　　　　Odeon 6596

SCHUMACHER

Concert Suite in G, Op. 34 vln & pf
　　No. 2. Berceuse
　　with piano　　　　　1354°　Favorite 1–4056E

* Allegro or 1st mvt & Adagio or 2nd mvt is also on Classic MD9275.

SCHYTTE

(20) Promenades musicales, Op. 26 pf
　　No. 7. Berceuse arr. vln & pf Sitt
　　with piano　　　　　　Odeon 6596

WIENIAWSKI

(2) Mazurkas, Op. 12 vln & pf
　　No. 2. Mazurka No. 2, in g "Le Ménetrier"
　　with piano　　　　　　Odeon 6598
(2) Mazurkas, Op. 19 vln & pf
　　No. 1. Mazurka No. 1, in G "Obertass"
　　with piano　　　　　　Odeon 6598

Richard SCHUMACHER

VIVALDI

(12) Concerti, Op. 3 "L'Estro armonico" var. cbns & strs
　　Concerto No. 8, in a, P.2 (F.I, No. 177) 2 vlns, strs & c
　　with N. Petrović vln & Masterplayers　Amadeo AVRS6206
　　– Schumacher

Michél SCHWALBÉ (1919–)

BACH

(6) Brandenburg Concerti, BWV1046/51 (1721) strs & c
　　Brandenburg Concerto No. 1, in F, BWV1046 vln, 3 obs, bsn, 2 hrns, strs
　　& c
　　with K. Steins ob, A. Civil hrn, S.　Deutsche Grammophon
　　Hopkins hrn & Berlin Philharmonic　LPM18976, SLPM138976
　　Orch. – von Karajan
　　Brandenburg Concerto No. 2, in F, BWV1047 tpt, fl, ob, vln, strs & c
　　with A. Scherbaum tpt, K–H. Zöller fl,　Deutsche Grammophon
　　L. Koch ob & Berlin Philharmonic　LPM18976, SLPM138976
　　Orch. – von Karajan
　　Brandenburg Concerto No. 4, in G, BWV1049 vln, 2 fls, strs & c
　　with K–H. Zöller fl, M. Rütters fl &　Deutsche Grammophon
　　Berlin Philharmonic Orch. – von　LPM18977, SLPM138977
　　Karajan
　　Brandenburg Concerto No. 5, in D, BWV1050 clav, fl, vln, strs & c
　　with E. Picht–Axenfeld hpsi, K–H.　Deutsche Grammophon
　　Zöller fl & Berlin Philharmonic Orch.　LPM18977, SLPM138977
　　– von Karajan
Cantata No. 8 (Liebster Gott, wann werd' ich sterben?) BWV8*
　　with D. Fischer–Dieskau b, A. Nicolet　Angel 35698
　　fl, I. Poppen vlc, E. Picht–Axenfeld　Electrola E90022, E50496
　　hpsi & St. Hedwigs Cathedral Chorus,　HMV ALP1703, ASD342,
　　Berlin with Berlin Philharmonic Orch.　7ERW5365
　　– Forster
Cantata No. 13 (Meine Seufzer, meine Tränen) BWV13†
　　with D. Fischer–Dieskau b, A. Nicolet　Angel 35698
　　fl, I. Poppen vlc, E. Picht–Axenfeld　Electrola E50496, E90022
　　hpsi & St. Hedwigs Cathedral Chorus,　HMV ALP1703, ASD342,
　　Berlin with Berlin Philharmonic Orch.　7ERW5365
　　– Forster

* Aria only.
† Aria & chorale only.

BACH – *Continued*

Cantata No. 73 (Herr, wie du willst, so schick's mit mir) BWV73*
with D. Fischer–Dieskau b, A. Nicolet   Angel 35698
fl, I. Poppen vlc, E. Picht–Axenfeld   Electrola E50496, E90022
hpsi & St. Hedwigs Cathedral Chorus,   HMV ALP1703, ASD342
Berlin with Berlin Philharmonic Orch.
   – Forster

Cantata No. 157 (Ich lasse dich nicht, du segnest mich denn) BWV157*
with D. Fischer–Dieskau b, A. Nicolet   Angel 35698
fl, I. Poppen vlc, E. Picht–Axenfeld   Electrola E50496, E90022
hpsi & St. Hedwigs Cathedral Chorus,   HMV ALP1703, ASD342
Berlin with Berlin Philharmonic Orch.
   – Forster

Cantata No. 158 (Der Friede sei mit dir) BWV158
with D. Fischer–Dieskau b, A. Nicolet   Angel 35698
fl, I. Poppen vlc, E. Picht–Axenfeld   Electrola E50496, E90022
hpsi & St. Hedwigs Cathedral Chorus,   HMV ALP1703, ASD342
Berlin with Berlin Philharmonic Orch.
   – Forster

Cantata No. 159 (Sehet wir geh'n hinauf gen Jerusalem) BWV159†
with D. Fischer–Dieskau b, A. Nicolet   Angel 35698
fl, I. Poppen vlc, E. Picht–Axenfeld   Electrola E50496, E90022
hpsi & St. Hedwigs Cathedral Chorus,   HMV ALP1703, ASD342
Berlin with Berlin Philharmonic Orch.
   – Forster

BEETHOVEN

Mass in D, Op. 123 'Missa solemnis'
with G. Janowitz s, C. Ludwig a, F.   Deutsche Grammophon
Wunderlich t, W. Berry bs, J. Nebois   LPM39208/9, SLPM139208/9
org & Berlin Philharmonic Orch. –
von Karajan

BRAHMS

(16) Waltzes, Op. 39 pf duet
No. 15. Waltz No. 15, in A flat arr. vln & pf "in A" Hochstein
with G. Hengeveld pf   Philips A1106

MOZART

Quartet No. 1, in g, K478 pf, vln, vla & vlc
with I. Haebler pf, G. Cappone vla &   Philips 6500 098
O. Borwitzky vlc

Quartet No. 2, in E flat, K493 pf, vln, vla & vlc
with I. Haebler pf, G. Cappone vla &   Philips 6500 098
O. Borwitzky vlc

(Il) Re Pastore, K208 (1775) – opera
No. 10. L'amerò, sarò costante
with E. Köth s & Berlin Philharmonic   Electrola E70466, STE70466
Orch. – Klobucar   HMV BSDW8011, WBLP572

Serenade No. 6, in D, K239 "Serenata Notturna" orch.
with H. Westphal vln, D. Gerhardt   Deutsche Grammophon
vla, L. Wilhelm cbs & Berlin   LPE17101, EPL30442
Philharmonic Orch. – Böhm

* Recitative & aria only.
† Aria & chorale only.

PAGANINI

(24) Caprices, Op. 1 (1801/7) solo vln
Caprice No. 24, in a arr. vln & pf
with I. Rossican pf   Decca X10144

SARASATE

(8) Danzas españolas vln & pf
No. 3. Romanza andaluza, Op. 22, No. 1
with G. Hengeveld pf   Philips A1106
No. 6. Zapateado, Op. 23, No. 2
with I. Rossican pf   Decca X10144

STRAUSS, R.

Also Sprach Zarathustra, Op. 30 (1896) orch.
with Berlin Philharmonic Orch. –   Deutsche Grammophon
Böhm   LPEM19144, SLPEM136001

(Ein) Heldenleben, Op. 40 (1898) orch.
with Berlin Philharmonic Orch. – von   Deutsche Grammophon
Karajan   DGM12022, DGS712022,
   LPM18550, SLPM138025

Till Eulenspiegels lustige Streiche, Op. 28 (1895) orch.
with Berlin Philharmonic Orch. –   Electrola STE80438
Kempe   HMV ALP1759, ASD326,
   CSDW7054

STRAVINSKY

Apollon Musagète (1928) – ballet orch.
with Suisse Romande Orch. –   Decca LXT5169
Ansermet   London LL1401

Lucien SCHWARTZ

ANTIGA

Boîte à musique et pianola pf – arr. vln & orch.
with salon orch.   HMV K6248

d'AQUERRE

Maiténa
Demande aux roses arr. vln & orch.
with salon orch.   HMV K6611

BERVILY

Isabella v & pf – arr. vln & orch.
with salon orch.   HMV K6112

BILLI

Campane à sera vln or mand & pf – arr. vln & orch.
with salon orch.   HMV K6632

BOLZONI

Minuetto vln & pf
with salon orch.   HMV K6632

BOSC

Moss rose v & pf – arr. vln & orch.
with salon orch.   HMV K6719

BRANDL

(Der) Liebe Augustin – operetta
Du alter Stefansturm arr. vln & pf as "The old refrain" by Kreisler
with L. Petitjean pf   HMV L953

CAMOT

(Le) Carillon magique orch. – arr. vln & orch.
with salon orch.   HMV K6248

CHOPIN

(2) Nocturnes, Op. 27 pf
No. 2. Nocturne No. 8, in D flat arr. vln & pf Wilhelmj
with L. Petitjean pf   HMV L630

COPPOLA

Rêverie vln & pf
with L. Petitjean pf   HMV L751

CURILLIER

(La) Reine Joyeuse – musical
Troublante volupté arr. vln & orch.
with salon orch.   HMV K6112

DELIBES

Naïla valse (Pas des Fleurs) (1867) orch. – arr. vln & orch.
with salon orch.   HMV K6248

DURAND

Valse No. 1, in e flat, Op. 83 pf – arr. vln & orch. Mouten
with salon orch.   HMV K6194

FAURÉ

Berceuse, Op. 16 vln & pf
with L. Petitjean pf   HMV L881

GILLET

(Le) Lettre de Manon – valse pf – arr. vln & orch.
with salon orch.   HMV K6350

GODARD

Jocelyn (1888) – opera
Cachés dans cet asile "Berceuse" arr. vln & pf
with L. Petitjean pf   HMV L881

KREISLER

Liebesleid vln & pf
with L. Petitjean pf BFR 434[1]△ HMV K5164

LUCIANN

Serenade orch. – arr. vln & orch.
with salon orch.   HMV K6194

MASSENET

Thaïs (1894) – opera
Méditation arr. vln & pf Marsick
with L. Petitjean pf   HMV L751

MASSON–KIEK

(En) Relisant vos lettres – valse lente orch. – arr. vln & orch.
with salon orch.   HMV K6719

MONTI

Csárdas (1904) vln & pf
with L. Petitjean pf   HMV L649

RAVEL

Tzigane (Rapsodie de concert) (1924) vln & pf or orch.
with L. Petitjean pf 038043/4 HMV W1033

RIMSKY–KORSAKOV

(Le) Coq d'Or (1910) – opera
Hymn to the sun arr. vln & pf Kreisler
with L. Petitjean pf   HMV L953

SCHUBERT

(6) Moments musicaux, Op. 94 (D780) (1823/7) pf
No. 3. Moment musicale No. 3, in f "Air russe" arr. vln & pf Kreisler
with L. Petitjean pf BFR 435[1]△ HMV K5164

SILÉSU

Sérénade passionnée v & pf – arr. vln & orch.
with salon orch.   HMV K6350

TOSELLI

Serenade, Op. 6 vln & pf – arr. Gervasio
with L. Petitjean pf   HMV L649

VIVALDI

(12) Concerti, Op. 3 "L'Estro armonico" var. cbns & strs
Concerto No. 10, in b: Largo (2nd mvt) P.148 (F.IV, No. 10) 4 vlns, strs & c
with M. Crut vln, J. Dumont vln, H. Polydor 540002, 566275
Merckel vln & Pro Musica Orch. –
Goldschmidt

A. SCHWARZ

PURCELL

(10) Sonatas, Z802/11 (1697) 4 part – 2 vlns & c
Sonata No. 6, in g, Z807 "Chaconne"
with R. Bas vln, I. Nef hpsi & A. L'Oiseau–Lyre LD10
Navarra·vlc

Boris SCHWARZ (1906–)

AULIN

(4) Aquarelles vln & pf
No. 2. Humoresque
with J. Schwarz pf 52191 Homochord 4–8796

BACH, J.C.

(6) Trio–sonatas, Op. 4 (?1765) (T. P314) 2 vlns & vlc
Sonata No. 3, in E flat
with H. Merckel vln PART 1443/6 L'Oiseau–Lyre OL118/9
& A. Navarra vlc

BACH, J.S.

(6) Sonatas, BWV1014/9 vln & clav
Sonata No. 1, in b, BWV1014
with A. Ehlers hpsi 1824/7 Gamut 11, 12–117/8
Sonata No. 2, in A, BWV1015
with A. Ehlers hpsi 1828/31 Gamut 12, 12–119/20
Sonata No. 3, in E, BWV1016
with A. Ehlers hpsi 1832/6 Gamut 13, 12–121/2
Sonata No. 4, in c, BWV1017
with A. Ehlers hpsi 1837/40 Gamut 14, 12–123/4
Sonata No. 5, in f, BWV1018
with A. Ehlers hpsi 1841/4 Gamut 15, 12–125/6

BACH, J.S. – *Continued*

Sonata No. 6, in G, BWV1019
with A. Ehlers hpsi   1845/9   Gamut 16, 12–127/8

CORELLI
(12) Sonatas, Op. 5 vln & c
Sonata No. 12, in d "La Follia"
with J. Schwarz pf   52427/8   Homochord 4–8901

HAYDN
Sonata No. 1, in G, H.XV, No. 32 (1794) vln & hpsi
with A. Ehlers hpsi   Gamut 12–113, (in set MS6)
Sonata No. 2, in D, H.XVI, No. 24 (1773) vln & hpsi
with A. Ehlers hpsi   Gamut 12–114, (in set MS6)
Sonata No. 3, in E flat, H.XVI, No. 25 (1773) vln & hpsi
with A. Ehlers hpsi   Gamut 12–115, (in set MS6)
Sonata No. 6, in C, H.XVI, No. 15 (1767) vln & hpsi
with A. Ehlers hpsi   Gamut 12–116, (in set MS6)

LEO
Concerto in D 4 vlns & strs
with E. Brown vln, B.   US 1244/7   Royale 1826/7
Rabinoff vln, R. Totenberg vln, E.V.
Wolff hpsi & vlcs & cbs

PALMGREN
Romance in G vln & pf
with J. Schwarz pf   19598   Homochord 4–2473

RUBINSTEIN
(2) Melodies, Op. 3 pf
No. 1. Melody in F arr. vln & pf Auer
with J. Schwarz pf   52190   Homochord 4–8796

SPENDIAROV
Dance of the Tartars vln & pf
with J. Schwarz pf   19599   Homochord 4–2473

Margarete SCHWEYDA

HANDEL
(9) Sonatas, Op. 2 (1724) 2 vlns or obs & c
Sonata No. 4, in B flat
with W. Schweyda vln & J. Behr pf   Urania URLP7046
Sonata No. 8, in g
with W. Schweyda vln & J. Behr pf   Urania URLP7046
Sonata No. 9, in E
with W. Schweyda vln & J. Behr pf   Urania URLP7046
(7) Sonatas, Op. 5 (1739) 2 vlns & c
Sonata No. 3, in e
with W. Schweyda vln & J. Behr pf   Urania URLP7046

MARTINŮ
Sonata (1932) 2 vlns & pf
with W. Schweyda vln & J. Behr pf   Urania URLP5004
Sonatina (1931) 2 vlns & pf
with W. Schweyda vln & J. Behr pf   Urania URLP5004

Willi SCHWEYDA (1894–   )

HANDEL
(9) Sonatas, Op. 2 (1724) 2 vlns or obs & c
Sonata No. 4, in B flat
with M. Schweyda vln & J. Behr pf   Urania URLP7046
Sonata No. 8, in g
with M. Schweyda vln & J. Behr pf   Urania URLP7046
Sonata No. 9, in E
with M. Schweyda vln & J. Behr pf   Urania URLP7046
(7) Sonatas, Op. 5 (1739) 2 vlns & c
Sonata No. 3, in e
with M. Schweyda vln & J. Behr pf   Urania URLP7046

MARTINŮ
Sonata (1932) 2 vlns & pf
with M. Schweyda vln & J. Behr pf   Urania URLP5004
Sonatina (1931) 2 vlns & pf
with M. Schweyda vln & J. Behr pf   Urania URLP5004

Joseph SCRIPKA

HANDEL
(15) Sonatas, Op. 1 (?1731) fl or vln & c
Sonata No. 14, in A vln V
with E. Rich pf   Concert Hall CHC15
Sonata No. 15, in E vln VI
with E. Rich pf   Concert Hall CHC15

HAYDN
Concerto No. 2, in G, H.VIIa, No. 4 (1761) vln & orch.
with Concert Hall Symphony Orch. –   Concert Hall CHS8
Goehr

Antonio SCROSOPPI

ABACO
(12) Sonatas, Op. 3 (1714) 2 vlns & c
Sonata No. 2, in F
with L.G. des Combes vln, L. Sgizzi   Cycnus 30CM009
hpsi & E. Roveda vlc   Eurodisc 70908MK, 70909MK
                              Nonesuch (in sets HC3008 &
                              HC73008)

PORPORA
(6) Sinfonias da camera, Op. 2 (1735) 2 vlns & c
No. 4. Sinfonia da Camera No. 4, in D
with L.G. des Combes vln & L. Sgizzi   Eurodisc 70932MK, 70933MK
hpsi   Nonesuch (in sets HC3008 &
                              HC73008)

SCARLATTI, A.
Sonata in F rec, ob, vln or 2 vlns & c
with A. Zuppiger fl, L.G. des Combes   Eurodisc 70932MK, 70933MK
vln & L. Sgizzi hpsi   Nonesuch (in sets HC3008 &
                              HC73008

VIVALDI
(12) Sonatas, Op. 2 (1712) vln & c
Sonata No. 2, in A, F.XIII, No. 30
with L. Sgizzi hpsi   Cycnus 30CM029, 60CS529

VIVALDI – *Continued*

Sonata in c, F.XVI, No. 1 (P.7, No. 1) (Op. 24) vln, vlc & c
  with E. Roveda vlc & L. Sgizzi hpsi   Cycnus 30CM029, 60CS529
                                          Nonesuch H1088, H71088

Helen SEALY

ANONYMOUS

(The) Bonnie banks of Loch Lomond Traditional Scottish air – arr. vln & pf
  with P.B. Kiddle pf   HO 3425 ae   HMV 4–7926, B878

RUBINSTEIN

(6) Soirées de Saint–Pétersbourg, Op. 44 pf
  No. 1. Romance in E flat arr. vln & pf Wieniawski
  with P.B. Kiddle pf   HO 3428 ae   HMV 4–7923, B858

SEALY

Pekinese vln & pf
  with piano   HMV B798
Rosemary vln & pf
  with piano   HMV B798
Sybilla vln & pf
  with piano   HMV B798

Alexander SEBALD (1869–1934)

PAGANINI

(24) Caprices, Op. 1 (1801/7) solo vln
  Caprice No. 14, in E flat
  with J. Brinkman pf   Brunswick 3953, 4225

TARTINI

Sonata in g "Il Trillo del Diavolo" vln & c – arr. vln & pf Kreisler
  with J. Brinkman pf   Brunswick 3983/4, 4226/7

WIENIAWSKI

(2) Mazurkas, Op. 19 vln & pf
  No. 1. Mazurka No. 1, in G "Obertass"
  with J. Brinkman pf   Brunswick 3953, 4225

Pierre SECHIARI

BOCCHERINI

(6) Quintets, Op. 13 2 vlns, vla & 2 vlcs
  No. 5. Quintet No. 5, in E: Minuet (3rd mvt) "Bull" arr. vln & pf
  Kreisler
  with G. Catherine pf   HMV 237901
                                Zonophone X87922

BRAHMS

(21) Hungarian Dances pf duet
  Hungarian Dance No. 2, in d arr. vln & pf Joachim
  with G. Catherine pf   HMV 237908
                                Zonophone X87916

CATHERINE, A.

Berceuse vln & pf
  with G. Catherine pf   Zonophone X87918

CHAMPOREL

Berceuse vln & pf
  with G. Catherine pf   Zonophone X87914

GIORDANI

Caro mio ben v & pf – arr. vln & pf
  with G. Catherine pf   HMV 237909
                                Zonophone X87917

GODARD

Jocelyn (1888) – opera
  Cachés dans cet asile "Berceuse" arr. vln & pf
  with G. Catherine pf   HMV 77906, 237900
                                Zonophone X87921

LALO

Fantaisie norvégienne (1880) vln & orch.
  with G. Catherine pf   HMV 237911
                                Zonophone X87915

MASSENET

Ariane (1906) – opera
  Menuet des Graces arr. vln & pf
  with G. Catherine pf   HMV 237910
                                Zonophone X87915

  Rêverie d'Ariane arr. vln & pf
  with G. Catherine pf   HMV 237910
                                Zonophone X87915

RAFF

(6) Pieces, Op. 85 vln & pf
  No. 3. Cavatina in D
  with G. Catherine pf   Zonophone X87926

SAINT–SAËNS

(Le) Déluge, Op. 45 (1876) – oratorio
  Prélude vln & orch. – arr. vln & pf Saint–Saëns
  with G. Catherine pf   Zonophone X87925

SZULC

(3) Pieces vln & pf
  No. 3. Mélodie
  with G. Catherine pf   Zonophone X87920

WALTER–BEHRENS

Romance vln & pf
  with G. Catherine pf   Zonophone X87919

Carlos SEDANO

GOSSEC

Rosine (1786) – opera
  Gavotte arr. vln & pf Burmester
  with piano   Columbia J408

LOTTO

Fileuse (Romance sans paroles) Op. 8 vln & pf
  with piano   Columbia J408

Fritz SEDLAK (1895–   )

MOZART

(Il) Re Pastore, K208 (1775) – opera
  No. 10. L'amerò, sarò costante
          CHAX 259–1 & 260–2   Columbia LX1096
  with E. Schwarzkopff s & Vienna
  Philharmonic Orch. – Krips

Brigitte SEEGER

BACH

(6) Brandenburg Concerti, BWV1046/51 (1721) strs & c
  Brandenburg Concerto No. 3, in G, BWV1048 3 vlns, 3 vlas, 3 vlcs & cbs
  with W. Neuhaus vln, F–J. Maier vln,   Camden Classics (in set
  G. Lemmen vla, F. Beyer vla, D. Wolff VCCS6023)
  –Malm vla, R.J. Bühl vlc, R.   Victor (in set VICS6023)
  Mandalka vlc, H. Beckedorf vlc, P.
  Breuer cbs & G. Leonhardt hpsi of the
  Collegium Aureum

LOCATELLI

(12) Concerti, Op. 7 (1741) "Il pianto d'Arianna" strs & c
  Concerto No. 12, in F 4 vlns, strs & c
  with F–J. Maier vln, W. Neuhaus vln, Harmonia Mundi HMS30887
  G. Vollmer vln & Collegium Aureum

TORELLI

(12) Concerti, Op. 8 (1709) 1/6: 2 vlns, strs & c – 7/12: vln, strs & c
  Concerto No. 2, in a
  with E. Mayer–Schierning vln &   Mace M9031, SM9031
  Cologne Soloists Ensemble – Müller– Odeon O 80620, STO 80620
  Brühl

VIVALDI

(12) Concerti, Op. 3 "L'Estro armonico" var. cbns & strs
  Concerto No. 1, in D, P.146 (F.IV, No. 7) 4 vlns, vlc, strs & c
  with L. Käppeli vln, H. Scherz vln, T.   Archive SAPM198469
  Soh vln & Lucerne Festival Strings –
  Baumgartner

Heinz SEIDEL

VIVALDI

(12) Concerti, Op. 3 "L'Estro armonico" var. cbns & strs
  Concerto No. 2, in g, P.326 (F.IV, No. 8) 2 vlns, strs & c
  with S. Wagner vln, G. Kröll hpsi &   Volksplatte LDKS18011
  Cologne Chamber Orch. – Ellegiers
  Concerto No. 11, in d, P.250 (F.IV, No. 11) 2 vlns, vlc, strs & c
  with S. Wagner vln, K–H. Jommer vlc, Volksplatte LDKS18011
  G. Kröll hpsi & Cologne Chamber
  Orch. – Ellegiers

Toscha SEIDEL (1900–1962)

ACHRON

Hebrew melody, Op. 33 vln & pf – arr. Zimbalist
  with piano   98615   Columbia 9761, 9027M

d'AMBROSIO

Canzonetta, Op. 6 vln & pf
  with H. Kaufman pf   49689   Columbia 49689, 68072D, 9003M

ANONYMOUS

Eili, Eili Zionist hymn – arr. vln & pf Elman
  with L.T. Gruenberg pf   49526   Columbia 49526

BACH

(4) Suites, BWV1066/9 strs & c
  Suite No. 3, in D: Air (2nd mvt) BWV1068 2 obs, 3 tpts, drms, strs & c
  – arr. vln & pf as "Air on the G–string" by Wilhelmj
  with M. Rabinovich pf   98282   Columbia 09502, 7182M, 9031M,
                                 J9001

BALALEINIKOFF

Brahmsiana vln & pf
  with M. Rabinovitch pf   HMV ED188
                              Victor 18014

BEETHOVEN

(Die) Ruinen von Athen, Op. 113 – Incidental music orch.
  No. 4. Marcia alla turca arr. vln & pf Auer
  with piano   81282   Columbia 4033M

BRAGA

(7) Melodies (1867) v & pf
  No. 5. La serenata "Angel's serenade" arr. vln & pf Pollitzer
  with F. Longo pf   98046   Columbia 98046, 68031D

BRAHMS

(21) Hungarian Dances pf duet
  Hungarian dance No. 1, in g arr. vln & pf Joachim
  with E. Bay pf   98403   Columbia 9033M, J9007
  Hungarian dance No. 1, in g arr. vln & pf Joachim
  with H. Kaufman pf   49690   Columbia 09504, 49690, 68030D,
                                 9001M
  Hungarian dance No. 1, in g arr. vln & pf Joachim
  with E. Kusmiak pf   HMV AE2454
                              Victor 4458
  Sonata No. 1, in G, Op. 78 vln & pf
  with A. Loesser pf   Columbia 67815/8D, (set M155)
                              Perennial 2005
  Sonata No. 2, in A, Op. 100 vln & pf
  with A. Loesser pf   98188/93   Columbia 67180/2D, (set M36)

BURLEIGH

(8) Characteristic Pieces, Op. 6 vln & pf
  No. 4. Indian snake dance
  with F. Longo pf   80821   Columbia 33002D, 4001M

CHAMINADE

Sérénade espagnole pf – arr. vln & pf Kreisler
  with H. Kaufman pf   79488–2   Columbia 79488, 33027D

CHOPIN

Nocturne No. 19, in e, Op. 72, No. 1 pf – arr. vln & pf Auer
  with piano   49448   Columbia 49448, 68074D

CUI

Kaleidoscope, Op. 50 vln & pf
  No. 9. Orientale
    with orch.   78138   Columbia 78138, 33027D,
                                       4001M, X244, X315

DVOŘÁK

(8) Humoresques, Op. 101 pf
  No. 7. Humoresque No. 7, in G flat arr. vln & pf "in G" Wilhelmj
    with piano   49454   Columbia 49454, 68031D, 9003M
  No. 7. Humoresque No. 7, in G flat arr. vln & pf "in G" Wilhelmj
    with A. Loesser pf   98280   Columbia 09506, 7297M, 9028M,
                                      J9000
(8) Slavonic Dances, Op. 72 pf duet; orch.
  No. 2. Slavonic dance No. 10, in e arr. vln & pf Kreisler
    with H. Kaufman pf   Columbia 09504, 68076D, 9001M
  No. 2. Slavonic dance No. 10, in e arr. vln & pf Kreisler
    with E. Bay pf   98402   Columbia 9033M, J9007
Sonatina in G, Op. 100 vln & pf
  Larghetto (2nd mvt) arr. vln & pf as "Indian lament" by Kreisler
    with piano   Columbia 7238

GRIEG

Peer Gynt (Suite No. 1) Op. 46 orch.
  No. 3. Anitra's dance arr. vln & pf Sitt
    with piano   79835   Columbia 79835, 33042D, 4000M
Sonata No. 3, in c, Op. 45 vln & pf
  with A. Loesser pf   Columbia 67689/91D, (set
                    M127), J7894/6

HUBAY

(14) Scènes de la Csárda vln & pf
  No. 4. Hejre Kati, Op. 32
    with L.T. Gruenberg pf   49630   Columbia 49630, 68076D

KELLETTE

I'm forever blowing bubbles v & pf – arr. vln & pf
  with H. Kaufman pf   78798   Columbia 78798

KOŽELUH

(La) Ritrovata Figlia de Ottone, Op. 39 – ballet orch.
  Gavotte (Act IV) arr. vln & pf Kramer
    with H. Kaufman pf   79788   Columbia 79788, 33043D

KREISLER

Caprice viennois, Op. 2 vln & pf
  with L.T. Gruenberg pf   49449   Columbia 7362, 49449, 68029D
Liebesfreud vln & pf
  with H. Kaufman pf   49904–3   Columbia 09005, 49904, 68072D,
                                9002M
Liebesleid vln & pf
  with E. Bay pf   144862–1   Columbia 2128M, DB29, DV728
Polichinelle–serenade vln & pf
  with piano   81568   Columbia 4033M
Rondino on a theme by Beethoven vln & pf
  with piano   Columbia 30028D, 4002M
Schön Rosmarin vln & pf
  with E. Bay pf   144855–1   Columbia 09005, 80623, 33041D,
                                2128M, 4002M, DB29, DV728

LALO

Symphonie espagnole, Op. 21 vln & orch.
  Andante (4th mvt)
    with piano   Columbia 68021D, 9000M

MARGIS

Valse bleue vln & pf
  with H. Kaufman pf   78760   Columbia 78760, 33041D

MASSENET

Thaïs (1894) – opera
  Méditation arr. vln & pf Marsick
    with A. Loesser pf   98274   Columbia 09506, 7297M, 9028M,
                                J9000

MENDELSSOHN

Concerto in e, Op. 64 vln & orch.
  Allegro molto vivace (3rd mvt)
    with piano   Columbia 68021D, 9000M

MORRISON

Meditation vln & pf
  with H. Kaufman pf   49685–3   Columbia 49685, 68075D, 4000M

MOZART

Divertimento No. 17, in D, K334 2 hrns & strs
  Minuet (3rd mvt) arr. vln & pf Burmester
    with E. Kusmiak pf   Victor 4536
Idomeneo, re di Creta, K366 (1781) – opera
  Gavotte in G orch – arr. vln & pf Auer
    with E. Kusmiak pf   Victor 4536

PADEREWSKI

(6) Humoresques de concert, Op. 14 pf
  No. 1. Minuet in G arr. vln & pf Kreisler
    with H. Kaufman pf   49550–2   Columbia 49550, 68029D

PROVOST

Intermezzo (1940) vln & pf
  with E. Kusmiak pf   HMV AE2454
                    Victor 4458

RIMSKY–KORSAKOV

Scheherazade, Op. 35 (1888) orch.
  The young Prince & young Princesses (3rd mvt) arr. vln & pf as
  "Chanson arabe" by Kreisler
    with E. Bay pf   98281–6–A   Columbia 09505, 9035M, J9005
  The young Prince & young Princesses (3rd mvt) arr. vln & pf as
  "Chanson arabe" by Kreisler
    with F. Longo pf   80825   Columbia 33002D

SAINT–SAËNS

(Le) Déluge, Op. 45 (1876) – oratorio
  Prélude vln & orch. – arr. vln & pf Saint–Saëns
    with M. Rabinovitch pf   98276–4–C   Columbia 09505, 9035M, J9005

SARASATE

Zigeunerweisen, Op. 20 vln & pf or orch.
  with L.T. Gruenberg pf   49564   Columbia 7362, 49564, 68030D

SCARLATTI, D.

Sonata in e, L413 pf – arr. vln & pf as "Pastorale" by Bridgewater
  with piano   Columbia 33049D, 4023M

SCHARWENKA

(5) Polish Dances, Op. 3 pf
 No. 1. Polish dance No. 1, in E flat arr. vln & pf
  with H. Kaufman pf   78747   Columbia 78747, 33043D

SCHINDLER

Souvenir poétique (Paraphrase on Fibich's "Poem" Op. 41, No. 14) vln & pf
  with piano   Columbia 33028D

SCHUBERT

(16) Deutsche Tänze, Op. 33 (D783) pf
 No. 3. Deutscher Tanz No. 3, in B flat arr. vln & pf as "Valse sentimentale" by Franko
  with F. Longo pf   81006   Columbia 81006, 33013D
(7) Gesänge (set to Scott's "Lady of the Lake") Op. 52 v & pf
 No. 6. Ave Maria, D839 arr. vln & pf Wilhelmj
  with piano   98616   Columbia 9761, 9027M
(14) Schwanengesang, D957 (1828) v & pf
 No. 4. Ständchen "Serenade" arr. v, vln & orch.
  with C. Hackett t &   64384   Columbia 64384
  Columbia Symphony Orch.
 No. 4. Ständchen "Serenade" arr. vln & pf Elman
  with L.T. Gruenberg   49453–7   Columbia 7241, 7361, 49453,
                68075D, 9027M

SCHUMANN

(13) Kinderscenen, Op. 15 pf
 No. 7. Träumerei arr. vln & pf
  with piano   77899   Columbia 77899, 33013D, X251,
                X315

SIBELIUS

Kuolema, Op. 44 – Incidental music orch.
 Valse triste arr. vln & pf Franko
  with piano   Columbia 33049D, 4023M

SIMONETTI

Madrigale pf – arr. vln & pf
  with piano   78746   Columbia 78746, 33042D, 4000M

STRAUSS, J. (II)*

G'schichten aus dem Wiener Wald, Op. 325 orch. – arr. v, vln & orch. Tiomkin
  with M. Korjus s &   OA 026291/2△   Camden CAL427
  MGM Orch. – Finston   HMV B8862, K8275, 7EP7049
                Victor 4410

One day when we were young arr. v, vln & orch.
  with M. Korjus s &   OA 026294△   Camden CAE317, CAL279
  MGM Orch. – Finston   HMV B8863
                Victor 4411

There will come a time arr. v, vln & orch.
  with M. Korjus s &   OA 026293△   Camden CAE317, CAL279
  MGM Orch. – Finston   HMV B8863
                Victor 4411

TCHAIKOVSKY

Concerto in D, Op. 35 vln & orch.
 Canzonetta (2nd mvt)
  with orch.   49771–5   Columbia 49771, 68073D, 9002M

* The three Strauss items were all featured in the film "The Great Waltz."

TCHAIKOVSKY – *Continued*

Quartet No. 1, in D, Op. 11 2 vlns, vla & vlc
 Andante cantabile (2nd mvt) arr. vln & pf Kreisler
  with orch.   49624   Columbia 49624, 68074D

WAGNER

Albumblatt in C (1861) pf – arr. vln & pf Wilhelmj
  with M. Rabinovitch pf   98275   Columbia 09502, 7182M, 9031M,
                J9001

Albumblatt in C (1861) pf – arr. vln & pf Wilhelmj
  with M. Rabinovitch pf   HMV ED188
                Victor 18014

WIENIAWSKI

Concerto No. 2, in d, Op. 22 vln & orch.
 Romance (2nd mvt)
  with L.T. Gruenberg pf   49447   Columbia 49447, 68073D,
                7228M, 7361M

Bedřiška SEIDLOVÁ (1914–)

SARASATE

(8) Danzas españolas vln & pf
 No. 6. Zapateado, Op. 23, No. 2
  with A. Holeček pf   043295   Supraphon G22315
                Ultraphon G12666

SUK

(4) Pieces, Op. 17 vln & pf
 No. 3. Un poco triste
  with A. Holeček pf   043294   Supraphon G22315
                Ultraphon G12666

Emil SEILER (1906–)

TELEMANN

Concerto in B flat 3 obs, 3 vlns, hpsi & strs
  with H. Töttcher ob, F. Fest ob, F.   Archive APM14609, ARC3109
  Wagner ob, R. Schulz vln, G. Silzer
  vln, J. Wojciechowski bsn, W. Lutz
  vlc, G. Zschenker cbs & W. Meyer
  hpsi

Y. SEIMATOV

KALSONS

Sonata vln & pf
  with R. Kalsons pf   Mezhdunarodnaya Kniga
                D026049

Gerhard SEITZ

URAY

Variations in f vln & pf
  with E.L. Uray pf   Amadeo AVRS3007

Vladimir SELINSKY (1910–   )

ARENSKY

(4) Morceaux, Op. 30 vln & pf
  No. 2. Sérénade in G arr. vln & orch. Longey
  with string ensemble –   CO 28667   Columbia 35816, (in set C37)
  Selinsky

BOLDI

Chanson bohèmienne vln & pf
  with S. Itkis pf   Columbia DO2336

CHAMINADE

Sérénade espagnole pf –arr. vln & pf Kreisler
  with S. Itkis pf   Columbia DO2397

Sérénade espagnole pf – arr. vln & orch. Charmettes
  with string ensemble –   CO 28666   Columbia 35819, (in set C37)
  Selinsky

CUI

Kaleidoscope, Op. 50 vln & pf
  No. 9. Orientale
  with S. Itkis pf   Columbia 35750, DO2289

DRDLA

Serenade No. 1, in A vln & pf – arr. vln & orch. Hinrichs
  with string ensemble –   CO 28668   Columbia 35818, (in set C37)
  Selinsky

DRIGO

(Les) Millions d'Arlequin (1900) – ballet orch.
  Sérénade arr. vln & orch. Roberts
  with string ensemble –   CO 28658   Columbia 35818, (in set C37)
  Selinsky

HERBERT

Naughty Marietta (1910) – operetta
  selection
  with J. Peerce t, T.L. Thomas b, A.   Victor 12589, (in set C33)
  Jamieson s & Victor Salon Group

Sweethearts (1913) – operetta
  selection
  with J. Peerce t, A. Jamieson s &   Victor 12593
  Victor Salon Group

KREISLER

Rondino on a theme by Beethoven vln & pf
  with S. Itkis pf   Columbia 35975, DO2179

MOSZKOWSKI

(6) Klavierstücke, Op. 15 pf – 4 hands
  No. 1. Serenata arr. vln & pf
  with S. Itkis pf   Columbia 35750

  No. 1. Serenata arr. vln & orch.
  with string ensemble –   CO 28660   Columbia 35819, (in set C37)
  Selinsky

MOZART

Divertimento No. 17, in D, K334 2 hrns & orch.
  Minuet (3rd mvt) arr. vln & pf Burmester
  with S. Itkis pf   Columbia 35731, DO2205

PROVOST

Intermezzo (1940) vln & pf
  with S. Itkis pf   B 27200–2   Columbia 35886

RIMSKY–KORSAKOV

(4) Songs, Op. 2 (1865/6) v & pf
  No. 2. Enslaved by the rose & the nightingale arr. vln & pf as "Oriental
  Romance" by Gordon
  with S. Itkis pf   Columbia 35767, DO2336

ROMBERG

(The) Student Prince (1924) – operetta
  Serenade arr. vln & orch.
  with string ensemble –   CO 28657   Columbia 35817, (in set C37)
  Selinsky

SCHUBERT

(16) Deutsche Tänze, Op. 33 (D783) pf
  No. 3. Deutscher Tanz No. 3, in B flat arr. vln & pf as "Valse
  sentimentale" by Franko
  with S. Itkis pf   Columbia 35975, DO2179

(14) Schwanengesang, D957 (1828) v & pf
  No. 4. Ständchen "Serenade" arr. vln & orch.
  with string ensemble –   CO 28659   Columbia 35816, (in set C37)
  Selinsky

SILÉSU

(A) Little love, a little kiss (1912) v & pf – arr. vln & pf
  with S. Itkis pf   B 27484   Columbia 35886, DO2397

TCHAIKOVSKY

Souvenir d'un lieu cher, Op. 42 vln & pf
  No. 3. Mélodie
  with S. Itkis pf   Columbia 35731, DO2205

TOSELLI

Serenade, Op. 6 vln & pf – arr. vln & orch. Schmid
  with string ensemble –   CO 28665²   Columbia 35817, (in set C37)
  Selinsky

VALDEZ

Sérénade du Tzigane vln & pf
  with S. Itkis pf   Columbia DO2289

Vadim SELITSKY

HANDEL

(12) Concerti grossi, Op. 6 2 vlns, vlc & strs
  Concerto grosso No. 4, in a
  with L. Gozman vln, I. Ziss vlc &   Mezhdunarodnaya Kniga
  Leningrad Chamber Orch. – Gozman   D18357/8, S1307/8

HAYDN

Concerto No. 1, in C, H.VIIa, No. 1 vln & orch.
  with Leningrad Chamber Orch. –   Mezhdunarodnaya Kniga
  Gozman   D018859/60

Concerto No. 2, in G, H.VIIa, No. 4 vln & orch.
  with Leningrad Chamber Orch. –   Mezhdunarodnaya Kniga
  Gozman   D018859/60

Armida SENATRA (1889–)

BEETHOVEN

Romance No. 2, in F, Op. 50 vln & orch.
with piano   Anker E9444
Romance No. 2, in F, Op. 50 vln & orch.
with Berlin State Opera Orch. –   Columbia J8298, W269
Weissmann   Parlophone P56039, P57120

ELGAR

Salut d'amour, Op. 12 orch. – arr. vln & pf Elgar
with orch.   Parlophone 80228, B7777

GRÉTRY

Éphale et Procris (1773) – opera
Gavotte arr. vln & pf Franko
with orch.   43474   Decca G20644
                         Parlophone R22891

KREISLER

Tempo di minuetto (Pugnani) vln & pf
with orch.   Parlophone B7775

de MEGLIO

Fenesta che lucive v & pf – arr. vln & orch.
with orch.   Parlophone B7775

MENDELSSOHN

Concerto in e, Op. 64 vln & orch.
Andante (2nd mvt)
with piano   Anker E9486

PORPORA

Aria in E unid – arr. vln & pf Corti
with orch.   Parlophone B7777

RUBINSTEIN

(6) Soirées de Saint–Pétersbourg, Op. 44 pf
No. 1. Romance in E flat arr. vln & pf Wieniawski
with piano   Anker E9563

SAMMARTINI, G.

(6) Sonatas, Op. 1 2 vlns & c
Sonata No. 4, in A: Andante (3rd mvt) arr. vln & pf as "Canto amoroso"
by Elman
with orch.   43473   Decca G20644
                         Parlophone R22891

SIMONETTI

Berceuse vln & pf
with piano   Anker E9435

VIEUXTEMPS

Concerto No. 5, in a, Op. 37 vln & orch.
Adagio (2nd mvt)
with piano   Anker E9486

VIVALDI

(12) Concerti, Op. 3 "L'Estro armonico" var. cbns & strs
Concerto No. 6, in a, P.1 (F.I, No. 176) vln, strs & c
with organ & orch.   43469/72²   Columbia J5367/8
                                       Decca 20105/6
                                       Parlophone 28058/9, B7909/10,
                                         RO20371/2

WIENIAWSKI

Concerto No. 2, in d, Op. 22 vln & orch.
Romance (2nd mvt)
with piano   Anker E9435

Charles SENDEROVITZ (1916–)

CORELLI

(12) Sonatas, Op. 3 2 vlns & c
Sonata No. 7, in e
with L. Hansen vln, M. Wöldike org &   Haydn Society HSL2073
V. Norup vlc

RIISAGER

Sonata, Op. 55b 2 vlns
with W. Tworek vln   Decca LM4555
                               London LS785

SCHÜTZ

(21) Symphoniae Sacrae, Op. 12 (1650)
Concerto No. 5 (O Herr, hilf) a, s, t, vln & c
with V. Garde a, E. Brems s, A.   Metronome MCEP3055
Schiøtz t, L. Hansen vln, M. Wöldike
org & V. Norup vlc

Berl SENOFSKY (1927–)

BEETHOVEN

(10) Variations (on "Ich bin der Schneider Kakadu") Op. 121a pf, vln & vlc
with G. Graffman pf & S. Trepel vlc   Victor LM2715, LSC2715

BRAHMS

Concerto in D, Op. 77 (cadenza by Kreisler) vln & orch.
with Vienna Symphony Orch. – Moralt   Epic LC3291
                                       Philips GBL5592, SBL5222
Trio No. 2, in C, Op. 87 pf, vln & vlc
with G. Graffman pf & S. Trepel vlc   Victor LM2715, LSC2715

DEBUSSY

Sonata No. 3, in g (1917) vln & pf
with G. Graffman pf   Victor LM2488, LSC2488

FAURÉ

Sonata No. 1, in A, Op. 13 vln & pf*
with G. Graffman pf   Victor LM2488, LSC2488

* Allegro molto or 1st mvt is on Victor SPS133–52.

Adolph SENS

d'AMBROSIO

Serenade, Op. 4 vln & pf
  with piano   Polydor 12910

BACH

(4) Suites, BWV1066/9 strs & c
  Suite No. 3, in D: Air (2nd mvt) BWV1068 2 obs, 3 tpts, drms, strs & c
  – arr. vln & pf as "Air on the G–string" by Wilhelmj
  with harmonium   Polydor 12922

BAZZINI

(La) Ronde des lutins, Op. 25 vln & pf
  with piano   Polydor 13162

BRAHMS

(21) Hungarian Dances pf duet
  Hungarian dance No. 2, in d arr. vln & pf Joachim
  with piano   HMV AL196

di CAPUA

O sole mio v & pf – arr. vln & pf
  with piano   Polydor 15625

CHOPIN

(3) Nocturnes, Op. 9 pf
  No. 2. Nocturne No. 2, in E flat arr. vln & pf Sarasate
  with piano   Polydor 12821

DRDLA

Scherzando, Op. 62 vln & pf
  with piano   HMV X287988
                            Polydor 13318

Serenade No. 1, in A vln & pf
  with piano   1024 ab   HMV 107930, X287903
                            Zonophone X27901

Serenade No. 1, in A vln & pf
  with piano   Polydor 11461
Souvenir vln & pf
  with piano   Polydor 12821
Souvenir vln & pf
  with piano   Polydor 13162

EHRICH

Liebesfrühling – Ländler, Op. 32 pf & 2 vlns
  with G. Meine vln   1560 ak   HMV AL501, X287965

FLOTOW

Martha (1847) – opera
  selection arr. vln & pf as "Fantasia" by Sens
  with piano   HMV X287992/3
                            Polydor 13329

GODARD

Jocelyn (1888) – opera
  Cachés dans cet asile "Berceuse" arr. vln & pf
  with piano   14805½L   Polydor 12849
  Cachés dans cet asile "Berceuse" arr. vln & pf
  with piano   Polydor 15625

GOUNOD

Sérénade (Quand tu chantes) v & pf – arr. vln & pf
  with piano   Polydor 13318

GREEL

Laurbaer & Roser v & pf – arr. 2 vlns
  with G. Meine vln   HMV X287953

GUNGL

Oberländler (Country sounds) Op. 31 pf – arr. 2 vlns
  with G. Meine vln   HMV C1297

HAYDN

Klänge aus dem thüringer Wald v & pf – arr. vln & pf
  with piano   Polydor 12499
Klänge aus der Heimat v & pf – arr. vln & pf
  with piano   Polydor 12448

KREISLER

Andantino (Padre Martini) vln & pf
  with piano   Polydor 13389

LANGER

Grandmother, Op. 20 pf – arr. 2 vlns
  with G. Meine vln   15279 b   HMV X287927

MASCAGNI

Cavalleria Rusticana (1890) – opera
  Intermezzo orch. – arr. vln & pf
  with piano   1020 ab   HMV 107931, C396, X287904
                          Zonophone X27902

MASSENET

Thaïs (1894) – opera
  Méditation arr. 2 vlns & pf
  with G. Meine vln & piano   Polydor 12650

MELCHERT

Raslende Sølv, brusende Bølge v & pf – arr. 2 vlns
  with G. Meine vln   HMV X287954

MENDELSSOHN

(6) Duets, Op. 63 2 v's & pf
  No. 1. Ich wollt' meine Lieb' arr. 2 vlns
  with G. Meine vln   1561 ak   HMV AL501, X287966
(6) Songs without words, Op. 62 pf
  No. 6. Song without words No. 30, in A "Spring song" arr. vln & pf
  with piano   13672 I   HMV X287936
  No. 6. Song without words No. 30, in A "Spring song" arr. vln & pf
  with piano   Polydor 12369

MLYNARSKI

(3) Morceaux, Op. 4 vln & pf
  No. 1. Polonaise
  with piano   Polydor 15737

MOSZKOWSKI

(6) Klavierstücke, Op. 15 pf – 4 hands
  No. 1. Serenata arr. vln & pf
  with piano   HMV AL196
(2) Stücke, Op. 45 pf
  No. 2. Guitarre arr. vln & pf Sarasate
  with piano   Polydor 12922

OFFENBACH

(Les) Contes d'Hoffmann (1881) – opera
Belle Nuit, O nuit d'amour "Barcarolle" arr. 2 vlns
with G. Meine vln   15278½ b   HMV X287928

PIERNÉ

Sérénade in A, Op. 7 (1875) pf – arr. vln & pf
with piano   13671 I   HMV X287935

Sérénade in A, Op. 7 (1875) pf – arr. vln & pf
with piano   Polydor 12369

Sérénade in A, Op. 7 (1875) pf – arr. vln & pf
with piano   Polydor 12910

RAFF

(6) Pieces, Op. 85 vln & pf
No. 3. Cavatina in D
with piano   Polydor 11465

RENARD

(2) Berceaux, Op. 20 vln & pf
No. 2. Berceuse in F
with piano   15282 b   HMV X287910
                    Polydor 11466

RIES

Suite No. 3, in G, Op. 34 vln & pf
No. 4. Gondoliera
with piano   Polydor 13389

RUDÉNYI

Träumerei vln & pf
with piano   Polydor 12448

SCHMALSTICH

Elfenreigen, Op. 54 vln & pf
with piano   Polydor 13374

SCHUBERT

(7) Gesänge (set to Scott's "Lady of the Lake") Op. 52 v & pf
No. 6. Ave Maria, D839 arr. vln & pf Wilhelmj
with piano   HMV X287989
                    Polydor 13318

SCHUMANN

(13) Kinderscenen, Op. 15 pf
No. 7. Träumerei arr. vln & pf
with piano   15283 b   HMV C951, X287909

No. 7. Träumerei arr. vln & pf
with piano   Polydor 11466

SEIDLER–WINKLER

Romance in G vln & pf – arr. 2 vlns & pf
with G. Meine vln & piano   Polydor 12650

Scherzo in A vln & pf
with B. Seidler–Winkler   14804 L   Polydor 12849
pf

Wiegenliedchen vln & pf
with piano   Polydor 13374

SIMONETTI

Madrigale pf – arr. vln & pf
with piano   Polydor 13318

SINGALÉE

Fantasia (on themes from Verdi's opera "Il Trovatore") Op. 94 vln & pf
with piano   Polydor 13184

VERDI

Rigoletto (1851) – opera
Selection arr. vln & pf as "Fantasia" by Sens
with piano   Polydor 13341

(Il) Trovatore (1853) – opera
Selection arr. vln & pf as "Fantasia" by Sens
with piano   HMV AL195, X287986/7

WAGNER

(Die) Meistersinger von Nürnberg (1868) – opera
Morgenlich leuchtend "Prize song" arr. vln & pf Wilhelmj
with piano   HMV C951

Morgenlich leuchtend "Prize song" arr. vln & pf Wilhelmj
with piano   Polydor 11465, 15737

Selection arr. vln & pf as "Fantasia" by Sens
with piano   Polydor 13337

Tomislav ŠESTAK (1931–   )

BRAHMS

Sonata (1853) "Frei aber Einsam" vln & pf
Allegro (Scherzo) in c (3rd mvt) "Sonatensatz"
with R. Filjak pf   Jugoton 26340

CORELLI

(12) Sonatas, Op. 5 vln & c
Sonata No. 12, in d "La Follia"
with R. Filjak pf   Jugoton 26340

SCHUMANN

Sonata (1853) "Frei aber Einsam" vln & pf
Intermezzo (2nd mvt)
with R. Filjak pf   Jugoton 26340

Irma SEYDEL (1896–   )

GODARD

Concerto No. 1, Op. 35 "Concerto Romantique" vln & orch.
Canzonetta (2nd mvt)
with piano   (untraced)

KREISLER

Liebesleid vln & pf
with piano   Edison cylinder 4850

YRADIER

(La) Paloma (1877) v & pf – arr. vln & pf
with piano   (untraced)

Eudice SHAPIRO

BARTÓK

Rhapsody No. 2, in d (1928) vln & orch.
with R. Berkowitz pf   Vanguard VRS1023

(6) Rumanian folk dances (1915) pf – arr. vln & pf Székely
with R. Berkowitz pf   Vanguard VRS1023

BLOCH

Baal Shem (3 Pictures of Chassidic life) (1923) vln & pf
  with R. Berkowitz pf   Vanguard VRS1023

BRAHMS

Sonata No. 1, in G, Op. 78 vln & pf
  with R. Berkowitz pf
                   Amadeo AVRS6114
                   Vanguard VRS1009

Sonata No. 2, in A, Op. 100 vln & pf
  with R. Berkowitz pf
                   Amadeo AVRS6114
                   Vanguard VRS1009

Sonata No. 3, in d, Op. 108 vln & pf
  with R. Berkowitz pf
                   Amadeo AVRS6114
                   Vanguard VRS1009

DAHL

Concerto à tre (1947) vln, cl & vlc
  with M. Lurie cl & V. Gottlieb vlc   Columbia ML4493

FAURÉ

Quartet No. 1, in c, Op. 15 pf, vln, vla & vlc
  with L. Pennario pf, S. Schonbach vla   Capitol K80559, P8558, SP8558,
  & V. Gottlieb vlc   STK80559

KIRCHNER

Sonata concertante (1952) vln & pf
  with L. Kirchner pf   Epic LC3006

MILHAUD

Saudades do Brasil (1920/1) pf – arr. vln & pf Lévy
  with R. Berkowitz pf   Vanguard VRS1023

RAVEL

(2) Mélodies hébraïques v & pf
  No. 1. Kaddisch arr. vln & pf Garban
  with R. Berkowitz pf   Vanguard VRS1023

SCHUMANN

Quartet in E flat, Op. 47 pf, vln, vla & vlc
  with L. Pennario pf, S. Schonbach vla   Capitol K80559, P8558, SP8558,
  & V. Gottlieb vlc   STK80559

STRAVINSKY

(Le) Baiser de la Fée (1928) – ballet orch.
  Divertissement arr. vln & pf Dushkin & Stravinsky
  with B. Smith pf   Ava A/AS15
Duo concertante (1932) vln & pf
  with B. Smith pf   Ava A/AS15

Jan SHERMONT

HUBAY

(14) Scènes de la Csárda vln & pf
  No. 4. Hejre Kati, Op. 32
  with O. Schulhof pf   Remington YV2

ORTMANS

Concertino No. 1, in a, Op. 12 vln & pf
  with O. Schulhof pf   Remington YV3

RAFF

(6) Pieces, Op. 85 vln & pf
  No. 3. Cavatina in D
  with O. Schulhof pf   Remington YV2

SEITZ

Concertino No. 5, in D, Op. 22 vln & pf
  with O. Schulhof pf   Remington YV3

VIOTTI

Concerto No. 23, in G vln & orch.
  with O. Schulhof pf   Remington YV1

Zarius SHIKHMURZAYEVA

BIZET

Chanson d'avril (1866) v & pf – arr. vln & pf Tziganov
  with M. Muntyan pf   Mezhdunarodnaya Kniga
                        D17623/4

Pastorale (1868) v & pf – arr. vln & pf Tziganov
  with M. Muntyan pf   Mezhdunarodnaya Kniga
                        D17623/4

Vieille chanson (1865) v & pf – arr. vln & pf Tziganov
  with M. Muntyan pf   Mezhdunarodnaya Kniga
                        D17623/4

DEBUSSY

Valse romantique (1890) pf – arr. vln & pf Relain
  with S. Kokonina pf   Mezhdunarodnaya Kniga
                        D17623/4

PAGANINI

Moto perpetuo (Allegro di concert) Op. 11 (1830) vln & orch.
  with M. Muntyan pf   Mezhdunarodnaya Kniga
                        D17623/4

SAINT–SAËNS

Concerto No. 1, in A, Op. 20 "Konzertstück" vln & orch. – arr. vln & pf
Spiering
  with M. Muntyan pf   Mezhdunarodnaya Kniga
                        D17623/4

Zora SHIKHMURZAYEVA (1933–)

KREISLER

Grave (W.F. Bach) vln & pf
  with E. Fux pf   Mezhdunarodnaya Kniga D3963

MUZAFAROV

Concerto in B vln & orch.
  with Moscow Philharmonic Symphony   Mezhdunarodnaya Kniga
  Orch. – Dugashev   D026601

PAGANINI

(24) Caprices, Op. 1 (1801/7) solo vln
  Caprice No. 21, in A
  (unaccompanied)   Mezhdunarodnaya Kniga D3963

POLDINI

(7) **Marionnettes** pf
No. 2. Poupée valsante arr. vln & pf Kreisler
with E. Fux pf — Mezhdunarodnaya Kniga D3963

PROKOFIEV

(5) **Melodies,** Op. 35bis (1921)
with E. Fux pf — Mezhdunarodnaya Kniga D4300

RACHMANINOV

(2) **Pieces,** Op. 6 vln & pf
No. 1. Romance in d
with E. Fux pf — Mezhdunarodnaya Kniga D3963

TCHAIKOVSKY

Sérénade mélancolique in b flat, Op. 26 vln & orch. – arr. vln & pf
Wilhelmj
with E. Fux pf — Mezhdunarodnaya Kniga D4301
Waltz–scherzo, Op. 34 vln & pf or orch.
with E. Fux pf — Mezhdunarodnaya Kniga D4301

D. SHINDAREV

GRIGORYAN

Concerto in G vln & orch.
with USSR Bolshoi Theatre Orch. – Mezhdunarodnaya Kniga
Krivoshapko — D025207

Lev SHINDER

BACH, J.C.

Sinfonia concertante in E flat, TP284 (1770) 2 vlns, 2 fls, 2 hrns & orch.
with L. Oskotsky vln & Leningrad — Mezhdunarodnaya Kniga
Philharmonic Chamber Orch. – SM02197/8
Dmitriev

MARTINŮ

Concertino pf trio & str orch.
with G. Talrosé pf G. Ginovker vlc & — Mezhdunarodnaya Kniga
Leningrad Philharmonic Chamber — D22045/6, S1845/6
Orch. – Rozhdestvensky
Round dances 2 vlns, pf, ob, cl, bsn & tpt
with V. Ovcharek vln, G. Talrosé pf — Mezhdunarodnaya Kniga
V. Grigorovich ob, A. Veinblat cl, A. — D22045/6, S1845/6
Topol bsn & G. Krylov tpt

MOZART

Concertone in C, K190 2 vlns, ob, vlc & orch.
with V. Ovcharek vln & Leningrad — Mezhdunarodnaya Kniga
Philharmonic Chamber Orch. – D021255/6, S01597/8
Rabinovich
Sinfonia concertante in A, "Triple" vln, vla, vlc & orch.
with V. Solovyov vla, G. Ginovker vlc — Mezhdunarodnaya Kniga
& Leningrad Philharmonic Chamber — D021255/6, S01597/8
Orch. – Rabinovich

RACHMANINOV

Trio No. 2, in d, Op. 9 "Trio élégiaque" pf, vln & vlc
with G. Talrosé pf & G. Ginovker vlc — Mezhdunarodnaya Kniga
SM02233/4

VIVALDI

(6) **Concerti,** Op. 6 vln, strs & c
Concerto No. 1, in g, F.I, No. 192
with Leningrad Philharmonic Chamber — Mezhdunarodnaya Kniga
Orch. – Fedotov — SM02055/6

Yuko SHIOKAWA

REGER

Concerto in A, Op. 101 vln & orch.
with Nürnberg Symphony Orch. – — Colosseum MST514
Kloss

Nelli SHKOLNIKOVA (1927–)

BACH

(3) **Sonatas & 3 Partitas,** BWV1001/6 solo vln
Partita No. 3, in E, BWV1006
(unaccompanied) — Mezhdunarodnaya Kniga D9423

BEETHOVEN

(3) **Sonatas,** Op. 12 vln & pf
No. 2. Sonata No. 2, in A
with L. Yedlina pf — Mezhdunarodnaya Kniga
D17085
(3) **Sonatas,** Op. 30 vln & pf
No. 3. Sonata No. 8, in G
with L. Yedlina pf — Mezhdunarodnaya Kniga
D11063
Sonata No. 10, in G, Op. 96 vln & pf
with J. Gushanskaya pf — Mezhdunarodnaya Kniga
SM02471/2

COPLAND

Sonata (1943) vln & pf
with L. Yedlina pf — Mezhdunarodnaya Kniga D9424

DEBUSSY

Sonata No. 3, in g (1917) vln & pf
with J. Gushanskaya pf — Mezhdunarodnaya Kniga
SM02471/2

FALLA

(7) **Canciones populares españolas** (1914) v & pf
No. 1. El paño moruna arr. vln & pf Kochański
with J. Gushanskaya pf — Mezhdunarodnaya Kniga
SM02471/2
No. 3. Asturiana arr. vln & pf Kochański
with J. Gushanskaya pf — Mezhdunarodnaya Kniga
SM02471/2
No. 4 Jota arr. vln & pf Kochański
with J. Gushanskaya pf — Mezhdunarodnaya Kniga
SM02471/2
No. 5. Nana arr. vln & pf Kochański
with J. Gushanskaya pf — Mezhdunarodnaya Kniga
SM02471/2
No. 6. Canción arr. vln & pf Kochański
with J. Gushanskaya pf — Mezhdunarodnaya Kniga
SM02471/2

KHACHATURIAN

Chanson poème in e (1929) vln & pf
  with L. Yedlina pf
        Mezhdunarodnaya Kniga
        D22656/7

KREISLER

Sicilienne & Rigaudon (Francoeur) vln & pf
  with L. Yedlina pf
        Mezhdunarodnaya Kniga
        D5530/1

KUSS

Sonata in e vln & pf
  with L. Yedlina pf
        Mezhdunarodnaya Kniga
        D17086

MENDELSSOHN

Concerto in e, Op. 64 vln & orch.
  with Moscow Radio Symphony Orch. Mezhdunarodnaya Kniga S0838
  – Rozhdestvensky

MOZART

Concerto No. 4, in D, K218 (cadenzas by Joachim) vln & orch.
  with All–Union Radio Symphony Mezhdunarodnaya Kniga S0837
  Orch. – Rozhdestvensky

PAGANINI

Cantabile in D, Op. 17 vln & gtr
  with L. Yedlina pf
        Mezhdunarodnaya Kniga
        D5530/1

(24) Caprices, Op. 1 (1801/7) solo vln
Caprice No. 2, in b
(unaccompanied)
        Mezhdunarodnaya Kniga
        D6615/6

  Caprice No. 4, in c
  (unaccompanied)
        Mezhdunarodnaya Kniga
        D6615/6

  Caprice No. 16, in a
  (unaccompanied)
        Mezhdunarodnaya Kniga
        D6615/6

Minuet in F unid – vln & pf
  with L. Yedlina pf
        Mezhdunarodnaya Kniga
        D5530/1

(6) Sonatas, Op. 2 (1801/6) vln & gtr
No. 4. Sonata No. 4, in A
  with L. Yedlina pf
        Mezhdunarodnaya Kniga
        D6615/6

  No. 6. Sonata No. 6, in a
  with L. Yedlina pf
        Mezhdunarodnaya Kniga
        D6615/6

(6) Sonatas, Op. 3 (1801/6) vln & gtr
No. 6. Sonata No. 12, in e
  with L. Yedlina pf
        Mezhdunarodnaya Kniga
        D6615/6

Sonata a preghièra "Moses Fantasia" (on the aria "Dal tuo stellato soglio" from Rossini's opera "Mosè in Egitto") Op. 24 (1818 or 1819) vln & orch.
  with L. Yedlina pf
        Mezhdunarodnaya Kniga
        D6615/6

RAVEL

Pièce en forme d'Habanera v & pf – arr. vln & pf Catherine
  with L. Yedlina pf
        Mezhdunarodnaya Kniga
        D5530/1

TARTINI

Sonata in g "Il Trillo del Diavolo" vln & c – arr. vln & pf Kreisler
  with L. Yedlina pf
        Supraphon LPM457, SUF20361

TCHAIKOVSKY

Concerto in D, Op. 35 vln & orch.
  with USSR State Symphony Orch. –
  Kondrashin
        Mezhdunarodnaya Kniga
        D02175/6
Concerto in D, Op. 35 vln & orch.
  with Moscow Symphony Orch. –
  Kondrashin
        Mezhdunarodnaya Kniga
        D17341/2

VAINBERG

Sonatina in d, Op. 46 vln & pf
  with L. Yedlina pf
        Mezhdunarodnaya Kniga
        D11064

VERACINI

(12) Sonatas, Op. 2 (1744) "Sonate accademiche" vln & c
Sonata No. 8, in e
  with L. Yedlina pf
        Mezhdunarodnaya Kniga
        D5530/1

VITALI

Chaconne in g vln & c – arr. vln & pf Charlier
  with L. Yedlina pf
        Supraphon LPM457, SUF20361,
        FUK30037
        Ultraphon DM5375

WIENIAWSKI

(8) Étude–Caprices, Op. 18 solo vln & 2nd vln obb
Étude–Caprice No. 4, in a arr. vln & pf Kreisler
  with L. Yedlina pf
        Mezhdunarodnaya Kniga
        D5530/1

Scherzo–Tarantelle, Op. 16 vln & pf
  with L. Yedlina pf
        Mezhdunarodnaya Kniga
        D22627/8

Sadah SHUCHARI (1908–   )

GLAZOUNOV

(2) Pieces, Op. 20 vlc & pf
  No. 1. Mélodie arabe arr. vln & pf
  with A. Reginald pf
        Victor 4114

KREISLER

Sicilienne & Rigaudon (Francoeur) vln & pf
  with A. Reginald pf
        Victor 4114

Sylvan SHULMAN

VIVALDI

(12) Concerti, Op. 3 "L'Estro armonico" var. cbns & strs
  Concerto No. 10, in b, P.148 (F.IV, No. 10) 4 vlns, strs & c
  with F. Buldrini vln, A. Eidus vln, L.   Allegro ALG3146
  Graeler vln & Stradivari Ensemble   Concerteum CS194
    Stradivari STR604

Oscar SHUMSKY (1917–)

BACH

Mass in b, BWV232 (1733/7) s, a, t, b, cho, strs & c
  with S. Endich s, A. Addison s, F.   Victor (in sets LM6157 &
  Kopleff a, M. Walker t, A. Berberian   LSC6157)
  bs, P. Dunigan fl, R. Roseman ob
  d'amore, P. West ob d'amore, D.
  Sagarman bsn, H. Vogel bsn, J. Eger
  hrn, H. Shapiro vlc, R. Connelly org &
  Robert Shaw Chorale & Orch. – Shaw

BRAHMS

Concerto in D, Op. 77 (cadenzas by Kreisler) vln & orch.
  with Little Symphony Orch. –   Music Appreciation MAR1015
  Scherman

HAYDN

(Die) Sieben letzte Worte des Erlösers am Kreuze (1786)
  with J. Gingold vln, W. Primrose vla   Victor 17786/94
  & H. Shapiro vlc

MOZART

Concerto No. 5, in A, K219 "Turkish" (cadenzas by Joachim) vln & orch.
  with Little Symphony Orch. –   Music Appreciation MAR5613
  Scherman
(Il) Re Pastore, K208 (1775) – opera
  No. 10. L'amerò, sarò costante
    EO–RC 830/1–1A   HMV DB21495
  with E. Berger s & G. Schick pf
Sonata No. 16, in B flat, K570 pf – arr. vln & pf
  with L. Mittman pf   Allegro AL112
Sonata No. 21, in e, K304 vln & pf
  with L. Mittman pf   Allegro AL112
Sonata No. 22, in A, K305 vln & pf
  with L. Mittman pf   Allegro AL112
Sonata No. 32, in B flat, K454 vln & pf
  with L. Mittman pf   Allegro AL97
Sonata No. 34, in A, K526 vln & pf
  with L. Mittman pf   Allegro AL97

RAVEL

Sonata (1922) vln & vlc
    219–7 & 220/2–5   Amphion (set B6)
  with B. Greenhouse vlc   Classic CL6192
    Concert Hall 49/50, 1219/22,
    (set B4), CHS1123

RESPIGHI

Sonata in b (1917) vln & pf
  with A. Balsam pf   Concert Hall 61/3, (set B15)

RIMSKY–KORSAKOV

Capriccio espagnole, Op. 34 (1887) orch.
  with RCA Victor Symphony Orch. –   Victor LM2323, LSC2323,
  Kondrashin   RB16180, VIC1007

SCHUMANN

(13) Kinderscenen, Op. 15 pf
  No. 7. Träumerei arr. vln & orch.
  with orch. – Goodman   Victor 46–0008

VIVALDI

(6) Concerti, Op. 6 vln, strs & c
  Concerto No. 1, in g, F.I, No. 192*
  with Little Symphony Orch. –   Music Appreciation MAR5613
  Scherman

WIENIAWSKI

Polonaise brillante No 1, in D, Op. 4 vln & pf
  with Longine Symphonette – Piastro   Longine LW121

Edmund SIEJA

CORELLI

(12) Concerti grossi, Op. 6 orch.
  Concerto grosso No. 3, in c
  with F. Sadowski vln, A. Ciechański   Muza XL0191
  vlc & Warsaw National Philharmonic
  Chamber Orch. – Teutsch
  Concerto grosso No. 8, in g "Christmas Concerto"
  with F. Sadowski vln, A. Ciechański   Muza XL0191
  vlc & Warsaw National Philharmonic
  Chamber Orch. – Teutsch

Karl SIGMUND

BOCCHERINI

(6) Quintets, Op. 13 2 vlns, vla & 2 vlcs
  No. 5. Quintet No. 5, in E: Minuet (3rd mvt) arr. vln & pf Kreisler
  with piano   Panachord 25141

DVOŘÁK

(8) Humoresques, Op. 101 pf
  No. 7. Humoresque No. 7, in G flat arr. vln & pf "in G" Kreisler
  with piano   Panachord 25141

KREISLER

Liebesfreud vln & pf
  with piano   Panachord 25176

THOMAS

Mignon (1866) – opera
  Entr'acte (Gavotte) (Act II) orch. – arr. vln & pf Sarasate
  with piano   Panachord 25176

* Excerpts only.

Kenneth SILLITO

CORELLI

(12) Concerti grossi, Op. 6 orch.
  Concerto grosso No. 9, in F
    with J. Tunnell vln, K. Heath vlc &
    English Chamber Orch. – Leppard
    Electrola 1C053–02068
    HMV HQS1232

HANDEL

Sonata in B flat (1710) vln, strs & c
  with English Chamber Orch. –
  Leppard
    Philips 6500 240

HOLST

Concerto, Op. 49 (1929) 2 vlns & orch.
  with E. Hurwitz vln & English
  Chamber Orch. – I. Holst
    Lyrita SRCS44

Edward SILVERMAN

DVOŘÁK

Quartet No. 1, in D, Op. 23 pf, vln, vla & vlc
  with M. Good pf,   AR 5433/40–1 Decca K967/70
  W. Copperwheat vla & W. Pleeth vlc
Quartet No. 2, in E flat, Op. 87 pf, vln, vla & vlc
    AR 5695–4, 5696–1, 5720/1–1, Decca K971/4
    5722–2, 5723/4–1 & 5725–2
  with M. Good pf, W. Copperwheat vla
  & W. Pleeth vlc

GOUNOD

Ave Maria (Méditation on Bach's "Prelude No. 1, in C" from Book I of
  "Das Wohltemperirte Clavier") v & pf – arr. v, vln & pf
  with A. Desmond a & AR 6116–1 Decca K1014
  G. Moore pf

KHACHATURIAN

Chanson poème in e (1929) vln & pf
  with A. Bush pf   Topic TRC4
Trio in g (1932) cl, vln & pf
  Lento (1st mvt)
    with P. Cardew cl & B. Frankel pf   Topic TRC14

Joseph SILVERSTEIN (1932–)

BACH

(3) Sonatas & 3 Partitas, BWV1001/6 solo vln
  Sonata No. 1, in g, BWV1001
  (unaccompanied)
    Columbia ML5745, MS6345

BARTÓK

Concerto No. 2 (1938) vln & orch.
  with Boston Symphony Orch. –
  Leinsdorf
    Victor A635053, A645053,
    LM2852, LSC2852, RB6643,
    SB6643
Sonata in g (1944) solo vln
  (unaccompanied)
    Columbia ML5745, MS6345

BRAHMS

Trio in E flat, Op. 40 hrn, pf & vln
  with J. Stagliano hrn & C. Frank pf
    Victor (in sets LM6184 &
    LSC6184)

DEBUSSY

Sonata No. 3, in g (1917) vln & pf
  with M. Tilson Thomas pf
    Deutsche Grammophon 2530 049

IVES

Largo (1902) vln, cl & pf
  with H. Wright cl & R. Levin pf
    Deutsche Grammophon 2530 104

MOZART

Quartet No. 1, in g, K478 pf, vln, vla & vlc
  with C. Frank pf, B. Fine vla & J.
  Eskin vlc
    Victor (in sets LM6184 &
    LSC6184)

PORTER

Quintet ob, 2 vlns, vla & vlc
  with R. Gomberg ob, M. Hobart vln,
  B. Fine vla & J. Eskin vlc
    Deutsche Grammophon 2530 104

SCHUBERT

Trio in B flat, D471 ("Sonata" in one movement) vln, vla & vlc
  with B. Fine vla & J. Eskin vlc
    Victor (in sets LM6184 &
    LSC6184)

STRAUSS, R.

(Ein) Heldenleben, Op. 40 (1898) orch.
  with Boston Sympony Orch. –
  Leinsdorf
    Victor A635011, A645011,
    LM2641, LSC2641, RB6565,
    SB6565

STRAVINSKY

Concerto in D (1931) vln & orch.
  with Boston Symphony Orch. –
  Leinsdorf
    Victor A635053, A645053,
    LM2852, LSC2852, RB6643,
    SB6643

Giorgio SILZER

TELEMANN

Concerto in B flat 3 obs, 3 vlns, hpsi & strs
  with H. Töttcher ob, F. Fest ob, F.
  Wagner ob, R. Schulz vln, E. Seiler
  vln, J. Wojciechowski bsn, W. Lutz
  vlc, G. Zschenker cbs & W. Meyer
  hpsi
    Archive APM14609, ARC3109
Concerto in D 4 vlns & strs
  with W. Kirch vln, H-J. Westphal vln,
  R. Schulz vln & Chamber Orch. –
  Seiler
    Archive APM14609, ARC3109

Imre SIMKÓ

SÁRAI

Capriccio vln & pf
  with I. Szücs pf
    Qualiton LPX1188

András SIMOR (1931–   )

GRANADOS

(12) Danzas españolas, Op. 37 (1893) pf
  No. 5. Danza española No. 5, in e "Andaluza" arr. vln & pf Kreisler
  with M. Freymann pf   Qualiton LPX1124

HORVÁTH

Spring Waltz – operetta
  Intermezzo orch. – arr. vln & pf
  with M. Freymann pf   Qualiton LPX1124
Squirrel dance vln & pf
  with M. Freymann pf   Qualiton LPX1124

KREISLER

(La) Gitana vln & pf
  with M. Freymann pf   Qualiton LPX1124

TCHAIKOVSKY

(6) Pieces, Op. 51 pf
  No. 6. Valse sentimentale arr. vln & pf Grunes
  with M. Freymann pf   Qualiton LPX1124
Swan Lake, Op. 20 (1875/6) – ballet orch.
  Russian dance arr. vln & pf
  with M. Freymann pf   Qualiton LPX1124

WIENIAWSKI

Légende, Op. 17 vln & pf or orch.
  with M. Freymann pf   Qualiton LPX1124
(2) Mazurkas, Op. 19 vln & pf
  No. 1. Mazurka No. 1, in G "Obertass"
  with M. Freymann pf   Qualiton LPX1124

Boris SIMSKY

TCHAIKOVSKY

Suite No. 3, in G, Op. 55 orch.
  Theme & variations (4th mvt)
  with Moscow Philharmonic Symphony Eurodisc 76625KK
  Orch. – Kondrashin   Mezhdunarodnaya Kniga
    D013895 & D10042, S0907/8

Yulian Gregorevich SITKOVETSKY (1925–1958)

ANDRZEJOWSKI

Burleska vln & pf
  with I. Kollegorskaya pf   Muza X2064, XL0385
Burleska vln & pf
  with B. Davidovich pf   Mezhdunarodnaya Kniga
    D6089/90

BACH

(3) Sonatas & 3 Partitas, BWV1001/6 solo vln
  Partita No. 2, in d, BWV1004
  (unaccompanied)   Mezhdunarodnaya Kniga
    D2448/9

BARTÓK

Sonatina in D (on 3 Transylvanian peasant themes) (1915) pf – transcr. vln
& pf Gertler, 1931
  with B. Davidovich pf   Mezhdunarodnaya Kniga
    D6089/90

BAZZINI

(La) Ronde des lutins, Op. 25 vln & pf
  with piano   Mezhdunarodnaya Kniga D2165,
    D21386/7, D024483/4

BEETHOVEN

(3) Quartets, Op. 59 "Rasumovsky" 2 vlns, vla & vlc
  No. 1. Quartet No. 7, in F
  with A. Sharoyev vln, R. Barshai vla Mezhdunarodnaya Kniga
  & Y. Slobodkin vlc   D02673/4

ERNST

(6) Mehrstimmige Studien solo vln
  No. 6. Étude No. 6, in G (Variations on "The last rose of summer") (à
Bazzini)
  (unaccompanied)   Mezhdunarodnaya Kniga
    D07608

GLAZOUNOV

Concerto in a, Op. 82 vln & orch.
  with Moscow Symphony Orch. – Mezhdunarodnaya Kniga
  Kondrashin   D04258

LIPIŃSKI

(3) Caprices, Op. 29 solo vln
  Caprice No. 3, in D
  (unaccompanied)   Mezhdunarodnaya Kniga
    D025150, D07608

LYAPUNOV

Concerto in d, Op. 61 vln & orch.
  with USSR State Radio Symphony Mezhdunarodnaya Kniga
  Orch. – Gorohakov   D04259

MOSZKOWSKI

(2) Stücke, Op. 45 pf
  No. 2. Guitarre arr. vln & pf Sarasate
  with V. Yampolsky pf   Mezhdunarodnaya Kniga D863,
    D17550, D016873/4

MOZART

Sonata No. 26, in B flat, K378 vln & pf
  with B. Davidovich pf   Mezhdunarodnaya Kniga
    D07607

PAGANINI

Concerto No. 2, in b, Op. 7 vln & orch.
  Ronde à la clochette (3rd mvt) "La Campanella" arr. vln & pf Kreisler
  with piano   Mezhdunarodnaya Kniga D863,
    D0008366, D17200/1,
    D024483/4

Concerto No. 2, in b, Op. 7 vln & orch.
  with USSR State Radio Symphony Mezhdunarodnaya Kniga
  Orch. – Paverman   D1089/90
Moto perpetuo (Allegro di concert) Op. 11 (1830) vln & orch.
  with piano   Mezhdunarodnaya Kniga
    D17549

PAGANINI – *Continued*

Sonata a preghièra "Moses Fantasia" (on the aria "Dal tuo stellato soglio" from Rossini's opera "Mosè in Egitto") Op. 24 (1818 or 1819) vln & orch.
with piano   Mezhdunarodnaya Kniga D2168, D024483/4

(Le) Streghe (variations on a theme from Süssmeyer's opera "Il Noce di Benevento") Op. 8 (1813) vln & orch. – arr. vln & pf Kreisler
with piano   Mezhdunarodnaya Kniga D2804, D024483/4

RAKOV

Poem in e vln & pf
with B. Davidovich pf   Mezhdunarodnaya Kniga D07608

Scherzino in e (1945) vln & pf
with B. Davidovich pf   Mezhdunarodnaya Kniga D07608

SAINT-SAËNS

Concerto No. 1, in A, Op. 20 "Konzertstück" vln & orch. – arr. vln & pf Spiering
with A. Mitnik pf   Mezhdunarodnaya Kniga D1187, D016873/4

(6) Études, Op. 52 pf
No. 6. Étude No. 6, in D flat "Étude en forme de valse" arr. vln & pf Ysaÿe
with V. Yampolsky pf   Mezhdunarodnaya Kniga D864, D016873/4

SARASATE

(8) Danzas españolas vln & pf
No. 1. Malagueña, Op. 21, No. 1
with B. Davidovich pf   Mezhdunarodnaya Kniga D1188, D016873/4, D021759

No. 2. Habañera, Op. 21, No. 2
with B. Davidovich pf   Mezhdunarodnaya Kniga D1188, D016873/4, D021758

SHOSTAKOVICH

(24) Preludes, Op. 34 (1932/3) pf
Prelude No. 10, in c sharp arr. vln & pf Tziganov
with I. Kollegorskaya pf   Muza X2063, XL0385
Prelude No. 10, in c sharp arr. vln & pf Tziganov
with B. Davidovich pf   Mezhdunarodnaya Kniga D6089/90
Prelude No. 15, in D flat arr. vln & pf Tziganov
with I. Kollegorskaya pf   Muza X2063, XL0385
Prelude No. 15, in D flat arr. vln & pf Tziganov
with B. Davidovich pf   Mezhdunarodnaya Kniga D6089/90
Prelude No. 16, in b flat arr. vln & pf Tziganov
with I. Kollegorskaya pf   Muza X2063, XL0385
Prelude No. 16, in b flat arr. vln & pf Tziganov
with B. Davidovich pf   Mezhdunarodnaya Kniga D6089/90
Prelude No. 24, in d arr. vln & pf Tziganov
with B. Davidovich pf   Mezhdunarodnaya Kniga D6089/90

SHOSTAKOVICH – *Continued*

Quartet No. 3, in F, Op. 73 2 vlns, vla & vlc
with A. Sharoyev vln, R. Barshai vla & Y. Slobodkin vlc   Mezhdunarodnaya Kniga D2534/5
Parlophone PMA1040
Vanguard VRS6021

Quartet No. 4, in D, Op. 83 2 vlns, vla & vlc
with A. Sharoyev vln, R. Barshai vla & Y. Slobodkin vlc   Mezhdunarodnaya Kniga D2291/2
Parlophone PMA1040
Vanguard VRS6021

SIBELIUS

Concerto in d, Op. 47 vln & orch.
with Czech Philharmonic Orch. – Anosov   Parliament PLP148
Supraphon LPM418

SZYMANOWSKI

(3) Mythes, Op. 30 (1915) vln & pf
No. 1. La Fontaine d'Aréthuse
with B. Davidovich pf   Mezhdunarodnaya Kniga D6089/90

TARTINI

Sonata in g "Il Trillo del Diavolo" vln & c – arr. vln & pf Kreisler
with B. Davidovich pf   Mezhdunarodnaya Kniga D2805, D024483/4

TCHAIKOVSKY

(3) Souvenirs de Hapsal, Op. 2 pf
No. 3. Chant sans paroles in f arr. vln & pf Kreisler
with B. Davidovich pf   Mezhdunarodnaya Kniga D07608

VIEUXTEMPS

Suite in D, Op. 43 vln & pf*
with B. Davidovich pf   Mezhdunarodnaya Kniga D2167, D016873/4

WIENIAWSKI

(L') École moderne, Op. 10 (10 Études) solo vln
No. 4. Étude No. 4, in A "Le Staccato"
(unaccompanied)   Muza X2064, XL0385
No. 4. Étude No. 4, in A "Le Staccato"
(unaccompanied)   Mezhdunarodnaya Kniga D6089/90, D025150

Polonaise brillante No. 1, in D, Op. 4 vln & pf
with I. Kollegorskaya pf   Muza X2063, XL0385
Polonaise brillante No. 1, in D, Op. 4 vln & pf
with B. Davidovich pf   Mezhdunarodnaya Kniga D0008365, D6089/90

Alf SJÖEN (1914–)

GRIEG

Sonata No. 2, in G, Op. 13 vln & pf
with H. Salum pf   Telefunken E15070/1

* Gavotte or 4th mvt is also on Mezhdunarodnaya Kniga D00502.

Olga SKALAR

MOZART

Divertimento No. 15, in B flat, K287 2 hrns & strs
with F. Koch hrn, F. Hofmann hrn &   Erato STU70264
Vienna Baroque Ensemble –   Musical Heritage Society
Guschlbauer   MHS828

Max SKALKA

ANONYMOUS

Londonderry air Traditional Irish ballad – arr. vln & pf Kreisler
with V. Borggaard pf   Telefunken A5629

BOULANGER, G.

Avant de mourir, Op. 17 vln & pf
with piano   Triola T4247

CHOPIN

Polonaise No. 6, in A flat, Op. 53 pf – arr. vln & orch. Skalka
with orch.   Cupol 4269

DRDLA

Souvenir vln & pf
with V. Borggaard pf   ᴰ2063ᴮ Elite 5002
                                      Elite Special 8920

DVOŘÁK

(8) Humoresques, Op. 101 pf
  No. 7. Humoresque No. 7, in G flat arr. vln & pf "in G" Kreisler
  with V. Borggaard pf   Telefunken A5632

HARITO

Crysanteme vln & pf
with Ambassadeur taiteilijaork   Triola TS471

HENRIQUES

Romance in D, Op. 43 vln & pf
with V. Borggaard pf   Elite 9055
                                  Telefunken A5633

HUBAY

(14) Scènes de la Csárda vln & pf
  No. 4. Hejre Kati, Op. 32
  with orch.   Telefunken A5672

KREISLER

Liebesfreud vln & pf
with V. Borggaard pf   Telefunken A5629
Liebesleid vln & pf
with V. Borggaard pf   Elite 8919
                                  Telefunken A5628

Liebesleid vln & pf
with piano   Triola T4247
Schön Rosmarin vln & pf
with V. Borggaard pf   Telefunken A5628

MASCAGNI

Cavalleria Rusticana (1890) – opera
  Intermezzo orch. – arr. vln, vlc & pf
  with Z. Benatti vlc & A. Riis pf   Columbia J91

MASCAGNI – *Continued*

  Siciliana arr. vln, vlc & pf
  with Z. Benatti vlc & A. Riis pf   Columbia J91

MONTI

Csárdas (1904) vln & pf
with V. Borggaard pf   ᴰ2062ᴬ Elite 5002, 8920

RODRIGUEZ

(La) Cumparsita (1926) v & pf – arr. vln & orch. Skalka
with Ambassadeur taiteilijaork   Triola TS466

SCHUMANN

(13) Kinderscenen, Op. 15 pf
  No. 7. Träumerei arr. vln & pf
  with V. Borggaard pf   Telefunken A5632

WARNER

Scrub vln & pf
with V. Borggaard pf   Telefunken A5633

YRADIER

(La) Paloma (1877) v & pf – arr. vln & orch. Vasa
with Ambassadeur taiteilijaork   Triola TS466

ZELLER

(Der) Vogelhändler (1891) – operetta
  Noch einmal ... arr. vln & orch. Vasa
  with Ambassadeur taiteilijaork   Triola TS471

Erhard SKOGH

AULIN

(4) Aquarelles vln & pf
  No. 1. Idyll
  with piano   OT 551–II HMV*

Carlos SKOLNIK

MASCAGNI

Cavalleria Rusticana (1890) – opera
  Intermezzo orch. – arr. vln & pf
  with piano   10952 L Edison Bell 4784

OFFENBACH

(Les) Contes d'Hoffmann (1881) – opera
  Belle Nuit, O nuit d'amour "Barcarolle" arr. vln & pf
  with piano   10949 N Edison Bell 4784

Jenny SKOLNIK

DVOŘÁK

(8) Slavonic Dances, Op. 46 pf duet; orch.
  No. 2. Slavonic dance No. 2, in e arr. vln & pf "in g" Kreisler
  with piano   Polydor 14785

* Unissued.

KREISLER

Praeludium & Allegro (Pugnani) vln & pf
with piano — Polydor 19171

QUINN

Serenata vln & pf
with piano — Polydor 14785

SARASATE

(8) Danzas españolas vln & pf
No. 8. Danza española No. 8, in C, Op. 26, No. 2
with piano — Polydor 19171

Felix SLATKIN (1915–1963)

KAPLAN

Piece in the form of a Rhapsody vln & pf
with S. Kaplan pf — Co–Art 5024

Winifred SMALL (1896–   )

BRAHMS

(16) Waltzes, Op. 39 pf duet
No. 15. Waltz No. 15, in A flat arr. vln & pf "in A" Hochstein
with piano — Broadcast 5266

DVOŘÁK

(8) Slavonic Dances, Op. 46 pf duet; orch.
No. 2. Slavonic dance No. 2, in e arr. vln & pf "in g" Kreisler
with piano — Broadcast 5266

FRANCK

Sonata in A (1886) vln & pf
Allegro (2nd mvt)
with piano — Broadcast 5257

NACHÈZ

(4) Danses Tziganes, Op. 14 vln & pf
No. 1. Danse tzigane No. 1, in a
with piano — Broadcast 5254

SCHUBERT, François

(12) Bagatelles, Op. 13 vln & pf
No. 9. L'abeille
with piano — Broadcast 5266

SCHUBERT, Franz

Rosamunde von Cypern, Op. 26 (D797) (1823) – Incidental music orch.
No. 9. Ballet music II, in G arr. vln & pf Kreisler
with piano — Broadcast 5254

Miroslav SMEJKAL

SCHMIDEK

Rondo–Polonaise, Op. 49 "Konzertante" vln & strs
with Brünn Chamber Orch. — Preiser SPR3202

Eugen SMIRNOV

VIVALDI

(12) Concerti, Op. 8 (1725) "Il Cimento dell' Armonia e dell' Invenzione"
(Nos. 1/4: Le quattro Stagioni) vln & strs
Concerto No. 1, in E, F.I, No. 22 "La Primavera"
with Moscow Chamber Orch. – Barshai — Eurodisc 74607KK
Mezhdunarodnaya Kniga D08825/6, S0293/4

Concerto No. 2, in B flat, F.I, No. 23 "L'Estate"
with Moscow Chamber Orch. – Barshai — Eurodisc 74607KK
Mezhdunarodnaya Kniga D08825/6, S0293/4

Concerto No. 3, in F, F.I, No. 24 "L'Autunno"
with Moscow Chamber Orch. – Barshai — Eurodisc 74607KK
Mezhdunarodnaya Kniga D08825/6, S0293/4

Concerto No. 4, in f, F.I, No. 25 "L'Inverno"
with Moscow Chamber Orch. – Barshai — Eurodisc 74607KK
Mezhdunarodnaya Kniga D08825/6, S0293/4

Concerto in G, P.132 (F.I, No. 6) 2 vlns, strs & c
with A. Abramenkov vln & Moscow Chamber Orch. – Barshai — Le Chant du Monde LDX8326, LDX48326
Mercury MG50425, SR90425
Philips 835172AY, A02296L

Concerto in B flat, P.388 (F.IV, No. 2) (Op. 22, No. 2) vln, vlc, strs & c
with A. Vassolieva vlc & Moscow Chamber Orch. – Barshai — Le Chant du Monde LDX8326, LDX48326
Mercury MG50425, SR90425
Philips 835172AY, A02296L

Maureen SMITH

MENDELSSOHN

Concerto in e, Op. 64 vln & orch.
with London Philharmonic Orch. – Boult — Crossroads 22 16 0224
World Record Club ST680, T680

Sydney SMITH

BARNS

Swing song vln & pf
with piano — Pathé 699, 1320, 77178

BISHOP

Clari (1823) – opera
Home, sweet home arr. vln & pf
with piano — Pathé 701, 1322, 77181

DVOŘÁK

(8) Humoresques, Op. 101 pf
No. 7. Humoresque No. 7, in G flat arr. vln & pf "in G" Wilhelmj
with piano — Pathé 700, 1321, 77183

GOUNOD

Ave Maria (Méditation on Bach's "Prelude No. 1, in C" from Book I of "Das Wohltemperirte Clavier") v & pf – arr. vln & pf
with piano — Pathé 701, 1322, 77180

MENDELSSOHN

(6) Songs without words, Op. 62 pf
No. 6. Song without words No. 30, in A "Spring song" arr. vln & pf
with piano   Pathé 699, 1320, 77182

WIENIAWSKI

Mazurka in a, Op. 3 "Kujawiak" vln & pf
with piano   Pathé 700, 1321, 77179

Vaclav SNÍTIL (1928–)

KALABIS

Concerto (1959) vln & orch.
with Czech Philharmonic Orch. –   Supraphon MN20, SUA18502
Ančerl

MOZART

Quartet in F, K370 ob, vln, vla & vlc
with S. Duchoň ob, J. Kodousek vla &   Supraphon LPM320
V. Moučka vlc

Sonata No. 1, in E flat, K67 org, 2 vlns & vlc
with M. Šlechta org, J. Vlach vln & V.   Supraphon LPM320
Moučka vlc

Sonata No. 15, in C, K328 org, 2 vlns & vlc
with M. Šlechta org, J. Vlach vln & V.   Supraphon LPM320
Moučka vlc

Sonata No. 17, in C, K336 org, 2 vlns & vlc
with M. Šlechta org, J. Vlach vln & V.   Supraphon LPM320
Moučka vlc

SCHUBERT

Rondo brillante in b, Op. 70 (D895) vln & pf
with Z. Zichová–Lochmanová pf   Supraphon SV8325

(3) Sonatinas, Op. 137 (D384, D385 & D408) vln & pf
No. 2. Sonatina No. 2, in a, D385
with Z. Zichová–Lochmanová pf   Supraphon SV8325

No. 3. Sonatina No. 3, in g, D408
with Z. Zichová–Lochmanová pf   Supraphon SV8325

SRNKA

Concerto dramatique vln & orch.
with Czech Philharmonic Orch. –   Supraphon SUF28100
Neuman

VOŘÍŠEK

Rondo, Op. 8 vln & pf
with Z. Zichová–Lochmanová pf   Crossroads 22 16 0119, 22 16
0120
Supraphon MAB32, SUA19662,
SUAST59662, SV8313

Sonata in G, Op. 5 vln & pf
with Z. Zichová–Lochmanová pf   Crossroads 22 16 0119, 22 16
0120
Supraphon MAB32, SUA19662,
SUAST59662, SV8313

Semon SNITKOVSKY (1933–)

BACH

Prelude unid – arr. vln & pf Kodály*
with piano   Mezhdunarodnaya Kniga
D13427/8

(3) Sonatas & 3 Partitas, BWV1001/6 solo vln
Sonata No. 1, in g, BWV1001
(unaccompanied)   Mezhdunarodnaya Kniga
D18481/2

BARTÓK

Rhapsody No. 2, in d (1928) vln & orch.
with piano   Mezhdunarodnaya Kniga
D13427/8

BEETHOVEN

(3) Sonatas, Op. 30 vln & pf
No. 2. Sonata No. 7, in c
with L. Iossiovich pf   Mezhdunarodnaya Kniga
D08787

BRAHMS

(21) Hungarian Dances pf duet
Hungarian dance No. 8, in a arr. vln & pf Joachim
with piano   Mezhdunarodnaya Kniga
D022717/8

Sonata (1853) "Frei aber Einsam" vln & pf
Allegro (scherzo) in c (3rd mvt) "Sonatensatz"
with piano   Mezhdunarodnaya Kniga
D13427/8

CHOPIN

Nocturne No. 20, in c sharp, Op. posth pf – arr. vln & pf Rodionov
with I. Kollegorskaya pf   Electrecord ECD64
Mezhdunarodnaya Kniga
D05056/7

DEBUSSY

(La) Plus que lente – valse (1910) pf – arr. vln & pf Heifetz
with I. Kollegorskaya pf   Electrecord ECD64
Mezhdunarodnaya Kniga
D05056/7

Prélude à l'aprés–midi d'un faune (1894) orch. – arr. vln & pf Heifetz
with piano   Mezhdunarodnaya Kniga
D022717/8

DVOŘÁK

(7) Gypsy songs, Op. 55 v & pf
No. 4. Songs my mother taught me arr. vln & pf Kreisler
with I. Kollegorskaya pf   Electrecord ECD64
Mezhdunarodnaya Kniga
D05056/7

FALLA

(7) Canciones populares españolas (1914) v & pf
No. 4. Jota arr. vln & pf Kochański
with piano   Mezhdunarodnaya Kniga
D13427/8

* Possibly the Preludio or 1st mvt from the 3rd Partita for solo vln.

GLAZOUNOV

Concerto in a, Op. 82 vln & orch.
  with Moscow Radio Symphony Orch.   Eurodisc 76601KK
  – Rozhdestvensky   Mezhdunarodnaya Kniga
     D015643, S0995

HINDEMITH

Sonata No. 3, in E (1935) vln & pf
  with piano   Mezhdunarodnaya Kniga
     D18481/2

KREISLER

(La) Précieuse (L. Couperin) vln & pf
  with piano   Mezhdunarodnaya Kniga
     D022717/8

PAGANINI

(6) Sonatas, Op. 3 (1801/6) vln & gtr
  No. 6. Sonata No. 12, in e
  with piano   Mezhdunarodnaya Kniga
     D022717/8

SARASATE

Introduction & Tarantelle, Op. 43 vln & pf
  with I. Kollegorskaya pf   Electrecord ECD64
     Mezhdunarodnaya Kniga
     D05056/7

SCHUBERT

Sonata in A, Op. 162 (D574) 'Duo' vln & pf
  with L. Iosiovich pf   Mezhdunarodnaya Kniga
     D025267/8

SHCHEDRIN

(The) Hump–backed Horse (1959) – ballet orch.
  No. 1. Balalaika arr. vln & pf Snitkovsky
  with piano   Mezhdunarodnaya Kniga
     D022717/8

  No. 2. Adagietto arr. vln & pf Snitkovsky
  with piano   Mezhdunarodnaya Kniga
     D022717/8

  No. 3. Jesters' dance arr. vln & pf Snitkovsky
  with piano   Mezhdunarodnaya Kniga
     D022717/8

STRAVINSKY

Firebird (1910) ballet suite orch.
  No. 3. Jeu des princesses avec les pommes d'or arr. vln & pf as
  "Scherzo" by Dushkin & Stravinsky, 1933
  with piano   Mezhdunarodnaya Kniga
     D13427/8

Pétrouchka (1911) – ballet orch.
  Danse russe arr. vln & pf Dushkin & Stravinsky, 1933
  with piano   Mezhdunarodnaya Kniga
     D13427/8

SZYMANOWSKI

(3) Caprices (after Paganini) Op. 40 vln & pf
  No. 1. Caprice No. 20, in D
  with L. Iosiovich pf   Mezhdunarodnaya Kniga
     D18481/2

SZYMANOWSKI – *Continued*

  No. 2. Caprice No. 21, in A
  with L. Iosiovich pf   Mezhdunarodnaya Kniga
     D18481/2

  No. 3. Caprice No. 24, in a
  with piano   Mezhdunarodnaya Kniga
     D13427/8

Sonata No. 1, in d, Op. 9 vln & pf
  with L. Iosiovich pf   Mezhdunarodnaya Kniga
     D025267/8

TARTINI

Sonata in g "Il Trillo del Diavolo" vln & c – arr. vln & pf Kreisler
  with I. Kollegorskaya pf   Electrecord ECD64
     Mezhdunarodnaya Kniga
     D05056/7

VERACINI

(12) Sonatas, Op. 2 (1744) "Sonate accademiche" vln & c
  Sonata No. 8, in e
  with L. Iosiovich pf   Mezhdunarodnaya Kniga
     D08788

VIEUXTEMPS

Concerto No. 4, in d, Op. 31 vln & orch.
  with Moscow Radio Symphony Orch.   Eurodisc 76601KK
  – Rozhdestvensky   Mezhdunarodnaya Kniga
     D015644, C0996

VILLA–LOBOS

Sonata–Fantasia No. 2 (1914) vln & pf
  with piano   Mezhdunarodnaya Kniga
     D022717/8

WEINER

Latin–American suite vln & pf
  with L. Iosiovich pf   Mezhdunarodnaya Kniga
     D025267/8

WIENIAWSKI

Gigue, Op. 23 vln & pf
  with piano   Mezhdunarodnaya Kniga
     D022717/8

(2) Mazurkas, Op. 19 vln & pf
  No. 1. Mazurka No. 1, in G "Obertass"
  with piano   Mezhdunarodnaya Kniga
     D022717/8

Polonaise brillante No. 1, in D, Op. 4 vln & pf
  with I. Kollegorskaya pf   Mezhdunarodnaya Kniga
     D05056/7

YSAŸE

(3) Mazurkas, Op. 11 vln & pf
  No. 1. Mazurka No. 1, in G "Danse souvenir"
  with L. Iosiovich pf   Mezhdunarodnaya Kniga
     D08788

Rafael SOBOLEVSKY

BACH

(3) Sonatas & 3 Partitas, BWV1001/6 solo vln
Sonata No. 3, in C, BWV1005
(unaccompanied)

Mezhdunarodnaya Kniga
D016019/20

Sonata in d, BWV1036 2 vlns & c
with G. Barinova vln, T. Nikolayeva
pf & M. Rostropovich vlc

Mezhdunarodnaya Kniga
D01302

GRIEG

Sonata No. 2, in G, Op. 13 vln & pf
with A. Ginzburg pf

Mezhdunarodnaya Kniga
D018143

Sonata No. 3, in c, Op. 45 vln & pf
with A. Ginzburg pf

Mezhdunarodnaya Kniga
D018144

PAGANINI

Sonata a preghièra "Moses Fantasia" (on the aria "Dal tuo stellato soglio"
from Rossini's opera "Mosè in Egitto") Op. 24 (1818 or 1819) vln &
orch.
with E. Livchitz pf

Mezhdunarodnaya Kniga
D022047/8

SAINT-SAËNS

Havanaise, Op. 83 vln & orch.
with A. Mitnik pf

Mezhdunarodnaya Kniga
D016019/20

SARASATE

(8) Danzas españolas vln & pf
No. 1. Malagueña, Op. 21, No. 1
with I. Chernyshov pf

Mezhdunarodnaya Kniga
D016019/20

No. 3. Romanza andaluza, Op. 22, No. 1
with A. Mitnik pf

Mezhdunarodnaya Kniga
D016019/20

No. 6. Zapateado, Op. 23, No. 2
with I. Chernyshov pf

Mezhdunarodnaya Kniga
D016019/20

SHOSTAKOVICH

(24) Preludes, Op. 34 (1932/3) pf
Prelude No. 1, in C arr. vln & pf Tziganov
with E. Epstein pf

Mezhdunarodnaya Kniga
D022047/8

Prelude No. 2, in a arr. vln & pf Tziganov
with E. Epstein pf

Mezhdunarodnaya Kniga
D022047/8

Prelude No. 3, in G arr. vln & pf Tziganov
with E. Epstein pf

Mezhdunarodnaya Kniga
D022047/8

Prelude No. 5, in D arr. vln & pf Tziganov
with E. Epstein pf

Mezhdunarodnaya Kniga
D022047/8

Prelude No. 6, in b arr. vln & pf Tziganov
with E. Epstein pf

Mezhdunarodnaya Kniga
D022047/8

SHOSTAKOVICH – *Continued*

Prelude No. 8, in f sharp arr. vln & pf Tziganov
with E. Epstein pf

Mezhdunarodnaya Kniga
D022047/8

Prelude No. 10, in c sharp arr. vln & pf Tziganov
with E. Epstein pf

Mezhdunarodnaya Kniga
D022047/8

Prelude No. 11, in B arr. vln & pf Tziganov
with E. Epstein pf

Mezhdunarodnaya Kniga
D022047/8

Prelude No. 12, in g sharp arr. vln & pf Tziganov
with E. Epstein pf

Mezhdunarodnaya Kniga
D022047/8

Prelude No. 13, in F sharp arr. vln & pf Tziganov
with E. Epstein pf

Mezhdunarodnaya Kniga
D022047/8

Prelude No. 15, in D flat arr. vln & pf Tziganov
with E. Epstein pf

Mezhdunarodnaya Kniga
D022047/8

Prelude No. 16, in b flat arr. vln & pf Tziganov
with E. Epstein pf

Mezhdunarodnaya Kniga
D022047/8

Prelude No. 17, in A flat arr. vln & pf Tziganov
with E. Epstein pf

Mezhdunarodnaya Kniga
D022047/8

Prelude No. 18, in f arr. vln & pf Tziganov
with E. Epstein pf

Mezhdunarodnaya Kniga
D022047/8

Prelude No. 19, in E flat arr. vln & pf Tziganov
with E. Epstein pf

Mezhdunarodnaya Kniga
D022047/8

Prelude No. 20, in c arr. vln & pf Tziganov
with E. Epstein pf

Mezhdunarodnaya Kniga
D022047/8

Prelude No. 21, in B flat arr. vln & pf Tziganov
with E. Epstein pf

Mezhdunarodnaya Kniga
D022047/8

Prelude No. 22, in g arr. vln & pf Tziganov
with E. Epstein pf

Mezhdunarodnaya Kniga
D022047/8

Prelude No. 24, in d arr. vln & pf Tziganov
with E. Epstein pf

Mezhdunarodnaya Kniga
D022047/8

TARTINI

Sonata in g "Il Trillo del Diavolo" vln & c – arr. vln & pf Kreisler
with E. Epstein pf

Mezhdunarodnaya Kniga
D022047/8

Robert SOËTENS (1907–   )

BACH

(3) Sonatas & 3 Partitas, BWV1001/6 solo vln
Partita No. 2, in d, BWV1004
(unaccompanied)

Private*

* From a U.S. concert tour, 1967.

DEBUSSY

Sonata No. 3, in g (1917) vln & pf
with M. Roustcheva pf   Private†

FRANCK

Sonata in A (1886) vln & pf
with M. Roustcheva pf   Private*

MILHAUD

Sonata No. 1 (1911) vln & pf
with S. Roche pf   Ducretet–Thomson LPG8239

Sonata No. 2 (1917) vln & pf
with M. Roustcheva pf   Private†

RAVEL

Berceuse sur le nom de Gabriel Fauré (1922) vln & pf
with M. Roustcheva pf   Private†

Sonata (1927) vln & pf
with M. Roustcheva pf   Private*

ROUSSEL

Sonata No. 2, in A, Op. 28 vln & pf
with M. Roustcheva pf   Private*

Tomotada SOH

BACH

Concerto in D, BWV1064 3 clavs, strs & c – arr. 3 vlns, strs & c
with R. Barnert vln, W. Prystawski vln   Deutsche Grammophon
& Lucerne Festival Strings –   SLPM139432
Baumgartner

MENDELSSOHN

Concerto in d (1822) vln & strs
with Cologne Chamber Orch. – Müller   Musica Sacra VMS2025
–Brühl

SCHUBERT

Rondo in A, D438 vln & str orch.
with Cologne Chamber Orch. – Müller   Musica Sacra VMS2025
–Brühl

VIVALDI

(12) Concerti, Op. 3 "L'Estro armonico" var. cbns & strs
  Concerto No. 1, in D, P.146 (F.IV, No. 7) 4 vlns, vlc, strs & c
with L. Käppeli vln, H. Scherz vln, B.   Archive SAPM198469
Seeger vln & Lucerne Festival Strings
– Baumgartner

  Concerto No. 4, in e, P.97 (F.I, No. 174) 4 vlns, strs & c
with R. Barnert vln, W. Prystawski   Archive 2705 002, SAPM198469
vln, G. Ribeiro vln & Lucerne Festival
Strings – Baumgartner

  Concerto No. 7, in F, P.249 (F.IV, No. 9) 4 vlns, strs & c
with R. Barnert vln, W. Prystawski   Archive SAPM198470
vln, H. Scherz vln & Lucerne Festival
Strings – Baumgartner

  Concerto No. 8, in a, P.2 (F.I, No. 177) 2 vlns, strs & c
with W. Prystawski vln & Lucerne   Archive SAPM198470
Festival Strings – Baumgartner

* From a U.S. concert tour, 1967.
† From a November 29th 1967 concert at Oberlin College, Ohio.

VIVALDI – *Continued*

  Concerto No. 10, in b, P.148 (F.IV, No. 10) 4 vlns, strs & c
with R. Barnert vln, W. Prystawski   Archive SAPM198471
vln, H. Scherz vln & Lucerne Festival
Strings – Baumgartner

  Concerto No. 12, in E, P.240 (F.I, No. 179) vln, strs & c
with Lucerne Festival Strings –   Archive SAPM198471
Baumgartner

Marie SOLDAT (1864–1955)

SPOHR

Concerto No. 9, in d, Op. 55 vln & orch.
  Adagio (2nd mvt)
with O. Schulhof pf   Union A3000/1

Harry SOLLOWAY

BRUCH

Kol Nidrei, Op. 47 vlc or vln & orch.
with W. Liachovsky pf   Polydor 66488

DRIGO

(2) Airs de Ballet orch.
  No. 2. Valse bluette arr. vln & pf Auer
with piano   Polydor 62557

HUBAY

(Le) Luthier de Crémone, Op. 40 (1894) – opera
  Intermezzo orch. – arr. vln & pf Hubay
with piano   Polydor 66442

(3) Transcriptions, Op. 3 vln & pf
  No. 3. Carmen Fantasia (on themes from the opera by Bizet)
with piano   Polydor 66441

LALO

Symphonie espagnole, Op. 21 vln & orch.
  Andante (4th mvt)
with piano   T 5180   Homophone HD2139

RACHMANINOV

(5) Pieces, Op. 3 pf
  No. 1. Élégie arr. vln & pf Hubay
with piano   Polydor 62568

RIMSKY–KORSAKOV

(Le) Coq d'Or (1910) – opera
  Hymn to the sun arr. vln & pf Kreisler
with piano   Polydor 66567

SAINT–SAËNS

Introduction & Rondo Capriccioso, Op. 28 vln & orch.
with piano   Polydor 66566

SARASATE

(8) Danzas españolas vln & pf
  No. 3. Romanza andaluza, Op. 22, No. 1
with piano   T 5179   Homophone HD2139
  No. 3. Romanza andaluza, Op. 22, No. 1
with piano   Polydor 66442

SARASATE – *Continued*

No. 4. Jota navarra, Op. 22, No. 2
with piano   Polydor 66567
No. 5. Playera, Op. 23, No. 1
with piano   Polydor 66489
Zigeunerweisen, Op. 20 vln & pf or orch.
with piano   Homophone

SZYMANOWSKI

Notturno & Tarantella, Op. 28 vln & pf
Notturno
with piano   Polydor 66489

VECSEY

Caprice No. 1 "Le Vent" vln & pf
with piano   Homophone
Caprice No. 1 "Le Vent" vln & pf
with piano   Polydor 62557

WIENIAWSKI

Scherzo–Tarantelle, Op. 16 vln & pf
with piano   Homophone

ZSOLT

Valse–Caprice vln & pf
with piano   Polydor 62618

Miriam SOLOVIEV (1921–   )

BRAHMS

Sonata No. 1, in G, Op. 78 vln & pf
with J. Katchen pf   Decca SXL6209
Sonata No. 2, in A, Op. 100 vln & pf
with J. Katchen pf   Decca SXL6209
Sonata No. 3, in d, Op. 108 vln & pf
with J. Katchen pf   Decca SXL6209

CHAMINADE

Sérénade espagnole pf – arr. vln & pf Kreisler
with H. Ebert pf   CU–2852–A   Cupol 6038

DEBUSSY

Suite Bergamasque (1890) pf
No. 3. Clair de lune arr. vln & pf
with H. Ebert pf   CU–2855–A   Cupol 6038

KREISLER

Variations on a theme of Corelli (Tartini) vln & pf
with H. Ebert pf   CU–2852–A   Cupol 6038

LALO

Concerto in F, Op. 20 (1872) vln & orch.
with Vienna State Opera Orch. –   Classic CL6221
Swoboda   Concert Hall CHS1143

RIMSKY–KORSAKOV

Scheherazade, Op. 35 (1888) orch.
with Vienna State Opera Orch. – Rossi   Amadeo AVRS6058
                               CBS 51028
                               I Classici della Musica Classica
                               XAM4028
                               Fontana BIG302
                               Top Rank 35–006
                               Vanguard SRV103, SVR103SD

SCHUBERT

Rondo in A, D438 vln & str orch.
with Vienna State Opera Orch. –   Classic CL6221
Swoboda   Concert Hall CHS1176

Herbert SOMAN

BUTTERFIELD

When you and I were young, Maggie (1866) v & pf – arr. vln & pf
with piano   Edison cylinder 4422

CLESI

I'm sorry I made you cry (1918) v & pf – arr. vln & pf
with piano   Edison cylinder 3655

JEROME

Just a baby's prayer at twilight (1918) v & pf – arr. vln & pf
with piano   Edison cylinder 3633
Old pal (1920) v & pf – arr. vln & pf
with D. Lieberfeld pf   8008   Edison cylinder 4497
                               Edison Diamond Disc 50830

PENN

Smilin' through (1915) v & pf – arr. vln & pf
with J.F. Burckhardt pf   7448   Edison cylinder 5082
                               Edison Diamond Disc 50830

Eugen SONNTAG

PERGOLESI

Aria unid – arr. vln & pf
with H. Steinbrück pf   Ultraphon A397

TCHAIKOVSKY

(12) Pieces (of moderate difficulty) Op. 40 pf
No. 2. Chanson triste arr. vln & pf
with H. Steinbrück pf   Ultraphon A397

Denise SORIANO

BACH

(3) Sonatas & 3 Partitas, BWV1001/6 solo vln
Partita No. 3, in E: Preludio (1st mvt) BWV1006 arr. vln & pf Kreisler
with M. Tagliafero pf   Pathé PAT10

BIZET

(L') Arlésienne (Suite No. 1) (1872) orch.
No. 3. Adagietto arr. vln & pf Kreisler
with piano   Pathé PG31

FAURÉ

Andante, Op. 75 vln & pf
with M. Tagliafero pf   Pathé PAT10

Berceuse, Op. 16 vln & pf
with piano   Pathé PAT155

Sonata No. 1, in A, Op. 13 vln & pf
with M. Tagliafero pf   Pathé PAT3/5

HAHN

Romance in A vln & pf
with piano   Pathé PAT54

Sonata in C vln & pf
with D. Sternberg pf   Pathé PDT183/4

KREISLER

Rondino on a theme by Beethoven vln & pf
with piano   Pathé PG107

Minuet (Porpora) vln & pf
with piano   Pathé PAT54

MOZART

Concerto No. 3, in G, K216 (cadenzas by Enescu) vln & orch.
with orch. – Boucherit   Pathé PAT127/9

Concerto No. 7, in D, K271a (cadenzas by Enescu) vln & orch.
with orch. – Munch   Pathé PAT143/6

Divertimento No. 17, in D, K334 2 hrns & strs
Minuet (3rd mvt) arr. vln & pf Burmester
with A. Lermyte pf   Pathé PAT146

Sonata No. 26, in B flat, K378 vln & pf
with H. Pignari pf   Pathé PDT163/4

Sonata No. 32, in B flat, K454 vln & pf
CPTX 296–1 & 306/8–1   Columbia 69593/4D, (set X131),
with M. Tagliafero pf   DX856/7
                                 Pathé PAT84/5

PAGANINI

(24) Caprices, Op. 1 (1801/7) solo vln
Caprice No. 13, in B flat arr. vln & pf Kreisler
with A. Lermyte pf   Pathé PG107

PARADIES

Sicilienne vln & pf – arr. Dushkin
with piano   Pathé PG31

SCHUBERT, François

(12) Bagatelles, Op. 13 vln & pf
No. 9. L'abeille
with piano   Pathé PG31

TARTINI

(12) Sonatas, Op. 2 vln & c
Sonata No. 6, in C
with piano   Pathé PAT57

Sonata No. 12, in G: Adagio (2nd mvt)
with piano   Pathé PAT57

VIVALDI

(12) Concerti, Op. 3 "L'Estro armonico" var. cbns & strs
Concerto No. 9, in D, P.147 (F.I, No. 178) vln, strs & c – arr. Dandelot
with orch. – Munch   Pathé PAT154/5

Herbert SORKIN (1920–)

POWELL

Divertimento (1955) vln & hp
with M. Ross hp   Composers Recordings CRI121

Trio (1956) pf, vln & vlc
with L. Burnham pf & R. Schweitzer   Composers Recordings CRI121
vlc

STRAVINSKY

(L') Histoire du Soldat (1918) narrators & tpt, cbs, tbn, cl, vln, bsn & pcn
with D. Jandorf tpt, R. Jamitz cbs, J.   Westminster W–LAB7049
Thompson tbn S. Drucker cl, C. Segal
bsn, M. Lang pcn – cond. Mandell

Leonard SORKIN

VIVALDI

(12) Concerti, Op. 3 "L'Estro armonico" var. cbns & strs
Concerto No. 11, in d, P.250 (F.IV, No. 11) 2 vlns, vlc, strs & c
with Musical Arts Symphony Orch. –   Concert Disc C1031, CS31
Sorkin   Everest LPBR6121, SDBR3121

Spytihněv ŠORM (1914–)

PAUER

Sonatina vln & pf
with A. Holeček pf   Supraphon SUA10044

VYCPÁLEK

Sonata in D, Op. 19 "In praise of the violin" m–s, vln & pf
with S. Červena m–s & A. Holeček pf Supraphon SUA10044

Elsie SOUTHGATE (1889–1946)

ANONYMOUS

Auld Robin Gray (1780) Traditional Scottish ballad – arr. vln & org
with D. Southgate Mustel org   Zonophone 1569, X48043

Bonnie Mary of Argyle Traditional Scottish ballad – arr. vln & org
with D. Southgate Mustel org   Zonophone 1569, X48044

Coon melodies unid – arr. vln & org
with D. Southgate   HO 1257 e   HMV X288072
Mustel org   Zonophone 1554, X48042

Drink to me only with thine eyes (1762) Traditional – arr. vln & org
Hullah
with D. Southgate Mustel org   Zonophone 2028

Robin Adair (1750) Traditional Irish ballad – arr. vln & org
with D. Southgate Mustel org   Zonophone 1569, X48044

BALFE

Killarney (1862) v & pf – arr. vln & pf Moffat
with D. Southgate Mustel   y 19851 Zonophone 1880, X48062
org

BRUCH

Concerto No. 1, in g, Op. 26 vln & orch.
  Adagio (2nd mvt)*
    with D. Southgate   y 21852 e   HMV X871
    Mustel org   Zonophone 2070, X47958

CLARKE

Sincerity v & pf – arr. vln & org
  with D. Southgate Mustel org   Zonophone 1786

COWARD

Because (Berceuse Paysanne) v & pf – arr. vln & org
  with D. Southgate Mustel org   Zonophone 1325, X48032
Held in bondage v & pf – arr. vln & org
  with D. Southgate Mustel org   HMV X288074
                                  Zonophone 1634

DANKS

Silver threads among the gold (1873) v & pf – arr. vln & org
  with D. Southgate Mustel org   Zonophone 1820

DURANTE

Aria in d unid – arr. vln & org Southgate
  with D. Southgate org   Zonophone 2243

FORSTER

Rose in the bud vln & pf
  with D. Southgate cinema org   Zonophone 5109

FOSTER

Massa's in de cold, cold groun' (1852) v & pf – arr. vln & org
  with D. Southgate Mustel org   Zonophone 1820
(The) Old folks at home "Swanee River" (1851) v & pf – arr. vln & org
  with D. Southgate Mustel org   Zonophone 1820

GOODWIN

That wonderful mother of mine (1918) v & pf – arr. vln & org
  with D. Southgate Mustel org   Zonophone 2028

GOUNOD

Ave Maria (Méditation on Bach's "Prelude No. 1, in C" from Book I of "Das Wohltemperirte Clavier" v & pf – arr. vln & org
  with D. Southgate   HO 1258 e   Zonophone 1525, X49506
  Mustel org
Faust (1859) – opera
  Anges purs, anges radieux (Act V) arr. vln & org
  with D. Southgate Mustel org   Zonophone 1911
  Avant de quitter ces lieux (Act II) arr. vln & org
  with D. Southgate   Y 21232 e   Zonophone 1939, X47941
  Mustel org
  Faites–lui mes aveux (Act III) arr. vln & org
  with D. Southgate   Y 21229 e   Zonophone 1939, X47943
  Mustel org
  Salut! Demeure chaste et pure (Act III) arr. vln & org
  with D. Southgate Mustel org   Zonophone 1911
  (Il) Se fait tard (Act III) arr. vln & org
  with D. Southgate   H 20170 e   Zonophone 1848, X48068
  Mustel org

* Label states: "Adagio, Op. 57".

GOUNOD – *Continued*

  Versez vos chagrins (Act IV) arr. vln & org
  with D. Southgate   Y 79845 e   Zonophone 1848, X48059
  Mustel org

HANDEL

Serse (1738) – opera
  Ombra mai fu "Largo" arr. vln & pf Squire
  with D. Southgate Mustel org   Regal G8334
                                  Zonophone A168

d'HARDELOT

Because (1902) v & pf – arr. vln & org
  with D. Southgate   YR 1174[I]△ Zonophone 5024, X4961?
  cinema org

LOHR

Where my caravan has rested (1909) v & pf – arr. vln & org
  with D. Southgate Mustel org   Zonophone 1698

MARSHALL

I hear you calling me (1908) v & pf – arr. vln & org
  with D. Southgate cinema org   Zonophone 5109

MASCAGNI

Cavalleria Rusticana (1890) – opera
  Intermezzo orch. – arr. vln & org Southgate
  with D. Southgate   HO 1255 e   Zonophone 1525, X49505
  Mustel org

METCALF

Absent (1899) v & pf – arr. vln & org
  with D. Southgate Mustel   A 4036   Regal G8604
  org   Zonophone 1383

NEVIN

Mighty lak' a rose (1901) v & pf – arr. vln & org
  with D. Southgate   YR 1175[II]△ Zonophone 5024, X49613
  cinema org
(The) Rosary (1898) v & pf – arr. vln & org
  with D. Southgate Mustel org   HMV X288083
                                  Zonophone 1634

OFFENBACH

(Les) Contes d'Hoffmann (1881) – opera
  Belle Nuit, O nuit d'amour "Barcarolle" arr. vln & org Southgate
  with D. Southgate   HO 1256 e   HMV X288071
  Mustel org   Zonophone 1554, X48041

PAPINI

Idylle, Op. 96 vln & pf
  with D. Southgate   y 21778 e   Zonophone 1977, X48065
  Mustel org
(3) Morceaux lyriques, Op. 98 vln & pf
No. 2. Nocturne
  with D. Southgate   y 21778 e   Zonophone 1977, X48065
  Mustel org

PERGOLESI

Siciliano unid – arr. vln & cel
  with celeste   yy 1023[1]   Zonophone 2489, X47974

PINKARD

Mammy o' mine (1919) v & pf – arr. vln & org
  with D. Southgate   y 21787 e Zonophone 1977, X48066
  Mustel org

PUCCINI

(La) Bohème (1896) – opera
  Quando m'en vo soletta "Musetta's waltz song" (Act II) arr. vln & org
  Southgate
  with D. Southgate   y 21854[II]e Zonophone 2114, X47959
  Mustel org

RUBINSTEIN

(2) Melodies, Op. 3 pf
  No. 1. Melody in F arr. vln & pf Wilhelmj
  with D. Southgate Mustel org   Zonophone 1383, X49485

SAINT-SAËNS

(Le) Carnaval des animaux (1886) small orch.
  Le cygne arr. vln & cel
  with D. Southgate cel   y 20679 e Zonophone 2114, X47960

SCHUBERT

(14) Schwanengesang, D957 (1828) v & pf
  No. 4. Ständchen "Serenade" arr. vln & pf George
  with piano   yy 1025[II] Zonophone 2489, X47973

SCOTT, Lady John

Annie Laurie (Scottish ballad) (1838) v & pf – arr. vln & org
  with D. Southgate Mustel org   Zonophone 1325, X48031

SHARPE

One little hour v & pf – arr. vln & org
  with D. Southgate Mustel org   Zonophone 2352

SILÉSU

(A) Little love, a little kiss (1912) v & pf – arr. vln & org
  with D. Southgate Mustel org   Zonophone 1698

SOUTHGATE, D.

Dorothy's lullaby vln & org
  with D. Southgate Mustel org   Zonophone 2243
Mispah vln & org
  with D. Southgate Mustel org   Zonophone 2352
Sérénade espagnole vln & org
  with D. Southgate Mustel org   Zonophone 2143

SOUTHGATE, E.

Valse Egyptienne vln & org
  with D. Southgate org   y 21851 e Zonophone 2210, X47965

SOUTHGATE, E.D.

(The) Butterfly vln & org
  with D. Southgate org   y 21781 e Zonophone 2210, X47966

SOUTHGATE, E. & D.

Thanksgiving vln & org
  with D. Southgate Mustel org   Zonophone 1611

SOUTHGATE, F.S.

Dance of the elves, vln & org
  with D. Southgate Mustel org   Zonophone 1742

SOUTHGATE, F.S. – *Continued*

Pleading vln & org
  with D. Southgate Mustel org   Zonophone 1742
Rêve d'amour vln & org
  with D. Southgate Mustel org   Zonophone 1611 ·

SOUTHGATE, S.

Inspiration vln & org
  with D. Southgate Mustel org   Zonophone 2143

SULLIVAN

(The) Lost chord (1877) v & pf – arr. vln & org
  with D. Southgate Mustel org   Regal G8334
                          Zonophone A168

TATE

Somewhere a voice is calling (1911) v & pf – arr. vln & org
  with D. Southgate Mustel   A 4039 Regal G8604
  org   Zonophone 1383, X49486

THOMAS

Eileen Alannah (1873) v & pf – arr. vln & org
  with D. Southgate   y 19849 e Zonophone 1880, X48061
  Mustel org

THOMÉ

Andante religioso, Op. 70 pf – arr. vln & org
  with D. Southgate Mustel org   Regal G8568
(L') Extase pf – arr. vln & org
  with D. Southgate   y 19442 e HMV X288076
  cinema org   Zonophone 1667, 5040, X48049
Simple aveu, Op. 25 pf – arr. vln & org
  with D. Southgate   y 19440 e HMV X288075
  cinema org   Zonophone 1667, 5040, X48050

WAGNER

Tannhäuser (1845) – opera
  O du mein holder Abendstern (Act III) arr. vln & org Southgate
  with D. Southgate   y 21855 e HMV X871
  Mustel org   Regal G8568
                          Zonophone 2070, X47957

WOOD

Love's garden of roses v & pf – arr. vln & org
  with D. Southgate Mustel org   Zonophone 1786

WOODFORDE–FINDEN

(4) Indian Love Lyrics (1903) orch.
  No. 3. Kashmiri song arr. vln & org
  with D. Southgate   y 21856[II]e Zonophone 1995, X48067
  Mustel org
  No. 4. Till I wake arr. vln & org
  with D. Southgate   y 21897[I]e Zonophone 1995, X48068
  Mustel org

Albert SPALDING (1888–1953)

ALBÉNIZ

Malagueña, Op. 71, No. 6 pf – arr. vln & pf Kreisler
  with J. Wolffers pf   Allegro–Ultraphonic 1693
                    Halo 50296

ANONYMOUS

Drink to me only with thine eyes (1762) traditional arr. vln & pf Quilter
with A. Benoist pf   6951   Edison cylinder 29046
     Edison Diamond Disc 82184

Drink to me only with thine eyes (1762) Traditional – arr. vln & pf Quilter
with A. Benoist pf   Victor 1703

BACH

(3) Sonatas & 3 Partitas, BWV1001/6 solo vln
Partita No. 2, in d: Chaconne (5th mvt) BWV1004*
(unaccompanied)   Allegro–Ultraphonic 1675

(Das) Wohltemperirte Clavier, BWV846/93 clav
No. 38. Prelude & Fugue No. 14, in f sharp: Prelude, BWV882 – Book II
arr. vln & pf Spalding
with A. Kooiker pf   Concerteum CR281
     Remington R199–23

No. 38. Prelude & Fugue No. 14, in f sharp: Prelude, BWV882 – Book II
arr. vln & pf Spalding
with J. Wolffers pf   Allegro–Ultraphonic 1693
     Halo 50296

BEETHOVEN

Concerto in D, Op. 61 (cadenzas by Spalding) vln & orch.
with Austrian Symphony Orch. –   Concerteum CR218
Loibner   Remington R199–144

(6) Minuets, G167 pf
No. 2. Minuet No. 2, in G arr. vln & pf Burmester
with A. Benoist pf   5754   Edison Diamond Disc 82284

Romance No. 1, in G, Op. 40 vln & orch. – arr. vln & pf Flesch
with A. Benoist pf   Victor 1788

Romance No. 2, in F, Op. 50 vln & orch.
with A. Benoist pf   2A 89309/10 △   HMV ED76
     Victor 14579

Sonata No. 9, in A, Op. 47 "Kreutzer" vln & pf
with J. Wolffers pf   Allegro–Ultraphonic 1675

BÉRIOT

Concerto No. 2, in b, Op. 32 vln & orch.
Andante (2nd mvt)
with A. Benoist pf   7599   Edison Diamond Disc 82250

BIZET

(L') Arlésienne (Suite No. 1) (1872) orch.
No. 3. Adagietto arr. vln & pf Kreisler
with A. Benoist pf   5061   Edison Diamond Disc 82172

(L') Arlésienne (Suite No. 2) (1872) orch.
No. 2. Intermezzo arr. vln & pf Kreisler
with A. Benoist pf   2409   Edison Diamond Disc 82046

BOULANGER, L.

Cortège (1919) vln & pf
with A. Benoist pf   Victor 1740

BRAGA

(7) Melodies (1867) v & pf
No. 5. La serenata "Angel's serenade" arr. v, vln & pf
with F. Hempel s & R.   8005   Edison Diamond Disc 82240
Gayler pf

* Recorded live on Nov. 7th 1951 at Boston University.

BRAHMS

Concerto in D, Op. 77 (cadenza by Spalding) vln & orch.
with Austrian Symphony Orch. –   Concerteum CR216
Loibner   Remington R199–145

(21) Hungarian Dances pf duet
Hungarian dance No. 1, in g arr. vln & pf Joachim
with A. Benoist pf   Edison Diamond Disc 82263

Hungarian dance No. 1, in g arr. vln & pf Joachim
with J. Wolffers pf   Allegro–Ultraphonic 1693
     Halo 50296

Hungarian dance No. 1, in g arr. vln & pf Joachim
with A. Kooiker pf   Remington R199–24

Hungarian dance No. 2, in d arr. vln & pf Joachim
with A. Kooiker pf   Remington R199–24

Hungarian dance No. 2, in d arr. vln & pf Joachim
with J. Wolffers pf   Allegro–Ultraphonic 1693
     Halo 50296

Hungarian dance No. 3, in F, arr. vln & pf Joachim
with A. Kooiker pf   Remington R199–24

Hungarian dance No. 4, in f arr. vln & pf "in b" Joachim
with A. Kooiker pf   Remington R199–24

Hungarian dance No. 5, in f sharp arr. vln & pf "in g" Joachim
with A Benoist pf   2399   Edison cylinder 203
     Edison Diamond Disc 82048

Hungarian dance No. 5, in f sharp arr. vln & pf "in g" Joachim
with A. Kooiker pf   Remington R199–24

Hungarian dance No. 6, in D flat arr. vln & pf "in B flat" Joachim
with A. Kooiker pf   Remington R199–24

Hungarian dance No. 7, in A arr. vln & pf Joachim
with A. Benoist pf   4112   Edison cylinder 203
     Edison Diamond Disc 82046

Hungarian dance No. 7, in A arr. vln & pf Joachim
with A. Kooiker pf   Remington R199–24

Hungarian dance No. 8, in a arr. vln & pf Joachim
with A. Kooiker pf   Remington R199–24, R199–84

Hungarian dance No. 9, in e arr. vln & pf Joachim
with A. Kooiker pf   Remington R199–24, R199–84

Hungarian dance No. 14, in d arr. vln & pf Joachim
with A. Kooiker pf   Remington R199–24

Hungarian dance No. 15, in B flat arr. vln & pf "in A" Joachim
with A. Kooiker pf   Remington R199–24

Hungarian dance No. 16, in f arr. vln & pf "in g" Joachim
with A. Kooiker pf   Remington R199–24

Hungarian dance No. 17, in f sharp arr. vln & pf Joachim
with A. Kooiker pf   Remington R199–24

Hungarian dance No. 19, in b arr. vln & pf "in a" Joachim
with A. Kooiker pf   Remington R199–24

Hungarian dance No. 20, in e arr. vln & pf "in d" Joachim
with A. Kooiker pf   Remington R199–24

Hungarian dance No. 21, in e arr. vln & pf Joachim
with A. Kooiker pf   Remington R199–24

Sonata No. 1, in G, Op. 78 vln & pf
with E. von Dohnányi pf   Remington R199–84

Sonata No. 2, in A, Op. 100 vln & pf
with A. Benoist pf   Victor 8858 & 1724/5, (set M288)

Sonata No. 2, in A, Op. 100 vln & pf
with E. von Dohnányi pf   Remington RLP199–49

BRAHMS – *Continued*

Sonata No. 3, in d, Op. 108 vln & pf
  with E. Von Dohnányi pf   Remington RLP199–49
(16) Waltzes, Op. 39 pf duet
  No. 15. Waltz No. 15, in A flat arr. vln & pf "in A" Hochstein
  with A. Benoist pf   Brunswick 15127
  No. 15. Waltz No. 15, in A flat arr. vln & pf "in A" Hochstein
  with A. Benoist pf   Victor 1667

CASSADÓ

Danse du diable vert vln & pf
  with A. Benoist pf   Victor 1914

CHABRIER

(10) Pièces pittoresques (1880) pf
  No. 10. Scherzo–valse arr. vln & pf Loeffler
  with A. Benoist pf   Edison Diamond Disc 82168

CHAMINADE

Sérénade espagnole pf – arr. vln & pf Kreisler
  with A. Benoist pf   5061   Edison Diamond Disc 82172

CHOPIN

(3) Nocturnes, Op. 9 pf
  No. 2. Nocturne No. 2, in E flat arr. vln & pf Sarasate
  with A. Benoist pf   2408   Edison Diamond Disc 82062
  No. 2. Nocturne No. 2, in E flat arr. vln & pf Sarasate
  with A. Benoist pf   4113   Brunswick 30124, 50138
(2) Nocturnes, Op. 27 pf
  No. 2. Nocturne No. 8, in D flat arr. vln & pf Wilhelmj
  with A. Benoist pf   5752   Edison Diamond Disc 82212
(2) Nocturnes, Op. 37 pf
  No. 2. Nocturne No. 12, in G arr. vln & pf Spalding
  with A. Benoist pf   58   Brunswick 50099, A5102
                          Polydor 595011
(2) Waltzes, Op. 69 pf
  No. 2. Waltz No. 10, in b arr. vln & pf Spalding
  with A. Benoist pf   Victor 1703
(3) Waltzes, Op. 70 pf
  No. 1. Waltz No. 11, in G flat arr. vln & pf Spalding
  with A. Benoist pf   Edison Diamond Disc 82316

CORELLI

(12) Sonatas, Op. 5 vln & c
Sonata No. 1, in D
  with A. Kooiker pf   Concerteum CR281
                          Remington RLP199–23

Sonata No. 6, in A
  with A. Kooiker pf   Concerteum CR281
                          Remington RLP199–23

Sonata No. 12, in d "La Follia" arr. vln & pf Spalding
  with A. Kooiker pf   Concerteum CR281
                          Remington RLP199–23

COTTENET

Chanson méditation vln & pf
  with A. Benoist pf   Edison Diamond Disc 82206

CUI

Kaleidoscope, Op. 50 vln & pf
  No. 9. Orientale
  with A. Benoist pf   3394   Edison Diamond Disc 82064

DEBUSSY

(12) Préludes – Book I (1910) pf
  No. 12. Minstrels arr. vln & pf Hartmann
  with A. Benoist pf   Victor 1881
Suite Bergamasque (1890) pf
  No. 3. Clair de lune arr. vln & pf Spalding
  with J. Wolffers pf   Allegro–Ultraphonic 1693
                          Halo 50296

DELIBES

(Le) Roi s'amuse (1882) – Incidental music orch.
  No. 6. Passepied arr. vln & pf Gruenberg
  with A. Benoist pf   Brunswick 15211
  No. 6. Passepied arr. vln & pf Gruenberg
  with A. Benoist pf   Edison Diamond Disc 82192

DRDLA

Souvenir vln & pf
  with A. Benoist pf   5062   Edison Diamond Disc 82154

DRIGO

(2) Airs de Ballet orch.
  No. 2. Valse bluette arr. vln & pf Auer
  with A. Benoist pf   Edison Diamond Disc 82192
(Les) Millions d'Arlequin (1900) – ballet orch.
  Sérénade arr. vln & pf Auer
  with A. Benoist pf   Edison Diamond Disc 82263

DVOŘÁK

(8) Humoresques, Op. 101 pf
  No. 7. Humoresque No. 7, in G flat arr. vln & pf "in G" Wilhelmj
  with A. Benoist pf   4579–J–1–3   Edison Diamond Disc 82047
  No. 7. Humoresque No. 7, in G flat arr. vln & pf "in G" Wilhelmj
  with A. Benoist pf   Edison 47005*
(8) Slavonic Dances, Op. 72 pf duet; orch.
  No. 2. Slavonic dance No. 10, in e arr. vln & pf Kreisler
  with A. Benoist pf   Edison Diamond Disc 82311
Sonatina in G, Op. 100 vln & pf
  Larghetto (2nd mvt) arr. vln & pf as "Indian lament" by Kreisler
  with A. Benoist pf   8017   Edison Diamond Disc 82239

FALLA

(7) Canciones populares españolas (1914) v & pf
  No. 4. Jota arr. vln & pf Kochański
  with J. Wolffers pf   Allegro–Ultraphonic 1693
                          Halo 50296

  No. 5. Nana arr. vln & pf Kochański
  with J. Wolffers pf   Allegro–Ultraphonic 1693
                          Halo 50296

(La) Vida Breve (1913) – opera
  Danza española orch. – arr. vln & pf Kreisler
  with J. Wolffers pf   Allegro–Ultraphonic 1693
                          Halo 50296

* Electrical process, 1928.

FOSTER

My old Kentucky home v & pf – arr. vln & pf Spalding
with A. Benoist pf   Edison cylinder 28236
Edison Diamond Disc 82105

(The) Old folks at home "Swanee River" (1851) v & pf – arr. vln & pf
Zimbalist
with A. Benoist pf   7601   Edison Diamond Disc 82215

FRANCK

Sonata in A (1886) vln & pf
with A. Benoist pf   Victor 8274/7, (set M208)

GLUCK

Orphée et Eurydice (1762) – opera
Dance of the blessed spirits: Lento "Mélodie" (No. 2) arr. vln & pf Ries
with A. Benoist pf   Edison Diamond Disc 82206

GODARD

Concerto No. 1, Op. 35 "Concerto Romantique" vln & orch.
Canzonetta (2nd mvt)
with A. Benoist pf   5052   Edison Diamond Disc 82212

GOUNOD

Ave Maria (Méditation on Bach's "Prelude No. 1, in C" from Book I of
"Das Wohltemperirte Clavier") v & pf – arr. v, vln & orch.
with M. Rappold s & orch.   3815   Edison cylinder 28106
Edison Diamond Disc 82536

GRANADOS

(12) Danzas españolas, Op. 37 (1893) pf
No. 5. Danza española No. 5, in e "Andaluza" arr. vln & pf Kreisler
with A. Benoist pf   Edison Diamond Disc 82194

No. 5. Danza española No. 5, in e "Andaluza" arr. vln & pf Kreisler
with J. Wolffers pf   Allegro–Ultraphonic 1693
Halo 50296

HANDEL

Serse (1738) – opera
Ombra mai fu "Largo" arr. vln, pf & org Spalding
with A. Benoist pf & R.   7612   Edison Diamond Disc 82239
Gayler org

(15) Sonatas, Op. 1 (?1731) fl or vln & c
Sonata No. 15, in E vln VI
with A. Benoist pf   HMV DB3109
Victor 14029

(9) Sonatas, Op. 2 (1724) 2 vlns or obs & c
Sonata No. 9, in E: Adagio (2nd mvt)
with W. Primrose vla & A. Benoist pf   HMV DB6107*
Victor 18241, 18242, (in set
M838)

HARRIS

Poem vln & pf
with A. Benoist pf   Victor 8997

KETTEN

Caprice espagnole pf – arr. vln & pf Loeffler
with A. Benoist pf   5759   Edison Diamond Disc 82154

* Unissued.

KREISLER

Caprice viennois, Op. 2 vln & pf
with A. Benoist pf   3324   Edison Diamond Disc 82067

Liebesfreud vln & pf
with A. Benoist pf   Edison Diamond Disc 82323

Schön Rosmarin vln & pf
with A. Benoist pf   2409   Edison Diamond Disc 82046

MASCHERONI

Eternamente (1891) v & pf – arr. v, vln & pf
with C. Muzio s & R. Gayler pf   Contrepoint MC20010
Edison Diamond Disc 82243
Esoteric ES508

Eternamente (1891) v & pf – arr. v, vln & pf
with C. Muzio s & piano   7613   Edison Diamond Disc*

MASSENET

Thaïs (1894) – opera
Méditation arr. vln & pf Marsick
with A. Benoist pf   3762   Edison cylinder 28102
Edison Diamond Disc 82043

MENDELSSOHN

Concerto in e, Op. 64 vln & orch.
with Philadelphia   071271/3–1A†   Victor*
Orch. – Ormandy

(6) Gesänge, Op. 34 v & pf
No. 2. Auf Flügeln des Gesanges arr. vln & pf Achron
with A. Benoist pf   Brunswick 50066

(6) Songs without words, Op. 62 pf
No. 6. Song without words No. 3, in A "Spring song" arr. vln & pf
Spalding
with A. Benoist pf   5748   Edison Diamond Disc 82135

MOSZKOWSKI

(2) Stücke, Op. 45 pf
No. 2. Guitarre arr. vln & pf Sarasate
with A. Benoist pf   Brunswick 15107

MOZART

Divertimento No. 17, in D, K334 2 hrns & strs
Minuet (3rd mvt) arr. vln & pf Burmester
with A. Benoist pf   Brunswick 15127

Minuet (3rd mvt) arr. vln & pf Burmester
with A. Benoist pf   Victor 1667

Sinfonia concertante in E flat, K364 vln, vla & orch.
with W. Primrose vla & New Friends   Camden CFL105
of Music Orch. – Stiedry   HMV DB6104/7*
Victor 18238/41, 18242/5 (set
M838)

Sonata No. 28, in E flat, K380 vln & pf
with A. Benoist pf   Victor 18156/7, (set M819)

* Unissued.
† Sides 4 & 5 have no matrix or take numbers, nor the initials EO (Eugene
Ormandy) on them as do sides 1 to 3. These discs, numbering 5 in total,
are single–sided test pressings. The 2nd mvt is incomplete.

OPENSHAW

Love sends a little gift of roses (1919) v & pf – arr. vln & pf
with A. Benoist pf 9250 Edison Diamond Disc 82308

PAGANINI

(6) Sonatas, Op. 3 (1801/6) vln & gtr
No. 6. Sonata No. 12, in e arr. vln & pf Spalding
with J. Wolffers pf Allegro–Ultraphonic 1693
Halo 50296

PIERNÉ

Sérénade in A, Op. 7 (1875) pf – arr. vln & pf Haddock
with A. Benoist pf 5053 Edison Diamond Disc 82184

QUILTER

Three poor mariners v & pf – arr. vln & pf
with A. Benoist pf Edison Diamond Disc 82192

RAFF

(6) Pieces, Op. 85 vln & pf
No. 3. Cavatina in D
with A. Benoist pf Brunswick 50136
No. 3. Cavatina in D
with A. Benoist pf 3761–F–1–2 Edison Diamond Disc 82047

RANDEGGER

Pierrot serenade, Op. 33, No. 1 vln & pf
with A. Benoist pf Edison cylinder 28241
Edison Diamond Disc 82105

RAVEL

Pièce en forme d'Habanera v & pf – arr. vln & pf Catherine
with J. Wolffers pf Allegro–Ultraphonic 1693
Halo 50296

RUBINSTEIN

(2) Melodies, Op. 3 pf
No. 1. Melody in F arr. vln & pf Spalding
with A. Benoist pf 5747 Edison cylinder 28285
Edison Diamond Disc 82135

RUST

Gigue unid – arr. vln & pf
with A. Benoist pf Edison cylinder 28241
Edison Diamond Disc 82105

SAINT–SAËNS

(Le) Carnaval des animaux (1886) small orch.
Le cygne arr. vln & pf
with A. Benoist pf Edison cylinder 28185
Edison Diamond Disc 82316

(Le) Déluge, Op. 45 (1876) – oratorio
Prélude vln & orch. – arr. vln & pf Saint–Saëns
with A. Benoist pf & R. 5060 Edison Diamond Disc 82172
Gayler org

Introduction & Rondo Capriccioso, Op. 28 vln & orch.
with A. Benoist pf 3758 Edison Diamond Disc 82043

SARASATE

Carmen Fantasia (on themes from the opera by Bizet) Op. 25 vln & pf or orch.
with A. Benoist pf 8037 Edison Diamond Disc 82245

SARASATE – *Continued*

(8) Danzas españolas vln & pf
No. 2. Habañera, Op. 21, No. 2
with A. Benoist pf Edison Diamond Disc 82095
No. 3. Romanza andaluza, Op. 22, No. 1
with A. Benoist pf Brunswick 50136
No. 6. Zapateado, Op. 23, No. 2
with A. Benoist pf Brunswick 15211, A8854
No. 8. Danza española No. 8, in C, Op. 26, No. 2
with A. Benoist pf 2406 Edison Diamond Disc 82062
Introduction & Tarantelle, Op. 43 vln & pf
with A. Benoist pf 61 Brunswick 50099, A5102
Polydor 595011, A73087

Zigeunerweisen, Op. 20 vln & pf or orch.
with A. Benoist pf Edison cylinder 290
Edison Diamond Disc 82192

SCHERTZINGER

Marchéta (1913) v & pf – arr. vln & pf
with A. Benoist pf Edison Diamond Disc 82316

SCHINDLER

Souvenir poétique (Paraphrase on Fibich's "Poem" Op. 41, No. 14) vln & pf
with A. Benoist pf Edison Diamond Disc 82323

SCHUBERT

(16) Deutsche Tänze, Op. 33 (D783) pf
No. 3. Deutscher Tanz No. 3, in B flat, arr. vln & pf as "Valse sentimentale" by Franko
with A. Benoist pf Edison cylinder 29058
(7) Gesänge (set to Scott's "Lady of the Lake") Op. 52 v & pf
No. 6. Ave Maria, D839 arr. vln & pf Wilhelmj
with A. Benoist pf Brunswick 50066
No. 6. Ave Maria, D839 arr. vln & pf Wilhelmj
with J. Wolffers pf Allegro–Ultraphonic 1693
Halo 50296
No. 6. Ave Maria, D839 arr. v, vln & pf
with M. Rappold s & A. Benoist pf Edison Diamond Disc 82258
Horch! Horch! die Lerch, D889 (1826) v & pf – arr. vln & pf Spalding
with A. Benoist pf Edison 47005*
Horch! Horch! die Lerch, D889 (1826) v & pf – arr. vln & pf Spalding
with A. Benoist pf Victor 1667
(14) Schwanengesang, D957 (1828) v & pf
No. 4. Ständchen "Serenade" arr. vln & pf Reményi
with A. Benoist pf 7594 Edison cylinder 29070
Edison Diamond Disc 82222

SCHUMANN

(20) Albumblätter, Op. 124 pf
No. 16. Schlummerlied arr. vln & pf
with A. Benoist pf 5755 Edison Diamond Disc 82284
(12) Duets, Op. 85 pf – 4 hands
No. 3. Gartenmelodie arr. vln & pf
with A. Benoist pf Edison cylinder 217
No. 12. Abendlied arr. vln & pf Wilhelmj
with A. Benoist pf Victor 1727, JE36

* Electrical process, 1928.

SCHUMANN – *Continued*

(13) Kinderscenen, Op. 15 pf
No. 7. Träumerei arr. vln & pf
with A. Benoist pf   5749   Edison cylinder 29050
                                     Edison Diamond Disc 82188

No. 7. Träumerei arr. vln & pf
with A. Benoist pf   Victor 1727

(3) Romances, Op. 94 ob or vlc or vln or cl & pf
No. 2. Romance No. 2, in A arr. vln & pf Kreisler
with A. Benoist pf   Edison Diamond Disc 82168

SIBELIUS

Kuolema, Op. 44 – Incidental music orch.
Valse triste arr. vln & pf Franko
with A. Benoist pf   Edison Diamond Disc 82322

SPALDING

Alabama (Plantation melody) vln & pf
with A. Benoist pf   Edison Diamond Disc 82095

Dragonfly (A study in arpeggios) solo vln
(unaccompanied)   Victor 1914

Etchings, Op. 5 vln & pf
Books
with A. Benoist pf   Victor 1707/9, (in set M264)
Cinderella
with A. Benoist pf   Victor 1707/9, (in set M264)
Desert twilight
with A. Benoist pf   Victor 1707/9, (in set M264)
Dreams
with A. Benoist pf   Victor 1707/9, (in set M264)
Fireflies
with A. Benoist pf   Victor 1707/9, (in set M264)
Games
with A. Benoist pf   Victor 1707/9, (in set M264)
Ghosts
with A. Benoist pf   Victor 1707/9, (in set M264)
Happiness
with A. Benoist pf   Victor 1707/9, (in set M264)
Hurdy–gurdy waltz
with A. Benoist pf   8028   Edison Diamond Disc 82250
Hurdy–gurdy waltz
with A. Benoist pf   Victor 1707/9, (in set M264)
Impatience
with A. Benoist pf   Victor 1707/9, (in set M264)
October
with A. Benoist pf   Victor 1707/9, (in set M264)
Professor
with A. Benoist pf   Victor 1707/9, (in set M264)
Sunday morning bells
with A. Benoist pf   8028   Edison Diamond Disc 82250
Sunday morning bells
with A. Benoist pf   Victor 1707/9, (in set M264)

From the cottonfields, Op. 7, No. 3 vln & pf
with A. Benoist pf   7600   Edison Diamond Disc 82222

Sonata in e solo vln
(unaccompanied)   048982/5   Victor*

* Unissued – recorded Spring of 1940.

SPALDING – *Continued*

(The) Wind in the pines (Prelude) vln & pf
with A. Benoist pf   Victor 1881

SPOHR

Concerto No. 8, in a, Op. 47 "Gesangsscene" vln & orch.
with Philadelphia   2A 022377/80 △ HMV DB3831/2
Orch. – Ormandy   Victor 15355/6, (set M544)

SUK

(4) Pieces, Op. 17 vln & pf
No. 4. Burleska
with A. Benoist pf   Victor 1740

SVENDSEN

Romance in G, Op. 26 vln & orch. – arr. vln & pf Wilhelmj
with A. Benoist pf   Edison Diamond Disc 82194

TARTINI

(12) Sonatas, Op. 1 (1734) vln & c
Sonata No. 10, in g "Didone abandonata"
with A. Kooiker pf   Concerteum CR281
                                   Remington RLP199–23

Sonata in g "Il Trillo del Diavolo" vln & c – arr. vln & pf
with A. Benoist pf   Victor 14139 & 1787

TCHAIKOVSKY

Concerto in D, Op. 35 vln & orch.
Canzonetta (2nd mvt)
with A. Benoist pf   Brunswick 50100

Quartet No. 1, in D, Op. 11 2 vlns, vla & vlc
Andante cantabile (2nd mvt) arr. vln & pf Kreisler
with A. Benoist pf   Brunswick 50100

Sérénade mélancolique in b flat, Op. 26 vln & orch. – arr. vln & pf
Wilhelmj
with A. Benoist pf   3393   Edison Diamond Disc 82067

(3) Souvenirs de Hapsal Op. 2 pf
No. 3. Chant sans paroles in f arr. vln & pf Kreisler
with A. Benoist pf   3374   Edison Diamond Disc 82064

WAGNER

(Die) Meistersinger von Nürnberg (1868) – opera
Morgenlich leuchtend "Prize song" arr. vln & pf Wilhelmj
with A. Benoist pf   Edison cylinder 28177
                                   Edison Diamond Disc 82117

Morgenlich leuchtend "Prize song" arr. vln & pf Wilhelmj
with A. Benoist pf   842   Brunswick 30124, 50138

WHITE

Bandanna Sketches, Op. 12 vln & pf
No. 1. Nobody Knows de trouble I see (Negro spiritual)
with A. Benoist pf   Brunswick 15107

WIENIAWSKI

Capriccio–valse, Op. 7 vln & pf
with A. Benoist pf   9233   Edison Diamond Disc 82308

Concerto No. 2, in d, Op. 22 vln & orch.
Romance (2nd mvt)
with A. Benoist pf   Edison Diamond Disc 82117

Mazurka in a, Op. 3 "Kujawiak" vln & pf
with A. Benoist pf   8018   Edison Diamond Disc 82245

WIENIAWSKI – *Continued*

Polonaise brillante No. 1, in D, Op. 4 vln & pf
with A. Benoist pf   Edison cylinder 177

Polonaise brillante No. 2, in A, Op. 21 vln & pf
with A. Benoist pf   2395   Edison Diamond Disc 82048

Scherzo–Tarantelle, Op. 16 vln & pf
with A. Benoist pf   6975   Edison cylinder 29062
                                  Edison Diamond Disc 82188

Souvenir de Moscou, Op. 6 vln & pf or orch.
with A. Benoist pf   4327   Edison cylinder 28163
                                  Edison Diamond Disc 80071

Souvenir de Moscou, Op. 6 vln & pf or orch.
with A. Benoist pf   Edison cylinder 28102

WOOD

Roses of Picardy (1916) v & pf – arr. vln & pf Spalding
with A. Benoist pf   7595   Edison cylinder 29074
                                  Edison Diamond Disc 82215

Vladimir SPIVAKOV

BARTÓK

Rhapsody No. 1, in G (1928) vln & orch.
with V. Postnikova pf   Mezhdunarodnaya Kniga
                         SM02133/4

LOCATELLI

(12) Sonatas, Op. 6 (1737) vln & c
Sonata No. 1, in g (ed. David)
with V. Postnikova pf   Mezhdunarodnaya Kniga
                         SM02133/4

PAGANINI

(Le) Streghe (variations on a theme from Süssmeyer's opera "Il Noce di Benevento") Op. 8 (1813) vln & orch. – arr. vln & pf Kreisler
with V. Postnikova pf   Mezhdunarodnaya Kniga
                         SM02133/4

PROKOFIEV

(5) Melodies, Op. 35bis (1921) vln & pf
with V. Postnikova pf   Mezhdunarodnaya Kniga
                         SM02133/4

SHCHEDRIN

In imitation of Albéniz pf – arr. vln & pf Tziganov
with piano   Mezhdunarodnaya Kniga
                         D028103/4

Tossy SPIVAKOVSKY (1907–)

d'AMBROSIO

Serenade, Op. 4 vln & pf
with piano   Odeon 0–25087
                     Parlophone B48247

BACH

(3) Sonatas & 3 Partitas, BWV1001/6 solo vln
Sonata No. 1, in g, BWV1001
(unaccompanied)   Columbia (set MX326), ML2089

BARTÓK

(6) Rumanian folk dances (1915) pf – arr. vln & pf Székely
Nos. 1, 3, 4 & 6
with A. Balsam pf   20771   Concert Hall 1035, (in set CHS AA), CHC39

Sonata No. 2 (1922) vln & pf
with A. Balsam pf   31/5   Amphion (set B7)
                          Concert Hall 1030/4, (set CHS AA), CHC39

BAZZINI

(La) Ronde des lutins, Op. 25 vln & pf
with piano   2–21627   Decca 25786
                             Parlophone E11012

BEETHOVEN

(Die) Ruinen von Athen, Op. 113 – Incidental music orch.
No. 3. Chor der Derwische arr. vln & pf Auer
with piano   34162[3]   Decca 20003
                             Parlophone 44552, B7736, B12154, R3515

No. 4. Marcia alla turca arr. vln & pf Auer
with piano   34161[3]   Decca 20003
                             Parlophone 44552, B7736, B12154, R3515

(3) Sonatas, Op. 30 vln & pf
No. 3. Sonata No. 8, in G
with R. Cornman pf   Columbia ML2089

Sonata No. 10, in G, Op. 96 vln & pf
with R. Firkusny pf   Columbia ML4402

BLOCH

Baal Shem (3 Pictures of Chassidic life) (1923) vln & pf
No. 2. Nigun (Improvisation)
with piano   Decca 20020
                     Parlophone B12399, R1217

BRAHMS

(21) Hungarian Dances pf duet
Hungarian dance No. 1, in g arr. vln & pf Joachim
with piano   2–20801   Decca 25272
                             Parlophone 44512, 57500, B12318, E10985

Hungarian dance No. 4, in f arr. vln & pf "in b" Joachim
with piano   Columbia JX107
                     Decca 20666
                     Parlophone B28524

(16) Waltzes, Op. 39 pf duet
No. 15. Waltz No. 15, in A flat arr. vln & pf "in A" Hochstein
with piano   Parlophone 44512, B12154, R1414

CASTELNUOVO-TEDESCO

Chant hébraïque vln & pf
with piano   Parlophone P9574

DVOŘÁK

(8) Slavonic Dances, Op. 46 pf duet; orch.
No. 2. Slavonic dance No. 2, in e arr. vln & pf "in g" Kreisler
with piano   Parlophone 44746, B28514

DVOŘÁK – *Continued*

(8) Slavonic Dances, Op. 72 pf duet; orch.
No. 2. Slavonic dance No. 10, in e arr. vln & pf Kreisler
with piano   2–8302   Parlophone 64591, B28514,
              E10440
No. 2. Slavonic dance No. 10, in e arr. vln & pf Kreisler
with piano   2–21727   Decca 25379
              Parlophone E11185, P9548
No. 8. Slavonic dance No. 16, in A flat arr. vln & pf "in G" Kreisler
with piano   2–8301   Parlophone E10440

GLUCK

Orphée et Eurydice (1762) – opera
Dance of the blessed spirits: Lento "Mélodie" (No. 2) arr. vln & pf Kreisler
with piano   2–8481   Parlophone E10417

GRANADOS

(12) Danzas españolas, Op. 37 (1893) pf
No. 5. Danza española No. 5, in e "Andaluza" arr. vln & pf Kreisler
with piano   Parlophone B48203

HANDEL

(15) Sonatas, Op. 1 (?1731) fl or vln & c
Sonata No. 9, in b: Andante (1st mvt) arr. vln & pf as "Larghetto" by Hubay
with piano   Parlophone

JUON

(2) Violonstücke, Op. 52 vln & pf
No. 2. Arva "Valse mignonne"
with piano   Parlophone B12318

KIRCHNER

Concerto (1960) vln, vlc, 10 w–wnds & pcn
with A. Parisot vlc & Chamber Orch.   Epic BC1157, LC3830
– Kirchner

KREISLER

Caprice viennois, Op. 2 vln & pf
with piano   2–20802   Decca 25786
              Parlophone E11012
Caprice viennois, Op. 2 vln & pf
with A. Balsam pf   Columbia ML4402
Liebesfreud vln & pf
with piano   Decca 20030
Liebesleid vln & pf
with piano   Decca 20030
Tambourin chinois, Op. 3 vln & pf
with piano   2–20884   Parlophone E10914
Minuet (Porpora) vln & pf
with piano   2–8341   Parlophone E10472
Sicilienne & Rigaudon (Francoeur) vln & pf
with piano   Decca 20008
              Parlophone B48031, R1414

MENOTTI

Concerto (1952) vln & orch.
with Boston Symphony Orch. –   Victor A630275, A12R0115
Munch   LM1868

MOSZKOWSKI

(2) Stücke, Op. 45 pf
No. 2. Guitarre arr. vln & pf Sarasate
with piano   Odeon 0–25087
              Parlophone B48247

MOURET

(Le) Triomphe des Sens (1732) – ballet orch.
Sarabande in e arr. vln & pf Dandelot
with piano   2–21553[5]   Parlophone E11144, P9521

MOZART

Serenade No. 7, in D, K250 "Haffner" orch.
Rondo (4th mvt) arr. vln & pf Kreisler
with piano   2–21788[3]   Parlophone P9568

PAGANINI

(24) Caprices, Op. 1 (1801/7) solo vln
Caprice No. 20, in D arr. vln & pf Kreisler
with piano   2–20883   Decca 20666
              Parlophone B48203, E10914
Caprice No. 24, in a
(unaccompanied)   Columbia ML4402
(6) Sonatas, Op. 3 (1801/6) vln & gtr
No. 2. Sonata No. 8, in G arr. vln & pf Spivakovsky
with A. Balsam pf   Columbia ML4402
No. 5. Sonata No. 11, in A
with piano   2–20079   Decca 25049
              Odeon 0–7585
              Parlophone E10562, P9090
No. 6. Sonata No. 12, in e
with piano   2–20080   Decca 25049
              Odeon 0–7585
              Parlophone E10562, P9090

RAFF

(6) Pieces, Op. 85 vln & pf
No. 3. Cavatina in D
with piano   2–7708   Parlophone E10417

ROBERTSON

Concerto (1949) vln & orch.
with Utah Symphony Orch. –   Vanguard VRS1089, VSD2116
Abravanel

SARASATE

Carmen Fantasia (on themes from the opera by Bizet) Op. 25 vln & pf or orch.
with piano   Odeon 68094
              Parlophone P9577
(8) Danzas españolas vln & pf
No. 6. Zapateado, Op. 23, No. 2
with piano   2–21748[4]   Decca 25379
              Parlophone E11185, P9594
Introduction & Tarantelle, Op. 43 vln & pf
with piano   2–21605   Decca 25272
              Parlophone E10985, P9521
Introduction & Tarantelle, Op. 43 vln & pf
with A. Balsam pf   Columbia ML4402
Zigeunerweisen, Op. 20 vln & pf or orch.
       2–21807[5] & 2–21808   Odeon AA68097, 0–6875
with piano   Parlophone E10483

SCHUBERT

(7) Gesänge (set to Scott's "Lady of the Lake") Op. 52 v & pf
  No. 6. Ave Maria, D839 arr. vln & pf Wilhelmj
  with piano   2–21798[4] Parlophone P9568

SCHUMANN

(12) Duets, Op. 85 pf – 4 hands
  No. 12. Abendlied arr. vln & pf Wilhelmj
  with piano   Parlophone E10914

SIBELIUS

Concerto in d, Op. 47 vln & orch.
  with London Symphony Orch. –
  Hannikainen   Everest LPBR6045, SDBR3045
  Guilde Internationale du Disque
  SMS2559
  World Record Club ST94, T94

STRAVINSKY

Concerto in D (1931) vln & orch.
  with Utah Symphony Orch. –
  Abravanel   Vanguard VRS1089, VSD2116

TCHAIKOVSKY

Concerto in D, Op. 35 vln & orch.
  with London Symphony Orch. –
  Goehr   Adès (Florilège) 13010
  Everest LPBR6049, SDBR3049
Souvenir d'un lieu cher, Op. 42 vln & pf
  No. 3. Mélodie
  with piano   Parlophone 44746, B28514
  No. 3. Mélodie
  with London Symphony Orch. –
  Goehr   Adès (Florilège) 13010
  Everest LPBR6049, SDBR3049
Waltz–scherzo, Op. 34 vln & pf or orch.
  with A. Balsam pf   Columbia ML4402

WIENIAWSKI

Scherzo–Tarantelle, Op. 16 vln & pf
  with piano   2–8394 Parlophone 64591, E10472,
  P9548

Scherzo–Tarantelle, Op. 16 vln & pf
  with piano   2–21726[2] Parlophone E11144

Helmut SPRECHER

MOZART

Sinfonia concertante in E flat, K364 vln, vla & orch.
  with G. Weiss vla & Dresden Chamber Baroque BU1824
  Soloists – Bernard

Karel ŠROUBEK (1913–   )

BONPORTI

(10) Concerti, Op. 11 strs
  Concerto No. 5, in F: Adagio (2nd mvt) "Recitativo"
  with Czech Philharmonic Orch. –   Supraphon LPM35, SUF20210
  Pedrotti   Ultraphon D20111

BORODIN

Quartet No. 2, in D (1881/5) 2 vlns, vla & vlc
  Notturno (3rd mvt) arr. vln & pf
  with F. Maxián pf   044378 Supraphon 10600, G22175
  Ultraphon G14234

FIALA

Lord, O Lord, love pf – arr. vln & orch.
  with Prague Symphony Orch. –   Supraphon SUEC872
  Smetáček

(The) Talin pond (Folksong paraphrase) pf – arr. vln & orch.
  with Prague Symphony Orch. –   Supraphon SUEC872
  Smetáček

FIBICH

Concert–Polonaise in D, Op. posth vln & orch. – arr. Zich
  with Prague Radio Symphony Orch. – Ultraphon G12902
  Pařik
Concert–Polonaise in D, Op. posth vln & orch. – arr. Zich
  with Prague Radio Symphony Orch. – Supraphon LPV428
  Pinkas
Images, Impressions & Souvenirs, Op. 41 pf
  No. 14. Poem (from "Souvenirs", Part IV) arr. vln & pf Kubelík
  with F. Maxián pf   Supraphon SUEC820, SUK31294

GLAZOUNOV

Méditation, Op. 32 vln & pf
  with F. Maxián pf   044377 Supraphon G22175
  Ultraphon G14234

NEDBAL

Valse triste (1902) pf – arr. vln & pf Meyer
  with F. Maxián pf   Supraphon SUEC820, SUK31294

ONDŘIČEK

Fantasia (on "Dance of the comedians" from the opera "The Bartered Bride" by Smetana) Op. 15 vln & pf
  with F. Maxián pf   044355 Supraphon G22259
  Ultraphon G14204

PAGANINI

Moto perpetuo (Allegro di concert) Op. 11 (1830) vln & orch.
  with F. Maxián pf   044356 Supraphon G22259
  Ultraphon G14204

(6) Sonatas, Op. 2 (1801/6) vln & gtr
  No. 1. Sonata No. 1, in A
  with Z. Pitter gtr   Supraphon LPM373, SUF20334
  No. 2. Sonata No. 2, in C
  with Z. Pitter gtr   Supraphon LPM373, SUF20334
  No. 3. Sonata No. 3, in d
  with Z. Pitter gtr   Supraphon LPM373, SUF20334
  No. 4. Sonata No. 4, in A
  with Z. Pitter gtr   Supraphon LPM373, SUF20334
  No. 5. Sonata No. 5, in Đ
  with Z. Pitter gtr   Supraphon LPM373, SUF20334
  No. 6. Sonata No. 6, in a
  with Z. Pitter gtr   Supraphon LPM373, SUF20334
(6) Sonatas, Op. 3 (1801/6) vln & gtr
  No. 1. Sonata No. 7, in A
  with Z. Pitter gtr   Supraphon SUF20120

PAGANINI – *Continued*

No. 2. Sonata No. 8, in G
with Z. Pitter gtr   Supraphon SUF20120

No. 3. Sonata No. 9, in D
with Z. Pitter gtr   Supraphon SUF20120

No. 4. Sonata No. 10, in a
with Z. Pitter gtr   Supraphon SUF20120

No. 5. Sonata No. 11, in A
with Z. Pitter gtr   Supraphon SUF20120

No. 6. Sonata No. 12, in e
with Z. Pitter gtr   Supraphon SUF20120

RIMSKY–KORSAKOV

(The) Tale of Tsar Saltan (1900) – opera
Flight of the bumblebee (Act III) orch. – arr. vln & pf Hartmann
with F. Maxián pf   044377   Supraphon G22175
                     Ultraphon G14234

ŠEVČÍK

(6) Bohemian Dances, Op. 10 vln & pf
No. 3. Dance in f sharp
with F. Maxián pf   Supraphon LPM197
                     Ultraphon 5115C

No. 6. Furiant
with F. Maxián pf   Supraphon LPM135
                     Ultraphon 5115C

SZYMANOWSKI

(3) Mythes, Op. 30 (1915) vln & pf
No. 1. La Fontaine d'Aréthuse
with J. Hala pf   Supraphon SUA10580,
                  SUAST50580, SV8169

No. 2. Narcisse
with J. Hala pf   Supraphon SUA10580,
                  SUAST50580, SV8169

No. 3. Dryades et Pan
with J. Hala pf   Supraphon SUA10580,
                  SUAST50580, SV8169

TANEIEV

Concert Suite, Op. 28 vln & orch.
Tarantella (5th mvt)
with F. Maxián pf   044379   Supraphon G22176
                     Ultraphon G14235

TCHAIKOVSKY

Sérénade mélancolique in b flat, Op. 26 vln & orch. – arr. vln & pf
Wilhelmj
with F. Maxián pf   044380   Supraphon G22176
                     Ultraphon G14235

YSAŸE

Fantaisie, Op. 32 vln & pf
with J. Hala pf   Supraphon SUA10580,
                  SUAST50580, SV8169

Scène au Rouet (Poème No. 2) Op. 13 vln & pf or orch.
with J. Hala pf   Supraphon SUA10580,
                  SUAST50580, SV8169

Jelka STANIČ–KREK (1928–   )

CORELLI

(12) Concerti grossi, Op. 6 orch.
Concerto grosso No. 8, in g "Christmas Concerto"
with D. Hrdjok vln, A. Heiller hpsi, Z.   Bach Guild BG569, BGS5006
Pomykalo vlc & I Solisti di Zagreb –   Top Rank 40–003, TR5002
Janigro

TELEMANN

Concerto in a vln & strs
with I Solisti di Zagreb – Janigro   Amadeo AVRS6078,
                                     AVRS12005
                                     Bach Guild BG575, BGS5028
                                     Philips 906078ASY

TORELLI

(12) Concerti, Op. 8 (1709) 1/6: 2 vlns, strs & c – 7/12: vln, strs & c
Concerto No. 6, in g "Christmas Concerto"
with I. Pinkava vln, A. Heiller hpsi, Z.   Bach Guild BG569, BGS5006
Pomykalo vlc & I Solisti di Zagreb –   Top Rank 40–003, TR5002
Janigro

VIVALDI

Concerto in C, P.14 (F.I, No. 13) (Op. 54, No. 3) "Per la SS. Assunzione di
Maria Vergine" vln, strs & c
with H. Tachezi hpsi, D. Thune hpsi   Amadeo AVRS6325,
& I Solisti di Zagreb – Janigro   AVRS12100
                                     Bach Guild BG665, BGS70665

Heinz STANSKE (1913–   )

d'AMBROSIO

Canzonetta, Op. 6 vln & pf
with M. Raucheisen pf   Polydor 47417

BACH

(3) Sonatas & 3 Partitas, BWV1001/6 solo vln
Partita No. 3, in d: Chaconne (5th mvt) BWV1004
(unaccompanied)   Polydor 67891/2

BAZZINI

(La) Ronde des lutins, Op. 25 vln & pf
with H. Hidegheti pf   Polydor 57347

BEETHOVEN

(6) Minuets, G167 pf
No. 2. Minuet No. 2, in G arr. vln & pf Burmester
with H. Hidegheti pf   Polydor 47958

BLUME

Romance vln & pf
with H. Hidegheti pf   Polydor 57131

Valse–caprice "Schön Erika" vln & pf
with H. Hidegheti pf   Polydor 57131

BRUCH

Concerto No. 1, in g, Op. 26 vln & orch.*
          1751⅝GE 9, 1752½GE 9 &   Cetra RR8058/60
  with German Opera   1753/6¾GE 9   Polydor 67864/6
  House Orch. – Schuricht

CUI

Kaleidoscope, Op. 50 vln & pf
  No. 9. Orientale
  with M. Raucheisen pf   Polydor 47417

DAQUIN

Pièces de clavecin –Book I (1735) hpsi
  Le coucou arr. vln & pf Manén
  with G. Puchelt pf   Polydor 47529

FERRARI

Minuet unid – arr. vln & pf Corti
  with H. Hidegheti pf   Polydor 57347

GODARD

Jocelyn (1888) – opera
  Cachés dans cet asile "Berceuse" arr. vln & pf
  with G. Puchelt pf   1397½GE 9   Polydor 57273

HANDEL

Serse (1738) – opera
  Ombra mai fu "Largo" arr. vln & pf
  with H. Hidegheti pf   Polydor 57136

KREISLER

Liebesfreud vln & pf
  with FFB Orch. – Eisbrenner   Baccarola 77873ZK
Schön Rosmarin vln & pf
  with FFB Orch. – Eisbrenner   Baccarola 77873ZK

MOZART

Concerto No. 4, in D, K218 (cadenzas by Joachim) vln & orch.
  with Dresden Philharmonic Symphony   Polydor 67888/90
  Orch. – van Kempen

Divertimento No. 17, in D, K334 2 hrns & strs
  Minuet (3rd mvt) arr. vln & pf Burmester
  with H. Hidegheti pf   873⁴ GE 9   Polydor 57106

PARAY

Humoresque vln & pf
  with H. Hidegheti pf   Polydor 47847

PROKOFIEV

Concerto No. 2, in g, Op. 63 vln & orch.
  with Berlin Radio Symphony Orch. –   Le Chant du Monde LD8014
  Konwitschny

RAVEL

Pièce en forme d'Habanera v & pf – arr. vln & pf Catherine
  with H. Hidegheti pf   Polydor 47847

REGER

Romance in G vln & pf
  with H. Hidegheti pf   Polydor 47958

* Adagio or 2nd mvt is also on Polydor 68065.

RUBINSTEIN

(2) Melodies, Op. 3 pf
  No. 1. Melody in F arr. vln & orch.
  with FFB Orch. – Eisbrenner   Baccarola 77873ZK

SARASATE

(8) Danzas españolas vln & pf
  No. 2. Habañera, Op. 21, No. 2
  with H. Hidegheti pf   Polydor 57356
  No. 3. Romanza andaluza, Op. 22, No. 1
  with H. Hidegheti pf   Polydor 57356
  No. 6. Zapateado, Op. 23, No. 2
  with M. Raucheisen pf   Polydor 57104

SCHUBERT, F.

(7) Gesänge (set to Scott's "Lady of the Lake") Op. 52 v & pf
  No. 6. Ave Maria, D839 arr. vln & pf Wilhelmj
  with H. Hidegheti pf   Polydor 57136

SCHUBERT, H.

Concertante Suite vln & cha orch.
  with Berlin Philharmonic Symphony   Polydor 57358
  Orch. – Schubert

SUK

(4) Pieces, Op. 17 vln & pf
  No. 3. Un poco triste
  with M. Raucheisen pf   Polydor 57104
  No. 4. Burleska
  with G. Puchelt pf   Polydor 47529

SVENDSEN

Romance in G, Op. 26 vln & orch.
  with FFB Orch. – Eisbrenner   Baccarola 77873ZK

TCHAIKOVSKY

(6) Pieces, Op. 19 pf
  No. 4. Nocturne in c sharp arr. vln & pf Hartmann
  with M. Raucheisen pf   Polydor 47433
(3) Souvenirs de Hapsal, Op. 2 pf
  No. 3. Chant sans paroles in f arr. vln & pf Kreisler
  with G. Puchelt pf   1395½GE 9   Polydor 57273
Souvenir d'un lieu cher, Op. 42 vln & pf
  No. 3. Mélodie
  with M. Raucheisen pf   Polydor 47433

WEBER

Sonata No. 1, in C, Op. 24 (J138) pf
  Presto (Rondo) (4th mvt) "Perpetuum mobile" arr. vln & pf David
  with H. Hidegheti pf   871² GE 9   Polydor 57106

Gordon STAPLES (1929–)

DEBUSSY

Sonata No. 3, in g (1917) vln & pf
  with G. Silfies pf   McIntosh MM101

FALLA

(La) Vida Breve (1913) – opera
  Danza española orch. – arr. vln & pf Kreisler
  with G. Silfies pf   McIntosh MM101

KROLL

Banjo & fiddle vln & pf
   with G. Silfies pf   McIntosh MM101

PROKOFIEV

(The) Love for Three Oranges, Op. 33a (1919) – suite orch.
  No. 3. March arr. vln & pf Heifetz
    with G. Silfies pf   McIntosh MM101

SARASATE

(8) Danzas españolas vln & pf
  No. 1. Malagueña, Op. 21, No. 1
    with G. Silfies pf   McIntosh MM101

SZYMANOWSKI

(3) Mythes, Op. 30 (1915) vln & pf
  No. 1. La Fontaine d'Aréthuse
    with G. Silfies pf   McIntosh MM101

Steven STARYK (1932–)

ALBINONI

Adagio in g strs & org
  with A. de Klerk org & Amsterdam   CNR RS041
  Chamber Orch. – Rieu

BACH

Sonata in g, BWV1020 vln & clav
  with K. Gilbert hpsi   Baroque BC1858, BCS2858
                          Everest (in set SDBR3203)
                          Saga STXID5300

Sonata in G, BWV1021 vln & c
  with K. Gilbert hpsi   Baroque BC1858, BCS2858
                          Everest (in set SDBR3203)
                          Saga STXID5300

Sonata in F, BWV1022 vln & clav
  with K. Gilbert hpsi   Baroque BC1858, BCS2858
                          Everest (in set SDBR3203)
                          Saga STXID5300

Sonata in e, BWV1023 vln & c
  with K. Gilbert hpsi   Baroque BC1858, BCS2858
                          Everest (in set SDBR3203)
                          Saga STXID5300

BARTÓK

(2) Portraits, Op. 5 (1907) vln & orch.
  with Royal Philharmonic Orch. –   Capitol G7186, SG7186
  Kubelík   Electrola E91064, STE91064
                          HMV ALP1744, ASD312,
                          ASDF221, ASDW312,
                          FALP655, WALP1744

BEETHOVEN

(3) Sonatas, Op. 12 vln & pf
  No. 2. Sonata No. 2, in A
    with L. Boucher pf   Victor CC1016, CCS1016

BONPORTI

(10) Concerti, Op. 11 strs
  Concerto No. 8, in D
    with G. Leonhardt hpsi & Amsterdam Telefunken AWT9415,
    Chamber Orch. – Rieu   SAWT9415

BRAHMS

(21) Hungarian Dances pf duet
  Hungarian dance No. 4, in f arr. vln & ens Salzedo
    with Royal Tziganes – Staryk   Monitor MFS715
                            Philips 870034BFY
                            World Record Club SP929,
                            TT929

  Hungarian dance No. 17, in f sharp arr. vln & ens Salzedo
    with Royal Tziganes – Staryk   Monitor MFS715
                            Philips 870034BFY
                            World Record Club SP929,
                            TT929

Sonata No. 3, in d, Op. 108 vln & pf
  with M. Bernardi pf   CBC Radio Canada SM39

Sonata (1853) "Frei aber Einsam" vln & pf
  Allegro (Scherzo) in c (3rd mvt) "Sonatensatz"
    with E. Niwa pf   Everest (in set SDBR3203)
                          Orion ORS7027

Symphony No. 1, in c, Op. 68 orch.
  with Royal Philharmonic Orch. –   Columbia CX1573
  Kletzki

CORELLI

(12) Sonatas, Op. 5 vln & c
  Sonata No. 2, in B flat
    with K. Gilbert hpsi   Baroque BC2874
                            Columbia HRS1012EV
                            Everest (in set SDBR3203)

  Sonata No. 2, in B flat arr. Geminiani*
    with Baroque Chamber Orch. – Staryk Baroque BC1880, BC2880

COWARD

Bitter Sweet (1929) – operetta
  Zigeuner arr. vln & ens
    with Royal Tziganes – Staryk
                            Monitor MFS715
                            Philips 870034BFY
                            World Record Club SP929,
                            TT929

DANCLA

(24) Caprices, Op. 52 solo vln
  Caprice No. 9, in c (Allegro agitato)
  (unaccompanied)   Everest (in set SDBR3203)
                            HMV HQS1124
                            Imperial ILX1015
                            Virtuoso VIR1002

  Caprice No. 16, in b flat (Allegro vivace)
  (unaccompanied)   Everest (in set SDBR3203)
                            HMV HQS1124
                            Imperial ILX1015
                            Virtuoso VIR1002

DELIBES

Sylvia (1876) – ballet orch.
  Pas de deux (Act III)
    with Royal Philharmonic Orch. –   Capitol G7245, SG7245
    Irving   Electrola SME73956
                          HMV CLP1239

* Arranged by Geminiani as a concerto grosso which, in this recording, serves as an accompaniment for the violin thus becoming a violin concerto.

DINICU
Hora staccato vln & pf – arr. vln & ens
  with Royal Tziganes – Staryk

Monitor MFS715
Philips 870034BFY
World Record Club SP929,
TT929

DONT
(24) Caprices, Op. 35 solo vln
  Caprice No. 2, in a (Moderato)
  (unaccompanied)

Everest (in set SDBR3203)
HMV HQS1124
Imperial ILX1015
Virtuoso VIR1002

DVOŘÁK
Concerto in b, Op. 104 vlc & orch.
  with M. Rostropovich vlc & Royal
  Philharmonic Orch. – Boult

Capitol G7109
HMV ALP1595, ASD358
Seraphim S60136

FALLA
(La) Vida Breve (1913) – opera
  Danza española orch. – arr. vln & pf Kreisler
  with E. Niwa pf

Everest (in set SDBR3203)
Orion ORS7027

FARNON
Rhapsody vln & orch.
  with London Festival Orch. – Farnon   Polydor 2382 008

FIOCCO
Suite No. 1, in G hpsi
  Allegro (10th mvt) arr. vln & pf Bent & O'Neill
  with E. Niwa pf

Everest (in set SDBR3203)
Orion ORS7027

  Allegro (10th mvt) arr. vln & pf Bent & O'Neill
  with M. Bernardi pf   CBC Radio Canada SM39

FIORILLO
(36) Étude–Caprices, Op. 3 solo vln
  Caprice No. 3, in C (Allegro)
  (unaccompanied)

Everest (in set SDBR3203)
HMV HQS1124
Imperial ILX1015
Virtuoso VIR1002

  Caprice No. 8, in G (Largo)
  (unaccompanied)

Everest (in set SDBR3203)
HMV HQS1124
Imperial ILX1015
Virtuoso VIR1002

  Caprice No. 14, in g (Adagio)
  (unaccompanied)

Everest (in set SDBR3203)
HMV HQS1124
Imperial ILX1015
Virtuoso VIR1002

  Caprice No. 28, in D (Allegro assai)
  (unaccompanied)

Everest (in set SDBR3203)
HMV HQS1124
Imperial ILX1015
Virtuoso VIR1002

GEMINIANI
(6) Sonatas, Op. 5 (1738) solo vln
  Sonata in B flat (ed. Corti)
  (unaccompanied)

Baroque BC1851, BC2851
Everest (in set SDBR3203)
Hispavox HBR(S)380–03

GROFÉ
Grand Canyon (1931) – suite orch.
  On the trail (3rd mvt)
  with Capitol Symphony Orch. –   Capitol P8523, SP8523
  Dragon

HANDEL
(15) Sonatas, Op. 1 (?1731) fl or vln & c
  Sonata No. 9, in b: Andante (1st mvt) arr. vln & pf as "Larghetto" by
  Hubay
  with E. Niwa pf

Everest (in set SDBR3203)
Orion ORS7027

HAYDN
Sonata No. 1, in G, H.XV, No. 32 (1794) vln & clav
  with L. Boucher pf   CBC Transcription Program 243

Sonata No. 1, in G, H.XV, No. 32 (1794) vln & clav
  with L. Boucher pf   Orion ORS7027
    Select CC15069

Symphony No. 103, in E flat "Drum roll" orch.
  with Royal Philharmonic Orch. –   HMV ASD341
  Beecham

HINDEMITH
(2) Sonatas, Op. 31 (1924) solo vln
  Sonata No. 2
  (unaccompanied)

Baroque BC1851, BC2851
Everest (in set SDBR3203)
Hispavox HBR(S)380–03

HUBAY
(14) Scènes de la Csárda vln & pf
  No. 4. Hejre Kati, Op. 32 arr. vln & ens
  with Royal Tziganes – Staryk

Monitor MFS715
Philips 870034BFY
World Record Club SP929,
TT929

KÁLMÁN
Gräfin Mariza (1924) – operetta
  Komm, Zigany arr. vln as "Play, gypsy play" by Brammer & Grünwald –
  arr. vln & ens Grey & Foley
  with Royal Tziganes – Staryk

Monitor MFS715
Philips 870034BFY
World Record Club SP929,
TT929

KAYSER
(36) Elementary & Progressive Studies, Op. 20 solo vln
  Study No. 4, in C (Allegro)
  (unaccompanied)

Everest (in set SDBR3203)
HMV HQS1124
Imperial ILX1015
Virtuoso VIR1002

KREUTZER

(42) Etudes solo vln
Etude No. 2, in C (Allegro moderato)
(unaccompanied)

Everest (in set SDBR3203)
HMV HQS1124
Imperial ILX1015
Virtuoso VIR1002

Etude No. 8, in E (Allegro non troppo)
(unaccompanied)

Everest (in set SDBR3203)
HMV HQS1124
Imperial ILX1015
Virtuoso VIR1002

Etude No. 15, in B flat (Allegro non troppo)
(unaccompanied)

Everest (in set SDBR3203)
HMV HQS1124
Imperial ILX1015
Virtuoso VIR1002

LECLAIR

(12) Sonatas, Op. 9 – Book IV (1738) vln & c
Sonata No. 3, in D
with L. Boucher pf

CBC Transcription Program 243

Sonata No. 3, in D
with L. Boucher pf

Orion ORS7027
Select CC15069

LOCATELLI

(12) Sonatas, Op. 6 (1737) vln & c
Sonata No. 1, in g
with K. Gilbert hpsi

Baroque BC1874, BC2874
Columbia HRS1012EV
Everest (in set SDBR3203)

MAHLER

Symphony No. 4, in G (1900) orch.
with S. Stahlman s & Concertgebouw
Orch., Amsterdam – Solti

Decca LXT5638, SXL2276
London CM9286, CS6217

MARCELLO

(12) Concerti, Op. 1 (1708) vln, vlc obb & strs
Concerto No. 1, in D
with Baroque Chamber Orch. – Staryk   Baroque BC1880, BC2880

MASSENET

Thaïs (1894) – opera
Méditation
with Chicago Symphony Orch. –
Martinon

Victor 940040, LSC2939,
SB6741, VICS1358

MATHIEU

(12) Etudes solo vln
Etude No. 5
(unaccompanied)

CBC Transcription Program 243

Etude No. 6
(unaccompanied)

CBC Transcription Program 243

Etude No. 8
(unaccompanied)

CBC Transcription Program 243

MONTI

Csárdas (1904) vln & pf – arr. vln & ens
with Royal Tziganes – Staryk

Monitor MFS715
Philips 870034BFY
World Record Club SP929,
TT929

MOZART

Serenade No. 7, in D, K250 "Haffner" orch.
Rondo (4th mvt) arr. vln & pf Kreisler
with E. Niwa pf

Everest (in set SDBR3203)
Orion ORS7027

NARDINI

(6) Sonatas, Op. 2 (1765) vln & c
Sonata No. 5, in D
with K. Gilbert hpsi

Baroque BC1874, BC2874
Columbia HRS1012EV
Everest (in set SDBR3203)

NOVAČEK

(8) Concert caprices, Op. 5 vln & pf
No. 4. Perpetuum mobile
with E. Niwa pf

Everest (in set SDBR3203)
Orion ORS7027

PAGANINI

(24) Caprices, Op. 1 (1801/7) solo vln
Caprice No. 1, in E
(unaccompanied)

Musical Heritage Society
MHS1122
Select CC15076

Caprice No. 2, in b
(unaccompanied)

Musical Heritage Society
MHS1122
Select CC15076

Caprice No. 5, in a
(unaccompanied)

Musical Heritage Society
MHS1122
Select CC15076

Caprice No. 9, in E
(unaccompanied)

Musical Heritage Society
MHS1122
Select CC15076

Caprice No. 13, in B flat
(unaccompanied)

Musical Heritage Society
MHS1122
Select CC15076

Caprice No. 14, in E flat
(unaccompanied)

Musical Heritage Society
MHS1122
Select CC15076

Caprice No. 16, in g
(unaccompanied)

Musical Heritage Society
MHS1122
Select CC15076

Caprice No. 17, in E flat
(unaccompanied)

Musical Heritage Society
MHS1122
Select CC15076

PAGANINI – *Continued*

Caprice No. 19, in E flat
(unaccompanied)

Musical Heritage Society
MHS1122
Select CC15076

Caprice No. 20, in D
(unaccompanied)

Musical Heritage Society
MHS1122
Select CC15076

Caprice No. 21, in A
(unaccompanied)

Musical Heritage Society
MHS1122
Select CC15076

Caprice No. 24, in a
(unaccompanied)

Musical Heritage Society
MHS1122
Select CC15076

(6) Sonatas, Op. 3 (1801/6) vln & gtr
No. 6. Sonata No. 12, in e
with E. Niwa pf

Everest (in set SDBR3203)

PAPINEAU–COUTURE

Aria (1946) solo vln
(unaccompanied)

Baroque BC1851, BC2851
Everest (in set SDBR3203)
Hispavox HBR(S)380–03

(3) Caprices (1965) vln & pf
Caprice No. 1 "Nadia" (Allegro)
with L. Boucher pf

CBC Transcription Program 243

Caprice No. 2 "Ghilaine" (Adagio)
with L. Boucher pf

CBC Transcription Program 243

Caprice No. 3 "François" (Scherzando)
with L. Boucher pf

CBC Transcription Program 243

Suite (1956) solo vln
(unaccompanied)

Victor CC1016, CCS1016

PISENDEL

Sonata in a solo vln
(unaccompanied)

Baroque BC1851, BC2851
Everest (in set SDBR3203)
Hispavox HBR(S)380–03

PROKOFIEV

(5) Melodies, Op. 35bis (1921) vln & pf
No. 2
with E. Niwa pf

Everest (in set SDBR3203)
Orion ORS7027

Sonata in d, Op. 115 solo vln
(unaccompanied)

Baroque BC1851, BC2851
Everest (in set SDBR3203)
Hispavox HBR(S)380–03

Sonata No. 1, in f, Op. 80 vln & pf
with M. Bernardi pf

Ace of Diamonds SDD2152
Musical Heritage Society
MHS1135

Sonata No. 2, in D, Op. 94bis vln & pf
with M. Bernardi pf

Ace of Diamonds SDD2152
Musical Heritage Society
MHS1135

RAVEL

Daphnis et Chloe (1910) – ballet orch.*
with Chicago Symphony Orch. –
Martinon

Victor A635061, A645061,
LM2806, LSC2806

RIMSKY–KORSAKOV

Capriccio espagnol, Op. 34 (1887) orch.
with Royal Philharmonic Orch. –
Kurtz

HMV ALP1632

Easter Overture, Op. 36 "Grande Pâque Russe" orch.
with Royal Philharmonic Orch. –
Rodzinski

HMV ALP1711
Seraphim 60074

Scheherazade, Op. 35 (1888) orch.
with Royal Philharmonic Orch. –
Beecham

Angel 35505
HMV ALP1564, ASD251,
ASDF536, FALP536

Scheherazade, Op. 35 (1888) orch.
The sea and Sinbad's ship (1st mvt)
with Capitol Symphony Orch. –
Dragon

Capitol P8547

RODE

(24) Caprices, Op. 22 solo vln
Caprice No. 2, in a (Allegretto)
(unaccompanied)

Everest (in set SDBR3203)
HMV HQS1124
Imperial ILX1015
Virtuoso VIR1002

Caprice No. 8, in f sharp (Moderato assai)
(unaccompanied)

Everest (in set SDBR3203)
HMV HQS1124
Imperial ILX1015
Virtuoso VIR1002

Caprice No. 17, in A flat (Vivacissimo)
(unaccompanied)

Everest (in set SDBR3203)
HMV HQS1124
Imperial ILX1015
Virtuoso VIR1002

Caprice No. 21, in B flat (Tempo giusto)
(unaccompanied)

Everest (in set SDBR3203)
HMV HQS1124
Imperial ILX1015
Virtuoso VIR1002

ROUSSEL

Bacchus et Ariane, Op. 43 – ballet orch.†
with Chicago Symphony Orch. –
Martinon

Victor A635061, A645061,
LM2806, LSC2806

SAINT–SAËNS

Danse macabre, Op. 40 (1874) orch.
with Royal Philharmonic Orch. –
Collins

HMV ALP1649

Introduction & Rondo Capriccioso, Op. 28 vln & orch.
with London Festival Orch. – Gamley

Orion ORS7027
Select CC15069

* Suites 1 & 2.
† Suite No. 2.

SARASATE

Zigeunerweisen, Op. 20 vln & pf or orch. – arr. vln & ens*
  with Royal Tziganes – Staryk   Monitor MFS715
                                   Philips 870034BFY
                                   World Record Club SP929,
                                   TT929

Zigeunerweisen, Op. 20 vln & pf or orch.
  with London Festival Orch. – Gamley   Orion ORS7027
                                   Select CC15069

SCHUMANN

(3) Romances, Op. 94 ob or vln, or vlc or cl & pf
  No. 2. Romance No. 2, in A arr. vln & pf Kreisler
  with E. Niwa pf   Everest (in set SDBR3203)
                                   Orion ORS7027

SOMERS

Sonata No. 2 (1955) vln & pf
  with L. Boucher pf   Victor CC1016, CCS1016

STAMITZ, J.W.A.

Divertimento No. 2, in G solo vln
  Allegro moderato (1st mvt); **Minuetto**
  (unaccompanied)   Baroque BC1851, BC2851
                                   Everest (in set SDBR3203)
                                   Hispavox HBR(S)380–03

STRAUSS, R.

Don Juan, Op. 20 (1888) orch.
  with Concertgebouw Orch.,   Fontana 894119ZKY
  Amsterdam – Jochum   Philips PHC9106

(Ein) Heldenleben, Op. 40 (1898) orch.
  with Royal Philharmonic Orch. –   Capitol G7250, SG7250
  Beecham   HMV ALP1847, ASD421
                                   Seraphim 60041
                                   World Record Club ST664, T664

Till Eulenspiegels lustige Streiche, Op. 28 (1895) orch.
  with Concertgebouw Orch.,   Fontana 894119ZKY
  Amsterdam – Jochum   Philips PHC9106

SZYMANOWSKI

King Roger, Op. 46 (1926) – opera
  Chant de Roxane arr. vln & pf Kochański
  with E. Niwa pf   Everest (in set SDBR3203)
                                     Orion ORS7027

TCHAIKOVSKY

(12) Pieces (of moderate difficulty) Op. 40 pf
  No. 2. Chanson triste arr. vln & ens
  with members of the Concertgebouw   Imperial IPE5084
  Orch., Amsterdam – Staryk

Quartet No. 1, in D, Op. 11 2 vlns, vla & vlc
  Andante cantabile (2nd mvt) arr. vln & ens
  with members of the Concertgebouw   Imperial IPE5084
  Orch., Amsterdam – Staryk

Sleeping Beauty, Op. 66 (1888/9) – ballet orch.
  Pas de deux (Act III)
  with Royal Philharmonic Orch. –   Capitol G7245, SG7245
  Irving   HMV CLP1239

* Part I only.

TCHAIKOVSKY – Continued

Souvenir d'un lieu cher, Op. 42 vln & pf
  No. 3. Mélodie arr. vln & ens
  with members of the Concertgebouw   Imperial IPE5084
  Orch., Amsterdam – Staryk

Swan Lake, Op. 20 (1875/6) – ballet orch.
  Dance of the Queen of the swans (Act II)
  with Concertgebouw Orch.,   Decca LXT5648, SXL2285
  Amsterdam – Fistoulari   London CM9287, CS6218
  Pas de deux (Andante: Black swan variations) (Act III)
  with Concertgebouw Orch.,   Decca LXT5648, SXL2285
  Amsterdam – Fistoulari   London CM9287, CS6218

TORELLI

(12) Concerti, Op. 8 (1709) 1/6: 2 vlns, strs & c – 7/12: vln, strs & c
  Concerto No. 8, in c
  with Baroque Chamber Orch. – Staryk   Baroque BC1880, BC2880

VERACINI

(12) Sonatas, Op. 2 (1744) "Sonate accademiche" vln & c
  Sonata No. 8, in c
  with K. Gilbert hpsi   Baroque BC1874, BC2874
                                   Columbia HRS1012EV
                                   Everest (in set SDBR3203)

  Sonata No. 11, in E: Minuet; Gavotte
  with K. Gilbert hpsi   Baroque BC1874, BC2874
                                   Everest (in set SDBR3203)

VIVALDI

Concerto in A vln, strs & c
  with Baroque Chamber Orch. – Staryk   Baroque BC1880, BC2880

VLADIGEROV

Vardar (Rapsodie bulgare) Op. 16 vln & pf – arr. vln & ens
  with Royal Tziganes – Staryk   Imperial ILPT117
                                     Metronome HLP10082
                                   World Record Club TP339

WIENIAWSKI

(L') École moderne, Op. 10 (10 Études) solo vln
  No. 1. Étude No. 1, in c "Le Sautillé"
  (unaccompanied)   Everest (in set SDBR3203)
                                   HMV HQS1124
                                   Imperial ILX1015
                                   Virtuoso VIR1002

  No. 5. Étude No. 5, in E flat "alla Saltarella"
  (unaccompanied)   Everest (in set SDBR3203)
                                   HMV HQS1124
                                   Imperial ILX1015
                                   Virtuoso VIR1002

  No. 7. Étude No. 7, in A flat "La Cadenza"
  (unaccompanied)   Everest (in set SDBR3203)
                                   HMV HQS1124
                                   Imperial ILX1015
                                   Virtuoso VIR1002

WIENIAWSKI – *Continued*

(8) **Étude–Caprices**, Op. 18 solo vln & 2nd vln obb
No. 1. Étude–Caprice No. 1, in g
(playing both parts)

Everest (in set SDBR3203)
HMV HQM1139
Imperial ILX1016
Musical Heritage Society
MHS1131
Virtuoso VIR1001

No. 2. Étude–Caprice No. 2, in E flat
(playing both parts)

Everest (in set SDBR3203)
HMV HQM1139
Imperial ILX1016
Musical Heritage Society
MHS1131
Virtuoso VIR1001

No. 3. Étude–Caprice No. 3, in D
(playing both parts)

Everest (in set SDBR3203)
HMV HQM1139
Imperial ILX1016
Musical Heritage Society
MHS1131
Virtuoso VIR1001

No. 4. Étude–Caprice No. 4, in a
(playing both parts)

Everest (in set SDBR3203)
HMV HQM1139
Imperial ILX1016
Musical Heritage Society
MHS1131
Virtuoso VIR1001

No. 5. Étude–Caprice No. 5, in E flat
(playing both parts)

Everest (in set SDBR3203)
HMV HQM1139
Imperial ILX1016
Musical Heritage Society
MHS1131
Virtuoso VIR1001

No. 6. Étude–Caprice No. 6, in D
(playing both parts)

Everest (in set SDBR3203)
HMV HQM1139
Imperial ILX1016
Musical Heritage Society
MHS1131
Virtuoso VIR1001

No. 7. Étude–Caprice No. 7, in c
(playing both parts)

Everest (in set SDBR3203)
HMV HQM1139
Imperial ILX1016
Musical Heritage Society
MHS1131
Virtuoso VIR1001

No. 8. Étude–Caprice No. 8, in F
(playing both parts)

Everest (in set SDBR3203)
HMV HQM1139
Imperial ILX1016
Musical Heritage Society
MHS1131
Virtuoso VIR1001

WIENIAWSKI – *Continued*

Légende, Op. 17 vln & pf or orch.
with A. Kotowska pf

Everest (in set SDBR3203)
HMV HQM1139
Imperial ILX1016
Musical Heritage Society
MHS1131
Virtuoso VIR1001

(2) **Mazurkas**, Op. 19 vln & pf
No. 2. Mazurka No. 2, in D "Dudziarz"
with A. Kotowska pf

Everest (in set SDBR3203)
HMV HQM1139
Imperial ILX1016
Musical Heritage Society
MHS1131
Virtuoso VIR1001

Polonaise brillante No. 1, in D, Op. 4 vln & pf
with A. Kotowska pf

Everest (in set SDBR3203)
HMV HQM1139
Imperial ILX1016
Musical Heritage Society
MHS1131
Virtuoso VIR1001

Scherzo–Tarantelle, Op. 16 vln & pf
with A. Kotowska pf

Everest (in set SDBR3203)
HMV HQM1139
Imperial ILX1016
Musical Heritage Society
MHS1131
Virtuoso VIR1001

WILLAN

Sonata No. 2, in E (1923) vln & pf
with L. Boucher pf   CBC Transcription Program 243

Edward STATKIEWICZ

BACEWICZ
Sonata No. 4 vln & pf
with A. Utrecht pf   Muza XL0505

BERGSMA
Concerto vln & orch.
with Polish Radio & Television Orch.   Turnabout TV34428
– Szostak

PADEREWSKI
Sonata in a, Op. 13 (1880) vln & pf
with A. Utrecht pf   Muza XL0505

Wolfgang STAVONHAGEN (1916–   )

BARBER
Concerto, Op. 14 (1941) vln & orch.
with Imperial Philharmonic Symphony   Composers Recordings CRI137
of Tokyo – Strickland

KERR

Concerto (1950/1) vln & orch.
  with Imperial Philharmonic Symphony   Composers Recordings CRI142
  of Tokyo – Strickland

Jan ŠTĚDROŇ (1907–)

BENDA, F.

Sonata in A vln & pf – rev. J. & B. Stedron
  Allegro (2nd mvt); **Vivace** (3rd mvt)
  with B. Štědroň pf   Ultraphon MBA13050

Olga STEEB

CHOPIN

(5) Mazurkas, Op. 7 pf
  No. 1. Mazurka No. 5, in B flat arr. vln & pf
  with C. Valderrama pf   Edison Diamond Disc 51315

KREISLER

Schön Rosmarin vln & pf
  with A. Benoist pf   Edison Diamond Disc 50980

MacDOWELL

Air & Rigaudon, Op. 49 pf
  No. 2. Rigaudon arr. vln & pf
  with A. Benoist pf   Edison Diamond Disc 50980

MENDELSSOHN

(3) Fantasies, Op. 16 (1829) pf
  No. 2. Fantasy No. 2, in e arr. vln & pf
  with C. Valderrama pf   Edison Diamond Disc 51315

Angelo STEFANATO

VIVALDI

(12) Concerti, Op. 3 "L'Estro armonico" var. cbns & strs
  Concerto No. 3, in G, P.96 (F.I, No. 173) vln, strs & c
  with L.F. Tagliavini hpsi & Angelicum   Angelicum STA8911
  Orch., Milan – Zedda   Harmonia Mundi HM30664
  Concerto No. 4, in e, P.97 (F.I, No. 174) 4 vlns, strs & c
  with R. Ruotolo vln, F. Gulli vln, M.   HMV ALP1809, ASD391
  Benvenuti vln & Virtuosi di Roma –
  Fasano
  Concerto No. 5, in A, P.212 (F.I, No. 175) 2 vlns, strs & c
  with R. Ruotolo vln & Virtuosi di   HMV ALP1810, ASD392
  Roma – Fasano
  Concerto No. 8, in a, P.2 (F.I, No. 177) 2 vlns, strs & c
  with C. Ferraresi vln & Angelicum   Angelicum LPA5958, SLPA5958
  Orch., Milan – Zedda
  Concerto No. 10, in b, P.148 (F.IV, No. 10) 4 vlns, strs & c
  with L. Ferro vln, F. Gulli vln, E.   HMV ALP1811, ASD393
  Malanotte vln & Virtuosi di Roma –
  Fasano
  Concerto No. 10, in b, P.148 (F.IV, No. 10) 4 vlns, strs & c
  with C. Ferraresi vln, B. Salvi vln, M.   Angelicum LPA5911, STA8911
  Ceradini vln, L.F. Tagliavini hpsi &   Harmonia Mundi HM30664
  Angelicum Orch., Milan – Zedda

Andrea STEFFEN–WENDLING

VIVALDI

(12) Concerti, Op. 3 "L'Estro armonico" var. cbns & strs
  Concerto No. 1, in D, P.146 (F.IV, No. 7) 4 vlns, vlc, strs & c
  with R. Barchet vln, H. Endres vln, F.   Pathé–Vox (in set PV273)
  Hopfner vln, S. Barchet vlc, H. Elsner   Vox (in sets DL271, PL7243,
  hpsi & Pro Musica Orch., Stuttgart –   PL7420 & VBX20)
  Reinhardt
  Concerto No. 2, in g, P.326 (F.IV, No. 8) 2 vlns, strs & c
  with R. Barchet vln, H. Elsner hpsi &   Pathé–Vox (in set PV273)
  Pro Musica Orch., Stuttgart –   Vox (in sets DL271, PL7243,
  Reinhardt   PL7420 & VBX20)
  Concerto No. 4, in e, P.97 (F.I, No. 174) 4 vlns, strs & c
  with R. Barchet vln, H. Endres vln, F.   Pathé–Vox (in set PV273)
  Hopfner vln, H. Elsner hpsi & Pro   Vox (in sets DL271, PL7243,
  Musica Orch., Stuttgart – Reinhardt   PL7420 & VBX20)
  Concerto No. 7, in F, P.249 (F.IV, No. 9) 4 vlns, strs & c
  with R. Barchet vln, H. Endres vln, F.   Pathé–Vox (in set PV273)
  Hopfner vln, H. Elsner hpsi & Pro   Vox (in sets DL271, PL7243,
  Musica Orch., Stuttgart – Reinhardt   PL7420 & VBX20)
  Concerto No. 10, in b, P.148 (F.IV, No. 10) 4 vlns, strs & c
  with R. Barchet vln, H. Endres vln, F.   Pathé–Vox (in set PV273)
  Hopfner vln, H. Elsner hpsi & Pro   Vox (in sets DL271, PL7243,
  Musica Orch., Stuttgart – Reinhardt   PL7420 & VBX20)
  Concerto No. 11, in d, P.250 (F.IV, No. 11) 2 vlns, vlc, strs & c
  with R. Barchet vln, S. Barchet vlc, H.   Pathé–Vox (in set PV273)
  Elsner hpsi & Pro Musica Orch.,   Vox (in sets DL271, PL7243,
  Stuttgart – Reinhardt   PL7420 & VBX20)
(12) Concerti, Op. 9 (1728) "La Cetra" vln, strs & c
  Concerto No. 9, in B flat, P.341 (F.I, No. 57) with 2nd vln obb
  with R. Barchet vln, H. Elsner hpsi &   Vox (in sets DL203 & VBX30)
  Pro Musica Orch., Stuttgart –
  Reinhardt

George STEHL*

ANONYMOUS

Marie–Nocturne composer unid – arr. vln, fl & hp
  with M. Lufsky fl & C. Schuetze hp   Columbia A5222

Mazurka brillante composer unid – arr. 2 vlns & hp
  with H. von Wegern vln & hp   Columbia A705

Sounds from home composer unid – arr. vln, fl & hp
  with M. Lufsky fl & P. Sürth hp   Columbia A601

AVILÉS

A media noche v & pf – arr. vln, fl & hp
  with fl & hp   Columbia A1018, A5079

BALFE

(The) Bohemian Girl (1843) – opera
  Then you'll remember me arr. vln, fl & hp
  with Stanzione fl & C. Schuetze hp   Columbia A5238

BLON

Sérénade d'amour pf – arr. 2 vlns & pf
  with H. von Wegern vln & pf   4015   Columbia A657

* Labels occasionally state: George Steel. Stehl has also recorded various
  jigs and reels.

BRAGA

(7) Melodies (1867) v & pf
No. 5. La serenata "Angel's serenade" arr. vln, fl & hp
with M. Lufsky fl & C.   38398   Columbia A1250
Schuetze hp

BUTTSCHARDT

Christmas bells vln & pf
with C. Schuetze hp   Columbia A919

CORELLI

(12) Sonatas, Op. 5 vln & c
Sonata No. 1, in D: Adagio (4th mvt) arr. vln & pf as "O Sanctissima"
by Kreisler
with M. Lufsky fl & C.A. Prince pf   Columbia A5083

DELMET

(L') Etoile d'amour v & pf – arr. vln, fl & hp
with Henneberg fl & C. Schuetze hp   Columbia A5149

DVOŘÁK

(8) Humoresques, Op. 101 pf
No. 7. Humoresque No. 7, in G flat arr. vln, orch. & hp
with string orch. & harp   30521–2   Columbia 574, A5226
No. 7. Humoresque No. 7, in G flat arr. vln & orch.
with Prince's Orch.   Columbia A5704

EHRICH

Liebesfrühling – Ländler, Op. 32 pf & 2 vlns
with M. Lufsky fl & Pinto   3985–2   Columbia A631
hp

ELGAR

Salut d'amour, Op. 12 orch. – arr. vln & pf Elgar
with piano   Columbia 126, A5073

GRUBER

Stille Nacht, heilige Nacht (1818) v & pf – arr. vln, fl & pf
with M. Lufsky fl & C.A. Prince pf   Columbia A5083

GUNGL

Am Königssee, Op. 361 pf – arr. vln, fl & hp
with M. Lufsky fl & P.   39182   Columbia 127, A5079
Sürth hp

JUNGMANN

Heimweh (Longing for home) Op. 117 v & pf – arr. vln, fl & hp
with M. Lufsky fl & P. Sürth hp   Columbia A710

LABITZKY

In der Sennhütte (At the mountain inn) Op. 51 pf – arr. vln, fl & hp
with M. Lufsky fl & P.   30121–2   Columbia A5115
Sürth hp
(Der) Traum der Sennerin (Dream of the mountains – Idyll) Op. 45 orch. –
arr. vln, fl & hp
with M. Lufsky fl & P. Sürth hp   Columbia A587

LANGE

Flower song, Op. 39 vln & pf – arr. vln, fl & hp
with Henneberg fl & P. Sürth hp   Columbia A5134

LANGER

Grandmother, Op. 20 pf – arr. vln, fl & hp
with M. Lufsky fl & P. Sürth hp   Columbia A625

MacDOWELL

Woodland Sketches, Op. 51 pf
No. 1. To a wild rose arr. vln & orch.
with Prince's Orch.   Columbia A1030

MASSENET

Thaïs (1894) – opera
Méditation arr. vln, orch & hp
with string orch. & hp   30228–6   Columbia A5115

MOLLOY

Love's old sweet song v & pf – arr. vln, vlc & hp
with Richard vlc & C. Schuetze hp   Columbia A968

POTTER

Serenata amorosa arr. 2 vlns & pf
with W. Biederman vln & piano   Columbia A775

SCHUBERT

(14) Schwanengesang, D957 (1828) v & pf
No. 4. Ständchen "Serenade" arr. vln & 2 fls
with M. Lufsky fl & Pinto fl   Columbia 127, A5090

STEHL

Tyrolean echoes vln, fl & hp
with Henneberg fl & C. Schuetze hp   Columbia A5704

STEVENSON

Oft in the stilly night v & pf – arr. vln, fl & hp
with M. Lufsky fl & P. Sürth hp   Columbia A850

SVENDSEN

Romance in G, Op. 26 vln & orch.
with string orch.   Columbia 574

THOMÉ

Simple aveu, Op. 25 pf – arr. vln, fl & hp
with M. Lufsky fl & P. Sürth hp   Columbia A850

WALLACE

Maritana (1845) – opera
Scenes that are brightest arr. vln, fl & hp
with M. Lufsky fl & P. Sürth hp   Columbia A5159

Annie STEIGER–BETZAK

FIOCCO

Suite No. 1, in G hpsi
Allegro (10th mvt) arr. vln & pf Bent & O'Neill
with piano   Polydor 986

HANDEL

Cantata unid
Dank sei dir, Herr "Arioso" arr. vln & pf
with piano   Polydor 2035

LECLAIR

(12) Sonatas, Op. 9 – Book IV (1738) vln & c
Sonata No. 3, in D: Tambourin (3rd mvt) arr. vln & pf Sarasate
with piano   Polydor 986

LOHR

(The) Dancing violin v & pf – arr. vln & pf Markgraf
  with piano   Polydor 24732

PAGANINI

Moto perpetuo (Allegro di concert) Op. 11 (1830) vln & orch.
  with piano   Polydor 2035

RUBINOFF

Fiddlin' the fiddle vln & pf
  with piano   Polydor 24732

J. STEIN

HÁBA

Duo, Op. 49 (1936) 2 vlns
  Allegro moderato (1st mvt)
  with J. Weismeyer vln   CA 16635–1   Columbia DB1791, (in set
                                         CHM5)

Edith STEINBAUER

RUGGIERI

(10) Sonatas, Op. 3 (1693) 2 vlns, vlc & c
  Sonata No. 1, in e
  with E. Melkus vln, E. Knava gamba,   Society of Participating Artists
  A. Planyavsky cbs, K. Scheit gtr & K. SPA18
  Rapf org
  Sonata No. 2, in b
  with E. Melkus vln, E. Knava gamba,   Society of Participating Artists
  A. Planyavsky cbs & K. Rapf hpsi   SPA18
  Sonata No. 3, in B flat
  with E. Melkus vln, E. Knava gamba,   Society of Participating Artists
  A. Planyavsky cbs & K. Scheit lute   SPA18
  Sonata No. 4, in F
  with E. Melkus vln, E. Knava gamba,   Society of Participating Artists
  A. Planyavsky cbs, K. Scheit gtr & K. SPA18
  Rapf org
  Sonata No. 5, in g
  with E. Melkus vln, E. Knava gamba   Society of Participating Artists
  A. Planyavsky cbs & K. Scheit lute   SPA19
  Sonata No. 6, in A
  with E. Melkus vln, E. Knava gamba,   Society of Participating Artists
  A. Planyavsky cbs & K. Scheit gtr   SPA19
  Sonata No. 7, in a
  with E. Melkus vln, E. Knava vlc, A.   Society of Participating Artists
  Planyavsky cbs & K. Rapf pf   SPA18
  Sonata No. 8, in G
  with E. Melkus vln, E. Knava gamba,   Society of Participating Artists
  A. Planyavsky cbs & K. Rapf hpsi   SPA19
  Sonata No. 9, in d
  with E. Melkus vln, E. Knava vlc, A.   Society of Participating Artists
  Planyavsky cbs & K. Rapf pf   SPA18
  Sonata No. 10, in D
  with E. Melkus vln, E. Knava gamba,   Society of Participating Artists
  A. Planyavsky cbs & K. Rapf hpsi   SPA19

Simon STEINBERG

ANONYMOUS

Poschalej arr. vln & pf
  with piano   4826 ab   HMV X287961

JÄRNEFELT

Berceuse in g orch. – arr. vln & pf
  with piano   4827 ab   HMV X287962

Carl STEINER

HUBAY

(14) Scènes de la Csárda vln & pf
  No. 4. Hejre Kati, Op. 32
  with piano   Artiphon D03064/5

SARASATE

Zigeunerweisen, Op. 20 vln & pf or orch.
  with orch.   7329/30   Artiphon D07329/30

VIVALDI

(12) Concerti, Op. 3 "L'Estro armonico" var. cbns & strs
  Concerto No. 8, in a, P.2 (F.I, No. 177) 2 vlns, strs & c
  with R. Czerwonky vln & H. Steiner   Christschall 148/9
  pf

Arnold STEINHARDT

BACH

(3) Sonatas & 3 Partitas, BWV1001/6 solo vln
  Sonata No. 1, in g, BWV1001
  (unaccompanied)   Sheffield 7
  Partita No. 2, in d, BWV1002
  (unaccompanied)   Sheffield 7

MENDELSSOHN

Octet in E flat, Op. 20 4 vlns, 2 vlas & 2 vlcs
  with J. Laredo vln, A. Schneider vln,   CBS BRG72473, SBRG72473
  J. Dalley vln, M. Tree vla, S. Rhodes   Columbia ML6248, MS6848
  vla, L. Parnas vlc & D. Soyer vlc

SCHOENBERG

Fantasy, Op. 47 (1949) vln & pf
  with P. Serkin pf   Victor LSC3050, SB6816

Josef STEINHÄUSLER

TELEMANN

Concerto in G 2 vlns, strs & c
  with G. Retyi vln & Pro Arte   Christophorus CGLP75792,
  Chamber Orch., Munich – Redel   SCGLP75793
                                       Columbia SMC95066
                                       Erato LDE3243, STE50143,
                                       STU70143
                                       Westminster WST17042,
                                       XWN19042

Jarka Jaroslav ŠTĚPÁNEK (1905–)

DVOŘÁK

Mazurka in e, Op. 49 vln & pf
  with V. Řepková pf   42327   Ultraphon A12165

SUK

(7) Pieces, Op. 7 pf
  No. 2. Humoresque arr. vln & pf Ondřiček
  with V. Řepková pf   42330   Ultraphon A12166
  No. 4. Idyll arr. vln & pf Ondřiček
  with V. Řepková pf   42330   Ultraphon A12166
(4) Pieces, Op. 17 vln & pf
  No. 2. Appassionata
  with V. Řepková pf   42329   Ultraphon A12166

Joseph STEPANSKY

GLINKA

Quartet in F (1830) 2 vlns, vla & vlc
  with L. Kaufman vln, L. Kievman vla   Society for Forgotten Music
  & G. Neikrug vlc   SFM1001

MENDELSSOHN

Octet in E flat, Op. 20 4 vlns, 2 vlas & 2 vlcs
  with I. Baker vln, A. Belnick vln, J.   Victor A640761/3, (in sets
  Heifetz vln, W. Primrose vla, V.   LD6159 & LDS6159), LM2738,
  Majewski vla, G. Piatigorsky vlc & G.   LSC2738, SHP2322,
  Rejto vlc   SOR630761/3
Quartet No. 1, in E flat, Op. 12 2 vlns, vla & vlc
  with L. Kaufman vln, L. Kievman vla   Society for Forgotten Music
  & G. Neikrug vlc   SFM1001

TOCH

Quartet in D flat, Op. 18 (1909) 2 vlns, vla & vlc
  with L. Kaufman vln, L. Kievman vla   Contemporary C6002
  & G. Neikrug vlc
Serenade in G, Op. 25 (1917) 2 vlns & vla
  with L. Kaufman vln & L. Kievman   Contemporary C6002
  vla

Isaac STERN (1920–)

ANONYMOUS

Greensleeves Traditional English ballad – arr. vln & orch. Harris
  with Columbia Symphony Orch. –   CBS BRG72146, SBRG72146
  Katims   Columbia ML5896, MS6496

BACH

Concerto No. 1, in a, BWV1041 vln, strs & c
  with Prades Festival Orch. – Casals   Columbia CX1109, FCX325,
      ML4353
Concerto No. 1, in a, BWV1041 vln, strs & c
  with Philadelphia Orch. – Ormandy   Columbia ML5087
      Fontana 664019ER, 697203EL,
      EFL2501, EFR2027
      Philips A01239L, ABL3138
Concerto No. 1, in a, BWV1041 vln, strs & c
  with London Symphony Orch.   CBS BRG72531, SBRG72531
  members – Stern   Columbia ML6349, MS6949

BACH – *Continued*

Concerto No. 2, in E, BWV1042 vln, strs & c
  with New York Philharmonic   CBS BRG72531, SBRG72531
  Symphony Orch. members – Bernstein   Columbia ML6349, MS6949
Concerto in d, BWV1043 2 vlns, strs & c
  with A. Schneider vln & Prades   Columbia FCX155, ML4351,
  Festival Orch.   QCX155
Concerto in c, BWV1060 vln & ob or 2 vlns, strs & c
  with M. Tabuteau ob & Prades   Columbia ML4351, QCX155
  Festival Orch. – Casals   Philips L01511L
Concerto in c, BWV1060 vln & ob or 2 vlns, strs & c
  with H. Gomberg ob & New York   CBS BRG72531, SBRG72531
  Philharmonic Symphony Orch.   Columbia ML6349, MS6949
  members – Bernstein
(6) Sonatas, BWV1014/9 vln & clav
Sonata No. 3, in E, BWV1016
  with A. Zakin pf   Columbia ML4862
      Philips A01126L, ABL3011
Sonata in g, BWV1020 vln & clav
  with A. Zakin pf   Columbia ML4862
      Philips A01126L, ABL3011
Sonata in e, BWV1023 vln & c
  with A. Zakin pf   Columbia ML4862
      Philips A01126L, ABL3011
Sonata in G, BWV1038 fl, vln & c
  with J. Wummer fl & E. Istomin pf   Columbia CX1109, FCX325,
      ML4353

BARBER

Concerto, Op. 14 (1941) vln & orch.
  with New York Philharmonic   CBS BRG72345, SBRG72345
  Symphony Orch. – Bernstein   Columbia ML6113, MS6713

BARTÓK

Concerto No. 1, Op. posth (1908) vln & orch.
  with Philadelphia Orch. – Ormandy   CBS BRG72009, SBRG72009
      Columbia ML5677, MS6277
Concerto No. 2 (1938) vln & orch.
  with New York Philharmonic   Columbia ML5283, MS6002,
  Symphony Orch. – Bernstein   OS104
      Fontana 699020EL, 876000EZ,
      CFL1031, SCFL106
Rhapsody No. 1, in G (1928) vln & orch.
  with New York Philharmonic   CBS BRG72070, SBRG72070
  Symphony Orch. – Bernstein   Columbia ML5773, MS6373
Rhapsody No. 2, in d (1928) vln & orch.
  with New York Philharmonic   CBS BRG72070, SBRG72070
  Symphony Orch. – Bernstein   Columbia ML5773, MS6373
Sonata No. 1 (1921) vln & pf
  with A. Zakin pf   Columbia ML4376
Sonata No. 1 (1921) vln & pf
  with A. Zakin pf   Columbia M30944
Sonata No. 2 (1922) vln & pf
  with A. Zakin pf   Columbia M30944

BEETHOVEN

Concerto in C, Op. 56 "Triple" pf, vln, vlc & orch.
with E. Istomin pf, L. Rose vlc &   CBS BRG72346, SBRG72346
Philadelphia Orch. – Ormandy   Columbia ML6119, (in set
    D2L320), MS6719, (in set
    D2S720)

Concerto in D, Op. 61 (cadenzas to 1st mvt Kreisler: others by Joachim)
with New York Philharmonic   CBS BRG72092, SBRG72092
Symphony Orch. – Bernstein   Columbia ML5415, MS6093,
    OS115
    Fontana 699049CL, 876001EZ,
    CFL1051, SCFL120

(3) Sonatas, Op. 30 vln & pf
  No. 2. Sonata No. 7, in c
     XCO 34398–2, 34399–3, 34400/1   Columbia 71723/6D, 71727/30D,
      –2, 34402/3–3 & 34404–2   (set M604), LOX600/3, ML4326
   with A. Zakin pf

(3) Trios, Op. 1 pf, vln & vlc
  No. 1. Trio No. 1, in E flat
   with E. Istomin pf & L. Rose vlc   CBS S72852
    Columbia M30185, (in set M5
    30065)

  No. 2. Trio No. 2, in G
   with E. Istomin pf & L. Rose vlc   CBS S72852
    Columbia M30185, (in set M5
    30065)

  No. 3. Trio No. 3, in c
   with E. Istomin pf & L. Rose vlc   CBS S72854
    Columbia M30187, (in set M5
    30065), ML6483, MS7083

Trio in B flat, Op. 11 cl, vlc & pf – arr. vln, vlc & pf
with E. Istomin pf & L. Rose vlc   CBS S72854
    Columbia M30187, (in set M5
    30065)

(2) Trios, Op. 70 pf, vln & vlc
  No. 1. Trio No. 4, in D "Ghost"
   with E. Istomin pf & L. Rose vlc   CBS S72855
    Columbia M30188, (in set M5
    30065)

  No. 2. Trio No. 5, in E flat
   with E. Istomin pf & L. Rose vlc   CBS S72855
    Columbia M30188, (in set M5
    30065)

Trio No. 6, in B flat, Op. 97 "Archduke" pf, vln & vlc
wtih E. Istomin pf & L. Rose vlc   CBS BRG72434, SBRG72434
    Columbia ML6219, MS6819

Trio No. 6, in B flat, Op. 97 "Archduke" pf, vln & vlc
with E. Istomin pf & L. Rose vlc   CBS S72856
    Columbia M30189, (in set M5
    30065)

Trio in E flat, G153 (WoO.38) pf, vln & vlc
with E. Istomin pf & L. Rose vlc   CBS S72852
    Columbia M30185, (in set M5
    30065)

Trio in B flat, G154 (WoO.39) "In one movement" pf, vln & vlc
with E. Istomin pf & L. Rose vlc   CBS S72852
    Columbia M30187, (in set M5
    30065)

BEETHOVEN – *Continued*

(14) Variations in E flat, Op. 44 pf, vln & vlc
with E. Istomin pf & L. Rose vlc   CBS S72856
    Columbia M30189, (in set M5
    30065)

(10) Variations (on "Ich bin der Schneider Kakadu") Op. 121a pf, vln & vlc
with E. Istomin pf & L. Rose vlc   CBS S72853
    Columbia M30186, (in set M5
    30065)

BENJAMIN

(2) Jamaican Pieces (!940) orch.
  No. 2. Jamaican Rhumba arr. vln & orch. Harris
   with Columbia Symphony Orch. –   CBS BRG72146, SBRG72146
   Katims   Columbia ML5896, MS6496

BERG

Concerto (1935) vln & orch.
with New York Philharmonic   CBS BRG72070, SBRG72070
Symphony Orch. – Bernstein   Columbia ML5773, MS6373

BERNSTEIN

Serenade (1954) vln, hp, pcn & str orch.
with Symphony of the Air – Bernstein   Columbia ML5144

BLOCH

Baal Shem (3 Pictures of Chassidic life) (1923) vln & pf
  No. 2. Nigun (Improvisation)
   with A. Zakin pf   CO 39708/9   Columbia LB84, ML4324
Baal Shem (3 Pictures of Chassidic life) (1923) vln & pf
with A. Zakin pf   CBS BRG72354, SBRG72354
    Columbia ML6117, MS6717

Sonata No. 1 (1920) vln & pf
with A. Zakin pf   CBS BRG72354, SBRG72354
    Columbia ML6117, MS6717

BRAHMS

Concerto in D, Op. 77 (cadenza by Kreisler) vln & orch.
with Royal Philharmonic Orch. –   Columbia ML4530
Beecham   Fontana 699027CL
    Philips A01106L, ABL3023,
    G05612R, GBL5638

Concerto in D, Op. 77 (cadenza by Kreisler) vln & orch.
with Philadelphia Orch. – Ormandy   CBS BRG72094, SBRG72094
    Columbia ML5486, MS6153
    Fontana 699055CL, 876006EZ,
    CFL1060, SCFL129

Concerto in a, Op. 102 "Double" vln, vlc & orch.
with L. Rose vlc & New York   Columbia ML5076
Philharmonic Symphony Orch. –   Philips A01244L, ABL3139,
Walter   ABL3289, G05628R, GBL5614,
    GBR6534

Concerto in a, Op. 102 "Double" vln, vlc & orch.
with L. Rose vlc & Philadelphia Orch.   CBS BRG72295, SBRG72295
– Ormandy   S72786
    Columbia ML6118, (in set
    D2L320), MS6718, (in set
    D2S720), MS7217

BRAHMS – *Continued*

(21) Hungarian Dances pf duet
  Hungarian dance No. 5, in f sharp arr. vln & orch. "in g" Harris
  with Columbia Symphony Orch. –   CBS BRG72146, SBRG72146
  Katims   Columbia M31405, ML5896,
    MS6496

Quintet No. 2, in G, Op. 111 2 vlns, 2 vlas & vlc
  with A. Schneider vln, M. Katims vla, Columbia ML4701, (in set
  M. Thomas vla & P. Tortelier vlc SL185), ML4711, (in set SL182)
    Philips A01282L, ABL3184,
    L01294L

Sextet No. 1, in B flat, Op. 18 2 vlns, 2 vlas & 2 vlcs
  with A. Schneider vln, M. Katims vla, CBS BRG72324
  M. Thomas vla, P. Casals vlc & M. Columbia ML4703, (in set
  Foley vlc SL185), ML4711, (in set SL182)
    Fontana 409118AE
    Philips A01170L, ABL3085,
    G03599L, GBL5623

Sonata No. 1, in G, Op. 78 vln & pf
  with A. Zakin pf   CBS S61164
    Columbia ML4912, (in set
    SL202), ML2193
    Fontana 699047CL

Sonata No. 2, in A, Op. 100 vln & pf
  with A. Zakin pf   Columbia ML4913, (in set
    SL202)
    Fontana 699048CL
    Philips A01133L, ABL3068

Sonata No. 3, in d, Op. 108 vln & pf
          XCO 37051–2D, 37052–4B, Columbia 12735/7D, (set
  37053–2C, 37054/5–2B & 37056–4B MM730), LX1091/3, ML4363
  with A. Zakin pf

Sonata No. 3, in d, Op. 108 vln & pf
  with A. Zakin pf   CBS S61164
    Columbia ML4912, (in set
    SL202)
    Fontana 699047CL

Sonata (1853) "Frei aber Einsam" vln & pf
  Allegro (Scherzo) in c (3rd mvt) "Sonatensatz"
  with A. Zakin pf   Columbia ML4913, (in set
    SL202)
    Fontana 699048CL
    Philips A01133L, ABL3068

Trio No. 1, in B, Op. 8 pf, vln & vlc
  with M. Hess pf & P. Casals vlc
    Columbia ML4707, (in set
    SL185), ML4719, (in set SL184)
    Philips A01207L, ABL3113

Trio No. 1, in B, Op. 8 pf, vln & vlc
  with E. Istomin pf & L. Rose vlc CBS BRG72596, SBRG72596
    Columbia ML6383, (in set
    M2L360), MS6983, (in set
    M2S760)

Trio No. 2, in C, Op. 87 pf, vln & vlc
  with E. Istomin pf & L. Rose vlc CBS BRG72597, BRG77210,
    SBRG72597, SBRG77210
    Columbia ML6118, (in set
    D2L320), MS6718, (in set
    D2S720), ML6384, (in set
    M2L360), MS6984, (in set
    M2S760)

BRAHMS – *Continued*

Trio No. 3, in c, Op. 101 pf, vln & vlc
  with E. Istomin pf & L. Rose vlc CBS BRG72597, SBRG72597,
    BRG77210, SBRG77210
    Columbia ML6384, (in set
    M2L360), MS6984, (in set
    M2S760)

BRUCH

Concerto No. 1, in g, Op. 26 vln & orch.*
  with Philadelphia Orch. – Ormandy Columbia ML5097
    Fontana 664002CL, 699040CL,
    CFL1062, EFL2526, EFR2002
    Philips A01253L, ABL3168

Concerto No. 1, in g, Op. 26 vln & orch.
  with Philadelphia Orch. – Ormandy CBS BRG72612, SBRG72612
    Columbia ML6403, MS7003

COPLAND

Rodeo (1942) – ballet orch.
  No. 4. Hoe–down arr. vln & orch. Harris
  with Columbia Symphony Orch. – CBS BRG72146, SBRG72146
  Katims Columbia ML5896, MS6496

DEBUSSY

Sonata No. 3, in g (1917) vln & pf
  with A. Zakin pf   CBS BRG72454, SBRG72454
    Columbia ML5470, MS6139
    Fontana 699058CL, CFL1044

Suite Bergamasque (1890) pf
  No. 3. Clair de lune arr. vln & orch. Harris
  with Columbia Symphony Orch. – CBS BRG72146, SBRG72146
  Katims Columbia ML5896, MS6496

DIETRICH

Sonata (1853) "Frei aber Einsam" vln & pf
  Allegro in a (1st mvt)
  with A. Zakin pf   Columbia ML4913, (in set
    SL202)
    Fontana 699048CL
    Philips A01133L, ABL3068

DINICU

Hora Staccato vln & pf – arr. Heifetz
  with A. Zakin pf   CO 39705–1A Columbia 17541D, A1517, LB72,
    ML4324

DVOŘÁK

Concerto in a, Op. 53 vln & orch.
  with Philadelphia Orch. – Ormandy CBS BRG72457, SBRG72457
    Columbia ML6276, MS6876

(8) Humoresques, Op. 101 pf
  No. 7. Humoresque No. 7, in G flat arr. vln & orch. "in G" Waxman
  with orch. –   XCO 36759–1 Columbia 71881D, (in set M651),
  Waxman C16063, (in set D191), ML2103
  No. 7. Humoresque No. 7, in G flat arr. vln & orch. "in G" Harris
  with Columbia Symphony Orch. – CBS BRG72146, SBRG72146
  Katims Columbia M31405, ML5896,
    MS6496

* Adagio or 2nd mvt is also on Fontana 496035CE, CFE15036.

731

DVOŘÁK – *Continued*

Romance in f, Op. 11 vln & orch.
  with Philadelphia Orch. – Ormandy   CBS BRG72457, SBRG72457
                                       Columbia ML6276, MS6876

(8) Slavonic Dances, Op. 46 pf duet; orch.
  No. 2. Slavonic dance No. 2, in e arr. vln & pf "in g" Kreisler
  with A. Zakin pf   Columbia AAL23
                                       Fontana CFE15056
                                       Philips S06617R

(8) Slavonic Dances, Op. 72 pf duet; orch.
  No. 2. Slavonic dance No. 10, in e arr. vln & pf Kreisler
  with A. Zakin pf   Columbia A1517, ML4324

FALLA

(7) Canciones populares españolas (1914) v & pf
  No. 1. El paño moruno arr. vln & pf Kochański
  with A. Zakin pf   Columbia 72816/7D, (set
                                       MX314), ML2050

  No. 4. Jota arr. vln & pf Kochański
  with A. Zakin pf   Columbia 72816/7D, (set
                                       MX314), ML2050

  No. 5. Nana arr. vln & pf Kochański
  with A. Zakin pf   Columbia 72816/7D, (set
                                       MX314), ML2050

  No. 6. Canción arr. vln & pf Kochański
  with A. Zakin pf   Columbia 72816/7D, (set
                                       MX314), ML2050

FOSTER

I dream of Jeannie with the light brown hair v & pf – arr. vln & orch. Harris
  with Columbia Symphony Orch. –   CBS BRG72146, SBRG72146
  Katims   Columbia ML5896, MS6496

FRANCK

Sonata in A (1886) vln & pf
  with A. Zakin pf   Columbia ML2204
                                        Philips A01621R

Sonata in A (1886) vln & pf
  with A.Zakin pf   CBS BRG72454, SBRG72454
                                      Columbia ML5470, MS6139
                                      Fontana 699058CL, CFL1044

GERSHWIN

Porgy & Bess (1935) – opera
  Bess, you is my woman arr. vln & orch. Harris
  with Columbia Symphony Orch. –   CBS BRG72146, SBRG72146
  Katims   Columbia ML5896, MS6496

GLUCK

Orphée et Eurydice (1762) – opera
  Dance of the blessed spirits: Lento "Mélodie" (No. 2) arr. vln & pf Kreisler
  with A. Zakin pf   Columbia AAL23
                                       Fontana CFE15056
                                       Philips S06617R

HANDEL

(15) Sonatas, Op. 1 (?1731) fl or vln & c
  Sonata No. 13, in D: Allegro (2nd mvt) vln IV
  with A. Zakin pf   XCO 34634–1   Columbia 71726D, 71727D, (in
                                                      set M604)

HAYDN

Concerto No. 1, in C, H.VIIa, No. 1 (1765) (cadenza by Klengel) vln & orch.
  with A. Zakin hpsi & Columbia   Columbia 72730/2D, (in set
  Chamber Orch. – Stern   MM799), ML4301, ML5248
                                        Fontana 664025CL, 697203EL,
                                        EFL2501, EFR2027

HINDEMITH

Concerto in D (1940) vln & orch.
  with New York Philharmonic   CBS BRG72345, SBRG72345
  Symphony Orch. – Bernstein   Columbia ML6113, MS6713
Sonata No. 3, in C (1940) vln & pf
  with A. Zakin pf   Columbia ML2050

KREISLER

Liebesleid vln & pf – arr. vln & orch. Harris
  with Columbia Symphony Orch. –   CBS BRG72146, SBRG72146
  Katims   Columbia ML5896, MS6496

Schön Rosmarin vln & pf
  with A. Zakin pf   Columbia AAL23
                                        Fontana CFE15056
                                      Philips S06617R

LALO

Symphonie espagnole, Op. 21 vln & orch.*
  with Philadelphia Orch. – Ormandy   Columbia ML5097
                                        Fontana 664020ER, 699028EL
                                      Philips A01253L, ABL3168,
                                        S06640R

Symphonie espagnole, Op. 21 vln & orch.*
  with Philadelphia Orch. – Ormandy   CBS BRG72612, SBRG72612
                                          Columbia ML6403, MS7003

MENDELSSOHN

Concerto in e, Op. 64 vln & orch.
                  XCO 43646/51–1A   Columbia CX1071, FCX210,
  with Philadelphia Orch. – Ormandy   LNX8039/41, LX1445/7,
                                        LZX268/70, ML4363,
                                        QCX10042, (set A973), (set
                                        MM973)

Concerto in e, Op. 64 vln & orch.
  with Philadelphia Orch. – Ormandy   CBS BRG72083, SBRG72083
                                        Columbia ML5379, MS6062,
                                        MS7516, OL109, OS114
                                        Fontana 664021ER, 876004EZ,
                                        877700EZ, CFL1045, EFL2526,
                                        SCFL119

Concerto in e, Op. 64 vln & orch.
  with Israel Philharmonic Orch. –   Columbia ML6453, MS7053
  Bernstein
Trio No. 1, in d, Op. 49 pf, vln & vlc
  with E. Istomin pf & L. Rose vlc   Columbia ML6483, MS7083

* Including Intermezzo.

MILHAUD

Saudades do Brasil (1920/1) pf
No. 8. Tijuca arr. vln & pf Lévy
with A. Zakin pf   CO 39707–1B   Columbia 17541D, LB72,
                                         ML4324

MOZART

Concerto No. 1, in B flat, K207 (cadenzas by Joachim) vln & orch.
with Columbia Symphony Orch. –   CBS BRG72179, SBRG72179
Szell   Columbia ML5957, MS6557
Concerto No. 3, in G, K216 (cadenzas by Franko) vln & orch.
with Columbia Chamber Orch. – Stern   Columbia (set MM947), CX1071,
                                       FCX210, LZX271/3, ML4326,
                                       ML5248, WCX1071
                                       Fontana 664005CL, 697203EL,
                                       699012CL, 699025CL, CFL1013,
                                       EFL2501
Concerto No. 3, in G, K216 (cadenzas by Franko) vln & orch.
with members of Cleveland Orch. –   CBS S75662
Szell   Columbia ML6462, MS7062
Concerto No. 5, in A, K219 "Turkish" (cadenzas by Joachim) vln & orch.*
with Columbia Symphony Orch. –   CBS BRG72179, SBRG72179
Szell   Columbia ML5957, MS6557
Quartet No. 1, in D, K285 fl, vln, vla & vlc
with J–P. Rampal fl, A. Schneider vla   Columbia M30233
& L. Rose vlc
Quartet No. 2, in G, K285a fl, vln, vla & vlc
with J–P. Rampal fl, A. Schneider vla   Columbia M30233
& L. Rose vlc
Quartet No. 3, in C, K285b fl, vln, vla & vlc
with J–P. Rampal fl, A. Schneider vla   Columbia M30233
& L. Rose vlc
Quartet No. 4, in A, K298 fl, vln, vla & vlc
with J–P. Rampal fl, A. Schneider vla   Columbia M30233
& L. Rose vlc
Quartet in F, K370 ob, vln, vla & vlc
with M. Tabuteau ob, W. Primrose vla   Columbia CX1090, FCX227,
& P. Tortelier vlc   ML4566
Quartet No. 2, in E flat, K493 pf, vln, vla & vlc
with E. Istomin pf, A. Schneider vln &   Columbia ML5237
M. Katims vla
Serenade No. 7, in D, K250 "Haffner" orch.
Rondo (4th mvt) arr. vln & pf Kreisler
with A. Zakin pf   Columbia (in set M1087),
                          AAL23
                          Philips S06617R
Sinfonia concertante in E flat, K364 vln, vla & orch.
with W. Primrose vla & Perpignan   Columbia CX1089, FCX224,
Festival Orch. – Casals   ML4564, (in set SL170)
                                    Fontana 699012CL, CFL1013
Sinfonia concertante in E flat, K364 vln, vla & orch.
with W. Trampler vla & London   CBS S75662, SBRG72786
Symphony Orch. – Stern   Columbia ML6462, MS7062,
                                 MS7217
Sonata No. 26, in B flat, K378 vln & pf
with A. Zakin pf   Columbia (set MM915), ML4301

Tempo di menuetto: Allegro or 3rd mvt is also on Columbia M31405.

MUSSORGSKY

Sorochintsy Fair (1911/23) – opera
Gopak (Act III) orch. – arr. vln & pf Dushkin
with A. Zakin pf   Columbia PE21

NOVAČEK

(8) Concert caprices, Op. 5 vln & pf
No. 4. Perpetuum mobile
with A. Zakin pf   Columbia A1517, ML4324

PROKOFIEV

Concerto No. 1, in D, Op. 19 vln & orch.
with New York Philharmonic   Columbia ML5243
Symphony Orch. – Mitropoulos   Fontana 699014CL, CFL1036
Concerto No. 2, in g, Op. 63 vln & orch.
with New York Philharmonic   Columbia ML5243
Symphony Orch. – Bernstein   Fontana 699014CL, CFL1036
(10) Pieces (from the ballet "Romeo & Juliet") Op. 75 (1937) pf
No. 5. Masques arr. vln & pf Grunes
with A. Zakin pf   Columbia ML4324
Romeo & Juliet, Op. 64b (1935/6) – 2nd ballet suite orch.
No. 4. Danse de jeunes antillaises arr. vln & pf Grunes
with A. Zakin pf   Columbia ML4324
Sonata No. 1, in f, Op. 80 vln & pf
with A. Zakin pf   CBS BRG72203
                          Columbia ML4734
                          Fontana 699052CL
                          Philips A01205L
Sonata No. 2, in D, Op. 94bis vln & pf
with A. Zakin pf   CBS BRG72203
                          Columbia ML4734
                          Fontana 699052CL
                          Philips A01205L

PUGNANI

(6) Sonatas, Op. 8 vln & c
Sonata No. 3, in D: Largo expressivo (2nd mvt) arr. vln & pf Moffat
with A. Zakin pf   Columbia (in set MM915),
                          ML4324

RAVEL

Tzigane (Rapsodie de concert) (1924) vln & pf or orch.
with Philadelphia Orch. – Ormandy   Columbia ML5208
                                     Fontana 699020CL, CFE15012,
                                     CFL1031, EFF533

RIMSKY–KORSAKOV

(The) Tale of Tsar Saltan (1900) – opera
Flight of the bumblebee (Act III) orch. – arr. vln & orch. Waxman
with orch. –   XCO 36764–1   Columbia 71881D, (in set M657),
Waxman   C16064, (in set D191), ML2103
Flight of the bumblebee (Act III) orch. – arr. vln & orch. Harris
with Columbia Symphony Orch. –   CBS BRG72146, SBRG72146
Katims   Columbia M31405, ML5896,
                                  MS6496

SAINT–SAËNS

Introduction & Rondo Capriccioso, Op. 28 vln & orch.
with Philadelphia Orch. – Ormandy   Columbia ML5208
                                     Fontana 699028CL, CFE15012,
                                     EFF510

SARASATE

Caprice basque, Op. 24 vln & pf
with A Zakin pf — Columbia 72816D, (in set MX314), A1517, ML4324

Zigeunerweisen, Op. 20 vln & pf or orch.
XCO 36760–1 & 36761–2
with Columbia Symphony Orch. –
Waxman — Columbia 71883D, (in set M657), C16065/6, (in set D191), A1647, LFX890, LX1156, ML2103
Fontana 496035CE, CFE15036, EFF513, EFR2001

SCHUBERT, François

(12) Bagatelles, Op. 13 vln & pf
No. 9. L'abeille
with A. Zakin pf — Columbia AAL23
Fontana CFE15056
Philips S06617R

SCHUBERT, Franz

(7) Gesänge (set to Scott's "Lady of the Lake") Op. 52 v & pf
No. 6. Ave Maria, D839 arr. vln & orch. Harris
with Columbia Symphony Orch. – CBS BRG72146, SBRG72146
Katims — Columbia ML5896, MS6496

Quintet in C, Op. 163 (D956) 2 vlns, vla & 2 vlcs
with A. Schneider vln, M. Katims vla, Columbia ML4714, (in set
P. Casals vlc & P. Tortelier vlc — SL183)
Philips A01188L, ABL3100, G03600L, GBL5624

Trio No. 1, in B flat, Op. 99 (D898) pf, vln & vlc
with E. Istomin pf & L. Rose vlc — CBS BRG72344, SBRG72344
Columbia ML6116, MS6716

Trio No. 2, in E flat, Op. 100 (D929) pf, vln & vlc
with E. Istomin pf & L. Rose vlc — Columbia MS7419

SCHUMANN

Quintet in E flat, Op. 44 2 vlns, vla, vlc & pf
with M. Hess pf, A. Schneider vln, M. Columbia ML4701, (in set
Thomas vla & P. Tortelier vlc — SL185), ML4711, (in set SL182)
Philips A01282L, ABL3184

Sonata (1853) "Frei aber Einsam" vln & pf
Intermezzo (2nd mvt); **Finale** (4th mvt)
with A. Zakin pf — Columbia ML4913, (in set SL202)
Fontana 699048CL
Philips A01133L, ABL3068

(9) Waldscenen, Op. 82 pf
No. 7. Vogel als Prophet arr. vln & pf Auer
with A. Zakin pf — Columbia AAL23
Fontana CFE15056
Philips S06617R

SIBELIUS

Concerto in d, Op. 47 vln & orch.
CAX 11481–5A, 11482–4A, Columbia C1008, FC1022,
11483–3A, 11484–2A, 11485/6–3A & LX8947/50S, ML4550, QC5003
with Royal Philharmonic 11487–4A Fontana 664017ER, 699040CL
Orch. – Beecham — Philips G03630L, NBL5030

Concerto in d, Op. 47 vln & orch.
with Philadelphia Orch. – Ormandy — CBS S72885
Columbia M30068

STRAVINSKY

Concerto in D (1931) vln & orch.
with Columbia Symphony Orch. – CBS BRG72038, SBRG72038
Stravinsky — Columbia ML5731, MS6331, OS262

Firebird (1910) – ballet suite orch.
No. 5. Berceuse arr. vln & pf Dushkin & Stravinsky
with A. Zakin pf — Columbia PE21

TCHAIKOVSKY

Concerto in D, Op. 35 vln & orch.
with Philadelphia XCO 41137/44 Columbia 13037/40D, (set
Orch. – Hilsberg — MM863), (set A1087), C1022, FCX167, LX1316/9, ML4232, VC807

Concerto in D, Op. 35 vln & orch.
with Philadelphia Orch. – Ormandy — CBS BRG72083, SBRG72083
Columbia ML5379, MS6062, OL109, OS114
Fontana 664022ER, 699017CL, CFL1045, SCFL119
Philips S04634L

(6) Pieces, Op. 51 pf
No. 6. Valse sentimentale arr. vln & pf Zakin
with A. Zakin pf — Columbia AAL23
Fontana CFE15056
Philips S06617R

(6) Songs, Op. 6 v & pf
No. 6. None but the weary heart arr. vln & orch. Harris
with Columbia Symphony Orch. – CBS BRG72146, SBRG72146
Katims — Columbia ML5896, MS6496

VIOTTI

Concerto No. 22, in a (cadenzas by Ysaÿe) vln & orch.
with Philadelphia Orch. – Ormandy — CBS BRG72009, SBRG72009
Columbia ML5677, MS6277

VIVALDI

(12) Concerti, Op. 3 "L'Estro armonico" var. cbns & strs
Concerto No. 8, in a, P.2 (F.I, No. 177) 2 vlns, strs & c
with D. Oistrakh vln & Philadelphia Columbia ML5087
Orch. – Ormandy — Philips 409020AE, A01239L, ABE10181, ABL3138, G05650R

Concerto in D, P.189 (F.I, No. 41) 2 vlns, strs & c
with D. Oistrakh vln, W.R. Smith hpsi CBS BRG72082, SBRG72082
& Philadelphia Orch. – Ormandy — Columbia ML5604, MS6204
Fontana 699061CL, 876008EZ, CFL1070, SCFL136
Supraphon SUA10932, SUAST50932

Concerto in d, P.281 (F.I, No. 100) 2 vlns, strs & c
with D. Oistrakh vln, W.R. Smith hpsi CBS BRG72082, SBRG72082
& Philadelphia Orch. – Ormandy — Columbia ML5604, MS6204
Fontana 494100EE, 699061CL, 876008EZ, CFL1070, SCFL136
Supraphon SUA10932, SUAST50932

VIVALDI – *Continued*

Concerto in g, P.366 (F.I, No. 98) 2 vlns, strs & c
  with D. Oistrakh vln, W.R. Smith hpsi   CBS BRG72082, SBRG72082
  & Philadelphia Orch. – Ormandy   Columbia ML5604, MS6204
                                        Fontana 699061CL, 876008EZ,
                                        CFL1070, SCFL136
                                        Supraphon SUA10932,
                                        SUAST50932

Concerto in c, P.436 (F.I, No. 12) 2 vlns, strs & c
  with D. Oistrakh vln, W.R. Smith hpsi   CBS BRG72082, SBRG72082
  & Philadelphia Orch. – Ormandy   Columbia ML5604, MS6204
                                          Fontana 699061CL, 876008EZ,
                                        CFL1070, SCFL136
                                        Supraphon SUA10932,
                                        SUAST50932

WAGNER

Albumblatt in C (1861) pf – arr. vln & pf Wilhelmj
  with A. Zakin pf   Columbia ML4324

Tristan und Isolde (1865) – opera
  selection arr. vln & orch as "Fantasia" by Waxman
  with O. Levant pf   XCO 36764/6–1   Columbia 71882D, (in set M657),
  & orch. – Waxman   C16064/6, (in set D191),
                                          ML2103

WAXMAN

Carmen Fantasia (on themes from the opera by Bizet) vln & orch.
  with orch. –   XCO 36762/3–1   Columbia 71884D, (in set M657),
  Waxman   C16063/4, (in set D191),
                                          ML2103

WIENIAWSKI

Concerto No. 2, in d, Op. 22 vln & orch.*
  with New York Philharmonic   Columbia 12464/6D, (set M656),
  Symphony Orch. – Kurtz   C1013, LOX604/6, ML2012
                                    Philips S04634L

Concerto No. 2, in d, Op. 22 vln & orch.
  with Philadelphia Orch. – Ormandy   Columbia ML5208
                                    Fontana 699028CL, 699040CL,
                                    CFL1062

Louis STEVENS

BACH

Concerto No. 2, in E, BWV1042 vln, strs & c
  with Berlin Symphony Orch. – Ludwig   Royale 1367

BRAHMS

Concerto in D, Op. 77 (cadenza by Winkler) vln & orch.
  with Berlin Symphony Orch. –   Royale 1252
  Günther

KREISLER

Caprice viennois, Op. 2 vln & pf
  with piano
                            Festival CFR10–191
                            Royale 1245
                            Ultraphonic 50314

* Allegro moderato or 3rd mvt "alla Zingara" is also on Columbia A1647.

KREISLER – *Continued*

(La) Gitana vln & pf
  with piano
                            Festival CFR10–191
                            Royale 1245
                            Ultraphonic 50314

Liebesfreud vln & pf
  with piano
                              Festival CFR10–191
                            Royale 1245
                            Ultraphonic 50314

Liebesleid vln & pf
  with piano
                              Festival CFR10–191
                            Royale 1245, 6110
                            Ultraphonic 50314

Rondino on a theme by Beethoven vln & pf
  with piano
                            Festival CFR10–191
                            Royale 1245, 6110

Tambourin chinois, Op. 3 vln & pf
  with piano
                            Festival CFR10–191
                            Royale 1245
                            Ultraphonic 50314

Minuet (Porpora) vln & pf
  with piano   Royale 1245

MOZART

Serenade No. 7, in D, K250 "Haffner" orch.
  Rondo (4th mvt) arr. vln & pf Kreisler
  with piano   Royale 1245
                            Ultraphonic 50314

Kurt STIEHLER

BACH

(6) Brandenburg Concerti, BWV1046/51 (1721) strs & c
  Brandenburg Concerto No. 4, in G, BWV1049 vln, 2 fls, strs & c
  with Leipzig Gewandhaus Orch. –   Polydor 68191/3S
  Schmitz

Concerto in c, BWV1060 vln & ob or 2 vlns, strs & c
  with K. Kalmus ob & Ansbach   Polydor 2003/5S, 2402/3S
  Festival Orch. – Leitner

(3) Sonatas & 3 Partitas, BWV1001/6 solo vln
  Sonata No. 2, in a, BWV1003
  (unaccompanied)   Polydor 2008/10, PV2405/6

BEETHOVEN

Romance No. 2, in F, Op. 50 vln & orch.
  with Leipzig Gewandhaus Orch. –   Odeon 0–9159
  Schmitz

RESPIGHI

Concerto Gregoriano (1922) vln & orch.
  with Leipzig Radio Orch. – Borsamsky   Urania URLP7100

SPOHR

Concerto No. 8, in a, Op. 47 "Gesangsscene" vln & orch.
  with Leipzig Gewandhaus Orch. –   Urania URLP7049
  Schmitz

M. STIGLITZ

DVOŘÁK
(8) Slavonic Dances, Op. 72 pf duet; orch.
  No. 2. Slavonic Dance No. 10, in e arr. vln & pf Kreisler
  with piano   Hed Arzi 700

Leonora von STOSCH*

BOHM
(6) Pieces, Op. 314 vln & pf
  No. 4. Capriccio "Papillon"
  with piano   HMV 07918

  No. 6. Caprice en forme des variations
  with piano   HMV 07918

BRAHMS
(21) Hungarian Dances pf duet
  Hungarian Dance No. 1, in g arr. vln & pf Joachim
  with piano   HMV 07917

Albert Frederic STOESSEL (1894–1943)

STOESSEL
Suite antique (1922) 2 vlns & cha orch.
  with E. Brown vln &   US 1388/92   Royale 1854/6, (set 28)
  Sinfonietta – Schenkman

Jiří Jurenko STRAKA (1925–)

SMETANA
From my Homeland (1878) vln & pf
            2HC 236/8[1]☐ & 239[II]☐ HMV JX5/6
  with L. Straková pf

Ivan ŠTRAUS (1937–)

BERG
Chamber Concerto (1925) vln, pf & 13 w–wnds
  with Z. Kozina pf & Chamber   Erato STU70423
  Ensemble, Prague – Pešek   Eurodisc 80500PK
                           Parliament PLPS624
                           Supraphon 141 0122, SUA10679,
                           SUAST50679

KLUSÁK
Sonata vln & 11 w–wnds
  with Chamber Harmony – Pešek   Supraphon SUA18853,
                                SUAST58853, SV8427

SLAVICKÝ
Partita solo vln
  (unaccompanied)   Supraphon 141 0104

* Lady Edgar Speyer.

Jessie STRAUS

ERKEL
Himnusz (Hungarian national anthem) (1845) v & pf – arr. vln & orch.
  with orch.   Columbia A210

G. STRAUSS

BIBER
(16) Biblical Sonatas "Mysterien" (1674) vln & c
  Sonata No. 6, in c "Christ on the Mount of Olives"
  with P. Aubert   AS 211–1 & 212 L'Anthologie Sonore. 94
  hpsi

Ingeborg von STRELETZKY

BENATZKY
Ich weiss auf der Wieden ein kleines Hotel – walzer v & pf – arr. vln &
ens
  with ensemble   Imperial 19259

BOULANGER
Avant de mourir, Op. 17 vln & pf
  with ensemble   Imperial 19253

CZIBULKA
Gavotte (Stephanie) Op. 312 pf – arr. vln & pf
  with piano   Imperial 19282

FRIML
Rose Marie (1924) – operetta
  Indian love call arr. vln & ens
  with ensemble   Imperial 19279

GADE
Jealousy (1927) orch. – arr. vln & ens
  with ensemble   Imperial 19279

KÁLMÁN
Gräfin Mariza (1924) – operetta
  Komm' Zigany arr. vln & ens
  with ensemble   Imperial 19259

KREISLER
Schön Rosmarin vln & pf
  with piano   Imperial 19282

POLIAKIN
(Le) Canari (Concert–polka) vln & pf
  with ensemble   Imperial 19253

Rudolf STRENG

BACH
(6) Brandenburg Concerti, BWV1046/51 (1721) strs & c
  Brandenburg Concerto No. 3, in G, BWV1048 3 vlns, 3 vlas, 3 vlcs & cbs
  with J. Tomasow vln, A. Jilka vln, R.   Amadeo AVRS6043
  Harand vlc, G. Weis vlc W. Hübner   Bach Guild BG541
  vla, E. Rab vla, E. Kriss vla, L. Beinl
  vlc, O. Rühm cbs & A. Heiller hpsi

Leo STROCK

BACH

(3) Sonatas & 3 Partitas, BWV1001/6 solo vln
Partita No. 3, in E: Gavotte (3rd mvt) BWV1006
(unaccompanied)   Columbia 226
(4) Suites, BWV1066/9 strs & c
Suite No. 3, in D: Air (2nd mvt) BWV1068 2 obs, 3 tpts, drms, strs & c
– arr. vln & pf as "Air on the G–string" by Wilhelmj
with piano   Columbia 225

CHOPIN

(3) Nocturnes, Op. 9 pf
No. 2. Nocturne No. 2, in E flat arr. vln & pf Sarasate
with piano   6092   Columbia 227, D16054

PAGANINI

(24) Caprices, Op. 1 (1801/7) solo vln
Caprice No. 13, in B flat
(unaccompanied)   Columbia 226

SARASATE

Carmen Fantasia (on themes from the opera by Bizet) Op. 25 vln & pf or orch.
with piano   Columbia 224

SCHUBERT

(7) Gesänge (set to Scott's "Lady of the Lake") Op. 52 v & pf
No. 6. Ave Maria, D839 arr. vln & pf Wilhelmj
with piano   6091   Columbia 227, D16054

TCHAIKOVSKY

Sérénade mélancolique in b flat, Op. 26 vln & orch. – arr. vln & pf Wilhelmj
with piano   Columbia 228

WIENIAWSKI

Capriccio–valse, Op. 7 vln & pf
with piano   Columbia 225
Polonaise brillante No. 1, in D, Op. 4 vln & pf
with piano   Columbia 228

Leo STROCKOFF

BACH

(3) Sonatas & 3 Partitas, BWV1001/6 solo vln
Partita No. 2, in d: Allemande (1st mvt) BWV1004 arr. vln & pf Nachèz
with piano   Columbia 975
Partita No. 3, in E: Preludio (1st mvt) BWV1006 arr. vln & pf Nachèz
with piano   Columbia 975
Partita No. 3, in E: Gavotte (3rd mvt) BWV1006
(unaccompanied)   Columbia 2577
(4) Suites, BWV1066/9 strs & c
Suite No. 3, in D: Air (2nd mvt) BWV1068 2 obs, 3 tpts, drms, strs & c
arr. vln & pf as "Air on the G–string" by Wilhelmj
with string quartet   AX 126   Columbia 963

BEETHOVEN

(6) Minuets, G167 pf
No. 2. Minuet No. 2, in G arr. vln & pf Burmester
with piano   Columbia 2577

BEETHOVEN – *Continued*

(Die) Ruinen von Athen, Op. 113 – Incidental music orch.
No. 3. Chor der Derwische arr. vln & pf Auer
with piano   Columbia 3344

BOHM

(143) Lieder, Op. 326 v & pf
No. 27. Still wie die Nacht arr. vln & pf
with string quartet   AX 128   Columbia 947

DRDLA

Serenade No. 1, in A vln & pf
with piano   Columbia 2559

DRIGO

(2) Airs de Ballet orch.
No. 2. Valse bluette arr. vln & pf Auer
with piano   A 154   Columbia 3414

DVOŘÁK

(8) Humoresques, Op. 101 pf
No. 7. Humoresque No. 7, in G flat arr. vln & pf "in G" Wilhelmj
with piano   6454   Columbia 541
(8) Slavonic Dances, Op. 46 pf duet; orch.
No. 2. Slavonic dance No. 2, in e arr. vln & pf "in g" Kreisler
with piano   AX 273   Columbia 985

GRIEG

Peer Gynt (Suite No. 2) Op. 55 orch.
No. 4. Solveig's song arr. vln & pf Sitt
with string quartet   AX 129   Columbia 947

KREISLER

Caprice viennois, Op. 2 vln & pf
with piano   6445   Columbia 541
(La) Chasse (Cartier) vln & pf
with piano   A 155   Columbia 3414

LALO

Symphonie espagnole, Op. 21 vln & orch.*
with orch. – Harty   Columbia 67059/61D, (set M14)

MOSZKOWSKI

(2) Stücke, Op. 45 pf
No. 2. Guitarre arr. vln & pf Sarasate
with piano   A 1390   Columbia D1511

RIMSKY–KORSAKOV

(Le) Coq d'Or (1910) – opera
Hymn to the sun arr. vln & pf Kreisler
with piano   AX 272   Columbia 985
Sadko (1898) – opera
Chant hindou arr. vln & pf Kreisler
with string quartet   A 1388   Columbia D1511

SAINT–SAËNS

Introduction & Rondo Capriccioso, Op. 28 vln & orch.
with piano   Columbia 791

* Omitting intermezzo.

SARASATE

(8) Danzas españolas vln & pf
No. 6. Zapateado, Op. 23, No. 2
with piano   Columbia L1627

Zigeunerweisen, Op. 20 vln & pf or orch.
with piano   Columbia L1627

SCARLATTI, D.

Sonata in e, L413 pf – arr. vln & pf as "Pastorale" by Bridgewater
with string quartet   Columbia 975

SCHUBERT

(7) Gesänge (set to Scott's "Lady of the Lake") Op. 52 v & pf
No. 6. Ave Maria, D839 arr. vln & pf Wilhelmj
with piano   AX 120   Columbia 963

(6) Moments musicaux, Op. 94 (D780) (1823/7) pf
No. 3. Moment musicale No. 3, in f "Air russe" arr. vln & pf Kreisler
with piano   Columbia 2559

TCHAIKOVSKY

(3) Souvenirs de Hapsal, Op. 2 pf
No. 3. Chant sans paroles in f arr. vln & pf Kreisler
with piano   Columbia 3344

Ernest STRONG

MASCHERONI

Eternamente (1891) v & pf – arr. vln & pf
with piano   67551   Regal G6068

ROSENWEIG

Where the blue Danube flows v & pf – arr. vln & pf
with piano   Phoenix 0174

Wilhelm STROSS (1907–1966)

BACH

(6) Brandenburg Concerti, BWV1046/51 (1721) strs & c
Brandenburg Concerto No. 4, in G, BWV1049 vln, 2 fls, strs & c
with W. Theurer fl, W. Haag fl &   HMV DB11525/6
Chamber Orch. – Stross

Concerto in d, BWV1043 2 vlns, strs & c
with H. Endress vln & Berlin Radio   Le Chant du Monde LDXA8008
Chamber Orch. – Stross

BRAHMS

Trio No. 1, in B, Op. 8 pf, vln & vlc
with E. Ney pf & L. Hölscher vlc   Polydor 27316/9

Max STRUB (1900–1966)

BACH

Concerto No. 1, in a, BWV1041 vln, strs & c
with Berlin Collegium Musicum –   HMV DB5527/8
Stein

BEETHOVEN

Concerto in D, Op. 61 vln & orch.
     2RA 4130² A☐, 4131¹ A☐,   HMV DB5516/21
4132/4² A☐, 4135³ A☐, 4136/7¹ A
☐, 4138³ A☐ & 4139/40² A☐
with Saxon State Orch. – Böhm

(3) Trios, Op. 1 pf, vln & vlc
No. 3. Trio No. 3, in c: Minuetto
with E. Ney pf & L.   2RA 2031¹¹☐   HMV DB4590
Hölscher vlc

(2) Trios, Op. 70 pf, vln & vlc
No. 1. Trio No. 4, in D "Ghost"
     2RA 2678/9¹¹☐, 2680¹☐, 2681¹¹   Electrola E60564
     ☐, 2682/3¹☐ & 2684¹¹¹☐   HMV DB4587/90

BENDA, F.

Concerto in A vln & orch.
Presto
     OD 1705¹¹△ & 1707¹¹△   HMV B8119, EG2869
with Chamber Orch. – von Benda

HANDEL

(9) Sonatas, Op. 2 (1724) 2 vlns or obs & c
Sonata No. 1, in c: Andante (1st mvt)
with P. Luther fl, E.   OD 1709¹¹△   HMV EG2881
Kruttge hpsi & vlc

HAYDN

(31) Trios, H.XV, Nos. 1/31 pf, vln & vlc
Trio No. 25, in G, H.XV, No. 25 (Op. 73, No. 2)
with A. Aeschbacher pf & G. Cassadó   Polydor 68383/4
vlc

MOZART

Concerto No. 1, in D, K107 hpsi & orch.
Minuet (3rd mvt)
with B. Mazurat vln,   OD 1708¹¹△   HMV EG2881
H. Schrader vlc & E. Kruttge hpsi

PFITZNER

Duo, Op. 43 (1937) vln, vlc & orch.
with L. Hölscher vlc & orch. –   HMV DB4508/9
Pfitzner

REGER

Lyrisches Andante (1898) strs – arr. vln & pf Herman Unger
with E. Ney pf   2RA 1319²☐   HMV EH969

Suite in a, Op. 103a vln & pf
No. 4. Burleske
with E. Ney pf   2RA 1320¹☐   HMV EH969
No. 5. Menuett
with E. Ney pf   2RA 1320¹☐   HMV EH969

SCHUBERT

Trio No. 1, in B flat, Op. 99 (D898) pf, vln & vlc
     125½GO 8, 383½GO 8,   Decca X157/60
426½GO 8, 337½GO 8, 385 GO 8,   Polydor 57045/8
386½GO 8, 388 GO 8 & 389½GO 8
with E. Ney pf & L. Höslcher vlc

Trio No. 2, in E flat, Op. 100 (D929) pf, vln & vlc
Scherzo (3rd mvt)
with E. Ney pf & L. Hölscher vlc   HMV DB4537

Aïda STÜCKI

MOZART

Concerto No. 1, in B flat, K207 (cadenzas by Joachim) vln & orch.
   with Stuttgart Ton Studio Orch. –   Classic CL6131
   Lund   Nixa PLP549
                                             Period PLP549

Concerto No. 2, in D, K211 vln & orch.
   with Stuttgart Ton Studio Orch. –   Classic CL6131
   Lund   Nixa PLP549
                                             Period PLP549

Concerto No. 7, in D, K271 (cadenzas by Enescu) vln & orch.
   with Stuttgart Ton Studio Orch. –   Period PLP548
   Lund

SCHUMANN

Fantasia in C, Op. 131 vln & orch.
   with Stuttgart Pro Musica Orch. –   Vox PL7680
   Reinhardt

Willy STÜLKEN

BEETHOVEN

Sonata No. 8, in c, Op. 13 "Pathétique" pf
   Andante (2nd mvt) arr. vln & pf
   with piano   Favorite 1–14210

GLITZ

Larghetto vln & pf
   with piano   Favorite 1–14265

GOUNOD

Ave Maria (Méditation on Bach's "Prelude No. 1, in C" from Book I of
"Das Wohltemperirte Clavier") v & pf – arr. vln & pf
   with piano   Favorite 1–14210
Ave Maria (Méditation on Bach's "Prelude No. 1, in C" from Book I of
"Das Wohltemperirte Clavier") v & pf – arr. vln & pf
   with piano   Favorite 1–4029E

GUNGL

Oberländler, (Country sounds) Op. 31 pf – arr. vln & pf
   with piano   Favorite 1–14263

LANGE

Flower song, Op. 39 vln & pf
   with piano   Favorite 1–14265

LANGER

Grandfather, Op. 22 salon orch. – arr. vln & pf
   with piano   Favorite 1–14263

LEDERER

Mélodie, Op. 15 vln & pf
   with piano   Favorite 1–4029E

Karl STÜMMVOLL

BACH

(4) Suites, BWV1066/9 strs & c
   Suite No. 3, in D: Air (2nd mvt) BWV1068 2 obs, 3 tpts, drms, strs & c
   – arr. vln & pf as "Air on the G–string" by Wilhelmj
   with J. Messner org   Christschall 92

Jean Louis STUUROP

MANFREDINI

(12) Concerti, Op. 3 (1718) 2 vlns, strs & c
   Concerto No. 9, in D
   with H. Krebbers vln, L. van der Lee   CBS 51127
   hpsi & Amsterdam Chamber Orch. –
   Voorberg

VIVALDI

(12) Concerti, Op. 3 "L'Estro armonico" var. cbns & strs
   Concerto No. 11, in d, P.250 (F.IV, No. 11) 2 vlns, vlc, strs & c
   with H. Krebbers vln, K. Schouten   CBS 51125
   vla, H. Secrete vlc, L. van der Lee hpsi
   & Amsterdam Chamber Orch. –
   Voorberg

Eduard STYX

GODARD

Jocelyn (1888) – opera
   Cachés dans cet asile "Berceuse" arr. vln & orch.
   with orch.   Be 4541   Odeon A44832

RAFF

(6) Pieces, Op. 85 vln & pf
   No. 3. Cavatina in D arr. vln & orch.
   with orch.   Be 4540   Odeon A44832

Josef SUK (1929–   )

ALBÉNIZ

España (6 Feuilles d'album) Op. 165 pf
   No. 2. Tango in D arr. vln & pf Dushkin
   with A. Holeček pf   Epic BC1367, LC3967
                                            Supraphon 141 0101, SUA
                                            10882, SUA ST50882

BACH

(6) Brandenburg Concerti, BWV1046/51 (1721) strs & c
   Brandenburg Concerto No. 5, in D, BWV1050 clav, fl, vln, strs & c
   with Z. Ružičková (pf) J–P. Rampal fl   Erato STU70469
   & Prague Soloists – Fischer
Concerto No. 1, in a, BWV1041 vln, strs & c
   with Prague Symphony Orch. –   Bärenreiter Musicaphon BM30
   Smetáček   SL1219
                                            Crossroads 22 16 0037, 22 16
                                            0038
                                            Supraphon SUA10672, SUA
                                            ST50672, SV8396

BACH – *Continued*

Concerto No. 2, in E, BWV1042 vln, strs & c
   with Prague Symphony Orch. –   Bärenreiter Musicaphon BM30
   Smetáček   SL1219
        Crossroads 22 16 0037, 22 16
        0038
        Supraphon SUA10672, SUA
        ST50672, SV8396

Concerto in d, BWV1043 2 vlns, strs & c
   with L. Jásek vln & Prague Symphony   Bärenreiter Musicaphon BM30
   Orch. – Smetáček   SL1219
        Crossroads 22 16 0037, 22 16
        0038
        Supraphon SUA 10672, SUA
        ST50672, SV8396

Concerto in a, BWV1044 clav, fl, vln, strs & c
   with Z. Ružičková pf, J–P. Rampal fl   Erato STU70469
   & Prague Soloists – Fischer

(3) Sonatas & 3 Partitas, BWV1001/6 solo vln
   Sonata No. 1, in g, BWV1001
   (unaccompanied)   Electrola 1C183–02168
   Partita No. 1, in b, BWV1002
   (unaccompanied)   Electrola 1C183–02168
   Sonata No. 2, in a, BWV1003
   (unaccompanied)   Electrola 1C183–02169
   Partita No. 2, in d, BWV1004
   (unaccompanied)   Electrola 1C183–02169
   Sonata No. 3, in C, BWV1005
   (unaccompanied)   Electrola 1C183–02170
   Partita No. 3, in E: Preludio (1st mvt); **Loure** (2nd mvt) BWV1006
   (unaccompanied)   Supraphon SUA10741
   Partita No. 3, in E, BWV1006
   (unaccompanied)   Electrola 1C183–02170

(6) Sonatas, BWV1014/9 vln & clav
   Sonata No. 1, in b, BWV1014
   with Z. Ružičková hpsi   Epic BC1338, (in set BSC160),
        LC3938, (in set SL6060)
        Erato STU70531
        Supraphon SUA10549, SUA
        ST50549, SV8135

   Sonata No. 2, in A, BWV1015
   with Z. Ružičková hpsi   Epic BC1338, (in set BSC160),
        LC3938, (in set SL6060)
        Erato STU70532
        Supraphon SUA10549, SUA
        ST50549, SV8135

   Sonata No. 3, in E, BWV1016
   with Z. Ružičková hpsi   Epic BC1338, (in set BSC160),
        LC3938, (in set SL6060)
        Erato STU70531
        Supraphon SUA10549, SUA
        ST50549, SV8135

   Sonata No. 4, in c, BWV1017
   with Z. Ružičková hpsi   Epic BC1339, (in set BSC160),
        LC3939, (in set SL6060)
        Erato STU70532
        Supraphon SUA10550, SUA
        ST50550, SV8136

BACH – *Continued*

   Sonata No. 5, in f, BWV1018
   with Z. Ružičková hpsi   Epic BC1339, (in set BSC160),
        LC3939, (in set SL6060)
        Erato STU70531
        Supraphon SUA10550, SUA
        ST50550, SV8136

   Sonata No. 6, in G, BWV1019
   with Z. Ružičková hpsi   Epic BC1339, (in set BSC160),
        LC3939, (in set SL6060)
        Erato STU70532
        Supraphon SUA10550, SUA
        ST50550, SV8136

BARTÓK

(44) Duos (1931) 2 vlns
   with A. Gertler vln   Crossroads 22 16 0208
        Supraphon SUA10770, SUA
        ST50770, SV8345

BEETHOVEN

Concerto in D, Op. 61 (cadenzas by Příhoda) vln & orch.
   with Czech Philharmonic Orch. –   Eurodisc 80245ZK
   Konwitschny   Parliament PLP169
        Supraphon SUA10445, SV8064

Concerto in D, Op. 61 (cadenzas by Příhoda) vln & orch.
   with New Philharmonia Of London –   Electrola 1C063–02120
   Boult   HMV ASD2667

Romance No. 1, in G, Op. 40 vln & orch.
   with Academy of St. Martin–in–the–   Electrola 1C063–02096
   Fields – Marriner   HMV ASD2725

Romance No. 2, in F, Op. 50 vln & orch.
   with Academy of St. Martin–in–the–   Electrola 1C063–02096
   Fields – Marriner   HMV ASD2725

(3) Sonatas, Op. 12 vln & pf
   No. 1. Sonata No. 1, in D
   with J. Panenka pf   Eurodisc (in set 80193XK)
        Supraphon 1 11 0251, 1 11 0261,
        SUA10904, SUA ST50904

   No. 2. Sonata No. 2, in A
   with J. Panenka pf   Eurodisc (in set 80193XK)
        Supraphon 1 11 0252, 1 11 0262,
        SUA10905, SUA ST50905

   No. 3. Sonata No. 3, in E flat
   with J. Panenka pf   Eurodisc (in set 80193XK)
        Supraphon 1 11 0252, 1 11 0262,
        SUA10905, SUA ST50905

Sonata No. 4, in a, Op. 23 vln & pf
   with J. Panenka pf   Eurodisc (in set 80193XK)
        Supraphon 1 11 0253, 1 11 0263,
        SUA10906, SUA ST50906

Sonata No. 5, in F, Op. 24 "Spring" vln & pf
   with J. Panenka pf   Eurodisc (in set 80193XK)
        Supraphon 1 11 0253, 1 11 0263,
        SUA10906, SUA ST50906

(3) Sonatas, Op. 30 vln & pf
   No. 1. Sonata No. 6, in A
   with J. Panenka pf   Eurodisc (in set 80193XK)
        Supraphon 1 11 0254, 1 11 0264,
        SUA10907, SUA ST50907

BEETHOVEN – *Continued*

No. 2. Sonata No. 7, in c
with J. Panenka pf
Eurodisc (in set 80193XK)
Supraphon 1 11 0254, 1 11 0264,
SUA10907, SUA ST50907

No. 3. Sonata No. 8, in G
with J. Panenka pf
Eurodisc (in set 80193XK)
Supraphon 1 11 0255, 1 11 0265,
SUA10908, SUA ST50908

Sonata No. 9, in A, Op. 47 "Kreutzer" vln & pf
with J. Panenka pf
Eurodisc (in set 80193XK)
Supraphon 1 11 0255, 1 11 0265,
SUA10908, SUA ST50908

Sonata No. 10, in G, Op. 96 vln & pf
with J. Panenka pf
Eurodisc (in set 80193XK)
Supraphon 1 11 0251, 1 11 0261,
SUA10904, SUA ST50904

(3) Trios, Op. 1 pf, vln & vlc
No. 3. Sonata No. 3, in c
with J. Panenka pf & J. Chuchro vlc
Eurodisc 80234KK
Supraphon SUA10523, SUA
ST50523, SV8126

(2) Trios, Op. 70 pf, vln & vlc
No. 1. Trio No. 4, in D "Ghost"
with J. Panenka pf, & J. Chuchro vlc
Eurodisc 80234KK
Supraphon SUA10523, SUA
ST50523, SV8126

Trio No. 6, in B flat, Op. 97 "Archduke" pf, vln & vlc
with J. Panenka pf & M. Sadlo vlc
Supraphon SUA10410, SUA
ST50410

Trio No. 6, in B flat, Op. 97 "Archduke" pf, vln & vlc
with J. Panenka pf & J. Chuchro vlc
Crossroads 22 16 0021, 22 16
0022
Supraphon SV8129

BENJAMIN

(2) Jamaican Pieces (1940) orch.
No. 2. Jamaican Rhumba arr. vln & pf Primrose
with A. Holeček pf
Epic BC1367, LC3967
Supraphon 141 0101, SUA10882,
SUA ST50882

BERG

Concerto (1935) vln & orch.
with Czech Philharmonic Orch. –
Ančerl
Crossroads 22 16 0172
Erato STU70423
Eurodisc 80500PK
Supraphon SUA10804, SUA
ST50804, SV8429

BRAHMS

Concerto in a, Op. 102 "Double" vln, vlc & orch.
with A. Navarra vlc & Czech
Philharmonic Orch. – Ančerl
Eurodisc 0 080 237PK
Parliament PLP601, PLPS601
Supraphon SUA10573, SUA
ST50573, SV8121

Sonata No. 1, in G, Op. 78 vln & pf
with J. Hála pf
Elite CSLP6002
Supraphon LPV293

Sonata No. 1, in G, Op. 78 vln & pf
with J. Panenka pf
Supraphon SUA10275

BRAHMS – *Continued*

Sonata No. 1, in G, Op. 78 vln & pf
with J. Katchen pf
Decca LXT6321, SXL6321
London CM9549, CS6549

Sonata No. 2, in A, Op. 100 vln & pf
with J. Panenka pf
Supraphon SUA10474, SV8053

Sonata No. 2, in A, Op. 100 vln & pf
with J. Katchen pf
Decca LXT6321, SXL6321
London CM9549, CS6549

Sonata No. 3, in d, Op. 108 vln & pf
with J. Panenka pf
Supraphon SUA10474, SV8053

Sonata No. 3, in d, Op. 108 vln & pf
with J. Katchen pf
Decca LXT6321, SXL6321
London CM9549, CS6549

Sonata (1853) "Frei aber Einsam" vln & pf
Allegro (Scherzo) in c (3rd mvt) "Sonatensatz"
with J. Katchen pf
Decca (in set SDDA261/9)

Trio No. 1, in B, Op. 8 pf, vln & vlc
with J. Katchen pf & J. Starker vlc
Decca LXT6387, SAD22053,
SXL6387
London CS6611

Trio No. 3, in c, Op. 101 pf, vln & vlc
with J. Panenka pf & J. Chuchro vlc
Crossroads 22 16 0178
Supraphon SUA10815, SUA
ST50815, DV6313, SV8419

Trio No. 3, in c, Op. 101 pf, vln & vlc
with J. Katchen pf & J. Starker vlc
Decca LXT6387, SAD22053,
SXL6387
London CS6611

(16) Waltzes, Op. 39 pf duet
No. 15. Waltz No. 15, in A flat arr. vln & pf "in A" Hochstein
with J. Hála pf
Supraphon LPM482, SUEC840

BRUCH

Concerto No. 1, in g, Op. 26 vln & orch.
with Czech Philharmonic Orch. –
Ančerl
Epic BC1346, LC3946
Eurodisc 80224LK
Supraphon SUA10546, SUA
ST50546, SV8165

DEBUSSY

(La) Plus que lente – valse (1910) pf – arr. vln & pf Roques
with A. Holeček pf
Epic BC1367, LC3967
Supraphon SUA10882, SUA
ST50882

Sonata No. 3, in g (1917) vln & pf
with J. Panenka pf
Supraphon LPM498, SUF20380

Sonata No. 3, in g (1917) vln & pf
with J. Katchen pf
Decca 7022

Suite Bergamasque (1890) pf
No. 3. Clair de lune arr. vln & pf Roelens
with J. Hála pf
Supraphon LPM482, SUEC840

DVOŘÁK

Concerto in a, Op. 53 vln & orch.
with Czech Philharmonic Orch. –
Ančerl
Artia ALP193, ALPS193
Eterna 820578
Music for Pleasure MFP2115
Supraphon SUA10181, SV8022

DVOŘÁK – *Continued*

Romance in f, Op. 11 vln & orch.
  with Czech Philharmonic Orch. –
  Ančerl

Artia ALP193, ALPS193
Eterna 820578
Music for Pleasure MFP2115
Supraphon SUA10181, SV8022

(4) Romantic Pieces, Op. 75 vln & pf
  with J. Hála pf

Supraphon LPM348

Sonata in F, Op. 57 vln & pf
  with J. Panenka pf

Supraphon SUA10023

Sonatina in G, Op. 100 vln & pf
  with J. Panenka pf

Supraphon SUA10023

Trio No. 3, in f, Op. 65 pf, vln & vlc
  with J. Panenka pf & J. Chuchro vlc

CBS S75715
Supraphon SUA10817, SUA
ST50817, SV8420

Trio No. 4, in e, Op. 90 "Dumky" pf, vln & vlc
  with J. Panenka pf & M. Sadlo vlc

Deutsche Grammophon
LPE17150, SLPE133003

FALLA

(El) Amor Brujo (1915) – ballet m–s & orch.
  No. 14. Pantomime arr. vln & pf Kochański
    with A. Holeček pf

Epic BC1367, LC3967
Supraphon 141 0101, SUA10882,
SUA ST50882

(7) Canciones populares españolas (1914) v & pf
  No. 4. Jota arr. vln & pf Kochański
    with A. Holeček pf

Epic BC1367, LC3967
Supraphon 141 0101, SUA10882,
SUA ST50882

FAURÉ

Berceuse, Op. 16 vln & pf
  with J. Panenka pf

Supraphon 1 11 0227,
SUA10879, SUA ST50879

FOSTER

I dream of Jeannie with the light brown hair v & pf – arr. vln & pf Heifetz
  with A. Holeček pf

Epic BC1367, LC3967
Supraphon 141 0101, SUA10882,
SUA ST50882

FRANCK

Sonata in A (1886) vln & pf
  with J. Panenka pf

Supraphon 1 11 0227,
SUA10879, SUA ST50879

GERSHWIN

Porgy & Bess (1935) – opera
  Bess, you is my woman arr. vln & pf Heifetz
    with A. Holeček pf

Epic BC1367, LC3967
Supraphon 141 0101, SUA10882,
SUA ST50882

GRIEG

Sonata No. 3, in c, Op. 45 vln & pf
  with J. Hála pf

Elite CSLP6002
Supraphon LPV293

Sonata No. 3, in c, Op. 45 vln & pf
  with J. Panenka pf

Supraphon SUA10275

HANDEL

(15) Sonatas, Op. 1 (?1731) fl or vln & c
  Sonata No. 10, in g vln II
    with Z. Ružičková hpsi

Erato LDE3373, STE50273,
STU70273
Musical Heritage Society
MHS769

  Sonata No. 13, in D vln IV
    with Z. Ružičková hpsi

Erato LDE3373, STE50273,
STU70273
Musical Heritage Society
MHS769

  Sonata No. 14, in A vln V
    with Z. Ružičková hpsi

Erato LDE3373, STE50273,
STU70273
Musical Heritage Society
MHS769

  Sonata No. 15, in E vln VI
    with Z. Ružičková hpsi

Erato LDE3373, STE50273,
STU70273
Musical Heritage Society
MHS769

HONEGGER

Sonatina (1932) vln & vlc
  with A. Navarra vlc

Supraphon SUA10634, SUA
ST50634, SV8250

JANÁČEK

Sonata (1913/21) vln & pf
  with J. Panenka pf

Supraphon LPM498, SUF20380

JEŽEK

Sonata vln & pf
  with J. Panenka pf

Supraphon SV8344

KOCIÁN

(2) Pieces, Op. 17 vln & pf
  No. 2. Humoresque
    with Prague Chamber Orch. – Klima

Supraphon LPM348, SUEC818

(3) Pièces d'impression, Op. 18 vln & pf
  No. 1. Méditation du soir arr. vln & orch. Langey
    with Prague Chamber Orch. – Klima

Supraphon LPM348

  No. 2. Intermezzo pittoresque arr. vln & orch. Langey
    with Prague Chamber Orch. – Klima

Supraphon LPM348

KODÁLY

Duo, Op. 7 (1914) vln & vlc
  with A. Navarra vlc

Supraphon SUA10634, SUA
ST50634, SV8250

KREISLER

Caprice viennois, Op. 2 vln & pf
  with A. Holeček pf

Epic BC1367, LC3967
Supraphon 141 0101, SUA10882,
SUA ST50882

Rondino on a theme by Beethoven vln & pf
  with J. Panenka pf

Supraphon LPM482

KUBELÍK

Canzonetta vln & pf
  with A. Holeček pf

Epic BC1367, LC3967
Supraphon 141 0101, SUA10882,
SUA ST50882

MARTINŮ

Duo No. 1 (1927) vln & vlc
  with A. Navarra vlc

Supraphon SUA10634, SUA
ST50634, SV8250

Duo No. 2 (1958) vln & vlc
  with A. Navarra vlc

Supraphon 140 0101, SUA10877,
SUA ST50877

MENDELSSOHN

Concerto in e, Op. 64 vln & orch.
  with Czech Philharmonic Orch. –
  Ančerl

Epic BC1346, LC3946
Eurodisc 80224LK
Supraphon SUA10546, SUA
ST50546, SV8165

(6) Songs without words, Op. 62 pf
No. 1. Song without words No. 25, in G "May breezes" arr. vln & pf
Kreisler
  with A. Holeček pf

Epic BC1367, LC3967
Supraphon 141 0101, SUA10882,
SUA ST50882

Trio No. 1, in d, Op. 49 pf, vln & vlc
  with J. Panenka pf & J. Chuchro vlc

Crossroads 22 16 0178
Supraphon SUA10815, SUA
ST50815, SV6313

MÍČA

Concertino notturno in D vln & orch.
  with Prague Symphony Orch. –
  Smetáček

Supraphon LPM333

MOZART

Adagio in E, K261 vln & orch.
  with Academy of St. Martin–in–the–
  Fields – Marriner

Electrola 1C063–02096
HMV ASD2725

Duo No. 2, in B flat, K424 vln & vla
  with M. Škampa vla

Crossroads 22 16 0015, 22 16
0016
Supraphon SUA10427, SUA
ST50427, SV8087,

Rondo in C, K373 vln & orch.
  with Academy of St. Martin–in–the–
  Fields – Marriner

Electrola 1C063–02096
HMV ASD2725

Serenade No. 7, in D, K250 "Haffner" orch.
  with Prague Chamber Orch.

Guilde Internationale du Disque
SMS2562

Sinfonia concertante in E flat, K364 vln, vla & orch.
  with M. Škampa vla & Czech
  Philharmonic Orch. – Redel

Crossroads 22 16 0015, 22 16
0016
Supraphon SUA10427, SUA
ST50427, SV8087

PAGANINI

Cantabile e valzer in E, Op. 19 (1823 or 1824) vln & gtr
  with A. Holeček pf

Epic BC1367, LC3967
Supraphon 141 0101, SUA10882,
SUA ST50882

PODEŠVA

Sonata No. 2 (1958) vln & pf
  with J. Panenka pf

Supraphon MNB9, SUA10178

POLDINI

(7) Marionnettes pf
No. 2. Poupée valsante arr. vln & pf Hartmann
  with A. Holeček pf

Epic BC1367, LC3967
Supraphon 141 0101, SUA10882,
SUA ST50882

POULENC

Sonata in d (1943) "In memory of Garcia Lorca" vln & pf
  with J. Panenka pf

Supraphon 1 11 0227,
SUA10879, SUA ST50879

PROKOFIEV

(The) Love for Three Oranges, Op. 33 (1919) – opera
No. 3. March arr. vln & pf Heifetz
  with A. Holeček pf

Epic BC1367, LC3967
Supraphon 141 0101, SUA10882,
SUA ST50882

RAFF

(6) Pieces, Op. 85 vln & pf
No. 3. Cavatina in D
  with J. Hála pf

Supraphon LPM482, SUEC840
Ultraphon H24462

RAVEL

Pièce en forme d' Habanera v & pf – arr. vln & pf Catherine
  with A. Holeček pf

Epic BC1367, LC3967
Supraphon 141 0101, SUA10882,
SUA ST50882

RESPIGHI

Sonata in b (1917) vln & pf
  with J. Panenka pf

Supraphon SUA10018

SCHUBERT

(7) Gesänge (set to Scott's "Lady of the Lake") Op. 52 v & pf
No. 6. Ave Maria, D839 arr. vln & pf Wilhelmj
  with J. Hála pf
    Supraphon LPM482, SUEC818

Nocturne in E flat, Op. 148 (D897) pf, vln & vlc
  with J. Panenka pf & J. Chuchro vlc

Crossroads 22 16 0147, 22 16
0148
Erato STU70407
Supraphon SUA10624, SUA
ST50624, SV8245

Rondo in A, D438 vln & str orch.
  with Academy of St. Martin–in–the–
  Fields – Marriner

Electrola 1C063–02096
HMV ASD2725

Sonata in A, Op. 162 (D574) "Duo" vln & pf
  with J. Panenka pf

Supraphon SUA10464, SUA
ST50464, SV8132

(3) Sonatinas, Op. 137 (D384, D385 & D408) vln & pf
No. 1. Sonatina No. 1, in D, D384
  with J. Panenka pf

Supraphon SUA10464, SUA
ST50464, SV8132

SCHUBERT – *Continued*

Trio No. 1, in B flat, Op. 99 (D898) pf, vln & vlc
  with J. Panenka pf & J. Chuchro vlc   Crossroads 22 16 0147, 22 16
                                         0148
                                         Erato STU70407
                                         Supraphon SUA10624, SUA
                                         ST50624, SV8245

SCHUMANN

(12) Duets, Op. 85 pf – 4 hands
  No. 12. Abendlied arr. vln & pf Wilhelmj
  with J. Hála pf   Supraphon LPM482, SUEC840

(3) Romances, Op. 94 ob or vlc or vln or cl & pf
  No. 2. Romance No. 2, in A arr. vln & pf Kreisler
  with A. Holeček pf   Epic BC1367, LC3967
                                         Supraphon 141 0101, SUA10882,
                                         SUA ST50882

SMETANA

From my Homeland (1878) vln & pf
  with J. Panenka pf   Supraphon SUA10464, SUA
                                         ST50464, SV8132

Trio in g, Op. 15 pf, vln & vlc
  with J. Hála pf & J. Chuchro vlc   Supraphon LPV302

Trio in g, Op. 15 pf, vln & vlc
  with J. Panenka pf & J. Chuchro vlc   Supraphon 1 11 0448,
                                         SUA10863, SUA ST50863

SUK

Ballad, Op. 3b vln & pf
  with J. Panenka pf   Supraphon SUA10777, SUA
                                         ST50777, SV8346

Élégie, Op. 23 pf, vln & vlc
  with J. Hála pf & J. Chuchro vlc   Supraphon LPV302
                                         Ultraphon C12397

Élégie, Op. 23 pf, vln & vlc
  with J. Panenka pf & J. Chuchro vlc   Supraphon 1 11 0448,
                                         SUA10863, SUA ST50863

Fantasy in g, Op. 24 (1903) vln & orch.
  with Czech Philharmonic Orch. –   Supraphon SUA10777, SUA
  Ančerl   ST50777, SV8346

(4) Pieces, Op. 17 vln & pf
  with J. Panenka pf   Supraphon SUA10018

(4) Pieces, Op. 17 vln & pf
  with J. Panenka pf   Supraphon SUA10777, SUA
                                         ST50777, SV8346

Radúz & Mahulena, Op. 13 – Incidental music orch.
  Prologue arr. vln & pf
  with J. Panenka pf   Supraphon SUA10018

SVENDSEN

Romance in G, Op. 26 vln & orch. – arr. vln & pf Wilhelmj
  with J. Hála pf   Supraphon LPM482

TCHAIKOVSKY

Trio in a, Op. 50 "To the memory of a great artist" pf, vln & vlc
  with J. Panenka pf & J. Chuchro vlc   Supraphon SUA10485

Karl SUSKE

BACH

(6) Brandenburg Concerti, BWV1046/51 (1721) strs & c
  Brandenburg Concerto No. 4, in G, BWV1049 vln, 2 fls, strs & c
  with T. Waldbaur rec, E. Kästner rec   Amadeo AVRS6385
  & Leipzig Gewandhaus Orch. – Koch

HAYDN

Concerto No. 1, in C, H.VIIa, No. 1 (cadenzas by Flesch) vln & orch.
  with Staatskapelle Berlin – Suitner   Eterna 820560
                                         Fontana 894046ZKY

Concerto No. 2, in G, H.VIIa, No. 4 vln & orch.
  with Staatskapelle Berlin – Suitner   Eterna 820560
                                         Fontana 894046ZKY

Shinichi SUZUKI (1898–)

FRANCK

Sonata in A (1886) vln & pf
  with M. Gurlitt pf   Brunswick 90397/400
                                         Polydor 95216/9

VIVALDI

(6) Concerti, Op. 12 vln, strs & c
  Concerto No. 1, in g, P.343 (F.I, No. 211) (ed. Nachèz)
  with S. Suzuki pf   Columbia AK497/9

Juris ŠVOLKOVSKIS

CORELLI

(12) Sonatas, Op. 5 vln & c
  Sonata No. 8, in e
  with P. Sipolniek org   Mezhdunarodnaya Kniga
                                         D027489/90

DVOŘÁK

Trio No. 4, in e, Op. 90 "Dumky" pf, vln & vlc
  with V. Jancis pf & M. Villeruss vlc   Mezhdunarodnaya Kniga
                                         D24773/4

IVANOV

Concerto in e (1951) vln & orch.
  with Lithuanian Radio Symphony   Mezhdunarodnaya Kniga S01475
  Orch. – Tons

Quartet No. 2, in c 2 vlns, vla & vlc
  with L. Girska vln, A. Senakols vla & Mezhdunarodnaya Kniga
  M. Villeruss vlc   D24521/2

MEDYNS, Jasep

Latvian capriccio vln & pf
  with V. Cirule pf   Mezhdunarodnaya Kniga
                                         D022003, D025138

MEDYNS, Jekabs

Lettish caprice vln & pf
  with V. Cirule pf   Mezhdunarodnaya Kniga
                                         D022003

Romance vln & pf
  with V. Cirule pf   Mezhdunarodnaya Kniga
                                         D022003

VITALI

Chaconne in g vln & c – arr. vln & pf Charlier
 with P. Sipolniek org   Mezhdunarodnaya Kniga
              D027489/90

Sam SWAAP (1889–)

d'AMBROSIO

Canzonetta, Op. 6 vln & pf
 with piano   Favorite 669, 2–94096E
Canzonetta, Op. 6 vln & pf
 with piano   HMV B4851

ANONYMOUS

Eili, Eili Zionist hymn – arr. vln & pf Achron
 with piano   HMV C4866
Londonderry air Traditional Irish ballad – arr. vln & pf Tertis
 with piano   Bb 10790[1]△   HMV B4706

BACH

(4) Suites, BWV1066/9 strs & c
 Suite No. 3, in D: Air (2nd mvt) BWV1068 2 obs, 3 tpts, drms, strs & c–
 arr. vln & pf as "Air on the G–string" by Wilhelmj
 with piano   HMV C4866

BEETHOVEN

Romance No. 2, in F, Op. 50 vln & orch.
 with piano   Cc 11002[1]△   HMV C4856
Sonata No. 8, in c, Op. 13 "Pathétique" pf
 Adagio cantabile (2nd mvt) arr. vln & pf
 with piano   Cc 10773[1]△   HMV C4842

BRAGA

(7) Melodies (1867) v & pf
 No. 5. La serenata "Angel's serenade" arr. vln, vlc & pf
 with C. van Isterdael   Bb 10781[1]△   HMV B4711, K5587
 vlc & piano

BRAHMS

(5) Lieder, Op. 49 v & pf
 No. 4. Wiegenlied "Cradle song" arr. vln & org
 with H. Dawson org   OEA 7793[1]☐   HMV JF64
Sonata No. 3, in d, Op. 108 vln & pf
 Adagio (2nd mvt)
 with Andriessen pf   HMV D975
(16) Waltzes, Op. 39 pf duet
 No. 15. Waltz No. 15, in A flat arr. vln & pf "in A" Hochstein
 with piano   Bb 10774[V]△   HMV B4722

DVOŘÁK

Sonatina in G, Op. 100 vln & pf
 Larghetto (2nd mvt) arr. vln & pf as "Indian lament" by Kreisler
 with piano   Cc 11523[II]△   HMV C4856

ELGAR

Salut d'amour, Op. 12 orch. – arr. vln & pf Elgar
 with H. Dawson org   OEA 7794[1]☐   HMV JF62

ENGEL, J.

(29) Jüdische Volksmelodien Op. 41 pf
 No. 14. Freilachs arr. vln & pf
 with piano   HMV B4856

FALLA

(7) Canciones populares españolas (1914) v & pf
 No. 4. Jota arr. vln & pf Kochański
 with piano   HMV B4852

FAURÉ

Berceuse, Op. 16 vln & pf
 with piano   HMV B4852

FIORILLO

(36) Étude–Caprices, Op. 3 solo vln
 Caprice No. 28, in D (Allegro assai) arr. vln & pf Randegger
 with piano   Bb 11522[1]△   HMV B4722

FLIES

Wiegenlied (Schlafe, mein Prinzchen) v & pf – arr. vln & org
 with H. Dawson org   OEA 7789[1]☐   HMV JF64

FRANCK

Panis angelicus (1872) t, org, hp, vlc & cbs – arr. vln, vlc & pf
 with C. van Isterdael   Bb 10772[II]△   HMV B4713
 vlc & piano

FRANKLIN–PIKE

Idylle vln & pf
 with piano   Bb 11524[II]☐   HMV B4723

GLUCK

Orphée et Eurydice (1762) – opera
 Dance of the blessed spirits: Lento "Mélodie" (No. 2) arr. vln & pf
 Kreisler
 with piano   HMV B4856

GOUNOD

Ave Maria (Méditation on Bach's "Prelude No. 1, in C" from Book I of
"Das Wohltemperirte Clavier") v & pf – arr. vln & pf
 with piano   Bb 10797[II]△   HMV B4705, K5588

GRANADOS

(12) Danzas españolas, Op. 37 (1893) pf
 No. 5. Danza española No. 5, in e "Andaluza" arr. vln & pf Kreisler
 with piano   HMV B4704

GRIEG

Sonata No. 3, in c, Op. 45 vln & pf
 with Andriessen pf   HMV D974/5

HANDEL

Cantata (unid)
 Dank sei dir, Herr "Arioso" arr. vln, vlc & pf
 with C. van Isterdael   Bb 10771[V]△   HMV B4713
 vlc & piano
(The) Choice of Hercules (1750) – secular chorale
 There the brisk, sparkling nectar drain arr. vln & pf as "March" by
 Flesch
 with piano   HMV B4864

HANDEL – *Continued*

Solomon (1748) – oratorio
No. 40. Beneath the vine arr. vln & pf as "Pastorale" by Flesch
with H. Dawson org   OEA 7790[1]☐   HMV JF63
Te Deum, Dettingen (1743)
No. 17. Vouchsafe, O Lord arr. vln & pf as "Prayer" by Flesch
with piano   HMV B4864

KREISLER

Liebesfreud vln & pf
with piano   OB 1021[1]△   HMV B4857
Liebesleid vln & pf
with piano   OB 1022[II]△   HMV B4857
Rondino on a theme by Beethoven vln & pf
with piano   HMV B4704

MARTINI (Il Tedesco)

Plaisir d'amour v & pf – arr. vln & pf
with piano   Bb 11521[II]△   HMV B4723

MASSENET

Thaïs (1894) – opera
Méditation arr. vln & pf Marsick
with piano   Cc 10786[1]△   HMV C4842

MOSZKOWSKI

(6) Klavierstücke, Op. 15 pf – 4 hands
No. 1. Serenata arr. vln, vlc & pf
with C. van Isterdael   Bb 10782[1]△   HMV B4711, K5587
vlc & piano

MOZART

Ave verum corpus, K618 cho – arr. vln & org
with H. Dawson org   OEA 7792[1]☐   HMV JF63

PIERNÉ

Sérénade in A, Op. 7 (1875) pf – arr. vln & pf Haddock
with piano   Favorite 669, 2–94099E

RIMSKY–KORSAKOV

Sadko (1898) – opera
Chant hindou arr. vln & pf Kreisler
with piano   Bb 11001[1]△   HMV B4705, K5588

SARASATE

(8) Danzas españolas vln & pf
No. 3. Romanza andaluza, Op. 22, No. 1
with piano   Cc 10789[II]△   HMV C4843

SCHUBERT

(14) Schwanengesang, D957 (1828) v & pf
No. 4. Ständchen "Serenade" arr. vln & pf
with piano   Cc 10785[1]△   HMV C4843

SCHUMANN

(12) Duets, Op. 85 pf – 4 hands
No. 12. Abendlied arr. vln & pf Wilhelmj
with H. Dawson org   OEA 7791[1]☐   HMV JF62

TORELLI

Serenade, Op. 6 vln & pf
with piano   Bb 10794[II]△   HMV B4706

TOSTI

Good–bye v & pf – arr. vln, vlc & pf
with C. van Isterdael   Bb 10792[1]△   HMV B4712
vlc & piano
Idéale (1884) v & pf – arr. vln, vlc & pf
with C. van Isterdael   Bb 10791[1]△   HMV B4712
vlc & piano
(La) Serenata v & pf – arr. vln & pf
with piano   HMV B4851

VIEUXTEMPS

Ballade & Polonaise in G, Op. 38 vln & pf
with piano   HMV C4865

Gustave SWÄRDSTRÖM

MOZART

Adagio in E, K261 vln & orch.
with Stuttgart Ton Studio Orch. –   Classic CL6095
Lund   Period SPLP548
Rondo in B flat K269 vln & orch.
with Stuttgart Ton Studio Orch. –   Classic CL6095
Lund   Period SPLP548
Rondo in C, K373 vln & orch.
with Stuttgart Ton Studio Orch. –   Classic CL6095
Lund   Period SPLP548

Gustav SWOBODA

BACH

(Ein) Musikalisches Opfer, BWV1079 (1749) strs & c
with C. Wanausek fl, F. Wächter ob, J.   Nixa WLP5070
Noblinger E–hrn, K. Rapf hpsi, F.   Westminster W9005, WL5070,
Killinger bsn, A. Bog vln, A. Kreiner   XWN18375
vla, V. Gorlich vlc, cond. Scherchen
Sonata in C, BWV1037 2 vlns & c
with W. Schneiderhan vln, F. Holeček   Ducretet–Thomson LPG8717
hpsi & S. Benesch vlc   Westminster WL5036

BOCCHERINI

(6) Trios, Op. 34 2 vlns & vlc
Trio No. 1, in f
with W. Schneiderhan vln & S.   Westminster W9012, WL5046,
Benesch vlc   XWN18050
Trio No. 2, in G
with W. Schneiderhan vln & S.   Westminster W9012, WL5042,
Benesch vlc   XWN18050
Trio No. 3, in E flat
with W. Schneiderhan vln & S.   Westminster W9013, WL5046,
Benesch vlc   XWN18051
Trio No. 4, in D
with W. Schneiderhan vln & S.   Westminster W9013, WL5042,
Benesch vlc   XWN18051
Trio No. 5, in C
with W. Schneiderhan vln & S.   Westminster W9014, WL5042,
Benesch vlc   XWN18052
Trio No. 6, in E
with W. Schneiderhan vln & S.   Westminster W9014, WL5046,
Benesch vlc   XWN18052

DVOŘÁK

Quartet No. 3, in E flat, Op. 51 2 vlns, vla & vlc
with S. Rumpold vln A. Pioro vla &   Telefunken LGM65024
R. Harand vlc

HANDEL

(7) Sonatas, Op. 5 (1739) 2 vlns & c
Sonata No. 6, in F
with W. Schneiderhan vln, F. Holeček   Ducretet–Thomson LPG8717
hpsi & S. Benesch vlc   Westminster WL5036

HAYDN

(6) Quartets, Op. 20 (H.III, Nos. 31/6) 2 vlns, vla & vlc
No. 5. Quartet No. 35, in f, H.III, No. 35
with S. Rumpold vln, A. Pioro vla &   Telefunken LGX66034
R. Harand vlc

MENDELSSOHN

Octet in E flat, Op. 20 4 vlns, 2 vlas & 2 vlcs
with W. Boskovsky vln, P. Matheis   Decca LXT2858
vln, F. Leitermeier vln, G. Breitenbach   London LL859
vla, F. Strangler vla, N. Hübner vlc &
R. Harand vlc

SCHUBERT

(2) Quartets, Op. 125 2 vlns, vla & vlc
No. 1. Quartet No. 10, in E flat, D87
with S. Rumpold vln, A. Pioro vla &   Telefunken LGX66034
R. Harand vlc

Quartet No. 14, in d, D810 "Death & the maiden" 2 vlns, vla & vlc
with S. Rumpold vln, A. Pioro vla &   Telefunken LGX66016
R. Harand vlc

TELEMANN

Sonata No. 1, in a "Sonata Polonaise" 2 vlns & c
with W. Schneiderhan, vln F.   Ducretet–Thomson LPG8717
Holetschek hpsi & S. Benesch vlc   Westminster WL5036,
XWN18031

Sonata No. 3, in E 2 vlns & c
with W. Schneiderhan vln, F.   Ducretet–Thomson LPG8717
Holetschek hpsi & S. Benesch vlc   Westminster WL5036,
XWN18031

János SZABÓ

MOZART

Sonata No. 3, in B flat, K8 vln & pf
with E. Sellheim pf   Intercord 708–05SB
Sonata No. 4, in G, K9 vln & pf
with E. Sellheim pf   Intercord 708–05SB
Sonata No. 12, in G, K27 vln & pf
with E. Sellheim pf   Intercord 708–05SB
Sonata No. 16, in B flat, K31 vln & pf
with E. Sellheim pf   Intercord 708–05SB

Zoltan SZÉKELY (1903–   )

BARTÓK

(6) Rumanian folk dances (1915) pf – arr. vln & pf Székely
Nos. 1, 3, 4 & 6
with G. Frid pf   TA 3025–1   Decca K872

GLAZOUNOV

Concerto in a, Op. 82 vln & orch.
with Hague Residentie Orchestra – van   Decca X10110/2
Otterloo

MANÉN

Chanson–Adagietto, Op. A–8, No. 1 vln & pf
with G. Frid pf   TA 3024–1   Decca K872

PORPORA

(12) Sonatas (1754) vln & c
Sonata No. 2, in G (ed. David)
TA 3022–1 & 3023–11   Decca 25877, K863
with G. Frid pf

Magda SZEMERE

BRAGA

(7) Melodies (1867) v & pf
No. 5. La serenata "Angel's serenade" arr. vln & pf
with piano   110006   Polydor 50059, 67506

DRIGO

(Les) Millions d'Arlequin (1900) – ballet orch.
Sérénade arr. vln & pf Auer
with piano   26175   Polydor 30016

ELGAR

Salut d'amour, Op. 12 orch. – arr. vln & pf Elgar
with piano   26172   Polydor 30015

GLUCK

Gavotte pf – arr. vln & pf Burmester
with piano   26173   Polydor 30015

GODARD

Jocelyn (1888) – opera
Cachés dans cet asile "Berceuse" arr. vln & orch.
with orch. – Irmler   Parlophone E10031, P1509

HUBAY

(Le) Luthier de Crémone, Op. 40 (1894) – opera
Intermezzo orch. – arr. vln & pf Hubay
with piano   110007   Polydor 50059, 67506
(14) Scènes de la Csárda vln & pf
No. 4. Hejre Kati, Op. 32
with orch.   Parlophone P1527

NEVIN

(6) Water Scenes, Op. 13 pf
No. 4. Narcissus arr. vln & pf
with piano   26177   Polydor 30017

SAMMARTINI, G.

(6) Sonatas, Op. 1 2 vlns & c
Sonata No. 4, in A: Andante (3rd mvt) arr. vln & pf as "Canto amoroso"
by Elman
with piano   26174   Polydor 30016

SARASATE

Zigeunerweisen, Op. 20 vln & pf or orch.
with orch. – Irmler   Parlophone E10030, P1508
Zigeunerweisen, Op. 20 vln & pf or orch.
with piano   110004/5   Polydor 50058, 67504

WIENIAWSKI

Mazurka in a, Op. 3 "Kujawiak" vln & pf
with orch. – Irmler   Parlophone E10031, P1509
Mazurka in a, Op. 3 "Kujawiak" vln & pf
with piano   26176   Polydor 30017

Laszlö SZENTGYÖRGI (1910–)

BACH

(4) Suites, BWV1066/9 strs & c
Suite No. 3, in D: Air (2nd mvt) BWV1068 2 obs, 3 tpts, drms, strs & c
– arr. vln & pf as "Air on the G–string" by Wilhelmj
with piano   HMV EH412

BRAHMS

(16) Waltzes, Op. 39 pf duet
No. 15. Waltz No. 15, in A flat arr. vln & pf "in A" Hochstein
with piano   HMV EG1619

BRANDL

(Der) Liebe Augustin – operetta
Du alter Stefansturm arr. vln & pf as "The old refrain" by Kreisler
with C. Schmalstich pf   HMV AM1873, EG1133

HUBAY

(6) Blumenleben, Op. 30 vln & pf
No. 5. Der Zephir
with piano   HMV EG1619

PAGANINI

(24) Caprices, Op. 1 (1801/7) solo vln
Caprice No. 13, in B flat arr. vln & pf Kreisler
with C. Schmalstich pf   HMV AM2315, EG1442
Concerto No. 1, in D, Op. 6 vln & orch.
Allegro maestoso (1st mvt) arr. vln & orch. Wilhelmj
with Berlin State   CNR 794/7^{II}△   HMV AN486/7, C2457/8,
Opera Orch. – Schmalstich   EH418/9, S10326/7
Sonata a preghièra "Moses Fantasia" (on the aria "Dal tuo stellato soglio"
from Rossini's opera "Mosè in Egitto") Op. 24 (1818 or 1819) vln &
orch.
with piano   HMV EH254

SARASATE

(8) Danzas españolas vln & pf
No. 1. Malagueña, Op. 21, No. 1
with C. Schmalstich   CLR 5442^{II}△   HMV AN378, C2001, EH373
pf
No. 3. Romanza andaluza, Op. 22, No. 1
with piano   HMV EH254

SARASATE – *Continued*

No. 6. Zapateado, Op. 23, No. 2
with C. Schmalstich pf   HMV AM1873, EG1133

SCHUBERT

(7) Gesänge (set to Scott's "Lady of the Lake") Op. 52 v & pf
No. 6. Ave Maria, D839 arr. vln & pf Wilhelmj
with piano   HMV EH412
Sonata No. 17, in D, Op. 53 (D850) pf
Rondo (4th mvt) arr. vln & pf Friedberg
with C. Schmalstich   CLR 5441^{II}△   HMV AN378, C2001, EH373
pf

SCHUMANN

(9) Waldscenen, Op. 82 pf
No. 7. Vogel als Prophet arr. vln & pf Auer
with C. Schmalstich pf   HMV AM2315, EG1442

Miklós SZÉNTHELYI

JÁRDÁNYI

Variations (1955) 2 vlns & vlc
with T. Bokor vln & G. Eder vlc   Qualiton LPX1188

Henryk SZERYNG (1918–)

ALBÉNIZ

España (6 Feuilles d'album) Op. 165 pf
No. 2. Tango in D arr. vln & pf Kreisler
with T. Janopoulo pf   Odeon AOE1050, ODX129
No. 3. Malagueña in b arr. vln & pf Kreisler
with L. Schwarz pf   Orfeo 4001

BACH

Concerto No. 1, in a, BWV1041 vln, strs & c
with L'Association des Concerts,   CBS 51009
Pasdeloup – Bouillon   I CLassici della Musica Classica
     XAR4033
     Monitor MC2087, MCS2087
     Odeon ODX114, XOC112

Concerto No. 1, in a, BWV1041 vln, strs & c
with Collegium Musicum, Winterthur   Mercury MG50466, SR90466
– Szeryng   Philips 6526 028, 835331LY,
     A02462L, AL3540, SAL3540

Concerto No. 2, in E, BWV1042 vln, strs & c
with L'Association des Concerts,   CBS 51009
Pasdeloup – Bouillon   I Classici della Musica Classica
     XAR4033
     Monitor MC2087, MCS2087
     Odeon ODX114, XOC112

Concerto No. 2, in E, BWV1042 vln, strs & c
with Rumanian Radio Symphony   Electrecord ECD1018
Orch. – Conta

Concerto No. 2, in E, BWV1042 vln, strs & c
with Collegium Musicum, Winterthur   Mercury MG50466, SR90466
– Szeryng   Philips 835331LY, A02462L,
     AL3540, SAL3540

BACH – *Continued*

Concerto in d, BWV1043 2 vlns, strs & c
   with P. Rybar vln & Collegium   Mercury MG50466, SR90466
   Musicum, Winterthur – Szeryng   Philips (in set 6830 004),
                                      835331LY, A02462L, AL3540,
                                      SAL3540

(3) Sonatas & 3 Partitas, BWV1001/6 solo vln
  Sonata No. 1, in g, BWV1001
  (unaccompanied)   Angel HA5041
                                        CBS 51068
                                        Odeon O 80753, ODX122,
                                        XOC125
                                        Odyssey 32 16 0193 (in set 32 36
                                        0013)

  Sonata No. 1, in g, BWV1001
  (unaccompanied)   Deutsche Grammophon
                                          SLPM139270, (in set 2709 028)

  Partita No. 1, in b, BWV1002
  (unaccompanied)   Angel HA5041
                                        CBS 51068
                                        Odeon O 80753, ODX122,
                                        XOC125
                                        Odyssey 32 16 0193 (in set 32 36
                                        0013)

  Partita No. 1, in b, BWV1002
  (unaccompanied)   Deutsche Grammophon
                                          SLPM139270, (in set 2709 028)

  Sonata No. 2, in a, BWV1003
  (unaccompanied)   Angel HA5042
                                        CBS 51069
                                        Odeon O 80754, ODX123,
                                        XOC126
                                        Odyssey 32 16 0195 (in set 32 36
                                        0013)

  Sonata No. 2, in a, BWV1003
  (unaccompanied)   Deutsche Grammophon
                                          SLPM139271, (in set 2709 028)

  Partita No. 2, in d, BWV1004
  (unaccompanied)   Angel HA5042
                                        CBS 51069
                                        Odeon O 80754, ODX123,
                                        XOC126
                                        Odyssey 32 16 0195 (in set 32 36
                                        0013)

  Partita No. 2, in d: Chaconne (5th mvt) BWV1004
  (unaccompanied   Electrecord ECC545, ECD1018

  Partita No. 2, in d, BWV1004
  (unaccompanied)   Deutsche Grammophon
                                          SLPM139271, (in set 2709 028),
                                        SLPM139389

  Sonata No. 3, in C, BWV1005
  (unaccompanied)   Angel HA5043
                                        CBS 51070
                                        Odeon O 80755, ODX124,
                                        XOC127
                                        Odyssey 32 16 0197 (in set 32 36
                                        0013)

  Sonata No. 3, in C, BWV1005
  (unaccompanied)   Deutsche Grammophon
                                          SLPM139272, (in set 2709 028)

BACH – *Continued*

  Partita No. 3, in E, BWV1006
  (unaccompanied)   Angel HA5043
                                        CBS 51070
                                        Odeon O 80755, ODX124,
                                        XOC127
                                        Odyssey 32 16 0197 (in set 32 36
                                        0013)

  Partita No. 3, in E, BWV1006
  (unaccompanied)   Deutsche Grammophon
                                          SLPM139272, (in set 2709 028)

  (6) Sonatas, BWV1014/9 vln & clav
  Sonata No. 1, in b, BWV1014
  with H. Walcha hpsi   Philips 6526 028, 6700 017,
                                          802910/1AY, (in set C71
                                          AX223)

  Sonata No. 2, in A, BWV1015
  with H. Walcha hpsi   Philips 6700 017, 802910/1AY,
                                          (in set C71 AX223)

  Sonata No. 3, in E, BWV1016
  with H. Walcha hpsi   Philips 6700 017, 802910/1AY,
                                          (in set C71 AX223)

  Sonata No. 4, in c, BWV1017
  with H. Walcha hpsi   Philips 6700 017, 802910/1AY,
                                          (in set C71 AX223)

  Sonata No. 5, in f, BWV1018
  with H. Walcha hpsi   Philips 6700 017, 802910/1AY,
                                          (in set C71 AX223)

  Sonata No. 6, in G, BWV1019
  with H. Walcha hpsi   Philips 6700 017, 802910/1AY,
                                          (in set C71 AX223)

BARTÓK

Concerto No. 2 (1938) vln & orch.
  with Concertgebouw Orch. Amsterdam   Philips 6500 021
  – Haitink

Rhapsody No. 1, in G (1928) vln & orch.
  with Concertgebouw Orch.,   Philips 6500 021, 6526 028
  Amsterdam – Haitink

(6) Rumanian folk dances (1915) pf – arr. vln & pf Székely
  with C. Reiner pf   Mercury 120559MGL,
                                        130559MGY, MG50367,
                                        SR90367
                                        Philips 838427AY, GL5862,
                                        PHC9092, SFL14116, SGL5862

BEETHOVEN

Concerto in C, Op. 56 "Triple" vln, vlc, pf & orch.
  with J. Starker vlc, C. Arrau pf &   Philips 6500 129
  New Philharmonia Orch. – Inbal

Concerto in D, Op. 61 (cadenzas by Kreisler) vln & orch.
  with Paris Conservatory Orch. –   CBS 51004
  Thibaud   I Classici della Musica Classica
                                        XAR4029
                                        Monitor MC2093, MCS2093
                                        Odeon LDC7904, ODX109,
                                        XOC111

Concerto in D, Op. 61 (cadenzas by Kreisler) vln & orch.
  with Rumanian Radio Symphony   Electrecord ECE096
  Orch. – Conta

BEETHOVEN – *Continued*

Concerto in D, Op. 61 (cadenzas by Joachim & Flesch) vln & orch.
with London Symphony Orch. –
Schmidt–Isserstedt

Mercury MG50451/2, (in set
OL3–117), SR90451/2, (in set
SR3–9017)
Philips 8580 004, 835330LY,
A02461L, AL3538, SAL3538

Romance No. 1, in G, Op. 40 vln & orch.
with Concertgebouw Orch.,
Amsterdam – Haitink

Philips 6500 137

Romance No. 2, in F, Op. 50 vln & orch.
with Concertgebouw Orch.,
Amsterdam – Haitink

Philips 6500 137

Sonata No. 5, in F, Op. 24 "Spring" vln & pf
with A. Rubinstein pf

Victor LM2377, LSC2377,
RB16209, SB2084

(3) Sonatas, Op. 30 vln & pf
No. 3. Sonata No. 8, in G
with A. Rubinstein pf

Victor LM2620, LSC2620,
RB6513, SB6513

Sonata No. 9, in A, Op. 47 "Kreutzer" vln & pf
with A. Rubinstein pf

Victor LM2377, LSC2377,
RB16209, SB2084

(3) Trios, Op. 1 pf, vln & vlc
No. 1. Trio No. 1, in E flat
with W. Kempff pf & P. Fournier vlc

Deutsche Grammophon 643656,
(in set 2720 016)

No. 2. Trio No. 2, in G
with W. Kempff pf & P. Fournier vlc

Deutsche Grammophon
643656/7, (in set 2720 016)

No. 3. Trio No. 3, in c
with W. Kempff pf & P. Fournier vlc

Deutsche Grammophon 643657,
(in set 2720 016)

(2) Trios, Op. 70 pf, vln & vlc
No. 1. Trio No. 4, in D "Ghost"
with W. Kempff pf & P. Fournier vlc

Deutsche Grammophon 643658,
(in set 2720 016)

No. 2. Trio No. 5, in E flat
with W. Kempff pf & P. Fournier vlc

Deutsche Grammophon 643658,
(in set 2720 016)

Trio No. 6, in B flat, Op. 97 "Archduke" pf, vln & vlc
with W. Kempff pf & P. Fournier vlc

Deutsche Grammophon 643660,
(in set 2720 016)

Trio in B flat, G154 (WoO.39) "In one movement" pf, vln & vlc
with W. Kempff pf & P. Fournier vlc

Deutsche Grammophon 643659,
(in set 2720 016)

(14) Variations in E flat, Op. 44 pf, vln & vlc
with W. Kempff pf & P. Fournier vlc

Deutsche Grammophon 643659,
(in set 2720 016)

(10) Variations (on "Ich bin der Schneider Kakadu") Op. 121a pf, vln & vlc
with W. Kempff pf & P. Fournier vlc

Deutsche Grammophon 643659,
(in set 2720 016)

BERG

Concerto (1935) vln & orch.
with Bavarian Radio Symphony Orch.
– Kubelík

Deutsche Grammophon 2530 033

BRAHMS

Concerto in D, Op. 77 (cadenza by Joachim) vln & orch.
with London Symphony Orch. –
Monteux

Victor A630485, KV43, LM2281,
LSC2281, RB16168, SB2049,
VIC14, VIC1028, VICS1028

Concerto in D, Op. 77 (cadenza by Joachim) vln & orch.
with London Symphony Orch. –
Dorati

Mercury 120528MGL,
130528MGY, AMS16134,
MG50308, MMA11184, SR90308
Philips 838400MGY,
839545VGY, A04900L, AL3558,
SAL3558, SFM23021

Concerto in a, Op. 102 "Double" vln, vlc orch.
with J. Starker vlc & Concertgebouw
Orch., Amsterdam – Haitink

Philips 6500 137

(21) Hungarian Dances pf duet
Hungarian dance No. 17, in f sharp arr. vln & pf Kreisler
with L. Schwarz pf

Orfeo 4003

Hungarian dance No. 17, in f sharp arr. vln & pf Kreisler
with C. Reiner pf

Mercury 120559MGL,
130559MGY, MG50367,
SR90367
Philips 838427AY, GL5862,
PHC9092, SFL14116, SGL5862

Sonata No. 1, in G, Op. 78 vln & pf
with A. Rubinstein pf

Victor LM2620, LSC2620,
RB6513, SB6513

Sonata No. 2, in A, Op. 100 vln & pf
with A. Rubinstein pf

Victor LM2619, LSC2619,
RB6520, SB6520

Sonata No. 3, in d, Op. 108 vln & pf
with A. Rubinstein pf

Victor LM2619, LSC2619,
RB6520, SB6520

Trio in E flat, Op. 40 hrn, pf & vln
with J. Eger hrn & V. Babin pf

Victor LM2420, LSC2420

BRANDL

(Der) Liebe Augustin – operetta
Du alter Stefansturm arr. vln & pf as "The old refrain" by Kreisler
with C. Reiner pf

Mercury 120538MGL,
130538MGY, MG50348,
SR90348
Philips 838426AY, 839840GSY,
GL5868, SFL14117, SGL5868

CHÁVEZ

Concerto (1952) vln & orch.
with Orquestra Sinfonia Nacional
México – Chávez

CBS 32 11 0064

DEBUSSY

(La) Plus que lente – valse (1910) pf – arr. vln & pf Roques
with C. Reiner pf

Mercury 120559MGL,
130559MGY, MG50367,
SR90367
Philips 838427AY, GL5862,
PHC9092, SFL14116, SGL5862

DVOŘÁK

(8) Slavonic Dances, Op. 46 pf duet; orch.
No. 2. Slavonic dance No. 2, in e arr. vln & pf "in g" Kreisler
with R. Locatelli pf

Victor 11–8307

DVOŘÁK – *Continued*

No. 2. Slavonic dance No. 2, in e arr. vln & pf "in g" Kreisler
with M. Berthelier pf   Pacific EP90019, LDPC50
No. 8. Slavonic dance No. 8, in g arr. vln & pf Press
with L. Schwarz pf   Orfeo 4003

FALLA

(7) Canciones populares españolas (1914) v & pf
No. 1. El paño moruno arr. vln & pf Kochański
with L. Schwarz pf   Orfeo 4001
No. 1. El paño moruno arr. vln & pf Kochański
with M. Berthelier pf   Pacific LDPC50
                                         Telefunken A11116
No. 1. El paño moruno arr. vln & pf Kochański
with T. Janopoulo pf   Odeon AOE1050, ODX129
No. 3. Asturiana arr. vln & pf Kochański
with T. Janopoulo pf   Odeon AOE1050, ODX129
No. 4. Jota arr. vln & pf Kochański
with L. Schwarz pf   Orfeo 4001
No. 4. Jota arr. vln & pf Kochański
with M. Berthelier pf   Pacific LDPC50
                                         Telefunken A11116
No. 4. Jota arr. vln & pf Kochański
with T. Janopoulo pf   Everest LPBR6153, SDBR3153
                            Odeon AOE1050, ODX129
No. 5. Nana arr. vln & pf Kochański
with T. Janopoulo pf   Odeon AOE1050, ODX129
No. 6. Canción arr. vln & pf Kochański
with T. Janopoulo pf   Odeon AOE1050, ODX129
(La) Vida Breve (1913) – opera
Danza española orch. – arr. vln & pf Kreisler
with T. Janopoulo pf   Everest LPBR6153, SDBR3153
                            Odeon AOE1049, ODX129

GERSHWIN

(3) Jazz Preludes (1936) pf
No. 2. Prelude No. 2, in c sharp arr. vln & pf Heifetz
with M. Berthelier pf   Pacific LDPC50

GLUCK

Orphée et Eurydice (1762) – opera
Dance of the blessed spirits: Lento "Mélodie" (No. 2) arr. vln & pf
Kreisler
with C. Reiner pf   Victor LM2421, RB16240
Dance of the blessed spirits: Lento "Mélodie" (No. 2) arr. vln & pf
Kreisler
with C. Reiner pf   Mercury 120559MGL,
                            130559MGY, MG50367,
                            SR90367
                            Philips 838427AY, GL5862,
                            PHC9092, SFL14116, SGL5862

HALFFTER–ESCRICHE

Sonatina (1928) – ballet orch.
No. 4. Danza de la gitana arr. vln & pf Heifetz
with T. Janopoulo pf   Odeon ODX129
No. 4. Danza de la gitana arr. vln & pf Heifetz
with C. Reiner pf   Victor LM2421, RB16240

HALFFTER–ESCRICHE – *Continued*

No. 6. Danza de la pastora arr. vln & pf
with T. Janopoulo pf   Everest LPBR6153, SDBR3153
                            Odeon AOE1049, ODX129

JOLISCO

Danse indigène pf – arr. vln & pf Rolón
with T. Janopoulo pf   Everest LPBR6153, SDBR3153
                            Odeon AOE1049, ODX129

KHACHATURIAN

Concerto in D (1940) (cadenza by Khachaturian) vln & orch.
with Colonne Concerts Orch. –   Odeon OD1024, ODX167,
Dervaux   XOC110
Concerto in D (1940) (cadenza by Khachaturian) vln & orch.
with London Symphony Orch. –   Mercury MG50393, SR90393
Dorati   Philips 6585 002, 838418AY,
                                  AL3503, SAL3503

KREISLER

Caprice viennois, Op. 2 vln & pf
with C. Reiner pf   Mercury 120538MGL,
                            130538MGY, MG50348,
                            SR90348
                            Philips 838426AY, 839840GSY,
                            GL5868, SFL14117, SGL5868
Liebesfreud vln & pf
with C. Reiner pf   Mercury 120538MGL,
                            130538MGY, MG50348,
                            SR90348
                            Philips 838426AY, 839840GSY,
                            GL5868, SFL14117, SGL5868
Liebesleid vln & pf
with C. Reiner pf   Mercury 120538MGL,
                            130538MGY, MG50348,
                            SR90348
                            Philips 838426AY, 839840GSY,
                            GL5868, SFL14117, SGL5868
Recitative & Scherzo–caprice, Op. 6 solo vln
(unaccompanied)   Mercury 120538MGL,
                            130538MGY, MG50348,
                            SR90348
                            Philips 838426AY, 839840GSY,
                            GL5868, SFL14117, SGL5868
Rondino on a theme by Beethoven vln & pf
with C. Reiner pf   Mercury 120538MGL,
                            130538MGY, MG50348,
                            SR90348
                            Philips 838426AY, 839840GSY,
                            GL5868, SFL14117, SGL5868
Schön Rosmarin vln & pf
with C. Reiner pf   Mercury 120538MGL,
                            130538MGY, MG50348,
                            SR90348
                            Philips 838426AY, 839840GSY,
                            GL5868, SFL14117, SGL5868

KREISLER – *Continued*

Tambourin chinois, Op. 3 vln & pf
  with C. Reiner pf
    Mercury 120538MGL, 130538MGY, MG50348, SR90348
    Philips 838426AY, 839840GSY, GL5868, SFL14117, SGL5868

Allegretto (Boccherini) vln & pf
  with C. Reiner pf
    Victor LM2421, RB16240

Allegretto (Boccherini) vln & pf
  with C. Reiner pf
    Mercury 120538MGL, 130538MGY, MG50348, SR90348
    Philips 838426AY, 839840GSY, GL5868, SFL14117, SGL5868

Chanson Louis XIII & Pavane (L. Couperin) vln & pf
  with C. Reiner pf
    Mercury 120538MGL, 130538MGY, MG50348, SR90348
    Philips 838426AY, 839840GSY, GL5868, SFL14117, SGL5868

Grave (W.F. Bach) vln & pf
  with T. Janopoulo pf
    Everest LPBR6154, SDBR3154
    Odeon LDC7504, OD1008

Minuet (Porpora) vln & pf
  with C. Reiner pf
    Mercury 120538MGL, 130538MGY, MG50348, SR90348
    Philips 838426AY, 839840GSY, GL5868, SFL14117, SGL5868

Praeludium & Allegro (Pugnani) vln & pf
  with C. Reiner pf
    Mercury 120538MGL, 130538MGY, MG50348, SR90348
    Philips 838426AY, 839840GSY, GL5868, SFL14117, SGL5868

Tempo di minuetto (Pugnani) vln & pf
  with C. Reiner pf
    Mercury 120538MGL, 130538MGY, MG50348, SR90348
    Philips 838426AY, 839840GSY, GL5868, SFL14117, SGL5868

LALO

Symphonie espagnole, Op. 21 vln & orch* & †
  with Chicago Symphony Orch. – Hendl
    Camden Classics VCCS1064
    Victor LM2456, LSC2456, RB16251, SB2120, VIC1064, VICS1064

Symphonie espagnole, Op. 21 vln & orch.†
  with Orchestre de National de l'Opéra de Monte Carlo – van Remoortel
    Philips 6500 195

* Scherzando or 2nd mvt is also on Victor RB6543.
† Including Intermezzo.

LECLAIR

(12) Sonatas, Op. 9 – Book IV (1738) vln & c
  Sonata No. 3, in D
  with C. Reiner pf
    Mercury 120559MGL, 130559MGY, MG50367, SR90367
    Philips 838427AY, GL5862, PHC9092, SFL14116, SGL5862

LOCATELLI

(24) Caprices, Op. 3 solo vln
  Caprice No. 23, in D "Il laberinto armonico" arr. vln & pf as "Le Labyrinthe" by David
  with M. Berthelier pf
    Pacific LDPC50
    Telefunken E3887

  Caprice No. 23, in D "Il laberinto armonico" arr. vln & pf as "Le Labyrinthe" by David
  with C. Reiner pf
    Mercury 120559MGL, 130559MGY, MG50367, SR90367
    Philips 838427AY, GL5862, PHC9092, SFL14116, SGL5862

MARROQUÍN

Mexican lullaby vln & pf
  with T. Janopoulo pf
    Everest LPBR6153, SDBR3153
    Odeon ODX129

Mexican lullaby vln & pf
  with C. Reiner pf
    Mercury 120559MGL, 130559MGY, MG50367, SR90367
    Philips 838427AY, GL5862, PHC9092, SFL14116, SGL5862

MARTINON

Concerto No. 2, Op. 51 vln & orch.
  with Bavarian Radio Symphony Orch. – Kubelík
    Deutsche Grammophon 2530 033

MENDELSSOHN

Concerto in e, Op. 64 vln & orch.
  with London Symphony Orch. – Dorati
    Mercury 120575MGL, 130575MGY, MG50406, SR90406
    Philips 838417LY, AL3504, SAL3504

(6) Songs without words, Op. 62 pf
  No. 6. Song without words No. 30, in A "Spring song" arr. vln & pf
  with R. Locatelli pf
    Victor 10–1034

MOMPOU

(5) Scènes d'enfants (1915/8) pf
  No. 5. Jeunes filles au jardin arr. vln & pf Szigeti
  with M. Berthelier pf
    Nixa BZ2201
    Pacific LDPC50

MOZART

Adagio in E, K261 vln & orch.
  with New Philharmonia Orch. – Gibson
    Philips 6500 036, (in set 6707 011)

Concerto No. 1, in B flat, K207 (cadenzas by Erik Smith) vln & orch.
  with New Philharmonia Orch. – Gibson
    Philips 6500 035, (in set 6707 011)

MOZART – *Continued*

Concerto No. 2, in D, K211 (cadenzas by Erik Smith) vln & orch.
with New philharmonia Orch. –
Gibson
    Philips 6500 035, (in set 6707 011)

Concerto No. 3, in G, K216 (cadenzas by Franko) vln & orch.
with New Philharmonia Orch. –
Gibson
    Philips 6500 036, (in set 6707 011)

Concerto No. 4, in D, K218 (cadenzas by Joachim) vln & orch.
with New Philharmonia Orch. –
Gibson
    Philips 6500 036, (in set 6707 011)

Concerto No. 5, in A, K219 "Turkish" (cadenzas by Joachim) vln & orch.
with New Philharmonia Orch. –
Gibson
    Philips 6500 037, (in set 6707 011), 802709LY, AL3588, PHM500163, PHS900163, SAL3588

Concerto No. 7, in D, K271a (cadenzas by Enescu) vln & orch.
with New Philharmonia Orch. –
Gibson
    Philips 6500 037, (in set 6707 011), 802709LY, AL3588, PHM500163, PHS900163, SAL3588

Concertone in C, K190 2 vlns, ob, vlc & orch.
with G. Poulet vln, R. Morgan ob, N. Jones vlc & New Philharmonia Orch. – Gibson
    Philips 6500 038, (in set 6707 011)

Rondo in B flat, K269 vln & orch.
with New Philharmonia Orch. –
Gibson
    Philips 6500 035, (in set 6707 011)

Rondo in C, K373 vln & orch.
with New Philharmonia Orch. –
Gibson
    Philips 6500 035, (in set 6707 011)

Sinfonia concertante in E flat, K364 vln, vla & orch.
with B. Giuranna vla & New Philharmonia Orch. – Gibson
    Philips 6500 038, (in set 6707 011)

Sonata No. 17, in C, K296 vln & pf
with I. Haebler pf
    Philips 6500 053

Sonata No. 21, in e, K304 vln & pf
with I. Haebler pf
    Philips 6500 053

Sonata No. 25, in F, K377 vln & pf
with I. Haebler pf
    Philips 6500 054

Sonata No. 26, in B flat, K378 vln & pf
with I. Haebler pf
    Philips 6500 054

Sonata No. 32, in B flat, K454 vln & pf
with I. Haebler pf
    Philips 6500 055

Sonata No. 33, in E flat, K481 vln & pf
with I. Haebler pf
    Philips 6500 055

Sonata No. 34, in A, K526 vln & pf
with I. Haebler pf
    Philips 6500 053

NOVAČEK

(8) Concert caprices, Op. 5 vln & pf
No. 4. Perpetuum mobile
with M. Berthelier pf
    Nixa BY4023
    Pacific LDPC50
    Telefunken A11066

NOVAČEK – *Continued*

No. 4. Perpetuum mobile
with C. Reiner pf
    Mercury 120559MGL, 130559MGY, MG50367, SR90367
    Philips 838427AY, GL5862, PHC9092, SFL14116, SGL5862

PADEREWSKI

(6) Humoresques de concert, Op. 14 pf
No. 1. Minuet in G arr. vln & pf Kreisler
with R. Locatelli pf
    Victor 10–1035

PAGANINI

(24) Caprices, Op. 1 (1801/7) solo vln
Caprice No. 20, in D arr. vln & pf Kreisler
with R. Locatelli pf
    Victor 10–1034
Caprice No. 24, in a arr. vln & pf
with T. Janopoulo pf
    Everest LPBR6154, SDBR3154
    Odeon LDC7504, OD1008

Concerto No. 2, in b, Op. 7 vln & orch.
Ronde à clochette (3rd mvt) "La Campanella"
with L. Schwarz pf
    Orfeo 4004

Concerto No. 3, in E (cadenzas by Szeryng) vln & orch.
with London Symphony Orch. –
Gibson
    Philips 6500 175

PONCE

Concerto (1942) vln & orch.
with Colonne Concerts Orch. – Bour
    Odeon ODX159, XOC130

Estrellita (1913) v & pf – arr. vln & pf Heifetz
with T. Janopoulo pf
    Everest LPBR6153, SDBR3153
    Odeon AOE1049, ODX129

Sonata Breve (1933) vln & pf
with T. Janopoulo pf
    Everest LPBR6153, SDBR3153
    Odeon ODX129

Sonata Breve (1933) vln & pf
with C. Maillois pf
    Philips 6526 028

PROKOFIEV

Concerto No. 2, in g, Op. 63 vln & orch.
with Colonne Concerts Orch. –
Dervaux
    Odeon OD1025, ODX167, XOC110

Concerto No. 2, in g, Op. 63 vln & orch.
with London Symphony Orch. –
Rozdestvensky
    Mercury MG50453, (in set OL3–117), SR90453, (in set SR3–9017)
    Philips 6585 002, 835357AY, A02487L, AL3571, SAL3571

RAVEL

Tzigane (Rapsodie de concert) (1924) vln & pf or orch.
with Orchestre de National de l'Opéra de Monte Carlo – van Remoortel
    Philips 6500 195

RIMSKY-KORSAKOV

(The) Tale of Tsar Saltan (1900) – opera
Flight of the bumblebee (Act III) orch. – arr. vln & pf Hartmann
with L. Schwarz pf
    Orfeo 4002
Flight of the bumblebee (Act III) orch. – arr. vln & pf Hartmann
with M. Berthelier pf
    Nixa BY4023
    Pacific EP90018, LDPC50

RIMSKY–KORSAKOV – *Continued*

Flight of the bumblebee (Act III) orch. – arr. vln & pf Hartmann
with C. Reiner pf
Mercury 120559MGL, 130559MGY, MG50367, SR90367
Philips 838427AY, GL5862, PHC9092, SFL14116, SGL5862

ROLÓN

Mexican dance vln & pf
with T. Janopoulo pf
Everest LPBR6153, SDBR3153
Odeon AOE1049, ODX129

SAINT–SAËNS

Concerto No. 3, in b, Op. 61 vln & orch.
with Orchestre de National de l'Opéra de Monte Carlo – van Remoortel
Philips 6580 016

Havanaise, Op. 83 vln & orch.
with French Radio Symphony Orch. – Lindenberg
Everest LPBR6152, SDBR3152
Odeon FOC1012, LDG7502, OD1007

Havanaise, Op. 83 vln & orch.
with Orchestre de National de l'Opéra de Monte Carlo – van Remoortel
Philips 6526 028, 6580 016

Introduction & Rondo Capriccioso, Op. 28 vln & orch.
with French Radio Symphony Orch. – Lindenberg
Everest LPBR6152, SDBR3152
Odeon FOC1012, LDG7502, OD1007

Introduction & Rondo Capriccioso, Op. 28 vln & orch.
with Orchestre de National de l'Opéra de Monte Carlo – van Remoortel
Philips 6580 016

SARASATE

(8) Danzas españolas vln & pf
No. 3. Romanza andaluza, Op. 22, No. 1
with T. Janopoulo pf
Everest LPBR6152, SDBR3152
Odeon AOE1050, ODX129

No. 6. Zapateado, Op. 23, No. 2
with R. Locatelli pf
Victor 10–1035

No. 6. Zapateado, Op. 23, No. 2
with T. Janopoulo pf
Odeon AOE1049, ODX129

SCHUMANN

Concerto in d (1853) vln & orch.
with London Symphony Orch. – Dorati
Mercury 120575MGL, 130575MGY, MG50406, SR90406
Philips 838417LY, AL3504, SAL3504

(9) Waldscenen, Op. 82 pf
No. 7. Vogel als Prophet arr. vln & pf Auer
with C. Reiner pf
Victor LM2421, RB16240

SERRATOS

Etude in octaves vln & pf
with T. Janopoulo pf
Everest LPBR6152, SDBR3152
Odeon ODX129

SIBELIUS

Concerto in d, Op. 47 vln & orch.
with Colonne Concerts Orch. – Bour
Odeon ODX159, XOC130

SIBELIUS – *Continued*

Concerto in d, Op. 47 vln & orch.
with London Symphony Orch. – Rozdestvensky
Mercury MG50453, (in set OL3–117), SR90453, (in set SR3–9017)
Philips 835357AY, A02487L, AL3571, SAL3571

TARTINI

Sonata in g "Il Trillo del Diavolo" vln & c – arr. vln & pf Kreisler
with C. Reiner pf
Camden Classics VCCS1037
Victor ERA50–153, LM2421, RB16240, SMR8002, VIC15, VIC1037, VICS1037

(50) Variations on a theme of Corelli solo vln
Variations 13, 41, 24, 45 & 50 arr. vln & pf Francescatti
with T. Janopoulo pf
Everest LPBR6154, SDBR3154
Odeon LDC7504, OD1008

Variations 13, 41, 24, 45 & 50 arr. vln & pf Francescatti
with C. Reiner pf
Victor LM2421, RB16240

TCHAIKOVSKY

Concerto in D, Op. 35 vln & orch.
with Boston Symphony Orch. – Munch
Camden Classics VCCS1037
Victor LM2363, LSC2363, RB16204, SB2080, SMR8002, VIC15, VIC1037, VICS1037

Concerto in D, Op. 35 vln & orch.
with London Symphony Orch. – Dorati
Mercury MG50451/2, (in set OL3–117), SR90451/2, (in set SR3–9017), SR90527
Philips AL3503, SAL3503

(6) Pieces, Op. 51 pf
No. 6. Valse sentimentale arr. vln & pf Grunes
with L. Schwarz pf
Orfeo 4002

No. 6. Valse sentimentale arr. vln & pf Grunes
with M. Berthelier pf
Pacific EP90018, LDPC50
Telefunken A11066

VALLE

Ao pé da fogueira (Prelude XV) pf – arr. vln & pf Heifetz
with M. Berthelier pf
Nixa BY4023
Pacific LDPC50

VITALI

Chaconne in g vln & c – arr. vln & pf Charlier
with T. Janopoulo pf
Everest LPBR6154, SDBR3154
Odeon LDC7504, OD1008

Chaconne in g vln & c – arr. vln & pf Charlier
with C. Reiner pf
Victor LM2421, RB16240

Chaconne in g vln & c – arr. vln & pf Charlier
with C. Reiner pf
Mercury 120559MGL, 130559MGY, MG50367, SR90367
Philips 838427AY, GL5862, PHC9092, SFL14116, SGL5862

VIVALDI

(12) Concerti, Op. 8 (1725) "Il Cimento dell' Armonia e dell' Invenzione"
(Nos. 1/4: Le quattro Stagioni) vln & strs
  Concerto No. 1, in E, F.I, No. 22 "La Primavera"
    with English Chamber Orch. – Szeryng Philips 6500 076, 6580 002,
          88444DY
  Concerto No. 2, in B flat, F.I, No. 23 "L'Estate"
    with English Chamber Orch. – Szeryng Philips 6500 076, 6580 002,
          88444DY
  Concerto No. 3, in F, F.I, No. 24 "L'Autunno"
    with English Chamber Orch. – Szeryng Philips 6500 076, 6580 002,
          88444DY
  Concerto No. 4, in f, F.I, No. 25 "L'Inverno"
    with English Chamber Orch. – Szeryng Philips 6500 076, 6580 002,
          88444DY

WIENIAWSKI

Scherzo–Tarantelle, Op. 16 vln & pf
  with R. Locatelli pf   Victor 11–8307
Scherzo–Tarantelle, Op. 16 vln & pf
  with M. Berthelier pf   Nixa BZ2201
                            Pacific EP90018, LDPC50
                            Telefunken E3887
Scherzo–Tarantelle, Op. 16 vln & pf
  with T. Janopoulo pf   Everest LPBR6154, SDBR3154
                            Odeon AOE1049, OD1008
Scherzo–Tarantelle, Op. 16 vln & pf
  with C. Reiner pf   Victor LM2361, LM2421,
                            RB16240

Dezsö SZIGETI (–1963)

HUBAY

(6) Poèmes hongroise, Op. 27 vln & pf
  No. 1. Poème hongrois No. 1, in d
    with piano   Pathé 10390
  No. 2. Poème hongrois No. 2, in D
    with piano   Pathé 10390

Joseph SZIGETI (1892–1973)

ARNOLD

Nocturne vln & pf
  with H. Bird pf   Ab 13028 e   HMV 3–7934, C114

BACH

(6) Brandenburg Concerti, BWV1046/51 (1721) strs & c
  Brandenburg Concerto No. 5, in D, BWV1050 clav, fl, vln, strs & c
    with E. Istomin pf, J. Wummer fl &   Columbia ML4346
    Prades Festival Orch. – Casals
Cantata No. 156 (Ich steh' mit einem Fuss im Grabe) BWV156 (1730)
  Sinfonia arr. vln & orch. as "Arioso" by Szigeti
    with orch. – Goehr   CAX 8133–2 Columbia 69274D, (in set X103),
                                   GQX11517, LX711
                                   HMV HQM1127
  Sinfonia arr. vln & orch. as "Arioso" by Szigeti
    with CBS Symphony Orch. – Barlow   Armed Forces transcription disc
                                  11590B

BACH – *Continued*

Concerto in d, BWV1043 2 vlns, strs & c
  with C. Flesch vln   CAX8060/3–1 Columbia 69109/10D, (set X90),
  & orch. – Goehr   C15705/6, (set J12),
                                  GOX10887/8, LOX360/1,
                                  LX659/60
                                  HMV HQM1127
Concerto No. 3, in d, BWV1052 clav, strs & c – res. vln & orch. as
  "Concerto in d" by Reitz – arr. Szigeti
    XCO 27207/8–1, 27209–2, 27210 Columbia 11379/81D, (set
         –1, 27211–2 & 27212–1 M148), C15436/8, (set D77),
  with New Friends of Chamber Music LOX536/8, ML4286
  Orch. – Stiedry
Concerto No. 3, in d, BWV1052 clav, strs & c – res. vln & orch. as
  "Concerto in d" by Reitz – arr. Szigeti
  with Prades Festival Orch. – Casals   Columbia CX1113, ML4352
Concerto No. 5, in f, BWV1056 clav, strs & c – res. vln & orch. as
  "Concerto in g" by Schreck
  with orch. – Szell   Columbia ML4891
                            Philips A01140L, ABL3058
(3) Sonatas & 3 Partitas, BWV1001/6 solo vln
  Sonata No. 1, in g, BWV1001
         WAX 5958–1 & 5959/61–2 Columbia 67989/90D, (set X1),
  (unaccompanied)   LX127/8, SW91/2, (set 89)
  Sonata No. 1, in g, BWV1001
  (unaccompanied)   Amadeo AVRS6320
                            Bach Guild BG627
                            King MH5041
  Partita No. 1, in b: Bourrée (7th mvt) BWV1002
  (unaccompanied)   A 5807 Columbia 155M, 2073M, D1633,
                            J5018
  Partita No. 1, in b: Bourrée (7th mvt) BWV1002
  (unaccompanied)   XCO 30107–1 Columbia 71186D, (in set X202),
                            C15797, (in set J70)
  Partita No. 1, in b, BWV1002
  (unaccompanied)   Amadeo AVRS6320
                              Bach Guild BG627
                            King MH5041
  Sonata No. 2, in a, BWV1003
        CAX 6855/6–1, 6857–2 & 6858– Columbia 68152/3D, 70396/7D,
  (unaccompanied)   1 (set X2), LX259/60
  Sonata No. 2, in a, BWV1003
  (unaccompanied)   Amadeo AVRS6321
                              Bach Guild BG628
                            King MH5042
  Partita No. 2, in d, BWV1004
  (unaccompanied)   Amadeo AVRS6321
                              Bach Guild BG628
                            King MH5042
  Sonata No. 3, in C, BWV1005
  (unaccompanied)   Columbia (set MM901), ML4286
  Sonata No. 3, in C, BWV1005
  (unaccompanied)   Amadeo AVRS6322
                              Bach Guild BG629
                            King MH5043
  Partita No. 3, in E: Preludio (1st mvt) BWV1006
  (unaccompanied)   2611 f HMV 07911, 047914

BACH – *Continued*

Partita No. 3, in E: Gavotte (3rd mvt) BWV1006
(unaccompanied)   Columbia*

Partita No. 3, in E, BWV1006
(unaccompanied)   Amadeo AVRS6322
                                      Bach Guild BG629
                                      King MH5043

BARTÓK

Contrasts (1938) cl, vln & pf
          WXCO 26819/21–1 & 26822–3   Columbia 70362/3D, (set X178),
with B. Goodman cl & B. Bartók pf   LOX485/6, ML2213, SW190/1
                                      Odyssey 32 16 0220
                                      Philips L01517L

For Children (40 pieces) (1909) pf
Nos. 6, 13, 18, 25, 31, 36 & 40 arr. vln & pf as "Hungarian folk tunes"
by Szigeti
          WAX 5322–3 & 5323–1   Columbia 50318D, 7247M, LX31
with B. Bartók pf

(2) Portraits, Op. 5 vln & orch.
No. 1.
          CAX 9568–1 & 9569–2   Columbia LOX815, LX1531,
with Philharmonia Orch. – Lambert   ML2213

Rhapsody No. 1, in G (1928) vln & orch.
with B. Bartók pf   Columbia 11410D, LOX519,
                                      ML2213

Rhapsody No. 1, in G (1928) vln & orch.
with B. Bartók pf   Amadeo AVRS5048
                                      Philips AL3524
                                      Qualiton LPX11374
                                      Vanguard SRV305, VRS1131

(6) Rumanian folk dances (1915) pf – arr. vln & pf Székely
          A 9908–3 & 9909–4   Columbia 2293D, 17089D, LB6
with B. Bartók pf

Sonata No. 2 (1922) vln & pf
with R. Bogas pf   Mercury†

Sonata No. 2 (1922) vln & pf
with B. Bartók pf   Amadeo AVRS5048
                                      Philips AL3525
                                      Qualiton LPX11374
                                      Vanguard SRV305, VRS1131

BEETHOVEN

Concerto in D, Op. 61 (cadenzas by Joachim) vln & orch.
          CAX 6388–3, 6389/90–2, 6391–   Columbia 68070/4D, (set M177),
          1, 6392/5–2, 6396–1 & 6397–2   LFX293/7, LOX157/61,
with British Symphony Orch. – Walter   LX174/8, W212/6, (set 49)
                                        HMV HQM1224

Concerto in D, Op. 61 (cadenzas by Joachim) vln & orch.
          XCO 37589/93–1, 37594–2,   Columbia 12631/5D, (set
with New York   37597–1 & 37598–2   MM697), C16077/81, (set D194),
Philharmonic Symphony Orch. –   LX1298/302, ML4012, Z1/5,
Walter   (set 69)
                                      Philips L01459L

* Untraced Japanese number.
† To be released.

BEETHOVEN – *Continued*

Concerto in D, Op. 61 (cadenzas by Busoni) vln & orch.
with London Symphony Orch. –   Fontana 894021ZKY
Dorati   Mercury MG50358, SR90358

(6) Minuets, G167 pf
No. 2. Minuet No. 2, in G arr. vln & pf Burmester
with K. Ruhrseitz pf   WA 3540   Columbia 155M, 2073M, D1527,
                                      J5004

(3) Sonatas, Op. 12 vln & pf
No. 1. Sonata No. 1, in D
          XCO 36343–2A & 36344/6–1A   Columbia 72794/5D, (set X312),
with M. Horszowski pf   LX1018/9, ML4133

No. 1. Sonata No. 1, in D
with C. Arrau pf   Vanguard SRV300, VRS1109

No. 2. Sonata No. 2, in A
with C. Arrau pf   Vanguard SRV300, VRS1109

No. 3. Sonata No. 3, in E flat
with C. Arrau pf   Vanguard SRV300, VRS1109

Sonata No. 4, in f, Op. 23 vln & pf
with C. Arrau pf   Vanguard SRV301, VRS1110

Sonata No. 5, in F, Op. 24 "Spring" vln & pf
with M. Horszowski pf   Columbia ML4870

Sonata No. 5, in F, Op. 24 "Spring" vln & pf
with C. Arrau pf   Vanguard SRV302, VRS1111

Sonata No. 5, in F, Op. 24 "Spring" vln & pf*
with A. Schnabel pf   MJA MJA19691

(3) Sonatas, Op. 30 vln & pf
No. 1. Sonata No. 6, in A
with M. Horszowski pf   Columbia ML4870

No. 1. Sonata No. 6, in A
with C. Arrau pf   Vanguard SRV301, VRS1110

No. 2. Sonata No. 7, in c
with M. Horszowski pf   Columbia (set MM888), ML2097

No. 2. Sonata No. 7, in c
with C. Arrau pf   Vanguard SRV303, VRS1112

No. 3. Sonata No. 8, in G: Allegro vivace (3rd mvt)
with K. Ruhrseitz pf   A 5802   Columbia 17037D, D1630, J5045

No. 3. Sonata No. 8, in G
with C. Arrau pf   Vanguard SRV301, VRS1110

Sonata No. 9, in A, Op. 47 "Kreutzer" vln & pf
Andante con variazioni (2nd mvt)
with H. Bird pf   Ac 4736 f   HMV 07948, D74

Sonata No. 9, in A, Op. 47 "Kreutzer" vln & pf
with C. Arrau pf   Vanguard SRV302, VRS1111

Sonata No. 9, in A, Op. 47 "Kreutzer" vln & pf
with B. Bartók pf   Amadeo AVRS5048
                                      Philips AL3524
                                      Qualiton LPX11373
                                      Vanguard SRV304, VRS1130

Sonata No. 10, in G, Op. 96 vln & pf
with M. Horszowski pf   Columbia ML4642

Sonata No. 10, in G, Op. 96 vln & pf
with C. Arrau pf   Vanguard SRV303, VRS1112

Sonata No. 10, in G, Op. 96 vln & pf*
with A. Schnabel pf   MJA MJA29691

* Recorded at a recital at the Frick Museum on April 4th 1948.

BERLIOZ

Rêverie & Caprice, Op. 8 (1839) vln & orch.

CAX 9678–2 & 9679–1	Columbia 72869D, LX946
with Philharmonia Orch. – Lambert	HMV HQM1224

BLOCH

Baal Shem (3 Pictures of Chassidic life) (1923) vln & pf
No. 2. Nigun (Improvisation)

with K. Ruhrseitz pf A 3537/8	Columbia 2047M, D1557

Baal Shem (3 Pictures of Chassidic life) (1923) vln & pf

with A. Farkas XCO 27411/3–1 pf*	Columbia 70743/4D, 71129/3D, (set X188), LOX501/2, ML2122, ML4679

Concerto in a (1938) vln & orch.

CLX 2134/5–1, 2143/4–1, 2145– 2, 2146/7–1 & 2148–2 with Paris Conservatory Orch. – Munch	Columbia 69675/8D, 70039/41D, (set M380), LOX455/8, LX819/22, LX8445/8, A1648, ML4679

BRAHMS

Concerto in D, Op. 77 (cadenza by Joachim) vln & orch.

WAX 4420–2, 4421/3–3, 4424/5 –2, 4426–1 & 4427/8–2 with Hallé Orch. – Harty	Columbia 67608/12D, (set M117), C15377/81, (set D65), DWX1293/7, J7446/50, L2265/9, (set 246)

Concerto in D, Op. 77 (cadenza by Joachim) vln & orch.

XCO 34296–2 34297/304–1 with Philhadelphia Orch. – Ormandy	Columbia 12281/5D, (set M603), C16116/20, (set D205), LX983/7S, ML4015, SW8/12, (set 56)

Concerto in D, Op. 77 (cadenza by Joachim) vln & orch.

with London Symphony Orch. – Menges	Mercury AMS16034, MG50225, MMA11085, SR90225

(21) Hungarian Dances pf duet
Hungarian dance No. 5, in f sharp arr. vln & pf "in g" Joachim

with A. Földes CO 31950–1	Columbia 17340D, (in set M513), C10125, (in set D122), A1887, LO62 Philips 409506NE

Quartet No. 3, in c, Op. 60 pf, vln, vla & vlc

with M. Hess pf, M. Katims vla & P. Tortelier vlc	Columbia ML4712, (in set SL182) Philips A01647R, ABR4063

Sonata No. 1, in G, Op. 78 vln & pf

with M. Horszowski pf	Columbia ML5266

Sonata No. 2, in A, Op. 100 vln & pf

with M. Horszowski pf	Mercury AMS16076, MG50210, MMA11129, SR90210

Sonata No. 3, in d, Op. 108 vln & pf
Adagio (2nd mvt)

with K. Ruhrseitz pf AX 2930–2	Columbia 67612D, (in set M117), C15377, (in set D65), DWX1297, J7450, L2269

Adagio (2nd mvt)

with L. Hambro pf XCO 35392–1	Columbia 12285D, (in set M603), 72628D, C16116, (in set D205), SW12, (in set 56)

* Pseudonym for Andor Földes.

BRAHMS – *Continued*

Sonata No. 3, in d, Op. 108 vln & pf

CAX 8134/5–1, 8136/7–2, 8138– with E. Petri pf 3 & 8139–2	Columbia 69155/7D, (set M324), 70248/50D, LWX233/5, LX699/701, LX8374/6 HMV HQM1127

Sonata No. 3, in d, Op. 108 vln & pf

with M. Horszowski pf	Columbia ML5266

Trio No. 2, in C, Op. 87 pf, vln & vlc

with M. Hess pf & P. Casals vlc	Columbia ML4720, (in set SL184) Philips L01294L

Trio in E flat, Op. 40 hrn, pf & vln

with J. Barrows hrn & M. Horszowski pf	Mercury AMS16076, MG50210, MMA11129, SR90210 Olypienne S49028

BUSONI

Concerto in D, Op. 35a vln & orch.

with Little Orch. Society – Scherman	Columbia ML5224

Sonata No. 2, in e, Op. 36a vln & pf

with M. Horszowski pf	Columbia ML5224

CHABRIER

(10) Pièces pittoresques (1880) pf
No. 10. Scherzo–valse arr. vln & pf Loeffler

with N. de Magaloff pf AX 6849–2	Columbia 266162, 68162D, (in set M190), 72627D, C20058, (in set D51)

CORELLI

(12) Sonatas, Op. 5 vln & c
Sonata No. 12, in d "La Follia" arr. vln & pf Léonard

XCO 27422–1, 27423–2 & 27424–1 with A. Farkas pf*	Columbia 71185/6D, (set X202), C15797/8, (set J70)

COWELL

How old is song? vln & pf

with H. Cowell pf XCO 35331–1	Columbia 13095D, (in set MM920)

Sonata No. 1 (1945) vln & pf

with C. Bussotti pf	Columbia ML4841

DEBUSSY

Petite Suite (1889) pf – 4 hands
No. 3. Menuet arr. vln & pf Dushkin

with K. Ruhrseitz pf	Columbia 2073M

No. 3. Menuet arr. vln & pf Dushkin

with K. Ruhrseitz pf AX 2912	Columbia 04076, 7152M, GQX10485, J7252, L2037

Sonata No. 3, in g (1917) vln & pf

XCO 31998/32000–3 with A. Földes pf	Columbia 71590/1D, 71592/3D, (set X242)

Sonata No. 3, in g (1917) vln & pf

with B. Bartók pf	Philips AL3525 Qualiton LPX11374 Vanguard SRV305, VRS1131

Sonata No. 3, in g (1917) vln & pf

with R. Bogas pf	Mercury MG50442, SR90442

* Pseudonym for Andor Földes.

DEBUSSY – *Continued*

Suite Bergamasque (1890) pf
No. 3. Clair de lune arr. vln & pf Roelens
with A. Földes pf   XCO 32001–3   Columbia 71591D, 71592D, (in
                                               set X242), 72629D

No. 3. Clair de lune arr. vln & pf Roelens
with H. Kaufman pf   Columbia ML4338

DVOŘÁK
(8) Slavonic Dances, Op. 46 pf duet; orch.
No. 2. Slavonic dance No. 2, in e arr. vln & pf "in g" Kreisler
with K. Ruhrseitz pf   WAX 2913   Columbia 04129, 7144M, J7291,
                                              L2097

No. 2. Slavonic dance No. 2, in e arr. vln & pf "in g" Kreisler
with A. Földes pf   CO 30105–1   Columbia 17338D, (in set M513),
                                               C10125, (in set D122), LO75
                                               Philips 409506NE

(8) Slavonic Dances, Op. 72 pf duet; orch.
No. 2. Slavonic dance No. 10, in e arr. vln & pf Kreisler
with L. Barabeitschik pf   Muspred*

No. 2. Slavonic dance No. 10, in e arr. vln & pf Kreisler
with K. Ruhrseitz pf   WAX 1773–8   Columbia 50144D, 7278M,
                                              J7049, L1963

No. 2. Slavonic dance No. 10, in e arr. vln & pf Kreisler
with A. Földes pf   CO 31951–1   Columbia 17338D, (in set M513),
                                               A1887, C10126, (in set D122),
                                               LO75
                                               Philips 409506NE

ELGAR
Adieu pf – arr. vln & pf Szigeti
with N. de Magaloff   CA 14361–2   Columbia 2150M, GQ7201,
pf   J5399, LB14, LW9

Serenade pf – arr. vln & pf Szigeti
with N. de Magaloff   CA 14362–1   Columbia 2150M, GQ7201,
pf   J5399, LB14, LW9

FALLA
(El) Sombrero de Tres Picos (1919) – ballet orch.
No. 2. Danza del Molinero arr. vln & pf Szigeti
with A. Farkas pf†   XCO 27425–1   Columbia 70744D, (in set X188)

HANDEL
(15) Sonatas, Op. 1 (?1731) fl or vln & c
Sonata No. 9, in b: Andante (1st mvt) arr. vln & pf as "Larghetto" by
Hubay
with H. Bird pf   z 6948 f   HMV 07984

Sonata No. 13, in D Major vln IV
with N. de   CA 16265/8–1   Columbia 17098/9D, LB36/7,
Magaloff pf   LO22/3

Sonata No. 13, in D vln IV
with C. Bussotti pf   Columbia ML4891
                                          Philips A01140L, ABL3058

HINDEMITH
Sonata No. 3, in E (1935) vln & pf
with C. Bussotti pf   Columbia ML5178

* Number untraced.
† Pseudonym for Andor Földes.

HONEGGER
Sonata No. 1, in c sharp (1916/8) vln & pf
with R. Bogas pf   Mercury MG50442, SR90442

HUBAY
(6) Blumenleben, Op. 30 vln & pf
No. 5. Der Zephir
with H. Bird pf   z 6949 f   HMV 07913, D266, M4426

No. 5. Der Zephir
with H. Bird pf   2676 f   HMV 037912, 057903, W284

No. 5. Der Zephir
with K. Ruhrseitz pf   AX 1789   Columbia 7131M, GQX10344,
                                            L1788

No. 5. Der Zephir
with H. Kaufman pf   XCO 33947–1   Columbia 72734D

Nocturne in a, Op. 42 vln & pf
with H. Bird pf   2679 f   HMV 07912, 07916, 047915,
                                            057906, M4428

(2) Pieces, Op. 38 vln & pf
No. 2. Unter ihrem Fenster – serenade
with H. Bird pf   4113 f   HMV 07946
                                            Rococo 2001

(14) Scènes de la Csárda vln & pf
No. 3. Maros vize, Op. 18
with A. Földes pf   CO 31947/8–1   Columbia 17349D, (in set M513),
                                              C10127, (in set D122), LO60

No. 3. Maros vize, Op. 18
with N. de Magaloff pf   Columbia*

No. 5. Hullámzó balaton, Op. 33
with H. Bird pf   2608 f   HMV 07910, 047913, 057905,
                                            M4428

IVES
Sonata No. 4 (1916) "Children's day at the camp meeting" vln & pf
with A. Földes pf   New Music Quarterly Recordings
                                      1612

Sonata No. 4 (1916) "Children's day at the camp meeting" vln & pf
with R. Bogas pf   Mercury MG50442, SR90442

KODÁLY
Háry János (1926) – opera
No. 10. Intermezzo orch. – arr. vln & pf Szigeti
with A. Földes pf   CO 31949/50–1   Columbia 17340D, (in set M513),
                                               C10125/6, (in set D122), A1887,
                                               LO62
                                               Philips 409506NE

KREISLER
Caprice viennois, Op. 3 vln & pf
with L. Barabeitschik pf   Muspred†

Liebesfreud vln & pf
with M. Pirani pf   Columbia‡

Liebesleid vln & pf
with M. Pirani pf   Columbia‡

* Japanese & Australian numbers untraced.
† Number untraced.
‡ British & Australian numbers untraced.

KREISLER – *Continued*

Liebesleid vln & pf
  with A. Földes pf   AX 3742–2   Columbia 50144D, 7278M

Tambourin chinois, Op. 3 vln & pf
  with K. Ruhrseitz pf   AX 2917   Columbia 04076, 7144M, 7152M,
                                          GQX10485, J7252, L2037

Sicilienne & Rigaudon (Francoeur) vln & pf
  with K. Ruhrseitz pf   AX 1788   Columbia 7131M, A1887, L1788
                                          Philips 409506NE

LALO

(Le) Roi D'ys (1888) – opera
  Vainement, ma bien aimée – Aubade arr. vln & pf Szigeti
  with A. Farkas pf *   CO 30103–1   Columbia 17311D, C10114,
                                          LO65

LÁSZLÓ

Ungarische Weisen, Op. 5 vln & pf
  with H. Bird pf   3123 f   HMV 07921, 067902, D266
                                          Rococo 2001

LIE

Snow v & pf – arr. vln & pf Szigeti
  with N. de Magaloff   CA 16269–1   Columbia 17130D, LB38
  pf

MENDELSSOHN

Concerto in e, Op. 64 vln & orch.
            CAX 6932/3–2, 6934–1, 6935–2   Columbia 266388/91,
  with London   & 6936/8–1   68159/62D, (set M190),
  Philharmonic Orch. – Beecham   C20058/61, (set D51),
                                          GOX10739/42, LFX348/51,
                                          LX262/5, ML2217, W55/8, (set
                                          16)

MILHAUD

(Le) Printemps (1921) vln & pf
  with K. Ruhrseitz pf   WAX 1929   Columbia 7278M, J7049, L1963

(12) Saudades do Brasil (1920/1) pf
  No. 7. Corcavado arr. vln & pf Lévy
  with K. Ruhrseitz pf   WA 3587   Columbia 2073M, D1527, J5004
  No. 8. Tijuca arr. vln & pf Lévy
  with K. Ruhrseitz pf   A 5792   Columbia D1633, J5018
  No. 9. Sumare arr. vln & pf Lévy
  with A. Farkas pf*   XCO 27425–1 Columbia 70744D, (in set X188),
                                          72627D, LOX502

MOZART

Concerto No. 4, in D, K218 (cadenzas by Joachim) vln & orch.
            CAX 7288–2, 7289/91–1 &   Columbia 264686/8, 68339/41D,
  with London Philharmonic 7292/3–2   70112/4D, (set M224),
  Orch. – Beecham   LFX390/2, LOX220/2,
                                      LX386/8, LX8166/8, ML4533,
                                      W191/3

Divertimento No. 15, in B flat, K287 2 hrns & strs
  with orch. – Goberman   Columbia 266362/5, 69144/7D,
                                      (set M322), 70241/4D, JW555/8

* Pseudonym for Andor Földes.

MOZART – *Continued*

Divertimento No. 17, in D, K334 2 hrns & strs
  Minuet (3rd mvt) arr. vln & pf Burmester
  with H. Bird pf   2677 f   HMV 07915, 037913, 047916,
                                          W284

Sonata No. 17, in C, K296 vln & pf
  with M Horszowski pf   Vanguard SRV263SD
Sonata No. 18, in G, K301 vln & pf
  with M. Horszowski pf   Vanguard SRV262SD
Sonata No. 19, in E flat, K302 vln & pf
  with M. Horszowski pf   Vanguard SRV262SD
Sonata No. 20, in C, K303 vln & pf
  with M. Horszowski pf   Vanguard SRV265 SD
Sonata No. 21, in e, K304 vln & pf
  with N. de   CAX 7953/4–1   Columbia 69005D, LFX479,
  Magaloff pf   LWX188, LX604
Sonata No. 21, in e, K304 vln & pf
  with M. Horszowski pf   Vanguard SRV263SD
Sonata No. 22, in A, K305 vln & pf
  with M. Horszowski pf   Vanguard SRV263SD
Sonata No. 23, in D, K306 vln & pf
  with M. Horszowski pf   Vanguard SRV262SD
Sonata No. 24, in F, K376 vln & pf
  with M. Horszowski pf   Vanguard SRV265SD
Sonata No. 25, in F, K377 vln & pf
  with M. Horszowski pf   Vanguard SRV264SD
Sonata No. 26, in B flat, K378 vln & pf
  with M. Horszowski pf   Vanguard SRV266SD
Sonata No. 27, in G, K379 vln & pf
  with M. Horszowski pf   Vanguard SRV265SD
Sonata No. 28, in E flat, K380 vln & pf
  with M. Horszowski pf   Vanguard SRV264SD
Sonata No. 32, in B flat, K454 vln & pf
  with G. Szell pf   Columbia ML5005
                                          Vanguard SRV267SD
Sonata No. 33, in E flat, K481 vln & pf
  with G. Szell pf   Columbia ML5005
                                          Vanguard SRV267SD
Sonata No. 34, in A, K526 vln & pf
  with M. Horszowski pf   Vanguard SRV266SD

MUSSORGSKY

Sorochintsy Fair (1911/23) – opera
  Gopak (Act III) orch. – arr. vln & pf Dushkin
  with A. Farkas pf*   CO 30104–2   Columbia 17311D, C10114,
                                          LO65

PAGANINI

(24) Caprices, Op. 1 (1801/7) solo vln
  Caprice No. 2, in g
  (unaccompanied)   CAX 7588–1   Columbia 68555D, GQX10973,
                                          LFX404, LOX256, LX435
  Caprice No. 9, in E
  (unaccompanied)   CAX 6939–1   Columbia 68555D, LFX349,
                                          LOX188, LX263, W55, (in set
                                          16)

* Pseudonym for Andor Földes.

PAGANINI – *Continued*

Caprice No. 24, in a arr. vln & pf
with L. Barabeitschik pf — Muspred*

Caprice No. 24, in a
(unaccompanied) — A 3968/9 — Columbia 2059M, D1581, J5020

Caprice No. 24, in a arr. vln & pf
with K. Ruhrseitz pf — WAX 3744/5 — Columbia 264638, GQX10557, L2207, W242

PROKOFIEV

Concerto No. 1, in D, Op. 19 vln & orch.
CAX 7583–2, 7584–3 & 7585/7–2
with London
Philharmonic Orch. – Beecham — Columbia 266160/2, 68402/4D, (set M244), C15837/9, (set D129), LFX402/4 LX433/5, ML4533

Concerto No. 1, in D, Op. 19 vln & orch.
with London Symphony Orch. –
Menges — Mercury MG50419, SR90419

(5) Melodies, Op. 35bis (1921) vln & pf
with C. Bussotti
pf — Columbia ML5178

Sonata in d, Op. 115 solo vln
(unaccompanied) — Columbia ML5178

Sonata No. 1, in f, Op. 80 vln & pf
with J. Levine pf — Columbia 72889/91D, (set MM975), ML4257, WL5005

Sonata No. 1, in f, Op. 80 vln & pf
with A. Balsam pf — Mercury MG50319, SR90319 Philips SM7545

Sonata No. 2, in D, Op. 94bis vln & pf
XCO 33939/41–3A, 33942/3–2C
with L. Hambro pf & 33944–2A — Columbia 71787/9D, 71790/2D, (set M620), LOX612/4, ML4257, WL5005

Sonata No. 2, in D, Op. 94bis vln & pf
with A. Balsam pf — Mercury MG50319, SR90319 Philips SM7545

Symphony No. 1, in D, Op. 25 "Classical" orch.
Gavotte (3rd mvt) arr. vln & pf Grunes
with N. de Magaloff — CA 16269–1 — Columbia 17130D, LB38 LO24
pf

RAVEL

Pièce en forme d'Habanera v & pf – arr. vln & pf Leduc
with N. de Magaloff — CAX 7749–1 — Columbia 68922D, LOX323, LX575
pf

Sonata (1927) vln & pf
with C. Bussotti pf — Columbia ML5178

RIMSKY–KORSAKOV

(The) Tale of Tsar Saltan (1900) – opera
Flight of the bumblebee (Act III) orch. – arr. vln & pf Hartmann
with N. de Magaloff — CAX 6852–1 — Columbia 7304M, LOX162, LWX252, LX307
pf

RUBINSTEIN

(6) Soirées de Saint–Pétersbourg, Op. 44 pf
No. 1. Romance in E flat arr. vln & pf Wilhelmj
with H. Bird pf — 2674 f — HMV 07914, 057904, M4426

* Number untraced.

SCHUBERT, François

(12) Bagatelles, Op. 13 vln & pf
No. 9. L'abeille
with H. Bird pf — 2677 f — HMV 07915, 037913, 047916, W284

No. 9. L'abeille
with H. Kaufman pf — XCO 33948–1 — Columbia 72734D

SCHUBERT, Franz

Fantasia in C, Op. 159 (D934) vln & pf
with J. Levine pf — Columbia (set MM952), ML4338

(7) Gesänge (set to Scott's "Lady of the Lake") Op. 52 v & pf
No. 6. Ave Maria D839 arr. vln & pf Wilhelmj
with H. Bird pf — z 5467 f — HMV 07955, 047934, M0143

Rondo brillante in b, Op. 70 (D895) vln & pf
with C. Bussotti pf — Columbia ML4642

Sonata No. 17, in D, Op. 53 (D850) pf
Rondo (4th mvt) arr. vln & pf Friedberg
with N. de Magaloff — CAX 6850–1 — Columbia 69062D, LOX359, LX630
pf

Rondo (4th mvt) arr. vln & pf Friedberg
with A. Földes pf — XCO 32002–3 — Columbia 71488D, 71489D, (in set X238), 72628D

Sonata in A, Op. 162 (D574) "Duo" vln & pf
with M. Hess pf — Columbia ML4717, (in set SL185) Philips S06624R

(3) Sonatinas, Op. 137 (D384, D385 & D408) vln & pf
No. 1. Sonatina No. 1, in D, D384
with A. Földes pf — XCO 32003/5–2 — Columbia 71487/8D, 71489/90D, (set X238), LOX579/80, ML4133

SCRIABIN

(12) Etudes, Op. 8 pf
No. 10. Etude No. 10, in D flat arr. vln & pf as "Study in Thirds" by Szigeti
with N. de Magaloff — CAX 7749–1 — Columbia 68922D, LOX323, LX575
pf

SIBELIUS

Kuolema, Op. 44 – Incidental music orch.
Valse triste arr. vln & pf Franko
with H. Bird pf — A1 6217 f — HMV 07971, D74

STRAVINSKY

Duo concertante (1932) vln & pf
with I. Stravinsky pf — Columbia (set MM922), ML2122)

Duo concertante (1932) vln & pf
with R. Bogas pf — Mercury MG50419, SR90419

Mavra (1922) – opera
Russian maiden's song (Parasha's aria) arr. vln & pf Dushkin & Stravinsky
with I. Stravinsky — XCO 36310–1 — Columbia 72495D, CX1100, FCX212, LX1174, MO4398 Regal SEBL7022
pf

Pastorale (1908) v & pf – arr. vln & wnd qnt Dushkin & Stravinsky
with M. Miller ob, — XCO 35830–1 — Columbia 72495D, LX1174, R. McGinnis cl, B. Gassman ob, S. — ML2122
Schoenbach bsn, cond. Stravinsky

STRAVINSKY – *Continued*

Pastorale (1908) v & pf – arr. vln & pf Szigeti
  with N. de Magaloff   CAX 6852–1   Columbia 7304M, LOX162,
  pf   LX307
Pastorale (1908) v & pf – arr. vln & pf Dushkin & Stravinsky
  with H. Kaufman pf   XCO 33948–1   Columbia 72734D
Pétrouchka (1911) – ballet orch.
  Danse russe arr. vln & pf Dushkin & Stravinsky
  with N. de Magaloff   CA 16270–2   Columbia 17130D, LB38, LO24
  pf

SZYMANOWSKI

(3) Mythes, Op. 30 (1915) vln & pf
  No. 1. La Fontaine d'Aréthuse
  with N. de   CAX 6851/2–1   Columbia 266014, 7304M,
  Magaloff pf   LX630

TARTINI

Concerto in A vln & orch.
  Adagio (2nd mvt) arr. vln & pf Ondříček
  with N. de Magaloff   CAX 7750–1   Columbia 69062D, LOX359,
  pf   LX630
Concerto in d, D45 (C61) (cadenza by Szigeti) vln & orch.
            CAX 8130/1–1 & 8132–2   Columbia 69273/4D, (set X103),
  with string orch. & harpsichord   GQX11516/7, LWX261/2,
                                     LX710/11
                                     HMV HQM1127
Concerto in d, D45 (C61) (cadenza by Szigeti) vln & orch.
  with Columbia Symphony Orch. –   Columbia ML4891
  Szell   Philips A01140L, ABL3058
(12) Sonatas, Op. 2 vln & c
Sonata No. 12, in G
  with K. Ruhrseitz pf   A 5789/91   Columbia 17036/7D, D1629/30,
                                       GQ7206/7, J5044/5
Sonata No. 12, in G
  with C. Bussotti pf   Columbia ML4891
                                     Philips A01140L, ABL3058

TCHAIKOVSKY

(6) Pieces, Op. 51 pf
  No. 6. Valse sentimentale arr. vln & pf Grunes
  with H. Kaufman pf   XCO 33948–1   Columbia 72734D

VERACINI

(12) Sonatas, Op. 2 (1744) "Sonate accademiche" vln & c
Sonata No. 6, in A: Largo (2nd mvt) arr. vln & pf Corti
  with K. Ruhrseitz pf   WAX 2923   Columbia 04129, J7291, L2097

WARLOCK

Capriol Suite (1926) str orch.
  Basse danse; Pavane; Mattachins arr. vln & pf Szigeti
  with N. de   CA 15651/2–1   Columbia 17074D, LB32, LO44
  Magaloff pf

WEBER

(6) Sonatas, Op. 10 (J99/104) (1810) vln & pf
Sonata No. 3, in D, J101 "Thème russe & Rondo" arr. vln & pf Szigeti
  with N. de Magaloff   CAX 7748–1   Columbia 68922D, LOX323,
  pf   LX575

WEBERN

(4) Pieces, Op. 7 (1910) vln & pf
  with R. Bogas pf   Mercury MG50442, SR90442

Lajos SZIKRA (1899–)

d'AMBROSIO

Canzonetta, Op. 6 vln & pf
  with M. Raucheisen pf   Odeon 0–25431

BRAHMS

(16) Waltzes, Op. 39 pf duet
  No. 15. Waltz No. 15, in A flat arr. vln & pf "in A" Szikra
  with M. Raucheisen pf   Odeon 0–25431

CUI

Kaleidoscope, Op. 50 vln & pf
  No. 9. Orientale
  with M. Raucheisen pf   Odeon 0–25934

GOSSEC

Rosina (1786) – opera
  Gavotte arr. vln & pf Burmester
  with M. Raucheisen pf   Be 10955   Odeon 0–25448

HUBAY

(6) Poèmes hongroise, Op. 27 vln & pf
  No. 6. Poème hongrois No. 6, in B flat
  with M. Raucheisen pf   Be 10954–0   Odeon 0–25448
(14) Scènes de la Csárda vln & pf
  No. 4. Hejre Kati, Op. 32
  with M. Raucheisen pf   Be 10955   Odeon 0–25448

SCHUBERT, François

(12) Bagatelles, Op. 13 vln & pf
  No. 9. L'abeille
  with M. Raucheisen pf   Decca 20451
                                   Odeon 0–25400

SCHUBERT, Franz

(16) Deutsche Tänze, Op. 33 (D783) pf
  No. 6. Deutscher Tanz No. 6, in B flat arr. vln & pf
  with M. Raucheisen pf   Decca 20451
                                   Odeon 0–25400
(17) Ländler, Op. 18 (D145) (1815) pf
  No. 2. Ländler No. 2, in E flat arr. vln & pf as "Reigen" by Burmester
  with M. Raucheisen pf   Decca 20451
                                   Odeon 0–25400

TCHAIKOVSKY

Romance in f, Op. 5 pf – arr. vln & pf
  with M. Raucheisen pf   Be 11548   Decca 20287
                                       Odeon 0–25868, 0–26230

WEBER

(6) Sonatas, Op. 10 (J99/104) (1810) vln & pf
  Sonata No. 1, in F: Romanze (2nd mvt) J99
  with M. Raucheisen pf   Odeon 0–25934, 0–26230

WIENIAWSKI

Mazurka in a, Op. 3 "Kujawiak" vln & pf
  with M. Raucheisen pf   Be 11549   Decca 20287
                                      Odeon 0–25868

ZSOLT

Dragonflies vln & pf
  with M. Raucheisen pf   Decca 20451
                                      Odeon 0–25400

Mihály SZÜCS

BARTÓK

Contrasts (1938) cl, vln & pf
  with B. Kovács cl & E. Tusa pf   Qualiton LPX1280, SLPX1280

(44) Duos (1931) 2 vlns
  with W. Wilkomirska vln   Qualiton LPX11320

(2) Portraits, Op. 5 vln & orch.
  No. 1.
  with Budapest Philharmonic Orch. –   Qualiton LPX1302, SLPX1302
  Erdélyi

DURKÓ

Organismi vln & orch.
  with Hungarian Radio & TV Orch. – Qualiton LPX1298, SLPX1298
  Lehel

Bronislav SZULC (1881–1955)

SVENDSEN

Romance in G, Op. 26 vln & orch. – arr. vln & pf Wilhelmj
  with piano   Syrena 6789

Max TAK

BENATZKY

(Ein) Wiener Walzer orch. – arr. vln & pf
  with piano   Odeon 58047

TOSELLI

Serenade, Op. 6 vln & pf
  with piano   Odeon 57667

Glauco TALASSI

GEMINIANI

(6) Concerti grossi, Op. 7 (1746) orch.
  Concerto grosso No. 1, in D
  with P. Toso vln, C. Lardé fl, C.H.   Erato STU70546
  Scimone fl, S. Penazzi bsn & I Solisti
  Veneti – Scimone
  Concerto grosso No. 2, in d
  with P. Toso vln, C. Lardé fl, C.H.   Erato STU70546
  Scimone fl, S. Penazzi bsn & I Solisti
  Veneti – Scimone
  Concerto grosso No. 3, in C
  with P. Toso vln, C. Lardé fl, C.H.   Erato STU70546
  Scimone fl, S. Penazzi bsn & I Solisti
  Veneti – Scimone

  Concerto grosso No. 4, in d
  with P. Toso vln, C. Lardé fl, C.H.   Erato STU70546
  Scimone fl, S. Penazzi bsn & I Solisti
  Veneti – Scimone
  Concerto grosso No. 5, in c
  with P. Toso vln, C. Lardé fl, C.H.   Erato STU70546
  Scimone fl, S. Penazzi bsn & I Solisti
  Veneti – Scimone
  Concerto grosso No. 6, in B flat
  with P. Toso vln, C. Lardé fl, C.H.   Erato STU70546
  Scimone fl, S. Penazzi bsn & I Solisti
  Veneti – Scimone

Franco TAMPONI

VIVALDI

Concerto in F, P.278 (F.I, No. 34) 3 vlns, strs & c
  with F. Ayo vln, W. Gallozzi vln & I   Angel 35088
  Musici   Columbia CX1163, FCX305,
                                       QCX10039
                                       HMV LALP209

Concerto in F, P.278 (F.I, No. 34) 3 vlns, strs & c
  with F. Ayo vln, A.M. Cotogni vln &   Philips 835211AY, A02333L
  I Musici

Sergei TANENBAUM

BOUVARD

(12) Sonatas – Book I (1723) vln & c
  Sonata No. 8, in F
  with M. Charbonnier   AS 339/40–1   L'Anthologie Sonore 155
  hpsi

PAGIN

(6) Sonatas, Op. 1 (1748) vln & c
  Sonata No. 1, in D
  with M. Charbonnier   AS 341/2–1   L'Anthologie Sonore 150
  hpsi

Gerald TARACK

BRITTEN

Suite, Op. 6 (1935) vln & pf
  with T. Grubb pf   Lyrichord LL195, LLST7195

HINDEMITH

(2) Sonatas, Op. 31 (1924) solo vln
  Sonata No. 1
  (unaccompanied)   Nonesuch H1149, H71149

VIVALDI

Concerto in C, P.84 (F.XII, No. 14) "Per la Solennità di St. Lorenzo" 2 fls,
2 obs, 2 cls, 2 vlns, bsn, strs & c
  with Provincetown Symphony Orch. – Listening 6601
  Hawthorne

Blanche TARJUS (1932–)

MOZART

Serenade No. 7, in D, K250 "Haffner" orch.
  Rondo (4th mvt) arr. vln & pf Kreisler
  with M. Monard   OLA 4659/60–1   HMV DA5003
  pf

RAMEAU

(5) Suites hpsi
  Suite No. 2, in e: Le Rappal des oiseaux (4th mvt) arr. vln & pf Ysaÿe
  with M. Monard pf   HMV DA5011
  Suite No. 5, in G: Menuets I & II (4th mvt) arr. vln & pf Ysaÿe*
  with M. Monard pf   HMV DA5011

WIENIAWSKI

Capriccio–valse, Op. 7 vln & pf
  with M. Monard pf   OLA 4661/2–1   HMV DA5006

Carl TASCHKE

BÉRIOT

Scène de Ballet (Fantaisie–ballet No. 1) Op. 100 vln & orch.
  with Leipzig Philharmonic Orch. –   Urania URLP7166
  Kegel

Gerhard TASCHNER (1922–)

BACH

(3) Sonatas & 3 Partitas, BWV1001/6 solo vln
  Partita No. 2, in d: Chaconne (5th mvt) BWV1004
  (unaccompanied)   Odeon 0–8764/5

BEETHOVEN

Concerto in D, Op. 61 vln & orch.
  with Berlin Radio Symphony Orch. –   Regent LP5029, MG6063
  Rother

CHAMINADE

Sérénade espagnole pf – arr. vln & pf Kreisler
  with H. Giesen pf   Odeon 0–4673, OLA1006

FALLA

(La) Vida Breve (1913) – opera
  Danza española orch. – arr. vln & pf Kreisler
  with H. Giesen pf   Odeon 0–9184, OLA1006

FRANCK

Sonata in A (1886) vln & pf
        1 XXB 9124/9, 9130² & 9131⁴   Odeon 0–8793/6
  with C. de Groot pf

HANDEL

(15) Sonatas, Op. 1 (?1731) fl or vln & c
  Sonata No. 13, in D vln IV
  with C. de Groot pf   Odeon 50545/6

* Menuet No. 1 only.

KREISLER

Caprice viennois, Op. 2 vln & pf
  with H. Giesen pf   Odeon 0–9184, OLA1006
Praeludium & Allegro (Pugnani) vln & pf
  with H. Giesen pf   Odeon 0–9183, OLA1006
Variations on a theme of Corelli (Tartini) vln & pf
  with H. Giesen pf   Odeon 0–9183, OLA1006

MUSSORGSKY

Sorochintsy Fair (1911/23) – opera
  Gopak (Act III) orch. – arr. vln & pf Dushkin
  with H. Giesen pf   Odeon 0–4673, OLA1006

PAGANINI

(6) Sonatas, Op. 3 (1801/6) vln & gtr
  No. 6. Sonata No. 12, in e
  with G. Nette–Rothe   XXB 8919⁴   Odeon 0–8766
  pf

SARASATE

(8) Danzas españolas vln & pf
  No. 3. Romanza andaluza, Op. 22, No. 1
  with G. Nette–Rothe   XXB 8918²   Odeon 0–8766
  pf

Vilmós TÁTRAI (1912–)

BARTÓK

(2) Portraits, Op. 5 vln & orch.
  with Hungarian State Concert Orch. –   Qualiton LP1583
  Lehel

FARKAS

Fruit basket (10 songs) v, vln, vlc & cl
  with J. Sándor s, E. Banda vlc & F.   Qualiton EP3516
  Meizl cl

KODÁLY

Duo, Op. 7 (1914) vln & vlc
  with E. Banda vlc   Qualiton LPX1149
Serenade, Op. 12 (1919/20) 2 vlns & vla
  with I. Várkonyi vln & G. Konrad vla   Qualiton LPX11449

Arve TELLEFSEN (1936–)

ANONYMOUS

Sag du Nokke, Kjaeringa mi Norwegian folksong – arr. vln & pf Holger
  with R. Levin pf   Philips 839236NY

BULL

Säterjëntens søndag v & pf – arr. vln & pf Svendsen
  with R. Levin pf   Philips 839236NY

GRIEG

Sonata No. 2, in G, Op. 13 vln & pf
  with R. Levin pf   Philips 839240AY
Sonata No. 3, in c, Op. 45 vln & pf
  with R. Levin pf   Philips 839240AY

HALVORSEN

Air norvégien, Op. 31 vln & pf
with R. Levin pf   Philips 839236NY

(3) Danses norvégiennes (1914) vln & pf
No. 1. Danse norvégienne No. 1, in D
with R. Levin pf   Philips 839236NY
No. 2. Danse norvégienne No. 2, in A
with R. Levin pf   Philips 839236NY
No. 3. Danse norvégienne No. 3, in d
with R. Levin pf   Philips 839236NY

(4) Mosaïques (Suite des morceaux caractéristiques) vln & pf
No. 3. Scherzino
with R. Levin pf   Philips 839236NY
No. 4. Chant de Veslemøy
with R. Levin pf   Philips 839236NY

JENSEN

Bols vise vln & pf
with R. Levin pf   Philips 839236NY

LIE

(2) Norwegian Dances vln & pf
No. 1. Norsk dans No. 1, in G (Allegretto grazioso)
with R. Levin pf   Philips 839236NY
No. 2. Norsk dans No. 2, in A (Allegro con fuoco)
with R. Levin pf   Philips 839236NY

SINDING

(3) Pieces, Op. 89 vln & pf
No. 3. Abendlied
with R. Levin pf   Philips 839236NY
(2) Romances, Op. 79 vln & pf
No. 1. Romance No. 1
with R. Levin pf   Philips 839236NY

SVENDSEN

Romance in G, Op. 26 vln & orch. – arr. vln & pf Wilhelmj
with R. Levin pf   Philips 839236NY

VIVALDI

(12) Sonatas, Op. 1 2 vlns & c
Sonata No. 12, in d, F.XIII, No. 28 "La Follia"
with J. Thomsen vln, J.E. Hansen hpsi Bach Guild BG584
& B. Anker vlc

Emil TELMÁNYI (1892–   )

ALBÉNIZ

España (6 Feuilles d'album) Op. 165 pf
No. 2. Tango in D arr. vln & pf Kreisler
with A. Telmányi pf   2052   Tono K8010

BACH

(3) Sonatas & 3 Partitas, BWV1001/6 solo vln
Sonata No. 1, in g: Adagio (1st mvt) BWV1001 arr. vln & pf
with P. Kiss pf   Clangor M9323
Sonata No. 1, in g, BWV1001
(unaccompanied)   Decca LXT2951
                                     London LL1021, (in set LLA20)

BACH – *Continued*

Partita No. 1, in b, BWV1002
(unaccompanied)   Decca LXT2951
                                     London LL1021, (in set LLA20)

Sonata No. 2, in a, BWV1003
(unaccompanied)   Decca LXT2952
                                     London LL1022, (in set LLA20)

Partita No. 2, in d, BWV1004
(unaccompanied)   3729/34 Tono A170/3, LPA34002
Partita No. 2, in d, BWV1004
(unaccompanied)   Decca LXT2952
                                     London LL1022, (in set LLA20)
                                     Telefunken AWD8901

Sonata No. 3, in C, BWV1005
(unaccompanied)   Decca LXT2953
                                     London LL1023, (in set LLA20)

Partita No. 3, in E: Preludio (1st mvt); **Gavotte** (3rd mvt) BWV1006
(unaccompanied)   2066/7 Tono K8015
Partita No. 3, in E, BWV1006
(unaccompanied)   Decca LXT2953
                                     London LL1023, (in set LLA20)

(4) Suites, BWV1066/9 strs & c
Suite No. 3, in D: Air (2nd mvt) BWV1068 2 obs, 3 tpts, drms, strs & c
– arr. vln & pf as "Air on the G–string" by Wilhelmj
with A. Telmányi pf   1671   Tono A108

BEETHOVEN

(6) Minuets, G167 pf
No. 2. Minuet No. 2, in G arr. vln & pf Burmester
with A. Telmányi pf   3245   Tono K8053
Romance No. 1, in G, Op. 40 vln & orch.
with Danish State Radio   3313/4 Mercury MG15044
Orch. – Garaguly   Tono X25123
Romance No. 2, in F, Op. 50 vln & orch.
with Tivoli Orch. – Jensen   1673/4 Classic C2146
                                     Mercury MG15044
                                     Sonora K9510
                                     Tono X25004

Sonata No. 9, in A, Op. 47 "Kreutzer" vln & pf
with V. Schiøler pf   1669/76 Tono X25011/4

BRAHMS

(21) Hungarian Dances pf duet
Hungarian dance No. 1, in g arr. vln & pf Telmányi
with G. von   2RA 1041[1]☐   HMV DB2798
Vasarhelyi pf
Hungarian dance No. 5, in f sharp arr. vln & pf "in g" Joachim
with A. Telmányi pf   1506   Sonora K9506
                                     Tono A106

Sonata No. 1, in G, Op. 78 vln & pf
with G. von   2RA 3530/5   HMV DB4633/5
Vasarhelyi pf
Sonata No. 2, in A, Op. 100 vln & pf
                      2RA 3548[1]☐, 3549[II]☐ & HMV DB4640/1
with G. von   3550/1[1]☐
Vasarhelyi pf
Sonata (1853) "Frei aber Einsam" vln & pf
Allegro (Scherzo) in c (3rd mvt) "Sonatensatz"
with G. von   ORA 3891/2   HMV DA4464
Vasarhelyi pf

BRAHMS – *Continued*

(16) Waltzes, Op. 39 pf duet
  No. 15. Waltz No. 15, in A flat arr. vln & pf "in A" Hochstein
  with A. Telmányi pf   1506   Sonora K9506
                                      Tono A107

CHOPIN

(24) Preludes, Op. 28 pf
  No. 17. Prelude No. 17, in A flat arr. vln & pf Telmányi
  with P. Kiss pf   Clangor M9326

CIABRANO

(La) Caccia "The hunt" vln & pf
  with G. Moore pf   OEA 1350ᵛ☐   HMV DA1452

DINICU

Hora staccato vln & pf – arr. Heifetz
  with A. Telmányi pf   3243   Tono K8052

DOHNÁNYI

Ruralia Hungarica, Op. 32A pf
  No. 6. Adagio arr. vln & pf as "Gypsy Andante" by Kreisler
  with A. Telmányi pf   2050/1 Tono K8009

DVOŘÁK

(8) Humoresques, Op. 101
  No. 7. Humoresque No. 7, in G flat arr. vln & pf "in G" Kreisler
  with A. Telmányi pf   3240   Tono A136

ELGAR

(La) Capricieuse, Op. 17 vln & pf
  with A. Telmányi pf   3247   Tono A137

FALLA

(El) Amor Brujo (1915) – ballet m–s & orch.
  No. 14. Pantomime arr. vln & pf Kochański
  with A. Telmányi pf   1532   Tono A102

HANDEL

(15) Sonatas, Op. 1 (?1731) fl or vln & c
  Sonata No. 9, in b: Andante (1st mvt) arr. vln & pf as "Larghetto" by Hubay
  with A. Telmányi pf   1672   Tono A108
  Sonata No. 13, in D vln IV
  with A. Telmányi pf   2889/92 Tono A126/7

HUBAY

(?) Blumenleben, Op. 30 vln & pf
  No. 5. Der Zephir
  with A. Telmányi pf   Qualiton LP3527
(Le) Luthier de Crémone, Op. 40 (1894) – opera
  Intermezzo orch. – arr. vln & pf Hubay
  with A. Telmányi pf   Qualiton LP3527
(?) Poèmes hongroise, Op. 27 vln & pf
  No. 6. Poème hongrois No. 6, in B flat
  with A. Telmányi pf   Qualiton LP3527
(4) Scènes de la Csárda vln & pf
  No. 2. Scène de la Csárda, Op. 13
  with Budapest Municipal Orch. –   Radiola SP8028
  Fricsay
  No. 2. Scène de la Csárda, Op. 13
  with A. Telmányi pf   Qualiton LP3527

HUBAY – *Continued*

  No. 4. Hejre Kati, Op. 32
  with Telmányi Chamber   3042/3 Tono L28014
  Orch. – Jensen
  No. 4. Hejre Kati, Op. 32
  with A. Telmányi pf   Qualiton LP3527

KREISLER

Caprice viennois, Op. 2 vln & pf
  with A. Telmányi pf   1670   Sonora K9506
                                      Tono A107
(La) Gitana vln & pf
  with A. Telmányi pf   1533   Tono A102
Liebesfreud vln & pf
  with A. Telmányi pf   3241   Radiola RZ3043
                                      Tono A135
Liebesleid vln & pf
  with A. Telmányi pf   3246   Radiola RZ3043
                                      Tono K8053
Rondino on a theme by Beethoven vln & pf
  with A. Telmányi pf   1665   Tono K8003
Schön Rosmarin vln & pf
  with A. Telmányi pf   1668   Tono K8002
Chanson Louis XIII & Pavane (L. Couperin) vln & pf
  with A. Telmányi pf   3248   Tono A136

LECLAIR

(12) Sonatas, Op. 9 – Book IV (1738) vln & c
  Sonata No. 3, in D: Sarabande (1st mvt); **Tambourin** (3rd mvt) arr. vln & pf Sarasate
  with A. Telmányi pf   2895/6 Tono K8039

MASSENET

Thaïs (1894) – opera
  Méditation arr. vln & pf Marsick
  with A. Telmányi pf   3239   Tono A135

MENDELSSOHN

Concerto in e, Op. 64 vln & orch.
  with Telmányi Chamber   2883/8 Tono X25065/7
  Orch. – Jensen
(6) Songs without words, Op. 62 pf
  No. 1. Song without words No. 25, in G "May breezes" arr. vln & pf Telmányi
  with A. Telmányi pf   1666   Tono K8003

MOZART

Serenade No. 7, in D, K250 "Haffner" orch.
  Minuet (3rd mvt)
  with Copenhagen Royal   3025   Sonora K9533
  Opera Orch. – Tango   Tono X25085

NIELSEN

Concerto in D, Op. 33 (1911) vln & orch.
  with Copenhagen Royal   3016/24 Sonora K9529/33
  Opera Orch. – Tango   Tono X25081/5
(2) Fantasy pieces, Op. 2 (1889) ob & pf
  No. 1. Romance arr. vln & pf Telmányi
  with G. Moore pf   2EA 1347ᴵᴵ☐   HMV DB2503
                                      Victor 8829

NIELSEN – *Continued*

Sonata No. 1, in A, Op. 9 vln & pf
    2RA 800/1–2, 802/3³□, 804–2 HMV DB2732/4
with C. Christiansen pf   & 805–1

Sonata No. 1, in A, Op. 9 vln & pf
with V. Schiøler pf   HMV KALP6
                Odeon MOAK30003

Sonata No. 2, in g, Op. 35 vln & pf
with V. Schiøler pf   HMV KALP6
                Odeon MOAK30003

PAGANINI

(24) Caprices, Op. 1 (1801/7) solo vln
Caprice No. 9, in E
(unaccompanied)   Clangor M9325

PORPORA

Aria in E unid – arr. vln & pf Corti
with A. Telmányi pf   Tono K8040

RAFF

(6) Pieces, Op. 85 vln & pf
No. 3. Cavatina in D
with A. Telmányi pf   3242 Tono A137

RIMSKY–KORSAKOV

Sadko (1898) – opera
Chant hindou arr. vln & pf Kreisler
with A. Telmányi pf   3243 Tono K8052

SAINT-SAËNS

(Le) Carnaval des animaux (1886) small orch.
Le cygne arr. vln & pf
with A. Telmányi pf   2053 Tono K8010
Havanaise, Op. 83 vln & orch.
with Danish Radio Orch. – 3315/6 Classic C2152
  Garaguly   Mercury MG15044
                        Tono X25124
Introduction & Rondo Capriccioso, Op. 28 vln & orch.
with Copenhagen Royal   3030/1 Mercury MG15044
Opera Orch. – Jensen   Tono X25086

SARASATE

Zigeunerweisen, Op. 20 vln & pf or orch.
         1675 B & 1676 C Sonora K9509
with Tivoli Concert Orch. – Jensen Tono X25005

SCHUMANN

(13) Kinderscenen, Op. 15 pf
No. 7. Träumerei arr. vln & pf
with A. Telmányi pf   1667 Tono K8002

SIBELIUS

Concerto in d, Op. 47 vln & orch.
with Danish State Radio   4239/46 Mercury MG10131
Orch. – Jensen   Nera & Musica KE17518/21
                      Tono LPX35002, Y30003/6

(5) Danses champêtres, Op. 106 vln & pf
No. 1. Danse champêtre No. 1, in d
with G. von Vasarhelyi 2RA 1042¹ HMV DB2798, DB2893
pf

SIBELIUS – *Continued*

No. 2. Danse champêtre No. 2, in G
with G. Moore pf   2EA 1348ᴵᴵᴵ HMV DB2503, DB2893
                            Victor 8829

(4) Pieces, Op. 78 vln & pf
No. 2. Romance in F
with G. Moore pf   2EA 1348ᴵᴵᴵ HMV DB2503, DB2893
                            Victor 8829

TARTINI

(12) Sonatas, Op. 2 vln & c
Sonata No. 12, in G: Adagio arr. Corti
with A. Telmányi pf   2897/8 Tono K8040

VERACINI

(12) Sonatas, Op. 2 (1744) "Sonate accademiche" vln & c
Sonata No. 6, in A: Largo (2nd mvt) arr. vln & pf Corti
with G. Moore pf   OEA 1349ᴵᴵᴵ HMV DA1452

VIVALDI

(12) Concerti, Op. 3 "L'Estro armonico" var. cbns & strs
Concerto No. 11, in d, P.250 (F.IV, No. 11) 2 vlns, vlc, strs & c
with S. Forchhammer   2561/4 D Tono L28000/1
vln, J. Friisholm vlc & Telmányi
Chamber Orch. – Telmányi

Henri TEMIANKA (1906–)

ARENSKY

Trio No. 1, in d, Op. 32 pf, vln & vlc
        XE 9392/3–2 & 9396/9–2 Parlophone A4520/2, E11386/8
with E. Joyce pf & A. Sala vlc

BACH

(6) Sonatas, BWV1014/9 vln & clav
Sonata No. 4, in C: Siciliano BWV1017
with piano   XE 8402–2 Odeon O–7858
                          Parlophone A4549, E11445

BRIDGE

Cradle song in F (1911) vln & pf
with piano   XE 8403–1 Parlophone A4549, E11445
Moto perpetuo (1911) vln & pf
with piano   XE 8403–1 Parlophone A4549, E11445

DVOŘÁK

(4) Romantic pieces, Op. 75 vln & pf
with G. Robbins pf   Orion ORS7020
Sonata in F, Op. 57 vln & pf
with G. Robbins pf   Orion ORS7020
Sonatina in G, Op. 100 vln & pf
with G. Robbins pf   Orion ORS7020

HANDEL

(15) Sonatas, Op. 1 (?1731) fl or vln & c
Sonata No. 1, in e
with M. Hamilton hpsi   Everest (in sets LPBR6143 &
                           SDBR3143)

Sonata No. 2, in g
with M. Hamilton hpsi   Everest (in sets LPBR6143 &
                           SDBR3143)

HANDEL – *Continued*

Sonata No. 3, in A vln I
with M. Hamilton hpsi
Everest (in sets LPBR6143 &
SDBR3143)

Sonata No. 4, in a
with M. Hamilton hpsi
Everest (in sets LPBR6143 &
SDBR3143)

Sonata No. 5, in G
with M. Hamilton hpsi
Everest (in sets LPBR6143 &
SDBR3143)

Sonata No. 6, in g
with M. Hamilton hpsi
Everest (in sets LPBR6143 &
SDBR3143)

Sonata No. 7, in C
with M. Hamilton hpsi
Everest (in sets LPBR6143 &
SDBR3143)

Sonata No. 8, in c
with M. Hamilton hpsi
Everest (in sets LPBR6143 &
SDBR3143)

Sonata No. 9, in b: Andante (1st mvt) arr. vln & pf as "Larghetto" by
Hubay
with piano   XE 7982–2   Decca 25704
Odeon 0–7858
Parlophone E11312

Sonata No. 9, in b
with M. Hamilton hpsi
Everest (in sets LPBR6143 &
SDBR3143)

Sonata No. 10, in g vln II
with M. Hamilton hpsi
Everest (in sets LPBR6143 &
SDBR3143)

Sonata No. 11, in F
with M. Hamilton hpsi
Everest (in sets LPBR6143 &
SDBR3143)

Sonata No. 12, in F vln III
with M. Hamilton hpsi
Everest (in sets LPBR6143 &
SDBR3143)

Sonata No. 13, in D vln IV
with M. Hamilton hpsi
Everest (in sets LPBR6143 &
SDBR3143)

Sonata No. 14, in A vln V
with M. Hamilton hpsi
Everest (in sets LPBR6143 &
SDBR3143)

Sonata No. 15, in E vln VI
with M. Hamilton hpsi
Everest (in sets LPBR6143 &
SDBR3143)

PUGNANI

(6) Sonatas, Op. 6 vln & c
Sonata No. 1, in E arr. vln & pf Alard
with piano   XE 8263/4–3   Odeon 0–7868
Parlophone E11341

SAINT-SAËNS

Introduction & Rondo Capriccioso, Op. 28 vln & orch. – arr. vln & pf Bizet
with piano   XE 7275/6–1   Decca 25831
Odeon NLX20, 0–7867
Parlophone DPX4, E11298

SARASATE

(8) Danzas españolas vln & pf
No. 1 Malagueña, Op. 21, No. 1
with piano   XE 7583–2   Decca 25771
Odeon 0–7856
Parlophone E11304

No. 2. Habañera, Op. 21, No. 2
with piano   XE 7983–1   Decca 25704
Odeon 0–7856
Parlophone E11312

SCHUBERT

Rondo in A, D438 vln & str orch.
with chamber orch. –   XE 8424/6–1   Odeon 0–7323/4, 0–7869/70
Temianka   Parlophone A4500/1, DPX11/2,
E11331/2

SCHUMANN

(3) Romances, Op. 94 ob or vlc or vln or cl & pf
Romance No. 1, in a
with F. Reizenstein pf   XE 9742–1   Parlophone E11412
Romance No. 2, in A
with F. Reizenstein pf   XE 9743–3   Parlophone E11412

SIBELIUS

(4) Humoresques, Op. 89 vln & orch.
No. 4. Humoresque No. 6, in g
with chamber orch. –   XE 8427–1   Odeon 0–7324, 0–7870
Temianka   Parlophone DPX12, E11332

STRAUSS, R.

Don Quixote, Op. 35 (1897) vln & orch.
with G. Piatigorsky vlc, V.   Columbia 11790/4D, (set M506),
Bakaleinikoff vla & Pittsburgh   RL3027
Symphony Orch. – Reiner

SZYMANOWSKI

King Roger, Op. 46 (1926) – opera
Chant de Roxane arr. vln & pf Kochański
with piano   XE 8252–1   Decca 25737
Odeon 0–7857
Parlophone E11321

Romance in D, Op. 23 (1909) vln & pf
with piano   XE 8251–1   Decca 25737
Odeon 0–7857
Parlophone E11321

WIENIAWSKI

Polonaise brillante No. 2, in A, Op. 21 vln & pf
with piano   XE 7273/4–1   Decca 25770
Odeon 0–6989
Parlophone E11288

Scherzo–Tarantelle, Op. 16 vln & pf
with piano   XE 7584–2   Decca 25771
Parlophone E11304

Matla TEMKO (1908–   )

FRUMERIE

Sonata No. 2, in c sharp (1944) vln & pf
2SB 3464–3, 3465–1, 3466/8–2 &   HMV DB11050/2
with S. Ehrling pf   3469–1

György TEREBESI

ARENSKY

Trio No. 1, in a, Op. 32 pf, vln & vlc
with M. Littauer pf & H. Michel vlc . Candide CE31029

BACH

(6) Brandenburg Concerti, BWV1046/51 (1721) strs & c
Brandenburg Concerto No. 1, in F, BWV1046 vln, 3 obs, bsn, 2 hrns, strs & c
with H. Schneider ob, soloists & Europa E170
Südwestdeutsche Kammerorchester –
Tilegant

Brandenburg Concerto No. 2, in F, BWV1047 tpt, fl, ob, vln, strs & c
with M. André tpt, K.T. Dilloo fl, H. Europa E170
Schneider ob & Südwestdeutsche
Kammerorchester – Tilegant

Brandenburg Concerto No. 3, in G, BWV1048 3 vlns, 3 vlas, 3 vlcs & cbs
with Südwestdeutsche Europa E171
Kammerorchester – Tilegant

Brandenburg Concerto No. 4, in G, BWV1049 vln, 2 fls, strs & c
with K.T. Dilloo fl & Südwestdeutsche Europa E171
Kammerorchester – Tilegant

Brandenburg Concerto No. 5, in D, BWV1050 clav, fl, vln, strs & c
with H. Werdermann hpsi, K.T. Dilloo Europa E171
fl & Südwestdeutsche
Kammerorchester – Tilegant

Cantata No. 1 (Wie schön leuchtet der Morgensten!) BWV1
No. 1. Chorus
with P. Pierlot hrn, J. Chambon hrn, Erato STU70284
P. Kalt vln, E. Hölderlin hpsi, J.
Muckel vlc, Heinrich Schütz Chorale
of Heilbronn & Pforzheim Chamber
Orchestra – Werner

No. 5. Aria
with G. Jeldin t, P. Kalt vln, E. Erato STU70284
Hölderlin hpsi, J. Muckel vlc &
Pforzheim Chamber Orchestra –
Werner

Cantata No. 7 (Christ unser Herr zum Jordan kam) BWV7
No. 4. Aria
with G. Jeldin t, P. Kalt vln, E. Erato STU70342
Hölderlin hpsi & J. Muckel vlc

Cantata No. 32 (Liebster Jesu, mein Verlangen) BWV32
with A. Giebel s, B. McDaniel bs, P. Erato LDE3280, STE50180,
Pierlot ob, E. Hölderlin org, Heinrich STU70180
Schütz Chorale of Heilbronn &
Pforzheim Chamber Orch. – Werner

Cantata No. 53 (Schlage doch, gewünschte Stunde) BWV53
with C. Hellmann a, P. Pierlot ob, J. Erato LDE3281, STE50181,
Chambon ob, A. Wellez ob, E. STU70181
Hölderlin org & hpsi – Heinrich Musical Heritage Society
Schütz Chorale of Heilbronn & MHS1001
Pforzheim Chamber Orch. – Werner

Cantata No. 57 (Selig ist der Mann) BWV57
with A. Giebel s, B. McDaniel bs, P. Erato LDE3280, STE50180,
Pierlot ob, E. Hölderlin org & hpsi STU70180
Heinrich Schütz Chorale of Heilbronn
& Pforzheim Chamber Orch. – Werner

Cantata No. 68 (Also hat Gott die Welt geliebt) BWV68
with A. Giebel s, J. Stämpfli bs, P. Erato LDE3281, STE50181,
Pierlot ob, J. Chambon ob, A. Wallez STU70181
bsn, E. Hölderlin org & hpsi – Musical Heritage Society
Heinrich Schütz Chorale of Heilbronn MHS1001
& Pforzheim Chamber Orch. – Werner

Cantata No. 90 (Es reifet euch ein schrecklich Ende) BWV90
with C. Hellmann a, H. Krebs t, E. Erato LDE3282, STE50182,
Wenk bs, M. André tpt, Heinrich STU70182
Schütz Chorale of Heilbronn &
Pforzheim Chamber Orch. – Werner

Cantata No. 98 (Was Gott tut, das ist wohlgetan) BWV98
with A. Giebel s, C. Hellmann a, H. Erato LDE3281, STE50181,
Krebs t, E. Wenk bs, P. Pierlot ob, J. STU70181
Chambon ob, A. Wallez bsn, E. Musical Heritage Society MHS98
Hölderlin org & hpsi Heinrich Schütz
Chorale of Heilbronn & Pforzheim
Chamber Orch. – Werner

Cantata No. 103 (Ihr werdet weinen und heulen) BWV103
No. 3. Aria
with B. Scherler a, E. Hölderlin hpsi, Erato STU70342
& J. Muckel vlc

Cantata No. 147 (Herz und Mund und Tat und Leben) BWV147
with A. Giebel s, C. Hellmann a, H. Erato LDE3282, STE50182,
Krebs t, J. Stämpfli bs, P. Pierlot ob, STU70182
d'amour J. Muckel vlc, E. Hölderlin
org & hpsi Heinrich Schütz Chorale of
Heilbronn & Pforzheim Chamber
Orch. – Werner

Markus–Passion, BWV247
No. 6. Aria
with E. Lisken a, P. Kalt vln, H. Erato LDE3346, STE50246
Haferland gamba, A. Lessing gamba,
E. Hölderlin org & J. Muckel vlc

No. 10. Aria
with H. Erwin s, E. Hölderlin org, J. Erato LDE3346, STE50246
Muckel vlc & Pforzheim Chamber
Orch. – Gönnenwein

Ostern–Oratorium, BWV249 (1736)
with T. Zylis–Gara s, P. Johnson a, T. Angel 36322
Altmeyer t, D. Fischer–Dieskau b,
South German Madrigal Choir &
Südwestdeutsche Kammerorchester –
Gönnenwein

Weihnachts–Oratorium BWV248 (1734)
with A. Giebel s, C. Hellmann a, H. Erato LDE3240/2, STE50140/2
Krebs t, B. MacDaniel bs, P. Pierlot
ob, J. Chambon ob, P. Hongne bsn, M.
André tpt W. Strebel fl, E. Hölderlin
org, J. Muckel vlc – Heinrich Schütz
Chorale of Herlbronn & Pforzheim
Chamber Orch. – Werner

HAYDN

Concerto No. 2, in G, H.VIIa, No. 4 vln & orch.
with Südwestdeutsche Da Camera SM91401
Kammerorchester – Tilegant ORYX EXP24

LEO

Concerto in D 4 vlns & strs
    with D. Vorholz vln, E. Früh vln, H.   Archive APM14340, ARC3240,
    Schön vln & Berlin Chamber Music   ARC73240, SAPM198340
    Ensemble – Lange

P. TERPELYUK

TERPELYUK

Fantasy vln & orch.
    with Gutsul Folk Instruments Orch.   Mezhdunarodnaya Kniga
    D21203/4

Vernon TERTIS

WINNER

(The) Mocking bird vln & pf
    with R. Woods pf
    Aco G15142

Georges TESSIER

ALBÉNIZ

España (6 Feuilles d'album) Op. 165 pf
    No. 2. Tango in D arr. vln & pf Kreisler
    with T. Janopoulo pf   Pathé PD96

BACH

Sonata in c, BWV1079 fl, vln & c*
    with L. Lavaillotte fl & P. Aubert hpsi   Club français du Disque 29

BARSUKOV

Concerto No. 2, vln & orch.
    with Monte–Carlo National Opera   Everest LPBR6167, SDBR3167
    Orch. – Fremaux   Pathé ASTX344, DTX344

COUPERIN, F.

(Les) Nations – 4 suites (1726) 2 vlns & c
    No. 4. Suite No. 4, in g "La Piémontoise"
    with G. Alès vln, G. Schwartz vlc &   Club français du Disque 11
    D. Gouarne hpsi

DEBUSSY

(La) Plus que lente – valse (1910) pf – arr. vln & pf Roques
    with A. Collard pf   Pathé PDT175

Quartet in g, Op. 10 (1893) 2 vlns, vla & vlc
    with M. Hugon vln, J. Balout vla & R.   Club français du Disque 2
    Cordier vlc

OFFENBACH

(Les) Contes d'Hoffmann (1881) – opera
    Belle Nuit, O nuit o'amour "Barcarolle" arr. vln & pf
    with T. Janopoulo pf   Pathé PD96

RAVEL

Introduction & Allegro (1906) hp, fl, cl, 2 vlns, vla & vlc
    with A. Challan hp, F. Caratgé fl, A.   Angel 36290
    Boutard cl, P. Simon vln, C. Lequien   Columbia FCX1031, SAXF1031
    vla & R.Bex vlc

* Arr. fl, vln & c from "Ein Musikalische Opfer".

SCHMITT

Psalm XLVII, Op. 38 (1904) s, cho, orch. & org
    with D. Duval s, M.G. Duruflé org,   Angel 35020
    Elisabeth Brasseur Chorale & Paris   Columbia FCX171
    Conservatory Orch. – Tzipine

SCHUBERT

(4) Impromptus, Op. 90 (D899) pf
    No. 3. Impromptu No. 3, in G arr. vln & pf Tessier
    with A. Collard pf   Pathé PDT175

Teresa TESTA

FAWICK

Musicale (1969) 2 vlns *
    with S. Harth vln   143583   Pride

TELEMANN

(6) Sonatas, Op. 2 (1727) "Duets" 2 fls or vlns
    Sonata No. 1, in G "Canonic"
    with S. Harth vln   Allegro ALG3039
    Sonata No. 2, in b
    with S. Harth vln   Allegro ALG3039
    Sonata No. 4, in b
    with S. Harth vln   Allegro ALG3039
    Sonata No. 6, in E
    with S. Harth vln   Allegro ALG3039

Samuel THAVIA

PISTON

Partita (1944) vln, vla & org
    with K. Malno vla & V.W. Fillinger   Pittsburgh Festival of
    org   Contemporary Music CB190

Julius THEADOROWICZ

MANNA

Rachem orch. – arr. Zucca
    with R. Voisin tpt &   CS 023918   Victor 12536
    Boston "Pops" Orch. – Fiedler

SCHUBERT

(7) Gesänge (set to Scott's "Lady of the Lake") Op. 52 v & pf
    No. 6. Ave Maria, D839 arr. orch.
    with L. Cane hp, with   CS 023923   Victor 13589
    org & Boston "Pops" Orch. – Fiedler

Kurt THEINER

TELEMANN

Concerto in G 4 vlns, strs & c
    with A. Harnoncourt vln, W. Pfeiffer   Telefunken SAWT9483
    vln, P. Schuberwalter vln & Concentus
    Musicus, Vienna – N. Harnoncourt

* Variously scored for solo vln, vln & pf, & 2 vlns.

Alexander THEODORESCU

HEUBERGER

(Der) Opernball, Op. 40 (1898) – operetta
Im chambre séparée arr. vln & pf as "Midnight bells" by Kreisler
with M. Brunetti pf   Edison Bell F277

RIMSKY-KORSAKOV

(Le) Coq d'Or (1910) – opera
Hymn to the sun arr. vln & pf Kreisler
with M. Brunetti pf   Edison Bell F277

Marie–Claude THEUVENY

BARLOW

Sonata "Juventa" vln & pf
with G. Joy pf   Erato STU20174

DEBUSSY

Sonata No. 3, in g (1917) vln & pf
with F. Theuveny pf   Ducretet–Thomson EL93045

Jacques THIBAUD (1880–1953)

ALBÉNIZ

España (6 Feuilles d'album) Op. 165 pf
No. 2. Tango in D arr. vln & pf Kreisler
with T. Janopoulo pf   OB 6795¹ HMV DA13?

No. 3. Malagueña in b arr. vln & pf Kreisler
with T. Janopoulo pf   2B 6792¹¹ HMV DB2011

d'AMBROSIO

Canzonetta, Op. 6 vln & pf
with M. Amour pf   Pathé 9521

Orientale, Op. 24 vln & pf
with M. Amour pf   Pathé 9521

BACH

(6) Brandenburg Concerti, BWV1046/51 (1721) strs & c
Brandenburg Concerto No. 5, in D, BWV1050 clav, fl, vln, strs & c
2L 411¹¹△, 412¹△, 413¹¹¹□ & HMV DB1783/4
with A. Cortot pf, R. Cortet fl 414¹¹△ Victor 7863/4
& École Normale Orchestra – Cortot

Concerto No. 2, in E, BWV1042 vln, strs & c
with orch.   HMV DB789/91

(3) Sonatas & 3 Partitas, BWV1001/6 solo vln
Partita No. 3, in E: Gavotte (3rd mvt) BWV1006 arr. vln & pf Schumann
with piano   XPh 532¹¹¹ Fonotipia 39087
          Pearl GEM102

Partita No. 3, in E: Preludio (1st mvt); **Gavotte** (3rd mvt) BWV1006 arr.
vln & pf Schumann
with T. Janopoulo pf   Victor JE96

(4) Suites, BWV1066/9 strs & c
Suite No. 3, in D: Air (2nd mvt) BWV1068 2 obs, 3 tpts, drms, strs & c
– arr. vln & pf as "Air on the G–string" by Wilhelmj
with M. Amour pf   Pathé 9523

Suite No. 3, in D: Air (2nd mvt) BWV1068 2 obs, 3 tpts, drms, strs & c
– arr. vln & pf as "Air on the G–string" by Wilhelmj
with H. Craxton pf   Cc 9913¹¹△ HMV DB1017

BEETHOVEN

Romance No. 2, in F, Op. 50 vln & orch.
          Cc 7400¹¹△ & 7401¹△ HMV DB904
with H. Craxton pf   Victor 6606

Sonata No. 9, in A, Op. 47 "Kreutzer" vln & pf
CS 3716¹¹¹△, 3717¹¹△, 3718¹¹¹△, Angel COLH92
3719¹△, 3720¹¹△, 3721¹△, 3722¹¹△ & HMV COLH92, DB1328/31,
with A. Cortot pf   3723¹¹¹△ DB7013/6
          Victor 8166/9, (set M72)

Trio No. 6, in B flat, Op. 97 "Archduke" pf, vln & vlc
Cc 14759/60¹△, 14761/2¹¹△, HMV COLH29, DB1223/7,
14763¹ᴬ△, 14764¹¹¹ᴬ△, 14765¹ᴬ△, DB7452/6
14766/7¹¹△ & 14768ⱽ△ Victor 8196/200, (set M92)
with A. Cortot pf & P. Casals vlc

BRAHMS

Concerto in a, Op. 102 "Double" vln, vlc & orch.
CJ 2156¹¹△, 2157¹△, 2158/9¹¹△, Angel COLH75
2160¹△, 2161¹¹ᴬ△, 2162¹¹¹ᴬ□ & 2163¹¹△ HMV COLH75, DB1311/4,
with P. Casals vlc & Barcelona DB7423/6
Symphony Orch. – Cortot Seraphim (in set IC6043)
          Victor 8208/11, (set M99)

(16) Waltzes, Op. 39 pf duet
No. 15. Waltz No. 15, in A flat arr. vln & pf "in A" Hochstein
with H. Craxton pf   Bb 7366¹△ HMV DA866

BULL

Säterjëntens søndag v & pf – arr. vln & pf Svendsen
with piano   Pathé 9525

Säterjëntens søndag v & pf – arr. vln & pf Svendsen
with piano   Pathé 9565, 27503

CHAUSSON

Concerto in D, Op. 21 vln, pf & str qt
2G 973/6¹¹△ & 977/80¹△ HMV COLH313, DB1649/52,
with A. Cortot pf & string quartet (set 159)
          Victor 8240/4, (set M165)

Poème, Op. 25 vln & orch.
0027 ²GCP, 0028 ¹GCP, 0029 ³ Concerteum CVX358
with Lamoureux GCP & 0030 ¹GCP Polydor 566233/4
Orch. – Bigot   Turnabout TV4257
          Vox PL6450, PL8600, VIP45470

COUPERIN, F.

(Les) Chérubins, XX, No. 3 hpsi – arr. vln & pf Salmon
with piano   Pathé 9564, 60051

(Les) Chérubins, XX, No. 3 hpsi – arr. vln & pf Salmon
with piano   HMV DA647

DEBUSSY

Children's Corner Suite (1908) pf
No. 6. Golliwog's cake–walk arr. vln & pf
with H. Craxton pf   HMV DA758

Petite Suite (1889) pf
No. 1. En bateau arr. vln & pf Kreisler
with H. Craxton pf   HMV DA620

(12) Préludes – Book I (1910) pf
No. 8. La Fille aux cheveux de lin arr. vln & pf Hartmann
with H. Craxton pf   Bb 9911¹△ HMV DA866

No. 12. Minstrels arr. vln & pf Hartmann
with A. Cortot pf   Cc 16965¹¹△ HMV DB1323
          Victor 8184

DEBUSSY – *Continued*

Sonata No. 3, in g (1917) vln & pf
    Cc 16962^{IIA}△ & 16963/4^{II}△   HMV DB1322/3
  with A. Cortot pf   Victor 8183/4

DESPLANES

Intrada (Adagio) vln & c – arr. vln & pf Nachèz
  with piano   Cc 5314^{II} HMV DB791
Intrada (Adagio) vln & c – arr. vln & pf Nachèz
  with T. Janopoulo pf   2B 6798^{I}□ HMV DB2011

DVOŘÁK

(8) Humoresques, Op. 101 pf
  No. 7. Humoresque No. 7, in G flat arr. vln & pf "in G" Wilhelmj
  with piano   Pathé 9564, 60068
(8) Slavonic Dances, Op. 46 pf duet; orch.
  No. 2. Slavonic dance No. 2, in e arr. vln & pf "in g" Kreisler
  with piano   Bb 978^{III} HMV 5–7956, DA440
                          Victor 66209, 976

ECCLES

Sonata in g vln & c – arr. vln & pf Salmon
    Bb 19271^{II}△ & 19272^{I}△ HMV DA1184
  with T. Janopoulo pf   Trianon 2C 045–00887

FALLA

(7) Canciones populares españolas (1914) v & pf
  No. 4. Jota arr. vln & pf Kochański
  with T. Janopoulo pf   Cc 19146^{III}△ HMV DB1498
(La) Vida Breve (1913) – opera
  Danza española orch. – arr. vln & pf Kreisler
  with G. de Lausnay pf   CS 3733^{I}△ HMV DB1338
                          Trianon 2C 045–00887
                          Victor 7272

FAURÉ

Berceuse, Op. 16 vln & pf
  with piano   Pathé 9560
Berceuse, Op. 16 vln & pf
  with A. Cortot pf   2G 982^{I}△ HMV COLH313, DB1653
                          Victor 8244
Dolly, Op. 56 orch.
  Berceuse arr. vln & pf
  with T. Janopoulo pf   HMV DA4999
Quartet No. 2, in g, Op. 45 pf, vln, vla & vlc
  with M. Long pf, M. Vieux vla & P.   Columbia COLC76
  Fournier vlc   HMV DB5103/6
                          Seraphim (in set IC6044)
(3) Romances sans paroles, Op. 17 pf
  No. 3. Romance sans paroles No. 3, in A flat arr. vln & pf
  with piano   Pathé 9523
Sonata No. 1, in A, Op. 13 vln & pf
    CR 1420/3^{I}△ & 1424/5^{III}△ HMV COLH74, DB1080/2
  with A. Cortot pf

FIORILLO

(36) Étude–Caprices, Op. 3 solo vln
  Caprice No. 14, in g (Adagio) arr. vln & pf Mistowzky
  with piano   Pathé 9525

FRANCK

Sonata in A (1886) vln & pf
    Cc 3680/1^{I}, 3682^{IV}, 3683^{VII}, HMV DB785/8
    3684/5^{I}, 3686^{IV} & 3687^{III} Victor 6254/7
  with A. Cortot pf
Sonata in A (1886) vln & pf
    CS 3724^{I}△, 3725/6^{II}△, 3727^{I}△, HMV COLH74, DB1347/50
    3728/9^{II}△, 3730^{I}△ & 3731^{III}△
  with A. Cortot pf

GRANADOS

Danza originale unid vln & pf – ded. Thibaud
  with T. Janopoulo pf   Trianon 2C 045–00887
(12) Danzas españolas, Op. 37 (1893) pf
  No. 5. Danza española No. 5, in e "Andaluza" arr. vln & pf Kreisler
  with piano   Cc 980^{II} HMV 3–07959, DB518
  No. 5. Danza española No. 5, in e "Andaluza" arr. vln & pf Kreisler
  with H. Craxton pf   Cc 11714^{II}△ HMV DB1113
                        Trianon 2C 045–00887
  No. 5. Danza española No. 5, in e "Andaluza" arr. vln & pf Kreisler
  with T. Janopoulo pf   Cc 19145^{II}△ HMV DB1498
  No. 6. Danza española No. 6, in D arr. vln & pf Thibaud
  with piano   Cc 981^{II} HMV 3–07960, DB518
  No. 6. Danza española No. 6, in D arr. vln & pf Thibaud
  with H. Craxton pf   Cc 9912^{IV}△ HMV DB1113
                        Trianon 2C 045–00887
                        Victor 7250

GUIRAUD

Piccolino (1879) – opera
  Mélodrame arr. vln & pf
  with piano   Fonotipia 39209
  Mélodrame arr. vln & orch.
  with orch.   Pathé 9522, 60046

HAYDN

(31) Trios, H.XV, Nos. 1/31 pf, vln & vlc
  Trio No. 25, in G, H.XV, No. 25 (Op. 73, No. 2)
    BR 1331^{V}△, 1332^{II}△, 1333^{I}△ & Electrola 1C 047–01148, E80487
  with A. Cortot pf & P.   1334^{IIIA}△ HMV COLH12, DA895/6
  Casals vlc   Victor 3045/6

KREISLER

Liebesfreud vln & pf
  with piano   Pathé 5561

LECLAIR

(12) Sonatas, Op. 9 – Book IV (1738) vln & c
  Sonata No. 3, in D: Tambourin (3rd mvt) arr. vln & pf Kreisler
  with H. Craxton pf   HMV DA758

MARSICK

(2) Pieces, Op. 6 vln & pf
  No. 2. Scherzando
  with piano   XPh 697 Fonotipia 39222
  No. 2. Scherzando
  with M. Amour pf   Pathé 5708, 9524, 60051
  No. 2. Scherzando
  with T. Janopoulo pf   2B 6791^{II}□ HMV DB2006

MASSENET

Thaïs (1894) – opera
Méditation arr. vln & pf Marsick
with piano   XPh 524   Fonotipia 39054

Méditation arr. vln & pf Marsick
with piano   Pathé 9522, 60071

MENDELSSOHN

Concerto in e, Op. 64 vln & orch.
Andante (2nd mvt)
with orch. – Ruhlmann   Pathé 9526

Trio No. 1, in d, Op. 49 pf, vln & vlc
      CR 1385/6^{II}△, 1387^{I}△, 1389/90   HMV COLH75, DB1072/5
       ^{II}△, 1391^{IIIA}△ & 1392/3^{IA}△   Seraphim (in set IC6044)
with A. Cortot pf & P. Casals vlc

MOURET

(Le) Triomphe des Sens (1732) – ballet orch.
Sarabande in e arr. vln & pf Dandelot
with piano   HMV DA647

MOZART

Concerto No. 3, in G, K216 (cadenzas by Ysaÿe) vln & orch.
with Lamoureux Orch. – Paray   Celson DC1006/8
                             Concerteum CVX358
                             Polydor 566230/2
                             Turnabout TV4257
                             Vox (set 642), PL6420

Concerto No. 5, in A, K219 "Turkish" (Cadenzas by Joachim) vln & orch.
with orch. – Munch   HMV DB5142/4, FBLP25046,
                            FJLP5015

Concerto No. 6, in E flat, K268 (K365b) vln & orch.*
      Cc 9954/5^{II}△, 9956^{I}△ & 9957/9   HMV DB1018/20
with orch. – Sargent ^{II}△ Victor 6744/6

Serenade No. 7, in D, K250 "Haffner" orch
Rondo (4th mvt) arr. vln & pf Kreisler
with T. Janopoulo pf   HMV DA1649, FJLP5015

Sonata No. 26, in B flat, K378 vln & pf
with M. Long pf   HMV COLH312

Sonata No. 34, in A, K526 vln & pf
with M. Long pf   HMV COLH312, W1571/2

PARADIES

Sicilienne vln & pf – arr. Dushkin
with T. Janopoulo pf   Bb 19147^{II}△   HMV DA1191
                                Trianon 2C 045–00887

PENN

Smiling thru' (1915) v & pf – arr. vln & pf
with piano   Pathé 1459

POLDINI

(7) Marionnettes pf
No. 2. Poupée valsante arr. vln & pf Kreisler
with T. Janopoulo pf   OB 6793^{I}□   HMV DA1339

* Cadenza omitted.

RAMEAU

(Les) Fêtes d'Hébé (1739) – opera
Tambourin arr. vln & pf Kreisler
with piano   Bb 983^{I} HMV 5–7953, DA441
                       Victor 66066, 977

RAVEL

Pièce en forme d'Habanera v & pf – arr. vln & pf Catherine
with T. Janopoulo pf   HMV DA4999

RIMSKY–KORSAKOV

(Le) Coq d'Or (1910) – opera
Hymn to the sun arr. vln & pf Kreisler
with piano   HMV DB759

Hymn to the sun arr. vln & pf Kreisler
with H. Craxton pf   Cc 9945^{II}△   HMV DB1017

RODE

(24) Caprices, Op. 22 solo vln
Caprice No. 18, in f (Presto) "Minute" arr. vln & pf Thibaud
with piano   Bb 982^{II} HMV 5–7955, DA441
                       Victor 66065, 977

RUBINSTEIN

(2) Melodies, Op. 3 pf
No. 1. Melody in F arr. vln & pf Wilhelmj
with piano   Pathé 60046

SAINT–SAËNS

(Le) Carnaval des animaux (1886) small orch.
Le cygne arr. vln & pf
with piano   XPh 666   Fonotipia 39231

Le cygne arr. vln & pf
with piano   HMV DB759

(Le) Déluge, Op. 45 (1876) – oratorio
Prélude vln & orch. – arr. vln & pf Saint–Saëns
with piano   HMV DA620

Prélude vln & orch. – arr. vln & pf Saint–Saëns
with G. de Lausnay pf   CS 3732^{II}△   HMV DB1338
                            Trianon 2C 045–00887
                            Victor 7272

Havanaise, Op. 83 vln & orch.
with M. Amour pf   Pathé 5574, 5598, 9520

Havanaise, Op. 83 vln & orch.
      2B 6796^{II}□ & 6797^{I}□   HMV DB1990
with T. Janopoulo pf   Trianon 2C 045–00887

Introduction & Rondo Capriccioso, Op. 28 vln & orch.
with M. Amour pf   Pathé 5158

Introduction & Rondo Capriccioso, Op. 28 vln & orch.
with orch. – Ruhlmann   Pathé 9527, 60047

SCHUBERT

(7) Gesänge (set to Scott's "Lady of the Lake") Op. 52 v & pf
No. 6. Ave Maria, D839 arr. vln & pf Wilhelmj
with piano   Pathé 1467

(6) Moments musicaux, Op. 94 (D780) (1823/7) pf
No. 3. Moment musicale No. 3, in f "Air russe" arr. vln & pf Kreisler
with piano   Bb 982^{II} HMV 5–7955, DA441
                       Victor 66065, 977

SCHUBERT – *Continued*

(14) Schwanengesang, D957 (1828) v & pf
No. 4. Ständchen "Serenade" arr. vln & pf
with piano   Pathé 60071

Sonata No. 17, in D, Op. 53 (D850) pf
Rondo (4th mvt) arr. vln & pf Friedberg
with T. Janopoulo pf   HMV DB11104

(3) Sonatinas, Op. 137 (D384, D385 & D408) vln & pf
No. 3. Sonatina No. 3, in g, D408
with T. Janopoulo pf   HMV DB11103/4, FJLP5015

Trio No. 1, in B flat, Op. 99 (D898) pf, vln & vlc
          CR 533^I△, 534^{II}△, 535/6^I△,   Electrola 1C 047–01148
          537/8^{II}△, 539^I△ & 540^{IA}△   HMV COLH12, DB947/50,
with A. Cortot pf & P. Casals vlc   DB7000/3, DB7419/22

SCHUMANN

(13) Kinderscenen, Op. 15 pf
No. 7. Träumerei arr. vln & pf
with piano   Pathé 9565, 27503

Trio No. 1, in d, Op. 63 pf, vln & vlc
          Cc 14740^{IIA}△, 14741^I△, 14742/3   HMV DB1209/12, (set 95)
^{IA}△, 14744^{IIIA}△, 14756^I△, 14757^V☐   Victor 8130/3, (set M52)
with A. Cortot pf   & 14758^{IIA}△
& P. Casals vlc

SIMONETTI

Madrigale pf – arr. vln & pf
with piano   HMV DB759

SVENDSEN

Romance in G, Op. 26 vln & orch. – arr. vln & pf Wilhelmj
with piano   Pathé 60068

SZYMANOWSKI

(3) Mythes, Op. 30 (1915) vln & pf
No. 1. La Fontaine d'Aréthuse
with T. Janopoulo pf   2B 6794^I☐   HMV DB2006
                                              Victor JD305

TCHAIKOVSKY

(3) Souvenirs de Hapsal, Op. 2 pf
No. 3. Chant sans paroles in f arr. vln & pf Kreisler
with piano   Pathé 1467

VERACINI

(12) Sonatas, Op. 2 (1744) "Sonate accademiche" vln & c
Sonata No. 8, in e: Giga
with H. Craxton pf   HMV DB801
Sonata No. 8, in e: Giga
with T. Janopoulo pf   2A 8387△   HMV DB3111
                                              Victor 15564

Sonata No. 11, in E: Menuet; Gavotte
with H. Craxton pf   HMV DB801
Sonata No. 11, in E: Menuet; Gavotte
with T. Janopoulo pf   2A 8386△   HMV DB3111
                                              Victor 15568

VIEUXTEMPS

(3) Feuilles d'album, Op. 40 vln & pf
No. 2. Regrets
with M. Amour pf   Pathé 9524

VIEUXTEMPS – *Continued*

(6) Voix Intimes, Op. 45 vln & pf
No. 5. Sérénité
with piano   XPh 531   Fonotipia 39208
                                              Pearl GEM102

No. 5. Sérénité
with piano   Bb 979^{II} HMV 5–7954, DA440
                                              Victor 66064, 976

VITALI

Chaconne in g vln & c – arr. vln & pf Charlier
with T. Janopoulo   2LA 998/9^I☐   HMV DB2799
pf   Trianon 2C 045–00887
                                              Victor 15465

VIVALDI

(12) Concerti, Op. 3 "L'Estro armonico" var, cbns & strs
Concerto No. 11, in d: Largo (2nd mvt) P.250 (F.IV, No. 11) 2 vlns, vlc,
strs & c – arr. vln & pf Pochon
with T. Janopoulo pf   Bb 19150^{II}△   HMV DA1191

WAGNER

(Die) Meistersinger von Nürnberg (1868) – opera
Morgenlich leuchtend "Prize song" arr. vln & pf Wilhelmj
with piano   Pathé 5561

WIENIAWSKI

(8) Étude–Caprices, Op. 18 solo vln & 2nd vln obb
Étude–Caprice No. 4, in a arr. vln & pf Thibaud
with piano   Pathé 9525
Étude–Caprice No. 4, in a arr. vln & pf Thibaud
with piano   Bb 983^I HMV 5–7953, DA441
                                              Victor 66066, 977

Polonaise brillante No. 2, in A, Op. 21 vln & pf
with piano   Pathé 5708, 9560

Edmond THIELE (1853–1926)

DVOŘÁK

(8) Humoresques, Op. 101 pf
No. 7. Humoresque No. 7, in G flat arr. vln & pf "in G" Wilhelmj
with T. Frese pf   Paramount 30013

FRIML

Sometime (1918) – musical
Sometime arr. vln & pf
with piano   Pathé 22057

GILLESPIE

When you look in the heart of a rose v & pf – arr. vln & pf*
with piano   Pathé 22057

HERBERT

Maytime – operetta
Will you remember? arr. vln & pf
with piano   Pathé 20322

* From the British musical "The Better 'Ole."

KREISLER

Liebesfreud vln & pf
with T. Frese pf
Paramount 30013

MASCAGNI

Cavalleria Rusticana (1890) – opera
Intermezzo orch. – arr. vln & pf
with piano
Pathé 1299

MENDELSSOHN

(6) Songs without words, Op. 62 pf
No. 6. Song without words No. 30, in A "Spring song" arr. vln & pf
with piano
Pathé 1299

TOBANI

Hearts & flowers, Op. 245 (1899) v & pf – arr. vln & pf
with piano
Pathé 1162, 20322

Helga THOENE

KRIEGER, A.

Aria: Ich will es nicht achten, ich will es nicht tun v & strs
with C. Ocker b, W. Neuhaus vln, H.   Columbia C91111, STC91111
Jopen vla, E. Seiler vla, H. Hedler
gamba, A. Lessing gamba & W.
Thoene spin

ONDRAČEK

Sonata vln, fl & vlc
with V. Noack fl & H. Hedler vlc   Columbia C91113, STC91113

PISENDEL

Sonata in a solo vln
Largo (1st mvt)
(unaccompanied)
Columbia C91105, STC91105

ROSENMÜLLER

Sinfonia undecima 2 vlns, 2 vlas, 2 gambas, lute & hpsi
with W. Neuhaus vln, H. Jopen vla, E.   Columbia C91111, STC91111
Seiler vla, H. Hedler t-gamba, A.
Lessing bs-gamba, E. Müller-Dombois
lute & W. Thoene spin

STADEN

Pavane vln, 2 vlas & gamba
with H. Jopen vla, E. Seiler vlc & H.   Columbia C91110
Hedler gamba

Maria THOMAN

BACH

Cantata No. 156 (Ich steh' mit einem Fuss in Grabe) BWV156 (1730)
Sinfonia arr. vln & pf as "Arioso" by Szigeti
with piano   12022   Edison Bell H1054

(4) Suites, BWV1066/9 strs & c ·
Suite No. 3, in D: Air (2nd mvt) BWV1068 2 obs, 3 tpts, drms, strs & c
– arr. vln & pf as "Air on the G-string" by Wilhelmj
with piano   12023   Edison Bell H1054

Tessie THOMAS (1899–   )

ELGAR

(La) Capricieuse, Op. 17 vln & pf
with piano
HMV E154

ESPOSITO

Irish cradle song vln & pf
with piano
HMV E154

SARASATE

Carmen Fantasia (on themes from the opera by Bizet) Op. 25 vln & pf or orch.
with piano
HMV 2–07950/1, D357

VIEUXTEMPS

Ballade & Polonaise in G, Op. 38 vln & pf
Polonaise
with piano   HO 2760 af   HMV 2–07952, 2–087902, D356, M16

WIENIAWSKI

Capriccio–valse, Op. 7 vln & pf
with piano
HMV D358

Polonaise brillante No. 2, in A, Op. 21 vln & pf
with piano
HMV 2–07952, D358

Jakob THOMSEN

CORELLI

(12) Concerti grossi, Op. 6 orch.
Concerto grosso No. 1, in D
with K. Sambleben vln, I. Hermann   Bach Guild BG584
vlc, J.E. Hansen hpsi & Societas
Musica Chamber Orch. – Hansen

STRADELLA

(2) Sonatas "Sinfonias" vln, vlc & bs
Sonata No. 1, in d
with B. Anker vlc, E. Moseholm cbs,   Bach Guild BG582
J.E. Hansen hpsi & Societas Musica
Chamber Orch. – Hansen

TORELLI

(12) Concerti, Op. 8 (1709) 1/6: 2 vlns, strs & c – 7/12: vln, strs & c
Concerto No. 2, in a
with K. Sambleben vln, J.E. Hansen   Bach Guild BG584
hpsi & Societas Musica Chamber Orch.
– Hansen

VIVALDI

(12) Sonatas, Op. 1 2 vlns & c
Sonata No. 12, in d, F.XIII, No. 28 "La Follia"
with A. Tellefsen vln, J.E. Hansen hpsi Bach Guild BG582
& B. Anker vlc

Freya THRINIS

SARASATE

Zigeunerweisen, Op. 20 vln & pf or orch.
with piano
Odeon 250764

G. TINLOT

FAURÉ

Berceuse, Op. 16 vln & pf
with piano   HMV L283

Karl Maria TITZE (1908–   )

BRAHMS

(16) Waltzes, Op. 39 pf duet
No. 15. Waltz No. 15, in A flat arr. vln & pf "in A" Hochstein
with V. Pleasants pf   10755   Telefunken M5121, TPB238

BURMESTER

Staccato serenade vln & pf
with V. Pleasants pf   10839   Telefunken M5141

DRDLA

Serenade No. 1, in A vln & pf
with V. Pleasants pf   10838   Telefunken M5140
Souvenir vln & pf
with V. Pleasants pf   10754   Telefunken M5121, TPB238

FIBICH

Images, Impressions & Souvenirs, Op. 41 pf
No. 14. Poem (from "Souvenirs", Part IV) arr. vln & pf Kubelík
with V. Pleasants pf   10837   Telefunken M5140

SCHUMANN

(13) Kinderscenen, Op. 15 pf
No. 7. Träumerei arr. vln & pf
with V. Pleasants pf   10842   Telefunken M5141

A. TOLGANBAYEV

SHUBANOV

Aria vln & pf
with S. Kagan pf   Mezhdunarodnaya Kniga
                 D00018259/60

SHUBAYEV

Romance vln & pf
with S. Kagan pf   Mezhdunarodnaya Kniga
                 D00018259/60

TLENDIEV

Armandy Kiyal vln & pf
with I. Ivanova–Sokolskaya pf   Mezhdunarodnaya Kniga
                 D00018259/60

Jan TOMASOW (1914–1961)

ALBINONI

(12) Sonatas, Op. 6 (1711) "Trattenimenti armonia" vln & c
Sonata No. 11, in A
with A. Heiller hpsi   Amadeo AVRS6118
                 Bach Guild BG583, BGS5013
                 Top Rank 35–074
                 Vanguard SRV197, SRV197SD

BACH

(6) Brandenburg Concerti, BWV1046/51 (1721) strs & c
Brandenburg Concerto No. 1, in F, BWV1046 vln, 3 obs, bsn, 2 hrns, strs & c
playing vln–pic, with K. Mayrhofer ob,   Amadeo AVRS6042
A. Heiller hpsi & Vienna State Opera   Bach Guild BG540
Chamber Orch. – Prohaska   I Classici della Musica Classica
                                     XAM4012

Brandenburg Concerto No. 2, in F, BWV1047 tpt, fl, ob, vln, strs & c
with H. Wobisch tpt, H. Reznicek fl,   Amadeo AVRS6042
K. Mayerhofer ob, A. Heiller hpsi &   Bach Guild BG540
Vienna State Opera Chamber Orch. –   I Classici della Musica Classica
Prohaska   XAM4012
                                     Top Rank 35–009
                                     Vanguard SRV105

Brandenburg Concerto No. 3, in G, BWV1048 3 vlns, 3 vlas, 3 vlcs & cbs
with R. Streng vln, A. Jilka vln, W.   Amadeo AVRS6043
Hübner vla, E. Rab vla, E. Kriss vla,   Bach Guild BG541
R. Harand vlc, G. Weis vlc, L. Beinl
vlc, O. Rühm cbs, A. Heiller hpsi &
Vienna State Opera Chamber Orch. –
Prohaska

Brandenburg Concerto No. 4, in G, BWV1049 vln, 2 fls, strs & c
with K. Trotzmüller rec, P. Angerer   Amadeo AVRS6043
rec, A. Heiller hpsi & Vienna State   Bach Guild BG541
Opera Chamber Orch. – Prohaska   I Classici della Musica Classica
                                     XAM4013
                                     Vanguard PVL7016

Brandenburg Concerto No. 5, in D, BWV1050 clav, fl, vln, strs & c
with A. Heiller hpsi, H. Reznicek fl &   Amadeo AVRS6044
Vienna State Opera Chamber Orch. –   Bach Guild BG542
Prohaska   I Classici della Musica Classica
                                     XAM4013

Concerto No. 2, in E, BWV1042 vln, strs & c
with Vienna State Opera Orch. –   I Classici della Musica Classica
Tomasow   XAM4012
                                     Top Rank 35–009
                                     Vanguard SRV105

DEBUSSY

Ariettes oubliées (1888) v & pf
No. 2. Il pleure dans mon coeur arr. vln & pf Hartmann
with F. Holetschek pf   Amadeo AVRS6063
                 Top Rank 35–010
                 Vanguard VRS464

(La) Plus que lente – valse (1910) pf – arr. vln & pf Roques
with F. Holetschek pf   Amadeo AVRS6063
                 Top Rank 35–010
                 Vanguard VRS464

(12) Préludes – Book I (1910) pf
No. 12. Minstrels arr. vln & pf Hartmann
with F. Holetschek pf   Amadeo AVRS6063
                 Top Rank 35–010
                 Vanguard VRS464

Sonata No. 3, in g (1917) vln & pf
with F. Holetschek pf   Amadeo AVRS6063
                 Top Rank 35–010
                 Vanguard VRS464

FAURÉ

Sonata No. 1, in A, Op. 13 vln & pf
with F. Holetschek pf

Amadeo AVRS6063
Top Rank 35–010
Vanguard VRS464

MARCELLO, B.

(12) Sonatas, Op. 2 vln & c
Sonata No. 1, in F*
with A. Heiller hpsi

Amadeo AVRS6118
Bach Guild BG583, BGS5013
Top Rank 35–074

MENDELSSOHN

Concerto in e, Op. 64 vln & orch.
with orch. – Sherman

Music Appreciation Records
MAR92

MOZART

Divertimento No. 15, in B flat, K287 2 hrns & strs
with Vienna State Opera Orch. –
Prohaska

Amadeo AVRS6073
Vanguard VRS444

Divertimento No. 17, in D, K334 2 hrns & strs
with Vienna State Opera Orch. –
Prohaska

Amadeo AVRS6034
Top Rank 35–002
Vanguard VRS441

NARDINI

Concerto in e vln & orch.
with Vienna State Opera Chamber
Orch. – Tomasow

Amadeo AVRS6142
Bach Guild BG599, BGS5027
ı Classici della Musica Classica
XAM4008

STRAVINSKY

(L') Histoire du Soldat (1918) narrators & tpt, cbs, tbn, cl, vln, bsn & pcn
with J. Spindler tpt, O. Rühm cbs, F.
Wurzler tbn, A. Prinz cl, C. Ohlberger
bsn & A. Jonak pcn, – cond. Rossi

Amadeo AVRS6018
Vanguard PVL7009, VRS452

TARTINI

Concerto in d, D45 (C61) vln & orch.
with Vienna State Opera Chamber
Orch. – Tomasow

Amadeo AVRS6142
Bach Guild BG599, BGS5027
I Classici della Musica Classica
XAM4008

Sinfonia pastorale in D vln & strs
with Vienna State Opera Chamber
Orch. – Tomasow

Amadeo AVRS6142
Bach Guild BG599, BGS5027
I Classici della Musica Classica
XAM4008

(12) Sonatas, Op. 1 (1734) vln & c
Sonata No. 4, in G
with A. Heiller hpsi

Amadeo AVRS6118
Bach Guild BG583, BGS5013
Top Rank 15–012, 35–074
Vanguard SRV197, SRV197SD

* Occasionally published as Op. 1, No. 1, & transposed to D Major.

TARTINI – *Continued*

Sonata No. 10, in g "Didone abbandonata"
with A. Heiller hpsi

Amadeo AVRS6118
Bach Guild BG583, BGS5013
Top Rank 35–074
Vanguard SRV197, SRV197SD

VITALI

Chaconne in g vln & c – arr. vln & pf Charlier
with A. Heiller hpsi

Amadeo AVRS6118
Bach Guild BG583, BGS5013
Top Rank 35–074
Vanguard SRV197, SRV197SD

VIVALDI

(12) Concerti, Op. 3 "L'Estro armonico" var. cbns & strs
Concerto No. 1, in D, P.146 (F.IV, No. 7) 4 vlns, vlc, strs & c
with W. Boskovsky vln, W.
Hintermeyer vln, P. Matheis vln, H.
Nordberg hpsi, R. Harand vlc &
Vienna State Opera Chamber Orch. –
Rossi

Amadeo AVRS6088
Bach Guild BG572, BGS5016
I Classici della Musica Classica
XAM4023
Qualiton LPX1095
Top Rank 35–073
Vanguard SRV143

Concerto No. 2, in g, P.326 (F.IV, No. 8) 2 vlns, strs & c
with W. Boskovsky vln, H. Nordberg
hpsi & Vienna State Opera Chamber
Orch. – Rossi

Amadeo AVRS6088
Bach Guild BG572, BGS5016
I Classici della Musica Classica
XAM4023
Qualiton LPX1095
Top Rank 35–073
Vanguard SRV143

Concerto No. 4, in e, P.97 (F.I, No. 174) 4 vlns, strs & c
with W. Boskovsky vln, W.
Hintermeyer vln, P. Matheis vln, H.
Nordberg hpsi & Vienna State Opera
Chamber Orch. – Rossi

Amadeo AVRS6088
Bach Guild BG572, BGS5016
I Classici della Musica Classica
XAM4023
Qualiton LPX1095
Top Rank 35–073
Vanguard SRV143

Concerto No. 5, in A, P.212 (F.I, No. 175) 2 vlns, strs & c
with W. Boskovsky vln, H. Nordberg
hpsi & Vienna State Opera Chamber
Orch. – Rossi

Amadeo AVRS6089
Bach Guild BG573, BGS5017
I Classici della Musica Classica
XAM4024
Qualiton LPX1096
Top Rank 35–074
Vanguard SRV144

Concerto No. 6, in a, P.I (F.I, No. 176) vln, strs & c
with G. Leonhardt hpsi & Vienna
State Opera Chamber Orch. – Rossi

Amadeo AVRS6002
Bach Guild BG538
I Classici della Musica Classica
XAM4024
Qualiton LPX1096
Vanguard PVL7017, SRV144

VIVALDI – *Continued*

Concerto No. 7, in F, P.249 (F.IV, No. 9) 4 vlns, strs & c
with W. Boskovsky vln, W.   Amadeo AVRS6089
Hintermeyer vln, P. Matheis vln, H. Bach Guild BG573, BGS5017
Nordberg hpsi & Vienna State Opera   I Classici della Musica Classica
Chamber Orch. – Rossi   XAM4024
                                     Qualiton LPX1096
                                     Top Rank 35–074
                                     Vanguard SRV144

Concerto No. 8, in A, P.2 (F.I, No. 177) 2 vlns, strs & c
with W. Boskovsky vln, H. Nordberg   Amadeo AVRS6089
hpsi & Vienna State Opera Chamber   Bach Guild BG573, BGS5017
Orch. – Rossi   I Classici della Musica Classica
                                     XAM4024
                                     Qualiton LPX1096
                                     Top Rank 35–074
                                     Vanguard SRV144

Concerto No. 9, in D, P.147 (F.I, No. 178) vln, strs & c
with H. Nordberg hpsi & Vienna State Amadeo AVRS6090
Opera Chamber Orch. – Rossi   Bach Guild BG574, BGS5018
                                     I Classici della Musica Classica
                                     XAM4025
                                     Qualiton LPX1097
                                     Top Rank 35–075
                                     Vanguard SRV145, SRV145SD

Concerto No. 10, in b, P.148 (F.IV, No. 10) 4 vlns, strs & c
with W. Boskovsky vln, P. Matheis   Amadeo AVRS6090
vln, W. Hintermeyer vln, H. Nordberg Bach Guild BG574, BGS5018
hpsi & Vienna State Opera Chamber   I Classici della Musica Classica
Orch. – Rossi   XAM4025
                                     Qualiton LPX1097
                                     Top Rank 35–075
                                     Vanguard SRV145, SRV145SD

Concerto No. 11, in d, P.250 (F.IV, No. 11) 2 vlns, vlc, strs & c
with W. Boskovsky vln, G. Harand   Amadeo AVRS6090
vlc, H. Nordberg hpsi & Vienna State Bach Guild BG574, BGS5018
Opera Chamber Orch. – Rossi   I Classici della Musica Classica
                                     XAM4025
                                     Qualiton LPX1097
                                     Top Rank 35–075
                                     Vanguard SRV145, SRV145SD

Concerto No. 12, in E, P.240 (F.I, No. 179) vln, strs & c
with H. Nordberg hpsi & Vienna State Amadeo AVRS6090
Opera Chamber Orch. – Rossi   Bach Guild BG574, BGS5018
                                     I Classici della Musica Classica
                                     XAM4025
                                     Qualiton LPX1097
                                     Top Rank 35–075
                                     Vanguard SRV145, SRV145SD

(12) Concerti, Op. 8 (1725) "Il Cimento dell' Armonia e dell' Invenzione"
(Nos. 1/4: Le quattro Stagioni) vln & strs
Concerto No. 1, in E, F.I, No. 22 "La Primavera"
with I Solisti di Zagreb – Janigro   Amadeo AVRS6079
                                     Bach Guild BG564, BGS5001
                                     I Classici della Musica Classica
                                     XAM4001
                                     Fontana BIG328, BIG428
                                     Philips 906079ASY, GL5769,
                                     SGL5769
                                     Top Rank 40–002

VIVALDI – *Continued*

Concerto No. 2, in B flat, F.I, No. 23 "L'Estate"
with I Solisti di Zagreb – Janigro   Amadeo AVRS6079
                                     Bach Guild BG564, BGS5001
                                     I Classici della Musica Classica
                                     XAM4001
                                     Fontana BIG328, BIG428
                                     Philips 906079ASY, GL5769,
                                     SGL5769
                                     Top Rank 40–002

Concerto No. 3, in F, F.I, No. 24 "L'Autunno"
with I Solisti di Zagreb – Janigro   Amadeo AVRS6079
                                     Bach Guild BG564, BGS5001
                                     I Classici della Musica Classica
                                     XAM4001
                                     Fontana BIG328, BIG428
                                     Philips 906079ASY, GL5769,
                                     SGL5769
                                     Top Rank 40–002

Concerto No. 4, in f, F.I, No. 25 "L'Inverno"
with I Solisti di Zagreb – Janigro   Amadeo AVRS6079
                                     Bach Guild BG564, BGS5001
                                     I Classici della Musica Classica
                                     XAM4001
                                     Fontana BIG328, BIG428
                                     Philips 906079ASY, GL5769,
                                     SGL5769
                                     Top Rank 40–002

Concerto in g, P.343 vln, strs & c
with A. Heiller hpsi & Vienna State Bach Guild BG538
Opera Chamber Orch. – Tomasow   Vanguard PVL7018

(12) Sonatas, Op. 2 (1712) vln & c
Sonata No. 1, in g, F.XIII, No. 29
with A. Heiller hpsi   Amadeo AVRS6118
                                     Bach Guild BG583, BGS5013
                                     Top Rank 15–012, 35–074
                                     Vanguard SRV197, SRV197SD

Spiros TOMBRAS

PAPAIOANNOU

Suite (1954) vln & pf
with H. Tombras pf   Fidelity EP8866

Zlatko TOPOLSKI (1914–   )

MILOIERITSCH

Serbischer Tanz vln & pf
with A. Butakoff pf   2RA 4487[1]☐   HMV EH1292

TELEMANN

Quartet in e, T.III, No. 2 fl, vln, gamba & c
with H. Riessberger fl, J. Luitz vlc, H. Musical Heritage Society
Langford hpsi & R. Duerrer cbs   MHS642

TORELLI

(12) Concerti, Op. 8 (1709) 1/6: 2 vlns, strs & c – 7/12: vln, strs & c
Concerto No. 7, in d
with B. Zaczek gtr & members of the Musical Heritage Society
New Vienna String Quartet   MHS1053

TORELLI – *Continued*

Concerto No. 10, in A
with B. Zaczek gtr & members of the Musical Heritage Society
New Vienna String Quartet   MHS1053

VIVALDI

(12) Sonatas, Op. 1 2 vlns & c
Sonata No. 1, in g, F.XIII, No. 17
with R. Kalup vln, H. Langfort hpsi & Musical Heritage Society
R. Harand vlc   MHS804

Sonata No. 2, in e, F.XIII, No. 18
with R. Kalup vln, H. Langfort hpsi & Musical Heritage Society
R. Harand vlc   MHS804

Sonata No. 3, in C, F.XIII, No. 19
with R. Kalup vln, H. Langfort hpsi & Musical Heritage Society
R. Harand vlc   MHS804

Sonata No. 4, in E, F.XIII, No. 20
with R. Kalup vln, H. Langfort hpsi & Musical Heritage Society
R. Harand vlc   MHS804

Sonata No. 5, in F, F.XIII, No. 21
with R. Kalup vln, H. Langfort hpsi & Musical Heritage Society
R. Harand vlc   MHS804

Sonata No. 6, in D, F.XIII, No. 22
with R. Kalup vln, H. Langfort hpsi & Musical Heritage Society
R. Harand vlc   MHS804

(12) Sonatas, Op. 2 (1712) vln & c
Sonata No. 4, in F: Andante (2nd mvt) F.XIII, No. 32
with A. Butakoff pf 2RA 4488[1]□ HMV EH1292

Werner TORKANOWSKY (1926–)

ANTES

(3) Trios, Op. 3 2 vlns & vlc
Trio No. 1, in E flat
with I. Cohen vln, & S. Barab vlc New Records Incorporated
         NRI2016
         Society for the Preservation of
         the American Musical Heritage
         MIA99

Trio No. 2, in d
with I. Cohen vln & S. Barab vlc New Records Incorporated
         NRI2016
         Society for the Preservation of
         the American Musical Heritage
         MIA99

Trio No. 3, in C
with I. Cohen vln & S. Barab vlc New Records Incorporated
         NRI2016
         Society for the Preservation of
         the American Musical Heritage
         MIA99

PURCELL

(10) Sonatas, Z802/11 (1697) – 4 parts – 2 vlns & c
Sonata No. 1, in b, Z802
with G. Ciompi vln, H. Chessid hpsi & Contrepoint MC20053
G. Koutzen vlc   Dover HCR5224
         Period SPL572

PURCELL – *Continued*

Sonata No. 2, in E flat, Z803
with G. Ciompi vln, H. Chessid hpsi & Contrepoint MC20053
G. Koutzen vlc   Dover HCR5224
         Period SPL572

Sonata No. 4, in d, Z805
with G. Ciompi vln, H. Chessid hpsi Contrepoint MC20053
& G. Koutzen vlc   Dover HCR5224
         Period SPL572

Sonata No. 7, in G, Z808
with G. Ciompi vln, H. Chessid hpsi & Contrepoint MC20053
G. Koutzen vlc   Dover HCR5224
         Period SPL572

Sonata No. 8, in g, Z809
with G. Ciompi vln, H. Chessid hpsi & Contrepoint MC20053
G. Koutzen vlc   Dover HCR5224
         Period SPL572

Sonata No. 9, in F, Z810 "Golden Sonata"
with G. Ciompi vln, H. Chessid hpsi & Contrepoint MC20053
G. Koutzen vlc   Dover HCR5224
         Period SPL572

Sonata No. 10, in D, Z811
with G. Ciompi vln, H. Chessid hpsi & Contrepoint MC20053
G. Koutzen vlc   Dover HCR5224
         Period SPL572

Ernst–Reinhold TÖRNQVIST (1893–)

HALVORSEN

Andante religioso in g vln & pf
with orch. – Grevillius   Odeon D4817

Marta de la TORRE (1894–)

FRIML

Bygone days, Op. 65 vln & pf
with piano   Edison Diamond Disc 80615

KREISLER

Minuet (Porpora) vln & pf
with piano   Edison cylinder 4816

RIMSKY–KORSAKOV

Sadko (1898) – opera
Chant hindou arr. vln & pf Kreisler
with piano   Edison Diamond Disc 80615

SAMMARTINI, G.

(6) Sonatas, Op. 1 2 vlns & c
Sonata No. 4, in A: Andante (3rd mvt) arr. vln & pf as "Canto amoroso"
by Elman
with piano   Edison Diamond Disc 80653

YRADIER

(La) Paloma (1877) v & pf – arr. vln & gtr
with A. Valencia gtr   Edison cylinder 4705

Petar TOŠKOV (1920–)

HRISTIĆ

Ohridska Legenda – ballet orch.
with Belgrade Opera Orch. –   Jugoton LPY25
Zdravković

TARTINI

Sonata in g "Il Trillo del Diavolo" vln & c – arr. vln & pf Kreisler
with A. Preger pf   Jugoton 26360

Piero TOSO

ALBINONI

(12) Concerti, Op. 5 (1707) vln or ob & strs
Concerto No. 2, in F
with I Solisti Veneti – Scimone   CBS 32 11 0003, 32 11 0004,
            BRG72057, SBRG72057

(12) Concerti, Op. 9 (1722) var. cbns & strs
Concerto No. 1, in B flat vln & strs
with I Solisti Veneti – Scimone   Electrola C063–28275
            Erato STU70475
            Musical Heritage Society
            MHS1074

Concerto No. 7, in D vln & strs
with I Solisti Veneti – Scimone   Erato STU70476
            Musical Heritage Society
            MHS1075

Concerto No. 10, in F vln & strs
with I Solisti Veneti – Scimone   Erato STU70476
            Musical Heritage Society
            MHS1075

GEMINIANI

(6) Concerti grossi, Op. 3 (1755) orch.
Concerto grosso No. 2, in g
with R. Valpreda vln, F. Zampieri vln,   CBS 32 11 0003, 32 11 0004,
F. Sangiorgi vln & I Solisti Veneti –   BRG72057, SBRG72057
Scimone

(6) Concerti grossi, Op. 7 (1746) orch.
Concerto grosso No. 1, in D
with G. Talassi vln, C. Lardé fl, C.H.   Erato STU70546
Scimone fl, S. Penazzi bsn & I Solisti
Veneti – Scimone

Concerto grosso No. 2, in d
with G. Talassi vln, C. Lardé fl, C.H.   Erato STU70546
Scimone fl, S. Penazzi bsn & I Solisti
Veneti – Scimone

Concerto grosso No. 3, in C
with G. Talassi vln, C. Lardé fl, C.H.   Erato STU70546
Scimone fl, S. Penazzi bsn & I Solisti
Veneti – Scimone

Concerto grosso No. 4, in d
with G. Talassi vln, C. Lardé fl, C.H.   Erato STU70546
Scimone fl, S. Penazzi bsn & I Solisti
Veneti – Scimone

Concerto grosso No. 5, in c
with G. Talassi vln, C. Lardé fl, C.H.   Erato STU70546
Scimone fl, S. Penazzi bsn & I Solisti
Veneti – Scimone

GEMINIANI – *Continued*

Concerto grosso No. 6, in B flat
with G. Talassi vln, C. Lardé fl, C.H.   Erato STU70546
Scimone fl, S. Penazzi bsn & I Solisti
Veneti – Scimone

TARTINI

(6) Concerti, Op. 2 vln & strs
Concerto No. 2, in C, D2
with I Solisti Veneti – Scimone   Electrola 1C 063–28296
            Erato STU70625/7

Concerto in F, D67 vln & orch.
with I Solisti Veneti – Scimone   Electrola 1C 063–28296
            Erato STU70625/7

Concerto in A, D96 vln & orch.
with I Solisti Veneti – Scimone   Electrola 1C 063–28296
            Erato STU70625/7

Concerto in a, D115 (C76) vln & orch.
with I Solisti Veneti – Scimone   Erato STU70625/7

Concerto in b, D125 vln & orch.
with I Solisti Veneti – Scimone   Electrola 1C 063–28296
            Erato STU70625/7

(12) Sonatas, Op. 1 (1734) vln & c
Sonata No. 10, in g "Didone abbandonata"
with E. Farina hpsi & S. Zannerini vlc   Erato STU70625/7

Sonata in A vln & c
with E. Farina hpsi & S. Zannerini vlc   Erato STU70625/7

Sonata in d vln & c
with E. Farina hpsi & S. Zannerini vlc   Erato STU70625/7

Sonata No. 13, in A "Pastorale" vln & c
with E. Farina hpsi & S. Zannerini vlc   Erato STU70625/7

(50) Variations on a theme by Corelli vln & c
with E. Farina hpsi & S. Zannerini vlc   Erato STU70625/7

VIVALDI

(12) Concerti, Op. 8 (1725) "Il Cimento dell' Armonia e dell' Invenzione"
(Nos. 1/4: Le quattro Stagioni) vln & strs
Concerto No. 1, in E, F.I, No. 22 "La Primavera"
with I Solisti Veneti – Scimone   CBS BRG72676, SBRG72676

Concerto No. 2, in B flat, F.I, No. 23 "L'Estate"
with I Solisti Veneti – Scimone   CBS BRG72676, SBRG72676

Concerto No. 3, in F, F.I, No. 24 "L'Autunno"
with I Solisti Veneti – Scimone   CBS BRG72676, SBRG72676

Concerto No. 4, in f, F.I, No. 25 "L'Inverno"
with I Solisti Veneti – Scimone   CBS BRG72676, SBRG72676

Concerto No. 5, in E flat, F.I, No. 26 "La Tempesta di mare"
with I Solisti Veneti – Scimone   Erato STU70473

Concerto in C, P.14 (F.I, No. 13) (Op. 54, No. 3) "Per la SS. Assunzione di
Maria Vergine" vln, strs & c
with I Solisti Veneti – Scimone   CBS BRG75444, S72444,
            SBRG75444
            Columbia ML6221, MS6821

Concerto in C, P.16 (F.XII, No. 37) 2 mands, 2 obs, 2 fls, 2 cls, 2 vlns, vlc,
strs & c
with B. Bianchi mand, A. Pitrelli   Musical Heritage Society
mand, M. Schaffer ob, K. Gerwig ob,   MHS1100
C. Lardé fl, C.H. Scimone fl, A. Pecile
cl, A. Gerbi cl, A. Ferrari vln, M.
Cassoli vlc & I Solisti Veneti –
Scimone

VIVALDI – *Continued*

Concerto in D, P.163 (F.I., No. 133) vln, strs & c
  with I Solisti Veneti – Scimone   CBS BRG75444, S72444,
  SBRG75444
  Columbia ML6221, MS6821

Concerto in F, P.290 (F.I, No. 20) "per la solennità di S. Lorenzo" vln, strs & c
  with I Solisti Veneti – Scimone   CBS BRG75444, S72444,
  SBRG75444
  Columbia ML6221, MS6821

Concerto in B flat, P.367 (F.I, No. 59) 4 vlns, strs & c
  with R. Valpreda vln, F. Zampieri vln,   CBS 32 11 0003, 32 11 0004,
  F. Sangiorgi vln & I Solisti Veneti –   BRG72057, SBRG72057
  Scimone

Concerto in B flat, P.368 (F.I, No. 60) (Op. 28, No. 3) "Scordatura" vln, 2 str choruses & c
  with I Solisti Veneti – Scimone   Musical Heritage Society
  MHS1100

Concerto in B flat, P.385 (F.XII, No. 12) (Op. 41, No. 5) "Funebre" vln, strs & c
  with I Solisti Veneti – Scimone   CBS BRG75444, S72444,
  SBRG75444
  Columbia ML6221, MS6821

Concerto in B flat, P.406 (F.XII, No. 16) ob, vln, strs & c
  with I Solisti Veneti – Scimone   Musical Heritage Society
  MHS1076

Roman TOTENBERG (1911–   )

BACH

Concerto No. 1, in a, BWV1041 vln, strs & c
  with Musicraft Chamber Orch.   Musicraft (set MC78)

Concerto No. 1, in a, BWV1041 vln, strs & c
  with Poznan Philharmonic Symphony   Heliodor 89555, 478033
  Orch. – Wislocki   Muza XL0049

Concerto No. 2, in E, BWV1042 vln, strs & c
  with Poznan Philharmonic Symphony   Heliodor 89555, 478033
  Orch. – Wislocki   Muza XL0049

BARTÓK

Rhapsody No. 1, in G (1928) vln & orch.
  with Vienna State Opera Orch. –   Amadeo AVRS6281
  Golschmann   Philips A04303L
  Vanguard VRS1083, VSD2110

(6) Rumanian folk dances (1915) pf – arr. vln & pf Székely
  with R.D. Hanson pf   Heliodor 479018

BEETHOVEN

Concerto in D, Op. 61 (cadenzas by Joachim) vln & orch.
  with Poznan Philharmonic Symphony   Heliodor 89557, 479006
  Orch. – Wislocki   Muza XL0050
  Westminster P276

(3) Sonatas, Op. 12 vln & pf
  No. 1. Sonata No. 1, in D
  with A. Baller pf   3020/3   Allegro 2008/9, (set 3), AL2

Sonata No. 5, in F, Op. 24 "Spring" vln & pf
  with A. Baller pf   Allegro AL47

BEETHOVEN – *Continued*

(3) Sonatas, Op. 30 vln & pf
  No. 1. Sonata No. 6, in A
  with A. Baller pf   Allegro AL47

Sonata No. 10, in G, Op. 96 vln & pf
  with A. Baller pf   Allegro AL2

(3) Trios, Op. 1 pf, vln & vlc
  No. 1. Trio No. 1, in E flat
  with A. Baller pf & G. Rejto vlc   Allegro AL34

  No. 3. Trio No. 3, in c
  with A. Baller pf & G. Rejto vlc   Allegro AL40

(2) Trios, Op. 70 pf, vln & vlc
  No. 2. Trio No. 5, in E flat
  with A. Baller pf & G. Rejto vlc   Allegro AL4

Trio in B flat, Op. 11 cl, vlc & pf – arr. pf, vln & vlc
  with A. Baller pf & G. Rejto vlc   Allegro AL34

(10) Variations (on "Ich bin der Schneider Kakadu") Op. 121a pf, vln & vlc
  with A. Baller pf & G. Rejto vlc   Allegro AL40

BLOCH

Concerto in a (1938) vln & orch.
  with Vienna State Opera Orch. –   Amadeo AVRS6281
  Golschmann   Philips A04303L
  Vanguard VRS1083, VSD2110

BRAHMS

(21) Hungarian Dances pf duet
  Hungarian Dance No. 5, in f sharp arr. vln & pf "in g" Joachim
  with A. Baller pf   Sonora 4021, (in set M258)

Sonata No. 3, in d, Op. 108 vln & pf
  with A. Baller pf   Musicraft 1136/8, (set MC43)

Sonata (1853) "Frei aber Einsam" vln & pf
  Allegro (Scherzo) in c (3rd mvt) "Sonatensatz"
  with A. Baller pf   Musicraft 1138, (in set MC43)

Trio No. 2, in C, Op. 87 pf, vln & vlc
  with A. Baller pf & G. Rejto vlc   Allegro AL49
  Allegro–Elite ALG4035

DEBUSSY

(La) Plus que lente – valse (1910) pf – arr. vln & pf Roques
  with R.D. Hanson pf   Heliodor 479018

FASCH

Concerto in D, vln, strs & c
  with H. Langfort hpsi & Vienna   Musical Heritage Society
  Chamber Orch. – Topolski   MHS789

FRANCK

Sonata in A (1886) vln & pf
  with R.D. Hanson pf   Telefunken TW30228

HANDEL

Concerto in B flat vln, strs & c
  with H. Langfort hpsi & Vienna   Musical Heritage Society
  Chamber Orch. – Topolski   MHS789

(7) Sonatas, Op. 5 (1739) 2 vlns & c
  Sonata No. 5, in g
  with E. Brown vln, & E.V. Wolff hpsi   Royale 603

HAYDN

(6) Quartets, Op. 3 (H.III, Nos. 13/8) 2 vlns, vla & vlc
No. 5. Quartet No. 17, in F: Andante cantabile (2nd mvt) "Serenade" arr. vln & pf
    with A. Baller pf & string enemble   Sonora 4022, (in set 258)

(31) Trios, H.XV, Nos. 1/31 pf, vln & vlc
Trio No. 25, in G, H.XV, No. 25 (Op. 73, No. 2)
    with A. Baller pf & G. Rejto vlc   Allegro AL4

HEINICHEN

Concerto in D vln, strs & c
    with H. Langfort hpsi & Vienna   Musical Heritage Society
    Chamber Orch. – Topolski   MHS789

KREISLER

Liebesleid vln & pf
    with R.D. Hanson pf   Heliodor 479018

Praeludium & Allegro (Pugnani) vln & pf
    with piano   Parlophone 44818

LEO

Concerto in D 4 vlns & strs
    with E. Brown vln, B.   US 1244/7   Royale 1826/7
    Rabinoff vln, B. Schwarz vln, E.V.
    Wolff hpsi & vlcs & cbs

MOZART

Trio No. 4, in E, K542 pf, vln & vlc
    with K. Appelbaum pf & F. Magg vlc   Musicraft 1103/4, (set MC29)

Trio No. 5, in C, K548 pf, vln & vlc
    with K. Appelbaum pf & F. Magg vlc   Musicraft 1105/6, (set MC29)

NIN

(20) Cantos de España (1923) v & pf
No. 4. Montañesa arr. vln & pf Kochański
    with piano   Parlophone 44819

NOVÁČEK

(8) Concert caprices, Op. 5 vln & pf
No. 4. Perpetuum mobile
    with piano   Parlophone 44819

PISENDEL

Concerto in g vln, strs & c
    with H. Langfort hpsi & Vienna   Musical Heritage Society
    Chamber Orch. – Topolski   MHS789

RAVEL

Pièce en forme d'Habanera v & pf – arr. vln & pf Catherine
    with R.D. Hanson pf   Heliodor 479018

Trio in a (1915) pf, vln & vlc
    with A. Baller pf & G. Rejto vlc   Allegro AL77, ALG3091

Tzigane (Rapsodie de concert) (1924) vln & pf or orch.
    with R.D. Hanson pf   Heliodor 479018

RÓZYCKI

Melody, Op. 5 vln & pf
    with piano   Parlophone 44817

SARASATE

Navarra, Op. 33 2 vlns & pf or orch.
    with E. Brown vln &   US 121206/7   Royale 582
    string orch.

SCHUBERT

(14) Schwanengesang, D957 (1828) v & pf
No. 4. Ständchen "Serenade" arr. vln & pf
    with A. Baller pf   Sonora 4021, (in set M258)

Trio No. 2, in E flat, Op. 100 (D929) pf, vln & vlc
    with A. Baller pf & G. Rejto vlc   Allegro (set AR1), AL1

SINDING

Serenade No. 1, in G, Op. 56 2 vlns & pf
    with E. Brown vln & J. Zayde pf   Royale 1809/10

STRAVINSKY

Divertissement vln & pf
    with S. Stravinsky pf   Allegro AL46

Suite Italienne (on themes of Pergolesi) (1933) vln & pf
    with S. Stravinsky pf   Allegro AL46

SZYMANOWSKI

Concerto No. 1, in a, Op. 35 (1922) vln & orch.
    with Poznan Philharmonic Symphony   Eterna 820128
    Orch. – Wislocki   Muza XL0051

TCHAIKOVSKY

Quartet No. 1, in D, Op. 11 2 vlns, vla & vlc
Andante cantabile (2nd mvt) arr. vln, pf & str ens
    with A. Baller pf & string ensemble   Sonora 4022, (in set 258)

VIVALDI

(12) Concerti, Op. 3 "L'Estro armonico" var. cbns, & strs
Concerto No. 8, in a, P.2 (F.I, No. 177) 2 vlns, strs & c
        US 121127-2 & 121128/9-1   Royale 577/8, (set 26)
    with E. Brown vln & chamber orch.

Concerto No. 10, in b: Largo (2nd mvt) P.148 (F.IV, No. 10) 4 vlns, strs & c
    with M. Van den Berg vln, S. Frenkel   Telefunken SK1318, TF52
    vln, W. Hanke vln, G. Werthein hpsi
    & Berlin Philharmonic Orch. – Unger

WIENIAWSKI

Concerto No. 2, in d, Op. 22 vln & orch.
    with Poznan Philharmonic Symphony   Muza XL0051
    Orch. – Wislocki

(2) Mazurkas, Op. 19 vln & pf
No. 1. Mazurka No. 1, in G "Obertass"
    with piano   Parlophone 44817

Maurice TOUBAS (1902–)

FAURÉ

Berceuse, Op. 16 vln & pf
    with piano   Pathé–Actuelle 11166

KREISLER

Chanson Louis XIII & Pavane (L. Couperin) vln & pf
    with piano   Pathé–Actuelle 11166

Shigeru TOYAMA

MAMIYA
Sonata solo vln
  (unaccompanied)   Victor VX32

Koji TOYODA

BACH
Concerto in d, BWV1043 2 vlns, strs & c
  with A. Grumiaux vln, P. Ledger hpsi   Philips 6500 119
  & New Philharmonia Orch. – de
  Waart

Patricia TRAVERS (1927–   )

DELLO JOIO
Variations & Capriccio (1948) vln & pf
  with N. Dello Joio pf   Columbia ML4845

IVES
Sonata No. 2, (1910) vln & pf
  with O. Herz pf   Columbia ML2169

SESSIONS
Duo (1942) vln & pf
  with O. Herz pf   Columbia ML2169

Mario TRAVERSA

GRIEG
Peer Gynt (Suite No. 2) Op. 55 orch.
  No. 4. Solveig's song arr. vln & pf Sitt
  with orch.   Polydor 47438

SCHUBERT
(2) Lieder, Op. 98 (D498) v & pf
  No. 2. Wiegenlied (Schlafe, holder süsser Knabe) arr. vln & pf Elman
  with orch.   Polydor 47346
(14) Schwanengesang, D957 (1828) v & pf
  No. 4. Ständchen "Serenade" arr. vln & orch.
  with orch.   Polydor 47346

SIBELIUS
Kuolema, Op. 44 – Incidental music orch.
  Valse triste arr. vln & pf Franko
  with orch.   Polydor 47343

TCHAIKOVSKY
(6) Songs, Op. 6 v & pf
  No. 6. None but the weary heart arr. vln & orch.
  with orch.   Polydor 47343

Michael TREE (1934–   )

AMRAM
Dirge & Variations pf, vln & vlc
  with M. Andrews pf & D. Soyer vlc   Washington WR469, WS9469

CORELLI
(12) Sonatas, Op. 4 2 vlns & c
  Sonata No. 3, in A
  with M. Goberman vln, E. Earle hpsi   CBS–Odyssey 54028
  & J. Schneider vlc   Library of Recorded
                                        Masterpieces Vol. 2
                                        Odyssey 32 16 0073, (in set 32
                                        26 0005), 32 16 0074, (in set 32
                                        26 0006)

  Sonata No. 4, in D
  with M. Goberman vln, E. Earle hpsi   CBS–Odyssey 54029
  & J. Schneider vlc   Library of Recorded
                                        Masterpieces Vol. 1
                                        Odyssey 32 16 0075, (in set 32
                                        26 0005), 32 16 0076, (in set 32
                                        26 0006)

  Sonata No. 5, in a
  with M. Goberman vln, E. Earle hpsi   CBS–Odyssey 54029
  & J. Schneider vlc   Library of Recorded
                                        Masterpieces Vol. 3
                                        Odyssey 32 16 0075, (in set 32
                                        26 0005), 32 16 0076, (in set 32
                                        26 0006)

  Sonata No. 6, in E
  with M. Goberman vln, E. Earle hpsi   CBS–Odyssey 54029
  & J. Schneider vlc   Library of Recorded
                                        Masterpieces Vol. 3
                                        Odyssey 32 16 0075, (in set 32
                                        26 0005), 32 16 0076, (in set 32
                                        26 0006)

  Sonata No. 9, in B flat
  with M. Goberman vln, E. Earle hpsi   CBS–Odyssey 54029
  & J. Schneider vlc   Library of Recorded
                                        Masterpieces Vol. 2
                                        Odyssey 32 16 0075, (in set 32
                                        26 0005), 32 16 0076, (in set 32
                                        26 0006)

  Sonata No. 10, in G
  with M. Goberman vln, E. Earle hpsi   CBS–Odyssey 54028
  & J. Schneider vlc   Library of Recorded
                                        Masterpieces Vol. 1
                                        Odyssey 32 16 0073, (in set 32
                                        26 0005), 32 16 0074, (in set 32
                                        26 0006)

MENDELSSOHN
Octet in E flat, Op. 20 4 vlns, 2 vlas & 2 vlcs
  with J. Laredo vln, A. Steinhardt vln,   CBS BRG72473, SBRG72473
  A. Schneider vln, J. Dalley vln, S.   Columbia ML6248, MS6848
  Rhodes vla, L. Parnas vlc & D. Soyer
  vlc

MOZART
Concertone in C, K190 2 vlns, ob, vlc & orch.
  with J. Laredo vln & Marlboro   CBS BRG72435, SBRG72435
  Festival Orch. – Schneider   Columbia ML6248, MS6848

Paul TREFF

GOLTERMANN

Concerto No. 8, in A, Op. 130 vlc & orch.
  Andante (2nd mvt) arr. vln & pf
  with piano   HMV X947860

RUBINSTEIN

(2) Melodies, Op. 3 pf
  No. 1. Melody in F arr. vln & pf Wilhelmj
  with piano   HMV X947861

Charles TREGER (1935–)

JOACHIM

Concerto in d, Op. 11 "Hungarian" vln & orch.
  with Louisville Orch. – Mester   Louisville LS705

SZYMANOWSKI

Concerto No. 2, Op. 61 (1932/3) vln & orch.
  with Polish National Philharmonic   Muza XL0168
  Orch. – Satanowski

Viktor TRETYAKOV (1946–)

BACH

(3) Sonatas & 3 Partitas, BWV1001/6 solo vln
  Sonata No. 1, in g, BWV1001
  (unaccompanied)   Eurodisc 80026KK
                      Mezhdunarodnaya Kniga
                      D021491/2, SM02221/2

BRAHMS

Sonata No. 3, in d, Op. 108 vln & pf
  with M. Erokhine pf   HMV 1C 063–10876

PAGANINI

Cantabile in D, Op. 17 vln & gtr
  with L. Kurakova pf   Eurodisc 80026KK
                      Mezhdunarodnaya Kniga
                      D021491/2, SM02221/2

(24) Caprices, Op. 1 (1801/7) solo vln
  Caprice No. 17, in E flat
  (unaccompanied)   Eurodisc 80026KK
                      Mezhdunarodnaya Kniga
                      D021491/2, SM02221/2

  Caprice No. 24, in a
  (unaccompanied)   Eurodisc 80026KK
                      Mezhdunarodnaya Kniga
                      D021491/2, SM02221/2

Concerto No. 1, in D, Op. 6 vln & orch.
  with Moscow Philharmonic Symphony   Le Chant du Monde LDX78391
  Orch. – Järvi   Eurodisc 75739IK
                      Melodiya–Angel 40015
                      Mezhdunarodnaya Kniga
                      D018139/40, S01329/30

(I) Palpiti (variations on the aria "Di tanti palpiti" from Rossini's opera
  "Tancredi" Op. 13 (1819) vln & orch.
  with L. Kurakova pf   Eurodisc 80026KK
                      Mezhdunarodnaya Kniga
                      D021491/2, SM02221/2

PEIKO

Concert Fantasia No. 2, in g vln & pf
Prelude & Toccata
  with N. Peiko pf   Mezhdunarodnaya Kniga
                   D024121/2, SM02243/4

PROKOFIEV

Sonata No. 1, in f, Op. 80 vln & pf
  with M. Yerokhin pf   Mezhdunarodnaya Kniga
                   D024121/2, SM02243/4

RAVEL

Pièce en forme d'Habanera v & pf – arr. vln & pf Catherine
  with M. Erokhine pf   HMV 1C 063–10876

Tzigane (Rapsodie de concert) (1924) vln & pf or orch.
  with M. Erokhine pf   HMV 1C 063–10876

SHCHEDRIN

Humoresque pf – arr. vln & pf Tziganov
  with M. Yerokhin pf   Mezhdunarodnaya Kniga
                   D024121/2, SM02243/4

In imitation of Albéniz pf– arr. vln & pf Tziganov
  with M. Yerokhin pf   Mezhdunarodnaya Kniga
                   D024121/2, SM02243/4

TCHAIKOVSKY

Concerto in D, Op. 35 vln & orch.
  with Moscow Philharmonic Symphony   Eurodisc 75999XK
  Orch. – Järvi   Mezhdunarodnaya Kniga
                   D18167/8, S1349/50

VITALI

Chaconne in g vln & c – arr. vln & pf Charlier
  with M. Erokhine pf   HMV 1C 063–10876

Alfred TRIPPNER

GOLDBERG

Sonata in g 2 vlns & c
  with R. Amboden vln, M.G. Schneider   Da Camera SM92206
  hpsi & H. Schäfer vlc

KREBS

Trio in D fl, vln & c
  with L. Wehrung fl, M.G. Schneider   Da Camera SM92206
  hpsi & H. Schäfer vlc

Hendrika TROOSTWYCK

TROOSTWYCK

Springtime vln & pf
  with piano   Edison cylinder 2363

Jesse TRYON

BOTTESINI

Grand duo concertante in a vln, cbs & orch.
  with M. Anastasio cbs & H. Wingreen   Classic Editions CE1035
  pf

BURTON

Fiddlestick (1946) vln & pf
  with E. Burton pf   Classic Editions CE1006

Quintet (1945) pf & str qt
  with E. Burton pf, J. Maggid vln, B.   Classic Editions CE1006
  Kadinoff vla & G. Koutzen vlc

Sonatina (1946) vln & pf
  with E. Burton pf   Classic Editions CE1006

ELGAR

Sonata in e, Op. 82 vln & pf
  with J. la Montaine pf   Classic Editions CE1019

SCARLATTI, A.

Sonata in F rec, ob, vln or 2 vlns & c
  with L. Davenport rec, E. Schuster ob,   Classic Editions CE1051
  P. Davenport hpsi & M. Neal vlc

SCHUMANN

Sonata No. 1, in a, Op. 105 vln & pf
  with J. de Bonaventura pf   Classic Editions CE1028

Sonata No. 2, in d, Op. 121 vln & pf
  with J. de Bonaventura pf   Classic Editions CE1028

STRAUSS, R.

Sonata in E flat, Op. 18 vln & pf
  with J. la Montaine pf   Classic Editions CE1019

TELEMANN

Quartet in G, T.I, No. 2 fl, ob, vln & c
  with L. Davenport rec, E. Schuster ob,   Classic Editions CE1051
  P. Davenport hpsi & M. Neal vlc

Janine TRYSESSOONE

BARON

Concerto lute, vln & bs
  with M. Podolski lute & F. Terby bs   Orion ORS7032

HAYDN

Cassation in C, H.III, No. 6 lute, vln, & vlc*
  with M. Podolski lute & F. Terby bs   Orion ORS7032

SAINT–LUC

Partita lute, vln & bs
  with M. Podolski lute & F. Terby bs   Orion ORS7032

VIVALDI

(2) Trio–sonatas, P.7, Nos. 1/2 lute, vln & bs
  Trio No. 1
  with M. Podolski lute & F. Terby bs   Orion ORS7032

Anaid TSITSIKYAN

ARUTYUNYAN

Concert–Poem vln & orch.
  with Moscow Radio Symphony Orch.   Mezhdunarodnaya Kniga
  – Blazhkov   D012214, D15592, S0640

* Arrangement of Opus 1, No. 6.

John TUNNELL

BACH, J.C.

Quartet in G vln, pf, vla & vlc
  with C. Bizony pf, P. Howard vla &   Oryx ORYX1706
  O. Hegedus vlc

BACH, J.S.

(Ein) Musikalisches Opfer, BWV1079 (1749) strs & c
  with J. Francis fl, S. Francis ob & hrn,   Saga XID5237
  B. Davis vla, R. Birnstingl bsn, N.
  Jones vlc & M. Silver hpsi

BRAHMS

Trio in E flat, Op. 40 hrn, vln & pf
  with I. James hrn & S. Tunnell pf   Pye GSGC14132

CORELLI

(12) Concerti grossi, Op. 6 orch.
  Concerto grosso No. 9, in F
  with K. Sillito vln, K. Heath vlc &   Electrola 1C 053–02068
  English Chamber Orch. – Leppard   HMV HQS1232

HAYDN

Sonata in e flat (1795) "Derniere Sonate" vln & pf*
  with C. Bizony pf   Oryx ORYX1706

PURCELL

(12) Sonatas, Z790/801 (1683) 3 part – 2 vlns & c
  Sonata No. 1, in g, Z790
  with C. Pini vln, H. Lester hpsi & A.   Musical Heritage Society
  Pini vlc   MHS942

  Sonata No. 2, in B flat, Z791
  with C. Pini vln, H. Lester hpsi & A.   Musical Heritage Society
  Pini vlc   MHS942

  Sonata No. 3, in d, Z792
  with C. Pini vln, H. Lester hpsi & A.   Musical Heritage Society
  Pini vlc   MHS942

  Sonata No. 4, in F, Z793
  with C. Pini vln, H. Lester hpsi & A.   Musical Heritage Society
  Pini vlc   MHS943

  Sonata No. 5, in a, Z794
  with C. Pini vln, H. Lester hpsi & A.   Musical Heritage Society
  Pini vlc   MHS943

  Sonata No. 6, in C, Z795
  with C. Pini vln, H. Lester hpsi & A.   Musical Heritage Society
  Pini vlc   MHS943

  Sonata No. 7, in e, Z796
  with C. Pini vln, H. Lester hpsi & A.   Musical Heritage Society
  Pini vlc   MHS943

  Sonata No. 8, in G, Z797
  with C. Pini vln, H. Lester hpsi & A.   Musical Heritage Society
  Pini vlc   MHS943

  Sonata No. 9, in c, Z798
  with C. Pini vln, H. Lester hpsi & A.   Musical Heritage Society
  Pini vlc   MHS943

  Sonata No. 10, in A, Z799
  with C. Pini vln, H. Lester hpsi & A.   Musical Heritage Society
  Pini vlc   MHS942

* Identical with piano trio No. 31, in e flat, H.XV, No. 31.

PURCELL – *Continued*

Sonata No. 11, in f, Z800
with C. Pini vln, H. Lester hpsi & A. Pini vlc — Musical Heritage Society MHS942

Sonata No. 12, in D, Z801
with C. Pini vln, H. Lester hpsi & A. Pini vlc — Musical Heritage Society MHS942

(10) Sonatas, Z802/11 (1697) 4 parts – 2 vlns & c
Sonata No. 1, in b, Z802
with C. Pini vln, H. Lester hpsi & A. Pini vlc — Musical Heritage Society MHS 944

Sonata No. 2, in E flat, Z803
with C. Pini vln, H. Lester hpsi & A. Pini vlc — Musical Heritage Society MHS944

Sonata No. 3, in a, Z804
with C. Pini vln, H. Lester hpsi & A. Pini vlc — Musical Heritage Society MHS944

Sonata No. 4, in d, Z805
with C. Pini vln, H. Lester hpsi & A. Pini vlc — Musical Heritage Society MHS945

Sonata No. 5, in d, Z806
with C. Pini vln, H. Lester hpsi & A. Pini vlc — Musical Heritage Society MHS945

Sonata No. 6, in g, Z807 "Chaconne"
with C. Pini vln, H. Lester hpsi & A. Pini vlc — Musical Heritage Society MHS945

Sonata No. 7, in G, Z808
with C. Pini vln, H. Lester hpsi & A. Pini vlc — Musical Heritage Society MHS945

Sonata No. 8, in g, Z809
with C. Pini vln, H. Lester hpsi & A. Pini vlc — Musical Heritage Society MHS945

Sonata No. 9, in F, Z810 "Golden Sonata"
with C. Pini vln, H. Lester hpsi & A. Pini vlc — Musical Heritage Society MHS945

Sonata No. 10, in D, Z811
with C. Pini vln, H. Lester hpsi & A. Pini vlc — Musical Heritage Society MHS945

SCHOBERT

Trio in F pf, vln & vlc
with C. Bizony pf & O. Hegedus vlc — Oryx ORYX1706

VIVALDI

(12) Concerti, Op. 9 (1728) "La Cetra" vln, strs & c
Concerto No. 9, in B flat, P.341 (F. I, No. 57) with 2nd vln obb
with C. Pini vln, H. Lester hpsi, A. Pini vlc & Orch. of the Accademia Monteverdiana – Stevens — Orpheus OR336

Wandy TWOREK (1913–)

ALBÉNIZ

Suite española, Op. 47 pf
No. 1. Granada arr. vln & orch.
with orch. – Lampertz–Müller — Telefunken TW30090

No. 3. Savillanas arr. vln & orch.
with orch. – Lampertz–Müller — Telefunken TW30090

ANONYMOUS

Londonderry air Traditional Irish air – arr. vln & orch.
with string orch. & male choir – Reesen — HDK 2379 — Polyphon HA70009

BARTHOLDY

Strophe, Op. 30 pf – arr. vln & pf Lange
with E. Vagning pf — HDK 2901 — Polyphon HA70033

BARTÓK

Sonata in g (1944) solo vln
(unaccompanied) — AHDK 2915/20 — Decca LM4557
London LS711
Polyphon HM80062/4

BEETHOVEN

(6) Minuets, G167 pf
No. 2. Minuet No. 2, in G arr. vln & pf Burmester
with E. Vagning pf — HDK 2896 — Polyphon HA70004

BOCCHERINI

(6) Quintets, Op. 13 2 vlns, vla & 2 vlcs
No. 5. Quintet No. 5, in E: Minuet (3rd mvt) "Bull" arr. vln & pf Kreisler
with E. Vagning pf — HDK 2940 — Polyphon HA70038

BRAHMS

(5) Lieder, Op. 49 v & pf
No. 4. Wiegenlied "Cradle song" arr. vln & pf
with E. Vagning pf — HDK 2887 — Polyphon HA70032, HA70044

No. 4. Wiegenleid "Cradle song" arr. vln, orch. & cho
with orch. & Peter Knight Singers – Binge — HDKE 280 — London LB1121
Polyphon X51706

BULL

Säterjëntens søndag v & pf – arr. vln & pf Svendsen
with H. Aurvig pf — HDK 3289 — Polyphon HA70045

DINICU

Hora staccato vln & pf – arr. Heifetz
with E. Vagning pf — HDK 2899 — Polyphon HA70037

DRECHSEL

Ave Maria v & pf – arr. vln & orch. Reesen
with orch. — HDK 2735 — Polyphon X51316

DRIGO

(Les) Millions d'Arlequin (1900) – ballet orch.
Sérénade arr. vln & pf Auer
with E. Vagning pf — HDK 2902 — Polyphon HA70033

DVOŘÁK

(7) Gypsy songs, Op. 55 v & pf
No. 4. Songs my mother taught me arr. vln & pf
with string orch. & male choir – Reesen — HDK 2380 — Polyphon HA70009

No. 4. Songs my mother taught me arr. vln & pf Kreisler
with E. Vagning pf — HDK 2890 — Decca C16020
Polyphon HM80059

(8) Humoresques, Op. 101 pf
No. 7. Humoresque No. 7, in G flat arr. vln & pf "in G" Kreisler
with E. Vagning pf — HDK 2890 — Polyphon HM80059

DVOŘÁK – *Continued*

No. 7. Humoresque No. 7, in G flat arr. vln & orch.
with orch. – Binge   HDKE 278   London LB1121
                      Polyphon X51704

ELGAR

Salut d'amour, Op. 12 orch. – arr. vln & orch.
with orch. – Binge   HDKE 273   London LB1121
                      Polyphon X51703

FALLA

(La) Vida Breve (1913) – opera
Danza española orch. – arr. vln & pf Kreisler
with E. Vagning pf   HDK 2889   Polyphon HM80059

FIBICH

Images, Impressions & Souvenirs, Op. 41 pf
No. 14. Poem (from "Souvenirs", Part IV) arr. vln & pf Kubelík
            D.BHDKE 165–2   Polyphon HA70028
with E. Vagning pf
No. 14. Poem (from "Souvenirs", Part IV) arr. vln & pf Kubelík
with G. Hemmeshoi   HDK 1131   Polyphon NS90827
Frederiksen pf

FRANCK

Sonata in A (1886) vln & pf
                AHDKE 117/22–1   Decca AK2217/9
with E. Vagning pf   Polyphon HM80036/8

GADE

Jealousy (1927) v & pf – arr. vln & orch.
with Copenhagen   AHDKE 39–1   Decca K24005
Radio Symphony Orch. – Reesen   Polyphon Z60122
Jealousy (1927) v & pf – arr. vln & orch.
with orch. – Lampertz–Müller   Telefunken TW30089

GERSHWIN

Porgy & Bess (1935) – opera
Summertime arr. vln & orch. Heywood
with orch. – Lampertz–Müller   Telefunken TW30089

GODARD

Jocelyn (1888) – opera
Cachés dans cet asile "Berceuse" arr. vln & pf Tworek
with E. Vagning pf   HDK 2892   Polyphon HA70031
Cachés dans cet asile "Berceuse" arr. vln, orch. & cho
with orch. & Peter Knight Singers –   London LB1121
Binge   Polyphon X51705

GOSSEC

Rosine (1786) – opera
Gavotte arr. vln & pf Burmester
with E. Vagning pf   BHDKE 161   Polyphon HA70031

GOUNOD

Ave Maria (Méditation on Bach's "Prelude No. 1, in C" from Book I of
"Das Wohltemperirte Clavier") v & pf – arr. vln & orch.
            D.AHDKE 229–2   Polyphon HM80049
with Danish Radio Orch. – Reesen

GROSS

Tenderly (1946) v & pf – arr. vln & orch.
with orch. – Lampertz–Müller   Telefunken TW30089

HANDEL

Serse (1738) – opera
Ombra mai fu "Largo" arr. vln & orch.
            D.AHDKE 230–2   Polyphon HM80049
with Danish Radio Orch. – Reesen

HENRIQUES

Djaevledans (Devil dance) vln & pf
with E. Vagning pf   BHDKE 124   Decca C16019
                      Polyphon HA70020

Myggedans (Gnat's dance) Op. 20, No. 5 vln & pf
with E. Vagning pf   BHDKE 123   Decca C16019
                      Polyphon HA70020

(4) Songs, Op. 3 v & pf
No. 4. Agnetes Vuggevise arr. vln & pf Henriques
with E. Vagning pf   BHDKE 133–1   Polyphon HA70023

KÁLMÁN

Gräfin Mariza (1924) – operetta
Komm' Zigany arr. vln & orch.
with Copenhagen   AHDKE 40–2   Decca K24005
Radio Symphony Orch. – Reesen   Polyphon Z60122
Komm' Zigany arr. vln & orch.
with orch. – Lampertz–Müller   London 346012
                      Telefunken TW30089

KERN

All the things you are (1939) v & pf – arr. vln & orch.
with orch. – Lampertz–Müller   Telefunken TW30089

KREISLER

Caprice viennois, Op. 2 vln & pf
with orch. – Lampertz–Müller   Telefunken TW30090
Liebesfreud vln & pf
with E. Vagning pf   BHDKE 131–1   Polyphon HA70022
Liebesleid vln & pf
with E. Vagning pf   BHDKE 132–1   Polyphon HA70022
Schön Rosmarin vln & pf
with orch. – Binge   HDKE 279   London LB1121
                      Polyphon X51706

Allegretto (Boccherini) vln & pf
with orch. – Lampertz–Müller   Telefunken TW30090
Praeludium & Allegro (Pugnani) vln & pf
with orch. – Lampertz–Müller   Telefunken TW30090

LACOMBE

Aubade printanière, Op. 37 pf – arr vln & orch.
with orch.   D.BHDKE 255   Polyphon HA70034

LISZT

(3) Liebesträume, G326 pf
No. 3. Liebestraum No. 3, in A flat arr. vln & orch. Tworek
with orch. – Lampertz–Müller   Telefunken TW30090

MARTINI (Il Tedesco)

Plaisir d'amour v & pf – arr. vln & orch.
with orch. – Binge   HDKE 275   London LB1121
                      Polyphon X51704

MASSENET

Thaïs (1894) – opera
Méditation arr. vln, orch. & cho
with orch. & Peter Knight Singers –   London LB1121
Binge

MORTENSEN

Kitten on the strings vln & pf
with orch. – Lampertz–   HDK 2312   Polyphon X51094
Müller   Telefunken TW30089

MOSZKOWSKI

(6) Klavierstücke, Op. 15 pf – 4 hands
No. 1. Serenata arr. vln & pf
with E. Vagning pf   HDK 2904   Polyphon HA70037
No. 1. Serenata arr. vln & orch.
with orch. – Lampertz–Müller   Telefunken TW30090

NOVAČEK

(8) Concert caprices Op. 5 vln & pf
No. 4. Perpetuum mobile
with E. Vagning pf   HDK 2888   Polyphon HA70032

POLIAKIN

(Le) Canari (Concert–polka) vln & pf
with E. Vagning pf   BHDKE 168–1   Polyphon HA70027
(Le) Canari (Concert–polka) vln & pf
with G. Hemmeshøi   HDK 1130   Polyphon NS90827
Frederiksen pf

PONCE

Estrellita (1913) v & pf – arr. vln & pf Tworek & Reesen
with E. Vagning pf   HDK 2900   Polyphon HA70037

PORTER

Begin the beguine (1935) v & pf – arr. vln & orch.
with orch. – Lampertz–Müller   Telefunken TW30089

PREHN

Violinen synger vln & orch.
with string orch. –   HDK 2313   Polyphon X51094
Prehn

RIISAGER

Lullaby (Sovesang) vln & pf
with E. Vagning pf   HDK 2893   Polyphon HA70036
Palavas vln & pf
with H. Aurvig pf   HDK 3100   Polyphon HA70039
Sonata, Op. 55a vln, vlc & pf
with J. Hye–Knudsen vlc & E.   Decca LM4555
Vagning pf   London LS785
Sonata, Op. 55b 2 vlns
with C. Senderowitz vln   Decca LM4555
                              London LS785

RIMSKY–KORSAKOV

Sadko (1898) – opera
Chant hindou arr. vln & pf Kreisler
with E. Vagning pf   D.BHDKE 164   Polyphon HA70028
(The) Tale of Tsar Saltan (1900) – opera
Flight of the bumblebee (Act III) orch. – arr. vln & pf Hartmann
with E. Vagning pf   HDK 2891   Polyphon HA70027

SARASATE

Zigeunerweisen, Op. 20 vln & pf or orch.
with Danish Radio   AHDK 41/2–2   Polydor 516812
Orch. – Reesen   Polyphon HM80018
Zigeunerweisen, Op. 20 vln & pf or orch.
with orch. – Binge   HDKE 274   London LB1121
                                Polyphon X51706

SCHUBERT

(2) Lieder, Op. 98 (D498) v & pf
No. 2. Wiegenlied (Schlafe, holder süsser Knabe)
with E. Vagning pf   HDK 2895   Polyphon HA70004

SUK

(4) Pieces, Op. 17 vln & pf
No. 4. Burleska
with E. Vagning pf   HDK 2894   Polyphon HA70036

TARTINI

Sonata in g "Il Trillo del Diavolo" vln & c – arr. vln & pf Kreisler
with E. Vagning pf   Decca K28189/90

THOMÉ

Simple aveu, Op. 25 pf – arr. vln & orch.
with orch.   D.BHDKE 256   Polyphon HA70034

TOSELLI

Serenade, Op. 6 vln & pf
with E. Vagning pf   HDK 2898   Polyphon HA70045

TWOREK

Boogie for two vln & pf
with H. Aurvig pf   HDK 3101   Polyphon HA70039
Boogie for two vln & pf – arr. vln & orch. Aurvig
with orch. – Lampertz–Müller   Telefunken TW30089
Capriccietto vln & pf
with E. Vagning pf   BHDKE 134–1   Polyphon HA70023
Copenhagen joke vln & pf
with orch. – Lampertz–Müller   Telefunken TW30089
Gøglerens drøm (Gypsy dreams) – csárdas vln & pf
with orch.   BHDK 177/8   Polyphon X51250
(The) Talking violin vln & pf
with orch. – Lampertz–Müller   Telefunken TW30089

VILLA–LOBOS

(0) Canto do cysne negro (1917) vlc & pf – arr. vln & pf Villa–Lobos
with orch. – Lampertz–Müller   Telefunken TW30090

WIENIAWSKI

Concerto No. 2, in d, Op. 22 vln & orch.
          AHDKE 33–1, 34–2, 35–1 &   Decca AK24011/3
with Danish Radio Orch. –   36/7–2   Polyphon HM80015/7
Tuxen
Mazurka in a, Op. 3 "Kujawiak" vln & pf
with E. Vagning pf   AHDKE 38–2   Decca AK24011
                              Polyphon HM80015

Dmitri Mikhailovich TZIGANOV (1903–   )

ALABIEV

Sonata vln & pf
  with piano
                    Mezhdunarodnaya Kniga
                    D1125/6

Trio in a pf, vln & vlc
  with E. Gilels pf & S. Shirinsky vlc
                    Mezhdunarodnaya Kniga
                    D347/8, D16324/9

BEETHOVEN

Trio in B flat, Op. 11 cl, vlc & pf – arr. pf, vln & vlc
  with A. Goldenweiser pf & S.   Mezhdunarodnaya Kniga
  Shirinsky vlc   D07641/6

RAVEL

Trio in a (1915) pf, vln & vlc
  with A. Goldenweiser pf & S.   Mezhdunarodnaya Kniga
  Shirinsky vlc   D15960/3

George TZIPINE (1907–   )

BRUCH

Kol Nidrei, Op. 47 vlc or vln & orch.
  with piano   Pathé X9814

CHOPIN

(12) Etudes, Op. 10 pf
  No. 3. Etude No. 3, in E arr. vln & org
  with G. Ghestem org   Odeon 281331

COATES

Bird songs at eventide v & pf – arr. vln & org
  with organ   Parlophone F1496

GRIEG

Peer Gynt (Suite No. 2) Op. 55
  No. 4. Solveig's song arr. vln & pf Sitt
  with G. Ghestem org   Odeon 281353

MISRAKI

In my heart (Hungarian melody) v & pf – arr. vln & org
  with organ   Parlophone F1496

RAMEAU

(Les) Fêtes D'Hébé (1739) – opera
  Rondeau arr. vln & vlc
  with J. Tzipine vlc   Pathé X9832

  Tambourin arr. vln & vlc
  with J. Tzipine vlc   Pathé X9832

RIMSKY–KORSAKOV

Sadko (1898) – opera
  Chant hindou arr. vln & pf Kreisler
  with G. Ghestem org   Odeon 281353

VECSEY

Valse triste vln & pf
  with G. Ghestem org   Odeon 281331

Uto UGHI (1944–   )

KREISLER

Praeludium & Allegro (Pugnani) vln & pf
  with E. Lush pf   HMV 7EP7125, 7EPQ655,
                     PES5279, PESQ2009

TARTINI

Sonata in g "Il Trillo del Diavolo" vln & c – arr. vln & pf Kreisler
  with E. Lush pf   HMV 7EP7119, 7EPQ652,
                     PESQ2008

WIENIAWSKI

Scherzo–Tarantelle, Op. 16 vln & pf
  with E. Lush pf   HMV 7EP7125, 7EPQ655,
                     PES5279, PESQ2009

Eugenia UMINSKA (1910–   )

ANDRZEJOWSKI

Burleska vln & pf
  with J. Lefeld pf   WJ 544[2]   Columbia DM1846

BACEWICZ

Oberek No. 1 (1952) vln & pf
  with I. Newton pf   CXE 12965–1 Parlophone R20603

BACH, C.P.E.

Sonata in G, W157 2 vlns & c
  with I. Dubiska vln, J. Lefeld hpsi &   Muza XL0287
  K. Wilkomirska vlc

BACH, J.S.

Sonata in d, BWV1036 2 vlns & c
  with I. Dubiska vln, J. Lefeld hpsi &   Muza XL0287
  K. Wilkomirska vlc

HANDEL

(9) Sonatas, Op. 2 (1724) 2 vlns or obs & c
  Sonata No. 7, in g
  with I. Dubiska vln, J. Lefeld hpsi &   Muza XL0287
  K. Wilkomirska vlc

  Sonata No. 8, in g
  with I. Dubiska vln, J. Lefeld hpsi &   Muza XL0287
  K. Wilkomirska vlc

KARLOWICZ

Romance vln & orch.
  with Polish Radio Symphony Orch. –   Columbia DM1843
  Mzaurkiewicz

SZYMANOWSKI

Concerto No. 1, in a, Op. 35 (1922) vln & orch.
                CXE 12362–1, 12363–2 & Decca DL7516
  with Philharmonia   12364/7–1   Parlophone R20563/5
  Orch. – Fitelberg

Concerto No. 1, in a, Op. 35 (1922) vln & orch.
  with Polish Radio Symphony Orch. –   Muza XL1026
  Fitelberg

Concerto No. 2, Op. 61 (1932/3) vln & orch.
  with Polish Radio Symphony Orch. –   Bruno BR14069
  Fitelberg   Muza XL1026

SZYMANOWSKI – *Continued*

Harnasie, Op. 51 (1926) – ballet orch.
   Highland melody arr. vln & pf Kochański
    with Z. Dyget pf   Orpheon 143
   Highland melody arr. vln & pf Kochański
    with I. Newton pf   CXE 12965–1   Parlophone R20603
King Roger, Op. 46 (1926) – opera
   Chant de Roxane arr. vln & pf Kochański
    with J. Lefeld pf   WJ 538   Columbia DM1846
(3) Mythes, Op. 30 (1915) vln & pf
   No. 1. La Fontaine d'Aréthuse
    with Z. Dyget pf   Orpheon 141
   No. 2. Narcisse
    with Z. Dyget pf   Orpheon 139
   No. 3. Dryades et Pan
    with Z. Dyget pf   Orpheon 142
(12) Piesni kurpiowskie (Kurpian songs) Op. 58 (1931/2) v & pf
   Dance arr. vln & pf Kochański
    with Z. Dyget pf   Orpheon 143
   Polish folksong arr. vln & pf Kochański
    with I. Newton pf   CXE 12964–1   Parlophone R20603
Romance in D, Op. 23 (1909) vln & pf
    with Z. Dyget pf   Orpheon 138

Otilie UNGERMANNOVÁ (1907–)

ŘÍDKÝ

(3) Compositions, Op. 26 (1933) vln & pf
   No. 2. Lullaby
    with J. Řídký pf   045109   Supraphon G22845
                                   Ultraphon G14918
Polka–Fantasie, Op. 24 (1932) vln & pf
    with J. Řídký pf   045109/10 Supraphon G22845
                                     Ultraphon G14918

Yoshio UNNO (1936–)

BEETHOVEN

Romance No. 1, in G, Op. 40 vln & orch.
   with Tokyo CBS Symphony Orch. –   CBS/Sony SONC16004
   Mori   Columbia MS7411
Romance No. 2, in F, Op. 50 vln & orch.
   with Tokyo CBS Symphony Orch. –   CBS/Sony SONC16004
   Mori   Columbia MS7411
Sonata No. 9, in A, Op. 47 "Kreutzer" vln & pf
   with H. Kobayashi pf   King SKR1008

BRAHMS

Sonata No. 2, in A, Op. 100 vln & pf
   with H. Kobayashi pf   King SKR1008
(16) Waltzes, Op. 39 pf duet
   No. 15. Waltz No.15, in A flat arr. vln & pf "in A" Kreisler
    with H. Kobayashi pf   King SKR1008

MASSENET

Thaïs (1894) – opera
   Méditation vln & orch.
    with Tokyo CBS Symphony Orch. –   CBS/Sony SONC16004
    Mori   Columbia MS7411

SAINT–SAËNS

Introduction & Rondo Capriccioso, Op. 28 vln & orch.
   with Tokyo CBS Symphony Orch. –   CBS/Sony SONC16004
   Mori   Columbia MS7411

SARASATE

Zigeunerweisen, Op. 20 vln & pf or orch.
   with Tokyo CBS Symphony Orch. –   CBS/Sony SONC16004
   Mori   Columbia MS7411

TCHAIKOVSKY

Souvenir d'un lieu cher, Op. 42 vln & pf
   No. 3. Mélodie
    with Tokyo CBS Symphony Orch. –   CBS/Sony SONC16004
    Mori   Columbia MS7411

TOYAMA

Concerto (1963) vln & orch.
   with NHK Symphony Orch. – Toyama Columbia OS702, OS10061

Béla URBAN

DEBUSSY

Ariettes oubliées (1888) v & pf
   No. 2. Il pleure dans mon coeur arr. vln & pf Hartmann
    with V. Urban pf   Classic Editions CE1005

IBERT

(Le) Jardinier de Samos (1932) – Incidental music orch.
   Prélude
    with M. Hubert vlc   Classic Editions CE1005

KHACHATURIAN

Trio in g (1932) cl, vln & pf
   with S. Bellison cl & V. Urban pf   Classic Editions CE1002

MILHAUD

Sonata No. 2 (1917) vln & pf
   with V. Urban pf   Classic Editions CE1005

RAVEL

Sonata (1927) vln & pf
   with V. Urban pf   Classic Editions CE1002
Sonata (1922) vln & vlc
   with M. Hubert vlc   Classic Editions CE1005

Masuko USHIODA (1942–)

BARTÓK

Concerto No. 2 (1938) vln & orch.
   with Japan Philharmonic Symphony   Denon OS10024
   Orch. – Mori
Rhapsody No. 1, in G (1928) vln & orch.
   with N. Walter pf
                             Mezhdunarodnaya Kniga
                             D018121/2

BRUCH

Concerto No. 1, in g, Op. 26 vln & orch.
with Japan Philharmonic Symphony   HMV SXLP30137
Orch. – Ozawa

PAGANINI

(24) Caprices, Op. 1 (1801/7) solo vln
Caprice No. 11, in C
(unaccompanied)   Mezhdunarodnaya Kniga
D018121/2

SIBELIUS

Concerto in d, Op. 47 vln & orch.
with Japan Philharmonic Symphony   HMV SXLP30137
Orch. – Ozawa

TCHAIKOVSKY

Concerto in D, Op. 35 vln & orch.
with Japan Philharmonic Symphony   Denon OS10024
Orch. – Mori

Sérénade mélancolique in b flat, Op. 26 vln & orch. – arr. vln & pf
Wilhelmj
with N. Walter pf   Mezhdunarodnaya Kniga
D018121/2

Souvenir d'un lieu cher, Op. 42 vln & pf
No. 3. Mélodie
with N. Walter pf   Mezhdunarodnaya Kniga
D018121/2

TOYAMA

Sonata (1964) vln & pf
with N. Walter pf   Mezhdunarodnaya Kniga
D018121/2

Václav VAČÉK (1918–)

TARTINI

(12) Sonatas, Op. 1 (1734) vln & c
Sonata No. 10, in g "Didone abbandonata"
with F. Škvor pf   Supraphon LPM457, SUF20361

Agnès VADAS (1929–)

BARTÓK

(6) Rumanian folk dances (1915) pf – arr. vln & pf Székely
with piano   Qualiton SZK3352
Sonata in g (1944) solo vln
(unaccompanied)   Le Chant du Monde LDP8209

Mikhail Israilevich VAIMAN (1926–)

ARAPOV

Concerto (1964) vln & orch.
with Leningrad Philharmonic   Mezhdunarodnaya Kniga
Symphony Orch. – Jansons   D020567, S01589

BACH

Concerto No. 2, in E, BWV1042 vln, strs & c
with Leningrad Philharmonic   Mezhdunarodnaya Kniga
Symphony Orch. – Gozman   D014450, SM02287/8

BACH – *Continued*

Concerto in d, BWV1043 2 vlns, strs & c
with B. Gutnikov vln & Leningrad   Mezhdunarodnaya Kniga
Philharmonic Symphony Orch. –   D014449/50, SM02287/8
Gozman

BARTÓK

(6) Rumanian folk dances (1915) pf – arr. vln & pf Székely
with M. Karandashova pf   Electrecord ECE08
   Mezhdunarodnaya Kniga
   D00010233/4, D010325/8
Sonata No. 1 (1921) vln & pf
with M. Karandashova pf   Mezhdunarodnaya Kniga
   D019209

BEETHOVEN

(3) Sonatas, Op. 12 vln & pf
No. 1. Sonata No. 1, in D
with M. Karandashova pf   Electrecord ECE08
(3) Sonatas, Op. 30 vln & pf
No. 2. Sonata No. 7, in c
with M. Karandashova pf   Mezhdunarodnaya Kniga
   D017633
Sonata No. 10, in G, Op. 96 vln & pf
with M. Karandashova pf   Mezhdunarodnaya Kniga
   D017634

BRAHMS

(21) Hungarian Dances pf duet
Hungarian dance No. 7, in A arr. vln & pf Joachim
with M. Karandashova pf   Supraphon SUEC861, SUK30328

CHOPIN

Nocturne No. 20, in c sharp, Op. posth pf – arr. vln & pf Radionov
with M. Karandashova pf   Supraphon SUEC861, SUK30328

DINICU

Hora staccato vln & pf – arr. Heifetz
with M. Karandashova pf   Electrecord ECE08

HAYDN

Concerto No. 1, in C, H.VIIa, No. 1 (1765) vln & orch.
with Leningrad Philharmonic Chamber   Mezhdunarodnaya Kniga
Orch. – Shinder   D026057/8, SM02711/2

MATCHAVARIANI

Concerto in d (1950) vln & orch.
with USSR State Radio Symphony   Colosseum CRLP172
Orch. – Matchavariani   Mezhdunarodnaya Kniga
   D0536/7
   Westminster XWN18535

MILHAUD

(12) Saudades do Brasil (1920/1) pf
No. 7. Corcavado arr. vln & pf Lévy
with M. Karandashova pf   Supraphon SUEC861, SUK30328

MOZART

Concerto No. 5, in A, K219 "Turkish" vln & orch.
with Leningrad Philharmonic Chamber   Mezhdunarodnaya Kniga
Orch. – Shinder   D026057/8, SM02711/2

PROKOFIEV

Cinderella, Op. 87 (1941/4) – ballet orch.
  Waltz arr. vln & pf Fichtenholz
  with M. Karandashova pf   London LD9154, TW91068
Romeo & Juliet, Op. 64b (1935/6) – 2nd ballet suite orch.
  March arr. vln & pf Grunes
  with M. Karandashova pf   Electrecord ECE08
  No. 4. Danse de jeunes antillaises arr. vln & pf Grunes
  with M. Karandashova pf   Electrecord ECE08
Sonata No. 1, in f, Op. 80 vln & pf
  with M. Karandashova pf   Mezhdunarodnaya Kniga
                                   D3246/7

RAVEL

Sonata (1927) vln & pf
  with M. Karandashova pf   Mezhdunarodnaya Kniga D4832

SALMANOV

Sonata No. 2 (1962) vln & pf
  with M. Karandashova pf   Mezhdunarodnaya Kniga
                                   D019210

SARASATE

Zigeunerweisen, Op. 20 vln & pf or orch.
  with M. Karandashova pf   Electrecord ECE08
                                    Mezhdunarodnaya Kniga
                                    D00010233/4, D010325/8

SCHUBERT

Rondo brillante in b, Op. 70 (D895) vln & pf
  with M. Karandashova pf   Mezhdunarodnaya Kniga D4833

SHOSTAKOVICH

Trio No. 2, in e, Op. 67 "In memory of I.I. Sollertinsky" pf, vln & vlc
  with P. Serebryakov pf & M.   HMV ASD2718
  Rostropovich vlc   Melodiya–Angel SR40091
                                     Mezhdunarodnaya Kniga
                                     SM01805

SIBELIUS

Concerto in d, Op. 47 vln & orch.
  with Leningrad Philharmonic   Mezhdunarodnaya Kniga
  Symphony Orch. – Jansons   D017321/2, SM2201/2

TCHAIKOVSKY

Sérénade mélancolique in b flat, Op. 26 vln & orch. – arr. vln & pf
  Wilhelmj
  with M. Karandashova pf   London LD9154, TW91068
Waltz–scherzo, Op. 34 vln & pf or orch. – arr. Bezékirsky
  with M. Karandashova pf   London LD9154, TW91068
                                     Supraphon SUEC861, SUK30328

VOLOSHINOV

Sonata in e, Op. 17 vln & pf
  with N. Perelman pf   Mezhdunarodnaya Kniga
                                D03237

Dora VALESCA–BECKER

BRAHMS

(21) Hungarian dances pf duet
  Hungarian dance No. 2, in d arr. vln & pf Joachim
  with piano   Bettini cylinder

DELIBES

Sylvia (1876) – ballet orch.
  No. 16a. Pizzicato–scherzettino (Act III) arr. vln & pf
  with piano   Bettini cylinder

GABRIEL–MARIE

(La) Cinquantaine (1894) pf duet – arr. vln & pf
  with piano   Bettini cylinder

GRIEG

(4) Norwegian Dances, Op. 35 (1881) pf duet; orch.
  No. 2. Norwegian dance No. 2, in A arr. vln & pf Flesch
  with piano   Bettini cylinder

LÉONARD

Duo de Concert, Op. 25 vln & pf
  with piano   Bettini cylinder

MASCAGNI

Cavalleria Rusticana (1890) – opera
  Intermezzo orch. – arr. vln & pf
  with piano   Bettini cylinder

MENDELSSOHN

(6) Songs without words, Op. 62 pf
  No. 6. Song without words No. 30, in A "Spring song" arr. vln & pf
  with piano   Bettini cylinder

PIERNÉ

Sérénade in A, Op. 7 (1875) pf – arr. vln & pf
  with piano   Bettini cylinder

RAFF

(6) Pieces, Op. 85 vln & pf
  No. 3. Cavatina in D
  with piano   Bettini cylinder

RIES

Suite No. 3, in G, Op. 34 vln & pf
  No. 5. Perpetuum mobile
  with piano   Bettini cylinder

SARASATE

Zigeunerweisen, Op. 20 vln & pf or orch.
  with piano   Bettini cylinder

SCHUBERT

(14) Schwanengesang, D957 (1828) v & pf
  No. 4. Ständchen "Serenade" arr. vln & pf Reményi
  with piano   Bettini cylinder

SCHUMANN

(13) Kinderscenen, Op. 15 pf
  No. 7. Träumerei arr. vln & pf
  with piano   Bettini cylinder

THOMÉ

Simple aveu, Op. 25 pf – arr. vln & pf
  with piano   Bettini cylinder

WIENIAWSKI

Mazurka in a, Op. 3 "Kujawiak" vln & pf
  with piano   Bettini cylinder

(2) Mazurkas, Op. 19 vln & pf
  No. 1. Mazurka No. 1, in G "Obertass"
  with piano   Bettini cylinder

Ronald VALPREDA

GEMINIANI

(6) Concerti grossi, Op. 3 (1755) orch.
Concerto grosso No. 2, in g
with P. Toso vln, F. Zampieri vln, F.   CBS 32 11 0003, 32 11 0004,
Sangiorgi vln & I Solisti Veneti –   BRG72057, SBRG72057
Scimone

VIVALDI

Concerto in B flat, P.367 (F.I, No. 59) 4 vlns, strs & c
with P. Toso vln, F. Zampieri vln, F.   CBS 32 11 0003, 32 11 0004,
Sangiorgi vln & I Solisti Veneti –   BRG72057, SBRG72057
Scimone

Arthur VANCE

SAINT-SAËNS

(Le) Déluge, Op. 45 (1876) – oratorio
Prélude vln & orch. – arr. vln & pf Saint-Saëns
  with piano   38917 Regal G7160

Emanuel VARDI (1915–)

BARTÓK

Rhapsody No. 1, in G (1928) vln & orch.
  with New Symphony Orch. – Serly   Bartók BRS307
Rhapsody No. 2, in d (1928) vln & orch.
  with New Symphony Orch. – Autori   Bartók BRS307

K. VARENBERG

VIVALDI

(12) Concerti, Op. 3 "L'Estro armonico" var. cbns & strs
Concerto No. 10, in b, P.148 (F.IV, No. 10) 4 vlns, strs & c
with E. Boder vln, M. Furer vln, Y.   Mezhdunarodnaya Kniga
Milkis vln & Leningrad Chamber   D018097/8
Orch. – Gozman
Concerto No. 11, in d, P.250 (F.IV, No. 11) 2 vlns, vlc, strs & c
with L. Gozman vln & Leningrad   Mezhdunarodnaya Kniga
Chamber Orch. – Gozman   D018097/8

Ruben George VARGA (1928–)

BACH

(3) Sonatas & 3 Partitas, BWV1001/6 solo vln
Partita No. 2, in d, BWV1004
(unaccompanied)   Westminster WST17136,
                   XWN19136

BRAHMS

Concerto in D, Op. 77 (cadenzas by Joachim) vln & orch.
  with Vienna Chamber Orch. –   Orpheus OR364
  Topolski

Sonata No. 1, in G, Op. 78 vln & pf
  with G. Bennette pf   Musical Heritage Society
                   MHS923

Sonata No. 2, in A, Op. 100 vln & pf
  with G. Bennette pf   Musical Heritage Society
                   MHS923

Sonata No. 3, in d, Op. 108 vln & pf
  with G. Bennette pf   Musical Heritage Society
                   MHS934

FRANCK

Sonata in A (1886) vln & pf
  with J. Gurt pf   Musical Heritage Society
                   MHS934

PAGANINI

(24) Caprices, Op. 1 (1801/7) solo vln
Caprice No. 24, in a
(unaccompanied)   Westminster WST17136,
                   XWN19136

Nel cor più non mi sento "Sonata appassionata con variazioni" (on the aria
from Paisiello's opera "La bella molinara"), Op. 38 (1820 or 1821) solo
vln
(unaccompanied)   Westminster WST17136,
                   XWN19136

VARGA

Prelude & 4 Caprices solo vln
(unaccompanied)   Westminster WST17136,
                   XWN19136

Tibor VARGA (1921–)

BACH

Concerto No. 1, in a, BWV1041 vln, strs & c
  with   CAX 10545/8–1 Columbia DX1586/7
Philharmonia Orch. – Bernard
Concerto No. 1, in a, BWV1041 vln, strs & c
  with chamber orch. – Varga   Somerset SM607
Concerto No. 2, in E, BWV1042 vln, strs & c
  with Berlin Philharmonic Orch. –   Archive APM14050, PV2429/30
Lehmann
Concerto No. 2, in E, BWV1042 vln, strs & c
  with chamber orch. – Varga   Somerset SM607

BARTÓK

Concerto No. 2 (1938) vln & orch.
with Berlin Philharmonic Orch. –
Fricsay
Decca DL9545
Deutsche Grammophon 72075/7,
LPM18006

BEETHOVEN

Concerto in D, Op. 61 vln & orch.
with Zagreb Philharmonic Orch. –
Horvat
Musica et litera 8015

Romance No. 1, in G, Op. 50 vln & orch.
CAX 10549/50–1A   Columbia DX1615
with Philharmonia Orch. – Bernard

BRUCH

Concerto No. 1, in g, Op. 26 vln & orch.
with Philharmonia Orch. – Susskind
Columbia SX1017

Concerto No. 1, in g, Op. 26 vln & orch.
with Vienna Festival Orch. – Wallberg   Concert Hall SMSC2587
Guilde Internationale du Disque
SMS2587

CHOPIN

(3) Nocturnes, Op. 9 pf
No. 2. Nocturne No. 2, in E flat arr. vln & pf Sarasate
with piano
Radiola RBM159

Nocturne No. 20, in c sharp, Op. posth pf – arr. vln & pf Milstein
with piano
Radiola RBM159

DOHNÁNYI

Ruralia Hungarica, Op. 32A pf
No. 7. Moto vivace arr. vln & pf Kreisler
with piano
HMV HUC101

FALLA

(La) Vida Breve (1913) – opera
Danza española orch. – arr. vln & pf Kreisler
with G. Moore pf   CAX 10173–3   Columbia DX1533

FERRARA

Burleska vln & pf
with piano
HMV HUC100

GESZLER

(The) Humming top vln & pf
with G. Moore pf   CAX 10169–1   Columbia DX1481

HUBAY

(6) Blumenleben, Op. 30 vln & pf
No. 5. Der Zephir
with piano
Radiola RBM159

KREISLER

Sicilienne & Rigaudon (Francoeur) vln & pf
with piano
HMV HUC100

MENDELSSOHN

Concerto in e, Op. 64 vln & orch.
with Berlin Philharmonic Orch. –
Lehmann
Deutsche Grammophon 72125/6,
LPE16015, LPX29253
Heliodor 478409

MOZART

Adagio in E, K261 vln & orch.
with Tibor Varga Chamber Orch. –
Varga
Musica et litera 8021, 10013

Concerto No. 1, in B flat, K207 (cadenzas by Varga) vln & orch.
with Philharmonia Orch. – Susskind   Columbia SX1017

Concerto No. 2, in D, K211 vln & orch.
with chamber orch. – Varga
Somerset SM608

Concerto No. 3, in G, K216 vln & orch.
with chamber orch. – Varga
Somerset SM608

Concerto No. 4, in D, K218 vln & orch.
with Tibor Varga Chamber Orch. –
Varga
Musica et litera 8022

Concerto No. 5, in A, K219 "Turkish" vln & orch.
with Tibor Varga Chamber Orch. –
Varga
Musica et litera 8021

Rondo in C, K373 vln & orch.
with Tibor Varga Chamber Orch. –
Varga
Musica et litera 8021, 10013

NIELSEN

Concerto in D, Op. 33 (1911) vln & orch.
with Royal Danish Orch. – Semkow
Deutsche Grammophon
LPM39184, SLPM139184
Fona S1
Heliodor 89764
Turnabout TV4043, TV34043

PRINCIPE

(El) Campielo (1932) vln & pf
with G. Moore pf   CAX 10169–1   Columbia DX1481

SARASATE

Introduction & Tarantelle, Op. 43 vln & pf
with G. Moore pf   CAX 10172–1   Columbia DX1481

STRAVINSKY

Firebird (1910) – ballet orch.
No. 5. Berceuse arr. vln & pf Dushkin & Stravinsky
with piano
HMV HUC101

SZYMANOWSKI

(3) Mythes, Op. 30 (1915) vln & pf
No. 1. Le Fontaine d'Aréthuse
with G. Moore pf   CAX 10168–3   Columbia DX1533

TCHAIKOVSKY

Concerto in D, Op. 35 vln & orch.
with Vienna Festival Orch. – Auberson   Concert Hall SMSA3046

Istvan VARKONYI

KODÁLY

Serenade, Op. 12 (1919/20) 2 vlns & vla
with V. Tátrai vln & G. Konrad vla   Qualiton LPX11449

Cornelia VASILE (1949–   )

PAGANINI

(24) Caprices, Op. 1 (1801/7) solo vln
Caprice No. 5, in a
(unaccompanied)   Deutsche Grammophon 642106
Caprice No. 7, in a
(unaccompanied)   Deutsche Grammophon 642106
Caprice No. 9, in E
(unaccompanied)   Deutsche Grammophon 642106
Caprice No. 11, in C
(unaccompanied)   Deutsche Grammophon 642106
Caprice No. 13, in B flat
(unaccompanied)   Deutsche Grammophon 642106
Caprice No. 15, in e
(unaccompanied)   Deutsche Grammophon 642106
Caprice No. 19, in E flat
(unaccompanied)   Deutsche Grammophon 642106
Caprice No. 22, in F
(unaccompanied)   Deutsche Grammophon 642106
Caprice No. 23, in E flat
(unaccompanied)   Deutsche Grammophon 642106
Caprice No. 24, in a
(unaccompanied)   Deutsche Grammophon 642106

YSAŸE

(6) Sonatas, Op. 27 solo vln
Sonata No. 2, in a
(unaccompanied)   Deutsche Grammophon 642106

Ferenc von VECSEY (1893–1935)

BACH

(4) Suites, BWV1066/9 strs & c
Suite No. 3, in D: Air (2nd mvt) BWV1068 2 obs, 3 tpts, drms & strs –
arr. vln & pf as "Air on the G–string" by Wilhelmj
with piano   Delta TQD3035
                                    Fonotipia 62507
                                    Odeon 62507, 67774, 8022FXA,
                                    1597FXI, JX118522

Suite No. 3, in D: Air (2nd mvt) BWV1068 2 obs, 3 tpts, drms, strs & c
– arr. vln & pf as "Air on the G–string" by Wilhelmj
with K. Szreter pf   Vox 06295

Suite No. 3, in D: Air (2nd mvt) BWV1068 2 obs, 3 tpts, drms & strs –
arr. vln & pf as "Air on the G–string" by Wilhelmj
with G. Agosti pf   5745½ GR   Decca PO5115
                                    Polydor 10413, 62750

BAZZINI

(La) Ronde des lutins, Op. 25 vln & pf
with piano   XXph 4636   Fonotipia 74089
                                    Odeon 76430, 2042XX,
                                    8028FXXR, 8020XX, JXX81010
                                    Pearl GEM102

BEETHOVEN

(3) Sonatas, Op. 12 vln & pf
No. 3. Sonata No. 3, in E flat
              5738 GR, 5739/40½ GR, 5741   Cetra LL3005/7
with G.   GR & 5742/3½ GR   Decca DE7033/5
Agosti pf   Polydor 10318/20, 62717/9

DEBUSSY

Petite Suite (1889) pf – 4 hands
No. 1. En bateau arr. vln & pf Kreisler
with G. Agosti pf   5736½ GR   Polydor 10306, 62716

DVOŘÁK

(8) Humoresques, Op. 101 pf
No. 7. Humoresque No. 7, in G flat arr. vln & pf "in G" Wilhelmj
with piano   Fonotipia 74090
                                    Odeon 76431, 8028FXXF,
                                    2044XX, 8020XX, JXX81011

No. 7. Humoresque No. 7, in G flat arr. vln & pf "in G" Wilhelmj
with K. Szreter pf   2550   Vox 06294

HANDEL

(15) Sonatas, Op. 1 (?1731) fl or vln & c
Sonata No. 9, in B: Andante (1st mvt) arr. vln & pf as "Larghetto" by
Hubay
with piano   Xph 4523   Fonotipia 62506
                                    Odeon 67775, 8022FXA,
                                    1597FXI, JX118521, RX98086

HUBAY

(Le) Luthier de Crémone, Op. 40 (1894) – opera
Intermezzo orch. – arr. vln & pf Hubay
with piano   Xph 4628   Fonotipia 62498
                                    Odeon O–5604, 8025FXC,
                                    JX118517, RX98077
                                    Okey 72402

(3) Transcriptions, Op. 3 vln & pf
No. 3. Carmen Fantasia (on themes from the opera by Bizet)
with piano   Gramophone & Typewriter
                                    7965/6, 47956/7

No. 3. Carmen Fantasia (on themes from the opera by Bizet): Habañera
with piano   Gramophone & Typewriter
                                    07900

KREISLER

Grave (W.F. Bach) vln & pf
with piano   Kristall 05050

Praeludium & Allegro (Pugnani) vln & pf
with piano   Kristall 05050

MERKLER

Berceuse in F vln & pf
with piano   Gramophone & Typewriter 7963

MOSZKOWSKI

(2) Stücke, Op. 45 pf
No. 2. Guitarre arr. vln & pf Sarasate
with piano   Fonotipia 62509
                                    Odeon 2230, 8023FXA, 1598FXI

PAGANINI

(24) Caprices, Op. 1 (1801/7) solo vln
Caprice No. 2, in b
(unaccompanied)

Fonotipia 62502
Odeon 67770, 8027FXC, 8029X

Caprice No. 13, in B flat arr. vln & pf Baerwald
with G. Agosti pf   5733 GR   Cetra LL3004
Odeon JX118518
Parlophone OL6005
Polydor 62720

Caprice No. 14, in E flat
(unaccompanied)

Fonotipia 62499
Odeon 67767, 8025FXC, 8030X

PALMGREN

(4) Morceaux, Op. 43 vln & pf
No. 3. Canzonetta in F
with G. Agosti pf

Polydor 10686

REGER

(60) Schlichte Weisen – 6 Books, Op. 76 v & pf
No. 52. Maria–Wiegenlied arr. vln & pf
with G. Agosti pf

Polydor 10413, 62750

SARASATE

Zigeunerweisen, Op. 20 vln & pf or orch.
with K. Szreter pf

Vox 06295

SCHUBERT

(7) Gesänge (set to Scott's "Lady of the Lake") Op. 52 v & pf
No. 6. Ave Maria, D839 arr. vln & pf Wilhelmj
with piano   Xph 4632   Fonotipia 62504
Odeon 8021FXA, 8029X,
1596XFI, JX118519, RX98111,
X67772

No. 6. Ave Maria, D839 arr. vln & pf Wilhelmj
with piano

Vox 06332

SCHUMANN

(13) Kinderscenen, Op. 15 pf
No. 7. Träumerei arr. vln & pf
with piano   5447 b   Gramophone & Typewriter 7964
HMV B388

No. 7. Träumerei arr. vln & pf
with piano

Fonotipia 62505
Odeon 62501, 8021FXA,
1596XFI, JX118520, X67773

No. 7. Träumerei arr. vln & pf
with piano

Vox 06332

SIBELIUS

Pan & Echo, Op. 53 orch.
No. 3. Nocturne arr. vln & pf Press
with G. Agosti pf   5747½ GR   Cetra LL3012
Decca PO5115
Polydor 10686

SINIGAGLIA

(4) Kleine Stücke, Op. 25 vln & pf
No. 2. Capriccio all'antica
with piano   Xph 4629   Fonotipia 62501
Odeon O–5604, 67769, 8026FXC,
8030X

TARTINI

Sonata in g "Il Trillo del Diavolo" vln & c – arr. vln & pf Hubay
with piano

Fonotipia 74091
Odeon 6639, 8024FXXD,
1599XXFI

VECSEY

Caprice nostalgica vln & pf
with G. Agosti pf   5735½ GR   Cetra LL3004
Polydor 62720

Caprice No. 2 "Le Cascade" vln & pf
with G. Agosti pf   5734½ GR   Cetra LL3004
Polydor 10306, 62716

Caprice No. 2 "Le Cascade" vln & pf
with K. Szreter pf   2548   Vox 06294

Foglio d'album vln & pf
with piano   Xph 4535   Fonotipia 62500
Odeon 8026FXC, RX98078

(A) Toi vln & pf
with piano

Vox 6292

Valse triste vln & pf
with piano

Vox 6292

WIENIAWSKI

(Le) Carnaval russe (on the Russian air "Po ulicy mostovoj") Op. 11 vln & pf
with piano

Fonotipia 74092

Fantaisie brillante (on themes from the opera "Faust" by Gounod) Op. 20 vln & orch.
with piano

Fonotipia 62508
Odeon 2229, 8023FXA, 1598FXI

Souvenir de Moscou, Op. 6 vln & pf or orch.
with piano

Fonotipia 62503 & 74092
Odeon 6640, 6027FXC &
1599XXFI, 8024FXXD

Sándor VÉGH (1905–)

BACH

(3) Sonatas & 3 Partitas, BWV1001/6 solo vln
Sonata No. 1, in g, BWV1001
(unaccompanied)   Valois MB840/2

Partita No. 1, in b, BWV1002
(unaccompanied)   Valois MB840/2

Sonata No. 2, in a, BWV1003
(unaccompanied)   Valois MB840/2

Partita No. 2, in d, BWV1004
(unaccompanied)   Valois MB840/2

Sonata No. 3, in C, BWV1005
(unaccompanied)   Valois MB840/2

Partita No. 3, in E, BWV1006
(unaccompanied)   Valois MB840/2

Joseph de VELDER

d'AMBROSIO

Romance in D, Op. 9 vln & pf
   with piano   16493   Homochord H325

LANGER

Grandfather, Op. 22 salon orch. – arr. vln & pf
  with piano   Homochord H337

Grandmother, Op. 20 pf – arr. vln & pf
  with piano   Homochord H337

RIMSKY–KORSAKOV

(Le) Coq d'Or (1910) – opera
  Hymn to the sun arr. vln & pf Kreisler
  with piano   Homochord H310
Sadko (1898) – opera
  Chant hindou arr. vln & pf Kreisler
  with piano   Homochord H310

TOSELLI

Serenade, Op. 6 vln & pf
  with orch.   16492   Homochord H325

Jacob M. VELT

BENATZKY

(Ein) Wiener Walzer orch. – arr. vln & orch.
  with orch.   BE 2335–II   HMV X3428

VELT

Söndag pa sätern vln & pf
  with orch.   BE 2358–II   HMV X3428

Josef VENCLÛ

GASTALDON

Musica proibita, Op. 5 vln & pf
  with piano   Ultraphon A22248

Jacques VERDON

BEETHOVEN

(3) Sonatas, Op. 30 vln & pf
  No. 3. Sonata No. 8, in G
  with G. Manny pf   Janus–Pirouette JA19002

PRÉVOST

Sonata (1960/1) vln & pf
  with G. Manny pf   Janus–Pirouette JA19002

Emmy VERHEY (1949–   )

BACH

Concerto in d, BWV1043 2 vlns, strs & c
  with C. Bor vln & Kunstmaandorkest,   Philips 88129DY
  Amsterdam – Kersjes

BEETHOVEN

Romance No. 2, in F, Op. 50 vln & orch.
  with Kunstmaandorkest, Amsterdam –   Fontana D88483Y, (in set K71
  Kersjes   BC801)
                                    Philips 88129DY

Maria VERMES

WOHLEGEMUTH

Concerto (1963) vln & orch.
  with Rundfunk Symphony Orch.,   Eterna 820501
  Leipzig – Kegel

Joke VERMEULEN

BADINGS

Capriccio (1952) vln & 2 soundtracks
  with electronic equipment   Epic BC1118, LC3759
                                Philips 835056AY

Lavinio VIANELLI

VIVALDI

Concerto in C, P.54 (F.XII, No. 17) 2 fls, 2 obs, bsn, 2 vlns, strs & c – rev. Malipiero
  with G. Tassinari fl, C. Hoogendoorn   Angelicum LPA5929
  fl, L. Caroli ob, G. Cappello ob, V.
  Menghini bsn, B. Salvi vln &
  Angelicum Chamber Orch. – Suvini

Paul VIARDOT (1857–1941)

GRIEG

(8) Lyric Pieces – Book II, Op. 38 pf
  No. 1. Berceuse arr. vln & pf Sitt
  with piano   Gramophone & Typewriter
                                37924

WIENIAWSKI

Légende, Op. 17 vln & pf or orch.
  with piano   Gramophone & Typewriter
                                37927/8

Luciano VICARI

VIVALDI

(12) Concerti, Op. 3 "L'Estro armonico" var. cbns & strs
  Concerto No. 1, in D, P.146 (F.IV, No. 8) 4 vlns, vlc, strs & c
  with A.M. Cotogni vln, R. Michelucci   Philips 835162AY, A02277L
  vln, W. Gallozzi vln & I Musici

  Concerto No. 4, in e, P.97 (F.I, No. 174) 4 vlns, strs & c
  with A.M. Cotogni vln, R. Michelucci   Philips 835162AY, A02277L
  vln, W. Gallozzi vln & I Musici

  Concerto No. 7, in F, P.249 (F.IV, No. 9) 4 vlns, strs & c
  with A.M. Cotogni vln, R. Michelucci   Philips 835163AY, A02278L
  vln, W. Gallozzi vln E. Altobelli vlc &
  I Musici

VIVALDI – *Continued*

Concerto No. 10, in b, P.148 (F.IV, No. 10) 4 vlns, strs & c
with A.M. Cotogni vln, R. Michelucci Fontana 894075ZKY
vln W. Gallozzi vln, E. Altobelli vlc & Philips 802735AY, (in set C71
I Musici AX401), 835164AY,
  839526VGY, A02279L

Concerto in c, P.419 (F.I, No. 2) (Op. 51, No. 3) "Il Sospetto" vln, strs & c
with I Musici Epic BC1021, LC3486
  Philips 835002AY, A00476L,
  ABL3237

Raoul VIDAS (1901–   )

DIMITRESCU

Danse villageoise, Op. 15 vln & pf
with piano Columbia 6M, A3488

FIORILLO

(36) Étude–Caprices, Op. 3 solo vln
Caprice No. 14, in g (Adagio) arr. vln & pf – G String – Vidas
with W. Golde pf 79330 Columbia A3313

SARASATE

(8) Danzas españolas vln & pf
No. 4. Jota navarra, Op. 22, No. 2
with piano Columbia A3488

SCHUBERT

Rosamunde von Cypern, Op. 26 (D797) (1823) – Incidental music orch.
No. 9. Ballet music II, in G arr. vln & pf Kreisler
with W. Golde pf 79331 Columbia 6M, A3313

Germaine VIGNON

MASSENET

Thaïs (1894) – opera
Méditation arr. vln & pf Marsick
with piano Perfectaphone 3925

MONTI

Csárdas (1904) vln & pf
with piano Perfectaphone 3925

Valeria VILKER

JANÁČEK

Sonata (1913/21) vln & pf
with B. Rakova pf Mezhdunarodnaya Kniga
  D16213/4

SHOSTAKOVICH

(3) Danses fantastiques, Op. 5 (1922) pf – arr. vln & pf Glickman
with B. Rakova pf Mezhdunarodnaya Kniga
  D16213/4

STRAVINSKY

Mavra (1922) – opera
Russian maiden's song (Parasha's aria) arr. vln & pf Dushkin &
Stravinsky
with B. Rakova pf Mezhdunarodnaya Kniga
  D16213/4

Pétrouchka (1911) – ballet orch.
Danse russe arr. vln & pf Dushkin & Stravinsky
with B. Rakova pf Mezhdunarodnaya Kniga
  D16213/4

Suite Italienne (on themes of Pergolesi) (1933) vln & pf
No. 5. Scherzo
with B. Rakova pf Mezhdunarodnaya Kniga
  D16213/4

TCHAIKOVSKY

(2) Pieces, Op. 10 pf
No. 2. Humoresque in G arr. vln & pf Kreisler
with B. Rakova pf Mezhdunarodnaya Kniga
  D16213/4

Carlos VILLA

BACH

(6) Brandenburg Concerti, BWV1046/51 (1721) strs & c
Brandenburg Concerto No. 1, in F, BWV1046 vln, 3 obs, bsn, 2 hrns, strs
& c
with M. Winfield ob, R. Leppard hpsi, HMV SXLP20110
soloists & New Philharmonia Chamber
Orch. – Littaur

Brandenburg Concerto No. 2, in F, BWV1047 tpt, fl, ob, vln, strs & c
with D. Mason tpt, G. Morris fl, M. HMV SXLP20110
Winfield ob & New Philharmonia
Chamber Orch. – Littaur

Brandenburg Concerto No. 3, in G, BWV1048 3 vlns, 3 vlas, 3 vlcs & cbs
with members of the New HMV SXLP20110
Philharmonia Chamber Orch. – Littaur

Brandenburg Concerto No. 4, in G, BWV1049 vln, 2 fls, strs & c
with G. Morris fl & New Philharmonia HMV SXLP20111
Chamber Orch. – Littaur

Brandenburg Concerto No. 5, in D, BWV1050 clav, fl, vln, strs & c
with R. Leppard hpsi G. Morris fl & HMV SXLP20111
New Philharmonia Chamber Orch. –
Littaur

BEETHOVEN

Sonata No. 5, in F, Op. 24 "Spring" vln & pf
with G. Pryor pf Music for Pleasure MFP2071

Sonata No. 9, in A, Op. 47 "Kreutzer" vln & pf
with G. Pryor pf Music for Pleasure MFP2071

PERGOLESI

Concerto in B flat vln & strs
with Anglian Ensemble – Snashall Pye GGC4041, GSGC14041

Zinovi VINNIKOV

ESHPAI

Sonata in B flat (1963) vln & pf
with L. Pecherskaya pf   Mezhdunarodnaya Kniga
    D21386

MARCELLO, A.

(6) Concerti, Op. 1 ob or fl, strs & c
Concerto in d: Adagio (2nd mvt) arr. vln & pf from Bach edition by
Moffat
with L. Pecherskaya pf   Mezhdunarodnaya Kniga
    D21385

PROKOFIEV

(5) Melodies, Op. 35bis (1921) vln & pf
with L. Pecherskaya pf   Mezhdunarodnaya Kniga
    D21385

YSAYE

(6) Sonatas, Op. 27 solo vln
Sonata No. 3, in d
(unaccompanied)   Mezhdunarodnaya Kniga
    D21386

Mischa VIÓLIN (1902–)

BEETHOVEN

(6) Minuets, G167 pf
No. 2. Minuet No. 2, in G arr. vln & pf Burmester
with piano   Pathé 40118

KREISLER

Tambourin chinois, Op. 3 vln & pf
with piano   Pathé 40118

PAGANINI

Moto perpetuo (Allegro di concert) Op. 11 (1830) vln & orch.
with piano   Edison Diamond Disc 80828

RIES

Suite No. 3, in G, Op. 34 vln & pf
No. 5. Perpetuum mobile
with J. Adler pf   7695   Edison Diamond Disc 80683

SARASATE

(8) Danzas españolas vln & pf
No. 6. Zapateado, Op. 23, No. 2
with J. Adler pf   7651   Edison Diamond Disc 80622
Introduction & Tarantelle, Op. 43 vln & pf
with J. Adler pf   7652   Edison Diamond Disc 80641

Luben VLADIGEROV

BORODIN

Prince Igor (1890) – opera
Dance of the Polovtsian maidens arr. vln & pf P. Vladigerov
with W. Jäger pf   Polydor 25314

SPENDIAROV

Crimean sketches, Op. 9 orch.
No. 4. Kaitarna arr. vln & pf P. Vladigerov
with W. Jäger pf   Polydor 25313

VLADIGEROV, P.

(2) Bulgarian Paraphrases, Op. 18 vln & pf
No. 1. Choro arr. Casella
with P. Vladigerov   Polydor 19768
No. 2. Ratschenitza arr. Casella
with P. Vladigerov   Polydor 19768
Burlesque (on 2 Bulgarian national themes) Op. 14 vln & pf
with P. Vladigerov pf   Polydor 19764
Concert–foxtrot vln & pf
with P. Vladigerov pf   Polydor 21196
(10) Impressions, Op. 9 vln & pf
No. 4. Caressing
with P. Vladigerov pf   Polydor 21195
(2) Improvisations, Op. 7 vln & pf
No. 2. Popular tune (Im volkston)
with P. Vladigerov pf   Polydor 19765
(2) Morceaux, Op. 20 vln & pf
No. 1. Romanza
with P. Vladigerov pf   B 47563 P   Polydor 21194
No. 2. Oriental
with P. Vladigerov pf   B 47564 M   Polydor 21194
Orientalico (Concert shimmy) vln & pf
with P. Vladigerov pf   Polydor 21196
(4) Stücke, Op. 12 vln & pf
No. 4. Valse romantique
with P. Vladigerov pf   Polydor 21195
Suite bulgare, Op. 21 pf
No. 2. Chant arr. vln & pf P. Vladigerov
with P. Vladigerov pf   Polydor 21193
Vardar (Rapsodie bulgare) Op. 16 vln & pf
with P. Vladigerov pf   Polydor 19767

WEINBERGER

Svanda the Bagpiper (1927) – opera
Polka (Act I) orch. – arr. vln & pf P. Vladigerov
with W. Jäger pf   Polydor 25313

R. VLASOV

GLIÈRE

Romance in c, Op. 45, No. 3 vln & pf
with V. Vladimirova pf   Ultraphon H24039

GOENS

Scherzo, Op. 12, No. 2 vln & pf
with V. Vladimirova pf   Ultraphon H24039

F. VOELKER

MASCAGNI

Cavalleria Rusticana (1890) – opera
Intermezzo orch. – arr. vln & orch.
with orch.   11462 – A 511   HMV V27903

Ion VOICU (1925–)

BACH

(4) Suites, BWV1066/9 strs & c
Suite No. 3, in D: Air (2nd mvt) BWV1068 2 obs, 3 tpts, drms, strs & c
– arr. vln & pf as "Air on the G–string" by Wilhelmj
  with D. Buchholz pf   Electrecord ECE086

BRUCH

Concerto No. 1, in g, Op. 26 vln & orch.
  with London Symphony Orch. –   Decca LXT6184, SMD1081,
  Frühbeck de Burgos   SXL6184
                                London CM9450, CS6450

DEBUSSY

Sonata No. 3, in g (1917) vln & pf
  with M. Haas pf   Decca LXT6351, SXL6351

KREISLER

Schön Rosmarin vln & pf
  with D. Buchholz pf   Electrecord ECE086

LALO

Symphonie espagnole, Op. 21 vln & orch.*
  with Bucharest Philharmonic Orch. – Electrecord ECD73
  Georgescu   Eterna 820335

LOCATELLI

(12) Sonatas, Op. 6 (1737) vln & c
Sonata No. 1, in g (ed David)
  with D. Buchholz pf   Electrecord ECE086

MENDELSSOHN

Concerto in e, Op. 64 vln & orch.
  with Rumanian Philharmonic   Electrecord ECE0113, ECE0292
  Symphony Orch. "George Enescu" –
  Georgescu
Concerto in e, Op. 64 vln & orch.
  with London Symphony Orch. –   Decca LXT6184, SMD1081,
  Frühbeck de Burgos   SXL6184
                                London CM9450, CS6450

MILHAUD

Sonata No. 2, (1917) vln & pf
  with M. Haas pf   Decca LXT6351, SXL6351

PAGANINI

Concerto No. 1, in D, Op. 6 (cadenza by Ševčík) vln & orch.
  with Dresden Philharmonic Orch. Eterna 720179
  – Bongartz

(Le) Streghe (variations on a theme from Süssmeyer's opera "Il Noce di
Benevento") Op. 8 (1813) vln & orch.
  with D. Buchholz pf   Electrecord ECE086

PORUMBESCU

Ballade in e, Op. 29 vln & pf
  with Rumanian Radio Symphony Electrecord ECC286, ECD83
  Orch. – Conta

* Omitting Intermezzo.

PROKOFIEV

Concerto No. 2, in g, Op. 63 vln & orch.
  with Dresden Philharmonic Orch. – Eterna 820381
  Bongartz   Heliodor 89786
Sonata No. 2, in D, Op. 94bis vln & pf
  with M. Haas pf   Decca LXT6351, SXL6351

SARASATE

Zigeunerweisen, Op. 20 vln & pf or orch.
  with D. Buchholz pf   Electrecord ECC286, ECE086
Zigeunerweisen, Op. 20 vln & pf or orch.
  with Dresden Philharmonic Orch. – Eterna 520490
  Bongartz

VOICU

(The) Morning after the wedding solo vln
  (unaccompanied)   Electrecord ECE086

WIENIAWSKI

Concerto No. 2, in d, Op. 22 vln & orch.
  with Rumanian Radio Symphony Electrecord ECD83, ECE0292
  Orch. – Conta

YSAŸE

(6) Sonatas, Op. 27 solo vln
Sonata No. 6, in E
  (unaccompanied)   Electrecord ECE086

Henri VOLANT

d'AMBROSIO

Canzonetta, Op. 6 vln & pf
  with P. Raffit pf   Parlophone 80635

GODARD

Concerto No. 1, Op. 35 "Concerto Romantique" vln & orch.
Canzonetta (2nd mvt)
  with P. Raffit pf   Parlophone 80635

RIMSKY–KORSAKOV

Sadko (1898) – opera
Chant hindou arr. vln & pf Kreisler
  with L. Petitjean pf   Columbia DF958

SAINT–SAËNS

(Le) Déluge, Op. 45 (1876) – oratorio
Prélude vln & orch. – arr. vln & pf Saint–Saëns
  with L. Petitjean pf   Columbia DF958

STRAVINSKY

Ragtime (1918) fl, cl, hrn, tpt, tbn, cym, cymb, 2 vlns, vla & cbs
  with L. Lavailotte fl,   CLX 1810–1 Columbia 68300D, LFX357,
  Godeau cl, J. Deveny hrn, E. Foveau LX382
  tpt, R. Tudesq tbn, Racz cym, M.
  Morel ob, R. Charmy vln, E. Ginot vla
  & Juste cbs, – cond. Stravinsky

Günter VOLLMER

LOCATELLI

(12) Concerti, Op. 7 (1741) "Il pianto d'Arianna" strs & c
Concerto No. 12, in F 4 vlns, strs & c
  with F–J. Maier vln, W. Neuhaus vln,   Harmonia Mundi HMS30887
  B. Seeger vln & Collegium Aureum

Dieter VORHOLZ

BACH, C.P.E.

Sonata in D, W71 (1731) vln & hpsi
  with M.H. Hoffmann hpsi   Saba SB15041

BACH, J.S.

Concerto in d, BWV1043 2 vlns, strs & c
  with S. Lautenbacher vln & Mainz   Vox (in sets SVBX567 &
  Chamber Orch. – Kehr   VBX67), PL11540, STPL511540
Sonata in G, BWV1038 fl, vln & c
  with K. Pohlers fl & M.H. Hoffmann   Saba SB15041
  hpsi

BACH, W.F.

Duet in g vln & vla
  with G. Schmid vla   Vox DL463
Trio in D, F47 fl, vln or 2 vlns & c
  with K. Pohlers fl & M.H. Hoffmann   Saba SB15041
  hpsi

CORELLI

(12) Concerti grossi, Op. 6 orch.
Concerto grosso No. 1, in D
  with U. Grehling vln, K. Storck vlc,   Harmonia Mundi HM25140
  R. Ewerhart org & Collegium
  Musicum das Westdeutschen
  Rundfunks, Köln
Concerto grosso No. 3, in c
  with U. Grehling vln, K. Storck vlc,   Harmonia Mundi HM25140
  R. Ewerhart org & Collegium
  Musicum das Westdeutschen
  Rundfunks, Köln

HANDEL

(6) Concerti grossi, Op. 3 (1759) orch.
Concerto grosso No. 2, in B flat
  with U. Grehling vln, H. Schneider ob,   Archive APM14139
  H. Münch–Holland vlc, H. Müller vlc,
  F. Neumeyer hpsi, E. Müller hpsi &
  West German Radio Cappella
  Coloniensis – Wenzinger
Concerto in C (1736) "Alexander's Feast" 2 vlns, 2 obs & strs
  with U. Grehling vln, H. Münch–   Archive APM14140, EPA37195
  Holland vlc, F. Neumeyer hpsi, E.
  Müller hpsi & West German Radio
  Cappella Coloniensis – Wenzinger

LEO

Concerto in D 4 vlns & strs
  with E. Früh vln, G. Terebesi vln, H.   Archive APM14340,
  Schön vln & Berlin Chamber Music   SAPM198340, ARC3240,
  Ensemble – Lange   ARC73240

VIVALDI

Concerto in E flat, P.423 (F.I, No. 101) 2 vlns, strs & c
  with F–J. Maier vln & Collegium   Harmonia Mundi CVH333,
  Aureum – Reinhardt   HM30644

Andrée WACHSMUTH–LOEW (1911–)

FORNEROD

Concert 2 vlns & pf
  with A–M. Gründer vln & R. Dobos   Communauté de travail pour la
  pf   diffusion de la musique suisse
                    CT64–24

Siegfried WAGNER

VIVALDI

(12) Concerti, Op. 3 "L'Estro armonico" var. cbns & strs
Concerto No. 2, in g, P.326 (F.IV, No. 8) 2 vlns, strs & c
  with H. Seidel vln, G. Kröll hpsi &   Volksplatte LDKS18011
  Cologne Chamber Orch. – Ellegiers
Concerto No. 11, in d, P.250 (F.IV, No. 11) 2 vlns, vlc, strs & c
  with H. Seidel vln, K–H. Jommer vlc,   Volksplatte LDKS18011
  G. Kröll hpsi & Cologne Chamber
  Orch. – Ellegiers

Seymour WAKSCHAL

AMRAM

Sonata (1965) vln & pf
  with L. Parrott pf   Washington WR469, WS9469

Hugo WALDMAN

BEETHOVEN

Concerto in D, Op. 61 (cadenzas by Kreisler) vln & orch.
  with Berlin Philharmonia Orch. –   Summit LSU1019*
  Strauss

LALO

Symphonie espagnole, Op. 21 vln & orch.†
  with Paris Sinfonia – Dumont   Summit LSU1015

Jean–Pierre WALLEZ

BACH

Concerto No. 1, in a, BWV1041 vln, strs & c
  with Ensemble Instrumental de France   Classic 991081
  – Wallez
Concerto No. 2, in E, BWV1042 vln, strs & c
  with Ensemble Instrumental de France   Classic 991081
  – Wallez

---

* Label reads Otto Strauss as conductor whereas record jacket reads Gustav
Stolz.
† Including Intermezzo.

BACH – *Continued*

Concerto in d, BWV1043 2 vlns, strs & c
with A. Moglia vln & Ensemble   Classic 991081
Instrumental de France – Wallez

CORELLI

(12) Concerti grossi, Op. 6 orch.
Concerto grosso No. 8, in g "Christmas Concerto"
with N. Laroque vln, A. Queille vla,   Critère CRD186, SCRD5186
H. Martinerie vlc, L. Boulay hpsi &
Collegium Musicum, Paris – Douatte

TARTINI

(6) Concerti, Op. 2 vln & strs
Concerto No. 2, in C, D2
with Ensemble Instrumental de France   Classic 991089
– Wallez

Concerto in d, D.45 (C61) vln & orch.
with Ensemble Instrumental de France   Classic 991089
– Wallez

TELEMANN

Concerto in F, T.II, No. 3 3 vlns, strs & c
with R. Gendre vln, N. Laroque vln,   CBS SBRG75563
L. Boulay hpsi & Collegium Musicum,   Eurodisc 74225KK
Paris – Douatte   Nonesuch H1109, H71109

VIVALDI

(12) Concerti, Op. 3 "L'Estro armonico" var. cbns & strs
Concerto No. 10, in b, P.148 (F.IV, No. 10) 4 vlns, strs & c
with C. Jacquillat vln, N. Lepinte vln,   Christophorus SCGLP75896
Y. Carracilly vln, L. Boulay hpsi &   Critère CRD186, SCRD5186
Collegium Musicum, Paris – Douatte   Monitor MC2102, MCS2102
Concerto No. 10, in b, P.148 (F.IV, No. 10) 4 vlns, strs & c
with C. Crenne vln, A. Moglia vln,   Classic 991062
P.D. Pelaz vln, M. Roche hpsi &
Ensemble Instrumental de France –
Wallez
(12) Concerti, Op. 8 (1725) "Il Cimento dell' Armonia e dell' Invenzione"
(Nos. 1/4: Le quattro Stragioni) vln & strs
Concerto No. 1, in E, F.I, No. 22 "La Primavera"
with Ensemble Instrumental de France   Classic 991061
– Wallez

Concerto No. 2, in B flat, F.I, No. 23 "L'Estate"
with Ensemble Instrumental de France   Classic 991061
– Wallez

Concerto No. 3, in F, F.I, No. 24 "L'Autunno"
with Ensemble Instrumental de France   Classic 991061
– Wallez

Concerto No. 4, in f, F.I, No. 25 "L'Inverno"
with Ensemble Instrumental de France   Classic 991061
– Wallez

Arthur WALSH

BECKER

Romance in B flat, Op. 3, No. 1 vln & pf
with piano   Edison Diamond Disc 80336

Kertlu WANNE

FAURÉ

Berceuse, Op. 16 vln & pf
with A. Joutsens pf   Sto 6232   Odeon A255511, D2954

KREISLER

Tambourin chinois, Op. 3 vln & pf
with A. Joutsens pf   Sto 6231   Odeon A255511, D2954

Bohdan WARCHAL (1930–)

CORELLI

(12) Concerti grossi, Op. 6 orch.
Concerto grosso No. 1, in D
with V. Piatkowski vln, M. Capka vlc   Supraphon SUA10571, SUA
& Slovak Chamber Orch. – Warchal   ST50571, SV8183
Concerto grosso No. 2, in F
with V. Piatkowski vln, M. Capka vlc   Supraphon 140 0102, SUA10808,
& Slovak Chamber Orch. – Warchal   SUA ST50808
Concerto grosso No. 3, in c
with V. Piatkowski vln, M. Capka vlc   Supraphon SUA10571, SUA
& Slovak Chamber Orch. – Warchal   ST50571, SV8183
Concerto grosso No. 4, in D
with V. Piatkowski vln, M. Capka vlc,   Supraphon 140 0106, SUA10911,
& Slovak Chamber Orch. – Warchal   SUA ST50911
Concerto grosso No. 5, in B flat
with V. Piatkowski vln, M. Capka vlc,   Supraphon 140 0102, SUA10808,
& Slovak Chamber Orch. – Warchal   SUA ST50808
Concerto grosso No. 6, in F
with V. Piatkowski vln, M. Capka vlc   Supraphon SUA10571, SUA
& Slovak Chamber Orch. – Warchal   ST50571, SV8183
Concerto grosso No. 7, in D
with V. Piatkowski vln, M. Capka vlc   Supraphon SUA10571, SUA
& Slovak Chamber Orch. – Warchal   ST50571, SV8183
Concerto grosso No. 8, in g "Christmas Concerto"
with V. Piatkowski vln, M. Capka vlc   Supraphon 140 0102, SUA10808,
& Slovak Chamber Orch. – Warchal   SUA ST50808
Concerto grosso No. 9, in F
with V. Piatkowski vln, M. Capka vlc   Supraphon 140 0102, SUA10808,
& Slovak Chamber Orch. – Warchal   SUA ST50808
Concerto grosso No. 10, in C
with V. Piatkowski vln, M. Capka vlc   Supraphon 140 0106, SUA10911,
& Slovak Chamber Orch. – Warchal   SUA ST50911
Concerto grosso No. 11, in B flat
with V. Piatkowski vln, M. Capka vlc   Supraphon 140 0106, SUA10911,
& Slovak Chamber Orch. – Warchal   SUA ST50911
Concerto grosso No. 12, in F
with V. Piatkowski vln, M. Capka vlc   Supraphon 140 0106, SUA10911,
& Slovak Chamber Orch. – Warchal   SUA ST50911

VIVALDI

(12) Concerti, Op. 8 (1725) "Il Cimento dell' Armonia e dell' Invenzione"
(Nos. 1/4: Le quattro Stagioni) vln & strs
Concerto No. 1, in E, F.I, No. 22 "La Primavera"
with B. Čuberka hpsi & Slovak   Crossroads 22 16 0083, 22 16
Chamber Orch. – Warchal   0084
                      Supraphon SUA10767, SUA
                      ST50767, SV8394

VIVALDI – *Continued*

Concerto No. 2, in B flat, F.I, No. 23 "L'Estate"
with B. Čuberka hpsi & Slovak
Chamber Orch. – Warchal   Crossroads 22 16 0083, 22 16 0084
Supraphon SUA 10767, SUA ST50767, SV8394

Concerto No. 3, in F, F.I, No. 24 "L'Autunno"
with B. Čuberka hpsi & Slovak
Chamber Orch. – Warchal   Crossroad 22 16 0083, 22 16 0084
Supraphon SUA 10767, SUA ST50767, SV8394

Concerto No. 4, in f, F.I, No. 25 "L'Inverno"
with B. Čuberka hpsi & Slovak
Chamber Orch. – Warchal   Crossroads 22 16 0083, 22 16 0084
Supraphon SUA 10767, SUA ST50767, S8394

Helen WARE (1887–)

BRAHMS

(21) Hungarian Dances pf duet
Hungarian dance No. 2, in d arr. vln & pf Joachim
with F. Moore pf   4431   Edison Diamond Disc 80322

DRDLA

Souvenir vln & pf
with F. Moore pf   1287   Gennett 11000

DVOŘÁK

(8) Humoresques, Op. 101 pf
No. 7. Humoresque No. 7, in G flat arr. vln & pf "in G" Wilhelmj
with piano   Gennett 14004

GODARD

Jocelyn (1888) – opera
Cachés dans cet asile "Berceuse" arr. vln & pf
with piano   Gennett 14001
(6) Morceaux, Op. 128 vln & pf
No. 3. Adagio pathétique
with M. Eisner pf   1234   Gennett 11004

HUBAY

(Le) Luthier de Crémone, Op. 40 (1894) – opera
Intermezzo orch. – arr. vln & pf Hubay
with F. Moore pf   4015   Edison Diamond Disc 80322

KREISLER

Liebesfreud vln & pf
with piano   6022   Gennett 14002

MASSENET

Thaïs (1894) – opera
Méditation arr. vln & pf Marsick
with piano   Gennett 14004

NEVIN

Mighty lak' a rose (1901) v & pf – arr. vln & pf
with piano   Gennett 5148
(The) Rosary (1898) v & pf – arr. vln & pf
with piano   Gennett 14003

RUBINSTEIN

(2) Melodies, Op. 3 pf
No. 1. Melody in F arr. vln & pf Wilhelmj
with piano   Gennett 14001
No. 1. Melody in F arr. vln & pf Wilhelmj
with piano   Gennett 5148

SCHUBERT

(7) Gesänge (set to Scott's "Lady of the Lake") Op. 52 v & pf
No. 6. Ave Maria, D839 arr. vln & pf Wilhelmj
with piano   Gennett 14003
(6) Moments musicaux, Op. 94 (D780) (1823/7) pf
No. 3. Moment musicale No. 3, in f "Air russe" arr. vln & pf Kreisler
with piano   6015   Gennett 14002

WARE

Hungarian Fantasia, Op. 4 vln & pf
with piano   Edison Diamond Disc 80828

WIENIAWSKI

Capriccio–valse, Op. 7 vln & pf
with M. Eisner pf   1235a   Gennett 11004

Kathleen WASHBOURNE

RAWSTHORNE

Theme & Variations (1927) 2 vlns
    DTA3569–3, 3570–4, 3571–3 &   Decca K884/5
with J. Hinchcliffe vln   3572–4

WEBERN

Trio, Op. 20 vln, vla & vlc
    AR 3328–2 & 3329–1   Decca K904
with W. Copperwheat vla & W. Pleeth
vlc

Marek WEBER (1898–)

ADAM

Cantique de Noël v & pf – arr. vln & orch.
with orch.   HMV EG278

ANONYMOUS

O du Fröhliche, o du Selige (1819) v & pf – arr. vln & orch.
with orch.   BWR 331¹△   HMV AM714, EG277
Victor 80158

BRANDL

(Der) Liebe Augustin – operetta
Du alter Stefansturm arr. vln & orch. Weber
with orch.   Columbia GL514

BRUCH

Kol Nidrei, Op. 47 vlc or vln & orch.
with orch.   HMV EH403

GOUNOD

Ave Maria (Méditation on Bach's "Prelude No. 1, in C" from Book I of "Das Wohltemperirte Clavier") v & pf – arr. vln & orch.
with orch.   HMV EG919

GRUBER

Stille Nacht, heilige Nacht (1818) v & pf – arr. vln & orch.
  with orch.   BDR 4686[III]△   HMV AM714, EG269, EG277
                                        Victor 80158

HUMMEL

Hallelujah v & orch. – arr. v, vln & orch.
  with E. van Endert (s) & orch.   HMV EG919

REGER

(60) Schlichte Weisen – 6 Books, Op. 76 v & pf
No. 52. Maria–Wiegenlied arr. v, vln & orch.
  with E. van Endert s & orch.   HMV EG269

THOMÉ

Andante religioso, Op. 70 pf – arr. vln & orch.
  with orch.   HMV EG278

WAGNER

(Die) Meistersinger von Nürnberg (1868) – opera
  Morgenlich leuchtend "Prize song" arr. vln & orch. Mikulicz
  with orch.   HMV EG2952
                                  Victor 24773

Hans von WEGERN

ANDRÉ

On the high Alps arr. 2 vlns & pf
  with W. Biedermann vln & piano   Columbia A746

ANONYMOUS

Mazurka brillante composer unid – arr. 2 vlns & hp
  with G. Stehl vln & harp   Columbia A705

BLON

Sérénade d'amour pf – arr. 2 vlns & pf
  with G. Stehl vln & piano   4015 Columbia A657

John WEICHER (1904–1969)

STRAUSS, R.

Don Quixote, Op. 35 (1897) orch.
  with M. Preves vla, A. Janigro vlc &   Victor LM2384, LSC2384,
  Chicago Symphony Orch. – Reiner   SB2099, VICS1561

(Ein) Heldenleben, Op. 40 (1898) orch.
  with Chicago Symphony Orch. –   Camden Classics VCCS1042
  Reiner   HMV ALP1209
                                Victor LM1807, VIC1042

Stanley WEINER (1925–)

AUBERT

(6) Concerti, Op. 17 (1734/5) 4 vlns & strs
  Concerto No. 1, in D
  with Hamburg Chamber Orch. –   Turnabout TV34212
  Ludzuweit
  Concerto No. 2, in G
  with Hamburg Chamber Orch. –   Turnabout TV34212
  Ludzuweit

BEETHOVEN

Sonata No. 5, in F, Op. 24 "Spring" vln & pf
  with S. Guttmann pf   Oryx EXP59
                          Sastruphon SM007026

Sonata No. 9, in A, Op. 47 "Kreutzer" vln & pf
  with S. Guttmann pf   Oryx EXP59
                          Sastruphon SM007026

BRAHMS

Sonata No. 3, in d, Op. 108 vln & pf
  with M. Stoesser pf   McIntosh MM108

BRENTA

Mélopée vln & pf
  with L. Leveque pf   Alpha DB81

FRANCOEUR

(12) Sonatas – Book II (1733) vln & c
Sonata No. 6, in G
  with G. van Dijcke hpsi & A.   Discophiles français DF730066,
  Bauviens gamba   DF740016
Sonata No. 12, in E
  with G. van Dijcke hpsi & A.   Discophiles français DF730066,
  Bauviens gamba   DF740016

LECLAIR

(6) Concerti, Op. 7 (1737) vln & strs
Concerto No. 4, in F
  with Hamburg Chamber Orch. –   Turnabout TV34212
  Ludzuweit
(6) Concerti, Op. 10 (1744) vln & strs
Concerto No. 5, in e
  with Hamburg Chamber Orch. –   Turnabout TV34212
  Ludzuweit
(12) Sonatas, Op. 1 – Book I (1723) vln & c
Sonata No. 9, in A
  with G. van Dijcke hpsi & A.   Discophiles français DF730066,
  Bauviens gamba   DF740016
(12) Sonatas, Op. 5 – Book III (1734) vln & c
Sonata No. 6, in c
  with A. Geoffroy–Dechaume hpsi & H. Alpha DB86
  Kneihs vlc
Sonata No. 10, in C
  with A. Geoffroy–Dechaume hpsi & H. Alpha DB86
  Kneihs vlc
Sonata No. 11, in g
  with A. Geoffroy–Dechaume hpsi & H. Alpha DB86
  Kneihs vlc
(12) Sonatas, Op. 9 – Book IV (1738) vln & c
Sonatas No. 3, in D
  with A. Geoffroy–Dechaume hpsi & H. Alpha DB86
  Kneihs vlc

LEGLEY

Burlesque vln & pf
  with L. Leveque pf   Alpha DB81

LOEILLET

Sonata in D vln & c
  with G. van Dijcke hpsi & A.   Discophiles français DF730066,
  Bauviens gamba   DF740016

MARTINŮ

Sonata No. 3 (1944) vln & pf
 with M. Stoesser pf   McIntosh MM108

POOT

Ballade vln & pf
 with L. Leveque pf   Alpha DB81

PROKOFIEV

Sonata No. 1, in f, Op. 80 vln & pf
 with S. Guttmann pf   Da Camera SM93307

Sonata No. 2, in D, Op. 94bis vln & pf
 with S. Guttmann pf   Da Camera SM93307

REBEL

(12) Sonatas (1712) 2 & 3 part with figured bs
 Sonata No. 5, in D "La Pallas"
  with R. Bloch vln, A. Geoffroy– Discophiles français DF730076,
  Dechaume hpsi & J. Lamy gamba DF740076

 Sonata No. 6, in g "L'Immortelle"
  with R. Bloch vln, A. Geoffroy– Discophiles français DF730076,
  Dechaume hpsi & J. Lamy gamba DF740076

(12) Sonatas (1713) "Melées de Plusieurs Recits pour la Viole" vln & c
 Sonata No. 3, in a
  with A Geoffroy–Dechaume hpsi Discophiles français DF730076,
  & J. Lamy gamba   DF740076

 Sonata No. 4, in e
  with A. Geoffroy–Dechaume hpsi Discophiles français DF730076,
  & J. Lamy gamba   DF740076

 Sonata No. 6, in b
  with A. Geoffroy–Dechaume hpsi Discophiles français DF730076,
  & J. Lamy gamba   DF740076

 Sonata No. 11, in E
  with A. Geoffroy–Dechaume hpsi Discophiles français DF730076,
  & J. Lamy gamba   DF740076

REGER

Sonata No. 7, in c, Op. 139 vln & pf
 with G. Demoulins pf   Da Camera SM93309

(2) Sonatinas, Op. 103b vln & pf
 Sonatina No. 1, in d
  with G. Demoulins pf   Da Camera SM93309

SARASATE

Adios Montañas mias, Op. 37 vln & pf
 with H. McClure pf   McIntosh MM113

Caprice basque, Op. 24 vln & pf
 with H. McClure pf   McIntosh MM113

(8) Danzas españolas vln & pf
 No. 1. Malagueña, Op. 21, No. 1
  with H. McClure pf   McIntosh MM113

 No. 2. Habañera, Op. 21, No. 2
  with H. McClure pf   McIntosh MM113

 No. 3. Romanza andaluza, Op. 22, No. 1
  with H. McClure pf   McIntosh MM113

 No. 4. Jota navarra, Op. 22, No. 2
  with H. McClure pf   McIntosh MM113

 No. 5. Playera, Op. 23, No. 1
  with H. McClure pf   McIntosh MM113

 No. 6. Zapateado, Op. 23, No. 2
  with H. McClure pf   McIntosh MM113

SARASATE – Continued

 No. 7. Danza española No. 7, in a, Op. 26, No. 1
  with H. McClure pf   McIntosh MM113

 No. 8. Danza española No. 8, in C, Op. 26, No. 2
  with H. McClure pf   McIntosh MM113

Jota aragonesa, Op. 27 vln & pf
 with H. McClure pf   McIntosh MM113

TARTINI

Concerto in B flat vln & orch.
 with Chamber Orch. – Weiner Discophiles français DF730078,
            DF740078

Concerto in F vln & orch.
 with Chamber Orch. – Weiner Discophiles français DF730078,
            DF740078

Sonata in a vln & c
 with A. Geoffroy–Dechaume hpsi Discophiles français DF730078,
 & J. Lamy gamba   DF740078

Sonata in D vln & c
 with A. Geoffroy–Dechaume hpsi Discophiles français DF730078,
 & J. Lamy gamba   DF740078

WEINER

(9) Caprices (in hommage to celebrated violinists) solo vln
 Caprice No. 1, in b flat (Menuhin)
  (unaccompanied)   Alpha DB81

 Caprice No. 2, in c (Szigeti)
  (unaccompanied)   Alpha DB81

 Caprice No. 3, in A flat (Milstein)
  (unaccompanied)   Alpha DB81

 Caprice No. 4, in G (Grumiaux)
  (unaccompanied)   Alpha DB81

 Caprice No. 5, in g (Szeryng)
  (unaccompanied)   Alpha DB81

 Caprice No. 6, in b flat (Persinger)
  (unaccompanied)   Alpha DB81

 Caprice No. 7, in B flat (Stern)
  (unaccompanied)   Alpha DB81

 Caprice No. 8, in c (Galamian)
  (unaccompanied)   Alpha DB81

 Caprice No. 9, in B flat (Francescatti)
  (unaccompanied)   Alpha DB81

Isaac José WEINSTEIN

KREISLER

Concerto in C (Vivaldi) vln & strs
 with Argentine Chamber Orch. Victor 11–9273/4

Rachmael WEINSTOCK

LECLAIR

(12) Sonatas, Op. 4 (1732) 2 vlns & c
 Sonata No. 4, in A
  with H. Kohon vln & D. Walters hpsi Vox PL14000, STPL514000

Jacques WEINTRAUB

BACH

(3) Sonatas & 3 Partitas, BWV1001/6 solo vln
Partita No. 3, in E: Preludio (1st mvt) BWV1006
(unaccompanied)   Beka G12461

(4) Suites, BWV1066/9 orch.
Suite No. 3, in D: Air (2nd mvt) BWV1068 2 obs, 3 tpts, drms, strs & c
– arr. vln & pf as "Air on the G–string" by Wilhelmj
with orch.   Beka G40806

BLOM

Liebestraum (Romanze) vln & pf
with orch.   Beka G12460

BRAGA

(7) Melodies (1867) v & pf
No. 5. La serenata "Angel's serenade" arr. vln, fl & orch.
with flute & orch.   Beka 36, G11110

DELIBES

Sylvia (1876) – ballet orch.
No. 16a. Pizzicato–scherzettino (Act III) arr. vln & pf
with piano   Beka G11107

GOUNOD

Ave Maria (Méditation on Bach's "Prelude No. 1, in C" from Book I of "Das Wohltemperirte Clavier") v & pf – arr. vln, fl & orch.
with flute & orch.   Beka 36, G11111

HANDEL

Serse (1738) – opera
Ombra mai fu "Largo" arr. vln & orch.
with orch.   Beka G12458

HILL

(Das) Herz am Rhein v & pf – arr. vln & orch.
with orch.   Beka G12456

KAHNT

Romance in C, Op. 36 vln & pf
with flute & orch.   Beka G12452/3

MASCAGNI

Cavalleria Rusticana (1890) – opera
Intermezzo orch. – arr. vln fl & pf
with flute & piano   Beka 35, G11112

MENDELSSOHN

(6) Songs without words, Op. 62 pf
No. 1. Song without words No. 25, in G "May breezes" arr. vln & orch.
with orch.   Beka G40888

MOZART

Ave verum corpus, K618 cho – arr. vln & orch.
with orch.   Beka G12459

OFFENBACH

(Les) Contes d'Hoffmann (1881) – opera
Belle Nuit, O nuit d'amour "Barcarolle" arr. vln & orch.
with orch.   Beka G12455

SAINT–SAËNS

(Le) Carnaval des animaux (1886) small orch.
Le cygne arr. vln & orch.
with orch.   Beka 35, G11108

SCHUMANN

(13) Kinderscenen, Op. 15 pf
No. 7. Träumerei arr. vln & orch.
with orch.   Beka G12454

TITL

Serenade arr. vln & orch.
with orch.   Beka G12457

Vladimir WEISMAN (1931–   )

RESPIGHI

Sonata in b (1917) vln & pf
with E. Hancock pf   Nonesuch H71205

STRAUSS, R.

Sonata in E flat, Op. 18 vln & pf
with E. Hancock pf   Nonesuch H71205

Diez WEISMANN (1900–   )

ALBÉNIZ

España (6 Feuilles d'album) Op. 165 pf
No. 2. Tango in D arr. vln & pf Kreisler
with C. Schmalstich   BD 9114[II]△   HMV B4044, EG2206
pf

DRDLA

Guitarrero, Op. 88 vln & pf
with piano   HMV EG2439
Souvenir vln & pf
with piano   Bw 847[III]△   HMV AM974, EG717

DRIGO

(2) Airs de Ballet orch.
No. 2. Valse bluette arr. vln & pf Auer
with A. Sándor pf   Telefunken A3665

FIBICH

Images, Impressions & Souvenirs, Op. 41 pf
No. 14. Poem (from "Souvenirs", Part IV) arr. vln & pf Kubelík
with piano   HMV EG512

GODARD

Jocelyn (1888) – opera
Cachés dans cet asile "Berceuse" arr. vln & pf
with piano   HMV EH311

GOSSEC

Rosine (1786) – opera
Gavotte arr. vln & pf Burmester
with piano   HMV EG2439

GOUNOD

Ave Maria (Méditation on Bach's "Prelude No. 1, in C" from Book I of "Das Wohltemperirte Clavier") v & pf – arr. vln & pf
with piano   HMV EG1559

Ave Maria (Méditation on Bach's "Prelude No. 1, in C" from Book I of "Das Wohltemperirte Clavier") v & pf – arr. vln, vlc & pf
as member of trio   HMV X3498

HAYDN

Minuet unid – arr. vln & pf Friedberg
with piano   HMV EG2205

KREISLER

Rondino on a theme by Beethoven vln & pı
with piano   HMV EG2489

KŘENEK

Jonny Spielt Auf, Op. 45 (1927) – opera
Blues & triumphal song arr. vln & pf
with J. de Leur pf   HMV AM953, EG690

MASSENET

Élégie v & pf – arr. vln & pf
with C. Schmalstich   BD 9112^{II}△   HMV B4044, EG2206
pf

MENDELSSOHN

(6) Gesänge, Op. 34 v & pf
No. 2. Auf Flügeln des Gesanges arr. vln & pf Achron
with A. Sándor pf   Telefunken A1005, A3665
     Ultraphon A1005

MOSZKOWSKI

(6) Klavierstücke, Op. 15 pf – 4 hands
No. 1. Serenata arr. vln & pf
with piano   HMV EG1559

RAFF

(6) Pieces, Op. 85 vln & pf
No. 3. Cavatina in D arr. P. Hühn
with orch.   BLR 5053^{I}△   HMV B3770, EG1435, X3498

RIMSKY–KORSAKOV

Sadko (1898) – opera
Chant hindou arr. vln & pf Kreisler
with piano   HMV EH311

SCHUMANN

(20) Albumblätter, Op. 124 pf
No. 16. Schlummerlied arr. vln & pf
with piano   HMV EG2489

SPOLIANSKY

Serenade vln & pf
with piano   HMV EG802

Tango habañera vln & pf
with piano   HMV EG802

TCHAIKOVSKY

(The) Months (12 Characteristic pieces) Op. 37b pf
No. 6. Barcarole (June) arr. vln & pf
with C. Schmalstich pf   HMV EG2205

THOMAS

Mignon (1866) – opera
Entr'acte (Gavotte) (Act II) orch. – arr. vln & pf Sarasate
with piano   HMV EG2439

TOSELLI

Serenade, Op. 6 vln & pf
with orch.   BN 567^{II}△   HMV B3770, EG1435, X3498

TOSTI

For a kiss (Pour un baiser) v & pf – arr. vln & pf
with piano   HMV EG512

Melody v & pf – arr. vln & pf
with piano   Bw 846^{III}□   HMV AM974, EG717

J. WEISMEYER

HÁBA

Duo, Op. 49 (1936) 2 vlns
Allegro moderato (1st mvt)
with J. Stein vln   CA 16635–1   Columbia DB1791, (in set CHM5)

Andreas WEISSGERBER (1900–)

BACH

Minuet unid – arr. vln & pf Weissgerber
with piano   80835   Odeon 8034XX

(4) Suites, BWB1066/9 strs & c
Suite No. 3, in D: Air (2nd mvt) BWV1068 2 obs, 3 tpts, drms & strs – arr. vln & pf as "Air on the G–string" by Wilhelmj
with piano   Odeon 76234, 8032XX, 2009XXL, RXX80834

BEETHOVEN

Sonata No. 5, in F, Op. 24 "Spring" vln & pf
Scherzo: Allegro molto (3rd mvt)
with E. d'Albert pf   Odeon RXX80706

Rondo (Allegro ma non troppo) (4th mvt)
with E. d'Albert pf   Odeon RXX80706

BRAHMS

(21) Hungarian Dances pf duet
Hungarian dance No. 2, in d arr. vln & pf Joachim
with piano   Odeon 0–7512, 16237, 76237, 173110, 212033AA, 9305R, 2020XX, 8031XX, 8035XX, RXX80832

Hungarian dance No. 5, in f sharp arr. vln & pf "in g" Joachim
with piano   Odeon 0–7512, 16237, 76237, 173110, 212033AA, 9305R, 2020XX, 8031XX, 8035XX,

Hungarian dance No. 7, in A arr. vln & pf Joachim
with piano   Vox 6277

HUBAY

(14) Scènes de la csárda vln & pf
    No. 5. Hullámzó balaton, Op. 33
    with piano   Odeon 76236, 80831, 173110, 0–7512, 9305R, 2020XX, 8031XX, 8035XX, RXX80831

KREISLER

Liebesfreud vln & pf
    with piano   Odeon 173156, 212032AA, 0–7513

Liebesleid vln & pf
    with piano   Odeon 173156, 212032AA, 0–7513

MOZART

Sonata No. 26, in B flat, K378 vln & pf
    Andantino sostenuto e cantabile (2nd mvt)
    with E. d'Albert pf   Odeon RXX80707

PAGANINI

(Le) Streghe (variations on a theme from Süssmeyer's opera "Il Noce di Benevento") Op. 8 (1813) vln & orch.
    with piano   Odeon R55613/4

SARASATE

Zigeunerweisen, Op. 20 vln & pf or orch.
    with piano   XXB 7976[2]   Decca 25236
                               Odeon 173106, 0–7511, 212033AA, 8033XX, RXX80827
                               Parlophone A4105, E10801

SCHUMANN

(9) Waldscenen, Op. 82 pf
    No. 7. Vogel als Prophet arr. vln & pf Auer
    with piano   Vox 6277

WIENIAWSKI

Concerto No. 2, in d, Op. 22 vln & orch.
    Romance (2nd mvt)
    with piano   80836   Odeon 8034XX
Légende, Op. 17 vln & pf or orch.
    with piano   Odeon 8032XX, RXX80833
Souvenir de Moscou, Op. 6 vln & pf or orch.
    with piano   XXB 7975[4]   Decca 25236
                               Odeon 173106, 0–7511, 8033XX, RXX80827
                               Parlophone A4105, E10801

Ferdinand WEIST–HILL (1897–   )

BULL

Säterjëntens sondag v & pf – arr. vln & pf Svendsen
    with piano   Imperial 882

DRDLA

Serenade No. 1, in A vln & pf
    with piano   Imperial 883

HALVORSEN

(4) Mosaïques (Suite des morceaux caractéristiques) vln & pf
    No. 4. Chant de Veslemøy
    with piano   Imperial 881

MASSENET

Thaïs (1894) – opera
    Méditation arr. vln & pf Marsick
    with piano   Imperial 883

MENDELSSOHN

(6) Songs without words, Op. 62 pf
    No. 6. Song without words No. 30, in A "Spring song" arr. vln & pf
    with piano   Imperial 1027

RUBINSTEIN

(2) Melodies, Op. 3 pf
    No. 1. Melody in F arr. vln & pf Wilhelmj
    with piano   Imperial 881

SCHUMANN

(13) Kinderscenen, Op. 15 pf
    No. 7. Träumerei arr. vln & pf
    with piano   Imperial 882

THOMÉ

Simple aveu, Op. 25 pf – arr. vln & pf
    with piano   Imperial 1027

Feri WELTMANN

ALARD

(12) Duets, Op. 27 2 vlns
    No. 4. Duet No. 4, in d
    with R. Weltmann vlc   Pathé 51426

BEETHOVEN

(6) Minuets, G167 pf
    No. 2. Minuet No. 2, in G arr. vln & pf Burmester
    with piano   Edison Bell 1344

CSÁSZÁR

(A) Kunok (1848) – opera
    Aria unid – arr. 2 vlns Hubert
    with R. Weltmann vln   Pathé 1931, 39255

ERKEL*

GODARD

(6) Duettini, Op. 18 2 vlns & pf
    No. 6. Sérénade arr. 2 vlns
    with R. Weltmann pf   Pathé 2055, 51425

HUBAY

(14) Scènes de la Csárda vln & pf
    No. 3. Maros vize, Op. 18 arr. 2 vlns & pf
    with R. Weltmann vln & piano   Pathé 39252
    No. 6. Sárga Cserebogár, Op. 34 arr. 2 vlns & pf
    with R. Weltmann vln & piano   Pathé 1930/1, 39253

* See Vieuxtemps.

HUBAY – *Continued*

No. 8. Azt mondják, Op. 60 arr. 2 vlns & pf
with R. Weltmann vln & piano   Pathé 39254

(3) Transcriptions, Op. 3 vln & pf
No. 3. Carmen Fantasia (on themes from the opera by Bizet): Habañera
with piano   Odeon 97723
No. 3. Carmen Fantasia (on themes from the opera by Bizet): Habañera
with piano   Pathé 2056, 51428

KORÓLY

Fantaisie hongrois vln & pf – arr. 2 vlns & pf
with R. Weltmann vln & piano   Odeon 97723

PIERNÉ

Sérénade in A, Op. 7 (1875) pf – arr. vln & pf
with piano   Edison Bell 1344

RUBINSTEIN

(2) Melodies, Op. 3 pf
No. 1. Melody in F arr. vln & pf Wilhelmj
with piano   Pathé 2056, 51431

SARASATE

(8) Danzas españolas vln & pf
No. 3. Romanza andaluza, Op. 22, No. 1
with piano   Edison Bell 545
No. 7. Danza española No. 7, in a, Op. 26, No. 1
with piano   Edison Bell 545

SCHUMANN

(13) Kinderscenen, Op. 15 pf
No. 7. Träumerei arr. 2 vlns & pf
with R. Weltmann vln & piano   Pathé 2055, 51427

VIEUXTEMPS

Duo brillante en forme de fantaisie sur des airs hongrois, Op. 39 (1837) vln & pf*
with piano   Odeon 97721

Roszi WELTMANN

ALARD

(12) Duets, Op. 27 2 vlns
No. 4. Duet No. 4, in d
with F. Weltmann vln   Pathé 51426

CSÁSZÁR

(A) Kunok (1848) – opera
Aria unid – arr. 2 vlns Hubert
with F. Weltmann vln   Pathé 1931, 39255

GODARD

(6) Duettini, Op. 18 2 vlns & pf
No. 6. Sérénade arr. 2 vlns
with F. Weltmann vln   Pathé 2055, 51425

* Composed jointly with Erkel.

HUBAY

(14) Scènes de la Csárda vln & pf
Scène de la Csárda unid
with piano   Pathé 51429
No. 3. Maros vize, Op. 18 arr. 2 vlns & pf
with F. Weltmann vln & piano   Pathé 39252
No. 6. Sárga Cserebogár, Op. 34 arr. 2 vlns & pf
with F. Weltmann vln & piano   Pathé 1930/1, 39253
No. 8. Azt mondják, Op. 60 arr. 2 vlns & pf
with piano   Pathé 51429

KORÓLY

Fantaisie hongrois vln & pf – arr. 2 vlns & pf
with F. Weltmann vln & piano   Odeon 97723

SCHUMANN

(13) Kinderscenen, Op. 15 pf
No. 7. Träumerei arr. 2 vlns & pf
with F. Weltmann vln & piano   Pathé 2055, 51427

Mads WESTERGAARD

ALBINONI

(12) Sonatas, Op. 1 (1694) "Sinfonias" 2 vlns & c
Sonata No. 11, in e
with A. Lysy vln, G. Selmi vlc,   I Classici della Musica Classica
G. Levy fl & L. Cerroni hpsi   XAC4049

CORELLI

(12) Sonatas, Op. 1 2 vlns & c
Sonata No. 7, in C
with A. Lysy vln, G. Selmi vlc,   I Classici della Musica Classica
G. Levy fl & L. Cerroni hpsi   XAC4049

VIVALDI

(12) Sonatas, Op. 1 2 vlns & c
Sonata No. 8, in d, F.XIII, No. 24
with A. Lysy vln, G. Selmi vlc,   I Classici della Musica Classica
G. Levy fl & L. Cerroni hpsi   XAC4049

Albert WESTON

KNEASS

Ben Bolt (Oh! don't you remember sweet Alice?) (1848) v & pf – arr. vln & pf as "Fantasia" by Weston
with piano   Edison Diamond Disc 80116

WALLACE

Maritana (1845) – opera
Scenes that are brightest arr. vln & pf Weston
with piano   Edison Diamond Disc 80116

Hans–Joachim WESTPHAL

TELEMANN

Concerto in D 4 vlns & strs
with R. Schulz vln, G. Silzer vln,   Archive APM14609, ARC3109
W. Kirch vln & chamber orch. – Seiler

Norbert WETHMAR

BACH

(4) Suites, BWV1066/9 strs & c
  Suite No. 3, in D: Air (2nd mvt) BWV1068 2 obs, 3 tpts, drms strs & c –
  arr. vln & pf as "Air on the G–string" by Wilhelmj
  with piano   HMV EX64
               Zonophone 5727

BALFE

Killarney (1862) v & pf – arr. vln & pf Moffat
  with piano   Zonophone 5634

DRDLA

Souvenir vln & pf
  with piano   Zonophone 5931

KREISLER

Caprice viennois, Op. 2 vln & pf
  with piano   Zonophone 5810
Tambourin chinois, Op. 3 vln & pf
  with piano   Zonophone 5931

MASSENET

Thaïs (1894) – opera
  Méditation arr. vln & pf Marsick
  with piano   Zonophone 5810

PUCCINI

(La) Bohème (1896) – opera
  Quando me'en vo soletta "Musetta's waltz song" arr. vln & pf Wethmar
  with piano   Zonophone 5654

SAINT-SAËNS

(Le) Carnaval des animaux (1886) small orch.
  Le cygne arr. vln & pf
  with piano   Zonophone 5654

SCHUBERT, François

(12) Bagatelles, Op. 13 vln & pf
  No. 9. L'abeille
  with piano   HMV EX64
               Zonophone 5727

THOMAS, J.R.

Eileen Alannah (1873) v & pf – arr. vln & pf
  with piano   Zonophone 5634

Camilla WICKS (1928–)

ANONYMOUS

Norwegian dance arr. vln & pf Wicks
  with R. Levin pf   HMV DA11905

BENJAMIN

(2) Jamaican Pieces (1940) orch.
  No. 2. Jamaican Rhumba arr. vln & pf Primrose
  with K. Siem pf   Cupol 4054

BLOCH

Ball Shem (3 Pictures of Chassidic life) (1923) vln & pf
  No. 2. Nigun (Improvisation)
             OSB 3203–1 & 3204–1A   HMV DA11004
  with S. Ehrling pf

BORODIN

Petite Suite (1878/85) pf
  No. 6. Serenade arr. vln & pf Heifetz
  with S. Ehrling pf   HMV DA11004

CHOPIN

Nocturne No. 19, in e, Op. 72, No. 1 pf – arr. vln & pf Auer
  with K. Siem pf   Cupol 6004
Nocturne No. 20, in c sharp, Op. posth pf – arr. vln & pf Milstein
  with K. Siem pf   Cupol 6004

DVOŘÁK

(8) Slavonic Dances, Op. 46 pf duet; orch.
  No. 2. Slavonic dance No. 2, in e arr. vln & pf "in g" Kreisler
  with R. Levin pf   HMV DA11906
(8) Slavonic Dances, Op. 72 pf duet; orch.
  No. 2. Slavonic dance No. 10, in e arr. vln & pf Kreisler
  with K. Siem pf   Cupol 6002

EGGE

Concerto, Op. 26 vln & orch.
  with Oslo Philharmonic Orch. –   Philips 839238 DSY, PHS900210
  Fjeldstad

ELGAR

(La) Capricieuse, Op. 17 vln & pf
  with K. Siem pf   Cupol 4054

KABALEVSKY

Improvisation, Op. 21, No. 1 vln & pf
  with S. Ehrling pf   2SB 3205–1   HMV DB11025

KOCH

(4) Dances vln & pf
  No. 2. Dance No. 2, in A
            MR 337–A, RTJ–4636–MA   Metronome B607
  with R. Levin pf

KREISLER

Tambourin chinois, Op. 3 vln & pf
            MR 338–A, RTJ–4637–MA   Metronome B607
  with R. Levin pf

KROLL

Banjo & fiddle vln & pf
  with R. Levin pf   HMV DA11906

PAGANINI

(24) Caprices, Op. 1 (1801/7) solo vln
  Caprice No. 24, in a arr. vln & pf Auer
  with K. Siem pf   Cupol 4054

PONCE

Estrellita (1913) v & pf – arr. vln & pf Heifetz
  with K. Siem pf   Cupol 4035

PROKOFIEV

(The) Love for Three Oranges, Op. 33 (1919) – opera
  No. 3. March arr. vln & pf Heifetz
    with S. Ehrling pf   2SB 3198–1   HMV DB11025

SCHUBERT

(7) Gesänge (set to Scott's "Lady of the Lake") Op. 52 v & pf
  No. 6. Ave Maria, D839 arr. vln & pf Wilhelmj
    with K. Siem pf   Cupol 6002

SHOSTAKOVICH

(The) Age of Gold, Op. 22 (1930) – ballet orch.
  Polka arr. vln & pf Grunes
    with S. Ehrling pf   2SB 3198–1   HMV DB11025
(24) Preludes, Op. 34 (1932/3) pf
  Prelude No. 10, in c sharp arr. vln & pf Tziganov
    with S. Ehrling pf   OSB 3199–1   HMV DA11003
  Prelude No. 15, in D flat arr. vln & pf Tziganov
    with S. Ehrling pf   OSB 3199–1   HMV DA11003
  Prelude No. 16, in b flat arr. vln & pf Tziganov
    with S. Ehrling pf   OSB 3200–1   HMV DA11003
  Prelude No. 24, in d arr. vln & pf Tziganov
    with S. Ehrling pf   OSB 3200–1   HMV DA11003

SIBELIUS

Concerto in d, Op. 47 vln & orch.
  with Stockholm Radio Symphony   Capitol CTL7026, P8175, P8327
  Orch. – Ehrling   Metronome CLP510
    Telefunken LCSK8175

VALÉN

Concerto, Op. 37 vln & orch.
  with Oslo Philharmonic Symphony   HMV DB11908/9
  Orch. – Fjeldstad

WICKS*

Har du sett noko til Kjerringa mi vln & pf
  with R. Levin pf   HMV DA11905
Jeg lagde meg sa silde vln & pf
  with R. Levin pf   HMV DA11905
Jeg rodde meg ut vln & pf
  with R. Levin pf   HMV DA11905

Frances WIENER

BACH

(6) Sonatas, BWV1014/9 vln & clav
Sonata No. 4, in c, BWV1017
  with L. Shorr pf   Music Library Recordings
    MLR7094

HONEGGER

Sonata No. 2, in d (1919) vln & pf
  with L. Shorr pf   Music Library Recordings
    MLR7094

* Composed jointly with Rolf Hodger.

STRAUSS, R.

Sonata in E flat, Op. 18 vln & pf
  Improvisation (Andante cantabile) (2nd mvt)
    with L. Shorr pf   Music Library Recordings
    MLR7094

Hans WIESBECK

DRDLA

Serenade No. 1, in A vln & pf
  with FFB Orch. – Eisbrenner   Baccarola 77873ZK

FIBICH

Images, Impressions & Souvenirs, Op. 41 pf
  No. 14. Poem (from "Souvenirs", Part IV) arr. vln & pf Kubelík
    with FFB Orch. – Eisbrenner   Baccarola 77873ZK

MENDELSSOHN

Concerto in e, Op. 64 vln & orch.
  with Bavarian Symphony Orch. –   Classic Record Club MP29
  Wilhelm   Music Treasures of the World
    MT15
    Odeon XOC822

Jerome WIGLER

SWING

Sonata in c (1928) vln & pf
  with G. Reeves pf   Folkways FM3506

Maurice WILK (1922–1963)

BACH, J.C.

Sinfonia concertante in E flat, T. P284 (1770) 2 vlns, 2 fls, 2 hrns & orch.
  Andante (2nd mvt)
    with M. Miller ob & Little Symphony   Columbia ML4916
  Orch. – Saidenberg

BACH, J.S.

Cantata No. 59 (Ach Gott, wie manches Herzeleid) BWV59
  Ich bin vergnügt in meinem Leiden
    with E. Farrell s, P. Ulanowsky pf &   Decca DL9411, DL79411
  Bach Aria Group Orch. – Brieff
Cantata No. 68 (Also hat Gott die Welt geliebt) BWV68
  Mein Gläubiges Herz
    with E. Farrell s, B. Greenhouse vlc,   Decca DL9405, DL79405
  R. Bloom ob, P. Ulanowsky hpsi &
  Bach Aria Group – Scheide
Cantata No. 97 (In allen meinen Thaten) BWV97
  Ich traue seiner Gnaden
    with J. Peerce t, B. Greenhouse vlc, P.   Decca DL9405, DL79405
  Ulanowsky hpsi & Bach Aria Group –
  Scheide
Cantata No. 157 (Ich lasse dich nicht, du segnest) BWV157
  Ja, ja, ich halte Jesum feste
    with N. Farrow bs, J. Baker fl, B.   Decca DL9405, DL79405
  Greenhouse vlc, P. Ulanowsky hpsi &
  Bach Aria Group – Scheide

BACH, J.S. – Continued

Cantata No. 205 (Der zufriedengestellte Aeolus) BWV205
Angenehmer Zephyrus
with E. Farrell s, B. Greenhouse vlc,   Decca DL9409, DL79409
P. Ulanowsky pf & Bach Aria Group
– Scheide

Frische Schatten, meine Freude
with J. Peerce t, N. Farrow bs, B.   Decca DL9409, DL79409
Greenhouse vlc, P. Ulanowsky pf &
Bach Aria Group – Scheide

Concerto in c, BWV1060 vln & ob or 2 vlns, strs & c
Adagio (2nd mvt)
with M. Miller ob & Little Symphony   Columbia ML4916
Orch. – Saidenberg

Mass in F, BWV233 (1737)
Quoniam tu solus sanctus, tu solus Dominus
with C. Smith a, B. Greenhouse vlc, P.   Decca DL9411, DL79411
Ulanowsky pf & Bach Aria Group –
Brieff

Mass in A, BWV234
Domine Deus, Rex Coelestis, Deus Pater
with N. Farrow bs, B. Greenhouse vlc,   Decca DL9409, DL79409
P. Ulanowsky pf & Bach Aria Group
– Scheide

(4) Suites, BWV1066/9 strs & c
Suite No. 3, in D: Air (2nd mvt) BWV1068 2 obs, 3 tpts, drms, strs & c
– arr. vln & pf as "Air on the G–string" by Wilhelmj
with F. Kramer pf   Magic Tone MLP1002

BEETHOVEN

(3) Trios, Op. 1 pf, vln & vlc
No. 1. Trio No. 1, in E flat
with A. Baller pf & G. Rejto vlc   Decca DL10047, DL710047
(2) Trios, Op. 70 pf, vln & vlc
No. 1. Trio No. 4, in D "Ghost"
with A. Baller pf & G. Rejto vlc   Decca DL10064, DL710064
No. 2. Trio No. 5, in E flat
with A. Baller pf & G. Rejto vlc   Decca DL10047, DL710047

BRAHMS

Trio No. 2, in C, Op. 87 pf, vln & vlc
with A. Baller pf & G. Rejto vlc   Decca DL10047, DL710047

McBRIDE

Concerto (1954) vln & orch.
with Vienna Symphony Orch. – Hendl   American Recording Society
ARS27, ARS116
Desto D417, DS6417

PAGANINI

(24) Caprices, Op. 1 (1801/7) solo vln
Caprice No. 13, in B flat arr. vln & pf Kreisler
with F. Kramer pf   Magic Tone MLP1002
Caprice No. 14, in E flat
(unaccompanied)   Magic Tone MLP1002

SARASATE

(8) Danzas españolas vln & pf
Danza española No. 7, in a, Op. 26, No. 1
with F. Kramer pf   Magic Tone MLP1002

SCHUBERT

Trio No. 2, in E flat, Op. 100 (D929) pf, vln & vlc
with A. Baller pf & G. Rejto vlc   Decca DL10033, DL710033

SHOSTAKOVICH

(24) Preludes, Op. 34 (1932/3) pf
Prelude No. 10, in c sharp arr. vln & pf Tziganov
with F. Kramer pf   Magic Tone MLP1002
Prelude No. 24, in d arr. vln & pf Tziganov
with F. Kramer pf   Magic Tone MLP1002

WIENIAWSKI

Polonaise brillante No. 1, in D, Op. 4 vln & pf
with F. Kramer pf   Magic Tone MLP1002

Wanda WILKOMIRSKA (1929–   )

ALBÉNIZ

España (6 Feuilles d'album) Op. 165 pf
No. 2. Tango in D arr. vln & pf Kreisler
with A. Barbosa pf   Connoisseur Society CS2022

ANONYMOUS

Londonderry air traditional Irish ballad – arr. vln & pf Kreisler
with A. Barbosa pf   Connoisseur Society CS2022

BAIRD

Expressions (1959) vln & orch.
with Polish National Philharmonic   Muza XL0177
Orch. – Rowicki   Philips 835265AY, 839273DSY,
A02388L

BARTÓK

(44) Duos (1931) 2 vlns
with M. Szücs vln   Qualiton LPX11320

EGK

Geigenmusik (1936) vln & orch.
with Bavarian Radio Symphony   Deutsche Grammophon
Orch. – Egk   LPM39142, SLPM139142

GRIEG

Sonata No. 3, in c, Op. 45 vln & pf
with A. Barbosa pf   Connoisseur Society CS2038

HUEBERGER

(Der) Opernball, Op. 40 (1898) – operetta
Im chambre séparée arr. vln & pf as "Midnight bells" by Kreisler
with A. Barbosa pf   Connoisseur Society CS2022

KARLOWICZ

Concerto in A, Op. 8 vln & orch.
with Polish National Philharmonic   Muza XL0179
Orch. – Rowicki

KHACHATURIAN

Concerto in D (1940) vln & orch.
with Warsaw National Philharmonic   Musical Heritage Society
Symphony Orch. – Rowicki   MHS1102
Muza XL0513

KREISLER

Caprice viennois, Op. 2 vln & pf
with A. Barbosa pf   Connoisseur Society CS2022

Liebesfreud vln & pf
with A. Barbosa pf   Connoisseur Society CS2022

Liebesleid vln & pf
with A. Barbosa pf   Connoisseur Society CS2022

Schön Rosmarin vln & pf
with A. Barbosa pf   Connoisseur Society CS2022

Tamburin chinois, Op. 3 vln & pf
with A. Barbosa pf   Connoisseur Society CS2022

Praeludium & Allegro (Pugnani) vln & pf
with A. Barbosa pf   Connoisseur Society CS2022

Variations on a theme of Corelli (Tartini) vln & pf
with A. Barbosa pf   Connoisseur Society CS2022

MUSSORGSKY

Sorochintsy Fair (1911/23) – opera
  Gopak (Act III) orch. – arr. vln & pf Dushkin
  with J. Szamotulska pf   Muza X2062

PROKOFIEV

Sonata No. 1, in f, Op. 80 vln & pf
with A. Schein pf   Connoisseur Society CS2016

Sonata No. 2, in D, Op. 94bis vln & pf
with A. Schein pf   Connoisseur Society CS2016

RACHMANINOV

(2) Pieces, Op. 6 vln & pf
  No. 1. Romance in d
  with J. Szamotulska pf   Muza X2061, X2145

RAVEL

Pièce en forme d'Habanera v & pf – arr. vln & pf Catherine
with A. Barbosa pf   Connoisseur Society CS2038

Sonata (1927) vln & pf
with A. Barbosa pf   Connoisseur Society CS2038

SCOTT

Lotus land, Op. 47, No. 1 (1905) pf – arr. vln & pf Kreisler
with A. Barbosa pf   Connoisseur Society CS2022

SZYMANOWSKI

Concerto No. 1, in a, Op. 35 (1922) vln & orch.
  with Polish National Philharmonic   Heliodor 89672, HS25087
  Orch. – Rowicki   Muza XL0113, XL0116

Harnasie, Op. 51 (1926) – ballet orch.
  Highland melody arr. vln & pf Kochański
  with J. Szamotulska pf   Muza XL0385

(3) Mythes, Op. 30 (1915) vln & pf
  No. 1. La Fontaine d'Aréthuse
  with J. Szamotulska pf   Muza L0137

  No. 2. Narcisse
  with J. Szamotulska pf   Muza L0137

  No. 3. Dryades et Pan
  with J. Szamotulska pf   Muza L0137

Notturno & Tarantella, Op. 28 vln & pf
with J. Szamotulska pf   Muza L0137

WIENIAWSKI

Concerto No. 2, in d, Op. 22 vln & pf
  with Polish National Philharmonic   Heliodor 89672, HS25087
  Orch. – Rowicki   Muza XL0113, XL0382

(2) Mazurkas, Op. 19 vln & pf
  No. 1. Mazurka No. 1, in G "Obertass"
  with J. Szamotulska pf   Muza X2061, X2145

G. WILL*

CHAMINADE

Sérénade espagnole pf – arr. vln & pf Kreisler
with piano   Parlophone 80757, 85881

DVOŘÁK

(8) Humoresques, Op. 101 pf
  No. 7. Humoresque No. 7, in G flat arr. vln & pf "in G" Kreisler
  with piano   Parlophone 80757, 85881

Albert Gabrielle WILLAUME (1873–)

HUBAY

(6) Poèmes hongroise, Op. 27 vln & pf
  No. 4. Poème hongrois No. 4, in a
  with piano   Aerophon 845

PIERNÉ

Sérénade in A, Op. 7 (1875) pf – arr. vln & pf
with piano   Aerophon 844

SAINT–SAËNS

(Le) Déluge, Op. 45 (1876) – oratorio
  Prélude vln & orch. – arr. vln & pf Saint–Saëns
  with C. Saint–Saëns pf   03280 v   Audio Archives LA1203
                                        Gramophone & Typewriter
                                        037920
                                        HMV DB705
                                        Rococo 2001

Élégie, Op. 143 vln & pf
  with C. Saint–Saëns pf   03281 v   Gramophone & Typewriter
                                        037921
                                        HMV DB704

Havanaise, Op. 83 vln & orch.
  with piano   03392/3 v   Gramophone & Typewriter
                                        037922/3
                                        HMV W390

Charles WILLIAMS

MASCAGNI

Cavalleria Rusticana (1890) – opera
  Intermezzo orch. – arr. vln & org
  with cinema organ   Zonophone 5280

* Or G. Wullens.

RUBINSTEIN

(2) Melodies, Op. 3 pf
No. 1. Melody in F arr. vln & org
with cinema organ — HMV EX33; Zonophone 5194

SCOTT, Lady John

Annie Laurie (1838) v & pf – arr. vln & org
with cinema organ — Zonophone 5280

TATE

Somewhere a voice is calling (1911) v & pf – arr. vln & org
with cinema organ — Zonophone 5194

Victor WILLIS

MENDELSSOHN

(6) Songs without words, Op. 62 pf
No. 6. Song without words No. 30, in A "Spring song" arr. vln & pf
with piano — Apex 495; Edison Bell 2962; Gennett 10036

THOMÉ

Simple aveu, Op. 25 pf – arr. vln & pf
with piano — Apex 495; Edison Bell 2962; Gennett 10036

Gertrude WINCHESTER

COLERIDGE-TAYLOR

(4) African dances, Op. 58 vln & pf
No. 2. Andantino molto sostenuto
with piano — Beltona 811

DRDLA

Serenade No. 1, in A vln & pf
with piano — Beltona 467

Vision, Op. 28 vln & pf
with piano — Beltona 811

GOUNOD

Ave Maria (Méditation on Bach's "Prelude No. 1, in C" from Book I of "Das Wohltemperirte Clavier") v & pf – arr. vln & pf
with piano — Beltona 344

KREISLER

Liebesleid vln & pf
with piano — Beltona 467

MASSENET

Thaïs (1894) – opera
Méditation arr. vln & pf Marsick
with piano — Beltona 344

PADEREWSKI

(6) Humoresques de concert, Op. 14 pf
No. 1. Minuet in G arr. vln & pf Kreisler
with piano — Beltona 822

TCHAIKOVSKY

Souvenir d'un lieu cher, Op. 42 vln & pf
No. 3. Mélodie
with piano — Beltona 822

David WISE

d'AMBROSIO

Canzonetta, Op. 6 vln & pf
with piano — HMV EX44; Zonophone 5420

DVOŘÁK

(8) Humoresques, Op. 101 pf
No. 7. Humoresque No. 7, in G flat arr. vln & pf "in G" Kreisler
with orch. — Zz 17542[II]△ — Zonophone A371

MASCAGNI

Cavalleria Rusticana (1890) – opera
Siciliana arr. vln & pf
with piano — HMV EX44; Zonophone 5420

MOZART

Serenade No. 6, in D, K239 "Serenata Notturna" orch.
with M. Parikian vln, H. Downes vla, J.E. Merrett cbs & Philharmonia Orch. – Klemperer — Angel 35401; Columbia C90540, CX1438; HMV CLP1061, LALP539, 7ERL1426

VAUGHAN WILLIAMS

(The) Lark ascending (1914) vln & cha orch.
with Liverpool Philharmonic Orch. – Sargent — CAX 9863/6–1 — Columbia DX1386/7

WIENIAWSKI

Légende, Op. 17 vln & pf or orch.
with orch. — Zz 17543[IV]△ — Zonophone A371

Alma Rosengren WITEK

BACH

Concerto in d, BWV1043 2 vlns, strs & c
with A. Witek vln & Bayreuth Festival Orch. — WAX 3988/91 — Columbia 9681/2, J7435/6

Anton WITEK (1872–1933)

BACH

Concerto in d, BWV1043 2 vlns, strs & c
with A.R. Witek vln & Bayreuth Festival Orch. — WAX 3988/91 — Columbia 9681/2, J7435/6

Ludwig WITTELS (1896–1956)

BEETHOVEN

Romance No. 2, in F, Op. 50 vln & orch.
with L. Birkenfeld pf — Polydor 20204

HUBAY
(6) Blumenleben, Op. 30 vln & pf
No. 5. Der Zephir
  with L. Birkenfeld pf   3430 ar   Polydor 20203

KREISLER
Tambourin chinois, Op. 3 vln & pf
  with L. Birkenfeld pf   3429 ar   Polydor 20203

Alfred WITTENBERG (1880–)

BEETHOVEN
Romance No. 2, in F, Op. 50 vln & orch.
  with orch.   14005   Homochord B1366

BRAHMS
(21) Hungarian Dances pf duet
Hungarian dance No. 5, in f sharp arr. vln & pf "in g" Joachim
  with orch.   6648   Homochord 146, B1361

BROOKS
Children's song vln & pf
  with piano   15642/3   Homochord B1371

CHOPIN
(3) Nocturnes, Op. 9 pf
No. 2. Nocturne No. 2, in E flat arr. vln & pf Sarasate
  with orch.   6654   Homochord 381, B1361, B1368,
                          H274

DANIDERFF
Auf den wassern vln & pf
  with piano   15641   Homochord B1370

DELIBES
Sylvia (1876) – ballet orch.
No. 16a. Pizzicato–scherzettino (Act III) arr. vln & orch.
  with orch.   6647   Homochord 146, B1367

GOUNOD
Ave Maria (Méditation on Bach's "Prelude No. 1, in C" from Book I of "Das Wohltemperirte Clavier") v & pf – arr. vln & orch.
  with orch.   14007   Homochord B1369

HANDEL
Serse (1738) – opera
Ombra mai fu "Largo" arr. vln & orch.
  with orch.   6649   Homochord 381, B1368, H274

HAYDN
(6) Quartets, Op. 3 (H.III, Nos. 13/8) 2 vlns, vla & vlc
No. 5. Quartet No. 17, in F: Andante cantabile (2nd mvt) "Serenade", H.III, No. 17 arr. vln & orch.
  with orch.   6653   Homochord 383, B1363

HUBAY
(14) Scènes de la csárda vln & pf
No. 4. Hejre Kati, Op. 32
  with orch.   14009   Homochord B1365

LANGER
Grandfather, Op. 22 salon orch. – arr. vln & orch.
  with orch.   50516   Homochord B8036
Grandmother, Op. 20 pf – arr. vln & orch.
  with orch.   50517   Homochord B8036

MARRINER
Guten Abend, Herr Mond vln & pf
  with piano   15640   Homochord B1370

MENDELSSOHN
Concerto in e, Op. 64 vln & orch.
Andante (2nd mvt)
  with orch.   14008   Homochord B1366

MOZART
Divertimento No. 17, in D, K334 2 hrns & strs
Minuet (3rd mvt) arr. vln & pf Burmester
  with orch.   14006   Homochord B1369

RIES
Suite No. 3, in G, Op. 34 vln & pf
No. 5. Perpetuum mobile
  with orch.   6652   Homochord 383, B1363

SARASATE
Zigeunerweisen, Op. 20 vln & pf or orch.
  with orch.   6651   Homochord 382, B1362, B1367

WIENIAWSKI
Mazurka in a, Op. 3 "Kujawiak" vln & pf
  with orch.   6650   Homochord 382, B1362
Souvenir de Moscou, Op. 6 vln & pf or orch.*
  with orch.   12072   Homochord B1365

Herta WÖBBEL

TCHAIKOVSKY
Concerto in D, Op. 35 vln & orch.
  with Munich Symphony Orch. –   Fidelio ATL4018
  Havagesse

Petrescu WOIKU (1884–)

ANONYMOUS
Kol Nidrei Hebrew melody – arr. vln & pf Rosenfeld
  with piano   Vox 06109

BACH
(4) Suites, BWV1066/9 strs & c
Suite No. 3, in D: Air (2nd mvt) BWV1068 2 obs, 3 tpts, drms, strs & c – arr. vln & pf as "Air on the G-string" by Wilhelmj
  with piano   Vox 06109

BRAHMS
(21) Hungarian Dances pf duet
Hungarian dance No. 2, in d arr. vln & pf Joachim
  with F. Mück pf   2853 GN   Polydor 47060

* abridged.

HANDEL

Concerto No. 3, in g ob & orch.
  Sarabande (3rd mvt) arr. vln & pf Woiku
  with F. Mück pf   2852 GN   Polydor 47060

Endre WOLF (1913–)

ANONYMOUS

Londonderry air traditional Irish air – arr. vln & pf Kreisler
  with A. Wolf pf   Mercury EP1–5040
                                     Tono K8062

ATTERBERG

Suite No. 3, in c sharp, Op. 19, No. 1 vln, vla & orch.
  with T. Brostrom vla & Goteberg   Radiotjanst RC306 & RD538
  Radio Symphony Orch. – Mann

AULIN

(4) Aquarelles vln & pf
  No. 2. Humoresque
  with A. Wolf pf   OSB 2820–1   HMV X7379

BACH

Concerto No. 2, in E, BWV1042 vln, strs & c
  with Copenhagen Chamber Orch. –   Classic CL6015
  Tuxen   Mercury MG10023
                                     Sonora K9557/9
                                     Tono X25132/4

(3) Sonatas & 3 Partitas, BWV1001/6 solo vln
  Partita No. 2, in d: Sarabande (3rd mvt) BWV1004
  (unaccompanied)   OSB 2821–1   HMV X7379
  Partita No. 2, in d: Gigue (4th mvt) BWV1004
  (unaccompanied)   Tono X25128
  Sonata No. 3, in C: Largo (3rd mvt) BWV1004
  (unaccompanied)   Sonora K9559
                                     Tono X25134

BARTÓK

For Children (40 pieces) (1909) pf
  No. 6, 13, 18, 25, 31, 36 & 40 arr. vln & pf as "Hungarian folk tunes" by
  Szigeti
  with A. Wolf pf   Tono A150

BEETHOVEN

Sonata No. 5, in F, Op. 24 "Spring" vln & pf
  with A. Wolf pf   Mercury MG10120
                                     Tono X25157/9

Sonata No. 9, in A, Op. 47 "Kreutzer" vln & pf
  with A. Wolf pf   Mercury MG10120
                                     Tono LVA34001, X25170/3
                                     World Record Club R37

BRAHMS

Concerto in D, Op. 77 (cadenza by Kreisler) vln & orch.
  with Sinfonia of London – Collins Music Appreciation Records
                                     MAR15
                                     World Record Club T30

BRUCH

Concerto No. 1, in g, Op. 26 vln & orch.*
  with Danish Radio Orch. –   3343/8   Classic CL6017
  Tuxen   Mercury MG10064
                                     Sonora K9539/41
                                     Tono X25129/31

DVOŘÁK

(7) Gypsy songs, Op. 55 v & pf
  No. 4. Songs my mother taught me arr. vln & pf Kreisler
  with A. Wolf pf   Mercury EP1–5040
                                     Tono A149

FALLA

(El) Amor Brujo (1915) – ballet m–s & orch.
  No. 14. Pantomime arr. vln & pf Kochański
  with A. Wolf pf   OSB 2819–1   HMV X7378

GROBE

Sonata in g fl, 2 vlns, vla, vlc & cbs
  excerpt unid
  with H. Frenz fl, K. Knaak vln, B.E.   Decca 20497
  Urack vla, K. Kohnke vlc & M.   Odeon 0–25480
  Kastly cbs

HAYDN

(6) Quartets, Op. 64 (H.III, Nos. 63/8) 2 vlns, vla & vlc
  No. 5. Quartet No. 67, in D, H.III, No. 67 "Lark"
  with K. Knaak vln, B.E. Urack vla &   Odeon 25564/5
  K. Kohnke vlc

MENDELSSOHN

Concerto in e, Op. 64 vln & orch.
  with Danish Radio Orch. – Tuxen   Classic CL6017

MOZART

Concerto No. 5, in A, K219 "Turkish" (cadenzas by Joachim) vln & orch.
  with Copenhagen Chamber Orch. –   Classic CL6015
  Tuxen   Mercury MG10023
                                     Sonora K9542/5
                                     Tono X25125/8

PAGANINI

(24) Caprices, Op. 1 (1801/7) solo vln
  Caprice No. 5, in a arr. vln & pf Maciewski
  with A. Wolf pf   OSB 2818–1   HMV X7378
  Caprice No. 17, in E flat arr. vln & pf
  with A. Wolf pf   Mercury EP1–5040
                                     Tono A149

QUANTZ

Concerto in G fl & strs
  Allegro (1st mvt); **Arioso** (2nd mvt)
  with H. Frenz fl, K. Knaak vln, B.E.   Decca 20497/8
  Urack vla, K. Kohnke vlc & M.   Odeon 0–25480/1
  Kastly cbs

* Adagio or 2nd mvt. also on Tono X25144.

RIMSKY–KORSAKOV

(The) Tale of Tsar Saltan (1900) – opera
Flight of the bumblebee (Act III) orch. – arr. vln & pf Hartmann
with A. Wolf pf   Mercury EP1–5040
      Tono K8062

TARTINI

Sonata in g "Il Trillo del Diavolo" vln & c – arr. vln & pf Kreisler
with A. Wolf pf   Mercury EP1–5039
      Tono A151/2

TCHAIKOVSKY

Concerto in D, Op. 35 vln & orch.
with Danish State Radio Orch. –   Classic CL6017
Jensen   Mercury MG10064
      Tono X25153/6

Johannes WOLFF (1863–   )

BRAGA

(7) Melodies (1867) v & pf
No. 5. La serenata "Angel's serenade" arr. v, vln & pf
with B. Davies t & piano   Pathé cylinder 76003

GOUNOD

Ave Maria (Méditation on Bach's "Prelude No. 1, in C" from Book I of
"Das Wohltemperirte Clavier") v & pf – arr. vln & pf
with piano   Pathé cylinder 70104
Ave Maria (Méditation on Bach's "Prelude No. 1, in C" from Book I of
"Das Wohltemperirte Clavier") v & pf – arr. v, vln & pf
with B. Davies t & piano   Pathé 8510
      Pathé cylinder 76000

Faust (1859) – opera
Salut! demeure chaste et pure (Act III)
with B. Davies t & piano   Pathé 8510
      Pathé cylinder 76001

Sérénade (Quand tu chantes) v & pf – arr. v, vln & pf
with B. Davies t & piano   Pathé cylinder 76002

PIERNÉ

Sérénade in A, Op. 7 (1875) pf – arr. vln & pf Haddock
with piano   Pathé cylinder 70103

SAINT–SAËNS

Sérénade, Op. 15 pf, org, vln & vla – arr. vln & pf
with piano   Pathé cylinder 70101

THOMÉ

(L') Extase pf – arr. vln & pf
with piano   Pathé cylinder 70102

WIENIAWSKI

Polonaise brillante No. 1, in D, Op. 4 vln & pf
with piano   Pathé cylinder 70100

Louis WOLFF (1865–1926)

BEETHOVEN

(3) Trios, Op. 1 pf, vln & vlc
No. 2. Trio No. 2, in G: Presto (4th mvt)
with A.B.H. Verhey pf & J. Mosel vlc   Favorite 2–94002

MENDELSSOHN

Trio No. 1, in d, Op. 49 pf, vln & vlc
Scherzo (3rd mvt)
with A.B.H. Verhey pf & J. Mosel vlc   Favorite 2–94003

PIERNÉ

Sérénade in A, Op. 7 (1875) pf – arr. vln & pf Haddock
with A.B.H. Verhey pf   Favorite 2–94001D

M. A. WOLFF–ISRAEL

CUI

(5) Little Duets, Op. 56 fl & vln
No. 4. Nocturne
with V.F. Stepanov fl   Gramophone & Typewriter
      28000

SARASATE

(8) Danzas españolas vln & pf
Danza española*
with piano   Zonophone X67902

Doris WOLFF–MALM

PACHELBEL

Canon & Gigue in D 3 vlns & c
with U. Grehling vln, S. Lautenbacher   Archive EPA37256, SEPA181256
vln, F. Neumeyer hpsi & R. Buhl vlc
Partita No. 6, in B flat 2 vlns & c
with U. Grehling vln, S. Lautenbacher   Archive EPA37256, SEPA181256
vln & F. Neumeyer hpsi

G. WOLFGANG

DVOŘÁK

(8) Humoresques, Op. 101 pf
No. 7. Humoresque No. 7, in G flat arr. vln & pf "in G" Kreisler
with A. Marty hp   Guilde Européenne du
      Microsillon EGEX45103

GOUNOD

Ave Maria (Méditation on Bach's "Prelude No. 1, in C" from Book I of
"Das Wohltemperirte Clavier") v & pf – arr. vln & hp
with A. Marty hp   Guilde Européenne du
      Microsillon EGEX45103

MASSENET

Thaïs (1894) – opera
Méditation arr. vln & pf Marsick
with A. Marty hp   Guilde Européenne du
      Microsillon EGEX45103

* Unidentified.

Josef WOLFSTHAL (1899–1931)

BACH

(3) Sonatas & 3 Partitas, BWV1001/6 solo vln
  Partita No. 3, in E: Preludio (1st mvt) arr. vln & pf Kreisler
  with piano   Artiphon D7041

BEETHOVEN

Concerto in D, Op. 61 (cadenzas by Joachim) vln & orch.
                1534 BM 1, 1535½ BM 1,   Brunswick 90277/81
                1536/8 BM 1, 1547/8½ BM 1 &   Polydor 69789/94, 95243/7
  with Berlin   1549/51 BM 1
  Philharmonic Orch. – Gurlitt

Romance No. 2, in F, Op. 50 vln & orch.
  with Berlin State Opera Orch. –   Polydor 69794

(3) Trios, Op. 1 pf, vln & vlc
  No. 3. Trio No. 3, in c: Menuetto (3rd mvt)
  with L. Kreutzer pf & G. Piatigorsky   Polydor 66212
  vlc

Trio in B flat, Op. 11 cl, vlc & pf
  Adagio (2nd mvt)
  with L. Kreutzer pf & G. Piatigorsky   Polydor 66212
  vlc

BOHM

(143) Lieder, Op. 326 v & pf
  No. 27. Still wie die Nacht arr. vln, pf & org
  with I. van Pathy pf & C.   50642   Homochord B8083
  Stabernack org

BRAHMS

(21) Hungarian Dances pf duet
  Hungarian dance No. 2, in d arr. vln & pf Joachim
  with piano   Bw 52¹△   HMV B2601, EG233, R10158

Trio No. 1, in B, Op. 8 pf, vln & vlc
  Scherzo (2nd mvt)
  with L. Kreutzer pf & G. Piatigorsky   Polydor 66213
  vlc

(16) Waltzes, Op. 39 pf duet
  No. 15. Waltz No. 15, in A flat arr. vln & pf "in A" Byrd
  with piano   Bw 51¹△   HMV B2602, EG209, R10159

CHOPIN

(3) Nocturnes, Op. 9 pf
  No. 2. Nocturne No. 2, in E flat arr. vln & pf Sarasate
  with piano   Artiphon D7038
  No. 2. Nocturne No. 2, in E flat arr. vln & pf Sarasate
  with piano   50528   Homochord B8037

CUI

Kaleidoscope, Op. 50 vln & pf
  No. 9. Orientale
  with A. Sándor pf   Ultraphon A357

DVOŘÁK

(8) Humoresques, Op. 101 pf
  No. 7. Humoresque No. 7, in G flat arr. vln & pf "in G" Kreisler
  with piano   50527   Homochord B8037
  No. 7. Humoresque No. 7, in G flat arr. vln & pf "in G" Kreisler
  with piano   Artiphon D7034

FALLA

(7) Canciones populares españolas (1914) v & pf
  No. 3. Asturiana arr. vln & pf Kochański
  with piano   HMV EG333, R10158
  No. 4. Jota arr. vln & pf Kochański
  with piano   HMV EG333

GLUCK

Orphée et Eurydice (1762) – opera
  Dance of the blessed spirits: Lento "Mélodie" (No. 2) arr. vln & pf
  Kreisler
  with piano   HMV EG415, R10160

GODARD

Jocelyn (1888) – opera
  Cachés dans cet asile "Berceuse" arr. vln, pf & org
  with I. van Pathy pf & C.   50643   Homochord B8083
  Stabernack org

GOLDMARK

Concerto in a, Op. 28 vln & orch.
  Andante (2nd mvt) "Air"
  with Berlin Symphony   52222   Homochord 4–8819
  Orch. – Platen

GOUNOD

Ave Maria (Méditation on Bach's "Prelude No. 1, in C" from Book I of
"Das Wohltemperirte Clavier") v & pf – arr. vln, pf & org
  with I. van Pathy pf & C.   50641   Homochord B8082
  Stabernack org

GRIEG

Peer Gynt (Suite No. 2) Op. 55 orch.
  No. 4. Solveig's song arr. vln & pf sitt
  with piano   50554   Homochord B8049

HANDEL

Serse (1738) – opera
  Ombra mai fu "Largo" arr. vln, pf & org
  with I. van Pathy pf & C.   50639   Homochord B8082
  Stabernack org
  Ombra mai fu "Largo" arr. vln & pf
  with piano   Artiphon D7039

KARK

Nadjada (Intermezzo) vln & pf
  with I. von Pathy & C.   50648   Homochord B8066
  Stabernack org

KREISLER

Liebesfreud vln & pf
  with piano   Artiphon D7036

Liebesleid vln & pf
  with piano   Artiphon D7035

Polichinelle–serenade vln & pf
  with A. Sándor pf   Ultraphon A357

Schön Rosmarin vln & pf
  with piano   Artiphon D7036

Variations on a theme of Corelli (Tartini) vln & pf
  with piano   Artiphon D7040

LALO

Symphonie espagnole, Op. 21 vln & orch.
  Scherzando (3rd mvt)
    with Berlin Symphony Orch.   52218   Homochord 4–8835
  – Platen
  Andante (4th mvt)
    with Berlin Symphony Orch.   55219   Homochord 4–8835
  – Platen

MATTHESON

(12) Suites hpsi (1714)
  Suite No. 5, in c: Air arr. vln & pf Burmester
    with piano   Bw 49^1△ HMV B2602, EG209, R10159

MENDELSSOHN

Concerto in e, Op. 64 vln & orch.
  with Berlin State Opera House Orch. – Polydor 69819/22
  Liachowsky

MOZART

Concerto No. 5, in A, K219 "Turkish" (cadenzas by Joachim) vln & orch.
  2–20911, 2–20916, 2–20918/9, 2– Columbia 67757/60D
                20927/30 Decca 25102/5
                          Odeon 0–7635/8
                          Parlophone E10921/4, P9359/60
                          & P9457/8

(Il) Re Pastore, K208 (1775) – opera
  No. 10. L'amerò, sarò costante
    with M. Ivogün s & piano   Polydor 24234

RAFF

(6) Pieces, Op. 85 vln & pf
  No. 3. Cavatina in D arr. vln, pf & org
    with I. van Pathy pf & C.   50640   Homochord B8088
  Stabernack org

RIMSKY–KORSAKOV

(Le) Coq d'Or (1910) – opera
  Hymn to the sun arr. vln & pf Kreisler
    with A. Sándor pf   10248   Ultraphon A173, AP330
Sadko (1898) – opera
  Chant hindou arr. vln & pf Kreisler
    with piano   61037   Homochord B37
  Chant hindou arr. vln & pf Kreisler
    with A. Sándor pf   10249   Ultraphon A173, AP330

SAINT-SAËNS

(Le) Carnaval des animaux (1886) small orch.
  Le cygne arr. vln, pf & org
    with I. van Pathy pf & C.   50647   Homochord B8066
  Stabernack org
(Le) Déluge, Op. 45 (1876) – oratorio
  Prélude vln & orch. – arr. vln, pf & org
    with I. van Pathy pf & C.   50637   Homochord B8084
  Stabernack org
Introduction & Rondo Capriccioso, Op. 28 vln & orch.
  with Berlin Symphony   52220/1 Homochord 4–8881
  Orch. – Platen
Samson et Dalila, Op. 47 (1877) – opera
  Mon coeur s'ouvre ta voix arr. vln, pf & org
    with I. van Pathy pf & C.   50644   Homochord B8035
  Stabernack org

SARASATE

(8) Danzas españolas vln & pf
  No. 3. Romanza andaluza, Op. 22, No. 1
    with piano   Artiphon D7037
  No. 4. Jota navarra, Op. 22, No. 2
    with piano   HMV EG415, R10160

SCHUBERT

(7) Gesänge (set to Scott's "Lady of the Lake") Op. 52 v & pf
  No. 6. Ave Maria, D839 arr. vln, pf & org
    with I. van Pathy pf & C.   50636   Homochord B8084
  Stabernack org
(6) Moments musicaux, Op. 94 (D780) (1823/7) pf
  No. 3. Moment musicale No. 3, in f "Air russe" arr. vln & pf Kreisler
    with piano   Artiphon D7042
Trio No. 1, in B flat, Op. 99 (D898) pf, vln & vlc
  Andante un poco mosso (2nd mvt)
    with L. Kreutzer pf & G. Piatigorsky Polydor 66214
  vlc

SCHUMANN

(13) Kinderscenen, Op. 15 pf
  No. 7. Träumerei arr. vln & pf
    with I. van Pathy pf   50554   Homochord B8056, E8049
  No. 7. Träumerei arr. vln & pf
    with piano   Artiphon D7033
  No. 8. Am Camin arr. vln & pf
    with piano   Artiphon D7042

SIMONETTI

Madrigale pf – arr. vln, pf & org
  with I. van Pathy pf & C.   50638   Homochord B8088
  Stabernack org

SMETANA

From my Homeland (1878) vln & pf
  No. 2. Andantino
    with K. Szreter pf   HMV AM1273, EG416, R10161

TARTINI

Sonata in g "Il Trillo del Diavolo" vln & c – arr. vln & pf Kreisler
  with W. Liachowsky pf   2076/9 as Polydor 66191/2

TCHAIKOVSKY

Concerto in D, Op. 35 vln & orch.
  Canzonetta (2nd mvt)
    with Berlin Symphony Orch.   52223   Homochord 4–8819
  – Platen
Sérénade mélancolique in b flat, Op. 26 vln & orch. arr. vln, pf & org
  with I. van Pathy pf & C.   50645   Homochord B8035
  Stabernack org

TOSELLI

Serenade, Op. 6 vln, pf & org
  with I. van Pathy pf & C.   50518   Homochord B8056
  Stabernack org

Martin WOLTERS

BACH

(4) Suites, BWV1066/9 strs & c
Suite No. 3, in D: Air (2nd mvt) BWV1068 2 obs, 3 tpts, drms, strs & c
– arr. vln & pf as "Air on the G–string" by Wilhelmj
  with piano   Odeon A42906

DVOŘÁK

(8) Humoresques, Op. 101 pf
No. 7. Humoresque No. 7, in G flat arr. vln & pf "in G" Wilhelmj
  with piano   Odeon A42902

MASCHERONI

Rêverie pathétique vln & pf
  with piano   Odeon A42903

MASSENET

Thaïs (1894) – opera
Méditation arr. vln & pf Marsick
  with piano   Odeon A42904

SCHUBERT

(7) Gesänge (set to Scott's "Lady of the Lake") Op. 52 v & pf
No. 6. Ave Maria, D839 arr. vln & pf Wilhelmj
  with piano   Odeon A42900

SIMONETTI

Madrigale pf – arr. vln & pf
  with piano   Odeon A42909

Haydn WOOD (1882–1959)

PIERNÉ

Sérénade in A, Op. 7 (1875) pf – arr. vln & pf Haddock
  with piano   Pathé 728, 751, 76520

Mary WOODGATE

COTTENET

Chanson méditation vln & pf
  with piano   21695   Regal G7160

Tadeusz WROŃSKI

BERG

Concerto (1935) vln & orch.
  with Warsaw National Philharmonic   Muza XL0140
  Orch. – Wislocki

BRAHMS

Concerto in D, Op. 77 (cadenza by Kreisler) vln & orch.
  with Warsaw National Philharmonic   Muza XL0128
  Orch. – Krenz
Sonata No. 1, in G, Op. 78 vln & pf
  with W. Szpilman pf   Muza XL0035
Sonata No. 2, in A, Op. 100 vln & pf
  with W. Szpilman pf   Muza XL0034
Sonata No. 3, in d, Op. 108 vln & pf
  with W. Szpilman pf   Muza XL0034

CHOPIN

Trio in g, Op. 5 pf, vln & vlc
  with W. Szpilman pf & A. Ciechański   Muza XL0080
  vlc

DEBUSSY

Sonata No. 3, in g (1917) vln & pf
  with W. Szpilman pf   Muza XL0035

SCHUMANN

Quintet in E flat, Op. 44 2 vlns, vla, vlc & pf
  with B. Gimpel vln, S. Kamasa vlc, A.   Muza XL0270
  Ciechański vlc & W. Szpilman pf

SHOSTAKOVICH

Quintet in g, Op. 57 pf, 2 vlns, vla & vlc
  with W. Szpilman pf, B. Gimpel vln,   Muza XL0270
  S. Kamasa vla & A. Ciechański vlc

TURSKI

Concerto No. 1 vln & orch.
  with Warsaw National Philharmonic   Muza XL0140
  Orch. – Wislocki

ZAREBSKI

Quintet in g, Op. 34 (1885) pf, 2 vlns, vla & vlc
  with W. Szpilman pf, B. Gimpel vln,   Muza XL0178
  S. Kamasa vla & A. Ciechański vlc

Friedrich WÜHRER (1925–   )

BACH

(6) Brandenburg Concerti, BWV1046/51 (1721) strs & c
Brandenburg Concerto No. 1, in F, BWV1046 vln, 3 obs, bsn, 2 hrns, strs
& c
  with H. Kähne ob, F. Huth hrn, W.   Decca ND248
  Reuband hrn & Chamber Orch. –   Telefunken MD1001
  Richter

Brandenburg Concerto No. 2, in F, BWV1047 tpt, fl, ob, vln, strs & c
  with A. Scherbaum tpt, K. Schochow   Decca ND248
  fl, H. Nordbruch ob, F. Sommer vlc &   Telefunken MD1001
  Chamber Orch. – Richter

Brandenburg Concerto No. 4, in G, BWV1049 vln, 2 fls, strs & c
  with K. Schochow fl, B. Schaeffer fl, F.   Decca ND249
  Sommer vlc & Chamber Orch. –   Telefunken MD1002
  Richter

Brandenburg Concerto No. 5, in D, BWV1050 clav, fl, vln, strs & c
  with K. Richter hpsi, P. Meisen fl, F.   Decca ND248
  Sommer vlc & Chamber Orch. –   Telefunken MD1002
  Richter

VIVALDI

(12) Concerti, Op. 3 "L'Estro armonico" var. cbns & strs
Concerto No. 8, in a, P.2 (F.I, No. 177) 2 vlns, strs & c
  with G. Karpinski vln & Wührer   Somerset 554
  Chamber Orch. – Wührer
(12) Concerti, Op. 8 (1725) "Il Cimento dell' Armonia e dell' Invenzione"
(Nos. 1/4: Le quattro Stagioni) vln & strs
Concerto No. 1, in E, F.I, No. 22 "La Primavera"
  with Wührer Chamber Orch. –   Somerset 575
  Wührer

VIVALDI – *Continued*

Concerto No. 2, in B flat, F.I, No. 23 "L'Estate"
with Wührer Chamber Orch. –   Somerset 575
Wührer

Concerto No. 3, in F, F.I, No. 24 "L'Autunno"
with Wührer Chamber Orch. –   Somerset 575
Wührer

Concerto No. 4, in f, F.I, No. 25 "L'Inverno"
with Wührer Chamber Orch. –   Somerset 575
Wührer

Jewssey WULF (1888–1970)

BACH

(4) Suites, BWV1066/9 strs & c
Suite No. 3, in D: Air (2nd mvt) BWV1068 2 obs, 3 tpts, drms, strs & c
– arr. vln & pf as "Air on the G–string" by Wilhelmj
with piano   HMV HN212

GOSSEC

Rosine (1876) – opera
Gavotte arr. vln & pf Burmester
with piano   HMV HN212

Kathy WUNDER

BLOCH

Baal Shem (3 Pictures of Chassidic life) (1923) vln & pf
with G. Brough pf   CBC Radio Canada SM55

LECLAIR

(12) Sonatas, Op. 9 – Book IV (1738) vln & c
Sonata No. 3, in D
with G. Brough pf   CBC Radio Canada SM55

Anton YASHKIN

BEETHOVEN

Romance No. 1, in G, Op. 40 vln & orch.
with Pro Musica Orchestra, Berlin –   Falcon L–ST7029
Randolph

Romance No. 2, in F, Op. 50 vln & orch.
with Pro Musica Orchestra, Berlin –   Falcon L–ST7029
Randolph

MENDELSSOHN

Concerto in e, Op. 64 vln & orch.
with Pro Musica Orchestra, Berlin –   Falcon L–ST7029
Randolph

Marina YASHVILI

MATCHAVARIANI

Concerto in d (1950) vln & orch.
with Moscow Youth Orch. – Anosov   Mezhdunarodnaya Kniga
                                     D1726/7

SHAVERZASHVILI

Concerto in E vln & orch.
with Georgian Radio Symphony Orch.   Mezhdunarodnaya Kniga
– Kiladze   D23217

Luben YORDANOFF

BARTÓK

(6) Rumanian folk dances (1915) pf – arr. vln & pf Székely
with piano   Editions phonographiques
                              parisiennes APG115, APG120

CORELLI

(12) Concerti grossi, Op. 6 orch.
Concerto grosso No. 3, in c
with P. Doukan vln, A. Rémond vlc,   Ducretet–Thomson LA1018
M. de Lacour hpsi & Collegium   London EL93042
Musicum, Paris – Douatte   Telefunken LB6091

MANFREDINI

(12) Concerti, Op. 3 (1718) 2 vlns, strs & c
Concerto No. 12, in C "Christmas Concerto"
with P. Doukan vln, A. Rémond vlc,   Ducretet–Thomson LA1018
M. de Lacour hpsi & Collegium   London EL93042
Musicum, Paris – Douatte   Telefunken LB6091

SAINT-SAËNS

Danse macabre, Op. 40 (1874) orch.
with Orchestre de Paris – Jacquillat HMV C063–10107

SCHOENBERG

Pierrot Lunaire, Op. 21 (1912) speaker, pf, fl, pic, cl, bs–cl, vla & vlc
with H. Pilarczyk speaker, M.   Adès 15001, LA524
Bergman pf, J. Castagner fl & pic, G. Everest LPBR6171, SDBR3171
Deplus cl, L. Montaigne bs–cl, S.
Collot vla, J. Huchot vlc, cond. Boulez

Serenade, Op. 24 (1924) cl, bs–cl, mand, gtr, vln, vla, vlc & bs
with G. Deplus cl, L. Montaigne bs–cl, Adès LA525
P. Grund mand, P. Stingl gtr, S.   Everest LPBR6175, SDBR3175
Collot vla, J. Huchot vlc & L–J.
Rondeleux bs

TORELLI

(12) Concerti, Op. 8 (1709) 1/6: 2 vlns, strs & c – 7/12: vln, strs & c
Concerto No. 6, in g "Christmas Concerto"
with P. Doukan vln, A. Rémond vlc,   Ducretet–Thomson LA1018
M. de Lacour hpsi & Collegium   London EL93042
Musicum, Paris – Douatte   Telefunken LB6091

VIVALDI

(12) Concerti, Op. 3 "L'Estro armonico" var. cbns & strs
Concerto No. 1, in D, P.146, (F.IV, No. 8) 4 vlns, vlc, strs & c
with J. Champeil vln, L. Gali vln, R. Ducretet–Thomson LAG1014
Gendre vln & Pro Musica Orchestra –
Saguer

Concerto No. 7, in F, P.249 (F.IV, No. 9) 4 vlns, strs & c
with J. Champeil vln, L. Gali vln, R. Ducretet–Thomson LAG1014
Gendre vln & Pro Musica Orchestra –
Saguer

Concerto in A, P.227 vln, strs & c
with Pro Musica Orchestra – Saguer   Ducretet–Thomson 470C024,
                                      LAG1014

Eugène YSAŸE (1858–1931)

BRAHMS

(21) Hungarian Dances pf duet
Hungarian dance No. 5, in f sharp arr. vln & pf "in g" Joachim
with C. DeCreus pf　　　36524–2　Asco A123
　　　　　　　　　　　　　　　Columbia 7106, 36524, J3901
　　　　　　　　　　　　　　　Delta TQD3033
　　　　　　　　　　　　　　　Fondation Eugène Ysaÿe
　　　　　　　　　　　　　　　FEY3001

CHABRIER

(10) Pièces pittoresques (1880) pf
No. 10. Scherzo–valse arr. vln & pf Loeffler
with C. Decreus pf　　　36514　Columbia 7111, 36514, J3904
　　　　　　　　　　　　　　　Delta TQD3033

DVOŘÁK

(8) Humoresques, Op. 101 pf
No. 7. Humoresque No. 7, in G flat arr. vln & pf "in G" Wilhelmj
with C. Decreus pf　　　36908–1　Columbia 7102, 36908
　　　　　　　　　　　　　　　Delta TQD3033

FAURÉ

Berceuse, Op. 16 vln & pf
with C. DeCreus pf　　　36519–2　Columbia 7112, 36519, J3900
　　　　　　　　　　　　　　　Delta TQD3033

KREISLER

Caprice viennois, Op. 2 vln & pf
with C. DeCreus pf　　　36525–2　Columbia 7115, 36525, J3907
　　　　　　　　　　　　　　　Delta TQD3033

MENDELSSOHN

Concerto in e, Op. 64 vln & orch.
Allegro molto vivace (3rd mvt)
with C. DeCreus pf　　　36520–2　Columbia 7108, 36520, J3900
　　　　　　　　　　　　　　　Delta TQD3033
　　　　　　　　　　　　　　　Fondation Eugène Ysaÿe
　　　　　　　　　　　　　　　FEY3001
　　　　　　　　　　　　　　　Pearl GEM101

SCHUBERT

(7) Gesänge (set to Scott's "Lady of the Lake") Op. 52 v & pf
No. 6. Ave Maria, D839 arr. vln & pf
with C. DeCreus pf　　　36907–2　Columbia 7103, 36907
　　　　　　　　　　　　　　　Delta TQD3033

SCHUMANN

(12) Duets, Op. 85 pf – 4 hands
No. 12. Abendlied arr. vln & pf Wilhelmj
with C. DeCreus pf　　　36515　Columbia 36515

VIEUXTEMPS

(3) Salonstücke, Op. 32 vln & pf
No. 2. Rondino
with C. DeCreus pf　　　36523–1　Asco A123
　　　　　　　　　　　　　　　Columbia 7110, 36523, J3901
　　　　　　　　　　　　　　　Delta TQD3033
　　　　　　　　　　　　　　　Fondation Eugène Ysaÿe
　　　　　　　　　　　　　　　FEY3001
　　　　　　　　　　　　　　　Pearl GEM101

WAGNER

Albumblatt in C (1861) pf – arr. vln & pf Wilhelmj
with C. DeCreus pf　　　36526　Columbia 7114, 36526, J3904
　　　　　　　　　　　　　　　Delta TQD3033

(Die) Meistersinger von Nürnberg (1868) – opera
Morgenlich leuchtend "Prize song" arr. vln & pf Wilhelmj
with C. DeCreus pf　　　36513　Columbia 7107, 36513
　　　　　　　　　　　　　　　Delta TQD3033
　　　　　　　　　　　　　　　Fondation Eugène Ysaÿe
　　　　　　　　　　　　　　　FEY3001

WIENIAWSKI

(2) Mazurkas, Op. 19 vln & pf
No. 1. Mazurka No. 1, in G "Obertass"
with C. DeCreus pf　　　36521　Asco A123
　　　　　　　　　　　　　　　Columbia 7109, 36521
　　　　　　　　　　　　　　　Delta TQD3033
　　　　　　　　　　　　　　　Pearl GEM101

No. 2. Mazurka No. 2, in D "Dudziarz"
with C. DeCreus pf　　　36521　Asco A123
　　　　　　　　　　　　　　　Columbia 7109, 36521
　　　　　　　　　　　　　　　Delta TQD3033
　　　　　　　　　　　　　　　Pearl GEM101

YSAYE

(3) Mazurkas, Op. 11 vln & pf
No. 3. Mazurka No. 3, in b "Lointaine–passe"
with C. DeCreus pf　　　36516　Columbia 7113, 36516, J3907
　　　　　　　　　　　　　　　Delta TQD3033
　　　　　　　　　　　　　　　Fondation Eugène Ysaÿe
　　　　　　　　　　　　　　　FEY3001

Rêve d'enfant, Op. 14 vln & pf
with C. DeCreus pf　　　36522　Columbia 36522

Shen YUNG

HO

Concerto (1960) "Butterfly lovers" vln & orch.
with Chinese Conservatory Orch. –　　Everest SDBR3212
Cheng–Wu

Nikolai ZABAVNIKOV

DVOŘÁK

(8) Slavonic Dances, Op. 72 pf duet; orch.
No. 2. Slavonic dance No. 10, in e arr. vln & pf Kreisler
with N. Zabavnikova pf　　　Mezhdunarodnaya Kniga
　　　　　　　　　　　　　　D017439

No. 8. Slavonic dance No. 16, in A flat arr. vln & pf "in G" Kreisler
with N. Zabavnikova pf　　　Mezhdunarodnaya Kniga
　　　　　　　　　　　　　　D017439

Sonatina in G, Op. 100 vln & pf
with N. Zabavnikova pf　　　Mezhdunarodnaya Kniga
　　　　　　　　　　　　　　D017439

ENESCU

Sonata No. 2, in f, Op. 6 vln & pf
with N. Zabavnikova pf　　　Mezhdunarodnaya Kniga
　　　　　　　　　　　　　　D017440

Michael ZACHAREWITSCH (1879–1953)

ANONYMOUS

(The) Ash grove traditional Welsh song – arr. vln & pf Zacharewitsch
with piano   8176 A   Edison Bell 0192, 1099

ARENSKY

(4) Morceaux, Op. 30 vln & pf
No. 4. Scherzo in e
with piano   HMV B613

BACH

Notenbüchlein für Anna Magdalena Bach, BWV.Anh (1725) clav
No. 4. Minuet in G, BWV.Anh 114 arr. vln & pf Winternitz
with piano   Edison Bell 1200

No. 5. Minuet in g, BWV.Anh 115 arr. vln & pf Winternitz
with piano   Edison Bell 1200

(6) Sonatas, BWV1014/9 vln & clav
Sonata No. 4, in c: Adagio ma non tanto (3rd mvt) BWV1017
with J. Batten pf   9460 E   Edison Bell 1142

BAZZINI

(La) Ronde des lutins, Op. 25 vln & pf
with piano   HMV B613

BRAHMS

(16) Waltzes, Op. 39 pf duet
No. 15. Waltz No. 15, in A flat arr. vln & pf "in A" Hochstein
with piano   7849 B   Edison Bell 1076

DVOŘÁK

(8) Humoresques, Op. 101 pf
No. 7. Humoresque No. 7, in G flat arr. vln & pf "in G" Wilhelmj
with piano   X 1139 H   Edison Bell 583

FAURÉ

Berceuse, Op. 16 vln & pf
with piano   HMV B578

Berceuse, Op. 16 vln & pf
with piano   Edison Bell 1200

HAUSER

Rapsodie hongrois No. 1, in d, Op. 43 vln & pf
with piano   X 1320 C   Edison Bell 583

HAYDN

Minuet unid – arr. vln & pf Hartmann
with piano   Edison Bell 635

KREISLER

Rondino on a theme by Beethoven vln & pf
with piano   7850 C   Edison Bell 1076

MASCAGNI

Cavalleria Rusticana (1890) – opera
Intermezzo orch. – arr. vln & pf
with piano   7305 E   Edison Bell 1039

MENDELSSOHN

Concerto in e, Op. 64 vln & orch.
Allegro appassionato (1st mvt)
with piano   Edison Bell 652

MOZART

Serenade No. 7, in D, K250 "Haffner" orch.
Rondo (4th mvt) arr. vln & pf Kreisler
with piano   X 1321 A   Edison Bell 610

Sonata No. 21, in e, K304 vln & pf
     9562 J, 9563 E & 9564/5 C   Edison Bell 1155/6
with J. Batten pf

Suite in d, K399 (in the style of Handel) pf
Minuet arr. vln & pf
with piano   8177 B   Edison Bell 0192, 1099

OFFENBACH

(Les) Contes d'Hoffmann (1881) – opera
Belle Nuit, O nuit d'amour "Barcarolle" arr. vln & pf
with piano   7304 D   Edison Bell 1039

RAY

(The) Sunshine of your smile (1915) v & pf – arr. vln & pf
with piano   HMV B517

RIMSKY–KORSAKOV

(Le) Coq d'Or (1910) – opera
Hymn to the sun arr. vln & pf Kreisler
with piano   X 1259 A   Edison Bell 610

(The) Tale of Tsar Saltan (1900) – opera
Flight of the bumblebee (Act III) orch. – arr. vln & pf Hartmann
with J. Batten pf   9358 A   Edison Bell 1142

SAINT–LUBIN

Sextet (from the opera "Lucia di Lammermoor" by Donizetti) Op. 56 solo
vln
(unaccompanied)   HMV B578

SARASATE

Zigeunerweisen, Op. 20 vln & pf or orch.
     X 1171 C & 1172 B   Edison Bell 525
with piano

SCHUBERT

(7) Gesänge (set to Scott's "Lady of the Lake") Op. 52 v & pf
No. 6. Ave Maria, D839 arr. vln & pf Wilhelmj
with piano   X 11250   Edison Bell 509

SILÉSU

(A) Little love, a little kiss (1912) v & pf – arr. vln & pf
with piano   HO 1734 ab   HMV 3–7987, B560

SVENDSEN

Romance in G, Op. 26 vln & orch. – arr. vln & pf Wilhelmj
with piano   X 1123 B   Edison Bell 517

WIENIAWSKI

Légende, Op. 17 vln & pf or orch.
with piano   X 1122 D   Edison Bell 517

Polonaise brillante No. 1, in D, Op. 4 vln & pf
with piano   Edison Bell 635

Scherzo–Tarantelle, Op. 16 vln & pf
with piano   Edison Bell 716

ZACHAREWITSCH

Dance of Ivan Ivanovitch vln & pf
with piano   HMV B517

ZACHAREWITSCH – *Continued*

(A) Don Cossack's dance vln & pf
  with piano   HMV B517
Imagination (Romance) vln & pf
  with piano   X 11260   Edison Bell 509
Love & sorrow vln & pf
  with piano   Edison Bell 716

Helmut ZACHARIAS (1920–)

BRUCH

Concerto No. 1, in g, Op. 26 vln & orch.
  Adagio (2nd mvt)
  with orch. – Zacharias   Polydor 237335

HUBAY

(14) Scènes de la Csárda vln & pf
  No. 4. Hejre Kati, Op. 32
  with RIAS Symphony   06009²LGN   Deutsche Grammophon 72489,
  Orch. – Fricsay   EPL30089, LPE17071

KREISLER

Liebesfreud vln & pf – arr. Zacharias
  with Berlin Radio Symphony Orch. –   Deutsche Grammophon
  Zacharias   EPL30285
Liebesleid vln & pf – arr. Zacharias
  with Berlin Radio Symphony Orch. –   Deutsche Grammophon
  Zacharias   EPL30285

SARASATE

Zigeunerweisen, Op. 20 vln & pf or orch.
  with RIAS Symphony   06008 LGN   Deutsche Grammophon 72489,
  Orch. – Fricsay   EPL30089, LPE17071

SCHUBERT

(14) Schwanengesang D957 (1828) v & pf
  No. 4. Ständchen "Serenade" arr. vln & orch.
  with orch. – Zacharias   Polydor 237335

SVENDSEN

Romance in G, Op. 26 vln & orch.
  with orch. – Zacharias   Polydor 237335

David ZAFER (1934–)

CORELLI

(12) Concerti grossi, Op. 6 orch.
  Concerto grosso No. 1, in D
  with A. Benac vln & CBC Toronto   CBC Radio Canada SM3
  String Orch. – B. Brott

VIVALDI

(12) Concerti, Op. 3 "L'Estro armonico" var. cbns, strs & c
  Concerto No. 8, in a, P.2 (F.I, No. 177) 2 vlns, strs & c
  with A. Benac vln & CBC Toronto   CBC Radio Canada SM3
  String Orch. – B. Brott

Leon ZAKS

SHOSTAKOVICH

Pirogov (Suite from music to the film) Op. 76a orch.
  No. 1. Introduction
  with A. Levin vln & USSR Bolshoi   Melodiya Angel SR40160
  Theatre Orch. – Maxim Shostakovich   Mezhdunarodnaya Kniga
                                  D020135/6
Zoya (Suite from music to the film) Op. 64a orch.
  No. 1. Introduction (song about Zoya)
  with A. Levin vln & USSR Bolshoi   Melodiya Angel SR40160
  Theatre Orch. – Maxim Shostakovich   Mezhdunarodnaya Kniga
                                  D020135/6

THEODORAKIS

Sonatina No. 1 vln & pf
  with E. Liberman pf   Mezhdunarodnaya Kniga
                                  D00021805/6

Tamás ZALAY

SZELÉNYI

(8) Duo Sonatinas "Little Duos" 2 vlns
  No. 1. Chase
  with G. Albert vln   Qualiton LPX1188
  No. 2. Cuckoo chattering
  with G. Albert vln   Qualiton LPX1188
  No. 3. Rondino
  with G. Albert vln   Qualiton LPX1188

Louis ZÁMEČNÍK (1897–)

GOUNOD

Ave Maria (Méditation on Bach's "Prelude No. 1, in C" from Book I of
  "Das Wohltemperirte Clavier") v & pf – arr. vln & pf
  with F. Schauer pf   40486   Supraphon A22297
                                  Telefunken M6241

KOCIÁN

(2) Pieces, Op. 17 vln & pf
  No. 1. Serenade
  with piano   Ultraphon A11263

POLIAKIN

(Le) Canari (Concert–polka) vln & pf
  with F. Schauer pf   40485   Supraphon A22297
                                    Telefunken M6241

Franco ZAMPANI

VIVALDI

Concerto in A, P.222 (F.I, No. 139) "L'eco in lontano" 2 vlns & strs
  with W. Gallozzi vln & I Musici   Philips CXL15000

Fernando ZAMPIERI

GEMINIANI

(6) Concerti grossi, Op. 3 (1755) orch.
Concerto grosso No. 2, in g
with P. Toso vln, R. Valpreda vln, F.   CBS 32 11 0003, 32 11 0004,
Sangiorgi vln & I Solisti Veneti –   BRG72057, SBRG72057
Scimone

VIVALDI

Concerto in B flat, P.367 (F.I, No. 59) 4 vlns, strs & c
with P. Toso vln, R. Valpreda vln, F.   CBS 32 11 0003, 32 11 0004,
Sangiorgi vln & I Solisti Veneti –   BRG72057, SBRG72057
Scimone

Franz ZAPOTOCKI

DVOŘÁK

(8) Humoresques, Op. 101 pf
No. 7. Humoresque No. 7, in G flat arr. vln & pf "in G" Kreisler
with piano   Favorite 1–24033

MASCAGNI

Cavalleria Rusticana (1890) – opera
Intermezzo orch. – arr. vln & pf
with piano   Favorite 1–24032

Yuri ZARETSKY

SABITOV

Melody vln & pf
with piano   Mezhdunarodnaya Kniga
                                         D00013469/70

ZAIMOV

Allegretto vln & pf
with piano   Mezhdunarodnaya Kniga
                                         D00013469/70

Andante vln & pf
with piano   Mezhdunarodnaya Kniga
                                         D00013469/70

V. ZARINŠ

MEDYNS, Janis

Sonata in G vln & pf
with G. Braun pf   Mezhdunarodnaya Kniga
                                         D022008

Ede ZATHURECZKY (1903–1959)

BACH

(4) Suites, BWV1066/9 strs & c
Suite No. 3, in D: Air (2nd mvt) BWV1068 2 obs, 3 tpts, drms, strs & c
– arr. vln & pf as "Air on the G-string" by Wilhelmj
with G. Faragó pf   Radiola RBM106, SP8003

BARTÓK

For Children (40 pieces) (1909) pf – arr. vln & pf Zathureczky*
with A. Bálint pf   Qualiton M275/6, SZK3503

For Children (40 pieces) (1909) pf – arr. vln & pf Zathureczky*
with M. Karin pf   Supraphon LPM263, SUF20284
                                         Ultraphon H24263

Sonatina in D (on 3 Transylvanian peasant themes) (1915) pf – transc. vln
& pf Gertler, 1931
with M. Karin pf   Ultraphon 5185C, H24262

BEETHOVEN

Sonata No. 5, in F, Op. 24 "Spring" vln & pf
with G. Faragó pf   Radiola SP8031/3

(3) Sonatas, Op. 30 vln & pf
No. 3. Sonata No. 8, in G: Allegro vivace (3rd mvt)
with G. Faragó pf   Radiola SP8023
No. 3. Sonata No. 8, in G
with M. Pressler pf   Vox EZ1
Sonata No. 9, in A, Op. 47 "Kreutzer" vln & pf
with G. Faragó pf   Bartone LP502
                                         Radiola SP8024/7

BRAHMS

(16) Waltzes, Op. 39 pf duet
No. 15. Waltz No. 15, in A flat arr. vln & pf "in A" Hochstein
with M. Karin pf   Supraphon LPM263, SUH20284
                                         Ultraphon 5185C, H24240

CORELLI

(12) Sonatas, Op. 5 vln & c
Sonata No. 12, in d "La Follia" arr. vln & pf Léonard
with E. Petri pf   Qualiton LPX1051

DOHNÁNYI

Gavotte & Musette pf – arr. vln & pf Urai
with O. Herz pf   Radiola RBM107

FRANCK

Sonata in A (1886) vln & pf
with M. Pressler pf   Vox EZ1

FRESCOBALDI

Pastorale gentile unid – arr. vln & pf
with M. Karin pf   Supraphon LPM263, SUH20284
                                         Ultraphon H24264

GLUCK

Orphée et Eurydice (1762) – opera
Dance of the blessed spirits: Lento "Mélodie" (No. 2) arr. vln & pf
Kreisler
with O. Herz pf   Radiola RBM107

KODÁLY

Adagio in C (1905) vln & pf
with E. Petri pf   Qualiton MX586, SZN3053

KREISLER

Praeludium & Allegro (Pugnani) vln & pf
with O. Herz pf   Radiola RBM108

* Vol. I, nos. 3 & 6; Vol. II, nos. 33 & 35; Vol. III, nos. 6 & 7; Vol. IV,
No. 28.

LISZT

(6) Consolations, G172 (1849/50) "Tröstungen" pf
  Consolation No. 3, in D flat arr. vln & pf "in E flat" Milstein
    with E. Petri pf   Qualiton SZK3505

RAVEL

Pièce en forme d'Habanera v & pf – arr. vln & pf Catherine
  with O. Herz pf   Radiola RBM108

TCHAIKOVSKY

Concerto in D, Op. 35 vln & orch.
  with Budapest Philharmonic   Radiola SP8000/3
  Orch. – Ferencsik

VERESS

Nógrádi verbunkos (Hungarian dance) (1940) vln & pf
  with S. Veress pf   Magyar Muza MM107

VISKI

Concerto (1947) vln & orch.
  with Hungarian State Radio Symphony Qualiton LPX1051
  Orch. – Lukács

WEINER

Hungarian peasant songs vln & pf
  with E. Petri pf   Qualiton SKZ3505

ZSOLT

Dragonflies vln & pf
  with G. Faragó pf   Radiola RBM106
Dragonflies vln & pf
  with M. Karin pf   Supraphon LPM263, SUF20284
                    Ultraphon H24262

Jacob ZAYDE

MOZART

(Il) Re Pastore, K208 (1775) – opera
  No. 10. L'amerò, sarò costante
  with E. Rethberg s &   A 58139△ HMV DB1505
  orch.

George ZAZOFSKY (1914–)

LUMBYE

Concert–polka (1863) 2 vlns & orch.
  with A. Krips vln & Boston "Pops" Victor LM2885, LSC2885
  Orch. – Fiedler

MOZART

Cassation No. 1, in G, K63 str orch.
  with Zimbler Sinfonietta   Brunswick AXTL1001
                    Decca DCM3204, DL8520

VIVALDI

(12) Concerti, Op. 8 (1725) "Il Cimento dell' Armonia e dell' Invenzione"
  Nos. 1/4: Le quattro Stagioni vln & strs
  Concerto No. 1, in E, F.I, No. 22 "La Primavera"
  with Zimbler Sinfonietta   Argo RG108
                    Boston B400

VIVALDI – *Continued*

  Concerto No. 2, in B flat, F.I, No. 23 "L'Estate"
  with Zimbler Sinfonietta   Argo RG108
                    Boston B400
  Concerto No. 3, in F, F.I, No. 24 "L'Autunno"
  with Zimbler Sinfonietta   Argo RG108
                    Boston B400
  Concerto No. 4, in f, F.I, No. 25 "L'Inverno"
  with Zimbler Sinfonietta   Argo RG108
                    Boston B400

Věra ZEGZULKOVÁ

TROJAN

(The) Emperor's Nightingale (1948) vln & orch.
  with Radio Pops Orch. "BERO" –   Panton 01 0127, 11 0127
  Hudec

Robert ZEILER (1879–)

BEETHOVEN

Sonata No. 5, in F, Op. 24 "Spring" vln & pf
  with B. Seidler–Winkler pf   Polydor 65764/6
Sonata No. 9, in A, Op. 47 "Kreutzer" vln & pf
  with B. Seidler–Winkler pf   Polydor 65760/3
(3) Trios, Op. 1 pf, vln & vlc
  No. 3. Trio No. 3, in c: Andante cantabile con variazioni (2nd mvt)
  with B. Seidler–Winkler pf & H. Hopf Tri–Ergon 1025
  vlc
Trio in B flat, Op. 11 cl, vlc & pf – arr. pf, vln & vlc
  Adagio (2nd mvt)
  with B. Seidler–Winkler pf & H. Hopf Tri–Ergon 1023
  vlc
Trio No. 6, in B flat, Op. 97 "Archduke" pf, vln & vlc
  with B. Seidler–Winkler pf & H. Hopf Polydor 62417/8 & 65767/8
  vlc

LANNER

Waltz unid – arr. pf, vln & vlc*
  with B. Seidler–Winkler pf & H. Hopf Tri–Ergon 1024
  vlc

MASCHERONI

Ave Maria v & pf – arr. v, vln, pf & hp
  with C. Dux s, B. Seidler–Winkler pf HMV 03390
  & E. Wiesner hp

MENDELSSOHN

(3) Quartets, Op. 44 2 vlns, vla & vlc
  No. 2. Quartet No. 4, in e (1837): **Allegro di molto** (Scherzo) arr. pf, vln
  & vlc
  with B. Seidler–Winkler pf & H. Hopf Tri–Ergon 1023
  vlc

* Listed as Waltz momente No. 1 – edition Schütt.

STRAUSS, J. II

Waltz unid – arr. pf, vln & vlc*
  with B. Seidler–Winkler pf & H. Hopf Tri–Ergon 1024
  vlc

WAGNER

Albumblatt in C (1861) pf – arr. vln & pf Wilhelmj
  with Berlin State   CLR 5814[II]△ HMV C2185, EH431
  Opera Orch. – Schmalstich

Stanka ŽELEVA

VLADIGEROV

(2) Bulgarian Paraphrases, Op. 18 vln & pf
  No. 2. Ratschenitza
  with piano   Mezhdunarodnaya Kniga
                                D028103/4

Mary ZENTAY (1897–   )

DRDLA

Serenade No. 1, in A vln & pf
  with M. Smolen pf   Edison cylinder 28269

DRIGO

(Les) Millions d'Arlequin (1900) – ballet orch.
  Sérénade arr. vln & pf Auer
  with piano   Edison Diamond Disc

HUBAY

(14) Scènes de la Csárda vln & pf
  No. 8. Azt Mondják, Op. 60
  with J. Grunberg pf   4850   Edison cylinder 28281
                                  Edison Diamond Disc 80767

KREISLER

Tambourin chinois, Op. 3 vln & pf
  with J. Grunberg pf   4725   Edison cylinder 28246
                                  Edison Diamond Disc 80340

Praeludium & Allegro (Pugnani) vln & pf
  with piano   Edison Diamond Disc 80813

MASCAGNI

Cavalleria Rusticana (1890) – opera
  Intermezzo orch. – arr. v, vln & orch. as "Ave Maria"
  with F. Hempel s & orch.   5972   Edison cylinder 29027
                                  Edison Diamond Disc 82549

MASSENET

Élégie v & pf – arr. v, vln & pf
  with R. Stracciari b & piano   77261 Columbia 77261

MOZART

(Il) Re Pastore, K208 (1775) – opera
  No. 10. L'amerò, sarò costante
  with A. Verlet s & orch.   4853   Edison Diamond Disc 82217

---

* Listed as Waltz momente No. 2 – edition Schütt.

OFFENBACH

(Les) Contes d'Hoffmann (1881) – opera
  Belle Nuit, O nuit d'amour "Barcarolle" arr. vln & pf
  with P. Hauser pf   77473 Columbia A2503

PAGANINI

(24) Caprices, Op. 1 (1801/7) solo vln
  Caprice No. 13, in B flat arr. vln & pf Kreisler
  with J. Grunberg pf   4851 Edison Diamond Disc 80767

RUBINSTEIN

(2) Melodies, Op. 3 pf
  No. 1. Melody in F arr. vln & pf Wilhelmj
  with P. Hauser pf   77472 Columbia A2503

WIENIAWSKI

Scherzo–Tarantelle, Op. 16 vln & pf
  with J. Grunberg pf   4849 Edison Diamond Disc 80340

ZARZYCKI

Mazurka in G, Op. 26 vln & pf
  with piano   Edison Diamond Disc 80813

Fernando ZEPPARONI

BACH

Concerto in c, BWV1060 vln & ob or 2 vlns, strs & c
  with H. Winschermann ob &   L'Anthologie Sonore 3005LD,
  Augsbourg Chamber Orch. – Deyle AS35

CORELLI

(12) Sonatas, Op. 5 vln & c
  Sonata No. 1, in D
  with R. Veyron–Lacroix hpsi   L'Anthologie Sonore 3008LD,
                                  AS40

  Sonata No. 3, in C
  with R. Veyron–Lacroix hpsi   L'Anthologie Sonore 3008LD,
                                  AS40

TARTINI

(12) Sonatas, Op. 1 (1734) vln & c
  Sonata No. 10, in g "Didone abbandonata"
  with R. Veyron–Lacroix hpsi   L'Anthologie Sonore 3008LD,
                                  AS40

VERACINI

(12) Sonatas, Op. 1 (1721) vln & c
  Sonata No. 6, in e
  with R. Veyron–Lacroix hpsi   L'Anthologie Sonore 3008LD,
                                    AS40

VIVALDI

(12) Concerti, Op. 3 "L'Estro armonico" var. cbns & strs
  Concerto No. 11, in d, P.250 (F.IV, No. 11) 2 vlns, vlc, strs & c
  with R. Danz vln, W. Hillringhaus vlc Adès (Florilège) 13001
  & Augsbourg Chamber Orch. – Deyle

Helmut ZERNICK (1913–1970)

RIES

(La) Capricciosa vln & pf
with piano   KC 27922   Imperial 19143

Suite No. 3, in G, Op. 34 vln & pf
   No. 5. Perpetuum mobile
   with piano   KC 27921[2]   Imperial 19143

Lars ZETTERQVIST (1860–1946)

GRIEG

(3) Folkelivsbilleder (Scenes from peasant life) Op. 19 pf
   No. 2. Brudefølget drar forbi arr. vln & pf Sauret
   with piano   19867 b   HMV X2–287904

HALVORSEN

(4) Mosaïques (Suite des morceaux caractéristiques) vln & pf
   No. 4. Chant de Veslemøy
   with piano   19865 b   HMV X2–287905

Grigori ZHISLIN

BACH

(3) Sonatas & 3 Partitas, BWV1001/6 solo vln
   Partita No. 2, in d: Chaconne (5th mvt) BWV1004
   (unaccompanied)   Mezhdunarodnaya Kniga
                         D023973/4

LOCATELLI

(12) Sonatas, Op. 6 (1737) vln & c
   Sonata No. 1, in g (ed. David)
   with piano   Mezhdunarodnaya Kniga
                         D023973/4

PAGANINI

(24) Caprices, Op. 1 (1801/7) solo vln
   Caprice No. 1, in E
   (unaccompanied)   Mezhdunarodnaya Kniga
                         D023973/4

   Caprice No. 12, in A flat
   (unaccompanied)   Mezhdunarodnaya Kniga
                         D023973/4

   Caprice No. 19, in E flat
   (unaccompanied)   Mezhdunarodnaya Kniga
                         D023973/4

Nel cor più non mi sento "Sonata appassionata con variazioni" (on the aria from Paisiello's opera "La bella molinara") Op. 38 (1820 or 1821) solo vln
   (unaccompanied)   Mezhdunarodnaya Kniga
                         D023973/4

Valentin I. ZHUK (1934–)

BARTÓK

Rhapsody No. 1, in G (1928) vln & orch.
   with A. Rossokhatsky pf   Mezhdunarodnaya Kniga
                         D022039/40

BARTÓK – *Continued*

Rhapsody No. 2, in d (1928) vln & orch.
   with A. Rossokhatsky pf   Mezhdunarodnaya Kniga
                         D022039/40

BEETHOVEN

Sextet in E flat, Op. 81 2 vlns, vla, vlc & 2 hrns
   with Y. Daneman vln, M. Tolpygo vla,   Mezhdunarodnaya Kniga
   G. Ivanov vlc, A. Demin hrn & B.   SM02453/4
   Kharchenko hrn

BLOCH

Baal Shem (3 Pictures of Chassidic life) (1923) vln & pf
   No. 2. Nigun (Improvisation)
   with A. Rossokhatsky pf   Mezhdunarodnaya Kniga
                         D11020

CASELLA

Undici pezzi infantili, Op. 35 (1920) vln & pf
   No. 1. Preludio
   with A. Rossokhatsky pf   Mezhdunarodnaya Kniga
                         D017500

   No. 6. Siciliana
   with A. Rossokhatsky pf   Mezhdunarodnaya Kniga
                         D017500

DEBUSSY

Children's Corner Suite (1908) pf
   No. 6. Golliwog's cake–walk arr. vln & pf Choisnelle
   with A. Rossokhatsky pf   Mezhdunarodnaya Kniga
                         D016014

(La) Plus que lente – valse (1910) pf – arr. vln & pf Roques
   with A. Rossokhatsky pf   Mezhdunarodnaya Kniga
                         D016014

(12) Préludes – Book I (1910) pf
   No. 8. La Fille aux cheveux de lin arr. vln & pf Hartmann
   with A. Rossokhatsky pf   Mezhdunarodnaya Kniga
                         D016014

FAURÉ

Sonata No. 1, in A, Op. 13 vln & pf
   with A. Rossokhatsky pf   Mezhdunarodnaya Kniga
                         D017499

GERSHWIN

Porgy & Bess (1935) – opera
   Bess, you is my woman arr. vln & pf Heifetz
   with A. Rossokhatsky pf   Mezhdunarodnaya Kniga
                         D017500

   It ain't necessarily so arr. vln & pf Heifetz
   with A. Rossokhatsky pf   Mezhdunarodnaya Kniga
                         D017500

HANDEL

(15) Sonatas, Op. 1 (?1731) fl or vln & c
   Sonata No. 9, in b: Adagio (2nd mvt) arr. vln & pf as "Larghetto" by Hubay
   with A. Rossokhatsky pf   Mezhdunarodnaya Kniga
                         D11019

   Sonata No. 14, in A vln V
   with A. Rossokhatsky pf   Mezhdunarodnaya Kniga
                         D022039/40

KROLL

Banjo & fiddle vln & pf
    with A. Rossokhatsky pf   Mezhdunarodnaya Kniga
                                       D016014

LECLAIR

(12) Sonatas, Op. 5 – Book III (1734) vln & c
  Sonata No. 6, in c
    with A. Rossokhatsky pf   Mezhdunarodnaya Kniga
                                       D022039/40

NIN

(20) Cantos de España (1923) v & pf
  No. 1. Tonada de Valdovinos arr. vln & pf as "Vieja Castilla" by Nin & Gautier
    with A. Rossokhatsky pf   Mezhdunarodnaya Kniga
                                       D017500
  No. 4. Montañesa arr. vln & pf Kochański
    with A. Rossokhatsky pf   Mezhdunarodnaya Kniga
                                       D016014
  No. 5. Tonada murciana arr. vln & pf Kochański
    with A. Rossokhatsky pf   Mezhdunarodnaya Kniga
                                       D016014
  No. 7. Granadina arr. vln & pf Kochański
    with A. Rossokhatsky pf   Mezhdunarodnaya Kniga
                                       D016014
  No. 8. Saeta (Invocation) arr. vln & pf Kochański
    with A. Rossokhatsky pf   Mezhdunarodnaya Kniga
                                       D016014
  No. 15. Paño murciano arr. vln & pf as "Murciana" by Nin & Gautier
    with A. Rossokhatsky pf   Mezhdunarodnaya Kniga
                                       D017500
  No. 16. Villancico Catalán arr. vln & pf as "Catalana" by Nin & Gautier
    with A. Rossokhatsky pf   Mezhdunarodnaya Kniga
                                       D017500
  No. 18. El Vito arr. vln & pf as "Andaluza" by Nin & Gautier
    with A. Rossokhatsky pf   Mezhdunarodnaya Kniga
                                       D017500

PAGANINI

Cantabile in D, Op. 17 vln & gtr
    with A. Rossokhatsky pf   Mezhdunarodnaya Kniga
                                       D11020
Concerto No. 2, in b, Op. 7 vln & orch.
  Ronde à la clochette (3rd mvt) "La Campanella"
    with A. Rossokhatsky pf   Mezhdunarodnaya Kniga
                                       D016013
Moto perpetuo (Allegro di concert) Op. 11 (1830) vln & orch.
    with A. Rossokhatsky pf   Mezhdunarodnaya Kniga
                                       D016013
Nel cor più non mi sento "Sonata appassionata con variazioni" (on the aria from Paisiello's opera "La bella molinara") Op. 38 (1820 or 1821) solo vln
  (unaccompanied)   Mezhdunarodnaya Kniga
                                       D016013
Sonata a preghièra "Moses Fantasia" (on the aria "Dal tuo stellato soglio" from Rossini's opera "Mosè in Egitto") Op. 24 (1818 or 1819) vln & orch.
    with A. Rossokhatsky pf   Mezhdunarodnaya Kniga
                                     D11020

PORPORA

(12) Sonatas (1754) vln & c
  Sonata No. 2, in G (ed. David)
    with A. Rossokhatsky pf   Mezhdunarodnaya Kniga
                                     D016575/6

PROKOFIEV

Sonata No. 2, in D, Op. 94bis vln & pf
    with A. Rossokhatsky pf   Mezhdunarodnaya Kniga
                                     D016575/6

ROSSELINI

(La) Fontanna malata (1930) vln & pf
    with A. Rossokhatsky pf   Mezhdunarodnaya Kniga
                                     D017500

SAINT-SAËNS

Concerto No. 3, in b, Op. 61 vln & orch.
  with Moscow Radio Symphony Orch.   Mezhdunarodnaya Kniga
  – Khaikin   D025869, SM02345
Havanaise, Op. 83 vln & orch.
    with A. Rossokhatsky pf   Mezhdunarodnaya Kniga
                                     D11019
Introduction & Rondo Capriccioso, Op. 28 vln & pf
    with E. Fux pf   Mezhdunarodnaya Kniga
                                     D4292/3

SARASATE

(8) Danzas españolas vln & pf
  No. 6. Zapateado, Op. 23, No. 2
    with A. Rossokhatsky pf   Mezhdunarodnaya Kniga
                                     D11019

SCHUMANN

(3) Romances, Op. 94 ob or vlc or vln & cl & pf
  No. 2. Romance No. 2, in A arr. vln & pf Kreisler
    with A. Rossokhatsky pf   Mezhdunarodnaya Kniga
                                     D026143/4
Sonata No. 1, in a, Op. 105 vln & pf
    with A. Rossokhatsky pf   Mezhdunarodnaya Kniga
                                     D026143/4
Sonata No. 2, in d, Op. 121 vln & pf
    with A. Rossokhatsky pf   Mezhdunarodnaya Kniga
                                     D026143/4

SHEBALIN

Concerto in G, Op. 21 vln & orch.
  with Moscow Radio Symphony Orch.   Mezhdunarodnaya Kniga
  – Aranovich   D015389, S0975

SHOSTAKOVICH

(24) Preludes, Op. 34 (1932/3) pf
  Prelude No. 10, in c sharp arr. vln & pf Tziganov
    with E. Fux pf   Mezhdunarodnaya Kniga
                                     D4292/3
  Prelude No. 15, in D flat arr. vln & pf Tziganov
    with E. Fux pf   Mezhdunarodnaya Kniga
                                     D4292/3
  Prelude No. 16, in b flat arr. vln & pf Tziganov
    with E. Fux pf   Mezhdunarodnaya Kniga
                                     D4292/3

SHOSTAKOVICH – *Continued*

Prelude No. 24, in d arr. vln & pf Tziganov
with E. Fux pf   Mezhdunarodnaya Kniga
     D4292/3

TCHAIKOVSKY

Souvenir d'un lieu cher, Op. 42 vln & pf
No. 2. Scherzo
with E. Fux pf   Mezhdunarodnaya Kniga
     D4292/3

No. 3. Mélodie
with E. Fux pf   Mezhdunarodnaya Kniga
     D4292/3

VIVALDI

(12) Sonatas, Op. 2 (1712) vln & c
Sonata No. 2, in A, F.XIII, No. 30
with A. Rossokhatsky pf   Mezhdunarodnaya Kniga
     D016575/6

VLADIGEROV

Concerto in F, Op. 11 vln & orch.
with Moscow Radio Symphony Orch.   Mezhdunarodnaya Kniga
– Khaikin   D025870, SM02346

WIENIAWSKI

Légende, Op. 17 vln & pf or orch.
with E. Fux pf   Mezhdunarodnaya Kniga
     D4292/3

Léon ZIGHERA

ACHRON

Hebrew melody, Op. 33 vln & pf – arr. Auer
with piano   FMA 1835–1A   Decca TF138

BACH

Concerto No. 2, in E, BWV1042 vln, strs & c
   FMA 1585–1A, 1586–2A, 1587–   Decca TF135/6
with orch. – Bernard   3A & 1588–1A

(4) Suites, BWV1066/9 strs & c
Suite No. 3, in D: Air (2nd mvt) BWV1068 2 obs, 3 tpts, drms, strs & c
– arr. vln & pf as "Air on the G–string" by Wilhelmj
with piano   FMA 1380–1AX   Decca T134

BLOCH

Baal Shem (3 Pictures of Chassidic life) (1923) vln & pf
No. 2. Nigun (Improvisation)
with L. Heward pf
   Decca M144

CHOPIN

(3) Nocturnes, Op. 9 pf
No. 2. Nocturne No. 2, in E flat arr. vln & pf Sarasate
with piano   HMV L615

CORELLI

(12) Sonatas, Op. 5 vln & c
Sonata No. 12, in d "La Follia" arr. vln & pf Léonard
with L. Heward pf   Decca M154/5

DVOŘÁK

(8) Humoresques, Op. 101 pf
No. 7. Humoresque No. 7, in G flat arr. vln & pf "in G" Kreisler
with piano   HMV K5233

FAURÉ

Berceuse, Op. 16 vln & pf
with L. Heward pf   Decca M163

MASSENET

Thaïs (1894) – opera
Méditation arr. vln & pf Marsick
with piano   HMV L615

PIERNÉ

Sérénade in A, Op. 7 (1875) pf – arr. vln & pf Haddock
with piano   HMV K5233

PUGNANI

Gavotta variata in A unid – arr. vln & pf Corti
with piano   FMA 1377–2AX   Decca T134

RAVEL

Pièce en forme d'Habanera v & pf – arr. vln & pf Catherine
with piano   FMA 1836–1A   Decca TF138

RIMSKY–KORSAKOV

Sadko (1898) – opera
Chant hindou arr. vln & pf Kreisler
with L. Heward pf   Decca M163

SARASATE

(8) Danzas españolas vln & pf
No. 5. Playera, Op. 23, No. 1
with L. Heward pf   Decca M155

Ibolyka ZILZER

ALBÉNIZ

España (6 Feuilles d'album) Op. 165 pf
No. 2. Tango in D arr. vln & pf Kreisler
with orch.   Columbia DDX39, SCDK1
No. 3. Malagueña in b arr. vln & pf Kreisler
with F. Eberson pf   Columbia LDX18

BARTÓK

(6) Rumanian folk dances (1915) pf – arr. vln & pf Székely
with F. Schröder pf   Eterna 120043

BEETHOVEN

Romance No. 1, in g, Op. 40 vln & orch.
with M. Gurlitt pf   114/5 BO[IV]   Polydor 27132
Romance No. 2, in F, Op. 50 vln & orch.
with M. Raucheisen pf   713/4½ bi[IV]   Polydor 27077
(Die) Ruinen von Athen, Op. 113 – Incidental music orch.
No. 3. Chor der Derwische
with M Raucheisen pf   1081 BH[IV]   Polydor 22883

BOCCHERINI

(6) Quintets, Op. 13 2 vlns, vla & 2 vlcs
No. 5. Quintet No. 5, in E: Minuet (3rd mvt) "Bull" arr. vln, pf & vlc
Lochmann
with M. Gurlitt pf   B 49372△M Polydor 22542
H. Hopf vlc

BOULANGER

Avant de mourir, Op. 17 vln & pf
with orch.   Columbia SCDK2

BRAGA

(7) Melodies (1867) v & pf
No. 5. La serenata "Angel's serenade" arr. vln & pf
with M. Raucheisen pf   Polydor 27131

CHOPIN

(3) Nocturnes, Op. 9 pf
No. 2. Nocturne No. 2, in E flat arr. vln & pf Sarasate
with M. Raucheisen pf   Polydor 27160
No. 2. Nocturne No. 2, in E flat arr. vln & pf Sarasate
with F. Eberson pf   Columbia LDX17, SCBK1

DAQUIN

Pièces de clavecin – Book I (1735) hpsi
Le coucou arr. vln & pf Manén
with M. Raucheisen pf 1541 BH[IV] Polydor 22317

DRDLA

Serenade No. 1, in A vln & pf
with M. Raucheisen pf 1542 BH[IV] Polydor 22317

DUSSEK

Old dance unid – arr. vln & pf Burmester
with M. Raucheisen pf   Polydor 22859

DVOŘÁK

(8) Slavonic Dances, Op. 72 pf duet; orch.
No. 2. Slavonic dance No. 10, in e arr. vln & pf Kreisler
with F. Eberson pf   Columbia LDX17, SCBK1

EBERLÉ

Paraphrase on "A bird sang in the linden tree", Op. 7 vln & pf
with M. Raucheisen pf   Polydor 22132, 22600

FREIRE

Ay, ay, ay v & pf – arr. vln & orch.
with orch.   Columbia SCDK1

GOSSEC

Rosine (1786) – opera
Gavotte arr. vln & pf Burmester
with M. Raucheisen pf   Polydor 22861

GRANADOS

(12) Danzas españolas, Op. 37 (1893) pf
No. 5. Danza española No. 5, in e "Andaluza" arr. vln & pf Kreisler
with F. Eberson pf   Columbia LDX18

GRIEG

Peer Gynt (Suite No. 2) Op. 55 orch.
No. 4. Solveig's song arr. vln & pf Sitt
with orch.   Columbia DDX39, SCDK1

HUBAY

(14) Scènes de la Csárda vln & pf
No. 5. Hullámzó balaton, Op. 33
with M. Raucheisen pf   Polydor 15017

KÁLMÁN

Gräfin Mariza (1924) – operetta
Komm, Zigany arr. vln & pf
with piano   Columbia

KREISLER

Caprice viennois, Op. 2 vln & pf
with F. Schröder pf   Eterna 120044
Liebesfreud vln & pf
with M. Raucheisen pf   Imperial J17028
Liebesleid vln & pf
with M. Raucheisen pf   Imperial J17028
Schön Rosmarin vln & pf
with M. Raucheisen pf   Imperial J15024
    Kristall K416
Schön Rosmarin vln & pf
with F. Schröder pf   Eterna 120044
Tambourin chinois, Op. 3 vln & pf
with M. Raucheisen pf   Polydor 22861
Tambourin chinois, Op. 3 vln & pf
with F. Eberson pf   Columbia LD7
Sicilienne & Rigaudon (Francoeur) vln & pf
with M. Raucheisen pf   83 bs Polydor 27159

KUHLAU

Elverhøj (The Elves hill) Op. 100 (1828) – Incidental music orch.
No. 12. Menuetto in F (Act V) arr. vln & pf Burmester
with M. Raucheisen pf   Polydor 22860
Waltz unid – arr. vln & pf Burmester
with M. Raucheisen pf   Polydor 22860

LEONCAVALLO

Mattinata (1904) v & pf – arr. vln & orch.
with orch.   Columbia DDX40, SCDK2

MENDELSSOHN

(6) Gesänge, Op. 34 v & pf
No. 2. Auf Flügeln des Gesanges arr. vln & pf Achron
with M. Raucheisen pf   Polydor 19921
Trio No. 2, in c, Op. 66 pf, vln & vlc
Scherzo (3rd mvt)
with M. Gurlitt pf & H. Hopf vlc   Polydor 27231, 95333

MONTI

Csárdas (1904) vln & pf
with M. Raucheisen pf   Polydor 22132, 22600

MOSZKOWSKI

(2) Stücke, Op. 45 pf
No. 2. Guitarre arr. vln & pf Sarasate
with M. Raucheisen pf   Polydor 19921

PETERSON–BERGER

Frösöblomster, Op. 16 (1896) pf
Vid Frösö Kyrka arr. vln & orch.
with orch.   Columbia DDX39, SCDK1

POLIAKIN

(Le) Canari (Concert–polka) vln & pf
  with M. Raucheisen pf   Polydor 27131

PONCE

Estrellita (1913) v & pf – arr. vln & orch.
  with orch.   Columbia SCDK1

PROVOST

Intermezzo (1940) vln & pf
  with orch.   Columbia SCDK2

RAFF

(6) Pieces, Op. 85 vln & pf
  No. 3. Cavatina in D
  with M. Raucheisen pf   Polydor 15010, 27160

RIMSKY–KORSAKOV

(Le) Coq d'Or (1910) – opera
  Hymn to the sun arr. vln & pf Kreisler
  with M. Raucheisen pf   Brunswick 90366
        Polydor 19918

Sadko (1898) – opera
  Chant hindou arr. vln & pf Kreisler
  with M. Raucheisen pf   Brunswick 90366
        Polydor 19918

Scheherazade, Op. 35 (1888) orch.
  with Berlin Philharmonic   Polydor 95187/92
  Orch. – Fried

RUBINSTEIN

(2) Melodies, Op. 3 pf
  No. 1. Melody in F arr. vln, pf & vlc
  with M. Gurlitt pf & H. Hopf vlc   Brunswick 85051
        Polydor 22541

SARASATE

Carmen Fantasia (on themes from the opera by Bizet) Op. 25 vln & pf or
orch.
  with M. Raucheisen pf   Polydor 27059
(8) Danzas españolas vln & pf
  No. 1. Malagueña, Op. 21, No. 1
  with M. Raucheisen pf   Polydor 19919
  No. 2. Habañera, Op. 21, No. 2
  with M. Raucheisen pf   Polydor 19919

SCHUBERT, François

(12) Bagatelles, Op. 13 vln & pf
  No. 9. L'abeille
  with M. Gurlitt pf   116 BO[IV]   Polydor 27159

SCHUBERT, Franz

(2) Lieder, Op. 98 (D498) v & pf
  No. 2. Wiegenlied (Schlafe, holder süsser Knabe) arr. vln & pf Elman
  with M. Gurlitt pf   116 BO[IV]   Polydor 27159

SCHUMANN

(13) Kinderscenen, Op. 15 pf
  No. 7. Träumerei arr. vln, pf & vlc Lochmann
  with M. Gurlitt pf &   B 49371△M   Polydor 22542
  H. Hopf vlc

SIBELIUS

Kuolema, Op. 44 – Incidental music orch.
  Valse triste arr. vln & pf Franko
  with orch.   Columbia DDX39, SCDK1
(4) Pieces, Op. 78 vln & pf
  No. 2. Romance in F Major
  with F. Eberson pf   Columbia LD7

TCHAIKOVSKY

(3) Souvenirs de Hapsal, Op. 2 pf
  No. 3. Chant sans paroles in f arr. vln, pf & vlc
  with M. Gurlitt pf & H. Hopf vlc   Brunswick 85051
        Polydor 22541

TOSELLI

Serenade, Op. 6 vln & pf
  with M. Raucheisen pf   Imperial J15024
        Kristall K416

VECSEY

Valse triste vln & pf
  with M. Gurlitt pf   367 BT[VI]   Polydor 22883

WEBER

(18) Favoritenwalzer, J143/61 pf
  No. 5. Waltz No. 5, in B flat, J147 arr. vln & pf "in D" Burmester
  with M. Raucheisen pf   Polydor 22859

WIENIAWSKI

(2) Mazurkas, Op. 19 vln & pf
  No. 1. Mazurka No. 1, in G "Obertass"
  with M. Raucheisen pf   Polydor 22860

Efrem ZIMBALIST (1889–   )

ABT

When the swallows homeward fly v & pf – arr. v, vln & orch.
  with A. Gluck s & orch.   A 15908   HMV 7–43066
        Victor 87236, 87516, 3007

d'AMBROSIO

Serenade, Op. 4 vln & pf
  with S. Chotzinoff pf   HMV 4–7994, DA407
        Victor 64710, 891

ANONYMOUS

Hatikva Zionist hymn – arr. v, vln & orch Imber
  with A. Gluck s & orch.   A 22232   HMV 2–3333, DA448
        Victor 87296, 87522, 3003

Swedish cradle song folksong – arr. v, vln & pf
  with A. Gluck s & piano   Victor 87566, 3004

AULIN

(4) Aquarelles vln & pf
  No. 2. Humoresque
  with S. Chotzinoff pf   HMV 4–7988, DA405
        Victor 64241, 887

(4) Pieces, Op. 16 vln & pf
  No. 2. Impromptu in E
  with E. Bay pf   98562   Columbia 50090D, 7275M, J7356

BACH

Concerto in d, BWV1043 2 vlns, strs & c
  with F. Kreisler vln &   A 15560/2   HMV 2–07918, 2–07922 & 2–
  string quartet   07920, DB587/8
                             Rococo 2005
                             Victor 8040/1, (in set LM6099),
                             76028/30, A430569, RB6525

(4) Suites, BWV1066/9 strs & c
  Suite No. 3, in D: Air (2nd mvt) BWV1068 2 obs, 3 tpts, drms, strs & c
  – arr. vln & pf as "Air on the G–string" by Wilhelmj
  with E. Bay pf   Columbia 50289D, 7293M

BARNBY

Sweet & low mixed voices – arr. v, vln & orch.
  with A. Gluck s & orch.   Victor 87283

BEETHOVEN

(6) Minuets, G167 pf
  No. 2. Minuet No. 2, in G arr. vln & pf Burmester
  with piano   A 16088   HMV 2–07931, DB461
                             Victor 74444, 6332
  Romance No. 1, in G, Op. 40 vln & orch.
                NE 55004–2 & 55005–3   Columbia 68596D, DX772,
  with Japanese Broadcasting Symphony   J7696, W94
  Orch. – Schiferblatt

BETHIER

Petite serenade vln & pf
  with piano   Victor 66221, 988

van BIENE

Broken melody vlc & pf – arr. vln & pf
  with S. Chotzinoff pf   A 16078   HMV 2–07928, DB460
                             Victor 74445, 6331

BOWEN

Suite No. 1, in d (1909) pf
  No. 1. Humoresque arr. vln & pf Schott–Sohne
  with piano   HMV DB806
                             Victor 74884, 6451

BRAGA

(7) Melodies (1867) v & pf
  No. 5. La serenata "Angel's serenade"
  with A. Gluck s & E.   A 12995   HMV 03349, DB574
  Lutsky pf   Victor 88434, 89092, 8026

BRAHMS

(21) Hungarian Dances pf duet
  Hungarian dance No. 17, in f sharp arr. vln & pf Kreisler
  with T. Saidenberg pf   M 55084–3   Columbia 264619, DX785
  Hungarian Dance No. 20, in e arr. vln & pf "in d" Joachim
  with S. Chotzinoff pf   HMV 3–07908, DB462
                             Victor 74303, 6333
  Hungarian Dance No. 21, in e arr. vln & pf Joachim
  with S. Chotzinoff pf   HMV 3–07908, DB462
                             Victor 74303, 6333
  Sonata No. 3, in d, Op. 108 vln & pf
  with H. Kaufman pf   Columbia 67786/8D, (set M140),
                             J7655/7

CHOPIN

(3) Waltzes, Op. 64 pf
  No. 1. Waltz No. 6, in D flat "Minute Waltz" arr. vln & pf Zimbalist
  with S. Chotzinoff pf   A 12974   HMV 3–07907, DB461
                             Victor 74338, 6332

(3) Waltzes, Op. 70 pf
  No. 1. Waltz No. 11, in G flat arr. vln & pf Spalding
  with E. Bay pf   HMV DA788
                             Victor 1154

CORNELIUS

(6) Lieder, Op. 3 v & pf
  No. 3. Ein Ton (The monotone) arr. v, vln & pf
  with A. Gluck s & piano   Victor 87208

CUI

Kaleidoscope, Op. 50 vln & pf
  No. 9. Orientale
  with S. Chotzinoff pf   HMV 4–7991, DA404
                             Victor 64261, 886

  No. 9. Orientale
  with E. Bay pf   Columbia 181M, 2125M, J5041

DRDLA

Guitarerro, Op. 88 vln & pf
  with E. Bay pf   Victor 1056
Serenade No. 1, in A vln & pf
  with piano   Victor 64561
Souvenir vln & pf
  with F. Moore pf   HMV 4–7995, DA406
                             Victor 64813, 892

Souvenir vln & pf
  with T. Saidenberg   M 200208–1A   Columbia 17105D, DB1701,
  pf   DO1740, P10

DRIGO

(2) Airs de Ballet orch.
  No. 2. Valse bluette arr. vln & pf Auer
  with E. Bay pf   146918   Columbia 5314, 181M, 2125M,
                             J5041

(Les) Millions d'Arlequin (1900) – ballet orch.
  Sérénade arr. vln & pf Auer
  with orch.   HMV 2–07965, DB462
                             Victor 74467, 6333

  Sérénade arr. vln & pf Auer
  with E. Bay pf   98567–2   Columbia 9674, 50162D, 7279M,
                             J7348, P93

ELGAR

Salut d'amour, Op. 12 orch. – arr. vln & pf Elgar
  with H. Kaufman pf   Victor 66101, 890

FOSTER

Massa's in de cold, cold groun' (1852) v & pf – arr. vln & pf Pasternack
  with string orch. & celeste   A 18933   HMV 4–7927, DA493
                             Victor 64638, 888

Old black Joe (1860) v & pf – arr. vln & orch.
  with string orch.   A 18934   HMV 4–7921, DA493
                             Victor 64640, 888

FOSTER – *Continued*

(The) Old folks at home "Swanee river" (1851) v & pf*
with A. Gluck s & S.   A 12977   HMV 2–3107, DA450
Chotzinoff pf   Victor 87196, 87518, 3006

GLINKA

Farewell to Petersburg (1840) – 12 songs v & pf
No. 10. The lark arr. vln & pf Auer
with F. Moore pf   A 22235   HMV 3–07909, DB460
                                 Victor 74582, 6331

Ruslan & Ludmila (1842) – opera
Persian song arr. vln & pf Zimbalist
with E. Bay pf   HMV DA788
                                 Victor 1154

Persian song arr. vln & pf Zimbalist
with E. Bay pf   149719   Columbia 2191D, 2090M, J5118

GOODEVE

Fiddle & I v & pf – arr. v, vln & pf
with A. Gluck s & R.   A 16079   HMV 03565, DB573
Bourdon pf   Victor 88539, 89093, 8027

GOSSEC

Rosine (1786)– opera
Gavotte arr. vln & pf Burmester
with S. Chotzinoff pf   A 16088   HMV 2–07931, DB461
                                  Victor 74444, 6332

GOUNOD

Ave Maria (Méditation on Bach's "Prelude No. 1, in C" from Book I of
"Das Wohltemperirte Clavier") v & pf – arr. v, vln & pf
with A. Gluck s & E.   A 12975   HMV 03347, DB574
Lutsky pf   Victor 88433, 89091, 8026

GREENE

Sing me to sleep v & pf – arr. v, vln & str qt
with A. Gluck s & string   A 17834   HMV 03555, DB573
quartet   Victor 88573, 89094, 8027

HALVORSEN

(4) Mosaïques (Suite des morceaux caractéristiques) vln & pf
No. 4. Chant de Veslemøy
with S. Chotzinoff pf   A 20098   HMV 4–7985, DA402
                                  Victor 64737, 884

HANDEL

(15) Sonatas, Op. 1 (?1731) fl or vln & c
Sonata No. 9, in b: Andante (1st mvt) arr. vln & pf as "Larghetto" by
Hubay
with A. Lambert pf   HMV 4–7989, DA401
                                 Victor 64335, 883

HERBERT

(The) Fortune Teller (1898) – operetta
Gypsy love song arr. vln & pf
with E. Bay pf   Victor 1056

* Vln obbligato is Dvořák's "Humoresque".

HILDACH

(2) Lieder, Op. 15 v & pf
No. 1. Der Spielmann arr. v, vln & orch.
with A. Gluck s & orch.   A 18936   HMV 2–043018, DB593
                                    Victor 88583, 89095, 8046

HUBAY

(6) Blumenleben, Op. 30 vln & pf
No. 5. Der Zephir
with E. Bay pf   146916   Columbia 5314, 03623, 2123M,
                                       J5042

Concerto No. 3, in g, Op. 99 vln & orch.
Adagio (2nd mvt); **Scherzo** (3rd mvt)
with E. Bay pf   Columbia 50297D, 7235M

KRAMER

Chant nègre, Op. 32, No. 1 vln & pf
with piano   HMV 4–7986, DA402
                                       Victor 64736, 884

Entr'acte, Op. 46, No. 2 vln & pf
with E. Bay pf   Victor 1054

KREISLER

Liebesfreud vln & pf
with E. Bay pf   Columbia 50257D, 7287M, J7677
Liebesleid vln & pf
with E. Bay pf   98566–1   Columbia 9650, 7287M, J7627

LANE

In the hour of trial v & pf – arr. v, vln & org
with A. Gluck s & organ   A 22230   HMV 2–3399, DA449
                                     Victor 87300, 87523, 3005

LEROUX

(Le) Nil v & pf – arr. v, vln & pf Renaud
with A. Gluck s & piano   A 11601   HMV 2–033038, DB572
                                     Victor 88358, 89090, 8028

MacDOWELL

(4) Songs, Op. 56 (1898) v & pf
No. 1. Long ago arr. vln & pf
with S. Chotzinoff pf   HMV 4–7990, DA403
                                       Victor 64266, 885

MARSHALL

I hear you calling me (1908) v & pf – arr. vln & pf
with piano   Victor 64330

MASSENET

Élégie v & pf – arr. v, vln & pf
with A. Gluck s & piano   A 11603   HMV 7–33005, DA449
                                     Victor 87101, 87513, 3004

MENDELSSOHN

(6) Songs without words, Op. 62 pf
No. 6. Song without words No. 30, in A "Spring song" arr. vln & pf
with orch.   Victor 66034, 892

MOSZKOWSKI

(6) Klavierstücke, Op. 15 pf – 4 hands
No. 1. Serenata arr. vln & orch.
with orch.   HMV 4–7993, DA406
                                       Victor 64576, 891

NEVIN

(The) Rosary (1898) v & pf – arr. v, vln & orch.
with A. Gluck s & orch.   A 15909   HMV 2–3225, DA450
Victor 87237, 87517, 3006

PIERNÉ

Sérénade in A, Op. 7 (1875) pf – arr. vln & pf Haddock
with E. Balaban pf   Victor 64936, 890

RAVEL

(4) Chants populaires (1910) v & pf
No. 4. Chanson hébraïque arr. v, vln & orch. Pasternack
with A. Gluck s & orch.   Belcantodisc BC247
HMV 7–13360, DA448
Victor 87276, 87519, 3003

REGER

(4) Sonatas, Op. 42 solo vln
Sonata No. 2, in A: Andantino
(unaccompanied)   HMV 3–7996, DA403
Victor 64518

RIMSKY–KORSAKOV

(4) Songs, Op. 2 (1865/6) v & pf
No. 2. Enslaved by the rose & the nightingale arr. v, vln & pf
with A. Gluck s & piano   A 20087   HMV 7–33027, DA519
Victor 87146, 87251, 87287

SAINT–SAËNS

(Le) Bonheur est chose légère v & pf – arr. v, vln & pf
with A. Gluck s & piano   A 15387   Belcantodisc BC247
HMV 7–33011, DA519
Victor 87209, 87515

(Le) Carnaval des animaux (1886) small orch.
Le cygne arr. vln & pf
with S. Chotzinoff pf   A 12974   HMV 3–07907, DB461
Victor 74338, 6332

(Le) Déluge, Op. 45 (1876) – oratorio
Prélude vln & orch. – arr. vln & pf Saint–Saëns
with F. Moore pf   HMV DA404
Victor 64827, 886

SARASATE

Carmen Fantasia (on themes from the opera by Bizet) Op. 25 vln & pf or orch.
M 55086–2 & 55087–1   Columbia 9095M, DX765, W38
with T. Saidenberg pf

(8) Danzas españolas vln & pf
No. 6. Zapateado, Op. 23, No. 2
with piano   Victor 74883, 6451
No. 6. Zapateado, Op. 23, No. 2
with E. Bay pf   98561–1   Columbia 9650, 50162D, 7279M, J7348, W93
No. 7. Danza española No. 7, in a, Op. 26, No. 1
with piano   HMV DB806

Zigeunerweisen, Op. 20 vln & pf or orch.
with T. Saidenberg pf   Columbia 9101M, W95

SCHUBERT

(7) Gesänge (set to Scott's "Lady of the Lake") Op. 52 v & pf
No. 6. Ave Maria, D839 arr. vln & pf Wilhelmj
with E. Bay pf   98560–3   Columbia 9674, 266058, 50090D, 7275M, J7356

SCHUMANN

(13) Kinderscenen, Op. 15 pf
No. 7. Träumerei arr. vln & pf
with T. Saidenberg pf   M 200207–2   Columbia 17105D, DB1701, DO1740, P10

SCOTT

Tallahassee Suite, Op. 73 (1910) vln & pf
No. 2. After sundown
with E. Bay pf   146197   Columbia 03623, 167M, 2123M, J5042

SIMONETTI

Madrigale pf – arr. vln & pf
with piano   Victor 66220, 988

SPALDING

Alabama (Plantation melody) vln & pf
with S. Chotzinoff pf   Victor 74443

SUK

(4) Pieces, Op. 17 vln & pf
No. 4. Burleska
with E. Bay pf   149721   Columbia 2191D, 2090M, J5118

SULLIVAN

(The) Lost chord (1877) v & pf – arr. v, vln & orch.
with A. Gluck s & orch.   A 20673   HMV 03643, DB572
Victor 88593, 89096, 8028

TCHAIKOVSKY

(The) Months (12 characteristic pieces) Op. 37b pf
No. 10. Autumn song (October) arr. vln & pf Burmester
with orch.   HMV 4–7905, DA401
Victor 64577, 883

Quartet No. 1, in D, Op. 11 2 vlns, vla & vlc
Andante cantabile (2nd mvt) arr. vln & pf Kreisler
with T. Saidenberg pf   M 55085–1   Columbia 264619, DX785

(6) Songs, Op. 6 v & pf
No. 6. None but the weary heart arr. v, vln & orch.
with A. Gluck s & orch.   Victor 87244, 87518, 3007

(3) Souvenirs de Hapsal, Op. 2 pf
No. 3. Chant sans paroles in f arr. vln & pf Kreisler
with H. Kaufman pf   Victor 66119, 885

TOMER

God be with you 'til we meet again (1883) v & pf – arr. v, vln & orch. Rankin
with A. Gluck s & orch.   Victor 87278, 87520, 3005

WAGNER

(Die) Meistersinger von Nürnberg (1868) – opera
Morgenlich leuchtend "Prize song" arr. vln & pf Wilhelmj
with E. Bay pf   Columbia 50289D, 7293M

WIENIAWSKI

Légende, Op. 17 vln & pf or orch.
  with E. Lutsky pf
                               HMV 3–07910, DB586
                               Victor 74337, 6369

YSAŸE

(6) Sonatas, Op. 27 solo vln
  Sonata No. 1, in g
  (unaccompanied)
                               HMV ED263/4
                               Victor 16194/5, (set M669)

ZIMBALIST

Improvisation on a Japanese tune vln & pf
  with piano   Columbia 2087M, J5113
Improvisation on a Japanese tune vln & pf
  with E. Bay pf   Victor 1054
(3) Slavonic Dances vln & pf
  No. 1. Russian Dance
  with E. Balaban pf   Victor 64955, 889
  No. 2. Hebrew melody & dance
  with piano   HMV 4–7987, DA405
                               Victor 64455, 887
  No. 3. Polish dance
  with orch.   HMV 4–7992, DA407
                                 Victor 64562, 889
Suite dans la forme ancienne vln & pf
  No. 2. Sicilienne
  with S. Chotzinoff pf   HMV DB586
                                 Victor 74280, 6369
  No. 3. Minuet
  with S. Chotzinoff pf   HMV DB586
                                 Victor 74280, 6369

Louis ZIMMERMANN (1873–1954)

BACH

Concerto in d, BWV1043 2 vlns, strs & c
  with F. Hellmann vln &   Decca K20043/4
  Concertgebouw Orch., Amsterdam –
  Mengelberg
(4) Suites, BWV1066/9 strs & c
  Suite No. 3, in D: Air (2nd mvt) BWV1068 2 obs, 3 tpts, drms, strs & c
  – arr. vln & pf as "Air on the G–string" by Wilhelmj
  with piano   Columbia D15802

BEETHOVEN

Concerto in D, Op. 61 (cadenzas by Joachim) vln & orch.
        FX 77/8, 79–2, 80/5–1 & 86–2   Columbia DHX20/4
  with Concertgebouw Orch.,
  Amsterdam – Mengelberg
Romance No. 1, in G, Op. 40 vln & orch.
  with piano   FX 137   Columbia D15803, DHX28
Romance No. 2, in F, Op. 50 vln & orch.
  with piano   FX 75–1 & 76–2   Columbia DHX19
Sonata No. 8, in c, Op. 13 "Pathétique" pf
  Adagio (2nd mvt) arr. vln & pf
  with piano   FX134   Columbia D15805, DHX28

BRUCH

Concerto No. 1, in g, Op. 26 vln & orch.
  Adagio (2nd mvt)
  with piano   WFX 135/6   Columbia 9628, 02837, DHX29

CHOPIN

(3) Nocturnes, Op. 9 pf
  No. 3. Nocturne No. 3, in B arr. vln & pf Zimmermann
  with piano   Columbia DHX17

DVOŘÁK

(8) Slavonic Dances, Op. 72 pf duet; orch.
  No. 2. Slavonic dance No. 10, in e arr. vln & pf Kreisler
  with piano   Columbia D15802

ERNST

Élégie in c, Op. 10 vln & pf
  with piano   Columbia DHX17

GODARD

Jocelyn (1888) – opera
  Cachés dans cet asile "Berceuse" arr. vln & pf
  with piano   Columbia DHX27

GOUNOD

Hymne à Sainte–Cécile (1864) vln, org & pf – arr. vln & pf
  with piano   Columbia DHX30

GRANADOS

(12) Danzas españolas, Op. 37 (1893) pf
  No. 5. Danza española No. 5, in e "Andaluza" arr. vln & pf Kreisler
  with piano   Columbia D15801

GUIRAUD

Caprice (1884) vln & pf
  with piano   Columbia DHX18

HANDEL

Serse (1738) – opera
  Ombra mai fu "Largo" arr. vln & pf
  with piano   FX 124–1   Columbia D15829, DHX26
(15) Sonatas, Op. 1 (?1731) fl or vln & c
  Sonata No. 9, in b: Andante (1st mvt) arr. vln & pf as "Larghetto" by Hubay
  with piano   Columbia D15805
  Sonata No. 13, in D: Larghetto (1st mvt); **Allegro** (2nd mvt) vln IV
  with piano   Columbia D15801

LOCATELLI

(12) Sonatas, Op. 6 (1737) vln & c
  Sonata No. 1, in g: Giga (Allegro moderato) (ed. David)
  with piano   Columbia DHX16
  Sonata No. 5, in c: Siciliano (ed. David)
  with piano   Columbia DHX16

MENDELSSOHN

Concerto in e, Op. 64 vln & orch.
  Allegro molto vivace (3rd mvt)
  with piano   Columbia D15804

MOZART

Divertimento No. 17, in D, K334 2 hrns & strs
  Minuet (3rd mvt)
  with piano   Columbia D15803, DHX31

Serenade No. 7, in D, K250 "Haffner" orch.
  Minuet (3rd mvt) arr. vln & pf
  with piano   Columbia D15803

SAINT-SAËNS

(Le) Déluge, Op. 45 (1876) – oratorio
  Prélude vln & orch. – arr. vln & pf Saint-Saëns
  with piano   Columbia D15806

STRAUSS, R.

Sonata in E flat, Op. 18 vln & pf
  Improvisation (2nd mvt)
  with piano   Columbia DHX18

TARTINI

Sonata in g "Il Trillo del Diavolo" vln & c
  Larghetto affetuoso (1st mvt)
  with piano   Columbia D15804

TCHAIKOVSKY

Concerto in D, Op. 35 vln & orch.
  Canzonetta (2nd mvt)
  with piano   Columbia DHX31

THOMÉ

Adagio religioso, Op. 70 pf – arr. vln & pf
  with piano   FX 129   Columbia DHX26

VIEUXTEMPS

(6) Morceaux de salon, Op. 22 vln & pf
  No. 3. Rêverie
  with C. Raybould pf   FX 131/2   Columbia D15828, DHX25

VIVALDI

(12) Concerti, Op. 3 "L'Estro armonico" var. cbns & strs
  Concerto No. 8, in a, P.2 (F.I, No. 177) 2 vlns, strs & c
  with F. Hellmann vln & orch. –   Telefunken SK2401/2
  Mengelberg

WAGNER

(Die) Meistersinger von Nürnberg (1868) – opera
  Morgenlich leuchtend "Prize song" arr. vln & pf Wilhelmj
  with piano   Columbia DHX30

WIENIAWSKI

Concerto No. 2, in d, Op. 22 vln & orch.
  Romance (2nd mvt)
  with piano   Columbia DHX27

WILHELMJ

Romance, Op. 10 vln & pf
  with piano   Columbia D15806

ZIMMERMANN

Lento ma non troppo vln & pf
  with piano   Columbia D15807
Mazurka vln & pf
  with piano   Columbia D15807

Karel J. ZOUBEK (1902–1959)

SUK

(7) Pieces, Op. 7 pf
  No. 1. Love song arr. vln & pf Mařák
  with F. Holeček pf   Esta B7168

ZOUBEK

Valse–caprice vln & pf
  with F. Holeček pf   Esta B7168

Dĕnes ZSIGMONDY (1922–)

BACH

Concerto No. 2, in E, BWV1042 vln, strs & c
  with Masterplayers – Schumacher   Amadeo AVRS6175

BARTÓK

(6) Rumanian folk dances (1915) pf – arr. vln & pf Székely
  with A. Nissen pf   1773/4 KK   Deutsche Grammophon 62871,
                                           NL32208

BRAHMS

Sonata No. 3, in d, Op. 108 vln & pf
  with A. Nissen pf   Lyrichord LL145, LLST7145

DITTERSDORF

Concerto in G (1767) vln, strs & c
  with Vienna Chamber Orch. – Angerer   Amadeo AVRS6283
                                       Columbia OS3431
                                       Discapon 4225

KREISLER

Liebesfreud vln & pf
  with A. Nissen pf   1963[3] KK   Deutsche Grammophon 48408
Liebesleid vln & pf
  with A. Nissen pf   1964 KK   Deutsche Grammophon 48408

MOZART

Serenade No. 7, in D, K250 "Haffner" orch.
  with Bamberg Symphony Orch. –   Decca DL9636
  Leitner   Deutsche Grammophon 72165/8,
                                         LPM18041

Sonata No. 27, in G, K379 vln & pf
  with A. Nissen pf   02576/7 LWS   Deutsche Grammophon 72109

RAVEL

Tzigane (Rapsodie de concert) (1924) vln & pf or orch.
                 01948 KK & 01949[2] KK   Deutsche Grammophon 68446
  with Munich Philharmonic Orch. –
  Rieger

RÓZSA

Variations on a Hungarian peasant song, Op. 4 vln & orch.
  with Vienna State Opera Orch. –   Westminster XWN18805,
  Rózsa   WST14035

SCHUBERT

Fantasia in C, Op. 159 (D934) vln & pf
  with A. Nissen pf   Lyrichord LL145, LLST7145

SKORZENY

Fantasie–Sonata (in memoriam to Ginette Neveu) vln & pf
  with A. Nissen pf   Amadeo AVRS3010

Pinchas ZUKERMAN (1949–)

BEETHOVEN

(3) Trios, Op. 1 pf, vln & vlc
  No. 1. Trio No. 1, in E flat
    with D. Barenboim pf & J. Du Pré vlc   Angel 36745, (in set S3771)
    Electrola 3C 163–02046
    HMV SL789 /1

  No. 2. Trio No. 2, in G
    with D. Barenboim pf & J. Du Pré vlc   Angel 36746, (in set S3771)
    Electrola 3C 163–02047
    HMV SL789 /2

  No. 3. Trio No. 3, in c
    with D. Barenboim pf & J. Du Pré vlc   Angel 36745, (in set S3771)
    Electrola 3C 163–02046
    HMV SL789 /1

(2) Trios, Op. 70 pf, vln & vlc
  No. 1. Trio No. 4, in D "Ghost"
    with D. Barenboim pf & J. Du Pré vlc   Angel 36747, (in set S3771)
    Electrola 3C 163–02048
    HMV SL789 /3

  No. 2. Trio No. 5, in E flat
    with D. Barenboim pf & J. Du Pré vlc   Angel 36747, (in set S3771)
    Electrola 3C 163–02048
    HMV SL789 /3

Trio No. 6, in B flat, Op. 97 "Archduke" pf, vln & vlc
  with D. Barenboim pf & J. Du Pré vlc   Angel 36748, (in set S3771)
    Electrola 3C 163–02049
    HMV ASD2572, SL789 /4

Trio in E flat, G153 (Wo0.38) pf, vln & vlc
  with D. Barenboim pf & J. Du Pré vlc   Angel 36746, (in set S3771)
    Electrola 3C 163–02047
    HMV SL789 /2

Trio in B flat, G154 (Wo0.39) "In one movement" pf, vln & vlc
  with D. Barenboim pf & J. Du Pré vlc   Angel 36748, (in set S3771)
    Electrola C3 163–02049
    HMV SL789 /4

(14) Variations in E flat, Op. 44 pf, vln & vlc
  with D. Barenboim pf & J. Du Pré vlc   Angel 36749, (in set S3771)
    Electrola C3 163–02050
    HMV SL789 /5

(10) Variations (on "Ich bin der Schneider Kakadu") Op. 121a pf, vln & vlc
  with D. Barenboim pf & J. Du Pré vlc   Angel 36746, (in set S3771)
    Electrola C3 163–02047
    HMV SL789 /2

BLOCH

Baal Shem (3 Pictures of Chassidic life) (1923) vln & pf
  No. 2. Nigun (Improvisation)
    with Royal Philharmonic Orch. –   CBS SBRG72942
    Foster   Columbia M30644

CHAUSSON

Poème, Op. 25 vln & orch.
  with London Symphony Orch. –   CBS S72828
  Mackerras   Columbia MS7422

KABALEVSKY

Concerto in C, Op. 48 vln & orch.
  with Royal Philharmonic Orch. –   CBS SBRG72942
  Foster   Columbia M30644

MENDELSSOHN

Concerto in e, Op. 64 vln & orch.*
  with New York Philharmonic   CBS SBRG72768
  Symphony Orch. – Bernstein   Columbia MS7313

MOZART

Concerto No. 4, in D, K218 vln & orch.
  with English Chamber Orch. –   CBS S72859
  Barenboim   Columbia M30055
Concerto No. 5, in A, K219 "Turkish" vln & orch.
  with English Chamber Orch. –   CBS S72859
  Barenboim   Columbia M30055

SAINT–SAËNS

Introduction & Rondo Capriccioso, Op. 28 vln & orch.
  with London Symphony Orch. –   CBS S72828
  Mackerras   Columbia M31405, MS7422

TCHAIKOVSKY

Concerto in D, Op. 35 vln & orch.
  with London Symphony Orch. –   CBS SBRG72768
  Dorati   Columbia MS7313

VIEUXTEMPS

Concerto No. 5, in a, Op. 37 vln & orch.
  with London Symphony Orch. –   CBS S72828
  Mackerras   Columbia MS7422

WIENIAWSKI

Concerto No. 2, in d, Op. 22 vln & orch.
  with Royal Philharmonic Orch. –   CBS SBRG72942
  Foster   Columbia M30644
Polonaise brillante No. 1, in D, Op. 4 vln & pf
  with London Symphony Orch. –   CBS S72828
  Mackerras   Columbia MS7422

Oleg ZUKIN

TCHAIKOVSKY

Souvenir d'un lieu cher, Op. 42 vln & pf
  No. 3. Mélodie
    with N. Lichačeva pf   Panton 01 0254

Paul ZUKOFSKY (1943–)

BUSONI

Concerto in D, Op. 35a vln & orch.
  with New England Conservatory Orch.   Golden Crest NEC101
  – Prausnitz   New England Conservatory
    Vol. I

* Allegro molto appassionato or 1st mvt is also on Columbia M31405.

HOFFMANN

Trio (1963) vln, vla & vlc
with J. Dupouy vla & R. Sylvester vlc Composers Recordings
CRI240USD

IVES

Hallowe'en (pre–1908) str qt & pf
with R. Tecco vln, J. Dupouy vla, T. Columbia M30230
Eddy vlc & G. Kalish pf

In Re con moto et al (1913) str qt & pf
with R. Tecco vln, J. Dupouy vla, T. Columbia M30230
Eddy vlc & G. Kalish pf

Largo (1902) vln, cl & pf
with C. Russo cl & G. Kalish pf Columbia M30230

Largo (1901) vln & pf
with G. Kalish pf Columbia M30230

Largo Risoluto No. 1 (pre–1907) str qt & pf
with R. Tecco vln, J. Dupouy vla, T. Columbia M30230
Eddy vlc & G. Kalish pf

Largo Risoluto No. 2 (pre–1907) str qt & pf
with R. Tecco vln, J. Dupouy vla, T. Columbia M30230
Eddy vlc & G. Kalish pf

Set of three short pieces (1908) str qt, bs & pf
with R. Tecco vln, J. Dupouy vla, T. Columbia M30230
Eddy vlc, A. Brehm bs & G. Kalish pf

Sonata No. 1 (1903/8) vln & pf
with G. Kalish pf Folkways, FM3346

Sonata No. 2 (1910) vln & pf
with G. Kalish pf Folkways FM3346

Sonata No. 3 (1914) vln & pf
with G. Kalish pf Folkways FM3347

Sonata No. 4 (1916) "Children's day at the camp meeting" vln & pf
with G. Kalish pf Folkways FM3347

Trio (1904 – completed 1911) pf, vln & vlc
with R. Sylvester vlc & G. Kalish pf Columbia M30230

MARTINO

Fantasy variations (1962) solo vln
(unaccompanied) Composers Recordings
CRI240USD

Trio (1959) vln, cl & pf
with A. Bloom cl & G. Kalish pf Composers Recordings
CRI240USD

MYROW

Songs from the Japanese (1965) s, fl, a–fl, cl, bs–cl, vln, vla, vlc, cbs, pf, hpsi & pcn
with P. Bryn–Julson s, T. Nyfenger fl Nonesuch H71219
& a–fl, A. Bloom cl & bs–cl, R. Nagel
tpt, J. Swallow tbn, J. Glick vla, K.
Iwasaki vlc, J. Levine cbs, G. Kalish
pf & R. Desroches pcn

PAGANINI

(24) Caprices, Op. 1 (1801/7) solo vln
  Caprice No. 1, in E
  (unaccompanied) Cardinal VCS10093
  Caprice No. 2, in b
  (unaccompanied) Cardinal VCS10093
  Caprice No. 3, in e
  (unaccompanied) Cardinal VCS10093

PAGANINI – *Continued*

  Caprice No. 4, in c
  (unaccompanied) Cardinal VCS10093
  Caprice No. 5, in a
  (unaccompanied) Cardinal VCS10093
  Caprice No. 6, in g
  (unaccompanied) Cardinal VCS10093
  Caprice No. 7, in a
  (unaccompanied) Cardinal VCS10093
  Caprice No. 8, in E flat
  (unaccompanied) Cardinal VCS10093
  Caprice No. 9, in E
  (unaccompanied) Cardinal VCS10093
  Caprice No. 10, in g
  (unaccompanied) Cardinal VCS10093
  Caprice No. 11, in C
  (unaccompanied) Cardinal VCS10093
  Caprice No. 12, in A flat
  (unaccompanied) Cardinal VCS10093
  Caprice No. 13, in B flat
  (unaccompanied) Cardinal VCS10094
  Caprice No. 14, in E flat
  (unaccompanied) Cardinal VCS10094
  Caprice No. 15, in e
  (unaccompanied) Cardinal VCS10094
  Caprice No. 16, in g
  (unaccompanied) Cardinal VCS10094
  Caprice No. 17, in E flat
  (unaccompanied) Cardinal VCS10094
  Caprice No. 18, in C
  (unaccompanied) Cardinal VCS10094
  Caprice No. 19, in E flat
  (unaccompanied) Cardinal VCS10094
  Caprice No. 20, in D
  (unaccompanied) Cardinal VCS10094
  Caprice No. 21, in A
  (unaccompanied) Cardinal VCS10094
  Caprice No. 22, in F
  (unaccompanied) Cardinal VCS10094
  Caprice No. 23, in E flat
  (unaccompanied) Cardinal VCS10094
  Caprice No. 24, in a
  (unaccompanied) Cardinal VCS10094

PENDERECKI

Capriccio vln & orch.
with Buffalo Philharmonic Orch. – Nonesuch H71201
Foss

RANDALL

Lyric variations vln & computer
with computer Cardinal VCS10057

REICH

Violin phase (1967) vln & tape
with tape recorder Columbia MS7265

RHODES

Duo vln & vlc
  with R. Sylvester vlc   Acoustic Research 5

SAHL

Mitzvah for the dead vln & tape
  with tape recorder   Cardinal VCS10057

SCHUMAN

Concerto (1947) vln & orch.
  with Boston Symphony Orch. –   Deutsche Grammophon 2530 103
  Tilson–Thomas

SESSIONS

Concerto (1935) vln & orch.
  with French Radio Orch. – Schuller   Composers Recordings CRI220

SHIFRIN

Satires of Circumstance (1964) m–s, fl, pic, cl, vln, vlc, cbs & pf
  with J. DeGaetani m–s &   Nonesuch H71220
  Contemporary Chamber Ensemble –
  Weisberg

SYDEMAN

Concerto da camera No. 2 (1960) vln & orch.
  with Contemporary Chamber   Composers Recordings CRI181
  Ensemble – Weisberg

WOLPE

Chamber Piece No. 1 (1964) fl, ob, E–hrn, cl, bsn, hrn, tpt, tbn, 2 vlns, vla, cbs & pf
  with Contemporary Chamber   Nonesuch H71220
  Ensemble – Weisberg

WUORINEN

Duo vln & pf
  with C. Wuorinen pf   Acoustic Research 4

INDEX OF COMPOSERS

Abaco, Evaristo Felice dall' (1675–1742)
(12) Sonatas, Op. 3 (1714) (*2 vlns & c*)
  Sonata No. 1, in C *Burgin & Posselt*
  Sonata No. 2, in F *Combes & Scrosoppi –*
  Fournier & J. Pasquier
  Sonata No. 4, in G *Ayo & Cotogni*
Abbé (see: Vogler, Georg Joseph, 1749–1814)
Abbott, Lyman (1835–1922)
Wonderland of dreams (*v & pf*) *Ball*
Abel, Carl Friedrich (1723–1787)
(6) Quartets, Op. 12 (*fl or ob, vln, vla & vlc*)
  Quartet No. 2, in A *Kussmaul*
Abraham, Paul (1892–1960)
(Un) Chant d'amour (*v & pf*) *Curti*
Absil, Jean (1893–   )
Chaconne, Op. 69 (1949) (*solo vln*) *Raskin*
Fantaisie concertante, Op. 99 (1959) (*vln & orch.*)
Raskin
Abt, Franz (1819–1885)
When the swallows homeward fly (*v & pf*)
Zimbalist
Accordi, Pietro
(La) Seduzione (*Air de ballet*) (*orch*) *de Brayne –*
Curti – Mendels
Accoreti
(Die) Verführung (*vln & pf*) *André*
Achron, Joseph (1886–1943)
Dance (*Improvisation on a Hebrew folk tune*) Op.
37 (*vln & pf*) *Gimpel*
Hebrew dance, Op. 35, No. 1 (*vln & pf*) *R. Cohen*
– Gimpel – Heifetz
Hebrew lullaby, Op. 35, No. 2 (*vln & pf*) *Heifetz –*
Kálmán – Menges
Hebrew melody, Op. 33 (*vln & pf*)
  Barbieri (2) – Elman (3) – Erlih – Haendel –
  Hassid – Heifetz (3) – L. Kogan – Parnes – R.
  Ricci – T. Seidel – Zighera
Stimmungen, Op. 32 (*vln & pf*) *Eidus – A.*
Ferraresi – S. Furer – Heifetz – Kaufman
Ackernley, Mabel
(A) Dream song (*v & pf*) *Chemet*
Adam, Adolphe-Charles (1803–1856)
Cantique de Noël (*v & pf*) *Kulenkampff – Weber*
Adams, A. Emmett (–1938)
(The) Bells of St. Mary's (1917) (*v & pf*)
Andjelkovitch
Adams, Stephen (1844–1913)*
(The) Holy city (1892) (*v & pf*) *d'Almaine (2) –*
Rattay
Adaskin, Murray (1906–   )
Canzona & Rondo (1949) (*vln & pf*) *Hidy*
Sonata (1946) (*vln & pf*) *Adaskin*
Sonatina baroque (*solo vln*) *Adaskin*
Afanasyev, Nikolay Yakovlevich (1821–1898)
Concerto (*vln & orch*) *Grach*
d'Agostino, Alfonso (1883–   )
Flower of Italy (*Mazurka brillante No. 2*) Op. 10
(*vln & pf*) *Moskowitz*
Aguirre, Julián (1869–1924)
(2) Aires criollos (*vln & pf*) *Mus*
  No. 1. Aires criollo No. 1 *Inzaurraga*
Huella (*Canción argentina*) Op. 49 (*orch*) *Heifetz*
(5) Tristes (*pf*)

*Pseudonym for Michael Maybrick.

  No. 4. Triste No. 4, in B flat *Gendelman*
Akbarov, I. (1921–   )
Concerto No. 1, in G (*vln & orch*) *Grach*
Åkerlind, Curt
Romance (*vln & pf*) *Ericson*
Alabiev, Alexander (1787–1851)
(Le) Rossignol (*v & pf*)*
Erdenko – Lass
Sonata (*vln & pf*) *Tziganov*
Trio in a (*pf, vln & vlc*) *Tziganov*
Alard, Delphin (1815-1888)
(12) Duets, Op. 27 (*2 vlns*)
  Duet No. 4, in d *F. & R. Weltmann*
(10) Morceaux de salon, Op. 49 (*vln & pf*)
  No. 10. Brindisi *d'Almaine*
Alassio, Serafino
Montecarlo – march, Op. 515 (*mand & pf*) *May*
Albéniz, Isaac (1860–1909)
Canción catalan (*unid*) *Darrieux*
Cantos d'España, Op. 232 (*pf*)
  No. 4. Córdoba *Campoli*
(2) Danzas españolas, Op. 164 (*pf*)
  No. 1. Jota aragonesa *Dushkin – Lewkowitz*
España (*6 Feuilles d'album*) Op. 165 (*pf*)
  No. 2. Tango in D
  d'Aranyi – Bisztriczky – Campoli (2) – Candéla
  – Debruille – Dushkin – Elman (2) – Erlih –
  Filon – Flori – Fournier – Francescatti –
  Ghestem – Granchi – Grumiaux – Huppertz –
  Kreisler – Kulenkampff – Ludlow – Magyar –
  Novák – Quiroga – Rabinoff – Suk – Szeryng –
  Telmányi – Tessier – Thibaud – Weismann –
  Wilkomirska – Zilzer
  No. 3. Malagueña in b *Erlih – Haendel –*
  Kreisler – Leon-Ara – Szeryng – Thibaud –
  Zilzer
Ibéria – Book I (1906/9) (*pf*)
  No. 2. El puerto *Kogan*
  No. 6. Triana *Fichtenholz*
Love song (*unid*) *Komissarov – D. Oistrakh (2)*
Malagueña, Op. 71, No. 6 (*pf*) *Andrade –*
Spalding
Suite española, Op. 47 (*pf*)
  No. 1. Granada *Tworek*
  No. 3. Savillanas *Campoli – Goldstein – Heifetz*
  – L. Kogan – Tworek
Albicastro, Henricus (1670–1738)†
(9) Trio-sonatas, Op. 5 (*vln & c*)
  Trio sonata in B *Langbein*
  Trio Sonata in B flat *Leonhardt*
Albinoni, Tommaso (1674–1745)
Adagio in g (*strs & org*)‡
Hendel – Knowles – Lamacque – Leroy – Staryk
(12) Concerti, Op. 5 (1707) (*vln or ob, strs & c*)
  Concerto No. 2, in F *Toso*
  Concerto No. 3, in D *Lamacque*
  Concerto No. 5, in a *Cores – Kussmaul*
  Concerto No. 7, in D *Krebbers*

*See: 6 Divertissements, Op. 24 by Vieuxtemps.
†Also known as Heinrich Weisenburg.
‡A work by Giazzotto based on a concerto
movement by Albinoni & discovered at Dresden.

Concerto No. 9, in e *Lamacque*
Concerto No. 12, in C *Lamacque*
(12) Concerti, Op. 7 (1716) (*vln or ob, strs & c*)
  Concerto No. 1, in D *Lamacque*
(12) Concerti, Op. 9 (1722) (*var. cbns & strs*)
  Concerto No. 1, in B flat (*vln, strs & c*) *Ayo –*
  C. Ferraresi – Toso
  Concerto No. 4, in A (*vln, strs & c*) *Abbado –*
  Ayo – C. Ferraresi – A. Ferrari – Michelucci
  Concerto No. 7, in D (*vln , strs & c*) *Ayo (2) –*
  C. Ferraresi – Pelliccia – Toso
  Concerto No. 10, in F (*vln, strs & c*) *Ayo – C.*
  Ferraresi – Michelucci.– Toso
(12) Concerti, Op. 10 (*vln, strs & c*)
  Concerto No. 1, in B flat *Michelucci*
  Concerto No. 2, in g *Michelucci*
  Concerto No. 3, in C *Michelucci*
  Concerto No. 4, in G *Michelucci*
  Concerto No. 5, in A *Michelucci*
  Concerto No. 6, in D *Michelucci*
  Concerto No. 7, in F *Michelucci*
  Concerto No. 8, in g *Michelucci*
  Concerto No. 9, in C *Michelucci*
  Concerto No. 10, in F *Michelucci*
  Concerto No. 11, in E flat *Michelucci*
  Concerto No. 12, in B flat *Michelucci*
Concerto in C (1718) (*vln or ob, strs & c*)
Kussmaul – Lamacque – Liberman
(12) Sonatas, Op. 1 (1694) "Sinfonias"
  Sonata No. 3, in A (*2 vlns & c*) *Burgin &*
  Posselt – Elbaek & Kinch
  Sonata No. 11, in c (*2 vlns & c*) *Lysy &*
  Westergaard
(12) Sonatas, Op. 4 (1704) (*vln, vlc & c*)
  Sonata No. 3, in F *Guglielmo*
(12) Sonatas, Op. 6 (1711) "Trattenimenti
armonia" (*vln & c*)
  Sonata No. 11, in A *Kinch – Kussmaul –*
  Tomasow
Aletter, W. (1867–   )
Fantasy (*vln & pf*) *Anonymous*
Alexandri
My thoughts (*Trecui pe langa cruce*) (*vln & pf*)
Ionescu
Alfvén, Hugo (1872–1960)
Sonata in c, Op. 1 (*vln & pf*) *Saulesco*
Aliprandi, Bernardo (1710–1785)
Esquisses pyrénéennes (*vln & c*) *R. Quattrocchi*
Fantasia (*vln & c*) *R. Quattrocchi*
Allegri, Gregorio (1582–1652)
Symphonie à 4 (*2 vlns, vla d'amore & cbs*
d'amore) *Brix-Meinert – Kägi*
Almeida, H.
Cuban dance *Frolov*
Alpaerts, Jef (1904–   )
Concerto (1948) (*vln & orch*) *Neste*
Altermann, E.
Petite annonce (*vln & pf*) *Altermann*
Altunyan, R. (1939–   )
Concerto-Symphony (*vln, vla & orch*) *Mokatsyan*
Amani, Nicolai Nikolayevich (1872–1904)
(4) Pièces caractéristiques, Op. 7 (*pf*)
  No. 2. Orientale *Deman*
d'Ambrosio, Alfredo (1871–1914)
Aria, Op. 22 (*vln & pf*) *d'Ambrosio*

Canzonetta No. 1, Op. 6 (*vln & pf*)
  *Anonymous – Bleumers – Bonnemain – Bouillon
  – Breeskin – L. Cherniavsky – D. De Groot –
  Deman (2) – Dubois – Eidus – Elman – Frenkel
  – Gittelson – Godwin – M. Hall – Hayward (2)
  – Heermann – Kennedy – Knorre – Kocián –
  Koene – Kulenkampff – Ladschek – Lambert –
  Marcu – Morgan – Mossel – R. Pollack –
  Ranzato – Rèty – Rudényi – Sadler – T. Seidel
  – Stanske – Swaap (2) – Szikra – Thibaud –
  Volant – Wise*
Canzonetta No. 3, Op. 47 (*vln & pf*) *Herman*
Introduction & Humoresque, Op. 25 (*vln & pf*)
  Herman
Madrigal, Op. 26 (*vln & pf*) *Gregorowicz – Mossel*
(2) Morceaux, Op. 17 (*vln & pf*)
  No. 1. Aubade rêverie *d'Ambrosio – Dyke –
    Goni*
  No. 2. Nocturne *Goni*
Orientale, Op. 24 (*vln & pf*) *Thibaud*
Petit Chanson, Op. 28 (*vln & pf*) *d'Ambrosio –
  Asti – Clockers – Delmor – Lorenzo*
Petite Suite, Op. 37 (*vln & pf*)
  No. 1. Chanson napolitaine *d'Ambrosio –
    Sammons*
  No. 3. Valse *Hayward*
Primavera (*Intermezzo*) (*vln & pf*) *Curti*
Romance in D, Op. 9 (*vln & pf*) *d'Ambrosio –
  Chemet – M. Hall – Mittmann – Roeder – Velder*
Serenade, Op. 4 (*vln & pf*)
  *Asti – Borgani – Colombo – Cores – Dyke –
  Enescu – M. Hall – Heifetz – Jancowich –
  Kubelík – Rudényi – Wolfgang Schneiderhan –
  Sens – Spivakovsky – Zimbalist*
Sonnet allègre, Op. 53 (*vln & pf*) *Kálmán*
(A) Ton reveil (*vln & pf*) *Dubois*
Ames, William (1901–)
Dust of snow (*vln & pf*) *Fastofsky*
Amram, David (1930–)
Dirge & Variations (*pf, vln & vlc*) *Tree*
Sonata (1965) (*vln & pf*) *Wakschal*
Amy, Gilbert (1936–)
Trajectories (1965/6) (*vln & orch*) *Jarry*
Andolfi, Godfroy
Berceuse (*vln & pf*) *Curti*
Lorsque tu passes (*Sérénade appassionata*) (*vln &
  pf*) *Curti*
André, Ludwig
On the high Alps *Biedermann & von Wegern*
Andriessen, Hendrik (1892–)
(3) Inventions (*vln & vlc*) *J. Schröder*
Andrzejowski, Adam (1880–1920)
Burleska (*vln & pf*) *Sitkovetsky (2) – Uminska*
de Angelis, Girolamo (1858–1935)
Gigue, Op. 2 (*vln & pf*) *M. Hall*
Rêve d'amour (*vln & pf*) *Alessandro*
Anhalt, Istvan (1919–)
Sonata (1954) (*vln & pf*) *Bress*
Ankermann, H.
Cuban song (*vln & pf*) *Frolov*
Anonymous
Aa Ola, min Ola (*Norwegian melody*) *Haaland*
Ack Vårmeland du sköna (*Swedish folksong*) *W.
  Andersen*
(The) Admiral's galliard *Hayward*

Allemande No. 2 (*2 vlns & rec*)*
van den Hombergh & Leonhardt
Allemande No. 4 (*2 vlns & rec*)**van den*
Hombergh & Leonhardt
Ariettes & Airs (*18th century*) *Blot &
Ortmans-Bach*
Arkansas traveller (*traditional American folkong*)
Powell
(The) Ash grove (*traditional*) *Zacharewitsch*
Auld Robin Gray (1780) (*traditional Scottish
ballad*) *D. De Groot – Southgate*
(La) Ballo Lola (*La Seduzione*) *May*
Beautiful evening (*unid*) *Andjelkovitch*
(The) Bonnie banks of Loch Lomond (*traditional
Scottish air*) *Sealy*
Bonnie Mary of Argyle (*traditional Scottish
ballad*) *D. De Groot – Opfermann – Southgate*
(A) Borée (*traditional*) *M. Hall*
Brunswick medley (*unid*) *Gold*
(La) Carnevale di Venizia (*Italian folksong*)
d'Almaine (2) – Bucia (2)
Cherry ripe (*English folksong*) *Cochrane – Kreisler
– Sammons*
Christ Kindel (*Austrian carol*) (*v & pf*) *Pascal*
Concerto in A (*vln, fl, ob d'amore & c*) *Langbein*
Coon melodies (*unid*) *Southgate*
Deep river (*Negro spiritual*) *Campoli – Heifetz*
(A) Donegal air (*traditional*) *Hayward*
Drink to me only with thine eyes (1762)
(*traditional*) *Ball – D. De Groot – Menuhin –
Southgate – Spalding (2)*
Du grønne glitrende Tre (*vln & pf*) *Johansen*
Eili, Eili (*Zionist hymn*) *Elman (2) – Erlih –
Príhoda – Rosen – A. Sandler – T. Seidel – Swaap*
Esztergomi verbunkos (*Esztergom recruiting
dance*) (*solo vln*)†
Albert
Et barn er født i Betlehem (*vln & pf*) *Johansen*
Etude (*unid*) *Kubelík*
(The) Faithful bird (*Welsh air*) *Sammons (2)*
Fjorton år tror jag visst att jag var (*Swedish
folksong*) *W. Andersen*
Flowers o' the forest *Fellowes*
(The) Foggy, foggy dew (*American Folksong*)
Flesch
Gentle maiden (*English folksong*) *Heifetz – Kersey
– Pratz*
Greensleeves (*traditional English ballad*) *Leopold –
Stern*
(Die) Gute alte Zeit *R. Pollak*
Gypsy dance (*unid*) *Hager*
Harusame (*Japanese air*) *Lass*
Hatikva (*Zionist hymn*) *Zimbalist*
Heart's confession (*unid*) *Förster*
(The) Holly bush (*traditional*) *Chemet*
Hungarian potpourri *Dinicu*
Irish folksong (*unid*) *Lass*
Irish medley (*unid*) *Hager*
I saw from the beach (*folksong*) *Kreisler*
(An) Island sheiling song (*traditional*) *Hayward*
Japanese mother's lullaby (*Japanese air*) *Lass*

*From the volume "The Excellent Cabinet."
†Pre 1761 manuscript.

Jeg er så glad hver julekveld (*vln & pf*) *Johansen*
Jeg synger julekvad *Johansen*
Je vet e lita Jente (*Norwegian melody*) *Haaland*
Kol Nidrei (*Hebrew melody*) *Boulanger – A.
Sandler – Woiku*
Little red lark *Powell*
Loch Lomond (*traditional Scottish ballad*) *Bobbé*
Londonderry air (*traditional Irish ballad*)
  *Campoli – Darrieux – Francescatti (2) – Gold –
  Hayward – Kaufman – Kennedy – Kreisler (4) –
  Law – Morini – Sammons – A. Sandler (2) –
  Skalka – Swaap – Tworek – Wilkomirska –
  Wolf*
Marie-Nocturne (*unid*) *Stehl*
(The) Mason's apron – reel *Fellowes*
Mazurka brillante (*unid*) *Stehl & von Wegern*
(2) Mélodies catalanes *Casadesus*
Min Skat – waltz *Anonymous*
Minuet (*unid*) *Fogelberg*
Molly on the shore (*traditional Irish ballad*)
Hayward – Kreisler – Powell – Sammons
My love is like a red, red rose (*traditional*)
Hayward
Negro folksongs (*unid*) *F. Reuter*
Neuer Wien *R. Pollak*
Night of joy (*unid*) *Morino*
Norwegian dance (*unid*) *Wicks*
O du fröhliche, o du Selige (1819) (*v & pf*) *Dajos
– Horváth – Josephi – Lubow – R. Richter –
Weber*
Old English songs & dances (*unid*) *Sammons*
Old Irish song & dance (*unid*) *Elman*
Om dagen vid mitt arbete (*Swedish folksong*) *W.
Andersen*
Oshoro Takashima (*Japanese*) *Lass*
Paal paa Haugen (*traditional Norwegian melody*)
Haaland
Parasz-verbunkos (*Peasant recruiting dance*)*
Boross
Piquant stories (*unid*) *Ricci*
Polish national dance *d'Almaine*
Poschalej *Steinberg*
(The) Rakes of Mallow (*traditional*) *Bean*
Red butterfly (*Mazurka*) *Morino*
Réponse (*unid*) *Radics*
Robin Adair (1750) (*traditional Irish ballad*)
Southgate
Romance in C (*unid*) *Ricci*
Romance in F (*unid*) *Ricci*
(La) Romanesca (*16th century gaillarde*) *Menuhin
– Piastro*
Romanta tiganesti (*vln & pf*) *Dinicu*
(The) Rope dancer (*traditional*) *Hayward*
Sag du Nokke Kjaeringa mi (*Norwegian folksong*)
Tellefsen
Sehnsuchtsträume *Laue*
(The) Skye fisher's song (*traditional*) *Hayward*
Sleep baby sleep (*v & pf*) *Brown*
Slovenske a Ceske pisne (*unid*) *Lusk*
Smes Cesko (*Slavic song*) (*unid*) *Lusk*
Song of the Volga boatman (*traditional Russian
folksong*) *Curti – Kreisler – Menuhin*
Sounds from home (*unid*) *Stehl*

*1757 Manuscript.

*Arranged from the madrigal "Nous voyons que les hommes" by P.L. Dietsch, 1808–1865.

*The 1st violin dominates to the extent that these works are, in effect, solo concerti.

*Originally composed as Quartets.

Brandenburg Concerto No. 1, in F, BWV1046 (*vln, 3 obs, bsn, 2 hrns, strs & c*)
Barchet (3) – Bean (2) – Boskovsky – Burgin – A. Busch – Felicani – Frasca-Colombier – Goldberg (2) – Hamann – L. Hansen – Harnoncourt – L. Kogan – Kolberg – Krotzinger – Kussmaul – Kwalwasser – Lautenbacher – Maier – Menuhin – Pini – Schneeberger – Schneider – Wolfgang Schneiderhan – Schwalbé – Terebesi – Tomasow – Villa – Wührer
Brandenburg Concerto No. 2, in F, BWV1047 (*tpt, fl, ob, vln, strs & c*)
Barchet (4) – Baumgartner – Bean – Boskovsky – Burgin (2) – A. Busch – Frasca-Colombier – Goldberg (2) – Grinke – Hamann – L. Hansen – Harnoncourt – Heinemann – Krotzinger – Kussmaul – Kwalwasser – Lautenbacher (2) – Lehmann – Maier – Menuhin – Mischakoff – Parikian – Schneeberger – Schneider (2) – Schwalbé – Terebesi – Tomasow – Villa – Wührer
Brandenburg Concerto No. 3, in G, BWV1048 (*3 vlns, 3 vlas, 3 vlcs & cbs*)
Carter, Eitler & Pougnet – Frasca-Colombier – Galimir, N. Koutzen & Kwalwasser – Jilka, Streng & Tomasow – Maier, Neuhaus & Seeger – Schneeberger – Terebesi – Tomasow – Villa
Brandenburg Concerto No. 4, in G, BWV1049 (*vln, 2 fls, strs & c*)
Barchet (4) – Baumgartner – Bean – Bouillon – Boskovsky – Burgin (2) – A. Busch – Felicani – Frasca-Colombier – Goldberg (2) – Grinke – Hamann – L. Hansen – Harnoncourt – Heinemann – Jahn – Kolberg – Krotzinger – Kwalwasser – Lautenbacher (2) – Maier – Menuhin – Merckel – D. Oistrakh (2) – Rybar – Schneeberger – Schneider – Schwalbé – Stiehler – Stross – Suske – Terebesi – Tomasow – Villa – Wührer
Brandenburg Concerto No. 5, in D, BWV1050 (*clav, fl, vln, strs & c*)
Barchet (4) – Baumgartner – Bean – Borries – Boskovsky – Burgin (2) – A. Busch – I. Cohen – De Vito – Felicani – Ferras – Frasca-Colombier – Galimir – Gilels – Goldberg – Grinke – Hamann – L. Hansen – Harnoncourt – Heinemann – Kolberg – Krotzinger – Kussmaul – Lautenbacher (2) – Maier – Menuhin – Merckel – Parikian – Pougnet – Rybar – Schneeberger – Schneider – Schwalbé – Suk – J. Szigeti – Terebesi – Thibaud – Tomasow – Villa – Wührer
Brandenburg Concerto No. 6, in B flat, BWV1051 (*2 vlas, 2 gambas, vlc & cbs*) *A. Busch – Goberman – Goldberg – Menuhin*
Cantata No. 1 (*Wie schön leuchtet der Morgenstern!*) BWV1 (1740) (*s, t, b, cho, 2 obs d'amore, 2 hrns, strs & c*) *Kalt & Terebesi*
Cantata No. 7, (*Christ unser Herr zum Jordan kam*) BWV7 (1740) (*a, t, b, cho, 2 obs d'amore, bsn, 4 tpts, timp, strs & c*) *Kalt & Terebesi*
Cantata No. 8 (*Liebster Gott, wann werd' ich sterben?*) BWV8 (1725) (*s, a, t, b, cho, fl, ob, tpt, strs & c*) *Schwalbé*
Cantata No. 13 (*Meine Seufzer, meine Tränen*)

BWV13 (1736) (*s, a, t, b, cho, 2 fls, ob, strs & c*) *Schwalbé*
Cantata No. 21 (*Ich hatte viel Bekümmernis*) BWV21 (1714) (*s, t, b, cho, ob, bsn, 3 tpts, 4 tbns, timp, strs & c*) *Barchet*
Cantata No. 32 (*Liebster Jesu, mein Verlangen*) BWV32 (1740) (*s, b, cho, ob, strs & c*) *Terebesi*
Cantata No. 43 (*Gott faehret auf mit Jauchzen*) BWV43 (1735) (*s, a, t, b, cho, 2 obs, 3 tpts, timp, strs & c*) *Barchet*
Cantata No. 47 (*Wer sich selbst erhöhet, der soll ernierdriget werden*) BWV47 (1720) (*s, b, cho, 2 obs, org obb, strs & c*) *Abramenkov*
Cantata No. 53 (*Schlage doch, gewünschte Stunde*) BWV53 (1723/34) (*a, bell, strs & c*) *Terebesi*
Cantata No. 57 (*Selig ist der Mann*) BWV57 (1740) (*s, b, cho, 3 obs, strs & c*) *Terebesi*
Cantata No. 59 (*Ach Gott, wie manches Herzeleid*) BWV59 (1740) (*s, a, t, b, cho, 2 obs d'amore, hrn, tpt, strs & c*) *Wilk*
Cantata No. 68 (*Also hat Gott die Welt geliebt*) BWV68 (1735) (*s, b, cho, 3 obs, hrn, 3 tbns, vln-pic, strs & c*) *Catterall – Terebesi – Wilk*
Cantata No. 73 (*Herr, wie du willst, so schick's mit mir*) BWV73 (1725) (*t, b, cho, 2 obs, hrn, org obb, strs & c*) *Schwalbé*
Cantata No. 80 (*Ein feste Burg ist unser Gott*) BWV80 (1716/30) (*s, a, t, b, cho, 3 obs, 2 obs d'amore, 3 tpts, timp, strs & c*) *Barchet*
Cantata No. 84 (*Ich bin vergnügt mit meinem Glücke*) BWV84 (1731) (*s, cho, ob, strs & c*) *Grehling*
Cantata No. 85 (*Ich bin ein guter Hirt*) BWV85 (1735) (*s, a, t, b, cho, 2 obs, vln-pic, strs & c*) *Barchet*
Cantata No. 87 (*Bisher habt ihr nichts gebeten in meinem Namen*) BWV87 (?1735) (*a, t, b, cho, 2 obs, 2 obs d'amore, strs & c*) *Barchet*
Cantata No. 90 (*Es reifet euch ein schrecklich Ende*) BWV90 (1740) (*a, t, b, cho, tpt, strs & c*) *Terebesi*
Cantata No. 97 (*In allen meinen Taten*) BWV97 (1734) (*s, a, t, b, cho, fl, fl-pic, 2 obs d'amore, tpt, strs & c*) *Wilk*
Cantata No. 98 (*Was Gott tut, das ist wohlgetan*) BWV98 (1732) (*s, a, t, b, cho, 3 obs, strs & c*) *Terebesi*
Cantata No. 103 (*Ihr werdet weinen und heulen*) BWV103 (1735) (*a, t, cho, fl, fl-pic, 2 obs d'amore, spin, strs & c*) *Terebesi*
Cantata No. 129 (*Gelobet sei der Herr*) BWV129 (1732) (*s, a, b, cho, fl, 2 obs, ob d'amore, 3 tpts, timp, strs & c*) *Hellmann*
Cantata No. 130 (*Herr Gott, dich loben alle wir*) BWV130 (1740) (*s, a, t, b, cho, fl, 3 obs, 3 tpts, timp, strs & c*) *Barchet*
Cantata No. 137 (*Lobe den Herren, den mächtigen König der Ehren*) BWV137 (1732) (*s, a, t, b, cho, 2 obs, 3 tpts, timp, strs & c*) *Endres*
Cantata No. 140 (*Wachet auf, ruft uns die Stimme*) BWV140 (1731) (*s, t, b, cho, vln-pic, 3 obs, hrn, strs & c*) *Barchet – Endres – Fuchs*
Cantata No. 147 (*Herz und Mund und Tat und Leben*) BWV147 (1716) (*s, a, t, b, cho, 2 obs, ob d'amore, bsn, tpt, strs & c*) *Terebesi*

Cantata No. 156 (*Ich Steh' mit einem Fuss im Grabe*) BWV156 (1730) (*s, a, t, b, cho, ob, strs & c*) *Bean – Campoli – Morini – J. Szigeti (2) – Thoman*
Cantata No. 157 (*Ich lasse dich nicht, du segnest mich denn*) BWV157 (1727) (*t, b, cho, fl, ob, ob d'amore, strs & c*) *Wilk*
Cantata No. 158 (*Der Friede sei mit dir*) BWV158 (1708) (*s, b, cho, vln, ob, strs & c*) *Grehling – Schwalbé*
Cantata No. 159 (*Sehet wir geh'n hinauf gen Jerusalem*) BWV159 (1729) (*s, a, t, b, cho, ob, 2 bsns, strs & c*) *Schwalbé*
Cantata No. 171 (*Gott, wie dein Name, so ist dein Ruhm*) BWV171 (1730) (*s, a, t, b, cho, 2 obs, 3 tpts, timp, strs & c*) *Barchet*
Cantata No. 182 (*Himmelskönig, sei Willkommen*) BWV182 (1715) (*a, t, b, cho, fl, strs & c*) *Barchet*
Cantata No. 189 (*Meine Seele rühmt und preist*) BWV189 (1707) (*t, fl, ob, strs & c*) *Brix-Meinert*
Cantata No. 202 (*Weichet nur, betrübte Schatten*) BWV202 (1720) (*s, ob, strs & c*) *Krotzinger – Pougnet – Wolfgang Schneiderhan*
Cantata No. 205 (*Der Zufriedengestellte Aeolus*) BWV205 (1725) (*s, a, t, b, cho, 2 fls, 2 obs, ob d'amore, gamba, 2 hrns, 3 tpts, timp, strs & c*) *Wilk*
Cantata No. 206 (*Schleicht spielende Wellen*) BWV206 (1734) (*s, a, t, b, cho, 3 fls, 2 obs, 2 obs d'amore, 3 tpts, timp, strs & c*) *Krebbers*
Cantata No. 208 (*Was mir behagt, ist nur die muntre Jagd*) BWV208 (1716) "Hunting Cantata" (*s, t, b, cho, 2 fls, 3 obs, bsn, 4 hrns, strs & c*) *Borries – Krebbers – Lautenbacher*
Cantata No. 210 (*O holder Tag, erwünschte Zeit*) BWV210 (*s, fl, ob, vla d'amore, strs & c*) *Gavrilov*
Clavierübung – part III, BWV802/5 (*clav*)
Duetto No. 1, in e, BWV802 *L. Bobescu – Grinke*
Duetto No. 2, in F, BWV803 *L. Bobescu – Grinke*
Duetto No. 3, in G, BWV804 *L. Bobescu – Grinke*
Duetto No. 4, in a, BWV805 *Grinke*
Concerto No. 1, in a, BWV1041 (*vln, strs & c*)
Astruc – Barchet (2) – Barylli – Bernstein – Blecher – L. Bobescu – Cyroulnik – Erlih – Fernandez – Frasca-Colombier – Ganiev – Gertler – Goldberg – Grehling – Grumiaux (3) – Gutnikov – Harnoncourt – Heifetz – Hlaváček – Huberman – Jarry – Kalafusz – Laredo – Lautenbacher – Menuhin (2) – Michelucci – Milstein – Morini – D. Oistrakh (3) – Parikian – J. Pasquier – R. Ricci – Walther Schneiderhan – Wolfgang Schneiderhan (3) – Stern (3) – Strub – Suk – Szeryng (2) – Totenberg (2) – T. Varga (2) – Wallez
Concerto No. 2, in E, BWV1042 (*vln, strs & c*)
Ayo – Barchet (2) – Barylli – Blecher – Bratza – A. Busch – Cyroulnik – De Vito (2) – Elman (2) – Fernandez – Francescatti – Fujikawa – Garnier – Goldberg – Goldstein – Grehling – Grumiaux (2) – Harnoncourt – Heifetz – Jakowicz – Kalafusz – Kussmaul – Lautenbacher – Loveday – Menuhin (2) –

Merckel – Milstein – Morini – Odnoposoff – D. Oistrakh (4) – I. Oistrakh – Parikian – R. Ricci (2) – Rubenstein – Walther Schneiderhan – Wolfgang Schneiderhan – Schulz – Stern – Stevens – Suk – Szeryng (3) – Thibaud – Tomasow – Totenberg – Vaiman – T. Varga – Wallez – Wolf – Zighera – Zsigmundy

Concerto in d, BWV1043 (2 vlns, strs & c) d'Aranyi & Fachiri (2) – Armand & Cyroulnik – Ayo & Michelucci – Barchet & Beh – Barchet & van der Mueran – Baumgartner & Wolfgang Schneiderhan – Blanchard & Fernandez – Bor & Verhey – Bridge & Catterall – Bruun & Koppel – Büchner & Guntner – A. Busch & Magnes – Cron & Hofer – De Vito & Menuhin – Diener & Hampe – Diercks & W. Hansen – Endress & Stross – Enescu & Menuhin – Erlih & Merckel – Ferras & Menuhin – Flesch & J. Szigeti – Frasca-Columbier & Garnier – Friedman & Heifetz – Gilels & L. Kogan (2) – Grehling & Hendel – Grumiaux & Pougnet – Grumiaux & Toyoda – Gutnikov & Vaiman – Harnoncourt & Pfeiffer – Heifetz ₍playing both parts₎ – Heinemann & O. Schmidt – Hellmann & Zimmermann – Hermann & Kayser – Hoffner & Korn – Jásek & Suk – Jones & Pini – Kalafusz & Rösch – Krebbers & Olof – Kreisler & Zimbalist – Lautenbacher & Vorholz – Milstein & Morini – Moglia & Wallez – Munn & Petiot – Novello & Příhoda – D. & I. Oistrakh (4) – A.M. & A.J. Rose – Rybar & Szeryng – Schneider & Stern – A. & A.R. Witek

Concerto in a, BWV1044 (clav, fl, vln, strs & c) Barchet – Baumgartner – Felicani – Fernandez (2) – Ferras – Frydén – Hendel – Kroll – Kupiev – Lautenbacher (2) – Leonhardt – Menuhin – Merckel – Michelucci – R. Pasquier – Pinkava – Schneider – Suk

Concerto in D, BWV1045 (vln, tpts, strs & c)* Alès – Goren – Harnoncourt

Concerto No. 1, in d, BWV1052 (clav, strs & c) Bress – R. Ricci – J. Szigeti (2)

Concerto No. 5, in f, BWV1056 (clav, strs & c) Gavrilov – Grehling – I. Oistrakh – Rybar – J. Szigeti

Concerto in c, BWV1060 (vln & ob or 2 vlns, strs & c) Abramenkov – Alès – d'Aranyi & Fachiri – Barchet – Beh – Blot & Lovis – Bruun – Büchner (2) – Compinsky – Felicani – Fenyves – Fernandez – Fernandez & Lamacque – Frasca-Columbier & Garnier – Grehling – Grumiaux – Günther – Harnoncourt – Hendel – Hendriks – Kalafusz – Klima – Lehmann – Menuhin – Michelucci – Retyi – Rybar – Stern (2) – Stiehler – Wilk – Zepparoni

Concerto in C, BWV1064 ((3 clavs, strs & c) Bamert, Prystawski & Soh – Bünte, Hendel & Schlupp – Hendel – Isakadze, Kagen & Lubotsky

(6) English Suites, BWV806/11 (clav) English Suite No. 3, in g Heifetz

*One movement only. This "Sinfonia" is from a lost church cantata.

English Suite No. 6, in d Heifetz

Fugue in g, BWV578 "The Little G Minor" (org) Blot & Ortmans-Bach

Fugue in g, BWV1026 (vln & c) Doukan – Frenkel

(15) Inventions – 2 part, BWV772/86 (clav) Invention No. 2, in G, BWV773 Markov

Markus-Passion, BWV247 Kalt & Terebesi

Mass in b, BWV232 (1733/7) (s, a, t, b, cho, strs & c) Barchet – Koeckert – Parikian – Shumsky

Mass in F, BWV233 (1737) Barchet

Mass in A, BWV234 Wilk

Matthaeus-Passion, BWV244 (1729) Barchet – Barylli – Bean – Boskovsky – Fuchs – Krebbers – Menges – Walther Schneiderhan

Minuet (unid) Weissgerber

(Ein) Musikalisches Opfer, BWV1079 (1749) (strs & c) Barchet – Baumgartner & Harnoncourt – Bress – Büchner & Guntner – Endres & Lautenbacher – Godwin – Krotzinger – Marschner – Menuhin – Poltronieri – Swoboda – Tunnell

Notenbüchlein für Anna Magdalena Bach (1725) (clav) No. 4. Minuet in G, BWVAnh114 Kreisler – Zacharewitsch No. 5. Minuet in g, BWVAnh115 Kreisler – Zacharewitsch

Orgelbüchlein, BWV599/644 (org) No. 1. Nun komm', der Heiden Heiland, BWV599 Huberman

Ostern-Oratorium, BWV249 (1736) Lautenbacher – Terebesi

Prelude (unid)* Snitkovsky

(15) Sinfonias – 3 part Inventions, BWV787/801 (clav) Sinfonia No. 3, in D, BWV789 Heifetz Sinfonia No. 4, in d, BWV790 Heifetz Sinfonia No. 9, in f, BWV795 Heifetz

(3) Sonatas & 3 Partitas, BWV1001/6 (solo vln) Sonata No. 1, in g, BWV1001 Bress (2) – Champeil – Dahmen – Dumont – Enescu – Erlih – Eweler – J.C. Figueroa – Gimpel – Grumiaux – Gulli – Heifetz (2) – Joachim – Kocsis – Kreisler – Kulka – Lautenbacher – Marteau – Martzy – Menges – Menuhin (4) – Merckel – Milstein (2) – D. Oistrakh – I. Oistrakh – Olevsky – Renardy – R. Ricci – A.J. Rose – Schneider – R. Schroder – Silverstein – Snitkovsky – Spivakovsky – Steinhardt – Suk – Szeryng (2) – J. Szigeti (2) – Telmányi (2) – Tretyakov – Végh

Partita No. 1, in b, BWV1002 Arvesen – Bress (2) – Champeil – Chemet – Dessau – Dumont – Enescu – Erlih – Fachiri – J.C. Figueroa – Flesch – Gimpel – Grumiaux – Heifetz – Huberman – Joachim – Kaufman – Kim – L. Kogan – Lautenbacher – Martzy – Menuhin (4) – Milstein – Olevsky – Powell – R. Ricci – Schneider – R. Schroder – Suk – Szeryng (2) – J. Szigeti (3) – Telmányi – Végh

*Possibly the Preludio or 1st mvt. from the 3rd Partita for solo vln.

Sonata No. 2, in a, BWV1003 Abadiev – Bress (2) – Champeil – Dumont – Elman – Enescu – Erlih – Fichtenholz – J.C. Figueroa – Gimpel – Grumiaux – Heifetz – Huberman – Lautenbacher – Martzy – Menuhin (3) – Milstein – Olevsky – R. Ricci (2) – Schneider – R. Schroder – Stiehler – Suk – Szeryng (2) – J. Szigeti (2) – Telmányi – Végh

Partita No. 2, in d, BWV1004 Accardo – Alos – Bezrodny – Bress (3) – Büchner – A. Busch – Campoli – Champeil – Czerwonky – De Vito – Dumont – Enescu – Erduran – Erlih – J.C. Figueroa – Francescatti – Friedman – Gimpel – Gramatte – Gránát – Grumiaux (2) – Haendel – Heifetz (3) – Kocsis – Kozigyan – Lautenbacher – Magyar – Martzy – Menges – Menuhin (5) – Milstein (2) – Odnoposoff – Olevsky – Olof – Ortenberg – Porta – R. Ricci (3) – Schneider – Wolfgang Schneiderhan (2) – R. Schroder – Sitkovetsky – Soëtens – Spalding – Stanske – Steinhardt – Strockoff – Suk – Szeryng (3) – J. Szigeti – Taschner – Telmányi (2) – R. Varga – Végh – Wolf (2) – Zhislin

Sonata No. 3, in C, BWV1005 Ashkenazi – Bress (2) – Champeil – Dumont – Enescu – Erlih – J.C. Figueroa – Gimpel – Grumiaux – Heifetz (2) – L. Kogan – Lautenbacher – Martzy – Menuhin (3) – Milstein – Olevsky – Příhoda – Queling – Rabin – Renardy – R. Ricci – Schneider – R. Schroder – Sobolevsky – Suk – Szeryng (2) – J. Szigeti (2) – Telmányi – Végh – Wolf

Partita No. 3, in E, BWV1006 A. Bachmann – Benedetti – Bouillon – Bratza – Bress (2) – Brown – Büchner – Burmester – A. Busch – Champeil – Cillario – Dessau – Dumont – Dunn – Elman (2) – Enescu – Erlih – Eweler – Fachiri – Fichtenholz – Fidelmann – J.C. Figueroa – Francescatti (2) – Geyer – Gimpel – Goldin – Grumiaux – M. Hall – Heermann – Heifetz (2) – F.V. Henriques – Jarry – Kennedy – B. Koutzen – Kreisler (4) – Kubelík – Kulenkampff – Kulka – Laredo – Lautenbacher – Law – Loveday – Magyar – Marteau (2) – Martzy – Menges – Menuhin (4) – Merckel – Milstein – Mitnitzky – Olevsky – Parlow – Primrose – R. Ricci – Sarasate – Schneider – R. Schroder – Shkolnikova – Soriano – Strock – Strockoff (2) – Suk (2) – Szeryng (2) – J. Szigeti (3) – Telmányi (2) – Thibaud (2) – Végh – Weintraub – Wolfsthal

(6) Sonatas, BWV1014/9 (vln & clav) Sonata No. 1, in b, BWV1014 Auclair – Baloković – Barchet – Barinova – Buswell – Friedman – Frydén – Gerle – Grumiaux – Gutnikov – Hendel – Iwamoto – Lautenbacher – Lubotsky – Makanowitzky – Menuhin (2) – Merckel – Monosoff – D. Oistrakh – Pini – Schneeberger – Schneider – B. Schwarz – Suk – Szeryng

Sonata No. 2, in A, BWV1015 Auclair – Barchet – Buswell – Dubois – Friedman – Frydén – Gerle – Grumiaux – Hendel – Lautenbacher – Lubotsky –

Makanowitzky – Menuhin (2) – Merckel – Monosoff – D. Oistrakh – Pini – Primrose – Roberts – Schneeberger – Schneider – Wolfgang Schneiderhan – B. Schwarz – Suk – Szeryng
Sonata No. 3, in E, BWV1016
Auclair – Baloković – Barchet – Barinova – L. Bobescu – A. Busch – Buswell – Fernandez – Friedman – Frydén – Gerle – Grumiaux – Hendel – Klimov – Lautenbacher – Lubotsky – Makanowitzky – Malinin – Massia – Menges – Menuhin (4) – Monosoff – D. Oistrakh – Pach – Pini – Schneeberger – Schneider – B. Schwarz – Stern – Suk – Szeryng
Sonata No. 4, in c, BWV1017
Amar – Auclair – Barchet – A. Busch – Buswell – Dubois – Friedman – Frydén – Gerle – Godwin – Grumiaux – Hendel – L. Kogan – B. Koutzen – Lautenbacher – Lubotsky – Makanowitzky – Menuhin (2) – Merckel – Monosoff – D. Oistrakh – Pini – Powell – Schneeberger – Schneider – B. Schwarz – Suk – Szeryng – Temianka – Weiner – Zacharewitsch
Sonata No. 5, in f, BWV1018
Auclair – Barchet – Buswell – Dubois – Friedman – Frydén – Gerle – Grumiaux – Hendel – Lautenbacher – Lubotsky – Makanowitzky – Menuhin (2) – Monosoff – D. Oistrakh (2) – Pini – Schneeberger – Schneider – B. Schwarz – Suk – Szeryng
Sonata No. 6, in G, BWV1019
Auclair – Barchet – Buswell – Dubois – Friedman – Frydén – Gerle – Grumiaux – Hendel – Lautenbacher – Lubotsky – Makanowitzky – Menuhin (2) – Monosoff – D. Oistrakh (2) – Pini – Schneeberger – Schneider – B. Schwarz – Suk – Szeryng
Sonata in g, BWV1020 (*vln & clav*) *Barinova – Staryk – Stern*
Sonata in G, BWV1021 (*vln & c*) *Barchet – A. Busch – Fichtenholz – Friedmann – Grehling – Monosoff – Staryk*
Sonata in F, BWV1022 (*vln & clav*) *Barchet – Staryk*
Sonata in e, BWV1023 (*vln & c*)
   Barchet – Blot – A. Busch – Fichtenholz – Monosoff – Parikian – Rostal – Staryk – Stern
Sonata in c, BWV1024 (*vln & c*) *Barchet – Fichtenholz – Rybar*
(6) Sonatas, BWV1030/5 (*nos. 1/3: fl & clav – nos. 4/6: fl & c*)
   Sonata No. 2, in E flat, BWV1031 *Heber*
Sonata in d, BWV1036 (*2 vlns & c*)
   Altmann & Lardinois – Barinova & Sobolevsky – Blot & Ortmans-Bach – Dubiska & Uminska – Keltsch & Kussmaul – Kussmaul & Offner
Sonata in C, BWV1037 (*2 vlns & c*)
   Altmann & Lardinois – d'Aranyi & Fachiri – Blot & Ortmans-Bach – Fietz & Rybar – Hendel & Schlupp – Hurwitz & Liddell – Keltsch & Kussmaul – Milstein & Morini – D. & I. Oistrakh (2) – Walther Schneiderhan & Swoboda
Sonata in G, BWV1038 (*fl, vln & c*)*

*Doubtful.

Altmann & Lardinois – Doukan – Grehling – Hendel – Keltsch – Kussmaul – Posselt – Stern – Vorholz
Sonata in G, BWV1039 (*2 fls or vlns & c*) *Altmann & Lardinois*
Sonata in c, BWV1079 (*fl, vln & c*)* *Schneider – Tessier*
Suite in A, BWV1025 (*vln & clav*) *Frenkel*
(4) Suites, BWV1066/9 (*strs & c*)
   Suite No. 3, in D, BWV1068 (*2 obs, 3 tpts, drms, strs & c*)
   Accardo – Akos – Belov – Berg – Berkova – Boucherit – Burmester – Campoli – Dahman – Dessau – Dumont – Dunn – Elman (3) – Fairless – Farbmann – Fichtenholz – Francescatti – Gandini – Gold – Goldin – Gregorowicz – Heber – Høeberg – Hubay – Huberman (2) – Jancowich – Kennedy – Georg Kniestaedt – Kreisler – Kubelík – Kulenkampff – Laredo – J. Lasowski – Lederer – Levy – Manén – Marteau – Mendels – Menges – Menuhin – Meyer – Milstein – Moller – Mosley – Neaman – E.B. Nielsen – Ortenberg – Parlow – Příhoda – L. Quattrocchi – Quiroga – Ranzato – Rosand – A.J. Rose (2) – Sametini – T. Seidel – Sens – Strock – Strockoff – Stümmvoll – Swaap – Szentgyörgi – Telmányi – Thibaud (2) – Thoman – Vecsey (2) – Voicu – Weintraub – Weissgerber – Wethmar – Wilk – Woiku – Wolters – Wulf – Zathureczky – Zighera – Zimbalist – Zimmermann
Toccata, Adagio & Fugue in C, BWV564 (*org*) *d'Aranyi – Freund*
Weihnachts-Oratorium, BWV248 (1734) – oratorio *Bastien & Borries – Endres – Terebesi*
(Das) Wohltemperirte Clavier, BWV846/93 (*clav*)
   No. 38. Prelude & Fugue No. 14, in F sharp: Prelude, BWV882 – Book II *Spalding (2)*
Bach, Wilhelm Friedemann (1710–1784)
Air (*vln & clav*)†
Neveu
Duet in g (*vln & vla*) *Vorholz*
Sextet in E flat (*cl, 2 hrns, vln, vla & vlc*) *Brink – Ovcharek*
Sonata in F (*fl, vln & c*)‡
Brink
Trio in D, F47 (*fl, vln or 2 vlns & c*) *Vorholz*
Bachmann, Alberto (1875–1963)
Danse hongrois No. 3 (*vln & pf*) *A. Bachmann*
Mazurka brillante No. 2 "L'abeille" (*vln & pf*) *A. Bachmann*
Theme & Variations (*solo vln*) *A. Bachmann*
Zapateado (*vln & pf*) *A. Bachmann*
Bäck, Sven-Erik (1919–)
Quartet No. 2 (1947) (*2 vlns, vla & vlc*) *Barkel & Karpe*
Backer-Grøndahl, Agathe (1847–1907)
Barntes Vaardag (*cycle of 8 songs*) Op. 42 (*v & pf*)
   No. 7. Mot Kvaeld (*At eventide*) *W. Andersen –*

*Arrangement of "Ein Musikalisches Opfer."
†Unidentified.
‡Doubtful.

Brugman – Jelving
Sommarsång (*v & pf*) *W. Andersen*
Badings, Henk (1907–)
Capriccio (1952) (*vln & 2 soundtracks*) *Krebbers – Vermeulen*
Concerto (1954) (*2 vlns & orch*) *Krebbers & Olof*
Sonata No. 1 (1928) (*2 vlns*) *Krebbers & Olof*
Sonata No. 2 (1939) (*vln & pf*) *Juda*
Sonata (1940) (*solo vln*) *Juda (2)*
Baird, Tadeusz (1928–)
Expressions (1959) (*vln & orch*) *Wilkomirska*
Bajoras, F.
Dance (*vln & pf*) *Livontas*
Bakaleinikov, N. R.
Litosc miej! (*Habe mitleid mit mir*) (*v & pf*) *E. Kaufmann*
Balakirev, Mily Alexandrovich (1837–1910)
Octet in c, Op. 3 (*pf, fl, ob, hrn, vln, vla, vlc & cbs*) *Lubotsky*
Polka in f sharp (*pf*) *Goldstein*
(20) Songs (1858) (*v & pf*)
   No. 10. Oh, come to me *Elman*
Balaleinikoff, Vladimir (1885–1953)
Brahmsiana (*vln & pf*) *T. Seidel*
Balasanyan, S.
Shakuntala – ballet (*orch*)
   Lyric dance *Malinin*
   Shakuntala's variations *Malinin*
Balfe, Michael William (1808–1870)
(The) Bohemian Girl (1843) – opera
   Selection *Law*
   Then you'll remember me *d'Almaine (3) – Dolin – Stehl*
Killarney (1862) (*v & pf*) *Southgate – Wethmar*
Ball, Ernest R. (1878–1927)
Let the rest of the world go by (1919) (*v & pf*) *Chamberland*
Ball, Rae Eleanor
Creole serenade (*vln & pf*) *Ball*
Rufus on the Old Kent Road (*vln & pf*) *Ball*
Balogh, Ernö (1897–)
Caprice antique (*pf*) *Kreisler*
Dirge of the north (*pf*) *Kreisler*
Balsys, Edouardas (1919–)
Concerto No. 1, in a (*vln & orch*) *Livontas*
Concerto No. 2, in c (*vln & orch*) *Livontas*
Dramatic frescoes (*vln, pf & orch*) *Livontas*
Eglé, the Queen of Grass-snakes (1960) – ballet (*orch*)
   Adagio *Livontas*
   No. 1. Lament *Livontas*
   No. 2. Dryabulite, a naughty girl *Livontas*
   No. 3. Dance of little fishes *Livontas*
   No. 4. The mermaid *Livontas*
   No. 5. March *Livontas*
Baltin, A. (1931–)
Concerto in g (1964) (*vln & orch*) *Grach*
Bando, Gyula
Concerto hongrois (*vln & orch*) *Ferras*
Banks, Don (1923–)
Trio (*hrn, vln & pf*) *Langbein*
Banner, Michael (1868–)
Fantasia (*on themes by Léonard & Paganini*) (*vln & pf*) *Banner*
Barber, Samuel (1910–)

Concerto, Op. 14 (1941) (*vln & orch*) *Bernard – Gerle – Girdach – Kaufman – Stavonhagen – Stern*

Barbosa, Luiz
Romance (*vln & pf*) *Barbosa*

Barkauskas, V. (1931–   )
Partita (*solo vln*) *Livontas*

Barlow, Fred (1881–1951)
Sonata "Juventa" (*vln & pf*) *Theuveny*
Sonatina (*fl, vln & pf*) *Charmy*

Barnby, Joseph (1838–1896)
Sweet & low (*mixed voices*) *Brown – A. Schmidt – Zimbalist*

Barns, Ethel (1874–1948)
Humoresque (*vln & pf*) *Curti*
Swing song (*vln & pf*) *Chemet – Cochrane – Delmor – Elman – Kennedy – Lorenzo – Perutz – S. Smith*

Baron, Ernst Gottlieb (1696–1760)
Concerto (*lute, vln & bs*) *Trysessoone*

Barraud, Henri (1900–   )
Sonatina (1941) (*vln & pf*) *Garami – Reyes*

Barsukov, Sergei (1923–   )
Concerto No. 2 (*vln & orch*) *Tessier*

Bartholdy, Johan (1853–1904)
Strophe, Op. 30 (*pf*) *Tworek*

Barlett, James Carroll (1845–1920)
(A) Dream (1895) (*v & pf*) *Ball – Chemet – L. Rich*

Bartók, Béla (1881–1945)
Concerto No. 1, Op. posthumous (1908) (*vln & orch*) *Gertler – Kovács – Menuhin – D. Oistrakh – Stern*
Concerto No. 2 (1938) (*vln & orch*)
  Garay – Gertler – Gitlis – Kovács – Menuhin (4) – I. Oistrakh – Rostal – Silverstein – Stern – T. Varga – Ushioda
Concerto (1945) (*vla & orch*) *Menuhin*
Contrasts (1933) (*cl, vln & pf*)
  Altman – Fenyves –Gertler (2) – Grinke – Guilet – Latchem – R. Mann – Pauk – Pikaizen – Ritter – Rosoff – J. Szigeti – Szücs
(44) Duos (1931) (*2 vlns*)
  Aitay & Kuttner – Altmann & Lardinois – Fenyves & V. Martin – Gertler & Suk – Gotkovsky & Menuhin – Gravoin & Manzone – Gründer & Lengyel – Krebbers & Olof – Szücs & Wilkomirska
(10) Easy Pieces (1908) (*pf*)
  No. 5. Este à Székelyeknél *Gerle*
Élégie (*vln & orch*) *Madatov*
For Children (40 pieces) (1909)* (*pf*)
  Garay – Gerle – Gertler – Magyar – D. Oistrakh – I. Oistrakh – J. Szigeti – Wolf – Zathureczky (2)
(2) Portraits ,Op. 5 (1907) (*vln & orch*)
  Bouissinot – Brusilow – Fenyves – Pougnet – Ramor – Schulz – Staryk – J. Szigeti – Wolf – Zathureczky (2)
Quartet No. 2, in a, Op. 17 (1917) (*2 vlns, vla & vlc*) *Amar*
Quartet No. 6, in D (1939) (*2 vlns, vla & vlc*)

Gertler
Rhapsody No. 1, in G (1928) (*vln & orch*)
  Chernykhovsky – Erlih – Gertler – Kovács – Menuhin – Ney – Rubin – Ruha – Spivakov – Stern – J. Szigeti (2) – Totenberg – Ushioda – Vardi – Zhuk
Rhapsody No. 2, in d (1928) (*vln & orch*)
  Chernykhovsky – Erlih – Gertler – Menuhin – Rubin – Shapiro – Snitkovsky – Stern – Vardi – Zhuk
(6) Rumanian folk dances (1915) (*pf*)
  D'Andurain – Barinova – Beilina – Bezrodny – L. Bobescu – Chauveton – Erlih – Fenyves – Fujikawa – Garami – Garnier – Gerle – Gilels – Gimpel – Grumiaux – Haendel (3) – Hidy – Jarry – Kooper – Magyar – Marković – Menuhin (3) – Michelucci – D. Oistrakh – Rosoff – Wolfgang Schneiderhan – Shapiro – Spivakovsky – Székely – Szeryng – J. Szigeti – Totenberg – Vadas – Vaiman – Yordanoff – Zilzer – Zsigmondy
Sonata (1903) (*vln & pf*) *Gertler*
Sonata No. 1 (1921) (*vln & pf*)
  Bonaldi – Bress – Devries – Gertler (2) – Kagen – R. Mann – Menuhin (3) – Stern (2) – Vaiman
Sonata No. 2 (1922) (*vln & pf*)
  Banat – Bonaldi – Bress – Druian – Fenyves – Gertler (2) – Messiereur – Ney – Wolfgang Schneiderhan – Spivakovsky – Stern – J. Szigeti (2)
Sonata in g (1944) (*solo vln*)
  Aloume – Banat – Bress – Erlih – Fenyves – Gertler (2) – Gitlis – R. Mann– Menuhin (2) – Pikaizen – R. Ricci – Silverstein – Tworek – Vadas
Sonatina in D (*on 3 Transylvanian peasant themes*) (1915) (*pf*)*
  Garay – Gerle – Gertler – Komissarov – Sitkovetsky – Zathureczky

Bass, George
Chansonette (*v & pf*) *Fradkin – Kreisler*

Bavicchi, John (1922–   )
Sonata , Op. 39 (*vln & hpsi*) *Brink*
Sonata No. 1 (1956) (*vln & pf*) *Kobialka*

Bax, Arnold (1883–1953)
Ballad (1916) (*vln & pf*) *Holst*
Legend (1915) (*vln & pf*) *Holst*
Mediterranean (1921) (*pf; orch*) *Heifetz*
Sonata No. 1, in E (1910/5) (*vln & pf*) *Holst*
Sonata No. 2, in D (1915) (*vln & pf*) *Holst*
Sonata No. 3, in g (1927) (*vln & pf*) *Holst*

Bayly, Thomas Haynes (1797–1839)
Long, long ago (p.1843) (*v & pf*) *Gardner*

Bazzini, Antonio (1818–1897)
(6) Morceaux lyriques, Op. 35 (*vln & pf*)
  No. 1. Élégie *Goggi – Polo*
(La) Ronde des lutins, Op. 25 (*vln & pf*)
  Accardo – Barbosa – Benedetti – Campoli (2) – Culbertson – Dunn – A. Ferraresi – Francescatti – Gautier – M. Gordon – Haendel – Heifetz (2) – Huberman – Kubelík (2) – Mendels –

  Menuhin – Příhoda (2) – Quiroga – R. Ricci – Rode – Rostal – P. Sanchez – Sens – Sitkovetsky – Spivakovsky – Stanske – Vecsey – Zacharewitsch

Becce, Giuseppe (1881–   )
Légende d'amour, Op. 11 (*pf*) *Boulanger – Fritz-Crone – Galli – Manén*
Serenata Mignonne (*pf*) *Lensky*

Becker, Jean (1833–1884)
Romance in B flat, Op. 3, No. 1 (*vln & pf*) *Walsh*

Becucci, Ernesto (1845–1905)
Tesoro mio – waltz, Op. 228 (*orch*) *André – Anonymous – Dessau – Mánnok – May – Mendels*

Beethoven, Ludwig van (1770–1827)
Allegretto* *Principi*
(6) Allemandes, G171 (*WoO.42*) (*vln & pf*)
  Allemande No. 1, in F *Rosand*
  Allemande No. 2, in D *Rosand*
  Allemande No. 3, in F *Rosand*
  Allemande No. 4, in A *Rosand*
  Allemande No. 5, in D *Rosand*
  Allemande No. 6, in G *Rosand*
Andante in F, G170 "Andante favori" (*pf*) *Kreisler*
Concerto in C, Op. 56 "Triple" (*vln, vlc, pf & orch*)
  Corigliano – Erlih – Gimpel – Laredo – Odnoposoff – D. Oistrakh (5) – Wolfgang Schneiderhan – Stern – Szeryng
Concerto in D, Op. 61 (*vln & orch*)
  Balachowski – Belayeff – Bezrodny – Borgani – Borries – A. Busch – Campoli (2) – Carazza – Cyroulnik – Elman – Ferras (2) – Francescatti (2) – Freund – Gavrilov – Gimpel – Grumiaux (2) – Gulli – Haendel – Heifetz (2) – Huberman – Karpilowski – Klepper, Klimov, L. Kogan (4) – Kovács – Krebbers – Kreisler (2) – Kulenkampff – Lautenbacher – Loveday – Marschner – Menges – Menuhin (4) – Merckel – Milstein (2) – Mischakoff – D. Oistrakh (3) – I. Oistrakh (2) – Ozim – Queling (2) – R. Ricci – Rudényi – Wolfgang Schneiderhan (2) – Spalding – Stern – Strub – Suk (2) – Szeryng (3) – J. Szigeti (3) – Taschner – Totenberg – T. Varga – Waldman – Wolfsthal – Zimmermann
(12) Contretänze, G141 (*orch*)
  Contratanz No. 1, in C *Elman (2) – Goldstein*
(12) Deutsche Tänze, G140 (*WoO.8*) (*orch*)
  Deutscher Tanz No. 6, in G *Goldstein – Heifetz*
Duet in E flat, WoO.32 (1796) "2 obbligato eyeglasses" (*vla & vlc*) *Rosoff*
Élégie (*pf*)† *F.V. Henriques*
(25) Irish songs, G223 (1813) (*v, pf, vln & vlc*)
  No. 1. The return to Ulster *Frenkel*
  No. 3. Once more I hail thee *Frenkel*
  No. 4. The morning air *Frenkel*
  No. 5. The massacre of Glencoe *Frenkel*
  No. 21. Morning a cruel turmoiler is *Frenkel*
(20) Irish songs, G224 (1813) (*v, pf, vln & vlc*)

*Unidentified.
†Unidentified.

---

*Revised & re-numbered 1945.

*Transcribed for vln & pf in 1931 by André Gertler.

No. 4. The pulse of an Irishman *Frenkel*
No. 5. Oh! who, my dear Dermot *Frenkel*
Mass in D, Op. 123 "Missa Solemnis" *Corigliano*
– Hanke – Schwalbé
(6) Minuets, G167 (*pf*)
Minuet No. 2, in G
Aguiar – Andjelkovitch – Ball – Belov – Boshko
– Breeskin – Brown – D. De Groot – Elman (4)
– Eweler – Farbmann – Fradkin – Gade –
Goldin – Gootjes – Guidi – M. Hall – A.
Kaufmann – Kerekjarto – Kreisler – Lorand (2)
– MacMillen – Menuhin – Michaïlow – Nadien
– Noceti – D. Oistrakh – Parlow (3) – Polinski –
R. Pollak – Powell – Příhoda – Principi –
Reillie – K. Reuter – L. Rich – Sammons (2) –
Spalding – Stanske – Strockoff – J. Szigeti –
Telmányi – Tworek – Viólin – F. Weltmann –
Zimbalist
(6) Minuets, WoO.9 (*2 vlns & cbs*)
Minuet No. 1, in E flat *Holtman & Schröder*
Minuet No. 2, in G *Holtman & Schröder*
Minuet No. 3, in C *Holtman & Schröder*
Minuet No. 4, in F *Holtman & Schröder*
Minuet No. 5, in D *Holtman & Schröder*
Minuet No. 6, in G *Holtman & Schröder*
Quartet No. 4, in E flat, Op. 16 (*pf, vln, vla*
& vlc)* *Accardo – Eidus – Goldberg*
(6) Quartets, Op. 18 (*2 vlns, vla & vlc*)
No. 1. Quartet No. 1, in F *Catterall*
No. 2. Quartet No. 2, in G *Catterall*
No. 4. Quartet No. 4, in c *Galimir & Morini –*
A.J. Rose
No. 5. Quartet No. 5, in A *Catterall*
No. 6. Quartet No. 6, in B flat *Hayward*
(3) Quartets, Op. 59 "Rasumovsky" (*2 vlns, vla &*
vlc)
No. 1. Quartet No. 7, in F *Sitkovetsky*
No. 2. Quartet No. 8, in e *Hayward*
No. 3. Quartet No. 9, in C *Hayward*
Quartet No. 10, in E flat, Op. 74 "Harp" (*2 vlns,*
vla & vlc) *D. Oistrakh – A.J. Rose – Rybar –*
Wolfgang Schneiderhan
Quartet No. 11, in f, Op. 95 (*2 vlns, vla & vlc*)
Amar
Quartet No. 12, in E flat, Op. 127 (*2 vlns, vla &*
vlc) *Hayward*
Quartet No. 14, in c sharp, Op. 131 (*2 vlns, vla &*
vlc) *A.J. Rose*
Quartet No. 15, in a, Op. 132 (*2 vlns, vla & vlc*)
Peška
Romance No. 1, in G, Op. 40 (*vln & orch*)
Borries – Boskovsky – Chemet – Constantinescu
– Dumont – Elman – Ferras – Field –
Francescatti – Fuchs – Gavrilov – Geyer –
Gimpel – Grumiaux (2) – Heifetz – Iwamoto –
Kennedy – Georg Kniestaedt – Koeckert – Koene
– L. Kogan – Kovács – Kulenkampff –
Lautenbacher – Malinin – Marschner – Martzy
– Menuhin (3) – D. Oistrakh (2) – I. Oistrakh –
Olof – Ozim – Plocek – Röhn (2) – Rostal –
Walther Schneiderhan – Wolfgang Schneiderhan

*Arrangement of the quintet of the same opus for
pf, ob, cl, bsn & hrn.

– Spalding – Suk – Szeryng – Telmányi – Unno
– T. Varga – Verhey – Yashkin – Zilzer –
Zimbalist – Zimmermann
Romance No. 2, in F, Op. 50 (*vln & orch*)
Bor – Borries (2) – Boskovsky – Bouquet – Bress
– Constantinescu – De Vito – Dumont – Elman
– Ferras – Field – Francescatti – Fuchs –
Garnier – Gavrilov (2) – Gimpel – Grumiaux (2)
– Heifetz – Iwamoto – Kaul – Koeckert – L.
Kogan – Krachmalnick – Krebbers –
Kulenkampff – Lautenbacher – Lewkowitz –
Marschner – Martzy – Menuhin (3) – Milstein –
D. Oistrakh (4) – I. Oistrakh – Ozim – Plocek –
Röhn (2) – A.J. Rose – Rostal – Walther
Schneiderhan – Wolfgang Schneiderhan –
Senatra (2) – Spalding – Stiehler – Suk –
Swaap – Szeryng – Telmányi – Thibaud –Unno
– Wittels – Wittenberg – Wolfsthal – Yashkin –
Zilzer – Zimmermann
Rondo in G, G155 (*vln & pf*) *Grach – Menuhin*
(2) – Rosand – Rostal
(Die) Ruinen von Athen, Op. 113 – Incidental
music (*orch*)
No. 3. Chor der Derwische *Enescu – S. Furer –*
Heifetz – R. Ricci – Spivakovsky – Strokoff –
Zilzer
No. 4. Marcia alla turca
Accardo – Elman – Heifetz – L. Kogan –
Menuhin – Piastro – Příhoda (2) – T. Seidel –
Spivakovsky
(25) Scottish songs, Op. 108 (1815) (*v, pf, vln &*
vlc)
No. 2. Sunset (*The sun upon the Weirlaw Hill*)
Frenkel
No. 3. O sweet were the hours *Frenkel*
No. 7. Bonny laddie, highland laddie *Frenkel*
No. 8. The lovely lass of Inverness *Frenkel*
No. 14. O how can I be blithe & glad? *Frenkel*
No. 16. Could this ill world have been
contrived? *Frenkel*
No. 17. O Mary, at thy window be *Frenkel*
No. 20. Faithful Johnny *Frenkel*
No. 24. Again my lyre *Frenkel*
Septet in E flat, Op. 20 (*cl, hrn, bsn, vln, vla, vlc*
& cbs) *Catterall – L. Hansen*
Serenade in D, Op. 8 (*vln, vla & vlc*)
Fuchs – Goldberg – Grumiaux – Heifetz – Jarry
– Lautenbacher – Marschner – Pougnet – Röhn
Serenade in D, Op. 25 (*fl, vln & vla*)
Bruun – Darrieux – Fuchs – Grumiaux – Jarry
– Klingler – Koppel – D. Oistrakh – Schneider
Sextet in E flat, Op. 81 (*2 vlns, vla, vlc & 2 hrns*)
Daneman & Zhuk
Sonata No. 8, in c, Op. 13 "Pathétique" (*pf*)
Hayward – Ranzato (2) – Stülken – Swaap –
Zimmermann
Sonata No. 12, in A flat, Op. 26 (*pf*)
Marcia funebra (*3rd mvt*) *Gardner*
(2) Sonatas, Op. 27 (*pf*)
No. 2. Sonata No. 14, in c sharp "Moonlight"
Hager – Kerekjarto
(3) Sonatas, Op. 12 (*vln & pf*)
No. 1. Sonata No. 1, in D
Accardo – Boskovsky – Ferras (2) – Fournier –
Francescatti – Fuchs – Fujikawa – Gerle –

Grumiaux – Gulli – Heifetz – Kaul – L. Kogan
– Kreisler – Makanowitzky – Menuhin (3) – D.
Oistrakh (2) – I. Oistrakh – R. Pollak – Rosand
– Wolfgang Schneiderhan (2) – Suk – J. Szigeti
(2) – Totenberg – Vaiman
No. 2. Sonata No. 2, in A
Bernstein – Boskovsky – Ferras (2) – Fournier –
Francescatti – Fuchs – Gerle – Goldberg –
Grumiaux – Gulli – Hagen – Heifetz – Kreisler
– Lautenbacher – Makanowitzky – Menuhin (2)
– D. Oistrakh – I. Oistrakh – Plocek – Rosand
– Rostal – Walther Schneiderhan – Wolfgang
Schneiderhan (2) – Shkolnikova – Staryk – Suk
– J. Szigeti
No. 3. Sonata No. 3, in E flat
Ajemian – Boskovsky – A. Busch – Cyroulnik –
Feigin – Ferras (2) – Fournier – Francescatti (2)
– Fuchs – Gerle – Grumiaux – Gulli – Heifetz-
(2) – Kaul – Kim – Klimov – L. Kogan –
Kreisler – Makanowitzky – Menuhin (3) – D.
Oistrakh (2) – I. Oistrakh – Plocek – Rosand –
Wolfgang Schneiderhan (2) – Suk – J. Szigeti –
Vecsey
Sonata No. 4, in a, Op. 23 (*vln & pf*)
Bernstein – Boskovsky – Ferras (2) – Fournier –
Francescatti (2) – Fuchs – Gerle – Grumiaux –
Gulli – Heifetz – Kling – Kovács – Kreisler –
Makanowitzky – Menuhin (2) – Odnoposoff – D.
Oistrakh (2) – I. Oistrakh – Petrosyan – Plocek
– Rosand – Rostal – Wolfgang Schneiderhan (2)
– Suk – J. Szigeti
Sonata No. 5, in F, Op. 24 "Spring" (*vln & pf*)
Berg – Bernstein –E. Bloch – Borries –
Boskovsky – A. Busch – Catterall –
Constantinescu – Devries – Drescher – Elman –
Engels – Ferras (3) – Fournier – Francescatti –
Fuchs – Gavrilov – Gerle – Goldberg – Goldstein
– Grumiaux – Gulli (2) – Heifetz – Jarry –
Karpilowski – Kaul – Klijn – Kling – Kolberg –
Kreisler – Kulenkampff – Lautenbacher – Lener
– Lorand – Loveday – Makanowitzky –
Marschner – Massia – Menuhin (3) – Milstein
(2) – Moguilevski – Morini (2) – Nerini –
Oehler – D. Oistrakh (2) – I. Oistrakh – Plocek
– Rosand – Rostal – Sammons – Wolfgang
Schneiderhan (2) – Suk – Szeryng (2) – J.
Szigeti (3) – Totenberg – Villa – Weiner –
Weissgerber – Wolf – Zathureczky – Zeiler
(3) Sonatas, Op. 30 (*vln & pf*)
No. 1. Sonata No. 6, in A
Boskovsky – Fenyves – Ferras (2) – Fournier –
Francescatti – Fuchs – Gerle – Goldberg –
Grumiaux – Gulli – Heifetz – Klijn – Kreisler –
Lener – Makanowitzky – Menuhin (2) – D.
Oistrakh – I. Oistrakh – Rosand – Rostal –
Wolfgang Schneiderhan (2) – Suk – J. Szigeti
(2) – Totenberg
No. 2. Sonata No. 7, in c
Boskovsky – Bress – A. Busch – De Vito –
Dubois – Ferras (2) – Fournier – Francescatti
(2) – Fuchs – Gerle – Grumiaux – Gulli –
Heifetz – Isakadze – L. Kogan – Kreisler –
Krysa – Loveday – Makanowitzky – Menuhin
(4) – Morini – D. Oistrakh (2) – I. Oistrakh –
Plocek – R. Ricci – Rosand – Rostal – Walther

Schneiderhan – Wolfgang Schneiderhan (3) –
Snitkovsky – Stern – Suk – J. Szigeti (2) –
Vaiman
No. 3. Sonata No. 8, in G
Airoff – Bean – E. Bloch – Boskovsky –
Drescher – Ferras (2) – Fournier – Francescatti
(2) – Fuchs – Gerle – Grumiaux – Gulli –
Haendel – Heifetz (2) – Kreisler (2) – Loveday
– Makanowitzky – Martzy – Menuhin (3) –
Milstein (2) – Morini – Odnoposoff – D.
Oistrakh (2) – I. Oistrakh – Plocek – Rosand –
Rostal – Wolfgang Schneiderhan (2) –
Shkolnikova – Spivakovsky – Suk – Szeryng – J.
Szigeti (2) – Verdon – Zathureczky (2)
Sonata No. 9, in A, Op. 47 "Kreutzer" (*vln & pf*)
Accardo – Ajemian – Barbieri – Bean – E.
Bloch – Boskovsky – A. Busch – Catterall –
Colbentson – Crut – Cyroulnik – De Vito –
Drescher – Elman – Enescu – Fenyves – Ferras
(2) – Fournier – Francescatti (2) – Fuchs –
Gerle – Goldberg – Grumiaux – Gulli –
Hayward – Heifetz (2) – Huberman (2) – Klijn
– Klimov – L. Kogan – Kovács – Kreisler –
Kroll – Kulenkampff (3) – Lass – Lautenbacher
– Loveday – Makanowitzky – Marschner –
Menges – Menuhin (5) – Milstein – Oehler – D.
Oistrakh (3) – I. Oistrakh – Plocek – Polyakin –
Rosand – Rostal – Sammons – Walther
Schneiderhan – Wolfgang Schneiderhan (2) –
Spalding – Suk – Szeryng (2) – J. Szigeti (3) –
Telmányi – Thibaud – Unno – Villa – Weiner –
Wolf – Zathureczky – Zeiler
Sonata No. 10, in G, Op. 96 (*vln & pf*)
Boskovsky – Engels – Fachiri – Ferras (2) –
Fournier – Francescatti – Fuchs – Gerle –
Goldberg – Grumiaux – Gulli (2) – Hayward –
Heifetz – Kreisler – Makanowitzky – Menuhin
(5) – D. Oistrakh (2) – I. Oistrakh – Plocek –
R. Ricci – Rosand – Rostal – Wolfgang
Schneiderhan (2) – Shkolnikova – Spivakovsky –
Suk – J. Szigeti (2) – Totenberg – Vaiman
(3) Trios, Op. 1 (*pf, vln & vlc*)
No. 1. Trio No. 1, in E flat
Bělčík – Dessau – Diedrichsen – Feigin –
Fournier – Fuchs – Guilet – Hayward – Heifetz
– Stern – Szeryng – Totenberg – Wilk –
Zukerman
No. 2. Trio No. 2, in G
Diedrichsen – Guilet – Hayward – Posselt –
Sammons – Schneider – Stern – Szeryng – L.
Wolff – Zukerman
No. 3. Trio No. 3, in c
Benedetti – Catterall (2) – Diedrichsen –
Fournier – D. Oistrakh – Stern – Strub – Suk –
Szeryng – Totenberg – Wolfsthal – Zeiler –
Zukerman
Trio No. 1, in E flat, Op. 3 (*vln, vla & vlc*)
Grumiaux – Heifetz
L. Kogan – Lautenbacher – Pougnet
(3) Trios, Op. 9 (*vln, vla & vlc*)
No. 1. Trio No. 2, in G *Grumiaux – Heifetz –*
L. Kogan – Lautenbacher – Posselt – Pougnet
No. 2. Trio No. 3, in D *Grach – Grumiaux –*
Heifetz – L. Kogan – Lautenbacher – Pougnet
No. 3. Trio No. 4, in c *Fuchs – Grumiaux –*

Heifetz – L. Kogan – Lautenbacher – Pougnet
Trio in B flat, Op. 11 (*cl, vlc & pf*)
Accardo – Diedrichsen – Fournier – Grach –
Hayward – Pelliccia – Schneider – Stern –
Totenberg – Tziganov – Wolfsthal
(2) Trios, Op. 70 (*pf, vln & vlc*)
No. 1. Trio No. 4, in D "Ghost"
A. Busch – Diedrichsen – Fournier – Fuchs –
Gendre – Gruenberg – Menuhin (2) – D.
Oistrakh – Pelliccia – Poltronieri – Posselt –
Schneeberger – Stern – Strub – Suk – Szeryng –
Wilk – Zukerman
No. 2. Trio No. 5, in E flat
Diedrichsen – Feigin – Gendre – Grinke – L.
Kogan – Menuhin – Schneider – Stern –
Szeryng – Totenberg – Wilk – Zukerman
Trio No. 6, in B flat, Op. 97 "Archduke" (*pf, vln*
& vlc)
Bean – Diedrichsen – Feigin – Fournier – Grach
– Heifetz – Holst – Jarry – L. Kogan – Loveday
– D. Oistrakh – Pelliccia – Sammons –
Schneider – Stern (2) – Suk (2) – Szeryng –
Thibaud – Zeiler – Zukerman
Trio in E flat, G153 (WoO38) (*pf, vln & vlc*)
Diedrichsen – Feigin – L. Kogan – Stern –
Zukerman
Trio in B flat, G154 (WoO39) "In one
movement" (*pf, vln & vlc*) *Diedrichsen – Gendre –*
Gimpel – Guilet – Sammons – Stern – Szeryng –
Zukerman
(14) Variations in E flat, Op. 44 (*pf, vln & vlc*)
Diedrichsen – Feigin – Stern – Szeryng –
Zukerman
(6) Variations (*on very easy themes*) Op. 105 (*pf &*
vln or fl) *Glatte*
(10) Variations (*on national themes*) Op. 107 (*pf,*
vln or fl) *Glatte*
(10) Variations (*on "Ich bin der Schneider*
Kakadu") Op. 121a (*pf, vln & vlc*)
E. Bloch – Diedrichsen – Feigin – Pelliccia –
Senofsky – Stern – Szeryng – Totenberg –
Zukerman
(12) Variations in F (*on the aria "Se vuol ballare"*
from the opera "Le Nozze di Figaro" by Mozart)
G156 (*vln & pf*) *Menuhin – Rosand*
(11) Wiener Tänze, WoO17 (*orch*)
No. 1. Waltz in E flat *Brainin*
No. 3. Waltz in B flat *Brainin*
No. 11. Waltz in D *Brainin*
Bellini, Vincenzo (1801–1835)
(La) Sonnambula (1831) – opera
excerpt*
Fredericks
Prendi l'anel ti dono *Ranzato (2)*
Benatzky, Ralph (1884–1957)
Angoisse d'amour (*Einmal kommt der Tag*) (*orch*)
E. Kaufmann – Kellert
Ich muss wieder einmal in Grinzing sein
(*Walzerlied*) (*v & pf*) *A. Sandler*
Ich weiss auf der Wieden ein kleines Hotel –
walzer (*v & pf*) *Streletzky*
Im weissen Rössl (1936) – operetta†

*Unidentified.
†Composed jointly with Robert Stolz. The work is
better known as "The White Horse Inn."

Es muss was Wunderbares sein *Curti*
(Ein) Wiener Walzer (*orch*) *Tak – Velt*
Benda, František (1709–1786)
Concerto in A (*vln & orch*) *Strub*
Sonata in A (*vln & pf*) *Stědřon*
Benda, Jiří Antonín (*Georg*) (1722–1795)
Trio-sonata in E (*2 vlns & c*) *D. & I. Oistrakh*
Benedict, Julius (1804–1885)
(La) Carnevale di Venizia – variations (*v & pf*)
Rudenyi (2)
Ben-Haim, Paul (1897–   )
Berceuse (*vln & pf*) *Parnes*
Sonata in G (*vln & pf*) *Harth*
Benjamin, Arthur (1893–1960)
From San Domingo (1945) (*orch*) *Elman (2)*
(2) Jamaican pieces (1940) (*orch*)
No. 2. Jamaican rumba *Heifetz (2) – Stern –*
Suk – Wicks
Romantic Fantasy (1935) (*vln, vla & orch*) *Heifetz*
Sonatina (1925) (*vln & pf*) *Grinke*
Bennett, Robert Russell (1894–   )
Hexapoda (*5 Studies in Jitteroptera*) (1941) (*vln &*
pf) *Heifetz – Kaufman*
(A) Song Sonata (*vln & pf*) *Heifetz – Kaufman*
Bentoiu, Pascal (1927–   )
Concerto, Op. 9 (1958) (*vln & orch*) *Gheorghiu*
Bentzon, Niels Viggo (1919–   )
Capriccietta, Op. 28 (*vln & pf*) *Bohn*
V3, Op. 35 (1945) (*vln & pf*) *Bohn*
Berg, Alban (1885–1935)
Chamber Concerto (1925) (*pf, vln & 13 w-wnds*)
Baker – Charmy – Ferras – Gavrilov – Gitlis – I.
Štraus
Concerto (1935) (*vln & orch*)
Ferras – Garay – Gertler – Gitlis – Goldberg –
Grumiaux – L. Kogan – Krasner – Menuhin –
Stern – Suk – Szeryng – Wroński
Berger, Arthur (1912–   )
Duo No. 2 (*vln & pf*) *Erle*
Serenade concertante (1944 – *rev*. 1951) (*orch*)
Brink
Berger, Wilhelm Georg (1929–   )
Sonata (1964) (*solo vln*) *Berger*
Bergh, Arthur (1882–1962)
Evening (*vln & pf*) *Jacobsen*
Scherzo (*vln & pf*) *Bergh*
Bergsma, William (1921–   )
Concerto (*vln & orch*) *Statkiewicz*
Berio, Luciano (1925–   )
(2) Pieces (1951) (*vln & pf*) *Gavrilov*
Bériot, Charles August de (1802–1870)
Adagio* *Poltronieri*
(6) Airs varié, Op. 12 (*vln & pf*)
Air varié No. 6, in a *d'Almaine (3)*
Concerto No. 2, in b, Op. 32 (*vln & orch*)
d'Almaine – Gardner – Hager – Spalding
Concerto No. 7, in G, Op. 76 (*vln & orch*)
Fabroni – Law – Powell
Concerto No. 9, in a, Op. 104 (*vln & orch*)

*Unidentified. Possibly the 2nd mvt. from
"Concerto No. 7, in G," Op. 76.

Modern

Scène de Ballet (*Fantaisie-ballet No. 1*) Op. 100 (*vln & orch*) *Hager – Law – Luquin – Polo – Taschke*

Berkeley, Lennox Randal Francis (1903–   )

Sonatina in A, Op. 17 (1942) (*vln & pf*) *Davison – Grinke*

Theme & Variations, Op. 33, No. 1 (*solo vln*) *Grinke*

Trio (1944) (*vln, vla & vlc*) *Pougnet – Röhn*

Trio in e, Op. 19 (1952) (*vln, hrn & pf*) *Parikian*

Berlin, Irving (1888–   )

Always (1925) (*v & pf*) *Ball*

Because I love you (1926) (*v & pf*) *Andjelkovitch*

Blue skies (1927) (*v & pf*) *Kreisler*

Remember (1925) (*v & pf*) *Ball*

Rememb'ring (*Topsy & Eva*) (1923) (*v & pf*) *Förster*

Russian lullaby (*v & pf*) *Fradkin – Jacobsen*

What does it matter? (1927) (*v & pf*) *Fradkin*

What'll I do? (1924) (*v & pf*) *Ball*

When I lost you (1912) (*v & pf*) *d'Almaine*

White Christmas (1942) (*v & pf*) *Heifetz*

Berlioz, Hector (1803–1869)

Harold in Italy, Op. 16 (*vla & orch*) *Menuhin*

Rêverie & Caprice, Op. 8 (1839) (*vln & orch*) *Grumiaux – Menuhin – Rosand – J. Szigeti*

Bernhardt, Christoph (1627–1692)

Fürchtet euch Nicht – cantata (*s & strs*) *Bruun*

Berniaux, Désiré (1889–   )

Wenn ich dein Herz gewonnen (*vln & pf*) *Pinell*

Bernier, Nicolas (1664–1734)

Agréable Caffé "Coffee cantata" (1703) (*v, vln & c*) *Kohon*

Bacchus – cantata *Fernadez*

Bernstein, Leonard (1918–   )

Serenade (1954) (*vln, hp, pcn & str orch*) *Francescatti – Stern*

Bertali, Antonio (1605–1669)

Sonata in E (*2 vlns & c*) *Kiujken & Rubinlicht*

Bertheaume, Isidore (1752–1802)

(2) Sinfonia concertantes, Op. 6 (1787) (*2 vlns & orch*)

Sinfonia concertante No. 1, in G *Doukan & Gendre – Fiorito & Kempler*

Sinfonia concertante No. 2, in E flat *Fernandez & Germaine Raymond*

Bervily

Isabella (*v & pf*) *Schwartz*

Berwald, Johan (1787–1861)

Quartet No. 3, in E flat (1849) (*2 vlns, vla & vlc*) *Kyndel*

Quintet No. 1, in c, Op. 5 (*pf, 2 vlns, vla & vlc*) *Kyndel*

(3) Trios, Op. 1 (1845) (*pf, vln & vlc*)
No. 3. Trio No. 3, in d *Andreasson*

Bethier

Petite serenade (*vln & pf*) *Zimbalist*

Biber, Heinrich von (1644–1704)

(16) Biblical Sonatas (1674) "Mysterien" (*vln & c*)
Sonata No. 1, in d "The annunciation of the birth of Christ" *W. Koch – Lautenbacher – Melkus – Monosoff*
Sonata No. 2, in A "Visit of Mary to Elizabeth" *W. Koch – Lautenbacher – Melkus –*

Monosoff
Sonata No. 3, in b "Birth of Christ" *W. Koch – Lautenbacher – Melkus – Monosoff*
Sonata No. 4, in d "Christ in the temple" *W. Koch – Lautenbacher – Melkus – Monosoff*
Sonata No. 5, in A "The 12 year-old Jesus in the temple" *Lautenbacher – Melkus – Monosoff*
Sonata No. 6, in c "Christ on the Mount of Olives" *Grehling – Lautenbacher – Melkus – Monosoff – G. Strauss*
Sonata No. 7, in F "The Flagellation of Christ" *Lautenbacher – Melkus – Monosoff*
Sonata No. 8, in B flat "Christ's crowning with thorns" *Lautenbacher – Melkus – Monosoff*
Sonata No. 9, in a "Christ on the way to Calvary" *Grehling – Lautenbacher – Melkus – Monosoff*
Sonata No. 10, in g "The Crucifixion" *Grehling – Lautenbacher – Melkus – Monosoff*
Sonata No. 11, in G "The Resurrection" *Lautenbacher – Melkus – Monosoff*
Sonata No. 12, in C "The Ascension" *Lautenbacher – Melkus – Monosoff*
Sonata No. 13, in d "The Emanation of the Holy Ghost" *Lautenbacher – Melkus – Monosoff*
Sonata No. 14, in D "The Ascension of the Holy Virgin" *Lautenbacher – Melkus – Monosoff*
Sonata No. 15, in C "Coronation of the Virgin" *Lautenbacher – Melkus – Monosoff*
Sonata No. 16, in g "The Guardian Angel" (*solo vln*)*

Lautenbacher – Melkus – Monosoff – Rostal

(7) Partitas "Harmonia artificiosa-ariosa" (*2 vlns & c*)
Partita No. 1, in d *Harnoncourt & Pfeiffer*
Partita No. 3, in a *Harnoncourt & Pfeiffer*
Partita No. 5, in g *Harnoncourt & Pfeiffer*
Partita No. 6, in D *Harnoncourt & Pfeiffer*

Serenade in C "Der Nachtwächter" (*bs-v, 2 vlns, 2 vlas & c*) *Bünte & Hendel*

(8) Sonatas (1681) (*vln & c*)
Sonata No. 1, in A *Monosoff*
Sonata No. 2, in d *Monosoff*
Sonata No. 3, in F *Monosoff*
Sonata No. 4, in D *Monosoff – Roberts*
Sonata No. 5, in e *Monosoff*
Sonata No. 6, in c *Gabowitz – Monosoff*
Sonata No. 7, in g *Monosoff*
Sonata No. 8, in A *Monosoff*

van Biene, August (1850–1913)

Broken melody (*vlc & pf*) *Brown – Zimbalist*

Billi, Vincenzo (1869–1938)

Campane à sera (*vln or mand & pf*) *Curti – di Piramo – Rappaini – Schwartz*

Cintia (*vln or mand & pf*) *di Piramo*

Serenata alle rondini (*vln or mand & pf*) *di Piramo*

Topsy "Arabesca" (*vln or mand & pf*) *di Piramo*

Bishop, Henry Rowley (1786–1855)

Clari (1823) – opera
Home, sweet home *Kerekjarto – Opfermann –*

*Known as "Passacaglia."

S. Smith

Bizet, Georges (1838–1875)

Agnus Dei (*v & pf*)*
Debruille – Fradkin – Leopold

(L') Arlésienne (*Suite No. 1*) (1872) – Incidental music (*orch*)
No. 3. Adagietto *Kreisler – Soriano – Spalding*

(L') Arlésienne (*Suite No. 2*) (1872) – Incidental music (*orch*)
No. 2. Intermezzo *Kreisler – Spalding*
No. 7. Minuet *Fichtenholz*

Chanson d'avril (1866) (*v & pf*) *Zarius Shikhmurzayeva*

Pastorale (1868) (*v & pf*) *Zarius Shikhmurzayeva*

(Les) Pêcheurs de Perles (1863) – opera
A cette voix … Je crois entendre encore (*Romance de Nadir*) *Dinicu – Piastro*

Vieille chanson (1865) (*v & pf*) *Zarius Shikhmurzayeva*

Björkander, Nils (1893–   )

Cavatina (*vln & orch*) *Ericson*

Blaauw, Pierre

(The) Clock is playing (*pf*) *Dajos – Kellert*

Black, Johnny Stewart

Dardanella (1919) (*pf*) *Jacobsen*

Blackwood, Easley (1933–   )

Concerto , Op. 21 (*vln & orch*) *Kling*

Blake, Eubie (1883–   )

I'm just wild about Harry (1921) (*v & pf*) *Haxton*

Bland, James A. (1854–1911)

Carry me back to old Virginny (1878) (*v & cho*) *MacMurray*

Blaufuss, Walter E. (1883–1945)

My isle of golden dreams (1919) (*v & pf*) *Brown*

Your eyes have told me so (1919) (*v & pf*) *Brown*

Blech, Leo (1871–1958)

Alpenkönig and Menschenfiend, Op. 14 – opera
Prelude (*orch*) *Dessau*

Bleyle, Karl (1880–1969)

Quartet in a, Op. 37 (1925) (*2 vlns, vla & vlc*) *Havemann & Steiner*

Bliss, Arthur (1891–   )

Concerto (1953) (*vln & orch*) *Campoli*

Theme & Cadenza (1949) (*vln & orch*) *Campoli*

Bloch, Ernest (1880–1959)

Abodah (*God's worship*) (1929) (*vln & pf*) *Bress – Haendel – Menuhin*

Baal Shem (*3 Pictures of Chassidic life*) (1923) (*vln & pf*) *Bress – Neaman – Pavlovič – Stern – J. Szigeti*
No. 1. Vidui (*Contrition*) *Grumliková – Kash – Koene*
No. 2. Nigun (*Improvisation*)
Accardo – Beilina – Bezrodny – Castillo – R. Cohen – Elman (3) – Erlih – Ferras – Fournier – S. Furer – Haendel – Harth (2) – Hidy – Jásek – L. Kogan (2) – Kooper – Lewkowitz – Magyar – Menuhin – Milstein (2) – Olof – Spivakovsky – Stern – J. Szigeti – Wicks – Wunder – Zhuk – Zighera – Zukerman

Concerto in a (1938) (*vln & orch*) *Bress – J. Szigeti – Totenberg*

*Vocal arrangement of the Intermezzo or no. 2 from the "L'Arlésienne Suite No. 2."

Bozza, Eugène Joseph (1905–)
Rapsodie niçoise (*vln & orch*) *Merckel*
Braga, Gaetano (1829–1907)
Meditazione (*vlc or vln & pf*) *Ranzato (2)*
(7) Melodies (1867) (*v & pf*)
No. 5. La serenata "Angel's serenade"
Anonymous – de Brayne – Charmy – Dajos – F.
De Groot – Dessau (2) – Elman (2) – Fradkin –
Gittelson – B. Hall – Hayward (3) – Kreisler –
J.M. Lasowski – Livschakoff – Mendels –
Morino – Ranzato (3) – Rattay – Rosen –
Rudényi – Sänger – T. Seidel – Spalding – Stehl
– Swaap – Szemere – Weintraub – J. Wolff –
Zilzer – Zimbalist
Brahms, Johannes (1833–1897)
Concerto in D, Op. 77 (*vln & orch*)
Andrade – Auclair – De Vito (2) – Ferras (2) –
Francescatti (2) – Gimpel – Grumiaux –
Haendel – Heifetz (2) – Huberman – L. Kogan
(3) – Krebbers – Kreisler (2) – Kulenkampff (2)
– Lautenbacher – Manke – Martzy – Menuhin
(2) – Milstein (2) – Mischakoff – Morini –
Neveu – Odnoposoff – D. Oistrakh (4) – I.
Oistrakh – Olevsky – Renardy – Rybar –
Walther Schneiderhan – Wolfgang Schneiderhan
(3) – Senofsky – Shumsky – Spalding – Stern
(2) – Stevens – Szeryng (2) – J. Szigeti (3) – R.
Varga – Wolf – Wroński
Concerto in a, Op. 102 "Double" (*vln, vlc & orch*)
Campoli – De Vito – Erlih – Ferras – Fournier
– Francescatti – Gimpel – Heifetz (2) –
Kulenkampff – Milstein – Mischakoff – D.
Oistrakh (4) – Ozim – Prinz – Wolfgang
Schneiderhan (2) – Stern (2) – Suk – Szeryng –
Thibaud
(21) Hungarian dances (*pf duet*)
Hungarian dance*
d'Almaine – Gyarfas – Kneisel – Moll
Hungarian dance No. 1, in g
Auer – Bezrodny – Bress – Deutsch – Fain –
Fairhurst – Gerle – Goluboff – Heifetz –
Hoffman – Huberman (2) – Joachim – Klimov
– Kochański – L. Kogan – Komissarov –
Kozolupova – Lorand – Manuello – Menuhin –
Morini – Neumann – I. Oistrakh – Pierangeli –
T. Seidel (3) – Spalding (3) – Spivakovsky –
Stosch – Telmányi
Hungarian dance No. 2, in d
A. Busch – Catterall – Deman – Dessau (2) –
Fachiri – Garaguly – Gerle – Godwin – Gresser
– Hagen – Joachim – Kennedy – Kersey –
Georg Kniestaedt – L. Kogan – Kortschak –
Liberman – Mánnok – Manuello – Menges –
Milstein (2) – Minghetti – Mitnitzky –
Reittinger – Sechiari – Sens – Spalding (2) –
Valesca-Becker – Ware – Weissgerber – Woiku
– Wolfsthal
Hungarian dance No. 3, in F *Catterall – Gerle*
– Hagen – Hayward – D. Oistrakh – Schmuller
– Spalding
Hungarian dance No. 4, in f *Accardo – Gerle –*
C. Hansen – L. Kogan – Menuhin (2) –
Spalding – Spivakovsky – Staryk

*Unidentified

Hungarian dance No. 5, in f sharp
Alos – Anonymous – D'Aranyi – A. Busch –
Culbertson – M. De Groot (2) – Fredericks –
Gautier – Gerle – Ghestem – Godowsky –
Goldin – Guidi – Gyarfas – Hayward – Hegner
– Herman – Huberman – Gustav Kniestaedt –
Kreisler (2) – Kulenkampff – Lari – Maurice –
Menges – Menuhin – Morgagni – Morini – D.
Oistrakh – Pierangeli – Ranzato – A.J. Rose –
Wolfgang Schneiderhan (2) – Spalding (2) –
Stern – J. Szigeti – Telmanyi – Totenberg –
Weissgerber – Wittenberg – Ysaye
Hungarian dance No. 6, in D flat
Bilbe – Deman – S. Furer – Gerle – Ghestem –
Hagen – Kerekjarto – Gustav Kniestaedt –
Kooper – Marteau – Menuhin – Morini –
Sammons – Spalding
Hungarian dance No. 7, in A
Campoli – Elman – Gerle – Gittelson – Hagen –
Hegner – Heifetz (2) – Huberman –
Kulenkampff – Menges (2) – Menuhin – Morini
– Ranzato – Spalding (2) – Vaiman –
Weissgerber
Hungarian dance No. 8, in a
Anonymous – D'Aranyi – Gerle – Hagen –
Morini (2) – D. Oistrakh – Pikaizen – Sammons
– Snitkovsky – Spalding
Hungarian dance No. 9, in e *Akhtyamova –*
Gerle – D. Oistrakh – Spalding
Hungarian dance No. 10, in E *Gerle*
Hungarian dance No. 11, in d *Gerle – Heifetz –*
Menuhin – D. Oistrakh
Hungarian dance No. 12, in d *Gerle – Menuhin*
– D. Oistrakh
Hungarian dance No. 13, in D *Gerle –*
Schmuller
Hungarian dance No. 14, in d *Gerle – Spalding*
Hungarian dance No. 15, in B flat *Gerle –*
Spalding
Hungarian dance No. 16, in f *Akhtyamova –*
Gerle – L. Kogan – Spalding
Hungarian dance No. 17, in f sharp
Anonymous – Elman – Frolov – Gerle –
Gorokhov – Haendel (2) – Heifetz – Klimov –
L. Kogan – Kozolupova – Kreisler – Markov –
Menuhin – Morini – Plaeinitz – R. Ricci –
Spalding – Staryk – Szeryng (2) – Zimbalist
Hungarian dance No. 18, in D *Gerle*
Hungarian dance No. 19, in b *Gerle –*
Schmuller – Spalding
Hungarian dance No. 20, in e
Bezrodny – A. Busch – Campoli – Gerle –
Heifetz – Menges (2) – D. Oistrakh – Polyakin –
Rabinoff – R. Ricci – Spalding – Zimbalist
Hungarian dance No. 21, in e *Gerle – Spalding*
– Zimbalist
(5) Lieder, Op. 49 (*v & pf*)
No. 4. Wiegenlied "Cradle song"
d'Almaine – Brown – Ghestem – A. Kaufmann
– D. Oistrakh – Ranzato – A. Schmidt –
Schmied – Swaap – Tworek (2)
(5) Lieder , Op. 105 (*v & pf*)
No. 1. Wie Melodien zieht es *Goldstein*
Quartet No. 1, in g, Op. 25 (*pf, vln, vla & vlc*)

Goldberg – Pelliccia –Schneider
Quartet No. 2, in A, Op. 26 (*pf, vln, vla & vlc*)
Gimpel – Pelliccia
Quartet No. 3, in c, Op. 60 (*pf, vln, vla & vlc*)
Dyke – Goldberg – Heifetz – Pelliccia – Schneider
– J. Szigeti
(2) Quartets, Op. 51 (*2 vlns, vla & vlc*)
No. 1. Quartet No. 1, in c *Catterall – D.*
Oistrakh
Quartet No. 3, in B flat, Op. 67 (*2 vlns, vla & vlc*)
Catterall
Quintet in f, Op. 34 (*2 vlns, vla, vlc & pf*) *Bress –*
Rybar
Quintet No. 2, in G, Op. 111 (*2 vlns, 2 vlas & vlc*)
Schneider & Stern
Quintet in b, Op. 115 (*cl, 2 vlns, vla & vlc*)
Morbitzer – D. Oistrakh
Sextet No. 1, in B flat, Op. 18 (*2 vlns, 2 vlas & 2*
vlcs) *Dyke – Masters & Menuhin – Schneider &*
Stern
Sextet No. 2, in G, Op. 36 (*2 vlns, 2 vlas &*
2 vlcs) *Baker & Heifetz – Dyke – Masters &*
Menuhin
Sonata No. 1, in G, Op. 78 (*vln & pf*)
Abel – Bress – A. Busch – De Vito – Eto –
Ferras – Goldberg – Harth – Isakadze –
Kaufman – L. Kogan (2) – Krysa –
Kulenkampff – Loveday – Makanowitzky –
Menuhin (2) – Morbitzer – I. Oistrakh (2) –
Röhn – Rosand – Wolfgang Schneiderhan (2) –
T. Seidel – Shapiro – Soloviev – Spalding –
Stern – Suk (3) – Szeryng – J. Szigeti –
Telmányi – R. Varga – Wroński – Zsigmondy
Sonata No. 2, in A, Op. 100 (*vln & pf*)
A. Busch – De Vito – Druian – Eidus – Elman
– Fain – Ferras – Goldberg – Grumiaux –
Gutnikov – Heifetz – L. Kogan – Komlos –
Kulenkampff – Lorand – Loveday – Moss – I.
Oistrakh – Olof – R. Ricci – Rosand – M.
Scherzer – Wolfgang Schneiderhan – T. Seidel –
Shapiro – J. Szigeti – Telmányi – Unno – R.
Varga – Wroński
Sonata No. 3, in d, Op. 108 (*vln & pf*)
d'Albore – Bress – Catterall – Colbentson – De
Vito – Elman (2) – Eto – Farbmann – Ferras
(2) – Garay – Goldberg – Grach – Gutnikov –
Hagen – Harth – Heifetz – Kennedy – Kitain –
Klijn – Kochański – Kulenkampff – Laredo –
Loveday – Makanowitzky – Menges – Menuhin
(4) – Milstein – Morini (2) – Moss – D.
Oistrakh (3) – I. Oistrakh – Ozim – Polson – R.
Ricci – Wolfgang Schneiderhan (2) – Shapiro –
Soloviev – Spalding – Staryk – Stern (2) – Suk
(2) – Swaap – Szeryng – J. Szigeti (4) –
Totenberg – Tretyakov – R. Varga – Weiner –
Wroński – Zimbalist
Sonata (1853) "Frei aber Einsam" (*vln & pf*)
Allegro (*Scherzo*) in c (*3rd mvt*) "Sonatensatz"
Bakman – Barinova – Davison – Gottesmann –
Gyarmati – Kennedy – L. Kogan – Lubotsky –
Menuhin – Rybar – Wolfgang Schneiderhan –
Šestak – Snitkowsky – Staryk – Stern – Suk –
Telmányi – Totenberg
Symphony No. 1, in c, Op. 68 (*orch*) *Staryk*
Trio in E flat, Op. 40 (*hrn, pf & vln*)

Alès – Barylli – Bělčík – Brunet – A. Busch – Catterall – Dyke – Gimpel – Grumiaux – L. Kogan – Makanowitzky – Menuhin – Perlman – S. Scherzer – Schneider – Siverstein – Szeryng – J. Szigeti – Tunnell
Trio No. 1, in B, Op. 8 (*pf, vln & vlc*) *Bělčík – Feigin – Fournier – Kussmaul – Stern (2) – Stross – Suk – Wolfsthal*
Trio No. 2, in C, Op. 87 (*pf, vln & vlc*) *D'Aranyi – A. Busch – Gendre – Menuhin – Poltronieri – Senofsky – Stern – J. Szigeti – Totenberg – Wilk*
Trio No. 3, in c, Op. 101 (*pf, vln & vlc*) *Clebanoff – Dessau – Gendre – Stern – Suk (2)*
(14) Volkskinderlieder (1858) (*v & pf*)
No. 4. Sandmännchen *A. Schmidt*
(16) Waltzes, Op. 39 (*pf duet*)
Waltz No. 15, in A flat
Addash – W. Andersen – Barinova – Barylli – Benedetti – Borries – Bouillon (2) – Bratza – Campoli – Cesano – Chauveton – L. Cherniavsky – Culbertson – Eweler – Gautier – Gay – Ghestem – Goldin – Gorokhov – Hadjaje – Haendel (2) – Hochstein – Huberman – Jarry – Kalafusz – Kersey – B. Koutzen – Kreisler (2) – Lass – Menges (2) – Milstein – Mitnitzky – Morini – Nadien – Neste – Neumann – Ortenberg – Příhoda – Puig – Sachsenskjöld – Sammons – Schmied – Schwalbé – Small – Spalding (2) – Spivakovsky – Suk – Swaap – Szentgyörgi – Szikra – Telmányi – Thibaud – Titze – Unno – Wolfsthal – Zacharewitsch – Zathureczky
Brandl, Johann (1835–1913)
(Der) Liebe Augustin – operetta
Du alter Stefansturm
Alès – Auclair – Barstow – Bluestone – Breeskin – Brown – Carol – Druian – Eweler – Flesch – Fradkin (2) – Gorokhov – Kennedy – Kreisler (3) – Lass – Lorand (2) – Lorant – Menuhin – Michaïlow – Morini (2) – Odnoposoff – Olevsky – Rabin – Renardy – R. Ricci – Rubato – Wolfgang Scheiderhan – Schwartz – Szentgyörgi – Szeryng – Weber
Brant, Henry (1913–   )
Hieroglyphics (1966) (*solo vln*) *Kobialka*
Bražinskas, Algis (1937–   )
Sonata, Op. 7 (*vln & pf*) *Livontas*
Breau, Louis (1893–1928)
Humming (*v & pf*) *Brown*
Brenta, Gaston (1902–   )
Mélopée (*vln & pf*) *Weiner*
Brescianello, Giuseppe Antonio (1690–1757)
(12) Concerti (*2 vlns & c*)*
Concerto No. 1, in B flat *Ceradini & Redditi*
Bress, Hyman (1931–   )
Fantaisie electronique (*vln & tape recorder*) *Bress*
Bréton, Tomás (1850–1923)
(4) Escenas Andaluzas (*pf*)
No. 2. Polo gitano *H. Figueroa*
Bridge, Frank (1879–1941)
Cradle song in F (1911) (*vln & pf*) *Temianka*

*Manuscript is in the Biblioteca del Conservatorio di Musica di Firenze.

Gondoliera (1911) (*vln & pf*) *Hayward*
(3) Idylls (1906) (*2 vlns, vla & vlc*)
No. 1. Adagio molto espressivo *Hayward*
No. 2. Allegretto poco lento *Hayward*
No. 3. Allegro con moto *Hayward*
(9) Miniatures (*pf, vln & vlc*)
No. 1. Minuet *Sammons*
No. 8. Hornpipe *Sammons*
Moto perpetuo (1911) (*vln & pf*) *Temianka*
(3) Novelettes (1904) (*2 vlns, vla & vlc*) *Hayward*
Serenade (1910) (*vln & pf*) *Hayward*
Trio in c (1908) "Phantasie" (*pf, vln & vlc*) *Grinke*
Britten, Benjamin (1913–   )
Concerto No. 1, in d, Op. 15 (1939 – rev. 1958) (*vln & orch*) *Grumlíková – Kling – Lubotsky (2)*
Suite, Op. 6 (*vln & pf*) *Gutnikov – Jásek – Nemet – Tarack*
Brockman, James (1886–   )
Nightingale (*v & pf*) *Fradkin*
Brogi, Renato (1873–1924)
Mazurka (*vln & pf*) *Lari*
(2) Morceaux, Op. 34 (*vln & pf*)
No. 2. Arietta all'antica *Lari*
Broman, Sten (1902–   )
Romance (*vln & pf*) *O. Nielsen*
Brooks, Sydney
Children's song (*vln & pf*) *Wittenberg*
Brott, Alexander (1915–   )
Invocation & dance (1941) (*vln & pf*) *Lapenson*
Broustet, Edouard (1836–1901)
Airs populaires espagnole (*vln & pf*) *de Brayne*
Brown, Eddy (1895–   )
Rondino (*on a melody by J.B. Cramer*) (*vln & pf*)* *Brown*
Brown, Nacio Herb (1896–1964)
Paradise (*v & pf*) *A. Sandler*
Wedding of the painted doll (1929) (*v & pf*) *Fradkin*
Bruch, Max (1838–1920)
Concerto No. 1, in g, Op. 26 (*vln & orch*)
Auclair – Borries – Campoli (2) – Drdla – Drescher – Elman – Ferras – Field – Francescatti (2) – Gardi – Gitlis – Grumiaux (2) – Haendel – Heifetz (2) – Kayser – Krebbers – Kreisler – Kulenkampff (3) – Laredo – Lewkowitz – Manén (3) – Melcher – Menuhin (4) – Milstein (3) – Mischakoff – Morbitzer (2) – Morini – Odnoposoff – D. Oistrakh (2) – I. Oistrakh – Olevsky – Petronio – R. Ricci – Rudényi – Sammons – Wolfgang Schneiderhan – Southgate – Stanske – Stern (2) – Suk – Ushioda – T. Varga (2) – Voicu – Wolf – Zacharias – Zimmermann
Concerto No. 2, in d, Op. 44 (*vln & orch*) *Elman – Heifetz – Moris*
Kol Nidrei, Op. 47 (*vlc or vln & orch*)
Auclair – Barbieri – Condamine – Deman – Elman (2) – Gautier – Gold – Huberman (2) – Livontas – Pilzer – Powell – Rosen – Solloway – Tzipine – Weber

*Based on Cramer's "Rondo brilliant à la russe" for piano.

Scottish Fantasy, Op. 46 (*vln & orch*) *Campoli – Heifetz (2) – D. Oistrakh – Rabin*
(15) Swedish Dances, Op. 63 (*vln & pf*)
Swedish dance No. 1, in d *Rudényi*
Swedish dance No. 2, in D *Rudényi*
Swedish dance No. 3, in d *Rudényi*
Swedish dance No. 5, in g *Rudényi*
Swedish dance No. 6, in E flat *Rudényi*
Swedish dance No. 7, in B flat *Rudényi*
Brüll, Ignaz (1846–1907)
(3) Morceaux, Op. 90 (*vln & pf*)
No. 1. Scène espagnole *Elman*
Souvenir (*pf*) *Elman*
Brustad, Bjarne (1895–   )
Capricci (*vln & vla*) *B. Larsen*
Bucchi, Valentino (1916–   )
Concerto lirico (1959) (*vln & orch*) *Perez*
Buchbinder, Berndt
Příhoda-serenade (*vln & pf*) *Příhoda*
Bucia, Nicolas
Danse ruméne (*vln & pf*) *Bucia*
Imitation de Cornemuse (*vln & pf*) *Bucia (2)*
Popular Rumanian dance (*vln & pf*) *Bucia*
Bull, Ole (1810–1880)
Concerto in e (*vln & orch*) *Johannessen*
Et Säterbesøg (*Fantasy*) (*vln & pf*) *Johannessen*
I ensomme Stunde (*pf*) *Engelbretson – Johannessen*
Nocturne, Op. 2 (*vln & pf*) *Olsson-Föllinger*
Säterjëntens søndag (*v & pf*)
W. Andersen – Anonymous – Bartholdy – Engelbretson – Englund – Fritz-Crone – Gorensky – Groth – Haaland – Høeberg – Johansen – Knudsen – Maurice – Nilsson – Tellefsen – Thibaud (2) – Tworek – Weist-Hill
Burian, Emil František (1904–1959)
Quartet No. 2 (1929) (*2 vlns, vla & vlc*) *Peška*
Quartet No. 3 (1940) (*2 vlns, vla & vlc*) *Peška*
Sonata romantica (1938) (*vln & pf*) *Peška*
Burinskas, V.
Scherzino (*vln & pf*) *Livontas*
Burkhard, Willy (1900–1955)
Concerto, Op. 69 (1943) (*vln & orch*) *Schneeberger*
Quartet No. 2, Op. 68 (1943) "In one movement" (*2 vlns, vla & vlc*) *Geyer*
Burleigh, Cecil (1885–1941)
Caprice in a (*vln & pf*) *Farbmann*
(8) Characteristic pieces, Op. 6 (*vln & pf*)
No. 4. Indian snake dance *Farbmann – T. Seidel*
Natures voices, Op. 44 (*vln & pf*)
No. 1. Giant hills *Heifetz*
Plantation sketches, Op. 36 (*vln & pf*) *Margaret Harrison*
(4) Small concert pieces, Op. 21 (*vln & pf*
No. 4. Moto perpetuo *Heifetz*
Burmester, Willy (1869–1933)
Contretanze (*on a theme of Beethoven*) (*vln & pf*) *Francescatti*
Serenade (*vln & pf*) *Dinicu – Renardy*
Staccato serenade (*vln & pf*) *Titze*
Burton, Eldin (1913–   )
Fiddlestick (1946) (*vln & pf*) *Tryon*
Quintet (1945) (*pf, 2 vlns, vla & vlc*) *Tryon*
Sonatina (1946) (*vln & pf*) *Tryon*

& vlc) Gerle
Coppola, Piero (1888–   )
Rêverie (vln & pf) Schwartz
Corelli, Arcangelo (1653–1713)
(12) Concerti grossi, Op. 6 (orch)
  Concerto grosso No. 1, in D
  Apostoli & Ayo – E. Bachmann & Guilet –
  Benac & Zafer – Grehling & Vorholz –
  Hintermeyer & Melkus – Piatkowski & Warchal
  – Sambleben & Thomsen
  Concerto grosso No. 2, in F
  Apostoli & Ayo – E. Bachmann & Guilet –
  Hintermeyer & Melkus – Masters & Menuhin –
  Piatkowski & Warchal
  Concerto grosso No. 3, in c
  Apostoli & Ayo – E. Bachmann & Guilet –
  Doukan & Yordanoff – Grehling & Vorholz –
  Hintermeyer & Melkus – Piatkowski & Warchal
  – Sadowski & Sieja
  Concerto grosso No. 4, in D
  Apostoli & Ayo – Ayo & Gallozzi – E.
  Bachmann & Guilet – Malanotte & Mozzato –
  Piatkowski & Warchal
  Concerto grosso No. 5, in B flat
  Apostoli & Ayo – Ayo & Gallozzi – E.
  Bachmann & Guilet – Piatkowski & Warchal
  Concerto grosso No. 6, in F Apostoli & Ayo –
  E. Bachmann & Guilet – Piatkowski & Warchal
  Concerto grosso No. 7, in D
  Apostoli & Ayo – Ayo & Gallozzi – E.
  Bachmann & Guilet – Bruun & Koppel –
  Piatkowski & Warchal
  Concerto grosso No. 8, in g "Christmas
  Concerto"
  Apostoli & Ayo – Ayo & Gallozzi – Bruun &
  Koppel – Fernandez & Germaine Raymond –
  Grehling & Schärnack – Hamann & Kayser –
  Hrdjok & Stanič-Krek – Laroque & Wallez –
  Piatkowski & Warchal – Sadowski & Sieja
  Concerto grosso No. 9, in F
  Apostoli & Ayo – Ayo & Gallozzi – E.
  Bachmann & Guilet – Bünte & Hendel –
  Piatkowski & Warchal – Sillito & Tunnell
  Concerto grosso No. 10, in C Apostoli & Ayo –
  Ayo & Gallozzi – E. Bachmann & Guilet –
  Piatkowski & Warchal
  Concerto grosso No. 11, in B flat Apostoli &
  Ayo – E. Bachmann & Guilet – Piatkowski &
  Warchal
  Concerto grosso No. 12, in F Apostoli & Ayo –
  E. Bachmann & Guilet – Piatkowski & Warchal
Largo affettuoso* Bean
(12) Sonatas, Op. 1 (2 vlns & c)
  Sonata No. 7, in C Lysy & Westergaard
  Sonata No. 9, in G Fietz & Rybar
(12) Sonatas, Op. 2 (1685) (2 vlns & c)
  Sonata No. 4, in e Ceradini & Redditi
(12) Sonatas, Op. 3 (2 vlns & c)
  Sonata No. 1, in F Friisholm & Kassow
  Sonata No. 4, in b Bastien
  Sonata No. 5, in d Friisholm & Kassow
  Sonata No. 7, in e L. Hansen & Sendrovitz

  Unidentified.

  Sonata No. 9, in f Marriner & Roberts
(12) Sonatas, Op. 4 (2 vlns & c)
  Sonata No. 3, in A Goberman & Tree
  Sonata No. 4, in D Goberman & Tree
  Sonata No. 5, in a Goberman & Tree
  Sonata No. 6, in E Goberman & Tree
  Sonata No. 9, in B flat Goberman & Tree
  Sonata No. 10, in G Goberman & Tree
(12) Sonatas, Op. 5 (vln & c)
  Sonata No. 1, in D
  Biffoli & Magnani – Cores – Margaret Harrison
  – Kreisler – Kremer – Lack – Manzone –
  Monosoff – Plummer – Ranzato – Spalding –
  Stehl – Zepparoni
  Sonata No. 2, in B flat Biffoli & Magnani –
  Manzone – Plummer – Staryk (2)
  Sonata No. 3, in C Biffoli & Magnani – Brink –
  Cotogni – Eto – Manzone – Monosoff –
  Plummer – Zepparoni
  Sonata No. 4, in F Armuzzi-Romei – Biffoli &
  Magnani – Manzone – Plummer
  Sonata No. 5, in g Biffoli & Magnani – A.
  Busch – Friedman – Manzone – Plummer
  Sonata No. 6, in A Biffoli & Magnani – Brink –
  Manzone – Pincherle – Plummer – Spalding
  Sonata No. 7, in d Biffoli & Magnani –
  Geyrhalter – Manzone – Plummer
  Sonata No. 8, in e
  Biffoli & Magnani – Geyrhalter – Lack –
  Manzone – Monosoff – Plummer – Renardy –
  Švolkovskis
  Sonata No. 9, in A Bean – Biffoli & Magnani –
  Klijn – Manzone – Moss – Plummer
  Sonata No. 10, in F Biffoli & Magnani – Brink
  – Manzone – Plummer
  Sonata No. 11, in E Bastien – Biffoli &
  Magnani – Manzone – Plummer – Reynal
  Sonata No. 12, in d "La Follia"
  Accardo – Biffoli & Magnani – Bratza – Bress –
  Brink – Campoli – Comellas – Enescu –
  Fontanarosa – Grehling – Grumiaux – Haendel
  – Kulenkampff – Kussmaul – Manzone –
  Markov – Menuhin (2) – Milstein – Moguilevski
  – Plummer – Příhoda – Ranzato – B. Schwarz –
  Šestak – Spalding – J. Szigeti – Zathureczky –
  Zighera
Corigliano, John (Jr.) (1938–   )
Sonata (1963) (vln & pf) Corigliano
Cornelius, Peter (1824–1874)
(6) Lieder, Op. 3 (v & pf)
  No. 3. Ein Ton (The monotone) Zimbalist
Corrette, Michel (1709–1795)
(21) Concerti comique, Op. 8
  Concerto No. 6, in G "Le Plaisir du Dames"
  (fl, ob, vln, bsn & hpsi) Gendre
Sonata in D "Les jeux olympiques" (vln & hpsi)*
Kehr
Corti, Mario (1882–1957)
Grave (vln & pf) D'Aranyi
Cortopassi, Domenico
Canzone d'Aprile (vln & pf) di Piramo
Coslow, Sam (1902–   )

*Derived from Jean Joseph Mouret's comic opera
"Les Jeux Olympiques," 1729.

One summer night (v & pf) Fradkin
Costa, P. Mario (1858–   )
Frangesa march (v & pf) May – Polo
Cottenet, Richard
Chanson méditation (vln & pf) Komissarov –
Kreisler – Sammons – Spalding – Woodgate
Couperin, Armand-Louis (1725–1789)
(6) Sonates en Pièce de Clavecin, Op. 2 (1765)
(hpsi & vln obb)
  Sonata No. 2, in D Moss
Couperin, François (1668–1733)
(L') Apothéose de Lully (1725) (2 vlns & c) Alès
& Merckel – Melkus & Rantos
Audite, omnes (1706) – motet Brink
(Les) Chérubins, XX, No. 3 (hpsi) Fachiri –
Locatelli – Thibaud (2)
(4) Concerts Royaux (1722) (2 vlns, vla, fl & c)
  Concert Royale No. 1, in G Kussmaul
  Concert Royale No. 2, in D Kussmaul
  Concert Royale No. 3, in A Kussmaul
  Concert Royale No. 4, in e Kussmaul – Merckel
(La) Fleurie, ou la Tendre Nanette, I. No. 16
(hpsi) Dessau
(Les) Goûts-réunis, ou Nouveaux Concerts (unsp.
inst & c)
  Concert No. 9, in E "Ritratto dell' Amore"
  Merckel
  Concert No. 10, in a "La Tromba" (vln, vla
  & c) Fernandez – Gendre
(3) Leçons des Ténèbres (v & c) Fernandez
(La) Létiville, XVI, No. 7 (hpsi) Merckel
(Les) Nations – 4 Suites (1726) (2 vlns & c)
  Suite No. 1, in e "La Française" Fernandez,
  Gendre & J. Pasquier – Marriner & Pini
  Suite No. 2, in c "L'Espagnole" Fernandez,
  Gendre & J. Pasquier – Marriner & Pini
  Suite No. 3, in d "L'Impériale" Fernandez,
  Gendre & J. Pasquier – Lautenbacher –
  Marriner & Pini
  Suite No. 4, in g "La Piémontoise" Alès &
  Tessier – Fernandez, Gendre & J. Pasquier –
  Marriner & Pini
(Le) Parnasse, ou l'Apothéose de Corelli (1725) (2
vlns & c) Alès & Merckel – Lautenbacher –
Melkus & Rantos
(Les) Petits Moulins à vent, XVII, No. 2 (hpsi)
Heifetz – Press
Sonata No. 3, in g (1693) "L'Astrée" (2 vlns & c)
Blot & Ortmans-Bach – Gendre
Sonata No. 4, in d "L'Impériale" (1710/5)*
Coward, James M. (1824–1880)
Because (Berceuse Paysanne) (v & pf) Southgate
Held in bondage (v & pf) Southgate
Nina (v & pf) Andjelkovitch
Coward, Noël Pierce (1899–   )
Bitter Sweet (1929) – operetta
  Zigeuner Staryk
Cowell, Henry Dixon (1897–1965)
Homage to Iran (1959) (vln, pf & Persian drms)

*Same as number 3 of "Les Nations." The
Roman numerals in the François Couperin listing
refers to the "Ordre" to which the compositions
were assigned.

Avakian
How old is song? (*vln & pf*) *J. Szigeti*
Prelude (1955) (*vln & hpsi*) *Brink*
Set of Five (1952) (*vln, pf & pcn*) *Ajemian*
Sonata No. 1 (1945) (*vln & pf*) *J. Szigeti*
Cramer, Johann Baptist (1771–1858)
Waltz (*pf*) *Kennedy – Kobin*
Cristofaro, F. de
Love's nocturne, Op. 27 (*mand & pf*) *Dessau*
Croes, Henri-Jacques de (1705–1786)
(7) Concerti
    Concerto No. 6, in B flat (*fl, vln & strs*) *E. Koch*
    Concerto No. 7, in c (*vln, strs & c*) *L. Bobescu*
Croft, William (1678–1727)
Sonata in b (*vln & c*) *Lavers*
Sonata in g (*vln & c*) *Lavers*
Crosse, Gordon (1937–   )
Concerto da camera, Op. 6 (1962) (*vln, w-wnds & pcn*) *Parikian*
Crother, John (1895–   )
Gweedore Brae (*vln & pf*) *Collier – Heifetz – Kolberg – Mosley*
Császár, György (1813–1850)
(A) Kunok (1848) – opera
    aria* *F. & R. Weltmann*
Csermák, Antal
Lassú magyar (*Slow Hungarian dance*) (1826) (*dul, vlc & vln*) *Albert*
Cui, César Antonovich (1835–1918)
Kaleidoscope, Op. 50 (*vln & pf*)
    No. 5. Berceuse russe *Barinova – Bonis – Cochrane – Filon – Hayward*
    No. 9. Orientale
    Barinova – Berkova – Brown (2) – Debruille – Deman – Elman (4) – Erdenko – Farbmann – Fradkin – Frenkel – Godwin – Guidi – Hochstein – Moguilevski – Morrell – Press – Rosen – Rostal – T. Seidel – Selinsky – Spalding – Stanske – Szikra – Wolfsthal – Zimbalist (2)
    No. 11. Arioso *Beckwith*
    No. 12. Perpetuum mobile *Luboshutz*
    No. 21. Lettre d'amour *Elman*
(5) Little duets, Op. 56 (*fl & vln*)
    No. 2. Berceuse *Manasevich*
    No. 4. Nocturne *Manasevich – Wolff-Israel*
    No. 5. Valse *Manasevich*
(12) Miniatures, Op. 20 (*pf*)
    No. 8. Berceuse *Aranyi – Curti – M. Hall – C. Hansen – Kálmán*
Suite concertante, Op. 25 (*vln & orch*)
    No. 3. Cavatina *Petschnikoff*
Curci, Alberto (1886–   )
Concerto No. 1, Op. 21 "Concerto romantico" (*vln & orch*) *Gulli*
Concerto No. 2, Op. 30 (*vln & orch*) *Gulli*
Concerto No. 3, Op. 33 (*vln & orch*) *Gulli*
Suite italiana, Op. 34 (*vln & orch*) *Gulli*
Curillier
(La) Reine Joyeuse – musical
    Troublante volupté *Schwartz*

*Unidentified.

de Curtis, Giovanni Battista (1860–1926)
Carmé (*v & pf*) *Kreisler*
Torna a Sorrento (*v & pf*) *Förster*
Czerwonky, Richard (1886–1949)
Waltz (*vln & pf*) *Provinsky*
Czibulka, Alphons (1842–1894)
Gavotte (*Stephanie*) Op. 312 (*pf*) *Eweler – Streletzky*
Loin du Pays – valse (*pf*) *Moller*
Dahl, Ingolf (1912–   )
Concerto à tre (1947) (*vln, cl & vlc*) *Shapiro*
Dalberg, Friedrich Hugo von (1760–1812)
Sonata in F, Op. 28 (*vln & pf*) *Haag*
Dale, Benjamin James (1885–1943)
(3) Pieces, Op. 10 (1916/20) (*vln & pf*)
    No. 1. English dance *Grinke*
Dallapiccola, Luigi (1904–   )
(2) Studies (1947) (*vln & pf*)
    No. 1. Sarabanda *Materassi*
    No. 2. Fanfara e fuga *Materassi*
Tartiniana No. 1 (1951) (*vln & pf*) *Jásek – Posselt*
Tartiniana No. 2 (1955) (*vln & pf*) *Materassi*
Danbé, Jules (1840–1905)
Berceuse, Op. 17 (*vln & pf*) *Opfermann*
Dancla, Jean Charles (1818–1907)
Boléro & Romance, Op. 50 (*vln & pf*) *Kelly-Lange*
(24) Caprices, Op. 52 (*solo vln*)
    Caprice No. 9, in c (*Allegro agitato*) *Staryk*
    Caprice No. 16, in b flat (*Allegro vivace*) *Staryk*
Dandrieu, Jean-François (1682–1738)
(12) Trio-Sonatas, Op. 1 (1705) (*2 vlns & c*)
    Sonata No. 6, in e *Fernandez & Lamacque*
Daniderff, Leo
Auf den wassern (*vln & pf*) *Wittenberg*
Danks, Hart Pease (1838–1903)
Silver threads among the gold (1873) (*v & pf*)
Powell – Rostal – Southgate
Daquin, Louis Claude (1694–1772)
Pièces de clavecin – Book I (1735) (*hpsi*)
    Le coucou *Kozolupova – Lewkowitz – Manén (3) – Press – Stanske – Zilzer*
Darcy, Claude
Doleo (*v & pf*) *Pujol*
Darewski, Herman (1883–1947)
As you were – revue
    If you could care *Jacobsen*
Darewski, Max (1894–1929)
I might have known (*v & pf*) *Haxton*
I want a girl to foxtrot (*v & pf*) *Haxton*
(The) Nine O'Clock Revue – revue
    Shadow man *Haxton*
Snowball song (*v & pf*) *Haxton*
That's the time (*v & pf*) *Haxton*
Ting-ling (*Me lovee you*) (*v & pf*) *Haxton*
David, Johann Nepomuk (1895–   )
Concerto, Op. 45 (1952) (*vln & orch*) *David*
Sonata No. 2, Op. 58, No. 1 (1963) (*solo vln*) *Gavrilov*
David, Lee (1891–   )
Tonight you belong to me (1926) (*v & pf*) *Fradkin*
Davies, Henry Walford (1869–1941)
Psalm XXIII (The Lord is my shepherd) Op. 8 (1900) (*t, 2 vlns, vla, vlc & hp*) *Reillie*
Davis, Benny (1895–   )
see: Con Conrad

Dawes, Charles Gates (1865–   )
Improvisation (*vln & pf*) *MacMillen*
Melody in A (1912) (*vln & pf*) *Brown – Flesch – Fradkin – Kreisler – Příhoda*
Debussy, Claude Achille (1862–1918)
(6) Ariettes oubliées (1888) (*v & pf*)
    No. 2. Il pleure dans mon coeur *Heifetz – L. Kogan – Tomasow – Urban*
Beau soir (1878) (*v & pf*) *Heifetz (2) – L. Kogan*
(La) Boîte à joujoux (1913) – ballet (*orch*)
    Petite nigar *Bisztriczky*
(3) Chansons de Bilitis (1898) (*v & pf*)
    No. 2. La Chevelure *Goldstein – Heifetz (2)*
Children's Corner Suite (1908) (*pf*)
    No. 5. The little shepherd *Moguilevski*
    No. 6. Golliwogg's cake-walk *Goldstein – Heifetz (2) – Thibaud – Zhuk*
(2) Danses (1904) (*hp & str qt*)
    No. 1. Danse sacrée *Eidus – Jahn*
    No. 2. Danse profane *Eidus – Jahn*
(L') Enfant Prodigue (1884) – cantata (*v, cho & orch*)
    Prélude *Gorokhov – Heifetz – Mehta*
Images – Set I (1904) (*pf*)
    No. 3. Mouvement *A. Ferraresi*
Petite Suite (1889) (*pf – 4 hands*)
    No. 1. En bateau
    Bezrodny – Bustabo – Curti – Gorokhov – Kreisler – I. Oistrakh – Runnqvist – Thibaud – Vecsey
    No. 3. Menuet *Benedetti – Kulenkampff – J. Szigeti (2)*
(La) Plus que lente – valse (1910) (*pf*)
    Danchenko – Dubois – Elman – A. Ferraresi – Filon – Fournier – Gautier (2) – K. Gordon – Grach – Heifetz (2) – Kawaciuk – Komissarov – Ozim – Rabin – Snitkovsky – Suk – Szeryng – Tessier – Tomasow – Totenberg – Zhuk
Prélude à l'après-midi d'un faune (1894) (*orch*)
Bezrodny – Goldstein – L. Kogan – Snitkovsky
(12) Préludes – Book I (1910) (*pf*)
    No. 8. La Fille aux cheveux de lin
    Abussi – Accardo – Campoli – Cantrelle – Collier – Darrieux – Dubois – Eidus – A. Ferraresi – Francescatti – Garnier – Goluboff – Heifetz (3) – Kreisler – Laredo – Menuhin (4) – Milstein – Principi – Sachsenskjöld – Thibaud – Zhuk
    No. 12. Minstrels
    Campoli – Francescatti – Guarino – Menuhin – Milstein – Spalding – Thibaud – Tomasow
Quartet in g, Op. 10 (1893) (*2 vlns, vla & vlc*)
Catterall – Hayward – Tessier
Rêverie (1890) (*pf*) *Fachiri*
Sonata No. 3, in g (1917) (*vln & pf*)
    Auclair – Béan – Bress – Colbentson – Cyroulnik – Dubois – Elman – Ferras (2) – Fontanarosa – Fournier (2) – Francescatti – Friedman – Fuchs – Gavrilov – Grumiaux (3) – Heifetz – Hidy – Kagen – Mangeot – Nadien – Neveu – Odnoposoff – D. Oistrakh – Pavlović – Raskin – Röhn – Rostal – Senofsky – Shkolnikova – Silverstein – Soëtens – Staples – Stern – Suk (2) – J. Szigeti (3) – Theuveny – Thibaud – Tomasow – Voicu – Wroński

*Unidentified.

*Unidentified.

*Rewritten from the Andante con moto quasi
allegretto or 2nd mvt. of the Quartet in f, Opus 9.

*Pseudonym for Robert A. King.

*Later orchestrated.

Chamber Symphony (*vln, pf, ob, vla, vlc, cbs, fl, E-hrn, cbs, cl, hrn & tpt*) *Gheorghiu*
Impressions from childhood, Op. 28 (*vln & pf*) *Gheorghiu*
Octet in C, Op. 7 (*4 vlns, 2 vlas & 2 vlcs*) *Gendre, Geyre, Marchand & Ricros*
Quartet No. 2, in d, Op. 30 (*pf, vln, vla & vlc*) *Gheorghiu – Zabavnikov*
Sonata No. 2, in f, Op. 6 (*vln & pf*) *Enescu (2)*
Sonata No. 3, in a, Op. 25 "In the popular Rumanian style" (*vln & pf*) *Druian – Enescu (2) – Ferras – Fontanarosa – Gertler – Menuhin (2)*
Engel, Carl (1883–1944)
Elegy (*solo vln*) *Sagi*
Nachtgesang, Op. 7 (*v & pf*) *Fradkin*
Sea Shells (*v & pf*) *Rabin (2)*
Triptych (1920) (*vln & pf*) *Kroll*
Engel, Joel (1868–1927)
(29) Jüdische Volksmelodien, Op. 41 (*pf*)
   No. 14. Freilachs *Swaap*
Erhardt, Siegfried
Marfa (*vln & pf*) *Krämer*
Rumanian Rhapsody (*vln & pf*) *Krämer*
Eriksson, Josef (1872–   )
Aria, Op. 15 (*vln & pf*) *Rüthström*
Eriksson, Nils Fredrik (1902–   )
Concerto in g (1932) (*vln & orch*) *Kyndel*
Erkel, Ferenz (1810–1893)
Duo brillant en forme de fantaisie sur des airs hongrois (1837) (*vln & pf*)*
Himnusz (*Hungarian national anthem*) (1845) (*v & pf*) *J. Straus*
Erkin, Ulvi Djemal (1906–   )
Concerto (*vln & orch*) *Markov*
Quartet (*2 vlns, vla & vlc*) *Peška*
Erlanger, Camille (1863–1919)
Aphrodite (1905) – opera
   Prélude (*orch*) *Herman*
d'Erlanger, Frédéric (1868–1943)
Poème (*vln & pf*) *Fachiri*
Ernst, Heinrich Wilhelm (1814–1865)
Airs hongrois variés en A, Op. 22 (*vln & pf*) *Renardy – R. Ricci*
(La) Carnevale di Venizia – variations, Op. 18 (*vln & pf*) *Rudényi*
Concerto in f sharp, Op. 23 (*vln & orch*) *Rosand*
Élégie in c, Op. 10 (*vln & pf*) *Flesch – Rudényi – Zimmermann*
Fantasia brillante (*on themes from the opera "Otello" by Rossini*) Op. 11 (*vln & pf*) *Bezrodny – A.J. Rose (2)*
(6) Mehrstimmige Studien (*solo vln*)
   Étude No. 6, in G (*Variations on "The last rose of summer"*) (*à Bazzini*) *Ashkenazi – Kremer – R. Ricci – Sitkovetsky*
Nocturne, Op. 8 (*vln & pf*) *Heermann*
Erwin, Ralph†
I kiss your hand, madam (1929) (*v & pf*) *Curti – Rosen*
Eshpai, Andrei (1925–   )
Concerto (1956) (*vln & orch*) *Grach*

*See: Vieuxtemps.
†Pseudonym for Erwin Vogl.

Hungarian melodies (1958) (*vln & orch*) *Grach*
Sonata in B flat (1963) (*vln & pf*) *Grach – Vinnikov*
Espéjo, César (1892–   )
Airs tziganes, Op, 11 (1926) (*vln & pf*) *Elman (3) – Rubato*
(2) Pieces in ancient style (*vln & pf*) *L. Bobescu – Klimov*
Esperón, Ignacio Fernández
(La) Baerachita (*Mexican song*) (*v & pf*) *L. Cherniavsky*
Esposito, Michele (1855–1929)
Irish cradle song (*vln & pf*) *Thomas*
Fain, Sammy (1902–   )
Prologues (*orch*)*
   Près de la casçade *Curti*
Fairchild, Blair (1877–1933)
Canzonetta (*vln & pf*) *Farbmann*
Mosquitos (*vln & pf*) *Candéla*
Falla, Manuel de (1876–1946)
(El) Amor Brujo (1915) – ballet (*m-s & orch*)
   No. 7. Danza rituel del fuego *Fontanarosa – Mehta*
   No. 14. Pantomime *L. Bustabo – Heifetz – Suk – Telmányi – Wolf*
(7) Canciones Populares españolas (1914) (*v & pf*)†
   No. 1. El paño moruno
   Chemet – Flesch – Gautier – L. Kogan – Kooper – Moguilevski – Odnoposoff – D. Oistrakh – R. Ricci – Shkolníková – Stern – Szeryng (3)
   No. 3. Asturiana
   Benedetti – Gautier – Koene – L. Kogan – Kooper – Lorand – Milstein (2) – Moguilevski – Odnoposoff – D. Oistrakh – R. Ricci – Shkolníková – Szeryng – Wolfsthal
   No. 4. Jota
   Accardo – D'Aranyi – Barbieri – Benedetti – Chemet – Flesch (2) – Gautier – K. Gordon – Grumiaux – Heifetz (3) – L. Kogan – Kooper – Kreisler – Laredo – Lorand (2) – Milstein – Moguilevski – Odnoposoff – D. Oistrakh (3) – Petroni – Poltronieri – Quiroga – Rabinoff – R. Ricci – Shkolníková – Snitkovsky – Spalding – Stern – Suk – Swaap – Szeryng (3) – Thibaud – Wolfsthal
   No. 5. Nana
   Heifetz – L. Kogan – Kooper – Laredo – Moguilevski – Odnoposoff – D. Oistrakh – R. Ricci – Shkolníková – Spalding – Stern – Szeryng
   No. 6. Canción
   Abbado – Benedetti – Gautier – L. Kogan – Kooper – Kreisler – Lorand – Moguilevski – Odnoposoff – D. Oistrakh – R. Ricci – Shkolníková – Stern – Szeryng
   No. 7. Polo *Benedetti – Gautier*

*Film music.
†The arrangement by Paul Kochanski entitled "Suite populaire Espagnole" utilizes six of the seven Canciones, the sequence being: 1. El paño moruno – 2. Nana – 3. Canción – 4. Polo – 5. Asturiana – 6. Jota.

Concerto in D (1926) (*hpsi, fl, ob, cl, vln & vlc*)
   Alès – Darrieux – Nerini – Raimondi – Schneider
(El) Sombrero de Tre Picos (1919) – ballet (*orch*)
   No. 2. Danza del Molinero *Haendel – Pessina – J. Szigeti*
(La) Vida Breve (1913) – opera
   Danza española (*orch*)
   Andrade – D'Andurain – Auclair – Benedetti – Bouillon – Bouquet – Campoli – Danchenko – Erlih – Ferras – Fontanarosa – Friedman – Gautier (2) – Gimpel – Grach – Grumiaux – Haendel (3) – Heifetz – Isakadze – Jarry – Jásek – Kooper (2) – Kreisler (2) – Leon-Ara – Lorand (2) – Magyar – Malinin – Markov – Markovič – Martzy – Melsa – Menges – Menuhin (2) – Morini – Neaman – Neveu – Niemczyk – D. Oistrakh – Palulis – Rosen – Sachsenskjöld – Schmied – Wolfgang Schneiderhan – Spalding – Stanske – Staryk – Szeryng – Taschner – Thibaud – Tworek – T. Varga
Farina, Carlo (1600–1640)
(Il) Terzo libro primo della Pavane, Gagliarde ... (1626) (*var. cbns*)
   Sonata in f (*2 vlns & c*) *Kuijken & Rubinlicht*
Farkas, Ferenc (1905–   )
Fruit basket (*10 songs*) (*v, vln, vlc & cl*) *Tátrai*
Farnon, Robert (1917–   )
Rhapsody (*vln & orch*) *R. Cohen – Staryk*
Fasch, Johann Friedrich (1688–1758)
Concerto in D (*vln, strs & c*)*
Totenberg
Fauré, Gabriel Urbain (1845–1924)
Andante in B flat, Op. 75 (*vln & pf*) *Menuhin – Soriano*
Berceuse, Op. 16 (*vln & pf*)
   Alès – d'Ambrosio – Bas – Bastide – Bernardi – Bonnemain – Boucherit – Boussinot – Bress – Chauveton – Curti – Dony – Elman – Fabrizio – Ferras (2) – Flesch (2) – Gautier – Grumlíková – Isakadze – Jacobsen – Jarry – Krebbers – Levey – Mendels – Menges (2) – Menuhin – Merckel – Mossel – Nadien – T. Rich – Schwartz – Soriano – Suk – Swaap – Thibaud (2) – Tinlot – Toubas – Wanne – Ysaÿe – Zacharewitsch (2) – Zighera
(3) Chansons, Op. 7 (*v & pf*)
   No. 1. Après un rêve *Bratza – Curti – Dony – Elman – Knudsen (2) – Milstein (2) – Moguilevski*
(3) Chansons, Op. 23 (*v & pf*)
   No. 1. Les berceaux *Curti – Grumiaux*
Dolly, Op. 56 (*orch*)
   Berceuse *Thibaud*
Pelléas et Mélisande, Op. 80 (1898) – Incidental music (*orch*)
   No. 2. Fileuses *Bas*
Quartet No. 1, in c, Op. 15 (*pf, vln, vla & vlc*) *L. Kogan – Menuhin – Merckel – Shapiro*
Quartet No. 2, in g, Op. 45 (*pf, vln, vla & vlc*) *Raskin – Thibaud*

*The autograph of this concerto is in the Hessische Landes- und Hochschulbibliothek in Darmstadt.

Franci, Rinaldo (1854–1907)
Emma-Gavotte, Op. 60 (*vln & pf*) *Lari*
Franck, César (1822–1890)
Ave Maria (1863) (*s, t, bs & org*) *Reillie*
Panis angelicus (1872) (*t, org, hp, vlc & cbs*)
Flesch – Swaap
Quartet in D (1889) (*2 vlns, vla & vlc*) *Hayward*
Quintet in f (1878/9) (*pf, 2 vlns, vla & vlc*) *Baker
& Heifetz*
Sonata in A (1886) (*vln & pf*)
    *d'Albore – Allan – L. Bobescu – Cantrelle –
    Catterall (2) – Colbentson – De Vito – Doukan
    – Dubois – Elman (2) – Ferras (2) –
    Francescatti – Friedman – Fuchs – Gertler –
    Grumiaux – Gutnikov – Hayward – Heifetz –
    Kaufman – Kitain – Klimov – H. Koch –
    Komlós – Kulenkampff – Lantsman – Loveday
    – Mandel – Massia – Menuhin (3) – Morini –
    Nadien – D. Oistrakh (3) – I. Oistrakh – Olof –
    Onderet – Paulauskas – Perlman – Plocek –
    Renardy – Wolfgang Schneiderhan – Small –
    Soëtens – Spalding – Stern (2) – Suk – Suzuki –
    Taschner – Thibaud (2) – Totenberg – Tworek –
    R. Varga – Zathureczky*
Trio in f sharp, Op. 1, No. 1 (1841) (*pf, vln &
vlc*) *Raderman*
Francoeur, François (1698–1787)
(12) Sonatas – Book I (*vln & c*)
    Sonata No. 5, in c *Bonaldi*
    Sonata No. 6, in E *Bonaldi*
(12) Sonatas – Book II (1733) (*vln & c*)
    Sonata No. 1, in A *Bonaldi*
    Sonata No. 3, in e *Bonaldi*
    Sonata No. 6, in g *Cyroulnik – Grabowska –
    Weiner*
    Sonata No. 12, in E *Weiner*
Frankel, Benjamin (1906–   )
Sonata, Op. 13 (*solo vln*) *Rostal*
Franklin-Pike, Eleanor (1890–   )
Idylle (*vln & pf*) *Swaap*
Franko, Sam (1857–1937)
Irish lament (*vln & pf*) *Piastro*
Franz, Robert (1815–1892)
(6) Gesänge, Op. 17 (*v & pf*)
    No. 2. Ständchen (*Der Mond ist schlafen
    'gangen*) *Příhoda*
O Holy God, we praise Thy name! (*v & pf*) *A.
Schmidt*
Fraser, Jean (1920–   )
Élégie (*vln & pf*) *Leblanc*
Fraser, Norman George (1904–   )
Cueca (1926) (*vln & pf*) *D'Andurain – d'Aranyi &
Fachiri*
Freedman, Harry (1922–   )
(5) Pieces (1949) (*2 vlns, vla & vlc*) *Parlow*
Freire, Osman Pérez
Ay, ay, ay (*v & pf*) *Diaz – Dinicu – di Piramo –
Příhoda – Zilzer*
Frescobaldi, Girolamo (1583–1643)
(28) Canzoni da Sonari (*1/4 part*) (1628)
(*var. inst*)
    Canzona I "La Bonvisia" (*vln & c*)
    Armuzzi-Romei
    Canzona II "La Bernardina" (*vln & c*)
    Armuzzi-Romei

Pastorale gentile*
Zathureczky
Frešo, Tibor (1918–   )
Capriccio (1948) (*vln & pf*) *Gašparek*
Toccata, Op. 5 (*vln & pf*) *Gašparek*
de Freyne
Where the lazy Mississippi flows (*v & pf*) *Ball –
Jacobsen*
Fricker, Peter Racine (1920–   )
Sonata, Op. 12 (*vln & pf*) *Lidka*
Friedberg, Carl (1872–1955)
Old French Gavotte (*vln & pf*) *Kreisler – A.
Schmidt*
Friedman, Ignacy (1882–1948)
(6) Viennese Dances (*on themes by E. Gärtner*)
(*pf*)
    Wiener Tanz No. 1, in G flat *Eweler*
    Wiener Tanz No. 2, in G *Eweler*
Friml, Rudolph (1879–   )
(L') Amour, toujours l'amour (1922) (*v & pf*)
Fradkin – Jelving
Au soir (*At evening*) (*pf*) *Elman*
Bygone days, Op. 65 (*vln & pf*) *Torre*
Dance of the maidens, Op. 48 (*pf*) *Kreisler*
Mélodie, Op. 27 (*vln & pf*) *Davis*
Mignonette, Op. 59 (*vln & pf*) *Gardner*
Romance, Op. 17 (*vln & pf*) *Hayward*
Rose Marie (1916) – operetta
    Door of my dreams *Dobrinski – Sander*
    Indian love call *Bluestone – Crégut – Curti –
    Dobrinski – Kreisler – Sander – Streletzky*
Sometime (1918) – musical
    Sometime *Thiele*
(The) Vagabond King (1925) – operetta
    Only a rose *Jacobsen*
Fritz, Kaspar (1716–1782)
(6) Solos, Op. 2 (*vln & c*)
    Solo No. 4, in e *Langbein*
Frumerie, Gunnar Fredrik de (1908–   )
Sonata No. 1, in a (1934) (*vln & pf*) *Holst*
Sonata No. 2, in c sharp (1944) (*vln & pf*) *Holst –
Temko*
Trio No. 2, (1952) (*pf, vln & vlc*) *Berlin*
Fuchs, Lillian (1903–   )
Jota (*vln & pf*) *Bezrodny*
Fuchs, Robert (1847–1927)
Duet, Op. 60 (*vln & vla*) *Sammons*
Hungarian march (*vln & pf*) *Borries*
Fuga, Sandro (1906–   )
Sonata No. 5 (*vln & pf*) *V. Brun*
Funck, David (1630–1689)
Suite in g (*2 vlns, vla & c*) *Blot & Ortmans-Bach*
Gabriel-Marie (1852–1928)
(La) Cinquantaine (1894) (*pf duet*) *d'Almaine –
Elman – Jacobsen – Valesca-Becker*
Sérénade badine (*pf*) *Manuello*
Gabrinsky
Petite polonaise (*vln & pf*) *F.V. Henriques*
Gade, Jacob (1879–1963)
Canzonetta (*vln & pf*) *Collier*
Jealousy (1927) (*orch*) *Curti – Krips – Neaman –
Streletzky – Tworek (2)*
Gade, Niels Vilhelm (1817–1890)

*Unidentified.

(3) Noveletten in A, Op. 29 (*pf, vln & vlc*) *Kayser*
Trio in F, Op. 42 (*pf, vln & vlc*) *Sammons*
Gagnebin, Henri (1886–   )
Trio in D (1957) (*fl, vln & pf*) *Schneeberger*
Gaillard, Marius-François (1900–   )
Weekend (*vln & pf*) *Gautier*
Gajiev, Rauf (1922–   )
Concerto (*vln & orch*) *Aliev*
Gallatly, James M.
Fall o' day (*vln & pf*) *Haxton*
Galli, Mario
Serenata veneziana (*vln & pf*) *Galli*
Gallos, Mme.
(Le) Lac de Come – nocturne (*pf*) *Condamine*
Galuppi, Baldassare (1706–1785)
(12) Sonatas, Op. 1 (*hpsi*)
    Sonata No. 1, in C *D'Aranyi*
    Sonata No. 3, in a *D'Aranyi*
Ganne, Louis (1862–1923)
(L') Extase – Rêverie (*pf*) *Cochrane – Eweler –
Michaïlow – Sammons – A. Sandler*
Ganz, Wilhelm (1833–1914)
Sing, sweet bird (*v & pf*) *d'Almaine*
Garaguly, Carl (1900–   )
Csárdas (*vln & pf*) *Garaguly*
Hungarian fantasy (*vln & pf*) *Garaguly*
García, Eva
Reflections (*vln & pf*)* *Knudsen*
Gardner, Samuel (1892–   )
(2) Pieces, Op. 5 (*vln & pf*)
    No. 1. From the canebrake
    *Ball – Breeskin – Campoli – L. Cherniavsky –
    Fradkin – Hayward – Heifetz – Jacobsen –
    Perutz – Sammons (2)*
Garren
Just a girl that men forget (*v & pf*) *Ball*
Garrido, Pablo (1905–   )
Divertimento (1951) (*vln & pf*)
    Movimiento perpetuo *D'Andurain*
Gärtner, Eduard (1862–1918)
Aus Wien (*pf*)†
    Flesch – Kreisler – Lóránt
Gastaldon, Stanislao (1861–1939)
Musica proibita, Op. 5 (*v & pf*) *Venclů*
Gastoldi, Giovanni Giacomo (1556–1622)
(3) Balletti (1594) (*fl, vln, gamba & lute*)
    No. 1. L'Invaghito *C. Ferraresi*
    No. 2. Lo Spensierato *C. Ferraresi*
    No. 3. Lo Sdegnato *C. Ferraresi*
Gatti, Nicholas Comyn (1874–1946)
Bagatelle in D (*vln & pf*) *D'Aranyi*
Gaviniès, Pierre (1728–1800)
(6) Concerti, Op. 4 (1764) (*vln & orch*)
    Concerto No. 2, in F *Bernard*
    Concerto No. 5, in A *Bernard*
Gcki-Albi, G.N.
(L') Ours – valse (*orch*) *Moller*
Geehl, Henry Ernest (1881–1961)
For you alone (1909) (*v & pf*) *Hayward*

*Composed jointly with Gunnar Knudsen.
†Probably adapted from one of the six Viennese
dances.

Geminiani, Francesco (1687–1762)
(6) Concerti grossi, Op. 2 (1732) (*orch*)
Concerto grosso No. 1, in c *Biffoli & Giusto*
Concerto grosso No. 2, in c *Biffoli & Giusto*
Concerto grosso No. 3, in d *Biffoli & Giusto*
Concerto grosso No. 4, in D *Biffoli & Giusto*
Concerto grosso No. 5, in d *Biffoli & Giusto*
Concerto grosso No. 6, in A *Biffoli & Giusto*
(6) Concerti grossi, Op. 3 (1755) (*orch*)
Concerto grosso No. 2, in g *V. Brun &
Gramegna – Sangiorgi, Toso, Valpreda &
Zampieri*
(6) Concerti grossi, Op. 4 (1739) (*orch*)
Concerto grosso No. 1, in D *Biffoli & Giusto*
Concerto grosso No. 2, in b *Biffoli & Giusto*
Concerto grosso No. 3, in e *Biffoli & Giusto*
Concerto grosso No. 4, in a *Biffoli & Giusto*
Concerto grosso No. 5, in A *Biffoli & Giusto*
Concerto grosso No. 6, in c *Biffoli & Giusto*
(6) Concerti grossi, Op. 7 (1746) (*orch*)
Concerto grosso No. 1, in D *Ayo & Gallozzi –
Talassi & Toso*
Concerto grosso No. 2, in d *Ayo & Gallozzi –
Talassi & Toso*
Concerto grosso No. 3, in C *Ayo & Gallozzi –
Talassi & Toso*
Concerto grosso No. 4, in d *Talassi & Toso*
Concerto grosso No. 5, in c *Ayo & Gallozzi –
Talassi & Toso*
Concerto grosso No. 6, in B flat *Ayo & Gallozzi
– Talassi & Toso*
Introduction & Allegro (*vln & c*) *Bakman*
(12) Sonatas, Op. 4 (*vln & c*)*
Sonata No. 10, in A *Milstein – Odnoposoff*
(6) Sonatas, Op. 5 (1738) (*solo vln*)
Sonata in B flat *Janowski – Kremer –
Odnoposoff – Ostrovsky – Pikaizen – Staryk*
(12) Sonatas (1739) (*vln & c*)
Sonata in c *Belnick – A. Busch (2)*
Sonata in d "Sonata Impetuosa" *Jásek*
German, Edward (1862–1936)
Berceuse (*pf*) *Beckwith*
Henry VIII (1892) – Incidental music (*orch*)
d'Almaine – Hayward
Saltarelle (*vln & pf*) *Cochrane*
Gershwin, George (1898–1937)
(3) Jazz Preludes (1936) (*pf*)
Prelude No. 1, in B flat *Bezrondy – Heifetz (2)
– L. Kogan*
Prelude No. 2, in c sharp *Bezrodny – Heifetz
(2) – Szeryng*
Prelude No. 3, in E flat *Bezrodny – A. Ferraresi
– Heifetz (2)*
Porgy & Bess (1935) – opera
Bess, you is my woman *Gutnikov – Heifetz (2)
– Stern – Suk – Zhuk*
It ain't necessarily so *A. Ferraresi – Goldstein –
Heifetz (3) – Zhuk*
My man's gone now *A. Ferraresi – Goldstein –
Heifetz (2)*
Summertime *Heifetz (2) – Tworek*
Tempo di blues *Heifetz (2) – L. Kogan*
Woman is a sometime thing *Heifetz (2)*

*Actually concerti.

Short story (*vln & pf*) *Dushkin – Gautier – Grach*
Geszler, Györgi
(The) Humming top (*vln & pf*) *T. Varga*
Gheorghiu, Valentin (1928–   )
Trio in A (1950) (*pf, vln & vlc*) *Gheorghiu*
Ghrden
Mashiroki fujino ne (*vln & pf*)
Gilardi, Gilardo (1889–   )
Airs pampeanos (*vln & pf*) *Pessina*
Gilbert
Marionettes (*Scherzo*) (*vln & pf*) *Powell*
Gillespie, Haven
When you look in the heart of a rose (*v & pf*)*
Rattay – Thiele
Gillet, Ernest (1856–1940)
Babillage (*pf*) *Dessau – Ranzato (2) – Sadler*
Coeur Brisé (*pf*) *Haxton*
Entr'acte Gavotte, Op. 13 (*pf*) *Amrhein*
(Le) Lettre de Manon – valse (*pf*) *de Monge – di
Piramo – Ranzato – Schwartz*
Loin du Bal, Op. 36 – ballet (*orch*)
Intermezzo *Curti – Dessau – Moller – Ranzato
(2) – Sadler*
(6) Morceaux (*strs & pf*)
No. 2. Douce Caresse *Ranzato*
Polonaise (*vln & pf*) *Michaïlow*
Précieuse (*vln & pf*) *Michaïlow*
Rêve après le Bal – valse (*pf*) *Moller*
(Au) Village (*pf*) *Lorand*
Giltay, Berend (1910–   )
Concerto (1967) (*2 vlns & orch*) *B. & J. Lemkes*
Giordani, Tommaso (1730–1806)
Caro mio ben (*v & pf*) *Anonymous – Sechiari*
Giuliani, Giovanni Francesco (*18th century*)
Quartet No. 1, in A (*mand, vln, vla & lute*)
Pichler
Giuliani, Mauro (1781–1828)
Divertimento (*gtr & vln*) *Fontanarosa*
Sonata Grande, Op. 25 (*gtr & vln*) *Kocsis*
Gjerstrom, Gunnar (1891–1951)
(The) Myth (*vln & pf*) *Knudsen*
Glazounov, Alexander (1856–1936)
Concerto in a, Op. 82 (*vln & orch*)
*Candéla – Gabriël – Gimpel – Girdach –
Haendel – Heifetz (2) – Kulka – Magyar –
Milstein (3) – Morini – Odnoposoff – D.
Oistrakh – Polyakin – Rabin – Sitkovetsky –
Snitkovsky – Székely*
Mazurka-Oberek in D (*orch*) *D. Oistrakh*
Méditation, Op. 32 (*vln & pf*) *Beilina – Gautier –
Heifetz (2) – L. Kogan – Milstein (2) – D.
Oistrakh – Ranzato – Šroubek*
(5) Novellettes, Op. 15 (1888) (*2 vlns, vla & vlc*)
No. 2. Orientale *Hayward*
No. 3. Interludium in modo antico *Deman*
No. 4. Valse *Deman*
(2) pieces, Op. 20 (*vlc & pf*)
No. 1. Mélodie arabe *Shuchari*
No. 2. Sérénade espagnole *Kreisler –
Moguilevski*
Raymonda, Op. 57 (1897) – ballet (*orch*)
Entr'acte No. 1 *Bezrodny – Gutnikov – L.
Kogan*

*From the British musical "The Better 'Ole."

Grand Adagio *Heifetz – Kalinovsky – L. Kogan
– I. Oistrakh – Pratz*
Valse *Barinova – Heifetz – L. Kogan*
Glière, Reinhold Moritzovich (1875–1956)
(The) Bronze Horseman (1848/9) – ballet (*orch*)
ballet music *D. Oistrakh*
Concerto in g, Op. 100 "Concerto Allegro" (*vln &
orch*) *Goldstein*
(8) Pieces, Op. 39 (1909) (*vln & vlc*)
No. 1. Prelude *Rosoff*
No. 3. Lullaby *Rosoff*
No. 5. Intermezzo *Rosoff*
No. 7. Scherzo *Rosoff*
(The) Red Poppy, Op. 70 (1926/7) – ballet
(*orch*)
Romance *Kalinovsky*
Romance in D, Op. 3 (*vln & pf*) *Bezrodny*
Romance in c, Op. 45, No. 3 (*vln & orch*)
Barinova – D. Oistrakh – I. Oistrakh – Vlasov
Glinka, Mikhail Ivanovich (1804–1857)
Album leaf (*vln & pf*) *Goldstein*
Doubt (1838) (*v & pf*) *Manasevich*
Élégie* *Manasevich*
Farewell to Petersburg (1840) – 12 songs (*v & pf*)
No. 10. The lark *Barcewicz – Zimbalist*
Quartet in F (1830) (*2 vlns, vla & vlc*) *Catterall –
Kaufman & Stepansky*
Ruslan & Ludmila (1842) – opera
Persian song *D. Oistrakh – Zimbalist (2)*
Trio in d (1926/7) "Trio pathétique" (*pf, vln &
vlc*) *Feigin – D. Oistrakh*
Glitz, W.
Larghetto (*vln & pf*) *Stülken*
Glogau, Jack (1886–1953)
Moonlight lane (*v & pf*) *Ball*
Gloviritz
Polka brillante (*vln & pf*) *Ranzato*
Gluck, Christoph Willibald (1714–1787)
Concerto in G (*vln & orch*) *Lubotsky*
Gavotte (*pf*) *Szemere*
Orphée et Eurydice (1762) – opera
Dance of the blessed spirits: Andante (*No. 1*)
Powell
Dance of the blessed spirits: Lento "Mélodie"
(*No. 2*)
*Addash – d'Albore – Andrade – D'Aranyi –
Aranyi – Astruc – Auclair – Bratza – Chauveton
– Dajos – Deman – Eidus – Elman (2) – Fain –
Fairhurst – Feigin – A. Ferraresi – Fournier –
Goldstein – Grumlíková – Harth – Hayward –
Heifetz – Huberman – Jernou – B. Koutzen –
Kreisler – Kubelík – Kulenkampff – Leonidoff –
Livontas – Manén – Manuello – Michaïlow –
Milstein (2) – Morini (2) – Neaman – Neveu –
Powell – Rüthström – Sammons – Spalding –
Spivakovsky – Stern – Swaap – Szeryng (2) –
Wolfsthal – Zathureczky*
Paride ed Elena (1770) – opera
O del mio dolce ardor *Elman*
Godard, Benjamin (1849–1895)
Concerto No. 1, Op. 35 "Concerto Romantique"
(*vln & orch*)

*Unidentified.

Caterall – Grach – Hayward – F.V. Henriques –
Herman – Levey – Morini (2) – D. Oistrakh (2)
– Roeder – Rosand – Sandford – Seydel –
Spalding – Volant
Contemplation in F, Op. 2, No. 28 (v & pf) Hager
(6) Duettini, Op. 18 (2 vlns & pf)
   No. 1. Souvenir de campagne Sammons
   No. 5. Minuit D'Aranyi & Fachiri – Sammons
   No. 6. Sérénade D'Aranyi & Fachiri – F. & R.
   Weltmann
Jocelyn (1888) – opera
   Cachés dans cet asile "Berceuse"
   Anonymous (4) – Aranyi – Bergh – Blinder –
   Bonis – Capoulade – Chemet – Dajos – Dessau
   – Dinicu – Dunn – Dyke – Fradkin –
   Fritz-Crone – Ghestem – Godwin – Gygi –
   Hamowetskaya – Haxton (2) – Hayward –
   Heifetz – Huppertz – Jacobs – Jocobsen –
   Kreisler – Kun (2) – Lass – Laue – Livschakoff
   – Loránt – Mantovani – Maurice – Meier –
   Mendels – Morbitzer – Neaman – Opfermann –
   Polo – Post – Powell – Příhoda (2) – Quiroga –
   Ranzato (4) – Schwartz – Sechiari – Sens (2) –
   Stanske – Styx – Szemere – Tworek (2) – Ware
   – Weismann – Wolfsthal – Zimmermann
(3) Morceaux, Op. 78 – suite (vln & pf)
   No. 2. Berceuse in G Eisenberg
(6) Morceaux, Op. 128 (vln & pf)
   No. 3. Adagio pathétique Marteau – Ware
   No. 5. Sérénade andalouse Darrieux
   No. 6. Staccato-valse Menges
Trio in g, Op. 32 (pf, vln & vlc) Kayser
Godowsky, Leopold (1870–1938)
(12) Impressions (1916) (pf)
   No. 8. Waltz in D Heifetz
   No. 12. Viennese Heifetz – Kreisler
Triakontameron (30 moods & scenes in triple
measure) (1920) (pf)
   No. 11. Alt Wien A. Ferraresi – Heifetz (2) – L.
   Kogan
Goens, Daniel van (1904–   )
Scherzo, Op. 12, No. 2 (vln & pf) Rubato – Vlasov
Goeyens, Fernando (1892–   )
Humoresque (vln & pf) Dubois
Goldberg, Johann Gottlieb (1727–1756)
Sonata in g (2 vlns & c) Amboden & Trippner
Sonata No. 4, in a (2 vlns & c) Brandis & Rehm
Goldberg, Léon
Galante conversation (v & pf) Dony
Goldenweiser, Alexander (1875–1961)
Trio in e, Op. 31 (pf, vln & vlc) L. Kogan
Goldfaden, Abraham (1840–1908)
Raisins & almonds (v & pf) Elman
Goldmark, Karl (1830–1915)
Concerto in a, Op. 28 (vln & orch)
   Borgani – Catterall – Chemet – Garay – Geyer
   – Gimpel – Heifetz – MacMillen – Milstein –
   Morini – Příhoda – A.J. Rose – Rudényi –
   Rybar – Wolfsthal
Trio in e, Op. 33 (pf, vln & vlc) Lorand
Golestan, Stan (1876–1956)
Chant du berceau (1941) (vln & pf) L. Bobescu
(Le) Laoutar (1934) (vlc or vln & pf or orch)
   Danse moldave L. Bobescu – Damian
   Fantaisie L. Bobescu – Damian

(3) Pièces concertantes (1943) (vln & pf)
   No. 1. Romanesca L. Bobescu
Tzingarella (1943) (vln & pf) L. Bobescu –
Lewkowitz
Goltermann, Georg Eduard (1824–1898)
Concerto No. 8, in A, Op. 130 (vlc & orch) Treff
Gomez, José Soler (1875–   )
Habañera (vln & pf) Gomez
Goodeve, Mrs. William
Fiddle & I (v & pf) Jacobsen – Zimbalist
Goodman, Lillian Rosedale (1888–   )
Cherie, I love you (1926) (v & pf) Fradkin
Goodwin, Walter (1885–   )
That wonderful mother of mine (1918) (v & pf)
Southgate
Goossens, Eugene (1892–1962)
Old Chinese folksong, Op. 4, No. 1 (vln & pf)*
M. Hall
Sonata No. 1, in e, Op. 21 (1918) (vln & pf)
Mangeot – Michaelian
Gordon, Westell
Far-away bells (v & pf) Jacobsen
One little dream of love (v & pf) Brown – Chemet
Gossec, François Joseph (1734–1829)
(Le) Camp du Grand Pré (1793) – opera
   Tambourin Cantrelle – Elman – Hayward –
   Kulenkampff – Maurice
Rondo in D (fl, vln, hp & orch) Doukan
Rosine (1786) – opera
   Gavotte
   Berg – A. Busch – L. Cherniavsky – Elman (4)
   – Farbmann – Gade – Gyarfas (3) – Hayward –
   F.V. Henriques – Maurice – Michaïlow –
   Petersen – Příhoda – Rudényi – Sedano – Szikra
   – Tworek – Weismann – Wulf – Zilzer –
   Zimbalist
Goublier, Henri (1888–   )
Love's serenade (vln & pf) Anonymous
Gould, Glenn (1932–   )
Quartet No. 1 (1956) (2 vlns, vla & vlc) Bress &
Goodman
Gounod, Charles François (1818–1893)
Ave Maria (Méditation on Bach's "Prelude No. 1,
in C" from Book I of "Das Wohltemperirte
Clavier") (v & pf)
   Andjelkovitch – Anonymous (3) – Aranyi –
   Beneš – Berchmann – Bluestone – de Brayne –
   Carrodus – Cavalcabo – Czerwonky – D. De
   Groot (2) – M. De Groot – Dessau – Diaz –
   Dinicu – Dolin – Eidus – Elman – Eweler – A.
   Ferraresi (2) – Fischberg – Fradkin – Ghestem –
   Goldis – Guidi – Hager – Hamowetskaya –
   Haxton (2) – Hayward – F.V. Henriques –
   Huppertz – Ingen-Werts – Jacobsen – Kreisler –
   Kubelík – J.M. Lasowski – Lederer – Lewis –
   Lorand – Magyar – Mahlke – Mancke –
   Mánnok – May – Menges – Meyer – Morbitzer
   – Morino – Moskowitz – Neuri – Ormond –
   Pagani – Post – Prick – Příhoda – Ranzato (4)
   – Rosen – Sänger – Schmied – Silverman – S.
   Smith – Southgate – Spalding – Stülken (2) –
   Swaap – Tworek – Weber – Weintraub –
   Weismann (2) – Winchester – Wittenberg – J.

Wolff (2) – Wolfgang – Wolfsthal – Zámečník –
Zimbalist
Faust (1859) – opera
   Anges purs, anges radieux (Act V) Southgate
   Avant de quitter ces lieux (Act II) Southgate
   Faites-lui mes aveux (Act III) Southgate
   Il se fait tard (Act III) Southgate
   Nous nous retrouverons (Act II) Kubelík
   Salut! Demeure chaste et pure Dessau –
   Hayward (2) – Lynged – Southgate – J. Wolff
   Selection d'Almaine (2) – Bobbé – Jacobs –
   Opfermann
   Valse (Act II) Morena
   Versez vos chagrins (Act IV) Southgate
Hymne à Sainte-Cécile (1864) (vln, org & pf)
Dessau – Eweler – Zimmermann
Jeanne d'Arc (1873) – Incidental music (orch)
   Vision de Jeanne d'Arc Locatelli
Noël (v & pf) F.V. Henriques
Sérénade (Quand tu chantes) (v & pf) Aranyi –
Maurice – Moskowitz – Příhoda – Sens – J. Wolff
Gram, Peder (1881–1956)
Canzonetta, Op. 19, No. 1 (vln & pf) Mitnitzky
Gramatte, Sophie-Carmen (1902–   )
Concerto in a (1925) (vln & orch) Gramatte
Gramm, Arthur
Prelude (vln & pf) Gramm
Granados, Enrique y Campina (1867–1916)
(12) Danzas españolas, Op. 37 (1893) (pf)
   Danza española No. 5, in e "Andaluza"
   Bas – Campoli – Collier – Dukson – Eidus –
   Fachiri – Fontanarosa – Gautier – Godwin –
   Grumiaux (2) – Guidi – Heifetz – Kálmán –
   Kerekjarto – Kreisler – Lorand (3) – Lusk –
   Magyar – Menuhin (3) – Morini (2) – Niemczyk
   – Odnoposoff – Rabinoff – Robbins – Rosen –
   Ruggero – Simor – Spalding (2) – Spivakovsky –
   Swaap – Thibaud (3) – Zilzer – Zimmermann
   Danza española No. 6, in D Thibaud (2)
Danza originale (vln & pf)* Thibaud
Goyescas (1916) – opera
   Intermezzo Mus
Graniani, Filippo (1767-1812)
Duet in A (vln & gtr) L. Kogan
Grasse, Edwin (1884–1954)
Wellenspiel (Waves at play) (pf) Heifetz
Grassi, Antonio de (1880–   )
Berceuse (vln & pf) Fradkin
Gratton, Hector (1900–   )
Danse Canadienne No. 4 (inspired from Canadian
folklore) (1935) (vln & pf) Leblanc
Graun, Johann Gottlieb (1703–1771)
Trio-sonata in F (1741) (ob, vln & c) Grehling
Graunke, Kurt (1915–   )
Concerto (vln & orch) David
Greel
Laurbaer & Roser (v & pf) Meine & Sens
Green, Philip (1911–   )
Romance (on a theme by Paganini) (1946) (vln &
pf)† Menuhin

*Unidentified.

†The theme is from the 1st mvt. of Paganini's
"Concerto No. 1, in D" Op. 6. It was featured in
the 1946 J. Arthur Rank film "The Magic Bow."

*Opus 4, No. 2, or Opus 4a, is a serenade for fl &
pf.

Greene, Edwin
Sing me to sleep (*v & pf*) *Ball – Fradkin –
Gittelson – E. Kaufmann – Rubini – Zimbalist*
Grétry, André (1741–1813)
Éphale et Procris (1773) – opera
 Gavotte *Elman – Senatra*
Grieg, Edvard Hagerup (1843–1907)
(4) Albumblätter, Op. 28 (*pf*)
 No. 3. Albumleaf in A *Elman*
(4) Danish songs, Op. 5 (*v & pf*)
 No. 3. Jeg elsker dig (*Ich liebe dich*) *Michaïlow*
(2) Élégiac mélodies, Op. 34 (*str orch*)
 No. 2. Spring *Fritz-Crone – Halvorsen*
(3) Folkelivsbilleder (*Scenes from peasant life*) Op.
19 (*pf*)
 No. 2. Brudefølget drar forbi *Zetterqvist*
(8) Lyric pieces – Book I, Op. 12 (*pf*)
 No. 6. Norwegian melody *Mahlke*
 No. 7. Albumblatt *Mahlke*
(8) Lyric pieces – Book II, Op. 38 (*pf*)
 No. 1. Berceuse *Buchtele – Mahlke – Viardot*
 No. 6. Élégie *Mahlke*
 No. 7. Waltz *Mahlke*
(6) Lyric pieces – Book III, Op. 43 (*pf*)
 No. 2. Lonely wanderer *Mahlke – Piastro*
 No. 5. Erotik *Ranzato*
 No. 6. To the spring *Cravio – Dessau – de
 Grassi – Jacobsen – Kreisler – Lynch – Powell*
(7) Lyric pieces – Book IV, Op. 47 (*pf*)
 No. 3. Melody *Mahlke*
(6) Lyric pieces – Book V, Op. 54 (*pf*)
 No. 4. Nocturne *Elman*
(7) Lyric pieces – Book X, Op. 71 (*pf*)
 No. 3. Puck (*Småtrold*) *Heifetz*
(6) Moods, Op. 73 (*pf*)
 No. 2. Scherzo-Impromptu *Haendel – Heifetz*
(4) Norwegian Dances, Op. 35 (1881) (*pf duet;
orch*)
 Norwegian dance No. 1, in d *Bonis*
 Norwegian dance No. 2, in A *Flesch (2) –
 Knudsen – Valesca-Becker*
Peer Gynt, Op. 23 – opera
 Solveig's song (*Act I*) *Ranzato*
Peer Gynt (*Suite No. 1*) Op. 46 (*orch*)
 No. 3. Anitra's dance *Dessau – Livschakoff –
 Palinko – T. Seidel*
Peer Gynt (*Suite No. 2*) Op. 55 (*orch*)
 No. 4. Soveig's song
 *Akos – Alberti – W. Andersen – Anonymous (2)
 – Arany – Brown (2) – Englund – Eweler –
 Ghestem – Gorensky – Halvorsen – M. Hansen
 – Haxton – Johansen – Knudsen (2) – Lorand –
 Mahlke – Maurice – Michaïlow (3) – Palinko –
 Ranzato (2) – Strockoff – Traversa – Tzipine –
 Wolfsthal – Zilzer*
Quartet in g, Op. 27 (*2 vlns, vla & vlc*) *Hayward*
Sonata No. 1, in F, Op. 8 (*vln & pf*)
 *Csammer – Danchenko – Elman – Fuchs –
 Kennedy – L. Kogan – B. Larsen – Loveday –
 Menuhin – D. Oistrakh*

Sonata No. 2, in G, Op. 13 (*vln & pf*)
 *Brown – Godwin – Grumlíková – L. Hansen –
 Heifetz (2) – Kennedy – B. Larsen – Loveday –
 Menuhin – D. Oistrakh – Sammons – Sjöen –
 Sobolevsky – Tellefsen*
Sonata No. 3, in c, Op. 45 (*vln & pf*)
 *Astruc – Barbieri – Borgani – Doukan – Elman
 – Farbmann – Fuchs – Gabowitz – Gertler –
 Grumiaux – Hayward – Hidy – Knudsen – L.
 Kogan – Kreisler – Kulenkampff – Loveday –
 Menuhin – Rudényi – Sammons (3) – T. Seidel
 – Sobolevsky – Suk (2) – Swaap – Tellefsen –
 Wilkomirska*
(6) Songs, Op. 33 (*v & pf*)
 No. 3. Rundarne (*Vol. II*) *W. Andersen*
Griffis, Elliot (1893–   )
Sonata (1931) (*vln & pf*) *Chassman*
Grigoryan, G. (1919–1962)
Concerto in G (*vln & orch*) *Shindarev*
Grobe, Charles (1839–   )
Sonata in g (*fl, 2 vlns, vla, vlc & cbs*) *Wolf*
Grobet, Louis
(2) Gavottes (*vln & pf*)
 No. 1. Gavotte *Candéla*
Grofé, Ferde (1892–1972)
Grand Canyon (1931) – suite (*orch*)
 On the trail (*3rd mvt*) *Staryk*
Gronemann, Albert Johann (1710–1778)
(12) Sonatas, Op. 1 (*vln & c*)
 Sonata No. 12, in G *Noske*
Gross, Walter (1909–   )
Tenderly (1946) (*v & pf*) *Tworek*
Groth, Einar (1903–   )
Till rosorna (*vln & pf*) *Groth*
Grothe, Franz
Illusion – waltz (*vln & pf*) *Groth*
Groudis, Josas (1884–1948)
(3) Dances (*vln & pf*) *Paulauskas*
Oriental dance (*vln & pf*)*
Kalinauskaite
Sonata in d (*vln & pf*) *Paulauskas*
Grovlez, Gabriel (1879–1944)
(6) Mélodies sur les poèmes de Henri Bataille (*pf*)
 No. 2. Berceuse *Chemet*
Gruber, Franz Xaver (1787–1863)
Stille Nacht, heilige Nacht (1818) (*v & pf*) *Dajos –
Horvath – Josephi – Kulenkampff – Lubow – R.
Richter – Stehl – Weber*
Viennese song (*v & pf*) *Huppertz*
Gruber, Ludwig
Mei' Muatterl war a Wienerin, Op. 1000 (*v & pf*)
Huppertz
Gruenberg, Louis (1884–1964)
Concerto, Op. 47 (*vln & orch*) *Heifetz*
Guarnieri, Camargo Mozart (1907–   )
Sonata No. 2 (1947) (*vln & pf*) *Kaufman*
Sonata No. 4 (1956) (*vln & pf*) *Iacovino*
Guerra, Nicola (1865–   )
Capricho brasileiro (*vln & pf*) *Příhoda*
Gugel, Georg Anton (1743–1802)
Ballo (*vln & pf*) *Haag*
Gugo-Noris, J.
Valse d'or (*vln & pf*) *Curti – Pinell – Ranzato*

*May be one of the 3 dances listed above.

Guiraud, Ernest (1837–1892)
Caprice (1884) (*vln & pf*) *Zimmermann*
Piccolino (1879) – opera
 Mélodrame *Benedetti – Darrieux – Thibaud (2)*
Gullmar, Kai
Mon amour (*vln & pf*) *Groth*
Gungl, Josef (1810–1889)
Am Königssee, Op. 361 (*pf*) *Stehl*
Oberländler (*Country sounds*) Op. 31 (*pf*) *Meine &
Sens – Stülken*
Gurney, Ivor Bertie (1890–1937)
(The) Apple orchard (*vln & pf*) *Grinke*
Haaland, Ingebret (1878–1934)
Bøn (*vln & pf*) *Haaland – Johansen*
Norsk dance No. 1 (*vln & pf*) *Haaland*
Serenade (*vln & pf*) *Johansen*
Hába, Alois (1893–   )
Duo, Op. 49 (1936) (*2 vlns*) *Stein & Weismeyer*
Fantasy, Op. 9a (1921) (*solo vln*) *Bress – Peška*
Hacquart, Carolus (1640–1730)
(10) Sonatas, Op. 2 (*2 vlns, vlc & c*)
 Sonata No. 8, in e *Nijland & Noske*
Sonata (*2 vlns*)*
van den Hombergh & Leonhardt
Hageman, Richard (1882–   )
Do not go, my love (*v & pf*) *Fradkin*
Hahn, Reynaldo (1875–1947)
(7) Chansons grises (*pf*)
 No. 5. L'Heure exquise *A. Sandler*
Ciboulette (1923) – operetta
 Comme frère et soeur *Curti*
O Mon bel Inconnu (1933)
 Est-ce qu'il est mal *Charmy*
Paysage (*v & pf*) *Dony*
Romance in A (*vln & pf*) *Soriano*
Si mes vers avaient des aîles (*v & pf*) *Campoli –
Curti*
Sonata in C (*vln & pf*) *Soriano*
Hajdú, Mihály (1909–   )
Little Suite (*2 vlns & vlc*) *Menyhért & Párkányi*
Halaczinsky, Rudolf (1920–   )
Canzoni de sonas, Op. 39 (1968) (*vln & pf*)
Hagemann
(7) Stücke (*vln & pf*) *Hagemann*
Halévy, Jacques François (1799–1862)
(L') Éclair (1835) – opera
 Call me thine own (*Romance*) *d'Almaine (2)*
Halffter, Rodolfo (1900–   )
Concerto (1939/40) (*vln & orch*) *V. Martin*
Halffter-Escriche, Ernesto (1905–   )
Sonatina (1928) – ballet (*orch*)
 No. 4. Danza de la gitana *Heifetz – Perediaz –
 Szeryng (2)*
 No. 6. Danza de la pastora *Szeryng*
Halvorsen, Johan (1864–1935)
Air norvègien, Op. 31 (*vln & pf*) *Tellefsen*
Andante religioso in g (*vln & pf*) *Törnqvist*
(3) Danses norvègiennes (1914) (*vln & pf*)
 Danse norvègienne† *Parlow*

*From the volume "Harmonia Parnassia," 1686.
†Unidentified.

Danse norvègienne No. 1, in D *Halvorsen – Johannessen – Tellefsen*
Danse norvègienne No. 2, in A *Halvorsen – Tellefsen*
Danse norvègienne No. 3, in d *Tellefsen*
(4) Mosaïques (*Suite des morceaux caractéristiques*) (*vln & pf*)
  No. 3. Scherzino *Tellefsen*
  No. 4. Chant de Veslemøy
  W. Andersen – Arvesen – Barmas – Johannessen – Knudsen (3) – Parlow – Tellefsen – Weist-Hill – Zetterqvist – Zimbalist
Norsk bryllupsmarsch (*vln & pf*) *Arvesen*
Hanby, Benjamin Russell (1833–1867)
Darling Nellie Gray (1856) (*v & pf*) *Gardner*
Handel, George Frederic (1685–1759)
Adagio-Allegro in A (1750 or 1751) (*vln & org*) *Melkus*
Amadigi di Gaula (1715) – opera
  Ah! Spietato! *Sadowski*
Apollo e Dafne (*Cantata No. 16*) (*s, bs, fl, obs, bsn, strs & c*) *Alès*
Arioso* *Burmester – Olsson-Föllinger*
Armida abbandonata (*Cantata No. 13*) (*s, strs & c*)
  Dietro l'orme fugacci *Sadowski*
Berenice (1737) –opera
  Minuet *Hayward (3)*
Bourrée* *M. Hall*
Cantata*
  Dank sei dir, Herr "Arioso"†
  Elman – Georg Kniestaedt – L. Kogan – Steiger-Betzak – Swaap
(The) Choice of Hercules (1750) – secular chorale
  There the brisk, sparkling nectar drain *Flesch (2) – Swaap*
Concerto in B flat (*vln, strs & c*)‡
Menuhin – Totenberg
Concerto No. 3, in g (*ob, strs & c*) *Woiku*
(6) Concerti grossi, Op. 3 (1759) (*strs & c*)
  Concerto grosso No. 1, in B flat *Grehling – Lautenbacher*
  Concerto grosso No. 2, in B flat *Grehling & Vorholz – Lautenbacher*
  Concerto grosso No. 3, in G *Fernandez – Grehling – Lautenbacher – Schön*
  Concerto grosso No. 4, in F *Grehling – Lautenbacher*
  Concerto grosso No. 5, in d *Lautenbacher*
  Concerto grosso No. 6, in D *Lautenbacher*
  Concerto grosso No. 7, in F§
  Fernandez & Germaine Raymond
(6) Concerti, Op. 4 (1735/6) (*org, obs, strs & c*)

*Unidentified.
†Possibly a composition by Ochs.
‡Composed about 1710. Originally titled "Sonata a 5".
§This concerto is a reworking of thematic materials from the 4th organ concerto, Op. 4, which dates from 1735/6.

Concerto No. 3, in g *Barchet – Burmester*
(12) Concerti grossi, Op. 6 (1739) (*2 vlns, vlc, strs & c*)
  Concerto grosso No. 1, in G
  Barchet & Lautenbacher – F. Berger & Büchner – A. Busch & Drucker – Carles & Fernandez – Gaiser & Lautenbacher – Galimir & Schneider – Hurwitz & Keenlyside – Latchem & Marriner – Masters & Menuhin
  Concerto grosso No. 2, in F
  Barchet & Lautenbacher – Bastien & Borries – F. Berger & Büchner – A. Busch & Drucker – Carles & Fernandez – Gaiser & Lautenbacher – Galimir & Schneider – Grehling & Neininger – Hurwitz & Keenlyside – Latchem & Marriner – Masters & Menuhin
  Concerto grosso No. 3, in e
  Barchet & Lautenbacher – F. Berger & Büchner – A. Busch & Drucker – Carles & Fernandez – Gaiser & Lautenbacher – Galimir & Schneider – Grehling & Neininger – Hurwitz & Keenlyside – Latchem & Marriner – Masters & Menuhin
  Concerto grosso No. 4, in a
  Barchet & Lautenbacher – F. Berger & Büchner – A. Busch & Drucker – Carles & Fernandez – Gaiser & Lautenbacher – Galimir & Schneider – Gozman & Selitsky – Grehling & Neininger – Hurwitz & Keenlyside – Latchem & Marriner – Masters & Menuhin
  Concerto grosso No. 5, in D
  Barchet & Lautenbacher – F. Berger & Büchner – A. Busch & Drucker – Carles & Fernandez – Fukano & Nölting – Gaiser & Lautenbacher – Galimir & Schneider – Grehling & Neininger – Hurwitz & Keenlyside – Latchem & Marriner – Masters & Menuhin – Parikian & Salpeter
  Concerto grosso No. 6, in g
  Barchet & Lautenbacher – F. Berger & Büchner – A. Busch & Drucker – Carles & Fernandez – Gaiser & Lautenbacher – Galimir & Schneider – Grehling & Neininger – Hendel & Mayer-Schierning – Hurwitz & Keenlyside – Latchem & Marriner – Masters & Menuhin – Rybar
  Concerto grosso No. 7, in B flat
  Barchet & Lautenbacher – F. Berger & Büchner – A. Busch & Drucker – Carles & Fernandez – Gaiser & Lautenbacher – Galimir & Schneider – Gavrilov & Pietsch – Grehling & Neininger – Hurwitz & Keenlyside – Latchem & Marriner – Masters & Menuhin
  Concerto grosso No. 8, in c
  Barchet & Lautenbacher – F. Berger & Büchner – A. Busch & Drucker – Carles & Fernandez – Gaiser & Lautenbacher – Galimir & Schneider – Gavrilov & Pietsch – Grehling & Neininger – Hurwitz & Keenlyside – Latchem & Marriner – Masters & Menuhin
  Concerto grosso No. 9, in F
  Barchet & Lautenbacher – F. Berger & Büchner – A. Busch & Drucker – Carles & Fernandez – Gaiser & Lautenbacher – Galimir & Schneider – Grehling & Neininger – Hurwitz & Keenlyside – Latchem & Marriner – Masters & Menuhin
  Concerto grosso No. 10, in d

Barchet & Lautenbacher – F. Berger & Büchner – Boder & Gozman – A. Busch & Drucker – Carles & Fernandez – Fernandez & Germaine Raymond – Gaiser & Lautenbacher – Galimir & Schneider – Grehling & Neininger – Grinke & D. Martin – Hurwitz & Keenlyside – Latchem & Marriner – Masters & Menuhin
  Concerto grosso No. 11, in A
  Barchet & Lautenbacher – F. Berger & Büchner – A. Busch & Drucker – Carles & Fernandez – Gaiser & Lautenbacher – Galimir & Schneider – Grehling & Neininger – Hurwitz & Keenlyside – Latchem & Marriner – Masters & Menuhin
  Concerto grosso No. 12, in b
  Barchet & Lautenbacher – Bastien & Borries – F. Berger & Büchner – A. Busch & Drucker – Carles & Fernandez – Gaiser & Lautenbacher – Galimir & Schneider – Grehling & Neininger – Grinke & D. Martin – Hurwitz & Keenlyside – Latchem & Marriner – Masters & Menuhin – Rybar
Concerto in C (1736) "Alexander's Feast" (*2 vlns, 2 obs, strs & c*)*
Grehling – Laurent & Petrović – Marriner & Pini
(9) Deutschen Arien (1729) (*v, vln, fl or ob & c*)
  No. 2. Das zitternde Glänzen der spielenden Wellen *Grehling*
  No. 4. Süsse Stille, sanfte Quelle *Bruun – Rybar*
  No. 6. Meine Seele hört im Sehen *Bruun*
  No. 7. Die ihr aus dunkeln Grüften *Grehling*
  No. 9. Flammende Rose, Zierde der Erden *Grehling*
(The) Messiah (1742) – oratorio
  No. 2. Comfort ye my people *Hayward*
  No. 3. Every valley shall be exalted *Hayward*
  No. 20a. He shall feed His flock *Barinova*
Minuet in F† *Menges*
Ottone, re di Germania (1723) – opera
  Overture *Hayward*
Rinaldo (1711) – opera
  Overture *Hayward*
Serse (1738) – opera
  Ombra mai fu "Largo"
  Akos – d'Almaine – Anonymous – Aranyi – Belov – W. Busch – Campoli – Chauveton – Elman – Fritz-Crone – Galli – Ghestem – Godwin – Heber – Herzl – Josephi – Georg Kniestaedt – Kreisler – Lass – Leopold – Leroy – Lorand – Marx – Menuhin – Meyer – Modern – Powell (2) – Prick – Příhoda (3) – Ranzato – Rattay – Ricci – A. Sandler – Sänger – A. Schmidt – Southgate – Spalding – Stanske – Tworek – Weintraub – Wittenberg – Wolfsthal (2) – Zimmermann
Solomon (1748) – oratorio
  No. 40. Am klaren Bach im stillen Tal *Flesch – Goldstein – Gutnikov – Haendel – Kozolupova – Swaap*
(15) Sonatas, Op. 1 (?1731) (*fl or vln & c*)

*Performed at the opening of Act II of the secular chorale "Alexander's Feast."
†Unidentified.

Sonata No. 1, in e *Olevsky – Temianka*
Sonata No. 1, in d* *Melkus*
Sonata No. 2, in g *Olevsky – Temianka*
Sonata No. 3, in A (*vln I*)
Barinova – Campoli – Casadesus – Chemet –
Fournier – Grumiaux – Hudeček –
Lautenbacher – Melkus – Menges – Menuhin –
Olevsky – Schneider – Temianka
Sonata No. 4, in a *Olevsky – Temianka*
Sonata No. 5, in G *Bratza – Burmester –*
Olevsky – Olsson-Föllinger – Temianka
Sonata No. 6, in g *Melkus – Olevsky –*
Temianka
Sonata No. 7, in C *Olevsky – Temianka*
Sonata No. 8, in c *Olevsky – Temianka*
Sonata No. 9, in b
Farbmann – Garaguly – Godwin – Hubay –
Ingen-Werts – Jacobsen – B. Koutzen – Lorand
– Milstein – Møller – Morini – Olevsky – Piastro
– R. Ricci – Spivakovsky – Staryk – J. Szigeti –
Telmányi – Temianka (2) – Vecsey – Zhuk –
Zimbalist – Zimmermann
Sonata No. 10, in g (*vln II*)
Bauer – Brix-Meinert – Campoli – Casadesus –
Fournier – Frasca-Colombier – Grumiaux –
Lautenbacher – Markov – Melkus – Menuhin –
Olevsky – Ruha – Schneider – Suk – Temianka
Sonata No. 11, in F *Olevsky – Temianka*
Sonata No. 12, in F (*vln III*)
Bauer – Campoli – Casadesus – Fournier –
Frenkel – Grumiaux – Lautenbacher – Melkus
– Menuhin – Michaïlow – Olevsky – Sammons –
Schneider – Temianka
Sonata No. 13, in D (*vln IV*)
Bezrodny – L. Bobescu – Boussinot – Campoli –
Casadesus – De Reus – De Vito – Dommett –
Elman (2) – Enescu – Flesch – Fournier –
Francescatti – Frasca-Colombier – Frolov –
Goldberg – Grumiaux – Gutnikov – Jásek –
Klijn – Klimov – Lautenbacher – Melkus –
Menges – Menuhin (3) – Milstein – Moss –
Olevsky – Röhn – Schneider – Stern – Suk – J.
Szigeti (2) – Taschner – Telmányi – Temianka
– Zimmermann
Sonata No. 14, in A (*vln V*)
Bauer – C. Bobescu – Campoli – Casadesus –
Elman – Flesch – Fournier – Frasca-Colombier
– Frenkel – Friedmann – Gautier – Grumiaux –
Lautenbacher – Melkus – Menuhin – Olevsky –
Petronio – Schneider – Scripka – Suk –
Temianka – Zhuk
Sonata No. 15, in E (*vln VI*)
Bauer – Bezrodny – Campoli – Casadesus –
Chemet – Demkeck – Dubois
– Elman – Farbmann – Flesch – Fournier –
Frasca-Colombier – Grumiaux – Gutnikov –
Heifetz – L. Kogan – Kubel ík– Lautenbacher –
Melkus – Menuhin (2) – Olevsky – Schneider –
Scripka – Spalding – Suk – Temianka
(9) Sonatas, Op. 2 (1724) (*2 vlns or obs & c*)
Sonata No. 1, in c *Strub*
Sonata No. 1b, in b (*fl, vln & c*) *Harnoncourt*

*Opus 1, No. 1b.

Sonata No. 2, in g *Blot & Ortmans-Bach*
Sonata No. 3, in g *G. & W. Beal – Harnoncourt*
& Pfeiffer
Sonata No. 4, in B flat *M. & W. Schweyda*
Sonata No. 5, in F (*rec, vln & c*) *Harnoncourt*
Sonata No. 7, in g *D'Aranyi & Fachiri –*
Dubiska & Uminska – D. & I. Oistrakh
Sonata No. 8, in g *Dubiska & Uminska – De*
Vito & Menuhin – Sammons – M. & W.
Schweyda
Sonata No. 9, in E *M. & W. Schweyda –*
Spalding
(7) Sonatas, Op. 5 (1739) (*2 vlns & c*)
Sonata No. 1, in A *Friisholm & Kassow*
Sonata No. 2, in D *De Vito & Menuhin –*
Friisholm & Kassow – Hurwitz & Liddell
Sonata No. 3, in e *Friisholm & Kassow – M. &*
W. Schweyda
Sonata No. 4, in G *Fietz & Rybar – Friisholm*
& Kassow
Sonata No. 5, in g *Brown & Totenberg –*
Friisholm & Kassow
Sonata No. 6, in F *Friisholm & Kassow –*
Walther Schneiderhan & Swoboda
Sonata No. 7, in B *Friisholm & Kassow*
Sonata in B flat (1710) (*vln, strs & c*) *Jarry –*
Sillito
Sonata in d (*ob, vln & c*) *Harnoncourt*
Sonata in G (*vln & hpsi*)* *Melkus*
Suite (*vln & pf*)† *Hayward*
Suite (*vln & pf*)‡
  No. 1. Rigaudon *Menges*
  No. 3. Hornpipe *Menges*
  No. 4. Passacaglia *Menges*
(16) Suites (1720/33) (*hpsi*)
  Suite No. 7, in g: Passacaglia (*6th mvt*)
  Asselin – L. Bobescu – Brown – Heifetz – L.
  Kogan – Persinger – Richards – Sammons (2)
  Suite No. 11, in d *Grinke*
  Suite No. 14, in G *Elman*
Te Deum, Dettingen (1743)
  No. 17. Gebet ('*Verlieh uns Herr, zu schirmen*
  . . .) *Flesch (2) – Magyar – Menuhin (2) –*
  Renardy – Swaap
(6) Trio-sonatas (1696) (*2 obs or 2 vlns & c*)
  Trio-sonata No. 3, in E flat *Geissmar – Gendre*
Hanley, James Frederick (1892–1942)
Just a cottage small by a waterfall (1925) (*v & pf*)
Fradkin – Jacobsen
Hannikainen, Arvo (1897–1942)
Spring wagon (*vln & pf*) *Hannikainen*
Hanousek, Karel (1902–   )
Capriccietto (*vln & pf*) *Hanousek*

*Attributed to Handel
†Arrangement of Minuet & Musette from
"Alcina"; Andante from "Alexander's Feast" &
the Gavotte from "Ottone, re di Germania" by
Walford Davies.
‡Arranged from miscellaneous movements by
Hamilton Harty.

Valse-caprice (*vln & pf*) *Hanousek*
Hansen, Adolf Johannes Waldemar (1852–1911)
Wiegenlied (*vln & pf*) *Aranyi*
Haquinius, Johan Algot (1886–   )
Sonata in c sharp (*vln & pf*) *Karpe*
Svensk dans (*vln & pf*) *Karpe – Runnqvist*
d'Hardelot, Guy (1858–1936)*
Because (1902) (*v & pf*) *d'Almaine – Chemet – D.*
De Groot – Southgate
I know a lovely garden (*v & pf*) *Haxton*
Wait (*v & pf*) *Lensky – A. Sandler*
Harito, E.
Crysanteme (*vln & pf*) *Skalka*
Harris, Roy (1898–   )
Poem (*vln & pf*) *Spalding*
Sonata (1941) (*vln & pf*) *Gingold*
Trio (1934) (*pf, vln & vlc*) *Gerle – Poltronieri*
Harrison, Julius Allan Greenway (1885–1963)
Widdicombe fair, Op. 22 "Humoresque" (*2 vlns,*
vla & vlc) *Hayward*
Harrison, Lou (1917–   )
Suite (1951) (*vln, pf & small orch*) *Ajemian*
Hartley, Lloyd
Sérénade mélancolique (*vln & pf*) *Sammons*
Hartmann, Emil (1836–1898)
Agnetes Vuggevise (*pf*) *Petersen*
Hartmann, Karl Amadeus (1905–1963)
Concerto funèbre (1939) (*vln & str orch*) *Gertler –*
Lehmann
Harty, Hamilton (1879–1941)
Irish Fantasia (*vln & pf*) *Kelly-Lange*
Haslinde, Paul
Abendwind in Sevilla (*vln & pf*) *Eweler*
(Die) Galanten (*vln & pf*) *Eweler*
Hasse, Johann Adolph (1699–1783)
Abendlied (*vln & org*) *Josephi*
Hauser, Miska (1822–1887)
(2) Lieder ohne Worte, Op. 11 (*vln & pf*)
  No. 2. Wiegenlied *Freeman*
Rapsodie hongrois No. 1, in d, Op. 43 (*vln & pf*)
Lari – Liebman – Moller – Zacharewitsch
Hayashi, Hikaru
Rhapsody "Winter on 72nd Street" (*vln & pf*)
Kuronuma
Haydn, Franz Josef (1732–1809)
Capriccietto-Presto† *Elman*
Cassation in G, H.II, No. 9 (*2 vlns, 2 obs, 2 hrns,*
2 vlas, vlc & cbs) *Grehling & Maier*
Cassation in F, H.II, No. 20 (*2 vlns, 2 obs, 2 hrns,*
2 vlcs, vlc & cbs) *Grehling & Maier*
Cassation in C, H.III, No. 6 (*lute, vln & vlc*)‡
Trysessoone
Concerto in F, H.XVIII, No. 6 (1765) (*vln, hpsi &*
orch)
  Barchet – Chauveton – Glenn – Hertz – Jarry –
  Manzone – Melkus – Pougnet – Rybar – J.
  Schröder

*Pseudonym for Helen Guy Rhodes.
†Unidentified.
‡Arrangement of opus 1, No. 6.

Concerto No. 1, in C, H.VIIa, No. 1 (1765) (*vln & orch*)

Auclair – Ayo – Comellas – Frasca-Colombier – Geyer (2) – Goldberg – Gotkovsky – Grumiaux – Kempler – Krebbers – Menuhin – Rüman – Stern – Suske – Vaiman

Concerto No. 2, in G, H.VIIa, No. 4 (1761) (*vln & orch*)

Bertschinger – Grumiaux – Kempler – Krebbers – Melkus – Scripka – Selitsky – Suske – Terebesi

Concerto No. 3, in A, H.VIIa, No. 3 (1765) "Melk" (*vln & orch*) *Bertschinger – Gerle – Gotkovsky – Grumiaux – Hitzker – J. Schröder*

(6) Divertimenti, H.II, Nos. 9/14 (*Op. 5*) (*fl, vln, vla & vlc*)

Quartet No. 1, in D, H.II, No. 9 *Jarry*
Quartet No. 2, in G, H.II, No. 10 *Jarry*
Quartet No. 3, in D, H.II, No. 11 *Jarry – Lautenbacher*
Quartet No. 4, in G, H.II, No. 12 *Jarry*
Quartet No. 5, in D, H.II, No. 13 *Jarry*
Quartet No, 6, in C, H.II, No. 14 *Jarry*

(6) Divertimenti, H.IV, Nos. 6/11 (*Op. 100*) (*fl, vln & vlc*)

Divertimento No. 1, in D, H.IV, No. 6 *Frühauf – J. Pasquier*
Divertimento No. 2, in G, H.IV, No. 7 *J. Pasquier*
Divertimento No. 4, in G, H.IV, No. 9 *J. Pasquier*
Divertimento No. 6, in D, H.IV, No. 11 *J. Pasquier (2)*

(3) Duos, H.III, Nos. 25/7 (1769) (*vln & vlc*)
Duo No. 3, in B flat, H.III, No. 27 *D. & I. Oistrakh*
(3) Duos, H.III, Nos. 28/30 (1769) (*vln & vlc*)
Duo No. 4, in D, H.III, No. 28 *Posselt*

Klänge aus dem thüringer Wald (*v & pf*) *Sens*
Klänge aus der Heimat (*v & pf*) *Sens*
Minuet* *Petroni – Weismann – Zacharewitsch*
Minuet in F* *Brown – Elman*

(6) Quartets, Op. 1 (*H.III, Nos. 1/6*) (*2 vlns, vla & vlc*)

No. 6. Quartet No. 6, in C, H.III, No. 6 *Brix-Meinert*

(6) Quartets, Op. 2 (*H.III, Nos. 7/12*) (*2 vlns, vla & vlc*)

No. 2. Quartet No. 8, in E, H.III, No. 8 *Grach – Kehr – Loveday*

(6) Quartets, Op. 3 (*H.III, Nos. 13/18*) (*2 vlns, vla & vlc*)

No. 5. Quartet No. 17, in F, H.III, No. 17 *Hayward – Kalki – Lutsky & Ovcharek – Totenberg – Wittenberg*

(6) Quartets, Op. 20 (*H.III, Nos. 31/6*) (*2 vlns, vla & vlc*)

No. 4. Quartet No. 34, in D, H.III, No. 34 *Michaïlow & Pietsch*
No. 5. Quartet No. 35, in f, H.III, No. 35 *Swoboda*

(6) Quartets, Op. 33 (*H.III, Nos. 37/42*) (*2 vlns,*

*Unidentified.

vla & vlc*)
No. 2. Quartet No. 38, in E flat, H.III, No. 38 *Knudsen*

(7) Quartets, Op. 51 (*H.III, Nos. 50/6*) (*2 vlns, vla & vlc*)*

No. 1. Pater, dimmitte illis, non enim sciunt quid faciunt, H.III, No. 50 *Gingold & Shumsky*
No. 2. Amen, dico tibi, hodie mecum eris in Paradiso, H.III, No. 51 *Gingold & Shumsky*
No. 3, Muller ecce filius tuus, et tu, ecce mater tua!, H.III, No. 52 *Gingold & Shumsky*
No. 4. Eli, Eli lama asabthani?, H.III, No. 53 *Gingold & Shumsky*
No. 5. Sitio, H.III, No. 54 *Gingold & Shumsky*
No. 6. Consumatum est!, H.III, No. 55 *Gingold & Shumsky*
No. 7. Pater, in manus tuus commendo spiritum meum, H.III, No. 56 *Gingold & Shumsky*

(3) Quartets, Op. 54 (*H.III, Nos. 57/9*) (*2 vlns, vla & vlc*)

No. 2. Quartet No. 58, in C, H.III, No. 58 *Goldstein*

(6) Quartets, Op. 64 (*H.III, Nos. 63/8*) (*2 vlns, vla & vlc*)

No. 5. Quartet No. 67, in D, H.III, No. 67 "The Lark" *Dyke – Heifetz – Kalki – Kayser – Queling – Wolf*

(3) Quartets, Op. 74 (*H.III, Nos. 72/4*) (*2 vlns, vla & vlc*)

No. 1. Quartet No. 72, in C, H.III, No. 72 *Gertler – Hayward*

(6) Quartets, Op. 76 (*H.III, Nos. 75/80*) (*2 vlns, vla & vlc*)

No. 1. Quartet No. 75, in G, H.III, No. 75 *Catterall*
No. 2. Quartet No. 76, in d, H.III, No. 76 "Quinten" *Elman – Morbitzer*
No. 3. Quartet No. 77, in C, H.III, No. 77 "Emperor"†
Elman (2) – Hayward – Kayser – Kreisler
No. 5. Quartet No. 79, in D, H.III, No. 79. *Catterall*

Quartet No. 83, in B flat, Op. 103 (*H.III, No. 83*) "Unfinished" (*2 vlns, vla & vlc*) *Bress & Goodman*
Sextet "Divertimento" in E flat, H. II, No. 39 "Echo" (*4 vlns & 2 vlcs*) *Lautenbacher*
(Die) Sieben letzte Worte des Erlösers am Kreuze (1786) (*orch*)‡
Sinfonia concertante in B flat, Op. 84 (*H.I, No. 105*) (*vln, vlc, ob, bsn & orch*)
Alès – Barchet – Charmy – Gulli – L. Hansen – Hendel – Hurwitz – Krachmalnick – Lautenbacher (2) – Neuhaus – Schnitzer
Sonata No. 3, in C, H.XVI, No. 3 (*pf*) *Chemet*
Sonata No. 51, in D, H.XVI, No. 51 (*Op. 93*) (*pf*) *Posselt*

*Die Sieben letzte Worte des Erlösers am Kreuze, 1786.

†The Oesterreichische Bundeshymne or Austrian hymn is from this work.

‡See: 7 Quartets, Op. 51 (*H.III, Nos. 50/6.*)

Sonata in B flat, Op. 4 (*H.XIV, No. 1*) "Divertimento" (*2 hrns, vln, vlc & hpsi*) *Jarry*
(6) Sonatas, H.VI, Nos. 1/6 (*vln & vla*)
Sonata No. 1, in C, H.VI, No. 1 *Kovács*
Sonata No. 2, in A, H.VI, No. 2 *Kovács*
Sonata No. 3, in E flat, H.VI, No. 3 *Kovács*
Sonata No. 4, in F, H.VI, No. 4 *Kovács*
Sonata No. 5, in D, H.VI, No. 5 *Kovács*
Sonata No. 6, in B flat, H.VI, No. 6 *Kovács*

Sonata No. 1, in G, H.XV, No. 32 (1794) (*vln & hpsi*) *Franke – Gabowitz – Nemet – B. Schwarz – Staryk (2)*
Sonata No. 2, in D, H.XVI, No. 24 (1773) (*vln & hpsi*) *Nemet – B. Schwarz*
Sonata No. 3, in E flat, H.XVI, No. 25 (1773) (*vln & hpsi*) *Kremer – Nemet – B. Schwarz*
Sonata No. 4, in A, H.XVI, No. 26 (*vln & hpsi*)* *L. Kogan*
Sonata No. 5, in E flat, H.XVI, No. 43 (1785) (*vln & hpsi*) *Nemet*
Sonata No. 6, in C, H.XVI, No. 15 (1767) (*vln & hpsi*) *B. Schwarz*
Sonata No. 7, in F, H.III, No. 82 (*vln & hpsi*)† *Bernard – Lubotsky*
Sonata in e flat (1795) "Derniere Sonate" (*vln & pf*)‡ *Tunnell*
Symphony No. 6, in D "Le Matin" (*orch*) *V. Martin*
Symphony No. 7, in C "Le Midi" (*orch*) *V. Martin*
Symphony No. 8, in G "Le Soir" (*orch*) *V. Martin*

Symphony No. 96, in D (1791) "Miracle" (*orch*) *Chemet – Elman – Kreisler*
Symphony No. 103, in E flat "Drum roll" (*orch*) *Staryk*
Trio in E flat, H.IV, No. 5 (1767) (*hrn, vln & vlc*) *Walther Schneiderhan*
Trio No. 34, in D, H.XI, No. 34 (*baryton, vla & cbs*) *Eweler*
Trio No. 78, in D, H.XI, No. 78 (baryton, vla & cbs) *Eweler*
(31) Trios, H.XV, Nos. 1/31 (*pf, vln & vlc*)§
Trio No. 1, in g, H.XV, No. 1 (*Op. 70, No. 2*) (*L16; P19; U21*) *Fournier*
Trio No. 4, in F, H.XV, No. 4 (*Op. 40, No. 2*) (*L27*) *Fournier*
Trio No. 5, in G, H.XV, No. 5 (*Op. 40, No. 3*) (*L28*) *Fournier*

*Arrangement of the piano sonata, H.XVI, No. 26 – ed. David.
†Arrangement of the string quartet No. 82, in F, Op. 77, H.III, No. 82.
‡Identical with the piano trio No. 31, in e flat, H.XV, No. 31.
§The piano trios are at some variance with regard to numbering in all editions. The following publications relate to the abbreviations listed in parentheses following normal entry procedure. L = Litolff; P = Peters; U = Universal.

Trio No. 12, in e, H.XV, No. 12 (*Op. 57, No. 2*) (*L10; P71*) *Fournier*

Trio No. 14, in A flat, H.XV, No. 14 (*Op. 61*) (*L24, P11; U16*) *Fournier*

Trio No. 16, in D, H.XV, No. 16 (*Op. 63*) (*L30*) *Fournier – L. Kogan*

Trio No. 17, in F, H.XV, No. 17 (*Op. 68*) (*L29*) *Fournier*

Trio No. 19, in g, H.XV, No. 19 (*Op. 70, No. 2*) (*L14; P17; U19*) *L. Kogan*

Trio No. 21, in C, H.XV, No. 21 (*Op. 75, No. 1*) (*L18; P21*) *D. Oistrakh (2)*

Trio No. 22, in E flat, H.XV, No. 22 (*Op. 75, No. 3*) (*L20; P23*) *Fournier – Melkus*

Trio No. 25, in G, H.XV, No. 25 (*Op. 73, No. 2*) (*L1*)
Catterall – Feigin – Fournier – Holst – Kreisler – Melkus – F. Reuter – Sammons – Strub – Thibaud – Totenberg

Trio No. 26, in f sharp, H.XV, No. 26 (*Op. 73, No. 3*) (*L2*) *Gendre – Goldberg – Gruenberg – Melkus*

Trio No. 27, in C, H.XV, No. 27 (*Op. 75, No. 1*) (*L3*) *Anonymous – Goldberg*

Trio No. 28, in E, H.XV, No. 28 (*Op. 75, No. 2*) (*L4; U23*) *Fournier – Gendre (2) – Goodman – D. Oistrakh*

Trio No. 29, in E flat, H.XV, No. 29 (*Op. 75, No. 3*) (*L5*) *Goldberg*

Trio No. 30, in E flat, H.XV, No. 30 (*Op. 42, No. 3*) (*L12; P8; U11*) *Fournier*

Trio No. 31, in e flat, H.XV, No. 31 (*L15; P18; U20*) *Melkus*

(3) Trios, H.XVI, Nos. 40/2 (*Op. 53*) (*vln, vla & vlc*)

Trio No. 1, in G, H.XVI, No. 40 *Grumiaux – Pougnet*

Trio No. 2, in B flat, H.XVI, No. 41 *Grumiaux – Pougnet*

Trio No. 3, in D, H.XVI, No. 42 *Gendre – Grumiaux – Pougnet*

Haydn, Michael (1737–1806)

Concerto in A (*vln & orch*)*
Armon – Grumiaux

Concerto in B flat (1760) (*vln & orch*) *Gerle – Walther Schneiderhan – Schröder*

Divertimento in D, P93 (*2 vlns, vla & cbs*) *Redditi*

Divertimento in C, P99 (*vln, vlc & cbs*) *Pougnet*

Hays, William Shakespeare (1837–1907)

Molly darling (1871) (*v & pf*) *Gusikoff*

Hegar, Friedrich (1841–1927)

(6) Waltzes, Op. 14 (*vln & pf*)

Waltz No. 2 *Marteau*

Waltz No. 4 *Marteau*

Heilmann, Harald (1924–   )

Sonata No. 1 (*vln & pf*) *Hagemann*

Heinichen, Johann David (1683–1729)

Concerto in D (*vln, strs & c*)†
Totenberg

Heinsius, Michael Ernst

---

*Discovered 1964.

†Manuscript is in the Hessische Landes- und Hochschulbibliothek in Darmstadt.

(6) Concerti (*vln & strs*)

Concerto in G *Noske*

Helf, J. Fred

(A) Picture no artist can paint (1899) (*v & pf*) *Hager*

Hellendaal, Pieter (1721–1799)

(6) Sonatas, Op. 1 (*vln & c*)

Sonata No. 3, in g *Noske*

Helm, Everett (1913–   )

Comment on 2 spirituals (*vln & pf*) *Kaufman (2)*

Hemel, Oscar van (1892–   )

Concerto (1943/4) (*vln & orch*) *Olof*

Henderson, Ray (1896–   )

So blue (*v & pf*) *Fradkin*

Henkemans, Hans (1913–   )

Concerto (1948) (*vln & orch*) *De Reus*

Concerto (1954) (*vln & orch*) *Olof*

Henley, William (1874–1957)

Variations hongroise, Op. 55 (*vln & pf*) *Henley*

Variations on the Austrian Hymn, Op. 33, No. 1 (*vln & pf*) *Henley*

Henri, Jacques

Légende amoureuse (*Mélodie sentimentale*) (*vln & pf*) *MacMillen*

Henriques, Fini Valdemar (1867–1940)

Ballerina (*vln & pf*) *Leth*

Canzonetta, Op. 27 (*vln & pf*) *F.V. Henriques*

Djaevledans (*Devil dance*) (*vln & pf*) *Tworek*

(Det) Døende barn (*The dying child*) (1899) (*v & pf*) *F.V. Henriques*

(5) Erotic pieces, Op. 15 (*pf*)

No. 4. Petite romance *F.V. Henriques*

Merry dance (*vln & pf*) *Barmas*

Myggedans (*Gnat's dance*) Op. 20, No. 5 (*vln & pf*) *F.V. Henriques (2) – Tworek*

(10) Pieces (*pf*)

No. 3. Bryllupsdans (*Gavotte*) *F.V. Henriques*

Romance in D, Op. 43 (*vln & pf*) *F.V. Henriques & Pedersen – Skalka*

Sammenspil (*10 character pieces*) Op. 22 (*vln & pf*)

No. 6. Vuggesang *F.V. Henriques*

(4) Songs, Op. 3 (*v & pf*)

No. 4. Agnetes Vuggevise *Baranowski – Brugman – M. Hansen – F.V. Henriques (2) – Tworek*

To maa man vaere (*There must be two*) (1920) (*v & pf*) *F.V. Henriques*

Wiegenlied (*vln & pf*) *F.V. Henriques*

Hentschel, Erwin

Liebesreigen-serenade (*vln & pf*) *Lorand*

Hentschel, George (1850–1934)

Illusion tango (*vln & pf*) *Asti – Jelving*

Henze, Hans Werner (1926–   )

Concerto (1948) (*vln & orch*) *Wolfgang Schneiderhan*

Herbert, Victor (1859–1924)

À la valse (*vln & pf*) *Elman – Heifetz*

Babes in Toyland (1903) – musical comedy

Toyland *Raderman*

Bandinage (*pf*) *Chemet*

(The) Fortune Teller (1898) – operetta

Gypsy love song *Alberti – Ball (2) – Chemet – Fradkin – Morell – Zimbalist*

Heart o' mine (*v & pf*) *Fradkin*

Mademoiselle Modiste (1905) – comic opera

Kiss me again *Chemet – Fradkin – Lipschultz – Morrell*

Maytime – operetta

Will you remember? *Thiele*

Naughty Marietta (1910) – operatta

Ah! sweet mystery of life *Andjelkovitch – Jelving – Mantovani*

selection *Selinsky*

Orange Blossoms (1922) – opera

A kiss in the dark *Fradkin – Kreisler*

Petite valse (*vln & pf*) *Brown – Powell*

Suite in F, Op. 3 (*vln & pf*)

No. 4. Serenade (*Andante grazioso*) *Drdla – Jacobsen*

Sweethearts (1913) – musical comedy*

selection *Chemet – Selinsky*

Hermann, Adolf (1823–1903)

Boléro sur des motifs espagnols, Op. 52 (*vln & pf*) *Polo*

Hermite, Maurice

Evening in the desert (*v & pf*) *Manuello*

(The) Nights of Erzeroum (*v & pf*) *Lensky*

Hérold, Louis Joseph Ferdinand (1791–1833)

(Le) Pré aux Clercs (1832) – opera

Cadenza *de Monge*

Jours de mon enfance *Manén*

O Dieu du jeunge âge *Manén*

Herrando, José (18*th century*)

(10) Pieces (1750) (*clav*)

No. 9. Movemento perpétuel *L. Bobescu*

Herrmann, Thomas

Canzonetta, Op. 57 (*vln & pf*) *Alessandro*

Hess, Ernst (1912–   )

Quartet, Op. 50 (2 *vlns, vla & vlc*) *Rybar*

Hessenberg, Kurt (1908–   )

Trio, Op. 48 (1949) (*vln, vla & vlc*) *Kehr*

Heuberger, Richard (1850–1914)

(Der) Opernball, Op. 40 (1898) – operetta

Im chambre séparée
Brückner – Campoli (2) – Cochrane – Colombo – Druian – Eweler – Flesch – Huppertz – Jacobsen – Jelving – Kreisler (3) – Morini – Rubato – A. Sandler – Theodorescu – Wilkomirska

Heykens, Jonni (1884–   )

(The) Child & his dancing doll (*orch*) *A. Sandler*

Serenade, Op. 21 (*orch*) *W. Andersen*

Spanish serenade (*orch*) *A. Sandler*

Heymann, Werner Richard (1896–   )

Je ne sais (*v & pf*)† *Curti*

Hidas, Frigyes (1928–   )

Concertino (1957) (*vln & orch*) *Kovács*

Hierro

Jota capricho (*vln & pf*) *Mus*

Hildach, Eugen (1849–1924)

(2) Lieder, Op. 15 (*v & pf*)

No. 1. Der Spielmann *Rattay – Zimbalist*

Hill, Wilhelm (1838–1902)

(Das) Herz am Rhein (*v & pf*) *Weintraub*

---

*Later a film score.

†From the film "Le rêve blond."

Hindemith, Paul (1895–1963)
Concerto in C sharp (1939) (*vln & orch*) *Gertler – Merckel*
Concerto in D (1940) (*vln & orch*) *Fuchs – Gitlis – D. Oistrakh (2) – Stern*
(4) Kammermusik, Op. 36 (*var. cbns*)
    No. 3. Kammermusik No. 4 (1925) (*vln & cha orch*) *I. Oistrakh*
Nobilissima Visione (1938) – ballet (*orch*)
    Méditation *Bakman*
Quartet No. 3, in C, Op. 22 (1922) (*2 vlns, vla & vlc*) *Amar (2)*
Schulwerk, Op. 44 (1927) (*var. inst*)
    No. 4. 5 Pieces in the first position for more advanced players *Gozman – Menuhin**
(6) Sonatas, Op. 11†
    Sonata No. 1, in E flat (1920) (*vln & pf*)
    Dembeck – Gutnikov – Krysa – Messiereur – D. Oistrakh
    Sonata No. 2, in D (1920) (*vln & pf*) *Kaufman – Komissarov – Lack – Schiavina*
(2) Sonatas, Op. 31 (1924) (*solo vln*)
    Sonata No. 1 *Bochková – Merckel – R. Ricci – Schmahl – Tarack*
    Sonata No. 2 *Lewkowitz – Petrosyan – R. Ricci (2) – Schiavina – Staryk*
Sonata No. 3, in E (1935) (*vln & pf*) *Endres – I. Oistrakh – Ortenberg – Posselt – R. Ricci – Rosoff – Snitkovsky – J. Szigeti*
Sonata No. 3, in C (1940) (*vln & pf*) *Schiavina – Wolfgang Schneiderhan – Stern*
Symphonic Metamorphosis on themes by Weber "Four Temperaments" (1946) (*orch*) *Gieseler*
Trauermusik (*for the death of King George V*) (1936) (*vla*) *Grach*
Trio No. 1, Op. 34 (1924) (*vln, vla & vlc*) *Amar – Pougnet*
Trio No. 2 (1934) (*vln, vla & vlc*) *Goldberg – Grach – Pougnet*

Hirota
Chikuma-Gawa Ryojo no Uta (*vln & pf*) *Lass*
Shikararete *Lass*

Hirsch, Louis Achille (1881–1924)
Colorado (*v & pf*) *Fradkin*
Mary (1920) – musical
    The love nest *Chamberland – Jacobsen – Kreisler*

Hjelt, August
(6) Eteläpohjalaisia tansee, Op. 17a (*vln & pf*) *Pohjola*

Ho, Chan-hao
Concerto (1960) "Butterfly lovers" (*vln & orch*) *Li-Na – Yung*

Høeberg, Georg Valdemar (1872–1950)
Romance in G, Op. 3 (*vln & pf*) *Nilsson*

Hoffmann, Johann (*18th century*)
Quartet in F (*mand, vln, vla & lute*) *Pichler*

Hoffmann, Richard (1925–   )
Trio (1963) (*vln, vla & vlc*) *Zukofsky*

*5th piece only – "Lebhaft".
†Only sonatas 1 & 2 are for vln & pf. Number 3 is for vlc & pf; No. 4 is for vla & pf; No. 5 is for solo vla & No. 6 is for solo vln.

Hoffmeister, Franz Anton (1754–1812)
(3) Duets, Op. 6 (*vln & vla*)
    Duet No. 3, in G *Grumiaux*
Holland, Theodore Samuel (1878–1947)
(4) Fancies, Op. 18 (*vln & pf*) *Fellowes*
Hollman, Josef (1852–1927)
Chanson d'amour (*v & pf*) *Elman – Förster*
Holmboe, Vagn (1909–   )
Quartet No. 3, Op. 48 (*2 vlns, vla & vlc*) *Bruun*
Holst, Gustav (1874–1934)
Concerto, Op. 49 (1929) (*2 vlns & orch*) *Hurwitz & Sillito*
St. Paul's Suite (1913) (*orch*)
    Intermezzo *Parikian*
(4) Songs, Op. 35 (*v, vln & pf*)
    No. 1. Jesu sweet *Brainin – Reed*
    No. 2. I sing of a maid *Brainin – Reed*
    No. 3. My soul has nought but fire & ice *Brainin – Reed*
    No. 4. My leman is so true of love *Brainin – Reed*
Valse-Étude (*vln & pf*) *M. Hall*
Honegger, Arthur (1892–1955)
(La) Danse des Morts (1938) – oratorio
    Lamento *Pascal*
Petite Suite (1936) (*2 fls, cl, sax, vln & pf*) *Locatelli – Schneeberger*
Sonata No. 1, in c sharp (1916/8) (*vln & pf*) *Crut – Goldstein – J. Szigeti*
Sonata No. 2, in d (1919) (*vln & pf*) *Gertler – Rusin – Wiener*
Sonata (1940) (*solo vln*) *Ferras – Merckel (2)*
Sonatina (1920) (*2 vlns*) *G. & W. Beal – D. & I. Oistrakh*
Sonatina (1932) (*vln & vlc*) *Bas – Gendre – Schoenfeld – Suk*
von Hoop
Etude in e (*vln & pf*) *Kolársky*
Horváth, Josef Maria (1931–   )
Spring Waltz – operetta
    Intermezzo (*orch*) *Simor*
Squirrel dance (*vln & pf*) *Simor*
Hovhaness, Alan (1911–   )
Concerto No. 2, Op. 89A (1957) (*vln & orch*) *Ajemian*
Duet (1954) (*vln & hpsi*) *Brink*
Kirgiz Suite, Op. 93 (1951) (*vln & pf*) *Ajemian*
Shatakh (*vln & pf*) *Ajemian*
Suite, Op. 99 (1952) (*vln, pf & pcn*) *Ajemian*
Tzaikerk (*vln, fl & orch*) *Ajemian*
Howells, Herbert Norman (1892–   )
Lady Audrey's Suite, Op. 19 (1916) (*2 vlns, vla & vlc*)
    The little girl & the shepherd *Catterall*
    The old shepherd *Catterall*
Hristič, Stevan (1885–1958)
Ohridska Legenda – ballet (*orch*) *Toškov*
Hubay, Jenö (1858–1937)
(6) Blumenleben, Op. 30 (*vln & pf*)
    No. 5. Der Zephir
    Barbieri – Beckwith – Bisztriczky (3) – Campoli – A. Ferraresi – Gautier – Gorokhov – Kubelík (2) – Law – Menges – Morini – Moszkowski – D. Oistrakh – Powell – Příhoda – Quiroga – R. Ricci (2) – Szentgyörgi – J. Szigeti (4) –

Telmányi – T. Varga – Wittels – Zimbalist
Concerto No. 3, in g, Op. 99 (*vln & orch*) *Rosand – Zimbalist*
Hungarian fantasy "Kunok abrand" (*vln & pf*) *Dessau*
Impression de la Puszta (*3 Morceaux caractéristiques hongrois*) Op. 44 (*vln & pf*)
    No. 2. Les fileuses (*A Fonòban*) *d'Albert*
(Le) Luthier de Crémone, Op. 40 (1894) – opera
    Intermezzo (*orch*)
    d'Albert – Asti – Garay – Gyarfas – Hayward – Hubay – Kersey – R. Ricci – Sándor – Szemere – Telmányi – Vecsey – Ware
(2) Mazurkas, Op. 45 (*vln & pf*)
    Mazurka No. 1, in a "Madame Leopold Horowitz" *Galli – Gyarfas*
(3) Morceaux, Op. 10 (*vln & pf*)
    No. 1. Arioso *d'Albert*
    No. 2. Danse diabolique *Ranzato*
Nocturne in a, Op. 42 (*vln & pf*) *Galli – J. Szigeti*
(6) Nouveaux Poèmes (*on popular themes*) Op. 76 (*vln & pf*)
    No. 4. Magyar Költemény *d'Albert*
(2) Pieces, Op. 38 (*vln & pf*)
    No. 1. A Képe elött *d'Albert*
    No. 2. Unter ihrem Fenster (*Serenade*) *J. Szigeti*
(6) Pieces (*Pusztai hangok Hat zenedarab eredeti magyar dalokután*) Op. 57 (*vln & pf*)
    No. 6. Magyar Cigány dal *d'Albert*
(10) Poèmes caractéristiques, Op. 79 (*vln & pf*)
    No. 9. Berceuse *Hubay*
(6) Poèmes hongroise, Op. 27 (*vln & pf*)
    Poème hongrois* *Sándor*
    Poème hongrois No. 1, in d *D. Szigeti*
    Poème hongrois No. 2, in D *D. Szigeti*
    Poème hongrois No. 3, in A *Lorand*
    Poème hongrois No. 4, in a *Lorand – Willaume*
    Poème hongrois No. 6, in B flat *Anemoyanni – D'Aranyi – Condamine – Hubay – Lorand – Szikra – Telmányi*
Romance, Op. 25 (*vln & pf or orch*) *Ricci*
(14) Scènes de la Csárda (*vln & pf*)
    Scène de la Csárda* *Moller – R. Weltmann*
    No. 2. Scène de la Csárda, Op. 13 *Kerekjarto – Michel – Telmányi (2)*
    No. 3. Maros vize, Op. 18 *d'Albert – Michel – J. Szigeti (2) – F. & W. Weltmann*
    No. 4. Hejre Kati, Op. 32
    d'Albert – Barcewicz – Bergh – Bild – Boucherit – Campoli – L. Cherniavsky – Cochrane – Elman – Flesch – Gyarfas (2) – C. Hansen – Hayward – Heermann – Horvath – Georg Kniestaedt – Law – Lessmann – Linz – Livschakoff – Lorand – Melsa – Menges – Modern – Morbitzer – Powell – Robbins – Sammons (2) – Schmüller – T. Seidel – Shermont – Skalka – Staryk – Steiner – Szemere – Szikra – Telmányi (2) – Wittenberg – Zacharias
    No. 5. Hullámzó balaton, Op. 33
    d'Albert – Bisztriczky – Fachiri – Geczy –

*Unidentified.

Hubay – Kobin – Kolberg – J. Szigeti –
Weissgerber – Zilzer
No. 6. Sárga Cserebogár, Op. 34 *Michel – F. &*
R. Weltmann
No. 7. Kossuth-Nóta, Op. 41 *Michel*
No. 8. Azt mondják, Op. 60 *F. & R. Weltmann*
– Zentay
No. 12, Piczi tubiczám (*little dove*) Op. 83
Hubay
(3) Transcriptions, Op. 3 (*vln & pf*)
No. 2a. Crépuscule (*Massenet*) *Arvesen – Powell*
No. 3. Carmen Fantasia (*on themes from the*
opera by Bizet) *Solloway – Vecsey (2) – F.*
Weltmann (2)
Ugy-e Jani (*Clever Jack*) Op. 92 (*v, pf & vln obb*)
Hubay
Variations sur un thème hongrois, Op. 72 (*vln &*
pf) *Ricci*
Hubbell, Raymond (1879–1954)
(The) Big Show (1916) – musical
Poor butterfly *Kreisler*
Hubeau, Jean (1917–   )
Concerto in C (1938) (*vln & orch*) *Merckel*
Huber, Hans (1852–1921)
Quartet "Waldlieder" (*pf, vln, vla & vlc*)
Schneeberger
Huert, Pata
Mon coeur (*vln & pf*) *Georg Kniestaedt*
Hüllmandel, Nikolaus Joseph (1751–1823)
(3) Sonatas, Op. 6 (*vln & pf*)
Sonata No. 3, in B *Haag*
Humel, Gerald R. (1931–   )
Sonata "Journey to Praha" (*vln & pf*) *Gross*
Hummel, Jan Nepomuk (1778–1837)
Concerto in G, Op. 17 "Le Grande" (*vln, pf &*
orch) *Lautenbacher*
Hallelujah (*v & orch*) *Weber*
Rondo in E flat, Op. 11 "Rondo favori" (*pf*)
Campoli – Feigin – Grach – Heifetz
Waltz in A (*pf*) *Aranyi – Elman – Gyarfas (2) –*
Lorand
Waltz in E flat (*pf*) *Elman*
Huybrechts, Albert (1899–1938)
Sonata in G (1925) (*vln & pf*) *Neste*
Hyde, Cicely
Slumber song (*vln & pf*) *Carrodus*
Ibert, Jacques (1890–1962)
Entr'acte (*fl or vln & gtr*) *Fontanarosa*
(10) Histoires (*pf*)
No. 2. Le Petit âne blanc *Haendel – Heifetz –*
Neaman
(2) Interludes (*fl, vln & hp*) *Jahn*
(Le) Jardinier de Samos (1932) – Incidental music
(*orch*)
Prélude *Urban*
Jeux Sonatina (1926) (*fl & pf*) *Kulenkampff*
Trio (1944) (*vln, vlc & hp*) *Charmy – J. Sanchez*
Ikenouchi, Tomojiro (1906–   )
Sonatina No. 2 (*vln & pf*) *Kubo*
d'Indy, Vincent (1851–1931)
Sonata in C, Op. 59 (*vln & pf*) *Bistesi*
Infante, Manuel (1883–1958)
Chanson gitane (*vln & pf*) *Bouquet*
Innocenzi, Carlo (1906–   )
Dal pincio (*Intermezzo*) (*vln & orch*) *Beneš*

Ionescu, Constantin A. (1912–   )
Dream of roses (*Visul florilor*) (*vln & pf*) *Ionescu*
Russian Gypsy romance (*Malerco*) (*vln & pf*)
Ionescu
Ireland, John (1879–1962)
Bagatelle (1911) (*vln & pf*) *Hayward*
Sonata No. 1, in d (1909) (*vln & pf*) *Grinke –*
Loveday
Sonata No. 2, in a (1917) (*vln & pf*) *Catterall –*
Robbins
Trio No. 1, in a (1908) "Phantasy-Trio" (*pf, vln &*
vlc) *Grinke*
Trio No. 3, in E (1938) (*pf, vln & vlc*) *Grinke*
Isaacs, Edward
Sonata in A (*vln & pf*) *Holst*
Ivanov, Janis (1906–   )
Concerto in e (1951) (*vln & orch*) *Švolkovskis*
Quartet No. 2, in c (*2 vlns, vla & vlc*) *Švolkovskis*
Ivanovici, Ion (1845–1902)
Valurile Dunării "Danube waves" (*orch*) *Paget*
Ives, Charles (1874–1954)
Hallowe'en (pre-1908) (*str qt & pf*) *Zukofsky*
In re con moto et al (1913) (*str qt & pf*) *Zukofsky*
Largo (1902) (*vln, cl & pf*) *Silverstein – Zukofsky*
Largo (1901) (*vln & pf*) *Zukofsky*
Largo Risoluto No. 1 (pre-1907) (*str qt & pf*)
Zukofsky
Largo Risoluto No. 2 (pre-1907) (*str qt & pf*)
Zukofsky
Set of three short pieces (1908) (*str qt, bs & pf*)
Zukofsky
Sonata No. 1 (1903/8) (*vln & pf*) *Druian – Field –*
Zukofsky
Sonata No. 2 (1910) (*vln & pf*) *Babitz – Druian –*
Field – Magaziner – M. Sandler – Travers –
Zukofsky
Sonata No. 3 (1914) (*vln & pf*) *Druian – Zukofsky*
Sonata No. 4 (1916) "Children's day at the camp
meeting" (*vln & pf*) *Ajemian – Druian – J. Szigeti*
(2) – Zukofsky
Trio (1904 – completed 1911) (*pf, vln & vlc*)
Zukofsky
Trio (1901/3) (*vln, cl & pf*) *Magaziner*
Jacobi, Frederick (1891–1952)
Ballade (1942) (*vln & pf*) *Lack*
Concerto (1937) (*vln & orch*) *Gertler*
Jacobi, Victor (1883–1921)
On Miami shore (1919) (*v & pf*) *Brown – Kreisler*
Jakobowsky, E.
Erminie – musical
Lullaby *Brown*
Janáček, Leoš (1854–1928)
Concertino (1925) (*pf, 2 vlns, vla, cl, hrn & bsn*)
Abramenkov & Poleess – Barylli – Baxa &
Kolouch – J. Gordon – Krachmalnick
Dumka (1880) (*vln & pf*) *Barylli*
Quartet No. 2 (1927/8) "Intimate pages" (*2 vlns,*
vla & vlc) *Plocek*
Sonata (1913/21) (*vln & pf*)*
Barylli – R. Bloch – Druian – D. Oistrakh – Olof
– Plocek – Suk – Vilker
Jaques-Dalcroze, Émile (1865–1950)

*Four versions exist of this work. The various
performances remain unidentified.

Danse frivole (*vln & pf*) *Darrieux*
Járdányi, Pál (1920–   )
Concertino (1953) (*vln & pf*) *Diós*
Variations (1955) (*2 vlns & vlc*) *Bokor &*
Szenthelyi
Jarnach, Philipp (1892–   )
Musik zum Gedächtnis der Einsamen (1952) (*2*
vlns, vla & vlc) *Hamann & Köhnsen*
(3) Rhapsodies, Op. 20 (1927) (*vln & pf*)
Hagemann
Järnefelt, Armas (1869–1958)
Berceuse in g (*orch*)
W. Andersen – Andreasson – Barinova –
Bornfors – Cochrane – Fritz-Crone – C. Hansen
– Hayward – F.V. Henriques – Lessmann –
Raderman – Romberg – Sänger – Steinberg
Jenkinson, Ezra
(6) Lyrical pieces (*vln & pf*)
No. 2. Elfentanz *Dessau – Dyke*
Jenson, Ludvig Irgens (1894–   )
Bols vise (*vln & pf*) *Tellefsen*
Jeral, Wilhelm (1861–1935)
Sérénade viennois, Op. 18 (*vln & pf*) *Kreisler – R.*
Pollak
Jerome, Maurice Kraus (1894–   )
Just a baby's prayer at twilight (1918) (*v & pf*)
Soman
Old pal (1920) (*v & pf*) *Soman*
Ježek, Jaroslav (1906–1941)
Sonata (*vln & pf*) *Peška – Suk*
Joachim, Joseph (1831–1907)
Concerto in d, Op. 11 "Hungarian" (*vln & orch*)
Treger
Romance in C (*vln & pf*) *D'Aranyi – Joachim*
Joachim, Otto (1910–   )
Quartet No. 1 (1956) (*2 vlns, vla & vlc*) *Bress &*
Goodman
Johnson, James Weldon (1871–1938)
Intermezzo (*Marcella*) (*v & pf*) *Haxton (2) –*
Hayward
Since you went away (*v & pf*) *Kreisler*
Jolisco
Danse indigene (*pf*) *Szeryng*
Jolivet, André (1905–   )
Chant de Linos (1944) (*fl, vln, vla, vlc & hp*) *J.*
Sanchez
Suite rapsodique (1965) (*solo vln*) *Erlih*
Jones, Isham (1894–1956)
Indiana moon (1923) (*v & pf*) *Jacobsen*
Jones, Kelsey (1922–   )
Introduction & Fugue (1959) (*vln & pf*) *Bress –*
Pach
Suite (*fl & strs*) *Bress & Goodman*
Jongen, Joseph (1873–1953)
(2) Aquarelles, Op. 59 (*vln & pf*)
No. 1. Légende naïve *Bratza*
Serenata (*vln & pf*) *Grumiaux*
Jora, Mihail (1891–   )
Quartet in c, Op. 9 (1926) (*2 vlns, vla & vlc*) *Ruha*
Jordá, Luis (1898–   )
Romántica mazurca (*vln & pf*) *Rocabruna*
Joseph

Hebrew legend (*vln & pf*) *Rosen*
Josten, Werner (1885–1963)
Sonatina (1939) (*vln & pf*) *Elman*
Jungmann, Albert (1823–1892)
Heimweh (*Longing for home*) Op. 117 (*v & pf*)
Stehl
Juon, Paul (1882–1940)
(8) Bagatellen, Op. 36 (*vln & pf*)
   No. 8. Swedish airs *Link*
Humoresque, Op. 72 (*vln & pf*) *Havemann*
(9) Miniatures, Op. 18 "Satyre und Nymphen"
(*pf*)
   No. 3. Rêverie *Freund*
   No. 6. Élégie *Freund*
   No. 7. Humoresque *Freund*
(5) Neue Tanzrhytmen, Op. 24 (*vln & pf*)
   No. 2. Danse fantastique *Freund*
(4) Pieces, Op. 28 (*vln & pf*)
   No. 3. Berceuse *Ast – Farbmann – Heifetz –*
   Morini
Sonata in a, Op. 7 (*vln & pf*) *Barkel*
(2) Violinstücke, Op. 52 (*vln & pf*)
   No. 1. Arietta *Barkel*
   No. 2. Arva "Valse mignonne" *Havemann –*
   Poltronieri – Sammons – Spivakovsky
Jurmann, Walter (1903–)
Vivons l'amour, vivons la vie – tango (*orch*)*
Curti
Jurovský, Šimon (1912–)
Romance (1933) (*vln & pf*) *Bauer – Gašparek*
Juzeliunas, Julius (1916–)
Concerto (*vln, org & orch*) *Paulauskas*
Kabalevsky, Dmitri (1904–)
Concerto in C. Op. 48 (*vln & orch*) *Bezrodny – D.*
Oistrakh – Zukermann
Improvisation, Op. 21, No. 1 (*vln & pf*)
   Castillo – Gilels – Grumlíková – Kozolupova –
   Markov – D. Oistrakh – I. Oistrakh (2) – R.
   Ricci – Wicks
Rondo in C. Op. 69 (*vln & pf*) *Bochková –*
Gutnikov
Kahn, Percival Benedict (1880–1966)
Ave Maria (*v & pf*) *Elman – Eweler – Fradkin*
Kahnt, Maurizio (1836–1904)
Romance in C, Op. 36 (*vln & pf*) *Weintraub*
Kalabis, Viktor (1923–)
Concerto (1959) (*vln & orch*) *Snítil*
Kálmán, Emmerich (1882–1953)
Gräfin Mariza (1924) – operetta
   Komm, Zigany *Curti – Staryk – Streletzky –*
   Tworek (2) – Zilzer
Kalnins, Alfred (1879–1951)
Latvian folk song suite (*vln & orch*) *Birznieks*
Kalomiris, Manolis (1883–1962)
Oblivion (*v, 2 vlns, vla, vlc & pf*) *Kolassis*
Kalsons, R. (1936–)
Sonata (*vln & pf*) *Seimatov*
Kaminsky, D. (1907–)
Concerto No. 2, in A (*vln & orch*) *L. Gorelik*
Kämpf, Karl (1874–1950)
Bagatelle (*vln & pf*) *Galli*
Kaper, Bronislau (1902–)†

*Composed jointly with Bronislau Kaper.
†See: Walter Jurmann.

Kaplan, Sol
Piece in the form of a Rhapsody (*vln & pf*)
Slatkin
Karayev, K. (1918–)
Sonata in d (*vln & pf*) *Ganiev*
Kark, Frederick
Bramosia (*vln & pf*) *Ortenberg*
Nadjada (*Intermezzo*) (*vln & pf*) *Wolfsthal*
Karlowicz, Mieczyslaw (1876–1909)
Concerto in A, Op. 8 (*vln & orch*) *Barinova –*
Wilkomirska
Romance (*vln & orch*) *Uminska*
Karnavičius, Jurgis (1884–1941)
(2) Caprices (*vln & pf*) *Livontas*
Karosas, Josas (1890–)
Sonata "Legend of the sea" (*vln & pf*) *Livontas*
Suite (*vln & pf*) *Livontas*
Karpilowski, Daniel
Berceuse (*vln & pf*) *Karpilowski*
Kaschubec, Erich (1899–)
Konzertstück in G (*vln & orch*) *Geczy*
Kasemets, Udo (1919–)
Sonata (*vln & pf*) *Garami*
Kayser, Heinrich Ernst (1815–1888)
(36) Elementary & Progressive Studies, Op. 20
(*solo vln*)
   Study No. 4, in C (*Allegro*) *Staryk*
Kazandzhiev, Vasil (1934–)
Sonata (*solo vln*) *Leshev*
Kellette, John William
I'm forever blowing bubbles (*v & pf*) *T. Seidel*
Kelly, Frederick Septimus (1881–1916)
Suite, Op. 7 (*fl & pf*)
   No. 5. Jig *D'Aranyi*
Kepitis, Janis (1908–
Trio No. 3, in G (*pf, vln & vlc*) *Dalmanis*
Kerekjarto, Duci de (1900–1962)
Child's dream (*vln & pf*) *Kerekjarto*
Kerker, Gustav A. (1857–1923)
(The) Belle of New York (1897) – musical
   I'm the belle of New York *Moller*
Kern, Jerome (1885–1945)
All the things you are (1939) (*v & pf*) *Tworek*
(The) Cat and the Fiddle (1931) – musical
   The night was made for love *Curti*
Ka-lu-a (*v & pf*) *Haxton*
Kern, Kurt
Sarabande in c sharp (*vln & pf*) *Frenkel (2)*
Kerr, Harrison (1897–)
Concerto (1950/1) (*vln & orch*) *Stavonhagen*
Sonata (1955) (*vln & pf*) *Joseph*
Trio in a (1941) (*pf, vln & vlc*) *Gerle*
Ketèlbey, Albert William (1875–1959)
Algerian scene (*orch*) *A. Sandler*
Phantom melody (*orch*) *A. Sandler*
Ketlar, Jetvan
Monte Cristo – valse-tzigane (*orch*) *Anonymous –*
Moller
Ketten, Henri (1848–1883)
Caprice espagnole (*pf*) *Spalding*
Khachaturian, Aram (1903–)
Ballade, Op. 2 (1927) (*vln & pf*) *Feigin*
Chanson poème in e (1929) (*vln & pf*)
   Ajemian – L. Kogan – Malinin – Markov – D.

   Oistrakh (3) – I. Oistrakh – Petronio –
   Shkolnikova – Silverman
Concerto in D (1940) (*vln & orch*)
   Bernard – Elman – Erlih – Kaufman – L.
   Kogan (2) – Magyar – D. Oistrakh (4) – I.
   Òistrakh – R. Ricci – Schmahl – Szeryng (2) –
   Wilkomirska
Concerto-Rhapsody (*vln & orch*) *L. Kogan*
Dance in B flat (1927) (*vln & pf*) *D. Oistrakh (3)*
Gayaneh (*Suite No. 1*) (1942) – ballet (*orch*)
   No. 1. Sabre dance *Heifetz – L. Kogan*
   No. 2. Dance of Ayshe *Agaronyan – L. Kogan*
   (2)
Gayaneh (*Suite No. 2*) (1942) – ballet (*orch*)
   No. 11. Gayaneh's Adagio *Corigliano – L.*
   Kogan
Masquerade (1939) – Incidental music to the
ballet (*orch*)
   Mazurka *L. Kogan*
   Nocturne *Corigliano – L. Kogan*
Trio in g (1932) (*cl, vln & pf*) *Silverman – Urban*
Khachaturian, Karen (1920–)
Sonata in g, Op. 1 (*vln & pf*) *Heifetz – Mikhlin –*
D. Oistrakh
Khaitbayev
Concerto (*vln & orch*) *Sarkisyan*
Khadoshkin, Ivan (1747–1804)
Variations on Russian themes (*vln & vlc*) *L.*
Kogan
Khrennikov, Tikhon (1913–)
Concerto in C, Op. 14 (*vln & orch*) *L. Kogan (2)*
Kiel, Alfredo
Guitarra (*vln & pf*) *Barbosa*
King, Reginald (1904–)
Daybreak (*pf*) *A. Sandler*
Melody at dusk (*Intermezzo*) (*pf*) *A. Sandler*
Song of paradise (*pf*) *Campoli – Groth – Jelving –*
A. Sandler
Kinze
Canzonetta (*vln & pf*) *Levey*
Kirchner, Leon (1919–)
Concerto (1960) (*vln, vlc, 10 w-wnds & pcn*)
Spivakovsky
Duo (1947) (*vln & pf*) *Kobialka*
Sonata concertante (1952) (*vln & pf*) *Shapiro*
Trio (1954) (*pf, vln & vlc*) *Rubin*
Kirman, Paul
Chanson palestinienne (*pf*) *Knorre*
Kiyose, Yasuji (1900–)
(2) Movements (1959) (*vln & pf*) *Iwamoto*
Klasen, Willy
Berceuse, Op. 18 (*pf*) *Wolfgang Schneiderhan*
Mazurka, Op. 14 (*pf*) *Wolfgang Schneiderhan*
Klebe, Giselher (1925–)
Sonata, Op. 14 (*vln & pf*) *Hagemann*
Kletzki, Paul (1900–)
Trio in d, Op. 16 (*pf, vln & vlc*) *Freund*
Klickmann, F. Henri (1885–1966)
Waters of the Perkiomen (1925) (*v & pf*) *Lensky –*
Manuello
Klova, Vitautas (1926–)
Nocturne Prelude (*vln & pf*) *Livontas*
Klupsch, Siegfried
In a little rendezvous (*v & pf*) *Fradkin*
Klusák, Jan (1934–)

Sonata (1964/5) (*vln & 11 w-wnds*) *I. Štraus*
Kneass, Nelson (–1869)
Ben Bolt (*Oh! don't you remember sweet Alice?*)
(1848) (*v & pf*)* *d'Almaine (2) – Weston*
Kneisel, Franz (1865–1926)
Mazurka, Op. 27 (*vln & pf*) *Kneisel (2)*
Serenade, Op. 28 (*vln & pf*) *Kneisel*
Knipper, L. (1898–   )
Concerto in D "Little" (*vln & str orch*) *Futer*
Concert scherzo (*vln & pf*) *Pikaizen*
Knudsen, Gunnar (1907–   ) ,
Norwegian Rhapsody (*vln & pf*) *Knudsen*
Reflections (*vln & pf*)† *Knudsen*
Kobin, Otto
(Die) Quelle (*vln & pf*) *Lessmann*
Koch, Erland von (1910–   )
(4) Dances (*vln & pf*) *Berlin – Karpe – Wicks*
Kochan, Günter (1930–   )
Concerto in D, Op. 1 (*vln & orch*) *Morbitzer*
Kocián, Jaroslav (1883–1950)
(2) Pieces, Op. 17 (*vln & pf*)
   No. 1. Serenade *Zámečník*
   No. 2. Humoresque *Příhoda – Suk*
(3) Pièces d'impression, Op. 18 (*vln & pf*)
   No. 1. Méditation du soir *Suk*
   No. 2. Intermezzo pittoresque *Suk*
Kodály, Zoltan (1882–1967)
Adagio in C (1905) (*vln & pf*) *Gerle – Hidy –*
   Kaufman – Kovács – Zathureczky
Duo, Op. 7 (1914) (*vln & vlc*) *Eidus – Heifetz –*
   V. Martin – Suk – Tátrai
Epigramm (1954) (*vln & pf*) *Bisztriczky*
Háry János (1926) – opera
   No. 10. Intermezzo *Gerle – J. Szigeti*
Kallo (1952) (*orch*)
   (3) Hungarian dances *D. Oistrakh (3)*
Serenade, Op. 12 (1919/20) (*2 vlns & vla*) *Tátrai*
   & Varkonyi
Valsette (1907) (*pf*) *Bisztriczky*
(7) Zongoramuzsika, Op. 11 (1908/10) (*pf*)
   No. 3. It is raining in the village *Milstein (2)*
Kohaut, Carl (1726–1782)
Divertimento (*vln, gtr & vlc*) *Klasinc*
Kohs, Ellis B. (1916–   )
Chamber Concerto (1949) (*vln, vla & strs*) *R.*
   Mann
Kókay, Rezsö (1906–   )
Concerto (1950) (*vln & orch*) *Gertler*
Verbunkos rapszódia (*Recruiting rhapsody*) (1955)
(*vln & pf*) *Garay*
Kokoiti, A.
Rhapsody (*vln & orch*) *Brailovsky*
Kolman, Peter
Monumento per 6,000,000 (*orch*) *Moži*
Komitas, Solomon (1869–1935)
Keler Tsoler (*pf*) *Agaronyan*
Krunk (*Crane*) (*pf*) *Agaronyan*
Vagarshapat dance (*pf*) *Agaronyan*
Kondor, Ernst

*Based on a German air.
†Composed jointly with Eva García.

Vanha mustalainen (*The old Gypsy*) (*v & pf*)
Jussila
Königsberger, Josef
Rêverie (*vln & pf*) *Eweler*
Konstantinidis
Suite (*on Greek themes of the Dodecanese*) (*vln &
pf*) *Kolassis*
Kontski, Anton (1817–1899)
Mazurka No. 1, Op. 7 (*vln & pf*) *Barcewicz*
Kopylow, Alexander Alexandrovich (1854–1911)
(14) Kleine Charakterstücke, Op. 52 (*pf*)
   No. 9. Bein Einschlummern (*To slumberland*)
   Elman
Kornauth, Egon (1891–1959)
Trio in b, Op. 27 (*pf, vln & vlc*) *Freund*
Korngold, Erich Wolfgang (1897–1957)
Concerto in D, Op. 35 (*vln & orch*) *Heifetz*
(Die) Tote Stadt, Op. 12 (1920) – opera
   Meine sehnen, mein Wähnen (*Pierrotlied*)
   Kreisler – R. Pollak
Viel Lärmen um Nichts (*Much ado about nothing*)
Op. 11 (1919) – Incidental music (*orch*)
   No. 1. Mädchen im Brautgemach *Elman –*
   Rostal
   No. 2. Holzapfel und Schlehwein *Elman –*
   Heifetz (2) – J. Pollak – Rostal
   No. 3. Gartenszene *Elman – Eweler – Heifetz –*
   J. Pollak – Rostal
   No. 4. Mummenschanz (*Hornpipe*) *Elman –*
   Eweler – J. Pollak – Rostal
Koróly
Fantaisie hongrois (*vln & pf*) *F. & R. Weltmann*
Koschat, Thomas (1845–1914)
Forsaken (*v & pf*) *Brown – Kreisler – Morini*
Koscki
Sendo Kawaiya – variations (*vln & pf*) *Lass*
Kosenko, Viktor Stepanovich
Sonata, Op. 18 (*vln & pf*) *Parkhomenko*
Trio, Op. 17 "Classical" (*pf, vln & vlc*) *Budovsky*
Kosha, D. (1897–   )
Trio (1946) (*2 vlns & vla*) *Lutsky & Ovcharek*
Kosloff, Hilarion
Idylle finnoise, Op. 5 (*vln & pf*) *Kennedy*
Mélodie tartare (*vln & pf*) *Kennedy*
Koštál, Erno (1889–   )
Minuet (*vln & pf*) *Beregowsky*
de Koven, Reginald (1859–1920)
Oh! Promise me (1889) (*v & pf*) *Chemet*
Kox, Hans (1930–   )
Concerto (1963) (*vln & orch*) *Olof*
Koželuh, Leopold Antonín (1752–1818)
(La) Ritrovata Figlia de Ottone, Op. 39 – ballet
(*orch*)
      No. 22. Gavotte (*Act IV*) *Brown – Gorokhov –*
      Kreisler – A. Schmidt – T. Seidel
Kraft, William (1923–   )
Concerto grosso (1962) (*fl, bsn, vln, vlc & orch*)
Kling
Krakauer, Alexander
Im Paradies (1926) (*pf*) *Kreisler – Moguilevski*
Kramer, Arthur Walter (1890–1969)
Chant nègre, Op. 32, No. 1 (*vln & pf*) *Jacobsen –*
Zimbalist
Entr'acte, Op. 46, No. 2 (*vln & pf*) *Kreisler –*
Zimbalist

(The) Last hour (*v & pf*) *Kreisler*
Silhouette (*O Kaiserstadt du schöne*) (*v & pf*)
D'Aranyi
Kramer, Wilhelm (1745–1799)
Adagio in g (*vln & pf*) *Haag*
Kraus, Joseph Martin (1756–1792)
Quintet in D (*fl, 2 vlns, vla & vlc*) *Kussmaul*
Sonata No. 2, in D (*vln & pf*) *Haag*
Krebs, Johann Ludwig (1713–1780)
Trio in D (*fl, vln & c*) *Trippner*
Krein, Alexander Abramovich (1883–1951)
Dance No. 4 (*vln & pf*) *Heifetz – L. Kogan*
Kreisler, Fritz (1875–1962)
Apple Blossoms (1919) – operetta
   Who can tell? *Kreisler*
Aucassin & Nicolette (*Canzonetta medievale*) (*vln
& pf*) *Kreisler*
Aus Wien (*vln & pf*)* *Berg – Farbmann*
Berceuse romantique, Op. 9 (*vln & pf*) *Grach –
Kreisler*
Caprice viennois, Op. 2 (*vln & pf*)
   *Alès – Aranyi – Arschensky – Auclair – Bean –
   Benedetti – Berg – Blinder – Campoli (2) –
   Caponi – L. Cherniavsky – Culbertson – Dajos –
   Debruille – Druian – Elman – Ferras – Filon –
   Fournier – Fradkin – Francescatti (4) – Fuchs –
   Garnier – Gautier – Gay – Gimpel – Gittelson –
   Grach – Grumiaux – Guidi – Gyarfas –
   Haendel – Hassid – Hood – Georg Kniestaedt –
   L. Kogan (2) – Kooper – Kreisler (6) – Krips –
   Lass – Linz – Lorand – Magyar – Manuello –
   Marschner – Melsa – Menuhin (3) – Morbitzer
   (2) – Morini – Odnoposoff – Olevsky – Pilzer –
   Polinski – Pougnet – Poulet – Příhoda (3) –
   Rabin – Renardy – R. Ricci – Robbins –
   Rosand – Rostal – Sammons – B. Scherzer –
   Wolfgang Schneiderhan (2) – T. Seidel –
   Spalding – Spivakovsky (2) – Stevens – Strockoff
   – Suk – Szeryng – J. Szigeti – Taschner –
   Telmányi – Tworek – Wethmar – Wilkomirska
   – Ysaÿe – Zilzer*
Cavatina (*vln & pf*) *L. Kogan*
(La) Gitana (*vln & pf*)
   *Aranyi – Berg – Brown – Campoli – Elman –
   Francescatti – Fuchs – Gimpel – Grach –
   Gutnikov – Kochański – L. Kogan – Kreisler (3)
   – Krips – Markov – Michaïlow – Neumann – D.
   Oistrakh – Piastro-Borisoff – Pougnet – Rabinoff
   – R. Ricci – Rosen – Sammons – Simor –
   Stevens – Telmányi*
Gypsy caprice (*vln & pf*) *Bezrodny – A. Ferraresi
– Grach – Kreisler – Markov – Rabinoff*
(The) King Steps Out – film (*orch*)
   Stars in my eyes *Kreisler*
Liebesfreud (*vln & pf*)
   *Akos – Alès – Auclair – Bean – Berg –
   Bluestone – Campoli (2) – Carol – Chauveton –
   Cochrane – Culbertson – Czerwonky – Dajos –
   Debruille – Deman – Dessau (2) – Druian –
   Elman – Eweler – Fabrizio – Fain – Ferras –
   Fradkin – Francescatti (3) – Fritz-Crone –
   Ghestem – Gimpel – Godwin – Grach –*

*Unidentified.

Grumiaux – Guidi – Kennedy – Kreisler (4) –
Lorand (2) – Lorenzo – Magyar – Marschner –
Morbitzer (2) – E.B. Nielsen – Odnoposoff –
Olevsky – Palulis – Parlow – Pougnet – Příhoda
(2) – Renardy – R. Ricci – Rosand – Wolfgang
Schneiderhan – Schwartz – T. Seidel – Sigmund
– Skalka – Spalding – Spivakovsky – Stanske –
Stevens – Swaap – Szeryng – J. Szigeti –
Telmányi – Thibaud – Thiele – Toubas –
Tworek – Ware – Weissgerber – Wilkomirska –
Wolfsthal – Zilzer – Zimbalist – Zsigmondy

Liebesleid (vln & pf)
  Akos – Alès – W. Andersen – Andersson –
Auclair – Bean – Berg – Bluestone – Boulanger
– Bratza – C. Brosa – Campoli (2) – Carol –
Cochrane – Collier – Dajos – Darrieux –
Debruille – Deman – Dessau (2) – Druian –
Elman (2) – Erlih – Eweler – Ferras –
Francescatti (4) – Frenkel – Fritz-Crone – Fuchs
– Gade – Gautier – Ghestem – Gimpel –
Godwin – K. Gordon – Grach – Grumiaux –
Hegner – Hochstein – Jacobsen – Jernou –
Kersey – Kreisler (4) – Kutcher – Lorand –
Loránt – Magyar – Marschner – Menuhin –
Michaïlow – Morbitzer (2) – Morini – Neaman
– E.B. Nielsen – Nissen – Odnoposoff – Olevsky
– Palulis – Poltronieri – Příhoda (3) – Renardy
– R. Ricci – Rosand – Rudényi – Sammons –
Wolfgang Schneiderhan (2) – Schwartz – T.
Seidel – Seydel – Skalka (2) – Spivakovsky –
Stern – Stevens – Swaap – Szeryng – J. Szigeti
(2) – Telmányi – Totenberg – Tworek –
Weissgerber – Wilkomirska – Winchester –
Wolfsthal – Zacharias – Zilzer – Zimbalist –
Zsigmondy

Marche miniature viennoise (vln & pf) Grach –
Huppertz – Kreisler (2) – Lorand

Negro folk tune (vln & pf)* Grach

Paraphrase on 2 Russian folksongs (vln & pf)
Lorand – Moguilevski – Morini

Polichinelle-serenade (vln & pf)
  Campoli – Cochrane – Deman – Farbmann –
Gimpel – Grach – Gresser – Koene – Kooper –
Kreisler (2) – Kutcher – Locatelli – T. Seidel –
Wolfsthal

Quartet in a (1919) (2 vlns, vla & vlc) Kreisler

Recitative & Scherzo-caprice, Op. 6 (solo vln)
  Accardo – Benedetti – Dubois – Francescatti (2)
– S. Furer – Grach – Harth – Menuhin –
Nadien – Odnoposoff – R. Ricci (2) – Rostal (2)
– Szeryng

Romance, Op. 4 (vln & pf) Olevsky

Rondino on a theme by Beethoven (vln & pf)†
  Andrade – D'Aranyi – Auclair – Benedetti –
Berg – Bratza (2) – Brückner – Campoli (2) –
Chauveton – Delmor – Deru – Elman (2) –
Ferras – Flesch (2) – Francescatti (4) – Gautier

*Unidentified. This piece may be the transcription
of the Largo from Dvořák's symphony "From the
New World."
†The theme is from Beethoven's "Rondo in G,"
G.155 for vln & pf.

– Godwin – Goldin – K. Gordon – Grach –
Grumiaux – Jovanovič – Kreisler (4) – Kremer –
Loránt – Milstein – Morini – T. Nielsen – D.
Oistrakh – Olevsky – Pilzer – Quiroga – R.
Ricci – Ruha – Sachsenskjöld – A. Sander (2) –
T. Seidel – Selinsky – Soriano – Stevens – Suk –
Swaap – Szeryng – Telmányi – Weismann –
Zacharewitsch

Schön Rosmarin (vln & pf)
  Alès – W. Andersen – Auclair – Barbieri – Bean
– Berg – Bleumers – Bluestone – Bress –
Campoli (2) – Carol – Chauveton – Curti –
Debruille – Delmor – Druian – Elman – Eweler
– Farbmann – Fradkin – Francescatti (2) –
Geyer – Gimpel – Godwin (2) – Gorokhov –
Grach – Grumiaux – Guidi – Gyarfas –
Haendel (2) – B. Hall – Georg Kniestaedt (2) –
Koene – B. Koutzen – Kreisler (4) – Lensky –
Lindblom – Lorand (2) – Marschner – Menuhin
(2) – Michaïlow – Modern – Morbitzer –
Renardy – R. Ricci – Robbins – Rosand –
Rostal – Rudényi – A. Sandler – Schmied (2) –
Wolfgang Schneiderhan – T. Seidel – Skalka –
Spalding – Stanske – Steeb – Stern – Streletzky
– Szeryng – Telmányi – Tworek – Voicu –
Wilkomirska – Wolfsthal – Zilzer (2)

Shepherd's madrigal (vln & pf) S. Furer – Kreisler

Slavonic Fantasia in b (on themes by Dvořák) (vln
& pf) Elman (3) – Kreisler – Lorand

Syncopation (vln & pf) Grach – Kreisler

Tambourin chinois, Op. 3 (vln & pf)
  Alès – Aranyi – Auclair – A. Bachmann –
Beckwith – Benedetti – Bratza – Brugman –
Bucia – Campoli (2) – Carol – Druian – Erlih –
Farbmann – Francescatti (3) – Fuchs – Gautier
– Gay – Gimpel – Gold – Grach – Grumiaux –
Guidi – Gulli – Haendel – Jacobsen – Jarry –
Kawaciuk – B. Koutzen – Kreisler (4) –
Kulenkampff – Lorand – Ludlow – Magyar –
Melsa – Menuhin – Olevsky – Parlow – Poulet –
R. Quattrocchi – Renardy – R. Ricci – Rosand
– Sammons – A. Sandler – Spivakovsky –
Stevens – Szeryng – J. Szigeti – Víolin – Wanne
– Wethmar – Wicks – Wilkomirska – Wittels –
Zentay – Zilzer (2)

Toy soldier's march (vln & pf) Kreisler

Viennese Rhapsodic Fantasietta (vln & orch)
Kreisler

(in the style of other composers)

Allegretto (Boccherini) (vln & pf)
  Catterall – Elman – Francescatti (3) – Gautier –
B. Koutzen – Kreisler – Kulenkampff – Markov
– Szeryng (2) – Tworek

Andantino (Padre Martini) (vln & pf)
  Allan – Barbosa – Boussinot – Dahmen – Dajos
– Druian – Fogelberg – Gautier – Geyer – Heber
– Huttenbach – Koene – Kozolupova – Kreisler
– Leonidoff – Levey – Mossel – Paget –
Poltronieri – Ruminelli – Sens

Aubade provençale (L. Couperin) (vln & pf)
Enescu – Kreisler – A. Schmidt

Chanson Louis XIII & Pavane (L. Couperin) (vln
& pf)
  Benedetti – Bochková – Chemet – Druian –
Elman – Fournier – Gorokhov – Kreisler (4) –

Olevsky – Petronio – R. Ricci – Rostal –
Szeryng – Telmányi – Toubas

(La) Chasse (Cartier) (vln & pf)
  Campoli – Fairhurst – Fournier – Gautier –
Gyarfas – Kreisler – Menuhin – Rabin – R.
Ricci – Strockoff

Concerto in C (Vivaldi) (vln & strs) Campajola –
Kreisler – Pougnet – Weinstein

Grave (W.F. Bach) (vln & pf)
  Andrade – Barkel – Blinder – Bratza – Deman
– A. Ferraresi – Fournier – Francescatti – Grach
– Kroyt – I. Oistrakh – Pierangeli – Zora
Shikhmurzayeva – Szeryng – Vecsey

Minuet (Porpora) (vln & pf)
  Andrade – Druian – Elman – Fournier –
Francescatti (2) – Friedman – M. Hall – Heifetz
– Porta – Soriano – Spivakovsky – Stevens –
Szeryng – Torre

Praeludium & Allegro (Pugnani) (vln & pf)
  Auclair – Barbosa – Barinova – Barkel – A.
Busch – Bustabo – Campoli – Chemet – Druian
– Elman – Erlih – Ferras – Fournier –
Francescatti (2) – Gautier – Gimpel – Haendel
(2) – Kalmer – Lorand (2) – Magyar –
Menuhin – Milstein – Møller – Morini – Mosley
– Nadien – Neaman – Olevsky – Pougnet (2) –
Poulet – R. Ricci – Salpeter – Sammons – J.
Skolnik – Szeryng – Taschner – Totenberg –
Tworek – Ughi – Vecsey – Wilkomirska –
Zathureczky – Zentay

(La) Précieuse (L. Couperin) (vln & pf)
  Cochrane – Deman – Druian – Elman – Fain –
Francescatti – Gimpel – Grach – M. Hall – B.
Koutzen – Kreisler (2) – Livontas – Locatelli –
Morini – Olevsky – Snitkovsky

Preghièra (Padre Martini) (vln & pf) Elman

Scherzo (Dittersdorf) (vln & pf)
  D'Aranyi – A. Busch – Cantrelle – Dessau –
Dinicu – Elman – Gorokhov – Hegner – Koene
– Kreisler (2)

Sicilienne & Rigaudon (Francoeur) (vln & pf)
  Andrade – Barbosa – Berkova – Campoli –
Catterall – Charmy – Druian – Elman (2) –
Erlih – Farbmann – Fournier – Gardner –
Gilels – Godowsky – Grach – Haendel – Hamza
– Hegner – Heifetz – Jarry – B. Koutzen – Linz
– Magyar – Menuhin – Michaïlow – Milstein –
Olevsky – R. Ricci – Shkolníková – Shuchari –
Spivakovsky – J. Szigeti – T. Varga – Zilzer

Tempo di minuetto (Pugnani) (vln & pf)
  Aranyi – Astruc – Catterall – Enescu – Fournier
– Levey – Primrose – Senatra – Szeryng

Variations on a theme of Corelli (Tartini) (vln &
pf)
  Benedetti – Bezrodny – Blinder – Bouillon –
Boussinot – Bratza – Brown – A. Busch –
Campoli (2) – Carol – Dahmen – Elman –
Fachiri – Fournier – Francescatti – Fuchs –
Gardner – Garnier – Gautier – Gold – Gyarfas
– Jarry – Kreisler – Law – Loránt – Luquin –
Magyar – Morini (2) – Mosley – Nadien – Neste
– Neveu – Odnoposoff – D. Oistrakh (2) –
Příhoda – R. Ricci (2) – Rudényi – Soloviev –
Taschner – Wilkomirska – Wolfsthal

Křenek, Ernst (1900–   )

*Unidentified.
†More correctly: At the Alpine chalet.

*Also known as "Herd girl's dream."

*Unidentified.

Concerto No. 5, in e *Fernandez – Weiner*
Concerto No. 6, in g *Auclair – Fernandez*
Concerto in d "L'Infant" (*vln, strs & c*) *L. Bobescu*
Gavotte ancienna*
Boucherit
(12) Sonatas, Op. 1 – Book I (1723) (*vln & c*)
Sonata No. 8, in G *Alès – Fernandez – J. Pollak*
Sonata No. 9, in A *Weiner*
(12) Sonatas, Op. 2 – Book II (1728) (*vln & c*) ·
Sonata No. 1, in e *Alès*
Sonata No. 3, in C *Ciompi*
Sonata No. 5, in G *Pougnet*
Sonata No. 8, in D *Schlupp*
Sonata No. 9, in E flat *Gravoin*
Sonata No. 12, in g *Alès*
(6) Sonatas, Op. 3 (1730) (*2 vlns*)
Sonata No. 1, in G *Gilels & L. Kogan*
Sonata No. 2, in A *D'Aranyi & Fachiri*
Sonata No. 3, in C *Gilels & L. Kogan*
Sonata No. 4, in B flat *D'Aranyi & Fachiri*
(12) Sonatas, Op. 4 (1732) (*2 vlns & c*)
Sonata No. 2, in B flat *Blot & Ortmans-Bach*
Sonata No. 3, in d *Lacrouts & Germaine Raymond*
Sonata No. 4, in A *Blot & Ortmans-Bach – Kohon & Weinstock*
(12) Sonatas, Op. 5 – Book III (1734) (*vln & c*)
Sonata No. 1, in A *Alès*
Sonata No. 3, in e *Gravoin*
Sonata No. 4, in B flat *Alès – Fernandez*
Sonata No. 6, in c "Le Tombeau" *Grehling – Melkus – Weiner – Zhuk*
Sonata No. 10, in C *Gravoin – Weiner*
Sonata No. 11, in g *Weiner*
(12) Sonatas, Op. 9 – Book IV (1738) (*vln & c*)
Sonata No. 3, in D
Amar – d'Ambrosio – Andreasson – D'Aranyi – L. Bobescu – Boucherit – Bratza – Bress – Deman – Dubois – Erlih – Friedmann – Gautier – Gendre – Gold – Gorokhov – Gyarmati – Haendel – M. Hall – F.V. Henriques – Menuhin – Milstein – D. Oistrakh (3) – Petronio – R. Pollak – Polson – Powell – Germaine Raymond – Sammons – Staryk (2) – Steiger-Betzak – Szeryng – Telmányi – Thibaud – Weiner – Wunder
Sonata No. 4, in A *Alès – Fernandez*
Sonata No. 9, in E *Gravoin*
(12) Sonatas, Op. 12 (*2 vlns & c*)
Sonata No. 4, in B flat *Fernandez & Lamacque*
Sonata (*vln & c*)* *Bress*
Lederer, Desző (1858–   )
Mélodie, Op. 15 (*vln & pf*) *Lederer – Stülken*
(2) Poèmes hongroise, Op. 16 (*vln & pf*)
Poème hongrois No. 1, in e *MacMillen*
Poème hongrois No. 2, in D *Gladys Raymond*
Scène de la Csárda No. 1 (*vln & pf*) *Fradkin*
Lefort, Augustin (1852–   )
Danse mauresque (*vln & pf*) *Boucherit*
Legley, Victor (1915–   )
Burlesque (*vln & pf*) *Weiner*

*Unidentified.

Legrenzi, Giovanni (1626–1690)
(12) Sonatas, Op. 2 (1655) (*2 vlns & c*)
Sonata in G "La Raspona" *Franzetti & Porta*
(12) Sonatas, Op. 10 (1673) (*2 vlns & c*)
Sonata No. 5, in D *C. Ferraresi & Gulli*
Leguerney, Jacques (1906–   )
Sonatina (*vln & pf*) *Chauveton*
Lehár, Franz (1870–1948)
Frasquita (1923) – operetta
Hab' ein blaues Himmelbett *Campoli – L. Cherniavsky – Curti – Fradkin (2) – Kreisler – Quiroga*
Friederike (1928) – operetta
selection *Eweler*
Giuditta (1934) – operetta
selection *d'Albert (2)*
(Der) Graf von Luxemburg (1909) – operetta
selection *d'Albert*
Hungarian Dance (*vln & pf*) *Gerard*
(Das) Land des Lächelns (1923) – operetta
Boston Walzer *Curti*
Dein ist mein ganzes Herz *Curti*
selection *d'Albert*
Libellentanz (1922) – operetta
Intermezzo *Ranzato (3)*
(Die) Lustige Witwe (1905) – operetta
Ez waren zwei Königskinder *Fassbander & Rohr*
S'flüstern Geigen ... Lippen schweigen (*waltz*) *Dobrinski*
Viljalied *Eweler*
Paganini (1925) – operetta
Gern hab' ich die Frau'n geküsst *Curti*
selection *d'Albert (2)*
Zigeunerfest (*Act II*) *Garay – R. Pasquier*
Leigh, Frank
Lovely Lucerne (*v & pf*) *Fradkin*
Lekeu, Guillaume (1870–1894)
Quartet in b (1893) "Unfinished" (*pf, vln, vla & vlc*)* *H. Koch*
Sonata in G (1892) (*vln & pf*) *Ferras – Grumiaux – Iwamoto – H. Koch (2) – Menuhin (2)*
Trio in c (1891) (*pf, vln & vlc*) *Baker*
Lemaire, Jean Eugèn Gaston (1854–   )
Dansez marquise (*vln & pf*) *Filon*
Lemare, Edwin Henry (1865–1934)
Andantino, Op. 83, No. 2 (*pf*) *Kreisler – Ludlow*
Lenz, F.
Concert mazurka (*vln & pf*) *F.V. Henriques*
Leo, Leonardo Oronzo Salvatore di (1694–1744)
Concerto in D (*4 vlns, strs & c*)
Brown, Rabinoff, B. Schwarz & Totenberg – Früh, Schön, Terebesi & Vorholz
Leonard, Harold
Iyone, my own Iyone (*v & pf*) *Ball*
Léonard, Hubert (1819–1890)
Austrian Hymn – variations "Souvenir de Haydn" Op. 2 (*vln & pf*) *Rudényi (2)*
Duo de concert, Op. 25 (*vln & pf*) *Valesca-Becker*
Fantaisie militaire, Op. 15 (*vln & pf*) *d'Almaine – Buchtele – Drdla*
(5) Scènes humoristiques, Op. 61 (*vln & pf*)

*Completed by Vincent d'Indy.

No. 1. Coq et poules *Krettly*
No. 3. Chatte et souris *Krettly*
No. 4. L'Ane et l'Anier (*Donkey & driver*) *d'Almaine*
No. 5. Sérénàde du lapin belliqueux *Brown, Mischakoff & Rabinoff*
Leoncavallo, Ruggiero (1858–1919)
Mattinata (1904) (*v & pf*) *Condamine – Fuchs – Heermann – Manuello – Ranzato – Ricci – Zilzer*
(I) Pagliacci (1892) – opera
selection *Lensen*
Vesti la giubba *Moller*
Sérénade française (*v & pf*) *Elman*
Sérénade napolitaine (*v & pf*) *Elman*
Lepnurm, H. (1914–   )
Variations (*vln & org*) *Rannap*
Leroux, Xavier (1863–1919)
(Le) Nil (*v & pf*) *Kreisler – Zimbalist*
Leutjens, Christopher
Caresse de fleurs (*Intermezzo*) (*vln & pf*) *Leutjens (2)*
Chant de brise (*Valse lente*) (*vln & pf*) *Leutjens*
Charme secret (*Valse lente*) (*vln & pf*) *Leutjens*
Heimliche Reize (*vln & pf*) *Leutjens*
Intermezzo (*valse*) (*vln & pf*) *Leutjens*
Simple aubade (*vln & pf*) *Leutjens*
Levitin, Yuri Abramovich (1912–   )
Sonata in c, Op. 43 (*vln & pf*) *D. Oistrakh*
Variations, Op. 45 (*solo vln*) *Pikaizen*
Levy, Sol Paul (1881–1920)
That naughty waltz (1920) (*v & pf*) *Ball – Brown*
Lewis, Robert Hall (1926–   )
Toccata (1963) (*vln & pcn*) *Banat*
Leybach, Ignace (1817–1891)
Nocturne No. 5, in A flat, Op. 52 (*pf*) *Ludlow – Powell – Rattay – K. Reuter – A. Schmidt*
Liadov, Anatol Konstantinovich (1855–1914)
Prelude* *Lorand (2)*
(Les) Vendredis "Fridays" (*pf*)†
No. 2. Sarabande in g *Goldstein*
No. 3. Polka in D *Catterall*
Lie, Sigurd (1871–1904)
(2) Norwegian Dances (*vln & pf*)
Norsk dans No. 1, in G (*Allegretto grazioso*) *Tellefsen*
Norsk dans No. 2, in A (*Allegro con fuoco*) *Tellefsen*
Snow (*v & pf*) *J. Szigeti*
Lieurance, Thurlow (1878–1963)
By the waters of the Minnetonka (1914) (*v & pf*)
Campoli – Chemet – Cochrane – Grinke – Lipschultz – Mantovani
Liliuokalani (1838–1917)‡
Aloha Oe (1892) (*v & pf*) *Akos – Campoli – Kreisler*
Lincke, Paul (1866–1946)
Amina (*Egyptian serenade*) (*pf*) *Anonymous*
Lipiński, Karol Józef (1790–1861)
(3) Caprices, Op. 29 (*solo vln*)

*Unidentified.
†Composed jointly with Glazounov & Sokolov.
‡Queen of Hawaii.

Caprice No. 3, in D *Castillo – Sitkovetsky*
Concerto No. 2, in D, Op. 21 "Military" *(vln & orch) Iwanow*
Lipovšek, Marijan (1910–   )
Rhapsody *(vln & pf) Ozim*
Liszt, Franz (1811–1886)
(6) Consolations, G172 (1849/50) "Tröstungen" *(pf)*

Consolation No. 3, in D flat *Milstein – Zathureczky*

Duo Sonata *(on Chopin's "Mazurka in c sharp" Op. 6, No. 2) R127 (1832/5) (vln & pf) Campoli – Garay*
Hungarian Rhapsody, G383 *(paraphrase on N. Lenau's poem "Die Drei Zigeuner" by Hubay) (vln & orch) Glenn – Moss*
(3) Liebesträume, G326 *(pf)*

Liebestraum No. 3, in A flat *A. Ferraresi – Leopold – A. Sandler – Tworek*

Soirées italiennes *(6 amusements sur des motifs de Mercadante) G411 (1838) (pf)*

No. 1. La primavera *L. Kogan*

(3) Valses oubliées, G215 (1881/3) *(pf)*

Valse oubliée No. 1 *Bisztriczky*

Locatelli, Pietro (1693–1764)
(24) Caprices, Op. 3 *(solo vln)**

Caprice No. 23, in D "Il laberinto armonico" *Menuhin – F. Reuter – R. Ricci – Szeryng (2)*
Caprice No. 24, in D *Neste*

(12) Concerti grossi, Op. 1 (1721) *(2 vlns, vla, vlc, strs & c)*

Concerto grosso No. 2, in c *Krebbers*
Concerto grosso No. 8, in f *Ayo & Cotogni*
Concerto grosso No. 9, in D *Ayo & Cotogni*
Concerto grosso No. 11, in c *Ayo & Cotogni*
Concerto grosso No. 12, in g *Ayo & Cotogni*

(12) Concerti, Op. 3 (1733) "L'Arte del Violino" *(vln, strs & c)*†

Concerto No. 1, in D *Lautenbacher – Michelucci – J. Schröder*
Concerto No. 2, in c *Fernandez – Lautenbacher*
Concerto No. 3, in F *Lautenbacher*
Concerto No. 4, in E *Lautenbacher*
Concerto No. 5, in C *Lautenbacher*
Concerto No. 6, in g *Lautenbacher*
Concerto No. 7, in B flat *Lautenbacher*
Concerto No. 8, in e *Lautenbacher – Michelucci*
Concerto No. 9, in G *Lautenbacher – Michelucci*
Concerto No. 10, in F *Lautenbacher*
Concerto No. 11, in A *Lautenbacher*
Concerto No. 12, in D *Lautenbacher*

(12) Concerti, Op. 7 (1741) "Il pianto d'Arianna" *(strs & c)*

Concerto No. 6, in E flat *(vln, strs & c) Fernandez*
Concerto No. 12, in F *(4 vlns, strs & c) Maier, Neuhaus, Seeger & Vollmer*

*These caprices are usually played as cadenzas to the 12 concerti of opus 3 which are entitled "L'Arte del Violino."
†These concerti contain, as cadenzas, the 24 Caprices for solo vln.

(12) Sonatas, Op. 6 (1737) *(vln & c)*
Sonata* *Morse*
Sonata No. 1, in g *Fain – Klijn – Spivakov – Staryk – Voicu – Zhislin – Zimmermann*
Sonata No. 5, in c *Zimmermann*
Sonata No. 7, in f "Au Tombeau" *Bezrodny – L. Kogan – Kremer – Leon-Ara – Michaelian – D. Oistrak (2)*
Sonata in G (c. 1736) *(2 vlns & c) Geyrhalter & Kuhn*
Tema con variazione *(vln, gtr & vlc) Klasinc*
Loeffler, Charles Martin (1861–1935)
(10) Mélodies, Op. 10 *(v & pf)*
No. 2. Adieu pour jamais *J. Gordon*
No. 4. Les paons *J. Gordon*
Partita (1930) *(vln & pf) J. Gordon*
Loeillet, Jean Baptiste (1680–1730)
(12) Sonatas, Op. 2 *(nos 1/6: 2 vlns & c – 7/9: 2 fls & c – 10/12: ob, fl & c)*
Sonata No. 1, in B flat *Alès*
Sonata No. 2, in F *Alès – Fontanarosa & Ponticelli*
Sonata No. 5, in c *Fontanarosa & Ponticelli*
Sonata No. 6, in c *Alès – Clebanoff – Fontanarosa & Ponticelli*
Sonata No. 9, in g *Fontanarosa & Ponticelli*
Sonata in D *(vln & c) Weiner*
Suite de danses *(vln & c) Fontanarosa*
Logan, Frederick Knight (1871–1929)
Missouri waltz (1914) *(v & pf)*† *Fradkin*
Pale moon (1920) *(v & pf) Campoli – Cillario – Fradkin – Jacobsen – Kreisler – A. Sandler (2)*
Lohr, Herman (1872–   )
(The) Dancing violin *(v & pf) Steiger-Betzak*
Little grey home in the west (1911) *(v & pf) Andjelkovitch – Förster – Haxton – Lensky*
Star of the east *(v & pf) Ludlow*
Where my caravan has rested (1909) *(v & pf) Heifetz – Southgate*
Lopatnikoff, Nikolai (1903–   )
Sonata No. 2, Op. 32 *(vln & pf) Fuchs*
Lorenzo, Ange (1894–   )
Sleepytime gal (1925) *(v & pf)*‡ *Fradkin*
Loret, Charles
Berceuse *(vln & pf) Ranzato*
Loth, Louis Leslie (1888–   )
Firelight fancies *(v & pf) Rubini*
Lotka, Fran (1883–1962)
Croatian Rhapsody *(vln & pf) S. Furer*
Lotti, Antonio (1667–1740)
Arminio (1714) – pasticcio
Pur dicesti *Flesch (3) – F. V. Henriques – Petroni*
Lotto, Izydor (1840–   )

*Unidentified.
†From an original melody procured by John Valentine Eppell.
‡Composed jointly with Richard A. Whiting.

Fileuse *(Romance sans paroles) Op. 8 (vln & pf) Sedano*
Louis Ferdinand (1772–1806)*
Suite romantique *(vln & orch) Hetzel*
Lovenskjold, Hermann *(19th century)*
(La) Sylphide (1836) – ballet *(orch)*
Scène de la Sylphide *(Act II) Gruenberg*
Lubbe, K.
Erinnerung *(Réminiscence) Eweler*
Lübeck, Vincentius (1654–1740)
Willkommen, süsser Bräutigam "Christmas Cantata" *(s, a & strs) Bruun & Koppel*
Lucantoni, Giovanni (1825–1902)
Tarantelle *(vln & pf) Rocabruna*
Lucchesi, Andrea (1741–1800)
Sérénade à une belle *(vln & pf) Aguiar*
Luciann
Serenade *(orch) Schwartz*
Luening, Otto (1900–   )
Gargoyles (1962) *(vln & synthesized sound) Pollikoff*
Sonata No. 3, (1945) *(vln & pf) Gavrilov*
Lully, Jean Baptiste (1632–1687)
Ballet du Roy (1659)†

Gavotte *Cores – Garaguly – Kulenkampff – Morini – R. Pollack – Pratz – Ranzato (2)*
Rondeau *Cores – Kulenkampff*

(Le) Bourgeois Gentilhomme (1670) – Comédie-ballet *(orch)*
Menuet *Ghestem – Gladys Raymond*
Suite No. 3, in B *(orch) Gendre*
Suite No. 7, in g *(orch) Gendre*
Lumbye, Hans Christian (1810–1874)
Concert-polka (1863) *(2 vlns & orch)*
C. Andersen & K.P. Andersen – C. Andersen & Lynged – Christiansen & Kjeldsen – Elbaek & Madsen – L. Hansen & Preil – Krips & Zazofsky
Luz, Ernest
(The) Four Horsemen of the Apocalypse – musical
I have a rendezvous with you *B. Scherzer*
Luzzi, Luigi (1828–1876)
Ave Maria, Op. 80 *(v & pf) Ranzato*
Lyapunov, Sergei (1859–1924)
Concerto in d, Op. 61 *(vln & orch) Sitkovetsky*
Lyatoshinsky, Boris Nikolayevich (1895–   )
Trio No. 2, Op. 41 *(pf, vln & vlc) Budovsky*
Lysenko, Nikolai Vitalievich (1842–1912)
Capriccio élégiaque, Op. 32 *(vln & pf) d'Albert*
Élégie in a (1912) *(vln & pf) d'Albert*
Fantasia, Op. 21 *(vln & pf) d'Albert*
Low sinks the sun *(vln & pf) d'Albert*
Moment of disappointment (1901) *(vln & pf) d'Albert*
Rhapsody No. 2 *(on Ukrainian themes)* "Dumka-Shoomka", Op. 18 *(vln & pf) d'Albert*
Romance in A flat, Op. 27 *(vln & pf) d'Albert*
Trio in A *(2 vlns & vla) Barinova & Goldstein*
MacBeth, Allan (1856–1910)

*Prince of Prussia
†Unidentified.

Love in idleness (*vln & pf*) *Godwin*
McBride, Robert Guryn (1911–   )
Aria & Toccata in Swing (1946) (*vln & pf*)
Kaufman (2)
Concerto (1954) (*vln & orch*) *Wilk*
MacDowell, Edward (1861–1908)
Air & Rigaudon, Op. 49 (1894) (*pf*) *Steeb*
(4) Songs, Op. 56 (1898) (*v & pf*)
  No. 1. Long ago *Zimbalist*
Woodland sketches, Op. 51 (*pf*)
  No. 1. To a wild rose
    Ball – Brown (2) – Fradkin – Grach – Guidi –
    Gusikoff (2) – Jacobsen – Leopold – Mantovani
    – Morrell – Stehl
  No. 7. From uncle Remus *Grach*
MacKenzie, Alexander Campbell (1847–1935)
(6) Pieces, Op. 37 (*vln & pf*)
  No. 3. Benedictus *Jacob – Menges*
MacMillen, Francis (1885–   )
Barcarolle (*vln & pf*) *MacMillen*
Causerie "Prairy flowers" (*vln & pf*) *MacMillen*
(2)
MacMurrough, Dermot (1872–1943)*
Macushla (1910) (*v & pf*) *Chemet*
Macho, Gustav†
Staccato-serenade, Op. 10 (*vln & pf*) *Příhoda*
Mägi, Esther (1922–   )
Serenade (*vln & orch*) *Lippus*
Magine, Frank (1888–   )
Venetian moon (*v & pf*) *Ball*
Magnard, Albéric (1865–1914)
Sonata in G, Op. 13 (*vln & pf*) *Bress*
Mahaut, Antonio
Duets, Op. 4 (*2 vlns*)
  Duet No. 6 *Nijland & Noske*
Mahler, Gustav (1860–1911)
Symphony No. 3, in d (1895) (*soloists, cho*
& orch) *Corigliano – Juda – Walther*
Schneiderhan
Symphony No. 4, in G (1900) (*orch*) *Staryk*
Makarova, Nina (1908–   )
Melody, Op. 18, No. 1 (*vln & pf*) *Pikaizen*
Scherzo in B flat, Op. 18, No. 2 (*vln & pf*)
Pikaizen
Malderen, Edward van
(Le) Tango de rêve (*vln & pf*) *Groth*
Malipiero, Gian Francesco (1882–   )
Concerto (1932) (*vln & orch*) *Kirmse*
Mamedov, Ibragim (1928–   )
Symphonic Variations (*vln & orch*) *Aliev*
Mamiya, Michio (1929–   )
Concerto (1959) (*vln & orch*) *Eto*
Sonata (*solo vln*) *Toyama*
Mancini, Francesco (1679–1739)
Concerto a quattro in e (1729) (*fl, 2 vlns & hpsi*)
Alès & Doukan
Mancini, Henry (1924–   )
Cameo (*vln & orch*) *Carol*
Manén, Juan (1883–   )
Chanson-Adagietto, Op. A-8, No. 1 (*vln & pf*)
Manén – Michaïlow – Székely

*Pseudonym for Harold Robert White.
†Surname is sometimes spelled Maho.

Toccata (*vln & pf*) *Manén*
Turkey in the straw (*Morceau sur un thème*
américain) (*vln & pf*) *Barinova*
Manfredini, Francesco (1680–1748)
(12) Concerti, Op. 3 (1718) (*2 vlns, strs & c*)
  Concerto No. 1, in F *Biffoli & Magnani*
  Concerto No. 2, in a *Biffoli & Magnani –*
  Cotogni & Michelucci
  Concerto No. 3, in e *Biffoli & Magnani –*
  Cotogni & Michelucci
  Concerto No. 4, in B flat *Biffoli & Magnani*
  Concerto No. 5, in d *Biffoli & Magnani*
  Concerto No. 6, in D *Biffoli & Magnani*
  Concerto No. 7, in G *Biffoli & Magnani –*
  Cotogni & Michelucci
  Concerto No. 8, in F *Biffoli & Magnani –*
  Cotogni & Michelucci
  Concerto No. 9, in D *Biffoli & Magnani –*
  Krebbers & Stuurop
  Concerto No. 10, in g *Biffoli & Magnani –*
  Cotogni & Michelucci
  Concerto No. 11, in c *Biffoli & Magnani*
  Concerto No. 12, in C "Christmas Concerto"*
  Biffoli & Magnani – Cotogni & Michelucci –
  Doukan & Yordanoff – Fietz & Kaufman
Mansuryan, T.
Sonata No. 1 (1962) (*vln & pf*) *Agaronyan*
Marais, Marin (1656–1728)
(5) Danses anciennes (*vln & c*) *Davison – Kooper*
Sonnerie de Sainte Geneviève du Mont de Paris
(1723) (*vln, gamba & hpsi*) *Harnoncourt*
Marcello, Alessandro (1684–1750)
(6) Concerti, Op. 1 (*ob or fl, strs & c*)
  Concerto in d† *Vinnikov*
Marcello, Benedetto (1686–1739)
(12) Concerti, Op. 1 (1708) (*vln, vlc obb,*
strs & c) ‡
  Concerto No. 1, in D *Fantini – Staryk*
  Concerto No. 2, in e *Fantini*
  Concerto No. 3, in E *Bacchetta*
  Concerto No. 4, in F *Fantini – Krebbers*
  Concerto No. 5, in b *Bacchetta*
  Concerto No. 6, in B flat *Bacchetta*
  Concerto No. 7, in f *Bacchetta*
  Concerto No. 8, in F *Bacchetta*
  Concerto No. 9, in A *Bacchetta*
  Concerto No. 10, in C *Bacchetta*
  Concerto No. 11, in E flat *Bacchetta*
  Concerto No. 12, in G *Bacchetta*
Concerto in D (*vln, strs & c*)§
Glenn – N. Roth
Introduzione, Aria & Presto (*vln, strs & c*)
Krebbers

*The Pastorale or 1st mvt. is also known as
"Sinfonia da chiesa, con una pastorale."
†Arranged by Moffat from a solo hpsi version
edited by J.S. Bach
‡Originally for strs. & hpsi.
§The manuscript is in the Biblioteca del
Conservatorio di Musica di Firenze.

(12) Sonatas, Op. 2 (*vln & c*)
  Sonata No. 1, in F* *Tomasow*
Marcheselli, Domenico (*17th century*)
Concerto No. 1, in D (*vln, ob, vlc, strs & c*) *Ferro*
Marchetti, Filippo D. (1831–1902)
Coeur affolé! ... andante appassionato (*pf*)
Michaïlow
Fascination (*Valse tzigane*) (*orch*) *Dyke*
Marco, Sano (1898–   )
Humoresque (*vln & pf*) *Rudényi*
Marenco, Romualdo (1841–1907)
(La) Incognito – mazurka (*pf*) *Ranzato*
Margis, Alfred (1874–   )
Valse bleue (*vln & pf*) *Moller – T. Seidel*
Margutti
Canzone appassionata (*vln & pf*) *di Piramo*
Mariani, Angelo (1822–1873)
(L') Abbandono, voce del core (*mand or vln*
& pf) *Ranzato*
Marini, Biagio (1595–1665)
(La) Gardana (1617) (*vln, cbs, spin & lute*) *C.*
Ferraresi
Romance, Gaillarde & Courante (*vln, strs & c*)
Blot & Ortmans-Bach
Sonata (*vln & c*) *A. Ferraresi*
Markaitis, Bruno (1922–   )
Sonata in D (1960) (*vln & pf*) *d'Albert*
Markov, Albert (1933–   )
Variations on a theme of Paganini's "La
Carnevale di Venizia" (*vln & pf*) *Markov*
Marks, Florence Mary
When dreams come true (*v & pf*) *Gusikoff*
Marriner, P.
Guten abend, Herr Mond (*vln & pf*) *Wittenberg*
Marroquín, José Sabre (1910–   )
Mexican lullaby (*vln & pf*) *Szeryng (2)*
Marsaglia, V.A.
Pas du cygne (*vln & pf*) *di Piramo*
Marshall, Charles (1857–1927)
I hear you calling me (1908) (*v & pf*) *Chemet –*
Southgate – Zimbalist
Marsick, Martin Pierre Joseph (1848–1924)
(2) Pieces, Op. 6 (*vln & pf*)
  No. 2. Scherzando *D'Aranyi – Thibaud (3)*
Martin, Easthope (1887–1925)
Evensong (*v & pf*) *Mantovani*
From the Rialto (*vln & pf*) *Allan*
Morning song (*vln & pf*) *Allan*
Martin, Frank (1890–   )
Concerto (1951) (*vln & orch*) *Kling – Wolfgang*
Schneiderhan (2)
Martini, Giovanni Battista "Padre" (1706–1784)
Concerto in F (*vln, strs & c*) *Guglielmo*
Sinfonia concertante (*vln, hpsi, strs & c*) *Redditi*
(12) Sonatas, Op. 2 (1741) (*hpsi*)
  Sonata No. 2, in D† *D'Aranyi*
  Sonata No. 12, in F†
  Flesch – Manén – Newe
Martini (*Il Tedesco*) (1741–1816)

*Published in some editions as Opus 1, No. 1 &
transposed to "D."
†Vitali edition.

Plaisir d'amour (v & pf) Aguiar – Dinicu –
Ghestem – Powell – Swaap – Tworek
Martino, Donald (1929–   )
Fantasy variations (1962) (solo vln) Kobialka –
Zukofsky
Trio (1959) (vln, cl & pf) Zukofsky
Martinon, Jean (1910–   )
Concerto No. 2, Op. 51 (vln & orch) Szeryng
Sonatina No. 5, Op. 32, No. 1 (solo vln) Fournier
– Merckel
Martinů, Bohuslav (1890–1959)
Concertino (pf trio & str orch) Shinder
Concerto da camera (1941) (vln, pf, pcn & strs)
Lehmann
Concerto No. 2 (1943) (vln & orch) Bělčík
Duo No. 1 (1927) (vln & vlc) Heifetz – Posselt –
Rithère – Suk
Duo No. 2 (1958) (vln & vlc) Suk
(7) Études rhythmiques (1931) (vln & pf)
  Étude rhythmique No. 4 Wolfgang
  Schneiderhan
(3) Madrigals (1948) (vln & vla) L. Bobescu –
Fuchs – Novák
(5) Madrigal Stanzas (1943) (vln & pf) Kuronuma
– Michaelian
(5) Pièces Brèves (1930) (vln & pf)
  No. 2. Andante Kaufman
  No. 5. Allegro Kaufman
Round dances (2 vlns, pf, ob, cl, bsn & tpt)
Ovcharek & Shinder
Sonata No. 1 (1930) (vln & pf) Beilina – Loveday
Sonata No. 2 (1933) (vln & pf) Parnes
Sonata No. 3 (1944) (vln & pf) Kuronuma –
Plocek –Weiner
Sonata (1932) (2 vlns & pf) Kaufman & Rybar –
M. & W. Schweyda
Sonatina (1938) (vln & pf) Jásek
Sonatina (2 vlns & pf) M. & W. Schweyda
Mascagni, Pietro (1863–1945)
(L') Amico Fritz (1891) – opera
  Air Gomez
  selection May
  Serenade di Piramo
  Violinista A. Ferraresi – Ranzato (2)
  Zingaresca Genesini
Cavalleria Rusticana (1890) – opera
  Intermezzo (orch)
  d'Almaine – L. André – Anonymous (2) –
  Benavente – D. De Groot (2) – Dyke – Gautier
  – Hager – B. Hall – Haxton (2) – Huppertz –
  Jacobs – Kreisler – Ledru – Mantovani – Moller
  – Paget – Parlow – Ranzato – Ricci – R.
  Richter – Rubini – Rudényi – Sammons – Sens
  – Skalka – C. Skolnik – Southgate – Thiele –
  Valesca-Becker – Voelker – Weintraub –
  Williams – Zacharewitsch – Zapotocki – Zentay
  selection Dyke – Lorand – Manuello – Meier
  Siciliana Ranzato – Skalka – Wise
Mascheroni, Angelo (1855–1905)
Ave Maria (v & pf) Zeiler
Cavezze (Melodia) (vln & pf) di Piramo
Eternamente (1891) (v & pf)*

*Also known as: "For all eternity"; "A Jamais";
& "In alle Ewigkeit."

Haxton – Spalding (2) – Strong
Rêverie pathétique (vln & pf) Wolters
Mason, Daniel Gregory (1873–1953)
(3) Pieces. Op. 13 (fl, hp & str qt) Brown
Massenet, Jules (1842–1914)
Ariane (1906) – opera
  Menuet des Graces Sechiari
  Rêverie d'Ariane Sechiari
Élégie (v & pf)
  Aguiar – W. Andersen – Ball – Brown – De Vito
  – Eidus – Elman (2) – Fradkin – Fritz-Crone –
  Hayward – Jacobsen – Powell – Robbins –
  Rosen – Sammons (2) – Weismann – Zentay –
  Zimbalist
(Les) Erinnyes (1873) – Incidental music (orch)
  Entr'acte Marteau
Italian Christmas Pastorale * MacMillen
Scène pittoresques (1874) (orch)† Lorand
Thaïs (1894) – opera
  Méditation
  Abadiev – Andjelkovitch – R. André –
  Anonymous (3) – Arschensky – A. Bachmann –
  Ball – Barcewicz – Barinova – Barylli – Bild –
  Bisztriczky – Boucherit – Brückner – Brusilow –
  Campoli – Cavalcabo – Chauveton – Chemet –
  Cochrane – Culbertson – Curti – Czerwonky –
  Darrieux – Eidus – Elman (4) – A. Ferraresi –
  Ferras (2) – Fleming – Fradkin – Francescatti –
  S. Furer – Gali – Gautier – Ghestem – Gittelson
  – Godwin – Gomez – Gramegna – Guidi –
  Gundersen – Haendel – B. Hall – Hassid –
  Haxton – Hayward – Jacobsen – Jarry – Kalki
  – Kaufman – Kolberg – Kortschak – Kreisler
  (2) – Lass – Law – Lederer – Leutjens – Levey
  – Livontas – Lorand – Luquin – Lusk – Magyar
  – Meine – Mendels – Menges – Meyer –
  Milstein (3) – Moller – Møller – Morbitzer –
  Nadien – Parikian – Parlow – Pessina – Phal –
  Pilzer (2) – Powell – Prick – Příhoda – Rabin –
  Ranzato (4) – Rattay – Reillie – Romberg –
  Rosen – Rudényi – Sammons (3) – Sandford –
  A. Sandler – Schmied – Schwartz – T. Seidel –
  Sens – Spalding – Staryk – Stehl – Swaap –
  Telmányi – Thibaud (2) – Unno – Vignon –
  Ware – Weist-Hill – Wethmar – Winchester –
  Wolfgang – Wolters – Zighera
(La) Vierge (1880) – oratorio
  Le Dernier Sommeil de la Vierge Locatelli –
  Phal
Masson-Kiek, F.
(En) Relisant vos lettres – Valse lente (orch) Dony
– Schwartz
Matchavariani, Alexei Davidovich (1913–   )
Concerto in d (1950) (vln & orch) Vaiman –
Yashvili
Doluri (solo vln) Grach
Mathé, Edouard (1863–1936)
(Le) Petit savoyard (vln & pf) Leutjens
Mathieu, André (1929–   )

*Unidentified
†Orchestral Suite No. 4.

Quintet No. 1 (2 vlns, vla, vlc & pf) Bress
Mathieu, Rodolphe (1896–1962)
(12) Etudes (solo vln)
  Etude No. 5 Staryk
  Etude No. 6 Staryk
  Etude No. 8 Staryk
Mattei, Tito (1841–1914)
Non è ver (v & pf) Kreisler
Mattheson, Johann (1681–1764)
(12) Sonatas (1720) (fl or vln & clav)
  Sonata No. 6, in e Kaufman
(12) Suites (1714) (hpsi)
  Suite No. 5, in c Andrade – Grach – Heber –
  Příhoda – R. Ricci – Wolfsthal
Mattullath, Alice
Cradle song (1915) (based on Kreisler's "Caprice
viennois") (v & pf) Ball
Matúška, Janko (1821–1877)
Variations (vln & pf) Gašparek
Maury, Lowndes (1911–   )
Sonata (1952) "In memory of the Korean war
dead" (vln & pf) M. Sandler
Medtner, Nicolai Raslovich (1879–1951)
(2) Fairytales, Op. 20 (1910) (pf)
  Fairytale No. 1, in b flat Heifetz
(4) Fairytales, Op. 34 (1916) (pf)
  Fairytale No. 2, in e Malinin
(3) Nocturnes, Op. 16 (vln & pf)
  Nocturne No. 1, in f sharp D. Oistrakh
Quintet in C (1950) (pf, 2 vlns, vla & vlc)
Danchenko & Grach
Sonata No. 1, in b, Op. 21 (vln & pf) Malinin
Sonata No. 3, in e, Op. 57 (1936) "Sonata epica"
(vln & pf) Labko – D. Oistrakh
Medyns, Janis (1890–1966)
Prelude (vln & pf) Bulavinov
Romance (vln & pf) Švolkovskis
Sonata in G (vln & pf) Zariņš
Medyns, Jasep (1877–1947)
Latvian capriccio (vln & pf) Švolkovskis
Medyns, Jekabs (1885–   )
Concert polka (vln & pf) L. Rubens
Lettish caprice (vln & pf) L. Rubens – Švolkovskis
Poem in b (vln & orch) Bergs
Romance (vln & pf) L. Rubens
Rondino (vln & pf) L. Rubens
Meglio, Vincenzo de
Fenesta che lucive (v & pf) Senatra
Meisel, Will
Maria-Louise (Sérénade) (vln & pf) Curti
Melartin, Erkki (1875–1937)
(2) Songs, Op. 3 (v & pf)
  No. 2. Élégie Moguilevski
Melchert, J.
Raslende Sølv, brusende Bølge (v & pf) Meine &
Sens
Melfi, Mario (1905–   )
Remembrance (pf) A. Sandier
Menasch, Jacques de (1905–1960)
Sonata No. 1 (1940) (vln & pf) Fuchs
Mendelssohn, Alfred (1910–1966)
Partita on a theme of Bach (1957) (solo vln)
Danchenko
Mendelssohn, Felix (1809–1847)
Concerto in d (1822) (vln & strs) Menuhin (2) –

Michelucci – Soh
Concerto in d (1823) "Double" (*vln, pf & strs*)
Glenn – Gulli
Concerto in e. Op. 64 (*vln & orch*)
Accardo – Anonymous (4) – Auclair – Belayeff – Borries – A. Brosa – Brown – Campoli (2) – Carrodus – Cochrane – De Vito – Elman (2) – Erlih – Farbmann – Ferras – Field – Francescatti (2) – Friedman – Gavrilov – Gimpel – Gitlis – Godowsky – Goldstein – Grumiaux (3) – Gulli – Haendel – M. Hall (2) – Heifetz (3) – Huberman – Jacobs – Kaufman – Klimov – L. Kogan – Kovács – Kreisler (2) – Kulenkampff – Kulky – Lack – Laredo – Law – List – Lorand – Malachowsky – Manén (3) – Marschner – Martzy – Melcher – Menuhin (3) – Milstein (3) – Mischakoff – Odnoposoff – D. Oistrakh (3) – I. Oistrakh – Olevsky – Parlow – Persinger – Petronio – Pikaizen – Powell – Příhoda – Rabin – R. Ricci – A.J. Rose – Rudényi – Ruppert – Rybar – Walther Schneiderhan (2) – Wolfgang Schneiderhan – T. Seidel – Senatra – Shkolníková – M. Smith – Stern (3) – Suk – Szeryng – J. Szigeti – Telmányi – Thibaud – Tomasow – T. Varga – Voicu (2) – Weisbeck – Wittenberg – Wolf – Wolfsthal – Yashkin – Ysaÿe – Zacharewitsch – Zimmermann – Zukerman
(6) Duets, Op. 63 (*2 v's & pf*)
No. 1. Ich wollt' meine Lieb' *Meine & Sens*
Elijah, Op. 70 (1846) – oratorio
No. 31. O rest in the Lord *Hayward*
(3) Fantasies, Op. 16 (1829) (*pf*)
No. 2. Fantasy No. 2, in e *Steeb*
(6) Gesänge, Op. 34 (*v & pf*)
No. 2. Auf Flügeln des Gesanges
Accardo – Ball – Barbieri – Bean – Bustabo – Campoli (2) – Candéla – Granchi – Grumlíková – Haendel – Heifetz (3) – Komissarov – Milstein – Nadien – D. Oistrakh – Příhoda (3) – Robbins – Spalding – Weismann – Zilzer
Hymn: Hear my prayer "O for the wings of a dove" (*Psalm 55*) (1844) (*s, mix-cho & org*) *Elman*
Octet in E flat, Op. 20 (*4 vlns, 2 vlas & 2 vlcs*)
Baker, Belnick, Heifetz & Stepansky – Boskovsky, Matheis & Swoboda – Laredo, Schneider & Steinhardt
Quartet No. 1, in c, Op. 1 (*pf, vln, vla & vlc*)
Guilet
Quartet No. 1, in E flat, Op. 12 (*2 vlns, vla & vlc*)
Brown – Elman – Kaufman & Stepansky – D. Oistrakh – Primrose
Quartet No. 2, in a, Op. 13 (*2 vlns, vla & vlc*)
Catterall
(3) Quartets, Op. 44 (*2 vlns, vla & vlc*)
No. 2. Quartet No. 4, in e (1837) *Dyke – Pessina*
No. 3. Quartet No. 5, in E flat (1838) *Hayward*
Sonata in f, Op. 4 (1825) (*vln & pf*) *Guilet – Juda*
Sonata in F (1838) (*vln & pf*) *Gulli – Lysy – Menuhin*
(6) Songs without words, Op. 19 (*pf*)
No. 1. Song without words No. 1, in E "Sweet remembrance" *Dumont – Heifetz*

No. 6. Song without words No. 6, in g "Venezianisches Gondellied" *R. Pollak*
(6) Songs without words, Op. 62 (*pf*)
No. 1. Song without words No. 25, in G "May breezes"
Bratza – Carpi – Chauveton – Dessau – Dukson – Elman (4) – A. Ferraresi – Ferras – Flesch – Ghestem – Gorokhov – Guidi – Jovanovič – L. Kogan – Kreisler (2) – Milstein – R. Ricci – Suk – Telmányi – Weintraub
No. 6. Song without words No. 30, in A "Spring song"
d'Almaine (2) – Ball – Chauveton – Chemet – Dumont – Hager – B. Hall – Haxton – Hayward – Herman – Jacob – Jacobsen – Kalafusz – J.M. Lasowski – Maurice – Ormond – Pilzer – R. Pollak – Polo – L. Quattrocchi – Ranzato – K. Rubens – Rudényi – Sammons – Sens (2) – S. Smith – Spalding – Szeryng – Thiele – Valesca-Becker – Weist-Hill – Willis – Zimbalist
(6) Songs without words, Op. 67 (*pf*)
No. 6. Song without words No. 36, in E "Serenade" *Elman – Příhoda*
Trio No. 1, in d, Op. 49 (1839) (*pf, vln & vlc*)
Catterall – Guilet – Heifetz – Jarry – Lorand – D. Oistrakh – Pelliccia – Sammons – Schneeberger – Schneider – Stern – Suk – Thibaud – L. Wolff
Trio No. 2, in c, Op. 66 (1845) (*pf, vln & vlc*)
Catterall – Heifetz – D. Oistrakh – Sammons (2) – Zilzer
Menotti, Gian Carlo (1911–   )
Concerto (1952) (*vln & orch*) *Spivakovsky*
Menzel, Franz
Romanze, Op. 40 "Sweet longing" (*fl & var. inst*) *d'Almaine – Biedermann – Rattay*
Merikanto, Oscar (1868–1924)
Intermezzo (*vln & pf*) *Bezrodny*
Mustalainen (*pf*) *W. Andersen*
Valse lente (*pf*) *Andreasson – Asti – Hannikainen – Mossel*
Merkler, Andro
Berceuse in F (*vln & pf*) *Vecsey*
Merkur
I lost my heart to you (*v & pf*)* *Jacobsen*
Merula, Tarquinio (1595–1665)
Canzone la Loda (*2 vlns & c*) *A. Ferraresi & Franzetti*
de Mesquita, Carlos (1864–1953)
Chanson de l'Esmeralda, Op. 104 (*vln & pf*) *Curti*
Messiaen, Olivier (1908–   )
Quartet (1940) "For the end of time" (*vln, cl, vlc & pf*) *Fernandez – J. Pasquier*
Metcalf, John W. (1856–1926)
Absent (1899) (*v & pf*) *Benavente – Southgate*
Meyer, Ernst Hermann (1905–   )
Concerto (1963/4) (*vln & orch*) *D. Oistrakh*
Meyer-Helmund, Erik (1861–1932)
Intermezzo, Op. 28 (*pf*) *Laue*
Leaves & buds "Sérénade Rococo" (1896) (*2 mands & pf*) *Dyke*

*Composed jointly with Benny Davis.

(3) Lieder, Op. 21 (*v & pf*)
No. 2. Das Zauberlied *Huppertz – Michaïlow*
(3) Lieder, Op. 73 (*v & pf*)
No. 2. Ballgeflüster "Flirtation" *Kreisler*
Waltz, Op. 14 (*pf*) *Laue*
Mezzacapo, E.
Sympathie – valse (*pf*) *Moller*
Miaskovsky, Nikolai Yakovlevich (1881–1950)
Concerto in d, Op. 44 (1938) (*vln & orch*) D. Oistrakh
Míča, Jan Adam (1746–1811)
Concertino notturno in D (*vln & orch*) *Suk*
Michaïlow, Max
(La) Carnevale di Venizia (*Italian folksong*) (*vln & pf*) *Michaïlow (2)*
Gavotte, Op. 2 (*vln & pf*) *Dajos – Michaïlow*
Micheli
Rêverie (*vln & pf*) *di Piramo*
Serenata (*vln & pf*) *di Piramo*
Michiels, Gustav (1845–   )
(6) Csárdas (*on national Hungarian airs*) (*vln & pf*)
Csárda No. 1 "Piroska" *Dumont – Maurice*
Mielczewski, Marcin (1600–1651)
Canzona (*2 vlns & c*) *Iwanow & Murawski*
Mignone, Francisco (1897–   )
Berceuse (*vln & pf*) *Borgerth*
Cançao brasileira (*vln & pf*) *Borgerth*
Lenda Sertaneja No. 2 (*vln & pf*) *Borgerth*
Tango capriccio (*vln & pf*) *Borgerth*
Migot, Georges Elbert (1891–   )
Sonata (1951) (*solo vln*) *Fueri*
Mihalovici, Marcel (1898–   )
Sonata No. 2, Op. 45 (*vln & pf*) *Rostal*
Mihály, Andreas (1917–   )
Concerto (1959) (*vln, orch & pf obb*) *Kovács*
Milandre, Louis-Toussaint (1770– ?)
Minuetto* *Kennedy*
Miles, Percy Hilder
Idyll (*vln & pf*) *Rudényi*
Milaud, Darius (1892–   )
Aspen-Serenade (1957) (*fl, ob, cl, bsn, tpt, vln, vla & cbs*) *Jarry*
Cinéma-Fantaisie (*on "Le Boeuf sur le toit"*) (1919) (*vln & orch*) *Benedetti*
Concertino de printemps (1934) (*vln & cha orch*) *Astruc – Goldberg – Kaufman*
Concerto No. 2 (1946) (*vln & orch*) *Bernard – Kaufman*
Danses de Jacarémirim (1921) (*vln & pf*) *Kaufman*
(Le) Printemps (1921) (*vln & pf*) *Lewkowitz – J. Szigeti*
(12) Saudades do Brasil (1920/1) (*pf*)
No. 3. Leme *Beilina – Koene – Shapiro*
No. 4. Copacabana *Beilina – Shapiro*
No. 5. Ipanema *Beilina – Kaufman – Koene – Martzy – Shapiro*
No. 7. Corcavado *Beilina – Heifetz – L. Kogan – Shapiro – J. Szigeti – Vaiman*
No. 8. Tijuca *Beilina – Shapiro – Stern – J. Szigeti*

*Unidentified.

No. 9. Sumare *Beilina – Heifetz – L. Kogan – Shapiro – J. Szigeti*
Scaramouche (1937) (*2 pfs*)*
   No. 3. Brasileira *Goldstein (2)*
Septet (1964) (*2 vlns, 2 vlas, 2 vlcs & cbs*) *Ghestem & Jarry*
Sonata No. 1 (1911) (*vln & pf*) *Soëtens*
Sonata No. 2 (1917) (*vln & pf*) *Gertler (2) – Montbrun – Soëtens – Urban – Voicu*
Sonatina (1940) (*2 vlns*) *G. & W. Beal*
Suite (1936) (*vln, cl & pf*)† *Ritter*
Suite de quatrains (1962) (*narrator, fl, s-sax, bs-cl, hp, vln, vlc & cbs*) *Jarry*
Miller, Charles
Cubanaise (1951) (*vln & pf*) *Elman*
Millöcker, Karl (1842–1899)
(The) Blue lagoon (*v & pf*) *Elman*
Miloieritsch, M.D.
Serbischer Tanz (*vln & pf*) *Topolski*
Milstein, Nathan (1904–   )
Paganiniana (*solo vln*) *Accardo – Milstein*
Mimaroglu, Ilhan Kemaleddin (1926–   )
Music plus one (1970) (*vln & electromagnetic tape*) *Banat*
Minkus, Ludwig (1827–1890)
(La) Bayadère (1877) – ballet (*orch*)
   Grand pas de deux (*Act IV*) *Gruenberg*
Mirzoyev, M.
Adagio & waltz-scherzo (*vln & pf*) *Malinin*
Misraki, Paul (1908–   )
In my heart (*Hungarian melody*) (*v & pf*) *Tzipine*
Mistowski, Alfred
Suite of 7 Pieces (*vln & pf*)
   Hornpipe *Kennedy*
Mitsukuri, Shukichi (1895–   )
Sonata in F (*vln & pf*) *Iwamoto*
Miyagi, Michio (1894–1956)
Haru no umi (*The sea in springtime*) (1929) (*v & pf*) *Chemet*
Miyoshi, Akira
Sonata (*vln & pf*) *Kuronuma*
Mlynarski, Emil (1870–1935)
Mazurka in G, Op. 26 (*vln & pf*) *Barinova – Berchmann – Hundt – Irmer – Mossel*
(3) Morceaux, Op. 4 (*vln & pf*)
   No. 1. Polonaise *Sens*
Moeran, Ernest John (1894–1950)
Trio in G (1931) (*vln, vla & vlc*) *Pougnet*
Moeschinger, Albert (1897–   )
Sonata No. 1, Op. 62 (*vln & pf*) *Schneeberger*
Molloy, James Lyman (1837–1909)
Love's old sweet song (*v & pf*) *Brown – Colombo – D. De Groot – Sammons – A. Sandler – Stehl*
Mompou, Federico (1893–   )
(5) Scènes d'enfants (1915/8) (*pf*)
   No. 5. Jeunes filles au jardin *Bezrodny – Rabin – Szeryng*
Monasterio, Jesús de (1836–1903)
Serenata Andaluza (*vln & pf*) *S. Furer – Menuhin*
Sierra Morena (*vln & pf*) *Barinova*

de Mondonville, Joseph (1711–1772)
(6) Sonatas, Op. 3 (*vln & c*)
Sonata No. 1, in g *Frydén*
Sonata No. 2, in F *Frydén*
Sonata No. 3, in B flat *Frydén*
Sonata No. 4, in C *Andrade – Frydén*
Sonata No. 5, in G *Frydén*
Sonata No. 6, in A *Frydén*
Sonata in G (*fl, vln & clav*) *Gendre*
Moniuszko, Stanislav (1819–1872)
Halka (1854) – opera
   air* *Leutjens*
   The wind whistles (*Jontek's aria*) *Leutjens*
Monk, William Henry (1823–1889)
Abide with me (1861) (*v & pf*) *Campoli – A. Sandler*
Monn, Mathias Georg (1717–1750)
   Concertino fugato in G (1742) (*vln & strs*) *Melkus*
Monsigny, Pierre-Alexandre (1729–1817)
Aline, Reine de Golconde (1766) – opera
   Rigaudon *Elman – Kersey – Menuhin*
Montavani
Impromptu serenade (*vln & pf*) *Gandino*
Montbrun, Raymond Gallois (1918–   )
Symphonie concertante in E (1951) (*vln & orch*) *Montbrun*
Monteverdi, Claudio (1567–1643)
Madrigals – Book VII (1619)
   I lettera amorosa *Brink*
Madrigals – Book IX (1651)
   La mia turca *Brink*
   Ohimé ch'io cado *Brink*
   Si dolce è il tormento *Brink*
Scherzi musicali (1632)
   Et è pur dunque vero *Brink*
   Quel sguardo sdegnosetto *Brink*
Vespers of the Blessed Virgin (1610) *Barchet*
Monti, Vittorio (1868–   )
Aubade d'amour (*vln & pf*) *Curti – Darrieux – L. Quattrocchi*
Csárdas (1904) (*vln & pf*)
   W. Andersen – Barbosa – Benedetti – Bleumers – Brugman – Buckingham – Campoli – Curti (2) – Darrieux – M. De Groot – Dumont – Hayward (2) – Kantrovitch – Kawaciuk – Ladscheck – Lensky – Michaïlow – Morbitzer – Morgagni – Philippot – Robbins – P. Sanchez – A. Sandler (2) – Schwartz – Skalka – Staryk – Vignon – Zilzer
(Il) Natale di Pierrot (*orch*) – mime-drama
   Serenata *Ranzato*
Moore, Thomas (1779–1852)
Believe me if all those endearing young charms (*v & pf*) *Gardner*
(The) Last rose of summer (*v & pf*) *Elman – Fradkin – Gardner – Hoffman – Parlow (2) – A. Sandler*
Morawetz, Oscar (1917–   )
Duo (1946) (*vln & pf*)†

Hidy – Kash – Pach – Pratz
Sonata No. 1 (1956) (*vln & pf*) *Pratz*
Morgan, Harold
Variations on the Austrian Hymn (*vln & pf*) *Morgan*
Morrison, C. S.
Meditation (*vln & pf*) *T. Seidel*
Mortari, Virgilio (1902–   )
Largo in d (1928) (*vln & pf*) *Abbado*
Mortensen, Kai (1908–   )
Humoresque (*vln & pf*) *Leth*
Kitten on the strings (*vln & pf*) *Tworek*
Moss, Lawrence (1927–   )
Sonata (1959) (*vln & pf*) *Raimondi*
Mostras, Constantin (1886–   )
Caprice, Recitative & Toccata (*vln & pf*) *Pikaizen*
Moszkowski, Moritz (1854–1925)
(5) Danzas españolas, Op. 12 (*pf – 4 hands*)
   Danza española No. 5, in D (*con spirito*) *Barcewicz – Jacobsen – Lorand*
(6) Klavierstücke, Op. 15 (*pf – 4 hands*)
   No. 1. Serenata
   Andjelkovitch – Asti – Beneter – Campoli – D. De Groot – Deman – Dessau – Dyke – Guidi – Henley – Jacobs – Kerekjarto – Kreisler – J.M. Lasowski – Lass – Law – Lorand – Mánnok – Michaïlow – Powell – Rattay – Rubini – Rudényi – A. Sandler – Selinsky (2) – Sens – Swaap – Tworek (2) – Weismann – Zimbalist
(6) Nachtstücke, Op. 56 (*pf*)
   No. 2. Sarabande *Herman*
   No. 3. Passepied *Herman*
(3) Stücke, Op. 29 (*vlc & pf*)
   No. 3. Berceuse in F *Příhoda*
(2) Stücke, Op. 45 (*pf*)
   No. 2. Guitarre
   Barbieri – Bean – Benedetti – Bezrodny – Bratza – Campoli – Clockers – Culbertson – Farbmann – Godowsky – Gomez – Heifetz (2) – Jancowich – Menuhin – Pratz – Quiroga – R. Ricci – Sens – Sitkovetsky – Spalding – Spivakovsky – Strockoff – Vecsey – Zilzer
Tanz-Momente, Op. 89 (*pf*)
   No. 2. Valse mignonne *Link*
Mouret, Jean-Joseph (1682–1738)
(Le) Triomphe des Sens (1732) – ballet (*orch*)
   Sarabande in e *Spivakovsky – Thibaud*
Moya*
(The) Song of songs (1914) (*v & pf*) *Chemet – Groth – Jacobsen*
Moyzes, Alexander (1906–   )
Concerto, Op. 53 (*vln & orch*) *Bauer*
Suite poetique, Op. 35 (*vln & pf*) *Bauer – Gašparek*
Mozart, Leopold (1719–1787)
Suite aus dem Jahre (1762) (*vln & hpsi*) *Franke*
Mozart, Wolfgang Amadeus (1756–1791)
Adagio in E, K261 (*vln & orch*)
   Feigin – Fuchs – Geyer – Grumiaux – Gyarmati – Harth – Haendel – Klijn – Krysa – Kulenkampff (3) – Milstein (2) – Petrosyan – Pougnet – Renardy – Wolfgang Schneiderhan – Suk – Swärdström – T. Varga

(6) Adagios & 6 Fugues, K404a (*vln, vla & vlc*)
   Adagio No. 6, in f* *Kehr*
Ave verum corpus, K618 (*cho*) *Catterall – Ricci –
Swaap – Weintraub*
Cassation No. 1, in G, K63 (*orch*) *Langbein –
Richter-Steiner – Zazofsky*
Concerto No. 1, in D, K107 (*hpsi & orch*)†
Strub
Concerto in D, KAnh294a "Princess Adelaide"
(*vln & orch*) *Kaufman – Menuhin*
Concerto No. 1, in B flat, K207 (*vln & orch*)
   *Boskovsky – Erlih – Grumiaux (2) – Menuhin –
   D. Oistrakh – Parikian – Wolfgang
   Schneiderhan – Stern – Stücki – Szeryng – T.
   Varga*
Concerto No. 2, in D, K211 (*vln & orch*)
   *Erlih – Francescatti – Grumiaux (2) – Kalafusz
   – Menuhin – Wolfgang Schneiderhan – Stücki –
   Szeryng – T. Varga*
Concerto No. 3, in G, K216 (*vln & orch*)
   *D'Aranyi – Barchet – Borsody – Boskovsky – De
   Vito (2) – Ferras – Fontanarosa – Fournier –
   Francescatti – Fuchs – Goldberg – Grumiaux
   (2) – Gulli (2) – Hendel – Huberman – Kagen
   – Klimov – L. Kogan (3) – Laredo – Maazel –
   Makanowitzky – Martzy – Menuhin (4) –
   Mischakoff – D. Oistrakh (4) – Parikian –
   Poulet – Příhoda – Wolfgang Schneiderhan –
   Soriano – Stern (2) – Szeryng – Thibaud – T.
   Varga*
Concerto No. 4, in D, K218 (*vln & orch*)
   *Auclair – Barchet (2) – Borsody – Boskovsky –
   Bress – Elman – Fain – Ferras – Francescatti –
   George – Goldberg – Grumiaux (2) – Gulli –
   Heifetz (2) – Janowski – Georg Kniestaedt –
   Kreisler (2) – Makanowitzky – Martzy –
   Menuhin (3) – Milstein – Morini – Novak – D.
   Oistrakh (2) – Parikian – Pauk – Poulet –
   Příhoda (2) – Queling – Schneider – Wolfgang
   Schneiderhan (3) – Shkolnikova – Stanske –
   Szeryng – J. Szigeti – T. Varga – Zukerman*
Concerto No. 5, in A, K219 "Turkish" (*vln &
orch*)
   *Auclair – Barchet – L. Bobescu – Boucherit – A.
   Busch – Catterall – Dahmen – Elman –
   Fassbander – Ferras – Field – Fournier –
   Francescatti – George – Goldberg – Grinke –
   Grumiaux (2) – Gulli – Heifetz (3) – Hitzker –
   Kagen – Kayser – L. Kogan (3) – Kovács –
   Kozolupova – Kulenkampff – Maazel – Menuhin
   (2) – Milstein (2) – Morini (2) – D. Oistrakh (3)
   – Olof – Parikian – Parkhomenko – Pauk –
   Wolfgang Schneiderhan (3) – Shumsky – Stern
   – Szeryng – Thibaud – Vaiman – T. Varga –
   Wolf – Wolfsthal – Zukerman*
Concerto in G, K250 (*vln & orch*)‡ *Hendel*

*Fugue by W.F. Bach.
†After J.C. Bach's opus 5, number 2.
‡The 2nd, 3rd & 4th mvts. from the "Haffner"
Serenade constitute this work.

Concerto No. 6, in E flat, K268 (*K365b*) (*vln &
orch*) *Barchet (2) – Chemet – Constantinescu –
Dubois – Ferras – Menuhin – Thibaud*
Concerto No. 7, in D, K271a (*vln & orch*) *Airoff –
Bress – Grumiaux – Menuhin (2) – D. Oistrakh –
Soriano – Stücki – Szeryng*
Concerto in D, K315 "Unfinished" (*vln, pf
& orch*) *Dumont*
Concertone in C, K190 (*2 vlns, ob, vlc & orch*)
   *Büchner & Hendel – Goren & Hurwitz – Hendel
   & Makanowitzky – Keltsch & Lautenbacher –
   Laredo & Tree – Lysy & Menuhin – Ovcharek
   & Shinder – Poulet & Szeryng*
(6) Deutsche Tänze, K600 (*orch*)
   Deutscher Tanz No. 1, in C "Ländler" *Gyarfas
   – Kulenkampff*
   Deutscher Tanz No. 4, in C *Barmas – Petroni*
Divertimento in D, K136 (*str orch*) *Geyer*
Divertimento No. 10, in F, K247 (*2 hrns & strs*)
Grehling & Maier
Divertimento No. 11, in D, K251 (*2 hrns, ob &
strs*) *Grehling & Maier – Schneider*
Divertimento No. 15, in B flat, K287 (*2 hrns &
strs*) *Burgin – Skalar – J. Szigeti – Tomasow*
Divertimento No. 17, in D, K334 (*2 hrns & strs*)
Druian – Tomasow
   Minuet (*3rd mvt*)
   *Addash – Andjelkovitch – D'Aranyi – Bas –
   Beckwith – Benedetti – Boucherit – Bratza –
   Cantell – Catterall – Chauveton – Deman –
   Dubois – Dumont – Fischberg – Ghestem – Gygi
   – M. Hall – M. Hansen – Heifetz (2) –
   Jovanovic – Kolberg – B. Koutzen – Ladscheck
   – Lorand – MacMillen – Menuhin – Meyer –
   Mittmann – Morini (2) – Noceti – R. Pollak –
   Powell – Příhoda (2) – Ranzato (5) – F. Roth –
   T. Seidel – Selinsky – Soriano – Spalding (2) –
   Stanske – J. Szigeti – Wittenberg –
   Zimmermann*
   Adagio (*4th mvt*) *Fachiri*
Divertimento in E flat, K563 (*vln, vla & vlc*)
   *Grumiaux – Gulli – Heifetz – Jarry – Kehr –
   Posselt – Pougnet*
Don Giovanni, K527 (1787) – opera
   No. 14. Minuet *Rubini*
Duo No. 1, in G, K423 (*vln & vla*)
   *L. Bobescu – Brainin – Dyke – Fuchs –
   Goldberg – Grehling – Grinke – Grumiaux –
   Kovács – D. & I. Oistrakh – I. Oistrakh – J.
   Pasquier – Persinger*
Duo No. 2, in B flat, K424 (*vln & vla*)
   *L. Bobescu – Fuchs (2) – Goldberg – Grehling –
   Grinke – Grumiaux – Gulli – Heifetz – Klingler
   – Kovács – Novák – I. Oistrakh – J. Pasquier –
   Suk*
Exsultate, jubilate, K165 (*s & orch*) *Barylli*
Idomeneo, Re di Creta, K366 (1781) – opera
   Gavotte in G*
   Elman – Kersey – B. Koutzen (2) – T. Seidel
   Non temer, amato bene *Boskovsky – Wolfgang
   Schneiderhan*

*The Gavotte is the 4th piece in the ballet
music of Act III. The ballet music is assigned
to K367.

(6) Ländler, K606 (*orch*)
   Ländler No. 1, in B flat *Elman – A. Schmidt*
   Ländler No. 3, in B flat *A. Schmidt*
(Ein) Musikalischer Spass in F, K522 (*strs & 2
hrns*)* *Gulli*
(Le) Nozze di Figaro, K492 (1786) – opera
   No. 17. Vedro mentr'io sospiro *Aguiar*
Quartet No. 1, in D, K285 (*fl, vln, vla & vlc*)
   *Grumiaux – Kehr – A. Schneider & Stern –
   Walther Schneiderhan*
Quartet No. 2, in G, K285a (*fl, vln, vla & vlc*)
   Grumiaux – A. Schneider & Stern
Quartet No. 3, in C, K285b (*fl, vln, vla & vlc*)
   Grumiaux – A. Schneider & Stern
Quartet No. 4, in A, K298 (*fl, vln, vla & vlc*)
   Grumiaux – A. Schneider & Stern
Quartet in F, K370 (*ob, vln, vla & vlc*) *Bruun &
Koppel – Kehr – Klijn – Snítil – Stern*
Quartet No. 1, in g, K478 (*pf, vln, vla & vlc*)
   Menuhin – Schneider – Schwalbé – Silverstein
Quartet No. 2, in E flat, K493 (*pf, vln, vla & vlc*)
   Menuhin – Schneider – Schwalbé – Stern
Quartet No. 11, in E flat, K171 (*2 vlns, vla & vlc*)
D. Oistrakh
Quartet No. 14, in G, K387 (*2 vlns, vla & vlc*)
Catterall
Quartet No. 15, in d, K421 (*2 vlns, vla & vlc*)
Amar – Catterall – Elman
Quartet No. 16, in E flat, K428 (*2 vlns, vla & vlc*)
Amar (2) – Elman
Quartet No. 18, in A, K464 (*2 vlns, vla & vlc*)
Michaïlow & Pietsch
Quartet No. 19, in C, K465 (*2 vlns, vla & vlc*)
Deman
Quartet No. 20, in D, K499 (*2 vlns, vla & vlc*)
Klijn & J. Schröder
Quartet No. 21, in D, K575 (*2 vlns, vla & vlc*)
Michaïlow & Pietsch
Quartet No. 22, in B flat, K589 "King of Prussia"
(*2 vlns, vla & vlc*) *Klijn & J. Schröder*
Quartet No. 23, in F, K590 (*2 vlns, vla & vlc*)
Amar – Galimir & Morini
Quintet in A, K581 (*cl, 2 vlns, vla & vlc*) *Burgin
& Krips – I. Cohen & Schneider – Dyke – Eidus –
Kussmaul*
Quintet in E flat, K407 (*hrn, vln, 2 vlas & vlc*)
Burgin – Eidus
Quintet in C, K515 (*2 vlns, 2 vlas & vlc*) *Baker &
Heifetz*
Quintet in g, K516 (*2 vlns, 2 vlas & vlc*) *Baker &
Heifetz*
(Il) Re Pastore, K208 (1775) – opera
   No. 10. L'amerò, sarò costante
   *Barylli – Hayward – Kubelík – J. Pasquier –
   Piastro – Wolfgang Schneiderhan – Schwalbé –
   Sedlak – Shumsky – Wolfsthal – Zayde –
   Zentay*
Romance in A flat, KAnh205 (*pf*)† *Kubelík*
Rondo in B flat, K269 (*vln & orch*) *Klijn –*

*"The Musical Joke."
†Not by Mozart.

Wolfgang Schneiderhan – Swärdström
Rondo in C, K373 (*vln & orch*)
   Fain – Friedman – Fuchs – Grumiaux – Hendel
   – Klijn – Milstein (2) – Pougnet – Wolfgang
   Schneiderhan – Suk – Swärdström – T. Varga
Serenade No. 3, in D, K185 "Andretter" (*orch*)
Kalup – Kempler – Schröcksnadel
Serenade No. 4, in D, K203 (*orch*) Grehling –
Kempler – Lautenbacher
Serenade No. 5, in D, K204 (*orch*) Schnitzer
Serenade No. 6, in D, K239 "Serenata notturna"
(*orch*)
   A. Busch – Ceredini & Redditi – Höver –
   Maguire & Marriner – Parikian & Wise –
   Pougnet – Prystawski – Schwalbé
Serenade No. 7, in D, K250 "Haffner" (*orch*)
Boskovsky – Hendel – Koeckert – Lautenbacher –
Menuhin – Rybar – Suk – Zsigmondy
   Andante (*2nd mvt*) Crut
   Minuet (*3rd mvt*) D'Aranyi – Telmányi –
   Zimmermann
   Rondo (*4th mvt*)
   Andrade – Benedetti – Bezrodny – Boskovsky –
   Bress – Bruckbauer – Chemet (2) – Fournier –
   Goldberg – Grumiaux – Gutnikov – Hagen –
   Heifetz (2) – Jarry – Kreisler – Kubo – Lorand
   – Niemczyk – I. Oistrakh (2) – Rostal –
   Sammons – Spivakovsky – Staryk – Stern –
   Stevens – Tarjus – Thibaud – Zacharewitsch
Sinfonia concertante in A, K.* (*2 vlns, ob, vlc &
orch*) Shinder
Sinfonia concertante in E flat, K364 (*vln, vla &
orch*)
   Barchet – Barylli – L. Bobescu – Brainin (2) –
   Brandis – Bruun & Koppel – Büchner – Druian
   – Fontanarosa – Fuchs (2) – Grumiaux – Gulli
   – Heifetz – Klijn – Lautenbacher (2) – Menuhin
   – D. Oistrakh – D. & I. Oistrakh – J. Pollak –
   Richter-Steiner – Romascano – Sammons –
   Walther Schneiderhan – Spalding – Sprecher –
   Stern (2) – Suk – Szeryng
Sonata No. 1, in E flat, K67 (*org, 2 vlns & vlc*)
Snítil
Sonata No. 15, in C, K328 (*org, 2 vlns & vlc*)
Snítil
Sonata No. 17, in C, K336 (*org, 2 vlns & vlc*)
Snítil
Sonata No. 4, in E flat, K282 (*pf*)
   Adagio (*2nd mvt*) Elman – R. Ricci
Sonata No. 11, in A, K331 (*pf*)
   Rondo alla turca (*3rd mvt*) Příhoda
Sonata No. 16, in B flat, K570 (*pf*) Shumsky
Sonata No. 1, in C, K6 (*vln &pf*) Boskovsky –
Dumont – Haag
Sonata No. 2, in D, K7 (*vln & pf*) Bernard –
Dumont – Franke – Melcher
Sonata No. 3, in B flat, K8 (*vln & pf*) Dumont –
Szabó
Sonata No. 4, in G, K9 (*vln & pf*) Dumont –
Szabó
Sonata No. 5, in e, K10 (*vln & pf*) Bernard
Sonata No. 6, in G, K11 (*vln & pf*) Haag – Klijn
Sonata No. 8, in F, K13 (*vln & pf*) Haag

*Unidentified.

Sonata No. 11, in E flat, K26 (*vln & pf*) Haag
Sonata No. 12, in G, K27 (*vln & pf*) Boskovsky –
Melcher – Szabó
Sonata No. 13, in C, K28 (*vln & pf*) Bernard –
Haag
Sonata No. 15, in F, K30 (*vln & pf*) Haag
Sonata No. 16, in B flat, K31 (*vln & pf*) Szabó
Sonata No. 17, in F, K55 (KAnh209c) (*vln & pf*)
* Boskovsky
Sonata No. 18, in C, K56 (KAnh209d) (*vln
& pf*)* Boskovsky
Sonata No. 19, in F, K57 (KAnh209e) (*vln & pf*)
Boskovsky
Sonata No. 20, in E flat, K58 (KAnh209f) (*vln &
pf*)* Barylli – Boskovsky
Sonata N. 21, in c, K59 (KAnh209g) (*vln & pf*)*
Boskovsky
Sonata No. 22, in e, K60 (KAnh209h) (*vln & pf*)*
Boskovsky
Sonata in E flat, K293b (*vln & pf*) Kovács
Sonata No. 17, in C, K296 (*vln & pf*)
   Barylli – Boskovsky – V. Brun – Druian –
   Goldberg – Heifetz – Kovács – Kroll – Menuhin
   – Milstein (2) – Pauk – Roberts – Schneider –
   Wolfgang Schneiderhan – Szeryng – J. Szigeti
Sonata No. 18, in G, K301 (*vln & pf*)
   Barylli – Boskovsky – Druian – Gabowitz –
   Grumiaux (2) – Klijn – Kovács – Kyndel –
   Menuhin – Milstein – Pauk – Plocek –
   Wolfgang Schneiderhan – J. Szigeti
Sonata No. 19, in E flat, K302 (*vln & pf*)
Boskovsky – Kovács – Paul – Schneider – J.
Szigeti
Sonata No. 20, in C, K303 (*vln & pf*) Boskovsky –
Menuhin – Pauk – J. Szigeti
Sonata No. 21, in e, K304 (*vln & pf*)
   Barylli – Boskovsky – Bress – V. Brun –
   Charmy – Druian – Franke – Grumiaux (2) –
   Klijn – Klopčič – Kroll – Langbein – Lubotsky
   – Olof – Pauk – Plocek – F. Roth – Wolfgang
   Schneiderhan – Shumsky – Szeryng – J. Szigeti
   (2) – Zacharewitsch
Sonata No. 22, in A, K305 (*vln & pf*)
   Anonymous – Barylli – Boskovsky – V. Brun –
   Ferras – Haag – Kroll – Malinin – Pauk – F.
   Roth – Schneider – Wolfgang Schneiderhan –
   Shumsky – J. Szigeti
Sonata No. 23, in D, K306 (*vln & pf*)
Benedetti – Boskovsky – Klijn – Langbein –
Neste – Pauk – Schneider – J. Szigeti
Sonata in G, K373a (*vln & pf*) Kovács
Sonata No. 24, in F, K376 (*vln & pf*)
   Barylli – Boskovsky – Druian – Eweler – Ferras
   – Fournier – Grumiaux – Jarry – L. Kogan –
   Kovács – Martzy – Menuhin – Milstein – Pauk
   – Schneider – Wolfgang Schneiderhan – J.
   Szigeti
Sonata No. 25, in F, K377 (*vln & pf*)
   Barylli – Boskovsky – A. Busch – Gertler –
   Goldberg – Pauk – Wolfgang Schneiderhan –
   Szeryng – J. Szigeti
Sonata No. 26, in B flat, K378 (*vln & pf*)
   Boskovsky – Cillario – Cyroulnik – Diedrichsen

*Doubtful authenticity.

   – Fichtenholz – Flesch – Goldberg – Grumiaux
   – Hayward – Heifetz (2) – Klijn – Kolářský –
   Langbein – Menuhin – Moss – I. Oistrakh –
   Pauk – R. Ricci – Schneider – Wolfgang
   Schneiderhan – Sitkovetsky – Soriano – Stern –
   Szeryng – J. Szigeti – Thibaud – Weissgerber
Sonata No. 27, in G, K379 (*vln & pf*)
   Barylli – Boskovsky – V. Brun – Constantinescu
   – Dommett – Goldberg – Klijn – Kovács – Kroll
   – Melkus – D. Oistrakh (2) – Pauk – Schneider
   – Wolfgang Schneiderhan – J. Szigeti –
   Zsigmondy
Sonata No. 28, in E flat, K380 (*vln & pf*) E. Bloch
   – Boskovsky – Goldberg – Pauk – Wolfgang
   Schneiderhan – Spalding – J. Szigeti
Sonata No. 29, in A, K402 (*vln & pf*) Barylli –
Boskovsky – V. Brun – Pauk
Sonata No. 30, in C, K403 (*vln & pf*) Boskovsky –
V. Brun
Sonata No. 31, in C, K404 (*vln & pf*) d'Albore –
Boskovsky – Goldberg
Sonata No. 32, in B flat, K454 (*vln & pf*)
   Barylli – Boskovsky – V. Brun – Cyroulnik –
   Elman – Grinke – Grumiaux – Hayward –
   Heifetz (2) – Kovács – Kroll – Kulenkampff –
   Malinin – Melkus – Menuhin (2) – Merckel –
   Morini – Moss – Neaman – D. Oistrakh (3) –
   Pauk – Peters – Plocek – Reynal – Wolfgang
   Schneiderhan – Shumsky – Soriano – Szeryng –
   J. Szigeti
Sonata No. 33, in E flat, K481 (*vln & pf*)
   Asselin – Barylli – Boskovsky – Dommett –
   Goldberg – Grumiaux – Klijn – Kroll –
   Langbein – Morini – Pauk – Peters – Wolfgang
   Schneiderhan – Szeryng – J. Szigeti
Sonata No. 34, in A, K526 (*vln & pf*)
   Boskovsky – Catterall – Fuente – Grinke –
   Grumiaux – Klijn – Komissarov – Langbein –
   Menuhin (2) – Pauk – Schneider – Wolfgang
   Schneiderhan – Shumsky – Szeryng – J. Szigeti
   – Thibaud
Sonata No. 35, in F, K547 (*vln & pf*) Boskovsky –
Pauk
Sonata in F, K244 (*2 vlns & c*) Harnoncourt &
Pfeiffer
Sonata in C, K328 (*2 vlns & c*) Harnoncourt &
Pfeiffer
Suite in d, K399 (*in the style of Handel*) (*pf*)
Zacharewitsch
Trio in E flat, K498 (*pf, cl & vla*) Sammons
Trio No. 1, in B flat, K254 (*pf, vln & vlc*)
Boskovsky – Fournier
Trio in d, K442 (*pf, vln & vlc*) Boskovsky
Trio No. 2, in G, K496 (*pf, vln & vlc*) Boskovsky
– Fournier – Gruenberg
Trio No. 3, in B flat, K502 (*pf, vln & vlc*)
Boskovsky – Fournier – Goldberg – Laredo –
Posselt
Trio No. 4, in E, K542 (*pf, vln & vlc*) Boskovsky –
Catterall – Fournier – Goodman – Menuhin –
Posselt – Sammons – Totenberg
Trio No. 5, in C, K548 (*pf, vln & vlc*) Bezrodny –
Boskovsky – Fournier – Goldberg – Sammons –
Totenberg
Trio No. 6, in G, K564 (*pf, vln & vlc*) Boskovsky

*The theme is from the 1st 16 measures of the Ciacona from Sammartini's 4th Sonata of opus 3 for 2 vlns & c.

*This concerto is arranged from a viola sonata in f, which in turn, was made up from the final mvt. of the 3rd sonata plus the 1st & last mvts. from the 4th sonata of the set as appears in the Schirmer edition Vol. 1852 which was published in 1967.

Bělčík
Novello, Franko (1929–   )
Malinconia (*vln & pf*) *Novello*
Nyaga, Georgi Stepanovich (1922–   )
Sonata in b (*vln & pf*) *Brushtein*
Očenáš, Andrej (1911–   )
Children's Suite (*vln & pf*) *Gašparek*
Offenbach, Jacques (1819–1880)
(La) Chanson de Fortunio (1861) – opéra-comedie
    No. 6bis. La chanson de fortunio (*Si vous croyez*
    que je vais dire) *Dessau*
(Les) Contes d'Hoffmann (1881) – opera
    Belle Nuit, O nuit d'amour "Barcarolle"
    W. Andersen – Benavente – Elman – Hayward
    – Kreisler – Livschakoff – Mantovani – Meine &
    Sens – Mendels – Powell – Ricci – C. Skolnik –
    Southgate – Tessier – Weintraub –
    Zacharewitsch – Zentay
Orphée aux Enfers (1858) – opera
    Overture *Horvath*
(La) Périchole (1868) – opéra-bouffe
    No. 3. La lettre (*O mon cher amant, je te jure*)
    Dessau
Ogarew, M. (1857–   )
Caprice in a, Op. 51, No. 2 (*vln & pf*) *Powell – A.*
Schmidt
O'Hara, Geoffrey (1882–   )
(The) Blush rose (*v & pf*) *Rubini*
Olcott, Chauncey (1858–1932)
Mother Machree (*v & pf*) *d'Almaine*
My wild Irish rose (1899) (*v & pf*) *Fradkin*
Olsson-Föllinger, Gøran (1886–   )
(3) Karaktärsstycke (*vln & pf*)
    No. 1. Polska (*Lapp Nils*)*
    Olsson-Föllinger
    No. 2. Polska *Olsson-Föllinger*
    No. 3. Gammal bondmarsch (*Lapp Nils'*
    "Jämtland") *Olsson-Föllinger*
Nejlikan (*vln & pf*) *Olsson-Föllinger*
Spelmansvals (*vln & pf*) *Olsson-Föllinger*
Ondraček, Johann (–1743)
Sonata (*vln, fl & vlc*) *Thoene*
Ondříček, Frantisek (1857–1922)
(15) Etudes (*solo vln*)
    Etude No. 2 *Ondříček*
Fantasia (*on themes from the opera "The Bartered*
Bride" by Smetana) Op. 9 (*vln & pf*) *Frait*
Fantasia (*on "Dance of the comedians" from the*
opera "The Bartered Bride" by Smetana) Op. 15
(*vln & pf*) *Frait – Hayward – Šroubek*
Rapsodie bohème, Op. 21 (*vln & orch*) *Frait*
Scherzo Capriccio, Op. 18 (*vln & pf*) *Frait –*
Gutnikov
Openshaw, John (1880–   )
June brought the roses (1924) (*v & pf*) *Fradkin*
Love sends a little gift of roses (1919) (*v & pf*)
Curti – Debruille – Kreisler – Spalding
Opraem, Gilbert Michl (1750–1828)
Benedictus in E flat (*bs, vln, hrn & strs*)
Ninomiya
Orr, Robin (1909–   )
Sonatine (1948) (*vln & pf*) *Rostal*
Ortmans, René (1866–   )

*Folk specialist Nils Jonasson, 1804–1870.

Concertino No. 1, in a, Op. 12 (*vln & pf*)
Shermont
Ostrčil, Otakar (1879–1935)
Sonatina, Op. 22 (1925) (*vln, vla & pf*) *Hlaváček*
Ostrovsky, Fredy (1922–   )
Capriccio orientale (*solo vln*) *Ostrovsky*
Impromptu (*solo vln*) *Ostrovsky*
Je Pense à mon amour (*solo vln*) *Ostrovsky*
Oteo, Alfonso Esparza (1896–   )
Mi viejo amour (*v & pf*) *Ludlow*
Ovchinnikov, Viatcheslav (1936–   )
Ballade (*vln & pf*) *Beilina*
Melody (*vln & pf*) *Feigin*
Owen, Elwyn
Invocation (*pf*) *Kreisler*
Pacchierotti, Gasparo (1740–1821)
(L') Albatro
    Assollo *Ranzato*
    Danza delle Algho *Ranzato*
(Il) Re Olaf (*v & pf*)
    Ballata *Ranzato*
Pachelbel, Johann (1653–1706)
Canon & Gigue in D (*3 vlns & c*) *Feliciani, Lahrs*
& Brix-Meinert – Grehling, Lautenbacher &
Wolff-Malm
Partita No. 2, in c (*2 vlns & c*) *Grehling &*
Lautenbacher
Partita No. 6, in B flat (*2 vlns & c*) *Felicani &*
Brix-Meinert
Paderewski, Ignace Jan (1860–1941)
(6) Humoresques de concert, Op. 14 (*pf*)
    No. 1. Minuet in G
    Anonymous – Berkova – Brown – Campoli (2) –
    Candéla – L. Cherniavsky – Cochrane – Eweler
    – Gyarfas – Kalmer – Kreisler – Lensen –
    Lorand – Opfermann – Ranzato (2) – T. Seidel
    – Szeryng – Winchester
(7) Miscellanea, Op. 16 (*pf*)
    No. 2. Mélodie *Barcewicz (2) – Eweler –*
    Kreisler
(6) Polish Dances, Op. 9 – Book II (*pf*)
    No. 5. Krakowiak in A *Niemczyk*
Sonata in a, Op. 13 (1880) (*vln & pf*) *Statkiewicz*
Padureano
Eyes of sin (*Sund Ochii Adinci ca un pacat*) (*vln*
& pf) *Ionescu*
Paganetti, C.
Méditation (*vln & pf*) *Benedetti*
Scherzo (*vln & pf*) *Benedetti*
Paganini, Niccolo (1782–1840)
Cantabile e valzer in E, Op. 19 (1823 or 1824)
(*vln & gtr*) *Grach – R. Ricci – Suk*
Cantabile in D, Op. 17 (*vln & gtr*)
    Accardo – Beilina – Csaba – Gitlis – Gulli –
    Isakadze – L. Kogan – Kremer – Krysa –
    Ostrovsky – Shkolníková – Tretyakov – Zhuk
(24) Caprices, Op. 1 (1801/7) (*solo vln*)
    Caprice* *Jarry – Melsa*
    Caprice No. 1, in E
    Accardo – Erlih – Kawaciuk – Pikaizen – Rabin
    (2) – Renardy (2) – R. Ricci (2) – Staryk –
    Zhislin – Zukofsky

*Unidentified.

Caprice No. 2, in b
Accardo – Beilina – Gorokhov – Kawaciuk –
Pikaizen (2) – Rabin – Renardy (2) R. Ricci (2)
– Shkolníková – Staryk – J. Szigeti – Vecsey –
Zukofsky
Caprice No. 3, in e *Accardo – Kawaciuk –*
Pikaizen – Rabin – Renardy (2) – R. Ricci (2) –
Zukofsky
Caprice No. 4, in c
Accardo – Kawaciuk – Kremer – Pikaizen –
Rabin – Renardy (2) – R. Ricci (2) –
Shkolníková – Zukofsky
Caprice No. 5, in a
Accardo – Bress (2) – Bustabo – Erlih – F.C.
Ferrari – Kawaciuk – Michaels – Pikaizen –
Rabin (2) – Renardy (2) – R. Ricci (2) – Staryk
– Vasile – Wolf – Zukofsky
Caprice No. 6, in g
Accardo – Erlih – Kawaciuk – Kubelík –
Menuhin (2) – Montbrun – Pikaizen – Rabin –
Renardy (2) – R. Ricci (2) – Zukofsky
Caprice No. 7, in a
Accardo – Kawaciuk – Markov – Pikaizen –
Rabin – Renardy (2) – R. Ricci (2) – Vasile –
Zukofsky
Caprice No. 8, in E flat
Accardo – Kawaciuk – Pikaizen – Rabin –
Renardy (2) – R. Ricci (2) – Zukofsky
Caprice No. 9, in E
Abadiev – Accardo – Beilina (2) – Boussinot –
Dichterow – Erlih – Francescatti – Kawaciuk –
L. Kogan – Menuhin – Merckel – Montbrun –
Pikaizen – Poulet – Rabin (2) – Renardy (2) –
F. Reuter – R. Ricci (2) – Staryk – J. Szigeti –
Telmányi – Vasile – Zukofsky
Caprice No. 10, in g
Accardo – Kawaciuk – Pikaizen – Rabin –
Renardy (2) – R. Ricci (2) – Zukofsky
Caprice No. 11, in C
Accardo – Kawaciuk – Pikaizen – Rabin (2) –
Renardy (2) – R. Ricci (2) – Ushioda – Vasile –
Zukofsky
Caprice No. 12, in A flat
Accardo – Kawaciuk – Pikaizen – Rabin –
Renardy (2) – R. Ricci (2) – Zhislin – Zukofsky
Caprice No. 13, in B flat
Accardo – Alos – Ambrose – Barbieri –
Boussinot – Campoli – Catterall – Dunn – Erlih
– Flesch – Fournier – Francescatti – Garay –
Gitlis – Grach – Gulli – Heifetz (3) – Herman –
Kawaciuk – Laredo – Menuhin – Merckel – D.
Oistrakh – Pikaizen – Poulet – R. Quattrocchi –
Rabin (2) – Renardy (2) – F. Reuter – R. Ricci
(3) – Soriano – Staryk – Strock – Szentgyörgi –
Vasile – Vecsey – Wilk – Zentay – Zukofsky
Caprice No. 14, in E flat
Accardo – Barbieri – Beilina – Erlih –
Francescatti – Kawaciuk – Pikaizen – Rabin (2)
– Renardy (2) – R. Ricci (2) – Ruha – Sebald –
Staryk – Vecsey – Wilk – Zukofsky
Caprice No. 15, in e
Accardo – Barbieri – Erlih – Francescatti –
Kawaciuk – Lantsman – Pikaizen – Rabin –
Renardy (2) – R. Ricci (2) – Vasile – Zukofsky

Caprice No. 16, in g
*Accardo – Barbieri – Gulli – Kawaciuk –
Pikaizen – Porta – Rabin (2) – Renardy (2) –
R. Ricci (2) – Shkolníková – Staryk – Zukofsky*
Caprice No. 17, in E flat
*Accardo – Agaronyan – Agoston – Barbieri –
Bochková – Erlih – Friedman – Gulli –
Kawaciuk – Kremer – Liberman – D. Oistrakh
– Pikaizen – Porta – Rabin (2) – Renardy (3) –
R. Ricci (2) – Staryk – Tretyakov – Wolf –
Zukofsky*
Caprice No. 18, in C
*Accardo – Barbieri – Kawaciuk – Pikaizen –
Rabin (2) – Renardy (2) – R. Ricci (2) –
Zukofsky*
Caprice No. 19, in E flat
*Accardo – Barbieri – Erlih – Kawaciuk –
Pikaizen – Rabin – Renardy (2) – R. Ricci (2) –
Staryk – Vasile – Zhislin – Zukofsky*
Caprice No. 20, in D
*Accardo – Barbieri – Bleier – Campoli – Erlih –
Francescatti – Garnier – Gitlis – Gulli – Heifetz
(3) – Huttenbach – Kawaciuk – Menuhin –
Nadien – Pikaizen – Rabin – Renardy (2) – R.
Ricci (3) – Spivakovsky – Staryk – Szeryng –
Zukofsky*
Caprice No. 21, in A
*Accardo – Barbieri – Erlih – Francescatti –
Friedman – Grach – Kawaciuk – Pikaizen –
Rabin (2) – Renardy (2) – R. Ricci (2) – Zora
Shikhmurzayeva – Staryk – Zukofsky*
Caprice No. 22, in F
*Accardo – Barbieri – Francescatti – Kawaciuk –
Pikaizen – Rabin – Renardy (2) – R. Ricci (2) –
Vasile – Zukofsky*
Caprice No. 23, in E flat
*Accardo – Barbieri – Grach – Kawaciuk – L.
Kogan – Menuhin – Pikaizen (2) – Rabin –
Renardy (2) – R. Ricci (2) – Vasile – Zukofsky*
Caprice No. 24, in a
*Accardo – D'Aranyi – Barbieri – Beilina – Bress
– Cillario – Elman – Erlih – Francescatti –
Gitlis – Haendel – Heifetz – Herman –
Kawaciuk – Menuhin – Pikaizen – Poulet –
Rabin (2) – Renardy (3) – F. Reuter – R. Ricci
(2) – Schwalbé – Spivakovsky – Staryk –
Szeryng – J. Szigeti (3) – Tretyakov – R. Varga
– Vasile – Wicks – Zukofsky*
(La) Carnevale di Venezia – variations, Op. 10
(1829) (*solo vln*) *Francescatti – Haxton – Mendels*
(18) Centone di sonate, Op. 64 (1828) (*vln & gtr*)
Sonata No. 1, in A *Grach – Ostrovsky – R.
Pasquier*
Sonata No. 2, in D *Grach – Ostrovsky – R.
Pasquier*
Sonata No. 3, in C *Grach – Ostrovsky – R.
Pasquier*
Sonata No. 4, in A *Grach – Ostrovsky – R.
Pasquier*
Sonata No. 5, in E *Ostrovsky – R. Pasquier*
Sonata No. 6, in A *Ostrovsky – R. Pasquier*
Concerto No. 1, in D, Op. 6 (*vln & orch*)
*Abadiev – Ashkenasi – Benedetti – Brandt –
Brückner – Bustabo – Campoli (2) –
Francescatti – Friedman – Gilels – Gimpel –*

*Gitlis (2) – Hudeček – L. Kogan (2) – Krebbers
– Kreisler – Kubelík – Menuhin (3) – Novák –
Novello – Odnoposoff – Pikaizen – Příhoda –
Rabin (2) – R. Ricci (2) – Rudényi – Ruha –
Szentgyörgi – Tretyakov – Voicu*
Concerto No. 2, in b, Op. 7 (*vln & orch*)
*Accardo – Ashkenasi – Gitlis – Markov –
Menuhin (2) – Odnoposoff – R. Ricci (2) –
Sitkovetsky*
Ronde à la clochette (*3rd mvt*) "La
Campanella"
*Andrade (2) – Banat – Beilina – Campoli (2) –
Farbmann – Garnier – Gilels – Gitlis –
Huberman – Leon-Ara – Menuhin – Milstein –
Nerini – Odnoposoff – F. Reuter – R. Ricci (3)
– Rode – Sitkovetsky – Szeryng – Zhuk*
Concerto No. 3, in E (1826) (*vln & orch*) *Szeryng*
Concerto No. 4, in d (1829) (*vln & orch*)
Grumiaux – R. Ricci
Concerto No. 5, in a (1830) (*vln & orch*) *Gulli*
Gavotte variata* *R. Pollak*
God save the King – variations, Op. 9 (1829) (*vln
& orch*) *Accardo – Francescatti – Kubelík – R.
Ricci (2)*
Grande Sonata in A, Op. 39 (*gtr with vln acc*)
Klasinc – R. Pasquier
Minuet in F (*vln & gtr*)* *Gitlis – Shkolnikova*
Moto perpetuo (*Allegro di concert*) Op. 11 (1830)
(*vln & orch*)
*Accardo – Campoli – Garami – M. Hall –
Heifetz – Kubelík – Lewkowitz – Manén (2) –
Menuhin – Nadien – Parlow – Rabin (2) – R.
Ricci (2) – Rostal – Zarius Shikhmurzayeva –
Sitkovetsky – Šroubek – Steiger-Betzak – Viólin
– Zhuk*
Nel cor più non mi sento "Sonata appassionata
con variazioni" (*on the aria from Paisiello's opera
"La bella molinara"*) Op. 38 (1820 or 1821) (*solo
vln*)
*Accardo – Agaronyan – A. Ferraresi –
Fidelmann – L. Kogan – Kubelík – Menuhin
(2) – Příhoda (3) – R. Ricci (2) – R. Varga –
Zhislin – Zhuk*
(I) Palpiti (*variations on the aria "Di tanti palpiti"
from Rossini's opera "Tancredi"*) Op. 13 (1819)
(*vln & orch*)
*Accardo – Francescatti (2) – Gitlis – Grumiaux
– Gulli – L. Kogan – Příhoda – R. Ricci –
Tretyakov*
(3) Quartets, Op. 4 (1806/16) (*vln, vla, vlc & gtr*)
Quartet No. 2, in C *Grach*
(6) Sonatas, Op. 2 (1801/6) (*vln & gtr*)
No. 1. Sonata No. 1, in A *Kocsis – L. Kogan –
Kohon – Michel – Šroubek*
No. 2. Sonata No. 2, in C *Fastofsky – Kocsis –
Kohon – Michel – Šroubek*
No. 3. Sonata No. 3, in d *Kohon – Michel –
Šroubek*
No. 4. Sonata No. 4, in A *Kocsis – Kohon –
Lantsman – Michel – Shkolníková – Šroubek*
No. 5. Sonata No. 5, in D *Fastofsky – Kohon –
Michel – Šroubek*

*Unidentified.

No. 6. Sonata No. 6, in a *Fastofsky – Kohon –
Lantsman – Markov – Michel – Shkolníková –
Šroubek*
(6) Sonatas, Op. 3 (1801/6) (*vln & gtr*)
No. 1. Sonata No. 7, in A *Kohon – Michel – R.
Pasquier – Šroubek*
No. 2. Sonata No. 8, in G *Kohon – Michel – R.
Pasquier – Spivakovsky – Šroubek*
No. 3. Sonata No. 9, in D *Kohon – Michel – R.
Pasquier – Šroubek*
No. 4. Sonata No. 10, in a *Grach – Kohon –
Markov (2) – Michel – R. Pasquier – Šroubek*
No. 5. Sonata No. 11, in A *Kohon – Michel –
R. Pasquier – Spivakovsky – Šroubek*
No. 6. Sonata No. 12, in e
*Accardo – Alos – Barbieri – Borries – A.
Ferraresi – Gitlis – Granchi – Harth – Kalafusz
– Kohon – Madle – Michel – R. Pasquier –
Příhoda (3) – Ranzato – Renardy – R. Ricci (2)
– Ruminelli – Shkolníková – Snitkovsky –
Spalding – Spivakovsky – Šroubek – Taschner*
Sonata a preghièra "Moses Fantasia" (*on the aria
"Dal tuo stellato soglio" from Rossini's opera
"Mosè in Egitto"*) Op. 24 (1818 or 1819) (*vln &
orch*)
*Accardo – Barylli – Garnier – Haendel (2) –
Kawaciuk – Loránt – Menuhin – D. Oistrakh –
F. Reuter – R. Ricci (3) – Shkolníková –
Sitkovetsky – Sobolevsky – Szentgyörgi – Zhuk*
Sonata concertante in A, Op. 61 (1804) (*vln
& gtr*) *Dawes – Fontanarosa – Klasinc*
Sonata con Variazioni (*on the theme "Prig ch'io
l'impegno" from Weigl's opera "L'Amor
marinaro"*) (1828) (*vln & orch*) *R. Ricci*
Sonata in A, Op. posthumous (*vln & gtr*) *Csaba –
Klasinc – Ranzato – Renardy*
(Le) Streghe (*variations on a theme from
Süssmeyer's opera "Il Noce di Benevento"*) Op. 8
(1813) (*vln & orch*)
*Accardo – Agaronyan – A. Bachmann – Barbieri
– A. Ferraresi (2) – Grumiaux – Markov –
Marschner – Příhoda (2) – Renardy – R. Ricci
(3) – Sitkovetsky – Spivakov – Voicu –
Weissgerber*
Tarantella in a, Op. 33 (*vln & small orch*) *R.
Pasquier*
Trio in D, Op. 66 (1833) (*vln, vlc & gtr*) *Drolc –
Loveday*
(60) Variations (*on the Genoese air "Barucaba"*)
Op. 14 (1835) (*vln & gtr or pf*) *Accardo*
Pagin, André-Noël (1721–1785)
(6) Sonatas, Op. 1 (1748) (*vln & c*)
Sonata No. 1, in D *Tanenbaum*
Pakalnis, J.
(The) Bride – ballet (*orch*)
Grand Adagio *Livontas*
Palmgren, Selim (1878–1951)
Berceuse in A flat (*vln & pf*) *Ignatius-Hirvensalo*
(7) Compositions, Op. 78 (*vln & pf*)
No. 5. Finnish romance *Hannikainen*
Illusion (*solo vln*) *Hurstinen*
Jugend (*6 lyric pieces*) Op. 28 (*pf*)
No. 5. Der Schwan *Moguilevski*
(4) Morceaux, Op. 43 (*vln & pf*)
No. 3. Canzonetta in F *Vecsey*

Romance in G (*vln & pf*) *Bratza – B. Schwarz*
Panella, Louis
Carolina lullaby (*vln & pf*) *Ball*
Panizza, Héctor Ettore (1875–   )
Quartet in c (*2 vlns, vla & vlc*) *Pessina*
Papaioannou
Suite (1954) (*vln & pf*) *Tombras*
Papineau-Couture, Jean (1916–   )
Aria (1946) (*solo vln*) *Hagen – Staryk*
(3) Caprices (1965) (*vln & pf*)
    Caprice No. 1 "Nadia" (*Allegro*) *Staryk*
    Caprice No. 2 "Ghilaine" (*Adagio*) *Staryk*
    Caprice No. 3 "François" (*Scherzando*) *Staryk*
Concerto (*vln & orch*) *Brunet*
Sonata in G (1944) (*vln & pf*) *Brunet*
Suite (1956) (*solo vln*) *Staryk*
Papini, Guido (1847–1912)
Idylle, Op. 96 (*vln & pf*) *Southgate*
(4) Morceaux, Op. 28 (*vln & pf*)
    No. 1. Souvenir du Tage (*Larghetto*)
    Anonymous
(2) Morceaux de salon, Op. 55 "Souvenir di
Sorrento" (*vln & pf*)
    No. 2. Saltarella *Anonymous – Haxton (2)*
(3) Morceaux Lyriques, Op. 98 (*vln & pf*)
    No. 2. Nocturne *Southgate*
Paradies, Maria Theresa von (1759–1824)
Sicilienne (*vln & pf*)
    *d'Arco – Barbieri – Barinova – L. Bobescu – W.
    Busch – Garami – Goldberg – Grumlíková –
    Jarry – Kulenkampff – Laredo – Magyar –
    Milstein – Minghetti – Morini – Neveu – E.B.
    Nielsen (2) – R. Ricci – Richards – Soriano –
    Thibaud*
Paray, Paul (1886–   )
Humoresque (*vln & pf*) *Stanske*
Parelli
(L') Alba nascente (*v & pf*) *Ranzato*
Parmegiani, Bernard (1927–   )
Violostries (1964) (*vln & 4 channels*) *Erlih*
Partos, Ödön (1907–   )
Sonia (*Russian ballad*) (*v & pf*) *Benavente*
Pascal, Claude (1921–   )
Sonata No. 2, in A (1963) (*vln & pf*) *Lantsman*
Pasquini, Bernardo (1637–1710)
Arietta (*vln & str orch*) *Lemaire*
Erminia in riva del Giordano – aria (*v & c*)
Sadowski
Patáky, Hubert
Auf dem Flusse (*v & pf*) *Georg Kniestaedt*
Pauer, Jiří (1919–   )
Sonatina (*vln & pf*) *Šorm*
Pechotsch, Raimund
Caprice (*vln & pf*) *Rudényi*
Cradle song (*vln & pf*) *Rudényi (2)*
Légende (*vln & pf*) *Rudényi*
Rapsodie hongrois (*vln & pf*) *Rudényi*
Serenade (*vln & pf*) *Rudényi*
Tarantella romantique (*vln & pf*) *Rudényi*
Wiegenleid (*vln & pf*)* *Rudényi*
Peiko, Nicolai (1916–   )
Concert Fantasia No. 2, in g (*vln & pf*) *Tretyakov*

*May be the same work as "Cradle song."

Fantasia on Finnish folk themes (*vln & orch*)
Grach
Penderecki, Krzysztof (1933–   )
Capriccio (*vln & orch*) *Zukofsky*
Miniatury (1959) (*vln & pf*) *Banat*
Penn, Arthur A. (1875–1941)
Smilin' through (1915) (*v & pf*) *Soman – Thibaud*
Pente, Emilio (1860–1929)
(2) Pieces, Op. 12 (*vln & pf*)
    No. 2. Les farfadets *Elman*
Pentland, Barbara (1912–   )
Quartet No. 1 (1944) (*2 vlns, vla & vlc*) *Bress &
Goodman*
Pepusch, Johann Christopf (1667–1752)
Sonata in a (*vln, gamba & c*) *Lautenbacher*
Sonata in C (*fl, gamba, vln & org*) *Cron*
Sonata in d (*fl, gamba & c*) *Cron*
Pergament, Moses (1893–   )
Dibbuk Fantasia (*vln & orch*) *Ericson*
Serenade (*vln or vlc & pf*) *Dobrinski*
Pergolesi, Giovanni (1710–1736)
Aria*
D'Aranyi – Noceti – Příhoda
Sonntag
(6) Concertini "Concerti armonici" (*strs & c*)
    Concertino No. 1, in G *Krebbers*
    Concertino No. 2, in G *L. Bobescu*
Concerto in B flat (*vln, strs & c*) *Abbado – Fain –
Laurent – Pelliccia – Villa*
Sicilianok† *Southgate*
(14) Sonatas (1770) (*2 vlns & c*)
    Sonata No. 1, in G *Andrade – Araki & Jahn –
    Morini*
    Sonata No. 2, in B *Araki & Jahn*
    Sonata No. 3, in c *Araki & Jahn*
    Sonata No. 4, in G *Araki & Jahn*
    Sonata No. 5, in C *Araki & Jahn – Ayo &
    Cotogni*
    Sonata No. 6, in D *Araki & Jahn*
    Sonata No. 7, in g *Araki & Jahn*
    Sonata No. 8, in E flat *Araki & Jahn*
    Sonata No. 9, in A *Araki & Jahn*
    Sonata No. 10, in F *Araki & Jahn*
    Sonata No. 11, in d *Araki & Jahn*
    Sonata No. 12, in E *Araki & Jahn – Milstein
    (2)*
    Sonata No. 13, in g *Araki & Jahn*
    Sonata No. 14, in C *Araki & Jahn*
Sonata (*in the style of a concerto*) (*vln, strs & c*)
Perez
Tre giorni son che Nina (*v & c*)‡
Jacobsen – Kreisler – Manuello – Pelliccia
Perlman, George
Suite Hebraïque (1929) (*vln & pf*)
    No. 2. Dance of the Rebbitzen *Elman*
Perrault, Michel (1925–   )
Sextet (1955) (*2 vlns, vla, vlc, cl & hp*) *Bress &*

*Possibly "Tre giorni son che Nina" for voice &
continuo.
†Unidentified
‡Doubtful authenticity.

Goodman
Trio (1954) (*pf, vln & vlc*) *Bress*
Petersen, David
Sonata in d (*vln & c*) *Noske*
Peterson-Berger, Wilhelm (1867–1942)
Concerto in f sharp (1928) (*vln & orch*) *Pierrou*
Frösöblomster, Op. 16 (1896) (*pf*)
    Vid Frösö Kyrka *Zilzer*
Fyra danspoem (1900) (*pf*)
    Serenade *O. Nielsen*
Romance (1915) (*vln & orch*) *Pierrou*
Petrie, Henry W. (1857–1925)
(Los) Seemans (*v & pf*) *Lensky*
Pfitzner, Hans 1869–1949)
Concerto in b, Op. 34 (1923) (*vln & orch*)
Lautenbacher
Duo, Op. 43 (1937) (*vln, vlc & orch*) *Strub*
Phillips, Gerald
Chanson Tzigane (*vln & pf*) *Sammons*
Pianelli, Antonio de (1747–1803)
Villanelle *D'Aranyi*
Piastro-Borisoff, Josef (1889–   )
Valse staccato, Op. 60, No. 3 (*vln & pf*)*
Elman
Pieltain, Dieudonné-Pascal (1754–1833)
Concerto in G (*vln & orch*) *E. Koch*
Pierné, Gabriel (1863–1937)
Cydalise et le Chèvre-Pied (1923) – ballet (*orch*)
    Marche des petits faunes *Candéla*
Impressions de Music Hall (1927) – ballet suite
(*orch*) *Merckel*
Scherzo de concert, Op. 29bis (*pf*) *May*
Sérénade à Colombine, Op. 32 (1894) (*pf*)
MacMillen
Sérénade in A, Op. 7 (1875) (*pf*)
    *d'Almaine – Barmas – Bas – Breeskin – Chemet
    (2) – Curti – Darrieux – Deru – Drdla – Eweler
    – Fidelmann – Flesch – Gautier – Goggi –
    Gusikoff – Gygi – Haxton (2) – J.F. Henriques
    – Jacobsen – Jancowich – Kochański – Kocián –
    Levey – Manuello – Maurice – May – Mendels
    – Ranzato (2) – Rudényi – Sens (3) – Spalding
    – Swaap – Valesca-Becker – F. Weltmann –
    Willaume – J. Wolff – L. Wolff – Wood –
    Zighera – Zimbalist*
Sonata in D, Op. 36 (1900) (*vln & pf*) *Candéla –
J.C. Figueroa*
Pijper, Willem (1898–1947)
Concerto (1939) (*vln & orch*) *Olof*
Sonata No. 2 (1922) (*vln & pf*) *Salomon*
Pinkard, Maceo (1897–   )
Mammy o' mine (1919) (*v & pf*) *Southgate*
Pinkham, Daniel (1923–   )
Cantilena (1956) (*vln & hpsi*) *Brink*
Capriccio (1956) (*vln & hpsi*) *Brink*
Concertante No. 1 (1954) (*vln, hpsi & strs*) *Brink*
Pinsuti, Ciro (1829–1888)
(II) Libro santo (*v & pf*) *Ranzato*
When life is brightest (*v & pf*) *Rattay*
Piot, Julien (1850–1923)
Danza española (*vln & pf*) *Curti*
Pipkov, Ljubomir (1904–   )

*Based on "Étude Mignonne" by Jean Henri
Ravina, 1818–1906.

Sonata (1929) (*vln & pf*) *Leshev*

Pisendel, Johann Georg (1687–1755)

Concerto in D (*vln, 2 obs, strs & c*) *Melkus – Schröder*

Concerto in g (*vln, strs & c*)* *Totenberg*

Sonata in a (*solo vln*) *Staryk – Thoene*

Piston, Walter (1894–   )

Concerto (1939) (*vln & orch*) *Kolberg*

Partita (1944) (*vln, vla & org*) *Thavia*

Sonata (1939) (*vln & pf*) *Fuchs – Krasner*

Sonatina (1945) (*vln & hpsi*) *Schneider*

Pizzetti, Ildebrando (1880–1968)

Aria in D (1906) (*vln & pf*) *Poltronieri*

(3) Canti ad una giovane fidanzata (1924) (*vln & pf*) *Poltronieri*

    No. 1. Affettuoso *Milstein (2)*

    No. 3. Appassionato *d'Albore*

Sonata No. 1, in A (1918) (*vln & pf*) *Menuhin*

Platti, Giovanni Benedetto (1690–1763)

(6) Sonatas, Op. 3 (1743) (*fl & c*)

    Sonata No. 1, in e *Renardy*

Pleyel, Ignaz (1757–1831)

(6) Duets, Op. 24 (*vln & vla*)

    Duet No. 1, in C *Rosoff*

    Duet No. 2, in g *Rosoff*

(3) Quartets, Op. 17 – Book III (*fl, vln, vla & vlc*)

    Quartet No. 1, in D *Gendre*

Podešva, Jaromír (1927–   )

Sonata No. 2 (1958) (*vln & pf*) *Suk*

Podkovyrov, Piotr (1910–   )

Concert-poème in G (*vln & orch*) *P. Gorelik*

Poggis

Amor (*v & pf*) *Morino*

Laura (*v & pf*) *Morino*

Poldini, Ede (1869–1957)

(7) Marionnettes (*pf*)

    No. 2. Poupée valsante

    Accardo – Boussinot – Candéla – Chauveton – Chemet – Hamza – Hayward (2) – Jacobsen – Kreisler (2) – Ladscheck – Mantovani – Milstein (2) – Powell – Zora Shikhmurzayeva – Suk – Thibaud

Poldowski, Lady Dean Paul (1880–1932)†

Tango (*vln & pf*) *Heifetz*

Polgár, Tibor (1907–   )

Serenade (1924) (*vln & pf*) *Garay*

Poliakin, F.

(Le) Canari (Concert-polka) (*vln & pf*)

    Anonymous – Boulanger – Campoli – Colombo – Dinicu – Frey – Haxton (2) – A. Kaufmann – Kellert – Parnes – P. Sanchez – Schmied – Streletzky – Tworek (2) – Zámečník – Zilzer

Marche des petits tambours (*vln & pf*) *Gerard*

Pollack, Lew (1896–1946)

Diane (1927) (*v & pf*)‡ *Morino*

*Pre-1720 manuscript is in the Saxon State Library at Dresden.

†Irene Regine Wienieawska, daughter of Henryk Wieniawski.

‡Composed jointly with Erno Rapée.

Polson, Arthur (1934–   )

Fantasy "Dracula" (*vln & pf*) *Polson*

Ponce, Manuel (1882–1948)

Concerto (1942) (*vln & orch*) *Szeryng*

Estrellita (1913) (*v & pf*)

    Bean – Campoli – Collier – Frolov – Ghestem – Heifetz (2) – L. Kogan – Lipschultz – Ludlow – Rubato – Sammons – Szeryng – Tworek – Wicks – Zilzer

Sonata Breve (1933) (*vln & pf*) *D'Andurain – Szeryng*

Poot, Marcel (1901–   )

Ballade (*vln & pf*) *Weiner*

Popov

(2) Septets, Op. 2 (*fl, cl, bsn, tpt, vln, vlc & cbs*)

    Septet in a *Brushtein*

    Septet in C *Brushtein*

Popper, David (1843–1913)

Elfentanz, Op. 39 (*vlc & pf*) *Luboshutz*

Nocturne, Op. 22 (*vlc & pf*) *A.J. Rose (2)*

(3) Stücke, Op. 64 (*vln & pf*)

    No. 1. Wie einst in schönern Tagen (*Fond recollections*) *Elman*

Popy, Francis

Suite orientale (*vln & pf*) *Lorand*

Porpora, Niccolo (1686–1766)

Aria in E*

A. *Busch – Gandini – Meyer – E.B. Nielsen – Senatra – Telmányi*

(6) Sinfonias da camera, Op. 2 (1735) (*2 vlns & c*)

    Sinfonia da camera No. 4, in D *Combes & Scrosoppi*

(12) Sonatas (1754) (*vln & c*)

    Sonata No. 2, in G *Accardo – Székely – Zhuk*

Porter, Cole (1897–1963)

Begin the beguine (1935) (*v & pf*) *Tworek*

Porter, Quincy (1897–1966)

Quintet (*ob, 2 vlns, vla & vlc*) *Silverstein*

Sonata No. 2, in a (1929) (*vln & pf*) *Druian – Flissler – Kaufman*

Porumbescu, Cyprian (1853–1883)

Ballade in e, Op. 29 (*vln & pf*) *Barinova – Voicu*

Potter, Philip Cipriani (1792–1871)

Serenata amorosa* *Biedermann & Stehl*

Poulenc, Francis (1899–1963)

(Le) Bal masqué (1932) – secular cantata (*b, septet & pcn*) *Merckel*

(3) Mouvements perpétuels (1918) (*pf*)

    Mouvement perpétuel No. 1, in C *Gautier – Heifetz (2)*

(3) Pieces (1934/5) (*pf*)

    No. 1. Presto in B flat *Campoli – Francescatti – Heifetz – L. Kogan – Krebbers*

Sonata in d (1943) "In memory of Federico Garcia Lorca" (*vln & pf*) *Goldstein – Kash – Kaufman – Rubin – Suk*

Pousseur, Henri (1929–   )

Madrigal III (1962) (*cl, vln, vlc, 2 pcn & pf*) *Jarry*

Powell, John (1882–1963)

Sonata Virginianesque, Op. 7 (*vln & pf*) *Brown*

Powell, Maud (1868–1920)

Plantation melodies (*vln & pf*)

*Unidentified.

Powell, Mel (1923–   )

Divertimento (1955) (*vln & hp*) *H. Sorkin*

Trio (1956) (*pf, vln & vlc*) *H. Sorkin*

Praetorius, Michael (1571–1621)

Es ist ein Rös' entsprungen (*choral setting*) *Godwin*

Prats, R.

Maria's song (*vln & pf*) *Frolov*

Predieri, Luca Antonio (1688–1767)

Concerto in C (*vln, strs & c*) *Liberman*

Prehn, Ernst

Violinen synger (*vln & orch*) *Tworek*

Pressman, Samuel

Caprice de la Balerine (*vln & pf*) *Doré*

Prévost, André (1934–   )

Sonata (1960/1) (*vln & pf*) *Verdon*

Příhoda, Váša (1900–1960)

Caprice in E (1926) (*vln & pf*) *Novello – Příhoda*

Minuet in olden style (*vln & pf*) *Příhoda*

Romance élégiaque (*vln & pf*) *Příhoda*

Serenata (*vln & pf*) *Příhoda*

Slavonic melody (*vln & pf*) *Příhoda (2)*

Waltz in A (*vln & pf*) *Novello – Příhoda*

Prince, Charles A.

(The) White cockade (*vln & orch*) *d'Almaine*

Principi, Remy (1889–   )

(El) Campielo (1932) (*vln & pf*) *Barbieri – Collier – Principi – T. Varga*

Canti siciliani (*vln & pf*) *Principi*

Prohaska, Carl (1869–1927)

Arietta (*vln & pf*) *Příhoda*

Prokofiev, Sergei (1891–1953)

Cinderella, Op. 87 (1941/4) – ballet (*orch*)

    Gavotte *Kaufman – Kozigyan – D. Oistrakh (2)*

    Mazurka *D. Oistrakh (2) – Parkhomenko*

    Passepied *D. Oistrakh*

    Waltz *Bochková – Kozigyan – D. Oistrakh – Parkhomenko – Vaiman*

    Winter fairytale *Grumlíková – D. Oistrakh (2) – Pratz*

Concerto No. 1, in D, Op. 19 (*vln & orch*)

    Bernard – Drescher – Friedman – Milstein (2) – Odnoposoff – D. Oistrakh (3) – I. Oistrakh – R. Ricci – Stern – J. Szigeti (2)

Concerto No. 2, in g, Op. 63 (*vln & orch*)

    Drescher – Francescatti – Heifetz (2) – Jásek – L. Kogan (2) – Milstein – D. Oistrakh (2) – Perlman – R. Ricci – Stanske – Stern – Szeryng – Voicu

(The) Duenna (*Betrothal in the Monastery*) Op. 86 (1940/1) – opera

    Andantino *Grach*

    Moment musicale *Grach*

    Serenade *Grach*

(The) Love for Three Oranges, Op. 33 (1919) – opera

    No. 3. March*

    D'Andurain – Bezrodny – Erlih – Heifetz (2) – Hidy – Komissarov – Mikhlin – Neaman – D. Oistrakh – Rabin – Staples – Suk – Wicks

(5) Melodies, Op. 35bis (1921) (*vln & pf*)†

*Transcribed from Prokofiev's piano arrangement entitled "Suite" Op. 33a.

†Composed in 1920 for v & pf – rewritten in 1921 for vln & pf.

Beilina – Gradov – Holst – Kneller – Knudsen – D. Oistrakh (2) – I. Oistrakh – Posselt – Zora Shikhmurzayeva – Spivakov – Staryk – J. Szigeti – Vinnikov

Overture on Hebrew themes, Op. 34 (1919) (*cl, pf, 2 vlns, vla & vlc*) *Goberman & Miksovsky*

Peter & the Wolf, Op. 66 (1936) (*narrator & orch*)
Theme & processional *Bezrodny (2) – Odnoposoff*

(10) Pieces, Op. 12 (1908/13) (*pf*)
No. 1. March in f *Heifetz – L. Kogan*

(4) Pieces, Op. 32 (1918) (*pf*)
No. 3. Gavotta *Goldstein – Heifetz – Malinin – Mikhlin*

(10) Pieces (*from the ballet "Romeo & Juliet"*) Op. 75 (1937) (*pf*)
No. 5. Masques *Gutnikov – Heifetz –Klimov – L. Kogan (2) – Stern*

Quintet, Op. 39 (1924) (*ob, cl, vln, vla & cbs*) *Dumont*

Romeo & Juliet, Op. 64b (1935/6) – 2nd ballet suite (*orch*)
March* *Vaiman*
No. 1. Montagues & Capulets *Klimov – L. Kogan*
No. 4. Danse de jeunes antillaises *Gutnikov – Klimov – Stern – Vaiman*

Sonata in d, Op. 115 (*solo vln*) *Barinova – Jásek – Markov – R. Ricci – Staryk – J. Szigeti*

Sonata No. 1, in f, Op. 80 (*vln & pf*)
Bader – Barbieri – Flissler – Menuhin – D. Oistrakh (4) – Perlman – Staryk – Stern – J. Szigeti (2) – Tretyakov – Vaiman – Weiner – Wilkomirska

Sonata No. 2, in D, Op. 94bis (*vln & pf*)†
Bader – Grach – Gradov – Klimov – L. Kogan (2) – Milstein – Nemet – D. Oistrakh (3) – Perlman – R. Ricci – Wolfgang Schneiderhan – Staryk – Stern – J. Szigeti (2) – Voicu – Weiner – Wilkomirska – Zhuk

Sonata in C, Op. 56 (*2 vlns*) *Eidus & Persinger – Nadien & R. Ricci – D. & I. Oistrakh (3)*

Suite of Waltzes, Op. 110 (1946) (*pf*)
No. 1. Since I met you *Chernyakhovsky*
No. 3. Mephisto waltz *Chernyakhovsky*

Symphony No. 1, in D, Op. 25 "Classical" (*orch*)
Gavotte (*3rd mvt*) *J. Szigeti*

Provazník, Anatol (1887–   )
Caprice d'une femme (*vln & pf*) *Příhoda*
Hindoo song, Op. 140 (*vln & pf*) *Kawaciuk – Příhoda*
Valse joyeuse, Op. 137 (*vln & pf*) *Příhoda*
Valse triste (*vln & pf*) *Příhoda*
Valzer con brio (*vln & pf*) *Příhoda*

Provinciali, Emilio
Aubade (*vln & pf*) *Herman*
Provost, Heinz (1891–   )
Intermezzo (1940) (*vln & pf*)

*Unidentified
†Originally composed for fl & pf.

W. Andersen – Clebanoff – Eidus – Fuchs – Jelving – Kerry – Kyndel (2) – Mantovani (2) – Robbins – Rubato – T. Seidel – Selinsky – Zilzer

Prume, François Hubert (1816–1849)
Fantaisie & Variations sur un thème d'Hérold, Op. 9 (*vln & pf*) *F.V. Henriques*
(La) Mélancolie (*Pastorale*) Op. 1 (*vln & pf*) *Post*

Puccini, Giacomo (1858–1924)
(La) Bohème (1896) – opera
Che gelida manina *Eweler*
Quando me'n vo soletta "Musetta's waltz song" *Filon – Michaïlow – Ranzato – Southgate – Wethmar*
selection *Lorand – Manuello – Moller – Powell*
Madama Butterfly (1904) – opera
Un bel di, vedremo *Ranzato*
Tosca (1900) – opera
E lucevan le stelle *Eweler*
selection *Lorand – Michaïlow*

Pugnani, Gaetano (1731–1798)
Gavotta variata in A* *Zighera*
(6) Sonatas, Op. 1 (*2 vlns & c*)
Sonata No. 6, in C *D'Aranyi & Fachiri*
(6) Sonatas, Op. 6 (*vln & c*)
Sonata No. 1, in E *Temianka*
(6) Sonatas, Op. 8 (*vln & c*)
Sonata No. 3, in D *C. Bobescu – Chailley – Cores – Curti – Enescu – Lorand – Stern*

Pugni, Cesare (1805–1870)
Pas de quatre (1845) – ballet (*orch*) *Gruenberg*
Purcell, Henry (1659–1695)
Aria in a† *S. Furer*

(The) Fairy Queen, Z629 (1692) – opera
O let me weep "The plaint" *Alès – Brink*
(15) Fantasias, Z731/45 (*4 & 5 part*) (*orig. viols*)
Fantasia No. 1, in F, Z731 (*3 parts upon a ground*) (? 1679) *Gibbs, Jones & Marriner – Marriner & Pini*
Fantasia No. 4, in g, Z735 (1680) *Menuhin*
Fantasia No. 7, in c, Z738 (1680) *Menuhin*
Fantasia No. 8, in d, Z739 (1680) *Masters & Menuhin*
Fantasia No. 11, in G. Z742 (1680) *Masters & Menuhin*
Fantasia No. 15, in F, Z745 (? 1679) "Upon one note" *Masters & Menuhin*
(The) Indian Queen, Z630 (1695) – opera
Act tune "Air" (*Act IV*) *D'Aranyi*
(5) Pavanes, Z748/52 (pre–1680) (*Nos. 1/4: 3 part – No. 5: 4 part*)
Pavane No. 5, in g, Z752 (? 1677) *Gibbs, Jones & Marriner – Gibbs, Marriner & Pini – Lysy, Masters & Menuhin*
Sonata in g, Z780 (*vln & c*) *Gautier – Grinke – Holst – Marriner – Pini*
(12) Sonatas, Z790/801 (1683) (*3 part – 2 vlns & c*)
Sonata No. 1, in g, Z790 *Alès & Merckel –*

*Unidentified.
†Unidentified.

Gibbs & Marriner – Pini & Tunnell
Sonata No. 2, in B flat, Z791 *Alès & Merckel – Gibbs & Marriner – Pini & Tunnell*
Sonata No. 3, in d, Z792 *Alès & Merckel – Gibbs & Marriner – Pini & Tunnell*
Sonata No. 4, in F, Z793 *Alès & Merckel – Gibbs & Marriner – Hurwitz & Liddell – Pini & Tunnell*
Sonata No. 5, in a, Z794 *Alès & Merckel – Gibbs & Marriner – Pini & Tunnell*
Sonata No. 6, in C, Z795 *Alès & Merckel – Gibbs & Marriner – Lysy & Menuhin – Pini & Tunnell*
Sonata No. 7, in e, Z796 *Alès & Merckel – Gibbs & Marriner – Pini & Tunnell*
Sonata No. 8, in G, Z797 *Alès & Merckel – Gibbs & Marriner – Lysy & Menuhin – Pini & Tunnell*
Sonata No. 9, in c, Z798 *Alès & Merckel – Gibbs & Marriner – Hurwitz & Liddell – Pini & Tunnell*
Sonata No. 10, in A, Z799 *Alès & Merckel – Gibbs & Marriner – Pini & Tunnell*
Sonata No. 11, in f, Z800 *Alès & Merckel – Gibbs & Marriner – Pini & Tunnell*
Sonata No. 12, in D, Z801 *Alès & Merckel – Gibbs & Marriner – Pini & Tunnell*
(10) Sonatas, Z802/11 (1697) (*4 parts – 2 vlns & c*)
Sonata No. 1, in b, Z802 *Ciompi & Torkanowsky – Gibbs & Marriner – Pini & Tunnell*
Sonata No. 2, in E flat, Z803 *Ciompi & Torkanowsky – Gibbs & Marriner – Pini & Tunnell*
Sonata No. 3, in a, Z804 *Gibbs & Marriner – Grinke & Pougnet – Pini & Tunnell*
Sonata No. 4, in d, Z805 *Ciompi & Torkanowsky – Gibbs & Marriner – Pini & Tunnell*
Sonata No. 5, in d, Z806 *Gibbs & Marriner – Knorre – Pini & Tunnell*
Sonata No. 6, in g, Z807 "Chaconne" *Bas & A. Schwarz – Frenkel – Gibbs & Marriner – Hurwitz & Liddell – Lysy & Menuhin – Pini & Tunnell*
Sonata No. 7, in G, Z808 *Ciompi & Torkanowsky – Gibbs & Marriner – Pini & Tunnell*
Sonata No. 8, in g, Z809 *Ciompi & Torkanowsky – Gibbs & Marriner – Hayward – Pini & Tunnell*
Sonata No. 9, in F, Z810 "Golden Sonata" *D'Aranyi & Fachiri – Ciompi & Torkanowsky – De Vito & Menuhin – Ferrit & J. Pasquier – Gibbs & Marriner – Grinke & Pougnet – Menges & Primrose (2) – Pini & Tunnell*
Sonata No. 10, in D, Z811 *Ciompi & Torkanowsky – Gibbs & Marriner – Pini & Tunnell*
Timon of Athens, Z632 (1694) – opera *Alès*
Quantz, Johann Joachim (1697–1773)
Concerto in G (*fl & strs*) *Wolf*
Quilter, Roger (1877–1953)
(3) Pastoral songs, Op. 22 (*v, vln, vlc & pf*)

No. 2. Cherry valley *Grinke*

(3) Shakespeare songs, Op. 6 (*v, vln, vlc & pf*)

   No. 1. Come away death *Grinke*

(5) Shakespeare songs, Op. 23 (*v, vln, vlc & pf*)

   No. 4. Take, o take those lips away *Grinke*

Three poor mariners (*v & pf*) *Spalding*

Where the Rainbow Ends (1911) – Incidental music (*orch*)

   Fairy Frolic *Hayward*

   Rosamund *Hayward*

Quinn

Serenata (*vln & pf*) *J. Skolnik*

Souvenir de Venise (*vln & pf*) *Rubini*

Quiroga, Manuel (1890–1961)

Canto amoroso (*vln & pf*) *Quiroga*

Danza española (*vln & pf*) *Quiroga*

Rondalla (*Jota*) (*vln & pf*) *Quiroga*

Segunda Guajira (*vln & pf*) *Quiroga*

Rääts, Jan (1932–   )

Concerto, Op. 21 (*vln & cha orch*) *Erendi*

Rabey, René (1878–   )

Dans tes yeux en pleurs (*v & pf*) *Elman*

Rachmaninov, Sergei Vassilievich (1873–1943)

(9) Études-Tableaux, Op. 39 (*pf*)

   Étude-tableau No. 2, in a (*Lento assai*) *Heifetz*

(2) Pieces, Op. 2 (1892) (*pf*)

   No. 2. Danse orientale *Goldstein – Heifetz (2)*

(5) Pieces, Op. 3 (1892) (*pf*)

   No. 1. Élégie in e flat *Biszticzky – Solloway*

   No. 5. Mélodie in E *Curti – Fastofsky – Grinke*

(2) Pieces, Op. 6 (*vln & pf*)

   No. 1. Romance in d *Beilina – Bezrodny (3) – D. Oistrakh – Zora Shikhmurzayeva – Wilkomirska*

(10) Preludes, Op. 23 (*pf*)

   Prelude No. 4, in D *Bezrodny*

   Prelude No. 5, in G *Goldstein*

(6) Songs, Op. 4 (*v & pf*)

   No. 3. In the silent night *Kreisler – Menuhin*

   No. 4. O cease thy singing, maiden fair *Kreisler*

(12) Songs, Op. 21 (*v & pf*)

   No. 7. How fair this spot *Kreisler*

(15) Songs, Op. 26 (1906) (*v & pf*)

   No. 7. To the children *Kreisler*

   No. 10. Before my window *Kreisler*

(14) Songs, Op. 34 (1912) (*v & pf*)

   No. 14. Vocalise

   Brown – Elman – Fain – Heifetz – Knorre – Kochański – Milstein – D. Oistrakh – R. Ricci

(6) Songs, Op. 38 (1916) (*v & pf*)

   No. 3. Daisies *Gimpel – Goldstein – Heifetz (3) – Kreisler – D. Oistrakh*

Trio No. 2, in d, Op. 9 "Trio élégiaque" (*pf, vln & vlc*) *Compinsky – D. Oistrakh – Shinder*

Raff, Joseph Joachim (1822–1882)

(6) Pieces, Op. 85 (*vln & pf*)

   No. 3. Cavatina in D

   d'Almaine (3) – W. Andersen – Anonymous – Ast – Breeskin – Brown – Catterall – G. Cherniavsky – Cochrane – Curti – Darrieux – Debruille – D. De Groot – Dessau – Dyke – Elman (2) – Farbmann – Fidelmann – Galli – Gittelson – Godwin – Gomez (2) – Governale – M. Hall – Haxton (2) – F.V. Henriques – F.V. & J.F. Henriques – Høeberg – Isaacs – Jacobsen

   – Kalki – A. Kaufmann – Georg Kniestaedt – Kochański – Krengel – Kubelík – Lambert – Larysz – J.M. Lasowski – Law – Liebman – Mahlke – Mahn – Manuello – Modern – Moller – Morbitzer – Nadien – Opfermann – Pillitz – Polo – Powell – Příhoda (2) – Ranzato – Rattay – Gladys Raymond – Reillie – T. Rich – Rudényi – Sammons – A. Schmidt – Sechiari – Sens – Shermont – Spalding (2) – Spivakovsky – Styx – Suk – Telmányi – Valesca-Becker – Weismann – Wolfsthal – Zilzer

   No. 6. Tarantella *Rudényi*

(3) Quartets, Op. 192 (*2 vlns, vla & vlc*)

   No. 2. Quartet No. 7, in D "The Mill" *Pessina*

Serenade, Op. 1 (*pf*) *Kreisler*

Rainger, Ralph (1901–1942)

Love in bloom (1934) (*v & pf*)* *Curti*

Rakov, Nikolai Petrovich (1908–   )

Concerto in e (1948) (*vln & orch*) *Gavrilov – D. Oistrakh (2) – I. Oistrakh*

(5) Pieces (*2 vlns & pf*) *I. Oistrakh & Pikaizen*

Poem in e (*vln & pf*) *D. Oistrakh – I. Oistrakh – Sitkovetsky*

Scherzino in e (1945) (*vln & pf*) *Sitkovetsky*

Sonata in e (1951) (*vln & pf*) *D. Oistrakh*

Rameau, Jean Philippe (1683–1764)

Andante† *Law*

Castor et Pollux (1737) – opera

   Gavotte (*Act IV*) *Burmester – Gade – Johannessen – Koene – Law – Link – Lorand*

(6) Concerts en Sextuor (*3 vlns, vla & 2 vlcs*)

   Concert No. 5 *Freund*

   Concert No. 6, in g *L. Kogan*

Dardanus (1739) – opera

   Rigaudon (*Act I*) *Cores*

(Les) Fêtes d'Hébé (1739) – opera

   Rondeau *Tzipine*

   Tambourin *Farbmann – Kreisler – Thibaud – Tzipine*

Orphée (1721) – cantata *Grehling*

(Les) Paladins (1760) – opera

   Ballet suites 1 & 2 *Gravoin*

(5) Pièces de Clavecin en Concerts (1741) (*hpsi, vln & c*)

   Concert No. 1, in c *Feigin – Lautenbacher*

   Concert No. 2, in G *Feigin*

   Concert No. 3, in A *Feigin*

   Concert No. 4, in B flat *Blot & Ortmans-Bach – Feigin – Lautenbacher*

   Concert No. 5, in d *Feigin – J. Pasquier*

(5) Suites (*hpsi*)

   Suite No. 2, in e *Tarjus*

   Suite No. 5, in G *Tarjus*

(Le) Temple de la Gloire (1745) – opera

   Gavotte in D (*Act III*) *Andrade*

Randall, J.K. (1929–   )

Lyric variations (*vln & computer*)‡ *Zukofsky*

---

*Composed jointly with Leo Robin.

†Unidentified.

‡ The program notes state: "The computer has been exploited in this piece solely as an instrument of performance, and not as a composer-surrogate."

Randegger, Alberto (*Jr.*) (1880–1918)

Bohemian dance, Op. 22 (*vln & pf*) *MacMillen*

Pierrot sérénade, Op. 33, No. 1 (*vln & pf*) *Candéla – Kubelík (2) – Spalding*

Saltarello-Caprice, Op. 17, No. 2 (*vln & pf*) *MacMillen*

Ranzato, Virgilio (1883–1937)

Allegro alla zingareska (*vln & pf*) *Ranzato*

Berceuse (*vln & pf*) *Ranzato*

Cin-ci-la (*Romanza*) (*vln & pf*) *Ranzato*

Città Rosa (*romanza*) (*vln & pf*) *Ranzato*

(Il) Cuculo (*vln & pf*) *Ranzato*

(La) Danza del Globo (*vln & pf*) *Ranzato*

(La) Danza di Nonnina (*vln & pf*) *Ranzato (2)*

(La) Duchessa di Hollywood (*vln & pf*) *Ranzato*

(A) Galoppo (*vln & pf*) *Ranzato (2)*

Mazurka-caprice (*vln & pf*) *Ranzato*

(I) Monelle fiorentini (*vln & pf*) *Ranzato*

(4) Morceaux, Op. 12 (*vln & pf*)

   No. 3. Berceuse *Ranzato (2)*

(L') Organetto di Barberia (*vln & pf*) *Ranzato*

(Il) Paese dei Campanelli (*Romanza di Nola*) (*vln & pf*) *Ranzato*

Pasquinade (*vln & pf*) *Ranzato*

(La) Pattuglia delgli tzigani (*vln & pf*) *Ranzato*

(La) Prieghiera della sera (*vln & pf*) *Ranzato*

Rapsodie russe (*vln & pf*) *Ranzato*

Romanza sans paroles (*vln & pf*) *Ranzato*

Scherzo in d (*vln & pf*) *Ranzato*

Scherzo in e (*vln & pf*) *Ranzato (2)*

Serenata (*vln & pf*) *Ranzato (2)*

Serenata galante (*vln & pf*) *Andreasson – Ranzato (2)*

Valse des diamants (*vln & pf*) *Ranzato*

Valse des rubis (*vln & pf*) *Ranzato*

Rapée, Erno (1891–1945)*

Rasse, François (1873–1955)

Concerto in C (*vln & orch*) *Hosselet*

Rathaus, Karol (1895–   )

Suite in f (*vln & orch*) *Frenkel*

Rautio, Roine (1934–1961)

Sonatina in c (*vln & pf*) *Kutsovsky*

Ravel, Maurice (1875–1937)

Berceuse sur le nom de Gabriel Fauré (1922) (*vln & pf*)

   Banat – Darrieux – Doukan – Francescatti (2) – Garnier – Kooper – Lewkowitz – Lubotsky – V. Martin – Martzy – Milstein – Soëtens

(7) Chants populaires (1910) (*v & pf*)

   No. 4. Chanson hébraïque *Zimbalist*

Daphnis et Chloe (1910) – ballet (*orch*)†

Staryk

(L') Enfant et les Sortilèges (1925) – opera-ballet

   Pastourelle *Merckel*

Introduction & Allegro (1906) (*hp, fl, cl, 2 vlns, vla & vlc*) *Dejean – Eidus – Hayward – Pougnet – P. Sanchez – Tessier*

Ma Mère l'Oye (1908) (*pf duet; orch*)

---

*See: **Pollack**, Lew

†Suites 1 & 2.

No. 2. Petit Poucet *Fournier*
(2) Mélodies hébraïques (*v & pf*)
   No. 1. Kaddisch *Francescatti – Menuhin (2) –*
   Ozim – Shapiro
Pavane pour une infante défunte (1899) (*orch*)*
Asselin – Curti – Ferras – Raderman
Pièce en forme d'Habanera (*v & pf*)
   Andrade – L. Bobescu – Campoli – Darrieux –
   Eidus – Elman – Erlih – Francescatti –
   Grumiaux (3) – Guarino – Gutnikov – Gyarmati
   – Haendel (2) – Heifetz – Jarry – L. Kogan –
   Kozigyan – Lantsman – Lewkowitz – Magyar –
   Martzy – Menuhin (3) – Morini – Nadien –
   Neaman – Neveu – E.B. Nielsen – Ozim –
   Petroni – Rabin – Shkolníková – Spalding –
   Stanske – Suk – J. Szigeti – Thibaud –
   Totenberg – Tretyakov – Wilkomirska –
   Zathureczky – Zighera
Quartet in F (1910) (*2 vlns, vla & vlc*) *Champeil –*
Hayward
Sonata (1927) (*vln & pf*)
   Auclair – Bonaldi – Doukan – Druian – Eidus –
   Erlih – Fain – Francescatti – Gautier –
   Grumiaux – Kaufman – Komlós – V. Martin –
   Merckel – Montbrun – D. Oistrakh – Raskin –
   Renardy – Rostal – Rubin – Soëtens – J. Szigeti
   – Urban – Vaiman – Wilkomirska
Sonata (1922) (*vln & vlc*) *Gautier – V. Martin –*
Raskin – Schoenfeld – Shumsky – Urban
Sonatina in f sharp (1905) (*pf*) *A. Ferraresi –*
Garnier – Heifetz – Kulenkampff
(Le) Tombeau de Couperin (1914/7) (*pf*)
   No. 4. Rigaudon *Fain*
Trio in a (1915) (*pf, vln & vlc*)
   Bean – Benedetti – Bonaldi – Eidus – Erlih –
   Gautier – Gendre – Heifetz – Menuhin –
   Merckel – D. Oistrakh – Plocek – Totenberg –
   Tziganov
Tzigane (*Rapsodie de concert*) (1924) (*vln & pf or*
orch)
   Anonymous – Barbieri – Bezrodny – Boussinot –
   Doukan – Erlih – Feigin – Ferras (3) – Fournier
   – Francescatti (4) – Friedman – Garnier (2) –
   Gimpel – Grach – Grumiaux (4) – Haendel (2)
   – Heifetz (2) – Hudeček – Jásek – Kimber – L.
   Kogan – Kóté – Krysa – Lockhart – Lozada –
   Magyar – Menuhin – Neveu – E.B. Nielsen – D.
   Oistrakh – I. Oistrakh – Peinemann – Perlman
   – Rabin – Rabinoff – Raskin – R. Ricci (2) –
   Röhn – Rosand – Schwartz – Stern – Szeryng –
   Totenberg – Tretyakov – Zsigmondy
(7) Valses nobles et sentimentales (1911) (*pf*)
Heifetz (2)
Ravini, E.
Serenade (*Sans les étoiles*) (*vln & pf*) *Curti*
Rawsthorne, Alan (1905–1971)
Sonata (1959) (*vln & pf*) *Parikian*
Theme & Variations (1927) (*2 vlns*) *Hinchliffe &*
Washbourne
Ray, Lillian†
(The) Sunshine of your smile (1915) (*v & pf*)

*Originally for piano.

†Pseudonym for John Neat.

Rubini – Zacharewitsch
Your gentle smile (*v & pf*) *Curti*
Reading, John (1640–1692)
O come all ye faithful (*Adeste Fideles*) (*hymn*)
d'Almaine
Rebel, Jean-Ferry (1663–1747)
(12) Sonatas (1712) (*2 & 3 part with figured bs*)
   Sonata No. 5, in D "La Pallas" *R. Bloch &*
   Weiner
   Sonata No. 6, in g "L'Immortelle" *R. Bloch &*
   Weiner
(12) Sonatas (1713) "Melées de Plusieurs Recits
pour la Viole" (*vln & c*)
   Sonata No. 3, in a *Weiner*
   Sonata No. 4, in e *Weiner*
   Sonata No. 6, in b *Weiner*
   Sonata No. 11, in E *Weiner*
Regamey, Constantin (1907–   )
Quartet No. 1 (1949) (*2 vlns, vla & vlc*) *Rybar*
Reger, Max (1873–1916)
Concerto in A, Op. 101 (*vln & orch*) *Shiokawa*
(14) Lose Blätter, Op. 13 (*pf*)
   No. 5. Petite caprice in b flat *Havemann*
Lyrisches Andante (1898) (*strs*) *Strub*
(3) Pieces, Op. 79d (*vln & pf*)
   No. 1. Wiegenlied in G *Barmas – Havemann –*
   Keller – Wolfgang Schneiderhan (2)
   No. 2. Capriccio in b *Keller*
   No. 3. Burla in a *Keller*
(8) Preludes & Fugues, Op. 117 (*solo vln*)
   No. 7. Prelude & Fugue No. 7, in a *Keller –*
   Schmahl
Quartet No. 5, in F sharp, Op. 121 (*2 vlns, vla &*
vlc) *Parlow*
Romance in G (*vln & pf*) *Barmas – Barylli –*
Minghetti – Queling – Stanske
(60) Schlichte Weisen – 6 Books, Op. 76
(*v & pf*)
   No. 52. Maria-Wiegenlied *Livschakoff –*
   Mitnitzky – Wolfgang Schneiderhan – Vecsey –
   Weber
Serenade in D, Op. 77a (*fl, vln & vla*) *J.C.*
Figueroa – Klingler
Serenade in G, Op. 141a (*fl, vln & vla*) *J.C.*
Figueroa
(4) Sonatas, Op. 42 (*solo vln*)
   Sonata No. 2, in A *Juda – Zimbalist*
Sonata No. 5, in f sharp, Op. 84 (*vln & pf*) *A.*
Busch – Holst
(7) Sonatas, Op. 91 (*solo vln*)
   Sonata No. 1, in a *Bress – Grumlíková –*
   Kulenkampff
   Sonata No. 3, in B flat *Bress*
   Sonata No. 7, in a (*with Chaconne*) *Bress*
Sonata No. 7, in c, Op. 139 (*vln & pf*) *Weiner*
(2) Sonatinas, Op. 103b (*vln & pf*)
   Sonatina No. 1, in d *Weiner*
   Sonatina No. 2, in A *Lapenson*
Suite in F, Op. 93 "Im alten stil" (*vln & pf*)
Bakman – Holst – Keller
Suite in a, Op. 103a (*vln & pf*) *Geyer – Knudsen –*
Kulenkampff – Rostal – Strub
Trio in b, Op. 2 (*pf, vln & vla*) *Kash*
Trio in a, Op. 77b (*vln, vla & vlc*) *Amar – J.C.*
Figueroa – Keller – Klingler

Trio in d, Op. 141b (*vln, vla & vlc*) *J.C. Figueroa*
Rehfeld, Fabian (1842–1920)
(2) Konzertstücke, Op. 58 (*vln & pf*)
   No. 1. Spanish dance *Barbosa – Gramm – Pilzer*
   (2) – Příhoda – Rattay
Reich, Steve (1936–   )
Violin phase (1967) (*vln & tape*) *Zukofsky*
Reizenstein, Franz (1911–1968)
Prologue, Variations & Finale (1939) (*vln & pf*)
Rostal
Suite (1936) (*pf*) *Rostal*
Renard, Felix
(2) Berceuse, Op. 20 (*vln & pf*)
   No. 2. Berceuse in F *de Brayne – Curti –*
   Jacobsen – Lambert – Sens
Renö, Seress
Sorgens söndag (*vln & pf*) *W. Andersen*
Reske
Amor segrets (*v & pf*) *Ranzato*
Respighi, Ottorino (1879–1936)
Berceuse (*vln & pf*) *Bezrodny*
Concerto Gregoriano (1922) (*vln & orch*) *Richartz*
– Stiehler
Sonata in b (1917) (*vln & pf*) *Beilina – Heifetz –*
Kaufman – Shumsky – Suk – Weisman
Valse caressante (*vln & pf*) *Cochrane*
Reuter, Florizel von (1893–   )
American melody (*vln & pf*) *Barylli*
Reuter, Fritz (1896–1963)
Sonata in e "Lausitzer Sonata" (*vln & pf*)
Reuter-Rau
Revueltas, Silvestre (1899–1940)
(3) Pieces (1932) (*vln & pf*) *Ajemian*
Revutsky, Lev Nikolayevich (1889–   )
Intermezzo (*vln & pf*) *Parkhomenko*
Rhodes, Phillip (1940–   )
Duo (*vln & vlc*) *Zukofsky*
Rice, Gitz Ingraham (1891–1947)
Dear old pal of mine (1918) (*v & pf*) *Fisberg –*
Jacobsen
Rich, Louis
Venetian love dance (*vln & pf*) *L. Rich*
Richards, Brinley (1817–1885)
(La) Canzone degli Uccelletti (*v & pf*) *A.*
Kaufmann
Richardson, Alan (1904–   )
Dreaming spires (*vln & pf*) *Grinke*
Sonnet (*vln & pf*) *Grinke*
Richardson, T.
Mary (*v & pf*) *Hayward*
Richartz, Willy (1900–   )
Romance, Op. 49 (*vln & orch*) *Borries*
Richepin, Tiarko
(Le) Sommeil d'Antinéa (*pf*) *Curti*
Richter, Franz Xaver (1709–1789)
Trio No. 3, in A (*pf, vln & vlc*) *Fournier*
Rico, J.
Primo Bachio (*vln & pf*) *Darrieux*
Řidký, Jaroslav (1897–1956)
(3) Compositions, Op. 26 (1933) (*vln & pf*)
   No. 2. Lullaby *Ungermannová*
Polka-fantasie, Op. 24 (1932) (*vln & pf*)
Ungermannová
Riegger, Wallingford (1885–1961)
Sonatina (1947) (*vln & pf*) *Ajemian*

Trio, Op. 1 (1920) (*pf, vln & vlc*) *Kroll*
Variations, Op. 71 (1959) (*vln & orch*) *Harth*
del Riego, Teresa (1876–1968)
O dry those tears! (*v & pf*) *Elman*
Ries, Franz (1846–1932)
(La) Capricciosa (*vln & pf*)
  Borries – Campoli – Dahmen – Georg
  Kniestaedt (2) – Kulenkampff (2) – Livontas –
  Menuhin – Zernick
Suite No. 1, Op. 26 (*vln & pf*)
  No. 5. Gavotte *d'Almaine*
Suite No. 3, in G, Op. 34 (*vln & pf*)
  No. 3. Adagio *Havemann – Lambert*
  No. 4. Gondoliera *Dessau – Elman – Law –*
  Sens
  No. 5. Perpetuum mobile
  Andrade – Barbosa – Benedetti – Bratza – Cores
  – M. Hall – Jarry – Kerekjarto – Kubelík –
  Milstein – Wolfgang Schneiderhan (2) –
  Valesca-Becker – Violin – Wittenberg – Zernick
Riisager, Knudåge (1897–   )
Lullaby (*Sovesang*) (*vln & pf*) *Tworek*
Palavas (*vln & pf*) *Tworek*
Serenade, Op. 26b (*vln, fl & vlc*) *E. Bloch*
Sonata, Op. 55a (*vln, vlc & pf*) *Tworek*
Sonata, Op. 55b (*2 vlns*) *Senderovitz & Tworek*
Rimsky-Korsakov, Nicolas (1844–1908)
Capriccio espagnole, Op. 34 (1887) (*orch*) *Bean –*
Maguire – Piastro – Shumsky – Staryk
(Le) Coq d'Or (1910) – opera
  Hymn to the sun
  Brown – Cochrane – Curti – Elman (2) –
  Francescatti – Gresser – Heifetz – Kaufman –
  Kreisler (2) – Lass (2) – Lorand (2) – Magyar –
  Menges (2) – Ormandy – Piastro – Příhoda (2)
  – Sammons – P. Sanchez – Schwartz – Solloway
  – Strockoff – Theodorescu – Thibaud (2) –
  Velder – Wolfsthal – Zacharewitsch – Zilzer
Easter Overture, Op. 36 "Grande Pâque Russe"
(*orch*) *Staryk*
Fantasia on Russian themes, Op. 33 (1886) (*vln &*
orch) *Kozolupova – Milstein*
(La) Nuit de Mai (1877/9) – opera
  selection *Elman*
Sadko (1898) – opera
  Chant hindou
  Addash – Andjelkovitch – Barbieri – Barthalay –
  Bleumers – Borries – Boulanger – Bratza (2) –
  Brown – Chauveton – Cochrane – Colombo –
  Crégut – Curti – Debruille – D. De Groot –
  Deman – Farbmann – Ferras – Gautier –
  Ghestem – Godwin – Guidi – Gyarfas – Haikala
  – Jovanović – Kálmán – Karpilowski – Kreisler
  (2) – Lass (2) – Lorand – Marcu – Menges –
  Michaïlow – Mittmann – Ormandy – Příhoda
  (2) – Puig – Ranzato – Reillie – Sammons (2) –
  Strockoff – Swaap – Telmányi – Torre – Tworek
  – Tzipine – Velder – Volant – Weismann –
  Wolfsthal (2) – Zighera – Zilzer
Scheherazade, Op. 35 (1888) (*orch*)
  Aitay – Bean – Brusilow – Corigliano – Dahmen
  – Druian – Fenyves – Francescatti – Fridheim –
  Gimpel – Gramegna – Gruenberg (2) – Harth –
  Jarvis – Kalinovsky – L. Kogan – Kreisler (2) –
  Loveday – Maguire (2) – Nerini – D. Oistrakh –

  Parikian – Pollikoff – Robbins – Sammons –
  Walther Schneiderhan – T. Seidel (2) – Soloviev
  – Staryk (2) – Zilzer
(The) Snow Maiden (1882) – opera
  Dance of the tumblers *S. Furer*
(4) Songs, Op. 2 (1865/6) (*v & pf*)
  No. 2. Enslaved by the rose & the nightingale
  Elman – Kreisler – Selinsky – Zimbalist
(The) Tale of Tsar Saltan (1900) – opera
  Flight of the bumblebee (*Act III*) (*orch*)
  Candéla – Erlih – Friedman – Garami – Heifetz
  (2) – Menuhin (2) – Milstein (3) – Rabin – P.
  Sanchez – San-Malo – Schulz – Šroubek – Stern
  (2) – Szeryng (3) – J. Szigeti – Tworek – Wolf –
  Zacharewitsch
Trio in c (1897) (*pf, vln & vlc*) *D. Oistrakh*
(The) Tsar's Bride (1899) – opera
  Haste thee, mother mine *Menuhin*
Rissland, Rudolf (1868–1960)
Valse-caprice, Op. 16 (*vln & pf*) *Elman*
Rivilis, P. (1936–   )
Suite, Op. 9 (*vln & pf*) *Niaga*
Roberts, Jeremy Dale
Capriccio (*vln & pf*) *Mason*
Roberts, Lee S. (1884–1949)
Lonesome, that's all (*v & pf*) *Fradkin*
Robertson
Violin d'amour (*vln & pf*) *Jelving*
Robertson, Leroy J. (1896–   )
Concerto (1949) (*vln & orch*) *Spivakovsky*
Robin, Leo (1895–   )*
Robinson, Joseph (1816–1898)
Snowy-breasted pearl (*v & pf*) *Hayward – Ludlow*
Robledo, Julian
Three o'clock in the morning (1922) (*v & pf*)
Fradkin – Haxton
Rochberg, George (1918–   )
Duo concertante (1955 – rev. 1959) (*vln & vlc*)
Kobialka
Roche, Gustav
Bandinage (*vln & pf*) *de Brayne*
Rode, Alfredo (1905–   )
(La) Carnevale di Venizia – variations (*vln & pf*)
Rode
Rode, Pierre Jacques Joseph (1774–1830)
(24) Caprices, Op. 22 (*solo vln*)
  Caprice No. 2, in a (*Allegretto*) *Staryk*
  Caprice No. 8, in f sharp (*Moderato assai*)
  Staryk
  Caprice No. 17, in A flat (*Vivacissimo*) *Elman –*
  Staryk
  Caprice No. 18, in f (*Presto*) "Minute Caprice"
  Thibaud
  Caprice No. 21, in B flat (*Tempo giusto*) *Staryk*
Trio in D (*vln, vla & gtr*) *Csaba*
Rodrigo, Joaquin (1902–   )
Capriccio (1944) "Ofrenda a Sarasate" (*solo vln*)
Leon-Ara
Concerto (1943) (*vln & orch*) *Ferras*
(2) Esbozas, Op. 1 (1923) (*vln & pf*)
  No. 1. La enamorada junto al pequeño surtidor
  Bouquet – Leon-Ara – Mus
  No. 2. Pequeña ronda *Bouquet – Leon-Ara*

*See: **Rainger**, Ralph

Sonata Pimpante "Homage to Joaquin Turina"
(*vln & pf*) *Leon-Ara*
Rodriguez, G. H. Matos
(La) Cumparsita (1926) (*v & pf*) *Skalka*
Roesgen-Champion, Marguerite (1894–
Pièces (*vln & pf*) *Merckel*
Rogister, Jean (1879–1964)
Concerto in G (1945) (*vln & orch*) *H. Koch*
Rolf, Irving
Sehnsucht (*v & pf*) *Dajos*
Rolón, José (1883–1945)
Mexican dance (*vln & pf*) *Szeryng*
Roman, Johan Helmich (1694–1758)
(6) Assaggi (*solo vln*)
  Assagio No. 6, in b, B324 *Frydén*
Concerto No. 3, in d (*vln & orch*) *Berlin –*
Liljefors
Romberg, Sigmund (1887–1951)
Blossom Time (1921) – operetta
  Song of love *Ball – Rosen – B. Scherzer*
(The) Rose of France – operetta
  Tango *Curti*
(The) Student Prince (1924) – operetta
  Deep in my heart, dear *Dobrinski – Fradkin –*
  Kreisler
  Serenade *Dobrinski – Fradkin – Kreisler*
Ronald, Landon Russell (1873–1938)
Garden of allah (1921) – Incidental music (*orch*)
  In an eastern garden *Beckwith*
  Prelude *Beckwith*
Summertime – 4 songs (1901) (*v & pf*)
  No. 4. O lovely night *Hayward*
Ropartz, Guy (1864–1955)
Sonata in D (1907) *Erlih*
Sonata No. 3, in A (*vln & pf*) *Bress*
Ropp, J-B.
(I) Canto per te (*v & pf*) *Dony*
de Rose, Peter (1900–1953)
When you're gone I won't forget (*pf*) *Debruille*
Rose, Fred (1897–   )
Underneath Hawaiian skies (*v & pf*) *Ball*
Rosenberg, Hilding (1892–   )
Concerto (1955) "Louisville" (*vln & orch*) *Harth*
Rosenbloom, Sydney (1889–   )
Gavotte in D (*vln & pf*) *Doré*
Lament (*vln & pf*) *Kennedy*
Waltz–scherzo (*vln & pf*) *Kennedy*
Rosenfeld, Gerhard (1931–   )
Concerto (1963) (*vln & orch*) *Schmahl*
Rosenmüller, Johann (1619–1684)
Sinfonia undecima (*2 vlns, 2 vlas, 2 gambas, lute*
& hpsi) *Neuhaus & Thoene*
(12) Sonatas (1670) (*var. cbns*)
  Sonata in e *Blot & Ortmans-Bach*
Rosenweig, Florence
Where the blue Danube flows (*v & pf*) *Strong*
Ross, A.
(Le) Chant du Rossignol (*v & pf*) *Gerard*
Rosselini, Renzo (1908–   )
(La) Fontanna malata (1930) (*vln & pf*) *Cillario –*
Zhuk
Rossi, Salomone (1570–1639)
Sonata in f (1613) (*2 vlns & c*) *Kuijken &*
Rubinlicht
Rossini, Gioacchino (1792–1868)

Guillaume Tell (1829) – opera
  selection *Law*
Stabat Mater (1842) (*s, a, t, b, cho & orch*)
  No. 2. Cujus animam *Ranzato*
Rousseau, L. Julien
Incanto valse (*pf*) *Michaïlow*
Rousseau, Samuel (1853–1904)
Berceuse (*Hush, my baby*) (*v & pf*) *A. Schimdt*
(Les) Promis (*v & pf*) *Curti*
Roussel, Albert (1869–1937)
Bacchus et Ariane, Op. 43 – ballet (*orch*)
  Suite No. 2 *Staryk*
Serenade in C, Op. 30 (*fl, vln, vla, vlc & hp*) *Futer
  – P. Sanchez*
Sonata No. 2, in A, Op. 28 (*vln & pf*) *Devries –
Doukan – Soëtens*
Rozsa, Miklós (1907–   )
Concerto, Op. 24 (*vln & orch*) *Heifetz*
Concerto (1964) "Double" (*vln, vlc & orch*)
Heifetz
North Hungarian peasant songs & dances, Op. 5
(1929) (*vln & orch*) *Colbentson*
Variations on a Hungarian peasant song, Op. 4
(*vln & orch*) *Zsigmondy*
Rózycki, Ludomir (1883–1953)
Melody, Op. 5 (*vln & pf*) *Totenberg*
Rubbra, Edmund (1901–   )
Improvisation, Op. 89 (1955) (*vln & orch*) *Harth*
Sonata No. 2, Op. 31 (1931) (*vln & pf*) *Grinke –
Holst – Sammons*
Trio, Op. 68 "In one movement" (*pf, vln & vlc*)
Gruenberg
Rubens, Paul Alfred (1875–1917)
(The) Blue Moon – musical
  Mother dear *Ricci*
Tina – musical
  The violin song *A. Sandler (2)*
Rubinoff, David (1897–   )
Fiddlin' the fiddle (*vln & pf*) *Steiger-Betzak*
Rubinstein, Anton (1830–1894)
Bal costumé (*20 pieces*) Op. 103 (*pf duet*)
  No. 7. Toréador et Andalouse *A. Sandler*
(6) Lieder, Op. 72 (*v & pf*)
  No. 1. Es blinkt der Tau (*The dew is sparkling*)
  Bustabo – Elman
(2) Melodies, Op. 3 (*pf*)
  No. 1. Melody in F
  *Anonymous – Ball (2) – Curti – Dajos – E.
  Dubois – Elman – Eweler – Förster – Ghestem –
  Hager – Haxton (3) – Kalafusz – Lorand –
  Maurice – Moskowitz (2) – Nadien – Parlow –
  K. Rubens – Rudényi – B. Schwarz – Southgate
  – Spalding – Thibaud – Treff – Ware (2) –
  Weist-Hill – F. Weltmann – Williams – Zentay
  – Zilzer*
(6) Soirées de Saint-Pétersbourg, Op. 44 (*pf*)
  No. 1. Romance in E flat
  *Bezrodny – Elman – Flesch – Herman –
  Kubelík – Michaïlow – Příhoda – A.J. Rose –
  Sealy – Senatra – J. Szigeti*
Trio No. 3, in B flat, Op. 52 (*pf, vln & vlc*)
Manasevich
(12) Two-part songs, Op. 48 (*cho & pf*)
  No. 5. Wanderess Nachtlied *Dessau*
Rudényi, Jan (–1914)

Chanson de Venise (*vln & pf*) *Rudényi*
Fantaisie hongrois (*vln & pf*) *Rudényi*
Rêverie (*vln & pf*) *Rudényi*
Romance in A (*Chant à Mélisande*) (*vln & pf*)
Rudényi
Sérénade d'amour (*vln & pf*) *Rudényi*
Sérénade amoureuse (*vln & pf*) *Rudényi*
Träumerei (*vln & pf*) *Sens*
Ruggieri, Giovanni Maria
(10) Sonatas, Op. 3 (1693) (*2 vlns & c*)
  Sonata No. 1, in e *Melkus & Steinbauer*
  Sonata No. 2, in b *Melkus & Steinbauer*
  Sonata No. 3, in B flat *Melkus & Steinbauer*
  Sonata No. 4, in F *Melkus & Steinbauer*
  Sonata No. 5, in g *C. Ferraresi & Gulli –
  Melkus & Steinbauer*
  Sonata No. 6, in A *Melkus & Steinbauer*
  Sonata No. 7, in a *Melkus & Steinbauer*
  Sonata No. 8, in G *Melkus & Steinbauer*
  Sonata No. 9, in d *Melkus & Steinbauer*
  Sonata No. 10, in D *Melkus & Steinbauer*
Rupp, Carl (1892–   )
Arizona stars (*v & pf*) *Ball*
Just an ivy-covered shack (*v & pf*) *Ball*
Russell, James J.
Serenade to Nicolette (*vln & pf*) *Arschensky –
Godowsky*
Rust, Friedrich Wilhelm (1739–1796)
Gigue* *Spalding*
Sonata in G (*vln & gtr*) *Klasinc*
Rüthström, Julius (1877–1944)
(En) Gammal – waltz (*vln & pf*) *Galli*
Ruyneman, Daniël (1886–1963)
Sonata in G (*vln & pf*) *Moszkowski*
Rzayev, Azer (1930–   )
Concerto No. 1, in a (*vln & orch*) *Goldstein*
Saar, Louis Victor (1868–1937)
(5) Klavierstücke, Op. 23 (*pf*)
  No. 1. Intermezzo *Brown*
(6) Klavierstücke, Op. 52 (*pf*)
  No. 4. Gondoliera *Powell*
Sabitov, Nariman (1925–   )
Melody (*vln & pf*) *Zaretsky*
Sabo, F. (1902–   )†
Trio (1927) (*2 vlns & vla*) *Lutsky & Ovcharek*
Sadan
Serenade to spring (*vln & pf*) *di Piramo*
Saenger, Gustav (1865–1935)
(3) Concert Miniatures, Op. 130 (*vln & pf*)
  No. 2. Scotch pastorale *Elman – Menuhin*
Improvisation (*vln & pf*) *Provinsky*
Sahl, Michael (1934–   )
Mitzvah for the dead (*vln & tape*) *Zukofsky*
Saint-Georges, Joseph de (1739–1799)
(Les) Caquets (*Rondeau en staccato*) (*hpsi*)
Casadesus
(2) Sinfonia concertantes, Op. 9 (1778) (*2 vlns &
strs*)
  Sinfonia concertante No. 2, in G‡

*Unidentified.
†Also spelled Szabo.

‡It is now generally accepted that the above
sinfonia is actually from opus 13 & was
composed in 1782.

  *Blanchard & Germaine Raymond – Carles &
  Fernandez*
Saint-Lubin, Léon de (1805–1850)
Sextet (*from the opera "Lucia di Lammermoor" by
Donizetti*) Op. 56 (*solo vln*) *Kubelík (2) – Příhoda
– F. Reuter – Zacharewitsch*
Saint-Luc, Jacques (1616– ?)
Partita (*lute, vln & bs*) *Trysessoone*
Sainton, Prosper Philippe Cathérine (1813–1890)
Fantaisie Ecossaise, Op. 27 (*vln & pf*)*
Fellowes
Saint-Saëns, Charles Camille (1835–1921)
(Le) Bonheur est chose légère (*v & pf*) *Zimbalist*
(Le) Carnaval des animaux (1886) (*small orch*)
  Le cygne
  *d'Ambrosio – W. Andersen – Aranyi – d'Arco –
  Asti – A. Bachmann (2) – Barbieri – Barmas –
  Bisztriczky – Boucherit – Boulanger – Curti –
  Dajos – Davis – D. De Groot – Elman –
  Fradkin – M. Gordon – M. Hall (2) – Heifetz
  (2) – J.F. Henriques – Hood – Jarry – L. Kogan
  – Kubelík – Lambert (2) – Law – Mendels –
  Meyer – de Monge – Opfermann – Pessina –
  Petschnikoff (2) – Phal – R. Pollak – Powell –
  Příhoda – Ranzato (2) – Rudényi – A. Sandler
  – Wolfgang Schneiderhan (3) – Southgate –
  Spalding – Telmányi – Thibaud (2) –
  Weintraub – Wethmar – Wolfsthal – Zimbalist*
Concerto No. 1, in A, Op. 20 "Konzertstück" (*vln
& orch*) *Combarieu – Renardy – R. Ricci – Zarius
Shikhmurzayeva – Sitkovetsky*
Concerto No. 2, in C, Op. 58 (*vln & orch*) *Gitlis*
Concerto No. 3, in b, Op. 61 (*vln & orch*)
*Bělčík – Campoli – Candéla – Francescatti –
Grumiaux (2) – Kaufman (2) – Menuhin –
Merckel – Milstein – R. Ricci – Rosand –
Szeryng – Zhuk*
Concerto No. 4, in G, Op. 62 "Unfinished" (*vln &
orch*)†
Danse macabre, Op. 40 (1874) (*orch*)
  *Bean – Bělčík – Corigliano – Gramegna –
  Hilsberg – Krebbers – Merckel – Nadien –
  Staryk – Yordanoff*
(Le) Déluge, Op. 45 (1876) – oratorio
  Prélude (*orch*)
  *Aranyi (2) – Asselin – Bas – A. Brun – Charmy
  – Chauveton – Dessau – Gramm – Herman –
  Kerekjarto – Marteau – Mendels – Pessina –
  Phal – Sechiari – T. Seidel – Spalding –
  Thibaud (2) – Vance – Volant – Willaume –
  Wolfsthal – Zimbalist – Zimmermann*
Élégie, Op. 143 (*vln & pf*) *Willaume*
(6) Études, Op. 52 (*pf*)
  Étude No. 6, in D flat "Étude en forme de
  valse" *Benedetti – Gitlis – Isakadze –
  Komissarov – D. Oistrakh – Sitkovetsky*
Fantaisie in A, Op. 124 (1907) (*vln & hp*) *Eidus*

*This work consists of 1 Auld Robin Gray & 2.
Duncan Gray.

†See: Morceau de concert, Op. 62.

R. Ricci
Havanaise, Op. 83 (*vln & orch*)
Campoli – Candéla – Charmy – Filon –
Francescatti (2) – Friedman – Grach –
Grumiaux (2) – Heifetz (3) – Kaufman – L.
Kogan (2) – Krebbers – Menuhin – Odnoposoff
– I. Oistrakh – Petronio – Rabin – R. Ricci –
Rosand – Sobolevsky – Szeryng (2) – Telmányi
– Thibaud (2) – Willaume – Zhuk
Introduction & Rondo Capriccioso, Op. 28 (*vln &*
orch)
Barbieri – Campoli (2) – Chemet – Elman (3) –
Fain (2) – Francescatti (3) Friedman –
Grumiaux (2) – Gutnikov – Haendel – Heifetz
(2) – Jacobs – Jacobsen – Kennedy – L. Kogan
– Kóté – Krebbers – Kubo – Kulka – Menuhin
– Milstein – Odnoposoff – D. Oistrakh (2) – I.
Oistrakh (4) – Petronio – Piastro – Primrose –
Rabin (2) – R. Ricci – Rosand – Schmied –
Solloway – Spalding – Staryk – Stern –
Strockoff – Szeryng (2) – Telmányi – Temianka
– Thibaud (2) – Unno – Wolfsthal – Zhuk –
Zukerman
Morceau de concert, Op. 62 (*vln & orch*)*
Gitlis
Oratorio de Noël, Op. 12 (1863) – oratorio
No. 7. Tecum principium *de Brayne – Darrieux*
Quartet in B flat, Op. 41 (*pf, vln, vla & vlc*)
Hayward
Quintet in a, Op. 14 (*pf, 2 vlns, vla & vlc*) *Gali*
Samson et Dalila, Op. 47 (1877) – opera
Mon coeur s'ouvre ta voix *Ball – D. De Groot –*
Eweler – Indig – Lorand – Moller – Wolfsthal
selection *Aranyi – de Monge – Radics*
Septet in E flat, Op. 65 (*tpt, 2 vlns, vla, vlc, cbs &*
pf) *Gali*
Sérénade, Op. 15 (*pf, org, vln & vla*) *Mossel – J.*
Wolff
Sonata No. 1, in d, Op. 75 (*vln & pf*) *Heifetz (2) –*
Komissarov – Pascal
Trio No. 1, in F, Op. 18 (*pf, vln & vlc*) *Sammons*
Salesski
Rêverie triste (*vln & pf*)
Salieri, Antonio (1750–1825)
Concerto in D "Triple" (*vln, ob, vlc & orch*)
Redditi
Salinen, A.
Cadenza (*solo vln*) *Petrosyan*
Salmanov, Vadim (1912–   )
Sonata No. 2 (1962) (*vln & pf*) *Vaiman*
Samazeuilh, Gustav Marie Victor Fernand (1877–
1967)
Chant d'Espagne (*vln & pf*) *Menuhin*
Sammartini, Giuseppe (1693–1750)
Concerto in F (*vln, strs & c*) *Salvi*
(6) Sonatas, Op. 1 (*2 vlns & c*)
Sonata No. 4, in A†
W. Busch – Cillario – Curti – Elman (2) –

*This is the popular name for the Concerto No.
4, in G, "Unfinished."

†The Andante or 3rd mvt. is better known in
the arrangement by Mischa Elman entitled
"Canto amoroso."

Kerekjarto – Kozolupova – Mus – Senatra –
Szemere – Torre
Sammartini, Giovanni Battista (1701–1775)
Concerto No. 2, in C (*vln & orch*) *Abussi – Glenn*
(12) Sonatas, Op. 1 (*2 vlns & c*)
Sonata No. 6, in D *D'Aranyi*
Sammons, Albert (1886–1953)
Bagatelle (*vln & pf*) *Sammons*
Bourrée, Op. 12 (*vln & pf*) *Sammons*
Canzonetta, Op. 20 (*vln & pf*) *Sammons*
Cradle song (*Berceuse*) Op. 6 (*vln & pf*) *Sammons*
Danse hongrois (*vln & pf*) *Sammons*
Fantasia on Irish airs (*vln & pf*) *Sammons*
Humoresque (*vln & pf*) *Sammons*
Intermezzo (*vln & pf*) *Sammons*
Rêve d'enfant (*vln & pf*) *Sammons*
Theme & Variations in the olden style (*vln & pf*)
Sammons
Sanders, Erl
Once (*v & pf*) *Lensky – Manuello*
Sanderson, Wilfred Ernest (1878–   )
Looking for you (*v & pf*) *A. Sandler*
Until (1918) (*v & pf*) *Hayward – A. Sandler*
Santly, Joseph H. (1886–   )
Hawaiian butterfly (*v & pf*) *Rubini*
Sárai, Tibor (1919–   )
Capriccio (*vln & pf*) *Simkó*
Sarasate, Pablo Martín Melitón Sarasate y
Navascues (1844–1908)
Adios montañas mias, Op. 37 (*vln & pf*)
Komissarov – Renardy – Weiner
Caprice basque, Op. 24 (*vln & pf*)
Asiain – Ball – Brown – Elman – Fain –
Farbmann – Godowsky (2) – Isakadze – Klimov
– L. Kogan (2) – Leon-Ara – Lewkowitz –
Malinin – Menuhin – Nadien – R. Ricci (2) –
Rosand – Ruha – Sarasate – Stern – Weiner
Carmen Fantasia (*on themes from the opera by
Bizet*) Op. 25 (*vln & pf or orch*)
Benedetti – Bernard – Bratza (2) – Dessau –
Haendel – Heifetz – Huberman – L. Kogan –
Kubelík – Laredo – Marteau (2) – Morini – D.
Oistrakh – Parlow – Rabin – R. Ricci – Rosand
– Spalding – Spivakovsky – Strock – Thomas–
Zilzer – Zimbalist
(Le) Chant du rossignol, Op. 29 (*vln & pf*) *F.
Reuter*
(8) Danzas españolas (*vln & pf*)
Danza española*
Fredericks – Wolff-Israel
No. 1. Malagueña, Op. 21, No. 1
Asiain – Benedetti – Debruille – Farbmann –
Flesch – Heifetz – Jacobsen – Kochański – L.
Kogan – B. Koutzen – Magyar – V. Martin –
Menges (2) – Menuhin (3) – Odnoposoff – D.
Oistrakh – R. Ricci (2) – Rosand – Rostal –
Sitkovetsky – Sobolevsky – Staples – Szentgyörgi
– Temianka – Weiner – Zilzer
No. 2. Habañera, Op. 21, No. 2
Asiain – Banat – Benedetti – Bernard –
Bochková – Bustabo – Eidus – Goni –
Grumlíková – Heifetz – Leon-Ara – Marteau –
V. Martin – Menuhin (5) – Nadien –

*Unidentified

Odnoposoff – D. Oistrakh – Pikaizen – Polyakin
– R. Quattocchi – Rabin – R. Ricci (3) –
Rosand – Rostal – Sarasate – Sitkovetsky –
Spalding – Stanske – Temianka – Weiner –
Zilzer
No. 3. Romanza andaluza, Op. 22, No. 1
Accardo – Aloume – Asiain – Barbieri – Berg –
Berkova – Bisztriczky – Brugman – Culbertson –
Dessau – Dunn – Elman – Erlih – A. Ferraresi
– Ferras (2) – Fontanarosa – Goni – Gramegna
– Grumlíková – Heifetz (2) – Huberman (2) –
Kawaciuk – Kerekjarto – L. Kogan – Kubelík –
Lass – Leon-Ara – Linz – Locatelli – Loránt –
V. Martin – Menuhin (3) – Milstein (2) –
Morini (2) – Moskowitz (2) – Mus – Onderet –
Perediaz – Pikaizen – Plaeinitz – R. Pollak –
Příhoda (2) – Renardy – R. Ricci (2) – Rosand
– San-Malo – Schwalbé – Sobolevsky – Solloway
(2) – Spalding – Stanske – Swaap – Szentgyörgi
– Szeryng – Taschner – Weiner – F. Weltmann
– Wolfsthal
No. 4. Jota navarra, Op. 22, No. 2
Cillario – Erlih – Gimpel – Huberman –
Leon-Ara – V. Martin – Příhoda (3) – Quiroga
(3) – Renardy – F. Reuter – R. Ricci (2) –
Rosand – Solloway – Vidas – Weiner –
Wolfsthal
No. 5. Playera, Op. 23, No. 1
W. Busch – Erlih – Hassid – Markov – V.
Martin – Mus – Reis – R. Ricci (2) – Rosand –
Solloway – Weiner – Zighera
No. 6. Zapateado, Op. 23, No. 2
Accardo – Asiain – Banat – Barbieri – Barleben
– Benedetti – Bress – Bustabo – Culbertson (2)
– Dunn – Erlih (2) – A. Ferraresi – Haendel –
Hassid – Heifetz (4) – Kerekjarto – L. Kogan –
Kubelík (2) – Leon-Ara – Losowsky – Markov –
V. Martin – Melsa – Menuhin – Nadien –
Nerini – D. Oistrakh – R. Quattrocchi –
Quiroga – Rabin – Renardy – R. Ricci (2) –
Rosand – Sarasate – Schwalbé – Seidlová –
Sobolevsky – Spalding – Spivakovsky – Stanske
– Strockoff – Szentgyörgi – Szeryng (2) – Víolín
– Weiner – Zhuk – Zimbalist (2)
No. 7. Danza española No. 7, in a, Op. 26,
No. 1
Asiain – Dunn – Hegner – Loránt – V. Martin
– R. Ricci (2) – Rosand – Weiner – F.
Weltmann – Wilk – Zimbalist
No. 8. Danza española No. 8, in C, Op. 26,
No. 2
L. Cherniavsky – Kubelík – V. Martin – Powell
– R. Ricci (2) – Rosand – A.J. Rose – J.
Skolnik – Spalding – Weiner
Faust Fantasia (*on themes from the opera by
Gounod*) (*vln & pf or orch*)
d'Almaine (2) – Anonymous – Barcewicz –
Bernard – Dessau – Farbmann – Gygi – May –
Morini (3) – A.J. Rose – Schelz
Guernikako Arbola (*vln & pf*) *Gomez*
Introduction & Caprice-Jota, Op. 41 (*vln & pf*)
*Sarasate**
Introduction & Tarantelle, Op. 43 (*vln & pf*)

*Caprice-Jota only.

897

(12) Bagatelles, Op. 13 (*vln & pf*)
No. 9. L'abeille
*Barbosa – Campoli – Cantrelle – Curti –
Debruille – Dunn – Eidus – Erlih – Fairhurst –
Garami – Gautier – Gregorowicz – Gyarmati –
M. Hall – Jarry – Kreisler – Kulenkampff –
Law – Madle – Neste – Noack – R. Pollak –
Porta – Powell – A. Schmidt – Wolfgang
Schneiderhan – Small – Soriano – Stern – J.
Szigeti (2) – Szikra – Wethmar – Zilzer*

Schubert, Franz Peter (1797–1828)
Allegretto grazioso* *Freund*
(5) Deutsche Tänze (*Minuets*) & 6 Trios, D89
(1813) (*orch*) *Deman*
(16) Deutsche Tänze, Op. 33 (D783) (*pf*)
Deutscher Tanz No. 3, in B flat *Elman (2) –
Morini – Pessina – Polyakin – T. Seidel –
Selinsky – Spalding*
Deutscher Tanz No. 6, in B flat *Szikra*
Fantasia in C, Op. 159 (D934) (*vln & pf*)
*Accardo – Ajemian – Auclair – E. Bloch – R.
Bloch – A. Busch – Druian – Fain –
Francescatti – Heifetz – Klimov – Lautenbacher
– Martzy – Menuhin – D. Oistrakh – Pauk –
Rostal – Wolfgang Schneiderhan – J. Szigeti –
Zsigmondy*
(7) Gesänge (*set to Scott's "Lady of the Lake"*)
Op. 52 (*v & pf*)
No. 6. Ave Maria, D839
*Ambrose – W. Andersen – Ball – Barbieri –
Benes – Blinder – Borries – Boussinot – Campoli
– Caponi – Chauveton – Culbertson – Driffield –
Dunn – Elman (4) – Falk – Farbmann – Ferras
– H. Figueroa – Flesch – Francescatti –
Heifetz (3) – Huberman – Jacobs – Kalmer –
Kaufman – Kooper – Kreisler – Kubelík (2) –
Kubo – Kulenkampff (2) – Lorand – Mariani –
Markov – Menges – Menuhin (3) – Meyer – de
Monge – Morini – Nadien – E.B. Nielsen –
Nilsson – Opfermann – Post – Powell – Prick –
Příhoda (3) – Puig – Ranzato – Renardy –
Roeder – Rosand – Rosen (2) – K. Kubens – T.
Seidel – Sens – Spalding (3) – Spivakovsky –
Stanske – Stern – Strock – Strockoff – Suk –
Szentgyörgi – J. Szigeti – Theadorowicz –
Thibaud – Vecsey (2) – Ware – Wicks –
Wolfsthal – Wolters – Ysaÿe – Zacharewitsch –
Zimbalist*
Horch! Horch! die Lerch, (D889) (*pf*) *Piastro –
Spalding*
(4) Impromptus, Op. 90 (D899) (*pf*)
Impromptu No. 3, in G *Collier – Heifetz (2) –
Klimov – L. Kogan – Tessier*
Introduction & Variations on "Trockne Blumen"
(*from "Die Schöne Müllerin"*) Op. 160 (D802)
(*fl & pf*) *Accardo*
Konzertstück in D, D345 (1816) (*vln & orch*)
Eitler
(17) Ländler, Op. 18 (D145) (1815) (*pf*)
Ländler No. 2, in E flat *Szikra*
(4) Lieder, Op. 3 (D257) (*v & pf*)

*Unidentified

No. 3. Heidenröslein *d'Arco*
(2) Lieder, Op. 98 (D498) (*v & pf*)
No. 2. Wiegenlied "Schlafe, holder süsser
Knabe"
*Blinder – Bratza – Jacobsen – Jovanovič –
Kennedy – Morini – Poltronieri – Příhoda – A.
Schmidt – Traversa – Tworek – Zilzer*
Litanei auf das Fest aller Seelen, D343 (*v & pf*)
*Borries – Dessau – Elman – Hayward – T.
Nielsen – Nilsson – Příhoda*
(3) Marches militaires, Op. 51 (D733) (*pf duet*)
Marche militaire No. 1, in D *Dessau –
Sammons*
(6) Moments musicaux, Op. 94 (D780) (1823/7)
(*pf*)
Moment musicale No. 3, in f "Air russe"
*Alès – Bratza – Candéla – Catterall –
Chauveton – Elman (2) – Fairhurst – Farbmann
– Francescatti – Gautier – Granchi – Guidi –
Gyarfas (2) – M. Hall – Hayward – Huberman
– Jovanovič – B. Koutzen – Kreisler – Law –
Parlow (2) – Příhoda – Ranzato – Sammons (2)
– Schwartz – Strockoff – Thibaud – Ware –
Wolfsthal*
Nocturne in E flat, Op. 148 (D897) (*pf, vln
& vlc*) *Barchet – Gimpel – Menuhin – Suk*
Octet in F, Op. 166 (D803) (*cl, hrn, bsn, 2 vlns,
vla, vlc & cbs*) *Cantell – Dessau – Kennedy – D.
Oistrakh (2) – Wolfgang Schneiderhan*
(2) Quartets, Op. 125 (*2 vlns, vla & vlc*)
No. 1. Quartet No. 10, in E flat, D87 *Deman –
Swoboda*
No. 2. Quartet No. 11, in E, D353 *Rybar*
Quartet No. 12, in c, D703 "Quartettsatz" (*2 vlns,
vla & vlc*) *Rybar*
Quartet No. 13, in a, Op. 29, No. 1 (D804) (*2
vlns, vla & vlc*) *Deman – Dyke – Elman*
Quartet No. 14, in d, D810 "Death & the
Maiden" (*2 vlns, vla & vlc*) *Hamza –
Deman – Lorand – A.J. Rose – Swoboda*
Quintet in A, Op. 114 (D667) "Trout" (*pf, vln,
vla, vlc & cbs*)
*Dumont – Goldberg – Grumiaux – Hanke –
Klijn – Komlós – Kussmaul – Laredo – Lorand
– Môži – Raskin – Rybar – Schneider*
Quintet in C, Op. 163 (D956) (*2 vlns, vla
& 2 vlcs*) *Baker & Heifetz – Schneider & Stern*
Romance* *Rocabruna*
Rondo brillante in b, Op. 70 (D895) (*vln & pf*)
*Accardo – Auclair – Lantsman – Martzy –
Menuhin – Pauk – Pierangeli – Rostal –
Schneider – Wolfgang Schneiderhan – Snítil – J.
Szigeti – Vaiman*
Rondo in A, D438 (*vln & str orch*) *Ayo –
Fernandez – Grumiaux – Kamper – Ozim – Röhn
– Soh – Soloviev – Suk – Temianka*
Rosamunde von Cypern, Op. 26 (D797) (1823) –
Incidental music (*orch*)
No. 5. Entr'acte III, in B flat *Bratza –
Manuello – Powell – Sammons*
No. 9. Ballet music II, in G
Barstow – Benedetti – Bouillon – Chauveton –

*Unidentified.

*Fournier – Haendel – Kreisler (2) – Lorand –
Manuello – Press – Příhoda (2) – Puig – Rostal
– Small – Vidas*
Scherzo in B flat, D953 (*pf*) *Eweler*
(14) Schwanengesang, D957 (1828) (*v & pf*)
No. 4. Ständchen "Serenade"
*d'Almaine (4) – W. Andersen – Anonymous –
Beneš – Candéla – Dinicu – Elman (3) – Eweler
– Farbmann – Fradkin – Gerard – Ghestem –
Guidi – Hager – Georg Kneistaedt (2) – Kreisler
– Laue – Lichtenberg – Livschakoff – Marteau
– Michaïlow – Milstein – Nadien – Nilsson –
Opfermann – Ranzato – K. Rubens – Sammons
– A. Sandler – Sänger – B. Scherzer – T. Seidel
(2) – Selinsky – Southgate – Spalding – Stehl –
Swaap – Thibaud – Totenberg – Traversa –
Valesca-Becker – Zacharias*
Sonata in a, D821 (1824) "Arpeggione"
(*arpeggione & pf*) *Barinova*
Sonata No. 17, in D, Op. 53 (D850) (*pf*)
Rondo (*4th mvt*)
*Gorokhov – Heifetz (2) – Liberman – Malinin –
Markov – Szentgyörgi – J. Szigeti (2) – Thibaud*
Sonata in B, D28 (*pf, vln & vlc*) *Menuhin*
Sonata in A, Op. 162 (D574) "Duo" (*vln & pf*)
*Accardo – Auclair – Borries – Devries – Druian
– Fuchs – Grumiaux – Gulli – Hagen – Harth –
Kaufman – Kreisler – Lack – Lautenbacher –
Martzy – Menuhin – Merckel – D. Oistrakh (2)
– I. Oistrakh – Pauk – Rostal – Schneider –
Wolfgang Schneiderhan (2) – Snitkovsky – Suk
– J. Szigeti*
(3) Sonatinas, Op. 137 (D384, D385 & D408) (*vln
& pf*)
Sonatina No. 1, in D, D384
*Accardo – d'Albore – Auclair – Borries –
Boskovsky – Bress – Chilingirian – Francescatti
– Fuchs – Grumiaux – Harth – Komlós –
Kozolupova – Markov – Martzy – Menuhin –
Merckel – Mischakoff – Pauk – Renardy –
Roche – Rostal – Sammons – Schneider –
Wolfgang Schneiderhan (2) – Suk – J. Szigeti*
Sonatina No. 2, in A, D385
*Accardo – Auclair – Chilingirian – Grumiaux –
Gulli – Harth – Martzy – Mischakoff – Pauk –
Roche – Rostal – Schneider (2) – Wolfgang
Schneiderhan (2) – Snítil*
Sonatina No. 3, in g, D408
*Accardo – Auclair – Boskovsky – Chilingirian –
Francescatti – Freund – Fuchs – Grumiaux –
Haendel – Harth – Heifetz – Lubotsky – Martzy
– Matthews – Menges – Mischakoff – Pauk –
Renardy – Roche – Rostal – Sammons –
Schneider – Wolfgang Schneiderhan (2) – Snítil
– Thibaud*
Trio No. 1, in B flat, Op. 99 (D898)
(*pf, vln & vlc*)
*D'Aranyi – Benedetti – Catterall – Fournier –
Heifetz – Holst – Menuhin – D. Oistrakh –
Pelliccia – Sammons – Schneider – Stern (2) –
Strub – Suk – Thibaud – Wolfsthal*
Trio No. 2, in E flat, Op. 100 (D929) (*pf, vln &
vlc*)
*A. Busch (2) – Fournier – Menuhin – D.
Oistrakh – Plocek – Röhn – Schneider – Strub –*

Totenberg – Wilk
Trio in B flat, D471 "Sonata in one movement"
(*vln, vla & vlc*) *Grumiaux – Kamper – Menuhin –
Silverstein*
Trio in B flat, D581 (*vln, vla & vlc*) *Grumiaux –
Kamper*
(12) Walzer, D145 (1815/21) (*pf*)
    Waltz No. 3, in a *Komissarov*
Schubert, Heinz (1908–1945)
Concertante Suite (*vln & cha orch*) *Stanske*
Schulhoff, Erwin (1894–1942)
Quartet No. 1 (*2 vlns, vla & vlc*) *Peška*
Schumacher, Paul
Concert Suite in G, Op. 34 (*vln & pf*)
    No. 2. Berceuse *P. Schumacher*
Schuman, William (1910–   )
Concerto (1947) (*vln & orch*) *Zukofsky*
Schumann, Clara (1819–1896)
Trio in g, Op. 17 (*pf, vln & vlc*) *Gimpel*
Schumann, Robert (1810–1856)
(20) Albumblätter, Op. 124 (*pf*)
    No. 6. Wiegenliedchen *Farbmann*
    No. 16. Schlummerlied *C. Brosa – W. Busch –
    Kersey – Ladscheck – Sänger – Spalding –
    Weismann*
Concerto in d (1853) (*vln & orch*) *Anonymous –
Kulenkampff – Menuhin – Rybar – Szeryng*
(4) Duets, Op. 34 (*s, t & pf*)
    No. 1. Liebesgarten *Sammons*
(4) Duets, Op. 78 (*s & t*)
    No. 4. Wiegenlied *Barmas – Buchtele*
(12) Duets, Op. 85 (*pf – 4 hands*)
    No. 3. Gartenmelodie *D'Aranyi – Hayward –
    Queling – Sammons – Spalding*
    No. 9. Am Springbrunnen *Morini*
    No. 12. Abendlied
    *Arany – Barmas – Darrieux – Deman – Elman
    – Fradkin – M. Hansen – Heller – F.V.
    Henriques – F.V. & J.F. Henriques – Josephi –
    Georg Kniestaedt – Kreisler – Kulenkampff –
    Lari – Lessmann – Menges – Milstein (2) –
    Ondříček – Přihoda – Queling – Spalding –
    Spivakovsky – Suk – Swaap – Ysaÿe*
Fantasia in C, Op. 131 (*vln & orch*) *Klimov – L.
Kogan – Stücki*
(3) Fantasiestücke, Op. 73 (*cl & pf*) *Akhtyamova –
Rybar*
Fantasiestücke, Op. 88 (*pf, vln & vlc*) *Asselin –
Catterall*
(13) Kinderscenen, Op. 15 (*pf*)
    No. 1. Von fremden Ländern und Menschen
    Barmas – Farbmann
    No. 7, Träumerei
    *Akos – d'Almaine (2) – d'Ambrosio –
    Andjelkovitch – Anemoyanni – Anonymous (2) –
    Barbieri – Berchmann – Bornfors – Breeskin –
    Buchtele – A. Busch – Catterall – Chauveton –
    Cochrane – Culbertson – Dajos – Darrieux – D.
    De Groot – Deman – Elman (5) – Eweler –
    Falk – Ferras – Flesch – Fradkin – Ghestem –
    Goldis – Gomez – Hager – Haxton (3) – Heber
    – F.V. Henriques – Herman – Iwamoto –
    Jacobsen – Josephi – Kaufman – Georg
    Kniestaedt – Kubelík – Kun – Lessmann –
    Levey – Lewis – Lichtenberg – Losowsky – Lusk*

*– Manén – Mantovani – Mariani – Michaïlow –
Milstein (2) – Modern – Moller – Nachèz –
Nadien – Neumann – Newe – Paget –
Plamondon – Powell – Příhoda (2) – Ranzato
(2) – Rattay – Reillie – R. Richter – Rosand –
A.J. Rose – Rosen – K. Rubens – Rudényi –
Sammons – Schmied – T. Seidel – Sens (2) –
Shumsky – Skalka – Spalding (2) – Telmányi –
Thibaud – Titze – Valesca-Becker – Vecsey (3) –
Weintraub – Weist-Hill – F. Weltmann –
Wolfsthal (2) – Zilzer – Zimbalist*
    No. 8. Am Camin *Wolfsthal*
(26) Myrthen, Op. 25 (*v & pf*)
    No. 1. Widmung *Heifetz*
    No. 3. Der Nussbaum *Debruille*
Quartet in E flat, Op. 47 (*pf, vln, vla & vlc*)
Goldberg – F. Reuter – Schneider – Shapiro
(3) Quartets, Op. 41 (*2 vlns, vla & vlc*)
    Quartet No. 2, in F *Catterall*
    Quartet No. 3, in A *Rybar*
Quintet in E flat, Op. 44 (*2 vlns, vla, vlc & pf*)
*Bress & Goodman – Gimpel & Wroński – Guidi –
Hayward – Pauk – Schneider & Stern*
(3) Romances, Op. 94 (*ob or vln, or vlc or cl & pf*)
    Romance* *Breeskin*
    Romance No. 1, in a *Ferras – Temianka*
    Romance No. 2, in A
    *Cochrane – Ferras – Gilels – Gorokhov –
    Grumlíková – Hamza – Kreisler – Menuhin –
    R. Ricci – Spalding – Staryk – Suk – Temianka
    – Zhuk*
    Romance No. 3, in a *Ferras*
Sonata (1853) "Frei aber Eisam" (*vln & pf*)
    Intermezzo (*2nd mvt*) *Bakman – Gottesmann –
    Milstein – Rybar – Šestak – Stern*
    Finale (*4th mvt*) *Bakman – Gottesmann – Stern*
Sonata No. 1, in a, Op. 105 (*vln & pf*)
    *Ajemian – Bonaldi – Bress – A. Busch –
    Chauveton – Doukan – Druian – Goldberg –
    Grumlíková – Hagen – Jarry – Kaufman –
    Kennedy – Komissarov – Morbitzer – Petroni –
    Rostal – Rybar – Wolfgang Schneiderhan (2) –
    Tryon – Zhuk*
Sonata No. 2, in d, Op. 121 (*vln & pf*)
    *Bonaldi – Bress – Doukan – Enescu –
    Komissarov – Menuhin – Rybar – Tryon –
    Zhuk*
Trio No. 1, in d, Op. 63 (*pf, vln & vlc*)
    *Gheorghiu – Gimpel – L. Kogan – Merckel –
    Schneider – Thibaud*
Trio No. 2. in F. Op. 80 (*pf, vln & vlc*) Bělčík –
Gruenberg
Trio No. 3, in g, Op. 110 (*pf, vln & vlc*) *Asselin –
Merckel*
(9) Waldscenen, Op. 82 (*pf*)
    No. 7. Vogel als Prophet
    *Anonymous – Brown (2) – Elman (2) –
    Francescatti – Heifetz – Ignatius-Hirvensalo – B.
    Koutzen – Stern – Szentgyörgi – Szeryng –
    Weissgerber*
Wie glücklich sie wardeln* *Press*

*Unidentified.

Schütt, Eduard (1856–1933)
(3) Marches, Op. 54 (*vln & pf*)
    Waltz No. 3 (*Allegro vivace*) *Sammons*
(4) Morceaux, Op. 52 (*vln & pf*)
    No. 2. Serenata *Dessau*
    No. 4. Mazurka *Dessau*
(3) Morceaux, Op. 53 (*vln & pf*)
    No. 1. Élégie slave *Kreisler*
Schütz, Heinrich (1585–1672)
(20) Symphoniae sacrae, Op. 6 (1629)
    Concerto No. 3, (*In te, Domine, speravi*)
    SWV259 (*a, vln, tbn & c*) *Lautenbacher*
    Concerto No. 5 (*Venite ad me*) SWV261 (*t, 2
    vlns & c*) *Keltsch & Lautenbacher*
    Concerto No. 9 (*O quam tu pulchra es*)
    SWV265 (*2 t's, 2 vlns & c*) *Borries – Keltsch &
    Lautenbacher*
    Concerto No. 10 (*Veni de Libano*) SWV266 (*2
    t's, 2 vlns & c*) *Borries – Keltsch &
    Lautenbacher*
(27) Symphoniae sacrae, Op. 10 (1647)
    Concerto No. 2 (*Singet dem Herren ein neues
    Lied*) SWV342 (*t, 2 vlns & c*) *Keltsch &
    Lautenbacher*
    Concerto No. 6 (*Ich werde nicht sterben*)
    SWV346 (*s, 2 vlns & c*) *Gunderson – Keltsch &
    Lautenbacher*
    Concerto No. 7 (*Ich danke dir, Herr*) SWV347
    (*s, 2 vlns & c*) *Keltsch & Lautenbacher*
    Concerto No. 8 (*Herzlich lieb hab ich dich, o
    Herr*) SWV348 (*a, 2 vlns or obs & c*) *Keltsch &
    Lautenbacher*
    Concerto No. 27 (*Freuet euch des Herrn, ihr
    Gerechten*) SWV367 (*2 t's, bs, 2 vlns & c*)
    Keltsch & Lautenbacher
(21) Symphoniae sacrae, Op. 12 (1650)
    Concerto No. 5 (*O Herr, hilf*) (*a, s, t, vln & c*)
    L. Hansen & Senderovitz
Schuurmann, Melchert
Vision (*vln & pf*) *Georg Kniestaedt*
Schwartz, Elliott (1936–   )
Aria No. 2 (*vln & drms*) *Furney*
Schytte, Ludwig (1848–1909)
(20) Promenades musicales, Op. 26 (*pf*)
    No. 7. Berceuse *P. Schumacher*
Scott, Cyril Meir (1879–1971)
Danse nègre, Op. 58, No. 5 (*pf*) *Heifetz –
Kennedy – Menuhin*
(5) Impressions from the Jungle Book (1912) (*pf*)
    No. 2. Dawn *Grach*
Lotus land, Op. 47, No. 1 (1905) (*pf*) *Fuchs –
Gorokhov – Gutnikov – Klimov – Kreisler (2) –
Markov – Wilkomirska*
Lullaby, Op. 57, No. 2 (*v & pf*) *Levey*
(2) Preludes, Op. 57 (1914) (*vln & pf*)
    No. 2. Danse *Kulenkampff*
Tallahassee Suite, Op. 73 (1910) (*vln & pf*)
    No. 1. Bygone memories *Heifetz*
    No. 2. After sundown *Zimbalist*
Valse triste, Op. 73, No. 3 (*vln & pf*) *Hayward –
Link*
Scott, Lady John Douglas (1810–1900)*

*Alicia Ann Spottiswoode.

Annie Laurie (1838) (*v & pf*) *Campoli – Gardner
– Hager – Kreisler – Rudényi (2) – Southgate –
Williams*

Scriabin, Alexander Nikolayevich (1872–1915)
(12) Etudes, Op. 8 (*pf*)
  Etude No. 10, in D flat "Etude in thirds" *D.
  Oistrakh – Rabin – J. Szigeti*
  Etude No. 11, in B flat *Fichtenholz – I.
  Oistrakh – Pikaizen*
(8) Etudes, Op. 42 (*pf*)
  Etude No. 7, in f sharp *Fichtenholz*
(9) Mazurkas, Op. 25 (*pf*)
  Mazurka No. 1, in f *Malinin*
(2) Nocturnes, Op. 5 (*pf*)
  Nocturne No. 1, in f sharp *Goldstein –
  Liberman – Malinin – D. Oistrakh (3) –
  Pikaizen*
(3) Pieces, Op. 45 (1907) (*pf*)
  No. 1. Album leaf in E flat *Malinin*
Waltz in A flat, Op. 38 (*pf*) *Malinin*

Sculthorpe, Peter (1929–   )
Irkanda IV (1961) (*vln & orch*) *Dommett*

Sealy, Helen
Pekinese (*vln & pf*) *Sealy*
Rosemary (*vln & pf*) *Sealy*
Sybilla (*vln & pf*) *Sealy*

Seidler-Winkler, Bruno (1880–1960)
Gavotte in C (*vln & pf*) *Dessau – Gyarfas*
Romance in G (*vln & pf*) *Meine & Sens*
Scherzo in A (*vln & pf*) *Dessau – Sens*
Wiegenliedchen (*vln & pf*) *Dessau – Sens*

Seitz, Ernest (1893–   )
(The) World is waiting for the sunrise (1919) (*v &
pf*) *Kreisler – Morrell*

Seitz, Friedrich (1848–1918)
Concertino No. 5, in D, Op. 22 (*vln & pf*)
Shermont

Semenoff, Ivan (1917–   )
Concerto "Double" (*vln, pf & orch*) *Ferras*

Senaillié, Jean-Baptiste (1687–1730)
(10) Sonatas – Book I (1710) (*vln or fl & c*)
  Sonata No. 4, in E *Grabowska*
  Sonata No. 9, in g *Klijn*

Serly, Tibor (1900–   )
Sonata (1947) "In Modus Lascivus" (*solo vln*)
Magnes

Serradell, Narciso
(La) Golondrina (*v & pf*) *Lipschultz*

Serrano, Emilio (1850–1939)
(La) Canción del Olvido (1916) – zarzuela
  Canción de Marinella *Menuhin*

Serratos
Etude in octaves (*vln & pf*) *Szeryng*

Sessions, Roger (1896–   )
Concerto (1935) (*vln & orch*) *Zukofsky*
Duo (1942) (*vln & pf*) *Travers*
Sonata (1953) (*vln & pf*) *Bress*

Ševčík, Otakar (1852–1934)
(6) Bohemian Dances, Op. 10 (*vln & pf*)
  No. 1. Blue-eyed maiden (*Holka modrooká*)
  Kawaciuk (2)
  No. 2. Dance in G *Bělčík*
  No. 3. Dance in f sharp *Šroubek*
  No. 4. Fantasia in G *Bělčík*
  No. 5. Czech song (*Bretislav*) *Bratza –*

Kawaciuk
  No. 6. Furiant *Šroubek*

Sgambati, Giovanni (1841–1914)
(2) Pieces, Op. 24 (*vln & pf*)
  No. 2. Serenata napoletana *Collier – Heifetz –
  Kubelík – Lorand – Pilzer – Poltronieri*

Shamo, Igor Naumovich (1925–   )
Sinfoniette-Concerto (*vln, pf, bayan, cel & cha
orch*) *Kushnir*

Shankar, Ravi (1920–   )
Prabhāti (*based on Rāga Gunkali*) (*vln & tabla*)*
Menuhin
Raga Piloo (*vln, sitar & tabla*)† *Menuhin*
Swara-Kakali (*based on Raga Tilang*)
(*vln & sitar*)* *Menuhin*

Shannon, James Royce (1881–1946)
That's an Irish lullaby (*Too-ra-loo-ra-loo-ral*)
(1914) (*v & pf*) *Brown*

Shapey, Ralph (1921–   )
Evocation (1959) (*vln, pf & pcn*) *Raimondi*

Sharpe, Anna Wright (1914–   )
One little hour (*v & pf*) *Southgate*

Shaverzashvili, Alexander (1919–   )
Concerto in E (*vln & orch*) *Yashvili*

Shchedrin, Rodion Konstantinovich
(1932–   )
Humoresque (*pf*) *Malinin – Tretyakov*
(The) Hump-backed Horse (1959) – ballet (*orch*)
  No. 1. Balalaika *Grach – Snitkovsky*
  No. 2. Adagietto *Snitkovsky*
  No. 3. Jesters' dance *Snitkovsky*
In imitation of Albéniz (*pf*) *Kremer – Malinin –
Spivakov – Tretyakov*

Shebalin, Vissarion Yakovlevich (1902–1963)
Concerto in G, Op. 21 (*vln & orch*) *Zhuk*

Sher, V.
Fantasia (*on themes from Prokofiev's opera "War
& Peace"*) (*vln & pf*) *Komissarov*

Shifrin, Seymour (1926–   )
Satires of Circumstance (1964) (*m-s, fl, pic, cl, vln,
vlc, cbs & pf*) *Zukofsky*

Shnitke, A. (1934–   )
Sonata (1965) (*vln & pf*) *Lubotsky*

Shostakovich, Dmitri (1906–   )
(The) Age of Gold, Op. 22 (1930) – ballet (*orch*)
  Polka *Erlih – Francescatti – Wicks*
Concerto No. 1, in a, Op. 99 (1955) (*vln & orch*)
L. Kogan – D. Oistrakh (2)
Concerto No. 2, in c sharp, Op. 129 (1967) (*vln &
orch*) *D. Oistrakh*
(3) Danses fantastiques, Op. 5 (1922) (*pf*) *Feigin –
Heifetz – Pratz – Vilker*
(The) Gadfly – film music (*orch*)
  Romance *Kemlin*
Pirogov (*Suite from music to the film*) Op. 76a

*Cadenza in 2nd mvt. improvised by Menuhin.

†Composed for the United Nations Human Rights
Day concert, December 10th 1967 where it was
first performed by Shankar & Menuhin.

(*orch*)
  No. 1. Introduction *A. Levin & Zaks*
(24) Preludes, Op. 34 (1932/3) (*pf*)
  Prelude No. 1, in C *Lantsman – Mikhlin –
  Sobolevsky*
  Prelude No. 2, in a *Gutnikov – Malinin –
  Sobolevsky*
  Prelude No. 3, in G *Lantsman – Mikhlin –
  Sobolevsky*
  Prelude No. 5, in D *Lantsman – Mikhlin –
  Sobolevsky*
  Prelude No. 6, in b *Gutnikov – Malinin –
  Sobolevsky*
  Prelude No. 8, in f sharp *Lantsman – Mikhlin –
  Sobolevsky*
  Prelude No. 10, in c sharp
  *Gutnikov – Heifetz – Klimov (2) – L. Kogan (2)
  – Korsakov – Mikhlin – Sitkovetsky (2) –
  Sobolevsky – Wicks – Wilk – Zhuk*
  Prelude No. 11, in B *Lantsman – Mikhlin –
  Sobolevsky*
  Prelude No. 12, in g sharp *Gutnikov – Malinin
  – Sobolevsky*
  Prelude No. 13, in F sharp *Gutnikov – Malinin
  – Sobolevsky*
  Prelude No. 15, in D flat *Gutnikov – Heifetz –
  Klimov (2) – L. Kogan (2) – Korsakov –
  Mikhlin – Sitkovetsky (2)*
  Prelude No. 16, in b flat *Klimov – L. Kogan (2)
  – Korsakov – Mikhlin – Sitkovetsky (2) –
  Sobolevsky – Wicks – Zhuk*
  Prelude No. 17, in A flat *Gutnikov – Malinin –
  Sobolevsky*
  Prelude No. 18, in f *Gutnikov – Malinin –
  Sobolevsky*
  Prelude No. 19, in E flat *Gutnikov – Malinin –
  Sobolevsky*
  Prelude No. 20, in c *Gutnikov – Malinin –
  Sobolevsky*
  Prelude No. 21, in B flat *Gutnikov – Malinin –
  Sobolevsky*
  Prelude No. 22, in g *Gutnikov – Malinin –
  Sobolevsky*
  Prelude No. 24, in d
  *Gutnikov – Klimov – L. Kogan (2) – Korsakov –
  Mikhlin – Sitkovetsky – Sobolevsky – Wicks –
  Wilk – Zhuk*
Quartet No. 1, in C, Op. 49 (*2 vlns, vla & vlc*)
Klijn
Quartet No. 2, in A, Op. 69 (*2 vlns, vla & vlc*)
Schulz
Quartet No. 3, in F, Op. 73 (*2 vlns, vla & vlc*)
Sitkovetsky
Quartet No. 4, in D, Op. 83 (*2 vlns, vla & vlc*)
Danchenko → Malinin – Sitkovetsky
Quintet in g, Op. 57 (*pf, 2 vlns, vla & vlc*) *Gimpel
& Wroński*
Satirical dance (*vln & pf*) *Kolberg*
Sonata, Op. 134 (*vln & pf*) *D. Oistrakh*
Trio No. 2, in e, Op. 67 "In memory of I.I.
Sollertinsky" (*pf, vln & vlc*) *Bezrodny – Compinsky
– D. Oistrakh – Plocek – Vaiman*
Zoya (*Suite from music to the film*) Op. 64a
(*orch*)
  No. 1. Introduction (*Song about Zoya*) *A. Levin*

& Zaks

Shtogarenko, Andrei Yakovlevich
(1902–   )
Trio "Youth" (*pf, vln & vlc*) *Gorokhov*
Shubanov, A.
Aria (*vln & pf*) *Tolganbayev*
Shubayev
Romance (*vln & pf*) *Tolganbayev*
Shulman, Alan M. (1915–   )
Suite American "Folksong suite" (*vln & pf*)
    Cod liver 'ile *Heifetz*
Sibelius, Jean Julian Christian (1865–1957)
Belshazzar's Feast, Op. 51 – Incidental music
(*orch*)
    No. 3. Nocturne "Night song" *Heifetz –*
    Ladscheck – Press
(4) Compositions, Op. 115 (*vln & pf*)
    No. 1. Moods of the moor *Ignatius-Hirvensalo*
Concerto in d, Op. 47 (*vln & orch*)
    Andrade – Bustabo – Chung – Dahmen – Eidus
    – Ferras – Francescatti – Gimpel – Gitlis –
    Heifetz (2) – Ignatius-Hirvensalo – Kóté –
    Kulenkampff – Magyar – Menuhin – Neveu –
    D. Oistrakh (4) – Perlman – R. Ricci –
    Rüthström – Sitkovetsky – Spivakovsky – Stern
    (2) – Szeryng (2) – Telmányi – Ushioda –
    Vaiman – Wicks
(5) Danses champêtres, Op. 106 (*vln & pf*)
    Danse champêtre No. 1, in d *Telmányi*
    Danse champêtre No. 2, in G *Telmányi*
(2) Humoresques, Op. 87b (*vln & orch*)
    No. 1. Humoresque No. 1, in d *D. Oistrakh –*
    Rosand
    No. 2. Humoresque No. 2, in D *D. Oistrakh –*
    Rosand
(4) Humoresques, Op. 89 (*vln & orch*)
    No. 1. Humoresque No. 3, in g *Rosand*
    No. 2. Humoresque No. 4, in g *Gimpel –*
    Rosand
    No. 3. Humoresque No. 5, in E flat *Rosand*
    No. 4. Humoresque No. 6, in g *Rosand –*
    Temianka
King Christian II, Op. 27 – Incidental music
(*orch*)
    Musette *Powell*
Kuolema, Op. 44 – Incidental music (*orch*)
    Valse triste
    Elman – Law – Powell – Schmied – T. Seidel –
    Spalding – J. Szigeti – Traversa – Zilzer
Novelette, Op. 102 (*vln & pf*) *Krysa*
Pan & Echo, Op. 53 (*orch*)
    No. 3. Nocturne *Krysa – Moguilevski – Vecsey*
(2) Pieces, Op. 2 (*vln & pf*)
    No. 2. Epilogue *Kaufman*
(4) Pieces, Op. 78 (*vln & pf*)
    No. 2. Romance in F *Aro – Asti – Cronvall –*
    Eweler – Gimpel – Ignatius-Hirvensalo –
    Telmányi – Zilzer
(5) Pieces, Op. 81 (*vln & pf*)
    No. 1. Mazurka *Elman – Gimpel –*
    Ignatius-Hirvensalo (2) – E.B. Nielsen
    No. 3. Valse *Cronvall*
(2) Serenades, Op. 69 (*vln & orch*)
    Serenade No. 1, in d (1912) *Bezrodny*
    Serenade No. 2, in g (1913) *Bezrodny*

Sonatina in E, Op. 80 (*vln & pf*) *Holst*
(The) Tempest, Op. 109 (1926) – Incidental music
(*orch*) *Cronvall*
Sieczynski, R.
Wien, mina drömmars stad (*v & pf*) *Jelving*
Siegmeister, Elie (1909–   )
Sonata No. 3 (1965) (*vln & pf*) *I. Cohen*
Silésu, Lao (1883–   )
(A) Little love, a little kiss (1912) (*v & pf*)
    Andjelkovitch – Dobrinski – Förster – Haxton –
    Mantovani – Selinsky – Southgate – Zacharewitsch
Love, here is my heart (*v & pf*) *Rubini*
Sérénade passionnée (*v & pf*) *Schwartz*
Star of my life (*v & pf*) *Lensky*
Silvestri, Giuseppe (1841–1921)
Sérénade d'autrefois (*pf*) *Rappaini – di Piramo*
Serenata medioevale (*pf*) *Ranzato*
Simbriger, Heinrich (1903–   )
Sonata, Op. 110 (1965) (*vln & pf*) *Hagemann*
Simon, Anton (1850–1916)
(2) Pieces, Op. 17 (*vln & pf*)
    No. 2. Berceuse *Kobin – Maurice – Ranzato*
Simonetti, Achille (1859–1928)
Berceuse (*vln & pf*) *Senatra*
Madrigale (*pf*)
    Ahberg – d'Albore – Aranyi – Asti – Bonnemain
    – Borries – Buchtele – Chemet – Curti (2) –
    Darrieux – F. De Groot – Eweler – Falk –
    Farbmann – Galli – Hayward – Ladscheck –
    Lass – Maurice – Mossel – R. Pollak – Příhoda
    – Ranzato (2) – Rattay – A.J. Rose (2) – T.
    Seidel – Sens – Thibaud – Wolfsthal – Wolters
    – Zimbalist
Recitativo, Chorale & Cadenza (*vln & pf*)
Pierangeli
Simons, Moisés (1888–1944)
Marta (1931) (*v & pf*) *A. Sandler*
Sinding, Christian (1856–1941)
(3) Elegiac pieces, Op. 106 (*vln & pf*)
    No. 3. Andante religioso (*Canto patetico*)
    Burmester
(6) Pieces, Op. 32 (*pf*)
    No. 3. Frühlingsrauschen "Rustle of spring"
    Hayward – Michaïlow
(4) Pieces, Op. 61 (*vln & pf*)
    No. 1. Prelude *Link*
    No. 2. Elegy *Link*
(3) Pieces, Op. 89 (*vln & pf*)
    No. 2. Alte Weise *Barkel*
    No. 3. Abendlied *Tellefsen*
(2) Romances, Op. 79 (*vln & pf*)
    No. 1. Romance *M. Hall – Tellefsen*
Serenade No. 1, in G, Op. 56 (*2 vlns & pf*)
    D'Aranyi & Fachiri – Brown & Totenberg – F.V.
    & J.F. Henriques
Suite in a, Op. 10 (*vln & pf or orch*) *Heifetz*
Singalée, Jean Baptiste (1812–1875)
Fantasia (*on themes from Bellini's opera "I*
Lombardi") Op. 28 "Jérusalem Fantaisie" (*vln &*
pf) *Kneisel*
Fantasia (*on themes from Hérold's opera "Le Pré*
aux Clercs") Op. 24 (*vln & pf*) *Mendels*
Fantasia (*on themes from Verdi's opera "Il*
Trovatore") Op. 94 (*vln & pf*) *Sens*
Sinigaglia , Leone (1868–1944)

(4) Kleine Stücke, Op. 25 (*vln & pf*)
    No. 2. Capriccio all'antica *Cochrane – Elman –*
    M. Hall – Vecsey
    No. 3. Bagatelle *Elman*
Rapsodie piemontese, Op. 26 (*vln & pf*)
Havemann – Sammons
Sitt, Hans (1850–1922)
Souvenir Suite, Op. 105 (*vln & pf*)
    Saltarella (*4th mvt*) *Link*
(3) Trios, Op. 63 (*pf, vln & vlc*)
    Trio No. 1, in G *Kayser*
Sivori, Ernesto Camillo (1815–1894)
(2) Romanzas senza paroles, Op. 23 (*vln & pf*)
F.V. Henriques – Kneisel – Lari
Sjöberg, Carl Leopold (1861–1900)
Tonerna (*vln & pf*) *W. Andersen – Bornfors*
Sjögren, Emil (1853–1918)
Sonata No. 1, in g, Op. 19 (*vln & pf*) *Baranowski*
Sonata No. 2, in e, Op. 24 (*vln & pf*) *Andreasson*
– Baranowski – Berlin – Jelving
Skalkottas, Nikos (1904–1949)
(4) Greek dances (*vln & pf*) *Kolassis*
(8) Variations on a Greek folk tune (1938) (*vln,*
vlc & pf) *Masters*
Sköld, Sven (1899–1956)
Canzonetta (*vln & pf*) *Reinholdsson*
Melodi (*vln & pf*) *Kyndel*
Skorzeny, Fritz (1900–   )
Fantasie-Sonata (*in memoriam to Ginette Neveu*)
(*vln & pf*) *Zsigmondy*
Škroup, František Jan (1801–1862)
Kde domov muj (1834) (*v & pf*)* *Lusk*
Skulte, A. (1909–   )
Symphonic pictures (*from the film "Rainis"*) (*vln*
& orch with cl obb) *Birznieks*
Slavenski, Josip (1896–
Sonata, Op. 5 (*vln & pf*) *Baloković – Pavlovic*
Slavický, Klement (1910–   )
Partita (*solo vln*) *I. Štraus*
Slavik, Josef (1806–1833)
Concerto No. 2, in a "Unfinished" (*vln & orch*)
    Allegro (*1st mvt*)† *Gutnikov – Plocek*
Smetana, Bedřich (1824–1884)
(The) Bartered Bride (1866) – opera
    No. 5. As my mother blessed me ... Faithful
    love *Mánnok*
    No. 28. Think it over, Mařenka *Lusk*
From my Homeland (1878) (*vln & pf*) *Baloković –*
Kawaciuk – Plocek – Straka – Suk
    No. 1. Moderato *Elman – Kulenkampff*
    No. 2. Andantino
    Ast – Barinova – Bezrodny – Bratza – Buchtele
    – Elman (3) – Flesch – Fuchs – Godwin –
    Grinke – Gutnikov – Margaret Harrison –
    Kreisler – Milstein (2) – Odnoposoff – Pikaizen
    – Příhoda – R. Ricci – Wolfsthal
Quartet No. 1, in e (1876) "From my life" (*2 vlns,*
vla & vlc) *Bucia – Eidus – Klijn*
Trio in g, Op. 15 (*pf, vln & vlc*) *Eidus – Freund –*

*Czech National anthem.

†Only the Allegro exists.

Kaufman – D. Oistrakh – Plocek – Suk (2)
Smith, K.L.
Puritan Lullaby – musical
   Always *A. Sandler*
Smith, Leland (1925–   )
Trio (*vln, vla & vlc*) *Rubin*
Smith, Walter (1887–   )
Havana moon (*v & pf*) *Ball*
Smith, William O. (1926–   )
Capriccio (1952) (*vln & pf*) *Rubin*
Ecloque (*vln & pf*) *Loft*
Suite (1952) (*vln & cl*) *Rubin*
Söderman, August Johann (1832–1870)
Swedish wedding march, Op. 12 (*vln & pf*) *de Grassi*
Soler, Padre Antonio (1729–1783)
(6) Quintets (*2 vlns, vla, vlc & org or pf*)
   Quintet No. 6, in g *Fernandez & Germaine Raymond*
(3) Sonatas (*vln & pf*)* *Kooper*
Somers, Harry Stewart (1925–   )
Rhapsody (1948) (*vln & pf*) *Pach*
Sonata No. 1 (1953) (*vln & pf*) *Hidy*
Sonata No. 2 (1955) (*vln & pf*) *Staryk*
Sommer, Vladimír (1921–   )
Concerto in g, Op. 10 (*vln & orch*) *Jásek*
Soproni, Jozsef (1930–   )
Ovidii Metamorphoses (*v, vln, cho & orch*) *Ney*
Sorbi, J.B. (15th century)
Fiori sparsi (*Scattered flowers*) *Curti*
Soro, Enrique (1884–   )
Serenatella (*vln & pf*) *D'Andurain*
Souris, André (1899–   )
(3) Ancient pieces (*vln & vla*) *L. Bobescu*
Southgate, Dorothy (1889–1946)
Dorothy's lullaby (*vln & org*) *Southgate*
Mispah (*vln & org*) *Southgate*
Sérénade espagnole (*vln & org*) *Southgate*
Thanksgiving (*vln & org*)† *Southgate*
Southgate, Elsie
Thanksgiving (*vln & org*)‡ *Southgate*
Valse Egyptienne (*vln & org*) *Southgate*
Southgate, E.D.
(The) Butterfly (*vln & org*) *Southgate*
Southgate, F.S.
Dance of the elves (*vln & org*) *Southgate*
Pleading (*vln & org*) *Southgate*
Rêve d'amour (*vln & org*) *Southgate*
Southgate, S.
Inspiration (*vln & org*) *Southgate*
Spalding, Albert (1888–1953)
Alabama (*Plantation melody*) (*vln & pf*) *Spalding – Zimbalist*
Dragonfly (*A study in arpeggios*) (*solo vln*) *Spalding*
Etchings, Op. 5 (*vln & pf*)

*Unidentified.

†Composed jointly with Elsie Southgate.

‡Composed jointly with Dorothy Southgate.

Books *Spalding*
Cinderella *Spalding*
Desert twilight *Spalding*
Dreams *Spalding*
Fireflies *Spalding*
Games *Spalding*
Ghosts *Spalding*
Happiness *Spalding*
Hurdy-gurdy waltz *Spalding (2)*
Impatience *Spalding*
October *Spalding*
Professor *Spalding*
Sunday morning bells *Spalding (2)*
From the cottonfields, Op. 7, No. 3 (*vln & pf*) *Spalding*
Sonata in e (*solo vln*) *Spalding*
(The) Wind in the pines (*Prelude*) (*vln & pf*) *Spalding*
Spencer, Herbert (1878–1944)
Underneath the stars (*v & pf*) *Kreisler*
Spendiarov, Alexander Afanasievich (1871–1928)
Crimean sketches, Op. 9 (*orch*)
   No. 4. Kaitarna *Vladigerov*
Dance of the Tartars (*vln & pf*) *B. Schwarz*
(2) Stücke, Op. 3 (*orch*)
   No. 2. Berceuse *Lorand*
Spier, Larry (1901–1956)
Memory lane (1924) (*v & pf*)* *Fradkin*
Spies, Ernst
Elfentanz in D, Op. 62 (*vln & pf*) *Kocián*
Polonaise, Op. 34 (*vln & pf*) *Amrhein*
Spohr, Ludwig (1784–1859)
Concerto No. 7, in e, Op. 38 (*vln & orch*) *Shulz*
Concerto No. 8, in a, Op. 47 "Gesangsscene" (*vln & orch*)
   Borries – Bress – Field – Heifetz – Koeckert – Kulenkampff – Lautenbacher – Spalding – Stiehler
Concerto No. 9, in d, Op. 55 (*vln & orch*) *Bress – Soldat*
(3) Duets, Op. 39 (*2 vlns*)
   Duet No. 1, in d *D'Aranyi & Fachiri – Bridge & Catterall – Menuhin*
(3) Duets, Op. 67 (*2 vlns*)
   Duet No. 2, in D *D'Aranyi & Fachiri – De Vito & Menuhin*
   Duet No. 3, in g *De Vito & Menuhin – D. & I. Oistrakh*
Grand Duo in e, Op. 13 (*vln & vla*) *Lautenbacher*
Nonet in F, Op. 31 (*fl, cl, ob, bsn, hrn, vln, vla, vlc & 2 cbs*) *Eidus*
(2) Potpourris (*on airs from the opera "Jessonda"*) Op. 64 (*vln, vlc & orch*) *Lautenbacher*
Quartet No. 1, in d, Op. 65 "Double Quartet" (*4 vlns, 2 vlas & 2 vlcs*) *Baker & Heifetz*
Trio in F, Op. 123 (*pf, vln & vlc*) *Csaba*
Spoliansky, Mischa (1898–   )
Serenade (*vln & pf*) *Weismann*
Tango habañera (*vln & pf*) *Weismann*
Squire, William Henry (1871–1963)
Fantaisie hongrois (*vlc & pf*) *Levey*
Srnka, Jiří (1907–   )

*See: **Conrad**, Con

Concerto dramatique (*vln & orch*) *Snítil*
Staden, Johann (1581–1634)
Pavane (*vln, 2 vlas & gamba*) *Thoene*
Stadlmair, Hans (1929–   )
Concerto (*vln & strs*) *David*
Stainer, John (1840–1901)
(The) Daughter of Jairus (1878) – oratorio
   Love divine, all love excelling *Elman*
Stamitz, Johann Wenzl Anton (1717–1757)
Divertimento No. 2, in G (*solo vln*) *Staryk*
Stamitz, Karl (1745–1801)
Concerto in B flat (*vln & orch*) *Milstein*
Concerto in D (*vln, vla, ob & orch*) *Mayer-Schierning*
(6) Duets, Op. 18 (*vln & vla*)
   Duet No. 5, in F *Kussmaul*
(6) Quartets, Op. 4 (1787) (*2 vlns, vla & vlc*)
   Quartet No. 4, in F *Fournier*
(4) Quartets, Op. 8 (*ob or cl, vln, vla & vlc*)
   Quartet No. 4, in E flat *Kussmaul (2)*
Sinfonia in E flat (*vln, vla & orch*) *Grehling*
Sinfonia concertante in A (*vln, vla, vlc & orch*) *Maier*
Sinfonia concertante in D (*vln, vla & orch*) *Grehling – Hendel & Makanowitzky – Lautenbacher*
(3) Trios, Op. 14 (*fl, vln & c*)
   Trio No. 1, in G *Kussmaul*
Trio in G (*2 fls & vlc*) *Nölting*
Stanford, Charles Villiers (1852–1924)
(4) Irish Dances, Op. 89 (*vln & pf*)
   No. 3. Leprechaun's dance *Menges*
Starer, Robert (1924–   )
Variants (*vln & pf*) *Buswell*
Statkovski, Roman (1859–1925)
Cracovienne, Op. 7 "Krakowiak" (*vln & pf*) *S. Furer – Parkhomenko*
Steane, Bruce Harry Dennis (1866–   )
Love's pleading (*v & pf*) *Hayward*
Steffani, Agostino (1654–1728)
Enrico Leone (1689) – opera
   Lo consolo i cori amanti *Sadowski*
Stehl, George
Tyrolean echoes (*vln, fl & hp*) *Stehl*
Stein, Leon (1910–   )
Sonata (*solo vln*) *Moll*
Sonata (*vln & pf*) *Moll*
Stenhammar, Vilhelm Eugen (1871–1927)
(2) Sentimental romances, Op. 28 (1910) (*vln & orch*)
   Sentimental romance No. 1, in A *Asti*
   Sentimental romance No. 2, in f *Kyndel*
Sonata in a, Op. 19 (*vln & pf*) *Saulesco*
Stevens, Bernard George (1916–   )
Fantasia on a theme of Dowland, Op. 23 (1953) (*vln & pf*) *Holst*
Stevenson, Sir John Andrew (1761–1833)
Oft in the stilly night (*v & pf*) *Stehl*
Stewart, Sir Robert Prescott (1825–1894)
Capriccietto (*vln & pf*) *Allan*
Ecstasy (*vln & pf*) *Allan*
(La) Lettre d'amour – valse tzigane (*vln & pf*) *de Monge*
Stich, Jan Václav (1746–1803)
Quartet (*hrn, vln, vla & vlc*) *Posselt*

Quintet (*3 fls, vln & vlc*) *Pougnet*
Still, William Grant (1895–   )
Carmela *Kaufman*
Lenox Avenue Suite (1937) (*orch*) *Kaufman (2)*
Pastorela (1946) (*vln & orch*) *Kaufman*
Suite (1943) (*vln & pf*) *Kaufman*
(3) Visions (1936) (*pf*)
    No. 2. Summerland *Kaufman*
Stoessel, Albert Frederic (1894–1943)
Suite antique (1922) (*2 vlns & cha orch*) *Brown & Stoessel*
Stolz, Robert (1880–   )
Donne-moi ton coeur ce soir (*v & pf*) *Curti*
(The) Melody that haunts my heart (*orch*) *Corigliano*
Stone, David (1922–   )
(8) Pieces (*in the 3rd position*) (*vln & pf*)
    Festive dance *Bean*
    March in D *Bean*
Storey, Buddy*
Stoyanov, Veselin (1902–   )
Sonata in f sharp (*vln & pf*) *Schneidermann*
Stradella, Alessandro (1642–1682)
Preghiera (*v & viols*) *Ranzato*
(2) Sonatas "Sinfonias" (*vln, vlc & bs*)
    Sonata No. 1, in d *Gulli – Thomsen*
(8) Sonatas "Sinfonias" (*2 vlns & concertino*)
    Sonata No. 1, in a (*2 vlns, vlc, cbs, lute & hpsi*) *Carles & Fernandez*
    Sonata No. 2, in G (*2 vlns, vlc, strs & org*) *Carles & Fernandez*
    Sonata No. 3, in D (*2 vlns, vlc, hpsi, 2 tpts, tbn & org*) *Carles & Fernandez*
    Sonata No. 5, in F (*2 vlns, vlc & lute*) *Carles & Fernandez*
Strange, Paul
Birds in the forest (*pf*) *Levy & Rattay*
Stransky, Josef (1872–1936)
Kaddisch (*vlc & pf*) *Boulanger*
Straus, Ĥugo
Frühlings-serenade, Op. 52 (*vln & pf*) *Georg Kniestaedt*
Straus, Oscar (1870–1954)
Suite, Op. 4 (*pf, vln & vlc*) *Dessau*
(Ein) Walzertraum (1907) – operetta
    selection *Curti*
Strauss, Johann (II) (1825–1899)
An der schönen, blauen Donau – waltz, Op. 314 (*orch*) *Manuello*
(Die) Fledermaus (1874) – operetta
    Trinke Liebchen, trinke schnell *Curti*
G'schichten aus dem Wiener Wald, Op. 325 (*orch*) *Godowsky – T. Seidel*
Morgenblätter – waltz, Op. 279 (*orch*) *Manuello*
One day when we were young (*v & orch*)†
T. Seidel
There will come a time (*v & orch*)†*T. Seidel*
Waltz† *Zeiler*
Wiener Blut, Op. 354 (*orch*) *Dinicu*
Strauss, Richard (1864–1949)

*See: **Caddigan,** Jack J.
†These adaptations were featured in the 1939 film "The Great Waltz."

Also sprach Zarathustra, Op. 30 (1896) (*orch*)
Boskovsky – Nadien – Schwalbé
Concerto in d, Op. 8 (1882) (*vln & orch*) *Borries – Glenn*
Don Juan, Op. 20 (1888) (*orch*) *Georg Kniestaedt – Staryk*
Don Quixote, Op. 35 (1897) (*orch*) *Borries – Burgin – Druian – Guilet – Hilsberg – Nadien – Piastro – Temianka – Weicher*
(Ein) Heldenleben, Op. 40 (1898) (*orch*)
    Boskovsky – Brusilow – Chernyakhovsky – Druian – Frisina – Guidi – Hilsberg – Krachmalnick – Krebbers – Maguire – Morasch – Schwalbé – Silverstein – Staryk – Weicher
(8) Lieder, Op. 10 (*v & pf*)
    No. 8. Allerseelen *Jacobs*
(4) Lieder, Op. 27 (*v & pf*)
    No. 4. Morgen *A. Brosa – Campoli – Eweler – Margaret Harrison – Kreisler – Menges – Sänger*
(3) Lieder, Op. 29 (*v & pf*)
    No. 1. Traum durch die Dämmerung *Bisztriczky*
Quartet in A, Op. 2 (*2 vlns, vla & vlc*) *Danchenko & Grach*
Quartet in c, Op. 13 (*pf, vln, vla & vlc*) *J.C. Figueroa – Grach*
(Der) Rosenkavalier, Op. 59 (1911) – opera
    Suite (*Überreichung der Silber-Rose*) (*orch*) *A.J. Rose*
    Waltzes (*Act II*) *Borries – Dessau – A. Ferraresi – Příhoda (2)*
Sonata in E flat, Op. 18 (*vln & pf*)
    Agaronyan – Campoli – Deman – Fuchs – Glenn – Heifetz (2) – Kaufman – Koeckert – L. Kogan – Neveu – R. Ricci (2) – Wolfgang Schneiderhan – Tryon – Weisman – Wiener – Zimmermann
(5) Stimmungsbilder, Op. 9 (*pf*)
    No. 2. An einsamer Quelle *Heifetz*
Till Eulenspiegels lustige Streiche, Op. 28 (1895) (*orch*) *Borries – Schwalbé – Staryk*
Stravinsky, Igor (1882–   )
Apollon Musagète (1928) – ballet (*orch*) *Schwalbé*
(Le) Baiser de la Fée (1928) – ballet (*orch*)
    Ballade *Gautier*
(Le) Chant du rossignol (1919) – ballet (*orch*) *Dushkin*
Concertino (1920) (*2 vlns, vla & vlc*) *Amar*
Concerto in D (1931) (*vln & orch*)
    Bress – Dushkin – Gitlis – Grumiaux – D. Oistrakh – Wolfgang Schneiderhan – Silverstein – Spivakovsky – Stern
Divertissement (*vln & pf*)*
Akhtyamova – Goldstein – Haendel (2) – Shapiro – Totenberg
Double Canon (1939) (*2 vlns, vla & vlc*) *Baker*
Duo concertante (1932) (*vln & pf*)
    Bress – Devries – Dushkin – Fuchs – Gitlis – Kaufman – Messiereur – Pikaizen – Rostal – Schmahl – Wolfgang Schneiderhan – Shapiro –

* An arrangement by Dushkin & Stravinsky of the Concert Suite from the ballet "Le Baiser de la Fée."

J. Szigeti (2)
Élégie (1944) (*solo vla or vln*) *Erlih – Gautier – Ostrovsky – R. Ricci*
Firebird (1910) – ballet suite (*orch*)
    No. 3. Jeu des princesses avec les pommes d'or *Dushkin – Snitkovsky*
    No. 5. Berceuse*
    Dushkin – Heifetz – Milstein (2) – Stern – T. Varga
(L') Histoire du Soldat (1918) (*narrators, tpt, cbs, tbn, cl, vln, bsn & pcn*)†
Alès – Baker – Chumachenko – Darrieux – Maguire – V. Martin – Schneider – H. Sorkin – Tomasow
In Memoriam Dylan Thomas (1954) (*t, 4 tbns, 2 vlns, vla & vlc*) *Babitz & Baker*
(3) Japanese Lyrics (1913) (*s, 2 fls, 2 cls, 2 vlns, vla, vlc & pf*) *Baker*
Mavra (1922) – opera
    Russian maiden's song (*Parasha's aria*)
    Accardo – Barinova – Beilina – L. Bobescu – A. Ferraresi – Grach – Lewkowitz – Milstein (2) – Neste – E.B. Nielsen – Wolfgang Schneiderhan – J. Szigeti – Vilker
Orphée (1947) – ballet (*orch*) *Gruenberg*
Pastorale (1908) (*v & pf*) *Dushkin – Erlih – J. Szigeti (3)*
Pétrouchka (1911) – ballet (*orch*)
    Danse russe
    Barinova – Dushkin – Erlih – Gimpel – Haendel (3) – Wolfgang Schneiderhan – Snitkovsky – J. Szigeti – Vilker
(3) Pieces (1914) (*2 vlns, vla & vlc*) *Ghestem*
(2) Poems of Balmont (1911) (*s, 2 fls, 2 cls, 2 vlns, vla, vlc & pf*) *Baker*
Rag-time (1918) (*fl, cl, hrn, tpt, tbn, cym, cymb, 2 vlns, vla & cbs*) *Charmy & Volant*
Suite Italienne (*on themes of Pergolesi*) (1933) (*vln & pf*)‡
L. Bobescu – Bress – Dushkin – Fournier – Grach – Magnes – I. Oistrakh (2) – Totenberg
Strecker, Heinrich
Drunt' in der Lobau (*v & pf*) *Huppertz*
Sturestep, Voldemar (1909–   )
(Le) Moulin (*The mill*) (*vln & pf*) *Dalmanis*
Struzenegger, Richard (1905–   )
Quartet (1940) (*2 vlns, vla & vlc*) *Rybar*
Suchoň, Evžen (1908–   )
Fantasy & Burlesque, Op. 7 (*vln & orch*) *Gašparek*
Sonata, Op. 11 (*vln & pf*) *Gašparek*
Sugár, Rezsö (1919–   )
Little Suite (*pf, vln & vlc*) *Boker*
Sugiyama
Debune *Lass*
Suk, Josef (1874–1935)
Ballad, Op. 3b (*vln & pf*) *Suk*
Élégie, Op. 23 (*pf, vln & vlc*) *Suk (2)*

*Revised from the orchestral suite, 1919.
†The violin pieces in this work are: Tango, Waltz & Ragtime.
‡From the ballet "Pulcinella."

Fantasy in g, Op. 24 (1903) (*vln & orch*) *Plocek –*
Rybar – Suk
(7) Pieces, Op. 7 (*pf*)
No. 1. Love song *Barinova – Bratza – A.*
Ferraresi – Kawaciuķ – Mehta – D. Oistrakh (3)
– Zoubek
No. 2. Humoresque *Štěpánek*
No. 4. Idyll *Štěpánek*
No. 5. Dumka *Příhoda (2)*
(4) Pieces, Op. 17 (*vln & pf*) *Bochková – Fournier*
– Neveu – Suk (2)
No. 1. Quasi ballata *Aloume – D. Oistrakh*
No. 2. Appassionata *Aloume – Neveu –*
Štěpánek
No. 3. Un poco triste *Bratza – Frenkel –*
Lorand (2) – Marković – Neveu – D. Oistrakh –
Seidlová – Stanske
No. 4. Burleska
Bustabo – Grumlíková – Kolberg – Kubelík –
Marković – Milstein (2) – D. Oistrakh – Rabin
– R. Ricci (2) – Spalding – Stanske – Tworek –
Zimbalist
Radúz & Mahulena, Op. 13 – Incidental music
(*orch*) *Suk*
Sullivan, Arthur Seymour (1842–1900)
(The) Gondoliers (1889) – operetta
selection *Law*
Iolanthe (1882) – operetta
selection *Law*
(The) Lost chord (1877) (*v & pf*) *Leopold –*
Southgate – Zimbalist
(The) Mikado (1885) – operetta
selection *Law*
(The) Pirates of Penzance (1880) – operetta
selection *Law*
Ruddigore (1887) – operetta
selection *Law*
Yeomen of the Guard (1888) – operetta
selection *Law*
Sulzer, Joseph (1850–1926)
Sarabande, Op. 8 (*vln or vlc & pf*) *Elman (2) –*
Kreisler – Manuello
Surinach, Carlos (1915–   )
Doppio Concertino (1954) (*vln, pf & cha orch*)
Ajemian
Suter, Robert (1919–   )
Quartet No. 1 (*2 vlns, vla & vlc*) *Rybar*
Svendsen, Johan (1840–1911)
(4) Melodies, Op. 24 (*v & pf*)
No. 3. Venetian serenade *Borries*
Romance in G, Op. 26 (*vln & orch*)
C. Andersen – W. Andersen – Beckwith –
Bernardi – Brown – Curti – Gardi – Grumiaux
– Hekking – F.V. Henriques – Kalafusz – Kaul
– Kayser – Knudsen – Krebbers – Kulenkampff
– B. Larsen – Levey – Lewis – Marschner –
Meisel (2) – Menges – Morbitzer (2) – Morini –
Mosley – Parlow – Příhoda – Ranzato (2) –
Rudényi – Sammons (2) – Spalding – Stanske –
Stehl – Suk – Szulc – Tellefsen – Thibaud –
Zacharewitsch – Zacharias
Svetlanov, Y. (1928–   )
(2) Sonatinas (*vln & pf*)
Sonatina No. 1, in C *Labko*
Sonatina No. 2, in e *Labko*

Sviridov, Georgi Vasilyevich (1915–   )
Trio in a (1945 – ed. 1955) (*pf, vln & vlc*) *Grach*
Swing, Raymond Gram (1887–   )
Sonata in c (1928) (*vln & pf*) *Wigler*
Sydeman, William (1928–   )
Concerto da camera No. 1 (1958) (*vln & orch*)
Pollikoff
Concerto da camera No. 2 (1960) (*vln & orch*)
Zukofsky
Trio (1958) (*fl, vln & cbs*) *Kobialka*
Sylva, George Gard "Buddy" de (1896–1950)
Arcady (*v & pf*) *Ball*
Sylvain, Jules (1900–1968)
Canzonetta (*vln & pf*) *Kyndel*
Rêverie de Printemps (*vln & pf*) *Kyndel*
Sylviano, René (1903–   )*
Je n'ai que mon coeur (*v & pf*) *Curti*
Szelényi, István (1904–   )
(8) Duo-sonatinas "Little Duos" (*2 vlns*)
No. 1. Chase *G. Albert & Zalay*
No. 2. Cuckoo chattering *G. Albert & Zalay*
No. 3. Rondino *G. Albert & Zalay*
Szopowicz, Henryk
(4) Mazurkas, Op. 1 (*pf*)
Mazurka No. 3, in A flat *Bacewicz*
Szulc, Josef Zygmunt (1875–1956)
(3) Pieces (*vln & pf*)
No. 3. Melody *Sechiari*
Szymanowski, Karol (1883–1937)
(La) Berceuse d'Aitacho Enia, Op. 52 (1925) (*vln*
& pf) *Niemczyk*
(3) Caprices (*after Paganini*) Op. 40 (*vln & pf*)
No. 1. Caprice No. 20, in D *Snitkovsky*
No. 2. Caprice No. 21, in A *Borries –*
Snitkovsky
No. 3. Caprice No. 24, in a *Bezwierchnyi –*
Snitkovsky
Concerto No. 1, in a, Op. 35 (1922) (*vln & orch*)
Janowski – D. Oistrakh – Totenberg – Uminska
(2) – Wiłkomirska
Concerto No. 2, Op. 61 (1932/3) (*vln & orch*)
Jásek – Palulis – Treger – Uminska
Harnasie, Op. 51 (1926) – ballet (*orch*)
Highland melody *Uminska (2) – Wilkomirska*
King Roger, Op. 46 (1926) – opera
Chant de Roxane *Haendel – Heifetz – Pratz –*
Staryk – Temianka – Uminska
(3) Mythes, Op. 30 (1915) (*vln & pf*) *Jakowicz –*
Rusin – Šroubek – Uminska – Wilkomirska
No.1. La Fontaine d'Aréthuse
Benedetti – Cillario – Komissarov – Lewkowitz
(2) – Milstein – D. Oistrakh – I. Oistrakh –
Sitkovetsky – Staples – J. Szigeti – Thibaud – T.
Varga
Notturno & Tarantella, Op. 28 (*vln & pf*)
Accardo – Bezrodny – Grumiaux – Haendel –
Hagen – Jásek – L. Kogan – Martzy – Menuhin
– Milstein (2) – Solloway – Wilkomirska
(12) Pieśni kurpiowskie (*Kurpian songs*) Op. 58
(1931/2) (*v & pf*)
Dance *Uminska*
Polish folksong *Dubiska – Uminska*
(9) Preludes, Op. 1 (1900) (*pf*)

*Pseudonym for Sylvere Victor Joseph Caffot.

Prelude No. 1, in b *Bacewicz – Barinova*
Romance in D, Op. 23 (1909) (*vln & pf*) *Bezrodny*
– Friedman – Temianka – Uminska
Sonata No. 1, in d, Op. 9 (*vln & pf*) *Goldstein –*
Nemet – D. Oistrakh (2) – Snitkovsky
Tailleferre, Germaine (1892–   )
Pastorale (1921) (*vln & pf*) *Pratz*
Taki
Kojo no Tsuki (*Song of the ruined castle*) (*v & pf*)
Lass
Taktakishvili, Otar Vasilevich (1924–   )
Concertino (*vln & orch*) *D. Oistrakh*
Taneiev, Sergei Ivanovich (1856–1915)
Concert Suite, Op. 28 (*vln & orch*) *Bezrodny (2) –*
Klimov – L. Kogan – Liberman – D. Oistrakh (2)
– Šroubek
(10) Immortelles, Op. 26 (1909) (*v & pf*)
No. 1. Birth of a harp *Pratz*
Quartet No. 4, in a, Op. 11 (*2 vlns, vla & vlc*)
Catterall
Romance (*vln & pf*) *D. Oistrakh*
Trio in D, Op. 21 (*2 vlns & vla*) *Lutsky &*
Ovcharek – D. Oistrakh
Trio in D, Op. 22 (*pf, vln & vlc*) *D. Oistrakh*
Tanguay, Georges-Emile (1893–   )
Romance (*vln & pf*) *Onderet*
Tansman, Alexandre (1897–   )
(5) Pieces (*vln & pf or small orch*)
No. 3. Mouvement perpétuel *Heifetz – Pratz*
Tapray, Jean François (1738–1819)
Sinfonia concertante in E flat, Op. 9 (*hpsi, pf, vln*
& orch) *Gendre*
Tarenghi, Mario (1870–1938)
(5) Morceaux, Op. 51 (*pf*)
No. 3. Berceuse *Ranzato*
Tarp, Svend Erik (1908–   )
Serenade, Op. 28b (*fl, vln, vla & vlc*) *L. Hansen*
Tartini, Giuseppe (1692–1770)
(6) Concerti, Op. 2 (*vln & strs*)
Concerto No. 1, in G, D73 *Biffoli*
Concerto No. 2, in C, D2 *Biffoli – Toso –*
Wallez
Concerto No. 3, in b, D124 *Biffoli*
Concerto No. 4, in F, D62 *Biffoli*
Concerto No. 5, in C, D3 *Biffoli*
Concerto No. 6, in E, D46 *Biffoli*
Concerto in F, C63 (*vln & orch*) *Gulli*
Concerto in D, C78 (*vln & orch*) *Combes*
Concerto in D, D24 (*vln & orch*) *Gertler*
Concerto in D, D30 (*vln & orch*) *Gertler*
Concerto in d, D45 (C61) (*vln & orch*)
Francescatti – Principi – Rybar – Walther
Schneiderhan – J. Szigeti (2) – Tomasow – Wallez
Concerto in E, D53 (C84) (*vln & orch*) *Ferro –*
Gertler – Ribaupierre – Rüthström
Concerto in F, D67 (*vln & orch*) *Wolfgang*
Schneiderhan – Toso
Concerto in F, D68 (*vln & orch*) *Gertler*
Concerto in G, D75 (*vln & orch*) *Gertler – Melkus*
Concerto in G, D83 (*vln & orch*) *Gertler*
Concerto in g, D86 (C6) (*vln & orch*) *Rostal*
Concerto in A, D95 (*vln & orch*) *Gertler*
Concerto in A, D96 (*vln & orch*) *Toso*
Concerto in a, D115 (C76) (*vln & orch*) *Bozzini –*
Ceradini & Salvi – Walther Schneiderhan – Toso

Concerto in b, D125 (*vln & orch*) *Toso*
Concerto in A (*vln & orch*) *J. Szigeti*
Concerto in B flat (*vln & orch*) *Weiner*
Concerto in e (*vln & orch*) *Redditi*
Concerto in F (*vln & orch*) *Redditi – Weiner*
Sinfonia Pastorale in D (*vln & strs*) *Ceradini – Tomasow*
(12) Sonatas, Op. 1 (1734) (*vln & c*)
  Sonata No. 1, in A *Belnick – Geyer – Gimpel – Kulenkampff – Lack – Pierangeli*
  Sonata No. 3, in A *Abbado – Bonaldi*
  Sonata No. 4, in G *Tomasow*
  Sonata No. 10, in g "Didone abbandonata" *Barinova – C. Bobescu – L. Bobescu – Bonaldi – Campoli (2) – Candéla – Chemet – Eto – Flesch – Kamilarov – Klijn – Lack – Lütschg – Lysy – Magyar – Morini (2) – Spalding – Tomasow – Toso – Vaček – Zepparoni*
  Sonata No. 12, in F *Bonaldi*
(12) Sonatas, Op. 2 (*vln & c*)
  Sonata No. 6, in C *Soriano*
  Sonata No. 12, in G *A. Busch (2) – Soriano – J. Szigeti (2) – Telmányi*
(12) Sonatas, Op. 3 (*2 vlns & c*)
  Sonata No. 1, in D *Ayo & Cotogni*
  Sonata No. 4, in F *D'Aranyi & Fachiri – D. & I. Oistrakh (3)*
  Sonata No. 7, in g *Rybar*
(12) Sonatas, Op. 5 (*vln & c*)
  Sonata No. 3, in B flat *Campoli – Carol – Haendel*
(12) Sonatas, Op. 7 (*vln & c*)
  Sonata No. 5, in g *Haendel*
Sonata in A (*vln & c*) *Toso*
Sonata in a (*vln & c*) *Roberts – Rybar – Weiner*
Sonata in b, P14 (*vln & c*) *Rybar*
Sonata in B flat (*vln & c*) *Kaufman*
Sonata in c (*vln & c*) *Lütschg*
Sonata in D (*vln & c*) *Rybar – Weiner*
Sonata in d (*vln & c*) *Toso*
Sonata in E (*vln & c*) *Rybar*
Sonata in e (*vln & c*) *Rybar*
Sonata in g "Il Trillo del Diavolo" (*vln & c*)
Accardo – Agaronyan – Ambrose – Barbieri – Bratza – Bress – Campoli (2) – Candéla – Comellas – Eto – Fain – Flesch – Fuente – Garay – Grumiaux – Gulli – Haendel – Jarry – Kneisel – Komlós – Lari – Lütschg – Menuhin (3) – Milstein (2) – Morini – Niemczyk – Odnoposoff – D. Oistrakh (2) – Příhoda (2) – Ranzato – F. Reuter – Rostal – Sammons (2) – Sebald – Shkolníková – Sitkovetsky – Snitkovsky – Sobolevsky – Spalding – Szeryng – Toškov – Tworek – Ughi – Vecsey – Wolf – Wolfsthal – Zimmermann
Sonata No. 13, in A "Pastorale" (*vln & c*) *Bonaldi – Lütschg – Toso*
(50) Variations on a theme of Corelli (*solo vln*)*
A. Ferraresi – Francescatti – Friedman – Szeryng (2) – Toso

*This is the Francescatti arrangement which utilizes the theme plus variations 13, 41, 24, 45 & 50 respectively. The theme is from Corelli's Gavotte from the "Sonata in F" Op. 5, No. 10.

Tate, Arthur Frank (1880–   )
Somewhere a voice is calling (1911) (*v & pf*)
Andjelkovitch – Benavente – Southgate – Williams
Tavares, Hekel (1896–   )
Concerto No. 4, Op. 107 "em formas brasileiras" (*vln & orch*) *Borgerth*
Tchaikovsky, Boris (1925–   )
Sonata in A (*vln & pf*) *I. Oistrakh*
Tchaikovsky, Peter Ilyitch (1840–1893)
Children's Album, Op. 39 (*pf*)
  No. 22. Song of the lark *Fairhurst*
Concerto in D, Op. 35 (*vln & orch*)
Accardo – Andrade – Anonymous – Auclair (2) – Barcewicz – Barylli – Belayeff – Blinder – Bress – Campoli – Chung – Elman (2) – Erlih (2) – Farbmann – Feliciant – Ferras (2) – Flesch – Francescatti (2) – Friedman – Gavrilov – Gimpel – Gitlis – Grumiaux (2) – Gutnikov – Haendel (2) – Heifetz (4) – Holmes – Huberman (2) – Jacobsen – Klimov – Koene – L. Kogan (3) – Kozolupová – Kremer – Kubelík – Kulenkampff – Laurane – List – Malachowsky – Marcel – Milstein (3) – Mischakoff – Moguilevski – Morini (2) – Odnoposoff – D. Oistrakh (6) – I. Oistrakh (2) – Ozim – Pauk – Perlman – Petschnikoff – Rabin – Ranzato – R. Ricci (2) – Ruha – Rybar – Schulz – T. Seidel – Shkolníková (2) – Spalding – Spivakovsky – Stern (2) – Szeryng (2) – Tretyakov – Ushioda – T. Varga – Wöbbel – Wolf – Wolfsthal – Zathureczky – Zimmermann – Zukerman
Eugene Onegin, Op. 24 (1877/8) – opera
  Faint echo of my youth (*Lensky's aria*) *Farbmann*
(The) Months (*12 Characteristic pieces*) Op. 37a (*pf*)
  No. 2. Carnival time (*February*) *Anonymous – Kulenkampff – Morini*
  No. 6, Barcarolle (*June*) *Cesano – Lorand – Mendels – Morini – Ranzato – Weismann*
  No. 10. Autumn song (*October*) *Candéla – Fuchs – Příhoda – Zimbalist*
(3) Pieces, Op. 9 (*pf*)
  No. 3. Mazurka de salon in d *Leth – Lorand*
(2) Pieces, Op. 10 (*pf*)
  No. 2. Humoresque in G *Hayward – Kreisler – Morini – Vilker*
(6) Pieces, Op. 19 (*pf*)
  No. 4. Nocturne in c sharp *Chemet – Lass – Stanske*
(12) Pieces (*of moderate difficulty*) op. 40 (*pf*)
  No. 2. Chanson triste
Barinova – Barmas – Bratza – Crégut – Curti – D. De Groot – Eweler – Guilevitch – Henley – Jovanović – Law – Sammons – Sonntag – Staryk
  No. 10. Russian dance *Barinova – Elman (3)*
(6) Pieces, Op. 51 (*pf*)
  No. 6. Valse sentimentale *Bisztriczky – Elman – Goldstein – Scholz – Simor – Stern – Szeryng (2) – J. Szigeti*
Pique Dame, Op. 68 (1890) – opera
  Romance *Buchtele*
Quartet No. 1, in D, Op. 11 (*2 vlns, vla & vlc*)

D'Aranyi – Catterall – Elman (3) – Fischberg – Goberman & Miksovsky – Hayward – Kaufman – Kreisler (2) – Lewkowitz – D. Oistrakh (2) – A.J. Rose – A. Schmidt – T. Seidel – Spalding – Staryk – Totenberg – Zimbalist
Quartet No. 2, in F, Op. 22 (*2 vlns, vla & vlc*)
Catterall (2)
Quartet No. 3, in e flat, Op. 30 (*2 vlns, vla & vlc*)
Burgin
Romance in f, Op. 5 (*pf*) *Borries (2) – Kyndel – Poulet – Příhoda (2) – Szikra*
Serenade in C, Op. 48 (*str orch*)
  Valse (*2nd mvt*) *Elman – Heifetz (2) – Příhoda*
Sérénade mélancolique in b flat, Op. 26 (*vln & orch*)
Abadiev – Anonymous – Barinova – Beilina – Blinder – Bochková – Campajola – Elman – Flesch – Friedman – Fuchs – Fujikawa – Grumiaux – Heifetz – Kayser – Kimber – L. Kogan (3) – Moguilevski – D. Oistrakh – R. Ricci – Rosand – Rudényi – Ruha – Zora Shikhmurzayeva – Spalding – Šroubek – Strock – Ushioda – Vaiman – Wolfsthal
Sextet, Op. 70 "Souvenir de Florence" (*2 vlns, 2 vlas & 2 vlcs*) *Gilels & L. Kogan*
Sleeping Beauty, Op. 66 (1888/9) – ballet (*orch*)
Druian – Menuhin – Staryk
(6) Songs, Op. 6 (*v & pf*)
  No. 5. Why? *Fradkin*
  No. 6. None but the weary heart *Bleumers – Elman (3) – Milstein – E.B. Nielsen – Rattay – Stern – Traversa – Zimbalist*
Souvenir d'un lieu cher, Op. 42 (*vln & pf*)
Barinova – Beilina – Ladscheck
  No. 1. Méditation *Gutnikov (2) – Klimov – L. Kogan (2) – Krysa – Milstein – D. Oistrakh (2) – Ruha*
  No. 2. Scherzo *Elman – Heifetz – Kubo – Milstein (2) – R. Ricci – Ruha – Zhuk*
  No. 3. Mélodie
Accardo – Alós – Ashkenazi – Asti – Auer – Baranowski – Barbieri – Bean – Bress – Cochrane – Collier – Dinicu – Dolin – Eidus – Elman (4) – Fuchs – Gittelson – Grindenko – Hassid – Havemann – Heifetz – Huberman (2) – Kimber – Kochański – Krengel – Lorand – Lubotsky – Milstein – Mosley – Moszkowski – E. B. Nielsen – D. Oistrakh – Palulis – Parlow (2) – Petschnikoff – R. Ricci – Rosen – Rudényi – Selinsky – Spivakovsky (2) – Stanske – Staryk – Unno – Ushioda – Winchester – Zhuk – Zukin
(3) Souvenirs de Hapsal, Op. 2 (*pf*)
  No. 3. Chant sans paroles in f
Andrade – Bleier – Bonnemain – Chauveton – Cochrane (2) – Corigliano – Driffield – Elman – Fradkin – Fuchs – Gautier – Gilels – Goldstein – B. Hall – Hayward – Herman – Kerekjarto – Kochański – Kreisler (3) – Law – Levey – Maurice – Morini (2) – Petroni – Gladys Raymond – Rudényi – Sadler – Sitkovetsky – Spalding – Stanske – Strockoff – Thibaud – Zilzer – Zimbalist
Suite No. 3, in G, Op. 55 (*orch*)
  Theme & variations *Barylli – Bean – Nerini –*

R. Ricci – Simsky

Suite No. 4, in G, Op. 71 "Mozartiana" (orch) R. Ricci

Swan Lake, Op. 20 (1875/6) – ballet (orch)
A. Brosa – Campoli – G. Cherniavsky – L. Cherniavsky – M. Chernyakhovsky – R. Cohen – Druian – Farbmann – Fuchs – Goldstein – Grumiaux – Kalinovsky – L. Kogan – Maguire – Menuhin – Simor – Staryk

Trio in a, Op. 50 "To the memory of a great artist" (pf, vln & vlc)
Bezrodny – Catterall – Dessau – Hayward – Heifetz – Kaufman – L. Kogan – V. Martin – Menuhin (2) – D. Oistrakh – Sammons – Suk

Waltz-scherzo, Op. 34 (vln & pf or orch)
Beilina – Gutnikov – Isakadze – Kalafusz – Klimov – L. Kogan – Kremer – Milstein – D. Oistrakh (2) – I. Oistrakh – Pikaizen – Polyakin – Zora Shikhmurzayeva – Spivakovsky – Vaiman

Ye who have yearned alone (v & pf) Moskowitz

Tcherepnin, Alexander (1899–   )

Trio in D, Op. 34 (1925) (pf, vln & vlc) Clebanoff

Telemann, Georg Philipp (1681–1767)

Cantata No. 19 (Gott will Mensch und sterblich werden) Borries – Schneider

Concerto in E (fl, ob d'amore, vla d'amore, strs & c) Retyi

Concerto in A, T.I, No. 3 (fl, vln, vlc, strs & c) Gendre

Concerto in E Flat (2 fls, ob, vln, strs & c) Melkus

Concerto in B flat (3 obs, 3 vlns, hpsi & strs) Abramenkov, Barshai & Poleess – Carol – Schulz, Seiler & Silzer

Concerto in a (rec, ob, vln, hpsi & strs)* Kohon

Concerto in A (rec, vln, strs & c) J. Schröder

Concerto in D (tpt, vln, strs & c) Mayer-Schierning

Concerto in a (vln, strs & c) Mayer-Schierning – Stanič-Krek

Concerto in a (vln, strs & c)† N. Roth

Concerto in B flat "Pisendel" (vln, strs & c) N. Roth – J. Schröder

Concerto in F (vln, strs & c) Kaufman

Concerto in G (vln, strs & c) Armand

Concerto in D (vln concertato, tpt, 3 vlns, 2 vlas & vlc obb) Carol

Concerto in B flat "Polonaise" (2 vlns, vla, hpsi & c) Melkus & Rantos

Concerto in C (2 vlns, strs & c) Bünte & Hendel

Concerto in G (2 vlns, strs & c) Retyi & Steinhäusler

Conceerto in G "alla Polonaise" (2 vlns, vla, hpsi & c) Melkus & Rantos

Concerto in F, T.II, No. 3 (3 vlns, strs & c) Apostoli, Ayo & Colandrea – Egger,

*From a manuscript in the Hessian State Library.

†This was written as the overture to the opera "Emma und Eginhard" and produced in Hamburg in 1728. It was rewritten as a violin concerto by the composer.

Lautenbacher & Schäfer – Fietz, Kaufman & Rybar – Frydén, Mayer-Schierning & Melkus – Gendre, Laroque & Wallez – Geyrhalter, Kakuska & Kalup – Holtman, Leohardt & Schröder

Concerto in C (4 vlns, strs & c) Hori, Kortner, Nägele & Ohnheiser

Concerto in D (4 vlns, strs & c) Dejean, Gaunet, Geyr & J. Pasquier – Kirch, Schulz, Silzer & Westphal

Concerto in G (4 vlns, strs & c) Harnoncourt, Pfeiffer, Schuberwalter & Theiner

Essercizii Musici (1721)
No. 3. Trio-sonata in F (vln, gamba & c) Lautenbacher
No. 9. Trio-sonata in E (fl, vln & c) Gendre – Goodman

(12) Fantasias (1735) (solo vln)
Fantasia No. 1, in b Grumiaux – Lysy
Fantasia No. 2, in G Grumiaux
Fantasia No. 3, in f Grumiaux
Fantasia No. 4, in D Grumiaux – Koppel
Fantasia No. 5, in A Grumiaux
Fantasia No. 6, in e Grumiaux
Fantasia No. 7, in E flat Grumiaux
Fantasia No. 8, in E Friedmann – Grumiaux
Fantasia No. 9, in b Grumiaux
Fantasia No. 10, in D Grumiaux
Fantasia No. 11, in b Grumiaux
Fantasia No. 12, in a Friedmann – Grumiaux

(6) Partitas (var. cbns)
Partita No. 3, in c (vln & c) Lautenbacher
Partita No. 6, in E flat (vln & c) Lautenbacher

Quartet in G (fl, ob, vln & c) Gendre

Quartet in G, T.I., No. 2 (fl, ob, vln & c) Brandis – Gendre – Tryon

Quartet in e, T.III, No. 2 (fl, vln, gamba & c) Felicani – Lamacque – Topolski

Quartet in d, T.II, No. 2 (fl, vln, ob, bsn & hpsi) Gendre

Quartet in b (fl, vln, vlc, bsn & hpsi) Kussmaul

Quartet in b (fl, vln, vlc, bsn & hpsi) Kussmaul

Quartet in D (fl, vln, vlc, bsn & hpsi) Kussmaul

Quartet in g (fl, vln, vlc, bsn & hpsi) Haag

Quartet in e (1733) (fl, vln, vlc & c) Gendre – Gutnikov – Kussmaul

(6) Quartets "Paris" (fl, vln, vlc & c)
Quartet No. 1, in D Jahn
Quartet No. 3, in G Jahn
Quartet No. 4, in b Jahn
Quartet No. 6, in e "Chaconne" Jahn

Quartet in G (rec, vln, vlc & c) J. Schröder

Solo in A, T.II, No. 5 (solo vln) Kalup – Melkus – J. Schröder

(6) Sonatas, Op. 2 (1727) "Duets" (2 fls or vlns)
Sonata No. 1, in G "Canonic" Gilels & L. Kogan – Harth & Testa
Sonata No. 2, in b Harth & Testa
Sonata No. 4, in b Harth & Testa – Lysy
Sonata No. 6, in E Harth & Testa

Sonata in F (rec, vln & c) Fagerlund & Kinch

Sonata in a (vln & c) Kaufman

Sonata in g (vln & c) Kaufman

Sonata in e (2 vlns & c) Mell

Sonata No. 1, in a "Sonata Polonaise" (2 vlns

& c) Walther Schneiderhan & Swoboda

Sonata No. 2, in a "Sonata Polonaise" (2 vlns & c) Melkus & Rantos

Sonata No. 3, in E (2 vlns & c) Walther Schneiderhan & Swoboda

(6) Suites (fl, vln & c)
Suite No. 6, in d Büchner

Suite in F "Konzertsuite" (2 hrns, 2 vlns & c) Harnoncourt

Suite in D, T.II, No. 1 (ob, tpt, strs & c) Kaufman

Suite in B flat, T.III, No. 1 (2 obs, strs & c) Barchet & Lautenbacher – Lamacque – Oguse

Suite in F (vln, strs & c) J. Schröder

Suite No. 1, in a (1725) (2 vlns, vla & c) Grach & Kaptsan

Suite No. 2, in g (1730) (2 vlns, vla & c) Grach & Kaptsan

Trio-sonata in d (rec, vln & c) Olsen

Trio-sonata in B flat (rec, hpsi & c) Gendre

Trio in E flat, T.I, No. 4 (2 vlns & c) G. & W. Beal – Holtman & J. Schröder

Telesfor, S.
Hungarian song* Lorand

Tellam, Heinrich
(En) Sourdine sur les motifs d'une sérénade de J. Tellam (vln & pf) Leutjens

Tenaglia, Antonio Francesco (1650– ?)
Have pity, sweet eyes (v & c)†
Cores – Flesch – Morse – R. Pollak – Powell

Terperlyuk, P.
Fantasy (vln & orch) Terpelyuk

Theodorakis, M. (1925–   )
Sonatina No. 1 (vln & pf) Zaks

Thielmann, Per
Canzonetta (vln & pf) W. Andersen

Thomas, Ambroise (1811–1896)
Mignon (1866) – opera
Connais-tu le pays? Eweler – Kreisler – Ranzato
Entr'acte (Gavotte) (Act II)
d'Almaine – Brown – W. Busch – Debruille – Dessau – Hayward – Law – Levy & Rattay – Maurice – Mendels – Powell – Rudényi – Sigmund – Weismann
Je suis Titania "Polonaise" May
selection Eweler – Indig – Lorand – May

Thomas, John Rogers (1826–1913)
Eileen Alannah (1873) (v & pf) Southgate – Wethmar

Thomé, Francis (1850–1909)
Andante religioso, Op. 70 (pf) de Brayne – Dyke – Law – Modern – Rudényi – Southgate – Weber – Zimmermann

(L') Extase (pf) Hayward – Lewis – Southgate – J. Wolff

Simple aveu, Op. 25 (pf)
Altermann – Andjelkovitch – L. Andre – Anonymous – Ball – Breeskin – Carrodus – Chauveton – Cochrane – Curti – Debruille –

*Unidentified.

†Arranged for vln & pf as "Aria in f" by Franz Ries.

Dyke – Elman (2) – Eweler – Filon – M.
Gordon – Hayward – Jacobs – Kalmer –
Leutjens – Luquin – Manuello – Maurice –
Mendels – Michaïlow – Opfermann – Roeder –
Rudényi – Sammons (3) – Southgate – Stehl –
Tworek – Valesca-Becker – Weist-Hill – Willis
Sous la feuillée, Op. 29 (pf) Chemet – de Monge
Thomson, Virgil (1896–   )
Sonata (1930) (vln & pf) Fuchs
Thuillier, Edmund
(Le) Sommeil d'un ange – cantabile (pf) de Brayne
Tichý, Rudolf
Triton – valse (pf) Anonymous
Walzer-Zauber (Intermezzo) Op. 66 (vln & pf)
André – Mastny
Tiessen, Heinz
Totentanz-Melodie, Op. 29 (vln & pf) Frenkel
Tippett, Michael (1905–   )
Fantasia concertante on a theme of Corelli (1953)
(2 vlns, vlc & strs) Masters & Menuhin
Tirindelli, Pietro Adolfo (1858–1937)
Mistica in G (vln & pf) Ranzato
(6) Morceaux de concert, Op. 1 (vln & pf)
No. 3. Histoire Ranzato
No. 4. Airs hongrois Dessau
No. 6. Pasquinade Barbosa – Caponi – Lari
Serenata (vln & pf) Ranzato
Titl, Anton Emil (1809–1882)
Serenade Flesch – Rudényi – Weintraub
Tlendiev, N.
Armandy Kiyal (vln & pf) Tolganbayev
Tobani, Theodore Moses (1855–1933)
Hearts & flowers, Op. 245 (1899) (v & pf)*
Carrodus – Haxton (3) – Jacobs – Morini – Thiele
Tobias, Charles (1897–   )
Just another day wasted away (1927) (v & pf)†
Fradkin
Toch, Ernst (1887–1964)
(2) Divertimenti, Op. 37‡
Divertimento No. 2 (vln & vla) Heifetz
Quartet in D flat, Op. 18 (1909) (2 vlns, vla & vlc)
Kaufman & Stepansky
Serenade in G, Op. 25 (1917) (2 vlns & vla)
Kaufman & Manasevitch – Kaufman & Stepansky
Toeschi, Carlo Giuseppe (1724–1788)
Concerto in D (vln & orch) Hendel
Tomasini, Luigi (1741–1808)
Concerto in A (vln, 2 hrns & strs) Melkus
Tomer, William Gould
God be with you till we meet again (1883)
(v & pf) Zimbalist
Tomkins, Thomas (1572–1656)
Fantasy (2 vlns, vla & vlc) Bress & Goodman
Tomlinson, Ernest
Lament (2 vlns, vla & vlc) Dyke
Torch, Sydney
Dr. Watson meets Sherlock Holmes – Incidental
music (orch) Campoli
Torelli, Giuseppe (1658–1708)

*Based on a tune by Czibulko.
†Composed jointly with Roy Turk.
‡Divertimento No. 1 is for vln & vlc.

(12) Concerti, Op. 8 (1709) (1/6: 2 vlns, strs & c –
7/12: vln, strs & c)
Concerto No. 1, in C Alès & Kaufman –
Barchet & Beh – Ceradini & Redditi
Concerto No. 2, in a
Alès & Kaufman – Armuzzi-Romei & Rossi –
Barchet & Beh – Beguin & Fernandez – Cotogni
& Michelucci – Mayer-Schierning & Seeger –
Sambleben & Thomsen
Concerto No. 3, in E Alès & Kaufman –
Barchet & Beh – Ceradini & Redditi – Cotogni
& Michelucci – Kaufman & unid. vln
Concerto No. 4, in B flat Alès & Kaufman –
Barchet & Beh
Concerto No. 5, in G Alès & Kaufman –
Barchet & Beh
Concerto No. 6, in g "Christmas Concerto"
Alès & Kaufman – Barchet & Beh – Cotogni &
Michelucci – Doukan & Yordanoff – Pinkava &
Stanič-Krek
Concerto No. 7, in d Barchet – Kaufman –
Redditi (2) – Topolski
Concerto No. 8, in c Barchet – Fernandez –
Glenn – Kaufman – Liberman – Lubotsky –
Staryk
Concerto No. 9, in e Barchet – Kaufman –
Liberman – Michelucci – Redditi
Concerto No. 10, in A Barchet – Kaufman –
Topolski
Concerto No. 11, in f Barchet – Kaufman
Concerto No. 12, in D Barchet – Kaufman –
Michelucci
Concerto in D (vln, gtr, strs & c) Pichler
Ricercate, o mie speranze – aria (v & c) Sadowski
(12) Sonatas, Op. 3 (vln & c)
Sonata No. 7, in e C. Ferraresi & Gulli
Toselli, Enrico (1883–1926)
Serenade, Op. 6 (vln & pf)
W. Andersen – Arlt – Bleumers – Bornfors –
Cesano – Chauveton – Chemet – Curti (2) –
Darrieux – De Vito – Dinicu – Dolin – Eweler –
Fradkin – Fritz-Crone – Gaillard – J.F.
Henriques – Hlaváček – Horvath – Jacobsen –
Kawaciuk – Kayser – Georg Kniestaedt –
Lipschultz – Lorand – Manuello – Mendels –
Mittmann (2) – Morini – Příhoda (3) – Ranzato
– Reis – Rubato – A. Sandler – Schmied –
Schwartz – Selinsky – Swaap – Tak – Tworek –
Velder – Weismann – Wolfsthal – Zilzer
Tosti, Francesco Paolo (1846–1916)
For a kiss (Pour un baiser) (v & pf) Huppertz –
Michaïlow – Weismann
Good-bye (v & pf) Swaap
Idéale (1884) (v & pf) Manuello – Swaap
Invanno (mand & pf) Arany
(The) Last kiss (Dernier baiser) (v & pf) Cesano
Melody (v & pf) Weismann
My dreams (v & pf) Haxton
Parted (v & pf) D. De Groot – A. Sandler
(La) Serenata (v & pf) Kreisler – Livschakoff –
Michaïlow – Swaap
Townsend, Pearl Dea Etta (Madame Lawrence)
(1886–   )
Berceuse (vln & pf) Bezrodny – Kreisler – Polyakin

Toyama, Yuzo
Concerto (1963) (vln & orch) Unno
Sonata (1964) (vln & pf) Ushioda
Triggs, Harold (1900–   )
Danza brasiliana (vln & pf) Bezrodny – Kaufman
(2)
Troiani, Gaetano (1873–1942)
Estilo, de Motivos de la sierra y la llanura (vln &
pf) Pessina
Trojan, Václav (1907–   )
(The) Emperor's Nightingale (1948) (vln & orch)
Kawaciuk – Zegzulková
Troostwyck, Hendrika
Springtime (vln & pf) Troostwyck
Tzintsadze, Sulkhan (1925–   )
Melody (vln & pf) Grach
Tureček, Eduard (1899–   )
Menuet (vln & pf) Madle
Turina, Joaquin (1882–1949)
Sonata No. 1, in d, Op. 51 (1929) (vln & pf)
Leon-Ara – V. Martin
Sonata No. 2, Op. 82 (1934) "Sonata española"
(vln & pf) V. Brug – J.C. Figueroa – V. Martin –
Pessina – Sammons
Trio No. 1, in d, Op. 35 (pf, vln & vlc) Heifetz –
V. Martin
Turini, Francesco (1595–1656)
Madrigali ... con alcune Sonate, Libro Primo
(1624)
Sonata in a (2 vlns & c) van den Hombergh &
Leonhardt
Turk, Roy (1892–1934)*
Turner, Charles (1921–   )
Serenade for Icarus (1960) (vln & pf) Kroll
Turner, Robert Comrie (1920–   )
Sonata (1956) (vln & pf) Pratz
Turski, Zbigniew (1908–   )
Concerto No. 1 (vln & orch) Wroński
Tveitt, Nils Geirr (1908–   )
Baldurs draumar – ballet (orch)
Dance Knudsen
Tworek, Wandy (1913–   )
Boogie for two (vln & pf) Tworek (2)
Capriccietto (vln & pf) Tworek
Copenhagen joke (vln & pf) Tworek
Gøglerens drøm (Gypsy dreams) – csárdas (vln &
pf) Tworek
(The) Talking violin (vln & pf) Tworek
Ugarte, Floro Manuel (1884–   )
Sonata (1928) (vln & pf) Pessina
Uray, Ernst Ludwig (1906–   )
Variations in f (vln & pf) Seitz
Vainberg, Moysey (1919–   )
Concerto in g, Op. 67 (vln & orch) L. Kogan
Moldavian Rhapsody in g, Op. 47 (vln & pf)
Beilina – D. Oistrakh
Sonatina in d, Op. 46 (vln & pf) Mikhlin –
Shkolníková
Vainiunas, Stasis (1909–   )
Rhapsody on Lithuanian themes, Op. 30 (vln &
orch) Livontas
Valdez, Charles Robert
Sérénade du Tzigane (vln & pf) Brown – S. Furer

*See: **Tobias**, Charles

– *Kreisler – Lorand – Morini – Morell – Příhoda (2) – Rosen – Selinsky*

Valén, Fartein (1887–1952)
Concerto, Op. 37 (*vln & orch*) *Wicks*

Valensin, Georges (1844–   )
Symphony No. 1, in G (*orch*)
  Minuet *Ladscheck*

Valentini, Giuseppe (1681–1746)
(12) Concerti, Op. 6 (*orch*)
  Concerto No. 3, in C *Ferro*
(12) Sonatas, Op. 8 (1714) "Alletamenti" (*vln & c*)
  Sonata in D *Krebbers*

Valiullin, K.
Lyric dance (*vln & pf*) *Akhmetov*

Valle, Francisco
Ao pé de fogueira (*Prelude XV*) (*pf*) *Bean – Francescatti – Heifetz – Szeryng*

Vallerand, Jean (1915–   )
Quartet No. 1 (*2 vlns, vla & vlc*) *Bress & Goodman*
Sonata (1950) (*vln & pf*) *Brunet*

Vandersloat
Dreamy Hawaii (*v & pf*) *Kerekjarto*

Varga, Ruben Georg (1928–   )
Prelude & 4 Caprices (*solo vln*) *R. Varga*

Varvoglis, Mario (1885–   )
Pastoral Suite (*2 vlns, vla & vlc*) *Kolassis*

Vaughan Williams, Ralph (1872–1958)
Concerto in d (1925) "Concerto accademico" (*vln & orch*) *Buswell – Fuchs – Grinke – Grumlíková – Kaufman*
Job (1930) (*orch*)
  Elihu's dance of youth & beauty *Datyner*
(The) Lark ascending (1914) (*vln & orch*) *Bean – Chausow – Druian – Grinke – Menges – Pougnet – Wise*
On Wenlock edge – song cycle (1909) (*t, 2 vlns, vla, vlc & pf*) *Grinke*
Quintet (1914) "Phantasy" (*3 vlns, vla & vlc*) *Mangeot & Pougnet*
Serenade to Music (1937/8) (*soloists, cho & orch*) *Knitzer*
Sonata in a (*vln & pf*) *Grinke*

Vecsey, Franz von (1893–1935)
Caprice nostalgica (*vln & pf*) *Vecsey*
Caprice No. 1 "Le Vent" (*vln & pf*) *R. Ricci (3) – Solloway (2)*
Caprice No. 2 "La cascade" (*vln & pf*) *Renardy – Vecsey (2)*
Foglio d'album (*vln & pf*) *Vecsey*
(A) Toi (*vln & pf*) *Link – Vecsey*
Valse triste (*vln & pf*)
  Bisztriczky – Deman – S. Furer – Garaguly – Garay – Moguilevski – Rèty – F. Roth – Rubato – Tzipine – Vecsey – Zilzer

Velt, Jacob M.
Söndag pa sätern (*vln & pf*) *Velt*

Veracini, Francesco (1690–1750)
Concerto No. 7 in D (*vln, strs & c*) *Glenn*
(12) Sonatas, Op. 1 (1721) (*vln & c*)
  Sonata No. 1, in g *Bress*
  Sonata No. 2, in a *Bress*
  Sonata No. 3, in b *Bress*
  Sonata No. 4, in C *Bress*

Sonata No. 5, in d *Bress*
Sonata No. 6, in e *L. Bobescu – Bress – Zepparoni*
Sonata No. 7, in A *Bress – Grumiaux*
Sonata No. 8, in B flat *Bress – Guglielmo*
Sonata No. 9, in C *Bress*
Sonata No. 10, in D *Bress*
Sonata No. 11, in E *Bress*
sonata No. 12, in F *Bress*
(12) Sonatas, Op. 2 (1744) "Sonate accademiche" (*vln & c*)
  Sonata No. 6, in A *d'Albore – Caponi – Cillario – Gandini – Guarino – Krebbers – Mikhlin – Nadien – R. Ricci – Ruggero – J. Szigeti – Telmányi*
  Sonata No. 8, in e *Amar – Klijn – Komissarov – Moguilevski – Shkolníková – Snitkovsky – Staryk – Thibaud (2)*
  Sonata No. 11, in E *Moguilevski – R. Ricci – Staryk – Thibaud (2)*

Verbrugghen, Henri (1874–1934)
Berceuse (*Sommeil d'un ange*) (*vln & pf*) *de Brayne*

Verdi, Giuseppe (1813–1901)
Aïda (1871) – opera
  selection *Law*
(La) Forza del Destino (1862) – opera
  selection *Ranzato*
  Solenne in quest'ora *Livschakoff*
(I) Lombardi (1843) – opera
  Prelude (*Act III*) *Ranzato*
  selection *Goggi*
Quartet in e (1873) (*2 vlns, vla & vlc*) *Amar*
Rigoletto (1851) – opera
  Caro nome *Ranzato*
  selection *Haxton – Law – de Monge – Sens*
(La) Traviata (1853) – opera
  aria* *Eweler*
  Prelude (*Acts I or III*) *Pagani*
  selection *Law – Manuello – May*
  Waltz *May*
(Il) Trovatore (1853) – opera
  Miserere d'Almaine (3) – *Morena*
  potpourri *Dessau*
  selection *Anonymous – Bobbé – Law – Manuello – May – Opfermann – Sens*

Veress, Sándor (1907–   )
Nógrádi verbunkos (*Hungarian dance*) (1940) (*vln & pf*) *Zathureczky*

Vicars, Harold (–1922)†

Vieuxtemps, Henri (1820–1881)
Ballade & Polonaise in G, Op. 38 (*vln & pf*)
  Aranyi – Beckwith – Berg – Clockers – Eisenberg – Fidelmann – M. Gordon – Huberman – Law – Octors – Powell – Sammons – Swaap – Thomas
(6) Bouquet Américain, Op. 33 (*solo vln*)
  No. 2. La Fête de St. Patrice *Powell – Rudényi*
Caprice burlesque (*Souvenir d'Amérique*) Op. 17
  "Yankee Doodle" (*vln & pf*) *Breeskin – Rudényi*

*Unidentified.
† See: **Moya**

Concerto No. 2, in f, Op. 19 (*vln & orch*) *Gerle*
Concerto No. 4, in d, Op. 31 (*vln & orch*)
  Francescatti – Grumiaux – Heifetz – Irmer – Krebbers – Law – Menuhin – Morse – Příhoda (2) – Rudényi – Snitkovsky
Concerto No. 5, in a, Op. 37 (*vln & orch*) *Dubois – Grumiaux – Heifetz (2) – L. Kogan – Menuhin – Senatra – Zukerman*
(6) Divertissements d'Amateurs sur des Mélodies russes, Op. 24 (*vln & pf*)
  No. 1. Romance (*Otgadaj, moja rodnaja*) (*after Alexander Lvovich Gurilyov, 1803–1858*) *Barinova – S. Furer*
  No. 2. Le rossignol (*after Alexander Alabiev, 1787–1851*) *Erdenko – Lass*
  No. 3. Romance (*after Alexander Sergeyevich Dargomizhsky, 1813–1869*) *S. Furer*
Duo brillante en forme de fantaisie sur des airs hongrois, Op. 39 (1837) (*vln & pf*)*
  F. Weltmann
Fantasia-appassionata, Op. 35 (*vln & pf*) *Berg – Clockers – Petschnikoff*
(3) Feuilles d'album, Op. 40 (*vln & pf*)
  No. 1. Romance *Sadler*
  No. 2. Regrets *Nadien – Thibaud*
(6) Morceaux de salon, Op. 20 (*vln & pf*)
  No. 4. Souvenir *D. Oistrakh*
(6) Morceaux de salon, Op. 22 (*vln & pf*)
  No. 3. Rêverie *Aranyi – Flesch – Zimmermann*
  No. 4. Tarantelle in a *Danchenko – Malinin – Morse – I. Oistrakh*
(4) Romances, Op. 8 (*vln & pf*)
  No. 4. Air savoyard *Ranzato*
(7) Romances sans paroles, Op. 7 (*vln & pf*)
  Romance No. 1, in D flat "Chant d'amour" *Kalafusz*
  Romance No. 2, in c "Désespoir" *Gulli – D. Oistrakh*
  Romance No. 3, in C "Reminiscence" *D. Oistrakh*
(3) Salonstücke, Op. 32 (*vln & pf*)
  No. 2. Rondino *Flesch – C. Hansen – L. Kogan (2) – Ysaÿe*
Suite in D, Op. 43 (*vln & pf*) *Sitkovetsky*
(6) Voix Intimes, Op. 45 (*vln & pf*)
  No. 5. Sérénité *Chemet – Thibaud (2)*

Villa-Lobos, Heitor (1887–1959)
(O) Canto do cysne negro (1917) (*vlc & pf*)
  Bezrodny – Francescatti – Odnoposoff – Tworek
Chôros No. 1 (1920) (*gtr*) *Borgerth – San-Malo*
Chôros No. 2 (1924) (*fl & cl*) *Borgerth – San-Malo – Schoenfeld*
Chôros No. 7 (1924) (*fl, ob, cl, sax, bsn, vln & vlc*) *Baker*
Duo (1946) (*vln & vla*) *Persinger*
Fantasia de movimentos mixtos (1922) (*vln & pf*) *Borgerth*
Sonata-Fantasia No. 1, in c (1912) "Déspespérance" (*vln & pf*) *Beilina – Iacovino – Posselt*
Sonata-Fantasia No. 2 (1914) (*vln & pf*) *Iacovino – Snitkovsky*
Sonata-Fantasia No. 3 (1915) (*vln & pf*) *Iacovino –*

*Composed jointly with Ferenz Erkel, 1810–1893.

Odnoposoff
Suite (1923) (*v & vln*) *R. Ricci*
Trio (1945) (*vln, vla & vlc*) *Schneider*
Viotti, Giovanni Battista (1753–1824)
Concerto in E flat "Double" (*pf, vln & str orch*)
Abussi – Glenn – Lautenbacher
Concerto No. 3, in A (*pf, vln obb & strs*) *Gulli*
Concerto No. 3, in a (*vln & orch*) *Prencipe*
Concerto No. 4, in D (*vln & orch*) *Abussi*
Concerto No. 22, in a (*vln & orch*) *Accardo –
Grumiaux – Georg Kniestaedt – Lautenbacher –
Morini – D. Oistrakh – Rybar – Stern*
Concerto No. 23, in G (*vln & orch*) *Shermont*
(3) Duets, Op. 2 (*2 vlns*)
    Duet No. 3, in G *De Vito & Menuhin*
(6) Duets, Op. 20 (*2 vlns*)
    Duet No. 3, in G *Cotogni & Michelucci*
(3) Duets, Op. 29 (*2 vlns*)
    Duo concertante No. 1, in g *Novello & Příhoda*
    Duo concertante No. 2, in d *Ceradini &
    Pignatelli*
    Duo concertante No. 3, in D *Gulli*
Duet No. 2 (*2 vlns*)* *Koluch & Novosad*
(3) Quartets, Op. 22 (*fl & vln or 2 vlns, vla & vlc*)
    Quartet No. 1, in B flat *Baker & Belnick*
    Quartet No. 3, in c *Baker & Belnick – Gendre*
Viski, Janós (1906–1961)
Concerto (1947) (*vln & orch*) *Zathureczky*
Vitali, Giovanni Battista (1644–1692)
Artifici musicali, Op. 13 (1689) (*vln & c*)
    Caprice No. 1, in D *Armuzzi-Romei*
    Caprice No. 2, in g *Armuzzi-Romei*
(12) Sonatas, Op. 5 (1669) (*vln & c*)
    Sonata No. 1, in D *Armuzzi-Romei – Franzetti*
Vitali, Tommaso Antonio (1665–1735)
Chaconne in g (*vln & c*)
    *Accardo – D'Aranyi – Armuzzi-Romei – C.
    Bobescu – De Vito – Elman – Francescatti (2) –
    Frolov – Garami – Grumiaux – Heifetz – Klijn
    – Kozolupova – Lorand – Lubotsky – Milstein
    (2) – Odnoposoff (2) – D. Oistrakh – I. Oistrakh
    – Ozim – Příhoda (2) – Ruha – Sammons –
    Shkolníková – Svolkovkis – Szeryng (3) –
    Thibaud – Tomasow – Tretyakov*
(12) Concerti di Sonate, Op. 4 (*vln, vlc & c*)
    Sonata No. 11, in b *C. Ferraresi & Gulli*
Sonata in D (1689) (*vln & c*) *Cotogni*
Vitol, Yazep (1863–1948)
Romance in d, Op. 15 (*vln & pf*) *Dalmanis*
Vivaldi, Antonio (1678–1741)
Adagio* *Bezrodny*
(12) Concerti, Op. 3 "L'Estro armonico" (*var.
cbns, strs & c*)
    Concerto No. 1, in D, P.146 (*F.IV, No. 7*) (*4
    vlns, vlc, strs & c*)
    *Barchet, Endres, Hopfner & Steffen-Wendling –
    Benvenuti, Gulli, Malanotte & Poltronieri –
    Boskovsky, Hintermeyer, Matheis & Tomasow –
    Carles, Déat, Jarry & Molard – Champeil, Gali,
    Gendre & Yordanoff – Cotogni, Gallozzi,*

*Unidentified.

*Michelucci & Vicari – Gavrilov, Hermann,
Karolyi & Schilling – Käppeli, Scherz, Seeger &
Soh – Redditi & soloists*
Concerto No. 2, in g, P.326 (*F.IV, No. 8*) (*2
vlns, strs & c*)
    *Barchet & Steffen-Wendling – Boskovsky &
    Tomasow – Colandrea & Michelucci – Ferro &
    Mozzato (2) – Gavrilov & Hermann – Prystawski
    & Scherz – Redditi & unid. vln – H. Seidel &
    Wagner*
Concerto No. 3, in G, P.96 (*F.I, No. 173*) (*vln,
strs & c*) *Barchet – Gavrilov – Gulli – Kempler
– Michelucci – Prystawski – Redditi – Salvi –
Stefanato*
Concerto No. 4, in e, P.97 (*F.I, No. 174*) (*4
vlns, strs & c*)
    *Barchet, Endres, Hopfner & Steffen-Wendling –
    Barnert, Prystawski, Ribeiro & Soh – Benvenuti,
    Gulli, Ruotolo & Stefanato – Boskovsky,
    Hintermeyer, Matheis & Tomasow – Carles,
    Déat, Jarry & Molard – Cotogni, Gallozzi,
    Michelucci & Vicari – Gavrilov, Hermann,
    Karolyi & Schilling – Redditi & soloists*
Concerto No. 5, in A, P.212 (*F.I, No. 175*) (*2
vlns, strs & c*)
    *Barchet & Endres – Boskovsky & Tomasow –
    Colandrea & Michelucci – Gavrilov & Karolyi –
    Mozzato & Ruotolo – Prystawski & Scherz –
    Redditi & unid. vln – Ruotolo & Stefanato*
Concerto No. 6, in a, P.I (*F.I, No. 176*) (*vln,
strs & c*)
    *Barchet – Bernstein – Bress – Chemet (2) –
    Cores – Fachiri – Gavrilov – Grumiaux – Gulli
    – Hendel – Liberman – Meyer – Michelucci –
    Prystawski – Redditi – Senatra – Tomasow*
Concerto No. 7, in F, P.249 (*F.IV, No. 9*) (*4
vlns, strs & c*)
    *Barchet, Endres, Hopfner & Steffen-Wendling –
    Barnert, Prystawski, Scherz & Soh – Benvenuti,
    Ferro, Gulli & Malanotte – Boskovsky,
    Hintermeyer, Matheis & Tomasow – Carles,
    Déat, Jarry & Molard – Champeil, Gali, Gendre
    & Yordanoff – Cotogni, Gallozzi, Michelucci &
    Vicari – Gavrilov, Hermann, Karolyi & Schilling
    – Redditi & soloists*
Concerto No. 8, in a, P.2 (*F.I, No. 177*) (*2 vlns,
strs & c*)
    *Armand & Giordano – Barchet & Endres –
    Benac & Zafer – Boskovsky & Tomasow –
    Brouwer & Rombouts – Brown & Totenberg –
    Cotogni & Michelucci (2) – Czerwonky &
    Steiner – Dejean & Gendre – Doukan & Gendre
    – C. Ferraresi & Stefanato – Gavrilov & Karolyi
    – Gulli & Malanotte – Hellmann &
    Zimmermann – Karpinsky & Wührer –
    Malanotte & Mozzato – D. & I. Oistrakh (3) –
    D. Oistrakh & Stern – Petrovik & R.
    Schumacher – Pezzani & Salvi – Pierangeli –
    Prystawski & soh – Redditi & unid. vln*
Concerto No. 9, in D, P.147 (*F.I, No. 178*) (*vln,
strs & c*)
    *Barchet – Cervera – Ferro – Fournier – Gavrilov
    – Michelucci – Prystawski – Redditi – Soriano –
    Tomasow*
Concerto No. 10, in b, P.148 (*F.IV, No. 10*) (*4

vlns, strs & c)
    *Armand, Auriacombe, Giordano & Muhlberger –
    Bakowski, Iwanow, Komosiński & Radek –
    Barchet, Endres, Hopfner & Steffen-Wendling –
    Barnert, Prystawski, Scherz & Soh – Boder,
    Furer, Milkis & Varenberg – Boskovsky,
    Hintermeyer, Matheis & Tomasow – Buldrini,
    Eidus, Graeler & Shulman – Carles, Déat, Jarry
    & Molard, – Carracilly, Jacquillat, Lepinte &
    Wallez – Ceradini, C. Ferraresi, Salvi &
    Stefanato – Connah, Howard, Marriner &
    Nelson – Cotogni, Gallozzi, Michelucci & Vicari
    – Crenne, Moglia, Pelaz & Wallez – Crut,
    Dumont, Merckel & Schwartz – Dejean, Gendre,
    Marchand & Plešzonich – Ferro, Gramegna,
    Malanotte & Pelliccia – Ferro, Gulli, Malanotte
    & Stefanato – Fietz, Kaufman, Piraccini &
    Rybar – Frenkel, Hanke, Totenberg & van der
    Berg – Gavrilov, Hermann, Karolyi & Schilling
    – Goren, Humphreys, Masters & Menuhin –
    Redditi & soloists – Retyi & soloists*
Concerto No. 11, in d, P.250 (*F.IV, No. 11*) (*2
vlns, vlc, strs & c*)
    *Asselin – E. Bachmann & Schneider – Barchet
    & Steffen-Wendling – Baumgartner & Wolfgang
    Schneiderhan – Boskovsky & Tomasow –
    Cotogni & Michelucci – Danz & Zepparoni –
    Ferro & Malanotte (2) – Forchhammer &
    Telmányi – Gavrilov & Karolyi – Gozman &
    Varenberg – Holtman & Krachmalnick –
    Krebbers & Stuurop – Milstein & Morini –
    Pezzani & Salvi – Prystawski & Scherz – Redditi
    & unid. vln – L. Sorkin – Thibaud*
Concerto No. 12, in E, P.240 (*F.I, No. 179*)
(*vln, strs & c*) *Barchet – Bress – Ferro (2) –
Gavrilov – Michelucci – Redditi – Soh –
Tomasow*
(12) Concerti, Op. 4 "La Stravaganza" (*vln, strs
& c*)
    Concerto No. 1, in B flat, F.I, No. 180 *Ayo –
    Barchet – Fantini*
    Concerto No. 2, in E, F.I, No. 181 *Ayo –
    Barchet – Fantini – Retyi*
    Concerto No. 3, in G, F.I, No. 182 *Ayo –
    Barchet – Fantini*
    Concerto No. 4, in a, F.I, No. 183 *Ayo –
    Bacchetta – Barchet – Lamacque*
    Concerto No. 5, in A, F.I, No. 184 *Alès – Ayo
    – Bacchetta – Barchet – Malanotte*
    Concerto No. 6, in g, F.I, No. 185 *Alès – Ayo –
    Bacchetta – Barchet – Bress – Kaufman*
    Concerto No. 7, in C, F.I, No. 186 *Alès – Ayo –
    Barchet – Fantini – Kaufman*
    Concerto No. 8, in d, F.I, No. 187 *Alès – Ayo –
    Barchet – Fantini*
    Concerto No. 9, in F, F.I, No. 188 *Alès – Ayo –
    Barchet – Fantini – Kaufman*
    Concerto No. 10, in c, F.I, No. 189 *Alès – Ayo
    – Bacchetta – Barchet*
    Concerto No. 11, in D, F.I, No. 190 *Alès – Ayo
    – Bacchetta – Barchet – Kaufman*
    Concerto No. 12, in G, F.I, No. 191 *Alès – Ayo
    – Bacchetta – Barchet*
(6) Concerti, Op. 6 (*vln, strs & c*)
    Concerto No. 1, in g, F.I, No. 192 *Ferraris –*

Shinder – Shumsky
Concerto No. 2, in B flat, F.I, No. 193 *Ferraris*
Concerto No. 3, in g, F.I, No. 194 *Ferraris*
Concerto No. 4, in D, F.I, No. 195 *Fantini*
Concerto No. 5, in e, F.I, No. 196 *Fantini*
Concerto No. 6, in d, F.I, No. 197 *Fantini*
(12) Concerti, Op. 7 (*vln, strs & c*)*
  Concerto No. 11, in D *Salvi*
(12) Concerti, Op. 8 (1725) "Il Cimento dell'
Armonia e dell' Invenzione" (*Nos. 1/4: Le quattro
Stagioni*) (*vln, strs & c*)
  Concerto No. 1, in E, P.241 (*F.I, No. 22*) "La
  Primavera"
  *Accardo – Alès – Armand – Ayo (2) – Bacchetta
  – Barchet (3) – Bean – Biffoli – L. Bobescu –
  Bronne – Brusilow – Büchner – Combes –
  Corigliano (2) – Emanuele – Fantini – A.
  Ferrari – Ferro (3) – Frasca-Colombier – Gulli –
  Jarry – Kaufman (2) – Kovács – Krebbers –
  Krotzinger – Lautenbacher – Loveday –
  Michelucci – Milanova – Molinari – Nadien –
  Olevsky – Ozim – Parikian – Pavella –
  Puschacher – R. Ricci – Ruha – Wolfgang
  Schneiderhan – J. Schröder – Smirnov – Szeryng
  – Tomasow – Toso – Wallez – Warchal –
  Wührer – Zazofsky*
  Concerto No. 2, in B flat, P.336 (*F.I, No. 23*)
  "L'Estate"
  *Accardo – Alès – Armand – Ayo (2) – Bacchetta
  – Barchet (3) – Bean – Biffoli – L. Bobescu –
  Brusilow – Büchner – Combes – Corigliano (2) –
  Emanuele – Fantini – A. Ferrari –
  Frasca-Colombier – Gulli – Jarry – Kaufman
  (2) – Kovács – Krotzinger – Lautenbacher –
  Loveday – Michelucci – Milanova – Molinari –
  Monosoff – Mozzato (2) – Nadien – Olevsky –
  Ozim – Parikian – Pavella – Puschacher – R.
  Ricci – Ruha – Wolfgang Schneiderhan – J.
  Schröder – Smirnov – Szeryng – Tomasow –
  Toso – Wallez – Warchal – Wührer – Zazofsky*
  Concerto No. 3, in F, P.257 (*F.I, No. 24*)
  "L'Autunno"
  *Accardo – Alès – Armand – Ayo (2) – Bacchetta
  – Barchet (2) – Bean – Biffoli – L. Bobescu –
  Brusilow – Büchner – Combes – Corigliano (2) –
  Emanuele – Fantini – A. Ferrari – Ferro (3) –
  Frasca-Colombier – Gulli – Jarry – Kaufman
  (2) – Kovács – Krebbers – Krotzinger –
  Kwalwasser – Lautenbacher – Loveday –
  Michelucci – Milanova – Molinari – Nadien –
  Olevsky – Ozim – Parikian – Pavella –
  Puschacher – R. Ricci – Ruha – Wolfgang
  Schneiderhan – J. Schröder – Smirnov – Szeryng
  – Tomasow – Toso – Wallez – Warchal –
  Wührer – Zazofsky*
  Concerto No. 4, in f, P.442 (*F.I, No. 25*)
  "L'Inverno"
  *Accardo – Alès – Armand – Ayo (2) – Bacchetta
  – Barchet (3) – Bean – Biffoli – L. Bobescu –
  Brusilow – Büchner – Combes – Corigliano (2) –
  Emanuele – Fantini – A. Ferrari –
  Frasca-Colombier – Gulli (2) – Jarry –
  Kaufman (2) – N. Koutzen – Kovács – Krebbers*

*Numbers 1 & 7 are for oboe.

*– Krotzinger – Lautenbacher – Loveday –
Michelucci – Milanova – Molinari – Mozzato (2)
– Nadien – Olevsky – Ozim – Parikian – Pavella
– Puschacher – R. Ricci – Ruha – Wolfgang
Schneiderhan – J. Schröder – Smirnov – Szeryng
– Tomasow – Toso – Wallez – Warchal –
Wührer – Zazofsky*
Concerto No. 5, in E flat, P.415 (*F.I, No. 26*)
"La Tempesta di mare" *Ayo – Barchet –
Kaufman – Levan – Malanotte (2) – Olevsky –
Ozim – Redditi – Toso*
Concerto No. 6, in C, P.7 (*F.I, No. 27*) "Il
piacere" *Ayo – Barchet – Kaufman – Menuhin
– Olevsky – Ozim – Redditi – Ruotolo*
Concerto No. 7, in d, P.258 (*F.I, No. 28*) *Ayo –
Barchet – Gulli – Kaufman – Milstein – Olevsky
– Ozim – Redditi*
Concerto No. 8, in g, F.I, No. 16 *Ayo – Barchet
– Gulli – Kaufman – Olevsky – Ozim – Redditi*
Concerto No. 9, in d, F.VII, No. 1 *Ayo –
Barchet – Kaufman – Olevsky – Ozim – Redditi*
Concerto No. 10, in B flat, P.338 (*F.I, No. 29*)
"La Caccia" *Ayo – Barchet – Fernandez –
Kaufman – Malanotte (2) – Olevsky – Ozim –
Redditi*
Concerto No. 11, in D, P.153 (*F.I, No. 30*) *Ayo
– Barchet – Gulli – Kaufman – Olevsky – Ozim
– Redditi*
Concerto No. 12, in C, P.8 (*F.I, No. 31*) *Ayo –
Barchet – Kaufman – Olevsky – Ozim – Redditi*
(12) Concerti, Op. 9 (1728) "La Cetra" (*vln, strs
& c*)
  Concerto No. 1, in C, P.9 (*F.I, No. 47*) *Ayo –
  Barchet – Kaufman – Makanowitzky – Pini*
  Concerto No. 2, in A, P.214 (*F.I, No. 51*) *Ayo –
  Barchet – Kaufman – Makanowitzky – Pini*
  Concerto No. 3, in g, P.339 (*F.I, No. 52*) *Ayo –
  Barchet – Ceradini – Kaufman – Makanowitzky
  – Pini*
  Concerto No. 4, in E, P.242 (*F.I, No. 48*) *Ayo –
  Barchet – Kaufman – Makanowitzky – Pini*
  Concerto No. 5, in a, P.10 (*F.I, No. 53*) *Ayo –
  Barchet – Kaufman – Makanowitzky – Pini*
  Concerto No. 6, in A, P.215 (*F.I, No. 54*) (*with
  solo vln scordato*) *Ayo – Barchet – Kaufman –
  Makanowitzky – Pini*
  Concerto No. 7, in B flat, P.340 (*F.I, No. 55*)
  *Ayo – Barchet – Kaufman – Makanowitzky –
  Pini*
  Concerto No. 8, in d, P.260 (*F.I, No. 56*) *Ayo –
  Barchet – Kaufman – Makanowitzky – Pini*
  Concerto No. 9, in B flat, P.341 (*F.I, No. 57*)
  (*with 2nd vln obb*) *Ayo & Cotogni – Barchet &
  Steffen-Wendling – Boskovsky & Makanowitzky
  – Kaufman – Pini & Tunnell*
  Concerto No. 10, in G, P.103 (*F.I, No. 49*) *Ayo
  – Barchet – Kaufman – Makanowitzky – Pini*
  Concerto No. 11, in c, P.416 (*F.I, No. 58*) *Ayo
  – Barchet – Kaufman – Makanowitzky – Pini*
  Concerto No. 12, in b, P.154 (*F.I, No. 50*) (*with
  solo vln scordato*) *Ayo – Barchet – Fernandez –
  Kaufman – Makanowitzky – Pini*
(6) Concerti, Op. 10 (*fl, 2 vlns, vla, org & vlc*)
  Concerto No. 3, in D, P.155 (*F.VI, No. 14*)
  Goberman

(6) Concerti, Op. 11 (*vln, strs & c*)
  Concerto No. 2, in e, P.106 (*F.I, No. 208*) "Il
  Favorito" *Michelucci*
(6) Concerti, Op. 12 (*vln, strs & c*)
  Concerto No. 1, in g, P.343 (*F.I, No. 211*)
  *Elman (2) – Fantini – Gertler – L. Kogan (2) –
  Rybar – Suzuki*
  Concerto No. 2, in d, F.I, No. 212 *Fantini*
  Concerto No. 3, in D *Fantini*
  Concerto No. 4, in C, F.I, No. 213 *Fantini*
  Concerto No. 5, in E flat, F.I, No. 86 *Fantini*
  Concerto No. 6, in E flat, F.I, No. 214 *Fantini*
Concerto in B flat, F.I, No. 40 (*2 vlns, strs & c*)
Iwanow & Kucharski
Concerto in E flat, F.I, No. 231 "Il Ritiro" (*vln,
strs & c*) *Maier – Milstein*
Concerto in B flat, 7.XI, No. 24 (P.342) (*vln, strs
& c*) *Krebbers*
Concerto in g, F.XI, No. 21 (*vln, strs & c*)
Krebbers
Concerto in F, F.XI, No. 29 (*vln, strs & c*)
Krebbers
Concerto in g, F.XII, No. 6 (*vln, strs & c*)
Krebbers
Concerto in e, F.XII, No. 13 (*vln, strs & c*)
Krebbers
Concerto in d, F.XII, No. 31 (*Op. 41, No. 1*) (*2
fls, 2 obs, bsn, 2 vlns, strs & c*) *Ceradini & Salvi*
Concerto in a, P.13 (*vln, strs & c*) *Blot*
Concerto in C, P.14 (*F.I, No. 13*) (*Op. 54, No. 3*)
"Per la SS. Assunzione di Maria Vergine" (*vln,
strs & c*) *L. Bobescu – Ferro – Redditi –
Stanič-Krek – Toso*
Concerto in C, P.16 (*F.XII, No. 37*) (*2 mands, 2
obs, 2 fls, 2 cls, 2 vlns, vlc, strs & c*) *A. Ferrari &
Toso*
Concerto in a, P.28 (*F.I, No. 61*) (*2 vlns, strs & c*)
*Ayo & Michelucci – Benedetti Michelangeli &
Biffoli – Brandis & Maas – Malanotte & Scaglia*
Concerto in C, P.54 (*F.XII, No. 17*) (*2 fls, 2 obs,
bsn, 2 vlns, strs & c*) *Gershman & Manzella –
Salvi & Vianelli*
Concerto in C, P.58 (*vln, 2 vlcs, strs & c*) *L.
Bobescu – Pelliccia*
Concerto in C, P.74 (*F.XII, No. 4*) (*vln, rec, strs
& c*) *Krebbers*
Concerto in a, P.77 (*F.XII, No. 11*) (*2 vlns, fl, vlc,
strs & c*) *Galimir & Kwalwasser*
Concerto in C, P.82 (*F.XII, No. 24*) (*fl, ob, vln,
bsn & c*) *Goberman*
Concerto in C, P.84 (*F.XII, No. 14*) "Per la
Solennità di St. Lorenzo" (*2 fls, 2 obs, 2 cls, 2
vlns, bsn, strs & c*) *Benedetti Michelangeli &
Pasquali – Bolotine & Galimir – Tarack*
Concerto in C, P.87 (*F.XII, No. 23*) (*2 fls, ob,
E-hrn, 2 tpts, vln, 2 vlas & 2 hpsi*) *Kalup*
Concerto in D, P.88 (*F.I, No. 3*) (*vln, strs & c*)
Magaziner – Milstein
Concerto in G, P.105 (*fl, vln, ob, bsn & c*)
Goberman
Concerto in B flat, P.112 (*F.I, No. 163*)
"Posthorn" (*vln, strs & c*) *Gerle – Jakowicz*
Concerto in G, P.132 (*F.I, No. 6*) (*2 vlns, strs
& c*) *Abramenkov & Smirnov – Benedetti
Michelangeli & Biffoli*

Concerto in G, P.135 (*F.IV, No. 1*) (*2 vlns, 2 vlcs, strs & c*) *Alès & Gendre – Carles & Fernandez – Galimir & N. Koutzen*

Concerto in D, P.146 (*F.IV, No. 7*) (*4 vlns, vlc, strs & c*) *L. Bobescu*

Concerto in D, P.159 (*2 vlns, strs & c*) *Kaufman & Rybar*

Concerto in D, P.163 (*F.I, No. 133*) (*vln, strs & c*) *Milstein – Toso*

Concerto in D, P.164 (*F.I, No. 62*) "Per la SS Assunzione di Maria Vergine" (*vln & 2 str. choruses*) *Fantini*

Concerto in D, P.165 (*F.I, No. 136*) "Fatto per la solennità della S. Lingua di S. Antonio" (*vln, strs & c*) *Fantuzzi*

Concerto in D, P.185 (*vln, strs & c*) *Fernandez*

Concerto in D, P.188 (*F.IV, No. 4*) (*2 vlns, 2 vlcs, strs & c*) *Ceradini & Redditi – Guglielmo & Toso*

Concerto in D, P.189 (*F.I, No. 41*) (*2 vlns, strs & c*) *Hendel & Schlupp – D. Oistrakh & Stern*

Concerto in D. P.195 (*F.I, No. 162*) (*vln, strs & c*) *Milstein*

Concerto in D, P.198 (*F.XII, No. 7*) (*vln, fl & c*) *Gendre*

Concerto in D, P.204 (*F.XII, No. 29*) "La Pastorella" (*fl, ob, vln, bsn & c*) *Gendre – Goberman*

Concerto in D. P.206 (*vln, fl, bsn, strs & c*) *Kwalwasser*

Concerto in D, P.207 (*F.XII, No. 25*) (*fl, ob, vln, bsn & c*) *Fernandez – Gendre*

Concerto in D, P.208 (*F.I, No. 10*) (*Op. 51, No. 1*) "L'Inquietudine" (*vln, strs & c*) *Brandis – Gallozzi – Milstein*

Concerto in D, P.209 (*F.XII, No. 15*) (*2 vlns, lute, strs & c*) *Goberman & Manzella*

Concerto in A, P.222 (*F.I, No. 139*) "L'eco in lontano" (*2 vlns, strs & c*) *Gallozzi & Zampani – Giaccone & Gramegna – Höver & Prystawski – Lautenbacher & Mampaey*

Concerto in A, P.227 (*vln, strs & c*) *Yordanoff*

Concerto in A, P.228 (*F.I, No. 141*) "Pisendel" (*vln, strs & c*) *Bress – Milstein – Quick*

Concerto in A, P.229 (*F.I, No. 39*) (*vln, strs & c*) *Milstein*

Concerto in A, P.234 (*F.I, No. 106*) (*vln, strs & c*) *Milstein*

Concerto in A, P.236 (*F.I, No. 5*) (*vln, strs & c*) *Kwalwasser – Milstein*

Concerto in A, P.238 (*vln, vlc, strs & c*) *Abbado – Gulli*

Concerto in E, P.246 (*F.I, No. 127*) (*Op. 35, No. 6*) "L'Amoroso" (*vln, strs & c*) *Ayo – Barchet – Brandis*

Concerto in E, P.248 (*F.I, No. 4*) "Il Riposo" (*vln, strs & c*) *Cotogni – Glenn – Gramegna*

Concerto in F, P.273 (*Op. 46, No. 2*) (*vln, 2 obs, 2 hrns, bsn, strs & c*) *Bolotine – Fantuzzi*

Concerto in F, P.274 (*F.XII, No. 41*) (*vln, org, strs & c*) *Fernandez*

Concerto in F, P.278 (*F.I, No. 34*) (*3 vlns, strs & c*)

Abbado, d'Annibale & Borgo – Ayo, Cotogni & Tamponi – Ayo, Gallozzi & Tamponi – Bronne, N. Koutzen & Monosoff – Bünte, Hendel & Schlupp – Larner, N. Roth & Rozsa

Concerto in d, P.281 (*F.I, No. 100*) (*2 vlns, strs & c*) *Blanchard & Fernandez – D. Oistrakh & Stern*

Concerto in F, P.290 (*F.I, No. 20*) "Per la solennità di S. Lorenzo" (*vln, strs & c*) *Toso*

Concerto in F, P.301 (*vln, ob, strs & c*) *Manzella*

Concerto in d, P.310 (*F.I, No. 11*) "Senza cantin" (*vln, 2 fls, 2 obs & 2 bsns*) *Gendre – Gershman – Kaufman*

Concerto in d, P.311 (*Op. 22, No. 4*) (*vln, strs & c*) *Anonymous*

Concerto in F, P.322 (*F.XII, No. 21*) (*fl, ob, vln & c*) *Gendre*

Concerto in F, P.323 (*F.XII, No. 26*) (*fl, ob, vln, bsn & c*) *Gendre – Goberman*

Concerto in F, P.325 (*vln, strs & c*) *Alès*

Concerto in B flat, P.342 (*F.XI, No. 5*) (*vln, strs & c*) *Krebbers*

Concerto in g, P.343 (*vln, strs & c*) *Tomasow*

Concerto in B flat, P.349 (*vln, strs & c*) *Champeil*

Concerto in g, P.359 (*F.XII, No. 33*) "Per S.A.R. di Sassonia" (*3 obs, bsn, vln, 2 hrns, strs & c*) *Gabowitz*

Concerto in g, P.360 (*F.XII, No. 5*) (*fl, ob, vln, bsn & c*) *Fernandez – Gendre – Goberman*

Concerto in g, P.366 (*F.I, No. 98*) (*2 vlns, strs & c*) *D. Oistrakh & Stern*

Concerto in B flat, P.367 (*F.I, No. 59*) (*4 vlns, strs & c*)

Abbado, d'Annibale, Borgo & Pasquali – Carles, Déat, Jarry & Molard – Sangiorgi, Toso, Valpreda & Zampieri

Concerto in B flat, P.368 (*F.I, No. 60*) (*Op. 28, No. 3*) "Scordatura" (*vln, 2 str choruses & c*) *L. Bobescu – Gerle – Redditi – Toso*

Concerto in B flat, P.373 (*vln, strs & c*) *Alès*

Concerto in g, P.383 (*F.XII, No. 3*) "Per l'orchestra di Dresda" (*vln, 2 fls, 2 obs, 2 bsns & c*)

Anonymous – Fernandez – Gershman – Gieseler – Glenn – Glenn & Grötzer – Kaufman – Melkus – Salvi

Concerto in B flat, P.385 (*F.XII, No. 12*) (*Op. 41, No. 5*) "Funebre" (*vln, strs & c*) *Fantuzzi – Toso*

Concerto in B flat, P.388 (*F.IV, No. 2*) (*Op. 22, No. 2*) (*vln, vlc, strs & c*) *Alès – Ayo – Heifetz – Kempler – Pelliccia – Salvi – Smirnov*

Concerto in B flat, P.391 (*2 vlns, strs & c*) *Lamacque & Oguse*

Concerto in g, P.403 (*F.XII, No. 20*) (*fl, ob, vln, bsn & c*) *Goberman*

Concerto in g, P.404 (*F.XII, No. 8*) (*vln, fl, bsn, strs & c*) *Kwalwasser*

Concerto in B flat, P.405 (*vln, strs & c*) *Magaziner*

Concerto in B flat, P.406 (*F.XII, No. 16*) (*vln, ob, strs & c*) *Alès – Artur – Fernandez – Galimir – Hendel – Pelliccia – Roberts – Toso*

Concerto in g, P.407 (*vln, strs & c*) *Alès*

Concerto in c, P.419 (*F.I, No. 2*) (*Op. 51, No. 3*) "Il Sospetto" (*vln, strs & c*) *Bress – Glenn – Milstein – Pelliccia – Vicari*

Concerto in E flat, P.423 (*F.I, No. 101*) (*2 vlns, strs & c*) *Maier & Vorholz*

Concerto in E flat, P.428 (*Op. 33, No. 1*) (*vln, strs & c*) *Rybar*

Concerto in E flat, P.429 (*Op. 33, No. 2*) (*vln, strs & c*) *Kaufman – Minetti*

Concerto in c, P.436 (*F.I, No. 12*) (*2 vlns, strs & c*) *N. Koutzen & Kwalwasser – D. Oistrakh & Stern*

Concerto in A (*gtr, vln, vla & vlc*) *Corigliano*

Concerto in C (*lute, vln & c*) *Corigliano*

Concerto in A (*vln, strs & c*) *Staryk*

Concerto in e (*vln, strs & c*) *Ceradini*

Concerto in D "Accademico formato" (*vln, ob, vlc, strs & c*) *Ferro*

Concerto (*2 vlns, strs & c*)*

Kaufman & unid. vln

(12) Sonatas, Op. 1 (*2 vlns & c*)

Sonata No. 1, in g, F.XIII, No. 17 *Ferraris & Molinaro – Kalup & Topolski*

Sonata No. 2, in e, F.XIII, No. 18 *Ferraris & Molinaro – Gendre – Kalup & Topolski*

Sonata No. 3, in C, F.XIII, No. 19 *Ferraris & Molinari – Kalup & Topolski*

Sonata No. 4, in E, F.XIII, No. 20 *Ferraris & Molinaro – Kalup & Topolski – Kuijken & Maier*

Sonata No. 5, in F, F.XIII, No. 21 *Ferraris & Molinaro – Kalup & Topolski*

Sonata No. 6, in D, F.XIII, No. 22 *Ferraris & Molinaro – Kalup & Topolski*

Sonata No. 7, in E flat, F.XIII, No. 23 *Ferraris & Molinaro*

Sonata No. 8, in d, F.XIII, No. 24 *Ferraris & Molinaro – Lysy & Westergaard*

Sonata No. 9, in A, F.XIII, No. 25 *Ferraris & Molinaro*

Sonata No. 10, in B flat, F.XIII, No. 26 *Ferraris & Molinaro*

Sonata No. 11, in b, F.XIII, No. 27 *Ferraris & Molinaro*

Sonata No. 12, in d, F.XIII, No. 28 "La Follia" *Ferraris & Molinaro – Tellefsen & Thomsen*

(12) Sonatas, Op. 2 (1712) (*vln & c*)

Sonata No. 1, in g, F.XIII, No. 29 *Akos – Fontanarosa – Kovács – Tomasow*

Sonata No. 2, in A, F.XIII, No. 30 *Akos – Bernstein – A. Busch – Eto – J.C. Figueroa – Gabowitz – Heifetz – Herman – Klijn – Kovács – Laredo – Milstein (2) – Odnoposoff – R. Ricci – Scrosoppi – Zhuk*

Sonata No. 3, in d, F.XIII, No. 31 *Akos – Blot – Kovács*

Sonata No. 4, in F, F.XIII, No. 32 *Akos – Kovács – Topolski*

Sonata No. 5, in b, F.XIII, No. 33 *Akos – Kovács*

Sonata No. 6, in C, F.XIII, No. 34 *Akos – Kovács*

Sonata No. 7, in c, F.XIII, No. 35 *Kovács – R. Ricci*

Sonata No. 8, in G, F.XIII, No. 36 *Kovács*

Sonata No. 9, in e, F.XIII, No. 37 *Fernandez – Kinch – Kovács*

Sonata No. 10, in f, F.XIII, No. 38 *Kovács*

Sonata No. 11, in D, F.XIII, No. 39 *Blot – Kovács*

Sonata No. 12, in a, F.XIII, No. 40 *Blot – Kovács*

*Unidentified.

(6) Sonatas, Op. 5 "Fatte per Monsieur Pisendel" (*vln & c*)
    Sonata No. 1, in F *Gulli*
    Sonata No. 2, in A *Gulli*
    Sonata No. 3, in B flat *Gulli*
    Sonata No. 4, in e *Gulli*
    Sonata No. 5, in E flat *Gulli*
    Sonata No. 6, in g *Gulli*
(6) Sonatas, Op. 13 (1737) "Il Pastor Fido" (*fl, ob, vln, strs & c*)
    Sonata No. 4, in A, F.XVI, No. 8 *Asselin – Kohon – Quick*
    Sonata No. 6, in g, F.XVI, No. 10 *Kohon*
Sonata in d, Op. 18 (*vln & c*) *Fain*
(4) Sonatas, Op. 19 (*2 vlns & c*)
    Sonata No. 1, in F *Goberman & Manzella*
    Sonata No. 2, in G *Goberman & Manzella*
    Sonata No. 3, in F *Goberman & Manzella*
    Sonata No. 4, in B flat *Goberman & Manzella*
(2) Sonatas, Op. 55 (*lute, vln & c*)
    Sonata No. 2, in C *Goberman* ·
Sonata in D, F.XII, No. 6 (*vln & c*)
    Accardo – Comellas – Fain – Kolberg – Livontas – Marković – Milstein – Morini (2)
Sonata in c, F.XVI, No. 1 (*P.7, No. 1*) (*Op. 24*) (*vln, vlc & c*) *Galimir – Scrosoppi*
Sonata a quattro in E flat, F.XVI, No. 2 (*P.441*) "Al Santo Sepolcro" (*2 vlns, vla & c*) *C. Ferraresi & Gulli – Goberman & Manzella*
(2) Sonatas, P.7, Nos. 1 & 2 (*lute, vln & bs*)
    Trio No. 1 *Trysessoone*
Sonata in C "Mauro Foà" (*lute, vln & c*) *Redditi*
Sonata in c (*vln & c*) *Blot*
Viviani, Giovanni Buonaventura (17th century)
(12) Capricci armonici, Op. 4 (1678) (*vln & c*)
    No. 2. Symphonia *Armuzzi-Romei*
    No. 4. Aria *Armuzzi-Romei*
Vladigerov, Panchu (1899–)
(2) Bulgarian Paraphrases, Op. 18 (*vln & pf*)
    No. 1. Choro *Goldstein – D. Oistrakh – Vladigerov*
    No. 2. Ratschenitza *Vladigerov – Želeva*
Burlesque (*on 2 Bulgarian national themes*) Op. 14 (*vln & pf*) *Vladigerov*
Concert-foxtrot (*vln & pf*) *Vladigerov*
Concerto in F, Op. 11 (*vln & orch*) *Zhuk*
Danse, Op. 37 (*pf*) *Bezrodny*
(10) Impressions, Op. 9 (*vln & pf*)
    No. 4. Caressing *Vladigerov*
(2) Improvisations, Op. 7 (*vln & pf*)
    No. 2. Popular tune (*Im volkston*) *Vladigerov*
(2) Morceaux, Op. 20 (*vln & pf*)
    No. 1. Romanza *Vladigerov*
    No. 2. Oriental *Vladigerov*
Orientalico (*Concert-shimmy*) (*vln & pf*) *Vladigerov*
(4) Stücke, Op. 12 (*vln & pf*)
    No. 4. Valse romantique *Vladigerov*
Suite bulgare, Op. 21 (*pf*) *Grach – Petronio – Vladigerov*
Vardar (*Rapsodie bulgare*) Op. 16 (*vln & orch*) *Bezrodny – Garay – D. Oistrakh – Staryk – Vladigerov*
Vlasov, Vladimir (1903–)
Asel – ballet (*orch*) *Reyentovich*
Vocht, Lodewijk de (1887–)

Concerto in E (*vln & orch*) *Neste*
Voglein
Old Viennese dance (*vln & pf*) *Godowsky*
Vogler, Georg Joseph (1749–1814)
Aria, Chasse & Minuetto (*vln & pf*) *Dubois*
Caprice in E flat (*vln & pf*) *Haag*
Sonata in C "The Matrimonial Tiff" (*2 vlns, vla & c*) *Felicani & Kägi*
Vogrich, Max Wilhelm Karl (1852–1916)
Dans le Bois (*based on "Caprice No. 9, in E", Op. 1 by Paganini*) (*vln & pf*) *Elman*
Voicu, Ion (1925–)
(The) Morning after the wedding (*solo vln*) *Voicu*
Voigt, G. Bernhard
Abendgedanken "An meine Mutter" (*vln, vla & pf*) *Biedermann*
Volkmann, Robert (1815–1883)
Waltz (*vln & pf*) *Příhoda*
Voloshinov, Viktor (1911–1960)
Sonata in e, Op. 17 (*vln & pf*) *Vaiman*
Voříšek, Jan Hugo (1791–1825)
Rondo, Op. 8 (*vln & pf*) *Snítil*
Sonata in G, Op. 5 (*vln & pf*) *Snítil*
Vorrei
Could I? (*v & pf*) *Morino*
Vycpálek, Ladislav (1882–1969)
Sonata in D, Op. 19 "In praise of the violin" (*m-s, vln & pf*) *Šorm*
Wagner, Joseph Frederick (1900–)
Concert piece (1966) (*vln & vlc*) *Schoenfeld*
Preludes & Toccata (1964) (*hp, vln & orch*) *Schoenfeld*
Wagner, Richard (1813–1883)
Albumblatt in C (1861) (*pf*)
    Bezrodny – Elman (2) – Enescu – Kolberg – Kozolupova – Kulenkampff – Lorand – Mehta – D. Oistrakh – Poulet – Příhoda – Schöne – T. Seidel (2) – Stern – Ysaÿe – Zeiler
(5) Gedichte "Wesendonck-Lieder" (*v & pf*)
    No. 5. Träume *Krips – Schöne*
(Die) Meistersinger von Nürnberg (1868) – opera
    Morgenlich leuchtend "Prize song"
    Allan – Aranyi (2) – Bild – Cochrane – Elman (2) – Kochański – Ranzato (2) – Sens (2) – Spalding (2) – Thibaud – Weber – Ysaÿe – Zimbalist – Zimmermann
    selection *Sens*
Siegfried (1876) – opera
    Gönntest du mir wohl (*Waldweben*) (*Act II*) *Guidi*
Tannhäuser (1845) – opera
    O du mein holder Abendstern (*Act III*) *Bluestone – Southgate*
Tristan und Isolde (1865) – opera
    selection *Stern*
Wagner, Siegfried (1869–1930)
Concerto (1915) (*vln & orch*) *Abel*
Waldteufel, Emil (1837–1915)
Dolores – waltz, Op. 170 (*orch*) *A. Sandler*
Estudiantina, Op. 191 (*orch*) *May – Pinell – Ranzato – A. Sandler*
Wallace, William Vincent (1812–1865)
Lurline (1860) – opera
    Sweet spirit, hear my prayer *d'Almaine*
Maritana (1845) – opera
    Scenes that are brightest *d'Almaine (3)* –

    Fredericks – Stehl – Weston
    selection *Law*
Waller, Jack (1886–)
Princess Charming – musical
    I want you so *Andjelkovitch*
Walter-Behrens
Romance (*vln & pf*) *Sechiari*
Walther, Johann Jakob (1650– ?)
Aria in e (1676) (*vln & c*)* *Neuhaus*
Sonata No. 2, in A (1676) (*vln & c*)* *Friedman*
Walton, William (1902–)
Concerto (1929) (*vla & orch*) *Menuhin*
Concerto (1939) (*vln & orch*) *Francescatti – Heifetz (2) – Menuhin*
Sonata (1939) (*vln & pf*) *Menuhin – Nemet – Rostal*
Wangemann, Otto Carl Eugen (1848–)
Oberlandler (*Tyrolean airs*) (*pf*) *Amrhein*
Ware, Helen (1887–)
Hungarian Fantasia, Op. 4 (*vln & pf*) *Ware*
Warlock, Peter (1894–1930)
Capriol Suite (1926) (*str orch*) *J. Szigeti*
Warner, Harry Waldo (1874–1945)
Intermezzo (*vln & pf*) *Levey*
Lullaby (*vln & pf*) *Levey*
Scrub (*vln & pf*) *Skalka*
Serenade (*vln & pf*) *Elman*
Warren, Harry (1893–)
(The) Gold diggers of 1933 – musical
    The gold diggers song *Curti*
Waxman, Franz (1906–1967)
Carmen Fantasia (*on themes from the opera by Bizet*) (*vln & orch*) *Heifetz – L. Kogan – Stern*
Wayne, Mabel (1904–)
Chiquita (1928) (*v & pf*) *Rosen*
In a little Spanish town (*v & pf*) *Fradkin*
Ramona (1927) (*v & pf*) *Curti – Kaufman – Morino*
Weber, Carl Maria Friedrich Ernst von (1786–1826)
Contretanz in D (1815) (*orch*) *Elman – Farbmann*
(18) Favoritenwalzer, J143/60 (1812) (*pf*)
    Waltz No. 5, in B flat, J147 *Bean – Chemet – Kobin – Zilzer*
Ländlichen Tanz†. *C. Hansen*
Quintet in B flat, Op. 34 (*cl, 2 vlns, vla & vlc*) *Rybar*
Sonata No. 1, in C, Op. 24 (J138) (*pf*) *Stanske*
(6) Sonatas, Op. 10 (J99/104) (1810) (*vln & pf*)
    Sonata No. 1, in F, J99
    Aranyi – d'Arco – Bockhová – Fachiri – Flesch (2) – Haag – Kreisler (2) – L. Kogan – Markov – Neaman – R. Ricci – Szikra
    Sonata No. 2, in G, J100 *Haag – L. Kogan – R. Ricci*
    Sonata No. 3, in D, J101 *E. Bloch – A. Ferraresi – Haag – R. Ricci – J. Szigeti*
    Sonata No. 4, in E flat, J102 *Haag – R. Ricci*

*From a collection of 12 works entitled "Scherzi da Violino solo con il basso continuo" – 1676.

†Unidentified.

Sonata No. 5, in A, J103 *Haag – L. Kogan – R. Ricci*

Sonata No. 6, in C, J104 *Haag – R. Ricci*

Webern, Anton (1883–1945)

(4) Pieces, Op. 7 (1910) (*vln & pf*) *Ajemian – Bress – Hagemann – Jarry – Messiereur (2) – Schaeffer – J. Szigeti*

Trio, Op. posthumous (*vln, vla & vlc*) *Jarry*

Trio, Op. 20 (*vln, vla & vlc*) *Jarry – Washbourne*

Weill, Kurt (1900–1950)

Concerto, Op. 12 (1926) (*vln & w-wnds*) *Ajemian*

(Die) Dreigroschenoper (1928) – opera

Morität *Heifetz*

Suite (*vln & pf*)* *Frenkel*

Weinberger, Jaromir (1896–1967)

Švanda the Bagpiper (1927) – opera

Polka (*act I*) *Vladigerov*

Weiner, Leo (1885–1960)

Hungarian peasant songs (*vln & pf*) *Zathureczky*

Weiner, Stanley (1925–   )

(9) Caprices (*in hommage to celebrated violinists*) (*solo vln*)

Caprice No. 1, in b flat (*Menuhin*) *Weiner*

Caprice No. 2, in c (*Szigeti*) *Weiner*

Caprice No. 3, in A flat (*Milstein*) *Weiner*

Caprice No. 4, in G (*Grumiaux*) *Weiner*

Caprice No. 5, in g (*Szeryng*) *Weiner*

Caprice No. 6, in b flat (*Persinger*) *Weiner*

Caprice No. 7, in B flat (*Stern*) *Weiner*

Caprice No. 8, in c (*Galamian*) *Weiner*

Caprice No. 9, in B flat (*Francescatti*) *Weiner*

Latin-American suite (*vln & pf*) *Snitkovsky*

Weinzweig, John Jacob (1913–   )

Concerto (1954) (*vln & orch*) *Pratz*

Wellesz, Egon (1885–   )

Concerto, Op. 84 (1962) (*vln & orch*) *Melkus*

Weninger, Leopold (1879–   )

Auf Wiederhören

selection *Eweler*

Westendorf, Thomas Paine (1848–1923)

I'll take you home again Kathleen (1876) (*v & pf*) *Gusikoff*

Westermann

Resignation, Op. 27 (*vln & pf*) *Asti*

Westphal, Frank C. (1889–1948)

Broken dreams (*v & pf*) *Ball*

White, Clarence Cameron (1880–1960)

Bandana Sketches, Op. 12 (*vln & pf*)

No. 1. Nobody knows de trouble I see (*Negro spiritual*) *Barinova – Kreisler – Lass – Lynch – Pratz – Spalding*

Levee dance, Op. 27, No. 2 (*vln & pf*)† *Heifetz*

Whiting, Richard A. (1891–1938)‡

Song of Persia (*v & pf*) *Ball*

'Till we meet again – musical

Where was I? *Kerry*

Whittemore, Thomas (1880–1861)

*Based on songs from "Die Dreigroschenoper."

†Based on "Go down Moses."

‡See: **Lorenzo, Ange**

In a little garden (*v & pf*) *Fradkin*

Wicks, Camilla (1929–   )

Har du sett noko til Kjerringa mi (*vln & pf*)* *Wicks*

Jeg lagde meg sa silde (*vln & pf*)* *Wicks*

Jeg rodde meg ut (*vln & pf*)* *Wicks*

Widor, Charles Marie (1844–1937)

Serenade in B flat, Op. 10 (*orch*) *Eweler – Marx – Sammons*

Wieniawski, Henryk (1835–1880)

Adagio élégiaque in a, Op. 5 (*vln & pf*) *L. Kogan*

Capriccio-valse, Op. 7 (*vln & pf*)

Gilels – Heifetz – F.V. Henriques – Huberman – Jacobsen – B. Koutzen – Morini (3) – Perutz – Powell – Rubato – Rudényi – Spalding – Strock – Tarjus – Thomas – Ware

(Le) Carnaval russe (*on the Russian air "Po ulicy mostovoj"*) Op. 11 (*vln & pf*) *Kochański – Piastro – Vecsey*

Concerto No. 1, in f sharp, Op. 14 (*vln & orch*)

Gitlis – Krysa – Pikaizen – Rabin

Concerto No. 2, in d, Op. 22 (*vln & orch*)

Ambrose – Bilbe – Bratza – Brown – Brückner – Buchtele – Culbertson – Elman (2) – Fain (2) – Farbmann – Gimpel – Gitlis – Grumiaux – Haendel – Halik – Heifetz (3) – Herman – Huberman – Irmer – Kubelík – Lass – Law (2) – MacMillen – Menges – Milstein – Mischakoff – Morini (2) – Mosley – I. Oistrakh (2) – Olevsky – Powell – Příhoda – Rabin – T. Seidel – Senatra – Spalding – Stern (2) – Totenberg – Tworek – Voicu – Weissgerber – Wilkomirska – Zimmermann – Zukerman

(L') École moderne, Op. 10 (*10 Études*) (*solo vln*)

Étude No. 1, in c "Le Sautillé" *Staryk*

Étude No. 4, in A "Le Staccato" *R. Ricci*

Étude No. 5, in E flat "alla Saltarella" *Barinova – Campoli – Eidus – Elman – D. & I. Oistrakh – Staryk*

Étude No. 7, in A flat "La Cadenza" *Danczowska – Sitkovetsky (2) – Staryk*

(8) Étude-Caprices, Op. 18 (*solo vln & 2nd vln obb*)

Étude-Caprice No. 1, in g *Staryk*

Étude-Caprice No. 2, in E flat *Staryk*

Étude-Caprice No. 3, in D *Feigin – Staryk*

Étude-Caprice No. 4, in a

Campoli – Eidus – Fain – Francescatti – Kremer – D. Oistrakh – Rabin (2) – Shkolníková – Staryk – Thibaud (2)

Étude-Caprice No. 5, in E flat *D. Oistrakh – D. & I. Oistrakh – Staryk*

Étude-Caprice No. 6, in D *Staryk*

Étude-Caprice No. 7, in c *Staryk*

Étude-Caprice No. 8, in F *Staryk*

Fantaisie brillante (*on themes from Gounod's "Faust"*) Op. 20 (*vln & orch*)

d'Almaine – Elman (2) – Gimpel – Jacobsen – L. Kogan – Lorand – Melsa – Parlow – Piastro – Příhoda – Vecsey

Gigue, Op. 23 (*vln & pf*) *Snitkovsky*

Légende, Op. 17 (*vln & pf or orch*)

Accardo – Barinova – Beckwith – Campoli –

*Composed jointly with Rolf Hodger.

Castillo – Catterall – Czerwonky – Dessau – Elman (2) – Flesch – Friedman – Frolov – Gimpel – Grumiaux – M. Hansen – Jacobs – Jussila – Kalafusz – Kerekjarto – Kneisel – L. Kogan – Law – Manén – Mendels – Menuhin (2) – Milstein – D. Oistrakh (2) – Onderet – R. Pollak – Rudényi – Sammons – Simor – Staryk – Viardot – Weissgerber – Wise – Zacharewitsch – Zhuk – Zimbalist

Mazurka* *R. Pollak*

Mazurka in a, Op. 3 "Kujawiak" (*vln & pf*)

Barcewicz – Barinova – Brown – Buchtele – Carrodus – M. De Groot – Elman – Frolov – Gimpel – Gyarfas – C. Hansen – F.V. Henriques – Herzl – Høeberg – Ignatieff – Kerekjarto – Georg Kniestaedt – Krengel – Law – Luquin – Mossel – Neumann – Powell – Roeder – Schmied – S. Smith – Spalding – Szemere (2) – Szikra – Tworek – Valesca-Becker – Wittenberg

(2) Mazurkas, Op. 12 (*vln & pf*)

Mazurka No. 1, in D "Sielanka" *Barinova – Posselt*

Mazurka No. 2, in g "Le Ménetrier" *Barinova – Carrodus – Elman (2) – Opfermann – Plaeinitz – P. Schumacher*

(2) Mazurkas, Op. 19 (*vln & pf*)

Mazurka No. 1, in G "Obertass"

Anonymous – Bartholdy – Bonis – Borgerth – Dessau – Dunn – Dyke – Fischberg – Fontova – Frenkel – Gimpel – Gregorowicz – C. Hansen – Heermann – Jacobs – Kantrovitch – L. Kogan (2) – Manuello – Mendels – Moller – Moszkowski – Ranzato (2) – P. Schumacher – Sebald – Simor – Snitkovsky – Totenberg – Valesca-Becker – Wilkomirska – Ysaÿe – Zilzer

Mazurka No. 2, in D "Dudziarz"

Barinova – Elman – Fabroni – Flesch (2) – Fredericks – Gimpel (2) – Godwin – Heermann – Huberman – Jacobs – Georg Kniestaedt – L. Kogan – Kubelík – Kulenkampff – W. Meyer – Milstein (2) – Powell – Ranzato – Staryk – Ysaÿe

Polonaise brillante No. 1, in D, Op. 4 (*vln & pf*)

Accardo – Barbieri – Boussinot – Chemet – Eidus – Elman – Erduran – Fain – Garnier (2) – Gimpel – Haendel – Heifetz (2) – Jásek – Lewkowitz – Lubotsky – Mendels – Menges – Milstein (2) – I. Oistrakh – A.J. Rose – Shumsky – Sitkovetsky (2) – Snitkovsky – Spalding – Staryk – Strock – Wilk – J. Wolff – Zacharewitsch – Zukerman

Polonaise brillante No. 2, in A, Op. 21 (*vln & pf*)

Cantrelle – Eidus – Gimpel – Haendel – Jacobs – Janowski – Jarry – Kamilarov – L. Kogan – Liberman – Spalding – Temianka – Thibaud – Thomas

Scherzo-Tarantelle, Op. 16 (*vln & pf*)

Accardo – Ambrose – Barylli – Bean – Bochkova – Bress – Danczowska – Eidus – Fain (2) – Fairless – Friedman – Garnier – Gimpel – M. Gordon – Haendel (2) – Heifetz (3) – Jarry – Kálmán – Kolberg – Kubelík – Laredo –

*Unidentified.

Menuhin (4) – Milstein (2) – D. Oistrakh – I. Oistrakh – Pillitz – Příhoda – Renardy – R. Ricci – Rostal – Shkolníková – Solloway – Spalding – Spivakovsky (2) – Staryk – Szeryng (4) – Temianka – Ughi – Zacharewitsch – Zentay

Souvenir de Moscou, Op. 6 (*vln & pf or orch*)
A. Bachmann – Barinova – Benedetti – Carrodus – Eidus (2) – Elman (2) – Francescatti – Fuchs – Gregorowicz – Grumiaux – Kerekjarto – Law – Menuhin – Piastro – Quiroga – Rudényi – A. Schmidt – Spalding (2) – Vecsey – Weissgerber – Wittenberg

Variations in A (*on an original theme*) Op. 15 (*vln & pf*) *L. Kogan – Kremer*

Variations in G (*on the Austrian National Anthem*) (1853) (*solo vln*) *R. Ricci*

Wijdeveld, Wolfgang (1910–　　)
Sonata (1952) (*vln & pf*) *Klijn – Olof*

Wilhelmj, August (1845–1908)
Berceuse (*vln & pf*) *Newe*

Parsifal Fantasia (*on themes from the opera by Wagner*) (*vln & pf*) *Dessau*

Romance, Op. 10 (*vln & pf*) *Zimmermann*

Swedish melody (*vln & pf*) *Fabrizio – Hayward – Press*

Wilhite, Monte (1899–1961)
Yesterday (*v & pf*) *Ball*

Willan, Healey (1880–1968)
Sonata No. 1, in e (1922) (*vln & pf*) *Pratz (2)*
Sonata No. 2, in E (1923) (*vln & pf*) *Staryk*

Willaume, Gabriel (1873–　　)
(La) Noce bretonne (*vln & pf*) *Curti*

Williams, Alberto (1862–1952)
En la sierra, Op. 32 (*pf*)
　No. 4. El Rancho abandonado *Scholz*
Sonata No. 2, in d, Op. 51 (*vln & pf*) *Pessina*

Wilson, Richard (1941–　　)
Music for Violin & Violincello (1969) (*vln & vlc*) *Matsuda*

Wilton, Charles Henry (17 ?–18 ?)
(6) Trios (1783) (*vln, vla & vlc*)
　Trio No. 1, in A *Pougnet*
　Trio No. 3, in C *Pougnet*
　Trio No. 6, in F *Pougnet*

Winner, Septimus (1827–1902)
(The) Mocking bird (*vln & pf*) *d'Almaine (2) – Hager – Tertis*

Winter, Fred
Inga orkideer (*v & pf*) *Groth*

Winternitz, Felix (1872–1948)
Dance of the marionettes (*vln & pf*) *Collier – Kreisler – Rubato*

Dream of youth (*vln & pf*) *Kreisler*

Wirén, Dag (1905–　　)
Quartet No. 2, in C, Op. 9 (1936) (*2 vlns, vla & vlc*) *Kyndel*

Suite miniature, Op. 8a (*vlc & orch*) *Karpe*

Woestijne, David van de (1915–　　)
Concerto (*vln & 12 solo inst*) *Putters*

Wohlegemuth, Gerhard (1920–　　)
Concerto (1963) (*vln & orch*) *Vermes*

Wolf, Ernst Wilhelm (1735–1792)
Vom Sekt sind die Geigen berauscht (*v & pf*) *E. Kaufmann*

Wolf, Hugo (1860–1903)
Italienische Serenade in G (*2 vlns, vla & vlc*) *Wolfgang Schneiderhan*

Wolff, Christian (1934–　　)
Duo (*vln & pf*) *Kobayashi*
Summer (*2 vlns, vla & vlc*) *Kobayashi & Raimondi*

Wolpe, Stefan (1902–　　)
Chamber Piece No. 1 (1964) (*fl, ob, E-hrn, cl, bsn, hrn, tpt, tbn, 2 vlns, vla, cbs & pf*) *Zukofsky*
Piece (*in 2 parts for 6 players*) (*vln, cl, tpt, vlc, hp & pf*) *Datyner*
Pieces (*in 2 parts*) (*solo vln*) *Harbison*
Sonata (1949) (*vln & pf*) *Magnes*

Wolstenholm, William (1865–1931)
Allegretto (*vln & pf*) *Cochrane*
(The) Answer *Andjelkovitch*

Wood, Haydn (1882–1959)
Bird of love divine (*v & pf*) *Andjelkovitch*
(2) Little pieces (*vln & pf*)
　No. 1. Slumber song *Hayward – Kutcher – Lewis – Opfermann*
Love's garden of roses (*v & pf*) *Chemet – D. De Groot – Förster – Lensky – Manuello – Southgate*
Roses of Picardy (1916) (*v & pf*)
　Andjelkovitch (2) – Ball – Chemet – Crégut – Curti – Fradkin – Jelving – Lensky – Manuello – Spalding
World of love (*v & pf*) *Lensky*

Woodforde-Finden, Amy (　　–1919)
(4) Indian Love Lyrics (1903) (*orch*)
　No. 1. The temple bells *Cochrane*
　No. 3. Kashmiri song *Cochrane – Southgate*
　No. 4. Till I wake *Southgate*
(A) Lover in Damascus – song cycle (*v & pf*)
　No. 1. Far across the desert sands *Cochrane*
　No. 2. Where the Abana flows *Cochrane*
　No. 3. Beloved in your absence *Cochrane*
　No. 4. How many a lonely caravan *Cochrane*
　No. 5. If in the great bazaars *Cochrane*
　No. 6. Allah be with us *Cochrane*

Work, Henry Clay (1832–1884)
Kingdom coming (*v & pf*) *Powell*

Wuorinen, Charles (1938–　　)
Duo (*vln & pf*) *Zukofsky*

Wyner, Yehudi (1929–　　)
Concert Duo (1956) (*vln & pf*) *Raimondi*

Yamada, Kôsçaku (1886–　　)
Karatachi no Hana (*vln & pf*) *Lass*
Kismit (*Orientale characteristique*) (*vln & pf*) *Godwin*
Nobara (*vln & pf*) *Lass*
Suite Japonaise (*vln & pf*) *Lass*
Tomari-bune (*vln & pf*) *Lass*
Yuko Haru (*vln & pf*) *Lass*

Yardumian, Richard (1917–　　)
Concerto (*vln & orch*) *Brusilow*

Yearsley, Claude Blakesley
Siesta (*v & pf*) *D. De Groot*

Yellen, Jack (1892–　　)
I'm waiting for ships that never come in (*v & pf*) *Fradkin*

Yradier, Sebastián (1809–1865)
(La) Paloma (1877) (*v & pf*) *D. De Groot – Ghestem – Gomez – Huppertz – Morino – Seydel – Skalka – Torre*

Ysaÿe, Eugéne (1858–1931)
Berceuse in f, Op. 20 (*vln & pf*) *Bezrodny*
Chant d'Hiver, Op. 15 (*vln & cha orch*) *Rosand*
Extase in E flat (*Poème No. 4*) Op. 21 (*vln & pf or orch*) *Fain (2) – D. Oistrakh (2)*
Fantaisie, Op. 32 (*vln & pf*) *Šroubek*
Harmonies du soir, Op. 31 (*2 vlns, vla, vlc & strs*) *E. & H. Koch*
(3) Mazurkas, Op. 11 (*vln & pf*)
　Mazurka No. 1, in G "Danse souvenir" *Danchenko – Snitkovsky*
　Mazurka No. 2, in a *Danchenko – L. Kogan*
　Mazurka No. 3, in b "Lointaine-passé" *Boussinot – Danchenko – Odnoposoff – I. Oistrakh – Pikaizen (2) – Ysaÿe*
Poème élégiaque in d (*Poème No. 1*) Op. 12 (*vln & pf or orch*) *Markov – Mikhlin – D. Oistrakh – Petrosyan – Raskin*
Rêve d'enfant, Op. 14 (*vln & pf*) *D. De Groot – Dubois – Elman – Odnoposoff – R. Ricci – Ysaÿe*
Scène au Rouet (*Poème No. 2*) Op. 13 (*vln & pf or orch*) *L. Kogan – Šroubek*
(6) Sonatas, Op. 27 (*solo vln*)
　Sonata No. 1, in g (*à Joseph Szigeti*) *Bress – Danchenko – Octors – Zimbalist*
　Sonata No. 2, in a (*à Jacques Thibaud*) *Bress – Castillo – Grumlíková – Isakadze – Jakowicz – Mikhlin – Vasile*
　Sonata No. 3, in d "Ballade" (*à Georges Enescu*) *Accardo – Bress – Dembeck – Dubois – Gutnikov – Gyarmati – Harth – Jakowicz – Lubotsky – Odnoposoff – D. Oistrakh (2) – I. Oistrakh – Rabin – Raskin – Vinnikov*
　Sonata No. 4, in e (*à Fritz Kreisler*) *Bress – Kocsis – Malinin – Odnoposoff (2) – Rabin*
　Sonata No. 5, in G (*à Mathieu Crickboom*) *Bress*
　Sonata No. 6, in E (*à Manuel Quiroga*) *Bress – Klimov – Lubotsky – Mikhlin – Petronio – Voicu*
Sonata No. 1, in C (*2 vlns*) *Gilels & L. Kogan*

Yun, Isang (1917–　　)
Gaza (1963) (*vln & pf*) *Gavrilov*

Zacharewitsch, Michael (1879–1953)
Dance of Ivan Ivanovitch (*vln & pf*) *Zacharewitsch*
(A) Don Cossack's dance (*vln & pf*) *Zacharewitsch*
Imagination (*Romance*) (*vln & pf*) *Zacharewitsch*
Love & sorrow (*vln & pf*) *Zacharewitsch*

Zaimov, Khailik (1914–　　)
Allegretto (*vln & pf*) *Zaretsky*
Andante (*vln & pf*) *Zaretsky*

Zamecnik, J.S. (1872–　　)
Only a smile (*v & pf*) *Lensky*

Zarebski, Juliusz (1854–1885)
Quintet in g, Op. 34 (1885) (*pf, 2 vlns, vla & vlc*) *Gimpel & Wroński*

Zarzycki, Aleksander (1834–1895)
Mazurka in G, Op. 26 (*vln & pf*)
　Barinova – Francescatti – S. Furer – Garnier – Gutnikov – Herman – Huberman (2) – Kalafusz – Kennedy – Menges – Morini – D. Oistrakh (2) – Powell – Renardy – Zentay

Zavateri, Lorenzo (18th century)
(12) Concerti, Op. 1 (1735) (*vln & strs*)
    Concerto No. 12 "Tempesta di mare" *C.*
    Ferraresi
Zeisl, Eric (1905–1959)
Sonata (1949) "Brandeis" (*vln & pf*) *Baker*
Železný, Lubomír (1925–   )
Concerto (*vln & orch*) *Bělčík*
Zeller, Carl (1842–1898)
(Der) Vogelhändler (1891) – operetta
    Mir scheint, ich Kenn' dich spröde Fee – waltz
    Moller
    Noch einmal ... *Skalka*
    Der Schmoller *Moller*
Zerkovitz, Béla
Schwalbe, wu fliegst du bin (*v & pf*) *Földes*

Zimbalist, Efrem (1889–   )
Fantasia (*on themes from Rimsky-Korsakov's opera
"Le Coq d'or"*) (*vln & pf*) *Bezrodny – Feigin*
Improvisation on a Japanese tune *vln & pf*)*
Zimbalist (2)
(3) Slavonic dances (*vln & pf*)
    No. 1. Russian dance *Kennedy – Zimbalist*
    No. 2. Hebrew melody & dance *Breeskin –
    Kennedy – Zimbalist*
    No. 3. Polish dance *Zimbalist*
Suite dans la forme ancienne (*vln & pf*) *Zimbalist*
Zimmermann, Louis (1873–1954)
Lento ma non troppo (*vln & pf*) *Zimmermann*
Mazurka (*vln & pf*) *Zimmermann*

Zlatev-Cherkin
Svevdana, Op. 28 (*vln & pf*) *Kamilarov*
Znosko-Borowsky, Alexandre (1908–   )
Concerto (*vln & orch*) *Budovsky*
Zoubek, Karol J. (1902–1959)
Valse-caprice (*vln & pf*) *Zoubek*
Zsolt, Nándór (1887–1937)
Berceuse in D flat (1908) (*vln & pf*) *Garay*
Dragonflies (*vln & pf*) *Bisztriczky – Bratza –
Kennedy – Losowsky – Ludlow – Szikra –
Zathureczky (2)*
Herbstblätter (*vln & pf*) *Bisztriczky*
Satyre et Dryades (*vln & pf*) *Bisztriczky – Garay*
Valse-caprice (*vln & pf*) *Solloway*

*Tune: Kuruka-kuraka by Yamada.

INDEX OF POPULAR TITLES

(L') Abeille
Bachmann, Mazurka brillante No. 2 (*vln & pf*)

Accademico formato
Vivaldi, Concerto in D (*vln, ob, vlc & strs*)

Air
Purcell, (The) Indian Queen, Z630 (1695) - opera
  –Act tune "Air" (Act IV)

Air on the G-string
J.S. Bach (4) Suites, BWV 1066/9 (*orch*)
  Suite No. 3, in D: Air (2nd mvt) BWV 1068 (*2 obs, 3 tpts, drums & strs* - arr *vln & pf* as "Air on the G-string" by Wilhelmj)

Air russe
Schubert, (6) Moments musicaux, Op. 94 (D780) (1823/7) (*pf*)
  No. 3. Moment musicale No. 3, in f "Air russe"

à la Zingara
Wieniawski, Concerto No. 2, in d, Op. 22 (*vln & orch*)
  Allegro moderato (3rd mvt) "à la Zingara"

Alexander's Feast
Handel, Concerto in C (1736) "Alexander's Feast" (*2 vlns, 2 obs & strs*)

alla Saltarella
Wieniawski, (L') École moderne, Op. 10 (10 Études) (*solo vln*)
  No. 5. Étude No. 5, in E flat "alla Saltarella"

Alletamenti
Valentini, (12) Sonatas, Op. 8 (1714) "Alletamenti" (*vln & c*)

All souls day
Lassen, (6) Lieder, Op. 85 (*v & pf*)
  No. 3. Allerseelen "All souls day"

Al Santo Sepolcro
Vivaldi, Sonata a quattro in E flat, F.XVI, No. 2 (P.441) "Al Santo Sepolcro" (*2 vlns, vla & c*)

American
Dvořák, Quartet No. 6, in F, Op. 96 "American" (*2 vlns, vla & vlc*)

(L') Amoroso
Vivaldi, Concerto in E, P.246 (F.I, No. 127) (Op. 35, No. 6) "L'Amoroso" (*vln, strs & c*)

Andaluza
Granados, (12) Danzas españolas, Op 37 (1893) (*pf*)
  –No. 5. Danza española No. 5, in e "Andaluza"

Andretter
Mozart, Serenade No. 3, in D, K.185 "Andretter" (*orch*)

Angel's serenade
Braga, (7) Melodies (1867) (*v & pf*)
  No. 5. La serenata "Angel's serenade"

(The) Annunciation of the birth of Christ
Biber, (16) Biblical Sonatas "Mysterien" (*vln & c*)
  Sonata No. 1, in d "The annunciation of the birth of Christ"

Archduke
Beethoven, Trio No. 6, in B flat, Op. 97 "Archduke" (*pf, vln & vlc*)

Arioso
J.S. Bach, Cantata No. 156 (Ich steh' mit einem Fuss im Grabe) BWV156
  –Sinfonia (arr *vln & pf* as "Arioso" by Franko)

Arioso
J.S. Bach, Cantata (unid)
  –Dank sei dir, Herr "Arioso"

(L') Arte del Violino
Locatelli, (12) Concerti, Op. 3 (1733) "L'Arte del violino" (*vln & strs*)

(The) Ascension
Biber, (16) Biblical Sonatas "Mysterien" (*vln & c*)
  –Sonata No. 12, in C "The Ascension"

(L') Astrée
Couperin, Sonata No. 3, in g (1693) "L'Astrée" (*2 vlns & c*)

Au Tombeau
Locatelli (12) Sonatas, Op. 6 (1737) (*vln & c*)
  –Sonata No. 7, in f "Au Tombeau"

(L') Autunno
Vivaldi, (12) Concerti, Op. 8 (1725) "Il Cimento dell' Armonia e dell' Invenzione" (Nos 1/4: Le quattro Stagioni) (*vln & strs*)
  –Concerto No. 3, in F, F.I, No. 24 "L'Autunno"

Barcarolle
Offenbach, (Les) Contes d'Hoffmann (1881) - opera
  –Belle Nuit, O nuit d'amour "Barcarolle"

Berceuse
Godard, Jocelyn (1888) - opera
  –Cachés dans cet asile "Berceuse"

(La) Bernardina
Frescobaldi, (28) Canzoni da Sonari (1/4 part) (1628) (*var inst.*)
  –Canzona II "La Bernardina" (*vln & c*)

Birth of Christ
Biber, (16) Biblical Sonatas "Mysterien" (*vln & c*)
  –Sonata No. 3, in b "Birth of Christ"

(The) Black swan
Tchaikovsky, Swan Lake, Op. 20 (1875/6) - ballet (*orch*)

(La) Bonvisia
Frescobaldi, (28) Canzoni da Sonari (1/4 part) (1628) (*var inst*)
  –Canzona I "La Bonvisia" (*vln & c*)

Bull
Boccherini (6) Quintets, Op. 13 (*2 vlns, vla & 2 vlcs*)
  –No. 5. Quintet No. 5, in E "Bull"

Butterfly lovers
Ho, Concerto (1960) (*vln & orch*)

(La) Caccia
Vivaldi, (12) Concerti, Op. 8 (1725) "Il Cimento dell' Armonia e dell' Invenzione" (*vln & strs*)
  –Concerto No. 10, in B flat, F.I, No. 29 "La Caccia"

(La) Cadenza
Wieniawski, (L') École moderne, Op. 10 (10 Études) (*solo vln*)
  –No. 7. Étude No. 7, in A flat "La Cadenza"

(La) Campanella
Paganini, Concerto No. 2, in b, Op. 7 (*vln & orch*)
  –Ronde à la clochette (3rd mvt) "La Campanella"

Canonic
Telemann, (6) Sonatas, Op. 2 (1727) "Duets" (*2 fls or vlns*)
  –Sonata No. 1, in G "Canonic"

Canto amoroso
Sammartini, (6) Sonatas, Op. 1 (*2 vlns & c*)
  –Sonata No. 4, in A: Andante (3rd mvt) "Canto amoroso"

(Du) Carillon
J Aubert, Concerto No. 13, in e "du Carillon" (*vln & strs*)

(La) Cascade
Vecsey, Caprice No. 2 "La Cascade" (*vln & pf*)

Chaconne
Purcell, (10) Sonatas, Z.802/11 (1697) (*4 parts - 2 vlns & c*)
  –Sonata No. 6, in g, Z.807 "Chaconne"

Children's day at the camp meeting
Ives, Sonata No. 4 (1916) "Children's day at the camp meeting" (*vln & pf*)

Christ in the temple
Biber, (16) Biblical Sonatas "Mysterien" (*vln & c*)
  –Sonata No. 4, in d "Christ in the temple"

Christmas cantata
Lübeck, Willkommen, süsser Bräutigam "Christmas cantata" (*s, a & strs*)

Christmas Concerto
Corelli, (12) Concerti grossi, Op. 6 (*orch*)
  –Concerto grosso No. 8, in g "Christmas Concerto"

Christmas Concerto
Manfredini, (12) Concerti, Op. 3 (1718) (*2 vlns, strs & c*)
  –Concerto No. 12, in C "Christmas Concerto"

Christmas Concerto
Torelli, (12) Concerti, Op. 8 (1709) (*1/6: 2 vlns, strs & c; 7/12: vln, strs & c*)
  –Concerto No. 6, in g "Christmas Concerto"

Christ on the Mount of Olives
Biber, (16) Biblical Sonatas "Mysterien" (*vln & c*)
  –Sonata No. 6, in c "Christ on the Mount of Olives"

Christ on the way to Calvary
Biber, (16) Biblical Sonatas "Mysterien" (*vln & c*)
  –Sonata No. 9, in a "Christ on the way to Calvary"

Christ's crowning with thorns
Biber, (16) Biblical Sonatas "Mysterien" (*vln & c*)
  –Sonata No. 8, in B flat "Christ's crowning with thorns"

(Il) Cimento dell' Armonia e dell' Invenzione
Vivaldi, (12) Concerti, Op. 8 (1725) "Il Cimento dell' Armonia e dell' Invenzione" (*vln & strs*)

Coffee cantata
Bernier, Agréable Caffé "Coffee cantata" (1703) (*v, vln, & c*)

Concert Allegro
Glière, Concerto in g, Op. 100 "Concert Allegro" (*vln & orch*)

Concerto accademico
Vaughan Williams, Concerto in d (1925) "Concerto accademico" (*vln & orch*)

Concerto romantique
Godard, Concerto No. 1, Op. 35 "Concerto

Romantique" (*vln & orch*)

Concerto russe

Lalo, Concerto in g, Op. 29 "Concerto russe" (*vln & orch*)

Coronation of the Virgin

Biber, (16) Biblical Sonatas "Mysterien" (*vln & c*)
  –Sonata No. 15, in C "Coronation of the Virgin"

Cradle song

Brahms, (5) Lieder, Op. 49 (*v & pf*)
  –No. 4. Wiegenlied "Cradle song"

(The) Crucifixion

Biber, (16) Biblical Sonatas "Mysterien" (*vln & c*)
  –Sonata No. 10, in g "The Crucifixion"

Danse souvenir

Ysaÿe, (3) Mazurkas, Op. 11 (*vln & pf*)
  –No. 1. Mazurka No. 1, in G "Danse souvenir"

Danube waves

Ivanovici, Valurile Dunării "Danube waves" (*orch*)

Death & the maiden

Schubert, Quartet No. 14, in d, D.810 "Death & the maiden" (*2 vlns, vla & vlc*)

Delirium Amoris

Muffat, (12) Concerti grossi (1701) (*2 vlns, vlc, strs & c*)
  –Concerto grosso No. 11, in e "Delirium Amoris"

Désespoir

Vieuxtemps, (7) Romances sans paroles, Op. 7 (*vln & pf*)
  –No. 2. Romance No. 2, in c "Désespoir"

Déspespérance

Villa-Lobos, Sonata-Fantasia No. 1, in c (1912) "Déspespérance" (*vln & pf*)

Devil's trill

Tartini, Sonata in g "Il Trillo del Diavolo" (*vln & c*)

Didone abbandonata

Tartini, (12) Sonatas, Op. 1 (1734) (*vln & c*)
  –Sonata No. 10, in g "Didone abbandonata"

Double

Boyce, Concerto in b "Double" (*2 vlns & strs*)

Double

Brahms, Concerto in a, Op. 102 "Double" (*vln, vlc & orch*)

Double

Mendelssohn, Concerto in d (1823) "Double" (*vln, pf & strs*)

Double

Rozsa, Concerto (1964) "Double" (*vln, vlc & orch*)

Double

Semenoff, Concerto "Double" (*vln, pf & orch*)

Double

Viotti, Concerto in E flat "Double" (*pf, vln & str orch*)

Double Quartet

Spohr, Quartet No. 1, in d, Op. 65 "Double Quartet" (*4 vlns, 2 vlas & 2 vlcs*)

Drum roll

Haydn, Symphony No. 103, in E flat "Drum roll" (*orch*)

Dudziarz

Wieniawski, (2) Mazurkas, Op. 19 (*vln & pf*)
  –No. 2. Mazurka No. 2, in D "Didziarz"

Duets

(6) Sonatas, Op. 2 (1727) "Duets" (*2 fls or vlns*)

Dumky

Dvořák, Trio No. 4, in e, Op. 90 "Dumky" (*pf, vln & vla*)

Duo

Schubert, Sonata in A, Op. 162 (D.574) "Duo" (*vln & pf*)

(L') Eco in lontana

Vivaldi, Concerto in A, P.222 (F.I, No. 139) "L'eco in lontana" (*2 vlns, strs & c*)

(The) Emanation of the Holy Ghost

Biber, (16) Biblical Sonatas "Mysterien" (*vln & c*)
  –Sonata No. 13, in d "The Emanation of the Holy Ghost"

Em formas brasíleiras

Tavares, Concerto No. 4, Op. 107 "Em formas brasíleiras" (*vln & orch*)

Emperor

Haydn, (6) Quartets, Op. 76 (H.III, Nos. 75/80) (*2 vlns, vla & vlc*)
  –No. 3. Quartet No. 77, in C, H.III, No. 77 'Emperor'

(L') Espagnole

Couperin, (Les) Nations - 4 Suites (1726) (*2 vlns & c*)
  –Suite No. 2, in c "L'Espagnole"

(L') Estate

Vivaldi, (12) Concerti, Op. 8 (1725) "Il Cimento dell' Armonia e dell' Invenzione" (*vln & strs*)
  –Concerto No. 2, in B flat, F.I, No. 23 "L'Estate"

(L') Estro armonico

Vivaldi, (12) Concerti, Op. 3 "L'Estro armonico" (*var cbns & strs*)

Étude en forme de valse

Saint-Saëns, (6) Études, Op. 52 (*pf*)
  –Etude No. 6, in D flat "Étude en forme de valse"

Etude in thirds

Scriabin, (12) Etudes, Op. 8 (*pf*)
  –No. 10. Etude No. 10, in D flat "Etude in thirds"

Fatto per la solennità della S. Lingua di S. Antonio

Vivaldi, Concerto in D. P.165 (F.I, No. 136) "Fatto per la solennità della S. Lingua di S. Antonio" (*vln, strs & c*)

(The) Flagellation of Christ

Biber, (16) Biblical Sonatas "Mysterien" (*vln & c*)
  –Sonata No. 7, in F "The Flagellation of Christ"

Folksong suite

Shulman, Suite American "Folksong suite" (*vln & pf*)

(La) Follia

Corelli, (12) Sonatas, Op. 5 (*vln & c*)
  –Sonata No. 12, in d "La Follia"

(La) Follia

Vivaldi, (12) Sonatas, Op. 2 (1712) (*vln & c*)

  –Sonata No. 12, in d, F.XIII, No. 28 "La Follia"

Forellen

Schubert, Quintet in A, Op. 114 (D.667) "Trout" (*pf, vln, vla, vlc & cbs*)

(The) Four seasons

Vivaldi, (12) Concerti, Op. 8 (1725) "Il Cimento Dell' Armonia e dell' Invenzionne" (*vln & strs*)

Françoise

Papineau-Couture, (3) Caprices (1965) (*vln & pf*)
  –Caprice No. 3 "Françoise" (Scherzando)

(La) Françoise

Couperin, (Les) Nations - 4 Suites (1726) (*2 vlns & c*)
  –Suite No. 1, in e "la Françoise"

Frei aber Einsam (FAE):

Brahms, Schumann & Dietrich, Sonata (1853) (*vln & pf*)

Fridays

Liadov, (Les) Vendredis "Fridays" (*pf*)

From my life

Smetana, Quartet No. 1, in e (1876) "From my life" (*2 vlns, vla & vlc*)

From the New World

Dvořák, Symphony No. 9, in e, Op. 95 "From the New World" (*orch*)

Funebre

Vivaldi, Concerto in B flat, P.385 (F.XII, No. 12) (Op. 41, No. 5) "Funebre" (*vln, strs & c*)

Gesangsscene

Spohr, Concerto No. 8, in a, Op. 47 "Gesangsscene" (*vln & orch*)

Ghilaine

Papineau-Couture, (3) Caprices (1965) (*vln & pf*)
  –Caprice No. 2 "Ghilaine" (Adagio)

Ghost

Beethoven, (2) Trios, Op. 70 (*pf, vln & vlc*)
  –No. 1. Trio no. 4, in D "Ghost"

God's worship

Bloch, Adodah (God's worship) (1929) (*vln & pf*)

Golden Sonata

Purcell, (10) Sonatas, Z.802/11 (1697) (*4 parts - 2 vlns & c*)
  –Sonata No. 9, in F, Z.810 "Golden Sonata"

(Le) Grande

Hummel, Concerto in G, Op. 17 "Le Grande" (*vln, pf & orch*)

(The) Guardian Angel

Biber, (16) Biblical Sonatas "Mysterien" (*vln & c*)
  –Sonata No. 16, in g "The Guardian Angel" (*solo vln*)

Haffner

Mozart, Serenade No. 7, in D, K.250 "Haffner" (*orch*)

Harmonia artificiosa-ariosa

Biber, (7) Partitas "Harmonia artificiosa-ariosa" (*2 vlns & c*)

Homage to Joaquin Turina

Rodrigo, Sonata Pimpante "Homage to Joaquin Turina" (*vln & pf*)

Humoresque

J.A.G. Harrison, Widdicombe Fair, Op. 22

"Humoresque" (*2 vlns, vla & vlc*)

Hungarian folk tunes
Bartok, For Children (40 pieces) (1909) (*pf*)

(The) Hunt
Cibrano, (La) Caccia "The Hunt" (*vln & pf*)

Hunting cantata
J.S. Bach, Cantata No. 208 (Was mir behagt, ist nur die muntre Jagd) BWV.208 (1716) "Hunting cantata" (*s, t, b, cho, 2 fls, 3 obs, bsn, 4 hrns, strs & c*)

Im alten stil
Reger, Suite in F, Op. 93 "Im alten stil" (*vln & pf*)

(L') Immortelle
Rebel, (12) Sonatas (1712) (*2 & 3 part with figured bs*)
  –Sonata No. 6, in g "L'Immortelle"

(L') Impériale
Couperin, (Les) Nations - 4 Suites (1726) (*2 vlns & c*)
  –Suite No. 3, in d "L'Impériale"

In memory of Garcia Lorca
Poulenc, Sonata in d "In memory of Garcia Lorca" (1943) (*vln & pf*)

In memory of I.I. Sollertinsky
Shostakovich, Trio No. 2, in e, Op. 67 "In memory of I.I. Sollertinsky" (*pf, vln & vlc*)

In modus Lascivus
Serly, Sonata (1947) "In Modus Lascivus" (*solo vln*)

In one movement
Burkhard, Quartet No. 2, Op. 68 (1943) "In one movement" (*2 vlns, vla & vlc*)

In one movement
Beethoven, Trio in B flat, G.154 (WoO.39) "In one movement" (*pf, vln & vlc*)

In praise of the violin
Vycpálek, Sonata in D, Op. 19 "In praise of the violin" (*m-s, vln & pf*)

(L') Inquietudine
Vivaldi, Concerto in D. P.208, (FI, No. 10) (Op. 51, No. 1.) "L'Inquietudine" (*vln, strs & c*)

In the popular Rumanian style
Enescu, Sonata No. 3, in a, Op. 25 "In the popular Rumanian style" (*vln & pf*)

Intimate pages
Janácek, Quartet No. 2 (1927/8) "Intimate pages" (*2 vlns, vla & vlc*)

(L') Inverno
Vivaldi, (12) Concerti, Op. 8 (1725) "Il Cimento dell' Armonia e dell' Invenzione" (*vln & strs*)
  –Concerto No. 4, in f, F.I, No. 25 "L'Inverno"

Jérusalem Fantaisie
Singalée, Fantasia (on themes from Bellini's opera "I Lombardi") Op. 28, Jérusalem Fantaisie" (*vln & pf*)

(Les) Jeux olympiques
Corrette, Sonata in D "Les jeux olympiques" (*vln & hpsi*)

King of Prussia
Mozart, Quartet No. 22, in B flat, K.589 "King

of Prussia" (*2 vlns, vla & vlc*)

Konzertstück
Saint-Saëns, Concerto No. 1, in A, Op. 20 "Konzertstück" (*vln & orch*)

Konzertsuite
Telemann, Suite in F "Konzertsuite" (*2 hrns, 2 vlns & c*)

Krakowiak
Statkovski, Cracovienne, Op. 7 "Krakowiak" (*vln & pf*)

Kreisler serenade
Lehár, Frasquita (1923) - operetta
  –Hab' ein blaues Himmelbett

Kreutzer
Beethoven, Sonata No. 9, in A, Op. 47 "Kreutzer" (*vln & pf*)

Kujawiak
Wieniawski, Mazurka in a, Op. 3 "Kujawiak" (*vln & pf*)

(Il) Laberinto armonico
Locatelli, (24) Caprices, op. 3 (*solo vln*)
  –Caprice No. 23, in D "Il laberinto armonico"

Largo
Handel, Serse (1738) - opera
  –Ombra mai fu "Largo"

(The) Lark
Haydn, (6) Quartets, Op. 64 (H.III, Nos. 63/8) (*2 vlns, vla & vlc*)
  –No. 5. Quartet No. 67, in D, H.III, No. 67 "The Lark"

Lausitzer Sonata
Reuter, Sonata in e "Lausitzer Sonata" (*vln & pf*)

Little
Knipper, Concerto in D "Little" (*vln & str orch*)

(The) Little G-minor
J.S. Bach, Fugue in g, BWV.578 "The Little G-minor" (*org*)

Lontaine-passe
Ysaÿe, (3) Mazurkas, Op. 11 (*vln & pf*)
  –No. 3. Mazurka No. 3, in b "Lointaine-passe"

Louisville
Rosenberg, Concerto (1955) "Louisville" (*vln & orch*)

Madame Leopold Horowitz
Hubay, (2) Mazurkas, Op. 45 (vln & pf)
  –Mazurka No. 1, in a "Madame Leopold Horowitz"

(The) Maiden's wish
Chopin, (17) Polish songs, Op. 74 (*v & pf*)
  –No. 1. Zyczenie "The maiden's wish"

(Le) Matin
Haydn, Symphony No. 6, in D "Le Matin" (*orch*)

(The) Matrimonial Tiff
Vogler, Sonata in C "The matrimonial tiff" (*2 vlns, vla & vlc*)

May breezes
Mendelssohn, (6) songs without words, Op. 62 (*pf*)
  –No. 1. Song without words No. 25, in G "May breezes"

Melées de Plusieurs Recits pour la Viole
Rebel, (12) Sonatas (1713) "Melées de Plusieurs Recits pour la Viole" (*vln & c*)

Melk

Haydn, Concerto No. 3, in A, H.VIIa, No. 3 (1765) "Melk" (*vln & orch*)

Mélodie
Gluck, Orphée et Eurydice (1762) – opera
  –Dance of the blessed spirits: Lento "Mélodie" (No. 2)

(Le) Ménetrier
Wieniawski, (2) Mazurkas, Op. 12 (*vln & pf*)
  –Mazurka No. 2, in g "Le Ménetrier"

(Le) Midi
Haydn, Symphony No. 7, in C "Le midi" (*orch*)

Midnight bells
Heuberger, (Der) Opernball, Op. 40 (1898) - operetta
  –Im chambre séparée (arr. *vln & pf* as "Midnight bells" by Kreisler)

Military
Lipiński, Concerto No. 2, in D, Op. 21 "Military" (*vln & orch*)

Minute waltz
Chopin, (3) Waltzes, Op. 64 (*pf*)
  –No. 1. Waltz No. 6, in D flat "Minute waltz"

Miracle
Haydn, Symphony No. 96, in D (1791) "Miracle" (*orch*)

Missa solemnis
Beethoven, Mass in D, Op. 123 "Missa Solemnis"

Moonlight
Beethoven, (2) Sonatas, Op. 27 (*pf*)
  –No. 2. Sonata No. 14, in c sharp "Moonlight"

Moses Fantasia
Paganini, Sonata a preghière "Moses Fantasia" (on the aria "Dal tuo stellato soglio" from Rossini's opera "Mosè in Egitto") Op. 24 (1818 or 1819) (*vin & orch*)

(La) Musica Notturna di Madrid
Boccherini, (6) Quintets, Op. 30 (1780) (*2 vlns, vla & 2 vlcs*)
  –No. 6. Quintet No. 6, in C "La Musica Notturna di Madrid"

Mysterien
Biber, (16) Biblical Sonatas "Mysterien" (*vln & c*)

(Der) Nachtwächter
Biber, Serenade in C "Der Nachtwächter" (*bs-v, 2 vlns, 2 vlas & c*)

Nadia
Papineau-Couture, (3) Caprices (1965) (*vln & pf*)
  –Caprice No. 1 "Nadia" (Allegro)

Negro spiritual melody
Dvořák, Symphony No. 9, in e, Op. 95 "From the New World" (*orch*)

Night song
Sibelius, Belshazzar's Feast, Op. 51 - Incidental music (*orch*)
  –No. 3. Nocturne "Night song"

(2) Obbligato eyeglasses
Beethoven, Duet in E flat, WoO.32 (1796) "2 Obbligato eyeglasses" (*vla & vlc*)

Obertass
Wieniawski, (2) Mazurkas, Op. 19 (*vln & pf*)
  –No. 1. Mazurka No. 1, in G "Obertass"

Ofrenda a Sarasate
Rodrigo, Capriccio (1944) "Ofrenda a sarasate" (*solo vln*)

On wings of song
Mendelssohn, (6) Gesänge, Op. 34 (*v & pf*)
  –No. 2. Auf Flügeln des Gesanges
O Sanctissima
Corelli, (12) Sonatas, Op. 5 (*vln & c*)
  –Sonata No. 1, in D

(La) Pallas
Rebel, (12) Sonatas (1712) (*2 & 3 part with figured bs*)
  –Sonata No. 5, in D "La Pallas"
Papillon
Bohm, (6) Pieces, Op. 314 (*vln & pf*)
  –No. 4. Capriccio (Papillon)
Passacaglia
Biber, (16) Biblical Sonatas "Mysterien" (*vln & c*)
  –Sonata No. 16, in g "The Guardian Angel" (*solo vln*)
Pastoral
Coleman, Sonata in A "Pastoral" (*vln & pf*)
(La) Pastorella
Vivaldi, Concerto in D, P.204 (F.XII, No. 29) "La Pastorella" (*fl, ob, vln, bsn & c*)
(Il) Pastor Fido
Vivaldi, (6) Sonatas, Op. 13 (1737) "Il Pastor Fido" (*fl, ob, vln, strs & c*)
Pathétique
Beethoven, Sonata No. 8, in c, Op. 13 "Pathétique" (*pf*)
Per l'orchestra di Dresda
Vivaldi, Concerto in g, P.383 (F.XII, No. 3) "Per l'orchestra di Dresda" (*vln, 2 fls, 2 obs, 2 bsns & c*)
Per la Solennità di St. Lorenzo
Vivaldi, Concerto in C, P.84 "Per la Solennità di St. Lorenzo" (*2 fls, 2 obs, 2 cls, 2 vlns, bsn & strs*)
Per la SS. Assunzione di Maria Vergine
Vivaldi, Concerto in C, P.14 (F.I, No. 13) (Op. 54, No. 3) "Per la SS. Assunzione di Maria Vergine" (*vln, strs & c*)
Perpetuum mobile
Weber, Sonata No. 1, in C, Op. 24 (*pf*)
  Presto (4th mvt) "Perpetuum mobile"
Per S.A.R. di Sassonia
Vivaldi, Concerto in g, P.359 "Per S.A.R. di Sassonia" (*3 obs, bsn, vln, 2 hrns, strs & c*)
Phantasy
Vaughan Williams, Quintet (1914) "Phantasy" (*3 vlns, vla & vlc*)
Phantasy-Trio
Ireland, Trio No. 1, in a (1908) "Phantasy-Trio" (*pf, vln & vlc*)
(Il) Piacere
Vivaldi, (12) Concerti, Op. 8 (1725) "Il Cimento dell' Armonia e dell' Invenzione" (*vln & strs*)
  –Concerto No. 6, C, F.I, No. 27 "Il piacere"
(Il) Pianto d'Arianna
Locatelli, (12) Concerti, Op. 7 (1741) "Il pianto d'Arianna" (*strs & c*)
(La) Piémontoise
F. Couperin, (Les) Nations - 4 Suites (1726) (*2 vlns & c*)
  –Suite No. 4, in g "La Piémontoise"
Pisendel

Telemann, Concerto in B flat "Pisendel" (*vln, strs & c*)
Pisendel
Vivaldi, Concerto in A, P.228 (F.I, No. 141) "Pisendel" (*vln, strs & c*)
(The) Plaint
Purcell, (The) Fairy Queen, Z.629 (1692) - opera
  –O let me weep "The plaint"
(Le) Plaisir du Dames
Corrette, (21) Concerti comique, Op. 8
  –Concerto No. 6, in G "Le Plaisir du Dames" (*fl, ob, vln, bsn & hpsi*)
Polonaise
Thomas, Mignon (1866) - opera
  –Je suis Titania "Polonaise"
Posthorn
Vivaldi, Concerto in B flat, P.112 "Posthorn" (*vln, strs & c*)
Presto
Scarlatti, Sonata in G, L.487 "Presto" (*pf*)
(La) Primavera
Vivaldi, (12) Concerti, Op. 8 (1725) "Il Cimento dell' Armonia e dell' Invenzione" (*vln & strs*)
  –Concerto No. 1, in E, F.I, No. 22 "La Primavera"
Princess Adelaide
Mozart, Concerto in D, K.Anh. 294a "Princess Adelaide" (*vln & orch*)
Prize song
Wagner, (Die) Meistersinger von Nürnberg (1868) - opera
  –Morgenlich leuchtend "Prize song"
(I) Profeti
Castelnuovo-Tedesco, Concerto No. 2 (1933) "I Profeti" (*vln & orch*)

Quartettsatz
Schubert, Quartet No. 12, in c, D.703 "Quartettsatz" (*2 vlns, vla & vlc*)
(Le) Quattro Stagioni
Vivaldi, (12) Concerti, Op. 8 (1725) "Il Cimento dell' Armonia e dell' Invenzione" (Nos. 1/4: Le quattro Stagioni) (*vln & strs*)
Quinten
Haydn, (6) Quartets, Op. 76 (H.III, Nos. 75/80) (*2 vlns, vla & vlc*)
  –No. 2. Quartet No. 76, in d, H.III, No. 76 "Quinten"

(La) Raspona
Legrenzi, (12) Sonatas, Op. 2 (1655) (*2 vlns & c*)
  –Sonata in G "La Raspona"
Rasumovsky
Beethoven, (3) Quartets, Op. 59 "Rasumovsky" (*2 vlns, vla & vlc*)
Reminiscence
Vieuxtemps, (7) Romances sans paroles, Op. 7 (*vln & pf*)
  –No. 3. Romance No. 3, in C "Reminiscence"
(The) Resurrection
Biber, (16) Biblical Sonatas "Mysterien" (*vln & c*)
  –Sonata No. 11, in G "The Resurrection"
(Il) Riposo
Vivaldi, Concerto in E, P.248 (F.I, No. 4) "Il

Riposo" (*vln, strs & c*)
(La) Ritirata di Madrid
Boccherini, (6) Quintets, Op. 57 (1799) (*pf, 2 vlns, vla & vlc*)
  –No. 6. Quintet No. 6, in C "La Ritirata di Madrid"
(Il) Ritiro
Vivaldi, Concerto in E flat, F.I, No. 231 "Il Ritiro" (*vln, strs & c*)
Ritratto dell' Amore
Couperin, (Les) Gouts-réunis, ou Nouveaux Concerts (*unsp inst & c*)
  –Concert No. 9, in E "Ritratto dell' Amore"
Rondo favori
Hummel, Rondo in E flat, Op. 11 "Rondo favori" (*pf*)
Rustle of spring
Sinding, (6) Pieces, Op. 32 (*pf*)
  –No. 3. Frühlingsrauschen "Rustle of spring"

Satyre und Nymphen
Juon, (9) Miniatures, Op. 18 "Satyre und Nymphen" (*pf*)
(Le) Sautillé
Wieniawski, (L') École moderne, Op. 10 (10 Études) (*solo vln*)
  –No. 1. Étude No. 1, in c "Le Sautillé"
Schön Erika
Blume, Valse-caprice "Schön Erika" (*vln & pf*)
Senza cantin
Vivaldi, Concerto in d, P.310 (F.I, No. 11) "Senza cantin" (*vln, 2 fls, 2 obs & 2 bsns*)
Serenade
Schubert, (14) Schwanengesang, D.957 (1828) (*v & pf*)
  –No. 4. Ständchen "Serenade"
Serenade
Mendelssohn, (6) Songs without words, Op. 67 (*pf*)
  –No. 6. Song without words No. 36, in E "Serenade"
Sérénade appassionata
Andolfi, Lorsque tu passes (sérénade appassionata) (*vln & pf*)
Serenata lirica
Blume, Florida "Serenata lirica" (*vln & pf*)
Serenata Notturna
Mozart, Serenade No. 6, in D, K.239 "Serenata notturna" (*orch*)
Sielanka
Wieniawski, (2) Mazurkas, Op. 12 (*vln & pf*)
  –No. 1. Mazurka No. 1, in D "Sielanka"
Sinfonias
Albinoni, (12) Sonatas, Op. 1 (1694) "Sinfonias"
(Le) Soir
Haydn, Symphony No. 8, in G "Le Soir" (*orch*)
Sonata appassionata con variazioni
Paganini, Nel cor più non mi sento "Sonata appassionata con variazioni" (on the aria from Paisiello's opera "La bella molinara") Op. 38 (1820 or 1821) (*solo vln*)
Sonata española
Turina, Sonata No. 2, Op. 82 (1934) "Sonata española" (*vln & pf*)
Sonata Impetuosa

Geminiani, (12) Sonatas (1739) (*vln & c*)

Sonata Polonaise
Telemann, Sonata No. 1, in a "Sonata Polonaise"
(*2 vlns & c*)

Sonata Polonaise
Telemann, Sonata No. 2, in a "Sonata Polonaise"
(*2 vlns & c*)

Sonate accademiche
Veracini, (12) Sonatas, Op. 2 (1744) "Sonate
accademiche" (*vln & c*)

Sonatensatz
Brahms, Sonata (1853) "Frei aber Einsam" (*vln &
pf*)
    —Allegro (Scherzo) in c (3rd mvt)
    "Sonatensatz"

(Il) Sospetto
Vivaldi, Concerto in c, P.419 (F.I, No. 2) (Op. 51,
No. 3) (*vln, strs & c*)

Souvenir de Florence
Tchaikovsky, Sextet, Op. 70 "Souvenir de
Florence" (*2 vlns, 2 vlas & 2 vlcs*)

Souvenir di Sorrento
Papini, (2) Morceaux de salon, Op. 55 "Souvenir
di Sorrento" (*vln & pf*)

Spring
Carrillo, Quartet "Spring" (*2 vlns, vla & vlc*)

Spring
Beethoven, Sonata No. 5, in F, Op. 24 "Spring"
(*vln & pf*)

Spring song
Mendelssohn, (6) Songs without words, Op. 62
(*pf*)
    —No. 6. Song without words No. 30, in A
    "Spring song"

(La) Stravaganza
Vivaldi, (12) Concerti, Op. 4 "La Stravaganza"
(*vln, strs & c*)

Swanee river
Foster, (The) Old folks at home "Swanee River"
(1851) (*v & pf*)

Sweet longing
Menzel, Romanze, Op. 40 "Sweet longing" (*fl &
var inst*)

Sweet remembrance
Mendelssohn, (6) Songs without words, Op. 19
(*pf*)
    —No. 1. Song without words No. 1, in E "Sweet
    remembrance"

(4) Temperaments
Hindemith, Symphonic Metamorphosis on themes

by Weber "Four Temperaments" (1946) (*orch*)

(La) Tempesta di mare
Vivaldi, (12) Concerti, Op. 8 (1725) "Il Cimento
dell' Armonia e dell' Invenzione" (*vln & strs*)
    —Concerto No. 5, in E flat, F.I, No. 26 "La
    Tempesta di mare"

(La) Tempesta di mare
Zavateri, (12) Concerti, Op. 1 (1735) (*vln & strs*)
    —Concerto No. 12 "Tempesta di mare"

Tercer
Carrillo, Quartet "Tercer" (*2 vlns, vla & vlc*)

(Der) Tod und das Mädchen
Schubert, Quartet No. 14, in d, D.810 "Death &
the Maiden" (*2 vlns, vla & vlc*)

To the memory of a great artist
Tchaikovsky, Trio in a, Op. 50 "To the memory
of a great artist" (*pf, vln & vlc*)

Trattenimenti armonio
Albinoni, (12) Sonatas, Op. 6 (1711)
"Trattenimenti armonio" (*vln & c*)

(Il) Trillo del Diavolo
Tartini, Sonata in g "Il Trillo del Diavolo" (*vln &
c*)

Trio élégiaque
Rachmaninov, Trio No. 2, in d, Op. 9 "Trio
élégiaque" (*pf, vln & vlc*)

Triple
Beethoven, Concerto in C, Op. 56 "Triple" (*vln,
vlc, pf & orch*)

Triple
Carrillo, Concerto, (1918) "Triple" (*vln, fl, vlc &
orch*)

Triple
Constantinescu, Concerto "Triple" (*vln, vlc, pf &
orch*)

(La) Tromba
Couperin (Les) Goûts-réunis, ou Nouveaux
Concerts (*unsp inst & c*)
    —Concert No. 10, in a "La Tromba" (vln, vla &
    c)

Tröstungen
Liszt, (6) Consolations, G.172 (1849/50)
"Tröstungen" (*pf*)

Trout
Schubert, Quintet in A, Op. 114 (D.667) "Trout"
(*pf, vln, vla, vlc & cbs*)

Turkish
Mozart, Concerto No. 5, in A, K.219 "Turkish"
(*vln & orch*)

(The) Twelve-year old Jesus in the temple
Biber, (16) Biblical Sonatas "Mysterien" (*vln & c*)

    —Sonata No. 5, in A "The twelve-year old Jesus
    in the temple"

Unfinished
Mozart, Concerto in D, K.315 "Unfinished" (*vln,
pf & orch*)

Unfinished
Slavík, Concerto No. 2, in a "Unfinished" (*vln &
orch*)

Unfinished
Lekeu, Quartet in b (1893) "Unfinished" (*pf, vln,
vla & vlc*)

Unfinished
Haydn, Quartet No, 83, in B flat, Op. 103 (H.III,
No. 83) "Unfinished" (*2 vlns, vla & vlc*)

Upon one note
Purcell, (15) Fantasias, Z.731/45 (4 & 5 part)
(*orig viols*)
    —Fantasia No. 15, F, Z.745 (?1679) "Upon one
    note"

Valse sentimentale
Schubert, (16) Deutsche Tänze, Op. 33 (D.783)
(*pf*)
    —No. 3. Deutscher Tanz No. 3, in B flat (arr
    vln & pf as "Valse sentimentale")

Venezianisches Gondellied
Mendelssohn, (6) Songs without words, Op. 19
(*pf*)
    —No. 6. Song without words No. 6, in g
    "Venezianisches Gondellied"

(Le) Vent
Vecsey, Caprice No. 1 "Le vent" (*vln & pf*)

Visit of Mary to Elizabeth
Biber, (16) Biblical Sonatas "Mysterien" (*vln & c*)
    —Sonata No. 2, in A "Visit of Mary to
    Elizabeth"

Will-o-the-wisp
Sauret, (4) Morceaux, Op. 40 (*vln & pf*)
    —No. 3. Farfalla-caprice "Will-o-the-wisp"

Witches' dance
Paganini, (Le) Streghe (variations on a theme
from Süssmeyer's opera "Il Noce di Benevento")
Op. 8 (1813) (*vln & orch*)

Yankee Doodle
Vieuxtemps, Caprice burlesque "Souvenir
d'Amérique) Op. 17 "Yankee Doodle" (*vln & pf*)

Youth
Shtogarenko, Trio "Youth" (*pf, vln & vlc*)

MANUFACTURERS

Label	Series	33 1/3 rpm (LP)	78 rpm	45 rpm standard & extended play
ACADEMY (USA)	ALP	12″		
ACADIA (Canada)	3000	12″		
ACE OF CLUBS (Gt. Britain)	ACL	12″		
ACE OF DIAMONDS (Gt. Britain)	ADD	12″		
	SDD (S)	12″		
ACO (Gt. Britain)	F		12″	
	G		10″	
ACOUSTIC RESEARCH (USA)	AR	12″		
ACTUELLE (see: Pathé-Actuelle)				
ADAM (Italy)	C		10″	
ADÈS (France)	15000	12″		
	LA	12″		
ADLER (Germany)	5000		10″	
ADVANCE (USA)	FGR	12″		
AEROPHON (France)	800		10″	
ALBION (Gt. Britain)	1000		10″	
ALCO (USA)	A		12″	
	AC	12″		
	ALP	12″		
	AR		12″	
	T[1]	12″		
	Y	12″		
ALLEGRO (USA)	2000		12″	
	4000[2]	12″		
	Al	10″ & 12″		
	ALG	12″		
	ALX	12″		
	ALY	12″		
	AR (set)		12″	
	LDAD[2]	12″		
	LEG[3]	12″		
ALLEGRO-ULTRAPHONIC (USA)	1600	12″		
ALPHA (France)	CL2000	10″		
	CL3000	12″		
	CL4000 (S)	12″		
	CM (C)	12″		
	DB	12″		
ALSHIRE (Germany)	S800	12″		
AMADEO (Austria)	AVR12000	12″		
	AVRS5000/6000	12″		
	AVRS12000 (S)	12″		
	AVRS6-6000	12″		
	EP			7″ (extended)
AMERICAN GRAMOPHONE SOCIETY (USA)	AGSA		10″	
AMERICAN LIBRARY IN PARIS (USA)[4]		12″		
AMERICAN RECORDING SOCIETY (USA)	200		12″	
	ARS	12″		
AMIGA (Germany, DDR)	740000	10″		
AMPHION (France)	500		12″	
	A (set)		12″	

---

1 Experimental 16″ LP	4 Private recording for the American Library in Paris	7 = 17 cm
2 Elite series	(C) = compatible	10 = 25 cm
3 Reissues	(S) = stereophonic	12 = 30 cm

Label	Series	33 1/3 rpm (LP)	78 rpm	45 rpm standard & extended play
AMPHION (France) — *Continued*	AD		12″	
	B (set)		12″	
AMPRIA (USA)[5]		12″		
ANGEL (USA)				
South America	292700	12″		
	AB	12″		
	ASC	12″		
	GR	12″		
	HA	12″		
	LPC	12″		
	SCBAE	12″		
U.S.A.	3500/3700 (sets)	12″		
	35000/36000	12″		
	45000	12″		
	COLH[6]	12″		
ANGELICUM (Italy)	CALP (S)	12″		
	LPA900/1000	10″ & 12″		
	LPA1700	12″		
	LPA5900	12″		
	LPA7000			7″ (extended)
	SLPA (S)	12″		
	STA (S)	12″		
ANKER (Germany)	100		12″	
	E		10″	
L'ANTHOLOGIE SONORE (France)	(no prefix)		12″	
	3000 (suffix LD)	12″		
	AS		12″	
	AS	12″		
ANTROCHORD (Italy)	AK		12″	
APEX (Canada)	400/500		10″	
APOLLO SOUND (Gt. Britain)	AS	12″		
APPLAUDANDO (Denmark)	1300		10″	
	31300		12″	
ARCHIVE (Germany)[7]	2533 000	12″		
	2705 000	12″		
	2710 000 (set)	12″		
	2714 000 (set)	12″		
	APM	10″		
	EPA			7″ (extended)
	SAPM (S)	12″		
	SEPA (S)			7″ (extended)
North American series	ARC3000	12″		
	ARC73000 (S)	12″		
ARCOPHON (Italy)	AC (C)	12″		
	AM (S)	12″		
ARGO (Gt. Britain)	ARL	12″		
	ARS	12″		
	ATC	12″		
	ATM	12″		
	EAF			7″ (extended)
	RG	12″		
	TM	12″		
	ZRG (S)	12″		

5   Private issue   7   Product of Deutsche Grammophon
6   Great Recordings of the Century series

Label	Series	33 1/3 rpm (LP)	78 rpm	45 rpm standard & extended play
ARIEL (Germany)	1000		10"	
ARIOLA (Germany)	11300K	10"		
	AR16000D			7" (extended)
ARS NOVA/ARS ANTIQUA (USA)	AN	12"		
ARTIA (USA)[8]	ALP	12"		
	ALPS (S)	12"		
ARTIPHON (France, Germany & Scandinavia)	(3 digit – no prefix)		10"	
	11200		10"	
	D 000/7000		10"	
	D 03000/07000		12"	
ARTONE (Netherlands)	EPDE			7" (extended)
ASCO (USA)[9]	A	12"		
ASSOCIATION PHONIQUE DE GRANDE ARTISTE – APGA (France)	150000		10½"	
AUDIO ARCHIVES (USA)	LA	12"		
	LP	10"		
AUDIO FIDELITY (USA)	FCS (C)	12"		
	FSC	12"		
AVA (USA)	A/AS	12"		
B & C RECORDINGS INC. (USA)[10]	BC	12"		
B & F BUDAPEST (USA)	B	12"		
	SG	12"		
	ST (S)	12"		
BACCAROLA (Germany)	60100UK	10"		
	77800ZK			7" (extended)
BACH (Gt. Britain)	300	12"		
BACH GUILD (USA)	BG	12"		
	BGS (S)	12"		
BALKANTON (Bulgaria)	400	12"		
BANNER (Gt. Britain)	900		10"	
	2000		10"	
BÄRENREITER-MUSICAPHON (Germany)	BM25	10"		
	BM30	12"		
BAROQUE (USA)	BC1800	12"		
	BC2800 (S)	12"		
	BU	12"		
BARTÓK (USA)	BRS	10" & 12"		
BARTONE (USA)	LP	10"		
BEKA (Germany)	000/800		10"	
	5000		10"	
	40500		10"	
	G		10"	
	M		10"	
BELCANTODISC (Gt. Britain)	BC	12"		
	LR			7" (extended)
BELGIAN CONSERVATORY OF MUSIC (Belgium)	4000		10"	
BELL (USA)	1000		10"	
BELTONA (Gt. Britain)	(3 digits)		10"	
	6000		10"	

8   North American outlet for Czech Ultraphon   9   American Stereophonic Corporation   10   Private limited edition

Label	Series	33 1/3 rpm (LP)	78 rpm	45 rpm standard & extended play
BELVÉDÈRE (France)	ELY	12″		
BELVOX (Gt. Britain & USA)	500		10″	
BERLINER (Gt. Britain)	7900[11]		7″ & 10″	
BETTINI (USA)[12]	2200		10″	
BLUEBIRD (Canada)[13]	10000		10″	
(La) BOÎTE À MUSIQUE (France)	(no prefix – 1 to 3 digits)		12″	
	LD (& 2 digits)	12″		
BOSTON (USA)	B	12″		
	BST (S)	12″		
BRAZILIAN CONTINENTAL (Brazil)	20000		10″	
BROADCAST (TWELVE) (Gt. Britain)	(3 digits)		7″	
	5000/6000		10″	
	B		10″	
BRUDER-BUSCH (Germany)	12PAL	12″		
BRUNO (USA)	BR	12″		
	SBR (S)	12″		
BRUNSWICK – International				
Germany & Austria	62000		10″	
	73000		12″	
Gt. Britain	100		10″	
	03000		10″	
	7000/8000		10″	
	15000		10″	
	20000		12″	
	AXA	12″		
	AXL	10″		
	AXTL	12″		
	SA		10″	
	SXA (S)	12″		
U.S.A.	2000/5000		10″	
	10000		10″	
	13000		10″	
	15000		10″	
	20000		12″	
	30000[11]		12″	
	50000		12″	
	73000		12″	
	80000/85000		10″	
	90000/95000		12″	
BYRON (USA)		12″		
CALIG (Germany)	CAL	12″		
CAMBRIDGE (USA)	CRM	12″		
	CRS (S)	12″		
CAMDEN (USA)[14]				
Gt. Britain	CDN	12″		
	CFL	12″		
Italy	ML	12″		
U.S.A.	CAE			7″ (extended)
	CAL	12″		
	CBL (set)	12″		
CAMDEN CLASSICS (Canada)[15]	VCCS	12″		

11 Single-sided
12 Also cylinders
13 Product of Victor
14 Product of Victor
15 Same numbering as U.S. Victrola series on Victor

Label	Series	33 1/3 rpm (LP)	78 rpm	45 rpm standard & extended play
CAMDEN CLASSICS (Canada) — *Continued*	VICS	12″		
CAMEO (Canada)	N L	10″		
CAMEO (USA)	S		10″	
CANDIDE (USA)	CE	12″		
CANTATE (Germany)	047700	12″		
	057700 (S)	12″		
	640200	12″		
	641200	12″		
	642200	10″		
	643200	12″		
	650200 (S)	12″		
	651200 (S)	12″		
	T72000	12″		
CANTORIA (France)	MD		10″	
CAPITOL (USA)				
Germany	K	12″		
	STK (S)	12″		
Gt. Britain	CCL	10″		
	CEC			7″ (extended)
	CTL	12″		
U.S.A.	6F87000			7″ (standard)
	ABO (2 rec set)	12″		
	ECL (set)			7″ (standard)
	FAP	12″		
	G	12″		
	GBR (2 rec set)	12″		
	KCF (set)			7″ (extended)
	KCM (set)			7″ (standard)
	L	10″		
	LC	10″		
	LCB	12″		
	P	12″		
	PBR (2 rec set)	12″		
	PCR (3 rec set)	12″		
	SABO (S)	12″		
	SFP (S)			7″ (extended)
	SG (S)	12″		
	SGBR (S) (2 rec set)	12″		
	SP (S)	12″		
	SPBR (S) (2 rec set)	12″		
CARDINAL (USA)[16]	VCS	12″		
CARISCH (Italy)	BCA	12″		
	MCA		12″	
	MCA28000	12″		
CBC RADIO CANADA (Canada)[17]	SM	12″		
CBC TRANSCRIPTION (Canada)[18]	Program	12″		
CBS (USA)[19]				
Germany (CBS-Odyssey)	54000 (S)	12″		
Gt. Britain	77000 (S)	12″		
	BRG	12″		

16   Product of Vanguard
17   Domestic Service of the Canadian Broadcasting Corporation
18   International Service of the Canadian Broadcasting Corporation
19   International division of the Columbia Broadcasting System, New York

Label	Series	33 1/3 rpm (LP)	78 rpm	45 rpm standard & extended play
CBS – *Continued*				
Gt. Britain — *Continued*	SBRG (S)	12″		
Italy	51100 (S)	12″		
Japan (CBS/Sony)	SONC	12″		
CELSON (Italy)	DC		12″	
	NY		10″	
CENTURY (USA)	31300	12″		
CETRA (Italy)[20]	AT		10″	
	BB		12″	
	CB		12″	
	CC		12″	
	CS	12″		
	LL		10″	
	LP	12″		
	LPC	12″		
	LPS	12″		
	LPU	12″		
	LPV	10″		
	OL		10″	
	PE		12″	
	RR		12″	
	TI		10″	
(Le) CHANT DU MONDE (France)	500		10″	
	GA5000 (or 5000)		12″	
	LD	10″		
	LDX	12″		
	LDXA	12″		
	LDYA	12″		
	LDZM	12″		
	MEL	12″		
CHARLIN (France)	SLC	12″		
CHRISTOPHORUS (Germany)	CGLP	12″		
	CLP	12″		
	SCGLP (S)	12″		
CHRISTSCHALL (Germany & Austria)	(3 digits – no prefix)		12″	
CHUNG KUO CH'ANG B'IEN CH'ANG (China)	M-	12″		
CIRCLE (USA)	L51-100	12″		
CITIZEN (Gt. Britain)	600		10″	
CLANGOR (Germany)	M		10″	
	MD		12″	
CLASSIC (France)	990000 (C)	12″		
	C2000	10″ & 12″		
	CL6000	12″		
	CL11000	10″		
	MD	12″		
	RSCL (S)	12″		
CLASSIC EDITIONS (USA)	CE	12″		
(I) CLASSICI DELLA MUSICA CLASSICA (Italy)				
	SXAE (S)	12″		
	SXVA (S)	12″		
	SXVG (S)	12″		
	XAC	12″		
	XAM	12″		
CLASSIC RECORD CLUB (USA)	AACMP	12″		

20   See also: Parlophone (Italy)

Label	Series	33 1/3 rpm (LP)	78 rpm	45 rpm standard & extended play
CLASSIC RECORD CLUB — *Continued*	MP	12″		
CLASSICS CLUB (Gt. Britain)	CCHN	10″ & 12″		
	SMP	12″		
	X (1/3 digits)	10″		
	X1000	10″		
	X3000/4000	12″		
CLASSICS FOR PLEASURE (Gt. Britain)	CFP	12″		
CLUB FRANÇAIS DU DISQUE (France)	(digits only)	12″		
CLUB NATIONAL DU DISQUE (France)	CND	12″		
CNR (Netherlands)	RS	12″		
CO-ART (USA)	5000		12″	
COLOSSEUM (Germany)	M	12″		
	MST (S)	12″		
	SM (S)	12″		
COLOSSEUM (USA)	CRLP	12″		
	CRLPX	12″		
COLUMBIA – International				
Argentina	264500		12″	
	266000		12″	
	292000		12″	
	500000		12″	
Australia	0501/1999		10″	
	01000		10″	
	02501/2999		12″	
	03000		10″	
	09500		12″	
	DO		10″	
	DOX		12″	
	LO		10″	
	LOX		12″	
	M		10″	
Austria	D8101/8699		10″	
	D30701		10″	
	DV		10″	
	DVX		12″	
	FPX	12″		
Belgium	D2001		10″	
	D13001		10″	
	D15000		12″	
	D19001		10″	
	DF		10″	
	DFX		12″	
	FC	10″		
	FCX	12″		
	GFX		12″	
	LF		10″	
	LFX		12″	
	LNX		12″	
Brazil	AG		12″	
Canada	C10000		10″	
	C15000/16000		12″	
	C20000		12″	
	D (set)[21]		12″	
	J (set)[22]		12″	

21 A set of 3 or more discs   22 A set of 2 discs

Label	Series	33 1/3 rpm (LP)	78 rpm	45 rpm standard & extended play
COLUMBIA – International – *Continued*				
Czechoslovakia	OD		10″	
Denmark	DDX		12″	
	FP	10″		
	LDX		12″	
	SCBK			7″ (standard)
	SCDK			7″ (extended)
Finland	DY		10″	
France	CXH	12″		
	D2001		10″	
	D13001		10″	
	D15000		12″	
	D19001		10″	
	DF		10″	
	DFX		12″	
	FC	10″		
	FCS	12″		
	FCX	12″		
	GFX		12″	
	LF		10″	
	LFX		12″	
	LNX		12″	
	SAFX	12″		
Germany	ASDW	12″		
	C50500			7″ (extended)
	C70000	10″		
	C80000/90000	12″		
	DW		10″	
	DWX		12″	
	EPC			7″ (extended)
	EPSTC (S)			7″ (extended)
	LW		10″	
	LWX		12″	
	SBOW	10″		
	SCXW	12″		
	SMC (C)	12″		
	STC50500 (S)			7″ (extended)
	STC70000 (S)	10″		
	STC80000/90000 (S)	12″		
	WC	10″		
	WCX	12″		
	WSX	12″		
Gt. Britain	1000/5999		10″	
	7100[23]		10″	
	9001/9999		12″	
	14001[24]		12″	
	16001[24]		10″	
	70001/49[24]		10″	
	C	10″		
	CHM (set)		10″	
	CX	12″		
	D1325/1700		10″	
	DB		10″	
	DC[24]		10″	
	DCX[24]		12″	

23   Single-sided
24   Export International series

Label	Series	33 1/3 rpm (LP)	78 rpm	45 rpm standard & extended play
COLUMBIA – International – *Continued*				
Gt. Britain — *Continued*	DX		12″	
	FB		10″	
	L		12″	
	LB		10″	
	LCX[24]		12″	
	LX		12″	
	RO[25]		10″	
	ROX[25]		12″	
	SAX	12″		
	SED	12″		7″ (extended)
	WT[26]		10″	
	X		10″	
Hungary	D8101/8699		10″	
	D30701		10″	
	DV		10″	
	DVX		12″	
	LVX		12″	
Italy	CQ		10″	
	D13001[27]		10″	
	DQ		10″	
	ELSQ			7″ (extended)
	GQ		10″	
	GQX		12″	
	QC	10″		
	QCX	12″		
	SAXQ (S)	12″		
	SEBQ (S)			7″ (extended)
Japan	28600		10″	
	AK		12″	
	G		12″	
	HRS	12″		
	J2000		10″	
	J5000		10″	
	J7500/9000		12″	
	J55000		12″	
	JD		10″	
	JS		12″	
	JW		10″	
	JX		10″	
	NH		12″	
	OS	12″		
	SW		12″	
	W		12″	
Netherlands	CXH	12″		
	D9725/10999		10″	
	D17000/17199		12″	
	DH			7″ (standard)
	DHX		12″	
	HRS	12″		
Norway	DN		10″	
	GN		10″	
Poland (& Baltic countries)	DM		10″	
	LMX		12″	
Spain	AB[28]		10″	

24 Export & international series
25 British Society & private issues
26 Test pressing

27 Duplicates French series
28 Product of a Spanish firm – *not* EMI

Label	Series	33 1/3 rpm (LP)	78 rpm	45 rpm standard & extended play
COLUMBIA – International – *Continued*				
Spain — *Continued*	AG[28]		12″	
	CCL	12″		
	N		10″	
	RG[28]		12″	
	SCLL (S)	12″		
Sweden	8401		10″	
	18351		10″	
Switzerland	DZX		12″	
	LZ		10″	
	LZX		12″	
U.S.A.[29]	0/200		10″	
	1000/3000		10″	
	5000		10″	
	27000		10″	
	30000		10″	
	31400		10″	
	35000/36000		12″	
	49000[30]		12″	
	78000/81000[30]		10″	
	1000/2000 D		10″	
	11000/12000 D		12″	
	17000 D		10″	
	4-13000 D			7″ (standard)
	20000 D		10″	
	33000 D		10″	
	50000/60000D		12″	
	67000/72000D		12″	
	14000F		10″	
	1/153M		10″	
	2000M		10″	
	4000M		10″	
	5000M		12″	
	7000M		12″	
	9000M		12″	
	3000R		10″	
	1/100S		10″	
	A0/4999		10″	
	A1500			7″ (extended)
	A5000/6000		12″	
	AAL	10″		
	C (set)		10″	
	C6000		10″	
	D (digit L) (set)	12″		
	D (digit S) (S) (set)	12″		
	E (set)		10″	
	E3000[31]		10″	
	GL	12″		
	K (digit L) (set)	12″		
	KL	12″		
	M (C)	12″		
	M (digit L) (set)	12″		
	M (digit S) (S) (set)	12″		
	ML2000	10″		
	ML4000/6000	12″		

28 Product of a Spanish firm – *not* EMI
29 Originally Columbia Graphophone Company of Washington, D.C., and now CBS – *not* EMI

30 Single-sided
31 International series

Label	Series	33 1/3 rpm (LP)	78 rpm	45 rpm standard & extended play
COLUMBIA – International – *Continued*				
USA — *Continued*	MM[32]		˙ 12″	
	MS (S)	12″		
	PE	7″		7″ (extended)
	RL[33]	12″		
	SL (set)	12″		
	X		10″	
	X (set)[34]		12″	
COMMUNAUTE DE TRAVAIL POUR LA DIF-FUSION DE LA MUSIQUE SUISSE (Switzerland)	CT	12″		
	CTS (S)	12″		
COMPANIA GENERALE DEL DISCO (Italy)	PV		10″	
COMPASS (USA)	C (set)		12″	
COMPOSERS RECORDINGS (USA)	CRI	12″		
CONCERT ARTIST (Gt. Britain)	LPA	12″		
CONCERT CLASSICS (USA)	4000	12″		
	CC4100			7″ (extended)
CONCERT DISC (USA)	C	12″		
	CS (S)	12″		
CONCERTEUM (France)	CCX	12″		
	CLP	12″		
	CR	12″		
	CS	12″		
	CVX	12″		
	TCR	10″		
CONCERT HALL SOCIETY (USA)				
Gt. Britain	CM	12″		
	DL	12″		
	E	12″		
	F	12″		
	G	12″		
	M	12″		
	MCS	12″		
	SMSA (S)	12″		
	SMSC (S)	12″		
U.S.A.	(1 to 3 digits)		12″	
	1000		12″	
	AA (set)		12″	
	AG (set)		12″	
	AR (set)		12″	
	CHC	12″		
	CHS	12″		
	D (set)	12″		
	G (set)	12″		
CONNOISSEUR SOCIETY (USA)	CS	12″		
CONTEMPORARY (USA)	7000/8000 (S)	12″		
	C	12″		
CONTINENTAL (USA)	CLP	12″		
CONTREPOINT (France)	EXPT			7″ (extended)
	MC	12″		
	STMC (S)	12″		
CORONA (Germany)	30000	12″		

---

32 A set of 3 or more discs
33 Entre series
34 A set of 2 discs

Label	Series	33 1/3 rpm (LP)	78 rpm	45 rpm standard & extended play
COUNTERPOINT (USA)	C	12″		
	CPT	12″		
	CPTS (S)	12″		
	CS (S)	12″		
CRITÈRE (France)	CRD	12″		
	SCRD (S)	12″		
CROSSROADS (USA)	22 16 0000[35]	12″		
CROWELL-COLLIER RECORD GUILD (USA	RG	12″		
CROYDON (Gt. Britain)	CX			7″ (extended)
	EP			7″ (extended)
CRYSTAL (USA)	M	12″		
	S (S)	12″		
CULTURA (Belgium)	5000	12″		
CUPOL (Sweden)	4000		10″	
	6000		12″	
CURCI (Italy)	LP	12″		
CUTTY WREN (USA)	CWR	12″		
CYCNUS (France)	30CM	12″		
	60CS (S)	12″		
DA CAMERA (Germany)	HB	10″ & 12″		
	HKO			7″ (extended)
	M	10″		
	SM (S)	12″		
	SV			7″ (extended)
	WK			7″ (extended)
DACAPO (Germany)	(2 & 3 digits)		10″	
	2000		12″	
	8800		10″	
	E		10″	
DECCA (Gt. Britain)				
Australia	Y		10″	
	Z		12″	
Austria	HD	12″		
	LXT	12″		
	MD	12″		
	SMD (S)	12″		
	VD			7″ (extended)
Belgium	BA133000	10″		
	BAT133000	12″		
Denmark[36]	NS	10″		
	X51000	12″		
France	7600	12″		
	EUA108500			7″ (extended)
	FA143000	10″		
	FAT143000/173000	12″		
	FM133000	10″		
	FST153000	12″		
	GAG		12″	
	TF		12″	
	UA243000	10″		
	UAT273000	12″		
	UM233000	10″		

35 If the final digit is even, the disc is stereo; if it is odd, the disc is monaural. The 3rd digit from the left indicates either a single record or a set. E.g.: 16 (1 disc), 26 (2 discs), 36 (3 discs).

36 See Polyphon for balance of production

Label	Series	33 1/3 rpm (LP)	78 rpm	45 rpm standard & extended play
DECCA – *Continued*				
France – *Continued*	UMT263000	12″		
	UST253000	12″		
	UW333000	10″		
Germany	F43000		10″	
	HD	12″		
	K23000		12″	
	LW50000	10″		
	LXT2000	12″		
	MD	12″		
	NLK	12″		
	SMD (S)	12″		
	VD			7″ (extended)
	X53000		12″	
Gt. Britain	AK[37]		12″	
	AX		12″	
	CA[38]		12″	
	CEP			7″ (extended)
	D		12″	
	DE[38]		10″	
	F		10″	
	K		12″	
	LK	12″		
	LM	10″		
	LW	10″		
	LXT	12″		
	LY[38]		12″	
	M		10″	
	MET	12″		
	PO[38]		10″	
	PSF	12″		
	SEC			7″ (extended)
	SET (S)	12″		
	SXL (S)	12″		
	X		12″	
Netherlands	M32000		10″	
	XP6000		12″	
Spain	215000	12″		
	CCL38000	12″		
Sweden	K24000		12″	
Switzerland	K28000		12″	
	LXY	12″		
U.S.A.[39]	23000/24000		10″	
	25000		12″	
	29000		12″	
	40000[40]		10″	
	60000		10″	
	45-72000			7″ (standard)
	216000		10″	
	DCM	12″		
	DL4000[41]	10″		
	DL7000	10″		
	DL7500	10″		

37 Automatic sequence
38 Polydor series
39 A U.S. company owned by MCA – *not* the English Decca Group
40 Celebrity series
41 Medium play classical discs. *Not* to be confused with the popular music 10″ DL4000 series.

Label	Series	33 1/3 rpm (LP)	78 rpm	45 rpm standard & extended play
DECCA – *Continued*				
U.S.A. – *Continued*	DL8500	12″		
	DL9000/10000[42]	12″		
	DX (set)	12″		
	DXE	12″		
	DXSE (S)	12″		
	ED			7″ (extended)
	G20000		10″	
DELTA (Gt. Britain)	DEL	12″		
	TQD	12″		
DELYSE (Gt. Britain)	ECB	12″		
DENON (Japan)	OS	12″		
DESIGN (USA)	DLP	12″		
DESTO (USA)	DC	12″		
DEUTSCHE GRAMMOPHON[43]	600	12″		
	800	12″		
	135000[44]	12″		
	642000[45]	12″		
	643000	12″		
	2530 000	12″		
	2538 000	12″		
	2555 000	12″		
	2705 000 (set)	12″		
	2709 000 (set)	12″		
	2720 000 (set)	12″		
	EPA			7″ (extended)
	EPL			7″ (extended)
	LP	10″		
	LPE	10″		
	LPEM	12″		
	LPM	12″		
	SEPA (S)			7″ (extended)
	SLPEM (S)	12″		
	SLPM (S)	12″		
DEVA (France)	45A			7″ (extended)
	M7			7″ (extended)
DIADEL (Germany)	D		10″	
DIAL (USA)	LP	12″		
DIAMOND (Gt. Britain)	(no prefix)		10″	
DIRECCIÓN GENERAL DE INFORMACIONES Y CULTURE (Chile)	V-S		12″	
DISC (USA)	(1 to 3 digits) (set)		12″	
	4000		12″	
DISCAPON (USA)	4000	12″		
DISCOFIL (Sweden)	A		12″	
	LT	12″		
	TR	12″		
DISCOPHILES FRANÇAIS (France)	(1 & 2 digits – no prefix)		12″	
	225000	10″		
	525000	10″		
	DF	12″		
	DF730000	12″		
	DF740000 (S)	12″		
	EX			7″ (extended)

---

42 If preceded by the digit 7, it is a stereo disc   44 Privilege series
43 For 78 rpm discs see Polydor   45 Debut series

Label	Series	33 1/3 rpm (LP)	78 rpm	45 rpm standard & extended play
DISCOPHILES FRANÇAIS (France) – *Continued*	KLDC	12″		
DOMINION (Gt. Britain)	B		10″	
DONEMUS (Netherlands)	DAVS	12″		
DORIAN (USA)	1000	12″		
DOT (USA)	DLP	12″		
DOVER (USA)	HCR	12″		
	HCRST (S)	12″		
DUCRETET-THOMSON (France)[46]				
France	250V	10″		
	255C			7″ (extended)
	260V	10″		
	270C	10″		
	300V	12″		
	320C	12″		
	370C	12″		
	470C			7″ (extended)
	LAG	12″		
	LAP			7″ (extended)
	LP	12″		
	LPG	12″		
Gt. Britain	DTL	12″		
	EL	10″		
DUOPHONE (Gt. Britain)	B		10″	
	D		10″	
	GS		12″	
DURIUM (Italy)	A		10″	
	E		12″	
DUROSOIR (France)	SM		10″	
ECLIPSE (Gt. Britain)	ECM	12″		
	ECS (S)	12″		
EDISON (USA)[47]	47000[48]		10″	
	50000/52000		10″	
	80000		10″	
	82000		10″	
EDISON BELL (Gt. Britain)[49]	100		10″	
	0200		10″	
	500/600		12″	
	800		10″	
	1000/5000		10″	
	10000		10″	
	F		7″	
	H		10″	
	SH		7″	
EDITION MODERN (Switzerland)	TLPE	12″		
EDITION RHODOS (Hungary)	ERS 1200	12″		
EDITIONS PHONOGRAPHIQUES PARISIENNES (France)	APG[50]	12″		
	SLP	12″		
EDUCO (USA)	4000	12″		
EGMONT (Gt. Britain)	EGM	12″		
EKOPHON (Sweden)	300		10″	
	NS		10″	

---

46 Product of the Decca Group, England
47 Vertical-cut "Hill-and-dale" discs. Also cylinders
48 Electrical process
49 Main series were the "Velvet Face" & "Winner"
50 Allegro series

Label	Series	33 1/3 rpm (LP)	78 rpm	45 rpm standard & extended play
ELECTRECORD (Rumania)	ECC			7″ (extended)
	ECD	10″		
	ECE	12″		
ELECTROLA (see: His Master's Voice, Germany)				
ELITE (Switzerland, Germany, etc.)	3000	12″		
	5000	10″		
	7000	12″		
	9000	10″		
	CSLP	12″		
ELITE SPECIAL (Switzerland)	8000		10″	
	SMLP5000	12″		
	TLPE	12″		
EMBASSY (Gt. Britain)	WLP	12″		
EMERSON (USA)	(3 digits)		7″	
	7000		10″	
	02000X		10″	
ENCORE (Gt. Britain)	ENC	12″		
(L') ENCYCLOPEDIE SONORE (France)	320E	12″		
ENSAYO (Spain)	ENY	12″		
EPIC (USA)	BC (S)	12″		
	BSC (S)	12″		
	LC	12″		
	SC (set)	12″		
ERATO (France)	20000	12″		
	DP	12″		
	EFM8000	12″		
	EFM42000			7″ (extended)
	ERG	12″		
	LDE	12″		
	LPE	10″		
	STE (S)	12″		
	STU (C)	12″		
ESOTERIC (USA)	ES	12″		
ESQUIRE (Gt. Britain)	TN	12″		
	TW4000		12″	
	TW14000	12″		
ESTA (Czechoslovakia)	B		10″	
	H		12″	
	K		10″	
ETERNA (Germany, DDR)	120000/121000		12″	
	520000			7″ (extended)
	720000	10″		
	820000	12″		
EUROCHORD (Germany)	LPC	12″		
	LPG	12″		
	TAI		12″	
EURODISC (Germany)	40000/41000CK			7″ (extended)
	60000GE & GK			7″ (extended)
	70000KK, LP & MK	12″		
	73000/74000KK	12″		
	78000ZK	12″		
	79000KK (S)	12″		
	80000XK & ZK (S)	12″		
	LP55000	12″		
	S60000GE (S)			7″ (extended)

Label	Series	33 1/3 rpm (LP)	78 rpm	45 rpm standard & extended play
EURODISC (Germany) – *Continued*	S70000XK (set)	12″		
EUROPA (Germany)	E100	12″		
EUROPAISCHE FONOCLUB (Germany)	2000 (S)	12″		
EVEREST (USA)	LPBR	12″		
	SDBR (S)	12″		
EXCELSIUS (Italy)	UN	12″		
FALCON (Germany)	L-ST (C)	12″		
FAMOUS (Gt. Britain)	700		10″	
FANTASY (USA)	5000	12″		
	8000 (S)	12″		
	85000 (C)	12″		
FAVORITE (International)[51]				
France	1-4000E		10″	
	2-4000E		12″	
	2-94000E		12″	
Germany	1-14000E		10″	
	D		10″	
Gt. Britain	(1 to 3 digits – no prefix)		10″	
Italy	1-34000		10″	
Poland	1-74000D		10″	
Russia	1-24000		10″	
Spain	1-64000E		10″	
Sweden	1-84000		10″	
FELSTED (USA)	L	12″		
FENNICA (Finland)	ST		10″	
FESTIVAL (Australia)	CFR	12″		
	FES	12″		
	FLD	12″		
	FLP	12″		
FIDELIO (Gt. Britain)	ATL	12″		
FIDELITY (Greece)	EP			7″ (extended)
FILMOPHONE (Gt. Britain)[52]	100		7″	
FINLANDIA (Finland)	PEP		12″	
FLORILÈGE (France)[53]	(2 digits)		12″	
	13000	12″		
	HP		12″	
FOLKWAYS (USA)	FM	12″		
FONA (Denmark)	S	12″		
FONDATION EUGEN YSAYE (Belgium)	FEY	12″		
FONIT (Italy)	13000		10″	
	LP	10″		
	LPU	12″		
FONO (Switzerland)	25-	10″		
	30-	12″		
	FGL	12″		
	FGLS (S)	12″		
FONOTIPIA (Italy)	39000		10¾″	
	62000		10¾″	
	69000		13″	
	74000		12″	

---

51 A "1-" = 10″ disc; a "2-" = 12″ disc. A "4" appearing as the 4th digit from the right indicates "violin."

52 Celluloid disc
53 Product of Adès

Label	Series	33 1/3 rpm (LP)	78 rpm	45 rpm standard & extended play
FONOTIPIA (Italy) – *Continued*	152000		10¾″	
	172000		12″	
FONTANA (Netherlands)				
France	200000WGL	12″		
	665000EE			7″ (extended)
	699000CL & EL	12″		
	700000WGY (S)	12″		
Germany	494000EE			7″ (extended)
Gt. Britain	BIG300	12″		
	BIG400 (S)	12″		
	CFE			7″ (extended)
	CFL	12″		
	EFF			7″ (extended)
	EFL	12″		
	EFR			7″ (extended)
	SCFL (S)	12″		
	SFON (S)	12″		
Netherlands (& international)	88400DY	12″		
	496000CE	12″		
	663000ER	12″		
	664000ER	12″		
	675000KR	12″		
	695000KL	12″		
	697000EL	12″		
	698000CL & FL	12″		
	875000CY	12″		
	876000EZ	12″		
	877000EZ	12″		
	894000ZKY	12″		
	K71 BC800 (set)	12″		
FORUM (USA)	F	12″		
FOUNDATION FOR THE RECORDING OF AUSTRALIAN MUSIC (Australia)	FRAM	12″		
	SFRAM (S)	12″		
FOURFRONT (Gt. Britain)	848100DKY	12″		
	4FM (S)	12″		
FRIENDS OF CHAMBER MUSIC (USA)	(2 digits – no prefix)	12″	12″	
FUNDACION MITO JUAN PRO-MUSICA (Venezuela)	(Vol.)	12″		
GALA (USA)	GLP	12″		
GALLERY (USA)		12″		
GAMUT (USA)	12-		12″	
	GT		12″	
	MS (set)		12″	
GEMINI (Gt. Britain)	GME	12″		
GENERAL (USA)			12″	
GENNETT (USA)	2000/4000		10″	
	9000/11000		10″	
	14000		12″	
	C		10″	
GLORIA (Germany)	GO		10″	
GOLDEN CREST (USA)	CR	12″		
	GC	12″		
	NEC[54]	12″		

54 New England Conservatory series

Label	Series	33 1/3 rpm (LP)	78 rpm	45 rpm standard & extended play
GOLDEN CREST (USA) – *Continued*	RE	12″		
GOLDEN MUSIC SOCIETY (USA)	GMS	12″		
	LP	12″		
GRAMMAVOX (Gt. Britain)	6000		10″	
	C		10″	
GRAMOLA (Belgium)	GLP	10″		
GRAMOPHONE (USA)[55]	2000	12″		
GRAMOPHONE & TYPEWRITER (Gt. Britain)[56]				
France	37900		10″	
	037900		12″	
Germany	47900		10″[57]	
	047900		12″	
Gt. Britain	3500		10″	
	7900		10″[57]	
	07900		12″	
	08000		12″	
Italy	057900		12″	
U.S.S.R.	23400		10″	
	24300		10″	
	27900		10″	
	28000		10″	
	027900		12″	
GRAMOPHONE SHOP (USA)	GS (set)		12″	
	GSC		12″	
GREAT MUSICIANS (Gt. Britain)	(Vol.)	12″		
	TGM	12″		
GRIFFON (USA)	LP	12″		
GUILDE EUROPÉENNE DU MICROSILLON (France)	EGEX			7″ (extended)
	GEM	12″		
GUILDE INTERNATIONALE DU DISQUE (France)	M	12″		
	SMA	12″		
	SMS (S)	12″		
HALLMARK (Canada)	RS	10″		
HALLMARK (Gt. Britain)	HM	12″		
HALL OF FAME (USA)	HOF	12″		
HALO (USA)	50000	12″		
HARGAIL (USA)	MW (set)		12″	
HARMONIA MUNDI (Germany)	CVH	12″		
	HM25000	10″		
	HM30000	12″		
	HMB[58]	12″		
	HMS30000 (S)	12″		
	HMST530000 (S)	12″		
HARMONY (USA)[59]	HL	12″		
HARMONY (USA)	(H suffix)		10″	
HARMONY MUSIC (Sweden)	(2 digits – no prefix)		10″	
HAYDN SOCIETY (USA)	AS[60]	12″		
	HS	12″		

---

55 Mastered by Radio Corporation of America (RCA)
56 English numberings continue in sequence from Berliner discs
57 The same series covers the occasional 7″ disc

58 Balkanton series
59 Product of U.S. Columbia
60 L'Anthologie Sonore series

Label	Series	33 1/3 rpm (LP)	78 rpm	45 rpm standard & extended play
HAYDN SOCIETY (USA) – *Continued*	HSL	12″		
	HSLC	12″		
	HSLN	12″		
	HSLP	12″		
HED ARZI (Germany)	700		10″	
	(no prefix)		12″	
HELIODOR (Germany)[61]				
Belgium & France	428000(S)	12″		
	478000	12″		
Germany	466000	12″		
	478000	12″		
	480000	12″		
Gt. Britain	89500	12″		
	428000 (S)	12″		
	479000	12″		
USA	H	12″		
	HS (S)	12″		
HERALD (Gt. Britain)	RPL	12″		
HI-FI STEREO REVIEW (USA)	(special pressing)	12″		
HIS MASTER'S VOICE – HMV (Gt. Britain)				
Australia	EA		10″	
	ED		12″	
Austria	ES		12″	
	GA		10″	
	GB		12″	
	VALP	12″		
	VBLP	10″		
Belgium	ASDF (S)	12″		
	ASDW (S)	12″		
	AU		12″	
	CVA	12″		
	CVB	12″		
	CVC	12″		
	DA4700/4799		10″	
	DB4700/4799		12″	
	EX		10″	
	F		10″	
	FALP	12″		
	FBLP	10″		
	FJLP	12″		
	GHLP	10″		
	7ERF			7″ (extended)
	7RF			7″ (extended)
Czechoslovakia	ER		10″	
	JX		12″	
Denmark	KALP	12″		
	KBLP	10″		
France (Voix de son Maître)	30700		10″	
	37900[62]		10″	
	037900[62]		12″	
	237900		10″	
	0237900		12″	
	2-033000		12″	

61 Branch of Deutsche Grammophon
62 French numberings continue in sequence from Gramophone & Typewriter

Label	Series	33 1/3 rpm (LP)	78 rpm	45 rpm standard & extended play
HMV – *Continued*				
France – *Continued*	ASDF (S)	12″		
	CVA	12″		
	CVB	12″		
	CVC	12″		
	CVD	12″		
	DA4800/5199		10″	
	DB4800/5199		12″	
	DB11100		12″	
	FALP	12″		
	FBLP	10″		
	FJLP	12″		
	GHLP	10″		
	K		10″	
	L		12″	
	P		10″	
	W		12″	
	X77000		12″	
	7ERF			7″ (extended)
	7RF			7″ (extended)
Germany (Electrola)	2-43000		10″	
	104900		10″	
	947900		10″	
	1C047- (C)	12″		
	1C053- (C)	12″		
	2C063- (C)	12″		
	ASDW (S)	12″		
	BSDW (S)	12″		
	CSDW (S)	12″		
	DA4400/4699		10″	
	DA5500/5699		10″	
	DB4400/4699		12″	
	DB5500/5699		12″	
	DB7600		12″	
	DB11500		12″	
	DSDW (S)	12″		
	E20000/40000			7″ (extended)
	E60000	10″		
	E70000	10″		
	E80000/90000	12″		
	EG		10″	
	EH		12″	
	EJ		12″	
	EW		10″	
	GESW			7″ (extended)
	I41300	12″		
	J60000	12″		
	RESW			7″ (extended)
	SHZE	12″		
	SHZEL	12″		
	SME (S)	12″		
	STE70000 (S)	10″		
	STE80000/90000 (S)	12″		
	WALP	12″		
	WBLP	10″		
	WCLP	12″		
	WDLP	10″		
	7EGW			7″ (extended)
	7ERW			7″ (extended)

Label	Series	33 1/3 rpm (LP)	78 rpm	45 rpm standard & extended play
HMV – *Continued*				
Germany (Electrola) – *Continued*	7PW			7″ (Standard)
	7RW			7″ (standard)
Gt. Britain	4000		10″	
	7900[63]		10″	
	02400		12″	
	03000		12″	
	07900[63]		12″	
	3-7900		10″	
	4-7900		10″	
	5-7900		10″	
	6-7900		10″	
	7-7900		10″	
	2-07900		12″	
	3-07900		12″	
	ALP	12″		
	ASD (S)	12″		
	B		10″	
	B4700[64]		10″	
	BD		10″	
	BLP	10″		
	C		12″	
	C4800[64]		12″	
	CLP	12″		
	COLH[65]	12″		
	CSLP (S)	12″		
	D		12″	
	DA100/3999		10″	
	DB100/4099		12″	
	DB6100/6999		12″	
	DB7000/9999[66]		12″	
	DB21000		12″	
	DK[67]		12″	
	DLP	10″		
	E		10″	
	HLP	12″		
	HMS		12″	
	HOM	12″		
	HQS (S)	12″		
	IR		10″	
	JF		10″	
	JG[68]		12″	
	JO[69]		10″	
	JOX[69]		12″	
	MH[69]		10″	
	SAN (S)[70]	12″		
	SLS[71]	12″		
	SXLP (S)	12″		
	TJ[69]		10″	
	TK[69]		12″	
	XLP	12″		

63 British numberings continue in sequence from Gramophone & Typewriter
64 Export & international series
65 Great Recordings of the Century series
66 Automatic couplings
67 Pre-electric reissue – Celebrity series
68 Private issue
69 Export & international series
70 Angel series
71 U.S.S.R. series

Label	Series	33 1/3 rpm (LP)	78 rpm	45 rpm standard & extended play
HMV – *Continued*				
Gt. Britain – *Continued*	7EB			7″ (extended)
	7EG			7″ (extended)
	7EP			7″ (extended)
	7ER			7″ (extended)
	7P			7″ (standard)
	7R			7″ (standard)
Hungary	AM		10″	
	AN		12″	
	HUC		10″	
India	N100		10″	
	P30000		10″	
Italy (La Voce del Padrone)	057900[72]		12″	
	7-257900		12″	
	ASDQ (S)	12″		
	AV		10″	
	AW		12″	
	DA5350/5449		10″	
	DA11300		10″	
	DB5350/5449		12″	
	DB05350		12″	
	DB11300		12″	
	GW		10″	
	HN		10″	
	QALP	12″		
	QBLP	10″		
	QCLP	12″		
	QDLP	10″		
	QFLP	10″		
	R		10″	
	RESQ			7″ (extended)
	S		12″	
	7EPQ			7″ (extended)
	7ERQ			7″ (extended)
	7RQ			7″ (standard)
Netherlands	B4700/4900		10″	
Scandinavia (Norway, Denmark & Sweden)[73]	900		10″	
	277900		10″	
	2-083000		12″	
	2-087900		12″	
	7-53000		10″	
	7-82000		10″	
	7-87900		10″	
	32-		10″	
	AL		10″	
	B (6 digits)		10″	
	DA5200/5299		10″	
	DA10500		10″	
	DA11900		10″	
	DB1		12″	
	DB5200/5299		12″	
	DB10000[74]		12″	
	DB10500		12″	
	DB11000/11099[75]		12″	

72 Italian numberings continue in sequence from Gramophone & Typewriter
73 78 rpm only
74 Repressings
75 Local pressings

Label	Series	33 1/3 rpm (LP)	78 rpm	45 rpm standard & extended play
HMV — *Continued*				
SCANDINAVIA (Norway, Denmark & Sweden) – *Cont.*	DB11900		12″	
	DB20100		12″	
	K87900/88000		10″	
	M		12″	
	V		10″	
	X		10″	
	Z		12″	
Spain (La Voz de su Amo)	067900		12″	
	AB		12″	
	AE		10″	
	AF		10″	
	DA4200/4399		10″	
	DB4200/4399		12″	
	LALP	12″		
	LBLP	10″		
	7ERL			7″ (extended)
Sweden	CSDS (S)	12″		
	SCLP	12″		
Switzerland	DB6000/6099		12″	
	DB10000		12″	
U.S.S.R. (& Baltic countries)	27900[76]		10″	
	027900[76]		12″	
	EK		10″	
HISPAVOX (Spain)	HBR (S)	12″		
	HH10-	12″		
	HH16			7″ (extended)
HISTORICAL RECORD SOCIETY (USA)	1000		10″	
HOMOCHORD (Gr. Britain & Germany)				
France	B		10″	
Gt. Britain & Germany	(2 & 3 digits)		10″	
	4-		10″	
	2000/3000		10″	
	6000		10″	
	9000		12″	
	4-0000		12″	
	B 8000		10″	
	H		10″	
	H4000		12″	
	HB		12″	
	P		10″	
HOMOPHONE (Gt. Britain)	25-100		10″	
	HD		12″	
HUNGAROTON (Hungary)[77]	SHLX	12″		
	SLPX	12″		
IDEAL (Gt. Britain)	7000		10″	
IKAR (USA)	IK (suffix M)	12″		
	IK (suffix S) (S)	12″		
IMPERIAL (International)				
Germany	(begins zero)		12″	
	I			7″ (extended)
	ILP	10″		
	IPE		10″	
	J		10″	

76 Soviet numberings continue in sequence from Gramophone & Typewriter
77 Replaces Qualiton

Label	Series	33 1/3 rpm (LP)	78 rpm	45 rpm standard & extended play
IMPERIAL (International) – *Continued*				
Gt. Britain	(3 digits)		10″	
	1000/2000		10″	
	19000		10″	
	45000[78]		10″	
Netherlands	ILPT			7″ (extended)
	ILX	12″		
	IPE	10″		
INTERCORD (Germany)	061-00K	12″		
	700-09	12″		
	708-09	12″		
	709-00SB	12″		
	710-00Z	12″		
	713-00MH	12″		
	716-00SB	12″		
	928-00Z (set)	12″		
	939-00Z	12″		
	947-00K	12″		
	973-00Z (set)	12″		
	978-00K	12″		
	989-00K	12″		
INTERNATIONAL RECORD COLLECTOR'S CLUB (USA)	(2 digits)		12″	
IRAMAC (Netherlands)	6500	12″		
JANUS (Denmark)	1000		10″	
JANUS-PIROUETTE (USA)	J	12″		
	JA	12″		
	JAS (S)	12″		
JOHN BULL (Gt. Britain)	B		10″	
JOKER (Germany)	M	12″		
JUGOTON (Yugoslavia)[79]	200	10″		
	2200	12″		
	26000			7″ (extended)
	213100	12″		
	LPY	12″		
	LPYV	12″		
JUMBO (Gt. Britain)	(3 digits)		10″	
	A		10″	
KALLIOPE (Germany)	K		10″	
KANTOREI (Germany)	(1 digit)		12″	
KAPP (USA)	KC	12″		
	KCL (S)	12″		
	KL	12″		
	KS (S)	12″		
KASKADE (Germany)	8000	12″		
KEYNOTE (USA)	K		12″	
KING (Japan)	MH	12″		
	SKR	12″		
KINGSWAY (USA)	KL	12″		
KRISTALL (Germany)	5000		10″	
	05000		12″	
	21000		10″	
	021000		12″	

---

78 Single-sided
79 Radio Televizije Beograd – RTB

Label	Series	33 1/3 rpm (LP)	78 rpm	45 rpm standard & extended play
KRISTALL (Germany) – *Continued*	SMVP	12″		
KUULA LEVYT (Finland)	TK-S	12″		
LEEDS (USA)	4000		10″	
LIBRARY OF RECORDED MASTERPIECES (USA)	(Vol.)	12″		
	BB	12″		
	LRM	12″		
LINCOLN (USA)	2000		10″	
LION (USA)	CL	12″		
LISTENING, Inc. (USA)	6600	12″		
LITTLE WONDER (USA)	1000		5½″	
LIZARD (USA)	C	12″		
LONDON (USA)[80]	CHA (set)	12″		
	CM	12″		
	CS (S)	12″		
	CSA (S) (set)	12″		
	EL[81]	12″		
	LA (set)		10 & 12″	
	LB	10″		
	LD[82]	10″		
	SMVP	12″		
KUULA LEVYT (Finland)	TK-S	12″		
LEEDS (USA)	4000		10″	
LIBRARY OF RECORDED MASTERPIECES (USA)	(Vol.)	12″		
	BB	12″		
	LRM	12″		
LINCOLN (USA)	2000		10″	
LION (USA)	CL	12″		
LISTENING, Inc. (USA)	6600	12″		
LITTLE WONDER (USA)	1000		5½″	
LIZARD (USA)	C	12″		
LONDON (USA)[80]	CHA (set)	12″		
	CM	12″		
	CS (S)	12″		
	CSA (S) (set)	12″		
	EL[81]	12″		
	LA (set)		10″ & 12″	
	LB	10″		
	LD[82]	10″		
	LL	12″		
	LLP	12″		
	LPS	10″		
	LS	10″		
	PM	12″		
	R		10″	
	SLC	12″		
	SPC (S)	12″		
	ST (S)	12″		
	T		12″	

80 North American subsidiary of the English Decca group
81 International series
82 Medium-play disc

Label	Series	33 1/3 rpm (LP)	78 rpm	45 rpm standard & extended play
LONDON – *Continued*	TC	12″		
	TCS (S)	12″		
	TW[81]	12″		
	TWV[81]	12″		
	W[81]	12″		
LONDON-GLOBE (Gt. Britain)	GLB	12″		
LONGINE (USA)	LW	12″		
LOUISVILLE (USA)	LOU	12″		
	LS (S)	12″		
LUMEN (France)	30000		10″	
	30100		10″	
	206000		10″	
	208000		10″	
	LD1-400			7″ (extended)
	LD3-400	12″		
LYRICHORD (USA)	LL	12″		
	LLST (S)	12″		
LYRITA (Gt. Britain)	SRCS (S)	12″		
McINTOSH (USA)	MM	12″		
MACE (USA)	M	12″		
	MCS (S)	12″		
	MXX (C)	12″		
	SM (S)	12″		
MADISON (USA)	14000		10″	
MAESTRO (Belgium)	OAT	12″		
MAGIC TONE (USA)	MLP	10″		
MAGYAR MUZA (Hungary)	MM		10″	
MANHATTAN (USA)	SRO	10″		
MARATHON (Gt. Britain)	100/300		10″	
MARBLE ARCH (Gt. Britain)	MAL	12″		
	MALS (S)	12″		
MARLBORO RECORDING SOCIETY (USA)	MRS	12″		
MARSPEN (Germany)	200		10″	
MASTERPIECE (USA)	8500		10″	
MASTERSEAL (USA)	MSLP	12″		
MAYOR (Italy)	500		12″	
MCA (Gt. Britain)[83]	MACS (S)	12″		
	MUC	12″		
	MUCS (S)	12″		
MEDEA (USA)	1000	12″		
MELODISC (Germany)	80000K	12″		
MELODIYA-ANGEL (USA)[84]	R	12″		
	SR (S)	12″		
MELOMANES FRANÇAIS (France)	MF	12″		
MERCURY (USA)				
France	131000MSY	12″		
Gt. Britain	AMS (S)	12″		
	MMA	12″		
Netherlands	120500MGL	12″		
	130500MGY	12″		

83   British outlet for U.S. Decca releases
84   North American outlet for Soviet MK releases

Label	Series	33 1/3 rpm (LP)	78 rpm	45 rpm standard & extended play
MERCURY – *Continued*				
Netherlands – *Continued*	DS641900L	12″		
	DS836900Y (S)	12″		
U.S.A.	14000		12″	
	16000		12″	
	DM (set)		12″	
	EP1-5000			7″ (extended)
	MEP			7″ (extended)
	MG10000	12″		
	MG15000	10″		
	MG50000	12″		
	MGL (set)	12″		
	MGW[85]	12″		
	MPT	12″		
	SR (S)	12″		
	SRW (S)[85]	12″		
	WL[85]	12″		
	XEP			7″ (extended)
MERIT (USA)	1-	12″		
MERRICK (Gt. Britain)[86]	FMS	12″		
METRO-GOLDWYN-MAYER - MGM (USA)	9500		10″	
	30000		10″	
	E	12″		
	F6	12″		
	GC	12″		
METRONOME (Denmark)				
Denmark	B		10″	
	CLP	12″		
	MCEP			7″ (extended)
	MCLP	12″		
Netherlands	HLP			7″ (extended)
METROPOLE (Gt. Britain)	1000		10″	
MEZHDUNARODNAYA KNIGA (U.S.S.R.)[87]	D			
	S (S)			
	SM (C)			
MICHEL-ANGE (France)	(no prefix)	12″		
MJA (USA)[88]	MJA	12″		
MODE (France)	CMDINT (S)	12″		
	MDINT	12″		
MONARCH (Gt. Britain)	MEL			7″ (extended)
	MWL	12″		
MONITOR (USA)	MC	12″		
	MCS (S)	12″		
	MFS (S)	12″		
MORGAN (Gt. Britain)	M100 IL	12″		
MUSICA (Denmark)	A		10″	
MUSICA BAVARICA (Germany)	MB	12″		
MUSICA BRASILEIRA (Brazil)	SLP	12″		
MUSICA ET LITERA (France)	8000	12″		
	10000			7″ (extended)
	00300ALK	12″		

85 Wing series
86 Frank Merrick Society
87 78 rpm: 7″ & 8″ discs begin with 2 zeros; 10″ discs begin with a digit; 12″ discs begin with a zero. LP's: 7″ discs begin with 3 zeros; 10″ discs begin with a digit; 12″ discs begin with a zero

88 Private issue

Label	Series	33 1/3 rpm (LP)	78 rpm	45 rpm standard & extended play
MUSICAL HERITAGE SOCIETY (USA)	CC	12″		
	DRM	12″		
	MHS	12″		
MUSICAL MASTERPIECE SOCIETY (USA)	(2 & 3 digits)	10″		
	MMS (1 to 3 digits)	10″		
	MMS2000	12″		
	POP	10″		
MUSICA MUNDI (Germany)	VMS	12″		
MUSICAPHON	25R900	10″		
MUSIC APPRECIATION RECORDS (USA)	CM		12″	
	MAR	10″ & 12″		
	S (set)		12″	
MUSICA RARA (Gt. Britain)	MUR	12″		
	MUS (S)	12″		
MUSICA SACRA (Germany)	AMS	12″		
MUSIC FOR PLEASURE (Gt. Britain)	MFP	12″		
MUSIC GUILD (USA)	M	12″		
	MG	12″		
	MS (S)	12″		
	S (S)	12″		
MUSIC HALL (USA)	MH	12″		
MUSICIANS FOUNDATION OF AMERICA (USA)	(no prefix)	12″		
MUSIC IN OUR TIME (Gt. Britain)	MIOT	12″		
MUSIC LIBRARY (USA)	MLR (1 & 2 digits)		10″ & 12″	
	MLR5000	10″		
	MLR7000	12″		
MUSICRAFT (USA)	1000		12″	
	8500		10″	
	MC (set)		12″	
MUSIC TREASURES OF THE WORLD (USA)	MT	12″		
MUSIDISC (France)	RC	12″		
MUSIK PRODUCTION SCHWARZWERK – BASF (Germany)	CRO	12″		
MUSIQUE AU VATICAN (France)	1000		12″	
MUSIQUE DE TOUS LES TEMPS (France)	EP			7″ (extended)
MUSIQUE ROYALE (Germany)[89]	199000	12″		
MUSPRED (U.S.S.R.)			12″	
MUZA (Poland)	1400/1500		12″	
	L	10″		
	SXL (S)	12″		
	X		10″	
	XL	12″		
	XW	12″		
NATIONAL GRAMOPHONIC SOCIETY (Gt. Britain)[90]	NGS		12″	
NERA & MUSICA (Norway)	KE		12″	
NEW EDITIONS (USA)	(no prefix)	12″		

89 Product of Deutsche Grammophon
90 10 & 12 inch sizes are intermixed in an alphabetized numbering system utilizing A/Z, AA/ZZ & AAA/ZZZ

Label	Series	33 1/3 rpm (LP)	78 rpm	45 rpm standard & extended play
NEW MUSIC QUARTERLY RECORDINGS (USA)	1-		12″	
	1000		12″	
NEW RECORDS INC. (USA)	NRI	12″		
	NRLP200 (set)	12″		
	NRLP400	12″		
	NRLP2000	12″		
NIXA (Gt. Britain)[91]	BLP	12″		
	BY			7″ (extended)
	BZ			7″ (extended)
	HLP	12″		
	LLP	12″		
	MLPY	10″		
	PLP	12″		
	QLP	12″		
	SPLP	12″		
	WLP	12″		
NONESUCH (USA)	H1000	12″		
	H71000 (S)	12″		
	H73000 (S) (set)	12″		
NORDISKA MUSIKFÖRLAGET (Norway)	AEP			7″ (extended)
OCTACROS (Gt. Britain)	100/300		10″	
ODEON – International				
Argentina	51800		10″	
	55000/57000		10″	
	64000		12″	
	76000		12″	
	124000/125000		12″	
	177000		12″	
	195000/196000		10″	
	263000		12″	
	LDM		10″	
Austria	A186000		10″	
Belgium	BSOA			7″ (extended)
	BSOAE			7″ (extended)
	FOC	10″		
	LDC	12″		
	OD	10″		
	ODX	12″		
	ZOC	12″		
	7AOE			7″ (extended)
Brazil	66000		12″	
	285000		12″	
	286000		10″	
	288000		10″	
	A3000		10″	
	C7000		12″	
Denmark	600A		12″	
	3300AA		12″	
	D6000		12″	
	D6400		12″	
	DO7000		12″	
	MOAK	12″		
	PASK	12″		

---

91 Division of Pye Corporation

Label	Series	33 1/3 rpm (LP)	78 rpm	45 rpm standard & extended play
ODEON – *Continued*				
Finland	228000		10″	
	PLD		10″	
France	3700		7″	
	33000		10¾″	
	36000		10¾″	
	56000		12″	
	123000		12″	
	165000/166000		10″	
	171000		12″	
	188000		10″	
	238000		10″	
	282000		10″	
	311000		10″	
	BSOA			7″ (extended)
	BSOAE			7″ (extended)
	FOC	10″		
	LDC	12″		
	OD	12″		
	ODX	12″		
	XOC	12″		
	7AOE			7″ (extended)
Germany	2000		10¾″	
	0-2000		10″	
	0-3300		10″	
	0-4000		10″	
	0-6000		12″	
	0-7200/7800		12″	
	0-8400		12″	
	0-8700		12″	
	0-9100		12″	
	0-11000		10″	
	0-25000/26000		10″	
	0-28000		10″	
	0-50500		12″	
	(N suffix)		12″	
	8000FXB		10¾″	
	8000FXC		10¾″	
	8000FXXE		12″	
	AA		12″	
	BEOW			7″ (extended)
	EP90000			7″ (extended)
	O 60000	10″		
	O 80000	12″		
	STO60000 (S)	10″		
	STO80000 (S)	12″		
Gt. Britain	700		10¾″	
	0100/0700		10¾″	
	5000		10″	
	30000		10¾″	
	32000		10¾″	
	44000		10¾″	
	51000		10¾″	
	(R suffix)		12″	
	A		12″	
	JX		12″	
	LX		10¾″	
	LXX		12″	

Label	Series	33 1/3 rpm (LP)	78 rpm	45 rpm standard & extended play
ODEON – *Continued*				
Gt. Britain – *Continued*	R		12″	
	RX		10¾″	
	RXX		12″	
	UA		10¾″	
	UX		12″	
	X		12″	
	XX		12″	
Italy	110000		10″	
	A		10″	
	C		10″	
	GO		10″	
	O		10″	
	P		10″	
	R		12″	
Norway	60400		12″	
	79000		12″	
Rumania	199000		12″	
Spain	121000		12″	
	183000/184000		10″	
	OLAL			7″ (extended)
	OLAX	12″		
Sweden	A160000		12″	
	A162000		10″	
	A210000		12″	
	D1000		10″	
	D3000/4000		10″	
	D6000		12″	
U.S.A.	3000		12″	
ODYSSEY (USA)[92]	32 16 0000	12″		
	Y30000	12″		
L') OISEAU-LYRE (France & Gt. Britain)	200		12″	
	LD	12″		
	OL (1 to 3 digits)		10″ & 12″	
	OL50000	12″		
	OLP (set)		12″	
	SOL (S)	12″		
OKEY (USA)	4000		10″	
	41000		10″	
	52000		12″	
	72000		10¾″	
OLYPIENNE (France)	S49000	12″		
OMNIA (France)	27000		7″	
OPERA DISC (USA)[93]	07900		12″	
ORFEI (Bulgaria)	1300		12″	
ORFEO (Argentina)	4000		10″	
ORIOLE (USA)	400		10″	
ORION (USA)	OR	12″		
	ORS (S)	12″		
ORPHÉE (France)	150000			7″ (extended)
	LDP-D50000	12″		
	LDP-D60000 (S)	12″		
ORPHEON (France)	(3 digits – no prefix)		10″	

92 If the final digit is even, the disc is stereo; if it is odd, the disc is monaural. The 3rd digit from the left indicates either a single record or a set. E.g.: 16 (1 disc), 26 (2 discs), 36 (3 discs).

93 Pirate label

Label	Series	33 1/3 rpm (LP)	78 rpm	45 rpm standard & extended play
ORPHEUS (USA)	OR	12″		
ORYX (Gt. Britain)	3C300	12″		
	EXP	12″		
	ORYX	12″		
PACIFIC (France)	3000		12″	
	150000			7″ (extended)
	A	10″		
	E			7″ (extended)
	EP			7″ (extended)
	LDAD	12″		
	LDFC	10″		
	LDO-E	12″		
	LDPC	10″		
	LDP-D50000	12″		
	LDP-D60000 (S)	12″		
	LDPF	12″		
	PIZ		12″	
PAN (Gt. Britain)[94]	PAN	12″		
	SPAN (S)	12″		
PANACHORD (Gt. Britain)	25000		10″	
PANTHÉON (France)[95]	XPV	12″		
PANTON (Czechoslovakia)	01 0000	12″		
	11 0000 (S)	12″		
PARAGON (USA)	9000		10″	
PARAMOUNT (USA)	33000		10″	
PARLIAMENT (USA)	PLP	12″		
	PLPS (S)	12″		
PARLOPHONE (Gt. Britain)				
Australia	A4000		12″	
	A7000		10″	
	AR1100		12″	
France[96]	22000		10″	
	44000		10″	
	57000		12″	
	80000		10″	
	85000		10″	
Germany	500		12″	
	7000		10″	
	B5000		10″	
	B27000		10″	
	B37000		10″	
	B48000/49000		10″	
	P1000		10″	
	P9000		12″	
	UA40000		10″	
	UX52000		10″	
Gt. Britain	CGEP[97]			7″ (extended)
	DP[98]		10″	
	DPX[98]		12″	
	E6000		10″	

94 Product of Saga
95 Product of Vox
96 Exported discs are prefixed "B" & "P"
97 International series
98 Export series

Label	Series	33 1/3 rpm (LP)	78 rpm	45 rpm standard & extended play
PARLOPHONE – *Continued*				
Gt. Britain – *Continued*	E10000		12″	
	F		10″	
	PMA	12″		
	PMB	10″		
	PMC	12″		
	PXO[98]		12″	
	R2000		10″	
	R20000		12″	
	SW1/8000[99]		12″	
Italy	AT[100]		10″	
	B		10″	
	BB[100]		12″	
	C		10″	
	CB[100]		12″	
	CC[100]		12″	
	ESLO			7″ (extended)
	LL[101]		10″	
	OL[101]		10″	
	P		12″	
	P56000		12″	
	PE[100]		12″	
	PES			7″ (extended)
	PESQ			7″ (extended)
	RR[100 & 101]		12″	
	SEBQ			7″ (extended)
	TI[102]		10″	
Netherlands	PHD			7″ (extended)
Sweden	B41000		10″	
PATHÉ (France)[103]				
Austria	19000/19999		10″	
Belgium	9000		10″	
	X9000		10″	
Czechoslovakia	900		12″	
France	500		11½″	
	1000		10″	
	2000		14″	
	3000		10″	
	5000		11½″	
	6000		11½″	
	8000		10″	
	8500		7″ & 10″	
	9000		11½″	
	9500		12″	
	40000		11½″	
	ADTX	12″		
	ASTX (S)	12″		
	DTX	12″		
	EA		10″	
	PA		10″	
	PAT		12″	

99 SW8000 series begins automatic couplings
100 Cetra series
101 Cetra-Polydor series
102 Cetra series
103 The letter "X" indicates a lateral-cut disc which, in all cases, is a re-recording of a vertical-cut "hill-and-dale" disc. The numbers remain identical.

Label	Series	33 1/3 rpm (LP)	78 rpm	45 rpm standard & extended play
PATHÉ – *Continued*				
France – *Continued*	PD		10″	
	PDT		12″	
	PG		10″	
	PGT		12″	
	X		10″	
Germany	6000		10″	
	54000/54499		12″	
Gt. Britain	1000		10″	
	5000		11½″	
	5000/70100[104]			
	78000		11½″	
	79000		9½″	
Hungary	16000		10″	
Italy	80000		11½″	
	84000		10″	
	86000		10″	
Netherlands	X90000		10″	
Poland	26000		10″	
Rumania	100		10″	
Spain	DMX	12″		
	EMD			7″ (extended)
U.S.A.	10000		12″	
	20000		10½″	
	25000		10″	
	27000		10″	
	30000/40000		11½″	
	60000		11½″	
	70000		14″	
	82000		14″	
unidentified origin	D		12″	
	FC		10″	
	K		10″	
	M		10″	
	0-100		12″	
PATHÉ-ACTUELLE (France)[105]				
Austria	52000		10″	
Germany	15000/15499		10″	
Gt. Britain & U.S.A.	10000/11000		10″	
	15000		10″	
	020500		10″	
PATHÉ-VOX (France)	PV (set)	12″		
PAX (Sweden)	(digits only)		10″	
PEARL (Gt. Britain)	GEM	12″		
	SHE	12″		
PERFECT (France)[106]	11500		10″	
PERFECTAPHONE (France)	1000		10″	
	3000		10″	
PERIOD (USA)	PRST (S)	12″		
	SHO	12″		
	SHOST (S)	12″		
	SPL	12″		
	SPLP	12″		
	TE (set)	12″		

104 Cylinders

105 Transfers from original Pathé hill-and-dale discs

106 Vertical-cut

Label	Series	33 1/3 rpm (LP)	78 rpm	45 rpm standard & extended play
PHILHARMONIC (USA)	0100	12″		
PHILHARMONIC FAMILY LIBRARY OF GREAT MUSIC (USA)	(album)	12″		
PHILIPS (Netherlands)				
France	802000DXY & LY	12″		
	820000DTY	12″		
	835000AY	12″		
	836000DSY	12″		
	837900LY	12″		
	839000EGY & GSY	12″		
	A00000/00500L	12″		
	A00000/00700R	10″		
	G03000L	12″		
	L00000	12″		
Germany	40000AE & AY			7″ (extended)
	836000GY	12″		
	837000GY	12″		
	838000AY & HGY	12″		
Gt. Britain	ABE			7″ (extended)
	ABL	12″		
	ABR	10″		
	AL	12″		
	AXA	12″		
	CPC	12″		
	FL	12″		
	GBL	12″		
	GL	12″		
	NBE			7″ (extended)
	NBL	10″		
	NBR	10″		
	SAB	12″		
	SABE			7″ (extended)
	SABL (S)	12″		
	SAL (S)	12″		
	SBF			7″ (extended)
	SBL	12″		
	SBR	12″		
	SFL (S)	12″		
	SGL (S)	12″		
Netherlands	6500 000[107]	12″		
	6504 000[107]	12″		
	6515 000[107]	12″		
	6525 000[107]	12″		
	6526 000[107]	12″		
	6580 000[107]	12″		
	6585 000[107]	12″		
	6641 000 (set)[107]	12″		
	6700 000 (set)[107]	12″		
	6707 000 (set)[107]	12″		
	88000DY			7″ (extended)
	313000SF			7″ (extended)
	409000AE			7″ (extended)
	412000AE			7″ (extended)
	610000BL, VR & VL	12″		

107 International series

Label	Series	33 1/3 rpm (LP)	78 rpm	45 rpm standard & extended play
PHILIPS – *Continued*				
Netherlands – *Continued*	641000AXL & LL	12″		
	741000LL	12″		
	836000DSY & VZ	12″		
	838000DXY & VY	12″		
	870000BFY	12″		
	A00000/00500L [107]	12″		
	A00000/00700R [107]	10″		
	C71 AX 300 (set)	12″		
	G 03000 L [107]	12″		
	N 00000 L [107]	12″		
	NH 17800			7″ (standard)
	P 10000 R			7″ (extended)
	PE 422000			7″ (extended)
	PF 317800			7″ (extended)
	PH 17000			7″ (extended)
	PR 10000			7″ (standard)
	S 06000 R	12″		
	SC71 AX 300 (S) (set)	12″		
	XPY855800	12″		
Norway	839000NY	12″		
U.S.A.	PHC (C)	12″		
	PHM2/3-500 (set)	12″		
	PHM500000	12″		
	PHS2/3-900 (set)	12″		
	PHS900000	12″		
PHOENIX (Gt. Britain)	0/0000		10″	
PHONO-CUT (USA) [108]	5000		10″	
PICCADILLY (Gt. Britain)	300/700		10″	
	5000		10″	
PICKWICK (usa)	PC4000 (S)	12″		
PITTSBURGH FESTIVAL OF CONTEMPORARY MUSIC (USA)	CB	12″		
PLAISIR MUSICAL (France)	25000	10″		
	30000	12″		
PLÉIADE (France)	P		10″	
	P100/200	10″		
	P3000	12″		
PLYMOUTH (USA)	P10-	10″		
	P12-	12″		
POLSKIE NAGRANIA (Poland)	200	12″		
POLYDOR (Germany) [109]				
Denmark	13000/14000		10″	
	30000 [110]		10″	
	C [111]		12″	
France	516000		12″	
	522000		10″	
	524000		10″	
	540000		12″	
	566000		12″	
	595000		12″	
	A6000 [112]		12″	

108 Vertical-cut
109 Includes Deutsche Grammophon & Gramophone Company pressings
110 German issue
111 Decca repressing
112 The first two digits are replaced by letter "A" for automatic couplings

Label	Series	33 1/3 rpm (LP)	78 rpm	45 rpm standard & extended play
POLYDOR – *Continued*				
Germany[113]	900		10″	
	2000[114]		12″	
	4000[114]		12″	
	10000		10″	
	12000		10″	
	15000		12″	
	19000		12″	
	20000/25000		10″	
	27000		12″	
	30000		10″	
	36000		10″	
	47000/49000		10″	
	57000/59000		12″	
	61000/62000		10″	
	65000		12″	
	66000/69000		12″	
	70000		10″	
	72000		12″	
	90000		10″	
	95000		12″	
	237000	12″		
	2382 000	12″		
	EPH21000			7″ (extended)
	PV[114]		12″	
Japan	1000		10″	
	5000		12″	
	40000		12″	
	D		10″	
Switzerland	13000/14000		10″	
POLYMUSIC (USA)	PR	12″		
POLYPHON (Denmark)[115]	30000		10″	
	HA70000		10″	
	HM80000		12″	
	X51000		10″	
	XS47500		10″	
	Z60000		12″	
POPULAR (Gt. Britain)	P		10″	
PREISER (Austria)	SPR	12″		
PREMIER (USA)	8800		10″	
PRÉTORIA (France)	CL	12″		
PRIDE (USA)[116]		12″		
PRO MUSICA (France)	PMR		12″	
	PMT	12″		
PURITAN (USA)	9000		10″	
PYE (Gt. Britain)	CEC			7″ (extended)
	GGC[117]	12″		
	GSGC (S)[117]	12″		
QUALITON (Hungary)	BLP	10″		

113 Pre-war domestic pressings bore the "Grammophon" label while export pressings were "Polydor." Some wartime pressings bore "Siemens-Spezial" while post-war pressings were issued on "Deutsche Grammophon."
114 Archive series
115 Brunswick repressings
116 Private issue
117 Golden Guinea series

Label	Series	33 1/3 rpm (LP)	78 rpm	45 rpm standard & extended play
QUALITON (Hungary) – *Continued*	EP			7″ (extended)
	HLP	12″		
	HLPX	12″		
	LP	10″		
	LPX	12″		
	MK		12″	
	QKM		12″	
	QNM		12″	
	SLPX (S)	12″		
	SZK		12″	
	SZN		10″	
(LE) QUATRE SAISONS (France)	AR	12″		
	LQS	12″		
QUE (USA)	LP	12″		
RADIOLA (Hungary)	RBM		10″	
	RZ		10″	
	SP		12″	
RÁDIO MINISTÉRIO DA EDUCAÇAO E CULTURA (Brazil)	CFX		12″	
	DVX		12″	
RADIO NEDERLAND (Netherlands)[118]	109000	10″ & 12″		
	DR	10″		
	RN	10″ & 12″		
RADIOPROM (Bulgaria)	1300		12″	
RADIOTJÄNST (Sweden)	RC		10″	
	RD		12″	
	RE		12″	
REALM (Gt. Britain)	RM	12″		
RECITAL HALL (USA)	RH (set)	12″		
RECORD HUNTER (USA)	TRH	12″		
RECORD SOCIETY (Gt. Britain)	RS	12″		
	RSS (S)	12″		
REDWOOD (USA)	RRES	12″		
REGAL (Spain)[119]	QRX	12″		
	SREG	12″		
REGAL (Gt. Britain)	G1000		12″	
	G6000/8000		10″	
REGAL (USA)	9000		10″	
REGAL-ZONOPHONE (Gt. Britain)	EE		10″	
	G		10″	
	T		10″	
REGENT (USA)	LP	12″		
	MG	12″		
REMINGTON (USA)	PL	10″		
	R	12″		
	RLP149-	10″		
	RLP199-	12″		
	YV	12″		
RENA (USA)[120]	1000		10″	
RENAISSANCE (USA)	X	12″		

118 Broadcast performances drawn from the reserves of radio stations AVRO, KRO, NCRN
   & VARA at Hilversum
119 Product of EMI
120 Product of U.S. Columbia

Label	Series	33 1/3 rpm (LP)	78 rpm	45 rpm standard & extended play
REVOLUTION (Gt. Britain)	RCB	12″		
REX (Gt. Britain)	9000		10″	
RICHMOND (USA)[121]	B	12″		
	S (S)	12″		
ROCOCO (Canada)	2000	12″		
ROMANY (USA)	LP	12″		
	RR	10″		
RONDOLETTE (USA)	SA	12″		
ROYALE (USA)	500/600		12″	
	1000	12″		
	1200/1500	12″		
	1800		10″	
	6900	12″		
RS (USA)[122]	RS	12″		
RYMUSE (Sweden)	SALR	12″		
RYTMI (Finland)	2000		10″	
	R		10″	
SABA (Germany)	MPS	12″		
	SB	12″		
SAGA (Gt. Britain)	EFID			7″ (extended)
	ERO	12″		
	EROS (S)	12″		
	STXID (S)	12″		
	XID	12″		
SASTRUPHON (Germany)[123]	SM (S)	12″		
SATURN (France)	LDG	12″		
	LP	12″		
	M		10″	
SCALA (Gt. Britain)	000/1500		10″	
	4000		12″	
	DL		10″	
SCHIRMER (USA)	2500		12″	
SELECT (Canada)	CC (C)	12″		
	SSC (S)	12″		
SERAPHIM (USA)	60000 (& S60000) (S)	12″		
	IC (set)	12″		
	SIC (S) (set)	12″		
SEVEN SEAS (Japan)	SH	12″		
SHEFFIELD (USA)	M	12″		
	S (S)	12″		
SILVERTONE (USA)	2000		10″	
SKANDIA (Sweden)	SG		10″	
	SV		10″	
SOCIÉTÉ FRANÇAISE DE PRODUCTIONS PHONOGRAPHIQUES (France)	CVS	12″		
SOCIÉTÉ FRANÇAISE DU SON (France)	174000	12″		
	SXL (S)	12″		
SOCIETY FOR FORGOTTEN MUSIC (USA)	7000 (S)	12″		
	S (S)	12″		
	SFM	12″		

121 Product of London
122 Private issue by Robert Staub
123 Product of Da Camera

Label	Series	33 1/3 rpm (LP)	78 rpm	45 rpm standard & extended play
SOCIETY FOR THE PRESERVATION OF THE AMERICAN MUSICAL HERITAGE (USA)	MIA	12″		
SOCIETY OF PARTICIPATING ARTISTS – SPA (USA)	SPA	12″		
SOMERSET (Germany)	500	12″		
	SM	12″		
SONATA (Sweden)	(1 to 3 digits)		10″	
SONIDO (Brazil)	(1 & 2 digits)	12″		
SONORA (Sweden)	1/100		10″	
	1000		10″	
	6000		10″	
	9000		10″	
	K		12″	
SONORA (USA)	1000		10″	
	4000		10″	
	MS (set)		10″	
SOUND RECORDING COMPANY (USA)	(no prefix)	12″		
STARR (Gennett) (USA)[124]	500		10″	
	9000		10″	
STEREO-FIDELITY (USA)[125]	14500	12″		
STINSON (USA)	5000		10″	
STORIA DELLA MUSICA (Italy)	MdM			7″ (extended)
	SdM (S)			7″ (extended)
STRADIVARI (USA)	SLP		10″	
	STR		12″	
STUDIO (Netherlands)	33 20000	12″		
STUDIO TWO (Gt. Britain)	STWO (S)	12″		
SUMMIT (Gt. Britain)	LSU	12″		
SUPERMAJESTIC (Italy)	BBH	12″		
	SBBH (S)	12″		
SUPERTONE (USA)	S		10″	
SUPRAPHON (Czechoslovakia)[126]	3000		12″	
	3800		10″	
	0 10 0000	12″		
	1 10 0000 (S)	12″		
	1 11 0000 (S)	12″		
	1 41 0000 (S)	12″		
	20Z (2 digits)	12″		
	A		10″	
	B		10″	
	C		10″	
	D		10″	
	DV[127]	12″		
	E		12″	
	F		12″	
	FUK			7″ (extended)
	G		12″	
	H		12″	
	LPM	10″		
	LPV	12″		

124 Product of Gennett
125 Product of U.S. Somerset
126 Post-war export label for Czech Ultraphon
127 Test pressing

Label	Series	33 1/3 rpm (LP)	78 rpm	45 rpm standard & extended play
SUPRAPHON – *Continued*	MBA[128]		12″	
	SUA	12″		
	SUAST (S)	12″		
	SUB	12″		
	SUEC			7″ (extended)
	SUF	10″		
	SUG	10″		
	SUH	12″		
	SUK			7″ (extended)
	SUL			7″ (extended)
	SUN	12″		
	SV[129]	12″		
	TA[130]		10″	
	TE[130]		12″	
	TF[130]		12″	
SVERIGES RADIO (Sweden)	RELP	12″		
SYMPHONIC (USA)	SR	12″		
SYRENA (Poland)	6000		12″	
	8000		10″	
	(no prefix)	12″		
TAP (USA)	T	12″		
TECHNICHORD (USA)	T (set)		10″	
	TC		10″	
TELEFUNKEN (Germany)				
Czechoslovakia	TE		12″	
France	205TC	10″		
	270TC	10″		
	FT	10″		
Germany	A		10″	
	A10000		10″	
	AWD	12″		
	AWT	12″		
	B		10″	
	BLE	10″		
	BLP	10″		
	C047-	12″		
	DK	12″		
	E		12″	
	F		12″	
	GMA	12″		
	HT	12″		
	LA	10″		
	LB	10″		
	LT	12″		
	M		10″	
	NLB	10″		
	NT	12″		
	SAT	12″		
	SAWD (S)	12″		
	SAWT (S)	12″		
	SK		12″	
	SLT	12″		
	SMD	12″		

128 Anthology series. Later adapted to LP's
129 Domestic series
130 Telefunken repressings

Label	Series	33 1/3 rpm (LP)	78 rpm	45 rpm standard & extended play
TELEFUNKEN – *Continued*	SMT	12″		
Germany – *Continued*	STEL (S)			7″ (standard)
	STW (S)	12″		
	SUV (S)			7″ (extended)
	TEL			7″ (standard)
	TPB		10″	
	TW	10″		
	U			7″ (standard)
	UV			7″ (extended)
Gt. Britain	LGM	10″		
	LGX	12″		
	TM	10″		
Sweden	A		10″	
Switzerland	A		10″	
	A10000		10″	
	B		10″	
	E		12″	
	F		12″	
	M		10″	
	SK		12″	
	TPB		10″	
U.S.A.	TC	12″		
	TCS (S)	12″		
TEMPO (Spain)	TIL	12″		
TEMPO (USA)	4600	12″		
	MTT	12″		
TIME (USA)	8000 (S)	12″		
	58000	12″		
TONO (Denmark)	A		10″	
	K		10″	
	L		10″	
	LPA	12″		
	LPX	12″		
	LPY		12″	
	X		12″	
	Y		12″	
TOP CLASSIC (Germany)[131]	TC	12″		
TOPIC (Gt. Britain)	TRC		10″	
TOP RANK (Gt. Britain)	35-000	12″		
	40-000	12″		
	TR	12″		
	XRK	12″		
TOSHIBA (Japan)	JSC	12″		
TOWER (Gt. Britain)	1000		10″	
TREASURY OF MUSIC (Gt. Britain)	T		12″	
TRIANGLE (USA)	15000		10″	
TRIANON (France)	2C045-	12″		
	CTRE	12″		
	TRX	12″		
TRI-ERGON (Germany)	1000		12″	
	5000		10″	
	10000		10″	
TRIOLA (Finland)	RNLP	12″		

131 Product of Metronome

Label	Series	33 1/3 rpm (LP)	78 rpm	45 rpm standard & extended play
TRIOLA (Finland) – *Continued*	T		10″	
	TS		10″	
TROPHY (USA)		12″		
TUDOR (Germany)	TUD	12″		
TURNABOUT (USA)	TV4000	12″		
	TV34000 (S)	12″		
TWENTIETH (20th) CENTURY FOX (USA)	TFM	12″		
ULTRAPHON (Czechoslovakia)				
Czechoslovakia	5100C	10″		
	A		10″	
	B		10″	
	C		10″	
	D		10″	
	DM	12″		
	E		12″	
	F		12″	
	G		12″	
	H		12″	
	MBA	12″		
France	AP		10″	
	BP		10″	
	FP		12″	
ULTRAPHONIC (USA)	50300	12″		
UNICORN (Gt. Britain)	RHS	12″		
	UNI	12″		
	UNS (S)	12″		
UNICORN (USA)	UNLP	12″		
UNION (Germany)	A		12″	
UNITED STATES EVERLASTING INDE-STRUCTIBLE CYLINDER (USA)[132]				
UNIVERSITY OF OKLAHOMA (USA)	(1 digit)	12″		
URANIA (USA)	RS7-	12″		
	URLP5000	10″		
	URLP7000	12″		
VALOIS (France)	MB400	12″		
	MB800/900 (S)	12″		
VANGUARD (USA)				
Gt. Britain	PVL	12″		
U.S.A.	SD	12″		
	SD (& suffix S) (S)	12″		
	SRV	12″		
	SRV (& suffix SD) (S)	12″		
	VRS	12″		
	VSD (S)	12″		
VARSITY (USA)	2000	12″		
V-DISC (USA)	(1 to 3 digits)		12″	
VEDETTE (Italy)	VSC	12″		
VEGA (France)	19000	12″		
	C30	12″		
	C37	12″		
	C37a			7″ (extended)
	MT	12″		

132 Cylinder

Label	Series	33 1/3 rpm (LP)	78 rpm	45 rpm standard & extended play
VEGA (France) – *Continued*	ST (S)	12″		
VERITAS (USA)	VM	12″		
VERITON (Hungary)	XV	12″		
VICTOR (USA)				
Argentina	P (2 digits)		10″	
Brazil	13000		10″	
Canada	216000		10″	
	CC	12″		
	CCS (S)	12″		
France	A95000			7″ (extended)
	A430000	12″		
	A630000	12″		
	A640000 (S)	12″		
	RCX	12″		
	VIC (2 digits)	12″		
Germany	LM[133]	12″		
	LSC[133]	12″		
	MD	12″		
	SMR	12″		
Gt. Britain	RB	12″		
	SB (S)	12″		
	SBS (S)	12″		
	VIC[133]	12″		
	VICS (S)[133]	12″		
Italy	A12R	12″		
	INTS	12″		
	KV	12″		
	KVIS	12″		
	LM20000	12″		
	ML20000	12″		
	ML40000 (set)	12″		
	ML61000 (Set)	12″		
	MLD (set)	12″		
	MLDS (S) (set)	12″		
	SL	12″		
	V		10″	
Japan	EP			7″ (extended)
	JAS (set)		12″	
	JD	12″		
	JE		12″	
	LS	12″		
	ND		12″	
	NH		12″	
	SD		12″	
	SHP	12″		
	SJX	10″		
	VX	12″		
Netherlands	26000	12″		
Sweden	LM10000	12″		
	LSC10000 (S)	12″		
U.S.A.	0/1000		10″	
	2000		10″	
	3000/5000		10″	
	6000/8000		12″	

133 Identical to U.S. series

Label	Series	33 1/3 rpm (LP)	78 rpm	45 rpm standard & extended play
VICTOR – *Continued*				
U.S.A. – *Continued*	11000/12000		12″	
	14000/16000		12″	
	16000[134]		10″	
	17000/19000		12″	
	20000/22000		10″	
	24000		10″	
	26000/27000		10″	
	31000		10″	
	35000		12″	
	61000[135]		10″	
	62000/63000[136]		10″	
	64000[135]		10″	
	66000[135]		10″	
	68000		12″	
	71000[135]		12″	
	74000[135]		12″	
	80000/81000[135]		10″	
	87000[135]		10″	
	88000/89000[135]		12″	
	91000[135]		10″	
	120000		10″	
	150000		10″	
	10-0000		10″	
	11-0000/12-0000		12″	
	17-0000			7″ (standard)
	18-0000[137]		12″	
	20-0000		10″	
	46-0000			7″ (standard)
	49-0000			7″ (standard)
	56-0000		10″	
	CP (set)		10″	
	DM (set)[138]		12″	
	DPS (set)		12″	
	ECS			7″ (extended)
	ERA			7″ (extended)
	ERB (2 rec set)			7″ (extended)
	L[139]	12″		
	LBC[140]	12″		
	LCT (under 1000)	10″		
	LCT (over 1000)	12″		
	LD	12″		
	LDS (S)	12″		
	LHMV[141]	12″		
	LM (under 1000)	10″		
	LM (over 1000)	12″		
	LRM	10″		
	LSC (S)	12″		
	LVT	12″		
	M (set)[142]		12″	
	MO (set)		10″	

134 Early accoustic discs. Later, the series was duplicated but as 12″ red seal discs
135 Single-sided
136 South American series
137 Red vinyl
138 Automatic couplings
139 Transcription disc
140 Bluebird series
141 HMV series
142 Manual couplings

Label	Series	33 1/3 rpm (LP)	78' rpm	45 rpm standard & extended play
VICTOR – *Continued*				
U.S.A. – *Continued*	P (3 digits)		10″	
	P (set)		10″	
	SMR	12″		
	SOR[143]	12″		
	SPS[144]	12″		
	T[145]	12″		
	V (set)		12″	
	VCM (set)	12″		
	VIC[146]	12″		
	VICS (S)[146]	12″		
	WBC (set)[140]			7″ (standard)
	WCT (set)			7″ (standard)
	WDM (set)			7″ (standard)
	WEPR (set)			7″ (extended)
VIENÖLA (Austria)	LPR	10″		
VIRTUOSO (Gt. Britain)	TPLS (S)	12″		
VIRTUOSO (USA)	VIR	12″		
VOCALION (Gt. Britain)				
Gt. Britain	A0100		12″	
	A24000		10″	
	B70000		12″	
	D02000		12″	
	K05000		12″	
	R6000		10″	
	X9000		10″	
U.S.A.	14000/15000		10″	
	30000[147]		12″	
	38000		12″	
	46000		12″	
	60000		10″	
	70000		12″	
VOIX DES NÔTRES (France)	MLP	10″		
VOLKSPLATTE (Germany)	LDKS	12″		
VOX (Germany)	6000		10″	
	06000		12″	
VOX (USA)				
Gt. Britain	GBY	12″		
	STGBY (S)	12″		
U.S.A.	600		10″ & 12″	
	12000		12″	
	16000		10″	
	DL (set)	12″		
	DL400	12″		
	EZ	12″		
	PL	12″		
	STDL (S)	12″		
	STPL (S)	12″		
	SVBX (S) (3 rec set)	12″		
	VBX (3 rec set)	12″		
	VIP			7″ (extended)

143 Soria series
144 Sampler
145 Private pressing
146 Victrola series
147 Single-sided

Label	Series	33 1/3 rpm (LP)	78 rpm	45 rpm standard & extended play
VOX – *Continued*				
U.S.A. – *Continued*	VP	12″		
	VSPS (set)	12″		
	VUX (2 rec set)	12″		
	VXL [148]	12″		
	XPV	12″		
W & G (Australia)	WB-BS	12″		
WASHINGTON (USA)	WR	12″		
	WS (S)	12″		
WEBSTER (USA)	(Vol.)	12″		
WEINBERGER (Italy)	W		12″	
WERGO (Germany)	300			7″ (extended)
	WER	12″		
WESTMINSTER (USA)				
Germany	21000	12″		
	P	12″		
	PWN	12″		
	PWS (S)	12″		
U.S.A.	OPW (set)	12″		
	W	12″		
	WAL (set)	12″		
	WL	12″		
	W-LAB	12″		
	WM (set)	12″		
	WMS (S) (set)	12″		
	WST (S)	12″		
	XWN	12″		
WHITEHALL (USA)	5000	12″		
	WH	12″		
	WHS (S)	12″		
WORLD RECORD CLUB (Gt. Britain)	CM	12″		
	SC	10″		
	SCM (S)	12″		
	SP	12″		
	ST (S)	12″		
	T	12″		
	TP			7″ (extended)
	TT	12″		
ZONOPHONE - International [149]				
France	X80500		10″	
	X87900/88000		10″	
Germany	X47900/49000		10″	
	X507900		10″	
Gt. Britain	100/700		10″	
	1000/2000		10″	
	5000		10″	
	A		12″	
	GO		10″	
Italy	X1000		10″	
Spain	X67900		10″	
U.S.S.R.	X27900		10″	

148 A 16 2/3 rpm disc
149 Five & six digit numbers are Gramophone Company pressings

INDEX OF ARTISTS

Brandt, Karl
Bratza, Yovanovitch (1904–   )
de Brayne, H.
Breeskin, Elias (1895–1969)
Bress, Hyman (1931–   )
Bridge, John S.
Brink, Robert (1924–   )
Brix-Meinert, Ilse
Bronne, Ariana
Brosa, Antonio (1896–   )
Brosa, C.
Brouwer, Henk
Brown, Eddy (1895–   )
Bruckbauer, Franz
Brückner, Karl (1893–   )
Brugman, Anne
Brun, Alfred Alphonse (1888–1963)
Brun, Virgilio
Brunet, Noël (1916–   )
Brushtein, L.
Brusilow, Anshel (1929–   )
Bruun, Elsa Maria (1911–   )
Büchner, Otto (1924–   )
Buchtele, Jan (1874–1941)
Bucia, Nicolae
Budovsky, N.
Bulavinov, E.
Buldrini, Fred
Bünte, Hans
Burgin, Richard (1892–   )
Burmester, Willy (1869–1933)
Busch, Adolf (1891–1952)
Busch, Willy
Bustabo, Guila (1919–   )
Buswell, James Oliver (1947–   )
Campajola, Enrico (1899–   )
Campoli, Alfredo (1906–   )
Candéla, Miguel (1914–   )
Cantell, Frank (1901–1963)
Cantrelle, William (1888–   )
Caponi, Eugenio
Capoulade, F.
Carazza, André
Carles, Ginette
Carlier, Carl*
Carol, Norman (1930–   )
Carpi, Giannino
Carracilly, Yvon
Carrodus, Bernard Molique (1867–1936)
Carter, T.
Casadesus, Marius Robert Max (1892–   )
Castillo, José Francisco d'el
Catterall, Arthur (1883–1943)
Cavalcabo, Cesare
Čeleda, Jaroslav (1890–   )
Ceradini, Margherita
Cerha, Friedrich (1926–   )
Cervera, Montserrat
Cesano, Louis
Chailley, Eleves de Marcel (1891–1936)
Chamberland, Albert (1886–   )
Champeil, Jean (1910–   )
Charmy, Roland (1908–   )

*Pseudonym for Karl Bornfors.

Chassman, Joachim
Chausow,
Chauveton, Michel (1929–   )
Chemet, Renée (1888–   )
Chenski, Ivan
Cherniavsky, Gregor
Cherniavsky, Leo (1890–   )
Chernyakhovsky, Mikhail
Christiansen, Niels Simon
Chung, Kyung-Wha (1948–   )
Cillario, Carlo Felice (1915–   )
Ciompi, Georgio
Cisyk, Volodymyr
Clebanoff, Herman (1917–   )
Clockers, Hector
Cochrane, Peggy (1907–   )
Cohen, Isidore
Cohen, Raymond Hyam (1919–   )
Colandrea, Italo
Colbentson, Oliver (1927–   )
Collier, Derek (1929–   )
Colombo, Emilio (1874–1937)
Combarieu, Mlle.
Combes, Louis Gay de
Compinsky, Manuel (1901–   )
Condamine, Henry
Connah, Trevor
Constantinescu, Mihai
Cores, Alexander
Corigliano, John (1901–   )
Corvino
Cotogni, Anna Maria
Crafoord, Gert
Cravio
Cregut, Émile
Crenne, Christian
Cron, Michael
Cronvall, Erik Johan (1904–   )
Crut, Maurice
Csaba, Jerry (1940–   )
Csammer, Alfred
Culbertson, Sascha (1894–1944)
Curti, Yvonne
Cyroulnik, Charles
Czerwonky, Richard (1886–1949)
Dahmen, Jan (1898–1957)
Dajos, Béla (1897–   )
Dalmanis, Indulis (1922–   )
Damian, Benone
Danchenko, Viktor
Danczowska, Kaja (1949–   )
Daneman, Julian
Danz, Rith
Darrieux, Marcel (1891–   )
Datyner, Henry (1917–   )
David, Lukas (1934–   )
Davis, Rosalynd
Davison, Arthur
Dawes, Andrew (1940–   )
Déat, Huguette
Debruille, Alexander
De Groot, David (1881–1933)
De Groot, Frida
De Groot, Max
Dejean, Jacques

Delmor, Mary
Deman, Rudolf
Dembeck, John
De Reus, Dick (1923–   )
Deru, Edouard (1875–1928)
Desarzens, George
Desarzens, Victor (1908–   )
Dessau, Bernhard (1861–1923)
Deutsch, Emery (1907–   )
De Vito, Gioconda (1907–   )
Devriès, Gabrielle
Diaz, Celso
Diaz-Pelaz, Patrick (See Pelaz)
Dichterow, Glenn (1948–   )
Diedrichsen, Annegret
Diener, Hanns Hermann (1897–1955)
Diercks, Helga
Dinicu, Grigoras (1889–1949)
Diös, Nelly
Dobrinski, Mischa
Dolin, Max
Dommett, Leonard (1929–   )
Dony, Paul
Dore, Michael
Dorson, Charles (1882–   )
Doukan, Pierre
Drdla, Franz (1868–1944)
Drescher, Helmut
Driffield, Henry
Drucker, Ernest
Druian, Rafael (1922–   )
Dubiska, Irena (1899–   )
Dubois, Alfred (1898–1949)
Dubois, Eugene
Dukson, R.
Dumont, Jacques (1913–   )
Dunn, John (1866–1940)
Durosoir, L.
Dushkin, Samuel (1891–   )
Dyke, Spencer (1880–1946)
Egger, Georg
Eidus, Arnold (1922–   )
Eisenberg, Harold
Eitler, Marta (1922–   )
Elbaek, Peter
Elman, Mischa (1891–1967)
Emanuele, Vittorio
Endres, Heinz
Enescu, Georges (1881–1955)
Engelbretson, Hallvor
Engels, Wolfgang
Englund, Folke (1907–   )
Erdenko, Mikhail
Erduran, Ayla (1936–   )
Erendi, L.
Ericson, Ivan (1911–   )
Erle, Broadus
Erlih, Devy (1928–   )
Eto, Toshita (1927–   )
Eweler, Grete
Fabrizio, Carmine
Fabroni, Pietro
Fachiri, Adila (D'Aranyi) (1886–1962)
Fagerlund, Lis
Fain, Roza (1929–   )

Fairless, Margaret (1897–   )
Fairhurst, Harold (1903–   )
Falk, Jules (1875–1928)
Fantini, Franco
Fantuzzi, Reno
Farbmann, Harry
Fassbander, Hedwig (1897–1939)
Fastofsky, Stuart (1927–1964)
Feigin, Grigory (1937–   )
Feik, Herman
Felicani, Rodolfo (1902–   )
Feliciant, Boris
Fellowes, Edmund Horace (1870–1951)
Fenyves, Lorand (1918–   )
Fernandez, Huguette
Ferraresi, Aldo (1906–   )
Ferraresi, Cesare (1918–   )
Ferrari, Astorre
Ferrari, Franco Claudio
Ferraris, Mario
Ferras, Christian (1933–   )
Ferrit, Pierre
Ferro, Luigi (1903–   )
Fichtenholz, Mikhail (1920–   )
Fidelmann, Samuel
Field, Joan
Fietz, Anton (1926–   )
Figueroa, Hermanos
Figueroa, José C. (1905–   )
Filon, Simonne
Fiorito, Ursula
Fisberg, A.
Fischberg, Jascha
Fleming, Ethel
Flesch, Carl (1873–1944)
Flissler, Joyce (1929–   )
Flori
Fogelberg, Gösta (1892–   )
Földes, Bela
Fontanarosa, Patrice (1943–   )
Fontova, Léon (1875–   )
Forchhammer, Sverre
Förster, P.
Fournier, Jean (1913–   )
Fradkin, Fredrick (1892–1963)
Frait, Vojtěch (1894–   )
Francescatti, Zino (1905–   )
Franke, Karlheinz
Frankl, Paul Josef (1892–   )
Franzetti, Giulio
Frasca-Colombier, Monique
Fredericks, Wallace
Freeman, Grace
Frenkel, Stefan (1902–   )
Freund, Karl (1904–   )
Frey, William
Fridheim, Henrick
Friedman, Erick (1940–   )
Friedmann, Lilli
Friisholm, Lavard (1912–   )
Frisina, David
Fritz-Crone, Harry
Frolov, Igor
Früh, Elfriede
Frühauf, Herbert

Frydén, Lars
Fuchs, Joseph Philip (1900–   )
Fuente, James de la (1914–1963)
Fueri, Maurice
Fujikawa, Mayumi (1946–   )
Fukano, Hideko
Furer, M.
Furer, Shmuel Isaakovich (1909–   )
Furney
Futer, Arkady
Gabowitz, Louis (1909–   )
Gabriel, André
Gade, Jacob H.
Gaillard, Jules
Gaiser, Michael
Gali, Lionel
Galimir, Felix
Galli, Mario (1901–1937)
Gallozzi, Walter
Gandini, Ettore
Gandino, Leonelli
Ganiev, S.
Garaguly, Carl (1900–   )
Garami, Arthur (1921–
Garay, György (1909–   )
Gardi, Mario
Gardner, Samuel (1892–   )
Garnier, Liliane
Gašparek, Tibor (1913–   )
Gaunet, G.
Gautier, Jeanne (1898–   )
Gauvovetskaya
Gavrilow, Saschko (1929–   )
Gay, Sylvia de
Geczy, Barnabas von (1897–   )
Geissmar, Martha
Gendelman, A.
Gendre, Robert
Genesini, Alessandro
George
Gerard, Nina
Gerle, Robert (1924–   )
Gershman, Paul
Gertler, André (1907–   )
Geyer, Stefi (1893–1958)
Geyr, F.
Geyrhalter, Manfred
Gheorghiu, Stepan
Ghestem, Jacques
Giaccone, Ercole
Gibbs, Peter (1921–   )
Gieseler, Hans
Gilels, Elizaveta (1919–   )
Gimpel, Bronisław (1911–   )
Gingold, Josef (1909–   )
Giordano, Oreste
Girdach, Hans
Gitlis, Ivry (1922–   )
Gittelson, Frank (1896–   )
Giusto, Pio
Glase-Schirin, O. M.
Glatte, Peter
Glenn, Carol (1922–   )
Goberman, Max (1911–1962)
Godowsky, Louis (1900–   )

Godwin, Paul (1902–   )
Goggi, O.
Gold, Maude
Goldberg, Szymon (1909–   )
Goldin, Milton
Goldis, M. L.
Goldstein, Boris (1922–   )
Goluboff, Grisha
Gomez, José Soler (1875–   )
Goni, Christeta (1900–   )
Goodman, Mildred
Gootjes, Derk
Gordon, Jacques (1899–1948)
Gordon, Kenneth
Gordon, Mayer
Gorelik, Lev
Gorelik, Pavel
Goren, Eli (1923–   )
Gorensky, Paul
Gorokhov, Alexei
Gotkovsky, Nell (1939–   )
Gottesmann, Hugo
Governale, F.
Gozman, Lazar
Grabowska, J.
Grach, Eduard
Gradov, V.
Gradsky, Victor
Graeler, Louis
Gramatte, Sophie-Carmen (1902–   )
Gramegna, Armando
Gramm, Arthur
Gránát, Endre
Granchi, Marco
Grassi, Antonio de (1880–   )
Gravoin, Jean-René
Gregorowicz, Karol (1867–1920)
Grehling, Ulrich (1917–   )
Gresser, Emily (1894–   )
Grey, Frederick
Grindenko, Tatyana (1946–   )
Grinke, Frederick (1911–   )
Gross, Robert (1914–   )
Groth, Einar (1903–   )
Grötzer, Hans
Gruenberg, Erich (1924–   )
Grumiaux, Arthur (1921–   )
Grumlíková, Nora (1930–   )
Gründer, Anne-Maria
Grünfarb, Josef (1920–   )
Guarino, Gian Mario (1900–   )
Guglielmo, Giovanni
Guidi, Scipione (1884–1966)
Guilet, Daniel (1899–   )
Guilevitch, Daniel
Gulli, Franco (1926–   )
Gundersen, Robert
Günther, Max
Guntner, Kurt
Gusikoff, Michel (1895–   )
Gutnikov, Boris (1931–   )
Gyarfas, Ibolyka
Gyarmati, Vera (1936–   )
Gygi, Ota
Haag, Hanno

Haaland, Ingebret (1878–1934)
Hadjaje, Paul
Haendel, Ida (1928–)
Hagemann, Sophie
Hagen, Betty-Jean (1930–)
Hager, Frederick W.* (1841–1927)
Haikala, P.
Halik, Mieczyslaw (1902–)
Hall, Bernard
Hall, Marie (1884–1947)
Halvorsen, Leif Fritjof (1887–)
Hamann, Bernhard (1909–)
Homowetskaya
Hampe, Charlotte (1910–)
Hamza, Gheorghe
Hanke, Winifred
Hannikainen, Arvo (1897–1942)
Hanousek, Karel (1902–)
Hansen, Cecilia (1898–)
Hansen, Leo (1911–)
Hansen, Marius
Hansen, Werner
Harbison, Rosemary
Harnoncourt, Alice
Harrison, Margaret
Harrison, May (1891–1959)
Harth, Sydney (1925–)
Hassid, Joseph (1924–1946)
Havemann, Gustav (1882–1960)
Haxton, A. Stroud
Hayward, Marjorie (1885–1953)
Heber, Richard
Heermann, Hugo (1844–1935)
Hegedüs, Ferenc
Hegner, Anna (1881–1963)
Heifetz, Jascha (1899–)
Heinemann, Adolf
Hekking, Hans
Heller, Amely
Hellmann, Ferdinand
Hellmann, Ruth
Hendel, Georg Friedrich
Hendriks, Marc
Henley, William (1874–1957)
Henriques, Fini Valdemar (1867–1940)
Henriques, Johan Fini (1892–)
Herman, Charles
Hermann, Karl Albrecht
Hertz, Yaela
Herzl, Max
Hetzel, Gerhard
Heurtevant, Yvonne
Hidy, Marta
Hilsberg, Alexander (1900–1961)
Hinchliffe, Jessie
Hintermeyer, Walter (1892–)
Hitzker, Eva
Hlaváček, Libor (1926–)
Hlouňová, Maria (1912–)
Hochstein, David (1892–)
Høeberg, Georg
Hofer, Pierre

Hoffman, Michel
Hoffner, P.
Holmes, Ralph Francis (1937–)
Holst, Henry (1899–)
Holtman, Jacques
Hombergh, Antoinette van den
Hood, Florence
Hopfner, Franz
Hori, Masafumi
Horvath, Johan
Hosselet, Robert
Höver, Herbert
Howard, Anthony
Hrdjok, Dragutin
Hubay, Jenö (1858–1937)
Huberman, Bronislaw (1882–1947)
Hudeček, Václav (1953–)
Humphreys, Sydney (1926–)
Hundt, Hugo
Huppertz, Heinz
Hurstinen, Sulo (1881–)
Hurwitz, Emanuel (1919–)
Huttenbach
Iacovino, Mariuccia
Ignatieff, Mischa (1910–)
Ignatius-Hirvensalo, Anja (1911–)
Indig, Alfred
Ingen-Werts, C. van
Inzaurraga, A.
Ionescu, Gica
Irmer, Hermann
Isaacs, Lila
Isakadze, Liana (1946–)
Iwamoto, Marito (1926–)
Iwanow, Igor (1923–)
Jacob, Joseph
Jacobs, George (1880–)
Jacobsen, Sascha (1895–)
Jacquillat, Cécile
Jahn, Jörg-Wolfgang
Jakowicz, Krzysztof (1939–)
Jancowich, Augusto (1878–1937)
Janesi, Rigo (1863–1927)
Janowski, Piotr (1951–)
Jarry, Gérard
Jarvis, Gerald (1930–)
Jásek, Ladislav (1929–)
Jelving, Åke (1908–)
Jernou, François
Jilka, Alfred
Joachim, Joseph (1831–1907)
Johannessen, Jim
Johansen, Willy
Jones, Granville (1922–1968)
Jongen, Charles
Joseph
Josephi, Wolfgang
Jovanovič, Milan-Braca (1904–)
Juda, Jo (1909–)
Jussila, Wolde
Kagen, Oleg (1946–)
Kägi, Walter (1901–)
Kakuska, Thomas
Kalafusz, Hans
Kalinauskaite, E.

Kalinovsky, Simon
Kalki, Max
Kalman, Lilla
Kalmer, Henry
Kalt, Percy
Kalup, Rudolf
Kamilarov, Emil
Kamper, Anton
Kantrovitch, Julius
Käppeli, Lisbeth
Kaptsan, A.
Karolyi, Sándor
Karpe, Sven (1908–)
Karpinski, Günther
Kash, Eugene (1912–)
Kassow, Hans (1902–)
Kaufman, Louis (1905–)
Kaufmann, Adolf
Kaufmann, Erich
Kaul, Paul (1902–)
Kawaciuk, Ivan (1913–)
Kayser, Max
Keenlyside, Raymond (1928–)
Kehr, Günter (1920–)
Keller, Erich
Kellert, Raphael
Kelly-Lange, Edith
Keltsch, Werner
Kemlin, G.
Kempler, Hans
Kennedy, Daisy (1893–)
Kerekjarto, Duci di (1900–1962)
Kerry, Albert
Kersey, Eda (1904–1944)
Kim, Young Uck (1947–)
Kimber, Beryl
Kinch, Ole
Kirch, Willi
Kirmse, Fritz
Kitain, Robert
Kjeldsen, Eyvind Sand
Klasinc, Walter (1924–)
Klepper, Wilhelm
Klijn, Nap de (1909–)
Klima, Josip (1927–)
Klimov, Valery (1931–)
Kling, Paul
Klingler, Karl (1879–1971)
Klopčič, Rok (1933–)
Kneisel, Franz (1865–1926)
Kneller, Georgi
Kniestaedt, Georg
Kniestaedt, Gustav
Knitzer, Joseph (1913–1967)
Knorre, Anatol
Knowles, Clifford
Knudsen, Gunnar (1907–)
Kobayashi, Kenji
Kobialka, Daniel (1943–)
Kobin, Otto
Koch, Emmanuel
Koch, Henri (1903–1969)
Koch, Walter
Kochański, Paul (1887–1934)
Kocián, Jaroslav (1883–1950)

*Pseudonym for Wallace Fredericks.

Kocsis, Albert
Koeckert, Rudolf (1913–)
Koene, Francis (1900–1935)
Kogan, I.
Kogan, Leonid Borisovich (1924–)
Kohon, Harold
Kolářský, Zdeněk (1898–)
Kolassis, Byron (1922–)
Kolberg, Hugo .1898–)
Koldofsky, Adloph (1905–1951)
Kolouch, Václav
Komissarov, Mark (1928–)
Komlós, Peter (1935–)
Komosiński, Edmund
Kooper, Kees
Koppel, Julius (1910–)
Korn, M.
Korsakov, André
Kortner, Ottavia
Kortschak, Hugo (1884–1957)
Kóté, László (1941–)
Koutzen, Boris (1901–1966)
Koutzen, Nadia (1930–)
Kovács, Dénes (1930–)
Kozigyan, Varuzhan
Kozoulupova, Marina (1918–)
Krachmalnick, Jacob (1922–)
Krämer, Curt (1904–1963)
Krasner, Louis (1903–)
Krebbers, Herman (1923–)
Kreisler, Fritz (1875–1962)
Kremer, Guidon (1947–)
Krengel, Editha
Krettly, Robert (1891–)
Krips, Alfred
Kroll, William (1901–)
Krotzinger, Werner
Kroyt, Boris (1897–1969)
Krysa, Oleg (1942–)
Kubelík, Jan (1880–1940)
Kubo, Yoko
Kucharski, Janusz
Kuhn, Manfred
Kuijken, Sigiswald
Kulenkampff, Georg (1898–1948)
Kulka, Konstanty (1947–)
Kun, Arpad
Kupiev, B.
Kuronuma, Yuriko
Kushnir, I.
Kussmaul, Rainer (1946–)
Kutcher, Samuel (1899–)
Kutsovsky, Emmanuel
Kuttner, Michael
Kwalwasser, Helen (1927–)
Kyndel, Otto (1904–)
Labko, Alexander
Lack, Fredell
Lacrouts, Jean
Ladscheck, Max (1889–)
Lahrs, Rosemarie
Lamacque, Philippe
Lambert, Lucien (1859–)
Langbein, Brenton (1928–)
Lantsman, Vladimir (1942–)
Lapenson, George

Lardinois, Jean-Louis
Laredo, Jaime (1941–)
Lari, Fanfulla (1876–1931)
Larner, Reginald
Laroque, Nicole
Larsen, Bjarne (1922–)
Larsen, Jørgen Fisher
Larysz, Eduard
Lasowski, Johannes Michael (1894–)
Lasowoski, Joseph
Lass, Boris
Latchem, Malcolm
Laue, O.
Laurane, Marcel
Laurent, Jacques
Lauricella, Remo (1912–)
Laursen, Kai
Lautenbacher, Suzanne (1932–)
Lavers, Marjorie (1916–)
Law, Mary (1890–1919)
Leblanc, Arthur (1906–)
Lederer, Deszö (1858–)
Ledru, Jacques (1922–)
Lehmann, Ulrich (1928–)
Lemaire, Géry
Lemkes, Bouw
Lemkes, Jeanne
Lenaerts, Valère
Lener, Jenö (1894–1948)
Lengyel, Gabrielle (1920–)
Lensen, Jean
Lensky, Boris
Leon-Ara, Augustin (1936–)
Leonhardt, Marie
Leonidoff, Leon (1895–)
Leopold, Reginald
Lepinte, Nicole
Leroy, Marcelle
Leshev, Boyan
Lessmann, Bernard
Leth, Ivan
Leutjens, Christopher
Levan, Michel
Levey, James (1887–1955)
Levin, Anatoli
Levin, D.
Levy, Theodore
Lewis, Philip
Lewkowitz, Henri
Liberman, Viktor
Lichtenberg, Leopold (1861–1935)
Liddell, Nona
Lidka, Maria
Liebman, Alice
Liljefors, Mats
Li-Na, Yu
Lindblom, Alice
Link, Gustav (1894–)
Linz, Marta (1898–)
Lippus, Endel
Lipschultz, George
Lipsky, Alexander (1900–)
List, Karl (1902–)
Livontas, Alexandras
Livschakoff, Ilja
Locatelli, Albert

Lockhart, Elizabeth (1921–)
Loft, Abram
Lorand, Edith
Loránt, Ferry
Lorenzo, Margaret
Losowsky, Isaak
Loveday, Alan Raymond (1928–)
Lovis, Sonia (1924–1947)
Lozada, Carmenzita
Luboshutz, Léa (1885–1965)
Lubotsky, Mark
Lubow, Georg
Ludlow, Godfrey R. (1893–1956)
Luquin, Fernand
Lusk, Milan (1898–)
Lütschg, Andrej
Lutsky, Grigori
Lynch, Albert
Lynged, Peder (1886–)
Lysy, Alberto (1935–)
MacGuigan, Madeleine
MacMillen, Francis (1885–)
McMorrow, L.
MacMurray, Frederick
Maas, Emil
Maazel, Lorín (1930–)
Madatov, S.
Madle, Alexander Peter (1928–)
Madsen, Borge
Magaziner, Elliot
Magnani, Giuseppe
Magnes, Frances (1922–)
Maguire, Hugh (1927–)
Magyar, Tamás Aurel (1913–)
Mahlke, Hans
Mahn, Frederick L.
Maier, Franz-Josef (1925–)
Makanowitzky, Paul (1920–)
Malachowsky, Fritz*
Malanotte, Edmondo (1912–)
Malinin, Vladimir (1935–)
Mampaey, Ernesto
Manasevich, N. T.
Mancke, Grete
Mandel, Henri
Manén, Juan (1883–)
Mangeot, André Louis (1883–1970)
Manke, Gerhard (1910–)
Mann, Robert (1920–)
Mann, Sydney Malcolm (1939–)
Mánnok, Julius Maria von
Mantovani, Annunzio Paulo (1905–)
Manuello
Manzella, Fred
Manzone, Jacques-Francis
Marcel, Renée
Marcu, Jean
Margolies, Jacques
Markov, Albert (1933–)
Marković, Vladimir (1917–)
Marriner Neville (1924–)
Marschner, Wolfgang (1926–)

*Pseudonym chosen for issuance of broadcast
performances of Bronisław Huberman.

Marteau, Henri (1874–1934)
Martin, David (1911–)
Martin, Victor (1940–)
Martzy, Johanna (1924–)
Marx, Marguerite
Mason, Frances Gillian (1939–)
Massia, Joan
Masters, Robert Henderson (1917–)
Mastney, Karl
Materassi, Sandro (1904–)
Mathe, Blain (1907–1967)
Matheis, Philipp
Matsuda, Yoko
Matthews, Thomas (1907–1969)
Maurice, H.
May, Ariodante
Mayer-Schierning, Ernst
Mazzionetta
Mehta, Mehli (1908–)
Meier, Eugene (1880–)
Meine, Gustav
Meisel, Ferdinand
Melcher, Wilhelm
Melkus, Eduard
Mell, Albert
Melsa, Daniel (1892–1952)
Melser, Franz
Mendels, Emile
Menges, Isolde (1893–)
Menuhin, Yehudi (1916–)
Menyhért, Emöke
Merckel, Henri (1897–)
Messiereur, Petr (1937–)
Meyer, Claud de
Meyer, William
Michaelian, Ernest
Michaels, Geoffrey (1944–)
Michaïlow, Max
Michel, Ted
Michelucci, Roberto
Mikhlin, Alexei (1938–)
Miksovsky, Friedrich
Milanova, Stoika (1946–)
Milkis, Y.
Milstein, Nathan (1904–)
Minetti, Enrico (1900–)
Minghetti, Lisa (1912–)
Mischakoff, Mischa (1895–)
Mitnitzky, Issay (1887–)
Mittmann, Bronisław
Modern, Max
Moglia, Alain
Moguilevsky, A.
Mokatsyan, Villi
Molard, Jean-Noël
Molinari, Bernardino
Molinario, Ermanno
Moll, David
Moller
Møller, Peder
Monasevitch, Grischa
Monge, Ferdinand de
Monosoff, Sonya
Montbrun, Raymond Gallois (1918–)
Morasch, Placidus

Morbitzer, Egon (1927–)
Morena
Morgagni, Vincent
Morgan, Harold
Morini, Erica (1906–)
Morino, Guilietta
Moris, Eugen
Morrell, Marie Dawson
Morse, Earl Williams
Moskowitz, Isadore
Mosley, Raymond
Moss, Marshall
Mossel, Max (1871–1929)
Moszkowski, Alexander M. (1851–1934)
Móži, Aladar (1923–)
Mozzato, Guido
Mueren, Guido van der
Muhlberger, Klaus
Munn, Peter
Murawski, Zygmunt
Mus, Abel
Musin, Ovide (1854–1929)
Nachèz, Tivadár (1859–1930)
Nadien, David (1928–)
Nägele, Philipp
Neaman, Yfrah (1923–)
Neininger, Wolfgang
Nelson, Norman
Nemet, Mary Ann (1936–)
Nerini, Pierre (1915–)
Neste, Carlo van (1914–)
Neuhaus, Werner
Neuman, Laszlo
Neuri, Adolphe
Neveu, Ginette (1919–1949)
Newe, Heinrich (1886–)
Ney, Tibor (1906–)
Niaga, G. (1922–)
Nielsen, Ellen Birgithe (1924–)
Nielsen, Olaf (1898–1972)
Nielsen, Thorvald (1891–1965)
Niemczyk, Wacław (1907–)
Nijland, Piet
Nilsson, Johann (1893–)
Ninomiya, Miwako
Nissen, Ebba
Noack, Sylvain (1881–1953)
Noceti, Jean
Nölting, Peter
Nordin, Mona
Noske, Willem (1918–)
Novák, Jiří (1924–)
Novello, Franco (1929–)
Novosad, Rudolf
Octors, Georges (1923–)
Odnoposoff, Riccardo (1914–)
Oehler
Offner, Werner
Oguse, Francis
Ohnheiser, Gerhard
Oistrakh, David Fedorovich (1908–)
Oistrakh, Igor Davidovitch (1931–)
Olevsky, Julian (1927–)
Olof, Theo (1924–)
Olowski, J.

Olsen, Henrik Gotthardt
Olsson-Folliger, Gøran (1886–1969)
Onderet, Maurice (1899–)
Ondříček, František (1857–1922)
Opfermann, Victor
Ormandy, Eugene (1899–)
Ormond, Harold
Ortenberg, Edgar
Ortmans-Bach, Edmée (1896–1947)
Oskotsky, L.
Ostrovsky, Fredy (1922–)
Ovcharek, Vladimir
Ozim, Igor (1931–)
Pach, Joseph
Pagani, Emanuel
Paget, David
Pálinkó, Ferenc
Palulis, Henryk (1920–)
Parikian, Manoug (1920–)
Párkányi, István
Parkhoimenko, Olgar
Parlow, Kathleen (1890–1963)
Parnes, Sascha (1909–)
Parshin, G.
Pascal, André (1894–)
Pasquali, Teresa
Pasquier, Jean (1903–)
Pasquier, Régis (1915–)
Pauk, György (1936–)
Paulauskas, Eugenius
Pavella, Benedetto
Pavlović, Aleksandar (1929–)
Pedersen, Knud
Peinemann, Edith (1937–)
Pelaz, P.D.
Pelliccia, Arrigo (1912–)
Perediaz, Manuel
Perez, Antonio (1936–)
Perlman, Itzhak (1945–)
Persinger, Louis (1887–1967)
Perutz, Robert (1886–)
Peška, Joseph (1906–)
Pessina, Carlos (1897–)
Peters, Reinhard
Petersen, Frederick Schnedler
Petiot, Jeanne
Petroni, Leo (1903–)
Petronio, Frédéric
Petrosyan, Isabella
Petrović, Nikola
Petschnikoff, Alexander (1873–1949)
Pezzani, Romano
Pfeiffer, Walter
Phal
Philippot, Georges
Piastro, Mishel (1892–1970)
Piastro-Borisoff, Josef (1889–)
Piatkowski, Vladimir
Pichler, Günter
Pierangeli, Enrico
Pierrou, Nilla
Pietsch, Helmut
Pignatelli, N.
Pikaizen, Viktor Alexandrovich (1933–)
Pillitz, Imre
Pilzer, Maximilian (1890–1958)

Pincherle, Marc (1888–   )
Pinell, M. J.
Pini, Carl
Pinkava, Ivan (1912–   )
Piraccini, G.
Piramo, Armando di
Plaeinitz, Konstantin
Plamondon, Ernest Gill (1896–   )
Plocek, Alexander (1914–   )
Plummer, Stanley
Pohjola, Paavo
Poleess, Leonid
Polinski, Juan
Pollak, J.
Pollak, Robert (1880–1962)
Pollikoff, Max
Polo, Enrico (1868–1953)
Polson, Arthur (1934–   )
Poltronieri, Alberto (1894–   )
Polyakin, Myron (1895–1939)
Ponticelli, Joseph
Porta, Enzo
Porta, José (1890–   )
Portnoff, Vassilij (1900–   )
Posselt, Ruth (1914–   )
Post, Hermann (1880–   )
Pougnet, Jean (1907–1968)
Poulet, Gérard Georges (1938–   )
Powell, Maud (1868–1920)
Pratz, Albert (1914–   )
Preil, Louis (1901–   )
Prencipe, Giuseppe
Press, Michael (1872–1938)
Prick, Rudolf
Příhoda, Váša (1900–1960)
Primrose, William (1904–   )
Principi, Remy (1889–   )
Prinz, Ernst
Provinsky, Victor
Prystawski, Walter
Pucci, Eldon
Puig, Roland (1919–   )
Pujol, Marcel
Puschacher, Walter
Putters, Joseph
Quattrocchi, Lucian
Quattrocchi, Robert
Queling, Riele
Quick, Robert
Quiroga, Manuel (1890–1961)
Rabin, Michael (1936–1972)
Rabinoff, Benno (1910–   )
Radek, Ludwik
Raderman, Lou
Radics, Béla (1867–1930)
Raimondi, Matthew
Ramor, Erwin
Rannap, I.
Rantos, Spiros
Ranzato, Virgilio (1883–1937)
Rappaini
Raskin, Maurice (1906–   )
Rašković, Fern
Rattay, Howard
Raymond, Germaine

Raymond, Gladys
Redditi, Aldo
Reed, William Henry (1876–1942)
Rehm, Helga
Reillie, Bernard
Reinholdsson, Folke (1905–   )
Reis, Lamy
Reittinger, Pierre
Renardy, Ossy (1921–1953)
Rèty, Røzsy
Retyi, Georg
Reuter, Florizel von (1893–   )
Reuter, Karl
Reuter-Rau, Barbara
Reyentovich, Julian
Reyes, Angel (1919–   )
Reynal, Marcel
Ribaupierre, André de (1893–1955)
Ribeiro, Gerardo
Ricci
Ricci, Ruggiero (1918–   )
Rich, Louis
Rich, Thaddeus (1884-1969)
Richards, Irene (1911–1965)
Richartz, Paul
Richter, Karl Arthur (1883–1957)
Richter, Rolf
Richter-Steiner, Christa (1903–   )
Riemann, Paul
Riphahn, Hans
Rithère, O.
Ritter, Melvin (1923–   )
Robbins, Tessa (1930–   )
Roberts, Winifred
Rocabruna, José (1870–   )
Roche, Joseph
Rode, Alfredo (1905–   )
Roeder, Sofie
Röhn, Andreas (1945–   )
Röhn, Erich (1910–   )
Röhr, Hanns
Romascano, Stephan
Romberg, Joseph
Rombouts, Ad
Rosand, Aaron (1929–   )
Rösch, Wolfgang
Rose, Alma Marie (1905–   )
Rose, Arnold Josef (1863–1946)
Rosen, Max (1900–1956)
Rosenthal, Paul (1942–   )
Rosoff, Elliott
Rossi, Christiano
Rostal, Max (1905–   )
Roth, Feri (1899–1969)
Roth, Nicholas (1910–   )
Rozsa, Suzanne (1927–   )
Rubato, Romano *
Rubens, Karl
Rubens, Lida
Rubenstein, Jerrold
Rubin, Nathan
Rubini, Jan (1900–   )
Rubinlicht, Janine

*Pseudonym for Herman Krebbers.

Rubinoff, David (1897–   )
Rudényi, Jan (–1914)
Ruggero, Astolfi
Ruha, Stefan (1931–   )
Rüman, Angelika
Ruminelli, Mario (1907–   )
Runnqvist, Axel (1880–1947)
Ruotolo, Renato (1912–   )
Ruppert, Christa
Rusin, Miroslav
Rüthström, Julius (1877–1944)
Rybar, Peter (1913–   )
Sachsenskjold, Henryk
Sadler, Georg
Sadowski, Fryderyk
Sagi, Carmela
Salomon, Herman
Salpeter, Max (1910–   )
Salvi, Bruno
Samaroff, Toscha
Sambleben, Kanny
Sametini, Léon (1886–   )
Sammons, Albert (1886–1953)
Sanchez, José
Sanchez, Pepito
Sander, Alex
Sandford, Robert
Sandler, Albert (1906–1948)
Sandler, Myron
Sándor, Georg
Sänger, Bruno
Sangiorgi, Ferruccio
San-Malo, Alfredo (1898–   )
Sarasate, Pablo de (1844–1908)
Sarkisyan, A.
Saulesco, Mircea
Scaglia, Feruccio (1921–   )
Schaeffer, Ralph
Schäfer, Adelheid
Schärnack, Otto
Schelz, Josef
Scherz, Herbert
Scherzer, Benjamin
Scherzer, Manfred (1933–   )
Schiavina, Gian Piero
Schilling, E.
Schiøler, Marie Louise
Schlupp, Klaus
Schmahl, Gustav (1929–   )
Schmidt, Alexander
Schmidt, Otto
Schmied, Jaro
Schmuller, Alexander (1880–1933)
Schneeberger, Hansheinz (1926–   )
Schneider, Alexander (1908–   )
Schneiderhan, Walther (1901–   )
Schneiderhan, Wolfgang (1915–   )
Schneidermann, Dina (1931–   )
Schnitzler, Michael
Schoenfeld, Alice
Scholz, Alejandro
Schön, Helga
Schröcksnadel, Joseph
Schröder, Jaap (1925–   )
Schroder, Rolf (1901–   )

Schuberwalter, Peter
Schulz, Rudoloph (1911–   )
Schumacher, Paul
Schumacher, Richard
Schwalbé, Michel (1919–   )
Schwartz, Lucien
Schwarz, A.
Schwarz, Boris (1907–   )
Schweyda, Margarete
Schweyda, Willi (1894–   )
Scripka, Joseph
Scrosoppi, Antonio
Sealy, Helen
Sebald, Alexander (1869–1934)
Sechiari, Pierre
Sedano, Carlos
Sedlak, Fritz (1895–   )
Seeger, Brigitte
Seidel, Heinz
Seidel, Toscha (1900–1962)
Seidlová, Bedřiška (1914–   )
Seiler, Emil (1906–   )
Seimatov, Y.
Seitz, Gerhard
Selinsky, Vladimir (1910–   )
Selitsky, Vadim
Senatra, Armida (1889–   )
Senderovitz, Charles (1916–   )
Senofsky, Berl (1927–   )
Sens, Adolph
Šestak, Tomislav (1931–   )
Seydel, Irma (1896–   )
Shadwick, Joseph
Shapiro, Eudice
Shermont, Jan
Shikhmurzayeva, Zarius
Shikhmurzayeva, Zora (1933–   )
Shindarev, D.
Shinder, Lev
Shiokawa, Yuko (1946–   )
Shkolnikova, Nelli (1927–   )
Shuchari, Sadah (1908–   )
Shulman, Sylvan
Shumsky, Oscar (1917–   )
Sieja, Edmund
Sigmund, Karl
Sillito, Kenneth
Silverman, Edward
Silverstein, Joseph (1932–   )
Silzer, Giorgio
Simko, Imre
Simor, András (1931–   )
Simsky, Boris
Sitkovetsky, Yulian Gregorevich (1925–1958)
Sjöen, Alf (1914–   )
Skalar, Olga
Skalka, Max
Skogh, Erhard
Skolnik, Carlos
Skolnik, Jenny
Slatkin, Felix (1915–1963)
Small, Winifred (1896–   )
Smejkal, Miroslav
Smirnov, Eugen
Smith, Maureen Felicity
Smith, Sydney

Snítil, Václav (1928–   )
Snitkovsky, Semen (1933–   )
Sobolevsky, Rafael
Soetens, Robert (1907–   )
Soh, Tomotada
Soldat, Marie (1864–1955)
Solloway, Harry
Soloviev, Miriam (1921–   )
Soman, Herbert
Sonntag, Eugen
Soriano, Denise
Sorkin, Herbert (1920–   )
Sorkin, Leonard
Šorm, Spytihněv (1914–   )
Southgate, Elsie (1889–1946)
Spalding, Albert (1888–1953)
Spivakov, Vladimir (1944–   )
Spivakovsky, Tossy (1907–   )
Sprecher, Helmut
Šroubek, Karel (1913–   )
Stanić-Krek, Jelka (1928–   )
Stanske, Heinz (1913–   )
Staples, Gordon (1929–   )
Staryk, Steven (1932–   )
Statkiewicz, Edward
Stavonhagen, Wolfgang (1916–   )
Štědroň, Jan (1907–   )
Steeb, Olga
Stefanato, Angelo
Steffen-Wendling, Andrea
Stehl, George
Steiger-Betzak, Annie
Stein, J.
Steinbauer, Edith
Steinberg, Simon
Steiner, Carl
Steinhardt, Arnold
Steinhäusler, Josef
Štěpanek, Jarka Jaroslav (1905–   )
Stepansky, Joseph
Stern, Isaac (1920–   )
Stevens, Louis
Stiehler, Kurt
Stiglitz, M.
Stoessel, Albert Frederic (1894–1943)
Stosch, Leonora von (Lady Speyer)
Straka, Jiří Jurenko (1925–   )
Štraus, Ivan (1937–   )
Straus, Jessie
Strauss, G.
Streletzky, Ingeborg von
Streng, Rudolf
Strock, Leo
Strockoff, Leo
Strong, Ernest
Stross, Wilhelm (1907–1966)
Strub, Max (1900–1966)
Stücki, Aida
Stülken, Willy
Stümmvoll, Karl
Stuurop, Jean Louis
Suk, Josef (1929–   )
Suske, Karl
Suzuki, Shinichi (1898–   )
Švolkovskis, Juris

Swaap, Sam (1889–   )
Swärdström, Gustave
Swoboda, Gustav
Szabó, János
Szekély, Zoltan (1903–   )
Szemere, Magda
Szentgyörgi, Laszlö (1910–   )
Szenthèlyi, Miklós
Szeryng, Henryk (1918–   )
Szigeti, Dezsö (–1963)
Szigeti, Joseph (1892–1973)
Szikra, Lajos (1899–   )
Szücs, Mihály
Szulc, Bronislav (1881–1955)
Tak, Max
Talassi, Glauco
Tamponi, Franco
Tanenbaum, Sergei
Tarack, Gerald
Tarjus, Blanche (1932–   )
Taschke, Carl
Taschner, Gerhard (1922–   )
Tátrai, Vilmós (1912–   )
Tellefsen, Arve (1936–   )
Telmányi, Emil (1892–   )
Temianka, Henri (1906–   )
Temko, Matla (1908–   )
Terebesi, György
Terpelyuk, P.
Tertis, Vernon
Tessier, Georges
Testa, Teresa
Thaviu, Samuel
Theadorowicz, Julius
Theiner, Kurt
Theodorescu, Alexander
Theuveny, Marie-Claude
Thibaud, Jacques (1880–1953)
Thiele, Edmond (1853–1926)
Thoene, Helga
Thoman, Marie
Thomas, Tessie (1899–   )
Thomsen, Jakob
Thrinis, Freya
Tinlot, Gustav (1887–   )
Titze, Karl Maria (1908–   )
Tolganbayev, A.
Tomasow, Jan (1914–1961)
Tombras, Spiros
Topolski, Zlatko (1914–   )
Torkanowsky, Werner (1926–   )
Törnqvist, Ernst-Reinhold (1893–   )
Torre, Marta de la (1894–   )
Toškov, Petar (1920–   )
Toso, Piero
Totenberg, Roman (1911–   )
Toubas, Maurice Alexis (1902–   )
Toyama, Shigeru
Toyoda, Koji
Travers, Patricia (1927–   )
Traversa, Mario
Tree, Michael (1934–   )
Treff, Paul
Treger, Charles (1935–   )
Tretyakov, Viktor (1946–   )

Trippner, Alfred
Troostwyck, Hendrika
Tryon, Jesse
Trysessoone, Janine
Tsitsikyan, Anaid
Tunnell, John (1936–   )
Tworek, Wandy (1913–   )
Tziganov, Dmitri Mikhailovich (1903–   )
Tzipine, George (1907–   )
Ughi, Uto (1944–   )
Uminska, Eugenia (1910–   )
Ungermannova, Otilie (1907–   )
Unno, Yoshio (1936–   )
Urbán, Béla
Ushioda, Masuko (1942–   )
Vaček, Václav (1918–   )
Vadas, Agnés (1929–   )
Vaiman, Mikhail Israelevich (1926–   )
Valesca-Becker, Dora
Valpreda, Ronald
Vance, Arthur
Vardi, Emanuel (1915–   )
Varenberg, K.
Varga, Ruben George (1928–   )
Varga, Tibor (1921–   )
Varkonyi, István
Vasile, Cornelia (1949–   )
Vecsey, Ferenc von (1893–1935)
Vegh, Sándor (1905–   )
Velder, Joseph de
Velt, Jacob M.
Venclû, Josef
Verdon, Jacques
Verhey, Emmy (1949–   )
Vermes, Maria
Vermeulen, Joke
Vianelli, Lavinio
Viardot, Paul (1857–1941)
Vicari, Luciano
Vidas Raoul (1901–   )
Vignon, Germaine
Vilker, Valeria
Villa, Carlos (1939–   )
Vinnikov, Zinovi
Viólin, Mischa (1902–   )
Vladigerov, Luben (1899–   )
Vlasov, R.
Voelker, F.
Voicu, Ion (1925–   )
Volant, Henri
Vollmer, Günter

Vorholz, Deiter
Vos, Jeanne *
Wachsmuth-Loew, Andrée (1911–   )
Wagner, Siegfried
Wakshal, Seymour
Waldman, Hugo
Wallez, Jean-Pierre
Walsh, Arthur
Wanne, Kerttu (1905–   )
Warchal, Bohdan (1930–   )
Ware, Helen (1887–   )
Washbourne, Kathleen
Weber, Marek (1898–   )
Wegern, Hans von
Weicher, John (1904–1969)
Weiner, Stanley Milton (1925–   )
Weinstein, Isaac José
Weinstock, Rachmael
Weintraub, Jacques
Weisman, Vladimir (1931–   )
Weismann, Diez (1900–   )
Weismeyer, J.
Weissgerber, Andreas (1900–   )
Weist-Hill, Ferdinand (1897–   )
Weltmann, Feri
Weltmann, Roszi
Westergaard, Mads
Weston, Albert
Westphal, Hans-Joachim
Wethmar, Norbert
Wicks, Camilla (1928–   )
Wiener, Frances
Wiesbeck, Hans
Wigler, Jerome
Wilk, Maurice (1922–1963)
Wilkomirska, Wanda (1929–   )
Will, G.
Willaume, Albert Gabrielle (1873–   )
Williams, Charles
Willis, Victor
Winchester, Gertrude
Wise, David
Witek, Alma Rosengren-
Witek, Anton (1872–1933)
Wittels, Ludwig (1896–1956)
Wittenberg, Alfred (1880–   )
Wöbbel, Herta
Woiku, Petrescu (1884–   )
Wolf, Endré (1913–   )
Wolff, Johannes (1863–   )
Wolff, Louis (1865–1926)

Wolff-Israel, M.A.
Wolff-Maim, Doris
Wolfgang, G.
Wolfsthal, Josef (1899–1931)
Wolters, Martin
Wood, Haydn (1882–1959)
Woodgate, Mary
Wroński, Tadeusz (1915–   )
Wührer, Friedrich (1925–   )
Wulf, Jewssey (1888–1970)
Wullens, G.
Wunder, Kathy
Yashkin, Anton
Yashvili, Marina
Yordanoff, Luben
Ysaÿe, Eugène (1858–1931)
Yung, Shen
Zabavnikov, Nikolai
Zacharewitsch, Michael (1879–1953)
Zacharias, Helmut (1920–   )
Zafer, David (1934–   )
Zaks, Leon
Zalay, Tamás
Zámečník, Louis (1897–   )
Zampani, Franco
Zampieri, Fernando
Zapotocky, Franz
Zaretsky, Yuri
Zarinš, V.
Zathureczky, Ede (1903–1959)
Zayde, Jacob
Zazofsky, George (1914–   )
Zegzulková, Véra
Zeiler, Robert (1879–   )
Želeva, Stanka (1944–   )
Zentay, Mary (1897–   )
Zepparoni, Fernando
Zernick, Helmut (1913–1970)
Zetterqvist, Lars (1860–1946)
Zhislin, Grigori (1946–   )
Zhuk, Valentin I. (1934–   )
Zighera, Léon
Zilzer, Ibolyka
Zimbalist, Efrem (1889–   )
Zimmermann, Louis (1873–1954)
Zoubek, Karel J. (1902–1959)
Zsigmondy, Dénes (1922–   )
Zukerman, Pinchas (1948–   )
Zukin, Oleg
Zukofsky, Paul (1943–   )

*Maiden name of Jean Lemkes.